David Lampe
Jan. '91

CONTEMPORARY NOVELISTS

Contemporary Writers of the English Language

Contemporary Poets

Contemporary Novelists
  (including short story writers)

Contemporary Dramatists

CONTEMPORARY NOVELISTS

FOURTH EDITION

PREFACE TO THE FIRST EDITION
WALTER ALLEN

PREFACE TO THE THIRD EDITION
JEROME KLINKOWITZ

EDITOR
D.L. KIRKPATRICK

CONSULTING EDITOR
JAMES VINSON

ST. MARTIN'S PRESS
NEW YORK

© 1986 by St. James Press

All rights reserved. For information, write:
Scholarly & Reference Division,
St. Martin's Press, Inc., 175 Fifth Avenue, New York, NY 10010

First published in the United States of America in 1986

Printed in the U.S.A.

ISBN 0-312-16731-8

Library of Congress Cataloging-in-Publication Data

Contemporary novelists.

   (Contemporary writers of the English language)
   On t.p. of earlier ed. (2nd, 1976) editors'
names are in reverse order.
   Includes bibliographies and index.
   1. English fiction—20th century—Bio-bibliography.
2. American literature—20th century—Bio-bibliography.
I. Kirkpatrick, D.L.   II. Vinson, James, 1933-
III. Series: Contemporary writers of the English
language.
PR883.C64   1986   823'.914'09   86-13904
ISBN 0-312-16731-8

CONTENTS

PREFACE
to the First Edition

The novel, we have been told many times in recent years, is dying: the news, as the appearance of this book shows, doesn't seem to have reached novelists themselves. But I don't recall that the assertion was made until about 1945, and perhaps it ought to be examined. We might at least discover why it is made. Ironically, it seems to have been first propounded at just about the time when the study of novels as a serious form of writing was being taken up in the universities. Today, one sometimes has the impression that little else but novels are studied there. The only ones I remember meeting in prescribed courses when I was an undergraduate studying English at the beginning of the Thirties were Jane Austen's—and, of all things, *The Castle of Otranto*, which must have had something to do with something else. I suppose one might cynically say that the very fact that novels are studied so seriously now in the universities is a sign that the form is dying.

If this were so, there would be nothing intrinsically remarkable about it. Literary forms, or significant variations of them, have disappeared before. For the best part of half a century the verse play was the great glory of English literature. Its death was certainly protracted, but for a hundred years it got steadily weaker until it ended not with a bang but a whimper in the closet poetic drama of the Romantics and the Victorians; and attempts to resurrect it in our time have not been conspicuously successful. Literary forms die or dwindle in importance as a result, I think we can say, of technological changes or of changes in men's interests. The novel itself had its origin in both kinds of change.

One thing it seems to me can be said with some certainty: the novel no longer has the central place in current literature and culture that it had in the nineteenth century. Having made the generalisation with some certainty, I find myself drawing back from it. On second thoughts, I suspect that Tennyson and Ruskin, for instance, were regarded with greater awe, as poets and prophets, than Dickens or George Eliot, who, as novelists, were merely entertainers. But *we* see the novel as central to nineteenth-century literature—it may be for reasons that are much the same as those that lead some people to think the novel is dying.

For one thing, as entertainers the Victorian novelists had virtually no competitors except one another. There were no films, no television, no radio. Dickens, indeed, was almost a Hollywood in himself. If you wanted to be beguiled, taken out of yourself, where could you turn but to the novel? And in the novel, in Dickens, Thackeray, George Eliot, Trollope, you could find a synoptic view of society; English life, depicted on a large enough scale, with enough contrast between social classes to suggest the whole of English life, was spread out in front of you. And there was something else, which is indicated by the historian G.M. Young. Writing on the Victorian age, Young has said: "It was part of the felicity of the fifties to possess a literature which was at once topical, contemporary, and classic; to meet the Immortals in the street and to read them with added zest for the encounter." Among these Immortals, even as young men, were Dickens and Thackeray. But the main emphasis, in my view, has to go on the word "classic"; the role was forced upon the great novelists almost by the situation of the times, which enabled them to identify themselves with their public, to speak for it, to an extent that is impossible for a novelist today. They shared the assumptions about the age common to the age, and when they criticised them they did so in much the same way as their readers were doing. In other words, they were the spokesmen of their age, or at least of the most important section of their public, the middle class. But this was not a serious limitation on them, for middle-class values were dominant. The society they wrote for was more homogeneous than ours. Middle-class culture, perhaps even upper middle-class culture was supreme, and seriously to read was to become part of that culture. The notion of cultural splits, the division into highbrow, middle-brow, low-brow, did not exist. And the novelists' identification with their society and their public gave them an authority denied, I suspect, to novelists of our time. Not that the synoptic novelist is unknown today. One thinks of C.P. Snow, whose *Strangers and Brothers* sequence takes in large and diverse areas of experience embracing a whole range of social class from lower-middle to aristocracy. I suspect that Snow's ideal of the novel is the Victorian at the height of its power. But there is a difference, and I think it is fundamental. Snow presents his synoptic, panoramic view of our society through the experiences of his narrator Lewis Eliot, whose life and career bear distinct resemblances to Snow's own. He is pretty obviously a persona for his creator. What Snow gives us, in other words, is one man's view of society. But when Thackeray, Trollope and George Eliot drop into the first person singular we read and accept, I believe, their "I" as "we". We assume an identification with their readers, and for all his idiosyncrasy, we do this with Dickens too. The novelists are not speaking for themselves, but for the consensus of opinion of their age. This is one of the factors that gives their novels a universal quality.

It was such novelists as these that Lionel Trilling had in mind when he wrote his famous passage in *The Liberal Imagination*:

> For our time the most effective agent of the moral imagination has been the novel of the last two hundred years. It was never, either aesthetically or morally, a perfect form and its faults and failures can be quickly enumerated. But its greatness and its practical usefulness lie in its unremitting work of involving the reader himself in the moral life, inviting him to put his own motives under examination, suggesting that reality is not as his conventional education has led him to see it. It taught us, as no other genre ever did, the extent of human variety and the value of this variety. It was the literary form to which the emotions of understanding and forgiveness were indigenous, as if by the definition of the form itself.

For me, these words of Trilling's constitute the great main justification of the novel. I know, though I had not realized until I read Trilling, that this is where my first interest in the novel began, both as reader and as someone who aspired to be a novelist himself. It is not, of course, the end of my interest in the novel. In our time, however, I feel it is increasingly difficult for the novelist to fulfil Trilling's expectations. Why this is so is indicated by Kingsley Amis's hero in *I Like It Here*, as he contemplates the memorial to Henry Fielding in Lisbon:

> Perhaps it was worth dying in your forties if two hundred years later you were the only non-contemporary novelist who could be read with unaffected and whole-hearted interest, the only one who never had to be apologized for or excused on the grounds of changing taste. And how enviable to live in the world of his novels, where duty was plain, evil arose from malevolence and a starving wayfarer could be invited indoors without hesitation and without fear. Did that make it a simplified world? Perhaps, but that hardly mattered beside the existence of a moral seriousness without the aid of evangelical puffing and blowing.

Well, today duty is not plain, and we can no longer confidently say that evil arises from malevolence. Our faith in our moral judgments has been sapped, principally I suppose by the findings of Freud and his followers. But we also live in a world that presses on us in all its intensity of evil so remorselessly as to seem unassimilable in the novel. The paradigm of the evil is the concentration camps of Nazi Germany; but the evil—at the moment of writing in Vietnam, in Ulster, in East Bengal, and God knows where it will be next year—leaps at us nightly from the television screen. It was something the great Victorians didn't have to take into account, or there was less of it to take into account. Equally, it is something we and our contemporaries must. The difficulty of doing so, perhaps indeed the impossibility, has been stated by George Steiner in *Language and Silence*. That even sixty-five years ago the difficulty could be overcome was shown by Conrad in what now seems his prophetic novel *Nostromo*; and we can see it can be handled in our time from Golding's *Lord of the Flies*, from Graham Greene throughout his career and from Saul Bellow's *Mr. Sammler's Planet*. But novels of this order seem almost special cases.

I am putting forward a number of things that differentiate the contemporary novel from the classic novel, by which in the end rightly or wrongly we tend to judge contemporary work. Briefly, the novel is no longer the main medium of entertainment and instruction. The film tells a story at least as well; and a good part of what, even as late as Lawrence, was taken for granted as belonging to the content of the novel, what may be called the journalistic or documentary and argumentative content, has been taken over by television and the non-fiction book. Best-sellers are no longer, as they were fifty years ago, generally novels. The books that are most widely read and argued about are works of non-fiction, works of reportage, scientific theory and speculation, and controversy. The discussion of current ideas and affairs, the exposures of current abuses, these are now presented to us on television. This is a consequence of technological development, and perhaps nothing can be done about it. But the result is a loss to the novel—and also, I think, to the quality of our response to what is happening everywhere in the world. The world, simply, is too much with us, and too immediately so: we lack the filter of fiction and must suffer instead the immediate brutal impact upon us of events and new ideas. In the past, the writing of a novel was a comparatively leisurely affair. It may still be so. To write a novel takes anything from one year to ten: but now, by the time it is published, and irrespective of the length of time in its writing, it may seem to refer to a world that is irredeemably past.

One consequence of this speeding up of life and the decay between the event and the novelist's assimilation of and reaction towards it is, it seems to me, a distrust of fiction, which is seen almost as a luxury. There is perhaps some evidence of this in the large number of *romans fleuves* which has been so striking a feature of the British novel since the war, sequences like those of Snow, Waugh, Powell, Doris Lessing, Durrell and Olivia Manning. Vastly different from one another though these works are, they have one thing in common: the narrator of each one of them seems to be uncommonly close to his creator, so that there appears in these sequences to be a narration of events akin to those the novelist has himself experienced. It is a short step beyond this to something that, though in many ways comparable to the novel, is not the novel. I am thinking of what has been called the "non-fiction novel," notably Truman Capote's *In Cold Blood* and Norman Mailer's *The Armies of the Night*, a work of reporting of personal experience that only a novelist of great brilliance could have written.

But there is another kind of book, which does not profess in any way to relate to the novel, that all the same seems to cater to the interests of readers who half a century ago would have been reading novels or would have had a comparable experience from reading novels. The books I have in mind are a disparate lot; it includes books like Kate Millett's and Germaine Greer's on Woman's Lib., White's *The Organization Man*, Watson's *The Double Helix*, anthropological and sociological works based on taped interviews, Desmond Morris's *The Naked Ape*, the books of Bruno Bettelheim and the psychological writings of R.D. Laing. All in one way or another are about people. And there are two points here. They are in some sense specialised works the contents of which novelists themselves will generally have no more first-hand knowledge of than the non-specialist reading public. And they also appear to be based on recorded fact or what looks like it. They appeal, in other words, to a curiosity that in the past the novelist could satisfy but that now he cannot.

These books may be seen as case-histories. They are of the stuff of fiction but *true*; and it may be that we are in a period when readers prefer to read what they think is history rather than the imaginative re-creation of history that is the novel.

It could also be that this interest in history and in what seems to be the scientifically provable is being counterbalanced by an interest in a fiction of what might be called an extreme kind, one that goes beyond the novel and is akin to the romance that we all thought the novel had displaced two and a half centuries ago. It seems significant that for the past four or five years the works of fiction most eagerly devoured by university students in the United States, and I suspect in Britain too, have been the fantasies of Tolkien and the works of Hermann Hesse, works of fiction that lie outside the novel as I conceive it.

What that is will be apparent. For me, though I recognise variants such as the novels of Melville, the novel is a broadly realistic representation of man's life in society which is also a criticism of life and of society. This, as I see it, makes up the mainstream of the English novel from Fielding to Joyce and Lawrence. All the evidence—and it comes from novels themselves—suggests that during the past two or three decades the contemporary novelist has been forced by pressures of circumstances—technological change, change in men's attitudes towards themselves and towards the universe, the simple facts of history in our time, and the sheer increase of knowledge in many fields from which as a non-specialist he is barred—to yield much of his former territory to other literary forms and media. Despite himself, he has become more subjective, much less sure of himself. He has lost much of the authority his forbears could take for granted. It seems less possible for the novelist to put forward the mimic world he has invented as a convincing paradigm of the world in which he and his readers live.

There is, I am well aware, a factor that so far I have ignored. Invoking the past, I have referred to the very great novelists of the language. We in this second half of the twentieth century follow in the wake of very great novelists. The years from roughly 1900 to 1949 form one of the peak periods in our literature, in poetry and the novel alike. The great names are obvious enough: in the novel,

Conrad, Joyce, Lawrence, Virginia Woolf; Dreiser, Fitzgerald, Hemingway perhaps, Faulkner; and a host of smaller but very significant figures flank them. What impresses us in them today is the scope of their ambitions and their success in realising them. If we have no one to set against them, the same seems to me to be true of the novel throughout the world. But history shows that similar situations have existed before, that an age of intense flowering is often followed by one comparatively barren or in which the growths are smaller. The emergence of a new novelist of the calibre of Conrad or Faulkner could change the literary scene as an earthquake changes a landscape and make nonsense of all my generalisations. Figures of Conrad's and Faulkner's stature can't be produced to order—and it may be worth pointing out that the true greatness of some of the novelists of our century, Conrad among them, was not seen until after their deaths and that their influence, which we now take for granted, was posthumous.

Meanwhile, until that monster the new great novelist arrives, we must put up with what we have. If that sounds churlish, it is not meant to be. Our contemporary novelists are ours, they belong to us, the problems that face them face us their readers too. Their fragmentation reflects ours. But much more can be said than that. If I do not believe that we live in one of the peak periods of the novel, I do emphatically believe that we live in a time distinguished by a bigger concentration of talented men and women only less than the great than has ever been seen before in the history of the novel in English. I have spent almost all my life reading novels (and trying to write them) and I could write down the names of I suspect two score and probably more from Britain and America who have given me pleasure, aesthetic or intellectual, of a keenness that makes it almost impossible for me to think they won't be read at least with interest a century hence. The temptation is to write the names down, but it must be resisted.

No, the novel is not dead or dying, even though its stature may be smaller than a century ago—and that, as I have suggested, the arrival of my monster may change. And there is another reason, besides the prodigality of talent on all sides, which shows no sign of drying up, for believing the novel is not dying. This is the sudden and unexpected appearance of the novel within the past three decades or so in the new countries where English is spoken, the Caribbean islands, India, the countries of Africa. For a congenital reader and student of the novel it has been a moving experience to watch these new literatures come into existence during one's reading lifetime, for they are surely signs of life, not of death. The task of these men and women making these new literatures is, no doubt, different from that of contemporary English and American white novelists, for it is to forge, in Joyce's words, the uncreated conscience of their race. But their novels testify to the variety and diversity of human experience and to the human need to set it down and rejoice in it. It is in the consciousness precisely of that variety and diversity that the novel had its origins; and so long as it remains, so long as men are curious about their fellows and themselves, it seems to me unlikely the novel will die.

—WALTER ALLEN

PREFACE
to the Third Edition

Fiction constitutes a way of looking at the world. What a rich and potentially troublesome definition that is! One cannot imagine a novelist from Cervantes to Beckett (himself the last Quixote) who would disagree, yet its very philosophy of form makes fiction the most volatile and controversial literary genre we are likely to encounter.

For example: when we read *Bleak House* or *Great Expectations* we are getting more than just a picture of 19th-century England, rich with documentary material complementary to our social and political histories of the time. In a Dickens novel we are privileged to the author's *way of seeing* the England (and its people) of his day. That view was certainly different from Samuel Butler's or either of the Brontës'. Standing behind the contents of their novels are entire philosophies social, moral, and aesthetic—which determine each author's sense of what should be recorded, and how.

When the world changes, controversies of form are even more pronounced. "In or about December, 1910", Virginia Woolf once remarked, "human character changed." She was referring to the first London exhibition of post-impressionist paintings, in themselves a radical statement on the act of seeing. But those works were part of an emerging world view which influenced her own way of writing novels and the entire culture's manner of judging itself. Painting still remains painting, even though its physical form—from impressionism through cubism and surrealism to abstract expressionism and beyond—changes so radically. It must be the world, then, and our way of seeing it that are transformed. And even more immediately than painting, the novel is there to respond to and express this violent alteration.

To survey the status of the novel in English these days is to describe a battle of the books, both critical and creative, such as has not existed in Anglo-American letters for nearly a century. That long-distant conflict was the H.G. Wells–Henry James debate over the future course of fiction: Was the novel to enter the 20th century as a documentary record of social action, the "novel of saturation" which by its refusal to tamper with reality placed highest value in the writer's ability to perceive and report, or would modern times begin with the Jamesian "novel of selection," picking and choosing among the materials of life to present not the world itself but rather an illusory representation of it?

Both novels, of course, continued to be written. Novelists of saturation (Arnold Bennett, Theodore Dreiser, John Steinbeck) satisfied a wide range of interests from popular entertainment to social advocacy, while the selectivists (Joseph Conrad, Virginia Woolf, F. Scott Fitzgerald) pursued a more formally modernist fiction which helped prepare an aesthetic for such newly invented media as film and an ethic open to the discoveries of psychology and psychoanalysis.

But by midcentury a curious discomfort with the world itself became evident among novelists and critics alike. Reviewing the absurdly ridiculous events of the American 1950's, Philip Roth complained ("Writing American Fiction," in *Reading Myself and Others*, 1975):

> The American writer in the middle of the 20th century has his hands full in trying to understand, and then describe, and then make *credible* much of the American reality. It stupefies, it sickens, it infuriates, and finally it is even a kind of embarrassment to one's meager imagination. The actuality is continually outdoing our talents and the culture tosses up figures almost daily that are the envy of any novelist.

Critics were quick to agree, proclaiming "the death of the novel" on the evidence of form as well as of content, for philosophy and social history had discredited the world view upon which conventions of fiction had been based, as Ronald Sukenick explained in his own short story "The Death of the Novel":

> Realistic fiction presupposed chronological time as the medium of plotted narrative, an irreducible individual psyche as the subject of its characterization, and, above all, the ultimate, concrete reality of things as the object and rationale of its description. In the world of post-realism, however, all of these absolutes have become absolutely problematic.
>
> The contemporary writer—the writer who is acutely in touch with the life of which he is a part—is forced to start from scratch: Reality doesn't exist, time doesn't exist, personality doesn't exist. God was the omniscient author, but he died; now no one knows the plot, and since our reality lacks the sanction of a creator, there's no guarantee as to the authenticity of the received version. Time is reduced to presence, the content of a series of discontinuous moments. Time is no longer purposive, and so there is no destiny, only chance. Reality is, simply, our experience, and objectivity is, of course, an illusion. Personality, after having passed through a phase of awkward self-consciousness, has become, quite minimally, a mere locus for our experience. In view of these annihilations, it should be no surprise that literature, also, does not exist—how could it? There is only reading and writing, which are things we do, like eating and making love, to pass the time, ways of maintaining a considered boredom in the face of the abyss.

Again, conventionally realistic novels continued to be written—in America by the commercial entertainers but also by such craftsmen and women as John Updike, Saul Bellow, and Joan Didion, and in Britain by Kingsley Amis, Margaret Drabble, and many others. But never again could realism proceed with such confidence and naivety, for in the face of the disruptions just described even simple characterization and linear plotting became necessarily experimental techniques.

The 1960's and 1970's in particular witnessed a sometimes bitter debate over fiction's new aesthetic. Was it to be a vehicle for commentary on man's existence, or simply an artifact of his own making and nothing more? Whether the novel was "about" reality or "about" itself (and hence an addition to experience rather than a report of it) set the terms for a squabble both trans-Atlantic and domestic. "It seems a country-headed thing to say," the novelist William H. Gass admits ("The Medium of Fiction," in *Fiction and the Figures of Life*, 1970), "that literature is language, that stories and the places and the people in them are merely made of words as chairs are made of smoothed sticks and sometimes of cloth and metal tubes.... It seems incredible," he readily agrees, "the ease with which we sink through books quite out of sight, pass clamorous pages into soundless dreams." His own style of metafic- tion—works whose subject is its own making, its product nothing but its own process—is indeed disrup- tively revolutionary, especially startling not just for what it does in itself but for what it discredits in the conventional novel. "That novels should be made of words, and merely words, is shocking, really," he concludes. "It's as if you had discovered that your wife were made of rubber: the bliss of all those years, the fears ... from sponge."

Opposed to Gass (and to the French theoreticians of literary language—Barthes, Derrida, and Kris- teva—who support him) are the moral fictionist John Gardner and the truth-centered critic Gerald Graff. Does literature have a duty beyond its own self-apparency of form? Most certainly, Gardner replies (in *On Moral Fiction*, 1978), citing Tolstoy: God instructs, heroes enact, and writers record. Is writing simply a commentary on other writing, as philosophers from Hegel onward would suggest? Not at all, Graff insists (in *Literature Against Itself*, 1978): "Most theories of the nature of literature are more or less concealed theories of the nature of man and of the good society. In this sense, literary thinking is inseparable from moral and social thinking." The rub is, Graff dismisses entirely the post- modern theory of Derrida, Gass & Co. Fiction still makes truth-claims, he believes, and those claims are just as creditable as the bottom line statements from a bank.

This battle of the books now raging in America bears close resemblance to the stand-off many critics have claimed exists between the contemporary British and American novels. Comparing their states of criticism (and behind them the style of fiction each advocates), Ihab Hassan (in *Georgia Review*, Fall 1980) sees the best elements in America reflecting the French philosophy of deconstruction (truth in textuality alone) while "England offers nothing bracing in criticism now." Meanwhile in a British symposium for *The New Review* on "The State of Fiction" (Summer 1978) John Braine is asked How Are Things Going? and What's New? and glowers in reply, "A bad time," acknowledging little from the UK and "From the USA, nothing at all, now that John O'Hara's dead." What Malcolm Bradbury calls "a depressing and outdated folklore" informs both views: that since the start of the 19th century American fiction has been vitalized by a searchingly romantic disposition, while the British novel rests smugly within the confidence of Lockean empiricism and the comforts of a hearty life sustained by beef and ale. Is Hassan aware of John Fowles, Lawrence Durrell and the later works of Doris Lessing? Of course, just as Braine must know of William H. Gass, Ronald Sukenick, Donald Barthelme, and the fuss they have caused at home among supporters and detractors alike. But each chooses to discount such work as either unrepresentative or unworthy of notice, so that the old distinctions might live one more day.

Indeed, the characteristics of British, American, and Commonwealth fiction in the 1980's suggests that novelists are eager to grow beyond such narrowly national groupings and confront the aesthetic issues of their times—and also to acknowledge that simply performing in character and writing what might be expected of them is no longer a satisfactory or rewarding approach to fiction. In Britain romancers such as John Fowles and Lawrence Durrell are eclipsing D.H. Lawrence's belief that Americans have prior claim to license of imagination. As Chris Bigsby explains (*Granta*, Fall 1980), Fowles is still a storyteller who uses most devices of conventional narration, drawing upon all the traditional strengths of the English novel; yet he also appreciates that "the process of invention is itself the source of values. But it is also the origin of coercion," and so involves himself in the metafictional drama described by William H. Gass. In Canada, Margaret Atwood has crafted a series of novels at once womanly and universal, transcending the narrow issues of sexual politics in order to shape a fictive world responsive to the genuinely new lives being led in this era. In America, the moral fiction debate has continued, and the controversy has lent its themes and structures to novels themselves, such as Clarence Major's *Emergency Exit* (which deconstructs a simple narrative into its semiological and linguistic components) and John Gardner's *October Light*, a self-proclaimed moral fiction which contains within itself a parodistic experimental novel.

A common complaint against postwar British fiction is that it was shaped by its contents—an argument summarized in the title of Rubin Rabinovitz's study *The Reaction Against Experiment in the English Novel 1950–1960*, in which "experiment" implies the determinacy of aesthetic form. The newer work of Angus Wilson, Doris Lessing, and many others (as we shall see) in fact turns this assertion on its head: novels such as *No Laughing Matter* and *The Golden Notebook* adopt new forms which twist content beyond the old habitual patterns of understanding—an exercise in which John Fowles also takes delight. The irony is that so many recent American novelists have distinguished themselves by seeking the very informing-sort of content previously reserved for their British colleagues. Sometimes the same historical event must do double duty, as the execution of accused atom-spies Julius and Ethel Rosenberg serves for E.L. Doctorow's *The Book of Daniel* (where the names are changed but events remain closely factual) and Robert Coover's masterful *The Public Burning* (where the names stay the same but events are subjected to unrestrained fancy). Ishmael Reed turns to black folklore and the mythology of popular culture for his novels *Flight to Canada* and *The Last Days of Louisiana Red*, and in *Mumbo Jumbo* constructs a virtual epic from historical sources dating from the present back to ancient Egypt—all as a way of putting contemporary life in sharper focus and revealing the aesthetic structures of existence. Norman Mailer's *The Executioner's Song* and Doctorow's *Ragtime* mark the extremes of this para-historical approach: the absolute weight of experience forming its own phenomeno-logical poetry, or the delicate dance of several wispy historical threads to create both the spirit of an era and the joy of textual play. At its best, in the hands of Guy Davenport, history yields itself to collage: Kafka at an airshow in Brescia brushing shoulders with Ludwig Wittgenstein (*Tatlin!*), Lenin photographed in a Zurich cafe, self-consciously and properly posed, while undetected (at the time) in the background may be seen James and Nora Joyce haggling with a taxi driver (*DaVinci's Bicycle*). Rather than being shaped by such contents, recent American fiction of this style uses form itself to reshape history, believing that in any contest between the ethics and aesthetic of truth, the latter must always win.

The alleged conservatism of British fiction against which so many critics, both English and American, have complained, was actually a short-lived and readily explainable phenomenon. Joyce, Woolf, and Lawrence had, of course, helped create the modern novel. Solidly grounded in psychology and myth, its formal experimentalism was scarcely a cause for complaint, for all bases, moral and aesthetic, were covered. In the postwar years, however, a younger generation of university men and women reacted against what they considered the romantic excesses of writers such as Dylan Thomas and Henry Treece, taking counsel from critics F.R. Leavis and William Empson that the goals of literature should be a "marked moral intensity" distinguished by rationalism, realism, empiricism, and above all clarity of expression. Loosely called "The Movement" and more famous for its poetry, it nevertheless included novelists so disposed as Kingsley Amis, Philip Larkin, and John Wain, who believed fiction was not so much a textual display as an instrument of persuasion, what Jonathan Raban called "the nicest and kindest form of paternal dictatorship" (*The Society of the Poem*, 1971) and which Blake Morrison sums up as "a strong determinism to inform, instruct, even manipulate" (*The Movement*, 1980). Behind it all was a new attitude expressed by a new style of hero, the central character of such books as Amis's *Lucky Jim* and Wain's *Hurry on Down*, as described by Walter Allen (*New Statesman*, 30 January 1954):

> A new hero has risen among us. Is he the intellectual tough, or the tough intellectual? He is consciously, even conscientiously, graceless. His face, when not dead-pan, is set in a snarl of exasperation. He has one skin too few, but his is not the sensitiveness of the young man in earlier twentieth-century fiction: it is the phoney to which his nerve-ends are tremblingly exposed, and at the least suspicion of the phoney he goes tough. He is at odds with his conventional university education, though he comes generally from a famous university: he has seen through the academic racket as he sees through all the others.... The Services, certainly,

helped to make him; but George Orwell, Dr. Leavis and the Logical Positivists—all contributed to his genesis.

It is in reaction to this very coercion and manipulation that the most recent British fiction has defined itself. A conservative attitude is itself coercive, rejecting new ideas as smugly as Dr. Johnson kicking Bishop Berkeley's stone. The novels of Doris Lessing challenge this position. Raised in Southern Rhodesia, she seems to have adopted this colonial displacement for her own posture as a novelist. As Lorna Saga explains (*Granta*, Fall 1980), "Deliberately, traumatically (and now it at last seems serenely) she has mislaid her sense of humour, her sense of proportion, her 'English' personality. The science fiction and fantasy she's writing in her new 'Canopus in Argos' sequence reveals a fragmented cosmos seen by a composite, coolly impersonal eye." Traditional values no longer boast a unifying effect—indeed, the center has not held—but for British fiction this readjustment to the world has proved a godsend. The novels of Angus Wilson, for example, become more lively year by year as they turn to parody and pastiche (rather than social reportage) for their structure. In Malcolm Bradbury's work, the comedy is so hilariously extreme that no predictable form can hold it. The emerging nation of womanhood, as Lorna Sage calls it, provides genuinely new material for the works of Angela Carter, Beryl Bainbridge, and Caroline Blackwood in Britain and Margaret Atwood in Canada—material of a reality previous generations might not have known existed. In Australia Patrick White abandons conventional wisdom and familiar views to present a totally unstereotyped view of his world. And at the far side of such ethical and aesthetic ponderings, John Fowles writes novels which examine their own structures, particularly those which determine reality, even as their stories continue on. In a fully legitimate manner, British novelists are having it both ways, celebrating what Alan Kennedy calls (in *The Protean Self*, 1974) "the dramatic actions" of a "Protean self" which "testify to a reality underlying, but they do not by any means give the whole of that reality."

Where lies fiction's reality: in its contents or in its form? This has been the central question for debate in our times. If fiction is indeed a way of looking at the world, it lies in each, and the Protean selves of John Fowles's characters and the reinventive and imaginatively transforming heroes of such American novelists as Kurt Vonnegut (*Slaughterhouse-Five*) and Jerzy Kosinski (*The Painted Bird*) are the truest fictions of our age. Virginia Woolf's world changed in 1910, as signalled by the post-impressionist painters. If we are to believe the reactions of our finest novelists today, their world changed with the abstract expressionists, who taught that the painter's canvas is not so much a surface upon which to represent but rather an arena within which to act. The contemporary novelist's page shows evidence of this same ethic: what we read is not so much a report of experience as a sample of experience itself, yet in this very activity still reflective of the moral spirit. The last Quixote, as Robert Coover calls him, is still among us, counselling that despite all obstacles we must continue, that even as we say "I can't go on" we *have* gone on to make another statement. Samuel Beckett offers a way of going on without making an affirmation of anything but that creative, continuing act—an act, of course, which speaks volumes and offers hope beyond rational belief.

—JEROME KLINKOWITZ

EDITOR'S NOTE

The selection of writers included in this book is based on the recommendations of the advisers listed on page xvii, a number of whom have helped with all four editions.

The entry for each writer consists of a biography, a complete list of separately published books, and a signed essay. In addition, entrants were invited to comment on their work.

Original British and United States editions of all books have been listed; other editions are listed only if they are first editions. All uncollected short stories published since the entrant's last collection, plus others mentioned by the entrant, have been listed; in those cases where an uncollected story was originally published in a magazine and later in an anthology, we have tended to list the anthology. As a rule all books written about the entrant are listed in the Critical Studies section; the reviews and essays listed have been recommended by the entrant.

An appendix of entries has been included for some 11 writers who have died since 1960 but whose reputations are essentially contemporary.

We would like to thank the entrants and contributors for their patience and cooperation in helping us compile this book.

ADVISERS

Walter Allen
Bernard Bergonzi
Earle Birney
Elmer Borklund
Anthony Burgess
D.D.C. Chambers
Margaret Drabble
Leslie A. Fiedler
Roy Fuller
Albert Guerard
James B. Hall
John Hawkes
Susan Hill
A. Norman Jeffares
Bruce King
Jerome Klinkowitz
James Korges
Hermione Lee
John Lehmann

Harry T. Moore
J.E. Morpurgo
Stephen Murray-Smith
Cynthia Ozick
Desmond Pacey
Marge Piercy
Hal Porter
Anthony Powell
Arthur Ravenscroft
John M. Reilly
Kenneth Rexroth
H. Winston Rhodes
Alan Ross
Barney Rosset
Mark Schorer
Tony Tanner
Fay Weldon
Michael Wood
George Woodcock

CONTRIBUTORS

Walter Allen
Patricia Altner
Richard Andersen
Alvin Aubert
Jane S. Bakerman
William C. Bamberger
John Barnes
Bruce Bennett
Sally H. Bennett
Alice Bensen
Bernard Bergonzi
Marshall A. Best
William Bittner
William Borden
Elmer Borklund
Frederick Bowers
Malcolm Bradbury
M. E. Bradford
Laurence Brander
Lloyd W. Brown
Herbert C. Burke
Mary Cadogan
Silver Donald Cameron
Frank Campenni
Charles Caramello
Frederic I. Carpenter
Hayden Carruth
D.D.C. Chambers
Gerda Charles
Ann Charters
Shirley Chew
Paul Seiko Chihara
Laurie Clancy
Anderson Clark

Ruby Cohn
John Colmer
Mary Conroy
Judy Cooke
Richard Corballis
George Core
John Cotton
David M. Craig
Hallvard Dahlie
Barrie Davies
Terence Dawson
Leon de Kock
Peter Desy
Margaret Dick
R.H.W. Dillard
Dale K. Doepke
Jay Dougherty
Paul A. Doyle
Deborah Duckworth
Ursula Edmands
Chester E. Eisinger
James A. Emanuel
Michel Fabre
Richard J. Fein
Brenda R. Ferguson
John J. Figueroa
M. J. Fitzgerald
Barbara Foley
Roberta J. Forsberg
Ruel E. Foster
Warren French
Alan Warren Friedman
Melvin J. Friedman
Lucy Frost

John Fuegi
David Galloway
Norman T. Gates
David J. Geherin
James Gindin
Lois Gordon
William Goyen
Robert Greacen
Richard Greenleaf
George Grella
Albert Guerard
Prabhu S. Guptara
Jay L. Halio
James B. Hall
Cherry A. Hankin
Maurice Harmon
S.C. Harrex
James A. Hart
David M. Heaton
Jacqueline Hoefer
Jan Hokenson
Janis Butler Holm
Craig Hudziak
Van Ikin
Louis James
A. Norman Jeffares
Annibel Jenkins
William M. Karis
Margaret Keith
Wendy Robbins Keitner
Peter Kemp
Sandra Kemp
Burton Kendle
Brian Kiernan
Robert F. Kiernan
Bruce King
H. Gustav Klaus
H.M. Klein
Marcus Klein
Jerome Klinkowitz
James Korges
Martin L. Kornbluth
Richard Kostelanetz
Mary M. Lay
Robert Lecker
Thomas LeClair
Anastasia Leech
Margaret B. Lewis
Naomi Lewis
Peter Lewis
Stanley W. Lindberg
Bernth Lindfors
Jack Lindsay
John Lucas
Robert E. Lynch
Clinton Machann
David Madden
Hena Maes-Jelinek
Irving Malin
Paul Marx
Roland Mathias
Brian E. Matthews
Frank D. McConnell
John McCormick
Frederick P.W. McDowell
Margaret B. McDowell

George McElroy
John Mepham
Patricia Merivale
Robert E. Mielke
Naomi Mitchison
John Montague
David Montrose
Gerald Moore
Harry T. Moore
Robert A. Morace
Anne Morddel
J.E. Morpurgo
Robert K. Morris
Christopher Murray
Kay J. Mussell
Shyamala A. Narayan
W.H. New
Leslie Norris
Robert Nye
D.J. O'Hearn
John P. O'Neill
John Ormond
Bridget O'Toole
Desmond Pacey
Malcolm Page
Joseph Parisi
William Peden
Marian Pehowski
Barbara M. Perkins
George Perkins
Frank T. Phipps
Marge Piercy
Sanford Pinsker
Marco Portales
Jeremy Poynting
Isabel Quigly
Arthur Ravenscroft
J.C. Reid
John M. Reilly
H. Winston Rhodes
Trevor Royle
Louis D. Rubin, Jr.
Geoff Sadler
Hana Sambrook
David Sanders
Stewart F. Sanderson
William J. Schafer
Alexander Scott
Cynthia Secor
Kathryn Lee Seidel
Alan R. Shucard
Ben Siegel
Angela Smith
Christopher Smith
Curtis C. Smith
Grahame Smith
Eric Solomon
Radcliffe Squires
Derek Stanford
Jane W. Stedman
Carol Simpson Stern
James R. Stevens
Joan Stevens
Victor Strandberg
W.J. Stuckey
Judith Summers

Fraser Sutherland
John Sutherland
Alrene Sykes
Roy Thomas
Chris Tiffin
H.M. Tiffin
Philippa Toomey
Shirley Toulson
Richard Tuerk
Roland Turner
Peter G. W. van de Kamp

Thomas A. Vogler
William Walsh
Val Warner
Harold H. Watts
John A. Weigel
Robert L. Welker
Perry D. Westbrook
Peter R. Weston
Margaret Willy
George Woodcock
Leopoldo Y. Yabes

CONTEMPORARY NOVELISTS

Ahmad Abbas
Walter Abish
Peter Abrahams
Chinua Achebe
Peter Ackroyd
Alice Adams
Richard Adams
Renata Adler
Brian Aldiss
James Aldridge
Ahmed Ali
Walter Allen
Lisa Alther
T.M. Aluko
A. Alvarez
Elechi Amadi
Eric Ambler
Kingsley Amis
Martin Amis
Mulk Raj Anand
Rudolfo A. Anaya
Jessica Anderson
I.N.C. Aniebo
Michael Anthony
Ayi Kwei Armah
Harriette Arnow
Isaac Asimov
Thea Astley
Margaret Atwood
Louis Auchincloss

Murray Bail
Paul Bailey
Beryl Bainbridge
Elliott Baker
James Baldwin
David Ballantyne
J.G. Ballard
Lynne Reid Banks
Russell Banks
John Banville
A.L. Barker
Julian Barnes
Stan Barstow
John Barth
Donald Barthelme
Frederick Barthelme
Jonathan Baumbach
Nina Bawden
Ann Beattie
David Beaty
Stephen Becker
Samuel Beckett
Barry Beckham
Sybille Bedford
Saul Bellow
David Benedictus
John Berger
Thomas Berger
Chaim Bermant
Bhabani Bhattacharya
Graham Billing
Rachel Billington
Earle Birney
Caroline Blackwood
Clark Blaise

Burt Blechman
Fred Bodsworth
Vance Bourjaily
John Bowen
Paul Bowles
William Boyd
Clare Boylan
Kay Boyle
Malcolm Bradbury
Ray Bradbury
David Bradley
Melvyn Bragg
John Braine
Sasthi Brata
Errol Brathwaite
André Brink
John Broderick
Harold Brodkey
E.M. Broner
Christine Brooke-Rose
Anita Brookner
Brigid Brophy
George Mackay Brown
Frederick Buechner
Charles Bukowski
Anthony Burgess
Alan Burns
William S. Burroughs
Janet Burroway
Frederick Busch
A.S. Byatt

Erskine Caldwell
Hortense Calisher
Morley Callaghan
Philip Callow
Peter Carey
J.L. Carr
Angela Carter
Raymond Carver
R.V. Cassill
David Caute
Gerda Charles
Jerome Charyn
Eleanor Clark
Arthur C. Clarke
Austin C. Clarke
Jon Cleary
J.M. Coetzee
Leonard Cohen
Matt Cohen
Barry Cole
Isabel Colegate
Cyrus Colter
Alex Comfort
Richard Condon
Evan S. Connell, Jr.
David Cook
Lettice Cooper
William Cooper
Robert Coover
Jack Cope
Peter Cowan
Harry Crews
Ian Cross

Roald Dahl
O.R. Dathorne
Guy Davenport
Lionel Davidson
Robertson Davies
Dan Davin
Jennifer Dawson
Ralph de Boissière
Len Deighton
Samuel R. Delany
Don DeLillo
Nigel Dennis
Anita Desai
G.V. Desani
Peter De Vries
Monica Dickens
Joan Didion
Stephen Dixon
E.L. Doctorow
J.P. Donleavy
Margaret Drabble
Robert Drewe
C.J. Driver
Allen Drury
Maureen Duffy
Daphne du Maurier
Elaine Dundy
Nell Dunn
Lawrence Durrell
Geoffrey Dutton

William Eastlake
Cyprian Ekwensi
Stanley Elkin
Alice Thomas Ellis
Ralph Ellison
David Ely
Buchi Emecheta
Isobel English
Vincent Eri
Ahmed Essop

Zoë Fairbairns
Nuruddin Farah
Howard Fast
Irvin Faust
Raymond Federman
Elaine Feinstein
Leslie A. Fiedler
Gabriel Fielding
Eva Figes
Timothy Findley
Roderick Finlayson
Penelope Fitzgerald
Thomas Flanagan
Shelby Foote
Jesse Hill Ford
Leon Forrest
Margaret Forster
Frederick Forsyth
David Foster
John Fowles
Janet Frame
Dick Francis
Michael Frayn
Nicolas Freeling

Gillian Freeman
Bruce Jay Friedman
Daniel Fuchs
Roy Fuller

William Gaddis
Ernest J. Gaines
Mavis Gallant
Helen Garner
George Garrett
William H. Gass
Maggie Gee
Maurice Gee
Martha Gellhorn
Zulfikar Ghose
Stella Gibbons
Ellen Gilchrist
Brendan Gill
Penelope Gilliatt
Brian Glanville
Julian Gloag
Rumer Godden
Dave Godfrey
Gail Godwin
Herbert Gold
William Golding
William Goldman
Nadine Gordimer
Giles Gordon
Mary Gordon
Robert Gover
Patricia Grace
Winston Graham
Shirley Ann Grau
Alasdair Gray
Graham Greene
Alfred Grossman
Albert Guerard
A.B. Guthrie, Jr.

William Haggard
Arthur Hailey
Nancy Hale
James B. Hall
Clifford Hanley
Gerald Hanley
Barry Hannah
Barbara Hanrahan
Elizabeth Hardwick
Frank Hardy
Mark Harris
Wilson Harris
Elizabeth Harrower
Nicholas Hasluck
Epeli Hau'ofa
John Hawkes
Shirley Hazzard
Bessie Head
John Hearne
Roy A.K. Heath
Robert A. Heinlein
Joseph Heller
David Helwig
James Leo Herlihy
John Hersey
Aidan Higgins

George V. Higgins
Patricia Highsmith
Carol Hill
Susan Hill
Noel Hilliard
Thomas Hinde
Barry Hines
Edward Hoagland
Russell Hoban
Laura Z. Hobson
Jack Hodgins
Alice Hoffman
Desmond Hogan
John Clellon Holmes
Hugh Hood
Peter Hooper
Christopher Hope
Paul Horgan
Geoffrey Household
Elizabeth Jane Howard
Maureen Howard
David Hughes
William Bradford Huie
Keri Hulme
William Humphrey
Emyr Humphreys
Evan Hunter
Kristin Hunter

Witi Ihimaera
Hammond Innes
David Ireland
John Irving

Dan Jacobson
C.L.R. James
P.D. James
Storm Jameson
Robin Jenkins
Ruth Prawer Jhabvala
Colin Johnson
Denis Johnson
Diane Johnson
Josephine Johnson
Jennifer Johnston
Elizabeth Jolley
Gayl Jones
Glyn Jones
Gwyn Jones
Madison Jones
Marion Patrick Jones
Mervyn Jones
Erica Jong
Neil Jordan
Gabriel Josipovici

Johanna Kaplan
Steve Katz
William Melvin Kelley
Thomas Keneally
William Kennedy
Ken Kesey
Ismith Khan
Benedict Kiely
John Oliver Killens
Richard E. Kim

Jamaica Kincaid
Francis King
W.P. Kinsella
Fletcher Knebel
John Knowles
C.J. Koch
Bernard Kops
Jerzy Kosinski
Richard Kostelanetz
Uys Krige
Robert Kroetsch

George Lamming
Margaret Laurence
Mary Lavin
John le Carré
Ursula K. Le Guin
Rosamond Lehmann
Fritz Leiber
Alan Lelchuk
Doris Lessing
Ira Levin
Norman Levine
Janet Lewis
Jack Lindsay
Emanuel Litvinoff
David Lodge
Earl Lovelace
Jack Ludwig
Alison Lurie
Morris Lurie
Andrew Lytle

Robie Macauley
Hugh MacLennan
David Madden
Norman Mailer
Clarence Major
Bernard Malamud
Manohar Malgonkar
David Malouf
Frederick Manfred
Jerre Mangione
Wolf Mankowitz
Dambudzo Marechera
Kamala Markandaya
Wallace Markfield
Bruce Marshall
Paule Marshall
Allan Massie
Peter Mathers
Jack Matthews
Peter Matthiessen
Elizabeth Mavor
William Maxwell
Mary McCarthy
Joseph McElroy
Ian McEwan
John McGahern
Thomas McGuane
Larry McMurtry
James A. McPherson
John Metcalf
Leonard Michaels
James A. Michener
O.E. Middleton

Stanley Middleton
Margaret Millar
Mark Mirsky
Joseph Mitchell
Julian Mitchell
W.O. Mitchell
Naomi Mitchison
N. Scott Momaday
Brian Moore
Frank Moorhouse
Wright Morris
Toni Morrison
Penelope Mortimer
Nicholas Mosley
Es'kia Mphahlele
John Munonye
Alice Munro
Iris Murdoch

Chaman Nahal
V.S. Naipaul
R.K. Narayan
Bill Naughton
Gloria Naylor
Jay Neugeboren
P.H. Newby
C.J. Newman
Charles Newman
Ngugi wa Thiong'o
Abioseh Nicol
Robert Nye

Joyce Carol Oates
Edna O'Brien
Julia O'Faolain
Sean O'Faolain
Tillie Olsen
Cynthia Ozick

Grace Paley
Alan Paton
Orlando Patterson
Bill Pearson
Walker Percy
Kathrin Perutz
Jerzy Peterkiewicz
Harry Mark Petrakis
Ann Petry
Gilbert Phelps
Jayne Anne Phillips
Marge Piercy
David Plante
James Plunkett
Frederik Pohl
Chaim Potok
Anthony Powell
J.F. Powers
David Pownall
Reynolds Price
V.S. Pritchett
Frederic Prokosch
James Purdy
Mario Puzo
Thomas Pynchon

Thomas Head Raddall

Raja Rao
Frederic Raphael
Simon Raven
Piers Paul Read
John Rechy
Ishmael Reed
Vic Reid
Mordecai Richler
Tom Robbins
Marilynne Robinson
Mary Robison
Daphne Rooke
Sinclair Ross
Judith Rossner
Leo Rosten
Henry Roth
Philip Roth
Bernice Rubens
Jane Rule
Michael Rumaker
Salman Rushdie
Joanna Russ

Nayantara Sahgal
Garth St. Omer
J.D. Salinger
Andrew Salkey
May Sarton
Susan Fromberg Schaeffer
Budd Schulberg
Hubert Selby, Jr.
Samuel Selvon
Maurice Shadbolt
Margery Sharp
Tom Sharpe
Wilfrid Sheed
Clancy Sigal
Leslie Marmon Silko
Alan Sillitoe
Andrew Sinclair
Jo Sinclair
Isaac Bashevis Singer
Khushwant Singh
F. Sionil Jose
Elizabeth Smart
Emma Smith
Iain Crichton Smith
Susan Sontag
Gilbert Sorrentino
Terry Southern
Muriel Spark
Colin Spencer
Elizabeth Spencer
Wallace Stegner
James Stern
Richard G. Stern
J.I.M. Stewart
Irving Stone
Robert Stone
David Storey
Randolph Stow
Francis Stuart
William Styron
Ronald Sukenick
Glendon Swarthout
Graham Swift

Julian Symons

Peter Taylor
Emma Tennant
Kylie Tennant
Alexander Theroux
Paul Theroux
Audrey Thomas
D.M. Thomas
Gillian Tindall
Peter Tinniswood
Honor Tracy
Rose Tremain
William Trevor
Rachel Trickett
Niccolò Tucci
Frank Tuohy
George Turner
Amos Tutuola
Anne Tyler

John Updike
Edward Upward
Leon Uris
Fred Urquhart

Laurens van der Post
Peter Vansittart
Gore Vidal
Kurt Vonnegut, Jr.

David Wagoner
John Wain
Dan Wakefield
Alice Walker
Margaret Walker
Rex Warner
Robert Penn Warren
Keith Waterhouse

David Watmough
Jerome Weidman
Fay Weldon
Eudora Welty
Albert Wendt
Glenway Wescott
Anthony West
Anthony C. West
Morris West
Paul West
William Wharton
Patrick White
John Edgar Wideman
Rudy Wiebe
Michael Wilding
John Williams
John A. Williams
Raymond Williams
Wirt Williams
Calder Willingham
A.N. Wilson
Angus Wilson
Colin Wilson
Sloan Wilson
Adele Wiseman
Larry Woiwode
Douglas Woolf
Herman Wouk
Charles Wright
Rudolph Wurlitzer

James Yaffe
Richard Yates
Frank Yerby
Helen Yglesias
Jose Yglesias
Al Young
Marguerite Young
Sol Yurick

APPENDIX

Truman Capote
John Cheever
J.G. Farrell
John Gardner
James Jones
Jack Kerouac

Ross Macdonald
Olivia Manning
Carson McCullers
Flannery O'Connor
Paul Scott

ABBAS, (Khwaja) Ahmad. Indian. Born in Panipat, Punjab, 7 June 1914. Educated at Hali Muslim High School; Aligarh Muslim University, B.A. 1933, LL.B. 1935. Married Mujtabai Khatoon in 1942 (died, 1958); one daughter. Reporter and sub-editor, 1936–39, and editor of the Sunday edition, and columnist, 1939–47, Bombay *Chronicle*. Since 1947, contributing columnist ("Last Page"), *Blitz* magazine, Bombay. Since 1951, proprietor, Naya Sansar film production company, Bombay. Leader, Indian Film Delegation, U.S.S.R., 1954. Recipient: *Hindustan Times* prize, 1950; President of India's Gold Medal, for film, 1964; Padma Shree, 1969; Haryana State Robe of Honour, 1969. Address: Philomena Apartment, Church Road, Juhu, Bombay-49, India.

PUBLICATIONS

Novels

Tomorrow Is Ours! Bombay, Popular Book Depot, 1943; as *Divided Heart*, New Delhi, Paradise, 1968.
Defeat for Death: A Story Without Names. Baroda, Padmaja, 1944.
Blood and Stones. Bombay, Hind Kitabs, 1947.
Inqilab. Bombay, Jaico, 1955.
When Night Falls. New Delhi, Hind, 1968.
Mera Naam, Joker. New Delhi, Hind, 1970.
Maria. New Delhi, Hind, 1972.
Boy Meets Girl. New Delhi, Sterling, 1973.
Bobby. New Delhi, Sterling, 1973.
Distant Dream. New Delhi, Sterling, 1975.
The World Is My Village. New Delhi, Ajanta, 1983.

Short Stories

Not All Lies! Privately printed, 1945.
Rice and Other Stories. Bombay, Kutub, 1947.
Cages of Freedom and Other Stories. Bombay, Hind Kitabs, 1952.
One Thousand Nights on a Bed of Stones and Other Stories. Bombay, Jaico, 1957.
The Black Sun and Other Stories. Bombay, Jaico, 1963.
The Most Beautiful Woman in the World. New Delhi, Paradise, 1968.
The Walls of Glass. New Delhi, Himalaya, 1977.
Men and Women. New Delhi, NV, 1977.

Plays

Zubeida (produced Bombay, 1944).
Invitation to Immortality. Bombay, Padma, 1944.
Lal Gulab Ki Wapsi (produced Bombay, 1964).
Barrister-at-Law: A Play about the Early Life of Mahatma Gandhi. New Delhi, Orient, 1977.

Screenplays: *Naya Sansar*, 1941; *Dr. Kotnis*, 1945; *Dharti Ke Lal*, 1946; *Awara*, 1951; *Anhonee*, 1951; *Rahi*, 1952; *Munna*, 1954; *Shri 420*, 1955; *Pardesi*, 1957; *Chardil Char Rahen*, 1959; *Shehar Aur Sapna*, 1963; *Hamara Gaar*, 1964; *Aasman Bahal*, 1966; *Bambai Raat Ki Bahon Mein*, 1968; *Saat Hindustani*, 1969; *Mera Naam Joker*, 1970; *Do Boond Pani*, 1971; *Bobby*, 1973; *Achanak*, 1973; *Faaslah*, 1974.

Other

Outside India: The Adventures of a Roving Reporter. New Delhi, Hali, 1938.

Let India Fight for Freedom. Bombay, Sound Magazine, 1943.
An Indian Looks at America. Bombay, Thacker, 1943.
And One Did Not Come Back: The Story of the Congress Medical Mission to China. Bombay, Sound Magazine, 1944.
Report to Gandhiji, with N.G. Yog. Bombay, Hind Kitabs, 1944.
I Write as I Feel (selections from Bombay *Chronicle*). Bombay, Hind Kitabs, 1948.
Kashmir Fights for Freedom. Bombay, Kutub, 1948.
China Can Make It. Bombay, Bhatt, 1952.
In the Image of Mao Tse-tung. Bombay, Peoples Publishing House, 1953.
Face to Face with Khrushchev. New Delhi, Rajpal, 1960.
Till We Reach the Stars: The Story of Yuri Gagarin. London, Asia Publishing House, 1961; New York, Asia Publishing House, 1962.
Indira Ghandi: Return of the Red Rose. Bombay, Popular Prakashan, 1966.
That Woman: Her Seven Years In Power. New Delhi, Indian Book Company, 1973; revised edition, as *That Woman: Indira Gandhi's Ten Years in Power*, 1976.
Face to Face with Indira Gandhi, with R.K. Karanjia. New Delhi, Chetana, 1974.
Jawaharlal Nehru: Portrait of an Integrated Indian. New Delhi, National Council of Educational Research and Training, 1974.
I Am Not an Island: An Experiment in Autobiography. New Delhi, Vikas, and Columbia, Missouri, South Asia Books, 1977.
The Mad, Mad, Mad World of Indian Films. New Delhi, Hind, 1977.
Four Friends. New Delhi, Arnold-Heinemann, 1977.
20th March 1977: A Day Like Any Other. New Delhi, Vikas, 1978.
Janata in a Jam? Bombay, Jaico, 1978.
The Naxalites. New Delhi, Lok, 1979.
Sarojini Naidu: An Introduction to a Fascinating Personality. Bombay, Bharatiya Vidya Bhavan, 1980.
Bread, Beauty and Revolution, Being a Chronological Selection from the Last Pages 1947 to 1981. New Delhi, Marwah, 1982.

Translator, *I Cannot Die*, by Krishnan Chandar. Poona, Kutub, 1943 (?).
Translator, *Shadows Speak*, by A.H. Sahir Ludhianvi. Bombay, P.P.H. Bookstall, 1958.

*

Ahmad Abbas comments:

Highbrow literary critics in India have sometimes sneeringly labelled my novels and short stories as "mere journalese." The fact that most of them are inspired by aspects of the contemporary historical reality, as sometimes chronicled in the press, is sufficient to put them beyond the pale of literary creation. I have no quarrel with the critics. Maybe I am an unredeemed journalist and reporter, masquerading as a writer of fiction. But I have always believed that while the inner life of man undoubtedly is, and should be, the primary concern of literature, this inner personal life impinges upon the life of the community—and of humanity—at every critical turning point of human experience. "No man is an island ..." said John Donne, and one may add that even if he was, no island is free from the inroads of the sea, as no man is free from the impact of social forces and the life around him.

This inter-action of the individual society, both in its psychological and social complexity, is of particular interest to me as a writer. It has inspired, provoked, or coloured most of what I have written.

Mirrored in my works are many fragments of our recent history—the war, the religious riots and the killings, the partition, the post-freedom years of disillusionment, of the new hopes engendered, and problems raised, by the industrialization and mechanization of agriculture. But I do hope I have also revealed glimpses of the "inner life" of my contemporaries, the people of a new India, in their moments of tenderness and passion, of frustration and exultation, as they evolve from the passive (but by no means ignoble) fatalism, so characteristic of the Indian peasant rooted in tradition, towards the hopeful dynamism, the remarkable adaptability and the willingness to change, which, paradoxically enough, is also an Indian characteristic.

If there is one thing that I have tried consistently to do in my novels and stories, it is to give the readers a little peep into the hearts and minds, the inner life, of my contemporaries and fellow Indians, to show that their life is being influenced and changed and re-shaped by the historical and social forces that are greater than us and our "destiny."

*　　　*　　　*

Ahmad Abbas is one of the most popular Indian writers in English. He is, however, one of the least regarded of them from a scholarly point of view. This is due partly to the uneven quality of the large amount of material he has produced, and partly to the popular forms in which he works. His populist orientation is evident from the fact that he has chosen to write much of his work in English specifically because he wants to communicate with Indians from all linguistic backgrounds (according to the last census, India has over a thousand languages: Hindi and English are the two official languages, but Hindi, though used by 40 per cent of the country, is the mother-tongue of only one region; English, though used by a far smaller number—only around ten per cent of the country—has the "advantage" of being equally foreign to all parts of the country! All educated Indians know English, but not all educated Indians know Hindi, despite considerable governmental pressure to learn the language). Indian intellectuals like to pride themselves on their secularism. Abbas has not been greatly helped by the fact that he comes from a Muslim background.

The forms in which Abbas has written include short stories, novels, plays, and Hindi-language filmscripts for the huge Indian film industry. Elite snobbishness toward Indian films—with their song-and-fight formulas and their pastiche of fabulous Indian (rather than realist Western) conventions—has no doubt helped to deprive Abbas of the right credentials to be taken seriously by literary scholars. Abbas's favourite genre, the short story, does not have an enthusiastic following among Indian literary critics either, and his use of English is not marked by that Oxbridge ease so beloved of some Indian critics; nor does he seem to have had the inclination to theorize about his linguistic experiments in the way of other writers, such as Mulk Raj Anand and Raja Rao. What Abbas has been trying to produce is genuinely home-grown work which speaks to the people. In a hierarchical country like India, it is not surprising that his work should, then, not speak to scholars and critics. If it is pastiche the people want, as in the Indian cinema, he is willing to work within the enormous constraints imposed by the conventions of Indian pastiche in order to get his message across.

The message is not easy to decipher, because he has been a Gandhian, is now better-known for his sympathy with the Soviet Union and, in an article published not long ago, he summed up his position as consisting in the almost Romantic words, "Bread, Beauty and Revolution." The first of Abbas's collections of short stories in English, *Not All Lies!*, typifies his output. It is primarily satirical, and attacks hypocrisy and the unscrupulously mercenary character of the middle classes. Several of the stories are sharply anti-British. But his anti-British sentiments are consequent upon his concern with the social and political issues facing the country. In this sense, Abbas has remained a Gandhian: all his work is rooted in a concern for India; patriotism and the unity and welfare of the country seem to be the driving force of all of his work. Abbas is an Indian even before he is a Gandhian. The different way in which he has at various times put his beliefs shows, not a change in fundamentals, but his view of what is of greatest concern to the country at that moment. No other English-language writer in the country uses its history so fully. No other writer knows so well the currents and moods of contemporary India. No one else speaks so effectively to them. He turned the script of his successful film *Saat Hindustani* (Seven Indians) into a novel, *Maria*, which features companions in an undercover operation who help liberate the Portuguese colony of Goa in 1961 and reunite it with India. After the success of the operation, six of them scatter to other parts of India. Seven years later, Maria is ill, and, feeling herself near death, sends telegrams to the others to ask them to see her one last time. Caught up in their own lives, it takes them some time to respond and, by the time they arrive, Maria is already dead. When they meet at the graveside, they are alienated from each other by the sorts of concerns and tensions that have fuelled regionalist politics in India but, recalling their mutual affection in the past and their comradeship in the struggle to liberate Goa, they are brought to a reconciliation. *The Naxalites* is one of the few attempts by an Indian writer to explore the history, psychology, and relative success of the Maoist revolutionary movement which attracted some of the most intelligent and well-educated young Indians to its cadres and required extensive operations by the Indian Army before it was suppressed.

What saves Abbas's work from being merely propagandist is precisely his love for his subjects, for he loves them in their strengths as well as their weaknesses. Mulk Raj Anand once said that Abbas "grasps the weaknesses of his characters amid their strengths." That is Abbas's strength as a writer. His strength as an *Indian* writer is that he brings to India, similarly, "the only kind of love which can redeem its present wretchedness and stretch out to its unexplored future."

Abbas's first English-language novel, *Tomorrow Is Ours!*, celebrates a twenty year-old heroine, Parvati. Beautiful and sharply conscious of social problems, she is forced to give up her medical studies because of the death of her mother. Becoming a dancer in a different part of the country, she falls in love with one of the regular patrons, Dr. Shrikant. Shrikant's rather conservative mother, Ramadevi, does not approve of Parvati. However, the couple get married in a civil ceremony, and Ramadevi needs to be almost at death's door from injury during the bombardment of Calcutta (the action is set during the Second World War) before she relents. The novel's bold opposition to caste prejudice was, at that time, fairly new in Indian literature. In creating a modern couple who ignore tradition and get away with it, and in making the conservative Ramadevi give up her beliefs in the face of circumstances, the novel was inverting the usual way in which such themes were handled.

The anti-imperial and anti-fascist theme in the novel is subordinated to the story, and to the immediate problems faced by the characters.

Inqilab (Revolution) is a more ambitious novel which attempts to portray the whole history of the national movement. The novel took some seven years to write, for the idea for the novel came to Abbas after 8 August 1942 when the Indian National Congress passed its famous "Quit India" resolution. The novel's protagonist, Anwar, is a young Muslim intellectual committed to the nationalist struggle, and the novel plainly draws on Abbas's childhood in a traditional Muslim family, his student days at university, and his life as a journalist and as someone slowly drawn into the freedom struggle. However, key events in Anwar's life have been movingly reconstructed from history: the Amritsar massacre in 1919, the Salt March, the declaration of Independence, the proceedings of the Congress Working Party. When Anwar rebukes some Muslim separatists, his uncle reveals the family secret of Anwar's parentage to deflate him: Anwar is not in fact a Muslim but the illegitimate son of a Hindu. The novel concludes: "Could it be that he who by birth was neither a Hindu nor wholly a Muslim or, rather, who was both, an oddly symbolic Son of India, was in a peculiarly advantageous position to understand both the communities and to work for the synthesis that was already symbolized in his person." That clumsily multisyllabic ending is symptomatic of the points in Abbas's work where his literary judgment is subverted by his idealism.

Abbas's work has also been accused of being too political, too journalistic, too crowded, too crammed with incidental detail, too sweeping, too sentimental. But there is, in all his work, an attempt to contain and recreate the whole experience of modern India, an attempt undertaken by few others.

—Prabhu S. Guptara

ABISH, Walter. American. Born in Vienna, Austria, 24 December 1931; became American citizen, 1960. Married Cecile Gelb (i.e., the sculptor Cecile Abish). Adjunct Professor, Empire State College, New York, 1975; Writer-in-Residence, Wheaton College, Norton, Massachusetts, 1976; Visiting Butler Professor, State University of New York, Buffalo, 1977. Since 1979, Lecturer in English and Comparative Literature, Columbia University, New York. Visiting Professor, Yale University, New Haven, Connecticut, 1985. Recipient: New Jersey Council on the Arts fellowship, 1972; Rose Isabel Williams Foundation grant, 1974; Ingram Merrill Foundation grant, 1977; National Endowment for the Arts fellowship, 1980, 1985; PEN-Faulkner Award, 1981; Guggenheim fellowship, 1981; Creative Artists Public Service grant, 1981; D.A.A.D. fellowship (West Berlin), 1986. Agent: Candida Donadio, 231 West 22nd Street, New York, New York 10011. Address: P.O. Box 485, Cooper Station, New York, New York 10276, U.S.A.

PUBLICATIONS

Novels

Alphabetical Africa. New York, New Directions, 1974.
➤*How German Is It.* New York, New Directions, 1980; Manchester, Carcanet, 1982.

Short Stories

Minds Meet. New York, New Directions, 1975.
➤*In the Future Perfect.* New York, New Directions, 1977; London, Faber, 1984.

Uncollected Short Stories

"Inside Out," in *Personal Injury Magazine 4* (New York), 1978.
"Happiness," in *Parenthèse* (Brewster, New York), 1979.
"Ninety-nine: The New Meaning," in *Renegade 1* (New York), 1979.
"Auctioning Australia," in *Text-Sound Texts,* edited by Richard Kostelanetz. New York, Morrow, 1980.
"Alphabet of Revelations," in *New Directions 41.* New York, New Directions, 1980.
"The Idea of Switzerland," in *The Best American Short Stories 1981,* edited by Hortense Calisher and Shannon Ravenel. Boston, Houghton Mifflin, 1981.
"What Else?" in *Conjunctions* (New York), Winter 1981–82.

Verse

Duel Site. New York, Tibor de Nagy, 1970.

*

Critical Studies: "Through a Continent Darkly," in *Picked-Up Pieces* by John Updike, New York, Knopf, 1975, London, Deutsch, 1976; interview with Jerome Klinkowitz, in *Fiction International* (Canton, New York), Fall 1975, and *The Life of Fiction,* Urbana, University of Illinois Press, 1977, "Walter Abish and the Surfaces of Life," in *Georgia Review* (Athens), Summer 1981, and *The Self-Apparent Word,* Carbondale, Southern Illinois University Press, 1984, all by Klinkowitz; "Restrictive Fiction" by Kenneth Baker, in *New Directions 35,* New York, New Directions, 1977; "Self-Portrait" by Abish, in *Individuals: Post Movement Art in America,* New York, Dutton, 1977; "In So Many Words" by Irving Malin, in *Ontario Review* (Windsor), Winter 1978–79; "Present Imperfect" by Tony Tanner, in *Granta* (Cambridge), 1979; "The Writer-to-Be: An Impression of Living" by Abish, and "The Puzzle of Walter Abish" by Alain Arias-Misson, in *Sub-Stance 27* (Madison, Wisconsin), Winter 1980; interview with Sylvère Lotringer, in *Semiotext(e)* (New York), 1982; *Silverless Mirrors: Book, Self, and Postmodern American Fiction* by Charles Caramello, Tallahassee, Florida State University Press, 1983; "Walter Abish's Fictions: Perfect Unfamiliarity, Familiar Imperfections" by Richard Martin, in *Journal of American Studies 17* (Norwich), 1983; *The Novel in Motion* by Richard Pearce, Athens, Ohio University Press, 1983; "The Disposition of the Familiar" by Régis Durand, and "Postromantic Irony in Postmodernist Times" by Heide Ziegler, in *Delta* (Montpellier, France), 1983; *American Fictions 1940–1980* by Frederick Karl, New York, Harper, 1983.

Walter Abish comments:

The innovative novel is, in essence, a novel of defamiliarization—a novel that has ceased to concern itself with the mapping of the "familiar" world, for to do so would compel the characters to adopt a perception of the everyday predicated on an unquestioning affirmation of the function and role of the "self" in society. This role is as rigidly governed by the "Reality Principle" (as defined by Freud) and as subsumed by the reality of everyday existence as we are. What the innovative novel must disavow is the self-centered world in which the "self" continues to reign supreme. Arnheim speaks of order as any-thing the human mind is to understand. I think by undermining order writers bring about a new understanding.

*   *   *

Walter Abish—born in Vienna, raised in China, settled in Israel, and trained as a city planner, the occupation which first brought him to America and a job in New York City—began publishing fiction in 1970. His major work has appeared in the semi-annual anthologies produced by New Directions, the publisher who has also issued his two collections of short fiction and two novels. A master of the stiff-upper lip, self-consciously presentational prose style made famous by Donald Barthelme, Abish has devised his own techniques by which the language of his stories explores itself in search of the ironies of human communication and behaviour.

His first novel, *Alphabetical Africa*, is a tour de force demonstration of how words can refer to their own artificiality at the same time they operate as linguistic signifiers. The first chapter is titled "A," and every word therein begins with that letter ("Ages ago, Alex, Allen and Alva arrived at Antibes, and Alva allowing all, allowing anyone, against Alex's admoni-tion, against Allen's angry assertion: another African amuse-ment," etc.). The second-chapter, "B," adds words beginning with the letter *B*, and so forth until the book expands to its full linguistic possibilities. Such a self-apparent structure makes the reader painfully aware of the words themselves, and of how an artificial discipline of language determines just what reality may transpire. For example, a character named Herman can't appear until chapter "H"; the first person narrator must keep his comments to himself until chapter "I"; and the char-acters cannot travel to Jedda until chapter "J." By chapter "Z" the full exercise of language may have lulled the reader into complacency. But the book is only half done, for the 27th chapter is titled "Z" once more, followed by "Y," "X," and so forth back through the now-contracting alphabet. Familiar persons, places, and things are lost at each receding chapter as the book's mimetic action literally effaces itself in one's hands, until at the end one is left with the solemn toiling at the minimally expressive letter *A*. Like breathing in and then breathing out, the reader has experienced the expansion and contraction, the life and death of a work of fiction. At no point can one suspend disbelief and sink into the pantomime of suspended disbelief, for at all times attention is riveted to the self-conscious making and unmaking of the physical book.

Minds Meet collects 12 of Abish's short fictions from the early 1970's. The title piece is based upon improvisations with the theme of human communication: "Taken Aback by the Message," "The Abandoned Message," Abased by the Mes-sage," and so forth. Another story, "This Is Not a Film. This is a Precise Act of Disbelief," employs the semiology of con-temporary American culture, whereby the needs of people are served by an assortment of surface details ("pure signifiers" as the structuralists would say). Abish's most characteristic style in these shorter pieces is to write sentences composed of radically different thoughts which collide at the caesura; readers are thus aware of content and linguistic form at the same time, and especially how syntax presupposes judgment—an irony Abish enjoys exploiting with his humor of sexual innuendo. By these collisions, the story moves forward; its real subject is nothing other than itself.

The stories of *In the Future Perfect* are distinguished by their mechanical structures which call attention to their component words. "Ardor/Awe/Atrocity" consists of block paragraphs headed by three superscripted words, their presence in the

following sections numbered in alphabetical order. One is thus aware of the 78 key words which will be featured long before they pop up in the narrative; when they do, the reader should be more inclined to treat them as signifiers—as creatures of the writer's invention—than as signified in the outside world of associations. "In So Many Words" assembles the words of each paragraph in alphabetical order before those same terms are repeated in syntactic sense, making attention to the writer's artifice (and the words themselves) more pronounced. Even the apparently conventional stories in this volume, by virtue of their circular technique, return to key elements ("perfec-tion," "repetition") which the author selects at the start of each section.

How German Is It, Abish's second novel, is disarmingly con-ventional. But only on the surface is it a simple story of a writer's return to "the new Germany." A story from *In the Future Perfect*, "The English Garden," is actually its prolegom-ena, and the epigraph from John Ashbery indicates Abish's deeper interests in the linguistically contrived nature of human behaviour: "Remnants of the old atrocity subsist, but they are converted into ingenious shifts in scenery, a sort of 'English Garden' effect, to give the required air of naturalness, pathos and hope."

—Jerome Klinkowitz

ABRAHAMS, Peter (Henry).   South African.   Born in Vre-dedorp, near Johannesburg, in 1919. Educated at Church of England mission schools and colleges. Married Daphne Eliza-beth Miller; three children. Merchant seaman, 1939–41; then lived in England: regular contributor to *The Observer*, London, and the *Herald Tribune*, New York and Paris, 1952–64; Editor, *West Indian Economist*, and Controller, *West Indian News*, Jamaica, 1955–64; Chairman, Radio Jamaica, Kingston, 1977–80. Address: Red Hills, St. Andrew, Jamaica.

PUBLICATIONS

Novels

Song of the City.   London, Crisp, 1945.
Mine Boy.   London, Crisp, 1946; New York, Knopf, 1955.
The Path of Thunder.   New York, Harper, 1948; London, Faber, 1952.
Wild Conquest.   New York, Harper, 1950; London, Faber, 1951.
A Wreath for Udomo.   New York, Knopf, and London, Faber, 1956.
A Night of Their Own.   New York, Knopf, and London, Faber, 1965.
This Island Now.   London, Faber, 1966; New York, Knopf, 1967.
The View from Coyaba.   London, Faber, 1985.

Short Stories

Dark Testament.   London, Allen and Unwin, 1942.

Verse

A Blackman Speaks of Freedom!   Durban, Universal Printing Works, 1938 (?).

Other

Return to Goli (reportage).   London, Faber, 1953.
Tell Freedom: Memories of Africa.   London, Faber, and New York, Knopf, 1954.
Jamaica: An Island Mosaic.   London, Her Majesty's Stationery Office, 1957.
The World of Mankind, with others.   New York, Golden Press, 1962.

*

Critical Studies: *Peter Abrahams* by Michael Wade, London, Evans, 1972; *The Writing of Peter Abrahams* by Kolawole Ogungbesan, London, Hodder and Stoughton, 1979.

*   *   *

Peter Abrahams left South Africa in 1939, when he was only 20 years old, but the racial and political problems of that troubled land for many years continued to dominate his imagination. All but the last two of his eight novels have been set entirely or in part in South Africa, and even the exceptions, *This Island Now* and *The View from Coyaba*, deal with problems in plural societies in which there is great friction between blacks and whites. Abrahams has also written two autobiographical books, *Tell Freedom* and *Return to Goli*, both of which focus on his experiences as a mulatto in South Africa.

Abrahams's early novels were influenced by Marxist ideas so they tend to be concerned more with race and economics than with politics. *Song of the City* and *Mine Boy* tell of the consequences of urbanization and industrialization on the lives of young black workers who move from the country to the city. *Song of the City* takes place at the time of the second world war, *Mine Boy* against the backdrop of booming gold mines in Johannesburg. In both novels nonwhites are mistreated and oppressed by whites.

In his next novel, *The Path of Thunder*, Abrahams turned to the theme of interracial love, exploring its impact on a young Coloured schoolteacher and an Afrikaner girl whose passionate affair ultimately ends in tragedy when the Afrikaner community discovers they are lovers. Two years later Abrahams moved in yet another direction, this time reconstructing the era of the Afrikaner migration or "Great Trek" in *Wild Conquest*, an historical novel in which he made an effort to be fair to all the major ethnic groups in South Africa—Bantu, Boer and Briton.

After these early works, all of which were written in the 1940's, Abrahams's fiction became more political. *A Wreath for Udomo*, published just before Ghana attained its independence, was an attempt to predict what might happen when independent black African nations were confronted with the choice between the financial advantages of collaborating with the white regimes in southern Africa and the moral imperative of opposing them by actively supporting black liberation movements. *A Night of Their Own* carried the revolutionary theme further by detailing the adventures of an African underground agent involved in smuggling funds to an Indian resistance organization in South Africa. *This Island Now* told of racial tensions and internal power struggles in a small, black-ruled Caribbean island-state, and *The View from Coyaba*, certainly his most ambitious historical novel, covered more than 150 years of black experience in tropical Africa, the Caribbean and the deep south of the United States. In each successive novel Abrahams moved further and further away from a depiction of South African social realities to the construction of hypothetical situations which afforded greater elbow room. Even *A Night of*

Their Own, though set in South Africa, had elements of fantasy and wishful thinking in it. Abrahams's increased independence on his imagination in these later novels may reflect how far out of touch he is with contemporary conditions in his native land.

Abrahams has always written in a simple, direct prose style which wavers between superior reportage and maudlin romanticizing. He is at his best when transcribing newsworthy events which have a basis in fact; his autobiographical and travel writings, for instance, are superb. But he has a regrettable tendency to sentimentalize personal relationships between men and women, especially if they are of different races, as they so often are in his novels. His accounts of miscegenated love are nearly always literary disasters because they are bathed in lachrymose artificiality.

Yet when he writes of exciting happenings such as spontaneous labor strikes, bloody frontier battles, underground resistance campaigns, or the highly-charged political debates at a Pan-African congress, Abrahams can carry the reader along swiftly and persuasively, building up a spell-binding momentum which is broken only when he suddenly veers from the external world of his characters into the internal world of their thoughts and dreams. Abrahams has not yet learned to write a decent interior monologue, and his novels would be more aesthetically satisfying if his heroes and heroines were less inclined to moments of moody introspection. His surface sketches are much more convincing than his psychological probings.

Because Abrahams was one of the first African writers to achieve international recognition, his works received a good deal of patronizing attention at first. European and American critics were all too eager to embrace him as a literary phenomenon—a nonwhite South African who could not only write but could actually write fairly well!—so they wrote glowing reviews of his early novels, emphasizing their strong points and ignoring obvious flaws. Today, in the midst of an African literary awakening, Abrahams tends to be regarded with less enthusiasm, for his novels are recognized as far less interesting and accomplished than those produced in West Africa by such talented artists as Chinua Achebe, Wole Soyinka, and Ayi Kwei Armah. Abrahams has certainly carved a niche for himself in African literary history, but it is a small niche somewhere at the base of the monument, passionately but clumsily hewn.

—Bernth Lindfors

ACHEBE, Chinua.   Nigerian.   Born Albert Chinualumogu in Ogidi, 16 November 1930. Educated at Government College, Umuahia, 1944–47; University College, Ibadan, 1948–53, B.A. (London) 1953. Married Christiana Okoli in 1961; two sons and two daughters. Talks producer, Lagos, 1954–57, Controller, Enugu, 1958–61, and Director, Lagos, 1961–66, Nigerian Broadcasting Corporation; Chairman, Citadel Books Ltd., Enugu, 1967; Senior Research Fellow, 1967–73, and Professor of English, 1973–81, University of Nigeria, Nsukka; since 1984, Emeritus Professor. Visiting Professor, University of Massachusetts, Amherst, 1972–75, and University of Connecticut, Storrs, 1975–76; Regents' Lecturer, University of California, Los Angeles, 1984. Founding Editor, Heinemann African Writers series, 1962–72, and since 1970, Director, Heinemann Educational Books (Nigeria) Ltd., and Nwankwo-Ifejika Ltd., later Nwamife, publishers, Enugu; since 1971, Editor, *Okike*, an African journal of new writing. Member, University of Lagos Council, 1966; Chairman, Society of Nigerian Authors, 1966, and since 1982 President, Association of Nigerian Authors. Recipient: Margaret Wrong Memorial Prize, 1959; Nigerian National Trophy, 1960; Rockefeller fellowship, 1960; Unesco fellowship, 1963; Jock Campbell Award (*New Statesman*), 1965; Commonwealth Poetry Prize, 1972; Neil Gunn International Fellowship, 1974; Nigerian National Merit Award, 1979; Commonwealth Foundation Senior Award, 1983. D. Litt.: Dartmouth College, Hanover, New Hampshire, 1972; University of Southampton, 1975; University of Ife, 1978; University of Nigeria, 1981; University of Kent, Canterbury, 1982; Mount Allison University, Sackville, New Brunswick, 1984; University of Guelph, Ontario, 1984; Franklin Pierce College, Rindge, New Hampshire, 1985; D. Univ.: University of Stirling, 1975; LL.D.: University of Prince Edward Island, Charlottetown, 1976; D.H.L.: University of Massachusetts, 1977. Honorary Fellow, Modern Language Association (USA), 1975; Member, Order of the Federal Republic of Nigeria, 1979; Honorary Member, American Academy, 1982; Fellow, Royal Society of Literature, 1983. Address: P.O. Box 53, University of Nigeria, Nsukka, Anambra State, Nigeria.

PUBLICATIONS

Novels

Things Fall Apart. London, Heinemann, 1958; New York, McDowell Obolensky, 1959.
No Longer at Ease. London, Heinemann, 1960; New York, Obolensky, 1961.
Arrow of God. London, Heinemann, 1964; New York, Day, 1967.
A Man of the People. London, Heinemann, and New York, Day, 1966.

Short Stories

The Sacrificial Egg and Other Stories. Onitsha, Etudo, 1962.
Girls at War. London, Heinemann, and New York, Doubleday, 1972.

Verse

Beware, Soul-Brother and Other Poems. Enugu, Nwankwo-Ifejika, 1971; revised edition, Enugu, Nwamife, and London, Heinemann, 1972.
Christmas in Biafra and Other Poems. New York, Doubleday, 1973.

Other (for children)

Chike and the River. London and New York, Cambridge University Press, 1966.
How the Leopard Got His Claws, with John Iroaganachi. Enugu, Nwamife, 1972; New York, Third Press, 1973.
The Flute. Enugu, Fourth Dimension, 1977.
The Drum. Enugu, Fourth Dimension, 1977.

Other

Morning Yet on Creation Day: Essays. London, Heinemann, and New York, Doubleday, 1975.
In Person: Achebe, Awoonor, and Soyinka at the University of Washington. Seattle, University of Washington African Studies Program, 1975.

The Trouble with Nigeria. Enugu, Fourth Dimension, 1983; London, Heinemann, 1984.

Editor, with Dubem Okafor, *Don't Let Him Die: An Anthology of Memorial Poems for Christopher Okigbo.* Enugu, Fourth Dimension, 1978.
Editor, with C.L. Innes, *African Short Stories.* London, Heinemann, 1984.

*

Bibliography: in *Africana Library Journal* (New York), Spring 1970.

Critical Studies: *The Novels of Chinua Achebe* by G.D. Killam, London, Heinemann, and New York, Africana, 1969, revised edition, as *The Writings of Chinua Achebe*, Heinemann, 1977; *Chinua Achebe* by Arthur Ravenscroft, London, Longman, 1969, revised edition, 1977; *Chinua Achebe* by David Carroll, New York, Twayne, 1970, revised edition, London, Macmillan, 1980; *Chinua Achebe et la tragédie de l'histoire* by Thomas Melone, Paris, Présence Africaine, 1973; *Chinua Achebe* by Kate Turkington, London, Arnold, 1977; *Critical Perspectives on Chinua Achebe* edited by Bernth Lindfors and C.L. Innes, London, Heinemann, and Washington, D.C., Three Continents, 1978; *Achebe's World: The Historical and Cultural Context of the Novels of Chinua Achebe* by Robert M. Wren, Washington, D.C., Three Continents, 1980, London, Longman, 1981; *The Four Novels of Chinua Achebe: A Critical Study* by Benedict C. Njoku, Bern, Switzerland, Lang, 1984; *L'Oeuvre de Chinua Achebe* by Denise Coussy, Paris, Présence Africaine, 1985.

Chinua Achebe comments:
I am a political writer. My politics is concerned with universal human communication across racial and cultural boundaries as a means of fostering respect for all people. Such respect can issue only from understanding. So my primary concern is with clearing the channels of communication in my own neighborhood by hacking away at the thickets that choke them.
Africa's meeting with Europe must be accounted a terrible disaster in this matter of human understanding and respect. The nature of the meeting precluded any warmth of friendship. First Europe was an enslaver; then a colonizer. In either role she had no need and made little effort to understand or appreciate Africa; indeed she easily convinced herself that there was nothing there to justify the effort. Today our world is still bedevilled by the consequences of that cataclysmic encounter.
I was born into the colonial era, grew up in the heady years of nationalist protest and witnessed Africa's resumption of independence. (It was not, however, the same Africa which originally lost her freedom that now regained it, but a different Africa created in the image of Europe—but that's another story.) So I have seen in my not very long lifetime three major eras in precipitate succession, leaving us somewhat dazed. My response as a writer has been to try to keep pace with these torrential changes. First I had to tell Europe that the arrogance on which she sought to excuse her pillage of Africa, i.e., that Africa was the Primordial Void, was sheer humbug; that Africa had a history, a religion, a civilization. We reconstructed this history and civilization and displayed it to challenge the stereotype and the cliché. Actually it was not to Europe alone I spoke. I spoke also to that part of ourselves that had come to accept Europe's opinion of us. And I was not alone nor even the first.

But the gauntlet had barely left our hands when a new historic phase broke on us. Europe conceded independence to us and we promptly began to misuse it, or rather those leaders to whom we entrusted the wielding of our new power and opportunity. So we got mad at them and came out brandishing novels of disenchantment. Actually we had all been duped. No independence was given—it is never given but taken, anyway. Europe had only made a tactical withdrawal on the political front and while we sang our anthem and unfurled our flag she was securing her iron grip behind us in the economic field. And our leaders in whose faces we hurled our disenchantment neither saw nor heard because they were not leaders at all but marionettes.

So the problem remains for Africa, for black people, for all deprived peoples and for the world. And so for the writer, for he is like the puppy in our proverb: that stagnant water in the potsherd is for none other but him. As long as one people sit on another and are deaf to their cry, so long will understanding and peace elude all of us.

*   *   *

For technical inventiveness both in language and novelistic technique, for profound insight into tragic human experience, for satirical sophistication, and for sustained creative energy, Chinua Achebe must still be regarded as the Anglophone African novelist of most considerable stature. The success of his first novel, *Things Fall Apart*, has led to some underestimation of the books that followed. Because Obi in *No Longer at Ease* is a grandson of Okonkwo in the first novel, the second has been regarded as not only a sequel but an attempt at essentially the same kind of tragic novel, and there has been disappointment that expectations aroused by *Things Fall Apart* are not fulfilled in *No Longer at Ease*. Because *Arrow of God* deals with the same sort of traditional Igbo society as forms the setting of *Things Fall Apart*, it has been seen as a less concise exercise over the same ground. Because there is a surface opposition between the young Odili and the corrupt political boss, Chief Nanga, in *A Man of the People*, much of the subtle satire and moral judgement in this novel has been missed.

Things Fall Apart is rightly praised as a taut, economically written novel that examines the period of the first Igbo contact with white missionaries and colonial officials in terms that are reminiscent of Greek tragedy. The rise of the self-made man, Okonkwo, in such a society, and his ignominious end are often regarded as the peculiar strength of the novel. Yet what happens to Okonkwo is the result of neither blind fate nor inevitable psychological bias. Okonkwo's very warrior-strength comes from his conscious will; he pursues a particular course from deliberate choice, and suppresses all his humaner tendencies so that his natural affections become warped. Other alternatives are open to him, and taken by others equally valiant. His career parallels and illumines the tragedy that overcomes his people; Igbo society is too inflexible to cope with the imperial power. Although Achebe presents traditional African society and his hero Okonkwo with great sympathy, he retains an admirable artistic objectivity about them. He does not allow his desire to show that the pre-colonial African past had a highly developed culture to obscure its weaknesses—precisely those that enabled the missionaries to get a toehold among the Igbos. The point of view is sympathetic, yet delicately balanced, and complex in the means by which it is conveyed. For instance, the most marked linguistic characteristic is Achebe's use of literal English translations of Igbo proverbs. This device not only makes for surface authenticity, but is a

means of indicating how Igbo society is simultaneously strengthened and severely limited by its traditional wisdom inherited through gnomic folk sayings. In an oral culture, the spoken word is extraordinarily utilitarian, but also a form of continuing ritual. While the tragedy is the destruction of an admirable, self-contained society by an intrusive culture, the victim is also seen to have serious inadequacies. Achebe's story is not a lament for the past but an analysis of a process of historical change. The blindnesses of those involved on both sides are revealed with a detachment on the novelist's part that is intimately related to his satirical methods in *No Longer at Ease* and *A Man of the People*.

Although *Arrow of God* provides an even richer evocation of traditional culture than *Things Fall Apart* does, it is more than a similar novel on a grander scale. The organic daily life of the Umuaro clan is drawn in great detail, but not simply to anatomize traditional culture. It is necessary for realizing fully the part of the priest Ezeulu in that society, for Ezeulu is the most complex and ambitious study in characterization that Achebe has yet produced, and his tragedy grows out of the conflict within him between the demands of his semi-divine office as priest of the clan's protective deity and his very human desire for personal power. The theme is a man's attitude to the power he already wields, what he does with that power, and the effects of his misuse of it upon himself and his people. In *Arrow of God*, too, Achebe uses Igbo proverbs, but now not merely to suggest the ordinary rituals of traditional life, but also as means of conveying that twilit area between a man's terrestrial life and his function as a semi-spirit mediating on his people's behalf with a deity. It is here that Ezeulu loses his way. Achebe directs the intricate drama with great sympathy and human understanding yet maintains an extraordinary detachment, best illustrated by the sardonic last paragraph of the novel, which casts doubts on the people's over-simple interpretation of Ezeulu's downfall.

In *No Longer at Ease* the characteristics of pre-colonial Igbo culture have become hollow mockeries, just as Obi's youthful idealism is seen to be without foundation before the harsh realities of corruption in modern Lagos. What is satirically laid bare is the chaotic, rootless bewilderment of West African city life, again fully reflected in the character's speech, as they switch from Igbo to pidgin or to English, according to their relationships with other people. The general crisis of culture is particularized—and humanized—in Obi's career, but Achebe's satire underlines the absence of any larger mode for personal integrity to work within.

In *A Man of the People* Achebe attacks political corruption and thuggery, not by conventional means, but by using Odili as an anti-hero who lucidly analyses the evils around him, while taking a share in them himself. The only clue to Odili's real fictional function lies in the false, pseudo-sophisticated speech that Achebe places in his mouth. The novel is a brilliant creation, a superb satirical farce.

Achebe's experience of the Nigerian Civil War (1967–70), in which he worked for the Biafran government, has been expressed in two compassionate stories in *Girls at War* and some very fine, somber, caustic poems about the dark side of human behavior in war in *Beware, Soul Brother*.

Perhaps Achebe's greatest strength as a novelist is the steady refinement of his control over language as a means of conveying rather than stating moral insights.

—Arthur Ravenscroft

ACKROYD, Peter. British. Born in London, 5 October 1949. Educated at Clare College, Cambridge, 1968–71, M.A.; Yale University, New Haven, Connecticut, 1971–73. Literary editor, *The Spectator*, London, 1973–77; television critic, *The Times*, London. Recipient: Maugham Award, 1984; Whitbread Award, 1985; Royal Society of Literature Heinemann Award, for non-fiction, 1985; *Guardian* Fiction Prize, 1985. Lives in London. Agent: Anthony Sheil Associates Ltd., 43 Doughty Street, London WC1N 2LF, England.

PUBLICATIONS

Novels

The Great Fire of London. London, Hamish Hamilton, 1982.
The Last Testament of Oscar Wilde. London, Hamish Hamilton, and New York, Harper, 1983.
Hawksmoor. London, Hamish Hamilton, 1985; New York, Harper, 1986.

Uncollected Short Stories

"The Inheritance," in *London Tales*, edited by Julian Evans. London, Hamish Hamilton, 1983.
"Ringing in the Good News," in *The Times* (London), 24 December 1985.

Verse

London Lickpenny. London, Ferry Press, 1973.
Country Life. London, Ferry Press, 1978.

Other

Notes for a New Culture: An Essay on Modernism. London, Vision Press, and New York, Barnes and Noble, 1976.
Dressing Up: Transvestism and Drag: The History of an Obsession. London, Thames and Hudson, and New York, Simon and Schuster, 1979.
Ezra Pound and His World. London, Thames and Hudson, and New York, Scribner, 1981.
T.S. Eliot (biography). London, Hamish Hamilton, and New York, Simon and Schuster, 1984.

Editor, *PEN New Fiction.* London, Quartet, 1984.

*   *   *

By the time Peter Ackroyd published his first novel in 1982, he was already well known in the literary world as a poet, critic, literary theorist, and cultural historian, and since his début as a novelist he has further enhanced his reputation as a non-fiction writer with his award-winning biography of T.S. Eliot. Before the appearance of his first novel, it seemed that his writing career was likely to develop in the fields of literary criticism and biography, but with three novels in quick succession between 1982 and 1985 he has established himself as one of the most gifted and imaginative English novelists to have emerged during the current decade. Critical opinion may differ about whether his strikingly original talent is taking the right direction, but there is no disagreement about his potential.

Ackroyd's polemical book, *Notes for a New Culture*, contains a relentless attack on the parochialism and impoverishment of contemporary English culture, especially literature and the academic literary establishment; he makes clear his intellectual allegiance to Continental (primarily French and German)

models and theories descending from such figures as de Sade, Nietzsche, Mallarmé, and Husserl, in opposition to what he sees as the stultifying tradition of empiricism, positivism, and humanism still dominant in English artistic and intellectual life. He insists on the autonomy and formal absoluteness of language, on the way in which language constitutes meaning only within itself, and he therefore challenges the philosophical basis of orthodox realistic fiction, regarding its conventions as no longer having any validity for the modern writer. As might be expected, his three novels are not conventionally realistic, but his innovatory approach to fiction has not led him into the cul-de-sacs of hyper-selfconscious experimentalism or navel-gazing phenomenology. On the contrary, all three books possess a strong narrative drive and are highly readable, demonstrating that he has not felt the need to reject storytelling in order to develop his own type of literary fiction. At the same time, the three novels are very different from each other: Ackroyd is a novelist who likes to try something new with every book.

There is an element of deception in the titles of Ackroyd's novels, especially as all three, *The Great Fire of London*, *The Last Testament of Oscar Wilde*, and *Hawksmoor*, could be the titles of historical or biographical studies rather than works of fiction. The fire in *The Great Fire of London* is not that of 1666, an event referred to in *Hawksmoor*, but an apocalyptic fictional one that begins with the burning of a film set for a screen adaptation of *Little Dorrit*. As if to substantiate his theoretical point that writing emerges from other writing rather than from life, Ackroyd draws on Dickens's novel in many ways, thus emphasizing the fictionality of his own fictional world, however realistic it may appear in some respects. Indeed, Ackroyd's novel is centrally concerned with the perpetual human activity of creating fictions in life as well as in art. The short opening section of *The Great Fire of London*, "the story so far," outlines the plot of *Little Dorrit* and ends: "although it could not be described as a true story, certain events have certain consequences"—including, of course, the writing of Ackroyd's novel. Dickens's eponymous heroine and the novel itself feature prominently in the minds of many of Ackroyd's characters, including Spenser Spender (a filmmaker with two poets' names who is determined to put the novel on the screen), Rowan Phillips (a Canadian homosexual and Cambridge don currently working on Dickens), and Audrey Skelton (a telephone operator who is possessed by the spirit of Little Dorrit during a séance). The setting of much of *Little Dorrit*, the Marshalsea Prison, also provides a link between the two novels because its site is visited by several of Ackroyd's characters. With its panorama of London in the 1980's from left-wing activists to gay bars, *The Great Fire of London* is at least as much a London novel as *Little Dorrit*. Ackroyd's narrative structure, in which several strands begin in parallel and gradually intertwine and coalesce, is itself derived from Dickens's methods and techniques, especially in his later novels such as *Little Dorrit*. By using one of the greatest of English novels as his point of departure, Ackroyd inevitably takes the risk of being unflatteringly compared with Dickens, but *The Great Fire of London* must be taken on its own terms, not Dickens's, and as such it is an exuberant, inventive, and accomplished piece of writing.

Ackroyd's second novel draws its inspiration not from a major mid-Victorian novel but from an important late Victorian writer. *The Last Testament of Oscar Wilde* is the testament that Wilde himself did not write but that Ackroyd has written for him in the form of a journal-cum-memoir covering that last few months of Wilde's life in Paris in 1900. The book therefore purports to be Wilde's autobiographical confessions in the tradition of such writing that connects St. Augustine with Rousseau and De Quincey. To write *The Last Testament of Oscar Wilde* Ackroyd must have steeped himself in Wilde's biography as well as his writing, and presumably could have written yet another study of the man and his work. Instead Ackroyd has chosen the freedom of fiction to enter imaginatively into Wilde's mind as he lives through his last weeks in France and simultaneously offers an explanation of his famous rise and infamous fall. The obvious danger with a novel of this type, not only about an historical personage but written from his point of view, is that readers will be tempted to compare the "facts" with the fictional re-creation, but this would be to approach the novel in far too literal-minded a way. As a fictional character, Ackroyd's Wilde cannot be the historical Wilde: for all its "factual" content, *The Last Testament of Oscar Wilde* is primarily a work of the imagination about the relationship between the artist and the world and about the difference between fictional and historical truth.

The skill with which Ackroyd creates a style and tone of voice for his narrator and sustains it throughout *The Last Testament of Oscar Wilde* is a remarkable technical achievement, but it pales beside the ludic and verbal virtuosity of his most ambitious and complex novel to date, *Hawksmoor*, in which he plays far more elaborate games with fact and fiction, history and imagination. The title is the name of Sir Christopher Wren's most distinguished assistant, Nicholas Hawksmoor, the great architect responsible for some of London's finest churches (referred to in *The Great Fire of London*), but in the novel these churches are attributed to Nicholas Dyer while Hawksmoor himself is a modern Detective Chief Superintendent investigating a series of murders in the East End. Although *Hawksmoor* contains characters who belong to history, such as Wren and Vanbrugh, and draws heavily on various historical sources, it is not an historical novel in the usual sense; indeed, it radically subverts the conventions of historical fiction. In a concluding note Ackroyd states that "this version of history is my own invention" and that "any relation to real people, either living or dead, is entirely coincidental." The six odd-numbered chapters in a book in which numerology plays a significant part are set in the early 18th century and are narrated by Dyer in a contemporary idiom, complete with old spellings and the initial capitalization of many words. Although a builder of churches, Dyer is secretly a Satanist and devotee of black magic, as well as being an opponent of the new scientific empiricism of the Royal Society, and dedicates his buildings to the dark powers by ensuring a human sacrifice in connection with each one. The six even-numbered chapters, set about two and a half centuries later, provide a third-person narration of the bizarre and puzzling killings associated with the same churches and of Hawksmoor's attempt to track down the culprit. Ackroyd creates mystery and suspense, but unlike orthodox writers of crime and detection he does not provide a solution. Despite the time shift between the two narratives, they flow smoothly into each other and run strictly in parallel. The last words of the first chapter are also the first words of the second chapter, for example, and the name of Dyer's first sacrificial victim is the same as that of the first person murdered in the 20th-century narrative. Time dissolves so that the modern policeman is, in a sense, investigating crimes of the past. One of Ackroyd's central concerns is the human continuity associated with place, specifically the East End of London, in spite of all the changes wrought by the passage of time. *Hawksmoor* is as multi-layered as the archaeological heritage beneath the baroque churches built by Dyer, a gothic figure in a landscape of rationalism, enlightenment, and superficial optimism. The dazzling erudition and ingenuity of Ackroyd's third novel brings to mind such authors as Borges, Nabokov, Pynchon, and Eco without seeming derivative in the pejorative sense.

—Peter Lewis

ADAMS, Alice (Boyd). American. Born in Fredericksburg, Virginia, 14 August 1926. Educated at Radcliffe College, Cambridge, Massachusetts, A.B. 1946. Married in 1946 (divorced, 1958); one son. Has worked as secretary, clerk, and bookkeeper; now full-time writer. Recipient: National Endowment for the Arts grant, 1976; Guggenheim fellowship, 1978. Lives in San Francisco. Address: c/o Knopf Inc., 201 East 50th Street, New York, New York 10022, U.S.A.

PUBLICATIONS

Novels

Careless Love. New York, New American Library, 1966; as *The Fall of Daisy Duke*, London, Constable, 1967.
Families and Survivors. New York, Knopf, 1975; London, Constable, 1976.
Listening to Billie. New York, Knopf, and London, Constable, 1978.
Rich Rewards. New York, Knopf, 1980.
Superior Women. New York, Knopf, 1984; London, Heinemann, 1985.

Short Stories

Beautiful Girl. New York, Knopf, 1979.
To See You Again. New York, Knopf, 1982.
Molly's Dog. Concord, New Hampshire, Ewert, 1983.
Return Trips. New York, Knopf, 1985.

*   *   *

Alice Adams, in her collections of short stories and her several novels, is an investigator of the plight (and the good fortunes) of American women: women living in a period extending from the early 1940's to the present. Adams's women have a variety of histories and follow many different careers—most of these careers are, however, more or less "creative." But the histories take place within certain limits: limits that can be easily experienced by a reading of Adams's short stories—*Beautiful Girl*, *To See You Again*, and *Return Trips*. As both the stories and the novels suggest, the Adams world is peopled by women who have "made it." Some have "arrived" with practically no effort at all. These women have rich parents who, usually after some delay, die and leave a heroine with money to redecorate her house and do whatever else comes to her mind (and this usually involves getting rid of a husband and finding a new love). Occasionally, however, a heroine has to seek a job and is even a little hampered by the presence of a child or so.

Not unimportant in the fictions is the "space" in which the heroines seek self-knowledge and self-realization. Three geographical regions "count"; the women have often, like Adams herself, been brought up in the south, have completed their educations in the Boston area, and more often than not follow careers that take them to San Francisco.

Against such backgrounds are acted out the dramas that are Adams's preoccupations: the passing of "interesting" women through several decades, from a time when self-realization for women was looked at with suspicion to later eras when orgasms can be talked about over a cup of coffee or a glass of tea. But none of the Adams women suffers unduly from the social reprisals free life-styles once stirred up. Instead, in ambiances where people are quite often "rich" (a recurrent word in the novels) women advance to meet new partners or retreat in order to meditate on the lovers they have left behind. Marriages are dissolved without much ado, and it is usually harder to say goodbye to a lover than to a husband. The novels in particular offer many examples of women measuring the value of what they have endured with this man or that one.

Although the Adams women are well-read, the chief intellectual resource the heroines draw on is a schematic version of Freudian analysis. Many a woman understands her present troubles by recalling her attachment to her father or her opposition to her mother. All heroines worth their salt can discover latent homosexuality in their female friendships, and women can pass a pleasant afternoon speculating about the "real" sexual orientation of men near to them.

This is a general description of Adams's work. Each of the novels mentioned below operates as a terrain of vigorous action, but not as an area of surprise and innovation. A quick passage through the novels supports this point.

The heroine of *Careless Love*, Daisy Duke, has rejected her husband (too weak) and her lover (too mundane), and is finally delighted with a lover who has some of the élan of Valentino. The tale is a presage of the later narratives. *Families and Survivors* is primarily the history of a privileged Southern girl, Louisa Calloway, who is surrounded by a typical Adams clientele: a Jewish psychiatrist, a failed novelist (he becomes an English professor), and female friends who aid Louisa as she scans her life and who expect the same service from her. In this novel, which covers thirty-odd years of Louisa's life, there are brief references to current events: these work quite well for a person who has lived through the period. Adams appears to count on such a reader. The pace, in this novel and others, varies. Years are dismissed in a paragraph, and then the novel slows down while Louisa attends a party or prepares a meal for a new lover.

Listening to Billie is, again, the selective life-history of a woman, Eliza Hamilton Quarles (and her half-sister Daria as well). The girls are daughters of a famous woman writer. Daria makes a marriage that ends after a couple of decades of "success." Eliza, in contrast, strikes out for herself boldly, after the early death of her husband. (Husbands frequently disappear in this way.) Her most successful love-affair unites her to a famous film-director; her most painful one entangles her with an epicene antiques dealer who (it turns out characteristically) was deeply attractive years before to Eliza's husband. Across these and other complexities Eliza passes with some success; she is aided by a vivid recollection of a night-club performance by Billie Holiday.

Rich Rewards is essentially the tale of a long wait. Daphne Matthiessen (a product of Wisconsin, for a change) has, early in her marriage, a brief relationship with a young Frenchman, Jean-Paul. This done, she returns to America with her husband, leaves him, becomes an interior decorator . . . and waits. Passing lovers help her endure her solitude. But all this dissolves in happiness when Jean-Paul comes to America to lecture. Twenty years have passed, but Jean-Paul says to Daphne, as she passes him: "Daphne."

Superior Women is fuller and more coherent than some of the novels. In it, Adams goes into the lives of four schoolmates

of the 1940's, and does so with a thoroughness that her previous glancing methods did not always permit. In this novel, at least, the chief characters are intimately connected with their own pasts and loves and with those of their friends. The four girls are, of course, still thoroughly creatures of Adams's particular vision in which women reckon the worth of their lives in terms of the various loves they have known. And, as in the other novels, this worth is analyzed in terms that Freudian psychiatry has made familiar. Indeed, *Superior Women* is a clear reminder of all that Adams has seen from coast to coast.

—Harold H. Watts

ADAMS, Richard (George). British. Born in Newbury, Berkshire, 9 May 1920. Educated at Bradfield College, Worcester; Worcester College, Oxford, B.A. in modern history 1948, M.A. 1953. Served in the British Army, 1940–45. Married Barbara Elizabeth Acland in 1949; two daughters. Worked in the Ministry of Housing and Local Government, London, 1948–68; Assistant Secretary, Department of the Environment, London, 1968-74. Writer-in-Residence, University of Florida, Gainesville, 1975, and Hollins College, Virginia, 1976. President, Royal Society for the Prevention of Cruelty to Animals, 1980–82 (resigned). Independent Conservative candidate for Spelthorne, 1983. Recipient (for children's book): Library Association Carnegie Medal, 1972; *Guardian* award, 1973. Fellow, Royal Society of Literature, 1975. Agent: David Higham Associates Ltd., 5–8 Lower John Street, London WIR 4HA. Address: 26 Church Street, Whitchurch, Hampshire, England.

PUBLICATIONS

Novels

-*Watership Down.* London, Collings, 1972; New York, Macmillan, 1974.
-*Shardik.* London, Allen Lane-Collings, 1974; New York, Simon and Schuster, 1975.
-*The Plague Dogs.* London, Allen Lane, 1977; New York, Knopf, 1978.
The Girl in a Swing. London, Allen Lane, and New York, Knopf, 1980.
Maia. London, Viking, 1984; New York, Knopf, 1985.

Fiction (for children)

The Bureaucrats. London, Viking Kestrel, 1985.

Verse (for children)

The Tyger Voyage. London, Cape, and New York, Knopf, 1976.
The Ship's Cat. London, Cape, and New York, Knopf, 1977.

Other

Voyage Through the Antarctic, with Ronald Lockley. London, Allen Lane, 1982; New York, Knopf, 1983.
A Nature Diary. London, Viking, 1985.

Other (for children)

Nature Through the Seasons with Max Hooper. London,

Kestrel, and New York, Simon and Schuster, 1975.
Nature Day and Night, with Max Hooper. London, Kestrel, and New York, Viking Press, 1978.
The Watership Down Film Picture Book. London, Allen Lane, and New York, Macmillan, 1978.
The Iron Wolf and Other Stories (folktales). London, Allen Lane, 1980; as *The Unbroken Web*, New York, Crown, 1980.

Editor, *Grimm's Fairy Tales*. London, Routledge, 1981.
Editor, *Richard Adams's Favourite Animal Stories*. London, Octopus, 1981.
Editor, *The Best of Ernest Thompson Seton*. London, Fontana, 1982.

*   *   *

Originally published as a book for children, *Watership Down* made Richard Adams's name as a novelist by becoming one of the leading bestsellers of the 1970's. Set in the rabbit world of the English countryside, it is primarily an adventure story, original in conception, but with excellent natural descriptions and evocations of such human virtues as courage, loyalty, and modesty. The story begins when a peaceful rabbit warren in Berkshire is destroyed by a new housing development and a party of young bucks escape, thanks to the ability of one of their number, Fiver, to foresee the future. What follows is an odyssey to find a new home, during which the rabbits encounter many strange and terrifying adventures. Danger comes from human beings, poisoned fields, machines, and also from another group of rabbits led by the despotic General Woundwort. "In combat he was terrifying, fighting entirely to kill, indifferent to any wounds he received himself and closing with his adversaries until his weight overbore and exhausted them. Those who had no heart to oppose him were not long in the feeling that here was a leader indeed." Eventually, the rabbits achieve their goal but have to fight a fiercely contested battle to protect their new territory.

Adams, a senior civil servant when he wrote *Watership Down*, admitted that many parts of the novel were created as stories to please his children during long car journeys and that much of the factual information came from R.M. Lockley's study *The Private Life of the Rabbit*, but his work is very much a fictional unity. Some critics have suggested that *Watership Down* is an allegory on man's indifference to the natural life of his planet and, taken that way, it presents a grimly satirical view; but the novel is best seen as part of the fantastic strain in English literature, in line with the work of C.S. Lewis, J.R.R. Tolkien, and Kenneth Grahame.

In his second novel, *Shardik*, Adams shifted his centre of literary influences to the adventure genre of H. Rider Haggard and John Buchan. The action and setting are timeless and the background imaginary—the Beklan empire which has been over-run, and its inhabitants, the Ortelgans, enslaved. When a large bear is driven from their forests, the Ortelgans take him to be an ancient bear-god called Shardik. With his help they are able to drive off their oppressors and are returned to power. Kelderek, "a simple foolish fellow," becomes king of the Ortelgans but idleness and luxury lures him into wickedness. Once again the country is threatened but is redeemed by Shardik's blood sacrifice. Although Adams centered most of his attention on the bear, the humans are real enough and his ability to create an imaginary world may be considered the novel's great strength. In parts overwritten—a trap for any adventure novel—*Shardik* is, nevertheless, a powerful statement about man's inhumanity to man.

Adams was more successful when he returned to the animal world in *The Plague Dogs*, which is, among other things, a hard-hitting attack on the world of animal research. Snitter, a throughbred terrier, and Rowf, a mongrel, escape from a government research station in the Lake District and the novel is an account of their adventures to keep out of man's way before they escape to the mystical Isle of Dog. As in *Watership Down*, Adams gives his animals human characteristics but they are not men in dogs' guise. When Snitter and Rowf decide to live off the land, for example, it is a fox who teaches them the necessary tricks and they have difficulty understanding his thick local dialect. When they are seen, men appear only as the enemy and the animals themselves have little understanding of their world.

Although he has also written adventure novels in the style of *Shardik*, Adams is at his happiest in the animal world. The arcadian worlds of the rabbits' Berkshire and the dogs' Lake District are peopled by an organised society of idealised, largely peaceful animals but this is not simple anthropomorphosis. The animals might be able to speak and to rationalise like human beings but they have not lost their animal characteristics. The rabbits of *Watership Down* even have the remnants of an ancient rabbit language with its own words like *n-Frith* for noon and *hrududu* for tractor or any other man-made machine. It is his ability to create the rabbits and dogs as sensible and sensitive creatures and not as animals-in-man's-clothing or as lovable furry creatures which gives Adams his greatest strength as a novelist.

—Trevor Royle

ADLER, Renata. American. Born in Milan, Italy, 19 October 1938. Educated at Bryn Mawr College, Pennsylvania, A.B. 1959; the Sorbonne, Paris, D.D'E.S. 1961; Harvard University, Cambridge, Massachusetts, M.A. 1962. Since 1962, writer and reporter, *The New Yorker*. Film critic, New York *Times*, 1968–69; member of the editorial board, *American Scholar*, Washington, D.C., 1968–73. Fellow, Trumbull College, Yale University, New Haven, Connecticut, 1969–72. Recipient: Guggenheim fellowship, 1973; O. Henry Award, for short story, 1974; Hemingway Foundation award, 1977; American Academy award, 1979. Agent: Lynn Nesbit, International Creative Management, 40 West 57th Street, New York, New York 10019. Address: The New Yorker, 25 West 43rd Street, New York, New York 10036, U.S.A.

PUBLICATIONS

Novels

Speedboat. New York, Random House, 1976; London, Hamish Hamilton, 1977.
Pitch Dark. New York, Knopf, and London, Hamish Hamilton, 1983.

Uncollected Short Stories

"Collect Calls," in *New Yorker*, 24 October 1970.
"Downers and Séances," in *New Yorker*, 13 February 1971.
"Castling," in *New Yorker*, 30 December 1972.
"Brownstone," in *Prize Stories 1974*, edited by William Abrahams. New York, Doubleday, 1974.

"Agency," in *New Yorker*, 16 February 1976.
"Drowning Nanny and an Aces Fellow," in *Vogue* (New York), October 1976.

Other

A Year in the Dark: Journal of a Film Critic 1968–69. New York, Random House, 1969.
Toward a Radical Middle: Fourteen Pieces of Reporting and Criticism. New York, Random House, 1970.

*   *   *

"What is extraordinary about each of these writers is her complete consistency, her strict attention to only that psychological level that she has chosen to study ... each manages to convey more truth by means of her polygraph than we are getting from many writers of cataclysmic aspiration, the seismologists among contemporary novelists." Speaking here of Nathalie Sarraute and Iris Murdoch, Renata Adler could just as well have been describing her own fiction. In her two novels, *Speedboat* and *Pitch Dark*, she has proven herself an adept practitioner of the polygraph method, which characterizes the fiction of a number of other contemporary American writers as well: Raymond Carver, Joan Didion, Leonard Michaels, and others. Theirs is a fiction as bleak, as anonymous, and as disjunctive as the modern world in which their stories are set. Yet despite the brittle syntax and jagged surface of her novels, Adler has been highly critical of the "unearned nihilism" and apocalyptic posturing of many contemporary writers, artists, and composers, whose avant-garde experiments she has judged pretentious and often boring. Adler prefers what she has termed "a radical middle," a delicate balance of hope and risk, tradition and innovation, in which the possibility of gain must be weighed against the remembrance of one's personal losses; it is this elusive state that Adler's female protagonists long for but fail to attain.

As the title of her first novel suggests, Adler's is a fiction about motion as well as a fiction that is itself *in* motion. Her characters work but never accomplish anything important or even substantive; they travel but never reach any clear, final destination, any still point in the whirling universe of transatlantic flights, rented cars, and speedboats. Adler's syntax reflects her characters' sensibility, a kind of emotional jet lag: "Things have changed very much, several times, since I grew up, and like everyone else in New York except the intellectuals, I have led several lives and I still lead some of them." This is a fiction of juxtaposed elements structured on the basis of coordination rather than (as in conventional fiction) subordination; it is a prose in which positions are stated only to be qualified and finally either contradicted or cancelled altogether. Makeshift transitional phrases pretend to connect random events that do not so much define as overwhelm the novel's characters. A drift in time and space, they suddenly appear and just as suddenly disappear, known to the reader (and, one suspects, to the narrator-protagonist as well) merely as names or generic epithets—Bill, Maggie, "the young construction worker," "the wife of the Italian mineral-water tycoon."

As narrator of her own story-in-the-making, *Speedboat*'s Jen Fain fares somewhat better. For the 35-year-old Fain, whose biography resembles Adler's in many ways and whose name suggests willingness and contentment as well as deception and artifice, storytelling is a psychological necessity, the means by which she attempts to order her life retrospectively, to transform what she now sees as discrete and disjunctive events into a seamless and sensible narrative: a life story. Unfortunately,

the story she tells becomes not a means to this end but instead an endless labyrinth from which she finds occasional release as the result of her ironic (often self-reflexively ironic) sensibility and, more importantly, her refusal to heed the drunken voice whose advice is "'Forget it ... What's it for? Throw it away.'"

The end of a love affair (not, as in a cataclysmic writer like Pynchon, the end of the world) is the event, or "it," which causes Fain to tell her story and in this way to bridge the sudden chasm that has opened before her. The end of another love affair serves a similar purpose in Adler's second novel. As in *Speedboat*, *Pitch Dark*'s narrator, Kate, prefers not to deal directly with her loss but instead to turn her and the reader's attention to what at first glance appear to be unrelated matters. However, what seems unrelated to the novel's minimal plot turns out to be central to the novel's overall minimalist effect, which, as in the poetic fiction of John Hawkes, depends much less on the sequence of events than on the pattern of images: the various islands, for example, which suggest to the reader Kate's lonely isolation, or the "pitch dark" through which she travels both literally and metaphorically.

For Kate even more than for Jen, the problem of living without her lover merges with the problem of how to tell the story of this loss, a story which is at once personal and representative. Once upon a time, Adler has pointed out, there were daring stories of daring lives that ended interestingly and conclusively; now there are only questions and complications, false starts rather than new beginnings, repetitions rather than denouements. With good reason, Kate sees herself as a latter-day Scheherazade wondering whether she will be able to please her lover/reader for another day, for another story. Her storytelling is, therefore, like Jen's, as much a necessity as a choice, as is her decision to adopt Emily Dickinson's dictum and tell all the truth but tell it slant. For the reader this means having to travel through a pitch dark narrative, of barely distinguished characters, unassigned dialogue, a narrator who refers to herself in both the first and third persons and of lines that propel the reader ahead and simultaneously turn him back to the beginning, or, more accurately, to *a* beginning. Lines repeat, becoming refrains that echo Kate's confusion and despair: "Here I am, for the first time, and yet again, alone at last on Orcas Island." Adler's flat, colorless prose embodies her characters' bleak existence, but against that grim vision Adler posits her narrators' efforts to work their way through to something better, to that viable middle ground between affirmation and apocalypse, between the wholeness of conventional fiction and the dislocations of contemporary existence.

—Robert A. Morace

ALDISS, Brian (Wilson). British. Born in East Dereham, Norfolk, 18 August 1925. Educated at Framlingham College, Suffolk, 1936–39; West Buckland School, 1939–42. Served in the Royal Signals in the Far East, 1943–47. Married Margaret Manson in 1965 (second marriage); four children, two from previous marriage. Bookseller, Oxford, 1947–56; literary editor, *Oxford Mail*, 1958–69; science-fiction editor, Penguin Books, London, 1961–64; art correspondent, *Guardian*, London, 1969–71. President, British Science Fiction Association, 1960–65; co-founder, 1972, and Chairman, 1976–78, John W.

Campbell Memorial Award; Co-President, Eurocon Committee, 1975–79; Chairman, Society of Authors, London, 1978–79; member, Arts Council Literature Panel, 1978–80. Since 1975, Vice-President, Stapledon Society; since 1977, founding trustee, World Science Fiction, Dublin; since 1982, President, World SF; since 1983, Vice-President, H.G. Wells Society. Recipient: World Science Fiction Convention citation, 1959; Hugo Award, 1962; Nebula Award, 1965; Ditmar Award (Australia), 1970; British Science Fiction Association award, 1972, 1982, and Special Award, 1974; Eurocon award, 1976; James Blish Award, for non-fiction, 1977; Cometa d'Argento (Italy), 1977; Prix Jules Verne, 1977; Pilgrim Award, 1978; John W. Campbell Memorial Award, 1983. Guest of Honour, World Science Fiction Convention, London, 1965, 1979. Agent: A.P. Watt Ltd., 26–28 Bedford Row, London WC1R 4HL. Address: Woodlands, Foxcombe Road, Boars Hill, Oxfordshire OX1 5DL, England.

PUBLICATIONS

Novels

The Brightfount Diaries.   London, Faber, 1955.
Non-Stop.   London, Faber, 1958; as *Starship*, New York, Criterion, 1959.
Vanguard from Alpha.   New York, Ace, 1959; as *Equator* (includes "Segregation"), London, Digit, 1961.
Bow Down to Nul.   New York, Ace, 1960; as *The Interpreter*, London, Digit, 1961.
The Male Response.   New York, Galaxy, 1961; London, Dobson, 1963.
The Primal Urge.   New York, Ballantine, 1961; London, Sphere, 1967.
The Long Afternoon of Earth.   New York, New American Library, 1962; expanded edition, as *Hothouse*, London, Faber, 1962; Boston, Gregg Press, 1976.
The Dark Light Years.   London, Faber, and New York, New American Library, 1964.
Greybeard.   London, Faber, and New York, Harcourt Brace, 1964.
Earthworks.   London, Faber, 1965; New York, Doubleday, 1966.
An Age.   London, Faber, 1967; as *Cryptozoic!*, New York, Doubleday, 1968.
Report on Probability A.   London, Faber, 1968; New York, Doubleday, 1969.
Barefoot in the Head.   London, Faber, 1969; New York, Doubleday, 1970.
The Hand-Reared Boy.   London, Weidenfeld and Nicolson, and New York, McCall, 1970.
A Soldier Erect; or, Further Adventures of the Hand-Reared Boy.   London, Weidenfeld and Nicolson, and New York, Coward McCann, 1971.
Frankenstein Unbound.   London, Cape, 1973; New York, Random House, 1974.
The Eighty-Minute Hour.   London, Cape, and New York, Doubleday, 1974.
The Malacia Tapestry.   London, Cape, 1976; New York, Harper, 1977.
Brothers of the Head.   London, Pierrot, 1977; New York, Two Continents, 1978.
Enemies of the System.   London, Cape, and New York, Harper, 1978.
A Rude Awakening.   London, Weidenfeld and Nicolson, 1978; New York, Random House, 1979.

Brothers of the Head, and Where the Lines Converge.   London, Panther, 1979.
Life in the West.   London, Weidenfeld and Nicolson, 1980.
Moreau's Other Island.   London, Cape, 1980; as *An Island Called Moreau*, New York, Simon and Schuster, 1981.
The Helliconia Trilogy.   New York, Atheneum, 1985.
    Helliconia Spring.   London, Cape, and New York, Atheneum, 1982.
    Helliconia Summer.   London, Cape, and New York, Atheneum, 1983.
    Helliconia Winter.   London, Cape, and New York, Atheneum, 1985.

Short Stories

Space, Time, and Nathaniel: Presciences.   London, Faber, 1957; abridged edition, as *No Time Like Tomorrow*, New York, New American Library, 1959.
The Canopy of Time.   London, Faber, 1959; revised edition, as *Galaxies Like Grains of Sand*, New York, New American Library, 1960.
The Airs of Earth.   London, Faber, 1963.
Starswarm.   New York, New American Library, 1964; London, Panther, 1979.
Best Science Fiction Stories of Brian Aldiss.   London, Faber, 1965; as *Who Can Replace a Man?*, New York, Harcourt Brace, 1966; revised edition, Faber, 1971.
The Saliva Tree and Other Strange Growths.   London, Faber, 1966.
Intangibles Inc. London, Faber, 1969.
A Brian Aldiss Omnibus 1–2.   London, Sidgwick and Jackson, 2 vols., 1969–71.
Neanderthal Planet.   New York, Avon, 1970.
The Moment of Eclipse.   London, Faber, 1970; New York, Doubleday, 1972.
The Book of Brian Aldiss.   New York, DAW, 1972; as *The Comic Inferno*, London, New English Library, 1973.
Excommunication.   London, Post Card Partnership, 1975.
Last Orders and Other Stories.   London, Cape, 1977.
New Arrivals, Old Encounters: Twelve Stories.   London, Cape, 1979; New York, Harper, 1980.
Seasons in Flight.   London, Cape, 1984; New York, Atheneum, 1986.

Play

Distant Encounters, adaptation of his own stories (produced London, 1978).

Verse

Pile: Petals from St. Klaed's Computer.   London, Cape, and New York, Holt Rinehart, 1979.
Farewell to a Child.   Berkhamsted, Hertfordshire, Priapus, 1982.

Other

Cities and Stones: A Traveller's Jugoslavia.   London, Faber, 1966.
The Shape of Further Things: Speculations on Change.   London, Faber, 1970; New York, Doubleday, 1971.
Billion Year Spree: A History of Science Fiction.   London, Weidenfeld and Nicolson, and New York, Doubleday, 1973.
Science Fiction Art, illustrated by Chris Foss.   New York, Bounty, 1975; London, Hart Davis, 1976.
Science Fiction as Science Fiction.   Frome, Somerset, Bran's Head, 1978.

This World and Nearer Ones: Essays Exploring the Familiar. London, Weidenfeld and Nicolson, 1979; Kent, Ohio, Kent State University Press, 1981.

Science Fiction Quiz. London, Weidenfeld and Nicolson, 1983.

The Pale Shadow of Science. Seattle, Serconia Press, 1985.

Editor, *Penguin Science Fiction.* London, Penguin, 1961; *More Penguin Science Fiction*, 1963; *Yet More Penguin Science Fiction*, 1964; 3 vols. collected as *The Penguin Science Fiction Omnibus*, 1973.

Editor, *Best Fantasy Stories.* London, Faber, 1962.

Editor, *Last and First Men*, by Olaf Stapledon. London, Penguin, 1963.

Editor, *Introducing SF.* London, Faber, 1964.

Editor, with Harry Harrison, *Nebula Award Stories 2.* New York, Doubleday, 1967; as *Nebula Award Stories 1967*, London, Gollancz, 1967.

Editor, with Harry Harrison, *All about Venus.* New York, Dell, 1968; enlarged edition, as *Farewell, Fantastic Venus*, London, Macdonald, 1968.

Editor, with Harry Harrison, *Best SF 1967* [to *1975*]. New York, Berkley and Putnam, 7 vols., and Indianapolis, Bobbs Merrill, 2 vols., 1968–75; as *The Year's Best Science Fiction 1–9*, London, Sphere, 8 vols., 1968–76, and London, Futura, 1 vol., 1976.

Editor, with Harry Harrison, *The Astounding-Analog Reader.* New York, Doubleday, 2 vols., 1972–73; London, Sphere, 2 vols., 1973.

Editor, *Space Opera.* London, Weidenfeld and Nicolson, 1974; New York, Doubleday, 1975.

Editor, *Space Odysseys.* London, Futura, 1974; New York, Doubleday, 1976.

Editor, with Harry Harrison, *SF Horizons* (reprint of magazine). New York, Arno Press, 1975.

Editor, with Harry Harrison, *Hell's Cartographers: Some Personal Histories of Science Fiction Writers.* London, Weidenfeld and Nicolson, and New York, Harper, 1975.

Editor, with Harry Harrison, *Decade: The 1940's, The 1950's, The 1960's.* London, Macmillan, 3 vols., 1975–77; *The 1940's* and *The 1950's*, New York, St. Martin's Press, 2 vols., 1978.

Editor, *Evil Earths.* London, Weidenfeld and Nicolson, 1975; New York, Avon, 1979.

Editor, *Galactic Empires.* London, Weidenfeld and Nicolson, 2 vols., 1976; New York, St. Martin's Press, 2 vols., 1977.

Editor, *Perilous Planets.* London, Weidenfeld and Nicolson, 1978; New York, Avon, 1980.

*

Bibliography: *Brian W. Aldiss: A Bibliography 1954–1984* by Margaret Aldiss, San Bernardino, California, Borgo Press, 1986.

Manuscript Collections: Bodleian Library, Oxford University; Dallas Public Library.

Critical Studies: "Generic Discontinuities in SF: Brian Aldiss' *Starship*" by Fredric Jameson, in *Science-Fiction Studies* (Terre Haute, Indiana), vol. 1, no. 2, 1973; *Aldiss Unbound: The Science Fiction of Brian W. Aldiss* by Richard Mathews, San Bernardino, California, Borgo Press, 1977; *Apertures: A Study of the Writings of Brian Aldiss* by Brian Griffin and David Wingrove, Westport, Connecticut, Greenwood Press, 1984;

article by Aldiss in *Contemporary Authors Autobiography Series 2* edited by Adele Sarkissian, Detroit, Gale, 1985.

Brian Aldiss comments:

Time is the spectre haunting the stage of most of my books: Time in its own right and in one of its nastier disguises, as Change. The characters cope with this as best they can. Sometimes, Time has only a walk-on role, as in *Barefoot in the Head*; sometimes, it even consents to play the fool, as in my series of contemporary novels, *The Hand-Reared Boy*, *A Soldier Erect*, and *A Rude Awakening*.

By nature I'm an obsessive writer. Whatever I am writing at present pleases me most, or else I give it up. My science fiction represents a spectrum moving from extreme science-fiction situations in the early novels towards situations merely coloured by the presence of the future; by the time I reached *Report on Probability A* and *Barefoot*, I was writing a fiction that bears only slight resemblance to traditional SF. The Horatio Stubbs novels are a logical extension of this process; here the gaze is directed towards the past, but emphasis is still on Change—change, in this case, as it relates to one man's life. The emphasis in this series is on comedy, with sorrow as a light zither accompaniment; in my science fiction, the arrangement has generally been the other way round.

As the titles indicate, time is a considerable element in the Helliconia novels, although here the emphasis is on human beings and their intricate relationships with the biosphere and politics. The large canvas of this trilogy became accessible to me only after I had written the contemporary novel *Life in the West*. *Life in the West* prompted me to write of the same problems (I hoped more powerfully) within a more metaphorical context, and encompassing a few minor irritants—like religion.

After this considerable labour I am resting—revising *Billion Year Spree* with David Wingrove, planning a near-historical novel at present entitled *Whitehall*, and writing an account of the book world as I see it: which was where I began, 30 years ago.

*   *   *

The great contribution Brian Aldiss has made to the art of science fiction is to help to raise it to the point where it is now accepted, by all but the chronically bigoted, as a literary form worthy of serious consideration. I suspect that this has much to do with the fact that Aldiss has always looked upon himself primarily as a novelist rather than as a writer of SF, and he has written several novels other than those on science-fiction themes.

His first full length science-fiction novel was *Non-Stop* which was based on the almost classic SF theme of a giant space-ship adrift in space. As a piece of story telling it is first class, and it displays all the excellences that are to be found in his later work: the ability to establish by carefully selected detail a convincing atmosphere of place and time, and a logical development of situations so that even the most outlandish become acceptable to the reader. In *Hothouse*, for example, Aldiss creates a world dominated by vegetation where we can sense the continual and overwhelming growth, even breathe the vegetable air, and in *Greybeard* the experience of being in post-atomic Oxford is remarkably vivid. But in *Non-Stop*, while the exploration of the ship (once built by giants) by Roy Complain and his companions has parallels with the sense of awe and wonder experienced by the Old English poets when they encountered the ruins of Roman cities, the space ship becomes a microcosm of Earth which, too, can be seen as a giant ship itself endlessly adrift in space, and the exploration develops into a search for destination and purpose.

A quality which informs Brian Aldiss's work, and which should not be overlooked, is his sense of humour. In *Non-Stop* one aspect of this can be seen in his pursuit of the idea that in the future psychology will develop its own theology and superstitions and replace our present religions. It is a plausible thesis and at the same time an amusing one, and often Aldiss's humour helps to save his SF novels from the over-seriousness that has engulfed other practitioners in this genre. It has been responsible too for the excellent humorous novels. The logical consequences of the invention and universal use of an "Emotional Register" are used in *The Primal Urge* to create a fantastic and hilarious story.

In recent years Brian Aldiss has striven to extend the boundaries of his art. In *Report on Probability A* he attempted the first SF anti-novel, a study in relative phenomena which proved a tour de force, and in *Barefoot in the Head* he produced another "first" where groups of poems and "pop-songs" reflect and comment on the preceding prose chapters. In a Europe reeling psychodelically from an attack by an Arab state with Psycho-Chemical Aerosol Bombs, Chateris, the hero of *Barefoot in the Head*, gradually absorbs the acid-head poison in the atmosphere to find himself a new Messiah. As social and thought patterns disintegrate so does the language, and Aldiss develops a stunning-punning prose reminiscent of the verbal pyrotechnics of Joyce's *Finnegans Wake*. At the same time he creates a nightmare world reflecting trends observable in the situation already with us.

Though not strictly within a discussion of Brian Aldiss's novels, we should not overlook his collections of short stories, *Space, Time, and Nathaniel* and *The Canopy of Time*, of which he is justly proud. A recent enterprise, planned as a group of novels, constitutes a fictional autobiography covering the years from the 1930's to the 1960's, where through the sexual and spiritual development of Horatio Stubbs are examined certain aspects of the poverty of English middle-class life. The first, *The Hand-Reared Boy*, begins with Horatio as a boy, his masturbatory fantasies and his first sexual encounters. The direct and extremely realistic style of the first part of this novel might not be to everyone's taste, but it flowers into a most beautifully controlled story of Horatio's first and hopeless love for an older woman. In the second novel, *A Soldier Erect*, we find Horatio still hard at it in the army and serving in India and Burma where his sexual and social education is broadened. The coarse brutality of wartime soldiering in the Far East is accurately and as brutally portrayed, but redeemed by humour and set in contrast with Horatio's growing awareness of values beyond the more immediately erotic, a theme continued and brought to conclusion in the third novel in the series, *A Rude Awakening*, where Horatio encounters the Dutch, Indian, Japanese, Chinese, and Indonesian forces in Sumatra and finds himself with two girls.

On the SF side, Aldiss's *Frankenstein Unbound* breaks new ground again. As a result of the indiscriminate use of nuclear weapons within the ambits of the Earth-Lunar system the infrastructure of space is seriously damaged to the point where time and space go "on the brink." The consequent "time shifts" find Joe Boderland suddenly transported to Switzerland in the year 1816 where he encounters not only Mary Shelley, the creator of Frankenstein, but Frankenstein himself in a world where reality itself is equally unstable and the dividing line between the real and the imagined world has become confused. In this situation Boderland finds himself unsure of his own role, and it is the discovery and fulfilment of his mission which constitutes the central theme of the narrative. It is a measure

of Aldiss's powers as a novelist that he persuades the reader of the *reality* of this fantastic situation. The theme, I suspect, was suggested by his researches into the origins of science fiction which he undertook to produce his history of the genre, *Billion Year Spree*, and in which he makes a powerful case for Mary Shelley's *Frankenstein* as the first true SF novel.

More recent novels increase one's admiration for Brian Aldiss's versatility and unflagging powers of invention. *Brothers of the Head*, the story of Siamese twin boys with a third dominant head which becomes increasingly demanding, is a brilliant if disturbing excursion into the macabre, while *The Malacia Tapestry* almost defies definition. Set in an age old city state, riddled with rival philosophies, under the spell of magicians, and where change is forbidden, it presents the reader with a panorama of dukes, wealthy merchants, thespians, courtesans, spongers, and soldiers. What we are never sure of is whereabouts in the time scale we are. Is it a medieval town? Then just a glimpse of something tells us no. An alternative world? But never explicitly so. The way in which Aldiss makes this totally imaginary world a reality is remarkable, a superb example of how to induce the suspension of disbelief.

Given Aldiss's run of the gamut of fictional styles and structures it was almost inevitable that sooner or later he would attempt a saga. In *The Helliconia Trilogy* he does just that and in inventing an entire solar system with its own history, dynasties, religions, mythologies, and cultures it is one of epic proportions. While parallels with life on Planet Earth can be observed, the chief and fundamental difference is in the length of Helliconia's seasons. Centuries long the whole of life changes as the seasons wear on, dormant life forms emerge and dynasties rise and fall. At the heart of this, nevertheless, is the struggle between the Humans and the Phagors, and a stroke of genius is to have hovering in the background an Earth Observation Platform which is itself declining into disaster, thus adding a further perspective to this cosmic vision. The other remarkable aspect of Aldiss's invented universe is that it is not, as is so often the case in science fiction, an ideal world held up in criticism of our own. Helliconia's history is as messy, corrupt, illogical, and confused as Earth's. If there is a message it is in Helliconia's acceptance of and adjustment to its even harsher physical environment, while the Earth Platform's disaster is directly related to Earth's attempt to over-control its environment.

The books themselves, *Spring, Summer*, and *Winter*, are full of action and incident: picaresque journeys, hierarchical struggles, natural disasters, feats of endurance, bravery, loyalty and affection, and dynastic warfare which make them each, in an old-fashioned phrase, a gripping read. They are in addition a remarkable achievement.

—John Cotton

ALDRIDGE, (Harold Edward) James. Australian. Born in White Hills, Victoria, 10 July 1918. Educated at Swan Hill High School; London School of Economics. Married Dina Mitchnik in 1942; two sons. Writer, Melbourne *Herald* and *Sun*, 1937–38, and London *Daily Sketch* and *Sunday Dispatch*, 1939; European and Middle East war correspondent for the Australian Newspaper Service and the North American Newspaper Alliance, 1939–44; Teheran correspondent, for *Time* and *Life*, 1944. Recipient: Rhys Memorial Prize, 1945; World Peace Council Gold Medal; International Organization of

Journalists prize, 1967; Lenin Memorial Peace Prize, 1972; Australian Children's Book Council Book of the Year Award, 1985. Agent: Curtis Brown, 162–168 Regent Street, London W1R 5TA, England.

PUBLICATIONS

Novels

Signed with Their Honour.   London, Joseph, and Boston, Little Brown, 1942.
The Sea Eagle.   London, Joseph, and Boston, Little Brown, 1944.
Of Many Men.   London, Joseph, and Boston, Little Brown, 1946.
The Diplomat.   London, Lane, 1949; Boston, Little Brown, 1950.
The Hunter.   London, Lane, 1950; Boston, Little Brown, 1951.
Heroes of the Empty View.   London, Lane, and New York, Knopf, 1954.
I Wish He Would Not Die.   London, Bodley Head, 1957; New York, Doubleday, 1958.
The Last Exile.   London, Hamish Hamilton, and New York, Doubleday, 1961.
A Captive in the Land.   London, Hamish Hamilton, 1962; New York, Doubleday, 1963.
The Statesman's Game.   London, Hamish Hamilton, and New York Doubleday, 1966.
My Brother Tom.   London, Hamish Hamilton, 1966; as *My Brother Tom: A Love Story,* Boston, Little Brown, 1967.
A Sporting Proposition.   London, Joseph, and Boston, Little Brown, 1973; as *Ride a Wild Pony*, London, Penguin, 1976.
Mockery in Arms.   London, Joseph, 1974; Boston, Little Brown, 1975.
The Untouchable Juli.   London, Joseph, 1975; Boston, Little Brown, 1976.
One Last Glimpse.   London, Joseph, and Boston, Little Brown, 1977.
Goodbye Un-America.   London, Joseph, and Boston, Little Brown, 1979.

Short Stories

Gold and Sand.   London, Bodley Head, 1960.

Uncollected Short Stories

"Braver Time," in *Redbook* (New York), May 1967.
"The Unfinished Soldiers," in *Winter's Tales 15,* edited by A.D. Maclean.   London, Macmillan, 1969; New York, St. Martin's Press, 1970.
"The Black Ghost of St. Helen," in *After Midnight Ghost Book*, edited by James Hale.   London, Hutchinson, 1980.

Plays

The 49th State (produced London, 1947).
One Last Glimpse (produced Prague, 1981).

Television Plays: scripts for *Robin Hood* series.

Other

Undersea Hunting for Inexperienced Englishmen.   London,

Allen and Unwin, 1955.
The Flying 19 (for children).   London, Hamish Hamilton, 1966.
Living Egypt, photographs by Paul Strand.   London, MacGibbon and Kee, and New York, Horizon Press, 1969.
Cairo: Biography of a City.   Boston, Little Brown, 1969; London, Macmillan, 1970.
The Marvelous Mongolian (for children).   Boston, Little Brown, and London, Macmillan, 1974.
The Broken Saddle (for children).   London, MacRae, 1982; New York, Watts, 1983.
The True Story of Lilli Stubek.   South Yarra, Victoria, Hyland House, 1984.
The True Story of Spit MacPhee.   Ringwood, Victoria, Viking, 1986.

*

Critical Studies: "It All Comes Out Like Blood: The Novels of James Aldridge," in *Australians* by John Hetherington, Melbourne, Cheshire, 1960; "Man of Action, Words in Action" by Eric Partridge, in *Meanjin* (Melbourne), 1961.

*   *   *

James Aldridge left Australia when quite a young man as a war correspondent; and this fact has largely determined the material and the angle of approach in his work. He went through the Greek campaign and wrote two books based directly on his experiences in it. Here his method was strongly affected by Hemingway; but the books were saved from being mere imitations by the genuine freshness and truth of his presentation. He was learning how to build a narrative full of stirring events and based on historical developments which he knew at first-hand, and at the same time to link the story with the personal problems and struggles of his protagonists. With his next book, a collection of stories, came a break from the Hemingway influence. What he had gained from his apprenticeship was now integrated in his own method and outlook. The tales showed how well he was able to grasp situations with very diverse settings and convincingly to define aspects of national character in a compact form. Still drawing on his wartime experiences as a correspondent, he wrote *The Diplomat*, an ambitious large-scale work, dealing with both the Soviet Union and the region of the Kurds in northern Mesopotamia. With much skill he explored the devious world of diplomacy in the postwar world, making the issues concrete by their basis in the difficult national question of the Kurds. Aldridge emerged as an important political novelist. He showed himself able to handle complicated political themes without losing touch with the essential human issues. The political aspects were removed from triviality or narrowness by being linked with the painful struggles of the protagonist to understand the world in which he found himself an actor. Thus what gave artistic validity to the work, beyond any particular conclusions reached in the search for truth, was the definition of that search itself.

In *The Hunter* Aldridge next refreshed himself by dropping all large themes and turning to Canada in a work more concerned with immediacies of experience; his theme was the world of the hunter, a direct relationship to nature; and he showed he could conjure up a dimension of sheer physical living. But it was perhaps significant that when he turned from the theme of contemporary history and politics, it was to the sphere of nature he looked, not to everyday life in some specific society. For good and bad his uprooting through the war had made him into a novelist of the large national conflicts of our age. His material has thus been born of his journalism, but in transforming it into fiction he has overcome the journalistic limitations and been able to penetrate to deep human issues. He sees the problem in terms of real people and has never been guilty of inventing puppets to represent national or political positions.

He now turned again to the Near East, in *Heroes of the Empty View, I Wish He Would Not Die*, and *The Last Exile*, not dealing with such a remote issue as that of the Kurds, but taking up the problems of the Arab world, with special reference to Egypt. He has been helped by having many direct connections and sources of information; but despite his sympathy for the Arabs he has not oversimplified issues or made his works into tracts for a particular point of view. The stories clarify things and deepen one's understanding of the human beings entangled in vast conflicts. In his latest works he has again taken up the question of the Soviet Union but with less force and artistic success than in *The Diplomat* or the books on the Near East. It would be hard to point to any contemporary novelist who has dealt more directly with postwar political problems on the international plane with such success, uniting a warm sympathy for the persons he writes about, with, in the last resort, a true artistic detachment.

—Jack Lindsay

ALI, Ahmed. Pakistani. Born in New Delhi, India, 1 July 1910. Educated at Aligarh Muslim University, 1925–27; Lucknow University, 1928–31, B.A. (honours) in English 1930, M.A. in English 1931. Married Bilquees Jehan in 1950; three sons and one daughter. Lecturer in English, Lucknow University, 1931–32 and 1936–42; Professor, Agra College, 1933–34; Lecturer, Allahabad University, 1934–36; representative and listener-research director, BBC, New Delhi, 1942–44; Professor of English and Head of the English Department, Presidency College, Calcutta, 1945–47; with East Pakistan Senior Educational Service, 1947–60; British Council Visiting Professor, National Central University of China, Nanking, 1947–48; Visiting Professor, Michigan State University, East Lansing, Summer 1975, University of Karachi, 1977–79, and other universities; Fulbright-Hays Professor of History, Western Kentucky University, Bowling Green, and Fulbright Professor of English, Southern Illinois University, Carbondale, 1978–79. Director of Foreign Publicity, Government of Pakistan, Karachi, 1948–49; senior posts with Pakistan Foreign Service, Karachi, Peking, and Rabat, 1950–60 (established diplomatic relations with People's Republic of China and Morocco). Public relations adviser to business and industry, 1960–70. Since 1970, Chairman, Lomen Fabrics Ltd., Karachi. Editor, *Indian Writing*, London, 1933–41, *Tomorrow*, Bombay, 1941–42, and *PEN Miscellany*, Karachi, 1948–50. Proprietor, Akrash Publishing, New Delhi, 1940–47, and Karachi since 1963. Founder, Indian Progressive Writers Movement, 1932; Founding Fellow, Pakistan Academy of Letters; represented Pakistan at 18th International Meeting of Writers, Belgrade, 1981. Recipient: Sitara-e-Imtiaz (Star of Distinction), Government of Pakistan, 1980. Address: 21-A Faran Society, Hyder Ali Road, Karachi 5, Pakistan.

PUBLICATIONS

Novels

Twilight in Delhi.   London, Hogarth Press, 1940; New York and London, Oxford University Press, 1967.
Ocean of Night.   London, Owen, 1964.
Of Rats and Diplomats.   New Delhi, Orient Longman, 1985.

Short Stories

The Prison-House.   Karachi, Akrash, 1985.

Short Stories (in Urdu)

Angaray.   Lucknow, Nizam Press, 1932.
Sholay.   Allahabad, Naya Sansar, 1934.
Hamari Gali.   New Delhi, Insha Press, 1944.
Qaid Khana.   New Delhi, Insha Press, 1944.
Maut Se Pahlay.   New Delhi, Insha Press, 1945.

Plays

The Land of Twilight (produced Lucknow, 1931). Lucknow, Sreshta, 1937.
Break the Chains (produced Lucknow, 1932).

Verse

Purple Gold Mountain: Poems from China.   London, Keepsake Press, 1960.

Other

Mr. Eliot's Penny-World of Dreams.   Lucknow, Lucknow University, 1941.
Muslim China.   Karachi, Institute of International Affairs, 1949.
Problem of Style and Technique in Ghalib.   Karachi, American Centre, 1969.
Shadow and the Substance: Principles of Reality, Art and Literature.   Karachi, Karachi University, 1977.

Editor and Translator, *The Flaming Earth: Poems from Indonesia.*   Karachi, Friends of the Indonesia Society, 1949.
Editor and Translator, *The Bulbul and the Rose: An Anthology of Urdu Poetry.*   Karachi, Jamia, 1962.
Editor and Translator, *Selections from Ghalib.*   Rome, ISMEO, 1969.
Editor and Translator, *The Golden Tradition: An Anthology of Urdu Poetry.*   New York, Columbia University Press, 1973.

Translator, *The Falcon and the Hunted Bird* (Urdu poetry).   Karachi, Kitab, 1950.
Translator, *Al-Qur'an.*   Karachi, Akrash, 1984; revised edition, 1985.

*

Critical Studies: "Two Novels of Ahmed Ali" by Laurence Brander, in *Journal of Commonwealth Literature* (Leeds), July 1967; "Ahmed Ali and *Twilight in Delhi*" by David D. Anderson, in *Mahfil* (East Lansing, Michigan), Spring-Summer 1971; "*Twilight in Delhi*: A Study in Lyricism" by Anita S. Kumar, in *Indian Literature* (New Delhi), March-April 1976; "The Short Stories of Ahmed Ali" by Carlo Coppola, in *Center for South and Southeast Asian Studies Publications* (Madison, Wisconsin), series 5, 1979; "Historical Imagination in the Novels of Ahmed Ali" by Alastair Niven, in *Journal of Indian Writing in English* (Gulbarga), January–July 1980.

Ahmed Ali comments:

Starting with poetry and belles lettres as a young student, I moved on with growing awareness of the state of a society riddled with superstition, slavery, and hunger, indifferent to the human condition, to an expression of purpose and protest in writing. This led me to short fiction, and the founding, with two other friends, of the Progressive Writers Movement in 1932 with a volume of short stories, *Angaray* (Burning Coals), in Urdu, which so shocked a section of society that the book was banned within three months of publication. This set me on the course of a literary career, with four more volumes of short stories in Urdu. But the canvas of short fiction being limited, it ceased to have an appeal. At the same time, search for a wider public led to the writing of *Twilight in Delhi* in English, depicting the decay of a culture and way of life, in 1938–39 as war clouds were gathering over Asia and Europe.

A second novel, *Ocean of Night*, dealing with life between the two Wars, was written in 1943–44, but was put aside and forgotten in the momentous changes, social and psychological, that left no time for the good things of life, and was published only in 1964. It explored the decay of culture in the struggle between feudalism and the modern spirit. The feeling heart, still alive in the world of *Twilight in Delhi*, is here half atrophied, half searching in utter confusion. During the decades between *Ocean of Night* and *Of Rats and Diplomats*, many intellectual barriers intervened which cleft and divided the past from the present. For the society I was depicting, this came in the shape of the splitting up of India into two in 1947, the new part empty of the past, the old replete with more History as the new disowned what naturally belonged to it. The direction of life was thus utterly lost in the mazes of change, and any speculation became almost impossible. The mist began to clear only after 20 years, 12 of which, in my case, were spent in the curative interlude of diplomatic life which took me over half the world, and regions of the mind till then unfamiliar. When I came back to my life as a private citizen and a writer, I realised that the social order I was chronicling was not the same, and the process of decay had changed its direction and form with the shifting of the geographical scene, and its character from an empire to a state, with new problems, the motivating forces confined into narrow grooves and egotistic impulses, going backwards instead of seeking new avenues.

Thus, when I took up the thread in *Of Rats and Diplomats*, the canvas was not the same, and the palette had lost its primary colours, the quality of background so threadbare and thin as to require the use of the scalpel to fill in the features and the landscape. It could not but be different, denuded of expanse. The mind had developed, but the heart had died in the madness of power and greed for self. Only a faint, far echo is heard, and even that in memory of something undefined in a world from which the Big Idea seemed to have fled. It had to take me, naturally, into quite a different field, rich with symbol and allegory—the translation of the Qur'an; and now into the realm of history replete of vistas into the sources of the rise and fall of nations and civilisation.

*   *   *

The Muslim civilization of India is centred in Delhi and Agra and Lucknow. Delhi and Agra provide the great monuments. Delhi and Lucknow provide the language and the poetry. In its decline the poetry is drenched in remembrance of things past and this agony before the British went was mingled with

prophecy of their going and hope that the ancient Moghul splendour would be revived. In the event, the memories have become shadows of shades and the exquisitely civilized Muslims from the great Moghul cities live in exile in Pakistan,

The first two novels of Ahmed Ali are the finest celebration we have in novel form of the nostalgia for former glories and that accompanying Muslim belief in the vanity of earthly life. They are expressions of the pain of our human condition and of the agonized sense of the transitory nature of its happiness. They celebrate aspects of Muslim life in two of the great centres of Muslim culture. The Delhi novel came first. In time, it is set in the early decades of the century. From the old house in a by-lane of Old Delhi we go out to see the Great Durbar held by the King-Emperor in 1911, we see Delhi's reactions during the 1914 War, we glimpse the horror of the influenza epidemic in 1919 which decimated the population and we hear of the political unrest which swept across Northern India in 1920. But these things are on the fringe. At the centre is an old Muslim feudal family, generation following generation in gentle, dignified decay. The essential atmosphere of the novel is of the emptiness of the days as life passes by: the want of meaning. It is a special aspect of the despair which saturated the Gangetic Plain—the earth and air stale with the pain of existence, every atom of dust anguished and exhausted after being so many times vegetable, animal and human.

The story outline is simple and sad. Not tragic; it does not attempt that dimension. Two young people fall in love and for a time their union is thwarted—the girl is of a mere Moghul family, Asian from beyond the Himalayas, while the boy is Arabic, straight from the great families. The difficulties are overcome but eventually his love falters and he is unfaithful. The girl pines but before she dies their love is renewed. The value of the novel is in what is embroidered round this simple tale. The father's delight in the great Delhi pastime of pigeon flying, life in the zenana, the ceremonies at the wedding and the descriptions of all the people in the lanes who must play their part. It is a picture of energetic life and brilliant colour, the energy and colour which make life tolerable with its aching background of despair. Then later, the blows of fate, inevitable and cruel. On one side, the Muslim exuberance; on the other, the acceptance of fate: "Who can meddle in the affairs of God?" *Twilight in Delhi* is the most imaginative picture we have of the old Muslim life in Delhi which disappeared when the British went away; it is a fragment of Muslim history written with the pride of deep affection.

The second novel, *Ocean of Night*, was drafted soon afterwards though put aside and published much later. Instead of the colourful vigour of the first novel we have the mood appropriate to Lucknow, where the story is set. Again we have the Muslim celebration, but this time of the Muslim ideas of love and peace and friendship. The action is sordid, taking place in the house of a dissolute Nawab and the house of his mistress, an accomplished dancing girl. Lucknow is famous as a training ground of courtesans and we see the dancing master and the pimps, and the protector being bled of all his possessions. Sordid, the balancing excess to the expression of another excess, the intensity of mystical Islamic thinking. This more interesting theme is presented as the private search of a Muslim intellectual, a lawyer, for the traditional spiritual fulfillment of Islam. The intensity of this emotion is intellectual, a vivid glimpse of the mystical core of Islam. Religions normally reflect man's search for peace and harmony and in his search this Muslim lawyer had a vision in which the inhabitants of his dream tell him that peace is both love and glory, that friendship and love are what matter and the Muslim must subdue his natural pride for he will experience them only in humility. (Ali develops this theme in his fascinating anthology of Urdu poetry, *The Golden Tradition*.) So are we reconciled with God and man. In these two novels a distinguished Urdu poet offers imaginative glimpses of the grace and glory of Islam as it flourished once on the Gangetic Plain.

—Laurence Brander

ALLEN, Walter (Ernest). British. Born in Birmingham, Warwickshire, 23 February 1911. Educated at King Edward's Grammar School, Birmingham; Birmingham University, B.A. (honours) in English 1932. Married Peggy Yorke Joy in 1944; two sons and two daughters. Assistant Master, King Edward's Grammar School, Birmingham, 1934; Visiting Lecturer in English, University of Iowa, Iowa City, 1935; features editor, Cater's News Service, Birmingham, 1935–37; assistant technical officer, Wrought Light Alloys Development Association, Birmingham, 1943–45; Margaret Pilcher Visiting Professor of English, Coe College, Cedar Rapids, Iowa, 1955–56; assistant literary editor, 1959–60, and literary editor, 1960–61, *New Statesman*, London; Visiting Professor of English, Vassar College, Poughkeepsie, New York, 1963–64, University of Kansas, Lawrence, 1967, and University of Washington, Seattle, 1967; Professor and Chairman of English Studies, New University of Ulster, Coleraine, 1967–73; Berg Professor of English, New York University, 1970–71; Visiting Professor, Dalhousie University, Halifax, Nova Scotia, 1973–74; Miles Professor of English, Virginia Polytechnic Institute and State University, Blacksburg, 1974–75. Fellow, Royal Society of Literature, 1960. Address: 4-B Alwyne Road, London N1 2HH, England.

PUBLICATIONS

Novels

Innocence Is Drowned. London, Joseph, 1938.
Blind Man's Ditch. London, Joseph, 1939.
Living Space. London, Joseph, 1940.
Rogue Elephant. London, Joseph, and New York, Morrow, 1946.
Dead Man over All. London, Joseph, 1950; as *Square Peg*, New York, Morrow, 1951.
All in a Lifetime. London, Joseph, 1959; as *Threescore and Ten*, New York, Morrow, 1959.

Uncollected Short Stories

"At Aunt Sarah's," in *New Writing* (London), Spring 1938.
"You Hit Me," in *New Writing* (London), Christmas 1939.
"Hotel Hudson-Potomac," in *English Story*, edited by Woodrow and Susan Wyatt. London, Collins, 1941.

Other

The Black Country (topography). London, Elek, 1946.
The Festive Baked-Potato Cart and Other Stories (for children). London, Muller, 1948.
Arnold Bennett. London, Home and Van Thal, 1948; Denver, Swallow, 1949.
Reading a Novel. London, Phoenix House, and Denver, Swallow, 1949; revised edition, Phoenix House, 1956, 1963.
Joyce Cary. London, Longman, 1953; revised edition, 1963, 1971.

The English Novel: A Short Critical History. London, Phoenix House, 1954; New York, Dutton, 1955.
Six Great Novelists: Defoe, Fielding, Scott, Dickens, Stevenson, Conrad. London, Hamish Hamilton, 1955.
The Novel Today. London, Longman, 1955; revised edition, 1960.
George Eliot. New York, Macmillan, 1964; London, Weidenfeld and Nicolson, 1965.
Tradition and Dream: The English and American Novel from the Twenties to Our Time. London, Phoenix House, 1964; as *The Modern Novel in Britain and the United States*, New York, Dutton, 1964.
The British Isles in Colour. London, Batsford, and New York, Viking Press, 1965.
The Urgent West: An Introduction to the Idea of the United States. London, Baker, 1969; as *The Urgent West: The American Dream and Modern Man*, New York, Dutton, 1969.
Some Aspects of the American Short Story (lecture). London, Oxford University Press, 1973.
The Short Story in English. Oxford, Clarendon Press, and New York, Oxford University Press, 1981.
As I Walked Down New Grub Street: Memories of a Writing Life. London, Heinemann, 1981; Chicago, University of Chicago Press, 1982.

Editor, *Writers on Writing*. London, Phoenix House, 1948; as *The Writer on His Art*, New York, McGraw Hill, 1949.
Editor, *Transatlantic Crossing: American Visitors to Britain and British Visitors to America in the Nineteenth Century*. London, Heinemann, and New York, Morrow, 1971.
Editor, *The Roaring Queen*, by Wyndham Lewis. London, Secker and Warburg, and New York, Liveright, 1973.

*

Walter Allen comments:
    My first three novels seem now to have been the outcome of a single impulse, or rather a twin impulse. One side of it was to set down the nature of working-class life as I saw it all about me in the Midland city of Birmingham in a time of industrial depression, the rise of fascism and the threat of war. To this extent, these three novels are very much of the late 1930's. The other side of the impulse was formal: I was concerned with economy, with limits, with unity, almost indeed the Unities, believing that the most intense writing came from a narrow but powerful focus. I found myself unable to write fiction during the war and turned to the writing of criticism, and my first postwar novel, *Rogue Elephant*, turned out to be very different from my earlier work, though it had formal elements in common. I set out to write a work almost of classical comedy. At this time and for a long time to come I was caught up with the novel, as reviewer, publisher's reader and as a historian of the form, to the almost total exclusion of other interests, and this, I am sure, had its consequences. One was that I came increasingly to value what might be called the historical aspects of the novel. I was conscious, writing *Dead Man over All*, that I was attempting a number of disparate things. I wanted to show the influence on individuals of history, heredity, family tradition and so on; to say something about what seemed to me the changing nature of industrialism; to describe life in a factory geared to production for war during war (and that itself would be a contribution of a sort to the history of industry and the recent war); and also to depict a man in what I called an impossible position, impossible because willed for him, as it were, by others, by tradition.

All the same, in that novel, I largely retained the narrative pattern of my earlier books. I broke away from it in *All in a Lifetime*. Writing that novel, I was conscious that I was trying to do several things simultaneously: to trace the rise of the British Labour Party through a working man in some sort representative, to adumbrate the growth of a city through half a century, to show the rise to political and cultural awareness of the working class. There was also a personal factor that was probably fundamental to these: I wanted to celebrate my father, who became the model in the novel of my "in some sort representative" working man. But I had to satisfy myself that he might have written what I have him write in the novel—it is in fact the novel—and this dictated the narrative technique of the long letter/Defoe-esque pseudo-autobiographical novel. This emerged only after many false starts.

I don't think my novels have appeared to be particularly playful works; but in the writing of them it is the element of play that I have found most pleasurable, the making of a mimic world through the arrangement, both studied and "accidental," of one's characters. I wouldn't, though, have found much point in the play if it hadn't resulted from time to time in what seemed an acceptable paradigm of the real world.

*   *   *

The title of Walter Allen's novel *Innocence Is Drowned* comes from Yeats's well-known lines beginning: "Things fall apart; the centre cannot hold/The blood-dimmed tide is loosed, and everywhere/The ceremony of innocence is drowned." Allen had in mind not only the approach of the Second World War but also the manner in which his characters came to recognise not only the cruelty and indifference of others but also the cruelty and indifference in themselves. The novel can be seen as their attempt to come to terms with reality.

Innocence Is Drowned, Allen's first novel, has presumably his home-town of Birmingham for its setting, although no name is given to the place in the book. He introduces us to a working-class family. It is one in which the father, Dick Gardiner, is conscientious, hard-working, politically committed: a man who made the mistake of setting up as a master toolmaker instead of remaining a secure employee. The novel—like *Dead Man over All* and *Living Space*—covers only a few days in time: Tuesday, Wednesday and Thursday.

The narrative is largely conveyed through the minds of Mr. Gardiner, his wife and three sons, Ralph, Eric, and Sydney. One forms a vivid picture of each character and a clear impression of his (or her) relationships both within and outside the family. The actual events are trivial enough—for instance, the detention at school of the youngest boy causes quite a bit of fuss in the family circle—but they are skillfully built up into a convincing re-creation of pre-War life in the Midlands.

Innocence Is Drowned marked the emergence of a writer who has made more impact, perhaps, as a literary critic (he has a specialised knowledge of the English novel from its beginnings to the present day) than as a novelist. It shows, too, how Allen, while not standing aside from the Left-wing current of his time, knew from the start that propaganda and art are ill-sorted bedfellows.

Rogue Elephant represents a considerable advance on the earlier novels. The style is more supple and fluent, and contains less pedestrian writing. Allen, like all true artists, obviously learned from his first experiments in his craft as well as from the twentieth-century masters about whom he has written so perceptively.

The central character of *Rogue Elephant* is called Henry Ashley, a fat, clever but unintegrated young man who ambles through the novel; a schemer with a soft core in his personality. This is how he looks at himself: "Mr. Henry Ashley ... saw himself as the enemy, as miching mallecho which means mischief, as the test-tube of cholera bacillus that is broken into the water supply." For a while Ashley wreaks havoc among two girls (they are cousins) in an upper-class household in Devonshire. Ashley lives for and through his writing. A rising young novelist and critic, he copes with life through ideas and word-spinning. He keeps reality at arm's length. Henry Ashley comes across as a real person, not just as a target for satirical rifle-practice.

Allen's most solid achievement in the novel is undisputably *All in a Lifetime*. It came out, in 1959, at a time when regionalism was beginning to be a potent force in post-War English fiction. That same year saw the publication, for instance, of Keith Waterhouse's *Billy Liar* and Alan Sillitoe's *The Loneliness of the Long-Distance Runner*. Brash, ill-mannered young working-class heroes (or, rather, anti-heroes) without religious, political or moral conviction became fashionable. Allen, an older man than writers such as John Braine, Stan Barstow and the others, stood foursquare against the new gospel of revolt for its own sake.

Billy Ashted, the narrator of *All in a Lifetime*, is in his middle seventies. He looks back calmly on his life and the changes he has lived through. He is portrayed as a man with a strong political faith—a kind of substitute, it may be, for religion—a man who tended to look outward rather than into his own ego. Allen accurately analyses the place held by religion in the Black Country when Billy Ashted was young: the Nonconformist chapel where the preacher was a "great populariser" who "talked of new ideas and movements of ideas in such a way that your curiosity was stimulated to find out about them at first hand." Opposed to the plain services and Christian Socialism of the chapel, there is the High Anglicanism that repels Billy Ashted because it smacks of Popery and aristocracy.

In a comment on the novel Allen says that Billy Ashted is based on his father who, like Ashted, was "a working silversmith in Birmingham all his life and never earning at any time more than £5 a week from his craft." Nevertheless, Allen's father "had a very considerable learning in philosophy and, in the opinion of people much better qualified than me to judge, had genuine ability as a philosopher." Billy Ashted's brief migration to the U.S. was paralleled by Allen's own father's experience in that country. The author tells us that his father had lived in Philadelphia whereas Billy Ashted goes to New York for the good reason that the novelist is more familiar with the topography of New York.

Allen had two aims in writing the novel: first, he wanted to write a chronicle novel in which social change would be explored and the rise of the Labour Party outlined; and second, he wished to write about an old man and so project himself "imaginatively into the experience of old age as it faces death." Already he had, in *Rogue Elephant* and *Dead Man over All*, drawn the portraits of very old men: but they were minor characters and he was determined to essay a major portrait. This he does here with great success, taking care to balance the essentially contemplative Billy Ashted with the more active and politically committed George Thompson.

The novel consists of a "letter" Billy Ashted writes to his sister at a time of family crisis: the ostensible reason for it is to discover how to cope with the present difficulty. He feels this can be achieved by dredging incidents and people from his long life. Thus past and present are intermingled, and the novel takes on a reality and naturalness it might lack had it been written in the third person.

All in a Lifetime did not create much of a stir in the literary world when it appeared. Unlike other novels of the time with a strong regional flavour it has not been filmed or adapted for television. What it lacks in newsworthiness it makes up in sincerity and warmth and, not least, in sheer skill. It will probably be more durable than those novels that have a hard, glittering shell but are soft and cold at the center.

—Robert Greacen

ALTHER, Lisa (née Reed). American. Born in Kingsport, Tennessee, 23 July 1944. Educated at Wellesley College, Massachusetts, 1962–66, B.A. 1966. Married Richard Alther in 1966; one daughter. Editorial assistant, Atheneum Publishers, New York, 1966; staff writer, Garden Way Publishers, Charlotte, Vermont, 1969–72; Visiting Lecturer, St. Michael's College, Winooski, Vermont, 1980. Lives in Hinesburg, Vermont. Address: c/o Knopf Inc., 201 East 50th Street, New York, New York 10022, U.S.A.

PUBLICATIONS

Novels

Kinflicks. New York, Knopf, and London, Chatto and Windus, 1976.
Original Sins. New York, Knopf, and London, Women's Press, 1981.
Other Women. New York, Knopf, 1984; London, Viking, 1985.

Uncollected Short Stories

"Encounter," in *McCall's* (New York), August 1976.
"Termites," in *Homewords.* Knoxville, University of Tennessee Press, 1986.

Other

Non-Chemical Pest and Disease Control for the Home Orchard. Charlotte, Vermont, Garden Way, 1973.

*

Critical Studies: "Condemned to Survival: The Comic Unsuccessful Suicide" by Marilynn J. Smith, in *Comparative Literature Studies* (Urbana, Illinois), March 1980; "Alther and Dillard: The Appalachian Universe" by Frederick G. Waase, in *Appalachia/America: The Proceedings of the 1980 Appalachian Studies Conference* edited by Wilson Somerville, Johnson City, Tennessee, Appalachian Consortium Press, 1981; article in *Women Writers of the Contemporary South* edited by Peggy Whitman Prenshaw, Jackson, University Press of Mississippi, 1984.

*   *   *

Lisa Alther comments with shrewdness, insight—and a hefty measure of irony—upon American types, their trendy habits, and their dreams. Typical though they be, Alther's protagonists are, nevertheless, fully realized individuals who are sometimes despairing, prickly, dense, or self-destructive, but who are also unfailingly interesting folk, often surprisingly courageous survivors. These factors, along with Alther's keen sense of place, her clever manipulation of point of view, and her exploitation of various levels of comedy are the chief strengths of *Kinflicks*, *Original Sins*, and *Other Women*.

Alther's manipulation of point of view contributes to the sprawling effect of her bulky novels even as it helps control them. The picaresque *Kinflicks* alternates between third-person narration of the present moment as Ginny Babcock Bliss keeps vigil at her mother's deathbed and first-person flashbacks which hilariously and satirically recount Ginny's penchant for redesigning herself to suit those who successively dominate her affections—parents, gum-chewing football hero, motorcycle hood, lesbian reformer, snow-mobile salesman, disturbed Viet vet, baby daughter. Ultimately, alone but rather more determined, she sets out to suit herself. The distancing effect of Ginny's memories facilitates the bald, raucous humor of the book for, in effect, Ginny is laughing at herself *with* her readers; the detachment of the third-person narrator in the alternate chapters legislates against melodrama or shallow sentimentality.

Though *Original Sins* is told in the third person, major sections allow readers to share the consciousness of five protagonists. Members of a huge extended family, sisters Emily and Sally Prince, brothers Jed and Raymond Tatro, and Donny Tatro are inseparable as children, but are later driven apart by circumstances of sex, social class, personal ambition, and race (Donny is black). A *bildungsroman*, *Original Sins* depicts youngsters who believe they can do anything becoming adults who often wonder if anything worthwhile can be done—but who don't stop trying. *Other Women*, a "delayed *bildungsroman*," also uses the third person throughout and shifts between the consciousness of its protagonists, Carolyn Kelley, a single mother whose lesbian relationship is dissolving, and her therapist, Hannah Burke. As Hannah counsels Carolyn toward acceptance of herself, adulthood, and responsibility, some of her own very old, deep wounds begin to heal, and the novel concludes with a note of genuine hope symbolized by the women's developing friendship. In *Other Women* and *Original Sins*, the availability of each protagonist's thought processes lends immediacy and realism as it arouses empathy. Readers may not fully endorse the protagonists' decisions, but they remain involved and concerned with the characters because their motivations are so clearly drawn. Suitably, the humor in these novels is quieter, developing more from quirks of personality and wry social comment than from the slapstick situations of *Kinflicks*.

Because both *Kinflicks* and *Original Sins* are set primarily in Tennessee, her home state, Alther has been dubbed a regionalist. She recognizes the influence of fellow Southerner Flannery O'Connor upon her literary sensibilities and freely acknowledges the usefulness and attraction of the "ready-made social context" available to Southerners writing about their area (see her article "Will the South Rise Again?," *New York Times Book Review*, 16 December 1979). It is equally important, however, to note that Alther's settings range across the eastern United States. Her assessment of college life on a New York City campus, her stringent portrayal of the power struggles among supposedly egalitarian Northern civil rights workers (*Original Sins*), her lovingly drawn Vermont landscapes in *Other Women*—as well as her acknowledgement that conducting a private life privately is just as difficult in any closed Northern community as it is in a Southern one (*Kinflicks*)—attest to her understanding of several locales and make explicit the wide scope of her social commentary. In this way, Alther differs a bit from regionalists who imply rather than dramatize the larger applications of their social comment.

Considered by many to be a feminist writer, Alther focuses primarily upon contemporary American women, giving great attention to the limitations thrust upon them, but she also details their self-imposed restrictions and stresses the need for each to assume responsibility for her own life. In an interview with Andrew Feinberg (*Horizon*, May 1981), she comments, "People are assigned roles because of their external characteristics and then are forced to play them out ... unless they are lucky enough to figure out what is going on and get out." The process of getting out, always painful, sometimes unsuccessful, is the motivational force in Alther's plots and functions as effectively for several male characters as it does for females. Alther's awareness that despite the deep social divisions which exist between many contemporary women and men, there are also shared problems—such as the constrictions of traditionalism, the desire to escape from parents' demands, the difficulties of assimilation into another cultural-geographic region— demonstrates the universality of feminist fiction just as her humor reveals that feminist writers can treat serious subjects without being deadly dull. By modifying critical categories, Lisa Alther produces novels incorporating strong plots and intriguing characterizations with effective social commentary.

—Jane S. Bakerman

ALUKO, T(imothy) M(ofolorunso). Nigerian. Born in Ilesha, 14 June 1918. Educated at primary schools in Ilesha, 1926–32; Government College, Ibadan, 1933–38; Yaba Higher College, 1939–42; University of London, 1946–50, B.Sc. in engineering and diploma in town planning 1950; University of Newcastle-upon-Tyne (Unesco Fellow), 1968–69, M.Sc. in engineering 1969; University of Lagos, Ph.D. in public health engineering 1976. Married Janet Adebisi Fajemisin in 1950; six children. Engineer, Public Works Department, Lagos, 1943–46; executive engineer, Public Works Department, Ibadan and Lagos, 1950–56; town engineer, Lagos Town Council, 1956–60; Director and Permanent Secretary, Ministry of Works and Transport, Western Nigeria, 1960–66; Senior Lecturer, University of Ibadan, 1966; Senior Research Fellow in Municipal Engineering, 1966–78, and Associate Professor of Public Health Engineering, 1978, University of Lagos. Since 1979, Resident Partner, Scott Wilson Kirkpatrick, consulting engineers and transportation planners, Lagos. Commissioner of Finance, Government of Western Nigeria, 1971–73. Fellow, Institution of Civil Engineers, Institution of Municipal Engineers, and Nigerian Society of Engineers. O.B.E. (Officer, Order of the British Empire), 1963; O.O.N. (Officer, Order of the Niger), 1964. Address: 53 Ladipo Oluwote Road, Apapa, Lagos, Nigeria.

PUBLICATIONS

Novels

One Man, One Wife. Lagos, Nigerian Printing and Publishing Company, 1959; London, Heinemann, 1967; New York, Humanities Press, 1968.
One Man, One Matchet. London, Heinemann, 1964; Mystic, Connecticut, Verrey, 1965.

Kinsman and Foreman. London, Heinemann, 1966; New York, Humanities Press, 1967.
Chief the Honourable Minister. London, Heinemann, 1970.
His Worshipful Majesty. London, Heinemann, 1973.
Wrong Ones in the Dock. London, Heinemann, 1982.

Uncollected Short Story

"The New Engineer," in *African New Writing.* London, Lutterworth Press, 1947.

*

Critical Study: *Long Drums and Cannons* by Margaret Laurence, London, Macmillan, and New York, Praeger, 1968.

*   *   *

T.M. Aluko's *One Man, One Wife* was the first African novel in English to be published in Nigeria, and in following it up with five more books Aluko became one of the more productive African novelists. Aluko is, however, a much under-rated writer whose very intelligent comic sense has been out of tune with the serious-mindedness of West African fiction generally and has thus caused his work to be overlooked or summarily dismissed. In his first three novels he applies a wry, comic detachment to the stresses between modern and traditional life among the Yoruba people.

Most reviewers and commentators have seen this detachment as a complete lack of commitment in social problems, about which they believe all African writers should be committed, and one suspects that they have sometimes mistaken for Aluko's own the clichés, grandiloquences, and superficial attitudes which, with considerable linguistic sophistication, he mocks by embedding them even in authorial narration; for instance, this bemused reflection upon the Christian catechist Royasin's message on Christmas Day: "How could this same Baby have founded a religion nearly two thousand years old? And how could this same mysterious Baby rule all the world? The invitation to all the faithful to come to Bethlehem, the geographical location of which even the great Royasin could not tell ..." (*One Man, One Wife*). In this novel Aluko captures the very accents of various levels of English used in Yorubaland, as he satirizes with amused impartiality the foibles of both Christians and polygamists, of both followers of the new faith who retain a toehold in the old, like Elder Joshua, and the blindly committed converts, like Bible Jeremiah. The comedy is largely verbal and cerebral, the mode dead-pan, like that of the silent-film comedian, Buster Keaton, but it is never malicious, and even as satire it finds cause for celebration in the rich absurdities of human behaviour.

One Man, One Matchet plays upon the differences between the unprincipled, rabble-rousing Benjamin Benjamin, who is no more than a spiv with the gift of the gab, and the newly appointed Nigerian-born administrators trying to do an honest job but suspected by the traditionalists because of their command of "the White Man's language." The purpose is not anti-Nationalist but exposure of the spurious and the absurd wearing Nationalist garb. *Kinsman and Foreman* explores the trials and embarrassments of an overseas-trained Nigerian engineer who is employed by the Public Works Department in his home town and finds that his relations expect him to use his official position for their private benefit. It is a book that bubbles with cross-cultural misunderstandings.

Perhaps as a result of meagre critical attention, Aluko tries to swim in the mainstream of Nigerian writing with *Chief the*

Honourable Minister, a novel which, somewhat in the manner of Achebe's *A Man of the People*, deals with post-Independence political developments in Nigeria. This more "serious" venture confirms that Aluko's real gift is a judicious response to the comic, though the presentation of the idealistic Alade Moses's transformation into a corrupt politician is very skillfully done; Moses is for ever putting off as untimely the decision to resign on principle as a Minister in the government, and always succeeds in finding good principles to justify his continuing in office.

With some success *His Worshipful Majesty* treats tragically the inability of an *oba* or traditional king to make the transition from autocratic rule to mere Chairmanship of a Local Government Council hemmed in by bureaucratic regulations. In the details of the story, however, there is a muted return to Aluko's earlier comic manner, and he does achieve an uneasy poise in modulating the comic with the tragic within the same novel.

With *Wrong Ones in the Dock* Aluko seems to have abandoned the comic. He returns to the social satire of *Chief the Honourable Minister* with an indignant attack upon the inept workings of the machinery of justice in Nigeria, the general tone of which is captured in this extract from the final paragraph of the novel:

> What the Judge handed down was judgment without justice. It was unfortunately all that he was competent to give in the circumstances of the cumbersome judicial system which he operated . . .. Real justice was impossible under a truth-inhibiting judicial system which had been imported from a foreign clime and which, in spite of over a century of nursing in the inhospitable soil of an indigenous society, has yet, in that society, to grow roots that will reach down to the ground water of true justice.

It is a solemnity that sits uneasily on Aluko's pen and makes his full and detailed court-room scenes, for instance, awkward and lumbering, despite some telling satirical touches, rather than deft exposures of absurdity, ineptitude, hypocrisy, immorality, and injustice.

—Arthur Ravenscroft

ALVAREZ, A(lfred). British. Born in London, 5 August 1929. Educated at Oundle School, Northamptonshire; Corpus Christi College, Oxford (Senior Research Scholar and Research Scholar of Goldsmiths' Company, 1952–53, 1954–55), B.A. 1952, M.A. 1956; Princeton University, New Jersey (Procter Visiting Fellow, 1953–54). Married 1) Ursula Barr in 1956 (marriage dissolved, 1961), one son; 2) Anne Adams in 1966, one son and one daughter. Gauss Lecturer, Princeton University, 1957–58; Visiting Professor, Brandeis University, Waltham, Massachusetts, 1960, and State University of New York, Buffalo, 1966. Advisory poetry editor, *The Observer*, London, 1956–66; poetry critic and editor, *Journal of Education*, London, 1957; drama critic, *New Statesman*, London, 1958–60; advisory editor, Penguin Modern European Poets in Translation, 1965–75; presenter, *Voices* programme, Channel 4 television, 1982. Recipient: Rockefeller fellowship, 1955, 1958; D.H. Lawrence Fellowship, 1958; Vachel Lindsay Prize (*Poetry*, Chicago), 1961. Agent: Deborah Rogers Ltd., 49 Blenheim Crescent, London W11 2EF; or, Candida Donadio and Associates, 231 West 22nd Street, New York, New York 10011, U.S.A. Address: c/o The Observer, 8 St. Andrew's Hill, London EC4V 5JA, England.

PUBLICATIONS

Novels

Hers. London, Weidenfeld and Nicolson, 1974; New York, Random House, 1975.
Hunt. London, Macmillan, 1978; New York, Simon and Schuster, 1979.

Uncollected Short Stories

"The Smile," in *Cosmopolitan* (New York), December 1970.
"Laughter," in *Winter's Tales 17*, edited by Caroline Hobhouse. London, Macmillan, 1971; New York, St. Martin's Press, 1972.
"Summertime," in *Daily Telegraph Magazine* (London), 16 July 1971.
"Night Out," in *New Yorker*, 4 September 1971.
"Veterans," in *The Times Saturday Review* (London), 24 January 1976.

Play

Screenplay: *The Anarchist*, 1969.

Verse

(*Poems*). Oxford, Fantasy Press, 1952.
The End of It. Privately printed, 1958.
Twelve Poems. London, The Review, 1968.
Lost. London, Turret, 1968.
Penguin Modern Poets 18, with Roy Fuller and Anthony Thwaite. London, Penguin, 1970.
Apparition. St. Lucia, University of Queensland Press, 1971.
The Legacy. London, Poem-of-the-Month Club, 1972.
Autumn to Autumn and Selected Poems 1953–1976. London, Macmillan, 1978.

Other

The Shaping Spirit: Studies in Modern English and American Poets. London, Chatto and Windus, 1958; as *Stewards of Excellence: Studies in Modern English and American Poets*, New York, Scribner, 1958.
The School of Donne. London, Chatto and Windus, 1961; New York, Pantheon, 1962.
Under Pressure: The Artist and Society: Eastern Europe and the U.S.A. London, Penguin, 1965.
Beyond All This Fiddle: Essays 1955–1967. London, Allen Lane, 1968; New York, Random House, 1969.
The Savage God: A Study of Suicide. London, Weidenfeld and Nicolson, 1971; New York, Random House, 1972.
Beckett. London, Fontana, and New York, Viking Press, 1973.
Life after Marriage: Scenes from Divorce. London, Macmillan, 1982; as *Life after Marriage: Love in an Age of Divorce*, New York, Simon and Schuster, 1982.
The Biggest Game in Town (on gambling). London, Deutsch, and Boston, Houghton Mifflin, 1983.
Offshore: A North Sea Journey. London, Hodder and Stoughton, and Boston, Houghton Mifflin, 1986.

Editor, *The New Poetry: An Anthology*. London, Penguin, 1962; revised edition, 1966.

*

Critical Study: interview with Ian Hamilton, in *New Review* (London), March 1978.

* * *

A. Alvarez's reputation rests primarily upon his criticism. *The Savage God*, with its perceptive essay on Plath, and *Beyond All This Fiddle* express Alvarez's temper, the breadth of his literary interests, and the subtlety of his mind. His poetry and his novels suffer from some of the faults typical of a literary-critic-turned-creative writer: his style is derivative, and a little too self-conscious; he lacks the freedom of invention characteristic of the best writers. Nonetheless, he writes well and is always eminently readable. His poetry suffers from its compression and adherence to formal conventions. His novels at times create a scene or person with life-like vividness, but generally his characters are thin and the plot is slight.

His first novel, *Hers*, is voguish in its subject. It is the story of a middle-aged woman's affair with one of her husband's students, a man some 12 years her junior. Julie, the wife of German extraction with a painful past, is married to the stereotypical university professor of letters, an older man who married her to capture the youth he neglected for his books. Alvarez's caricature of academia is not as rich as Kingsley Amis's in *Lucky Jim*, nor does he have the flair that Iris Murdoch and Joyce Carol Oates have for this subject, but his portrait of Charles, the Professor, is often entertaining. Charles, with his unspeakable air of self-assurance, with his inability to register any emotion without filtering it through the language of literary characters—when he discovers his wife has cuckolded him, he mutters Othello's words—is a perfectly realized representative of a "preordained academic." At one point, he lectures his student, who is his wife's lover, talking to him on morality and literature, quoting his lecture notes, calling upon Arnold and Tolstoy, Wellek and Warren, Eliot and Hume rather than simply confronting him directly with his anger. Julie is a complicated person. Blond, youthful in appearance, fragile and Germanic, she is the mother of two children and a woman who took an older husband to forget the abuse heaped on her by the Russians and the murder of her father by the Nazis. Julie provides Sam every pleasure but the pleasure of being inside her, fearing that the final act will somehow mark her as an infidel. Once she becomes Sam's mistress in every sense, she is driven back into her past. Returning to a sanitorium in Germany, she comes to terms with herself in a fairly predictable way. Probably the best scenes in the novels are those when Charles behaves paranoically, venting his hostility upon the young, and making himself the prey of a motorcycle gang, and when he violently retakes possession of his wife, making her share in the complicity of their mutual violence.

Hunt is a thriller, written in a manner very like Arthur La Bern's *Goodbye Piccadilly, Farewell Leicester Square*. The drab life of Conrad Jessup, a man dulled by his marriage and tedious job, is depicted with a naturalism typical of Greene at his best. Jessup's quest for excitement and a moment that will give value to his life takes him to the gambling tables and then out into the park, late in the night, where he discovers the body of a woman who has been assaulted. His discovery leads to his arrest on suspicion of murder. Once released, he cannot resist finding the woman and he becomes caught up in her web of international espionage. The plot is slow, and

rather obvious. The best moments in the novel are the scenes at the poker table where Conrad's compulsive gambling is so convincingly portrayed that the reader vicariously experiences his excitement and disillusion. The world of pubs, gambling clubs, and boutiques is presented with a good sense of detail. But the story itself has been told before.

It is too early to judge Alvarez as a novelist. He is clever and has a good sense of the modern. His next novel may well surprise us.

—Carol Simpson Stern

AMADI, Elechi. Nigerian. Born in Aluu, 12 May 1934. Educated at University College, Ibadan, 1955–59, B.Sc. in mathematics and physics 1959. Served in the Nigerian Federal Army, 1963–66, 1968–69. Married Dorah Ohale in 1957; eight children. Government survey assistant, Calabar, 1953–55, and surveyor, Enugu, 1959–60; science teacher in mission schools, Oba and Ahoada, 1960–63; Principal, Asa Grammar School, 1967. Administrative Officer, 1970–74, and Permanent Secretary, 1975–83, Government of Rivers State, Port Harcourt. Since 1984, Writer-in-Residence and Dean of the Faculty of Arts, College of Education, Port Harcourt. Recipient: International Writers Program grant, University of Iowa, 1973. Address: Box 331, Port Harcourt, Nigeria.

PUBLICATIONS

Novels

The Concubine. London, Heinemann, 1966.
The Great Ponds. London, Heinemann, 1969; New York, Day, 1973.
The Slave. London, Heinemann, 1978.
Estrangement. London, Heinemann, 1986.

Plays

Isiburu (in verse; produced Port Harcourt, Nigeria, 1969). London, Heinemann, 1973.
Peppersoup (produced Port Harcourt, Nigeria, 1977). Included in *Peppersoup, and The Road to Ibadan*, 1977.
The Road to Ibadan (produced Port Harcourt, Nigeria, 1977). Included in *Peppersoup, and The Road to Ibadan*, 1977.
Peppersoup, and The Road to Ibadan. Ibadan, Onibonoje Press, 1977.
Dancer of Johannesburg (produced Port Harcourt, Nigeria, 1979).

Other

Sunset in Biafra: A Civil War Diary. London, Heinemann, 1973.
Ethics in Nigerian Culture. Ibadan and London, Heinemann, 1982.

Translator, with Obiajunwo Wali and Greensille Enyinda, *Okwukwo Eri* (hymnbook). Port Harcourt, Nigeria, CSS Printers, 1969.

Translator, *Okupkpe* (prayerbook). Port Harcourt, Nigeria, CSS Printers, 1969.

*

Critical Study: *The Concubine: A Critical View* by Alastair Niven, London, Collings, 1981.

Elechi Amadi comments:

I like to think of myself as a painter or composer using words in the place of pictures and musical symbols. I consider commitment in fiction a prostitution of literature. The novelist should depict life as he sees it without consciously attempting to persuade the reader to take a particular viewpoint. Propaganda should be left to journalists.

In my ideal novel the reader should feel a sense of aesthetic satisfaction that he cannot quite explain—the same feeling he gets when he listens to a beautiful symphony. For those readers who insist on being taught, there are always things to learn from a faithful portrayal of life in a well-written novel.

*   *   *

From his first appearance as a novelist, with *The Concubine* in 1966, Elechi Amadi established himself as a unique figure in African fiction. He was not alone in attempting to convey the day-to-day texture of traditional, pre-colonial life in an African village (Chinua Achebe's *Things Fall Apart* had already done this, at least in its earlier pages), but he distinguished himself by not offering any explicit contrasts between that traditional world and the one that replaced it. Whereas *Things Fall Apart* and many other African novels are concerned, in part at least, with the coming of the white man and the effect of that coming, Amadi's novels have never adverted to alien influences at all. The action of any of his three novels could have taken place either five years or a century before the colonial intrusion upon the area; the dilemmas which confront and finally destroy his heroes or heroines derive entirely from the beliefs, practices, and events of their indigenous culture.

The Concubine was followed by *The Great Ponds* and *The Slave*. Although not thematically related, all three novels take place in what is recognizably the same Ikweore environment. The action of all three appears to turn upon the working out of a fate which falls upon the characters from without, but which it would be meaningless, in this traditional and godfearing environment, to call unjust. Iheoma, heroine of *The Concubine*, is powerless to avert her spiritual marriage to the sea-king which prevents her having any successful human relationship. Her attraction thus becomes a fatal one, resulting in the deaths of all those who seek to free her from her condition. Likewise, the hero of *The Slave* leaves the shrine of Amadioha to which his late father was bound as an *osu* (cult-slave) and appears to have right on his side in arguing for his emancipation, since he was not actually conceived there. Nevertheless, his brief career in freedom has an obstinately circular form curving through initial success to a series of disasters which brings him, friendless and alone, back to the shrine he had so hopefully deserted.

Amadi maintains a nicely judged ambiguity about the meaning of these events, which must depend entirely upon the reader himself. The society of which he writes would have rejected, perhaps still rejects, any clear distinction between the natural and spiritual orders of existence. These interpenetrate to such an extent that man cannot demand the mastery of his fate through will alone. The highest he can aspire to is to know his fate and tune his soul to its acceptance. Tragedy springs as much from failure to do this, as from the nature of that fate itself.

—Gerald Moore

AMBLER, Eric. British. Born in London, 28 June 1909. Educated at Colfe's Grammar School, London; University of London, 1925–28. Served in the Royal Artillery, 1940–46; Assistant Director of Army Kinematography, 1944–46; Lieutenant Colonel; Bronze Star (U.S.A.). Married 1) Louise Crombie in 1939 (divorced, 1958); 2) Joan Harrison in 1958. Engineering apprentice, 1928; advertising copywriter, 1929–37; director of an advertising agency, 1937–38. Created *Checkmate* TV series, 1959. Recipient: Crime Writers Association Award, 1959, 1962, 1967, 1972; Mystery Writers of America Edgar Allan Poe Award, 1964, and Grand Master Award, 1975; Svenska Deckarakademins Grand Master, 1975. O.B.E. (Officer, Order of the British Empire), 1981. Agent: Campbell Thomson and McLaughlin Ltd., 31 Newington Green, London N16 9PY, England.

PUBLICATIONS

Novels

The Dark Frontier. London, Hodder and Stoughton, 1936.
Uncommon Danger. London, Hodder and Stoughton, 1937; as *Background to Danger*, New York, Knopf, 1937.
Epitaph for a Spy. London, Hodder and Stoughton, 1938; New York, Knopf, 1952.
Cause for Alarm. London, Hodder and Stoughton, 1938; New York, Knopf, 1939.
The Mask of Dimitrios. London, Hodder and Stoughton, 1939; as *A Coffin for Dimitrios*, New York, Knopf, 1939.
Journey into Fear. London, Hodder and Stoughton, and New York, Knopf, 1940.
Judgment on Deltchev. London, Hodder and Stoughton, and New York, Knopf, 1951.
The Schirmer Inheritance. London, Heinemann, and New York, Knopf, 1953.
The Night-Comers. London, Heinemann, 1956; as *State of Siege*, New York, Knopf, 1956.
Passage of Arms. London, Heinemann, 1959; New York, Knopf, 1960.
The Light of Day. London, Heinemann, 1962; New York, Knopf, 1963; as *Topkapi*, New York, Bantam, 1964.
A Kind of Anger. London, Bodley Head, and New York, Atheneum, 1964.
Dirty Story. London, Bodley Head, and New York, Atheneum, 1967.
The Intercom Conspiracy. New York, Atheneum, 1969; London, Weidenfeld and Nicolson, 1970.
The Levanter. London, Weidenfeld and Nicolson, and New York, Atheneum, 1972.
Doctor Frigo. London, Weidenfeld and Nicolson, and New York, Atheneum, 1974.
Send No More Roses. London, Weidenfeld and Nicolson, 1977; as *The Siege of the Villa Lipp*, New York, Random House, 1977.
The Care of Time. London, Weidenfeld and Nicolson, and New York, Farrar Straus, 1981.

Novels as Eliot Reed (with Charles Rodda)

Skytip. New York, Doubleday, 1950; London, Hodder and
  Stoughton, 1951.
Tender to Danger. New York, Doubleday, 1951; as *Tender
  to Moonlight,* London, Hodder and Stoughton, 1952.
The Maras Affair. London, Collins, and New York, Double-
  day, 1953.
Charter to Danger. London, Collins, 1954.
Passport to Panic. London, Collins, 1958.

Uncollected Short Stories

"The Army of the Shadows," in *The Queen's Book of the
  Red Cross.* London, Hodder and Stoughton, 1939.
"The Intrusions of Dr. Czissar" ("A Bird in the Tree," "Case
  of the Gentleman Poet," "Case of the Landlady's Brother,"
  "Case of the Overheated Flat," "The Case of the Pinchbeck
  Locket"), in *The Sketch* (London), 1940.
"The Blood Bargain," in *Winter's Crimes 2,* edited by George
  Hardinge. London, Macmillan, 1970.
"The Case of the Emerald Sky," in *The Arbor House Treasury
  of Mystery and Suspense,* edited by Bill Pronzini, Barry N.
  Malzberg, and Martin H. Greenberg. New York, Arbor
  House, 1981.

Plays

Screenplays: *The Way Ahead,* with Peter Ustinov, 1944; *United
States,* 1945; *The October Man,* 1947; *The Passionate Friends
(One Woman's Story),* 1949; *Highly Dangerous,* 1950; *The
Magic Box,* 1951; *Gigolo and Gigolette,* in *Encore,* 1951; *The
Card (The Promoter),* 1952; *Rough Shoot (Shoot First),* 1953;
The Cruel Sea, 1953; *Lease of Life,* 1954; *The Purple Plain,*
1954; *Yangtse Incident (Battle Hell),* 1957; *A Night to
Remember,* 1958; *The Wreck of the Mary Deare,* 1960; *Love
Hate Love,* 1970.

Other

The Ability to Kill and Other Pieces. London, Bodley Head,
  1963.
Here Lies: An Autobiography. London, Weidenfeld and
  Nicolson, 1985.

Editor, *To Catch a Spy: An Anthology of Favourite Spy Stories.* London, Bodley Head, 1964; New York, Atheneum,
  1965.

*

Manuscript Collection: Mugar Memorial Library, Boston
University.

Critical Studies: "Eric Ambler Issue" of *Hollins Critic* (Hollins
College, Virginia), February 1971; *Über Eric Ambler* (includes
bibliography) edited by Gerd Haffmans, Zurich, Diogenes,
1979.

Eric Ambler comments:

  I have found that every statement I have ever tried to make
on the subject of my work later seems either pretentious or
meaningless. Besides, I am an unreliable witness. When *Über
Eric Ambler* was published on my 70th birthday I gave a
number of interviews to European journalists. One of them
pointed out that I had answered a standard question (where

do you get your ideas?) in two entirely different ways. Which
answer was the right one? I explained that I always tried to
avoid giving an interviewer the same answer as I had given
his colleague so that each had something exclusive. He was
deeply shocked. Did I not distinguish between truth and false-
hood? I could have said, "Not when answering dull or unanswerable questions." Instead, I mumbled something about
only trying to be helpful. It failed to satisfy him. I stood convicted of frivolity.

*   *   *

  In Graham Greene's view Eric Ambler is Britain's best
thriller writer and there are many reasons for supporting this
judgment. The most important is Ambler's capacity for telling
a story. He wastes no words; his narrative is economical yet
evocative; his grasp of detail matches his control of suspense.
  His ability to vary the tempo of a story is subtle. He is a
master of reconstruction without boredom. This technique is
one of the reasons for the success of an early book, *The Mask
of Dimitrios,* where his character Latimer, a detective story
writer, becomes obsessed with the mysterious life of a man
called Dimitrios whose supposed body he sees in a Turkish
morgue. He decides to find out something of the man's odd
past, and discovers more and more of his intrigues in many
countries, his altering identity, his capacity for murder, pimp-
ing, political assassination, drug trafficking, and double crossing. Latimer's own search unfolds slowly, then follows his
unwilling cooperation with a former associate and victim of
Dimitrios. Gradually the narration speeds up until Latimer
is confronted by the fact that Dimitrios is alive, and not only
alive but deadly dangerous. The reader is involved in Latimer's
searching, in the gradual building up of a biography, in the
factual details which reveal the ruthless cleverness of this professional crook. The narration gives us a clear picture of
Latimer's thoughts and shows him building up theories about
Dimitrios as his knowledge of the man's past increases. Not
only does the tension of a search which is progressing steadily
despite the inevitable setbacks keep the reader's attention
clearly focused on the details of the story, but the relationship
between Latimer and the mysterious Mr. Peters also heightens
the intensity.
  In *The Mask of Dimitrios* no sympathy is evoked for the
successful, ruthless criminal, nor indeed for Mr. Peters, the
unsuccessful one. There is some alteration of viewpoint in some
of Ambler's later novels. For instance, in *Dirty Story,* the main
character, Arthur Simpson (he first appeared in *The Light of
Day*), is described in an Interpol dossier as interpreter, chauffeur, waiter, pornographer, and guide. He is also a pimp, and
the story begins with his urgent need for a passport. His stormy
interview with Her Majesty's Vice-Consul in Athens leaves
us no possibility for illusions about the man whose life, according to the Vice-Consul, is nothing but a long dirty story. Driven
by lack of money (with which to buy a Panlibhoncan passport)
into acting as a casting director of blue films, he eventually
becomes a mercenary in Central Africa. He does not cover
himself with credit but eventually escapes to Tangier. One of
Ambler's particular skills is a capacity to create modern rogue
literature. Morally we despise his character, but such is the
power of the tense narration that we follow his adventures
with an interest which verges between sympathy, as things go
hopelessly wrong, and a wry sense of the sheer comedy latent
in Arthur Simpson's incongruous, unscrupulous, and ridiculous
nature.

The whole unscrupulous world of espionage occupies some of Ambler's attention. In *The Intercom Conspiracy* the protagonist is Theodore Carter, editor of *Intercom*, a journal owned by a retired, somewhat crackpot American general of anti-Communist views. When the general dies the journal is bought by a mysterious Arnold Bloch, who supplies material for the journal which offends west and east alike. Various intelligence agencies become interested in Carter's sources, and eventually, after being, in the space of a few hours, snatched, interrogated under duress, roughed up, threatened, burgled, and gassed, he runs. We know that two clever and unscrupulous colonels have got disgruntled with their role in their respective intelligence services; their plot to play off the major powers and cash in on the situation involves Carter as cats-paw—and, of course, Latimer, Ambler's author character, created much earlier, who is busily writing up the story. The inclusion of Latimer, and his disappearance at the beginning of the book, allows Ambler to tell the story at different levels and from different viewpoints. As usual the tension heightens, the pace speeds up, as the reader becomes sufficiently *au fait* with the complex linkage of events. The story is realistic; its portrayal of the cynicism, indeed the theatrically self-conscious seediness and secrecy of the world of military and political intelligence, is convincing in its detail. Ambler's characters have sufficient depth and individuality to match this superb handling of plot. Carter, the journalist, is given to drink; his marriage has broken up earlier; and he is "a man of undoubted ability who takes pleasure in misusing it." Again, the central character is no orthodox hero, and must be taken with blemishes and all: and the two colonels realise he will have dangerous moments. This is a calculated risk and he must take his chance. And take it he does in the respectable surroundings of Geneva.

Ambler has two kinds of story, the simple and the complex. In *The Night-Comers* he unfolds a simple story of an English consulting engineer who is unwillingly involved in a military coup d'état in an island near Indonesia. He is on his way home, staying for a few days in a friend's flat on the top of the local radio station when the revolution begins. His situation is complicated, indeed endangered by the presence of an Eurasian girl with whom he is having a brief affair when the rebels make this their headquarters. The government forces close in on the radio station, and the novel describes the fighting with skilled economy. Tension is built up, the waiting alternates with hope and despair. Again Ambler's realism keeps the story convincing. At one period, when the Englishman realises that one of the insurgent's leaders is a government agent and that his own life and the girl's are in danger, he is compelled to repair a generator so that the rebel general can broadcast his programme to the outside world. This sudden involvement with the mechanical problems of drying out a generator, damaged by water seeping into the power house after a bomb blast, gives the story an authenticity which is compelling. It adds an extra dimension to the simple narrative by, as it were, describing one aspect of the situation of the insurgents in some depth. The effect of the rising on the hapless spectators, the Englishman and the Eurasian girl, gives the story the necessary counterpointing, and again is used to involve the reader's sympathy, to sharpen and hold his attention.

For Ambler's ability to juggle with a complex plot there is *A Kind of Anger* where a newspaperman becomes involved in the search for a missing girl, the mistress of a murdered Iraqi colonel, a Kurdish conspirator. Here there are rival buyers for the colonel's papers, which the girl possesses, and which the newspaperman, lonely, neurotic, suicidal, eventually helps her to sell. Here the mixture of cross purposes is skilfully woven into the tapestry of the story. This is ingeniously done,

and the suspense mounts steadily as the various motives are brought together. *The Care of Time* is a good example of how Ambler can hold the reader's attention by the characters' conversations until the story erupts into action. Gradually the reasons emerge for the choice of Robert Halliday as a go-between in delicate negotiations between NATO and a Middle Eastern leader; they are subtle and complex but credible because the reader has been involved in their unfolding. While Ambler's plots require sex and violence there is no excess of them, and when they do arise there is a touch of inevitability about them which adds to the conviction his narration has already established in the reader's mind. He is indeed a skilled, professional writer of the highest order.

—A. Norman Jeffares

AMIS, Kingsley (William). British. Born in London, 16 April 1922. Educated at City of London School; St. John's College, Oxford, M.A. Served in the Royal Corps of Signals, 1942–45. Married 1) Hilary Ann Bardwell in 1948 (marriage dissolved, 1965), two sons, including Martin Amis, *q.v.*, and one daughter; 2) the writer Elizabeth Jane Howard in 1965 (divorced, 1983). Lecturer in English, University College, Swansea, Wales, 1949–61; Fellow in English, Peterhouse, Cambridge, 1961–63. Visiting Fellow in Creative Writing, Princeton University, New Jersey, 1958–59; Visiting Professor, Vanderbilt University, Nashville, Tennessee, 1967. Recipient: Maugham Award, 1955; *Yorkshire Post* award, 1974, 1984; John W. Campbell Memorial Award, 1977. Honorary Fellow, St. John's College, 1976; University College, Swansea, 1984. C.B.E. (Commander, Order of the British Empire), 1981. Agent: Jonathan Clowes Ltd., 22 Prince Albert Road, London NW1 7ST, England.

PUBLICATIONS

Novels

Lucky Jim. London, Gollancz, and New York, Doubleday, 1954.
That Uncertain Feeling. London, Gollancz, 1955; New York, Harcourt Brace, 1956.
I Like It Here. London, Gollancz, and New York, Harcourt Brace, 1958.
Take a Girl Like You. London, Gollancz, 1960; New York, Harcourt Brace, 1961.
One Fat Englishman. London, Gollancz, 1963; New York, Harcourt Brace, 1964.
The Egyptologists, with Robert Conquest. London, Cape, 1965; New York, Random House, 1966.
The Anti-Death League. London, Gollancz, and New York, Harcourt Brace, 1966.
Colonel Sun: A James Bond Adventure (as Robert Markham). London, Cape, and New York, Harper, 1968.
I Want It Now. London, Cape, 1968; New York, Harcourt Brace, 1969.
The Green Man. London, Cape, 1969; New York, Harcourt Brace, 1970.
Girl, 20. London, Cape, 1971; New York, Harcourt Brace, 1972.
The Riverside Villas Murder. London, Cape, and New York, Harcourt Brace, 1973.

Ending Up. London, Cape, and New York, Harcourt Brace, 1974.
▪*The Alteration.* London, Cape, 1976; New York, Viking Press, 1977.
▪*Jake's Thing.* London, Hutchinson, 1978; New York, Viking Press, 1979.
Russian Hide-and-Seek: A Melodrama. London, Hutchinson, 1980.
Stanley and the Women. London, Hutchinson, 1984; New York, Summit, 1985.

Short Stories

My Enemy's Enemy. London, Gollancz, 1962; New York, Harcourt Brace, 1963.
Penguin Modern Stories 11, with others. London, Penguin, 1972.
Dear Illusion. London, Covent Garden Press, 1972.
The Darkwater Hall Mystery. Edinburgh, Tragara Press, 1978.
Collected Short Stories. London, Hutchinson, 1980.

Plays

Radio Play: *Something Strange*, 1962.

Television Plays: *A Question about Hell*, 1964; *The Importance of Being Harry*, 1971; *Dr. Watson and the Darkwater Hall Mystery*, 1974; *See What You've Done* (*Softly, Softly* series), 1974; *We Are All Guilty* (*Against the Crowd* series), 1975.

Verse

Bright November. London, Fortune Press, 1947.
A Frame of Mind. Reading, Berkshire, University of Reading School of Art, 1953.
(*Poems*). Oxford, Fantasy Press, 1954.
A Case of Samples: Poems 1946–1956. London, Gollancz, 1956; New York, Harcourt Brace, 1957.
The Evans Country. Oxford, Fantasy Press, 1962.
Penguin Modern Poets 2, with Dom Moraes and Peter Porter. London, Penguin, 1962.
A Look round the Estate: Poems 1957–1967. London, Cape, 1967; New York, Harcourt Brace, 1968.
Wasted, Kipling at Bateman's. London, Poem-of-the-Month Club, 1973.
Collected Poems 1944–1978. London, Hutchinson, 1979; New York, Viking Press, 1980.

Recordings: *Kingsley Amis Reading His Own Poems*, Listen, 1962; *Poems*, with Thomas Blackburn, Jupiter, 1962.

Other

Socialism and the Intellectuals. London, Fabian Society, 1957.
New Maps of Hell: A Survey of Science Fiction. New York, Harcourt Brace, 1960; London, Gollancz, 1961.
The James Bond Dossier. London, Cape, and New York, New American Library, 1965.
Lucky Jim's Politics. London, Conservative Political Centre, 1968.
What Became of Jane Austen? and Other Questions. London, Cape, 1970; New York, Harcourt Brace, 1971.
On Drink. London, Cape, 1972; New York, Harcourt Brace, 1973.

Rudyard Kipling and His World. London, Thames and Hudson, 1975; New York, Scribner, 1976.
An Arts Policy? London, Centre for Policy Studies, 1979.
Every Day Drinking. London, Hutchinson, 1983.
How's Your Glass? A Quizzical Look at Drinks and Drinking. London, Weidenfeld and Nicolson, 1984.

Editor, with James Michie, *Oxford Poetry 1949.* Oxford, Blackwell, 1949.
Editor, with Robert Conquest, *Spectrum [1–5]: A Science Fiction Anthology.* London, Gollancz, 5 vols., 1961–65; New York, Harcourt Brace, 5 vols., 1962–67.
Editor, *Selected Short Stories of G.K. Chesterton.* London, Faber, 1972.
Editor, *Tennyson.* London, Penguin, 1973.
Editor, *Harold's Years: Impressions from the New Statesman and the Spectator.* London, Quartet, 1977.
Editor, *The New Oxford Book of Light Verse.* London and New York, Oxford University Press, 1978.
Editor, *The Faber Popular Reciter.* London, Faber, 1978.
Editor, *The Golden Age of Science Fiction.* London, Hutchinson, 1981.

*

Bibliography: *Kingsley Amis: A Checklist* by Jack Benoit Gohn, Kent, Ohio, Kent State University Press, 1976; *Kingsley Amis: A Reference Guide* by Dale Salwak, Boston, Hall, and London, Prior, 1978.

Manuscript Collection (verse): State University of New York, Buffalo.

Critical Study: *Kingsley Amis* by Philip Gardner, Boston, Twayne, 1981.

Kingsley Amis comments:
(1972) Anything a novelist (or any other artist) says about his own work should be regarded with suspicion. It will depend, at least partly, on his mood, the reception of his latest book, whether the one he is working on at the moment is coming well or badly (actually my own always come well, i.e. slowly but—so far—surely). And a novelist is far from being his own best critic, if only because, as Christopher Isherwood once remarked (in effect), no writer is aware of more than about two-thirds of what he is actually doing and saying. Nor should he be.
Well, anyhow: what I think I am doing is writing novels within the main English-language tradition. That is, trying to tell interesting, believable stories about understandable characters in a reasonably straightforward style: no tricks, no experimental foolery. As the tradition indicates, my subject is the relations between people, and I aim at the traditional wide range of effects: humour, pathos, irony, suspense, description, action, introspection. If I had to find a label for my novels, I should call them serio-comedies, though I like to venture now and again into a kind of genre fiction that has always interested me, and have written a straight espionage thriller, a mainstream novel with espionage and science-fiction elements, and a mainstream novel with a large ghost-story interest. One day I may tackle a straight science-fiction novel and a straight detective story.
What I do not think I am doing, despite what some critics have said, is making any kind of statement about "society." As a private citizen I am deeply interested in politics; as a novelist I merely use political material along with domestic,

personal, sexual, farcical, social, and other material. The novelist must always try to get the reader to believe that his story and characters are very probable. To do this he must get his background right, or right as he sees it, which means he must try to describe his times; but this is not his prime object. That object is to portray human nature as it has always been, the permanent human passions of love, sorrow, ambition, fear, anger, frustration, joy, and the rest. No "commitment" for me, except to literature.

*   *   *

Kingsley Amis's principal distinction, in all his novels and other writings, is the sharp comic texture of his prose. Full of mimicry, elaborate satire of ordinary experience (like the bad taste of food or the pains of waking up with a hangover), stock characters tagged by occupation (dentists' mistresses about in the early fiction), pseudological analyses of experience, satire of contemporary fads and social attitudes, Amis's prose is generally funny. At times, in works like *The Anti-Death League* or *Girl, 20*, the prose is flatter and less referential, the list of grievances less ebullient, but farcical events and sharply observed improbabilities keep the tone and texture comic. And some of the later work, like *Jake's Thing*, displays a biting wit directed against contemporary sex therapy and other fashionable distortions of relationships between the sexes. In some of the later fiction, what was, in Amis, an initial attitude of iconoclasm, mocking pretensions to culture, tourist-like enthusiasms for foreign lands, or attempts by characters to transcend themselves, has come to sound like a perverse grumble. Particularly in novels like *One Fat Englishman* or *Girl, 20*, or the more recent *Ending Up*, the spirited and farcical antics of the protagonists, originally, as in *Lucky Jim*, self-protective, turn into a series of aggressive and hostile tricks. Amis sometimes shades the line between the persona of the plain Englishman, fooled by neither the old-fashioned non-sense of faith in official or religious verities nor the contemporary nonsense of various rebellious or international fads, and the persona of the curmudgeon.

Amis is a careful craftsman in a wide variety of literary forms. He has always demonstrated a strong interest in science fiction and the novel of espionage. Within the last two decades, he has written a ghost story (*The Green Man*), a who-done-it (*The Riverside Villas Murder*), a novel dependent on the imaginative historical assumption, detailed in terms of 1976, that Martin Luther became Pope instead of founding a new religion (*The Alteration*), and a futuristic novel set 50 years hence in a Russia that has abandoned Marxism to return to autocratic Czarist control while retaining the exploitive and brutal qualities Amis sees as endemic to both regimes (*Russian Hide-and-Seek*). The novels set in the more familiar contemporary world are also constructed carefully. Frequently, thematic strands, embodied in different satirically symbolic characters, are gradually drawn together toward a climactic scene that involves almost everyone in the novel. These culminating scenes, like the drunken lecture in *Lucky Jim*, the party in *Take a Girl Like You*, or the therapy workshop week-end in *Jake's Thing*, often take place in public, emphasizing the resolution of the novel in terms that are publicly and socially visible. For Amis, the novel is a rational construction, and he has frequently demonstrated his respect for the traditional novels of the 18th century, both explicitly, as in the great admiration for Fielding shown in *I Like It Here*, and implicitly, as in all the parallels followed by an ironically reversed conclusion between Richardson's *Pamela* and Amis's *Take a Girl Like You*. Amis's rational constructions lampoon deviation, excessive complexity, or

eccentricity, and they resolve mystery, either directly in a novel like *The Riverside Villas Murder* or metaphorically, in social and psychological terms, in a novel like *That Uncertain Feeling*. Amis's fictional structures are seldom open-ended, containing little of the thematic corollaries of the open-ended, of introspection, self-doubt, emotional turbulence, indecision, or romanticism.

In spite of all the journalistic declarations in the late 1950's about "Angry Young Men," a rebellion he supposedly led, Amis has never been or claimed to be an iconoclast about society. Rather, the novels, whatever the setting, demonstrate an acceptance, no matter how ironic or grudging, of the social status quo. Frequently, as in *One Fat Englishman* and *I Want It Now*, Amis begins by satirizing a character who pretends to be iconoclastic by showing the iconoclasm as merely modish opportunism. As the novel develops, in a characteristic switch, Amis depicts the opportunism as much like everyone else's, perhaps slightly less selfish and self-deluding than that of others. The energetic iconoclast often learns to adjust in contemporary society, earns the rewards of jobs and good women by sensibly squelching deviation or insistence on self and following the axioms audible around him. Often, in the early novels like *Lucky Jim*, *Take a Girl Like You*, and *I Want It Now*, the central character is helped materially by an aristocrat, a symbolic representative of the pinnacle of society who leans down, like a fairy-godfather, to reward the deserving. Committed social rebels, those who would transform society in terms of a new or resurrected vision, are either peripheral fools or non-existent in Amis's fiction.

Amis's attitude toward the social adjustment he endorses has altered in the course of his fictional career. Initially, in *Lucky Jim* and *That Uncertain Feeling*, the value of adjustment was debatable, although the process inevitable for a talented young man. *That Uncertain Feeling*, Amis's least certain, least consoling novel, and one that seems to catch contemporary social references strikingly, even develops sympathy for the man who is unable to adjust and must retreat to the provincial society he came from. Later, in *I Like It Here* and *Take a Girl Like You*, questions about the value of adjustment become more a matter of superficial comedy and the worth of adjustment, like that of learning to order a meal, drive a car, or lose virginity, is taken for granted. In *I Want It Now* adjustment becomes a positive virtue contrasted to the selfish deviation of eccentrics who are eventually exposed; in *Girl, 20*, the most curmudgeonly novel, the eccentrics can despoil and destroy contemporary London and can only be countered by a rigid adherence to a non-permissive social code. In some recent fiction, like *Jake's Thing*, adjustment is somewhat gentler, the 60-year-old protagonist's recognition that, although the social forms of sex therapy and the new female consciousness are ludicrous (including the theory that Hamlet was really a woman in disguise), he has learned to modify somewhat and accept the uncomfortable consequences of the male chauvinism by which he has lived. In other recent examples, like *Stanley and the Woman*, adjustment is more difficult, requiring the protagonist to accept and attempt to understand both his son's breakdown and his second wife's lies and emotional explosions, both forms of "madness" against which he tries to pose the solid though very limited certainties of his origins in the lower-middle class of South London. Stanley is less the authorial voice of a nastily misogynistic sexism he has been accused of being than the example of a sane, too simple man in retreat from the psychological and social complexities of the modern world he can no longer absorb. The emphasis on the rightness of adjustment or accommodation in Amis's fiction is stated negatively, casually. At the end of *Lucky Jim* Jim Dixon, less arid and phony as a teacher than are the other academics, is rewarded because "It's not that you've got the qualifications . . . You haven't got the disqualifications, though, and that's much rarer"; at the end of *I Want It Now* the hero and heroine acknowledge that all they can do is help "each other not to be as bad as we would be on our own"; Jake, at the end of *Jake's Thing*, learns that the "loss of libido" that propelled his excursion into the ludicrous new psychological world to which he partially adjusted may have been physical in origin after all. In other words, Amis characteristically wraps his resolving accommodations in layers of irony.

Amis's forms, his attitudes, and his ironic resolutions work against any sympathetic presentation of depth or intensity in human emotions. For example, in many of the novels, especially the early ones, sexual encounters are almost always material for comedy. Potentially emotional love-making is interrupted by mosquitoes, wasps, a pseudological analysis of how to defend different parts of the anatomy, or a manual of sexual technique to demonstrate the protagonist's social skills. Often, the actual scene generating emotion is omitted or severely compressed; at other times, it is subservient to another irony, as in *The Green Man*, in which the protagonist has wanted most to be in bed with his wife and his mistress simultaneously and arranges it only to find that the two women shut him out entirely. A similar irony resolves the plot of *The Alteration*, in which the imaginary contemporary theocratic world (brilliantly depicted in sharply semi-anachronistic prose) propounds the central question of castrating an exceptionally talented young church singer. Just as the talented boy is about to escape, a sudden illness makes castration medically necessary. When, as in *I Want It Now* and *The Anti-Death League*, Amis tries to depict sexuality or love directly, the comedy disappears, the prose becomes flat and banal, and the scene is sentimental. Only occasionally does the implicit Puritanism surface from underneath the irony. In *The Riverside Villas Murder*, in which the resolution is ratiocinatively clever and all the ends neatly tied but the motivation sketchy and unconvincing, the murderer is the woman who sexually initiated the young narrator in a long and conventionally steamy scene. Here, uncharacteristically, the introduction of Eve, the sensual woman who imposes evil on the innocent boy, overwhelms the design of the novel.

Although less skilfully comic than many of his novels, *The Anti-Death League* (in which L.S. Caton, the rather slimy editor and lecturer who writes in green ink and appears in almost all the earlier novels, is finally killed off) is one of Amis's most interesting and illustrative. A group of characters at and near a military base recognize the prospect of death and confront the issues of survival in their political, occupational, personal, and psychological ramifications. But the lovers, facing the possible death of one, are simply silent, as if all talk, all human articulation, is futile or pretentiously silly. The other characters spin off into farce, tricks, or deliberate evasion in order to survive. Similarly, in *Ending Up*, in which five old people share Tupenny-Hapenny cottage, Bernard, the most intelligent of them, learns that he has only a few months to live. He indulges in a series of malicious tricks on the others, expresses his defiance of death in hostility, and begins a chain of events that kills all five. *Stanley and the Women* does not fully face or resolve all the difficult psychological material about families and relationships it so sharply and effectively introduces. Often, Amis's protagonists assume a comic belligerent pose, as if potential humanity and sensitivity are hiding behind the masks, the tricks, all the paraphernalia of the comic survival kit (one that includes the capacity for self-satire as well), and the professional sharpness and skill. When the pose slips or

is discarded, the books are suddenly silent, as if nothing else is there and we can infer sensitivity only from its negation. For the most part, Amis's characteristic virtue, as well as his characteristic limitation, is his sense of distance, his capacity for seeing clearly a great deal of what is ludicrous and pretentious even at the price of omitting what is most profoundly or intensely human.

—James Gindin

AMIS, Martin (Louis).   British.   Born in Oxford, 25 August 1949; son of Kingsley Amis, *q.v.*. Educated at Exeter College, Oxford, B.A. (honours) 1971. Married Antonia Phillips in 1984; one son. Editorial assistant, *Times Literary Supplement*, London, 1972–75; assistant literary editor, 1975–77, and literary editor, 1977–79, *New Statesman*, London. Since 1979, full-time writer; since 1980, special writer, *The Observer*, London. Recipient: Maugham Award, 1974. Agent: A.D. Peters, 10 Buckingham Street, London WC2N 6BU, England.

PUBLICATIONS

Novels

The Rachel Papers.   London, Cape, 1973; New York, Knopf, 1974.
Dead Babies.   London, Cape, 1975; New York, Knopf, 1976; as *Dark Secrets*, London, Triad, 1977.
Success.   London, Cape, 1978.
Other People: A Mystery Story.   London, Cape, and New York, Viking Press, 1981.
Money.   London, Cape, 1984; New York, Viking, 1985.

Uncollected Short Stories

"Denton's Death," in *Encounter* (London), October 1976.
"Heavy Water," in *Winter's Tales 25*, edited by Caroline Hobhouse.   London, Macmillan, 1979; New York, St. Martin's Press, 1980.
"Vernon," in *Penthouse* (London), December 1980.
"The Time Sickness," in *Granta 13* (Cambridge), 1984.
"Bujack and the Strong Force," in *London Review of Books*, 6 June 1985.
"The Little Puppy That Could," in *Literary Review* (London), August–September 1985.

Play

Screenplay: *Saturn 3*, 1980.

Other

Invasion of the Space Invaders.   London, Hutchinson, 1982.

*

Theatrical Activities:
Actor: **Film**—*A High Wind in Jamaica*, 1965.

*   *   *

Martin Amis has been celebrated as the foremost novelist of his generation; his success has been so rapid that it is sometimes hard to see how good he really is. His theme of rotten sweetness is rooted in the decaying idealism of his time but he takes it far beyond the merely topical. He writes taut, satiric prose; he can sketch a scene and sum up a character with economy and style; his sombre observations on cruelty are balanced by an underlying optimism, a bubbling well of comic energy. As a moralist, he is on God's side, and probably knows it.

The Rachel Papers introduced his self-seeking, self-doubting protagonist; clever, young, ambitious, Charles is the essential survivor. He cuts a swathe through the chaos around him and ends up with the prizes, in this case, a place at Oxford and the right girl. Inevitably, his progress was compared to that of a 1950's picaresque hero, Lucky Jim. Jim was always on the way up, true, but by virtue of his own innocence; he could never have been labelled "whiz kid."

Quentin, the central character in *Dead Babies*, is like a rocket fuelled by fashion, the darling of gossip columnists, blonde-haired, green-eyed, literary show biz. This novel shows the full range of Amis's talent; like Burroughs's *Naked Lunch*, the title is meant to shock and the text is thoroughly shocking. It describes a country house party at Appleseed Rectory, home of Quentin and the aristocratic Celia, refuge to a group of English eccentrics, the neurotic Giles, the dwarfish Keith, the simple stud Andy Adorno. A hell hole of degradation and deceit, in fact. Left to themselves, the gilded English might have kept within the sentimentalities of flower power; enter an American trio, Skip, Roseanne, and their spokesman, Dr. Marvell Buzhardt, chemist and philosopher: "We've agreed that life is a rat's ass and it's no fun being yourself at the time. . . . Fuck all this dead babies about love, understanding, compassion . . . we have drugs to make you euphoric, sad, horny, lucid, tender." Thus begins the lost weekend of the 1970's, an unremittingly asexual orgy in which the characters destroy themselves. A psychopath is on the loose, an outsider who breaks in, wreaks havoc, and signs himself "Johnny." When his identity is revealed the reader recognises that, on one level, it has been known all along. The narrative is so savage that one had hoped, against all the odds, for a last minute reprieve, a glimpse of the heroic.

After this triumph, black and dazzling, *Success* seemed unresolved, incomplete. It is a study of the relationship between two foster-brothers, Terence and Gregory, neither very likeable and at times indistinguishable. A deeply melancholy book, it ends on one of the author's best lines: "The wind will never cease to craze the frightening leaves."

The cast list preceding *Dead Babies* described Johnny as "a practical joker." He may be the author of *Other People*, a self-styled mystery story in which nothing else is clear, not even the divisions between life and death. Mary Lamb, the central character, exists on a metaphysical seesaw, the focus of both good and evil. We meet her in hospital, dazed, amnesiac, the victim of "special damage"; she wanders out into the city, is rescued, raped, hunted down, and seduced by a sinister saviour, Prince. Is he the devil, the prince of darkness? Does he take her to be murdered? Or is she dead anyway, in hell right from the start of the story? The book invites, but defies, interpretation. Mary seems unavoidably guilty, inextricably bound up with suffering. Like the figure in a Francis Bacon painting, she compels our sympathy and puzzles our understanding. It is a compelling piece of writing.

—Judy Cooke

ANAND, Mulk Raj. Indian. Born in Peshawar, 12 December 1905. Educated at Khalsa College, Amritsar; Punjab University, 1921–24, B.A. (honours) 1924; University College, University of London, 1926–29, Ph.D.; Cambridge University, 1929–30; League of Nations School of Intellectual Cooperation, Geneva, 1930–32. Married 1) Kathleen Van Gelder in 1939 (divorced, 1948); 2) Shirin Vajifdar in 1950, one daughter. Lecturer, School of Intellectual Cooperation, Summer 1930, and Workers Educational Association, London, intermittently 1932–45; has also taught at the universities of Punjab, Benares, and Rajasthan, Jaipur, 1948–66; Tagore Professor of Literature and Fine Art, University of Punjab, 1963–66; Visiting Professor, Institute of Advanced Studies, Simla, 1967–68. Fine Art Chairman, Lalit Kala Akademi (National Academy of Art), New Delhi, 1965–70. Since 1946, Editor *Marg* magazine, and Director, Kutub Publishers, both Bombay. Since 1970, President of the Lokayata Trust, for creating a community and cultural centre in Hauz Khas village, New Delhi. Recipient: Leverhulme Fellowship, 1940–42; World Peace Council prize, 1952; Padma Bhushan, India, 1968; Sahitya Academy award, 1974. Member, Indian Academy of Letters. Address: 25 Cuffe Parade, Bombay 400 005, India.

PUBLICATIONS

Novels

Untouchable. London, Wishart, 1935; revised edition, London, Bodley Head, 1970.
The Coolie. London, Lawrence and Wishart, 1936; as *Coolie*, London, Penguin, 1945; New York, Liberty Press, 1952; revised edition, London, Bodley Head, 1972.
Two Leaves and a Bud. London, Lawrence and Wishart, 1937; New York, Liberty Press, 1954.
The Village. London, Cape, 1939.
Lament on the Death of a Master of Arts. Lucknow, Naya Sansar, 1939.
Across the Black Waters. London, Cape, 1940.
The Sword and the Sickle. London, Cape, 1942.
The Big Heart. London, Hutchinson, 1945; revised edition, edited by Saros Cowasjee, New Delhi, Arnold-Heinemann, 1980.
Seven Summers: The Story of an Indian Childhood. London, Hutchinson, 1951.
Private Life of an Indian Prince. London, Hutchinson, 1953; revised edition, London, Bodley Head, 1970.
The Old Woman and the Cow. Bombay, Kutub, 1960; as *Gauri*, New Delhi, Orient, 1976.
The Road. Bombay, Kutub, 1961.
Death of a Hero. Bombay, Kutub, 1963.
Morning Face. Bombay, Kutub, 1968.
Confession of a Lover. New Delhi, Arnold-Heinemann, 1976.
The Bubble. New Delhi, Arnold-Heinemann, 1984.

Short Stories

The Lost Child and Other Stories. London, J.A. Allen, 1934.
The Barber's Trade Union and Other Stories. London, Cape, 1944.
The Tractor and the Corn Goddess and Other Stories. Bombay, Thacker, 1947.
Reflections on the Golden Bed. Bombay, Current Book House, 1947.
The Power of Darkness and Other Stories. Bombay, Jaico, 1958.
Lajwanti and Other Stories. Bombay, Jaico, 1966.
Between Tears and Laughter. New Delhi, Sterling, 1973.
Selected Short Stories of Mulk Raj Anand, edited by M.K. Naik. New Delhi, Arnold-Heinemann, 1977.

Play

India Speaks (produced London, 1943).

Other

Persian Painting. London, Faber, 1930.
Curries and Other Indian Dishes. London, Harmsworth, 1932.
The Golden Breath: Studies in Five Poets of the New India. London, Murray, and New York, Dutton, 1933.
The Hindu View of Art. Bombay, Asia Publishing House, and London, Allen and Unwin, 1933; revised edition, Asia Publishing House, 1957.
Letters on India. London, Routledge, 1942.
Apology for Heroism: An Essay in Search of Faith. London, Drummond, 1946.
Homage to Tagore. Lahore, Sangam, 1946.
Indian Fairy Tales: Retold (for children). Bombay, Kutub, 1946.
On Education. Bombay, Hind Kitabs, 1947.
The Bride's Book of Beauty, with Krishna Hutheesing. Bombay, Kutub, 1947; as *The Book of Indian Beauty*, Rutland, Vermont, Tuttle, 1981.
The Story of India (for children). Bombay, Kutub, 1948.
The King-Emperor's English; or, The Role of the English Language in the Free India. Bombay, Hind Kitabs, 1948.
Lines Written to an Indian Air: Essays. Bombay, Nalanda, 1949.
The Indian Theatre. London, Dobson, 1950; New York, Roy, 1951.
The Story of Man (for children). New Delhi, Sikh Publishing House, 1952.
The Dancing Foot. New Delhi, Ministry of Information, 1957.
Kama Kala: Some Notes on the Philosophical Basis of Hindu Erotic Sculpture. London, Skilton, 1958; New York, Lyle Stuart, 1962.
India in Colour. Bombay, Taraporevala, London, Thames and Hudson, and New York, McGraw Hill, 1959.
Homage to Khajuraho, with Stella Kramrisch. Bombay, Marg, 1960.
More Indian Fairy Tales (for children). Bombay, Kutub, 1961.
Is There a Contemporary Indian Civilisation? Bombay, Asia Publishing House, 1963.
The Story of Chacha Nehru (for children). New Delhi, Rajpal, 1965.
Bombay. Bombay, Marg, 1965(?).
The Third Eye: A Lecture on the Appreciation of Art. Patiala, University of Punjab, 1966.
Design for Living. Bombay, Marg, 1967.
The Humanism of M.K. Gandhi: Three Lectures. Chandigahr, University of Panjab, 1967(?).
Konorak, with others. Bombay, Marg, 1968.
The Volcano: Some Comments on the Development of Rabindranath Tagore's Aesthetic Theories. Baroda, Maharaja Sayajirao University, 1968.
Delhi, Agra, Sikri. Bombay, Marg, 1968.
Indian Ivories. Bombay, Marg, 1970.
Ajanta, photographs by R.R. Bhurdwaj. Bombay, Marg-McGraw Hill, 1971.
Roots and Flowers: Two Lectures on the Metamorphosis of Technique and Content in the Indian-English Novel. Dharwar, Karnatak University, 1972.
Mora. New Delhi, National Book Trust, 1972.

Author to Critic: The Letters of Mulk Raj Anand, edited by Saros Cowasjee. Calcutta, Writers Workshop, 1973.
Album of Indian Paintings. New Delhi, National Book Trust, 1973.
Folk Tales of Punjab. New Delhi, Sterling, 1974.
Lepakshi. Bombay, Marg, 1977(?).
Seven Little-Known Birds of the Inner Eye. Rutland, Vermont, Tuttle, 1978.
The Humanism of Jawaharlal Nehru. Calcutta, Visva-Bharati, 1978.
The Humanism of Rabindranath Tagore. Aurangabad, Marathwada University, 1979.
Maya of Mohenjo-Daro (for children). New Delhi, Children's Book Trust, n.d.
Conversations in Bloomsbury (reminiscences). New Delhi, Arnold-Heinemann, and London, Wildwood House, 1981.
Pilpali Sahab: The Story of a Childhood under the Raj. New Delhi, Arnold-Heinemann, 1985.

Editor, *Marx and Engels on India.* Allahabad, Socialist Book Club, 1933.
Editor, with Iqbal Singh, *Indian Short Stories.* London, New India, 1947.
Editor, *Introduction to Indian Art*, by A.K. Coomaraswamy. Madras, Theosophical Publishing House, and Wheaton, Illinois, Theosophical Press, 1956.
Editor, *Experiments: Contemporary Indian Short Stories.* Agra, Kranchalson, 1968.
Editor, *Annals of Childhood.* Agra, Kranchalson, 1968.
Editor, *Contemporary World Sculpture.* Bombay, Marg, 1968.
Editor, *Grassroots.* Agra, Kranchalson, 1968(?).
Editor, *Homage to Jaipur.* Bombay, Marg, 1977.
Editor, *Homage to Amritsar.* Bombay, Marg, 1977.
Editor, *Tales from Tolstoy.* New Delhi, Arnold-Heinemann, 1978.
Editor, *Alampur.* Bombay, Marg, 1978(?).
Editor, *Homage to Kalamkari.* Bombay, Marg, 1979.
Editor, *Splendours of Tamil Nadu.* Bombay, Marg, 1980.
Editor, *Splendours of Kerala.* Bombay, Marg, 1980.
Editor, *Golden Goa.* Bombay, Marg, 1980.
Editor, *Treasures of Everyday Art.* Bombay, Marg, 1981.
Editor, *Splendours of the Vijayanagara.* Bombay, Marg, 1980.
Editor, *Maharaja Ranjit Singh as Patron of the Arts.* Bombay, Marg, 1981; Atlantic Highlands, New Jersey, Humanities Press, 1982.
Editor, with Lance Dane, *Kama Sutra of Vatsyayana* (from translation by Sir Richard Burton and F.F. Arbuthnot). New Delhi, Arnold-Heinemann, and Atlantic Highlands, New Jersey, Humanities Press, 1982.

*

Critical Studies: *Mulk Raj Anand: A Critical Essay* by Jack Lindsay, Bombay, Hind Kitabs, 1948, revised edition, as *The Elephant and the Lotus*, Bombay, Kutub, 1954; "Mulk Raj Anand Issue" of *Contemporary Indian Literature* (New Delhi), 1965; *An Ideal of Man in Anand's Novels* by D. Riemenschneider, Bombay, Kutub, 1969; *Mulk Raj Anand: The Man and the Novelist* by Margaret Berry, Amsterdam, Orienta Press, 1971; *Mulk Raj Anand* by K.N. Sinha, New York, Twayne, 1972; *Mulk Raj Anand* by M.K. Naik, New Delhi and London, Arnold-Heinemann, and New York, Humanities

Press, 1973; *Anand: A Study of His Fiction in Humanist Perspective* by G.S. Gupta, Bareilly, Prakash, 1974; *So Many Freedoms: A Study of the Major Fiction of Mulk Raj Anand* by Saros Cowasjee, New Delhi and London, Oxford University Press, 1978; *Perspectives on Mulk Raj Anand* edited by K.K. Sharma, Atlantic Highlands, New Jersey, Humanities Press, 1978; *Yoke of Pity: A Study of the Fictional Writings of Mulk Raj Anand* by Alastair Niven, New Delhi, Arnold-Heinemann, 1979; *The Sword and the Sickle: A Study of Mulk Raj Anand's Novels* by K.V. Suryanarayana Murti, Mysore, Geetha, 1983.

Mulk Raj Anand comments:

I began to write early—a kind of free verse in the Punjabi and Urdu languages, from the compulsion of the shock of the death of my cousin when she was nine years old. I wrote a letter to God telling him He didn't exist. Later, going through the dark night of another bereavement, when my aunt committed suicide because she was excommunicated for interdining with a Muslim woman, I wrote prose. Again, when I fell in love with a young Muslim girl, who was married off by arrangement, I wrote calf love verse. The poet-philosopher, Muhammad Iqbal, introduced me to the problems of the individual through his long poem "Secrets of the Self." Through him, I also read Nietzsche to confirm my rejection of God. After a short term in jail, my father, who was pro-British, punished my mother for my affiliations with the Gandhi Movement. I went to Europe and studied various philosophical systems and found that these comprehensive philosophies did not answer life's problems. I was beaten up for not blacklegging against workers in 1926, in the coal-miner's strike. I joined a Marxist worker's study circle with Trade Unionist Alan Hutt, and met Palme-Dutt, John Strachey, T.S. Eliot, Herbert Read, Bonamy Dobrée, Harold Laski, Leonard Woolf. During that time I fell in love with a young Welsh girl painter, Irene, whose father was a biologist. For her I wrote a long confession about the break-up of my family, the British impact, and my later life. Nobody would publish the 2,000 word narrative. So I began to rewrite portions, as allegories, short stories, and novels. On a tour with Irene, in Paris, Rome, Vienna, Berlin, Brussels, I discovered Rimbaud, Dante, and Joyce. My first attempt at a novel was revised in Gandhi's Sabarmati Ashram in Ahmedabad, but was turned down by 19 publishers in London. The 20th offered to publish it if E.M. Forster wrote a Preface. This the author of *A Passage to India* did.

Since the publication of this first novel, I have written continuously on the human situation in the lives of people of the lower caste, peasants, lumpen, and other eccentrics, thrown up during the transition from the ancient orthodox Indian society to the self-conscious modernist secular democracy.

I believe that creating literature is the true medium of humanism as against systematic philosophies, because the wisdom of the heart encourages insights in all kinds of human beings who grow to self-consciousness through the conflicts of desire, will, and mood. I am inclined to think that the highest aim of poetry and art is to integrate the individual into inner growth and outer adjustment. The broken bundle of mirrors of the human personality in our time can only become the enchanted mirror if the sensibility is touched in its utmost pain and sheer pleasure and tenderest moments. No rounded answers are possible. Only hunches, insights, and inspirations and the *karuna* that may come from understanding.

The novelist's task is that of an all-comprehending "God," who understands every part of his creation, through pity, compassion, or sympathy—which is the only kind of catharsis possible in art. The word is itself action of the still centre. The struggle to relate the word and the deed in the life of man is part of the process of culture, through which illumination comes to human beings. The world of art is a communication from one individual to another, or to the group through the need to connect. This may ultimately yield the slogan "love one another," if mankind is to survive (against its own inheritance of fear, hatred, and contempt, now intensified through money-power, or privileges, and large-scale violence) into the 21st century, in any human form.

*   *   *

Mulk Raj Anand is the champion of the underdog. All his novels deal with the underprivileged sections of Indian society. He was the first Indian novelist to make an untouchable the hero of a novel. *Untouchable* describes one day in the life of 18-year-old Bakha, who is treated as dirt by all Hindus just because his profession is to clean latrines. Artistically it is the most perfect of Anand's earlier novels. The distinction of Anand's writing lies in capturing Bakha's work ethic—Bakha tackles his odious job with a conscientiousness that invests his movements with beauty. The next novel, *The Coolie*, has a wider canvas and is more diffuse in structure. Munoo, a young orphan, works at a variety of odd jobs at Daulatpur, Bombay, and Simla till he dies aged 15 of tuberculosis brought on by undernourishment. Munoo is exploited not because of caste but because he is poor. *Two Leaves and a Bud* is about the plight of the labourers in a tea plantation in Assam; the novel fails because Anand's approach is too simplistic, the English owners are shown as unmitigated villains. Anand's next work was a trilogy with the young Lal Singh as hero. *The Village* is an authentic picture of a typical Punjabi village, and shows the adolescent Lal Singh rebelling against the narrow superstitions of the villagers—he goes so far as to cut his hair, unthinkable for a Sikh. *Across the Black Waters* shows Lal as a soldier fighting in the trenches of Flanders in the First World War; his contact with the French makes him realize that the white races too are human, and not demigods like the British in India. *The Sword and the Sickle* shows Lal engaged in revolutionary activities in India after eloping with the village landlord's daughter; it is not as well written as the earlier two volumes.

Anand is a prolific writer, and has written a large number of extremely varied short stories. They reveal his gift for humour, and deal in a lighter vein with the problems that engage him in his novels—the exploitation of the poor, the impact of industrialisation, colonialism, and race relations. One of Anand's best novels, *The Big Heart* deals with the traditional coppersmiths who feel threatened by mechanization. The large-hearted Ananta tries to weld them into a trade union; he tells them that it is not the machines but the owners who exploit them, but he dies in a scuffle before his ideals can be realised.

The Old Woman and the Cow (republished as *Gauri*) takes up the plight of another underprivileged section of society—women. The heroine, Gauri, is sold to an old money-lender by her own mother out of economic necessity. Gauri re-enacts the *Ramayana* myth of Sita by staying for some time in the house of the old banker, just as Sita had to stay with Ravana. Gauri is reunited with her husband Panchi just as Sita was reunited with Rama, and Panchi rejects her later, just as Rama rejected the pregnant Sita because of social pressures. At this point, Anand gives a new turn to the old myth: unlike Sita who bore her sufferings meekly, Gauri rejects her cowardly husband and goes on to build a new life for herself. The story is well conceived and the use of the myth original, but the writing is hurried and slipshod, and the harangues on social justice are not organic to the plot. *Private Life of an Indian Prince*, a study of a neurotic maharajah, is confused and disorganised; some critics, however, have defended the narrative as a true reflection of the hero's psyche, and consider it Anand's best novel.

Anand is now at work on an ambitious seven-volume autobiographical novel, *The Seven Ages of Man*. *Seven Summers*, published more than three decades ago, is a lyrical account of early childhood, primarily from the child's point of view. *Morning Face* describes the life of the protagonist, Krishan Chander Azad, up to the age of 15, and we get a vivid picture of the brutality that once passed for school-teaching. *Confession of a Lover* deals with Krishan's undergraduate days at Khalsa College, Amritsar. The novel is not only a moving human document, it is an authentic account of life in the Punjab in the 1920's, and records the ferment caused by Gandhi's *satyagraha*. The fourth volume, *The Bubble*, covers the period 1925–29; it shows Krishan as a student in England, obtaining a Ph.D. degree. He falls in love with Irene Rhys, and pours out his feelings by writing a long novel (just as Anand did in real life). When he returns to India, Krishan plans to go to Gandhi's Ashram to work on a novel with an untouchable as hero. Most of Anand's works have a linear structure, but *The Bubble* departs from this convention. This novel is in the form of letters, diary entries, and excerpts from the novel Krishan is writing; it also includes numerous philosophical discussions. The life of an Indian student in the England of the time, and particularly Krishan's loneliness, are impressively portrayed. But, like *Morning Face* and *Confession of a Lover*, *The Bubble* is too long (600 pages). If only the "outpourings" had been sensitively edited, *The Bubble* would have been Anand's best work, and a triumph in terms of technique.

Anand attempts to capture the ambience of Punjabi life by literally translating words and phrases, but this device does not always succeed. Readers outside the Punjab may find it difficult to make anything of phrases like "there is no talk," and "May I be your sacrifice." However, he is successful in presenting a vivid picture of the Punjabi peasant and the problems of the poor. The range of his novels is impressive, covering not only the Punjab but life in towns like Bombay and Simla, the trenches of Flanders, and the tea gardens of Assam. His concern for the underdog does not take the form of communism—he is above all a humanist, and his humanism embraces all aspects of life, from contemporary slums to ancient Indian art and philosophy.

—Shyamala A. Narayan

ANAYA, Rudolfo A(lfonso). American. Born in Pastura, New Mexico, 30 October 1937. Educated at Albuquerque High School, graduated 1956; Browning Business School, Albuquerque, 1956–58; University of New Mexico, Albuquerque, B.A. in literature 1963, M.A. in literature 1968, M.A. in guidance and counseling 1972. Married Patricia Lawless in 1966. Teacher, Albuquerque public schools, 1963–70. Director of Counseling, 1972–74, and since 1974, Associate Professor of English, University of New Mexico. Lecturer, Universidad Anahuac, Mexico City, Summer 1974; teacher, New Mexico Writers Workshop, Albuquerque, summers 1977–79. Associate Editor, *American Book Review*, New York, 1980–85. Vice-President, Coordinating Council of Literary Magazines, 1974–80. Recipient: Quinto Sol prize, 1971; University of New

Mexico Mesa Chicana award, 1977; City of Los Angeles award, 1977; New Mexico Governor's award, 1978, 1980; National Chicano Council on Higher Education fellowship, 1978; National Endowment for the Arts fellowship, 1979; Before Columbus Foundation award, 1980; Corporation for Public Broadcasting Script Development award, 1982; Kellogg Foundation fellowship, 1983. D.H.L.: University of Albuquerque, 1981; Marycrest College, Davenport, Iowa, 1984. Address: 5324 Canada Vista N.W., Albuquerque, New Mexico 87120, U.S.A.

PUBLICATIONS

Novels

Bless Me, Ultima. Berkeley, California, Quinto Sol, 1972.
Heart of Aztlán. Berkeley, California, Justa, 1976.
Tortuga. Berkeley, California, Justa, 1979.
The Legend of La Llorona. Berkeley, California, Tonatiuh-Quinto Sol, 1984.

Short Stories

The Silence of Llano. Berkeley, California, Tonatiuh-Quinto Sol, 1982.

Uncollected Short Story

"The Captain," in *A Decade of Hispanic Literature.* Houston, Revista Chicano-Riqueña, 1982.

Plays

The Season of La Llorona (produced Albuquerque, 1979).

Screenplay (documentary): *Bilingualism: Promise for Tomorrow*, 1976.

Verse

The Adventures of Juan Chicaspatas. Houston, Arte Publico Press, 1985.

Other

Editor, with Jim Fisher, *Voices from the Rio Grande.* Albuquerque, Rio Grande Writers Association, 1976.
Editor, with Antonio Márquez, *Cuentos Chicanos.* Albuquerque, New America, 1980.
Editor, with Simon J. Ortiz, *A Ceremony of Brotherhood 1680–1980.* Albuquerque, Academia, 1981.

Translator, *Cuentos: Tales from the Hispanic Southwest, Based on Stories Originally Collected by Juan B. Rael*, edited by José Griego y Maestas. Santa Fe, Museum of New Mexico Press, 1980.

*

Manuscript Collection: Zimmerman Library, University of New Mexico, Albuquerque.

Critical Studies: "Extensive/Intensive Dimensionality in Anaya's *Bless Me, Ultima*" by Daniel Testa, in *Latin American Literary Review* (Pittsburgh), Spring–Summer 1977; "Degradacion y Regeneracion en *Bless Me, Ultima*" by Roberto

Cantu, in *The Identification and Analysis of Chicano Literature* edited by Francisco Jimenez, New York, Bilingual Press, 1979; *Chicano Authors: Inquiry by Interview* edited by Juan Bruce-Novoa, Austin, University of Texas Press, 1980; *The Magic of Words: Rudolfo A. Anaya and His Writings* (includes bibliography by Teresa Marquez) edited by Paul Vassallo, Albuquerque, University of New Mexico Press, 1982.

*   *   *

Rudolfo A. Anaya is best known for a trilogy of novels published during the 1970's. Although *Bless Me, Ultima*, *Heart of Aztlán*, and *Tortuga*, offer separate worlds with different characters, there are suggestions and allusions in the second and third novels which loosely connect the three works.

Bless Me, Ultima, a first-person narrative, details the childhood and coming of age of young Antonio Marez, a boy who grows up in the rural environs of Las Pasturas and Guadalupe, New Mexico in the late 1940's and early 1950's. Behind almost every experience and adventure Antonio undergoes there is Ultima, a "cuarandera" who comes to live with the Marez family at the start of the novel. She is a miracle-worker who heals the sick through her extensive knowledge of the herbs and remedies of the ancient New Mexico settlers. Guided by her unseen but pervasively felt presence, Antonio moves through a series of incidents which show him the greed, evil, and villainy of men. The novel is significant mainly because it introduced characters and a type of writing not seen before in Chicano literature.

Heart of Aztlán, despite winning the Before Columbus Foundation American Book award, fared less well than its predecessor. The main character is Clemente Chavez, a farmer who loses his land at the start of the narrative and is forced to move into a barrio in Albuquerque. In the city, the Chavez family see their teenage children lose themselves in drugs, sex, and violence. Prompted by a desire to preserve his family, Clemente undertakes a soul-searching quest for an identity and a role for himself and the Chicanos in the barrio. The writing here is noticeably more labored than in *Ultima*. The book ends with a Chicano march against the oppressive Santa Fe Railroad, an attempt to provide a fictive analogue to the Chicano consciousness-raising efforts of the 1970's.

In *Tortuga*, Anaya engagingly captures life in a sanatorium for terminally-ill teenagers. There is much ado in this labyrinthine ward in the desert, and the novel shows that Anaya is particularly adept at plausibly instilling life, vigor, and reasons to live into characters abandoned by society.

Anaya has also published work in other genres. For some time he has been interested in using the media to advance the interests of Spanish-speaking American citizens, and in 1976 he wrote a screenplay, *Bilingualism: Promise for Tomorrow*, which was produced as a documentary and aired on prime-time television. He is a tireless promoter of Chicano and other ethnic literatures and has edited a number of anthologies.

Anaya's latest book is something of a departure. *The Adventures of Juan Chicaspatas* is a 48-page mock-heroic epic poem which employs the same type of search motif used in *Heart of Aztlán*. Anaya's tone and attitude here are quite different from those in his earlier work. In *Heart of Aztlán*, he was seriously engaged in creating a language appropriate to rendering one character's quest for self-definition, but *Juan Chicaspatas* (literally, John Smallfeet) is written in the language of the "vatos locos," or crazy barrio Chicanos who jest at virtually everything. In passing, Anaya points out that there are "many tribes of Chicanos," which, of course, suggests that there are different languages as well. The prime message of the 16th-century Aztlán goddess he depicts is: "Go and tell your people about Aztlán. Tell them I live. Tell them the españoles will come and a new people will be born. Tell them not to become like the tribes of the Anglos, and remind them not to honor King Arthur. Tell them their Eden and their Camelot are in Aztlán. Their covenant is with the earth of this world." Anaya's message has not changed, but now the appeal is made not to the more middle-class Chicanos as in the earlier work, but in a language that is closer to the work of Alurista and Sergio Elizondo, two other writers who take great relish in Chicano slang.

Anaya has written several books that are widely appreciated and is still young enough to write quite a few more wonderful tales.

—Marco Portales

ANDERSON, Jessica (Margaret, née Queale).   Australian. Born in Gayndah, Queensland. Educated at schools in Brisbane; Brisbane Technical College, 1 year. Married 1) Ross McGill (divorced), one daughter; 2) Leonard Culbert Anderson in 1954 (divorced). Recipient: Miles Franklin Award, 1979; New South Wales Premier's award, 1981. Agent: Elaine Markson Literary Agency, 44 Greenwich Avenue, New York, New York 10011, U.S.A.

PUBLICATIONS

Novels

An Ordinary Lunacy.   London, Macmillan, 1963; New York, Scribner, 1964.
The Last Man's Head.   London, Macmillan, 1970.
The Commandant.   London, Macmillan, and New York, St. Martin's Press, 1975.
Tirra Lirra by the River.   Melbourne, Macmillan, 1978; London and New York, Penguin, 1984.
The Impersonators.   Melbourne, Macmillan, 1980; as *The Only Daughter*, New York and London, Viking, 1985.

Uncollected Short Story

"Under the House," in *Bulletin Literary Supplement* (Sydney), 30 September 1980.

Plays

Radio Plays: *The American*, 1966, *The Aspern Papers*, 1967, and *Daisy Miller*, 1968, all from works by Henry James; *The Maid's Part*, 1967; *The Blackmail Caper*, 1972; *Quite Sweet, Really*, 1972; *Tirra Lirra by the River*, 1975; *The Last Man's Head*, from her own novel, 1983; *A Tale of Two Cities* (serial), from the novel by Dickens; *Outbreak of Love* (serial), from the novel by Martin Boyd.

*

Manuscript Collections: Mitchell Library, Sydney; Australian National Library, Canberra.

Critical Studies: "Tirra Lirra by the Brisbane River" by Donat Gallager, in *Literature in Northern Queensland*, vol. 10, no.

1, 1981; "The Expatriate Vision of Jessica Anderson" by Elaine Barry, in *Meridian* (Melbourne), vol. 3, no. 1, 1984.

*   *   *

In one of the more quietly startling moments of Jessica Anderson's *Tirra Lirra by the River* Nora, the elderly narrator/ protagonist, tells us almost off-handedly that in middle age she tried to commit suicide. One reason for the attempt was the failure of a face-lift operation, and she links this with the horrifying revelations coming out of post-war Germany: ". . . if I leap to explain that the weakness resulting from six bronchial winters, and the approach of menopause, left me morbidly defenceless against the postwar revelations of the German camps, it is because I am ashamed to admit that in the same breath as that vast horror, I can speak of the loss of my looks." Jessica Anderson's novels do not tackle broad social, political or historical issues head-on, but always the large event, the major issue, is in the background, while her characters move in a world where small personal experiences, experiences which are as nothing on a world scale, profoundly influence them.

Tirra Lirra by the River is one of three novels by Anderson which begin with a woman arriving in Australia from "overseas." In *The Commandant* the woman is 17-year-old Frances, arriving from Ireland in the 1830's to live with her sister and brother-in-law, Captain Patrick Logan, the commandant of the title, who is remembered in Australian history as a fanatical and brutal disciplinarian, loathed by the convicts under his charge at Moreton Bay. Frances has initially the traditional role of innocent observer, until events make her unwillingly responsible for a young convict receiving 50 lashes—thus drawing her into "the system." In *Tirra Lirra by the River* and *The Impersonators*, however, the role of one-who-arrives is more complex, as both elderly Nora (*Tirra Lirra*) and middle-aged Sylvia (*The Impersonators*) are Australians returning home after many years of absence in Europe, bearing the accretions and conflicts of two cultures. The arrivals in these three books provide a promising opening, with their inherent possibilities of movement and change, but they also provide a direct entry into several of Anderson's major themes. (Her two earlier novels, *An Ordinary Lunacy* and *The Last Man's Head*, open with smaller but portentous visits.) Anderson is fascinated by the tug between the old culture (Europe) and the new (Australia). In her novels, arrival is always part of a longer journey, an inner journey as well as a physical one, and thus relates to the getting of wisdom and our conflicting desires for flight and sanctuary. To arrive at an unfamiliar place normally sharpens our awareness of environment, and descriptions of place—particularly of houses, and the harbour and gardens of Sydney, shown as being deeply part of the consciousness of the women characters in particular—are among the strengths of Anderson's most recent novels.

Tirra Lirra by the River, the most highly regarded of Anderson's novels, has in fact been written in three forms: as a short story, as a radio play, and finally as a prize-winning novel. By no means overtly feminist, it has been praised by feminist critics as showing the difficulties of women's lives from the point of view of a woman born early in the century. As the title suggests, the novel has links with Tennyson's poem, "The Lady of Shallott." In the poem, the Lady, generally accepted as artist or perhaps anima, lives secluded in a tower on an island, weaving her magic web and watching the world indirectly through a mirror. When she hears Lancelot pass by, singing, she looks down for the first time on the "real" world; the mirror cracks, the web flies out the window, and the Lady, dying, floats in her boat down to Camelot. Nora relates to

the Lady in a quite complex way, which has at its base the idea of her as artist seeing the world indirectly, through the mirror of a culture (European) not her own. The process begins when she is a child, and a flaw in the glass of a window transforms as she looks through it ordinary sticks, stones, bits of grass, into the magic landscape, with rivulets, castles, lakes, of her story books; enchanted, she fails even to see the "real river" near her home. After a failed marriage, she goes to London, working there for many years making theatre costumes; finally, she returns to Australia, and like the Lady of the poem, faces the "real": for her, suppressed memories, mistaken beliefs, a real river instead of the river running down to Camelot, and the discovery that embroidered hangings she made before she left Australia are the most promising things she ever did. Like the Lady, she becomes very sick, but unlike the Lady, recovers, and the novel ends with her globe of memory (one of the recurrent images of the book) in full spin, with no dark sides hidden. The book is not as simplistic as this thematic sketch probably suggests; Anderson habitually tests and qualifies her themes, and in *Tirra Lirra* Nora's spiritual/physical journey is counterbalanced by the lives of other women, who are partly defined, though not judged, by the journeys they make—or do not make.

In *The Impersonators*, a more diffuse and less successful book than *Tirra Lirra*, the debate sparked by the return of Sylvia after nearly twenty years is one that was current until the 1970's but has less cogency for Australians today: essentially it is a debate between what is seen as the cultural richness of Europe and the raw discontinuity of Australia, and whether there is a moral imperative for Australians who have been abroad to centres where culture is more securely consolidated to "come home and use what they've learned." In the end Sylvia, like Nora accepting what for her is "real," recognises that she has been yearning over "other people's rituals," and decides to stay in Sydney with her lover. An equally important theme is signalled by the title of the book: in materialistic, fractured Sydney of 1977, most of the characters are in some sense impersonators, living part of their lives behind protective masks. Jessica Anderson's portrait is sharp-eyed, unsentimental, but compassionate rather than satiric.

—Alrene Sykes

ANIEBO, I(feanyichukwu) N(dubuisi) C(hikezie). Nigerian. Born in Nigeria, in 1939. Educated at Government College, Umuahia; University of California, Los Angeles, B.A., C.Phil., M.A. Joined the Nigerian Army in 1959: attended cadet schools in Ghana and England; officer in the United Nations peace-keeping force in the Congo; at Command and General Staff College, Fort Leavenworth, Kansas; fought on the Biafran side in the Nigerian civil war; discharged from army, 1971. Currently, Senior Lecturer in English, University of Port Harcourt. Address: Department of English, University of Port Harcourt, P.M.B. 5523, Port Harcourt, Rivers State, Nigeria.

PUBLICATIONS

Novels

The Anonymity of Sacrifice.   London, Heinemann, 1974.

The Journey Within.   London, Heinemann, 1978.

Short Stories

Of Wives, Talismans and the Dead.   London, Heinemann, 1983.

Uncollected Short Stories

"The Jealous Goddess," in *Spear* (Lagos), October 1963.
"My Mother," in *Sunday Times* (Lagos), 22 December 1963.
"The Ring," in *Nigeria Magazine* (Lagos), December 1964.
"The Peacemakers," in *Nigeria Magazine* (Lagos), December 1965.
"Shadows," in *Black Orpheus 20* (Lagos), 1966.
"Mirage," in *Nigeria Magazine* (Lagos), March 1966.
"The Outing," in *Happy Home and Family Life* (Lagos), May 1972.
"Happy Survival, Brother," in *Ufahamu* (Los Angeles), vol. 7, no. 3, 1977.

*   *   *

Since 1963 I.N.C. Aniebo has been the author of a steady succession of short stories written for various periodical publications, a selection of them at last appearing as *Of Wives, Talismans and the Dead* as recently as 1983. Most of them deal with the problems of Igbo people in Eastern Nigeria trying to cope with the transition from rural to urban living and with other pressures of accelerating social change, including that most hectic of such changes, war itself. The commonest experience in Aniebo's fiction is the bewilderment that results from lack of trust in other people and lack of faith in the efficacy of the gods, whether traditional African or imported Christian. He often plunges his characters into some variety of spiritual emptiness or near-despair after they have been betrayed by those closest to them in childhood, adolescence, work, or marriage. The acrid taste of defeat is perhaps Aniebo's most distinctive contribution to West African Literature in English—his ability to record convincingly instances of human strength wilting and shrivelling, usually as the indirect outcome of large social processes. If Aluko's writing captures the comedy of Nigerian life acclimatizing itself to the modern world, and Achebe's the tragedy of it within an historical perspective, and Soyinka's the human spirit refusing to be broken by it, then what Aniebo records is the intense pain that afflicts people when social change halts, trips, nonplusses, or defeats them.

In the story "Dilemma," the priestess addresses her wayward son: "The earth has never changed. The winds still continue to blow, the rains to fall, and men to be born and die. Only little things that don't matter change. Don't say because things change, you'll stop believing in God and believe in the Devil." Her words pronounce the traditional wisdom that many Nigerians today mock, or cannot accept, or covet, when it appears in others, or deliberately reject for the pursuit of personal ambition and the acquisition of consumer goods. Aniebo, however, presents such evaporation of faith not as an ordinary clash-of-cultures matter but as the heavy price that Nigerians pay for entry into the modern world. While it is more pervasive in large towns, like Port Harcourt in the novel *The Journey Within*, it characterizes also the stories in *Of Wives, Talismans and the Dead*, most of which are set in rural Igbo villages. Thus, in the privacy of their tender incestuous love, widowed father and devoted daughter and only surviving child, in "Maruma," find the true fulfilment of giving to another, but when her pregnancy makes their love public, their having broken

a powerful social taboo destroys first their relationship and then themselves and their line. Yet, years later, their ruined, crumbling compound is symmetrically matched at the other end of the village by another as desolate, whose respectable and fecund owners had committed no "abomination." This even-handed "levelling" at the end of the story is the author's explicit comment, and it makes one wonder whether the dark views of the human condition that many of Aniebo's characters express aren't also his own, as in the war story, "In the Front Line": "The war had proved that no matter what one did or worshipped one died all the same, and more often than not like a rat." Similarly, in the thoughts of Christian Okoro in *The Journey Within*: ". . . his family had fought for survival, always getting up after a fall, always continuing to fight after a defeat. So, was life merely a getting-up after a fall?"

Aniebo's first published book, *The Anonymity of Sacrifice*, is a novel about the bitterness of successive Biafran "falls" during the Nigerian Civil War. It is a collection of very vivid, rapidly sketched illustrations of, admittedly, some heroical improvizations against great odds, but chiefly of betrayals, misunderstandings, personal defeats, frustration, and distrust, with the estrangement of the two major characters, and their pointless deaths, inadequately exploited novelistically. While the details of the narrative do indeed convey disillusion and corruption, there is little sense of their being worked into a firm design, and the title promises more significance than the book delivers.

The second novel, *The Journey Within*, is altogether more relaxed in execution, but again more ambitious in the endeavour than in the realization. It is centred upon the stories of two marriages, one traditional, the other Christian. In probing, to some depth, the joys, sorrows, tensions, struggles, love, and hatred that are generated between husband and wife, Aniebo is clearly arguing that marriage (whatever its kind) is a very thorny experience. Unfortunately, by making the two marriages progressively less distinctive, he throws away the opportunity to treat his larger theme with finer shades and more delicate ironies. Yet the novel is full of sardonic instances of human folly, as individuals seek their own fulfilments in an urban environment of free and selfish enterprise. While there is much mature observation of love and sexuality, some of the scenes between lovers are rendered with more mere titillation than the tone of the narration elsewhere strives after.

The collection of short stories is certainly the most successful of Aniebo's books, for under the pressure of brevity and pithiness, his particular gift, the rapid but accurate sketching of a scene without having to sustain its implications across a large design, is revealed as professional and complete in its own right. In the novels his transitions from one emotion to another are often incongruous, but in the stories he can move without inhibition or oddity across a gamut of emotions—anger at the exploitation of dockers in "Rats and Rabbits," self-confidence without moral crutches in "Godevil" (intentionally ambiguous as "Go devil" or "God evil"?), self-gratification in "Moment of Decision," the horror of murder within the family in "The Quiet Man" and "A Hero's Welcome," and, rarely, the consolation of faith in "Four Dimensions." The bleakness of Aniebo's vision is tempered, in his best writing, by a wry ironic sense that does not exclude muted compassion.

—Arthur Ravenscroft

ANTHONY, Michael. Trinidadian. Born in Mayaro, 10 February 1932. Educated at Mayaro Roman Catholic School; Junior Technical College, San Fernando, Trinidad. Married Yvette Francesca in 1958; two sons and two daughters. Lived in England, 1954–68: journalist, Reuters News Agency, London, 1964–68; lived in Brazil, 1968–70; assistant editor, Texaco Trinidad, Pointe-à-Pierre, 1970–72. Since 1972, researcher, National Cultural Council (now Ministry of Culture), Port-of-Spain. Address: 99 Long Circular Road, St. James, Port-of-Spain, Trinidad.

PUBLICATIONS

Novels

The Games Were Coming. London, Deutsch, 1963; Boston, Houghton Mifflin, 1968.
The Year in San Fernando. London, Deutsch, 1965.
Green Days by the River. Boston, Houghton Mifflin, and London, Deutsch, 1967.
Streets of Conflict. London, Deutsch, 1976.
All That Glitters. London, Deutsch, 1981.
Bright Road to El Dorado. Walton-on-Thames, Surrey, Nelson, 1982.

Short Stories

Sandra Street and Other Stories. London, Heinemann, 1973.
Cricket in the Road. London, Deutsch, 1973.
Folk Tales and Fantasies. Port-of-Spain, Trinidad, Columbus, 1976.

Other

Glimpses of Trinidad and Tobago, with a Glance at the West Indies. Port-of-Spain, Trinidad, Columbus, 1974.
Profile Trinidad: A Historical Survey from the Discovery to 1900. London, Macmillan, 1975.
The Making of Port of Spain 1757–1939. Port-of-Spain, Trinidad, Key Caribbean, 1978.

Editor, with Andrew Carr, *David Frost Introduces Trinidad and Tobago.* London, Deutsch, 1975.

*

Critical Studies: in *London Magazine*, April 1967; "Novels of Childhood" in *The West Indian Novel and Its Background* by Kenneth Ramchand, London, Faber, and New York, Barnes and Noble, 1970.

Michael Anthony comments:

I see myself principally as a story-teller. In other words, I am not aware that I have any message. I think both the past life and the fascination of landscape play a most important part in my work.

My infancy has been very important in my literary development and so far almost everything I have written—certainly my novels—are very autobiographical.

It is strange that I have never had the desire to write about England, although I spent 14 years there. To some people, judging from my writing alone, I have never been out of Trinidad. And this is true in some sort of way.

I feel a certain deep attachment to Trinidad and I want to write about it in such a way that I will give a faithful picture of life here. But when I am writing a story I am not aware that I want to do anything else but tell the story.

*   *   *

Michael Anthony's most successful novels are set in Southern Trinidad, deal with the experiences of childhood and youth, and are simple in structure. Where Anthony steps outside that framework, as he does in *Streets of Conflict*, and attempts explicit social comment, the results are disastrous. Yet it would be absurd to conclude, as some critics have done, that Anthony has nothing to say, and that his books are merely charming but naive semi-autobiographical remembrances of childhood.

His first novel, *The Games Were Coming*, subtly explores the need for a balance between restraint and joyful abandon. In a society where order has been a colonial imposition and the anarchic spirit of fete embraced as the only true guarantee of freedom, these are important issues. Anthony contrasts the cycling championships, for which the novel's hero, Leon, is training with self-denying discipline, and the approach of carnival which is associated with "fever," "chaos," and "release." Leon becomes so obsessed by the need for restraint that he neglects his girl friend, Sylvia, and nearly loses her. She in turn suffers for failing to know herself. She prides herself on being cool, controlled, and pure, but is embarrassed by indelicate thoughts which spring unbidden to her mind. She disapproves of carnival, but is willing to "jump-up" at night when no-one will see. She ignores these promptings of sexual energy and as a result is swept away by her feelings and Leon's neglect into the calculating arms of her middle-aged employer. Anthony suggests a resolution of these forces first in the character of Leon's younger brother, Dolphus, who is attracted equally to the Games and to carnival, and second by a subtle pattern of imagery which hints at the complementarity of these events, so that the "madness and wildness" of jouvert morning is shown as the energy which is disciplined into the "richness and splendour" of Grand Carnival.

The Year in San Fernando is also much more than a sensitive novel about growing up. Although Anthony scrupulously adheres to the unfolding perceptions of 12-year-old Francis, from puzzled naivety towards the growth of sympathetic understanding, what he creates in the novel is a richly textured and moving portrayal of the growth and disappearance in time of what is human. Set against the passage of the seasons is Francis's relationship with Mrs. Chandles, the old woman for whom he is brought as a companion from his impoverished village home in return for his board and schooling. Initially, she is all dominant will, a self-contained, bitter old lady who treats Francis as a virtual slave. He, when the year begins, is cowed and passive, scarcely more than a bundle of sensations. As the year passes, he observes Mrs. Chandles's spirit and flesh wilt in the drought of crop-season and comes to understand the reasons for her ill-temper. At the same time, Francis's self is growing powerfully as he begins to acknowledge his feelings, both positive and negative. There is a brief season of rain when Mrs. Chandles is released from her pain and the two meet as open and giving personalities. But then as Francis continues his growth to personhood, the personality of Mrs. Chandles disintegrates as she begins to die. Yet there is more for Francis to learn than his part in the cycle of life and death, and this is contained in a puzzling comment Mrs. Chandles makes. Throughout the dry season he has painstakingly tended her shrivelling flowers and oiled and massaged her protesting limbs. She comments on his "willing mind" and bemuses him by telling him that she "connected willingness of mind with sacredness." It is through this "sacredness" that Francis redeems his year in San Fernando from time.

None of Anthony's other novels quite achieves the same degree of understated but unflawed art. *Green Days by the River* evokes another passage from adolescent freedom to adult responsibility in the countryside around Mayaro in prose of great beauty. But the novel seems to escape from Anthony's control, in a way which is interesting but damaging to its coherence, in the central relationship between Shellie, the youth, and Mr. Gidharee the Indian farmer who lures him into marriage with his daughter. Here the meeting is complicated by its Trinidadian ethnic resonances. In portraying Gidharee as a creolised Jekyll who charms Shellie into his confidence, and an Indian Hyde who sets his dogs to savage him as a warning about what will happen if he fails to marry his daughter, Anthony unavoidably appears to be making a veiled statement about ethnic relations. Two kinds of irony tangle. One is the dramatic irony that Shellie fails to see the twig being limed to catch him, the other is the irony of Shellie's racial innocence when so much of Gidharee's behaviour adds up to a Creole stereotype of the Indian as an economic threat. The second irony leads to inconsistencies in the portrayal of Shellie, who is bright and sensitive in all respects except in his dealings with Gidharee, where he appears spineless and impercipient. It is hard to know in a somewhat evasive novel quite what Anthony intended.

Anthony's one attempt to deal with broader social issues, in *Streets of Conflict*, is an outright failure. It is an inept performance, inconsistent and shallow in characterisation, broken-backed in plot and embarrassingly naive in its portrayal of society and politics in Brazil.

All That Glitters is at least a partial return to excellence. In some respects it can be seen as a return to familiar territory, to the growing awareness of young Horace Lumpres of the complications of the adult world around him, of the jealousies and deceptions provoked by the return of his sophisticated Aunty Roomeen to the village of Mayaro. In a more intense way than in any earlier novel, Anthony focuses on a child's attempt to discern whether people are being sincere or false. Words such as trickster, genuine, hypocrite, acting, feigned, frankoment, and pretensive act as leitmotifs in the text and Horace has to learn that being adult means wearing different faces. This play on truth and falsity is linked through the novel's two complementary mottoes ("Gold Is Where You Find It" and "All That Glitters") to Anthony's most conscious exploration of the nature of his art. The distinction is caught in the contrast between Horace's joy in discovering through writing what he thinks and feels, when he writes about the golden day with the fishermen or the sordid saga of the stolen golden chain, and the way that the adult clichés which his teacher Myra uses embalm experience. Nevertheless, for all her circumlocutions, she recognises the child's magical directness, and it is her advice, "Make it colourful and vivid—and true" which both Horace and Michael Anthony follow.

—Jeremy Poynting

ARMAH, Ayi Kwei. Ghanaian. Born in Takoradi in 1938. Educated at Achimota College. Accra; Groton School, Massachusetts; Harvard University, Cambridge, Massachusetts, A.B. in social studies; Columbia University, New York. Translator, *Révolution Africaine* magazine, Algiers; scriptwriter for Ghana Television; English teacher, Navrongo School, Ghana, 1966; editor, *Jeune Afrique* magazine, Paris, 1967–68; teacher at Teacher's College, Dar es Salaam, and universities of Massachusetts, Amherst, Lesotho, and Wisconsin, Madison. Address: c/o Heinemann Ltd., 10 Upper Grosvenor Street, London W1X 9PA, England.

PUBLICATIONS

Novels

The Beautyful Ones Are Not Yet Born. Boston, Houghton Mifflin, 1968; London, Heinemann, 1969.
Fragments. Boston, Houghton Mifflin, 1970; London, Heinemann, 1975.
Why Are We So Blest? New York, Doubleday, 1972; London, Heinemann, 1975.
Two Thousand Seasons. Nairobi, East African Publishing House, 1973; London, Heinemann, 1979; Chicago, Third World Press, 1980.
The Healers. Nairobi, East African Publishing House, 1978; London, Heinemann, 1979.

Uncollected Short Stories

"A Short Story," in *New African* (London), December 1965.
"Yaw Manu's Charm," in *Atlantic* (Boston), May 1968.
"The Offal Kind," in *Harper's* (New York), January 1969.

*

Critical Study: *The Novels of Ayi Kwei Armah: A Study in Polemical Fiction* by Robert Fraser, London, Heinemann, 1980.

*   *   *

Ayi Kwei Armah's masterly control over language forces his reader to suspend his disbelief, however reluctant he may be to do so. The comic or horrific distortion of what is nearly recognisable reality in the first three novels has extraordinary imaginative power.

The title of the first novel refers to an inscription which the central character, known only as "the man," sees on a bus. By implication it refers back to the Teacher's story of Plato's cave, where the one man who escapes from the cave and returns to tell his fellow sufferers of the beautiful world outside is thought to be mad by those in the "reassuring chains." The man is anonymous because he is regarded as mad in his society, modern Accra. His family suffers from his refusal to take bribes in his position as a railway clerk, and his honesty is incomprehensible to "the loved ones." His former friend, Koomson, has become a Minister through corruption, and, though the regime of which he is a part falls, an equally corrupt one takes its place. The fusion of styles in *The Beautyful Ones* can be seen in the first few pages, which give a realistic account of a bus journey but also introduce the controlling symbol in the novel, that of money as decay, or excrement. The bus conductor smells a cedi note and finds it has "a very old smell, very strong, and so very rotten that the stench itself of it came with a curious, satisfying pleasure." This anticipates the comic and horrible way in which Koomson has to escape the new regime, by wriggling through a latrine. The depravity of the society is suggested by the manner in which a young man confesses he has made money in a lottery "in the embarrassed way of a young girl confessing love"; if he escaped from his society the man would only mirror his broken pencil sharpener, whose handle "sped round and round with the futile freedom of a thing connected to nothing else."

Armah's ability to invest apparently insignificant objects or scenes with meanings is clear in *Fragments*. Early in the novel there is a detailed account of the destruction of a mad dog by a man with a gross sexual deformity, while the little boy who loves the dog looks on helplessly. It is so vivid that it prepares the reader for the destruction of the central character, Baako, who returns to Ghana from New York wanting to write film scripts because "Film gets to everyone." He finds that his society wants material evidence of his "been-to" status. The new element in this novel is represented by Naana, Baako's blind grandmother, who is the voice of the traditional culture. Traditional ceremonies, such as Baako's baby nephew's outdooring, have lost their spiritual significance and become an opportunity for ostentation and avarice; the plot suggests that Naana's fears for the baby as the victim of this irreligious display are justified, for he dies in the course of it. The fragments of the title seem to be the members of the new society, placed within the opening and closing sections of the novel which express Naana's sense of meaningful community. The only other hopeful element is the growing love between Baako and the sensitive Puerto Rican, Juana.

Why Are We So Blest? is a more fragmented novel than *Fragments*, jumping between three narrators with no obvious narrative line, though we eventually discover that Solo, a failed revolutionary, is using the notebooks of Aimée, a white American, and Modin, a Ghanaian, intercut with his own text. The savage irony of the title is sustained throughout the novel, which lacks the cynical comedy of the two previous works and is much more overt in its distortion of reality. All the white women in the novel prey on the black men: Modin, a student who drops out of Harvard to go to Laccryville in North Africa as a would-be revolutionary, is used primarily by Aimée, who epitomises the sexual sickness of all the white women. She is frigid when she meets Modin, and uses him as an object to stimulate her sexual fantasies of intercourse with a black servant. Modin's attempt to liberate her into a fuller sensitivity destroys him. The horrific scene, in which Aimée is raped and Modin castrated by white men, fully enacts Aimée's fantasy. She is sexually aroused and kisses Modin's bleeding penis, asking him to say that he loves her. Solo sees Modin as an African who does not know "how deep the destruction has eaten into himself, hoping to achieve a healing juncture with his destroyed people."

Armah's most recent novels are historical. *Two Thousand Seasons* is written in a new style, in its repetitiveness and long leisurely sentences suggesting that it is folk myth: "With what shall the utterers' tongue stricken with goodness, riven silent with the quiet force of beauty, with which mention shall the tongue of the utterers begin a song of praise whose perfect singers have yet to come?" Its narrator is not identified, though he participates in the action. The violation of his people's way of life by Arab and then European invaders is depicted powerfully but the ideal of "the way, our way" remains nebulous. *The Healers* is stylistically much more vigorous, and is set at a precise time in the past, during the Second Asante War. The idea of "inspiration" is gradually defined in the course of the novel as being a healing and creative force which can only work slowly, and Armah perhaps sees himself as one of

those prophesied by Damfo in the novel, "healers wherever our people are scattered, able to bring us together again."

—Angela Smith

ARNOW, Harriette (Louisa, née Simpson). American. Born in Wayne County, Kentucky, 7 July 1908. Educated at St. Helen's Academy; Stanton Academy; Burnside High School, graduated 1924; Berea College, Kentucky, 1924–26; University of Louisville, B.S. 1931. Married Harold B. Arnow in 1939 (died, 1985); one daughter and one son. Teacher in Pulaski County, Kentucky, 1926–28, 1931–34, and Louisville, 1934; waitress, Cincinnati, 1934–39. Recipient: Berea College Centennial Award, 1955; Friends of American Writers award, 1955; American Association for State and Local History award, 1971; University of Louisville Outstanding Alumni Award, 1979. D.Litt.: Albion College, Michigan, 1955; Transylvania University, Lexington, Kentucky, 1979; University of Kentucky, Lexington, 1981. *Died in March 1986.*

PUBLICATIONS

Novels

Mountain Path. New York, Covici Friede, 1936.
Hunter's Horn. New York, Macmillan, 1949; London, Collins, 1950.
The Dollmaker. New York, Macmillan, 1954; London, Heinemann, 1955.
The Weedkiller's Daughter. New York, Knopf, 1970.
The Kentucky Trace: A Novel of the American Revolution. New York, Knopf, 1974.

Uncollected Short Stories

"Marigolds and Mules," in *Kosmos* (Philadelphia), August–September 1934.
"A Mess of Pork," in *The New Talent* (New York), October–December 1935.
"Washerwoman's Day," in *An Anthology of Stories from the Southern Review*, edited by Cleanth Brooks and Robert Penn Warren. Baton Rouge, Louisiana State University Press, 1953.
"Fra Lippi and Me," in *Georgia Review* (Athens), Winter 1979.

Other

Seedtime on the Cumberland. New York, Macmillan, 1960.
Flowering of the Cumberland. New York, Macmillan, 1963.
Some Musings on the Nature of History (lecture). Ann Arbor, Historical Society of Michigan, 1968.
Old Burnside. Lexington, University Press of Kentucky, 1978.

*

Manuscript Collection: Margaret I. King Library, University of Kentucky, Lexington.

Critical Studies: by Joyce Carol Oates, in *Rediscoveries* edited by David Madden, New York, Crown, 1971; *Harriette Arnow* by Wilton Eckley, New York, Twayne, 1974.

Harriette Arnow comments:

Judging from critical studies, reviews, and letters the main features of my novels are the characters, sometimes praised, but often damned. Perhaps the most notable characters are in *Hunter's Horn* and *The Dollmaker*; at least more has been written of them, particularly of Gertie Nevels in *The Dollmaker*, the story of a rural family's migration to an industrial city during World War II. While I was writing that novel I felt no one would care to read the story of an ugly, inarticulate, secretive woman who couldn't understand that the industry she hated was trying to help with the war as had her dead brother Henley. Most of the characters in *The Weedkiller's Daughter*, set in modern suburbia, were damned. The main character in *The Kentucky Trace*, an historical novel, did somewhat better.

*   *   *

Harriette Arnow's reputation as an artist rests on three significant volumes: two—*Seedtime on the Cumberland* and *Flowering of the Cumberland*—are cultural histories; one—*The Dollmaker*—is a novel. The histories are remarkable for the brilliant, often lyrical, narrative techniques and for the accuracy and wealth of detail relating the every-day domestic life of the early settlers of the Cumberland. The same attention to life-as-lived detail and to strong prose distinguishes *The Dollmaker*, which Joyce Carol Oates called "a legitimate tragedy, our most unpretentious American masterpiece."

Discounting possible overstatement, most critics would agree with Oates: *The Dollmaker* is a masterpiece, one which does with the folk of Appalachia what Steinbeck's *The Grapes of Wrath* does with the Okies, one which gives the plight of a displaced family heroic stature and epic sweep. Following the archetype of flight from the ruined Eden to the new promised land, the novel dramatizes with authentic precision the collision of two cultures. The mountain family's agrarian values of independence, self-sufficiency, love of the land, and aesthetic based on closeness to the beauty and harshness of nature are epitomized in the mother. Gertie, who with the soul of an artist is a marvel of physical and spiritual strength, ingenuity, and endurance. Rather than the dust bowl and rapacity of landholders, the calamity that springs the exodus from her Eden is World War II which took the men from the mountains and lured them to death in combat or to death-in-life in industrial Detroit. Seduced in part by her own traditions of family loyalty, the mother follows her man's dream of better life in progressive Detroit which promised affluence, untold luxuries, and marvelous conveniences. The incipient callousness and bigotry of Gertie's mountain society also follow to Detroit where they are mass-produced and manufactured on a scale of overwhelming vulgarity. With a fate as persistent, inevitable, finely wrought, and devastating as pursued Jude the Obscure, the horrors of industrialized society are exposed: the family disintegrates and sinks to the lowest levels of violence and misery. Even the artistic soul of Gertie is sacrificed to mass production, standardization, mechanization, and crass commercialism.

Overlaid on the superb rendering of the minutiae of life in Appalachia and Detroit are the same mythic and epic elements as Steinbeck's novel. Ultimately the novel becomes a search for Christ in the world, a Christ freed from the dogma and bigotry of established institutions. Certainly as successful in this attempt as Steinbeck, Arnow shows that beneath the selfishness and ignorance, beneath the degrading impersonalization of modernism, the suppressed folk have a genuine human care for each other that binds them together and gives them the strength to endure their crucifixions. *En masse* they can endure and perhaps overcome the enemy: organized religion, industrialism, false aristocracy, mass media, standardization, public education—anything that depersonalizes and dehumanizes. Salvation seems to be in the mass rather than in the individuals. Thus, finally, Arnow turns from agrarian novelist to proletariat novelist. This paradox or ambiguity is seen in the ending of *The Dollmaker*. Throughout the trials that Gertie endures, the chief sustainer and symbol of her dream of spirituality and human truth has been a block of wood which she has carved, but which she has not finished, awaiting the revelation that will give the figure a face. The figure is amorphous, even to Gertie, and is sometimes a man, sometimes a woman, sometimes a Judas, sometimes a virgin, but ultimately it is to be Christ. In the final pages of the novel, in a pointed counterpart of a religious procession of a holy image, the block of wood is hauled to the saw mill in the midst of crowds of on-lookers. It is cut into blocks to make mass-produced dolls for commercial sale. Her vision is thus sacrificed to the cheap vulgarity and needs of a materialistic and meaningless existence. However, at the last Gertie sees that unseen face of Christ could have been the face of her neighbors—"millions and millions of faces fine enough for him." Christ is to be found in the mass, in the millions of those who are the folk, to which the individual vision must be relinquished.

Arnow's earlier novels, *Mountain Path* and *Hunter's Horn*, are less ambitious and *au courant* with the times, but they are indicative of her skill in depicting mountain scenes and characters. They also show her lesser skill at realistic plotting, especially *Mountain Path*, which indulges in plot clichés and situations common to stereotyped hillbilly life. *The Weedkiller's Daughter* and *The Kentucky Trace* are barely satisfactory for serious reading. *The Weedkiller's Daughter* sets a group of nature-loving, arrogantly deceitful, pseudo-sophisticated, precocious teenagers against a plastic society of stupid and vulgar newly-rich parents. The plot is negligible and a contrivance merely to hold together a narrative designed to deliver every stance posed by the 1960's liberal. *The Kentucky Trace* returns to some of the materials of Arnow's earlier work, but the narrative is a creaking vehicle to utilize her detailed knowledge of the pioneer ways and means of the mountain settlers.

—Robert L. Welker

ASIMOV, Isaac.   American.   Born in Petrovichi, U.S.S.R., 2 January 1920; emigrated to the United States in 1923; became citizen, 1928. Educated at Columbia University, New York, B.S. 1939, M.A. 1941, Ph.D. in chemistry 1948. Served in the United States Army, 1945–46. Married 1) Gertrude Blugerman in 1942 (divorced), one son and one daughter; 2) Janet Opal Jeppson in 1973. Instructor in Biochemistry, 1949–51, Assistant Professor, 1951–55, Associate Professor, 1955–79, and since 1979 Professor, Boston University School of Medicine. Recipient: Edison Foundation National Mass Media Award, 1958; Blakeslee Award, for non-fiction, 1960; World Science Fiction Convention citation, 1963; Hugo Award, 1963, 1966, 1973, 1977, 1983; American Chemical Society James T. Grady Award, 1965; American Association for the Advancement of Science-Westinghouse Science Writing Award, 1967; Nebula Award, 1972, 1976; *Locus* award, for non-fiction, 1981, for fiction, 1983. Guest of Honor, World Science Fiction Convention, 1955. Address: 10 West 66th Street, Apartment 33-A, New York, New York 10023, U.S.A.

PUBLICATIONS

Novels

Triangle. New York, Doubleday, 1961; as *An Isaac Asimov Second Omnibus*, London, Sidgwick and Jackson, 1969.
Pebble in the Sky. New York, Doubleday, 1950; London, Corgi, 1958.
The Stars, Like Dust. New York, Doubleday, 1951; London, Panther, 1958; abridged edition, as *The Rebellious Stars*, New York, Ace, 1954.
The Currents of Space. New York, Doubleday, 1952; London, Boardman, 1955.
Foundation Trilogy. New York, Doubleday, 1963(?); as *An Isaac Asimov Omnibus*, London, Sidgwick and Jackson, 1966.
 Foundation. New York, Gnome Press, 1951; London, Weidenfeld and Nicolson, 1953; abridged edition, as *The Thousand-Year Plan*, New York, Ace, 1955.
 Foundation and Empire. New York, Gnome Press, 1952; London, Panther, 1962; as *The Man Who Upset the Universe*, New York, Ace, 1955.
 Second Foundation. New York, Gnome Press, 1953.
The Caves of Steel. New York, Doubleday, and London, Boardman, 1954.
The End of Eternity. New York, Doubleday, 1955; London, Panther, 1958.
The Naked Sun. New York, Doubleday, 1957; London, Joseph, 1958.
The Death Dealers. New York, Avon, 1958; as *A Whiff of Death*, New York, Walker, and London, Gollancz, 1968.
Fantastic Voyage (novelization of screenplay). Boston, Houghton Mifflin, and London, Dobson, 1966.
The Robot Novels (includes *The Caves of Steel* and *The Naked Sun*). New York, Doubleday, 1971.
The Gods Themselves. New York, Doubleday, and London, Gollancz, 1972.
Murder at the ABA. New York, Doubleday, 1976; as *Authorized Murder*, London, Gollancz, 1976.
The Collected Fiction: The Far Ends of Time and Earth, Prisoners of the Stars. New York, Doubleday, 2 vols., 1979.
Foundation's Edge. New York, Doubleday, 1982; London, Granada, 1983.
The Robots of Dawn. New York, Doubleday, 1983; London, Granada, 1984.
Robots and Empire. New York, Doubleday, and London, Granada, 1985.

Short Stories

I, Robot. New York, Gnome Press, 1950; London, Grayson, 1952.
The Martian Way and Other Stories. New York, Doubleday, 1955; London, Dobson, 1964.
Earth Is Room Enough. New York, Doubleday, 1957; London, Panther, 1960.
Nine Tomorrows: Tales of the Near Future. New York, Doubleday, 1959; London, Dobson, 1963.
The Rest of the Robots. New York, Doubleday, 1964; London, Dobson, 1967.
Through a Glass, Clearly. London, New English Library, 1967.
Asimov's Mysteries. New York, Doubleday, and London, Rapp and Whiting, 1968.
Nightfall and Other Stories. New York, Doubleday, 1969; London, Rapp and Whiting, 1970.

The Early Asimov; or, Eleven Years of Trying. New York, Doubleday, 1972; London, Gollancz, 1973.
The Best of Isaac Asimov (1939–1972). London, Sidgwick and Jackson, 1973; New York, Doubleday, 1974.
Have You Seen These? Cambridge, Massachusetts, NESFA Press, 1974.
Tales of the Black Widowers. New York, Doubleday, 1974; London, Gollancz, 1975.
Buy Jupiter and Other Stories. New York, Doubleday, 1975; London, Gollancz, 1976.
The Dream, Benjamin's Dream, Benjamin's Bicentennial Blast: Three Short Stories. Privately printed, 1976.
The Bicentennial Man and Other Stories. New York, Doubleday, 1976; London, Gollancz, 1977.
More Tales of the Black Widowers. New York, Doubleday, 1976; London, Gollancz, 1977.
Good Taste. Topeka, Kansas, Apocalypse Press, 1977.
Casebook of the Black Widowers. New York, Doubleday, and London, Gollancz, 1980.
3 by Asimov. New York, Targ, 1981.
The Complete Robot. New York, Doubleday, and London, Granada, 1982.
The Winds of Change and Other Stories. New York, Doubleday, and London, Granada, 1983.
The Union Club Mysteries. New York, Doubleday, 1983; London, Granada, 1984.
Banquets of the Black Widowers. New York, Doubleday, 1984; London, Gollancz, 1985.
The Edge of Tomorrow (stories and essays). New York, Tor, 1985.
Alternative Asimovs. New York, Doubleday, 1986.

Verse

Lecherous Limericks. New York, Walker, 1975; London, Corgi, 1977.
More Lecherous Limericks. New York, Walker, 1976.
Still More Lecherous Limericks. New York, Walker, 1977.
Asimov's Sherlockian Limericks. Yonkers, New York, Mysterious Press, 1978.
Limericks: Too Gross, with John Ciardi. New York, Norton, 1978.
A Grossery of Limericks, with John Ciardi. New York, Norton, 1981.
Limericks for Children. New York, Caedmon, 1984.

Other (fiction for children) as Paul French

David Starr, Space Ranger. New York, Doubleday, 1952; Kingswood, Surrey, World's Work, 1953.
Lucky Starr and the Pirates of the Asteroids. New York, Doubleday, 1953; Kingswood, Surrey, World's Work, 1954.
Lucky Starr and the Oceans of Venus. New York, Doubleday, 1954; as *The Oceans of Venus* (as Isaac Asimov), London, New English Library, 1973.
Lucky Starr and the Big Sun of Mercury. New York, Doubleday, 1956; as *The Big Sun of Mercury* (as Isaac Asimov), London, New English Library, 1974.
Lucky Starr and the Moons of Jupiter. New York, Doubleday, 1957; as *The Moons of Jupiter* (as Isaac Asimov), London, New English Library, 1974.
Lucky Starr and the Rings of Saturn. New York, Doubleday, 1958; as *The Rings of Saturn* (as Isaac Asimov), London, New English Library, 1974.

Other

Biochemistry and Human Metabolism, with Burnham Walker and William C. Boyd.   Baltimore, Williams and Wilkins, 1952; revised edition, 1954, 1957; London, Ballière Tindall and Cox, 1955.

The Chemicals of Life: Enzymes, Vitamins, Hormones.   New York, Abelard Schuman, 1954; London, Bell, 1956.

Races and Peoples, with William C. Boyd.   New York, Abelard Schuman, 1955; London, Abelard Schuman, 1958.

Chemistry and Human Health, with Burnham Walker and M.K. Nicholas.   New York, McGraw Hill, 1956.

Inside the Atom.   New York and London, Abelard Schuman, 1956; revised edition, Abelard Schuman, 1958, 1961, 1966, 1974.

Building Blocks of the Universe.   New York, Abelard Schuman, 1957; London, Abelard Schuman, 1958; revised edition, 1961, 1974.

Only a Trillion.   New York and London, Abelard Schuman, 1957; as *Marvels of Science,* New York, Collier, 1962.

The World of Carbon.   New York and London, Abelard Schuman, 1958; revised edition, New York, Collier, 1962.

The World of Nitrogen.   New York and London, Abelard Schuman, 1958; revised edition, New York, Collier, 1962.

The Clock We Live On.   New York and London, Abelard Schuman, 1959; revised edition, New York, Collier, 1962; Abelard Schuman, 1965.

The Living River.   New York and London, Abelard Schuman, 1959; revised edition, as *The Bloodstream: River of Life,* New York, Collier, 1961.

Realm of Numbers.   Boston, Houghton Mifflin, 1959; London, Gollancz, 1963.

Words of Science and the History Behind Them.   Boston, Houghton Mifflin, 1959; London, Harrap, 1974.

Breakthroughs in Science (for children).   Boston, Houghton Mifflin, 1960.

The Intelligent Man's Guide to Science.   New York, Basic Books, 2 vols., 1960; revised edition, as *The New Intelligent Man's Guide to Science*, 1 vol., 1965; London, Nelson, 1967; as *Asimov's Guide to Science*, Basic Books, 1972; London, Penguin, 2 vols., 1975; as *Asimov's New Guide to Science*, Basic Books, 1984.

The Kingdom of the Sun.   New York and London, Abelard Schuman, 1960; revised edition, New York, Collier, 1962; Abelard Schuman, 1963.

Realm of Measure.   Boston, Houghton Mifflin, 1960.

Satellites in Outer Space (for children).   New York, Random House, 1960; revised edition, 1964, 1973.

The Double Planet.   New York, Abelard Schuman, 1960; London, Abelard Schuman, 1962; revised edition, 1966.

The Wellsprings of Life.   New York and London, Abelard Schuman, 1960.

Realm of Algebra.   Boston, Houghton Mifflin, 1961; London, Gollancz, 1964.

Words from the Myths.   Boston, Houghton Mifflin, 1961; London, Faber, 1963.

Fact and Fancy.   New York, Doubleday, 1962.

Life and Energy.   New York, Doubleday, 1962; London, Dobson, 1963.

The Search for the Elements.   New York, Basic Books, 1962.

Words in Genesis.   Boston, Houghton Mifflin, 1962.

Words on the Map.   Boston, Houghton Mifflin, 1962.

View from a Height.   New York, Doubleday, 1963; London, Dobson, 1964.

The Genetic Code.   New York, Orion Press, 1963; London, Murray, 1964.

The Human Body: Its Structure and Operation.   Boston, Houghton Mifflin, 1963; London, Nelson, 1965.

The Kite That Won the Revolution.   Boston, Houghton Mifflin, 1963.

Words from the Exodus.   Boston, Houghton Mifflin, 1963.

Adding a Dimension: 17 Essays on the History of Science.   New York, Doubleday, 1964; London, Dobson, 1966.

The Human Brain: Its Capacities and Functions.   Boston, Houghton Mifflin, 1964; London, Nelson, 1965.

Quick and Easy Math.   Boston, Houghton Mifflin, 1964; London, Whiting and Wheaton, 1967.

A Short History of Biology.   Garden City, New York, Natural History Press, 1964; London, Nelson, 1965.

Planets for Man, with Stephen H. Dole.   New York, Random House, 1964.

Asimov's Biographical Encyclopedia of Science and Technology.   New York, Doubleday, 1964; London, Allen and Unwin, 1966; revised edition, Doubleday, 1972, 1982; London, Pan, 1975.

An Easy Introduction to the Slide Rule.   Boston, Houghton Mifflin, 1965; London, Whiting and Wheaton, 1967.

The Greeks: A Great Adventure.   Boston, Houghton Mifflin, 1965.

Of Time and Space and Other Things.   New York, Doubleday, 1965; London, Dobson, 1967.

A Short History of Chemistry.   New York, Doubleday, 1965; London, Heinemann, 1972.

The Neutrino: Ghost Particle of the Atom.   New York, Doubleday, and London, Dobson, 1966.

The Genetic Effects of Radiation, with Theodosius Dobzhansky.   Washington, D.C., Atomic Energy Commission, 1966.

The Noble Gases.   New York, Basic Books, 1966.

The Roman Republic.   Boston, Houghton Mifflin, 1966.

From Earth to Heaven.   New York, Doubleday, 1966.

Understanding Physics.   New York, Walker, 3 vols., 1966; London, Allen and Unwin, 3 vols., 1967; as *The History of Physics*, Walker, 1 vol., 1984.

The Universe: From Flat Earth to Quasar.   New York, Walker, 1966; London, Penguin, 1967; revised edition, Walker and Penguin, 1971; revised edition, as *The Universe: From Flat Earth to Black Holes—and Beyond*, Walker, 1980, Penguin, 1983.

The Roman Empire.   Boston, Houghton Mifflin, 1967.

The Moon (for children).   Chicago, Follett, 1967; London, University of London Press, 1969.

Is Anyone There? (essays).   New York, Doubleday, 1967; London, Rapp and Whiting, 1968.

To the Ends of the Universe.   New York, Walker, 1967; revised edition, 1976.

The Egyptians.   Boston, Houghton Mifflin, 1967.

Mars (for children).   Chicago, Follett, 1967; London, University of London Press, 1971.

From Earth to Heaven: 17 Essays on Science.   New York, Doubleday, 1967; London, Dobson, 1968.

Environments Out There.   New York, Abelard Schuman, 1967; London, Abelard Schuman, 1968.

Science, Numbers, and I: Essays on Science.   New York, Doubleday, 1968; London, Rapp and Whiting, 1969.

The Near East: 10,000 Years of History.   Boston, Houghton Mifflin, 1968.

Asimov's Guide to the Bible: The Old Testament, The New Testament.   New York, Doubleday, 2 vols., 1968–69.

The Dark Ages.   Boston, Houghton Mifflin, 1968.

Galaxies (for children).   Chicago, Follett, 1968; London, University of London Press, 1971.

Stars (for children). Chicago, Follett, 1968.
Words from History. Boston, Houghton Mifflin, 1968.
Photosynthesis. New York, Basic Books, 1968; London, Allen and Unwin, 1970.
The Shaping of England. Boston, Houghton Mifflin, 1969.
Twentieth Century Discovery (for children). New York, Doubleday, and London, Macdonald, 1969.
Opus 100 (selection). Boston, Houghton Mifflin, 1969.
ABC's of Space (for children). New York, Walker, 1969.
Great Ideas of Science (for children). Boston, Houghton Mifflin, 1969.
To the Solar System and Back. New York, Doubleday, 1970.
Asimov's Guide to Shakespeare: The Greek, Roman, and Italian Plays; The English Plays. New York, Doubleday, 2 vols., 1970.
Constantinople. Boston, Houghton Mifflin, 1970.
The ABC's of the Ocean (for children). New York, Walker, 1970.
Light (for children). Chicago, Follett, 1970.
The Best New Thing (for children). Cleveland, World, 1971.
The Stars in Their Courses. New York, Doubleday, 1971; London, White Lion, 1974.
What Makes the Sun Shine? Boston, Little Brown, 1971.
The Isaac Asimov Treasury of Humor. Boston, Houghton Mifflin, 1971; London, Vallentine Mitchell, 1972.
The Sensuous Dirty Old Man (as Dr. A.). New York, Walker, 1971.
The Land of Canaan. Boston, Houghton Mifflin, 1971.
ABC's of Earth (for children). New York, Walker, 1971.
The Space Dictionary. New York, Starline, 1971.
More Words of Science. Boston, Houghton Mifflin, 1972.
Electricity and Man. Washington, D.C., Atomic Energy Commission, 1972.
The Shaping of France. Boston, Houghton Mifflin, 1972.
Asimov's Annotated "Don Juan." New York, Doubleday, 1972.
ABC's of Ecology (for children). New York, Walker, 1972.
The Story of Ruth. New York, Doubleday 1972.
Worlds Within Worlds. Washington, D.C., Atomic Energy Commission, 1972.
The Left Hand of the Electron (essays). New York, Doubleday, 1972; London, White Lion, 1975.
Ginn Science Program. Boston, Ginn, 5 vols., 1972–73.
How Did We Find Out about Dinosaurs [*The Earth Is Round, Electricity, Vitamins, Germs, Comets, Energy, Atoms, Nuclear Power, Numbers, Outer Space, Earthquakes, Black Holes, Our Human Roots, Antarctica, Coal, Oil, Solar Power, Volcanoes, Life in the Deep Sea, Our Genes, the Universe, Computers, Robots, the Atmosphere*] (for children). New York, Walker, 25 vols., 1973–85; 6 vols. published London, White Lion, 1975–76; 1 vol. published London, Pan, 1980; 7 vols. published (as *How We Found Out . . .* series), London, Longman, 1982.
The Tragedy of the Moon (essays). New York, Doubleday, 1973; London, Abelard Schuman, 1974.
Comets and Meteors (for children). Chicago, Follett, 1973.
The Sun (for children). Chicago, Follett, 1973.
The Shaping of North America from the Earliest Times to 1763. Boston, Houghton Mifflin, 1973; London, Dobson, 1975.
Please Explain. Boston, Houghton Mifflin, 1973; London, Abelard Schuman, 1975.
Physical Science Today. Del Mar, California, CRM, 1973.
Jupiter, The Largest Planet (for children). New York, Lothrop, 1973; revised edition, 1976.

Today, Tomorrow, and . . . New York, Doubleday, 1973; London, Abelard Schuman, 1974; as *Towards Tomorrow*, London, Hodder and Stoughton, 1977.
The Birth of the United States 1763–1816. Boston, Houghton Mifflin, 1974.
Earth: Our Crowded Spaceship. New York, Day, and London, Abelard Schuman, 1974.
Asimov on Chemistry. New York, Doubleday, 1974; London, Macdonald and Jane's, 1975.
Asimov on Astronomy. New York, Doubleday, and London, Macdonald, 1974.
Asimov's Annotated "Paradise Lost." New York, Doubleday, 1974.
Our World in Space. Greenwich, Connecticut, New York Graphic Society, and Cambridge, Patrick Stephens, 1974.
The Solar System (for children). Chicago, Follett, 1975.
Birth and Death of the Universe. New York, Walker, 1975.
Of Matters Great and Small. New York, Doubleday, 1975.
Our Federal Union: The United States from 1816 to 1865. Boston, Houghton Mifflin, and London, Dobson, 1975.
The Ends of the Earth: The Polar Regions of the World. New York, Weybright and Talley, 1975.
Eyes on the Universe: A History of the Telescope. Boston, Houghton Mifflin, 1975; London, Deutsch, 1976.
Science Past—Science Future. New York, Doubleday, 1975.
The Heavenly Host (for children). New York, Walker, 1975; London, Penguin, 1978.
Alpha Centauri, The Nearest Star (for children). New York, Lothrop, 1976.
I, Rabbi (for children). New York, Walker, 1976.
Asimov on Physics. New York, Doubleday, 1976.
The Planet That Wasn't. New York, Doubleday, 1976; London, Sphere, 1977.
The Collapsing Universe: The Story of Black Holes. New York, Walker, and London, Hutchinson, 1977.
Asimov on Numbers. New York, Doubleday, 1977.
The Beginning and the End. New York, Doubleday, 1977.
Familiar Poems Annotated. New York, Doubleday, 1977.
The Golden Door: The United States from 1865 to 1918. Boston, Houghton Mifflin, and London, Dobson, 1977.
The Key Word and Other Mysteries (for children). New York, Walker, 1977.
Mars, The Red Planet (for children). New York, Lothrop, 1977.
Life and Time. New York, Doubleday, 1978.
Quasar, Quasar, Burning Bright. New York, Doubleday, 1978.
Animals of the Bible (for children). New York, Doubleday, 1978.
Isaac Asimov's Book of Facts. New York, Grosset and Dunlap, 1979; London, Hodder and Stoughton, 1980; abridged edition (for children), as *Would You Believe?* and *More . . . Would You Believe?*, Grosset and Dunlap, 2 vols., 1981–82.
Extraterrestrial Civilizations. New York, Crown, 1979; London, Robson, 1980.
A Choice of Catastrophes. New York, Simon and Schuster, 1979; London, Hutchinson, 1980.
Saturn and Beyond. New York, Lothrop, 1979.
Opus 200 (selection). Boston, Houghton Mifflin, 1979.
In Memory Yet Green: The Autobiography of Isaac Asimov 1920–1954. New York, Doubleday, 1979.
The Road to Infinity. New York, Doubleday, 1979.
In Joy Still Felt: The Autobiography of Isaac Asimov 1954–1978. New York, Doubleday, 1980.
The Annotated Gulliver's Travels. New York, Potter, 1980.
Opus (includes *Opus 100* and *Opus 200*). London, Deutsch, 1980.
Change! Seventy-One Glimpses of the Future. Boston, Houghton Mifflin, 1981.

Visions of the Universe, paintings by Kazuaki Iwasaki. Montrose, California, Cosmos Store, 1981.

Asimov on Science Fiction. New York, Doubleday, 1981; London, Granada, 1983.

Venus, Near Neighbor of the Sun (for children). New York, Lothrop, 1981.

The Sun Shines Bright. New York, Doubleday, 1981; London, Granada, 1984.

In the Beginning: Science Faces God in the Book of Genesis. New York, Crown, and London, New English Library, 1981.

Exploring the Earth and the Cosmos. New York, Crown, 1982; London, Allen Lane, 1983.

Counting the Eons. New York, Doubleday, 1983; London, Granada, 1984.

The Measure of the Universe. New York, Harper, 1983.

Those Amazing Electronic Thinking Machines! (for children). New York, Watts, 1983.

The Roving Mind. Buffalo, Prometheus, 1983.

Norby the Mixed-Up Robot (for children), with Janet Asimov. New York, Walker, 1983; London, Methuen, 1984.

X Stands for Unknown. New York, Doubleday, 1984; London, Granada, 1985.

Opus 300. Boston, Houghton Mifflin, 1984; London, Hale, 1985.

Norby's Other Secret (for children), with Janet Asimov. New York, Walker, 1984; London, Methuen, 1985.

Robots: Where the Machine Ends and Life Begins, with Karen A. Frenkel. New York, Crown, 1985.

The Exploding Suns: The Secrets of the Supernovas. New York, Dutton, and London, Joseph, 1985.

Asimov's Guide to Halley's Comet. New York, Walker, 1985.

The Subatomic Monster: Essays on Science. New York, Doubleday, 1985.

Norby and the Lost Princess (for children), with Janet Asimov. New York, Walker, 1985.

Editor, *Soviet Science Fiction* [and *More Soviet Science Fiction*]. New York, Collier, 2 vols., 1962.

Editor, *The Hugo Winners 1–4*. New York, Doubleday, 4 vols., 1962–85; *1* and *3*, London, Dobson, 2 vols., 1963–67; *2*, London, Sphere, 1973.

Editor, with Groff Conklin, *Fifty Short Science Fiction Tales*. New York, Collier, 1963.

Editor, *Tomorrow's Children: 18 Tales of Fantasy and Science Fiction*. New York, Doubleday, 1966; London, Futura, 1974.

Editor, *Where Do We Go from Here?* New York, Doubleday, 1971; London, Joseph, 1973.

Editor, *Nebula Award Stories 8*. New York, Harper, and London, Gollancz, 1973.

Editor, *Before the Golden Age: A Science Fiction Anthology of the 1930's*. New York, Doubleday, and London, Robson, 1974.

Editor, with Martin H. Greenberg and Joseph D. Olander, *100 Great Science Fiction Short-Short Stories*. New York, Doubleday, and London, Robson, 1978.

Editor, with Martin H. Greenberg and Charles G. Waugh, *The Science Fictional Solar System*. New York, Harper, 1979; London, Sidgwick and Jackson, 1980.

Editor, with Martin H. Greenberg and Charles G. Waugh, *The Thirteen Crimes of Science Fiction*. New York, Doubleday, 1979.

Editor, with Martin H. Greenberg, *The Great SF Stories 1–14*. New York, DAW, 1979–86.

Editor, with Martin H. Greenberg and Joseph D. Olander, *Microcosmic Tales: 100 Wondrous Science Fiction Short-*

Short Stories. New York, Taplinger, 1980.

Editor, with Martin H. Greenberg and Joseph D. Olander, *Space Mail 1*. New York, Fawcett, 1980.

Editor, with Martin H. Greenberg and Joseph D. Olander, *The Future in Question*. New York, Fawcett, 1980.

Editor, with Alice Laurance, *Who Done It?* Boston, Houghton Mifflin, 1980.

Editor, with Martin H. Greenberg and Charles G. Waugh, *The Seven Deadly Sins of Science Fiction*. New York, Fawcett, 1980.

Editor, with Martin H. Greenberg and Joseph D. Olander, *Miniature Mysteries: 100 Malicious Little Mystery Stories*. New York, Taplinger, 1981.

Editor, with Martin H. Greenberg and Charles G. Waugh, *Science Fiction Shorts* series (for children; includes *After the End*, *Thinking Machines*, *Travels Through Time*, *Wild Inventions*, *Mad Scientists*, *Mutants*, *Tomorrow's TV*, *Earth Invaded*, *Bug Awful*, *Children of the Future*, *The Immortals*, *Time Warps*). Milwaukee, Raintree, 12 vols., 1981–84.

Editor, *Fantastic Creatures*. New York, Watts, 1981.

Editor, with Charles G. Waugh and Martin H. Greenberg, *The Best Science Fiction* [*Fantasy, Horror and Supernatural*] *of the 19th Century*. New York, Beaufort, 3 vols., 1981–83; *Science Fiction*, London, Gollancz, 1983; *Fantasy* and *Horror and Supernatural*, London, Robson, 2 vols., 1985.

Editor, *Asimov's Marvels of Science Fiction*. London, Hale, 1981.

Editor, with Carol-Lynn Rössell Waugh and Martin H. Greenberg, *The Twelve Crimes of Christmas*. New York, Avon, 1981.

Editor, with Charles G. Waugh and Martin H. Greenberg, *The Seven Cardinal Virtues of Science Fiction*. New York, Fawcett, 1981.

Editor, with Martin H. Greenberg and Charles G. Waugh, *TV: 2000*. New York, Fawcett, 1982.

Editor, with Martin H. Greenberg and Charles G. Waugh, *Last Man on Earth*. New York, Fawcett, 1982.

Editor, with Charles G. Waugh and Martin H. Greenberg, *Tantalizing Locked Room Mysteries*. New York, Walker, 1982.

Editor, with Martin H. Greenberg and Charles G. Waugh, *Space Mail 2*. New York, Fawcett, 1982.

Editor, with J.O. Jeppson, *Laughing Space: Funny Science Fiction*. Boston, Houghton Mifflin, and London, Robson, 1982.

Editor, with Alice Laurance, *Speculations*. Boston, Houghton Mifflin, 1982.

Editor, with Charles G. Waugh and Martin H. Greenberg, *Science Fiction from A to Z: A Dictionary of the Great Themes of Science Fiction*. Boston, Houghton Mifflin, 1982.

Editor, with Martin H. Greenberg and Charles G. Waugh, *Flying Saucers*. New York, Fawcett, 1982.

Editor, with Martin H. Greenberg and Charles G. Waugh, *Dragon Tales*. New York, Fawcett, 1982.

Editor, *Asimov's Worlds of Science Fiction*. London, Hale, 1982.

Editor, with Martin H. Greenberg and Charles G. Waugh, *Hallucination Orbit: Psychology in Science Fiction*. New York, Farrar Straus, 1983.

Editor, with Martin H. Greenberg, *Magical Worlds of Fantasy* series (*Wizards*, *Witches*). New York, New American Library, 2 vols., 1983–84.

Editor, with Martin H. Greenberg and Charles G. Waugh, *Caught in the Organ Draft: Biology in Science Fiction*. New York, Farrar Straus, 1983.

Editor, *The Big Apple Mysteries.* New York, Avon, 1983.
Editor, with George R.R. Martin and Martin H. Greenberg, *The Science Fiction Weight-Loss Book.* New York, Crown, 1983.
Editor, with Martin H. Greenberg and Charles G. Waugh, *Starships.* New York, Ballantine, 1983.
Editor, *Asimov's Wonders of the World.* London, Hale, 1983.
Editor, with George Zebrowski and Martin H. Greenberg, *Creations: The Quest for Origins in Story and Science.* New York, Crown, 1983; London, Harrap, 1984.
Editor, with Martin H. Greenberg and Charles G. Waugh, *Computer Crimes and Capers.* Chicago, Academy, 1983; London, Viking, 1985.
Editor, with Patricia S. Warrick and Martin H. Greenberg, *Machines That Think.* New York, Holt Rinehart, and London, Allen Lane, 1984.
Editor, with Terry Carr and Martin H. Greenberg, *100 Great Fantasy Short Short Stories.* New York, Doubleday, and London, Robson, 1984.
Editor, with Charles G. Waugh and Martin H. Greenberg, *The Great Science Fiction Firsts.* New York, Beaufort, 1984; London, Robson, 1985.
Editor, with others, *Murder on the Menu.* New York, Avon, 1984.
Editor, with Martin H. Greenberg and Charles G. Waugh, *Sherlock Holmes Through Time and Space.* New York, Bluejay, 1984.
Editor, with Martin H. Greenberg, *Isaac Asimov's Wonderful World of Science Fiction 2: The Science Fictional Olympics.* New York, New American Library, 1984.
Editor, with Martin H. Greenberg and Charles G. Waugh, *Young Mutants* [*Extraterrestrials, Ghosts, Monsters*] (for children). New York, Harper, 4 vols., 1984–85.
Editor, with Martin H. Greenberg, *Election Day 2084: Stories about the Politics of the Future.* Buffalo, Prometheus, 1984.
Editor, with Martin H. Greenberg and Charles G. Waugh, *Great Science Fiction Stories by the World's Great Scientists.* New York, Fine, 1985.
Editor, *Living in the Future.* New York, Beaufort, 1985.
Editor, with Martin H. Greenberg and Charles G. Waugh, *Giants.* New York, New American Library, 1985.
Editor, with Martin H. Greenberg, *Amazing Stories: 60 Years of the Best Science Fiction.* Lake Geneva, Wisconsin, TSR, 1985.

*

Bibliography: *Isaac Asimov: A Checklist of Works Published in the United States March 1939–May 1972* by Marjorie M. Miller, Kent, Ohio, Kent State University Press, 1972; in *In Joy Still Felt*, 1980.

Manuscript Collection: Mugar Memorial Library, Boston University.

Critical Studies: *Asimov Analyzed* by Neil Goble, Baltimore, Mirage Press, 1972; *The Science Fiction of Isaac Asimov* by Joseph F. Patrouch, Jr., New York, Doubleday, 1974, London, Panther, 1976; *Isaac Asimov* edited by Joseph D. Olander and Martin H. Greenberg, New York, Taplinger, and Edinburgh, Harris, 1977; *Asimov: The Foundations of His Science Fiction* by George Edgar Slusser, San Bernardino, California, Borgo Press, 1980; *Isaac Asimov: The Foundations of Science Fiction* by James Gunn, New York and Oxford, Oxford University Press, 1982; *Isaac Asimov* by Jean Fiedler and Jim Mele, New York, Ungar, 1982.

Isaac Asimov comments:
If there is any category of human being for whom his work ought to speak for itself, it is the writer. If people *insist* on hearing from me, there are my books *Opus 100, Opus 200, The Early Asimov, Before the Golden Age, In Memory Yet Green,* and *In Joy Still Felt,* in which I tell people far more about me than they probably want to know.

*   *   *

In the long writing career that began in his teen years, Isaac Asimov has been credited with the most inventive mind in science fiction. He has also been declared a masterful psychological writer, skillful puzzlist, and the shaper of contemporary popular expectations for robots (the very term "robotics" is his). Called a Renaissance humanist despite being an academic biochemist, he is also regarded as a facile propagandist for mankind's survival—or revival—and the most prolific author of modern times.

Only the final title is unassailable. Along with Asimov's unequalled torrent of words in the forms of novels, short stories, essays, verse, reviews, columns, articles and other non-fiction (largely science and history) there is his growing role as a lecturer and television personality and his public acceptance as a scientific seer with particular insight into the future of the universe. To call him a one-man industry strikes too sour a note, but since it is likely that all works in an immense body are not equal, evaluating Asimov involves the choice of works which are influential even though brief, as well as of what may endure over what simply exists.

Asimov's single greatest contribution to science fiction is not so much that he has made millions of uninquiring readers aware of the scientific underpinnings of existence—although he has done that. More important, Asimov is the writer who most clearly established the science fiction thesis that the future is one of alternatives—good or bad—and that there are choices to be made by beings along the way. This sets him apart from most of his peers in science fiction's Golden Age, from a Robert Meinlein whose serene optimism holds that Man will live forever, or an Arthur C. Clarke who regards Man as fixed in place at the top of a hierarchy. Asimov's long-popular Foundation novels (*Foundation, Foundation and Empire,* and *Second Foundation*) bear out his favorite proposal that there is a way to survive, but first there must be a will to do so—the first of all good choices.

Other Asimov works reflect such scientifically based proposals as that while the struggle for survival may mean overpowering enemies through wit or might, it is also just as likely to mean adapting to an environment, as in *The Caves of Steel.* An even more obvious choice and perhaps science fiction's most famous story is Asimov's "Nightfall." In that story, a civilization doomed to see its four suns fade and slowly die, moves from near-despair to rekindled hope when it awakens from darkness to find a sky abloom with stars, then gropingly turns to its own resources and invents that tiniest of man-made stars, the candle.

This story, like even his least successful novels, probably provides the clue to why Asimov is an undeniably popular writer. Not only is he scientifically in touch with his time, but he is morally gratifying to readers. The "lessons" of alien life in far-off galaxies in future time also fit today's Main Street, the office, the club, the college dorm. The facts that Asimov characters generally avoid the mangled English assumed to be Futurespeak in favor of current usage and that they are physically recognizable as human, if "advanced," also cement the strong identity of Asimov readers with Asimov characters.

As the author once put it, "I couldn't make a character who speaks through his ears."

Perhaps too much has been made of Asimov's robots whose computered brains serve humans in line with Asimov's Three Laws of Robotics—in summary: robots cooperate with humans. Asimov himself has not precisely settled the question of free will in an inanimate object which nontheless partakes of an artificial intelligence. Thus his Three Laws add up to a single dodge of the issue. Through uncritical readers, however, the "laws" have filtered into popular if unfounded expectations for robots. The most widely read robot works are probably the stories which form *I, Robot.*

Another popular collection which shows his varying success at melding the traditional detective story with science fiction is *Asimov's Mysteries.* Among his best delineations of character are those in *Pebble in the Sky* and *The Stars, Like Dust. Prisoners of the Stars* is perhaps the most convenient sampler for readers new to his fiction.

Asimov is not widely regarded as much of a stylist, thus denying him the literary stature of a Clarke or a Ray Bradbury. Having learned to write by imitating, then outdoing, the early science-fiction writers he read in the magazines sold at his father's candy shop, Asimov actually had many good teachers in them. He retains their simple, readable, strongly-plotted style and his imagination twists old plots easily. The situations (speculations like "What if—") which send him off on a story are scientifically sound. Yet without gifts of evocative language or even a particularly good ear for dialogue, Asimov has increasingly fallen back on his interest in psychology to lace his works with behavioral insights, some simply too predictable or too pat. Oddly enough, just as Asimov had a good editor in his youth, John W. Campbell, he himself has proven to be a discriminating editor in his choices for the many science-fiction anthologies which he has produced.

Asimov's reputation clearly rests on the works written when both he and science fiction were younger. His recent novels tend to pontificate needlessly and have slowed to a pace at times deliberate if not turgid. In his 1985 *Robots and Empire,* Asimov attempts to link his robot novels with his Foundation series through a few surviving characters from each. This synthesis of the robots Daneel and Giskard with Lady Gladia, the stranded lover of a Foundation hero, into a new threesome may serve Asimov's sweeping Hegelian views of history. However such out-of-their-element leaders are unlikely to convince readers that the trio could ever stop the book's impending interstellar war.

Fortunately Asimov's reputation is not likely to suffer from his later fiction. He is justly respected for the spontaneous stories that he spun out so readily when the young scientist's "What if —" became the young writer's exhilarating look into distant time and space.

—Marian Pehowski

ASTLEY, Thea (Beatrice May). Australian. Born in Brisbane, Queensland, 25 August 1925. Educated at the University of Queensland, Brisbane, 1943–47, B.A. 1947. Married Edmund John Gregson in 1948; one son. English teacher in Queensland, 1944–48, and in New South Wales, 1948–67. Since 1968, Senior Tutor, then Fellow in English, Macquarie University, Sydney; now retired. Recipient: Commonwealth Literary Fund fellowship, 1961, 1964; Miles Franklin Award, 1963, 1966, 1973; Moomba Award, 1965; *The Age* Book of the Year Award, 1975. Address: P.O. Box 213, Kuranda, North Queensland 4872, Australia.

PUBLICATIONS

Novels

Girl with a Monkey.   Sydney, Angus and Robertson, 1958.
A Descant for Gossips.   Sydney and London, Angus and Robertson, 1960.
The Well-Dressed Explorer.   Sydney and London, Angus and Robertson, 1962.
The Slow Natives.   Sydney, Angus and Robertson, 1965; London, Angus and Robertson, 1966; New York, Evans, 1967.
A Boat Load of Home Folk.   Sydney and London, Angus and Robertson, 1968; New York, Penguin, 1983.
The Acolyte.   Sydney and London, Angus and Robertson, 1972.
A Kindness Cup.   Melbourne, Nelson, 1974.
An Item from the Late News.   St. Lucia, University of Queensland Press, 1982; New York, Penguin, 1984.
Beachmasters.   Ringwood, Victoria, Penguin, 1985.

Short Stories

Hunting the Wild Pineapple.   Melbourne, Nelson, 1979.

Uncollected Short Stories

"Cubby," in *Coast to Coast.*   Sydney, Angus and Robertson, 1961.
"The Scenery Never Changes," in *Coast to Coast.*   Sydney, Angus and Robertson, 1963.
"Journey to Olympus," in *Coast to Coast.*   Sydney, Angus and Robertson, 1965.
"Seeing Mrs. Landers," in *Festival and Other Stories,* edited by Brian Buckley and Jim Hamilton.   Melbourne, Wren, 1974; Newton Abbot, Devon, David and Charles, 1975.

Other

Editor, *Coast to Coast, 1969–1970.*   Sydney, Angus and Robertson, 1971.

*

Critical Study: "The Idiot Question" by Astley, in *Southerly 1* (Sydney), 1970.

Thea Astley comments:

(1972) My main interest (and has been through my five published and current unpublished novels) is the misfit. Not the spectacular outsider, but the seedy little non-grandiose nonfitter who lives in his own mini-hell. Years ago I was impressed at eighteen or so by *Diary of a Nobody,* delighted by the quality Grossmith gave to the non-achiever and the sympathy which he dealt out. My five published novels have always been, despite the failure of reviewers to see it, a plea for charity—in the Pauline sense, of course—to be accorded to those not ruthless enough or grand enough to be gigantic tragic figures, but which, in their own way, record the same *via crucis.*

*   *   *

Towards the end of Thea Astley's fifth novel (*A Boat Load of Home Folk*) a hurricane descends upon Port Lena and rages violently while the problems and personal crises of the various characters draw towards some sort of resolution. The hurricane as a destructive natural phenomenon is slightly unusual in the imaginative world of Thea Astley, but, as a symbol, it is not at all unfamiliar. For her characters seem to move perpetually in the artificially calm eye of the universe's innate anarchy: a symbolic storm encloses, yet also by its very existence and threatening nature, divides them. Moving in this constantly endangered pseudo-equilibrium, they brush often the edges of disaster, succumb to it occasionally, make what order they can with the opportunities that offer.

The impending, eager-to-consume anarchy of Astley's world is manifested variously: it can materialise as the chaos of the emotional life, that destroys identity, reduces "to a spineless receptivity" (*Girl with a Monkey*); it may take the form of spiritual annihilation by human viciousness exquisitely applied and cravenly veiled (*A Descant for Gossips*); or act through the confusing yet endlessly fascinating impulses of the uncomprehended self (*The Well-Dressed Explorer*); or emerge as that fatal disjunction from an intolerable world, experienced by those who, like "the wandering islands" of A.D. Hope's poem, ply "the long isolation of the heart" (*The Slow Natives*). Anarchy of a kind crowds in upon Astley's characters and they have few resources with which to resist it.

Because the action is caught, as it were, in the eye of the symbolic storm, her novels, especially the earlier ones, seem at times highly, even excessively, deliberated: characters move in a real enough world, yet often with fleetingly dream-like deliberateness, islands of intense self-consciousness seeking, in assertive almost desperate avowals of identity, bastions against encroaching chaos. Thus Elsie, in *Girl with a Monkey*, is "caught static in a complete island of twenty-four hours"—a metaphor which continually reinforces a sense of extreme deliberation in action and thought. When she hears, at Mass "as through walls of water," it is an apt and summary image for the action of the whole book; similarly, Mrs. Crozier is pictured as moving "Almost epileptically . . . pruning as she went the ambient roses . . . ." In *A Descant for Gossips* the tragic relationship between Helen, Miller, and Vinny is captured, with momentary statuesqueness at its vey inception, as "a dangerous montage," while at the end of the book, Vinny, coming to her crucial decision, is described as seeing everything with "an amazing clarity . . . the grass stood in millions of separate blades, green and sharp . . . " This has that quality of the dream that is not blurred and vague but horrifically more real than real. Again, George Brewster, hero of *The Well-Dressed Explorer*, builds his life on fantasy views of himself and dies in a "dream-streaked sleep" in which that life is paraded, insanely truncated, yet paradoxically illuminating and immensely moving. A similar quality is discoverable, though it is admittedly less obvious amidst a growing complexity, in the remaining two books.

This deliberation, even if it is occasionally overdone, is no mere quirk of "style," it is a quality, a condition, in the characters' lives and an element in the Astley universe. And it is necessary, indeed indispensable, if the people are to affirm identity and a concept of order in the face of a chaos of evil, sordidness, deadly triviality, and cavernous loneliness.

It is difficult to determine what real weapons her characters have in this essentially rearguard action against a universe morally and spiritually anarchic. Perhaps love, but that is plagued by infidelity, impediment, or possessiveness; perhaps the child's innocence, but in this world, that innocence, followed out, brings Vinny Lalor and Keith Leverson to tragedy or near tragedy; perhaps religion. Thea Astley is certainly preoccupied with Catholic experience and upbringing, with Catholicism as

an influence on personality and intellect and with the guilt and neurosis traditionally associated with Catholic sexual morality. But religion is not much comfort in the eye of the storm: it is at best irrelevant, at worst grotesque. Indeed grotesquerie and corruption become inseparable from Catholicism in Astley's vision, even if she suggests, in a way reminiscent of Greene, a road to sanctity through intimate knowledge of sin. A deeply personal conflict between religious commitment and revulsion against unhealthy inhibition and veiled corruption seems to be involved. It may be that in *A Boat Load of Home Folk*, where almost excessive sordidness and grotesqueness seem to suggest something like purgation, this conflict has reached a resolution.

Following that novel, Astley published *The Acolyte*—a brilliant, complex portrayal of the egocentric artist who enslaves and preys upon everyone around him, the more exquisitely and ruthlessly because he is blind. Like Brewster, but with much greater sophistication and intent, he creates chaos everywhere. *The Acolyte*, together with *A Kindness Cup*—a tense, remorseless study of fear and guilt which won *The Age* Book of the Year Award—marks one of the peaks of Astley's continuing achievements in the novel form.

After Astley retired from her position at Macquarie University in Sydney she returned to North Queensland. With greater leisure and remote from interruptions in her tropical eyrie, she turned her attention to short stories, reflecting her new surroundings and perspective in a collection entitled *Hunting The Wild Pineapple*. These witty, engaging but sometimes savagely pungent stories are told in a characteristically dense, sometimes staccato style which never slips into tortuousness. The wounded and the misfits are all there; life is as uncontrollable as always. But the occasional straining for effect of earlier books is replaced by a marvellous confidence and control as a now middle-aged, quizzical Keith Leverson (of *The Slow Natives*) casts a tolerant eye over life in an ambiguous, tropical "Eden."

Two further books followed in quick succession. *An Item from the Late News* depicts events in the unlovely township of "Allbut"—classic Astley country where tensions, violence, and corrosive resentments stirred up by an eccentric anti-nuclear protester wait poised for the trigger that will release them. *Beachmasters* looks outward into the Pacific where a brief, unsuccessful revolution on a small island stands as that haunting hurricane presence that decides the fates of so many of Astley's struggling, vulnerably human characters.

Astley's work, now a major and substantial presence in contemporary Australian literature, still receives less attention than it merits from professional critics. But this does not alter the fact that she is one of the most significant and innovative of Australian writers.

—Brian E. Matthews

ATWOOD, Margaret (Eleanor). Canadian. Born in Ottawa, Ontario, 18 November 1939. Educated at Victoria College, University of Toronto, B.A. 1961; Radcliffe College, Cambridge, Massachusetts, A.M. 1962; Harvard University, Cambridge, Massachusetts 1962–63, 1965–67. Divorced; one daughter. Lecturer in English, University of British Columbia, Vancouver, 1964–65; Instructor in English, Sir George Williams University, Montreal, 1967–68; Assistant Professor of English, York University, Toronto, 1971–72. Writer-in-

Residence, University of Toronto, 1972–73. Recipient: E.J. Pratt Medal, 1961; President's Medal, University of Western Ontario, 1965; Governor-General's Award, 1966; Centennial Commission prize, for poetry, 1967; Union League Civic and Arts Foundation Prize, 1969, and Bess Hokin Prize, 1974 (*Poetry*, Chicago); City of Toronto award, 1976; St. Lawrence Award, 1977; Radcliffe Medal, 1980; Molson Award, 1981; Guggenheim fellowship, 1981; Welsh Arts Council International Writers Prize, 1982. D.Litt.: Trent University, Peterborough, Ontario, 1973; Concordia University, Montreal, 1980; LL.D.: Queen's University, Kingston, Ontario, 1974. Companion, Order of Canada, 1981. Agent: Phoebe Larmore, 2814 Third Street, Santa Monica, California 90405, U.S.A. Address: c/o Oxford University Press, 70 Wynford Drive, Don Mills, Ontario M3C 1J9, Canada.

PUBLICATIONS

Novels

The Edible Woman. Toronto, McClelland and Stewart, London, Deutsch, and Boston, Little Brown, 1969.
Surfacing. Toronto, McClelland and Stewart, 1972; London, Deutsch, and New York, Simon and Schuster, 1973.
Lady Oracle. Toronto, McClelland and Stewart, and New York, Simon and Schuster, 1976; London, Deutsch, 1977.
Life Before Man. Toronto, McClelland and Stewart, 1979; New York, Simon and Schuster, and London, Cape, 1980.
Bodily Harm. Toronto, McClelland and Stewart, 1981; New York, Simon and Schuster, and London, Cape, 1982.
The Handmaid's Tale. Boston, Houghton Mifflin, 1986.

Short Stories

Dancing Girls and Other Stories. Toronto, McClelland and Stewart, 1977; New York, Simon and Schuster, and London, Cape, 1982.
Encounters with the Element Man. Concord, New Hampshire, Ewert, 1982.
Murder in the Dark: Short Fictions and Prose Poems. Toronto, Coach House Press, 1983; London, Cape, 1984.
Bluebeard's Egg. Toronto, McClelland and Stewart, 1983.
Unearthing Suite. Toronto, Grand Union Press, 1983.

Plays

Television Plays: *The Servant Girl*, 1974; *Snowbird*, 1981.

Verse

Double Persephone. Toronto, Hawkshead Press, 1961.
The Circle Game (single poem). Bloomfield Hills, Michigan, Cranbrook Academy of Art, 1964.
Talismans for Children. Bloomfield Hills, Michigan, Cranbrook Academy of Art, 1965.
Kaleidoscopes: Baroque. Bloomfield Hills, Michigan, Cranbrook Academy of Art, 1965.
Speeches for Doctor Frankenstein. Bloomfield Hills, Michigan, Cranbrook Academy of Art, 1966.
The Circle Game (collection). Toronto, Contact Press, 1966.
Expeditions. Bloomfield Hills, Michigan, Cranbrook Academy of Art, 1966.
Who Was in the Garden. Santa Barbara, California, Unicorn, 1969.
The Animals in That County. Boston, Little Brown, 1969.

Five Modern Canadian Poets, with others, edited by Eli Mandel. Toronto, Holt Rinehart, 1970.
The Journals of Susanna Moodie. Toronto, Oxford University Press, 1970.
Procedures for Underground. Boston, Little Brown, 1970.
Power Politics. Toronto, Anansi, 1971; New York, Harper, 1973.
You Are Happy. New York, Harper, 1974.
Selected Poems. Toronto, Oxford University Press, 1976; New York, Simon and Schuster, 1978.
Marsh, Hawk. Toronto, Dreadnaught, 1977.
Two-Headed Poems. Toronto, Oxford University Press, 1978; New York, Simon and Schuster, 1980.
True Stories. Toronto, Oxford University Press, 1981; New York, Simon and Schuster, and London, Cape, 1982.
Notes Towards a Poem That Can Never Be Written. Toronto, Salamander Press, 1981.
Snake Poems. Toronto, Salamander Press, 1983.
Interlunar. Toronto, Oxford University Press, 1984.

Recording: *The Poetry and Voice of Margaret Atwood*, Caedmon, 1977.

Other

Survival: A Thematic Guide to Canadian Literature. Toronto, Anansi, 1972.
Days of the Rebels 1815–1840. Toronto, Natural Science of Canada, 1977.
Up in the Tree (for children). Toronto, McClelland and Stewart, 1978.
Anna's Pet (for children), with Joyce Barkhouse. Toronto, Lorimer, 1980.
Second Words: Selected Critical Prose. Toronto, Anansi, 1982; Boston, Beacon Press, 1984.

Editor, *The New Oxford Book of Canadian Verse in English.* Toronto, New York, and Oxford, Oxford University Press, 1983.

*

Bibliography: "Margaret Atwood: An Annotated Bibliography (Prose)" and "(Verse)" by Alan J. Horne, in *The Annotated Bibliography of Canada's Major Authors 1–2* edited by Robert Lecker and Jack David, Downsview, Ontario, ECW Press, 2 vols., 1979–80.

Manuscript Collection: Fisher Library, University of Toronto.

Critical Studies: *Margaret Atwood: A Symposium* edited by Linda Sandler, Victoria, British Columbia, University of Victoria, 1977; *A Violent Duality* by Sherril Grace, Montreal, Véhicule Press, 1979, and *Margaret Atwood: Language, Text, and System* edited by Grace and Lorraine Weir, Vancouver, University of British Columbia Press, 1983; *The Art of Margaret Atwood: Essays in Criticism* edited by Arnold E. and Cathy N. Davidson, Toronto, Anansi, 1981; *Margaret Atwood* by Jerome H. Rosenberg, Boston, Twayne, 1984; *Margaret Atwood: A Feminist Poetics* by Frank Davey, Vancouver, Talonbooks, 1984.

*   *   *

Margaret Atwood is one of Canada's most versatile writers, a fine poet with several collections to her credit, a critic whose *Survival* and *Second Words* offer significant insights into Canadian writers and writing, and the author of six novels.

The capillary links between Atwood's poetry, fiction, and criticism are many and clear. The relationship between her first novel, *The Edible Woman*, and her poems of the same period is so close that the best way of saying what the novel is about is to quote a verse from her early collection *The Circle Game*:

> These days we keep
> our weary distances
> sparring in the vacant spaces
> of peeling rooms
> and rented minutes, climbing
> all the expected stairs, our voices
> abraded with fatigue
> our bodies weary.

The Edible Woman too is about distances and defences between human beings, necessary because all are predators. *The Edible Woman* deals with emotional cannibalism; its title names the central image. The edible woman is a cake shaped like a woman and iced for verisimilitude, which the heroine—Marian McAlpin—eats at the key point of the novel, when she is released from the doggedly conventional life she has been following. Having trapped a highly normal young man into a proposal of marriage, Marian feels herself the victim of his emotional anthropophagy. Victor and victim are one. Marian's recognition of her situation takes the form of a symbolic neurosis. First her tongue closes against meat as she associates it with the living animal, then against vegetables whose agonies she imagines; finally, having tried to escape her marriage and found that escape only makes her another kind of victim, she bakes the edible women, offers the cake to her shocked fiancé, and then eats it herself. In consuming the artificial "normal" being she tried to become, she is made whole.

If one associates *The Edible Woman* with Atwood's early poems, one associates *Surfacing* with the similarly titled critical work, *Survival*, which explores the theme of the victim and his evasion of destruction as exemplified in Canadian writing. *Surfacing* resembles *The Edible Woman* in being an account of a *rite de passage*; it is a novel of self-realization, hence of life-realization, but it also contains a strong element of self-mockery. Hearing of her father's disappearance from his cabin on a northern lake, the narrator goes there with three companions, all fake *emancipés*. It is a journey into her past, but also, though she does not recognize this immediately, into her true self. She is significantly nameless, though she names her companions. "I" is at first in a state of inner apathy; she cannot absorb or generate human feeling. She describes herself as just a head, untouched and untouching. Yet, through events that explode out of her return to childhood's scenes, she recovers herself as a whole being. It is a process of surfacing, but only after submersion. The metaphors of drowning recur. Her brother is almost drowned as a child; her father, she discovers, drowned searching for Indian paintings on a rock wall falling sheer to the lake; her own crisis is precipitated when, diving to locate the paintings, she encounters her father's floating corpse; her surfacing becomes almost literally a rising from death into life.

By this time other realizations have surfaced. "I" must shed all she had acquired, unlearn adulthood, return through childhood, and become like the victim animals, as she is when, fleeing from her companions and living like a beast, she returns to a consciousness beyond the animistic. The gods have departed; she is alone: "The lake is quiet, the trees surround me, asking and giving nothing." One senses, as the novel ends, that benign indifference of the universe of which Camus spoke.

In many ways *Lady Oracle* resembles its predecessors. Joan Foster, alias Louisa K. Delacourt, is obsessed with food and morbidly dominated by her parents. Her life exemplifies the abrasive nature of sexual relations; during the whole period of the novel Joan is in flight from marriage, hiding in a sordid Italian coast resort town, pretending to be dead. *Lady Oracle* differs from the earlier novels in the sureness of its comedy and the satirical intensity of its portrayal of Canadian bourgeois life, both philistine and bohemian. An obsessive eater who slims to win an inheritance that will liberate her, Joan has her fat and thin personalities. Out of them emerge both the romantic novelist, Louisa K. Delacourt, and Joan Foster the psychic poet, in which role she becomes involved in the vagaries of the Canadian literary world. Perhaps most impressive in *Lady Oracle* is the way Atwood has parodically reused old themes and devices, the divided personality, the resentment of child against parent, the inherent hostility in long relations between men and women, and has raised them to a higher level through a remarkable adeptness in the devices of comedy. Indeed, it is the sustained and uninhibited comic tone that secures Atwood's fictional achievement in *Lady Oracle* from any doubt that she can maintain her role as a novelist and avoid being caught in a groove of merely poetic fiction.

Life Before Man, a muted narrative of emotional conflicts among employees of the Royal Ontario Museum, seems a marking of time. It has all the virtues Wilde once attributed to James—"his neat literary style, his felicitous phrases, his swift and caustic satire"—but it disturbingly tends to negate the presupposition on which the novel has been traditionally based, that the lives of men and women necessarily have a value worth cherishing. All such assumptions are thrown into doubt in a book that rejects the illusions of hope. I suspect *Life Before Man* does not reject compassion as well, but Atwood is strangely reticent about declaring it in this curiously reserved book.

In both Atwood's most recent novels, *Bodily Harm* and *The Handmaid's Tale*, the inclination towards parody already shown in *Lady Oracle* is further developed, for in each the author uses in an ironic way a type of fiction that has become popular in recent times—*Bodily Harm* the quasi-political thriller and *The Handmaid's Tale* the futurist fantasy, and both are largely saved by the sophistication with which parody is used to create the structure but never to subvert the meaning.

Bodily Harm, though it is not in intent a political tract, undoubtedly originated from the feelings generated when Atwood became for a period involved in near-political activity as a volunteer for Amnesty International; the place in which the heroine finds her life turning awry is one of the areas in which the victims Amnesty cares for are likely to be found. She flees from a consumer-oriented Canadian urban environment rather like that of *The Edible Woman* to what she feels must be the more natural existence of a small Caribbean island. There she becomes involved in a brutal political coup described with such stark authenticity that when the Grenada crisis occurred shortly after its publication, *Bodily Harm* read like a prophecy. Her life is imperilled, her sensibilities are violated, but she had learnt the lessons about the realities of power and suffering in most of the modern world, from which contemporary North American society had insulated her. While Atwood's earlier novels dealt with private problems, *Bodily Harm* deals largely with public ills, and this fact and the book's narrative strength make it arguably her best novel to date.

The Handmaid's Tale is a futurist story with a twist, since the future Atwood envisages in fact turns resolutely towards the past in a Republic of Gilead, not too many years ahead; there all the hopes of contemporary religious fundamentalists are realized in a society where the family is sanctified and in the name of Christianity women find the kind of place Hitler once allotted to them, attending the kitchen and the cradle. Satire, in *The Handmaid's Tale*, is expressed in the deadpan descriptiveness with which the absurd rules and customs of Gilead are shown in action, but in the absence of credible human conflict *The Handmaid's Tale* shows a defect shared by most futurist function, and the novel can best be considered an ingenious but tentative exercise by a versatile writer.

—George Woodcock

AUCHINCLOSS, Louis (Stanton). American. Born in Lawrence, New York, 27 September 1917. Educated at Groton School, Massachusetts, graduated 1935; Yale University, New Haven, Connecticut, 1935–38; University of Virginia Law School, Charlottesville, LL.B. 1941; admitted to the New York Bar, 1941. Served in the United States Naval Reserve, 1941–45: Lieutenant. Married Adèle Lawrence in 1957; three sons. Associate Lawyer, Sullivan and Cromwell, New York, 1941–51. Associate, 1954–58, and since 1958 Partner, Hawkins Delafield and Wood, New York. Since 1966, President of the Museum of the City of New York. Trustee, Josiah Macy Jr. Foundation, New York; former member of the Executive Committee, Association of the Bar of New York City. D.Litt.: New York University, 1974; Pace College, New York, 1979. Member, American Academy. Agent: Curtis Brown, 10 Astor Place, New York, New York 10003. Address: 1111 Park Avenue, New York, New York 10028, U.S.A.

PUBLICATIONS

Novels

The Indifferent Children (as Andrew Lee). New York, Prentice Hall, 1947.
Sybil. Boston, Houghton Mifflin, 1951; London, Gollancz, 1952.
A Law for the Lion. Boston, Houghton Mifflin, and London, Gollancz, 1953.
The Great World and Timothy Colt. Boston, Houghton Mifflin, 1956; London, Gollancz, 1957.
Venus in Sparta. Boston, Houghton Mifflin, and London, Gollancz, 1958.
Pursuit of the Prodigal. Boston, Houghton Mifflin, 1959; London, Gollancz, 1960.
The House of Five Talents. Boston, Houghton Mifflin, 1960; London, Gollancz, 1961.
Portrait in Brownstone. Boston, Houghton Mifflin, and London, Gollancz, 1962.
The Rector of Justin. Boston, Houghton Mifflin, 1964; London, Gollancz, 1965.
The Embezzler. Boston, Houghton Mifflin, and London, Gollancz, 1966.
A World of Profit. Boston, Houghton Mifflin, 1968; London, Gollancz, 1969.
I Come as a Thief. Boston, Houghton Mifflin, 1972; London, Weidenfeld and Nicolson, 1973.
The Partners. Boston, Houghton Mifflin, and London, Weidenfeld and Nicolson, 1974.
The Winthrop Covenant. Boston, Houghton Mifflin, and London, Weidenfeld and Nicolson, 1976.

The Dark Lady. Boston, Houghton Mifflin, and London, Weidenfeld and Nicolson, 1977.
The Country Cousin. Boston, Houghton Mifflin, and London, Weidenfeld and Nicolson, 1978.
The House of the Prophet. Boston, Houghton Mifflin, and London, Weidenfeld and Nicolson, 1980.
The Cat and the King. Boston, Houghton Mifflin, and London, Weidenfeld and Nicolson, 1981.
Watchfires. Boston, Houghton Mifflin, and London, Weidenfeld and Nicolson, 1982.
Exit Lady Masham. Boston, Houghton Mifflin, 1983; London, Weidenfeld and Nicolson, 1984.
The Book Class. Boston, Houghton Mifflin, and London, Weidenfeld and Nicolson, 1984.
Honorable Men. Boston, Houghton Mifflin, 1985.

Short Stories

The Injustice Collectors. Boston, Houghton Mifflin, 1950; London, Gollancz, 1951.
The Romantic Egoists: A Reflection in Eight Minutes. Boston, Houghton Mifflin, and London, Gollancz, 1954.
Powers of Attorney. Boston, Houghton Mifflin, and London, Gollancz, 1963.
Tales of Manhattan. Boston, Houghton Mifflin, and London, Gollancz, 1967.
Second Chance. Boston, Houghton Mifflin, 1970; London, Gollancz, 1971.
Narcissa and Other Fables. Boston, Houghton Mifflin, 1983.

Uncollected Short Stories

"The Adventures of Johnny Flashback," in *Saturday Review* (New York), 22 October 1955.
"The Trial of Mr. M.," in *Harper's* (New York), October 1956.

Play

The Club Bedroom (produced New York, 1967).

Other

Edith Wharton. Minneapolis, University of Minnesota Press, 1961.
Reflections of a Jacobite. Boston, Houghton Mifflin, 1961; London, Gollancz, 1962.
Ellen Glasgow. Minneapolis, University of Minnesota Press, 1964.
Pioneers and Caretakers: A Study of 9 American Women Novelists. Minneapolis, University of Minnesota Press, 1965; London, Oxford University Press, 1966.
Motiveless Malignity (on Shakespeare). Boston, Houghton Mifflin, 1969; London, Gollancz, 1970.
Henry Adams. Minneapolis, University of Minnesota Press, 1971.
Edith Wharton: A Woman in Her Time. New York, Viking Press, 1971; London, Joseph, 1972.
Richelieu. New York, Viking Press, 1972; London, Joseph, 1973.
A Writer's Capital (autobiography). Minneapolis, University of Minnesota Press, 1974.
Reading Henry James. Minneapolis, University of Minnesota Press, 1975.
Persons of Consequence: Queen Victoria and Her Circle. New York, Random House, and London, Weidenfeld and Nicolson, 1979.

Life, Law, and Letters: Essays and Sketches. Boston, Houghton Mifflin, 1979; London, Weidenfeld and Nicolson, 1980.
Three "Perfect Novels" and What They Have in Common. Bloomfield Hills, Michigan, Bruccoli Clark, 1981.
Unseen Versailles. New York, Doubleday, 1981.
False Dawn: Women in the Age of the Sun King. New York, Doubleday, 1984.

Editor, *An Edith Wharton Reader.* New York, Scribner, 1965.
Editor, *The Warden, and Barchester Towers*, by Trollope. Boston, Houghton Mifflin, 1966.
Editor, *Fables of Wit and Elegance.* New York, Scribner, 1975.
Editor, *Maverick in Mauve: The Diary of a Turn-of-the-Century Aristocrat*, by Florence Adele Sloane. New York, Doubleday, 1983.

*

Bibliography: *Louis Auchincloss and His Critics: A Bibliographical Record* by Jackson R. Bryer, Boston, Hall, 1977.

Manuscript Collection: University of Virginia, Charlottesville.

Critical Studies: *The Novel of Manners in America* by James W. Tuttleton, Chapel Hill, University of North Carolina Press, 1972; *Louis Auchincloss* by Christopher Dahl, New York, Ungar, 1985.

Louis Auchincloss comments:

(1972) I do not think in general that authors are very illuminating on their own work, but in view of the harshness of recent (1970) reviewers, I should like to quote from a letter of Edith Wharton in my collection. It was written when she was 63, ten years older than I now am, but the mood is relevant. She is speaking of critics who have disliked her last novel: "You will wonder that the priestess of the life of reason should take such things to heart, and I wonder too. I never have minded before, but as my work reaches its close, I feel so sure that it is either nothing or far more than they know. And I wonder, a little desolately, which." Mrs. Wharton's work was far from its close, and I hope mine may be!

*   *   *

Louis Auchincloss is among the few dedicated novelists of manners at work in contemporary America. He is a successor to Edith Wharton as a chronicler of the New York aristocracy. In this role he necessarily imbues his novels with an elegiac tone as he observes the passing beauties of the city and the fading power of the white Anglo-Saxon Protestants of old family and old money who can no longer sustain their position of dominance in the society or their aristocratic ideals. His principal subject is thus the manners and morals, the money and marriages, the families and houses, the schools and games, the language and arts of the New York aristocracy as he traces its rise, observes its present crisis, and meditates its possible fall and disappearance. The point of vantage from which he often observes the aristocracy is that of the lawyer who serves and frequently belongs to this class.

The idea of good family stands in an uneasy relation to money in Auchincloss's fiction. Auchincloss dramatizes the dilemma of the American aristocracy by showing that it is necessary to possess money to belong to this class but fatal to one's standing within the class to pursue money. People who have connections with those who are still in trade cannot themselves fully

qualify as gentlemen, as the opportunistic Mr. Dale in *The Great World and Timothy Colt* shows. On the other hand, Auchincloss is clearly critical of those aristocrats like Bertie Millinder or Percy Prime who do nothing constructive and are engaged simply in the spending of money. Auchincloss recognizes that the family is the most important of aristocratic institutions and that its place in its class is guaranteed by the conservation of its resources. This task of preserving the family wealth falls to the lawyers, and his fiction is rich in the complexities, both moral and financial, of fiduciary responsibility; *Venus in Sparta* is a novel in point. The paradox that Auchincloss reveals but does not seem sufficiently to exploit is that the conservative impulse of the aristocracy, which emphasizes the past, is concerned ultimately with posterity, which of course emphasizes the future.

Auchincloss does, however, fully exploit the conflict between the marriage arranged for the good of the family, often by strong women, and romantic or sexual impulses that are destructive of purely social goals, as *Portrait in Brownstone* illustrates. Sex and love are enemies to the organicism of conservative societies, in which the will of the individual is vested in the whole. Auchincloss observes the workings of this organic notion in the structure of family and marriage as well as in institutions like the school and the club where a consensus judgment about value and behaviour is formulated and handed down. Such institutions preserve a way of life and protect those who live by it from those on the outside who do not. *The Rector of Justin* is the most obvious of Auchincloss's novels to deal with an institution, or with a man as an institution, that performs this function.

Auchincloss's fiction does more than present us with a mere record of the institutions that support the American aristocracy. The dramatic interest in his novels and whatever larger importance may be accorded them lies in his recognition that the entire class is in jeopardy and that individual aristocrats are often failures. The closed, unitary life of the aristocracy is sometimes threatened by outsiders—Jews, for example, as in *The Dark Lady* and *The House of the Prophet*—who must be repelled or at worst absorbed. Sometimes Auchincloss sees problems arising within the context of aristocracy itself, as when individual will or desire comes in conflict with the organicism; perhaps Rees Parmalee, in *Pursuit of the Prodigal*, makes the most significant rebellion of all Auchincloss's characters, but he is rejecting a decadent aristocracy and not aristocracy itself. Auchincloss is severely critical of the idea of the gentleman when it is corrupted by allegiance to superficial qualities, like Guy Prime's capacity to hold his liquor or to behave with virile cordiality in *The Embezzler*. But the real failures are those aristocrats who suffer, as so many of Auchincloss's male characters do, from a sense of inadequacy and insecurity that leads them to self-destructiveness. They are not strong and tough-fibred, as so many of the women are; they seem too fastidious and over-civilized, and they are failing the idea of society and their class. In this way, and in others, Auchincloss regretfully chronicles the passing of the aristocracy, which cannot sustain its own ideals in the contemporary world: *A World of Profit* is the most explicit recognition of this failure.

Auchincloss has made his record of the New York aristocracy in a style which is clear and simple, occasionally elegant and brilliant, and sometimes self-consciously allusive. He has a gift for comedy of manners, which he has not sufficiently cultivated, and a fine model in Oscar Wilde. Other influences upon him include Edith Wharton, in ways already mentioned; Henry James, from whom he learned the manipulation of point of view and the faculty of endowing things, art objects for example, with meaning; and St. Simon, a memorialist who did for the French court what Auchincloss wishes to do for Knicker-bocker New York. Yet among his faults as a novelist, especially evident because of the particular genre he has chosen, is a failure to give the reader a richness of detail; he does well with home furnishings but is far less successful with the details of institutions. Furthermore, he sometimes loses control of his novels and permits action to overwhelm theme. The most serious criticism to be made of his work is that while he does indeed pose moral dilemmas for his characters, he too easily resolves their problems for them. He does not sufficiently convey a sense of the bitter cost of honesty or courage or moral superiority, a continuing difficulty for him, as *The Country Cousin* demonstrates. He has given us, on balance, a full enough record of upper-class life in New York, but he has fallen short of the most penetrating and meaningful kinds of social insight that the best of the novelists of manners offer.

—Chester E. Eisinger

BAIL, Murray. Australian. Born Adelaide, South Australia, 22 September 1941. Educated at Norwood Technical High School, Adelaide. Married Margaret Wordsworth in 1965. Member of the Council, Australian National Gallery, Canberra, 1976–81. Recipient: *The Age* Book of the Year Award, 1980; National Book Council award, 1980. Address: 47 Darling Street, East Balmain, New South Wales 2041, Australia.

PUBLICATIONS

Novel

Homesickness. Melbourne and London, Macmillan, 1980.

Short Stories

Contemporary Portraits and Other Stories. St. Lucia, University of Queensland Press, 1975; as *The Drover's Wife*, London, Faber, 1986.

Uncollected Short Stories

"Healing," in *New Yorker*, 16 April 1979.
"Home Ownership," in *Winter's Tales 27*, edited by Edward Leeson. London, Macmillan, 1981; New York, St. Martin's Press, 1982.

Other

Ian Fairweather. Sydney, Bay, 1981.

*   *   *

With Peter Carey and to a lesser extent Frank Moorhouse, Murray Bail was one of the chief revivers of the tradition of the Australian short story during the early and mid-1970's. As well as reviving it, they also transformed its nature. Bail is one of the comparatively few Australian writers who have experimented successfully with new aesthetic forms, who have rebelled against what Patrick White castigated as "journalistic, dun-coloured realism."

The tricks in his first book begin with the title; there is no story called "Contemporary Portraits." Bail's interest in the relationship between language and reality is present in all the stories, and is most obvious in "Zoellner's Definition" and the final story, "A, B, C, D, E, F, G, H, I, J, K, L, M, N, O, P, Q, R, S, T, U, V, W, X, Y, Z." The opening and longest story, "Heubler," concerns a man who decides to "photographically document . . . the existence of everyone alive." He has begun with a list of 23 people, and the unnamed narrator (most of these stories are written in the first person) obligingly assists him with one example of each type. For instance, there is "At least one person who always has the last word"; the preoccupation with language is immediately evident when this proves to have a literal application. Leslie Aldridge is determined to coin a word beginning with z which will be the last in the dictionary, and comes up with zynopic, zythm, and zyvxatiate—to sway or revolve with feet fixed to one spot while under the influence of alcohol—but so far has not managed to introduce them into general usage.

The most famous story in the collection is "The Drover's Wife," which has been frequently anthologised. Here Bail takes the classic story by Henry Lawson and re-interprets it: his version is a monologue, based on Russell Drysdale's famous painting, by the deserted drover, who gazes at the painting and speculates on what has happened to his wife. The story "Portrait of Electricity" proceeds by absence. It contains the embryo out of which Bail's novel *Homesickness* grows. A great man is defined in terms of the evidence of his existence contained in a museum devoted to him, these beginning with an ashtray and culminating in an example of his excrement. The story displays the same strange mixture of surrealistic fantasy and broad satire of Australian customs that characterises Bail's novel.

Bail's first and to date only novel, *Homesickness*, won both the National Book Council award and *The Age* Book of the Year Award when it was published in 1980. It is a coldly written but brilliantly inventive and original novel which recounts the experiences of a group of 13 Australians on a package tour of the world. The characters are stereotypical Australians and no great attempt is made to render them with psychological complexity; the real interest of the novel lies in the startling elaborations on its central metaphor. "The world itself is a museum; and within its circumference the many small museums, the natural and the man-built, represent the whole." The novel turns this insight into a literal one. The tourists travel the world, visiting successively an unnamed city in Africa, London, Quito in Ecuador, New York, and Moscow and in each focus on bizarre kinds of museums. In Africa, for instance, they inspect the MUSEU OF HANDICRAFTS (the M at the end of the first word has fallen off and not been replaced) which is full of incongruous and undistinguished artifacts: an early Singer sewing machine, an umbrella, an empty soda syphon. In London there is a museum of Found Objects, those recovered by the Lost Property Office and displayed for the benefit of tourists in a redundant old railway station. In Ecuador there is a Museum of Legs and in New York they watch actual muggings and rapes.

Bail satirises the tourists and their cultural assumptions and mores, especially the ingenuous but aggressive nationalism of some of them, in a flat, de-humanising tone which seems to owe something to the satiric mode of Patrick White. But Bail's real interest lies in finding imaginative ways of conveying the absurdity of the anthropological patterns of the universe they wander aimlessly through. The writing contains surprises and unexpected information or insights on every page.

—Laurie Clancy

BAILEY, Paul. British. Born Peter Henry Bailey in Battersea, London, 16 February 1937. Educated at Sir Walter St. John's School, London, 1948–53; Central School of Speech and Drama, London, 1953–56. Actor, 1956–63. Literary Fellow, University of Newcastle-upon-Tyne and University of Durham, 1972–74; Visiting Lecturer, North Dakota State University, Fargo, 1977–79. Recipient: Maugham Award, 1968; Arts Council award, 1968; Authors' Club award, 1970; E.M. Forster Award (U.S.A.), 1974; Bicentennial Arts Fellowship, 1976; Orwell Memorial Prize, for essay, 1978. Fellow, Royal Society of Literature, 1982. Address: 79 Davisville Road, London W12 9SH, England.

PUBLICATIONS

Novels

At the Jerusalem. London, Cape, and New York, Atheneum, 1967.
Trespasses. London, Cape, 1970; New York, Harper, 1971.
A Distant Likeness. London, Cape, 1973.
Peter Smart's Confessions. London, Cape, 1977.
Old Soldiers. London, Cape, 1980.

Plays

A Worthy Guest (produced Newcastle-upon-Tyne, 1973; London, 1974).
Alice (produced Newcastle-upon-Tyne, 1975).
Crime and Punishment, adaptation of a novel by Dostoevsky (produced Manchester, 1978).

Radio Play: *At Cousin Harry's*, 1964.

Television Play: *We Think the World of You*, with Tristram Powell, 1980.

Other

An English Madam: The Life and Work of Cynthia Payne. London, Cape, 1982.

Theatrical Activities:
Actor: **Plays**—roles in *The Sport of My Mad Mother* by Ann Jellicoe, London, 1958; *Epitaph for George Dillon* by John Osborne and Anthony Creighton, London, 1958; and other plays.

*

Paul Bailey comments:
    I write novels for many reasons, some of which I have probably never consciously thought of. I don't like absolute moral judgments, the "placing" of people into types—I'm both delighted and appalled by the mysteriousness of my fellow creatures. I enjoy "being" other people when I write, and the

novels I admire most respect the uniqueness of other human beings. I like to think I show my characters respect and that I don't sit in judgment on them. This is what, in my small way, I am striving for—to capture, in a shaped and controlled form, something of the mystery of life. I am writing, too, to expand and stimulate my own mind. I hope I will have the courage to be more ambitious, bolder and braver in my search for the ultimately unknowable, with each book I write.

*   *   *

Paul Bailey's first novel, *At the Jerusalem*, has been rightly acknowledged as one of the outstanding literary debuts of the 1960's in England, and among the reasons why it attracted attention when it appeared was that it departed so markedly from our usual expectations of first novels—autobiographies in thin disguise. What came as a surprise was to find a first novel by a young man in his twenties about old age and its attendant tribulations. Yet Bailey's achievement did not, of course, lie in merely writing about the elderly and their problems, but in doing so with such sympathetic understanding and sensitivity while maintaining sufficient detachment and objectivity to avoid any trace of sentimentality. There is no falsification, no whimsy, none of that awkwardness and emotional uncertainty that tend to afflict writers when dealing with the old. Bailey's depiction of an old people's home, the Jerusalem of the title, and especially of the central character, Mrs. Gadny, whose fairly rapid decline after entering the home is charted, carries complete conviction. Quiet and unpretentious as *At the Jerusalem* is, it is also an extraordinary feat of the imagination.

    In retrospect, we can now see that *At the Jerusalem* introduced many of the themes and preoccupations which have come to be integral components of the Bailey world: isolation, suffering, death, suicide, old age, the pain of loss, psychological collapse, role-playing in an attempt to bear or ward off reality. If *At the Jerusalem* is mainly a study of disintegration—Mrs. Gadny's fate is to be taken to a mental hospital—Bailey's second novel, *Trespasses*, partly set in a mental hospital, is about an attempt at reintegration after personal breakdown and fragmentation. Surprisingly for a Bailey novel, *Trespasses* ends on a note of muted optimism, but much of the book is pervaded by anguish, leading to suicide in the case of one character and mental collapse in the case of another. Technically, *Trespasses* is a much more adventurous work than the fairly orthodox and straightforward *At the Jerusalem*. Some sections of the novel are collages of short, fragmented monologues, appropriate enough for the subject but demanding considerable concentration and imaginative involvement on the part of the reader, who has to construct the total picture from the pieces like a jig-saw puzzle. This intricate cross-cutting between different minds is a most economical way of revealing characters and events; narrated in a conventional way, the novel would be very much longer and far less intense than it is, and the technique justifies itself as the pieces finally cohere into a highly organized pattern.

    Bailey's pursuit of poetic concentration, a concomitant of his increasing technical sophistication and artistic discipline, is taken a stage further in his third novel, *A Distant Likeness*. Like *Trespasses*, the novel is fragmented and elliptical so that the reader again has to work hard to piece the information together. Bailey is almost as sparing of words as Webern was of musical notes. The book, about a policeman in charge of a murder investigation, is another study in disintegration, resulting in this case from the policeman's inner contradictions. Many critics have felt the "distant likeness" to be between the policeman and the murderer, but the sentence from Simone Weil's *Notebooks* that provides the novel with its title, "Privation is a distant likeness of death," is perhaps the key to the interpretation of this complex book. Bailey's subject is privation, and it appears in various forms. *A Distant Likeness* has been compared to *Crime and Punishment*, but Bailey's novel is not so much like Dostoevsky as a distillation of a super-refined Dostoevskian essence. The extreme compression can be likened to T.S. Eliot's miniaturization of epic form in *The Waste Land*, a parallel that suggests itself because of similarities between the imagery of the two works.

After the minimalist austerity and purity, as well as human bleakness, of *A Distant Likeness*, Bailey altered course somewhat, producing a much more relaxed novel in a comic, even picaresque, vein, *Peter Smart's Confessions*. Here the Dickensian side of his talent, evident but not prominent in his earlier books, is given freer rein, although he maintains his usual technical and stylistic control, never wasting words. *Peter Smart's Confessions* is a kind of *bildungsroman*, dealing with the development of a sensitive and artistic boy surrounded by philistinism and other forms of paralysing opposition. Yet much of the interest lies in the gallery of eccentrics and extraordinary characters with whom Peter comes into contact rather than in Peter himself. The later stages of the novel are more desultory and less subtle than the brilliant first half, but the novel as a whole opened up new possibilities for Bailey.

His most recent novel, *Old Soldiers*, is his most completely satisfying since *At the Jerusalem*, and is also about old age, the two main characters being men in their seventies with unforgettable memories of the First World War—hence the title. Technically, the novel is not as "difficult" as *Trespasses* or *A Distant Likeness*, but it resembles them in its brevity, imagistic density, and dependence on suggestion rather than statement. As usual, much is left unsaid. Bailey's treatment of the two very different men, who are nevertheless drawn together after their paths cross, again reveals one of his central concerns as a novelist to be the essential isolation of human beings, the way in which everyone lives and dies alone. He exposes the vulnerable core at the heart of all individuals, the strategies by which people try to disguise their vulnerability and protect themselves from the daily assault of reality, including the inevitability of death. This marks him as a descendant of Conrad, a novelist he greatly admires. Yet if Bailey peels away the deceptions and self-deceptions, the masks and pretences, by which his characters live, he does so with enormous sympathy for their predicament. Bailey respects the uniqueness of individuals, and possesses the true novelist's fascination with people of every description. His novels succeed in widening our sympathy, extending our imagination, and expanding our consciousness.

—Peter Lewis

BAINBRIDGE, Beryl (Margaret). British. Born in Liverpool, Lancashire, 21 November 1934. Educated at Merchant Taylors' School, Liverpool; ballet school in Tring, Hertfordshire. Married Austin Davies in 1954 (divorced, 1959); one son and two daughters. Actress with repertory theatres in Liverpool, Windsor, Salisbury, London, and Dundee, 1949–60; cellar women in a bottle factory, London, 1970; clerk, Gerald Duckworth Ltd., publishers, London, 1961–73. Recipient: *Guardian* Fiction Prize, 1974; Whitbread Award, 1977.

Fellow, Royal Society of Literature, 1978. Address: 42 Albert Street, London NW1 7NU, England.

PUBLICATIONS

Novels

A Weekend with Claude.   London, Hutchinson, 1967; revised edition, London, Duckworth, 1981; New York, Braziller, 1982.
Another Part of the Wood.   London, Hutchinson, 1968; revised edition, London, Duckworth, 1979; New York, Braziller, 1980.
Harriet Said.   London, Duckworth, 1972; New York, Braziller, 1973.
The Dressmaker.   London, Duckworth, 1973; as *The Secret Glass*, New York, Braziller, 1974.
The Bottle Factory Outing.   London, Duckworth, 1974; New York, Braziller, 1975.
Sweet William.   London, Duckworth, 1975; New York, Braziller, 1976.
A Quiet Life.   London, Duckworth, 1976; New York, Braziller, 1977.
Injury Time.   London, Duckworth, 1977; New York, Braziller, 1978.
Young Adolf.   London, Duckworth, 1978; New York, Braziller, 1979.
Winter Garden.   London, Duckworth, 1980; New York, Braziller, 1981.
Watson's Apology.   London, Duckworth, 1984; New York, McGraw Hill, 1985.

Short Stories

Mum and Mr. Armitage.   London, Duckworth, 1985.

Plays

Screenplay: *Sweet William*, 1980.

Television Plays: *Tiptoe Through the Tulips*, 1976; *Blue Skies from Now On*, 1977; *The Warrior's Return* (*The Velvet Glove* series), 1977; *Words Fail Me*, 1979; *The Journal of Bridget Hitler*, with Philip Saville, 1981; *Somewhere More Central*, 1981.

Other

English Journey; or, The Road to Milton Keynes.   London, Duckworth, and New York, Braziller, 1984.

Editor, *New Stories 6*. London, Hutchinson, 1981.

*

Beryl Bainbridge comments:

(1976) As a novelist I am committing to paper, for my own satisfaction, episodes that I have lived through. If I had had a camera forever ready with a film I might not have needed to write. I am not very good at fiction ... It is always me and the experiences I have had. In my last three novels I have used the device of accidental death because I feel that a book has to have a strong narrative line. One's own life, whilst being lived, seems to have no obvious plot and is therefore without tension.

I think writing is a very indulgent pastime and I would probably do it even if nobody ever read anything.

I write about the sort of childhood I had, my parents, the landscape I grew up in: my writing is an attempt to record the past. I am of the firm belief that everybody could write books and I never understand why they don't. After all, everyone speaks. Once the grammar has been learnt it is simply talking on paper and in time learning what not to say.

*   *   *

With the exception of *Sweet William* and *Winter Garden*, all Beryl Bainbridge's novels are centered on a death or act of violence. Her novels are also overshadowed by generalized violence, usually the Second World War. *The Dressmaker* evokes the Liverpudlian home front during the war, while *A Quiet Life* is set in the immediate postwar period, with German prisoners-of-war waiting to be repatriated, and *Harriet Said* slightly later, amid vivid memories of Italian prisoners-of-war. In *A Weekend with Claude*, the old Jewess may not forget the concentration camps, which in a sinisterly different way obsess the "Commandant" of the camping site in the earlier version of *Another Part of the Wood*. Since *Young Adolf* takes off from the possibility that Hitler may have lived in Liverpool in 1909, the book's very conception foreshadows the Holocaust and the war. *Winter Garden* is set against the Cold War. *Injury Time* draws on a background of terrorism and armed crime in contemporary London, while another London novel, *The Bottle Factory Outing*, relies for its effect on the build-up of a violently foreboding atmosphere in and around the bottle factory, without any political cause. *Watson's Apology* examines a clergyman's murder of his wife; it is based on an actual case of 1871. Bainbridge's novels in fact work largely by the build-up of violent atmosphere, drawn from both external circumstances and the characters themselves; this typically erupts in a death, albeit apparently accidental.

In *A Weekend with Claude*, the central act of violence is a shooting, innocuous in its effect whatever its intention. Like her second novel, *Another Part of the Wood*, which Bainbridge later rewrote, it lacks the taut spareness which distinguishes her work from *Harriet Said* on.

The questions of responsibility which her novels often beg so stylishly are twofold in *Harriet Said*; not only is the killing accidental, but it is done by a 13-year-old. On one level, the book is an amusing portrayal by a girl of her friend's sexuality and unnatural "wisdom": "We both tried very hard to give our parents love, and security, but they were too demanding." In *The Dressmaker*, a young girl's pathetic first love for an American G.I. unfolds toward death against the stark symbolism of the work of the dressmaker, who "dreamed she was following mother down a country garden, severing with sharp scissors the heads of roses." Through the more flamboyant black comedy of *The Bottle Factory Outing* flickers the rare lyricism that as elsewhere in Bainbridge's work is a measure of her Joycean acceptance of her characters. This lyrical quality derives from the setting; the garden in *A Weekend with Claude* has become Windsor Great Park in the later novel. But the death precludes total acceptance.

In *Sweet William*, a girl living in a London bedsit falls disastrously in love with the Don Juan of the title, a philandering playwright who moves nonchalantly among the human wreckage he creates. Outstanding here is the portrait of the girl's mother; it was in reaction against her vicious pettiness that the daughter was vulnerable to William. *A Quiet Life* takes an archetypal nuclear family to focus devastatingly again on what children become in reaction to their parents and, as is

hinted, in turn cause any children they have to react against. Bainbridge begins several novels with a Chapter 0, implying what is to come, and here she both begins and ends with this device, as brother and sister meet 15 years later.

Injury Time describes the unorthodox dinner-party of a middle-aged quartet, accidentally taken as hostages in a siege, to the especial embarrassment of a married man dining *chez* his mistress. Beneath the black comedy, and as moulded by formative early experiences, the meaner and more generous impulses of the two main characters come through, in all their ambivalence.

Young Adolf is Bainbridge's most ambitious book, with the tension deriving from our knowledge of what is to come, historically. Against this appalling factual scenario, details like the brown shirt made for the penniless Adolf by his sister-in-law— so that "he needn't sit wrapped in a blanket while his other one was in the wash"—are the blackest black comedy imaginable, though some readers may feel the subject ultimately precludes any such treatment.

Winter Garden hilariously follows an accident-prone civil servant masquerading as an artist to accompany his mistress in a delegation to the Soviet Union. In *Watson's Apology* Bainbridge traces a 26-year-old marriage to suggest how Rev. Watson came to murder his wife. Contemporary documents are used in a narrative remarkable for its authentic reconstruction of Victorian London, culminating in moving impressions of the aged Watson. Beside the new depth in *Watson's Apology*, the accidental deaths in her earlier brilliant novels seem all the more mistaken, for by sensationalizing they distract attention from the composite picture of egotisms pilloried so unnervingly by her black comedy.

—Val Warner

———

BAKER, Elliott. American. Born in Buffalo, New York, 15 December 1922. Educated at Indiana University, Bloomington, B.S. 1944. Served in the United States Army Infantry, 1943–46. Writer for television progams *U.S. Steel Hour* and *Robert Montgomery Show*; script supervisor, *Zero One* series, BBC Television, London. Address: c/o Times Books, 201 East 50th Street, New York, New York 10022, U.S.A.

PUBLICATIONS

Novels

A Fine Madness. New York, Putnam, and London, Joseph, 1964.
The Penny Wars. New York, Putnam, 1968; London, Joseph, 1969.
Pocock and Pitt. New York, Putnam, 1971; London, Joseph, 1972.
Klynt's Law. New York, Harcourt Brace, and London, Joseph, 1976.
And We Were Young. New York, Times, 1979; London, Joseph, 1980.

Short Stories

Unrequited Loves. New York, Putnam, and London, Joseph, 1974.

Plays

The Delinquent, The Hipster, and *The Square* (broadcast, 1959). Published in *The Delinquent, The Hipster, The Square, and the Sandpile Series,* edited by Alva I. Cox, Jr., St. Louis, Bethany Press, 1962.
The Penny Wars (produced New York, 1969).

Screenplays: *A Fine Madness,* 1966; *Luv,* 1967; *Viva Max,* 1970.

Radio Plays: *The Delinquent, The Hipster,* and *The Square,* 1959.

Television Plays: *The Right Thing,* 1956 (U.K.); *Crisis in Coroma* (*U.S. Steel Hour*), 1957; *The Entertainer,* from play by John Osborne, 1976.

*

Manuscript Collection: Indiana University, Bloomington.

* * *

Elliott Baker's first novels, *A Fine Madness* and *The Penny Wars,* demonstrate a diversity of ideas and themes but focus on moral and psychological growth and the life of the imagination. They are comic views of modern America informed by an underlying sense of tragedy or tragic potential. Baker's later works continue to present this tension.

A Fine Madness depicts the triumph of an artist, a kind of American Gulley Jimson, over the forces of conformity and death-in-life. Samson Shillitoe, a working-class hero, a Blakean poet driven by powerful artistic and sexual urges, is pursued and seized by a group of psychiatric experimenters. He is analyzed, institutionalized, and lobotomized but emerges whole, sane, and uncastrated, his creative (and procreative) energies intact. Baker uses his inside knowledge of modern psychotherapy to show the artist at war with a mechanical world and the mechanized minds of clinical psychology. Shillitoe is obsessed by imagination, driven by forces beyond his control. He is amoral, anti-social, unconcerned with "adjustment" or mental health. The psychologists view him only as a specimen, a sample of neurosis or psychosis. Shillitoe's view triumphs: he conceives and produces an epic-sized poem and his common-law wife conceives his child. Life and creation vanquish death and destruction.

In *The Penny Wars* Baker creates a nostalgic vision of adolescence on the eve of World War II. Tyler Bishop, another rebel, grows up in 1939 in squalor and confusion of values. An unreconstructed liberal, Tyler worries about the Nazis while America's smugness and isolationism seem invincible, worries about his budding sexuality, worries about the world he will inherit. Himself a WASP, he stands up for Jews and Negroes, fights bigotry and ignorance—and loses. Through a series of social confrontations, Tyler begins to find his way toward a self-sufficient individualism.

Unrequited Loves, a set of related novellas, documents the youth (1939–45) of a persona named "Elliott Baker," especially initiations into love and sex. Each story is a comic odyssey wherein the young man discovers the battles and truces in the war between men and women. It is Baker's most genial and optimistic book, focusing the nostalgia of *The Penny Wars* on our national pastimes—love, war, baseball, growing up.

Pocock and Pitt is a satirical exploration of identity and childhood in the modern world. Wendell Pocock, American middle-class victim of repeated heart attacks, becomes Winston Pitt, British worker in an organ bank. A pawn in an international espionage duel, he discovers genuine love and redemption after exhausting the cold consolations of history and philosophy. The novel develops the slapstick mediations of *A Fine Madness* and widens Baker's scope to the state of the whole modern world.

Klynt's Law is a *tour de force* in combining genres—a satirical "college novel," a thriller of Las Vegas criminal shenanigans, a study of parapsychology and gambling compulsions. In it, Tobias Klynt (a.k.a. Kleinmann), an archetypal *klutz,* breaks with his shrewish wife, his university career, and the straight world to put the para-normal talents of four students to work on roulette wheels. They have evolved the perfect "system" to beat Las Vegas but fail to understand that gambling is not for winners. The irony is alternately black and farcical, and, as in all good gambling stories, winners are losers.

The same is true in *And We Were Young,* which traces four ex-rifle-squad members in the red-scare years after World War II. A tangle of coincidences—or synchronistic ironies—brings them together in New York City, where each betrays his youthful desires and beliefs in the enveloping glaciers of the Cold War. The book extends Baker's picture of the generation that grew up with World War II, begun in *The Penny Wars* and *Unrequited Loves,* and develops his vision of our society as it changed radically in a new internationalist world.

—William J. Schafer

BALDWIN, James (Arthur). American. Born in New York City, 2 August 1924. Educated at Public School 139, Harlem, New York, and DeWitt Clinton High School, Bronx, New York, graduated 1942. Worked as handyman, dishwasher, waiter, and office boy in New York, and in defense work, Belle Meade, New Jersey, in early 1940's; lived in Europe, mainly in Paris, 1948–56. Member, Actors Studio, New York; National Advisory Board of CORE (Congress on Racial Equality); and National Committee for a Sane Nuclear Policy. Recipient: Saxton Fellowship, 1945; Rosenwald Fellowship, 1948; Guggenheim fellowship, 1954; American Academy award, 1956; Ford fellowship, 1958; National Conference of Christians and Jews Brotherhood Award, 1962; George Polk Award, 1963; Foreign Drama Critics Award, 1964; Martin Luther King, Jr., Award, City University of New York, 1978. D.Litt.: University of British Columbia, Vancouver, 1963. Member, American Academy, 1964. Lives in New York City and St.-Paul, near Vence, France. Agent: Edward L. Acton, 928 Broadway, New York, New York 10010, U.S.A.

PUBLICATIONS

Novels

Go Tell It on the Mountain. New York, Knopf, 1953; London, Joseph, 1954.
Giovanni's Room. New York, Dial Press, 1956; London, Joseph, 1957.
Another Country. New York, Dial Press, 1962; London, Joseph, 1963.
Tell Me How Long the Train's Been Gone. New York, Dial Press, and London, Joseph, 1968.

If Beale Street Could Talk. New York, Dial Press, and London, Joseph, 1974.
Just above My Head. New York, Dial Press, and London, Joseph, 1979.

Short Stories

Going to Meet the Man. New York, Dial Press, and London, Joseph, 1965.

Uncollected Short Stories

"Any Day Now," in *Partisan Review* (New Brunswick, New Jersey), Spring 1960.
"Exodus," in *American Negro Short Stories*, edited by John Henrik Clarke. New York, Hill and Wang, 1966.
"Equal in Parts," in *Travelers.* New York, Macmillan, 1972.

Plays

The Amen Corner (produced Washington, D.C., 1955; New York, Edinburgh, and London, 1965). New York, Dial Press, 1968.
Blues for Mr. Charlie (produced New York, 1964; London, 1965). New York, Dial Press, 1964; London, Joseph, 1965.
One Day, When I Was Lost: A Scenario Based on "The Autobiography of Malcolm X." London, Joseph, 1972; New York, Dial Press, 1973.
A Deed from the King of Spain (produced New York, 1974).

Screenplay: *The Inheritance*, 1973.

Verse

Jimmy's Blues: Selected Poems. London, Joseph, 1983.

Other

Notes of a Native Son. Boston, Beacon Press, 1955; London, Joseph, 1964.
Nobody Knows My Name: More Notes of a Native Son. New York, Dial Press, 1961; London, Joseph, 1964.
The Fire Next Time. New York, Dial Press, and London, Joseph, 1963.
Nothing Personal, photographs by Richard Avedon. New York, Atheneum, and London, Penguin, 1964.
A Rap on Race, with Margaret Mead. Philadelphia, Lippincott, and London, Joseph, 1971.
No Name in the Street. New York, Dial Press, and London, Joseph, 1972.
A Dialogue: James Baldwin and Nikki Giovanni. Philadelphia, Lippincott, 1973; London, Joseph, 1975.
Little Man, Little Man (for children). London, Joseph, 1976; New York, Dial Press, 1977.
The Devil Finds Work: An Essay. New York, Dial Press, and London, Joseph, 1976.
The Price of a Ticket: Collected Nonfiction 1948–1985. New York, St. Martin's Press, and London, Joseph, 1985.
The Evidence of Things Not Seen. New York, Holt Rinehart, 1985.

*

Bibliography: "James Baldwin: A Checklist 1947–1962" by Kathleen A. Kindt, and "James Baldwin: A Bibliography 1947–1962" by Russell G. Fischer, both in *Bulletin of Bibliography* (Boston), January–April 1965; *James Baldwin: A Reference Guide* by Fred L. and Nancy Standley, Boston, Hall, 1979.

Critical Studies: *The Furious Passage of James Baldwin* by Fern Eckman, New York, Evans, 1966, London, Joseph, 1968; *James Baldwin: A Critical Study* by Stanley Macebuh, New York, Third Press, 1973, London, Joseph, 1975; *James Baldwin: A Collection of Critical Essays* edited by Keneth Kinnamon, Englewood Cliffs, New Jersey, Prentice Hall, 1974; *James Baldwin: A Critical Evaluation* edited by Therman B. O'Daniel, Washington, D.C., Howard University Press, 1975; *James Baldwin* by Louis H. Pratt, Boston, Twayne, 1978; *James Baldwin* by Carolyn W. Sylvander, New York, Ungar, 1981; *Baldwin: Three Interviews* by Kenneth B. Clarke and Malcolm King, Middletown, Connecticut, Wesleyan University Press, 1985.

Theatrical Activities:
Director: **Film**—*The Inheritance*, 1973.

James Baldwin comments:
I have always found it difficult to speak of my own work. I am not altogether certain that I can identify my "subjects" and "themes." The life that I was born into, or the life that I have lived—which are not, necessarily, the same—certainly account, to some degree, for the structure of my mind. I have made a certain conscious effort to avoid sentimentality. I am still making that effort.

*   *   *

James Baldwin, the most eloquently intense and morally insistent essayist in midcentury America has published six novels and a book of short stories. Some of his fiction, like some of his drama, has stimulated controversy; but there is general agreement that he has done masterful work in both the novel and the short story forms.

Go Tell It on the Mountain, Baldwin's first and best novel, centered upon the religious conversion of John Grimes the night of his 14th birthday, is divided into three parts. Part I, "The Seventh Day," introduces the Grimes family in Harlem in March 1935. John feels locked in by the repressive, doom-ridden preachments of his father Gabriel, head deacon of the store-front Temple of the Fire Baptized, and is guiltily aware of sex. He hates his father reciprocally, sometimes hates his mother, and will soon hate all white people—whom his father despises—"if God did not change his heart."

Part II, "The Prayers of the Saints," which comprises in flashbacks well over half the novel, provides background for the family dilemma of John. His 60-year-old Aunt Florence, driven by her fear of death from cancer, recalls in her prayer the following: the slavery-time memories of her and Gabriel's mother, who envisioned a dominant masculine role in Black family life; Florence's departure from the South in 1900 after her white employer "proposed that she become his concubine"; and the marital love between her and caramel-colored Frank—ended after ten years by her disdain for his "common nigger" friends and by her jars of skin-whitener (despite Frank's reminder that "black's a mighty pretty color"). Florence ends her prayer bitterly asking why God "preferred her mother and her brother, the old, black woman, and the low, black man, while she, who had sought only to walk upright, was come to die, alone and in poverty, in a dirty, furnished room?"

Gabriel, in the long section on his prayer, relives highlights of his 21st through 40th years, mainly his affair with Esther and the birth and death at 18 of their son Royal. This affair, preceded by wild young Gabriel's marriage of repentance to bony, "sexless" Deborah, humanizes him as trapped in contradictory pietistic and lustful urges so delicately balanced within him as to demand rigid, defensive behavior. Significant are young Gabriel's criticism of "big, comfortable, ordained" ministers at the Twenty-Four Elders Revival Meeting; the intimation of the perfect coincidence of death and life at the burial of Esther and later at the news of her son Royal's death; and John's sense of the artistic value of hatred: "He did not *want* to love his father; he wanted to hate him, to cherish that hatred, and give his hatred words one day." Stylistically notable are the poetic prose description of Gabriel's autumn flight after deserting Esther, and the use of sound, silence, and group movement to signal flashbacks.

Elizabeth, in her section, recalls what love has meant to her. Deprived of her sick mother's questionable love by death, and of her disreputable father's evident love by her aunt's prudishness, Elizabeth finds idyllic love when she and Richard go to New York. But Richard commits suicide after humiliation and beating by police. After the birth of their illegitimate son John, she finds redemption in marriage to Gabriel (Deborah having died), who promises to love her son. In this section about love, the antithesis has its role: Richard's quest for knowledge is energized by hatred of whites; and Elizabeth, after Richard's death, "hated it all—the white city, the white world."

Part III, "The Threshing-Floor," engrossingly describes John's conversion on the floor before the altar, the tortured probings and exhilarations of his mind sharpened by guilt and expanded by hope for salvation. At dawn, the smiling boy, facing an unsmiling father, is confident of his future.

Plainly autobiographical, this novel about a boy's anguished choice between church and jail metaphorically opposes the demands of those institutions as the forces that have long constricted but spiritualized Black people. The "saints" of the store-front church are all martyrs, Florence having been undone by normal ambition, Gabriel by duties too spiritual for his normal flesh, and Elizabeth by love. Jailed within body, family, church, and country, they vacillate between varieties of surrender and feel no sinless ecstasy or power other than singing the mysteries of God. The Biblical enchantment of Baldwin's prose rhythm elevates even his scenes of animal love, and the speech of his characters is vividly true to their heritage.

In *Giovanni's Room*, Baldwin's major fictional deviation from the racial theme, he melodramatically but profoundly explores love as illuminated and defined by homosexuality. The action, set in Paris and recalled by David on the eve of homosexual Giovanni's execution for murdering his exploiter Guillaume, concerns David's love and responsibility for Giovanni, whom he deserts to return to his fiancée Hella. Giovanni's indictment of David is central: "You are not leaving me for a *woman*. If you were really in love with this little girl, you would not have had to be so cruel to me" and "You want to *kill* [me] in the name of all your lying little moralities." Baldwin emphasizes that love inspires magnanimity and charity and that morality begins in honesty about oneself.

Another Country is Baldwin's major attempt to dramatize the racist destruction of interracial affections. In Book I, Rufus Scott, the jazz musician who turns his drums and his Southern white girl friend into objects for the dazzling release of his frustrations over racism, dives suicidally off the George Washington Bridge. His white friends, who failed to imagine his despair, live under its shadow as victims of a loveless, divisive New York. His sister Ida uses Vivaldo Moore's love to hasten her vengeance upon the white world. Vivaldo, loving her partly to shorten the distance that his whiteness maintains, pays in pain the dues that Cass Silenski offers less riskily. In Books II and III, Eric Jones, a young Southern actor who in France

discovers his reality homosexually with Yves, moves therapeutically among other characters, teaching as existential man sexual liberation from the chaos of life, love, racism, and death. *Another Country*, although weakened by talkiness, occasionally inconsistent diction, and a questionable ending, is morally keyed to a remark by the preacher at Rufus's funeral: "Try to understand . . . we got to try to be better than the world."

Tell Me How Long the Train's Been Gone follows Leo Proudhammer from the age of ten in Harlem through his years as a famous actor. More to be noted than the typical inclusion of heterosexual, homosexual, and interracial lovemaking are young Leo's despairing father and idolized brother Caleb. Too much black rum and servility before white men destroy Leo's respect for the former; then police and prison guard brutality, followed by conversion to the ministry during his service in World War II, saps the once admirable militance in Caleb. Leo's affections turn to Christopher, who enters his life as his body-guard and who closes the novel telling him "I think you got to agree that we [Black people] need us some guns." Although Leo, like Christopher, considers religion useless in the racial struggle, he demurs at the thought of violence. This novel is occasionally powerful—in the summer workshop and police station scenes, for example—but it is Baldwin's least impressive long work.

Of the eight stories in *Going to Meet the Man*, the first three focus upon father–son relationships: "The Rockpile" and "The Outing" (both using characters and situations seen in his first novel) and "The Man Child." Three others show people trying to accept their Blackness: "Previous Condition," "Come Out the Wilderness," and the excellent "This Morning, This Evening, So Soon." The other two are also exceptional: "Sonny's Blues," the best story, and "Going to Meet the Man." The former brilliantly probes the failure of sympathy between two brothers, one an addict, and the latter traces the growth of psychopathetic race hatred in an impotent deputy sheriff.

In *If Beale Street Could Talk* there is neither love nor mercy in the Black church, neither truth nor justice in American law, and neither hope nor sanctuary in anything but familial and personal love. Probing the racist-fomented dilemmas of his young Harlem narrator, Tish Rivers, and her falsely jailed fiancé, Fonny Hunt, Baldwin transcends his earlier renderings of Black men: the lovers' fathers here, like Fonny, are strong men precisely because they accept as a masculine challenge their Black ancestry and the needs of their children. Tish's narrative style does not fully demand Baldwin's sophisticated powers (although his love scenes and proverbial wisdom are memorable); but his new cynicism and deepened affinities foretell added significance in his later themes.

Those themes appear comprehensively in his longest novel, *Just above My Head*, its five books narrated by Hall Montana, shocked into memories by the death in London of his younger brother Arthur, a famous gospel singer. Hall recreates in flashbacks the entangled lives of Julia, the Harlem child evangelist trapped in incest and liberated only in Africa; of Jimmy, her younger brother and Arthur's final, providential lover; and of two other homosexual partners of Arthur's (his fellow-musician Crunch and his Parisian lover, Guy).

Set mostly in New York and in the civil-rights inferno of the South, the novel reasons out long-standing Baldwinian themes. Whatever its weaknesses—to some, its profanity and sexual details—it uniquely and memorably imbeds the rhythms, idioms, and philosophy of Black music into each main character's consciousness, talk, and action—increasingly as he or she approaches a true ability to love. This final humanness (Baldwin's wish for the U.S.A.) comes only when lovers knowingly act like jazz musicians: taking off on faith alone, they listen for the inaudible note, cross the invisible bridge, obey the felt signal to "step out on the promise," into their own song.

Baldwin's fiction, even when it falters, aims high, grappling with problems by which people measure themselves as humans and lovers. Unsparing but hopeful in its societal and racial criticism, urging self-acceptance and love in personal relations, his novels and stories pain and elevate the consciousness of his vast audience.

—James A. Emanuel

BALLANTYNE, David (Watt). New Zealander. Born in Auckland, 14 June 1924. Educated at Gisborne High School. Served in the New Zealand Army, 1942–43. Married Vivienne Heise in 1949; one child. Journalist, Auckland *Star*, 1943–47, *Southern Cross*, Wellington, 1947–48, Auckland *Star*, 1949–54, and London *Evening News*, 1955–63; editor, *Finding Out*, London, 1964; journalist, London *Evening Standard*, 1965; feature writer, 1966–77, and literary editor, 1977–84, Auckland *Star*. Member of the Literary Fund Advisory Committee, 1976–82. Recipient: Hubert Church Prose Award, 1949; ATV prize, for television play, 1961; New Zealand Scholarship in Letters, 1968. Address: 4 Lincoln Street, Auckland, New Zealand.

PUBLICATIONS

Novels

The Cunninghams. New York, Vanguard Press, 1948; London, Hale, 1963.
The Last Pioneer. Christchurch, Whitcombe and Tombs, and London, Hale, 1963.
A Friend of the Family. Christchurch, Whitcombe and Tombs, and London, Hale, 1966.
Sydney Bridge Upside Down. Christchurch, Whitcombe and Tombs, and London, Hale, 1968.
The Talkback Man. Palmerston North, Dunmore Press, and London, Hale, 1978.
The Penfriend. Palmerston North, Dunmore Press, and London, Hale, 1980.

Short Stories

And the Glory. Christchurch, Whitcombe and Tombs, and London, Hale, 1963.

Uncollected Short Stories

"Only a Kid of Course," in *New Zealand Weekly News* (Auckland), 21 January 1942.
"A Child's Day," in *New Zealand New Writing 2* (Wellington), October 1943.
"A Couple of Hacks," in *Arena* (Wellington), 1962.

Plays

Television Plays: *Passing Through*, 1963 (U.K.); *The Night of the Leopard*, 1963 (U.K.); *Twice upon a Time*, 1965 (U.K.); *Frances Hodgkins* (documentary), 1969; *Arthur K. Frupp*, 1970; *A Last Look*, 1971.

Other

Editor, *Around the World: Looking at Other Lands* (for children). London, Purnell, 1964; Boston, Ginn, 1966.

*

Critical Studies: *New Zealand Literature* by E.H. McCormick, London, Oxford University Press, 1959; *Islands of Innocence* by M.H. Holcroft, Wellington, Reed, 1964; *New Zealand Fiction since 1945* by H. Winston Rhodes, Wellington, McIndoe, 1968; "Whimsical Losers" by C.K. Stead, in *Landfall 132* (Christchurch), December 1979.

David Ballantyne comments:

(1972) I took my earliest themes from what I knew of the ways of life of my fellow countrymen. I wanted to write truthfully about their attitudes and their behaviour. I thought of myself as a realist, in the tradition of writers like Zola, Dreiser, Joyce, Hemingway, and Farrell. I drew upon my own experiences for my fiction, but tried for a detachment that would allow me to see the humour and warmth in life as well as the anxiety and pain. I thought a lean writing style, free of pretty phrases and philosophical flourishes, best suited to what I had to say. This was my approach in my first novel, *The Cunninghams*, and in my short stories. In a later novel, *A Friend of the Family*, written after I had lived in London several years, I used satire to suggest how I viewed certain aspects of contemporary life. And in another novel, *Sydney Bridge Upside Down*, I found parody a useful device. Mainly, though, I have told stories. Some more eventful than others.

*   *   *

David Ballantyne's distinctive quality as a writer of fiction is his fidelity to the details, however trivial, of day to day life as it is (or might be) lived by lower-middle-class New Zealanders. With the exception of *A Friend of the Family*, whose setting might be either Auckland or London, all his novels are set in New Zealand. But Ballantyne's work does not evoke a strong sense of place; his characters are more observant of their own feelings than they are of their surroundings. Perhaps this is because the environment, both mental and physical, inhabited by typical Ballantyne characters is itself colourless, if not dreary.

Greatly influenced by the American writer James T. Farrell and to a lesser extent by Frank Sargeson, Ballantyne seems to have set out deliberately to write in the naturalist tradition. Accordingly, his style is bare and unadorned, echoing (with all their limitations) the thought-processes of his characters. It is through the characters' reported thoughts, and their dialogue, that the story of their lives is mostly told. Ballantyne gives us not literary language, then, but a fairly accurate representation of the sometimes colourful colloquialisms and turns of phrase used by working class and lower-middle-class New Zealanders. Although the use of slang runs the risk of dating a novel, its strength in Ballantyne's work is the liveliness and veracity it imparts to his characterization.

Ballantyne's novels have been justly criticized for an absence of intellectual and philosophical depth. Their pre-occupation with characters who are essentially losers, eking out spiritually empty lives in an atmosphere of seediness and boredom, offers little of the transcendence that characterizes great literature. But Ballantyne is never sentimental: we like his characters because they accept themselves and their lot, however unsatisfactory, without self pity.

Of the six novels, three stand out: *The Cunninghams*, *Sydney Bridge Upside Down* and *The Talkback Man*. The *Cunninghams* focuses on the vicissitudes of three members of a family struggling to cope with the hardships of the Depression in a provincial town. Gil, the father, is slowly dying of war injuries aggravated by his work in the local slaughterhouse. His youngish wife, Helen, is torn between a genuine love for her sick husband and her very human need for a little bit of fun. Their eldest son, Gilbert, puzzles over the problems of adolescence as well as his feelings for his parents. This is New Zealand's best naturalist novel, remarkable for its objectivity—and for the skill and feeling with which Ballantyne evokes the woman's point of view.

And the Glory is a creditable collection of short stories about provincial life. *The Last Pioneer* tells of the failed attempt of an English immigrant to make a life for himself and his young son in a town where inertia and the cult of mediocrity infect even the ambitious. In an acerbic commentary on New Zealand attitudes, the would-be pioneer is told: "The New Zealander's highest tribute! You realise that? I mean a decent joker's an ordinary joker, and *that's* what we want. But you'll have to stay ordinary, you know. Go easy on the ideas, or you'll be called a crackpot."

The amount of dialogue and the frequent shifts backwards and forwards in time make *A Friend of the Family*, a novel about a young male clerical worker in a large city company, difficult to follow. *The Penfriend* is less technically complex. Set in a provincial town, it centres on a young journalist who pursues, besides attractive women, mysterious clues to recent UFO sightings.

Sydney Bridge Upside Down is Ballantyne's best novel. Probably influenced by Ian Cross's *The God Boy* and R.H. Morrieson's *The Scarecrow*, it is set in a small town and narrated in the first person by an adolescent boy whose mother has run off to the city with the local school teacher. There is a hint of the gothic in the gradually unfolding story of a summer during which the protagonist is responsible for two deaths in the town's abandoned slaughterhouse. Intermingled with the boy's ingenuous revelation of his amoral personality is the story of his awakening sexual awareness—and his awareness of the power exerted by sex on the lives of those around him.

Ballantyne's other memorable novel is *The Talkback Man*. The simple but effective plot-line focuses on a former journalist who runs a lustreless radio talkback show. The protagonist is a likeable character, and the author's handling of distance ensures that we follow his decline into alcohol and casual sexual encounters with sympathy and concern.

If there is a certain sameness about Ballantyne's characters, with their tendency to seek escape from life's problems through casual (if affectionate) sex and the camaraderie of the pubs, there is also a genuine compassion that irradiates his novels and invites us to suspend judgement of our fellow human beings.

—Cherry Hankin

BALLARD, J(ames) G(raham). British. Born in Shanghai, China, 15 November 1930. Educated at Leys School, Cambridge; King's College, Cambridge. Served in the Royal Air Force. Married Helen Mary Matthews in 1954 (died, 1964); three children. Recipient: *Guardian* Fiction Prize, 1984; James Tait Black Memorial Prize, 1985. Agent: Margaret Hanbury, 27 Walcot Square, London SE11 4UB. Address: 36 Old Charlton Road, Shepperton, Middlesex TW17 8AT, England.

PUBLICATIONS

Novels

The Wind from Nowhere. New York, Berkley, 1962; London, Penguin, 1967.
The Drowned World. New York, Berkley, 1962; London, Gollancz, 1963.
The Burning World. New York, Berkley, 1964; revised edition, as *The Drought*, London, Cape, 1965.
The Crystal World. London, Cape, and New York, Farrar Straus, 1966.
Crash. London, Cape, and New York, Farrar Straus, 1973.
Concrete Island. London, Cape, and New York, Farrar Straus, 1974.
High-Rise. London, Cape, 1975; New York, Holt Rinehart, 1977.
The Unlimited Dream Company. London, Cape, and New York, Holt Rinehart, 1979.
Hello America. London, Cape, 1981.
Empire of the Sun. London, Gollancz, and New York, Simon and Schuster, 1984.

Short Stories

The Voices of Time and Other Stories. New York, Berkley, 1962.
Billenium and Other Stories. New York, Berkley, 1962.
The Four-Dimensional Nightmare. London, Gollancz, 1963.
Passport to Eternity and Other Stories. New York, Berkley, 1963.
Terminal Beach. London, Gollancz, 1964; abridged edition, New York, Berkley, 1964.
The Impossible Man and Other Stories. New York, Berkley, 1966.
The Disaster Area. London, Cape, 1967.
The Day of Forever. London, Panther, 1967.
The Overloaded Man. London, Panther, 1967.
Why I Want to Fuck Ronald Reagan. Brighton, Unicorn Bookshop, 1968.
The Atrocity Exhibition. London, Cape, 1970; as *Love and Napalm: Export USA*, New York, Grove Press, 1972.
Chronopolis and Other Stories. New York, Putnam, 1971.
Vermilion Sands. New York, Berkley, 1971; London, Cape, 1973.
Low-Flying Aircraft and Other Stories. London, Cape, 1976.
The Best of J.G. Ballard. London, Futura, 1977.
The Best Short Stories of J.G. Ballard. New York, Holt Rinehart, 1978.
The Venus Hunters. London, Panther, 1980.
News from the Sun. London, Interzone, 1982.
Myths of the Near Future. London, Cape, 1982.

*

Bibliography: *J.G. Ballard: A Primary and Secondary Bibliography* by David Pringle, Boston, Hall, 1984.

Critical Studies: *J.G. Ballard: The First Twenty Years* edited by James Goddard and David Pringle, Hayes, Middlesex, Bran's Head, 1976; *Re Search: J.G. Ballard* edited by Vale, San Francisco, Re Search, 1983.

J.G. Ballard comments:

I believe that science fiction is the authentic literature of the 20th century, the only fiction to respond imaginatively to the transforming nature of science and technology. I believe that the true domain of science fiction is that zone I have termed inner space, rather than outer space, and that the present, rather than the future, is now the period of greatest moral urgency for the writer. In my own fiction I have tried to achieve these aims.

*   *   *

As in the case of his acknowledged partial inspiration Graham Greene, J.G. Ballard seems to divide his distinguished canon into novels and "entertainments": serious, challenging prose that makes new demands upon us as readers, and breezier productions that serve as aesthetic holding actions. In the former category, one would find in chronological order *The Drowned World*, *The Atrocity Exhibition*, *Crash*, *The Unlimited Dream Company*, and *Empire of the Sun*. Ballard's "entertainments" include *The Wind from Nowhere*, *The Drought*, *The Crystal World*, the short story cycle *Vermilion Sands*, *Concrete Island*, *High-Rise*, and *Hello America*. Ballard's voluminous short fiction could profitably be divided along similar lines, with far greater debate concerning what works best. Ballard's own selection of his best fiction is very reliable: sympathetic readers of Ballard will share his enthusiasm for "The Voices of Time" and "Terminal Beach." Nonetheless, he has consistently produced rewarding short prose since the last exhaustive anthology, most of which has been collected in *Low-Flying Aircraft*, *The Venus Hunters*, and *Myths of the Near Future*. ("The Air Disaster" remains hard to obtain outside of its appearance in *Bananas*.)

This bare listing does not get at the delightful, harsh truth that easy, accessible Ballard is apt to strike the casual reader as more than a bit outré on first glance. One has to absorb 200 pages of erotic car crash fantasies (*Crash*) to curl up cozily with a novel that begins with its protagonist devouring a dog in a housing complex reduced to savagery (*High-Rise*). Any Ballard work is intimidating to the uninitiated, and one might do well to start reading an "entertainment" before venturing into the major canon. What one will find upon perusing that canon is its creator's brilliant, grasping imagination, his densely ironic voice, and a genuine moral vision.

Although it is his most recent work, *Empire of the Sun* provides the kindest entry into the major canon. This novel is both boy-book, a work written for adults about childhood, and war memoir. Jim, the protagonist, has received inevitable comparisons with his author. Both were interred in Japanese prisoner-of-war camps in China during World War II; Ballard admits these related events were his own in the foreword. *Empire of the Sun* allows us as a result to "solve" the case of J.G. Ballard. The young author's separation from his parents, radical dislocation, and struggle for survival produce the traumatic scene of the Ballardian text: a world of flat affect where setting predominates over character and action (unless a generic formula is being ruthlessly parodied), a landscape littered with aircraft fuselages, automobiles, miasmas, and tarmac, all aching to burn under the silent, bone-revealing glare of the Nagasaki explosion Jim witnesses in the ontological climax of the novel: "the light was a premonition of his death, the sight of his small soul joining the larger soul of the dying world." Thus begins the death-in-life of Jim Ballard.

This youth, our mythic construction of the ideal Ballard-author, grows up to become a science-fiction writer: the world he experienced did not match the conventions of 19th-century fiction, so he turned to visions of the future, reading pulp magazines while an airman in Canada. W. Warren Wagar in *Terminal Visions* offers us a helpful paradigm for reading Ballard's science fiction and experimental canon through time. Ballard, roughly, has moved from an obsession with feminized natural landscape in the quartet of so-called disaster novels (the world imperiled by the four elements, approximately), to an obsession with homoeroticized technological artifacts (*The Atrocity Exhibition* through *High-Rise*), to an achieved polymorphous perversity (*The Unlimited Dream Company*). Only after this long therapeutic journey could he return to the traumatic scene and write his war memoir, even as Vonnegut had to work up to *Slaughterhouse-Five*. He is cured; he need never write again. If he does, it will be mainstream. One could also use Ballard's own statements to posit his work as progressing, and usefully regressing, from more distant future worlds to our present world of apartment complexes and flyovers, and ultimately to his Shanghai past. *Empire of the Sun* gives the critic marvelous ammunition for familiarizing an unsettling fictional presence. That flat affect Ballard shares with kindred maverick William S. Burroughs can be traced to the Japanese camps, even as Burroughs owes his style, ostensibly, more to the neurophysiological effects of heroin than to a Swiftian spirit.

Such reductive remarks could pass for an accurate assessment of Ballard's work. Nonetheless, something is lost in the neatness of it all; most notably, the unescapable belatedness of this late mainstream work. We read it in the light of the science fiction and experimental writing: the cramped cubicles of Lunghua C.A.C. irresistibly invoke the locales of "Billennium" and *High-Rise*. Ballard values the fabulative powers of science fiction too greatly to allow his summating work to stand outside them. The ultimate joke on the reader may be that *Empire of the Sun* is history revealed as the ultimate science-fiction text, especially as Ballard writes either. As Gould remarks in "Low-Flying Aircraft," "The ultimate dystopia is the inside of one's own head." *Empire of the Sun* is an immense and real achievement, but only partially enlightening as a key to the canon. Other, less reductive structures can be suggested to illuminate Ballard's strategies.

The most helpful perspective I have found for enjoying Ballard can be located in Roland Barthes's explication of bourgeois myth. Myth is a secondary order of signification, a higher code of accepted meaning. The image of an oak tree in an insurance company advertisement, by a theft of the sign, becomes a signifier of longevity, dependability, etc. The artist has two strategies for attacking the conventional accretions of myth: she or he, according to Barthes, can either restore to physical objects their uncanniness and historicity or create a third order of signification by looking behind the myth for its concealed signification.

A fairly plausible case can be made that Ballard has always attacked conventional signification, progressing from Barthes's first strategy to an increasing use of his second strategy. The early novels restore to things their non-mythic materiality: especially the heightened elemental powers in the quartet, but also the technological flotsam and jetsam being blown about or floating by. The crystallization process in *The Crystal World* provides an almost perfect allegory of the defamiliarization of bourgeois nature.

But Ballard has been honing his skills at discovering the third order of signification (which Barthes infelicitously terms "Bouvard and Pecuchetity" in honor of Flaubert's ironic skills) since *The Wind from Nowhere*. One of the few nice things one say about this work—produced in two short weeks, it remains Ballard's worst novel—is that it knows at all points that it's formulaic junk, a parody of the John Wyndham school of disaster writing. Its successor, *The Drowned World*, is playing similar games with its transparent allusiveness, but there is far greater interest in the code behind the code of disaster fiction. For Ballard and his protagonist Kerans, disaster is concealed psychic opportunity. In the clearly indicated "happy" ending of the work, Kerans embraces the destructive principle, the chthonic, by heading South into greater heat. As in most later Ballard, such self-destruction is always a symbolic invitation to transformation, a relentless reiteration that the old order is dying and a new one is coming up—and such a transformation won't look like liberal reform. (How puzzling that Marxists dismiss Ballard as neo-colonial or reactionary given such a recurrent stance of critical surrealism.) In Foucault's terminology, we are in a shifting episteme; writers like Ballard and Burroughs have their ears pressed closest to the rails, listening to the eschatological murmur. Such, after all, is the requisite stance for a survivor. Ballard reveals in *Empire of the Sun* that "a code within a code" always intrigued Jim. He would watch bridge games for this reason; later, such skills would keep him alive.

In *The Atrocity Exhibition*, Ballard's talents as a reader of bourgeois myth emerge strikingly. The book dissects some of the psychoanalytic significance behind the overdetermination of 1960's culture: television coverage of the Vietnam War, the assassination of John F. Kennedy, Marilyn Monroe, the automobile, cancer victims all converge in a terrifying psychedelic hellbroth of image, redeemed, like *Naked Lunch*, only by its abiding ironic humor, its Swiftian critical distance and its undeniable prophecy. The obsessional accuracy of this series of "condensed novels" has aged remarkably well, as a chapter title like "Why I Want to Fuck Ronald Reagan" indicates.

For some readers, *Crash* is even rougher going, a semilogical anatomy of the automobile accident that exchanges breadth (in *The Atrocity Exhibition*) for depth of analysis. As in the later *Empire of the Sun*, Ballard toys with the reader by giving the narrator his own name. Ballard the character's quest for "the keys to a new sexuality born from a perverse technology" horrifies, delights, and enlightens. At his best, Ballard's imagination risks the unimaginable, even as his clunky, chunky prose—with its transparent allusions and similes, its hardboiled rhythms, and its vague redundancies—acquires a paradoxical grace all its own: a bombed-out, flat affect poetry that perfectly ensnares our era. His sinister replication of medical school textbook argot in this second phase assures us Ballard has a good ear; he knows exactly what effects he's achieving in this minatory technological pornography.

Ballard's recent polymorphous phase has given us some of his finest writing, in *The Unlimited Dream Company* and *Empire of the Sun* (and his funniest in the overlooked *Hello America*). Ballard will undoubtedly continue to grow along the amazing and original course he has charted. Much of his supposed classism and racism seems unfounded; his use of formulaic heroines, though parodic and appropriate for his gender-bound, extreme loners, has drawn greater and more justified criticism from feminists. Recent stories like "Having a Wonderful Time" and "The Smile" adumbrate his own interest in correcting these misperceptions. Thematically, he will continue to gesture towards a problematic social transformation, hoping for its arrival but uncertain of its shape, wishing for it to resemble the community in *Vermilion Sands*, but ever the survivor, willing to settle for anything shy of Eniwetok. As long as we avoid choosing the latter (and perhaps for a bit on the day after if we do not manage that), J.G. Ballard will continue to interest us as our bravest explorer of the psychic contours of post-nuclear humanity, the fabulist chronicler of our overlooked median strips.

—Robert E. Mielke

BANKS, Lynne Reid. British. Born in London, 31 July 1929. Educated at the Royal Academy of Dramatic Art, London. Married Chaim Stephenson in 1965; three sons. Actress in British repertory companies, 1949–53; secretary to the writer Wolf Mankowitz, 1953–54; interviewer, reporter and scriptwriter, Independent Television News, London, 1954–61; English teacher, Kibbutz Yasur School and Na'aman High School, Israel, 1962–71. Recipient: Yorkshire Arts Association award, 1977. Lives in Beaminster, Dorset. Agent: Watson Little Ltd., Suite 8, 26 Charing Cross Road, London WC2H 0DG, England.

PUBLICATIONS

Novels

The L-Shaped Room. London, Chatto and Windus, 1960; New York, Simon and Schuster, 1961.
An End to Running. London, Chatto and Windus, 1962; as *House of Hope*, New York, Simon and Schuster, 1962.
Children at the Gate. London, Chatto and Windus, and New York, Simon and Schuster, 1968.
The Backward Shadow. London, Chatto and Windus, and New York, Simon and Schuster, 1970.
Two Is Lonely. London, Chatto and Windus, and New York, Simon and Schuster, 1974.
Dark Quartet: The Story of the Brontës. London, Weidenfeld and Nicolson, 1976; New York, Delacorte Press, 1977.
Path to the Silent Country: Charlotte Brontë's Years of Fame. London, Weidenfeld and Nicolson, 1977; New York, Delacorte Press, 1978.
Defy the Wilderness. London, Chatto and Windus, 1981.
The Warning Bell. London, Hamish Hamilton, 1984.

Fiction (for children)

One More River. London, Vallentine Mitchell, and New York, Simon and Schuster, 1973.
Sarah and After: The Matriarchs. London, Bodley Head, and New York, Doubleday, 1975.
The Adventures of King Midas. London, Dent, 1976.
The Farthest-Away Mountain. London, Abelard Schuman, 1976; New York, Doubleday, 1977.
My Darling Villain. London, Bodley Head, and New York, Harper, 1977.
I, Houdini: The Autobiography of a Self-Educated Hamster. London, Dent, 1978.
The Indian in the Cupboard. London, Dent, 1980; New York, Doubleday, 1981.
The Writing on the Wall. London, Chatto and Windus, 1981; New York, Harper, 1982.
Maura's Angel. London, Dent, 1984.
The Fairy Rebel. London, Dent, 1985.
Return of the Indian. London, Dent, and New York, Doubleday, 1986.

Plays

It Never Rains (televised, 1954; produced Keighley, Yorkshire, 1954). London, Deane, 1954.
Miss Pringle Plays Portia, with Victor Maddern. London, Deane, 1955.
The Killer Dies Twice. London, Deane, 1956.
All in a Row. London, Deane, and Boston, Baker, 1956.
The Unborn (produced London, 1962).
Already It's Tomorrow (televised, 1962). London, French, 1962.
The Gift (produced London, 1965).

Radio Plays: *The Stowaway,* 1967; *Lame Duck,* 1978; *Purely from Principle,* 1984.

Television Plays: *It Never Rains,* 1954; *Already It's Tomorrow,* 1962; *The Wednesday Caller,* 1963; *Last Word on Julie,* 1964; *The Eye of the Beholder* (*She* series), 1977.

Other

The Kibbutz: Some Personal Reflections (address). London, Anglo-Israel Association, 1972.
Letters to My Israeli Sons: The Story of Jewish Survival. London, W.H. Allen, 1979; New York, Watts, 1980.
Torn Country: An Oral History of the Israeli War of Independence. New York, Watts, 1982.

*

Manuscript Collection: Boston University.

Theatrical Activities:
Actress: **Radio**—*Purely from Principle,* 1984.

Lynne Reid Banks comments:

I've never gone in much for analysing my work or my work-processes. As a writer, and as a person, I tend to be lazy and disorganised. If my characters do not "take over" and direct my typing fingers, it is nothing but drudgery for me—I write in order to have written. I find out what I had to say after I have said it. But in any case, "things to say" are not my primary driving-force. I am a story-teller. That to me is what fiction is—it is not a subtle way of communicating one's political, social, or any other opinions to a host of faceless readers. Praise, to me, is not "How I agreed with you about such-and-such!" but "How I cared about this or that character...."

Although the great rallying-cry to writers these days is "Truth for Truth's sake," objective truth, the chronicling of reality, is not my metier. If it were, I should not write fiction. Fiction means, to me, a reflection of life so "doctored" that its only relationship to truth is an illusion in the reader's mind. The reader must receive this illusion of reality, of course, or else the one binding commandment of the novel-writer—"Involve thy reader"—is broken; but this is not to say that the story need be "true" in the sense of reflecting ordinary, typical people or events.

Jane Austen is the only novelist I know whose peculiar genius lies in taking perfectly ordinary people through ordinary situations, and transmogrifying them into fascinating fiction. Every other great novelist I can think of has either created exceptional characters or has devised for them abnormal events—often both. Dickens, Tolstoi, the Brontës, Victor Hugo—all were allowed their outrageous coincidences, their larger-than-life heroes, their impossible denouements and neat, incredible resolutions. Nobody in those days queried the fiction-writers' right to write *fiction,* and not fiction parading as fact.

Characters in novels may not go beyond the possible. But they should—the principal ones, anyway—be exceptional people. Jane (*The L-Shaped Room*) did not behave like an ordinary girl. Her reactions and decisions were those of, let us say, one girl in ten, or fifty, or a hundred in her situation. Perhaps the others would have liked to do what she did; perhaps that explains why the book was widely read. Her exceptional qualities made her interesting and stimulating. The same with Kofi, the Arab in *Children at the Gate.* Some Israelis complained that he was not a typical Arab. I never thought he was. He was not even a typical human being. I made him rare on purpose. I reject the criticism of those who demand that I point out his living counterpart before they will accept him.

However, themes are another matter. The themes one writes about must be true—not objectively true, but true to one's deepest convictions. My fourth novel, *The Backward Shadow,* was criticised by one American woman for its underlying assumption that women need men and cannot live full lives without them. But I believe this. It is in accordance with my own experience and observation. I doubt if I could write a convincing novel about a happy, single, "liberated" woman, not only because I have never met one but because, rightly or wrongly, deep down I don't believe they exist.

One of my recurring themes is women alone. This theme is drawn from the secret places of my own life. I was not, myself, exceptional in my reaction to singleness, but then I am an ordinary woman. My heroines may either react to loneliness with greater courage, awareness, and resourcefulness than I did, or sink to lower depths; but they must be more *extreme,* otherwise I cannot be bothered with them, nor can I see why any reader should.

In short, fiction should grow out of life; but the operative word is "out." It should be an extension, an underlining, a highlighting. Above all, it must involve the reader in a process of identification. My novels are not for everyone. They are only for those who are similar enough to me to sympathise with the characters I create. To any reader who turns away, in boredom, irritation, or revulsion, from my heroines, however real they may seem to him, I owe an apology for failure.

*   *   *

Lynne Reid Banks acquired sudden literary fame with her first novel, *The L-Shaped Room.* Despite her considerable output of fiction since then, she has remained best known for that one book. This may be partly because of Bryan Forbes's film, which starred Leslie Caron as Jane, the heroine waiting for the birth of her illegitimate child in a Fulham bedsit. The novel shows Jane coming to know the range of sleazy, eccentric, and ordinary characters in the house, and learning to be at peace with her plight. *The L-Shaped Room* was regarded as highly daring in its time, and though that frisson has worn off by now, the book is still notable for its originality and its compassionate observation of people. It can be faulted on construction: the room never acquires the dominant place it is clearly meant to have because there is too much happening outside it that engages our attention, and some of the other characters are tantalizingly sketchy. Jane's lover is a writer, Toby Cohen, and he remains a cameo of a type of person who was then considered fashionable. However, these faults are insignificant, because the story grips us. We care about the girl's dilemma, we worry about the future of the baby. One critic pointed out that the best things in this novel remind us of Orwell's *Down and Out in Paris and London;* the worst remind us of *Rebecca of Sunnybrook Farm.*

The Backward Shadow was the sequel to *The L-Shaped Room.* This has Jane enjoying motherhood and temporary isolation in a country cottage not far from London. Though she still loves Toby, she has decided not to burden him with responsibility for herself as this will interfere with his writing. Jane's nobility is rewarded by Toby's falling for a nymphet, and the story really becomes concerned with Jane's relationship with Dotty and Henry, partners in a boutique. Jane's friendship with them also collapses, because of her lack of confidence in herself and her occasional guardedness. The novel examines love and friendship, and the necessity of knowing when to offer your presence and when to withdraw it, when to express need of other people and when to leave it unexpressed. Jane is a thoroughly good sort of person, endearingly ready to discuss her feelings and her emotional development with the reader. However, her lack of irony, malice, and humour contribute to making the book somewhat duller than it might have been if Jane had not been the narrator.

The final novel in the trilogy about Jane, *Two Is Lonely*, has Jane still unmarried and finding it increasingly difficult to handle her son David who is now eight. Obsessed with his need for a father, he asks questions constantly, cannot sleep at night, and suffers from nightmares. Finally, he runs away from home and disappears. The focus of the novel is on Jane's relationships with men in the past and in the present, for she has continued her search for a mate. Banks believes that a woman is superior to a man in many ways, but does need a man (just as a man needs a woman). Jane is being wooed by a handsome widower, a rich and successful architect; however, she still dreams of Toby who has emigrated to Israel, but whose marriage is foundering. The architect wisely encourages Jane to look Toby up, and she goes to Israel with John, the black friend from *The L-Shaped Room*. Jane eventually finds Toby, but ends up rejecting him when he fails to make love to her. Jane returns to London when she hears of her son's disappearance; she discovers that another flame, Terry, has indulged in a face-lift and dye-job, so she rejects him too, leaving the field finally clear for the architect. Though a postscript hints at the continuation of the saga, Banks has not written one so far.

The strengths and weaknesses of the trilogy typify Banks's strengths and weaknesses in general: one always feels that her heart is in the right place, and she commands a fine economy in evoking scenes—especially those that involve the emotions. However, she has never mastered the architectonics of fiction, and her language veers from the over-rich to the monotonous. Her chief drawback, however, is that she treats in a curiously old-fashioned way the paradoxes of being a woman who is both thoroughly modern and yet sensitive to questions of truth, morality, and commitment. But it is also true that Banks negotiated the journey from outrageous amorality to seeing its problems far more quickly and less spectacularly than Germaine Greer.

However, such preoccupations are not prominent in all of Banks's novels. For she went to Israel and found both a cause and a husband in that country. Though she, her husband, and her children eventually settled in Britain again, they decided to leave Israel for pragmatic considerations of making a living, and Banks has written several books in praise of Israel, for children, teenagers, and adults. The best known of these books is *Defy the Wilderness*, in which a woman writer is researching a book on contemporary right-wing Israel, hoping to make it a fairly objective account. However, as one critic put it, "her liberal principles are overwhelmed by a rogue-male Attila of Zionism for whom she falls." The intensifying need of the Jews to distinguish between those who are for Israel and those who are against it tears her irrevocably away from her insipid family life back home in England. Discursive, weighty, and frankly committed, the book failed to arouse any

enthusiasm among critics, though it has been as popular with the public as any of her other works.

Banks's principal fault in the eyes of critics has been the ultimate sin of earnestness; there is nothing so damning as being described in the fashionable periodicals as a "bore." Banks is not a great novelist, but she does offer effective satire, the illuminating detail, and pithy dialogue. It is her misfortune that the gatekeepers of culture themselves typify the values with which she initially sympathized and on which she has now turned her back. She continues to defy them with her latest weapon, *The Warning Bell*, a frank exploration of what fashionable people find to be the most terrifying of timebombs, conscience.

—Prabhu S. Guptara

BANKS, Russell (Earl). American. Born in Newton, Massachusetts, 28 March 1940. Educated at Colgate University, Hamilton, New York, 1958; University of North Carolina, Chapel Hill, A.B. 1967 (Phi Beta Kappa). Married 1) Darlene Bennett in 1960 (divorced, 1962); 2) Mary Gunst in 1962; 3) Kathy Walton in 1982; four daughters. Plumber in New Hampshire, 1959–64; publisher and editor, Lillabulero Press, and co-editor, *Lillabulero* magazine, Chapel Hill, North Carolina, and Northwood Narrows, New Hampshire, 1966–75; taught at Emerson College, Boston, 1968 and 1971, University of New Hampshire, Durham, 1968–75, and New England College, Henniker, New Hampshire, 1975 and 1977–81. Since 1981 has taught at New York University and Princeton University, New Jersey. Recipient: Woodrow Wilson Fellowship, 1968; St. Lawrence award, 1975; Guggenheim fellowship, 1976; National Endowment for the Arts grant, 1977, 1982; Merrill Foundation award, 1983. Lives in Brooklyn, New York. Agent: Ellen Levine Literary Agency, 432 Park Avenue South, Suite 1205, New York, New York 10016. Address: c/o Harper and Row Publishers, 10 East 53rd Street, New York, New York 10022, U.S.A.

PUBLICATIONS

Novels

Family Life.   New York, Avon, 1975.
Hamilton Stark.   Boston, Houghton Mifflin, 1978.
The Book of Jamaica.   Boston, Houghton Mifflin, 1980.
The Relation of My Imprisonment.   Washington, D.C., Sun and Moon Press, 1983.
Continental Drift.   New York, Harper, and London, Hamish Hamilton, 1985.

Short Stories

Searching for Survivors.   New York, Fiction Collective, 1975.
The New World.   Urbana, University of Illinois Press, 1978.
Trailerpark.   Boston, Houghton Mifflin, 1981.
Success Stories.   New York, Harper, 1986.

Verse

15 Poems, with William Matthews and Newton Smith. Chapel Hill, North Carolina, Lillabulero Press, 1967.

30/6. New York, The Quest, 1969.
Waiting to Freeze. Northwood Narrows, New Hampshire, Lillabulero Press, 1969.
Snow: Meditations of a Cautious Man in Winter. Hanover, New Hampshire, Granite, 1974.

*   *   *

Russell Banks's novels and stories are various, ranging from the problematic intricacies of postmodernism of his early work to the semi-realism of his latest. However, though his techniques and forms vary, his work shows a remarkable thematic progress from an often convoluted questioning of the human predicament in the early novels to a lucid answering in *Continental Drift.* Banks early on experimented with a number of styles, forms, and types—fable, "relation," tale, parable, mannered avant-garde, stories-within-stories, realistic narrative. But always he has been primarily interested in the human predicament and modern man's place within and outside his traditions. His settings range from New England to Haiti, and places in between.

Family Life, Banks's first novel, is a self-conscious fabulistic romance that takes place in an imaginary kingdom and concerns the fates of King Egress, Queen Naomi Ruth, and their sons Orgone, Egress, Jr., and Dread. The novel is seriously marred by obscure literary references and jokes and nearly impenetrable passages of allusion alternating with farcical scenes. The "relevance" of the novel appears to be something on the order that we fight nameless wars in nameless countries, that we are misplaced and displaced persons searching for identity.

Hamilton Stark is told from an avant-garde point of view—shifting, multi-faceted, and fragmented, with long philosophical monologues, radical time shifts, psychological digressions, and tales-within-tales, often put together, again, self-consciously and often not convincingly. The real strength of the novel, and it is considerable, derives chiefly from the several points of view from which Stark is viewed by a number of the other characters. There is no definitive attempt to piece together these fragments, for that is, indeed, the theme of the novel—that there is no defining "self" mediating among the various understandings that would guarantee a static, comforting identity.

The Book of Jamaica concerns a novelist and professor from New England (Banks is a professor at Princeton who spent 18 months in Jamaica) who receives a grant to study the Jamaican Maroons, whose forebears were escaped African slaves who in the 17th and 18th centuries took to the mountains to fight the British. The main character is a liberal, guilt-ridden because of his identification with the wealthy, racist islanders and other whites. The narrator, on his own journey into the heart of darkness, is afflicted with the modern, overly analytical mind, suffers from alienation and loneliness, and attempts to find among the Maroons a self unburdened by 20th-century culture and tradition and to refashion himself both as a social creature and "natural" man. The narrator becomes "Johnny," among the Maroons, a name they give to friendly whites. He is assumed into Otherness, a kind of forgetfulness necessary to eliminate old cultural prejudices and the shackling of character and personality by the intellectual life that obscures elementary experience.

The Relation of My Imprisonment is told in the form of a "relation," a form popular with 17th-century Puritans; it is a first hand account of an imprisoned man's deviance from religious orthodoxy and is embellished by Scripture and sermon. The unnamed prisoner, a builder of coffins, has been sentenced to 12 years for illegally plying his trade as coffin maker; he is a heretic. The book's larger theme involves the persecution of Puritan Dissenters in England, but its real concern is contemporary man's imprisonment, his fragmentation and consequent loss of self. The prison itself is a metaphor for the modern situation. While the ostensible form is old, the style and language are postmodernist, and the tale is told "expressly for the living."

Continental Drift, undoubtedly Banks's best novel, is also his most approachable. For the first time in the novel form (he has written more conventionally in his short fiction) his narrative is straightforward and the style unadorned and lucid; it is Banks's apparent break with postmodernism, and in this work he finds the full flowering of his talent. Bob Dubois is a $137.44-a-week 30 year-old oil-burner repairman in Catamount, New Hampshire who suddenly sees into his awful predicament: "He loves his wife and children. He has a girlfriend. He hates his life." He vows to start over, packs up his family and leaves for Florida to work for his brother in a liquor store. Dubois's story is alternated with and parallel to another, that of Vanise Dorsinville, an impoverished Haitian and her son and nephew who leave their country for the promise of America. Both main characters are united by the novel's central concern, the drifting quality of life in America in the last half of the 20th century and how individual life everywhere is as determined as are the tectonic plates of continents, by movements imperceptible to those affected by them. From a more distant perspective than that allowed to men living through the drift, the planet is seen "as an organic cell," a metaphor for human life and the futility of escape from constant motion. At the heart of the novel is a great sympathy for the characters, not hope for the transformation of this life: "Books get written—novels, stories and poems stuffed with particulars that try to tell us what the world is, as if our knowledge of people like Bob Dubois and Vanise and Claude Dorsinville will set people like them free. It will not. Knowledge of the facts of Bob's life changes nothing in the world. Our celebrating his life and grieving over his failure will."

—Peter Desy

BANVILLE, John. Irish. Born in Wexford, 8 December 1945. Educated at Christian Brothers School, and St. Peter's College, both Wexford. Married Janet Dunham in 1969; two sons. Copy editor, *Irish Press*, Dublin, 1970–83. Recipient: Allied Irish Banks prize, 1973; Arts Council of Ireland Macaulay Fellowship, 1973; Irish-American Foundation Award, 1976; James Tait Black Memorial Prize, 1977; *Guardian* Fiction Prize, 1981. Agent: Anthony Sheil Associates Ltd., 43 Doughty Street, London WC1N 2LF, England. Address: Dunamase, Balkill Road, Howth, County Dublin, Ireland.

PUBLICATIONS

Novels

Nightspawn. London, Secker and Warburg, and New York, Norton, 1971.
• *Birchwood.* London, Secker and Warburg, and New York, Norton, 1973.
• *Doctor Copernicus.* London, Secker and Warburg, and New York, Norton, 1976.

• *Kepler*. London, Secker and Warburg, 1981; Boston, Godine, 1983.
• *The Newton Letter: An Interlude*. London, Secker and Warburg, 1982.

Short Stories

Long Lankin. London, Secker and Warburg, 1970.

Uncollected Short Stories

"The Party," in *Kilkenny Magazine*, Spring-Summer 1966.
"Mr. Mallin's Quest" and "Nativity," in *Transatlantic Review* (London), Autumn-Winter 1970–71.
"Into the Wood," in *Esquire* (New York), March 1972.
"De rerum natura," in *Transatlantic Review 50* (London), 1975.
"Rondo," in *Transatlantic Review 60* (London), 1977.

Play

Screenplay: *Reflections*, 1984.

*

Critical Studies: "John Banville Issue" of *Irish University Review* (Dublin), Spring 1981.

*   *   *

John Banville writes about writing. His characters are marionettes, entangled in self-reflexive explorations of the relationship between creation and reality. Banville's fiction is full of borrowings, from Marvell to Sir Arthur Eddington, yet it is saved from intellectualism and narcissism by its disciplined structure and Nabokovian narrative voice, deliberately uneasy and emotionally strained.

Its third-person narrative distinguishes *Long Lankin* from Banville's later books. Like *Dubliners*, this debut collection presents different stages in the lives of Irish characters in sets of episodic stories dealing with childhood, adolescence, and adulthood respectively. "The Possessed," a novella, is added as a coda. Each story centres on two dispossessed characters who frustrate each other's initial sense of freedom and end up in a state of arrest, wholly unable to fathom the "whatness of things." Ominously prominent background noises and shadows continually hint at Long Lankin, the leper from the old English ballad, whose cure depended on a ritual murder. He materialises in the novella as Ben White and radically upsets the tenor, chronology, and fictional level of the book. White's transformation into "Black Fang" intermediates his appearance in two preceding stories: in "Summer Voices" as a boy, bullied by his sister and fascinated with death; and in "Island" as an unproductive writer who stares at Delos and is accused of murder by his demanding girlfriend. In "The Possessed," Ben demands a blood-sacrifice for creative freedom, metaphorically kills his sister by severing their—almost incestuous—ties, and lifts himself to the status of implied author, unleashing a savagery that reflects the author's urge to finish off the book.

Nightspawn is a sequel to "The Possessed" and exploits the metafictional effects of coalescing hero, narrator, and writer. Ben imitates Yeats, Prufrock, and Shelley, and in the best *nouveau roman* tradition he soon becomes a pawn in his own cliché thriller. His Greek island gets crowded with his stock characters who emotionally involve White beyond his narrative control and are to blame for the novel's doubles, double plots, and obscurity. Eager to get to "the real meat,"

but checked by "the conventions," White becomes the first of Banville's Beckettian heroes who must go on, or perish in silence and who are doomed at the end to return to the first sentence.

In *Birchwood*, Banville refutes many of his fabulations. Gabriel Godkin, the narrator, is once again autocratic and conditioned by his own narrative. His genre is the Irish big house with all its familiar trappings and stock characters. There are slapstick humour and morbid fun: Granny Godkin finds her end in the summerhouse by spontaneous combustion. Intermingled with the big house is the external world of romance, Prospero's circus, which Gabriel joins on his quest for a sister who is in fact an imaginative character created to deprive him of his inheritance by the aunt who proves to be his mother. Gabriel's anachronistic narrative is determined by his "search for time misplaced"; like the antics of Birchwood's grandfather clock, it transcends boundaries of time as deftly as Proust's *Recherches*. But the book's shifting frames of reference are firmly fixed in its philosophical observation that the expression of the memories of things is at best a two-dimensional mirror-image in which much is consistently reversed.

In his classical tetralogy, Banville translates his fascination for the relationship between creation and reality into eminent scientists' quests for truth. He even appends bibliographies with references to works on theoretical physics. In *Doctor Copernicus*, Duke Albrecht claims that he and Copernicus are "the makers of . . . supreme fictions." And indeed, Coppernigk is time and again likened to Wallace Stevens in order to show how science is art and how art cannot express truth, but only embody it. Coppernigk's quest leads from conceptualisation to cognition, a unification with his anti-self, his syphilitic brother Andreas who repeats verbatim Eddington's "We *are* the truth." Although the book recreates the cruelty and stench of the Renaissance, it is not an historical novel. Copernicus is a protégé of a writer's consciousness which is informed by Einstein, Kierkegaard, Wittgenstein, Max Planck, Yeats, and Stevens—who are all quoted in a pandemonium of opposing philosophical contentions. Banville feels free to introduce a mad-cap, manic depressive paranoid called Rheticus, who claims responsibility for Copernicus's *De Revolutionibus*, lies like mad, lays bare the irrational undertones of the book and provides a delightfully comic interlude. Ultimately *Doctor Copernicus* is another metafiction; all characters may be figments of Copernicus's own mind; and he, in turn, acts and thinks as part of the literary creation. Every book of the novel is a closed entity, revolving within itself and resolving in a restatement of the first paragraph, with the very last sentence being a return to the very first. The narrative reads like a fugue, but despite its insistence on form it is immensely realistic in its depiction of a nightmarish era, where total chaos is just around the corner.

The structure of *Kepler* is a reflection of the hero's belief that "in the beginning is the shape." The five chapters are shaped like the polygons that Kepler envisaged within the intervals of the six planetary orbits; the sections acrostically spell out the names of famous scientists, and the shifts of time in each section reflect Kepler's discovery that the planets move in ellipses. In his Quixotic quest for a truthful order, Kepler the man becomes conditioned by the entropy that Kepler the scientist creates, with a paradoxical anti-hero as the result.

At the basis of *The Newton Letter* lies von Hofmannsthal's *Ein Brief*; the Nabokovian first sentence aptly reads "Words fail me, Clio." The epistolary form grants the narrator more autonomy than any of Banville's protagonists and emphasises his treacherous subjectivity. The novel is the satire of the tetralogy and details the consequences of immersing an historian with a Newtonian mechanistic view in the common world of the big house, where Goethe's humanity reigns supreme. The hero is constantly baffled and blinded, misinterprets the inhabitants of Ferns and is Banville's most convincing example that truth is perhaps inhuman.

—Peter G.W. van de Kamp

BARKER, A(udrey) L(ilian). British. Born in St. Paul's Cray, Kent, 13 April 1918. Educated at schools in Beckenham, Kent, and Wallington, Surrey. Worked for Amalgamated Press, London, 1936; reader, Cresset Press, London, 1947; secretary and sub-editor, BBC, London, 1949–78. Member of the Executive Committee, English PEN, 1981–85. Recipient: Atlantic Award, 1946; Maugham Award, 1947; Cheltenham Festival Award, 1963; Arts Council Award, 1970; South East Arts Award, 1981. Agent: Jennifer Kavanagh, 39 Camden Park Road, London NW1 9AX. Address: 103 Harrow Road, Carshalton, Surrey MS5 3QF, England.

PUBLICATIONS

Novels

Apology for a Hero. London, Hogarth Press, and New York, Scribner, 1950.
A Case Examined. London, Hogarth Press, 1965.
The Middling: Chapters in the Life of Ellie Toms. London, Hogarth Press, 1967.
John Brown's Body. London, Hogarth Press, 1969.
A Source of Embarrassment. London, Hogarth Press, 1974.
A Heavy Feather. London, Hogarth Press, 1978; New York, Braziller, 1979.
Relative Successes. London, Chatto and Windus, 1984.

Short Stories

Innocents: Variations on a Theme. London, Hogarth Press, 1947; New York, Scribner, 1948.
Novelette with Other Stories. London, Hogarth Press, and New York, Scribner, 1951.
The Joy-Ride and After. London, Hogarth Press, 1963; New York, Scribner, 1964.
Lost upon the Roundabouts. London, Hogarth Press, 1964.
Penguin Modern Stories 8, with others. London, Penguin, 1971.
Femina Real. London, Hogarth Press, 1971.
Life Stories. London, Chatto and Windus, 1981.
No Word of Love. London, Chatto and Windus, 1985.

Play

Television Play: *Pringle,* 1958.

*   *   *

The theme of A.L. Barker's work is the ambivalence of love and the dangers of egoism. She examines those relationships which exist between victor and victim, he who eats and he who is eaten. This material is handled lightly and skilfully; she has the satirist's ability to select detail, placing her characters socially as well as psychologically. Her territory covers childhood, the worlds of the outcast and the ill and the impover-

ished lives of the lonely. She is close to the English tradition of the comic novel and like Angus Wilson, a major writer in this genre, she often indulges in caricature.

Many of her short stories reveal a fondness for the macabre, introducing elements of horror into seeming calm. Her first collection, *Innocents,* begins with a study of a boy testing his courage in swimming; he becomes involved in a scene of adult violence that is far more dangerous to him than the tree-roots in his river. Innocence in these stories is seen as inexperience, as the blinkered vision of the mad and as the selfishness of the egoist. *Lost upon the Roundabouts* is a further exploration of these ideas and contains two very fine short stories, "Miss Eagle"' and "Someone at the Door."

The central characters in Barker's novels are parasites, dependent on other people for a sense of their own identity. For Ellie in *The Middling* love means "turning another person into a colony of myself." Charles Candy, the central character of *Apology for a Hero,* loves his wife Wynne "because she could give him himself." After Wynne's death he acquires a housekeeper and finds that "when he was with her he felt located." He meets death on a reckless voyage, persuaded that sea-trading will, at last, show him the real Mr. Candy.

The egoist in *A Case Examined* is Rose Antrobus, the chairman of a charity committee with the power to allocate money either to a destitute family or to the church hassock fund. Rose has always insulated herself against suffering. She remembers a childhood friend, Solange, whom she credits with the understanding of despair: Solange provokes violence, she feels, by her own wickedness. This fantasy is shattered by a visit to Paris and a meeting with the real Solange, whose account of Nazi persecution shakes Rose into compassion. A bridge has been made between the worlds of the two women, between the petty and the tragic, and the committee decision is altered accordingly.

Femina Real, is an entertaining set of portraits, nine studies of the female character. In many of the situations an apparent vulnerability hides an underlying strength. A frail woman dominates those around her; adolescence vanquishes middle-age; a ten-year-old cripple turns the tables on the man holding her prisoner. As always, Barker's clear prose style matches the accuracy of her observations. Hers is a talent to be treasured.

—Judy Cooke

BARNES, Julian (Patrick). British. Born in Leicester, 19 January 1946. Educated at City of London School, 1957–64; Magdalen College, Oxford, 1964–68, B.A. (honours) in modern languages 1968. Editorial assistant, *Oxford English Dictionary* supplement, 1969–72; assistant literary editor, 1977–79, and television critic, 1977–81, *New Statesman,* London; deputy literary editor, *Sunday Times,* London, 1980–82. Since 1982, television critic, *The Observer,* London. Contributing editor, *New Review,* London, 1977–78. Recipient: Maugham Award, 1981; Faber Memorial Prize, 1985. Agent: A.D. Peters, 10 Buckingham Street, London WC2N 6BU, England.

PUBLICATIONS

Novels

Metroland. London, Cape, 1980; New York, St. Martin's Press, 1981.

Before She Met Me.   London, Cape, 1982.
Flaubert's Parrot.   London, Cape, 1984; New York, Knopf, 1985.

Novels as Dan Kavanagh

Duffy.   London, Cape, 1980.
Fiddle City.   London, Cape, 1981.
Putting the Boot In.   London, Cape, 1985.

Uncollected Short Story as Dan Kavanagh

"The 50p Santa," in *Time Out* (London), 19 December 1985–1 January 1986.

*   *   *

Julian Barnes's wry and accomplished first novel, *Metroland*, charts the progress to adulthood of its narrator, Christopher Lloyd, and the divergence of him and his abiding friend, Toni Barbarowski, from kindred spirits to near-opposites. In 1963, as adolescents, they are would-be bohemians: their heroes are the French symbolists, their watchwords "*écraser l'infâme*" and "*épater la bourgeoisie.*" By 1977, Chris is married with a young daughter. He has a well-paid job with a publisher of popular reference books. And he has returned to the "bourgeois dormitory" where he grew up: "Metroland," that "thin corridor" of outer suburbia connected to London by the Metropolitan Line. Toni, by contrast, is an academic and author heavily involved in "street politics." He lives with a girl "in the least fashionable part of the borough of Kensington he could find." Chris claims to have attained maturity and happiness; Toni considers him a complacent philistine. Chris's version seems the more immediately persuasive, not least because Toni cuts such an unattractive, unexemplary figure. He retains the preoccupation with image of their adolescence and youth: his life appears to be a sequence of radical-chic gestures. Chris, on the other hand, has apparently acquired the confidence to be himself, has outgrown the need to strike prose. But *Metroland* is more subtle than that. In fact, Toni's criticisms are not entirely unjustified, and Chris does experience sneaking reservations about certain aspects of his development. For Chris, growing up has not been a straightforward process of either education or corruption, but a combination—difficult to distinguish—of both.

Barnes's novels are linked by Francophilia, notably a passion for French literature, and preoccupation with marriage and fidelity. The former permeates the first two parts of *Metroland*—the second of which sees Chris in Paris—while the latter comprises a bone of contention between Chris, faithful husband, and the promiscuous Toni in the third. In *Before She Met Me*, though, the latter overshadows all else: Graham Hendrick, an historian, becomes obsessed with the lovers his second wife, Ann, had before him. His fixation begins when he sees Ann, once a bit-part film actress, in a "five-year-old British comedy flop." She admits that her lover in the film was also, briefly, her actual lover. Thereafter, increasingly consumed by retrospective jealousy, Graham probes Ann's sexual history, pestering her for names, dates, recollections. She keeps secret only her long-gone affair with the novelist, Jack Lupton: he is Graham's friend and confidante. Meanwhile, Graham frequents backwater cinemas to witness Ann's fleeting appearances, to see the actors who were her onscreen and/or offstage lovers. He drinks more; he will take holidays only in places

she has not visited with other men; his dreams are lurid exaggerations of her past "adulteries." Finally, by analysing some of Lupton's novels (which borrow freely from life), Graham uncovers Ann's affair with him. Mistakenly, though, he believes it to be still going on. This provokes the blood-letting which closes the book—disappointingly. Dealing with a little-explored contemporary subject—the problem of jealousy in an age of sexual freedom—Barnes constructs an authoritative portrait of a cracking personality only to embrace finally the all-too-convenient (and, in this case, melodramatic) device of death. *Before She Met Me* remains, though, a praiseworthy novel, memorable also for Barnes's deadly portrayal of the emotional war of attrition waged by Graham's first wife during and after their marriage.

Geoffrey Braithwaite, the retired general practitioner and widower who narrates *Flaubert's Parrot*, is a man obsessed, too. A fervent admirer of the eponymous author, he wants to know everything about the man behind the books. The title alludes to his attempt to discover which of two stuffed parrots was the one Flaubert kept on his desk during the writing of "Un coeur simple." Investigation, though, confuses rather than resolves the issue: in fact, the parrot could have been any one of fifty. And if, Braithwaite asks, it proves impossible to discover the facts about this one small thing, how can we ever "seize the past"? Certainly, truth—apropos of questions both large and small—is throughout elusive and incomplete: a chapter devoted to considering the colour of Emma Bovary's eyes reaches no firm conclusion, for instance, while in another—a self-contained twist-in-the-tail story—a cache of newly-unearthed letters providing definitive proof of Flaubert's true relationship with the shadowy Juliet Herbert are burned before Braithwaite can read them. As a consequence of this prevailing uncertainty, the novel is, in part, a compendium of different ways—Braithwaite's and others'—of regarding Flaubert and his work, all half-truths (or less) that never amount to a whole.

Graham Hendrick's obsession was destructive; Braithwaite's, conversely, offers solace: his quest for Flaubert distracts him from the subject of his beloved late wife, a compulsive adultress of whose "secret life" he knows nothing beyond its existence and whose suicide he cannot understand. Seeking to know her instead would not only be a painful and possibly (given Graham's example) dangerous task, but an intractable one also:

My wife: someone I feel I understand less well than a foreign writer dead for a hundred years … Books say: she did this because. Life says: she did this. Books are where things are explained to you; life is where things aren't. I'm not surprised some people prefer books.

Serious and playful, often simultaneously, *Flaubert's Parrot* is a *tour de force* of fiction, criticism, and biography combined. Admittedly, there are occasional *longueurs*, and Braithwaite's character is rather insubstantial. Furthermore, some of its devices—which include a cod exam-paper and a glossary of conventional wisdom on Flaubertian matters—can seem flashy on second reading. But for all that, it is a thoroughly absorbing work.

Barnes's "Dan Kavanagh" novels are detective stories featuring Nick Duffy, a bisexual ex-policeman. The earliest, *Duffy*, is the most successful, compensating for an unexceptional plot with its semi-humorous protagonist and an evocation of Soho's "Golden Mile" praised for its realism by the reviewer for *Police World*. Despite some fascinating glimpses into the arcana of smuggling through airports, *Fiddle City* is less impressive, while *Putting the Boot In* is an outright disappointment: a lacklustre picture of lower division football coupled with a familiar plot.

—David Montrose

BARSTOW, Stan(ley). British. Born in Horbury, Yorkshire, 28 June 1928. Educated at Ossett Grammar School. Married Constance Mary Kershaw in 1951; one son and one daughter. Draftsman and sales executive in the engineering industry, 1944–62. Recipient: Writers Guild award, 1974; Royal Television Society award, 1975. M.A.: Open University, Milton Keynes, Buckinghamshire, 1982. Honorary Fellow, Bretton Hall College, Wakefield, Yorkshire, 1985. Agent: Harvey Unna and Stephen Durbridge Ltd., 24–32 Pottery Lane, London W11 4LZ. Address: Goring House, Goring Park Avenue, Ossett, West Yorkshire WF5 0HX, England.

PUBLICATIONS

Novels

A Kind of Loving: The Vic Brown Trilogy. London, Joseph, 1981.
  A Kind of Loving. London, Joseph, 1960; New York, Doubleday, 1961.
  The Watchers on the Shore. London, Joseph, 1966; New York, Doubleday, 1967.
  The Right True End. London, Joseph, 1976.
Ask Me Tomorrow. London, Joseph, 1962.
Joby. London, Joseph, 1964.
A Raging Calm. London, Joseph, 1968; as *The Hidden Part*, New York, Coward McCann, 1969.
A Brother's Tale. London, Joseph, 1980.
Just You Wait and See. London, Joseph, 1986.

Short Stories

The Desperadoes. London, Joseph, 1961.
The Human Element and Other Stories, edited by Marilyn Davies. London, Longman, 1969.
A Season with Eros. London, Joseph, 1971.
A Casual Acquaintance and Other Stories, edited by Marilyn Davies. London, Longman, 1976.
The Glad Eye and Other Stories. London, Joseph, 1984.

Plays

Ask Me Tomorrow, with Alfred Bradley, adaptation of the novel by Barstow (produced Sheffield, 1964). London, French, 1966.
A Kind of Loving, with Alfred Bradley, adaptation of the novel by Barstow (broadcast, 1964; produced Sheffield, 1965). London, Blackie, 1970.
An Enemy of the People, adaptation of a play by Ibsen (produced Harrogate, Yorkshire, 1969). London, Calder, 1977.
Listen for the Trains, Love, music by Alex Glasgow (produced Sheffield, 1970).
Stringer's Last Stand, with Alfred Bradley (produced York, 1971).

We Could Always Fit a Sidecar (broadcast, 1974). Published in *Out of the Air: Five Plays for Radio*, edited by Alfred Bradley, London, Blackie, 1977.
Joby, adaptation of his own novel (televised, 1975). London, Blackie, 1977.
The Human Element, and Albert's Part (televised, 1977). London, Blackie, 1984.

Radio Plays: *A Kind of Loving*, from his own novel, 1964; *The Desperadoes*, from his own story, 1965; *The Watchers on the Shore*, from his own novel, 1971; *We Could Always Fit a Sidecar*, 1974; *The Right True End*, from his own novel, 1978.

Television Plays: *The Human Element*, 1964; *The Pity of It All*, 1965; *A World Inside* (documentary), with John Gibson, 1966; *A Family at War* (1 episode), 1970; *Mind You, I Live Here* (documentary), with John Gibson, 1971; *A Raging Calm*, from his own novel, 1974; *South Riding*, from the novel by Winifred Holtby, 1974; *Joby*, 1975; *The Cost of Loving*, 1977; *The Human Element*, 1977; *Albert's Part*, 1977; *Travellers*, 1978; *A Kind of Loving*, from his own novels, 1981; *A Brother's Tale*, from his own novel, 1983.

Other

Editor, *Through the Green Woods: An Anthology of Contemporary Writing about Youth and Children.* Leeds, E.J. Arnold, 1968.

*

Stan Barstow comments:
  Came to prominence about the same time as several other novelists from North of England working-class backgrounds, viz. John Braine, Alan Sillitoe, David Storey, Keith Waterhouse, and saw with satisfaction, and occasional irritation, the gains made in the opening up of the regions and the "elevation" of the people into fit subjects for fictional portrayal absorbed into the popular cultures of the cinema and TV drama series and comedy shows. Still, living in the provinces and using mainly regional settings, consider myself non-metropolitan oriented. The publication of some of my work in the U.S. and its translation into several European languages reassures me that I have not resisted the neurotic trendiness of much metropolitan culture for the sake of mere provincial narrowness; and the knowledge that some of the finest novels in the language are "regional" leads me to the belief that to hoe one's own row diligently, thus seeking out the universal in the particular, brings more worthwhile satisfactions than the frantic pursuit of a largely phoney jet-age internationalism.

*   *   *

  "What's happening is bloody life, Gordon!"
  Eileen's angry outburst at her bewildered husband in *A Brother's Tale* provides us, in a recent novel, with a succinct appraisal of Stan Barstow's work. Life, with its tangle of messy conflicts and uncertainties, is Barstow's chosen subject, rather than the neat half-truths of escapist fiction. The lives he investigates are those of ordinary men and women, and through their experiences he depicts—keenly, but with compassion—the sad essence of human frailty, the lack of permanent relationships, and the growing challenge of the young to the established attitudes of their elders.
  A Kind of Loving, the book which marked Barstow's arrival as a writer, in many ways foreshadows the novels and stories

to come. Its account of a young man blinded by physical and romantic infatuation into thinking himself in love, and subsequently forced to marry the pregnant girl as that imagined love fades, remains a classic today. Told in the first person and the present tense, it engages the reader with its immediacy, Vic Brown's personality coming through in the racy narrative, its naivety sheltering behind a rough northern humour. Vic emerges as a believable character, brash and a touch aggressive, yet at the same time brooding and vulnerable, not as grown up as he at first appears. *A Kind of Loving*, like most Barstow novels, ends with its future unsettled. Vic's search for a lasting relationship—"I want something I can't bear to be without, because anything else must be in constant jeopardy"—is explored in two sequels, *The Watchers on the Shore* and *The Right True End*, describing the break-up of Vic's marriage and his hope of a new life with a woman for whom he feels genuine love. It could be argued that these two books lack something of the freshness of *A Kind of Loving* and *The Watchers on the Shore* especially seems to negate much of the message of its predecessor, but both are strong, well-crafted works eminently able to stand on their own merits. Maturity replaces the exuberance of the first novel, and a remarkable continuity is maintained, which ensures that the three books fit together. Barstow sticks to the first-person present tense narrative and manages with the minimum number of flashbacks. He offers several swift, adroit character sketches, and captures perfectly the speech of the different protagonists.

Barstow's own philosophy infuses most of his work, emerging through the characters, as when blunt, no-nonsense Vic Brown condemns apartheid in South Africa. Similarly, Vic's love of classical music and mainstream jazz is clearly shared by his creator. Sometimes, as in *Ask Me Tomorrow*, the autobiographical element tends to be too intrusive, and this novel—strong in many respects—suffers from too much introspective analysis of the writer and his problems. Philosophy is more effectively worked into the body of the novels in the Vic Brown trilogy, and in subsequent works. This is nowhere more apparent than in *A Raging Calm*, where the middle-aged Tom Simpkins embodies most of the Barstow virtues while remaining credible as a character. The story pivots on two love affairs—that of Simpkins himself for a married woman, and that of his young secretary for a married teacher—and their consequence, measured against the background of local politics in Cressley, the fictitious northern town which provides the setting for most Barstow novels and several short stories. The author weaves the threads of character storyline capably and without fuss, the work coming together as a satisfying whole. *A Raging Calm* once more studies the challenge to established mores on marriage, adultery, and divorce, and the telling is shot through with the human socialism of its author.

Shorter and sharper are *Joby* and *A Brother's Tale*, the former in particular unlike the normal Barstow novel. *Joby* is the story of a young boy whose world undergoes a crisis of its own in the summer of 1939, with the threatened destruction of his parents' marriage and his own involvement in petty crime. Simply but delicately told, it ranks as one of Barstow's outstanding works, the world-view and perceptions of the child beautifully caught in a number of understated passages. *A Brother's Tale* follows the other novels more closely, but shares with *Joby* and the rest the basic theme of a fancied stability suddenly removed, in this case the narrator's apparently secure marriage falling away to leave him contemplating a terrible void.

A born storyteller, Barstow also excels in the short story form, where his sharpness of line and ear for dialogue are put to good use. *The Desperadoes* and *A Season with Eros*

portray working-class lives for the most part, and some of the stories are almost Lawrentian in tone. *The Glad Eye* shows a greater depth of perception, Barstow presenting flawed men in need of women, or tragic women stricken by catastrophe, in efforts more finished and mature than in previous collections. The novella-length "Rue," with its study of ill-fated attraction, is something of a new departure.

Barstow views life clearly and honestly. He doesn't look away, or pretend that things are other than they are. Detesting such modern trends as the TV culture and bingo-addiction, he nevertheless retains his belief in progress. Though the relationships of his characters are uncertain and fraught with danger, one senses that they will endure. More even than his honesty, Barstow shares his humanity with the reader.

"And if you say well what is life about I'll say it's about life, and that's all."

—Geoff Sadler

BARTH, John (Simmons). American. Born in Cambridge, Maryland, 27 May 1930. Educated at the Juilliard School of Music, New York; Johns Hopkins University, Baltimore, A.B. 1951, M.A. 1952. Married 1) Anne Strickland in 1950 (divorced, 1969), one daughter and two sons; 2) Shelly Rosenberg in 1970. Junior Instructor in English, Johns Hopkins University, 1951–53; Instructor 1953–56, Assistant Professor, 1957–60, and Associate Professor of English, 1960–65, Pennsylvania State University, University Park; Professor of English, 1965–71, and Butler Professor, 1971–73, State University of New York, Buffalo. Since 1973, Centennial Professor of English and Creative Writing, Johns Hopkins University. Recipient: Brandeis University Creative Arts Award, 1965; Rockefeller grant, 1965; American Academy grant, 1966; National Book Award, 1973. Litt.D.: University of Maryland, College Park, 1969. Member, American Academy, 1977, and American Academy of Arts and Sciences, 1977. Agent: International Creative Management, 40 West 57th Street, New York, New York 10019. Address: c/o Writing Seminars, Johns Hopkins University, Baltimore, Maryland 21218, U.S.A.

PUBLICATIONS

Novels

The Floating Opera. New York, Appleton Century Crofts, 1956; revised edition, New York, Doubleday, 1967; Secker and Warburg, 1968.
The End of the Road. New York, Doubleday, 1958; London, Secker and Warburg, 1962; revised edition, Doubleday, 1967.
The Sot-Weed Factor. New York, Doubleday, 1960; London, Secker and Warburg, 1961; revised edition, Doubleday, 1967.
Giles Goat-Boy; or, The Revised New Syllabus. New York, Doubleday, 1966; London, Secker and Warburg, 1967.
Letters. New York, Putnam, 1979; London, Secker and Warburg, 1980.
Sabbatical: A Romance. New York, Putnam, and London, Secker and Warburg, 1982.

Short Stories

Lost in the Funhouse: Fiction for Print, Tape, Live Voice.
New York, Doubleday, 1968; London, Secker and Warburg,
1969.
~*Chimera.* New York, Random House, 1972; London,
Deutsch, 1974.

Other

*The Literature of Exhaustion, and The Literature of Replenish-
ment* (essays).   Northridge, California, Lord John Press, 1982.
The Friday Book: Essays and Other Nonfiction.   New York,
Putnam, 1984.
Don't Count on It: A Note on the Number of the 1001 Nights.
Northridge, California, Lord John Press, 1984.

*

Bibliography: *John Barth: A Descriptive Primary and Annotated Secondary Bibliography* by Joseph Weixlmann, New
York, Garland, 1975; *John Barth: An Annotated Bibliography*
by Richard Allan Vine, Metuchen, New Jersey, Scarecrow
Press, 1977; *John Barth, Jerzy Kosinski, and Thomas Pynchon:
A Reference Guide* by Thomas P. Walsh and Cameron Northouse, Boston, Hall, 1977.

Manuscript Collection: Library of Congress, Washington,
D.C.

Critical Studies: *John Barth* by Gerhard Joseph, Minneapolis,
University of Minnesota Press, 1970; *John Barth: The Comic
Sublimity of Paradox* by Jac Tharpe, Carbondale, Southern
Illinois University Press, 1974; *The Literature of Exhaustion:
Borges, Nabokov, and Barth* by John O. Stark, Durham, North
Carolina, Duke University Press, 1974; *John Barth: An Intro-
duction* by David Morrell, University Park, Pennsylvania State
University Press, 1976; *Critical Essays on John Barth* edited
by Joseph J. Waldmeir, Boston, Hall, 1980; *Passionate Virtuo-
sity: The Fiction of John Barth* by Charles B. Harris, Urbana,
University of Illinois Press, 1983.

*   *   *

Often hailed as the best fiction writer of our time, John
Barth is undoubtedly one of the most important American
novelists of the 20th century. He combines the kind of experimentation associated with postmodernist writing with a firm
mastery of the skills demanded of the traditional novelist. A
progression toward postmodernism may easily be traced in his
works from the more traditional treatments of his earlier
books—*The Floating Opera, The End of the Road,* and *The
Sot-Weed Factor*—to the wild experimentation that characterizes such works as *Giles Goat-Boy, Chimera, Letters,* and especially *Lost in the Funhouse.* In *Sabbatical,* he returns to the
more traditional kind of narrative, with the added postmodernist twist that the novel itself is supposed to be a work produced
by the two central characters in it.

Although Barth denies that he engages in experimentation
for its own sake, the stories in *Lost in the Funhouse* certainly
give that appearance. Subtitled *Fiction for Print, Tape, Live
Voice,* the work marks Barth's wholehearted embrace of the
world of the postmodern in which fiction and reality, fictitious
characters and the authors that produce them, become indistinguishable. Barth's insistence that some of the stories in this
"series," as he calls it, were not composed "expressly for print"
and thus "make no sense unless heard in live or recorded

voices" is questionable, since, after all, they are in print and
presumably the author did compose them by writing them on
paper. Nonetheless, they clearly show Barth's versatility with
various fictitious forms. Still, even if we can assume that a
story like "Echo," the eighth in the series, is intended only
for live or recorded voice and must not be read silently, it
is difficult to determine whether it is profound or merely full
of gimmickry.

Barth calls *Letters* "an old time epistolary novel," yet it is
anything but old-fashioned. In this monumental work the
author himself becomes a fictitious character with whom his
"fictitious drolls and dreamers," many of whom are drawn
from Barth's earlier works, correspond concerning their often
funny, sometimes horrifying problems. The letters they
exchange gradually reveal to the reader a convoluted plot that
involves such things as abduction, possible incest, and suicide.
That postmodernism may have reached its dead-end in this
book is something Barth himself seems to have recognized
in his return to a more traditional form in *Sabbatical,* a novel
with a fairly easily summarizable plot involving fairly clearly
defined characters.

Along with his movement from modernism to postmodernism may be traced a movement from what Barth calls "the
literature of exhaustion" to what he calls "the literature of
replenishment." The anti-heroes of his earlier works—Todd
Andrews, Jake Horner, and Ebenezer Cooke—give way to
the genuinely heroic protagonist of *Giles Goat-Boy,* a book
of epic dimensions containing a central figure and plot modeled
largely on myths of various heroes, both pagan and Christian.
This work is Barth's most important. The central character,
Giles himself, lacks a human father (quite probably he was
fathered by the computer that controls the world of the novel).
As the book unfolds, he proceeds without hesitation to fulfill
his typically heroic destiny to *Pass All Fail All.* Whatever victories he achieves are, of course, ambiguous, and his very
existence is left in doubt.

The part of the book involving the actual narrative of events
in the life of George Giles is entitled "*R.N.S.: The Revised
New Syllabus of George Giles OUR GRAND TUTOR,* Being
the Autobiographical and Hortatory Tapes Read Out at New
Tammany College to His Son *Giles (,) Stoker* by the West
Campus Automatic Computer and by Him Prepared for the
Furtherment of the Gilesian Curriculum." It contains a kind
of comic, cosmic new testament, a collection of sacred-profane
writings designed to serve as a guide for future students in
this university world. Narrating the life and adventures of
George Giles, the goat-boy of the title, it recounts his intellectual, political, and sexual exploits. The introductory material
to the "Revised New Syllabus," consisting of a "Publisher's
Disclaimer," with notes from Editors A through D and written
by "The Editor-in-Chief"; the "Cover-Letter to the Editors
and Publisher," written by "This regenerate Seeker after
Answers, J.B."; the "Posttape" as well as the "Postscript to
the Posttape," again written by J.B.; and the "Footnote to
the Postscript," written by "Ed.," are all, of course, part of
this fiction that extends its boundaries out into the world in
which we all live.

From the paralysis of a Jacob Horner in *The End of the
Road* to the action of a Giles is a long stride indeed. Horner
is paralyzed, he claims, because he suffers from "cosmopsis,"
"the cosmic view" in which "one is frozen like the bullfrog
when the hunter's light strikes him full in the eyes, only with
cosmopsis there is no hunter, and no quick hand to terminate
the moment—there's only the light." An infinite number of
possibilities leads to an inability to choose any one, thus leading
to paralysis. The same kind of cosmic view, however, causes

no paralysis for Giles, who, when unable to choose between existing possibilities, unhesitatingly creates his own, as he does when he first leaves the barn to seek his destiny in the outside world. Heroically, George realizes that he even "had invented myself as I'd elected my name," and he is willing to accept responsibility not only for himself but also for the world in which he lives.

In *Sabbatical* Barth returns to a more traditional form. Drawing heavily on folklore of the Chesapeake Bay, as well as of the CIA, he writes of the end of a year-long sailing voyage taken by Fenwick, an ex-CIA agent, and Susan, a college professor, in order to decide what they will do with their lives. Although the resolution of their problem seems rather trite and unconvincing, their path toward that resolution is worth following. Like *Chimera, Sabbatical* is a kind of 20th-century fairytale. It even ends with the statement about the two central characters "that they lived

> Happily after, to the end
> Of Fenwick and Susie. . . .*"

The rhyme is completed in the footnote: "*Susan./Fenn." Obviously, in this work too it is often difficult to distinguish between gimmickry and profundity.

Barth has consistently been at the forefront of literary experimentation, producing works occasionally uneven and, as a result of his particular type of experimentation, occasionally too self-consciously witty. Still, he has produced some works that are now ranked and probably will continue to be ranked among the best of his time.

—Richard Tuerk

BARTHELME, Donald. American. Born in Philadelphia, Pennsylvania, 7 April 1931; brother of Frederick Barthelme, *q.v.* Educated at the University of Houston. Served in the United States Army, 1953–55. Married 1) Birgit Barthelme; 2) Marion Knox in 1978; two daughters. Reporter, *Houston Post*, 1951, 1955–56; worked on public relations and news service staff, and founding editor of the university literary magazine *Forum*, University of Houston, 1956–59; director, Contemporary Arts Museum, Houston, 1961–62; managing editor, *Location* magazine, New York, 1962–64. Visiting Professor, State University of New York, Buffalo, 1972, and Boston University, 1973. Since 1974, Distinguished Visiting Professor, City College, New York; since 1981, Visiting Professor, University of Houston. Recipient: Guggenheim fellowship, 1966; National Book Award, 1972; American Academy Morton Dauwen Zabel Award, 1972. Member, American Academy. Address: Department of English, University of Houston, 4800 Calhoun Road, Houston, Texas 77004, U.S.A.

PUBLICATIONS

Novels

Snow White. New York, Atheneum, 1967; London, Cape, 1968.
The Dead Father. New York, Farrar Straus, 1975; London, Routledge, 1977.
Paradise. New York, Putnam, 1986.

Short Stories

Come Back, Dr. Caligari. Boston, Little Brown, 1964; London, Eyre and Spottiswoode, 1966.
Unspeakable Practices, Unnatural Acts. New York, Farrar Straus, 1968; London, Cape, 1969.
City Life. New York, Farrar Straus, 1970; London, Cape, 1971.
Sadness. New York, Farrar Straus, 1972; London, Cape, 1973.
Guilty Pleasures. New York, Farrar Straus, 1974.
Amateurs. New York, Farrar Straus, 1976; London, Routledge, 1977.
Great Days. New York, Farrar Straus, and London, Routledge, 1979.
The Emerald. Los Angeles, Sylvester and Orphanos, 1980.
Presents, collages by the author. Dallas, Pressworks, 1980.
Sixty Stories. New York, Putnam, 1981.
Overnight to Many Distant Cities. New York, Putnam, 1983.

Uncollected Short Stories

"Man's Face," in *New Yorker*, 30 May 1964.
"Then," in *Mother 3* (Northfield, Minnesota), November–December 1964.
"Philadelphia," in *New Yorker*, 30 November 1968.
"Newsletter," in *New Yorker*, 11 July 1970.
"Adventure," in *Harper's Bazaar* (New York), December 1970.
"The Story Thus Far:," in *New Yorker*, 1 May 1971.
"Natural History," in *Harper's* (New York), August 1971.
"Three," in *Fiction 1* (New York), 1972.
"Edwards, Amelia," in *New Yorker*, 9 September 1972.
"A Man," in *New Yorker*, 30 December 1972.
"The Inauguration," in *Harper's* (New York), January 1973.
"The Bill," in *Viva* (New York), November 1973.
"The Bed," in *Viva* (New York), March 1974.
"The Dassaud Prize," in *New Yorker*, 12 January 1976.
"Monumental Folly," in *Atlantic* (Boston), February 1976.
"The Short Story Contest," in *New York Times Magazine*, 1 February 1976.
"Manfred," with Karen Snow, in *New York Times Magazine*, 18 April 1976.
"The Great Debate," in *New Yorker*, 3 May 1976.
"Chablis," in *New Yorker*, 12 December 1983.
"Sindbad," in *New Yorker*, 27 August 1984.
"Simon," in *New Yorker*, 24 September 1984.
"Opening," in *New Yorker*, 22 October 1984.
"Construction," in *New Yorker*, 29 April 1985.

Other

The Slightly Irregular Fire Engine; or, The Thithering Dithering Djinn (for children). New York, Farrar Straus, 1971.

*

Bibliography: *Donald Barthelme: A Comprehensive Bibliography and Annotated Secondary Checklist* by Jerome Klinkowitz, Asa Pieratt, and Robert Murray Davis, Hamden, Connecticut, Shoe String Press, 1977.

Critical Studies: "Donald Barthelme Issue" of *Critique* (Atlanta), vol. 16, no. 3, 1975; *Donald Barthelme* by Lois Gordon, Boston, Twayne, 1981; *Donald Barthelme* by Maurice Courturier and Régis Durand, London, Methuen, 1982; *The*

Metafictional Muse: The Works of Robert Coover, Donald Barthelme, and William H. Gass by Larry McCaffery, Pittsburgh, University of Pittsburgh Press, 1982; *Donald Barthelme's Fiction: The Ironist Saved from Drowning* by Charles Molesworth, Columbia, University of Missouri Press, 1982.

*   *   *

Since the mid-1960's a new literary movement has appeared on both sides of the Atlantic. Given a variety of labels—including postmodernism, surfiction, metafiction, superfiction, and parafiction—this avant-garde rejects all the traditions of the conventional novel form and takes as its subject the very act of writing fiction and the difficulties of using language to reflect a reality that in itself may be unknowable. In America the movement includes Donald Barthelme, William Gass, Robert Coover, Ronald Sukenick, Raymond Federman, Ishmael Reed, Steve Katz, John Hawkes, and Gilbert Sorrentino, and the earlier-known and earlier-established John Barth and Vladimir Nabokov. Abroad it includes Julio Cortázar, Italo Calvino, Robert Pinget, Claude Simon, Philippe Sollers, Jean Richardou, and J.M.G. Le Clézio, with Beckett and Borges its earliest practitioners.

Like the other writers of this "movement," Barthelme rejects the conventional mimetic form—traditional linear plot and characterization, the unities of time and space, and the assumption that the novel can reflect and comment upon reality. Numerous themes recur throughout his work, which has often, at least up through *The Dead Father*, been described as verbal collage: the hypereducated society brainwashed by packaged slogans and media-marketed expertise ("The Viennese Opera Ball"), the political and social pathology of American life ("The President"), and the inhuman and grotesque mentality of its warmongers ("Report"). Barthelme also writes about more personal matters, like the endless war between the sexes ("Indian Uprising"), the father-son relationship ("See the Moon"), and aging ("The New Jazz"). Throughout, his most persistent theme is the difficulty of using language in both a personal and creative way—not only as an artistic vehicle but also as a satisfactory way of connecting with the world and the human community ("The Balloon"). Some of his best stories treat how "signs sometimes lie" ("Me and Miss Mandible") and how one's experience is always private, and one's efforts to *translate it into words* is always inadequate ("Shower of Gold," "Marie, Marie, Hold On Tight," "Robert Kennedy Saved from Drowning").

In his earliest volumes, Barthelme was especially concerned with social issues—the contemporary, brainwashed society bent on mounting technology and texts, a world totally indifferent to "meaning" and feeling (*Come Back, Dr. Caligari* and *Unspeakable Practices, Unnatural Acts*). In *City Life* and *Sadness*, while these concerns persisted, Barthelme turned to irony as a defense against the spiritually sordid world. What he discovered, however, was that irony permitted only a pyrrhic victory. One wants, in fact, not a denial of reality (or annihilation of it through irony) but reconciliation with the world. These two volumes, and stories like "At the Tolstoy Museum," "The Glass Mountain," "Kierkegaard Unfair to Schlegal," "The Temptation of St. Anthony," and "Daumier" are among his most provocative works.

Guilty Pleasures, which the dust-jacket calls "non-fiction," is Barthelme's funniest book and a good introduction to his variety of parodic forms. It is a wild excursion through the corroded soul of contemporary America. In *Amateurs* Barthelme introduces a new fable form, and in *Great Days* he turns to an entirely new dialogue form to explore larger and more basic issues like time and morality. He creates more human figures with whom one can feel a certain personal kinship. These are not the earlier exaggerated comic creations of *Come Back, Dr. Caligari* or *Unspeakable Practices, Unnatural Acts*.

Barthelme's novels are his most interesting works. In his ingenious characterization of the modern young woman in the contemporary world, in *Snow White*, he concentrates on the difficulties of role-playing, of communicating with words, and of playing out "scripts"—that is, of being born, say, as Snow White, with a code of expectations from another era. In *The Dead Father* he focuses on the human compulsion both toward and away from "authority" (here, the dead father), and he projects on to his central figure any number of literary, mythic, historical, political, and linguistic meanings. The book has an encyclopedic scope and incorporates a variety of techniques from art, music, and film.

Throughout, one is overwhelmed by Barthelme's inventive use of language. As though to offer an alternative to our immersion in fixed roles and clichés, and our inevitable imprisonment in the fixed structures of language, he subjects the written and spoken forms of language to endless parody and experimentation. Through his various verbal arrangements he evokes a universe—unborn until then—in his reader's consciousness. He creates (until *The Dead Father*) a unique form of comedy, with language an emblem of man's relationship to the universe.

In the more recent work, Barthelme writes in a more poetic style. One associates the verbal collage with the earlier and main body of his work, and the more ineffable and polyphonic techniques of poetry and musical composition with the later work, like *Great Days*. The most recent collection, *Overnight to Many Distant Cities*, alternates short stories (there are 24) with dialogue/arias (there are 12). "Conversations with Goethe," one of the volume's best stories, is filled with typical Barthelmean wit: "Youth, Goethe said, is the silky apple butter on the good brown bread of possibility," and "Food is the top most taper on the golden candelabrum of existence."

Barthelme illustrates how words, with all the difficulties (and one's inevitable "failure") in using them, are our only link with the universe, all we have as a barter against annihilation. In "Nothing: A Preliminary Account" he illustrates his central thesis that one must never capitulate to nothingness. He punctuates an unending list of negatives with the phrase "Hurry on" as he embraces life: "How joyous the notion that, try as we may, we cannot do other than fail and fail absolutely and that the task will remain always before us, like a meaning for our lives. Hurry. Quickly. Nothing is not a nail."

—Lois Gordon

BARTHELME, Frederick. American. Born in Houston, Texas, 10 October 1943; brother of Donald Barthelme, *q.v.* Educated at Tulane University, New Orleans, 1961–62; University of Houston, 1962–65, 1966–67; Johns Hopkins University, Baltimore, (teaching fellow; Coleman Prose Award, 1977), 1976–77, M.A. 1977. Architectural draftsman, Jerome Oddo and Associates, and Kenneth E. Bentsen Associates, both Houston, 1965–66; exhibition organizer, St. Thomas University, Houston, 1966–67; assistant to director, Kornblee Gallery, New York, 1967–68; creative director, BMA Advertising, Houston, 1971–73; senior writer, GDL & W Advertising, Houston, 1973–76. Since 1977, Professor of

English, Director of the Center for Writers, and Editor of *Mississippi Review*, University of Southern Mississippi, Hattiesburg. Visual artist: exhibitions at galleries in Houston, Norman, Oklahoma, New York, Seattle, Vancouver, Buenos Aires, and Oberlin, Ohio, 1965–74. Recipient: National Endowment for the Arts fellowship, 1979; University of Southern Mississippi research grant, 1980. Address: 203 Sherwood Drive, Hattiesburg, Mississippi 39401, U.S.A.

PUBLICATIONS

Novels

War and War.   New York, Doubleday, 1971.
Second Marriage.   New York, Simon and Schuster, 1984; London, Dent, 1985.
Tracer.   New York, Simon and Schuster, 1985.

Short Stories

Rangoon.   New York, Winter House, 1970.
Moon Deluxe.   New York, Simon and Schuster, 1983; London, Penguin, 1984.

Uncollected Short Stories

"Export" 23 April 1984, "Pupil" 5 August 1985, "Driver" 23 September 1985, and "Cleo" 18 November 1985, all in *New Yorker*.

*   *   *

Frederick Barthelme's early fiction—*Rangoon* and *War and War*—is self-consciously experimental, overly influenced (and greatly overshadowed) by the far more successful work of writers like his older brother Donald. It wasn't until more than a decade later, in the 17 stories that comprise *Moon Deluxe*, that he would begin writing the kind of fiction that would establish him as one of the most interesting of current American writers.

Barthelme's stories have the familiar look of the real world; they are meticulously detailed in such matters as the make and color of the cars the characters drive, the brand names of the products they buy, the names of the places where they live and the restaurants where they eat. On the other hand, they are eerily vague and indistinct about such matters as their location (the general setting is the Sun Belt states along the Gulf Coast), background information about the characters' jobs, their past, sometimes about their own names. Barthelme's fictional world is filled with real objects but empty of meaningful experience; his characters talk about things but seldom about things that matter.

The stories are typically narrated in present tense by men in their late 30's, either single or divorced, who live alone. Like Camus's Meursault, they report events in a detached, disengaged, almost affectless manner. (Several of the stories are told in second person, which distances the narrator even from himself.) Passive individuals, these men are watchers rather than doers; it is usually the women who are the aggressors, the men responding almost willy-nilly to their advances.

These characters reveal so little of their real selves that they are virtually interchangeable from one story to another.

The emptiness of the characters' lives and the dead tone in which the tales are narrated combine to make a powerful statement about the loneliness that infects the lives of many who inhabit the modern shopping malls, fast food restaurants, and singles apartment complexes of contemporary suburban America. However, Barthelme avoids making his stories as bleak as his characters' lives by presenting incidents and dialogue with a decidedly comic touch. The stories also transmit a strong sense of expectation, an unsettling feeling that something dramatic is about to happen (it seldom does). In *Moon Deluxe* the dull and the routine seem charged with mystery.

Second Marriage is a brilliant comedy of contemporary social and sexual manners, rich in offbeat characters and wickedly funny dialogue. The novel tells the story of a man named Henry (no last name) whose ex-wife Clare moves in with him and his current wife Theo. The two women soon discover they like each other more than they like Henry, so they ask him to move out. The book records with wry humor his goofy experiences following his eviction by his wives.

Henry is in many ways a typical Berthelme character: decent but ineffectual, he finds himself pushed aside, a casualty of the sexual revolution; bewildered, he passes the time watching TV, vacuuming his apartment, cleaning the refrigerator, aimlessly reading magazine articles he doesn't understand. One activity that usually rouses him from his torpor is eating, a favorite pastime for all of Barthelme's characters. None of them especially savors food; going out to eat is simply something to do, a safe way of filling up time, though the fast food they routinely consume is as lacking in nutrition as the tentative relationships they stumble in and out of.

Martin, the narrator of *Tracer*, moves into the Florida motel-condo operated by his wife Alex's sister Dominica following the breakup of his marriage. He is soon sleeping with Dominica, which complicates matters when both Alex and Dominica's estranged husband Mel show up. Out of this tangled web of relationships Berthelme fashions another of his quirky comedies of modern life.

Tracer is rich in details, incidents, and dialogue which underscore Barthelme's favorite themes of displacement and failed connections. The central symbol of the novel is a P-38 Night Fighter plane which, like Martin, has come to rest on Dominica's property like a lost bird. The dialogue, composed largely of humorous yet pointless monologues, conversational non-sequiturs, and misunderstood statements, is as disconnected as the characters' lives. Even incidents (such as the bizarre episode involving a stranger who takes out a gun and inexplicably begins shooting at the P-38) seem to have become unglued from any sort of logical context.

Tracer differs from its predecessors in one important respect: it communicates greater feeling and emotion. Unlike most of Barthelme's narrators who act lost in a world they fail to understand, Martin is better able to understand and articulate his situation and his feelings. He reveals an almost lyric sensitivity in his poignant reminiscences and his descriptions disclose the hidden beauty to be found in even the commonest objects and scenes, which nicely balances the absurdities the novel so deftly depicts.

In *Second Marriage* Henry describes a movie in which "ordinary life is at once ridiculed and shown to be strange and wonderful." This is an apt description of Barthelme's own fiction. He is a poet of the mundane who combines a satirist's skill in exposing the ridiculous in contemporary society with a photographer's ability to isolate the quotidian details of everyday life. His fiction, situated somewhere between good-humored social satire and documentary realism, both captures the absurdity and celebrates the wondrous beauty of the ordinary.

—David J. Geherin

BAUMBACH, Jonathan. American. Born in New York City, 5 July 1933. Educated at Brooklyn College, New York, 1951–55, A.B. 1955; Columbia University, New York, 1955–56, M.F.A. 1956; Stanford University, California, 1958–61, Ph.D. 1961. Served in the United States Army, 1956–58. Married 1) Elinor Berkman in 1956 (divorced, 1967), one son and one daughter; 2) Georgia A. Brown in 1968, two sons. Instructor, Stanford University, 1958–60; Instructor, 1961–62, and Assistant Professor, 1962–64, Ohio State University, Columbus; Assistant Professor, New York University, 1964–66. Associate Professor, 1966–70, 1971–72, and since 1972, Professor of English, Brooklyn College, City University of New York. Visiting Professor, Tufts University, Medford, Massachusetts, 1970–71, and University of Washington, Seattle, 1978–79. Film critic, *Partisan Review*, New Brunswick, New Jersey, and Boston, 1974–83. Co-founder, 1974, co-director, 1974–78, and currently member of the Board of Directors, Fiction Collective, New York; Chairman, National Society of Film Critics, 1982–84. Recipient: *New Republic* Award, 1958; Yaddo grant, 1963, 1964, 1965; National Endowment for the Arts fellowship, 1967; Guggenheim fellowship, 1978; Ingram Merrill Foundation Fellowship, 1983. Agent: Robert Cornfield, 5 West 73rd Street, New York, New York 10023. Address: 320 Stratford Road, Brooklyn, New York 11218, U.S.A.

PUBLICATIONS

Novels

A Man to Conjure With. New York, Random House, 1965; London, Gollancz, 1966.
What Comes Next. New York, Harper, 1968.
Reruns. New York, Fiction Collective, 1974.
Babble. New York, Fiction Collective, 1976.
Chez Charlotte and Emily. New York, Fiction Collective, 1979.
My Father More or Less. New York, Fiction Collective, 1982.

Short Stories

The Return of Service. Urbana, University of Illinois Press, 1979.

Uncollected Short Stories

"You Better Watch Out," in *Seems* (Sheboygan, Wisconsin), Fall 1978.
"Passion?," in *Prize Stories 1979: The O. Henry Awards*, edited by William Abrahams. New York, Doubleday, 1979.
"Mother and Father," in *Iowa Review* (Iowa City), Winter 1979.
"A West Coast Story," in *New York Arts Journal*, Spring 1980.
"The Conference," in *North American Review* (Cedar Falls, Iowa), Spring 1980.
"Errant Melancholy," in *Canto* (Andover, Massachusetts), Winter 1980.

"How You Play the Game," in *New York Arts Journal*, Spring 1981.
"Familiar Games," in *Antaeus* (New York), Fall 1981.
"Who Shall Escape Whipping," in *Mississippi Review* (Hattiesburg), Winter 1981.
"From the Life of the President," in *Seattle Review*, Fall 1982.
"Children of Divorced Parents," in *Fiction International* (San Diego, California), Spring 1983.
"The Life and Times of Major Fiction," in *Prize Stories 1984: The O. Henry Awards*, edited by William Abrahams. New York, Doubleday, 1984.

Play

The One-Eyed Man Is King (produced New York, 1956).

Other

The Landscape of Nightmare: Studies in the Contemporary American Novel. New York, New York University Press, 1965; London, Owen, 1966.

Editor, with Arthur Edelstein, *Moderns and Contemporaries: Nine Masters of the Short Story.* New York, Random House, 1968; revised edition, 1977.
Editor, *Writers as Teachers / Teachers as Writers.* New York, Holt Rinehart, 1970.
Editor, *Statements: New Fiction from the Fiction Collective.* New York, Braziller, 1975.
Editor, with Peter Spielberg, *Statements 2: New Fiction.* New York, Fiction Collective, 1977.

*

Manuscript Collection: Boston University Library.

Critical Study: *The Life of Fiction* by Jerome Klinkowitz, Urbana, University of Illinois Press, 1977.

Jonathan Baumbach comments:

Novels are an attempt to make sense out of experience and to make experience out of sense, to eschew the illusion of verisimilitude, to give form to what never existed, not to imitate life but to re-invent it out of language, to imagine the processes of the imagination, to imagine the imagining of the processes of the imagination, involved with cinema, dream, and memory, and the underground landscape of their conjunction.

No theory informs the work. It is what it comes to. My fiction is the illusion of itself.

*   *   *

A helpful preface to Jonathan Baumbach's fiction is his critical study, *The Landscape of Nightmare: Studies in the Contemporary American Novel.* Baumbach is representative of a new style of novelist (which includes Ronald Sukenick, Jerzy Kosinski, and William H. Gass), having earned a graduate degree before writing fiction himself. Baumbach's thesis, that "To live in this world, to live consciously in this world in which madness daily passes for sanity is a kind of madness in itself," describes a problem for literary art against which he poses his own fiction as solution. "Unable to believe in the surface (the *Life* magazine reality) of our world," he argues, "the best of the post-Second-World-War novelists have taken as their terrain the landscape of the psyche." Yet for that "landscape of nightmare" writers such as Bernard Malamud and William

Styron were still using techniques more appropriate to social realism. In his own work Baumbach has striven to find a new style suitable for the innovative fiction he writes. As he emphasized to an interviewer in 1973, "I'm not just using the dream in the traditional sense, in the psychological sense where it's an almost compacted parable, with special symbols. I'm just trying to find another way of getting at reality. I mean, my sense is that the conventional novel, for me, anyway, is on its way to a dead end. And I'm trying to get at the way things are in a way that no one has ever seen them before."

Baumbach's first novel, *A Man to Conjure With*, synthesizes various trends outlined in his critical study. Much like William Styron's *Lie Down in Darkness*, Baumbach's work has a protagonist who moves simultaneously backward and forward in time, carefully orchestrating revelations of plot and character so that the present is gradually understood in a plausible and convincing way. As a result, the narrative is assembled as a psychological collage; only in the protagonist's final act do all the elements become clear. Baumbach's technical achievement has been to find a structural form which reflects this psychological state: a thoroughly spatial novel.

What Comes Next is a more tightly written exploration of this same structural theme. Again the situation is psychological: a young college student, beset by sexual and parental problems, is "flipping out," and Baumbach's novel expresses this confusion by its very form. Violence erupts on every page, though primarily as mental device, since it is usually sparked by newspaper headlines and fantasized incidents. The book organizes itself as a literal landscape of nightmare, as all reference points for the character's reality are located within his own disjointed perceptions. As far as temporal narrative, "what comes next" is created from the workings of his mind.

Baumbach's subsequent work has been even more strongly experimental. His third novel, *Reruns*, abandons plot and character entirely in favor of dream-like images from movies rerun page by page. *Babble*, a novel made up of several "baby stories" written through the mid-1970's, is more playful but no less daring in its technical achievement. In order to explore the workings of narrative, Baumbach records the stories his infant son allegedly tells him ("His second story is less fresh than the first, though of greater technical sophistication"; "The robot is after him again, this time disguised as a soda vending machine. 'You can't have any Coke,' the robot says, 'until you wash your face'"). Once more Baumbach has become the critic in order to fashion a new mode for fiction.

Throughout the 1970's Baumbach continued to experiment with various structures for fiction, including the sub-genre parodies, movie mythologies, and dreamlike obsessions featured throughout his story collection *The Return of Service*. But it is his fifth novel, *Chez Charlotte and Emily*, which displays his greatest facility as a writer. Ostensibly the device by which a bored husband and wife communicate with each other (by proposing a narrative and then critiquing it), the novel is actually an excuse (à la *The Canterbury Tales*) for the telling of stories. Freed from the necessity of plausible context, Baumbach is able to spin out fantasies of shipwreck, sexual adventure, intrigue, and the complexity of human relationships—all as pure writing, justified by the arrangement of the couple's critical debate. Soon the two contexts, critical and fictional, merge—as they must, Baumbach would argue, for it is through works of the imagination that we preserve our consciousness of the world.

His sixth novel, *My Father More or Less*, experiments with forms of intertextuality to make this same point. Alternately narrated by Tom Terman and by a third-person narrator reflecting the actions of his father Lukas, the novel shows how Tom's visit to his father in London is shaped by the son's memory of his earlier abandonment, while the father's own coming to terms with his son, his mistress, and his employer becomes interwoven with the detective-story screenplay he's been working on. Lukas only superficially controls his film narrative, as its development toward the protagonist's death is impelled by the pressure of events unfolding in Terman's life. But these same events are enriched by the textual experience with his script. At times the writer's role takes over, as when Terman extricates himself from an unhappy situation by "writing himself a few lines of dialogue." For his part, Tom finds himself in a film script situation enhanced by the fact that actual movies have been shot on location in his father's house; but when events threaten, he is able to telephone his father for a rescue, much like a character calling upon the author for relief. That the father is creator of the son helps establish the naturalized quality of Baumbach's narrative. Although as experimentally intertextual as the most sophisticated literary experiments, *My Father More or Less* reads as accessibly as the most realistic fiction, indicating that Baumbach has found a useful device for bringing innovative fiction back within the literary mainstream.

—Jerome Klinkowitz

BAWDEN, Nina (née Mabey). British. Born in London, 19 January 1925. Educated at Ilford County High School; Somerville College, Oxford, B.A. 1946, M.A. 1951; Salzburg Seminar in American Studies, 1960. Married 1) H.W. Bawden in 1946, two sons (one deceased); 2) A.S. Kark in 1954, one daughter. Assistant, Town and Country Planning Association, 1946–47. Since 1969, Justice of the Peace for Surrey. Regular reviewer, *Daily Telegraph*, London. Member, P.E.N. Executive Committee, 1968–71; President, Society of Women Writers and Journalists. Recipient: *Guardian* award, for children's book, 1976; *Yorkshire Post* award, 1976. Fellow, Royal Society of Literature, 1970. Agent: Curtis Brown, 162–168 Regent Street, London W1R 5TA. Address: 22 Noel Road, London N1 8HA, England.

PUBLICATIONS

Novels

Who Calls the Tune. London, Collins, 1953; as *Eyes of Green*, New York, Morrow, 1953.
The Odd Flamingo. London, Collins, 1954.
Change Here for Babylon. London, Collins, 1955.
The Solitary Child. London, Collins, 1956; New York, Lancer, 1966.
Devil by the Sea. London, Collins, 1957; Philadelphia, Lippincott, 1959; abridged edition (for children), London, Gollancz, and Lippincott, 1976.
Just Like a Lady. London, Longman, 1960; as *Glass Slippers Always Pinch*, Philadelphia, Lippincott, 1960.
In Honour Bound. London, Longman, 1961.
Tortoise by Candlelight. London, Longman, and New York, Harper, 1963.
Under the Skin. London, Longman, and New York, Harper, 1964.
A Little Love, A Little Learning. London, Longman, 1965; New York, Harper, 1966.

A Woman of My Age. London, Longman, and New York, Harper, 1967.

The Grain of Truth. London, Longman, and New York, Harper, 1968.

The Birds on the Trees. London, Longman, 1970; New York, Harper, 1971.

Anna Apparent. London, Longman, and New York, Harper, 1972.

George Beneath a Paper Moon. London, Allen Lane, and New York, Harper, 1974.

Afternoon of a Good Woman. London, Macmillan, 1976; New York, Harper, 1977.

Familiar Passions. London, Macmillan, and New York, Morrow, 1979.

Walking Naked. London, Macmillan, 1981; New York, St. Martin's Press, 1982.

The Ice-House. London, Macmillan, and New York, St. Martin's Press, 1983.

Fiction (for children)

The Secret Passage. London, Gollancz, 1963; as *The House of Secrets*, Philadelphia, Lippincott, 1964.

On the Run. London, Gollancz, 1964; as *Three on the Run*, Philadelphia, Lippincott, 1965.

The White Horse Gang. London, Gollancz, and Philadelphia, Lippincott, 1966.

The Witch's Daughter. London, Gollancz, and Philadelphia, Lippincott, 1966.

A Handful of Thieves. London, Gollancz, and Philadelphia, Lippincott, 1967.

The Runaway Summer. London, Gollancz, and Philadelphia, Lippincott, 1969.

Squib. London, Gollancz, and Philadelphia, Lippincott, 1971.

Carrie's War. London, Gollancz, and Philadelphia, Lippincott, 1973.

The Peppermint Pig. London, Gollancz, and Philadelphia, Lippincott, 1975.

Rebel on a Rock. London, Gollancz, and Philadelphia, Lippincott, 1978.

The Robbers. London, Gollancz, and New York, Lothrop, 1979.

Kept in the Dark. London, Gollancz, and New York, Lothrop, 1982.

Princess Alice. London, Deutsch, 1985.

The Finding. London, Gollancz, and New York, Lothrop, 1985.

Other (for children)

William Tell. London, Cape, and New York, Lothrop, 1981.

St. Francis of Assisi. London, Cape, and New York, Lothrop, 1983.

*

Critical Study: article by Gerda Seaman, in *British Novelists since 1960* edited by Jay L. Halio, Detroit, Gale, 1983.

Nina Bawden comments:

I find it difficult to comment on my adult novels. I suppose one could say that the later books, from *Just Like a Lady* onwards, are social comedies with modern themes and settings; the characters moral beings, hopefully engaged in living. People try so hard and fail so often, sometimes sadly, sometimes comically; I try to show how and why and to be accurate about relationships and motives. I have been called a "cryptomoralist with a mischievous sense of humour," and I like this description: it is certainly part of what I aim to be.

This quotation, from the *Christian Science Monitor*, though not the most flattering, might be useful:

Nina Bawden is a writer of unusual precision who can depict human foibles with an almost embarrassing accuracy. Yet for all that she centres dead on target, there is always a note of compassion in her stories. The light thrown on her characters, clear though it is, is no harsh spotlight. It is a more diffuse beam that allows one to peer into the shadows and see causes even while it focuses on effects.

*   *   *

The world of the English middle classes is the focal point for most of Nina Bawden's fiction. In *The Birds on the Trees*—a key novel in her development—she observes life as she sees it, centering on an entirely believable middle-class family, with children who puzzle and dismay their parents, because these are the people she sees every day, and these are the children who interest and baffle her, too. She captures the capricious intensity of sibling love, rivalry, and loyalty; she is reluctant to pin blame and quick to display compassion; she is also logical enough to offer no easy solutions, but sufficiently warm-hearted to include realistic sprinklings of hope. Above all, she brings a sympathetic ear to the cadences of everyday speech, a virtue which heightens the intensity of the plot—a story of alienation and the betrayal by the pampered Toby of his vain self-righteous parents.

Her no-nonsense, no-holds-barred approach to contemporary social problems is taken a stage further in *Walking Naked*, a chillingly precise novel about people unable to come to grips with the worlds they inhabit. Laura is a novelist whose method of dealing with difficulties is to retreat into the realm of her imagination. These problems are induced by guilt—guilt about her parents, her first marriage, her son who is in jail, her friends, and her present husband. "I write because I am afraid of life," is her easy palliative to life's ills. Now life is taking its revenge. In the course of one fraught day Laura struggles to come to terms with what she has made of her life, to strip away the layers of anxiety which give her nightmares that her house is falling down about her ears, to avoid the self-deception which has made a mockery of her art, to walk naked and alone. The timescale gives the novel a sharp narrative vigour and the dialogue is always slyly intelligent and believable, but what gives *Walking Naked* its authority is Bawden's precise analysis of middle-class mores and the way in which they are brought to bear on a woman's life.

As in all her later fiction Bawden excels at revealing the tensions and hidden currents at work beneath the calm and humdrum exteriors of her characters. She is no mere moralist; rather, the matter of relationships is her main concern. In *The Ice-House*, a caustic glance at the complexities of modern marriage, friendship, and loyalty, she examines the unlikely friendship of Daisy and Ruth who have been friends since their schooldays. As girls, Daisy was boisterous and extrovert; Ruth withdrawn and frightened, a victim of an overbearing father. Thirty years later Ruth has a successful career and, on the surface at least, has a happy marriage; Daisy, though, is less content. When a tragedy rocks the lives of the two women and their families, its repercussions force them out of uneasy self-deception into a new and painful reality which they both have to accept. *The Ice-House* is an unusual and subtle novel about familiar themes—love, marriage, friendship, adultery—in which the emotional lives of the two female protagonists are viewed with a mixture of sympathy and disconcerting accuracy. No less tangled are their moral confusions and the task of unravelling them gives the novel is central narrative line. To her adult novels Bawden has brought psychological depth and a humorous focus on human moods, resignations and self-deceptions, tempered only by her powers of observation and discrimination.

Nina Bawden is one of the very few authors who will admit to making a conscious adjustment to writing for children. She has said: "I consider my books for children as important as my adult work, and in some ways more challenging." In all her children's novels childhood is seen with a special clarity and she has the gift of not only understanding childhood but also the childhoods of her own characters. *The Peppermint Pig*, for example, explores the reactions of a family of Edwardian children to their new and reduced circumstances and it is through their eyes that we see their reactions to the world around them. We can understand their hopes and fears, their relationships with each other and with the adult world: this is felt most clearly in a profound episode dealing with the inevitable death of Johnny, the children's pet pig. Bawden's secret is that her sympathy for the children never flags—she thereby retains her readers' sympathies, too.

—Trevor Royle

* * *

BEATTIE, Ann. American. Born in Washington, D.C., 8 September 1947. Educated at American University, Washington, D.C., B.A. 1969; University of Connecticut, Storrs, 1970–72, M.A. 1970. Married David Gates in 1973; one son. Visiting Lecturer, 1976–77 and 1980, University of Virginia, Charlottesville; Briggs Copeland Lecturer in English, Harvard University, Cambridge, Massachusetts, 1977–78. Recipient: Guggenheim fellowship, 1977; American University Distinguished Alumnae Award, 1980; American Academy award, 1980. Agent: Lynn Nesbit, International Creative Management, 40 West 57th Street, New York, New York 10019. Address: c/o Random House, 201 East 50th Street, New York, New York 10022, U.S.A.

PUBLICATIONS

Novels

Chilly Scenes of Winter. New York, Doubleday, 1976.
Falling in Place. New York, Random House, 1980; London, Secker and Warburg, 1981.
Love Always. New York, Random House, and London, Joseph, 1985.

Short Stories

Distortions. New York, Doubleday, 1976.
Secrets and Surprises. New York, Random House, 1978; London, Hamish Hamilton, 1979.
Jacklighting. Worcester, Massachusetts, Metacom Press, 1981.
The Burning House. New York, Random House, 1982; London, Secker and Warburg, 1983.

Uncollected Short Stores

"Mr. B. and the Miraculous Christmas Tree," in *House and Garden* (New York), December 1981.
"Moving Water," in *New Yorker*, 8 November 1982.
"Coney Island," in *New Yorker*, 24 January 1983.
"Television," in *New Yorker*, 28 March 1983.
"Lofty," in *New Yorker*, 8 August 1983.
"One Day," in *New Yorker*, 29 August 1983.
"Heaven on a Summer Night," in *New Yorker*, 28 November 1983.
"Times," in *New Yorker*, 26 December 1983.
"A Shaggy Love Story," in *Ladies Home Journal* (New York), June 1984.
"In the White Night," in *New Yorker*, 4 June 1984.
"Summer People," in *New Yorker*, 24 September 1984.
"Janus," in *New Yorker*, 27 May 1985.
"On the Radio," in *Harper's* (New York), June 1985.

Other

Spectacles (for children). New York, Workman, 1985.

* * *

Ann Beattie's *Chilly Scenes of Winter* and *Distortions* were published simultaneously, and, to the author's consternation, she was quickly celebrated as the chronicler of the disillusioned 1960's counterculture. She was praised as a narrator of the ennui and disillusion of the postlapsarian love children, the generation that turned on in the 1960's but totally dropped out in the 1970's. Of this Beattie has said: "That's a horribly reductive approach. ... What I've always hoped for is that somebody will then start talking more about the meat and bones of what I'm writing about," and one shares Beattie's sentiment. While it is true that many of her stories use the manners and jargon of the post-counterculture era as a backdrop—particularly its songs and culture heroes—these details function in much the same way as Raymond Carver's Pacific Northwest, or Donald Barthelme's New York City—to create a concrete setting from which to abstract more general human dilemmas—in Beattie's case, the difficulties of adjusting to the modern world, the growing distance between one's youthful dreams and present responsibilities, and in particular, the fragility and difficulty of sustaining relationships and the despair of loneliness. What persists in Beattie's fiction is the focus upon the common decency and generosity of people, and the bonds of friendship that survive the worst of times. Beattie's men and women have an indefatigable selflessness about them. They are capable of extending themselves to others, despite their most difficult personal circumstances.

The novel *Chilly Scenes of Winter*, more than any of her subsequent works, has as its background the dreams and values of the 1960's. The story concerns a 27-year-old disaffected, ex-love child who despairs over his girlfriend's return to her husband. Charles is virtually obsessed with Laura, and the novel traces what is in fact his paralysis in going after her. Instead, Charles busies himself with a cast of other needy people including his childhood friend Sam, now mourning the death of his dog; his neurotic, suicidal mother and her husband Pete; his ex-girlfriend Pamela Smith, who has begun experimenting with lesbianism; and his naive sister, Susan (she doesn't even understand the significance of Janis Joplin). At the end of the novel, Charles learns that Laura has left her husband and he visits her; the two prepare to go off into the sunset.

Although this is the plot, the novel is actually about the loss of innocence and first love—as they are tied to the qualities of optimism, passion, and unflagging hope, characteristic of the 1960's youth culture. It is a study, through Charles and his friend Sam, of the aimlessness and ennui of the 1970's lost generation. Throughout is the sense that "You could be happy to . . . if you hadn't had your eyes opened in the sixties." That the 1960's was not, however, to Beattie, a hallowed time is clear, as she retains an extraordinary balance between an objective (sometimes critical) and affectionate (slightly mocking) portrayal of that time. There is, for example, something ridiculous about Charles's wistfulness toward the past. Everyone has died, he repeats—not just Janis Joplin and Brian Jones, but also Jim Morrison's widow, Amy Vanderbilt, Adele Davies, and maybe even Rod Stewart (about whom, of course, he is wrong). Charles, in his quest for Laura, is a self-proclaimed poor man's Gatsby, and he and Sam live with a paralyzing world weariness. But many of their laments are hilarious. Times have grown worse, they commisserate, since "women put their brassieres back on and want you to take them to Paul Newman movies." Even Susan says of her brother: "You deliberately make yourself suffer all the time because then you can be aware of yourself."

That you can't go home again, even if you want to—to the 1960's—is extended to the notion that you can't return anywhere, and one feels kindly toward Charles when he speculates that maybe his relationship with Laura might have worked better in the 1950's (when they could have danced to "Rock around the Clock") or in the 1940's when they could have enjoyed strawberry shortcake desserts together (like the people in Norman Rockwell posters). Furthermore, if the 1960's weren't all that solid a time, neither are the 1970's. Charles's ex-girlfriend goes off to California (she cans cauliflower in Menolena) and hears some disillusioning scuttlebutt. Dylan is hanging around with Cher; Peter Fonda "has screwed" a girl on the floor of an all-night health food restaurant. Young people get stoned and actually believe what Dylan says on his records.

Charles is a dreamer, out of place and time now, but also out of place in any time. He is afraid of the present (he is obsessed with illness and death), and like many others in the book, he longs to be a child again. But he is earnest, sympathetic, generous, and always kind. And to these important human qualities Beattie conveys a sense of respect, although she never leaves her subtle humor far behind. The novel, nevertheless, ends bitterly. Sam gets a new dog, which Charles says is the ugliest dog he has ever seen, "a terrible genetic mistake," and one can't help thinking the same of his reunion with Laura.

The stories in *Distortions*, like the majority of the later stories, focus on the empty relationships of married and single couples, on the terrible need for companionship and definition that drives most people. Especially moving are the figures in "Dwarf House," "The Parking Lot," "A Platonic Relationship," "Snakes' Shoes," and "Vermont." Although these characters are only peripherally aware of their drab lives, the reader feels deeply for them. More fully characterized are the people in *Secrets and Surprises*, men and women once again trapped in unfulfilling jobs and personal relationships. A more affluent group, they are into gourmet cooking, jogging, health foods, weekends in the country, and the usual fare of the 1970's upper-middle-class mobile society. What they share is a terrible sense of emptiness, although friendship and pets (particularly dogs) are once more their only comfort. Some of Beattie's most memorable evocations of loneliness and yearning are in the title story, "A Vintage Thunderbird," "A Reasonable Man," "Distant Music," and "The Lawn Party." Lines that summarize

a lifetime—like one character's remark that people smile because they don't understand each other—resound throughout. Another woman explains: "If you have something to say about the weather, you will always be able to make conversation with people." These people are trapped but they lack self-pity; they are lost but they still extend a hand.

An even more sophisticated society inhabits *The Burning House*, but it is the juxtaposition of the characters' loneliness and selflessness that continues to move the reader. Little occurs in the way of change, although there are occasional moments of muted insight; once again, the stories are evocations of mood, descriptive of states of being. There remains very little trace of the 1960's past. Of particular interest is the title story and "Learning to Fall," where Beattie concretizes two characters' remarks: "What will happen can't be stopped" and "I'm sick of hearing how things might have been worse, when they might also have been better." "Girl Talk" is about two women, one young, unmarried, and pregnant, and the other, the unborn child's grandmother, many times married, wealthy, still beautiful but no longer capable of bearing children. It is about how "pain is relative." "The Cinderella Waltz," one of Beattie's most evocative stories, is about the complex of emotions exchanged between a mother and daughter and their estranged husband-father and his new male lover.

Falling in Place, Beattie's second novel, portrays the small amount of control one has over one's destiny—how life just seems to fall in place. Once again, she measures the fragility of relationships, here focusing on the disintegration of a family and the guilt that falls to both parents and children. The book lacks a traditional plot; rather, Beattie shifts from character to character and then combines events from each chapter into brief mood interludes. Set in Connecticut and New York in the summer of 1979, the novel focuses on the surrogate emotional relationships each member of the John Knapp family sets up. The climax revolves around the son's quasi-accidental shooting of his sister and how the family members finally face one another; things fall into place. Although the book ends with a positive resolution, like *Chilly Scenes of Winter*, it is bitter and the prognosis for future happiness is bleak.

Lucy Spenser, in Beattie's most recent novel, *Love Always*, is a 40-year-old, modern-day Miss Lonelyhearts ("Cindi Coeur"), and she writes hilarious letters (actually both the letter and the answer) for a counterculture magazine, *Country Doze*. The novel follows the madcap experiences of her 14-year-old niece who comes to visit her for the summer. The girl, Nicole, who portrays an adolescent alcoholic on a popular soap opera, brings into Lucy's beautiful Vermont existence a number of bizarre, sad, and eccentric adventures, and Lucy gains another level of experience about the world about her. The novel is wildly funny, highly sophisticated, and totally enjoyable.

—Lois Gordon

BEATY, (Arthur) David. British. Born in Hatton, Ceylon, 28 March 1919. Educated at Kingswood School, Bath, Somerset; Merton College, Oxford, 1938–40, M.A. in history 1940; University College, London, 1964–67, 1974–77, M. Phil. in psychology 1977. Served in the Royal Air Force, in the United Kingdom and the Middle East, 1940–46: Squadron Leader; Distinguished Flying Cross and Bar. Married Betty Smith (i.e., the writer Betty Beaty) in 1948; three daughters. Senior Captain, BOAC (British Overseas Airways Corporation), 1946–53. Instructor, College of Air Training, Hamble, Hampshire, 1963. Principal, Administrative Civil Service, 1966–70; Administrative Secretary, Centre for Education Development Overseas, London, 1970–72; Principal, Overseas Development Administration, London, 1972–74. Member, Royal Aeronautical Society. Agent: A.P. Watt Ltd., 26–28 Bedford Row, London WC1R 4HL. Address: Woodside, Hever, Edenbridge, Kent TN8 7LR, England.

PUBLICATIONS

Novels

The Take Off. London, Laurie, 1948; as *The Donnington Legend*, New York, Morrow, 1949.
The Heart of the Storm. London, Secker and Warburg, 1954; as *The Four Winds,* New York, Morrow, 1955.
The Proving Flight. London, Secker and Warburg, 1956; New York, Morrow, 1957.
Cone of Silence. London, Secker and Warburg, and New York, Morrow, 1959.
The Wind Off the Sea. London, Secker and Warburg, and New York, Morrow, 1962.
The Siren Song. London, Secker and Warburg, and New York, Morrow, 1964.
Sword of Honour. London, Secker and Warburg, 1965; New York, Morrow, 1966.
The Temple Tree. London, Secker and Warburg, and Boston, Houghton Mifflin, 1971.
Electric Train. London, Secker and Warburg, 1975.
Excellency. London, Secker and Warburg, 1977; New York, Morrow, 1978.
The White Sea-Bird. London, Secker and Warburg, 1979; New York, Morrow, 1980.
Wings of the Morning, with Betty Beaty. London, Macmillan, and New York, Coward McCann, 1982.
The Stick. London, Secker and Warburg, 1984.

Novels as Paul Stanton

Call Me Captain. London, Joseph, 1959; New York, Mill, 1960.
Village of Stars. London, Joseph, and New York, Mill, 1960.
The Gun Garden. London, Joseph, and New York, Mill, 1965.

Uncollected Short Story

"Kid's Stuff," in *Pick of Today's Short Stories*, edited by John Pudney. London, Putnam, 1954.

Plays

Radio Plays: *The Magic Carpet* serial, 1983.

Other

Milk and Honey: Travails with a Donkey (as Paul Stanton). London, Joseph, 1964; New York, Mill, 1965.
The Human Factor in Aircraft Accidents. London, Secker and Warburg, 1969; New York, Stein and Day, 1970.
The Water Jump: The Story of Transatlantic Flight. London, Secker and Warburg, and New York, Harper, 1976.

The Complete Skytraveller. London, Methuen, 1979.
Strange Encounters: Mysteries of the Air. London, Methuen, 1982; New York, Atheneum, 1984.

*

Critical Studies: *The World of David Beaty*, New York, Twayne, 1971, and *Antoine de Saint-Exupéry and David Beaty: Poets of a New Dimension*, Boston, Hall, 1974, both by Roberta J. Forsberg.

David Beaty comments:

(1972) In my view, the main purpose of a novel is to search out and exhibit truth, illuminating at the same time human behaviour. This should be executed in a way that is both informative and interesting. The reader must be absorbed by what he reads in order to turn the page. The motivation behind the characters' actions, the interacting of their personalities within the plot are most important. I am interested in "why," not simply in the events themselves. My novels are built up on a plan, almost a blueprint. "Belief" is all important, and the sustaining of belief is one of the most difficult things to do. Without belief, the novel is nothing—though belief is of course still possible within fantasy and fairy stories. I see the plot as a symphony composed of incidents, complete in themselves, all with their own note and colour. An incident is "wrong" when it is out of tune or clashes with the colour of its neighbour. Every novel is an attempt to capture time, to weave something solid out of air. The author knows it is an impossible task—that is why he keeps on trying.

(1981) As far as I know, I am the only professional novelist who is qualified in psychology. My characters follow very closely present-day thinking in psychology and human behaviour.

(1986) My main interest in psychology is the psychology of "mistakes"—why we make "mistakes," the ambiguity of what a "mistake" is, the consequences of "mistakes," and the whole misconception on the subject of "mistakes" in our upbringing, education, and society. This interest is of course reflected in my novels.

*   *   *

David Beaty, like Saint-Exupéry, makes his fiction out of the world of commercial aviation. And like his predecessor, his poetic insight enables him to add the symbolic dimension to the realism of his characterization and action. That realism centres on the contemporary dilemma, the human being trapped more and more by his own technology. The novelist particularizes this theme in *The Siren Song* by putting a question, "What is going to happen now that a machine can land an aeroplane a thousand times more safely than a human operator?"

The Beaty concern with man vs. machine has qualities which differentiate his work from that of other writers who discuss the same problem. As reference to the biography will indicate, he is a professional with a distinguished career as a pilot. In addition, he is an expert in certain areas of flying. His most recent research was published in 1969 in *The Human Factor in Aircraft Accidents*. This study of the psychological factors affecting pilot performance was so highly regarded by an international airline that the management wished to serialize it in their house organ. The importance of his past work is that it has an essential bearing on his art, on its emotional depth. In short Beaty draws upon his experience for more than a life-like milieu and professionally performing men and women.

Many facets of his work reveal the ties between his technology and his poetic fiction, but only two of these can be indicated in a short summary essay. The first aspect one can only call fundamental love of the instrument. Like the ship of the sea, the airship is regarded as a living creature. "As always on a runway, he had a sense of having no right to be there; as though this was the property of the machines that came tearing down it, to lift themselves up just before where he was now standing, and launch themselves into their own element." Obviously David Beaty does not belong to the back-to-nature school of critics, those who would denounce what they see as dirty, ugly, caricatures of birds. To airmen like him they are the vital tools for casting off earth's fetters, for seeing a new beauty, and for finding peace of mind and soul. Man and machine, "each dead without the other," must make their lives together, struggle with the elements together. Often the novelist sees the survival of each as equally important.

But man can use this instrument for bringing about his own damnation, even as the path to hell goes down from the gate to paradise. Thus, in the Beaty world of multiple images, the man-machine twinning becomes a warning symbol of ultimate destruction, as well as a sign of the way to a better world on the humanistic level and of joy on the transcendental level. In *The Wind Off the Sea* Gavin Gallagher, the Commander of a nuclear rocket base, has gloried in his god-sized power. "Marching along like this he had a sudden feeling of wisdom and elevation. . . . He was a giant. God. And he looked on it, and it was Good. . . . He said . . . let there be Life. And there was Life. . . . Let there be Death. . . . And there was Death. At the turn of a switch. . . . Quick as God." But a combination of factors culminating in the chilling experience of thinking that he has, through his right-left confusion, accidentally released the rocket, brings him to conversion:

> He walked away down the gravel path, out of the rocket site. Overhead the thin cloud cleared, and the sky was luminous with light. . . . He had the distinct impression that he had been suffocating in a million fragmented thoughts, the metabolism of a life-time's mental processes, a dark pit, a deep sea. And that suddenly he had swum upwards towards a chink of light. . . . He learned against what had once been a blast wall to protect aircraft. He seemed to see every blade of grass, every branch of every tree, every patch of field and hedge and roadway, every iridescent particle of moonlight in some warm and loving radiance.

Beaty's most recent novel, *The Stick*, shows how the misapplication of the science of psychology can destroy. The overconfidence of an aviation psychologist in using the data from a simulator in his analysis of a pilot's personality proves deadly. Once again, the Beaty warning note is struck. But the symbolic "stick" points to a healing process that ends a dark story with a spark of light.

Beaty continues to write in two fields, fictional and technical. On the technical side, *The Water Jump* discusses the conquering of the North Atlantic route, and *The Complete Skytraveller* answers in detail the questions asked by the passenger. In fiction, two later novels, *Excellency*, on a newly formed independent African government, and *The White Sea-Bird*, a moving depiction of sacrifice in World War II, unite his interests, for here he is concerned, as always, to show the human problems connected with the new technological environment man is creating.

—Roberta J. Forsberg

BECKER, Stephen (David). American. Born in Mount Vernon, New York, 31 March 1927. Educated at Harvard University, Cambridge, Massachusetts, 1943–47, B.A. 1947; Yenching University, Peking, 1947–48. Served in the United States Marine Corps, 1945. Married Mary Elizabeth Freeburg in 1947; two sons and one daughter. Instructor, Tsing Hua University, Peking, 1947–48; Teaching Fellow, Brandeis University, Waltham, Massachusetts, 1951–52; Lecturer, University of Alaska, College, 1967, Bennington College, Vermont, 1971, 1977, 1978, and University of Iowa, Iowa City, 1974. Editor, Western Printing Company, New York, 1955–56. Recipient: Paul Harris Fellowship, 1947; Guggenheim fellowship, 1954; National Endowment for the Arts grant, for translation, 1984. Agent: Russell and Volkening Inc., 50 West 29th Street, New York, New York 10001, U.S.A.; or, Deborah Rogers Ltd., 49 Blenheim Crescent, London W11 2EF, England. Address: Box 536, East End, Tortola, British Virgin Islands.

PUBLICATIONS

Novels

The Season of the Stranger. New York, Harper, and London, Hamish Hamilton, 1951.
Shanghai Incident (as Steve Dodge). New York, Fawcett, 1955; London, Fawcett, 1956.
Juice. New York, Simon and Schuster, 1958; London, Muller, 1959.
A Covenant with Death. New York, Atheneum, and London, Hamish Hamilton, 1965.
The Outcasts. New York, Atheneum, and London, Hamish Hamilton, 1967.
When the War Is Over. New York, Random House, 1969; London, Hamish Hamilton, 1970.
Dog Tags. New York, Random House, 1973; London, Barrie and Jenkins, 1974.
The Chinese Bandit. New York, Random House, 1975; London, Chatto and Windus, 1976.
The Last Mandarin. New York, Random House, and London, Chatto and Windus, 1979.
The Blue-Eyed Shan. New York, Random House, and London, Collins, 1982.

Uncollected Short Stories

"To Know the Country," in *Harper's* (New York), August 1951.
"The Town Mouse," in *The Best American Short Stories 1953*, edited by Martha Foley. Boston, Houghton Mifflin, 1953.
"A Baptism of Some Importance," in *Story.* New York, McKay, 1953.
"Monsieur Malfait," in *Harper's* (New York), June 1953.
"The New Encyclopaedist," in *The Year's Best SF 10*, edited by Judith Merril. New York, Delacorte Press, 1965.
"Rites of Passage," in *Florida Review* (Orlando) Autumn 1984.

Other

*Comic Art in America: A Social History of the Funnies, the
Political Cartoons, Magazine Humor, Sporting Cartoons,
and Animated Cartoons.* New York, Simon and Schuster,
1959.
Marshall Field III: A Biography. New York, Simon and
Schuster, 1964.

Translator, *The Colors of the Day*, by Romain Gary. New
York, Simon and Schuster, and London, Joseph, 1953.
Translator, *Mountains in the Desert*, by Louis Carl and Joseph
Petit. New York, Doubleday, 1954; as *Tefedest*, London,
Allen and Unwin, 1954.
Translator, *The Sacred Forest*, by Pierre-Dominique Gais-
seau. New York, Knopf, 1954.
Translator, *Faraway*, by André Dhôtel. New York, Simon
and Schuster, 1957.
Translator, *Someone Will Die Tonight in the Caribbean*, by
René Puissesseau. New York, Knopf, 1958; London,
W.H. Allen, 1959.
Translator, *The Last of the Just*, by André Schwarz-Bart.
New York, Atheneum, and London, Secker and Warburg,
1961.
Translator, *The Town Beyond the Wall*, by Elie Wiesel. New
York, Atheneum, 1964; London, Robson, 1975.
Translator, *The Conquerors*, by André Malraux. New York,
Holt Rinehart, 1976.
Translator, *Diary of My Travels in America*, by Louis-Philippe.
New York, Delacorte Press, 1977.
Translator, *Ana No*, by Agustín Gomez-Arcos. London,
Secker and Warburg, 1980.

*

Critical Study: by Becker, in *Contemporary Authors Autobiography Series 1* edited by Dedria Bryfonski, Detroit, Gale,
1984.

*   *   *

Equally distinguished as a translator, a biographer, a commentator on the popular arts, and a novelist, Stephen Becker
bring to his fiction a breadth of experience with world culture
and human behavior which yields moral complexity and psychological verity in his work. Two major themes intertwine
through his novels—the problems of justice and the necessity
for self-knowledge and self-fulfillment.

Beginning most clearly with *Juice*, Becker concentrates on
the moral and social complexities of law and justice, continuing
this theme in *A Covenant with Death* and *When the War Is
Over*. The problem Becker's protagonists face is to distinguish
between the arbitrary and mechanical justice of the law and
true human justice. The rigidity and absoluteness of law collide
with human values—especially the need for expiation, mercy
and compassion. The characters' dilemma is to choose between
true justice and simple retribution and to use the mechanism
of blind justice to solve difficult moral problems. Against this
theme is developed another—an existential concept of the self,
men struggling with themselves, with nature and with circumstances to become fully alive and functioning beings. This
theme is isolated most clearly in *The Outcasts*, which describes a group of engineers building a bridge deep in a primeval
jungle. There they must overcome the indifferent force of
nature, their own weaknesses, their fears and prejudices.

In *Juice* the theme of human and mechanical justice arises
when the central character, Joseph Harrison, kills a pedestrian
in an auto accident. His friends and employer try to use the
law and the power of money and position ("juice") to white-
wash the occurrence, while Harrison demands an absolute
judgment to redeem his error. The tensions between views
of law and truth reshape Harrison's whole existence. In *A Covenant with Death* a young judge is confronted with a difficult
decision in a murder case; through detective work, insights
into motivation and a complete understanding of the limits
of the law, Judge Lewis is able to render a humane verdict
and still satisfy the meaning of law. The forces of procrustean
and draconian legalism are averted through the judge's efforts,
through an intense moral revaluation which ultimately changes
the judge's own life. In this novel, humanity triumphs through
the action of the law.

The tragedy of the law is exposed in *When the War Is Over*,
Becker's most satisfying novel. It is the story of the last victim
of the Civil War, a boy executed as a Confederate guerilla
long after hostilities had ceased. The moral struggle is embodied in Lt. Marius Catto, a young career officer caught
between a genuine love of peace and justice and a natural
inclination toward the arts of war. He works to prevent General
Hooker from wreaking vengeance through law on the boy but
fails and is left scarred and embittered by disillusionment. The
novel, based on historical fact, is a brilliant reconstruction of
the time and place and an intense scrutiny of moral and social
values. It convincingly examines the mechanism of military
order, social justice and our conflicting views of violence and
law. The story uncovers basic contradictions in our organization of legal murder.

Dog Tags is another densely detailed chronicle of man at
war and his ability to survive it humanly and intelligently. It
focuses on Benjamin Beer, a Jew wounded in World War II
and later interned in North Korea. His response to war is to
become a skilled and humane doctor, as if in expiration for
the universal crime of war. His life is a moral struggle for
self-knowledge and understanding of man's limitless potentials:
"You're worried about good and bad," he says, "well, I'm
worried about good and evil." In his quest, Benjamin learns
his own abilities and limitations and achieves peace and grace
within himself.

The Chinese Bandit, The Last Mandarin, and *The Blue-Eyed
Shan* are finely-wrought and highly atmospheric Asian tales
which focus on the collision of Western adventurers with oriental culture. Each story details the effect of American mercenaries in search of action in China and Southeast Asia after
World War II and develops the moral and social conflicts
between the two cultures through tales of violence and individual struggles for survival. The landscape and social patterns
of a changeless East are refracted through the sensibilities of
self-sufficient and resourceful Americans who find themselves
alone in the crowds of the orient.

Becker's examination of society's structure and limitations
and his portrayal of men seek ng "grace under pressure" is
a significant contribution to contemporary fiction. The existential premises of the works—individuals finding meaning inside
the arbitrary bounds of social order—reflect our acceptance
of the civilization we have built.

—William J. Schafer

BECKETT, Samuel (Barclay).   Irish.   Born near Dublin, 13 April 1906. Educated at Portora Royal School, County Fermanagh; Trinity College, Dublin, B.A. in French and Italian 1927, M.A. 1931. Worked at the Irish Red Cross Hospital, St. Lô, France, 1945. Married Suzanne Deschevaux-Dumesnil in 1961. French teacher, Campbell College, Belfast, 1928; Lecturer in English, Ecole Normale Supérieure, Paris, 1928–30; Lecturer in French, Trinity College, Dublin, 1930–31. Closely associated with James Joyce in Paris in the late 1920's and 1930's. Settled in Paris in 1937 and has written chiefly in French since 1945; translates his own work into English. Recipient: *Evening Standard* award, for drama, 1955; Obie award, for drama, 1958, 1960, 1962, 1964; Italia Prize, 1959; International Publishers Prize, 1961; Prix Filmcritice, 1965; Tours Film Prize, 1966; Nobel Prize for Literature, 1969; National Grand Prize for Theatre (France), 1975. D.Litt.: Dublin University, 1959. Member, German Academy of Art; Companion of Literature, Royal Society of Literature, 1984. Address: c/o Editions de Minuit, 7 rue Bernard-Palissy, 75006 Paris, France.

PUBLICATIONS

Novels

Murphy.   London, Routledge, 1938; New York, Grove Press, 1957.
Molloy.   Paris, Minuit, 1951; translated by the author and Patrick Bowles, Paris, Olympia Press, and New York, Grove Press, 1955; London, Calder, 1959.
Malone meurt.   Paris, Minuit, 1951; translated by the author as *Malone Dies*, New York, Grove Press, 1956; London, Calder, 1958.
L'Innommable.   Paris, Minuit, 1953; translated by the author as *The Unnamable*, New York, Grove Press, 1958; London, Calder, 1959.
Watt (written in English). Paris, Olympia Press, 1953; New York, Grove Press, 1959; London, Calder, 1963.
Comment C'Est.   Paris, Minuit, 1961; translated by the author as *How It Is*, New York, Grove Press, and London, Calder, 1964.
Mercier et Camier.   Paris, Minuit, 1970; translated by the author as *Mercier and Camier*, London, Calder and Boyars, 1974; New York, Grove Press, 1975.

Short Stories and Texts

More Pricks Than Kicks.   London, Chatto and Windus, 1934; New York, Grove Press, 1970.
Nouvelles et Textes pour Rien.   Paris, Minuit, 1955; translated by the author and Richard Seaver as *Stories and Texts for Nothing*, New York, Grove Press, 1967; in *No's Knife: Selected Shorter Prose 1945–66*, 1967.
From an Abandoned Work.   London, Faber, 1958.
Imagination morte imaginez.   Paris, Minuit, 1965; translated by the author as *Imagination Dead Imagine*, London, Calder and Boyars, 1965.
Assez.   Paris, Minuit, 1966; translated by the author as *Enough*, in *No's Knife*, 1967.
Bing.   Paris, Minuit, 1966; translated by the author as *Ping*, in *No's Knife*, 1967.
Têtes-Mortes (includes *D'Un Ouvrage Abandonné, Assez, Bing, Imagination morte imaginez*). Paris, Minuit, 1967; translated by the author, in *No's Knife*, 1967.

No's Knife: Selected Shorter Prose 1945–1966 (includes *Stories and Texts for Nothing, From an Abandoned Work, Imagination Dead Imagine, Enough, Ping*). London, Calder and Boyars, 1967.
L'Issue.   Paris, Georges Visat, 1968.
Sans.   Paris, Minuit, 1969; translated by the author as *Lessness*, London, Calder and Boyars, 1971.
Séjour.   Paris, Georges Richard, 1970.
Premier Amour.   Paris, Minuit, 1970; translated by the author as *First Love,* London, Calder and Boyars, 1973.
Le Dépeupleur.   Paris, Minuit, 1971; translated by the author as *The Lost Ones*, London, Calder and Boyars, and New York, Grove Press, 1972.
The North.   London, Enitharmon Press, 1972.
First Love and Other Shorts.   New York, Grove Press, 1974.
Fizzles.   New York, Grove Press, 1976.
For to End Yet Again and Other Fizzles.   London, Calder, 1976.
All Strange Away.   New York, Gotham Book Mart, 1976; London, Calder, 1979.
Four Novellas (*The Expelled, The Calmative, The End, First Love*).   London, Calder, 1977; as *The Expelled and Other Novellas*, London, Penguin, 1980.
Six Residua.   London, Calder, 1978.
Company.   London, Calder, and New York, Grove Press, 1980.
Mal vu mal dit.   Paris, Minuit, 1981; translated by the author as *Ill Seen Ill Said*, London, Calder, and New York, Grove Press, 1982.
Worstward Ho.   London, Calder, and New York, Grove Press, 1983.

Plays

Le Kid, with Georges Pelorson (produced Dublin, 1931).
En Attendant Godot (produced Paris, 1953). Paris, Minuit, 1952; translated by the author as *Waiting for Godot: Tragicomedy* (produced London, 1955; Miami and New York, 1956), New York, Grove Press, 1954; London, Faber, 1956.
Fin de Partie: Suivi de Acte sans Paroles (produced London, 1957). Paris, Minuit, 1957; translated by the author as *Endgame: A Play in One Act; Followed by Act Without Words: A Mime for One Player* (*Endgame*, produced New York and London, 1958; *Act Without Words*, produced New York, 1960), New York, Grove Press, and London, Faber, 1958.
All That Fall (broadcast, 1957).   New York, Grove Press, and London, Faber, 1957.
Krapp's Last Tape (produced London, 1958; New York, 1960).   Included in *Krapp's Last Tape and Embers*, 1959; in *Krapp's Last Tape and Other Dramatic Pieces*, 1960.
Embers (broadcast, 1959).   Included in *Krapp's Last Tape and Embers*, 1959; in *Krapp's Last Tape and Other Dramatic Pieces*, 1960.
Krapp's Last Tape and Embers.   London, Faber, 1959.
Act Without Words II (produced New York, 1959; London, 1960).   Included in *Krapp's Last Tape and Other Dramatic Pieces*, 1960; in *Eh Joe and Other Writings*, 1967.
Krapp's Last Tape and Other Dramatic Pieces (includes *All That Fall, Embers, Act Without Words I and II*). New York, Grove Press, 1960.
Happy Days (produced New York, 1961; London, 1962).   New York, Grove Press, 1961; London, Faber, 1962; bilingual edition, edited by James Knowlson, Faber, 1978.

Words and Music, music by John Beckett (broadcast, 1962). Included in *Play and Two Short Pieces for Radio*, 1964; in *Cascando and Other Short Dramatic Pieces*, 1968.

Cascando (broadcast, in French, 1963). Paris, Minuit, 1963; translated by the author as *Cascando: A Radio Piece for Music and Voice* (broadcast, 1964; in *Beckett 3*, produced London, 1970; New York, 1976), included in *Play and Two Short Pieces for Radio*, 1964; in *Cascando and Other Short Dramatic Pieces*, 1968.

Play (as *Spiel*, produced Ulm-Donau, 1963; as *Play*, New York and London, 1964). Included in *Play and Two Short Pieces for Radio*, 1964; in *Cascando and Other Short Dramatic Pieces*, 1968.

Play and Two Short Pieces for Radio (includes *Words and Music* and *Cascando*). London, Faber, 1964.

Eh Joe (televised, 1966; produced New York, 1978). Included in *Eh Joe and Other Writings*, 1967; in *Cascando and Other Short Dramatic Pieces*, 1968.

Come and Go: Dramaticule (produced Paris, 1966; Dublin and London, 1968; New York, 1974). London, Calder and Boyars, 1967; in *Cascando and Other Short Dramatic Pieces*, 1968.

Eh Joe and Other Writings (includes *Act Without Words II* and *Film*). London, Faber, 1967.

Cascando and Other Short Dramatic Pieces (includes *Words and Music, Eh Joe, Play, Come and Go, Film*). New York, Grove Press, 1968.

Film. New York, Grove Press, 1969; London, Faber, 1972.

Breath (part of *Oh! Calcutta!*, produced New York and Glasgow, 1969; London, 1970). Included in *Breath and Other Shorts*, 1971.

Breath and Other Shorts (includes *Come and Go, Act Without Words I* and *II*, and the prose piece *From an Abandoned Work*). London, Faber, 1971.

Not I (produced New York, 1972; London, 1973). London, Faber, 1973; in *First Love and Other Shorts*, 1974.

Tryst (televised, 1976). Included in *Ends and Odds*, 1976.

That Time (produced London and Washington, D.C., 1976; New York, 1977). London, Faber, 1976; in *Ends and Odds*, 1976.

Footfalls (also director: produced London and Washington, D.C., 1976; New York, 1977). London, Faber, 1976; in *Ends and Odds*, 1976.

Ends and Odds: Dramatic Pieces (includes *That Time, Footfalls, Tryst, Not I*). New York, Grove Press, 1976; as *Ends and Odds: Plays and Sketches* (includes *Not I, That Time, Footfalls, Ghost Trio, . . . but the clouds . . ., Theatre I* and *II, Radio I* and *II*), London, Faber, 1977.

Rough for Radio (broadcast, 1976). As *Radio II*, included in *Ends and Odds*, 1977.

Shades (televised, 1977). Included in *Ends and Odds*, 1977.

Theatre I and II (produced London, 1985). Included in *Ends and Odds*, 1977.

A Piece of Monologue (produced New York, 1980). Included in *Rockaby and Other Short Pieces*, 1981; in *Three Occasional Pieces*, 1982.

Rockaby (produced Buffalo, New York, and New York City, 1981; London, 1982). Included in *Rockaby and Other Short Pieces*, 1981; in *Three Occasional Pieces*, 1982.

Rockaby and Other Short Pieces. New York, Grove Press, 1981.

The Ohio Impromptu (produced Columbus, Ohio, 1981; New York, 1983; Edinburgh and London, 1984). Included in *Rockaby and Other Short Pieces*, 1981; in *Three Occasional Pieces*, 1982.

Catastrophe et autres dramaticules: Cette fois, Solo, Berceuse,

Impromptu d'Ohio. Paris, Minuit, 1982.

Three Occasional Pieces. London, Faber, 1982.

Quad (televised, 1982). Included in *Collected Shorter Plays*, 1984.

Catastrophe (produced Avignon, 1982; New York, 1983; Edinburgh and London, 1984). Included in *Collected Shorter Plays*, 1984.

Nacht und Träume (televised, 1983). Included in *Collected Shorter Plays*, 1984.

What Where (produced in German, Graz, 1983; in English, New York, 1983; Edinburgh and London, 1984). Included in *Collected Shorter Plays*, 1984.

Collected Shorter Plays. London, Faber, and New York, Grove Press, 1984.

Ohio Impromptu, Catastrophe, and What Where. New York, Grove Press, 1984.

Screenplay: *Film*, 1965.

Radio Plays: *All That Fall*, 1957; *Embers*, 1959; *Words and Music*, 1962; *Cascando*, 1963; *Rough for Radio*, 1976.

Television Plays: *Eh Joe*, 1966; *Tryst*, 1976; *Shades* (*Ghost Trio, Not I, . . . but the clouds . . .*), 1977; *Quad*, 1982; *Nacht und Träume*, 1983.

Verse

Whoroscope. Paris, Hours Press, 1930.

Echo's Bones and Other Precipitates. Paris, Europa Press, 1935.

Gedichte (collected poems in English and French, with German translations). Wiesbaden, Limes, 1959.

Poems in English. London, Calder, 1961; New York, Grove Press, 1963.

Collected Poems in English and French. London, Calder, and New York, Grove Press, 1977; revised edition, as *Collected Poems 1930–1978*, Calder, 1984.

Other

"Dante . . . Bruno. Vico . . Joyce," in *Our Exagmination round His Factification for Incamination of Work in Progress*. Paris, Shakespeare and Company, 1929; London, Faber, 1936; New York, New Directions, 1939.

Proust. London, Chatto and Windus, 1931; New York, Grove Press, 1957; with *Three Dialogues with Georges Duthuit*, London, Calder, 1965.

Bram von Welde, with others. Paris, Georges Fall, 1958; translated by the author and Olive Classe, New York, Grove Press, 1960.

A Samuel Beckett Reader. London, Calder and Boyars, 1967.

I Can't Go On: A Selection from the Work of Samuel Beckett, edited by Richard Seaver. New York, Grove Press, 1976.

Disjecta: Miscellaneous Writings and a Dramatic Fragment, edited by Ruby Cohn. London, Calder, 1983; New York, Grove Press, 1984.

Collected Shorter Prose 1945–1980. London, Calder, 1984.

Translator, *Anthology of Mexican Poetry*, edited by Octavio Paz. Bloomington, Indiana University Press, 1958; London, Thames and Hudson, 1959.

Translator, *The Old Tune*, by Robert Pinget. Paris, Minuit, 1960; in *Plays 1*, by Pinget, London, Calder, 1963; in *Three Plays*, by Pinget, New York, Hill and Wang, 1966.

Translator, *Zone*, by Guillaume Apollinaire. Dublin and

London, Dolmen Press-Calder and Boyars, 1960.

Translator, with others, *Selected Poems*, by Alain Bosquet. Athens, Ohio University Press, 1973.

Translator, *Drunken Boat*, by Arthur Rimbaud, edited by James Knowlson and Felix Leakey. Reading, Whiteknights Press, 1977.

*

Bibliography: *Samuel Beckett: His Work and His Critics: An Essay in Bibliography* by Raymond Federman and John Fletcher, Berkeley, University of California Press, 1970 (through 1966); *Samuel Beckett: Checklist and Index of His Published Works 1967–1976* by Robin John Davis, privately printed, 1979.

Manuscript Collections: University of Texas, Austin; Ohio State University, Columbus; Washington University, St. Louis; Dartmouth College, Hanover, New Hampshire; Reading University, England.

Critical Studies (selection): *Samuel Beckett: A Critical Study*, New York, Grove Press, and London, Calder, 1962, revised edition, Berkeley, University of California Press, 1968, and *A Reader's Guide to Samuel Beckett*, New York, Farrar Straus, and London, Thames and Hudson, 1973, both by Hugh Kenner; *Samuel Beckett: The Comic Gamut*, New Brunswick, New Jersey, Rutgers University Press, 1962, and *Back to Beckett*, Princeton, New Jersey, Princeton University Press, 1974, both by Ruby Cohn, and *Samuel Beckett: A Collection of Criticism* edited by Cohn, New York, McGraw Hill, 1975; *Samuel Beckett* by William York Tindall, New York, Columbia University Press, 1964; *Samuel Beckett* by Richard N. Coe, New York, Grove Press, 1964; *The Novels of Samuel Beckett* by John Fletcher, London, Chatto and Windus, and New York, Barnes and Noble, 1964; *Samuel Beckett: A Collection of Critical Essays* edited by Martin Esslin, Englewood Cliffs, New Jersey, Prentice Hall, 1965; *Journey to Chaos: Samuel Beckett's Early Fiction* by Raymond Federman, Berkeley, University of California Press, 1965, and *Samuel Beckett: The Critical Heritage* edited by Federman and Lawrence Graver, London, Routledge, 1979; *Beckett at 60: A Festschrift* edited by John Calder, London, Calder and Boyars, 1967; *Samuel Beckett* by Ronald Hayman, London, Heinemann, 1968, New York, Ungar, 1974, revised edition, Heinemann, 1980; *Samuel Beckett Now: Critical Approaches to His Novels, Poetry, and Plays* edited by Melvin J. Friedman, Chicago, University of Chicago Press, 1970; *Samuel Beckett: A Study of His Novels* by Eugene Webb, Seattle, University of Washington Press, 1970; *The Fiction of Samuel Beckett: Form and Effect* by H. Porter Abbott, Berkeley, University of California Press, 1973; *Samuel Beckett* by John Pilling, London, Routledge, 1976, and *Frescoes of the Skull: The Later Prose and Drama of Samuel Beckett* edited by Pilling and James Knowlson, London, Calder, 1979, New York, Grove Press, 1980; *Beckett/Beckett* by Vivian Mercier, New York, Oxford University Press, 1977, London, Oxford University Press, 1979; *Samuel Beckett: A Biography* by Deirdre Bair, New York, Harcourt Brace, and London, Cape, 1978; *The Samuel Beckett Manuscripts: A Study* by Richard L. Admussen, London, Prior, 1979; *Beckett and the Voice of Species: A Study of His Prose Fiction* by Eric P. Levy, Dublin, Gill and Macmillan, and New York, Barnes and Noble, 1980; *Abysmal Games in the Novels of Samuel Beckett* by Angela B. Moorjani, Chapel Hill, University of North Carolina Department of Romance Languages, 1982; *Samuel Beckett:*

Humanistic Perspectives edited by Morris Beja, S.E. Gontarski, and Pierre Astier, Columbus, Ohio State University Press, 1983; *Samuel Beckett* by Charles Lyons, New York, Grove Press, 1983; *Samuel Beckett's Real Silence* by Hélène L. Baldwin, University Park, Pennsylvania State University Press, 1983; *Samuel Beckett and the Meaning of Being: A Study in Ontological Parable* by Lance St. John Butler, London, Macmillan, 1984; *The Development of Samuel Beckett's Fiction* by Rubin Rabinovitz, Urbana, University of Illinois Press, 1984.

Theatrical Activities:
Director: **Plays**—*Come and Go*, Paris, 1966; *Endgame*, Berlin, 1967; *Krapp's Last Tape*, Berlin, 1969; *Krapp's Last Tape* and *Act Without Words*, Paris, 1970; *Krapp's Last Tape* and *Endgame*, London, 1971; *Happy Days*, Berlin, 1971, London, 1979; *Waiting for Godot*, Berlin, 1975, New York, 1977, London, 1984; *Krapp's Last Tape* and *Not I*, Paris, 1975; *Footfalls*, London, 1976; *Krapp's Last Tape*, Berlin, 1977, and London, 1978. **Television**—*Eh Joe*, 1966 (Germany).

*　　　*　　　*

Poet, playwright, and occasional critic, Samuel Beckett considers his most valid work to be the fiction which has changed radically from the modish English written in his twenties, to the dense French written in his seventies.

Beckett's first published short story, "Assumption," appeared in the June 1929 issue of *transition*, along with his essay on Joyce's *Work in Progress*. Beckett then began his own Work in Progress, a novel entitled *Dream of Fair to Middling Women*. After 214 pages, he abandoned it, although he published two excerpts in 1932. More importantly, he salvaged the novel's protagonist, Belacqua Shuah, for a series of short stories, *More Pricks Than Kicks*. The exotic name of the Dublin-based hero is borrowed from Canto IV of Dante's *Purgatorio*, where he sits in fetal position "more indolent than if sloth were his sister." Like his namesake, Beckett's Belacqua inclines to indolence, but circumstances and fair to middling women conspire against him, so that he leads an active short life. Thrice married. Beckett's Belacqua dies in surgery and is replaced by his best friend in the arms of his widow. The book closes in a cemetery, where the ground keeper forgets about Belacqua's remains. "So it goes in the world." For the way of the world is not a way of lingering compassion.

After the 1934 publication of these ten stories that constitute a picaresque novel, Beckett began the novel *Murphy*, more traditionally plotted. In name and spirit, Belacqua was a foreigner in his native Dublin; Murphy the Irishman is a foreigner in London, where Beckett was living when he wrote the novel. Like Belacqua, Murphy cherishes indolence, and like Beckett's Belacqua, Murphy finds that Woman is the main obstacle to the indolent life of the mind. Belacqua's several women crystallize into Murphy's Celia Kelly, a kind-hearted whore about whom the hero's mind and body are in conflict. Despite reluctance on the part of the former, she prevails upon the latter to seek employment so that she need not continue hers. At his place of employment, the Magdalen Mental Mercyseat, Murphy renounces the outside world, including Celia. While this ironic reversal is taking place, a virtual posse has set out in search of Murphy—from Cork through Dublin to London, where they converge upon a Murphyless Celia. Murphy, having retired to a garret, is burned to death in an explosion. Murphy's various hunters find only his charred remains, and they go on with their separate lives. For the way of the world is not a way of lingering compassion.

Murphy was not published until 1938, after Beckett had moved to Paris, where he still lives. His first French fiction was the translation of *Murphy* into French, undertaken with Alfred Péron and completed before the outbreak of World War II. After fleeing from the Nazis to Free France, while working as an agricultural laborer Beckett completed *Watt*. The naive titular hero expects language to explain phenomena. Using his senses, "his most noble faculties," and his mind, "whatever that may be," Watt seeks to make sense of thing, event, and person at Mr. Knott's establishment, where he undertakes service. But reason and senses are incommensurate with Mr. Knott, and Watt leaves Mr. Knott's house. At a later date, Watt moves and speaks in inversions; he lives in a mansion where he meets Sam who lives in his own mansion, and it is Sam who purports to be the recorder of Watt's adventures are narrated by their hero. It is presumably Sam who divides the novel into four numbered parts and an Addendum. Part 2 is the core of Watt's tragedy—his inability to come to terms with the phenomena of Mr. Knott's establishment. Part 2 of *Watt* also contains the precursor of Beckett's French fiction—his predecessor Arsene's alogical, first-person narration.

Although Beckett had written poems in French and translated *Murphy* into French, it was not until his return to Paris after World War II that he adopted French as his major writing language. The bulk of Beckett's fiction should be classified as *French* fiction. With an occasional collaborator, however, he has translated his French fiction into English, whose literature he thereby enriches.

After four long stories (*La Fin, L'Expulsé, Premier amour,* and *Le Calmant*) and a novel (*Mercier et Camier*), Beckett embarked on the trilogy, often considered his major work. *Molloy, Malone Dies,* and *The Unnamable,* published separately, are not a trilogy in the usual sense of developing a plot through time. Rather, they progressively concentrate events and characters through heightened intensity of the first-person narrations. *Molloy* is divided into two parts. In the first a grotesque old cripple, hat fastened to his buttonhole by a lace, having arrived mysteriously in his mother's room, writes a disconnected tale of his disconnected voyage toward his mother. In the second part Jacques Moran, a middle-aged Catholic father of an only namesake son, having returned from a mission to seek Molloy, writes a report for his employer Youdi. In *Malone Dies* the paralytic hero, confined to his bed, tries to order the time of his dying by writing an inventory of his possessions, a description of his present state, and stories. The titular speaker-protagonist of *The Unnamable* seeks to penetrate behind fictional and linguistic formulae to himself. His utterances, stripped of Moran's determination, Molloy's passion, and Malone's purpose, attain an incantatory anguish of meaning made music.

After the trilogy, genre designations are difficult for Beckett's non-dramatic work, and plots crumble before any effort at summary. His *Texts for Nothing*, spare of event, might be called prose poems or thematic monologues; Beckett calls them "texts." *How It Is*, whose three parts might be called a novel, traces the itineraries of characters who meet and part, naked in the mud. The grammatical first person dissolves into unpunctuated phrases in irregular verses which, repeated and permuted, carry the burden of a narration climaxed by the tender yet terrifying encounter of Pim and Bom. *How It Is* is the verbal distillation of anguished reaching for a self.

After *How It Is*, Beckett's mainly French fiction is more frankly fiction as it recedes further and further from referential reality, the quasi-mathematical *Residua* leading to *The Lost Ones*. *How It Is* reached for an infinite series of Pims and Boms, but the protagonist of *The Lost Ones* is a tiny town—two hundred five inhabitants of a desiccated cylinder. These inferno-dwellers manoeuvre fifteen ladders in their vain search for an exit from the cylinder. Searchers, climbers, and vanquished form a perpetual motion machine that (distortedly?) mirrors human societies. Beckett depersonalizes narration, only to create another analogue of suffering.

Company is Beckett's first extended English fiction since *Watt*—after 35 years—and it is marked by lyrical cadences of rich language for dim scenes. "You," a man on his back in the dark, has for "company" a voice—the voice that resonates as early as *Watt*, and that attains full diapason in the post-*Godot* fiction. Further even than *How It Is* from specific setting, *Company* coalesces drama and fiction; *Company* is a dialogue between an inert "you" and an observing "he." *Company* blends autobiographical traces with phrases, themes, incidents of earlier Beckett works—the whole company. *Company* is its own salute to man's capacity for conceiving company.

As though to disdain that capacity, Beckett retreated to French for *Mal vu mal dit*. A Venus-haunted, white-haired woman in black is intermittently perceived in her own perceptions. Alerting the reader by calls of "Attention," the narrative imagination endows her with a dozen disciples, a suffering lamb, and shards of biblical landscapes. No longer goal-oriented as in *How It Is* and *The Lost Ones, Ill Seen Ill Said* fragments the myths of our culture by coming to us "ill seen ill said."

By *Worstward Ho* our very perceptions are misseen, missaid. Beckett's boldest foray into uncharted prose at once summons and shrinks from human trace—a head sunk on crippled hands, an old man and a child plodding hand in hand, a kneeling old woman. In an incantation of monosyllables, negatives, contradictions, and qualifications, scene precipitates to image, being to saying, "no" to "on." And that monosyllable—on—may serve as the watchword of Beckett's ever searching, ever exploring wordward ho.

—Ruby Cohn

BECKHAM, Barry (Earl). American. Born in Philadelphia, Pennsylvania, 19 March 1944. Educated at Brown University, Providence, Rhode Island, 1962–66, A.B. 1966; Columbia University Law School, New York. Married 1) Betty Louise Hope in 1966 (divorced, 1977), one son and one daughter; 2) Geraldine Lynne Palmer in 1979. Public relations consultant, 1966–67, and urban affairs associate, 1969–70, Chase Manhattan Bank, New York; public relations consultant, YMCA National Council, New York, 1967–68, and Western Electric Company, New York, 1968–69. Lecturer, 1970–72, Assistant Professor, 1972–78, since 1979 Associate Professor of English, and since 1980 Director of Graduate Program in Creative Writing, Brown University. Agent: William Morris Agency, 1350 Avenue of the Americas, New York, New York 10019. Address: Department of English, Brown University, Providence, Rhode Island 02912, U.S.A.

PUBLICATIONS

Novels

My Main Mother. New York, Walker, 1969; London, Wingate, 1970; as *Blues in the Night*, London, Tandem, 1974.

Runner Mack.   New York, Morrow, 1972.
Double Drunk.   Los Angeles, Holloway House, 1981.

Play

Garvey Lives! (produced Providence, Rhode Island, 1972).

Other

Editor, *The Black Student's Guide to Colleges.*   New York, Dutton, 1982.

*

Manuscript Collection: Mugar Memorial Library, Boston University.

Critical Studies: reviews by Peter Rowley, 30 November 1969, and Mel Watkins, 17 September 1972, both in *New York Times Book Review*; interview with Sanford Pinsker, in *Black Images 3* (Toronto), Autumn 1974.

*   *   *

Barry Beckham's reputation rests modestly on two small novels published within the three-year period of 1969–72. Both are flawed and somewhat derivative, yet Beckham's talents suggest promising developments in fiction about black experience in America, a field which he thinks "has been inadequately treated for the most part." In both novels, Beckham moves decisively away from the ghetto novel of social protest and literary naturalism to the psychological effects of neglect and exploitation, portrayed in a blend of verbal impressionism and surrealism.

In *My Main Mother* Mitchell Mibbs tells his own story of how he came to murder his beautiful mother, Pearl, in their home in Chatsworth, Maine, where Mitch's grandparents were born. In this tragi-comic "confession of the soul," or "proclamation of my own emancipation," Mitchell plans an imaginary press release, a self-mocking and ironic outline-summary of Beckham's first novel: "A young black genius, sitting comfortably in an abandoned auto on the outskirts of town, announced today that he has killed his mother for the best of all concerned. His testimony is a novel, profound manuscript of some eighty thousand words, listing various and sundry acts alleged to have prompted the macabre slaying. The acts have been arranged in narrative form, and the manuscript has been cited by leading authorities as extremely accomplished."

Perhaps the cruelest of mother Pearl's "various and sundry acts" is the exploitation and betrayal of old Mervin Pip, an honest, kindly uncle who serves Mitch *in loco parentis* and is his one true friend. The title is therefore a triple play on the shaping environment: "main" refers to the geographical location, to Uncle Melvin and to Pearl, all of whom have made Mitchell what he is. Throughout, racial themes are both present and understated, while authentic portrayal of main characters, skillful use of point-of-view, and vivid imagery earn our attention. The title phrase is, of course, "black," and so are the idiom, characterizations, and occurrences of the novel without the stridency of naturalism or the "race novel." Present, nevertheless, are the props and concerns found in *Native Son* and *Black Boy*, the ur-works of modern black literary art: besides the title similarities, combined in this one work are Wright's dual depictions of the fatherless boy who murders a beautiful woman, the suppression of aspiration in a bright black boy, the hypocrisy of liberal or well-meaning whites, and the sense of entrapment, betrayal, and waste of youth.

Runner Mack is indebted to that other seminal and symbolic black novel, *Invisible Man*, by Ralph Ellison. Beckham's Henry Adams, not a New England patrician but a poor Mississippi baseball player, comes to New York ostensibly for a baseball try-out ("this is the national past-time, they've got to be fair with me"), and then remains to be educated in the true national sport of "keeping this nigger running." Cheated by a midget manager of his fair chance in athletics (a prime source of upward mobility for American blacks), Henry tries the subtler game of American business, where he is given token opportunity in a dead-end job. In dreamlike sequences, he is hit by a Mack truck (before encountering "Runner Mack," the title character); a heedless Spanish building "super" steals his pajamas; Henry's wife is raped in his presence; a crippled corporation president delivers an inaudible Christmas speech; and a summons arrives requiring Henry to leave at once "to fight for my country." Like Ellison, Barry Beckham casts his young innocent in a picaresque narrative reprise of black-American history, with emphasis on the absurdity of American rituals and the indecencies of American institutions.

Thus, the stage is set for the novel's second half, Henry's army adventures in a twin parody of war and revolution. Institutionalized racism is patriotically turned against "slopes" and "gooks" instead of blacks, so that even Henry may become both a racist and a good American. The Vietnam war is mysteriously transposed to the white Alaskan wilderness and since no "slopes" are ever found, the men slay seals and herds of Caribou, the ecological equivalent of defoliation. The young soldiers are terrified by the Pentagon mentality of Captain Nevins and the fierce, foul intensity of his need to kill. Then Henry encounters Runnington Mack, a cynical, honest black hipster, who becomes his mentor in a revolutionary plot to bomb the White House. "Runner" Mack, loose as a halfback and solid as a truck, stands in obvious contrast to the hysterical, murderous Captain Nevins, to the deformed baseball manager and corporation president and to the other obsessive, obscene whites whom Henry has had to follow. Swiftly, he learns from Mack of the hypocrisy of American leadership, the futility of reform in a death-directed culture, and the need for violent revolution. Henry Adams' "education" is poignantly completed when Runner Mack's thought-out plan fails abysmally because no one cares and Mack commits suicide in despair.

Although his main characters are believable in both novels, Beckham's characterizations sometimes divide humanity into wholly good or wholly despicable specimens, and nearly all white characters are negatively drawn. Despite this side-choosing, he elicits our sympathy for his good guys, such as Mitch, Henry, and Runner, and hostility toward Mitch's mother, her husband Julius, and assorted villains. His success at evoking reader empathy is largely attributable to Beckham's small-scale scenic method, whereby we see and feel the misery of a rustic old man lost in Harlem, the loneliness of a boy in a rusty, abandoned car in the woods, the isolation of a housewife deafened by television, the panic of a man running to a job interview. These and other carved images become slide-projections or backdrops in the larger enactments of black absurd theatre.

—Frank Campenni

BEDFORD, Sybille.   British.   Born in Charlottenburg, Germany, 16 March 1911. Educated privately. Married Walter Bedford in 1935. Has worked as a law reporter: covered the

Auschwitz Trial at Frankfurt for the *Observer*, London, and the *Saturday Evening Post*, Philadelphia, 1963–65, and the trial of Jack Ruby at Dallas for *Life*, New York, 1964. Vice-President, PEN, 1979. Fellow, Royal Society of Literature, 1964. O.B.E. (Officer, Order of British Empire), 1981. Address: c/o Coutts Bank, 1 Old Park Lane, London W1Y 4BS, England.

PUBLICATIONS

Novels

A Legacy. London, Weidenfeld and Nicolson, 1956; New York, Simon and Schuster, 1957.
A Favourite of the Gods. London, Collins, and New York, Simon and Schuster, 1963.
A Compass Error. London, Collins, 1968; New York, Knopf, 1969.

Uncollected Short Story

"Compassionata at Hyde Park Corner," in *23 Modern Stories*. New York, Knopf, 1963.

Other

The Sudden View: A Mexican Journey. London, Gollancz, and New York, Harper, 1953; revised edition, New York, Atheneum, 1963; as *A Visit to Don Otavio: A Traveller's Tale from Mexico*, London, Collins, 1960.
The Best We Can Do: An Account of the Trial of John Bodkin Adams. London, Collins, 1958; as *The Trial of Dr. Adams*, New York, Simon and Schuster, 1959.
The Faces of Justice: A Traveller's Report. London, Collins, and New York, Simon and Schuster, 1961.
Aldous Huxley: A Biography. London, Chatto and Windus-Collins, 2 vols., 1973–74; New York, Knopf, 1 vol., 1974.

*

Critical Studies: by Evelyn Waugh, in *The Spectator* (London), 13 April 1956; V.S. Pritchett, in *New Statesman* (London), 11 January 1963; P.N. Furbank, in *Encounter* (London), April 1964; Bernard Levin, in London *Daily Mail*, 12 September 1966; Constantine FitzGibbon, in *Irish Times* (Dublin), 19 October 1968; introductions by Peter Vansittart to *A Favourite of the Gods* and *A Compass Error*, both London, Virago Press, 1984.

*   *   *

A first glance at Sybille Bedford's fiction suggests the genre of social history, perhaps the subordinate form of the family novel. Yet, although the accoutrements of history and generation are present, strongest in the first novel and diminishing in the next two, the actual core of interest resides in the individual character as such and the validity of his action.

The first novel, *A Legacy*, might have commented on the unification of Germany through a parallelling of the events of the Felden Scandal or the marriages that occupy much of the action. The novel might also have commented on the degeneration of the twin dynamos of the early modern age, Voltaire and Rousseau, through the description of the two major families of the book: the Merzes, "wealthy" Berlin Jews whose retiring and bourgeois interests belie their originating ancestor's intellectual passions; and the von Feldens, petty South

German barons who are vaguely agrarian and on occasion Catholic. However, the ties are too tenuous and the long build-up accorded the families only serves as an interesting forepiece to the corrupt morality and inadequate vitality that are revealed in the marriages of Julius von Felden to Melanie Merz and later to Caroline Trafford, the generous-spirited English woman who suddenly appears more than half way through the novel and serves as the reader's sounding board.

A Favourite of the Gods, running from the turn of the century into the period between the World Wars in Italy and England, draws less extensively on social and historical matters, although the characters reflect regional stereotypes and there is some mention made of the First World War and of the opposition to Mussolini. Principally, however, the novel contrasts Anna, a sexually ingenuous and probably repressed blue-stocking from New England, who marries a Roman prince, with Constanza, her sexually free, liberal-minded, but intellectually poorly-developed daughter.

A Compass Error, which takes place in Southern France, is the least socio-historical, having only peripheral mention of anti-fascism and the Second World War. An enlargement of an incident in *A Favourite of the Gods*, it details a hybristic error made by Flavia, the daughter of Constanza, and her short-lived English husband. Within the frame of a backward look the middle-aged Flavia recounts her young belief that she could chart out her life, and her subsequent manipulation by the wife of her mother's lover that changed her own as well as her mother's life.

The socio-historical settings of the novels, although never essential to the action, are often fascinating in themselves. Further, they suggest, as a consideration of the characters will show, the possible mastership of Henry James. Besides the indirection of comment, that sometimes maddening characteristic of James, each of the characters who pair off in the novels' action derives from a different country, again typical. In addition each pair exhibits the contrast between fresh, energetic innocence and degenerate, if attractive, worldliness leading to moral insight that James modulated from *The American* to *The Golden Bowl*. Yet, if the characterization is Jamesian, the shifting point of view of the narrator is not. Nor is the large structure of the novels, as evidenced by the overweighted early part of *A Legacy* and the background that Flavia relates in *A Compass Error*, at the end of which her fictional auditor is quite understandably asleep.

Although Sybille Bedford's is a modest talent we can recognize her civilized and informed attitude and the skillfully drawn characters, the delightful evocation of place and time, and the witty well-rendered scenes that have won her deserved attention.

—John P. O'Neill

BELLOW, Saul. American. Born in Lachine, Quebec, Canada, 10 June 1915; grew up in Montreal, moved with his family to Chicago, 1924. Educated at Tuley High School, Chicago, graduated 1933; University of Chicago, 1933–35; Northwestern University, Evanston, Illinois, 1935–37, B.S. (honors) in sociology and anthropology 1937; did graduate work in anthropology at University of Wisconsin, Madison, 1937. Served in the United States Merchant Marine, 1944–45. Married 1) Anita Goshkin in 1937 (divorced), one son; 2) Alexandra Tschacbasov in 1956 (divorced), one son; 3) Susan Glassman in 1961 (divorced), one son; 4) Alexandra Ionescu Tulcea in 1975. Teacher, Pestalozzi-Froebel Teachers College, Chicago, 1938–42; member of the Editorial Department, "Great Books" Project, *Encyclopaedia Britannica*, Chicago, 1943–46; Instructor, 1946, and Assistant Professor of English, 1948–49, University of Minnesota, Minneapolis; Visiting Lecturer, New York University, 1950–52; Creative Writing Fellow, Princeton University, New Jersey, 1952–53; member of the English faculty, Bard College, Annandale-on-Hudson, New York, 1953–54; Associate Professor of English, University of Minnesota, 1954–59; Visiting Professor of English, University of Puerto Rico, Rio Piedras, 1961. Since 1962, Professor, and Chairman, 1970–76, Committee on Social Thought, University of Chicago; now Grunier Distinguished Services Professor. Co-editor, *The Noble Savage*, New York, then Cleveland, 1960–62. Fellow, Academy for Policy Study, 1966; Fellow, Branford College, Yale University, New Haven, Connecticut. Recipient: Guggenheim fellowship, 1948, 1955; American Academy grant, 1952, and Gold Medal, 1977; National Book Award, 1954, 1965, 1971; Ford grant, 1959, 1960; Friends of Literature Award, 1960; James L. Dow Award, 1964; Prix International de Littérature, 1965; Jewish Heritage Award, 1968; Formentor prize, 1970; Nobel Prize for Literature, 1976; Pulitzer Prize, 1976; Neil Gunn International Fellowship, 1977; Brandeis University Creative Arts Award, 1978. D.Litt.: Northwestern University, 1962; Bard College, 1963; Litt.D.: New York University, 1970; Harvard University, Cambridge, Massachusetts, 1972; Yale University, 1972; McGill University, Montreal, 1973; Brandeis University, Waltham, Massachusetts, 1974; Hebrew Union College, Cincinnati, 1976; Trinity College, Dublin, 1976. Commandant, Order of Arts and Letters, 1968, and Chevalier, Legion of Honor (France); Member, American Academy, 1970. Agent: Harriet Wasserman Literary Agency, 137 East 36th Street, New York, New York 10016. Address: Committee on Social Thought, University of Chicago, 1126 East 59th Street, Chicago, Illinois 60637, U.S.A.

PUBLICATIONS

Novels

Dangling Man.   New York, Vanguard Press, 1944; London, Lehmann, 1946.
The Victim.   New York, Vanguard Press, 1947; London, Lehmann, 1948.
The Adventures of Augie March.   New York, Viking Press, 1953; London, Weidenfeld and Nicolson, 1954.
Henderson the Rain King.   New York, Viking Press, and London, Weidenfeld and Nicolson, 1959.
Herzog.   New York, Viking Press, 1964; London, Weidenfeld and Nicolson, 1965.
Mr. Sammler's Planet.   New York, Viking Press, and London, Weidenfeld and Nicolson, 1970.
Humboldt's Gift.   New York, Viking Press, and London, Secker and Warburg, 1975.
The Dean's December.   New York, Harper, and London, Secker and Warburg, 1982.

Short Stories

Seize the Day, with Three Short Stories and a One-Act Play (includes *The Wrecker*).   New York, Viking Press, 1956; London, Weidenfeld and Nicolson, 1957.
Mosby's Memoirs and Other Stories.   New York, Viking Press, 1968; London, Weidenfeld and Nicolson, 1969.

Him with His Foot in His Mouth and Other Stories.   New York, Harper, and London, Secker and Warburg, 1984.

Uncollected Short Stories

"The Mexican General," in *Partisan Reader*, edited by William Phillips and Philip Rahv.   New York, Dial Press, 1946.
"Dora," in *Harper's Bazaar* (New York), November 1949.
"A Sermon by Dr. Pep," in *The Best American Short Stories 1950*, edited by Martha Foley.   Boston, Houghton Mifflin, 1950.
"The Trip to Galena," in *Partisan Review* (New York), November–December 1950.
"Address by Gooley MacDowell to the Hasbeens Club of Chicago," in *Nelson Algren's Book of Lonesome Monsters*, edited by Nelson Algren.   New York, Lancer, 1962; London, Panther, 1964.
"The Old System," in *Playboy* (Chicago), January 1968.
"Burdens of a Lone Survivor," in *Esquire* (New York), December 1974.

Plays

The Wrecker (televised, 1964).   Included in *Seize the Day*, 1956.
Scenes from Humanitas: A Farce, in *Partisan Review* (New Brunswick, New Jersey), Summer 1962.
The Last Analysis (produced New York 1964; Derby, 1967).   New York, Viking Press, 1965; London, Weidenfeld and Nicolson, 1966.
Under the Weather (includes *Out from Under*, *A Wen*, and *Orange Soufflé*) (produced Edinburgh and New York, 1966; as *The Bellow Plays*, produced London, 1966).   *A Wen* published in *Esquire* (New York), January 1965; in *Traverse Plays*, edited by Jim Haynes, London, Penguin, 1966; *Orange Soufflé* published in *Traverse Plays*, 1966; in *Best Short Plays of the World Theatre 1968–1973*, edited by Stanley Richards, New York, Crown, 1973.

Television Play: *The Wrecker*, 1964.

Other

Dessins, by Jesse Reichek; text by Bellow and Christian Zervos.   Paris, Editions Cahiers d'Art, 1960.
Recent American Fiction: A Lecture.   Washington, D.C., Library of Congress, 1963.
Like You're Nobody: The Letters of Louis Gallo to Saul Bellow, 1961–62, Plus Oedipus-Schmoedipus, The Story That Started It All.   New York, Dimensions Press, 1966.
Technology and the Frontiers of Knowledge, with others.   New York, Doubleday, 1973.
The Portable Saul Bellow, edited by Gabriel Josipovici.   New York, Viking Press, 1974; London, Penguin, 1977.
To Jerusalem and Back: A Personal Account.   New York, Viking Press, and London, Secker and Warburg, 1976.
Nobel Lecture.   Stockholm, United States Information Service, 1977.

Editor, *Great Jewish Short Stories.*   New York, Dell, 1963; London, Vallentine Mitchell, 1971.

*

Bibliography: *Saul Bellow: A Comprehensive Bibliography* by B.A. Sokoloff and Mark E. Posner, Norwood, Pennsylvania,

Norwood Editions, 1973; *Saul Bellow, His Works and His Critics: An Annotated International Bilbiography* by Marianne Nault, New York, Garland, 1977; *Saul Bellow: A Bibliography of Secondary Sources* by F. Lercangée, Brussels, Center for American Studies, 1977; *Saul Bellow: A Reference Guide* by Robert G. Noreen, Boston, Hall, 1978.

Manuscript Collections: Regenstein Library, University of Chicago; University of Texas, Austin.

Critical Studies (selection): *Saul Bellow* by Tony Tanner, Edinburgh, Oliver and Boyd, 1965, New York, Barnes and Noble, 1967; *Saul Bellow* by Earl Rovit, Minneapolis, University of Minnesota Press, 1967, and *Saul Bellow: A Collection of Critical Essays* edited by Rovit, Englewood Cliffs, New Jersey, Prentice Hall, 1975; *Saul Bellow: A Critical Essay* by Robert Detweiler, Grand Rapids, Michigan, Eerdmans, 1967; *The Novels of Saul Bellow* by Keith Michael Opdahl, University Park, Pennsylvania State University Press, 1967; *Saul Bellow and the Critics* edited by Irving Malin, New York, New York University Press, and London, University of London Press, 1967, and *Saul Bellow's Fiction* by Malin, Carbondale, Southern Illinois University Press, 1969; *Saul Bellow: In Defense of Man* by John Jacob Clayton, Bloomington, Indiana University Press, 1968, revised edition, 1979; *Saul Bellow* by Robert R. Dutton, New York, Twayne, 1971, revised edition, 1982; *Saul Bellow* by Brigitte Scheer-Schäzler, New York, Ungar, 1973; *Saul Bellow's Enigmatic Laughter* by Sarah Blacher Cohen, Urbana, University of Illinois Press, 1974; *Whence the Power? The Artistry and Humanity of Saul Bellow* by M. Gilbert Porter, Columbia, University of Missouri Press, 1974; *Saul Bellow: The Problem of Affirmation* by Chirantan Kulshrestha, New Delhi and London, Arnold-Heinemann, 1978, Atlantic Highlands, New Jersey, Humanities Press, 1979; *Critical Essays on Saul Bellow* edited by Stanley Trachtenberg, Boston, Hall, 1979; *Quest for the Human: An Exploration of Saul Bellow's Fiction* by Eusebio L. Rodrigues, Lewisburg, Pennsylvania, Bucknell University Press, 1981; *Saul Bellow* by Malcolm Bradbury, London, Methuen, 1982; *Saul Bellow's Moral Vision: A Critical Study of the Jewish Experience* by L.H. Goldman, New York, Irvington, 1983; *Saul Bellow: Vision and Revision* by Daniel Fuchs, Durham, North Carolina, Duke University Press, 1984; *Saul Bellow and History* by Judie Newman, New York, St. Martin's Press, and London, Macmillan, 1984; *A Sort of Columbus: The American Voyages of Saul Bellow's Fiction* by Jeanne Braham, Athens, University of Georgia Press, 1984.

*   *   *

Saul Bellow is the most distinguished novelist of the post-war period in America. He is the most intellectual of American novelists, but one who, paradoxically, relies finally upon imagination and feeling; in his penultimate novel at this writing, *Humboldt's Gift*, he moves more surely than ever before toward intuition and mysticism, toward a non-rational epistemology. He may be the staunchest defender of the idea of the self in American fiction, but he frequently recognizes claims of brotherhood and love that limit the egoistic pursuit of the self. His fiction rests upon a conception of becoming or possibility, yet he recognizes the human initiative in creating and pursuing process is limited by powerful determinants beyond human control. Bellow is an optimist, despite the prevailing climate of pessimism and despair. His novels are built on these dichotomies and paradoxes and written in a language that is almost always vibrant and resourceful.

The evolution of Bellow's style is a key to the understanding of his fiction. He began, in *Dangling Man* and *The Victim*, was a tight conception of both language and structure, using Flaubert as his model. Both books are disciplined and spare; Bellow has said that he strove for a kind of correctness that would be acceptable to the Anglo-Saxon Protestant world that seemed to dominate American literature. But by the time he came to write *The Adventures of Augie March*, he had discovered rhetoric, he had gained confidence as a writer and as an American, and he had recognized the weakening of the WASP hold on literature in the United States. The result is that the language of this novel streams out of Bellow in a fine, free flow; it is as larky as its protagonist and as various as the many levels of its discourse demand, ranging in its versatility from the talk of Jewish immigrants to the intercourse of University of Chicago intellectuals. As the language expanded, so did the book, and *Augie* is a sprawling, picaresque work in contrast to the carefully contained earlier novels. Succeeding novels show a curbing of rhetorical extravagance, but *Augie* established the essential mode of expression for the fiction Bellow has done since.

Bellow's taste for a vital and even eccentric language is related, first, to his conviction that words are a form of power, and second, to his hope that character can be preserved in contemporary fiction. With respect to the latter, he has made a considerable contribution by assembling in his novels a gallery of ill assorted oddballs, misfits, geniuses, and cranks, like Einhorn in *Augie*, or confidence men, like Dr. Tamkin in *Seize the Day*. Bellow commands Dickensian comic energies in the depiction of character, but he can also give us characters of size, power, subtlety, and cunning like Julius in *Humboldt's Gift*, who has the presence and imperious will of a Medici prince. The idea of character, furthermore, is associated with the survival of the self. Nothing is more important in Bellow's fiction, and Augie March, Henderson, and Tommy Wilhelm, among his protagonists, are all committed to the quest for identity and the salvation of the self. Bellow knows that, beginning in the 19th century, many forces, from Darwinism and Marxism to the Nazis and the logical positivists of the 20th century, have conspired to eliminate the self, and that writers like Joyce and Beckett have joined in this campaign. He believes, as he has said repeatedly in his fiction, that the main business of a man's life is to carry the burden of his personality or "to be the carrier of a load which was his own self," as he puts it in *Seize the Day*. By realizing the self, one asserts his humanity, that is, lays a claim to sharing in human suffering and joy, in the human destiny.

Realization of the self means surrender of the self. Bellow has always recognized this paradox, which he dramatizes nowhere more effectively than in *Henderson the Rain King*. Henderson begins as a man overwhelmed by the demands of his own ego. Neighbors, wives, children—nothing and nobody is permitted to stand in the way of his self gratification as he listens to an inner voice intoning, "I want! I want!" At the end of the book, his African experience has taught him that what men need is a right relation with the world of nature and with humanity as a whole. The guardianship he assumes of the lion cub and the little boy is an expression of love in both realms of being that signifies Henderson's surrender of the ego in order to realize the self through immersion in the order of nature and in the community of man. Similarly, Tommy Wilhelm in *Seize the Day* finds the consummation of his heart's need in the abandonment of self concern and the substitution of a generalized love for mankind.

Mr. Sammler's Planet, however, a novel of the 1970's, is far more critical of the idea of the self than any previous work. It is a book that documents Bellow's conviction that the conception of individualism or the self that we took first from Christianity and then from the Enlightenment has degenerated, in our time, into self-indulgence and license. But even in the face of this bitter revision of the optimistic history of the West, Bellow is unwilling to abandon in this novel the possibility that good may be found in human beings, and he persists in showing the need to pursue definition in one's life.

This hedged optimism in the face of his own pessimistic conclusions about the nature and fate of man is one of the most difficult situations that Bellow must confront in his fiction. Like Charlie Citrine in *Humboldt*, Bellow wonders whether Americans have a theory of evil and speculates that the American experience is "uncorrected by the main history of human suffering." The evidence tells him that man is depraved. Observation shows that men tend to behave, in crisis, like rats in a sack, as H.G. Wells said. Reason crowds him to an acceptance of absurdity as the prime condition of man and the world. But Bellow simply refuses to credit what observation, reason, and ideas thrust before him. He knows that man is less than what the Golden Age promised us, but he refuses to believe that man is nothing. He is something, Bellow says, and saying it he performs an act of faith. He rests his conviction on his feelings, and like the Transcendentalists upon whom he calls so often in his fiction, he resorts to his intuition. *Herzog* is a clear-cut illustration of Bellow's rejection of pessimistic philosophies. Everyone believes that man is a sick animal, says the protagonist of this novel, but he himself refuses to acquiesce in this judgment or to accept such dark interpretations of human experience as are contained in Kierkegaardian despair and absurdity, Spengler's decline of the West, or Eliot's wasteland complex. Herzog is himself a victim in modern America, but he simply refuses to accept his fate. He refuses to accept the empirical evidence. Persisting in his quest for love, he comes at the end to a restoration of sanity and hope for the future.

As Bellow accepts the epistemological implications of feeling, he also accepts or indeed advocates openness to feeling as sentiment. *Dangling Man* contained a rejection of the stiff-lipped Hemingway code which demands the suppression of emotion, and in all subsequent work he tended to expand the role given to emotion. He believes in the power of feeling and thinks that the novel must show a sympathetic devotion to the life of someone else, that the reader, in other words, must be asked to respond with sympathetic devotion to the life of the characters. In this way, Bellow works toward human connection between author and reader, between reader and characters; these are the connections that will lead to understanding. This emphasis upon emotion in Bellow is to be traced, in part, to the influence of Wilhelm Reich, who related the liberation of the emotions to the struggle for life fulfillment, and in part to the influence of Hasidism, the Jewish creed in which the central proposition is that life is holy joy.

The emphasis upon the self, optimism, and feeling must be understood in relation to Bellow's attitude toward death. He believes that one cannot understand life until one comes to terms with death. He treats the theme everywhere in his fiction, but it is enough here to remark it in four of his books. In *Seize the Day*, Tommy Wilhelm is able to come fully into possession of life, to seize the day, only after he confronts death itself and undergoes a symbolic drowning. Death brings him to the recognition of the heart's ultimate need, which is love. Bellow is equally concerned with death in *Henderson the Rain King* but less successful with it. Henderson insists that we hate

and fear death, but that there is nothing like it. He means that we all know we must face it and that we learn from facing it, as he learned from facing the lion, the meaning of life. In *Humboldt*, Citrine says repeatedly that Whitman was right: the important question is the death question. One of the major attractions of Rudolf Steiner's anthroposophy for Citrine is that in death the soul will liberate itself from the body. *Mr. Sammler's Planet* is Bellow's most extensive treatment of death. It is an elegiac mediation, first, on the approaching death of Western culture, brought on by a new barbarism represented by those who surrendered traditional concepts of value. And it is, further, the story of a man who has come back from the dead, as it were, whose authority as a spokesman rests upon his knowledge of death: he had dug what was supposed to be his own grave but had, by chance, crawled out of it; he had seen the Arab dead rotting at Gaza; he had himself killed a man. Throughout the novel he watches his friend and benefactor die. To have known death is to know the meaning of life and to know what it means to be a human being.

The Dean's December is a static novel in which the themes, substantial in themselves, lose some of their force because they have lost the urgency and novelty of initial revelation; we have heard them before from Bellow. The Dean is a humanistic journalist like Sammler attacking the violence and degeneracy of urban life and the collapse of standards, especially among the dirty, rebellious youth of the 1960's. Or the Dean is an academic like Herzog and must contend, like the latter, with a variety of "reality instructors," shrewd, hard, brutal, successful Chicago types who have contempt for the "moral excitement" that the Dean brings to his observation and assessment of American life. The novel is a meditation on death, as in so many previous Bellow fictions. Here it is death in Bucharest, an "Oppressive socialist wonderland" and in Chicago, and the protagonist is a man whose predilection is for philosophizing and whose tendency is toward an ill-controlled didacticism.

Him with His Foot in His Mouth, a collection of five pieces, recalls us to the boundless vitality and originality of the Jewish family members in *Augie*, an old Bellow subject that in this volume, like its other concerns, he makes new again. Here, as in "Cousins," the family center is an intellectual whose decision-making power affects nations, and the family ties expand to the cousinhood of mankind. In "What Kind of a Day Did You Have?" Bellow gives us perhaps the most compelling portrait of the intellectual in all his work thus far. Victor Wulpy, ill and living in the presence of death, staves off the end because "the excitement of thought . . . prevent[s] decay." He is the intellectual as a dying god, the descendant of Hercules, who addresses the ultimate questions about art and morality, sex and death, that define our humanity. Working in a full apprehension of the sense of an ending, of the impending moral and intellectual apocalypse (for which Chicago stands often as a symbol), Bellow has given us in this volume reason once more to regard him as the premier philosophical fiction writer of his time in America and as one in a select company of great writers in the 20th century.

Bellow's achievement is to have imposed upon the contending forces in his fiction—life and death, optimism and despair, reason and feeling, self and brotherhood—an idea of order. He has always known that the novelist begins at a great depth of distraction and disorder. Out of the chaos of experience and the tensions of conflicting claims, he has sought to create a coherent and compelling vision of experience. But it has been a tentative endeavor marked by a sad, sane, comic skepticism about the power of the artist or intellectual to affect the world in any way. Near the end of *Humboldt* Citrine says an extraordinary poetry is buried in America, "but none of the conventional means known to culture can even begin to extract it. . . . The agony is too deep, the disorder too big for art enterprises to be undertaken in the old way." The implication is not that we must, in despair, fall into silence, but that we must find another way to express delight and reveal beauty, to listen "in secret to the sound of truth that God puts into us," and achieve in the midst of disorder a framework of order willed by the artist.

—Chester E. Eisinger

BENEDICTUS, David (Henry). British. Born in London, 16 September 1938. Educated at Eton College; Balliol College, Oxford, B.A. in English 1959; University of Iowa, Iowa City. Married in 1971. Assistant trainee, BBC Radio, London, 1963–64; drama director, 1964–65, and story editor, "Wednesday Play," 1967, for BBC Television; trainee director, Thames Television, Bristol, 1969–70; assistant director, Royal Shakespeare Company, London, 1970–71; Writer-in-Residence, Central Library, Sutton, Surrey, 1976, and Kibbutz Gezer, Israel, 1980. Address: 20 Alexandra Road, East Twickenham, Middlesex, England.

PUBLICATIONS

Novels

The Fourth of June. London, Blond, and New York, Dutton, 1962.
You're a Big Boy Now. London, Blond, 1963; New York, Dutton, 1964.
This Animal Is Mischievous. London, Blond, 1965; New York, New American Library, 1966.
Hump; or, Bone by Bone, Alive. London, Blond, 1967.
The Guru and the Golf Club. London, Blond, 1969.
A World of Windows. London, Weidenfeld and Nicolson, 1971.
The Rabbi's Wife. London, Blond and Briggs, and New York, Evans, 1976.
A Twentieth-Century Man. London, Blond and Briggs, 1978.
Whose Life Is It Anyway? (novelization of play). London, Weidenfeld and Nicolson, 1981.
Lloyd George (novelization of television series). London, Weidenfeld and Nicolson, 1981.
Who Killed the Prince Consort? London, Macmillan, 1982.
Local Hero (novelization of screenplay). London, Penguin, 1983.
Floating Down to Camelot. London, Macdonald, 1985.

Uncollected Short Stories

"Mother Love," in *Seventeen* (New York), September 1963.
"E-Type Charlie," in *Seventeen* (New York), September 1964.
"The Unworthiness of Caspar," in *Queen* (London), 1 September 1965.
"Eat Me!," in *Status* (New York), November 1968.
"Nose-Job," in *Pointer* (London), 1970.
"Dreamboat," in *Penthouse* (London), 1971.
"The Torture Chambers of the Mind," in *Men Only* (London), 1974.

Plays

The Fourth of June, adaptation of his own novel (produced London, 1964).
Angels (Over Your Grave) and Geese (Over Mine) (produced Edinburgh, 1967).
Dromedary, adaptation of his novel *Hump* (produced Newcastle-upon-Tyne, 1969).
The Happy Hypocrite, music by Tony Russell, adaptation of the work by Max Beerbohm (produced Bristol, 1969).
What a Way to Run a Revolution!, music by Guy Woolfenden (produced London, 1971).
Betjemania (also director: produced Richmond, Surrey, 1978).

Radio Plays: *Fortune and the Fishmonger*, 1981; *The Golden Key*, 1982.

Other

Junk! How and Where to Buy Beautiful Things for Next to Nothing. London, Macmillan, 1976.
The Antique Collector's Guide. London, Macmillan, 1980; New York, Atheneum, 1981.
The Essential Guide to London: The Best of Everything and Some of the Worst. London, Sphere, 1984.

*

Theatrical Activities:
Director: **Play**—*Betjemania*, Richmond, Surrey, 1978.

David Benedictus comments:
Given peace of mind, financial independence, and a modicum of luck, I may produce a novel to be proud of one day. But then, who wouldn't? In the meantime, I continue to rehearse in public.

*   *   *

The range of David Benedictus's novels is very broad. Beginning as a penetrating social satirist in his first works—*The Fourth of June, You're a Big Boy Now, This Animal Is Mischievous*—he has become increasingly serious and experimental over the past decade. Throughout his fiction, Benedictus is concerned with British society's most rigid conventions of sexual and political behavior and with the many kinds of victims caused by the abrasions of caste and class. His caustic ironic vision is perhaps closer to that of Nathanael West than that of Evelyn Waugh, to whom he has been compared.

Benedictus poses the stock characters of social comedy—bishops, clubmen, schoolmasters—against individuals often maimed, deranged, or outcasts by society. A Kafkaesque quality of irony emerges in the novels. *Hump* is a dystopian fantasy about a hump-back who loves his deformity in a world of increasing uniformity. *A World of Windows* is a dialectical drama between a voyeur and his wife, exploring the reciprocal madness of observed and observer. *The Guru and the Golf Club* poses a caricature of Eastern mysticism against a parallel caricature of British middle-class pretensions and aspirations.

The Rabbi's Wife and *A Twentieth-Century Man* are mordant and tragic investigations of our times through the refracting prism of Jewish experience. Each contrasts norms of British behavior with the catastrophes of the Holocaust and contemporary terrorism against Jews. In *The Rabbi's Wife* Palestinian terrorists separate a young mod rabbi and his wife, murdering children in a synagogue on the Day of Atonement. The terrorists, modern British Jews, and the indifferent mass of the population are detailed against the horrifying events of political diabolism. *A Twentieth-Century Man* establishes the same mordant ironies by juxtaposing scenes from the marriage of a Tory M.P. and his Dutch wife, whom he rescued from Bergen-Belsen in 1945. Bitter, disturbing comparisons arise between the destruction of the human spirit in the death camps and in contemporary urban civilization.

In *Who Killed the Prince Consort?* the answer to the title question is "practically everyone." The novel is a sly and highly comic satire on Victorian life and mores, focusing on the death of "dear Albert" and the internal politics of the royal family in 1861. The cast of characters includes Karl Marx, a young Sherlock Holmes, the royal physicians and servants, a 97-year-old Scots Pretender, and other parodic figures. Behind the bizarre satire is a serious investigation of hypocrisy, corruption, and mental aberration as the true basis of the Victorian ethos. In many ways, this is Benedictus's funniest work, full of quirky historical data and mock-tushery.

In recent years, Benedictus has worked with film scripts and "novelizations" of films (Brian Clark's *Whose Life Is It Anyway?* and his own *Local Hero*), and he has created increasingly dramatic renderings in his fiction. The vision of his satire has covered our main cultural foibles and dissected the darker anatomy of British class and power.

Benedictus's *forte* in his fiction is the creation of vivid, complex characters that represent basic assumptions of our culture. His satire is Swiftian in intensity and in its distorted images of sexuality, violence, and brutality. Moving from the sublimated prison system of the quintessential British public school (Eton) to the torments of urban life, the death camps, and warfare by terrorism, Benedictus has compiled a sardonic catalogue of our century's ills. The collision between dead tradition and the anarchy of the present instant is Benedictus's entree into his characters.

These novels also demonstrate a measure of compassion for individuals trapped by the failures of our culture. Even when afflicted by bizarre sexual compulsions, failures of will and nerve, or base selfishness, many of his characters rise to small moments of love and heroism. If Benedictus's satire does not exempt many from its ironies, it also allows room for individual's virtues. The survivors of our varied holocausts still struggle to live and love one another.

—William J. Schafer

BERGER, John (Peter). British. Born in Stoke Newington, London, 5 November 1926. Attended the Central School of Art and the Chelsea School of Art, London. Served in the Oxford and Buckinghamshire Infantry, 1944–46. Married twice; three children. Painter and drawing teacher, 1948–55; contributor, *Tribune* and *New Statesman*, both London, 1951–60. Narrator, *About Time* television series, 1985. Art exhibited at Wildenstein, Redfern, and Leicester galleries, London. Recipient: Booker Prize, 1972; *Guardian* Fiction Prize, 1972; James Tait Black Memorial Prize, 1973; New York Critics prize, for screenplay, 1976; George Orwell Memorial Prize, 1977. Address: Quincy, Mieussy, 74440 France.

PUBLICATIONS

Novels

A Painter of Our Time. London, Secker and Warburg, 1958; New York, Simon and Schuster, 1959.

The Foot of Clive. London, Methuen, 1962.
Corker's Freedom. London, Methuen, 1964.
G. London, Weidenfeld and Nicolson, and New York, Viking Press, 1972.

Short Stories

Pig Earth. London, Writers and Readers, 1979; New York, Pantheon, 1980.

Plays

Jonas qui aura 25 ans en l'an 2000 (screenplay), with Alain Tanner. Lausanne, Cinémathèque Suisse, 1978; translated by Michael Palmer, as *Jonah Who Will Be 25 in the Year 2000*, Berkeley, California, North Atlantic, 1983.
Question of Geography, with Nella Bielski (produced Marseille, 1984).
Les Trois Chaleurs (produced Paris, 1985).
Boris, translated into Welsh by Rhiannon Ifans (produced Cardiff, 1985).

Screenplays, with Alain Tanner: *La Salamandre* (*The Salamander*), 1971; *Le Milieu du monde* (*The Middle of the World*), 1974; *Jonas* (*Jonah Who Will Be 25 in the Year 2000*), 1976.

Other

Marcel Frishman, with George Besson. Oxford, Cassirer, 1958.
Permanent Red: Essays in Seeing. London, Methuen, 1960; as *Towards Reality*, New York, Knopf, 1962.
The Success and Failure of Picasso. London, Penguin, 1965; New York, Pantheon, 1980.
A Fortunate Man: The Story of a Country Doctor, photographs by Jean Mohr. London, Allen Lane, and New York, Holt Rinehart, 1967.
Art and Revolution: Ernst Neizvestny and the Role of the Artist in the U.S.S.R. London, Weidenfeld and Nicolson, and New York, Pantheon, 1969.
The Moment of Cubism and Other Essays. London, Weidenfeld and Nicolson, and New York, Pantheon, 1969.
The Look of Things, edited by Nikos Stangos. London, Penguin, 1972; New York, Viking Press, 1974.
Ways of Seeing, with others. London, BBC-Penguin, 1972; New York, Viking Press, 1973.
A Seventh Man: Migrant Workers in Europe, photographs by Jean Mohr. London, Penguin, and New York, Viking Press, 1975.
About Looking. London, Writers and Readers, and New York, Pantheon, 1980.
Another Way of Telling (on photography), with Jean Mohr. London, Writers and Readers, and New York, Pantheon, 1982.
And Our Faces, My Heart, Brief as Photos. London, Writers and Readers, and New York, Pantheon, 1984.
The White Bird. London, Chatto and Windus, 1985.
The Sense of Sight: Writings, edited by Lloyd Spencer. New York, Pantheon, 1986.

Translator, with Anya Bostock, *Poems on the Theatre*, by Bertolt Brecht. London, Scorpion Press, 1961; as *The Great*

Art of Living Together: Poems on the Theatre, Bingley, York-
shire, Granville Press, 1972.
Translator, with Anya Bostock, *Helene Weigel, Actress*, by
Bertolt Brecht. Leipzig, Veb Edition, 1961.
Translator, with Anya Bostock, *Return to My Native Land*,
by Aimé Césaire. London, Penguin, 1969.
Translator, with Lisa Appignanesi, *Oranges for the Son of
Asher Levy*, by Nella Bielski. London, Writers and
Readers, 1982.

*   *   *

John Berger does not like one to divide his work up into
categories; but if one is to consider the three novels published
between 1959 and 1964 in isolation from his other published
work then what immediately stands out is that he is a very
skilful entertainer as well as a Marxist and a painter. Those
two last attributes do, however, have a strong, if indirect, bearing on the novels. Berger is far too much of an artist to mix
fiction and polemic, but he is concerned with how his characters
behave in a social setting, whether the society is confined to
the men's ward of a general hospital, as in *The Foot of Clive*,
or a sleazy employment agency in Clapham (*Corker's Freedom*). It is how these microcosms of civilisation affect and shape
his characters that matters. For although individuals may have
strong ideas about how they intend to fashion their lives, the
entrenched structures of society, which somehow always seem
to be in a league with their own habitual weaknesses, always
prove too much for them.

As a painter, Berger brings to his novels a sensual awareness
that is not entirely visual. Reviewing *The Foot of Clive* for
The Observer, Francis Wyndham wrote, "He can make us smell
the ward (lemons and sour milk), taste the tea, hear the Light
Programme through the earphones, see the sick men's bodies,
above all feel the texture of the sheets, pyjamas, human skin."
He also has an artist's awareness of structures and of the various
complimentary levels on which all facets of life operate. For
instance in the act of speaking, we have at one level the words
that actually emerge, but behind these in the speaker's mind
are the words he would like to say, his feelings, his fantasies,
and his instinctively accurate, and usually highly disturbing,
knowledge about the existential facts of the immediate situation. All these levels come clear in the illustrated lecture on
Vienna which Corker, the seedy, aged bachelor from Clapham,
gives to a Church social gathering.

To both these attributes must be added Berger's skill as an
entertainer. He can hold his audience's attention by his dexterity in dealing with his subject matter, and with the wit with
which he brings to light the absurd juxtapositions of the human
situation.

All these qualities are deepened and extended in *G*. This
work is written more in the form of a film script than an orthodox work of fiction, each paragraph (and some of them only
contain one short sentence) being sharp and complete in itself,
and often setting a precise visual scene. G is the illegitimate
son of a wealthy Italian merchant and rather advanced American girl who later develops Fabian leanings. He was born four
years after Garibaldi's death, and the initial by which his author
calls him refers equally to that, and to his father's name Giovanni. He was killed in Trieste on the day that Austria declared
war on Italy on account of that city. Although G is intrinsically
bound up with the historical events of his time, he is almost
a-political himself. In this chronicle, Berger has set himself
the vast task that Tolstoy undertook: that of depicting how
each one of us is history in that we are both monumentally
shaped by events and, in small measure, by the mere act of
inhabiting our skins, influence their course.

—Shirley Toulson

———

BERGER, Thomas (Louis). American. Born in Cincinnati,
Ohio, 20 July 1924. Educated at the University of Cincinnati,
B.A. 1948; Columbia University, New York, 1950–51. Served
in the United States Army, 1943–46. Married Jeanne Redpath
in 1950. Librarian, Rand School of Social Science, New York,
1948–51; staff member, *New York Times Index*, 1951–52; asso-
ciate editor, *Popular Science Monthly*, New York, 1952–54;
film critic, *Esquire*, New York, 1972–73; Writer-in-Residence,
University of Kansas, Lawrence, 1974; Distinguished Visiting
Professor, Southampton College, New York, 1975–76; Visiting
Lecturer, Yale University, New Haven, Connecticut, 1981–82;
Regents' Lecturer, University of California, Davis, 1982. Recip-
ient: Dial fellowship, 1962; Western Heritage Award, 1965;
Rosenthal Award, 1965. Agent: Don Congdon Associates, 177
East 70th Street, New York, New York 10021, U.S.A.

PUBLICATIONS

Novels

Crazy in Berlin. New York, Scribner, 1958.
Reinhart in Love. New York, Scribner, 1962; London, Eyre
and Spottiswoode, 1963.
Little Big Man. New York, Dial Press, 1964; London, Eyre
and Spottiswoode, 1965.
Killing Time. New York, Dial Press, 1967; London Eyre and
Spottiswoode, 1968.
Vital Parts. New York, Baron, 1970; London, Eyre and Spot-
tiswoode, 1971.
Regiment of Women. New York, Simon and Schuster, 1973;
London, Eyre Methuen, 1974.
Sneaky People. New York, Simon and Schuster, 1975; Lon-
don, Methuen, 1980.
Who Is Teddy Villanova? New York, Delacorte Press, and
London, Eyre Methuen, 1977.
Arthur Rex: A Legendary Novel. New York, Delacorte Press,
1978; London, Methuen, 1979.
Neighbors. New York, Delacorte Press, 1980; London,
Methuen, 1981.
Reinhart's Women. New York, Delacorte Press, 1981; Lon-
don, Methuen, 1982.
The Feud. New York, Delacorte Press, 1983; London, Meth-
uen, 1984.
Nowhere. New York, Delacorte Press, 1985; London, Meth-
uen, 1986.

Short Story

Granted Wishes. Northridge, California, Lord John Press,
1984.

Uncollected Short Stories

"Professor Hyde," in *Playboy* (Chicago), December 1961.
"A Monkey of His Own," in *Saturday Evening Post* (Philadelphia), 22 May 1965.

"Fatuous Fables," in *Penthouse* (London), March 1973.

"Envy," in *Oui* (Chicago), April 1975.

"The Achievement of Dr. Poon," in *American Review 25*, edited by Theodore Solotaroff. New York, Bantam, 1976.

"Tales of the Animal Crime Squad," in *Playboy* (Chicago), December 1980.

"The Methuselah Factor," in *Gentlemen's Quarterly* (New York), September 1984.

Play

Other People (produced Berkshire Theatre Festival, Massachusetts, 1970).

*

Manuscript Collection: Boston University Library.

Critical Studies: "Bitter Comedy" by Richard Schickel, in *Commentary* (New York), July 1970; "Thomas Berger's *Little Big Man* as History" by Leo Oliva, in *Western American Literature* (Fort Collins, Colorado), vol. 8, nos. 1–2, 1973; "Thomas Berger's Elan" by Douglas Hughes, in *Confrontation* (New York), Spring–Summer 1976; "The Radical Americanist" by Brooks Landon, and "The Second Decade of *Little Big Man*" by Frederick Turner, both in *The Nation* (New York), 20 August 1977; "Berger and Barth: The Comedy of Decomposition" by Stanley Trachtenberg, in *Comic Relief* edited by Sarah Blacher Cohen, Urbana, University of Illinois Press, 1978; "Thomas Berger Issue" (includes bibliography) of *Studies in American Humor* (San Marcos, Texas), Spring and Fall 1983; "Reinhart as Hero and Clown" by Gerald Weales, in *Hollins Critic* (Hollins College, Virginia), December 1983.

Thomas Berger comments:

I write to amuse and conceal myself.

*   *   *

Thomas Berger's novels exhibit an extraordinary comic sensibility, a satiric talent for wild caricature, and a concern for the quality of middle-class life in middle America. His novels chronicle the decline and fall of the Common Man in 20th-century America and meticulously detail the absurdities of our civilization. Berger is one of the subtlest and most accurate parodists writing today, with a flawless sense of style and proportion that is charged with comic vitality.

His Reinhart saga (*Crazy in Berlin*, *Reinhart in Love*, *Vital Parts*, and *Reinhart's Women*) follows Carlo Reinhart from adolescence to middle age, detailing his career as a soldier in occupied Germany, a GI Bill student, and a failed wage-slave and decrepit father in the bewildering America of the 1980's. Reinhart epitomizes the failure of good intentions. A believer in the American Dream as purveyed in magazines, high-school classrooms, and advertisements, Carlo is a constant victim of deceit and fraud. Like the Good Soldier Schweik, Carlo takes the world at face value and assumes that appearance is reality; unlike Schweik, Carlo is guileless and incapable of hypocrisy, so he is perpetually victimized and disillusioned. The comedy arises in the gulf between Carlo's expectations and his experience.

In *Crazy in Berlin* Carlo is swept up in conspiracy, involved with spies and criminals dividing the spoils of the fallen Nazi state. A good-natured slob and summer soldier, Carlo survives, but he is driven to murder and madness, shattered not by war but by the lunacy of peace. The novel exudes the bitter ironies of sophisticated slap-stick comedy, similar to Preston Sturges's films. Carlo, a bewildered, optimistic average man, is driven mad by the Hobbesian nightmare of Occupied Germany.

The second novel, *Reinhart in Love*, continues the mock-heroic saga. Carlo returns to the purported normality of peacetime America to continue college on the GI Bill. Again he is duped, exploited, and betrayed as Orlando himself, charged with cosmic love: "*Reinhart was in love with everything.*" But as his boss tells him, the world is still a Hobbesian jungle, with every man's hand raised against his fellows: "life, real life, is exactly like the fighting, except in the latter you use guns and therefore don't destroy as many people." The novel ends with Carlo married by deception to a shrew, failed even at suicide and bereft of ideals and ambitions, ready to move upward and onward.

Vital Parts moves ahead 20 years to reveal Reinhart still married to his shrew and father to a fat, mooning daughter and a vicious ne'er-do-well son. He has failed at every capitalistic venture, lost his hair and youth, gained debts and a paunch. Again in suicidal despair, he becomes involved in a bizarre cryogenics scheme—to immortality via technology. He becomes the guinea pig in a scheme to freeze and revive a human being. Carlo feels he has little to choose between an absurd life, an absurd death, and a remote hope of immortality.

In *Reinhart's Women*, Carlo achieves a degree of peace with his wife and daughter, and he takes on a new role as a gourmet cook. Berger makes Carlo here less the ever-ready butt of slapstick and more the master of his destiny, as if Carlo were growing in later middle age into himself. The book's comedy is mellower and less acerbic than the view of corrupt post-World War II culture from which Berger began the saga.

In *Little Big Man* Berger also uses mock-heroic satire, here on the elaborate mythology of the Old West. A tale of cowboys and Indians told from *both* views, the novel describes the only white survivor of the Battle of the Little Big Horn—111-year-old Jack Crabb, victim of Indian attacks, Indian, Indian-fighter, gunfighter, gambler, con man, etc. The novel follows the "half-man, half-alligator" tradition of frontier humor, bursting with gigantic hyperbole. It is also a detailed, convincing picture of prairie life, both with the Cheyenne (the "Human Beings") and with the white settlers. The violence, squalor, and monotony of life in raw nature are as intensely realized as the farce. Jack Crabb is a frontier Carlo Reinhart, with the same insecurities, the same propensities for confusion and cowardice, the same common humanity.

Arthur Rex may be the finest redaction of the legend since Malory. It is a labor of love for pure story and style in which Berger's brilliant prose is honed like Excalibur itself. A straightforward rendering of the Arthurian material, the novel is a tribute to romance, adventure, and storytelling as the roots of our literature. Berger makes the characters come sharply alive in vigorous, dramatic scenes and retains the mixture of exuberance and nostalgia which defines the ancient cycle.

A theme inherent in Berger's work is that of metamorphosis—transformation, counterfeiting, deception, the shiftiness of reality. *Who Is Teddy Villanova?*, *Nowhere*, and *Neighbors* focus on this theme. Detective fiction and cold-war thrillers are parodied in the first two novels, which follow the hapless adventures of Russel Wren, an inept semi-pro detective who is constantly overwhelmed by violent events beyond his perception. *Who Is Teddy Villanova?* caricatures the conventions of the tough-guy detective novel, and *Nowhere* brilliantly combines the spy story and the utopian romance. An atmosphere of bizarre paranoia suffuses both installments of the Wren romance. In *Neighbors* the same mode is applied to suburban realities. Earl Keese, prone to hallucinations, is subjected to a series of emotional and mental assaults by a man and woman who move in next door. The story turns on paradoxes and illusions, an increasingly grotesque feeling that things are never what they seem. In Berger's view, our culture has crashed through the looking glass, where absurdity rules all and everything turns by subtle and malicious irony into its opposite.

Sneaky People and *The Feud* also anatomize middle-class American life; both are set in the 1930's and deal with the peculiar conflation of acquisitiveness and sexuality which creates the ethos for the people-next-door culture described in *Neighbors*. A mixture of healthy cynicism and obvious nostalgia makes the narratives attractive as satires on the conventional American success story.

—William J. Schafer

BERMANT, Chaim (Icyk). British. Born in Breslev, Poland, 26 February 1929. Educated at Queen's Park School, Glasgow, 1938–48; Glasgow Yeshiva (rabbinical college), 1949–51; Glasgow University, 1952–55, 1959–61, M.A. 1955, M.Litt. 1960; London School of Economics, 1955–57, M.Sc. 1957. Married Judith Weil in 1962; two sons and two daughters. Schoolmaster, 1955–57; economist, 1957–58; scriptwriter, Scottish Television, Glasgow, 1958–59, and Granada Television, London, 1959–60; features editor, *Jewish Chronicle*, London, 1964–66. Recipient: Wingate Award (*Jewish Chronicle*), for non-fiction, 1977. Agent: A.P. Watt Ltd., 26–28 Bedford Row, London WC1R 4HL. Address: 18 Hill Rise, London NW11 6NA, England.

PUBLICATIONS

Novels

Jericho Sleep Alone.   London, Chapman and Hall, 1964.
Berl Make Tea.   London, Chapman and Hall, 1965.
Ben Preserve Us.   London, Chapman and Hall, 1965; New York, Holt Rinehart, 1966.
Jericho Sleep Alone, and Berl Make Tea.   New York, Holt Rinehart, 1966.
Diary of an Old Man.   London, Chapman and Hall, 1966; New York, Holt Rinehart, 1967.
Swinging in the Rain.   London, Hodder and Stoughton, 1967.
Here Endeth the Lesson.   London, Eyre and Spottiswoode, 1969.
Now Dowager.   London, Eyre and Spottiswoode, 1971.
Roses Are Blooming in Picardy.   London, Eyre Methuen, 1972.
The Last Supper.   London, Eyre Methuen, and New York, St. Martin's Press, 1973.
The Second Mrs. Whitberg.   London, Allen and Unwin, and New York, St. Martin's Press, 1976.
The Squire of Bor Shachor.   London, Allen and Unwin, and New York, St Martin's Press, 1977.
Now Newman Was Old.   London, Allen and Unwin, and New York, St. Martin's Press, 1978.
The Patriarch.   London, Weidenfeld and Nicolson, and New York, St. Martin's Press, 1981.
The House of Women.   London, Weidenfeld and Nicolson, and New York, St. Martin's Press, 1983.
Dancing Bear.   London, Weidenfeld and Nicolson, 1984; New York, St. Martin's Press, 1985.

Play

Television Play: *Pews*, 1980.

Other

Israel.   London, Thames and Hudson, and New York, Walker, 1967.
Troubled Eden: An Anatomy of British Jewry.   London, Valentine Mitchell, 1969; New York, Basic Books, 1970.
The Cousinhood: The Anglo-Jewish Gentry.   London, Eyre and Spottiswoode, 1971; New York, Macmillan, 1972.
The Walled Garden: The Saga of Jewish Family Life and Tradition.   London, Weidenfeld and Nicolson, 1974; New York, Macmillan, 1975.
Point of Arrival: A Study of London's East End.   London, Eyre Methuen, 1975; as *London's East End: Point of Arrival*, New York, Macmillan, 1976.
Coming Home.   London, Allen and Unwin, 1976.
The Jews.   London, Weidenfeld and Nicolson, and New York, Times, 1977.
Ebla: An Archaeological Enigma, with Michael Weitzman. London, Weidenfeld and Nicolson, and New York, Times, 1979.
Belshazzar: A Cat's Story for Humans.   London, Allen and Unwin, 1979; New York, Avon, 1982.
On the Other Hand.   London, Robson, 1982.
What's the Joke: A Study of Jewish Humour Through the Ages. London, Weidenfeld and Nicolson, 1986.

Editor, with Murray Mindlin, *Explorations: An Annual on Jewish Themes.*   London, Barrie and Rockliff, 1967; Chicago, Quadrangle, 1968.

*

Manuscript Collection: Mugar Memorial Library, Boston University.

Chaim Bermant comments:

My characters are mainly Jewish, hapless but not helpless, beset by many small calamities which somehow never amount to an irreversible disaster and which certainly do not diminish their hope that even if the worst is not over the best is yet to come. The treatment is humorous, but the intention is serious.

*   *   *

Of Chaim Bermant's novels the one word consistently used by every reviewer is "funny." And so they are, with a crisp, snip-snap style based largely on wordplay and repetition, the one-line sentences tripping down the page in a way which makes the easiest of easy reading. Yet, although this accolade is almost the greatest a writer can receive today, one must look for other criteria when attempting judgment. However jokey and ephemeral the fashion of our time, the novel is still a serious art form and its most important task is still the creation of character.

By this standard, Bermant's first novel, *Jericho Sleep Alone*, is genuinely alive and kicking. Its hero is a young Jewish boy living with his Orthodox family and friends in Glasgow. So far, so autobiographical. His growing up, his uncertainty about himself, his bewilderment as to what makes personality, what qualities bring success, his infatuation with (inevitably) the "most popular girl" in his group (the best and most believable female character in the whole of his work)—all this is conveyed in a brisk, lively style. It is a most agreeable book, not sweet, not sour, but tart and fresh and truthful.

With *Berl Make Tea*, that well-known hazard, the second novel, the author, it must be said, doesn't quite make it. Berl is a squat philosophical little Jew, the eternal rubberball, taking all misfortunes and bouncing back every time. He (thankfully) loses his wife, loses his job, drifts from place to place encountering odd people and odd goings on. The characters are—as so often in this writer's work—line drawings rather than people; escapes from a sort of 19th-century, Yiddish, comic strip.

It is perhaps a pity that it was this book rather than *Jericho* which set the pattern for many of Bermant's subsequent novels (mostly written in the first person). *Ben Preserve Us*: the central character a young Rabbi in a Scottish town, eligible and, it is discovered, very rich but also Jewish-mother-ridden. *Swinging in the Rain*: central figure a rich chocolate manufacturer with business worries, a flighty daughter and an oafish son, and so on. (This author, apart from his archetypal Jewish parents, appears to be equally fascinated by the very rich and the oafs. They appear in practically every one of his novels.)

Of the six or seven books of the "middle period" perhaps *Now Dowager*, though written in exactly the same style and tone as the rest is probably the most enjoyable. The "I" character this time is a very rich, old Jewish widow trying to convert a non-Jewish girl to the faith. It is as wildly unbelievable as all his other books but is somehow more attractive and exhibits his abilities at their sparkling best. These abilities are a gift for endless but sometimes very amusing dialogue which, like salted biscuits or crisp celery, one can go on eating—or reading—forever; a real talent for economical, physical description; and powers of invention, shallow perhaps, but so quick and skilful and lively that the critical faculty invariably takes a holiday while actually reading. There is also very often a genuine touch of pathos. It is this last which gives the impression that if Bermant, instead of producing books which can be read in an hour and forgotten in twenty minutes (a fair example of Bermant's style of comment) were to forget what appears to have been an over-exposure to P.G. Wodehouse in his youth (since he has neither the ultimate flair nor the meticulous sense of structure which underlies the great, classic comedy writers) he would be not only a much better novelist but also a true humorist rather than a jokester.

About midway in his career Bermant published a very slender book, hardly a novel, more a *conte*, entitled *Diary of an Old Man*. It is a simple account of one freezing, wintry month in the life of an old man living in one room. Yet, perhaps because of its very brevity, the author was able to give his tale the concentrated care really good fiction demands and the result was an imperfect but very moving little gem; imperfect because too often this author has a slapdash approach which leaves loose, contradictory bits of character and a handful of short ends lying around every novel.

The Last Supper is an ambitious attempt to break out of the snap, crackle and pop formula of his previous fiction. It is the story of the week's mourning which Jewish families observe when a close member—in this case the mother—dies. Again the milieu is that of a very rich, Anglo-Jewish aristocratic family but this time the author has made a genuine try at distinguishing between his characters; brothers and sisters, aunts and uncles, in-laws. . . . During the week revelations are made, old scandals revived, sub-plots inserted. The book is a failure but the attempt is an honourable one; the characters emerging half-hewn as it were from the stone.

It is only fair to add that though up till now Bermant cannot be claimed as a novelist really to be reckoned with, he is an admirable and often brilliant journalist and also a respectable hard-backed sociologist, specialising in aspects of Anglo-Jewish life. Both *Troubled Eden* and *The Cousinhood*, a study of the rich, interweaved families of Jewish aristocracy in England have been much praised—as have two other books, *Point of Arrival*, a history of the East End of London, and *The Walled Garden*, a study of Jewish family groupings and traditions.

As book succeeds book Bermant's writing grows ever more concerned with his abiding, not to say obsessive, interest in the English upper classes. This, since it still runs in harness with his equal obsession with his Jewishness has produced at least two more volumes of slightly uneasy alliance. *Dancing Bear* is a novel about a young man brought up in a rich, Gentile family (or are they Gentile?) who is uncertain about his grandfather's origins (or was he his grandfather?) and sleeps with his aunt (or was she his mother?) and throughout is attempting to discover whether he is Jewish or not. Smallish sections of this book are very well done. Bermant is excellent, as always, on tiny vignettes of place: Germany, Egypt, Oxford, Arabia, to say nothing of America and Russia. On character he is occasionally both vivid and good. But the larger part is so convoluted, so dizzying with plot and maze that its smaller virtues are submerged.

The House of Women, by far his best novel to date, was written before *Dancing Bear* which seems to argue a slightly retrograde step. This one is again about an upper-middle-class family which hardly knows it is Jewish. There are a father; four daughters (the second, a clever, knowing girl named Ducks, is the narrator—a first-person mode which Bermant, in drag so to speak, carries off splendidly); and a son by a second marriage. Here, for almost the first time nearly all of Bermant's more trying mannerisms, inversions, and tedious wordplay have disappeared. The tone, the dialogue, the development of real character are quite remarkably sustained. And *here* is where this author must, at this stage in his career, return. On the evidence of *The House of Women* we are at last being made aware that Bermant's potentiality as a really good novelist has as yet hardly been tapped.

—Gerda Charles

BHATTACHARYA, Bhabani. Indian. Born in Bhagalpur, Bihar, 22 October 1906. Educated at Patna University, B.A. (honours) in English 1927; University of London, 1929–34, B.A. (honours) in history 1931, Ph.D. 1934. Married Salila Mukerji in 1935; one son and two daughters. Press attaché, Embassy of India, Washington, D.C., 1949–50; assistant editor, *Illustrated Weekly of India*, Bombay, 1950–52; secretary, Tagore Commemorative Society, New Delhi, 1959–60; consultant, Ministry of Education, New Delhi, 1961–67; senior specialist, East-West Center, Honolulu, 1969–70. Since 1970, Visiting Professor, University of Hawaii, Honolulu, University of Washington, Seattle, and other universities. Delegate, International Seminar, Harvard University, Cambridge, Massachusetts, 1959, and Harvard Japanese Seminar, Tokyo, 1960; lectured as a guest of the government in New Zealand, 1962, Australia, 1962, and West Germany, 1963; British Council lecturer, 1963, 1969. Recipient: Universities of New Zealand Prestige Award, 1962; Asia Foundation grant, 1966; Sahitya Academy award, 1968; Ford grant, 1968, 1969; American Institute of Indian Studies-Indian Council for Cultural Relations grant, 1980. Member of the Advisory Board, Indian National

Academy of Letters. Address: 252-B Glandore Drive, Manchester, Missouri 63021, U.S.A.

PUBLICATIONS

Novels

So Many Hungers!   London, Gollancz, 1947.
Music for Mohini.   New York, Crown, 1952; London, Angus and Robertson, 1959.
He Who Rides a Tiger.   New York, Crown, 1954; London, Angus and Robertson, 1960.
A Goddess Named Gold.   New York, Crown, 1960.
Shadow from Ladakh.   New York, Crown, 1966; London, W.H. Allen, 1967.
A Dream in Hawaii.   New Delhi, Macmillan, 1979.

Short Stories

Steel Hawk and Other Stories.   New Delhi, Hind, 1968.

Other

Some Memorable Yesterdays.   Patna, Pustak Bhandar, 1941; revised edition, as *Indian Cavalcade*, Bombay, Nalanda, 1948; as *Glimpses of Indian History*, New Delhi, Sterling, 1975.
Gandhi the Writer: The Image as It Grew.   New Delhi, National Book Trust, 1969; revised edition, as *Mahatma Gandhi*, New Delhi, Arnold-Heinemann, 1976.
Socio-Political Currents in Bengal: A Nineteenth Century Perspective.   New Delhi, Vikas, 1980.

Editor, *Contemporary Indian Short Stories*, series 2.   New Delhi, Sahitya Akademi, 1967.

Translator, *The Golden Boat*, by Tagore.   London, Allen and Unwin, 1932; New York, Macmillan, 1933.
Translator, *Towards Universal Man*, by Tagore.   Bombay, London, and New York, Asia Publishing House, 1961.

*

Manuscript Collection: Boston University.

Critical Studies: *Bhabani Bhattacharya* by K.R. Chandrasekharan, New Delhi, Arnold-Heinemann, 1974; *Bhabani Bhattacharya* by Dorothy B. Shimer, Boston, Twayne, 1975; *Bhabani Bhattacharya: His Vision and Themes* by K.K. Sharma, New Delhi, Abhinav, 1979; *Perspectives on Bhabani Bhattacharya* edited by R. Srivastava, New Delhi, Vimal, 1984.

Bhabani Bhattacharya comments:

How did I happen to become a novelist? When I was a student in London in the 1930's, I started writing a novel. Halfway through, I thought it was no good and I was not destined to be a creative writer—I was not a student of Literature anyway. I tore up the manuscript. However, I wrote some short sketches for *The Spectator*. I translated Tagore. Back in India, I found other preoccupations. Early in the 1940's I tried to do a novel again. When half-written, it found its way into a heap of unwanted papers.

Then the great famine swept down upon Bengal. The emotional stirrings I felt (more than two million men, women and children died of slow starvation amid a man-made scarcity)

were a sheer compulsion to creativity. The result was the novel *So Many Hungers!* (The story was concerned with all the intensified hungers of the historic years 1942–43—not food alone: the money hunger, the sex hunger, the hunger to achieve India's political freedom.) Again I tucked the manuscript away. But my wife Salila forced me to have faith in my work. Acceptance by a publisher, and success, were quick.

I have no big literary output, as you see. I have not believed in writing for the sake of writing. I seldom planned a story structure. Each story grew in my subconscious mind, as it were. When it had grown enough, I had to give it a physical form. The characters, even when I had decided how they were going to behave, moved by their own volition, often defeating my purpose.

Finally, why did I choose English as my medium of expression? I have loved writing in English. The creative writer must have full freedom to use the language of his choice. If he decides on a foreign tongue, he will have to cross immense technical hurdles, but that is *his* headache. I have enjoyed the challenge of this literary problem—expressing Indian life in the idiom of an alien tongue.

*   *   *

Bhabani Bhattacharya has stated that he regards art as a criticism of life which reviews current values, and that he conceives the novel as an "idiom of compassion" which is designed to have a curative social effect. His own novels conscientiously reflect these views. Their subject-matter and themes derive from modern Indian history and the problems of contemporary Indian society, and they embody programmes of reform as well as stinging social criticism. This approach, initiated in modern Indian fiction in English by the early novels and short stories of Mulk Raj Anand (from 1935–47), is a feature of the majority of Indian post-Independence novels. Bhattacharya's contributions to the contemporary Indian novel demonstrates that, for literate Indians, fiction is a good medium in which to examine such problems as caste, poverty, ignorance, political injustice, communal intolerance and economic inequality. Many Indian novelists, including Bhattacharya, have revealed how these and many other aspects of Indian life relate to the course of modern Indian history, particularly the Independence struggle. Partition, and "free" India's attempt to create a new social order.

Like many other Indians, Bhattacharya celebrated Independence with the publication of a first novel: *So Many Hungers!* This novel is a harrowing account of famine in Bengal (unfortunately ever-relevant) and a passionate indictment of the human culpability involved, particularly of the grasping parasites (mostly upper-class) who exploit the famine to make black-market fortunes. The story is told from the point of view of the starving peasants who migrated to Calcutta where they died in the streets, and is calculated to shock the reader's sense of humanity in scenes such as that which describes a jackal perched on the thigh of a pregnant woman, tearing at her swollen belly while her screams slash the air.

Bhattacharya's second novel, *Music for Mohini*, is the story of an arranged marriage and the adjustment which the modern city girl, Mohini, has to make to fit into the traditional patterns of life in her husband Jayadev's "Big House," presided over by his aristocratic iron-willed mother. The main theme of the novel is the idea of "synthesis," "a profound union of today with yesterday," whereby the conflict between tradition and modernity will be resolved. Synthesis is achieved in practice as well as theory: finally Mohini and her mother-in-law are agreeably reconciled and Jayadev is transformed, through conjugal and moral stimuli, from ascetic intellectual into village reformer. *Shadow from Ladakh*, set against the background of the Indo-Chinese border conflict following China's annexation of Tibet, is also a variation on the theme of synthesis. Through the relationships of the main characters Bhattacharya advocates for present-day India a cultural fusion based on a love-match between Gandhian idealism and a progressive people's technology.

He Who Rides a Tiger and *A Goddess Named Gold* are social fables and as such are Bhattacharya's most formally sophisticated works. The former is the story of an untouchable who successfully poses as a Brahmin holy man; the plot of the latter is a variation of fairytale in which the heroine and her fellow villagers believe that her amulet has the magical power to transform copper into gold whenever she performs a true act of kindness. In *He Who Rides a Tiger* the social theme is developed in terms of irony in order to dramatise the iniquities and hypocrises of the caste system, while in *A Goddess Named Gold* the moral supremacy of communal unity over landlord selfishness is proposed as a model for independent India.

Although Bhattacharya has a tendency to load his novels with mechanical sociology, over-simplified philosophies, and naively symbolic relationships (as in *Shadow from Ladakh*), these defects are compensated for by the sincerity of his compassion and the relevance of his vision.

—S.C. Harrex

BILLING, Graham (John). New Zealander. Born in Dunedin, 12 January 1936. Educated at Otago Boys High School, 1948–52; Otago University, Dunedin, 1953–58; studied for Presbyterian ministry for 1 year. Married 1) Atanui Ellison in 1959; 2) Diane Farmer in 1965, one daughter and one son; 3) Rowan Cunningham in 1978. Cadet officer, Shaw Saville Line, 1953–54; able seaman, Union Steam Ship Company, 1956; construction worker, 1956–58; junior reporter, later senior reporter, Dunedin *Evening Star*, 1958–62; information officer, New Zealand Antarctic Research Programme, Wellington and Ross Dependency, Antarctica, 1962–64; chief reporter, Radio New Zealand News, Christchurch, 1964–65; free-lance writer, 1965–67, 1969–73, and 1975–76; broadcast media editor and columnist, *New Zealand Sunday Times*, Wellington, 1967–68; parliamentary correspondent, *New Zealand Truth*, 1968–69; Lecturer in English, Mitchell College of Advanced Education, Bathurst, New South Wales, 1974–75; current affairs producer, Radio New Zealand, 1977. Free-lance writer since 1978. Writer-in-Residence, University of Canterbury, Christchurch, 1985. Recipient: Cowman Memorial Prize, for journalism, 1962; New Zealand Literary Fund grant, 1965, 1983, 1984, and scholarship, 1971, 1981; Otago University Robert Burns Fellowship, 1973; Hubert Church Prose Award, 1975. Agent: Elaine Markson Literary Agency, 44 Greenwich Avenue, New York, New York 10011, U.S.A.; or, Abner Stein, 10 Roland Gardens, London SW7 3PH, England. Address: 89 Mersey Street, St. Albans, Christchurch 1, New Zealand.

PUBLICATIONS

Novels

Forbush and the Penguins. London, Hodder and Stoughton, 1965; New York, Holt Rinehart, 1966.

The Alpha Trip. Christchurch, Whitcombe and Tombs, and London, W.H. Allen, 1969.
Statues. London, Hodder and Stoughton, 1971.
The Slipway. New York, Viking Press, 1973; London, Quartet, 1974.
The Primal Therapy of Tom Purslane. Dunedin, Caveman Press, 1980.

Plays

Radio Plays: *Forbush and the Penguins*, 1966; *Mervyn Gridfern versus the Baboons*, 1966; *The Slipway*, from his own novel, 1977.

Verse

Changing Countries. Dunedin, Caveman Press, 1980.

Other

South: Man and Nature in Antarctica. Wellington, Reed, 1964; London, Hodder and Stoughton, and Seattle, University of Washington Press, 1965; revised edition, Reed, 1969.
New Zealand, The Sunlit Land, photographs by R.J. Griffith. Wellington, Reed, 1966.
The New Zealanders, photographs by Robin Smith and Warren Jacobs. Auckland, Golden Press, 1975; revised edition, Christchurch, Kowhai, 1979.

Editor, *Wellington Town Plan: A Commentary on the District Planning Scheme 1967*. Wellington, Wellington City Council, 1967.

*

Manuscript Collection: Turnbull Library, Wellington.

Critical Studies: interview with Richard Corballis, in *Landfall 135* (Christchurch), September 1980; article by Howard McNaughton, in *Landfall 139* (Christchurch), September 1981.

Graham Billing comments:

I am one of the few New Zealanders who write about middle- and upper-middle-class people and intellectuals. Such subjects tend to be ignored here and I have always had to sell my novels in London or New York first rather than to the local industry. This has made me more determined to survive as an outsider in my own society and to be uncompromising in my choice of themes.

My first 16 years straddled World War II. They were privileged. My father was Professor of Economics at the world's most remote university—Otago at Dunedin. Until the post-war graduates flooded in from overseas it was more a family than a university. I didn't get educated, I grew. My mother's eccentricities and temperament affected me deeply. She taught me to sew and cook and made me learn the piano and elocution. I rebelled then but am now glad. My father countered by teaching me the rudiments of hunting, shooting, fishing, dog-handling, and sailing. It is out of such tensions that I create. But I lived in Paradise for a while, the only Worm being that I did slowly inherit my mother's manic-depressive condition. It would lead me into a deep search of my unconscious mind in middle life. I was not untouched either by her religious passions. Having fallen out with the patriarch God I turned in my early 20's to a contemplation of the Goddes sustained in turns by Robert Graves and C.G. Jung. These references abound in my writing. In my mid-life quest these ideas have been severely modified as I have found time to research original material instead of other writers' conclusions. People amaze me. I'm a slow thinker. Books come out whole mostly without need for revision. I still grieve that I didn't have the chance to work in a war. Antarctica was the closest thing and rather more dangerous then than it is now. I am watching myself with deep interest to see what happens next.

*   *   *

Graham Billing's novels are remarkable for the intensity with which the central characters' inner lives are realized. He has no peer in New Zealand—and few world-wide—when it comes to evoking strong emotional and physical sensations.

He often has difficulty, however, in inventing a plot which can contain this rampant sensuousness. *The Primal Therapy of Tom Purslane* (published in 1980 but written as early as 1973) illustrates the problem very well. All that happens is that Purslane has a brief, unsatisfactory love affair which jeopardizes his marriage. It is not even clear just why the affair is unsatisfactory or what will become of the marriage. Billing seems scarcely interested in the story or the ancillary characters; it is Purslane's responses that fascinate him, and these are underlined by a cloying welter of symbols, symbolic episodes, dreams, and allusions.

Purslane is an extreme example—partly, no doubt, because Billing had the Romantics very much in mind (Hazlitt's *Liber Amoris* in particular) and therefore endeavoured to "load every rift with ore." But *Statues* (which is Billing's own favorite among his novels to date) is another clear case of texture run wild and plot neglected. The other three novels are better balanced, but the same old problems recur to some extent. The plots seldom provide an adequate objective correlative to the central characters' responses, and nobody except the central character (who is always a man and always remarkably like Graham Billing) comes completely to life.

His first novel, *Forbush and the Penguins*, is still probably his best known—partly because it spawned a feature film and a radio play. Forbush goes to Antarctica to undertake a study of a penguin rookery at Cape Royds. Antarctica becomes for him a kind of laboratory—rather like Renaissance pastoral—where nature's extremes (the self-sacrificing love of the penguins and the violence of the predatory skuas and sea-leopards) are closely juxtaposed. This juxtaposition prompts him to reflect on the conflict between love and hate in his own experience, and he draws this conclusion from his observations and recollections:

If all the penguins died and were eaten by all the sea-leopards, nothing would change. If no skua gull ever nested on the Cape again, nothing would change. Life is not an individual thing but a total thing, a volume like the sea. Therefore I am a victim. But if I know I am a victim I am a victim no longer. I am free.

This moral sounds rather too neat to be true, and its credibility is further undermined by the lack of any adequate background to Forbush's sense of himself as a victim. Billing's subsequent comments about the book have emphasized the "wounds" which Forbush's parents inflicted on him, but there is scarcely any sign of these in the published text. So although Forbush's present experiences (at Cape Royds) are well documented, the coverage of the past is too skimpy to justify his deeper reflections.

The Alpha Trip was written while Billing was working as an investigative journalist in Wellington. In the news at the time (1968–69) was a widely-held suspicion that certain American communication bases in New Zealand were crucial links in America's nuclear strategy. The novel elaborates this idea and focusses on a communist plot to destroy a base near Blenheim. But the plot itself is less important than the character at the center of it—Strachan, a New Zealand patriot who cannot accept the hegemony of either the Americans or the communists. As usual Billing becomes so preoccupied with his protagonist that nobody else really comes to life. The two characters who suffer most from this neglect are Laetitia, who loves Strachan beyond the call of (communist) duty but shows no real sign of the anxiety—danger even—that ought to result from this conflict, and Percival, the communist super-mole, whose motives are dishonestly disguised early in the book. Still *The Alpha Trip* is a competent thriller as well as an eloquent plea for national self-awareness.

Billing's finest work to date is *The Slipway*, a compelling study of the agonies and ecstasies, the deceptions and delusions of an alcoholic (Geoffrey Targett). The protrait is so powerful that one scarcely notices that there is a characteristic discrepancy between Geoffrey's predicament and the plot which is woven about it. Like many of Billing's characters, Geoffrey undergoes an intensely evoked descent into hell, and we expect him to emerge a changed man. But no; he goes straight back into a pub, as excruciatingly alcoholic and deluded as ever. (The problems Billing had with the book's structure are elaborated in the interview published in *Landfall 135*.)

Billing's novels—the last four of the five anyway—were written in rapid succession, and they have much in common besides the structural weaknesses and textual excellence discussed above. The descent-into-hell motif recurs frequently. And certain symbolic characters pop up again and again. For example, there is often an old salt-of-the-earth fellow (Collis in *Statues*, Chivers in *The Primal Therapy of Tom Purslane*) who embodies the normality from which the protagonist has departed. And there is generally a dog or some other animal who seems in some way to represent the protagonist's soul. Many of the protagonists have an important characteristic in common too. They are often artists—photographers for the most part. And when they are at their most creative they tend to see life in terms of circles. Likewise, as the *Landfall* interview indicates, Billing himself got the impulse to write both *Forbush and the Penguins* and *The Slipway* from an initial circular image (Forbush standing in a ring of stones; Geoffrey gazing at a radarscope).

These recurrent circles are a symptom of the closed world inhabited by Billing's protagonists, who generally do not develop significantly or interact meaningfully with other characters. (Billing tried to break the circle in *Statues* by dividing the narration between two characters—Bracken and his ex-wife Miriam—but the result is really just two closed circles instead of one.)

It is interesting and encouraging to find that in his forthcoming novel *Terra Incognita*, the central symbol is to be a nautilus shell (spiral-shaped) rather than a circle. This promises a more dynamic plot than he has achieved so far.

—Richard Corballis

BILLINGTON, (Lady) Rachel (Mary, née Pakenham). British. Born in Oxford, 11 May 1942; daughter of the writers Lord Longford and Elizabeth Longford; sister of the writer Antonia Fraser. Educated at the University of London, B.A. (honours) 1963. Married the film and theatre director Kevin Billington in 1967; two sons and two daughters. Free-lance writer: reviewer and feature writer for *Financial Times*, *The Times*, and BBC Radio, all London and *New York Times*. Agent: David Higham Associates Ltd., 5–8 Lower John Street, London W1R 4HA. Address: 30 Addison Avenue, London W11 4QP, England.

PUBLICATIONS

Novels

All Things Nice. London, Heinemann, 1969.
The Big Dipper. London, Heinemann, 1970.
Lilacs Out of the Dead Land. London, Heinemann, 1971; New York, Saturday Review Press, 1972.
Cock Robin; or, A Fight for Male Survival. London, Heinemann, 1972.
Beautiful. London, Heinemann, and New York, Coward McCann, 1974.
A Painted Devil. London, Heinemann and New York, Coward McCann, 1975.
A Woman's Age. London, Hamish Hamilton, 1979; New York, Summit, 1980.
Occasion of Sin. London, Hamish Hamilton, 1982; New York, Summit, 1983.
The Garish Day. London, Hamish Hamilton, 1985; New York, Morrow, 1986.

Plays

Radio Plays: *Mrs. Bleasdale's Lodger*, 1976; *Mary, Mary*, 1977; *Sister, Sister*, 1978; *Have You Seen Guy Fawkes?*, 1979.

Television Plays: *Don't Be Silly*, 1979; *Life after Death*, 1981.

Other (for children)

Rosanna and the Wizard-Robot. London, Methuen, 1981.
The First Christmas. London, Collins, 1983.
Star-Time. London, Methuen, 1984.

*   *   *

On a surface level the novels of Rachel Billington reflect the conventions of the upper-class comedy of manners. Her works are invariably set within an aristocratic milieu, their central characters a privileged churchgoing elite of country or London gentry, whose condescension towards the lower orders seems a natural response. Billington's books are distinguished by an adroit use of language, personalities revealed through conversations which display a keen, often caustic wit. Yet beneath the outward show of humour lurks a strong tendency to violence, which manifests itself in the conflicts of obsessional love.

In *All Things Nice* and *The Big Dipper* the wit and comedy predominate, these early novels emerging as vehicles for the author's stylistic skills. *Lilacs Out of the Dead Land* is both deeper and more dark. April, the younger daughter of moneyed parents, travels to Italy with her married lover. During their time together, she is forced to reassess their relationship in the context of her elder sister's death. The infatuation which draws her to the lover is slowly countered by the fear of being smothered by his love. As the tension builds inside her, events move swiftly to the cathartic act of violence. More complex and unsettling than its predecessors, *Lilacs Out of the Dead Land* shows considerable narrative skill, the author switching fluently from April's time with her lover to scenes with her parents, at the school where she teaches, and her last encounter with her sister. Dialogue fits the dovetailed scenes, each character perfectly matched by his or her patterns of speech. This novel is an early indication of the psychological depths which lie under the surface glitter of Billington's work.

Beautiful and *Cock Robin* are lighter, but accomplished creations, the elegant prose and polite behaviour merely masking the pathological impulses deeper down. *Cock Robin* centres on the male narrator's passion for three girls at his university, all of them seemingly unattainable. The book follows the four of them in their careers, where the young man gradually emerges as the dominant figure, while the three goddesses prove to be tragic failures. The bitchy wit is in evidence, the story itself eminently credible, if marked by a heartless gloss. In *Beautiful*, obsessive passion again appears as a destructive force. Lucy, the flawless, amoral heroine of the novel, has thus far been able to shape the world in her image as it revolves around her. Alex, the discarded lover unwilling to let go, threatens to shatter that world and its fake stability: "Lucy prided herself on her understanding of the human psyche; with the unmentionable exception of Alex, no-one had ever stepped out of the role in which she had cast them." Once more the course is set for a violent resolution. A light, tautly-written work, with short terse scenes and skilful dialogue, *Beautiful* shows the author at her most assured, the hard sheen of the surface and the murky underlying depths in perfect balance.

A Painted Devil is altogether more sinister, revealing Billington's vision at its grimmest. Obsessional love is again the agent of destruction, embodied in Edward, the negative central character. A painter of genius, Edward draws unquestioning adoration from his wife and friends, while giving nothing in return. His cold, remote personality, its inhuman quality symbolized by his hatred of physical love, is subtly glimpsed in conversation and unuttered thoughts. In *A Painted Devil* the glittering crust of civilized behaviour is thin indeed, the novel becoming increasingly horrific as one tragedy follows another. Cruellest of all Billington's works, it is nevertheless a memorable achievement.

A Woman's Age is a new departure, the comedy of manners forsaken for an epic novel spanning a period of 70 years. It focuses mainly on the figure of Violet Hesketh, who survives a difficult childhood and broken marriages to find a successful career in politics. A mammoth undertaking, the novel shows its author's ability to convey the essence of the passing years, but one cannot help feeling that it lacks the bite and conviction of some of her shorter works, and it is in the latter that her main strength as a writer lies.

With *Occasion of Sin* is another experiment, this time a contemporary retelling of Tolstoy's *Anna Karenina*, Billington's account of the lawyer's wife who falls for a computer software executive follows the original closely, both in characters and incidents, but avoids too slavish an interpretation, particularly in some of its solutions. A worthy variant of the classic novel, the depth of this novel's theme is matched by a highly effective use of language, with Billington's mastery of dialogue well to the fore. Her latest book, *The Garish Day*, is an ambitious saga covering two generations of diplomats at the time of the British Raj.

Billington is an accomplished and elegant writer; her blending of stylistic flair and complex themes clearly indicates a continuing development.

—Geoff Sadler

BIRNEY, (Alfred) Earle. Canadian. Born in Calgary, North West Territories (now Alberta), 13 May 1904. Educated at the University of British Columbia, Vancouver (Editor, *The Ubyssey*, 1923–26), 1922–26, B.A. (honours) in English 1926; University of Toronto (Leonard Scholar, 1926–27), M.A. 1927, Ph.D. 1936; University of California, Berkeley, 1927–30; Queen Mary College, London (Royal Society of Canada Research Fellow, 1934–35). Served in the Canadian Army, in the reserves, 1940–41, and on active duty, 1942–45: Major-in-Charge, Personnel Selection, Belgium and Holland, 1944–45. Married 1) Sylvia Johnstone in 1933 (marriage annulled, 1936); 2) Esther Bull in 1940 (divorced, 1977), one son. Summer school lecturer, University of British Columbia, 1927–37; Instructor in English, University of Utah, Salt Lake City, 1930–34; Lecturer, 1936–40, and Assistant Professor of English, 1940–42, University of Toronto; supervisor, European Foreign Language Broadcasts, Radio Canada, Montreal, 1945–46; Professor of Medieval English Literature, 1946–63, and Professor and Chairman of the Department of Creative Writing, 1963–65, University of British Columbia. Visiting Professor, University of Oregon, Eugene, 1961; Writer-in-Residence, University of Toronto, 1965–67, and University of Waterloo, Ontario, 1967–68; Regents' Professor in Creative Writing, University of California, Irvine, 1968; Writer-in-Residence, University of Western Ontario, London, 1981–82, and University of Alaska, Fairbanks, 1984. Since 1968, freelance writer and lecturer. Editor, Point Grey *Gazette*, 1925; literary editor, *Canadian Forum*, Toronto, 1936–39; editor, *Canadian Poetry Magazine*, Vancouver, 1946–48; guest editor (Canadian issues), *Outposts*, Manchester, 1948, *Poetry Commonwealth*, London, 1951, and *Envoi*, Cheltenham, 1964; editor, *Prism International*, Vancouver, 1964–65; advisory editor, *New: American and Canadian Poetry*, Trumansburg, New York, 1966–70. Recipient: Governor-General's Award, for poetry, 1942, 1945; Leacock Award, 1949; Borestone Mountain Poetry Award, 1951; University of Western Ontario President's Medal, 1951, 1954; Canadian Government Overseas Fellowship, 1953, and Service Medal, 1970; Lorne Pierce Medal, 1953; Nuffield fellowship, 1958; Canada Council Senior Arts Fellowship, 1962, 1974, Travel Award, 1962, 1971, 1974, Medal, 1968, and Special Fellowship, 1968, 1978. LL.D.: University of Alberta, Edmonton, 1965; D.Litt.: McGill University, Montreal, 1979; University of Western Ontario, 1984. Fellow, Royal Society of Canada, 1954; Member, 1970, and Officer, 1981, Order of Canada. Address: 484 Church Street, Suite 414, Toronto, Ontario M4Y 2C7, Canada.

PUBLICATIONS

Novels

• *Turvey: A Military Picaresque.* Toronto, McClelland and Stewart, 1949; London, Abelard Schuman, 1958; New York,

Abelard Schuman, 1959; as *The Kootenay Highlander*, London, Four Square, 1960; complete version, McClelland and Stewart, 1976.
Down the Long Table. Toronto, McClelland and Stewart, 1955; London, Abelard Schuman, 1959.

Short Stories

Big Bird in the Bush: Selected Stories and Sketches. Oakville, Ontario, Mosaic/Valley, 1978.

Uncollected Short Story

"The Reverend Eastham Discovers Life," in *The Ubyssey* (Vancouver), March 1924.

Plays

The Damnation of Vancouver: A Comedy in Seven Episodes (broadcast, 1952). Included in *Trial of a City*, 1952; revised version (produced Seattle, 1957; Vancouver, 1978), Toronto, McClelland and Stewart, 1977.
Words on Waves (radio plays), edited by Howard Fink. Kingston, Ontario, Quarry Press, 1985.

Radio Play: *The Damnation of Vancouver*, 1952.

Verse

David and Other Poems. Toronto, Ryerson Press, 1942.
Now Is Time. Toronto, Ryerson Press, 1945.
The Strait of Anian: Selected Poems. Toronto, Ryerson Press, 1948.
Trial of a City and Other Verse. Toronto, Ryerson Press, 1952.
Ice Cod Bell or Stone. Toronto, McClelland and Stewart, 1962.
Near False Creek Mouth. Toronto, McClelland and Stewart, 1964.
Selected Poems 1940–1966. Toronto, McClelland and Stewart, 1966.
Memory No Servant. Trumansburg, New York, New Books, 1968.
The Poems of Earle Birney. Toronto, McClelland and Stewart, 1969.
Pnomes, Jukollages and Other Stunzas, edited by B.P. Nichol. Toronto, Ganglia Press, 1969.
Rag and Bone Shop. Toronto, McClelland and Stewart, 1971.
Four Parts Sand: Concrete Poems, with others. Ottawa, Oberon Press, 1972.
The Bear on the Delhi Road: Selected Poems. London, Chatto and Windus, 1973.
What's So Big about Green? Toronto, McClelland and Stewart, 1973.
The Collected Poems, edited by John Newlove. Toronto, McClelland and Stewart, 2 vols., 1975.
The Rugging and the Moving Times: Poems New and Uncollected 1976. Coatsworth, Ontario, Black Moss Press, 1976.
Alphabeings and Other Seasyours, edited by Jamie Hamilton. London, Ontario, Pikadilly Press, 1976.
Ghost in the Wheels: Selected Poems 1920–1976. Toronto, McClelland and Stewart, 1977.
Fall by Fury and Other Makings. Toronto, McClelland and Stewart, 1978.
The Mammoth Corridors. Okemos, Michigan, Stone Press, 1980.
Copernican Fix. Downsview, Ontario, ECW Press, 1985.

One Muddy Hand. Toronto, McClelland and Stewart, 1986.

Recordings: *David*, 1964; *Earle Birney Reads His Poems*, Barnet, 1970; *Birney*, Ontario Institute for Studies in Education, 1971; *Nexus and Earle Birney*, Nexus, 3 albums, 1984.

Other

Canada Calling. Montreal, CBC, 1946.
The Creative Writer. Toronto, CBC, 1966.
The Cow Jumped over the Moon: The Writing and Reading of Poetry. Toronto, Holt Rinehart, 1972.
Spreading Time: Remarks on Canadian Writing and Writers 1: 1926–1949. Montreal, Véhicule Press, 1980.
Essays on Chaucerian Irony. Toronto, University of Toronto Press, 1985.

Editor, *20th Century Canadian Poetry.* Toronto, Ryerson Press, 1953.
Editor, *Record of Service in the Second World War.* Vancouver, University of British Columbia, 1955.
Editor, with others, *New Voices: Canadian Writing of 1956.* Toronto, Dent, 1956.
Editor, with Margerie Lowry, *Selected Poems of Malcolm Lowry.* San Francisco, City Lights, 1962.
Editor, with Margerie Lowry, *Lunar Caustic*, by Malcolm Lowry. London, Cape, 1968.

*

Bibliography: by Peter Noel-Bentley, in *The Annotated Bibliography of Canada's Major Authors 4* edited by Robert Lecker and Jack David, Downsview, Ontario, ECW Press, 1983.

Manuscript Collections: Fisher Library, University of Toronto; Queen's University, Kingston, Ontario; University of British Columbia, Vancouver.

Critical Studies: review of *Turvey* by Malcolm Lowry, in *Thunderbird* (Vancouver), December 1949; "Earle Birney and the Compound Ghost" by Paul West, in *Canadian Literature* (Vancouver), Summer 1962; introduction by George Woodcock to *Turvey*, Toronto, McClelland and Stewart, 1963; *Earle Birney* by Frank Davey, Toronto, Copp Clark, 1971; *Earle Birney* by Richard Robillard, Toronto, McClelland and Stewart, 1971; *Earle Birney* edited by Bruce Nesbitt, Toronto, McGraw Hill Ryerson, 1974; *Earle Birney* by Peter Aichinger, Boston, Twayne, 1979; *Perspectives on Earle Birney* edited by Jack David, Downsview, Ontario, ECW Press, 1981; "Earle Birney Issue" of *Essays on Canadian Writing* (Toronto), Spring 1981; *A Reader's Guide to the Canadian Novel* by John Moss, Toronto, McClelland and Stewart, 1981.

Earle Birney comments:

My short stories have been extensions of my work as a poet. More relaxed in style than my best-known poem *David*, they are nevertheless equally symbolic in technique, and unified around a two-person relationship and a definite action.

My novels, on the other hand, are attempts to contain within one fairly complex form a multitude of experiences none of which seemed to me naturally separable, and much more likely to be effective if handled together. They are to some extent "documentary," aiming at accuracy in dialogue and in reference to the historic frame; but their over-all preoccupations have been with the mores and philosophy of North American society.

Turvey, my first novel, was written out of things that happened to me, or stories told to me, during the Second World War. For the last three years of it my job was interviewing soldiers: in Canada, volunteers, draftees, deserters, or men in sick bays or cells; in England, officer candidates, paratroopers, commandos, psychotics in hospital or psychopaths in detention; in Belgium and Holland, officers and soldiers in every arm and service of an Army, wanting to get into action or out of it, to change their job or their wife, to see a psychiatrist or just to make it back home. This kind of job taught me a lot about the bureaucratic complexity of a modern Army, its capacity for muddle and waste, especially of its human material. The job taught me also something about soldiers in general and the young Canadian one in particular. I came out of the army determined to write a novel whose central character would be a soldier both absurd and eccentric (like me) and wild, funny, naive, and long-suffering (like the average Canadian soldier—and perhaps civilian). *Turvey* is my attempt. His only literary cousin, of whom I was conscious, was the Good Soldier Schweik, Hasek's dumb wily Czech private caught in the Austro-Hungarian army of World War One.

My second novel, *Down the Long Table*, is laid in the Depressed Thirties, its scene shifting from Salt Lake City to Toronto to Vancouver. Like *Turvey* it is somewhat picaresque in form but the tone is more serious and the theme more involved in confrontations of ideas. It is not an autobiographical novel, but many of the characters are based on my acquaintance with young American and Canadian radicals of the Thirties, leaders of mine strikes, organizers of the unemployed, Trotskyist theoreticians, Stalinist bureaucrats, and some plain workers and workless of forty years ago, who were honest and brave and helpless and doomed.

*   *   *

Earle Birney is best known as one of Canada's finest contemporary poets, and, especially outside Canada, his reputation in this role has tended to obscure his achievements in fiction. He is the author of two novels, *Turvey* and *Down the Long Table*. Both of them, if not autobiographical, deal with times and settings in which the author was deeply and passionately involved: the Canadian army in the Second World War in the case of *Turvey*, and the social despair and political idealism of the 1930's in the case of *Down the Long Table*. Both novels share with Birney's poetry an inclination towards social satire and a preoccupation with colloquial speech patterns; *Down the Long Table* also shares with Birney's later verse an experimental use of the verbal detritus of political propaganda and the mass media in general.

Turvey is described accurately by its author as "a military picaresque." It narrates the adventures of a simple, rustic-minded Canadian, Turvey, who is anxious to serve his country in his local regiment, but becomes involved in a bureaucratic hurdle race which leads him into a series of comic predicaments, out of which in the end he emerges—never having seen a German soldier—to hail with joy his return to civilian life. Inevitably, *Turvey* calls to mind *The Good Soldier Schweik*, but there is a slyness in Schweik which Turvey does not possess. Where from the beginning Schweik seems to use the pretense of stupidity as a subversive weapon, Turvey is throughout the naive enthusiast, and it is the army that condemns itself by its bureaucratic unintelligence. The fighting war is always distant; the real war that Birney invites us to follow is the burlesque combat between a mindless collective machine and Turvey's irrepressible individuality. That Turvey emerges undefeated makes this a statement of faith in the victory of man over the inhumanity of mass organization.

Down the Long Table is a novel of memory, projected from the silent 1950's into the troubled 1930's. The basic structure is Proustian; Professor Gordon Saunders, a Canadian teaching in the United States, is brought before a committee investigating Communist affiliations. Before him at the long table he sees a face from the past, that of an ex-Communist turned informer, and this provokes the chain of memories which forms the substance of the book. Gordon remembers the fatal interconnection between personal relationships and political actions, weaving into a rope that shifts his sentimental idealism into militancy, takes him in and rapidly out of the Communist party, and culminates in a brief, violent, and disillusioning period as the would-be organizer of a Trotskyist movement among the unemployed and skidroad derelicts of Vancouver.

The greatest merit of *Down the Long Table* is the vividness with which the spirit and even the physical feel of the 1930's are recreated. It is when one considers the book as more than an evocative document that its defects become evident. There is an unassimilable implausibility about Professor Saunders sitting at the long table and, in that instant of time which is undoubtedly all the inquisiting senators would allow him, plunging into almost three hundred pages of chronologically sequential recollection, interrupted, not by the impinging voices of the present, but by the chapter-dividing extracts from contemporary newspapers, which enhance the documentary verisimilitude, but which in fictional terms are out of pitch with the essentially romantic tone of the rest of the novel, with its dark but poetic vision of what happens to ideals when they must find expression through human beings twisted and battered by existence. *Turvey* has a wholly convincing comic unity; *Down the Long Table* is divided by the conflict between the historical impulse to reconstruct authentically time past, and the fictional impulse to establish a self-confident imaginary world.

—George Woodcock

BLACKWOOD, Caroline (Lady Caroline Hamilton-Temple-Blackwood). British. Born in Ireland, 16 July 1931; daughter of the Marquis and Marchioness of Dufferin and Ava. Attended a boarding school in England. Married 1) the painter Lucian Freud (divorced); 2) Israel Citkovitz, three daughters (one deceased); 3) the poet Robert Lowell in 1972 (died, 1977), one son. Recipient: Higham Award, 1976. Address: c/o Heinemann Ltd., 10 Upper Grosvenor Street, London W1X 9PA, England.

PUBLICATIONS

Novels

The Stepdaughter. London, Duckworth, 1976; New York, Scribner, 1977.
Great Granny Webster. London, Duckworth, and New York, Scribner, 1977.
The Fate of Mary Rose. London, Cape, and New York, Summit, 1981.
Corrigan. London, Heinemann, 1984; New York, Viking, 1985.

Short Stories

For All That I Found There (includes essays). London, Duckworth, 1973; New York, Braziller, 1974.
Goodnight Sweet Ladies. London, Heinemann, 1983.

Other

Darling, You Shouldn't Have Gone to So Much Trouble (cookbook), with Anna Haycraft. London, Cape, 1980.
On the Perimeter (on the Greenham Common nuclear protest). London, Heinemann, 1984; New York, Penguin, 1985.

*   *   *

Caroline Blackwood's first book, *For All That I Found There*, has a threefold division into "Fiction," "Fact," and "Ulster," which deals mostly with what seems to be autobiographical material. The rationale for the final section's form is given in the short story "The Interview" by the famous painter's widow, who criticizes a film about her husband as "a little too factual ... One should only ever be linked to the past through one's memory. Luckily memory is the most miserable, and unreliable, old muscle." It is perhaps the same rationale that underlies the "novel" form of *Great Granny Webster*, with its unnamed narrator and possibly autobiographical material.

Highlighting relationships in contemporary materialistic society, Blackwood's short stories were hard-hitting from the start. In her later collection, *Goodnight Sweet Ladies*, the title of each of the five stories is a female name or occupation. Whether written in the third or first person, in each story the central, rather unattractive figure (a woman except in "Taft's Wife") is shown obsessively analysing her predicament; after all, "Self-obsessed people can suffer just as much as unselfish ones." The "horrible fascination" of Blackwood's work lies in her inexorable probing of motivation, leavened by black humour. In the longest piece, "Angelica," an ex-actress imagines herself in love with a long-dead major in Brompton Cemetery in an attempt to recover from her abandonment by her young lover.

Blackwood is writing her own version of the novel of motivation as written by James, Proust, Anthony Powell—without their intricacy of social setting, and in black comedy. *The Stepdaughter* is told entirely in the form of letters to an imaginary friend from a woman who rarely leaves her claustrophobic Manhattan penthouse. She is, understandably, obsessed by the repulsive stepdaughter whom her ex-husband has foisted on her. The letters consist mainly of the woman's analysis of herself, her stepdaughter, and her ex-husband. The technique throws the focus of interest onto the woman, as we learn about her between the lines. This technique also allows Blackwood to manipulate dextrously the reader's sympathy as we respond to the woman's changing moods.

Great Granny Webster is, apparently, a loosely linked account of the selfish woman of the title, who by force of sheer longevity "had managed to be both the start of a line and the end of a line," and of the main characters in this line—the narrator's grandmother, once mistress of the decaying ancestral home in Ulster, but long in a mental hospital, her flighty Aunt Lavinia, and her father, who died when she was nine. The blurred figure of the narrator's father is at the heart of the novel, doubly lost to her because he died before "the beginning of my memory's photography." The book's *pièce de résistance* is the final description of Great Granny Webster's funeral, actualizing the imagery of black and white running all through the book, one purpose of which is to blur certainties and whose first word is the "I" of the narrator and last word the "eye" of one of the narrated.

In *The Fate of Mary Rose*, by the brilliant structural device of making the narrator apparently the rapist and murderer of a child, although he does not remember this, Blackwood can deploy her extraordinary gift for minute analysis of motivation in a novel of suspense, beset by multiple ironies. She also probes the mass psychology in the Kent village after the killing. Though it grips like a thriller, through Blackwood's analysis of the narrator, his estranged, increasingly sick wife, and his friends among the London rich and talented, this novel transcends the form in a way comparable to John Fowles's *The Collector*.

Corrigan hinges on the same structural device as *The Fate of Mary Rose*; uncertainty is created in the reader's mind at the outset to engender mounting suspense—in this book regarding the honesty of the energetic wheelchair-bound charity fund-raiser, Corrigan, in his dealings with the naïve widow Devina Blunt, whose sad, petty life he revolutionizes. Blackwood's characteristic unflinching and witty examination of the effects of Corrigan yet begs one basic question. Even if Corrigan turns out a con-man, Mrs. Blunt has emotionally still been given a good run for her money. But Corrigan has raised huge sums elsewhere for the supposed benefit of people who desperately need help; though Corrigan may be exonerated *vis-à-vis* Mrs. Blunt, this the larger question remains.

Recently, Blackwood's ironic style has reached a new pitch of *faux-naïf*, generally devastating, but occasionally inadequate, as sometimes in *On the Perimeter*, her account of the Greenham Common Peace Camps. Generally, Caroline Blackwood's wide-eyed, confrontational style is part of the honesty which often leads her to take as subject the uglier aspects of human relationships, while leaving open as many of the possibilities as one human being's perception can apprehend. Her voice is unique.

—Val Warner

BLAISE, Clark (Lee). Canadian. Born in Fargo, North Dakota, United States, 10 April 1940; became Canadian citizen, 1973. Educated at Denison University, Granville, Ohio, 1957–61, A.B. 1961; University of Iowa, Iowa City, 1962–64, M.F.A. 1964. Married Bharati Mukherjee in 1963; two sons. Acting Instructor, University of Wisconsin, Milwaukee, 1964–65; teaching fellow, University of Iowa, 1965–66; Lecturer, 1966–67, Assistant Professor, 1967–69, Associate Professor, 1969–72, and Professor of English, 1973–78, Sir George Williams University, later Concordia University, Montreal; Professor of Humanities, York University, Toronto, 1978–80; Professor of English, Skidmore College, Saratoga Springs, New York, 1980–81, 1982–83. Visiting Lecturer or Writer-in-Residence, University of Iowa, 1981–82, Saskatchewan School of the Arts, Saskatoon, Summer 1983, David Thompson University Centre, Nelson, British Columbia, Fall 1983, Emory University, Atlanta, 1985, Bennington College, Vermont, 1985, and Columbia University, New York, Spring 1986. Recipient: University of Western Ontario President's Medal, for short story, 1968; Great Lakes Colleges Association prize, 1973; Canada Council grant, 1973, 1977, and travel grant, 1985; St. Lawrence award, 1974; Fels award, for essay, 1975; *Asia Week* award, for non-fiction, 1977; *Books in Canada* prize,

1979; National Endowment for the Arts grant, 1981; Guggenheim grant, 1983. D.Litt.: Denison University, 1979. Agent: Timothy Seldes, Russell and Volkening Inc., 50 West 29th Street, New York, New York 10001. Address: 804 Ronalds Street, Iowa City, Iowa 52240, U.S.A.

PUBLICATIONS

Novels

Lunar Attractions. New York, Doubleday, 1979.
Lusts. New York, Doubleday, 1983.

Short Stories

New Canadian Writing 1968, with Dave Godfrey and David Lewis Stein. Toronto, Clarke Irwin, 1969.
A North American Education. Toronto and New York, Doubleday, 1973.
Tribal Justice. Toronto and New York, Doubleday, 1974.
Personal Fictions, with others, edited by Michael Ondaatje. Toronto, Oxford University Press, 1977.

Uncollected Short Stories

"The Sense of an Ending," in *76: Best Canadian Stories*, edited by John Metcalf and Joan Harcourt. Ottawa, Oberon Press, 1976.
"Man and His World," in *Moral Fictions*, edited by Joe David Bellamy. Canton, New York, Fiction International Press, 1980.
"Prying," in *Toronto Life*, 1983.

Other

Days and Nights in Calcutta, with Bharati Mukherjee. New York, Doubleday, 1977.
Resident Alien (autobiography). Toronto, Penguin, 1986.

Editor, with John Metcalf, *Here and Now*. Ottawa, Oberon Press, 1977.
Editor, with John Metcalf, *78 [79, 80]: Best Canadian Stories*. Ottawa, Oberon Press, 3 vols., 1978–80.

*

Manuscript Collection: Calgary University Library, Alberta.

Critical Studies: *On the Line* by Robert Lecker, Downsview, Ontario, ECW Press, 1982; article by Blaise, in *Contemporary Authors Autobiography Series 3*, Detroit, Gale, 1986.

Clark Blaise comments:

(1981) My fiction is an exploration of threatened space; the space has been geographically and historically defined as French–Canada and French–America (New England), as well as extremely isolated areas of the deep South. Most of my fiction has been concerned with the effects of strong and contrasting parents, with the memory of Europe and of Canada, and the very oppressive reality, rendered minutely, of America. I am concerned with nightmare, terror, violence, sexual obsession, and the various artistic transformations of those drives. The tone of the work is not gothic or grotesque, however; I am devoted to the close observation of the real world, and to hold the gaze long enough to make the real world seem distorted. My work is also involved with the growth of the mind, the coming on of ideas about itself and the outside world. I would agree with critics who see my work as courting solipsism, and much of my own energy is devoted to finding ways out of the vastness of the first person pronoun.

*   *   *

Clark Blaise's short stories and novels are marked by their preoccupation with the tensions between a host of metaphorical extremes. Blaise is attracted to raw experience, spontaneous impulse, grotesque realism, uncultured thought: simultaneously, he is a polymath who needs reason, order, intellect, and learning in order to survive. For Blaise, these two worlds can never coincide; yet his fiction is driven by the strategies he employs in his attempt to *make* them coincide. The most obvious strategy involves doubling and superimposition. Blaise's characters are often two-sided, and their stories detail, through extended use of archetype and symbol, a profound desire to discover an integrated and authentic self. A list of the authors who influenced Blaise—including Pascal, Flaubert, Proust, Faulkner, and Céline—suggests that his work is philosophical, realistic, epic, eschatological, and existential. It is important to note this range, if only because Blaise has been viewed as a purely realistic writer involved with the tragic implications of his age. This perspective seems curious when one considers the extent to which Blaise's stories become self-conscious explorations of their own mode of articulation. Their ultimate reality is internal, psychological, personal, and self-reflective. To trace Blaise's growing preoccupation with this self-reflective mode is to describe the evolution of his fiction.

A North American Education, Blaise's first collection of linked short stories, is marked by the multi-levelled revelation of the fears, obsessions, and aesthetic values informing its three central narrators. In the final group of tales—"The Montreal Stories"—Norman Dyer begins to comment on the cosmopolitan milieu he inhabits from the removed and condescending perspective of an intellectual elitist who appears to be in full, if arrogant, control. But as the three stories comprising this section develop, panic sets in; the distanced third-person perspective of the opening eventually gives way to a revealingly fragmented first-person mode that details Dyer's personal and narrative collapse as he confesses that "I who live in dreams have suffered something real, and reality hurts like nothing in the world." In the "Keeler Stories" we hear the confessions of "a writer, a creator" who "would learn to satisfy himself with that." But here, as in the closing "Thibidault Stories," Blaise makes it clear that his narrators will never be satisfied with their creations, or with themselves. Yet they continue to deceive themselves in the belief that "anything dreamt had to become real, eventually."

The dreams shared by Blaise's narrators are always highly symbolic and archetypal in form, a conclusion supported by even the most cursory reading of Blaise's second short story collection, *Tribal Justice*. Here, in some of his richest and most evocative fiction, Blaise returns again and again to his narrators' meditations on their art. If there is a paradigmatic Blaise story—one that reveals the various tensions I have described—it is surely "Grids and Doglegs." It begins with its narrator recalling his interest in creativity, maps, education, history, archaeology, and cultural life; but no sooner is this interest articulated than it is ruthlessly undercut by hints of isolation and impending doom. Other stories—I think particularly of "Notes Beyond a History" and "At the Lake"—are framed by the same kind of divided opening, and by the same suggestion that the narrator who inhabits that opening is psychologically split.

Blaise's first two books established him as one of the finest short story writers in Canada at the very time he decided to explore a different genre. While *Lunar Attractions* proved that Blaise could master the novel form, it also demonstrated that his fundamental attraction to self-reflective writing remained central to his art. After all, *Lunar Attractions* is a semi-autobiographical account of a writer's development: David Greenwood insists on seeing himself in every aspect of his creation, so much so that his fiction becomes an intricate confession about his failure to get beyond himself. Yet *Lunar Attractions* is by no means purely solipsistic: it is a book about our times, about growing up in our times, and about the symbols and systems we use to explain our lives. Blaise has written that he wanted "to create the portrait of the authentically Jungian or even Freudian whole mind," which "sees every aspect of the natural and historical world being played out in its own imagination, and it literally creates the world that it sees."

These words suggest that for Blaise the writer can never be merely a recorder or even the interpreter of events. He must give form to experience and must be responsible to that form. The nature of this responsibility is the focus of Blaise's second and most recent novel—*Lusts*. Here the nature of writing is explored through Richard Durgin's struggle to understand the suicide of his wife, a successful poet who challenged Durgin's assumptions about the social and political implications of art.

If Rachel is Richard's "other self" then her death is doubly significant: it suggests that Blaise may have overcome the personal divisions that kept his successive narrators from becoming whole. Does this mean that he has found the integrated self he has sought throughout his work? A forthcoming volume of autobiographical essays may answer this question. But Blaise has written autobiography before—most notably in *Days and Nights in Calcutta*—only to return to the story of his personal and aesthetic search. The search is essential to his art, for the quality of his writing—its permutations, obsessions, and complex use of voice—is tragically dependent on Blaise's constant inability to find himself or his final story.

—Robert Lecker

BLECHMAN, Burt. American. Born in Brooklyn, New York, 2 March 1927. Educated at the University of Vermont, Burlington, B.A. 1949 (Phi Beta Kappa). Formerly, Instructor, New York University Medical School. Recipient: Ingram Merrill Foundation Award, 1965. Address: 200 Waverly Place, New York, New York 10014, U.S.A.

PUBLICATIONS

Novels

How Much? New York, Obolensky, 1961; London, Eyre and Spottiswoode, 1963.
The War of Camp Omongo. New York, Random House, 1963.
Stations. New York, Random House, 1963; London, Owen, 1966.
The Octopus Papers. New York, Horizon Press, 1965; London, Owen, 1966.

Maybe.   Englewood Cliffs, New Jersey, Prentice Hall, and London, Owen, 1967.

*

Critical Studies: article by Alfred Kazin in *The Great Ideas Today*, Chicago, Encyclopaedia Britannica, 1962; essay by Jacques Cabau in *L'Express* (Paris), December 1965; *The Jewish Writer in America* by Allen Guttman, New York, Oxford University Press, 1971.

*   *   *

> For Armageddon is frightening only to those who fear progress. (*Maybe*)

Though his first books, *How Much?* and *The War of Camp Omongo*, treated the same self-searching adolescents, ineffectual fathers, domineering mothers, and crass value systems as the work of other young Jewish novelists of the period, Burt Blechman focused on the total social picture rather than on a young male protagonist and created mothers whose comic vulgarity paradoxically earns them the compassion with which Blechman views all his characters (Mrs. Halpern's obsessive search for candlesticks in *How Much?* and boast of "Creative Shopping" during her brief appearance in *Omongo*, and Mrs. Levine's matching her quarter-carat ring against the three and two-and-one-half carat competition of the wealthier *Omongo* mothers). Just as these characters flesh out their caricature outlines, Blechman's entire fictional world transcends, without denying, the episodic structure and rapid pacing of the comic strip. *Stations*, which dramatizes the surrealistic world of a Catholic homosexual, was even stronger proof of Blechman's individuality, as were *The Octopus Papers* and *Maybe*, though all three books have stylistic and thematic parallels with his earlier novels.

Dramatizing their compulsions, Blechman's characters frantically fear and court the destruction that threatens either as individual confinement to perpetually shrinking spaces or as universal annihilation. "Little Normy Greenberg, the lousiest kid in the whole camp, paddling for all he was worth ..." in a desperate attempt to triumph by the camp code he has always despised, achieves the goal he unconsciously sought: "The water was up to his ankles. Faster. Faster. His arms digging, digging, digging. A spade. A shovel. A grave" (*The War of Camp Omongo*). And the atmosphere of the novel tends to reinforce the belief of Eagle, the Indian caretaker, that his fellow Omongos are plotting the total slaughter of the white men who have usurped their land and who encourage catastrophe by the ritual war games they enact at the boys' camp.

In *How Much?* Jenny Stern's desire for independence in the home of her daughter and son-in-law, the Halperns, predictably traps her in a converted closet: "A drape, so Mama will think there's a window. We can even put a light behind so when she pulls the drape, open sesame, a little electric sun." Next Jenny inhabits the morgue, the cheapest room in Dr. Zatz's nursing home, where she must play dead during an inspector's visit. As the Halperns continually cry the title question in the face of bankruptcy, war, failure, and unresponsive auctioneers. "How much, dear God, how much does it cost to be happy?" they hasten the fate they profess to fear.

Myra Russell of *Maybe*, compulsively wasting money and time ("Maybe the biggest problem in life is how to spend it") while she calculates her shrinking future by her dwindling investments ironically resists her son's advice to move into a maisonette that has both a kitchenette and bathroomette, but

is too small for a bedroomette. As the enemy's Tyranny Tests, countered by America's Freedom Tests, threaten to explode Myra's world, the newspapers stress the plight of the trapped Cave Girl. The two alternatives converge.

901, the homosexual voyeur of *Stations*, is driven by a conviction of the impending doom embodied in the vice-detective, Dom, to travel the Via Dolorosa of his confining subway "chapels" for what he believes to be the last time. His menacing universe, peopled by Madonna and Mother Superior, and filled with altars and confessionals, depends on a parody of Catholicism that combines elements of Genet with the science fiction-*cum*-paranoia of William Burroughs, Blechman employs a more general biblical parody in *How Much?*, *Maybe*, and in items like Steiner's commandments in *Omongo*: "Thou shalt have no other loyalties before me for I am the Lord Steiner who hath led thee from bondage in the land of thy parents. ..." Though often brash and crude, Blechman's parody manages to ridicule both modern perversions of religious creeds and the original creeds themselves. Simultaneously, the parody laments a lost pattern of meaning that prevented or at least explained the chaos that perpetually waits to undo the universe. 901's abortive aspirations toward various careers parallel young Bernard Halpern's strivings in *How Much?* (Since Bernard appears in *The Octopus Papers* as B. Halpern, photographer, and in *Maybe* as B. Halpern, caricaturist, he apparently made a choice of a sort. His role as young Fat Stuff Halpern in *Omongo* reinforces the shared world view and tone of the books.)

The Octopus Papers, a collage of documents "selected, adapted, compiled, and annotated by Burt Blechman," is a literary hoax in the manner of *Gulliver's Travels* or *The Dunciad*, though the "Author's Apology" claims to be aping the style of Restoration Comedy. The book traces the history of Arsyn, an organization committed to the synthesis and marketing of the arts. Blechman has more tellingly satirized this tendency in *Omongo*, when a businessman attributed the widespread popularity of Van Gogh's "Sunflowers," in copies with simulated brushstrokes (cf. the "little electric sun" of Jenny's closet), to the artist's brilliant advertising ploy of self-mutilation. Moreover, the shadowy characterizations, thin texture, and surprisingly slow pace of *Octopus* make obtrusive Blechman's perpetual punning, as in the name of the trendsetting Newvoes, while this device seems venial amid the gusto and speed of the other books.

Pathetic little Norman Greenberg (*Omongo*), whose often hilarious obscenity helps define his loveless misery, epitomizes the combination of comic horror and pathos that is Blechman's major achievement. Similarly the humor in Jenny Stern's struggle against the senile amorousness of Mr. Lazar at the nursing home balances the compassionate responses she and her fellow inmates give to the news of their nurse's pregnancy, while they continue their litany of familiar complaints about their own children. What insures Blechman's status as a comic novelist, despite his often horrifying subject-matter is his complex parody, his word play that exposes an undercutting level of wit, his stylized handling of realistic dialogue, and, ultimately, in Rabbi Yeslin's lament for his failure as a marriage broker a prose that mocks an absurdity otherwise too painful to endure: "Nowadays, men wanted a special type, the kind you found late at night, alone in a delicatessen, waiting" (*The War of Camp Omongo*).

—Burton Kendle

BODSWORTH, (Charles) Fred(erick). Canadian. Born in Port Burwell, Ontario, 11 October 1918. Educated at Port Burwell public and high schools. Married Margaret Neville Banner in 1944; two daughters and one son. Reporter, St. Thomas *Times-Journal*, Ontario, 1940–43; reporter and editor, Toronto *Daily Star* and *Weekly Star*, 1943–46; staff writer and editor, *Maclean's Magazine*, Toronto, 1947–55. Since 1955, free-lance writer. Director, and former President (1965–67), Federation of Ontario Naturalists: leader of worldwide ornithological tours. Since 1970, Honorary Director, Long Point Bird Observatory; since 1975, Chairman of the Board of Trustees, James L. Baillie Memorial Fund for ornithology; editor, Natural Science of Canada series, 1980–81, and since 1980, member of the Board of Directors, Natural Science of Canada. Recipient: Doubleday Canadian Novel Award, 1967. Agent: Curtis Brown, 10 Astor Place, New York, New York 10003, U.S.A. Address: 294 Beech Avenue, Toronto, Ontario M4E 3J2, Canada.

PUBLICATIONS

Novels

The Last of the Curlews. Toronto and New York, Dodd Mead, 1955; London, Museum Press, 1956.
The Strange One. Toronto and New York, Dodd Mead, 1959; London, Longman, 1960.
The Atonement of Ashley Morden. Toronto and New York, Dodd Mead, 1964; as *Ashley Morden*, London, Longman, 1965.
The Sparrow's Fall. New York, Doubleday, and London, Longman, 1967.

Other

The People's Health: Canada and WHO, with Brock Chisholm. Toronto, Canadian Association for Adult Education, 1949.
The Pacific Coast. Toronto, Natural Science of Canada, 1970.
Wilderness Canada, with others. Toronto, Clarke Irwin, 1970.

*

Critical Studies: introduction by James Stevens to *The Last of the Curlews*, Toronto, McClelland and Stewart, 1963; in *The Oxford Companion to Canadian History and Literature* edited by Norah Story, Toronto, New York, and London, Oxford University Press, 1967; Don Gutteridge, in *Journal of Canadian Studies* (Peterborough, Ontario), August 1973; Olga Dey, in *Canadian Author and Bookman* (Toronto), Fall 1981; *A Reader's Guide to the Canadian Novel* by John Moss, Toronto, McClelland and Stewart, 1981.

Fred Bodsworth comments:

The major part of my work has been novels linking human and animal characters in a fiction format with strong natural history content and wilderness backgrounds. The nature storyteller who uses birds or mammals in fictional situations treads a narrow path if he wishes to be scientifically authentic and portray them as they really are. On the one hand, he has to personalize his animal as well as his human characters or he simply has not dramatic base for his story. Yet if the personalizing of animal characters goes too far and begins turning them into furry or feathered people—the nature writer's sin of anthropomorphism—the result is maudlin nonsense that is neither credible fable nor fiction. I enjoy the challenge of presenting wildlife characters as modern animal behaviour studies are showing them to be—creatures dominated by instinct, but not enslaved by it, beings with intelligence very much subhuman in some areas yet fascinatingly superhuman in others. Out of this blending of human and animal stories comes the theme that I hope is inherent in all my books: that man is an inescapable part of all nature, that its welfare is his welfare, that to survive he cannot continue acting and regarding himself as a spectator looking on from somewhere else.

*   *   *

Fred Bodsworth, writing in imaginative, uncomplicated prose, has used the Canadian Shield of pine-tree laden granite for the setting of his novels. He calls it "a benign land sometimes amiable, even indulgent, but at other times a land of perverse hostility." These sparsely, Indian-populated lands provide a unique characteristic which distinguishes Canada from its gargantuan neighbor to the south. Bodsworth is then readily identifiable as a Canadian novelist.

The strength of his writing is the skillful portrayal of characters who are dependent upon the milieu and the forces within it. He is able to make his birds and humans unpredictable because of unforeseen but crucial subtleties in the environmental settings. Bodsworth's naturalist and ornithological knowledge fosters such keen insight. Atook, a native hunter in *The Sparrow's Fall*, seems doomed because Christian myth interferes with his hunting prowess. But the will to survive, which resides in all his characters, eventually causes Atook to cast aside his alien beliefs and adjust to his natural surroundings.

The Last of the Curlews is his most stimulating and moving novel. Bodsworth reveals the brutal and senseless slaughter of a bird that has not developed a fear of the earth's most irrational creature, man. In sensitive prose, the tiny bird becomes personalized but not human; thus he avoids sham. The theme of this novel has increased in importance since its writing because of the growing awareness of our threatened environment.

While Bodsworth commits the occasional transgression by allowing his creatures to reason, it does not seriously detract from his animal characters.

In *The Strange One*, he adroitly interweaves the mating of an alien Hebridean Barra goose with a native Canada goose and the love of a young biologist for a Cree maiden, who has been socialized in the whiteman's world. Indian-white miscegenation is as old as Canada itself and this theme intertwined with the geese is unusual in Canadian literature. Bodsworth is the first to write about it. The parallel between man and bird in this novel clearly reveals the interrelationship of man with animal when Rory, the scientist, follows what appear to be almost instinctual feelings, disregards social convention and returns to the beautiful Cree, Kanina.

The Strange One and *The Atonement of Ashley Morden* involve what may be melodramatic relationships between men and birds, but the two themes are drawn together skillfully, and are quite effectively written. An underlying theme in both these novels, as well as the others, is the complicated, often contradictory behaviour of men contrasted with the logical, conditioned instincts of animals and birds.

In the context of Canadian literature, Bodsworth is one of the leading traditional novelists.

—James R. Stevens

BOURJAILY, Vance (Nye). American. Born in Cleveland, Ohio, 17 September 1922. Educated at Bowdoin College, Brunswick, Maine, B.A. 1947. Served in the American Field Service, 1942–44, and in the United States Army, 1944–46. Married Bettina Yensen in 1946; three children (one deceased). Taught at the Writers Workshop, 1957–58, and Associate Professor, 1960–64, 1966–67, 1971–72, University of Iowa, Iowa City; Visiting Professor, University of Arizona, Tucson, 1977–78. Served on the United States Department of State mission to South America, 1959. Distinguished Visiting Professor, Oregon State University, Corvallis, Summer 1968. Agent: William Morris Agency, 1350 Avenue of the Americas, New York, New York 10019, U.S.A.

PUBLICATIONS

Novels

The End of My Life. New York, Scribner, 1947; London, W.H. Allen, 1963.
The Hound of Earth. New York, Scribner, 1955; London, Secker and Warburg, 1956.
The Violated. New York, Dial Press, 1958; London, W.H. Allen, 1962.
Confessions of a Spent Youth. New York, Dial Press, 1960; London, W.H. Allen, 1961.
The Man Who Knew Kennedy. New York, Dial Press, and London, W.H. Allen, 1967.
Brill among the Ruins. New York, Dial Press, 1970; London, W.H. Allen, 1971.
Now Playing in Canterbury. New York, Dial Press, 1976.
A Game Men Play. New York, Dial Press, 1980.

Uncollected Short Stories

"The Poozle Dreamers," in *Dial* (New York), Fall 1959.
"Fractional Man," in *New Yorker*, 6 August 1960.
"Goose Pits," in *New Yorker*, 25 November 1961.
"Varieties of Religious Experience," in *The Esquire Reader*, edited by Arnold Gingrich and others. New York, Dial Press, 1967.
"A Lover's Mask," in *Saturday Evening Post* (Philadelphia), 6 May 1967.
"The Amish Farmer," in *Great Esquire Fiction*, edited by L. Rust Hills. New York, Viking Press, 1983.

Play

$4000: An Opera in Five Scenes, music by Tom Turner (produced Iowa City, 1969). Published in *North American Review* (Cedar Falls, Iowa), Winter 1969.

Other

The Girl in the Abstract Bed (text for cartoons). New York, Tiber Press, 1954.
The Unnatural Enemy (on hunting). New York, Dial Press, 1963.
Country Matters: Collected Reports from the Fields and Streams of Iowa and Other Places. New York, Dial Press, 1973.

Editor, *Discovery 1–6.* New York, Pocket Books, 1953–55.

*

Manuscript Collection: Bowdoin College Library, Brunswick, Maine.

Critical Studies: *After the Lost Generation* by John W. Aldridge, New York, McGraw Hill, 1951, London, Vision Press, 1959; by Bourjaily in *Afterwords* edited by Thomas McCormack, New York, Harper, 1969; *The Shaken Realist* by John M. Muste, Baton Rouge, Louisiana State University Press, 1970.

*   *   *

Vance Bourjaily's first three novels trace the effects of World War II on his generation of Americans, people who were undergraduates at the time of Munich and Benny Goodman's rendition of "I Got It Bad and That Ain't Good." In the looser structure of his fourth book, *Confessions of a Spent Youth*, the war becomes one of several stages in the narrator's growing up, and Bourjaily attempts moods and situations, humor and introspection that had not entered his more rigid earlier work. The novels that have followed this pivotal book have displayed a remarkable variety of subject and technique without gaining for Bourjaily the popularity or critical recognition that many have thought his due over the past 30 years.

The End of My Life recalls another slender novel of wartime ambulance service, Dos Passos's *One Man's Initiation—1917*. Skinner Galt, Bourjaily's hero, is another young man who believes in a few friends; any larger society or idea more complex than those relationships repels him. His accounting for this emptiness makes him sift through his slight reading and slighter experience to understand why he has "no principles, no truths, no ethics, no standards." For all of his, however, Skinner has some of the appeal of Fitzgerald's Amory Blaine struggling in *This Side of Paradise* to know himself in the mists of his general ignorance, and when the friendship theme is pursued in action beyond Skinner's disquisitions the book comes to life.

The Hound of Earth is a parable of American responsibility for nuclear power. It describes the last days of the seven-year flight of an atomic scientist, who has left his work and family because these ties constantly remind him of the people he has helped to kill. He adopts a life of bare subsistence only to be run down by his "hound of earth," a nagging humanitarian impulse that compels him to perform small acts of kindness to everyone he meets. *The Violated*, a far more ambitious novel, shows how four characters violate those whom they would love, and are, in turn, violated in the emptiness of their rapacious lives. The child of one of them (or perhaps two of them) plays the lead and directs other children in her own production of *Hamlet* before the parents, who sit as so many kings and queens, stupefied or wary until when, "frightened with false fire," a Claudius rises to end the show. This most sustained and complicated of Bourjaily's early plots thus ends with his first striking outburst of fictional invention.

Confessions of a Spent Youth is a re-telling of *The End of My Life* that relieves the narrator, Quincy Quince, of the burden of philosophical exposition and allows him to reminisce easily about his young life: friendships, drinking, brushes with drugs, his loves, and his war service. The autobiographical element, admitted by Bourjaily, is clearest in Quincy's statement that "to recall is a pleasure," for these stories show the writer let loose with craft he had begun to tap with the children's play in *The Violated*. His earlier writing seems narrow and solemn alongside Quincy's adventures, his detailed observation of ordinary existence and the pathos of meeting a girl "so beautiful you wanted to believe your eyes."

In *The Man Who Knew Kennedy*, Bourjaily examines the crises that overtake two friends in the months following the President's assassination. The connection between history and private lives is not altogether clear. Kennedy, according to the narrator, was killed by the psychotic force of someone writhing out of an abyss of frustration. A generation's illusions of invulnerability were smashed on impact. The gifted, graceful victim of this novel is, on the other hand, destroyed by his inexplicable ties to a woman as depraved as she is helpless. This man had traded on his talent, instead of developing it, while the surviving friend realizes that he is the stronger of the two for such reasons as "making necessary items out of wood—not fiberglass." *Brill among the Ruins* is Bourjaily's richest novel, and Brill, a middle-aged lawyer from southern Illinois, is his most fully realized character. He stands among two kinds of ruins, the hard bargain of his life and the archaeological sites of Oaxaca, developing on that line an understanding of himself that finally arrests his flight from responsibility. The accounts of digging are superb, surpassed only by the hunting scene when Brill is "sculling" for ducks alone on the Mississippi before dawn. Among the ruins, he confirms his own integrity.

Now Playing in Canterbury follows Chaucer to the extent of having characters tell tales within a framework like a pilgrimage. Their journey is the progress from planning to performing an opera commissioned for the opening of a university theatre. It is an exciting mixture of extravagant tales and breathless frame narrative. In the troubled early 1970's, Bourjaily implies, only artistic collaboration could draw such people together. Only their talents could withstand the blows of circumstance on their characters.

A Game Men Play concerns yet another combat veteran, this one a poetic, reflective man trained as a killer and conditioned as a victim. *Is there anything at all that I can do?* he wires an old friend and tormentor upon learning of a family catastrophe. What he can and cannot do to help is lost in the novel's (perhaps deliberate) loose ends, although the last glimpse of him in exile is utterly clear, recalling his moments decades before when he helped free the inmates of a death camp and confronted a ragged German warden: " '*Bitte.* Please.' He was the last man Chink killed in the Second World War. Chink did not stop to wonder if the man was asking for his life or for his death." If not Bourjaily's great novel, *A Game Men Play* is closer than any other to his summing up.

—David Sanders

BOWEN, John (Griffith). British. Born in Calcutta, India, 5 November 1924. Educated at Queen Elizabeth's Grammar School, Crediton, Devon; Pembroke College, Oxford (Editor, *Isis*), 1948–51; St. Antony's College, Oxford (Frere Exhibitioner in Indian Studies), 1951–53; M.A. 1953; Ohio State University, Columbus, 1952–53. Served in the Mahratha Light Infantry, 1943–47: Captain. Assistant editor, *The Sketch* magazine, London, 1953–56; copywriter, J. Walter Thompson Company, London, 1956–58; head of the copy department, S.T. Garland Advertising, London, 1958–60; script consultant, Associated Television, London, 1960–67; drama producer, Thames Television, London, 1978–79, London Weekend Television, 1981–83, and BBC, 1984. Agent: (fiction) Elaine Greene Ltd., 31 Newington Green, London N16 9PU; (theatre) Margaret Ramsay Ltd., 14-A Goodwin's Court, London WC2N 4LL. Address: Old Lodge Farm, Sugarswell Lane, Edgehill, Banbury, Oxfordshire OX15 6HP, England.

PUBLICATIONS

Novels

The Truth Will Not Help Us: Embroidery on an Historical Theme. London, Chatto and Windus, 1956.
After the Rain. London, Faber, 1958; New York, Ballantine, 1959.
The Centre of the Green. London, Faber, 1959; New York, McDowell Obolensky, 1960.
Storyboard. London, Faber, 1960.
The Birdcage. London, Faber, and New York, Harper, 1962.
A World Elsewhere. London, Faber, 1965; New York, Coward McCann, 1967.
Squeak: A Biography of NPA 1978A 203. London, Faber, 1983; New York, Viking, 1984.
The McGuffin. London, Hamish Hamilton, 1984; Boston, Atlantic Monthly Press, 1985.
The Girls. London, Hamish Hamilton, 1986.

Uncollected Short Stories

"Another Death in Venice," in *London Magazine*, June 1964.
"The Wardrobe Mistress," in *London Magazine*, January 1971.
"Barney," in *Mae West Is Dead*, edited by Adam Mars-Jones. London, Faber, 1983.

Plays

The Essay Prize, with A Holiday Abroad and The Candidate: Plays for Television. London, Faber, 1962.
I Love You, Mrs. Patterson (produced Cambridge and London, 1964). London, Evans, 1964.
The Corsican Brothers, based on the play by Dion Boucicault (televised, 1965; revised version, produced London, 1970). London, Methuen, 1970.
After the Rain, adaptation of his own novel (produced London, 1966; New York, 1967). London, Faber, 1967; New York, Random House, 1968; revised version, Faber, 1972.
The Fall and Redemption of Man (as *Fall and Redemption*, produced London, 1967; as *The Fall and Redemption of Man*, produced New York, 1974). London, Faber, 1968.
Silver Wedding (televised, 1967; revised version, produced in *We Who Are about to . . .*, later called *Mixed Doubles*, London, 1969). London, Methuen, 1970.
Little Boxes (includes *The Coffee Lace* and *Trevor*) (produced London, 1968; New York, 1969). London, Methuen, 1968; New York, French, 1970.
The Disorderly Women, adaptation of a play by Euripides (produced Manchester, 1969; London, 1970). London, Methuen, 1969.
The Waiting Room (produced London, 1970). London, French, 1970; New York, French, 1971.
Robin Redbreast (televised, 1970; produced Guildford, Surrey, 1974). Published in *The Television Dramatist*, edited by Robert Muller, London, Elek, 1973.
Diversions (produced London, 1973). Excerpts published in *Play 9*, edited by Robin Cook, London, Arnold, 1981.
Young Guy Seeks Part-Time Work (televised, 1973; produced London, 1978).
Roger, in *Mixed Blessings* (produced Horsham, Sussex, 1973). Published in *London Magazine*, 1976.
Florence Nightingale (as *Miss Nightingale*, televised, 1974; revised version, as *Florence Nightingale*, produced Canterbury, 1975). London, French, 1976.

Heil Caesar!, adaptation of *Julius Caesar* by Shakespeare (televised, 1974). London, BBC Publications, 1974; revised version (produced Birmingham, 1974), London, French, 1975.
Which Way Are You Facing? (produced Bristol, 1976). Excerpts published in *Play 9*, edited by Robin Cook, London, Arnold, 1981.
Singles (produced London, 1977).
Bondage (produced London, 1978).
The Inconstant Couple, adaptation of a play by Marivaux (produced Chichester, 1978).
Spot the Lady (produced Newcastle-upon-Tyne, 1981).

Radio Plays: *Digby* (as Justin Blake, with Jeremy Bullmore), 1959; *Varieties of Love* (revised version of television play *The First Thing You Think Of*), 1968.

Television Plays: created the *Garry Halliday* series; episodes in *Front Page Story*, *The Power Game*, *The Guardians* (7 episodes), *Wylde Alliance*, and *The Villains* series; *A Holiday Abroad*, 1960; *The Essay Prize*, 1960; *The Jackpot Question*, 1961; *The Candidate*, 1961; *Nuncle*, from the story by John Wain, 1962; *The Truth about Alan*, 1963; *A Case of Character*, 1964; *Mr. Fowlds*, 1965; *The Corsican Brothers*, 1965; *Finders Keepers*, 1967; *The Whole Truth*, 1967; *Silver Wedding*, 1967; *A Most Unfortunate Accident*, 1968; *Flotsam and Jetsam*, 1970; *Robin Redbreast*, 1970; *A Woman Sobbing*, 1972; *The Emergency Channel*, 1973; *Young Guy Seeks Part-Time Work*, 1973; *Miss Nightingale*, 1974; *Heil Caesar!*, 1974; *The Treasure of Abbot Thomas*, 1974; *The Snow Queen*, 1974; *A Juicy Case*, 1975; *Brief Encounter*, from the film by Noël Coward, 1976; *A Photograph*, 1977; *Rachel in Danger*, 1978; *A Dog's Ransom*, from the novel by Patricia Highsmith, 1978; *Games*, 1978; *The Ice House*, 1978; *The Letter of the Law*, 1979; *Dying Day*, 1980; *The Specialist*, 1980; *Dark Secret*, 1981; *Honeymoon*, 1985.

Other (for children)

Pegasus. London, Faber, 1957; New York, A.S. Barnes, 1960.
The Mermaid and the Boy. London, Faber, 1958; New York, A.S. Barnes, 1960.
Garry Halliday and the Disappearing Diamonds [*Ray of Death*; *Kidnapped Five*; *Sands of Time*; *Flying Foxes*] (as Justin Blake, with Jeremy Bullmore). London, Faber, 5 vols., 1960–64.

*

Manuscript Collections: Mugar Memorial Library, Boston University; (television works) Temple University Library, Philadelphia.

Critical Studies: *Postwar British Fiction*, Berkeley, University of California Press, 1962, and "The Fable Breaks Down," in *Wisconsin Studies in Contemporary Literature* (Madison), vol. 8, no. 7, 1967, both by James Gindin.

Theatrical Activities:
Director: **Plays**—at the London Academy of Music and Dramatic Art since 1967; *The Disorderly Women*, Manchester, 1969, London, 1970; *Fall and Redemption*, Pitlochry, Scotland, 1969; *The Waiting Room*, London, 1970.

Actor: **Plays**—in repertory in North Wales, summers 1950–51; Palace Theatre, Watford, Hertfordshire, 1965.

John Bowen comments:
I have always been interested in problems of form. Thus, in my first novel, *The Truth Will Not Help Us*, I wanted to try to tell a story of an historical occurrence of 1705 in Britain in terms of the political atmosphere and activities of the U.S.A. in 1953; in both those years political witch-hunting caused injustice and harm to innocent persons. My second novel, *After the Rain*, began as an attempt to do for science fiction what Michael Innes had done for the detective story: I failed in this attempt because I soon became more interested in the ideas with which I was dealing than in the form, and anyway made many scientific errors. My third novel was straightforwardly naturalistic, but in my fourth, *Storyboard*, I used an advertising agency as a symbol of a statement about public and private life, just as Zola used a department store in *Au Bonheur des Dames*. In my fifth novel, *The Birdcage*, I attempted to use a 19th-century manner—the objective detachment of Trollope, who presents his characters at some distance, displays and comments on them. In my sixth novel, *A World Elsewhere*, the hero, himself a wounded and needed politician, is writing a fiction about Philoctetes, the wounded archer, and until he has found his own reasons for returning to political life in London, cannot conclude his fiction, because he does not see why Philoctetes should allow himself to accompany Odysseus to Troy. In *Squeak*, the biography of a pigeon I once helped to rear, the story is told sometimes from Squeaks point of view, sometimes from that of her owners. In *The McGuffin* I tried to tell the story as the first-person narrative of one of the characters *inside* the kind of film Hitchcock might have made, the character himself being a reviewer of films. The same interest in different problems of form can be seen in my plays—the first Ibsenesque, the second borrowing from Brecht, Pirandello, and the Chinese theatre, the third a pair of linked one-acters, designed as two halves of the same coin, the fourth an attempt to rework the myth of *The Bacchae* as Sartre, Giraudoux, and Anouilh had used Greek myths, and to blend verse and prose, knockabout comedy, high tragedy, and Shavian argument. My full-length play *The Corsican Brothers* (an expansion of my earlier television play) has songs set within the play to music pirated from 19th-century composers, and I tried to make, from the melodramatic fantasies of Dumas and Dion Boucicault, a kind of Stendhalian statement about a society based on ideas of honour. In two of my television plays, *Miss Nightingale* and *The Emergency Channel*, I experimented with a narrative method that was associative, not lineal.

In this commentary, I am more confident in writing of form than of theme. One's themes are for the critics to set out neatly on a board: one is not always so clearly conscious of them oneself. There is a concern with archetypical patterns of behaviour (therefore with myth). There is a constant war between reasonable man and instinctive man. There is the pessimistic discovery that Bloomsbury values don't work, but that there seem to be no others worth holding. There is a statement of the need for Ibsen's "Life Lie" even when one knows it to be a lie, and Forster's "Only connect" becomes "Only accept" in my work. There is, particularly in *The McGuffin*, a concern with—and sorrow over—the ways in which human beings manipulate others of their kind.

I believe that novels and plays should tell a story, that the story is the mechanism by which one communicates one's view of life, and that no symbolism is worth anything unless it also works as an element in the story, since the final symbol is the story itself.

Inasmuch as the influences on one's style are usually those writers whom one has discovered in one's adolescence and early twenties, I might be said to have been influenced as a novelist by Dickens, Trollope, E.M. Forster, Virginia Woolf, E. Nesbit, P.G. Wodehouse, and Evelyn Waugh—perhaps a little also by Hemingway and Faulkner. As a playwright, I have been influenced by Ibsen, Tchekov, Shaw, Pirandello, Anouilh, Giraudoux, and Noël Coward. Most of these names, I am sure, would be on any lists made by most of my contemporaries.

*   *   *

John Bowen has always been an intelligent and didactic novelist. His first novel, *The Truth Will Not Help Us*, uses a story of English seamen charged with piracy in a Scottish port in 1705 as a metaphor for the political evil of assuming guilt by rumor or association. *A World Elsewhere* uses the myth of Philoctetes as a parallel to complicated speculation about hypocrisy and engagement in contemporary political life. *The Birdcage* contains a long essay giving an account of the history and development of commercial television; a defense of advertising is not necessarily more corrupt than any other institution in urban, capitalistic society introduces *Storyboard*. Although Bowen's fictional lessons are invariably complex and thoughtful, the author's presence is always visible arranging, blocking out, and connecting the material. Myth is made pointedly and explicitly relevant; symbols, like the lovebirds in *The Birdcage* or the breaking of a bronze chrysanthemum at a funeral in *The Centre of the Green*, sometimes seem attached heavy-handedly and literally. Bowen always acknowledges his own presence in his fiction, at times addressing the reader directly and becoming playful and intelligently skeptical about the complexities that prevent him from making any easy disposition of the characters and issues he has developed. The author is conspicuously articulate and instructive, but he does not attempt to play God; in fact, the danger of human substitutions for a non-existent or unknowable deity comprises part of the message of *After the Rain* and the skepticism underlying *The Birdcage* and *A World Elsewhere*.

Bowen's novels contain sharply memorable and effective scenes: the retired colonel expressing his style and his strength through his garden in *The Centre of the Green*, the nocturnal trip around Soho in which a character is beaten in *The Birdcage*, the picnic on a Greek island in *A World Elsewhere*. Often the best scenes involve a witty and comic treatment of dramatic conflict between two characters involved in close relationship, like the familial and sexual relationships in *The Centre of the Green* and *Storyboard*, the brilliantly handled quarrel between two contemporary London lovers who have lived together too long that takes place in the Piazza San Marco in *The Birdcage*, or the play with switching gender identities in *The McGuffin*. Bowen's comedy, however, no matter how strident initially, invariably turns into sympathy for his characters because they are unable to be more dignified or to match their own conceptions of a fuller humanity. This characteristic switch from satire to sympathy is emblematic of most of Bowen's fiction which works on reversals, on dramatically presented and thematically central violations of expected conclusions. The simple, muscle-flexing athlete, not the expected sensitive intellectual, finally defies and defeats the tyrant who would make himself God in *After the Rain*. Humanity and integrity appear in just those places most easily and generally thought the most corrupt in modern society in *Storyboard*. The family in which all members seem, superficially, most selfish and isolated can understand and respect each other in *The Centre of the Green*. This engagingly perverse positivism is often applied to social or political clichés, as in the forceful and complicated treatment of E.M.

Forster's "Only connect" in *The Birdcage* or the ramifications on "politics is the art of the possible" developed in *A World Elsewhere*. Such clichés, in Bowen's fictional world, never honestly express the concerns or dilemmas of the characters who use them so glibly, although they may yet be partially true in ways the characters never intend and can seldom comprehend. The fact that people, in Bowen's novels, generally haven't a very good idea of what they're about is no warrant for denying their humanity or their capacity to invoke sympathy.

In the mid-1960's, Bowen turned to writing and producing plays for stage and television. Some of these, like adaptations of Euripides' *The Bacchae*, Shakespeare's *Julius Caesar*, and Dion Boucicault's *The Corsican Brothers*, compress the use of myth and symbol in dramatic confrontation, and suggest darker and more tragic versions of experience than do the novels. Recently, after nearly 20 years away from novels, Bowen has published two, *Squeak* and *The McGuffin*. Both depend on formal devices, dramatic fictional artifice: *Squeak* on the reconstruction of the knowable world through the carefully limited attention to a pigeon's perspective; *The McGuffin* on applying Alfred Hitchcock's term for the device in his films that triggered the action without itself being part of the plot to a more intricately locked version of menacing violations of expected identities. These novels function less as implicit social commentary than do some of Bowen's earlier ones, although, beneath the wit, they still convey humane and thoughtful lessons concerning the need to accept human deficiency and to respect forms of being, in oneself and in others, that one could not have initially imagined.

—James Gindin

BOWLES, Paul (Frederick). American. Born in New York City, 30 December 1910. Educated at the University of Virginia, Charlottesville, 1928–29; studied music with Aaron Copland in New York and Berlin, 1930–32, and with Virgil Thomson in Paris, 1933–34. Married Jane Sydney Auer (i.e., the writer Jane Bowles) in 1938 (died, 1973). Music critic, New York *Herald-Tribune*, 1942–46; also composer. Recipient: Guggenheim fellowship, 1941; American Academy award, 1950; Rockefeller grant, 1959; Translation Center grant, 1975; National Endowment for the Arts grant, 1977. Since 1947 has lived in Tangier. Agent: William Morris Agency, 1350 Avenue of the Americas, New York, New York 10019, U.S.A. Address: 2117 Tanger Socco, Tangier, Morocco.

PUBLICATIONS

Novels

The Sheltering Sky.   London, Lehmann, and New York, New Directions, 1949.
Let It Come Down.   London, Lehmann, and New York, Random House, 1952.
The Spider's House.   New York, Random House, 1955; London, Macdonald, 1957.
Up above the World.   New York, Simon and Schuster, 1966; London, Owen, 1967.

Short Stories

The Delicate Prey and Other Stories. New York, Random House, 1950.
A Little Stone. London, Lehmann, 1950.
The Hours after Noon. London, Heinemann, 1959.
A Hundred Camels in the Courtyard. San Francisco, City Lights, 1962.
The Time of Friendship. New York, Holt Rinehart, 1967.
Pages from Cold Point and Other Stories. London, Owen, 1968.
Three Tales. New York, Hallman, 1975.
Things Gone and Things Still Here. Santa Barbara, California, Black Sparrow Press, 1977.
Collected Stories 1939–1976. Santa Barbara, California, Black Sparrow Press, 1979.
Midnight Mass. Santa Barbara, California, Black Sparrow Press, 1981; London, Owen, 1985.

Uncollected Short Stories

"The Eye," in *Missouri Review* (Columbia), 1978.
"Here to Learn," "The Dismissal," "Madame and Ahmed," and "Kitty," in *Antaeus* (New York), 1979–80.
"The Husband," in *Michigan Quarterly Review* (Ann Arbor), 1980.
"At the Krungthep Plaza," in *Ontario Review* (Windsor), 1980.
"Monologue (Massachusetts 1931)," in *Conjunctions* (New York), 1983.
"Monologue (Tangier 1975)," in *Threepenny Review* (Berkeley, California), 1983.
"Hugh Harper," in *Threepenny Review* (Berkeley, California), Spring 1985.
"Julian Vreden," in *Threepenny Review* (Berkeley, California), Autumn 1985.

Verse

Scenes. Los Angeles, Black Sparrow Press, 1968.
The Thicket of Spring: Poems 1926–1969. Los Angeles, Black Sparrow Press, 1972.
Next to Nothing. Kathmandu, Starstreams, 1976.
Next to Nothing: Collected Poems 1926–1977. Santa Barbara, California, Black Sparrow Press, 1981.

Other

Yallah (travel). Zurich, Manesse, 1956; New York, McDowell Obolensky, 1957.
Their Heads Are Green (travel). London, Owen, 1963; as *Their Heads Are Green and Their Hands Are Blue*, New York, Random House, 1963.
Without Stopping: An Autobiography. London, Owen, and New York, Putnam, 1972.
In the Red Room. Los Angeles, Sylvester and Orphanos, 1981.
Points in Time (on Morocco). London, Owen, 1982; New York, Ecco Press, 1984.

Translator, *No Exit*, by Jean-Paul Sartre. New York, French, 1946.
Translator, *Lost Trail of the Sahara*, by Roger Firson-Roche. London, Hale, 1956; Englewood Cliffs, New Jersey, Prentice Hall, 1962.
Translator, *A Life Full of Holes*, by Driss ben Hamed Charhadi. New York, Grove Press, 1964; London, Weidenfeld and Nicolson, 1965.
Translator, *Love with a Few Hairs*, by Mohammed Mrabet. London, Owen, 1967; New York, Braziller, 1968.

Translator, *The Lemon*, by Mohammed Mrabet. London, Owen, 1969; New York, McGraw Hill, 1972.
Translator, *Mhashish*, by Mohammed Mrabet. San Francisco, City Lights, 1969.
Translator, *The Boy Who Set the Fire and Other Stories.* Los Angeles, Black Sparrow Press, 1974.
Translator, *For Bread Alone*, by Mohamed Choukri. London, Owen, 1974.
Translator, *Jean Genet in Tangier*, by Mohamed Choukri. New York, Ecco Press, 1974.
Translator, *The Oblivion Seekers*, by Isabelle Eberhardt. San Francisco, City Lights, 1975.
Translator, *Hadidan Aharam*, by Mohammed Mrabet. Los Angeles, Black Sparrow Press, 1975.
Translator, *Harmless Poisons, Blameless Sins*, by Mohammed Mrabet. Santa Barbara, California, Black Sparrow Press, 1976.
Translator, *Look and Move On*, by Mohammed Mrabet. Santa Barbara, California, Black Sparrow Press, 1976.
Translator, *The Big Mirror*, by Mohammed Mrabet. Santa Barbara, California, Black Sparrow Press, 1977.
Translator, *Five Eyes: Short Stories by Five Moroccans.* Santa Barbara, California, Black Sparrow Press, 1979.
Translator, *Tennessee Williams in Tangier*, by Mohamed Choukri. Santa Barbara, California, Cadmus, 1979.
Translator, *The Beach Café, and The Voice*, by Mohammed Mrabet. Santa Barbara, California, Black Sparrow Press, 1980.
Translator, *The Chest*, by Mohammed Mrabet. Bolinas, California, Tomboctou, 1983.
Translator, *She Woke Me Up So I Killed Her.* Tiburon, California, Cadmus, 1985.
Translator, *The Beggar's Knife*, by Rodrigo Rey Rosa. San Francisco, City Lights, 1985.

Published Music: *Tornado Blues* (chorus); *Music for a Farce* (chamber music); *Piano Sonatina*; *Huapango 1* and *2*; *Six Preludes for Piano*; *El Indio*; *El Bejuco*; *Sayula*; *La Cuelga*; *Sonata for Two Pianos*; *Night Waltz* (two pianos); *Songs: Heavenly Grass*; *Sugar in the Cane*; *Cabin*; *Lonesome Man*; *Letter to Freddy*; *The Years*; *Of All the Things I Love*; *A Little Closer, Please*; *David*; *In the Woods*; *Song of an Old Woman*; *Night Without Sleep*; *Two Skies*; *Que te falta?*; *Ya Llego*; *Once a Lady Was Here*; *Bluebell Mountain*; *Three*; *On a Quiet Conscience*; *El Carbonero*; *Baby, Baby*; *Selected Songs*, Santa Fe, Soundings Press, 1984.

Operas: *Denmark Vesey*, 1937; *The Wind Remains*, 1941.

Ballets: *Yankee Clipper*, 1937; *Pastorella*, 1941; *Sentimental Colloquy*, 1944; *Blue Roses*, 1957.

Incidental Music, for plays: *Horse Eats Hat*, 1936; *Dr. Faustus*, 1937; *My Heart's in the Highlands*, 1939; *Love's Old Sweet Song*, 1940; *Twelfth Night*, 1940; *Liberty Jones*, 1941; *Watch on the Rhine*, 1941; *South Pacific*, 1943; *Jacobowsky and the Colonel*, 1944; *The Glass Menagerie*, 1945; *Twilight Bar*, 1946; *On Whitman Avenue*, 1946; *The Dancer*, 1946; *Cyrano de Bergerac*, 1946; *Land's End*, 1946; *Summer and Smoke*, 1948; *In the Summer House*, 1953; *Edwin Booth*, 1958; *Sweet Bird of Youth*, 1959; *The Milk Train Doesn't Stop Here Anymore*, 1963; for films: *Roots in the Soil*, 1940; *Congo*, 1944.

Recordings: *The Wind Remains*, M.G.M.; *Café Sin Nombre*, New Music; *Sonata for Two Pianos*, Concert Hall; *Night Waltz*, Columbia; *Scènes d'Anabase*, Columbia; *Music for a Farce*,

Columbia; *Song for My Sister*, Disc; *They Cannot Stop Death*, Disc; *Night Without Sleep*, Disc; *Sailor's Song*, Disc; *Rain Rots the Wood*, Disc; *Sonata for Flute and Piano*, Art of This Century; *Six Preludes*, Golden Crest; *Huapango 1* and *2*, New Music; *A Picnic Cantata*, lyrics by James Schuyler, Columbia, 1955; *El Bejuco* and *El Indio*, Art of This Century; *Blue Mountain Ballads*, Music Library; *Concerto for Two Pianos, Winds and Percussion*, Columbia; *Once a Lady Was Here, Song of an Old Person*, New World; *Six Latin American Pieces*, Etcetera, 1984; *Five Songs*, GSS, 1984.

*

Manuscript Collection: Humanities Research Center, University of Texas, Austin.

Critical Studies: "Paul Bowles and the Natural Man" by Oliver Evans, in *Recent American Fiction*, Boston, Houghton Mifflin, 1963; *Paul Bowles: The Illumination of North Africa* by Lawrence D. Stewart, Carbondale, Southern Illinois University Press, 1974; *Paul Bowles: Staticity and Terror* by Eric Mottram, London, Aloes, 1976; *The Fiction of Paul Bowles: The Soul Is the Weariest Part of the Body* by Hans Bertens, Amsterdam, Rodopi, and Atlantic Highlands, New Jersey, Humanities Press, 1979; "Paul Bowles Issue" of *Review of Contemporary Fiction* (Elmwood Park, Illinois), vol. 2, no. 3, 1982; *Paul Bowles: The Inner Geography* by Wayne Pounds, Bern, Switzerland, Lang, 1985.

Paul Bowles comments:

All I can find of interest to say about my work is to mention the key role in the process of writing played by my subconscious. It knows far better than I what should be written and how it should sound in words.

*   *   *

Since the publication of his first novel, *The Sheltering Sky*, Paul Bowles has provoked sharply partisan feelings in his readers. To some he is a major prophet for our times; to others his work rather luridly exploits the fashionable themes of nihilism, violence, and despair. Few, however, are able to deny the insistent power of his prose—its urgency, clarity, and lyric compactness. Bowles's subtly acute sense of language no doubt owes a major debt to his training as a musician, his work as a translator, and his life-long interest in poetry. The intricate web of language in which his novels are contained often seems the only protection against the horror and despair which threaten to overwhelm his characters.

The Sheltering Sky sounded the major theme with which Bowles was to be concerned in all his work: the elemental clash between the primitive and the civilized. Bowles's central characters, Kit and Port Moresby, arrive in North Africa without any clear past, and make their way through a series of grotesque adventures. They are spiritual somnambulists, exiles, ambassadors from the wasteland of the modern world, and their veneer of civilization is slowly stripped away as they confront the primitive realities of the barren Sahara. *The Sheltering Sky* owes a debt, in its precise rendering of the violence and poverty of the Arab world, to the naturalist tradition, but beneath the novel's precisely rendered surface are undercurrents of symbol and insinuation which continually extend the meaning of the work. Like Edgar Allan Poe, the American writer whom he most admires, Bowles is primarily interested in probing the human soul, and to do so he must first strip it naked. That process most often reveals a spiritual emptiness, a sense of the void which links him to European existentialist writers like Sartre, whose *No Exit* Bowles translated in 1946. As Bowles remarks of one of his own characters, "in order to deal with relative values, he had long since come to deny all purpose to the phenomenon of existence—it was more expedient and more comforting."

Some reviewers felt that *The Sheltering Sky* was merely a retelling of the story of spiritually bankrupt expatriates that Hemingway had recorded in *The Sun Also Rises*. In his second novel, *Let It Come Down*, Bowles made it clear that his interest in *nada* went far beyond Hemingway's essentially romantic attitude toward the dispossessed. The atmosphere of this work is even more stark, malevolent, and absurd than that of the first novel. A sober, sheltered clerk in a New York bank gives up his position in order to work in a friend's travel agency in Tangier; there he discovers the business to be a front for currency black-marketeering, and following that revelation he himself becomes involved in smuggling, narcotics traffic, sexual perversion, espionage, and murder, ultimately absconding with an Arab companion and a bundle of stolen currency. Despite the obvious sensationalism of plot, Bowles is again concerned with the psychic disintegration and moral decay which overtake so-called civilized man when he confronts the primitive, the theme pervades his major writing as it does that of Joseph Conrad.

The hero (or anti-hero) of *Let It Come Down* seeks some place in the world to cancel out his meaningless existence, to find self by losing it; rejecting all conventional ideas of order, he acts in a chaotic way that creates and invites violence. Violence also overtakes and destroys the central characters of *Up above the World* who celebrate their second wedding anniversary with a trip to an obscure plantation republic. As they wander through wild landscapes, their adventures become increasingly feverish, compulsive, and agonized until hallucination and death overtake them.

The world of Paul Bowles's fiction is morally uninhabitable; it closes down on his characters like a hypnotic spell, as it closes down on the reader willing to grant the author's *donnée*: that there is within each of us the capacity for violence, irrational behavior, and madness, and that modern culture proves increasingly ineffective in giving check to those abysses. Nonetheless, Bowles's most memorable characters struggle for some kind of definition and often gamble for meaning with their very souls. Such concerns are equally present in Bowles's poetry, his travel books, and such edited "translations" as *Love with a Few Hairs*, the autobiography of the young Moroccan, Mohammed Mrabet. Many readers will find his vision discomforting, but it has significant parallels in the work of Sartre and Genet, Camus's *L'Etranger*, and the later work of Norman Mailer. Few modern writers have explored so memorably the contrasts between naivety and guile, Puritan restraint and pagan indulgence, Western sophistication and ancient superstition.

Nonetheless, it is difficult to escape the sense that Bowles's agonized vision, his extraordinary range of talent and his richly international experience have never coalesced to produce the single great work on which a major reputation might be established. The hypnotic atmosphere of *The Sheltering Sky* has been equalled in later work, but never surpassed, and while *The Spider's House* and *Up above the World* demonstrate a refinement of narrative power, they seem finally like somewhat redundant variations on long-established gothic themes.

—David Galloway

BOYD, William (Andrew Murray). British. Born 7 March 1952. Educated at Gordonstoun School, Elgin, Morayshire; Glasgow University, M.A. (honours) in English and philosophy; Jesus College, Oxford. Married Susan Anne Wilson in 1975. Lecturer in English, St. Hilda's College, Oxford, 1980–83. Television critic, *New Statesman*, London, 1981–83. Recipient: Whitbread Award, 1981; Maugham Award, 1982; Rhys Memorial Prize, 1982. Fellow, Royal Society of Literature, 1983. Lives in Fulham, London. Agent: Deborah Rogers Ltd., 49 Blenheim Crescent, London W11 2EF, England.

PUBLICATIONS

Novels

A Good Man in Africa. London, Hamish Hamilton, 1981; New York, Morrow, 1982.
An Ice-Cream War. London, Hamish Hamilton, 1982; New York, Morrow, 1983.
Stars and Bars. London, Hamish Hamilton, 1984; New York, Morrow, 1985.

Short Stories

On the Yankee Station and Other Stories. London, Hamish Hamilton, 1981; New York, Morrow, 1984.

Uncollected Short Story

"The Airport Hotel," in *Harper's* (New York), May 1983.

Plays

School Ties (includes the TV plays *Good and Bad at Games* and *Dutch Girls*, and an essay). London, Hamish Hamilton, 1985.
Care and Attention of Swimming Pools, and Not Yet Jayette (produced London, 1985).

Radio Play: *On the Yankee Station*, from his own story, 1985.

Television Plays: *Good and Bad at Games*, 1983; *Dutch Girls*, 1985.

*   *   *

But for *An Ice-Cream War*, William Boyd would be firmly labelled an exponent of that familiar comic genre, the accident-prone hero novel, as practised by, among others, Kingsley Amis (*Lucky Jim*), Anthony Burgess (the Enderby series), and Tom Sharpe (the Wilt series). Both *A Good Man in Africa* and *Stars and Bars* feature protagonists—Morgan Leafy and Henderson Dores, respectively—entrusted with crucial assignments only to be hampered and finally thwarted by proliferating complications. Foreign locations enable Boyd to add occasional culture shock to their predicaments.

Morgan Leafy is a minor diplomat stationed in a provincial backwater in the "not-very-significant" West African nation of Kinjanja. For three years, his stupefying boredom has been palliated only by readily available alcohol and sex. Then, unexpectedly, his boss, Fanshawe, deputes him to cultivate, on behalf of H.M. Government, a local politician (Samuel Adekunle) who is a bigwig in the party set to win Kinjanja's forthcoming elections. At the same time, Morgan begins to court Priscilla, Fanshawe's attractive daughter. Initially, the outlook

seems promising: both Adekunle and Priscilla respond to Morgan's overtures. Subsequently, things deteriorate inexorably. Distractions and indignities dog him. Through a misunderstanding, he loses Priscilla to a hated underling. Then he finds himself being blackmailed by Adekunle. To secure his silence, Morgan must suborn an expatriate Scot, Dr. Murray, who is obstructing a lucrative swindle the politician hopes to transact. Unfortunately, Murray is a model of rectitude: Morgan's proposition only worsens matters. In the final pages, though, providence apparently rescues him.

Henderson Dores is an art expert who has recently left England to join the fledgling New York branch of Mulholland, Melhuish, a London auction house. Already he has become simultaneously involved with two alluring, imperious women: his former wife, Melissa, with whom he is discussing remarriage, and his mistress, Irene. Henderson's assignment entails travelling to the Deep South to talk Loomis Gage, a reclusive millionaire, into letting Mulholland, Melhuish handle the sale of his paintings: a coup that would "signal their arrival." Inconveniently, Bryant, Henderson's teenage stepdaughter-to-be, invites herself along, thereby jeopardising his plans to meet Irene while away. Then the Gage household proves to be chock-full of confusing and/or intimidating oddballs. Nevertheless, braving the violent opposition of Gage's elder son and assorted misadventures, Henderon brings matters to a successful conclusion. Gage, however, promptly suffers a fatal coronary, leaving him with only an unwitnessed oral agreement. Furthermore, Bryant announces her intention of eloping with Duane, the son of Gage's housekeeper. Abducting Bryant, Henderson decamps to New York. After further misadventures, the novel closes with him fleeing a vengeful Duane. By this time, Henderson has lost his job (perhaps temporarily) and both his women (probably permanently). The paintings, meanwhile, have been destroyed.

Stars and Bars contains various inventive comic flights, but several others seem decidedly routine, poking fun at soft targets like American speech, American cuisine (especially the down-home kind), radio "sermonettes," country and western music. Elsewhere, bedroom farce ensues when Henderson and Irene rendezvous at Atlanta's swishest hotel. *A Good Man in Africa* generally avoids such lapses into the familiar. In addition, the world created in *Stars and Bars* is distinctly cartoon-like: Henderson is a two-dimensional character whose pratfalls provide entertainment alone. Morgan's mishaps also arouse some sympathy: the reader discerns his real desperation as Adekunle turns the screw, his pricks of conscience at engaging, albeit unavailingly, in corruption.

At one stage in Julian Barnes's *Flaubert's Parrot* the narrator proposes that certain types of fiction be no longer written, including ". . . novels about small hitherto forgotten wars in distant parts of the British Empire, in the painstaking course of which we learn . . . that war is very nasty indeed." *An Ice-Cream War* is clearly one of the novels that has prompted this injunction: it is set mainly in East Africa during World War I, when the adjacent British and German colonies became a secondary battlefield. The description, though, is unjust: Boyd's point about the nature of war is a deeper one—he believes that literature has not only glossed over the bloodiness of war, but also its contingency.

Boyd's humour is altogether more grim here than in his other novels. Destiny is again antipathetic towards his characters, but the tricks of fate are now brutal rather than mischievous. An incongruous episode in *Stars and Bars* concerns Henderson's discovery that his father's death during World War II occurred when he was struck by a tin of pineapple chunks dropped from a supply plane. In *An Ice-Cream War*, death and injury from comparably absurd causes are commonplace; accident rather than design is throughout the motive force behind events. One of the principal characters, Captain Gabriel Cobb, takes part in the sea-borne invasion of German East Africa, during which military order and discipline degenerate into chaos. Later, as an escaping POW, he is killed by German askaris who have misunderstood their commander's orders. In the novel's penultimate section, Gabriel's revenge-bent younger brother, Felix, tracks down the commander only to find that he has just died from influenza. Elsewhere, Felix and his brother-in-law are severely wounded in training botch-ups.

The action of the novel is witnessed through several centres of consciousness. The main ones—in addition to Gabriel and Felix—are (in Britain) Gabriel's wife, Charis, and (in Africa) an American planter, Temple Smith, whose martial activities are simply a means of continuing his quest to recover a prized farm machine confiscated by the Germans. *An Ice-Cream War* is easily Boyd's most substantial work, even if he rather over-does the ironies and also perpetrates some false notes, notably the employment—decidedly old-hat—of a Scottish sergeant with an impenetrable accent.

The stories in *On the Yankee Station* do not represent Boyd at his best, several might have been written for the glossy magazine market. The remainder feature some fine ideas, but they are developed perfunctorily and without the stylistic verve of the novels. "Next Boat from Douala" and "The Coup," however, are noteworthy for the presence of Morgan Leafy, while "Hardly Ever" deals with the public school world also explored in the screenplays of *School Ties*.

—David Montrose

BOYLAN, Clare. Irish. Born in Dublin, in 1948. Educated at schools in Dublin. Married Alan Wilkes in 1970. Reporter, 1968–69, and staff feature writer, 1973–78, Dublin *Evening Press*; Editor, *Young Woman* magazine, 1969–71, and *Image* magazine, 1978–81, both Dublin. Presenter, Radio Telefís Eireann radio and television, book reviewer, *Cosmopolitan*, London, and contributor, *Good Housekeeping*, London, and *Vogue*, New York. Recipient: Journalist of the Year Award (Dublin), 1983. Lives in Kilbride, County Wicklow. Agent: Gill Coleridge, Anthony Sheil Associates, 43 Doughty Street, London WC1N 2LF, England.

PUBLICATIONS

Novels

Holy Pictures. London, Hamish Hamilton, and New York, Summit, 1983.
Last Resorts. London, Hamish Hamilton, 1984; New York, Summit, 1986.

Short Stories

A Nail on the Head. London, Hamish Hamilton, 1983; New York, Penguin, 1985.

*   *   *

Clare Boylan chronicles the struggles of the personality under threat. Her novels and short stories describe the search of lonely individuals for love and freedom in a hostile environment, where acquiescence to its soul-destroying rules is tacitly assumed. Met by society's concerted pressures, her heroines' search is often vain, but sometimes one manages to find a chink in the world's armour, casting off the role that has been chosen for her.

In *Holy Pictures* it is the society of adults which dominates. To Nan and Mary, growing up in Dublin in 1925, the world of their elders is marked out by rules specifically designed to thwart the dreams and desires of the young, its unyielding rigidity typified by the old-fashioned corset produced by the workers in their father's factory. Nan, coming painfully and uncomprehendingly to adolescence in a strict convent school, is lured by the dream-world of the cinema with its promises of fame and beauty, finding a welcome glamour in the Jewish Schweitzer family, whose walls bear the cut-out pictures of the movie stars she worships at a distance. Inwardly Nan longs to escape from the drab, routine life which fate has allocated to her, glimpses of freedom coming to her in the brief moments of joy she finds, such as her dance as the fairy at a school concert: "She was a star, elevated as the lovely ladies of America who wore coatees of mink and ermine and walked on spirals of celestial stairs." Such dreams as she has, however—like Mary's money-making schemes—break down before the order of the adult world, met by a blind wall of indifference and rejection. Through the eyes of the teenage girls, Boylan reveals a grown-up universe appalling in its brutal, crass stupidity and pettiness, remarkable only for its ability to crush youthful ideals. To Nan and Mary, adulthood offers years of drudgery, and initiation into the more squalid activities of the human race. The author presents their rites of passage quietly, without sensationalism deftly contrasting the innocence of her central characters against the flawed, often grotesque figures of their elders. Touches of humour lighten the story at times, notably with the comic servant Nellie and her amusing distortion of language. Such moments, however, only serve to emphasize the prevailing darkness of what is in essence a tragic work.

Holy Pictures is a skilfully-achieved creation, Boylan's outwardly simple style concealing the depth of her insights. Visual imagery is subtly but continually used throughout the book—family photographs, pictures of film stars, the religious cards that give the novel its title and which Mary handles like talismans. Taken together, they provide a series of ikons which serve as a focus for the dreams and longings of the characters. Unreal as the images themselves are, they are shown as calling out the purest qualities in those who worship them.

Last Resorts reverses the vision of *Holy Pictures*, its single-parent heroine dominated by her teenage children and their selfish needs. Foul-mouthed, crude, and unpleasant, the youngsters are exact counterparts of the adults in the previous novel, callously using their mother for their own convenience. Their tyranny is echoed by the brutal "modernising" and milling tourists of a Greek island next to the one on which the family are holidaying. Harriet, the heroine of the book, is shown as essentially a conventional person who longs for the domesticity shorn from her by the desertion of her husband. "Contentment was more nourishing than joy. Being in love was not very peaceful." Snatching at happiness with a married lover who refuses to supply it, and thwarted when the needs of her children are compounded by the return of her husband and an additional set of demands, Harriet is forced to choose between the satisfaction of others and her own freedom. Boylan portrays her inward and outer struggles in a clear, restrained prose whose quietness occasionally startles with the sharp single-line image, as when Harriet visualizes the bare breasts of a woman as captive white rabbits. The reader comes to know the heroine gradually, encountering with her the monstrous dependence of her family, and the seeming reasonableness of their outrageous demands. Set in the present and in a more exotic location than *Holy Pictures*, *Last Resorts* nevertheless shows the exploration of a closely allied theme.

The stories of *A Nail on the Head* again pursue the search for love in all its forms. "The Wronged Woman" is a witty portrayal of the differing perceptions of a husband by his two wives, and in the generation clash of "Bad Natured Dog" the author displays considerable skill in showing the conflict of outward appearance and inner reality. The stories range from the frivolity of "Ears" to the bedroom tragedy of "Married," and the macabre atmosphere of "Mama" and "For Your Own Bad," both of which are peopled by grotesques akin to those of *Holy Pictures*. In each story the quiet, understated style creeps stealthily up on the reader, surprising and shocking by sudden twists of plot and startling revelations.

—Geoff Sadler

* * *

BOYLE, Kay. American. Born in St. Paul, Minnesota, 19 February 1902. Educated at the Cincinnati Conservatory of Music; Ohio Mechanics Institute, 1917–19. Married 1) Richard Brault in 1922 (divorced); 2) Laurence Vail in 1931 (divorced), five daughters and one son; 3) Baron Joseph von Franckenstein in 1943 (died, 1963). Lived in Europe for 30 years. Foreign correspondent, *The New Yorker*, 1946–53. Professor of English, San Francisco State University, 1963–80; since 1980 Professor Emerita. Lecturer, New School for Social Research, New York, 1962; Fellow, Wesleyan University, Middletown, Connecticut, 1963; Director, New York Writers Conference, Wagner College, New York, 1964; Fellow, Radcliffe Institute for Independent Study, Cambridge, Massachusetts, 1964–65; Writer-in-Residence, University of Massachusetts, Amherst, 1967, Hollins College, Virginia, 1970–71, and Eastern Washington University, Cheney, 1984. Recipient: Guggenheim fellowship, 1934, 1961; O. Henry Award, for short story, 1935, 1941; San Francisco Art Commission award, 1978; National Endowment for the Arts grant, 1980; Before Columbus Foundation award, 1983; Celtic Foundation award, 1984. D.Litt: Columbia College, Chicago, 1971; Southern Illinois University, Carbondale, 1982; D.H.L.: Skidmore College, Saratoga Springs, New York, 1977. Member, American Academy, 1979. Agent: Watkins Loomis Agency, 150 East 35th Street, New York, New York 10016, U.S.A.

PUBLICATIONS

Novels

Plagued by the Nightingale.   New York, Cape and Smith, and London, Cape, 1931.
Year Before Last.   New York, Smith, and London, Faber, 1932.
Gentlemen, I Address You Privately.   New York, Smith, 1933; London, Faber, 1934.
My Next Bride.   New York, Harcourt Brace, 1934; London, Faber, 1935.
Death of a Man.   New York, Harcourt Brace, and London, Faber, 1936.
Monday Night.   New York, Harcourt Brace, and London, Faber, 1938.

Primer for Combat.   New York, Simon and Schuster, 1942; London, Faber, 1943.
Avalanche.   New York, Simon and Schuster, and London, Faber, 1944.
A Frenchman Must Die.   New York, Simon and Schuster, and London, Faber, 1946.
1939.   New York, Simon and Schuster, and London, Faber, 1948.
His Human Majesty.   New York, McGraw Hill, 1949; London, Faber, 1950.
The Seagull on the Step.   New York, Knopf, and London, Faber, 1955.
Generation Without Farewell.   New York, Knopf, 1960.
The Underground Woman.   New York, Doubleday, 1975.

Short Stories

Short Stories.   Paris, Black Sun Press, 1929.
Wedding Day and Other Stories.   New York, Cape and Smith, 1930; London, Pharos, 1932.
The First Lover and Other Stories.   New York, Smith and Haas, 1933; London, Faber, 1937.
The White Horses of Vienna and Other Stories.   New York, Harcourt Brace, 1936; London, Faber, 1937.
The Crazy Hunter: Three Short Novels.   New York, Harcourt Brace, 1940; as *The Crazy Hunter and Other Stories*, London, Faber, 1940.
Thirty Stories.   New York, Simon and Schuster, 1946; London, Faber, 1948.
The Smoking Mountain: Stories of Post War Germany.   New York, McGraw Hill, 1951; London, Faber, 1952.
Three Short Novels.   Boston, Beacon Press, 1958.
Nothing Ever Breaks Except the Heart.   New York, Doubleday, 1966.
Fifty Stories.   New York, Doubleday, 1980; London, Penguin, 1981.

Uncollected Short Story

"St. Stephen's Green," in *Prize Stories 1981: The O. Henry Awards*, edited by William Abrahams.   New York, Doubleday, 1981.

Verse

A Statement.   New York, Modern Editions Press, 1932.
A Glad Day.   New York, New Directions, 1938.
American Citizen: Naturalized in Leadville, Colorado.   New York, Simon and Schuster, 1944.
Collected Poems.   New York, Knopf, 1962.
Testament for My Students and Other Poems.   New York, Doubleday, 1970.
This Is Not a Letter and Other Poems.   College Park, Maryland, Sun and Moon Press, 1985.

Other

The Youngest Camel (for children).   Boston, Little Brown, and London, Faber, 1939; revised edition, New York, Harper, 1959; Faber, 1960.
Breaking the Silence: Why a Mother Tells Her Son about the Nazi Era.   New York, Institute of Human Relations Press-American Jewish Committee, 1962.
Pinky, The Cat Who Liked to Sleep (for children).   New York, Crowell Collier, 1966.
Pinky in Persia (for children).   New York, Crowell Collier, 1968.

Being Geniuses Together 1920–1930, with Robert McAlmon. New York, Doubleday, 1968; London, Joseph, 1970; revised edition, London, Hogarth Press, 1984.
The Long Walk at San Francisco State and Other Essays. New York, Grove Press, 1970.
Four Visions of America, with others. Santa Barbara, California, Capra Press, 1977.
Words That Must Somehow Be Said: Selected Essays of Kay Boyle 1927–1984, edited by Elizabeth S. Bell. Berkeley, California, North Point Press, and London, Chatto and Windus, 1985.

Editor, with Laurence Vail and Nina Conarain, *365 Days.* New York, Harcourt Brace, and London, Cape, 1936.
Editor, *The Autobiography of Emanuel Carnevali.* New York, Horizon Press, 1967.
Editor, with Justine Van Gundy, *Enough of Dying! An Anthology of Peace Writings.* New York, Dell, 1972.

Translator, *Don Juan*, by Joseph Delteil. New York, Cape and Smith, 1931.
Translator, *Mr. Knife, Miss Fork*, by René Crevel. Paris, Black Sun Press, 1931.
Translator, *The Devil in the Flesh*, by Raymond Radiguet. New York, Smith, 1932; London, Grey Walls Press, 1949.
Translator, *Babylon*, by René Crevel. Berkeley, California, North Point Press, 1985.

Ghost-writer for the books *Relations and Complications, Being the Recollections of H.H. the Dayang Muda of Sarawak* by Gladys Palmer Brooke, London, Lane, 1929, and *Yellow Dusk* by Bettina Bedwell, London, Hurst and Blackett, 1937.

*

Manuscript Collection: Morris Library, Southern Illinois University, Cardondale.

*   *   *

What is most memorable in the writing of Kay Boyle are specific scenes—the sight of the sea tide building and crashing through the mouth of a river; a young man, sick with tuberculosis, leaning over a basin to vomit blood; a bus-driver arguing recklessly with his passengers while the bus careens along a cliff road; a run-over dog pulling itself forward, as its spilled-out entrails drag and turn white in the dust; Americans and Germans waiting over real fox holes in a German forest, ready to club the young foxes as they come out, and underground, moving through the tunnels, now near, now distant, the sound of the yelping pack and pursing dog.

Boyle's concern here is to heighten our responses to these events. She asks us not only to respond to the vivid and extreme sensations which they present, but to see them in sharp moral and aesthetic terms, as beautiful or dangerous or agonizingly brutal.

It is this intense kind of involvement that Boyle asks from us generally. She offers very little neutral ground on which we may look at these scenes on our own. The youthful idealists, who play a major role in her novels, will give us, I think, the right emotional cues for appreciating her work. Inexperienced in the ways of the world, their feelings are open and unmitigated; they do not quite believe in evil and yet they are deeply troubled by pain and injustice. Bridget, Victoria John, Mary Farrant, Milly Roberts—young Americans whose destinies are connected with Europe—are such figures. If the

fictional situation would seem to echo James, there are major differences in its development, for Kay Boyle's morality is active rather than introspective.

Indeed, whether her heroes be young Americans in Europe or former German soldiers, they express themselves in concrete acts—Mary Farrant makes her way up a rocky cliff to save the dwarf Marrakech; a middle-aged dandy, terrified of horses, enters the stall of a blind horse, and, for his daughter's sake, stays there while it kicks and rears in fright; Jaeger, a German journalist and ex-POW from the Afrika Corps, crawls over a heap of sliding rubble to give a cigarette to a power shovel driver trapped inside his cab.

What her heroes have in common is the courage to act—it is the only thing people ever remember, one character says. But action is, of course, no guarantee of success. Involved in every human venture, it would seem, are elements that bring about its destruction. Those elements may be physical in nature —not malevolent but merely indifferent—stupid accident, or man's incapacity to make a social world that is supportive and helpful.

Thus, in *Plagued by the Nightingale*, the closely bound world of a French family becomes so destructive that three daughters and a son wait desperately for an escape. Only Charlotte, the fourth daughter, loves her richly domestic life and her place within the family; and only Charlotte is deprived of it by death. In *Year Before Last* Martin, a young poet, dying of tuberculosis, and Eve, his aunt, are bound together by their dedication to art. Yet the emotion that shapes their lives is Eve's cruel jealousy of Hanah, whom Martin loves and who would shield him from the agonies of poverty and illness. In *My Next Bride* the artist, Sorrel, uses the common funds of the art colony to buy a magnificent and expensive automobile. In this shallow attempt to escape poverty and ugliness, he betrays the destitute craftsmen who work for him, as well as the artistic creed he has professed to live by.

Boyle's novels have a potentially tragic feeling. The qualities she projects in her strongest characters—courage to act as a counter to failure, energy rather than hopeless despair—offer this possibility. Very often, it seems wasted, for although Boyle insists upon courageous action, the possible choices she sees in such action are limited. Also, perhaps equally harmful, these choices do not necessarily grow out of the fictional situation; they seem fixed from the beginning. It is for this reason, perhaps, that her characters sometimes take unreal positions—in *Avalanche* the mountain men are total in their dedication to a good cause, the German agent, total in his dedication to a bad one; in *The Seagull on the Step* the doctor commits melodramatic villainies, the teacher-reformer, heroic deeds; in *Generation Without Farewell* the American colonel is brutal and gross, his wife and daughter are gentle and sensitive. Such extreme divisions in realistic novels are unconvincing. In relation to this kind of fictional situation, we are no longer active readers but spectators, waiting for the author to tell us what is right, what is sad and pitiable, what is mean.

There is a problem, also, in Boyle's wish to discover in technology and social reform, the elements of high moral adventure. In *Generation Without Farewell*, for example, Jaeger, the German journalist, and his fellow-townsmen drive through the night to pick up an iron lung for Christoph Horn, dying of bulbar polio, and arrive back in time to save Horn's life, if only for a few days. Later, after Horn's death, the director of America House, Honerkamp, erects a huge thermometer in the town square to register donations for an iron lung that, hopefully, the town will now buy for itself. In both instances, we are expected to share the emotions of the major figures, of Jaegar, who sees the journey as "keeping death at bay," and of Honerkamp, who believes that the Germans will learn something about democracy from this community chest effort.

The focus here is on technical solutions—the iron lung for saving a life; the thermometer, for registering a common social effort. Both are stock images that offer very little opportunity for a fresh response. More important, perhaps, they are mechanical and static. Our involvement with them is necessarily limited, for they have no power to draw us into a situation in which our feelings may be deepened and extended. The best we can offer is a set response.

Yet, I am sure that Boyle would never exclude these social possibilities, whatever the literary risks. In an early poem, she uses the phrase "tough taste." It is a good phrase to describe her conception of what she is doing.

What gives her work strength are not these special interests, but her understanding that our human connections lies finally in our limitations, most of all in our common morality. From the beginning, she has had this kind of knowledge.

At moments we see it expressed with startling clarity. In her first novel, Charlotte's family is hastily called to her bedside. Those who have waited through the day—Charlotte's young children, her sisters—make their way through the dark, wet fall night, to Charlotte's house, up the great stairs and to her room. There, they wait in silence until the door is opened, and the children walk "calmly into the roar of Charlotte's death." In her novel of postwar Germany, a power shovel in downtown Frankfurt accidentally unearths an underground air raid shelter and releases a single survivor, entombed there since the war. As the mad, tattered figure runs wildly across the upturned ground, bewildered by his resurrection, any ideals we may hold about nationality, military success, moral justification, diminish into nothingness. Only a sense of our common inhumanity persists.

In the short stories also, Boyle shows us the complicated devastation that human beings can work on one another and on themselves. Among the best are the stories of postwar Germany in *The Smoking Mountain*. The scale is modest—an American army wife shops in a PX supermarket, three boys search out a center for lost children, a group of local actors put on a play at a Weinstube—the right dimension to make us understand such a catastrophe as an individual, day-to-day experience. Likewise, in the brilliant reportorial piece that opens the collection, on the murder trial of a minor Gestapo official, Heinrich Baab, nothing is obscured by the blare of historical significance. Baab, accused of 57 murders, was, as Boyle says, a "small criminal." For those who sometimes have doubts about the relationship between art and the direct observation of experience, these stories should give a clear answer.

—Jacqueline Hoefer

BRADBURY, Malcolm (Stanley). British. Born in Sheffield, Yorkshire, 7 September 1932. Educated at West Bridgford Grammar School, Nottingham, 1943–50; University College, Leicester, 1950–53, B.A. (1st class honours) 1953; Queen Mary College, University of London (Research Scholar), 1953–55, M.A. in English 1955; Indiana University, Bloomington (English-Speaking Union Fellow), 1955–56; University of Manchester, 1956–58, Ph.D. in American Studies 1962; Yale University, New Haven, Connecticut (British Association for American Studies Fellow), 1958–59. Married Elizabeth Salt in 1959; two sons. Staff Tutor in Literature and

Drama, Department of Adult Education, University of Hull, Yorkshire, 1959–61; Lecturer in English, University of Birmingham, 1961–65. Lecturer, 1965–67, Senior Lecturer, 1967–69, Reader in English, 1969–70, and since 1970, Professor of American Studies, University of East Anglia, Norwich. Visiting Professor, University of California, Davis, 1966; Visiting Fellow, All Souls College, Oxford, 1969; Visiting Professor, University of Zurich, 1972; Fanny Hurst Professor, Washington University, St. Louis, 1982; Davis Professor, University of Queensland, Brisbane, and Visiting Professor, Griffith University, Nathan, Queensland, 1983. Series editor, Stratford-upon-Avon Studies, for Arnold publishers, London, 1971–84, and Contemporary Writers series for Methuen publishers, London. Recipient: American Council of Learned Societies fellowship, 1965; Royal Society of Literature Heinemann Award, 1976. D.Litt.: University of Leicester, 1986. Fellow, Royal Society of Literature, 1975; Honorary Fellow, Queen Mary College, 1984. Agent: Curtis Brown, 162–168 Regent Street, London W1R 5TA; or, 10 Astor Place, New York, New York 10003, U.S.A. Address: School of English and American Studies, University of East Anglia, Norwich, Norfolk NR4 7TJ, England.

PUBLICATIONS

Novels

Eating People Is Wrong. London, Secker and Warburg, 1959; New York, Knopf, 1960.
Stepping Westward. London, Secker and Warburg, 1965; Boston, Houghton Mifflin, 1966.
The History Man. London, Secker and Warburg, 1975; Boston, Houghton Mifflin, 1976.
Rates of Exchange. London, Secker and Warburg, and New York, Knopf, 1983.

Short Stories

Who Do You Think You Are? Stories and Parodies. London, Secker and Warburg, 1976; augmented edition, London, Arena, 1984.

Plays

Between These Four Walls (revue), with David Lodge and James Duckett (produced Birmingham, 1963).
Slap in the Middle (revue), with others (produced Birmingham, 1965).
The After Dinner Game, with Christopher Bigsby (televised, 1975). Included in *The After Dinner Game*, 1982.
Love on a Gunboat (televised, 1977). Included in *The After Dinner Game*, 1982.
Standing In for Henry (televised, 1980). Included in *The After Dinner Game*, 1982.
The After Dinner Game: Three Plays for Television. London, Arrow, 1982.

Radio Plays: *Paris France* (documentary), 1960; *This Sporting Life*, with Elizabeth Bradbury, from the novel by David Storey, 1974; *Scenes from Provincial Life* and *Scenes from Married Life*, with Elizabeth Bradbury, from the novels by William Cooper, 1975–76; *Patterson*, with Christopher Bigsby, 1981; *Congress*, 1981; *See a Friend This Weekend*, 1984.

Television Plays: *The After Dinner Game*, with Christopher Bigsby, 1975; *Stones* (*The Mind Beyond* series), with Christopher Bigsby, 1976; *Love on a Gunboat*, 1977; *The Enigma*, from the story by John Fowles, 1980; *Standing In for Henry*, 1980; *Blott on the Landscape* series, from the novel by Tom Sharpe, 1985.

Verse

Two Poets, with Allan Rodway.   Nottingham, Byron Press, 1966.

Other

All Dressed Up and Nowhere to Go (revised editions).   London, Pavilion-Joseph, 1982.
  Phogey! How to Have Class in a Classless Society.   London, Parrish, 1960.
  All Dressed Up and Nowhere to Go: The Poor Man's Guide to the Affluent Society.   London, Parrish, 1962.
Evelyn Waugh.   Edinburgh, Oliver and Boyd, 1964.
What Is a Novel?   London, Arnold, 1969.
The Social Context of Modern English Literature.   Oxford, Blackwell, and New York, Schocken, 1971.
Possibilities: Essays on the State of the Novel.   London, Oxford University Press, 1973.
The Outland Dart: American Writers and European Modernism (lecture).   London, Oxford University Press, 1978.
Saul Bellow.   London, Methuen, 1982.
The Expatriate Tradition in American Literature.   Durham, British Association for American Studies, 1982.
The Modern American Novel.   Oxford and New York, Oxford University Press, 1983.

Editor, *Forster: A Collection of Critical Essays.*   Englewood Cliffs, New Jersey, Prentice Hall, 1966.
Editor, *Pudd'nhead Wilson, and Those Extraordinary Twins*, by Mark Twain.   London, Penguin, 1969.
Editor, *E.M. Forster: A Passage to India: A Casebook.*   London, Macmillan, 1970.
Editor, with Eric Mottram, *U.S.A.*, in *The Penguin Companion to Literature 3.*   London, Penguin, and New York, McGraw Hill, 1971.
Editor, with James McFarlane, *Modernism 1890–1930.*   London, Penguin, 1976; Atlantic Highlands, New Jersey, Humanities Press, 1978.
Editor, *The Novel Today: Contemporary Writers on Modern Fiction.*   Manchester, Manchester University Press, and Totowa, New Jersey, Rowman and Littlefield, 1977.
Editor, with Howard Temperley, *Introduction to American Studies.*   London, Longman, 1981.

*

Manuscript Collection: Nottingham Public Library.

Critical Studies: "Fictions of Academe" by George Watson, in *Encounter* (London), November 1978; "Images of Sociology and Sociologists in Fiction" by John Kramer, in *Contemporary Sociology* (Washington, D.C.), May 1979; "The Business of University Novels" by J.P. Kenyon, in *Encounter* (London), June 1980; "Malcolm Bradbury's *The History Man*: The Novelist as Reluctant Impresario" by Richard Todd, and interview with Todd, in *Dutch Quarterly Review* (Amsterdam), vol. 2, 1981–83; article by Melvin J. Friedman, in *British Novelists since 1960* edited by Jay L. Halio, Detroit, Gale, 1983; interviews in *The Radical Imagination and the Liberal Tradition* edited by Heide Ziegler and Christopher Bigsby, London, Junction, 1982, with Ronald Hayman, in *Books and Bookmen* (London), April 1983, with Alastair Morgan, in *Literary Review* (London), October 1983, and in *Novelists in Interview* by John Haffenden, London, Methuen, 1985.

Malcolm Bradbury comments:

My fiction—four novels and a volume of short stories written over 30 years—seems to me to have followed the evolving pattern of postwar British fiction generally. I started writing when novelists in Britain and America were showing a new moral confidence and a hope for humanity, following the defeat of Fascism and the fading of some of the disorders of the earlier part of the century. Despite the Holocaust and the coming of the atomic age, there was a liberal spirit strong in fiction, and I began writing in its mood of humanism and realism. If my books have a consistent theme, it is that they treat—with a growing irony and harshness, but always in the spirit of comedy—the problems of liberalism and moral responsibility. In the early novels the characters are concerned but confused moral agents, liberal less in a political than a moral sense. Their values were always subject to their own doubt and the novelist's irony, and the comedy turned toward pathos or tragedy as their confusions increased. Over time my irony, my sense of lost moral certainties, and my concern with fiction as form have increased. My first book, *Eating People Is Wrong*, written mostly when I was an undergraduate, but revised a little later, is largely about the academic world as world of decency, goodwill, and humanism. In *Stepping Westward* I started to explore the feeling that moral liberalism was in conflict with an age often indifferent to humanism and concerned with hard politics, reason and decency constantly at odds with interest and desire. By *The History Man* this theme became central, as the new radicalism made its post-humanist bid to claim the world. Howard Kirk, the central character, is a sociologist, but also a "history man" because he believes he can act to change history and transform individual lives, challenging humanism as an old philosophy of individualism and innocence. With *Rates of Exchange* I tried to show the fading sense of authenticity available to the individual in any modern state, though I trust I left a measure of hope that can come from the elusive, alternative power that is possessed by fiction-makers themselves.

Because my books have been largely set around universities—I began the first as a first-generation student fascinated by the academic world, for someone of my background anutter novelty—I have often been thought of as a "campus novelist" and a progenitor of the "university novel." But, though my first book is set around a British red-brick, the second around an American campus, and the third around a new university—I feel any setting which allowed me intelligent characters and intellectual and humanist issues would do as well. This perhaps is one reason why I set *Rates of Exchange* in an imaginary hardline Eastern European country. Another was that it marks a move away from the limited and provincial settings and the general self-protective Britishness in which I think English fiction becomes too easily encased. And this is a further reason why my books have changed. Happily, British fiction has shown signs of moving away from provincial realism toward a sense of membership in a larger, more dangerous contemporary world of writing. My books show this shift, and in particular *The History Man* and *Rates of Exchange*. Harsher in tone and more experimental technically, they challenge (as the novel, in responding to contemporary ideas, must) the old stable ideas of character, of realism of presentation, and moral confidence in which much fiction has been written. *Rates of Exchange* also deals with the problem of the contemporary British writer who uses a language much changed by its role as a world language, and for many people a second language. Again, the sense of authenticity of older, more certain meanings is lost, and stories become more dangerous and ambiguous. I realize that this makes my more recent books less companionable, but it also, I believe, makes them better.

The novel is a changing form for every writer who sees it as a mode of enquiry and not simply a conventional genre of entertainment. I see my books as works of comic and satirical observation on the decades in which they are set, but also displaying the stylistic pressures that change the form of fiction. Socially they cover the period from the moral 1950's through the liberation-seeking 1960's to the radical extremism of the early 1970's and then to the economically tight, bleak, and indifferent world of the 1980's. And in form they move from moral comedy through to a much greater technical concern and a harder tone in which the comic moves closer to the tragic. I am fascinated by the fictionality of fiction—which, for me, takes its power from the fact that I see all certain truths as fictions, and fiction as the form of scepticism which understands how fictions can become approximate forms of truth. The novelist must be concerned with responsibility to the real world, the historical world, in its immediate existence, but must also retain his or her scepticism. We live in the world where the real seems to have lost all authenticity, and style all substance, but in which the novelist, responsible for fiction, has to find a respect for truth and humanity. My own books have grown both bleaker and more concerned with such formal problems. But at the same time they are comedies of contemporary uncertainty, confusion, and pain, and if they find liberalism difficult and at times absurd they do not find it impossible. Like many writers I have moved away from naive realism to a greater sense of fictionality, but in the belief that fiction can bring us back toward historical awareness and a greater sense of what is of human value.

*   *   *

Ever since the 1959 publication of his first novel, *Eating People Is Wrong*, Malcolm Bradbury has been regarded as an extremely witty satirist, lampooning topical phenomena and issues. He excels in group scenes: the cautiously wild and slapstick university party that mixes faculty and students in *Eating People Is Wrong*; the American faculty committee meeting to choose a writer-in-residence that begins *Stepping Westward* and is ironically contrasted with the concluding one a year later; the department meeting that combines haggling over procedure, trivia, several forms of self-seeking, and genuine academic concerns in *The History Man*; the adult education class that was apparently cut from *Eating People Is Wrong* and, in revised form, printed in the collection of *Who Do You Think You Are?*; the guest lectures of and alcoholic lunches for the English linguist on a two-week tour of the country in "central Eastern Europe" that prides itself on "clean tractors" and a "reformed watercress industry" in *Rates of Exchange*. All these pieces bring people, representing various points of view on some current question of politics or communal definition, into sharp, comically outrageous conflict or misunderstanding.

Bradbury often castigates a whole contemporary millieu through scenes like with "with-it," consciously "existential" party, a license for free self-definition, arranged by the "new university" sociologist, Howard Kirk, in *The History Man*. Bradbury also exploits his talent for mimicry of current attitudes, modes of speech (like the variety of ways to mangle English in *Rates of Exchange*), and the style and themes of other writers. A long section of *Who Do You Think You Are?*,

for example, contains astringent parodies of Snow, Amis, Murdoch, Braine, Sillitoe, and others, along with less biting and salient echoes of Angus Wilson and Lawrence Durrell. The use of Amis (with whose early work Bradbury's has often been compared) is particularly resonant. Like Amis, Bradbury sometimes includes characters from one fiction in another, like the free-loving psychologist, Flora Beniform, who is both Howard Kirk's uncommitted mistress in *The History Man* and a central character on the television panel concerning modern sexual mores satirized in the story "Who Do You Think You Are?" As an in-joke, Bradbury even appropriates the Amis character who doesn't appear, the fraudulent L.S. Caton used in a number of novels until Amis finally killed him off in *The Anti-Death League*. Bradbury makes him a professor, scheduled to visit Benedict Arnold University in the U.S. to give a lecture on the "angry young men," who never arrives. In spite of all the critical comparisons and interlocking references, Bradbury's satire is different from Amis's, Bradbury generally more concerned with issues and ideas, less implicitly committed to pragmatic success in the world or, until the recent *Rates of Exchange*, to mocking various forms of contemporary incompetence.

Much of Bradbury's fiction takes place within a university setting: the provincial red-brick during the 1950's in *Eating People Is Wrong*, the American university in the flat wilderness of the Plains states in *Stepping Westward*, the new south coast university in 1972 in *The History Man*. Yet, as Bradbury himself has rightly insisted, the applications of his fiction extend beyond the university, just as the implications of his moral treatments of contemporary experience are far from slapstick comedy. In *Stepping Westward* the Englishman, James Walker, who becomes writer-in-residence at the "moral supermarket" of the American university, begins with his own "decent modest radicalism" and tries to extend himself to assimilate more of the modern world, looking for "sense and design." The plot depends on Walker's public refusal to sign an American loyalty oath, part of his English "faith in unbelief," and the America he finds is one of "violence and meaninglessness and anarchy." In *The History Man* Howard Kirk, seen far less sympathetically than James Walker is, seeks "liberation" and "emancipation" in the new university for himself and others, ignoring or condescending to his old friend, Beamish, a rather bumbling locus of value in the novel, who claims "there is an inheritance of worthwhile life in this country." In this novel, written entirely in the rush of the present tense, Kirk chooses instead to redevelop the town, to lie, to manipulate others in the name of the "now" and the "new," and to ignore the voice of a young English teacher who sees her function as simply reading and talking about books. In both novels Bradbury's moral focus is clear and searching, although it sometimes seems slightly provincial. He attacks the self-seeking, the self-deceptive, and the meretricious, like a career academic named Froelich who becomes chairman in *Stepping Westward* and Kirk himself in *The History Man*. Yet some of Bradbury's work has more complexity and distance than outlining the moral framework might suggest. Sometimes, as in *The History Man*, which ends with Kirk's wife deliberately pushing her arm through the window, an act of self-destruction like that more ambivalently performed by Beamish at an earlier party, or in a short story entitled "A Very Hospitable Person," the satire seems brittle, almost cruel, in denying the central figures any humanity or self-doubt. At other times, as in an excellent story called "A Breakdown," about a student having a futile affair with a married man in Chesterfield who runs off to Spain to punish herself, or as in *Stepping Westward*, where James Walker recognizes that America has defeated him, that, in spite of all his morality, he could not really handle his own freedom to define himself, Bradbury's perspective is more sympathetic without diluting the moral concern. A prefatory note to *Rates of Exchange* characterizes the novel as "a paper fiction, offered for exchange" that illustrates "our duty to lie together, in the cause, of course, of truth." Beneath its comic texture of constant mutual misunderstanding and incompetence (sometimes overdone), Bradbury sensitively questions the comfortable assumption of virtue or truth in any of the various national, political, intellectual, or sexual languages that form systems of human exchange.

—James Gindin

BRADBURY, Ray(mond Douglas). American. Born in Waukegan, Illinois, 22 August 1920. Educated at Los Angeles High School, graduated 1938. Married Marguerite Susan McClure in 1947; four daughters. Since 1943, full-time writer. President, Science-Fantasy Writers of America, 1951–53. Member of the Board of Directors, Screen Writers Guild of America, 1957–61. Recipient: O. Henry Prize, 1947, 1948; Benjamin Franklin Award, 1954; American Academy award, 1954; Boys' Clubs of America Junior Book Award, 1956; Golden Eagle Award, for screenplay, 1957; Ann Radcliffe Award, 1965, 1971; Writers Guild award, 1974; Aviation and Space Writers award, for television documentary, 1979; Gandalf Award, 1980. D.Litt.: Whittier College, California, 1979. Agent: Harold Matson Company, 276 Fifth Avenue, New York, New York 10001. Address: 10265 Cheviot Drive, Los Angeles, California 90064, U.S.A.

PUBLICATIONS

Novels

Fahrenheit 451.   New York, Ballantine, 1953; London, Hart Davis, 1954.
Dandelion Wine.   New York, Doubleday, and London, Hart Davis, 1957.
Something Wicked This Way Comes.   New York, Simon and Schuster, 1962; London, Hart Davis, 1963.
Death Is a Lonely Business.   New York, Knopf, 1985.

Short Stories

Dark Carnival.   Sauk City, Wisconsin, Arkham House, 1947; abridged edition, London, Hamish Hamilton, 1948; abridged edition, as *The Small Assassin*, London, New English Library, 1962.
The Martian Chronicles.   New York, Doubleday, 1950; as *The Silver Locusts*, London, Hart Davis, 1951.
The Illustrated Man.   New York, Doubleday, 1951; London, Hart Davis, 1952.
The Golden Apples of the Sun.   New York, Doubleday, and London, Hart Davis, 1953.
The October Country.   New York, Ballantine, 1955; London, Hart Davis, 1956.
A Medicine for Melancholy.   New York, Doubleday, 1959.
The Day It Rained Forever.   London, Hart Davis, 1959.
The Machineries of Joy.   New York, Simon and Schuster, and London, Hart Davis, 1964.

The Vintage Bradbury.   New York, Random House, 1965.
The Autumn People.   New York, Ballantine, 1965.
Tomorrow Midnight.   New York, Ballantine, 1966.
Twice Twenty Two (selection).   New York, Doubleday, 1966.
I Sing the Body Electric!   New York, Knopf, 1969; London, Hart Davis, 1970.
Bloch and Bradbury, with Robert Bloch.   New York, Tower, 1969; as *Fever Dreams and Other Fantasies*, London, Sphere, 1970.
(*Selected Stories*), edited by Anthony Adams.   London, Harrap, 1975.
Long after Midnight.   New York, Knopf, 1976; London, Hart Davis MacGibbon, 1977.
The Best of Bradbury.   New York, Bantam, 1976.
To Sing Strange Songs.   Exeter, Devon, Wheaton, 1979.
The Stories of Ray Bradbury.   New York, Knopf, and London, Granada, 1980.
The Last Circus, and The Electrocution.   Northridge, California, Lord John Press, 1980.
Dinosaur Tales.   New York, Bantam, 1983.
A Memory for Murder.   New York, Dell, 1984.

Uncollected Short Stories

"Hollerbochen's Dilemma," in *Imagination* (Evanston, Illinois), January 1938.
"Pendulum," with Henry Hasse, in *Super Science* (Kokomo, Indiana), November 1941.
"Eat, Drink, and Be Wary," in *Astounding* (New York), July 1942.
"The Candle," in *Weird Tales* (New York), November 1942.
"The Piper," in *Thrilling Wonder Stories* (New York), February 1943.
"Gabriel's Horn," with Henry Hasse, in *Captain Future* (New York), Spring 1943.
"Subterfuge," in *Astonishing* (Chicago), April 1943.
"Promotion to Satellite," in *Thrilling Wonder Stories* (New York), Fall 1943.
"And Watch the Fountains" and "Doodad," in *Astounding* (New York), September 1943.
"The Ducker," in *Weird Tales* (New York), November 1943.
"The Sea Shell," in *Weird Tales* (New York), January 1944.
"The Monster Maker," in *Planet* (New York), Spring 1944.
"I, Rocket," in *Amazing* (New York), May 1944.
"Morgue Ship," in *Planet* (New York), Summer 1944.
"Bang! You're Dead!," in *Weird Tales* (New York), September 1944.
"Lazarus Come Forth," in *Planet* (New York), Winter 1944.
"Undersea Guardians," in *Amazing* (New York), December 1944.
"The Poems," in *Weird Tales* (New York), January 1945.
"The Watchers," in *Weird Tales* (New York), May 1945.
"Final Victim," with Henry Hasse, in *Amazing* (New York), February 1946.
"Defense Mech," in *Planet* (New York), Spring 1946.
"Rocket Skin," in *Thrilling Wonder Stories* (New York), Spring 1946.
"Lorelei of the Red Mist," with Leigh Brackett, in *Planet* (New York), Summer 1946.
"Rocket Summer," in *Planet* (New York), Spring 1947.
"Tomorrow and Tomorrow," in *Fantastic Adventures* (New York), May 1947.
"The Irritated People," in *Thrilling Wonder Stories* (New York), December 1947.
"The October Game," in *Weird Tales* (New York), March 1948.

"The Black Ferris," in *Weird Tales* (New York), May 1948.
"The Square Pegs," in *Thrilling Wonder Stories* (New York), October 1948.
"Asleep in Armageddon," in *Planet* (New York), Winter 1948.
"The Silence," in *Super Science* (Kokomo, Indiana), January 1949.
"Changeling," in *Super Science* (Kokomo, Indiana), July 1949.
"The Lonely Ones," in *Startling* (New York), July 1949.
"Holiday," in *Arkham Sampler* (Sauk City, Wisconsin), Autumn 1949.
"A Blade of Grass," in *Thrilling Wonder Stories* (New York), December 1949.
"Payment in Full," in *Thrilling Wonder Stories* (New York), February 1950.
"Forever and the Earth," in *Planet* (New York), Spring 1950.
"Punishment Without Crime," in *Other Worlds* (Evanston, Indiana), March 1950.
"Death Wish," in *Planet* (New York), Fall 1950.
"The Fireman," in *Galaxy* (New York), February 1951.
"A Little Journey," in *Galaxy* (New York), August 1951.
"Bright Phoenix," in *Fantasy and Science Fiction* (New York), May 1963.
"The Year the Glop-Monster Won the Golden Lion at Cannes," in *Cavalier*, July 1966.
"The Hour of Ghosts," in *Saturday Review* (New York), 25 October 1969.
"The Parrot Who Met Papa," in *Playboy* (Chicago), January 1972.
"Trapdoor," in *Omni* (New York), April 1985.

Plays

The Meadow, in *Best One-Act Plays of 1947–48*, edited by Margaret Mayorga. New York, Dodd Mead, 1948.
The Anthem Sprinters and Other Antics (produced Los Angeles, 1968). New York, Dial Press, 1963.
The World of Ray Bradbury (produced Los Angeles, 1964; New York, 1965).
The Wonderful Ice-Cream Suit (produced Los Angeles, 1965). Included in *The Wonderful Ice-Cream Suit and Other Plays*, 1972.
The Day It Rained Forever. New York, French, 1966.
The Pedestrian. New York, French, 1966.
Christus Apollo, music by Jerry Goldsmith (produced Los Angeles, 1969).
The Wonderful Ice-Cream Suit and Other Plays (includes *The Veldt* and *To the Chicago Abyss*). New York, Bantam, 1972; London, Hart Davis, 1973.
The Veldt (produced London, 1980). Included in *The Wonderful Ice-Cream Suit and Other Plays*, 1972.
Leviathan 99 (produced Los Angeles, 1972).
Pillar of Fire and Other Plays for Today, Tomorrow, and Beyond Tomorrow (includes *Kaleidoscope* and *The Foghorn*). New York, Bantam, 1975.
The Foghorn (produced New York, 1977). Included in *Pillar of Fire and Other Plays*, 1975.
That Ghost, That Bride of Time: Excerpts from a Play-in-Progress. Glendale, California, Squires, 1976.
The Martian Chronicles, adaptation of his own stories (produced Los Angeles, 1977).
Fahrenheit 451, adaptation of his own novel (produced Los Angeles, 1979).
Dandelion Wine, adaptation of his own story (produced Los Angeles, 1980).
Forever and the Earth (radio play). Athens, Ohio, Croissant, 1984.

Screenplays: *It Came from Outer Space*, with David Schwartz, 1952; *Moby-Dick*, with John Huston, 1956; *Icarus Montgolfier Wright*, with George C. Johnston, 1961; *Picasso Summer* (as Douglas Spaulding), with Edwin Booth, 1972.

Television Plays: *Shopping for Death*, 1956, *Design for Loving*, 1958, *Special Delivery*, 1959, *The Faith of Aaron Menefee*, 1962, and *The Life Work of Juan Díaz*, 1963 (all *Alfred Hitchcock Presents* series); *The Marked Bullet* (*Jane Wyman's Fireside Theater* series), 1956; *The Gift* (*Steve Canyon* series), 1958; *The Tunnel to Yesterday* (*Trouble Shooters* series), 1960; *I Sing the Body Electric!* (*Twilight Zone* series), 1962; *The Jail* (*Alcoa Premier* series), 1962; *The Groom* (*Curiosity Shop* series), 1971.

Verse

Old Ahab's Friend, and Friend to Noah, Speaks His Piece: A Celebration. Glendale, California, Squires, 1971.
When Elephants Last in the Dooryard Bloomed: Celebrations for Almost Any Day in the Year. New York, Knopf, 1973; London, Hart Davis MacGibbon, 1975.
That Son of Richard III: A Birth Announcement. Privately printed, 1974.
Where Robot Mice and Robot Men Run round in Robot Towns: New Poems, Both Light and Dark. New York, Knopf, 1977; London, Hart Davis MacGibbon, 1979.
Twin Hieroglyphs That Swim the River Dust. Northridge, California, Lord John Press, 1978.
The Bike Repairman. Northridge, California, Lord John Press, 1978.
The Author Considers His Resources. Northridge, California, Lord John Press, 1979.
The Aqueduct. Glendale, California, Squires, 1979.
The Attic Where the Meadow Greens. Northridge, California, Lord John Press, 1980.
Imagine. Northridge, California, Lord John Press, 1981.
The Haunted Computer and the Android Pope. New York, Knopf, and London, Granada, 1981.
The Complete Poems of Ray Bradbury. New York, Ballantine, 1982.
Two Poems. Northridge, California, Lord John Press, 1982.
The Love Affair. Northridge, California, Lord John Press, 1983.

Other

Switch on the Night (for children). New York, Pantheon, and London, Hart Davis, 1955.
R Is for Rocket (for children). New York, Doubleday, 1962; London, Hart Davis, 1968.
S Is for Space (for children). New York, Doubleday, 1966; London, Hart Davis, 1968.
Teacher's Guide: Science Fiction, with Lewy Olfson. New York, Bantam, 1968.
The Halloween Tree (for children). New York, Knopf, 1972; London, Hart Davis MacGibbon, 1973.
Mars and the Mind of Man. New York, Harper, 1973.
Zen and the Art of Writing, and The Joy of Writing. Santa Barbara, California, Capra Press, 1973.
The Mummies of Guanajuato, photographs by Archie Lieberman. New York, Abrams, 1978.
Beyond 1984: Remembrance of Things Future. New York, Targ, 1979.
About Norman Corwin. Northridge, California, Santa Susana Press, 1979.

The Ghosts of Forever, illustrated by Aldo Sessa.   New York, Rizzoli, 1981.
Los Angeles, photographs by West Light.   Port Washington, New York, Skyline Press, 1984.
Orange County, photographs by Bill Ross and others.   Port Washington, New York, Skyline Press, 1985.

Editor, *Timeless Stories for Today and Tomorrow*.   New York, Bantam, 1952.
Editor, *The Circus of Dr. Lao and Other Improbable Stories*.   New York, Bantam, 1956.

*

Critical Studies: interview in *Show* (New York), December 1964; introduction by Gilbert Highet to *The Vintage Bradbury*, 1965; "The Revival of Fantasy" by Russell Kirk, in *Triumph* (Washington, D.C.), May 1968; "Ray Bradbury's *Dandelion Wine*: Themes, Sources, and Style" by Marvin E. Mengeling, in *English Journal* (Champaign, Illinois), October 1971; *The Ray Bradbury Companion* (includes bibliography) by William F. Nolan, Detroit, Gale, 1975; *The Drama of Ray Bradbury* by Benjamin P. Indick, Baltimore, T-K Graphics, 1977; *The Bradbury Chronicles* by George Edgar Slusser, San Bernardino, California, Borgo Press, 1977; *Ray Bradbury* (includes bibliography) edited by Joseph D. Olander and Martin H. Greenberg, New York, Taplinger, and Edinburgh, Harris, 1980; *Ray Bradbury* by Wayne L. Johnson, New York, Ungar, 1980; *Ray Bradbury and the Poetics of Reverie: Fantasy, Science Fiction, and the Reader* by William F. Toupence, Ann Arbor, Michigan, UMI Research Press, 1984.

Ray Bradbury comments:

I am not so much a science-fiction writer as I am a magician, an illusionist. From my beginnings as a boy conjurer I grew up frightening myself so as to frighten others so as to cure the midnight in our souls. I have grown into a writer of the History of Ideas, I guess you might say. Any idea, no matter how large or small, that is busy growing itself alive, starting from nowhere and at last dominating a town, a culture, or a world, is of interest. Man the problem solver is the writer of my tales. Science fiction becoming science fact. The machineries of our world putting away and keeping our facts for us so they can be used and learned from. Machines as humanist teachers. Ideas of men built into those machines in order to help us survive and survive well. That's my broad and fascinating field, in which I will wander for a lifetime, writing past science fictions one day, future ones another. And all of it a wonder and a lark and a great love. I can't imagine writing any other way.

*   *   *

Although he has written the novels *Something Wicked This Way Comes* and *Fahrenheit 451*, Ray Bradbury is primarily a writer of short stories. Ever the storyteller, Bradbury aims in each story at producing the horror, the surprise, or the single dominant effect of Poe, one of his principal mentors. Nonetheless, his short story collections—notably *The Martian Chronicles* and *Dandelion Wine*—have an overall meaning which exceeds the meaning of the parts. Although he often seems to write about disparate bits of experience, Bradbury does have an identifiable view of life.

"Here There Be Tygers" (*R Is for Rocket*) contains several of the elements of that view. Astronauts land on a previously unknown planet. One of them fears that there are dangers ("tygers") on the planet, and he wishes to kill whatever is

alive and to exploit the remaining dead matter. He fulfills his own prophecy: the planet kills him. There *are* tygers on this pastoral world, but the other astronauts are drawn to them. The planet is not dead but alive, and when the astronauts dare to dream their favourite forbidden dreams into it, they awake to find them true. Bradbury follows Wordsworth, Coleridge, and Keats in believing that the childlike imagination can create a wonderful but also terrifying, and temporary, pleasure dome. All but one of the astronauts leave the strange Eden.

In *The Martian Chronicles*, the Eden is Mars. The ancient, delicate Martian civilization is destroyed by crass, polluting, materialistic American invaders. Bradbury the dystopian never entirely shuts out Bradbury the believer in fresh starts, however. "The Million Year Panic" concerns a family which escapes from nuclear war on Earth and uses the psychic energy or imaginative force of the dead Martians to make themselves into "Martians," capable of starting a new and more humane civilization.

The Illustrated Man and *Fahrenheit 451* continue the theme of the imagination threatened but ultimately triumphant. In "The Exiles" Poe, Bierce, and other writers of the fantastic and the macabre perish with their creations on Mars. Fahrenheit 451 is the temperature which the firemen of the future generate to burn all books. Both works point ways out, however. In *Fahrenheit 451* a rebel band memorizes books. "The Rocket," last story in *The Illustrated Man*, concerns a junkman who makes a rocket ship out of tin cans, which creates for his children the illusion of going to Mars.

Thus Bradbury believes that the imagination may operate in humble and private places as well as in space, and that it is as important to make familiar things new as to make the new things of the space age familiar. *Dandelion Wine* grafts suggestions of horror and science-fiction machines onto "Green Town," Illinois (presumably a version of the Waukegan, Illinois, of Bradbury's childhood). A man who can remember the Civil War past becomes a "time machine" to the boys who listen to his stories. Electric cars, lawnmowers, and trolleys become as mysterious as spaceships. Each day of the summer of 1928 a flask of dandelion wine—a noble thing made from a common plant—is put away for winter use. Bradbury's short stories are flasks of this wine: each day, or each story, is a little different and must be tasted separately. No single flask of wine contains all the wonders and terrors of our kaleidoscopic world.

The stories of *A Medicine for Melancholy* and *The Machineries of Joy* use terror and delight to purge the reader of melancholy. In "The Day It Rained Forever" 71-year-old Miss Hillgood, who has let her life pass by while she attended only to music, arrives at Joe Terle's Desert Hotel, where for years past there has been rain only one day of the year. When she begins to play, her music suddenly ceases to be sterile, and it magically causes a permanent end of the drought. To Bradbury, the unexpected can always happen. Life can always take a new turn precisely when and where you think of giving it up.

Both *The Machineries of Joy* and *I Sing the Body Electric!* contain Mars stories and others in the familiar Bradbury manner. But (particularly in the latter book) Bradbury experiments with replacing fantasy and plot twists with atmosphere, interior emotion, and character development. Too often the resulting stories lack the motivation and the logic which the fantastic never required. But Bradbury is a flexible and resourceful writer, and he may yet make successful use of the techniques of mainstream fiction.

Perhaps Bradbury's greatest value is as a social critic and a commentator on technology. Perceiving the madness of expansionist technology, Bradbury no longer shares the teen-age boy's worship of the astronaut corps in "R Is for Rocket." But his Martians have a more advanced technology than Earth's, in many respects—their cities last, and Earthmen's do not. "Space travel has made children of us all," says the philosopher on the verso of *The Martian Chronicles*. The American astronauts are childish idiots, but space travel also makes possible the childlike wonder of the million-year picnic. In "The End of the Beginning" (*A Medicine for Melancholy*) a man pauses from mowing his lawn to watch his son rocket into the twilight air to make the first space station. Bradbury suggests the unity of all technology: Ezkiel's wheel in the middle of the air, the wheeling space station and lawnmower, and the wheels in the man's watch. Moreover, life and technology are interrelated. The amoeba's climb from water to land prepared for man's climb from Earth. It is now a new age, but the man finishes mowing the lawn after watching the rocket launching. Bradbury is not against technology. He simply believes that man must look around and back at the same time he looks forward.

In the 1960's and 1970's Bradbury's career took an entirely new turn. Few of his recent stories are science fiction or fantasy. Instead, Bradbury now concentrates solely on what was always present in his writing, his compassion for likeable but inadequate people struggling against the tragic ironies of life, and often being successful in ways they did not expect. "The Parrot Who Met Pappa" is about the theft of a parrot who knew Hemingway by a writer, Hemingway's contemporary, whose life is still filled with jealousy of the great man. In "The Utterly Perfect Murder" Douglas returns to Green Town, Bradbury's fabled childhood world, to kill someone he hated as a child. But when Douglas finds this changed and almost pitiful person, his murderous feelings melt. "Have I Got a Chocolate Bar for You!" is the tale of a Catholic priest who saves an Irish Jew from the sin of chocolate addiction. His writing in the late 1970's and 1980's has been chiefly stories for children, crime fiction, and poetry.

As we can tell from his essay "Zen and the Art of Writing," Bradbury is an ambitious writer with a theory behind what he is doing. He is trying to convey the zest that life can have in a less-than-ideal universe. Bradbury's early science fiction now seems dated, and the emotion in his more recent fiction is at times overdone. but Bradbury's compassion for his characters and for his readers deserves respect.

—Curtis C. Smith

BRADBURY, David (Henry, Jr.). American. Born in Bedford, Pennsylvania, 7 September 1950. Educated at Bedford Area High School, graduated 1968; University of Pennsylvania, Philadelphia (Franklin Scholar, Presidential Scholar), 1968–72, B.A. (summa cum laude) in creative writing 1972; King's College, University of London (Thouron Scholar), 1972–74, M.A. in area studies 1974. Reader and assistant editor, J.B. Lippincott, publishers, Philadelphia, 1974–76; Visiting Lecturer in English, University of Pennsylvania, 1975. Visiting Instructor, 1976–77, Assistant Professor, 1977–82, and since 1982, Associate Professor of English, Temple University, Philadelphia. Editorial consultant, Lippincott, 1977–78, and Ace Science Fiction, New York, 1979; Visiting Lecturer, San Diego State University, 1980–81. Member of the Executive Board, PEN American Center, 1982–84. Recipient: American Academy award, 1982; PEN-Faulkner Award, 1982. Agent: Wendy Weil, Julian Bach Literary Agency, 747 Third Avenue, New York, New York 10017. Address: Department of English, Temple University, Philadelphia, Pennsylvania 19122, U.S.A.

PUBLICATIONS

Novels

South Street.   New York, Grossman, 1975.
-*The Chaneysville Incident.*   New York, Harper, 1981.

Play

Sweet Sixteen (produced Louisville, Kentucky, 1983).

*

David Bradley comments:

I believe a work of fiction ought to more or less speak for itself—certainly the author ought to keep his mouth shut about it; he's *had* his chance. On the other hand, I have noticed a few things about my own attitudes that might bear mentioning. Nothing so deliberate as a "what I am trying to do with my writing" statement (which I find pretentious and usually wrong), but just observations about what I tend to think is good. I am, first of all, an Aristotelian writer. Meaning that I believe in the Gospel as laid down in *The Poetics*. Plot is paramount, and I do not like *anything* that does not have one. Second, I do not believe in a sharp distinction between fiction and non-fiction. Most of my writing is grounded in real places and people. I always find myself "adapting" reality to the writing, as one might "adapt" a novel for a film. Third, I do not believe in art for art's sake. Art *has* no sake; people do. A work of art that cannot be understood is a voice crying in the wilderness. Fourth, I demand a lot from readers. I do not write "easy" things; they require effort and emotional commitment from me—and they require the same from readers. I hope only that readers feel their time and sweat are well spent.

*   *   *

For David Bradley, place matters, and history haunts. If the Stephen Dedalus of James Joyce's *A Portrait of the Artist as a Young Man* tries desperately to fly over the nets of family, church, and state, Bradley speaks lyrically of those cords that bind him to his birthplace (the rural community of Bedford, Pennsylvania), to the black church in which he grew up, and to the family that nurtured his early interest in history, and in writing about that history. As he put it in "A Personal View from the Third Generation" (*New York Times Sunday Magazine*):

For he [Bradley] realizes this is *his* church. Three generations of his family have occupied Mt. Pisgah's pulpit and worshiped in its pews. A plaque on the wall dedicates the 1960's redecoration to his grandmother. The Bible on the lectern was an offering by his father when his mother survived a dangerous illness. In the truest sense, he, not the denomination, owns Mt. Pisgah. And owes it.

For, in a day when and a place where opportunities were restricted, Mt. Pisgah gave him the chance to speak, to lead, to learn the history of his people. When opportunities became available, it was the experience gained at Mt. Pisgah that equipped him to take advantage of them. But, after taking advantage of them, he abandoned the church that had nurtured him. He walked from Mt. Pisgah down into the Promised Land and never really looked back. Perhaps the time has come to turn around.

These are eloquent, confessional words. For Bradley has moved with astonishing speed from the raw, lusty talent that described the "street people" who hold forth on Philadelphia's *South Street* (published in 1975, when Bradley was only 24) to the sweep and ambition of *The Chaneysville Incident*, the novel that brought Bradley national recognition.

South Street is a novel anchored in the naturalism of "ele-phantine cockroaches and rats the size of cannon shells," but it is also a novel that reaches well beyond the geography of urban despair. Bradley's South Street poises itself at the border of Philadelphia's black ghetto, where it ties "the city's rivers like an iron bracelet or a wedding band, uniting the waters, sewer to sewer, before they meet at the city's edge." Place matters deeply, of course—in this case, the locus seems to be Lightnin' Ed's Bar—but it is the people, and Bradley's ear for their colorful language, that matters even more:

Leo, the two-hundred-and-fifty-eight-pound owner-bar-tender-cashier-bouncer of Lightnin' Ed's Bar and Grill, looked up from the glass he was polishing to see a one-hundred-and-fifty-eight-pound white man walk into his bar. Leo's mouth fell open and he almost dropped the glass. One by one the faces along the bar turned to stare at the single pale face, shining in the dimness. "Yes, sir, cap'n," Leo said uneasily, "what can we be doin' for you?"

George looked around nervously. "I, ah, had a little accident. I, ah, ran over a cat in the street, and I, uh, don't know what to do about it."

"Whad he say?" a wino at the far end of the bar, who claimed to be hard of hearing, whispered loudly.

The jukebox ran out and fell silent just as somebody yelled to him, "Paddy says he run over some cat out in the street." The sound echoed throughout the bar. Conversation died.

"Goddamn!" said the wino.

Leo leaned over the bar, letting his gigantic belly rest on the polished wood. "Yeah?" he said to George. "Didja kill him?"

"Oh yes," George assured him. "I made certain of that."

Bradley is at his best when he moves inside the set pieces, the extended anecdotes, that give *South Street* its resonance. What might well have become yet another unrelenting grim account of sordid conditions and despairing lives transmogrifies itself into a high, more humane key. It was, in short, a novel that prompted reviewers to say "Keep your eye on Mr. Bradley." In this case, they were righter than they knew.

The Chaneysville Incident both widened and deepened the scope of Bradley's obvious talents. His postgraduate research in American history at the University of London sent him back, ironically enough, to a story he had heard in Bedford about 13 escaped slaves who asked to be killed rather than recaptured and about the 13 unmarked graves his mother once discovered.

The Chaneysville Incident tells this story from the perspective of John Washington, a black man who has bootstrapped himself from humble, rural origins to become a history professor at a Philadelphia university and who lives with Judith, a white psychologist. The question the book raises is simply, and per-plexingly, how should a black man live in a world white men have made. The result is a thickly textured, multi-layered book,

one that inextricably combines theory, historical research, and domestic tension. As Washington, the historian, puts it: "The key to the understanding of any society lies in the observation and analysis of the insignificant and the mundane ... If you doubt it [i.e. that America is a classed society], consider the sanitary facilities employed in America's three modes of public long-distance transportation: airplanes, trains, and buses."

Washington, however, not only discovers the historical truth of the "Chaneysville incident," but also that the truth is more complex, more riddling than he had imagined. If part of his character serves as Bradley's mouthpiece, part of him must, finally, be rejected by Bradley, the novelist. Luckily, it is the latter part that matters most, when one has recovered from the anger and whitey-baiting that gives this important novel much of its initial energy.

—Sanford Pinsker

BRAGG, Melvyn. British. Born in Carlisle, Cumberland, 6 October 1939. Educated at Nelson-Thomlinson Grammar School, Wigton, Cumberland, 1950–59; Wadham College, Oxford, M.A. (honours) in modern history 1961. Married 1) Lise Roche in 1961 (died, 1971), one daughter; 2) Catherine Mary Haste in 1973, one daughter and one son. Producer, BBC Radio and Television, London, from 1961: presenter, *Second House*, 1973–77, and *Read All about It*, 1976–77. Since 1978, presenter and editor, *South Bank Show*, and since 1982, Head of Arts, London Weekend Television. Since 1983, General Editor, Piatkus Arts series. Since 1969, member, and Chairman, 1977–80, Arts Council Literature Panel. Recipient: Writers Guild award, for screenplay, 1966; Rhys Memorial Prize, 1968; Northern Arts Association prose award, 1970; Silver Pen Award, 1970; Broadcasting Press Guild award, 1984. Fellow, Royal Society of Literature, 1970. Address: 12 Hampstead Hill Gardens, London N.W. 3, England.

PUBLICATIONS

Novels

For Want of a Nail. London, Secker and Warburg, and New York, Knopf, 1965.
The Second Inheritance. London, Secker and Warburg, 1966; New York, Knopf, 1967.
Without a City Wall. London, Secker and Warburg, 1968; New York, Knopf, 1969.
The Cumbrian Trilogy. London, Coronet, 1984.
  The Hired Man. London, Secker and Warburg, 1969; New York, Knopf, 1970.
  A Place in England. London, Secker and Warburg, 1970; New York, Knopf, 1971.
  Kingdom Come. London, Secker and Warburg, 1980.
The Nerve. London, Secker and Warburg, 1971.
The Hunt. London, Secker and Warburg, 1972.
Josh Lawton. London, Secker and Warburg, and New York, Knopf, 1972.
The Silken Net. London, Secker and Warburg, and New York, Knopf, 1974.
Autumn Manoeuvres. London, Secker and Warburg, 1978.
Love and Glory. London, Secker and Warburg, 1983.

Short Story

A Christmas Child. London, Secker and Warburg, 1976.

Uncollected Short Story

"The Initiation," in *Winter's Tales 18*, edited by A.D. Maclean. London, Macmillan, and New York, St. Martin's Press, 1972.

Plays

Mardi Gras, music by Alan Blaikley and Ken Howard (produced London, 1976).
The Hired Man, adaptation of his own novel, music and lyrics by Howard Goodall (produced Southampton and London, 1984).

Screenplays: *Play Dirty*, with Lotte Colin, 1968; *Isadora* with Clive Exton and Margaret Drabble, 1969; *The Music Lovers*, 1970; *Jesus Christ Superstar*, with Norman Jewison, 1973.

Radio Play: *Robin Hood*, 1971.

Television Plays: *The Debussy File*, with Ken Russell, 1965; *Charity Begins at Home*, 1970; *Zinotchka*, 1972; *Orion*, music by Ken Howard and Alan Blaikley, 1977; *Clouds of Glory*, with Ken Russell, 1978.

Other

Speak for England: An Essay on England 1900–1975. London, Secker and Warburg, 1976; revised edition, London, Coronet, 1978; as *Speak for England: An Oral History of England 1900–1975*, New York, Knopf, 1977.
Land of the Lakes. London, Secker and Warburg, 1983; New York, Norton, 1984.
Laurence Olivier. London, Hutchinson, 1984.

Editor, *My Favourite Stories of Lakeland*. Guildford, Surrey, Lutterworth Press, 1981.
Editor, *Cumbria in Verse*. London, Secker and Warburg, 1984.

*

Critical Studies: by Rodney Pybus, in *Stand* (Newcastle-upon-Tyne), Summer 1970; Kenneth John Achuty, in *Kenyon Review 127* (Gambier, Ohio), 1971.

Melvyn Bragg comments:
(1972) The ways in which I came to write are sketched in the last chapters of *A Place in England*: they are made the notions of a fictional self—Douglas Tallentire.
Present ideas on fiction are represented in the novel *The Nerve* and in an essay "Class and the Novel" in *Times Literary Supplement* (London), 15 October 1971.

*   *   *

Melvyn Bragg began with two good novels about wasted human potential, *For Want of a Nail* and *The Second Inheritance*. But it was *Without a City Wall* which secured for him a deserved reputation as one of the best contemporary novelists. Theme and structure reinforce each other as Bragg traces, first, the awakening of passion in Richard Godwin, a self-imposed exile from the chaos of London, for Janice Beattie, a Cumberland girl of unusual intelligence and powerful ambition; and then, the challenges that the life of consummated

passion entails for both of them. The drama develops principally from Janice whose ambition and fastidiousness prove stronger than sexual passion or her sense of responsibility to others. Her passion for Richard contracts, while his for her continues to expand. Richard is driven to the brink of self-destruction but recoils in time to force Janice to some kind of modus vivendi between the claims of his passion and the claims of her individuality. Bragg's more recent novel, *The Silken Net*, also develops the theme of sexual struggle. This book focuses on a restless intellectual, Rosemary Lewis, whose energy alienates her from life in the Cumberland village of Thurston. Her vigor is admirable but her egoism is destructive as she attempts to breed in her husband the same intensities that motivate her. The resulting conflict registers with less authority, however, than that developed in *Without a City Wall*.
The alternation of intensity and apathy in the passional life is again one subject explored in *The Hired Man*. Covering the years 1898 to 1920 in the life of John and Emily Tallentire, the novel articulates the nuances of their emotions. Communication between a man and a woman becomes a function of the body; and estrangement develops when perfect physical accord is broken. After Emily's death at forty John is where he was at the beginning, a man for casual hire on the great farms but now with all zest gone. Bragg's artistry is at its best in his honest portrayal of the hard lives of agricultural laborers in the early 20th century. *A Place in England* has for protagonist Joseph Tallentire, John's son. Bragg is less close to Joseph than to John; in fact, the most memorable pages of the novel feature the now patriarchal John. After much struggle Joseph is able to "be his own man" as owner of a public house; but his success is undercut by the disintegration of his marriage, a loss to him for which he cannot account.
Kingdom Come reveals much of the power found in *The Hired Man* and has much interest for the modern reader, as Bragg presents the contemporary generation of the Tallentire men. Lester, a con man and cousin, and Douglas, the son of Joseph and a writer of talent, lack the purposiveness and inner strength of their ancestors, though Harry, the adopted son who stays in Thurston, retains these qualities in large part. Douglas is the sympathetically presented protagonist who can neither be satisfied with the stern ancestral morality nor get clear of the claims of responsibility which derive from it. His divided nature defeats him because it leads him to betray the woman he loves and whose real worth he realizes too late.
In two other recent novels Bragg has again had recourse to Cumberland and its people. In *Josh Lawton*, a moving parable, Lawton has overtones of a Biblical patriarch and suffers the predictable fate of those who are too good for this world. In *Autumn Manoeuvres* Bragg traces the destructive and self-destructive career of Gareth Johnson. His violent loathing of his stepfather and his own violent self-loathing are linked to the violence of his begetting (his mother had been gang raped in World War I). Is he the victim of fatality or is he his own victim—more the second than the first, Bragg implies.
London figures more than Cumberland in *The Nerve* and *Love and Glory*. In *The Nerve* Bragg traces, in a first-person narrative, the stages in the mental breakdown of his protagonist, Ted. Power accrues when Ted, the narrator, actualizes some of his experiences of physical and mental pain, but the breakdown which is a "breakthrough" is not precisely characterized. In *Love and Glory* Bragg explores the various forms of love from self-serving passion to selfless devotion. The conflict centers in the relationship between Ian Grant, an actor of genius, and Caroline, his Scottish mistress, who loves him with greater devotion than he can reciprocate. The central character is a writer for television, Willie Armstrong, who is Grant's

BRAINE 129

best friend and who comes to love Caroline to distraction but gives her up when she fails to respond to his advances and when he realizes the claims of his wife, Joanna, upon him. Willie thus gains in insight and understanding while Ian Grant retrogresses spiritually and becomes even more submerged in his egotism.

The immediacy of Bragg's Cumberland milieu is, at least superficially, the quality that impresses most in his fiction. As in Thomas Hardy and D.H. Lawrence, milieu is integrally fused with the fortunes and development of the characters. Like Hardy he has in unusual degree insight into human beings who confront the elemental realities of nature, and like Hardy's his people encounter problems difficult to resolve when they lose rapport with nature. Bragg's eye for detail, his compelling sense of drama, his penetration into the emotional and psychic life of his characters, his sense of the moral verities, and his supple and luminous prose have all contributed to his standing as a distinguished novelist.

—Frederick P.W. McDowell

BRAINE, John (Gerard). British. Born in Bradford, Yorkshire, 13 April 1922. Educated at St. Bede's Grammar School, Bradford; Leeds School of Librarianship, A.L.A. 1949. Served as a telegraphist in the Royal Navy, 1942–43. Married Helen Patricia Wood in 1955; one son and three daughters. Assistant Librarian, 1940–49, and Chief Assistant Librarian, 1949–51, Bingley Public Library, Yorkshire; free-lance writer, London and Yorkshire, 1951–54. Branch Librarian, Northumberland County Library, 1954–56, and West Riding County Library, Darton, Yorkshire, 1956–57. Writer-in-Residence, Purdue University, Lafayette, Indiana, Fall 1978. Member, BBC North Regional Advisory Council, 1960–64. Agent: David Higham Associates Ltd., 5–8 Lower John Street, London W1R 4HA. Address: c/o Methuen Ltd., 11 New Fetter Lane, London EC4P 4EE, England.

PUBLICATIONS

Novels

Room at the Top. London, Eyre and Spottiswoode, and Boston, Houghton Mifflin, 1957.
The Vodi. London, Eyre and Spottiswoode, 1959; revised edition, London, Eyre Methuen, 1978; as *From the Hand of the Hunter*, Boston, Houghton Mifflin, 1960.
Life at the Top. London, Eyre and Spottiswoode, and Boston, Houghton Mifflin, 1962.
The Jealous God. London, Eyre and Spottiswoode, 1964; Boston, Houghton Mifflin, 1965.
The Crying Game. London, Eyre and Spottiswoode, and Boston, Houghton Mifflin, 1968.
Stay with Me till Morning. London, Eyre and Spottiswoode, 1970; as *The View from Tower Hill*, New York, Coward McCann, 1971.
The Queen of a Distant Country. London, Methuen, 1972; New York, Coward McCann, 1973.
The Pious Agent. London, Eyre Methuen, 1975; New York, Atheneum, 1976.
Waiting for Sheila. London, Eyre Methuen, 1976.
Finger of Fire. London, Eyre Methuen, 1977.

One and Last Love. London, Eyre Methuen, 1981.
The Two of Us. London, Methuen, 1984.
These Golden Days. London, Methuen, 1985.

Plays

The Desert in the Mirror (produced Bingley, Yorkshire, 1951).

Television Plays: *Man at the Top* series, 1970, 1972; *Waiting for Sheila*, from his own novel, 1977; *Queen of a Distant Country*, from his own novel, 1978; *Stay with Me till Morning*, from his own novel, 1980.

Other

Writing a Novel (textbook). London, Eyre Methuen, and New York, McGraw Hill, 1975.
J.B. Priestley. London, Weidenfeld and Nicolson, 1978; New York, Barnes and Noble, 1979.

*

Bibliography: *John Braine and John Wain: A Reference Guide* by Dale Salwak, Boston, Hall, 1980.

Manuscript Collection: Central Public Library, Bradford, Yorkshire.

Critical Study: *John Braine* by James W. Lee, New York, Twayne, 1968.

John Braine comments:

What I care about the most is telling the truth about human beings and the world they live in. I'm not interested in making moral judgements as a novelist. I'm not interested in making any sort of propaganda. I do have very strong political beliefs and in a sense can't separate them from my religious beliefs. I'll put it this way: I believe in parliamentary democracy, majority rule, the rule of law, and a fixed morality. I would rather die than live under a government which denied me the freedom to write exactly as I want to. It isn't for me to say whether I write well or badly. But this at least I can say: I have never thought of being anything else but a writer and will never be anything else but a writer. And every word I write is a celebration of my love for the created world and everyone and everything within it.

* * *

John Braine burst upon the literary scene in 1957 with *Room at the Top*, an instantaneous success which enrolled him among "the angry young men," writers who protested the discriminations imposed upon those who came from the working class or the lower middle class. Joe Lampton derives from the wrong class for worldly success to come easily to him. He is cynical of the establishment but determined to exploit it. At this time he does not realize that he may be absorbed by the class whose wealth he intends to share. Against his will he falls in love with Alice Aisgill, an unhappily married middle-aged woman. Out of opportunism he gives her up but feels guilt for her violent death. He marries Susan Brown, his fairy princess, with painful lack of enthusiasm. Braine implies that any society which demands the sacrifice of integrity as the price of "success" is corrupt.

Life at the Top, a sequel, is equally fine. Joe Lampton has by now joined the establishment and become a minor administrator in his father-in-law's firm. He finds that life at the top is empty and that affluence entails severe liabilities. Joe, the rebel against the drabness of Dufton (his native town), now realizes that life at the top can be just as drab, certainly more corrupt, than life in Dufton. Joe reaches beyond torment and materialist values to spiritual triumph when he accepts the child with love whom he discovers is not his own.

The Jealous God is a religious novel which traces the ramifications of Catholicism upon the personal life. Vincent Dungarvan has for long been poised between life as priest and life in the world. His possessive mother is more anxious than Vincent for him to become a priest. In the upshot the church and Mrs. Dungarvan win out over Vincent's desire to marry a divorcee whose husband had been homosexual. Braine depicts with urgency and strength the conflicts inherent in Vincent, the sensual man of deep religious commitment. And life in the provincial town is rendered with knowledge, finesse, and sympathy. *The Vodi* is Braine's least significant novel and chronicles the successful revolt of Dick Corvy against malign supernatural presences (the Vodi).

The Crying Game is a kind of "morality," depicting Frank Batcombe's oscillating attitudes toward the glamor and easy rewards of London, the intense yet transitory quality of its pleasures. The conflicts do not register clearly because Braine fails to keep his characters at a sufficient ironic distance for him to judge them adequately and the values they embody. Like Milton, Braine at times seems to be of the devil's party, represented in the book by Adam Keelby and his sleazy values. Braine, however, seems to be as fascinated by the great world of finance and intrigue as he is critical of it. Frank, a journalist, sees in time the corruption which is about to engulf him as a result of Adam's influence. He turns to his "good angel," Theresa, whom he had thought earlier of being the right girl met at the wrong time. *The Crying Game* does capture the texture of decadent urban life, the corruptness of its luxury, the opportunism inherent in its human relationships, especially in the realm of sex.

In *Stay with Me till Morning* Braine analyzes marital discord for the first time since *Life at the Top*. The protagonists, Robin and Clive Lendrick, have everything: a fine home in a Yorkshire town, economic security, healthy children, mutual affection and understanding. Yet after 20 years together they feel that something has gone from their relationship if ever it were there. Infidelity, Braine seems to imply, is preferable to spiritual lassitude. The difficulties inherent in marriage, and its general inflexibility, are principal themes in this disquieting dissection of modern mores. These themes are again predominant in *The Two of Us*, a sequel to *Stay with Me till Morning*. The Lendrick marriage again bleakly survives the challenges to it of outside influences: first, the intrusion of Stephen Belgard who again captivates for a short period the disaffected Robin, and second, the defection of the pregnant Ruth Inglewood, Clive's mistress, who in leaving him deprives him of ongoing emotional and personal stability. More constricted in its reach and less impressive generally is *Waiting for Sheila* which is a painful and hardly significant first-person analysis by its lower class protagonist of his sexual difficulties, largely the result of his ignorance and of his lack of imagination.

In *The Queen of a Distant Country* a successful novelist from the provinces, Tom Matfield, becomes aware, finally, that a demanding professional career need not exclude a meaningful personal life. He also faces honestly his indebtedness to Miranda, once among the most acclaimed of writers.

More recently Braine has ventured into the spy novel, with considerable flair and structural expertise. *The Pious Agent* is an intense, disturbing, and sinister book, in which Braine presents the insistent claims made by governmental departments upon the efficient agents which they must use. Whether such departments are justified in exploiting these men for the common political good is one question explored in the book. The agent, Colonel Xavier Flynn, is torn between conflicting impulses: religion, patriotism, moral decency, sexual ardor, desire for serene domesticity, contempt for and fascination with international power politics, compulsion to wield power, and violence. *Finger of Fire* recounts Flynn's confrontations with FIST, an organization dedicated to the penetration of British politics and to the violent overthrow of British democratic government.

In the recent *One and Last Love* Braine chronicles how Tim Harnforth, a novelist, finds love in middle age, a fulfilment that he had never found before in two marriages and many casual affairs. Braine celebrates here genuine and understanding love, which includes but transcends sex, as the supreme human experience.

Braine has emerged as a writer alternately fascinated and repelled by the present-day upper middle class, especially that segment of it which enjoys prosperity but lacks spiritual stamina. He is a master at analyzing the antagonisms of people thrown together in close association in marriage, friendship, government, and professional life. Some of his characters, satirically treated, never attain awareness: for them sex has none but a perfunctory significance. Others do attain enlightenment, but with much pain, sometimes even with regret. The acknowledgement of the claims of other people upon them coincides with an acknowledgement of their own personal deficiencies. The unregenerate are those whose egotism is impervious to the influence of others. As a creator of characters who embody the tensions existing between themselves and others and between themselves and social institutions and conventions, he achieves his greatest distinction.

—Frederick P.W. McDowell

BRATA, Sasthi (Sasthibrata Chakravarti). British. Born in Calcutta, India, 16 July 1939. Educated at Calcutta Boys School; Presidency College, Calcutta University. Married Pamela Joyce Radcliffe (divorced). Has worked in Europe as a lavatory attendant, kitchen porter, barman, air-conditioning engineer, and postman, and in New York as a free-lance journalist; London columnist, *Statesman*, 1977–80. Recipient: Arts Council grant, 1979. Agent: Barbara Lowenstein, 250 West 57th Street, Suite 701, New York, New York 10107, U.S.A. Address: 33 Savernake Road, London NW3 2JU, England.

PUBLICATIONS

Novels

Confessions of an Indian Woman Eater. London, Hutchinson, 1971; as *Confessions of an Indian Lover*, New Delhi, Sterling, 1973.
She and He. New Delhi, Orient, 1973.
The Sensuous Guru: The Making of a Mystic President. New Delhi, Sterling, 1980.

Short Stories

Encounter. New Delhi, Orient, 1978.

Verse

Eleven Poems. New Delhi, Blue Moon, 1960.

Other

My God Died Young (autobiography).   London, Hutchinson, and New York, Harper, 1968.
A Search for Home (autobiography).   New Delhi, Orient, 1975.
Astride Two Worlds: Traitor to India.   New Delhi, B.I. Publications, 1976; as *Traitor to India: A Search for Home*, London, Elek, 1976.
Labyrinths in the Lotus Land (on India).   New York, Morrow, 1985.

*

Sasthi Brata comments:

My first published book, *My God Died Young*, was a self-professed autobiography, written at the age of 28, before I had made any kind of a name for myself as a writer, or anything else. This led a good few publishers, readers, and finally critics to utter the exasperated cry: "What makes you think that the story of your life (woefully unlived-in up to that time) deserves to be told? Or that people will want to read it?" The answer to these questions was within the book itself, of course. But in a sense *all* of my writing, fiction, non-fiction, and journalism, has been an attempt to refute the assumptions lurking behind those superficially plausible and innocent-sounding queries. For they presume that only the heroic and the grand deserve artistic exploration and autobiographical treatment. While I believe, very firmly, that everyone, but everyone has *a* story to tell. The difference between the true artist and the pub bore is that the writer has a sure grasp over the instruments of his trade—words, sentences, paragraphs, syntax, metaphor, melody—and is then able to select, assemble, and present a somewhat more ordered and appetising version of the world than the chaotic, often repetitive jumble of experiences from external reality which make up his raw material.

All my fiction has been supremely autobiographical. Even in those books which are listed as non-fiction on library shelves, I have used fictional devices, and equally freely introduced reportage techniques in books which profess to be novels. I should warn the prospective reader however not to deduce from this that every hero in every one of my novels is an exactly congruent picture of the man I am. In a review of the late Yukio Mishima's novels I wrote: "The obsessionally autobiographical writer may be an invisible man." For while he may not be telling lies, he is not necessarily telling the *truth* either, at least not of the kind the law courts would accept. Since he is an artist, he *has* used his imagination, but he has not necessarily let you into the secret of where the fictive imagination begins or where empirically verifiable reality ends.

There was a time when I used to be irked by attacks on the high sexual content in my writing. I am no longer. Few addicts of hardcore porn would find any of my books satisfactory. Prurient sensibilities, with a cavalier indifference to style and linguistic resonances, might equally be put off by their subject matter. Apologies to neither group.

I would call myself a "radical traditionalist" as a novelist, if only because to be a successful "experimental" writer, in the sense that Joyce and Borges are, requires *a* poetic sensibility I do not possess. It is easy to descend into the wholly bogus or deliberately pedantic in trying to achieve effects about which one is not totally sure. There are no rules in the use of language of course, but I would rather stick within certain wide but strictly defined limits, than stray into those unexplored territories where the arcane, obscure, or simply fraudulent vendors ply their wares. I believe that all my books can be read simply as good tales.

Labyrinths in the Lotus Land was my first commissioned work. I wrote it specifically for a Western audience. It was an ambitious attempt to inform a western reader, within the compass of a single book, everything that he or she might wish to know about the country, spanning the whole gamut of history, religion, art, politics etc. Critics who complained about the apparent incongruity of introducing *personal* experiences into a book which purports to portray a picture of contemporary India were not aware of my long-held belief that by relating a particular incident or episode in a graphic and authentic manner, the universal is illuminated more poignantly than any amount of dry didactic scholarship can ever do.

*   *   *

Most of Sasthi Brata's books are written in the first person, and all his heroes seem to be modelled after the novelist himself. The hero is always a Bengali Brahmin, from a well-to-do family, who lives in Calcutta and studies physics at college. He leaves home in protest after the girl of his choice is married off to someone whom her parents have chosen. He drifts into a number of jobs, including journalism, and finally establishes himself comfortably in Hampstead. His chief hobby is haunting pubs. The narrator of his first novel, *Confessions of an Indian Woman Eater*, differs only in name from the narrator of the autobiographies *My God Died Young* and *Astride Two Worlds*. The physical characteristics remain the same, even if the hero is Zamir Ishmael of *She and He*: he is dark, of medium height, with dark eyes and an attractive smile; his success with women is unlimited. Brata's books are quite readable; his style is racy and adequate for his purpose, which is generally limited to describing the exploits of his hero in bed. The exception is *Astride Two Worlds*, the second part of his autobiography, which touches upon many serious topics like racial discrimination in Britain, the involvement of the Indian government in the guerilla activities of the Mukti Bahini in Bangledesh in 1971, and the growing disillusionment of the young with established politicians in India. A couple of chapters, written in the third person, serve to give a proper perspective to this autobiography.

Brata's best selling novel, *Confessions of an Indian Woman Eater*, begins where his first book, *My God Died Young*, an autobiography, let off: Amit Ray, like Sasthi Brata, runs away from his Calcutta home. Amit recounts his varied sexual experiences in a number of capitals—New Delhi, Rome, London, Paris, Copenhagen. He finally ends up in Hampstead with a steady job, and becomes a successful writer. For a certain readership the chief attraction of the book would lie in the step-by-step accounts of copulation, found almost every ten pages. The next novel, *She and He*, has a hero born of an Arab father and a French mother; he is at home in England and lands a good job because he can speak the language with the proper accent. He always talks about writing the "Great English Novel," but does nothing about it until one of his ex-girl friends sends him an unfinished novel, having written her side of the story, with blank pages for the hero to fill in. The first person account of Zamir alternating with the third person narrative of Sally is an interesting stylistic innovation, but the hero's mindless drifting from bed to bed is ultimately boring.

The Sensuous Guru: The Making of a Mystic President, perhaps the most imaginative of Brata's works, recounts the rise of Ram Chukker (short for Ram Chakravarti, just as Sasthi

Brata is the shortened form of Sasthibrata Chakravarti). Chukker initially sets himself up as a Guru in New York, and makes a good living. He writes a short autobiographical novel, *The Making of a Guru*, which outdoes the worst that America can produce in pornography. Through high-pressure promotion with the help of an influential literary agent Chukker wins the Pulitzer Prize, is nominated for the Nobel Prize, manages one for Peace, and is ultimately elected President of the United States.

Brata has also published a collection of stories; most of them are like his novels (some have appeared, with modifications, as chapters in his novels). One very good story is "Smiles among the Bric-a-Brac," about a young Oxford graduate from a rich English family, comfortably settling down to the girl and the job his parents have chosen for him, though he earlier loves the beautiful Nina Fernandez, of mixed parentage. The first person account, with the hero justifying the way he drops Nina, is a beautiful psychological study of the hero's lack of principles. It is significant that Robert Lomax, from an old English family, is very different from the usual Bengali hero. On feels that Brata could write better fiction, especially if he got rid of his autobiographical obsession.

—Shyamala A. Narayan

BRATHWAITE, Errol (Freeman). New Zealander. Born in Clive, Hawkes Bay, 3 April 1924. Educated at Waipukurau District High School, 1929–37; Timaru Boys' High School, 1938–39. Served in the New Zealand Army in the City of Wellington's Own, 1942–43; Royal New Zealand Air Force, 1943–45, 1947–55; Royal New Zealand Signals, 1955–58. Married Alison Irene Whyte in 1948; one son and one daughter. Cadet, New Zealand Railways, 1940–42, 1945; farm trainee, Rehabilitation Department, King Country, 1946; copywriter, New Zealand Broadcasting Corporation, Christchurch, 1959–62, and Dobbs-Wiggins-McCann-Erickson, Christchurch, 1962–66. Since 1969, copywriter, and manager, 1971–73, Carlton Carruthers du Chateau, Christchurch. Recipient: Otago *Daily Times* Centennial Novel Prize, 1961; New Zealand Award for Achievement, 1962. Address: 12 Fulton Avenue, Fendalton, Christchurch 1, New Zealand.

PUBLICATIONS

Novels

Fear in the Night. Christchurch, Caxton Press, 1959.
An Affair of Men. Auckland and London, Collins, 1961; New York, St. Martin's Press, 1964.
Long Way Home. Christchurch, Caxton Press, 1964.
The Flying Fish. Auckland and London, Collins, 1964; San Francisco, Tri-Ocean, 1969.
The Needle's Eye. Auckland and London, Collins, 1965; San Francisco, Tri-Ocean, 1969.
The Evil Day. Auckland and London, Collins, 1967; San Francisco, Tri-Ocean, 1969.
The Flame Box. Auckland, Collins, 1978.

Uncollected Short Story

"Williams and Christmas," in *New Zealand Weekly* (Auckland), 1968.

Plays

Radio Plays: *An Affair of Men*, 1962; *Long Way Home*, 1966; *The Needle's Eye*, 1969; *Marnot*, 1978; *Marnot and the Power Game*, 1979; *The Rehabilitation of Captain Marnot*, 1979; *Shape Up or Ship Out*, 1979; *Holes in the Air*, 1980.

Other

Morning Flight. Wellington, Commemoration Committee, 1970.
The Companion Guide to the North [South] Island of New Zealand. Auckland and London, Collins, 2 vols., 1970–72.
New Zealand and Its People. Wellington, New Zealand Government Printer, 1974.
The Beauty of New Zealand, photographs by Robin Smith. Auckland, Golden Press, 1974.
Historic New Zealand. Christchurch, Kowhai, 1979.
New Zealand. Christchurch, Kowhai, 1980.
Sixty Red Nightcaps and Other Curiosities of New Zealand History. Auckland, Bateman, 1980.
The Companion Guide to Westland. Auckland, Collins, 1981.
The Beauty of Waikato, Bay of Plenty, photographs by Warren Jacobs and Robin Smith. Christchurch, Kowhai, 1981.
Dunedin, photographs by Warren Jacobs. Christchurch, Kowhai, 1981.
The Beauty of New Zealand's North Island, photographs by Warren Jacobs and Robin Smith. Christchurch, Kowhai, 1982.
The Beauty of New Zealand's South Island, photographs by Warren Jacobs. Christchurch, Kowhai, 1982.
The Companion Guide to Otago, Southland, and Stewart Island. Auckland, Collins, 1982.
Just Looking: A View of New Zealand, illustrated by John Haycraft. Auckland, Bateman, 1982.
Beautiful New Zealand. Auckland, Bateman, 1985.

*

Errol Brathwaite comments:
It is difficult for me to comment on my own novels, since I never write with any other end in view than to tell a good story.

I regard life as a constant battle between good and evil, albeit a highly complex warfare, since both sides in any given encounter have within them leanings towards both good and evil. I strive to make my characters positive, though not necessarily strong—never clean-cut good or evil, though tending infinitely more strongly in one direction (usually towards good) than the other. I acknowledge the complexity of the battle by giving my creations multifaceted characters; and while I comment on life, I try to allow the commentary to grow as a by-product of observations and reportage. I do not deliberately attack attitudes or situations, but merely use them. To do otherwise would be to obtrude, to force myself and my opinions on the reader.

If I want a particular character to be a hero, I make him progress towards an obviously desirable goal somewhat in spite of himself, sometimes fortuitously and always with much stumbling and a modicum of obtuseness. I try to let the reader see the desirable objective, as it were from a height, observing the hero's ground-level side-tracking and stumbling progress. I do this in an attempt to involve the reader, which I regard as being a first principle of good entertainment.

I suppose that this is why war has so often been, if not the subject, then the setting of my novels. It is a pattern, in bold relief, of life itself. It is full of dramatic possibilities. It can face ordinary good/evil man with a rapid series of searing moral and other dilemmas.

I don't expect that I shall always write about war, but I regard conflict as being one of the two major dramatic themes, the other being the "Robinson Crusoe" situation, wherein man overcomes circumstance and bends it to his will.

What else is there to say? I believe that life itself is seldom tidy, and that its conclusion inevitably leaves a number of more or less untidy loose ends flapping around. I realise that in a novel there must be a rather greater degree of contrivance than in life, but I don't care to make my novels too unlifelike.

I suppose, to sum it all up, that I regard myself as an entertainer; a teller, as Kai Lung used to say, of imagined tales. I have, therefore, one source of material, which is human behaviour, and three forms of presentation, which are drama, romance and comedy. Drama and comedy call for high, bold colouring techniques—the dash and splash of bright oils. Romance calls for water-colour treatment, and I don't think that my brushwork is subtle enough. Therefore, I suppose that the highly dramatic will continue to be my chosen form, and that if there is any change, it will be to comedy.

*   *   *

In Errol Brathwaite's novels, the basic formula is that of men in a dangerous war-situation, submitted to physical and mental stress, which strips them down to basic responses and confronts them with moral dilemmas. His work represents an endeavour to add to the war-novel an extra dimension of moral significance and to highlight the complexity of circumstances which are usually treated in terms of mere physical endurance. His strength lies in his keen historical sense, his ability to tell exciting stories, his understanding of the psychology of fighting men (women make very rare appearances in his fiction) and his clean-cut, unfussy style. His weaknesses are seen in his tendency to view his characters at times as human beings, at others as representing abstract qualities, and his slightly mechanical organisation of moments of tension. But he is one of the most readable of New Zealand novelists and at the same time sets his sights high.

His first two novels were *Fear in the Night* and *Long Way Home*. (Despite the publication date of *An Affair of Men*, 1961, it was written after *Long Way Home*.) Both come from the author's own aviation experience. In *Fear in the Night*, the crew of a bomber forced down in Japanese territory are under pressure to repair the plane before they are captured. Brathwaite's technical knowledge and his eye for detail combine with his skill in exploring the minds of his characters under the strain to create a convincing situation remarkable for its concentration of effect. *Long Way Home*, which deals with a search and rescue operation in New Zealand's Southern Alps, is similarly organised.

There is a real advance in *An Affair of Men*. This time the suspense story does not so much include the moral attitudes as dramatise them. Allied airmen who have crashed on the Pacific island Bougainville are pursued by the Japanese under Captain Itoh. His search is frustrated by a Christian-educated headman, Sedu, who insists on remaining neutral. The clash of wills and ideologies is handled with continual invention and boldness and is resolved in terms of the psychology and background of the antagonists. The drama reflects modern man's dilemma in his choice between two different sets of values, between peace and violence.

Brathwaite's trilogy, *The Flying Fish*, *The Needle's Eye*, and *The Evil Day*, follows the experiences of the fictional Major

Williams in the Maori Wars of the 1860's and is the most ambitious treatment of this subject so far written. Again, it is not only the details of strategy and battles which engage Brathwaite and the various kinds of military sensibility which he analyses, although these are treated with careful attention to historical fact, but the personal and moral problems posed by war itself. A further theme is the development of mutual understanding, paradoxically, between Maori and European through the wars and the question of where the real blame for the conflict lay. The characterisation is firm and varied and Major Williams is one of the most completely realised characters in New Zealand fiction.

—J.C. Reid

BRINK, André (Philippus). South African. Born in Vrede, Orange Free State, 29 May 1935. Educated at Lydenburg High School; Potchefstroom University, Transvaal, B.A. 1955, M.A. in English 1958, M.A. in Afrikaans and Dutch 1959; the Sorbonne, Paris, 1959–61. Married 1) Estelle Naudé in 1959 (divorced), one son; 2) Salomi Louw in 1965 (divorced), one son; 3) Alta Miller in 1970, one son and one daughter. Lecturer, 1963–73, Senior Lecturer, 1974–75, Associate Professor, 1976–79, and since 1980 Professor and Head of the Department of Afrikaans and Dutch Literature, Rhodes University, Grahamstown. Editor, *Sestiger* magazine, Pretoria, 1963–65. Since 1986, Editor, *Standpunte* magazine, Cape Town. President, Afrikaans Writers Guild, 1978–80. Recipient: Geerlings prize, 1964; CNA award, 1965, 1979, 1983; South African Academy award, for translation, 1970; Medicis prize (France), 1980; Martin Luther King Memorial Prize (UK), 1980. D.Litt.: Rhodes University, 1975; University of the Witwatersrand, Johannesburg, 1985. Agent: Faber and Faber Ltd., 3 Queen Square, London WC1N 3AU, England. Address: Department of Afrikaans and Dutch Literature, Rhodes University, Grahamstown, Cape Province 6140, South Africa.

PUBLICATIONS

Novels (translated into English by the author)

Die gebondenes. Johannesburg, Afrikaanse Pers, 1958.
Die eindelose weë. Cape Town, Tafelberg, 1960.
Lobola vir die lewe (Dowry for Life). Cape Town, Human & Rousseau, 1962.
Die ambassadeur. Cape Town, Human & Rousseau, 1963; as *The Ambassador*, Johannesburg, CNA, 1964; London, Faber, 1985; New York, Summit, 1986; as *File on a Diplomat*, London, Longman, 1967.
Orgie (Orgy). Cape Town, Malherbe, 1965.
Miskien nooit: 'n Somerspel. Cape Town, Human & Rousseau, 1967.
Kennis van die aand. Cape Town, Buren, 1973; as *Looking on Darkness*, London, W.H. Allen, 1974; New York, Morrow, 1975.
'n Oomblik in die wind. Johannesburg, Taurus, 1975; as *An Instant in the Wind*, London, W.H. Allen, 1976; New York, Morrow, 1977.
Gerugte van reën. Cape Town, Human & Rousseau, 1978; as *Rumours of Rain*, London, W.H. Allen, and New York, Morrow, 1978.

'n Droë wit seisoen. Johannesburg, Taurus, 1979; as *A Dry White Season*, London, W.H. Allen, 1979; New York, Morrow, 1980.
Houd-den-bek. Johannesburg, Taurus, 1982; as *A Chain of Voices*, London, Faber, and New York, Morrow, 1982.
Die muur die pes. Cape Town, Human & Rousseau, 1984; as *The Wall of the Plague*, London, Faber, 1984; New York, Summit, 1985.

Short Stories and Novellas

Die meul teen die hang. Cape Town, Tafelberg, 1958.
Rooi, with others. Cape Town, Malherbe, 1965.
Oom Kootjie Emmer. Cape Town, Buren, 1973.
'n Emmertjie wyn: 'n versameling dopstories. Cape Town, Saayman & Weber, 1981.
Oom Kootjie Emmer en die nuwe bedeling: 'n stinkstorie. Johannesburg, Taurus, 1983.
Loopdoppies: Nog dopstories. Cape Town, Saayman & Weber, 1984.

Plays

Die band oms ons harte (The Bond Around Our Hearts). Johannesburg, Afrikaanse Pers, 1959.
Caesar (in verse; produced Stellenbosch, Cape Province, 1965). Cape Town, Nasionale, 1961.
Die beskermengel en ander eenbedrywe (The Guardian Angel and Other One-Act Plays), with others. Cape Town, Tafelberg, 1962.
Bagasie (Baggage; includes *Die koffer*, *Die trommel*, *Die tas*) (produced Pretoria, 1965). Cape Town, Tafelberg, 1965.
Elders mooiweer en warm (Elsewhere Fair and Warm) (produced Bloemfontein, 1969). Cape Town, Malherbe, 1965.
Die verhoor (The Trial) (produced Pretoria, 1975). Cape Town, Human & Rousseau, 1970.
Die rebelle (The Rebels). Cape Town, Human & Rousseau, 1970.
Kinkels innie kabel (Knots in the Cable), adaptation of *Much Ado About Nothing* by Shakespeare. Cape Town, Buren, 1971.
Afrikaners is plesierig (Afrikaners Make Merry). Cape Town, Human & Rousseau, 1973.
Pavane (produced Pretoria, 1980). Cape Town, Human & Rousseau, 1974.
Die Hamer van die hekse (The Hammer of the Witches). Cape Town, Tafelberg, 1976.
Toiings op die langpad (Toiings on the Long Road). Pretoria, Van Schaik, 1979.

Other

Die bende (The Gang; for children). Johannesburg, Afrikaanse Pers, 1961.
Platsak (Broke; for children). Johannesburg, Afrikaanse Pers, 1962.
Orde en chaos: 'n Studie oor Germanicus en die tragedies van Shakespeare (Order and Chaos: A Study of *Germanicus* and the Tragedies of Shakespeare). Cape Town, Nasionale, 1962.
Pot-pourri: Sketse uit Parys (Pot-pourri: Sketches from Paris). Cape Town, Human & Rousseau, 1962.
Die verhaal van Julius Caesar (for children). Cape Town, Human & Rousseau, 1963.

Sempre diritto: Italiaanse reisjoernaal (Sempre diritto: Italian Travel Journal). Johannesburg, Afrikaanse Pers, 1963.
Olé: Reisboek oor Spanje (Olé: A Travel Book on Spain). Cape Town, Human & Rousseau, 1965.
Aspekte van die nuwe prosa (Aspects of the New Fiction). Pretoria, Academica, 1967; revised edition, 1969, 1972, 1975.
Parys–Parys: Retoer (Paris–Paris: Return). Cape Town, Human & Rousseau, 1969.
Midi: Op reis deur Suid-Frankryk (Midi: Travelling Through the South of France). Cape Town, Human & Rousseau, 1969.
Fado: 'n reis deur Noord-Portugal (Fado: A Journey Through Northern Portugal). Cape Town, Human & Rousseau, 1970.
Die poësie van Breyten Breytenbach (The Poetry of Breyten Breytenbach). Pretoria, Academica, 1971.
Portret van die vrou as 'n meisie (Portrait of a Woman as a Young Girl). Cape Town, Buren, 1973.
Aspekte van die nuwe drama (Aspects of the New Drama). Pretoria, Academica, 1974.
Brandewyn in Suid-Afrika. Cape Town, Buren, 1974; as *Brandy in South Africa*, 1974.
Dessertwyn in Suid-Afrika. Cape Town, Buren, 1974; as *Dessert Wine in South Africa*, 1974.
Die Klap van die meul (A Stroke from the Mill). Cape Town, Buren, 1974.
Die Wyn van bowe (The Wine from Up There). Cape Town, Buren, 1974.
Ik ben er geweest: Gesprekken in Zuid-Afrika (I've Been There: Conversations in South Africa), with others. Kampen, Kok, 1974.
Voorlopige rapport: Beskouings oor die Afrikaanse literatuur van sewentig (Preliminary Report: Views on Afrikaans Literature in the 1970's). Cape Town, Human & Rousseau, 1976; *Tweede voorlopige rapport* (Second Preliminary Report), 1980.
Jan Rabie se 21. Cape Town, Academica, 1977.
Why Literature?/Waarom literatuur? Grahamstown, Rhodes University, 1980.
Heildronk uit Wynboer saamgestel deur AB ter viering van die blad se 50ste bestaansjaar. Cape Town, Tafelberg, 1981.
Die fees van die malles. Cape Town, Saayman & Weber, 1981.
Mapmakers: Writing in a State of Siege. London, Faber, 1983; as *Writing in a State of Siege*, New York, Summit, 1984.
Literatuur in die strydperk (Literature in the Arena). Cape Town, Human & Rousseau, 1985.

Editor, *Oggendlied: 'n bundel vir Uys Krige op sy verjaardag 4 Februarie 1977.* Cape Town, Human & Rousseau, 1977.
Editor, *Klein avontuur*, by Top Naeff. Pretoria, Academica, 1979.

Translator, *Die brug oor die rivier Kwaï*, by Pierre Boulle. Cape Town, Tafelberg, 1962.
Translator, *Reisigers na die Groot Land*, by André Dhôtel. Cape Town, Tafelberg, 1962.
Translator, *Die wonderhande*, by Joseph Kessel. Cape Town, HAUM, 1962.
Translator, *Nuno, die visserseun*, by L.N. Lavolle. Cape Town, HAUM, 1962.
Translator, *Verhale uit Limousin*, by Léonce Bourliaguet. Cape Town, Human & Rousseau, 1963.
Translator, *Die slapende berg*, by Léonce Bourliaguet. Cape Town, Human & Rousseau, 1963.

Translator, *Land van die Farao's*, by Leonard Cottrell.   Cape Town, Malherbe, 1963.

Translator, *Die bos van Kokelunde*, by Michel Rouzé.   Cape Town, Malherbe, 1963.

Translator, *Moderato Cantabile*, by Marguerite Duras.   Cape Town, HAUM, 1963.

Translator, *Die goue kruis*, by Paul-Jacques Bonzon.   Cape Town, Malherbe, 1963.

Translator, *Land van die Twee Riviere*, by Leonard Cottrell.   Cape Town, Malherbe, 1964.

Translator, *Volke van Afrika*, by C.M. Turnbull.   Cape Town, Malherbe, 1964.

Translator, *Alice se avonture in Wonderland*, by Lewis Carroll.   Cape Town, Human & Rousseau, 1965.

Translator, *Die mooiste verhale uit die Arabiese Nagte*.   Cape Town, Human & Rousseau, 1966.

Translator, *Die avonture van Don Quixote*, retold by James Reeves.   Cape Town, HAUM, 1966.

Translator, *Ek was Cicero*, by Elyesa Bazna.   Johannesburg, Afrikaanse Pers, 1966.

Translator, *Koning Babar*, by Jean de Brunhoff.   Cape Town, Human & Rousseau, 1966.

Translator, *Die Swerfling*, by Colette.   Johannesburg, Afrikaanse Pers, 1966.

Translator, *Die vindingryke ridder, Don Quijote de la Mancha*, by Cervantes.   Cape Town, Human & Rousseau, 1966.

Translator, *Speuder Maigret, Maigret en sy dooie, Maigret en die Lang Derm*, and *Maigret en die Spook*, by Simenon.   Johannesburg, Afrikaanse Pers, 4 vols., 1966–69.

Translator, *Die mooiste sprokies van Moeder Gans*, by Charles Perrault.   Cape Town, Human & Rousseau, 1967.

Translator, *Die eenspaaier*, by Ester Wier.   Cape Town, Human & Rousseau, 1967.

Translator, *Die eendstert* (Brighton Rock), by Graham Greene.   Johannesburg, Afrikaanse Pers, 1967.

Translator, *Mary Poppins in Kersieboomlaan*, by P.L. Travers.   Cape Town, Malherbe, 1967.

Translator, *Die Leeu, die heks en die hangkas*, by C.S. Lewis.   Cape Town, Human & Rousseau, 1967.

Translator, with others, *Die groot boek oor ons dieremaats*.   Cape Town, Human & Rousseau, 1968.

Translator, with others, *Koning Arthur en sy ridders van die Ronde Tafel*.   Cape Town, Human & Rousseau, 1968.

Translator, *Die Kinders van Groenkop*, by Lucy Boston.   Cape Town, Human & Rousseau, 1968.

Translator, *Alice deur die spieël*, by Lewis Carroll.   Cape Town, Human & Rousseau, 1968.

Translator, *Die Botsende rotse, Die Bul in die doolhoof, Die Horing van ivoor*, and *Die Kop van die gorgoon*, by Ian Serraillier.   Cape Town, HAUM, 4 vols., 1968.

Translator, *Bontnek*, by Dhan Gopal Mukerji.   Cape Town, HAUM, 1968.

Translator, *Die Draai van die skroef* (The Turn of the Screw), by Henry James.   Johannesburg, Afrikaanse Pers, 1968.

Translator, *Die Gelukkige prins en ander sprokies*, by Oscar Wilde.   Cape Town, Human & Rousseau, 1969.

Translator (into Afrikaans), *Richard III*, by Shakespeare.   Cape Town, Human & Rousseau, 1969.

Translator, *Die Gestewelde kat*, by Charles Perrault.   Cape Town, Human & Rousseau, 1969.

Translator, *Die groot golf*, by Pearl S. Buck.   Cape Town, Human & Rousseau, 1969.

Translator, *Die Nagtegaal*, by H.C. Andersen.   Cape Town, HAUM, 1969.

Translator, *Die Terroriste*, by Camus.   Johannesburg, Dramatiese Artistieke en Letterkundige Organisasie, 1970.

Translator, *Eskoriaal*, by Michel De Ghelderode.   Johannesburg, Dramatiese Artistieke en Letterkundige Organisasie, 1971.

Translator, *Ballerina*, by Nada Ćurčija-Prodanović.   Cape Town, Malherbe, 1972.

Translator, *Die Seemeeu* (The Seagull), by Chekhov.   Cape Town, Human & Rousseau, 1972.

Translator, *Die Bobaas van die Boendoe* (The Playboy of the Western World), by Synge.   Cape Town, Human & Rousseau, 1973.

Translator, *Jonathan Livingston Seemeeu*, by Richard Bach.   Cape Town, Malherbe, 1973.

Translator, *Hedda Gabler*, by Ibsen.   Cape Town, Human & Rousseau, 1974.

Translator, *Die Wind in die wilgers*, by Kenneth Grahame.   Cape Town, Human & Rousseau, 1974.

Translator, *Die Tragedie van Romeo en Juliet*, by Shakespeare.   Cape Town, Human & Rousseau, 1975.

Translator, *Die Tierbrigade*, and *Nuwe avontuur van die Tierbrigade*, by Claude Desailly.   Cape Town, Tafelberg, 2 vols., 1978–79.

Translator, *Die Nagtegaal en die roos*, by Oscar Wilde.   Cape Town, Human & Rousseau, 1980.

Translator, *Rot op reis*, by Kenneth Grahame.   Cape Town, Human & Rousseau, 1981.

Translator, *Adam van die pad*, by Elizabeth Janet Gray.   Cape Town, Human & Rousseau, 1981.

Translator, *Klein Duimpie*, by Charles Perrault.   Cape Town, Human & Rousseau, 1983.

*

Manuscript Collections: University of the Orange Free State, Bloemfontein; National English Literary Museum, Grahamstown.

André Brink comments:
   My early work revealed the influence of existentialism (notably of Camus) and was largely a matter of technical exploration. Ever since a year-long stay in Paris in 1968 a deep awareness of the responsibility of the novelist towards his society has shaped my work: not in the sense of "using" the novel for propaganda purposes, which degrades literature, but as a profound evaluation of social and interpersonal relationships as they affect the individual: the individual doomed to solitude and to more or less futile attempts to break out of this spiritual "apartheid" by trying to touch others—which means that the sexual experience is of primary importance to my characters.

*   *   *

   André Brink is an Afrikaner dissident who has chosen to remain inside the South African apartheid society which he regards as morally insupportable. His powerful political and historical novels have been translated into 20 languages, while in South Africa he is regarded with a highly sceptical eye by writers and academics alike.
   Brink is a prodigious, multi-talented literary figure. In addition to plays, travel writing, and critical work, he has written 12 novels and translated a great many works into Afrikaans. Presently a professor at Rhodes University, he is one of the country's foremost critics of Afrikaans literature. Despite three nominations for the Nobel Prize for literature, Brinks is reviled by many Afrikaans writers and critics in South Africa, not so much (or not only) because of his outright moral opposition

to apartheid, but for what is regarded as sentimentality and sensationalism in his writing. There is no doubt that Brink's writing is extremely uneven. His novels are almost always flawed in some respect, and they are often overwritten. Also, Brink has a singular penchant for placing gauche and inane statements in the mouths of his characters, while his rendition of sexual experience is cliché-ridden and tasteless. Yet he has written some of the most powerful stories to emerge in recent South African writing, and he commands impressive narrative skills (though here too he sometimes tries too hard).

As an emerging Afrikaans novelist in the late 1950's and early 1960's, Brink almost singlehandedly modernised Afrikaans novel-writing. Arguably the most eclectic South African writer at the time, he knocked the conservative Afrikaans literary tradition out of complacency with themes and techniques drawn from writers like Camus, Beckett, Sartre, Nabokov, Henry Miller, Faulkner, Greene, and Durrell. In 1974, the Afrikaner establishment was hit by the sensational news that Brink's *Kennis van die aand*, later translated into English as *Looking on Darkness*, had been banned. The banning created a major division between the State and many of the country's Afrikaans writers, and introduced a new era of increasingly vocal dissidence from within the establishment. After a Supreme Court hearing and a further two appeals, the novel was finally unbanned in 1982, but given an age restriction which is impossible to enforce.

For Brink, expulsion from the laager was an important juncture. Capitalising on sudden international fame as South Africa's first Afrikaans writer to be banned under the country's comprehensive 1963 censorship legislation—usually reserved for girlie calendars, Communist publications, and morally and politically perverse writing in English—Brink translated *Kennis van die aand* into English and became, thenceforth, an international novelist writing in English. He has since produced five weighty novels, roughly one every two years.

By his own admission Brink remains, in essence, an Afrikaner, but his recent novels are not "translated." Brink maintains that he produces the novels in both languages more or less simultaneously, starting out in Afrikaans, but completing the first "final" draft in English. However, Brink is far more idiomatic and comfortable in Afrikaans, and his English versions sometimes suffer from a certain rigidity of style.

Looking on Darkness is a compelling but uneven novel. As Nadine Gordimer has observed, it suffers from the "defiant exultation and relief" of Brink's first major cry of rebellion. The novel veers recklessly from profound historical reconstruction and metaphoric statement to the slushiest of sexual and emotional scenes. This book tells the story of Joseph Malan, a coloured man and a descendant of slaves who makes good as an actor after winning a grant to study at RADA in London, and who then comes home to launch a full-on cultural assault against apartheid. A passionate love affair with a white (British) woman develops, and Joseph is caught between the impossibility of love across the colour line, and the sinister manoeuvres of the Security Police against his theatre group. In a contrived and somewhat unconvincing denouement, Joseph murders his lover, whereupon the Security Police half kill him in unspeakably brutal fashion. He is sentenced to death, and the narrative is written from the death cell on sheets of paper which (we are asked to believe) Joseph daily flushes down the toilet, so determined is he to escape the scrutiny of his gaolers.

Looking on Darkness sets the pattern for Brink's later novels in several important respects. There is an uncompromising engagement with issues of race and politics, an insistence on exposing the sinister, vicious, and hypocritical elements at the heart of the apartheid system, an ability to rediscover the present in terms of a rich and violent frontier history, and a persistent fictional exploration of sexual love as a framework for a higher form of enquiry into the state of modern existence, subject to the peculiar restraints of apartheid society.

In *An Instant in the Wind*, Brink's first "English" novel following *Looking on Darkness*, a runaway slave escorts an 18th-century Cape lady back to civilisation after her husband and their party come to grief in an expedition into the interior. The story is a rich investigation into pertinent South African themes, and has a strong romantic appeal, but the love story between the erstwhile slave and the fallen lady constantly verges on a kind of sentiment more appropriate to popular romance fiction.

However, Brink's best talents come to the fore powerfully in his next—arguably his best—novel, *Rumours of Rain*. Like its successor, *A Dry White Season*, the novel examines the moral options of a contemporary Afrikaner who is rooted to a potent nationalistic history, but who is vulnerable to the shortcomings and hypocrisy of Afrikaner nationalism. *Rumours of Rain* achieves remarkable depth and complexity, and contains some of Brink's best characterisation.

The narrative inventiveness of *Rumours of Rain* and *A Dry White Season* is taken further in Brink's other *tour de force*, *A Chain of Voices*. This is a major novel which fictionalises a slave revolt in the early 19th century in the Cape. Brink gives each of his several characters a narrating voice, and out of the overlapping narratives a story of great force and interlocking complexity emerges. Brink's exceptional ability to re-animate the past—especially that of slavery in South Africa—enables him to establish the recurrent motifs of a frontier history in which South Africa remains confined.

True to form, Brink has followed up this success with a work which is thoroughly mediocre. *The Wall of the Plague* is a particularly clumsy attempt at metaphorically associating the Black Death plague of medieval Europe with modern apartheid. The novel degenerates into a lengthy and tired implied debate between three South African expatriates about the merits of exile as opposed to active engagement in the country itself, expressed in terms of black versus white sexual potency (there is a coloured girl in the middle) with a great deal of melodrama and sheer inanity thrown in. The sterility and creaking artifice of this novel truly make one wonder whether Brink has much more to say. But his is a reckless, unpredictable, and adventurous talent, with, no doubt, some surprises still in store.

—Leon de Kock

BRODERICK, John. Irish. Born in Athlone, 30 July 1927. Has lived in France, Italy, 1951–54, Morocco, 1960–61, and Mexico, 1976–77; now lives in Bath, England. Recipient: Irish Academy of Letters award, 1975. Agent: John Johnson Ltd., 45–47 Clerkenwell Green, London EC1R 0HT, England.

PUBLICATIONS

Novels

The Pilgrimage. London, Weidenfeld and Nicolson, 1961; as *The Chameleons*, New York, Obolensky, 1961.
The Fugitives. London, Weidenfeld and Nicolson, and New York, Obolensky, 1962.

Don Juaneen.   London, Weidenfeld and Nicolson, 1963; New York, Obolensky, 1965.
The Waking of Willie Ryan.   London, Weidenfeld and Nicolson, 1965.
An Apology for Roses.   London, Calder and Boyars, 1973.
The Pride of Summer.   London, Harrap, 1976.
London Irish.   London, Barrie and Jenkins, 1979.
The Trial of Father Dillingham.   London, Boyars, 1982.
A Prayer for Fair Weather.   London, Boyars, 1984.
The Rose Tree.   London, Boyars, 1985.

Plays

Radio Plays: *The Enemies of Rome*, 1979; *A Share of the Light*, 1981.

*

Manuscript Collection: Longford/Westmeath County Library.

Critical Study: "The Town: A Study of the Novels of John Broderick" by Sean McMahon, in *Eire-Ireland* (St. Paul), 1975.

John Broderick comments:

The novels of John Broderick deal with many themes: the difficulty of loving; the predicament of homosexuals in a hostile society; the strength of genuine religious feeling, and the weaknesses of its opposite; the frequency with which the strong overcome the weak; the apparent triumph, in many cases, of the unworthy. But the real theme, which dominates all the novels, with the exception of the two spy stories, *The Fugitives* and *A Prayer for Fair Weather*, is the power of money. Harsh, brutal, and pervading, it moulds the lives of nearly all the characters, and shapes their way of life. If Willie Ryan, in the novel about him, had been financially independent, he would not have spent 20 years in a mental asylum; if Phillip O'Connor in *Don Juaneen* had been a poor man, he would have been a better one.

Few of the people in Broderick's novels escape the enslavement of money, a corruption which is particularly malignant in a society, like the well-to-do middle class in Ireland during the years 1950 to 1980. This is still dominated, publicly at least, by the standards and shibboleths of a fiercely puritanical peasant tribe. Although sympathetic to Catholicism, and obviously possessing a strong religious sense, the author has not spared the attitudes of a church which has adapted itself to the narrow-mindedness and rapacity of this society.

Money then is the key to all the novels of John Broderick. It is a subject which is rarely examined in modern literature. Since it has very largely taken the place of God, it is treated with caution and even fear. Few critics have perceived this major theme in Broderick, allowing themselves to be distracted by other variations more obvious and less embarrassing. So much so that hardly any of them have noticed the strong vein of humour which, with the exception of the first novel, *The Pilgrimage* is present in all these books.

Don Juaneen is essentially a comic novel, so is *An Apology for Roses*, which has been taken with deadly earnestness by almost every critic. *The Pride of Summer* is certainly more comedy than tragedy. While *London Irish* with its complete cast of characters dominated by money is black comedy from beginning to end.

*   *   *

Up to *London Irish*, his seventh novel, all of John Broderick's books were set in the Irish midlands, around his native

Athlone. In these early novels he staked out a territory with an assuredness of style and purpose. With courage and sensitivity, Broderick made room for the naturalistic novel of provincial life, that essentially 19th-century form, in post-Joycean Ireland. Most Irish naturalism is urban, with the exception of such occasional novels as Brinsley MacNamara's *The Valley of the Squinting Windows* (1918) or John McGahern's *The Dark* (1965). Ireland is still a small country, and holding the mirror up to a rural community can mean big trouble for an author. Broderick never suffered public attack to the same degree as MacNamara or McGahern but by his continuing focus on the repressiveness of provincial society he can be said to have achieved the sort of moral effect that these writers undoubtedly, and painfully, attained. Although he is, to some extent, a "popular" writer, Broderick shared in a literary movement in Ireland in the 1960's, when a changing society was honestly and powerfully depicted, questioned, and explored.

In a prefatory note to *The Waking of Willie Ryan* Broderick defines the Irish Catholic scene which forms the landscape of his fiction: "From their lives, at first sight ordinary and parochial, the author reveals the meaning and hypocrisy which is part of the comedy and kind of tragedy." The atmosphere is invariably claustrophobic. Julia Glynn, the typical Broderick heroine, ponders her surroundings in *The Pilgrimage*: "Out there in the town, behind some window she had passed, somebody knew something which could bring her comfortable, secure life toppling about her." It is a society where anonymous letters are sent, describing in ill-spelled detail the sexual adventures of respectable, affluent, married women like Julia Glynn. Broderick's leading characters have always much to lose, much to be found out on. Their lives, accordingly, are furtive, their stratagems ignominious as well as (in essence) ludicrous.

Broderick treats heterosexual and homosexual love in much the same way. That is, his major theme is "forbidden love," forced upon the self by the urgencies of the flesh born into a narrow-minded culture. His women are of two kinds: one, like Julia Glynn or like Marie Fogarty in *An Apology for Roses*, of powerful sexuality thwarted by a sickly husband or a Puritan mother; the other a dried-up, over-pious woman with a hatred of sex and a malice towards women who display an appetite for it. Besides Mrs. Fogarty, in *An Apology for Roses*, Mrs. Reid in *London Irish* provides an example. But when one sees how homosexual love is depicted, in *The Waking of Willie Ryan* and *The Trial of Father Dillingham* in particular, it is clear that Broderick's concern is less psychological (as in D.H. Lawrence, for example) than sociological. He deals again and again with the vulnerability of the homosexual in a society dominated by conservative Roman Catholic mores. It is the secrecy of love that provides the drama of a Broderick novel.

In several of his novels there is a priest, whom Broderick humanizes in an interesting way. Father Mannix in *The Waking of Willie Ryan* opposes Ryan's homosexuality and tries to obliterate its history in the community from which Ryan has for some 20 years been barred, literally, in a mental asylum. Though he is depicted as a conventional cleric, Father Mannix is also treated sympathetically, as a man trapped in his own way within the rituals of his church. In *An Apology for Roses* Broderick breaks new ground by depicting a priest as the lover of Marie Fogarty, a young rich girl whose house he visits regularly on the pretext of teaching her German. Father Tom Moran is, of course, a scandal, as the poison-pen letters soon tell his superiors; but his human need, his loneliness, is given more attention in the book than his deceitfulness. There is no spite in Broderick's revelation of priestly weakness. He is, in fact, deeply interested in the plight of the priest in a changing society, and deals with it in detail in *The Trial of*

Father Dillingham. Here the priest has left the church, not for woman but for intellectual reasons, because a book he wrote met opposition from the Irish hierarchy. His struggle in the novel is parallelled by that of the homosexual Eddie Doyle: a struggle to find some kind of meaning in life after a disabling experience. This ambitious book ends with Father Dillingham's finding some kind of mission, of however tentative a nature, in South America. In *A Prayer for Fair Weather* there is a priest, Father Pat McMahon, who is rather more like Father Moran in *An Apology for Roses*, involved in an affair with a woman. But now it is clear that the priest is not merely pitiably satisfying natural desires but much more sympathetically caught up in a relationship with a woman who needs his love.

Religion is a significant theme in Broderick's novels. While he writes of sexual desire and social hypocrisy he maintains always a concern for the larger question of salvation. This is what lends detachment to his work, for he can view provincial life *as* provincial, as part of the human comedy, because it lacks the love that casts out fear. He derides false religion repeatedly. The joke in *The Pilgrimage* is directed at the hypocrisy of a family planning a trip to Lourdes while cheating on each other in a variety of ways; indeed, the trip will provide the sick man's wife added opportunity to continue her affair with her husband's nephew. That the invalid should actually be cured is the last thing anybody going on the pilgrimage really anticipates. But the last sentence in the book is: "In this way they set off on their pilgrimage, from which a week later Michael returned completely cured." We are left to imagine the shock of this miracle on all concerned. In *The Waking of Willie Ryan* Broderick claims that there is, in fact, very little religion, as opposed to convention, in Ireland. In *London Irish* he shows how the Irish in Britain keep at bay the realities (such as death and passion) by transplanting rituals from Ireland. Ritual, habit, is what these people live by. Their deadliness is suggested by their interest in funerals. Broderick measures them and finds them comically lacking, as when old Pollard loses his nerve, abandons his engagement to a sexy non-believer, and turns instead to the insufferable Mrs. Reid, a Catholic widow, whom he invites to share the graveplot he has just bought in Ireland. Ironically, the true meaning of love, which eludes this well-matched couple, is found by the sexy non-believer, Nancy Cook. This theme occupies *The Trial of Father Dillingham* more theologically, and it is here that Broderick's meditative preoccupation with relationships ambiguously viewed by society finds its most religious expression.

Having severed his connection with the Irish midlands Broderick looked for a wider, more cosmopolitan setting in his more recent novels. At the same time, he has begun to make use of the thriller genre. That, indeed, is the subtitle he gives to *A Prayer for Fair Weather*. It is as if suddenly Broderick had entered the world of John le Carré, where international spies, ruthless double agents, and political double-dealing abound. Yet there always was an element of the detective thriller in Broderick's work, in the relationship of secrecy and subterfuge to the form itself, with its suspense over who knew the secret and when or how it might be exposed. It could be said that Broderick is merely expanding his field of interest now, and using the form of the thriller to make his moral statement on a wider plane. In *A Prayer for Fair Weather* the one thing on which the various factions agree is that England is "deeply decadent." A great deal of detail, of London life, of contemporary politics and so on, is used to provide a realistic basis for this view. The result is a rather lifeless book, where the characters seem abstract. It may well be that the earlier novels, with their narrow scope, have in them an intensity,

a vitality, and a significance which the later, more sophisticated and ambitious work fails to attain.

—Christopher Murray

BRODKEY, Harold. American. Born in Alton, Illinois, 25 October 1930. Educated at Harvard University, Cambridge, Massachusetts, 1947–52, B.A. (cum laude) 1952. Married 1) Joanna Brown in 1952 (divorced, 1960), one daughter; 2) Ellen Schwamm in 1980. Associate Professor of English, Cornell University, Ithaca, New York, 1977–78, Spring 1979, and Fall 1981. Recipient: American Academy in Rome fellowship, 1959; Creative Artists Public Service grant, 1972; National Magazine award, 1974; Brandeis University Creative Arts Award, 1975; Pushcart prize, 1975; O. Henry Award, 1975, 1976; National Endowment for the Arts grant, 1984. Agent: Lynn Nesbit, International Creative Management, 40 West 57th Street, New York, New York 10019. Address: 255 West 88th Street, New York, New York 10024, U.S.A.

PUBLICATIONS

Short Stories

First Love and Other Sorrows. New York, Dial Press, 1957; London, Hamish Hamilton, 1958.
Women and Angels. Philadelphia, Jewish Publication Society of America, 1985.

Uncollected Short Stories

"The Abundant Dreamer," in *New Yorker*, 23 November 1963.
"On the Waves," in *New Yorker*, 4 September 1965.
"Bookkeeping," in *New Yorker*, 27 April 1968.
"Hofstedt and Jean—and Others," in *New Yorker*, 25 January 1969.
"Shooting Range," in *New Yorker*, 13 September 1969.
"Innocence," in *American Review 16*, edited by Theodore Solotaroff. New York, Bantam, 1973.
"Play," in *American Review 17*, edited by Theodore Solotaroff. New York, Bantam, 1973.
"Intro," in *American Poetry Review* (Philadelphia), May–June 1975.
"Manipulations," in *Ms.* (New York), October 1975.
"Puberty," in *Esquire* (New York), December 1975.
"His Son, in His Arms, in Light, Aloft," in *Prize Stories 1976: The O. Henry Awards*, edited by William Abrahams. New York, Doubleday, 1976.
"The Pain Continuum," in *Partisan Review* (New Brunswick, New Jersey), vol. 43, no. 1, 1976.
"Largely an Oral History of My Mother," in *New Yorker*, 26 April 1976.
"Two Soliloquies and Several Obsenities," in *American Review 26*, edited by Theodore Solotaroff. New York, Bantam, 1977.
"Verona: A Young Woman Speaks," in *Prize Stories 1978: The O. Henry Awards*, edited by William Abrahams. New York, Doubleday, 1978.
"Egypt and Fleshpots, Johnno and Wiley," in *Partisan Review* (Boston), vol. 51, 1984.
"Nonie," in *New Yorker*, 5 March 1984.
"What Going Out Without Ora Is Like: Johnno: 1956," in *Partisan Review* (Boston), vol. 52, no. 4, 1985.

"Falling and Ascending Bodies," in *Vanity Fair* (New York),
  March 1985.
"S.L.," in *New Yorker*, 9 September 1985.

*   *   *

Like a saint prematurely canonized before his martyrdom,
Harold Brodkey is in the delicate position of being declared
a novelist without having produced a novel. His early published
works are creditable if slender, although it was assumed—especially by awards committees—that his 1957 collection of nine
short stories, *First Love and Other Sorrows*, forecast a luminous
literary career.

The stories themselves were fresh, modest reprises of growing-up—puppy love to parenthood—not uncommon territory
for a young writer. *First Love* assured Brodkey's welcome on
college campuses where he has also read from his occasional
later works. In the three decades since his story collection,
however, Brodkey has produced only a few stories and a small
scattering of poems and comment. Two stories were the 1975
and 1976 O. Henry first prize winners nonetheless. "His Son,
in His Arms, in Light, Aloft," the 1976 selection, is a toddler-
narrated reflection on a father-son relationship and is an
obvious precursor of the recent sketch entitled "S.L."

Brodkey's creativity is said to be directed into a lengthy
novel-in-progress, *A Party of Animals*. In recent years, two
selections, "Lila" and "Ceil" were printed in the *New Yorker*,
then were reprinted along with another segment, "Angel,"
collectively called *Women and Angels*. A fourth exerpt, "S.L.,"
has appeared in the *New Yorker*. Since these four pieces—
character sketches of sorts—are the only glimpses of what has
been suggested is a life-work, they may not reliably define
the novel to come. They little suggest a novel at all, except
that they, again, cover a man's early years and are more or
less set in the Jewish family milieu in a small Illinois town.
Actually the excerpts have little to do with either being young
or being Jewish; they may be autobiographical and therefore
have much to do with being Brodkey. Whether that compels
readers may depend on how they share the every-life-a-novel
view which he presumably meant in a 1980 comment scoring
those who feel "that our lives are perhaps not worth writing
about."

A cyclonic tangle of recollections by Wiley Silenowicz about
his Russian-Jewish birth-mother, Ceil, and his American Jewish adoptive-parents, Lila and S.L. Silenowicz compete with
a one-hour appearance in the Harvard Yard by an Angel, who
may be God or Truth or "Sheer Otherness."

Wiley was utterly egocentric even as a toddler with perfect
recall of such trivia as shirt fabrics. His mean-spirited evalua-
tions of his not one, but two Jewish mothers inevitably invites
categorizing Brodkey's work in the Knock Mom school of fiction. It is also patronizingly Knock Dad in "S.L." and slides
down the slippery (and obviously unfamiliar) slopes of philosophy into incomprehensibility in "Angel." If Wiley is too
smart to Knock God in the quasi-interview that is "Angel",
he again settles for patronizing as in "I suddenly wanted to
be like It."

It is in narrative style that Brodkey insists on playing on
all the keys at once. A cacophony of effects results. There
is outrageous posturing and poetizing, eccentric syntax, arbitrary capitalizations, italics and incremental repetition, heaped
into overloaded sentences sagging under the weight of clause
upon clause. This excess obscures the undeniable poetic gifts
of language and rhythm that do manage to avoid inundation.
A line like "The air, the masked rainlight, the wind pounding,
hissing, pecking and pushing as if with a ruffled-feather breast—

it is monstrous" suddenly soars out. Even the spontaneous
burst of blabby, nervous S.L.'s compliment to baby Wiley
"You are really something; you are a bouquet on two legs—you
know that?" is a delight. Yet, enamored of the sound of words,
Brodkey too often tends to let meaning fall where it will, as
in the aphoristic "Child flesh in its brevity and shine is witty."

Excessive shifts in time and point of view compound confusion. Wiley, hooked on interior monologue when knee-high,
also narrates as himself at different ages, although in adult
language. He even makes room for another voice to speak
of him in the third person. Moreover, Wiley knows best what
other characters mean despite what they say and interprets
for the reader.

Brodkey has a way of melding narrative infelicities that does
appear unique. The nuances of advertising copy join awkward
syntax in ". . . no resistance emerges outward from me as my
own statement from the auditoriums of awe that much of my
personal consciousness is." Or here the sociological simplism
pairs with a poor pun: "We have here a landscape of envy
and emptiness—a place of temporary and embattled *comforts*,
an American beauty (that which results from a meeting of what
was here and a society of grand acquisitors)."

It is probably enough to say that when, or if, Brodkey
chooses to complete *A Party of Animals* that will be time for
a judgment on its entirety. As compulsive as a familiar exercise
or as necessary as an exorcism—who but Brodkey would
know?—the work completed may free him to go on to the
great creativity long expected of him. Or, less likely, prove
that Brodkey is already there.

—Marian Pehowski

BRONER, E(sther) M(asserman). American. Born in
Detroit, Michigan, 8 July 1930. Educated at Wayne State
University, Detroit, B.A. 1950, M.A. 1962; Union Graduate
School, New York, Ph.D. 1978. Married to Robert Broner;
four children. Since 1963, Member of the English Department,
currently Professor of English, Wayne State University. Visiting Professor, Haifa University, Israel, 1972 and 1975, and
at Hebrew Union College, Cincinnati, Oberlin College, Ohio,
and University of California, Los Angeles; Guest Professor,
Sarah Lawrence College, Bronxville, New York, 1982–85.
Recipient: Bicentennial Playwriting prize, 1976; National
Endowment for the Arts grant, 1979; Wonder Woman award,
1983; Wayne State University Distinguished Alumna award,
1984. Address: Department of English, Wayne State University, Detroit, Michigan 48202, U.S.A.

PUBLICATIONS

Novels

Her Mothers. New York, Holt Rinehart, 1975.
A Weave of Women. New York, Holt Rinehart, 1978.

Short Stories

Journal/Nocturnal and Seven Stories. New York, Harcourt
  Brace, 1968.

Uncollected Short Stories

"Traveler and His Telling," in *Commentary* (New York), September 1970.
"Is Fred Dead," in *Mother Jones* (San Francisco), January 1983.
"The Dancers," in *Ms.* (New York), November 1983.

Plays

Summer Is a Foreign Land (produced Detroit, 1967). Detroit, Wayne State University Press, 1966.
Colonel Higginson, with M. Zieve (produced Detroit, 1968).
The Body Parts of Margaret Fuller (produced Detroit and New York, 1976).
Letters to My Television Past (produced New York, 1985).

Television Play: *Wait Till I Swallow My Saliva*, 1968.

Other

Editor, with Cathy N. Davidson, *The Lost Tradition: Mothers and Daughters in Literature*. New York, Ungar, 1981.

*

Critical Studies: "Of Holy Writing and Priestly Voices" by Nancy Jo Hoy, Summer 1983, and interview, Winter 1984, both in *Massachusetts Review* (Amherst).

*   *   *

E.M. Broner is an original novelist. Except for a short story or two and her novella *Journal/Nocturnal*, she has never worked in a realistic mode. Even her first published play, *Summer Is a Foreign Land* (she has written others produced in university and community theaters), includes a character who is both a doctor and the angel of death, and a grandmother with an inheritance of three magical wishes because she descended from a wonder-working Hassidic rabbi in Poland. The matter of that play is clear and pragmatic enough: assimilation, the loss of traditional values, the weakening of generational ties, family expectations in conflict with personal freedom, but the world of the play is one of ordinary marvels.

It is not entirely accurate to call *Journal/Nocturnal* realistic, although there are no wonder-working rabbis or angels of death to be found. The setting is an urban university; we have a double journal by a faculty wife who has been having an affair with a right-wing student of her husband's, during the years of the Vietnam war, the split in the nation reflected in the split in the psyche of the protagonist and in the journal itself. One journal, running down the left half of the page, contains what she is willing to cede to the world, the surface of realism; the other side is her secret emotional life, verging into madness and finally into an accident we cannot help but see as willful death.

Journal/Nocturnal and the other stories in that volume are interesting, even arresting, but *Her Mothers* represents a leap of mastery, breadth, emotional range and power. A strong narrative voice emerges, in this case the partially throttled, often uproarious, and extremely intelligent voice of Beatrix Palmer. The book begins with a datum, the 1944 high school yearbook page of photographs. Through the novel, a vaudeville routine runs.

"Mother, I'm pregnant with a girl."
"How old is she?"
"Seventeen."

"Then you're giving birth to me."

or

"Mama, I'm giving birth to a baby girl."
"What is she?"
"Patient."
"Then leave her in the hospital."

We have the dreadful misadventures of Beatrix's high school girl friends. We have the adventures of her elective foremothers, Margaret Fuller, Louisa May Alcott, Emily Dickinson, and Charlotte Forten, about whom Bea is writing a book. The other foremothers of her search for identity are the Biblical matriarchs, Sara, Rivka, Lea, and Rahel (Sarah, Rebecca, Leah, and Rachel, in the usual English versions), whose stories Broner retells.

Bea is in search of her lost and estranged daughter Lena, trying to place herself in history with a set of foremothers who lead to her and a daughter who will carry on from her. She wanders through history and through the world in search of her ancestors and progeny, in Detroit, Florida, California, sea to sea, in Israel, in dreams. She has an affair with a ghost on a Georgia sea island, where foremother Charlotte Forten taught former slaves. Finally her daughter comes to her and in a scene that takes place obliquely, they quarrel, Bea tries to return her to the salty womb of the sea, and they reach a bumpy and fragile reconciliation.

A Weave of Women is a novel about a group of women, friends in Israel who try to reclaim the female and lunar side of Judaism, to place themselves again in history and also in the holy cosmos that always underlies Broner's work, in an ancient stone house in Jerusalem across the street from a home for wayward girls. The book is full of rituals the women invent, rediscover, create together to celebrate the times, the seasons, the crises of women's lives.

The women are sharply individuated, yet seen as a collective. The highly imagistic, rhythmic, and often wry narrative voice carries us in and out of their diverse experiences. Many disasters befall. At a Purim celebration where Simah (Joy) is retelling the myth of Esther from a woman-centered viewpoint, her baby daughter is murdered by an Arab who thinks she is someone else. Tsipporah, one of the wayward girls whose name means bird, is unable to survive the lures of the underside of religious and criminal life in the old city and becomes a pigeon instead. Shula, a wayward girl rescued by the women and sent to art school, goes abroad to study and is raped and murdered in a closed train compartment and literally eaten alive. Others of the women find strength to change their lives and become politically and religiously potent.

Broner's world-view is thoroughly Judaic and religious, a living and sensuous and intelligent battle fought with her religion through all of her books with the intent of making Judaism extend justice to and become a home for women. The world created in her novels is very much the modern world, full of the threats, the perils, the problems of modern life, a life of jetting about, trying to get grants, single motherhood, racism, antisemitism, wars, and threats of global wars; yet it is also a world never merely natural. It is a world in which demons enter women who are frustrated and soured, and can be expelled by wise and caring friends. It is a world in which a tormented girl can become a pigeon. It is a world in which myths embody themselves for good or evil in men and women and walk the earth to be encountered and wrestled with.

The women of *A Weave of Women* are even more ambitious than Bea in *Her Mothers*, for they want not only to locate themselves and their daughters in history, but to re-experience the cosmos, to re-invent godhead and the law, to make a new heaven and a new earth. Broner is not a prolific writer, but, like some of the characters she invents, she is passionate, serious, and ambitious. Her concern with women's descent, foremothers, mothers and daughters, runs through her strongest work, along with a consciously priestly or rabbinical function of reinterpreting the law and ritual in the service of women's dignity. She is a writer in whom a passionate experimentation comes together with serious political and religious inquiry.

—Marge Piercy

BROOKE-ROSE, Christine. British. Born in Geneva, Switzerland. Educated at Somerville College, Oxford, 1946–49, B.A., M.A. 1953; University College, London, 1950–54, B.A., Ph.D. 1954. Married Jerzy Peterkiewicz, *q.v.*, in 1948 (divorced, 1975). Free-lance literary journalist, London, 1956–68. Maitre de Conférences, 1969–75, and since 1975, Professor, University of Paris VIII, Vincennes. Recipient: Society of Authors travelling prize, 1965; James Tait Black Memorial Prize, 1967; Arts Council translation prize, 1969. Address: c/o Cambridge University Press, Edinburgh Building, Shaftesbury Road, Cambridge CB2 2RU, England.

PUBLICATIONS

Novels

The Languages of Love. London, Secker and Warburg, 1957.
The Sycamore Tree. London, Secker and Warburg, 1958; New York, Norton, 1959.
The Dear Deceit. London, Secker and Warburg, 1960; New York, Doubleday, 1961.
The Middlemen: A Satire. London, Secker and Warburg, 1961.
Out. London, Joseph, 1964.
Such. London, Joseph, 1966.
Between. London, Joseph, 1968.
Thru. London, Hamish Hamilton, 1975.
Amalgamemnon. Manchester, Carcanet, 1984.

Short Stories

Go When You See the Green Man Walking. London, Joseph, 1970.

Verse

Gold. Aldington, Kent, Hand and Flower Press, 1955.

Other

A Grammar of Metaphor. London, Secker and Warburg, 1958.
A ZBC of Ezra Pound. London, Faber, 1971; Berkeley, University of California Press, 1976.
A Structural Analysis of Pound's Usura Canto: Jakobson's Method Extended and Applied to Free Verse. The Hague, Mouton, 1976.
A Rhetoric of the Unreal: Studies in Narrative and Structure, Especially of the Fantastic. Cambridge and New York, Cambridge University Press, 1981.

Translator, *Children of Chaos*, by Juan Goytisolo. London, MacGibbon and Kee, 1958.
Translator, *Fertility and Survival: Population Problems from Malthus to Mao Tse Tung*, by Alfred Sauvy. New York, Criterion, 1960; London, Chatto and Windus, 1961.
Translator, *In the Labyrinth*, by Alain Robbe-Grillet. London, Calder and Boyars, 1968.

*   *   *

Christine Brooke-Rose teaches American literature at the University of Paris, and this fact is important in considering the work of this cosmopolitan writer, whose later novels are much influenced by the French *avant-garde* of the late 1950's. Her early, biting satires are constructed in the usual manner of plot and character, but when she came to consider the work of such French writers as Robbe-Grillet, her style changed radically. She virtually discarded metaphor, and started to use language more as a concrete artefact than as a vehicle of communication and information.

In its least subtle forms, this manner of writing comes close to word games. At its best it pushes the reader into a new awareness of semantics and logical absurdities. The words are built up round a single theme, which acts as a prism for a multitude of facets. There is no plot in the conventional sense, and no character is sufficiently realised for the reader's emotions to become entangled. Even when Brooke-Rose treats of a global disaster, as she does in *Out* (the first novel of her new genre) she is careful to distance her reader, in this instance by the technical language of advanced science.

The next novel, *Such*, deals with a near-death experience, in which the central character, an astronomer called Larry (a deliberate echo of Lazarus) sees people in the same way as he had once seen the emerging and degenerating heavenly bodies. The protagonist of *Between* works as an interpreter from French to German, a circumstance that presents a natural occasion for the linguistic kaleidoscopes which are the meat of Brooke-Rose's cerebral work.

Thru is probably the most accessible, and certainly the funniest of these concrete novels. Here Brooke-Rose turns again to satire, taking for her target the faculty of a modern university, running courses in various aspects of linguistics, creative writing, and all sorts of fashionable sociological and feminist topics. The students' essays are matched against the discussions endlessly going on among the faculty members; and the triangular relationship that snakes its way through the work of the apprentice novelists is shadowed by the affairs taking place among the staff. The reader is not allowed to disentangle any of this too easily. Once again the main purpose of the novel is the exploration of language, and this is done even to the extent of discarding anything resembling conventional syntax in favour of pseudo-diagrams and concrete patterns. From time to time the reader is thrown a joke to ease the struggle for meaning. So a teaching method is defined as one in which "you peripatate along in ancient sunshine (known also as the peripatetic fallacy)." But anything as explicit as that is rare. The reader must be prepared to approach these novels with the same sort of expectations that one brings to surrealist painting.

Although Brooke-Rose's work up to the mid-1970's was acclaimed by Angus Wilson, and Frank Kermode, she kept a nine-year silence after the publication of *Thru*. When *Amalgamemnon* finally appeared, the reader was once again plunged into the academic world, although in this instance there is a single protagonist, a woman teacher of literature and history, who becomes redundant. This character is as fluid as one would expect, and as her world and assumptions disintegrate around her in a collage of classical texts, radio weather forecasts, phone-ins only a little less awful than the real thing, anticipated conversations and the world of ancient myth and modern violence, we are presented with a kaleidoscope of wit and invention. Yet the play on words can pall. The joke of placing an initial "s" before almost every word beginning with "ex" struck me as sexasperating; but the skill with which Brooke-Rose can mimic voices and so create the cast which forms the background of this near-abstract novel is a source of admiration and pleasure.

With *Xorandor* (forthcoming) the reader leaves academe for the world of science fiction in which the explosive development of the computer and the micro-chip (a marvellous opportunity for linguistic gymnastics) is combined with the urgent problem of nuclear waste disposal. The computer, which gives its name to the title, actually feeds off alpha-particles from fissile materials. Its story is told by two children, who dictate it to a word processor, which presents them with all kinds of linguistic experiences, except the vital one which comes from the communication between non-programmed, frequently irrational human beings.

—Shirley Toulson

BROOKNER, Anita. British. Born in London, 16 July 1928. Educated at James Allen's Girls' School; King's College, University of London; Courtauld Institute of Art, London, Ph.D. in art history. Visiting Lecturer, University of Reading, Berkshire, 1959–64; Slade Professor, Cambridge University, 1967–68. Lecturer, 1964, and since 1977, Reader, Courtauld Institute of Art. Fellow, New Hall, Cambridge. Recipient: Booker Prize, 1984. Address: 68 Elm Park Gardens, London SW10 9PB, England.

PUBLICATIONS

Novels

A Start in Life. London, Cape, 1981; as *The Debut*, New York, Linden Press, 1981.
Providence. London, Cape, 1982; New York, Pantheon, 1984.
Look at Me. London, Cape, and New York, Pantheon, 1983.
Hotel du Lac. London, Cape, 1984; New York, Pantheon, 1985.
Family and Friends. London, Cape, and New York, Pantheon, 1985.

Other

Watteau. London, Hamlyn, 1968.
The Genius of the Future: Studies in French Art Criticism: Diderot, Stendahl, Baudelaire, Zola, the Brothers Goncourt, Huysmans. London and New York, Phaidon Press, 1971.
Greuze: The Rise and Fall of an Eighteenth-Century Phenomenon. London, Elek, and Greenwich, Connecticut, New York Graphic Society, 1972.
Jacques-Louis David: A Personal Interpretation (lecture). London, Oxford University Press, 1974.

Jacques-Louis David. London, Chatto and Windus, 1980; New York, Harper, 1981.

Translator, *Utrillo*. London, Oldbourne Press, 1960.
Translator, *The Fauves*. London, Oldbourne Press, 1962.
Translator, *Gauguin*. London, Oldbourne Press, 1963.

*   *   *

There are times when nothing but the cliché will do. In the extraordinary case of Anita Brookner, the unavoidable phrase is a meteoric rise to success. Five novels in four years. Reviews ranging from excellent to lyrical for all of them. The fourth, *Hotel du Lac* wins the Booker Prize, together with an avalanche of publicity (to say nothing of huge sales) such as even this controversy-arousing award has never received before.

Does she deserve it? Like Brookner, the majority of our women novelists today have high educational backgrounds and only too often their intellectual slips show. The surprise about this author is that all her novels pulse with the blood of ordinary, everyday experience. It's true, her principal characters live and work in that almost obligatory, cultivated, middle-class, fairly sophisticated society which produces so much contemporary fiction. But vividly, if lightly, evoked is also an ordinary world of clothes, cooking, encounters in streets and cafes, landladies, staff rooms, and what used to be called "servants." She has an almost magical gift for making important what can only be described, with the pleasure of recognition, as the trivia of day to day living. But this is only a part of the periphery round her main themes . . . or perhaps one should say "theme" since all five of her novels are really different slices of what appears to be largely autobiography. Brookner herself in various interviews and with a singular openness has volunteered this information.

What is this theme? It is one which hardly any woman writer since Charlotte Brontë has had the courage to express: the plight of the clever, feeling woman of great sensibility who longs all too humanly for love and companionship with a man of particular quality but has neither the beauty to attract him nor the coarseness of temperament to grab for him. A secondary, but important theme is revealed as a progress from belief in the triumph of the good and the decent to the painful discovery that virtue is useless.

In Brookner's first novel, *A Start in Life*, we have the childhood and young womanhood of Ruth Weiss, her quietness and discipline set against a slightly raffish family background. (In all her books Brookner appears to draw very freely upon her own central European, vaguely artistic, rather rich, family history.) Ruth ends up at 40, a lecturer in literature—but alone. Brookner's second book, *Providence*, carries the heroine, this time called Kitty, rather further into the region of disillusionment. She is let down by the kind of "unselfish" man she should have seen through. But he is physically beautiful (all the men fancied by Brookner's women are intelligent, tall, have handsome or distinguished faces with long mouths, are either married already or choose someone else) and Kitty is exceptionally susceptible to masculine good looks. It must be said that in this respect Brookner's heroines are amazingly old-fashioned if not downright Victorian. Has she not learned that most contemporary women don't fall for well-mannered, handsome types (if they ever did) and are far more likely to go for squat, ugly, demanding men? Charlotte Brontë got it right with Rochester and even more so with the short, peppery professor in *Villette*. Where both writers converge is in their characters' longing for nobility, for moral rectitude. Jane Eyre found it.

Brookner's heroines do not. Indeed, in her clear, bitter, final understanding of the way we are now can be seen, almost in a sentence, the crucial difference between the last century and our own.

Look at Me, her third novel and her best to date, continues the search for love, and also glamour. This hard, relentless exposure of another largely unchronicled area of the human psyche—its violent longing for some more marvellous life—constitutes Brookner's greatest claim on our attention. Frances, again a quiet-seeming, bookish spinster falls for the entrancing, brilliant personalities of a married couple, beautiful and lively, who take her up into their delightful orbit and as inevitably drop her. There is a possible lover who does the same. But the strength and depth of the book, the revelation of the greed and selfishness of these careless, heartless children (for this is how Frances, rightly, comes to see them) is done with a degree of psychological insight which is breathtaking. It ends on a note of heart-breaking betrayal.

Hotel du Lac, set in an elegant Swiss hotel and done with immaculate observation and exquisite detail, takes the Brookner heroine's experience a stage further—but with one important difference. Her continually being cold-shouldered by life is having its effect. Edith Hope, while still vulnerable, here shows for the first time signs of a corruption inevitable upon so much betrayal. She has become cruel; much as Henry James's heroine in *Washington Square* becomes cruel. She has behaved very badly—and, worse, shows no sign of remorse—to a decent, good if dull man and, somewhat inexplicably, throws away her later chance of dignity in marriage, for a continuing, futile relationship with a married man. All for love! It is possible to see here for the first time why a few critics have accused Brookner of sentimentality.

And finally, *Family and Friends*; something of a departure since the form has changed. Written in the historic present, with practically no dialogue, this is more a rumination than a novel; again exact and beautifully written but somehow strangely misty. It is the first of her novels not to have one woman at the precise centre but is woven around a family: a widowed mother of central European and obviously Jewish origin and her two sons and two daughters. Once more we have the contrast between the lucky and the unlucky, the dazzling and the dull. And again the author reaches the firm conclusion that the prizes of life go not to the good but to the vulgar and unscrupulous.

Are the praise and the critical fuss justified? Certainly ... but not with an unqualified Yes. This novelist has determinedly thrown into harsh light aspects of human, feminine (*not* feminist) experience which needed to be thrust before us. People should know what this kind of suffering is like, she says. Look at me. *Look* at me. But it is when looking for classic status that one or two awkward questions arise. Though Brookner's insight goes very deep, her canvas so far is very narrow. The five books are really only one, with one central character. Ruth is Kitty is Frances is Edith. And there really isn't all that much difference between her faithless men either. Also the five novels are all very short and somehow one feels the need for more abundance. We are *told* a great deal. But a truly great novel really requires *presentation*; actuality on the page. Frances, in *Look at Me* describes herself as capable of being an amusing companion, witty and sharp-tongued. But we never actually hear her being either. Her creator handles gesture and body language with something near genius. But is that enough? And finally, perhaps, the most important question of all. She has made one, admittedly desperately important statement, five times. Has she anything to say about anything else?

But this is carping. We should simply be grateful for the emergence of so subtle and searing a perception, so blessed with a talent for expressing itself.

—Gerda Charles

BROPHY, Brigid (Antonia). British. Born in London, 12 June 1929. Educated at St. Paul's Girls' School; St. Hugh's College, Oxford (Jubilee Scholar), 1947–48. Married Sir Michael Levey in 1954; one daughter. Co-organiser, Writers Action Group, 1972–82; Executive Councillor, Writers Guild of Great Britain, 1975–78; Vice-Chairman, British Copyright Council, 1976–80. Since 1974, Vice-President, Anti-Vivisection Society of Great Britain. Recipient: Cheltenham Festival prize, 1954; *London Magazine* prize, 1962; Tony Godwin Award, 1985. Fellow, Royal Society of Literature, 1973. Address: Flat 3, 185 Old Brompton Road, London SW5 0AN, England.

PUBLICATIONS

Novels

Hackenfeller's Ape. London, Hart Davis, 1953; New York, Random House, 1954.
The King of a Rainy Country. London, Secker and Warburg, 1956; New York, Knopf, 1957.
Flesh. London, Secker and Warburg, 1962; Cleveland, World, 1963.
The Finishing Touch. London, Secker and Warburg, 1963.
The Snow Ball. London, Secker and Warburg, 1964.
The Snow Ball, with The Finishing Touch. Cleveland, World, 1964.
In Transit. London, Macdonald, 1969; New York, Putnam, 1970.
The Adventures of God in His Search for the Black Girl: A Novel and Some Fables. London, Macmillan, 1973; Boston, Little Brown, 1974.
Palace Without Chairs: A Baroque Novel. London, Hamish Hamilton, and New York, Atheneum, 1978.

Short Stories

The Crown Princess and Other Stories. London, Collins, and New York, Viking Press, 1953.

Uncollected Short Stories

"Pilgrimage," in *Winter's Tales 3.* London, Macmillan, and New York, St. Martin's Press, 1957.
"De Bilbow," in *Shakespeare Stories*, edited by Giles Gordon. London, Hamish Hamilton, 1982.
"Singled Out," in *Short Story Monthly*, 1982.

Plays

The Waste-Disposal Unit (broadcast, 1964). Published in *London Magazine*, April 1964; in *Best Short Plays of the World Theatre 1958–67*, New York, Crown, 1968.
The Burglar (produced London, 1967). London, Cape, and New York, Holt Rinehart, 1968.

Radio Play: *The Waste-Disposal Unit*, 1964.

Other

Black Ship to Hell. London, Secker and Warburg, and New York, Harcourt Brace, 1962.
Mozart the Dramatist: A New View of Mozart, His Operas, and His Age. London, Faber, and New York, Harcourt Brace, 1964.
Don't Never Forget: Collected Views and Reviews. London, Cape, 1966; New York, Holt Rinehart, 1967.
Religious Education in State Schools. London, Fabian Society, 1967.
Fifty Works of English and American Literature We Could Do Without, with Michael Levey and Charles Osborne. London, Rapp and Carroll, 1967; New York, Stein and Day, 1968.
Black and White: A Portrait of Aubrey Beardsley. London, Cape, 1968; New York, Stein and Day, 1969.
The Longford Threat to Freedom. London, National Secular Society, 1972.
Prancing Novelist: A Defence of Fiction in the Form of a Critical Biography in Praise of Ronald Firbank. London, Macmillan, and New York, Barnes and Noble, 1973.
Beardsley and His World. London, Thames and Hudson, and New York, Crown, 1976.
Pussy Owl (for children). London, BBC Publications, 1976.
The Prince and the Wild Geese. London, Hamish Hamilton, and New York, St. Martin's Press, 1983.
A Guide to Public Lending Right. Aldershot, Hampshire, Gower, 1983.

*

Manuscript Collection: Lilly Library, University of Indiana, Bloomington.

*   *   *

In the agreeably self-dramatizing preface to her play *The Burglar*, Brigid Brophy provides a definitive statement of her aims and methods as a critic and novelist. Like Saw (whom she sees, along with Freud, as one of the "two mainstays of the twentieth century"), Brophy is an evolutionary vitalist, essentially optimistic despite a sharp eye for human failings and hypocrisies. And like Shaw she assumes the existence of a driving Life Force which strives to express itself in ever more competent and complex forms.

Art itself is a "function of the life instinct," which by its potent illusions brings us "into accord with reality" (unlike religion, which makes the mistake of taking its illusions as literal truths). The human race is a species "uniquely capable of imagination, rationality and moral choice," and therein lies man's justification and perilous responsibility. For Brophy, like Shaw once more, knows full well that our powers may be misused, that the human race is frighteningly capable of undoing what the Life Force has accomplished thus far. From Freud Brophy takes over the conception of life as a dynamic struggle between Eros, the binding and civilizing force, and Thanatos, the death instinct which seeks to destroy the work of Eros. Thus *Black Ship to Hell* has as its theme "man as a destructive and, more particularly, a self-destructive animal" and is in effect an encyclopedic investigation of the interrelationships of the two opposing principles in war, politics, art and religion. Brophy sees her work, finally, in the life-affirming tradition of Shaw and Freud: "I too am aiming to reform civilization."

The necessary balance between Eros and Thanatos, the integration of work, love, and responsibility, gives Brophy the theme of her fiction: in the long run there may be reason to hope for civilization, but in the short run of individual lives there are failures as well as successes, an infinite fund of dramatic possibilities to be exploited.

Brophy's didacticism is apparent at once in her first collection of short stories, *The Crown Princess*, many of which are no more than fictionalized statements of a thesis or problem. But there is one story here, "Fordie," which unmistakably reveals a writer of remarkable power and intelligence. An intricate fable about the differences between the true creator and the self-seeking failure, "Fordie" belongs in the company of Henry James's great series of artist-parables. *Hackenfeller's Ape*, Brophy's first novel, is a disappointingly thin version of one of her persistent concerns, the treatment of animals "whom we have no right to maim, torture or kill." Embedded here, however, is a dialogue between opposing forces which illustrates clearly the truth of Brophy's statement that all of her works are "baroque," that is, they all "proceed by contraposition; and in a reductive analysis the elements contraposited are always Eros and Thanatos." *The King of a Rainy Country*, a much more engaging novel, dramatizes the disordered forms Eros may assume in individual lives—in regressive, homo-erotic relationships and more specifically in doomed, infantile quests for the "perfect moment." In this comic anti-romance the heroine learns at some painful cost that the static ideal is impossible: "you give from one person and take from another—give and take vitality, I mean. Nobody is a reservoir. It's just an exchange. It goes round in an endless cycle." *Flesh* continues to explore this vital give and take, dramatizing with splendid economy and wit the way in which love reclaims a diffident young man. Brophy avoids sentimentality, however, by indicating that in this particular relationship the cost of investigation has been high; the young man brought to life by Eros is now an object of both horror and desire for his wife; pain becomes a sinister bond in "a hostile and perhaps perverted situation."

The baroque method of construction is increasingly important in Brophy's later work, "deploying masses in such a way that each, as well as performing its own function, constitutes a funnel down which one gets a sharply unexpected view—ironic, tragic or comic." *The Snow Ball* is architectural with a vengeance: its complexity, Brophy boasts, "defies even my own intellectual analysis." But unfortunately the opposite is true: in this brittle, pretentious reworking of the Don Juan–Donna Anna theme (to which Brophy is addicted, seeing in the myth a paradigm of the human sexual emotions), only the contrived and quite obvious design engages the reader's attention. Man is not only *homo faber* and *homo artifax* for Brophy, but *homo Fabergé* as well, and hence her fascination with Beardsley, Firbank, and other aesthetes and dandies. *The Finishing Touch*, besides providing another example of Eros distorted, is an homage to Ronald Firbank, an imitative recreation of the very highest order.

In Transit is a radical departure from the quasi-naturalistic style of the earlier books. In "Fordie" the narrator had reflected that "perhaps the personality surrenders some of its philosophic right to be called a personality when the babbling to oneself, which is the mark of human identity, is halted. I would write a book on the subject, if anyone would attend to it." *In Transit* is that book, and a good deal more, anatomizing the layers of individual personality in a wild, punning Joycean flow of rhetoric which defies coherent description. The hero–heroine (we are hurled into a vortex where sexual differences are superficial) is "in transit," literally waiting to board a plane, but psychically in transit as well, pulled and pushed by a host of new energies. The secondary or simultaneous protagonist of *In Transit* is language itself, which is extended, inverted, parodied, and finally blown to bits by the onslaught of modern life. "I am," the psyche insists, but "communication is broken." In a sleight-of-hand finale, however, which is typical of Brophy's invincible optimism, the psyche is reintegrated "for Love of You"—the "You" being (apparently) the expectant interlocutor our consciousness by necessity posits and the eternal "you" of the audience, waiting for the voice of the artist to bring it back into accord with even the most disruptive modern reality.

The sub-title of *The Adventures of God in His Search for the Black Girl* is misleading. The first section of the book is made up of short fables, very much in the style of *The Crown Princess* and making many of the same points. The long title piece, however, is not really a novel at all, but a kind of philosophic dialogue in the manner of Lucian and Shaw. The chief character, God, is anxious to establish once and for all his "fictitious" nature as a being wholly created by man. The problems arise, he argues, when men take this fiction—or any of their other guiding fictions—as literal, historic truth. The issue here is a familiar one these days: all human beliefs and ideals are, like works of art, purely imaginative constructs. Some are benign, some are not. The implied goal, then, is to construct fictions which will be recognized as such and will still have the power to work for the benefit of mankind. The "Godifesto" is released in a dove-like shower over Rome, but in a wry epilogue Brophy seems to be suggesting that those receiving it will fail to understand what is at stake.

Palace Without Chairs is a novel of sorts, an extended if not entirely clear political allegory. The King and Queen of Evarchia and four of their five children kill themselves or disappear in a series of ludicrous accidents, and a military dictatorship promptly takes over; but the last of the royal children, Heather, a "pachydermous" lesbian, manages to reach London, where our final glimpse of her is an ambiguous one. Drunk in a small hotel bar and happily pursuing another ample lady, she still seems to her former governess (who may not be a reliable witness) to offer "some just cause for hope. ... The very elements in her personality that most people condemned were ... the sources of a vitality that should surmount both guilt and nostalgia." *Palace Without Chairs* is amusing enough at times but takes few risks and as a result is considerably less impressive than *In Transit*.

—Elmer Borklund

BROWN, George Mackay. British. Born in Stromness, Orkney, Scotland, 17 October 1921. Educated at Stromness Academy, 1926–40; Newbattle Abbey College, Dalkeith, Midlothian, 1951–52, 1956; Edinburgh University, 1956–60, 1962–64, B.A. (honours) in English 1960, M.A. Recipient: Society of Authors travel award, 1968; Scottish Arts Council prize, 1969; Katherine Mansfield-Menton Prize, 1971. M.A.: Open University, 1976; LL.D.: University of Dundee, 1977; D.Litt.: University of Glasgow, 1985. Fellow, Royal Society of Literature, 1977. O.B.E. (Officer, Order of the British Empire), 1974. Address: 3 Mayburn Court, Stromness, Orkney KW16 3DH, Scotland.

PUBLICATIONS

Novels

Greenvoe. London, Hogarth Press, and New York, Harcourt Brace, 1972.
Magnus. London, Hogarth Press, 1973.
Time in a Red Coat. London, Chatto and Windus, 1984; New York, Vanguard Press, 1985.

Short Stories

A Calendar of Love. London, Hogarth Press, 1967; New York, Harcourt Brace, 1968.
A Time to Keep. London, Hogarth Press, 1969; New York, Harcourt Brace, 1970.
Hawkfall and Other Stories. London, Hogarth Press, 1974.
The Sun's Net. London, Hogarth Press, 1976.
Witch and Other Stories. London, Longman, 1977.
Andrina and Other Stories. London, Chatto and Windus, 1983.
Christmas Stories. Oxford, Perpetua Press, 1985.
The Masked Fisherman. Pitlochry, Perthshire, Duval, 1985.
Selected Stories. New York, Vanguard Press, 1986.

Plays

Witch (produced Edinburgh, 1969). Included in *A Calendar of Love*, 1967.
A Spell for Green Corn (broadcast, 1967; produced Edinburgh, 1970). London, Hogarth Press, 1970.
The Loom of Light (produced Kirkwall, 1972). Included in *Three Plays*, 1984.
The Storm Watchers (produced Edinburgh, 1976).
The Martyrdom of St. Magnus (opera libretto), music by Peter Maxwell Davies, adaptation of the novel *Magnus* by Brown (produced Kirkwall and London, 1977; Santa Fe, 1979). London, Boosey and Hawkes, 1977.
The Two Fiddlers (opera libretto), music by Peter Maxwell Davies, adaptation of the story by Brown (produced London, 1978). London, Boosey and Hawkes, 1978.
The Well (produced at St. Magnus Festival, 1981). Included in *Three Plays*, 1984.
The Voyage of Saint Brandon (broadcast, 1984). Included in *Three Plays*, 1984.
Three Plays. London, Chatto and Windus, 1984.

Radio Plays: *A Spell for Green Corn*, 1967; *The Voyage of Saint Brandon*, 1984.

Television Plays: three stories from *A Time to Keep*, 1969; *Orkney*, 1971; *Miss Barraclough*, 1977; *Four Orkney Plays for Schools*, 1978; *Andrina*, 1984.

Verse

The Storm. Kirkwall, Orkney Herald Press, 1954.
Loaves and Fishes. London, Hogarth Press, 1959.
The Year of the Whale. London, Hogarth Press, 1965.
The Five Voyages of Arnor. Falkland, Fife, Duval, 1966.
Twelve Poems. Belfast, Festival, 1968.
Fishermen with Ploughs: A Poem Cycle. London, Hogarth Press, 1971.
Poems New and Selected. London, Hogarth Press, 1971; New York, Harcourt Brace, 1973.
Lifeboat and Other Poems. Crediton, Devon, Gilbertson, 1971.
Penguin Modern Poets 21, with Iain Crichton Smith and Norman MacCaig. London, Penguin, 1972.

Winterfold.   London, Hogarth Press, 1976.
Selected Poems.   London, Hogarth Press, 1977.
Voyages.   London, Chatto and Windus, 1983.
Christmas Poems.   Oxford, Perpetua Press, 1984.

Recording: *George Mackay Brown*, Claddagh, 1977.

Other

Let's See the Orkney Islands.   Fort William, Inverness, Thomson, 1948.
Stromness Official Guide.   London, Burrow, 1956.
An Orkney Tapestry.   London, Gollancz, 1969.
The Two Fiddlers (for children).   London, Chatto and Windus, 1974.
Letters from Hamnavoe (essays).   Edinburgh, Wright, 1975.
Edwin Muir: A Brief Memoir.   West Linton, Peeblesshire, Castlelaw Press, 1975.
Pictures in the Cave (for children).   London, Chatto and Windus, 1977.
Under Brinkie's Brae.   Edinburgh, Wright, 1979.
Six Lives of Fankle the Cat (for children).   London, Chatto and Windus, 1980.
Portrait of Orkney, photographs by Werner Forman.   London, Hogarth Press, 1981.

*

Manuscript Collections: Scottish National Library, Edinburgh; Edinburgh University.

Critical Study: *George Mackay Brown* by Alan Bold, Edinburgh, Oliver and Boyd, and New York, Barnes and Noble, 1978.

George Mackay Brown comments:

(1972) I find it very difficult to comment on my own work, except in some imaginery context. I have recently finished a short story called "Seal Skin" about a musician. He reads, in Dublin, an old Celtic manuscript, about "the intricate web of creation" that men are mindlessly exploiting and tearing; and he is much moved by it. The last paragraphs are as follows:

He [Magnus Olafson the musician] thought of the men who have thrown off all restraint and were beginning now to raven in the most secret and delicate and precious places of nature. They were the new priesthood; the world went down on its knees before every tawdry miracle—the phonograph, the motor car, the machine-gun, the wireless—that they held up in triumph. And the spoliation had hardly begun.

Was this then the task of the artist: to keep in repair the sacred web of creation—that cosmic harmony of God and beast and man and star and plant—in the name of humanity, against those who in the name of humanity are mindlessly and systematically destroying it?

If so, what had been taken from him was a necessary sacrifice.

*   *   *

The ancient undulating landscape of the Orkney islands forms more than a backcloth to the work of George Mackay Brown: it provides motif after motif for his novels and short stories, informing them with a sense of grandeur and venerable antiquity. A favourite description is "very ancient," and this phrase recurs again and again to build up a sense of timelessness

where chronology becomes unimportant. In his novel *Greenvoe* Brown views time as "not a conflagration; it is a slow grave sequence of grassblade, fish, apple, star, snowflake," and the natural symbolism is continued in the inevitable demise of the community of Greenvoe and the promise of its resurrection: "The sun rose. The stars were warm. They broke the bread." Although there is death in the novel, the death of a human community, Brown uses the potent concept of renewal through the planting of seed both as a reminder of the island's heritage and as a reiteration of the doctrine of salvation through resurrection. Skarf, the Marxist fisherman, imagines the founding of the Orkney islands with strange visitors from the Mediterranean and Scandinavia bringing with them jars of seed to ensure their survival in a new life.

The descendants of those early invaders are the crofters and fishermen of Orkney who are the life-blood of Brown's fiction. It is they who are the integral part of the circle of life and death and it is they who move inexorably in its rhythm of seedtime, birth, harvest, and death. Their participation and their knowledge of the historical inter-twining of their present with their ancestors' past give a dignity to their lives and also prevents Brown's interest in them from sliding into sentimentality or nostalgia for the irretrievable past.

The theme of renewal is continued in *Hawkfall*, a collection of five related pieces which contemplate the survival of human characteristics in an Orkney family from the Bronze Age to the present day. Through the long sweep of history Brown traces both the story of his islands and the personal relationships that exist between succeeding generations of its people. The stories in *Hawkfall* are in the minor key, sombre and suffused with the ancient heritage of Orkney, and it is fitting that the collection should end with "The Interrogator," a story that examines not the finality and pain of death but its impossible mystery. That same sense of the mystery of creation is present in *The Sun's Net*, a collection of stories imbued with Brown's religious belief that each birth is the re-enactment of the nativity; in "A Winter Tale" the ancient ritual of the sun king and the corn queen is contrasted with the simple birth of a child in mid-winter at a deserted croft. Children grow up to renew the community and in any season are blessed, but this child born at Christmas is seen by all, except the minister who has become blind to miracles, as a promise of the island's salvation. In *Andrina*, Brown shows that he has perfected a narrative style of great simplicity, its virtues drawn more from the traditional art of telling tales than from any experimental form of fiction.

Brown's fascination with the Christian theme of redemption finds its most vigorous form in his second novel, *Magnus*, which tells the story of the 12th-century Earl of Orkney who was later sanctified for his martyrdom at the hands of his cousin Haakon. The terrible contemplation of Magnus's torment lies at the heart of this deeply religious work, a novel so dense and committed to its central theme that it lacks the simple narrative structure of the best short stories. More successful is *Time in a Red Coat*, a densely packed novel which offers a moving parable on the stupidity of war. Set in an eastern kingdom, the novel is a kaleidoscope of images, stereotypes, and freakish landscapes, all described with Brown's customary inventiveness and economy of language. The atmosphere is timeless, yet fantasy and fact are mingled persuasively in evocations of past and present as they exist in the mind of the central character, a young girl charged with the mission of destroying the dragon of war before it engulfs the world in flames and death.

Despite this new departure, the central pre-occupation in Brown's fiction remains Orkney, its history and traditions, the people who have contributed to its story and to its regeneration over succeeding generations: these are the central strands with which Brown has woven a seamless literature, deceptively simple yet universal in its appeal.

—Trevor Royle

BUECHNER, (Carl) Frederick. American. Born in New York City, 11 July 1926. Educated at Lawrenceville School, New Jersey, graduated 1943; Princeton University, New Jersey, A.B. 1947; Union Theological Seminary, New York, B.D. 1958; ordained a Minister of the United Presbyterian Church, 1958. Served in the United States Army, 1944–46. Married Judith Friedrike Merck in 1956; three children. English Master, Lawrenceville School, 1948–53; Instructor in Creative Writing, New York University, summers 1953–54; head of the employment clinic, East Harlem Protestant Parish, New York, 1954–58; Chairman of the Religion Department, 1958–67, and School Minister, 1960–67, Phillips Exeter Academy, New Hampshire. William Belden Noble Lecturer, Harvard University, Cambridge, Massachusetts, 1969; Russell Lecturer, Tufts University, Medford, Massachusetts, 1971; Lyman Beecher Lecturer, Yale Divinity School, New Haven, Connecticut, 1976; Harris Lecturer, Bangor Seminary, Maine, 1979; Smyth Lecturer, Columbia Seminary, New York, 1981; Zabriskie Lecturer, Virginia Seminary, Lynchburg, 1982. Recipient: O. Henry Prize, 1955; Rosenthal Award, 1959; American Academy award, 1982. D.D.: Virginia Seminary, 1983; Lafayette College, Easton, Pennsylvania, 1984. Agent: Harriet Wasserman, 137 East 36th Street, New York, New York 10016. Address: Box 1160, Pawlet, Vermont 05761, U.S.A.

PUBLICATIONS

Novels

A Long Day's Dying. New York, Knopf, 1950; London, Chatto and Windus, 1951.
The Seasons' Difference. New York, Knopf, and London, Chatto and Windus, 1952.
The Return of Ansel Gibbs. New York, Knopf, and London, Chatto and Windus, 1958.
The Final Beast. New York, Atheneum, and London, Chatto and Windus, 1965.
The Entrance to Porlock. New York, Atheneum, and London, Chatto and Windus, 1970.
The Book of Bebb. New York, Atheneum, 1979.
  Lion Country. New York, Atheneum, and London, Chatto and Windus, 1971.
  Open Heart. New York, Atheneum, and London, Chatto and Windus, 1972.
  Love Feast. New York, Atheneum, 1974; London, Chatto and Windus, 1975.
  Treasure Hunt. New York, Atheneum, 1977; London, Chatto and Windus, 1978.
Godric. New York, Atheneum, 1980; London, Chatto and Windus, 1981.

Uncollected Short Story

"The Tiger," in *Prize Stories 1955: The O. Henry Awards*, edited by Paul Engle and Hansford Martin. New York, Doubleday, 1955.

Other

The Magnificent Defeats (meditations). New York, Seabury Press, 1966; London, Chatto and Windus, 1967.
The Hungering Dark (meditations). New York, Seabury Press, 1969.
The Alphabet of Grace (autobiography). New York, Seabury Press, 1970.
Wishful Thinking: A Theological ABC. New York, Harper, and London, Collins, 1973.
The Faces of Jesus, photographs by Lee Boltin. Croton-on-Hudson, New York, Riverwood, 1974.
Telling the Truth: The Gospel as Tragedy, Comedy, and Fairy Tale. New York, Harper, 1977.
Peculiar Treasures: A Biblical Who's Who. New York, Harper, 1979.
The Sacred Journey (autobiography). New York, Harper, and London, Chatto and Windus, 1982.
Now and Then (autobiography). New York, Harper, 1983.
A Room Called Remember: Uncollected Pieces. New York, Harper, 1984.

*

Manuscript Collection: Wheaton College, Illinois.

Critical Study: *Laughter in a Genevan Gown: The Works of Frederick Buechner 1970–1980* by Marie-Hélène Davies, Grand Rapids, Michigan, Eerdmans, 1983.

Frederick Buechner comments:
  When I started out writing novels, my greatest difficulty was always in finding a plot. Since then I have come to believe that there is only one plot. It has to do with the way life or reality or God—the name is perhaps not so important—seeks to turn us into human beings, to make us whole, to make us Christs, to "save" us—again, call it what you will. In my fiction and non-fiction alike, this is what everything I have written is about.

*   *   *

  The novels of Frederick Buechner represent a movement from a consideration of psychological textures to an assessment of the religious values that are expressed by those textures. The fact that Buechner is an ordained Presbyterian clergyman may not strike the reader of the earlier novels—*A Long Day's Dying*, *The Seasons' Difference*, and *The Return of Ansel Gibbs* —as particularly relevant to the interpretation of those novels. His early novels, indeed, may impress the casual reader as works that are in the tradition of Henry James, concerned as they are with the rather delicate and tenuously resolved relations among cultivated and privileged Americans. The characters in these novels are preoccupied with resolutions of their difficulties, but these resolutions go no farther than clarification of their identities in relation to each other. This clarification is conveyed in a style that was regarded, at the time of the novels' appearance, as oblique and over-worked. The actual course of event in the early novels issues, as indicated, in changes of orientation that can be spoken of as a clearing out of the psychological undergrowth that impedes the discovery of purpose and self-knowledge on the part of the chief characters. The course of the narratives is marked by a taste for ironic comedy—a comedy that records the experience of living in a world that, unlike the world of some older comedy, is bare of generally shared values. The values that are to be detached are values for a particular person and do not have much wider relevance.

It is in later novels—*The Final Beast*, *The Entrance to Porlock*, and *Lion Country*—that one can see Buechner moving, in an ironic and quite self-protective way, toward concerns that his ordination as a clergyman would suggest. He moves from concern with particular persons in special situations toward more inclusive concerns which announce that lives of individual characters are oblique annunciations of the general constraint and opportunity which all human beings can, if they are responsive, encounter. The psyche is also a soul—a focus of energy that achieves fulfillment by coming into relation with patterns that religion and mythology testify to. The style of the later work becomes simpler, and Buechner delights in reporting farcical aspects of American experience that found little place in his earlier work. And these farcical elements are organized by invocation of narrative patterns that are widely known. The narrative pattern that underpins *The Entrance to Porlock* is drawn from that item of popular culture, *The Wizard of Oz*; the motley company of his novel repeats and varies the quest that took Dorothy Gale and her companions along the Road of Yellow Bricks.

In *Lion Country* and the three novels that succeed it—*Open Heart*, *Love Feast*, and *Treasure Hunt*—the grotesque menagerie of characters has experiences that are organized by nothing less than the traditional patterns of the Christian religion itself. (The four novels are published together under the title of *The Book of Bebb*.) In this series, the Christian religion undergoes parody that on the surface is blasphemous, is offered variation that is ironical rather than confirming, and yet—in the long run—achieves the only kind of validation that is possible at the present time. At the very least the series is a successful counter-weight to novels that confirm conventional piety by exercises in conventional piety. Yet beneath the adultery, farce, and sheer violence of the Bebb series is a set of insights that are very close to the assertions of conventional Christianity. The conventionality—and the sincerity—of Buechner's views can be sampled in the theological ABC contained in *Wishful Thinking* and other meditations.

In summary Buechner can be seen as a novelist who at first was challenged by the sheer complexity of human behavior and who later finds that complexity comprehensible when linked with popular myth-work like the Oz books and, finally, with the self-mastery and self-discovery offered by the Christian religion.

—Harold H. Watts

BUKOWSKI, Charles. American. Born in Andernach, Germany, 16 August 1920; brought to the United States in 1922. Attended Los Angeles City College, 1939–41. Divorced; one daughter. Post office worker, Los Angeles, for 12 years. Formerly, Editor, *Harlequin*, Wheeler, Texas, then Los Angeles, and *Laugh Literary* and *Man the Humping Guns*, both Los Angeles; columnist ("Notes of a Dirty Old Man"), *Open City*, Los Angeles, then Los Angeles *Free Press*. Recipient: Loujon Press award; National Endowment for the Arts grant, 1974. Address: P.O. Box 132, San Pedro, California 90731, U.S.A.

PUBLICATIONS

Novels

Post Office. Los Angeles, Black Sparrow Press, 1971; London, London Magazine Editions, 1974.
Factotum. Los Angeles, Black Sparrow Press, 1975; London, W.H. Allen, 1981.
Women. Santa Barbara, California, Black Sparrow Press, 1978; London, W.H. Allen, 1981.
Ham on Rye. Santa Barbara, California, Black Sparrow Press, 1982; London, Airlift, 1983.

Short Stories

Notes of a Dirty Old Man. North Hollywood, California, Essex House, 1969.
Erections, Ejaculations, Exhibitions and General Tales of Ordinary Madness. San Francisco, City Lights, 1972; abridged edition, as *Life and Death in the Charity Ward*, London, London Magazine Editions, 1974; selections, edited by Gail Chiarello, as *Tales of Ordinary Madness* and *The Most Beautiful Woman in Town and Other Stories*, City Lights, 2 vols., 1983.
South of No North. Los Angeles, Black Sparrow Press, 1973.
Bring Me Your Love. Santa Barbara, California, Black Sparrow Press, and London, Airlift, 1983.
Hot Water Music. Santa Barbara, California, Black Sparrow Press, and London, Airlift, 1983.
There's No Business. Santa Barbara, California, Black Sparrow Press, and London, Airlift, 1984.

Verse

Flower, Fist and Bestial Wail. Eureka, California, Hearse Press, 1959.
Longshot Poems for Broke Players. New York, 7 Poets Press, 1961.
Run with the Hunted. Chicago, Midwest, 1962.
Poems and Drawings. Crescent City, Florida, Epos, 1962.
It Catches My Heart in Its Hands: New and Selected Poems 1955–1963. New Orleans, Loujon Press, 1963.
Grip the Walls. Storrs, Connecticut, Wormwood Review Press, 1964.
Cold Dogs in the Courtyard. Chicago, Chicago Literary Times, 1965.
Crucifix in a Deathhand: New Poems 1963–65. New Orleans, Loujon Press, 1965.
The Genius of the Crowd. Cleveland, 7 Flowers Press, 1966.
True Story. Los Angeles, Black Sparrow Press, 1966.
On Going Out to Get the Mail. Los Angeles, Black Sparrow Press, 1966.
To Kiss the Worms Goodnight. Los Angeles, Black Sparrow Press, 1966.
The Girls. Los Angeles, Black Sparrow Press, 1966.
The Flower Lover. Los Angeles, Black Sparrow Press, 1966.
Night's Work. Storrs, Connecticut, Wormwood Review Press, 1966.
2 by Bukowski. Los Angeles, Black Sparrow Press, 1967.
The Curtains Are Waving. Los Angeles, Black Sparrow Press, 1967.
At Terror Street and Agony Way. Los Angeles, Black Sparrow Press, 1968.
Poems Written Before Jumping Out of an 8-Story Window. Berkeley, California, Litmus, 1968.
If We Take . . . . Los Angeles, Black Sparrow Press, 1969.

The Days Run Away Like Wild Horses over the Hills. Los Angeles, Black Sparrow Press, 1969.
Penguin Modern Poets 13, with Philip Lamantia and Harold Norse. London, Penguin, 1969.
Another Academy. Los Angeles, Black Sparrow Press, 1970.
Fire Station. Santa Barbara, California, Capricorn Press, 1970.
Mockingbird Wish Me Luck. Los Angeles, Black Sparrow Press, 1972.
Me and Your Sometimes Love Poems. Los Angeles, Kisskill Press, 1972.
While the Music Played. Los Angeles, Black Sparrow Press, 1973.
Love Poems to Marina. Los Angeles, Black Sparrow Press, 1973.
Burning in Water, Drowning in Flame: Selected Poems 1955–1973. Los Angeles, Black Sparrow Press, 1974.
Africa, Paris, Greece. Los Angeles, Black Sparrow Press, 1975.
Weather Report. North Cambridge, Massachusetts, Pomegranate Press, 1975.
Winter. Evanston, Illinois, No Mountain, 1975.
Touch Company, with *The Last Poem*, by Diane Wakoski. Santa Barbara, California, Black Sparrow Press, 1976.
Scarlet. Santa Barbara, California, Black Sparrow Press, 1976.
Maybe Tomorrow. Santa Barbara, California, Black Sparrow Press, 1977.
Love Is a Dog from Hell: Poems 1974–1977. Santa Barbara, California, Black Sparrow Press, 1977.
Legs, Hips, and Behind. Los Angeles, Wormwood Review Press, 1979.
Play the Piano Drunk Like a Percussion Instrument until the Fingers Begin to Bleed a Bit. Santa Barbara, California, Black Sparrow Press, 1979.
A Love Poem. Santa Barbara, California, Black Sparrow Press, 1979.
Dangling in the Tournefortia. Santa Barbara, California, Black Sparrow Press, 1981.
The Last Generation. Santa Barbara, California, Black Sparrow Press, 1982.
Sparks. Santa Barbara, California, Black Sparrow Press, 1983.
War All the Time: Poems 1981–1984. Santa Barbara, California, Black Sparrow Press, 1984.

Other

Confessions of a Man Insane Enough to Live with Beasts. Bensenville, Illinois, Mimeo Press, 1965.
All the Assholes in the World and Mine. Bensenville, Illinois, Open Skull Press, 1966.
A Bukowski Sampler, edited by Douglas Blazek. Madison, Wisconsin, Quixote Press, 1969.
Art. Santa Barbara, California, Black Sparrow Press, 1977.
What They Want. Santa Barbara, California, Neville, 1977.
We'll Take Them. Santa Barbara, California, Black Sparrow Press, 1978.
You Kissed Lilly. Santa Barbara, California, Black Sparrow Press, 1978.
Shakespeare Never Did This. San Francisco, City Lights, 1979.
The Bukowski/Purdy Letters: A Decade of Dialogue 1964–1974, with Al Purdy, edited by Seamus Cooney. Sutton West, Ontario, Paget Press, 1983.

Editor, with Neeli Cherry and Paul Vangelisti, *Anthology of L.A. Poets.* Los Angeles, Laugh Literary, 1972.

*

Bibliography: *A Bibliography of Charles Bukowski* by Sanford Dorbin, Los Angeles, Black Sparrow Press, 1969.

Manuscript Collection: University of California, Santa Barbara.

Critical Studies: *Charles Bukowski: A Biographical Study* by Hugh Fox, Somerville, Massachusetts, Abyss, 1968; *Bukowski: Friendship, Fame, and Bestial Myth* by Jory Sherman, Augusta, Georgia, Blue Horse Press, 1982; "Charles Bukowski Issue" of *Review of Contemporary Fiction* (Elmwood Park, Illinois), Fall 1985.

*   *   *

Charles Bukowski's world, as John William Corrington aptly stated in the introduction to *It Catches My Heart in Its Hands* (1963), "is an alley, a dark hallway; it is a park or a trashlittered road alongside the Pacific—or the Mississippi. And its tenants are not actors. They are derelicts, convicts, whores, dogs, paupers, roaches, drunks, and the rest of the lower end of the American spectrum." This is both a fair assessment of the world represented through Bukowski's prose and poetry (Bukowski is most famous as a poet) and representative itself of the "compliments" that Bukowski's admirers pay him. Bukowski writes of the "lower end" of America and the people who inhabit this sphere perhaps more honestly and bluntly—sparing no four-lettered words, no unpleasant detail—than any American writer ever has. "The spoken word nailed to the page" is how Corrington describes Bukowski's style. It is because of his no-holds-barred depiction of a heretofore ignored stratum of America that Bukowski has come to be loved particularly by those bored with the "safe" subjects and the formal, etiquette-burdened prose of most of Bukowski's contemporaries. Bukowski has never been supported by a university or a large publisher; he has come from and largely remained in the world of which he writes. Published by small, underground presses and ephemeral mimeographed little magazines, Bukowski has gained popularity, in a sense, through word of mouth.

Bukowski's first full-length book of short stories was called *Erections, Ejaculations, Exhibitions and General Tales of Ordinary Madness.* The themes in this early book are perhaps best described by Thomas Edward of the *New York Review*, who paraphrases Bukowski's attitude as, "Politics is bullshit, since work is as brutalizing and unrewarding in a liberal order as in any totalitarian one; artists and intellectuals are mostly fakes, smugly enjoying the blessings of the society they carp at; the radical young are spiritless asses, insulated by drugs and their own endless cant from any authentic experience of mind or body; most women are whores, though *honest* whores are good and desirable; no life finally works, but the best one possibly involves plenty of six packs, enough money to go to the track, and a willing woman of any age and shape in a good old-fashioned garter belt and high heels."

Bukowski despises phoniness and pretension on any level, and his style, accordingly, is simple and straightforward, shunning the ornate or "literary" usage, Bukowski's sentences are mostly short and direct (no metaphor, no allusion, no "devices"), and he prefers, like Hemingway, with whom he is sometimes compared, the simple adjective. But *Erections,*

Ejaculations also reveals a Bukowski who, while maintaining a simple, direct prose style, is experimenting on other levels. In the book there are stories in third person and first person (in later books Bukowski will stay with first-person narration), stories in which no capitalization of proper nouns is used, and stories in which every letter of dialogue is capitalized; there are also stories—clearly autobiographical—in which Bukowski will use his own name for the protagonist and others, also autobiographical, in which the protagonist is named Henry Chinaski, a name Bukowski will use solely in all later stories and novels. They are clearly the stories of a still-developing writer.

An important element in *Erections, Ejaculations*, as in all of Bukowski's writings, is humor. Bukowski's is a lowbrow, tough-guy humor which belittles and degrades just about anything or anyone—from feminists to homosexuals to writers to politicians. Many do not find Bukowski funny at all, but, for others, Bukowski's humor is the main attraction of his writing, enlivening his otherwise utterly depressing outlook. A few lines of one story in *Erections, Ejaculations*, "Great Poets Die in Steaming Pots of Shit," give a taste of the humor and the way in which Bukowski uses it to make serious statements. At the beginning of the story, Bukowski is in a typical condition: "with sick hangover I crawled out from under the sheets the other day to get to the store, buy some food, place food inside of me and make the job I hate." He gets to the grocery store and meets a man who recognizes Bukowski as the great underground poet. The man insists on starting a conversation with Bukowski, who, as usual, is not interested but tolerates the man while Bukowski, hungover, throws food into his basket. The story is made up mostly of their dialogue, signified throughout by upper case letters, and through the dialogue Bukowski's position concerning himself and others who have "made it" comes through in one-line quips. The man nagging Bukowski, recognizing Bukowski's deplorable condition, asks, "CAN'T YOU GET A GRANT OR SOMETHING." Bukowski says, "I TRIED LAST YEAR. THE HUMANITIES. ALL I GOT BACK WAS A FORM-LETTER OF REJECTION." "BUT EVERY ASS IN THE COUNTRY IS LIVING ON A GRANT," the man says. "YOU FINALLY SAID SOMETHING," Bukowski replies.

Bukowski's first novel, *Post Office*, shows, if not a change in overall attitude or "theme," a coalescing of style and point of view which Bukowski maintains to the present day. His protagonist is Henry Chinaski, a thinly-disguised alter-ego, and the novel is, as usual, roughly autobiographical, since Bukowski did work for a post office in Los Angeles as, first, a substitute carrier and, later, a clerk for nearly 12 years—his only steady job, other than that of writer. The tale begins when Chinaski, a drunk, needing a temporary job (again), learns from "the drunk up the hill" that the post office will hire "damned near anybody" near Christmas as a temporary carrier. The novel ends when, many hassles with the supervisors, drunken days and nights, and several women later, Chinaski, finally leaving the post office for good, decides to write his first novel. *Post Office* is, like all of Bukowski's novels, very episodic, written in short sections of often little more than a page which recount, for instance, a mail-carrying mishap, a run-in with the boss, a drunken spree, or a fight with the woman. Yet the novel coheres because of its overall purpose of telling the story of Chinaski's days with the post office, and each section, though a little "episode" in itself, depends upon the others to complete the overall story.

Post Office makes clear that Chinaski/Bukowski is a terminal loner. And it brings out a recurring theme in Bukowski: that human relationships, because of inevitably conflicting egos and

desires, never work. Chinaski, time and again, begins alone, encounters others (usually a woman), with whom he begins a relationship. But the relationships inevitably fail, and Chinaksi ends up alone, again. Chinaski is not rueful about this inevitability; he is accepting. He is a supreme existentialist, and the words which end the chapters of *Post Office* often illuminate this attitude: "I got up, walked to the car and I rented the first place I saw with a sign. I moved in that night. I had just lost 3 women and a dog"; "She even helped me pack . . . I got into the car and began cruising up and down the streets looking for a For Rent sign. It didn't seem to be an unusual thing to do"; "We drank a little and then we went to bed, but it wasn't the same, it never was . . . We slept without touching. We had both been robbed." *Post Office* is, appropriately, "dedicated to nobody."

After reading much Bukowski (and there is much to read: though he has written only four novels, his output thus far has been over 60 books, including poetry and short fiction), one senses that, behind this inexorable existential stoicism, there is a Bukowski who has indeed, somewhere along the way, "been robbed" emotionally himself. Bukowski's most recent novel, *Ham on Rye*, confirms this suspicion, as it recounts the story of Henry Chinaski as a child and adolescent. It is autobiographical, and its mixture of poignance, humor, and honesty have made it Bukowski's most highly acclaimed work. It also marks the first time Bukowski has written about his childhood.

The story is told, as usual, by Chinaski himself, starting with his earliest memories of his childhood. As in *Huckleberry Finn* and *The Catcher in the Rye*, the vantage point of a young person is perhaps the best one from which to expose the hypocrisy, pretensions, and vanity of a "grown-up" world, the main things Bukowski sets out to expose. *Ham on Rye* takes on a much more touching, human dimension than his earlier works, for here it is the young, impressionable, and vulnerable Chinaski having to cope with the evils and sicknesses of grown-up people.

Ham on Rye takes place mostly during the Depression years and ends at the outbreak of World War II. Chinaski is raised in a household where the father, chronically unemployed, is stereotypically stern and overbearing ("He didn't like me. 'Children should be seen and not heard,' he told me") and the mother is characterless and obeying ("'The father,' she said, 'is always right'"). Chinaski's parents—like most grown-ups in the novel—live their lives based on false ideals and erroneous perceptions of how life "should be." Their ideals and perceptions have little to do with reality and they make life, for those who, like Chinaski, see the phoniness and wish for truth and honesty, a game of little interest. The novel unfolds as a series of incidents—often tragic, often hilarious—through which Chinaski sees these shortcomings in his parents and people of the "real" world and comes to accept his situation as hopeless. Chinaski first fully understands the phoniness with which people cloak themselves when he fabricates what was supposed to be a factual account of President Hoover's visit to Los Angeles and submits it to his English teacher. After his English teacher discovers that his supposedly "factual" paper—a paper she had read to the class and praised as exemplary—is a fraud, she, to save face, praises Chinaski anyway, saying "That makes it all the more remarkable." Chinaski comments: "So that's what they wanted: lies. Beautiful lies. That's what they needed. People were fools."

Knowing that people prefer the comfortable lie to the uncomfortable truth makes encounters with all but understanding outsiders (like himself) unbearable for Chinaski. With the "outsiders" Chinaski finds himself inevitably allied. Because, however, the human relationship—even among outsiders like Chinaski—is ineluctably ephemeral, Chinaski soon finds that the only things that make life bearable are masturbating, dreaming of sex (Chinaski never does, in *Ham on Rye*, actually have intercourse with a woman), and, above all, alcohol: "'Without drink,' Chinaski says to his buddy near the end of the novel, 'I would have long ago cut my god-damned throat.'" Charles Bukowski's ability to present in a language directly from the people about whom he writes the hypocrisies, the intellectual shortcomings, and the sadness of those trying to live out the American Dream makes *Ham on Rye*—and most of Bukowski's fiction—relevant and moving.

—Jay Dougherty

BURGESS, Anthony. Pseudonym for John Anthony Burgess Wilson. British. Born in Manchester, Lancashire, 25 February 1917. Educated at Xaverian College, Manchester; Manchester University, B.A. (honours) in English 1940. Served in the British Army Education Corps, 1940–46: Sergeant-Major. Married 1) Llewela Isherwood Jones in 1942 (died, 1968); 2) Liliana Macellari in 1968, one son. Lecturer, Extra-Mural Department, Birmingham University, 1946–48; Education Officer and Lecturer, Central Advisory Council for Adult Education in the Forces, 1946–48; Lecturer in Phonetics, Ministry of Education, 1948–50; English Master, Banbury Grammar School, Oxfordshire, 1950–54; Senior Lecturer in English, Malayan Teachers Training College, Khata Baru, 1954–57; English Language Specialist, Department of Education, Brunei, Borneo, 1958–59. Writer-in-Residence, University of North Carolina, Chapel Hill, 1969–70; Professor, Columbia University, New York, 1970–71; Visiting Fellow, Princeton University, New Jersey, 1970–71; Distinguished Professor, City University of New York, 1972–73; Literary Adviser, Guthrie Theatre, Minneapolis, 1972–75. Also composer. Recipient: National Arts Club award, 1973; Foreign Book Prize (France), 1981. D.Litt.: Manchester University, 1982. Fellow, Royal Society of Literature, 1969. Address: 44 rue Grimaldi, Monaco.

PUBLICATIONS

Novels

Time for a Tiger. London, Heinemann, 1956.
The Enemy in the Blanket. London, Heinemann, 1958.
Beds in the East. London, Heinemann, 1959.
The Right to an Answer. London, Heinemann, 1960; New York, Norton, 1961.
The Doctor Is Sick. London, Heinemann, and New York, Norton, 1960.
The Worm and the Ring. London, Heinemann, 1961; revised edition, 1970.
Devil of a State. London, Heinemann, 1961; New York, Norton, 1962.
One Hand Clapping (as Joseph Kell). London, Davies, 1961; as Anthony Burgess, New York, Knopf, 1972.
A Clockwork Orange. London, Heinemann, 1962; New York, Norton, 1963.
The Wanting Seed. London, Heinemann, 1962; New York, Norton, 1963.

Honey for the Bears. London, Heinemann, 1963; New York, Norton, 1964.
Inside Mr. Enderby (as Joseph Kell). London, Heinemann, 1963.
The Eve of Saint Venus. London, Sidgwick and Jackson, 1964; New York, Norton, 1967.
Nothing Like the Sun: A Story of Shakespeare's Love-Life. London, Heinemann, and New York, Norton, 1964.
The Malayan Trilogy (includes *Time for a Tiger, The Enemy in the Blanket, Beds in the East*). London, Heinemann, 1964; as *The Long Day Wanes,* New York, Norton, 1965.
A Vision of Battlements. London, Sidgwick and Jackson, 1965; New York, Norton, 1966.
Tremor of Intent. London, Heinemann, and New York, Norton, 1966.
Enderby Outside. London, Heinemann, 1968.
Enderby (includes *Inside Mr. Enderby* and *Enderby Outside*). New York, Norton, 1968.
MF. London, Cape, and New York, Knopf, 1971.
Napoleon Symphony. London, Cape, and New York, Knopf, 1974.
The Clockwork Testament; or, Enderby's End. London, Hart Davis MacGibbon, 1974; New York, Knopf, 1975.
Beard's Roman Women. New York, McGraw Hill, 1976; London, Heinemann, 1977.
Abba Abba. London, Faber, and Boston, Little Brown, 1977.
1985. London, Hutchinson, and Boston, Little Brown, 1978.
Man of Nazareth. New York, McGraw Hill, 1979; London, Magnum, 1980.
Earthly Powers. London, Hutchinson, and New York, Simon and Schuster, 1980.
Enderby (includes *Inside Mr. Enderby, Enderby Outside, The Clockwork Testament*). London, Penguin, 1982.
The End of the World News. London, Hutchinson, 1982; New York, McGraw Hill, 1983.
Enderby's Dark Lady; or, No End to Enderby. London, Hutchinson, and New York, McGraw Hill, 1984.
The Kingdom of the Wicked. London, Hutchinson, and New York, Arbor House, 1985.

Short Story

Will and Testament: A Fragment of Biography. Verona, Plain Wrapper Press, 1977.

Uncollected Short Stories

"From 'It Is the Miller's Daughter,'" in *Transatlantic Review* (London), Spring 1967.
"Somebody's Got to Pay the Rent," in *Partisan Review* (New Brunswick, New Jersey), Winter 1968.
"An American Organ," in *Splinters,* edited by Alex Hamilton. New York, Walker, 1969.
"A Benignant Growth," in *Transatlantic Review* (London), Summer 1969.
"I Wish My Wife Was Dead," in *Transatlantic Review* (London), Winter 1969–70.
"The Muse," in *Best SF 1969,* edited by Brian Aldiss and Harry Harrison. New York, Putnam, and London, Sphere, 1970.

Plays

Cyrano de Bergerac, adaptation of the play by Rostand (produced Minneapolis, 1971). New York, Knopf, 1971; musical version, as *Cyrano,* music by Michael Lewis, lyrics by Burgess (produced New York, 1972).

Oedipus the King, adaptation of a play by Sophocles (produced Minneapolis, 1972; Southampton, Hampshire, 1979). Minneapolis, University of Minnesota Press, 1972; London, Oxford University Press, 1973.

The Cavalier of the Rose (story adaptation), in *Der Rosenkavalier*, libretto by Hofmannsthal, music by Richard Strauss. Boston, Little Brown, 1982; London, Joseph, 1983.

Cyrano de Bergerac (not same as 1971 version), adaptation of the play by Rostand (produced London, 1983). London, Hutchinson, 1985.

Screenplay: special languages for *Quest for Fire*, 1981.

Radio Play: *Blooms of Dublin*, music by Burgess, 1983.

Television Plays: *Moses—The Lawgiver*, with others, 1975; *Jesus of Nazareth*, with others, 1977; *A Kind of Failure* (documentary; *Writers and Places* series), 1981; *The Childhood of Christ*, music by Berlioz, 1985.

Verse

Moses: A Narrative. London, Dempsey and Squires, and New York, Stonehill, 1976.

A Christmas Recipe. Verona, Plain Wrapper Press, 1977.

Other

English Literature: A Survey for Students (as John Burgess Wilson). London, Longman, 1958.

The Novel Today. London, Longman, 1963.

Language Made Plain (as John Burgess Wilson). London, English Universities Press, 1964; New York, Crowell, 1965; revised edition, London, Fontana, 1975.

Here Comes Everybody: An Introduction to James Joyce for the Ordinary Reader. London, Faber, 1965; revised edition, London, Hamlyn, 1982; as *Re Joyce*, New York, Norton, 1965.

The Novel Now: A Student's Guide to Contemporary Fiction. London, Faber, and New York, Norton, 1967; revised edition, Faber, 1971.

Urgent Copy: Literary Studies. London, Cape, and New York, Norton, 1968.

Shakespeare. London, Cape, and New York, Knopf, 1970.

Joysprick: An Introduction to the Language of James Joyce. London, Deutsch, 1973; New York, Harcourt Brace, 1975.

Obscenity and the Arts (lecture). Valletta, Malta Library Association, 1973.

A Long Trip to Teatime (for children). London, Dempsey and Squires, and New York, Stonehill, 1976.

New York, with the editors of Time-Life books. New York, Time-Life, 1976.

Ernest Hemingway and His World. London, Thames and Hudson, and New York, Scribner, 1978.

The Land Where Ice Cream Grows (for children). London, Benn, and New York, Doubleday, 1979.

On Going to Bed. London, Deutsch, and New York, Abbeville, 1982.

This Man and Music. London, Hutchinson, 1982; New York, McGraw Hill, 1983.

Ninety-Nine Novels: The Best in English since 1939: A Personal Choice. London, Allison and Busby, and New York, Summit, 1984.

Flame into Being: The Life and Work of D.H. Lawrence. London, Heinemann, and New York, Arbor House, 1985.

Homage to "Qwertyuiop." London, Hutchinson, 1985; as *But Do Blondes Prefer Gentlemen?*, New York, McGraw Hill, 1986.

Editor, *The Coaching Days of England 1750–1850.* London, Elek, and New York, Time-Life, 1966.

Editor, *A Journal of the Plague Year*, by Daniel Defoe. London, Penguin, 1966.

Editor, *A Shorter Finnegans Wake*, by James Joyce. London, Faber, and New York, Viking Press, 1966.

Editor, with Francis Haskell, *The Age of the Grand Tour.* London, Elek, and New York, Crown, 1967.

Editor, *Malaysian Stories*, by W. Somerset Maugham. Singapore, Heinemann, 1969.

Translator, with Llewela Burgess, *The New Aristocrats*, by Michel de Saint-Pierre. London, Gollancz, 1962; Boston, Houghton Mifflin, 1963.

Translator, with Llewela Burgess, *The Olive Trees of Justice*, by Jean Pelegri. London, Sidgwick and Jackson, 1962.

Translator, *The Man Who Robbed Poor Boxes*, by Jean Servin. London, Gollancz, 1965.

*

Bibliography: *Anthony Burgess: A Bibliography* by Jeutonne Brewer, Metuchen, New Jersey, Scarecrow Press, 1980.

Manuscript Collection: Mills Memorial Library, Hamilton, Ontario.

Critical Studies: in *The Red Hot Vacuum* by Theodore Solotaroff, New York, Atheneum, 1970; *Shakespeare's Lives* by Samuel Schoenbaum, Oxford, Clarendon Press, 1970; *Anthony Burgess* by Carol M. Dix, London, Longman, 1971; *The Consolations of Ambiguity: An Essay on the Novels of Anthony Burgess* by Robert K. Morris, Columbia, University of Missouri Press, 1971; *Anthony Burgess* by A.A. DeVitis, New York, Twayne, 1972; *The Clockwork Universe of Anthony Burgess* by Richard Mathews, San Bernardino, California, Borgo Press, 1978; *Anthony Burgess: The Artist as Novelist* by Geoffrey Aggeler, University, University of Alabama Press, 1979; *Anthony Burgess* by Samuel Coale, New York, Ungar, 1981.

Anthony Burgess comments:

I hesitate to say much about my own work, which I can lay less claim to understanding than a really perceptive professional critic. I was shocked to be told that the name of the hero of *A Vision of Battlements* (R. Ennis) spells sinner backwards—a fact it took me fifteen years to realise. Since then, I have become so used to my unconscious mind dictating not only the themes of my novels but also the names and symbols that I regard myself as a mere hen, non-ovivorous. But the novels are probably all about the same thing—man is a sinner, but not sufficiently a sinner to deserve the calamities that are heaped upon him. I suppose I try to make comic novels about man's tragic lot.

*   *   *

Anthony Burgess's first novel, *A Vision of Battlements*, was written in 1949 but remained unpublished until 1965. As a young man he had been interested in composing music rather than writing books, but he produced *A Vision of Battlements* as an attempt to exercise the oppressive memory of his war service in Gibraltar. It makes a good starting point for the discussion of his work, as it already displays, if in an undeveloped form, many of the characteristics of his later novels.

Its hero, Richard Ennis, a sergeant in an education branch of the British Army in Gibraltar, is a victim of his environment—in this case the military hierarchy—but although he suffers many defeats he fights back resiliently, and wins the occasional tactical victory. He is a lapsed Catholic and the burden of his religious upbringing weighs heavily upon him. Ennis has fairly strong libidinous urges but he is also fastidious in his attitudes to sex, being as much repelled by the flesh as drawn to it; he is at home in squalid surroundings, while aspiring to a materially comfortable life. Life presents itself to him as a rapid alternation of comic and melodramatic incidents. Basically *A Vision of Battlements* is a semipicaresque novel that draws heavily on Burgess's memories of wartime Gibraltar. Yet it is characteristic that he complicated his story by underpinning it with the plot of the *Aeneid* ("Ennis" = Aeneas) in a manner directly imitative of Joyce's use of the *Odyssey* in *Ulysses*. The influence of Joyce is pervasive, too, in Burgess's endless fascination with language and his love of verbal games, an influence reinforced in his later fiction by that of Nabokov. The other dominant influence is that master of cruel comedy, Evelyn Waugh, particularly his early work.

It was to be several more years before Burgess emerged as a novelist. In the 1950's he published his *Malayan Trilogy* which drew on his experiences as a Colonial Civil Servant in Malaya during the final phase of British rule. Here, too, one finds a sad, comic, victimised hero, and a highly episodic story line. The essential nature of Burgess's fiction has not changed since then, though his particular effects have become increasingly sophisticated. He can reasonably be described as a writer of black comedy, who is preoccupied with certain quasi-religious themes. Burgess himself is what he has called a "renegade Catholic," who comes from an old Lancashire Catholic family and attended a Catholic school in Manchester; in the opening of *Tremor of Intent* he describes the terrifyingly repressive atmosphere of such a school, in what reads like an autobiographical account, and which is reminiscent of Joyce's *Portrait of the Artist*. He has remarked that "The God my religious upbringing forced upon me was a God wholly dedicated to doing me harm.... A big vindictive invisibility." If he has abandoned the practice of Catholicism, Burgess has certainly not turned to the agnostic liberal humanism professed by most English-speaking intellectuals. He remains preoccupied in a Jansenist way by the separation between Nature and Grace, and is deeply suspicious of progressive social ideals and movements. This Augustinian pessimism, which is more convinced of the depravity of man than of the likelihood of transcendent goodness, has antecedents in Baudelaire and Graham Greene and T.S. Eliot, and it pervades Burgess's finest novel, *A Clockwork Orange*.

This novel is an anti-utopian fable about the near future, when teenage gangs habitually terrorize the inhabitants of a shabby metropolis. The story is told in the first person by a young criminal, Alex, in a superb piece of impersonatory writing by Burgess. Alex may be morally vicious but he is mentally alert, and through his flow of complicated slang (much of it of Russian origin) one distinguishes a coherent though desperate view of life. Alex is cruel and ruthless, though usually cheerful, given to beating up older citizens and raping girls and destroying books. And if he acts in this way it is not because he has had an unhappy childhood or lives in an under-privileged community, as liberal-minded psychologists might say, but because he has deliberately chosen evil, as an assertion of spiritual freedom in a world of sub-human conformists. Like all Burgess's novels, *A Clockwork Orange* has a largely episodic plot, but it rises to a powerful climax when Alex is subjected by the state to a form of psychological conditioning that removes his capacity to engage in criminal acts. Here Burgess touches on a question of great philosophical importance: in what sense is a man who has been *forced* to be good better than a man who deliberately asserts his humanity by choosing evil? *A Clockwork Orange* works brilliantly as a metaphysical thriller. It has thematic affinities with another accomplished novel, *The Right to an Answer*, which Burgess has described as "a study of provincial England, as seen by a man on leave from the East, with special emphasis on the decay of traditional values in an affluent society." It is one of Burgess's funniest books, but it is pervaded by a profound distaste for the contemporary English scene, where the comic elements are held in tension with a sense that England is a flat and dismal place of petty lusts and feeble adulteries, drawing all its values from the mass media. in *The Wanting Seed* Burgess draws another pessimistic vision of the future, this time of a society grappling with overpopulation, where history moves cyclically, a severe Augustinian ideology persisting for a while, then giving place to a relaxed Pelagian one, and so on indefinitely. These three novels of the early 1960's are full of wit and inventiveness, and are convincing as novels of ideas.

Burgess's later novels are numerous, for he is an extraordinarily prolific writer. They develop the characteristics of his early fiction, notably the combination of verbal brilliance and loose, episodic structure. Although Burgess is sympathetic to experimental fiction, his own work is basically conventional, despite his taste for Joycean manipulations of language. He has become increasingly more ingenious and has turned to a variety of themes or models. *Nothing Like the Sun* is a novel about Shakespeare, who is treated in a very unromantic way, and where Burgess uses Elizabethan language with great finesse. *Tremor of Intent* is an attempt to use the conventions of the sensational spy-story to write a serious novel, though it is little more than a series of bravura episodes. In *Inside Mr. Enderby* and its sequel *Enderby Outside* Burgess returns to familiar Joycean ground; its hero, the middle-aged poet, F.X. Enderby, can only compose in the lavatory. He is a lapsed Catholic, who associates the Catholic religion with his frightful stepmother who has frightened him off women for life. Enderby prefers solitary sex, but in the later part of the story he marries, against his will, and gets involved in a series of fast-moving if incredible adventures. Here, as elsewhere in his fiction, Burgess has devised a convincing and interesting character, but can do nothing with him except thrust him into a rapid episodic narrative. Almost all of Burgess's novels reflect this basic weakness in maintaining and developing a large-scale structure. In his recent novels Burgess has appeared to make a virtue of this limitation, deliberately using external devices as a way of ensuring a sustained fictional structure. Thus, *MF* draws heavily on the anthropology of Lévi-Strauss, mixing riddles and incest myths and identical twins and bird symbolism, with a dazzling range of puns and word-play, spanning many languages. And in *Napoleon Symphony* Burgess brings together his musical and literary interests in a formidably intricate novel about Napoleon whose form closely imitates Beethoven's "Eroica" symphony. Such works show Burgess's ceaseless ingenuity and inventiveness; but they provide few of the ordinary satisfactions of fiction. Burgess remains a uniquely clever and energetic novelist, but his recent development is not encouraging.

—Bernard Bergonzi

BURNS, Alan. British. Born in London, 29 December 1929. Educated at the Merchant Taylors' School, London; Middle Temple, London: called to the Bar, 1956. Served in the Royal Army Education Corps, 1949–51. Married 1) Carol Lynn in 1954, one son and one daughter; 2) Jean Illien in 1980, one daughter. Practised as barrister, London, 1956–59; research assistant, London School of Economics, 1959; Assistant Legal Manager, Beaverbrook Newspapers, London, 1959–62; First Holder, Henfield Fellowship, University of East Anglia, Norwich, 1971; Senior Tutor in Creative Writing, Western Australian Institute of Technology, South Bentley, 1975; Arts Council Writing Fellow, City Literary Institute, London, 1976. Since 1977, Associate Professor and Professor of English, University of Minnesota, Minneapolis. Recipient: Arts Council grant, 1967, 1969, and bursary, 1969, 1973; C. Day Lewis Fellowship, 1973; Bush Foundation Arts Fellowship, 1984. Agent: Deborah Rogers Ltd., 49 Blenheim Crescent, London W11 2EF, England. Address: Department of English, University of Minnesota, Minneapolis, Minnesota 55455, U.S.A.

PUBLICATIONS

Novels

Buster, in *New Writers One.*   London, Calder, 1961; published separately, New York, Red Dust, 1972.
Europe after the Rain.   London, Calder, 1965; New York, Day, 1970.
Celebrations.   London, Calder and Boyars, 1967.
Babel.   London, Calder and Boyars, 1969; New York, Day, 1970.
Dreamerika! A Surrealist Fantasy.   London, Calder and Boyars, 1972.
The Angry Brigade: A Documentary Novel.   London, Allison and Busby, 1973.
The Day Daddy Died.   London, Allison and Busby, 1981.
Revolutions of the Night.   London, Allison and Busby, 1986.

Uncollected Short Story

"Wonderland," in *Beyond the Words.*   London, Hutchinson, 1975.

Play

Palach, with Charles Marowitz (produced London, 1970). Published in *Open Space Plays*, edited by Marowitz, London, Penguin, 1974.

Other

To Deprave and Corrupt: Technical Reports of the United States Commission on Obscenity and Pornography.   London, Davis Poynter, 1972.
The Imagination on Trial: British and American Writers Discuss Their Working Methods, with Charles Sugnet.   London, Allison and Busby, 1981.

*

Critical Studies: articles by Robert Nye in *The Scotsman* (Edinburgh), 17 April 1965 and 7 October 1967; profile in *The Guardian* (London), 30 April 1970; interview in *Times Educational Supplement* (London), 18 September 1970; *Times Literary Supplement* (London), 18 December 1981; *San Francisco Review of Books*, May 1982; article by David W. Madden, in *British Novelists since 1960* edited by Jay L. Halio, Detroit, Gale, 1983.

*   *   *

Alan Burns's novels deserve the attention of serious readers. The first, *Europe after the Rain*, taking its title from a painting by Max Ernst, established him as a kind of infra-realist. Set in the unspecified future, in a Europe devastated by internecine strife within "the party," it deals with ruined figures in a ruined landscape, purposelessly dedicated to "the work" which is the only thing the party will reward with the food necessary to keep alive. The unnamed narrator alone possesses any genuine purpose. His quest to find and take care of the daughter of the Trotskyite leader of the rebel forces is inspired by something like love, doubtfully implicit in his actions, later developed into a statement of hope which comes as the one redeeming human fact in a world blasted beyond the usual trappings of humanity, but arrived at only after much violence: a woman is flogged, a dog stabbed and its legs dislocated, people fight over corpses for the gold fillings in the teeth, a leg is wrenched off a corpse and eaten by a woman, other women pursue and stone and half-crucify and eventually beat to death the commander of the forces who are in power at the book's beginning. To this nightmarish action Burns applies a style which may be described as burntout. His sentences are mostly short, or built up of short phrases resting on commas where one might have expected full-stops, the total effect being slipped, stripped, and abrupt.

Celebrations is similarly uncompromising, with six characters and seven funerals. Williams, boss of a factory, has two sons, Michael and Phillip, whom he dominates. A hero to himself, Williams is a most uncertain personality, inconstant in his psychological attributes, extravagant in behaviour which is nevertheless always reported in the same flat and colourless prose. Phillip's death, following an accident which necessitates the amputation of his leg, leaves an even sharper taste of doubt in the reader's mind—for while it throws his father and his brother into grim rivalry for the attention of his widow, Jacqueline, these affairs are chronicled with such irony that they hardly seem to occur. All the time, it appears, we are meant to be reminded of Kierkegaard's dictum, "The thought of death condenses and intensifies life," as Burns piles violence on violence, and funeral on funeral, abbreviating whole lives to a tapestry of gesture.

With *Babel* Burns seemed to have reached a dead end, though it confirms him in his role as infra-realist, anti-poet, steely perceiver of disconnections, writing as though he looks down on the rest of us from a private spaceship in unwilling orbit. Here he has assembled an ice-cold report on a world in chaos, stitching together clichés from the newspapers, fragments of misunderstood conversation, a babble of jokes and warnings. The cunningly fragmented styles owe too much to Burroughs and Ballard, and the comedy cannot quite conceal something merely self-disgusted in such furious insistence on unmeaning.

—Robert Nye

BURROUGHS, William S(eward). American. Born in St. Louis, Missouri, 5 February 1914. Educated at John Burroughs

School and Taylor School, St. Louis; Los Alamos Ranch School, New Mexico; Harvard University, Cambridge, Massachusetts, A.B. in anthropology 1936; studied medicine at the University of Vienna; Mexico City College, 1948–50. Served in the United States Army, 1942. Married Jean Vollmer in 1945 (died, 1951); one son (deceased). Has worked as a journalist, private detective, and bartender; now a full-time writer. Heroin addict, 1944–59. Recipient: American Academy award, 1975. Member, American Academy, 1983. Lived for many years in Tangier; now lives in New York City. Agent: Andrew Wylie Agency, 250 West 57th Street, New York, New York 10107. Address: William Burroughs Communications, Box 147, Lawrence, Kansas 66044, U.S.A.

PUBLICATIONS

Novels

Junkie: Confessions of an Unredeemed Drug Addict (as William Lee). New York, Ace, 1953; London, Digit, 1957; complete edition, London, Penguin, 1977.
The Naked Lunch. Paris, Olympia Press, 1959; London, Calder, 1964; as *Naked Lunch*, New York, Grove Press, 1962.
The Soft Machine. Paris, Olympia Press, 1961; New York, Grove Press, 1966; London, Calder and Boyars, 1968.
The Ticket That Exploded. Paris, Olympia Press, 1962; revised edition, New York, Grove Press, 1967; London, Calder and Boyars, 1968.
Dead Fingers Talk. London, Calder, 1963.
Nova Express. New York, Grove Press, 1964; London, Cape, 1966.
The Wild Boys: A Book of the Dead. New York, Grove Press, 1971; London, Calder and Boyars, 1972; revised edition, London, Calder, 1979.
Short Novels. London, Calder, 1978.
Blade Runner: A Movie. Berkeley, California, Blue Wind Press, 1979.
Port of Saints. Berkeley, California, Blue Wind Press, 1980; London, Calder, 1983.
Cities of the Red Night: A Boy's Book. London, Calder, and New York, Holt Rinehart, 1981.
The Place of Dead Roads. New York, Holt Rinehart, 1983; London, Calder, 1984.
Queer. New York, Viking, 1985; London, Pan, 1986.

Short Stories

Exterminator! New York, Viking Press, 1973; London, Calder and Boyars, 1974.
Early Routines. Santa Barbara, California, Cadmus, 1981.
The Streets of Chance. New York, Red Ozier Press, 1981.

Play

The Last Words of Dutch Schultz. London, Cape Goliard Press, 1970; New York, Viking Press, 1975.

Other

The Exterminator, with Brion Gysin. San Francisco, Auerhahn Press, 1960.
Minutes to Go, with others. Paris, Two Cities, 1960; San Francisco, Beach, 1968.
The Yage Letters, with Allen Ginsberg. San Francisco, City Lights, 1963.

Roosevelt after Inauguration. New York, Fuck You Press, 1964.
Valentine Day's Reading. New York, American Theatre for Poets, 1965.
Time. New York, "C" Press, 1965.
Health Bulletin: APO-33: A Metabolic Regulator. New York, Fuck You Press, 1965; revised edition, as *APO—33 Bulletin*, San Francisco, Beach, 1966.
So Who Owns Death TV?, with Claude Pelieu and Carl Weissner. San Francisco, Beach, 1967.
The Dead Star. San Francisco, Nova Broadcast Press, 1969.
Ali's Smile. Brighton, Unicorn, 1969.
Entretiens avec William Burroughs, by Daniel Odier. Paris, Belfond, 1969; translated as *The Job: Interviews with William S. Burroughs* (includes *Electronic Revolution*), New York, Grove Press, and London, Cape, 1970.
The Braille Film. San Francisco, Nova Broadcast Press, 1970.
Brion Gysin Let the Mice In, with Brion Gysin and Ian Somerville, edited by Jan Herman. West Glover, Vermont, Something Else Press, 1973.
Mayfair Academy Series More or Less. Brighton, Urgency Press Rip-Off, 1973.
White Subway, edited by James Pennington. London, Aloes, 1974.
The Book of Breeething. Ingatestone, Essex, OU Press, 1974; Berkeley, California, Blue Wind Press, 1975; revised edition, Blue Wind Press, 1980.
Snack: Two Tape Transcripts, with Eric Mottram. London, Aloes, 1975.
Sidetripping, with Charles Gatewood. New York, Strawberry Hill, 1975.
The Retreat Diaries, with *The Dream of Tibet*, by Allen Ginsberg. New York, City Moon, 1976.
Cobble Stone Gardens. Cherry Valley, New York, Cherry Valley Editions, 1976.
The Third Mind, with Brion Gysin. New York, Viking Press, 1978; London, Calder, 1979.
Roosevelt after Inauguration and Other Atrocities. San Francisco, City Lights, 1979.
Ah Pook Is Here and Other Texts (includes *The Book of Breeething, Electronic Revolution*). London, Calder, 1979; New York, Riverrun, 1982.
A William Burroughs Reader, edited by John Calder. London, Pan, 1982.
Letters to Allen Ginsberg 1953–1957. New York, Full Court Press, 1982.
New York Inside Out, photographs by Robert Walker. Port Washington, New York, Skyline Press, 1984.
The Burroughs File. San Francisco, City Lights, 1984.
The Adding Machine: A Summation of Comments, edited by James Grauerholz. New York, Arbor House, 1985.
Mind Wars. London, Calder, 1985.

*

Bibliography: *William S. Burroughs: An Annotated Bibliography of His Works and Criticism* by Michael B. Goodman, New York, Garland, 1976; *William S. Burroughs: A Bibliography 1953–73* by Joe Maynard and Barry Miles, Charlottesville, University Press of Virginia, 1978.

Critical Studies: *William Burroughs: The Algebra of Need* by Eric Mottram, Buffalo, Intrepid Press, 1971; *Contemporary Literary Censorship: The Case History of Burroughs' Naked Lunch* by Michael B. Goodman, Metuchen, New Jersey, Scarecrow Press, 1981; *With William Burroughs: A Report from the*

Bunker edited by Victor Bokris, New York, Seaver, 1981, London, Vermilion, 1982; "William Burroughs Issue" of *Review of Contemporary Fiction* (Elmwood Park, Illinois), vol. 4, no. 1, 1984; *William Burroughs* by Jennie Skerl, Boston, Twayne, 1985.

*   *   *

William S. Burroughs is an American novelist who is deeply involved with experimental writing and the investigation of his unconscious mind. In the years between his first book, *Junkie*, published in 1953 under the pseudonym of William Lee, and his most recent fiction, his narrative has been shaped by a series of intensely personal, sometimes eccentric ideas and unconventional prose techniques. Obsessively directed as a writer by what he calls the "dark side" of his mind, he feels invaded by what he describes as "the Ugly Spirit and maneuvered into a lifelong struggle" in which he says he has no choice except to write his way out.

The more than 20 books comprising Burroughs's published fiction reflect his homosexuality and his 15 years of experience as a morphine and heroin addict. The motivation for *Junkie* was simple: he wanted to render in the most accurate and precise terms his experiences as a drug addict. This was the first time in American literature that drug addiction was presented nonjudgmentally as an individual choice, a type of solitary conditioning that was an alternative to the mass conditioning of conventional society. *Queer*, his next book, unpublished until 1985 but written 30 years earlier, was also autobiographical, created with a more complex intention during a brief period of withdrawal from junk after he accidentally shot and killed his wife in Mexico City. In his recent introduction to *Queer* Burroughs analyzes the creative process in which he initially became a writer, inventing what he calls the form of the "routine" to shock and amuse his audience during this period of his life when he felt himself "disintegrated, desperately in need of contact, completely unsure of himself and his purpose." Expressionistic routines became the basic structure of Burroughs's narrative style in much of his subsequent prose, a series of frantic, hallucinated, surreal episodes whose witheringly humorous tone masks a deadly serious commitment to writing. *The Yage Letters* is an epistolary "novel" based on his letters to Allen Ginsberg describing a journey to the Amazon jungle in search of the "final fix." It forms with *Junkie* and *Queer* what the poet Robert Creeley calls "a trilogy of despair" exploring sensory experience as an alternative to conventional social behaviour and morality. It wasn't until after Burroughs moved from Mexico to Tangier and was cured of his heroin addiction in 1959 that he created the book generally regarded as his masterpiece, *Naked Lunch*.

The title of this volume was given to him by his friend Jack Kerouac, who helped type the manuscript from the thousand pages of notes Burroughs had kept during his addiction. The words "naked lunch" were meant to suggest what Burroughs sees as the book's theme: "That frozen moment when everyone sees what is on the end of every fork"—or as the critic Eric Mottram translates the image, "The moment a man realizes his cannibalism, his predatory condition, and his necessary parasitism and addictive nature." In *Naked Lunch* Burroughs engages himself totally with his nightmare experience, descending into the horrors of human physical disintegration and degradation with an unsettling calm and cold descriptive power reminiscent of Swift, entering the absolute nadir of existence where the physical tyranny of the junk habit has stripped bare what Burroughs envisions as the socio-political tyranny that controls our lives.

The Ticket That Exploded, The Soft Machine, and *Nova Express,* a trilogy assembled in Paris over the next few years from the remaining pages of notes accumulated in Tangier, strengthened Burroughs's literary reputation after *Naked Lunch.* The unnerving, sometimes viscerally disturbing routines involving sex and sadism in his work were admired by some readers—Anthony Burgess said, "Mr. Burroughs joins a small body of writers who are willing to look at hell and report what they see"—but his books also provoked violent critical response from many others. This controversy intensified during his next experimental phase of writing after he moved to London in 1966 and began to practice the cut-up method of composition with the American poet and painter Brion Gysin, introduced to him by Paul Bowles. Burroughs and Gysin collaborated on the books *Minutes to Go, The Exterminator,* and *The Third Mind.*

Burroughs regarded the cut-up method as an important evolutionary advance in the development of literature, a step beyond his narrative routines and Kerouac's technique of "spontaneous prose" composition. It was another way to help free the writer from the control of the standard sentence, which Burroughs (deadpan) told an interviewer from the *Paris Review* was "one of the great errors of Western thought" because it encouraged the conscious, rational mind and inhibited creativity. The technique of the cut-up was basically a juxtaposition of heterogeneous material; Burroughs felt that Eliot had used the method earlier in "The Waste Land." Experimenting with tapes and printed material, one of Burroughs's favorite procedures was to tape his own voice reading at random from magazines, newspapers, and books; then he would run the tape back and forth, inserting new material wherever it happened to stop, continuing until all the phrases were cut-up. Burroughs's English publisher John Calder realized that the cut-up was another way of producing mechanically what the writer's own creative processes had previously evoked by random association. Years later Burroughs was startled when Samuel Beckett told him that cut-ups weren't writing; they were plumbing. At the same time Burroughs was experimenting with cut-ups he also used his earlier narrative style in the other books he wrote in London: *The Wild Boys, Port of Saints,* the film script *The Last Words of Dutch Schultz,* and *Exterminator!,* a collection of short prose sketches that contains (along with *Junkie* and *Queer*), some of his most accessible writing.

Since Burroughs's return to live in the United States in 1974, he has continued experimenting with tapes and written cut-up collages, influencing a number of young writers and musicians. Under his influence, his son William Burroughs, Jr., wrote two fine autobiographical novels about addiction, *Speed* and *Kentucky Ham.* Burroughs's recent major fiction, *Cities of the Red Night* and *The Place of Dead Roads,* are long picaresque expressionistic novels in which several characters from his previous books appear—Doctor Benway, Clem Snide the Private Asshole, and the Wild Boys—along with new characters, as Burroughs experiments with satires of science fiction and the western. The form of the short, episodic, hallucinated routine still usually provides the basic structure of his narrative.

Burroughs is essentially a satirist who wants to reveal ways in which anyone in a position of authority exercises control over others. His routines dramatize his conviction that since our moral values are askew, police have a vested interest in crime, doctors in illness, governments in war, and the Drug Enforcement Administration in addiction. Believing that human nature is evil throughout history, Burroughs feels the only possibility for good to evolve is through each individual's understanding his own nature and exorcising the cruelty and sadism that is innate in all of us; he says he exorcises the evil in his own mind by writing his routines.

Both Allen Ginsberg and Jack Kerouac credit him as a strong influence on their writing. The critic John Tytell recognizes that "Ginsberg's and Kerouac's pathway to beatitude stemmed from Burroughs's nightmare of devastation." Ginsberg feels that Burroughs's work, like his own, expresses "the change of consciousness that overcame the United States in the last two decades [since the 1960's] which resulted in disillusionment on the part of the general public with self-mystifying government. That was the first theme I picked up from him back in the 1940's—his contempt for the trappings of authoritarianism and his humor in seeing through military-police uniforms to the hairy cancerous body-corpse inside. And that leads later on to his cynicism about the outward forms and trappings of the ego itself."

If the farcical caricatures in Burroughs's brutal routines are a projection of his general cynicism about human nature, his attitude as a homosexual is sometimes specifically misogynistic. He said in *The Job*, "Women are a perfect curse. I think they were a basic mistake, and the whole dualistic universe evolved from this error. ... Love is a con put down by the female sex." Yet while he feels he can make such sweeping statements, he is impatient with generalizations made by critics about his work. Burroughs insists that as a black humorist and writer he is transcribing "the still sad music of humanity." Of his writing he says, "I just make a little skit, that's all."

—Ann Charters

BURROWAY, Janet (Gay). American. Born in Tucson, Arizona, 21 September 1936. Educated at the University of Arizona, Tucson, 1954–55; Barnard College, New York, B.A. (cum laude) 1958; Cambridge University, B.A. (honours) 1960, M.A. 1965; Yale School of Drama, New Haven, Connecticut, 1960–61. Married 1) Walter Eysselinck in 1961 (divorced, 1973), two sons; 2) William Dean Humphries in 1978. Supply teacher and music director, Binghamton public schools, New York, 1961–63; costume designer, Belgian National Theatre, Ghent, 1965–70, and Gardner Centre for the Arts, University of Sussex, Brighton, 1965–71; Lecturer in American Studies, University of Sussex, 1965–72; Assistant to the Writing Program, University of Illinois, Urbana, 1972. Associate Professor, 1972–77, and since 1977, Professor of English, Florida State University, Tallahassee. Visiting Lecturer, Writers Workshop, University of Iowa, Iowa City, 1980. Fiction reviewer, *New Statesman*, London, 1970–71, 1975. Recipient: Amoco Award, for teaching, 1974; National Endowment for the Arts grant, 1976; Florida Fine Arts Council grant, 1983. Agent: Gail Hochman, Brandt and Brandt Inc., 1501 Broadway, New York, New York 10036. Address: 240 De Soto Street, Tallahassee, Florida 32303, U.S.A.

PUBLICATIONS

Novels

Descend Again. London, Faber, 1960.
The Dancer from the Dance. London, Faber, 1965; Boston, Little Brown, 1968.

Eyes. London, Faber, and Boston, Little Brown, 1966.
The Buzzards. Boston, Little Brown, 1969; London, Faber, 1970.
Raw Silk. Boston, Little Brown, and London, Gollancz, 1977.
Opening Nights. New York, Atheneum, and London, Gollancz, 1985.

Uncollected Short Stories

"Embalming Mom," in *Apalachee Quarterly* (Tallahassee, Florida), Spring 1985.
"Winn Dixie," in *New Letters* (Kansas City), January 1986.

Plays

Garden Party (produced New York, 1958).
The Fantasy Level (produced New Haven, Connecticut, 1961; Brighton, Sussex, 1968).
The Beauty Operators (produced Brighton, Sussex, 1968).
Poenulus; or, The Little Carthaginian, adaptation of a play by Plautus, in *Five Roman Comedies*, edited by Palmer Boive. New York, Dutton, 1970.

Television Plays: *Hoddinott Veiling*, 1970; *Due Care and Attention*, 1973.

Verse

But to the Season. Weston super Mare, Somerset, Universities' Poetry, 1961.
Material Goods. Tallahassee, University Presses of Florida, 1981.

Other

The Truck on the Track (for children). London, Cape, 1970; Indianapolis, Bobbs Merrill, 1971.
The Giant Ham Sandwich (verse only; for children), with John Vernon Lord. London, Cape, 1972; Boston, Houghton Mifflin, 1973.
Writing Fiction: A Guide to Narrative Craft. Boston, Little Brown, 1982.

*

Manuscript Collection: Florida State University, Tallahassee.

Critical Study: article by Elisabeth Muhlenfeld, in *American Novelists since World War II*, 2nd series, edited by James E. Kibler, Jr., Detroit, Gale, 1980.

*   *   *

Janet Burroway depicts contemporary social issues through multiple points-of-view to convey strong, and sometimes nebulous, moral messages. Complicated relationships are neatly interconnected within sharply defined domestic and urban settings, as contrasting characters try to work out crises of conscience. The author's penchant for epigrams and symbols further unifies her narratives, but at the cost of excessive, self-conscious rhetoric. Likewise, while her abrupt and usually ambiguous endings avoid blatant didacticism, they also seriously mar the proportions of her careful structures. Stories do not seem to conclude so much as merely come to a halt. She also favors theatrical surprises which do not proceed necessarily from exigencies of plot but facilely exploit the sensational. These linguistic artifices and narrative ploys intrude more than they enlighten, weakening her otherwise admirable craftsmanship. Burroway's novels are well-paced, however, and she further enhances their popular appeal by providing plenty of practical information.

Eyes views the problems of race prejudice and of ethics in medicine and journalism through the individual perspectives of the four principal characters. Set in the South, the novel examines one day in the life of Dr. Rugg, an eye surgeon; his wife Maeve, who is pregnant at 40; their somewhat estranged son Hilary, a liberal reporter on a conservative paper; and Hilary's fiancée Jadeen, a junior high school teacher. Skillfully Burroway evokes the Southern atmosphere and delineates the elaborate rituals of black-white relations as enacted by her sensitive protagonists. As a newly liberal and insecure daughter of an old Southern family, Jadeen's dilemma becomes acute: to refuse to teach an outrageously biased textbook and thus lose her job and alienate her genteel but bigotted mother, or to cave in and betray her recent convictions and lose her fiancé. Dr. Rugg, awkward in his charity and family relations and preoccupied in his profession, unwittingly destroys his career by casually mentioning his war-time experiments. Hilary, frustrated in his job and resentful of his famous father, carelessly misses the major scandal his father's seemingly innocuous lecture turns out to be—ironically, sent out on the national wires by Dodds, Rugg's soon-to-be-blind patient—which costs him and his mentor their positions. No totally satisfactory solution to these complications is possible. But Rugg heroically refuses to recant to save face for the State Department, and he serenely awaits his final heart-attack. Hilary, given a last chance, refuses to compromise his principles, or betray his father. Jadeen, however, is not strong enough for the sacrifice and buckles under to the "system"; she resigns herself (somewhat illogically) to being a subservient, dull teacher, without Hilary. Only Maeve, always understanding if inarticulate, and calm, maintains stability amid the domestic chaos. At the end, Jadeen points a moral of sorts: "Thoughts are complex. Actions are not. That is the subject of tragedy." Burroway's vignettes are telling, especially when she describes racial tension in a black bar or the techniques of surgery, reporting, teaching. But that's the rub: she prefers to tell more than to show. Dialogue is often wooden, and despite the neat plotting, the separate thematic strands don't quite mesh. The melodrama ends slightly out of focus.

The Dancer from the Dance is an ambitious and often subtle attempt at a novel of manners, in which the young, strangely innocent yet wise Prytania naively brings about the destruction and near-collapse of the older and more sophisticated people irresistibly drawn to her. 60-year-old Powers, the sensitive but detached narrator, gives the hapless girl a job in his UNICEF office in Paris and entrée into his elegant world. Soon Prytania holds all in thrall. Stoddard, a young and unimaginative medical student, she leads on but finally cannot marry. Old Riebenstahl, a primitive sculptor and curious sage, finally commits suicide, because he has acted as go-between for her illicit affair with the talented mime Jean-Claude. Even the worldly wise Mme. de Verbois, with whom she stays, and finally Powers himself are cruelly touched by her strange power. The nuances of social behavior, the curious transformations of character, and the complex emotional entanglements are deftly portrayed in several delicately drawn scenes. Yet, for all that, Prytania remains a shadowy figure, and the narrative barely escapes incredibility. Further, although the pages are cluttered with more witticisms and aphorisms than a Restoration comedy, the general tone is more that of a middling French film about yet another blighted romance. The several ironies and crises come off as contrived and formulaic, and ultimately the novel sadly disappoints: such an anticlimax after so much art.

In *The Buzzards* Burroway turns to the political realm, employing, yet again, several narrators. But as we follow the campaign trail of Alex, the conservative but likeable Senator from Arizona, the multiple perspectives—interior monologues, set speeches, newspaper articles, letters—soon become redundant and tedious. Especially so are the fatuous epigrams which clog the journal of the sententious and most implausible manager, Galcher (he calls them Axioms of God; e.g., "We are not subtle enough to contrive a machine in which disintegration contributes to maintenance and manufacture"). Alex's cold, brittle, and marvelously inept wife, his disaffected son, and neurotic daughter Eleanor (whose near-suicide and Mexican abortion pose serious threats to his chances), like the "allegorical" Galcher, are definite liabilities—not only for Alex but for the reader, who has little reason to be interested in them, let alone to like them. Younger daughter Evie, a vivacious, all-American, plastic pom-pom girl, is equally off-putting, though depicted as an asset in Alex's uphill struggle for re-election. Nonetheless, Burroway still has incisive power to reveal the moral ambiguities, contradictions, and rationalizations of her characters, especially the women. But beyond showing the hectic pace and many stratagems of modern politicking, the novel's rationale is not quite clear. And when Evie is precipitously assassinated in the last few pages, the event seems not tragic but merely expedient in terminating a journey that has no real destination. That a writer of Janet Burroway's obvious talents in use of detail and perspective should ultimately be defeated by a lack of control or malfunction of these very elements is an unfortunate irony of her otherwise impressive work.

—Joseph Parisi

BUSCH, Frederick. American. Born in Brooklyn, New York, 1 August 1941. Educated at Muhlenberg College, Allentown, Pennsylvania, 1958–62, A.B. 1962; Columbia University, New York (Woodrow Wilson Fellow, 1962), 1962–63, M.A. 1967. Married Judith Burroughs in 1963; two sons. Writer and editor, North American Précis Syndicate, New York, 1964–65, and *School Management* magazine, Greenwich, Connecticut, 1965–66. Instructor, 1966–67, Assistant Professor, 1968–72, Associate Professor, 1973–76, and since 1976, Professor of English, Colgate University, Hamilton, New York. Recipient: National Endowment for the Arts grant, 1976; Guggenheim fellowship, 1980; Ingram Merrill Foundation fellowship, 1981. Agent: Elaine Markson Literary Agency, 44 Greenwich Avenue, New York, New York 10011. Address: R.D. 1, Box 31-A, New Turnpike Road, Sherburne, New York 13460, U.S.A.

PUBLICATIONS

Novels

I Wanted a Year Without Fall. London, Calder and Boyars, 1971.
Manual Labor. New York, New Directions, 1974.
The Mutual Friend. New York, Harper, and Hassocks, Sussex, Harvester Press, 1978.
Rounds. New York, Farrar Straus, and London, Hamish Hamilton, 1980.

Take This Man. New York, Farrar Straus, 1981.
Invisible Mending. Boston, Godine, 1984.
Sometimes I Live in the Country. Boston, Godine, 1986.

Short Stories

Breathing Trouble and Other Stories. London, Calder and Boyars, 1974.
Domestic Particulars: A Family Chronicle. New York, New Directions, 1976.
Hardwater Country. New York, Knopf, 1979.
Too Late American Boyhood Blues. Boston, Godine, 1984.

Other

Hawkes: A Guide to His Fictions. Syracuse, New York, Syracuse University Press, 1973.
When People Publish (essays). Iowa City, University of Iowa Press, 1986.

*

Manuscript Collection: Ohio State University, Columbus.

Frederick Busch comments:

I write about characters I want to matter more than my own theories and more than my own delights. The great problem is to face the fullest implications of one's insights and fears—and to sustain the energy to make a usable shape from them. No: the great problem is to sit and write something worthy of the people on the page, and the good reader.

*   *   *

Frederick Busch is a humanist with an eagle eye fixed on the family. His are not like da Vinci's harmonious figure, however. They suggest Ted Hughes's more primal man: "Shot through the head with balled brains/ . . . Clubbed unconscious by his own heart/ . . .He managed to hear faint and far—'It's a boy!' " Pre-eminently, Busch celebrates that tenacity, somehow of the blood, by which we refuse to junk the perplexing intimacies in our lives.

Few writers attempt, let alone so effectively, to narrate from as many points of view. When his persona is a child or a woman, we do not disbelieve. Nor is there any bias in his work for male or female, or for adults as against children. Busch's descriptions are delineated with imagistic exaction and his conviction that work is grace allows him to particularize every type of labor with care. He is equally alert to the countryside or the city, to the barn or the hospital. Natural settings can be saving, as in "Trail of Possible Bones" (*Domestic Particulars*), or fearsome, as in "What You Might as Well Call Love" (*Hardwater Country*). Either way they are fixed in minutely apt detail. Likewise with work. Prioleau making a television hook-up (*Take This Man*), or Silver and Hebner at their pediatrics (*Rounds*; *Domestic Particulars*)—always, the enterprise is vividly present.

Frequently Busch's architecture renders plot in sundered pieces. One must be patient, wait for the late integration of narrative lines. It is time ill-spent with the too cryptic "You Have Been Warned" (*Breathing Trouble*); it is worthwhile with the adroit *Take This Man*. Busch's syntax is also significant. It can be terse, but is more often transcontinental. The goal is to let phrasing embody a character's thought process or immediate realization of place. A weakness is that Busch's

dialogue has tended to repartee. Characters spontaneously produce the *mot juste*. Because their phrasing is closely woven into the works' *leitmotifs*, this seems a requirement. But in fiction so realistic, the pressure upon every utterance to be resonant has damaged plausible conversation, with its inevitable flatness. The problem lessens in *Rounds* and *Take This Man*. In *Invisible Mending*, Busch's best novel, such speech is germane.

I Wanted a Year Without Fall is legend passing from a father to his sleeping infant son. Its comic absurdity resides in parallels with *Pilgrim's Progress* and *Beowulf*. Ben recounts his adventures with Leo, who hits the road to escape urban destitution and a cuckold who wants his hide. Ben's complementary poverty is rural. *He* is fleeing a dead woman's voice. In a typical parody, Ben plays the Green Knight to an army of cockroaches. Here is the heroism of flight, not of the quest. Busch's anxious and ongoing preoccupation with the act of writing is central to the conclusion. Ben's last bardic utterance to his uncomprehending boy, "I will ask you to listen to an old time lay," is absurd indeed. Few will doubt this is a first novel.

Manual Labor concerns the struggle of Anne and Phil Sorenson to overcome the death of their unborn child. All three narrate the story, the immanent baby as the guiding voice. Anne writes an endless letter to her mother, but only in her mind. Phil keeps a journal, often contemplating the uses of narrative in the control of chaos. Death pervades their lives, including the suicide of a vagrant, Abe, whom they befriend in Maine. He had become an unhealthy focus of Anne's own suicidal attention. The novel esteems the victory of the couple over the nearly ubiquitous disintegration surrounding them. The key is labor, the manual labor of the two rebuilding an old house following the ruined labor of a childless mother. Phil's dictum, "You forget with your hands," is provided at the outset by the "child." Some, ponders Saul Maloff in *The New Republic*, will find the persona of the "bled away fetus" an "insuperable obstacle to . . . reading on."

Domestic Particulars is nearly a collection of stories, but its thirteen chapters are an integrated, episodic revelation of a family, as it endures between 1919 and the 1970's. Brooklyn, the Upper West Side, and Greenwich Village are extraordinarily detailed here. All conditions of the great national social ambience hover pointedly over time and place. Again, domestic strife and the unexpected power of family affection are the essence. But the key figures, Claire and Mac and their son Harry, are much more tenuously bonded than the Sorensons. And the peace they make does not much alleviate the reader's sense of their limited natures and chary good will.

Pondering Busch's canon, one could not anticipate *The Mutual Friend*. It is, of course, about Dickens, but only the lonely figure of 1867 to 1870. No single Dickens emerges, however, because narrators vary. Dickens speaks through his own writing—including his entire will—but the "Chief's" companion, George Dolby, takes over and allows that it is difficult to guarantee precise accounts. And when he dies in a Fulham charity hospital, the Asian servant, Moon, tells us he'll be changing what we've had from Dolby. Busch, who believes we must accommodate the past narratively, nevertheless displays fiction's inevitable mutation of it.

Rounds joins the Sorensons, Elizabeth Bean (a school psychologist), and Eli Silver, M.D. The Sorensons still need children. Elizabeth is pregnant, unmarried, and unwilling to abort the fetus. At the outset, Silver is all but ruined. His inadvertance has cost his son's life and, in the disastrous aftermath of the tragedy, his marriage. Busch separates and eventually intersects his characters' stories, a common strategy in his work. Silver intends to save himself from alcohol and emotional collapse by unflagging and expert attention to his pediatric practice, which is presented with surpassing realism. But only the Sorensons' affectionate regard and Elizabeth's love for him finally achieve that. Silver's scrupulous decision to initiate the death of a little girl in her final agony is realized with superb ethical authenticity.

Gus has two fathers. At ten he goes to Anthony Prioleau, the biological one. His mother follows suit. The three are a family, strangely but abidingly. Tony and Ellen never marry. Hence, *Take This Man*. The novel gradually sketches in backgrounds—why Tony was a Conscientious Objector, why Ellen had a taste for leavetaking. The other father remains in emotional but not physical range, never betrayed by Gus, who nonetheless comes to love Ellen and Tony unreservedly. Gus's first meeting with Tony and Tony's passing are Busch at his emotional best. Two ministers, the Reverends Van Eyck and Billy Horsefall (a parody of Billy Joe Hargis), are Busch at his comic best.

Invisible Mending is equally hilarious and poignant. Though Zimmer, a "Jew manqué," fears loneliness, his Gentile wife shows him the door. Her love isn't equal to his self absorption. For the first four pages it is 1980; it requires 214 pages to get back there. Meanwhile, Zimmer recollects his wondrous days with Rhona Glinksy, librarian and Nazi hunter, and his marriage with Lillian. Lil avers that Zimmer "can make a secular mystery out of the holiest simplicity." Zimmer recollects himself as "the treacherous amphibian who waddled on the Christian sands and swam in the blood of Jews." When Rhona reappears in 1980, times past and present merge. But Zimmer's young son provides a new and imperative focus. *Invisible Mending* brings Philip Roth to mind, both *Portnoy's Complaint* and *The Ghost Writer*. The novel is entirely up to the comparison.

—David M. Heaton

BYATT, A(ntonia) S(usan, née Drabble). British. Born in Sheffield, Yorkshire, 24 August 1936; sister of Margaret Drabble, *q.v.* Educated at Sheffield High School; The Mount School, York; Newnham College, Cambridge (open scholarship), B.A. (honours) in English 1957; Bryn Mawr College, Pennsylvania (English-Speaking Union Fellow), 1957–58; Somerville College, Oxford, 1958–59, B.A. Married 1) I.C.R. Byatt in 1959 (divorced, 1969), one daughter and one son (deceased); 2) Peter J. Duffy in 1969, two daughters. Teacher, Westminster Tutors, London, 1962–65; Lecturer, Central School of Art and Design, London, 1965–69; Extra-Mural Lecturer, 1962–71, Lecturer, 1972–81, and Senior Lecturer in English, 1981–83, University College, London (Assistant Tutor, 1977–80, and Tutor for Admissions, 1980–82, Department of English). British Council lecturer in Spain, 1978, India, 1981, and Korea, 1985. Since 1977, Associate of Newnham College; since 1985, Deputy Chairman of the Committee of Management, Society of Authors. Recipient: Arts Council grant, 1968. Fellow, Royal Society of Literature, 1983. Address: 37 Rusholme Road, London S.W. 15, England.

PUBLICATIONS

Novels

Shadow of a Sun. London, Chatto and Windus, and New York, Harcourt Brace, 1964.

The Game. London, Chatto and Windus, 1967; New York, Scribner, 1968.
The Virgin in the Garden. London, Chatto and Windus, 1978; New York, Knopf, 1979.
Still Life. London, Chatto and Windus, and New York, Scribner, 1985.

Uncollected Short Stories

"Daniel," in *Encounter* (London), April 1976.
"The July Ghost," in *Firebird 1*, edited by T.J. Binding. London, Penguin, 1982.
"On the Day That E.M. Forster Died," in *Encounter* (London), December 1983.
"The Changeling," in *Encounter* (London), May 1985.

Other

Degrees of Freedom: The Novels of Iris Murdoch. London, Chatto and Windus, and New York, Barnes and Noble, 1965.
Wordsworth and Coleridge in Their Time. London, Nelson, 1970; New York, Crane Russak, 1973.
Iris Murdoch. London, Longman, 1976.

Editor, *The Mill on the Floss*, by George Eliot. London, Penguin, 1979.

*

A.S. Byatt comments:

My novels are about habits of thought and imagination: the quartet I am writing combines a partly parodic "realist" first and last volumes, with a more experimental second and third. I am presently writing a novel, *Possession*, not in this quartet, and partly to do with history and the history of ideas, in the 19th century.

*   *   *

Although A.S. Byatt is among the best-known literary figures in England today, she has published only four creative (as opposed to critical) books—all novels—since her writing career began over 20 years ago. Until the publication of her third novel, *The Virgin in the Garden*, in 1978, her reputation owed more to her scholarly and critical writing, including the first book-length study of Iris Murdoch, *Degrees of Freedom*, and to the high quality of her literary journalism and reviewing than to her fiction; this was somewhat overshadowed by the very popular output of her younger and more prolific sister, Margaret Drabble. However, with *The Virgin in the Garden*, Byatt's first novel in over a decade and one of the most rewarding works of English fiction in the second half of the 1970's, she established herself as an important novelist in her own right, and confirmed this status in 1985 with *Still Life*, the first of three planned sequels to *The Virgin in the Garden*.

Byatt's first two novels do not aim as high as *The Virgin in the Garden* and *Still Life*, but both are substantial books, and they reveal a development towards the fusion of realism and symbolism in her more recent work. *Shadow of a Sun*, her first work of fiction, is essentially a straightforward piece of orthodox realism, whereas *The Game* makes extensive use of mythical and symbolic elements within a realistic framework.

The action of *Shadow of a Sun*—the title comes from a Ralegh poem—takes place in the shadow cast by Henry Severell, a major English novelist of visionary intensity who is prone to bouts of manic insanity. His teenage daughter, Anna, is the character most dominated by his overpowering personality, and the novel explores Anna's attempt to define herself as an independent being by liberating herself from parental, especially paternal, control and from her own conventionality. The book is a kind of *bildungsroman*, tracing Anna's development from a very immature schoolgirl, who makes a protest by running away from school, to a Cambridge undergraduate made pregnant by one of her father's friends and most enthusiastic critics, Oliver Canning. In the inconclusive and open-ended final chapter, Anna, having rejected the possibility of a marriage of convenience with a well-to-do, kind-hearted, and mother-dominated fellow-student, asserts her new-found independence and maturity, and confronts the future.

Despite its ample scale, *Shadow of a Sun* concentrates on a very small, tightly knit group of characters, Henry Severell and his wife, Oliver Canning and his wife, and Anna herself. Byatt's second novel, *The Game*, is less claustrophobic in this respect, taking in a much wider spectrum of characters, from academics at Oxford and a Quaker community in Northumberland to fashionable television people in London and a homeless problem family. This range is one reason for the novel being more impressive than its predecessor, although there are obvious resemblances: a novelist is again a major participant, for example, and the erosion of a marriage features prominently. At the heart of *The Game* is the complex and basically antagonistic relationship between two sisters in their thirties, the unmarried Cassandra Corbett, an Oxford don specializing in medieval romance literature, and Julia Eskelund (her husband is Norwegian), a popular novelist who writes about the problems of contemporary women. Cassandra, a convert to Anglo-Catholicism from her family's Quakerism, is otherworldly; Julia, who becomes a participant in a regular arts programme on television and also has an affair with the producer, is decidedly modish. The game that gives the book its title is their elaborate Brontë-like childhood invention, which had literary analogues and opened up an entire imaginary world. Indeed, Cassandra, unlike her much more down-to-earth sister, still lives to a considerable extent in the realm of the imagination and has only a tenuous grasp of reality; the Arthurian imagery and symbolism—she is actually editing Malory—help to convey this. It is the re-entry into their lives of another part of their shared childhood experience, the now-famous zoologist and television personality Simon Moffitt, that revitalizes their teenage conflict over him and leads to Julia rapidly writing a cruel novel based on Cassandra and Simon. This in turn precipitates the tragic denouement of Byatt's novel with a mortally humiliated Cassandra finally retreating completely from reality by killing herself. Sibling rivalry finally culminates in death 20 years later. While the surface of *The Game* is realistic, Byatt introduces a mythic level by cleverly employing the symbolism of the Garden of Eden in relation to her characters; Simon's snakes, for example, clearly bring to mind the serpent.

Although much larger in scale than either of its predecessors, *The Virgin in the Garden* is but the first novel in an as yet untitled tetralogy in progress, which promises to be one of the most ambitious fictional undertakings of the postwar period, comparable to Lawrence Durrell's *Alexandria Quartet*, Doris Lessing's *The Children of Violence*, and Anthony Powell's *A Dance to the Music of Time*. The tetralogy aims to follow the lives of a group of characters during the second Elizabethan age, from the accession of the Queen in 1952 until the major Post-Impressionist Exhibition held in London in 1980, but each novel, while advancing the chronology, is expected to have its own dominating motif or central symbol and was originally intended to be technically and stylistically distinctive. However, Byatt has found this latter plan very difficult, perhaps impossible, to implement for reasons explained in the second volume, *Still Life*.

After a short but complex and symbolically rich Prologue set in 1968, *The Virgin in the Garden* narrates events in 1952–53, with occasional and brief forward-flashes that illuminate the characters from the advantageous perspective of hindsight. The novel, set in North Yorkshire, mainly in and around a public school, concentrates on the three children of the senior English master, Bill Potter, and the person each of them is most involved with: the eldest, Stephanie, a schoolteacher, and the curate she marries, much to the annoyance of her militantly agnostic father; Frederica, a brilliant and precocious schoolgirl, and the English teacher, poet, and playwright Alexander Wedderburn she falls in love with; the strange schoolboy, Marcus, and the biology teacher, a religious maniac, with whom he indulges in a lunatic, quasi-spiritual experiment.

One of the things the novel captures best is the festive atmosphere of Coronation year with its sense of promise and rebirth, of release from postwar privations, of a new Elizabethan age with just as much potentiality as that of the first Elizabeth. A main strand of the book is the production of Alexander's verse play about the Virgin queen, *Astraea*, in the garden of an Elizabethan country house—hence the title, although it also refers to Frederica, another virgin until the closing pages. The novel is, in fact, full of quotations and literary and mythological allusions, and is concerned with both English history and the English cultural tradition. While *The Virgin in the Garden* possesses an almost Victorian leisureliness in its depiction of detail and its analysis of characters, it is also a decidedly modernist work in the wake of *Ulysses*, since its meticulous realism is fused with symbolism. More conspicuously than in her previous fiction, Byatt draws her inspiration from Proust, one of her favourite novelists and a major influence on her work. Significantly, two of the three epigraphs to her next novel, *Still Life*, are from Proust.

If, as the title indicates, Elizabethan iconography plays an important part in structuring and unifying *The Virgin in the Garden*, the art of painting, as the title against suggests, performs an equivalent role in *Still Life*. The novel opens at the Post-Impressionist Exhibition in 1980, and is pervaded by reference to the life and work of van Gogh, including a number of quotations from his famous letters. In *Still Life*, Alexander Wedderburn's new verse play, parallel to *Astraea* in its predecessor, is *The Yellow Chair*, which dramatizes the last phase of van Gogh's life and appropriates the title of one of his best-known paintings for its own title. The intrusive authorial "I," who must be equated with Byatt herself rather than interpreted as a deceptive metafictional device, comments reflexively on *Still Life* on several occasions, and describes her failure to achieve a style for the novel using the analogy of painting, as she had hoped. She had wanted to follow William Carlos Williams's injunction about "no ideas but in things" and to write "a novel of naming and accuracy" by using a language shorn of metaphor and figures of speech, an ambition shared by her character Alexander Wedderburn in writing *The Yellow Chair*. Like Wedderburn, she found that language, being inherently metaphorical and figurative, was against her, and she had to abandon her experimental aspirations for the book. As a result, *Still Life* is more of an orthodox sequel to *The Virgin in the Garden* than originally planned, and in some respects conforms to the traditional family saga, even though the use of flash-forward techniques and self-reflecting analysis, along with her intellectual arguments and philosophical speculations, ensure that its underlying realism is qualified by postmodernist perspectives on language, art, and reality itself.

As in *The Virgin in the Garden*, the narrative of *Still Life* has three main strands, one for each of the Potter children, and follows their lives during the mid and late 1950's, ending catastrophically with the accidental death of the eldest, Stephanie, electrocuted in her own kitchen. The closing chapters, dealing with this absurd yet horrific incident and its aftermath, are among the best in the book and are characterised by sombre intensity. In parallel with Stephanie's life as curate's wife and young mother are Marcus's development into a young scientist with a mystical apprehension of the world, and Frederica's career as an undergraduate at Newnham College, Cambridge, replete with intellectual and sexual adventures. Much of the vitality of the novel belongs to this part of the book, where Byatt's interest in ideas can be incorporated as an essential part of her academic characters' lives. Elsewhere the writing is at times laboured and lacks the freshness and dynamism of *The Virgin in the Garden*, perhaps because the major figures were so thoroughly described there. Byatt is, in fact, faced with the old, familiar problem confronting all writers of sequels and series: how to maintain the original momentum and avoid staleness. She anticipated the difficulty by resolving to write the novel in a totally different way from *The Virgin in the Garden*, but in the event found herself unable to do so.

—Peter Lewis

CALDWELL, Erskine (Preston). American. Born in Moreland, Georgia, 17 December 1903. Educated at Erskine College, Due West, South Carolina, 1920–21; University of Virginia, Charlottesville, 1922, 1925–26; University of Pennsylvania, Philadelphia, 1924. Married 1) Helen Lannigan in 1925 (divorced), two sons and one daughter; 2) the photographer Margaret Bourke-White in 1939 (divorced, 1942); 3) June Johnson in 1942 (divorced, 1955), one son; 4) Virginia Moffett Fletcher in 1957. Played professional football, Wilkes-Barre, Pennsylvania, in the 1920's; reporter, Atlanta *Journal*, 1925; screenwriter, Hollywood, 1930–34, 1942–43; foreign correspondent in Mexico, Spain, Czechoslovakia, Russia, and China, 1938–41; editor, American Folkways series, 1941–55. Recipient: *Yale Review* award, 1933; Order of Cultural Merit (Poland), 1981. Member, National Institute of Arts and Letters, 1942, and American Academy, 1984; Commandant, Order of Arts and Letters (France), 1984. Agent: McIntosh and Otis, 475 Fifth Avenue, New York, New York 10017. Address: P.O. Box 4550, Hopi Station, Scottsdale, Arizona 85258, U.S.A.

PUBLICATIONS

Novels

The Bastard. New York, Heron Press, 1930.
Poor Fool. New York, Rariora Press, 1930.
Tobacco Road. New York, Scribner, 1932; London, Cresset Press, 1933.
God's Little Acre. New York, Viking Press, and London, Secker, 1933.
Journeyman. New York, Viking Press, 1935; revised edition, Viking Press, and London, Secker, 1938.
Trouble in July. New York, Duell, and London, Cape, 1940.
All Night Long: A Novel of Guerrilla Warfare in Russia. New York, Duell, 1942; London, Cassell, 1943.

Tragic Ground. New York, Duell, 1944; London, Falcon Press, 1947.
A House in the Uplands. New York, Duell, 1946; London, Falcon Press, 1947.
The Sure Hand of God. New York, Duell, 1947; London, Falcon Press, 1949.
This Very Earth. New York, Duell, 1948; London, Falcon Press, 1949.
Place Called Estherville. New York, Duell, 1949; London, Falcon Press, 1951.
Episode in Palmetto. New York, Duell, 1950; London, Falcon Press, 1951.
A Lamp for Nightfall. New York, Duell, and London, Falcon Press, 1952.
Love and Money. New York, Duell, 1954; London, Heinemann, 1955.
Gretta. Boston, Little Brown, 1955; London, Heinemann, 1956.
Claudelle Inglish. Boston, Little Brown, 1959; as *Claudell*, London, Heinemann, 1959.
Jenny by Nature. New York, Farrar Straus, and London, Heinemann, 1961.
Close to Home. New York, Farrar Straus, and London, Heinemann, 1962.
The Bastard, and Poor Fool. London, Bodley Head, 1963.
The Last Night of Summer. New York, Farrar Straus, and London, Heinemann, 1963.
Miss Mamma Aimee. New York, New American Library, 1967; London, Joseph, 1968.
Summertime Island. Cleveland, World, 1968; London, Joseph, 1969.
The Weather Shelter. Cleveland, World, 1969; London, Joseph, 1970.
The Earnshaw Neighborhood. Cleveland, World, 1971; London, Joseph, 1972.
Annette. New York, New American Library, 1973; London, Joseph, 1974.

Short Stories

American Earth. New York, Scribner, 1931; London, Secker, 1935; as *A Swell-Looking Girl*, New York, New American Library, 1951.
Mama's Little Girl. Privately printed, 1932.
A Message for Genevieve. Privately printed, 1933.
We Are the Living: Brief Stories. New York, Viking Press, 1933; London, Secker, 1934.
Kneel to the Rising Sun and Other Stories. New York, Viking Press, 1935; London, Heinemann, 1961.
The Sacrilege of Alan Kent. Portland, Maine, Falmouth Book House, 1936.
Southways. New York, Viking Press, 1938; London, Falcon Press, 1953.
Jackpot: The Short Stories of Erskine Caldwell. New York, Duell, 1940; London, Falcon Press, 1950; abridged edition, as *Midsummer Passion*, New York, Avon, 1948.
Georgia Boy. New York, Duell, 1943; London, Falcon Press, 1947.
A Day's Wooing and Other Stories. New York, Grosset and Dunlap, 1944.
Stories by Erskine Caldwell: 24 Representative Stories, edited by Henry Seidel Canby. New York, Duell, 1944; as *The Pocket Book of Erskine Caldwell Stories*, New York, Pocket Books, 1947.
Where the Girls Were Different and Other Stories, edited by Donald A. Wollheim. New York, Avon, 1948.

A Woman in the House. New York, New American Library, 1949.

The Humorous Side of Erskine Caldwell, edited by Robert Cantwell. New York, Duell, 1951; as *Where the Girls Were Different and Other Stories*, New York, New American Library, 1962.

The Courting of Susie Brown. New York, Duell, and London, Falcon Press, 1952.

The Complete Stories. New York, Duell, 1953.

Gulf Coast Stories. Boston, Little Brown, 1956; London, Heinemann, 1957.

Certain Women. Boston, Little Brown, 1957; London, Heinemann, 1958.

When You Think of Me. Boston, Little Brown, 1959; London, Heinemann, 1960.

Men and Women: 22 Stories. Boston, Little Brown, 1961; London, Heinemann, 1963.

Stories. Franklin Center, Pennsylvania, Franklin Library, 1980.

Stories of Life: North and South. New York, Dodd Mead, 1983.

The Black and White Stories of Erskine Caldwell. Atlanta, Peachtree, 1984.

Plays

Screenplays: *A Nation Dances* (documentary), 1943; *Volcano*, 1953.

Other

In Defense of Myself. Privately printed, 1930.

Tenant Farmer. New York, Phalanx Press, 1935.

Some American People. New York, McBride, 1935.

You Have Seen Their Faces, photographs by Margaret Bourke-White. New York, Viking Press, 1937.

North of the Danube, photographs by Margaret Bourke-White. New York, Viking Press, 1939.

Say! Is This the U.S.A.?, photographs by Margaret Bourke-White. New York, Duell, 1941.

All-Out on the Road to Smolensk. New York, Duell, 1942; as *Moscow Under Fire: A Wartime Diary, 1941*, London, Hutchinson, 1942.

Russia at War, photographs by Margaret Bourke-White. New York and London, Hutchinson, 1942.

The Caldwell Caravan: Novels and Stories. Cleveland, World, 1946.

Call It Experience: The Years of Learning How to Write. New York, Duell, 1951; London, Hutchinson, 1952.

Molly Cottontail (for children). Boston, Little Brown, 1958; London, Heinemann, 1959.

Around About America. New York, Farrar Straus, and London, Heinemann, 1964.

In Search of Bisco. New York, Farrar Straus, and London, Heinemann, 1965.

The Deer at Our House (for children). New York, Collier, and London, Collier Macmillan, 1966.

In the Shadow of the Steeple. London, Heinemann, 1966.

Writing in America. New York, Phaedra, 1967.

Deep South: Memory and Observation (includes *In the Shadow of the Steeple*). New York, Weybright and Talley, 1968.

Afternoons in Mid-America: Observations and Impressions. New York, Dodd Mead, 1976.

*

Manuscript Collection: Baker Library, Dartmouth College, Hanover, New Hampshire.

Critical Studies: *The Southern Poor White from Lubberland to Tobacco Road* by Shields McIlwaine, Norman, University of Oklahoma Press, 1939; introduction by Carvill Collins to *Men and Women* by Caldwell, Boston, Little Brown, 1961, London, Heinemann, 1963; *Erskine Caldwell* by James Korges, Minneapolis, University of Minnesota Press, 1969; *Black Like It Is/Was: Erskine Caldwell's Treatment of Racial Themes* by William A. Sutton, Metuchen, New Jersey, Scarecrow Press, 1974; *Critical Essays on Erskine Caldwell* edited by Scott Mac-Donald, Boston, Twayne, 1981; *Erskine Caldwell* by James E. Devlin, Boston, Twayne, 1984.

*   *   *

Balzac notoriously claimed that anyone wanting to know trades, manners, or business in the France of his time could learn about them by reading his novels. Erskine Caldwell, good as some of his novels are, is not Balzac's equal; precious few writers are. Yet the social historian as well as the literary critic will in the future turn to Caldwell's novels finding in them a representation of the Southern region of the United States, a representation in its own way unequalled by the other great writers of the region—Flannery O'Connor, William Faulkner, Robert Penn Warren, Eudora Welty, and others. For Caldwell has been observing and writing for longer than any other great writer in the region, his novels taken as a whole coming to produce one of the most fascinating measures of the life and times, attitudes and temperaments of the area. One has only to set the recent *The Weather Shelter* beside the earlier *Trouble in July* to have one of the most graphic and moving indications of the changes taking place in the Southern region of the United States. Indeed, in his autobiography of his public career, *Call It Experience*, Caldwell suggests that his novels form a "cyclorama of the South." To argue for long in this manner, however, would seem to indicate that Caldwell's novels are a mere adjunct to social studies (sometimes called "science"). Caldwell closely observes the social scene, but he is also a literary artist of high quality and the author of some splendid novels.

This brief essay is not the place to consider the wide range of his achievements as a writer—and indeed as editor of the invaluable *American Folkways* series of regional books. His achievements in reporting and analysis would alone place him in the front rank of contemporary prose writers in the English language. I have written elsewhere (*Erskine Caldwell*, University of Minnesota Press) about Caldwell's tact and his success in the forms of biography and autobiography. In each mode he undertook a very difficult subject. His biographical writing ranges from scaldingly satirical chapters in, especially, his early political, social, and economic commentary, to the tender and affecting memoir of his father, a well-known Presbyterian minister, which is full of sentiment without being sentimental—surely one of the most difficult kinds of writing. In the autobiographical mode, Caldwell undertook to write about the most banned and censored writer of his time, without being vindictive; and at the same time about the most financially successful writer of his time, without being pompous. As in his autobiography he keeps this perilous balance between self-justification and righteous scorn, so in his travel books he is both objective in his reports yet compassionate; and his eye for detail is shrewdly discerning. These qualities which mark his non-fiction are abundantly clear also in his best novels, as is his prose style which remains one of the most outstanding in this period of American literature. Every reader is impressed by the rich evocativeness of Faulkner's style, and the stylistic tension which contributes such force to Flannery O'Connor's great stories; yet not enough readers have noticed and praised the great lucid "plain" style of Erskine Caldwell. Some of his best writing is in his non-fiction, especially the Swiftian commentaries in *Some American People* (including Tenant Farmers) as well as the later and gentler *In Search of Bisco* and *Deep South*. And I will argue again while I have the opportunity for the great text-picture books he brought back into print, as the James Agee-Walker Evans *Let Us Now Praise Famous Men*; for the books Caldwell created with Margaret Bourke-White are among the greatest of the genre, especially *You Have Seen Their Faces*, *North of the Danube*, and *Say! Is This the U.S.A.?* These are masterpieces in an art form too often ignored. It required the happy conjunction of writer and photographer working as one author, not as one illustrating or explaining the work of the other.

When one considers Caldwell's prose fiction, one is confronted with a huge body of work; and as with all prolific writers, literary quality has ebbed and flowed in the novels and stories. Some of the novels are best read as groups or variations on themes. And despite his reputation as a writer of sexy and violent novels, Caldwell is often in the novels concerned with family relations, often tested by ideological or social conflicts. He presents resulting actions often in a comic way, which of course has the unfortunate tendency to make some readers suppose that the actions are therefore not "serious." The novels also disappoint readers who suppose that the "serious" novel must of necessity explore characters psychologically in the manner of Dostoevsky, James, or Faulkner, if the novel is to be given critical attention. Yet as Restoration comedy was once dismissed because it was not Shakespearean (and because it is sexy), and Joyce scorned because he did not write real novels as obviously Galsworthy did, so recently some simplistic notions about "the novel" have tended to lead critics to dismiss Caldwell's work because he does not write like Faulkner or Flannery O'Connor. Faulkner himself annoyed Hemingway no end by remarking his failure to risk much in his novels; and irritated his own admirers by placing himself second in achievement to Thomas Wolfe. Yet Faulkner's much publicised list of the five greatest American novelists of his generation has another surprise, for the currently much patronized Caldwell is on it: Wolfe, Faulkner, Dos Passos, Caldwell, Hemingway. (He was right about Dos Passos, also currently out of critical fashion.)

Though the whole of Caldwell's production—in fiction and non-fiction—will continue to be valuable to the student of Southern society and to the literary historian, the books that will survive as works of literary art are relatively few—as in the case of, say, Scott. Caldwell has in a way chronicled the South; his books if read in chronological succession show not just the author's mellowing into compassionate old age, but a South that slowly changes in mood and attitude. Yet Caldwell also produced three books of fiction that are masterpieces: *Tobacco Road*, *God's Little Acre*, and *Georgia Boy*. With these novels, 20 or 30 of his best short stories (some of this century's finest) will form a lasting body of prose fiction which, when set beside his considerable achievement in non-fiction, will clearly mark him one of the most important writers of our time.

Perhaps Caldwell's best-known work, *Tobacco Road*, almost failed to survive its initial publication. Sales were so small that Caldwell's advance was barely covered. Some time later Jack Kirkland dramatized the story; but the play almost closed after two weeks. By chance, the play survived, to run longer than any previous play; and *Tobacco Road* became a best-seller

book, second only to the Bible. These curiosities of publishing history are not in themselves important to literary criticism; though in this case the history of the book is especially ironic, since one of the themes of the novel is human tenacity in the face of rejection and failure. The physical hunger of Jeeter, the sexual appetites of Ellie May and Sister Bessie, the sterile marriage of Pearl and Tom, all are more than a comic presentation of low-life characters on land made sterile by cultivation of tobacco that once made the region's owners rich. The deformed characters (some physically, some mentally or spiritually) wait for God; as Jeeter says: "Him and me has always been fair and square with each other . . . . I don't know nothing else to do, except wait for Him to take notice." And they seem to act out a superior will, suggested more strongly in some of the later books.

God's Little Acre is a masterpiece. If, as many critics argue, it is less than *Absalom! Absalom!*, then it is less in the way that *Dead Souls* is less than *War and Peace*, or *Volpone* less than *King Lear*; but clearly at this level of literary competence, ranking becomes the parlor game of bored professors. Unfortunately all the censorship and banning gained *God's Little Acre* a reputation for being comic pornography; and some critics have continued to see the book as merely a comic exposé of Southern local color. The book is about southern mentality in about the same way as the typist at tea-time section of *The Waste Land* is about unfair labor practices in London. I do not make the comparison lightly; for *God's Little Acre* is a novel about sterility; it is a comic presentation of one of the most ancient moral problems, here stated in low country terms by Ty Ty Walden, the digger after gold: "There was a mean trick played on us somewhere. God put us in the bodies of animals and tried to make us act like people. That was the beginning of trouble." The book itself is structured on contrasts of characters, and on a progression of scenes alternating between farm and town and building to a climax of great technical brilliance.

Georgia Boy, on the other hand, is episodic, a series of closely related incidents narrated by a 12-year-old boy. It is equalled by only two other works in recent American fiction: Wright Morris's *My Uncle Dudley* and Faulkner's *The Reivers*. The earnestly innocent reports of adult behavior tend to transform what is said and done in the books, so that fictional strategy is itself a criticism of life.

The short stories present a problem by their very number; but a reader attempting to see Caldwell for the various and talented fictionist he is may be helped by this list of some of the best stories: "Country Full of Swedes," "The People v. Ake Lathan, Colored," "Candy-Man Beechum," "After-Image," "An Evening in Nuevo Leon," "We Are Looking at You, Agnes," "An Autumn Courtship," "A Swell-looking Girl," and "Meddlesome Jack." There are many other stories as good, or almost as good, in Caldwell's collections; and one suspects that we would have to go back to Maupassant to find his equal in short story writing.

—James Korges

CALISHER, Hortense. American. Born in New York City, 20 December 1911. Educated at Hunter College High School, New York; Barnard College, New York, A.B. in philosophy 1932. Married 1) H.B. Heffelfinger in 1935, one daughter and one son; 2) Curtis Harnack in 1959. Adjunct Professor of English, Barnard College, 1956–57; Visiting Professor, University of Iowa, Iowa City, 1957, 1959–60, Stanford University, California, 1958, Sarah Lawrence College, Bronxville, New York, 1962, and Brandeis University, Waltham, Massachusetts, 1963–64; Writer-in-Residence, 1965, and Visiting Lecturer, 1968, University of Pennsylvania, Philadelphia; Adjunct Professor of English, Columbia University, New York, 1968–70 and 1972–73; Clark Lecturer, Scripps College, Claremont, California, 1969; Visiting Professor, State University of New York, Purchase, 1971–72; Regents' Professor, University of California, Irvine, Spring 1976; Visiting Writer, Bennington College, Vermont, 1978; Hurst Professor, Washington University, St. Louis, 1979; National Endowment for the Arts Lecturer, Cooper Union, New York, 1983; Visiting Professor, Brown University, Providence, Rhode Island, 1986. Recipient: Guggenheim fellowship, 1952, 1955; Department of State American Specialists grant, 1958; American Academy award, 1967; National Endowment for the Arts grant, 1967. Litt.D.: Skidmore College, Saratoga Springs, New York, 1980. Member, American Academy, 1977. Lives in New York City. Agent: Candida Donadio and Associates, 231 West 22nd Street, New York, New York 10011, U.S.A.

PUBLICATIONS

Novels

False Entry. Boston, Little Brown, 1961; London, Secker and Warburg, 1962.
Textures of Life. Boston, Little Brown, and London, Secker and Warburg, 1963.
Journal from Ellipsia. Boston, Little Brown, 1965; London, Secker and Warburg, 1966.
The Railway Police, and The Last Trolley Ride. Boston, Little Brown, 1966.
The New Yorkers. Boston, Little Brown, 1969; London, Cape, 1970.
Queenie. New York, Arbor House, 1971; London, W.H. Allen, 1973.
Standard Dreaming. New York, Arbor House, 1972.
Eagle Eye. New York, Arbor House, 1973.
On Keeping Women. New York, Arbor House, 1977.
Mysteries of Motion. New York, Doubleday, 1983.
The Bobby-Soxer. New York, Doubleday, 1986.

Short Stories

In the Absence of Angels. Boston, Little Brown, 1951; London, Heinemann, 1953.
Tale for the Mirror: A Novella and Other Stories. Boston, Little Brown, 1962; London, Secker and Warburg, 1963.
Extreme Magic: A Novella and Other Stories. Boston, Little Brown, and London, Secker and Warburg, 1964.
The Collected Stories of Hortense Calisher. New York, Arbor House, 1975.
Saratoga, Hot. New York, Doubleday, 1985.

Other

What Novels Are (lecture). Claremont, California, Scripps College, 1969.
Herself (memoir). New York, Arbor House, 1972.

Editor, with Shannon Ravenel, *The Best American Short Stories 1981.* Boston, Houghton Mifflin, 1981.

*

Critical Studies: in *Don't Never Forget* by Brigid Brophy, London, Cape, 1966, New York, Holt Rinehart, 1967; Cynthia Ozick in *Midstream* (New York), 1969; "Ego Art: Notes on How I Came to It" by Calisher, in *Works in Progress* (New York), 1971; article by Kathy Brown, in *Current Biography* (New York), November 1973.

Hortense Calisher comments:

(1972) *False Entry* and *The New Yorkers* are connected novels; either may be read first; together they are a chronicle perhaps peculiarly American, according to some critics, but with European scope, according to others. *Journal from Ellipsia* was perhaps one of the first or the first serious American novel to deal with "verbal" man's displacement in a world of the spatial sciences; because it dealt with the possibility of life on other planets it was classed as "science fiction" both in the USA and in England. The *Dublin Times* understood it; its review does well by it. It also satirizes male-female relationships, by postulating a planet on which things are otherwise. In category, according to some, it is less an ordinary novel than a social satire akin to *Erewhon*, *Gulliver's Travels*, *Candide*, etc. *The Railway Police* and *The Last Trolley Ride*— the first is really a long short story of an individual, the second a novella built around an environs, a chorale of persons really, with four main parts, told in the interchanging voice of two men.

I usually find myself alternating a "larger" work with a smaller one, a natural change of pace. *Textures of Life*, for instance, is an intimate novel, of a young marriage, very personal, as *Journal* is not. After the latter, as I said in an interview, I wanted to get back to people. *The New Yorkers* was a conscious return to a "big" novel, done on fairly conventional terms, descriptive, narrative, leisurely, and inclusive, from which the long monologue chapters of the two women are a conscious departure. Its earlier mate, *False Entry*, has been called the only "metaphysical" novel in the America of its period—I'm not sure what that means, except perhaps that the whole, despite such tangible scenes as the Ku Klux Klan and courtroom episodes, is carried in the "mind" of one man. It has been called Dickensian, and in its plethora of event I suppose it is; yet the use of memory symbols and of psyche might just as well be French (Proust and Gide)—by intent it does both, or joins both ways of narration. *The New Yorkers* is more tied to its environs in a localized way; part of its subject *is* the environs.

Queenie is a satire, a farce on our sexual mores, as seen through the eyes of a "modern" young girl. As it is not yet out at this writing, I shall wait to be told what it is about.

(1986) *Standard Dreaming:* short novel narrated through the consciousness of a surgeon who believes the human race may be in process of dying off. *Herself:* the autobiography of a writer, rather than of the total life. Included are portions of critical studies, articles, etc., as well as several in toto (including one on the novel and on sex in American literature), and commentary on the writer's role in war, as a feminist, critic and teacher. *Eagle Eye:* the story of a young American non-combatant during and after the Vietnam War. Just as Queenie, in the novel of that name, confided in her tape-recorder, Bronstein addresses his computer. In 1974 some critics were bemused at this; time has changed that. *The Collected Stories:* Preface by author begins with the much-quoted "A story is an apocalypse, served in a very small cup." *On Keeping Women: Herself* had broken ground in some of its aspects of what feminists were to term "womanspeak." I was never to be a conventional feminist; conventional thought is not for writers. But I had always wanted to do a novel from within the female feelings I did have from youth, through motherhood and the wish for other creation. This is that book. *Mysteries of Motion:* as in *Journal from Ellipsia* I continue concern for the way we live daily with the vast efforts and fruits of the scientists, and the terrors, without much understanding. Begun in 1977, before shuttles had flown or manmade objects had fallen to earth from orbit, this story of the first civilians in space is I believe the first novel of character (rather than so-called "science fiction") to be set in space. Because of that intent, the lives of all six people before they embark are an essential part of the story. What may happen to people, personality—and nations—in the space race, is what I was after. Though I researched minimally—just enough to know the language, or some of it—one critic commented that its technical details could not be faulted. I imagined, rather than tried to be faithful to the momentary fact. And again, time has caught up with it, sadly so in the matter of "star wars." *Saratoga, Hot:* short works, called "little novels." Writing novels changes the short-story pen—the stories become novelistic, or mine do. The intent was "to give as much background as you can get in a foreground." *The Bobby-Soxer:* the story of the erotic and professional maturing of a young girl of the 1950's, as narrated by the woman she has become, it is also a legend of American provincial life, akin to the early novellas.

I have just completed a short novel called *Age,* and am resuming work on a novel set in Central Europe and the United States.

*   *   *

Many readers first encounter Hortense Calisher through her widely-anthologized short stories, then anticipate her novels. After reading them, however, they may come away vaguely unsatisfied though seldom quite dissatisfied. She is too gifted a writer for that.

It seems impossible for Calisher to write poorly: she is a master of language. Precise, powerful verbs give scenes life and immediacy. In "The Woman Who Was Everybody" an overqualified department store employee reluctantly faces the day: "She swung sideways out of bed, clamped her feet on the floor, rose and trundled to the bathroom, the kitchenette." Calisher's imagery is bountiful, original, and appropriate. In the same story, "the mornings crept in like applicants for jobs." Equal to language, Calisher has evidently observed and experienced how truth is revealed in the course of living and can reconstruct these epiphanies readily in characters.

Then why, since hers are among the best American short stories of this century, are Calisher's novels less successful? At least two reasons are likely. One is that it is impossible to sustain in the long form the power she packs into the short form. The small cast, limited setting, single problem of the short story let her build the work to a final revelation which suggests that, for better or worse, a life will never be quite the same again. This is the classic short story.

Calisher novels often merely elongate the story format. Substituting for traditional plot and sub-plot, there are series of revelations related to the central situation. (A young couple disclose aspects of themselves as they cope with an ill child in *Textures of Life.* Another couple, from the novella *Saratoga, Hot* actually reveal more about their horsey social set than themselves.) Whether the reader can sustain interest in longer works whose internal logic is random and whose continuity needs occasional propulsion by fortuitous revelation is a question. Certainly that *does* work in *The New Yorkers,* often called her most successful novel, an indulgent insight into family life. Ill-advised timing and treatment may have undercut Calisher's

satirical novel, *Queenie.* The late 1960's were not laughing times and for many the new sexual freedom which Queenie fumbles toward was no laughing matter. What may be her least successful novel, *Mysteries of Motion,* distracts as much as discloses since six lives are revealed, and on a space journey at that. Better a bus ride in Brooklyn.

That more modest approach to setting is exactly what makes her short stories seem instantly relevant to our ordinary lives, that and the fact that each story—however brief—is also a life history of sorts. Calisher examines that life at a time of crisis and the reader comes away instructed in valuable experience. In the classic "One of the Chosen" a successful Jewish lawyer, Davy Spanner, always popular in his college days, has believed lifelong that he never needed the support of fraternity life and had comfortably rejected the early overtures of the campus societies. At a class reunion, a gentile classmate blurts out the unsettling truth that Spanner would *never* have been offered a serious membership bid.

Calisher's long interest in psychology and the supernatural is evident. Her life spans Freudianism and beyond, but psychology—eclectic and non-systematic—as it appears in her work at times is close to fantasy, at other times follows accepted dogma. "Heartburn" centers on the power of suggestion; "The Scream on 57th Street" treats fear. Both "work" just as her general grasp of family relationships seems valid, however it was acquired. On the other hand, *Standard Dreaming,* Calisher's unfortunate excursion into a dream world of searching characters, could be taken for a parody of surrealism.

Calisher's short stories and novellas may initially appear to be peopled by fully-rounded characters, but an overview of the stories reveals a high proportion of well-done types: the educated misfit, the eccentric family member, the young innocent, the at-odds mother-daughter (or husband-wife), the displaced Southerner, the would-be radical. And type is all they need to be since hers are not primarily stories of character, but of complex situation, the result of long processes of cause and effect told in hints and subtleties. Where the Calisher protagonists have been, are now, and where they are probably going—or not going, depending on their revelations—*is* their story. Exactly *who* they are is incidental. Their external descriptions are often vivid, even witty, but their tastes and temperaments are revealed only to the degree that they serve the tale. If we flesh them out ourselves, it is a tribute to their creator's ability to write so that we *read* creatively.

The Collected Stories of Hortense Calisher, an enduring treasury of major works in her best genre, allows ready comparison of early and late works and reveals the consistency of Calisher's vision, even such traits as a vein of humor, a thread of the absurd, and a persistent interest in the power of the mind to direct fate. She is an eminently serious and concerned writer, despite the fatuous, the incompetents, the ditsy relatives, and the rattled authority figures who clamor for their share of attention in her works. Their truths are as true as anyone else's, Calisher suggests, and their numbers among us may be greater than we want to believe.

—Marian Pehowski

CALLAGHAN, Morley (Edward). Canadian. Born in Toronto, Ontario, 22 September 1903. Educated at St. Michael's College, University of Toronto, B.A. 1925; Osgoode Hall Law School, Toronto, LL.B. 1928; admitted to the Ontario Bar,

1928. Worked with the Royal Canadian Navy on assignment for the National Film Board during World War II; travelled across Canada as chairman of the radio forum "Of Things to Come," 1944. Married Lorrete Florence Dee in 1929; two sons. Worked on the Toronto *Star* while a student; full-time writer since 1928; lived in Paris, 1928–29. Recipient: Governor-General's Award, 1952; *Maclean's* award, 1955; Lorne Pierce Medal, 1960; Canada Council Medal, 1966, prize, 1970; Molson Prize, 1970; Royal Bank of Canada award, 1970. D.Litt.: University of Western Ontario, London, 1965; University of Windsor, Ontario, 1973; LL.D.: University of Toronto, 1966. Companion, Order of Canada, 1982. Address: 20 Dale Avenue, Toronto, Ontario M4W 1K4, Canada. *d. Aug. 1990*

PUBLICATIONS

Novels

Strange Fugitive.   New York, Grosset and Dunlap, 1928.
It's Never Over.   New York, Scribner, 1930.
A Broken Journey.   New York, Scribner, 1932.
Such Is My Beloved.   New York, Scribner, 1934.
They Shall Inherit the Earth.   New York, Random House, 1935; London, Chatto and Windus, 1936.
More Joy in Heaven.   New York, Random House, 1937.
The Varsity Story.   Toronto and London, Macmillan, and New York, Macmillan, 1948.
The Loved and the Lost.   New York, Macmillan, 1951; London, MacGibbon and Kee, 1961.
The Many Coloured Coat.   New York, Coward McCann, 1960; London, MacGibbon and Kee, 1963.
A Passion in Rome.   New York, Coward McCann, 1961; London, MacGibbon and Kee, 1964.
A Fine and Private Place.   New York, Mason Charter, 1975.
Close to the Sun Again.   New York, St. Martin's Press, 1977.
A Time for Judas.   Toronto, Macmillan, 1983; New York, St. Martin's Press, 1984.
Our Lady of the Snows.   New York, St. Martin's Press, 1986.

Short Stories

A Native Argosy.   New York, Scribner, 1929.
No Man's Meat.   Paris, Titus, 1931.
Now That April's Here and Other Stories.   New York, Random House, 1936.
Stories.   Toronto, Macmillan, 1959; London, MacGibbon and Kee, 2 vols., 1962–64.
An Autumn Penitent (includes *In His Own Country*).   Toronto, Macmillan, 1973.
No Man's Meat, and The Enchanted Pimp.   Toronto, Macmillan, 1978.

Uncollected Short Stories

"Lady in a Green Dress," in *Scribner's* (New York), August 1930.
"The Chiseller," in *New Yorker*, 16 August 1930.
"Poolroom," in *Scribner's* (New York), October 1932.
"Emily," in *Household Magazine* (New York), January 1933.
"Northern Summer Twilight," in *Household Magazine* (New York), September 1933.
"The Bridegroom," in *Esquire* (New York), January 1934.
"The Girl Who Was Easy," in *Esquire* (New York), May 1934.
"She's Nothing to Me," in *Story* (New York), June 1934.
"The Intellectual," in *Literary America* (New York), March 1935.

"In the Big Town," in *Esquire* (New York), April 1936.
"An Enemy of the People," in *Scribner's* (New York), September 1936.
"A Pair of Long Pants," in *Redbook* (New York), October 1936.
"The Fiddler on Twenty-Third Street," in *John O'London's Weekly* (London), 23 October 1936.
"Rendezvous with Self," in *Esquire* (New York), March 1937.
"This Man, My Father," in *Maclean's* (Toronto), 15 March 1937.
"Evening in Madison Square," in *Esquire* (New York), June 1937.
"A Little Beaded Bag," in *Harper's Bazaar* (New York), 1 September 1937.
"A Night Out," in *Household Magazine* (New York), October 1937.
"A Boy Grows Older," in *Esquire* (New York), December 1937.
"The Fugitive," in *North American Review* (Cedar Falls, Iowa), Summer 1938.
"The Consuming Fire," in *Harper's Bazaar* (New York), August 1938.
"The Sentimentalists," in *Harper's Bazaar* (New York), November 1938.
"The New Coat," in *Esquire* (New York), December 1938.
"The Thing That Happened to Uncle Adolphe," in *John O'London's Weekly* (London), 3 November 1939.
"Hello America," in *John O'London's Weekly* (London), 26 July 1940.
"Big Jules," in *Yale Review* (New Haven, Connecticut), September 1940.
"The Importance of Henry Bowman," in *Good Housekeeping* (New York), January 1945.
"Lilacs for Catherine," in *Seventeen* (New York), June 1946.
"Night of the Fire," in *Cosmopolitan* (New York), September 1946.
"I Knew Him When," in *American Magazine* (New York), April 1947.
"The Mexican Bracelets," in *Maclean's* (Toronto), 15 April 1947.
"This Man Couldn't Find a Fresh Angle on Xmas but He Did Find Peace and Good Will," in *New World* (Toronto), December 1947.
"With an Air of Dignity," in *Maclean's* (Toronto), 15 January 1948.
"All Right, Flatfoot," in *Maclean's* (Toronto), 15 August 1948.
"All the Doors Were Open," in *National Home Monthly* (Winnipeg), September 1948.
"The Indulgent Lady," in *Mademoiselle* (New York), November 1948.
"One Stormy Night," in *National Home Monthly* (Winnipeg), December 1948.
"The Bachelor's Dilemma," in *Maclean's* (Toronto), 1 August 1950.
"On the Edge of the World," in *Esquire* (New York), January 1951.
"Keep Away from Laura," in *Maclean's* (Toronto), 1 November 1952.
"The Way It Ended," in *Canadian Home Journal* (Toronto), September 1953.
"Something for Nothing," in *Canadian Home Journal* (Toronto), May 1954.
"We Just Had to Be Alone," in *Maclean's* (Toronto), 5 March 1955.
"The Doctor's Son," in *Ten for Wednesday Night*, edited by Robert Weaver.   Toronto, McClelland and Stewart, 1961.

"The Meterman, Caliban, and Then Mr. Jones," in *Exile* (Toronto), vol. 1, no. 3, 1973.

Plays

Turn Again Home, adaptation of his novel *They Shall Inherit the Earth* (produced New York, 1940; as *Going Home*, produced Toronto, 1950).
To Tell the Truth (produced Toronto, 1949).

Television Play: *And Then Mr. Jones*, 1974.

Other

Luke Baldwin's Vow (for children).   Philadelphia, Winston, 1948.
That Summer in Paris: Memories of Tangled Friendships with Hemingway, Fitzgerald, and Some Others.   New York, Coward McCann, and London, MacGibbon and Kee, 1963.
Winter, photographs by John de Visser.   Boston, New York Graphic Society, 1974.

*

Bibliography: by Judith Kendle, in *The Annotated Bibliography of Canada's Major Authors 5* edited by Robert Lecker and Jack David, Downsview, Ontario, ECW Press, 1984.

Critical Studies: *Morley Callaghan* by Brandon Conron, New York, Twayne, 1966, and *Morley Callaghan* edited by Conron, Toronto, McGraw Hill Ryerson, 1975; *Morley Callaghan* by Victor Hoar, Toronto, Copp Clark, 1969; *The Style of Innocence: A Study of Hemingway and Callaghan* by Fraser Sutherland, Toronto, Clarke Irwin, 1972; *Morley Callaghan* by Patricia Morley, Toronto, McClelland and Stewart, 1978; *The Callaghan Symposium* edited by David Staines, Ottawa, University of Ottawa Press, 1981.

*   *   *

The capacity which could produce Morley Callaghan's clipped, significant short stories, studies of the mysteriousness of the ordinary and the bewildering discrepancies of human fact, is not very evident in the early novels, *Strange Fugitive*, *It's Never Over*, and *A Broken Journey*, which are muddy in texture and melodramatic in action. It revealed itself first in *Such Is My Beloved*, a novel of which the whole air and idiom belong to the 1930's, the 1930's of the depression, of insecurity, unemployment, malnutrition, meanness.

The separation of two worlds, Christian and bourgeois, is the initiating contrast of the novel. Father Dowling speaks of it in his sermon in a lofty, generalising way. The novel shows it becoming biting and personal—"inevitable" in this way—in his own life. For all his spiritual and social conviction, and in spite of his working-class origins, he himself, because of his education, his status, his looks, his popularity with the parishioners, has a recognised position in the bourgeoisie. Officially he is on the side of religion against bourgeois convention; in reality he has at least one foot in both camps. The point at which the antagonism of the two orders becomes incorporated into his own life, the point at which he starts to be harrowed by the necessity for deciding between them, comes when he meets the two young prostitutes, Ronnie and Midge.

The economy of naturalness characteristic of Callaghan—which is a reconstruction of movement rather than a Zolaesque realism of detail—is best realised in this between Father Dowling and the prostitutes. Its growth, like that of all complex human feeling, is checked, troubled, backsliding, never wholly smooth or continuous; and yet it moves irresistibly onward, obeying and balancing an inward initiative as well as outer circumstances. At first, it is sympathetic but embarrassed on one side, suspect and then irritated on the other. As the priest begins to understand the economic forces beating on the young women his attention is less firmly concentrated on the rescue from prostitution and more on bringing a spontaneous human response from them. The contradiction between the donors and the deniers of life is at the heart of *Such Is My Beloved*. It is the conclusion to which the original division between the religious and the bourgeois worlds finally leads. Father Dowling in his efforts to be as richly a donor as he can becomes a scandal to the deniers. The novel makes it quite clear why; and not only clear but convincing. It has nothing to do with any sentimental falsification of the girls or of prostitution.

Poetry and religion have a universalising effect in *Such Is My Beloved*, making it appear to the British reader more accessible and less off-puttingly embedded in alien ground than, say, *More Joy in Heaven*, which wears an aspect—I can only put it like this—of continental parochialism. *More Joy in Heaven* is irremediably indigenous, North American in a limiting way. It is the story of a paroled criminal's effort to re-enter the society which has first punished and then forgiven him. Behind it stands an ethos of violence and the myth of the heroic gangster. Its setting is the brutal North-American city, ugly and unhistorical and very much "a machine for living," the sense of which is conveyed with confident incisiveness.

The paradox of one's reaction to *More Joy in Heaven* is that while its pure Americanism is so remote (it is, it seems to me, markedly more American than Canadian, unlike *Such Is My Beloved*) its cinematic conception, technique, imagery and characterisation are intimately familiar, part indeed of the history of one's own life. So much so that it is impossible to think about *More Joy in Heaven* without seeing it as a film and without casting its characters from those familiar names: Victor McLaglen, William Bendix, Janet Gaynor, Veronica Lake, Humphrey Bogart, Richard Widmark, Sidney Greenstreet, Franchot Tone, Edwin Arnold, Edward G. Robinson. *More Joy in Heaven* would make—perhaps, for all I know, it has already made—a superb film script.

I have stressed what I take to be the essential limitation in *More Joy in Heaven*, but it remains a strong piece of work and an impressive example of its genre. It is solid, vigorous, lean, and precise, the product of a serious mind. It has more weight than the documented but insubstantial study of a university institution, *The Varsity Story*, more bite than the more vaguely organised *A Passion in Rome*. *More Joy in Heaven* is a member of the group of novels which includes *Such Is My Beloved*, *The Many Coloured Coat*, and *The Loved and the Lost* to which I turn now. These novels, different in theme and setting, have in common a preoccupation with what I should like to call self-preservation, as long as I may remove from the term any hint of selfishness or over-personal concern. Callaghan is fascinated by what Henry James in the Preface to *What Maisie Knew* called a character's "truth of resistance," the gift or genius that some have for preserving intact the lineaments of their nature. It is a power which has at its heart a certain insistent simplicity: not self-confidence but trust in self. In Father Dowling it shows itself as a steady flame of goodness impervious even to the most high-minded opposition; in Kip Caley as the persistent, and finally desperate, trust of an abrasively independent identity. In *The Loved and the Lost* it is the girl Peggy Sanderson who possesses this faculty. It reveals itself in conduct which ignores or evades—rather than defies—the acceptable canons of behaviour in her world. The well-disposed think her capricious, the suspicious perverse. Her strangeness lies in her unpredictability, in her assumption that she is not caught in the same net as everybody else. She is described by his friend Foley to James McAlpine, a university teacher and would-be newspaper columnist, who is our source of awareness during this novel, in a fumbling conversation which tries to define her strangeness, as a blue jay, a bird which flies off at crazy and unpredictable angles.

The substance of the novel is the search for the true nature of the girl's odd, disconcerting individuality. It is conducted against the quietly insinuated but effectively established presence of Montreal. In no other novel of Callaghan is the city context so significantly part of the story and—at least to a British reader—so attractive. Incidentally, unobtrusively and, at every point, relevantly, the dimensions of the city appear.

The Many Coloured Coat is one of the finest of Callaghan's novels, and the one I take to represent his latest, and most developed work. The medium is in the same mode, quiet, unpretentious, close to speech and movement and with much of the flexibility and versatility of the spoken language. The medium, at once masculine and unpretentious, is in accord with Callaghan's attitude, which is, characteristically, both self-effacing and positive. The theme of *The Many Coloured Coat* is that of Joseph, the gifted and beloved young man. The novel rehearses the theme of the fortunes of the fortunate man. The biblical reference comes through, as the novel unfolds, without the least touch of impropriety or tactlessness, and it testifies to the steadiness Callaghan sees in human nature and to his perception of the permanent content of the varying crises it has to face.

The importance attributed in this novel to pride, not in any doctrinal way but by suggestive, concrete pointing, is justified not only by the facts of the case in this novel and the intelligent psychological investigation of them, but by a certain habit of sensibility in Callaghan himself. He has as Edmund Wilson pointed out in a perceptive and sympathetic essay, *O Canada*, "an intuitive sense of the meaning of Christianity." The human vision of these novels depends on a Christian style of feeling, of a particular tradition of religious sensibility which is present not as dogma or metaphysics but as a mode of perception and reaction.

I speak of Callaghan's Christian response, but, of course, that response and the whole economy of feeling of which it is a part, are sunk deep in the constitution of the novelist. If Callaghan is a Christian novelist, this is the way in which he is one. He is not the spokesman of religion, but the artist who possesses it as part of his personal nervous equipment. This traditional steadiness blends in Callaghan with that acute feeling for contemporary society, which, to a European at least, seems very natural to an artist working in the New World, and the combination makes him a novelist of an impressively serious quality. The contemporary flavour appears everywhere in his work, in themes, situations, characters and procedures. A single notable example of it in *The Many Coloured Coat* is his treatment of the life of the streets. The street in a modern industrial society presents itself to him as an image of that society and its experience. His skill in rendering the flow of life through the street, the brutality and ugliness, the glimpses the street provides of other, less tangible experiences, the altercations, the moments of communication, show the street not only as a place but as the analogue of human vitality and representativeness. "That night," he writes of Harry Lane after his fall, in words which are apt to describe the impression all Morley Callaghan's best work makes, "he walked through the streets for hours feeling he was wandering through his own life."

—William Walsh

CALLOW, Philip (Kenneth). British. Born in Birmingham, Warwickshire, 26 October 1924. Educated at Coventry Technical College, 1937–39; St. Luke's College, Exeter, Devon, 1968–70, Teacher's Certificate 1970. Married 1) Irene Vallance in 1953 (marriage dissolved, 1973), one daughter; 2) Penelope Jane Newman in 1974. Engineering apprentice and toolmaker, Coventry Gauge and Tool Company, 1940–48; clerk, Ministry of Works and Ministry of Supply, 1949–51; clerical assistant, South West Electricity Board, Plymouth, 1951–66; Arts Council Fellow, Falmouth School of Art, 1977–78; Creative Writing Fellow, Open University, 1979; Writer-in-Residence, Sheffield City Polytechnic, 1980–82. Recipient: Arts Council bursary, 1966, 1970, 1973, 1979; Society of Authors Travelling Scholarship, 1973; C. Day Lewis Fellowship, 1973; Southern Arts Association fellowship, 1974. Agent: MBA Literary Agents Ltd., 45 Fitzroy Street, London W1P 5HR. Address: Little Thatch, Haselbury, near Crewkerne, Somerset, England.

PUBLICATIONS

Novels

The Hosanna Man. London, Cape, 1956.
Common People. London, Heinemann, 1958.
A Pledge for the Earth. London, Heinemann, 1960.
Clipped Wings. Douglas, Isle of Man, Times Press, 1964.
Going to the Moon. London, MacGibbon and Kee, 1968.
The Bliss Body. London, MacGibbon and Kee, 1969.
Flesh of Morning. London, Bodley Head, 1971.
Yours. London, Bodley Head, 1972.
The Story of My Desire. London, Bodley Head, 1976.
Janine. London, Bodley Head, 1977.
The Subway to New York. London, Martin Brian and O'Keeffe, 1979.

Short Stories

Native Ground. London, Heinemann, 1959.
Woman with a Poet. Bradford, Yorkshire, Rivelin Press, 1983.

Uncollected Short Story

"Merry Christmas," in *New Statesman* (London), 22 December 1961.

Plays

The Honeymooners (televised, 1960). Published in *New Granada Plays*, London, Faber, 1961.

Radio Plays: *The Lamb*, 1971; *On Some Road*, 1979.

Television Play: *The Honeymooners*, 1960.

Verse

Turning Point.   London, Heinemann, 1964.
The Real Life: New Poems.   Douglas, Isle of Man, Times Press, 1964.
BareWires.   London, Chatto and Windus-Hogarth Press, 1972.
Cave Light.   Bradford, Yorkshire, Rivelin Press, 1981.
New York Insomnia and Other Poems.   Bradford, Yorkshire, Rivelin Grapheme Press, 1984.

Other

In My Own Land, photographs by James Bridgen.   Douglas, Isle of Man, Times Press, 1965.
Son and Lover: The Young D.H. Lawrence.   London, Bodley Head, and New York, Stein and Day, 1975.

*

Manuscript Collection: University of Texas Library, Austin.

Critical Study: by Callow in *Vogue* (New York), 1 September 1969.

Philip Callow comments:

All my writing up to now has been autobiographical in style and content. My aim has simply been to tell the story of my life as truthfully as possible. In fact, this is impossible, and in the attempt to do so one discovers that another, spiritual, autobiography is taking shape. I now realise that by devising a narrative about total strangers based on events reported in a newspaper I reveal myself as nakedly as in a personal confession. Perhaps more so.

*   *   *

In all his work Philip Callow is telling the same story—his life-story. His "autobiography" *In My Own Land* confirms a close approximation between himself and the "I" of the novels and the short stories in *Native Ground*. In his earlier novels he was seeking an idiom, which he found triumphantly in the freewheeling colloquialism of the trilogy *Going to the Moon*, *The Bliss Body*, and *Flesh of Morning*.

Callow's material is his working-class adolescence in the Midlands, the experience of factory and clerical work there and in the West country, his artistic leanings and adult relationships. Louis Paul, Nicky Chapman, and Alan Lowry, the narrators respectively of *The Hosanna Man*, *Common People*, and *Clipped Wings*, and Martin Satchwell, the central character of *A Pledge for the Earth*, are prototypes for the Colin Patten of the trilogy, and its sequel *The Story of My Desire*, when Patten has qualified as a teacher. Parallels exist in the earlier books for the trilogy's other important characters, while in subsequent work the lecturer David Lowry, the central figure in *Janine*, and the poet and writer-in-residence Jacob Raby, the narrator of *The Subway to New York*, recall Patten.

Callow gives a full account of adolescence, describing the development of sexuality—more freely in the later books—as the boy grows up at the end of the war when "there was a ration even on questions." Then he has to adjust to life on the factory floor. Patten's painting and writing lead him into provincial artistic circles, amateur of bohemian and anarchic—the "city nomads." Callow's outstanding portrayal is Jack Kelvin, "the hosanna man" himself, a drop-out like Albert Dyer in *Clipped Wings*, who "sits up on a cliff like a dirty old monk"; in *Common People* there is the drunken Sunday painter, Cecil Luce, leader of the "Birmingham Twelve." With the public

poetry-readings by the "Callow-figure" Jacob Raby, in *The Subway to New York*, the wheel has come full circle.

A Pledge for the Earth was the earlier of Callow's two third-person novels. The most overtly structured of his novels, it describes two generations of Satchwells, in a framework of natural imagery, and culminates in 20-odd pages in the first person written by Martin Satchwell. In *Clipped Wings* Callow returned to first-person narration: "I decided that the only way is to plant yourself down in the very centre of things, and then set out. In the same railway carriage, with all the others." With its new, forceful, colloquial idiom, *Clipped Wings* is the key book in Callow's stylistic development, and made possible the trilogy. At the same time, he'd begun to publish a good deal of poetry, which perhaps cross-fertilized his prose.

In the trilogy Callow ranged over his experiences freely with only a rough chronological surge onward: "Going back is pure instinct with me." The rationale of his method is in a sense anti-art: "Who believes in a book cut away from its writer with surgical scissors? I don't, I never did. I don't believe in fact and fiction, I don't believe in autobiography, poetry, philosophy, I don't believe in chapters, in a story." Callow's refusal to categorize is also embodied in his non-fiction *In My Own Land*, differentiated from his novels only by the use of real names.

Yours is an extended letter written by a young girl to her ex-lover, recalling that first unhappy love-affair. In *The Story of My Desire* Callow continued the trilogy, with Colin's affair with the married Lucy, both cause and effect of the breakdown of his own marriage, in turn inextricably linked in a nexus of guilt with his mental breakdown. *Janine* describes the middle-aged David Lowry's relationship with the mixed-up young girl of the title. It's written in the third person, and from the opening sentence, "His name was Lowry," the man is referred to throughout by surname. Until a key moment late in the novel, Janine never calls David by name, so that the third-person narration has an active structural role.

The structural rationale in *The Subway to New York* is circular: "always with a woman you go in circles." Thus Marjorie of *The Story of My Desire*, already resurrected as Kate in *Janine*, reappears as Carmel in *The Subway to New York*, and Lucy of *The Story of My Desire* is Nell in *Subway*. Sexuality runs all through Philip Callow's work, rooted in an understanding of life that he derives from D.H. Lawrence, but some readers may feel an insensitivity, especially in his two most recent novels.

—Val Warner

CAREY, Peter. Australian. Born in Bacchus Marsh, Victoria, in 1943. Educated at Geelong Grammar School; Monash University, Clayton, Victoria, 1 year. Married Alison Summers in 1985 (second marriage). Worked in advertising in Australia, 1962–68, and after 1970; lived in London, 1968–70. Currently, partner, McSpedden Carey Advertising Consultants, Chippendale, New South Wales. Recipient: New South Wales Premier's Award, 1980, 1982; Miles Franklin Award, 1981; National Book Council award, 1982; Australian Film Institute award, for screenplay, 1985; *The Age* Book of the Year Award, 1985. Lives in Sydney. Address: c/o University of Queensland Press, P.O. Box 42, St. Lucia, Queensland 4067, Australia.

PUBLICATIONS

Novels

Bliss. St. Lucia, University of Queensland Press, London, Faber, and New York, Harper, 1981.
Illywhacker.   London, Faber, and New York, Harper, 1985.

Short Stories

The Fat Man in History.   St. Lucia, University of Queensland Press, 1974; London, Faber, and New York, Random House, 1980; as *Exotic Pleasures*, London, Pan, 1981.
War Crimes.   St. Lucia, University of Queensland Press, 1979.

Play

Bliss: The Film.   London, Faber, 1985.

*   *   *

Peter Carey's short story collections, *The Fat Man in History* and *War Crimes*, established his reputation as one of Australia's most skilled and most innovative writers of short fiction. His stories break away from the Australian tradition of realism, experimenting with modes as diverse as absurdism, surrealism, science fiction, and the fable. "Report on the Shadow Industry" documents the terrors and addictions arising from a craze for buying packaged shadows; in "American Dreams" a man builds a mysterious replica of the town in which he lives, even sculpting the citizens' secrets and vices; and in "Peeling" a girl's clothing is unzipped and peeled away, followed by her flesh and her identity. . . . (Reviewers frequently compare Carey's work with that of Barthelme, Borges, García Márquez, and Vonnegut.)

Stylistically, Carey's stories are distinguished by the way in which his fantasy worlds are rendered with the specific, particularised detail that is typical of traditional realism (from "Peeling"):

She moves around the house on slow feet, her footsteps padding softly above me as I lie, on my unmade bed of unwashed sheets, listening. . . . The traffic crawls outside. There is a red bus, I can see the top of it, outside the window.

Thematically, the stories are concerned with contemporary social reality: the insignificance and helplessness of the average citizen, and the rapacious cynicism of those with power or influence. "A Windmill in the West" deals with a lonely soldier guarding a line drawn across the uninhabited wasteland of Central Australia; he has long ago forgotten the rationale for his task, but he has neither the courage nor the authority to protest at the futility of his plight. Twentieth-century *angst* is outlined in "Conversations with Unicorns" as a man tries to warn a cave of unicorns that they will soon be discovered and destroyed by the march of human progress. Believing themselves to be immortal, the unicorns refuse to listen, and the man who seeks to save them must kill one of their number in order to make his point. Such are Carey's metaphors for the plight of western man.

Because Carey's stories are lean and laconic, and employ fantastic or non-specific settings, they have left room for the criticism that the author is a pessimist who is unable to deal with day-to-day realities in a "real" setting. However, Carey's novels refute this criticism by dealing with characters living "normal" lives in familiar Australian settings.

Bliss is the sad-but-funny story of a middle-aged advertising executive, Harry Joy, who experiences clinical death after a heart attack and revives with a radically different perception of reality. Death leads him to a recognition of "the worlds of pleasure and pain, bliss and punishment, Heaven and Hell." His second chance at life forces him into the task of trying to cope with a world that now seems like Hell; a world in which his son pushes drugs and commits incest while his wife is addicted to adultery, a world in which affluent citizens choose tawdry "progress" and cancer-inducing food-additives above conservation and self-discipline.

Despite this description, *Bliss* is far from being a pessimistic novel. It is infused throughout with witty black humour, such as in Harry Joy's account of the caste system of "Hell," which ranges from Those in Charge (who inflict the torment) to the Actors (who robotically obey the orders they are given) to the Captives (who, like himself, can do nothing but suffer). Secondly, the characterisation of Honey Barbara establishes that man *can* at least try to manipulate his own destiny. (An honest but streetwise country girl, Honey Barbara divides her life between a primitive backwoods rainforest community and the hellish city in which she earns money from prostitution and drug-dealing.) Most importantly, the final section of the novel offers a vision of bliss on Earth as Harry Joy escapes from the lunatic-asylum to which his family has had him committed and joins Honey Barbara in her rainforest heaven.

Illywhacker (the word is slang for trickster, spieler, con-man) is the story of Herbert Badgery and three generations of his family, but the novel is also an examination of the lies and myths which underlie Australian history and culture. This is indicated by an epigraph from Mark Twain: "Australian history is almost always picturesque. . . . It does not read like history, but like the most beautiful lies. . . . It is full of surprises and adventures, the incongruities, and contradictions, and incredibilities; but they are all true, they all happened."

The central lie of Australian history is revealed to be the assertion that Australia had no original owners. But in two centuries of history this lie is shown to have spawned other lies, especially the belief that Australia is a free and independent land. The history of the Badgery family is a history of overseas domination continuing from one generation to another: Henry Badgery's 1920's dream of establishing an Australian aircraft industry is defeated by the importation of aircraft from overseas, his son's pet-shop only becomes successful because World War II brings American money into Australia, and the Badgery grandson can only continue the pet-shop business in the 1980's thanks to money invested by the Japanese. Yet Henry Badgery continues to believe (aggressively, pathetically) that with a few smooth lies, a bit of luck, and a confident swagger, he can be master of his own fate.

Though probably too long and fragmented, *Illywhacker* is an important work of Australian fiction. It celebrates the indomitable spirit of pioneers like Badgery, yet it also exposes the flaws in the nation and culture they helped to create.

—Van Ikin

CARR, J(ames Joseph) L(loyd).   British.   Born in Carlton Miniott, Yorkshire, 20 May 1916. Educated at village schools in North Riding, Yorkshire, and Castleford Secondary School, Yorkshire. Served as an Intelligence Officer in the Royal Air Force, 1940–46: Flight Lieutenant. Married Sally Sexton in 1945; one son. Schoolteacher, South Milford, Yorkshire,

1930–34; games master, Hedge End Senior School, Hampshire, 1933–35; teacher, school for sub-normal children, Birmingham, 1935–38; high school teacher, Huron, South Dakota, 1938–39; teacher in junior schools, Birmingham, 1946–51; head, Highfields Primary School, Kettering, Northamptonshire, 1951–67. Since 1967, publisher. Recipient: *Guardian* Fiction Prize, 1980. M.A.: Leicester University, 1981. Address: 27 Milldale Road, Kettering, Northamptonshire NN15 6QD, England.

PUBLICATIONS

Novels

A Day in Summer.   London, Barrie and Rockliff, 1963.
A Season in Sinji.   London, Ross, 1968.
The Harpole Report.   London, Secker and Warburg, 1972.
How Steeple Sinderby Wanderers Won the F.A. Cup.   London, London Magazine Editions, 1975.
A Month in the Country.   Brighton, Harvester Press, 1980; New York, St. Martin's Press, 1982.
The Battle of Pollocks Crossing.   London, Viking, 1985.

Other (for children)

The Red Windcheater.   London, Macmillan, 1970.
The Dustman.   London, Macmillan, 1972.
The Garage Mechanic.   London, Macmillan, 1972.
Red Foal's Coat.   London, Macmillan, 1974.
The Old Farm Cart.   London, Macmillan, 1974.
The Green Children of the Woods.   London, Longman, 1976.

Other

The Old Timers.   Privately printed, 1957.
Historical and Architectural Maps (*Hampshire, Suffolk, Wales, Sussex, Kent, Yorkshire, Wiltshire, Norfolk, Oxfordshire, Devon, Lincolnshire, Northamptonshire, Warwickshire, Lancashire, Gloucestershire, Somerset, Huntingdonshire, Essex, Northumberland, Leicestershire, Rutland, England and Wales, Herefordshire, Worcestershire, Berkshire, Cambridgeshire, Dorset, Durham, Shropshire, Cheshire, Bedfordshire, Buckinghamshire, Cornwall, Derbyshire, Hertfordshire, Middlesex, Nottinghamshire, Staffordshire, Surrey, Westmorland, Cumberland*).   Kettering, Northamptonshire, Carr, 41 vols., 1968–77.
Dictionary of Extra-ordinary English Cricketers.   Kettering, Northamptonshire, Carr, 1977.
Dictionary of English Queens, King's Wives, Celebrated Paramours, Handfast Spouses and Royal Changelings.   Kettering, Northamptonshire, Carr, 1977.
Final Catalogue of Paintings Done Between 1960–1978 and Usually Known as A Northamptonshire Record.   Kettering, Northamptonshire, Carr, 1978 (?).
Dictionary of English Kings.   Kettering, Northamptonshire, Carr, 1979.
Gidner's Brief Lives of the Frontier.   Kettering, Northamptonshire, Carr, 1985.

Editor, *A Selection from the Poems of Robert Bloomfield*.   Kettering, Northants Campaigner, 1966.
Editor, *Florin Poets* and *Mini-Poets* series (*William Blake, John Clare, Robert Herrick, Andrew Marvell, Dante Gabriel Rossetti, Matthew Arnold, John Donne, James Elroy Flecker, John Milton, Robert Louis Stevenson, Edward Thomas, William Wordsworth, William Cowper*).   Kettering, Northamptonshire, Carr, 13 vols., 1968–76.

Editor, *Lincolnshire Landscape*, by Tennyson.   Kettering, Northamptonshire, Carr, 1968.
Editor, *Twelve Poems*, by William Barnes.   Kettering, Northamptonshire, Carr, 1974.
Editor, *Portrait Miniatures*, by John Aubrey.   Kettering, Northamptonshire, Carr, 1976.
Editor, *Brief Lives*, by John Aubrey.   Kettering, Northamptonshire, Carr, 1976.
Editor, *Satirical Portraits*, by Dryden.   Kettering, Northamptonshire, Carr, 1976.
Editor, *Rubaiyat*, by Omar Khayyam.   Kettering, Northamptonshire, Carr, 1976.
Editor, *Hiawatha*, by Longfellow.   Kettering, Northamptonshire, Carr, 1977.

Other pamphlets and collections published.

*

Manuscript Collection: Pierpont Morgan Library, New York.

Critical Study: article by David Taylor, in *London Magazine*, November 1984.

J.L. Carr comments:

I have been novel-writing in spare time for about 23 years. Some of this time I supported my family by teaching and, later, by publishing a series of English county picture maps (which I drew) and about 80 very small (16-page) books, all of which I edited. All this was and still is done in the back bedroom. Last year I made £9000 by writing: this came from TV down payments and from paperback royalties. I think I could just about live on book-writing from now on.

I can't truthfully say that making money was at the back of my mind when writing the six novels because, right from the start, I believed this impossible. (Until *A Month in the Country*, although the novels had uniformly encouraging reviews, they were all in periodicals with small circulations; *The Battle of Pollocks Crossing* was the first to be reviewed in a Sunday newspaper.) So I entertained myself by trying to write each story in a different way. *A Day in Summer* is contrapuntal; *A Season in Sinji* has the chief character telling the story; *The Harpole Report* is a series of letters and extracts from a journal. And so on. Because I wasn't pressed for time, each of the books was rewritten, revised, edited, rewritten, revised, edited, etc. I took a lot of trouble over them: scissors and gum were my constant companions. I'm glad I wrote them.

*   *   *

Though his novels are written in various familiar forms, tell of facts not fantasy, and run properly clockwise in the matter of time, it is fair to call J.L. Carr a real original. Something of this comes from the content, its unusual kinds of expertise, its hidden idiosyncrasies, and the cunning way they are used. There's the angle too. Like *Wuthering Heights*, *Villette*, *The Woman in White*, *Great Expectations*, *The Go-Between*, *Rebecca*—add your own list—a novel by Carr is almost always a first-person narrative. This gives a particular slant, especially when that voice belongs to a loner, not as lead but observer or catalyst.

Since his best and also most characteristic book is *A Month in the Country*, it is worth outlining here. The year is 1920. The narrator, Tom Birkin, a shell-shocked survivor of the First World War, still in his mid-twenties, arrives at a remote north-country village on his first professional assignment. The late

Miss Laura Hebron, at the dwindling end of an ancient local family, has left a sum to the church when two conditions have been met. One is that a suspected mediaeval wall-painting hidden under wash in the church for centuries (why?) is to be uncovered. The other is that a family legend concerning an ancestor, Piers Hebron (d. 1373), is to be investigated. If he was buried, as seems the case, outside the hallowed stonework of the church (again, the question *why?*) are the bones still to be found?

The wall-job goes to Birkin. The pay is wretched but the interest great. (It grips the reader, too.) Through the long wonderful summer, July, August, the start of September, while he works at the huge astonishing mural, he becomes a part of the village, umpiring the week-end cricket (an essential Carr note, this), standing in for a lay preacher, parrying too the hostility of his reluctant employer, the embittered Rector in his huge and starveling Rectory, a bleak theologian marooned among peasants. And there is an element of love that the first cold wind might extinguish. September draws to a close.

If Birkin takes his time, so does the cheerful young archaeologist in charge of the other search. He has seen the answer straight away (he privately admits), but finds the whole rough field so fascinating that he delays the *coup*. For this, the unburying, he calls in Birkin. A marvellous climax! For the *coup* concerns him also; the double questions are one. Reading this book, with its several layers of plot, each at a different layer of time, is very much like the uncovering of the scene on the church wall.

Best to turn from here to the earlier book *A Season in Sinji*, a novel of the wartime 1940's. Chance—and the R.A.F.—bring three young men together: two allies and a third; their battle, which is dire, is fought out on the fields of love, of cricket, of military hierarchy. The narrator, Tom Flanders, comes of a line of farmers; except in the matter of cricket he is neither adventurous nor ambitious: he will later learn rather more about himself. Wakely, his companion in the slough (they are both very low level ground staff), is a mournful, scholarly type, as negative a warrior as Tom. Not so Turton, the third. Clever, elegant, assured, on the way to being commissioned, he easily snatches the girl they have treated over-politely. Drafted to West Africa, they find Turton more than ever their hornet and their bane. The final scene—a tremendous chapter—brings Tom and Turton into a rubber dinghy in the sea, sole survivors of a shot-down plane. Turton, woefully injured, has no defence counsel as Tom sets out the long term of his wrongs. But Carr has an unforeseen dark card still up his sleeve.

The satirical note, always evident in this book, is never overplayed. But it is a distinctive aspect of Carr's fiction, and is the mainstay of the earlier *The Harpole Report* and the most recent *The Battle of Pollocks Crossing*. The first, told through letters, memos, journal entries (the first-person angle again) is a preposterous comedy, often madly funny but with an awful ballast of truth, about teachers and teachership in a modern primary school—"the dust and battle in the front lines of English education." *The Battle of Pollocks Crossing*—different again, yet unmistakably Carr—is a grim black comedy, racing to tragedy, set in the American Midwest of 1929. George Gidner, a young Bradford schoolmaster wanting adventure, applies for a year's exchange, and with hazy thoughts of cowboys and Indians takes the place that the organisers have never been able to shift, in Pallisades, North Dakota. The train unloads him at last at a town in *nowhere*, "a prospect of false-fronted buildings, peeling paint, a mad muddle of power lines, a blank and brutal sky." Disaster looms from the start but is precipitated when George, teaching the obligatory Hiawatha ("an O.K. coloured American") offers the class the Indian view of Wounded Knee. This is Carr-comedy at its best. But thereafter, a mad muddle of power lines.

Still, it is *A Month in the Country* that will keep Carr's name alive. Already set in a series of yesterdays that seem like a living Now, it cannot date. The single egregious book, with a life of its own, is not peculiar to England. But the elements and attitudes—even the private clues and jokes—in all Carr's work are entirely English: his books could be usefully read for these alone. The metaphorical game of life is not visualised in terms of cards, or swordplay, or the gaming table. No indeed, it is cricket, always and absolutely.

If Carr has a weakness worth note it is his portrayal of desired and desirable young women; the more lush they are, the less they come to life. By contrast, the busy no-nonsense 12-year-old Methodist girl Kathy Ellerbeck, in *A Month in the Country*, is someone to be remembered. Those aspiring young novelists who write to authors in hope of a secret formula would do well to study this book, which contains so much so cunningly put together in its short space. They might learn that there are more sources of drama than one, even in human relationships, that craftsmanship is not to be undervalued, and—no less than these—that an expert knowledge of any kind is also an invaluable part of experience, and of writing.

—Naomi Lewis

CARTER, Angela (Olive, née Stalker). British. Born in Eastbourne, Sussex, 7 May 1940. Educated at the University of Bristol, 1962–65, B.A. in English 1965. Married Paul Carter in 1960 (divorced, 1972). Journalist, Croydon, Surrey, 1958–61. Arts Council Fellow in Creative Writing, University of Sheffield, 1976–78; Visiting Professor of Creative Writing, Brown University, Providence, Rhode Island, 1980–81; Writer-in-Residence, University of Adelaide, Australia, 1984. Recipient: Rhys Memorial Prize, 1968; Maugham Award, 1969; Cheltenham Festival Prize, 1979; Kurt Maschler Award, for children's book, 1982; James Tait Black Memorial Prize, 1985. Agent: Deborah Rogers Ltd., 49 Blenheim Crescent, London W11 2EF, England.

PUBLICATIONS

Novels

Shadow Dance. London, Heinemann, 1966; as *Honeybuzzard*, New York, Simon and Schuster, 1967.
The Magic Toyshop. London, Heinemann, 1967; New York, Simon and Schuster, 1968.
Several Perceptions. London, Heinemann, 1968; New York, Simon and Schuster, 1969.
Heroes and Villains. London, Heinemann, 1969; New York, Simon and Schuster, 1970.
Love. London, Hart Davis, 1971.
The Infernal Desire Machines of Dr. Hoffman. London, Hart Davis, 1972; as *The War of Dreams*, New York, Harcourt Brace, 1974.
The Passion of New Eve. London, Gollancz, and New York, Harcourt Brace, 1977.
Nights at the Circus. London, Chatto and Windus, 1984; New York, Viking, 1985.

Short Stories

Fireworks: Nine Profane Pieces. London, Quartet, 1974; New York, Harper, 1981.

The Bloody Chamber and Other Stories. London, Gollancz, 1979; New York, Harper, 1980.
Black Venus's Tale. London, Faber-Next, 1980.
Black Venus. London, Chatto and Windus, 1985.

Plays

Come unto These Yellow Sands (radio plays). Newcastle-upon-Tyne, Bloodaxe, 1984.

Screenplay: *The Company of Wolves*, with Neil Jordan, 1984.

Radio Plays: *Vampirella*, 1976; *Come unto These Yellow Sands*, 1979; *The Company of Wolves*, from her own story, 1980; *Puss in Boots*, 1982; *A Self-Made Man* (on Ronald Firbank), 1984.

Verse

Unicorn. Leeds, Location Press, 1966.

Other

Miss Z, The Dark Young Lady (for children). London, Heinemann, and New York, Simon and Schuster, 1970.
The Donkey Prince (for children). New York, Simon and Schuster, 1970.
Comic and Curious Cats, illustrated by Martin Leman. London, Gollancz, and New York, Crown, 1979.
The Sadeian Woman: An Exercise in Cultural History. London, Virago Press, 1979; as *The Sadeian Woman and the Ideology of Pornography*, New York, Pantheon, 1979.
Nothing Sacred: Selected Writings. London, Virago Press, 1982.
Moonshadow (for children). London, Gollancz, 1982.
Sleeping Beauty and Other Favourite Fairy Tales. London, Gollancz, 1982; New York, Schocken, 1984.

Translator, *The Fairy Tales of Charles Perrault.* London, Gollancz, 1977; New York, Avon, 1978.

*   *   *

Angela Carter's work reveals a notable energy, a flair for the comic, and an unusual diversity of imagination. Her style, with its emphasis on visual detail and imagery, is often poetic in effect. Vividly rendered sense impressions and purposefully distorted patterns of space and time account, in large part, for the strong effects produced in her tales (*Fireworks* and *The Bloody Chamber*) and in those novels laid in the future (*Heroes and Villains, The Infernal Desire Machines of Dr. Hoffman*, and *The Passion of New Eve*). She reveals her fascination with violence in scenes of mutilation, murder, rape, castration, cannibalism, incest, and flagellation, but at times she can also evoke the subtlest of psychological nuances.

Certain elements recur in her work: a claustrophobic enclosure of action in a small area; a charisma exerted by a demonic figure; a perverse need felt by an individual to cling tenaciously to another who both attracts and repels; and a discordant intermingling of horror and comedy.

Her books show her preoccupation with the frankly erotic, with the sadistic linking of sex with pain, and with the struggles for mastery between the powerful individual and the vulnerable. In *The Sadeian Woman* she finds in the Marquis de Sade's depiction of the tyrannical Juliette an anticipation of a "new pornography" in which women may be portrayed as dominant in a sexual relationship. On the other hand, she identifies his victimized Justine as the prototype of Marilyn Monroe, the Good-Bad Girl—innocent, very young, and comically surprised at her own sexual force. By implication, Carter's comments on de Sade interpret her own fiction, in which most of the female protagonists are Good-Bad Girls and in which the Amazons of *The Passion of New Eve* are Juliettes.

Shadow Dance has as its milieu a British slum where streets smell of urine, vomit, and stale beer. Here the beautiful and satanic Honeybuzzard and his woman, Ghislaine, have tyrannized over each other and over their associates, who regard them with admiration, dread, and resentment. The childlike Ghislaine with her "long yellow milkmaid hair . . . like moonlight on daisies" has moved from man to man like an exotic moth, but at the beginning of this novel the flamboyant Honeybuzzard, with a long slash of his knife, has, on impulse, mutilated her face. In pubs, junk shops, and abandoned building, all of the other characters—each one a comic grotesque marked by a single dominant characteristic—await her return, because they know she will return for vengeance.

In *The Magic Toyshop*, the most intense and claustrophobic of the novels, three orphaned children are sent to live with their cruel uncle above his dark London toyshop. Melanie, 15, through whose eyes the action is seen, is introduced in a superb comic prologue (laid in the country just before the parents' death) in which as an innocent she discovers the full range of her sexuality. In contrast, when she is virtually imprisoned for a year in the London shop, where even mirrors are forbidden and where her aunt was struck dumb on her wedding night, Melanie gradually loses her self-identity. Suspicion, guilt, cruelty, incestuous intrigue, and imminent rape become her realities. She finally escapes her prison by running through the flames which destroy the shop. She triumphs over malevolence, but that malevolence almost corrupts her in the process.

Love and *Several Perceptions*, two lesser novels, satirize aimlessness in British youth, the latter focusing on artists and students in a bohemian conclave.

Three other novels are set in the future. In *Heroes and Villains* she portrays Marianne, a 16-year-old runaway from the Land of the Professors, who finds herself—a century after the atomic holocaust—living in a bombed-out building and married to Jewel, a barbarian marauder who years before killed her brother and who more recently has raped her. The decor emphasizes the macabre and the horrible, and the desolation of the Land of the Barbarians is reflected in the barrenness of the human relationships between Jewel and a magician (his master) and between Jewel and Marianne. Horrible indeed are the dying infants, the pots of excrement, the lice women comb from the hair of their lovers, the cats grown monstrous, the graves to be dug at midnight, the roofs and walls half gone, the smokey fireplaces, and the floors oozing with filth.

As in *The Magic Toyshop* and *Heroes and Villains*, Carter thoroughly convinces the reader of the reality of her grotesque and macabre fable in *The Infernal Desire Machines of Dr. Hoffman*. The protagonist, Desiderio, journeys in search of Hoffman's secret for continuous generation of energy, a secret which will enable him to replace reality with ephemeral illusion. Hoffman's power, for example, allows him to create a cathedral in one instant and destroy it in the next; to transform an audience at the opera to a flock of peacocks; and to make pigeons atop a chimney quote Hegel. After many bizarre adventures, Desiderio discovers the secret in a huge laboratory where Hoffman has assembled wire cages from floor to ceiling in each of which a pair of lovers endlessly copulate. Sardonic and grotesque humor underlines the dehumanization of intimate relationships wherever these are exploited, as in this novel, for ulterior motives.

In *The Passion of New Eve* an arrogant man, stranded in the Arizona desert, encounters sophisticated Amazons who with their advanced technology change him into a woman in order that he may experience rape and unwanted pregnancy and understand the implications of his casual exploitation of women. The book closes with a bizarre orgy and massacre at the Hollywood mansion of an elderly film actress.

Nights at the Circus, set at the end of the 19th century, marks a shift from the futuristic settings of Carter's recent work. It recounts the picaresque adventures of the ebullient young Fevvers. She is a trapeze artist, billed as the Cockney venus, who has bright large wings and who claims to be able to fly. She both fascinates and repels Jack Walser, an American reporter who interviews her for his book, *Great Humbugs of the World*, and she almost convinces this cynic that she was "hatched" and left (with pieces of egg shell in her blanket) on the doorstep of a brothel. The prostitutes became her surrogate mothers, and when she sprouted her wings at puberty, they taught her to dye her feathers brilliantly, to attract business by standing on the stairway posing as Cupid, and to fly (by being pushed off the roof by one of her mothers). Impulsively, Walser joins the circus as it leaves London to tour Russia, Japan, and Seattle. In the euphoric ending, they marry just as he appears to have learned to understand women and as she acknowledges to him her amazement that he has almost believed her deceptions. Her laughter rings with delight through the cold midnight air, it seeps into cracks of neighboring houses, it makes babies smile in their sleep, and it rises like smoke in the air.

As in her other novels, Carter in *Nights at the Circus* blends the real and the surreal, makes unbelievable Dickensian eccentrics credible for the moment, and creates scenes of comic violence in fires and explosions and scenes of gothic horror and grotesque sexual encounter. What is new in this novel is the joy, the sympathetic development of a male, and the use of Fevvers as a symbol of the "New Woman" who may emerge in the approaching 20th century ("a New Age in which no woman will be bound to the ground").

—Margaret B. McDowell

* * *

CARVER, Raymond. *d 198* American. Born in Clatskanie, Oregon, 25 May 1938. Educated at Chico State College, California (Founding Editor, *Selection*), 1958–59; Humboldt State University, Arcata, California, 1960–63, A.B. 1963; University of Iowa, 1963–64, M.F.A. 1966. Married 1) Maryann Burk in 1957 (divorced, 1982), one daughter and one son; 2) the writer Tess Gallagher in 1982. Worked in various jobs, including janitor, saw mill worker, delivery man, and salesman, 1957–67; textbook editor, Science Research Associates, Palo Alto, California, 1967–70; Visiting Lecturer, University of California, Santa Cruz, 1970–71, and Santa Barbara, 1975; Visiting Professor of English, University of California, Berkeley 1971–72; Visiting Writer, University of Iowa, 1972–73, Goddard College, Vermont, 1977–78, and University of Texas, El Paso, 1978–79; Professor of English, Syracuse University, New York, 1980–84. Editor, *Quarry*, Santa Cruz, 1971. Recipient: National Endowment for the Arts fellowship, for poetry, 1971, for fiction, 1979; Stanford University Stegner Fellowship, 1973; Guggenheim fellowship, 1978; O. Henry Award, for short story, 1983; Strauss Living award, 1983. Agent: Amanda Urban, International Creative Management, 40 West 57th Street, New York, New York 10019. Address: 602 South B Street, Port Angeles, Washington 98362, U.S.A.

PUBLICATIONS

Short Stories

Put Yourself in My Shoes. Santa Barbara, California, Capra Press, 1974.
Will You Please Be Quiet, Please? New York, McGraw Hill, 1976.
Furious Seasons and Other Stories. Santa Barbara, California, Capra Press, 1977.
What We Talk about When We Talk about Love. New York, Knopf, 1981; London, Collins, 1982.
The Pheasant. Worcester, Massachusetts, Metacom Press, 1982.
Cathedral. New York, Knopf, 1983; London, Collins, 1984.
If It Please You. Northridge, California, Lord John Press, 1984.
The Stories of Raymond Carver. London, Pan, 1985.

Uncollected Short Stories

"The Aficionados" (as John Vale), "The Hair," and "Poseidon and Company," all in *Toyon* (Arcata, California), Spring 1963.
"Bright Red Apples," in *Gato* (Los Gatos, California), Spring-Summer 1967.

Plays

Carnations (produced Arcata, California, 1962).
Dostoevsky: A Screenplay, with Tess Gallagher; published with *Kind Dog* by Ursula K. LeGuin. Santa Barbara, California, Capra Press, 1985.

Verse

Near Klamath. Sacramento, California, Sacramento State College English Club, 1968.
Winter Insomnia. Santa Cruz, California, Kayak, 1970.
At Night the Salmon Move. Santa Barbara, California, Capra Press, 1976.
Two Poems. Salisbury, Maryland, Scarab Press, 1982.
Where Water Comes Together with Other Water. New York, Random House, 1985.
This Water. Concord, New Hampshire, Ewert, 1985.
Ultramarine. New York, Random House, 1986.

Other

Fires: Essays, Poems, Stories. Santa Barbara, California, Capra Press, 1983; London, Collins, 1985.

*

Critical Studies: "Voyeurism, Dissociation, and the Art of Raymond Carver" by David Boxer, in *Iowa Review* (Iowa City), Summer 1979; "Raymond Carver: A Chronicler of Blue-Collar Despair" by Bruce Weber, in *New York Times Magazine*, 24 June 1984; "Beyond Hopelessville: Another Side of Raymond Carver," in *Philological Quarterly* (Iowa City), Winter 1985, and article in *Dictionary of Literary Biography Yearbook 1984* edited by Jean W. Ross, Detroit, Gale, 1985, both by William

L. Stull; *European Views of Contemporary American Literature* edited by Marc Chénetier, Carbondale, Southern Illinois University Press, 1985.

*   *   *

In the ten or so years since the publication of his first collection of short stories, Raymond Carver has been called one of the most distinguished writers of the short story form. Frank Kermode called him "a full-grown master," Robert Towers, "one of the true contemporary masters." Stanley Elkin says that Carver's "rumpled men and ragged women will break your heart." The recipient and nominee of America's most prestigious awards and fellowships, Carver has worked in a number of forms but has been most widely acknowledged for his fiction, to which he has brought his gift for dramatic dialogue, poetic intensity, and linguistic purity. He has developed a unique and recognizable idiom.

Against the backdrop of the Pacific Northwest, Carver focuses on a society of the lower and middle class. These are hardworking, plain people—salesmen, high school teachers, factory workers—or they are people in a state of transition—husbands and wives in the process of separating, men and women between jobs, insomniacs in that state between sleep and wakefulness. All share a vaguely felt but unarticulated sense that life might be better. An emptiness and waste touches upon them, although they are not consciously aware of it. The drama of Carver's stories involves the moment that their vague sense of failure creeps into preconsciousness, the moment when their marginally happy lives are interrupted by an unfamiliar sense of desire, loneliness, fear, frustration, or violence.

What is unique to Carver's work is the manner in which his flat, meticulously unadorned though highly evocative style reflects his characters' subliminal revelations and the way in which these stories end just before epiphany—both the reader's and the characters'. Through this "implosive" technique—with understanding postponed beyond the story—both character and reader identify in a unique manner, as both participate in the existential act of creating private meaning within the void.

Many of the stories deal with the "dis-ease" (to use Camus's word) of marriage. Couples typically lie beside one another and make efforts to touch. They feign sleep and then remain awake, wondering what it's all about. In *Will You Please Be Quiet, Please?* the title story portrays a young man's inability to deal with his wife's sensuality. "What's in Alaska?" reports the uncommunicative language spoken by two couples who share some marijuana in an effort to be close. The widely anthologized "Neighbors" begins "Bill and Arlene Miller were a happy couple," but it is only when they take care of their vacationing neighbor's apartment—feeding the cat, watering the plants, trying on their clothes, eating their food, using their bathroom, and even lying in their bed—that they can express deep sexual passion for each other. The climax involves their leaving the key within the apartment, and their subsequent loss of identity as they remain wordless and helpless to respond to this entire event: "They held each other, leaned into the door as if against a void, and braced themselves."

Furious Seasons brings back familiar Carver subjects: marriages that don't work, the way people drink to escape, and the undercurrents of repressed violence and sexuality that intrude upon the ordinary life. Here once again are people with a deep compulsion to be free and yet that accompanying paralysis that prohibits action. "So Much Water So Close to Home" tells of a woman's repulsion at her husband's treatment of a young rape victim, a projection of herself.

Carver employs the minimalist techniques of condensation, precision, and objectivity in *What We Talk about When We Talk about Love*, where 17 of the 22 stories once again deal with hopeless marriage. The stories reveal Carver's ever-increasing concern with language, with the difficulty, if not the impossibility, of talking about what really matters, the emotional life. In the title story, two couples drink and talk of many sorts of love—spiritual, murderous, suicidal, carnal, and sentimental—but thoughts of death and time intrude, and, at the end, it is clear that no one can really say what love is: "I could hear my heart beating. I could hear everyone's heart. I could hear the human noise we sat there making, not one of us moving, not even when the room went dark." In "Why Don't You Dance?" a young couple sees what must be a yard sale. In fact, an old man, separated from his wife and drunk in an effort to escape his pain, has put his life—in the form of all his furnishings—out in the yard. The young girl bears witness to the man's despair but lacks the words of understanding. "Must be desperate or something," she says to him; at the end, although "she kept talking" and "told everyone . . ., there was more to it, and she kept trying to get it talked out. After a time, she quit trying." In "A Serious Talk," Carver reports the argument of a separated couple who, for just one moment, rekindle a deep affection as they handle "our ashtray," with which they shared many of their better moments.

The title story of *Cathedral* tells of a blind man's visit to a reluctant host who, when asked what a cathedral is, takes the blind man's hand on top of his and draws one. Once more, the failure of words is clear, but in this case, the host experiences a wordless affirmation. "So we kept on with it. His fingers rode my fingers. . . . It was like nothing else in my life up to now." There is a sense of religious connection here, as well as in one or two other stories of the volume, but most, like "Fever" and "Feathers," are portraits of emptiness and frustration. *Fires* consists of new versions of some earlier works and two new stories, as well as 50 poems arranged in four categories.

Throughout, in virtually all of Carver's work to date, is a remarkable use of precise image, an exact, photographic detailing of setting, a meticulous reportage of dialogue, and a uniquely disquieting turn of phrase. These help create the implosive technique mentioned above—a prose that has a lasting resonance upon the reader. Though plain and unadorned, Carver's terrain is the human soul, and as such, his landscapes insinuate themselves upon the reader's spirit to provoke an honesty about the self and the world reserved only for the most important of literatures. Carver, unlike the postmoderns who have occupied the literary avant-garde since the mid-1960's, acknowledges an obligation to separate the good from the bad, the admirable from the arrogant; he writes, to borrow his mentor John Gardner's term, "moral fiction." Carver says: "In the best novels and short stories, goodness is recognized as such. Loyalty, love, fortitude, courage, integrity may not always be rewarded, but they are recognized as good or noble actions or qualities; and evil or base or simply stupid behavior is seen and held up for what it is: evil, base, or stupid behavior. There are a few absolutes in this life, some verities, if you will, and we would do well not to forget them."

—Lois Gordon

CASSILL, R(onald) V(erlin). American. Born in Cedar Falls, Iowa, 17 May 1919. Educated at the University of Iowa, Iowa City, B.A. 1939 (Phi Beta Kappa), M.A. 1947; the Sorbonne, Paris (Fulbright Fellow), 1952–53. Served in the United States Army, 1942–46: Lieutenant. Married Karilyn Kay Adams in 1956; three children. Instructor, University of Iowa, 1948–52; editor, *Western Review*, Iowa City, 1951–52, *Collier's Encyclopedia*, New York, 1953–54, and *Dude* and *Gent*, New York, 1958; lecturer, Columbia University and New School for Social Research, both New York, 1957–59, and University of Iowa, 1960–65; Writer-in-Residence, Purdue University, West Lafayette, Indiana, 1965–66. Associate Professor, 1966–71, and Professor of English, 1972–83, Brown University, Providence, Rhode Island; now emeritus. U.S. Information Service Lecturer in Europe, 1975–76. Painter and lithographer: exhibitions—John Snowden Gallery, Chicago, 1946; Eleanor Smith Galleries, Chicago, 1948; Wickersham Gallery, New York, 1970. Recipient: *Atlantic* "Firsts" Prize, for short story, 1947; Rockefeller grant, 1954; Guggenheim grant, 1968. Agent: Candida Donadio and Associates, 231 West 22nd Street, New York, New York 10011. Address: 22 Boylston Avenue, Providence, Rhode Island 02906, U.S.A.

PUBLICATIONS

Novels

The Eagle on the Coin. New York, Random House, 1950.
Dormitory Women. New York, Lion, 1953.
The Left Bank of Desire, with Eric Protter. New York, Ace, 1955.
A Taste of Sin. New York, Ace, 1955; London, Digit, 1959.
The Hungering Shame. New York, Avon, 1956.
The Wound of Love. New York, Avon, 1956.
An Affair to Remember (novelization of screenplay; as Owen Aherne). New York, Avon, 1957.
Naked Morning. New York, Avon, 1957.
Man on Fire (novelization of screenplay; as Owen Aherne). New York, Avon, 1957.
The Buccaneer (novelization of screenplay). New York, Fawcett, 1958.
Lustful Summer. New York, Avon, 1958.
Nurses' Quarters. New York, Fawcett, 1958; London, Muller, 1962.
The Tempest (novelization of screenplay). New York, Fawcett, 1959.
The Wife Next Door. New York, Fawcett, 1959; London, Muller, 1960.
Clem Anderson. New York, Simon and Schuster, 1960.
My Sister's Keeper. New York, Avon, 1961.
Night School. New York, New American Library, 1961.
Pretty Leslie. New York, Simon and Schuster, 1963; London, Muller, 1964.
The President. New York, Simon and Schuster, 1964.
La Vie Passionée of Rodney Buckthorne: A Tale of the Great American's Last Rally and Curious Death. New York, Geis, 1968.
Doctor Cobb's Game. New York, Bantam, 1969.
The Goss Women. New York, Doubleday, 1974; London, Hodder and Stoughton, 1975.
Hoyt's Child. New York, Doubleday, 1976.
Labors of Love. New York, Arbor House, 1980.
Flame. New York, Arbor House, 1980.
After Goliath. New York, Ticknor and Fields, 1985.

Short Stories

15 x 3, with Herbert Gold and James B. Hall. New York, New Directions, 1957.
The Father and Other Stories. New York, Simon and Schuster, 1965.
The Happy Marriage and Other Stories. West Lafayette, Indiana, Purdue University Press, 1967.
Three Stories. Oakland, California, Hermes House Press, 1982.

Uncollected Short Stories

"To the Clear Mountains," in *American Prefaces* (Iowa City), June 1939.
"New Mexican Sun," in *American Prefaces* (Iowa City), 1940.
"Five Men and a Horse" (as Verlin Cassill), in *American Prefaces* (Iowa City), Autumn 1940.
"The Conditions of Justice," in *Atlantic* (Boston), December 1947.
"Convoy Sunday Morning," in *Perspective* (Louisville, Kentucky), Spring 1949.
"The Black Horse," in *Furioso* (New Haven, Connecticut), Summer 1951.
"The Waiting Room," in *Perspective* (Louisville, Kentucky), Autumn 1951.
"The Man Who Saw B-36s," in *Furioso* (New Haven, Connecticut), Spring 1952.
"The Kiss," in *New Story* (Paris), March 1952.
"The Puzzle Factory," in *Epoch* (Ithaca, New York), February 1954.
"The Hot Girl," in *New Directions 15*. New York, New Directions, 1955.
"Shadow of a Magnitude," in *University of Kansas City Review*, Winter 1956.
"A Question of Purity," in *Nugget* (New York), 1957.
"The Educational Process," in *Nugget* (New York), June 1957.
"Crisis of Love," in *Nugget* (New York), July 1957.
"The Squeaky Wheel," in *Epoch* (Ithaca, New York), Fall 1957.
"Hatcher's Devil," in *University of Kansas City Review*, October 1957.
"Fracture," in *The Beat Generation and The Angry Young Men*, edited by Gene Feldman and Max Gartenberg. New York, Citadel Press, 1958.
"The Pursuit of Happiness," in *Northwest Review* (Eugene, Oregon), 1958.
"The Play's the Thing," in *Dude* (New York), March 1958.
"Knight and the Hag," in *Dude* (New York), May 1958.
"May He Roast in Peace" (as Con Everling), in *Dude* (New York), July 1958.
"A Journey of the Magi," in *Texas Quarterly* (Austin), Summer-Autumn 1958.
"Ride for the Dark," in *What's New? 209*, Christmas 1958.
"The Chandelier," in *Dude* (New York), September 1959.
"The Greek Way," in *Gent* (New York), 1960.
"The Winchester Papers," in *Northwest Review* (Eugene, Oregon), Spring 1960.
"A Default," in *Southwest Review* (Dallas), Autumn 1960.
"Morning in Paris," in *Contact* (New York), May 1961.
"And in My Heart," in *Paris Review*, Winter-Spring 1965.
"My Brother Wilbur," in *Northwest Review* (Eugene, Oregon), Spring-Summer 1965.
"Date with a Winner," in *Dude* (New York), January 1966.
"This Lyf So Short," in *Bard* (Lafayette, Indiana), Spring 1966.
"In the Central Blue," in *Man and the Movies*, edited by W.R. Robinson and George Garrett. Baton Rouge, Louisiana State University Press, 1967.

"The Outer Island," in *Fiction as Process*, edited by Carl Hartman and Hazard Adams. New York, Dodd Mead, 1968.

"The Father," in *How We Live*, edited by Penney Chapin Hills and L. Rust Hills. New York, Macmillan, 1968.

"The Rationing of Love," in *New American Review 3*, edited by Theodore Solotaroff. New York, New American Library, 1968.

"The Gadfly," in *Jeopardy* (Bellingham, Washington), Spring 1969.

"The Invention of the Airplane," in *The Best Little Magazine Fiction*, edited by Curt Johnson. New York, New York University Press, 1971.

"Fragments for Reference," in *Accent: An Anthology 1940–1960*, edited by Daniel Curley and others. Urbana, University of Illinois Press, 1973.

"How I Live Through Times of Trouble," in *New and Experimental Literature*, edited by James P. White. Midland, Texas Center for Writers Press, 1975.

"Where Saturn Keeps the Years," in *Missouri Review* (Columbia), 1978.

"The Martyr," in *Ploughshares* (Cambridge, Massachusetts), vol. 5, no. 4, 1980.

"The Castration of Harry Bluethorn," in *Epoch* (Ithaca, New York), Spring-Summer 1980.

"The Suicide's Cat," in *December* (Chicago), vol. 23, nos. 1–2, 1981.

"Bring on the Poets," in *Massachusetts Review* (Amherst), Spring 1981.

Other

The General Said "Nuts." New York, Birk, 1955.
Writing Fiction. New York, Pocket Books, 1963; revised edition, Englewood Cliffs, New Jersey, Prentice Hall, 1975.
In an Iron Time: Statements and Reiterations: Essays. West Lafayette, Indiana, Purdue University Press, 1967.

Editor, *Intro 1–3.* New York, Bantam, 3 vols., 1968–70.
Editor, with Walton Beacham, *Intro 4.* Charlottesville, University Press of Virginia, 1972.
Editor, *Norton Anthology of Short Fiction.* New York, Norton, 1978; revised edition, 1981, 1985.

*

Manuscript Collection: Mugar Memorial Library, Boston University.

Critical Studies: "R.V. Cassill Issue" of *December* (Chicago), vol. 23, nos. 1–2, 1981 (includes bibliography).

R.V. Cassill comments:

(1972) My most personal statement is probably to be found in my short stories. If few of them are reliably autobiographical at least they grew from the observations, moods, exultations, and agonies of early years. If there is constant pattern in them, it is probably that of a hopeful being who expects evil and finds worse.

From my first novel onward I have explored the correspondences between the interior world—of desire and anxiety—and the public world of power—extra-social violences and politics. In *The Eagle on the Coin* I wrote of the ill-fated attempt of some alienated liberals, including a compassionate homosexual, to elect a Negro to the schoolboard in a small mid-western city. In *Doctor Cobb's Game* I used the silhouette of a major British political scandal as the area within which I composed

an elaborate pattern of occult-sexual-political forces weaving and unweaving. Between these two novels, almost 20 years apart, I have played with a variety of forms and subject matter, but the focus of concern has probably been the same, under the surface of appearances. In *Clem Anderson* I took the silhouette of Dylan Thomas's life and within that composed the story of an American poet's self-destructive triumph. It probably is and always will be my most embattled work, simply because in its considerable extent it replaces most of the comfortable or profitable clichés about an artist's life with tougher and more painful diagrams.

But then perhaps my whole productive life has been a swimming against the tide. A Midwesterner by origin, and no doubt by temperament and experience, I worked through decades when first the Southern and then the urban-Jewish novel held an almost monopolistic grip on the tastes and prejudices of American readers. In my extensive reviewing and lecturing I have tried more to examine the clichés, slogans, and rallying cries of the time than to oppose or espouse them—thus leaving myself without any visible partisan support from any quarter. To radicals I have appeared a conservative, to conservatives a radical—and to both a mystification or, I suppose, I would not have been tolerated as long as I have been. As I grow older I love the commonplace of traditional thought and expression with a growing fervor, especially as their rarity increases amid the indoctrinating forces that spoil our good lives.

*   *   *

From the first novel, *The Eagle on the Coin*, and the early stories, R.V. Cassill's art shows a steady development from the autobiographical and the imitative to the fully dramatic capabilities of the mature novelist and short story writer. The range of his talent is wide: from near-pastoral impressions of midwestern America, to urban life in Chicago and New York, to his most technically accomplished work, *Doctor Cobb's Game*, based on the Profumo scandals in London.

Cassill's most complex work relies on four broad kinds of material: stories and novels about the midwest, most notably Iowa as in *Pretty Leslie*; stories and novels concerning academic life, as in "Larchmoor Is Not the World" and *The President*; materials about art and the artist's life (*Clem Anderson*); and finally materials of a less regional nature which may be called the vision of modernity found in the short story "Love? Squalor?" and *Doctor Cobb*. A second lesser known order of Cassill's work consists of a dozen novels, "paperback originals" so-called because of the contractual circumstances of their first publication. For the most part *The Wound of Love, Dormitory Women*, and others await sophisticated literary evaluation. These shorter, often more spontaneous novels also exploit the same kinds of material. It should be well understood that these categories are intended to be only suggestive; the most ambitious work, for example, displays all these materials.

Beyond the technical accomplishments of any professional novelist, Cassill's most noteworthy literary quality is the "visual" nature of his prose fiction. There is a steady exploitation of color, of the precise, telling, visual detail, a sensitivity to proportion, and to the architectonics of scene. In fact Cassill began his artistic career as a painter, a teacher of art; from time to time he still exhibits his work. His fiction shows some of the same qualities as the Impressionists, the Post-Impressionists, and the German Expressionistic painters.

The literary influences are wide-ranging and interestingly absorbed. In general these influences are evoked when necessary rather than being held steadily as "models" in any neo-classic sense. Specifically, Cassill values Flaubert, James, Joyce, and especially D.H. Lawrence. Of a different order of specific influence would be *Madam Bovary*, Gissing's *New Grub Street*, and Benjamin Constant's *Adolphe* (1815). It is interesting that Cassill has written the best extant appreciation of *Adolphe*. Thus Cassill is a highly literary writer, with a broad, useful knowledge of American and European literatures; for many years he has been a teacher of contemporary literature and a writer-in-residence at universities, a professional reviewer, essayist, a discerning cultural commentator and critic.

The governing themes of Cassill's work are less easy to identify. A recurring situation is the nature and the resultant fate of a human pair, the destiny of a man or woman in the throes of new love, old love, marriage, or adultery. Closely bound to these concerns is the nature of love and responsibility; the implications of choice, loyalty, and liberty. Often there are conflicts generated between rationality and a merely emotional yearning—real or imagined—genuine affection as against the implied necessity of sexual aggression or the ironies of "modern love." At times these relationships are between teacher and pupil, lovers, man and wife; between artist and patron, mistress, or the world "out there."

A fascination with these and other difficult themes places a heavy obligation on the novelist, especially in the matter of plot-structures and the handling of sex scenes. Throughout Cassill's work there is the insistence on the centrality of the sexual aspect of all human relationships. If in real life such concerns are seldom finally resolved, so is it in many novelistic structures which tend to rely on sexual involvements as a central motivation. Often, therefore, a story or a novel will begin with a vivid, strong situation which in the end is obscured or vague rather than suggestive or resolved. The reliance on the sexual drive as a compelling motive becomes more insistent in the later work.

Although he is primarily a novelist, Cassill's most sustained work is often in the short fiction, of which he is a master. The best stories focus on domestic scenes, memories of youth, the pathos of age, the casual lost relationship, conversations on art, ideas, literature, and the meaning of life itself.

Taken together, the stories, novels, and criticism show a strongly unified sensibility, a dedicated, energetic artist, a man in a modern world imaginatively and at times romantically comprehended, a man whose powerful gifts are his best protection against his own vision of America and of the midwest where modernity is rampant and the end is nowhere in sight.

—James B. Hall

CAUTE, (John) David. British. Born in Alexandria, Egypt, 16 December 1936. Educated at Edinburgh Academy; Wellington College; Wadham College, Oxford, M.A. in modern history, D. Phil. 1962; Harvard University, Cambridge, Massachusetts (Henry Fellow), 1960–61. Served in the British Army, in Africa, 1955–56. Married 1) Catherine Shuckburgh in 1961 (divorced, 1970), two sons; 2) Martha Bates in 1973, two daughters. Fellow, All Souls College, Oxford, 1959–65; Visiting Professor, New York University and Columbia University, New York, 1966–67; Reader in Social and Political Theory, Brunel University, Uxbridge, Middlesex, 1967–70; Regents' Lecturer, University of California, 1974; Benjamin Meaker Visiting Professor, University of Bristol, 1985. Literary and arts editor, *New Statesman*, London, 1979–80. Deputy Chairman, 1979–80, and Co-Chairman, 1981–82, Writers Guild of Great Britain. Recipient: London Authors' Club award, 1960; Rhys Memorial Prize, 1960. Address: 41 Westcroft Square, London W6 OTA, England.

PUBLICATIONS

Novels

At Fever Pitch. London, Deutsch, 1959; New York, Pantheon, 1961.
Comrade Jacob. London, Deutsch, 1961; New York, Pantheon, 1962.
The Decline of the West. London, Deutsch, and New York, Macmillan, 1966.
The Occupation. London, Deutsch, 1971; New York, McGraw Hill, 1972.
The Baby Sitters (as John Salisbury). London, Secker and Warburg, and New York, Atheneum, 1978.
Moscow Gold (as John Salisbury). London, Futura, 1980.
The K-Factor. London, Joseph, 1983.

Plays

Songs for an Autumn Rifle (produced Edinburgh, 1961).
The Demonstration (produced Nottingham, 1969; London, 1970). London, Deutsch, 1970.
The Fourth World (produced London, 1973).

Radio Plays: *Fallout*, 1972; *The Zimbabwe Tapes*, 1983.

Television Documentary: *Brecht & Co.*, 1979.

Other

Communism and the French Intellectuals 1914–1960. London, Deutsch, and New York, Macmillan, 1964.
The Left in Europe since 1789. London, Weidenfeld and Nicolson, and New York, McGraw Hill, 1966.
Fanon. London, Fontana, and New York, Viking Press, 1970.
The Illusion. London, Deutsch, 1971; New York, Harper, 1972.
The Fellow-Travellers. London, Weidenfeld and Nicolson, and New York, Macmillan, 1973.
Collisions: Essays and Reviews. London, Quartet, 1974.
Cuba, Yes? London, Secker and Warburg, and New York, McGraw Hill, 1974.
The Great Fear: The Anti-Communist Purge under Truman and Eisenhower. New York, Simon and Schuster, and London, Secker and Warburg, 1978.
Under the Skin: The Death of White Rhodesia. London, Allen Lane, and Evanston, Illinois, Northwestern University Press, 1983.
The Espionage of the Saints. London, Hamish Hamilton, 1986.

Editor, *Essential Writings*, by Karl Marx. London, MacGibbon and Kee, 1967; New York, Macmillan, 1968.

*   *   *

David Caute is a rare breed among contemporary English novelists. Indeed, he is probably unique. For his novels are written out of a deep ideological commitment to Marxism, and they are thus attempts to explore and account for the nature of imperialism, bourgeois capitalism and Western liberal democracy. To say as much is to indicate how extraordinarily at odds they are with the customary modest scope and intention of the contemporary English novel.

It is a generally accepted, if unwritten, rule for the novelist that he can only write well about what he knows from first-hand experience. The raw material out of which he fashions his art must, that is, be familiar enough to him for him to be able to handle it with confidence and authority. In other words, one wants the "ring of truth" in all that is depicted, one expects authenticity of detail and verification of fact that will allow us as readers to have confidence that the author quite simply knows what he is talking about.

In so far as this is a demand we make of the novel, it is clear that Caute frequently falls short of meeting it. To look at his first novel is to see this. The handling of the African colonial life in *At Fever Pitch* quite lacks the kind of grasp of the sweaty actual that we find in the work of a master journalist-novelist like Graham Greene, for example, or that is so vividly present in Anthony Burgess's early and brilliant *Malayan Trilogy*. Caute very obviously cannot match their keenness of eye and ear for local colour, for realistic exactness. Yet he would no doubt reply that such veracity is unimportant for him and is finally unimportant to the novel as such. For what essentially matters is not how minutely you can detail all aspects of a way of life, but what deep and penetrative understanding you have of it; and for Caute such understanding can come only through Marxism. His novels are therefore living histories, analyses of societies which try to define their true nature through the historical and economic arguments of Karl Marx.

So far, so good. But then it may be argued, and indeed frequently *is*, that Caute's fictional writing is so much arid didacticism, a dressing-up of Marxist orthodoxy which succeeds only in suffocating the poor life of the novel itself. Caute, the argument runs, attempts to put a covering of skin over the bones of his theory, with the result that his novels can very clearly be seen to be skeletons, lifeless, inert, crucially artificial. None of his novels has suffered more from this criticism than the third one, *The Decline of the West*, and of none, perhaps, is the criticism more just. For as the un-ironic use of Oswald Spengler in the title implies, Caute is out to ram a thesis about capitalism in decay down our throats, and the consequence is that we turn away in irritation.

Yet to say this is not to question the validity of the novel of ideas. Sartre is an obvious and distinguished example of a novelist whose ideology is present in his fiction without constricting it, and what is true of him is true of others. But the difference between Sartre and Caute, at least in his early work, is that Sartre understands that to write a novel of ideas does not require the novelist to be impatient of anything *but* ideas. "No ideas but in things" the great American poet, William Carlos Williams said, and there is heartening evidence that David Caute is beginning to realise as much. Certainly *The Occupation* suggested that he had become aware of the problem that George Eliot formulated over a hundred years ago, when she remarked that her prime difficulty was "to make certain ideas incarnate, as if they had revealed themselves to me first in the flesh." Unfortunately, *The Occupation* did not produce the impetus to further fiction that one might have expected, and it now seems that the effort of composing it exhausted Caute's novelistic imagination, or at least put it under great strain. At all events, since its publication he has produced very little. There have been two indifferent crime thrillers, published under the pseudonym of John Salisbury, and most recently an attempted return to more serious fiction with *The K-Factor*. *The K-Factor* is, however, not a novel on which one would wish Caute's reputation to rest and it is to be hoped that at some time in the future he rediscovers those creative springs that made him so exciting a prospect in the early 1970's.

—John Lucas

CHARLES, Gerda. British. Born in Liverpool, Lancashire. Educated in Liverpool schools. Journalist and reviewer for *New Statesman, Daily Telegraph, New York Times, Jewish Chronicle*, and other periodicals; television critic, *Jewish Observer*, London, 1978–79. Recipient: James Tait Black Memorial Prize, 1964; Whitbread Award, 1971; Arts Council grant, 1972. Address: 22 Cunningham Court, London W9 1AE, England.

PUBLICATIONS

Novels

The True Voice. London, Eyre and Spottiswoode, 1959.
The Crossing Point. London, Eyre and Spottiswoode, 1960; New York, Knopf, 1961.
A Slanting Light. London, Eyre and Spottiswoode, and New York, Knopf, 1963.
A Logical Girl. London, Eyre and Spottiswoode, and New York, Knopf, 1967.
The Destiny Waltz. London, Eyre and Spottiswoode, 1971; New York, Scribner, 1972.

Uncollected Short Stories

"The Staircase," in *Vanity Fair* (London), April 1956.
"Rosh Hashanah in Five Weeks," in *Pick of Today's Short Stories 11.* London, Putnam, 1960.
"The Czech-Slovakian Chandelier," in *Modern Jewish Stories*, edited by Charles. London, Faber, 1963; Englewood Cliffs, New Jersey, Prentice Hall, 1965.
"A Mixed Marriage," in *Quest* (London), 1965.
"The Difference," in *Jewish Chronicle* (London), 24 November 1967.
"The Mitzvah," in *Jewish Chronicle* (London), March 1978.

Other

Editor, *Modern Jewish Stories.* London, Faber, 1963; Englewood Cliffs, New Jersey, Prentice Hall, 1965.

*

Critical Studies: "The World of Gerda Charles," in *Jewish Quarterly* (London), Summer 1967; "Facing the Music" by C.P. Snow, in *Financial Times* (London), 15 April 1971; "Revenge Is Sour," in *Guardian* (London), 27 May 1971; "Gerda Charles: A Visionary Realist," in *Jewish Quarterly* (London), Summer 1971.

Gerda Charles comments:
Though I am known primarily as an Anglo-Jewish writer, my five novels all deal in general with what I have described

(in my third book, *A Slanting Light*) as "the region of everyday hurt." My books are not concerned with extremes—which I believe to be largely unrelated to the real problems of living. They are not concerned with madness but rather with the job of maintaining sanity, dignity, and order. They advocate the unfashionable virtues of delicacy, tact, and generosity of heart within the context of day-to-day life.

*   *   *

The True Voice is an excellent first novel in which Gerda Charles develops a principal theme—the alienation felt by a person of talent when he is unable to articulate his aspirations and to communicate his inner intensities to others. After two disillusioning experiences with men, Lindy Frome finds that her only valid resource is the self, as she attains awareness of "the compassionate irony with which it was necessary to confront life; how flexibility, awareness and forgiveness were all."

With *The Crossing Point* Charles wrote her best book. She asserts through Rabbi Leo Norberg that Judaism is the most viable of religions for human beings since it is at "the crossing point" where opposites such as asceticism and sensuousness, mysticism and secularism, idealism and practicality converge. Boruch Gabriel is imposing as a presence but not as an influence since his conception of religion is literal and monolithic. His daughter, Sara, illustrates the true strength of Judaism as it gives her courage to face her father and her own life of impaired fulfilment. Rabbi Norberg is the novel's intellectual center. Humane and imaginative, he sometimes lacks the courage to act upon his insights. Knowing the best in Sara Gabriel, he chooses, out of a certain perversity and false pride, the second best, a calculating and fourth-rate woman, for wife. The characters, big with life, give the book its stature. They are human beings who also happen to be Jews, as they falter or triumph in achieving their destinies.

A Slanting Light is a notable if less arresting book. A psychically immolated American playwright, Bernard Zold, is protagonist. His chief antagonist is a power-hungry mother; his wife is superficial and his child unloving. He is a sufferer rather than a doer, a man of sympathetic imagination rather than of active confidence. For the narrator he is emblematic of "the whole role of the Jew in the historic life of the world's soul" and exemplifies "the human nature of society." Zold hardly achieves this archetypal dimension, and Charles's analysis of Zold as artist lacks immediacy and exactitude. But as a novel exploring entangled relationships it has distinction and force.

In *A Logical Girl*, Charles's best book since *The Crossing Point*, Rose Morgan's views of what ought to be are in abrupt contrast with the way things are. In World War II in a seaside town, she develops from naive adolescence to maturity while the town is "invaded" by European and American troops. Her sensitivity allows her to see how selfish, impersonal, and degrading her associates and family often are, while they impress the world as models of virtue and propriety. The elements of deceit, inconsiderateness, and cruelty which all too often determine human relationships are the reflection in little of the injustices and sadism in the Nazi regime on the continent. Rose learns that human beings do not behave consistently and logically, that impulse is often triumphant over honesty. Charles finely controls her irony as she demonstrates in Rose how the individual who sees the truth is disregarded by most other people in their reverence for the flashy, the meretricious, and the materialistic.

The Destiny Waltz is Charles's longest and least satisfactory novel. It concerns the surviving influence of Paul Salomon, a great poet from the 1920's who had been passed over in his lifetime. At the instigation of a television company, Jimmy Marchant, a retired band leader and Paul's closest friend, meets Michele Sandburg, a college teacher in her forties who has written the best life of the poet. They are to help make a documentary film about Salomon's life. Much pathos and intense feeling develop when Jimmy realizes that in Michele he may yet find the happiness that eluded him in his marriage and sexual affairs. Yet Jimmy lacks interest and presence, and his moralizing, while genuine, is frequently labored. Again, Charles fails to make her artist believable; we have, in short, little idea of what Salomon's poetry was like. She does depict with assuredness the studio milieu, wherein prudential motives and the requirements of art are in locked conflict. In sum, Charles has overextended her materials for the value which accrues to them.

Gerda Charles has analyzed with sympathy and comprehension the spiritual misfit in modern life. Her insight into human nature is penetrating; and her eccentrics, as well as her fully developed figures, are authentic. She establishes the outlines of her characters economically by concentrated analysis and persuasive dialogue. As a stylist her prose is always perspicuous and perfectly modulated to convey a sense of Jamesian complexities in character and situation. Her main preoccupation is with the painful incursion of moral knowledge. The process whereby her protagonists determine "how to be" is fraught with anguish, on occasion with muted triumph, always with the ring of truth.

—Frederick P.W. McDowell

CHARYN, Jerome. American. Born in New York City, 13 May 1937. Educated at Columbia University, New York, B.A. (cum laude) 1959 (Phi Beta Kappa). Married Marlene Phillips in 1965 (divorced). Recreation leader, New York City Department of Parks, early 1960's; English teacher, High School of Music and Art, and School of Performing Arts, both New York, 1962–64; Lecturer in English, City College, New York, 1965; Assistant Professor of English, Stanford University, California, 1965–68; Assistant Professor, 1968–72, Associate Professor, 1972–78, and Professor of English, 1978–80, Herbert Lehman College, City University of New York; Mellon Visiting Professor of English, Rice University, Houston, 1979. Visiting Professor, 1980, and since 1981, Lecturer in Creative Writing, Princeton University, New Jersey. Founding editor, *Dutton Review*, New York, 1970–72; executive editor, *Fiction*, New York, 1970–75. Since 1984, Member of the Executive Board, PEN American Center. Recipient: National Endowment for the Arts grant, 1979, 1984; Rosenthal Foundation award, 1981; Guggenheim grant, 1982. Address: 302 West 12th Street, Apartment 10-C, New York, New York 10014, U.S.A.

PUBLICATIONS

Novels

Once Upon a Droshky. New York, McGraw Hill, 1964.
On the Darkening Green. New York, McGraw Hill, 1965.
Going to Jerusalem. New York, Viking Press, 1967; London, Cape, 1968.
American Scrapbook. New York, Viking Press, 1969.

Eisenhower, My Eisenhower.   New York, Holt Rinehart, 1971.
The Tar Baby.   New York, Holt Rinehart, 1973.
The Isaac Quartet.   London, Zomba, 1984.
  Blue Eyes.   New York, Simon and Schuster, 1975.
  Marilyn the Wild.   New York, Arbor House, 1976.
  The Education of Patrick Silver.   New York, Arbor House, 1976.
  Secret Isaac.   New York, Arbor House, 1978.
The Franklin Scare.   New York, Arbor House, 1977.
The Seventh Babe.   New York, Arbor House, 1979.
The Catfish Man: A Conjured Life.   New York, Arbor House, 1980.
Darlin' Bill: A Love Story of the Wild West.   New York, Arbor House, 1980.
Panna Maria.   New York, Arbor House, 1982.
Pinocchio's Nose.   New York, Arbor House, 1983.
War Cries over Avenue C.   New York, Fine, 1985.

Short Stories

The Man Who Grew Younger and Other Stories.   New York, Harper, 1967.

Other

Editor, *The Single Voice: An Anthology of Contemporary Fiction.*   New York, Collier, 1969.
Editor, *The Troubled Vision.*   New York, Collier, 1970.

*

Critical Studies: introductions by Charyn to *The Single Voice*, 1969, and *The Troubled Vision*, 1970; "Notes on the Rhetoric of Anti-Realist Fiction" by Albert Guerard, in *Tri-Quarterly* (Evanston, Illinois), Spring 1974.

*   *   *

Few writers are as prolific as Jerome Charyn, or their fiction as restless. Many of his novels are picaresque, and this loose, episodic form suits him, for Charyn cannot imagine satisfaction or still the terror that he feels about American life. Even language itself becomes a source of dread for him. Characterizing the contemporary writer's predicament, Charyn cites Roland Barthes's idea that language has turned in on itself, "both as dream and menace." Indeed, menace is a constant in Charyn's fiction. To him, society's institutions press in on individuals, trying to mold them into social roles. So, typically, the novels are about misfits and their flight through a society that allows them no peace.

The city, usually New York City, serves as backdrop for the action and as metaphor for contemporary life. Neighborhoods come to life in the sinuous, evocative prose: Crotona Park, for instance, or the Jewish neighborhoods of lower Manhattan. Charyn characters partake of their urban context in the same way as Dickens characters do. Also like Dickens, Charyn lavishes attention on urban eccentrics: Patrick Silver, the former policeman, who goes about on pavement-blackened bare feet and in a rugby shirt that he never washes; or Pincus, the hunch-backed theater critic and lover of Russian literature and borsht. Such portraits always energize the novels.

Charyn's first three novels, *Once Upon a Droshky*, *On the Darkening Green*, and *Going to Jerusalem*, become increasingly picaresque in technique and theme; all use a first-person narrator who tells a tale of ineffectual rebellion or resistance. In *Once Upon a Droshky* Yankel tries to organize his fellow tenants to resist an eviction notice. In *On the Darkening Green* Nick Lapucci helps his young delinquent charges to rebel against Uncle Nate, the fascistic head of the Blattenburg Home for Wayward Jewish Boys. In *Going to Jerusalem*, an episodic account of a traveling chess exhibition, Ivan sympathizes with a whole series of down-and-out characters, most notably Kortz the ex-Nazi chess master. None of these novels is entirely successful, although individual passages and scenes display Charyn's considerable talents. The mock-heroic cafeteria confrontation of *Once Upon a Droshky* is antically memorable, revealing Charyn's identification with his eccentric characters as well as his depiction of their limitations.

The next three novels—*American Scrapbook*, *Eisenhower, My Eisenhower*, and *The Tar Baby*—mark Charyn's movement toward anti-realist fiction. Using a variety of points of view and narrative voices, *American Scrapbook* describes a Japanese-American family's detention during World War II. While in form the novel is similar to Faulkner's *As I Lay Dying*, Charyn's novel does not have the unity or narrative richness of Faulkner's. In *Eisenhower, My Eisenhower*, Charyn re-invents New York as a mythical city called Bedlam. Giving his gypsy characters their own language, history, and mythology, Charyn self-consciously calls attention to the fictionality of his story. *The Tar Baby* is a novel in the form of a college literary magazine, specifically of a commemorative issue to the fictitious, uneducated Wittgenstein specialist, Anatole Waxman-Weissman. This form allows Charyn to exercise his talent for parody and for writing in a variety of styles and voices. More importantly, it produces a remarkably unified and rhetorically innovative novel.

After *The Tar Baby*, Charyn again shifted direction, moving in the Isaac Sidel tetralogy (*Blue Eyes, Marilyn the Wild, The Education of Patrick Silver*, and *Secret Isaac*) toward a detective fiction that suggests the techniques of the American hard-boiled school. None of the novels is really a mystery though, for Charyn's chief interests lie in depicting the varied life of New York City streets, exploring the psychological complexities of his hero Isaac Sidel, and indulging his fondness for stylistic experimentation. In this tetralogy criminals and police represent different but interconnected aspects of human nature. We see this interconnectedness when Sidel gains physical and psychological nourishment in the Guzmanns' criminal lair at the same time that he is infected with a tapeworm that will torment him for the rest of his life. Or we see it in *Secret Isaac* when the mysterious criminal mastermind turns out to be a former police chief.

Charyn's recent novels show two different impulses at work: he uses the novel as a pseudo-autobiography, and he continues to experiment with form. In *The Catfish Man* and *Pinocchio's Nose*, Charyn gives his heroes his own name and tells of their development as writers. Both novels are highly ironic in that the heroes write pulp stories for mass consumption—while Charyn himself has tried throughout his career to establish his reputation as a serious writer. The subtitle of *The Catfish Man*, "A Conjured Life," and the title *Pinocchio's Nose* (evoking as it does the image of Pinocchio's lies) call attention to the self-parody in Charyn's imaginative creation of his life. In *The Seventh Babe* and *Darlin' Bill*, Charyn takes traditional novel types—the sports novel and the western romance—and injects his concerns. Thus *The Seventh Babe*, an account of a mythical baseball hero, Babe Ragland, becomes Charyn's usual story of non-conformity and rebellion. Notably, however, despite its parody of the form, this book has been much praised—as a baseball novel.

Charyn's most recent novel, *War Cries over Avenue C*, represents both a circling back and a synthesis, and as such allows us to generalize about his career. His account of ineffectual resistance and youthful self-definition is reminiscent of his first novels, though he fuses realist and anti-realist techniques in a new way; the resulting formal and thematic vision conjoins New York City streets and Vietnam as part of the same fictional landscape. In this fusion, both the admirable and the unfortunate in Charyn's fiction are evident: the playful, often self-mocking rhetoric and the memorably rendered urban eccentrics, together with the loose fictional form and the sameness of fictional vision. Fortunately, though, Charyn continues his fictional journeys. If they do not yield highly polished art, they do remind us that the pleasures of journeys often come in the new and unanticipated.

—David M. Craig

CLARK, Eleanor. American. Born in Los Angeles, California, 6 July 1913; grew up in Roxbury, Connecticut. Educated at Vassar College, Poughkeepsie, New York, B.A. 1934. Married Robert Penn Warren, *q.v.*, in 1952; two children. Editorial staff member, W.W. Norton and Company, publishers, New York, 1936–39. Worked for the United States Office of Strategic Services, Washington, D.C., 1943–45. Recipient: American Academy grant, 1947; Guggenheim fellowship, 1947, 1949; National Book Award, for non-fiction, 1965. Member, American Academy. Address: 2495 Redding Road, Fairfield, Connecticut 06430, U.S.A.

PUBLICATIONS

Novels

The Bitter Box. New York, Doubleday, 1946; London, Joseph, 1947.
Baldur's Gate. New York, Pantheon, 1970.
Gloria Mundi. New York, Pantheon, 1979.
Camping Out. New York, Putnam, 1986.

Short Stories

Dr. Heart: A Novella and Other Stories. New York, Pantheon, 1974.

Uncollected Short Story

"Fortress and Raggedy Ann," in *Georgia Review* (Athens), Spring 1982.

Other

Rome and a Villa. New York, Doubleday, 1952; London, Joseph, 1953; revised edition, New York, Pantheon, 1975; Henley on Thames, Ellis, 1976.
The Song of Roland (for children). New York, Random House, 1960; London, Muller, 1962.
The Oysters of Locmariaquer. New York, Pantheon, 1964; London, Secker and Warburg, 1965.
Eyes, Etc.: A Memoir. New York, Pantheon, 1977; London, Collins, 1978.

Tamrart: 13 Days in the Sahara. Winston-Salem, North Carolina, Palaemon Press, 1984.

Editor, with Horace Gregory, *New Letters in America.* New York, Norton, 1937.

Translator, *The Dark Wedding*, by Ramón Sender. New York, Doubleday, 1943; London, Grey Walls Press, 1948.

*

Critical Studies: "Eleanor Clark Issue" of *New England Review* (Hanover, New Hampshire), Winter 1979.

Eleanor Clark comments:

(1972) I do not feel it is wise or in most cases helpful for writers to analyze their own work. In any case, I find it impossible, except to remark that, concerning impulse, motive and kind of personal involvement, I find no clear line of demarcation between my novels and nonfiction books (*Rome* and *Oysters*). This does not of course refer to essays—a different job altogether.

Can a woman be a good writer (artist) and a good mother? I have no idea. Are the two in conflict? Of course—so is art and everything else. Do I love and value my two children above my books? Certainly. Would I have stopped writing altogether if necessary for the children's happiness? Well, yes, but it would perhaps not have been physically possible—in the sense that one eats when hungry and scratches when itching—and with a little sleight-of-hand it was never quite necessary for too fatally long at a time. However, these facts do relate to *Baldur's Gate* having been written over a period of many years. It was in gestation, with false starts, long before that, but the home-town scene (the usual first novel) was too close. I disposed of it when young in a story, "Hurry, Hurry," found a built-in distance for my first published novel, *The Bitter Box*, and came to the perspective for the original one only years later, possibly through the fact of having children.

*   *   *

Twenty-four years separate Eleanor Clark's first novel and her second and in comparison one gives the impression of looking backward and the other of looking forward. *The Bitter Box*, though published in 1946, reflects the leftist social ferment of the 1930's. The novel's center is a timid, punctilious bank clerk named Mr. Temple who in his teller's cage serves efficiently, almost worshipfully, the symbol of capitalism until driven by a sense of oppression to search out and embrace another god vaguely defined as "the party," the official organ of which is the *Word*. His ultimate realization that both gods are false and correupt is accompanied by an awakening to the redemptive influences of suffering and love. By painfully relinquishing the safety of a life of order and obedience he gradually learns to trust and to give of himself in concern for others. This theme of surrender into life, present also in *Baldur's Gate*, fails of effect in *The Bitter Box* largely because of a patronizing, detached point of view which creates a curiously remote and improbable hero whose political activism seems arbitrary rather than necessary and probable.

Baldur's Gate, an ambitious work rich in symbol and allusion, deals with a wealth of themes: the preservation of tradition, the search for values, the function of art, commercialism, ecology, among others. Eva Buckingham Hines relates the events in a complex style—disordered chronology, internal monologue, depth analysis—which complements her personal tortuous course out of the often painful and sometimes alluring memories of the past toward acceptance of the present and courage for the future. The memories derive from growing up in Jordan, an old Connecticut town rich in tradition and in the history of human weakness and error. And though she seems to be committed to the future, having married Lucas Hines and borne a son, in reality she is hostage to her past: to the pain and frustration of an indifferent and alcoholic mother, an ineffectual father, a corrupt brother, a once proud family socially disgraced, and to the memory of a love betrayed.

Her futile attempt to renew this early love affair with Jack Pryden and thus redeem the past is the motivating force behind many of the events, but it is the presence of the 70-year-old sculptor, Baldur Blake (the name suggesting his role as demigod and mystic), which lifts the novel above this rather trivial love affair. Having himself fought the battle of disillusionment with the heritage of the past, he returns to vision and creativity, like a fertility god in spring, revitalizing the whole community with promise that the future which destroys the past can also generate new beauty and harmony.

In the closing scene as Eva stands in the falling snow viewing the town dump, symbol of waste but also of change, the fundamental law of things, she reflects that his message had been "not to kid ourselves, about what art, home, love, Jordan, anything could ever mean to us again, and yet to keep capable of love, of work, of hope." The dream of a new community fails of realization, but the vision of the gate model Baldur never lived to complete remains, the "imitation of some large serenity always in the act of rising out of torment." The novel captures that torment and the courage to master it, but more frequently in the rhetoric than in the characters and situations. In the final analysis the plot and characters seem not quite the equal of the novel's deep philosophical vision.

—Dale K. Doepke

CLARKE, Arthur C(harles). British. Born in Minehead, Somerset, 16 December 1917. Educated at Huish's Grammar School, Taunton, Somerset, 1927–36; King's College, London, 1946–48, B.Sc. (honours) in physics and mathematics 1948. Flight Lieutenant in the Royal Air Force, 1941–46; served as Radar Instructor, and Technical Officer on the first Ground Controlled Approach radar; originated proposal for use of satellites for communications, 1945. Married Marilyn Mayfield in 1954 (divorced, 1964). Assistant auditor, Exchequer and Audit Department, London, 1936–41; assistant editor, *Physics Abstracts*, London, 1949–50. Since 1954, engaged in underwater exploration and photography of the Great Barrier Reef of Australia and the coast of Sri Lanka. Director, Rocket Publishing, London, Underwater Safaris, Colombo, and Spaceward Corporation, New York. Has made numerous radio and television appearances (most recently as presenter of the television series *Arthur C. Clarke's Mysterious World*, 1980, and *World of Strange Powers*, 1985), and has lectured widely in Britain and the United States; commentator, for CBS-TV, on lunar flights of Apollo 11, 12, and 15; Vikram Sarabhai Professor, Physical Research Laboratory, Ahmedabad, India, 1980. Recipient: International Fantasy Award, 1952; Hugo Award, 1956, 1969 (for screenplay), 1974, 1980; Unesco Kalinga Prize, 1961; Boys' Clubs of America award, 1961; Franklin Institute Ballantine Medal, 1963; Aviation-Space Writers Association Ball Award, 1965; American Association for the Advancement

of Science-Westinghouse Science Writing Award, 1969; *Playboy* award, 1971; Nebula Award, 1972, 1973, 1979; Jupiter award, 1973; John W. Campbell Memorial Award, 1974; American Institute of Aeronautics and Astronautics award, 1974; Boston Museum of Science Washburn Award, 1977; Marconi Fellowship, 1982. D.Sc.: Beaver College, Glenside, Pennsylvania, 1971. Chairman, British Interplanetary Society, 1946–47, 1950–53. Guest of Honor, World Science Fiction Convention, 1956. Fellow, Royal Astronomical Society; Fellow, King's College, London, 1977; Chancellor, University of Moratuwa, Sri Lanka, since 1979. Agent: David Higham Associates Ltd., 5–8 Lower John Street, London W1R 4HA, England; or, Scott Meredith Literary Agency, 845 Third Avenue, New York, New York 10022, U.S.A. Address: 25 Barnes Place, Colombo 7, Sri Lanka; or, Dene Court, Bishop's Lydeard, Taunton, Somerset TA4 3LT, England.

PUBLICATIONS

Novels

Prelude to Space. New York, Galaxy, 1951; London, Sidgwick and Jackson, 1953; as *Master of Space*, New York, Lancer, 1961; as *The Space Dreamers*, Lancer, 1969.
The Sands of Mars. London, Sidgwick and Jackson, 1951; New York, Gnome Press, 1952.
Against the Fall of Night. New York, Gnome Press, 1953; revised edition, as *The City and the Stars*, London, Muller, and New York, Harcourt Brace, 1956.
Childhood's End. New York, Ballantine, 1953; London, Sidgwick and Jackson, 1954.
Earthlight. London, Muller, and New York, Ballantine, 1955.
The Deep Range. New York, Harcourt Brace, and London, Muller, 1957.
Across the Sea of Stars (omnibus). New York, Harcourt Brace, 1959.
A Fall of Moondust. London, Gollancz, and New York, Harcourt Brace, 1961.
From the Oceans, From the Stars (omnibus). New York, Harcourt Brace, 1962.
Glide Path. New York, Harcourt Brace, 1963; London, Sidgwick and Jackson, 1969.
An Arthur C. Clarke Omnibus [and *Second Omnibus*]. London, Sidgwick and Jackson, 2 vols., 1965–68.
Prelude to Mars (omnibus). New York, Harcourt Brace, 1965.
2001: A Space Odyssey (novelization of screenplay). New York, New American Library, and London, Hutchinson, 1968.
The Lion of Comarre, and Against the Fall of Night. New York, Harcourt Brace, 1968; London, Gollancz, 1970.
Rendezvous with Rama. London, Gollancz, and New York, Harcourt Brace, 1973.
Imperial Earth. London, Gollancz, 1975; revised edition, New York, Harcourt Brace, 1976.
The Fountains of Paradise. London, Gollancz, and New York, Harcourt Brace, 1979.
2010: Odyssey Two. New York, Ballantine, and London, Granada, 1982.

Short Stories

Expedition to Earth. New York, Ballantine, 1953; London, Sidgwick and Jackson, 1954.
Reach for Tomorrow. New York, Ballantine, 1956; London, Gollancz, 1962.

Tales from the White Hart. New York, Ballantine, 1957; London, Sidgwick and Jackson, 1972.

The Other Side of the Sky. New York, Harcourt Brace, 1958; London, Gollancz, 1961.

Tales of Ten Worlds. New York, Harcourt Brace, 1962; London, Gollancz, 1963.

The Nine Billion Names of God: The Best Short Stories of Arthur C. Clarke. New York, Harcourt Brace, 1967.

The Wind from the Sun: Stories of the Space Age. New York, Harcourt Brace, and London, Gollancz, 1972.

Of Time and Stars: The Worlds of Arthur C. Clarke. London, Gollancz, 1972.

The Best of Arthur C. Clarke 1937–1971, edited by Angus Wells. London, Sidgwick and Jackson, 1973.

The Sentinel. New York, Berkley, 1983.

Uncollected Short Story

"Quarantine," in *Isaac Asimov's Science Fiction Magazine* (New York), Spring 1977.

Play

Screenplay: *2001: A Space Odyssey*, with Stanley Kubrick, 1968.

Other

Interplanetary Flight: An Introduction to Astronautics. London, Temple Press, 1950; New York, Harper, 1951; revised edition, 1960.

The Exploration of Space. London, Temple Press, and New York, Harper, 1951; revised edition 1959.

Islands in the Sky (for children). London, Sidgwick and Jackson, and Philadelphia, Winston, 1952.

The Young Traveller in Space (for children). London, Phoenix House, 1954; as *Going into Space*, New York, Harper, 1954; as *The Scottie Book of Space Travel*, London, Transworld, 1957; revised edition, with Robert Silverberg, as *Into Space*, New York, Harper, 1971.

The Exploration of the Moon. London, Muller, 1954; New York, Harper, 1955.

The Coast of Coral. London, Muller, and New York, Harper, 1956.

The Making of a Moon: The Story of the Earth Satellite Program. London, Muller, and New York, Harper, 1957; revised edition, Harper, 1958.

The Reefs of Taprobane: Underwater Adventures Around Ceylon. London, Muller, and New York, Harper, 1957.

Voice Across the Sea. London, Muller, 1958; New York, Harper, 1959; revised edition, London, Mitchell Beazley, and Harper, 1974.

Boy Beneath the Sea (for children). New York, Harper, 1958.

The Challenge of the Spaceship: Previews of Tomorrow's World. New York, Harper, 1959; London, Muller, 1960.

The First Five Fathoms: A Guide to Underwater Adventure. New York, Harper, 1960.

The Challenge of the Sea. New York, Holt Rinehart, 1960; London, Muller, 1961.

Indian Ocean Adventure. New York, Harper, 1961; London, Barker, 1962.

Profiles of the Future: An Enquiry into the Limits of the Possible. London, Gollancz, 1962; New York, Harper, 1963; revised edition, Harper, 1973; Gollancz, 1974, 1982; New York, Holt Rinehart, 1984.

Dolphin Island (for children). New York, Holt Rinehart, and London, Gollancz, 1963.

The Treasure of the Great Reef. London, Barker, and New York, Harper, 1964; revised edition, New York, Ballantine, 1974.

Indian Ocean Treasure, with Mike Wilson. New York, Harper, 1964; London, Sidgwick and Jackson, 1972.

Man and Space, with the editors of Life. New York, Time, 1964.

Voices from the Sky: Previews of the Coming Space Age. New York, Harper, 1965; London, Gollancz, 1966.

The Promise of Space. New York, Harper, and London, Hodder and Stoughton, 1968.

First on the Moon, with the astronauts. London, Joseph, and Boston, Little Brown, 1970.

Report on Planet Three and Other Speculations. London, Gollancz, and New York, Harper, 1972.

The Lost Worlds of 2001. New York, New American Library, and London, Sidgwick and Jackson, 1972.

Beyond Jupiter: The Worlds of Tomorrow, with Chesley Bonestell. Boston, Little Brown, 1972.

Technology and the Frontiers of Knowledge (lectures), with others. New York, Doubleday, 1973.

The View from Serendip (on Sri Lanka). New York, Random House, 1977; London, Gollancz, 1978.

1984: Spring: A Choice of Futures. New York, Ballantine, and London, Granada, 1984.

Ascent to Orbit: A Scientific Autobiography: The Technical Writings of Arthur C. Clarke. New York and Chichester, Sussex, Wiley, 1984.

The Odyssey File, with Peter Hyams. New York, Ballantine, and London, Granada, 1985.

Editor, *Time Probe: Sciences in Science Fiction.* New York, Delacorte Press, 1966; London, Gollancz, 1967.

Editor, *The Coming of the Space Age: Famous Accounts of Man's Probing of the Universe.* London, Gollancz, and New York, Meredith, 1967.

Editor, with George Proctor, *The Science Fiction Hall of Fame 3: The Nebula Winners 1965–1969.* New York, Avon, 1982.

*

Bibliography: *Arthur C. Clarke: A Primary and Secondary Bibliography* by David N. Samuelson, Boston, Hall, 1984.

Manuscript Collection: Mugar Memorial Library, Boston University.

Critical Studies: "Out of the Ego Chamber" by Jeremy Bernstein, in *New Yorker*, 9 August 1969; *Arthur C. Clarke* edited by Joseph D. Olander and Martin H. Greenberg, New York, Taplinger, and Edinburgh, Harris, 1977; *The Space Odysseys of Arthur C. Clarke* by George Edgar Slusser, San Bernardino, California, Borgo Press, 1978; *Arthur C. Clarke* (includes bibliography) by Eric S. Rabkin, West Linn, Oregon, Starmont House, 1979, revised edition, 1980; *Against the Night, The Stars: The Science Fiction of Arthur C. Clarke* by John Hollow, New York, Harcourt Brace, 1983.

Arthur C. Clarke comments:

I regard myself primarily as an entertainer and my ideals are Maugham, Kipling, Wells. My chief aim is the old SF cliché, "The search for wonder." However, I am almost equally interested in style and rhythm, having been much influenced by Tennyson, Swinburne, Housman, and the Georgian poets.

My main themes are exploration (space, sea, time), the position of Man in the hierarchy of the universe, and the effect of contact with other intelligences. The writer who probably had most influence on me was W. Olaf Stapledon (*Last and First Men*).

*   *   *

Arthur C. Clarke writes adventures of the near and far future, in which men seek knowledge and explore new environments. The most notable aspect of his fiction is the perfect welding of the expository passages, containing accurate but clear scientific explanations of how the adventures will sooner or later become possible, to the narrative passages.

Several of the adventures occur at or near the beginnings of exploration of a new environment. *Prelude to Space* fictionalizes what leads up to the first trip to the moon. *Earthlight* depicts the workings of the lunar colony, and *The Sands of Mars* does the same for that planet. *Islands in the Sky* explores the uses of space stations, and *The Deep Range* and *Dolphin Island* explore the uses of the sea, such as whale farming and cooperation with dolphins.

Three of Clarke's novels are primarily religious and philosophical. *Against the Fall of Night*, completed in 1946 and published in 1953, was rewritten as *The City and the Stars*. Diaspar, a city of the remote future, has (to paraphrase a favorite Clarke generalization) a technology so advanced that it cannot be distinguished from magic. But the city is a womb from which none of its citizens dare to escape until one courageous explorer goes on a quest for knowledge of the past, which opens up a new future for his society. In *Childhood's End* alien "Overlords" stop man's development of space travel until man, remade by his own unsuspected psychic powers, rises to a new level of childhood and moves toward the stars. The quest of David Bowman in *2001: A Space Odyssey* transforms him into Star-Child, who will "think of something" to move man up the ladder of evolution.

Clarke does in his short stories (such as those collected in *Reach for Tomorrow*, *The Other Side of the Sky*, *Tales of Ten Worlds*, and *Tales from the White Hart*) what he does elsewhere —plus some things which he does not do elsewhere. "Breaking Strain," for example, is a study of contrasting personalities in crisis; "Hate" is a moral fable; "Transcience" is a nearly plotless poem written in prose which compares and contrasts three stages of man's existence.

Rendezvous with Rama, about an alien spaceship's mysterious visit to the solar system, is in some ways unique among Clarke's novels in that it allows the mystery to remain unexplained. Astronauts from Earth visit the vast ship, which is apparently now devoid of intelligent lift and acting automatically; but they never do discover its origin and purpose. This is in contrast to *2001: A Space Odyssey*, in which the alien purpose is perhaps explained too thoroughly. Clarke's descriptive powers come marvellously to bear on the vast interior of the ship and the strange robotic forms which inhabit it.

What could Clarke do after *2001: A Space Odyssey* and *Rendezvous with Rama*? There is some, perhaps inevitable, deflation in *Imperial Earth*, a novel about the American Quincentennial in 2276. Clarke assumes an Americanized world—indeed, solar system—after a rather vague "time of troubles." The prestige of the MacKenzie family, derived from centuries of prominence in diplomacy, is more significant than any remaining national power. Duncan MacKenzie's visit to earth from his native Titan fails to provide enough plot to sustain a novel. There are only technological bits and pieces of interest, such as an excursion on the raised ship *The Titanic*.

Clarke's full imaginative powers return with *The Fountains of Paradise*, one of his best novels. Clarke fuses a general

technical idea of much interest—the space ladder as an alternative to rocketry—with the spirit of a particular place, a thinly disguised version of his homeland, Sri Lanka. A religious sect has inhabited the site of the space ladder for thousands of years, and Clarke lightly suggests a connection between their ancient presence and the scientific innovation which threatens them. The recent sequel to *2001*, called *2010*, is disappointing. Although the book does contain some arresting ideas and images, the plot lacks unity and the style is prosaic.

Although Clarke's style can be wordy and pedestrian at times (as when he overexplains), at other times it is sparse and poetic. His typical mode of narration—focusing all data through a first or second-person persona—generally facilitates his effective presentation of the concrete.

The universe challenges us, Clarke believes, by its inexhaustible beauty, strangeness, and richness. Unless we rise to the challenge by keeping our curiosity and extending our environment, both our art and our science will stagnate. The scientist is as likely to lack the necessary vision and spirit of adventure as the humanist; the romantic maverick is Clarke's protagonist. The eternal renewal of childhood in a never-ending expansion into the unknown is Clarke's theme.

—Curtis C. Smith

CLARKE, Austin C(hesterfield). Barbadian. Born in Barbados, 26 July 1934. Educated at Combermere Boys' School, Barbados; Harrison's College, Barbados; Trinity College, University of Toronto. Married Betty Joyce Reynolds in 1957; three children. Free-lance producer and broadcaster, Canadian Broadcasting Corporation, Toronto, from 1963; scriptwriter, Educational Television, Toronto; Ziskind Professor of Literature, Brandeis University, Waltham, Massachusetts, 1968–69; Hoyt Fellow, 1968, and Visiting Lecturer, 1969, 1970, Yale University, New Haven, Connecticut; Fellow, Indiana University School of Letters, Bloomington, 1969; Margaret Bundy Scott Visiting Professor of Literature, Williams College, Williamstown, Massachusetts, 1971; Lecturer, Duke University, Durham, North Carolina, 1971–72; Visiting Professor, University of Texas, Austin, 1973–74; Cultural and Press Attaché, Embassy of Barbados, Washington, D.C., 1974–75. Former General Manager, Caribbean Broadcasting Corporation, St. Michael, Barbados. Member, Board of Trustees, Rhode Island School of Design, Providence, 1970–75. Since 1984, Vice-Chairman, Board of Censors, Ontario. Recipient: Belmont Short Story Award, 1965; University of Western Ontario President's Medal, 1966; Canada Council Senior Arts Fellowship, 1967, 1970, and grant, 1977; Casa de las Americas prize, 1980. Agent: Harold Ober Associates, 40 East 49th Street, New York, New York 10017, U.S.A. Address: 432 Brunswick Avenue, Toronto, Ontario M5R 2Z4, Canada.

PUBLICATIONS

Novels

The Survivors of the Crossing. Toronto, McClelland and Stewart, and London, Heinemann, 1964.
Amongst Thistles and Thorns. Toronto, McClelland and Stewart, and London, Heinemann, 1965.
The Meeting Point. Toronto, Macmillan, and London, Heinemann, 1967; Boston, Little Brown, 1972.

Storm of Fortune.   Boston, Little Brown, 1973.
The Bigger Light.   Boston, Little Brown, 1975.
The Prime Minister.   Toronto, General, 1977; London, Routledge, 1978.

Short Stories

When He Was Free and Young and He Used to Wear Silks. Toronto, Anansi, 1971; revised edition, Boston, Little Brown, 1973.
When Women Rule.   Toronto, McClelland and Stewart, 1985.

Uncollected Short Stories

"I Hanging On, Praise God," in *From the Green Antilles*, edited by Barbara Howes.   New York, Macmillan, 1966; London, Souvenir Press, 1967.
"The Woman with the BBC Voice," in *Tamarack Review* (Toronto), 1966.
"Why Didn't You Use a Plunger," in *Tamarack Review* (Toronto), 1969.
"A Wedding in Toronto," in *Tamarack Review* (Toronto), 1970.
"What Happened?," in *Prejudice*, edited by Charles R. Larson.   New York, New American Library, 1971.
"They Heard the Ringing of Bells," in *Toronto Short Stories*, edited by Morris Wolfe and Douglas Daymond.   New York, Doubleday, 1977.

Other

The Confused Bewilderment of Martin Luther King and the Idea of Non-Violence as a Political Tactic.   Burlington, Ontario, Watkins, 1968.
Growing Up Stupid under the Union Jack: A Memoir.   Toronto, McClelland and Stewart, 1980.

*

Manuscript Collection: McMaster University, Hamilton, Ontario.

Critical Studies: "The West Indian Novel in North America: A Study of Austin Clarke" by Lloyd W. Brown, in *Journal of Commonwealth Literature* (Leeds), July 1970; interview with Graeme Gibson, in *Eleven Canadian Novelists*, Toronto, Anansi, 1974; "An Assessment of Austin Clarke, West Indian-Canadian Novelist" by Keith Henry in *CLA Journal* (Atlanta), vol. 29, no. 1, 1985.

Austin C. Clarke comments:

Whenever I am asked to give a statement about my work I find it difficult to do. All I can say in these situations is that I try to write about a group of people, West Indian immigrants (to Canada), whose life interests me because of the remarkable problems of readjustment, and the other problems of ordinary living. The psychological implications of this kind of life are what make my work interesting and I hope relevant to the larger condition of preservation. The themes are usually those of adjustment, as I have said, but this adjustment is artistically rendered in the inter-relationship of the two predominant groups of which I write: the host Jewish–Anglo Saxon group, and the black group (West Indian and expatriate black American).

*   *   *

Generally the discussion of West Indian fiction tends to focus exclusively on work written in England and the Caribbean. But the growing number of West Indian immigrants in Canada, especially over the last two decades, has given rise to a small but increasingly significant body of West Indian literature in that country. On the whole, West Indian literature in Canada is dominated by the predictable and familiar themes of exile, but the theme is integrated here with the West Indian's response to Canada's much-touted ideal of a cultural mosaic—the notion that the country is, or ought to be, a harmonious aggregation of distinctive cultures which maintain their distinctiveness while blending with each other to create a diversified cultural whole.

But for West Indians the ideal of a cultural mosaic is not quite as simple as it sounds to the Anglo-Canadians who often espouse it. Given the usual disadvantages of being black in a predominantly white society, West Indians must choose between being integrated into a strange culture—at the cost of their cultural uniqueness and racial integrity—or being so dedicated to maintaining their black, West Indian identity that they risk being cultural and economic outsiders in their adopted homeland. This dilemma, one that is explored by the growing number of writers in Canada, dominates the writings of Austin C. Clarke, unquestionably the major West Indian writer in Canada at this time.

These Canadian issues are not the major concern in his earliest novels, or in his most recent. *The Survivors of the Crossing* and *Amongst Thistles and Thorns* are set in Barbados and they explore the twin evils of colonial self-hatred and Caribbean poverty. *The Prime Minister* is centered on the experiences of a West Indian writer, John Moore, who has returned to Barbados, to a government appointment, after 20 years in Canada. Significantly, Moore does not stay in Barbados: he returns to his Canadian home after discovering, to his mortification, that he no longer has a real place in Barbados.

Moore's experiences can be viewed as a paradigm of West Indians including Clarke himself, now living and writing in Canada. And it is logical enough that the Canadian presence dominates Clarke's fiction as a whole. His first collection of short stories includes works which take a close look at Canada as the West Indians' El Dorado. In "They Heard a Ringing of Bells" a group of West Indians discuss their experiences as immigrants—delighting in the sense of being released from Caribbean poverty while lambasting the hostility and indifference of white Canada to the West Indian presence. "Waiting for the Postman to Knock" is less ambivalent, more openly hostile to the adopted homeland. Enid, the heroine, is one of the most typical and enduring symbols of West Indian life in Canada—the lonely and isolated West Indian domestic servant who feels equally exploited by her white employer and by her West Indian lover (if she is lucky enough to find a lover). For other West Indians in Clarke's short fiction the problems of loneliness are compounded by racial self-hatred, especially in the lives of those who are achieving some degree of economic success at the cost of their racial pride or cultural integrity ("Four Stations in His Circle" and "The Motor Car").

These related themes of loneliness, self-hatred, and cultural exclusion are the main concerns of Clarke's Canadian trilogy, *The Meeting Point, Storm of Fortune,* and *The Bigger Light.* The three works center on the lives of a group of West Indians in Toronto—especially Bernice Leach, her sister Estelle, Boysie Cumberbatch, his wife Dots, and Henry White. *The Meeting*

Point concentrates on Bernice's experiences as a maid in the home of the wealthy Burrmann family, and emphasizes the usual themes of sexual loneliness, cultural isolation, and the sense of economic exploitation.

Storm of Fortune shifts the focus to Estelle and her somewhat uneven struggle to gain a toehold in Canada. The novel also traces the failures of Henry White and his subsequent death, and, most important of all, it depicts the gradual emergence of Boysie Cumberbatch, from shiftless *bon vivant* to ambitious small businessman with his own janitorial company. His success-story is continued in *The Bigger Light* which, despite some uneven writing, remains Clarke's most ambitious novel to date. Having devoted much of the preceding novels to the failures and half-successes in the West Indian community, Clarke concentrates here on a successful man, but one whose economic successes have not protected him from emotional failure (the gradual breakdown of his marriage and his increasing isolation from his less fortunate West Indian friends). And in fact his success as a *Canadian* businessman, in the Anglo–Saxon mould, has had the effect of encouraging a certain snobbery and a marked reserve towards matters of cultural and racial significance. In short he becomes increasingly hostile towards the issue of racial identity.

But in spite of his extreme and increasing isolation in the novel, Boysie is not an entire failure as a human being. His very isolation becomes a catalyst for a certain perceptiveness which allows him to recognize the real nature of his choices and the limitations of the world in which he has chosen to live. And as a consequence he remains the typical Austin Clarke protagonist, one whose failures—economic and moral—are counterbalanced by a persistent ability to perceive their own lives, without self-deception or self-pity, as they really are. Given the persistent hostilities of the world in which they live, this kind of honest self-awareness is the most important quality of all—and Austin Clarke invariably presents and invites judgements on his characters on the basis of their ability to achieve such an awareness.

These themes of isolation and self-conflict have increasingly been integrated with the issue of Canadian society and Canadian identity in Clarke's more recent writing. Canada is no longer a temporary (and deeply resented) resting-place for immigrants with a strong sense of *transience*. Clarke's fictional world, in his second collection of short stories, *When Women Rule*, is firmly located in the much touted Canadian ideal of the social mosaic. These are stories about immigrants from Europe (Italians, "displaced" Central and Eastern Europeans), as well as from the Caribbean. They are almost all about middle-aged men whose familiar anxieties about aging, sexual relationships, and socio-economic success are interwoven with pervasive uncertainties about the directions of Canadian society—about the disruptive and challenging presence of "newer" immigrants, urban changes in metropolitan Canada, and the unsettling implications of female equality. And in one story, "Give It a Shot," these fears are shared even by a born-and-bred "Anglo–Canadian." Indeed, it is the central irony of this collection that the very idea of a Canadian mosaic, with its implicit promise of social harmony and individual success, binds Clarke's diverse Canadians together by virtue of its failure, rather than its fulfilment, in their lives. The ebullience and aggressive confidence of a Boysie Cumberbatch have given way to a middle-aged greyness, the newcomer's perpetual sense of youthfulness has been replaced by a depressing, numbing consciousness of death and aging. Canada, and the youthful idealism of its "mosaic" self-image, seem to have aged prematurely, like the anxious men who live and work in the anonymous apartment buildings of Clarke's Toronto.

Finally, it is noteworthy that Clarke's Canadian themes actually re-emphasize the most central, and universal, of all his themes—alienation. In their alienation from society, family, and even from their once-youthful selves, his middle-aged protagonists are the familiar isolates of much 20th-century fiction, ranging—in Clarke's work—from the canefields of Barbados to the chic boutiques and working-class bars of modern Toronto. And by way of emphasizing Clarke's insistence on the universality of alienation, it is only necessary to move from *When Women Rule* to his autobiography, *Growing Up Stupid under the Union Jack*. The title is no mere whimsy. The imperial reference sets the cultural theme—boyhood and adolescence in colonial Barbados. But the key word here is "stupid." It suggests the naivety, the stunted self-consciousness of the (well educated) colonial, a culturally ingrained, institutionally enforced ignorance of one's history, society, and ethnicity. And, drawing on the Caribbean connotations of "stupid/tchupidness," it connotes absurdity as well as mental dullness. The colonial situation is the essence of the absurd because it both causes and symbolizes the condition of being isolated from one's self, one's cultural and personal roots. To be a colonial is therefore to be both the unique product of a concrete, specific process—colonial culture—and another archetype of 20th-century alienation. "Tchupidness" is simultaneously a Caribbean condition and a universal experience.

—Lloyd W. Brown

CLEARY, Jon (Stephen). Australian. Born in Sydney, New South Wales, 22 November 1917. Educated at Marist Brothers School, Randwick, New South Wales, 1924–32. Served in the Australian Imperial Forces in the Middle East and New Guinea, 1940–45. Married Constantine Lucas in 1946; two daughters. Prior to 1939 worked as a commercial traveller, bush worker, and commercial artist. Since 1945, full-time writer. Journalist, Government of Australia News and Information Bureau, in London, 1948–49, and in New York, 1949–51. Recipient: Australian Broadcasting Commission prize, for radio drama, 1944; Australian Section Prize, *New York Herald-Tribune* World Short Story Contest, 1950; Crouch Gold Medal, 1950; Mystery Writers of America Edgar Allan Poe Award, 1974. Lives in New South Wales. Agent: John Farquharson Ltd., 162–168 Regent Street, London W1R 5TB. Address: c/o William Collins Ltd., 8 Grafton Street, London W1X 3LA, England.

PUBLICATIONS

Novels

You Can't See Around Corners. New York, Scribner, 1947; London, Eyre and Spottiswoode, 1949.
The Long Shadow. London, Laurie, 1949.
Just Let Me Be. London, Laurie, 1950.
The Sundowners. New York, Scribner, and London, Laurie, 1952.
The Climate of Courage. London, Collins, 1954; as *Naked in the Night*, New York, Popular Library, 1955.
Justin Bayard. London, Collins, 1955; New York, Morrow, 1956; as *Dust in the Sun*, New York, Popular Library, 1957.
The Green Helmet. London, Collins, 1957; New York, Morrow, 1958.

Back of Sunset. New York, Morrow, and London, Collins, 1959.
North from Thursday. London, Collins, 1960; New York, Morrow, 1961.
The Country of Marriage. New York, Morrow, and London, Collins, 1962.
Forests of the Night. New York, Morrow, and London, Collins, 1963.
A Flight of Chariots. New York, Morrow, 1963; London, Collins, 1964.
The Fall of an Eagle. New York, Morrow, 1964; London, Collins, 1965.
The Pulse of Danger. New York, Morrow, and London, Collins, 1966.
The High Commissioner. New York, Morrow, and London, Collins, 1966.
The Long Pursuit. New York, Morrow, and London, Collins, 1967.
Season of Doubt. New York, Morrow, and London, Collins, 1968.
Remember Jack Hoxie. New York, Morrow, and London, Collins, 1969.
Helga's Web. New York, Morrow, and London, Collins, 1970.
The Liberators. New York, Morrow, 1971; as *Mask of the Andes*, London, Collins, 1971.
The Ninth Marquess. New York, Morrow, 1972; as *Man's Estate*, London, Collins, 1972.
Ransom. New York, Morrow, and London, Collins, 1973.
Peter's Pence. New York, Morrow, and London, Collins, 1974.
The Safe House. New York, Morrow, and London, Collins, 1975.
A Sound of Lightning. New York, Morrow, and London, Collins, 1976.
High Road to China. New York, Morrow, and London, Collins, 1977.
Vortex. London, Collins, 1977; New York, Morrow, 1978.
The Beaufort Sisters. New York, Morrow, and London, Collins, 1979.
A Very Private War. New York, Morrow, and London, Collins, 1980.
The Golden Sabre. New York, Morrow, and London, Collins, 1981.
The Faraway Drums. London, Collins, 1981; New York, Morrow, 1982.
Spearfield's Daughter. London, Collins, 1982; New York, Morrow, 1983.
The Phoenix Tree. London, Collins, 1984.
The City of Fading Lights. London, Collins, 1985; New York, Morrow, 1986.

Short Stories

These Small Glories. Sydney, Angus and Robertson, 1946.
Pillar of Salt. Sydney, Horwitz, 1963.

Plays

Strike Me Lucky (produced Bromley, Kent, 1963).

Screenplays: *The Siege of Pinchgut*, with Harry Watt and Alexander Baron, 1959; *The Green Helmet*, 1961; *The Sundowners*, 1961; *Sidecar Racers* (*Sidecar Boys*), 1975.

Radio Play: *Safe Horizon*, 1944.

Television Plays: *Just Let Me Be*, 1957 (UK); *Bus Stop* series (2 episodes), 1961 (USA); *Spearfield's Daughter*, from his own novel, 1985 (USA).

*

Jon Cleary comments:
I write primarily to entertain, but, having stated that, I also write to inform about the world we live in. I have no overall theme, unless it is to affirm my belief that Man can, somehow, overcome the effects of his own disasters. I do my best not to be categorised, mainly because I want to keep fresh my enthusiasm for writing; but I'm afraid critics tend to overlook those books (such as *The Country of Marriage* and *The City of Fading Lights*) in which I do not write about adventure in exotic places and I'm resigned now to being classified as an "adventure" writer. I have a principle that I will not write about a place I have not visited—this involves me in a lot of travel and is, I hope, opening me up for a book or two of wider scope in the future. I am, I suppose, an old-fashioned story-teller—but I feel that stories, combining action with character, will always be read. I hope so—the job opportunities for out-of-work novelists in their late sixties are not too numerous.

*   *   *

Jon Cleary's conviction that he has been virtually "classified as an 'adventure' writer" despite books like *The Country of Marriage* and *Remember Jack Hoxie* should not come as a surprise. The great bulk of his work does, after all, invite such a classification: his characters confront ill-fortune, the elements, physical dangers, and personal ordeals in places as separated and contrasting as Bhutan and the Australian outback, New Guinea and Beirut. Yet it is in those relatively few novels in which neither locale nor the excitement of suspenseful action is paramount that Clearly does some of his best work.

He has a sensitive understanding of the fractional shifts in mood, the alterations in psychological atmosphere, the delicacy of the thread of communication that characterize—yet also in certain circumstances bedevil—the relationship between man and woman, and more particularly, husband and wife. Equally, he seems intuitively to grasp, and to be able to evoke with tact and controlled inference, that sense of the enduringly passionate undercurrent in successful love relationships; a passion which persists despite tangible and external vicissitudes. These are qualities which make *The Country of Marriage* such an impressive achievement; they also contribute significantly to the impact of *The Sundowners* which, for all its picaresque and unsophisticated sprawl, remains one of Cleary's most engaging successes—a Lawsonian picture of, among other things, a marriage weathering crises which are partly induced by the very nature of the "place," the bush environment.

But the full range of Cleary's work reveals emphatically that action not only suits his pen—he describes scenes of action with enormous zest and tough economy—but also his temperament. He is attracted to movement, suspense, resolution through decisive action. And it is this preoccupation which comes to predominate in his work. *Justin Bayard* is one of several novels in which conflicting forces in Cleary's artistic sensibility become evident: on the one hand there is a concern with marital tension, with the power of love and sexual passion to surmount external difficulties and with the alienating, corrosive effect of the outback upon the personality. On the other hand, the book is a disguised "country house thriller": the protagonists are virtually marooned in a homestead while evil and, ultimately, murder work among them. Violent action decides or overwhelms most of the personal dilemmas in Cleary's novels and resolves the human issues not by allowing them to be worked out but, as it were, by default.

Action and adventure, flavoured by exotic or dramatic geographical settings, thus emerge as important distinguishing features of Cleary's growing output. A characteristic Cleary "hero" evolves: a man of action plagued by an inner tentativeness, a fear of decision and responsibility. Paddy Carmody (*The Sundowners*), Vern Radcliffe (*The Climate of Courage*), Justin Bayard, Paul Tancred (*Season of Doubt*), Jack Marquis (*The Pulse of Danger*), Adam Nash (*The Country of Marriage*) are all recognizably in this mould. Scobie Malone, however—the hero of *The High Commissioner*, *Helga's Web* and *Ransom* —is not. And perhaps this is as good a way as any of pointing to the change that has come over Cleary's work in the last decade or so. He has dropped into his stride as a fully equipped writer of popular fiction. He is skilful in the economical creation of character, his plots are inventive without being outlandish, and he knows how to manipulate narrative pace. He is also very witty on occasions. Equally, he has an eye for the world stage as a source for fiction: the IRA (*Peter's Pence*), Third World tensions (*The Liberators*), political kidnap (*Ransom*), the resurgent interest in surviving Nazis (*The Safe House*) and, most recently and compulsively topical, a story that goes back to the last days of the war with Japan and the disasters of Hiroshima and Nagasaki (*The Phoenix Tree*). Cleary is extraordinarily prolific: *The Golden Sabre*, *The Faraway Drums*, and *Spearfield's Daughter* are all relatively recent and predate *The Phoenix Tree*. Yet, for all his high productivity, he remains a graceful and conscientious writer. *The Phoenix Tree*, as much as any of the Cleary novels that precedes it, has many finely wrought passages and memorable descriptions. Cleary has long since found his niche in the forefront of modern adventure writers but he has not sacrificed either his craftsmanship or his individuality in the process.

—Brian E. Matthews

COETZEE, J(ohn) M(ichael). South African. Born in Cape Town, 9 February 1940. Educated at the University of Cape Town, B.A. 1960, M.A. 1963; University of Texas, Austin, Ph.D. 1969. Married in 1963 (divorced, 1980); one son and one daughter. Applications programmer, IBM, London, 1962–63; systems programmer, International Computers, Bracknell, Berkshire, 1964–65; Assistant Professor, 1968–71, and Butler Professor of English, 1984, State University of New York, Buffalo. Lecturer, 1972–83, and since 1984, Professor of General Literature, University of Cape Town. Hinkley Professor of English, Johns Hopkins University, Baltimore, 1986. Recipient: CNA award 1978, 1980, 1983; James Tait Black Memorial Prize, 1980; Faber Memorial Award, 1980; Booker Prize, 1983; Fémina prize (France), 1985. D.Litt.: University of Strathclyde, Glasgow, 1985. Life Fellow, University of Cape Town. Agent: Murray Pollinger, 4 Garrick Street, London WC2E 9BH, England. Address: P.O. Box 92, Rondebosch, Cape Province 7700, South Africa.

PUBLICATIONS

Novels

Dusklands (two novellas). Johannesburg, Ravan Press, 1974; London, Secker and Warburg, 1982; New York, Viking, 1985.
In the Heart of the Country. Johannesburg, Ravan Press, and London, Secker and Warburg, 1977; as *From the Heart of the Country*, New York, Harper, 1977.
Waiting for the Barbarians. London, Secker and Warburg, 1980; New York, Penguin, 1982.
Life and Times of Michael K. London, Secker and Warburg, 1983; New York, Viking, 1984.

Other

Translator, *A Posthumous Confession*, by Marcellus Emants. Boston, Twayne, 1976.
Translator, *The Expedition to the Baobab Tree*, by Wilma Stockenström. Johannesburg, Ball, 1983; London, Faber, 1984.

*   *   *

J.M. Coetzee's first book, *Dusklands*, foreshadowed the main direction and emphasis of his work. *Dusklands* consists of two novellas, one set in the U.S. State Department during the Vietnam era, while the other gives accounts of exploration and conquest by, in particular, one Jacobus Coetzee in southern Africa of the 1760's. Very different in setting, and 200 years apart in time, they are juxtaposed to offer a scarifying account of the fear and paranoia of imperialists and aggressors and the horrifying ways in which dominant regimes, "empires," commit violence against "the other" through repression, torture, and genocide. In the first novella, "The Vietnam Project," Eugene Dawn, an expert in psychological warfare, sees himself as engaged in "a liberating creative act" while he is in fact a cog in the wheel of the contemporary United States machinery of destruction. The stresses of his project and his own associated psychological disturbances eventually drive him to kidnap and murder his own child. While Coetzee's work is firmly grounded in the violence and oppression of the South African situation out of which he writes, he regards it as "only one manifestation of a wider historical situation to do with colonialism, late colonialism, neo-colonialism."

Dusklands also shows Coetzee's interest in the interplay between fiction and fact, author and subject, and in the importance of text and intertextuality. He is concerned with "dissecting" the "myths of our culture" and has engaged in a complex intertextual dialogue with Defoe's *Robinson Crusoe* as part of this demythologising process. South Africa is usually the implied geographical and/or political setting of his novels, but whether his works are set in the past, the present, or the future, the desert is the pervading landscape. This provides an isolation comparable with that of the shipwrecked Robinson Crusoe, but one which produces very different results on individuals and even societies. Like Crusoe, Jacobus Coetzee must subdue the land and the people who inhabit it; but he does so by inflicting torture and death on the desert peoples who he feels have humiliated him and thwarted his imperial purpose. Magda, of *In the Heart of the Country* is obsessed, like Crusoe, with her father, but this obsession issues in violent fantasies in which she must destroy him in order to communicate with the servant-slaves, Klein Anna and Heindrick. Like Crusoe she realises that the isolate "must turn himself into an adventure," in her case the adventure of rejecting the "dangerous absolutism," of the "freedom in which to become god." The officials of the Empire in *Waiting for the Barbarians* live in armed dread of the pathetic barbarian footprints in the sand. Their entire *raison d'être* is aggression toward a "barbarian" enemy which has little reality outside their own projections. Only for Michael K of *Life and Times of Michael K* does the desert briefly bloom. More a persecuted Friday that a Crusoe imperialist, K has little time, however, to enjoy the fruits of his isolation before society attacks his peace. Coetzee thus rewrites the archetypal myth of Robinson Crusoe to comment on the nature of imperialism and colonialism, the conquest of "virgin" territory, the persecution of "the other," and the nature of totalitarian regimes. For Coetzee, too, the desert image has special relevance for South Africa in terms of "a lack of society and a lack of shared culture, a feeling of anomie, a feeling of solitariness, a feeling of not having human ties with the people around one."

In the Heart of the Country is narrated by the white South African spinster, Magda, who fantasises various bloody ways of disposing of the father with whom she lives on an isolated farm, and entering a new relationship, one not based on a gun and race superiority, with her erstwhile servants. But she cannot really dispose of the father or forge such a relationship however much she fictionally recreates her life. The "ghostly brown figures of the last people I knew" eventually abandon her. In this world where historical hatred and conflicts are irreconcilable, she cannot escape the polarities enshrined in the system to become "neither master nor slave, neither parent nor child but the bridge between."

Though the setting of *Waiting for the Barbarians* is unspecified, the novel can, like the earlier works, be read as a political fable of South Africa. A sympathetic but ineffectual liberal humanist, the narrator magistrate governs a frontier settlement at the edges of empire. A well-meaning man, he is nevertheless implicated in "the system" and is no match for the neo-Fascist torturer, Colonel Joll, who persecutes the few pathetic "barbarians" (actually from a local fishing tribe) the Empire has succeeded in capturing. The barbarians are almost invisible, being largely a product of that nameless fear that haunts all conquering empires. The Empire is threatened from within, not from without, but it projects its paranoia onto the unknown "other." The barbarians remain unknown, and neither Joll's brutalities nor the magistrate's feeble attempts at love and restitution can bring them closer.

If the earlier narratives are recounted from the perspectives of those who are implicated in the imperial purpose, most of *Life and Times of Michael K* is told from the perspective of those it controls. Michael K attempts, in this highly political novel, to live outside politics and history. As is clear in Coetzee's earlier work, the "real heroes" are those who attempt to escape history, not those who connive in its making. Formerly a gardener in Cape Town, Michael K attempts to return his dying mother by makeshift cart to the farm of her childhood. She dies during the journey, but her son continues to the destination with her ashes. Here he is insulated from the civil and military terror that are both cause and effect of the breakdown of social order. In complete isolation he is able to discover the joys of cultivation. Though his desert produce barely allows him to subsist it offers a thoroughly magnificent apprehension of life and living. Predictably his painful desert idyll is terminated when he is captured and incarcerated as a guerrilla, but his sense of that one "tip of vivid green," the potential of life outside a corrupt society and even outside the casual and violent compassion of other fringe dwellers remains with him to the end.

Though complex and disorienting, Coetzee's novels are brilliant allegories (or quasi-allegories to use George Lamming's term), fables whose South African roots demythologise and decode the historical and contemporary myths of imperialism.

—H.M. Tiffin

COHEN, Leonard (Norman). Canadian. Born in Montreal, Quebec, 21 September 1934. Educated at McGill University, Montreal, B.A. 1955; Columbia University, New York. Composer and singer: has given concerts in Canada, the United States, and Europe. Artist-in-Residence, University of Alberta, Edmonton, 1975–76. Recipient: McGill University literary award, 1956; Canada Council award, 1960; CBC award, 1962; Quebec literary award, 1964. D.Litt.: Dalhousie University, Halifax, Nova Scotia, 1971. Lives in Montreal. Address: c/o McClelland and Stewart Ltd., 25 Hollinger Road, Toronto, Ontario M4B 3G2, Canada.

PUBLICATIONS

Novels

The Favorite Game. New York, Viking Press, and London, Secker and Warburg, 1963.
Beautiful Losers. Toronto, McClelland and Stewart, and New York, Viking Press, 1966; London, Cape, 1970.

Uncollected Short Stories

"Barbers and Lovers," in *Ingluvin 2* (Montreal), January-March 1961.
"Trade," in *Tamarack Review* (Toronto), Summer 1961.
"Luggage Fire Sale," in *Partisan Review* (New Brunswick, New Jersey), Winter 1961.
"Charles Axis," in *The Single Voice*, edited by Jerome Charyn. New York, Collier, 1969.

Plays

The New Step (produced Ottawa and London, 1972). Included in *Flowers for Hitler*, 1964; in *Selected Poems*, 1968.
Sisters of Mercy: A Journey into the Words and Music of Leonard Cohen (produced Niagara-on-the-Lake, Ontario, and New York, 1973).
A Man Was Killed, with Irving Layton, in *Canadian Theatre Review* (Downsview, Ontario), Spring 1977.

Verse

Let Us Compare Mythologies. Montreal, Contact Press, 1956.
The Spice-Box of Earth. Toronto, McClelland and Stewart, 1961; New York, Viking Press, 1965; London, Cape, 1971.
Flowers for Hitler. Toronto, McClelland and Stewart, 1964; London, Cape, 1973.
Parasites of Heaven. Toronto, McClelland and Stewart, 1966.
Selected Poems 1956–1968. New York, Viking Press, 1968; London, Cape, 1969.
Leonard Cohen's Song Book. New York, Collier, 1969.
Five Modern Canadian Poets, with others, edited by Eli Mandel. Toronto, Holt Rinehart, 1970.
The Energy of Slaves. London, Cape, 1972; New York, Viking Press, 1973.

Songs of Love and Hate.   London, Wise, 1972.
New Skin for the Old Ceremony.   New York, Amsco, 1975.
Death of a Lady's Man.   Toronto, McClelland and Stewart,
   1978; London, Deutsch, and New York, Viking Press, 1979.
Two Views/Seven Poems, lithographs by Gigino Falconi.
   Toronto, Madison Gallery, 1980.
Book of Mercy.   Toronto, McClelland and Stewart, London,
   Cape, and New York, Villard, 1984.

Recordings: *The Songs of Leonard Cohen*, 1968, *Songs from
a Room*, 1969, *Songs of Love and Hate*, 1971, *Live Songs*,
1973, *New Skin for the Old Ceremony*, 1974, and *The Best
of Leonard Cohen*, 1975, all Columbia; *Death of a Lady's Man*,
Warner Brothers, 1977; *Recent Songs*, CBS, 1979; *Various
Positions*, CBS, 1985.

*

Bibliography: by Bruce Whiteman, in *The Annotated Bibliography of Canada's Major Authors 2* edited by Robert Lecker
and Jack David, Downsview, Ontario, ECW Press, 1980.

Manuscript Collection: Fisher Library, University of Toronto.

Critical Studies: *Leonard Cohen* by Michael Ondaatje, Tor-
onto, McClelland and Stewart, 1970; *The Immoral Moralists:
Hugh MacLennan and Leonard Cohen* by Patricia Morley, Tor-
onto, Clarke Irwin, 1972; *Leonard Cohen: The Artist and His
Critics* edited by Michael Gnarowski, Toronto, McGraw Hill
Ryerson, 1976; *Leonard Cohen* by Stephen Scobie, Vancouver,
Douglas and McIntyre, 1978.

*   *   *

Few modern authors have presented critics so clearly as Leonard Cohen does with the problem of how to regard the writer
who personifies the Zeitgeist. With astonishing rapidity, in the
mid-1960's, Cohen passed from the obscurity of a romantic
Canadian poet into the celebrity of an international pop singer
who seemed to exemplify the decade's popular culture.

Time will decide how far, when fashion abandons him,
Cohen's real qualities will sustain his standing as a writer. What
the critic perceives even now is that the factors which made
Cohen popular are those he shares with modish culture: conventionalism masquerading as independence; a slightly acrid
romanticism merging into a solipsistic sentimentality; an echoing of past movements like the Decadence, Art Nouveau and
Dada, which elevated style above substance. The fiction such
movements have produced has usually been strained and eccentric. *The Picture of Dorian Gray*, the novels of Huysmans and,
later, Raymond Queneau, are examples.

Cohen stands in this company; his novels, *The Favorite Game*
and *Beautiful Losers*, are interesting examples of black
romance, and though *Beautiful Losers* projects a bizarre kind
of splendour, as the novels of poets often do, it is a work
of solitary fantasy that standards apart from the main stream
of fiction in our time.

A shallowness of feeling, a solipsistic passionlessness masquerading as stylized passion, infects almost all of Cohen's
writings. It is linked with the Pygmalion urge that is a dominant
theme in his novels, exemplified in F.'s delusions of godly crea-
tiveness in *Beautiful Losers* and in the fantasies of occult power
that haunt Breavman throughout *The Favorite Game*. "I want
to touch people like a magician," he says to one of his mistresses, "to change them or hurt them, leave my brand, make
them beautiful."

To be beautiful, and to be a loser; both desires find their
places in the romantic fancy; their juxtaposition in the title
of Cohen's second novel is neither accidental nor inappropriate. The solipsist creates beauty within the mind and that
is his only real world; he loses because the actual world does
not correspond with his visionary world yet impinges on his
life. F., the quasi-hero of *Beautiful Losers*, lives in flamboyant
style; he is killed, in true decadent tradition, by syphilis.

Cohen's first novel, *The Favorite Game*, tells the development of a rich Montreal Jewish boy into a poet and folk singer;
the resemblances to Cohen's life are close enough to justify
an assumption that this is the autobiographical novel with which
many writers make their finest sacrifice to the muse of fiction.
The Favorite Game is an episodic work, its shuffled time
sequences strung along the thread of Breavman's affair with
the all-American girl, Shell, most recent of his mistresses; the
account of his experience becomes a kind of dialogue with
Shell, from whom in the end he parts, as he has parted from
her predecessors. His life has been measured off by relationships with girls, yet in none has Breavman been able to evade
in passion that observing mind which is the alien participant.

Parallel to these uninvolved liaisons runs the continuing current of Breavman's friendship with Krantz, which survives all
the broken love affairs. But the moment of real involvement
comes when, working as a staff member in a Jewish summer
camp, Breavman encounters the boy Martin, "a divine idiot"
with a mathematical mania who spends his time counting grass
blades and pine needles, and dies grotesquely when he is
crushed by a bulldozer while killing and counting mosquitoes
in a marsh.

Martin represents the other pole in Cohen's world to profane
love. He is—albeit in disguise—of the company of saints, those
exalted and obsessed ones to whom Cohen is always drawn.
Destroyed saints appear often in his poems; Martin is one of
them. Yet he dies at the peak of joy, rating his days at "98
per cent"—and the joyful saint is always present in Cohen's
world:

Something about him so loves the world that he gives himself to the laws of gravity and chance. Far from flying
with the angels, he traces with the fidelity of a seismograph
needle the state of the solid bloody landscape. His house
is dangerous and finite, but he is at home in the world.
He can love the shapes of human beings, the fine and
twisted shapes of the human heart.

To the Cohen alive to the call of sainthood as the complement
of earthly love, the world takes on dual aspects. Breavman,
inexperienced, sees decay everywhere. "The works themselves
were corruption, the monuments were made of worms." But
in *Beautiful Losers*, when "I" puts the classic decadent point
about "the diamonds in the shit," F. replies, "It's all diamond."

It is the unity in duality of the erotic and the spiritual that
provides the bridge from *The Favorite Game* to *Beautiful
Losers*. But, though there are many ways in which—in details
of plot and imagery—the earlier novel anticipates its more
ambitious successor, *Beautiful Losers* moves into a quite different category. Young artist novels can only be written once,
and Cohen makes his escape in the same direction as Joyce,
in the aestheticist reconstruction of life. *Beautiful Losers* is
very much a work of artifice, and makes no concession to verisimilitude.

Of the three parts into which this novel is divided, the first
contains the erratic musings of the onanist "I." Edith, his wife
who has committed bizarre suicide, and F., the megalomaniac
lover of them both, move in memory within a pattern which

F. describes when he declares, "I was your journey and you were my journey and Edith was our holy star." Whether they have ever existed is not important, since they are absorbed in a timeless dream continuum where they are no more and no less real, no more and no less distant, than the Mohawk saint, Catherine Tekakwitha, three centuries dead, whose monumental holy masochiscm fascinates both F. and "I." F. becomes an industrialist who uses his unmanned factory for playing games, a member of Parliament quickly discredited, a leader of the Quebec underground, but these achievements are no more substantial than the grandiose fantasies which, one eventually realises, are the products of a brain rotted by the pox.

This becomes evident in the wild inventions of the "Long Letter from F." In the central episode described in this document, F. and Edith, after packing "I" off on an absurd research assignment, set off for Argentina with a bag of erotic devices, and indulge in a long orgy in which they are ravished in turn by the "Danish vibrator" (a machine that develops and fulfils desires of its own) and finally bathe "three in a tub" with a waiter who provides human soap and turns out to be Hitler in exile.

Book III, an "Epilogue in the Third Person," closes with a description of the last dissolving days of "I," who has learnt to combine F.'s debauchery and Catherine Tekakwitha's self-mortifications in a regressive tree-house existence; he is saint and sinner, at once himself and F. and Edith, and he disappears in a puff of ambiguity.

Beautiful Losers is filled with interesting experiments, some of which belongs to poetry rather than fiction; indeed there are passages which are actually concealed verse. But the burlesque element is overdone and the savage sexual comedy quickly palls. As a novel the book has no functioning unity; Cohen lacks the architectonic power with which Céline, for example, transformed similar material into self-consistent and convincing works of fiction.

—George Woodcock

COHEN, Matt(hew). Canadian. Born in Kingston, Ontario, 30 December 1942. Educated at Fisher Park and Nepean high schools, Ottawa; University of Toronto, B.A. 1964, M.A. in political science 1965. Lecturer in Religion, McMaster University, Hamilton, Ontario, 1967–68; Writer-in-Residence, University of Alberta, Edmonton, 1975–76; Visiting Professor, University of Victoria, British Columbia, 1979–80; Writer-in-Residence, University of Western Ontario, London, 1981; has also taught at York University, Toronto, and University of Bologna, Italy. Chairman, Canadian Writers' Union, 1985–86. Recipient: Canada Arts Council Senior Award, 1977. Lives in Verona, Ontario. Address: c/o McClelland and Stewart Ltd., 25 Hollinger Road, Toronto, Ontario M4B 3G2, Canada.

PUBLICATIONS

Novels

Korsoniloff. Toronto, Anansi, 1969.
Johnny Crackle Sings. Toronto, McClelland and Stewart, 1971.

The Disinherited. Toronto, McClelland and Stewart, 1974.
Wooden Hunters. Toronto, McClelland and Stewart, 1975.
The Colours of War. Toronto, McClelland and Stewart, 1977; New York, Methuen, 1978.
The Sweet Second Summer of Kitty Malone. Toronto, McClelland and Stewart, 1979.
Flowers of Darkness. Toronto, McClelland and Stewart, 1981.
The Spanish Doctor. Toronto, McClelland and Stewart, 1984; New York, Beaufort, 1985.

Short Stories

Columbus and the Fat Lady and Other Stories. Toronto, Anansi, 1972.
Too Bad Galahad. Toronto, Coach House Press, 1972.
Night Flights: Stories New and Selected. New York, Doubleday, 1978.
The Expatriate: Collected Short Stories. Toronto, General, 1981; New York, Beaufort, 1983.
Café le dog. Toronto, McClelland and Stewart, 1983; London, Penguin, 1985; as *Life on This Planet and Other Stories*, New York, Beaufort, 1985.

Verse

Peach Melba. Toronto, Coach House Press, 1974.

Other

The Leaves of Louise (for children). Toronto, McClelland and Stewart, 1978.

Editor, *The Story So Far 2.* Toronto, Coach House Press, 1973.
Editor, with David Young, *The Dream Class Anthology: Writings from Toronto High Schools.* Toronto, Coach House Press, 1983.

*

Manuscript Collection: Mills Memorial Library, McMaster University, Hamilton, Ontario.

*   *   *

In Matt Cohen's first book, *Korsoniloff*, a narrator possessed of dual consciousness confronts the reader with themes taken up and variously treated in Cohen's later work: that of the opacity of a character with little or no self-knowledge, and whose inner forces have been "misaligned." The novella is the journal of a schizophrenic professor of philosophy, Andre Korsoniloff, whose surname represents his alter ego. He does not yet "exist in the world," since his opposing selves together form a man who is essentially "unwhole and without judgement"; a man who is, however, wittily aware of this division within himself. We see Korsoniloff in the same way that he sees other characters, as being self-possessed and without need, but his one violent act—disturbing the peace at his mistress's wedding—renders credible his subsequent fantasies of suicide and murder.

Korsoniloff's potential for eruption also underscores the pop-hero of *Johnny Crackle Sings*, a star who cultivates "condition zero," his personal term for a state approaching Nirvana, as a retreat from pressure and decision. Rock idol of screaming schoolchildren, Johnny Crackle, born Johnny Harper, moves aimlessly, withdrawing into drug-induced illusions rather than reacting, another Cohen character "born without any destiny at all." He seems only subliminally aware that the rural landscape to which he continually returns has a calming effect upon him. When he moves to urban environments or travels abroad, he sinks back into his state of suspended animation. He and his girl-friend Jenny are finally married, and have a son, also Johnny. Crackle, in describing his reaction to the birth, sums himself up too: "Afterwards it was almost like I hadn't been there except like watching a movie."

Characters of Cohen's other books suffer from an uncultivated "condition zero," or (if one takes seriously *Too Bad Galahad*, distinguished more by Margaret Hathaway's illustrations than Cohen's literary merits), admit the quest for a Holy Grail of one sort or another, though they must perish finding it.

Cohen's short stories collected in *Columbus and the Fat Lady* can be whimsical, self-conscious, or embarrassingly weak. He is at his best with acutely observed psychological detail, as in "Janice"; stories with magical or fantastic elements are his least successful.

The Disinherited states what, in embryonic form, other books and characters have pointed to. The title applies to most of the characters in this novel, in which various forces of dispossession are at work. While it concentrates on the slow death of farmer Richard Thomas, and the alienation felt by his city-dwelling son, the novel flashes continually back and forth through four generations: young Erik Thomas and his adopted brother Brian, his father, his grandfather Simon Thomas, and his great-grandfather Richard, whose relative, a poet from England, had come to Canada as though to Canaan, like "Abraham being sent to father a new race of men." But those who came after him have been unable to accept the vision he wished them to inherit. The poet's son is mentally retarded and an outcast in the same way that other characters have been cast out, through human inadequacy or legal disheritance, from real and metaphoric promised lands. Richard is dying, Erik is not fully alive. With Erik begins the new breed; unlike his father, uncle or grandfather there is no heroic stance for him to assume: "A man has to know his own destiny," says Richard. Erik replies: "No-one has destinies any more. They live in apartments and breed goldfish."

The first and last chapters are the most successful of this book; here the basic dichotomy between the two generations and kinds of men stands out most clearly. As the book opens, Richard Thomas begins to succumb to the illness that kills him in the last pages, and is for the first time aware of the microscopic unknown workings of his body, an experience he explores in seemingly timeless detail throughout the rest of the book. Nature is revealed to him in an immediate and alarming fashion as he lies on the ground integrated into the landscape—a position symbolic of what Cohen makes him stand for in the book; and Richard Thomas has recurring dreams of being rooted in earth, hands and arms as branches growing up and out from soil. In the final chapter Erik returns to Toronto after his father's death, forcibly struck by the extent of his alienation from the city, sucking in peripheral lives like his. From his high-rise apartment he looks down aimlessly on the city, dispossessed of the farm, indispensable to no-one, not in pain, not even searching, but beginning to believe in the need for something other. *The Disinherited* is Cohen's most accomplished book, but he has not yet achieved balance, the kind of perspective that would allow him, instead of insisting on obscure eddies, to concentrate on the main currents he is obviously equipped to handle.

The Sweet Second Summer of Kitty Malone continues, in order to reverse, Cohen's earlier methods and preoccupations.

The technique of rambling discourse and apparent digression is here a means towards a fine sense of organic time serenely apprehended. Middle age is not a prelude to the bitter winter of discontented and unfulfilled old age, but to the wisdom of uncynical experience as astonishing as an Indian Summer. Each character seems on the brink of "re-possession," an almost biblical dying to oneself in order to live. Thus Pat Frank loses the physical fight and is badly beaten, but wins understanding of himself and of Kitty. The major archetypes at the end of the novel are a simultaneous and almost indistinguishable funeral and wedding.

Cohen's latest novel, *The Spanish Doctor*, is almost entirely a tumid pot-boiler. The horrors experienced by the Jews in 14th-century Spain are vitiated by the swash and buckle of the plot and the unlikely antics of the protagonist Avram Halevi. Son of a Jewish woman raped by Christians, a scientist in an age of superstition, fatally attractive to women, he would be redeemed, and the novel too, if he were played by Woody Allen.

—Barrie Davies

COLE, Barry. British. Born in Woking, Surrey, 13 November 1936. Educated at Balham Secondary School, London. Served in the Royal Air Force, 1955–57. Married Rita Linihan in 1958; three daughters. Reporter, 1965–70, and since 1974, senior editor, Central Office of Information, London. Northern Arts Fellow, universities of Newcastle-upon-Tyne and Durham, 1970–72. Address: Central Office of Information, Room 401, Hercules Road, London S.E.1, England.

PUBLICATIONS

Novels

A Run Across the Island. London, Methuen, 1968.
Joseph Winter's Patronage. London, Methuen, 1969.
The Search for Rita. London, Methuen, 1970.
The Giver. London, Methuen, 1971.
Doctor Fielder's Common Sense. London, Methuen, 1972.

Verse

Blood Ties. London, Turret, 1967.
Ulysses in the Town of Coloured Glass. London, Turret, 1968.
Moonsearch. London, Methuen, 1968.
The Visitors. London, Methuen, 1970.
Vanessa in the City. London, Trigram Press, 1971.
Pathetic Fallacies. London, Eyre Methuen, 1973.
The Rehousing of Scaffardi. Richmond, Surrey, Keepsake Press, 1976.
Dedications. Nottingham, Byron Press, 1977.

*

Barry Cole comments:

I have no general statement to make about my novels, but the epigraphs which precede *The Giver* may say more than any collected exegeses:

And down I set, abruptly I believe; what I had heard all in my head. (Fielding).

Aesthetics cannot exist because an artist never solves any problems except those which are entirely of his own creation. (Jean-François Revel).
The thought of the epistolary diary had long interested and troubled me. (Nabokov).
Everyone should read a book; to read two books shows intelligence; to read three is showing off. (Rita Linihan, 15).
A poet is the most unpoetical of anything in existence, because he has no identity; he is continually in for, and filling, some other body . . . (Keats).
No Costaguanero had ever learned to question the eccentricities of a military force. (Conrad).
He spoke in English and pronounced even the name "Boris" as if it were English. (Turgenev).
. . . getting the disorder of one's own mind in order . . . (Yeats).
Let not the critic ask how Corporal Trim could come by all this . . . (Sterne).
The Commissioner gazed at them with suspicion, almost with revulsion. Then he fell to laughing. (Jorge Luis Borges).
There is something funny about the human condition, and civilized intelligence makes fun of its own ideas. (Saul Bellow).
But Hetty's face had a language that transcended her feelings. (George Eliot).
Is it only that? said the willow-wren;
It's that as well, said the stars. (W.H. Auden).
Themes and thimes and habit reburns. To flame in you. (Joyce).
"Were you drunk?" asked Pleasant. (Dickens).

*   *   *

Barry Cole's novels have one striking thing in common. They are extremely well-written. It may, of course, be said that to write well is not so much a virtue in a novelist as a necessity. Yet the fact is that the majority of novelists lack Cole's gifts of verbal precision, wit, exact ear for conversation, and his feeling for the elastic possibilities of language, the way it can be stretched and twisted to provide unexpected meanings and insights. No doubt the fact that he is also a very fine poet accounts for much of his virtue as a writer of prose, but this should not be taken to mean that he writes poetic prose. On the contrary: his style is as free as possible from those encrustations of adjective and epithet that identify "fine" writing.
A Run Across the Island is a brilliant *tour de force* and for it Cole invented a form that he has found it possible to use for all his subsequent novels. Although by far the larger part of the novel is seen through the eyes of its hero, Robert Haydon, there is no straightforward narrative or division into chapters. Instead, we move about in time, each remembered detail or incident given a section, small or large, that is juxtaposed against others. By the end of the novel, however, the different incidents have been worked out and together compose one man's life, and it has been so resourcefully done that we have a much more *real* sense of a man's identity than we would have through a straightforward narrative.
The major theme of *A Run Across the Island* is, perhaps, of loneliness, of the difficulties of establishing relationships, of the slippery impermanence of friendship and love. And this theme is also present in the next novel. *Joseph Winter's Patronage* is, however, very different from *A Run Across the Island* in that its characters are almost exclusively old people. Indeed, the novel is mostly set in an Old People's Home, and the novelist manages with great sensitivity to create the feeling of

the Home itself and of its inhabitants. *Joseph Winter's Patronage* is the most touching and warmly sympathetic novel that Barry Cole has so far written.
By contrast, *The Search for Rita* is the most glittering. It is an extremely elegant novel, but the elegance is not one that marks how far its author stands fastidiously aloof from life. It is rather that the mess of life is met by a keen-eyed wit that can be ironic, self-deprecatory, satiric, and bawdy by turns. Style means everything in a novel of this kind, and the novelist's style does not let him down.

—John Lucas

COLEGATE, Isabel. British.   Born in Lincolnshire, 10 September 1931. Educated at boarding schools in Shropshire and Norfolk. Married Michael Briggs in 1953; one daughter and two sons. Worked for Anthony Blond, literary agent, London, in the 1950's. Recipient: W.H. Smith Literary Award, 1981. Agent: A.D. Peters, 10 Buckingham Street, London WC2N 6BU. Address: c/o Hamish Hamilton Ltd., 57–59 Long Acre, London WC2E 9JZ, England.

PUBLICATIONS

Novels

The Blackmailer.   London, Blond, 1958.
A Man of Power.   London, Blond, 1960.
The Great Occasion.   London, Blond, 1962.
Statues in a Garden.   London, Bodley Head, 1964; New York, Knopf, 1966.
The Orlando Trilogy.   London, Penguin, 1984.
   Orlando King.   London, Bodley Head, 1968; New York, Knopf, 1969.
   Orlando at the Brazen Threshold.   London, Bodley Head, 1971.
   Agatha.   London, Bodley Head, 1973.
News from the City of the Sun.   London, Hamish Hamilton, 1979.
The Shooting Party.   London, Hamish Hamilton, 1980; New York, Viking Press, 1981.
A Glimpse of Sion's Glory.   London, Hamish Hamilton, and New York, Viking, 1985.

*   *   *

The English will never turn Communist, they're such snobs. An English Communist could have a duke at gunpoint; if he asked him to stay for the weekend he'd drop the gun and dash off to Moss Bros to hire a dinner-jacket. (*Agatha*)

Isabel Colegate's fiction dramatizes the English obsession with aristocracy, even in the 20th century when its traditional power was declining. Against a backdrop of post-World War II global unrest, Colegate's first three novels, *The Blackmailer*, *A Man of Power*, and *The Great Occasion*, depict both the aristocrats' alliances with new sources of power and their incomprehension of the welfare state: ". . . a five-day week, holidays with pay, pensions, free this, free that .... There's no sense of values" (*The Blackmailer*). Her later novels, *Statues in a Garden*, *The Orlando Trilogy*, and *The Shooting Party*, root these changes in the disintegrating world immediately before and after World War I. *The Blackmailer*, a "self-making" man of lower-middle-class origins, extorts money from Judith, widow of Korean War hero Anthony Lane, primarily because he wants an entree to Lane's ancestral home and family to complete his identification with the dead man. These thriller elements are not a sound basis for Colegate's social satire, but her comedy supports the anti-romantic ending triggered by Judith's class loyalties.

The protagonist of *A Man of Power*, Lewis Ogden, a capitalist of lower-middle-class origins who has also risen through wartime opportunities, plans to wed Lady Essex, an impoverished beauty because of her "mystery" and ability to reshape his image; his first wife and former secretary is inadequate to the role: "It's always the wives that give them away." Upperclass characters respond as much to Lewis's mystique as to his money: Essex's daughter Vanessa experiences a painful initiation into his chaotic world through her love for Lewis. (Like the charismatic tycoon and the society beauty, the vulnerable young girl is a staple of Colegate's world.) The novel's sentimentality does not permit a serious treatment of its themes, however.

The Great Occasion focuses on middle-class vulnerability as it interweaves the lives of magnate Gabriel Dobson, whose success stemmed partly from an upper-class wife, and of his five daughters in a world that rejects his business integrity and his daughters' talents and idealism: "... I expect she'll soon level down to the others." The tone wavers because of Colegate's mixing Waughesque comedy with family saga, but her skill in maintaining several story lines anticipates *Statues in a Garden* and *The Shooting Party*. Like these works, *The Great Occasion* reveals the natural world as both ironical commentary on human futility and a source of reconciliation.

Developed cinematically in short scenes, *Statues in a Garden* portrays a group of aristocrats just before World War I and flashes forward to the futures implicit in their actions. A quasi-incestuous affair, one of many in Colegate's books, between society beauty Cynthia Weston and her nephew and adopted son Philip, suggests the destructive narcissism of their lives, though the immediate victim is Cynthia's Liberal MP husband. Philip and Cynthia proceed to dubious futures, his business speculations undermining the stability of the Weston world. Colegate controls detail and tone, Cynthia's uncomprehending "... not a very *close* sort of incest, surely?" perfectly defining her shallowness and ability to survive. Though Philip's schematic significance as disturber of both sexual and economic order seems obtrusive, the novel, a "fable," is free to endow private actions with larger meaning and uses symbolism more gracefully than *The Orlando Trilogy*.

The protagonist of *Orlando King*, raised on an island by an eccentric adoptive father to protect him from civilization, carries a heavy symbolic burden besides his name: his hammer toes and damaged eyesight link him with Oedipus, as do, more obviously, his partial responsibility for his father's death, and marriage to his aristocratic stepmother Judith. The participants learn the truth only many years later: " 'I suppose you really think ... that I look old enough to be Orlando's mother.' 'Could be,' he said.' " However amusing, this dialogue puzzles; surely Judith's resultant breakdown and death and the consequences for the next generation make this stress on her vanity misleading. Orlando's sense of guilt destroys his burgeoning business and political careers in the England of the 1930's that is increasingly dominated by men like his father who capitalize on wartime connections and marriages to aristocrats. If such outsiders lust after class status, aristocrats like Judith display equal fascination with the exciting challenge these newcomers represent. Orlando's initial success in emulating his father is presumably emblematic, but his other actions confuse the novel's political and social pattern. The incest motif seems especially intrusive: in *Orlando at the Brazen Threshold* he successfully pursues the mistress of his nephew Henry, whom his daughter Agatha later marries. Orlando's behavior seems ultimately mechanical and lacks the complexity that the interior monologues, letters, and searching dialogue initially promise. Similarly, the elliptical narration with flashforwards and allusions to incidents as yet unknown to the reader creates an atmosphere of elusive reality puzzling to the characters through whose voices we perceive it; but Colegate periodically destroys this rich ambiguity by over-explicit summary: "Stephen and Paul were Orlando's half-brothers. Their father Leonard had in the far-off and scarcely imaginable days of his youth also been the father of Orlando ...." Colegate's epigrams about the inevitable failure of Communism in a class-obsessed society clash with her serious treatment of radicals, who seem as futile and foolishly motivated as capitalists: Graham, who dies on the Loyalist side in Spain (*Orlando King*); Paul, who sells secrets to Russia during the Burgess era because of animosities against his family (*Agatha*). Set in the era of the Suez crisis, *Agatha* focuses on the girl's Forsteresque commitment to Paul rather than to England, perhaps in unconscious atonement for Orlando's earlier ruthlessness.

Negative aristocratic images abound in the trilogy, sometimes mocking the physical effects of reclusiveness: "his little eyes directed their feeble gaze down the long organ through which his frail tones appeared to emerge (eugenically speaking, his breeding was a disaster)." Judith's brother Conrad embodies a more damning inadequacy, from 1930's appeasement through Suez arrogance to betrayal of Agatha in the name of patriotism. He projects that fusion of charm, decency, and plaintive misunderstanding that characterize his class, but the trilogy fails to provide an adequate political context to explain the general malaise of English civilization by the mistakes of Conrad and his peers.

Like other Colegate characters, Sir Randolph Nettleby, protagonist of *The Shooting Party*, set in 1913, prophesies: "An age, perhaps a civilization, is coming to an end." The novel, Colegate's best, carefully places the Nettleby estate in its geographical and historical contexts and focuses on those details of dress and behavior that reveal the beauty and vulnerability of country life on the eve of destruction. Sir Randolph is at times over-generous in assessing his class: "If you take away the proper functions of an aristocracy, what can it do but play games too seriously?" But the novel's stress on the violence of these games redresses the balance: "It was hard to remember that the keen concentration of their hunting instinct was not directed at their fellow man." The callousness of a visiting Hungarian count, however, helps define, by contrast, the English commitment to their tenants and to their land. The highflown language and sentiments that impress servants have real substance. The narrowness of the aristocratic code, the complacency with which they experience their rituals is offset by their willingness to limit their freedom to embody standards: Gilbert Hartlib's agonizing headaches are the price his inbred nerves pay for his performance as a hunter. However foolish, the standards of these aristocrats give form and meaning to their lives, including the duty to sacrifice these lives in war.

Colegate's novels have developed these themes before, but never so deftly, never with the same control of complex narrative presented cinematically in vignettes that build suspense for the climax. Restraining the epigrammatical tendencies that unbalanced earlier works, Colegate fuses an ironical view of society with a moving appreciation of its painful pleasures. Her fiction offers an impressive demonstration of genuine talent finding its strengths and refining its craft.

—Burton Kendle

COLTER, Cyrus. American. Born in Noblesville, Indiana, 8 January 1910. Educated in Noblesville public schools; Youngstown University, Ohio; Ohio State University, Columbus; Kent College of Law, Illinois Institute of Technology, Chicago, J.D. 1940: admitted to the Illinois Bar, 1940. Served in the United States Army Field Artillery, Italy, 1942–46: Captain. Married Imogene Mackay Colter in 1943 (died, 1984). Worked for the YMCA, Youngstown, 1932–34, and Chicago, 1934–40; United States Government Deputy Collector of Internal Revenue, 1940–42; in private practice of law, Chicago, 1946–51; commissioner, Illinois Commerce Commission, Chicago, 1951–73. Professor of Creative Writing, 1973–76, and Chester D. Tripp Professor of Humanities, 1976–78, Northwestern University, Evanston, Illinois; now emeritus. Recipient: Iowa School of Letters award, 1970. D.Litt.: University of Illinois, Chicago, 1977. Address: 1115 South Plymouth Court, Chicago, Illinois 60605, U.S.A.

PUBLICATIONS

Novels

The Rivers of Eros.   Chicago, Swallow Press, 1972.
The Hippodrome.   Chicago, Swallow Press, 1973.
Night Studies.   Chicago, Swallow Press, 1980.

Short Stories

The Beach Umbrella.   Iowa City, University of Iowa Press, 1970.

Uncollected Short Stories

"The Amoralists," in *University Review* (Kansas City), June 1971.
"Macabre," in *New Letters* (Kansas City), Fall 1971.
"Frog Hunters," in *Chicago Review*, vol. 25, no. 1, 1973.

*   *   *

In his first volume of fiction, the stories collected as *The Beach Umbrella*, Cyrus Colter reveals a high purpose. The subject of each story, often an apparently small event, Colter recounts in the style of modern realism, keeping his authorial self unobtrusive while exploiting colloquial dialogue and entering briefly into the conscious minds of characters in order to develop the subject into a story intending no less than a dramatic *exemplum* of life in general. "The Lookout," for example, records the painful jealousy of a woman who discovers the frailty of what she had taken to be friendships; "Rescue," which tells of a woman finding herself unable to get out of a loveless relationship with a man agrees to marry him, has as a counterpart "Overnight Trip" in which a man becomes aware that he has lost his wife's love by sensing the joy she feels in going away from him ever so briefly. "An Untold Story" and "Moot"

tell of death, one in violence and the other by natural causes, but though the subject is larger than in the other stories, these do not differ in suggesting the essential human condition is isolation and powerlessness before fate.

The Rivers of Eros introduces into Colter's writing a wider variety of characters, and the greater length of the novel form permits him to range more widely in time. His theme also undergoes some development. Set in a Chicago rooming house, *The Rivers of Eros* is presided over by an aging woman named Clotilda and, more importantly, by an act of adultery she committed many years before. The granddaughter living with her is the offspring of the child she conceived in adultery, and the environment of Clotilda's house can offer no alternative when the girl becomes involved in dangerous love affairs herself. The other people in Clotilda's world, with the exception of a promising grandson, are eccentric outsiders, inadequate to mitigate a situation that drives the granddaughter to attempt suicide and Clotilda to insanity as a result of guilt for her sexual transgression and for the fact that it seemed to set in motion a series of events that caused her daughter to be murdered. The last link in the chain Clotilda forges by murdering her grandchild. The development of Colter's theme in this book amounts to a broadening of fate into a conception of determinism (he says that Hobbes has especially influenced him). Evidently Colter is agnostic about the possibility of a purpose in the deterministic universe, but he is sure that the pattern of living once set in the personalities and characters of human beings is irreversible and normally painful. Though the situations he describes occur in the humanly constructed world of social and personal relationships, Colter's determinism allows no modification through social change or human will, because he finds neither social status and its consequent material environment nor any historical experience to be the source of life's direction. One is tempted to say that, though Colter's deterministic view of human life appears to be metaphysical, he bases it upon empirical observation. Realist that he is in style, he could deny any selectiveness in his choice of fictional material and say that he only shapes the truth into an exemplary tale.

In his second novel, *The Hippodrome*, an additional factor appears to be suggested by epigraphs taken from Dostoevsky's "The Man Who Lived Underground," Sartre's *La Nausée*, and Genet's *Miracle of the Rose*. That factor is an interest in the emotions of fear and anguish which he describes in the mind of a man who brutally murders his wife in jealousy and through curious circumstances becomes imprisoned in a house (the hippodrome) engaged in the business of providing sex shows for a voyeuristic clientele. The peculiar setting, the alienating effect it has on characters, and the protagonist's obsession with his macabre crime provide an effective representation of human extremity. Again, however, the accomplishment occurs within the style of realism. The suggestions of philosophical reflection result in a scene of elementary pondering on such ideas as motives as always selfish and the appropriateness of uncertainty as a way of life.

In his chosen style Colter is masterly. His imagination for situation is fertile, and his representation of characters instills them with interest. Thematically, however, his conceptions offer no challenge. Many sources outside literature are available to assert the popular "wisdom" of restricted determinism. Like the traditional tale-teller Colter renders consensual views in narrative, but the view of fate held by this tale-teller is insufficiently complex for a world as fluid as ours has become.

—John M. Reilly

COMFORT, Alex(ander). British. Born in London, 10 February 1920. Educated at Highgate School, London, 1932–36; Trinity College, Cambridge (Styring Scholar; Senior Scholar), 1938–40, M.B., B.Ch. 1944, M.A. 1945; London Hospital (Scholar), M.R.C.S. and L.R.C.P. 1944, D.C.H. 1945, Ph.D. (biochemistry) 1949, D.Sc. (gerontology) 1963. Married 1) Ruth Muriel Harris in 1943 (marriage dissolved, 1973), one son; 2) Jane Tristram Henderson in 1973. House physician, London Hospital, 1944; resident medical officer, Royal Waterloo Hospital, London, 1944–45; Lecturer in Physiology, 1945–51; Honorary Research Associate, Department of Zoology, 1951–73, and Director of Research on the Biology of Ageing, 1966–73, University College, London; Professor of Pathology, University of California School of Medicine, Irvine, 1976–78. Since 1974, Lecturer in Psychiatry, Stanford University, California; since 1975, Senior Fellow, Institute for Higher Studies, Santa Barbara, California; since 1978, Consultant Psychiatrist, Brentwood Hospital, Los Angeles; since 1980, Adjunct Professor, Neuropsychiatric Institute, University of California, Los Angeles. Editor, with Peter Wells, Poetry Folios, Barnet, Hertfordshire, 1942–46. President, British Society for Research on Ageing, 1967. Recipient: Nuffield Research Fellowship, 1952; Ciba Foundation prize, 1958; Borestone Mountain Poetry award, 1962; Karger Memorial Prize in Gerontology, 1969. Address: 121 South Evergreen, Ventura, California 93003, U.S.A.; or, Windmill House, The Hill, Cranbrook, Kent TN17 3AH, England.

PUBLICATIONS

Novels

The Silver River, Being the Diary of a Schoolboy in the South Atlantic, 1936. London, Chapman and Hall, 1938.
No Such Liberty. London, Chapman and Hall, 1941.
The Almond Tree: A Legend. London, Chapman and Hall, 1942.
The Power House. London, Routledge, 1944; New York, Viking Press, 1945.
On This Side Nothing. London, Routledge, and New York, Viking Press, 1949.
A Giant's Strength. London, Routledge, 1952.
Come Out to Play. London, Eyre and Spottiswoode, 1961; New York, Crown, 1975.
Tetrarch. Boulder, Colorado, Shambhala, 1980; London, Wildwood House, 1981.

Short Stories

Letters from an Outpost. London, Routledge, 1947.

Plays

Into Egypt: A Miracle Play. Billericay, Essex, Grey Walls Press, 1942.
Cities of the Plain: A Democratic Melodrama. London, Grey Walls Press, 1943.

Television Play: *The Great Agrippa*, 1968.

Verse

France and Other Poems. London, Favil Press, 1941.
Three New Poets, with Roy McFadden and Ian Serraillier. Billericay, Essex, Grey Walls Press, 1942.

A Wreath for the Living. London, Routledge, 1942.
Elegies. London, Routledge, 1944.
The Song of Lazarus. Barnet, Hertfordshire, Poetry Folios, and New York, Viking Press, 1945.
The Signal to Engage. London, Routledge, 1947.
And All But He Departed. London, Routledge, 1951.
Haste to the Wedding. London, Eyre and Spottiswoode, 1962; Chester Springs, Pennsylvania, Dufour, 1964.
Poems for Jane. London, Mitchell Beazley, and New York, Crown, 1979.

Other

Peace and Disobedience. London, Peace News, 1946.
Art and Social Responsibility: Lectures on the Ideology of Romanticism. London, Falcon Press, 1946.
The Novel and Our Time. Letchworth, Hertfordshire, Phoenix House, and Denver, Swallow, 1948.
Barbarism and Sexual Freedom: Six Lectures on the Sociology of Sex from the Standpoint of Anarchism. London, Freedom Press, 1948.
First-Year Physiological Techniques. London, Staples Press, 1948.
The Pattern of the Future. London, Routledge, and New York, Macmillan, 1949.
The Right Thing to Do, Together with the Wrong Thing to Do. London, Peace News, 1949.
Authority and Delinquency in the Modern State: A Criminological Approach to the Problem of Power. London, Routledge, 1950; revised edition, as *Authority and Delinquency*, London, Sphere, 1970.
Sexual Behaviour in Society. London, Duckworth, and New York, Viking Press, 1950; revised edition, as *Sex in Society*, Duckworth, 1963; New York, Citadel Press, 1966.
Delinquency (lecture). London, Freedom Press, 1951.
Social Responsibility in Science and Art. London, Peace News, 1952.
The Biology of Senescence. London, Routledge, and New York, Rinehart, 1956; revised edition, as *Ageing: The Biology of Senescence*, 1964; revised edition, as *The Biology of Senescence*, Edinburgh, Churchill Livingston, and New York, Elsevier, 1979.
Darwin and the Naked Lady: Discursive Essays on Biology and Art. London, Routledge, 1961; New York, Braziller, 1962.
The Process of Ageing. New York, New American Library, 1964; London, Weidenfeld and Nicolson, 1965.
The Nature of Human Nature. New York, Harper, 1965; as *Nature and Human Nature*, London, Weidenfeld and Nicolson, 1966.
The Anxiety Makers: Some Curious Preoccupations of the Medical Profession. London, Nelson, 1967.
What Rough Beast? and What Is a Doctor? (lectures). Vancouver, Pendejo Press, 1971.
The Joy of Sex: A Gourmet's Guide to Love Making. New York, Crown, 1972; London, Quartet, 1973.
More Joy: A Sequel to "The Joy of Sex." London, Mitchell Beazley, 1973; New York, Crown, 1974.
A Good Age. New York, Crown, 1976; London, Mitchell Beazley, 1977.
The Facts of Love: Living, Loving, and Growing Up (for children), with Jane Comfort. New York, Crown, 1979; London, Mitchell Beazley, 1980.
I and That: Notes on the Biology of Religion. London, Mitchell Beazley, and New York, Crown, 1979.

What Is a Doctor? Essays on Medicine and Human Natural History. Philadelphia, Stickley, 1980.
Practice of Geriatric Psychiatry. New York, Elsevier, 1980.
What about Alcohol? (textbook), with Jane Comfort. Burlington, North Carolina, Carolina Biological Supply Company, 1983.
Reality and Empathy: Physics, Mind, and Science in the 21st Century. Albany, State University of New York Press, 1984.

Editor, with Robert Greacen, *Lyra: An Anthology of New Lyric.* Billericay, Essex, Grey Walls Press, 1942.
Editor, with John Bayliss, *New Road 1943* and *1944: New Directions in European Art and Letters.* London, Grey Walls Press, 2 vols., 1943–44.
Editor, *History of Erotic Art 1.* London, Weidenfeld and Nicolson, and New York, Putnam, 1969.
Editor, *Sexual Consequences of Disability.* Philadelphia, Stickley, 1978.

Translator, with Allan Ross Macdougall, *The Triumph of Death*, by C.F. Ramuz. London, Routledge, 1946.
Translator, *The Koka Shastra.* London, Allen and Unwin, 1964; New York, Stein and Day, 1965.

*

Bibliography: "Alexander Comfort: A Bibliography in Progress" by D. Callaghan, in *West Coast Review* (Burnaby, British Columbia), 1969.

Critical Studies: *The Freedom of Poetry* by Derek Stanford, London, Falcon Press, 1947; "The Scientific Humanism of Alex Comfort," in *The Humanist* (London), November-December 1951, and "Kafka and Alex Comfort," in *Arizona Quarterly* (Tucson), Summer 1952, both by Wayne Burns; "The Anarchism of Alex Comfort" by John Ellerby, "Sex, Kicks and Comfort" by Charles Radcliffe, and "Alex Comfort's Art and Scope" by Harold Drasdo, all in *Anarchy* (London), November 1963; "Alex Comfort as a Novelist" by John Doheny, in *Limbo* (Vancouver), November 1964; *Alex Comfort* by Arthur E. Salmon, Boston, Twayne, 1978.

*   *   *

During the Second World War Alex Comfort established a name for himself as a critic, poet, and playwright concerned with expounding an ethic and aesthetic of freedom, a morality of the Good Samaritan, and a policy of "direct action" and "mutual aid." The leading anarcho-pacifist of his own generation in letters, he presented his ideas through his fiction in such novels as *No Such Liberty*, *The Power House*, and *On This Side Nothing*. Since his pacifism and anarchism, however, derive from prior attitudes of pessimism and idealism, and since these latter attitudes are fully expressed in his early novel *The Almond Tree*, it is as well to consider this first.

For a certain type of mind, the pathos of life resides in recognizing the unattainable while helplessly committed, for all time, to the finite; and *The Almond Tree* may be regarded as an illustrated thesis upon this theme. Then, too, idealism in this novel is powerfully linked with pessimism, and references to *Ecclesiastes* and Solomon's doctrine of the vanity of all things are quite explicit. The story (like most of the author's fiction) has a European setting. Pyotr, the patriarch, is very old and dying. Through the death of his son, his grape-farm has passed to his grand-daughter Teresa and her German husband—a fact

which Pyotr resents but cannot alter. A family tyrant, though often kindly, Pyotr has constricted and warped the lives of his children who have found it difficult to break away from his parental possessiveness and authority. One by one they make their bid for freedom and independence, all of them in some sense failing. And, along with old Pyotr, all of them regard, or remember, the almond tree as a fixed symbol of beauty, the one constant in their world of flux, a visual—almost metaphysical—absolute. In this novel time and experience are seen as diminishing or destroying factors, giving rise to the pessimism which the characters respectively feel. On the other hand, the almond tree is equated with a feeling of idealism, a transcendental feature acting as a magnet or focus above the currents of mutability in which men's lives pass and flounder. In the vicious circle this novel traces—with its final return to the inevitable—there are certain parallels with Flaubert's great chronicle of emotional vanity, *Sentimental Education*. There is, though, one difference in the conclusions of these novels. The defeatism in Flaubert implies a cynicism whereas defeat in Alex Comfort's fiction never quite severs the connection which its characters maintain—through the tree—with the ideal.

Of his anarcho-pacifist novels *The Power House* is the most important. Set in occupied France, it preaches, through the words and actions of four young men, a message of civil disobedience and non-cooperation. "We are," remarks one of the characters, "the enemies of society, and we must learn disobedience. Then we shall probably inherit the earth by default when the maniacs have burnt each other to a cinder"; "The weak do a great deal—every woman who hides a deserter, every clerk who doesn't scrutinize a pass, every worker who bungles a fuse saves somebody's life for a while." Seven years later, *On This Side Nothing* again chose a wartime setting, and argued, in dramatic terms, the uncertain ethics of—in Auden's words—"the necessary murder."

In more recent years, Comfort's libertarianism has operated in the field of sexological writing, and his novel *Come Out to Play* reflects this interest in terms of a satirical fantasy about a biologist, Dr. George Goggins, deeply learned in the knowledge of human mating habits.

—Derek Stanford

CONDON, Richard (Thomas). American. Born in New York City, 18 March 1915. Educated in public schools in New York. Served in the United States Merchant Navy. Married Evelyn Hunt in 1938; two daughters. Worked briefly in advertising; publicist in the American film industry for 21 years: worked for Walt Disney Productions, 1936–41, Hal Horne Organization, Twentieth-Century Fox, 1941–45, Richard Condon Inc., 1945–48, Paramount, 1948–53, United Artists, 1953–57, and other firms; theatrical producer, New York, 1951–52. Agent: Harold Matson Company Inc., 276 Fifth Avenue, New York, New York 10001, U.S.A.; or, Abner Stein, 10 Roland Gardens, London SW7 3PH, England. Address: 3436 Asbury Avenue, Dallas, Texas 75205, U.S.A.

PUBLICATIONS

Novels

The Oldest Confession. New York, Appleton Century Crofts,

1958; London, Longman, 1959; as *The Happy Thieves*, New York, Bantam, 1962.

The Manchurian Candidate. New York, McGraw Hill, 1959; London, Joseph, 1960.

Some Angry Angel: A Mid-Century Faerie Tale. New York, McGraw Hill, 1960; London, Joseph, 1961.

A Talent for Loving; or, The Great Cowboy Race. New York, McGraw Hill, 1961; London, Joseph, 1963.

An Infinity of Mirrors. New York, Random House, 1964; London, Heinemann, 1967.

Any God Will Do. New York, Random House, 1964; London, Heinemann, 1967.

The Ecstasy Business. New York, Dial Press, and London, Heinemann, 1967.

Mile High. New York, Dial Press, and London, Heinemann, 1969.

The Vertical Smile. New York, Dial Press, 1971; London, Weidenfeld and Nicolson, 1972.

Arigato. New York, Dial Press, and London, Weidenfeld and Nicolson, 1972.

The Star-Spangled Crunch. New York, Bantam, 1974.

Winter Kills. New York, Dial Press, and London, Weidenfeld and Nicolson, 1974.

Money Is Love. New York, Dial Press, and London, Weidenfeld and Nicolson, 1975.

The Whisper of the Axe. New York, Dial Press, and London, Weidenfeld and Nicolson, 1976.

The Abandoned Woman. New York, Dial Press, 1977; London, Hutchinson, 1978.

Bandicoot. New York, Dial Press, and London, Hutchinson, 1978.

Death of a Politician. New York, Marek, 1978; London, Hutchinson, 1979.

The Entwining. New York, Marek, 1980; London, Hutchinson, 1981.

Prizzi's Honor. New York, Coward McCann, and London, Joseph, 1982.

A Trembling upon Rome. New York, Putnam, and London, Joseph, 1983.

Plays

Men of Distinction (produced New York, 1953).

Screenplays: *A Talent for Loving*, 1965; *The Summer Music*, 1969; *The Long Loud Silence*, 1969; *Prizzi's Honor*, with Janet Roach, 1985.

Other

And Then We Moved to Rossenarra; or, The Art of Emigrating. New York, Dial Press, 1973.

The Mexican Stove: A History of Mexican Food, with Wendy Bennett. New York, Doubleday, 1973.

*

Manuscript Collection: Mugar Memorial Library, Boston University.

Richard Condon comments:

A writer may call himself an artist but he cannot sit down and consciously create art. What is art is not likely to be decided for decades or longer after the work has been produced—and then is often redecided—so we must not feel badly if we think

of literature as entertainment rather than as transcendent enlightenment. The truest banner leading such a Children's Crusade should be blazoned: ENTERTAINMENT FOR THE SAKE OF LITERATURE. Any designation of any author's work as art, either by himself (shyly) or by his peers, is merely the kiss of a wish. Readers buy novels to be entertained, to be taken out of their own lives for a few hours, not to purchase the awe of the ages which will follow.

*   *   *

Richard Condon published his first novel, *The Oldest Confession*, at the age of 42; he had previously spent more than 20 years working as a publicist for the American film industry. Perhaps his fiction is best viewed in light of his prior Hollywood connection, for Condon is known primarily as the author of entertaining novels, novels that are what the public would term "good reads." Some of his more famous books (*The Manchurian Candidate* and *Winter Kills*, for example) have been made into successful movies, furthering Condon's own claim of "What I *am* is a professional entertainer."

Condon's first novel defines many of the trademarks of his later works. Although the characters are involved in a highly unlikely plot of art theft and intrigue and the book lacks a certain depth, the author's fine writing and the book's sheer readability save it from the dismal fate of many first novels. Condon proves himself a very able, if not excellent, satirist, parodying everything from the art world to American politics. His subtlest, yet most significant, satire, however, is that of the thriller novel itself. It would seem as if the author sets out to parody the very genre in which he is working; such is the humor and ingenuity of the early Condon.

With the publication of his second novel, *The Manchurian Candidate*, Condon gained an even larger readership, one which was drawn to his eccentric brand of satire and espionage. This novel of political intrigue, brainwashing, murder, and incest is perhaps the best of the author's earlier works. The plot centers around the brainwashing by the Chinese of Richard Shaw, an American GI during the Korean War. Upon returning to the United States, Shaw is recommended for a Medal of Honor, not realizing that he has been the victim of an international plot. He is now the pawn in a dangerous game of political murder. As if he didn't have enough problems, he is also faced with an incestuous relationship with his mother, and a step-father who bears a striking resemblance to Senator Joe McCarthy.

Condon's taking the absurd in any given situation to the extreme and examining the foibles and paranoia of modern American society soon won him wide public and critical acclaim. He became a type of cult novelist, being likened to Kerouac and Kafka. The novels published in the 1960's, although they still were read by avid fans, were greeted with less enthusiasm by critics. With each ensuing book, the mania and early satire gives way to an ever-increasing paranoia, a love of the too-grotesque, and an obsession with minute facts and statistics. This seeming divergence from his promising first novels lends credence to Condon's view of himself as the entertainer. Although the novels written in mid-career are neither satirical masterpieces nor realistic thrillers, they do combine moments of enjoyment with suspense.

Winter Kills re-established Condon's critical appeal. His best book since *The Manchurian Candidate*, *Winter Kills*, with its plot centering around the assassination of the wealthy, liberal Irish President Tim Kegan in 1960, could have back-fired in the hands of a less skillful novelist. The headline plot, as well as Condon's handling of it, raises paranoia to a high art, but

Condon controls it to a much better extent in *Winter Kills* than in any of his more recent works.

—Sally H. Bennett

CONNELL, Evan S(helby), Jr. American. Born in Kansas City, Missouri, 17 August 1924. Educated at Southwest High School, Kansas City; Dartmouth College, Hanover, New Hampshire, 1941–43; University of Kansas, Lawrence, 1946–47, A.B. 1947; Stanford University, California, 1947–48; Columbia University, New York, 1948–49. Served as an aviator in the United States Navy, 1943–45. Editor, *Contact* magazine, Sausalito, California, 1960–65. Recipient: Saxton fellowship, 1952; Guggenheim fellowship, 1962; Rockefeller grant, 1967. Agent: Elizabeth McKee, Harold Matson Company Inc., 276 Fifth Avenue, New York, New York 10001. Address: 487 Sherwood Drive, Apartment 310, Sausalito, California 94965, U.S.A.

PUBLICATIONS

Novels

Mrs. Bridge. New York, Viking Press, 1958; London, Heinemann, 1960.
The Patriot. New York, Viking Press, 1960; London, Heinemann, 1961.
The Diary of a Rapist. New York, Simon and Schuster, 1966; London, Heinemann, 1967.
Mr. Bridge. New York, Knopf, and London, Heinemann, 1969.
The Connoisseur. New York, Knopf, 1974.
Double Honeymoon. New York, Putnam, 1976.

Short Stories

The Anatomy Lesson and Other Stories. New York, Viking Press, 1957; London, Heinemann, 1958.
At the Crossroads: Stories. New York, Simon and Schuster, 1965; London, Heinemann, 1966.
St. Augustine's Pigeon: The Selected Stories, edited by Gus Blaisdell. Berkeley, California, North Point Press, 1980.

Uncollected Short Stories

"A Cross to Bear," in *Foreign Service* (Kansas City), April 1947.
"The Flat-Footed Tiger," in *American Mercury* (New York), May 1949.
"The Most Beautiful," in *Tomorrow* (New York), September 1949.
"Filbert's Wife," in *Today's Woman* (New York), Summer 1950.
"Cocoa Party," in *Paris Review*, Autumn 1953.
"The Succubus," in *Gent* (New York), August 1957.
"Death and the Wife of John Henry," in *Transatlantic Review* (London), Spring 1960.
"The End of Summer," in *Premiere 1* (Mobile, Alabama), n.d.
"Leon and Bebert Aloft," in *Carolina Quarterly* (Chapel Hill, North Carolina), Winter 1966.
"Puig's Wife," in *New Mexico Quarterly* (Albuquerque), Summer 1967.

"The Voyeur," in *Lillabulero* (Chapel Hill, North Carolina), Winter 1967.
"Undersigned, Leon and Bebert," in *Esquire* (New York), December 1969.
"Neil Dortu," in *Boston University Journal*, vol. 30, no. 1, 1977.

Verse

Notes from a Bottle Found on the Beach at Carmel. New York, Viking Press, 1963; London, Heinemann, 1964.
Points for a Compass Rose. New York, Knopf, 1973.

Other

A Long Desire. New York, Holt Rinehart, 1979.
The White Lantern. New York, Holt Rinehart, 1980.
Son of the Morning Star: Custer and the Little Bighorn. Berkeley, California, North Point Press, 1984; London, Pavilion, 1985.

Editor, *I Am a Lover*, by Jerry Stoll. Sausalito, California, Angel Island, 1961.
Editor, *Woman by Three*. Menlo Park, California, Pacific Coast Publishers, 1969.

*

Manuscript Collection: Boston University Library.

Critical Studies: "After Ground Zero" by Gus Blaisdell, in *New Mexico Quarterly* (Albuquerque), Summer 1966.

*   *   *

In a short story, "The Trellis" (*The Anatomy Lesson*), a murder suspect, in the course of talking rings around a bewildered and suspicious police inspector, observes of the dead man, "He felt that time was passing and he seemed vaguely baffled and resentful of the fact, for he knew he had not done much." The observation might be made of almost any of Evan S. Connell's characters who lead generally privileged but ineffectual lives in the almost hermetic worlds of their private preoccupations.

Connell's reputation rests principally on *Mrs. Bridge* and *Mr. Bridge*, tales of an affluent couple who live in the Country Club district of Kansas City, Missouri, where Connell grew up. The Bridges appeared first in several short sketches collected in *The Anatomy Lesson*; and the two books about them are in no sense traditional novels, but rather montages of many short sketches out of which the reader gradually constructs his own portraits. While they are comfortably wealthy and enjoy an unruffled family life, the Bridges are indeed "vaguely baffled" by life, which the husband has dealt with by following formulas while his wife has floundered around. Their story is summed up by the final episode of *Mrs. Bridge*, in which one December morning the now widowed wife finds herself stuck in her Lincoln, half-out of the garage, so that she cannot open the car doors. She calls, "Hello out there"; but no one answers, "unless it was the falling snow." The Bridges are the kind of earnest, upper-middle-class suburbanites found especially in the American midwest (and probably any provincial culture without a strong local tradition) who have become wealthy without achieving the sophistication to enjoy their lives. One inquiring why so many talented young Americans flee to New York and San Francisco need only read the Bridges' story to find out. (Connell himself now lives near San Francisco and writes mostly about New York.)

Between the Kansas City novels, Connell published *The Patriot*, a *bildungsroman* about a young man from Kansas City who becomes a Naval air cadet during World War II and at last breaks free of the suffocating obligations he feels to family and country. Though published after the success of *Mrs. Bridge*, the novel is so much more traditional in form than his others and so much in the convention of first novels by sensitive young Americans, it seems surely an early work.

Connell's most remarkable achievement is *The Diary of a Rapist*, a tour de force in the form of a calendar year's diary entries in which 26-year-old Earl Summerfield, alienated by his ambitious wife and spiteful fellow Civil Service bureaucrats, is "tempted to keep a scrapbook of monstrous events," occurring daily in San Francisco. Ultimately, he is tempted also to commit monstrous acts and finally, as he has observed others do, to betray himself in his pathetic quest for attention. The disconcerting novel is diminished only by the usual problems of a work limiting the reader's perspective to the paranoid revelations of an unreliable narrator.

Since abandoning the Bridges, Connell has focused on Muhlbach, a New York insurance executive (though with a name borrowed—like others in the books—from those prominent in Kansas City). Like the Bridges, Muhlbach—a widower with a young son and daughter and a domineering housekeeper—first appears in short stories (collected in *At the Crossroads*). The first novel about him, *The Connoisseur*, is, in fact, hardly more than a long short story about Muhlbach's developing an obsession for pre-Columbian art, extended to book length by virtuoso passages displaying the author's vast erudition about folk arts. *Obsession* is indeed the theme of all the Muhlbach stories (perhaps of all Connell's work), as this anti-hero realizes when he thinks, "I can't distinguish reality any longer, I'm gripped by an obsession. I suppose I should be alarmed, but as a matter of fact I'm not." Pre-Columbian art is entirely forgotten, however, in *Double Honeymoon*, in which Muhlbach becomes obsessed with an exotic young girl named Lambeth, whose erratic behavior culminates in suicide after she appears in the pornographic motion picture that gives the novel its title. The Muhlbach story—unlike the Bridges—remains unresolved as he disappears into a crowd.

Connell's book-length poems defy summary because, like most of the novels, they are a montage of fragments drawn from the author's vast readings about ancient peoples and their cultures that show how he shares the skill of his dazzling speaker in "The Trellis."

—Warren French

COOK, David. British. Born in Preston, Lancashire, 21 September 1940. Educated at the Royal Academy of Dramatic Art, London, 1959–61. Since 1961, professional actor. Writer-in-Residence, St. Martin's College, Lancaster, 1982–83. Recipient: Writers Guild award, 1977; American Academy E.M. Forster Award, 1977; Hawthornden Prize, 1978; Arts Council bursary, 1979; Southern Arts prize, 1985. Agent: Elaine Greene Ltd., 31 Newington Green, London N16 9PU. Address: 7 Sydney Place, London SW7 3NL, England.

PUBLICATIONS

Novels

Albert's Memorial.   London, Secker and Warburg, 1972.
Happy Endings.   London, Secker and Warburg, 1974.
Walter.   London, Secker and Warburg, 1978; Woodstock, New York, Overlook Press, 1985.
Winter Doves.   London, Secker and Warburg, 1979; Woodstock, New York, Overlook Press, 1985.
Sunrising.   London, Secker and Warburg, 1984; Woodstock, New York, Overlook Press, 1986.
Missing Persons.   London, Secker and Warburg, 1986.

Uncollected Short Story

"Finding Out," in *Mae West Is Dead*, edited by Adam Mars-Jones.   London, Faber, 1983.

Plays

Square Dance (produced London, 1968).
If Only (televised, 1984).   Published in *Scene Scripts 3*, edited by Roy Blatchford, London, Longman, 1982.

Television Plays: *Willy*, 1973; *Jenny Can't Work Any Faster*, 1975; *Why Here?*, 1976; *Couples* series, 1976; *A Place Like Home* series, 1976; *Lydia*, 1977; *Repent at Leisure*, 1978; *The Specialist*, 1979; *Mary's Wife*, 1980; *Walter*, 1982; *Walter and June*, 1982; *If Only*, 1984; *Singles Week-end*, 1984; also scripts for Schools Television.

*

David Cook comments:

I began writing because I was an out-of-work actor, and needed an occupation which would be creatively satisfying. From the beginning, therefore, I brought an actor's concern with character to the task of writing fiction, and all my work is based on the same sort of act of empathy by which any actor brings life to an invented person. My discovery was that I now had to make this empathetic act for all my characters, not just one, seeing through their eyes, thinking their thoughts, feeling their feelings, and to do it without the help of a text; creating the text was up to me.

So the questions for me always are "Who are you?" "How do you live?" "How have you arrived at this condition?", and from the answers, logic will make a narrative. My first novel was about an old bag-lady whom I used to see sitting in doorways near South Kensington Station. I did not write a story; I wrote little pieces of what the details of her life might be, and after a while they began to form themselves into a story. All my work since, both the novels and the TV plays, has been based on empathy and research, and with a strong bias to those who have been called "the walking wounded." When I decided that my fifth novel, *Sunrising*, should be set in a time which was not my own, the research became different in kind. I could no longer walk to Fleetwood or work with autistic children, but had to find my material in books, and while it is not exactly easy for someone with no academic education whatever to gain access to Oxford's Bodleian Library, it was done. Now that I have the taste, for it, I shall write a sequel to *Sunrising* one day, but I do not anticipate that

I shall abandon the walking wounded of the here and now; they press in too closely.

*   *   *

David Cook is a stage and television actor who began to write novels in the early 1970's. His first novel, *Albert's Memorial*, was acclaimed for its originality and its sharply detailed prose, and subsequent novels like *Happy Endings* and *Walter* won prestigious prizes. Finely and delicately crafted, Cook's novels build the interior perspectives of his characters with a meticulous sense of authenticity and convincing detail. Characteristically, Cook's characters are isolated, lonely, inward-dwelling creatures whose consciousness is limited by some form of impairment or crippling circumstance. Physical or emotional indigents, they wander through a world they perceive intensely, although never accurately, in only bits and pieces. The juxtaposition of their partial points of view, which Cook always sees sympathetically, with an assumed, seldom stated "normal" point of view provides the tension and the emotional energy of the novels. *Albert's Memorial*, for example, concentrates on two isolated creatures: Mary, who after her husband's death, tries to live in the cemetery where he is buried and later tramps to the seaside resort where they spent their honeymoon, interested only in the conversations she holds with him inside her head, and Paul, who establishes trivial routines in his more geographically circumscribed wanderings after his homosexual lover suddenly dies. In *Walter*, the world is seen through Walter's autistic point of view, tracing the origins and effects of the debility that has led to his being institutionalized. Cook's central characters are all dependent on others, or institutions, or fantasies, for a survival they cannot manage on their own.

Cook's characters welcome impingements on their isolation, respond to relationships that break through their defenses or their occluded and partial visions. In *Albert's Memorial*, Mary and Paul connect, finally living with each other and sharing the fantasy of Mary's phantom pregnancy (she has been raped while tramping, and mistakes symptoms because she and her husband had avoided having children by never fully consummating their love). The relationship exists in mutual dependency, as does that between Walter from the earlier novel and June, a more intellectually functioning although emotionally severely unstable resident of the mental institution, as they escape to wander England in *Winter Doves*.

Characters like Mary and Paul, Walter and June, are seen against the background of contemporary England. The reader is always aware of an ordinary England dimly seen through the distorted half-lens of the impaired, and Cook never explicitly and seldom even implicitly provides any significant social commentary. The understated conflict between the characters and the larger world is often effectively rendered as comedy, as in the scene in which Paul, consulting a doctor because he is worried that Mary's "pregnancy" may be endangered, is so haltingly unable to articulate his concern that the doctor tests him for gonorrhea and administers a preventive injection. Similarly, wandering characters, in *Winter Doves* and other novels, duplicate a muted version of the comic picaresque, as they clash with the society that they cannot understand. Cook frequently depicts representatives of the Welfare State who try to help or control the indigents. These representatives, nurses, social workers, custodians in mental hospitals, doctors, and bureaucrats, are generally benign and well-intentioned, although unable to touch or assuage the deeper disturbances of the central characters. England's postwar emphasis on the social services is seen as praiseworthy and humane, although

never finally relevant, as if no social issue or characterization is ever as significant as is the tenuous establishment of the individual identity.

Much of that identity in Cook's fictional world is physical and direct. He concentrates on immediate experience, describing with acute sensitivity how his characters touch, feel, reason, and communicate. Long passages detail the tiring efforts necessary to establish oneself as a squatter in an uncompleted office building or the elaborate preparation for and physical progress of the homosexual love affair. In the emphasis on the physical and emotional, the detailed representation of how the impaired see and feel, Cook is attempting to shape his carefully developed prose to get at a primal quality within the human creature. Cook's versions of the primal are never aggressive or animalistic; rather, his novels are most frequently populated by birds, pigeons and doves, in both plot and metaphor. The birds suggest the delicacy, fragility, and tenuousness of identity, the only kind of precarious existence these impaired creatures can manage. Cook sees the bird-like fragility and tenacity of the creatures of limited consciousness with enormous sympathy that, because of his writing's directness, specificity, and lack of pretense, never descends to sentimentality.

—James Gindin

COOPER, Lettice (Ulpha).   British.   Born in Eccles, Lancashire, 3 September 1897. Educated at St. Cuthbert's School, Southbourne; Lady Margaret Hall, Oxford, 1916–18, B.A. Editorial assistant and drama critic, *Time and Tide*, London, 1939–40. Public relations officer, Ministry of Food, London, 1940–45. President, Robert Louis Stevenson Club, 1958–74; Vice-Chairman, 1975–78, and President, 1979–81, English PEN Club. Recipient: Arts Council bursary, 1968, 1979; Eric Gregory Travelling Scholarship, 1977. O.B.E. (Officer, Order of the British Empire), 1980. Agent: A.P. Watt Ltd., 26–28 Bedford Row, London WC1R 4HL. Address: 95 Canfield Gardens, London NW6 3DY, England.

PUBLICATIONS

Novels

The Lighted Room.   London, Hodder and Stoughton, 1925.
The Old Fox.   London, Hodder and Stoughton, 1927.
Good Venture.   London, Hodder and Stoughton, 1928.
Likewise the Lyon.   London, Hodder and Stoughton, 1928.
The Ship of Truth.   London, Hodder and Stoughton, and Boston, Little Brown, 1930.
Private Enterprise.   London, Hodder and Stoughton, 1931.
Hark to Rover!   London, Hodder and Stoughton, 1933.
We Have Come to a Country.   London, Gollancz, 1935.
The New House.   London, Gollancz, and New York, Macmillan, 1936.
National Provincial.   London, Gollancz, and New York, Macmillan, 1938.
Black Bethlehem.   London, Gollancz, and New York, Macmillan, 1947.
Fenny.   London, Gollancz, 1953.
Three Lives.   London, Gollancz, 1957.
A Certain Compass.   London, Gollancz, 1960.
The Double Heart.   London, Gollancz, 1962.

Late in the Afternoon. London, Gollancz, 1971.
Tea on Sunday. London, Gollancz, 1973.
Snow and Roses. London, Gollancz, 1976.
Desirable Residence. London, Gollancz, 1980.

Uncollected Short Story

"Frowning Caryatid," in *London Calling*, edited by Storm Jameson. New York, Harper, 1942.

Fiction (for children)

Blackberry's Kitten. Leicester, Brockhampton Press, 1961; New York, Vanguard Press, 1963.
The Bear Who Was Too Big. London, Parrish, 1963; Chicago, Follett, 1966.
Bob-a-Job. Leicester, Brockhampton Press, 1963.
Contadino. London, Cape, 1964.
The Twig of Cypress. London, Deutsch, 1965; New York, Washburn, 1966.
We Shall Have Snow. Leicester, Brockhampton Press, 1966.
Robert the Spy Hunter. London, Kaye and Ward, 1973.
Parkin. London, Harrap, 1977.

Other (for children)

Great Men of Yorkshire (West Riding). London, Lane, 1955.
The Young Florence Nightingale. London, Parrish, 1960; New York, Roy, 1961.
The Young Victoria. London, Parrish, 1961; New York, Roy, 1962.
James Watt. London, A. and C. Black, 1963.
Garibaldi. London, Methuen, 1964; New York, Roy, 1966.
The Young Edgar Allan Poe. London, Parrish, 1964; New York, Roy, 1965.
The Fugitive King. London, Parrish, 1965.
A Hand upon the Time: A Life of Charles Dickens. New York, Pantheon, 1968; London, Gollancz, 1971.
Robert Louis Stevenson. London, Burns and Oates, 1969.
Gunpowder: Treason and Plot. London, Abelard Schuman, 1970.

Other

Robert Louis Stevenson. London, Home and Van Thal, 1947; Denver, Alan Swallow, 1948.
Yorkshire: West Riding. London, Hale, 1950.
George Eliot. London, Longman, 1951; revised edition, 1960, 1964.

*

Manuscript Collection: The Public Library, Eccles, Lancashire.

Lettice Cooper comments:

I want to write stories about people in depth, using the traditional form, but hoping to show how the unconscious pressures and situations are always there beneath the conscious pattern. I want to indicate both the inner and outer life of my characters, and to "explore the truth of the human situation."

*   *   *

Lettice Cooper has been writing novels for many years, and social historians of the future may well study them for their careful reflection of middle-class English life at various stages of this century. The worlds she described in her younger days may have gone, but this does not mean that the novels themselves have dated: technically and psychologically they still stand up well. Their settings are domestic, though their domesticity varies. In *Fenny*, one of the most ambitious and successful, we see some grandish Italian interiors; in *National Provincial*, lower middle-class North Country life; in *The Ship of Truth*, a young clergyman's home, penny-pinching through necessity; in *The New House*, an upper-middle-class family, suffocatingly cosy and financially quite secure; in *The Double Heart*, more townish and trendy people; in *Late in the Afternoon*, a smartish background in the main characters, very different ones in the others, who include a wandering hippy.

In some of the novels institutions stand behind the domesticity. In *Three Lives* it is an adult education college; in *We Have Come to a Country* an "occupational centre for unemployed men" (the time is the mid-1930's). In these cases, the institutions are not just decorative backgrounds, realistically painted flats; we get inside them, learn how they work. Nothing in Cooper's novels, is put in without a point or a place in the action, without being properly inserted and made familiar. Cooper is always professional, a writer whose care, and whose respect for her readers, deserve respect.

Two places are of primary importance in her novels—her native Yorkshire, standing rocklike and immoveable, often a symbol of stability in a shifting world, sometimes of narrowness in a wider one (London beckons the young); and the country for which she feels the deep love of the enchanted (though knowledgeable) outsider: Italy, and more specifically Tuscany. Again and again the novels are set in, or have excursions to, one or other of these places. Both, in a sense, seem to represent homecoming.

If the settings of the novels are domestic, the action, as a rule, is unadventurous, in the sense of undramatic—except in terms of feelings and personalities. But this might be said, of course, of the majority of English fiction written by women, from *Middlemarch* downwards, and implies no narrowness of outlook. Cooper has kept fairly firmly within the worlds she knows and understands, but that they have opened out with the years is clear from *Late in the Afternoon*, in which, from the standpoint of an elderly woman, she deals sympathetically with the new young, and makes a splendidly unpatronising excursion into a working-class household touched but not radically altered by the new prosperity. From her domestic settings she deals, in fact, with the basic issues and problems: love and indifference, parental selfishness, the young's longing for escape, moral dilemmas, varying standards of behaviour, of loyalty and truth. In what seems a straightforward way she concentrates much into seemingly simple scenes and passages; her strength lying in an intelligent understanding of human nature; in warmth tempered with briskness and humour, and in an intuitive interpretation of events, psychological and spiritual. At its simplest this concentration appears in her children's books, outstandingly good among which is *Bob-a-Job*, a small masterpiece of insight on that attractive menace, the predatory wolf-cub, out to help.

—Isabel Quigly

COOPER, William. Pseudonym for Harry Summerfield Hoff. British. Born in Crewe, Cheshire, 4 August 1910.

Educated at Christ's College, Cambridge, M.A. 1933. Served in the Royal Air Force, 1940–45. Married Joyce Barbara Harris in 1951; two daughters. Schoolmaster, Leicester, 1933–40; assistant commissioner, Civil Service Commission, London, 1945–58. Part-time personnel consultant, for the United Kingdom Atomic Energy Authority, 1958–72, the Central Electricity Generating Board, 1960–72, and the Commission of European Community, 1972–73; assistant director, Civil Service Selection Board, 1973–75; member of the Board, Crown Agents, 1975–77; adviser, Millbank Technical Services, 1975–77; personnel consultant, Ministry of Overseas Development, 1978. Since 1977, Adjunct Professor of English, Syracuse University, London Center. Fellow, Royal Society of Literature. Address: 22 Kenilworth Court, Lower Richmond Road, London SW15 1EW, England.

PUBLICATIONS

Novels

Trina (as H.S. Hoff).   London, Heinemann, 1934; as *It Happened in PRK*, New York, Coward McCann, 1934.
Rhéa (as H.S. Hoff).   London, Heinemann, 1937.
Lisa (as H.S. Hoff).   London, Heinemann, 1937.
Three Marriages (as H.S. Hoff).   London, Heinemann, 1946.
Scenes from Provincial Life.   London, Cape, 1950.
The Struggles of Albert Woods.   London, Cape, 1952; New York, Doubleday, 1953.
The Ever-Interesting Topic.   London, Cape, 1953.
Disquiet and Peace.   London, Macmillan, 1956; Philadelphia, Lippincott, 1957.
Young People.   London, Macmillan, 1958.
Scenes from Married Life.   London, Macmillan, 1961.
Scenes from Life (includes *Scenes from Provincial Life* and *Scenes from Married Life*).   New York, Scribner, 1961.
Memoirs of a New Man.   London, Macmillan, 1966.
You Want the Right Frame of Reference.   London, Macmillan, 1971.
Love on the Coast.   London, Macmillan, 1973.
You're Not Alone: A Doctor's Diary.   London, Macmillan, 1976.
Scenes from Metropolitan Life.   London, Macmillan, 1982.
Scenes from Later Life.   London, Macmillan, 1983.
Scenes from Provincial Life, and Scenes from Metropolitan Life.   New York, Dutton, 1983.
Scenes from Married Life, and Scenes from Later Life.   New York, Dutton, 1984.

Uncollected Short Stories

"Ball of Paper," in *Winter's Tales 1*.   London, Macmillan, and New York, St. Martin's Press, 1955.
"A Moral Choice," in *Winter's Tales 4*.   London, Macmillan, and New York, St. Martin's Press, 1958.

Plays

High Life (produced London, 1951).
Prince Genji (produced Oxford, 1968).   London, Evans, 1959.

Other

C.P. Snow.   London, Longman, 1959; revised edition, 1971.
Shall We Ever Know? The Trial of the Hosein Brothers for the Murder of Mrs. McKay.   London, Hutchinson, 1971; as *Brothers*, New York, Harper, 1972.

*

Manuscript Collection: Humanities Research Center, University of Texas, Austin.

Critical Studies: *Tradition and Dream* by Walter Allen, London, Phoenix House, 1964, as *The Modern Novel in Britain and the United States*, New York, Dutton, 1964; introduction by Malcolm Bradbury to *Scenes from Provincial Life*, London, Macmillan, 1969; *William Cooper the Novelist* by Ashok Kumar Sinha, New Delhi, Jnanada, 1977.

William Cooper comments:

(1972) I don't know that I specially believe in artists making statements about their own work. An artist's *work* is *his* statement. And that's that. The rest is for other people to say. Perhaps a writer whose original statement has turned out obscure may feel it useful to present a second that's more comprehensible—in that case I wonder why he didn't make the second one first.

Speaking for myself, *Scenes from Provincial Life* seems to me so simple, lucid, attractive, and funny that anyone who finds he can't read it probably ought to ask himself: "Should I be trying to read books at all? Wouldn't it be better to sit and watch television or something?" I write about the real world and real people in it. And I stick pretty close to what I've had some experience of. That's why *Scenes from Metropolitan Life*, which is also simple, lucid, attractive and funny, was suppressed. *Scenes from Married Life*, makes the third of a trilogy. *Albert Woods* and *Memoirs of a New Man* are about goings-on in the world of science and technology; *You Want the Right Frame of Reference* in the world of arts—they have an added touch of wryness and malice. An unusual marriage is the core of *Young People* and of *Disquiet and Peace*, the former set in the provinces in the '30's, the latter in Edwardian upperclass London—its small group of admirers think it's a beautiful book. *The Ever-Interesting Topic* is about what happens when you give a course of lectures on sex to a boarding school full of boys: what you'd expect. *Shall We Ever Know?* is a day-by-day account of a most surprising and mystifying murder trial, a kidnapping for ransom in which no trace whatsoever of the body was ever found, and two men were found guilty of murder.

(1981) *Love on the Coast*, my only novel to be set outside England, is about some former "flower children" in San Francisco who are working their way back into society by running an "experimental" theatre. And *You're Not Alone* is the diary of a London doctor, a retired GP of some distinction, to whom people come to confide their sexual quirks—as a start he tells them they are not alone.

(1986) In 1981 the 30-year suppression of *Scenes from Metropolitan Life* ended, allowing the trilogy to be published complete. The three novels fit together thus: *Provincial Life*—Boy won't marry Girl; *Metropolitan Life*—same Girl now won't marry Boy; *Married Life*—Boy meets another Girl and marries happily ever after. In 1983 I published *Scenes from Later Life* as a companion volume to the trilogy, with the characters in their sixties and seventies, learning to cope with old age—the final chapter, the best chapter I have ever written, can make you laugh and make you cry within seven pages. I am now three-quarters of the way through a new novel.

*   *   *

William Cooper is the pen-name of a novelist who had already published four novels under his own name, H.S. Hoff, when in 1950 he emerged with a new literary identity, and won a new literary reputation, with *Scenes from Provincial Life*—a book which quickly became a classic of a new kind of postwar realism and undoubtedly had a very powerful influence on the development of the English novel in the 1950's and since. A delightful and tough-minded story set among young provincial intellectuals, in a British midland town that bears a close resemblance to Leicester, over the crucial months of change and crisis leading up to the outbreak of the Second World War, *Scenes from Provincial Life*—published at a time when new fictional directions were uncertain and no real postwar movement had shown itself—became the forerunner of a whole sequence of novels which, in the postwar years, were to treat local English life, and the familiar and ordinary experience of recognizable people, with a fresh, youthful, exploratory, and critical curiosity. There can be little doubt that the book did encourage, and often considerably influence, a number of younger writers like John Braine, David Storey, Stanley Middleton, and Stan Barstow, some of whom directly expressed their indebtedness; and it certainly helped writers thereafter to find a sense of direction in the period after the decline both of Modernism and the political fiction of the 1930's. Its force was strengthened by the fact that Cooper—along with C.P. Snow, Pamela Hansford Johnson, and some other younger writers like Kingsley Amis, Philip Larkin, and John Wain—was deliberately reacting against the Bloomsbury-dominated climate of "cultured" and cosmopolitan experimentalism, and was seeking out a form of fiction much more social, empirical, realistic, and humanly substantial in character, and concerned with a felt sense of the texture and the issues of contemporary British life.

This spirit in writing has sometimes been characterized by critics as middlebrow, and it was self-defined as provincial. But it asserted a humanist vigour and a closeness to familiar life in the practice of serious British writing at a time when, in literary traditions in other countries, the break with the past was disquieting and the signs of literary strain were being felt. Joyce had seemed to bring the modern novel into a cul-de-sac, and Cooper and others pointed to the value of the native tradition, his argument clearly strengthened by the fact that his own novel was not just one of the first, but one of the best, of a kind. In time the tendency he represented was to come to seem a narrowed view of the direction of fiction, but Cooper represented this kind of novel in all its strength. *Scenes from Provincial Life* tells the story of Joe Lunn, the young science master at a provincial grammar school, and his friends, nonconforming emotional radicals who know they are distant witnesses to the world's great events, as a kind of conflict between the force of history and the force of the familiar. Fearful of a German occupation of Britain, they plan their exiles; but the day-to-day world of provincial life (especially their complex sexual relationships) seems all that matters, and they finally opt for it. The story was to go on through three more volumes, plotting the development of Joe's life as a scientific adviser to government, as a writer and a married man. *Scenes from Metropolitan Life*, written in the 1950's but not published for legal reasons until 1982, brings the story into the postwar world, the London scene, and the world of Whitehall, renewing Joe's relationship with his former mistress Myrtle in the context of urban sexual mores. *Scenes from Married Life*, which appeared in 1961, is, unusually in contemporary fiction, a celebration of marital life, reinforcing Cooper's gift for exploring the private underside of the public world in which Joe is now an important figure. *Scenes from Later Life* brings most of the characters forward into the world of the late 1970's, with Joe haunted by retirement and the ailments of his mother. But, despite a rising quota of pain, the characteristic Cooper good humour

and the sense of celebration of the familiar prevails, and the sequence sustains the spirit with which it started. As in the novels of C.P. Snow, but without Snow's stoical and even tragic pessimism, we see the new bloods turn into the men of place and power in an age in which the scientist and technologist become important public figures. But Cooper's social history gives way to a history of the domestic and the familiar, a comedy of daily life done with great luminosity and delicacy.

Cooper's other novels are all marked by the same commitment to familiar life, and the same luminous good humour. One, *Disquiet and Peace*, is an historical novel, set in the high-society milieu of Edwardian political and drawing-room life as the strange death of Liberal England is taking place; another, *Love on the Coast*, takes radical Californian life-style as its subject. But most of his books are, in an approving sense of the term, "banal" novels—concerned, that is, with the world of everyday social and emotional experience, and capable of evoking a strong, strange sense of recognition. Set in the provinces, the suburbs, or the world of the urban middle-classes with its clubs and appropriate restaurants—the pieces of social experience Cooper knows and details very well—they describe with affection and understanding the way ordinary things happen to intelligent and sceptical people as they marry, breed families, have affairs, work at recognizable jobs, and worry about their sexual lives, their mortality, and their salaries. Many of them indeed belong to the world of the "new men" (one book is called *Memoirs of a New Man*) whose meritocratic ascent forms an important story in British social life. Like that of his friend C.P. Snow (on whom he has written warmly), Cooper's fiction relates the life of ordinary origins to the commonsense decencies of public life, and, as with Snow, his realistic pleasure in the world seems to have to do with the fact that it is open to his mobility and talent. Like Snow's fiction, Cooper's achievement bears some relation to that desire for a better world that fed the postwar years, and also explores many of its ambiguities and disappointments.

But if one of Cooper's best qualities is his powerful realism, another is his comedy and wit. If he deals with familiar life, he lights it up with a striking sense of human oddity, and of the quirks and unexpected outrages that exist in his very recognizable characters. The outrage is often added to by the cool, undercutting tone of his narrators themselves. Like Muriel, who in *Disquiet and Peace* is provoked to stirring up disorder by donning an eyeglass and then dropping it in her soup, Cooper has a way of stirring up the surface of his world by his oblique vision. The struggles of the characters for sexual, social, or material success become matters for very cool irony. His plots often turn on conflicts between traditional and more liberal values, and he writes with a moral edge, but is also capable of moving lightly away from it all, leaving the chaos to itself, as in *The Ever-Interesting Topic*, about a headmaster who tries to bring lectures on sex education into his public school. All Cooper's books show a buoyant and vitalistic view of sexuality and an awareness of the way it undercuts so many of our social and moral pretensions. This comic vision is something he also handed on to his successors, and it makes his a realism of marvellous surprise, giving his books a sharp bite and clarity that distinguish them from Snow's sobered kind of realism. His Albert Woods and Joe Lunns may acquire influence, but they do not acquire sobriety. As a result they become attractive centres of vision, and that is especially true of Joe Lunn, who, in all the books where he is narrator, is both a performer in the chaotic and comic action and an artistic observer consciously knowing about fiction and busily interpreting, recalling, and shaping in a neat balance of sympathy and irony. Other narrative techniques are used in other novels, but they are usually distinguished by an adept mixture of sympathetic identification with lively characters and an ironic detachment from them.

Cooper's case for the novel that attends to daily life has indeed been very influential, and at times it has been inhibiting. But there can be no doubt about the value of his own contribution to contemporary British fiction. His novels possess a distinctive style and vision, even though they vary somewhat in quality, so that his gift for cutting deep into the flavour of life is stronger in some than in others. But what distinguishes his work from other writing superficially like it is his exact artistic control. This is most evident when he is capturing the flavour of some very distinctive ethos and observing and analyzing the behaviour of people in it, as he does in *Young People*. He can be compared with H.G. Wells, whom he admires ("I loved it, enshrining Wells's message of optimism," Joe Lunn writes in *Scenes from Later Life* of *The History of Mr. Polly*), and he has the same gift for capturing youthful, hopeful, buoyant pleasure in life. But at times, as in *Scenes from Provincial Life*, there is a powerful balance of reminiscence, irony, and sentiment so carefully composed as to recall major works of "artistic" realism, like Turgenev's. The technique is ostensibly simple but at best enormously self-conscious and adept. His novels, like much good realism, take their place as an important social record, of moods and mores, landscapes and cityscapes, social feelings and private emotions. But they are also comically and morally illuminating, and shot through with literary perspectives. It is this that has helped give *Scenes from Provincial Life* and its successors in the Joe Lunn tetralogy the status of modern classics that they now possess. Cooper's novels show us why the "new" novel of the 1950's, even in its traditionalism, still remains important and influential. They also tell us, like George Eliot's, that one thing that makes an artist is the power to have intelligently seen, known, and then been able to shape and illuminate the experiences of the ordinary world. In that aspect of fictional art, Cooper has been a very central contemporary performer.

—Malcolm Bradbury

COOVER, Robert (Lowell). American. Born in Charles City, Iowa, 4 February 1932. Educated at Southern Illinois University, Carbondale, 1949–51; Indiana University, Bloomington, B.A. 1953; University of Chicago, 1958–61, M.A. 1965. Served in the United States Naval Reserve, 1953–57: Lieutenant. Married Maria del Sans-Mallafré in 1959; two daughters and one son. Taught at Bard College, Annandale-on-Hudson, New York, 1966–67; University of Iowa, Iowa City, 1967–69; Columbia University, New York, 1972, Princeton University, New Jersey, 1972–73, Virginia Military Institute, Lexington, 1976, and Brandeis University, Waltham, Massachusetts, 1981. Since 1981, Writer-in-Residence, Brown University, Providence, Rhode Island. Fiction editor, *Iowa Review*, Iowa City, 1974–77. Recipient: Faulkner Award, 1966; Brandeis University Creative Arts Award, 1969; Rockefeller fellowship, 1969; Guggenheim fellowship, 1971, 1974; American Academy award, 1976. Agent: Georges Borchardt, 136 East 57th Street, New York, New York 10022, U.S.A.

PUBLICATIONS

Novels

The Origin of the Brunists.   New York, Putnam, 1966; London, Barker, 1967.

The Universal Baseball Association, Inc., J. Henry Waugh, Prop.   New York, Random House, 1968; London, Hart Davis, 1970.

The Public Burning.   New York, Viking Press, 1977; London, Allen Lane, 1978.

Spanking the Maid.   New York, Grove Press, 1982.

Gerald's Party.   New York, Linden Press, and London, Heinemann, 1986.

Short Stories

Pricksongs and Descants.   New York, Dutton, 1969; London, Cape, 1971.

The Water Pourer (unpublished chapter from *The Origin of the Brunists*).   Bloomfield Hills, Michigan, Bruccoli Clark, 1972.

Hair o' the Chine.   Bloomfield Hills, Michigan, Bruccoli Clark, 1979.

After Lazarus: A Filmscript.   Bloomfield Hills, Michigan, Bruccoli Clark, 1980.

Charlie in the House of Rue.   Lincoln, Massachusetts, Penmaen Press, 1980.

A Political Fable.   New York, Viking Press, 1980.

The Convention.   Northridge, California, Lord John Press, 1982.

In Bed One Night and Other Brief Encounters.   Providence, Rhode Island, Burning Deck, 1983.

Uncollected Short Stories

"Blackdamp," in *Noble Savage* (Cleveland), October 1961.

"Dinner with the King of England," in *Evergreen Review* (New York), November–December 1962.

"D.D., Baby," in *Cavalier* (New York), July 1963.

"The Duel," in *Evergreen Review* (New York), June 1967.

"The Square-Shooter and the Saint," in *Evergreen Review Reader*, edited by Barney Rosset.   New York, Grove Press, 1968.

"Some Notes about Puff," in *Iowa Review* (Iowa City), Winter 1970.

"McDuff on the Mound," in *Iowa Review* (Iowa City), Fall 1971.

"The Reunion," in *Iowa Review* (Iowa City), Winter 1971.

"Lucky Pierre and the Music Lesson," in *New American Review 14*, edited by Theodore Solotaroff.   New York, Simon and Schuster, 1972.

"The Dead Queen," in *Quarterly Review of Literature* (Princeton, New Jersey), 1973.

"Whatever Happened to Gloomy Gus of the Chicago Bears?," in *American Review 22*, edited by Theodore Solotaroff. New York, Bantam, 1974.

"You Must Remember This," in *Playboy* (Chicago), January 1985.

Plays

The Kid (produced New York, 1972; London, 1974).   Included in *A Theological Position*, 1972.

A Theological Position (includes *A Theological Position, The Kid, Love Scene, Rip Awake*).   New York, Dutton, 1972.

Love Scene (as *Scène d'amour*, produced Paris, 1973; as *Love Scene*, produced New York, 1974).   Included in *A Theological Position*, 1972.

Rip Awake (produced Los Angeles, 1975).   Included in *A Theological Position*, 1972.

A Theological Position (produced Los Angeles, 1977; New York, 1979).   Included in *A Theological Position*, 1972.

Other

Editor, with Kent Dixon, *The Stone Wall Book of Short Fiction*. Iowa City, Stone Wall Press, 1973.
Editor, with Elliott Anderson, *Minute Stories*.   New York, Braziller, 1976.

*

Manuscript Collection: Houghton Library, Harvard University, Cambridge, Massachusetts.

Critical Studies: *Fiction and the Figures of Life* by William H. Gass, New York, Knopf, 1970; "Robert Coover's Fiction" by Jackson I. Cope, in *Iowa Review* (Iowa City), vol. 2, no. 4, 1971; *Black Humor Fiction of the Sixties* by Max Schulz, Athens, Ohio University Press, 1973; "Robert Coover and the Hazards of Metafiction" by Neil Schmitz, in *Novel 7* (Providence, Rhode Island), 1974; "Humor and Balance in Coover's *The Universal Baseball Association, Inc.*" by Frank W. Shelton, in *Critique 17* (Atlanta), 1975; "Robert Coover, Metafictions, and Freedom" by Margaret Heckard, in *Twentieth Century Literature 22* (Los Angeles), 1976; "The Dice of God: Einstein, Heisenberg, and Robert Coover" by Arlen J. Hansen, in *Novel 10* (Providence, Rhode Island), 1976; "Structure as Revelation: Coover's *Pricksongs and Descants*" by Jessie Gunn, in *Linguistics in Literature*, vol. 2, no. 1, 1977; *The Metafictional Muse: The Works of Robert Coover, Donald Barthelme, and William H. Gass* by Larry McCaffery, Pittsburgh, University of Pittsburgh Press, 1982; *Robert Coover: The Universal Fictionmaking Process* by Lois Gordon, Carbondale, Southern Illinois University Press, 1983.

Robert Coover comments:
   In reply to the question: "Why Do You Write?":

   Because art blows life into the lifeless, death into the deathless.
   Because art's lie is preferable, in truth, to life's beautiful terror.
   Because, as time does not pass (nothing, as Beckett tells us, passes), *it* passes the time.
   Because death, our mirthless master, is somehow amused by epitaphs.
   Because epitaphs, well-struck, give death, our voracious master, heartburn.
   Because fiction imitates life's beauty, thereby inventing the beauty life lacks.
   Because fiction is the best position, at once exotic and familiar, for fucking the world.
   Because fiction, mediating paradox, celebrates it.
   Because fiction, mothered by love, loves love as a mother might her unloving child.
   Because fiction speaks, hopelessly, beautifully, as the world speaks.
   Because God, created in the storyteller's image, can be destroyed only by His maker.
   Because, in its perversity, art harmonizes the disharmonious.
   Because, in its profanity, fiction sanctifies life.
   Because, in its terrible isolation, writing is a path to brotherhood.
   Because in the beginning was the gesture, and in the end to come as well: in between what we have are words.

   Because, of all the arts, only fiction can unmake the myths that unman men.
   Because of its endearing futility, its outrageous pretensions.
   Because the pen, though short, casts a long shadow (upon, it must be said, no surface).
   Because the world is re-invented every day and this is how it is done.
   Because there is nothing new under the sun except its expression.
   Because truth, that elusive joker, hides himself in fictions and must therefore be sought there.
   Because writing, in all space's unimaginable vastness, is still the greatest adventure of all.
   And because, alas, what else?

*   *   *

The change that has overtaken American fiction, Robert Coover has said, came about for two reasons. One is the familiar notion that the novel as a literary form is exhausted. We therefore need new ideas concerning what story writing is about, and we must search for new principles of fiction. The other is equally familiar: we have been pushed, in the modern world, to a state of extremity in which we face the obliteration of the race. This condition raises questions about the value of religion and of history. If these are meaningless, as now appears to be the case, then writers have recourse to the grotesque or to a nightmarish fiction or to a form of comedy, but not to tragedy, which is an "adolescent response to the universe."

   In his own fiction Coover has accordingly turned away from traditional realism. What he demonstrates in *Pricksongs and Descants*, which represents his earliest writing although published subsequent to his first novel, and in everything written since, is the conviction that reality, history, and truth are "made" or invented, that appearances are everything, that forms are really substance, that poetry is the art of subordinating facts to the imagination, and that objectivity is an impossible illusion. These are matters that he actually discusses, in the self-reflexive mode of modernist fiction, in his novels; all the points above come specifically from *The Public Burning*. Coover's aim is to dis-establish dogmatic confidence in the nature of reality, as his well-known story, "The Babysitter," so clearly demonstrates. It is a goal which rests on the premise, to which both Vladimir Nabokov and William Gass have given voice, that the author is a dictator or a god. In "The Magic Poker" the authorial voice announces that *I* have invented these characters, have dressed them and may well undress them, have endowed them with physical attributes but need not be bound by any anatomical reality: they will have or not have organs exactly as I decree. Despite these assertions, however, Coover cannot altogether free himself in his fiction from the sense-apprehensible reality which most of us acknowledge.

   An alternative to the realistic novel which attempts to mirror life is a fiction which centers its attention upon language and technique. Language is a form of play, an expression of wit, and a source of joy. Language is an end in itself, rather than a means of expressing the ideas and feelings of characters and the culture. The magic of language becomes the supreme ordering principle of our existence. When Coover pushes these matters far enough, language transcends itself and becomes the culture. The play of language opens us to the literary strategies that are the means of defining and knowing the culture. The variety of techniques in *The Public Burning* offers the readiest example of Coover's conviction in this matter: he uses here, among others, the techniques of the drama, collage, montage, surrealism, opera, farce and slap-stick, the absurd, parody, and satire.

So much for Coover's version of the new ideas about fiction. Now as to history and religion, which are meaningless. Assuming the problematic nature of reality, Coover turns to myth in each of his first three novels. In *The Origin of the Brunists* a rational editor cynically invents a miracle which becomes the basis for a system of religious belief. This novel is an exercise in the creation of "truth"; the Brunist religion as an act of creation is a mirror-reflection of Coover's own creation of the novel itself. Coover is a myth-maker demonstrating how myth is made. In *The Universal Baseball Association, Inc., J. Henry Waugh, Prop.*, Coover's most successful book, "real" events pass into myth and are expressed in recurring ritual. The primacy of the imagined world is established as a result of conflict with the "real" world, which is Coover's way of asserting the primacy of fiction. "The world itself being a construct of fictions," he has said, "I believe the fiction maker's function is to furnish better fictions with which we can re-form our notions of things." In this novel, both real and invented realms are merged and coalesce in time; a system of belief emerges which passes into myth or religion. The reality upon which Coover builds here is the history of baseball. The reality in *The Public Burning* is the espionage trial of Ethel and Julius Rosenberg, which Coover transmutes by way of folklore and history into the myth of America. He provides initiation into evil and the threat of evil in the conflict with the Phantom; sacrifices of the victims, who are to be executed; spectacle and saturnalia, since the execution, an orgasmic occasion, is staged by Cecil B. De Mille and others in Times Square; purification by fire; and rescue and preservation of the sacred flame—the atomic bomb—by Uncle Sam, the archetypal American hero. But Uncle Sam is also Sam Slick, the Yankee Peddler, who has his dark side. And much of the novel is narrated by Vice-President Richard Nixon, portrayed as treacherous, cunning, ruthless, paranoid, mean-spirited, vengeful, repressed, self-pitying, sentimental, lonely, and alienated. The mythic world is a self-encapsulated fiction. The judgment about the American myth and American heroes—real or symbolic—takes us out of the hermetic world of myth. In this novel, Coover validates equally the two realms and thus undercuts his expressed belief in the supremacy of fiction and the imagination.

In Bed One Night and Other Brief Encounters consists of nine short exercises in modernist writing. The most elaborate of these is "Beginnings," which demonstrates in its very existence and form the difficulties of writing, now that time and history, logic and causation, sequence and linearity have all been invalidated. In another piece, the protagonist realizes that everything that has happened to him has happened in language, which confirms William Gass's view that all we have in fiction is language, because there is nothing else. And in addition to this language play, the volume offers some effective surrealistic satire.

Spanking the Maid is a modernist novella constructed as an unending series of repetitions in a sado-masochistic sexual fantasy. Coover's technique, like the mode of "The Babysitter," repeats the same action over and over again, with minor alterations, in order to convey a sense of the instability of reality and of the impossibility of capturing it exactly. Mimesis is undermined and fantasy legitimated as a replacement for verisimilitude. Thus literary realism is thrashed as compulsively as the maid is whipped. Further, cause and effect relationships are destroyed, since the whipping is done 1) in accordance with the principles in a manual which is never shown to us or identified, or 2) for stated reasons that vary from page

to page. In short, for no reason. Finally, the master and the maid, both nameless, are not characters in a fiction but automatons; or they are dream figures without being. The novella attacks the concept of ontology, as it does of rationality and reality. It lives, in no particularly vibrant way, in the rhythms of its repetition and in the sensuality of its male-oriented fantasy.

—Chester E. Eisinger

COPE, Jack (Robert Knox Cope). South African. Born in Mooi River, Natal, 3 June 1913. Educated at Durban High School. Married Lesley de Villiers in 1942 (divorced, 1956); two children. Reporter, *Natal Mercury*, Durban, 1931–35; correspondent in London for South African Morning Newspapers, 1936–40; farmer in Natal, 1941–42; engaged in shark-fishing enterprise, Cape Town, 1943–45; director, South African Association of the Arts, Cape Town, 1946–48. Since 1949, freelance writer and reporter: founding editor, *Contrast*, Cape Town, 1960–79; editor, Mantis Editions in the 1970's. Recipient: South African Arts and Sciences Prose Prize, 1959; British Council travel grant, 1960; Carnegie travel fellowship, 1966; South African Festival of the Soil award, 1970; CNA award, 1972; Argus Fiction Prize and Gold Medal, 1972. D.Litt.: Rhodes Univerity, Grahamstown, 1981. Agent: Shelley Power, INPRA, P.O. Box 149-A, Surbiton, Surrey KT6 5JH. Address: 21 Bearton Road, Hitchin, Hertfordshire SG5 1UB, England.

PUBLICATIONS

Novels

The Fair House.   London, MacGibbon and Kee, 1955.
The Golden Oriole.   London, Heinemann, 1958.
The Road to Ysterberg.   London, Heinemann, 1959.
Albino.   London, Heinemann, 1964.
The Dawn Comes Twice.   London, Heinemann, 1969.
The Rain-Maker.   London, Heinemann, 1971.
The Student of Zend.   London, Heinemann, 1972.
My Son Max.   London, Heinemann, 1977.

Short Stories

The Tame Ox.   London, Heinemann, 1960.
The Man Who Doubted.   London, Heinemann, 1967.
Alley Cat and Other Stories.   London, Heinemann, 1973.

Uncollected Short Stories

"The Little Stint," in *Contrast* (Cape Town), 1976.
"The Art Teacher," in *Contrast* (Cape Town), 1981.

Verse

Lyrics and Diatribes.   Cape Town, Stewart, 1948.
Marie: A South African Satire (as R.K. Cope).   Cape Town, Stewart, 1949.
Jack Cope/C.J. Driver.   Cape Town, Philip. 1979.

Other

Comrade Bill (biography).   Cape Town, Stewart, 1943.

The Adversary Within: Dissident Writers in Afrikaans. Cape Town, Philip, London, Collings, and Atlantic Highlands, New Jersey, Humanities Press, 1982.

Editor, with Uys Krige, *The Penguin Book of South African Verse.* London, Penguin, 1968.
Editor, *Seismograph: Best South African Writing from Contrast.* Cape Town, Reijger, 1970.
Editor, *Under the Horizon: Collected Poems of Charles Eglington.* Cape Town, Purnell, 1977.

Translator, with William Plomer, *Selected Poems of Ingrid Jonker.* London, Cape, 1968.

*

Jack Cope comments:
(1972) Raised by a farming family on the South African veld a long way from anywhere, I had made up my mind at about 10 years of age that I was going to be a writer. How to do it was another thing. I am still on that search. It has been said that the art of writing lies in the struggle against the inability to write. I was a third generation from settlers in a practically empty region of Natal; white, English-speaking. Zulus came up from the warm bush country to work on the cold high-veld and they were often the only playmates I and my brothers had. We got to know them, liked them, learnt from them.

In the old stone farmhouse there were thousands of books— sermons, religious tracts and poetry, Victorian novels by "Ouida," Disraeli, Mrs. Gaskell, Wilkie Collins, Mrs. Henry Wood, etc. But there were also Fenimore Cooper, Kingsley, Defoe, Mark Twain, Dickens, Ruskin, Scott, William Morris, Thackeray; there were Shakespeare and all the English poets up to Browning. The Bible was part of one's life, though we were too far away to go to church more than a few times. I knew that I couldn't model myself on any of the writers I read—we had no Redskins, no sea or pirates, no rivers, lakes, forests, no cities, no factories, no art, no stage. Living in a mental desert, what did one specially see and feel, let alone write about? We hunted and had guns and dogs and horses, but it was all so ordinary. At 12 I was sent 100 miles to boarding school into Durban, a seaport which seemed duller, more lonely even than the farm.

Then I left school, refused to enter university and went instead into a newspaper in Durban as an "apprentice." A mistake. I was ten years in journalism and never liked it. Learnt how not to write. One thing the newspaper business did for me—it got me out of South Africa and to London. I worked in Fleet Street. In four years I was almost flattened out into an Englishman. But there's the paradox, the nearer you are, the further you are away from a thing. Anyway I remained African. Language, blood, family, tradition were all on one side; but the break of nearly a century was too long. I belonged to Africa or to nowhere.

Of course I had long since made a mental holocaust of *white* race attitudes as no-one can like somebody born into them. Mad about Shaw and Morris, Russell, Marx, Ibsen, Pound(!), Eliot and O'Casey, I cultivated a polyglot creed, a sort of anarcho-social-communonihilist with a strong dash of pacifism. Wrote bad verse with an admiring eye on Yeats, Lawrence, or Pound, and my stories limped on crutches of Gorky, Bunin, Hemingway. No nationalism, no dogma, no traditionalism, I thought myself a citizen of that other country, The World. My time—the coming apocalypse.

The war drove me morosely from England home to Natal, to the farm, the loneliness. I tried to start writing consistently, seriously. To my astonishment and disgust I found I just couldn't. The novel I started with a family-historical background went through four re-writes over a period of 12 years— all torn up or burnt. Friends used to put down my typescript in embarrassment. The book was *The Fair House*. The fifth script I sent to London. Back came a cable from a young publisher, James MacGibbon: "Fair House is magnificent." I got very drunk. I'd like to believe it was true. But I know: it was shaky but a beginning. Meanwhile I was suddenly writing short stores that got accepted.

That was the break-out. I stumbled about after that but have made it a point not to get frozen into a "manner" (substitute for style) or be carried away by form. In each story and novel, as in my poems, I wanted all the elements, rhythm, structure, tone, to work separately and together within a different context and to be ruled by it. Each book, I hope, shifts a peg on. Seven novels so far, two books, and a lot of uncollected stories—the objective is still to produce one good book by the time I pack in, and then I'll feel there was something in my dreams at the age of ten.

Writing in South Africa is not easy. There's a high voltage of tension. There's Censorship, intimidation; one's books get banned. But I don't believe in quitting; you can't see things straight from too great a distance, from exile. I am against writing dirt for sales or for its own sake. Life's full enough of dirt and if it gets into a book the context must give it an absolute necessity. I remain an African, and Africa somehow keeps a certain innocence, a certain newness and strength. It's not a political slogan. Or a garbage dump.

To fight against isolation I've always tried to work back from my own experience and to draw together the younger writers, raise critical standards, demand sound craftsmanship. I make translations from Afrikaans, Zulu, Sotho, Xhosa, and this I feel helps create links in a multi-national society. Writers cannot get a wide enough readership in the developing languages and therefore aim to master English or Afrikaans. To command a new language and learn to write in it is a mammoth task—one can be helped or encouraged, but there are no short cuts. In 1960 I took part in starting a two-language literary quarterly, *Contrast*, and still edit it. The magazine has been a mouthpiece as well as workshop for many promising young poets, fiction writers, dramatists, artists.

South Africa still has a small enough population for writers living even thousands of miles apart to get to know each other. They come from every nationality, race, belief, outlook. Many are banned, exiled. But they form a kind of republic of talent rising above the jargon and propaganda, throwing shadows ahead.

(1986) In 1980 I came to England again, this time to write a novel from a new angle. My characters, although still African, have scattered outwards onto a wider stage. This has almost meant learning my craft all over again—a search for self. After more than five years I have already finished the task.

*   *   *

Jack Cope is a South African writer whose work has attracted attention not only for its intrinsic merit as fiction—and Cope is undeniably a competent and at times a compelling story-teller with the power to create wholly believable fictional worlds— but more significantly, perhaps, because of the way in which he uses his South African material. His novels and short stories present a romanticised and initially attractive view of contemporary South Africa, derived partly, it would appear, from his own privileged position in the class-ridden and rigidly divided structures of South African society. The product of a liberal education, and to a large extent removed by birth and upbringing from the political struggles which have dominated South African history for the past 70 years, Cope can afford to regard his fellow South Africans, both black and white, with a large degree of tolerance, seeing them as actors in the great human drama rather than—as so often happens in South African fiction—as victims or oppressors. The landscape is always an important element in Cope's fiction, and he is particularly adept at evoking the great spaces of the South African deserts, the rugged sea-coasts, and the lush sub-tropical settings of his native Natal. In his early stories, he also more than half seriously tends to invest the African landscape with a mystic quality, implying that powerful forces are at work helping to shape the destiny not only of the indigenous folk who still believe in witchcraft and sorcery but also of those more recent arrivals who have had the temerity to attempt to tame the wilderness.

Many of Cope's stories demonstrate a genuine concern for the sufferings of his black fellow citizens, whether such sufferings are caused by poverty or ignorance, or result from apartheid. Cope has however always avoided outright condemnation of this system, and has made it abundantly clear both in his critical writing and in his novels that he regards political involvement as an irrelevance at best, and at worst as exerting a corrupting influence on those who, like himself, should be concerned only with standards of excellence and with the republic of talent. Such views have ensured that Cope's work is free from the guilt-ridden breast-beating which characterises so much writing by white South Africans, particularly those of Cope's generation who believed that committed literature could play a part in the struggle against the apartheid system, but they are also responsible for the fact that much of his work appears remote from the historical and political realities of South Africa today, and lacks interest for contemporary readers.

Cope's first three novels tackle themes which can be broadly categorised as historical, while the more recent work focusses more directly on the contemporary situation. *The Fair House* recreates a significant episode from colonial history centering on the last armed rising of the Zulu in 1902 and on the subsequent consolidation of white power. *Albino* explores white and black relationships through a story of family feuds and guilts. *The Golden Oriole* describes the abortive attempts of a black writer to gain acceptance in the white literary world of the 1930's, and is set against a background of black political intrigue. In all these novels as in *The Road to Ysterberg* Cope presents his black characters with a degree of sympathy and insight, but the novels themselves suggest that he regards attempts at social integration as misguided; and although he is by no means overtly or intentionally racist, he suggests very strongly that only those who accept and share western cultural values can be considered truly civilised.

The Dawn Comes Twice, loosely based on events in the early 1960's, dramatises the efforts of a group of urban guerrillas to organise effective acts of sabotage. While this novel is relatively optimistic about the future of South Africa, *The Student of Zend* and *My Son Max* both demonstrate Cope's growing disillusion with the current political situation. Both novels are concerned with individuals who have tried to escape from a society which they perceive as narrow and personally frustrating. Both Jamie and Max are committed to a quest for personal fulfilment, which Cope presents in an almost romantic way as a "search for a goal beyond the self." Both men are, of course, doomed to failure; but while Jamie, the student of

ancient religions, can at least choose exile in Switzerland if he so desires, there is only one outcome for the young black man, Max, who refuses to commit himself to the freedom struggle in which his comrades are involved: death at the hands of these comrades. In his earlier novels Cope had suggested that white society denied black people the right to live in a civilised way. In *My Son Max* he appears to imply that while whites may now be ready to accept black people (particularly if they are as "civilised" as Max is), it is black people themselves who now seek to deny each other this right in the name of an illusory struggle for "freedom."

—Ursula Edmands

COWAN, Peter (Walkinshaw). Australian. Born in Perth, Western Australia, 4 November 1914. Educated at the University of Western Australia, Nedlands, B.A. 1940, Dip. Ed. 1946. Served in the Royal Australian Air Force, 1943–45. Married Edith Howard in 1941; one son. Clerk, farm labourer, and casual worker, 1930–39; teacher, 1941–42; member of the faculty, University of Western Australia, 1946–50; Senior English Master, Scotch College, Swanbourne, Western Australia, 1950–62. Since 1964, Senior Tutor in English, University of Western Australia. Recipient: Commonwealth Literary Fund fellowship, 1963; Australian Council for the Arts fellowship, 1974, 1980; University of Western Australia fellowship, 1982. Address: Department of English, University of Western Australia, Nedlands, Western Australia 6009, Australia.

PUBLICATIONS

Novels

Summer. Sydney and London, Angus and Robertson, 1964.
Seed. Sydney and London, Angus and Robertson, and San Francisco, Tri-Ocean, 1966.
The Color of the Sky. Fremantle, Western Australia, Fremantle Arts Centre Press, 1986.

Short Stories

Drift. Melbourne, Reed and Harris, 1944.
The Unploughed Land. Sydney, Angus and Robertson, 1958.
The Empty Street. Sydney and London, Angus and Robertson, and San Francisco, Tri-Ocean, 1965.
The Tins and Other Stories. St. Lucia, University of Queensland Press, 1973.
New Country, with others, edited by Bruce Bennett. Fremantle, Western Australia, Fremantle Arts Centre Press, 1976.
Mobiles. Fremantle, Western Australia, Fremantle Arts Centre Press, 1979.

Other

A Unique Position: A Biography of Edith Dircksey Cowan 1861–1932. Nedlands, University of Western Australia Press, 1978.
A Colonial Experience: Swan River 1839–1888. Privately printed, 1979.

Editor, *Short Story Landscape: The Modern Short Story.* Melbourne, Longman, 1964.

Editor, with Bruce Bennett and John Hay, *Spectrum 1–2.* Melbourne, Longman, 2 vols., 1970; London, Longman, 2 vols., 1971.

Editor, *A Faithful Picture: The Letters of Eliza and Thomas Brown at York in the Swan River Country 1841–1852.* Fremantle, Western Australia, Fremantle Arts Centre Press, 1977.

*

Critical Studies: "The Short Stories of Peter Cowan," 1960, and "New Tracks to Travel: The Stories of White, Porter and Cowan," 1966, both by John Barnes, in *Meanjin* (Melbourne); essay by Grahame Johnston in *Westerly* (Perth), 1967; "Cowan Country" by Margot Luke, in *Sandgropers* edited by Dorothy Hewett, Nedlands, University of Western Australia Press, 1973; "Behind the Actual" by Bruce Williams, in *Westerly* (Perth), no. 3, 1973; "Regionalism in Peter Cowan's Short Fiction" by Bruce Bennett, in *World Literature Written in English* (Guelph, Ontario), 1980.

Peter Cowan comments:

Up to the present time writing has been for me as much something I wanted to do to please myself as something aimed solely at publication and any kind of wide audience. Now, I don't think this kind of attitude is any longer possible, and the chances for this kind of fiction have greatly diminished.

My writing may have been concerned as much with place as with people, though I have tried to see people against a landscape, against a physical environment. If isolation is one of the themes that occur frequently, particularly in the short stories, this is perhaps enforced by the Australian landscape itself. I am deeply involved in everything to do with the physical Australia, the land, its shapes and seasons and colors, its trees and flowers, its birds and animals. And its coast and sea.

I have been more interested in the short story than the novel. The technical demands of a short story are high, and seldom met, and through the short story a writer has perhaps a better chance of trapping something of the fragmentary nature of today's living.

*   *   *

Peter Cowan is a quietly introspective writer, and consequently his intensity of vision and his scrupulous craftsmanship can easily be underrated. He has shown a particular talent for the short story or novella, in which he can focus on a single relationship and explore a single line of feeling. His stories, written in a spare, taut style, have as a recurring theme the relationship of a man and a woman seeking relief from their loneliness in sexual love. Cowan is intent upon an inner reality: his characters are seldom individualized very far; they seem almost anonymous, and the sensuous reality of the external world is only faintly felt. His imagination is compelled by a painful awareness of the feelings of loneliness and alienation that lie beneath the surface of commonplace lives; and in exploring this territory he has become, more than is generally recognized, a significant interpreter of Australian realities.

In Cowan's first collection of stories, *Drift*, the preoccupations of his mature work are merely sketched in. Uneven in quality and stylistically in debt to Hemingway, the book nevertheless has a coherence and a unity of impression unexpected in the work of a young writer. Cowan has known his subject right from the start. Most of these early stories are set in the poor farming country of southwestern West Australia before World War II, and they centre on the lives of people who are emotionally unfulfilled or unable to express themselves in normal relationships.

Over the next 14 years Cowan wrote little. In his second collection, *The Unploughed Land*, he reprinted seven of his stories from *Drift*, along with six new stories, which represent a distinct advance in technique. These new stories include the much-anthologized "The Redbacked Spiders," a powerful story of a boy whose resentment at his brutal father leads to the man's death. The title story is an extended treatment of that pre-war country life about which he writes in his first volume. In its evocation of that life it is one of his finest pieces, and it marks the end of the first phase of his development.

From this point onward Cowan has been more prolific and more varied—though compared with most writers he has a small and narrow output. In his third collection, *The Empty Street*, there is a noticeable shift in setting. Cowan now writes of people in suburbia, for whom the country is a refuge. The sense of being caught in an irresistible and disastrous historical process is expressed in a story like "The Tractor," which concerns the efforts of a hermit to stop the clearing of the land. Cowan's sympathies are with those who oppose "progress," but he sees their dilemma truly. "The Empty Street," a novella, is an impressive study of an unhappy middle-aged clerk, whose marriage is now a mere shell, and whose children are strangers to him: desperate to escape the pressures of a life that is meaningless to him, he collapses into schizophrenia and turns murderer. Cowan is especially responsive to the theme of the middle-aged, defeated, and desolate in marriage, groping for a way out. *The Tins and Other Stories* confirms the achievement of the earlier volumes, with stories like "The Rock" and "The Tins," in which Cowan is seen at his characteristic best.

In recent years Cowan has spent a great deal of time researching the history of his family, which has been prominent in the public life of West Australia since colonial times. This turning to the past has the appearance of being a retreat from the present, of which he takes such a bleak view in his fiction. But the collection, *Mobiles*, and, even more strikingly, his latest novel, *The Color of the Sky*, show, rather, that the sense of the past has sharpened and enlarged his sense of the present. Four of the seven stories in *Mobiles* are set in the stony northwest, beyond the limits of settlement or where settlement has failed. In these starkly rendered episodes human beings are no more than transitory figures in an enduring and inhospitable landscape. The longest story in the volume, "The Lake," reworks a favourite theme of 19th-century novelists—the "hidden valley" in the heart of the unexplored continent. In what is one of his most satisfying stories, the symbolic possibilities of the landscape—evoked here with more vividness than is usual in his writing—are subtly realized. This story points to a new strength in Cowan's writing which appears in his third and finest novel.

Peter Cowan's first two attempts at novels were not very successful. *Summer* is a short novel, more like two short stories that have been expanded and linked together. A businessman whose marriage has failed takes a job on the wheat bins, and in this lonely setting forms a relationship with the wife of the nearby storekeeper. The violent resolution is not well managed, and the central character tends to be a mouthpiece for Cowan's reflections on the spoiling of the natural environment. Yet there are some fine sequences establishing the relationship of the two lonely people in a solitary landscape.

In *Seed* Cowan set out to portray a group of middle-class families living in Perth. An Australian reader feels the force of his thesis about the boredom and frustration of suburban living, but it remains a thesis and seldom quickens into drama. It is a disappointing work, the result of Cowan's trying to write against the grain of his talent. He is not skilled at creating personalities or at suggesting the social facts of life, but in this rather old-fashioned, realistic novel the emphasis falls on just those aspects of his writing where he is weakest.

The Color of the Sky has the formal integrity and the imaginative vigour which the previous novels lacked. The narrator is a familiar enough Cowan creation–a man on his own, trying to make sense of his experience. In a visit to a place dimly remembered from a visit in childhood, the narrator is simultaneously exploring the past and the present, and much of the power of the narrative derives from the reader's realization of patterns only half-traced, elusive parallels, family likenesses, disturbing undercurrents and continuities. Both the past and the present contain events that could be sensationalized—drug-running, murder, illicit sexual liaisons—but Cowan's novel is a study of the consciousness of a man in search of himself. In the end, the narrator can no more complete the jigsaw puzzle of his family relationships than he can give shape to the incoherence of his own emotional and moral life, with its tangle of loose ends, evasions, and denials. This work is Cowan's most impressive treatment of (in his own words) "the fragmentary nature of today's living."

—John Barnes

CREWS, Harry (Eugene). American. Born in Alma, Georgia, 6 June 1935. Educated at the University of Florida, Gainesville, B.A. 1960, M.S.Ed. 1962. Served in the United States Marine Corps, 1953–56: Sergeant. Married Sally Ellis in 1960; two sons. English teacher, Broward Junior College, Fort Lauderdale, Florida, 1962–68. Associate Professor, 1968–74, and since 1974, Professor of English, University of Florida. Recipient: Bread Loaf Writers Conference Atherton Fellowship, 1968; American Academy award, 1972; National Endowment for the Arts grant, 1974. Address: Department of English, University of Florida, Gainesville, Florida 32601, U.S.A.

PUBLICATIONS

Novels

The Gospel Singer.   New York, Morrow, 1968.
Naked in Garden Hills.   New York, Morrow, 1969.
This Thing Don't Lead to Heaven.   New York, Morrow, 1970.
Karate Is a Thing of the Spirit.   New York, Morrow, 1971; London, Secker and Warburg, 1972.
Car.   New York, Morrow, 1972; London, Secker and Warburg, 1973.
The Hawk Is Dying.   New York, Knopf, 1973; London, Secker and Warburg, 1974.
The Gypsy's Curse.   New York, Knopf, 1974; London, Secker and Warburg, 1975.
A Feast of Snakes.   New York, Atheneum, 1976; London, Secker and Warburg, 1977.

Short Stories

The Enthusiast.   Winston-Salem, North Carolina, Palaemon Press, 1981.
Two.   Northridge, California, Lord John Press, 1984.

Uncollected Short Stories

"The Player Piano," in *Florida Quarterly* (Gainesville), Fall 1967.
"The Unattached Smile," in *Craft and Vision*, edited by Andrew Lytle.   New York, Delacorte Press, 1971.

Other

A Childhood: The Biography of a Place (on Bacon County, Georgia).   New York, Harper, 1978; London, Secker and Warburg, 1979.
Blood and Grits.   New York, Harper, 1979.
Florida Frenzy.   Gainesville, University Presses of Florida, 1982.

*

Critical Studies: *A Grit's Triumph: Essays on the Works of Harry Crews* edited by David K. Jeffrey, Port Washington, New York, Associated Faculty Press, 1983.

*   *   *

Harry Crews's eight novels establish him as the most astringent observer of contemporary good-old-boy culture, the grass roots of the South. An outrageous satirist of U.S. lie in general, Crews pits the empty materialism of our mainstream society against deep-South grotesques and misfits with results at once comic and horrific.

Beginning with *The Gospel Singer*, which probes the psychology of show-biz fundamentalism, Crews has invented a gallery of social, sexual, and spiritual outcasts who seek salvation in a civilization which offers them only *things*. The theme is expanded in *Naked in Garden Hills* . Fat Man, the 600-pound protagonist, lives in an abandoned phosphorus mine, where the earth has been eaten away, and he tries to eat the world itself. This is echoed in *Car*, in which Herman Mack vows to eat an entire 1971 Ford Maverick. A refugee from a junkyard, Mack revenges himself on the world by trying to consume and defecate it. *This Thing Don't Lead to Heaven* caricatures the old-folks industry, in which people are the used-up detritus of our society. In this novel, Jefferson Davis Munroe, a midget who works for a "graveyard chain," competes with Axel's Senior Club for the bodies (if not souls) of the dying.

In *Karate Is a Thing of the Spirit* Crews deals with the fads and obsessions of contemporary trendy culture. John Kaimon, its central character, wears a tee-shirt stenciled with William Faulkner's face and tries to find himself through an outlaw karate group. The story develops our sick fascination with sex and violence and the fear of love and belief which Crews sees as being at the focus of our lives. *The Hawk Is Dying* portrays a more positive, even heroic, obsession, George Gattling's desire to "man" (train) a hawk in the prescribed medieval ritual. His attempt to fuse his soul with the raptor's is another way out of the stylized hell of a technologically focused world. George's need for belief is satisfied by the vitality of his hawk, its innate freedom and dignity.

The Gypsy's Curse returns to a world of physical violence and action with Marvin Molar, born with stunted legs, who walks on his hands and develops his upper body through exercise. In his upside-down world, he becomes sexually obsessed with Hester, a normal woman. The connection between possessiveness, "normality," sexuality, and strength is a basic Crews theme. It appears also in the savage burlesque of *A Feast of Snakes*, in which high school football, baton-twirling, weightlifting, moonshine selling and rattlesnake hunting are intermixed as American rituals. The story ends, like *The Gospel*

Singer, in an explosion of mortal violence, as Joe Lon Mackey, ex-state-champ quarterback, loses his slender grip on his own life.

Crews's satire is directed toward the triviality and rootlessness of our culture, its lack of belief. His characters search frantically for salvation through money, sex, social status, physical strength, mystical rites, through sheer acquisitiveness. Crews shows how these are false paths, failures. John Kaimon, in *Karate Is a Thing of the Spirit*, thinks:

> . . . he also knew he did not believe. The breath of little children would leave his flesh only flesh.
> Belief could see through glass eyes, could turn flesh to stone or stone to flesh. But not for him, He would walk through the world naked. He would bruise and bleed. He saw it clearly.

Crews sees clearly, through his scathing satire, that the absence of faith leads to violence, madness, death. His creatures search through a world of junkyards and abandoned mines and prisons for their authenticity through belief, and our world fails and maims them in savage ways.

—William J. Schafer

CROSS, Ian (Robert). New Zealander. Born in Wanganui, in 1925. Educated at Wanganui Technical College. Married to Tui Tunnicliffe; four sons. Associate Nieman Fellow in Journalism, Harvard University, Cambridge, Massachusetts, 1954–55; Robert Burns Fellow, Otago University, Dunedin, 1959. Editor, *New Zealand Listener*, Wellington, 1973–77. Since 1977, Chairman and Chief Executive, Broadcasting Corporation of New Zealand, Wellington. Recipient: Hubert Church Prose Award, 1962. Address: Broadcasting Corporation of New Zealand, P.O. Box 98, Wellington, New Zealand.

PUBLICATIONS

Novels

The God Boy. New York, Harcourt Brace, 1957; London, Deutsch, 1958.
The Backward Sex. London, Deutsch, 1960.
After Anzac Day. London, Deutsch, 1961.

Uncollected Short Story

"Love Affair," in *Atlantic* (Boston), January 1958.

Play

Television Play: *The City of No*, 1970.

*   *   *

Ian Cross has written three novels of social concern, which explore the tensions in personal relationships, especially those given emphasis by the narrow experience of small communities. *The God Boy* presents this material through the eyes of a 13-year-old boy who has, two years previously, been a participant in a family tragedy which he observed but did not understand, and which has left its mark upon him. Torn between his father and his mother, young Jimmy reacts with violence and obsession, a classic case history. A clever child who has thought of himself as "chosen," he expects God to give him a helping hand, but no aid comes. He therefore sets up his own private "mutiny against God." The book is notable for its skilful handling of a difficult narrative mode, and for its successful evocation of the speech and ways of an average New Zealand boy. Irony thickens the texture. The reader is closely involved with Jimmy, and like the social worker whose concern this kind of situation so often becomes, begins to comprehend the disaster from within, with sympathetic insight.

The Backward Sex disappoints by being too similar in both manner and material. Raggleton, the coastal settlement of *The God Boy*, has become Albertville, but is otherwise the same place, with a wider range of wharves, sandhills, lupins, and suburban lives as befits the older teller, this time a boy of 17. The topic is the fumbling sexuality of adolescence, but the theme does not seem serious, and the novel is not far above the level of melodrama.

After Anzac Day is wider in both scope and narration. Four people share the telling: The Girl, whose life is going wrong (she is pregnant but unmarried); The Woman, wife of Rankin, ex-soldier and public servant, whose marriage has become a prison with "solitary cells' where the inmates do not even attempt to communicate; The Man, her husband; and The Old Man, her father. These four play out a domestic drama springing from the presence in The Woman's expensive well-oiled home of Jennie, The Girl, to whom her husband has unexpectedly extended a helping hand. Each narrator is given a short turn, which allows Cross to weave four different attitudes and backgrounds into the texture of his fictional world. Clearly, he means to raise wide social, personal, and even historical issues in the New Zealand of 1960. Had he succeeded fully, the elaborate narrative apparatus would have been justified, perhaps. But the problems of John and Margaret Rankin seldom lift above the level of private affairs; the story remains a family drama, without any transfer of significance to the wider issues. *The God Boy*, however, the best of these three novels, is a remarkable little work.

—Joan Stevens

DAHL, Roald. British. Born in Llandaff, Glamorgan, Wales, 13 September 1916. Educated at Repton School, Yorkshire. Served in the Royal Air Force, 1939–45: in Nairobi and Habbanyah, 1939–40; with a Fighter Squadron in the Western Desert, 1940 (wounded); in Greece and Syria, 1941; Assistant Air Attaché, Washington, D.C., 1942–43; Wing Commander, 1943; with British Security Co-ordination, North America, 1943–45. Married 1) the actress Patricia Neal in 1953 (divorced, 1983), one son and four daughters (one deceased); 2) Felicity Ann Crosland in 1983. Member of the Public Schools Exploring Society expedition to Newfoundland, 1934; member of the Eastern staff, Shell Company, London, 1933–37, and Shell Company of East Africa, Dar-es-Salaam, 1937–39. Recipient: Mystery Writers of America Edgar Allan Poe Award, 1953, 1959, 1980; Federation of Children's Book Groups award, 1983; Whitbread Award, 1983; World Fantasy Convention award, 1983. Agent: Murray Pollinger, 4 Garrick Street, London WC2E 9BH; or, Watkins Loomis Agency, 150 East 35th

Street, New York, New York 10016, U.S.A. Address: Gipsy House, Great Missenden, Buckinghamshire HP16 0PB, England.

PUBLICATIONS

Novels

Sometime Never: A Fable for Supermen.   New York, Scribner, 1948; London, Collins, 1949.
My Uncle Oswald.   London, Joseph, 1979; New York, Knopf, 1980.

Short Stories

Over to You: 10 Stories of Flyers and Flying.   New York, Reynal, 1946; London, Hamish Hamilton, 1947.
Someone Like You.   New York, Knopf, 1953; London, Secker and Warburg, 1954; revised edition, London, Joseph, 1961.
Kiss, Kiss.   New York, Knopf, and London, Joseph, 1960.
Twenty-Nine Kisses.   London, Joseph, 1969.
Selected Stories.   New York, Random House, 1970.
Penguin Modern Stories 12, with others.   London, Penguin, 1972.
Switch Bitch.   New York, Knopf, and London, Joseph, 1974.
The Best of Roald Dahl.   New York, Vintage, 1978; London, Joseph, 1983.
Tales of the Unexpected.   London, Joseph, and New York, Vintage, 1979.
More Tales of the Unexpected.   London, Joseph, 1980; as *Further Tales of the Unexpected*, Bath, Chivers, 1981.
A Roald Dahl Selection: Nine Short Stories, edited by Roy Blatchford.   London, Longman, 1980.

Fiction (for children)

The Gremlins.   New York, Random House, 1943; London, Collins, 1944.
James and the Giant Peach.   New York, Knopf, 1961; London, Allen and Unwin, 1967.
Charlie and the Chocolate Factory.   New York, Knopf, 1964; London, Allen and Unwin, 1967.
The Magic Finger.   New York, Harper, 1966; London, Allen and Unwin, 1968.
Fantastic Mr. Fox.   New York, Knopf, and London, Allen and Unwin, 1970.
Charlie and the Great Glass Elevator.   New York, Knopf, 1972; London, Allen and Unwin, 1973.
Danny, The Champion of the World.   London, Cape, and New York, Knopf, 1975.
The Wonderful Story of Henry Sugar and Six More.   London, Cape, 1977; as *The Wonderful World of Henry Sugar,* New York, Knopf, 1977.
The Complete Adventures of Charlie and Mr. Willy Wonka (omnibus).   London, Allen and Unwin, 1978.
The Enormous Crocodile.   London, Cape, and New York, Knopf, 1978.
The Twits.   London, Cape, 1980; New York, Knopf, 1981.
George's Marvellous Medicine.   London, Cape, 1981; New York, Knopf, 1982.
The BFG.   London, Cape, and New York, Farrar Straus, 1982.
The Witches.   London, Cape, and New York, Farrar Straus, 1983.

The Giraffe and the Pelly and Me.   London, Cape, and New York, Farrar Straus, 1985.

Plays

The Honeys (produced New York, 1955).

Screenplays: *You Only Live Twice*, with Harry Jack Bloom, 1967; *Chitty-Chitty-Bang-Bang*, with Ken Hughes, 1968; *The Night-Digger*, 1970; *The Lightning Bug*, 1971; *Willy Wonka and the Chocolate Factory*, 1971.

Television Play: *Lamb to the Slaughter* (*Alfred Hitchcock Presents* series), 1955.

Verse (for children)

Revolting Rhymes.   London, Cape, 1982; New York, Knopf, 1983.
Dirty Beasts.   London, Cape, and New York, Farrar Straus, 1984.

Other

Boy: Tales of Childhood (for children). London, Cape, and New York, Farrar Straus, 1984.

Editor, *Roald Dahl's Book of Ghost Stories.*   London, Cape, and New York, Farrar Straus, 1983.

*

Critical Studies: in *New York Herald-Tribune*, 7 February 1960; *Wilson Library Bulletin* (New York), February 1962; *Saturday Review* (New York), 17 February 1962.

Roald Dahl comments:
(1972) I am primarily a short-story writer. But a good plot is hard to find, and it gets harder all the time. No short-story writer should continue in this field when he has run out of plots, otherwise he finishes up producing indifferent work, as well as "mood-pieces" and essays all labelled "short stories"—which they are not.
I now write books for children. It gives me great pleasure.

*   *   *

Conventional human responses to bizarre circumstances domesticate Roald Dahl's carefully detailed, grotesque world. This shock of the familiar makes credible the logic of a cautionary tale in a universe that initially seems devoid of guidelines. "An African Story," which only tangentially develops the theme of Dahl's first adult book, *Over to You: Ten Stories of Flyers and Flying*, foreshadows the pattern dominating his later work. A neurotic's sensitivity to unpleasant animal habits causes an elderly Englishman to sacrifice him to a dead Mamba snake that can, in a characteristic Dahl touch, drink milk from a cow. Though the neurotic is punished rather more severely than he might be at home, the vengeful old man emerges as a champion of the typical English dedication to animals which operates even in the jungle. The snake's contented sip of milk after the killing produces a simultaneous effect of horror and conventional moral righteousness; in "The Visitor" (*Switch Bitch*) the discovery by Oswald, an antithetical blend of hypochondria and satyriasis, that an unscrupulous seduction has exposed him to leprosy produces a similar moral frisson.

Dahl's adult novel *Sometime Never: A Fable for Supermen*, which attempts to raise the war horrors and hallucinations of *Over to You* to the mythic level, effectively details some deadpan accounts of the discovery of gremlins, who "scraped platinum off the points and put it carefully into small leather purses which had zip-fasteners on them." However, Dahl's whimsical treatment of these creatures undercuts their lethal activities, which are "a bit too much like death to be funny . . . far too ridiculous to be amusing." And an atomic holocaust, that familiar feature of post-World War II novels, turns the gremlins of the second half of the book into rational thinkers contemptuous of the insanity of human war-making, though Dahl gives them Thurberish names like Snogs, Bogglers, and Hornswogglers. The final irony that equates total disappearance of human beings, an event long awaited by the gremlins, with the vanishing of these creatures themselves, since they are merely projections of the human imagination, does not resolve the contradictory roles of the gremlins and the resulting confusion in tone. The structural problems of this novel, and the only sporadic effectiveness of the long stories in *Switch Bitch*, suggest that Dahl's talent works best within the tightly plotted *short* story. Though he can create brilliant moments in which disturbed narrators reveal their lunatic obsessions, he seems unable to develop a consistent character who might unify a series of incidents. While Oswald's personality contributes to the atmosphere of "The Visitor," in his other appearance in "Bitch" he fades into a faceless, quirkless narrator whose part in the sexual climax would suit any non-senescent male.

The quintessential pattern of domesticated (often in both senses) horror was firmly established in the stories Dahl collected as *Someone Like You* and *Kiss, Kiss*. Frequently these stories focus on a bet or competition, usually rigged, and the perverse morality of Dahl's universe causes the dishonest victor to lose his status as a gourmet in "Taste," a Chippendale commode in "Parson's Pleasure," his money *and* his life in "Dip in the Pool," and the title of "Champion of the World" among partridge poachers. (Conversely, the children's novel *Charlie and the Chocolate Factory* utilizes the contest motif to stress the rewards of virtuous triumph.) Dahl gives verisimilitude to these situations by bombarding the reader with a wealth of detail involving such disciplines as wine lore, period furniture, and partridge trapping. Often, this almost statistical documentation simultaneously reinforces otherwise improbable anecdotes and ridicules self-styled expertise.

The many stories involving mutilation, either real or threatened, also depend on factual data both to mitigate and substantiate the horror. "Skin" seems so knowledgeable about the details of Soutine's life and technique, and so deadpan in its dialogue, that negotiations for the picture Soutine inconveniently painted on the back of an elderly beggar seem at once utterly absurd and frighteningly realistic. Apparently factual data similarly buttress Dahl's treatment of experiments in the monstrous, whether the sinister effects of feeding a sickly baby on "Royal Jelly," or a downtrodden wife's reaction to the survival of her dead husband's brain in "William and Mary." Her practical wifely stance parallels a husband's malevolently commonsense response in "Edward the Conqueror" to his wife's ecstatic discovery that stray cat houses the soul of Liszt.

Such mismatches occur frequently in Dahl's fiction and are often symbolized by the disproportionate physical dimensions of the partners: the diminutive husband and his "big rather than tall wife" in "My Lady Love, My Dove"; the tiny, repressed clergyman of "Georgy Porgy" and his amorous female parishioners, notably Miss Roach, ". . . a striking person—unusually muscular for a woman, with broad shoulders and powerful arms and a huge calf bulging on each leg." Dahl also stresses physiognomy, especially the mouth, as an index to character. People with "salmon" mouths ("Nunc Dimittis") and "caterpillar" mouths ("Mr. Hoddy") display the appropriate traits, and the gourmet's mouth in "Taste" functions not merely as the key to his character, but as the character itself: ". . . all mouth—mouth and lips—the full, wet lips of the professional gourmet, the lower lip hanging downward in the center, a pendulous, permanently open taster's lip, shaped open to receive the rim of a glass or a morsel of food. Like a keyhole, I thought, watching it; his mouth is like a large wet keyhole."

The symbolic possibilities of the mouth achieve fullest development in "Georgy Porgy," the title itself suggesting Dahl's gift for playing with the perverse implications of the childlike. The sex education given the protagonist by his progressive mother goes awry when the boy, witnessing the birth of rabbits, sees that the fondling, kissing mouth of the mother rabbit is devouring its offspring. Immediately, the child perceives his own mother's "huge red mouth opening wider and wider until it is just a great big round gaping hole with a black black centre. . . ." This regrettable epiphany foreshadows his response years later when Miss Roach attempts to kiss him: "I saw this great mouth of hers coming slowly down on top of me, starting to open, and coming closer and closer, and opening wider and wider . . . I had never in all my life seen anything more terrifying than that mouth. . . ." The clergyman's final insane conviction that he has been swallowed and now inhabits the woman's interior is made credible by his matter-of-fact tone: "It is all a trifle bizarre for a man of conservative tastes like myself. Personally, I prefer oak furniture and parquet flooring. . . ." Though Dahl avoids underlining the ultimate significance of his key symbol, he illuminates it obliquely through the clergyman's wonderfully detailed experiments with the sex drives of rats. In blending the ordinary and the grotesque, in ballasting both with convincing details and, especially, in preserving a delightfully ambivalent attitude toward the reader's credulity, "Georgy Porgy" might serve as the archetype for Dahl's fiction.

—Burton Kendle

DATHORNE, O(scar) R(onald).   British.   Born in Georgetown, Guyana, 19 November 1934. Educated at the University of Sheffield, Yorkshire, 1955–58, B.A. 1958, M.A. 1960, Ph.D. 1966; University of London, 1958–59, Cert.Ed. 1959, Dip.Ed. 1967; University of Miami, M.B.A., M.P.A. 1984. Married Hildegard Ostermaier in 1959; two children. Lecturer, Ahmadu Bello University, Zaria, Nigeria, 1959–63, and University of Ibadan, Nigeria, 1963–66; Unesco Consultant to the Government of Sierra Leone, 1967–68; Professor of English, Njala University College, University of Sierra Leone, Freetown, 1968–69; Professor, Afro-American Studies Department, University of Wisconsin, Madison, 1970, and Ohio State University, Columbus, 1971–77. Since 1977, Professor of English and Director of American Studies, University of Miami. Editor, *Journal of Caribbean Studies*, Coral Gables, Florida. Address: Department of English, University of Miami, Coral Gables, Florida 33124, U.S.A.

PUBLICATIONS

Novels

Dumplings in the Soup.   London, Cassell, 1963.

The Scholar-Man.   London, Cassell, 1964.

Uncollected Short Stories

"The Wintering of Mr. Kolawole," in *Stories from the Caribbean*, edited by Andrew Salkey.   London, Elek, 1965; as *Island Voices*, New York, Liveright, 1970.
"Hodge" and "The Nightwatchman and the Baby Nurse," in *Nigerian Radio Times* (Ibadan), 1967.
"Constable," in *Political Spider*.   London, Heinemann, 1969.

Verse

Kelly Poems.   Privately printed, 1977.

Other

The Black Mind: A History of African Literature.   Minneapolis, University of Minnesota Press, 1974; abridged edition, as *African Literature in the Twentieth Century*, University of Minnesota Press, and London, Heinemann, 1976.
Dark Ancestor: The Literature of the Black Man in the Caribbean.   Baton Rouge, Louisiana State University Press, 1981.

Editor, with others, *Young Commonwealth Poets '65.* London, Heinemann, 1965.
Editor, *Caribbean Narrative.*   London, Heinemann, 1966.
Editor, *Caribbean Verse.*   London, Heinemann, 1967.
Editor, with Willfried Feuser, *Africa in Prose.*   London, Penguin, 1969.
Editor, *African Poetry for Schools and Colleges.*   Yaba, Nigeria, Macmillan, 1969.
Editor, *Selected Poems*, by Derek Walcott.   London, Heinemann, 1977.
Editor, *Afro World: Adventures in Ideas.*   Milwaukee, University of Wisconsin Press, 1984.

*

Critical Studies: "Guyanese Writers" by Wilfred Cartey, in *New World* (Georgetown, Guyana), 1966; *The Islands in Between* by Louis James, London, Oxford University Press, 1968; *The Chosen Tongue* by Gerald Moore, London, Longman, 1969; *Homecoming* by James T. Ngugi, London, Heinemann, 1972, New York, Hill, 1973.

O.R. Dathorne comments:
(1972) My work has in general utilized situations which seemed near enough for me to handle. Black immigration in England, a Black man's quest for identity in Africa have been the starting points for what I hope have been larger involvements of the protagonist's new understanding of the world. Frequently, the "new" contact with reality cannot be resolved on a rational level and this is why in plays and poetry I have moved towards an intentionally "irrational" approach which expresses bewilderment.
I lived for ten years in Africa; they taught me to be wary of novelty, as did the creative urges of young African writers like myself. Only incidentally, I became a "critic" of the new African literature; only incidentally, I was forced to learn about a man's world-view (which I had to understand) before I spoke. Only incidentally this led me back to myself and the large interrogatives concerning my history. Now I am aware of the

manifestations of curious parallels in cultural experience and it is this I proclaim.

*   *   *

O.R. Dathorne as a novelist has two characteristics—an eye for comic idiosyncrasy, in particular African and West Indian, and a concern for the predicament of the expatriate. The first is uppermost in *Dumplings in the Soup*. Here John Jiffey Jacket gets a room in a London tenement crowded with immigrant lodgers. They are dominated by Boffo, a genial non-rent-paying confidence man who enlivens the religious devotions of the local Shakers club with strong drinks, and lets his landlord's cellar to a newcomer from Africa for fifty pounds in advance. The book is lively and readable, but the comic exaggeration undermines the more serious undertones, and, ultimately, some of the comedy itself.
The Scholar-Man is a more complex and successful book, Adam Questus, a West Indian, goes in search of Egor, an English-born mulatto who has had such a strong impression on his childhood that Adam looks to him for a meaning for his life. He teaches English at a University in an African state on the brink of independence. In his quest he visits a village where cult-drumming induces a trance in which he glimpses his slave-ancestry: at the same time the cult-whip inflicts a blow that would have been fatal but for the self-sacrifice of a University servant. He finds Egor has vanished, but making love to the mentally deficient girl Egor had run away with, he glimpses the highly ambiguous "reality" he had been seeking.
The search, with its echoes of Conrad's *Heart of Darkness*, is interwoven with satirical comedy about expatriate academic life and the political turmoil of a country exchanging one set of superstitions for another in its own search for identity. Some of the humour is again too forced, but the comedy also touches the wider theme, the absurdities of reality.

—Louis James

DAVENPORT, Guy (Mattison, Jr.).   American.   Born in Anderson, South Carolina, 23 November 1927. Educated at Duke University, Durham, North Carolina, B.A. 1948; Merton College, Oxford (Rhodes Scholar), 1948–50, B.Litt. 1950; Harvard University, Cambridge, Massachusetts, Ph.D. 1961. Served in the United States Army Airborne Corps, 1950–52. Instructor, Washington University, St. Louis, 1952–55; Assistant Professor, Haverford College, Pennsylvania, 1961–63. Since 1963, Professor of English, University of Kentucky, Lexington. Since 1962, contributing editor, *National Review*, New York. Also book and magazine illustrator and designer. Recipient: Blumenthal-Leviton Prize (*Poetry*, Chicago), 1967; American Academy Morton Dauwen Zabel Award, 1981. Address: 621 Sayre Avenue, Lexington, Kentucky 40508, U.S.A.

PUBLICATIONS

Novel

The Bicycle Rider.   New York, Red Ozier Press, 1985.

Short Stories

Tatlin!   New York, Scribner, 1974.

Da Vinci's Bicycle: Ten Stories. Baltimore, Johns Hopkins University Press, 1979.
Eclogues: Eight Stories. Berkeley, California, North Point Press, 1981; London, Pan, 1984.
Trois Caprices. Louisville, Pace Trust, 1981.
The Bowmen of Shu. New York, Grenfell Press, 1983.
Apples and Pears and Other Stories. Berkeley, California, North Point Press, 1984.

Uncollected Short Stories

"O Gadgo Niglo," in *Conjunctions 4* (New York), 1983.
"We Often Think of Lenin at the Clothespin Factory," in *Conjunctions 8* (New York), 1984.

Verse

Flowers and Leaves: Poema vel Sonata, Carmina Autumni Primaeque Veris Transformationum. Highlands, North Carolina, Jargon, 1966.
The Resurrection in Cookham Churchyard. New York, Davies, 1982.
Goldfinch Thistle Star. New York, Red Ozier Press, 1983.
Thasos and Ohio: Poems and Translations. Manchester, Carcanet, 1986.

Other

Cydonia Florentia. Cambridge, Massachusetts, Lowell Adams House Printers, 1966.
Pennant Key-Indexed Guide to Homer's Iliad [and *Odyssey*]. Philadelphia, Educational Research Associates, 2 vols., 1967.
Do You Have a Poem Book on E.E. Cummings? Highlands, North Carolina, Jargon, 1969.
Jonathan Williams, Poet. Cleveland, Asphodel Book Shop, 1969.
The Geography of the Imagination: Forty Essays. Berkeley, California, North Point Press, 1981; London, Pan, 1984.
Cities on Hills: A Study of I–XXX of Ezra Pound's "Cantos." Ann Arbor, Michigan, UMI Research Press, and Epping, Essex, Bowker, 1983.
The Art of Lafcadio Hearn, with Clifton Waller Bennett. Charlottesville, University of Virginia Library, 1983.

Editor, *The Intelligence of Louis Agassiz: A Specimen Book of Scientific Writings.* Boston, Beacon Press, 1963.

Translator, *Carmina Archilochi: The Fragments of Archilochos.* Berkeley, University of California Press, 1964.
Translator, *Sappho: Songs and Fragments.* Ann Arbor, University of Michigan Press, 1965.
Translator, *Archilochos, Sappho, Alkman: Three Lyric Poets of the Late Greek Bronze Age.* Berkeley, University of California Press, 1980.
Translator, *Herakleitos and Diogenes.* Berkeley, California, Grey Fox Press, 1980.
Translator, *The Mimes of Herondas.* Berkeley, California, Grey Fox Press, 1981.
Translator, *Maxims of the Ancient Egyptians*, by Boris de Rachewiltz. Louisville, Pace Trust, 1983.

*

Bibliography: "Guy Davenport: A Bibliographical Checklist," in *American Book Collector* (New York), March–April 1984.

Manuscript Collections: Rosenbach Library, Philadelphia; South Caroliniana Library, Columbia, South Carolina.

Critical Studies: "*Tatlin!*; or, The Limits of Fiction" by Richard Pevear, Spring 1975, and "Guy Davenport in Harmony," Autumn 1980, both in *Hudson Review* (New York).

Guy Davenport comments:
  My talent is minor, my prose unskilled and contrived, my ideas derivative. In my stories I shape anecdotes about real people much as Parson Weems made a folktale hero of George Washington. This is not my intention: it is what happens when anybody writes about things in ignorance and from a distance. I have Panait Istrati wearing a flowery embroidered shirt; Marguerite Dorian tells me that he wouldn't be caught dead in one. In spite of doing research, this wrong-shirt effect usually turns up in every detail. I read some 40 books about prehistory to write the story "Robot," visited the site of Lascaux, talked with Jacques Marsal, have heard first-hand accounts of refugees fleeing the Germans across that part of France; and yet my story (which is about the discovery of the prehistoric cave at Lascaux in 1941) could not possibly have a single sentence of truth in it. From five to ten years of such research go into every story; for one, fifteen. The stories are not what they seem to be about (what story is?), but I don't have any interpretation up my sleeve that I would insist on. My ambition is solely to get some effect, as of light on stone in a forest on a September day, that seems to me to be a duty to preserve, as a quality of our world, in a rhythm of words. I cannot write about myself or of emotions with which I am familiar. Fiction's essential activity is to imagine how others feel, what a Saturday afternoon in an Italian town in the second century looked like. I trust the world to speak for itself. If I write *rose*, there are roses to stand me good. When Louis Zukofsky wrote his *Eighty Flowers*, he went to the trouble to see each flower. Picture and description would not do. I have stood on my toes and touched Blériot's *Antoinette*, I've held Shelley's snuffbox in my hands, and have sat on the chair of Gertrude Stein's that Ezra Pound broke; I'll find a place for these encounters. I mention them because some such haptic event authenticates every detail in my writing. But for this invisible substantiality I would not write at all. In a sense my texts are translations of an obliterated original that can never be reconstituted. The story "Robot," for instance, is an afternoon looking for Indian arrowheads with my father in South Carolina (I feel certain). "The Dawn in Erewhon" is a translation and elaboration of a split second of a sunny morning in Amsterdam. "A Field of Snow on a Slope of the Rosenberg" is of course not about Robert Walser, but about Christopher Middleton's Robert Walser, and probably a translation of a moment in Paris 30 years ago, sitting in one of Joyce's *brasseries* (on the street where Rimbaud wrote *Les Illuminations*) when Chris and I saw a horse wearing a hat that made our day. "C. Musonius Rufus" is about Ezra Pound, or perhaps Vergil. "Au Tombeau de Charles Fourier" began in my head when I was reading Fourier on a bluff of the Ohio River and encountered the unknown word *quagga*. My feeling is that my stories just might, with luck, be included in the corporate attempt of writing in our time to understand how so hopeful a century as ours blundered so tragically as to be the most inhuman of them all.

*   *   *

  Guy Davenport's a critic, poet, classicist, translator, teacher, and book illustrator who with the publication of *Tatlin!*, *Da Vinci's Bicycle*, *Eclogues* and *Apples and Pears* has become a master fictionist as well. These collections include novellae treating the Soviet constructivist V. Tatlin, the Dutch philosopher Adriaan van Hovendaal and friends, and the Modernist circle surrounding Stein and Picasso. Other stories feature Leonardo Da Vinci inventing a bicycle (to be ridden in battle, "a phalanx of these *due rote* bearing lancers at full tilt"), Kafka and Max Brod attending an air show where they brush shoulders with Wittgenstein, and most remarkably (and fictionally) "A photograph of Lenin reading *Iskra* at a Zurich cafe" which "accidentally includes over to the left James and Nora Joyce haggling with a taxi driver about the fare."

What strange yet telling juxtapositions of the Moderns, the very makers of our century. The fact that half of them are made up takes nothing from Davenport's achievement; indeed, he considers such combinations of fact and fantasy "necessary fictions" which in their very form of delight tell us much about our Postmodern selves. Ezra Pound spinning a fable about Yeats's body lost at sea by a drunken navy crew? Nietzsche signing the guestbook at a Rapallo inn with the caution, "Beware the beefsteak"? These are snapshots of the Modern, crafted by the same aesthetic in which, as part of an early photographic plate of fossils at the Museum of Natural History, "two gentlemen stand in the background, spectators at the museum. One wears a top hat and looks with neurotic intelligence at the camera. He is Edgar Allan Poe. The other gentleman is cross-eyed and wears a beret. God knows who he is."

History is a dream that strays into innocent sleep. This motto, from the heart of Davenport's fiction, helps tell why he feels the two modes must be mixed. "The mind is what it knows!" one of his characters insists. "It is nothing else at all, at all." Can our very nature be formed by the way we view history? Consider how that relatively new and most typically Modern of aesthetic media, the camera, composes things for us. Poe caught posing with a dinosaur, Lenin and Joyce so casually compared in their own worlds of economics, all recorded by the chance photograph—"for the first time in the history of art," Davenport's story explains, "the accidental became the controlling iconography of a representation of the world."

Therefore *Tatlin!* and *Da Vinci's Bicycle* present imaginative exercises on characters who do not completely match up with our conventional readings of the past. The camera, by its very rigidity, rattles our perception and makes us see things we never knew were there; and so Davenport's fiction, using many of the same accidental and juxtapositional methods, attempts to do the same thing. Gertrude Stein is seen reading the Sunday comics to Picasso; ancient Greek philosophers invent a mechanical pigeon; President Richard Nixon, impressed by the Great Wall of China, bombs the DMZ to similarly impress his host. If any of these events did indeed happen, it was probably in other people's imaginations, for if history is a dream which strays into innocent sleep, so too may dreams contaminate (or perhaps enrich) history. In any event, Davenport concludes, we know reality only through our fictions, and his stories and novellae are attempts to structure those fictions according to the photographic, cinematic, and collagist natures of our time.

Eclogues and especially *Apples and Pears* are set in the world of Fourierist philosophy, and express Davenport's most complete vision. Adriaan van Hovendaal, the character whose sexual philosophy bloomed into the ménage à trois in *Tatlin!*'s "The Dawn in Erewhon," is now given a brood of children and network of friends within which to live his ideals of affection and sharing. The theme of apples and pears runs through this latter collection, providing a test of art against nature just as Adriaan's adventures allow philosophy to be measured against experience. As he and his friends establish an ideal

communal household of love and culture, so Davenport creates a fictive world in which the activities of making art and love combine in a natural philosophy for which belief need rarely be suspended.

Nature and intelligence form an ideal balance in Davenport's ideal world. His characters respond to Fourier's notion of Harmony, which is based on the attractions of desire; "Apples and Pears" brashly gives these desires free rein. Through the novella's four sections characters undress, share beds and clothes, and make love in all combinations of sex and age. "Poetry in the Harmony will be a system of analogies and correspondences noted by children and gifted adults," Adriaan writes, and as author Davenport reifies this aesthetic with boldly physical affection. His people paint, write, and love each other's bodies in the same spirit of unfettered creativity and exchange. Davenport's frankness tests the limits of a philosophical ideal by writing out all the possibilities. If prose can contain them, then the vision is sound, just as in Fourier's grand plan.

—Jerome Klinkowitz

DAVIDSON, Lionel. British. Born in Hull, Yorkshire, 31 March 1922. Served in the Royal Naval Submarine Service, 1941–46. Married Fay Jacobs in 1949; two sons. Free-lance magazine journalist and editor, 1946–59. Recipient: Crime Writers Association Gold Dagger, 1961, 1967, 1979. Agent: Curtis Brown, 162–168 Regent Street, London W1R 5TA, England.

PUBLICATIONS

Novels

The Night of Wenceslas. London, Gollancz, 1960; New York, Harper, 1961.
The Rose of Tibet. London, Gollancz, and New York, Harper, 1962.
A Long Way to Shiloh. London, Gollancz, 1966; as *The Menorah Men*, New York, Harper, 1966.
Making Good Again. London, Cape, and New York, Harper, 1968.
Smith's Gazelle. London, Cape, and New York, Knopf, 1971.
The Sun Chemist. London, Cape, and New York, Knopf, 1976.
The Chelsea Murders. London, Cape, 1978; as *Murder Games*, New York, Coward McCann, 1978.

Uncollected Short Stories

"Note to Survivors," in *Alfred Hitchcock's Mystery Magazine* (New York), May 1958.
"Where Am I Going? Nowhere!," in *Suspense* (London), February 1961.
"Indian Rope Trick," in *Winter's Crimes 13*, edited by George Hardinge. London, Macmillan, 1981.
"I Do Dwell," in *Winter's Crimes 16*, edited by Hilary Hale. London, Macmillan, 1984.

Fiction (for children) as David Line

Soldier and Me. New York, Harper, 1965.
Run for Your Life. London, Cape, 1966.
Mike and Me. London, Cape, 1974.
Under Plum Lake (as Lionel Davidson). London, Cape, and New York, Knopf, 1980.
Screaming High. London, Cape, and Boston, Little Brown, 1985.

*   *   *

A novelist in various genres and a screenwriter, Lionel Davidson has become most widely known as a writer of mysteries, winning the Crime Writers Association Gold Dagger, an annual prize, three different times. His mystery stories are intricate and full of social and historical detail. *The Chelsea Murders* (published as *Murder Games* in the United States), for example, uses clues drawn from 19th-century literary and pre-Raphaelite figures. Each of the seven victims has the initials of one of the luminaries who lived in Chelsea, figures like Dante Gabriel Rossetti, Oscar Wilde, and Algernon Charles Swinburne; the mass killer, like one of the victims, has the initials of the satirist W.S. Gilbert. In addition, the clues, mailed to the police through different ingenious guises, are quotations from the writers, emphasizing the novel's resemblance to an intricate game. No clue is, in itself, more relevant than any of the others. *The Chelsea Murders* is also, like much of Davidson's fiction, socially referential, containing quick depictions of London porno clubs, film-making, language lessons for the acculturation of Arabs, a gay disco, and a jeans store on the King's Road. Within his quickly shifting and often comic scenes, Davidson pays deference to traditional elements in crime fiction, the establishment of time frame, the police procedure, and the use of disguise to confuse identity, although he allows himself little space for the treatment of motive, psychology, or any interior quality. His characterizations, like his characters themselves, are likely to operate in groups, and the most common theme in the mysteries is that of betrayal, the violation by one member of the ethos, the standards, or the lives of other members of the group.

Other of Davidson's novels shade the line dividing the mystery from the novel of espionage. One espionage novel is *Making Good Again* in which three lawyers in the 1960's, an Englishman, a German, and an Israeli, combine in an effort to find a long-missing German-Jewish banker or to decide what to do with the million Swiss francs still left in his name. Using various costumes and guises as they travel through the Bavarian forest and other parts of Europe, and shifting allegiances to various governments and national interests, they constantly confront echoes of Nazi feeling and raise questions about German guilt and possible reparations for crimes against the Jews and the rest of humanity. Again, the theme is betrayal; but the notion of a new international combination of responsibilities cannot sustain itself in a plot that involves a good deal of action and adventure. Another novel, published as *A Long Way to Shiloh* in England and *The Menorah Men* in the United States, combines adventure with a depiction of Israel in the 1960's. This novel places the search for a religious symbol originally lost or stolen from the Temple at Jerusalem against a background of contemporary Israel trying to develop a national identity through current forms of economic, social, sexual, and religious behavior.

Davidson manifests a considerable range among fictional genres, almost never writing the same kind of novel twice. *The Rose of Tibet* is pure adventure and travelogue, evoking that strange and isolated land held in by mountains. *Smith's*

Gazelle, with considerable delicacy and sensitivity, deals with the excitements and problems of preserving a nearly extinct herd of deer, working its implicit argument for conservation into suggestions of a mythic statement about the origins of species. *Under Plum Lake* is a fantasy for children in which a young boy discovers a whole subterranean civilization underneath a familiar lake. Different as they are in genre and setting, all Davidson's novels depend on action and adventure, externalizing their themes and concerns into a constant involvement with a difficult, various, and morally confusing contemporary world.

Davidson's moral statements, however, never become obvious or heavy-handed. His humor and games are always visible, his social commentary more a matter of reference to or passing jabs at contemporary social phenomena than any sustained social social criticism or analysis. His references, too, like those in *The Chelsea Murders*, are often literary, historical, or topical, references to other works or quick echoes of other styles that make the novels, especially those like *The Sun Chemist*, about the possible existence among Chaim Weitzmann's forgotten papers of a chemical formula that will free the world's industry from its dependence on Arab oil, sound derivative. Davidson has, as a novelist, not yet developed a strong or distinctive literary identity, but his protean skill, his deftness, his humor, and the excitement of the action and cleverness visible in all his novels, along with settings that always illustrate a responsiveness to the contemporary social and political world, have earned him a considerable and growing reputation.

—James Gindin

DAVIES, (William) Robertson. Canadian. Born in Thamesville, Ontario, 28 August 1913. Educated at Upper Canada College; Queen's University, Kingston, Ontario; Balliol College, Oxford, 1936–38, B.Litt. 1938. Married Brenda Mathews in 1940; three children. Teacher and actor, Old Vic Theatre School and Repertory Company, London, 1938–40; literary editor, *Saturday Night*, Toronto, 1940–42; editor and publisher, *Examiner*, Peterborough, Ontario, 1942–63. Since 1960, Professor of English, since 1962, Master of Massey College, and since 1981, Master Emeritus, University of Toronto. Formerly, Governor, Stratford Shakespeare Festival, Ontario; member, Board of Trustees, National Arts Centre. Recipient: Ottawa Drama League prize, 1946, 1947; Dominion Drama Festival prize, for play, 1948, 1949, for directing, 1949; Leacock Medal, 1955; Lorne Pierce Medal, 1961; Governor-General's Award, 1973; World Fantasy Convention award, 1984. LL.D.: University of Alberta, Edmonton, 1957; Queen's University, 1962; University of Manitoba, Winnipeg, 1972; University of Toronto, 1981; D.Litt.: McMaster University, Hamilton, Ontario, 1959; University of Windsor, Ontario, 1971; York University, Toronto, 1973; Mount Allison University, Sackville, New Brunswick, 1973; Memorial University of Newfoundland, St. John's, 1974; University of Western Ontario, London, 1974; McGill University, Montreal, 1974; Trent University, Peterborough, Ontario, 1974; University of Lethbridge, Alberta, 1981; University of Waterloo, Ontario, 1981; University of British Columbia, Vancouver, 1983; University of Santa Clara, California, 1985; D.C.L.: Bishop's University, Lennoxville, Quebec, 1967; D.U.C.: University of Calgary, Alberta, 1975; D.Hum.Litt.: Rochester University, New York, 1983. Fellow, Royal Society of Canada, 1967, and Royal

Society of Literature, 1984; Honorary Member, American Academy, 1981 (first Canadian elected). Companion, Order of Canada, 1972. Agent: Curtis Brown, 10 Astor Place, New York, New York 10003, U.S.A. Address: Massey College, 4 Devonshire Place, Toronto, Ontario M5S 2E1, Canada.

PUBLICATIONS

Novels

Tempest-Tost. Toronto, Clarke Irwin, 1951; London, Chatto and Windus, and New York, Rinehart, 1952.
Leaven of Malice. Toronto, Clarke Irwin, 1954; London, Chatto and Windus, and New York, Scribner, 1955.
A Mixture of Frailties. Toronto, Macmillan, London, Weidenfeld and Nicolson, and New York, Scribner, 1958.
The Deptford Trilogy. London, Penguin, 1983.
  Fifth Business. Toronto, Macmillan, and New York, Viking Press, 1970; London, Macmillan, 1971.
  The Manticore. Toronto, Macmillan, and New York, Viking Press, 1972; London, Macmillan, 1973.
  World of Wonders. Toronto, Macmillan, 1975; New York, Viking Press, 1976; London, W.H. Allen, 1977.
The Rebel Angels. Toronto, Macmillan, 1981; New York, Viking Press, and London, Allen Lane, 1982.
What's Bred in the Bone. Toronto, Macmillan, and New York, Viking, 1985.

Short Stories

High Spirits: A Collection of Ghost Stories. Toronto and London, Penguin, 1982; New York, Viking Press, 1983.

Uncollected Short Stories

"The All Hallows Horrors," in *City* (Toronto), 30 October 1977.
"A Christmas Carol Reharmonized," in *Washington Post Book World*, 1982.

Plays

A Play of Our Lord's Nativity (produced Peterborough, Ontario, 1946).
Overlaid (produced Peterborough, Ontario, 1947). Included in *Eros at Breakfast and Other Plays*, 1949.
The Voice of the People (produced Montreal, 1948). Included in *Eros at Breakfast and Other Plays*, 1949.
At the Gates of the Righteous (produced Peterborough, Ontario, 1948). Included in *Eros at Breakfast and Other Plays*, 1949.
Hope Deferred (produced Montreal, 1948). Included in *Eros at Breakfast and Other Plays*, 1949.
Fortune, My Foe (televised; produced Ottawa, 1948). Toronto, Clarke Irwin, 1949.
Eros at Breakfast (produced Ottawa, 1948). Included in *Eros at Breakfast and Other Plays*, 1949.
Eros at Breakfast and Other Plays (includes *Hope Deferred, Overlaid, At the Gates of the Righteous, The Voice of the People*). Toronto, Clarke Irwin, 1949.
At My Heart's Core (produced Peterborough, Ontario, 1950). Toronto, Clarke Irwin, 1950.
King Phoenix (produced Peterborough, Ontario, 1950). Included in *Hunting Stuart and Other Plays*, 1972.

A Masque of Aesop (produced Toronto, 1952). Toronto, Clarke Irwin, 1952; in *Five New One-Act Plays*, edited by James A. Stone, London, Harrap, 1954.
A Jig for the Gypsy (broadcast; produced Toronto and London, 1954). Toronto, Clarke Irwin, 1954.
Hunting Stuart (produced Toronto, 1955). Included in *Hunting Stuart and Other Plays*, 1972.
Love and Libel; or, The Ogre of the Provincial World, adaptation of his novel *Leaven of Malice* (produced Toronto and New York, 1960; revised version, as *Leaven of Malice*, produced Toronto, 1973).
A Masque of Mr. Punch (produced Toronto, 1962). Toronto, Oxford University Press, 1963.
Centennial Play, with others (produced Lindsay, Ontario, 1967). Ottawa, Centennial Commission, 1967.
Hunting Stuart and Other Plays (includes *King Phoenix* and *General Confession*), edited by Brian Parker. Toronto, New Press, 1972.
Brothers in the Black Art (televised, 1974). Vancouver, Alcuin Society, 1981.
Question Time (produced Toronto, 1975). Toronto, Macmillan, 1975.
Pontiac and the Green Man (produced Toronto, 1977).

Radio Plays: *A Jig for the Gypsy*, and others.

Television Plays: *Fortune, My Foe; Brothers in the Black Art*, 1974; and others.

Other

Shakespeare's Boy Actors. London, Dent, 1939; New York, Salloch, 1941.
Shakespeare for Young Players: A Junior Course. Toronto, Clarke Irwin, 1942.
The Diary of Samuel Marchbanks (essays). Toronto, Clarke Irwin, 1947.
The Table Talk of Samuel Marchbanks (essays). Toronto, Clarke Irwin, 1949; London, Chatto and Windus, 1951.
Renown at Stratford: A Record of the Shakespearean Festival in Canada 1953, with Tyrone Guthrie. Toronto, Clarke Irwin, 1953.
Twice Have the Trumpets Sounded: A Record of the Stratford Shakespearean Festival in Canada 1954, with Tyrone Guthrie. Toronto, Clarke Irwin, 1954; London, Blackie, 1955.
Thrice the Brinded Cat Hath Mew'd: A Record of the Stratford Shakespearean Festival in Canada 1955, with Tyrone Guthrie. Toronto, Clarke Irwin, 1955.
A Voice from the Attic. New York, Knopf, 1960.
The Personal Art: Reading to Good Purpose. London, Secker and Warburg, 1961.
Marchbanks' Almanack. Toronto, McClelland and Stewart, 1967.
Stephen Leacock. Toronto, McClelland and Stewart, 1970.
What Do You See in the Mirror? Agincourt, Ontario, Book Society of Canada, 1970.
The Revels History of Drama in English VI: 1750–1880, with others. London, Methuen, 1975.
One Half of Robertson Davies: Provocative Pronouncements on a Wide Range of Topics. Toronto, Macmillan, 1977; New York, Viking Press, 1978.
The Enthusiasms of Robertson Davies, edited by Judith Skelton Grant. Toronto, McClelland and Stewart, 1979.

The Well-Tempered Critic: One Man's View of Theatre and Letters in Canada, edited by Judith Skelton Grant. Toronto, McClelland and Stewart, 1981.
The Mirror of Nature (lectures). Toronto, University of Toronto Press, 1983.

Editor, *Feast of Stephen: An Anthology of Some of the Less Familiar Writings of Stephen Leacock*. Toronto, McClelland and Stewart, 1970.

*

Bibliography: by John Ryrie, in *The Annotated Bibliography of Canada's Major Authors 3* edited by Robert Lecker and Jack David, Downsview, Ontario, ECW Press, 1981.

Manuscript Collection: Massey College, University of Toronto.

Critical Studies: *Robertson Davies* by Elspeth Buitenhaus, Toronto, Forum House, 1972; *Conversations with Canadian Novelists 1* by Silver Donald Cameron, Toronto, Macmillan, 1975; "Robertson Davies Issue" of *Journal of Canadian Studies* (Peterborough, Ontario), February 1977; *Robertson Davies* by Judith Skelton Grant, Toronto, McClelland and Stewart, 1978; *Here and Now 1* edited by John Moss, Toronto, NC Press, 1979; "The Master of the Unseen World" by Judith Finlayson, in *Quest* (Toronto), vol. 8, no. 4, 1979; *Studies in Robertson Davies' Deptford Trilogy* edited by Robert G. Lawrence and Samuel L. Macey, Victoria, British Columbia, English Literary Studies, 1980; *The Smaller Infinity: The Jungian Self in the Novels of Robertson Davies* by Patricia Monk, Toronto, University of Toronto Press, 1982; in *Canadian Writers and Their Work* edited by Robert Lecker, Jack David, and Ellen Quigley, Downsview, Ontario, ECW Press, 1985.

Theatrical Activities:
Actor: **Plays**—Lord Norfolk in *Traitor's Gate* by Morna Stuart, London, 1938; Stingo in *She Stoops to Conquer* by Oliver Goldsmith, London, 1939; Archbishop of Rheims in *Saint Joan* by Shaw, London, 1939; roles in *The Taming of the Shrew* by Shakespeare, London, 1939.

Robertson Davies comments:
   The theme which lies at the root of all my novels and several of my plays is the isolation of the human spirit. This sounds somewhat gloomy but I have not attempted to deal with it in a gloomy fashion but rather to demonstrate that what my characters do that might be called really significant is done entirely on their own volition and usually contrary to what is expected of them. This theme, which might be called in C.G. Jung's phrase "The Search for the Self," is worked out in terms of characters, usually young, who are trying to escape from early influences and find their own place in the world, but who are reluctant to do so in a way that will bring pain and disappointment to others, and particularly to people of the previous generation. As I say, this may not look like a theme for comedy but I find it so, and many readers of my books have assured me that they agree.

*   *   *

An essayist in the satiric manner of Stephen Leacock, one of the few Canadian playwrights of stature, scholar and literary critic, Robertson Davies came to international attention with *Fifth Business*, the first of his trilogy of Deptford novels. It showed that his virtues as a novelist include strong characters,

surprising events, boldness in treating ideas, serious questioning of how people should live, fascination with curious information, and an ability to imagine a world in high relief. If the ideas are outrageous, Davies seldom bores; at his best he is a showman who prefers extravagance, deception, energy, at the expense of finesse, as means of creating illusions of wonder, amazement, awe. Myth, legend, the occult, angel and devil, saint and sinner, rich and poor, interest him, whereas the middle class gains his attention only for satire or to reveal how the repression of potentialities results in malice and evil disguised as social judgment. Evil is "the revenge of the unlived life." While Davies is an excellent satiric novelist, with a witty, sharp tongue and with knowledge of the world to puncture social, spiritual, and moral pretences, his fiction lacks texture, polish, form, consistency of character and action, and probability. Although the domestic is usually satirized, great passions are recommended but not portrayed. He is conscious of the art of the novel and uses a variety of narrators, but his characters seem mouthpieces for his opinions.

   While the extremes and grand gestures in the novels reflect his demand that life be lived fully, actively, and his dislike of mean-spirited caution, there is a more specific structure of ideas than is usual in modern fiction. As his early novels show, he is concerned with the puritanism, penny-pinching, pettiness and greyness of provincial Canada—the colonial Calvinist Canada still found in many towns and cities until the 1960's. If Davies shows there is a more spiritual, enlarged life elsewhere, he also feels that the drab surface of Canada masks a dynamic inner emotional turmoil. The novels have a Blakean romanticism—it is necessary to fall to be saved—an Ibsenite belief in the absolute necessity of being true to yourself, denial of which causes evil, and the double vision of the nationalist who idealizes while berating the lack of sophistication of his society.

   The powerful Deptford trilogy evolved from the witty satire of the earlier three Salterton novels. Salterton, an imagined Ontario city analogous to Kingston, is dominated by its old families, Anglican church, military school, university, and belief in the virtues of England and the English; underneath its mannered veneer there is evil caused by inhibiting full expression of the spirit. Social and cultural discriminations are forms of revenge in which the dead hand of the past stifles as it was stifled.

   Tempest-Tost, the first of the Salterton trilogy, appears a comedy of the provincial bourgeoisie in which the weak passions, narrow vision, and petty behavior of local society are represented by an amateur theatre group. While the parallels between Shakespeare's great romance and the players are humorously satiric, they imply that the play is a representation of universal patterns of experience and behavior. *Leaven of Malice* recognizes the dark side of human nature disguised by morals and manners, eccentricities, gossip, and provinciality. Although Davies shows that small-town poverty, puritanism, and cultural isolation inhibit the Canadian soul, turning its repressed energies to meanness, he says, through the voice of one of his characters, that it is necessary for Canadians to "know that whatever happens to them has its roots in what they are." *A Mixture of Frailties* illustrates both the burden of the past and the artist's need for growth, experiment, and experience to become an artist. The main character is given opportunities which require changing her views about life and her family if she is to achieve. In this novel Davies's use of Jungian archetypes for characters, symbols, and themes becomes apparent. Along with the increased depth of characterization—in contrast to the flat satiric characters of the previous two novels—Davies points to the central theme of his work, "the metamorphosis of life itself, in which man moves from confident inexperience through the bitterness of experience, towards the rueful wisdom of self-knowledge."

Although having dark depths, the Salterton trilogy is written within the British tradition of social comedy. With the Deptford novels Davies breaks out of this mode and reveals himself a natural story teller of large-scale, imaginative plots with larger-than-life, energetic, interesting characters. The trilogy treats of the transformations and interweaving of several lives over half a century and is filled with the miraculous. These novels are unpredictable, take unexpected directions while exploring the relations between the physical and spiritual; both satire and romance predominate over social comedy to reveal the saints, devils, magicians, and other profound, universal archetypes that Davies sees within Canada. The tremendous energy, excitement, and depth of experience first expressed in *Fifth Business*, and continued through the later novels, has its probable origins in Davies's study of Jung which allows him to go beyond the tightly controlled surfaces of the earlier trilogy. He traces through the three novels the way a childhood incident has affected the lives of the characters and their descendants. The satire is harsher and there are such extremes of character as absolute goodness, saintliness, and wisdom. Davies uses Jungian ideas to show that timeless universals found in folklore, myths, and religion are present, although often unrecognized in contemporary Canada; Jungian archetypes are part of a neglected spiritual reality. Although Dunstan Ramsay, the narrator and one of the author's mouthpieces in *Fifth Business*, claims that religion is closer in spirit to the *Arabian Nights* than to the modern Presbyterian Church, there is a strong element of Calvinist determinism in these novels. Magnus Eisengrim, the Canadian-born international magician whose life is the focus of *World of Wonders*, says that people eventually get what is coming to them.

Davies's novels progress from studies in repression of passion, through the recognition of evil and the need to experience life fully, to the assertion of wonder in the later fiction. Rather than remaining strangers in their own land, the Canadians of Davies's novels are on the way to self-discovery of who they are. Such a significance can be seen in the way *Fifth Business* recounts the story of an aged schoolmaster whose life is shown to be surprisingly cosmopolitan and a witness (the "fifth business" is the necessary observer) for other complex, full Canadian lives. Perhaps the most significant example Davies offers is Mackenzie King. A national leader for most of 30 years, King has usually been viewed as the embodiment of Canadian mediocrity, blandness, and dull, grey caution. In *The Manticore* Boy Staunton, whose story spans the trilogy, complains:

Do you realize that man never calls an election without getting a fortune-teller in Kingston to name a lucky day? Do you realize that he goes in for automatic writing? And decides important things—nationally important things—by opening his Bible and stabbing at a verse with a paper-knife, while his eyes are shut? And that he sits with the portrait of his mother and communes—*communes* for God's sake!—with her spirit and gets her advice?

Ramsay replies: "Mackenzie King rules Canada because he himself is the embodiment of Canada—cold and cautious on the outside, dowdy and pussy in every overt action, but inside a mass of intuition and dark intimations." The snowball which, in *Fifth Business*, Boy Staunton throws at Dunstan Ramsay, but which hits Magnus Eisengrim's mother, causing his premature birth and her craziness, is the beginning of a long history of Canadian small-town guilt and hypocrisy that Davies wants

to uncover. More than a half-century of Canadian social, cultural, political, and spiritual history is sketched in the trilogy to show that alongside pettiness there is a *World of Wonders*.

Useful introductory comments about Davies's novels can be found in prefaces he has been contributing to various books, including recent reprintings of his novels. His theory of the novel is clearly expressed in *The Rebel Angels*; besides its literal meaning, a novel is an allegory of man's pilgrimage to discover himself and anagogically expresses the spiritual processes of the universe. This tendency to philosophize and explain his work makes Davies's later novels both very old-fashioned in their wordiness and yet curiously modern in their self-referentiality. His claims that personal destiny is fated and that the necessity to escape the horrors of a provincial Canadian childhood is the best start are discussed by the two *daimons* who narrate part of *What's Bred in the Bone*, another novel in which a Canadian is revealed to have had a surprisingly eventful life. Literary and cultural allusions, especially to the Quest for the Grail, show that Davies's imagination is increasingly more concerned with mythology, fable, and astrology than with a rationalist and scientific vision of reality. Davies is an original mixture of romantic myth-maker, modern psychologist, and nationalist. That his use of archetypes, myths, and legends, and his preference for romance and allegory make his novels readily available to the dominant mode of a Canadian literary criticism originated by Northrop Frye is often cited by younger Canadians as evidence that there is indeed a distinctive national culture.

—Bruce King

DAVIN, Dan(iel Marcus). British. Born in Invercargill, New Zealand, 1 September 1913. Educated at Marist Brothers' School, Invercargill; Sacred Heart College, Auckland; Otago University, Dunedin, M.A. in English, Dip.M.A. in Latin 1935; Balliol College, Oxford (Rhodes Scholar), B.A. in classics 1939, M.A. 1945. Served in the Royal Warwickshire Regiment, 1939–40, and in the New Zealand Division, 1940–45: Major; M.B.E. (Member, Order of the British Empire), 1945. Married Winifred Gonley in 1939; three daughters. Junior Assistant Secretary, 1946–48, and Assistant Secretary, 1948–69, Clarendon Press, Oxford; Deputy Secretary to the Delegates, 1970–78, and Director of the Academic Division, 1974–78, Oxford University Press: retired 1978. Fellow of Balliol College, 1965, emeritus since 1978. D.Litt.: Otago University, 1984. Fellow, Royal Society of Arts. Agent: Bruce Hunter, David Higham Associates Ltd., 5–8 Lower John Street, London W1R 4HA. Address: 193 Southmoor Road, Oxford OX2 6RE, England.

PUBLICATIONS

Novels

Cliffs of Fall. London, Nicholson and Watson, 1945.
For the Rest of Our Lives. London, Nicholson and Watson, 1947; revised edition, London, Joseph, 1965.
Roads from Home. London, Joseph, 1949; edited by Lawrence Jones, Auckland, Auckland University Press, 1976.
The Sullen Bell. London, Joseph, 1956.
No Remittance. London, Joseph, 1959.

Not Here, Not Now.   London, Hale, 1970.
Brides of Price.   London, Hale, 1972; New York, Coward
McCann, 1973.

Short Stories

The Gorse Blooms Pale.   London, Nicholson and Watson,
1947.
Breathing Spaces.   London, Hale, 1975.
Selected Stories.   Wellington, Victoria University Press–Price
Milburn, and London, Hale, 1981.

Uncollected Short Story

"When Mum Died," in *The Summer Book: A New Zealand
Miscellany*, edited by Bridget Williams and Roy Parsons.
Wellington, Port Nicholson Press, 1982.

Other

An Introduction to English Literature, with John Mulgan.
London, Oxford University Press, 1947; New York, Oxford
University Press, 1948.
Crete.   Wellington, New Zealand Government War History
Department, and London and New York, Oxford University
Press, 1953.
Writing in New Zealand: The New Zealand Novel, with W.K.
Davin.   Wellington, School Publications Board, 2 vols.,
1956.
Katherine Mansfield in Her Letters.   Wellington, School Publi-
cations Board, 1959.
Closing Times (memoirs).   London, Oxford University Press,
1975.
*Snow upon Fire: "A Dance to the Music of Time": Anthony
Powell* (lecture).   Swansea, University College of Swansea,
1976.

Editor, *New Zealand Short Stories.*   Wellington and London,
Oxford University Press, 1953.
Editor, *Selected Stories*, by Katherine Mansfield.   Wellington
and London, Oxford University Press, 1953.
Editor, *English Short Stories of Today*, second series.   Lon-
don, Oxford University Press, 1958.
Editor, *Short Stories from the Second World War.*   Oxford,
Oxford University Press, 1982.

*

Critical Studies: *New Zealand Literature* by Eric McCormick,
London, Oxford University Press, 1959; review by Michael
Beveridge, in *Landfall* (Christchurch), September 1970; "Dan
Davin, Novelist of Exile," in *Meanjin* (Melbourne), June 1973,
and *Dan Davin*, Auckland and Oxford, Oxford University
Press, 1983, both by James Bertram.

Dan Davin comments:

(1972) *Not Here, Not Now* more or less concluded, as far
as I can at present project, a sequence of novels that I had
in mind as long ago as 1939. The war and the turn my career
subsequently took gave the novels I intended to write a different cast and brought in new themes and substance. Thus *Not
Here, Not Now*, the last of the sequence, is the one I originally
intended to have done first.

My work has suffered and gained from the fact that so large
a share of my energies has had to go into an exacting and
very responsible job.

My most recent novel, *Brides of Price*, makes a new departure (for me) in subject and technique.

(1986) I have two novels in progress, delayed by travel to
New Zealand and by two serious illnesses. I am also at work
on a second series of memoirs, which will deal mainly with
soldiers and scholars who were my friends.

*   *   *

On the evidence of his short stories and novels, Dan Davin
might well echo Katherine Mansfield's nostalgic cry: "New
Zealand is in my very bones." Despite his long residence as
an expatriate in England, he returns continually to the haunts
of his childhood and youth. As a New Zealander who has
left his country, an Irish Catholic who has lost both creed and
community, as a soldier in the New Zealand Division who
cannot retain the comradeship he found in the service, he has
kept faith with his memories, relives his estrangement from
early allegiances and, with sympathetic if critical understanding, contemplates his fellow-countrymen wherever they may
be found. By so doing he has discovered a starting-point for
much wider human explorations than the search for national
identity, a starting-point not an anchorage.

Yet the anchorage is suggested if only because no writer
has walked more consistently on his own shadow and in the
places where that shadow has appeared. It is tempting, but
inaccurate, to describe him as a regional novelist or perhaps
as the historian and cartographer of a small enclave of Irish
Catholics, farming and labouring within the confines of Southland and sending some of their children northwards as far as
the University of Otago. His characters bear such names as
Mark Burke, Ned Hogan, Tom O'Dwyer, Frank Fahey, Hugh
Egan and Martin Cody; they have an assortment of qualities
and fortunes that are not very dissimilar to Davin's. Whether
they are in London, North Africa, or more commonly in New
Zealand, their Southland backgrounds travel with them and
are described with loving care and great accuracy; their experiences and conflicts provide material for discussion and meditation; but the shadow of Dan Davin is always present, and
his *Roads from Home* turn back towards the homeland that
fires his imagination.

Nevertheless, that much of Davin's writing is comprised of
incidents, places, and people recollected in tranquillity is less
important than his possession of the historian's eye for the
appropriate detail and the artist's instinct for a workable situation. By remaining true to his memories he is able to give
authenticity to his glimpses of provincial life, and by remaining
true to himself fits them into a pattern of human change and
struggle. His collection of short stories *The Gorse Blooms Pale*
contains clear and vivid evidence both of his biographical
dependence and of his ability to recreate and select from the
local minutiae those features that best serve his purpose, for
it is not the scene but the aim of his endeavour that becomes
significant. Davin's provincial studies of an earlier Southland
have not been undertaken as a simple act of piety of former
days, but because he had discovered the fascination that the
retracing of steps holds for those who are more than usually
conscious of the continuity of life and know that the future
is contained in the womb of the past.

It is in *Roads from Home* rather than in his earlier or later
novels dedicated to his memories of Southland that the thematic structure rivets attention and indicates some of his major
preoccupations. The plot serves, but no more than serves, the
purpose. Davin is concerned with the implications of his title—
the roads down which men travel from youth to age, the many
roads they might have taken, the changing ways of the world,
the old paths followed by established traditions and the new
that excite the young and disturb their seniors. Southland has

provided him with a microcosm of community life and aspiration, and with provincial material sufficient to reanimate old themes. Family relationships, complicated by a protestant daughter-in-law, unsettled by a son's loss of faith, the slow secularisation of life, the pathos of the clash between generations, the failure of communications between parents and children, husbands and wives, together with the threats of separation and departure, are unified by recurrent imagery associated with the walls that divide human beings and the roads that lead in different directions.

A characteristic feature of Davin's writing, not unconnected with his biography, is his ability to switch from a simple and unaffected language which catches the casual accents and speech habits of New Zealanders to a more complex and literary style. In his use of the interior monologue he combines the inward thoughts with indirect authorial elaboration that becomes metaphorical and allusive, and is able to suggest wider implications than the bare narrative can supply. This is most apparent in his fictional record of the New Zealand Division in North Africa. Some have been inclined to dismiss *For the Rest of Our Lives* because it attempts, in the author's words, "to combine history and fiction in order to produce the illusion of reality," but fails to give that illusion through defects in its rendering of the fragments of dislocated lives and in the creation of character. It remains, however, an impressive novel, not because it achieves aims imposed on the writer from outside, but because its thematic structure serves another function, prescribed by its subject of war for the rest of our lives. By imagery, related episodes, by description and meditation, the emphasis is placed on the appalling insignificance of the individual in the immensity of time, on his feelings of helplessness and guilt in the midst of heroic exploits and the unbreakable unity of the Division, on the centuries-old martyrdom of man and the frightful continuity of history in pain and suffering.

Davin has not always done justice to his capabilities as a novelist. He has tended to rely too heavily on reflective monologue and dramatised discussions about "things that matter" at the cost of plot structure and character portrayal. His preoccupation with Southland memories has given his work an air of provinciality, in keeping with his themes, but ill-adapted to the exercise of his gifts as a writer. However his latest novel, *Brides of Price*, is a much more sophisticated narrative, both in matter and manner. He seems to have freed himself from the burden of memories and produced a witty, ironic comedy of contemporary life in which plot, character, and style are in harmony with the theme. The first-person narrator is a middle-aged anthropologist who, in his involvement with a series of women and his desire to escape appointment to a University Chair, comes no nearer to Southland than Sydney and Auckland. Whereas in his earlier novels, Davin was concerned with memories of "a man young," he is now intent on "a man old," continually surprised that experience has not enabled him to overcome the deficiencies of his own character, and increasingly conscious that communication with a younger generation is more difficult than he had imagined. *Brides of Price* only emphasises at a more sophisticated level that Davin's "period pieces" were not the result of nostalgia but rather an outcome of his wish to explore all the roads down which men pass as they seek to know and understand "the warp and woof of things."

—H. Winston Rhodes

DAWSON, Jennifer. British. Educated at Mary Datchelor School, London; St. Anne's College, Oxford, M.A. 1952. Married to Michael Hinton. Has worked for Clarendon Press, Oxford, as a social worker in a mental hospital, and as a teacher. Recipient: James Tait Black Memorial Prize 1962; Cheltenham Festival award, 1963. Lives in Charlbury, Oxfordshire. Address: c/o Virago Press, 41 William IV Street, London WC2N 4DB, England.

PUBLICATIONS

Novels

The Ha-Ha. London, Blond, and Boston, Little Brown, 1961.
Fowler's Snare. London, Blond, 1962.
The Cold Country. London, Blond, 1965.
Strawberry Boy. London, Quartet, 1976.
A Field of Scarlet Poppies. London, Quartet, 1979.

Short Stories

Penguin Modern Stories 10, with others. London, Penguin, 1972.
Hospital Wedding. London, Quartet, 1978.

*

Jennifer Dawson comments:
My greatest passion in life has always been music. I regard writing as a last resort, a *faute de mieux* for me. In a world where language has been eroded, gutted ("pre-emptive strike," "take-out" for the murder of eight million civilians, etc.) all art "aspires to the condition of music," which cannot be exploited, interpreted, which explores the lost places of the heart, which makes all things new. Two of my novels have had musicians as their main characters—studies of the composer/musician who for social and political reasons experiences dryness, aridity, and cannot play any more. Politics creep, burst inevitably into my novels. They then become shrill, rhetorical, routine, etc.

One feeling that has haunted me all my life is that life, social life as we know it, is a kind of game with correct moves, correct remarks and replies, correct procedures. I do not know the rules. I have struggled in vain to solve this problem, the real life as opposed to the game of men-and-women.

But the thing that obsesses me most, and which I feel I shall never put into language, is the strangeness of life, its accidentalness. Here we all are on a tiny, precious blue-green balloon in the midst of space, naked gases, chambers of violence. The planet as an accident that has produced music, literature, art, and the extraordinary theme-and-variations of religions. Here we are, with our fitted carpets and Mixmasters and spin-dryers, stilted above the world, talking about mock O-levels, who is to be next Master of St. Judas's, how all the cars in St. John's Street seemed badly parked today. Here we are in the midst of nothingness, in the midst of a mystery, accidental and yet behaving politically and socially as though the bizarre nature of our life on this planet has not hit us yet. To me this freak of life (like a purple flower growing out of the dumped tippings of a hoover-bag) is the invitation to a new kind of freedom. Only art can introduce us to this. But my art? *No!* It must be someone else's. I shall never succeed in saying what I want to say.

*   *   *

Novels which explore madness have certain qualities in common. They describe a world which is enclosed, static and ruled by obsessions; they are vivid, fragmented, highly personal documents in which only one character can be fully realised. This intensity is double-edged. It can exclude, and ultimately bore, the reader or it can provide him with a vision of life which has a relevance beyond the barriers of mental illness. Kafka's metaphors have been readily accepted and understood. Jennifer Dawson's *The Ha-Ha* is one of the few contemporary novels significant enough to deserve the appellation Kafkaesque.

The Ha-Ha is set in a mental hospital where the narrator, Jean, is slowly recovering from a breakdown. She has progressed from the ward and the company of the irretrievably mad; she is now allowed her own room and promised a suitable job, an eventual regrading. Even as the nurse explains these steps towards freedom, we see their sad irrelevance. Jean's private world is ready to obtrude at any moment; her existence is precarious, threatened by the anarchy in her own imagination. One of the most moving illustrations of her plight is given in the description of her work as a librarian. She happily catalogues books for an elderly couple in the nearby town but is nonplussed by their casual, friendly conversation. When fine weather is mentioned she remarks "I wonder whether the monkeys would be better at the tops or the bottoms of the trees." Her own company of animals, spotted, sleek, furred and quilled, wait relentlessly for the time when she will step back into their universe.

The inevitable relapse is brought about by her first real relationship, a love relationship, a love affair with another patient. Alastair is critical of doctors and routines; he alarms Jean by telling her the true nature of her illness and she panics when he leaves the hospital. She runs away, is picked up by the police and brought back to face "the black box crashing down around my head." It is at this point that the novel changes direction. Jean remembers Alastair for his anger; she begins to share his indignation, rejects the doctors and escapes for good, feeling that her own identity is worth more than any medical tag of health.

Schizophrenia is a disease that has received much attention from modern writers. It has been used to symbolise the artist's alienation from society and, by extension, presented as the condition of modern man, lost, lonely, unable to communicate. The schizophrenic is sometimes hailed as a prophet, whose view of life is not only as valid as that of his doctors but also morally superior to the standards they uphold. Dawson shares this fashionable, essentially romantic, attitude but her writing is without the stridency of propaganda. The parallels with Sylvia Plath's *The Bell Jar* are many and the prose is equally fine. Dawson has written further explorations of her subject but has not yet matched the sustained brilliance of this first novel.

—Judy Cooke

---

de BOISSIÈRE, Ralph (Anthony Charles). Australian. Born in Port-of-Spain, Trinidad, 6 October 1907; moved to Australia, 1947; became citizen, 1970. Educated at Queen's Royal College, Port-of-Spain, 1916–22. Married Ivy Alcántara in 1935; two daughters. Accounts clerk, 1927–28, and salesman, Standard Brands, 1929–39, both Trinidad; clerk, Trinidad Clay Products, 1940–47; auto assembler, General Motors-Holden, 1948, cost clerk in car repair shops, 1949–55, free-lance writer, 1955–60, and statistical clerk, Gas and Fuel Corporation, 1960–80, all in Melbourne. Agent: Reinhard Sander, Bayreuth University, Postfach 3008, 8580 Bayreuth, West Germany. Address: 10 Vega Street, North Balwyn, Victoria 3104, Australia.

PUBLICATIONS

Novels

Crown Jewel. Melbourne, Australasian Book Society, 1952; London, Allison and Busby, 1981.
Rum and Coca-Cola. Melbourne, Australasian Book Society, 1956; London, Allison and Busby, 1984.
No Saddles for Kangaroos. Sydney, Australasian Book Society, 1964.

Uncollected Short Stories

"Booze and the Goberdaw" and "The Woman on the Pavement," in *From Trinidad*, edited by Reinhard Sander. New York, Africana, 1979.

Play

Calypso Isle, music by the author (produced Melbourne, 1955).

*

Critical Study: "The Trinidad Awakening: West Indian Literature of the 1930's" by Reinhard Sander, unpublished dissertation, University of Texas, Austin, 1979.

Ralph de Boissière comments:

I began writing *Crown Jewel* in 1935. As I am a slow writer who has rarely had much time to write I was still at it when the uprising took place in the oilfields of South Trinidad on 19 June 1937. I saw I was writing the wrong novel. The oil workers had lighted a torch to signal the breaking of the first bonds of colonialism, bonds which we novelists, short story writers, poets and artists who made up *The Beacon* group (after the name of the now-defunct magazine) had dared to dream would fall before our hatred of foreign masters and our urge to independence. A salesman at the time, I had come to know much of the oilfield area. From two of the important activists in the uprising I got important inside information on its origins, and I began again, discarding much of what I had already written.

I come from one of the best-known French-Creole families, families which, in days long gone, when cocoa was king, had been the real rulers of this British colonial outpost. But with 19 June 1937 my detestation of colonialism, simmering from childhood, and crudely expressed in a few short stories, now became clearly defined.

The second novel of the trilogy, *Rum and Coca-Cola*, deals with the war years when tens of thousands of American soldiers and civilians were building military bases on the island. The American military had in effect become our rulers. There is not the same tension as in *Crown Jewel* because everyone had a job and many had two. The conflicts were of a more subtle sort—the breaking down of British prestige, the mockery of former British might, under American occupation.

The third book of the trilogy, *Homeless in Paradise* (not yet published), covers the approach to Independence in 1962 and its immediate aftermath.

Readers sometimes want to know who was the real-life basis for such and such a character. It is both unwise and impossible to say because I am continually adding to and subtracting from people I have known and, what is more, putting myself into them as characters. The characters may have some resemblance to certain originals, that is all. It is in important crises that people truly reveal themselves: for the most part of our everyday lives we exhibit aspects of character that give only superficial insights into what we are made of. I chose a Black servant girl, Cassie, as one of the main figures in *Crown Jewel* because in Trinidad her class were the most oppressed, ill-paid, and despised among Blacks. In all of us there is potential of one kind or another, but I am thinking particularly of the potential of the human spirit to achieve greatness, something unsuspected by the individual until he or she is flung by events into a crucial situation which demands the utmost. Cassie has that potential. It made her a leader when the time came. There was no such woman as Cassie, but the point is, *there could have been*. In other more stable parts of the world there are fewer possibilities for the appearance of such characters because the social conflicts are not extreme or the time for their resolution is not ripe. This is evident in my third novel, *No Saddles for Kangaroos*, set largely in an automobile factory in Melbourne during the years of the Korean war; here I am dealing with different people at a different historical time.

In technology we have taken great leaps forward, but morally we lag far behind these attainments—which sometimes even threaten to destroy us. But under the surface of life there is always some urge, some movement to rise out of the mire, and it is this movement the writer should try to grasp, this spiritual strength that has to be encouraged. While a writer may profit greatly by displaying the potential for evil he fails if he does not also indicate the potential for creativity as well. The world does not need more hatred, gore, and contempt for life—especially now. It needs belief in the powers of ordinary people to achieve.

No Saddles for Kangaroos is based on experiences I and others had in the early 1950's. Those experiences, those times could produce a novel full of drama. But I find myself unable to write about other, quieter times in Australia because I wasn't born and schooled in that country. At the same time I am a West Indian who has become partly Australian without knowing it. Australia is in my blood, but home is still Trinidad, a home I intuitively, instinctively, emotionally understand as I do not understand Australia.

*   *   *

Ralph de Boissière's *Crown Jewel* and *Rum and Coca-Cola*, both published without much remark three decades ago in Australia, have rightly been reissued in the 1980's and received with justified acclaim. They remain relevant because they give an unrivalled portrayal of two moments in Trinidad's recent past which are still very much alive in shaping its present. De Boissière's third novel, *No Saddles for Kangaroos*, deals with Cold-War politics in the Australian trade union movement, but it lacks the social inwardness and the shaping coherence that his own personal vantage point, as a white creole in a society moving towards black majority rule, gives his two Trinidadian novels.

Crown Jewel depicts Trinidadian society in the years between 1935 and 1937 when the black working class briefly threw aside the middle-class leaders who had diverted its power to their own ends and, through a series of bitter strikes and demonstrations began the process which led to universal suffrage, and political independence. *Rum and Coca-Cola* is set just before the end of World War II when the dollars from the American military presence changed Trinidad from a neglected and quasi-feudal British colony into a competitive market economy in which "we is all sharks, the stronger feedin' on the weaker." Both forces remain alive in Trinidadian society, the unfinished revolts of 1937 and 1970, and the individualistic consumer materialism which was fuelled by the oil boom. Now that the boom has gone and social tensions rise, de Boissière's novels seem more relevant than ever.

Both novels are, in a Caribbean context, rare and largely successful attempts to create fictional models which give a panoramic view of their society. They give not merely a static or descriptive background against which characters perform, but a dynamic image of society created by the actions and social relationships of the characters. And, particularly in *Crown Jewel*, de Boissière shows individuals who are aware that it is they who make history.

There are limitations, both social and fictional in origin, to de Boissière's portrayal of his society. His portrayal of the Indian role in the social conflicts is inadequate and stereotyped, a consequence perhaps both of ignorance and his concern with coming to terms with his own denied black ancestry, which leads to the exclusion of the more significant relationship between people of African and Indian origin. De Boissière also has a naturalistic concern with narrative plausibility which condemns him to providing each of the major characters with some link of blood, service, or mutual acquaintance. This gives an image of Trinidad as a much more comfortable though quarrelling social family than is, I think, intended by the overt picture of class warfare.

However, while most critics have agreed that *Crown Jewel* gives a detailed and vigorous social and historical portrayal of Trinidad, some have felt that its attempts at the development of a coherent literary design are undermined by its commitment to documentary realism. In fact, its relationship to historical reality is of a different kind. If one compares the fictional character of Le Maitre, the black trade union leader, with the historical person of "Buzz" Butler on whom it is based, one sees not the pursuit of topical detail but the simplification of the character in response to the needs of the novel's shaping pattern. Thus Le Maitre becomes a character of massive moral certainty and clear historical consciousness as a touchstone against which to measure the confused and tentative leanings of the three central intermediary characters towards the black working class.

It is de Boissière's concern with the moral choices facing this group, in particular the character of André de Coudray, like the author an idealistic and socially concerned French Creole, which shapes the novel. And because de Boissière is refreshingly honest in his recognition that de Coudray's commitment involved the destruction of his comfortably privileged world without any guarantee of a place in the new, he is convincing in making de Coudray's journey towards self-knowledge, social responsibility, and cultural pride an image for that of the whole society.

As befitting his perception of the individualism that the power of the American dollar stimulated in Trinidadian society, *Rum and Coca-Cola* places much greater emphasis on the inner lives of its major characters. In this period moral commitment is not so much a question of social action but of the attempt to stay true to one's perceptions of what one is and to principles which are being swept aside in a society engaged in a competitive struggle for survival, money and power.

In this novel the issue of choice is focused on the triangular relationship of three characters confused about who they are and how they should act in a Trinidad which denies their ideals. Fred Collingwood, a principled black working-class socialist is doomed because of his "moral strength in all its beauty" and he destroys the relationship with Marie, the woman he most loves, because he displaces his desire to change society onto her and in the process destroys her sense of worth. Indra, the part-Indian girl from a lower-middle-class family, struggles against a "terrible division of spirit" which affects her social and racial sensibilities. Even though she makes a commitment to the working-class movement she still feels cut off, "doomed at this time to a lonely pursuit of the dust they raised in their forward marching." But it is the character of Marie, trapped by the lightness of her colour into believing that she can escape into whiteness, which provides the novel's tragic focus. Of the three main characters, she is the one to benefit most materially from the war-time boom, but her unremitting efforts to escape from her past of poverty and casual prostitution are made at the expense of her inner self. Her fate is tragic because she sees herself engaged in a battle for individual self-hood, but in the process becomes separated from what she most truly is and disintegrates as a personality.

Yet *Rum and Coca-Cola* does not succumb to pessimism. Indra's cry, "O my God! But what am I capable of" is agonised, but the possibilities of moral choice and the issues of human capacity remain central to de Boissière's vision. He sees Trinidad moving in a direction which he detests, but when he has Fred reflect on what has occurred, he shows him capable of taking something positive from it. He sees a society which is not yet free, but one in which old colonial illusions have been destroyed. "Now that walls had fallen, what lay exposed was a life of untrustworthy promises, treachery by those you trusted, servility...." And in this process of laying bare, Fred sees the generation of a new disabused awareness and "ideas which could be weapons."

—Jeremy Poynting

DEIGHTON, Len (Leonard Cyril Deighton). British. Born in London, 18 February 1929. Educated at Marylebone Grammar School, St. Martin's School of Art, and Royal College of Art, all London. Served in the Royal Air Force. Married Shirley Thompson in 1960. Has worked as a railway lengthman, pastry cook, dress factory manager, waiter, illustrator, teacher, and photographer; art director of advertising agencies in London and New York; steward, British Overseas Airways Corporation, 1956–57; wrote a weekly comic strip on cooking for *The Observer*, London, in the 1960's; founder of Continuum One literary agency, London. Lives in Ireland. Address: c/o Century Hutchinson, 62–65 Chandos Place, London WC2N 4NW, England.

PUBLICATIONS

Novels

The Ipcress File. London, Hodder and Stoughton, 1962; New York, Simon and Schuster, 1963.
Horse under Water. London, Cape, 1963; New York, Putnam, 1968.
Funeral in Berlin. London, Cape, 1964; New York, Putnam, 1965.

Billion-Dollar Brain. London, Cape, and New York, Putnam, 1966.
An Expensive Place to Die. London, Cape, and New York, Putnam, 1967.
Only When I Larf. London, Joseph, 1968.
Bomber. London, Cape, and New York, Harper, 1970.
Close-Up. London, Cape, and New York, Atheneum, 1972.
Spy Story. London, Cape, and New York, Harcourt Brace, 1974.
Yesterday's Spy. London, Cape, and New York, Harcourt Brace, 1975.
Twinkle, Twinkle, Little Spy. London, Cape, 1976; as *Catch a Falling Spy*, New York, Harcourt Brace, 1976.
SS-GB: Nazi-Occupied Britain 1941. London, Cape, 1978; New York, Knopf, 1979.
XPD. London, Hutchinson, and New York, Knopf, 1981.
Goodbye Mickey Mouse. London, Hutchinson, and New York, Knopf, 1982.
Game, Set and Match. London, Hutchinson, 1985.
  Berlin Game. London, Hutchinson, 1983; New York, Knopf, 1984.
  Mexico Set. London, Hutchinson, 1984; New York, Knopf, 1985.
  London Match. London, Hutchinson, 1985; New York, Knopf, 1986.

Short Stories

Declarations of War. London, Cape, 1971; as *Eleven Declarations of War*, New York, Harcourt Brace, 1975.

Plays

Screenplay: *Oh! What a Lovely War*, 1969.

Television Plays: *Long Past Glory*, 1963; *It Must Have Been Two Other Fellows*, 1977.

Other

Action Cook Book: Len Deighton's Guide to Eating. London, Cape, 1965; as *Cookstrip Cook Book*, New York, Geis, 1966.
Où Est Le Garlic; or, Len Deighton's French Cook Book. London, Penguin, 1965; New York, Harper, 1977; revised edition, as *Basic French Cooking*, London, Cape, 1979.
Len Deighton's Continental Dossier: A Collection of Cultural, Culinary, Historical, Spooky, Grim and Preposterous Fact, compiled by Victor and Margaret Pettitt. London, Joseph, 1968.
Fighter: The True Story of the Battle of Britain. London, Cape, 1977; New York, Knopf, 1978.
Airshipwreck, with Arnold Schwartzman. London, Cape, 1978; New York, Holt Rinehart, 1979.
Blitzkrieg: From the Rise of Hitler to the Fall of Dunkirk. London, Cape, 1979; New York, Knopf, 1980.
Battle of Britain. London, Cape, and New York, Coward McCann, 1980.

Editor, *London Dossier.* London, Cape, 1967.
Editor, with Michael Rund and Howard Loxton, *The Assassination of President Kennedy.* London, Cape, 1967.
Editor, *Tactical Genius in Battle*, by Simon Goodenough. Oxford, Phaidon Press, and New York, Dutton, 1979.

*   *   *

Partly as a result of the work of Len Deighton the spy story has replaced the formal detective novel as the relevant thriller for its time. While continuing the tradition of literary excellence that has distinguished espionage fiction since the days of Somerset Maugham, Eric Ambler, and Graham Green, both he and his gifted contemporary John le Carré have contributed a new energy, intelligence, and meaning to the novel of espionage. Ever since his first novel, *The Ipcress File*, Deighton has instructed a large reading public in some of the factual and emotional realities of espionage and counterespionage. Writing with a lively wit, a keen eye for the surfaces of modern life, a convincing sense of authenticity, and a genuine intellectual concern for what the dark side of governmental practice can mean, Deighton has revealed, in all of his novels, some of the sham and self-delusion of contemporary politics.

In his spy novels Deighton employs a nameless first-person narrator who owes something to Raymond Chandler's Philip Marlowe in his breezy wisecracks and his sometimes strained metaphors; beneath the wiseguy surface, however, he possesses also some of Marlowe's decency and compassion. Resolutely working-class in background, education, and point of view, Deighton's hero is a professional spy who must do constant battle with the forces of the British Establishment in their full and whinnying glory as well as with whatever is on the other side. Frequently, in fact, his spy never knows precisely which side he is on, and is so often betrayed by his colleagues and superiors that it sometimes doesn't matter. Professional and personal betrayal mesh perfectly in his "game, set, match" trilogy, where the protagonist's wife, who is also a colleague, turns out to be a Soviet agent, giving a new dimension to the spy novel's necessary questioning of loyalty.

Accompanying the energetic style and disillusioned outlook is a complicated sense of novelistic architecture. Deighton's books frequently reveal at their conclusions both their method and their meaning. As the protagonist solves whatever mystery has been confronting him, or wraps up a long and tangled investigation, the book reaches the end of a usually puzzling and complicated narrative structure. The complications of its subject and of its fictional development appear to blend perfectly: the construction becomes, very artfully, an emblem of the meaning of espionage, as much as the usual anonymity of the narrator suggests something about the problem of identity in this troubled world.

Deighton's fictional and nonfictional researches into the history of World War II reflect some of the same concerns and interests of his espionage fiction. Like his spy novels, his war novels, *Bomber* and *Goobye Mickey Mouse*, demonstrate his passion for authenticity along with a bittersweet attitude toward a past that is both glorious and ignoble. He mingles his love for the great airplanes of the war with admiration for the brave men who flew them, and a moving realization of the horror and futility of war itself.

Like John le Carré again, Deighton has done much to advance our knowledge of the way spies and spying work and what they really mean in our time. For both writers the novel of espionage serves an emblematic function. It shows, all too convincingly, the sad history of treason that marks the real battle in the shadows—a spy seems always to betray one cause, one country, one person or another in order to do his task. The contemporary reality of the Western world provides the necessary historical context for Deighton's novels; daily headlines indicate the truth of his fictional perceptions, and the Kafkaesque quality of international politics and modern life itself reflects the deeper truth of his books.

Because Deighton's novels invariably show the folly, imbecility, and corruption of the wealthy and privileged classes in England, they have some of the satiric flavor of the Angry Young Men, and his hero is somewhat of a Lucky Jim of espionage. Because they present a labyrinthine picture of undeclared war, conflicting loyalties, multiple betrayals, and complicated national alignments, they provide a useful image of the world we all inhabit. Their dominant ideas and emotions are those of our time—puzzlement, anxiety, cynicism, and guilt. They recognize, further, one of the major lessons of the modern English spy novel, that an entire class, long protected by its own sense of unity and privilege, has sold its birthright, as the sordid history of Burgess, Maclean, Philby, and Blunt, among others, has proved.

In his own flip, entertaining, and exciting style, Deighton treats essentially the same problem that haunts a great deal of English fiction, the timeless question of who will inherit the virtue of the nation, who will save England from itself. His works thus show some connections with such books as *Adam Bede*, *Tess of the d'Urbervilles*, and *Lady Chatterley's Lover*, carrying on in a highly unlikely form the theme of a nation and a class that, ultimately, has betrayed itself. His novels indicate that the continuing vitality of the English novel may very well depend upon the popular and subliterary genres. As a spy novelist and as a British author of fiction, he deserves sympathetic reading and consideration with some of the better writers of the time.

—George Grella

DELANY, Samuel R(ay).   American.   Born in New York City, 1 April 1942. Educated at the Dalton School and Bronx High School of Science, both New York; City College of New York (poetry editor, *The Promethean*), 1960, 1962–63. Married the poet Marilyn Hacker in 1961 (divorced, 1980); one daughter. Butler Professor of English, State University of New York, Buffalo, 1975; Fellow, Center for Twentieth Century Studies, University of Wisconsin, Milwaukee, 1977. Recipient: Nebula Award, 1966, 1967 (twice), 1969; Hugo Award, 1970. Address: c/o Bantam Books Inc., 666 Fifth Avenue, New York, New York 10019, U.S.A.

PUBLICATIONS

Novels

The Jewels of Aptor.   New York, Ace, 1962; revised edition, Ace, and London, Gollancz, 1968; London, Sphere, 1971; Boston, Gregg Press, 1977.
The Fall of the Towers (revised texts).   New York, Ace, 1970; London, Sphere, 1971.
    Captives of the Flame.   New York, Ace, 1963; revised edition, as *Out of the Dead City*, London, Sphere, 1968; Ace, 1977.
    The Towers of Toron.   New York, Ace, 1964; revised edition, London, Sphere, 1968.
    City of a Thousand Suns.   New York, Ace, 1965; revised edition, London, Sphere, 1969.
The Ballad of Beta-2.   New York, Ace, 1965.
Babel-17.   New York, Ace, 1966; London, Gollancz, 1967; revised edition, London, Sphere, 1969; Boston, Gregg Press, 1976.
Empire Star.   New York, Ace, 1966.

The Einstein Intersection. New York, Ace, 1967; London, Gollancz, 1968.
Nova. New York, Doubleday, 1968; London, Gollancz, 1969.
The Tides of Lust. New York, Lancer, 1973; Manchester, Savoy, 1979.
Dhalgren. New York, Bantam, 1975; revised edition, Boston, Gregg Press, 1977.
Triton. New York, Bantam, 1976; London, Corgi, 1977.
The Ballad of Beta-2, and Empire Star. London, Sphere, 1977.
Empire: A Visual Novel, illustrated by Howard V. Chaykin. New York, Berkley, 1978.
Neveryóna; or, The Tale of Signs and Cities. New York, Bantam, 1983.
Stars in My Pocket Like Grains of Sand. New York, Bantam, 1984.
The Splendor and Misery of Bodies, of Cities. New York, Bantam, 1985.
Flight from Nevèryon. New York, Bantam, 1985.

Short Stories

Driftglass: 10 Tales of Speculative Fiction. New York, Doubleday, 1971; London, Gollancz, 1978.
Tales of Nevèryon. New York, Bantam, 1979.
Distant Stars. New York, Bantam, 1981.

Other

The Jewel-Hinged Jaw: Notes on the Language of Science Fiction. Elizabethtown, New York, Dragon Press, 1977.
The American Shore: Meditations on a Tale of Science Fiction by Thomas M. Disch—"Angouleme." Elizabethtown, New York, Dragon Press, 1978.
Heavenly Breakfast: An Essay on the Winter of Love (memoir). New York, Bantam, 1979.
Starboard Wine: More Notes on the Language of Science Fiction. Pleasantville, New York, Dragon Press, 1984.

Editor, with Marilyn Hacker, *Quark 1–4.* New York, Paperback Library, 4 vols., 1970–71.
Editor, *Nebula Winners 13.* New York, Harper, 1980.

*

Manuscript Collection: Mugar Memorial Library, Boston University.

Critical Studies: *The Delany Intersection: Samuel R. Delany Considered as a Writer of Semi-Precious Words* by George Edgar Slusser, San Bernardino, California, Borgo Press, 1977; *Worlds Out of Words: The SF Novels of Samuel R. Delany* by Douglas Barbour, Frome, Somerset, Bran's Head, 1979; *Samuel R. Delany* by Jane Weedman, Mercer Island, Washington, Starmont House, 1982; *Samuel R. Delany* by Seth McEvoy, New York, Ungar, 1983.

*   *   *

Samuel R. Delany's first novel, *The Jewels of Aptor,* is a novel of quests, both physical and philosophical, with mythological overtones, but is hardly distinguishable from other science-fiction novels of its time. In the three novels that followed (known collectively as *The Fall of the Towers*), Delany's strongly anti-war stance, his warning that a government can

control, by manipulation of information, a citizenship that is metaphorically/literally asleep, were clear indications that Delany would become a writer who sets his narratives in the future in order to (as he recently wrote of Ursula Le Guin) "force a dialogue with the here and now, a dialogue generally called science fiction." But Delany is not only a social thinker; he has immersed himself and his writings in the sciences, with archeology and linguistics uppermost among many.

A catchphrase from Delany's sixth published novel, *Empire Star,* best describes the layers of his work: "simplex, complex, multiplex." In the best of his work a complex question (the responsibilities of freedom, the shaping effect language has on thought) is worked through, and is interwoven with a fresh conception of a science (the study of myth, ethnomusicology) to produce a multiplex texture, a dense context that compels the reader to look at events in more than one light. Delany's greatest strength is as a conceptualist; his surfaces are kept deliberately simplex in most cases: adventure stories with daring heroes, strong beautiful women, and idiosyncratic aliens. *Empire Star,* probably the best point of entry into Delany's work, is very short, but has a complexity and a freshness that never flag, sustained by this multiplicity of levels, and particularly by many apparent paradoxes which Delany clears up on the last page by reminding the reader that human beings, their names, constructs, and actions, are very small parts of an infinite universe: "In this vast and multiplex universe there are almost as many worlds called Rhys as there are places called Brooklyn Bridge. It's a beginning. It's an end. I leave to you the problem of ordering your perceptions and making the journey from one to the other."

Between the Towers trilogy and *Empire Star* Delany wrote *The Ballad of Beta-2* and *Babel-17,* both of which revolve around linguistic puzzles. *Beta-2* is recognizably the work of a young author, while *Babel-17* is possessed of the mature Delany voice and complexity. The investigations reflect very different conceptions of the nature of language: in *Beta-2* language is a playful deceiver (even if the secrets it hides are tragic ones), while in *Babel-17* it is a threatening entity, an irresistible tyrant that shapes its users' thoughts.

The Einstein Intersection is a fascinating novel, and a very dense one. It is set in a highly mutated, possibly post-invasion, future. The plot is a variation on the Orpheus myth, but the subject of the novel's deepest probing is the author himself, his view of mythology, his ideas of how legendary figures from the Minotaur to Billy the Kid can be manipulated, and how their archetypal power can be used to charge a narrative. Notes from Delany's own journal serve as epigraphs for the chapters. And if the focus of *The Einstein Intersection* is on how Delany will use common experience and symbols, the space opera *Nova* is an investigation into how personal experience can become fiction. One character is trying to figure out how to write a novel from his experiences—the experiences we read about in this novel by Samuel R. Delany. Capt. Lorq von Ray filters ambivalent (multiplex) facts to sustain a subjective reality (fiction) that allows him to sustain his obsession to possess the powerful element Illyrion.

Introspective and self-referential elements are allowed to dominate the massive, though less successful, *Dhalgren.* Seven years in the making (the story collection *Driftglass* and the erotic novel *The Tides of Lust* appeared during the interval), *Dhalgren* appeared in 1975, but in its preoccupation with the idea of total freedom in the collapse of ordered civilization, and in the ways information is presented to the reader, this novel is a direct descendant of the experimental fictions of the 1960's. Parts of *Dhalgren* are presented in disruptive ways—text in double columns on a page, for example. Unfortunately, these techniques unbalance the work as a whole. The setting is vaguely mid-Armageddon, and the textual manipulations lack the emotional weight of the story elements. The reader is in effect asked to accept that a writer's notebook is as important as the end of civilization. Many readers remain unconvinced.

Triton concerns itself with sexual identity and role, but the depiction of the Triton colony, at once so alien and so close to our own experience, is undisrupted by authorial manipulations and the novel as a whole buoys up Delany's ideas more successfully than does *Dhalgren*. Here the male protagonist's identity crisis results in his undergoing a sex-change operation, which finally solves none of his problems. Sexual problems run deeper than the physical body, Delany shows us; they are rooted in our language and our ways of ordering our existence.

Since 1979 Delany has delved deeper into the questions of sexual and/*vs.* individual identity in two universes, universes which portray similar struggles in very different terms. In the Nevèrÿon books and in *Stars in My Pocket Like Grains of Sand* Delany's science of choice is semiology, a more complex science than most he's previously investigated. In the Nevèrÿon trilogy the surface is very simplex: a sword and cart civilization. Here the reader is free to ride on top of the stories, or dip down into the role exploration aspects, or even deeper, into the underlay of the theory of linguistic sign generation. To each reader according to his abilities and ambitions. But in *Stars in My Pocket* (and in "Omegahelm," the related short story in *Distant Stars*) plot elements are sparse, and theoretical discussions and long strings of fabulous detail (details which actually succeed in reordering a reader's response to some words: for example, we soon come to read "tall" as meaning "unattractive," and "he" as meaning "a sexually stimulating individual") are pushed to the fore. There is no easy ride in this universe.

Delany is presently at work on more Nevèrÿon stories, and the other novel in the *Stars in My Pocket* universe diptych is presently "in the word processor." These, then, seem to be the universes which will carry Delany's work through the 1980's.

—William C. Bamberger

DeLILLO, Don. American. Born in New York City, 20 November 1936. Educated at Fordham University, Bronx, New York, 1954–58. Recipient: Guggenheim fellowship, 1979; American Academy award, 1984; American Book Award, 1985. Agent: Wallace and Sheil Agency, 117 East 70th Street, New York, New York 10021, U.S.A.

PUBLICATIONS

Novels

Americana. Boston, Houghton Mifflin, 1971.
End Zone. Boston, Houghton Mifflin, 1972; London, Deutsch, 1973.
Great Jones Street. Boston, Houghton Mifflin, 1973; London, Deutsch, 1974.
Ratner's Star. New York, Knopf, 1976.
Players. New York, Knopf, 1977.
Running Dog. New York, Knopf, 1978; London, Gollancz, 1979.

The Names. New York, Knopf, 1982; Brighton, Sussex, Harvester Press, 1983.
—*White Noise.* New York, Viking, 1985; London, Pan, 1986.

Uncollected Short Stories

"The River Jordan," in *Epoch* (Ithaca, New York), Winter 1960.
"Spaghetti and Meatballs," in *Epoch* (Ithaca, New York), Spring 1965.
"Take the 'A' Train," in *Stories from Epoch*, edited by Baxter Hathaway. Ithaca, New York, Cornell University Press, 1966.
"Coming Sun. Mon. Tues.," in *Kenyon Review* (Gambier, Ohio), June 1966.
"Baghdad Towers West," in *Epoch* (Ithaca, New York), Spring 1968.
"Game Plan," in *New Yorker*, 27 November 1971.
"In the Men's Room of the Sixteenth Century," in *The Secret Life of Our Times*, edited by Gordon Lish. New York, Doubleday, 1973.
"The Uniforms," in *Cutting Edges*, edited by Jack Hicks. New York, Holt Rinehart, 1973.
"Showdown at Great Hole," in *Esquire* (New York), June 1976.
"The Network," in *On the Job*, edited by William O'Rourke. New York, Random House, 1977.
"Creation," in *Antaeus* (New York), Spring 1979.
"Human Moments in World War III," in *Great Esquire Fiction*, edited by L. Rust Hills. New York, Viking Press, 1983.
"Walkmen," in *Vanity Fair* (New York), August 1984.

Play

The Engineer of Moonlight, in *Cornell Review* (Ithaca, New York), Winter 1979.

*   *   *

"What writing means to me is trying to make interesting, clear, beautiful language. Working at sentences and rhythms is probably the most satisfying thing I do as a writer. I think after a while a writer can begin to know himself through his language. He sees someone or something reflected back at him from these constructions. Over the years it's possible for a writer to shape himself as a human being through the language he uses. I think written language, fiction, goes that deep. He not only sees himself but begins to make himself or remake himself. Of course this is mysterious and subjective territory. Writing also means trying to advance the art. Fiction hasn't quite been filled in or done in or worked out. We make our small leaps" (interview in *Anything Can Happen*, edited by Thomas LeClair and Larry McCaffery, 1983).

Of American novelists who began publishing in the 1970's, Don DeLillo is one of the most prolific and compelling. DeLillo believes, with his subway inspector in *Ratner's Star*, that existence is "nourished from below, from the fear level, the place of obsession, the starkest tract of awareness." His eight novels are a spelunker's guide to American life, cool explorations of undergrounds and subcultures where the powers once housed in churches may now exist; football, rock music, film, terrorism, espionage, pure mathematics, technology. His characters experiment with crime and violence, burrow into bat caves and esoterica, travel to deserts and shut themselves in empty rooms to seek what can be called "subcendence," a private being far beneath the strictures, conditioning, and boredom of ego and ordinary life. Paralleling their quest is DeLillo's experiment with specialized languages, his search for a precision of style that will imply what he quotes Hermann Broch as calling "the word beyond speech."

Consistent in motive and theme, DeLillo's work has a virtuoso variety of subject, form, and style. Like Pynchon, DeLillo knows the new modular man, component of large systems, consumer of banalities enlarged and projected by electronic media. His features are boredom, game-playing, narcissism, paranoia. Like Barth, DeLillo turns popular forms—the thriller, science fiction, the sports novel, the disaster book—against themselves and the reader's expectations. His books move toward vanishing points, not conclusions. Like Barthelme, DeLillo records the babble of jargons—scientific, military, entertainment, and many others—that compete for power over silent reality. He can do aphorisms and slapstick, irony and meditation, linear plots and recursive structures. But for DeLillo, learning and craft are always the means to mystery, ways to manifest and pass through filters and occlusions, manufactured passions and trained gestures toward "the starkest tract of awareness," the primal and unnameable.

DeLillo thinks of his work as two parts: *Ratner's Star* and the seven realistic novels preceding and following this hybrid of *Alice in Wonderland* and science fiction. *Americana* is an extravagant, yet rather conventional, first novel, an on-the-road book full of observation and notebook philosophizing. Its protagonist, David Bell, leaves the politics of the New York City television industry to tour his small-town past and to cross the continent. As he travels, he both stores up and empties out experience, a signature of the DeLillo hero. In *End Zone* Gary Harkness, like Bell, moves West, away from civilization and towards an atavistic existence playing football for Logos College. The novel becomes a struggle between word (logos) and act, symbol systems and signal behavior, as the characters who surround Harkness try to claim him within their very different discourses. Probably DeLillo's best-known work, *End Zone* skilfully compresses into its football metaphor social, linguistic, and religious themes. *Great Jones Street* completes the protagonist's retreat. Bucky Wunderlick, a Mick Jagger-like rock star, drops out of his group to become "the least of what he was." Although *Great Jones Street* was largely unnoticed by reviewers, I think DeLillo's presentation of rock music, its motives, excesses, and voids, compares with West's treatment of the movies in *The Day of the Locust*.

Ratner's Star, like other encyclopedic novels of the 1970's—Barth's *Letters*, Gaddis's *JR*, Coover's *The Public Burning*—is more about processes than people, the paradoxical process of learning uncertainty. Trying to decipher a message from space, mathematical prodigy Billy Twillig finds that all abstract structures must be thought through and that a meta-language ("Have you emptied your system of meaning?" one character asks him) must be constructed. Dervish philosophers, inhabitants of holes, and other Alice-like creatures rise up to give the reader a history of mathematics and a Godelian lesson: in "our press to measure and delive . . . we implicate ourselves in endless uncertainty." A fiction about all fiction-making, *Ratner's Star* is a conceptual monster, a tail- and tale-eating beast worthy of Sterne, Carroll, or Escher.

The two short novels—*Players* and *Running Dog*—that follow *Ratner's Star* are more modest, scaled down to show the meager ways contemporaries try to fill up rather than map out voids. Conspirators in excitement, the protagonists hunt extremity in terrorism, sexual adventure, and pornography. The books, though, are subtracting machines, showing how little becomes less, a gradual divestment of humanness. DeLillo's more recent novels—the widely praised *The Names* and *White Noise*—synthesize realistic observation with the intellectual range of his earlier fiction. *The Names* is an international novel, set in Greece and the Mideast, that explores terror in all its manifestations—political, religious, family, and linguistic. *White Noise*, a disaster book about a toxic spill in mid-America, probes deep into "the fear level"—the fear of death and its ironically destructive defenses. Called "our wittiest writer" by John Leonard, DeLillo in his latest work fuses his usual diagnostic clarity with greater sympathy for the fears humans impose upon themselves, giving this work a new emotional depth and accessibility.

—Thomas LeClair

DENNIS, Nigel (Forbes). British. Born in Bletchingley, Surrey, 16 January 1912. Educated at Plumtree School, Southern Rhodesia; Odenwaldschule, Germany. Married 1) Mary-Madeleine Massias; 2) Beatrice Ann Hewart Matthew in 1959; two daughters. Secretary, National Board of Review of Motion Pictures, New York, 1935–36; assistant editor, and book reviewer, *New Republic*, New York, 1937–38; staff book reviewer, *Time*, New York, 1940–59; drama critic, 1960–63, and joint editor, 1967–70, *Encounter*, London; staff book reviewer, *The Sunday Telegraph*, London, 1961–82. Recipient: Houghton Mifflin-Eyre and Spottiswoode award, 1950; Royal Society of Literature Heinemann Award, for non-fiction, 1966. Fellow, Royal Society of Literature, 1966. Address: c/o A.M. Heath, 40–42 William IV Street, London WC2N 4DD, England.

PUBLICATIONS

Novels

Boys and Girls Come Out to Play.   London, Eyre and Spottiswoode, 1949; as *A Sea Change*, Boston, Houghton Mifflin, 1949.
Cards of Identity.   London, Weidenfeld and Nicolson, and New York, Vanguard Press, 1955.
A House in Order.   London, Weidenfeld and Nicolson, and New York, Vanguard Press, 1966.

Uncollected Short Stories

"Poor Signora," in *New Yorker*, 13 May 1961.
"Blocked Feed," in *Harper's* (New York), December 1961.
"The Pukey," in *Anti-Story*, edited by Philip Stevick.   New York, Free Press, 1971.

Plays

Cards of Identity, adaptation of his own novel (produced London, 1956).   Included in *Two Plays and a Preface*, 1958.
The Making of Moo (produced London, 1957; New York, 1958).   Included in *Two Plays and a Preface*, 1958.
Two Plays and a Preface (includes *Cards of Identity* and *The Making of Moo*).   London, Weidenfeld and Nicolson, 1958; New York, Vanguard Press, 1959.
August for the People (produced Edinburgh and London, 1961).   London, French, 1962.

Radio Play: *Swansong for 7 Voices*, 1985.

Verse

Exotics: Poems of the Mediterranean and the Middle East.
   London, Weidenfeld and Nicolson, 1970; New York, Vanguard Press, 1971.

Other

Dramatic Essays.   London, Weidenfeld and Nicolson, 1962;
   Westport, Connecticut, Greenwood Press, 1978.
Jonathan Swift: A Short Character.   New York, Macmillan,
   1964; London, Weidenfeld and Nicolson, 1965.
An Essay on Malta.   London, Murray, 1972; New York, Van-
   guard Press, 1974.

*   *   *

Although Nigel Dennis has published only three novels, their
quality is high enough to give him a place as one of the best
English novelists of his generation. He lived in America for
many years and in fact the principal characters of his first novel,
Boys and Girls Come Out to Play, are all American. It is set
in the summer of 1939, on the eve of the Second World War,
and the action takes place partly in America and partly in
Poland. A liberal journalist, Max Divver, goes to Poland to
report on the political situation for a progressive magazine,
accompanied by Jimmy Morgan, the adolescent son of the rich
woman who owns and edits the magazine. Jimmy is a difficult
boy, who is liable to fits, but the visit proves the making of
him, whereas it is the undoing of Max, a forceful but insecure
character, who is consumed by self-loathing. Nigel Dennis
develops the relationship between them in a leisurely fashion
that allows for much indulgence in psychological nuance but
results in a long book that has rather a lot of static passages.
There is a slightly uneasy contrast between the reflective sections and the element of adventure that builds up as Max and
Jimmy try to escape from Poland just before the German invasion. The interest is essentially in the characters and the Polish
setting never really seems convincing. The novel leaves no
doubt, however, of the quality of Dennis's writing, shown for
instance in the dazzling account of the attempts by a mechanic
to start a large and ancient car (a vehicle which much later
comes to play a crucial part in the plot). It also shows a satirical
inclination, and a tendency to allegory or fable in that Max
Divver is clearly meant to embody the insufficiencies of the
liberal intellectual at a time of great historical crisis.

These tendencies were fully developed in Dennis's next
novel, *Cards of Identity*, which established his reputation and
remains one of the most brilliant works of post-war English
fiction. It is about the "problem of identity" which is so much
discussed in the modern world, and the essence of the novel
lies in the characters' difficulty in knowing who they are supposed to be. Yet *Cards of Identity* also indicates the time and
place of its composition. The setting is an English country house
where a body called the Identity Club is holding its annual
meeting, at which the members listen to papers describing the
case-histories of interesting identity problems. Much of the
detail reflects English life in the late 1940's and early 1950's,
a period of ration-books and identity cards and continuing post-
war privations. One of the case-histories is about an ex-communist turned monk who is writing his memoirs in a monastery,
all of whose inmates have had a similar communist past; it
is very entertaining, but inevitably seems rather dated now.

On the other hand, the story of the Co-Wardens of the Badger-
ies, and the sad farcical events that took place while ceremo-
niously leading a symbolic stuffed badger across London in
the funeral procession of the Lord Royal, is still a valid satire
on the more absurd manifestations of English public traditionalism. The case histories are told with great verve and are full
of Dennis's imaginative exuberance. But where *Cards of Identity* transcends the treatment of individual forms of identity
crisis and looks at the problem of English cultural identity as
a whole, is not in the separate case-histories but in the narrative
framework of the novel. The setting of the events is a traditional
country house of the kind familiar in innumerable English
novels. But it has been empty for a long time, and in order
to find staff for it the local representatives of the Identity Club
abduct various of the local inhabitants and by unspecified but
infallible means transform them into typical denizens of the
English country house, such as the butler, the cook and the
eccentric gardener. In fact they construct, specially for the
Club, a model of the comfortable timeless milieu of much traditional English fiction, though it proves in the end no more
than a house of cards, and identity-cards at that. In this brilliantly comic and ingenious novel Nigel Dennis probes at many
contemporary problems. The satirical examination of the way
in which the familiar symbols of English cultural identity have
been losing their validity is an important part of the meaning
of *Cards of Identity*.

Dennis's third novel, *A House in Order*, also dwells on the
question of identity, though it is more personal and less culturally specific than its predecessor. The subject is deliberately
narrow and intensely treated: during a war between two
unnamed powers a prisoner is kept confined in a greenhouse
by the soldiers of one side. He cannot be moved as he is an
object of contention between two branches of the military
establishment, though neither of them is interested in his personal welfare. With enormous patience the man cultivates the
small plants he finds in the greenhouse and in the yard outside
where he is allowed to exercise; he thereby keeps not only
his house but his mind in order, and preserves his sense of
self. At the end of the story, when he has been released and
returned to his own country and a greenhouse of his own,
he even looks back nostalgically to the days of his imprisonment
as to some vanished ideal order. The story has of course many
obviously allegorical implications about the human condition,
but Dennis embodies them in a detailed convincing narrative
that never becomes thinly symbolic, and where the humour
that distinguished *Cards of Identity* is still noticeable. *A House
in Order* is remarkable for the way in which it works as a
novel, even while being an evident moral fable.

—Bernard Bergonzi

DESAI, Anita (née Mazumdar).   Indian.   Born in Mussoorie,
24 June 1937. Educated at Queen Mary's Higher Secondary
School, New Delhi; Miranda House, Delhi University, B.A.
in English literature 1957. Married Ashvin Desai in 1958; four
children. Since 1972, Member of the Sahitya Academy English
Board. Recipient: Royal Society of Literature Winifred Holtby
Prize, 1978; Sahitya Academy award, 1979; *Guardian* award,
for children's book, 1982. Fellow, Royal Society of Literature,
1978. Address: c/o Heinemann Ltd., 10 Upper Grosvenor
Street, London W1X 9PA, England.

PUBLICATIONS

Novels

Cry, The Peacock. Calcutta, Rupa, n.d.; London, Owen, 1963.
Voices in the City. London, Owen, 1965.
Bye-Bye, Blackbird. New Delhi, Hind, and Thompson, Connecticut, InterCulture, 1971.
Where Shall We Go This Summer? New Delhi, Vikas, 1975.
Fire on the Mountain. New Delhi, Allied, London, Heinemann, and New York, Harper, 1977.
Clear Light of Day. New Delhi, Allied, London, Heinemann, and New York, Harper, 1980.
In Custody. London, Heinemann, 1984; New York, Harper, 1985.

Short Stories

Games at Twilight and Other Stories. New Delhi, Allied, and London, Heinemann, 1978; New York, Harper, 1980.

Uncollected Short Stories

"Circus Cat, Alley Cat," in *Thought* (New Delhi), 1957.
"Tea with the Maharani," in *Envoy* (London), 1959.
"Grandmother," in *Writers Workshop* (Calcutta), 1960.
"Mr. Bose's Private Bliss," in *Envoy* (London), 1961.
"Ghost House," in *Quest* (Bombay), 1961.
"Descent from the Rooftop," in *Illustrated Weekly of India* (Bombay), 1970.

Other (for children)

The Peacock Garden. Bombay, India Book House, 1974; London, Heinemann, 1979.
Cat on a Houseboat. Bombay, Orient Longman, 1976.
The Village by the Sea. London, Heinemann, 1982.

*

Critical Studies: *Indian Writing in English* by Paul Verghese, Bombay, Asia Publishing House, 1970; *Anita Desai: A Study of Her Fiction* by Meena Belliappa, Calcutta, Writers Workshop, 1971; *The Twice-Born Fiction* by Meenakshi Mukherjee, New Delhi, Arnold-Heinemann, 1972; *Indian Writing in English* by Srinivas Iyyengar, Bombay, Asia Publishing House, 1972; *The Novels of Mrs. Anita Desai* by B.R. Rao, New Delhi, Kalyani, 1977; *Anita Desai the Novelist* by Madhusudan Prasad, Allahabad, New Horizon, 1981.

Anita Desai comments:

I have been writing, since the age of 7, as instinctively as I breathe. It is a necessity to me: I find it is in the process of writing that I am able to think, to feel, and to realize at the highest pitch. Writing is to me a process of discovering the truth—the truth that is nine-tenths of the iceberg that lies submerged beneath the one-tenth visible portion we call Reality. Writing is my way of plunging to the depths and exploring this underlying truth. All my writing is an effort to discover, to underline and convey the true significance of things. That is why, in my novels, small objects, passing moods and attitudes acquire a large importance. My novels are no reflection of Indian society, politics, or character. They are part of my private effort to seize upon the raw material of life—its shapelessness, its meaninglessness, that lack of design that drives one

to despair—and to mould it and impose on it a design, a certain composition ad order that pleases me as an artist and also as a human being who longs for order.

While writing my novels, I find I use certain images again and again and that, although real, they acquire the significance of symbols. I imagine each writer ends by thus revealing his own mythology, a mythology that symbolizes his private morality and philosophy. One hopes, at the end of one's career, to have made some significant statement on life—not necessarily a water-tight, hard-and-fast set of rules, but preferably an ambiguous, elastic, shifting, and kinetic one that remains always capable of further change and growth.

Next to this exploration of the underlying truth and the discovery of a private mythology and philosophy, it is style that interests me most—and by this I mean the conscious labour of uniting language and symbol, word and rhythm. Without it, language would remain a dull and pedestrian vehicle. I search for a style that will bring it to vivid, surging life. Story, action, and drama mean little to me except insofar as they emanate directly from the personalities I have chosen to write about, born of their dreams and wills. One must find a way to unite the inner and the outer rhythms, to obtain a certain integrity and to impose order on chaos.

*   *   *

Whereas earlier Indian novelists were concerned with nationalist politics, protest and cultural assertion, Anita Desai is interested in the various changes which have affected lives since independence. Although her novels differ radically in subject matter, they attempt to find patterns in the chaos of modern India and modern life. At times this can result in the simplified optimism of *The Village by the Sea*: "You are going to give up your traditional way of living and learn a new way to suit the new environment that the factory will create at Thul so as to survive. Yes, you will survive." More complexly *In Custody* notes the decay of the great Muslim Urdu-language culture of north India since colonialism and partition; the last remaining great poet, carrier of the tradition, grows senile in a Delhi where Urdu poetry is used for the lyrics of sentimental cinema music.

An excellent stylist whose impressionistic sentences move the mind to imagine visual scenes, Desai is a less patient, less tolerant, more questioning social satirist than R.K. Narayan. She sees the same comedy of oversize characters, inefficiency, and deflated ambition as Narayan, but with less sympathy. Her up-beat, hopeful endings often seem imposed, a forced, formal drawing of the curtains on a farce or comedy which was leading towards a revelation of a dark world. Other novels reveal unsatisfied lives filled with illusions, lack of will, pettiness, misplaced duty, false ideals, and self-deception. The relationships between the characters and their lives are filled with subtexts; several of her novels are about the tensions between people related through family, childhood, friendship, admiration, or need. These people never live up to their ambitions, while the larger-than-life are small when seen closely. Desai's stories explore character through inaction; usually there is a wastage of the self, false choices, illusions, lack of will. Time takes it toll and those we have sympathized with are found to be foolish or wrong, while those who have been previously judged as superficial or weak are now seen in a better light. The novels unexpectedly change direction. *Bye-Bye, Blackbird* appears a better written version of the Third World immigrant to England novel, but surprisingly veers off into the English countryside where epiphanies of the main characters lead to changed lives. *Voices in the City* starts as a Dostoevskian study in a young man's anguish and resentment, set in Calcutta, but becomes a record of a woman's search for purpose. *Clear Light of Day*, like Desai's previous books, first gives the impression of being about its male characters and then its focus shifts to the various roles, problems, and disillusionments of women.

In post-colonial India women have been radically affected by such matters as the increase of western-style education, choice in marriage partner, career expectations, and the loosening of the joint family. Desai, being an educated woman of half-European descent, is sensitively situated to record the crisis of the Indian colonial bourgeoisie after independence. This crisis leads to a sense of drifting lives, a general alienation and nostalgia. Each of Desai's novels focuses on a life at a particular stage. These lives, although set in a social context, are puzzling as more is implied than the stories offered about them. They are often marked by failure, withdrawals into the self, or self-assertions which at best are mediocre. The main characters have escaped confining limitations, but liberated they create an even more sterile existence. Desai's concern is with the lives of women, the limitations and handicaps placed on them by society and, as in *Where Shall We Go This Summer?* and *Clear Light of Day*, the difficulties they face in giving their lives purpose when they attempt to assert their identity.

Many of the lives she portrays are of wives, older women, sisters who are unable to break with their family, those who take responsibility for others, widows who want to be left alone. They are from the bourgeoisie, the upper-middle classes, or families which have gone down in the world economically since British rule without losing their English ways; they are from westernized families in which choice of life and independence for a woman is a moral and financial possibility. At first such women seem morally, although not financially, superior; they appear independent and have chosen their fate. As we read further, however, their choices seem traps and they are less free than others who were less favoured, less able to choose, more corrupted by realities. Are such lives grey because they are so misleadingly free and because they are so responsible? Virtue, sensitivity, fineness of perception, even freedom may not be as important as relationships, success, and adjustment. We are offered portraits of women trying to salvage dignity or hope from their lives only to be crushed by their own mediocrity. By contrast a few of the characters, usually artists, have a naturally irresponsible spirit, which allows them a true freedom in realizing themselves, far different from those of the failures.

Desai writes two basic novels, often mixing them together; there are novels about what men do and novels about what women feel. Although women also act, that is less relevant than the choices which lead to quiet desperation. In *Fire on the Mountain* we are inside the mind of an older woman who, after withdrawing from the family and social pressures of her former life, is unexpectedly made responsible for an independent, interesting great-granddaughter with whom ironically she is unable to make contact and who causes her death. When Desai writes of men it may be done very well and with great care, but it is external. *Bye-Bye, Blackbird* and *Voices in the City* begin with the lives of men and are focused on their actions, but the perspective shifts from the outside into the mind of a woman whose emotional life is a major concern of each novel. *In Custody* uses R.K. Narayan's comic territory of well-meaning, bumbling incompetence made more absurd when unexpectedly confronted by possibilities of achievement and fame. If males are judged by their successful actions in the public realm, the male poet and male teacher here are among the two most feminine characters Desai has created. While the comedy of *In Custody* shows the impossibility of returning

to the womb of ambitionless resignation, the novel has its post-partition political-cultural dimension. Hindi-speaking Hindu India is now responsible for the preservation of the great Urdu culture of its former Muslim rulers.

On the evidence of Desai's recent books the long apprenticeship of her earlier novels was worthwhile. Her concerns have not changed, but whereas her early work seemed cluttered, arbitrary in form, and over-polished in style, the novels are now better structured, plotted and more implicit in psychology and characterization; instead of calling attention to her symbols, Desai now uses images functionally as part of a description of a scene.

—Bruce King

DESANI, G(ovindas) V(ishnoodas). American. Born in Nairobi, Kenya, 8 July 1909; became United States citizen, 1979. Came to Britain in 1926; journalist after 1928; correspondent for *Times of India*, Reuters, and Associated Press, 1935–45; lecturer on antiquities for Bombay Baroda and Central India Railway in late 1930's; lecturer, Imperial Institute, Council for Adult Education in the British Armed Forces, London and Wiltshire County Councils, and Royal Empire Society, and BBC broadcaster, during World War II; lived in Hindu and Buddhist monasteries in India, 1952–66, and Burma, 1960; special contributor and columnist ("Very High and Very Low"), *Illustrated Weekly of India*, Bombay, 1962–68. Fulbright-Hays Lecturer, 1968, Professor of Philosophy, 1969–79, and since 1979, Professor Emeritus, University of Texas, Austin. Visiting Professor, Boston University, Summer 1979, and 1981. Agent: Stephen Greenberg, 707 West 10th Street, Austin, Texas 78701. Address: Department of Philosophy, W.H. 316, University of Texas, Austin, Texas 78712, U.S.A.

PUBLICATIONS

Novel

All about Mr. Hatterr: A Gesture. London, Aldor, 1948; as *All about H. Hatterr: A Gesture*, London, Saturn Press, 1950; revised edition, New York, Farrar Straus, 1951; revised edition, London, Bodley Head, and Farrar Straus, 1970; revised edition, New York, Lancer, 1972; London, Penguin, 1973.

Uncollected Short Stories

"A New Bridge of Plenty," "Mephisto's Daughter," "The Lama Arupa," "Trade Winds," "A Border Incident," "The Fall of G.M. Haii, In Memoriam," "The Sticky Affair," "Goan, Meet a Samoan," "With Malice Aforethought," "The Second Mrs. Was Wed in a Nightmare," "Sutta Abandoned," "The Last Long Letter," "The Fiend Screams 'KYA CHAHATE HO?,'" all in *Illustrated Weekly of India* (Bombay), 1957–67.
"The Explanation," in *Hindi Review* (Benares), July 1959.
"Mephisto's Daughter," in *Noble Savage 4* (Cleveland), 1961.
"With Malice Aforethought," in *Noble Savage 5* (Cleveland), 1962.
"The Second Mrs. Was Wed in a Nightmare," in *Transatlantic Review 9* (London), Spring 1962.

Play

Hali. London, Saturn Press, 1950; revised edition, Calcutta, Writers Workshop, 1967.

Other

Mainly Concerning Kama and Her Immortal Lord. New Delhi, Indian Council on Cultural Relations, 1973.

*

Critical Studies: *A Note ... on G.V. Desani's "All about H. Hatterr" and "Hali"* edited by Khushwant Singh and Peter Russell, London and Amsterdam, Szeben, 1952; "The Dialogue in G.V. Desani's *All about H. Hatterr*" by D.M. Burjorjee, in *World Literature Written in English* (Arlington, Texas), November 1974.

*   *   *

G.V. Desani's published fiction consists of a small number of short stories and one novel, *All about H. Hatterr.* In addition, he has published a prose poem, in dramatic form, titled *Hali,* which some critics consider his most significant work. *Hali* has also been called a "story of passion"; but whatever its classification, it serves as companion piece for Desani's novel. In both works the author is taking the measure of man—in *Hali,* ideal man, and in *All about H. Hatterr,* everyman or man as he really is in a far-from-perfect world. *Hali* is written in the prophetic and exalted style that its subject demands. In it the young hero, Hali, passes through fear, defeat, and sorrow to achieve a selfless, changeless, Christlike love for all humanity. Discarding deities that he had revered earlier, he now worships only his newly found God of Love, who is "eternally incarnated" in the human form.

H. Hatterr in *All about H. Hatterr* has accurately been described as "the mathematical opposite of Hali." The same may be said of the styles and the tones of the two works. A Eurasian born in Penang but a resident for long periods in India and England, H. Hatterr is indeed fitted for the role of everyman that Desani intends him to fill. The language employed by H. Hatterr as he narrates his "Autobiographical" is a mixture, wholly unique in literature, of cockney and babu English with liberal infusions of American slang, the argot of criminals, the jargon of the medical and legal professions, and literal translations from Hindi, the whole being sprinkled with quotations and misquotations from Shakespeare and other poets. Desani has aptly been called "a playboy of the English language, a juggler with words." His virtuosity in this respect is one of the chief pleasures and wonders of his novel: e.g., "Only a few days ago ... I was sitting in my humble belle-vue-no view, cul-de-sack-the-tenant, a landlady's up-and-do-'em opportunity apartment-joint in India." H. Hatterr's incessant flow of vulgarisms, cynicisms, sarcasms, and malapropisms reflects the vulgarity-cum-naivety of his character as a 20th-century everyman. In contrast to Hali's reglion of selfless love, H. Hatterr phrases his philosophy as follows: "To be easy and comfortable appears to be the aim of all man: even at the expense of the other feller." H. Hatterr's application of this simple rule of conduct in seven "life-encounters" supplies the action of the novel. Each of the "encounters" is preceded by a humorous "Instruction," in which an eccentric guru voices some general truth about the human condition, and a "Presumption," which presents H. Hatterr's distortion of this truth. The "encounters" themselves are absurd and fantastic, and from each of them H. Hatterr emerges rather badly battered. But he always bounces back for more. "*Life,*" he avers, "is no one-way pattern. It's *contrasts* all the way. And *contrasts* by Law! ... I

am not fed up with *Life.* ...." The fact that H. Hatterr enjoys the absurdity of life, at least as he leads it, serves to raise him somewhat above the stature of a mere buffoon and to give the reader the sense that the author's purpose is one of life-affirmation.

In his short fiction, G. V. Desani writes in one or other of the two contrasting veins *Hali* and *All about H. Hatterr.* Thus "The Last Long Letter" records the ecstatic visions of a young man, a suicide, who casts his soul back into the opaque void of the universe, where it had been a light, as he has previously cast his jeweled ring into the depths of the sea to symbolize his belief that from time to time spirit illuminates matter but then withdraws, leaving all in chaos and darkness until its next coming. Other stories—"Mephisto's Daughter," "With Malice Aforethought," and "The Second Mrs. Was Wed in a Nightmare"—are fantasies, sometimes with a satiric sting, which further exemplify the talent that made *All about H. Hatterr* one of our century's major contributions to the literature of the absurd.

—Perry D. Westbrook

DE VRIES, Peter. American. Born in Chicago, Illinois, 27 February 1910. Educated at Englewood Christian School, 1916–23; Chicago Christian High School, 1923–27; Calvin College, Grand Rapids, Michigan (editor, *Calvin College Chimes,* 1931), 1927–31, A.B. in English 1931; Northwestern University, Evanston, Illinois, 1931. Married Katinka Loeser in 1943; four children (one deceased). Editor of community newspapers, Chicago, 1931; candy vending machine operator, lecturer, and radio actor, Chicago, 1931–38; associate editor, 1938–42, and co-editor, 1942–44, *Poetry,* Chicago. Since 1944, staff member, *New Yorker.* Balch Lecturer, University of Virginia, Charlottesville, 1962. Recipient: American Academy grant, 1946. D.H.L.: University of Bridgeport, Connecticut, 1968. Member, National Institute of Arts and Letters, 1969, and American Academy, 1983. Address: 170 Cross Highway, Westport, Connecticut 06880, U.S.A.

PUBLICATIONS

Novels

But Who Wakes the Bugler? Boston, Houghton Mifflin, 1940.
The Handsome Heart. New York, Coward McCann, 1943.
Angels Can't Do Better. New York, Coward McCann, 1944.
The Tunnel of Love. Boston, Little Brown, 1954; London, Gollancz, 1955.
Comfort Me with Apples. Boston, Little Brown, and London, Gollancz, 1956.
The Mackerel Plaza. Boston, Little Brown, and London, Gollancz, 1958.
The Tents of Wickedness. Boston, Little Brown, and London, Gollancz, 1959.
Through the Fields of Clover. Boston, Little Brown, and London, Gollancz, 1961.
The Blood of the Lamb. Boston, Little Brown, and London, Gollancz, 1962.
Reuben, Reuben. Boston, Little Brown, and London, Gollancz, 1964.
Let Me Count the Ways. Boston, Little Brown, and London, Gollancz, 1965.

The Vale of Laughter.   Boston, Little Brown, 1967; London, Gollancz, 1968.

The Cat's Pajamas, and Witch's Milk.   Boston, Little Brown, 1968.

Mrs. Wallop.   Boston, Little Brown, and London, Gollancz, 1970.

Into Your Tent I'll Creep.   Boston, Little Brown, 1971; London, Gollancz, 1972.

Forever Panting.   Boston, Little Brown, and London, Gollancz, 1973.

The Glory of the Hummingbird.   Boston, Little Brown, 1974; London, Gollancz, 1975.

I Hear America Swinging.   Boston, Little Brown, and London, Gollancz, 1976.

Madder Music.   Boston, Little Brown, 1977; London, Gollancz, 1978.

Consenting Adults; or, The Duchess Will Be Furious.   Boston, Little Brown, 1980; London, Gollancz, 1981.

Sauce for the Goose.   Boston, Little Brown, 1981; London, Gollancz, 1982.

Slouching Towards Kalamazoo.   Boston, Little Brown, and London, Gollancz, 1983.

The Prick of Noon.   Boston, Little Brown, 1985; London, Gollancz, 1986.

Short Stories

No, But I Saw the Movie.   Boston, Little Brown, 1952; London, Gollancz, 1954.

Without a Stitch in Time: A Selection of the Best Humorous Short Pieces.   Boston, Little Brown, 1972; London, Gollancz, 1974.

Uncollected Short Stories

"Come Down to Queue," in *New Yorker*, 11 March 1974.
"The Iridescence of Mrs. Pulsifer," in *New Yorker*, 26 March 1979.

Play

The Tunnel of Love, with Joseph Fields, adaptation of the novel by De Vries (produced New York and London, 1957). Boston, Little Brown, 1957.

*

Bibliography: *Peter De Vries: A Bibliography 1934–1977* by Edwin T. Bowden, Austin, University of Texas Humanities Research Center, 1978.

Manuscript Collection: Boston University Library.

Critical Studies: interviews with Roy Newquist in *Counterpoint*, Chicago, Rand McNally, 1964, and Richard B. Sale in *Studies in the Novel* (Denton, Texas), Fall 1969; *Peter De Vries* by Roderick Jellema, Grand Rapids, Michigan, Eerdmans, 1967; *Shriven Selves* by Wesley A. Kort, Philadelphia, Fortress Press, 1972; William Walsh, in *Encounter* (London), January 1973; *An Anatomy of Laughter* by Richard Boston, London, Collins, 1974; "The Case for Comic Seriousness" by Craig Challender, in *Studies in American Humor* (San Marcos, Texas), April 1974; "Peter De Vries: The Vale of Laughter" by Calvin De Vries, in *Theology Today* (Princeton, New Jersey), April 1975; "Tragicomedy and Saving Grace" by John Timmerman, in *Christian Century* (Chicago), 26 November 1975; Max Byrd, in *New Republic* (Washington, D.C.), 23 October 1976; *Peter De Vries* by J.H. Bowden, Boston, Twayne, 1983.

*   *   *

Peter De Vries is, first of all, a comic writer in the *New Yorker* tradition of James Thurber and S.J. Perelman. Like them he is funny, witty, and unfailingly clear. Wordplay, his inexhaustible talent and diversion, puts him next to Perelman among all American humorists, and the predicaments at the core of his plots recall the edginess in some of Thurber's stories and even his drawings ("That's my first wife up there" of a scowling termagant crouched on top of a bookcase, "and this is the *present* Mrs. Harris"). But while Thurber and Perelman spent their lives on their brilliant short pieces, De Vries soon turned such effort into episodes for his novels. In recent years his only contributions to the *New Yorker* are reported to be cartoon captions.

De Vries has published more than 20 novels, but now acknowledges only those that begin with *The Tunnel of Love* in 1954. This roaring farce, perhaps still his most popular work, was, for him, finally something that reflected his years of working by the exacting standards of the magazine that had brought him east from Chicago. In the *New Yorker's* mid-Manhattan offices he told a recent interviewer, he "learned the Charlie Chaplin principle—if what you're doing is funny don't horse around while you're doing it or you'll deprive it of its humor." This discipline has always made his timing precise, even when the narrator of *The Tunnel of Love* asks his hypochondriac doctor to give him a dose of sulfa and molasses. De Vries reels out strings of puns the length of a highwire, stopping just short of horsing around at the end. With Perelman's calculation and deftness he develops a non sequitur or "switcheroo" like the master's: "How choked my files were with letters beginning like that. How choked his own must be with my end of the correspondence. And how choked I was on this chicken." He is the virtuoso equally of epigrams and nonsense: "like the cleaning woman, we must all come to dust." All his work is laced with with literary allusions (most often to Eliot), and *The Tents of Wickedness* is a parody collection laced with narrative. Every De Vries novel is full of these considerable skills; they save his lesser efforts for his most devoted readers and give Chaplinesque point to the anguish of *The Blood of the Lamb*, his novel which shows how a comic writer may come to terms with personal tragedy.

He is decidedly not like the Phunny Phellers whom Mark Twain dismissed, for all their wit and wordplay, because they failed to teach or preach as he did, and were, thus, "mere" humorists. Since *The Mackerel Plaza* in 1958, De Vries has been periodically discovered as a serious writer. He covers the same suburbs and villages as another pair of *New Yorker* writers, John Cheever and John Updike, and often the three have seen the same follies and vices. Cheever and Updike do not lack humor, but they do not hold the essentially agnostic outlook common to De Vries and many other humorists, which De Vries stated in one of his "rejected" novels, *The Handsome Heart*, ". . . there is a scale of human values by which man lives, a hierarchy so to speak, within which there is much uncertainty and great variation in the light of each individual case."

He is a satirist of the upper-middle-class as it has settled in his fictional (or mythical) Avalon, Connecticut. This is a suburb of split-level churches peopled by consumers as much the prey of marriage counselors as of decorators and real estate agents. They have precarious city jobs or worse ones in the suburbs themselves. Chick Swallow, of *Comfort Me with Apples*, succeeds his father-in-law as advice columnist for the local *Picayune-Blade*. The early works flesh out or skewer the sociology outlined in *The Organization Man* and other treatises on the conformity of the 1950's, but even then readers saw these PTA frolics as so much mocking backdrop for the author's comedy of modern marriage. In *The Mackerel Plaza* the comedy is brilliantly joined to a satire on permissive suburban religion.

The Reverend Andrew Mackerel is a young widower as helpless as the young husbands in other De Vries novels. He has obviously been unable to handle, let alone fathom, the high-and public-spirited woman taken from him in a boating accident so suddenly that he has scarcely learned to grieve for her. His housekeeper happens to be his attractive sister-in-law obviously biding her time, which she can easily afford to do considering the naive man she lives with. Andrew is smitten instead with the imposing "bit of fluff" who tempts so many of De Vries's narrators. Mackerel's campaign with her fails guiltily (and as awkwardly as a schoolboy's), and the wily housekeeper, whose name is Hester, leads him to the point where she puts his stumbling apostasy into perspective as the most Calvinistic anti-Calvinism she has ever seen, only after which is Andrew able to note that "her body against me was like a bursting star." At least part of this ending is just deserts for the failed pastor of the People's Liberal Church, who had begun the story by calling city hall to demand removal of a garish "Jesus Saves" billboard.

De Vries rebelled early against the severity of the Dutch Reformed Church into which he had been born as the child of Dutch immigrants who settled in their own minuscule Chicago enclave. At college he became a mildly rakehell English major breaking out of a Puritan environment harsher than Hester's and Dimmesdale's Boston if only because it was surrounded by America's exploding popular culture instead of the earlier dark forests of red devils. *Slouching Towards Kalamazoo* springs from this background and continues De Vries's delightful harrowing of *The Scarlet Letter*. Fifteen-year-old Anthony Thrasher is held back in the eighth grade because he reads Proust and Joyce when he should be studying the prescribed courses. His teacher, Maggie Doubloon, would also fail him except that she is somehow persuaded to become his tutor, and, in a confusing sequence of actions, becomes impregnated by the boy the world has classified as an underachiever. He graduates, scraping by with a C−, and she leaves town wearing a swelling t-shirt that bears a brilliant A+. Back at her home in Kalamazoo she begins to make a fortune with such t-shirts just as Hester Prynne prospered as a seamstress. Young Thrasher predictably has a rougher road until years later he marries the bountiful Bubbles Breedlove, Maggie's step-daughter and step-sister to Anthony's own son, Ahab. He endures, for example, the results of a debate between his father, a fire-eating preacher, and the village atheist in which the antagonists convert each other with Dearest, Anthony's mother, moving along dutifully from one believer to another. Anthony's bride appears to him in breath-taking perspective as "one who might well combine elements of wife and bit of fluff all rolled into one." Another pleasing compromise leads him to proselyte, at his father's side, for The First Church of Christian Atheists, "the new persuasion that no evolutionary hypothesis could unsettle." The novel ends with a characteristic De Vries exchange that is probably not his last word on married love and guilt. "What about the matrimonial bark?" the *zaftig*

Mrs. Thralling asks Anthony. "I think it's worse than its bite," he tells her. "Would you pass me your plate, my dear?"

—David Sanders

DICKENS, Monica (Enid). British. Born in London, 10 May 1915. Educated at St. Paul's Girls' School, London. Married Roy Olin Stratton in 1951 (died, 1985); two adopted daughters. Worked as a maid and cook in private houses; as a factory worker, nurse, and with the Samaritans (founded Samaritans in the USA, 1974). Columnist ("The Way I See It"), *Woman's Own*, London, 1946–65. M.B.E. (Member, Order of the British Empire), 1981. Address: Lavender Cottage, Pudding Lane, Brightwalton, Berkshire RG16 0BY, England.

Publications

Novels

Mariana. London, Joseph, 1940; as *The Moon Was Low*, New York, Harper, 1940.
The Fancy. London, Joseph, 1943; as *Edward's Fancy*, New York, Harper, 1944.
Thursday Afternoons. London, Joseph, 1945.
The Happy Prisoner. London, Joseph, 1946; Philadelphia, Lippincott, 1947.
Joy and Josephine. London, Joseph, 1948; as *Portobello Road*, Toronto, Joseph, 1948.
Flowers on the Grass. London, Joseph, 1949; New York, McGraw Hill, 1950.
No More Meadows. London, Joseph, 1953; as *The Nightingales Are Singing*, Boston, Little Brown, 1953.
The Winds of Heaven. London, Joseph, and New York, Coward McCann, 1955.
The Angel in the Corner. London, Joseph, 1956; New York, Coward McCann, 1957.
Man Overboard. London, Joseph, 1958; New York, Coward McCann, 1959.
The Heart of London. London, Joseph, and New York, Coward McCann, 1961.
Cobbler's Dream. London, Joseph, and New York, Coward McCann, 1963.
Kate and Emma. London, Heinemann, 1964; New York, Coward McCann, 1965.
The Room Upstairs. London, Heinemann, and New York, Doubleday, 1966.
The Landlord's Daughter. London, Heinemann, and New York, Doubleday, 1968.
The Listeners. London, Heinemann, 1970; as *The End of the Line*, New York, Doubleday, 1970.
Last Year When I Was Young. London, Heinemann, 1974.

Uncollected Short Story

"A Modern Christmas Carol," in *Ladies Home Journal* (New York), December 1981.

Other

One Pair of Hands (autobiography). London, Joseph, and New York, Harper, 1939.

One Pair of Feet (autobiography).   London, Joseph, and New York, Harper, 1942.

Yours Sincerely (*Woman's Own* articles), with Beverley Nichols.   London, Newnes, 1949.

My Turn to Make the Tea (autobiography).   London, Joseph, 1951.

My Fair Lady (for children).   New York, Four Winds, 1967.

The Great Fire (for children).   London, Kaye and Ward, 1970; New York, Doubleday, 1973.

The House at World's End (for children).   London, Heinemann, 1970; New York, Doubleday, 1971.

The Great Escape (for children).   London, Kaye and Ward, 1971.

Summer at World's End (for children).   London, Heinemann, 1971; New York, Doubleday, 1972.

Follyfoot (for children).   London, Heinemann, 1971.

World's End in Winter (for children).   London, Heinemann, 1972; New York, Doubleday, 1973.

Dora at Follyfoot (for children).   London, Heinemann, 1972.

Cape Cod.   New York, Viking Press, 1972.

Follyfoot Farm (omnibus; for children).   London, Heinemann, 1973.

Spring Comes to World's End (for children).   London, Heinemann, 1973.

Talking of Horses.   London, Heinemann, 1973; Boston, Little Brown, 1974.

The Horses of Follyfoot (for children).   London, Heinemann, 1975.

Stranger at Follyfoot (for children).   London, Heinemann, 1976.

An Open Book (autobiography).   London, Heinemann, and New York, Mayflower, 1978.

The Messenger series (for children; *The Messenger, Ballad of Favour*).   London, Collins, 2 vols., 1985.

Miracles of Courage: How Families Meet the Challenge of a Child's Critical Illness.   New York, Dodd Mead, 1985.

Editor, with Rosemary Sutcliff, *Is Anyone There?* (on the Samaritans).   London, Penguin, 1978.

*

Monica Dickens comments:

(1972) My novels are mostly based on my own firsthand experience. Before I was married and had children, I used to go and do the jobs or join the communities in which I was interested. Now, not being able to throw up everything for an idea and start a new chapter of life every few years, I work more like a journalist, and research by observing and listening. Perhaps it will be helpful to name the backgrounds which led to each book:

Mariana. The first novel everyone writes sooner or later, about one's own childhood and growing up.

The Fancy. I worked in a factory that repaired Spitfires during the Battle of Britain.

Thursday Afternoons. I was a hospital nurse for most of the war.

The Happy Prisoner. I nursed a patient who was adjusting to amputation.

Joy and Josephine. I used my own background of Notting Hill and the Portobello Road where I was born and brought up.

Flower on the Grass. I did many of the various jobs that the central character tries (holiday camp, companion to sick boys, teaching, etc.).

No More Meadows. I used my own experiences in marrying into the US Navy and joining Washington Service society.

The Winds of Heaven. Observation of changing family patterns in which there is no room for the ageing parent.

Man Overboard. Observation of forcibly retired Service people.

The Heart of London. My own background again, of Notting Hill, plus months of research among the black community, social workers, police, teachers, churches, road construction gangs, midwives.

Cobbler's Dream. My own experiences with horses. Plus extensive work with the RSPCA.

Kate and Emma. Extensive field work with the NSPCC and juvenile courts.

The Room Upstairs. My own family experiences with the problems and terrors of an old lady, and with a nearby house in Massachusetts, USA, bisected by a highway.

The Listeners. My own experiences as a Samaritan.

My aim is to entertain, rather than instruct. I want readers to recognize life in my books, either as they know it, or as they are able to understand it, however alien the situation.

Increasingly, as I grow more prolific, my writing is for me the greater part of life. I live fully, surrounded by people and animals, but find more and more reality and interest in the people and worlds I create.

*   *   *

Monica Dickens's autobiographical books belong to a genre popular in the late 1930's and 1940's: amusing, mildly satiric, loosely organized personal experiences, usually written by a woman, a shrewd observer of the eccentricities of commonplace people, adroit at illuminating character with sudden flashes of insight, never herself top girl in any group, but always more radical and socially-conscious than most of the people she works or lives among. Thus, the heroine of *One Pair of Hands*, after picaresque adventures as a cook-general for a Dickensian series of employers, originally ended by making a speech at a Household Fair, suggesting improvements in the treatment of servants. With rueful irony she reports audience reaction: "'Words, words, words, and when you think of it, what did all that talk amount to?'"

This book gave Dickens the episodic structure for later plots as in *Flowers on the Grass, Man Overboard*, and *Last Year When I Was Young*, whose low-key heroes go from job to job, each with a cluster of satirically sketched personalities. Another favourite, closely related pattern, the concurrent picaresque, so to speak, is an intercutting from group to group of persons tenuously related by a common character as in *The Heart of London* and *The Listeners*. The incidents of these plots are often conventionally melodramatic, although they seem less stereotypic in her later novels where violence arises from urban slums and is the self-damage of the life-damaged.

Dickens, while prodigal in characterisation, has always been economical in subject matter. Her own experience while training as a nurse has, for example, produced both the autobiographical *One Pair of Feet* and the novel *Thursday Afternoons*, in which Dr. Sheppard, trapped by his own bedside manner, longs for active naval duty in the imminent Second World War. In *Flowers on the Grass* Daniel's rebellious adventures include a hospital episode in which Nurse Saunders recalls Nurse Dickens. Elizabeth (*The Happy Prisoner*) is a private nurse who married her patient; May (*The Heart of London*) is a district midwife who saves her best friend's premature illegitimate baby; the central character of *Last Year When I Was Young* is a male nurse. Even when it serves no useful plot function, a hospital may be a part of a character's background as it is in Christine Cope's (*No More Meadows*).

Likewise Dickens's wartime factory work provided material for *The Fancy* and for a long episode in *Joy and Josephine*, whose heroine prefers making airplanes to dilettante canteen service. Other books draw on Dickens's experiences as a reporter and as a Samaritan. Readers interested in seeing the facts of her fictions will find a great deal of material in Dickens's recent unfictionalized autobiography, *An Open Book*.

Certain characters also reappear: e.g., the slightly feeble-minded spinster, the married man with an affair, and especially the one-legged or lame man, who may be as engaging as Oliver (*Happy Prisoner*) or as selfish as David (*The Fancy*). In another group of novels these cripples become girls in wheelchairs or crippled boys. Naval officers recur, sometimes as minor as Uncle Tim (*Mariana*), married to "a walking Gieve's," or as crucial as Commander Vinson Gaegler, who inflicts American naval protocol on his English bride (*No More Meadows*). In *Man Overboard*, Commander Ben Francis, R.N., dismissed as redundant in postwar cutbacks, tries to find a civilian career. From this novel on, Dickens has generally turned more explicitly to social or socio-psychological themes: racial tension, schools, urban redevelopment, perversion, alcoholism (*Heart of London*); child abuse (*Kate and Emma*); old age (*The Winds of Heaven* and *The Room Upstairs*); the feeble-minded, the suicidal, the alone (*The Listeners*). Here she is interested in strange emotional liaisons, often touching but also grotesque. Emma Bullock, daughter of a Children's Court Magistrate, becomes the "blood comrade" of Kate, a mistreated adolescent who in turn beats and chains her own scapegoat child. The vulgarly sinister Dorothy Grue (*Room Upstairs*) adores Roger, a budgerigar. Charlotte (*The Landlord's Daughter*) welcomes Peter as a lover although he has killed and dismembered a former love, whose incriminating hank of hair Charlotte hides.

These books are grim, unlike the earlier, overflowing novels for which Dickens drew most heavily on family personalities and experiences. Minor personages of the later books are still likely to be humour characters, but their ruling passions lack ebullience—perhaps because the eccentricities of urban poverty, however pitiable, are rarely amiable ones. Still, all her novels show her eye for visual detail, her understanding of absurdities and values, petty satisfactions and hugged-tight rancors, and her assumption that not even the most minor and peripheral characters need lack identity and idiosyncrasy.

—Jane W. Stedman

DIDION, Joan. American. Born in Sacramento, California, 5 December 1934. Educated at California Junior High School and McClatchy Senior High School, both Sacramento; University of California, Berkeley, 1952–56, B.A. in English 1956. Married the writer John Gregory Dunne in 1964; one adopted daughter. Associate feature editor, *Vogue*, New York, 1956–63; moved to Los Angeles, 1964; columnist ("Points West"), with John Gregory Dunne, *Saturday Evening Post*, Philadelphia, 1967–69, and "The Coast," *Esquire*, New York, 1976–77; contributing editor, *National Review*, New York. Visiting Regents' Lecturer, University of California, Berkeley, 1975. Recipient: *Vogue* Paris Prize, 1956; Bread Loaf Writers Conference fellowship, 1963; American Academy Morton Dauwen Zabel Award, 1979. Lives in Brentwood Park, Los Angeles. Agent: Wallace and Sheil Agency, 177 East 70th Street, New York, New York 10021, U.S.A.

PUBLICATIONS

Novels

Run River.   New York, Obolensky, 1963; London, Cape, 1964.
Play It As It Lays.   New York, Farrar Straus, 1970; London, Weidenfeld and Nicolson, 1971.
A Book of Common Prayer.   New York, Simon and Schuster, and London, Weidenfeld and Nicolson, 1977.
Democracy.   New York, Simon and Schuster, and London, Chatto and Windus, 1984.

Uncollected Short Stories

"The Welfare Island Ferry," in *Harper's Bazaar* (New York), June 1965.
"When Did the Music Come This Way? Children Dear, Was It Yesterday?," in *Denver Quarterly*, Winter 1967.
"California Blue," in *Harper's* (New York), October 1976.

Plays

Screenplays: *Panic in Needle Park*, with John Gregory Dunne, 1971; *Play It As It Lays*, with John Gregory Dunne, 1972; *A Star Is Born*, with John Gregory Dunne and Frank Pierson, 1976; *True Confessions*, with John Gregory Dunne, 1981.

Other

Slouching Towards Bethlehem (essays).   New York, Farrar Straus, 1968; London, Deutsch, 1969.
Telling Stories.   Berkeley, California, Bancroft Library, 1978.
The White Album.   New York, Simon and Schuster, and London, Weidenfeld and Nicolson, 1979.
Salvador.   New York, Simon and Schuster, and London, Chatto and Windus, 1983.
Essays and Interviews, edited by Ellen G. Friedman.   Princeton, New Jersey, Ontario Review Press, 1984.

*

Critical Study: *Joan Didion* by Katherine Usher Henderson, New York, Ungar, 1981.

*   *   *

Though very much a California writer, Joan Didion is not provincial. She uses her immediate milieu to envision, simultaneously, the last stand of America's frontier values pushed insupportably to their limits and the manifestations of craziness and malaise which have initiated their finale. And while her novels invite a feminist critique, her understanding of sexual politics is beyond ideology. Each of her major characters struggles with a demonic nihilism which is corroding the individual, the family, and the social organism. Affluent and glib, her people endure a relatively privileged despair which may initially suggest a narrow purview. But a considerable ability to render social and physical environment broadly is saving.

In addition to dialogue which rivals Albee's, Didion's finest gifts are her talents for keeping clean of self-indulgence and for realizing a moral dimension in lives veering *inevitably* out of control. Certain recurring features of her work constitute leitmotifs germane to their interpretation. These include newspaper headlines, phrases from popular ballads, cinematic jargon, snakes, and the genteel Christian educations of her females. All pertain to the disintegration of an orderly past into a chaotic present, perhaps Didion's most irreducible theme.

Run River follows the eroding marriage of Everett and Lily (Knight) McClellan through 20 years. Concomitantly, it chronicles the collapse of a way of life and the betrayal of the land which had given an epoch its apparent order. Ryder Channing enters the McClellans' lives when he courts Everett's sister. Though Martha never misconceives his selfishness and venality, she kills herself when Channing quits her. Lily's many unfeeling liaisons express her isolation from her husband and fatally draw her into Channing's increasingly nihilistic orbit. In his futile attachment to their Northern California ranch, Everett lives at a tangent to Lily's very genuine crises. When Everett kills Channing, it is not simply because Channing and his sleazy economic machinations are the wave of California's future, the perverse energy which turns redwoods to taco stands. Everett's suicide ends an era. But Lily's justifiable conclusion that Channing is guiltless, because he is a "papier-mâché Mephistopholes," implies Didion's conviction that, however tawdry this interloper, he has only played upon a native tendency to ruin. Lily's survival implies her relatively greater, if tainted, adaptability and strength.

Play It As It Lays presents a culture beyond this metamorphosis. Consequently, it is set in Los Angeles where those tacky schemes of Ryder Channing are a *fait accompli* defining a whole state of being. Maria Wyeth's past is utterly disintegrated, her childhood home in Nevada having been detonated to oblivion by nuclear testing. Moribund, her marriage thins to extinction. With her brain-damaged daughter institutionalized and herself facing an abortion, Maria aimlessly drives the freeways to evade a ubiquitous dread.

Though Didion never politicizes abortion, she is morally obsessed with it. Lily and Maria endure the experience, but the treatment is fuller and more alarming here. A last straw, it pushes Maria closer to her counterpart and nemesis, B Z, another instance of modern demonic. Associated throughout with the serpent, this Hollywood Beelzebub tries with conscious nihilism to exploit Maria's drinking and sexual looseness. Maria's father, taking life as a crap game, had offered his case as a gambler and a cynic: "it goes as it lays, don't do it the hard way"; "overturning a rock [is] apt to reveal a rattlesnake." For Maria, this worldview is an affliction of passivity and anxiety, until she finally manages the small victory of rejecting B Z's invitation to join him in his successful suicide.

With *A Book of Common Prayer*, Didion suggests that the country is in the throes of metastasized California. So she invents an archetypal banana republic devoid of history. Boca Grande ("big mouth") yaps chamber of commerce propaganda and ingests North American residue. Charlotte Douglas, a San Francisco Pollyanna, weathers two difficult marriages: to a brilliant, callous and cynical opportunist, and to a well-heeled radical lawyer. What she doesn't quite weather is the loss (à la Patty Hearst) of her daughter, Marin, "to history." Marin's situation is really very simple. She suffers from severe cases of banality and political jargon. But her new way of life tests to the limit Charlotte's too selective memory of the girl in Easter dresses. With the FBI agents who litter her house and the futility of her marriages at her back, she makes it to Boca Grande and a marginal life of good works for the suffering masses. She continues to put the best light on dark matters: stateside things like her brother's miserable existence on the old homestead in Hollister; Grande things like the Army's confiscation, for profit, of the people's cholera serum. She becomes oddly Sisyphean but holds out for the idea that we all remember what we need. Charlotte dies in the crossfire between Army and revolutionary forces, the guerilleros having decided that for once their insurrection is not going to be a State-sponsored melodrama. We come to like her and to wonder about the future of such folks as the Simbianese Liberation Army.

Democracy concerns the long and amorous liaison between Inez Victor, a politician's wife, and Jack Lovett. The latter embodies personal and social values lacking in and inconceivable to the husband, a congressman aspiring to the presidency. Southern California recollected and contemporary Southeast Asia, particularly Kuala Lumpur, provide settings in which the fabulous quality of Boco Grande yields to realism. The novel clearly depicts American and international political life in the very fast lane, and its ruinous effect on familial relationships. But Inez Victor's moral tenacity and practical resolve to use the past ethically distinguish her from Didion's earlier protagonists. Technically the novel is fresh, if not unique, for cinematic effects which break linear narrative; and for including a narrator named Joan Didion, who remarks the discrete functions of journalism and fiction, both provinces of great success for the *real* author.

—David M. Heaton

DIXON, Stephen. American. Born in New York City, 6 June 1936. Educated at City College, New York, 1953–58, B.A. 1958. Married Anne Frydman in 1982; two daughters. Worked in various jobs, including bartender, waiter, junior high school teacher, technical writer, journalist, news editor, store clerk, and tour leader, 1953–79; lecturer, New York University School of Continuing Education, 1979–80. Assistant Professor, 1980–83, and since 1984, Associate Professor of English, Johns Hopkins University, Baltimore. Recipient: Stanford University Stegner Fellowship, 1964; National Endowment for the Arts grant, 1975; American Academy award, 1983; Train Prize (*Paris Review*), 1985; Guggenheim fellowship, 1985. Address: Writing Seminars, Gilman 135, Johns Hopkins University, Baltimore, Maryland 21218, U.S.A.

PUBLICATIONS

Novels

Work. Ann Arbor, Michigan, Street Fiction Press, 1977.
Too Late. New York, Harper, 1978.
Fall and Rise. Berkeley, California, North Point Press, 1985.

Short Stories

No Relief. Ann Arbor, Michigan, Street Fiction Press, 1976.
Quite Contrary: The Mary and Newt Story. New York, Harper, 1979.
14 Stories. Baltimore, Johns Hopkins University Press, 1980.
Movies. Berkeley, California, North Point Press, 1983.
Time to Go. Baltimore, Johns Hopkins University Press, 1984.

Uncollected Short Stories

"The Chess House," in *Paris Review*, Winter–Spring 1963.

"Pale Cheeks of a Butcher's Boy," in *Per Se* (Stanford, California), vol. 1, 1966.

"The Neighbors," in *Atlantic* (Boston), April 1966.

"The Bussed," in *Bennington Review* (Bennington, Vermont), vol. 3, no. 4, 1969.

"Berry Smashing Day at the C & L," in *Playboy* (Chicago), May 1969.

"What Is All This?" in *Playboy* (Chicago), November 1969.

"Love and Will," in *American Review 17*, edited by Theodore Solotaroff.   New York, Bantam, 1973.

"The Rehearsal," in *Transatlantic Review* (London), no. 48, 1974.

"A Parting," in *Confrontation* (New York), no. 10, 1974.

"An Outing," in *Genesis* (New York), May 1974.

"The New Era," "Grace Calls," "Making a Break," and "Ray," in *Making a Break*, edited by Robert and Rochelle Bonazzi.   Austin, Texas, Latitudes Press, 1975.

"Ez Is His Son, Till His Ex-Wife," in *Center* (Albuquerque), 1975.

"Game," in *Lowlands Review* (New Orleans), no. 5, 1975.

"End of a Friend," in *Big Moon* (Bellingham, Washington), vol. 1, no. 2, 1975.

"Closed Sylvia" and "Open Tisch," in *Center* (Albuquerque), no. 8, 1975.

"Buddy," in *Seneca Review* (Geneva, New York), vol. 6, no. 1, 1975.

"The Doctor," in *Confrontation* (New York), Fall–Winter 1975.

"The Young Man Who Read Brilliant Books," in *Just My Luck*.   Chicago, Playboy Press, 1976.

"The Chocolate Sampler," in *Sun and Moon* (College Park, Maryland), 1976.

"The Tellers," in *Agni Review* (Cambridge, Massachusetts), 1976.

"Evening," in *Mundus Artium* (Richardson, Texas), 1976.

"Speak," in *Bananas* (London), 1976.

"Heat," in *Carolina Quarterly* (Chapel Hill, North Carolina), vol. 28, no. 1, 1976.

"Shoelaces," in *Big Moon* (Bellingham, Washington), vol. 2, no. 1, 1976.

"Dog Days," in *South Carolina Review* (Clemson), vol. 8, no. 2, 1976.

"The Killer," in *Box 749* (New York), vol. 2, no. 1, 1976.

"Jackie," in *The Periodical Lunch* (Ann Arbor, Michigan), no. 7, 1976.

"The Leader," in *Iowa Review* (Iowa City), vol. 7, no. 4, 1976.

"Tails," in *Boundary 2* (Binghamton, New York), vol. 5, no. 1, 1976.

"Mourning Came," in *DeKalb Literary Arts Journal* (Clarkson, Georgia), vol. 10, no. 1, 1976.

"Knives," in *Pequod* (San Francisco), Summer 1976.

"Dawn," in *Westbere Review* (Tulsa, Oklahoma), 1977.

"Sylvia," in *Seven Stars* (San Jose, California), 1977.

"Meet the Natives," in *Sun and Moon* (College Park, Maryland), 1977.

"Speak," in *Seems* (Sheboygan, Wisconsin), no. 8, 1977.

"Sex," in *Chouteau Review* (Kansas City), 1978.

"Getting Lost," in *Quarry West* (Santa Cruz, California), no. 9, 1978.

"Try Again," in *Chouteau Review* (Kansas City), vol. 3, no. 1, 1978.

"A Home Away from Home," in *Fantasy and Science Fiction* (New York), February 1978.

"Paul's Dream," in *Confrontation* (New York), Spring–Summer 1978.

"The Village," in *Harper's* (New York), May 1978.

"She," in *Ohio Journal* (Columbus), Summer 1978.

"Getting a Contac," in *Grub Street* (New York), 1978(?).

"Next to Nothing," in *Departures* (Boulder, Colorado), 1979.

"Arrangements," in *Quarterly West* (Salt Lake City), no. 8, 1979.

"Question," in *Iowa Review* (Iowa City), vol. 9, no. 3, 1979.

"Ends," in *Appearances* (New York), no. 3, 1979.

"The Student," in *Mundus Artium* (Richardson, Texas), vol. 7, no. 1, 1979.

"A Sloppy Story," in *StoryQuarterly* (Northbrook, Illinois), vol. 10, 1979.

"A Lack of Space," in *Ohio Journal* (Columbus), Spring 1979.

"Overtime," in *North American Review* (Cedar Falls, Iowa), Winter 1979.

"Guests," in *Westbere Review* (Tulsa, Oklahoma), vol. 2, no. 2, 1980.

"Interest," in *Appearances* (New York), no. 4, 1980.

"The Stopover" and "Night," in *Brooklyn Sun*, vol. 1, no. 2, 1980.

"In Time," in *Ambit* (London), no. 81, 1980.

"The Good Woman," in *Chouteau Review* (Kansas City), vol. 4, no. 2, 1980.

"Said," in *Boundary 2* (Binghamton, New York), vol. 8, no. 3, 1980.

"The Last Resort," in *Chicago Review*, Autumn 1980.

"For a Quiet English Sunday," in *Montana Review* (Missoula), Winter 1980.

"Me," in *Neutral Repository* (Baltimore), no. 2, 1981.

"Storm," in *Washington Review* (Washington, D.C.), vol. 6, no. 5, 1981.

"My Dear," in *Literary Review* (Madison, New Jersey), vol. 25, no. 1, 1981.

"Capital Labor," in *Pendragon* (Denver), vol. 1, no. 1, 1981.

"The Argument," in *Little Magazine* (New York), vol. 13, nos. 1–2, 1981.

"Wrong Words," in *Appearances* (New York), nos. 5–6, 1981.

"The True Story," in *Confrontation* (New York), Summer 1981.

"Gifts," in *Paris Review*, Summer 1981.

"Yo-Yo," in *Pale Fire Review* (Providence, Rhode Island), vol. 2, no. 1, 1982.

"Never Ends," in *Ambit* (London), no. 88, 1982.

"The Dat," in *Appearances* (New York), no. 7, 1982.

"Knock Knock," in *Continental Drift* (Boulder, Colorado), vol. 1, no. 1, 1982.

"The Clean-Up Man," in *Iowa Review* (Iowa City), vol. 13, no. 2, 1982.

"Biff," in *Memphis State Review* (Memphis, Tennessee), vol. 3, no. 1, 1982.

"The Hairpiece," in *Michigan Quarterly Review* (Ann Arbor), Spring 1982.

"To Tom," in *Confrontation* (New York), Summer 1982.

"Magna Out of Earshot," in *Corona* (Bozeman, Montana), no. 3, 1983.

"Can't Win," in *New England Review* (Hanover, New Hampshire), vol. 5, no. 3, 1983.

"Magna . . . Reading," in *Chouteau Review* (Kansas City), vol. 6, no. 1, 1983.

"The Baby," "The Batterer," and "Stories," in *Ohio Journal* (Columbus), vol. 8, no. 1, 1983.

"PP 201–204," in *Appearances* (New York), no. 9, 1983.

"All Gone," in *Kansas Quarterly* (Manhattan), vol. 15, no. 2, 1983.

"Moving On," in *Ambit* (London), no. 94, 1983.

"Ten Years," in *Literary Review* (Madison, New Jersey), vol. 27, no. 1, 1983.

"The Burglars," in *Croton Review* (Croton-on-Hudson, New York), no. 6, 1983.

"The Second Part," in *StoryQuarterly* (Northbrook, Illinois), nos. 15–16, 1983.

"Only the Cat Escapes," in *South Carolina Review* (Clemson), vol. 16, no. 1, 1983.

"Training to Magna," in *Telescope* (Baltimore), vol. 13, no. 2, 1984.

"Fired," in *Appearances* (New York), no. 10, 1984.

"The Cove," in *2Plus2* (Lausanne, Switzerland), no. 2, 1984.

"Reinsertion," in *Washington Review* (Washington, D.C.), vol. 10, no. 2, 1984.

"The Painter" and "Down the Road," in *Tri-Quarterly* (Evanston, Illinois), no. 61, 1984.

"The Book Review," in *Threepenny Review* (Berkeley, California), no. 20, 1984.

"The Onlooker," in *South Carolina Review* (Clemson), vol. 17, no. 1, 1984.

"Garbage," in *Confrontation* (New York), nos. 27–28, 1984.

"The Wild Bird Reserve," in *Fiction Network* (San Francisco), Fall 1984.

"Frog in Prague," in *Secret Destinations*. New York, Persea, 1985.

"Friends," in *Fiction International* (San Diego), vol. 15, no. 2, 1985.

"The Writer" and "Starting Again," in *Other Voices* (Highland Park, Illinois), vol. 1, no. 1, 1985.

"The Last," "Scratch Scratch," and "Finished," in *Poet and Critic* (Ames, Iowa), vol. 16, no. 2, 1985.

"The Rescuer," in *Mississippi Review* (Hattiesburg), vol. 13, no. 3, 1985.

"The Visit," in *Confrontation* (New York), nos. 29–30, 1985.

"Paul" and "Magna as a Child," in *South Carolina Review* (Clemson), vol. 17, no. 2, 1985.

"The Postcard," in *2Plus2* (Lausanne, Switzerland), no. 4, 1985.

"A Friend's Death," in *Telescope* (Baltimore), Fall 1985.

"My Life Up till Now," in *Literary Review* (Madison, New Jersey), Winter 1985–86.

"The Letter," in *North American Review* (Cedar Falls, Iowa), vol. 270, no. 4, 1986.

"Cooked Goose," in *Florida Review* (Orlando), vol. 13, no. 2, 1986.

*

Critical Studies: "Stephen Dixon: Experimental Realism," in *North American Review* (Cedar Falls, Iowa), March 1981, and *The Self-Apparent Word*, Carbondale, Southern Illinois University Press, 1984, both by Jerome Klinkowitz; "Stephen Dixon Issue" of *Ohio Journal* (Columbus), Fall–Winter 1983–84 (includes bibliography); *The Dramaturgy of Style* by Michael Stephens, Carbondale, Southern Illinois University Press, 1985.

Stephen Dixon comments:

I've just about nothing to say about my work. I only write fiction. I don't write book reviews or any nonfiction. In fact the only book review I've written is a story called "The Book Review," about a character writing one. The only non-fiction work I've written since 1963, when I stopped writing news, and 1968, when I stopped being a technical writer, is a piece called "Why I Don't Write Nonfiction," which proves its point and appeared in the *Ohio Journal* issue devoted to my work. I write novels and short stories only and I like writing both but for different reasons. Novels because they continue, stories because they end. All my novels but the last one, *Fall and Rise*, started off as short stories and just grew. I would rather the reader interpret what I write than I interpret it for the reader. I don't want to give my life away in a statement. Not only is my life not very interesting but sometime in the future I might use, in my own way, part of my life for my fiction and then a reader might say "That comes from his uninteresting life." Better the reader know next to nothing about my life and how I write, where I get my ideas, and so on.

*   *   *

Stephen Dixon is a master of self-generating fiction. While eschewing the flamboyantly anti-realistic experiments of authors such as Ronald Sukenick and Robert Coover, Dixon nevertheless refuses to propel his narratives on the energy of represented action. Instead, he contrives circumstances so that everything that happens within his novels grows from the initial elements of his fiction. Developing from itself, his narrative ultimately has no pertinent reference beyond itself; yet that growth is so organic that it offers all the delight expectable from a more realistically referential piece of storytelling.

Dixon's method can be traced to his way of writing sentences. Often his action will take place grammatically, as subjects have to battle their way past intransigent verbs in order to meet their objects, and as modifying phrases pop up to thwart syntactic progress. There are always modifications to everything, Dixon has learned, and his genius has been to apply this insight to the making of narratives.

His first novel, *Work*, finds this scheme in the workplace, as an image for both how hard it is to find employment and what a struggle it is to keep it. Hunting down a job takes his narrator fully one-third of the novel, and that turns out to be the easy part. Once he has signed on as a bartender in a New York City chain of restaurants, he has to cope with a prime ingredient of Dixon's fictionally generative world: in this case a self-contained universe of rules and relationships, which include how to mix drinks, charge for special orders, move customer traffic, scan the papers for conversation items, spot company spies, handle rush hour jams, deal with the restaurant chain's union, thwart robberies, soothe tempers, counsel neurotics, and keep the whole mad dance of waiters, dishwashers, assistant managers, cashiers, and customers in step. And this is just three or four pages into the story. *Work* provides the ideal self-generating system for a Stephen Dixon novel.

Yet such a system also exists within the intimate relationship of a man and woman. *Too Late* borrows two favorite topics from Dixon's short stories—breaking off relationships and suffering through the endless complications of love—and rushes them through a breathless experience in the urban jungle, during which four days pass in an alternation of quick excitement and maniacal torture. The narrator's girl friend has left him in a movie, the violence of which has sickened her. But she never arrives home, and tracing her disappearance becomes a full-time job. Not for the police, who want to brush it off as a jilting. Instead, the narrator's capabilities for worry (another self-generating machine for fiction) run through all the lurid possibilities, from abduction and rape to murder. The very worst fears are just what happen, as the ghouls who feed on sensational news rush into the narrator's life, and he himself experiences a Jekyll-and-Hyde transformation which costs him job, friends, and peace of mind. *Too Late* succeeds as a tangled web of disruptions and distractions, the very stuff of Dixon's fiction which is shown to be a built-in potential of city life.

Quite Contrary: The Mary and Newt Story assembles 11 related stories to form something less than a novel but much more than a story collection. Their unity, although established by subject and circumstance of action, comes from their address to the main concerns of Dixon's work: the fragile stability of human relationships, and the danger reality has of running off into infinite digressions and qualifications. *Quite Contrary* treats the three-year off-and-on affair of a couple familiar to Dixon's fiction, whose involvement breeds complications upon themselves. Even their first meeting leads to a debate as to how they will leave to walk home. As their relationship develops, each finds fault: he is too demanding, she is too noncommittal. Even breaking up becomes an endless complication, for if Newt tells a friend that he and Mary are "this time really through," a friend reverses his syntax to show that "Nah, you two are never really through. You're a pair: Tom and Jerry, Biff and Bang. You just tell yourselves you're through to make your sex better and your lives more mythic and poetic and to repeatedly renew those first two beatific weeks you went through." Here is Dixon's method established in the form of his sentences: the declaration that the pair (one *and* another) are sundering their union leads directly to a restatement of that proposition in negative form, rebonding the relationship through a series of other conjunctions: mythic pairs, conjoined reasons, and most of all a grammatical structure which by virtue of more *ands* can string itself out indefinitely, just like their relationship which is commemorated in the final phrase.

Fall and Rise, Dixon's most ambitious novel, extends itself to its fullest fictional scope while requiring the least external circumstance. The affair which prompts it is the narrator's first sentence, "I meet her at a party." Its present tense is deliberate, for the narrator's voice moves through a constant set of possibilities to fill 245 closely-set pages with the action which devolves from just four or five hours of experience. Because so much of the narrator's action is made up of diffidence and fantasy, it has the character of fiction. In a Jamesian manner Dixon examines every nuance, even of situations yet to transpire, and as a result the reader is caught up in the narrator's own imaginative experience. For one chapter the narrative action is transferred to the object of these imaginative desires, and complications are amplified by having her point of view. The achievement of Dixon's work is that the smallest circumstance can expand to fill the space available, a reminder of fiction's infinite plenitude.

Stephen Dixon's reputation is built on his short stories, over 150 of which have been published and many of which fill his four collections. Here may be seen his method in highest profile, which establishes his talent for generative form. In "Said" he runs through the rise and fall of a relationship simply by dropping all content and running through the "he said/she said" rhythm of a fight. "Time to Go" uses fantasy to recapture the memory of a long-dead father, as an image of the old man accompanies his son and the young man's fiancée as they select wedding rings, the father forever hectoring about price and size. In all cases they are self-generating, perfectly made examples of fiction's ability to delight simply by its own working.

—Jerome Klinkowitz

DOCTOROW, E(dgar) L(awrence). American. Born in New York City, 6 January 1931. Educated at the Bronx High School of Science; Kenyon College, Gambier, Ohio, A.B.

(honors) in philosophy 1952; Columbia University, New York, 1952–53. Served in the United States Army, 1953–55. Married Helen Setzer in 1954; two daughters and one son. Editor, New American Library, New York, 1960–64; editor-in-chief, 1964–69, and publisher, 1969, Dial Press, New York; member of the faculty, Sarah Lawrence College, Bronxville, New York, 1971–78. Since 1982, Adjunct Professor of English, New York University. Writer-in-Residence, University of California, Irvine, 1969–70; Creative Writing Fellow, Yale School of Drama, New Haven, Connecticut, 1974–75; Visiting Professor, University of Utah, Salt Lake City, 1975; Visiting Senior Fellow, Princeton University, New Jersey, 1980–81. Director, Authors Guild of America, and American PEN. Recipient: Guggenheim fellowship, 1972; Creative Artists Public Service grant, 1973; National Book Critics Circle award, 1976; American Academy award, 1976. L.H.D.: Kenyon College, 1976; Litt.D.: Hobart and William Smith Colleges, Geneva, New York, 1979. Member, American Academy, 1984. Lives in New Rochelle, New York. Agent: International Creative Management, 40 West 57th Street, New York, New York 10019. Address: c/o Random House Inc., 201 East 50th Street, New York, New York 10022, U.S.A.

PUBLICATIONS

Novels

Welcome to Hard Times. New York, Simon and Schuster, 1960; as *Bad Man from Bodie*, London, Deutsch, 1961.
Big as Life. New York, Simon and Schuster, 1966.
The Book of Daniel. New York, Random House, 1971; London, Macmillan, 1972.
Ragtime. New York, Random House, and London, Macmillan, 1975.
Loon Lake. New York, Random House, and London, Macmillan, 1980.
World's Fair. New York, Random House, 1985; London, Joseph, 1986.

Short Stories

Lives of the Poets: Six Stories and a Novella. New York, Random House, 1984; London, Joseph, 1985.

Uncollected Short Story

"The Songs of Billy Bathgate," in *New American Review 2*, edited by Theodore Solotaroff. New York, New American Library, 1968.

Plays

Drinks Before Dinner (produced New York, 1978). New York, Random House, 1979; London, Macmillan, 1980.

Screenplay: *Daniel*, 1983.

Other

American Anthem, photographs by Jean-Claude Suarès. New York, Stewart Tabori and Chang, 1982.

*

Critical Studies: *E.L. Doctorow: Essays and Conversations* edited by Richard Trenner, Princeton, New Jersey, Ontario

Review Press, 1983; *E.L. Doctorow* (includes bibliography) by Paul Levine, London, Methuen, 1985.

* * *

E.L. Doctorow cannot be readily assimilated to any single school of contemporary fiction; rather, his works synthesize various important strains in post-modernist writing. Doctorow's formal inventiveness, wit, and covertly apocalyptic philosophy link him with such practitioners of metafiction as Pynchon, Barthelme, and Barth; his fascination with "facts"—invented or real—links him with new journalists and nonfiction novelists. But Doctorow decries the privatism of much contemporary fiction, which, he says, is lacking in "social reverberation." He is a serious historical novelist who weds experimental techniques with strong political convictions in an exploration of the historical roots of contemporary America.

Welcome to Hard Times, Doctorow's first novel, adopts the format of the Western to examine the illusory foundations of the American myth of progress. The town of Hard Times, devastated in one day by the rampaging Bad Man from Bodie, rebuilds itself and looks forward to a thriving future—only to be destroyed once again by its implacable antagonist. While in one sense the Bad Man exemplifies an archetypal evil that triumphs over weak humanity, in another sense the parable's judgments are specifically historical. Insofar as the town—read, the nation—is animated primarily by mutual exploitation, competition, and dreams of "hitting pay dirt," it is disarmed in its struggle with time and nature. Doctorow's implied critique of American false consciousness is reinforced by the first-person narration of Blue, the well-intentioned but shallow mayor, who chronicles the town's fate in his bookkeeping ledgers. Profit and loss, it would seem, provide no framework for grasping the realities of historical process. In *Big as Life*, a science-fiction satire, Doctorow restates this apocalyptic theme: New York City is shown in the grip of Brobdignagian monsters that threaten it with extinction, and the question of nuclear holocaust hovers in the not too distant background.

The Book of Daniel explores the recent past in greater depth and specificity and with greater formal complexity: it is Doctorow's first major work. Revolving around the fates of a family named the Isaacsons—who clearly resemble the Rosenbergs—the novel examines the lies, myths, and historical realities that shaped American consciousness from the McCarthy period to the 1960's. Structurally and thematically, the novel probes the relationship between past and present, as the Old Left is compared with the New, the parents with the children. Daniel Lewin/Isaacson's search for the truth about his parents is at once personal and general; his dissertation ("book") is an anatomy of contemporary culture and an exorcism of his own tortured past. The novel's form aptly bears out this dialectical theme: the blend of first- and third-person narration and the shifts in chronology underline the interplay of past and present, public and private, while the finale—which draws together Susan Isaacson's death in 1968, the parents' electrocution a decade and a half before, and Daniel's confrontation with his parents' betrayer in the mindless wilderness of Disneyland—effectively conveys the human cost of American historical myopia.

Ragtime is generally acknowledged to be Doctorow's tour de force. While Doctorow recreates the atmosphere of the Ragtime era with wit, accuracy, and a winsome nostalgia, he also examines its legacy for the present. Like the invented characters in much 19th-century historical fiction, Doctorow's invented characters represent social types who signal the dominant historical movements of the age—and thus undercut senti-

mental and complacent myths about American democracy and justice. The anonymous immigrant family reveals the harsh realities of working-class oppression. The anonymous middle-class WASP family exemplifies the impact of historical change upon the "mainstream" of American life—one direction represented by Mother's growing sexual liberation, another by Father's development of his fireworks factory into a munitions plant. Coalhouse Walker, a black ragtime pianist who is the novel's central character, confronts the racist establishment and is executed for his pride: his tale not only exposes some roots of contemporary racism but also (through its ingenious parallel with Kleist's story "Michael Kohlhaas") demonstrates the clashes that inevitably erupt when power relations are challenged by rising social forces. The public historical figures who appear in the novel—Emma Goldman, Evelyn Nesbit, Harry K. Thaw, Freud, Jung, Morgan, and Ford, to name a few—underline Doctorow's satire and introduce a note of hilarity. By placing real people in patently invented situations, indeed, Doctorow intentionally blurs the line between fact and fiction and thus leads us to question not only the content of the nation's historical myths but also the means by which these myths are constituted. In response to a fetishistic society that, Doctorow says, "deifies facts," he wittily proclaims the superiority of the imagination in arriving at a comprehensive vision of historical truth. Asked whether Morgan and Ford ever met, Doctorow has replied, "They have now."

While Doctorow's audacious confrontation with the substance and method of history is impressive, this last remark suggests the basis upon which his work is open to criticism: if historical truth is chimerical, then change is merely epiphenomenal, and progress is only a bourgeois myth that must be lampooned. Does Doctorow's breezy cynicism thus undercut the force of his social and historical critique? *Welcome to Hard Times* and *The Book of Daniel* can be seen as expressions of a cyclical and absurdist view of history, while *Ragtime* can be accused of reducing history to pastiche—as Doctorow puts it, "a tune on a player piano." Certainly Doctorow's intense awareness of historical injustice and obfuscation may yet take him to the threshold of absurdism, as is indicated in his recent play *Drinks Before Dinner*, where he examines the intense alienation and hollow liberalism of a group of middle-class intellectuals.

In *Loon Lake* Doctorow steps back somewhat from the threshold of the absurd and re-enters the realm of concrete historicity; but it is questionable whether this return is accompanied by a revived grasp of essential social realities. Returning to the themes of class struggle and economic and political injustice that animated *The Book of Daniel* and *Ragtime*, Doctorow proposes a biting portrait of the United States during the Depression. His ruthless and manipulative hero, Joseph Korzeniowski (shades of Joseph Conrad?), exemplifies the human cost that is involved in the capitalist scramble from rags to riches; his hero's counterpart, the failed poet Warren Penfield, poses an unflattering image of the romantic alternative. The novel's hybrid locale—part grim mining towns, part the rich man's Adirondack paradise of Loon Lake—underlines the breadth of Doctorow's social critique. Indeed, in one sense *Loon Lake* undertakes a more comprehensive exploration of the nation's past than any of the earlier novels, insofar as Doctorow refrains from the easier strategies of parodying national myth, evoking historical echoes, or playing fast and loose with facts, and instead fleshes out a past era by creating a microcosmic fictive world. *Loon Lake* also expands upon the technical achievement of Doctorow's earlier work, combining the rapid stylistic pace of *Ragtime* with the complex alternation of chronology and point of view of *The Book of Daniel*. Where *Loon*

Lake does not represent a movement ahead for Doctorow is in its essential failure of moral energy. While the novel is an exploration of national ethics that relies upon characterization to achieve its ends, Joe Korzeniowski and Warren Penfield constitute a composite protagonist with whom it is impossible to feel sympathy or even concern; Daniel Lewin/Isaacson and Coalhouse Walker involve the reader much more fully in Doctorow's implied system of beliefs. This weakness of characterization corresponds to another problem in *Loon Lake*—namely, its lack of a grand theme or even of a grand moment. The novel reveals a multitude of social ills rife with novelistic possibilities; but the suspenseful ending is contrived, and the hero's moral erosion is fundamentally uninteresting. The book's breathtaking style and complicated temporal structure cannot compensate for what we sense as an ethical absence: like the expanding circles produced by a loon's predatory descent into a lake, the novel's concentric circles of chronology and perspective ripple outward from a center that is disturbingly calm.

—Barbara Foley

DONLEAVY, J(ames) P(atrick). Irish. Born in Brooklyn, New York, United States, 23 April 1926; became Irish citizen, 1967. Educated at a preparatory school, New York; Trinity College, Dublin. Served in the United States Navy during World War II. Married 1) Valeria Heron (divorced), one son and one daughter; 2) Mary Wilson Price in 1970, one daughter and one son. Recipient: *Evening Standard* award, for drama, 1961; Brandeis University Creative Arts award, 1961; American Academy award, 1975. Address: Levington Park, Mullingar, County Westmeath, Ireland.

PUBLICATIONS

Novels

The Ginger Man. Paris, Olympia Press, and London, Spearman, 1955; New York, McDowell Obolensky, 1958; complete edition, London, Corgi, 1963; New York, Delacorte Press, 1965.
A Singular Man. Boston, Little Brown, 1963; London, Bodley Head, 1964.
The Saddest Summer of Samuel S. New York, Delacorte Press, 1966; London, Eyre and Spottiswoode, 1967.
The Beastly Beatitudes of Balthazar B. New York, Delacorte Press, 1968; London, Eyre and Spottiswoode, 1969.
The Onion Eaters. New York, Delacorte Press, and London, Eyre and Spottiswoode, 1971.
A Fairy Tale of New York. New York, Delacorte Press, and London, Eyre Methuen, 1973.
The Destinies of Darcy Dancer, Gentleman. New York, Delacorte Press, 1977; London, Allen Lane, 1978.
Schultz. New York, Delacorte Press, 1979; London, Allen Lane, 1980.
Leila. New York, Delacorte Press, and London, Allen Lane, 1983.
DeAlfonce Tennis: The Superlative Game of Eccentric Champions: Its History, Accoutrements, Conduct, Rules and Regimen. London, Weidenfeld and Nicolson, 1984; New York, Dutton, 1985.

Short Stories

Meet My Maker the Mad Molecule. Boston, Little Brown, 1964; London, Bodley Head, 1965.

Uncollected Short Stories

"A Friend" and "In My Peach Shoes," in *Queen* (London), 7 April 1965.
"Rite of Love," in *Playboy* (Chicago), October 1968.
"A Fair Festivity," in *Playboy* (Chicago), November 1968.
"A Small Human Being," in *Saturday Evening Post* (Philadelphia), 16 November 1968.

Plays

The Ginger Man, adaptation of his own novel (produced London and Dublin, 1959; New York, 1963). New York, Random House, 1961; as *What They Did in Dublin, with The Ginger Man: A Play*, London, MacGibbon and Kee, 1962.
Fairy Tales of New York (produced Croydon, Surrey, 1960; London, 1961; New York, 1980). London, Penguin, and New York, Random House, 1961.
A Singular Man, adaptation of his own novel (produced Cambridge and London, 1964; Westport, Connecticut, 1967). London, Bodley Head, 1965.
The Plays of J.P. Donleavy (includes *The Ginger Man*, *Fairy Tales of New York*, *A Singular Man*, *The Saddest Summer of Samuel S*). New York, Delacorte Press, 1972; London, Penguin, 1974.
The Beastly Beatitudes of Balthazar B, adaptation of his own novel (produced London, 1981; Norfolk, Virginia, 1985).

Radio Play: *Helen*, 1956.

Other

The Unexpurgated Code: A Complete Manual of Survival and Manners, drawings by the author. New York, Delacorte Press, and London, Wildwood House, 1975.

*

Bibliography: by David W. Madden, in *Bulletin of Bibliography* (Westport, Connecticut), September 1982.

Critical Studies: *J.P. Donleavy: The Style of His Sadness and Humor* by Charles G. Masinton, Bowling Green, Ohio, Popular Press, 1975; *Isolation and Protest: A Case Study of J.P. Donleavy's Fiction* by R.K. Sharma, New Delhi, Ajanta, 1983.

* * *

Perhaps because of his transatlantic and multinational character, J.P. Donleavy defies easy classification and may suffer from a certain critical neglect. His books blend some of the special literary qualities of all three—American, English, Irish —of his national traditions. He has a typically American zaniness, an anarchic and sometimes lunatic comic sense mingled with an undertone of despair. He possesses an English accuracy of eye and ear for the look and sound of things, for the subtle determinants of class in appearances and accents, a Jamesian grasp of density of specification. Finally, his novels display an Irish wit, energy, and vulgarity as well as a distinctly Irish sense of brooding and melancholy. Like any Irish writer, he is inevitably compared to Joyce, but in this case the comparison is appropriate—his tone, voice, and prose style have the comic brevity and particularity of many of Leopold Bloom's sections in *Ulysses*.

Ever since his great success with *The Ginger Man* Donleavy has followed a sometimes distressing sameness of pattern and subject in his books, whatever their individual differences may be. Roughly, they are serio-comic picaresques which mix a close attention to verifiable reality with an increasingly outrageous sense of fantasy. Although the fantasy is always strongly sexual—and Donleavy writes about sex with refreshingly carnal gusto—it also dwells on the sensuousness, perhaps even the eroticism of all materiality. When he sinks his teeth into the dense texture of life, Donleavy imparts an almost sexual appetite to his prose, glorying in the things of this world to the virtual exclusion of all else. He writes with the same zest about such matters as gentlemen's clothing, liquor, food, tobacco, women's bodies, the interior and exterior decorations of luxurious homes, all of the lovingly itemized concretions that represent the good life. In his recent novels, like *Schultz* and *Leila*, Donleavy records, with no diminution in his sense of awe, the dithyrambic praise of the appetitive view of life as fully and joyously as in *The Ginger Man*.

Because of the basic similarity of characters, events, style, and structures of his books, they often seem at first a mere continual rewriting of the first and most famous novel. They pile, often rather randomly and plotlessly, episode upon outrageous episode, repeat the scenes of sex, of comic violence, of pratfalls and ridicule in the same fragmented sentences, and often appear to run out of steam rather than end. Few of his books seem to have a real sense of closure: the protagonist most often is left, like the Ginger Man, suspended midway between triumph and ignominy, humor and sadness, still completely himself but also touched by despair and defeat. Their constant, most powerful note is elegiac—the protagonist may continue on his crazy way but he inevitably recognizes the most final and undeniable fact of all, the fact of death. The last perception of Sebastian Dangerfield in *The Ginger Man* is a vision of horses: "And I said they are running out to death which is with some soul and their eyes are mad and teeth out." In *The Destinies of Darcy Dancer, Gentleman* and its sequel, *Leila*, the fox hunt, which runs throughout the books, provides Dancer with the final metaphors of mortality—"Till the Huntsman's blowing his long slow notes. Turn home. At end of day." The one book that mixes the perception of death with some of the jaunty, lifeloving energy that pervades all his novels is *Schultz*, Donleavy's "Jewish" novel about a theatrical producer in London that caps the entire canon of Henry James in its portrait of an innocent American abroad. Contemplating the wreckage of all his lunatic schemes, Schultz perceives what is, for him, the structure of the universe. Out of his recognition of the enigma of infinitude and fatality, he concludes, "But if you can balance on top, you can not only scratch your fanny but touch the moon. But don't count on anything."

Like that of all good comic writers, Donleavy's vision is embedded in a dark view of the world; amid all his embracing vitality lies a perception of the need for comedy. His art derives from that perception—under the fully realized surfaces of life lie fear, guilt, and the dread of death. His books quite properly partake of the three traditions with which he has associated himself; all three converge in his mixture of solemnity and humor and in the same mixture of resolution and disintegration which invariably forms his conclusions. Life loving and death fearing, his novels end, at best, in a resounding "if." You may touch the moon, but don't count on anything. As Schultz responds to his own perception, "You bet/Your sweet/Rabbi ass/I won't." Good advice from a widely celebrated but insufficiently known novelist, and entirely appropriate as a commentary on the body of his work.

—George Grella

DRABBLE, Margaret. British. Born in Sheffield, Yorkshire, 5 June 1939; sister of A.S. Byatt, *q.v.* Educated at the Mount School, York; Newnham College, Cambridge, B.A. (honours) 1960. Married 1) Clive Swift in 1960 (divorced, 1975), two sons and one daughter; 2) the writer Michael Holroyd in 1982. Deputy Chairman, 1978–80, and Chairman, 1980–82, National Book League. Recipient: Rhys Memorial Prize, 1966; James Tait Black Memorial Prize, 1968; American Academy E.M. Forster Award, 1973. D.Litt.: University of Sheffield, 1976. C.B.E. (Commander, Order of the British Empire), 1980. Lives in London. Agent: A.D. Peters, 10 Buckingham Street, London WC2N 6BU, England.

PUBLICATIONS

Novels

A Summer Bird-Cage. London, Weidenfeld and Nicolson, 1962; New York, Morrow, 1964.
The Garrick Year. London, Weidenfeld and Nicolson, 1964; New York, Morrow, 1965.
The Millstone. London, Weidenfeld and Nicolson, 1965; New York, Morrow, 1966; as *Thank You All Very Much*, New York, New American Library, 1969.
Jerusalem the Golden. London, Weidenfeld and Nicolson, and New York, Morrow, 1967.
The Waterfall. London, Weidenfeld and Nicolson, and New York, Knopf, 1969.
The Needle's Eye. London, Weidenfeld and Nicolson, and New York, Knopf, 1972.
The Realms of Gold. London, Weidenfeld and Nicolson, and New York, Knopf, 1975.
The Ice Age. London, Weidenfeld and Nicolson, and New York, Knopf, 1977.
The Middle Ground. London, Weidenfeld and Nicolson, and New York, Knopf, 1980.

Short Stories

Penguin Modern Stories 3, with others. London, Penguin, 1969.
Hassan's Tower. Los Angeles, Sylvester and Orphanos, 1980.

Uncollected Short Stories

"A Voyage to Cytherea," in *Mademoiselle* (New York), December 1967.
"The Reunion," in *Winter's Tales 14*, edited by Kevin Crossley-Holland. London, Macmillan, and New York, St. Martin's Press, 1968.
"The Gifts of War," in *Winter's Tales 16*, edited by A.D. Maclean. London, Macmillan, 1970; New York, St Martin's Press, 1971.
"Crossing the Alps," in *Mademoiselle* (New York), February 1971.
"A Day in the Life of a Smiling Woman," in *In the Looking Glass*, edited by Nancy Dean and Myra Stark. New York, Putnam, 1977.

"A Success Story," in *Fine Lines*, edited by Ruth Sullivan. New York, Scribner, 1981.

Plays

Bird of Paradise (produced London, 1969).

Screenplays: *Isadora*, with Melvyn Bragg and Clive Exton, 1969; *A Touch of Love* (*Thank You All Very Much*), 1969.

Television Play: *Laura*, 1964.

Other

Wordsworth. London, Evans, 1966; New York, Arco, 1969.
Virginia Woolf: A Personal Debt. New York, Aloe, 1973.
Arnold Bennett: A Biography. London, Weidenfeld and Nicolson, and New York, Knopf, 1974.
For Queen and Country: Britain in the Victorian Age (for children). London, Deutsch, 1978; New York, Seabury Press, 1979.
A Writer's Britain: Landscape in Literature. London, Thames and Hudson, and New York, Knopf, 1979.

Editor, with B.S. Johnson, *London Consequences* (a group novel). London, Greater London Arts Association, 1972.
Editor, *Lady Susan, The Watsons, Sanditon*, by Jane Austen. London, Penguin, 1974.
Editor, *The Genius of Thomas Hardy.* London, Weidenfeld and Nicolson, and New York, Knopf, 1976.
Editor, with Charles Osborne, *New Stories 1.* London, Arts Council, 1976.
Editor, *The Oxford Companion to English Literature.* Oxford and New York, Oxford University Press, 1985.

*

Manuscript Collections: Boston University; University of Tulsa, Oklahoma.

Critical Studies: *Margaret Drabble: Puritanism and Permissiveness* by Valerie Grosvenor Myer, London, Vision Press, 1974; *Boulder-Pushers: Women in the Fiction of Margaret Drabble, Doris Lessing, and Iris Murdoch* by Carol Seiler-Franklin, Bern, Switzerland, Lang, 1979; *The Novels of Margaret Drabble: Equivocal Figures* by Ellen Cronan Rose, London, Macmillan, 1980, and *Critical Essays on Margaret Drabble* (includes bibliography by J.S. Korenman) edited by Rose, Boston, Hall, 1985; *Margaret Drabble: Existing Within Structures* by Mary Hurley Moran, Carbondale, Southern Illinois University Press, 1983; *Margaret Drabble* by Joanne V. Creighton, London, Methuen, 1985.

Margaret Drabble comments:

(1986) In this space I originally wrote that my books were mainly concerned with "privilege, justice and salvation," and that they were not directly concerned with feminism "because my belief in justice for women is so basic that I never think of using it as a subject. It is part of a whole." I stand by this, although the rising political consciousness of women has brought the subject more to the forefront in one or two of the later novels. I now see myself perhaps more as a social historian documenting social change and asking questions

rather than providing answers about society: but my preoccupation with "equality and egalitarianism" remains equally obsessional and equally worrying to me, and if anything I am even less hopeful about the prospects of change.

*   *   *

With the appearance of her first novels in the early 1960's, Margaret Drabble gained a sizeable audience who felt their own discoveries and dilemmas in the contemporary world depicted with intelligence and immediacy. *A Summer Bird-Cage* presents a young woman, just after graduation from Oxford, alternately drawn to and repelled by her older sister, seen as brilliant and attractive, who marries a rich novelist. The marriage is ultimately hollow, and the young protagonist uses her recognition of this, as well as that of the marriages, affairs, and occupations of friends, to sort out her own approach to mature experience. The protagonist of *The Garrick Year* is more intimately involved. Married to an actor in a company playing in a provincial town, she falls in love with the producer and finally is able to draw away from the thickets of staged infidelities in her realization of her responsibility for her child. Moral issues, increasingly, become part of the protagonists' examinations of experience, as in *The Millstone*, in which a young academic, initially feeling "free" of the inhibitions of sexual morality and class, and accidentally pregnant after a one-night stand, recognizes after the baby's birth that her concerns are her dependent on others, on community, and *Jerusalem the Golden*, in which a young graduate from the North, attracted to the cosmopolitan life represented by a London family, must sort out her own allegiances and responses to issues of love and class. Although *The Waterfall* is more internal, more exclusively concerned with the isolating emotions the protagonist feels in her affair with her cousin's husband, this novel, like the other early ones, reflects directly many of the problems concerning freedom, responsibility, sexual behavior, families, occupation, class, and geography confronted by young women in contemporay Britain.

Drabble's protagonists are invariably intelligent and literary, trying seriously (although not solemnly) to relate what they experience to what they've read. Often they define themselves, either positively or negatively, as characters within the fictions of the 19th-century middle classes, the heroines in George Eliot's world confronting moral dilemmas, or those in Hardy's measuring themselves in the metaphorical terms of landscape. *The Waterfall* rings changes on Jane Austen plots and attitudes; the protagonist in *The Millstone* superimposes Bunyan's allegorical geography on the dark streets of contemporary London. The frequency and the importance of the references indicate that Drabble has always seen herself as part of an English literary tradition, a consciousness of defining the self through fiction.

In Drabble's later novels, the consciousness and function of fiction change. Points of view are deliberately interrupted, fictionality is overtly proclaimed and manipulated, and, sometimes comically and sometimes not, Drabble relies on questions in literary criticism over the past 20 years as well as on the tradition of English literature. Library reference is likely to be more general and pervasive, as in the epigraph for *The Ice Age* which quotes Milton's *Areopagetica* about "the puissant Nation rousing herself like a strong man after sleep" to illustrate the possibility of British "recovery" from a debilitating period, or the literary party, explicitly connected to the one in Virginia Woolf's *Mrs. Dalloway*, which concludes *The Middle Ground*. The frame of moral reference in the later novels is much wider, more international or more a statement concerning the condition of England, and the novels are more amenable to metaphorical readings. *The Needle's Eye* establishes various gardens in unlikely places, the London slums, the North, and in Africa, gardens that are conscious devices to preserve and nourish the human spirit. *The Realms of Gold* depicts an archeologist who collects both the shards of a public past in excavations in Africa and those of the private past of her family amidst the local and class deprivations of East Anglia, trying to combine the implications of all the relics into a fuller public and private life. *The Ice Age* focuses on the depression, sterility, and violence of Britain in the mid-1970's, problems demonstrated as private in the particular characters and rendered public through the metaphors of property development and misuse that dominate the novel. National "recovery" is seen, perhaps equivocally, as possible. *The Middle Ground*, again combining the public and private, tries to collect representatives of various cultures and classes in a contemporary London reclaimed from the septic wastes of its origins, a metaphor like that in Dickens's *Our Mutual Friend*. Drabble's self-conscious play with fictional perspectives keeps these metaphors away from the potential solemnity of the grandiose, yet the moral implications of the metaphors, the statements judging both personal and public conditions in England, are serious and controlling.

—James Gindin

DREWE, Robert. Australian. Born in Melbourne, Victoria, 9 January 1943. Educated at Hale School, Perth, Western Australia, 1952–60. Married 1) Coral Prince; 2) Sandra Symons; three sons and two daughters. Cadet reporter, Perth *West Australian*, 1961–64; reporter, 1964–65, and head of Sydney bureau, 1965–70, *The Age*, Melbourne; daily columnist, 1970–73, features editor, 1971–72, and literary editor, 1972–74, *The Australian*, Sydney; special writer, 1975–76, and contributing editor, 1980–82, *The Bulletin*, Sydney; Writer-in-Residence, University of Western Australia, Perth, 1979; columnist, *Mode*, Sydney, 1981–82, and Sydney *City Monthly*, 1981–83. Recipient: Australia Council fellowship, 1973, 1974, 1976, 1978, 1983; U.S. Government Leader grant, 1978; Walkley award, 1976, 1981. Address: Jill Hickson Associates, 137 Regent Street, Chippendale, New South Wales 2008, Australia.

PUBLICATIONS

Novels

The Savage Crows. Sydney and London, Collins, 1976.
A Cry in the Jungle Bar. Sydney, Collins, 1979; London, Fontana, 1981.

Short Stories

The Bodysurfers. Darlinghurst, New South Wales, Fraser, 1983; London, Faber, 1984.

Uncollected Short Stories

"True West," in *Meanjin* (Melbourne), 1980.
"Cards of Identity," in *Bondi* (Sydney), 1984.

Play

Screenplay: *The Bodysurfers*, 1985.

*

Critical Studies: "Making Connections" by Veronica Brady, in *Westerly* (Perth, Western Australia), June 1980; "The Littoral Truth" by Jim Crace, in *Times Literary Supplement* (London), 24 August 1984; "Beaches and Bruised Loves" by Jill Smolowe, in *Newsweek* (New York), 29 October 1984.

Robert Drewe comments:
I find it difficult to talk about my work. May I be brief? *The Savage Crows* is an "ambitious" first novel about a young man's coming to terms with himself and Australian history, namely the genocide of the Tasmanian Aborigines. *A Cry in the Jungle Bar* is an allegory of the Australian experience in Asia, using elements of both farce and thriller. *The Bodysurfers* is a collection of inter-related stories, set around the Australian shoreline, which questions the national literary preoccupation with the outback. *Spargo* (forthcoming) is a novel about the dangers of heroism in an insecure society, especially one dominated by the American influence. *Overseas* (forthcoming) is a collection of stores about immigration, emigration, and compulsive travelling.

*   *   *

Robert Drewe is an important, highly original voice in Australian fiction. Like many other writers before him, Drewe deals with the plight of the Australian Aborigines, scrutinises Australia's uneasy relationship with Asia, and shows an overriding concern with questions of Australian national identity. But Drewe's approach to these issues is original and provocative.

Whereas a novel about the Australian Aborigines will usually be set among Aborigines, or at least involve white people who live in areas inhabited by Aborigines, *The Savage Crows* deals with a white youth whose contact with Aborigines is at first only theoretical. Stephen Crisp is researching the early 19th-century events which led to the extinction of the Aborigines living in the island state of Tasmania. His source material is a document titled "The Savage Crows: My Adventures Among the Natives of Van Diemen's Land." This is the diary-journal of the clergyman G.A. Robinson, whose attempts to bring Christianity and civilization to the Tasmanian natives led to cultural misunderstanding, the spread of disease, and death.

Though Robinson was an actual historical figure, the Robinson journal is based upon a number of 19th-century documents and newspaper reports. *The Savage Crows* has been described as a "documentary novel," but its concerns extend beyond the fictional recreation of history. Drewe presents a number of moral contrasts: Robinson's "good intentions" and their deplorable outcome; Crisp's clinical, academic approach and the dire human suffering to which it is directed; the petty "problems" of affluent 20th-century suburbia beside the plight of early colonists and Aborigines.

As the writing of his thesis progresses, Crisp becomes more personally involved with his material; his clinical approach is replaced by an awareness that his own life and times are the product of the Australian history he describes. Crisp sees that his fellow Australians have divorced themselves from their history and have chosen to ignore it (just as white Australians, in general, have chosen to live in ignorance of, and separation from, black Australians). But Crisp chooses to *confront* the past, compelling himself to react to the history he has uncovered, and in the final section of the novel Drewe implies that contemporary Australians *can* confront their past and cope with the legacy of guilt which history has handed them.

In his second novel, *A Cry in the Jungle Bar*, Drewe explores Australia's relationship with Asia, once again with focus upon the experiences of a single individual. The jungle bar is an attraction of the Asian Eden Hotel, and the "cry" of the title is an utterance of helpless western frustration in the face of Asian complexities. Australian Dick Cullen is a tall, beefy, former football player who now works for the United Nations in Manila. Like Stephen Crisp, Cullen is a researcher: an expert on animal husbandry, he is writing a book about water buffalo titled "The Poor Man's Tractor." More importantly, Cullen shares Crisp's desire to relate his own life to history (though Cullen is more interested in the future history of Australian-Asian relations), and he shares Crisp's struggle to come to terms with another race and culture.

Drewe presents a pessimistic, satirical view of the meeting of cultures. Cullen is marked indelibly as a foreigner because of his massive physique, but also because of his inability to understand the subtle political divisions of Asia. (His Bangladeshi colleague, Z.M. Ali, is an enigma to him, and Cullen is bewildered when Ali's political activities lead to his expulsion.)

In both of Drewe's novels there is an underlying concern with the malaise affecting suburban Australia. This is seen in the way in which both Crisp and Cullen are aloof and clinical about pressing human problems (each man addressing social issues through reports and documentation, rather than experiencing the problems directly), and it is evident in the failed sexual relationships portrayed in each novel. The 12 short stories in *The Bodysurfers* develop these concerns in more detail, exploring the conflicts and contradictions in the national character. The first of the book's epigraphs, from the polemical historian Manning Clark, is a statement about the loss of national values: "Just as Samson after being shorn of his hair was left eyeless in Gaza, was this generation, stripped bare of all faith, to be left comfortless on Bondi Beach?" Yet the second epigraph, quoting the words of the beach-inspector who arrested the first girl to wear a bikini on a public beach, is an almost contradictory assertion of the persistence of "values": "We'll pick up the bikini girls as soon as they take off their wraps, and we'll have their beach wraps back on them before the boys can let out a single *hubba bubba*." The stories reflect this conflict by contrasting the carefree sensuality of Australian beach life (the nude sunbathers, the smell of sun-tan oil) with the characters' unconscious prurience and uneasiness about sexuality, and with the mundane anxieties and problems of urban life.

Drewe's portrayal of the beach culture is superb; to quote one reviewer: "It's all here—the oiled bodies, the smell of the salt, the heat of the sun, the sensuality." But Drewe also offers a provocative analysis of Australian life, suggesting that the conflicts indicated by the book's epigraphs may stem from an inability to unite the "masculine" and "feminine" aspects of the national culture. In many stories the beach embodies the Australian myth of physical action and carefree hedonism, but these simplistic masculine values are often dispelled by the comments or actions of the female characters. And in the story called "The Last Explorer" an aged adventurer, slowly dying in hospital, symbolically turns his back on the sea (symbol of the young, feminine, new Australia) and faces the desert (symbol of the dead "macho" world of exploration and masculine deeds).

—Van Ikin

DRIVER, C(harles) J(onathan). British. Born in Cape Town, South Africa, 19 August 1939. Educated at St. Andrews College, Grahamstown; University of Cape Town, B.A. (honours) in English, B.Ed., and S.T.D. 1962; Trinity College, Oxford, M.Phil. 1967. Married Ann Elizabeth Hoogewerf in 1967; two sons and one daughter. President, National Union of South African Students, 1963–64; detained in 1964 under the "90 Day Law"; South African passport revoked, 1966. Assistant teacher, 1964–65 and 1967–68, and Housemaster, International Sixth Form Centre, 1968–73, Sevenoaks School, Kent; Director of 6th Form Studies, Matthew Humberstone Comprehensive School, Humberside, 1973–78; Principal, Island School, Hong Kong, 1978–83. Since 1983, Headmaster, Berkhamsted School, Hertfordshire. Resident Fellow, University of York, 1976. Fellow, Royal Society of Arts, 1984. Agent: John Johnson Ltd., 45–47 Clerkenwell Green, London EC1R 0HT. Address: Wilson House, Berkhamsted School, Berkhamsted, Hertfordshire HP4 2BE, England.

PUBLICATIONS

Novels

Elegy for a Revolutionary.   London, Faber, 1969; New York, Morrow, 1970.
Send War in Our Time, O Lord.   London, Faber, 1970.
Death of Fathers.   London, Faber, 1972.
A Messiah of the Last Days.   London, Faber, 1974.

Short Stories

Penguin Modern Stories 8, with others.   London, Penguin, 1971.

Uncollected Short Story

"Impossible Cry," in *London Magazine*, February 1966.

Verse

I Live Here Now.   Lincoln, Lincolnshire and Humberside Arts, 1979.
Jack Cope/C.J. Driver.   Cape Town, Philip, 1979.

Other

Patrick Duncan, South African and Pan-African.   London, Heinemann, 1980.

Editor, with H.B. Joicey, *Landscape and Light: Photographs and Poems of Lincolnshire and Humberside.*   Lincoln, Lincolnshire and Humberside Arts, 1978.

*

C.J. Driver comments:
I am a writer and a teacher; the order depends on whether I am writing or teaching, but I am Headmaster of an old and

quite celebrated independent secondary school. I write poems, though I do little about publishing them these days; I do quite a bit of reviewing, partly for the money, but more for my own enjoyment; I spent two years writing the biography of Patrick Duncan, one of the tragic heroes of recent South African history; and I write novels. I believe profoundly that the novel is the "great book of life," and I hope that all my concerns as a human being enter my work as a novelist—love, marriage, children, homes, money, food, work, leisure—though my predominant concerns are with politics—in the widest sense—the relation of self and society, and the relation of conscious and unconscious minds. I would, at the moment, regard myself more as a poet than a novelist; but I hope the picture may change before the final curtain.

*   *   *

C.J. Driver is a South African writer whose four novels have earned him a considerable reputation. Not exclusively South African in setting or in theme, the novels concentrate on issues which are both topical and popular, and offer a sometimes challenging and always recognisable view of contemporary society.

Elegy for a Revolutionary, the first and least satisfactory of the novels, uses Driver's own experience of underground political action in South Africa during the early 1960's. Like Nadine Gordimer's *The Late Bourgeois World*, it is an attempt to examine the motives and the fate of a group of young white "liberals" who turned to violence as a means of opposing the repressive Nationalist Government. Driver's analysis centres on the personality of the student leader, Jeremy, whom he sees as both traitor and, paradoxically, hero. The weakness of the novel lies in its excessively uncritical view of Jeremy. Unlike Nadine Gordimer, who presents her revolutionary as an integral part of a wider social setting, Driver fails to create a context in which Jeremy's actions can be understood. And, although he is much concerned with psychological motivation, the discussion of Jeremy's peculiar family relationships and obscure guilts remains too abstract to be really credible.

In *Send War in Our Time, O Lord* Driver's main theme is the examination of the liberal conscience under stress. His portrayal of Mrs. Allen, a middle-aged white widow, discovering the inadequacy of her life-long moral code based on decency and tolerance, demonstrates his ability to create a convincing character. The setting (an isolated missionary settlement on South Africa's northern border) is also well-presented. The major weakness of this novel lies in its melodramatic and somewhat far-fetched plot, which involves terrorist activity, much police brutality, madness and two or three suicides, all graphically described. In the welter of violent action, the central issues (the failure of liberal values, the need for dynamic leadership, the nature of political commitment) are almost submerged.

Death of Fathers and *A Messiah of the Last Days* are both set in England, and show a much surer grasp of technique and theme than the earlier books. Driver's interest in details of violence and suffering are still in evidence, but now become part of a general vision of modern life. *Death of Fathers* has a close affinity with *Elegy for a Revolutionary*, although it is set in the confines of an English public school. Its central character is a schoolmaster, and, as in the earlier novel, he is both "heroic" (larger in every way than his colleagues) and "treacherous" (he betrays the confidence of his most brilliant and difficult pupil, in an attempt to "save" him). Again, Driver explores the nature of guilt, and the concept of betrayal, which appears, in his view, to be an inherent part of human experi-

ence. Friendship between two different but complementary male characters forms another strand in the novel, and is more competently handled here than in the earlier book.

In *A Messiah of the Last Days* Driver returns to a contemplation of political action. This time he makes his anti-establishment figures a group of idealistic young anarchists, the Free People, who set up a commune in a disused warehouse in London. Their leader, charismatic John Buckleson, projects such a powerful and attractive vision of a new society that he wins the allegiance of a number of eminently respectable people, as well as exciting the younger members of society. The most ambitious of the four novels, *A Messiah of the Last Days* contrasts a number of different life styles, and presents a complex image of contemporay Britain. Through the fast-moving story runs what is clearly, by now, Driver's most persistent theme: the need society has for a "leader" with a compelling vision, and its equal need to destroy him. Buckleson, who ends his life as a "vegetable" in psychiatric ward, having been shot at close range by a former follower of his, is the latest version of Jeremy, sentenced to death for sabotage; of the terrorist leader, gunned down by the police; and of Nigel, the schoolboy who hanged himself. Skilled as Driver undoubtedly is in contriving variations on his theme, one hopes that his interest in leadership and betrayal will not become obsessive.

—Ursula Edmands

DRURY, Allen (Stuart). American. Born in Houston, Texas, 2 September 1918. Educated at Stanford University, California, B.A. 1939. Served in the United States Army, 1942–43. Editor, Tulare *Bee*, California, 1940–41; county editor, Bakersfield *Californian*, 1941–42; member, United Press Senate staff, Washington, D.C., 1943–45; national editor, *Pathfinder* magazine, Washington, D.C., 1947–53; member, Congressional staff, Washington *Evening Star*, 1953–54, and *New York Times*, 1954–59; political correspondent, *Reader's Digest*, 1959–63. Member, National Council on the Arts, Washington, D.C. Recipient: Sigma Delta Chi award, for journalism, 1941; Pulitzer Prize, for fiction, 1960. Lit.D.: Rollins College, Winter Park, Florida, 1961. Lives in Tiburon, California. Address: c/o Doubleday, 245 Park Avenue, New York, New York 10167, U.S.A.

PUBLICATIONS

Novels

Advise and Consent. New York, Doubleday, 1959; London, Collins, 1960.
A Shade of Difference. New York, Doubleday, 1962; London, Joseph, 1963.
That Summer. London, Joseph, 1965; New York, Coward McCann, 1966.
Capable of Honor. New York, Doubleday, 1966; London, Joseph, 1967.
Preserve and Protect. New York, Doubleday, and London, Joseph, 1968.
The Throne of Saturn. New York, Doubleday, and London, Joseph, 1971.

Come Nineveh, Come Tyre: The Presidency of Edward M. Jason. New York, Doubleday, 1973; London, Joseph, 1974.
The Promise of Joy: The Presidency of Orrin Knox. New York, Doubleday, and London, Joseph, 1975.
A God Against the Gods. New York, Doubleday, and London, Joseph, 1976.
Anna Hastings: The Story of a Washington Newspaperperson. New York, Morrow, 1977; London, Joseph, 1978.
Return to Thebes. New York, Doubleday, and London, Joseph, 1977.
Mark Coffin, U.S.S.: A Novel of Capitol Hill. New York. Doubleday, 1979; as *Mark Coffin, Senator*, London, Joseph, 1979.
The Hill of Summer. New York, Doubleday, 1981; London, Joseph, 1982.
Decision. New York, Doubleday, and London, Joseph, 1983.
The Roads of Earth. New York, Doubleday, 1984; London, Joseph, 1985.

Uncollected Short Stories

"Something," in *The Best from Fantasy and Science Fiction 10*, edited by Robert P. Mills. New York, Doubleday, 1961; London, Gollancz, 1963.
"No More Tears," in *Good Housekeeping* (New York), February 1971.

Other

A Senate Journal 1943–1945. New York, McGraw Hill, 1963.
Three Kids in a Cart: A Visit to Ike and Other Diversions. New York, Doubleday, 1965.
"A Very Strange Society": A Journey to the Heart of South Africa. New York, Simon and Schuster, 1967; London, Joseph, 1968.
Courage and Hesitation: Notes and Photographs of the Nixon Administration. New York, Doubleday, 1971; as *Courage and Hesitation: Inside the Nixon Administration*, London, Joseph, 1972.
Egypt: The Eternal Smile, photographs by Alex Gotfrydx. New York, Doubleday, 1980.

*

Manuscript Collection: Hoover Institution, Stanford, California.

*   *   *

Allen Drury's experiences as a journalist, especially as a political correspondent in Washington, D.C., have left their mark, for better or worse, on his novels and non-fiction. Almost all his fiction is concerned with political warfare in the United States, with attacks by the media upon politicians when in power and opposition, and with the external enemies of the United States. These enemies are shown as unprincipled, ungrateful, and malicious both when making their verbal assaults in the United Nations, an institution that is rarely shown in a flattering light, and when physically attacking American installations. Communist Russia, the arch-foe, is made completely villainous, particularly in *The Throne of Saturn* and *Come Nineveh, Come Tyre*. In the former, Russian astronauts try to destroy American space craft far above the earth; in the latter, Russia invades Alaska and humiliates a foolishly idealistic left-wing president.

Of his novels, *Advise and Consent* is the first published and the best. It would undoubtedly benefit from severe pruning,

but there is a momentum built upon a melodramatic presentation of events that carries the reader along, even if he is wary of the hysterical undertone of the book. In the detailing of Congressional infighting and the tension of significant debates in the Senate, Drury is at his strongest. Here his years as a member of the United Press Senate Staff are effectively used. He is not so strong, however, when presenting the actions of the president or the left-wingers. As in later books, many characters are stereotypes. Even in this book, a Pulitzer prize winner, he uses a plot that appears contrived (even though it has real life counterparts) and characters that are mere puppets.

Subsequent novels carry on the story of political struggles and national alarums through outbreaks of "liberal"-inspired violence and presidential assassination. Instead of refining and subtilizing the promising material and fictional technique of *Advise and Consent*, he seems to have been pushed by an increasing fear for the preservation of traditional American values and institutions into composing novels that are more overtly propagandistic statements of his conservative political beliefs than aesthetically pleasing books. Readers who share his deep distrust of liberals and his hatred of Communism may accept his fiction more readily, but they too probably find his prose heavy and his plots excessively sensational. Even characters such as Orrin Knox, who are interestingly depicted in the early novels, begin to pall in the later works. The use of melodramatic incident (often to compensate for feeble characterization) is strikingly exemplified in *Preserve and Protect*, which opens with the death of President Harley M. Hudson in a fiery plane crash and (on the last page) concludes with the assassination before a huge crowd of either the presidential or the vice-presidential nominee—in movie-serial fashion we are not told which one. The failure to identify the victims is deliberate since Drury is thereby able to give us two novels as sequels. In *Come Nineveh, Come Tyre*, Orrin Knox, the stalwart conservative, is identified as the victim. Thus Edward Montoya Jason, the liberal but too-malleable vice-presidential nominee assumes the highest office; but, exploited by NAWAC (National Anti-War Activities Congress) and Communist imperialists, he brings the country to abject international defeat. The alternative, with Jason dead and Knox alive, is given in *The Promise of Joy*.

The city is the same, but the focus has changed in *Anna Hastings*. The ruthless rise of the liberal newspaperwoman has interest and excitement, but the novel is often a sermon on the dangers of liberalism. In *Mark Coffin, U.S.S.* Drury comes back to the U.S. Senate, a scene he knows so well. The hero, the intelligent young senator from California, too naive to be completely credible, has to survive great political pressure and a scandal. The author's favourite, indeed obsessive, theme is dominant once again in *The Hill of Summer*. The usual elements of the realistic novel—plot, characterization, dramatic scene—are subordinated to the message that the United States is not sufficiently prepared to meet the Soviet menace. At the end of the novel, world war is temporarily averted. The theme is even more clearly and repetitiously sounded in *The Roads of Earth*, for both an authorial prefatory note and the novel itself monotonously declare that the Soviet Union is set on destroying the United States; pre-emptive strikes against Russian manifestations of power are advocated. The staunch incumbent American president forces the Russians to retreat. The characters are once again stereotyped as good or bad in *Decision*, but Drury centres this novel on the Supreme Court and the prevalence of violent crime in America: the highest court has to decide the case of a vicious Harvard graduate, a hippie, who has blown up an atomic power station and made the daughter of one of the judges hearing the case into a human vegetable. The issues are important, but the treatment is inadequately realistic.

Non-American readers are probably irritated by the obtrusive patriotism and the condescension shown for foreigners. Drury seems unable or unwilling to present foreigners with sympathy or in depth. Too often he resorts to stereotypes or caricatures in his fiction. Lord Claude Maudulayne, the British Ambassador, is an example. In addition, by failing to develop credible characters for the ambassadors at the UN or in Washington, he loses the chance to utilize them as a kind of Greek chorus commenting on American tragedies. On the other hand, a moderate and balanced view of foreigners is given in *"A Very Strange Society": A Journey to the Heart of South Africa.* Perhaps he is too ready to depreciate the achievements of black African nations, but he acknowledges the complex problems of a multi-racial society.

Two of Drury's novels of the late 1970's, *A God Against the Gods* and *Return to Thebes*, are set in ancient Egypt. In the former, Akhenaten and his beautiful wife Nefertitti are locked in a power struggle with the priesthood; in the sequel, Akhenaten is murdered, Tutankhaten succeeds him; then he too is murdered. Like most of Drury's novels, these two are concerned with the struggle for power. Both novels are well researched and have exciting scenes, but the characterization is simplistic and the dialogue insufficiently differentiated.

His main claim to fame, however, is his series of political novels, structured around the beliefs and actions of Americans during the 1960's, 1970's, and 1980's—some of the novels might indeed be read as *romans à clef*. In the 1970's American history betrayed Allen Drury: his right-wing heroes—at least their equivalents in real life—were found guilty through such investigations as Watergate of the very crimes he attributes to his left-wing villains. He was equally unfortunate in his non-fiction. *Courage and Hesitation: Notes and Photographs of the Nixon Administration* (1971) is a tribute, with only a few cautionary statements, to "a decent and worthy man, leading an administration composed, for the most part, of decent and worthy men." To overcome the unkind cuts of history, Drury must either develop a greater political sensitivity or take more seriously his role as a creator of fiction. Unfortunately, his recent fiction has become so melodramatic and hortatory in its insistence on the United States staunchly resisting the Russian threat that, even in the conservative era of the early 1980's, more readers will probably be alienated by the novelist's stridency than converted to his political creed.

—James A. Hart

DUFFY, Maureen (Patricia). British. Born in Worthing, Sussex, 21 October 1933. Educated at Trowbridge High School for Girls, Wiltshire; Sarah Bonnell High School for Girls; King's College, London, 1953–56, B.A. (honours) in English 1956. School teacher for five years. Co-founder, Writers Action Group, 1972; Joint Chairman, 1977–78, and since 1985, President, Writers Guild of Great Britain; Chairman, Greater London Arts Literature Panel, 1979–81; since 1981, Vice-Chairman, British Copyright Council; since 1982, Chairman, Authors Lending and Copyright Society. Recipient: City of London Festival Playwright's Prize, 1962; Arts Council bursary, 1963, 1966, 1975; Society of Authors travelling scholarship, 1976. Agent: Jonathan Clowes Ltd., 22 Prince Albert Road, London NW1 7ST. Address: 18 Fabian Road, London SW6 7TZ, England.

PUBLICATIONS

Novels

That's How It Was. London, Hutchinson, 1962; New York, Dial Press, 1984.
The Single Eye. London, Hutchinson, 1964.
The Microcosm. London, Hutchinson, and New York, Simon and Schuster, 1966.
The Paradox Players. London, Hutchinson, 1967; New York, Simon and Schuster, 1968.
Wounds. London, Hutchinson, and New York, Knopf, 1969.
Love Child. London, Weidenfeld and Nicolson, and New York, Knopf, 1971.
I Want to Go to Moscow: A Lay. London, Hodder and Stoughton, 1973; as *All Heaven in a Rage*, New York, Knopf, 1973.
Capital. London, Cape, 1975; New York, Braziller, 1976.
Housespy. London, Hamish Hamilton, 1978.
Gor Saga. London, Eyre Methuen, 1981; New York, Viking Press, 1982.
Scarborough Fear (as D.M. Cayer). London, Macdonald, 1982.
Londoners: An Elegy. London, Methuen, 1983.

Uncollected Short Story

"The Happy Bastard," in *One Parent Families*. London, Davis Poynter, 1975.

Plays

The Lay Off (produced London, 1962).
The Silk Room (produced Watford, Hertfordshire, 1966).
Rites (produced London, 1969). Published in *New Short Plays 2*, London, Methuen, 1969.
Solo, Olde Tyme (produced Cambridge, 1970).
A Nightingale in Bloomsbury Square (produced London, 1973). Published in *Factions*, edited by Giles Gordon and Alex Hamilton, London, Joseph, 1974.

Radio Play: *Only Goodnight*, 1981.

Television Play: *Josie*, 1961.

Verse

Lyrics for the Dog Hour. London, Hutchinson, 1968.
The Venus Touch. London, Weidenfeld and Nicolson, 1971.
Actaeon. Rushden, Northamptonshire, Sceptre Press, 1973.
Evesong. London, Sappho, 1975.
Memorials of the Quick and the Dead. London, Hamish Hamilton, 1979.
Collected Poems. London, Hamish Hamilton, 1985.

Other

The Erotic World of Faery. London, Hodder and Stoughton, 1972.
The Passionate Shepherdess: Aphra Behn 1640–1689. London, Cape, 1977; New York, Avon, 1979.
Inherit the Earth: A Social History. London, Hamish Hamilton, 1980.

Men and Beasts: An Animal Rights Handbook.   London, Paladin, 1984.

Editor, with Alan Brownjohn, *New Poetry 3.*   London, Arts Council, 1977.

Translator, *A Blush of Shame*, by Domenico Rea.   London, Barrie and Rockliff, 1968.

*

Manuscript Collection: King's College, University of London.

Critical Study: by Dulan Barber, in *Transatlantic Review 45* (London), Spring 1973.

*   *   *

Maureen Duffy is a prolific novelist, poet, and playwright whose work has developed rapidly in range and importance. *That's How It Was* won her immediate acclaim for its simplicity and forcefulness. It is a moving account of the relationship between a mother and daughter; their existence is poor, insecure, even brutal, but transcended by mutual love. "I grew six inches under the light touch of her hand," explains the narrator. The little girl has an acute sense of social isolation and a fierce loyalty to the one constant figure in her universe; her mother's death is thus cause for more than grief, it brings total despair. The loneliness, restlessness, and sexual hunger which spring from the situation are the dominating themes of each subsequent novel.

Realism is the touchstone of Duffy's style; like many other observers of working-class life, she is at her best when she relies on accurate, detailed reportage and at her weakest when tempted by sentiment. *The Paradox Players* is an example of her writing at its most compelling. It describes a man's retreat from society to live for some months in a boat moored on the Thames. The physical realities of cold, snow, rats, and flooding occupy him continually and the hardship brings him peace. He is a novelist, suffering from the hazards peculiar to that profession and has some pertinent comments to make about the vulnerability of the writer. "When I saw the reviews I could have cut my throat. You see they're very kind to first novels for some mistaken reason but when the poor bastard follows it up with a second and they see he really means it they tear its guts out." The experience of winter on the river restores his faith in his own ability to survive.

Duffy's observations are acute, her use of dialogue witty and direct; this authenticity is complemented by an interest in the bizarre, the fantastic. Her best-known book uses these qualities to great effect in a study of lesbian society which is both informative and original. *The Microcosm* begins and ends in a club where the central characters meet to dance, dress up, and escape from the necessity of "all the week wearing a false face." Their fantasies are played out in front of the juke box; then the narrative follows each woman back into her disguise, her social role. Steve is Miss Stephens, a schoolmistress; Cathy is a bus conductress; Matt works in a garage. Their predicament as individuals, the author suggests, extends beyond the interest of their own minority group. A plea is made for tolerance, understanding, and that respect without which the human spirit must perish. "Society isn't a simple organism with one nucleus and a fringe of little feet, it's an infinitely complex structure and if you try to suppress

any part . . . you diminish, you mutilate the whole." *Wounds* and *Love Child* reaffirm this belief.

—Judy Cooke

_____

du MAURIER, Daphne.   British.   Born in London, 13 May 1907; daughter of the actor/manager Sir Gerald du Maurier; granddaughter of the writer George du Maurier. Educated privately and in Paris. Married Lieutenant-General Sir Frederick Browning in 1932 (died, 1965); two daughters and one son. Recipient: Mystery Writers of America Grand Master Award, 1977. Fellow, Royal Society of Literature, 1952. D.B.E. (Dame Commander, Order of the British Empire), 1969. Address: Kilmarth, Par, Cornwall PL24 2TL, England.

PUBLICATIONS

Novels

The Loving Spirit.   London, Heinemann, and New York, Doubleday, 1931.
I'll Never Be Young Again.   London, Heinemann, and New York, Doubleday, 1932.
The Progress of Julius.   London, Heinemann, and New York, Doubleday, 1933.
Jamaica Inn.   London, Gollancz, and New York, Doubleday, 1936.
Rebecca.   London, Gollancz, and New York, Doubleday, 1938.
Frenchman's Creek.   London, Gollancz, 1941; New York, Doubleday, 1942.
Hungry Hill.   London, Gollancz, and New York, Doubleday, 1943.
The King's General.   London, Gollancz, and New York, Doubleday, 1946.
The Parasites.   London, Gollancz, 1949; New York, Doubleday, 1950.
My Cousin Rachel.   London, Gollancz, 1951; New York, Doubleday, 1952.
Mary Anne.   London, Gollancz, and New York, Doubleday, 1954.
The Scapegoat.   London, Gollancz, and New York, Doubleday, 1957.
Castle Dor, by Arthur Quiller-Couch, completed by du Maurier.   London, Dent, and New York, Doubleday, 1962.
The Glass-Blowers.   London, Gollancz, and New York, Doubleday, 1963.
The Flight of the Falcon.   London, Gollancz, and New York, Doubleday, 1965.
The House on the Strand.   London, Gollancz, and New York, Doubleday, 1969.
Rule Britannia.   London, Gollancz, 1972; New York, Doubleday, 1973.

Short Stories

Happy Christmas (story).   New York, Doubleday, 1940; London, Todd, 1943.
Come Wind, Come Weather.   London, Heinemann, 1940; New York, Doubleday, 1941.
Nothing Hurts for Long, and Escort.   London, Todd, 1943.

Consider the Lilies (story). London, Todd, 1943.
Spring Picture (story). London, Todd, 1944.
Leading Lady (story). London, Vallancey Press, 1945.
London and Paris (two stories). London, Vallancey Press, 1945.
The Apple Tree: A Short Novel, and Some Stories. London, Gollancz, 1952; as *Kiss Me Again, Stranger: A Collection of Eight Stories, Long and Short*, New York, Doubleday, 1953; as *The Birds and Other Stories*, London, Penguin, 1968.
Early Stories. London, Todd, 1954.
The Breaking Point: Eight Stories. London, Gollancz, and New York, Doubleday, 1959; as *The Blue Lenses and Other Stories*, London, Penguin, 1970.
The Treasury of du Maurier Short Stories. London, Gollancz, 1960.
The Lover and Other Stories. London, Ace, 1961.
Not after Midnight and Other Stories. London, Gollancz, 1971; as *Don't Look Now*, New York, Doubleday, 1971.
Echoes from the Macabre: Selected Stories. London, Gollancz, 1976; New York, Doubleday, 1977.
The Rendezvous and Other Stories. London, Gollancz, 1980.

Plays

Rebecca, adaptation of her own novel (produced Manchester and London, 1940; New York, 1945). London, Gollancz, 1940; New York, Dramatists Play Service, 1943.
The Years Between (produced Manchester, 1944; London, 1945). London, Gollancz, 1945; New York, Doubleday, 1946.
September Tide (produced Oxford and London, 1948). London, Gollancz, 1949; New York, Doubleday, 1950.

Screenplay: *Hungry Hill*, with Terence Young and Francis Crowdry, 1947.

Television Play: *The Breakthrough*, 1976.

Other

Gerald: A Portrait (on Gerald du Maurier). London, Gollancz, 1934; New York, Doubleday, 1935.
The du Mauriers. London, Gollancz, and New York, Doubleday, 1937.
The Infernal World of Branwell Brontë. London, Gollancz, 1960; New York, Doubleday, 1961.
Vanishing Cornwall, photographs of Christian Browning. London, Gollancz, and New York, Doubleday, 1967.
Golden Lads: Sir Francis Bacon, Anthony Bacon and Their Friends. London, Gollancz, and New York, Doubleday, 1975.
The Winding Stair: Francis Bacon, His Rise and Fall. London, Gollancz, 1976; New York, Doubleday, 1977.
Growing Pains: The Shaping of a Writer (autobiography). London, Gollancz, 1977; as *Myself When Young*, New York, Doubleday, 1977.
The Rebecca Notebook and Other Memories (includes short stories). New York, Doubleday, 1980; London, Gollancz, 1981.

Editor, *The Young George du Maurier: A Selection of His Letters 1860–1867.* London, Davies, 1951; New York, Doubleday, 1952.

Editor, *Best Stories*, by Phyllis Bottome. London, Faber, 1963.

*   *   *

Daphne du Maurier's enormous popularity can be traced in large part to extremely well-made plots, crammed with action, suspense, and mystery; she is also very adroit at capturing the atmosphere of her settings whether they be her beloved Cornwall or an imaginary but sharply rendered Italian city. Details of architecture, significant information about professions, chronicles of great historical events are combined with brief but telling identification of the flora of the area and particularly effective descriptions of weather. Frequently presented as the observations of her narrator and/or of her protagonist, these comments not only vivify the settings but also contribute to characterization.

Characterization is, in fact, of major interest in du Maurier's oeuvre. Her people seem breathtakingly vital during the course of the reading, but in retrospect are, often, almost unknowable. This seeming paradox arises from the types of personalities du Maurier explores and from the situations in which she examines them. Frequently she depicts men and women undergoing significant changes of personality and of life style, sometimes against their wills. Other characters display a startling duality of nature, seeming to some observers good and attractive, to others evil and corrupt.

Not surprisingly, the characters displaying this duality are the most fascinating. Rebecca de Winter (*Rebecca*) is known to most acquaintances as the brilliant, capable, perfect chatelaine of the family estate, but actually she leads a promiscuous, exploitative secret life. Rachel Ashley (*My Cousin Rachel*) is an even greater puzzle. She may be a loving, gentle, dreadfully unfortunate woman; she may also be a conniving fortune-hunting poisoner; du Maurier maintains that even she doesn't know the truth. Aldo Donati (*The Flight of the Falcon*) may be murderer and is certainly engaged in an alarmingly successful attempt at manipulating the students in the local university; his intentions may be noble or destructive. The action arises from other characters' attempts to understand, judge, and counter the behavior of these puzzling major figures, and in these three novels the plots are further complicated by the late maturation of the protagonist-narrators. In each instance, the action, centering on the paradoxical characters, is firmly resolved, yet the books are open-ended, for the newly emerged personalities of the protagonist-narrators are not fully dramatized, leaving the powerfully ironic conclusions deeply satisfying on one level, endlessly titillating on another.

In *The Scapegoat* du Maurier rings a change on the duality motif; the central characters, John, an indecisive Englishman, and Jean, a domineering Frenchman, represent the passive-innocent and the active-corrupt sides of one personality. It is a tribute to du Maurier's narrative skill that the improbable premise (that John can substitute for Jean in the midst of his family) proves viable, and the novel's theme, the effect of personal power upon its wielder, is neatly done. This theme is also apparent in *Hungry Hill* and *The Progress of Julius*, but each novel takes a different perspective, raises and suggests answers to slightly different questions.

Political power is a theme of some of du Maurier's historical novels—*The Glass-Blowers* (the French Revolution), *The King's General* (the Cromwellian era)—and of *Rule Britannia* (set in a U.S.-dominated future). Like *The Glass-Blowers*, *Mary Anne* and *The du Mauriers* depict the author's ancestors as well as their historical periods and are both fictional and biographical. *Jamaica Inn* and *Frenchman's Creek* highlight adventure and romance over history and are also notable because their female protagonists deny their vibrant personalities because of the men they love. Both Mary Yellan and Dona St. Columb make their decisions consciously; both know exactly what they are sacrificing, and each understands her motivations fully. The novels' thrilling climaxes leave the viability of the heroines' choices unresolved, their development unevaluated. These characters contrast sharply with the strong female protagonists of *The Loving Spirit* (like *Hungry Hill*, a family saga) and *The King's General*, women who behave consistently throughout. More contemporary settings figure in *I'll Never Be Young Again*, *The Progress of Julius*, and *The Parasites* which examine their protagonists' capacities to surmount or to be warped by personal error and cultural stress. *The House on the Strand* borders on science fiction, for its hero lives in both the present and the past. Like *Rebecca* and *Jamaica Inn*, it is a triumph of setting and mood.

Also a productive biographer, short story writer, and dramatist, Daphne du Maurier has successfully experimented with characterization and setting in her memorable novels.

—Jane S. Bakerman

DUNDY, Elaine. American. Born in New York City, in 1927. Educated at Sweet Briar College, Virginia. Married the writer Kenneth Tynan in 1951 (marriage dissolved, 1964); one daughter. Actress; worked for the BBC, London; directed the Winter Workshop of the Berkshire Festival; also journalist. Agent: Andrew Hewson, John Johnson Ltd., 45–47 Clerkenwell Green, London EC1R 0HT. Address: 570 Kings Road, London SW6 2DY, England.

PUBLICATIONS

Novels

The Dud Avocado. London, Gollancz, and New York, Dutton, 1958.
The Old Man and Me. London, Gollancz, and New York, Dutton, 1964.
The Injured Party. London, Joseph, 1974.

Uncollected Short Stories

"The Sound of a Marriage," in *Queen* (London), 1965.
"Death in the Country," in *Vogue* (New York), 1974.

Plays

My Place (produced London, 1962). London, Gollancz, 1962; New York, French, 1963.
Death in the Country, and The Drowning (produced New York, 1976).

Screenplay: *Life Sign*, 1975.

Other (biographies)

Finch, Bloody Finch (on Peter Finch). London, Joseph, and New York, Holt Rinehart, 1980.

Elvis and Gladys: The Genesis of the King (on Elvis Presley). New York, Macmillan, and London, Weidenfeld and Nicolson, 1985.

*   *   *

In *The Dud Avocado* and *The Old Man and Me*, Elaine Dundy employs first-person, reflective narrators who self-consciously and self-indulgently record and evaluate their experiences in Paris and Soho. The narrators relate their stories in a candid, energetic, witty style, spiced with parenthetical revelations, word association games, and sensory impressions. Their language is often the jargon of the Beat-hipster: audacious, flippant, nervous, saucy. Their tone is the good-humored self-mockery of the cocktail party confession, the stage whisper, the open diary. The narrators are deliberate storytellers, replaying moments from their pasts, exposing their naivety and limitations, and benefiting from hindsight.

Sally Jay in *The Dud Avocado* is the contemporary American innocent abroad, superficially hip to the decadent Left Bank and "running for her life." Caught in the ambiguity between naivety and sophistication, she is in pursuit of "freedom" and the ability "to be so sharp that I'll always be able to guess right . . . on the wing." She expends her time and innocence in a disorganized, impulsive debauch with the avant-garde of Paris.

Through a series of wrong guesses, she eventually is schooled in the ways of the world. The glamorous, daring, free world of Paris is revealed as pretentious, opportunistic, grotesque. Her romantic vision of the rebellious life is destroyed when she understands that her would-be lover is a pimp and that her life in Paris has exposed her to "too much prostitution." She declares herself a dud avocado—a seed without life potential.

In flight to Hollywood, the narrator confronts her runaway life strategy and determines that some "unrunning" is called for to "[lay] the ghost once and for all." She seeks out the role of librarian and schools herself in cynicism until she recognizes the life which she wishes to embrace. Giddy with optimism, she accepts the love and marriage proposal of a famous photographer and embarks on a new life with "an entirely new passport," the new self emerging from the old like the growth of an avocado seedling from the stone of the old fruit: "It's zymotic!" The narrator survives her initiation experience ready to "Make voyages. Attempt them. That's all there is."

Betsy Lou in *The Old Man and Me* is older and more experienced than Sally Jay, but like Sally Jay, she is on a quest which leads to greater self-knowledge. Motivated by puerile revenge, she journeys to London to recover her "stolen" inheritance from C.D. McKee. As his unknown heir, she plans to hasten the recovery of her money by any means necessary—lying, cheating, masquerading, or attempting murder. She partially achieves her declared end, and in the process realizes her injustice to those in her past, the reasons for the loss of her father's love, and her love for C.D. despite his age and possession of her money. Thus she corrects her mistaken view of her past and sees the futility of trying to salve emotional loss with money.

Betsy Lou's relationship to C.D. is never linear and controllable. The very complexity of the relationship betrays her ambiguity over her past, her present motives, and her unconscious needs. She loves/hates him, recognizes that he is/is not a father figure, accepts/rejects him as teacher, is repulsed/excited by his lust, and wishes him dead/fears for his life. This confusion drives her to abandonment in jazz, drink, dope, and sex, which results in C.D.'s collapse and her self-confrontation and confession.

Betsy Lou's declaration of her identity, her deceit, and her desire for C.D. comes too late. He rejects the contrite Betsy Lou, gives her fifty percent of her money, and leaves her with the advice that she "use it. See its power to corrupt or save . . . Learn from our stupidities." She is left with what she initially wanted "only . . . because it was mine."

In both novels the narrators are left at the point of departure. For Sally Jay the future appears glorious with possibility. She sees her new life as "the end. The end. The last word." However, the author implies that Sally Jay has ended one cycle of learning experiences and is beginning another with her marriage. One is reminded of Stefan's description of the Typical American Girl as the avocado, "So green—so eternally green." She has experienced growth and is more worldly wise, but her final pronouncement indicates that her maturation is not complete. The process has just begun. Similarly, Betsy Lou is left facing her future. She hasn't Sally Jay's confidence of joy, but rather experiences a sense of unreality. She has no delusions about the future, and the past "seems (to) never really (have) happened." She is no longer directed by spurious monetary goals; instead she suffers the bewilderment of a hollow victory. Thus, while both narrators experience an epiphany, that moment of awareness is tinged with irony.

Elaine Dundy is an entertaining novelist who rehearses the familiar theme of initiation with adeptness and flair. However, her craftsmanship and energy do not always compensate for her characters' lack of psychological depth nor for her rather formulaic situations. Her novels do not provoke new or refined insights, but they do provide moments of engaging and refreshing humor.

—Deborah Duckworth

DUNN, Nell (Mary). British. Born in London, in 1936. Educated at a convent school. Married the writer Jeremy Sandford in 1956; three children. Recipient: Rhys Memorial Prize, 1964; Susan Smith Blackburn Prize, for play, 1981; London *Standard* award, for play, 1982. Address: 10 Bell Lane, Twickenham, Middlesex, England.

PUBLICATIONS

Novels

Poor Cow. London, MacGibbon and Kee, and New York, Doubleday, 1967.
The Incurable. London, Cape, and New York, Doubleday, 1971.
I Want, with Adrian Henri. London, Cape, 1972.
Tear His Head off His Shoulders. London, Cape, 1974; New York, Doubleday, 1975.
The Only Child: A Simple Story of Heaven and Hell. London, Cape, 1978.

Short Stories

Up the Junction. London, MacGibbon and Kee, 1963; Philadelphia, Lippincott, 1966.

Plays

Steaming (produced London, 1981; New York, 1982).

Ambergate, Derbyshire, Amber Lane Press, 1981; New York, Limelight, 1984.
Sketches, in *Variety Night* (produced London, 1982).

Screenplay: *Poor Cow*, with Ken Loach, 1967.

Television Play: *Up the Junction*, from her own stories, 1965.

Other

Talking to Women. London, MacGibbon and Kee, 1965.
Freddy Gets Married (for children). London, MacGibbon and Kee, 1969.

Editor, *Living Like I Do.* London, Futura, 1977; as *Different Drummers*, New York, Harcourt Brace, 1977.

*   *   *

Nell Dunn begins with vignettes or fragmental episodes to build a picture of British urban life. Much like Charles Dickens, with his newspaper sketches and small portraits of London street life, she began her career with a set of brilliant realistic snapshots of the mod world. In *Up the Junction* she collected these sketches, which in effect are much like the 17th-century Theophrastan "character." They deal primarily with young working-class Britons in their milieu, incised in photographic reportage, built on their dialect, street signs, bits of popular music, the clichés and repetitious folk-wisdom of ghetto life. The feeling for the nagging, obstinate details of daily life is very strong—the sketches demonstrate how complex yet unrewarding most of these lives can be.

In *Poor Cow* Dunn develops the same method of terse, richly detailed sketches into a more unified form, a novel centering on the life of one young woman. Ironically named Joy, she becomes a "poor cow" through the constant erosion of her life. At 22 she has gone through one luckless marriage, and her life moves centrifugally around Jonny, her son. Joy drifts into casual prostitution, random affairs with anchorless men. She worries constantly about her looks, her body, her sexual responsiveness, the prospects of aging. Life is intractable, and wishes evaporate in the face of simple necessities. Joy's role as a mother is a transference of her egocentrism to Jonny, as an extension of her former hopes for herself. Her own life has run down a blind alley, but her son's life may be different. As she clings to Jonny, Joy invents a bitter epitaph for her youth: "To think when I was a kid I planned to conquer the world and if anyone saw me now they'd say, 'She's had a rough night, poor cow.' "

A vision of the confusion and oppressiveness of modern life is extended in *The Incurable*, which deals with a middle-class woman, Maro, whose life collapses in crisis. Maro's husband develops multiple sclerosis, and her formerly orderly and manageable existence is destroyed. She falls into a state of anomie which, like her husband's progressive disease, eats up her life. She too is "incurable," although her malaise is mental and spiritual. Her children's cannibalistic demands and the relentless pressure of everyday routine erode her will and energy: "She felt like some country that had been oppressed for a long time and was slowly rising up and throwing over its oppressors. She was making a revolution but the bloodshed was horrifying and how many lives would be lost and when was it going to end and would she ever make the country of the free spirits?"

Tear His Head off His Shoulders is another set of related vignettes and episodes in the lives of women. The narrative revolves around the sexual obsessions and conflicts of women, viewed in retrospect. The vernacular style and the complex combination of nostalgia and revulsion give a bittersweet flavor to the work. A strong "fascination of the abomination" feeling makes the stories of sexual compulsion convincing.

In *The Only Child* Dunn constructs a novel again focused on sexual obsession and possessiveness—of a mother for her son. We follow Esther Lafonte through Dunn's careful sensual details as she drifts from her over-comfortable marriage to a search for her identity—sexual and spiritual—in her 19-year-old son, Piers. At one point she speaks for all of Dunn's lost women: "I want to get in, I want to be somebody, I have a feeling that I could have done very much more with my life, that I could be doing more now, I want to be a part of things."

Nell Dunn's special province is the mind and spirit of the beleaguered woman—a view from the "oppressed country" of the woman trapped by circumstances. The vignettes she presents deal with developing sexuality, the allure of the pop world, the deadly immobility of domestic responsibilities. Her recent fiction extends this vision to the perimeters of middle-class life.

—William J. Schafer

DURRELL, Lawrence (George). British. Born in Julundur, India, 27 February 1912. Educated at the College of St. Joseph, Darjeeling, India; St. Edmund's School, Canterbury, Kent. Married 1) Nancy Myers in 1935 (divorced, 1947); 2) Eve Cohen in 1947 (divorced 1961 (died, 1967); 3) Claude Durrell in 1961 (died, 1967); 4) Ghislaine de Boysson in 1973 (divorced, 1979); two daughters. Has had many jobs, including jazz pianist (Blue Peter nightclub, London), automobile racer, and real estate agent. Lived in Corfu, 1934–40. Editor, with Henry Miller and Alfred Perlès, *The Booster* (later *Delta*), Paris, 1937–39; columnist, *Egyptian Gazette*, Cairo, 1941; editor, with Robin Fedden and Bernard Spencer, *Personal Landscape*, Cairo, 1942–45; special correspondent in Cyprus for *The Economist*, London, 1953–55; editor, *Cyprus Review*, Nicosia, 1954–55. Taught at the British Institute, Kalamata, Greece, 1940. Foreign Service Press Officer, British Information Office, Cairo, 1941–44; press attaché, British Information Office, Alexandria, 1944–45; Director of Public Relations for the Dodecanese Islands, Greece, 1946–47; Director of the British Council Institute, Cordoba, Argentina, 1947–48; press attaché, British Legation, Belgrade, 1949–52; Director of Public Relations for the British Government in Cyprus, 1954–56. Andrew Mellon Visiting Professor of Humanities, California Institute of Technology, Pasadena, 1974. Has lived in France since 1957. Recipient: Duff Cooper Memorial Prize, 1957; Foreign Book Prize (France), 1959; James Tait Black Memorial Prize, 1975; Fellow, Royal Society of Literature, 1954. Address: c/o Grindlay's Bank, 13 St. James's Square, London SW1Y 4LF, England.

PUBLICATIONS

Novels

Pied Piper of Lovers. London, Cassell, 1935.
Panic Spring (as Charles Norden). London, Faber, and New York, Covici Friede, 1937.

The Black Book: An Agon. Paris, Obelisk Press, 1938; New York, Dutton, 1960; London, Faber, 1973.
Cefalû. London, Editions Poetry London, 1947; as *The Dark Labyrinth*, London, Ace, 1958; New York, Dutton, 1962.
The Alexandria Quartet. London, Faber, and New York, Dutton, 1962.
   Justine. London, Faber, and New York, Dutton, 1957.
   Balthazar. London, Faber, and New York, Dutton, 1958.
   Mountolive. London, Faber, and New York, Dutton, 1958.
   Clea. London, Faber, and New York, Dutton, 1960.
White Eagles over Serbia. London, Faber, and New York, Criterion, 1957.
The Revolt of Aphrodite. London, Faber, 1974.
   Tunc. London, Faber, and New York, Dutton, 1968.
   Nunquam. London, Faber, and New York, Dutton, 1970.
The Avignon Quincunx:
   Monsieur; or, The Prince of Darkness. London, Faber, and New York, Viking Press, 1974.
   Livia; or, Buried Alive. London, Faber, 1978; New York, Viking Press, 1979.
   Constance; or, Solitary Practices. London, Faber, and New York, Viking Press, 1982.
   Sebastian; or, Ruling Passions. London, Faber, 1983; New York, Viking, 1984.
   Quinx; or, The Ripper's Tale. London, Faber, and New York, Viking, 1985.

Short Stories

Zero, and Asylum in the Snow. Privately printed, 1946; as *Two Excursions into Reality*, Berkeley, California, Circle, 1947.
Esprit de Corps: Sketches from Diplomatic Life. London, Faber, 1957; New York, Dutton, 1959.
Stiff Upper Lip: Life among the Diplomats. London, Faber, 1958; New York, Dutton, 1959.
Sauve Qui Peut. London, Faber, 1966; New York, Dutton, 1967.
The Best of Antrobus. London, Faber, 1974.
Antrobus Complete. London, Faber, 1985.

Plays

Sappho: A Play in Verse (produced Hamburg, 1959; Edinburgh, 1961; Evanston, Illinois, 1964). London, Faber, 1950; New York, Dutton, 1958.
Acte (produced Hamburg, 1961). London, Faber, 1964; New York, Dutton, 1965.
An Irish Faustus: A Morality in Nine Scenes (produced Hamburg, 1963). London, Faber, 1963; New York, Dutton, 1964.
Judith (shortened version of screenplay), in *Woman's Own* (London), 26 February–2 April 1966.

Screenplays: *Cleopatra*, with others, 1963; *Judith*, with others, 1966.

Radio Script: *Greek Peasant Superstitions*, 1947.

Television Scripts: *The Lonely Roads*, with Diane Deriaz, 1970; *The Alexandrians*, 1970; *The Search for Ulysses* (Canada); *Spirit of Place: Lawrence Durrell's Greece*, 1976, and *Lawrence Durrell's Egypt*, 1978.

Recordings: *The Love Poems*, Spoken Arts; *Ulysses Come Back: Sketch for a Musical* (story, music, and lyrics by Durrell), Turret Records, 1970.

Verse

Quaint Fragment: Poems Written Between the Ages of Sixteen and Nineteen. London, Cecil Press, 1931.
Ten Poems. London, Caduceus Press, 1932.
Ballade of Slow Decay. Privately printed, 1932.
Bromo Bombastes: A Fragment from a Laconic Drama by Gaffer Peeslake. London, Caduceus Press, 1933.
Transition. London, Caduceus Press, 1934.
Mass for the Old Year. Privately printed, 1935.
Proems: An Anthology of Poems, with others, edited by Oswald Blakeston. London, Fortune Press, 1938.
A Private Country. London, Faber, 1943.
The Parthenon: For T.S. Eliot. Privately printed, 1945 (?).
Cities, Plains, and People. London, Faber, 1946.
On Seeming to Presume. London, Faber, 1948.
A Landmark Gone. Privately printed, 1949.
Deus Loci. Ischia, Italy, Di Maio Vito, 1950.
Private Drafts. Nicosia, Cyprus, Proodos Press, 1955.
The Tree of Idleness and Other Poems. London, Faber, 1955.
Selected Poems. London, Faber, and New York, Grove Press, 1956.
Collected Poems. London, Faber, 1960; revised edition, Faber, and New York, Dutton, 1968.
Penguin Modern Poets 1, with Elizabeth Jennings and R.S. Thomas. London, Penguin, 1962.
The Poetry of Lawrence Durrell. New York, Dutton, 1962.
Beccaffico/Le Becfigue (English, with French translation by F.-J. Temple). Montpellier, France, La Licorne, 1963.
A Persian Lady. Edinburgh, Tragara Press, 1963.
Selected Poems 1935–1963. London, Faber, 1964.
The Ikons and Other Poems. London, Faber, 1966; New York, Dutton, 1967.
Faustus: A Poem. Privately printed, 1970.
The Red Limbo Lingo: A Poetry Notebook. London, Faber, and New York, Dutton, 1971.
On the Suchness of the Old Boy. London, Turret, 1972.
Vega and Other Poems. London, Faber, and Woodstock, New York, Overlook Press, 1973.
Lifelines. Edinburgh, Tragara Press, 1974.
Selected Poems, edited by Alan Ross. London, Faber, 1977.
Collected Poems 1931–1974, edited by James A. Brigham. London, Faber, and New York, Viking Press, 1980.

Published Lyrics (music by T.W. Southam): *Walking in My Sleep* (as Larry Dell), Athens, Gaetanos, 1945; *Nemea*, London, Augener, 1950; *Lesbos*, London, Oxford University Press, 1967; *Nothing Is Lost, Sweet Self*, London, Turret, 1967.

Other

Prospero's Cell: A Guide to the Landscape and Manners of the Island of Corcyra. London, Faber, 1945; with *Reflections on a Marine Venus*, New York, Dutton, 1960.
Key to Modern Poetry. London, Peter Nevill, 1952; as *A Key to Modern British Poetry*, Norman, University of Oklahoma Press, 1952.
Reflections on a Marine Venus: A Companion to the Landscape of Rhodes. London, Faber, 1953; with *Prospero's Cell*, New York, Dutton, 1960.
Bitter Lemons (on Cyprus). London, Faber, 1957; New York, Dutton, 1958.
Art and Outrage: A Correspondence about Henry Miller Between Alfred Perlès and Lawrence Durrell, with an Intermission by Henry Miller. London, Putnam, 1959; New York, Dutton, 1961.

Groddeck (on Georg Walther Groddeck). Wiesbaden, Limes, 1961.
Briefwechsel über "Actis", with Gustaf Gründgens. Hamburg, Rowohlt, 1961.
Lawrence Durrell and Henry Miller: A Private Correspondence, edited by George Wickes. New York, Dutton, and London, Faber, 1963.
La Descente du Styx (English, with French translation by F.-J. Temple). Montpellier, France, La Murène, 1964; as *Down the Styx*, Santa Barbara, California, Capricorn Press, 1971.
Spirit of Place: Letters and Essays on Travel, edited by Alan G. Thomas. London, Faber, and New York, Dutton, 1969.
Le Grand Suppositoire (interview with Marc Alyn). Paris, Belfond, 1972; as *The Big Supposer*, London, Abelard Schuman, 1973; New York, Grove Press, 1975.
The Happy Rock (on Henry Miller). London, Village Press, 1973; Belfast, Maine, Bern Porter, 1982.
The Plant-Magic Man. Santa Barbara, California, Capra Press, 1973.
Blue Thirst. Santa Barbara, California, Capra Press, 1975.
Sicilian Carousel. London, Faber, and New York, Viking Press, 1977.
The Greek Islands. London, Faber, and New York Viking Press, 1978.
A Smile in the Mind's Eye. London, Wildwood House, 1980; New York, Universe, 1982.
Literary Lifelines: The Richard Aldington-Lawrence Durrell Correspondence, edited by Harry T. Moore and Ian S. MacNiven. New York, Viking Press, and London, Faber, 1981.

Editor, with Robin Fedden and Bernard Spencer, *Personal Landscape: An Anthology of Exile.* London, Editions Poetry London, 1945.
Editor, *A Henry Miller Reader.* New York, New Directions, 1959; as *The Best of Henry Miller*, London, Heinemann, 1960.
Editor, *New Poems 1963.* London, Hutchinson, 1963.
Editor, *Poems*, by Wordsworth. London, Penguin, 1972.

Translator, *Six Poems from the Greek of Sekilianos and Seferis.* Privately printed, 1946.
Translator, with Bernard Spencer and Nanos Valaoritis, *The King of Asine and Other Poems*, by George Seferis. London, Lehmann, 1948.
Translator, *The Curious History of Pope Joan*, by Emmanuel Royidis. London, Verschoyle, 1954; revised edition, as *Pope Joan: A Romantic Biography*, London, Deutsch, 1960; New York, Dutton, 1961.
Translator, with others, *Selected Poems*, by Alain Bosquet. Athens, Ohio University Press, 1973.
Translator, *Three Poems of Cavafy.* Edinburgh, Tragara Press, 1980.

*

Bibliography: *Lawrence Durrell: An Illustrated Checklist* by Alan G. Thomas and James A. Brigham, Carbondale, Southern Illinois University Press, 1983.

Manuscript Collections: University of California, Los Angeles; University of Illinois, Urbana.

Critical Studies: *The World of Lawrence Durrell* edited by Harry T. Moore, Carbondale, Southern Illinois University Press, 1962; *Lawrence Durrell* by John Unterecker, New York, Columbia University Press, 1964; *Lawrence Durrell* by John

A. Weigel, New York, Twayne, 1965; *Lawrence Durrell: A Study* (includes bibliography by Alan G. Thomas), London, Faber, 1968, New York, Dutton, 1969, revised edition, Faber, 1973, and *Lawrence Durrell*, London, Longman, 1970, both by G.S. Fraser; *Sensation, Vision, and Imagination: The Problem of Unity in Lawrence Durrell's Novels* by Hartwig Isernhagen, Bamberg, Rodenbusch, 1969; *Art for Love's Sake: Lawrence Durrell and The Alexandria Quartet* by Alan Warren Friedman, Norman, University of Oklahoma Press, 1970, and *Critical Essays on Lawrence Durrell* edited by Friedman, Boston, Hall, 1986; *Alexandria Still: Forster, Durrell, and Cavafy* by Jane Lagoudis Pinchin, Princeton, New Jersey, Princeton University Press, 1977; *Deus Loci: Lawrence Durrell Newsletter* (Kelowna, British Columbia), since 1977; *The Muse of Science and The Alexandria Quartet* by Walter G. Creed, Norwood, Pennsylvania, Norwood Editions, 1977; "Lawrence Durrell Issue" of *Labrys 5* (London), 1979.

*   *   *

Prolific since writing his first novel, *Pied Piper of Lovers* (1935), Lawrence Durrell suddenly achieved commercial and critical success with *The Alexandria Quartet* in the late 1950's. Though protean and eclectic, Durrell displays a consistency of concerns and techniques: a lush, baroque style; a rich patterning of ideas (about personal relationships, politics, mysticism, relativity, etc.) and ideas about ideas; a multidimensional universe and vision transcending temporal and spatial barriers; an aesthetic dependent on personal mythos, on felt reality, on narrative perspectives and deceptions, on the interplay of art, love, and death. Also central to Durrell's writing are a sense of deracination and a concomitant need to belong somewhere (perhaps his most revealing book is a collection entitled *Spirit of Place*); for, like most placeless men, Durrell worships place: his landscapes embody, parallel, even motivate and control the workings of his characters. Their individuality seems often suffused, subordinated to some *deus loci*—as, on the largest scale, Alexandria dominates the *Quartet*: "Only the city is real." Durrell's writing is pervaded by the evanescent glow of place that functions as central metaphor, as touchstone, for the individual maturing into meaningful human involvement. Further, Durrell's early fiction, poetry, verse plays, and island books all anticipate the *Quartet's* theme of isolation and the individual's attaining full potential in both art and life only through total, active commitment to the creative process: art for love's sake. Thus, Justine associates work with love; Mountolive's failures in love are correlatives of his hating his work; Darley and Clea become lovers and artists only after long struggle. Most of Durrell's successful protagonists create an internal deity of selfhood, an analogue of the external *deus loci*.

In both *The Black Book* and *The Revolt of Aphrodite* demonically named protagonists reach beyond defining constrictions toward freedom and creativity. In *The Black Book* Lawrence Lucifer struggles to escape the spiritual sterility embodied by smug, dying England; he finally emerges into creative affirmation symbolized by Greece's warmth, color, and fertility. The book's style, like that of the contemporaneous *Zero, and Asylum in the Snow*, anticipates that of the *Quartet*, for its rich interweaving of naturalistic and poetic narratives transforms language into something fluid, unstructured, atemporal. In *Revolt*—a satire on science fiction, gothic, romantic, and business exposé novels—a master inventor, Felix Charlock, becomes ensnared in the international cartel, Merlin. He sells, and sells out, his work; love consequently becomes horrific, for, in Durrell, to deny the validity of one's work is to negate love. Charlock's ultimate task is to fashion an exact, "living"

replica of the beautiful Greek Io, deceased ex-prostitute and world-famous actress. But the wholly successful product (able even to copulate) cannot bear the world's reality and climactically "commits suicide."

Both *Revolt* and the recently completed five-volume novel, *The Avignon Quincunx* provoke comparisons with the earlier work. They too offer exotic settings peopled by improbable characters; multiple fictional and narrative layerings; a mixing of memory and desire in the meeting of retrospective and quest narrative structures; extensive mythical and metaphysical speculation on the nature of the universe and its creator, on the ego and personality, on the enterprises of being, becoming, and creating; a harsh critique of Western civilization and values; and an erotically charged prose style whose evocations and allusions overtly echo and invoke the *Quartet*. The underlying conception of the *Quincunx* derives from an ancient mystical design formed by placing one object, usually a tree, at each corner of a square and one at the center, like a five on a die. The figure forms an X (Roman numeral for ten), so the five objects magically double themselves. Further, the figure may be rotated to produce a circle, the geometrical sign of perfection; and, as a form of the Greek cross, it has come to symbolize Christ. Understandably, then, the quincunx is traditionally seen as having spiritual properties.

Durrell's Avignon series exploits the properties of the quincunx both in its five-part structure and in its thematic allusions to the Knights Templar, the richest and most powerful military force in Europe until the early 14th century. At that time, King Philip of France and Pope Clement V conspired to destroy them for motives that are not entirely clear: out of fear of their power, independence, and perhaps heterodoxy, out of a desire to seize their wealth, or perhaps both. In the event, the Knights Templar, for reasons never satisfactorily explained by historians, surrendered without a struggle, and no treasure was ever found. According to the legend Durrell evokes, the still lost treasure—which, depending on the version, is either a great cache of gold or the Holy Grail—is buried at the center of a quincunx located near Avignon, the home of Pope Clement during the schism with Rome. Durrell conceives of Hitler as seeking the treasure in order to establish a new knightly order on it and, thus, insure victory and world domination. At the climax of *Quinx*, the *Quincunx*'s final book, Durrell's surviving characters gather after the war at the Pont du Gard, the ancient Roman aqueduct outside of Avignon, to unearth neither gold nor Grail but, as at the end of the *Quartet*, the possibility of beginning anew.

In Durrell character becomes, in effect, anti-character: less imposing itself upon its surroundings than imposed upon, will-less, embodying Keats's notion of "negative capability" that is requisite for the creative act to occur. Durrell's fiction denies such conventional distinctions as those between major and minor characters, main and subplots, protagonist and antagonist. Every character becomes an independent fountainhead of actions multiplying in meaning and consequence. For Durrell, what man knows remains elusive, incessantly becoming; most of his survivors ultimately flee inhospitable surroundings and, as many of his poems suggest, seek meaning and selfhood in more conducive landscape and language. Durrell's series of island books most successfully represents his love of place, of landscape corresponding and responding to man's needs and proportions. Pre-war Corfu, war-devastated Rhodes, the incipient civil war of Cyprus, and the invader-dominated Sicily are all concomitants of failures in art and love. Yet the permanence and strength of Durrell's Mediterranean pattern undergird and inspirit his island books, making them not only fine travel reportage but also extended prose-poems.

All four books of the *Quartet* climax in death—which is almost always equivocal, other than what it seems. Durrell, among the most death-haunted and self-reflexive of contemporary novelists, is obsessed with death's creative, vitalizing power. In the *Quartet*, which was entitled "The Book of the Dead" during its genesis, death is incident, theme, motif, character, and setting. In Alexandria, city of death, virtually all its inhabitants, like those in *The Black Book*, are dead and kicking from the first. They are "playing-card characters of the living," shades partaking of the city's "obsessive rhythms of death." When Darley, the main narrator and maturing writer and lover, returns, it is "like a summons back to the Underworld," for "the dead are everywhere," he says.

Numerous characters disappear, then re-emerge in altered form. Chief among them is Pursewarden, Durrell's speaker for artistic vision and dedication *despite* his being a suicide of apparently minor significance in *Justine*. Pursewarden's death is equivocal because much of the *Quartet* attempts in various ways to explain its motivation; because large chunks of his posthumous papers are included and many characters quote him verbatim; and because he embodies the central themes of art, love, and death, as well as the *Quartet*'s ultimate focus on "resurrection from the dead." And so one character dies for another, a third apparently dies but returns after another is buried for him; one is resurrected as a saint, others as characters who seemed someone else, or they grow new parts to replace worn out ones.

Discussing the differences between Victorianism and modernism, Durrell in *Key to Modern Poetry* provides a "key" to himself. He maintains that human possibility, personality, values, validity, and time were transformed by Darwin, Einstein, and Freud, among others. Certainty's rock foundation has revealed itself as restive sand blown by winds of pluralism, relativity, subjectivity, indeterminacy. Like other impressionist novels, the *Quartet* dramatizes a limited narrator who seeks to understand a complex sequence of events. Yet truth's core remains forever elusive; everything is susceptible of, and receives, contradictory interpretations. In such novels the more "facts" we learn, the less significant they become; not despite but because *Mountolive* tells us most, depicts an "objective" reality, it says least about truth itself, the essence of reality captured, if anywhere, in the heart and mind of the interpreter. An early poem, "Eight Aspects of Melissa" (1946), anticipates the central devices of the *Quartet*—mirrors, prisms, lake water —and expresses Durrell's continuing concern with multifaceted personality, love, landscape, time. Both "Melissa" and the *Quartet*, like virtually all of Durrell's writings, are open-ended, implying that all aspects examined are equally valuable and that an indeterminate number of additional aspects await the seeker after truth. Neither pretends to exhaust the many questions it raises; each answer contains both additional questions and a proliferating chain of "truths." The open-endedness of the *Quartet* and the *Quincunx* suggests not that all has been arranged but that, past and present having somehow accommodated themselves to each other, the future can begin to begin. Pathways now exist where there had seemed only dead ends. With "Once upon a time . . ."—the ending of the *Quartet*—all avenues are open; no visionary world of man's imagination remains artificially precluded. At least for the moment—and therefore for all time, since each moment contains all time— impeding checks are removed; art and life are dynamically possible.

Durrell does not claim mastery of Einsteinian relativity or Freudian psychology, but he recognizes their radical influence upon literature; ranging widely, he has made uniquely his own and his art's all he has read and experienced. His finest achievement, despite much successful poetry, drama, and travel books, lies in experimental fiction. For like this century's supreme novelists, Durrell seeks both to create art of lasting significance and to proclaim new modes of thought, new ways of envisaging a world he too has helped imagine. He has assisted in our becoming what he says we must: our own contemporaries.

—Alan Warren Friedman

DUTTON, Geoffrey (Piers Henry). Australian. Born in Anlaby, South Australia, 2 August 1922. Educated at Geelong Grammar School, Victoria, 1932–39; University of Adelaide, 1940–41; Magdalen College, Oxford, 1946–49, B.A. 1949. Served in the Royal Australian Air Force, 1941–45: Flight Lieutenant. Married 1) Ninette Trott in 1944 (divorced, 1985), two sons and one daughter; 2) Robin Lucas in 1985. Senior Lecturer in English, University of Adelaide, 1954–62; Commonwealth Fellow in Australian Literature, University of Leeds, 1960; Visiting Professor, Kansas State University, Manhattan, 1962. Editor, Penguin Australia, Melbourne, 1961–65, and *Bulletin Literary Supplement*, Sydney, 1980–84. Since 1965, editorial director, Sun Books Pty. Ltd., Melbourne; since 1985, editor, *The Australian*, Sydney. Co-founder, *Australian Letters*, Adelaide, 1957, and *Australian Book Review*, Kensington Park, 1962. Member, Australian Council for the Arts, 1968–70, Commonwealth Literary Fund Advisory Board, 1972–73, and Australian Literature Board, 1973–78. Recipient: Grace Leven Prize, 1959. Officer, Order of Australia, 1976. Agent: Curtis Brown (Australia) Pty. Ltd., 27 Union Street, Paddington, New South Wales 2021. Address: 53 Regent Street, Paddington, New South Wales 2021, Australia.

PUBLICATIONS

Novels

The Mortal and the Marble. London, Chapman and Hall, 1950.
Andy. Sydney and London, Collins, 1968.
Tamara. Sydney and London, Collins, 1970.
Queen Emma of the South Seas. Melbourne and London, Macmillan, 1976; New York, St. Martin's Press, 1978.
The Eye-Opener. St. Lucia, University of Queensland Press, 1982.

Short Stories

The Wedge-Tailed Eagle. Melbourne, Macmillan, 1980.

Verse

Night Flight and Sunrise. Melbourne, Reed and Harris, 1944.
Antipodes in Shoes. Sydney, Edwards and Shaw, 1955.
Flowers and Fury. Melbourne, Cheshire, 1963.
On My Island: Poems for Children. Melbourne, Cheshire, 1967.
Poems Soft and Loud. Melbourne, Cheshire, 1968.
Findings and Keepings: Selected Poems 1940–1970. Adelaide, Australian Letters, 1970.
New Poems to 1972. Adelaide, Australian Letters, 1974.
A Body of Words. Sydney, Edwards and Shaw, 1977.

Selective Affinities. Sydney, Angus and Robertson, 1985.

Other

A Long Way South (travel). London, Chapman and Hall, 1953.
Africa in Black and White. London, Chapman and Hall, 1956.
States of the Union (travel). London, Chapman and Hall, 1958.
Founder of a City: The Life of William Light. Melbourne, Cheshire, and London, Chapman and Hall, 1960.
Patrick White. Melbourne, Lansdowne Press, 1961; revised edition, London and New York, Oxford University Press, 1971.
Walt Whitman. Edinburgh, Oliver and Boyd, and New York, Grove Press, 1961.
Paintings of S. T. Gill. Adelaide, Rigby, 1962.
Russell Drysdale (art criticism). London, Thames and Hudson, 1962; revised edition, as *Russell Drysdale: A Biographical and Critical Study*, Sydney and London, Angus and Robertson, 1981.
Tisi and the Yabby (for children). Sydney and London, Collins, 1965.
Seal Bay (for children). Sydney and London, Collins, 1966.
The Hero as Murderer: The Life of Edward John Eyre, Australian Explorer and Governor of Jamaica, 1815–1901. Melbourne, Cheshire, and London, Collins, 1967.
Tisi and the Pageant (for children). Adelaide, Rigby, 1968.
Australia's Last Explorer: Ernest Giles. London, Faber, 1970.
Australia since the Camera: From Federation to War 1901–14. Melbourne, Cheshire, 1972.
White on Black: The Australian Aborigine Portrayed in Art. Melbourne, Macmillan, 1974.
A Taste of History: Geoffrey Dutton's South Australia. Adelaide, Rigby, 1978.
Patterns of Australia, photographs by Harri Peccinotti. Melbourne, Macmillan, 1980; London, Macmillan, 1981.
Impressions of Singapore, photographs by Harri Peccinotti. Melbourne and London, Macmillan, 1981.
S. T. Gill's Australia. Melbourne, Macmillan, 1981.
The Australian Heroes. Sydney, Angus and Robertson, 1981; London, Angus and Robertson, 1982.
The Prowler (for children). Sydney, Collins, 1982.
Country Life in Old Australia. South Yarra, Victoria, O'Neill, 1982.
In Search of Edward John Eyre. Melbourne, Macmillan, 1982.
Snow on the Saltbush. Ringwood, Victoria, Viking, 1984.
The Australian Collection (100 classic Australian books). Sydney, Angus and Robertson, 1985.
The Beach. Melbourne, Oxford University Press, 1985.
The Squatters. South Yarra, Victoria, O'Neill, 1985.

Editor, *The Literature of Australia*. Melbourne, Penguin, 1964; revised edition, 1976.
Editor, *Modern Australian Writing*. London, Fontana, 1966.
Editor, *Australia and the Monarchy: A Symposium*. Melbourne, Sun, 1966.
Editor, with Max Harris, *The Vital Decade: 10 Years of Australian Art and Letters*. Melbourne, Sun, 1968.
Editor, with Max Harris, *Sir Henry Bjelke, Don Baby, and Friends*. Melbourne, Sun, 1971.
Editor, *Republican Australia?* Melbourne, Sun, 1977.

Translator, with Igor Mezhakoff-Koriakin, *Bratsk Station*, by Yevgeny Yevtushenko. Melbourne, Sun, 1966; New York, Doubleday, 1967; London, Hart Davis, 1968.

Translator, with Igor Mezhakoff-Koriakin, *Fever and Other New Poems*, by Bella Akhmadulina. Melbourne, Sun, 1968; New York, Morrow, 1969; London, Owen, 1970.
Translator, with Igor Mezhakoff-Koriakin, *Little Woods: Recent Poems*, by Andrei Voznesensky. Melbourne, Sun, 1972.
Translator, *Kazan University and Other New Poems*, by Yevgeny Yevtushenko. Melbourne, Sun, 1973.

*

Geoffrey Dutton comments:

(1972) My three novels, although completely different in characters and in settings, have all basically dealt with the same theme, that of Australian innocence as against the experience of "older" countries. In more detail, *The Mortal and the Marble* deals with the impact of European migrants on Australia after the second world war; *Andy* with the idiocy of war, especially in a country on whose soil it is never fought; *Tamara* with the impact on an intelligent but relatively unsophisticated Australian scientist of the complex world of Soviet Russian poetry.

(1986) *Queen Emma of the South Seas*, a fictionalized account of an historical figure, deals with Emma Coe, a Samoan-American, who in the late 19th century from a trading-post in what became German New Guinea established a commercial empire in the South-West Pacific. *The Eye-Opener* is a satirical novel about two confidence-men and the Adelaide Festival of Arts.

*   *   *

Geoffrey Dutton's reputation is that of an accomplished all-round man of letters—poet and critic, biographer and cultural historian, publisher, editor, and journalist—and his entertaining novels contribute to this general reputation. Although they vary widely in their settings and development, the four novels have some structural similarities, and all are concerned with conflicts between local and European values, individual freedom and social restriction, and the natural and the civilized worlds.

His first novel, *The Mortal and the Marble*, reveals its period by exhibiting what the Australian critic A.A. Phillips has called the "cultural cringe." With an eye on the overseas market, it explains local folkways in the obtrusive way that has characterized "colonial novels" for over a century, and even such hallowed clichés as the incongruity of eating Christmas pudding in the middle of summer find their place. The theme of the novel is Mark Vaughan's ambivalence towards two conflicting sets of values—the traditional culture of Europe he has never seen and the material comfort and natural beauty of his own "uncultured" country. And, the reader feels, *The Mortal and the Marble* is itself the author's attempt to resolve a similar conflict between his own "literary" notions of the novel and the incongruous, because "unliterary," actuality of his experiences in Australia.

Dutton attempts not only to work out dramatically the concern of the Australian novelist who feels his "complex fate" but also a more fundamental theme. As well as the encounters between the Vaughans and such representatives of European culture (and of the post-World War II immigration to Australia) as their Russian friend Alexey and the Germans Paul, Willi, and Professor Klein, there is contrast between personal and social life. The aridity of ordinary suburbia and the frigidity of Melbourne "Society" are both contrasted with the Vaughans' escapes to the bush. When the characters go to an island for a holiday the conflicts between Australian and European values and between the "natural" and the civilized life are explored in almost fable form, and action, rather than dialogue, becomes the vehicle of the theme.

The author is more successful with his description of the young married lovers in the bush than he is with them in Society, where his concerns become too overtly stated through the dialogue. Dutton has talents for describing action and natural setting (as his *The Hero as Murderer* reveals), and the passages of natural description draw with ease and enthusiasm on the English Romantic poetic tradition, while the most memorable sections of this first novel are accounts of body surfing and an interpolated story of stunt flying.

The resolution of Mark Vaughan's conflict is curious. His European friends, as in much New World writing, prove to be corrupt and degenerate beneath their charm and erudition. Dinkum Aussie values are finally vindicated but Mark also secures his ticket to the Europe he has idealized. The ending does not resolve his conflicts so much as allow him to have the best of both worlds. It is a novelettish ending to a book in which what is happening at the level of the author's own involvement with his characters (especially the impossibly stereotyped Professor Klein, embodiment of European degeneracy) proved more interesting than their involvement with each other.

In Dutton's second novel, *Andy*, nostalgia for the old Australia before the American alliance eroded the national virtues of independence and self-reliance lurks beneath the comic picaresque story of a young R.A.A.F. pilot's conflicts with authority. *Andy* is deliberately freer in form and more comic than the first novel, but again one senses personal experiences and responses to social change are being worked out through fantasies that are indistinguishable from those of the novelette. *Andy*, however, is not unequivocally an autobiographical projection. The author's merging with his hero is balanced by his merging with other characters as well—with the virginal and intellectual Ian Almond and with the idealized Tasmanian squire John Lydford.

More thematically than structurally organized, *Andy* is a free-wheeling comedy of the moral education of a pilot during World War II; but it is impossible to say what his moral education consists of because of a complete surrender to fantasy at the end. Like the first novel, *Andy* contains too much to be controlled and directed. It seems, appropriately for its hero, a cavalier enterprise, a deliberately off-handed indulgence in irresponsible *joie-de-vivre* accompanied by a nostalgia for youth and the past with which it is associated.

Dutton's third novel, *Tamara*, is his most satisfactory to date. Like the works of others, e.g., Malamud and Updike, who have visited the U.S.S.R. and attempted to come to grips with their own confused impressions through fiction, it presents the contradictions perceived in contemporary Russian society—warm humanity and cold bureaucracy, technological advance and bad plumbing, a national passion for literature and rigorous political censorship. Such contradictions offer possibilities for both social comedy and serious social concern and Dutton blends the two more successfully in this novel than in its predecessors. He is a fine travel writer and his descriptive powers are seen at their best in the scenes which present Russian, especially Georgian, life.

The story is one of a simple soil scientist from Kangaroo Island who is invited to Russia as Australian delegate to a literary conference and who falls in love with Russia's leading poetess. Through this romantic and not very probable story is expressed a serious concern with the position of the writer in the Soviet Union as a critical point for evaluating the whole direction of post-Stalinist Russia. The presentation of Russian society is vivid and sympathetic and, although it is a romantic comedy, *Tamara* avoids the wish-fulfilment endings of the earlier novels.

Queen Emma of the South Seas is a documentary fiction that presents, through multiple points of view, the life of the historical figure Emma Coe. The daughter of a U.S. commercial agent and one of his Samoan wives, she was educated in Australia and became unofficial queen of her island and a prosperous trader. The novel's early chapters evoke the lush natural setting and innocent Samoan life. With all of his romantic sympathies, Dutton presents Emma as beautiful, intelligent, and amorous, and his basic theme of innocence conflicting with experience is elaborated through the contrast between Samoan hedonism and the "civilization" brought by European colonizers and missionaries.

—Brian Kiernan

EASTLAKE, William (Derry). American. Born in New York City, 14 July 1917. Educated at Bonnie Brae School; Caldwell High School, New Jersey; Alliance Française, Paris, 1948–50. Served in the United States Army in World War II: Bronze Star. Married Martha Simpson in 1943 (divorced, 1971). Writer-in-Residence, Knox College, Galesburg, Illinois, 1967–68, University of New Mexico, Albuquerque, 1968–69, University of Southern California, Los Angeles, 1969, University of Arizona, Tucson, 1969–71, and United States Military Academy, West Point, New York, 1975. Vietnam correspondent, *Nation*, New York, 1968. Recipient: Ford grant, 1964; Rockefeller grant, 1966; Les Lettres Nouvelles award (France), 1972; Western Literature Association award, 1985. D.Litt.: University of Albuquerque, 1970. Agent: Harold Matson Inc., 276 Fifth Avenue, New York, New York 10001. Address: 15 Coy Road, Bisbee, Arizona 85603, U.S.A.

PUBLICATIONS

Novels

Go in Beauty. New York, Harper, 1956; London, Secker and Warburg, 1957.
The Bronc People. New York, Harcourt Brace, 1958; London, Deutsch, 1963.
Portrait of an Artist with Twenty-Six Horses. New York, Simon and Schuster, 1963; London, Joseph, 1965.
Castle Keep. New York, Simon and Schuster, 1965; London, Joseph, 1966.
The Bamboo Bed. New York, Simon and Schuster, 1969; London, Joseph, 1970.
Dancers in the Scalp House. New York, Viking Press, 1975.
The Long, Naked Descent into Boston: A Tricentennial Novel. New York, Viking Press, 1977.

Short Stories

Jack Armstrong in Tangier. Flint, Michigan, Bamberger, 1984.

Uncollected Short Stories

"Ishimoto's Land," in *Essai* (Geneva, Switzerland), Summer 1952.

"Two Gentlemen from America," in *Hudson Review* (New York), Fall 1954.

"Homecoming," in *Quarto* (New York), Fall 1954.

"The Barfly and the Navajo," in *Nation* (New York), 12 September 1959.

"A Long Day's Dying," in *The Best American Short Stories 1964*, edited by Martha Foley and David Burnett. Boston, Houghton Mifflin, 1964.

"Little Joe," in *The Best American Short Stories 1965*, edited by Martha Foley and David Burnett. Boston, Houghton Mifflin, 1965.

"Something Big Is Happening to Me," in *New American Story*, edited by Robert Creeley and Donald Allen. New York, Grove Press, 1965.

"What Nice Hands Held," in *Gallery of Modern Fiction*, edited by Robie Macauley. New York, Salem Press, 1966.

"Three Heroes and a Clown," in *Evergreen Review Reader 1957–1967*, edited by Barney Rosset. New York, Grove Press, 1968.

"Now Lucifer Is Not Dead," in *Evergreen Review* (New York), November 1968.

"The Message," in *New Mexico Quarterly* (Albuquerque), Winter 1968.

"The Hanging at Prettyfields," in *Evergreen Review* (New York), February 1969.

"The Biggest Thing since Custer," in *Prize Stories 1970: The O. Henry Awards*, edited by William Abrahams. New York, Doubleday, 1970.

"The Death of Sun," in *The Best American Short Stories 1973*, edited by Martha Foley. Boston, Houghton Mifflin, 1973.

"Mrs. Gage in Her Bed of Pain with a Nice Cup of Gin," in *Ms.* (New York), March 1977.

"Don't Be Afraid, The Clown's Afraid Too," in *South Shore* (Au Train, Michigan), vol. 1, no. 2, 1978.

"Inside the Belly of the Whale," in *Bisbee Times* (Bisbee, Arizona), March 1982.

Verse

A Child's Garden of Verses for the Revolution (includes essays). New York, Grove Press, 1971.

*

Critical Studies: "The Novels of William Eastlake" by Delbert W. Wylder, in *New Mexico Quarterly* (Albuquerque), 1965; "Of Cowboys, Indians and the Modern West" by Peter M. Kenyon, in *Sage* (Las Vegas, Nevada), Winter 1969; *William Eastlake* by Gerald Haslam, Austin, Texas, Steck Vaughn, 1970; "William Eastlake Issue" of *Review of Contemporary Fiction* (Elmwood Park, Illinois), Spring 1983; article by Eastlake, in *Contemporary Authors Autobiography Series 1* edited by Dedria Bryfonski, Detroit, Gale, 1984.

William Eastlake comments:

(1972) As long as we are serving a life sentence on this earth there has got to be something to make the time go easy. The thing to work at is to be the best writer on earth, or the best magician, for writing is magic, and like all the things that are important you do it all alone. As I expressed it in *The Bronc People*:

"You can't give anyone anything."
"You mean I've got to do it alone?"
"Yes."
"But the missionary says no man is an island."

"Well, he is."
"You think the missionary got that saying from another preacher?"
"Yes."
"We've got to go it all alone?"
"Yes, we do."

A Child's Garden of Verses for the Revolution, is a comment on the end of America and the west, the only part of the earth I really know. But the artist is sentenced and elected as medicine man because he holds out hope. That is his job. That is what he was hired for. My hope is in the youth of the world. The people of the earth turn more and more to the writer, the medicine man, as their tribal leaders fail them. And as our present tribal leaders are unworthy even of the dignity of death, the medicine man, through his novels, fulfills man through artistic re-enactment.

Once upon a time there was a time. The land here in the Southwest had evolved slowly and there was time and there were great spaces. Now a man on horseback from atop a bold mesa looked out over the violent spectrum of the Indian Country—into a gaudy infinity where all the colors exploded soundlessly. "There is not much time," he said.

The death of all of us worthy of death is enacted by the Indian medicine man. Death he calls "Something big is happening to me." Any place the writer, the medicine man, the shaman, lives is the center of the earth.

Below at the post, the exact center and the capital of the world for The People, two Indians crouched at the massive stone root of the petrified-wood house where it made its way into the ground.

"This crack," the Indian said, tracing it with his brown finger.

"They can fix it," Rabbit Stockings said.

"No. And perhaps even The People cannot stop something coming apart and beginning here at the center of the world."

The artist's job is to hold the world together. What the politicians cannot do with reality the artist does with magic, even if the artist is an epileptic Dostoievsky, a failed Melville working in a customs house, a wandering Walt Whitman peddling his *Leaves of Grass* from door to door. The artist finds life everlasting in his magic. William Shakespeare is still very much alive. God is pronounced dead.

*   *   *

At first glance William Eastlake appears to be America's most paradoxical literary artist. Although he was born in New York and grew up in New Jersey and although he traveled widely in Europe after World War II and for some years lived and worked in Los Angeles, he purchased land in an isolated, remote area of New Mexico and there for some years lived the life of the small-spread rancher and literary man. Eastlake thereby became a strongly committed regionalist and one of the most astute observers of present-day American Indian life. Although isolated, Eastlake's concerns were always with national policy, our establishment in Washington and in Vietnam, or the significance of American poverty at home as against American explorations of outer space. On the one hand he appears to seek a kind of peace in a remote area, yet he remains angry at fellow provincials of limited vision, the rednecks and unenlightened army colonels. If Eastlake protests the fate of Mexican, Indian, and Black persons in America, he cannot defend, in the name of a beloved democracy, the violence and the turmoil in our urban centers and on the country roads of out-yonder America. His life-style suggests the pursuit of calm by association with Nature; yet the work presents a sharp focus on the evils of modernity in an idiom which combines the sardonic and the realistic along with an acceptance of the implied values of both ritual and myth. If these paradoxes are real, then their resolution in Eastlake's work suggests an artist of uncommon personal stability and unusual dedication to his own view of the world. If there is tension implicit in these paradoxical roles, the result is artistic production of a high order.

From the centers of these contradictive conflicts emerge his most significant works. Ostensibly the materials are Indians and tourists; cattlemen and brute geography; the neon market towns and the sagebrush. Beneath this closely observed, naturalistic surface, however, the concern is the modes of right conduct, the normal propositions implicit in actions, the attitudes toward life of the protagonists. Irony, humor, and fantasy are everywhere, and thus the true position of the authorial voice behind the prose fictions is not always easy to discern. In moral considerations a continued reliance on irony is no position at all.

Nevertheless, the pervading irony—and compassion—suggest Eastlake's American literary tradition and major influence. His overt search for materials (the move to New Mexico), his stints as war correspondent in Vietnam, his running commentary on cultural and political policy suggest the tradition of the 19th-century correspondent/writer: Stephen Crane, Jack London, and more recently Hemingway. Likewise, the concern for a "moral center," for Justice, for the destiny of America and its people suggests Walt Whitman, poet, editor, "correspondent" of an earlier age. Of the direct literary influences, however, Hemingway is the most significant: the terse understatement, the stripped-down dialogue, the concept of the character, the close focus on the details of war, the sometimes anti-intellectual, anti-bookish, anti-cultural stances strongly suggest the Hemingway of the early novels and the war-correspondent years. Many commonplaces from the criticism of Hemingway, for example, the kind of commentary which identifies the strong romantic element in his work, could be applied as well to Eastlake. If the two men in a great many ways are comparable literary talents, Eastlake's exemplary management of his own talent may prove ultimately the more productive. Eastlake is a model of affirmative experience in the matter of attaining a balance between artistic necessity and humanitarian concern.

Of the novels *The Bronc People* and the short fictions in the same vein attract the most critical attention. Although *Castle Keep* became a successful film and was widely translated, the novel increasingly becomes an example of a book less effective as a whole than the sum of its sometimes brilliant episodes. The Vietnam materials, the journalistic snap shots and quasi-interviews, are repetitive and are less effective together than when they appeared singly in the *Nation*. The poetry of *A Child's Garden of Verses for the Revolution* purports to be "revolutionary" but on balance fails either to move the reader or to offer an effective program beyond the necessity of mutual respect, a change of heart, or other humanistic concerns. While the work varies in quality, the commitment is always firm, and a strong sensibility is apparent everywhere.

At full artistic maturity, Eastlake now lives in the country which was significant and stimulating to his early work: on the border of Arizona and Old Mexico. A recent collection of short fiction, *Jack Armstrong in Tangier*, is largely retrospective, a summary. The literary quality is high, the artistic intention lofty; at least four of the stories have claimed space in major anthologies. The cumulative effect of these stories is strong in large part because of the authorial voice behind them, this voice characterized by irony, humor, and wit; in addition, there is the sharp observation of the significant detail, and an unwavering—if often bleak—estimate of the human condition broadly considered.

—James B. Hall

EKWENSI, Cyprian (Odiatu Duaka). Nigerian. Born in Minna, Northern Nigeria, 26 September 1921. Educated at Government College, Ibadan; Achimota College, Ghana; School of Forestry, Ibadan; Higher College, Yaba; Chelsea School of Pharmacy, University of London. Married to Eunice Anyiwo; five children. Lecturer in Biology, Chemistry, and English, Igbodi College, Lagos, 1947–49; Lecturer in Pharmacognosy and Pharmaceutics, School of Pharmacy, Lagos, 1949–56; pharmacist, Nigerian Medical Service, 1956; head of features, Nigerian Broadcasting Corporation, 1957–61; director of information, Federal Ministry of Information, Lagos, 1961–66. Since 1966, director of information services in Enugu. Chairman, East Central State Library Board, Enugu, 1971; member, Nigerian Arts Council. Recipient: Dag Hammarskjöld International Award, 1968. Agent: David Bolt Associates, Cedar House, High Street, Ripley, Surrey GU23 6AE, England. Address: 12 Hillview, Independence Layout, P.O. Box 317, Enugu, Nigeria.

PUBLICATIONS

Novels

People of the City. London, Dakers, 1954; revised edition, London, Heinemann, 1963; New York, Fawcett, 1969.
Jagua Nana. London, Hutchinson, 1961; New York, Fawcett, 1969.
Burning Grass: A Story of the Fulani of Northern Nigeria. London, Heinemann, 1962.
Beautiful Feathers. London, Hutchinson, 1963.
Iska. London, Hutchinson, 1966.
Survive the Peace. London, Heinemann, 1976.
Divided We Stand. Enugu, Fourth Dimension, 1980.

Short Stories

Lokotown and Other Stories. London, Heinemann, 1966.
Restless City and Christmas Gold with Other Stories. London, Heinemann, 1975.

Fiction (for children)

When Love Whispers. Onitsha, Nigeria, Tabansi Bookshop, 1947.
The Leopard's Claw. London, Longman, 1950.
The Drummer Boy. London, Cambridge University Press, 1960.
The Passport of Mallam Ilia. London, Cambridge University Press, 1960.

Yaba Roundabout Murder. Lagos, Tortoise, 1962.
The Rainmaker and Other Stories. Lagos, African Universities Press, 1965.
Trouble in Form Six. London, Cambridge University Press, 1966.
Juju Rock. Lagos, African Universities Press, 1966.
Coal Camp Boy. Lagos, Longman, 1973.
Samankwe in the Strange Forest. Ikeja, Longman Nigeria, 1973.
The Rainbow-Tinted Scarf and Other Stories. London, Evans, 1975.
Samankwe and the Highway Robbers. London, Evans, 1975.
Motherless Baby. Enugu, Fourth Dimension, 1980.

Other (for children)

Ikolo the Wrestler and Other Ibo Tales. London, Nelson, 1947.
An African Night's Entertainment: A Tale of Vengeance. Lagos, African Universities Press, and London, Deutsch, 1962.
The Great Elephant-Bird (folktale). London, Nelson, 1965.
The Boa Suitor. London, Nelson, 1966.

Other

Editor, *Festac Anthology of Nigerian New Writing.* Lagos, Federal Ministry of Information, 1977.

*

Critical Study: *Cyprian Ekwensi* by Ernest Emenyona, London, Evans, 1974.

*   *   *

Granted much mawkish sentiment, an eye for the sensational, a technical naivety that allows abrupt transitions and unlikely coincidences, and a frequently banal use of English, Cyprian Ekwensi cannot be lightly dismissed as a Nigerian writer. His career began in the Onitsha market in Eastern Nigeria, where cheap, sentimental, moralistic stories in English catered for readers with an English-type primary education obtained in mission schools—and this Onitsha ethos can be detected in all his writings. Yet there are other characteristics also, chiefly a vivid sense of actuality, especially when he places his characters on the street and in the night clubs and slums of Lagos. Except for *Burning Grass* and stories written for children, Ekwensi's writings convey the heady experience of young Africans from the country being attracted, excited, bemused, usually destroyed by the glitter of city lights. Passing fashions of dress and undress are catalogues, highlife rhythms pulsate in the background, hips wiggle, and bosoms quiver alluringly, but with real understanding Ekwensi evokes the frustration, inner unhappiness, restlessness, and rootlessness of a new urbanized African generation. There is also a muted satirical tone. He attacks political jobbery and public scandal. He invents a Nigerian Ministry of Consolation to epitomize all that is corrupt and inefficient.

These qualities together suggest that Ekwensi's talent is that of a good journalist rather than a novelist, that he is the chronicler of modern West African urbanization, He clearly disapproves of much that he reports but, like a journalist, is so involved in the reporting that he also becomes excited by the things he would condemn. The banal dialogue of characters in moments of emotional intensity is the banality of the everyday speech of ordinary people—a dedication to the actual precludes any attempt at a literary artefact that would suggest the

"real" and yet transcend it. He has claimed that he is no "artist," simply a teller of entertaining tales. His historical position is clear enough: with *People of the City* he became the first Anglophone African writer who tried to present in fictional terms the human problems that confronted individuals in a time of rapid social and political change in Africa, as the mores of village culture came into conflict with westernized city life.

Though *Jagua Nana* is still episodic in construction, it gains from being a character-study in depth of a Lagos prostitute desperately trying to find stability before she has worked herself out. The book also probes the thuggery of Nigerian politics in the old Federation. *Beautiful Feathers* is the most successfully satirical of Ekwensi's books, with its wry treatment of politicians and civil servants. Its symbolic big-game hunt, when white observers get away with the quarry while the African delegates to a conference on African solidarity squabble among themselves, points to one of Ekwensi's genuine strengths—his sensitiveness to the larger political issues of the day. Despite its lingering Onitsha qualities, *Iska* warns with prophetic insistence of the dangers of tribal factionalism in Nigeria on the eve of the Biafran war, and shows a serious social purpose in its treatment of the 1966 Igbo massacres in Northern Nigeria. Ekwensi's role as vivid chronicler of change is confirmed in *Survive the Peace*, set in war-torn Eastern Nigeria as the Civil War ends.

—Arthur Ravenscroft

ELKIN, Stanley (Lawrence). American. Born in Brooklyn, New York, 11 May 1930. Educated at the University of Illinois, Urbana, 1948–60, B.A. 1952, M.A. 1953, Ph.D. in English 1961. Served in the United States Army, 1955–57. Married Joan Jacobson in 1953; two sons and one daughter. Instructor, 1960–62, Assistant Professor, 1962–66, Associate Professor, 1966–69, since 1969 Professor of English, and since 1983 Kling Professor of Modern Letters, Washington University, St. Louis. Visiting Lecturer, Smith College, Northampton, Massachusetts, 1964–65; Visiting Professor, University of California, Santa Barbara, Summer 1967, University of Wisconsin, Milwaukee, Summer 1969, Yale University, New Haven, Connecticut, 1975, and Boston University, 1976. Recipient: Longview Foundation award, 1962; *Paris Review* prize, 1965; Guggenheim fellowship, 1966; Rockefeller fellowship, 1968; National Endowment for the Arts grant, 1971; American Academy grant, 1974; Rosenthal Foundation award, 1980; *Southern Review* award, 1981; National Book Critics Circle award, 1983. Member, American Academy, 1982. Address: Department of English, Washington University, St. Louis, Missouri 63130, U.S.A.

PUBLICATIONS

Novels

Boswell. New York, Random House, and London, Hamish Hamilton, 1964.
A Bad Man. New York, Random House, 1967; London, Blond, 1968.
The Dick Gibson Show. New York, Random House, and London, Weidenfeld and Nicolson, 1971.
The Franchiser. New York, Farrar Straus, 1976.

George Mills.   New York, Dutton, 1982.
The Magic Kingdom.   New York, Dutton, 1985.

Short Stories

Criers and Kibitzers, Kibitzers and Criers.   New York, Random House, 1966; London, Blond, 1968.
The Making of Ashenden.   London, Covent Garden Press, 1972.
Searches and Seizures.   New York, Random House, 1973; as *Eligible Men*, London, Gollancz, 1974; as *Alex and the Gypsy*, London, Penguin, 1977.
The Living End.   New York, Dutton, 1979; London, Cape, 1980.
Early Elkin.   Flint, Michigan, Bamberger, 1985.

Play

The Six-Year-Old Man (filmscript), in *Esquire* (New York), December 1968.

Other

Stanley Elkin's Greatest Hits (omnibus).   New York, Dutton, 1980.
Why I Live Where I Live (essay).   University City, Missouri, Contre Coup Press, 1983.

Editor, *Stories from the Sixties.*   New York, Doubleday, 1971.
Editor, with Shannon Ravenel, *The Best American Short Stories 1980.*   Boston, Houghton Mifflin, 1980.

*

Manuscript Collection: Washington University Library, St. Louis.

Critical Studies: *Humanism and the Absurd* by Naomi Lebowitz, Evanston, Illinois, Northwestern University Press, 1971; *City of Words* by Tony Tanner, London, Cape, and New York, Harper, 1971; *The Jewish Writer in America* by Allen Guttman, New York, Oxford University Press, 1971; *Beyond the Wasteland* by Raymond Olderman, New Haven, Connecticut, Yale University Press, 1972; *The Fiction of Stanley Elkin* by Doris G. Bargen, Bern, Switzerland, Lang, 1980; *Reading Stanley Elkin* by Peter J. Bailey, Boston, Houghton Mifflin, 1985.

Stanley Elkin comments:

I don't know what to say about my work. What I like best about it, I suppose, are the sentences. What I like least about it is my guess that probably no one is ever moved by it.

*   *   *

"[Writing] is a matter of feeling one's way. It is not instinctive. It's a question of using a pencil, erasing, creating a palimpsest of metaphor right there on the page. One gets a notion of the conceit and one is inspired to work with it as a draftsman might work with some angle that he is interested in getting down correctly. That's where all the fun of writing is for me. I don't read much non-fiction because the non-fiction I do read always seems to be so badly written. What I enjoy about fiction—the great gift of fiction—is that it gives language an opportunity to happen. What I am really interested in after personality are not philosophic ideas or abstractions or patterns, but this superb opportunity for language to take place."

(Interview in *Anything Can Happen*, edited by Thomas LeClair and Larry McCaffery, 1983.)

"Surely the point of life was the possibility it always held out for the exceptional. The range of the strange," says Dick Gibson, Stanley Elkin's disc jockey and fellow word man. The point, too, of Elkin's fiction which is exceptional because sentence for sentence, metaphor for metaphor, no novelist in America writes as energetically and musically as Elkin. His books display the "range of the strange": not the exotic or esoteric, but ordinary life made extraordinary by his imaginative participation in it, the usual seen and said with unusual clarity. "The world is a miracle," adds franchiser Ben Flesh, but, he goes on for himself and for Elkin, you have to "Drive up and down in it.... Look close at it. See its moving parts, its cranes and car parks and theater districts." Elkin has pressed his nose to the American showcase, heard all the sellers of self and thing, has eaten Colonel Sanders chicken and slept in Holiday Inns. Everything—and this is the secret of Elkin's prose—is available for the sentences that turn us back to our franchised and media-furrowed land with new apprehension and appreciation.

"Drive drives the world," to quote Dick Gibson again. Elkin's heroes are obsessives, common men with uncommon appetites, bad men because they refuse to compromise, good men for the same reason. The professional wrestler in *Boswell*, Elkin's first novel, is obsessed with death and with what he calls "The Great." Like his predecessor James, Boswell seeks out the exceptional. Feldman, entrepreneur hero of *A Bad Man*, is driven to make the ultimate sale, either in his bargain basement or in the prison to which he is sent. Dick Gibson of *The Dick Gibson Show* and Ben Flesh of *The Franchiser* must have destinies, must feel chosen for the services they render: Gibson as a late-night Miss Lonelyhearts of the air, Flesh as provider of the goofy comfort of familiar franchises. For these characters, fixation turns an occupation a life, and Elkin turns their lives into success stories for a shrinking America: modest means transformed by the gaiety of will.

Like his characters, Elkin's prose is willful, obsessive, omnivorous. Here is Dick Gibson describing quiet: "I was in a trance, a catalepsy, a swoon, a brown study, a neutral funk. I was languid, gravid, the thousand-pound kid in Miriam's room, sensitized as human soup. And if I heard her at all it was in my ilium I listened—as deep as that—harkened in my coccyx, my pajama strings all ears, and my buttons and the Kleenex under my pillow." The series of synonyms tries to exhaust meaning as the extravagant metaphors, hyperbole, and refurbished clichés try to extend it. Elkin's models are oral and colloquial—the pitch of his salesman father, the oratory he wrote about in Faulkner's work, the shop talk he collects. His purposes are performance—Elkin loves the comic high-wire—and defamiliarization, the artistic recovery of "all the derelict and marooned, the ditched and scavenged. Debris, dregs, lees. Dregs addicts. All the multitudinous slag of the ordinary."

While Elkin's stories in *Criers and Kibitzers, Kibitzers and Criers* are widely anthologized, and the three novellas in *Searches and Seizures* are much admired, Elkin's gifts are those of the novelist. He describes himself as a "putter-inner." Because shorter forms do not allow Elkin room for the accretion of character that marks the novels, situations and people in the stories can seem simply eccentric. In the novels, repetition of image and action, rhetorical intensity, even digressions and included tales, have a cumulative effect. *The Living End*, a triad of long stories about heaven and hell, is an exception, for here a whole cosmos is created, laced and grained with detail. The most widely read of Elkin's books, *The Living End* ranges from the life of a Minneapolis-St. Paul liquor salesman to the secrets God held back from man ("why dentistry was a purer science than astronomy, biography a higher form than dance" and more), encompassing the banalities of conventional wisdom and the profundities of last things. Not since Melville shook Ahab's fist at heaven has as American novelist written so affectingly about the problem of Evil, the bugs in the divine "state of the art."

In the award-winning *George Mills* and in *The Magic Kingdom*, Elkin extends his imagination—to medieval Europe, Sultanic Turkey, and impoverished contemporary St. Louis in *George Mills*—and deepens his sensibility, treating with high comedy and passionate precision the holiday of terminally ill children in Disney's and Elkin's "Magic Kingdom." For a very long time a "writer's writer," Elkin has in these books brought his dense prose to bear on people's subjects, the strangeness of loss, the wearing down of life and lives, and, finally, in the face of the "sapped, the unsound, the impaired, the unfit," the ecstasy of creation, the very long-odds possibility of love.

—Thomas LeClair

ELLIS, Alice Thomas. Pseudonym for Anna Margaret Haycraft, née Lindholm. British. Married Colin Haycraft in 1957; four sons and one daughter (and one son and one daughter deceased). Director, Duckworth, publishers, London. Columnist ("Home Life"), *The Spectator*, London. Recipient: Welsh Arts Council award, 1977. Address: Duckworth, The Old Piano Factory, 43 Gloucester Crescent, London NW1 7DY, England.

PUBLICATIONS

Novels

The Sin Eater. London, Duckworth, 1977.
The Birds of the Air. London, Duckworth, 1980; New York, Viking Press, 1981.
The 27th Kingdom. London, Duckworth, 1982.
The Other Side of the Fire. London, Duckworth, 1983.
Unexplained Laughter. London, Duckworth, 1985.

Uncollected Short Story

"Away in a Niche," in *Spectator* (London), 21–28 December 1985.

Other

Natural Baby Food: A Cookery Book (as Brenda O'Casey). London, Duckworth, 1977; as Anna Haycraft, London, Fontana, 1980.
Darling, You Shouldn't Have Gone to So Much Trouble (cookbook; as Anna Haycraft), with Caroline Blackwood. London, Cape, 1980.

Editor, *Mrs. Donald*, by Mary Keene. London, Chatto and Windus, 1983.

*   *   *

In all her books Alice Thomas Ellis takes the form of the upper-class social comedy and turns it inside out, with mordant,

often uncomfortable wit, satire (some of it quite savage), and a gift for dialogue which means much more than is apparent, in a background which alternates between the country (usually Wales) and London, patches of which must be regarded as the author's own territory.

Her first novel, *The Sin Eater*, is set in Wales, where the Welsh have given up farming and taken to preying on the holidaymaker. In a country house, near a small resort which has declined since its pre-war heyday, the Captain, patriarch of the family, lies dying, unable to speak or move. Only a matter of time, says the doctor, cheerfully. Not much grief is shown by the family assembling to say goodbye to him. Henry, the eldest son and heir, lives with his wife Rose and the twins in the family home. Visiting are younger brother Michael, his wife Angela, and Edward, a Fleet Street literary journalist, object of Angela's love (or lust). Ministering incompetently to the household is Phyllis, her son Jack ("Jack the Liar") and Gomer, Phyllis's adored but highly unpleasant grandson. The outsider is Ermyn, youngest daughter of the house, back from a secretarial course in London, regarded by the rest as half-witted (in fact she is slightly deaf, following measles in childhood, but no one has noticed). Rose (like Ellis) is a Roman Catholic, a brilliant organiser, one who arranges food, houses, and circumstances to disconcert others. Angela (who hates her) is disoriented by being put in a room newly arranged in 1930's style. A killing meal is eaten shortly before the cricket match of village versus Squire. When the village wins, for the first time, there follows a vengeful and dismaying Welsh saturnalia. Rose loves only the twins (absent from all but the first and last page of the novel) and the terrifying denouement is a fitting end to the outpouring of spite and malice so deftly observed.

Christmas is a family time, and in *The Birds of the Air* Mrs. Marsh decides to invite all the family, to try to cheer Mary, whose grief will neither disappear, nor be assuaged. Mary's sister Barbara has just discovered her husband's infidelity by overhearing a sniggered comment that suddenly makes sense. She is on the way to a breakdown. Mary's grief is an indescribable agony, unhelped by her Catholicism, over the death of her illegitimate son, Robin. Everyone is embarrassed by Mary's grief. Barbara makes an exhibition of herself, getting drunk and pursuing Hunter, who rejects her. Social embarrassment to the last degree forms the basis for some hard, sharp things said about the nature of grief, love, and family life.

The 27th Kingdom (shortlisted for the Booker Prize in 1982) is set in Chelsea in the 1950's, where Aunt Irene (of distant Russian descent) lives with her nephew Kyril in a pretty little house. Chelsea is still very socially mixed, and the cast includes the O'Connors, a large family of criminal Cockneys, and a passing parade of casual lodgers. The outsider and new lodger is Valentine, who wishes to be a nun, but has been sent out to see more of the world by Reverend Mother, who is Aunt Irene's sister. Valentine is, most inconveniently, a saint, as well as being very beautiful, and black. As in all the novels, the four last things of the Catholic Church—death and judgement, heaven and hell—loom in the background. Aunt Irene loves Kyril, but recognises that he is evil and wicked. Both she and Mrs. O'Connor, the Cockney matriarch, recognise the goodness of Valentine. Once again, it's very funny, and slightly more gentle in tone. Food plays its part, and so does Focus, a charming, beautiful, and amusing cat.

The Other Side of the Fire brings together a number of themes which can be claimed as standard ingredients in the Ellis novel. Claudia Bohannon is the second wife of Charles—they have two children of their own (absent at boarding school). Claudia finds herself inexplicably and shamingly in love with her stepson, Philip. Her confidante is Sylvie (living in the country, there are few congenial people around). Sylvie has given up love, and company, and has become a witch—or not, depending on how you view her. Certainly she has a familiar in the dog Gloria, evil-tempered and a perfect nuisance, rather like Sylvie's ex-husband, as one of the characters points out. Evvie, Sylvie's daughter, is writing a romantic novel along very predictable lines, containing stock characters like a Scottish vet with a dull fiancée, a housekeeper, a beautiful promiscuous girl, a mad Laird. Unfortunately and hilariously the characters from the novel invade life, and vice versa. Claudia is sweet but dim—it takes a brick dropped by Evvie before she realises what everyone else knows—that Philip is a charming and unscrupulous homosexual. The book meditates on various forms of love—and its transitory nature—touching all but the maternal, which, as in *The Sin Eater*, is so important that it is never mentioned.

Unexplained Laughter is set in Wales, where Lydia, a tough London journalist, has retreated to get over a broken heart. With her is Betty, who is nice, but a bore. The only company (typically, a small group of characters at each other's throats) is a family. Hywel, a farmer, is married unhappily to Elizabeth; Angharad, his youngest sister, is speechless and considered mad, but is not as mad as all that; Beuno, the younger brother, is studying for the ministry. There is also the doctor, formerly Elizabeth's lover. Lydia is witty and cruel. It is only when she starts hearing unexplained laughter in the air round the cottage, and she talks to Beuno about the existence of God and the devil that she begins to develop into a more human being and allows herself to become fond of others. The devil is at work; they are a nasty bunch, with exceptions. Beuno is some kind of saint, Betty is pleasant and dull, Angharad is a visionary, and Lydia is improving her soul. Beuno exorcises the laughter, and it disappears. Whatever it was, he considered it evil.

These five short novels are written with an uncanny ear for contemporary dialogue, the flash of steel beneath the apparently harmless words. There is a great deal said about the Catholic church, life, death, food, love, children, and the existence of evil, the devil in our midst. "Stan" Lydia calls him, a nickname for "Satan." Only in the short story "Away in a Niche," in which a tired housewife swaps places with the local saint for the three worst days of Christmas, do we get anything like a cheerful, happy conclusion.

—Philippa Toomey

ELLISON, Ralph (Waldo). American. Born in Oklahoma City, Oklahoma, 1 March 1914. Educated at a high school in Oklahoma City, and at Tuskegee Institute, Alabama, 1933–36. Served in the United States Merchant Marine, 1943–45. Married Fanny McConnell in 1946. Writer from 1936; Lecturer, Salzburg Seminar in American Studies, 1954; Instructor in Russian and American Literature, Bard College, Annandale-on-Hudson, New York, 1958–61; Alexander White Visiting Professor, University of Chicago, 1961; Visiting Professor of Writing, Rutgers University, New Brunswick, New Jersey, 1962–64; Whittall Lecturer, Library of Congress, Washington, D.C., 1964; Ewing Lecturer, University of California, Los Angeles, 1964; Visiting Fellow in American Studies, Yale University, New Haven, Connecticut, 1966. Albert Schweitzer Professor in the Humanities, New York University 1970–79;

now emeritus. Chairman, Literary Grants Committee, American Academy, 1964–67; member, National Council on the Arts, 1965–67; member, Carnegie Commission on Educational Television, 1966–67; member of the editorial board, *American Scholar*, Washington, D.C., 1966–69; Honorary Consultant in American Letters, Library of Congress, Washington, D.C., 1966–72. Trustee, John F. Kennedy Center of the Performing Arts, Washington, D.C., New School for Social Research, New York, Bennington College, Vermont, Educational Broadcasting Corporation, and Colonial Williamsburg Foundation. Recipient: Rosenwald fellowship, 1945; National Book Award, 1953; National Newspaper Publishers Association Russwarm Award, 1953; American Academy Rome Prize, 1955, 1956; United States Medal of Freedom, 1969; National Medal of Arts, 1985. Ph.D. in Humane Letters: Tuskegee Institute, 1963; Litt.D.: Rutgers University, 1966; University of Michigan, Ann Arbor, 1967; Williams College, Williamstown, Massachusetts, 1970; Long Island University, New York, 1971; College of William and Mary, Williamsburg, Virginia, 1972; Wake Forest College, Winston-Salem, North Carolina, 1974; Harvard University, Cambridge, Massachusetts, 1974; L.H.D.: Grinnell College, Iowa, 1967; Adelphi University, Garden City, New York, 1971; University of Maryland, College Park, 1974. Commandant, Order of Arts and Letters (France), 1970. Member, American Academy, 1975. Agent: Owen Laster, William Morris Agency, 1350 Avenue of the Americas, New York, New York 10019. Address: 730 Riverside Drive, Apartment 8-D, New York, New York 10031, U.S.A.

PUBLICATIONS

Novel

Invisible Man. New York, Random House, 1952; London, Gollancz, 1953.

Excerpts from novel-in-progress: "The Roof, the Steeple and the People," in *Quarterly Review of Literature* (Princeton, New Jersey), 1960; "And Hickman Arrives," in *Noble Savage* (Cleveland), March 1960; "It Always Breaks Out," in *Partisan Review* (New Brunswick, New Jersey), Spring 1963; "Juneteenth," in *Quarterly Review of Literature 13*, 1965; "Night-Talk," in *Quarterly Review of Literature 16*, 1969; "Song of Innocence," in *Iowa Review* (Iowa City), Spring 1970; "Cadillac Flambé," in *American Review 16* edited by Theodore Solotaroff, New York, Bantam, 1973.

Uncollected Short Stories

"Slick Gonna Learn," in *Direction* (Darien, Connecticut), September 1939.
"Afternoon," in *American Writing*. Prairie City, Illinois, James A. Decker, 1940.
"The Birthmark," in *New Masses* (New York), 2 July 1940.
"Mister Toussan," in *New Masses* (New York), 4 November 1941.
"That I Had the Wings," in *Common Ground* (New York), Summer 1943.
"Flying Home," in *Cross Section*, edited by Edwin Seaver. New York, Fischer, 1944.
"In a Strange Country," in *Tomorrow* (New York), July 1944.
"King of the Bingo Game," in *Tomorrow* (New York), November 1944.
"Did You Ever Dream Lucky?," in *New World Writing 5*. New York, New American Library, 1954.

"A Coupla Scalped Indians," in *New World Writing 9*. New York, New American Library, 1956.
"Out of the Hospital and under the Bar," in *Soon, One Morning: New Writing by American Negroes, 1940–62*, edited by Herbert Hill. New York, Knopf, 1963.
"The Death of Clifton," in *Brothers and Sisters*, edited by Arnold Adoff. New York, Macmillan, 1970.
"Backwacking: A Plea to the Senator," in *Massachusetts Review* (Amherst), Autumn 1977.

Other

The Writer's Experience, with Karl Shapiro. Washington, D.C., Library of Congress, 1964.
Shadow and Act (essays). New York, Random House, 1964; London, Secker and Warburg, 1967.
The City in Crisis, with Whitney M. Young and Herbert Gnas. New York, Randolph Educational Fund, 1968.
Going to the Territory (essays). New York, Random House, 1986.

*

Bibliography: "A Bibliography of Ralph Ellison's Published Writings" by Bernard Benoit and Michel Fabre, in *Studies in Black Literature* (Fredericksburg, Virginia), Autumn 1971; *The Blinking Eye: Ralph Waldo Ellison and His American, French, German and Italian Critics 1952–1971* by Jacqueline Covo, Metuchen, New Jersey, Scarecrow Press, 1974.

Critical Studies: *The Negro Novel in America*, revised edition, by Robert A. Bone, New Haven, Connecticut, Yale University Press, 1958; "The Blues as a Literary Theme" by Gene Bluestein, in *Massachusetts Review* (Amherst), Autumn 1967; *Five Black Writers: Essays* by Donald B. Gibson, New York, New York University Press, 1970; *Twentieth-Century Interpretations of "Invisible Man"* edited by John M. Reilly, Englewood Cliffs, New Jersey, Prentice Hall, 1970; "Ralph Ellison Issue" of *CLA Journal* (Baltimore), March 1970; interview in *Atlantic* (Boston), December 1970; *The Merrill Studies in "Invisible Man"* edited by Ronald Gottesman, Columbus, Ohio, Merrill, 1971; *Ralph Ellison: A Collection of Critical Essays* edited by John Hersey, Englewood Cliffs, New Jersey, Prentice Hall, 1973; article by Leonard J. Deutsch, in *American Novelists since World War II* edited by Jeffrey Helterman and Richard Layman, Detroit, Gale, 1978; *Folklore and Myth in Ralph Ellison's Early Works* by Dorothea Fischer-Hornung, Stuttgart, Hochschul, 1979; *The Craft of Ralph Ellison*, Cambridge, Massachusetts, Harvard University Press, 1980, and "The Rules of Magic: Hemingway as Ellison's 'Ancestor,'" in *Southern Review* (Baton Rouge, Louisiana), Summer 1985, both by Robert G. O'Meally; *Ralph Ellison: The Genesis of an Artist* by Rudolf F. Dietze, Nuremberg, Carl, 1982; introduction by the author to 30th anniversary edition of *Invisible Man*, New York, Random House, 1982; "Ralph Ellison and Dostoevsky" by Joseph Frank, in *New Criterion* (New York), September 1983.

*   *   *

From the fact that he has published a single novel and that some 35 years ago, Ralph Ellison's reputation as a major American novelist seems phenomenal, but then his novel is a remarkable work. On one level the nameless protagonist of *Invisible Man* is a modern *picaro* moving through the realms of the Southern American black bourgeoise, Northern industrial society, and the radical political movement learning to survive the bewildering contradictions of racial stereotype and reality by converting the instability of personal identity, which he finds to be the normal state of a black person in the white world, into a condition for freedom. His triumph is less than the classical *picaro*'s, for it is conscious knowledge of the absurdity of the situations he has experienced that sustains him after his American progress rather than a tested capacity to determine his fate. In that fact, however, lies both Ellison's commentary on freedom in the modern world and his understanding of a philosophical role for fiction. The self-aware figure of the invisible man is liberated from external sanctions and, in the imagery of Camus, having seen the stage sets collapse knows there is no just authority to support the human inventions of caste. Crouched in his hole in the ground, mentally journeying through time and space while deliberating a responsible plan for living he gathers all of his being into potentiality. Only potentiality, though, because *Invisible Man*, published in 1952, announces the prerequisite mind set for liberation, not the tactics of the struggle.

The philosophical dynamics of Ellison's novel are embodied in its structure. The narrative of absurd experiences bound between a prologue and epilogue makes clear that the events have already happened to the invisible spokesman and are thus contained within his consciousness where he is free to shape them into significance as he wills. Where the realist or naturalist stresses the clarity of perception, saying he will record only what objectively happens in the world, the surrealist Ellison considers his tale to be an epistemological drama in which the active forces are the conceptions of race and society that determine what each character will perceive. Consequently, the stress upon sight in the title of the novel points not only to stereotypes that obscure our social vision but indicates as well the power of imagination to create a habitable reality.

Ellison's modernist esthetics have earned his novel high critical estimation. In 1965 *Book Week*, then a leading American weekly book review, conducted a poll of critics and found them choosing *Invisible Man* as the most distinguished American fiction of the post-war period. While the book undoubtedly merits its critical distinction, the nearly unanimous approval it receives from white critics often carries the implication that Ellison's universal *picaro*—"Who knows," he says, "but that I speak for you"—represents the transcendence of the invariable concerns of black writers. Clearly such sentiment is less an evaluation of Ellison's work than it is a product of the wish that the divisive issue of race could be verbally resolved without disturbing social arrangements or cultural commonplaces. Certainly, from the time of his earliest published writing Ellison has been interested in the universal theme of identity, but he has always conceived the theme in the context of black culture. "Did You Ever Dream Lucky?," which elaborates the story of Mary Rambo, and "Slick Gonna Learn," which tells of an aborted beating of a black workingman, describe experiences typified by their occurrence in the special circumstances of Afro—American life. Several stories ("Afternoon," "That I Had the Wings," "Mister Toussan," "A Coupla Scalped Indians") representing young black boys contending with fear and guilt, learning of sex, and fantasizing retaliation on whites who despise them might be tales of the invisible protagonist in adolescence, while the discovery by a young black aviator in "Flying Home" of his kinship to a black peasant employs race and culture as the basic terms for self discovery. If anything the attention to black life evident in these stories is more marked in *Invisible Man*, where the narrator's consciousness is provided substance by orations and jive sayings, Toms and race men, dreams and behavior from popular black culture.

So, too, does the surreal quality of the narrative manifest black experience. Caste restrictions seem reasonable perhaps to those who enforce them, but for those who experience them they are literally absurd. A society ordered by caste, therefore, can only be described adequately in narrative that departs from the decorum of rationality and insinuates that insanity is perceptive response, or a dream of anxiety a sound analysis.

Growing up in a black culture, and relishing it as he demonstrably does, Ellison found ready-to-hand the premise that would lead to the philosophical position of his invisible man; yet, his application of imagination to the story of the modern *picaro* is, in fact, a major achievement, for he has done nothing less than bring to its culmination a period of Afro-American literary history that had as its motif the sensation described by W.E.B. Du Bois in 1903 as a double-consciousness wherein "one ever feels his twoness—an American, a Negro ... two warring ideals in one dark body." By liberating his invisible protagonist of the ideals that, like an alien force, had invaded his ego, Ellison has prepared his narrator and those who, through influence, sympathy, or coincidence, will follow him to live with a unitary consciousness of themselves in the world.

—John M. Reilly

ELY, David. American. Born in Chicago, Illinois, 19 November 1927. Educated at the University of North Carolina, Chapel Hill, 1944–45; Harvard University, Cambridge, Massachusetts, 1947–49, B.A. 1949; St. Antony's College, Oxford (Fulbright Scholar), 1954–55. Served in the United States Navy, 1945–46, and the United States Army, 1950–52. Married Margaret Jenkins in 1954; four children. Reporter, St. Louis *Post-Dispatch*, 1949–50, 1952–54, 1955–56; administrative assistant, Development and Resources Corporation, New York, 1956–59. Recipient: Mystery Writers of America Edgar Allan Poe Award, for short story, 1962. Address: P.O. Box 1387, East Dennis, Massachusetts 02641, U.S.A.

PUBLICATIONS

Novels

Trot. New York, Pantheon, 1963; London, Secker and Warburg, 1964.
Seconds. New York, Pantheon, 1963; London, Deutsch, 1964.
The Tour. New York, Delacorte Press, and London, Secker and Warburg, 1967.
Poor Devils. Boston, Houghton Mifflin, 1970.
Walking Davis. New York, Charterhouse, 1972.
Mr. Nicholas. New York, Putnam, 1974; London, Macmillan, 1975.

Short Stories

Time Out. New York, Delacorte Press, 1968; London, Secker and Warburg, 1969.

Uncollected Short Stories

"The Wizard of Light," in *Amazing* (New York), March 1962.

"The Alumni March," in *Cosmopolitan* (New York), 1962.
"McDaniel's Flood," in *Elks Magazine* (Chicago), 1963.
"The Captain's Boarhunt," in *Saturday Evening Post* (Philadelphia), 21 March 1964.
"The Assault on Mount Rushmore," in *Cavalier* (New York), July 1966.
"The Language Game," in *Playboy* (Chicago), 1970.
"The Carnival," in *Antaeus* (New York), 1971.
"The Gourmet Hunt," in *Best Detective Stories of the Year 1973*, edited by Allen J. Hubin. New York, Dutton, 1973.
"The Many Faces of John Dobbler," in *Gallery* (Chicago), 1973.
"A Middleaged Nude," in *Cosmopolitan* (New York), 1974.
"A Place to Avoid," in *Playboy* (Chicago), 1974.
"The Light in the Cottage," in *Playboy* (Chicago), 1974.
"The Prince," in *Redbook* (New York), February 1974.
"Always Home," in *Playboy* (Chicago), 1975.
"Rockefeller's Daughter," in *Redbook* (New York), August 1975.
"Last One Out," in *Playboy* (Chicago), 1976.
"The Squirrel," in *Penthouse* (New York), 1976.
"Starling's Circle," in *Ellery Queen's Mystery Magazine* (New York), July 1976.
"The Running Man," in *Ellery Queen's Mystery Magazine* (New York), December 1976.
"The Partisan," in *Atlantic* (Boston), February 1977.
"The Weed Killer," in *Ellery Queen's Mystery Magazine* (New York), May 1977.
"The Temporary Daughter," in *Seventeen* (New York), April 1978.
"The Rich Girl," in *Seventeen* (New York), July 1978.
"The Looting of the Tomb," in *Ellery Queen's Scenes of the Crime*, edited by Ellery Queen. New York, Davis, 1979; London, Hale, 1981.
"Remember Me," in *Redbook* (New York), December 1979.
"Going Backward," in *Ellery Queen's Circumstantial Evidence*, edited by Ellery Queen. New York, Davis, 1980.
"The Marked Man," in *Best Detective Stories of the Year 1980*, edited by Edward D. Hoch. New York, Dutton, 1980.
"Methuselah," in *Atlantic* (Boston), March 1980.
"Summer Thick and Summer Green," in *Redbook* (New York), September 1981.
"Counting Steps," in *Ellery Queen's Eyewitnesses*, edited by Ellery Queen. New York, Davis, 1981.

*   *   *

David Ely's fiction describes the cost and conditions of freedom—what an ordinary man must do to understand himself and his world. His novels are shaped like thrillers; in each a man is driven onto a quest (initially for the wrong motives) which ultimately leads him to himself, to his unconscious mind, his heart. The novels describe with remarkable sensitivity individuals coping with worlds that are alien, inimical and all-powerful. The triumph of the individual spirit in hostile modern milieu is accompanied by pain and sorrow, loss of innocence and simple comfort, but it brings both self-knowledge and peace.

Trot, Ely's first novel, is subtitled "A Novel of Suspense" and predicates the world of all of Ely's fiction: an alien, minatory and hostile environment, in this case the Paris underworld after World War II. An Army CID man, Sergeant Trot, abruptly becomes the victim in a case on which he is assigned. Suspected of corruption and murder, he hides with the criminals he has stalked. The inversion of his world causes him to reassess his concepts of justice and freedom. Finally he is able to reinstate himself by breaking an extortion-murder plot by escaped Nazis. But the significant victory is Trot's own self-revelation.

In *Seconds*, probably Ely's best-known novel, a Babbitt-like man, a cipher known only by the code name "Wilson," abandons his comfortable but aimless upper-middle-class existence when a mysterious corporation offers him a new life, a second chance. He is surgically rehabilitated and supplied a total identity as a successful artist, but the new freedom proves too painful and challenging. Wilson disintegrates under the stress of his open and unfamiliar world of freedom and nonconformity. "I never had a dream," he says when he returns to the corporation to be erased.

The Tour deals with the same theme in a more terrifying form. A parable of American imperialism and military-scientific manipulation of other cultures, it describes a "tour" designed to provide jaded bourgeois travelers with ultimate thrills in a mythical central American banana republic. The tour includes episodes of sex, jungle survival and guerilla fighting, carefully staged for the fuddled gringos. Behind the scenes a test is made on an automated counter-insurgency weapon, a robot tank which wipes out a starveling guerilla band (and its builders) and nearly decimates the tour. The novel develops as an analogue for U.S. involvement in Southeast Asia and for other paramilitary "tours" of policy. It is similar in shape to Peter Matthiessen's important *At Play in the Fields of the Lord*.

Poor Devils attacks the sociological concepts of poverty and its alleviation. Another parable, it describes the slow education of a history professor, Aaron Bell, who stumbles onto a Project Nomad, a genocidal agency for a "final solution" to poverty, a technological bureau that fights poverty with coldly mechanical games theory and supertechnology. Bell's education leads him to discover the futility of his life and his career, the absurdity of history and ideals faced with amoral technology. The old man he has pursued, Lundquist, a "picaresque saint," teaches him finally that he must discover (or invent) his values himself. Bell opts out of the system of research and manipulation to become a Whitmanesque wanderer, following the "Lindquist heresy, the preamble written short for men in too big a hurry to read much: *Life, liberty, and the pursuit*."

An allegorical study of personality in existentialist terms, *Walking Davis* describes Pierce Davis, who decides to walk around the world. Setting out from Spark, Iowa, Davis makes a Robinson Crusoe voyage of survival and self-discovery, finally plumbing all his human resources and learning that "You can't build a monument to a hero. If a man's a hero, he builds his own." His walk leads him into a strange union with nature and himself, stripped of all pretense like Camus's Sisyphus, reduced to one essential human function—questing.

Mr. Nicholas describes the complete symptomology of paranoia, centering on an executive in the surveillance industry who becomes convinced that "He was being watched everywhere and all the time." The protagonist, Henry Haddock, eventually adjusts to a life without privacy, wherein his public function subsumes his whole personality, and he becomes reconciled to a world without privacy, without self. The story develops allegorically in that it describes a whole world pressed and overcrowded, when personal rights are lost to the pressure of the many.

Ely's novels are all parables of the New Babbitt redeemed, the affluent and self-satisfied "Executive Man" freed to make real, life-or-death decisions, to direct his life and test the morality of his society. The transformations are costly, painful and sometimes tragic, but they are real and significant actions, leaps of faith which give meaning to the small existences Ely depicts.

—William J. Schafer

EMECHETA, (Florence Onye) Buchi. British. Born in Lagos, Nigeria, 21 July 1944. Educated at Methodist Girls' High School, Lagos; University of London, B.Sc. (honours) in sociology 1972. Married Sylvester Onwordi in 1960 (separated, 1969); two sons and three daughters. Librarian, 1960–64; library officer, British Museum, London, 1965–69; youth worker and resident student, Race, 1974–76; community worker, Camden Council, London, 1976–78; visiting lecturer at 11 universities in the United States, 1979; Senior Research Fellow and Visiting Professor, University of Calabar, Nigeria, 1980–81; Lecturer, Yale University, New Haven, Connecticut, 1982. Since 1982, Lecturer, University of London. Proprietor, Ogwugwu Afo Publishing Company, London; since 1979, member of the Home Secretary's Advisory Council on Race. Address: 7 Briston Grove, Crouch End, London N8 9EX, England.

PUBLICATIONS

Novels

Adah's Story. London, Allison and Busby, 1983.
  In the Ditch. London, Barrie and Jenkins, 1972.
  Second-Class Citizen. London, Allison and Busby, 1974; New York, Braziller, 1975.
The Bride Price. London, Allison and Busby, and New York, Braziller, 1976.
The Slave Girl. London, Allison and Busby, and New York, Braziller, 1977.
The Joys of Motherhood. London, Allison and Busby, and New York, Braziller, 1979.
Destination Biafra. London, Allison and Busby, 1982.
Naira Power. London, Macmillan, 1982.
Double Yoke. London, Ogwugwu Afo, 1982; New York, Braziller, 1983.
The Rape of Shavi. London, Ogwugwu Afo, 1983; New York, Braziller, 1985.

Plays

Television Plays: *A Kind of Marriage*, 1976; *The Ju Ju Landlord*, 1976.

Other (for children)

Titch the Cat. London, Allison and Busby, 1979.
Nowhere to Play. London, Allison and Busby, 1980.
The Moonlight Bride. Oxford, Oxford University Press, 1980.
The Wrestling Match. Oxford, Oxford University Press, 1981; New York, Braziller, 1983.
Our Own Freedom (for adults), photographs by Maggie Murray. London, Sheba, 1981.

*   *   *

The title *Second-Class Citizen* which Buchi Emecheta chose for one of her most successful novels constitutes a very fair summary of the major theme which she explores. She always feels for the oppressed and presents their plight in a way that engages the reader's sympathy. From childhood on she observed life in Nigeria, and since her early twenties she has looked at the ways of the west through the sceptical, appraising eyes of a trained sociologist. And what she has seen, whether in Africa or England, has been a bleak picture of antagonisms and tyranny. There are flashes of humour and moments of happiness, but generally she depicts the scouring of human relationships by the desire of the powerful to dominate and exploit those who are weaker.

Married life she depicts as a battle of the sexes, and if some white males are shown in a bad light, that is nothing compared with the portrayal of the Nigerian men. Francis, in *Second-Class Citizen*, is a Nigerian immigrant in London whose thoughtlessness is the ruin of his more gifted wife; lazy, egotistical, and feckless, he compounds every problem that confronts the pair in their struggle to make ends meet, and his sexual demands and irresponsibility about parenthood leave Adah a physical wreck, distraught and without a penny in her pocket. In *The Joys of Motherhood* we become aware of the mordant irony of the title as the novel chronicles the misfortunes of Nnu Ego, a simple Nigerian girl who comes to Lagos to marry and suffers every kind of humiliation as her husband proves himself incapable of overcoming the admittedly difficult circumstances of his wretched existence. Her agony reaches its peak when, in accord with custom, he takes as his second wife the widow of his brother and thoroughly enjoys the tensions this naturally creates.

Tyranny and heartlessness outside the domestic sphere also rouse Emecheta's ire. For many young people in Nigeria education seems to offer a route towards self-fulfilment, but *Double Yoke* shows what the price can be when a young girl tries to cope with the rival claims of tradition and modernity within a system which fundamentally has little to offer that is really valid. The cynicism of the whole enterprise is revealed when the heroine realises she must trade sexual favours with her professor if she is to gain the examination results she covets. Once she has qualifications she will perhaps be able, like Adah in *Second-Class Citizen*, to go to the United Kingdom and enjoy what it has to offer. In fact, as *Second-Class Citizen* and its grim predecessor, *In the Ditch*, show, London is a hostile world where racialism is rife and housing is squalid. There is the welfare state, of course, yet it operates in such a way that a talented and qualified young woman is gradually but inexorably pauperised and deskilled. *Destination Biafra* is a chilling account of a different sort of horror, the disastrous civil war that rent Nigeria apart in the difficult times immediately after the withdrawal of the inadequate colonial powers. No atrocity is too cruel for men in brief authority, and though Emecheta has sympathy for everyone, it is natural that the women are shown as those who suffer the most.

Few will seek to deny that Emecheta has grounds for the complaints she makes about marital relationships in particular and about the interplay of social and political forces in general. Yet, to some degree, she loads the dice a little too much. The girls and women she takes as her heroines always possess something which places them above the ordinary run of those with whom they mix. Birth or superior intelligence makes them outstanding. But it also has the unfortunate consequence of making them atypical of the group they represent. There is too some idealisation of rural society in Nigeria in former times. It certainly had merits, which colonial powers were stupid not to recognise, yet by concentrating on the more advantaged members of such communities Emecheta distorts the picture. The problem becomes most acute in *The Rape of Shavi*, a somewhat mannered allegorical tale of Europeans who are fleeing from an impending cataclysm, and who have the privilege of insight into an almost Utopian Africa.

For the most part, however, Emecheta's mode is realistic, and though *Destination Biafra* contains some devastating pictures of the pretentiousness and luxurious life-style of upper-class Nigerians, she generally concerns herself with the straightforward portrayal of the underprivileged. There is some description of locales, with Nigerian names for plants, foodstuffs, and fabrics adding a dash of local colour which sometimes conrasts, especially in the earlier novels, a little too obviously with literary allusions in a dated English tradition. Dialogue is invariably crisp, highlighting important turns in the narrative or enhancing characterisation. Above all, Emecheta is a storyteller. The title of her novels, like the chapter headings, are direct and explicit, helping the reader to see the way forward through narratives that have the power to convince as well as the capacity to arouse sympathy with the misfortunes depicted.

—Christopher Smith

ENGLISH, Isobel. British. Born in London, 9 June 1925. Educated at a convent school in Somerset. Recipient: Katherine Mansfield-Menton Prize, 1974. Address: Grove House, Castle Road, Cowes, Isle of Wight, England.

PUBLICATIONS

Novels

The Key That Rusts. London, Deutsch, 1954.
Every Eye. London, Deutsch, 1956; New York, Crowell, 1959.
Four Voices. London, Longman, 1961.

Short Stories

Life after All and Other Stories. London, Martin Brian and O'Keeffe, 1973.

Uncollected Short Story

"Promises," in *New Stories 1*, edited by Margaret Drabble and Charles Osborne. London, Arts Council, 1976.

Play

Meeting Point, in *New Review* (London), 1976.

Other

The Gift Book, illustrated by Barbara Jones. London, Parrish, 1964.

*

Critical Study: interview in *Friends and Friendship* by Kay Dick, London, Sidgwick and Jackson, 1974.

*   *   *

Isobel English's particular angle of vision, focusing on the various implications of an action and intricate suppositions of hidden motivation, inclines her naturally towards first-person narration. For her, experience must necessarily be filtered through the eye of one particular observer, with an implicit question as to the nature of the filter in each case.

The Key That Rusts deals with the love-affair of the narrator's married step-brother and a friend, culminating in the latter's madness. The narrator both reveals much of herself in her account of this, and is insidiously affected by the action. The flashbacks to her childhood, as she revisits her old convent school, introduce another scale of values, though without necessarily any acceptance of "the security of faith," and complicated by the implications of the metamorphosis of her schoolgirl love, Felicity, into Mother Peter.

Confusion of time sequences to bring out thematic continuity is taken further in the more stylized *Every Eye*, with its exploitation of photographic imagery. Here, the narrator's holiday journey across Europe is accompanied by a journey through her memory, reconstructing her youthful love-affair with the middle-aged Jasper. Although in these memories the narrator is ostensibly one of the two chief protagonists, it yet seems appropriate for the journey through place to reveal that her role in Jasper's life was subsidiary to Cynthia's, whose presence has permeated the book. The closing factual substantiation of the relationship between Jasper and Cynthia is a highly skilful sleight-of-hand. English's quirky phrasing is well suited both to the piquant past and the contented present which her narrator juxtaposes; the style has shed the occasional overselfconsciousness of her previous book.

Middle-class characters similar to those of the earlier books reappear in *Four Voices*, but here English introduces the middle-class failures, Mona and Penry. Pentry has sunk to the level of a men's hostel, though the exigencies of the plot keep the setting mostly middle-class. In fact, the accidents of marriage unite the characters in the same family—an institution which fascinates English in all three novels. However, it is doubtful whether the slightly clumsy narrative technique—inspired by the radio?—justifies the wider range of characterization. In any case the technique of blending monologues "spoken" by the main characters, once used, is probably a dead end for this author.

English's stories, collected in *Life after All*, show an individual and accomplished use of the form. In general she dispenses with the first-person narrator on the smaller scale of the short story. An exception, "Running Away," describes a convent school childhood, while Sebastian's mother in "The Crucifix after Cellini" is cast in the same mould as the Catholic *dévoté* in *Four Voices*. English's preoccupation with the extended family runs through several stories, including the longest, "One of the Family," which like *The Key That Rusts* confronts mental illness. Her material ranges from the Jewish background of this story to an evocation of an American academic's homosexual haunts and cronies in "Saying Goodbye." Only one story, "Nobody Came," is unsuccessful, failing to avoid cliché in its treatment of lonely old age; but "Cousin Dot," partly in verse, is an interesting if light-weight attempt to handle a similar subject.

The middle-class ambience of English's work recalls Elizabeth Bowen and Elizabeth Taylor. Her power lies in her ironic control of nuance: "She frayed away the edges of her last days in the flat in a sadly distracted manner, that had behind it a great strength of purpose." There is a rare but all the more effective grotesqueness in her humor: "Then he said 'Granny,' and two heads reared up off their pillows like old tortoises, but fell back again when they saw him." This highly individual voice is only occasionally blurred by imprecision.

—Val Warner

ERI, Vincent (Serei). Papua New Guinean. Born in Moveave, 12 September 1936. Educated at Catholic mission schools, 1945–54; Sogeri High School, 1955; University of Papua New Guinea, Port Moresby, 1966–71, B.A. 1970. Married Margaret Karulaka; two daughters and four sons. Teacher, 1956–66; chief of operations, Education Department, 1972–73, and director, Information Department, 1973–74, both Port Moresby; with Papua New Guinea Foreign Service: Consul-General in Sydney, 1974–76, and High Commissioner in Canberra, 1976–79; Head of Department of Transport and Civil Aviation, 1980, and Department of Defence, 1981–82, both Port Moresby. Since 1982, personnel director, Harrisons and Crosfield Ltd. Address: P.O. Box 586, Lae, Papua New Guinea.

PUBLICATIONS

Novel

The Crocodile.   Milton, Queensland, Jacaranda Press, 1970; London, Longman, 1981.

*   *   *

Vincent Eri's *The Crocodile*, historically significant as the first Papua New Guinea novel, is a quiet but powerful record of the traditions, cultural confusions, and colonial humiliations of the Papuans during the 1930's and 1940's. As in many Third World novels we are early made aware that the central character belongs to an extended family, village, and clan with their own way of life, and tragedy results from the meeting of two different cultures with contrasting values. *The Crocodile* concerns a community which has superficially accommodated itself to missionary schools and to government by white Australian district officers, but which, like most of the Third World, was outside the mainstream of modern history until the Second World War.

The strengths of *The Crocodile* might be overlooked by readers expecting a fuller realization of society, customs, and characters; Eri's usual method is understatement, unassertive symbol, the leaving of events unexplained, and the avoidance of taking attitudes. The novel seems simplistic on the surface but has an interesting subtext of ironies and implications. A surprising quality of *The Crocodile* is Eri's irony:

There were no toilets. Why bother to build houses to house our waste? That is what the villagers would say to the medical orderlies who complained. The villagers agreed that it was necessary to build "small houses" for the Government officers, and the white missionaries. Their beautiful white skins looked too delicate to be allowed to use the bush. The teachers and students used the bush. So did all the village people. The teachers themselves did not believe in the story of the worms that made people sick. Nobody had seen these worms of destruction. The bush was kept clean by the pigs, who grew fat on it and trailed their bellies on the ground.

The narrator here is slightly distant from the narrative and while he can be felt in the sentence attributing the construction of outhouses to the delicacy of the whites, he has also, standing more at a distance, brought in ironies about the villagers' wrong beliefs concerning hygiene and infection. The apparent simplicity allows Eri not to choose between world views and kinds of explanation except when satiric. The narration usually subordinates protest to the depicting of a society and individuals under stresses that they do not understand.

The episodic structure of the novel both shows selectivity and is appropriate to the mentality of the main character, Hoiri. While many events take place, the storyline is slight, almost non-existent, as if there were no causes, no planned effects. Hoiri's mother is killed by one of the crocodiles that infest the rivers of the island. Although he is a Protestant deacon, the father believes, as do the villagers, that the crocodile embodies a magician who enslaves his victims. Later a large canoe is built to carry sago and betel nuts to Port Moresby, in exchange for pots. The attractions of the white man's city, with its undreamt-of comforts, goods, and wealth, are contrasted to the way Papuans do demeaning work for whites and are discriminated against. Other humiliations occur after Hoiri is made to become a carrier for a new, young, drunken Australian district officer. When his wife disappears, Hoiri is called home to hunt the crocodile which is presumed to have killed her. After the Second World War reaches the island, Hoiri is again made a carrier. He is taken to Huron Gulf, the first time he has seen New Guinea, where the various peoples of the island, despite their differing tongues, work peacefully together. They come into contact with Australian soldiers who treat them better than do the district officers; the Americans impress them with their generosity and wealth. As the Papuans believe that material goods are sent by their dead ancestors but that the whites have intercepted them for themselves, they are surprised to meet black American soldiers who have money. When they return to their villages after the war, the money they earned selling carvings to Americans is taken from them by the district officers. Instead they are paid humiliatingly small sums for their years as laborers and as compensation for relatives who died while working as government carriers. *The Crocodile* shows how little real impression Christianity and mission education made on the villagers, how the introduction of western products, such as sweet biscuits and clothing, created new desires and a new mythology (the cargo cult), and how the Second World War brought the various island groups together, initiating the process which led to national independence.

Eri's novel portrays cultural assertion, protest against colonialism, the unjust humiliating behavior of the white government officials, and the importance of education as a means of gaining equality—all topics familiar from literature written around the time of national independence. Other nationalist characteristics of the novel include representative characters, an attempt to create an indigenous style, the use of native words which are usually explained by the text, the transliteration of native linguistic expressions into English, the prominence of local vegetation, and use of local details in similes and metaphors ("like a sack of copra"). Addressed to a foreign readership, for whom the author is careful to explain local

customs, beliefs, and phrases, *The Crocodile* is filled with anthropological data concerning the feasts, sexual life, clan relations, traditions, funeral ceremonies, gender roles, food habits, myths, and economy of the clan.

The crocodile is a symbol of various kinds of power. When Hoiri impregnates his girlfriend, her mother calls him "a real crocodile . . . He has already made a kill." A powerful Australian is called a crocodile. The crocodile is also representative of the unknown, of sorcery, of colonialism, of the strangeness of the world which Hoiri must face and which defeats him. At the novel's conclusion Hoiri is arrested for bothering a woman whom he believes to be his bewitched wife; he feels in his pocket for the bank book recording his savings: "'Maybe this money will send Sevese to the white man's school, maybe he will grow up to understand the things that baffle me,' he thought numbly."

—Bruce King

ESSOP, Ahmed. Indian. Born in Dabhel, Surat, 1 September 1931. Educated at the University of South Africa, Pretoria, B.A. 1956, B.A. (honours) in English 1964. Married Farida Karim in 1960; four children. Teacher at a secondary school, Eldorado Park, Johannesburg, 1980–85. Recipient: English Academy of Southern Africa Schreiner Award, 1979. Address: P.O. Box 109, Lenasia, Johannesburg 1820, South Africa.

PUBLICATIONS

Novels

The Visitation. Johannesburg, Ravan Press, 1980.
The Emperor. Johannesburg, Ravan Press, 1984.

Short Stories

The Hajji and Other Stories. Johannesburg, Ravan Press, 1978.

Uncollected Short Stories

"Gemini" December 1979, "Two Dimensional" February 1980, "East/West" January 1981, "Full Circle" March 1982, "Jericho Again" June 1983, and "Initiation" September 1984, all in *Staffrider* (Johannesburg).
"Noorjehan," in *Forced Landing*, edited by Mothobi Mutloatse. Johannesburg, Ravan Press, 1980.
"Shakespeare's Image," in *English Academy Review* (Johannesburg), December 1983.

Verse

The Dark Goddess (as Ahmed Yousuf). London, Mitre Press, 1959.

*

Manuscript Collection: National English Literary Museum, Grahamstown, South Africa.

*   *   *

Ahmed Essop's fiction displays a marvellously realised sense of place and the ability to regard human nature, even at its most absurdly self-centred or viciously craven, as still worthy of some pity. Fordsburg, within metropolitan Johannesburg, is in Essop's writing what Malgudi is in R.K. Narayan's. Both are Indian places; their inhabitants have Indian names, often speak with similar accents, and would not feel entirely lost culturally if translated to each others' towns. In Fordsburg the women wear saris and there are "the raucous voices of vendors . . . the spicy odours of Oriental foods, the bonhomie of communal life." Older Fordsburgians usually speak Gujarati or Urdu and try to preserve traditional customs like arranged marriages. Hindu and Muslim religious observances exist side by side, with both rivalry and some merging at the edges (as in the Caribbean) rather than as potential sources of communal violence. As in Trinidad and Guyana, the Indian proletariat and the educated alike speak a regional variety of English, illustrated by this passage of invective from "Hajji Musa and the Hindu Fire-Walker":

"You liar! You come and tell me dat good-for-nutting Dendar boy, dat he good, dat he ejucated, dat he good prospect. My foot and boot he ejucated! He sleep most time wit bitches, he drink and beat my daughter. When you go Haj? You nutting but liar. You baster! You baster!"

The Afrikaans word "baster" (bastard) here signals the South African provenance of Essop's fiction about the largest population of Indian origin outside the sub-continent. Indeed Hindu and Muslim can taunt each other safely, in the knowledge that historically they have more in common than with members of other South African communities.

With its extension Newtown, Fordsburg seems to be based upon realities of Essop's childhood and youth before and during the 1950's campaign of passive resistance to apartheid, when there was a stronger sense of "Indianness," despite socialisings and sexual encounters across racial boundaries. More secular and less traditional is Lenasia, beyond the Johannesburg perimeter, where *The Emperor* is set, a government-built township for the decanting of Fordsburg Indians, thus allowing white suburbs around Fordsburg to expand conveniently and cheaply.

It is in *The Hajji and Other Stories* that the life of Fordsburg/Newtown is most engagingly and unpretentiously set forth. Nearly half the stories are satirisations of human beings falling short of the high standards of personal and social behaviour that they profess: Dr. Kamal's political cowardice in "The Betrayal," Yogi Khrishnasiva's covert fornication in his pursuit of spiritual liberation in "The Yogi," the holy men forced to seek refuge in the cinema and watch a film on "The Prophet" so as to escape the public violence they have stirred up as a protest against the screening of that film, the irrepressible Hajji Musa, in hospital with badly burned feet, dismissing Hindu fire-walking as "showmanship" after his own unsuccessful attempt. At his best, Essop strips pretence, hypocrisy, untruth, and deviousness from his characters and shows the naked humanity beneath, but with an imaginative and delicate understanding of the humiliation that people suffer when thus exposed, as in "The Hajji," where obdurate refusal to condone a brother's past apostasy results only in self-inflicted hurt and spiritual aridity, or the 70-year-old father's pathetic defeat when his new young second wife divorces him, Muslim-fashion, in preference for his own son. Some of the stories are competent psychological studies, as of the victim-figure in "The Target,' or of the self-important (unto insanity) high-school headmaster

in "Gladiators," or of the ambivalently dedicated political characters eventually left utterly isolated in "Ten Years" and "In Two Worlds." A frequent theme is the loss of human dignity, whether of the genuine or the merely outward kind. Occasionally Essop unnecessarily resorts to melodrama and sensationalism, as in "Labyrinth" and "Mr. Moonreddy."

The novel, *The Visitation*, sparkles with lively ideas and flashes of invention that on the whole don't quite coalesce. Mr. Sufi, a wealthy, complacent property owner, married but with a satisfying concubine discreetly housed in each of his apartment buildings, conducts his life quietly and respectably, even turning his monthly payment of protection money to the racketeer Gool into a polite little social ceremony. By the simple expedient of delivering large quantities of obviously stolen electric lamps to Sufi's home, Gool gains the blackmailer's firm hold upon a timid victim. Ironically, the lamps usher Sufi into an existence of darkness, fear, panic, and hallucination. As Gool and his thugs take over Sufi's very life, including his rent-collecting, like a supernatural visitation, he gradually realizes that they are doing crudely and violently what he has always done urbanely but equally ruthlessly. Even his love-life is reduced, when he witnesses Gool's sexual contortions with one of his former concubines. Clearly Gool is a doppelgänger, revealing to Sufi his own true nature, selfish, sensual, and sadistic, which he'd tried to cloak respectably. The weakness is that Gool becomes a mere caricature of criminality. The narrative might have been even more persuasive had Gool's wilder actions been incorporated in Sufi's hallucinations.

Caricature as a substitute for characterisation is a legitimate satirist's tool, though probably more successful within the narrower compass of a short story than in the fuller extent and more subtle shadings of a novel. The Lenasia headmaster, Mr. Dharma Ashoka, the central character in *The Emperor*, is a "stooge" Indian, a creature of the apartheid state with an unassuageable appetite for power. The ludicrous story of his rise and downfall is also the tragedy of his wrong-headedness. The author's ingenious schema isn't really credible—an analysis, in one persona, of both arrogance and its necessary pettinesses in exercising power, with Ashoka as a possible figuring of the apartheid state and his opponents as the resistance. But Essop's ultimate interest in human individuality undercuts such a reading, making Ashoka at the end (like Sufi in *The Visitation*), a man to be pitied in the hour of his humiliating self-knowledge.

—Arthur Ravenscroft

FAIRBAIRNS, Zoë (Ann). British. Born in Tunbridge Wells, Kent, 20 December 1948. Educated at St. Catherine's School, Twickenham, Middlesex, 1954–67; College of William and Mary, Williamsburg, Virginia, 1969–70; University of St. Andrews, Scotland, M.A. in modern history 1972. Editor, CND newspaper *Sanity*, London, 1973–75; Writer-in-Residence, Rutherford School, London, 1977–78, Bromley schools, Kent, 1981–82, Deakin University, Victoria, Australia, 1983, and Sunderland Polytechnic, 1983–85. Poetry editor, *Spare Rib*, London, 1978–82. Recipient: Fawcett Society Prize, 1985. Agent: A.M. Heath, 40–42 William IV Street, London WC2N 4DD, England.

PUBLICATIONS

Novels

Live as Family. London, Macmillan, 1968.

Down: An Explanation. London, Macmillan, 1969.
Benefits. London, Virago Press, 1979; New York, Avon, 1982.
Stand We at Last. London, Virago Press, and Boston, Houghton Mifflin, 1983.
Here Today. London, Methuen, and New York, Avon, 1984.

Short Stories

Tales I Tell My Mother, with others. London, Journeyman Press, 1978; Boston, South End Press, 1980.

Uncollected Short Stories

"Relics," in *Despatches from the Frontiers of the Female Mind*, edited by Jen Green and Sarah Lefanu. London, Women's Press, 1985.
"Spies for Peace: A Story of 1963," in *Voices from Arts for Labour*, edited by Nicki Jackowska. London, Pluto Press, 1985.

Play

Details of Wife (produced Richmond, Surrey, 1973).

Other

Study War No More. London, CND, 1974.
No Place to Grow Up, with Jim Wintour. London, Shelter, 1977.
Peace Moves: Nuclear Protest in the 1980's, with James Cameron, photographs by Ed Barber. London, Chatto and Windus, and Bridgeport, Connecticut, Merrimack, 1984.

Editor, *Women's Studies in the UK*, compiled by Oonagh Hartnett and Margherita Rendel. London, London Seminars, 1975.

*   *   *

Zoë Fairbairns is, deservedly, one of the most popular feminist fiction writers working in Britain. Her pacey novels are very much a part of mainstream fiction, making their appeal much broader than that of many more overtly polemical books. At first glance her work seems straight genre fiction: science fiction in *Benefits*; the multi-generational family saga in *Stand We at Last*; the crime thriller in *Here Today*. However, what Fairbairns does is to take each genre and transform it for her own use.

The main theme underlying each of these works is the gradual, irresistible raising of feminist consciousness. Other themes are the complexity of relationships between the sexes; loneliness; the powerlessness of need; and the ever-changing yet somehow constant problems faced by women, whether they be women of the future, the past, or today. Fairbairns approaches all her characters with realism, sympathy, and a great deal of wit. Though her male characters tend to be lightly sketched, her women make up for this lack of depth: they are humorous, deep-thinking, and self-critical; and whenever a character seems to be slipping close to social stereotype, the author quickly steps in with a touch of irony.

Take, for example, the two main characters in *Here Today*. On the one hand there is Catherine, a 30-year-old virgin, feminist, and teacher who, having been made redundant, finds herself thrown into the world of temporary office employment. Shocked by the exploitation of her fellow temps by the employers and job agencies, she sets about undermining the temping system. On the other hand there is fashion-conscious Antonia, one-time self-satisfied "Temp of the Year," who is shaken out of her complacency both by the advent of word-processing which threatens her livelihood and by a bad case of genital herpes which brings about the end of her marriage. Drawn together in an uneasy alliance through their loneliness and their common need to earn a living, the two women embark on an adventurous road to self-fulfilment, fraught with contrasts between the traditional middle- and working-class attitudes to love and work.

The concept of romantic love, though not a central theme, plays a part in Fairbairns's novels. Men tend to be either saints or sinners—and, surprisingly, the saints predominate. In *Here Today* Catherine forms a close relationship with Frank, a union leader extremely sympathetic to the women's movement. In *Benefits*, in many ways the most pessimistic of her books, we are presented with the enlightened, too-good-to-be-true Derek, who bends over backwards not to oppress his journalist wife, Lynn. However, the cold dictates of a superbureaucracy intent on controlling the reproductive rights of its women drives Lynn away from "the women's pages of the *Guardian*" towards a more radical feminism epitomised by Collindeane Tower, an abandoned block of council flats which has become home to a leaderless feminist community. As Lynn struggles with mixed feelings about her marriage and her own fertility, the women of Collindeane form ranks against Family, a political party dedicated to restoring so-called "family values" by methods of giving or holding back government benefits to those women who do or do not reproduce. The novel takes us from the late 1970's through to a 21st century where family planning has become government planning and the fabric of a once-prosperous society is, like Collindeane, crumbling away. Though *Benefits* is a science-fiction novel, the futuristic views of post-industrial Britain depicted in it are, at times, too close to aspects of present reality to be comfortable: poverty and decay are rife in all aspects of society; the Family Party eventually brings about its own destruction; and leaderless feminism seems to lead nowhere. The result is a powerful, chilling, somewhat depressing book.

Despite her preoccupation with the present lot of women, Fairbairns seems more at home when writing about the future or the past. Nowhere is this more evident than in *Stand We at Last*, perhaps the most ambitious of her novels. In her own words "a family saga with a feminist background," it traces the lives of a succession of women, starting in 1855 with the adventurous Sarah who emigrates to Australia hoping to make her fortune as a farmer, and ending with Jackie, a single parent living on a hippie commune in 1970's England. As in her other books, the writer remains true to the genre she has chosen: all of Life is present in this 600-page saga—births, suicides, miscarriages, abortions, raised hopes, dashed ambitions—not to mention love, passion, and sexual guilt. But this is no ordinary rags-to-riches saga: as in all Fairbairns's novels, ambitions are spiritual rather than material; children and men seem to be the rocks on which women's ambitions founder; and in order to break out of the cycle set up by her predecessors, the modern heroine must give up her man rather than get him in the end.

Though the themes in Zoë Fairbairns's writing are constant, each novel remains quite distinct in style. Her female characters, who are primarily ordinary people with ordinary problems, manage somehow to be extraordinarily interesting. Her plots are imaginative and gripping. One wonders with interest what genre she will choose to subvert next.

—Judith Summers

FARAH, Nuruddin. Somalian. Born in Baidoa, in 1945. Educated at Panjab University, Chandigarh, India; University of London; University of Essex, Wivenhoe. Divorced; one son. Clerk-typist, Ministry of Education, 1964–66, and secondary school teacher, 1969–71, both Mogadiscio, Somalia; Lecturer in Comparative Literature, Afgoi College of Education, 1971–74; Associate Professor, University of Ibadan, Jos, Nigeria. Recipient: Unesco fellowship, 1974; English-Speaking Union award, 1980. Address: c/o Allison and Busby Ltd., 6-A Noel Street, London W1V 3RB, England.

PUBLICATIONS

Novels

From a Crooked Rib.   London, Heinemann, 1970.
A Naked Needle.   London, Heinemann, 1976.
Sweet and Sour Milk.   London, Allison and Busby, 1979.
Sardines.   London, Allison and Busby, 1981.
Close Sesame.   London, Allison and Busby, 1983.

Play

A Dagger in Vacuum (produced 1969).

*   *   *

It is characteristic of Nuruddin Farah's writing that the reader reaches the end of his fourth novel, *Sardines*, and wonders what link there is between the title and the text. There is one, but it has to be teased out by a participating reader. The novels are, in the widest sense, political but are never simplistic or predictable. Farah is concerned to show the pressure of the Somalian regime on individual psyches; in three of his first four novels, all of which are set in Somalia, he concentrates on characters who are obsessed, or become obsessed, with the failure of the revolution or with the General, the head of the "revolutionary" state who has acquired ninety-nine names, like God, and is worshipped with such phrases as "there is no General but our General." In all his novels, Farah limits the narrative by using the partial and restricted point of view of his central characters, thus making the reader enact the characters' own frustrations and confusion in trying to make sense of a society whose leaders deliberately mislead, deceive, and betray their people.

Farah resembles no other African novelist in subject-matter or style. He is interested in experimental writers who portray extreme emotional and psychological states: Koschin's favourite novel in *A Naked Needle* is *Wuthering Heights* and he and Medina, in *Sardines*, refer to Soyinka's *The Interpreters*. Farah uses epigraphs in a stimulating manner, and they range from Somali proverbs to Beckett, Melville, Kafka, Ted Hughes, and Blake. Perhaps the most unusual aspect of Farah's fiction, especially in a writer who comes from a mainly Islamic society, is its sensitive depiction of women. The central characters in his two best novels, *From a Crooked Rib* and *Sardines*, are women; the dilemmas and pitfalls of a liberated woman in a profoundly reactionary society are explored brilliantly in *Sardines* though Farah has so far not extended his imaginative sympathy to white women: Nancy, in *A Naked Needle*, is lumpish and predatory. Women like Medina, in *Sardines*, are shown to bear the brunt of all the contradictory interwoven cultural strands that contribute to modern Somalia: tribalism, Islamic and Italian influences, a Marxist regime dominated by Soviet involvement, European culture imposed on an oral tradition. Medina thinks:

In this century, the African is a guest whether in Africa or elsewhere. A guest. The technology; the ideology; the living cells of power which throb with confidence; the intellectual make-up from which we derive our source of power; the contradictions which breathe life into us. If not a guest, then a slave to a system of thoughts, a system of a given economic rerouting.

Farah is not politically naive or specifically anti-Soviet; his implicit theme is the imprisoning effect of outside intervention in Somalian life. Loyaan, in *Sweet and Sour Milk*, sees "a nation regimented, militarised. A nation disciplined and forced to obey the iron-hand directing the orchestra of groans and moans."

One of the incidental pleasures of reading Farah's fiction is that characters recur in his imaginary world: *Sweet and Sour Milk* and *Sardines* are the first two parts of a trilogy but in *Sardines* we also discover what has become of the protagonists of *From a Crooked Rib* and *A Naked Needle*. *From a Crooked Rib* is the least political of the novels. The point of view is almost exclusively that of Ebla, a girl from a nomadic tribe who escapes from an arranged marriage only to become a victim of male sexual attitudes in Mogadiscio. Her naivety gradually disappears as she tries and fails to make her way in a man's world: "Why is it only the sons in the family who are counted? For sure this world is a man's—it is his dominion. It is his and is going to be his as long as women are oppressed, as long as women are sold and bought like camels, as long as this remains the system of life. Nature is against women . . . Aren't men the law?"

A Naked Needle takes place in one day in Mogadiscio during which Koschin passively accepts the arrival of an Englishwoman who is determined to marry him. Koschin himself is on the verge of a nervous breakdown, and is therefore rather too confusing a medium through which to communicate the situation to the reader. There are powerful passages, such as the chapter in which Koschin shows Nancy the city, but Koschin's are the only judgments given and he is so egotistical, bitter, and cruel to Nancy that the political issues are clouded by his diseased consciousness. In *Sweet and Sour Milk*, however, the reader is made acutely aware of the cunning of the post-revolutionary regime through Loyaan, a non-political innocent whose twin brother dies mysteriously at the beginning of the novel. The use of the plot is subtle: the reader expects to find out who killed Soyaan and shares Loyaan's experience as he gains wisdom and cynicism, and begins to unravel the mystery. But the answer is never found, and the reader's frustration mirrors that of the protagonist whose integrity cannot crack the manipulative power of the General and his minions. It is never clear who the minions and who the political activists are.

Sardines is similarly about people caught in a trap, or a tin. Our admiration of Medina, a journalist who has the courage to fight the General with all the weapons at her disposal, is tempered at the end when we see the precociousness of her daughter, Ubax, and the dangerous situation in which she has helped to place her husband, family, and friends. It is impossible to win in such a situation: Ubax embodies the difficulties for she, at eight, is charming and independent but also insolent and forlorn, longing for an ordinary mother. The language of the novel shows the weakness as well as the strengths of Farah's style. Even in a novel that explores the horrors of female circumcision this simile is strained: "the night which opened up like the teased lips of a vagina." There are persistent mixed metaphors which clutter a prose that, at its best, uses metaphor powerfully: "No, she wasn't a guest any more. She was a full and active participant in the history of her country."

—Angela Smith

FAST, Howard (Melvin). American. Born in New York City, 11 November 1914. Educated at George Washington High School, New York, graduated 1931; National Academy of Design, New York. Served with the Office of War Information, 1942–43, and the Army Film Project, 1944. Married Bette Cohen in 1937; one daughter and one son, the writer Jonathan Fast. War correspondent in the Far East for *Esquire* and *Coronet* magazines, 1945. Taught at Indiana University, Bloomington, Summer 1947. Imprisoned for contempt of Congress, 1947. Founder of the World Peace Movement and member of the World Peace Council, 1950–55. Operated Blue Heron Press, New York, 1952–57. Currently, member of the Fellowship for Reconciliation. American-Labor Party candidate for Congress for 23rd District of New York, 1952. Recipient: Bread Loaf Writers Conference award, 1933; Schomburg Race Relations Award, 1944; Newspaper Guild award, 1947; Jewish Book Council of America award, 1948; Stalin International Peace Prize (now Soviet International Peace Prize), 1954; Screenwriters award, 1960; National Association of Independent Schools award, 1962; Emmy Award, for television play, 1976. Agent: Sterling Lord Agency, 660 Madison Avenue, New York, New York 10021. Address: P.O. Box A, Redding Ridge, Connecticut 06876, U.S.A.

PUBLICATIONS

Novels

Two Valleys. New York, Dial Press, 1933; London, Dickson, 1934.
Strange Yesterday. New York, Dodd Mead, 1934.
Place in the City. New York, Harcourt Brace, 1937.
Conceived in Liberty: A Novel of Valley Forge. New York, Simon and Schuster, and London, Joseph, 1939.
The Last Frontier. New York, Duell, 1941; London, Lane, 1948.
The Unvanquished. New York, Duell, 1942; London, Lane, 1947.
The Tall Hunter. New York, Harper, 1942.
Citizen Tom Paine. New York, Duell, 1943; London, Lane, 1946.
Freedom Road. New York, Duell, 1944; London, Lane, 1946.
The American: A Middle Western Legend. New York, Duell, 1946; London, Lane, 1949.
The Children. New York, Duell, 1947.
Clarkton. New York, Duell, 1947.
My Glorious Brothers. Boston, Little Brown, 1948; London, Lane, 1950.
The Proud and the Free. Boston, Little Brown, 1950; London, Lane, 1952.
Spartacus. Privately printed, 1951; London, Lane, 1952.
Fallen Angel (as Walter Ericson). Boston, Little Brown, 1952; as *The Darkness Within*, New York, Ace, 1953; as *Mirage* (as Howard Fast), New York, Fawcett, 1965.
Silas Timberman. New York, Blue Heron Press, 1954; London, Lane, 1955.

The Story of Lola Gregg. New York, Blue Heron Press, 1956; London, Lane, 1957.
Moses, Prince of Egypt. New York, Crown, 1958; London, Methuen, 1959.
The Winston Affair. New York, Crown, 1959; London, Methuen, 1960.
The Golden River, in *The Howard Fast Reader.* New York, Crown, 1960.
April Morning. New York, Crown, and London, Methuen, 1961.
Power. New York, Doubleday, 1962; London, Methuen, 1963.
Agrippa's Daughter. New York, Doubleday, 1964; London, Methuen, 1965.
Torquemada. New York, Doubleday, 1966; London, Methuen, 1967.
The Hunter and the Trap. New York, Dial Press, 1967.
The Crossing. New York, Morrow, 1971; London, Eyre Methuen, 1972.
The Hessian. New York, Morrow, 1972; London, Hodder and Stoughton, 1973.
The Immigrants. Boston, Houghton Mifflin, 1977; London, Hodder and Stoughton, 1978.
Second Generation. Boston, Houghton Mifflin, and London, Hodder and Stoughton, 1978.
The Establishment. Boston, Houghton Mifflin, 1979; London, Hodder and Stoughton, 1980.
The Legacy. Boston, Houghton Mifflin, and London, Hodder and Stoughton, 1981.
Max. Boston, Houghton Mifflin, 1982; London, Hodder and Stoughton, 1983.
The Outsider. Boston, Houghton Mifflin, 1984; London, Hodder and Stoughton, 1985.
The Immigrant's Daughter. Boston, Houghton Mifflin, 1985.

Novels as E.V. Cunningham

Sylvia. New York, Doubleday, 1960; London, Deutsch, 1962.
Phyllis. New York, Doubleday, and London, Deutsch, 1962.
Alice. New York, Doubleday, 1963; London, Deutsch, 1965.
Lydia. New York, Doubleday, 1964; London, Deutsch, 1965.
Shirley. New York, Doubleday, and London, Deutsch, 1964.
Penelope. New York, Doubleday, 1965; London, Deutsch, 1966.
Helen. New York, Doubleday, 1966; London, Deutsch, 1967.
Margie. New York, Morrow, 1966; London, Deutsch, 1968.
Sally. New York, Morrow, and London, Deutsch, 1967.
Samantha. New York, Morrow, 1967; London, Deutsch, 1968.
Cynthia. New York, Morrow, 1968; London, Deutsch, 1969.
The Assassin Who Gave Up His Gun. New York, Morrow, 1969; London, Deutsch, 1970.
Millie. New York, Morrow, 1973; London, Deutsch, 1975.
The Case of the One-Penny Orange. New York, Holt Rinehart, 1977; London, Deutsch, 1978.
The Case of the Russian Diplomat. New York, Holt Rinehart, 1978; London, Deutsch, 1979.
The Case of the Poisoned Eclairs. New York, Holt Rinehart, 1979; London, Deutsch, 1980.
The Case of the Sliding Pool. New York, Delacorte Press, 1981; London, Gollancz, 1982.
The Case of the Kidnapped Angel. New York, Delacorte Press, 1982; London, Gollancz, 1983.

The Case of the Murdered Mackenzie. New York, Delacorte Press, 1984; London, Gollancz, 1985.
The Wabash Factor. New York, Delacorte Press, 1986.

Short Stories

Patrick Henry and the Frigate's Keel and Other Stories of a Young Nation. New York, Duell, 1945.
Departures and Other Stories. Boston, Little Brown, 1949.
The Last Supper and Other Stories. New York, Blue Heron Press, 1955; London, Lane, 1956.
The Edge of Tomorrow. New York, Bantam, 1961; London, Corgi, 1962.
The General Zapped an Angel. New York, Morrow, 1970.
A Touch of Infinity. New York, Morrow, 1973; London, Hodder and Stoughton, 1975.
Time and the Riddle: Thirty-One Zen Stories. Pasadena, California, Ward Ritchie Press, 1975.

Plays

The Hammer (produced New York, 1950).
Thirty Pieces of Silver (produced Melbourne, 1951; London, 1984). New York, Blue Heron Press, and London, Lane, 1954.
General Washington and the Water Witch. London, Lane, 1956.
The Crossing (produced Dallas, 1962).
The Hill (screenplay). New York, Doubleday, 1964.
Citizen Tom Paine, adaptation of his own novel (produced New York, 1985).

Screenplay: *The Hessian*, 1971.

Television Plays: *What's a Nice Girl Like You . . .?*, 1971; *The Ambassador* (*Benjamin Franklin* series), 1974; *21 Hours at Munich*, with Edward Hume, 1976.

Verse

Never to Forget the Battle of the Warsaw Ghetto, with William Gropper. New York, Jewish Peoples Fraternal Order, 1946.

Other

The Romance of a People (for children). New York, Hebrew Publishing Company, 1941.
Lord Baden-Powell of the Boy Scouts. New York, Messner, 1941.
Haym Salomon, Son of Liberty. New York, Messner, 1941.
The Picture-Book History of the Jews, with Bette Fast. New York, Hebrew Publishing Company, 1942.
Goethals and the Panama Canal. New York, Messner, 1942.
The Incredible Tito. New York, Magazine House, 1944.
Intellectuals in the Fight for Peace. New York, Masses and Mainstream, 1949.
Tito and His People. Winnipeg, Manitoba, Contemporary Publishers, 1950.
Literature and Reality. New York, International Publishers, 1950.
Peekskill, U.S.A.: A Personal Experience. New York, Civil Rights Congress, and London, International Publishing Company, 1951.
Korean Lullaby. New York, American Peace Crusade, n.d.
Tony and the Wonderful Door (for children). New York, Blue Heron Press, 1952; as *The Magic Door*, Culver City, California, Peace Press, 1979.

Spain and Peace. New York, Joint Anti-Fascist Refugee Committee, 1952.
The Passion of Sacco and Vanzetti: A New England Legend. New York, Blue Heron Press, 1953; London, Lane, 1954.
The Naked God: The Writer and the Communist Party. New York, Praeger, 1957; London, Bodley Head, 1958.
The Howard Fast Reader. New York, Crown, 1960.
The Jews: Story of a People. New York, Dial Press, 1968; London, Cassell, 1970.
The Art of Zen Meditation. Culver City, California, Peace Press, 1977.

Editor, *The Selected Work of Tom Paine.* New York, Modern Library, 1946; London, Lane, 1948.
Editor, *Best Short Stories of Theodore Dreiser.* Cleveland, World, 1947.

*

Manuscript Collections: University of Pennsylvania Library, Philadelphia; University of Wisconsin, Madison.

Howard Fast comments:

(1972) From the very beginning of my career as a writer, my outlook has been teleological. Since my first work was published at a very early age—my first novel at the age of eighteen—my philosophical position was naturally uncertain and in formation. Yet the seeds were there, and by the end of my first decade as a writer, I had clearly shaped my point of view. In the light of this, both my historical and modern novels (excepting the entertainments I have written under the name of Cunningham) were conceived as parables and executed as narratives of pace and, hopefully, excitement. I discovered that I had a gift for narrative in the story sense; but I tried never to serve the story, but rather to have it serve my own purpose—a purpose which I attempted in a transcendental sense.

In other words, I was—and am—intrigued by the apparent lunacy of man's experience on earth; but at the same time never accepted a pessimistic conclusion or a mechanical explanation. Thereby, my books were either examinations of moments or parables of my own view of history. As a deeply religious person who has always believed that human life is a meaningful part of a meaningful and incredibly wonderful universe, I found myself at every stage in my career a bit out of step with the current literary movement or fashion. I suppose that this could not have been otherwise, and I think I have been the most astounded of any at the vast audiences my work has reached.

Since I also believe that a person's philosophical point of view has little meaning if it is not matched by being and action, I found myself willingly wed to an endless series of unpopular causes, experiences which I feel enriched my writing as much as they depleted other aspects of my life. I might add that the more I have developed the parable as a form of literature, the more convinced I become that truth is better indicated than specified.

All of the above is of course not a critical evaluation of my work; and I feel that a writer is the last person on earth capable of judging his own work as literature with any objectivity. The moment I cease to feel that I am a good writer, I will have to stop writing. And while this may be no loss to literature, it would be a tragic blow to my income.

As for the dozen books I have written under the name of E.V. Cunningham, they are entertainments, for myself primarily and for all others who care to read them. They are also my own small contribution to that wonderful cause of women's liberation. They are all about wise and brave and gallant women, and while they are suspense and mystery stories, they are also parables in their own way.

*   *   *

Howard Fast has written in virtually every genre—novels, plays, poems, filmscripts, critical essays and short stories—and in a number of subgenres of fiction, including science fiction, social satire, historical and contemporary novels, spy thrillers, and moral allegories. He began publishing novels at the age of 18 and has kept up a brisk pace of production.

His strongest fictional gifts are a talent for swift, interesting narrative, the vivid portrayal of scenes of action, especially of violence, and an uncluttered style only occasionally marred by sentimental lapses. Although he became identified in the 1940's as a publicist for the Communist Party line, his novels reveal an intensely emotional and religious nature which eventually clashed with his left-wing allegiances. His ideals reflect a curious compound of slum-culture courage, Jewish concern for social justice, self-taught history, Cold-war Stalinism and, in his later years, Zen Buddhism. His entire literary career embodies his deepest beliefs: that life has moral significance, that the writer must be socially committed, that literature should take sides.

After two youthful blood-and-thunder romances, Fast found his métier in a series of class-conscious historical novels of the American Revolution. *Conceived in Liberty* heralded the loyalty of the common soldier; *The Unvanquished* celebrated the dogged persistence of George Washington (despite his aristocracy and wealth, Fast's favorite hero); and *Citizen Tom Paine* glorified our first professional revolutionary. Fast then championed anonymous heroes of other races: *The Last Frontier* is a spare but moving account of the heroic flight in 1878 of the Cheyenne Indians to their Powder River home in Wyoming; *Freedom Road* recounts the amazing social experiments of black Southern legislatures in the Reconstruction era. The best selling of the popular novels of the early 1940's, *Freedom Road* shows great power in its scenes of violent conflict but it is melodramatic and tendentious. By contrast, the poetically evocative *Last Frontier*, perhaps his best novel, enlists profound sympathy through great control and objectivity, and evades the pitfalls of "noble redskin" sentimentality.

In 1946 *The American* detailed the rise and fall of Illinois Governor John Peter Altgeld, who was politically defeated after he pardoned three anarchists convicted of bomb-throwing in Haymarket Square in 1886. Although Fast's novels had reflected Marxist thought since his youthful conversion to socialism, his propagandizing became too obtrusive with *Clarkton* in 1947. This proletarian strike novel of life in the Massachusetts textile mills revealed his inability to maintain the necessary distance to interpret contemporary events soundly. He returned in 1948 to the historical novel with *My Glorious Brothers*, a stirring account of the Maccabees and the 30-year Jewish resistance to Greek–Syrian tyranny. This success was duplicated with *Spartacus*, the largely imagined story of the gladiatorial revolt against Rome in 71 BC. *Spartacus* was self-published in 1951 after the author was blacklisted for Communist activities and had spent three months in federal prison for contempt of Congress. But, predictably, Fast's other works of the early 1950's were failures in proportion to their nearness to the present day: *The Passion of Sacco and Vanzetti* recounted sentimentally the last hours of the doomed Italian anarchists; *Silas Timberman* depicted an academic victim of a McCarthyite witchhunt; and *The Story of Lola Gregg* described the FBI

pursuit and capture of an heroic Communist labor leader. These self-published works of imprisoned martyrs, abounding in Christ-figures and symbolic Judases, reflect their author's bitter sense of entrapment and isolation, for he could neither publish with established houses nor leave the country.

In 1957 Fast publicly quit the Communist Party after the Hungarian revolution and then described his tortured apostasy in *The Naked God*. He soon revisited Jewish history as a favored novelistic subject with *Moses, Prince of Egypt; Agrippa's Daughter*; and *Torquemada*. He returned, with a more mature vision, thrice more to the American revolution in *April Morning, The Crossing*, and *The Hessian*. In other historical novels he continued to re-examine earlier themes: *The Winston Affair* deals with the court-martial of an American murderer, homosexual and anti-Semite who nevertheless deserves and wins justice in a military court, while *Power* shows the corruption by power of a John L. Lewis-type of labor leader; *Agrippa's Daughter* rejects the "just-war" theory of *My Glorious Brothers* in favor of Rabbi Hillel's pacifism.

Most readers saw Fast in two new guises (or disguises), as author of science-fiction stories and as a writer of "entertainments" in the manner of Graham Greene. These late science fiction or "Zen stories" include stories in *The Edge of Tomorrow, The Hunter and the Trap* and *The General Zapped an Angel* (late gathered into one volume, *Time and the Riddle*). The dozen or so "entertainments" are written under the pseudonym E.V. Cunningham, most built around the female title characters. Both the science fiction and the women-novels criticize American institutions and values with wit and humor, and all show the deft hand of the professional storyteller at work. A newer series of Cunningham thrillers stars Masao Masuto, a Japanese–American detective of the Beverly Hills Police Department and a Zen Buddhist. In these, character holds the main appeal, especially that of family-man Masuto.

Recently, Fast has achieved repeated bestsellerdom with an immigrant-saga that has grown to seven large novels, starting with *The Immigrants* and including, most recently, *The Immigrant's Daughter*. These volumes trace the Italian, Dan Lavette, and his family while newly arrived Italians, Jews, Orientals, and others struggle against the entrenched wealth and prejudice of old-line Americans. Beginning with the San Francisco earthquake of 1906, the series energetically sweeps across 20th-century American history and recent world events. No longer axe-grinding, Fast uses well his own rich experiences for the first time, and here he is at the top of his admirable narrative form.

—Frank Campenni

FAUST, Irvin.   American.   Born in New York City, 11 June 1924. Educated at City College of New York, B.S. 1949; Columbia University, New York, M.A. 1952, D.Ed. 1960. Served in the United States Army, 1943–46. Married Jean Satterthwaite in 1959. Teacher, Manhattanville Junior High School, New York, 1949–53; guidance counselor, Lynbrook High School, Long Island, 1956–60. Since 1960, Director of Guidance and Counseling, Garden City High School, Long Island. Taught at Columbia University, Summer 1963, New School for Social Research, New York, 1975, Swarthmore College, Pennsylvania, 1976, City College, 1977, and University of Rochester, New York, Summer 1978. Agent: Gloria Loomis, Watkins Loomis Agency Inc., 150 East 35th Street, New York,

New York 10016. Address: 417 Riverside Drive, New York, New York 10025, U.S.A.

PUBLICATIONS

Novels

The Steagle.   New York, Random House, 1966.
The File on Stanley Patton Buchta.   New York, Random House, 1970.
Willy Remembers.   New York, Arbor House, 1971.
Foreign Devils.   New York, Arbor House, 1973.
A Star in the Family.   New York, Doubleday, 1975.
Newsreel.   New York, Harcourt Brace, 1980.

Short Stories

Roar Lion Roar and Other Stories.   New York, Random House, and London, Gollancz, 1965.
The Year of the Hot Jock and Other Stories.   New York, Dutton, 1985.

Uncollected Short Story

"Action at Vicksburg," in *Black Mask Quarterly* (Orlando, Florida), Fall 1985.

Other

Entering Angel's World: A Student-Centered Casebook.   New York, Columbia Teachers College Press, 1963.

*

Critical Studies: by Richard Kostelanetz, in *The New American Arts*, New York, Horizon Press, 1965, in *Tri-Quarterly* (Evanston, Illinois), Winter 1967, and in *On Contemporary Literature*, New York, Avon, 1967; by R.V. Cassill, in *New York Times Book Review*, 29 August 1971; interview with Matthew Bruccoli, in *Conversations with Writers 2*, Detroit, Gale, 1978.

Irvin Faust comments:

(1972) It seems to me that thus far my work has dealt with the displacement and disorganization of Americans in urban life; with their attempt to find adjustments in the glossy attractions of the mass media—movies, radio, t.v., advertising, etc.—and in the image-radiating seductions of our institutions—colleges, sports teams, etc. Very often this "adjustment" is to the "normal" perception a derangement, but perfectly satisfying to my subjects.

Recently my work has moved out to include suburban America and also back in historical directions. My characters to this date have been outside of the white anglo–saxon milieu, but have included Jews, Blacks, Puerto Ricans and the so-called Ethnic Americans.

Both *Roar Lion Roar* and *The Steagle* were published in France (Gallimard) and I feel the reviews were most perceptive, leading me to muse that perhaps, unbeknownst to me, I am quite close to the French literary sensibility.

*   *   *

In his novels and short stories, Irvin Faust has attempted (as he said of one novel), "to show the rise and fall of this nation over the last forty years." Were this all, he would be essentially a social historian disguised as fictional chronicler of our times. Faust, however, has managed to weave together a substantial number of additional themes, drawing upon his background as Jew, New Yorker, veteran, husband, and professional guidance counselor. The integration of these materials, when successful, produces a rich tapestry of life in contemporary urban America, especially when played off against the past, both mythicized and actual.

His first fictional book, *Roar Lion Roar*. treated with sensitive compassion the interior lives of disturbed adolescents of minority backgrounds. In the title story, Ishmael Ramos, a janitor at Columbia University, so identifies with the "ivory leak" school that he kills himself when the football team loses. Most of the protagonists of these stories are insane but even the sane have been mind-molded by the mass media or warped by the pressures of recent history. Indeed, Faust's major theme of the forming and deforming of personality by an empty culture in a violent, chaotic world may here have found its most solid embodiment.

The broader canvas of the novel form permitted Faust the breadth and depth needed to convey the specificity of a conflicted culture in its dizzying impact upon the individual. In Faust's first novel, *The Steagle*, English Professor Harold Weissburg develops a multiple personality while his sense of self disintegrates during the Cuban missile crisis. The title is a composite-name formed from two football teams, the Steelers and the Eagles. Thus, as the United States shifts from "good neighbor" to threatening nuclear power, Weissburg, in desperate flight across the country, becomes Bob Hardy (brother of Andy, of the wholesome movie family), gangster Rocco Salvato, a football hero, a flying ace, and, finally Humphrey Bogart. In *The File on Stanley Buchta* his protagonist is an undercover policeman, Vietnam veteran, and college graduate who infiltrates both a para-military rightist group within the police department and a New Left organization. He is further divided in romantic loyalty to an all-American blonde beauty and a black militant on whom he is spying. Perhaps because the hero is not fully realized, or because the material lacks the historical density which the author prefers, this fairly conventional novel lacks impact.

Faust's next two novels, however, are probably his best to date. *Willy Remembers* features the redoubtable Willy Kleinhans, who at 93 is an embodiment and archive of America in the 19th century. The history he recalls is badly scrambled but curiously apt: Grover Cleveland is confused with baseball-pitcher Grover Cleveland Alexander; John F. Kennedy melds with McKinley, another assassinated President; Admiral and Governor Dewey, Franklin and Teddy Roosevelt likewise interchange. The Haymarket Riot, the frame-up of Tom Mooney, prohibition, and T.R. at San Juan Hill all whiz by as kaleidoscopic snapshots. Despite Willy's anti-Semitism, curmudgeonly judgments and angry confusion, he is a likable and likely representative of his time and place. Although R.V. Cassill rightly praised *Willy Remembers* for its "overlapping stereotypes of urban and national memory" and the novel's "Joycean complexity," Faust does not always guide the reader adequately along these high-speed, involuted memory-trips. The novel does display, nevertheless, a marked advance in control of point-of-view and the blend of fantasy and realism. With *Foreign Devils* Faust achieves mastery in weaving together the items of popular culture, the myths by which many Americans live, and the disintegrating personality of a Jewish writer. His hero, Sidney Benson (born Birnbaum), is separated from his wife and living partly off his mother's earnings from a candy store. Inspired by President Nixon's trip to China, Benson, who has suffered from writer's block, begins a novel about the Boxer rebellion. This melodrama, or novel-within-the novel, is an exquisite parody of the swashbuckling accounts of Richard Harding Davis, and is perhaps the chief attraction of *Foreign Devils*. The action in the present, except for Benson's reunion at the end with his father (who had deserted his family years ago), is cluttered with topical references, both a shortcoming and an attraction in Faust's fiction.

Faust's two most recent novels, *A Star in the Family* and *Newsreel*, show flashes of power as each book scans recent American history, but he is in danger of repeating himself. The tale of vaudevillian Bart Goldwine, protagonist of *Star in the Family*, consists of interviews conducted by Goldwine's biographer, plus longer memoiristic accounts by Goldwine. The reproduction of showbusiness patter, street talk, fan magazine prose, courtship, and family discussions is flawless in evoking the cynicism and innocence of the last generation. Showman Goldwine's impression of John F. Kennedy is abruptly ended by the assassination; his long decline thereafter is symbolically entwined with the decline of American vitality and national will. In *Newsreel* former Army Captain Manny "Speed" Finestone is again the victim of his times. Linked spiritually with his wartime "chief," Dwight Eisenhower, Speed cannot escape contrasting the purity of the great crusade against Hitler with the materialism of the affluent 1950's, the cold war mentality, and the slaying of President Kennedy (Chapter 29 is simply "11/22/63"). Finestone's inability to write, his failed romances with two Jewish women and an Irish girl, his unraveling into psychosis are all played against national deterioration in a cultural wasteland. Other previous themes and motifs are also present: sex and sports, the abandoning father, the Jew fighting his ethnic identity, the writer supported by his mother, the use of dialogues with other selves or fantasy-heroes. Although their repeated use suggests personal concerns that are insufficiently integrated into fiction, Faust continues to portray both interior individual lives and cultural tension with skill and sincerity.

—Frank Campenni

FEDERMAN, Raymond. American. Born in Paris, France, 15 May 1928; emigrated to the United States in 1947; became citizen, 1953. Educated at Columbia University, New York, 1954–57, B.A. (cum laude) 1957 (Phi Beta Kappa); University of California, Los Angeles, 1957–63, M.A. 1958, Ph.D. in French 1963. Served in the United States Army 82nd Airborne Division in Korea, 1951–54: Sergeant. Married Erica Hubscher in 1960; one daughter. Jazz saxophonist, 1947–50; Lecturer and Assistant Professor, University of California, Santa Barbara, 1959–64. Associate Professor of French, 1964–68, Professor of French and Comparative Literature, 1968–73, and since 1973, Professor of English and Comparative Literature, State University of New York, Buffalo. Visiting Professor, University of Montreal, 1970, and Hebrew University, Jerusalem, 1982–83. Co-editor, *Mica* magazine, Santa Barbara, 1959–64; co-director, Fiction Collective, 1977–80. Recipient: Guggenheim fellowship, 1966; *Panache* Experimental Fiction Prize, 1971; Steloff Prize, 1972; Camargo Foundation fellowship, 1977; Fulbright fellowship, 1982; National Endowment for the Arts fellowship, 1985; New York State Foundation for the Arts fellowship, 1985. Address: 46 Four Seasons West, Eggertsville, New York 14226, U.S.A.

PUBLICATIONS

Novels

Double or Nothing: A Real Fictitious Discourse.   Chicago, Swallow Press, 1971.
Amer Eldorado (in French).   Paris, Stock, 1974.
Take It or Leave It.   New York, Fiction Collective, 1976.
➤*The Voice in the Closet* (bilingual edition), with *Echos à Federman*, by Maurice Roche.   Madison, Wisconsin, Coda Press, 1979.
⊸*The Twofold Vibration.*   Bloomington, Indiana University Press, and Brighton, Harvester Press, 1982.
➤*Smiles on Washington Square.*   New York, Thunder's Mouth Press, 1985.

Uncollected Short Stories

"The Man on the Bridge" (as Robin St. Gill), in *Mica* (Santa Barbara, California), vol. 1, no. 1, 1960.
"False Evidence," in *Kolokon*, Summer 1966.
"Histoire du Ballon," in *West Coast Review* (Burnaby, British Columbia), Fall 1969.
"The Captain and the Kids," in *Assembling*, edited by Richard Kostelanetz.   New York, Assembling Press, 1970.
"Suspension," in *UCLAN Review Magazine* (Los Angeles), Winter 1970.
"Au pied du Livre," in *Sub-Stance 5-6* (Madison, Wisconsin), Summer 1973.
"An Impromptu Swim," in *Out of Sight* (Wichita, Kansas), April 1974.
"Inside the Thing," in *Oyez Review* (Berkeley, California), Fall 1974.
"Setting and Tripping," in *Statements*, edited by Jonathan Baumbach.   New York, Braziller, 1975.
"Self-Plagiaristic Autobiographical Poem in Form of a Letter from Here and Elsewhere," in *Oyez Review* (Berkeley, California), new series 5, 1977.
"Hat Missive," "Questionnaire," and "Hats Hats Hats," in *Milk 11-12*, 1978.
"Premembrance," in *Mississippi Review* (Hattiesburg), Fall 1978.
"Parcifal in Hamburg," in *Chicago Review*, Spring 1980.
"Moinous, Nam, and Dostoevsky," in *Paris Review*, Fall 1981.
"The Rigmarole of Contrariety," in *StoryQuarterly 15-16* (Northbrook, Illinois), 1982.
"Moinous and Sucette: A Love Story of Sorts," in *Sub-Stance* (Madison, Wisconsin), Spring 1983.
"Displaced Person," in *Denver Quarterly*, Spring 1984.

Verse

Among the Beasts (bilingual edition).   Paris, Millas Martin, 1967.
Me Too.   Reno, Nevada, West Coast Poetry Review Press, 1976.

Other

Journey to Chaos: Samuel Beckett's Early Fiction.   Berkeley, University of California Press, 1965.
Samuel Beckett: His Works and His Critics: An Essay in Bibliography, with John Fletcher.   Beckeley, University of California Press, 1970.

Editor, *Cinq Nouvelles Nouvelles*.   New York, Appleton Century Crofts, 1970.

Editor, *Surfiction: Fiction Now—and Tomorrow*. Chicago, Swallow Press, 1975; revised edition, Athens, Ohio University Press-Swallow Press, 1981.
Editor, with Tom Bishop, *Samuel Beckett*. Paris, L'Herne, 1976.
Editor, with Lawrence Graver, *Samuel Beckett: The Critical Heritage*. London, Routledge, 1979.

Translator, *Temporary Landscapes* (bilingual edition), by Yvonne Caroutch. Venice, Mica, 1965.

*

Critical Studies: *The End of Intelligent Writing* by Richard Kostelanetz, New York, Sheed and Ward, 1974; "The Choice of Invention" by Harris Dienstfrey, in *Fiction International 2* (Canton, New York), 1974; *Literary Disruptions* by Jerome Klinkowitz, Urbana, University of Illinois Press, 1975, revised edition, 1980; "Flushing Out 'The Voice in the Closet'" by Charles Caramello, in *Sub-Stance 20* (Madison, Wisconsin), 1978; interviews, with Charlotte Meyers in *StoryQuarterly* (Northbrook, Illinois), Fall 1982, with Larry McCaffery in *Contemporary Literature* (Madison, Wisconsin), Fall 1983, and in *Anything Can Happen: Interviews with Contemporary American Novelists* edited by McCaffery and Thomas LeClair, Urbana, University of Illinois Press, 1983.

Raymond Federman comments:

Although my work has been labelled "experimental" and "avant-garde," and it is true my fiction departs radically from conventional narrative forms, I do believe that it speaks to the reality of our modern times. That does not mean it is realistic; on the contrary, I am not interested in writing fiction which represents the world, but which improves reality. My main concern is with language, but not a language which reproduces meaning but which produces new meaning. I have expressed my position on fiction in several theoretical essays, in particular the essay/manifesto "Surfiction" (*Partisan Review*, 1973), and more recently in "Imagination as Playgiarism" (*New Literary History*, 1977). I believe that my novels form a coherent project which is an effort on my part to come to terms with both my personal experiences (especially during World War II, and as an immigrant in America) and the recent historical events in which I have participated as a writer and a human being. The distinction I make, however, is that I do not think that my life and history are the sources of my fiction, but that in fact my fiction is what invents my life and history. In other words, the stories I write are my life.

*   *   *

Raymond Federman established himself as a critic before he turned to novel-writing. His books and essays about Samuel Beckett seem to have shaped his career as a novelist just as surely as Beckett's early criticism on Joyce and Proust pointed the way to his fiction from *More Pricks Than Kicks* to the *Molloy* trilogy. Federman once called Beckett's fiction "le roman du langage." He was trying on this occasion to distinguish between André Gide's *Counterfeiters*, which he saw as "primarily a reflection on fiction by fiction," and Beckett's work, which is more "a reflection on fiction by its own language."
Federman's novels are, among other things, showcases for "linguistic play" and "narrative joy" (as Jerome Klinkowitz

points out in his *Literary Disruptions*). Like Beckett, Federman is enviably bilingual and moves with ease between English and French. His novels seem to profit from experiments—verbal, visual, and narrative—he has observed on both the American and French fictional scenes.

Double or Nothing, his first novel, is described on the dust-jacket as "a *concrete* novel—*concrete*, as in *concrete poetry*." Each page seems to go its own visual and verbal way. All classical distinctions between image and word appear to be rendered obsolete. *Double or Nothing* is what the French might call a "roman-en-train-de-se-faire." We witness the growing pains of writing a novel while we see the grudging, halting fleshing-out of a story which involves the arrival in America of a 19-year-old immigrant. Everything is tentative, every detail of the story is subject to the caprices of the narrator. Hence names change as they do in Beckett ("In fact I'll change all the names eventually. Has to be"), situations alter on retelling, digressions wear down the narrative at every turn. It seems to take the immigrant as long to disembark from his boat as it does Tristram Shandy to get born. Catalogues, inventories, all sorts of spatial devices slow down time and arrest any kind of forward movement.

The same complex, digressive, unlinear telling characterizes *Take It or Leave It*. This novel is more completely "a reflection on fiction by its own language" than *Double or Nothing*. This "exaggerated second-hand tale," as it is called on the title page, seems less eccentric typographically than its predecessor but much denser verbally and narratively. In a certain sense it is part of the tradition of the French voyage-of-discovery-of-America, a tradition which includes Céline's *Journey to the End of the Night* and Butor's *Mobile*. (There are even references to Céline in the text, such as "here go back and reread the arrival of Bardamu in New York in le Voyage.")

The telling of *Take It or Leave It* has more than its share of exhilaration (a word used appropriately as the title for the sixth chapter of the novel). Words seem to explode on the page as Frenchy's adventures are recounted from his days with the 82nd Airborne Division in North Carolina through his trip north to Camp Drum in early 1951. These adventures, which offer something of a narrative line, are eclipsed at every turn by an elaborate series of subtexts which comment on such unrelated matters as the differences between French and English, the theories of Derrida, and the terrible legacy of the Holocause. There is room in this unpaginated novel for almost anything its creator chooses to place within its covers. Titles of Federman's earlier works are paraded before us as well as a brief biographical sketch of the author when he retreats behind the mask of Hombre De La Pluma. This *opera aperta* (Umberto Eco's words) keeps opening-out and breaking down the walls of conventional fiction. The novelist freely enters the frame of his novel and creator and creatures come to confront one another on equal terms.

Even on this crowded canvas, with its "story that cancels itself as it goes," the presence of Beckett is unmistakable. Federman at one point embellishes a line from *Murphy*: "MUST I BITE THE HAND THAT STARVES ME SO THAT IT CAN STRANGLE ME BETTER?" At another he nods fondly to his mentor: "In complete LESSNESSness my friend Sam would say where nothing is even less than nothing."

The Voice in the Closet seems to honor Beckett at every turn. Just as the Irish writer achieved such remarkable economy of means in his recent prose, so has Federman realized a startling process of reduction here. *The Voice in the Closet*, which looks more like an art book than fiction, contains three texts: parallel English and French versions of a work by Federman

(*The Voice in the Closet/La Voix dans le Cabinet de Débarras*), with a piece by Maurice Roche, *Echos* (dedicated to Federman), sandwiched in between. The Federman work, with its disturbing hermetic words and cadences, is unpunctuated and unparagraphed in both languages. Here is the way the author described *The Voice in the Closet* in a recent letter: "A complex double book—system of mirrors, echoes, boxes within boxes to accommodate my plural voice."

Federman's career as writer and critic seems reduced to a few words and images in this text. A reading of the two earlier novels as well as a knowledge of his criticism and poetry would seem a prerequisite for any understanding of *The Voice in the Closet*. A forbidding Mallarméan density should keep away all but the most serious students of recent Franco–American literature. While the author hid behind a series of masks or disguises in *Double or Nothing* and *Take It or Leave It*, he emerges here as "federman" (or as "namredef" or "featherman") and Beckett quite simply as "sam." The matters of Jewishness ("the yellow star on my chest") and the experience of the Holocaust ("the empty skins already remade into lampshades") are perhaps more sharply focused here than anywhere else in Federman's work.

The focus continues into *The Twofold Vibration*, the title of which is taken from Beckett's *The Lost Ones*. The Irish writer's presence is once again everywhere in evidence, both in storytelling technique and in frequent reference, such as "… he sounded like old Winnie sinking into her mound of earth, you know in *Happy Days*, casually observing her own burial." The text is thickened by Federman's accustomed digressions to a variety of writers and works. Thus Dostoevsky's narrow escape from the firing squad in 1849 is given five pages and Henry James's ritualistic shaving of his beard as the 19th century ended is offered a lengthy paragraph. The present time of *The Twofold Vibration* is New Year's Eve 1999. An unnamed old man is about to be "deported to the space colonies." (This sounds like science fiction but we are assured it is something different: "call it exploratory or better yet extemporaneous fiction.") Three narrators tell this old man's story from his birth in 1918, through his Holocaust experiences, his amorous and gambling indulgences, his marriage and divorce, to the unlikely final happenings at the "spaceport." As with Federman's previous fiction, *The Twofold Vibration* is a constant witness to the frustrations and difficulties of writing a novel. Despite the eccentricities of telling, of composition, and even of typography and punctuation (commas everywhere, no periods), there is something agreeably old-fashioned about this work. It seems to be part of the leisurely picaresque tradition. It also, in an intriguing way, confronts contemporary issues and involves itself in the history of literature and thought.

Smiles on Washington Square offers a narrative which circles about an "initial encounter across a smile" between a man and a woman. This "almost" meeting between Moinous (a literary alter ego Federman has cultivated in his earlier fiction) and Sucette is precisely dated as occurring on March 15, 1954, during the McCarthy hearings. The rest of the text abounds in problematical turns, which feature words like should, would, could, perhaps, and if. Federman flirts with the device of the novel-within-the-novel, somewhat in the manner of Gide's *Counterfeiters*, when he has Sucette work on a short story which mirrors events in *Smiles on Washington Square*. The narrative is cleverly made to exist on a variety of levels, with fiction triumphing over fact, imagination over reality. Moinous, the French immigrant, and Sucette, the Bostonian with the social conscience, have a life together only when their creator posits hypothetical situations: "It would probably be a good place in the love story of Moinous & Sucette for her to suggest that perhaps they should go to her apartment where Sucette could then read her story to Moinous."

The typography, punctuation, and paragraphing here are all quite regular, suggesting perhaps that Federman has tired somewhat of his experiments with disrupting the appearance of his text. Yet the tentative nature of reality with a "story that cancels itself as it goes" (words from *Take It or Leave It*) seem to survive intact from the early fiction. Federman makes interesting use of the present tense through much of his narrative, capturing the illusion of what Gertrude Stein once called "a continuous present." There is less of Beckett in *Smiles on Washington Square* than in the rest of Federman's work. The writer who comes to mind is Marguerite Duras.

—Melvin J. Friedman

FEINSTEIN, Elaine.   British.   Born in Bootle, Lancashire, 24 October 1930. Educated at Wyggeston Grammar School, Leicester; Newnham College, Cambridge. Married Arnold Feinstein in 1956; three sons. Editorial staff member, Cambridge University Press, 1960–62; Lecturer in English, Bishop's Stortford Training College, Hertfordshire, 1963–66; Assistant Lecturer in Literature, University of Essex, Wivenhoe, 1967–70. Recipient: Arts Council grant, 1970, 1979, 1981; Daisy Miller Award, 1971; Kelus Prize, 1978. Fellow, Royal Society of Literature, 1980. Agent: (verse) Olwyn Hughes, 38 Stratford Villas, London NW1 9SG; (fiction) Gill Coleridge, Anthony Sheil Associates Ltd., 43 Doughty Street, London WC1N 2LF; (plays and film) Phil Kelvin, Goodwin Associates, 12 Rabbit Row, London W8 4DX. Address: c/o Century Hutchinson, 62–65 Chandos Place, London WC2N 4NW, England.

PUBLICATIONS

Novels

The Circle.   London, Hutchinson, 1970.
The Amberstone Exit.   London, Hutchinson, 1972.
The Glass Alembic.   London, Hutchinson, 1973; as *The Crystal Garden*, New York, Dutton, 1974.
Children of the Rose.   London, Hutchinson, 1975.
The Ecstasy of Dr. Miriam Garner.   London, Hutchinson, 1976.
The Shadow Master.   London, Hutchinson, 1978; New York, Simon and Schuster, 1979.
The Survivors.   London, Hutchinson, 1982.
The Border.   London, Hutchinson, 1984.

Short Stories

Matters of Chance.   London, Covent Garden Press, 1980.
The Silent Areas.   London, Hutchinson, 1980.

Plays

Radio Plays: *Echoes*, 1980; *A Late Spring*, 1982; *A Captive Lion*, 1984; *A Day Off*, from the novel by Storm Jameson, 1986.

Television Plays: *Breath* 1975; *Lunch*, 1982; *Country Diary of an Edwardian Lady* series, from work by Edith Holden, 1984; *A Brave Face*, 1985.

Verse

In a Green Eye. London, Goliard Press, 1966.
The Magic Apple Tree. London, Hutchinson, 1971.
At the Edge. Rushden, Northamptonshire, Sceptre Press, 1972.
The Celebrants and Other Poems. London, Hutchinson, 1973.
Some Unease and Angels: Selected Poems. London, Hutchinson, and University Center, Michigan, Green River Press, 1977.
The Feast of Euridice. London, Faber, 1980.

Other

Bessie Smith. London, Viking, 1985.

Editor, *Selected Poems of John Clare.* London, University Tutorial Press, 1968.
Editor, with Fay Weldon, *New Stories 4.* London, Hutchinson, 1979.
Translator, *The Selected Poems of Marina Tsvetayeva.* London, Oxford University Press, 1971; revised edition, Oxford and New York, Oxford University Press, 1981.
Translator, *Three Russian Poets: Margarita Aliger, Yunna Moritz, Bella Akhmadulina.* Manchester, Carcanet, 1979.

*

Manuscript Collection: Cambridge University.
Critical Study: article by Peter Conradi, in *British Novelists since 1960* edited by Jay L. Halio, Detroit, Gale, 1983.

Elaine Feinstein comments:
My earliest fiction was very much an extension of my poetry, but as the novels have moved away from a single narrative voice to explore a wider territory, I have largely abandoned those rhythms and have come to prefer the traditional clarity of prose.

*   *   *

Lena, in Elaine Feinstein's first novel, *The Circle*, realizes *à propos* her husband "that she would have to take it up again. Her separate life. Her lonely life, the music of words to be played with, the books ... they would be her refuge; her private world. As his was this of the laboratory. And she must now move as securely into that ... and find magic." However, in the general context of Feinstein's work, which shows a progressive widening of focus, this is broader than a feminist prescription. Subsequent novels are dominated by men and women in search of "magic," partly via illegitimate means in *The Ecstasy of Dr. Miriam Garner*, and both actively and contemplatively through religion in *The Shadow Master*. "Magic" may be partially embodied in people, as in *The Amberstone Exit*, with Emily's fascination with the glamorous Tyrenes, the local rich family, and in *The Ecstasy of Dr. Miriam Garner*, with Miriam's fascination with the brilliant but brutal Stavros; in both novels there is a strong erotic element in the fascination, and Emily's youthful hunger for sexual experience, which comes to focus on Max Tyrene, anticipates Miriam's more sophisticated desire for Stavres.
The fundamental source of "magic" is inevitably "the music of words," and Feinstein's definition of this develops. For Lena and Emily it is joy in intoxicating language and so it could be for the poet Hans in *The Border* were he not, as a part-Jew, persecuted by Hitler, while in the title story of *The Silent Areas*

poetry must be "the words that ran in the blood of freezing men without food. Or the minds of the half-mad in lonely cells." (This is an Englishman's thought in Russia; Feinstein, herself a poet, has translated Russian poets.) In *Shadow Master*, before the closing religious acceptance, the search for magic meant apocalyptic action. Thus, unfashionably, Feinstein is concerned with validation for people's lives outside as well as inside human relationships.
Perhaps drawing on her experience as a poet, in her first novel, *The Circle*, Feinstein used technical devices, notably spaces within paragraphs, intended for immediacy but in practice often distracting, and later abandoned. A staple technique throughout her work is the juxtaposition of different time sequences. In *The Circle* this is unstructured, while *The Amberstone Exit* opens in a maternity ward where Emily is having her baby and swings back over the events bringing her there, with the two time sequences running together toward the end.
The Amberstone Exit concerns a woman younger than Lena in *The Circle*, while *The Glass Alembic* is about a more mature woman, Brigid, and for the first time focuses on a group. Two passages from this novel are reworked with different names and alternative endings in the stories "Complicity" and "Strangers" (*The Silent Areas*). Brigid's arrival in Basel where her husband is a biochemist is a catalyst for various human reactions in the scientific community. The setting of Paracelsus-haunted Basel is merely coincidentally metaphoric of the action. By contrast, the settings are integral in *Children of the Rose*, which evokes Collaborationist tensions in present-day Provence and the reactions of Jews, once refugees, on revisiting Poland.
In *The Ecstasy of Dr. Miriam Garner*, Feinstein plaits a strand of narrative from medieval Toledo with a glamorous female academic's life into a mystery story with spiritual sidelights. *The Shadow Master* is set mainly in Turkey, where an international religious and political apocalyptic movement begins, leading indirectly to the explosion of "a small nuclear device." In *The Survivors*, Feinstein follows two Jewish *émigré* families in Liverpool, one rich and one poor, from 1914 to 1956, when Diana, the offspring of a surprising marriage linking the families, agonizes "So many had died in mud and fire for being Jewish. To give it up seemed a gross betrayal." This two-family saga not only describes the difficulties Jews found in Britain but also delineates both through the successor generations and within generations the characters' very different attitudes to their Jewishness. As the book ends, West Indians are moving into some of the old Jewish quarters.
The Border also draws on Feinstein's Jewish background. Through various narrative devices, notably the use of diaries kept by the scientist Inge and her husband the poet Hans, Feinstein highlights the personal and increasingly the political strains put upon the marriage. The book follows the part-Jewish couple's flight from Vienna to Paris and beyond, in 1938. In this powerful novella, where Walter Benjamin appears, "the border" is metaphoric as well as actual. The book is a technical *tour de force*, and a deeply moving human text. *The Border* brings together all Elaine Feinstein's greatest strengths—the examination of a long-term relationship between a man and a woman, where both are treated equally sympathetically, with a poet's use of language, and a witnessing to history, however dark.

—Val Warner

FIEDLER, Leslie A(aron). American. Born in Newark, New Jersey, 8 March 1917. Educated at New York University, B.A. 1938 (Phi Beta Kappa); University of Wisconsin, Madison, M.A. 1939, Ph.D. 1941; Harvard University, Cambridge, Massachusetts (Rockefeller Fellow), 1946–47. Served in the United States Naval Reserve, 1942–46: Lieutenant. Married 1) Margaret Ann Shipley in 1939 (divorced, 1973), six children; 2) Sally Smith Andersen, 1973, two step-children. Assistant Professor, 1947–48, Associate Professor, 1948–52, Professor of English, 1953–64, and Chairman of the Department, 1954–56, University of Montana, Missoula. Since 1965, Professor of English, currently Samuel Clemens Professor, State University of New York, Buffalo. Fulbright Lecturer, University of Rome, 1951–52, University of Bologna and Ca Foscari University, 1952–53, and University of Athens, 1961–62; Gauss Lecturer in Criticism, Princeton University, New Jersey, 1956–57; Lecturer, University of Sussex, Brighton, and University of Amsterdam, 1967–68; Visiting Professor, University of Vincennes, Paris, 1970–71. Fellow, Indiana University School of Letters, Bloomington, 1953; Associate Fellow, Calhoun College, Yale University, New Haven, Connecticut, 1969. Advisory editor, *Ramparts* magazine, New York, 1958–61; literary adviser, St. Martin's Press, New York, 1958–61. Recipient: *Furioso* poetry prize, 1951; *Kenyon Review* fellowship, for non-fiction, 1956; American Academy grant, 1957; American Council of Learned Societies grant, 1960, 1961; Guggenheim fellowship, 1970. Address: 154 Morris Avenue, Buffalo, New York 14214, U.S.A.

PUBLICATIONS

Novels

The Second Stone: A Love Story.   New York, Stein and Day, 1963; London, Heinemann, 1966.
Back to China.   New York, Stein and Day, 1965.
The Messengers Will Come No More.   New York, Stein and Day, 1974.

Short Stories

Pull Down Vanity and Other Stories.   Philadelphia, Lippincott, 1962; London, Secker and Warburg, 1963.
The Last Jew in America.   New York, Stein and Day, 1966.
Nude Croquet and Other Stories.   New York, Stein and Day, 1969; London, Secker and Warburg, 1970.

Uncollected Short Stories

"And We'll All Feel Gay," in *New Directions 10.*   New York, New Directions, 1948.
"Amphibious Operation," in *Harper's Bazaar* (New York), March 1948.
"Dear Friends and Gentle Hearts," in *Epoch* (Ithaca, New York), Fall 1949.
"For the Record," in *Quarterly Review of Literature* (Chapel Hill, North Carolina), Winter 1952.

Other

An End to Innocence: Essays on Culture and Politics.   Boston, Beacon Press, 1955.
The Jew in the American Novel.   New York, Herzl Press, 1959.
Love and Death in the American Novel.   New York, Criterion, 1960; London, Secker and Warburg, 1961; revised edition, New York, Stein and Day, 1966; London, Cape, 1967.

No! In Thunder: Essays on Myth and Literature.   Boston, Beacon Press, 1960; London, Eyre and Spottiswoode, 1963.
The Riddle of Shakespeare's Sonnets.   New York, Basic Books, 1962.
Waiting for the End.   New York, Stein and Day, 1964; as *Waiting for the End: The American Literary Scene from Hemingway to Baldwin,* London, Cape, 1965.
The Return of the Vanishing American.   New York, Stein and Day, and London, Cape, 1968.
Being Busted.   New York, Stein and Day, and London, Secker and Warburg, 1970.
The Collected Essays of Leslie Fiedler.   New York, Stein and Day, 2 vols., 1971.
The Stranger in Shakespeare.   New York, Stein and Day, 1972; London, Croom Helm, 1973.
To the Gentiles.   New York, Stein and Day, 1972.
Cross the Border, Close the Gap.   New York, Stein and Day, 1972.
A Fiedler Reader.   New York, Stein and Day, 1977.
Freaks: Myths and Images of the Secret Self.   New York, Simon and Schuster, 1978; London, Penguin, 1981.
The Inadvertent Epic: From Uncle Tom's Cabin to Roots.   Toronto, Canadian Broadcasting Corporation, 1979; New York, Simon and Schuster, 1980.
What Was Literature? Class Culture and Mass Society.   New York, Simon and Schuster, 1982.
Pity and Fear: Myths and Images of the Disabled in Literature Old and New, with others.   New York, International Center for the Disabled, 1982 (?).
Olaf Stapledon: A Man Divided.   New York and Oxford, Oxford University Press, 1983.

Editor, *The Art of the Essay.*   New York, Crowell, 1958; revised edition, 1969.
Editor, *Selections from "The Leaves of Grass,"* by Walt Whitman.   New York, Dell, 1959.
Editor, with Jacob Vinocur, *The Continuing Debate: Essays on Education.*   New York, St. Martin's Press, 1965.
Editor, with Arthur Zeiger, *O Brave New World.*   New York, Dell, 1968.
Editor, with Houston A. Baker, Jr., *English Literature: Opening Up the Canon.*   Baltimore, Johns Hopkins University Press, 1981.

*

Manuscript Collection: State University of New York, Buffalo.

Critical Study: *Leslie A. Fiedler* by Mark Royden Winchell, Boston, Twayne, 1985.

Leslie A. Fiedler comments:
My chief interest in the field of fiction has always been the exploration of the comic possibilities inherent in the elusive distinctions between races and generations, as well as between East and West, and Europe and America. I have also been deeply concerned with the difficulties of knowing who is one's father, or is not, for that matter. None of this, however, has seemed to me a proper occasion for tears.

*   *   *

There is no doubt that Leslie A. Fiedler aimed from his professional beginnings to be not just a critic but a genuine all-round man-of-letters, publishing not only controversial essays but also poetry and fiction soon after his literary debut; and he has followed all these muses, as well as a powerful one for public speaking, throughout his career. His fiction is, by common consent, less interesting and less original than his criticism (and his poetry even less substantial); and few critics of conscience have ever honored his imaginative work in print. In his opening critical essays, eventually collected as *An End to Innocence*, Fiedler established a knack for controversial argument, full of far-fetched connections and exaggerated remarks, all expressed in equally provocative prose; few since Mencken have provoked so much outrage. Rejecting the simple sentence along with the simplistic idea, Fiedler concocted a robust style composed of long and convoluted clause-compounded sentences riddled by paradoxes, parentheses, and charming self-ironies. However, only the tough-minded intelligence behind this forceful style, rather than the characteristic language, informs his fictions, which nonetheless reflect certain ideas in his criticism (which, in turn, sometimes mentions, if not quotes, his fiction!). The key theoretical text is the brilliant title essay opening his second collection, *No! In Thunder*, where Fiedler argues that the great modern writers have responded to ideals, institutions, and even people with uncompromised negation—the Melvillian cry of "No! in Thunder" indicating a complete stripping down that reveals inadequacy, deceit, failure, and the impossibility of perfection. "The No! in Thunder is never partisan," Fiedler writes, "it infuriates Our Side as well as Theirs, reveals that all Sides are one, insofar as they are all yea-sayers and hence all liars."

The title of his first collection of stories, *Pull Down Vanity*, announces the characteristic strategy of his fiction, for most of the pieces here are shaped around the uncovering of illusory images presented by a person or group; and in this stripping away of human artifice is unveiled another favorite Fiedler theme of universal culpability. Thus, these stories are structured around actions of exposure and embarrassment—a technique admittedly indebted to Nathanael West's *The Day of the Locust* (1939). Thus, should readers come to believe that one of Fiedler's characters might be honest and good, the rug is pulled out before the story is done, leaving that character too sprawled in the fundamental mud. In "Nude Croquet" a busty young thing darkens a party's room and then leads a group of middle-aging "intellectuals" in playing croquet in the buff. Not at all uncomfortable, she flaunts her fresh figure, forcing the others to uncover both their masked bodily defects and, then, their spiritual vanities. One has body hair different in color from that on her head, another a withered leg, a third is flat-chested, while on another level one is insanely jealous, another has never completed his projected and much-announced masterpiece, a third has "sold out" to the commercial theater. When the group's slightly older idol collapses from over-exertion and dies of a heart attack, the girl screams a long blast as the lights go on. "Molly-o," Fiedler writes, "confronted then in the classic pose of nakedness surprised, as if she knew for the first time what it meant to be really nude." Discovering one's nudity is, symbolically, recognizing comparable inadequacies and culpability.

Fiedler's first and best novel takes for its unusual subject the demonic attachment of unrelated twins who, once childhood friends, re-encounter each other over a dozen years. One character speaks of "a comedy of confused identities," and these confusions are not only witty, but also difficult to summarize. The novel's protagonist, Clem Stone, is an unsuccessful writer, while his friend is Mark Stone, an eminent TV intellectual and existentialist rabbi. In the past, Clem was named Mark Stone, and the present Mark's last name was Stein. But as the present Mark changed his surname, Clem, overshadowed by the most successful Mark, became known as Mark the second, or Mark Twain. As the historical author Twain's real

identity was Samuel Clemens, Stone takes the first name of Clem. The two Stones have always competed for the same goals, and before the novel is over, Clem seduces Mark's pregnant wife. The novel is similarly erudite in its joking, as in one scene Mark pummels his wife with a rolled-up copy of a magazine entitled *Thou*; and he is described, of course, as unable to stop stuttering "I-I-I-I." Long on such literary gags and arch symbols, *The Second Stone* is also short on credible surface and literary importance.

The protagonist of Fiedler's second novel, *Back to China*, is a college teacher in Montana, whose career in some respects parallels Fiedler's own—a Jew from the East teaching in the West, with a reputation for being the most famous radical on campus, the author of several books, a former wartime Japanese interpreter in the Far East; but whereas Fiedler himself has been a father several times over, Baro Finklestone's main problem is that he and his wife are childless. The reason, as we learn through a series of flashbacks, is that Finklestone's life, as well as the book's plot, turned upon a vasectomy, an irreparable voluntary sterilization, that he underwent in China. His reasons for doing this are never made entirely clear—indeed, the act itself is barely credible—and the novel never quite emerges from a mire of absurdities. Indeed, this slide toward preposterousness, which comes from mixing too much realistic, highly detailed, almost pedantic satire with more wholly symbolic fantasy—a mismating of Sinclair Lewis with Franz Kafka—becomes even more pronounced in the three novellas collected as *The Last Jew in America*; and Fiedler's next book of fiction, *Nude Croquet*, adds four slighter stories to those previously collected. A more suggestive step comes in *Being Busted*, an autobiographical memoir devoid of proper names, that successfully elevates to imaginative myth not only Fiedler's 1967 arrest on a marijuana related charge but also his responses to the life-styles of his children; for Fiedler ranks among the few writers of his post-fifty generation to suffer genuine confrontation and rebirth.

If Fiedler the critic is ambitious and original, as well as appreciative of eccentricity, the novelist is rather conventional in style, structure, and subject-matter—his own fiction scarcely acknowledging the innovative literature praised in his criticism; and the impact of his recent rebirth has so far been more intellectual than artistic. A truth of literature's past apparently unremembered in all this effort is that critics as major as Fiedler have rarely produced consequential fiction, try as much as they otherwise might. With his encompassing theme of deflation, Fiedler's fiction suggests that marriage is insufferable, that adultery is inevitable and just as inevitably disappointing; and his fictions deal as well with ambivalent attitudes toward paternity, slavish obsessions with seduction's ulterior motives, and the terrors of American professors and intellectuals. This rather limited range is, needless to say perhaps, closer to more prosaic writing than to what Fiedler the critic has defined as the great tradition of American imaginative prose.

—Richard Kostelanetz

FIELDING, Gabriel. Pseudonym for Alan Gabriel Barnsley. British. Born in Hexham, Northumberland, 25 March 1916. Educated at The Grange, Eastbourne, Sussex; Llangefni County School, Anglesey, Wales; St. Edward's School, Oxford; Trinity College, Dublin, B.A. 1940; St. George's Hospital, London B.A., T.C.D. Member of the Royal College of Surgeons, and Licentiate of the Royal College of Physicians, 1942. Served in the Royal Army Medical Corps, 1942–46: Captain. Married Edwina Eleanora Cook in 1943; three sons and two daughters. General medical practitioner, Maidstone, Kent, 1946–66; Deputy Medical Officer, Her Majesty's Training Establishment, 1954–64. Author-in-Residence, 1966–67, and Professor of English, 1967–81, Washington State University, Pullman; now emeritus. Recipient: St. Thomas More Association Gold Medal, 1963; W.H. Smith Literary Award, 1963; National Catholic Book Award, 1964. D.Litt.: Gonzaga University, Spokane, Washington, 1967. Address: 945 Monroe Street, N.E., Pullman, Washington 99163, U.S.A.

PUBLICATIONS

Novels

Brotherly Love.   London, Hutchinson, 1954; New York, Morrow, 1961.
In the Time of Greenbloom.   London, Hutchinson, 1956; New York, Morrow, 1957.
Eight Days.   London, Hutchinson, 1958; New York, Morrow, 1959.
Through Streets Broad and Narrow.   London, Hutchinson, and New York, Morrow, 1960.
The Birthday King.   London, Hutchinson, 1962; New York, Morrow, 1963; revised edition, Chicago, University of Chicago Press, 1985.
Gentlemen in Their Season.   London, Hutchinson, and New York, Morrow, 1966.
Pretty Doll Houses.   London, Hutchinson, 1979.
The Women of Guinea Lane.   London, Hutchinson, 1986.

Short Stories

Collected Short Stories.   London, Hutchinson, 1971.
New Queens for Old: A Novella and Nine Stories.   London, Hutchinson, and New York, Morrow, 1972.

Verse

The Frog Prince and Other Poems (as Alan Barnsley).   Aldington, Kent, Hand and Flower Press, 1952.
XXVIII Poems.   Aldington, Kent, Hand and Flower Press, 1955.

*

Manuscript Collections: McMaster University, Hamilton, Ontario; Georgetown University Library, Washington, D.C.

Critical Studies: interview in *Counterpoint* edited by Roy Newquist, Chicago, Rand McNally, 1964; *Gabriel Fielding* by Alfred Borrello, New York, Twayne, 1974.

Gabriel Fielding comments:

I am not a prolific writer, writing only where an obsession leads me. So far I have been led through the intricacies of family life in post-Evangelical northern England, to North Africa where the international drinking set settled for a while, to Germany during the Second World War and to England again where a restless postwar world was unsettling the old guard.

My short stories cover much the same ground: the alchemy of childhood, international and domestic misunderstandings and, again, the impact of the New Morality on the old middle and upper middle classes in England.

The Women of Guinea Lane, set in wartime London, continues the Blaydon sequence (also including *Brotherly Love, In the Time of Greenbloom,* and *Through Streets Broad and Narrow*) and examines the power of women in Western society.

*   *   *

Gabriel Fielding's growing reputation as a major serious novelist rests, in the main, on three of his novels—*In the Time of Greenbloom, The Birthday King*, and *Gentlemen in Their Season*. Throughout these novels, Fielding explores the theme of individual responsibility which has attracted European writers like Camus, Sartre, and Hesse, but which has been largely neglected by English novelists.

The narrative of *Greenbloom*, which forms, with *Brotherly Love* and *Through Streets Broad and Narrow*, a trilogy of the Blaydon family, concerns John Blaydon's growth to adolescence through a period of undeserved blame for the death of his friend Victoria Blount. Fielding presents a world devoted to finding sin in the young and innocent as a means of relieving its own sense of guilt. John only escapes acquiescence in a guilt which the world has persuaded him to own, through the intervention of Horat Greenbloom, an eccentric Jewish undergraduate follower of Wittgenstein and Sartre. Greenbloom's sympathetic interest is that of one scapegoat for another; his therapy, which is explicitly existential, subjective, and counterabstractive, is to make John see that the empty categorizations of adult society lead to personal irresponsibility and consequent feelings of guilt which have to be transferred to the innocent and vulnerable for punishment.

The same theme is further explored in *The Birthday King* which chronicles the rise and fall of Nazi Germany through the history of two Jewish brothers, Alfried and Ruprecht Waitzmann, co-directors of a large industrial group. The brothers are contrasted to present contrary reactions to the mechanistic Hitler society. Ruprecht chooses survival at all costs, running the factories on forced labour for the Nazi regime, betraying Alfried but preserving the family inheritance; Alfried, on the other hand, deliberately and ostentatiously ridicules the system, is imprisoned in a concentration camp and tortured to be "cured" of his eccentricity. Together, the brothers present the two faces of Jewishness, survival and sacrifice, and through them Fielding explores the extremes of human response to the absurdity of the world. Of all Fielding's novels, *The Birthday King* comes nearest to the work of Camus in its investigation of individual choice in a society dehumanized and wholly objective. Alfried's response is that of the mystic innocent whose honesty makes him rebel against the "rectitudes, mad superstitions and madder certainties" of romantic Nazism; he consciously and literally makes himself the scapegoat which might liberate others from their guilt. Ruprecht's response, which is that of the opportunist, aggressive, shrewd, and lucky, is just as "existential" as Alfried's, but takes the form of an unflamboyant endurance which makes him see Alfried's heroism as a luxury: "What difference does it make that he's in a camp when the whole country's a camp?" So Fielding's theme is no simple contrast between the kind of individual choice made in the face of Nazism; rather it is that the *fact* of choosing is important because we are still free to choose. In this, he echoes Sartre's "We were never more free than under the Nazi occupation. The choice that each of us made of his life and his being was a genuine choice because it was made in the presence of death." Both Ruprecht and Alfried make authentic decisions; they are contrasted with characters like the Kommandant, Baron von Hoffbach, Alexandra von Boehling, and Herr Grunwald who sleepwalk through the Hitler-time: "They must have been bored for years without ever knowing it and there must have been thousands like them, practically a whole generation."

Boredom provides the focus of analysis in *Gentlemen in Their Season*, but here it is the less dramatic though no less deadly boredom of marriage and adultery. The novel is, in many ways, more disturbing than either *Greenbloom* or *The Birthday King*: issues no longer look quite as clear-cut and the setting is too proximate to allow the reader to be uninvolved. The action concerns two middle-aged, middle-class men, Randell Coles and Bernard Presage, whose marriages (to a brisk humanist and devout Catholic, respectively) have entered the dark night of aimless stagnation and dishonest intellectualism which is characterized by "clever" parties, self-conscious devotion to the Third Program, unmotivated religious retreats, and rigorous partner criticism. Each of them drift into affairs which have disastrous consequences for an uninvolved third party, Hotchkis, who before finishing his sentence for the manslaughter of his wife's lover, breaks from prison to protect his marriage once more and is killed by the police.

Although the scapegoat figure appears, he is not given the centre of the novel. Fielding instead probes into the lives of the bystanders whose guilt causes, and is atoned by, Hotchkis's death; Coles and Presage are the von Hoffbachs and Grunwalds of the novel, somnambulistic puppets of their wives and of their own abstract preconceptions of marriage which prevent them from acting decisively. Hotchkis's night ends by his triumphant decision to break out of prison and force events by his own action. The dark night of Coles and Presage never ends and they remain hollow drifters, unable even to conduct their extra-marital affairs with pleasure or humanity.

Thus in all his major novels, Fielding presents the admonition that we are all, as humans, involved in the total of human activity; a man's choice is a choice for all men. But if this account might seem to imply that Fielding merely dramatizes a "message," the implication must be dispelled. The didactic conclusions drawn by the reader come not from editorial commentary but from the compelling narrative and evocative imagery which support each other so intimately that the novels transcend their parts to become themselves images of ideas which act on the reader directly, rather than merely persuade by explicit argument and apt illustration. Indeed, the texture of Fielding's novels is akin to that of good dramatic poetry; images cluster and iterate to form a depth of reference which sets up unconscious associations with the reader's conscious awareness of plot and character. The movement of his novels strongly recalls symphonic structure in its series of statements, repetitions, modifications, and juxtapositions of action and imagery.

—Frederick Bowers

FIGES, Eva (née Unger). British. Born in Berlin, Germany, 15 April 1932; came to England in 1939. Educated at Kingsbury Grammar School, 1943–50; Queen Mary College, University of London, 1950–53, B.A. (honours) in English 1953. Married John George Figes in 1954 (divorced, 1963); one daughter and one son. Editor, Longman, 1955–57, Weidenfeld and Nicolson, 1962–63, and Blackie, 1964–67, publishers, London. Recipient: *Guardian* Fiction Prize, 1967; C. Day Lewis Fellowship, 1973; Arts Council fellowship, 1977–79. Agent: Deborah Rogers

Ltd., 49 Blenheim Crescent, London W11 2EF. Address: 24 Fitzjohn's Avenue, London, N.W.3, England.

PUBLICATIONS

Novels

Equinox. London, Secker and Warburg, 1966.
Winter Journey. London, Faber, 1967; New York, Hill and Wang, 1968.
Konek Landing. London, Faber, 1969.
B. London, Faber, 1972.
Days. London, Faber, 1974.
Nelly's Version. London, Secker and Warburg, 1977.
Waking. London, Hamish Hamilton, 1981; New York, Pantheon, 1982.
Light. London, Hamish Hamilton, and New York, Pantheon, 1983.
The Seven Ages. London, Hamish Hamilton, 1986.

Uncollected Short Stories

"Obbligato, Bedsitter," in *Signature Anthology.* London, Calder and Boyars, 1975.
"On the Edge," in *London Tales*, edited by Julian Evans. London, Hamish Hamilton, 1983.

Plays

Radio Plays: *Time Regained*, 1980; *Days*, from her own novel, 1981; *Dialogue Between Friends*, 1982; *Punch-Flame and Pigeon-Breast*, 1983; *The True Tale of Margery Kempe*, 1985.

Other

The Musicians of Bremen: Retold (for children). London, Blackie, 1967.
The Banger (for children). London, Deutsch, and New York, Lion Press, 1968.
Patriarchal Attitudes: Women in Society. London, Faber, and New York, Stein and Day, 1970.
Scribble Sam (for children). London, Deutsch, and New York, McKay, 1971.
Tragedy and Social Evolution. London, Calder, and New York, Riverrun Press, 1976.
Little Eden: A Child at War (autobiography). London, Faber, 1978.
Sex and Subterfuge: Women Novelists to 1850. London, Macmillan, 1982.

Editor, *Classic Choice 1.* London, Blackie, 1965.
Editor, *Modern Choice 1* and *2.* London, Blackie, 2 vols., 1965–66.
Editor, with Abigail Mozley and Dinah Livingstone, *Women Their World.* Gisburn, Lancashire, Platform Poets, 1980.

Translator, *The Gadarene Club*, by Martin Walser. London, Longman, 1960.
Translator, *The Old Car*, by Elisabeth Borchers. London, Blackie, 1967.
Translator, *He and I and the Elephants*, by Bernhard Grzimek. London, Deutsch-Thames and Hudson, and New York, Hill and Wang, 1967.
Translator, *Little Fadette*, by George Sand. London, Blackie, 1967.

Translator, *A Family Failure*, by Renate Rasp. London, Calder and Boyars, 1970.

Translator, *The Deathbringer*, by Manfred von Conta. London, Calder and Boyars, 1971.

* * *

"I am using a different grid which I have first to construct by a painful process of trial and error," writes Eva Figes. In outright reaction against what she sees as the continuing conservative realist tradition of British fiction Figes resumes the Modernist task of reshaping the novel and questioning the assumptions on which it is built. In her novels, as in those of Virginia Woolf (surely the greatest influence on her work), Figes seeks to bring together the properties of formal art and the intensities of the inner self. Here, life takes place between the acts, and we catch it unawares in the lives of ordinary people: Janus, the old man dying alone in his council house in *Winter Journey*, or Lily, the spinster sister and aunt who measures the subtly shifting relationships in *Light*. As Figes explores the self concealed behind the artifice of manners, the most elusive moments of existence are redefined in her novels as the prerequisite for creative vitality, and continuity is found in the lyric hoard of memories through which her characters resist the flux of time. In *Winter Journey* the presentation of a series of psychological states in place of a continuous narrative or plot results in an intense poetic lyricism. The same kind of unbroken texture, or openness and continuity, is found in *Light* (Figes's finest work to date), where Claude, artist and philosopher, explains: "Everything is always in flux ... it was both his overriding difficulty and essential to him."

But there are darker realities here too. A sense of menace underlies the lyrical affirmation of the novels, and there is a corresponding sense that only a continuous style can soothe a narrative which is subject to unexpected disruptions and dislocations. "My starting-point is inevitably Kafka," Figes claims, and there are echoes of Beckett too in her novels' unresolved ambivalence about their own representational activity. The negative energies of solipsism and angst are inseparable from the moments of heightened consciousness in the fragmented autobiography of Janus' winter journey. And in *Light*, Claude's fragile images of perfection are troubled by the motifs of transience and death. In the final analysis, perhaps the most fascinating and complex aspect of Figes's novels is that they do follow the Modernist tradition of showing art and memory as creative of a new order of reality. But they also remain firmly located in the destructive elements of historical time that many classic modernists would seek to bypass. The power and potency of the recurrent images of holocaust in her novels seem to reveal the author's deepest motivations for writing: "I am a European wrestling with a different reality," she says. "A piece of shrapnel lodges in my flesh, and when it moves, I write."

—Sandra Kemp

FINDLEY, Timothy. Canadian. Born in Toronto, Ontario, 30 October 1930. Educated at Rosedale Public School, Toronto; St. Andrews College, Aurora, Ontario; Jarvis Collegiate, Toronto; Royal Conservatory of Music, Toronto, 1950–53; Central School of Speech and Drama, London. Stage, television, and radio actor, 1951–62: charter member, Stratford Shakespearean Festival, Ontario, 1953; contract player with H.M. Tennent, London, 1953–56; toured U.S. in *The Matchmaker*, 1956–57; studio writer, CBS, Hollywood, 1957–58; copywriter, CFGM Radio, Richmond Hill, Ontario. Playwright-in-Residence, National Arts Centre, Ottawa, 1974–75; Writer-in-Residence, University of Toronto, 1979–80, Trent University, Peterborough, Ontario, 1984, and University of Winnipeg, 1985. Recipient: Canada Council award, 1968, 1978; Armstrong Award, for radio writing, 1971; ACTRA award, for TV documentary, 1975; Toronto Book Award, 1977; Governor General's award, 1977; Anik award, for TV writing, 1980; Canadian Authors Association prize, 1985. D.Litt.: Trent University, 1982; University of Guelph, Ontario, 1984. Agent: Colbert Agency, 303 Davenport Road, Toronto, Ontario M5R 1K5. Address: Box 419, Cannington, Ontario L0E 1EO, Canada.

PUBLICATIONS

Novels

The Last of the Crazy People. New York, Meredith Press, and London, Macdonald, 1967.

The Butterfly Plague. New York, Viking Press, 1969; London, Deutsch, 1970.

The Wars. Toronto, Clarke Irwin, 1977; New York, Delacorte Press, and London, Macmillan, 1978.

Famous Last Words. Toronto, Clarke Irwin, and New York, Delacorte Press, 1981.

Not Wanted on the Voyage. Toronto, Viking, 1984; New York, Delacorte Press, and London, Macmillan, 1985.

Short Stories

Dinner Along the Amazon. Toronto and London, Penguin, 1984; New York, Penguin, 1985.

Uncollected Short Stories

"Island" and "The Long Hard Walk" in *The Newcomers*, edited by Charles E. Israel. Toronto, McClelland and Stewart, 1979.

Plays

The Paper People (televised, 1967). Published in *Canadian Drama* (Toronto), vol. 9, no. 1, 1983.

The Journey (broadcast, 1971). Published in *Canadian Drama* (Toronto), vol. 10, no. 1, 1984.

Can You See Me Yet? (produced Ottawa, 1976). Vancouver, Talonbooks, 1977.

John A., Himself (produced London, Ontario, 1979).

Strangers at the Door (radio script), in *Quarry* (Kingston, Ontario), 1982.

Daybreak at Pisa: 1945, in *Tamarack Review* (Toronto), Winter 1982.

Screenplays: *Don't Let the Angels Fall*, 1970; *The Wars*, 1983.

Radio Plays and Documentaries: *The Learning Stage* and *Ideas* series, 1963–73; *Adrift*, 1968; *Matinee* series, 1970–71; *The Journey*, 1971; *Missionaries*, 1973.

Television Plays and Documentaries: *Umbrella* series, 1964–66; *Who Crucified Christ?*, 1966; *The Paper People*, 1967;

The Whiteoaks of Jalna (7 episodes), from books by Mazo de la Roche, 1971–72; *The National Dream* series, with William Whitehead, 1974; *The Garden and the Cage*, with William Whitehead, 1977; *1832* and *1911* (*The Newcomers* series), 1978–79; *Dieppe 1942*, with William Whitehead, 1979; *Other People's Children*, 1981; *Islands in the Sun* and *Turn the World Around* (*Belafonte Sings* series), with William Whitehead, 1983.

Other

Imaginings, with Janis Rapaport, illustrated by Heather Cooper. Toronto, Ethos, 1982.

*

Critical Studies: *Eleven Canadian Novelists* by Graeme Gibson, Toronto, Anansi, 1973; *Conversations with Canadian Novelists* by Silver Donald Cameron, Toronto, Macmillan, 1973; "An Interview with Timothy Findley," in *University of Toronto Review*, 1980; "Timothy Findley Issue" of *Canadian Literature* (Vancouver), Winter 1981; *Timothy Findley* by Wilfred Cude, Toronto, Dundurn Press, 1982; "The Marvel of Reality" (interview) with Bruce Meyer and Brian O'Riordan, in *Waves* (Toronto), vol. 10, no. 4, 1982; "Prayers Against Despair" by Gilbert Drolet, in *Journal of Canadian Fiction 33* (Montreal), 1982; "Whispers of Chaos" by Eugene Benson, in *World Literature Written in English* (Guelph, Ontario), Autumn 1982; *Second Words: Selected Critical Prose* by Margaret Atwood, Toronto, Anansi, 1982, Boston, Beacon Press, 1984.

Timothy Findley comments:

There are some who say you should only and always write about what you know. If I had taken this advice, then all my books would be about the theatre, rabbits and cats, a fairly standard version of family life and the road between the farm where I live and the city of Toronto. The fact is, only the rabbits and the cats have made it into my fiction—in one book as the companions of a man in the First World War and in another as stowaways on Noah's Ark. Without apology, I must admit that I cannot imagine why I have written what I have. It does occur to me, however, that a thread runs through all my work that has to do with unlikely people being confronted with uncommon events.

*   *   *

Timothy Findley began writing fiction in his early twenties and contributed a story to the first issue of *Tamarack Review* in 1956, but during this earlier period he was largely involved in acting, playing at the first Stratford Shakespearean Festival (1953) and later touring in Britain and the United States. In several ways the theatrical career that he eventually abandoned had its effect on his later writing. His novels show him to be highly conscious of the dramatic potentialities in human relationships, and very often he seems in fiction to be moving in that area between actuality and illusion where we accept the backdrop for what it pretends to be and willingly allow the devices of *trompe-l'oeil* to go unchallenged. When he was acting in *The Matchmaker* its author, Thornton Wilder, encouraged Findley to continue writing fiction, advice that finally led him to devote himself full time to writing in the 1960's and his own early thirties.

Since that time Findley has published five novels and a volume of short stories, *Dinner Along the Amazon*. He has emerged as a historical novelist, for history is his favourite but not necessarily his most tractable material. In all his novels we look back into a past which for most of us is completed, finished business, but which for Findley is a stage on which to enact dramas in which his characters respond to the situation the world presents, accepting or reacting.

In his first novel, *The Last of the Crazy People*, he presents the 1960's in southern Ontario, where a child, obsessed by the futility of his family's existence in a world two wars have robbed of meaning, eventually kills the people he most loves as the logic of childhood and the logic of insanity blend together. In *The Butterfly Plague* he takes us to the late 1930's in Hollywood, where the fate of a family threatened with an inherited disease parallels the breakdown of civilization in Europe during the same decade; in *The Wars* he involves us in the pointless slaughters of the Great War as it was once called; in *Famous Last Words* he presents World War II with the bizarre and dread-ridden years that led up to it. Finally, in *Not Wanted on the Voyage*, he takes us back to Genesis and the world before history and rewrites the story of the Flood from the viewpoint of the humbler victims of Jehovah's caprices.

Rewriting is the key concept, for unlike past historical novelists, Findley is not seeking to present the past "as it must have been." He is taking history into the world of the imagination and in the process is creating his own myths by which the lessons of history are made more clear.

Findley's research is always impeccable. He knows the periods of which he writes in depth, and in *The Wars* he actually creates a deeper illusion of authenticity by presenting the story as the product of an intensive reconstruction of events, even to the extent of inventing taped interviews with the survivors who remember Robert, the hero, and his quixotic attempt to rescue a great troop of horses doomed to a pointless death on the western front. But *The Wars* is not merely the product of research, of vestigial records piled upon each other. It is a work of the imagination, of literature, and though history, as Auden once said, "cannot help or pardon," literature can offer understanding and compassion. When Clive, the soldier poet in *The Wars*, is asked "Do you think we'll ever be forgiven for what we've done?" ("we" meaning his generation) he answers: "I doubt we'll ever be forgiven. All I hope is—they'll remember we were human beings."

Famous Last Words is a work of elaborate artifice, in which fictional figures mingle with people who actually lived and were famous yet played such artificial roles that they become as manipulable as the puppets of the imagination. The narrator is actually an offspring of the mind of one of the characters, for Ezra Pound—who appears in the novel in one of his fascistic rages—invented Hugh Selwyn Mauberley, the narrator of *Famous Last Words*, as a minor figure in one of his poems. A fugitive collaborationist at the end of the war in a deserted Alpine hotel, Mauberley writes on the walls and ceilings the story of the bizarre plots in which he and his associates, including the Duke of Windsor and Mrs. Simpson, sought to make use of fascism for their own ends and merely became more deeply mired. Aestheticism and fascism, the lesson seems to read, lead to the same dead end. Yet finally, as a manifestation of the urge to live that lies at the heart of even the most extreme aestheticism, there is Mauberley's own remark, as he remembers the caves of Altamira and reproduces their smoke-ringed handprint above his own engraved message: "Some there are who never disappear. And I knew I was sitting at the heart of the human race—which is its will to say *I am*."

In such a statement—which echoes that of Clive in *The Wars*—style becomes its own morality, and understanding becomes more important than help or pardon.

—George Woodcock

FINLAYSON, Roderick (David). New Zealander. Born in Auckland, 26 April 1904. Educated at Ponsonby School; Seddon Memorial Technical College, 1918–21, diploma in engineering 1922; Auckland University School of Architecture 1922–24. Served in the New Zealand Home Guard, 1940–45. Married Ruth Evelyn Taylor in 1936; three daughters and three sons. Architectural draftsman, 1922–28; writer, Department of Education School Publications Branch, Wellington, 1950–60; printing-room assistant, Auckland City Council, 1958–66. Recipient: New Zealand Centennial Prize, 1940. Address: 46 McLeod Road, Weymouth, Manurewa, New Zealand.

PUBLICATIONS

Novels

Tidal Creek. Sydney and London, Angus and Robertson, 1948; revised edition, edited by Dennis McEldowney, Auckland, Auckland University Press-Oxford University Press, 1979.
The Schooner Came to Atia. Auckland, Griffin Press, 1953.

Short Stories

Brown Man's Burden. Auckland, Unicorn Press, 1938.
Sweet Beulah Land. Auckland, Griffin Press, 1942.
Brown Man's Burden and Later Stories, edited by Bill Pearson. Auckland, Auckland University Press-Oxford University Press, 1973.
Other Lovers (3 novellas). Dunedin, McIndoe, 1976.

Uncollected Short Stories

"Mr. Hake's Joyous Quest," in *Bulletin* (Sydney), 13 December 1944.
"A Nice Little Nest of Eggs," in *Bulletin* (Sydney), 30 April 1947.
"Mr. Stoke Had No Complaints," in *Bulletin* (Sydney), 5 November 1947.
"The Girl at the Golden Gate," in *Bulletin* (Sydney), 29 December 1948.
"The Morning for a Bargain," in *Arena 31* (Wellington), 1952.
"The Secret," in *New Zealand Listener* (Wellington), 23 May 1952.
"Fuel for the Fires of Love," in *New Zealand Listener* (Wellington), 18 July 1952.
"The Whole Mean Trick," in *New Zealand Listener* (Wellington), 24 October 1952.
"Sunday Outing," in *Arena 37* (Wellington), 1954.
"The Bulls," in *Landfall* (Christchurch), March 1956.
"A Nice Girl," in *Thursday* (Auckland), 1 May 1975.
"The Gift," in *Thursday* (Auckland), 22 March 1976.
"The Boomerang Boy," in *New Zealand Listener* (Wellington), 14 July 1979.

"Living and Dying in Dedwood," "The Holy Water," and "Three Widows," all in *Islands 33* (Auckland), July 1984.

Other

Our Life in This Land (essay). Auckland, Griffin Press, 1940.
The Coming of the Maori [*Musket, Pakeha*]. Wellington, Department of Education School Publications Branch, 3 vols., 1955–56.
The Golden Years. Wellington, Department of Education School Publications Branch, 1956.
The Return of the Fugitives. Wellington, Department of Education School Publications Branch, 1957.
Changes in the Pa. Wellington, Department of Education School Publications Branch, 1958.
The Maoris of New Zealand, with Joan Smith. London, Oxford University Press, 1959.
The New Harvest. Wellington, Department of Education School Publications Branch, 1960.
The Springing Fern (for children). Christchurch, Whitcombe and Tombs, 1965; San Francisco, Tri-Ocean, 1967.
D'Arcy Cresswell. New York, Twayne, 1972.

*

Manuscript Collection: Hocken Library, University of Otago, Dunedin.

Critical Studies: introduction to *Brown Man's Burden and Later Stories*, 1973, "The Maori and Literature 1938–1965," in *Essays in New Zealand Literature* edited by Wystan Curnow, Auckland, Heinemann, 1973, and "Attitudes to the Maori in Some Pakeha Fiction," in *Fretful Sleepers and Other Essays*, Auckland, Heinemann, 1974, all by Bill Pearson; "Narrative Stance in the Early Short Stories of Roderick Finlayson" by John Muirhead, in *World Literature Written in English 14* (Arlington, Texas), April 1975; *Maori e Pakeha: Due culture nella neozelandese* by Marinella Rocca Longo, Bologna, Patron, 1975.

Roderick Finlayson comments:

(1976) From the time I left school I had done occasional journalistic writing, mainly articles descriptive of the country and Maori traditions. But I suppose my work as a serious writer began when, after young manhood days among the Maori people of the Bay of Plenty, I found myself separated by city life from those friends. To give a more lasting form to my memories I began to embody them in short stories. The attention these attracted when published encouraged me to go on and to broaden the scope of my writing and to touch on all aspects of life in New Zealand. If, besides the literary, there is a social aim in my work, it could be said to be the hope to promote understanding between the races in New Zealand, and to take a hard look at our way of life in this land. I am now taking a new look at the relationship between the sexes, and am working on another series of short stories and two works of novella length.

*   *   *

When Roderick Finlayson began writing in the mid-1930's, the image of the Maori in Pakeha fiction was still confined to stereotypes which included the shiftless and unreliable native of the early settlers, the noble savage of romantic Victorians, and the comic foil to white superiority. He was exploited in fiction as well as in fact. At best he was patronised; at worst treated with contempt or open hostility. It is to Finlayson's credit that he was the first Pakeha writer to reveal the Maori as a human being with an identity that was both racial and individual, to reveal him with understanding, with sympathy, and with a determination to grasp the contemporary truth and not the historical illusion.

In this self-appointed task he was helped by an unusual combination of circumstances. As he has recorded, while still in his teens he rejected "our ruthless technological society," and sought the company of Maoris in remote country and coastal areas. He was accepted by them in their homes and became increasingly identified with their way of life. The depression of the 1930's only strengthened his attitudes both to the aggressive Pakeha world bent on self-destruction and to the dispossessed inheritors of ancient traditions, inheritors whose close relationship with the natural environment enabled them to survive in the present while cherishing their past. The desire to write about them was always uppermost in Finlayson's mind and, again as he records, his accidental discovery of Verga's Sicilian stories provided him with a convenient if distant model for his experiments. Their unaffected simplicity of style and vivid but unsentimental portrayal of peasant life admirably suited his purpose without tempting him to substitute imitation for observed experience. Moreover the beginning of his friendship with the New Zealand poet and prose-writer, D'Arcy Cresswell, who published *Eena Deena Dynamo; or, The Downfall of Modern Science* in 1936, reinforced his antagonism to civilised gadgetry, and gave him a sympathetic critic for his manuscript stories.

The title of his first collection of short stories drew attention to an important aspect of his writing. *Brown Man's Burden* suggested both an underlying theme and an authorial attitude. Nevertheless, Finlayson was always aware of the dangers of didacticism to artistic integrity and, although he could be described as a writer with a thesis, the thesis itself is the outcome of close observation and intense human experience among people whose customs and mode of existence have been sacrificed, as he believed, to the needs of a decadent civilisation and its idea of progress. The reader of *Brown Man's Burden and Later Stories*, which includes stories from his early collections together with a number written at various times through the last 45 years, will soon discover that he has kept in touch with the changing Maori world, and has continued with humour and insight, with sorrow as well as anger, to demonstrate the effects of that social pollution which sometimes goes under the name of race relations.

Finlayson is more concerned with the dramatic structure of his stories than with stylistic devices and the subtleties of language. As author he is aloof but compassionate, a master of ceremonies who takes no part in the proceedings, observant but uninvolved. The episode is chosen and so shaped that it generates its own ironies and moves swiftly to a climax without irrelevance or descriptive interruptions; and yet the reader is always made aware of implications that are likewise generated by action and setting. It would be a pity to use such well-worn phrases as "the cultural clash" or "the generation gap" to describe the major themes, because the incidents are brought to life in such a human way that sociological concepts seem to have no place in their development. The different values of Maori and Pakeha are laid bare by the logic of the narrative; and changes occurring as one set of values is more and more eroded by association with the other are revealed through character and circumstance. No attempt is made to idealise the Maoris, but the culture of traditional rural communities is keenly observed as it becomes submerged in the impoverished culture of cities.

Finlayson the novelist is less impressive than the short story writer. *Tidal Creek* is little more than a loosely strung series of humorous episodes and eccentric characters, among whom an elderly subsistence farmer exemplifies some of the rural virtues which Finlayson had stressed in his contentious *Our Life in This Land*. *The Schooner Came to Atia* is a slightly melodramatic tale of Europeans and Polynesians on a Pacific island, but its emphasis is not on the clash of cultures but on the soul-searching and vacillations of a missionary who has lost his faith. In some ways Finlayson has not fulfilled the expectations that his earlier work raised. Dependent on free-lance journalism, writing for School Publications and, latterly, on work for a City Council, he has found that time and energy have been insufficient to produce other than a handful of short stories which are not included in *Brown Man's Burden and Later Stories*. Nevertheless such books as his account of the history of the Maoris in *The Springing Fern* and his critical biography of his friend, the poet D'Arcy Cresswell, are useful contributions to the literature of New Zealand.

Of greater significance in relation to his earlier imaginative work was the appearance of three novellas under the title *Other Lovers*. Finlayson's preoccupations here, as elsewhere, revolve around ways of living and ways of loving in an environment where differing life-styles exert their pressures. His "other lovers" are by no means the usual protagonists of romantic fiction, for they include an elderly, disreputable tramp and a rebellious schoolgirl, a land-developer's agent seeking to purchase tribal land who becomes emotionally involved with a young Maori woman, and two frequenters of a small town milk-bar, one of whom is the daughter of an Island woman. From such unpromising material Finlayson is able to create a group of narratives in which the focus of his attention remains on the land and the people, on innocence and corruption, and on the social pollution that destroys or hinders spontaneous relationship. A sensitivity to change and difference in traditional modes of life together with the effects these have on individual attitudes and incentives cannot fail to give far more than romantic interest to these stories.

—H. Winston Rhodes

FITZGERALD, Penelope (Mary, née Knox). British. Born in Lincoln, 17 December 1916. Educated at Wycombe Abbey; Somerville College, Oxford, B.A. (honours) in English 1939. Married Desmond Fitzgerald in 1941 (died, 1976); one son and two daughters. Teacher with Westminster Tutors, London. Recipient: Booker Prize, 1979; British Academy Crawshay Prize, for non-fiction, 1985. Address c/o Collins Ltd., 8 Grafton Street, London W1X 3LA, England.

PUBLICATIONS

Novels

The Golden Child. London, Duckworth, 1977; New York, Scribner, 1978.
The Bookshop. London, Duckworth, 1978.
Offshore. London, Collins, 1979.
Human Voices. London, Collins, 1980.
At Freddie's. London, Collins, 1982.

Uncollected Short Story

"The Axe," in *The Times Anthology of Ghost Stories.*   London, Cape, 1975.

Other

Edward Burne-Jones: A Biography.   London, Joseph, 1975.
The Knox Brothers: Edmund ("Evoe") 1881–1971, Dillwyn 1883–1943, Wilfred 1886–1950, Ronald 1888–1957.   London, Macmillan, and New York, Coward McCann, 1977.
Charlotte Mew and Her Friends.   London, Collins, 1984.

Editor, *The Novel on Blue Paper*, by William Morris.   New York, AMS Press, and London, Journeyman Press, 1982.

*

Penelope Fitzgerald comments:

(1981) I've done short novels so far because I like economy and compression; I don't think long novels are necessarily better than short ones, any more than tall men are necessarily better than short men—it's a different form, that's all. Tolstoy's *Master and Man* is the great example.

I try to get the movement and counter-movement of the novel and its background to go together. *Offshore* was set in the Thames houseboat community and I wanted the movement of the novel to rise and ebb like the tidal river. *Human Voices* was set in Broadcasting House in the old days of wartime radio, and the narration as far as possible is through voices and music.

I write from my own experience and places where I've worked and from what I can judge of the feelings of other people, particularly when they are quiet by nature and prefer not to give away too much. Sometimes readers write and ask why I can't manage to produce a happy ending, but I don't see where to find one except in the considerate endurance of the human beings I have known.

*   *   *

Penelope Fitzgerald's first novel, *The Golden Child*, was a delightful, intelligent, and witty detective story. Even in a genre which does not call for such qualities, her characters are wholly believable—kind, vain, ambitious, or suffering. Her second, *The Bookshop*, was a "straight" novel, very short but beautifully composed and filled with flashing insights into the concealed, shaping currents of human behaviour. Her third novel, *Offshore*, equally short and memorable though not quite as outstanding as *The Bookshop* won the Booker Prize. But for this award and its attendant and focussing publicity, many people would never have discovered her, the best possible argument for the awarding of literary prizes, despite the absurdity of so many choices.

Before the novels, however, there were biographies of Edward Burne-Jones, the Victorian painter, and of the four famous Knox brothers, one of whom, Evoe (who became editor of *Punch*), was Fitzgerald's father. Both volumes are competently written, well researched, smoothly put together, and, above all, accurate. The author has that rare quality of engaging the reader's absolute trust. And though the biographies lack the acute and astonishing insights of the novels, Fitzgerald makes up for this by a brilliant ability to select other people's words: marvellously apt quotations which strikingly illuminate the narrative. Just one example from *Burne-Jones*, perfectly placed in context, is from a letter from his wife to George Eliot: "My heart smites me that I have somewhat resembled those friends who talk only of themselves to you." How revealing of the Victorian concept of good behaviour. That one phrase, in its delicacy, its self-accusation, is like a gleam of light shed on the entire English, upper-middle-class sensibility of the time.

It is, nevertheless, said by someone else. Fitzgerald's real talents only begin to reveal themselves in the novels. She evidently needs the imaginative freedom of fiction before she can take wing—though perhaps "plunge" would be a better word since she goes so deep. Give someone an enviably cultivated and civilised background, a First at Somerville, what seems to have been a wonderfully lively and interesting life, marriage and three bright children, and what kind of novels would one expect? Clever-academic? Grand-historical? The novel of manners? Even polished Women's Rights? Not a bit of it. Even in *The Golden Child*, for all its wit in portraying the jockeying for position of scholarly men in museums, she has an eye for the uncertainties which govern all our lives. She sees the tiny sources of terrible distress. In *The Bookshop*, about a pleasant, intelligent widow trying to run a bookshop in a small town, the theme is betrayal—sometimes from spite, sometimes from the baffling resentment always aroused by intelligence allied to modesty, sometimes from the equally inexplicable fury felt by the well-placed towards the less lucky, and sometimes from pure laziness. She sees the vast importance of small truths. Human beings, she says, are "divided into exterminators and exterminatees with the former, at any given moment, dominating." The book is a sad little masterpiece yet it sparkles with wit. And who could not admire a writer who can speak of an M.P. as "a brilliant, successful and stupid young man"?

Offshore deals with the fortunes, or rather misfortunes, of a variety of people living on houseboats on a stretch of the Thames. There are children who speak in a curiously formalised, almost Ivy Compton-Burnett style; their mother, beautiful and incapable; a stiff, competent, unhappily married man; and many others, all struggling to find a degree of fullness in their lives. Faced with the possibility of finally losing her estranged husband, the beautiful Nenna says: "I feel unemployed. I don't know what I'm going to think about if I'm not going to worry about him all the time." Fitzgerald sees with extraordinary perception what all our other women novelists, however famous, do not—that the root of love is not sex but occupation, the having something to do.

It is, again, startling to find that such a privileged life and nurturing should produce such understanding of what it is like to live on infinitely lower levels, socially, intellectually, and even emotionally. How did she manage to create a character like ten-year-old Christine, the working-class child in *The Bookshop*; perky, helpful, shrewd, impatient, and, in the end, like everyone else, a betrayer? Perhaps partly because, like her heroine in the same book: "In the end she valued kindness above everything."

These three novels are so good in their different ways that it is difficult to know how to avoid even further superlatives about the next two without sounding unbearably fulsome. *Human Voices* is set inside the BBC during World War II. The text abounds in that endemic BBC disease, initialitis: RPD, ADDG, RPA. They strew the pages but with such laughing satire that they do not irritate. The evocation of wartime London, the food, the black-outs, the people—from the irreproachable to the silly—is superb. Fitzgerald's style remains unique; at once broad and subtle, hilarious and heartbreaking, the whole laced with an astounding, psychological truth.

At Freddie's again exhibits her talents. It is set in a decrepit drama school, specialising in training children for the stage. The owner, Freddie (a sort of cross between Lilian Baylis and Joan Littlewood), is a monstrous, towering creation—and a survivor ("She knew that she was one of those people . . . whom society has mysteriously decided to support at all costs"). The children are impishly observed, as are the actors and the whole backstage world. But there are also desolation and failure. (Who else has noticed that shoulders, far more than faces, can speak of grief?)

The Booker Prize notwithstanding, Fitzgerald has never achieved the "flavour of the month" publicity of other winners. But compare her to some of our contemporary heavyweight women novelists, the politicos, the feminists, the sex-obsessed, the fairy-tale tellers, the working-class snapshotters, and she emerges with distinction. If one must find a fault it may be that people in real life do not so readily confess their faults and deficiencies as do her characters. Indeed, if they did, most of our lives would be spent in moments of horrified silence followed by rushed getaways. In this sense only does she swerve slightly from life as it is. But it is a small price to pay for such perception.

—Gerda Charles

FLANAGAN, Thomas (James Bonner). American. Born in Greenwich, Connecticut, 5 November 1923. Educated at Amherst College, Massachusetts, B.A. 1945; Columbia University, New York, M.A. 1948, Ph.D. in English 1958. Served in the United States Naval Reserve, 1942–44. Married Jean Parker in 1949; two daughters. Instructor, 1949–52, and Assistant Professor, 1952–59, Columbia University; Assistant Professor, 1960–67, Associate Professor, 1967–73, Professor, 1973–78, and Chairman of the Department of English, 1973–76, University of California, Los Angeles. Since 1978, Professor of English, State University of New York, Stony Brook. Recipient: American Council of Learned Societies grant, 1962; Guggenheim fellowship, 1962; National Book Critics Circle award, 1979. Address: Department of English, State University of New York, Stony Brook, New York 11794, U.S.A.

PUBLICATIONS

Novel

The Year of the French. New York, Holt Rinehart, and London, Macmillan, 1979.

Uncollected Short Stories

"The Cold Winds of Adesta" April 1952, "The Point of Honor" December 1952, "The Lion's Mane" March 1953, "This Will Do Nicely" August 1955, "The Customs of the Country" July 1956, and "Suppose You Were on the Jury" March 1958, all in *Ellery Queen's Mystery Magazine* (New York).
"The Fine Italian Hand," in *Ellery Queen's Book of First Appearances*, edited by Ellery Queen and Eleanor Sullivan. New York, Dial Press, 1982.

Other

The Irish Novelists 1800–1850. New York, Columbia University Press, 1959.

*   *   *

Thomas Flanagan spent 30 years researching and developing *The Year of the French*, his only novel to date. This narrative was based on an actual historical event in which a French military force landed at Killala, County Mayo, Ireland on 22 August, 1798. The French, who came ostensibly to free Ireland from British rule, were apparently more interested in embarrassing and harassing the English than in actually aiding the Irish. The French troops were joined by many peasants and various Irish rebel organizations. After marching through much of western and central Eire and winning several battles, they were eventually badly defeated at Ballinamuck, near Longford, by a vastly superior army led by Lord Cornwallis, whose success redeemed his tarnished experience in America. One of the most fascinating aspects of Flanagan's novel, which gives it an epic quality, is his attempt to portray in depth all sides and viewpoints in the conflict: the high born and the peasants, the Catholics and the Protestants, the French, Irish, and British military units, the clergy, the schoolmasters, the merchants— these and other groups are delineated with flesh and blood realization. At one point Flanagan even switches the scene to England and conveys a memorable portrait of an absentee landlord. Among the personages who beguile the reader are Arthur Broome, the local Anglican clergyman in Killala; Owen MacCarthy, the heavy drinking itinerant poet and hedgerow schoolmaster; Jean-Joseph Humbert, the wily, pragmatic French general; Malcolm Elliott, an upper-class Protestant estate holder committed to a more equitable economic order; and Captain Ferdy O'Donnell, a courageous, sensitive rebel leader.

Fictional characters are interrelated with real-life figures such as Wolfe Tone, George and John Moore, Dennis Browne, and Maria Edgeworth. The social, political, economic, and historical background and climate are presented and examined in thorough detail. Flanagan effectively intersperses dialogue and description with numerous imaginary diaries and memoirs of the era, and this technique adds immeasurably to the verisimilitude.

The novel is also distinguished by capturing the scene with marvellously rendered poetic lyricism exemplified in both the written and spoken language of the period. The book is a mellifluous delight—many of the pages are sheer poetry glowing with beauty and picturesque phrasing. Further, *The Year of the French* possesses considerable narrative drive. Although the use of journals and memoirs, frequent shifting from one character to another, and many scenic changes render the novel episodic, the pace never slows, and the movement is dynamic and pervasive.

The book's deficiencies center on three points. Flanagan presents a biased, hostile view of the Roman Catholic clergy (for example, if Flanagan's portrait of Father Murphy is compared with Liam O'Flaherty's Father Geelan in *Famine*, Flanagan's slant is evident; O'Flaherty too is anti-clerical, but his analysis of Geelan is balanced). On the other hand, Flanagan's Protestant clergymen appear to be wonderful, decent fellows. Secondly, Flanagan too often understates the sufferings and oppression which the common people endured; he strikes an unhealthy and distasteful note in describing the uneducated peasants. Thirdly, he fantasizes too unrealistically about a humanitarian union between Catholics and Protestants which could have somehow magically come about and solved all the country's problems. While this solution would have been highly desirable, Flanagan attempts unsuccessfully to make it appear within the realm of possibility.

Despite these weaknesses, *The Year of the French* is an epic saga of living history. It gives a panoramic view of one episode in the tragedy of English-Irish relations, reflected even today in the agony of Ulster. Flanagan is presently at work on another novel focusing on the late 19th-century Fenian Brotherhood era. If he can retain his combination of perceptive character portrayal, keen poetic sensibility, and gripping narrative force, and avoid his oversimplifications and a kind of upper-class long nose snobbism, he could secure for himself an important niche in the field of historical fiction.

—Paul A. Doyle

FOOTE, Shelby. American. Born in Greenville, Mississippi, 17 November 1916. Educated at the University of North Carolina, Chapel Hill, 1935–37. Served in the United States Army, 1940–44: Captain; and Marine Corps, 1944–45. Married Gwyn Rainer in 1956 (second marriage); two children. Novelist-in-Residence, University of Virginia, Charlottesville, November 1963; Playwright-in-Residence, Arena Stage, Washington, D.C., 1963–64; Writer-in-Residence, Hollins College, Virginia, 1968. Recipient: Guggenheim fellowship, 1955, 1956, 1957; Ford fellowship, for drama, 1963; Fletcher Pratt Award, for non-fiction, 1964, 1974; University of North Carolina award, 1975. D.Litt.: University of the South, Sewanee, Tennessee, 1981; Southwestern University, Memphis, Tennessee, 1982. Address: 542 East Parkway South, Memphis, Tennessee 38104, U.S.A.

PUBLICATIONS

Novels

Tournament. New York, Dial Press, 1949.
Follow Me Down. New York, Dial Press, 1950; London, Hamish Hamilton, 1951.
Love in a Dry Season. New York, Dial Press, 1951.
Shiloh. New York, Dial Press, 1952.
Jordan County: A Landscape in Narrative (includes stories). New York, Dial Press, 1954.
September September. New York, Random House, 1978.

Uncollected Short Story

"Rain Down Home," in *Stories from Tennessee*, edited by Linda Burton. Knoxville, University of Tennessee Press, 1983.

Play

Jordan County: A Landscape in the Round (produced Washington, D.C., 1964).

Other

The Civil War: A Narrative:
  1. *Fort Sumter to Perryville.* New York, Random House, 1958.
  2. *Fredericksburg to Meridian.* New York, Random House, 1963.
  3. *Red River to Appomattox.* New York, Random House, 1974.
The Novelist's View of History. Winston-Salem, North Carolina, Palaemon Press, 1981.

*

Manuscript Collection: Southern Historical Collection, Chapel Hill, North Carolina.

Critical Studies: *South* edited by Louis D. Rubin, Jr., and R.D. Jacobs, New York, Doubleday, 1961; "Shelby Foote Issue" (includes bibliography) of *Mississippi Quarterly* (State College), October 1971, and *Delta* (Montpellier, France), 1977; *Shelby Foote* by Helen White and Reading Sugg, Boston, Twayne, 1982; "Shelby Foote's Civil War" by James M. Cox, in *Southern Review* (Baton Rouge, Louisiana), Spring 1985.

*   *   *

Shelby Foote appears to succeed as a historian, not as a novelist; his multi-volume history *The Civil War: A Narrative* shows his ability to best advantage. However, one should remember that his entree into the literary world came as a promising novelist. His novels show a serious craftsman at work.

Foote experimented with technique. *Tournament* is a character study—approaching biography—with an objective omniscient point of view. *Follow Me Down* takes a single plot but incorporates a multiple point of view. This method is interesting because it allows eight characters—including protagonist and minor characters—to comment in a limited first person viewpoint on their reactions to a violent murder. *Love in a Dry Season* is a *tour de force* in which the author links two separate stories centered on the subject of money by a character who tries and fails to obtain a place in the financial elite of a small delta town. *Shiloh* enters the domain of historical fiction as the author recreates that Civil War battle through the eyes of six soldiers from both camps. Unlike the viewers in *Follow Me Down*, these narrators describe different aspects of the three-day confrontation, and only by adroit maneuvering does the author bring the respective narratives into contact. The battle, therefore, becomes the hero of the novel. *Jordan County* is a collection of seven tales or episodes ranging from 1950 backwards to 1797. In each case the locale is Bristol, Jordan County, Mississippi. As his previous novel focused on a single battle, so this chronicles human drama of a fictional area, which becomes the only constant in a world of flux.

With the exception of his historical novel, all of Foote's novels are located in his microcosm, the delta country around Lake Jordan. This fictive locale includes two counties. Issawamba and Jordan, Solitaire Plantation, and the town of Bristol on the Mississippi River. Through a habit of cross reference, Foote links episodes from one novel to another. For instance, the novella "Pillar of Fire" (*Jordan County*) relates the story of Isaac Jameson, founder of Solitaire Plantation and a patriarch of the delta, while *Tournament* supplies information about the man, Hugh Bart, who brought Solitaire back from devastation by war and reconstruction.

Foote's use of setting, as well as style, subject matter, themes, and characterization, invites comparison with his geographical neighbor, Faulkner, but Foote's accomplishments suffer thereby. Foote is competent, not great. Normally his style is simple, lean, and direct; it seldom takes on richly suggestive qualities. Most of his themes move in the negative, anti-social direction: violence instead of peace; lust rather than love; avarice, power, and pride instead of self-sacrifice; and loneliness rather than participation in community. At his best Foote deals effectively with dramatic situations and characterizations, for example, the concatenation of episodes in the life of Hugh Bart or Luther Eustis's murder (*Follow Me Down*); however, Harley Drew's career (*Love in a Dry Season*) of lust and avarice seems an exploitation of violence rather than art. Foote chronicles events in the realistic tradition without conveying a larger insight than the particular—an insight necessary for him to achieve a significant place in Southern literature.

—Anderson Clark

FORD, Jesse Hill (Jr.). American. Born in Troy, Alabama, 28 December 1928. Educated at Vanderbilt University, Nashville, B.A. 1951; University of Florida, Gainesville, M.A. 1955; University of Oslo (Fulbright Fellow), 1961. Served in the United States Navy, in the Far East, 1951–53. Married 1) Sally Davis in 1951 (divorced, 1975), two sons and two daughters; 2) Lillian Pellettieri in 1975. Reporter, Nashville *Tennesseean*, 1950–51; editorial news writer, University of Florida, 1953–55; medical news writer, Tennessee Medical Association, Nashville, 1955–56; public relations executive, American Medical Association, Chicago, 1956–57. Fellow, Center for Advanced Study, Wesleyan University, Middletown, Connecticut, 1965. Recipient: *Atlantic* "Firsts" Award, 1959; Guggenheim fellowship, 1966; Mystery Writers of America Edgar Allan Poe Award, for short story, 1976. D.Litt.: Lambuth College, Jackson, Tennessee, 1966. Agent: Harold Ober Associates, 40 East 49th Street, New York, New York 10017. Address: Box 43, Bellevue, Tennessee 37221, U.S.A.

PUBLICATIONS

Novels

Mountains of Gilead. Boston, Little Brown, 1961.
The Liberation of Lord Byron Jones. Boston, Little Brown, 1965; London, Bodley Head, 1966.
The Feast of Saint Barnabas. Boston, Little Brown, and London, Bodley Head, 1969.
The Raider. Boston, Little Brown, 1975.

Short Stories

Fishes, Birds, and Sons of Men: Stories. Boston, Little Brown, 1967; London, Bodley Head, 1968.

Uncollected Short Stories

"Collector," in *Atlantic* (Boston), February 1968.
"Doctor," in *Atlantic* (Boston), June 1969.
"Destruction," in *Esquire* (New York), July 1969.
"Debt," in *Atlantic* (Boston), June 1972.
"The Jail," in *The Edgar Winners*, edited by Bill Pronzini. New York, Random House, 1980.
"Big Boy," in *Stories from Tennessee*, edited by Linda Burton. Knoxville, University of Tennessee Press, 1983.

Plays

The Conversion of Buster Drumwright: The Television and Stage Scripts (televised, 1961). Nashville, Vanderbilt University Press, 1964; musical version, as *Drumwright!* (produced Knoxville, Tennessee, 1982).

Screenplay: *The Liberation of L.B. Jones*, with Sterling Silliphant, 1970.

Television Play: *The Conversion of Buster Drumwright*, 1961.

Other

Mister Potter and His Bank (biography of Edward Potter, Jr.). Nashville, Commerce Union Bank, 1977.

*

Bibliography: *Jesse Hill Ford: An Annotated Check List* by Helen White, Memphis, Tennessee, Memphis State University, 1974.

Manuscript Collection: Memphis State University, Tennessee.

Jesse Hill Ford comments:

(1981) In 1963 I found to my surprise that I had been working on the same story for ten years and that bits and pieces of it had by then appeared in several short stories, one play, and one novel. The second novel continued the story. In the third novel, *The Feast of St. Barnabas*, I tried, but failed to escape the one long story I began in 1953, the story I have, fitfully to be sure, been writing ever since. If one reads all my books and stories the pattern will emerge in tenuous connections sometimes indicated only by the appearance of a name carried forward, or backward, from one generation into another. The story begins in the western district of Tennessee in the American South and it probably will end there someday, far off in the future I hope, even though I am now 51 years old and still attempting to write it all down, not just the tragic events, but also the happy ones, and not just the earth-shaking things, but also the small moments that have been of such singular importance to the people I work to portray.

(1986) I owe special thanks to Edward Weeks and his wife, Phoebe-Lou Adams Weeks. Towards the end of his 35-year stint as editor of *The Atlantic Monthly* he and Phoebie-Lou, his associate editor, discovered and encouraged me, as did Peter Davison, who was then with the Atlantic Monthly Press. The unselfish efforts of these gifted people brought out the best in me. It is thanks to them that I've been privileged to devote the fresh hours of each day since 1957 to writing, and to live by and for it.

*   *   *

One generation removed from the modern Southern Renaissance, Jesse Hill Ford has begun to establish his legitimate place in that literary heritage. He has shown ability to treat universal themes embodied in the subjects—people, attitudes, events—of a particular geographic region, the American South. The greater portion of Ford's work—including two novels, *The Liberation of Lord Byron Jones* and *Mountains of Gilead*, and several short stories collected in *Fishes, Birds, and Sons of Men*—is set in the author's fictional 20th-century microcosm, Somerton, Sligo County, Tennessee. Through the continuity of locale and the cross reference to particularly prominent families and community events, the reader of Ford's fiction absorbs one writer's observation of the diversified southern consciousness.

Ford's observation covers an impressive range of themes. For example, the theme of innocence to experience has several dimensions. Simple childhood reminiscences in "The Cave" and "The Cow" respectively lead a child to intuit the fact of evil and of death, although the child can not articulate these experiences. In another short story, "A Strange Sky," Ford deals directly with the effects of this progression to experience in the life of his adult protagonist, Patsy Jo. She examines her past life, especially the seduction and manipulation by her irresponsible childhood lover, who has continually postponed marriage. Now past her marriageable prime, Patsy Jo reaches a point of maturity by severing her relationship as mistress. In the hunting story, "Savage Sound," the same theme is used differently. The protagonist does not move from innocence to experience; rather, he is responsible for teaching his young whippets to kill rabbits and, thereby, for changing the dogs' loving natures to that of vicious predators.

Violence as a theme pervades all of Ford's fiction. A catalogue of physical violence includes assault and battery, automobile wrecks, arson, rape, adultery, rusty coat hanger abortion, castration, cattle-prodding humans, drowning, man-slaughter in self-defense, premeditated murder, and even a bizarre homicide effected by the chomping jaws of a hay-bailing machine. Psychological violence, often a concomitant of the physical, makes Ford's characters also an emotionally mangled humanity. Both facets of violence show that in Ford's chaotic world egocentric modern man chooses to satisfy his own desires at the expense of his fellow man.

The violence in Ford's fiction is often an adjunct of the revenge theme. His drama, *The Conversion of Buster Drumwright*, produced first as a television play and later expanded for the stage, links murder, a desire for blood revenge, and religion. Ford's plot functions in such a way as to discredit the impulse toward revenge and sanction the worth, if not the authenticity, of the Christian message of repentance, forgiveness, and salvation. *Mountains of Gilead*, Ford's first novel, artistically uneven, offers a perceptive characterization of a Southern father caught in the dilemma of avenging his daughter's violated honor while remembering the unhappy consequences of his own early marital infidelity. That the father follows the code of revenge, despite his own moral inconsistency, allows the plot to resolve—after a blood bath, suicide, and time interval—in a melodramatic reunion and marriage of the estranged youthful lovers.

Another significant theme is racial injustice, prejudice, and discrimination in Ford's South. The short story "Bitter Bread" recounts the agony and humiliation of a black man whose wife dies in a hospital corridor because they have no money for admission. Ford continues this theme of racial injustice in his second novel, *The Liberation of Lord Byron Jones*. Somerton's respectable black mortician, L.B. Jones, in seeking a divorce from his young, promiscuous wife, precipitates his own violent "liberation," his murder by the white policeman involved in the miscegenous affair. Jones is a believably tragic character as well as a representative of the oppressed southern Negro. Other characters—with varying degrees of success—demonstrate typical attitudes including that of White Citizens' agitator, socially conservative and moderate whites, and simple and militant blacks. Ford takes another viewpoint in the third novel, *The Feast of Saint Barnabas*, by focusing on the forces operating in a southern racial riot. He shows a rich black man manipulating the violent elements in the community for selfish gains. While this novel contains plenty of action, it lacks dimensions of characterization and even psychological suffering which underscore themes of the two earlier impressive works.

As an imaginative craftsman, Ford writes especially well in the short story genre. In this particular genre, in contrast to a drift in his longer works toward the melodramatic or the maudlin, Ford welds dramatic action, effective characterization, and vivid imagery into a thematic unity. His talents in the short story are in the best of Southern Renaissance literary tradition. His narration is simple; his style is clear and direct. In the shorter pieces he handles point of view with strict control,

and while *The Liberation* offers a multiple point of view, Ford uses his short story technique of control from section to section. Of primary importance are his vivid eye for details, which often function both literally and symbolically, and his fine ear for dialogue. His sense of humor moves from the rockingly jovial to the grimly ironic, and his best characters possess the complexity and vitality of a gifted artist's imagination.

—Anderson Clark

FORREST, Leon. American. Born in Chicago, Illinois, 8 January 1937. Educated at Hyde Park High School, 1951–55, Wilson Junior College, 1955–56, and Roosevelt University, 1957–58, all Chicago; University of Chicago, 1959–60, 1962–64. Served in the United States Army, 1961–62: public information specialist. Editor of community newspapers, Chicago, 1965–69; associate editor, 1969–72, and managing editor, 1972–73, *Muhammad Speaks* (Black Muslim newspaper), Chicago. Associate Professor, 1973–84, since 1984 Professor, and since 1985, Chairman of the Department of African-American Studies, Northwestern University, Evanston, Illinois. President, Society of Midland Authors, 1981–82. "Leon Forrest Day" observed in Chicago, 1985. Address: Department of African-American Studies, Northwestern University, Arthur Andersen Hall, 2003 Sheridan Road, Evanston, Illinois 60201, U.S.A.

PUBLICATIONS

Novels

There Is a Tree More Ancient Than Eden. New York, Random House, 1973.
The Bloodworth Orphans. New York, Random House, 1977.
Two Wings to Veil My Face. New York, Random House, 1984.

Uncollected Short Stories

"Packwood's Sermon by Firelight," in *Massachusetts Review* (Amherst), Winter 1977.
"Oh Jeremiah of the Dreams," in *Callaloo* (Lexington, Kentucky), May 1979.
"Oh Say Can You See," in *StoryQuarterly* (Northbrook, Illinois), 1982.
"Inside the Body of a Green Apple Tree," in *Iowa Review* (Iowa City), vol. 14, no. 1, 1984.
"Sub-Rosa," in *Tri-Quarterly* (Evanston, Illinois), Summer 1984.

Plays (libretti)

Re-Creation, music by T.J. Anderson (produced Chicago, 1978).
Soldier Boy, Soldier, music by T.J. Anderson (produced Bloomington, Indiana, 1982).

*   *   *

Ralph Ellison's enthusiastic foreword to *There Is a Tree More Ancient Than Eden* helped to launch Leon Forrest as a novelist. The novel is a *tour de force*, not easy to get into and requiring constant participation from the reader, but offering great rewards. The narrator is Nathan Witherspoon, a mulatto boy attending his mother's funeral, although the five parts of the novel encompass a much wider scope. "The Lives" provides biographical information about the major characters and serves to start Nathan on his way to the confrontations in "The Nightmare" and "The Dream" which focus on his own experience. He then launches into "The Vision" and arrives at "Wakefulness." The influences of Faulkner's *The Sound and the Fury* and Joyce's *Ulysses* are discernible but the structure is more deeply informed by the patterns of oral narration in folk sagas. Recurring themes and symbols weave a vivid, complex texture of images and motifs in terms of violence, rapes, lynchings, and also ecstasies, flights, illuminations.

The past is all-important; it is seen as a burden, for the white branch of Nathan's family included slave traders and their Dupont relatives are still openly racist. Nathan wavers between the despairing voices of his own father and of Jamestown Fishbond and the hope embodied by his aunt and guide, Hattie Breedlove. Fishbond is Nathan's relative on the slave side and extreme poverty and racial oppression have made him a modern instance of the Africans transported during the Middle Passage. His sister Madge likewise tries to hold on to her Christian faith in spite of many setbacks but she is ultimately defeated.

Most of the narrative happens wholly within Nathan's consciousness (indeed the final monologue seems inspired by Molly Bloom's soliloquy in *Ulysses*), but a number of historical characters appear, such as Abraham Lincoln who is depicted as divided between his desire to keep the nation whole and his mission as the Emancipator. However, images and words are more important than themes: Forrest derives from black oral tradition his constant use of hymns, spirituals, church scenes, and biblical phrases typical of the black preacher. Folk sermon, lament, and chant mingle with angel-like apparitions and the sensation of being given a pair of wings. In the finale of the "Vision" section, a Christ figure is torn to pieces, crucified or lynched. The novel does not end in salvation but simply on the metaphorical road to it: the mulatto protagonist has taken stock of his divided heritage and one can hope his confidence will be restored by his acceptance of his, and his people's, history.

The mosaic-like composition makes the novel difficult reading, but, in a way similar to Ellison's *Invisible Man*, the juxtaposition of echoing episodes and characters makes them reverberate and enrich the whole. In his latest novel Forrest uses again a large number of characters and the same way of developing his story, which is centered around the symbolic image of the "bleeding tree," the Christian Cross and/or the instrument of lynching about which Billie Holiday sang in "Strange Fruit."

The Bloodworth Orphans pursues the exploration of American genealogy begun in *There Is a Tree More Ancient Than Eden* but extends it, by way of the Genesis myth of the lost children of Israel, into a complex metaphor of bastardy located at the heart of American national identity. The Bloodworths are, all of them, at least symbolically, orphans in search of ancestors: twelve chapters and many characters and episodes are united through the theme of abandonment. The descendants of P.F. Pourty Bloodworth are all more or less cast away and doomed to perish, but as in the Oedipus story, they are saved and raised by foster parents so that their prototypical experience becomes mirror for all the forsaken children in the novel, youngsters like Jonathan Bass or Rachel Flowers, all exposed to drift in quest of roots and anchorage in a chaotic world. Likewise, Regal Pettibone and LaDonna Scales are

heirs to a past of incest. Admittedly Noah Grandberry and Nathan find a baby right in the middle of a gang war, as though turmoil also produces the hope of regeneration. Violence, however, seems to prevail, and Carl Rae, the son of Rachel Flowers, is shot down, and nearly cut in two. Rachel herself is a dominant character, central in a scene of conversion and a dying soliloquy. Her strong Baptist faith leads her to self-denial and sacrifice. Contrasting with such well-meaning but disoriented characters is the scheming, all powerful con-man W.W.W. Ford. He is a sort of trickster straight from Afro-American folklore and creation myths alike, the leader who manipulates the crowd and deceives it as he pretends to act as its mentor. A hustler, he enacts his own entombment and resurrection in order to attract more followers. One finds echoes of *Invisible Man* in this elaborate novel, but also reference to the myths of Osiris, Oedipus, and Orpheus which transform episodes from Afro-American history and experience into metaphors for humanity at large. The strength of the novel derives from its superlative use of folk forms, notably the art of the black preacher represented by Reverend Packwood. Yet Forrest also employs, at times, a grotesque, surrealistic treatment.

Two Wings to Veil My Face uses similar types of characters and situations: is there a hint of Ishmael Reed's "neo hoodoo" aesthetics in Aunty Foisty, the conjure woman who has hexed I.V. Reed? Again, Forrest subtly draws upon the oral tradition of folk beliefs and projects black situations onto a wider framework through the half-veiled use of Greek myths. All Forrest's fictions seem to blend into one attempt at spinning a web of verbal connections. His novels are palimpsests, radical attempts to renew black fiction, not along metafictional and self-reflexive perspectives but by the contrapuntal arrangement of the timeless processes of popular tale-telling and the innovative techniques of modernism used by Joyce and Faulkner.

—Michel Fabre

FORSTER, Margaret. British. Born in Carlisle, Cumberland, 25 May 1938. Educated at Carlisle and County High School for Girls, 1949–56; Somerville College, Oxford (scholar), 1957–60, B.A. in modern history 1960. Married the writer Hunter Davies in 1960; two daughters and one son. Teacher, Barnsbury Girls' School, London, 1961–63; chief non-fiction reviewer, London *Evening Standard*, 1977–80. Fellow, Royal Society of Literature, 1975. Agent: Tessa Sayle Agency, 11 Jubilee Place, London SW3 3TE. Address: 11 Boscastle Road, London N.W.5, England.

PUBLICATIONS

Novels

Dames' Delight. London, Cape, 1964.
Georgy Girl. London, Secker and Warburg, 1965; New York, Berkley, 1966.
The Bogeyman. London, Secker and Warburg, 1965; New York, Putnam, 1966.
The Travels of Maudie Tipstaff. London, Secker and Warburg, and New York, Stein and Day, 1967.
The Park. London, Secker and Warburg, 1968.
Miss Owen-Owen Is at Home. London, Secker and Warburg, 1969; as *Miss Owen-Owen*, New York, Simon and Schuster, 1969.

Fenella Phizackerley. London, Secker and Warburg, 1970; New York, Simon and Schuster, 1971.
Mr. Bone's Retreat. London, Secker and Warburg, and New York, Simon and Schuster, 1971.
The Seduction of Mrs. Pendlebury. London, Secker and Warburg, 1974.
Mother Can You Hear Me? London, Secker and Warburg, 1979.
The Bride of Lowther Fell: A Romance. London, Secker and Warburg, 1980; New York, Atheneum, 1981.
Marital Rites. London, Secker and Warburg, 1981; New York, Atheneum, 1982.
Private Papers. London, Chatto and Windus, 1986.

Play

Screenplay: *Georgy Girl*, with Peter Nichols, 1966.

Other

The Rash Adventurer: The Rise and Fall of Charles Edward Stuart. London, Secker and Warburg, 1973; New York, Stein and Day, 1974.
William Makepeace Thackeray: Memoirs of a Victorian Gentleman. London, Secker and Warburg, 1978; as *Memoirs of a Victorian Gentleman*, New York, Morrow, 1979.
Significant Sisters: The Grassroots of Active Feminism 1839–1939. London, Secker and Warburg, 1984; New York, Knopf, 1985.

*   *   *

Since the publication of her first novel, *Dames' Delight*, more than twenty years ago Margaret Forster has written a dozen novels. In all of them she is preoccupied with human relationships or, to put it more precisely, with the impact of one person on another, with the possibility—or impossibility—of any real change in someone's character and outlook on life through emotional involvement with someone else. (She seems to declare her interest in character in the very choice of her titles; it is hardly an accident that so many of her novels carry someone's name, that badge of personal identity, in the title.)

Hers is a characteristically feminine preoccupation; even today love, whether within or outside marriage, or between those tied by the unbreakable blood knot, remains all-important to women, and Forster acknowledges this. Her perception of the impact of love seems to have changed somewhat, grown softer perhaps, over the years. In *Georgy Girl* behind all the clowning and laughter there hides a bleak, loveless little world, and George herself, so full of fierce, all-embracing love for children, has very little real lasting love to spare for her relationships with adults. In *The Travels of Maudie Tipstaff* Maudie, disappointed with her visits to her children, readily accepts the explanation of her disappointment offered in her son Robert's chilling words: "Two people are always two people ... I'm on my own, and you, Mother, are on your own." In *Mr. Bone's Retreat*, however, we sense a change; Mr. Bone retreats indeed from his position of determined non-involvement, and slowly and with hesitation comes to accept the possibility of receiving graciously the love that is offered: "Love had to be accepted. The quality of the gift was what mattered."

The process of change does not, however, culminate in the happy ending of a romantic novel. In *The Seduction of Mrs. Pendlebury* Alice Oram nearly destroys Mrs. Pendlebury by demanding love and reassurance for her own doubts and insecurities which Rose Pendlebury cannot give. Her demands cannot be met because a personality cannot change totally without

breaking in the violence of the change; the relationship between the two women sours into obsession and near madness. As in *Mr. Bone's Retreat* the young intruder acts as a catalyst, while remaining largely unchanged herself; her resilience and her strength in the possession of a future full of rich possibilities save her from disaster. For Mrs. Pendlebury salvation lies in flight to the isolation of a small seaside bungalow, set well back from its neighbours and screened so well by trees. However powerful human relationships are, they cannot radically alter a person's character, and tampering with people is a dangerous hobby.

In two recent novels, *The Bride of Lowther Fell* and *Marital Rites*, the note of cautious acceptance of love is sounded more clearly. Alexandra, the liberated young woman in *The Bride of Lowther Fell*, admits at the very end of her tale: "The lessons are learned. No man is an island, and no woman either." In *Marital Rites*, though Robert and Anna Osgood come through their marriage crisis shattered and diminished, marriage itself, the conventional and convenient symbol of lasting love, survives triumphant; the value of giving and accepting love, and being altered by it, is tacitly acknowledged.

There is always a touch of irony in a human relationship, in its misconceptions, its wishful attempts to make others see us as we see ourselves. Forster recognises this irony and uses it, sometimes as part of the very structure of her novels. Not always as overtly as in *Mother Can You Hear Me?* where Angela's struggle against the emotional demands of her elderly mother is counterpointed by italicised passages recording her vain attempts to bring up her own daughter free of the crushing burden of filial guilt. In *The Travels of Maudie Tipstaff*, too, Maudie's picture of herself and her children's perception of her behaviour are offered with silent irony, the mutual miscomprehensions stressing the theme of human isolation. In *The Seduction of Mrs. Pendlebury* and in *Mr. Bone's Retreat* the same technique is used more subtly, and instead of the juxtaposition of two contrasting pictures there are oblique backward glances, slowly altering a remembered incident or conversation.

In all her novels Forster's style is plain, deliberately downbeat, letting the pathos and the irony speak for themselves. The impersonal third-person narrator tells the story in short sentences, except when—as in *The Seduction of Mrs. Pendlebury*—she is voicing the thoughts of her characters. Then the sentences stretch and curl, following the course of thought.

Like so many women novelists writing today, Forster has a sharp eye for domestic detail, for the social comedy of our times. She is very much a town dweller (except in *The Bride of Lowther Fell* where she clearly draws on her Cumbrian memories, as well as—nostalgically—on those of North London). She can sum up in a few telling phrases the gentrification process in Islington ("large removal van, stacked with pine tables and brass bedsteads"), a council house in Cornwall ("The cheap cotton, flowered curtains had never fitted and let in too much light"), middle-class life in Highgate (instant coffee always offered with apologies, a sluttish daily help tolerated as a sop to social conscience). All this has been done often, but is done here extremely well.

She reproduces variants of speech with equal accuracy, and, it must be said, with equal facileness. Her characters come to us with full credentials of class and educational background. It is when she moves beyond the everyday that her skill fails her. Larger-than-life characters like the eponymous Miss Owen-Owen and Fenella Phizackerley may astonish us by their behaviour, but they do not convince. Over Miss Owen-Owen the shadow of Miss Jean Brodie lies very heavily indeed;

Fenella, the reader of popular women's magazines imprisoned inside a creature of breath-taking beauty, remains the impossible heroine of some extravagant fairy tale. The heroine of *The Bride of Lowther Fell* (a book subtitled "a Romance," and boldly inviting by its very title a comparison with the Victorian novel) is no more convincing than the contrived plot.

Margaret Forster is a skilful chronicler of the lifestyles of our times. Our pleasure in the recognition of a familiar domestic detail or an authentic snatch of dialogue is genuine and satisfying, but she lightens up for us a corner of the kitchen cupboard rather than the human condition.

—Hana Sambrook

FORSYTH, Frederick. British. Born in Ashford, Kent, in 1938. Educated at Tonbridge School, Kent. Served in the Royal Air Force. Married; two children. Journalist: with *Eastern Daily Press*, Norwich, and in King's Lynn, Norfolk, 1958–61; reporter for Reuters, London, Paris, and East Berlin, 1961–65; reporter, BBC Radio and Television, London, 1965–67; assistant diplomatic correspondent, BBC, 1967–68; free-lance journalist in Nigeria, 1968–70. Presenter, *Soldiers* television series, 1985. Recipient: Mystery Writers of America Edgar Allan Poe Award, 1971, 1983. Lives in London. Address: c/o Century Hutchinson, 62–65 Chandos Place, London WC2N 4NW, England.

PUBLICATIONS

Novels

The Day of the Jackal. London, Hutchinson, and New York, Viking Press, 1971.
The Odessa File. London, Hutchinson, and New York, Viking Press, 1972.
The Dogs of War. London, Hutchinson, and New York, Viking Press, 1974.
The Shepherd. London, Hutchinson, 1975; New York, Viking Press, 1976.
The Devil's Alternative. London, Hutchinson, 1979; New York, Viking Press, 1980.
The Fourth Protocol. London, Hutchinson, and New York, Viking, 1984.

Short Stories

No Comebacks: Collected Short Stories. London, Hutchinson, and New York, Viking Press, 1982.

Other

The Biafra Story. London, Penguin, 1969; as *The Making of an African Legend: The Biafra Story*, 1977.
Emeka (biography of Chukwuemeka Odumegwu-Ojukwu). Ibadan, Spectrum, 1982.

*   *   *

Frederick Forsyth achieved considerable commercial success with his first book, *The Day of the Jackal*, and in each of his subsequent novels he has followed the same basic formula. Start with a plausible international crisis, mix real historical personages with fictional characters, keep a number of narrative threads moving at all times, scatter violent and/or erotic incidents liberally through the story, explain the secrets of criminal and police activity in minute detail, build toward an explosive climax, end with an unexpected twist of plot. The formula has produced five bestsellers, all at least one notch above standard popular fare, all already made or likely to be made into profitable feature films.

The Day of the Jackal represents the best elements of the Forsyth formula. The main plot seems simple enough: a group of disgruntled veterans of the Algerian war hire a professional assassin from England, code-named the Jackal, to kill President de Gaulle for betraying the French cause in North Africa. Forsyth complicates the story by adding an abundance of peripheral plots and characters, many based on actual events of the time. We are jolted back and forth between two centers of intrigue: the solitary assassin meticulously planning each step of the murder and the special police unit trying to track him down. Forsyth's fascination with detail draws us into the story, details such as how to acquire false passports, how to obtain a custom-made rifle, how to travel around Europe under a variety of identities, and how, on the other hand, police forces of different nations cooperate to prevent the assassination. Facing a complex plot and an overabundance of characters, we see action without understanding the human motives behind it. But though we never get inside the main figure, the Jackal, we are willing to attribute this to the nature of the character: a professional assassin keeps his own counsel, revealing nothing of himself to anyone. Thus a fundamental shortcoming in Forsyth's work, an unwillingness or inability to create convincing characters, can be seen as a virtue in *The Day of the Jackal*.

The same flaw is more apparent, and less defensible, in the novels that followed. *The Odessa File* concerns a young German journalist's attempt to infiltrate an organization of influential former SS officers and to locate one war criminal in particular. The theme of hunter and hunted is repeated from the earlier book, but the lack of characterization seems glaring here. So too with *The Dogs of War*, a novel about mercenaries overthrowing an African dictator, and *The Devil's Alternative*, about a series of international events which brings the world to the brink of nuclear war. In *The Fourth Protocol*, however, as in *The Day of the Jackal*, the more shadowy the people, the more real they seem. The novel describes an ingeniously complex Soviet plot to undermine the British government, with intelligence experts from each side anticipating and thwarting the other's moves. The spies of *The Fourth Protocol*, like the professional assassin of *The Day of the Jackal*, are too special to be understood.

All Forsyth novels include a wealth of detail on matters well beyond the experience of their readers, yet they convey a compelling atmosphere of verisimilitude. We learn how experts make and plant bombs, smuggle weapons, infiltrate secret agencies; we learn how terrorists operate, how world leaders confer and conspire, how spies attend to their daily chores. But all of this detail does not produce convincing human beings. The events seem real, at least plausible, but not the people.

Forsyth himself is extremely candid about the strengths and weaknesses of his work. He recognizes the need for thorough research into his material, knowing that the credibility of his plots lies in his attention to realistic detail. He sees himself, moreover, as a strictly commercial writer, and his language is crisp and direct, without grace or pretention. Proficient within his genre, Forsyth has the intelligence and good taste not to stray beyond it.

—Robert E. Lynch

FOSTER, David (Manning). Australian. Born in Sydney, New South Wales, 15 May 1944. Educated at the University of Sydney, B.Sc. 1967; Australian National University, Canberra, Ph.D. 1970. Research Fellow, U.S. Public Health Service, Philadelphia, 1970–71; Senior Research Officer, University of Sydney Medical School, 1971–72. Recipient: Australian Literature Board fellowships, 1973–85; *The Age* award, 1974; Marten Bequest award, 1978; Australian National Book Council award, 1981. Address: Ardara, Victoria Street, Bundanoon, New South Wales 2578, Australia.

PUBLICATIONS

Novels

The Pure Land. Melbourne, Macmillan, 1974; New York, Penguin, 1985.
The Empathy Experiment, with D.K. Lyall. Sydney, Wild and Woolley, 1977.
Moonlite. Melbourne, Macmillan, 1981; London, Pan, 1982.
Plumbum. Ringwood, Victoria, Penguin, 1983.
Dog Rock: A Postal Pastoral. Ringwood, Victoria, and New York, Penguin, 1985.
Christian Rosy Cross. London, Penguin, 1986.

Short Stories

North South West: Three Novellas. Melbourne, Macmillan, 1973.
Escape to Reality. Melbourne, Macmillan, 1977.

Verse

The Fleeing Atalanta. Adelaide, Maximus, 1975.

*   *   *

One of Australia's most prolific and inventive contemporary writers, David Foster attracted considerable attention with his first full-length novel, *The Pure Land* (co-winner of *The Age* Book of the Year Award), but it is really with his more recent novels that he has emerged as a writer of originality and distinction. Most of the early fiction gives the impression of having been written by a talent of considerable, if somewhat cerebral, intelligence, deeply uncertain as to the direction in which it wants to move.

Foster studied as a scientist at the University of Sydney and the Australian National University before turning to fiction, and this background shows in his early as well as later work—in his interest in scientific and intellectual concepts such as entropy and his vast and eclectic vocabulary, which is full of technical and abstruse words. (He was co-author of a bizarre and unsuccessful science-fiction novel, *The Empathy Experiment*.) The early works are full of outsiders and drop-outs, fringe figures who search for a meaning and significance in life and finally settle more or less willingly for the conviction that they are not to be found. The most impressive of these books is *The Pure Land*, an unusual example of that familiar Australian fictive stand-by, the generational novel. Divided

into three parts, it tells the stories of three generations of a family, with only minor connecting links between the largely discrete sections. A Jewish photographer Manwaring, living in the Blue Hills of Sydney, is abandoned by his wife. He comes upon a couple making love, photographs them and sends the shots overseas, where they come into the hands of an American dealer in pornography, who writes offering a job. Manwaring abducts his unprotesting 12 year-old daughter Janet and flees. The second section deals with Janet (now Jean) in America and her somewhat uninspired marriage. Her son Danny is the subject of the last part. Danny disgraces himself at a scientific conference in Berkeley and drops out, quarrels with his lover Sylvia and stows away on a boat to Sydney. In the end the novel peters out with a series of letters from Danny in Sydney to Sylvia in Philadelphia but without replies. In structure the novel is triangular, with the eventual return to the original apex of Sydney, again by means of an illegal voyage. One cannot be sure at the end whether Danny has found his pure land or not.

Moonlite is a less coldly written but ingenious narrative of the picaresque adventures of one Finbar ("Moonbar") Mac-Duffie which seems to amount to something like an allegorical account of the history of immigration to Australia. It is divided into four "Acts" as Foster calls them. Act One is set on the distant island of Mugg, to the north of Scotland. By Act Two Finbar's mother Flora has moved to the nearby island of Hiphoray, which is subjected to the ravages of the Reverend Stewart Campbell, a parodic portrait of an evangelical preacher, who ruins the island and its inhabitants by introducing tourism. The young Finbar receives a revelation and is converted to a fervent Christianity. He travels south to Jesus Christ College where he attempts to convert the native heathens and somehow or other finds himself on a convict ship to Australia, where the most fanciful section of the novel takes place, culminating in an encounter with his alter ego, the Aboriginal Sunbeam. It is a very funny novel, reminiscent of John Barth's work, especially *The Sot-Weed Factor*. Foster displays his characteristic fascination with language for its own sake, using arcane or self-invented words, punning vigorously, giving characters names like the Marquis of Moneymore and Grog-strife and providing a variety of dialects as well as a multitude of satiric targets from academic scholarship and Christianity through advocates of temperance to Australian myths of heroism and identity.

Plumbum starts off coherently enough, with a group of young musicians gathering together to form the Blackman Brothers Band in Canberra. Despite the individual differences of temperament and the tensions among the members, the heavy metal rock band prospers. Inevitably they move to Sydney. Then, for reasons which like a great deal else in the novel are not very clear, they move to Bangkok. Then Calcutta. Then Utrecht. Long before their journey is ended they have left the reader far behind. The syncopated narrative becomes even more so, the medley of voices increasingly crowded, the exploits of the band increasingly bizarre and surreal.

Dog Rock is a country town, population 776; the narrator, D'Arcy D'Oliveres, has been postman there for ten years. A murderer known only as the Queen's Park Ripper is terrorising the town's citizens by progressively eliminating them. The novel is a parody of the detective quest, with an abundance of improbable clues and a plot whose complications would arouse the envy of Raymond Chandler. At the end, after D'Arcy has worked out the identity of the killer, he explains the solution in one of the novel's many long monologues, the killer is fatally wounded, he and D'Arcy forgive each other and the chapter ends with D'Arcy's statement, "Now I'll just tread on your chest to make it quicker for you."

Foster would seem on the face of it to have an imagination as original as almost any contemporary novelist and a good many other natural gifts. At the moment, though, that imagination seems difficult for him to harness. Like Barth and perhaps Thomas Pynchon, he reads better in bits and pieces than in toto. There are brilliantly original gags but no normative centre against which to place them. Perhaps he might do well to take note of one of his own brilliant scientific analogies from *Plumbum*: "You will sometimes see a middle-aged man holding the jaws of his mind open with every intellectual prop and pole at his disposal. In such a state, he resembles a bivalve mollusc, constrained to sup whatever shit floats by."

—Laurie Clancy

FOWLES, John (Robert). British. Born in Leigh-on-Sea, Essex, 31 March 1926. Educated at Bedford School, 1940–44; Edinburgh University, 1944; New College, Oxford, B.A. (honours) in French 1950. Served in the Royal Marines, 1945–46. Married Elizabeth Whitton in 1956. Lecturer in English, University of Poitiers, 1950–51; taught at Anargyrios College, Spetsai, Greece, 1951–52, and in London, 1953–63. Recipient: Silver Pen Award, 1969; W.H. Smith Literary Award, 1970; Christopher Award, 1981. Agent: Anthony Sheil Associates, 43 Doughty Street, London WC1N 2LF, England.

PUBLICATIONS

Novels

The Collector. London, Cape, and Boston, Little Brown, 1963.
The Magus. Boston, Little Brown, 1965; London, Cape, 1966; revised edition, Cape, 1977; Little Brown, 1978.
The French Lieutenant's Woman. London, Cape, and Boston, Little Brown, 1969.
Daniel Martin. Boston, Little Brown, and London, Cape, 1977.
Mantissa. London, Cape, and Boston, Little Brown, 1982.
A Maggot. London, Cape, and Boston, Little Brown, 1985.

Short Stories

The Ebony Tower: Collected Novellas. London, Cape, and Boston, Little Brown, 1974.

Plays

Don Juan, adaptation of the play by Molière (produced London, 1981).
Lorenzaccio, adaptation of the play by Alfred de Musset (produced London, 1983).
Martine, adaptation of a play by Jean Jacques Bernard (produced London, 1985).

Screenplay: *The Magus*, 1968.

Verse

Poems. New York, Ecco Press, 1973.
Conditional. Northridge, California, Lord John Press, 1979.

Other

The Aristos: A Self-Portrait in Ideas. Boston, Little Brown, 1964; London, Cape, 1965; revised edition, London, Pan, 1968; Little Brown, 1970.
Shipwreck, photographs by the Gibsons of Scilly. London, Cape, 1974; Boston, Little Brown, 1975.
Islands, photographs by Fay Godwin. London, Cape, 1978; Boston, Little Brown, 1979.
The Tree, photographs by Frank Horvat. London, Aurum Press, 1979; Boston, Little Brown, 1980.
The Enigma of Stonehenge, photographs by Barry Brukoff. London, Cape, and New York, Summit, 1980.
A Brief History of Lyme. Lyme Regis, Dorset, Friends of the Lyme Regis Museum, 1981.
A Short History of Lyme Regis. Wimborne, Dorset, Dovecote Press, 1982; Boston, Little Brown, 1983.
Land, photographs by Fay Godwin. London, Heinemann, and Boston, Little Brown, 1985.

Editor, *Steep Holm: A Case History in the Study of Evolution.* Sherborne, Dorset, Allsop Memorial Trust, 1978.
Editor, with Rodney Legg, *Monumenta Britannica*, by John Aubrey. Sherborne, Dorset Publishing Company, 2 vols., 1981–82; vol. 1, Boston, Little Brown, 1981.
Editor, *Thomas Hardy's England*, by Jo Draper. London, Cape, and Boston, Little Brown, 1984.

Translator, *Cinderella*, by Perrault. London, Cape, 1974; Boston, Little Brown, 1975.
Translator, *Ourika*, by Claire de Durfort. Austin, Texas, Taylor, 1977.

*

Bibliography: "John Fowles: An Annotated Bibliography 1963–76" by Karen Magee Myers, in *Bulletin of Bibliography* (Boston), vol. 33, no. 4, 1976; *John Fowles: A Reference Guide* by Barry N. Olshen and Toni A. Olshen, Boston, Hall, 1980; "John Fowles: A Bibliographical Checklist" by Ray A. Roberts, in *American Book Collector* (New York), September–October, 1980; "Criticism of John Fowles: A Selected Checklist" by Ronald C. Dixon, in *Modern Fiction Studies* (Lafayette, Indiana), Spring 1985.

Manuscript Collection: University of Tulsa, Oklahoma.

Critical Studies: *Possibilities* by Malcolm Bradbury, London, Oxford University Press, 1973; *The Fiction of John Fowles: Tradition, Art, and the Loneliness of Selfhood* by William J. Palmer, Columbia, University of Missouri Press, 1974; *John Fowles, Magus and Moralist* by Peter Wolfe, Lewisburg, Pennsylvania, Bucknell University Press, 1976, revised edition, 1979; *Etudes sur "The French Lieutenant's Woman" de John Fowles* edited by Jean Chevalier, Caen, University of Caen, 1977; *John Fowles* by Barry N. Olshen, New York, Ungar, 1978; *John Fowles, John Hawkes, Claude Simon: Problems of Self and Form in the Post-Modernist Novel* by Robert Burden, Würzburg, Königshausen & Neumann, and Atlantic Highlands, New Jersey, Humanities Press, 1980; *John Fowles* by Robert Huffaker, New York, Twayne, 1980; "John Fowles Issue" of *Journal of Modern Literature* (Philadelphia), vol. 8, no. 2, 1981; *Four Contemporary Novelists* by Kerry McSweeney, Montreal, McGill-Queen's University Press, London, Scolar Press, 1983; *John Fowles* by Peter J. Conradi, London, Methuen, 1982; *Fowles, Irving, Barthes: Canonical Variations on an Apocryphal Theme* by Randolph Runyon,

Columbus, Ohio State University Press, 1982; *The Timescapes of John Fowles* by H.W. Fawkner, Rutherford, New Jersey, Fairleigh Dickinson University Press, 1983; *Male Mythologies: John Fowles and Masculinity* by Bruce Woodcock, Brighton, Harvester Press, 1984; *The Romances of John Fowles* by Simon Loveday, London, Macmillan, 1985; "John Fowles Issue" of *Modern Fiction Studies* (Lafayette, Indiana), Spring 1985.

*   *   *

John Fowles is a highly allusive and descriptive novelist. In all his fictions, situations and settings are carefully and lavishly done: the French country landscape of "The Cloud" (*The Ebony Tower*); the blues and purples of the stark New Mexican mountains, the soft rainy contours of Devon in various greens and greys, the bleak and menacing deserts of Syria, all in *Daniel Martin*. Most frequently, Fowles's richly painted settings conceal a mystery, as in the title story of *The Ebony Tower*, in which an old English painter has created his "forest" in France, like that of Chrétien de Troyes, a "mystery island" to break away from the closed formal island into "love and adventure and the magical." The lush Greek island of *The Magus* conceals mystery and magic, a stage for the complicated and elaborate series of theatricals that enchant, enslave, and instruct a young Englishman who has taken a teaching job there. The five 18th-century travellers in *A Maggot* go through the deep vales and caverns near Exmoor, which leads to death for one, to a vision of paradise that may have helped establish a new religion for another, and to unknowable disappearance for a third. Often, Fowles's characters, like Nicholas Urfe in *The Magus* or the interrogating magistrate in *A Maggot*, try to solve the mysteries, to make sense of what happens as they confront new worlds, but they are not entirely successful. Frequently, as in the short story "The Enigma," in which a solid, stable, middle-aged Tory M.P. simply disappears, Fowles does not resolve the mystery and concentrates on the implications for others in living in terms of what is finally unknown.

In staging his mysteries, in choosing what to reveal and what to conceal, Fowles has often been seen by readers as manipulative. Such manipulation, however, is not merely a matter of tricks, ingenious switches, or "the God-game." Rather, the sense of "reality" as something that has to be manipulated, rearranged, in order to be understood is central to Fowles's conception of both the nature and the function of fiction. When victimized by a mock trial in the culminating theatrical invented for him, Nicholas Urfe realizes that he is only getting what he has deserved, for "all my life I had tried to turn life into fiction, to hold reality away." *Mantissa*, the title itself suggesting a trivial addition to literature, consists of a debate between the novelist and his erotic muse about the nature of fiction which satirizes simplistic solipsistic positions like "Serious modern fiction has only one subject: the difficulty of writing serious modern fiction." The novelist's manipulation is more complex and immediately recognizable in *The French Lieutenant's Woman*, which is full of parodies of old novelistic devices, switches in time and history, and frequent interruptions of the Victorian narrative that acknowledge the author's deliberate arrangements. The reader is constantly led to question what "Victorian" means, to recognize the texture of anachronism, parody, research, quotations from Marx, Darwin, Victorian sociological reports, Tennyson, Arnold, and Hardy as various means of demonstrating the conditional nature of time and history, the necessity of locating oneself in the present before one can understand anything of the past. The novel also has three endings, not simply as a form of prestidigitation, but as a demonstration that three different possible resolutions,

each characterizing a different possible perspective itself historically definable, are consistent with the issues and characters Fowles has set in motion. *A Maggot* deploys strategies of similar contemporary interruptions, like the child opening a gate for the travellers on horse-back who is thrown a farthing that falls "over her bent crown of no doubt lice-ridden hair," or the actor playing a London merchant who changes from "anachronistic skinhead" to "Buddhist monk," to present a conflict between legalistic dialogue and the origins of religion or art, later explained as a version of the universal conflict between the left-lobed brain and the right, in terms of its modern genesis in the socially static period of the 1730's. Only in *Mantissa* and in parts of *Daniel Martin* do Fowles's speculations about the nature of fiction become arid and modish.

The allusive references of Fowles's ingenious fictions have generally widened and deepened over the course of his development. In his first novel, *The Collector*, more sensational than those that followed, Fowles attempted to probe psychologically and sociologically on a single plane of experience, to demonstrate what in a young man of one class caused him to collect, imprison, and dissect the girl from another class he thought he loved. The fabrications of *The Magus* extend further into history, legend, and myth, exploring various kinds of Gods, of perspectives "real" and imaginary (one can never finally draw a line between the two) that negate human freedom. A number of the long stories of *The Ebony Tower*, like "Eliduc," retell ancient myths or recreate them in contemporary terms. *The French Lieutenant's Woman*, with all its literary, historical, and artistic allusions, shows what of the story is of the past, what of the present, and what indeterminate, for history, for Fowles, invariably includes much of the time and perspective of the historian. Thematically, *Daniel Martin* is, in some ways, an expansion of *The French Lieutenant's Woman*, an analysis of Fowles's own generation, the last in England that might still be characterized as Victorian, "brought up in some degree of the nineteenth century since the twentieth did not begin until 1945." *Daniel Martin* also makes explicit a theme implicit in Fowles's earlier fiction, the paralyzing and complicated effects of all the guilts originating in the Victorian past, what he calls "a pandemic of self-depreciation" that leads to emotional insularity and to the capacity to live gracefully with loss rather than expending effort to change. In this novel, which ranges geographically (America, Italy, and the Middle East, as well as England) and historically (past wars and cultural legends), the guilt and self-depreciation are also attached to attractions to lost civilizations, the American Indians, the Minoans, the Etruscans, and the contemporary English. *A Maggot*, following the metaphor of the "larval stage of a winged creature," but also, according to Fowles, meaning in the 18th century a "whim or quirk . . . an obsession," expands its terms historically into a vision of possible humanity, an "almost divine maggot" attempting social and religious change against "reason, convention, established belief."

Until the fictional focus on the mother and the creation of Ann Lee, the historical founder of the Shaker religion, in *A Maggot*, Fowles's central characters have been isolated, rational, self-punishing males who attempted to join with independent, passionate, and enigmatic women. As the voice of the author in *The French Lieutenant's Woman* claims, he may be simply transferring his own inabilities to understand the enigmatic female into the safety of his historically locatable Victorian story. The sexual focus, however, with its attendant guilts and metaphorical expansions, is characteristic, and the novels develop the rational and sometimes manipulative means the male uses to try to understand and control the amorphous and enigmatic female. The male is always limited, his formulations and understandings only partial. And, in his frustration, the necessity that he operate in a world where understanding is never complete, he acts so as to capture (*The Collector*), desert (*The Magus*), betray (*The French Lieutenant's Woman*), relate to through art (*Mantissa*), or both betray and finally recover (*Daniel Martin*) the female he can only partially comprehend. In *A Maggot*, the prestidigitating male finally disappears from the fiction entirely, leaving the woman, who incorporates both whore and saint, to bring forth significant life herself. Fowles has treated his constant metaphorical focus on relationships between the sexes with growing insight, sympathy, and intelligence, as well as with a fascinating complexity of sociological, historical, and psychological implications of the incessant human effort involved.

—James Gindin

FRAME, Janet (Paterson). New Zealander. Born in Dunedin, 28 August 1924. Educated at Oamaru North School; Waitaki Girls' High School; Otago University Teachers Training College, Dunedin. Recipient: Hubert Church Prose Award, 1952, 1964, 1974; New Zealand Literary Fund Award, 1960; New Zealand Scholarship in Letters, 1964, and Award for Achievement, 1969; Otago University Robert Burns Fellowship, 1965; Buckland Literary Award, 1967; James Wattie Award, 1983, 1985. D.Litt.: Otago University, 1978. C.B.E. (Commander, Order of the British Empire), 1983. Lives in Auckland. Agent: Brandt and Brandt, 1501 Broadway, New York, New York 10036, U.S.A.

PUBLICATIONS

Novels

Owls Do Cry. Christchurch, Pegasus Press, 1957; New York, Braziller, 1960; London, W.H. Allen, 1961.
Faces in the Water. Christchurch, Pegasus Press, and New York, Braziller, 1961; London, W.H. Allen, 1962.
The Edge of the Alphabet. Christchurch, Pegasus Press, New York, Braziller, and London, W.H. Allen, 1962.
Scented Gardens for the Blind. Christchurch, Pegasus Press, and London, W.H. Allen, 1963; New York, Braziller, 1964.
The Adaptable Man. Christchurch, Pegasus Press, New York, Braziller, and London, W.H. Allen, 1965.
A State of Siege. New York, Braziller, 1966; London, W.H. Allen, 1967.
The Rainbirds. London, W.H. Allen, 1968; as *Yellow Flowers in the Antipodean Room*, New York, Braziller, 1969.
Intensive Care. New York, Braziller, 1970; London, W.H. Allen, 1971.
Daughter Buffalo. New York, Braziller, 1972; London, W.H. Allen, 1973.
Living in the Maniototo. New York, Braziller, 1979; London, Women's Press, 1981.

Short Stories

The Lagoon: Stories. Christchurch, Caxton Press, 1952; revised edition, as *The Lagoon and Other Stories*, 1961.
The Reservoir: Stories and Sketches. New York, Braziller, 1963.

Snowman, Snowman: Fables and Fantasies. New York, Braziller, 1963.
The Reservoir and Other Stories. Christchurch, Pegasus Press, and London, W.H. Allen, 1966.
You Are Now Entering the Human Heart. Wellington, Victoria University Press, 1983; London, Women's Press, 1984.

Verse

The Pocket Mirror. New York, Braziller, and London, W.H. Allen, 1967.

Other

Mona Minim and the Smell of the Sun (for children). New York, Braziller, 1969.
An Autobiography:
 1. *To the Is-Land.* New York, Braziller, 1982; London, Women's Press, 1983.
 2. *An Angel at My Table.* Auckland, Hutchinson, New York, Braziller, and London, Women's Press, 1984.
 3. *The Envoy from Mirror City.* Auckland, Hutchinson, New York, Braziller, and London, Women's Press, 1985.

*

Bibliography: by John Beston, in *World Literature Written in English* (Arlington, Texas), November 1978.

Critical Studies: *An Inward Sun: The Novels of Janet Frame*, Wellington, New Zealand University Press, 1971, and *Janet Frame*, Boston, Twayne, 1977, both by Patrick Evans; *Janet Frame* by Margaret Dalziel, Wellington, Oxford University Press, 1981.

*   *   *

"All dreams," Janet Frame writes in her 1970 novel *Intensive Care*, "lead back to the nightmare garden." And all nightmares lead circuitously into truth. In all her novels, the looming threat of disorder, violent and disrupting, persistently attracts those that it frightens, for it proves more fertile, more imaginatively stimulating, more genuine, and more real than the too-familiar world of daily normality. The tension between safety and danger recurs as her characters—voyaging into strange geographies (like the epileptic Toby Withers in *The Edge of the Alphabet*), or madness (like Daphne in *Owls Do Cry*, or Istina Navet in *Faces in the Water*), or other people's identities (like Ed Glace in *Scented Gardens for the Blind*), or mirrors (like Vic in *The Adaptable Man*), or death (like Godfrey Rainbird in *The Rainbirds*)—discover both the mental debilitation that the safe state, in oxymoronic creativity, engenders, and the disembodying that danger contrives. The opening of *Faces in the Water* demonstrates the author's thematic density and sardonic touch:

They have said that we owe allegiance to Safety, that he is our Red-Cross God who will provide us with ointment and ... remove the foreign ideas, the glass beads of fantasy, the bent hair-pins of unreason embedded in our minds. On all the doors which lead to and from the world they have posted warning notices and lists of safety measures to be taken in extreme emergency. ... Never sleep

in the snow. Hide the scissors. Beware of strangers. . . .
But for the final day . . . they have no slogan. The streets
throng with people who panic, looking to the left and the
right, covering the scissors, sucking poison from a wound
they cannot find, judging their time from the sun's position
in the sky when the sun itself has melted and trickles down
the ridges of darkness into the hollows of evaporated seas.

Nightmares and madness, the education in the nature of Apocalypse and survival, become not mere metaphors of sanity,
but direct training in the reactivation of the mind's perceiving
eyes.

By "shipwrecking" oneself in mad geographies, however
(Frame speaks in one novel of "an affliction of dream called
Overseas"—as in another she observes that OUT is in man,
is what he fears, "like the sea"), one places oneself on "the
edge of the alphabet," in possession perhaps of insight, but
no longer capable of communicating with the people who stay
within regulated boundaries. Malfred Signal, in Janet Frame's
weakest novel, *A State of Siege*, for example, leaves her old
self to live on an island and to find the perspectives of "the
room two inches behind the eyes." What she discovers, when
the elements besiege her, is fear, but all she can do then is
silently utter the strange new language that she clutches, alone,
into seacalm and death. Like Ed Glace in *Scented Gardens*,
who researches the history of the surname *Strang* and (discovering *Strong*, *Strange*, and *Danger* along the way) wonders if
people are merely anagrams, Malfred lives in a mad mirror
world of intensely focused perception that anagrammatic Joycean punning—distorting day-to-day language—tries to
render. As *Owls Do Cry* had earlier specified, in the shallow
suburban character of Chicks, the "safe" world deals in language, too, as a defence against upset, hiding in the familiarity
of conventional clichés and tired similes. What the brilliant
punning passages of *The Rainbirds* show is what the title poem
of *The Pocket Mirror* implies: that convention will not show
ordinary men the "bars of darkness' that are optically contained
within the "facts of light"; "To undeceive the sight a detached
instrument like a mirror is necessary." Or her narratives. But
even that vantage point is fraught with deceit. Superstition,
like convention, and Platonic forms, like safe order, can all
interfere with true interpenetration with "actuality." And to
find the live language—the "death-free zone" of Thora Pattern,
in *Edge of the Alphabet*—as a novelist inevitably dealing with
day-to-day words becomes an increasingly difficult task the
stronger the visionary sense of the individual mind on its own.
Turnlung, the aging New Zealand writer in New York, in
Daughter Buffalo, finds the challenge particularly acute; his
exile to "a country of death" brings him into bizarrely creative
contact with a young doctor, but in the epilogue to the story,
he wonders if he has dreamed everything. What matters, as
Turnlung puts it, is that "I have what I gave." To conceive
is to create some kind of reality, however unconventional the
act, the result, and the language of rendering the experience
may seem.

There are passages in Frame that are reminiscent of Doris
Lessing—like the apocalyptic scenes of *Scented Gardens* and
Intensive Care, the one anticipating the atomic destruction of
Britain and the birth of a new language, the other observing
the destruction of animals in Waipori City (the computerized
enactment of the Human Delineation Act which will identify
the strong normal law-abiding "humans" and methodically,
prophylactically, eliminate the rest), and the ironic intensification of a vegetable human consciousness. In the earlier novel,
particularly, the author emphasizes the relationship between

the "safety dance of speech" and a kind of Coleridgean death-
in-life, and that between winter (the gardenless season) and
madness, life-in-death, "Open Day in the factory of the mind."
The Rainbirds, the writer's gentlest, most comic (however
hauntingly, macabrely, relentlessly discommoding) book,
takes up the metaphor in its story of a man *pronounced* dead
after a car accident. Though Godfrey Rainbird lives, the official
pronouncement, the conventional language, the public utterance, takes precedence over the individual spiritual actuality,
depriving him of his job, his children, public acceptance, and
so on. Indeed, he only becomes acceptable when he has "died"
a second time, when his story is sufficiently distanced into
legend and into the past to become a tourist attraction. But
if you visit the grave in the winter, Janet Frame adds, you
must create the summer flowers within yourself. Summer gardens are openly available even to the spiritually blind; winter
gardens are not. Her quiet acceptance, however, of that (mad,
winter) power to change seasons within the mind expresses
her most optimistic regard of humanity. And as *Living in the
Maniototo* reaffirms, there is an ordering potentiality in the
recognition of any person's several selves.

Intensive Care more broodingly evokes the same theme and
provokingly points out the difference between the hospitaliza-
tion of the body and the intensive care required to keep the
mind truly alive. When the second world war is long over and
the computer mentality takes over after the next impersonal
War, all fructifying abnormality seems doomed; Deciding Day
will destroy that which is not *named* human. Through the sharp
memory of the supposedly dull Milly Galbraith, who is one
of the few to appreciate an ancient surviving pear-tree, and
the damningly conciliatory (and then expiatory) attitudes of
Colin Monk, who goes along with the system, valuing Milly
too late to save her, the apocalyptic days of Waipori City are
told. Behind them both looms the mythical presence of Colin's
twin Sandy, the Reconstructed Man, made of metal and transplanted parts, who is also the Rekinstruckdead Man, a promise
of technological finesse and an accompanying sacrifice of man's
animal warmth and spiritual being. Milly is exterminated;
Sandy is myth; Colin, declared human, breathes:

I was safe, I had won.
I had lost. I began losing the first day, when the news
of the Act came to me and I signed the oath of agreement.
Why of course, I said, I'll do anything you ask, naturally,
it's the only way, the only solution, as I see it, to an impossible situation, as if situations needed solving, I mean,
looked at objectively, as it must be seen to be. . . .
The skimming words and phrases that need leave no
footprints; one might never have been there, but one had
spoken; and the black water lay undisturbed beneath the
ice; and not a blade of grass quivered or a dead leaf whispered; a race of words had lived and died and left no
relic of their civilization.
As it must be seen to be, looked at objectively. . . .

The ironies multiply around each other. Language reasserts
its fluid focus; the Society for the Prevention of Cruelty to
Vegetation plants new pear trees on the Livingstone estate;
the computer (not having been programmed for nostalgia) fails
to account for the new enthusiasm for old abnormalities; and
the Sleep Days cannot erase the time of the fires from the
mind of Colin Monk. The mind survives. That her commitment
to the spiritual independence of such perception is made so
provocative is a tribute to Janet Frame's arresting skill with

images. She has an uncanny ability to arouse the diverse sensibilities of shifting moods and to entangle in language the wordless truths of her inner eye.

—W.H. New

FRANCIS, Dick (Richard Stanley Francis). British. Born in Tenby, Pembrokeshire, 31 October 1920. Educated at Maidenhead County Boys' School, Berkshire. Served in the Royal Air Force, 1940–45: Flying Officer. Married Mary Margaret Brenchley in 1947; two sons. Amateur National Hunt (steeplechase) jockey, 1946–48; professional, 1948–57; National Hunt Champion, 1953–54. Racing correspondent, *Sunday Express*, London, 1957–73. Recipient: Crime Writers Association Silver Dagger, 1965, Golden Dagger, 1980; Mystery Writers of America Edgar Allan Poe Award, 1969, 1981. O.B.E. (Officer, Order of the British Empire), 1984. Agent: John Johnson, 45–47 Clerkenwell Green, London EC1R 0HT. Address: Penny Chase, Blewbury, Didcot, Oxfordshire OX11 9NH, England; or, 5100 North Ocean Boulevard, Apartment 609, Fort Lauderdale, Florida 33308, U.S.A.

PUBLICATIONS

Novels

Dead Cert. London, Joseph, and New York, Holt Rinehart, 1962.
Nerve. London, Joseph, and New York, Harper, 1964.
For Kicks. London, Joseph, and New York, Harper, 1965.
Odds Against. London, Joseph, 1965; New York, Harper, 1966.
Flying Finish. London, Joseph, 1966; New York, Harper, 1967.
Blood Sport. London, Joseph, 1967; New York, Harper, 1968.
Forfeit. London, Joseph, and New York, Harper, 1969.
Enquiry. London, Joseph, and New York, Harper, 1969.
Rat Race. London, Joseph, 1970; New York, Harper, 1971.
Bonecrack. London, Joseph, 1971; New York, Harper, 1972.
Smokescreen. London, Joseph, and New York, Harper, 1972.
Slay-Ride. London, Joseph, and New York, Harper, 1973.
Knock-Down. London, Joseph, 1974; New York, Harper, 1975.
High Stakes. London, Joseph, 1975; New York, Harper, 1976.
In the Frame. London, Joseph, 1976; New York, Harper, 1977.
Risk. London, Joseph, 1977; New York, Harper, 1978.
Trial Run. London, Joseph, 1978; New York, Harper, 1979.
Whip Hand. London, Joseph, 1979; New York, Harper, 1980.
Reflex. London, Joseph, 1980; New York, Putnam, 1981.
Twice Shy. London, Joseph, 1981; New York, Putnam, 1982.
Banker. London, Joseph, 1982; New York, Putnam, 1983.
The Danger. London, Joseph, 1983; New York, Putnam, 1984.
Proof. London, Joseph, 1984; New York, Putnam, 1985.
Break In. London, Joseph, 1985.

Uncollected Short Stories

"The Gift," in *Winter's Crimes 5*, edited by Virginia Whitaker. London, Macmillan, 1973.

"A Day of Wine and Roses," in *Sports Illustrated* (New York), May 1973.
"A Carrot for a Chestnut," in *Stories of Crime and Detection*, edited by Joan D. Berbrich. New York, McGraw Hill, 1974.
"The Big Story," in *Ellery Queen's Crime Wave*. New York, Putnam, and London, Gollancz, 1976.
"Nightmare," in *Ellery Queen's Searches and Seizures*. New York, Davis, 1977.
"Twenty-One Good Men and True," in *Verdict of Thirteen*, edited by Julian Symons. London, Faber, and New York, Harper, 1979.
"The Day of the Losers," in *Ellery Queen's Mystery Magazine* (New York), 9 September 1981.

Play

Screenplay: *Dead Cert*, 1974.

Other

The Sport of Queens: The Autobiography of Dick Francis. London, Joseph, 1957; revised edition, 1968, 1974, 1982; New York, Harper, 1969.
Lester: The Official Biography (on Lester Piggott). London, Joseph, 1986.

Editor, with John Welcome, *Best Racing and Chasing Stories 1–2*. London, Faber, 2 vols., 1966–69.
Editor, with John Welcome, *The Racing Man's Bedside Book*. London, Faber, 1969.

*

Critical Study: *Dick Francis* by Melvyn Barnes, New York, Ungar, 1985.

*   *   *

Wasting no time in a literary apprenticeship, Dick Francis established himself with *Dead Cert* as a master of action narrative, memorable characterization, and authentically detailed settings. Variations on character and milieu in subsequent novels have only freshened the curious pleasure we feel when our nerves are strained in the vicarious experiences of literature.

The only problem Francis provides his fans, and it appears to be a small problem indeed, is how to label his works. Does he write mysteries or novels of detection? His books have been featured by the Detective Book Club and the Mystery Guild, and he has won an award given to outstanding detective works. Is he a serious writer, then, or an entertainer? Various reviewers call him an outstanding author of suspense, mystery, or thriller writing, while others choose to say he writes bona fide novels. Of course determining a "correct" category for his works could never affect his reputation or our pleasure in his writing. Nevertheless, insisting that Dick Francis writes adventure stories as serious entertainment and not detective or mystery fiction has a critical point to it, because it clarifies the esthetic effect of his writing.

A threat to order jeopardizing life and honor forms the heart of each Francis novel. The order is usually associated with the sport of horse racing menaced by unscrupulous gamblers, as in *Dead Cert*, *Forfeit*, and *For Kicks*; hijacking of thoroughbreds as in *Blood Sport*, or those who would use the sport for their own psychological aggrandizement as in *Nerve* and

Bonecrack. In other novels proper business operation, whether of race tracks as in *Odds Against*, sportsmen's insurance as in *Rat Race*, or international petroleum development as in *Slay-Ride* represents the order besieged. Though the threats to order link the novels to all of crime literature, the stress in a Francis novel falls lightly upon ingenuity of method for commission of crime. Nor is the method given special significance by the central character, who usually narrates the story. He reasons and follows leads but never takes on the manner of a literary detective, because he is the person—and here is the chief point—to whom things happen rather than the ordained sleuth. Consequently, the focus is upon his overcoming adversity not merely to restore order but to survive.

The relative absence of the literary imperatives that would face him as the "rules of the game" if he were writing within the framework of detective or mystery stories permits Francis a wide range in which to develop narrative tensions. Often they are psychological and the result of a freedom to use varied characters: Sid Hally's struggle in *Odds Against* to regain his will to compete as a jockey, the conflicts between pairs of fathers and sons in *Bonecrack*, the identity problem of Henry Guy in *Flying Finish*, the difficulties of a chronic loser in *Rat Race*, or the compulsions of persecution complexes and mega-lomania among secondary characters. The greatest opportunity for narrative tension results, however, from Francis's concentration on external action rather than puzzle solving. The narrators' occupations as jockeys, pilots, investigators, or stars of action films necessarily require them to relate the regular adventures of their work. Then, their involvement in criminal plots subjects them to assault, torture, and murder attempts, so that finally the highpoint of nearly every novel combines occupational skill with the dangers caused by the criminal plot in top-flight scenes of chases and endurance of danger leading to a conclusive resolution. The very severity of others' hostility, and even the plausible weaknesses of the narrators' own personalities, strongly enforces the fact that the hero has survived to set things right and to go on to new life.

Francis has an apparently inexhaustible range of possibilities for lead characters and the plots that can be spun out of their occupations and personal skills: a loan manager with the instincts of an athlete ends an effort to destroy a stud farm to which he has provided capital in *Banker*; a physics teacher who is also an Olympic marksman blocks the theft of a computerized betting system in part one of *Twice Shy*, while his brother, a stock buyer, destroys the villain in part two; and the employee of a consulting firm specializing in protection against kidnapping lends his skills to the liberation of an Italian woman jockey and the Chief Steward of the Jockey Club in *The Danger*. In the face of this fecundity it might seem ungrateful to note that there is a Dick Francis story formula. Nevertheless, there is one, and the point of noting it is to say that it works. The heroes are natural aristocrats with a code of honor so deep in them that it rarely comes to consciousness. Surviving adverse circumstances and antagonists, who are properly considered villains because it is their character that is the source of the evil they do, Francis's heroes serve their sport, their employers, or their clients without regret or self-doubt. Their values are secure, the world they see about them is fundamentally healthy, so it can be the process of living adventurously that engages us and gratifies us.

The enthusiasm that readers have for Francis testifies to the quality of his formula, no apology necessary. Our dreams, if not enough of our lives, are much of the time devoted to the same themes of confronting danger or definite villainy, so the formula of the Francis novels resonates with deeply felt experiences in his audience. The adventure plots simplify our familiar sense of tension by representing it in external form. The stories entertain by giving us detail we readily accept as realistic in time and place, and they hearten us with positive resolution. Only a few people could undergo in actuality the experience of Francis's narrative events, but nearly everyone has that experience in mind.

—John M. Reilly

FRAYN, Michael. British. Born in Mill Hill, London, 8 September 1933. Educated at Sutton High School for Boys; Kingston Grammar School, Surrey; Emmanuel College, Cambridge, B.A. 1957. Served in the Royal Artillery and Intelligence Corps, 1952–54. Married Gillian Palmer in 1960; three daughters. Reporter, 1957–59, and columnist, 1959–62, *The Guardian*, Manchester and London; columnist, *The Observer*, London, 1962–68. Recipient: Maugham Award, 1966; Hawthornden Prize, 1967; National Press Award, 1970; *Standard* award, for play, 1976, 1981, 1983, 1985; Society of West End Theatre Award, 1977, 1982; British Theatre Association award, 1981, 1983; Olivier Award, for play, 1985. Address: c/o Elaine Greene Ltd., 31 Newington Green, London N16 9PU, England.

PUBLICATIONS

Novels

The Tin Men. London, Collins, 1965; Boston, Little Brown, 1966.
The Russian Interpreter. London, Collins, and New York, Viking Press, 1966.
Towards the End of the Morning. London, Collins, 1967; as *Against Entropy*, New York, Viking Press, 1967.
A Very Private Life. London, Collins, and New York, Viking Press, 1968.
Sweet Dreams. London, Collins, 1973; New York, Viking Press, 1974.

Plays

Zounds!, with John Edwards, music by Keith Statham (produced Cambridge, 1957).
The Two of Us (includes *Black and Silver*, *The New Quixote*, *Mr. Foot*, *Chinamen*) (produced London, 1970; Ogunquit, Maine, 1975; *Chinamen* produced New York, 1979). London, Fontana, 1970; *Chinamen* published in *The Best Short Plays 1973*, edited by Stanley Richards, Radnor, Pennsylvania, Chilton, 1973; revised version of *The New Quixote* (produced Chichester, Sussex, and London, 1980).
The Sandboy (produced London, 1971).
Alphabetical Order (produced London, 1975; New Haven, Connecticut, 1976). Included in *Alphabetical Order and Donkeys' Years*, 1977.
Donkeys' Years (produced London, 1976). Included in *Alphabetical Order and Donkeys' Years*, 1977.
Clouds (produced London, 1976). London, Eyre Methuen, 1977.
Alphabetical Order and Donkeys' Years. London, Eyre Methuen, 1977.
The Cherry Orchard, adaptation of a play by Chekhov (produced London, 1978). London, Eyre Methuen, 1978.

Balmoral (produced Guildford, Surrey, 1978; revised version, as *Liberty Hall*, produced London, 1980).
The Fruits of Enlightenment, adaptation of a play by Tolstoy (produced London, 1979). London, Eyre Methuen, 1979.
Make and Break (produced London, 1980; Washington, D.C., 1983). London, Eyre Methuen, 1980.
Noises Off (produced London, 1981; New York, 1983). London, Methuen, 1982.
Three Sisters, adaptation of a play by Chekhov (produced Manchester, 1985). London, Methuen, 1983.
Benefactors (produced London, 1984; New York, 1985). London, Methuen, 1984.
Wild Honey, adaptation of a play by Chekhov (produced London, 1984). London, Methuen, 1984.
Number One, adaptation of a play by Jean Anouilh (produced London, 1984).
Frayn Plays 1. London, Methuen, 1985.

Screenplay: *Clockwise*, 1985.

Television Plays and Documentaries: *Jamie, On a Flying Visit*, 1968; *One Pair of Eyes*, 1968; *Birthday*, 1969; *Imagine a City Called Berlin*, 1975; *Making Faces*, 1975; *Vienna: The Mask of Gold*, 1977; *Three Streets in the Country*, 1979; *The Long Straight*, 1980; *Jerusalem*, 1984.

Other

The Day of the Dog (*Guardian* columns). London, Collins, 1962; New York, Doubleday, 1963.
The Book of Fub (*Guardian* columns). London, Collins, 1963; as *Never Put Off to Gomorrah*, New York, Pantheon, 1964.
On the Outskirts (*Observer* columns). London, Fontana, 1967.
At Bay in Gear Street (*Observer* columns). London, Fontana, 1967.
Constructions (philosophy). London, Wildwood House, 1974.
Great Railway Journeys of the World, with others. London, BBC Publications, 1981; New York, Dutton, 1982.
The Original Michael Frayn: Satirical Essays, edited by James Fenton. Edinburgh, Salamander Press, 1983.

Editor, *The Best of Beachcomber*, by J.B. Morton. London, Heinemann, 1963.

*   *   *

Three of Michael Frayn's novels, the first, fourth, and fifth, are highly original, a satire and fantasies; the second and third, on the other hand, are conventional. The second, *The Russian Interpreter*, concerns an English research student in Moscow who serves as interpreter for a mysterious businessman (he seeks ordinary Russians for exchange visits), and the pair become involved with a Russian girl. Though Moscow's streets and weather are described, soon the action is moving swiftly. Books are stolen and sought, somebody is tricking somebody, espionage or smuggling is occurring, and we read on eagerly, awaiting explanations. Even when the student is imprisoned, Frayn focuses on his comic efforts to obtain a towel, and the novel remains a good, cheerful read.

The American title of the third novel points to opposing inertia and conformity; the English one, only a little more relevantly, to the subject of being in the mid-thirties (the hero "had spent his youth as one might spend an inheritance, and

he had no idea of what he had bought with it"). Frayn's 37-year-old is a Features Editor, worrying about repairs to his Victorian house with West Indian neighbours in S.W.23 and dreaming of escape, hopefully through appearance on a television panel. The plot is vehicle for comedy about a newspaper office, with a few shrewd observations, as when a girl reflects: "She wasn't a girl at all, in any sense that the fashion magazines would recognize. She was just a young female human being, fit only to be someone's cousin or aunt." Some passages suggest Frayn intends more, a fuller study of his hero's marriage and serious focus on the future of newspapers (a cynical, pushful graduate challenges the office's ways), but these are not pursued.

The Tin Men, the first book, is about the William Morris Institute of Automation Research and its eccentric scientists. A thin plot-line turns on a new wing, the arrangements for the Queen to open it, and the TV company that plans to finance it. Most of the fun is about computers: the automating of football results because the Director believes "the main object of organised sports and games is to produce a profusion of statistics," the programmed newspaper, which prints the core of familiar stories such as "I Test New Car" and "Child Told Dress Unsuitable by Teacher," and Delphic I, the Ethical Decision Machine, which expresses its moral processes in units called pauls, calvins, and moses. Amid clever jokes, Frayn shows anxiety about the dangerous possibilities of computers and the limitations of the men responsible for them.

A Very Private Life begins "Once upon a time there will be a little girl called Uncumber." In her world, "inside people" remain all their lives in windowless houses, supplied by tube and tap and using drugs—Pax, Hilarin and Orgasmin—for every experience. In very brief chapters, Frayn explains how life has grown more private, first physically, then through drugs to cope with anger and uncertainty. Dissatisfied Uncumber meets a man through a wrong number on "holovision" and goes to the other side of the world to visit him. The compelling story is part fairy tale, part fantasy, part morality, so that we ask "Is it plausible?" and "What is the moral?" Frayn's inspiration was contemporary America, where he noticed dark glasses used to hide feelings, and city people buying disused farmhouses to be alone in. He touches on penology, longevity, the treatment of personality, but concentrates on technology making possible a new kind of isolation which excludes uncomfortable realities. And Frayn the moralist never dominates Frayn the story-teller.

Even better is *Sweet Dreams*—clever, entertaining, dazzling. A typical middle-aged, middle-class Londoner is killed and finds himself in a Heaven where he can fly, speak any language, change his age, and retrieve long-lost possessions. He is set to invent the Matterhorn, returns to England and writes an official report on its condition, drops out to the simple country life and bounces back as righthand man to God (who proves to be a blend of Freddie Ayer and A.J.P. Taylor, and says "To get anything done at all one has to move in tremendously mysterious ways"). Slowly we realise the hero's Heavenly evolution is markedly similar to his earthly one. Frayn tells with wit and flourish his shrewd, sardonic and deceptively charming fable.

—Malcolm Page

FREELING, Nicolas. British. Born in London, 3 March 1927. Educated at schools in England, Ireland, and France;

attended University of Dublin. Served in the Royal Air Force, 1945–47. Married Cornelia Termes in 1954; four sons and one daughter. Hotel and restaurant cook throughout Europe, 1945–60. Recipient: Crime Writers Association Golden Dagger, 1964; Grand Prix de Roman Policier, 1964; Mystery Writers of America Edgar Allan Poe Award, 1966. Agent: Curtis Brown, 162–168 Regent Street, London W1R 5TA, England; or, 10 Astor Place, New York, New York 10003, U.S.A. Address: Grandfontaine, 67130 Schirmeck, France.

PUBLICATIONS

Novels

Love in Amsterdam. London, Gollancz, and New York, Harper, 1962; as *Death in Amsterdam*, New York, Ballantine, 1964.
Because of the Cats. London, Gollancz, 1963; New York, Harper, 1964.
Gun Before Butter. London, Gollancz, 1963; as *Question of Loyalty*, New York, Harper, 1963.
Valparaiso (as F.R.E. Nicolas). London, Gollancz, 1964; as Nicolas Freeling, New York, Harper, 1965.
Double-Barrel. London, Gollancz, 1964; New York, Harper, 1965.
Criminal Conversation. London, Gollancz, 1965; New York, Harper, 1966.
The King of the Rainy Country. London, Gollancz, and New York, Harper, 1966.
The Dresden Green. London, Gollancz, 1966; New York, Harper, 1967.
Strike Out Where Not Applicable. London, Gollancz, and New York, Harper, 1967.
This Is the Castle. London, Gollancz, and New York, Harper, 1968.
Tsing-Boum. London, Hamish Hamilton, 1969; as *Tsing-Boum!*, New York, Harper, 1969.
Over the High Side. London, Hamish Hamilton, 1971; as *The Lovely Ladies*, New York, Harper, 1971.
A Long Silence. London, Hamish Hamilton, 1972; as *Auprès de ma Blonde*, New York, Harper, 1972.
A Dressing of Diamond. London, Hamish Hamilton, and New York, Harper, 1974.
What Are Bugles Blowing For? London, Heinemann, 1975; as *The Bugles Blowing*, New York, Harper, 1976.
Lake Isle. London, Heinemann, 1976; as *Sabine*, New York, Harper, 1978.
Gadget. London, Heinemann, and New York, Coward McCann, 1977.
The Night Lords. London, Heinemann, and New York, Pantheon, 1978.
The Widow. London, Heinemann, and New York, Pantheon, 1979.
Castang's City. London, Heinemann, and New York, Pantheon, 1980.
One Damn Thing after Another. London, Heinemann, 1981; as *Arlette*, New York, Pantheon, 1981.
Wolfnight. London, Heinemann, and New York, Pantheon, 1982.
The Back of the North Wind. London, Heinemann, and New York, Viking Press, 1983.
No Part in Your Death. London, Heinemann and New York, Viking, 1984.
A City Solitary. London, Heinemann, and New York, Viking, 1985.

Cold Iron. London, Deutsch, and New York, Viking, 1986.

Uncollected Short Stories

"The Beach Murder" May 1969, "Van der Valk and the Old Seaman" August 1969, "Van der Valk and the Four Mice" November 1969, "Van der Valk and the Young Man" December 1969, "Van der Valk and the High School Riot" March 1970, "Van der Valk and the Great Pot Problem" April 1970, "Van der Valk and the Wolfpack" August 1970, "Van der Valk and the False Caesar" February 1972, "Van der Valk and the Man from Nowhere" May 1972, "Van der Valk: The Train Watcher" April 1973, "Van der Valk and the Cavalier" January 1974, and "Van der Valk and the Spanish Galleon" August 1975, all in *Ellery Queen's Mystery Magazine* (New York).
"Van der Valk and the Two Pigeons," in *Ellery Queen's Magicians of Mystery*. New York, Davis, 1976.

Other

Kitchen Book. London, Hamish Hamilton, 1970; as *The Kitchen*, New York, Harper, 1970.
Cook Book. London, Hamish Hamilton, 1971.

*

Nicolas Freeling comments:

I am known as a crime novelist, an expression meaningless unless preceded by the word "commercial," meaning one who writes a series on a similar theme purely for entertainment value and to make a living. This describes my activities accurately enough, but not my ideas, nor my ambitions.

The advantage of this method is that the public for crime novels is large, appreciative, faithful, and generous. For this I am extremely grateful. There is a corresponding large disadvantage: that one is held to and bound by a rigid formula. Any originality or variation in theme is severely discouraged by a sharp drop in sales; this rigidity is the enemy of progress and growth. The writer is expected to concentrate exclusively upon telling an entertaining story, which is indeed the first basic element of the novelist's craft, and to introduce elements of mystery and suspense, melodramatic and largely artificial. The crime novelist who attempts art, his natural function and legitimate ambition, is asking for trouble.

Few commercial crime novelists make the attempt. Most are content to work in purely mechanical fashion, with no artistic or literary pretension whatever. The result is that they receive no critical attention—indeed they need none, for their public rarely bothers with book reviews and has small interest in literary effort—and have small ambition, being content with a commercial operation and financial success.

It does not seem to me that the "crime" novelist should have such limited and materialistic ambitions.

Raymond Chandler agreed. He thought that it should be possible to write a crime "entertainment" which would rejoin the main stream of fiction. It would be about basic human themes and predicaments, of which crime, obviously a phenomenon of much social importance, with increasing impact upon the lives of any and all of us, would be the predominant subject, not necessarily the only subject.

I wish to attempt this ambitious design.

So far I have failed, and am not much ashamed because the ambition is high and the technical problems posed very considerable. Only the best European novelists—Stendhal, Dostoievsky, Conrad are the examples which come first to mind—have succeeded, and then often partially or imperfectly. A real human being, when involved in a traumatic situation such as a crime creates, behaves destructively—towards himself, towards society, and towards I may add the structure and coherence of a novel. This creates pitfalls for the novelist, the most obvious being to fall into mere sociological observation, documentary journalism in the interests of veracity. Also the behaviour of a criminal (a man by definition set at odds with his society) raises wide moral, metaphysical, and philosophic problems. To disregard these is to write a play with no third act. Many technically accomplished writers dodge ethical problems of right and wrong on the ground of "tolerance" and because their own ethical, not to say religious beliefs are vague, and often because they are frightened to appear unfashionable.

It has become too fashionable to disregard the craftsmanship of form, shape, and rhythm, on the ground that this is mere artificial mechanical contrivance. Such a notion is both immature and superficial: without form there is no art. The public insists, rightly, that a crime novel shall rebound continually in interest and excitement, and shall culminate, that is to say end in a climax.

I intend to keep trying.

*   *   *

Love in Amsterdam began Nicolas Freeling's career as a writer of novels which have an almost startling verisimilitude: their dialogue, setting, and action convey a feeling of exact observation at work. Freeling's Van der Valk is a Dutch detective who is human, individual, unorthodox. He has both compassion and a stern compulsion to solve the puzzles that are presented to him. His thoughts as he proceeds in his investigations are shown clearly to us; we share in his intellectual unravelling of problems of human behaviour; and we believe in the reflections and the actions because the characters are real and the locale so effectively re-created. The flavour of Dutch life, the tempo of Amsterdam, the attitudes of the Dutch emerge convincingly in *Love in Amsterdam*; they are consolidated in *Because of the Cats*, an unfolding of the terrifying ruthlessness displayed by a gang of Dutch teenagers, morally corrupted and warped. This story is set partially in a seaside town of about sixty thousand people, half an hour by train from Amsterdam, "a new town, the pride of Dutch building and planning." Here is where Van der Valk displays his intuition, becomes friendly with the local whore, and understands the parents' relations with their children as he probes into their activities. The tempo of the novel is skilfully varied, and the final speeding up comes with an inevitability which holds the reader's horrified attention. The effect of Freeling's narration is heightened by the sceptical comments, the iconoclastic attitude with which he invests his policeman. Van der Valk's humanity gains by his lack of illusion.

This Is the Castle showed a deepening in Freeling's powers of characterization. The story revolves around the Swiss ménage of a successful novelist, a neurotic yet likeable man, whose tensions and foibles are seen through his own eyes and his wife's. The relationship between the novelist and his wife (to whom he is God), his secretary–mistress, his Spanish servants, his sons and, above all, his teenage daughter are unfolded with skill and sympathy; the visiting publisher and the American journalist arrive in time for a shooting of a macabre kind. This novel explores the blurred edges between the writer's imagination and the real events of his life: it does much to convey the effort of writing, the nervous strain between books, the dangerous seductiveness of the daydream. It moves away from the genre of *roman policier*.

Freeling's next *roman policier*, *Tsing-Boum*, carries on this deeper interest in human nature. The parallel with Simenon's writing becomes clearer, and indeed Van der Valk mentions Maigret twice in his story of the murder of the wife of a dull Dutch sergeant. She is machine-gunned in her dull municipal flat during a television gangster serial. She leaves behind a daughter whose father is unknown, and as Van der Valk investigates he finds himself puzzling out the connections between this Mevrouw Zomerlust and Dien Bien Phu. This allows Freeling to explore the French surrender there and the complex aftermath: a case of cowardice, revenge, blackmail, jealousy, violence. The Dutch police Commissaire, older now (and suffering from wounds incurred in an earlier novel), regards his quarry with sympathy as well as severity, and the pathos of the story is effectively built up, with constant reminders of humanity's frailties as well as moments of bravery.

In *Valparaiso* Freeling develops further his uniting of person and place. Into Porquerolles he brings a second rank Parisian film star. Her coming has an explosive effect upon Raymond, who has drifted around the Mediterranean for years, nourishing a dream of crossing the Atlantic in his boat the *Olivia*. The need to refit the *Olivia* tempts Raymond into crime. The story has a seeming inexorability. The slow lazy tempo of life in Porquerolles gives way to an equally Mediterranean urgency, and the narrative tautens as Raymond becomes more deeply enmeshed in the consequences of what seemed a perfect plan for the quick acquisition of the money which would enable him to act out his dream. In *Valparaiso* Freeling again shows his Simenon-like capacity to absorb atmosphere, to assess how far it is created by and how much it affects the human beings whose lives he presents in such concentrated description, such revealing action and inaction.

After ten novels centering on Van der Valk, Freeling developed a French equivalent, Henri Castang. The new setting is an imaginary French city, and in *The Night Lords* Freeling explored differences between French and British legal institutions, for a British High Court Judge and his family on holiday in France are caught up in the machinery of the law when their Rolls-Royce is found to have a naked female corpse in its boot.

Strasbourg is the scene for *The Widow* in which Van der Valk's widow Arlette, now married to an Englishman, becomes a private detective, and tumbles into a narcotics racket. The suspense is, as usual, well maintained and Arlette's mental processes deftly sketched in, amid the continuous and sinister action. Freeling manages to mix the detail well; his city is alive, Arlette and her husband lucky to be so. *Castang's City*, however, is deliberately not Strasbourg: but it is a convincing French provincial city, in which Freeling's Commissaire Richard is an elegant foil to Castang, and his Colette Delavigne, the judge of instruction, a charming, intelligent French woman. There is a good deal of information in this novel about French provincial life, and French ways of dealing with crime; but this does not intrude unduly on the action. The action requires the detailed information supplied copiously in dialogue for the story to come alive, which, thanks to the careful creation not only of inanimate detail but of human idiosyncracies, it does, most convincingly too. Freeling's own attitudes burst out of his narration from time to time, and this gives his story an extra credibility since we are asked to share in his detached examination of characters who move through the novel with an apparent reality of their own.

A City Solitary is sensitive in its explorations of a writer's feelings, thoughts, ideals lost and regained. It moves swiftly in its tale of a ruthless robbery, the casual cruelty which later turns into a kidnapping in which the hostages aid their captor, convincingly, in a dash across France to the Belgian border. It tells its story well, as Freeling's novels always have; it blends realistic details evocatively with the emotional intensity engendered by the strange though entirely credible situation, in which Walter, his wife, and his son are involved, as well as Miriam Lebreton, an attractive young French woman who is a skilled advocate. This is, as is usual with Freeling's fiction, more than a crime novel; it is a penetrating psychological study of the main character whose memories blend with his reflections upon his own past and present, as well as on the nature of human life. This provides surprises, just as the narration provides the suspense to be expected as Freeling unrolls the actions of the story in his usual masterly way.

—A. Norman Jeffares

FREEMAN, Gillian.   British.   Born in London, 5 December 1929. Educated at the University of Reading, Berkshire, 1949–51, B.A. (honours) in English literature and philosophy 1951. Married Edward Thorpe in 1955; two children. Copywriter, C.J. Lytle Ltd., London, 1951–52; schoolteacher in London, 1952–53; reporter, *North London Observer*, 1953; literary secretary to Louis Golding, 1953–55. Lives in London. Agent: Richard Scott Simon Ltd., 32 College Cross, London N1 1PR, England.

PUBLICATIONS

Novels

The Liberty Man.   London, Longman, 1955.
Fall of Innocence.   London, Longman, 1956.
Jack Would Be a Gentleman.   London, Longman, 1959.
The Leather Boys (as Eliot George).   London, Blond, 1961; New York, Guild Press, 1962.
The Campaign.   London, Longman, 1963.
The Leader.   London, Blond, 1965; Philadelphia, Lippincott, 1966.
The Alabaster Egg.   London, Blond, 1970; New York, Viking Press, 1971.
The Marriage Machine.   London, Hamish Hamilton, and New York, Stein and Day, 1975.
Nazi Lady: The Diaries of Elisabeth von Stahlenberg 1933–1948.   London, Blond and Briggs, 1978; as *The Confessions of Elisabeth von S*, New York, Dutton, 1978; as *Diary of a Nazi Lady*, New York, Ace, 1979.
An Easter Egg Hunt.   London, Hamish Hamilton, and New York, Congdon and Lattès, 1981.
Love Child (as Elaine Jackson).   London, W.H. Allen, 1984.

Uncollected Short Stories

"The Soufflé," in *Courier* (London and New York), May 1955.
"Pen Friend," in *Woman's Own* (London), December 1957.
"The Changeling," in *London Magazine*, April 1959.
"The Polka (Come Dance with Me)," in *Woman's Own* (London), December 1962.
"Kicks," in *Axle Quarterly* (London), Summer 1963.
"Dear Fred," in *King* (London), June 1965.
"Venus Unobserved," in *Town* (London), July 1967.

Plays

Pursuit (produced London, 1969).

Screenplays: *The Leather Boys*, 1963; *That Cold Day in the Park*, 1969; *I Want What I Want*, 1970.

Radio Plays: *Santa Evita*, 1973; *Field Day*, 1974; *Commercial Break*, 1974.

Television Plays: *The Campaign*, 1965; *Man in a Fog*, 1984.

Ballet Scenarios: *Mayerling*, 1978; *Intimate Letters*, 1978; *Isadora*, 1981.

Other

The Story of Albert Einstein (for children).   London, Vallentine Mitchell, 1960.
The Undergrowth of Literature.   London, Nelson, 1967; New York, Delacorte Press, 1969.
The Schoolgirl Ethic: The Life and Work of Angela Brazil.   London, Allen Lane, 1976.

*

Manuscript Collection: University of Reading, Berkshire.

Critical Study: *Don't Never Forget* by Brigid Brophy, London, Cape, 1966; New York, Holt Rinehart, 1967.

Gillian Freeman comments:
I have always been concerned with the problems of the individual seen in relation to society and the personal pressures brought to bear because of moral, political or social conditions and the inability to conform. This is reflected in all my work to date, although I have never set out to propound themes, only to tell stories. After eleven novels I am able to make my own retrospective assessment, and I find recurring ideas and links of which I was unconscious at the time of writing.
My first six novels are in some way concerned with the class system in England, either as a main theme (*The Liberty Man*, *Jack Would Be a Gentleman*) or as part of the background (*The Leather Boys*). Although the rigid class patterns began to break up soon after the last war and have changed and shifted, they still retain subtle delineations that I find absorbing. In *The Liberty Man* there is the direct class confrontation in the love-affair between the middle-class school teacher and the cockney sailor. In *Fall of Innocence* I was writing about the sexual taboos of the middle class attacked by an outsider, a young American girl. This element, the planting of an alien into a tight social structure, reappears constantly in my novels —atheist Harry into the Church of England parish in *The Campaign*; the Prossers in *Jack Would Be a Gentleman* from one class area into an elevated one in the same town; the cross-visiting of Freda and Derek in *The Liberty Man*; strongest of all, Hannah in *The Alabaster Egg*, transplanted from Munich of the 1930's to post-war London. This is the theme pursued in *The Marriage Machine*, with Marion, from rural England, unable to adapt completely to life in the United States and battling against her in-laws (also uprooted from Europe) for the mind of her young son. In *Jack Would Be a Gentleman* the theme is the sudden acquisition of money without the middle- or upper-middle class conditioning which makes it possible to deal with it. *The Campaign* has the background of a seedy seaside parish, against which the personal problems of a cross-section of individuals (all involved in a fund-raising campaign) are exacerbated; God and Mammon, the permissive society,

the Christian ethics. *The Leather Boys* is the story of two work-ing-class boys who have a homosexual affair; *The Leader* explores fascism in a modern democracy, which, on both sides of the Atlantic, throws up a sufficient number of people who are greedy, ruthless, intolerant, bigoted and perverted enough to gravitate towards the extreme right. In *Nazi Lady* the socially climbing heroine, Elisabeth, records in her diary her joy in meeting Hitler. In *The Alabaster Egg*, which I consider my best work to date, Hannah also meets Hitler and there is another fictitious diary, an historical memoir of a lover of Ludwig II. This earlier novel contains several of my recurring themes—fascism, homosexuality, the main characters all victims of the prevailing political scenes. There are parallels between Hitler's Germany and Bismarck's reflecting in two love affairs which end in betrayal. I used real as well as imaginary characters, linking fiction and reality closely, and did so, too, in *Nazi Lady. An Easter Egg Hunt* is concerned with the disappearance of a schoolgirl during the First World War—another character wrenched from her normal environment, a refugee from France now living in England's Lake District where the war harshly changes the lives of the four main protagonists. *Love Child*, in the psychological thriller genre, is about the problems of surrogate motherhood in both England and the United States. Once more, the heroine, feckless and easygoing Gwen, is thrust into a new society.

My choice of Einstein for a children's biography—a highly individual man whose life was spent in trying to eliminate the frontiers of prejudice—and the thesis of *The Undergrowth of Literature* (the need for fantasy in the sexually disturbed) illustrate my interest in and compassion for those unable to conform to the accepted social mores. To some extent my film writing has also dealt with social and sexual distress, as did my short play for The National Theatre, *Pursuit*. The ballet scenarios for Kenneth MacMillan, although the subjects were not selected by me, again present individuals who are "outsiders" —Prince Rudolf in *Mayerling* and the strong, passionate and wayward Isadora Duncan.

*   *   *

Since her first novel, *The Liberty Man*, Gillian Freeman has shown an outstanding ability to get inside the skin of characters from very different social backgrounds. It should be remembered that *The Liberty Man* was considerably in advance of its time in its truly empathic conveyance of a working-class character (Derek, a naval rating) who becomes involved in an affair with an intellectual and middle-class woman. This book appeared when the prevailing literary method of portraying working-class people still tended to be by projecting the image of the well-intentioned but clumsy, scruffy, and inarticulate "little man." The unusual power of *The Liberty Man*, however, does not rest only in its portrait of Derek, but in his relationship with Freda, the middle-class school teacher, through which Freeman analyses resonances between people from extremely diverse social groups, and between the inner experiences of the individual and the externals that he sees in operation around him.

Freeman is, in a sense, the writer of the archetypal anti-Cinderella story. She has acute honesty and a flair for precise, almost wickedly unerring observation of detail and motive. In her novels, despite changes of fortune (*Jack Would Be a Gentleman* is a good example) people's lives are *not* transformed, and their basic inadequacies remain. Her novels are preoccupied with frustration and fallibility; she frequently manages, however, by well-timed injections of compassion, to lift a book's mood of inadequacy and doubt into warmth

and well-being that are almost physical in the strength of their expression.

Freeman observes and analyses the vagaries of human nature but rarely makes moral judgements. She highlights complexities in apparently "ordinary" or superficial characters, and makes her jaded sophisticates capable of sudden deep and challenging emotions. She explores conflicts between ambition and conscience, and the primitive feelings that underlie the veneer of our civilization. Permeating some of her narratives is a sense that the protective social structure we strive to perpetuate is deeply flawed. She is, in this context, extremely concerned with nonconformity—the healthily truculent attitudes of the working classes; the bewildered responses of the unconscious homosexual; the rootlessness of the young that can sometimes find expression only in violence (*The Leather Boys*).

Freeman's novels are synonymous with power and panache, though these qualities are often expressed in low-key and even throwaway language. She is in this respect quintessentially English, and until *The Alabaster Egg* her preoccupations were with issues particularly pertinent to English society. *The Alabaster Egg* is her most trenchant and telling work. It is about the pursuit of political power, and this is counterpointed by a probing of the exploitation of human beings at the personal level. Her setting is wider than in the earlier novels; it is no longer England but Europe—or the world—and the focus, significantly, is Germany—the vortex of 20th-century "civilization," corruption, and decay.

Her earlier stories were concerned with displacement, in particular with the catalytic effect of an alien presence in a close-knit and apparently secure social structure (*Fall of Innocence*, *The Campaign*). *The Alabaster Egg* highlights an ironic reversal of this theme of dissociation; Hannah, the book's heroine, has the misfortune to be a Jew in Nazi Germany. She does not, however, see herself as an alien. In her own estimation she is as much a German as a Jew. Her situation, of course, stresses one of the most pernicious effects of Nazi racist policies —the enforced separation of certain people from their own communities, from the only group to which they had felt a sense of belonging. Hannah's tragic but resilient story has parallels with happenings in the time of Bismarck. Her love affair with a "real" German is illuminated by her readings from the diary of the homosexual lover of King Ludwig II. This affair—like Hannah's—ends in bewilderment and betrayal.

Having written compellingly from the viewpoint of a sensitive and intelligent Jewish woman caught up in the hideousness of fascism, Freeman goes on to write as if from the inside about a passionate supporter of Hitler's ideologies in *Nazi Lady*. This originally appeared as a factual diary; it was so convincing that one critic pronounced it "unquestionably genuine." Genuineness, of course, does not have to be a matter of fact but of mood, and in this sense *Nazi Lady* is genuine, although it is a work of fiction. Freeman says that it was inspired by her publisher's observations on the extraordinary dichotomy between the anguishes of the battles of Stalingrad and the "good life" enjoyed at the same time by influential civilians in Germany.

In *Nazi Lady* the heroine's initial enthusiasm for Nazism is presented with subtlety and conviction. Elisabeth is German; to English readers she is possibly a slightly glamorized amalgam of Marlene Dietrich, Irma Greeser, and whatever the Nazi slogan "Strength Through Joy" suggested. As well as being brittle she is beautiful, and her experiences are macabrely fascinating.

Freeman combines fact and fiction with aplomb. (For example, Elisabeth has to accept expert but distasteful seduction by Goebbels in order to save her husband from the rigours of the Russian Front.) In the end, all her convictions are reduced to ashes, as both her son and her husband become victims of Nazi ruthlessness and fanaticism. But she survives—and marries an American from the liberating forces.

An Easter Egg Hunt, is set in a girls' school during the First World War, and it is not only an intriguing mystery story on its own account but memorable for its evocation of Angela Brazil's schoolgirl adventures. School was, of course, regarded by Angela Brazil as the (essentially neatly ordered) world in microcosm; but Freeman recognizes bizarre and eccentric elements even in the innately conservative and sheltered confines of school life. She adeptly creates and manipulates her adolescent characters without excesses or sentimentality, and they are in fact far removed from Brazil's colourful but artless embodiments of schoolgirlishness.

The narrative style of all Freeman's novels is perfectly suited to her sensitive but down-to-earth approach. Her prose is robust and direct; her plots are constructed with economy and excellence, and the stories seem to vibrate with energy and insight.

—Mary Cadogan

FRIEDMAN, Bruce Jay. American. Born in New York City, 26 April 1930. Educated at DeWitt Clinton High School, New York; University of Missouri, Columbia, 1947–51, Bachelor of Journalism 1951. Served in the United States Air Force, 1951–53: Lieutenant. Married Ginger Howard in 1954 (divorced, 1977); three children. Editorial director, Magazine Management Company, publishers, New York, 1953–66. Visiting Professor of Literature, York College, City University, New York, 1974–76. Address: P.O. Box 746, Water Mill, New York 11976, U.S.A.

PUBLICATIONS

Novels

Stern. New York, Simon and Schuster, 1962; London, Deutsch, 1963.
A Mother's Kisses. New York, Simon and Schuster, 1964; London, Cape, 1965.
The Dick. New York, Knopf, 1970; London, Cape, 1971.
About Harry Towns. New York, Knopf, 1974; London, Cape, 1975.
Tokyo Woes. New York, Fine, 1985.

Short Stories

Far from the City of Class and Other Stories. New York, Frommer-Pasmantier, 1963.
Black Angels. New York, Simon and Schuster, 1966; London, Cape, 1967.
Let's Hear It for a Beautiful Guy and Other Works of Short Fiction. New York, Fine, 1984.

Plays

23 Pat O'Brien Movies, adaptation of his own short story (produced New York, 1966).
Scuba Duba: A Tense Comedy (produced New York, 1967). New York, Simon and Schuster, 1968.

A Mother's Kisses, music by Richard Adler, adaptation of the novel by Friedman (produced New Haven, Connecticut, 1968).
Steambath (produced New York, 1970). New York, Knopf, 1971.
First Offenders, with Jacques Levy (also co-director: produced New York, 1973).
A Foot in the Door (produced New York, 1979).

Screenplay: *Stir Crazy*, 1980.

Other

The Lonely Guy's Book of Life. New York, McGraw Hill, 1978.

Editor, *Black Humor.* New York, Bantam, and London, Corgi, 1965.

*

Critical Study: *Bruce Jay Friedman* by Max F. Schulz, New York, Twayne, 1974.

Theatrical Activities:
Director: **Play**—*First Offenders* (co-director, with Jacques Levy), New York, 1973.

*   *   *

For good or ill, Bruce Jay Friedman seems destined to be forever linked with the literary phenomenon of the 1960's known as "black humor." In his foreword to *Black Humor*, an anthology he edited in 1965, Friedman ducks the business of rigid definition, insisting that each of the 13 writers represented is separate and unique, but he does suggest that "if there is a despair in this work, it is a tough, resilient brand and might very well end up in a Faulknerian horselaugh."

For Friedman, style is a function, an extension, of the disorderly world that surrounds him. As he puts it, there is a "fading line between fantasy and reality, a very fading line, a goddamned, almost invisible line." Friedman's slender fiction—as well as his drama and, increasingly, his screenplays—are pitched on this precarious edge. In such a world, the *New York Times* is "the source and fountain and bible of black humor," while television news convinces Friedman, perhaps too easily, that "there is a new mutative style of behavior afoot, one that can only be dealt with by a new, one-foot-in-the-asylum style of fiction."

We are hardly surprised when a contemporary novelist declines rather than develops, when he or she adds increasingly smaller additions to the original house of fiction. For Friedman, *Stern* doubled as his debut and his most accomplished novel. It's all there in *Stern*: the uneasy Jewishness, the ulcers, the suburban situation. But the sense of terror it generates is actualized, altogether convincing, located in a compactness that never quite appears again in Friedman's fiction.

Stern is, in short, the angst-ridden apartment dweller, nose pressed against suburbia while visions of extra rooms dance in his head: "As a child he had graded the wealth of people by the number of rooms in which they lived. He himself had been brought up in three in the city and he fancied people who lived in four were so much more splendid than himself." Alas, as Stern quickly discovers, he is not one of the Chosen People who can make the exodus from the bondage of crowded apartments to the Promised Land of suburban living. He is, at best, a reluctant pioneer, a man who misses the cop on the beat, the delicatessen at the corner.

Stern is a contemporary variation on the classical *schlemiel*, one victimized by darkly comic fantasies of his own making, rather than by accidents. Besieged by problems on all sides— caterpillars devour his garden, neighborhood dogs attack him on a nightly basis—Stern pictures the police as "large, neutral-faced men with rimless glasses who would accuse him of being a newcomer making vague troublemaking charges." Especially if he complains about the threatening dogs: "They would take him into a room and hit him in his large, white, soft stomach." And so he swallows his impulse to protest, only to imagine himself "fighting silently in the night with the two gray dogs, lasting eight minutes and then being found a week later with open throat by small Negro children."

Friedman's subsequent works confirmed two facts: that he is equally at home in the novel (*A Mother's Kisses*), the short story (*Far from the City of Class*), or the play (*Steambath*); and that he is a flashy writer of limited scope. For example, in *A Mother's Kisses*, the psychodynamics of black humor shrink to Momism and the difficulties of getting into college. As always, excess is the heart of Friedman's matter:

He [Joseph] saw himself letting a year go by, then reapply-ing only to find himself regarded as a suspicious leftover fellow, his application tossed onto a pile labeled "repeaters," not to be read until all the fresh new ones had been gone through. Year after year would slip away, until finally, at thirty-seven, he would enter night school along with a squad of newly naturalized Czechs, sponsored by labor unions and needing a great many remedial reading sessions. . . .

Joseph's American–Jewish mother begins as a vulgar cliché, and Friedman's touch merely raises it to a second power. When Joseph went away to summer camp, mother struck a camp of her own just across the lake; when Joseph finally sets off for Kansas Land Grant Agricultural (where courses like "the history and principles of agriculture" and "feed chemistry" comprise the curriculum) Mom insists on coming too.

And yet, there are moments in *A Mother's Kisses* when the terrors of contemporary life are rendered with sharp, metaphy-sical precision:

A long line had formed in the men's room, leading to a single urinal, which was perched atop a dais. When a fellow took too long, there were hoots and catcalls such as "What's the matter, fella, can't you find it?" As his turn came nearer, Joseph began to get nervous. He stepped before the urinal finally, feeling as though he had marched out onto a stage. He stood there a few seconds, then zipped himself up and walked off. The man in back of him caught his arm and said, "You didn't go. I watched."

Little of Kakfa's flavor is lost in the translation. And the hand that descends to unmask our smallest deception strikes us as real, all too real.

The problem, of course, is that Friedman throws off bril-liantly comic moments without the inclination to turn them into sustained, comic fictions. He remains the perennial sopho-more, chortling at what can only be called sophomoric jokes. In *The Dick*, for example, Friedman means to draw a parallel between sexuality and crime-fighting, as the title of the novel and the name of its beleaguered protagonist, LePeters, suggest.

One bad joke begets another. When LePeters has his psycholo-gical interview, the conversation owes more to Hollywood than to Henry James:

"What do you think all these guns around her repre-sent?" he asked LePeters in a lightning change of subject.

"Oh, I don't know," said LePeters. "Phalluses, I guess." Actually, he had dipped into a textbook or two and was taking a not-so-wild shot.

"Not bad," said Worthway, lifting one crafty finger in the Heidelberg style and making ready to leave. "But some of them are pussies, too."

About Harry Towns focuses on a moderately successful screenwriter, one given to verbal razzle-dazzle, urbane irony, and just enough innocence to be amazed about the money producers stuff into his pockets and the girls who fall into his bed. One shorthand way of putting it might be this: the Sexual Revolution caught Harry Towns with his pants up. The result is a man in his forties (formerly married, now anguishing through a permanent "temporary separation") trying too hard to be trendy and protesting too much about enjoying it. No doubt Friedman's biographer will, one day, point out just how "biographical" the stories in fact were.

Shortly after *About Harry Towns*, Friedman published a revealing piece in *Esquire* entitled "Hi, This Is Bruce Jay Fried-man, Reporting From Hollywood" (August 1976). After that, one learned to look quickly as his name, and the other credits, rolled over the silver screen. The heyday of the black humorist was over. Some, like Joseph Heller, continued to plug away at fiction nonetheless. Others, like Ken Kesey, dropped out. And some, like Bruce Jay Friedman, found the medium their "massage" had been looking for all along.

—Sanford Pinsker

FUCHS, Daniel. American. Born in New York City, 25 June 1909. Educated at Eastern District High School, Brook-lyn; City College of New York, B.A. 1930. Married Susan Chessen in 1932; two sons. Taught elementary school, New York, 1930–37. Since 1937, scriptwriter. Recipient: Oscar, for original screen story, 1956; American Academy award, 1962; National Jewish Book award, 1980. Agent: Irving Paul Lazar Agency, 211 South Beverly Drive, Beverly Hills, California 90212. Address: 430 South Fuller Avenue, Apartment 9-C, Los Angeles, California 90036, U.S.A.

PUBLICATIONS

Novels

The Williamsburg Trilogy.   New York, Avon, 1972.
 Summer in Williamsburg.   New York, Vanguard Press, 1934; London, Constable, 1935.
 Homage to Blenholt.   New York, Vanguard Press, and Lon-don, Constable, 1936.
 Low Company.   New York, Vanguard Press, 1937; as *Nep-tune Beach*, London, Constable, 1937.
West of the Rockies.   New York, Knopf, and London, Secker and Warburg, 1971.

Short Stories

Stories, with others.   New York, Farrar Straus, 1956; as *A Book of Stories*, London, Gollancz, 1957.

The Apathetic Bookie Joint. New York, Methuen, 1979; London, Secker and Warburg, 1980.

Plays

Screenplays: *The Day the Bookies Wept*, with Bert Granet and George Jeske, 1939; *The Big Shot*, with Bertram Millhauser and Abem Finkel, 1942; *The Hard Way*, with Peter Viertel, 1942; *Between Two Worlds*, 1944; *The Gangster*, 1947; *Hollow Triumph* (*The Scar*), 1948; *Criss Cross*, 1949; *Panic in the Streets*, with others, 1950; *Storm Warning*, with Richard Brooks, 1951; *Taxi*, with others, 1952; *The Human Jungle*, with William Sackheim, 1954; *Love Me or Leave Me*, with Isobel Lennart, 1955; *Interlude*, with Franklin Coen and Inez Cocke, 1957; *Jeanne Eagels*, with Sonya Levien and John Fante, 1957.

*   *   *

Of the young Jewish novelists who came of age in the 1930's, none depicted ghetto life more effectively than Daniel Fuchs, a Brooklyn schoolteacher who produced three novels in four years. *Summer in Williamsburg*, appearing when Fuchs was 24, was followed by *Homage to Blenholt* and *Low Company*. Each is given over more to private neuroses than public disorders; Fuchs touches rarely on politics—and then only to laugh. Even sex provides less motivation than does the obsessive desire for dignity, success, money.

All three are summer novels. Life then is more exposed, emotions more volatile, uncertainty more evident. Fuchs's hunched little people are not symbols or folk heroes enacting tribal myths; they are clamoring, sweating, lower-middle-class Jews who have inched from Ellis Island to Brooklyn across the East River's Williamsburg Bridge. There, locked into stifling little rooms, they are torn between Judaism's high principles and life's low facts. Most are natural losers attaining only anxiety and pain. *Summer in Williamsburg* catches the cosmic absurdity of their lives. Rejecting a linear narrative for a melange of contrapuntal scenes, Fuchs explores the moral choices confronting a dozen Ripple Street eccentrics during eight sweltering, explosive weeks. He focuses most clearly upon a young would-be writer, Philip Hayman, his family and friends. For Philip, at twenty, the summer is a time of choice and exploration. For several of his neighbors its proves life's end.

Even as a new novelist Fuchs opts for cinematic narrative; to avoid undue literary influence, he derives his structure less from Dos Passos's "Camera Eye" than from actual film-editing techniques. Leaning heavily upon dialogue, gesture, and setting, he bridges his imagistic scenes by a quick dissolve at points of greatest stress. Such mechanical crosspatching has its dangers; a sense of incompletion, fragmentary profiles rather than rounded portraits, characters abandoned with emotions exposed not explained, actions left dangling in mid-gesture. Yet his resolve to look anew at people and events too often glazed by familiarity and sentiment enables Fuchs to infuse *Summer in Williamsburg* with a self-sustaining vitality. It remains a hard, convincing montage of a Brooklyn summer.

Homage to Blenholt is an even more mocking commentary on the American dream. Here again, amid the airless redbrick tenements, are self-pitying little people shouting, slamming doors, overflowing kitchen and flat to cover fire-escape, sidewalk, and alley. Gleaning dreams from movie and tabloid,

they suffer from barren delusions, bad luck, and crushing conditions. The sad-funny narrative is spun of two hectic days in the lives of three young misfits—Max Balkan, Mendel Munves, and Coblenz—who, striving mightily to enrich their lives, only make them more frantic, comic, and pitiable. Yet each, by accepting without whining his inevitable fate, attains a measure of dignity. In Depression America few can expect much more.

Homage to Blenholt evoked charges of cynicism, but Fuchs's cynicism is that of the committed moralist or frustrated idealist who doubts man's ability to control his destiny. Life seems a cosmic burlesque comprised equally of the tragic and comic, sublime and ridiculous. With an eye for every reflex and ambiguity, an ear for every sigh, Fuchs shapes nuance, slang, gesture into telling revelations of character; in the process, he deftly fuses Yiddish-English and Brooklyn patois into a vernacular as idiomatic as Hemingway's, as native as Faulkner's or O'Hara's.

Low Company is the most somber and violent of the novels. It is also the best constructed, with plotting tighter, incidents more revealing, and characters more fully realized. Intensifying his caricatures, Fuchs moves from sour humor to greed and brutality, and from Williamsburg to Brooklyn's soggy fringe. Neptune Beach (a composite of Brighton Beach and Coney Island) is a marginal world of squalid beach cottages, sand, weeds, and flimsy boardwalk gaiety. Sun-soaked concessions hide a struggling, embittered world verging always on violence and disaster. Its human flotsam have been cast up on the sands by an inability to cope with city complexities. Maimed, brutalized, rejected, the Neptuners here spend three days messing-up their lives. Most damaged is Shubunka, the ugly, fat brothel operator; a childhood fall had bent both legs, heightened his apelike appearance, and rendered him a lonely grotesque. Intelligent, sensitive, and gentle, he arouses in those about him disgust and suspicion. Yet in the confused reader he evokes not only compassion but guilt for misplaced sympathy. Shubuanka at least recognizes his own evil, the peculiar justice of his pathetic fate, and his need for atonement.

Thus Fuchs touches notes long sounded by tragic poets, naturalists, and existentialists: the individual discovers little from experience but to exist and endure. He learns that all prayers are to a God indifferent to individual loss and collapse. Before such cosmic indifference, Fuchs insists, man can rely on what he can grab, steal or find. He himself neither condemns nor judges.

Time has not changed his ideas. *West of the Rockies*, Fuchs's long-awaited fourth novel, is a vigorous, but formless, distillation of three decades of accumulated movieland impressions. But despite the California locale, his scurrying hyperactives seem as scarred and self-pitying as their older New York cousins; caught up in the same savage ritual (the need to "make it"), they are propelled by similar anxieties and compulsions. Each is a survivor, with a proved ability to claw a limited victory from any defeat.

To Fannie Case's Palm Springs hotel, in the late 1950's, comes high-strung movie queen Adele Hogue, with three small children, a nervous skin disorder, an imperiled career, and a trail of scandals, broken marriages, and operations. In pursuit is a familiar Hollywood pack: her sinking producer, a torch-carrying ex-racketeer, and assorted talent agents. Among the last is Burt Claris, Fuchs's wry observer and commentator. A no-talent ex-athlete, a loser and "grifter," Burt, clinging desperately to the movie crowd's fringe, is now sexually involved with Adele. Also concerned for the actress is ex-rackets muscle man Harry Case; years back he had deserted his wife Fannie for Adele who, at the last moment, had spurned him.

Fuchs's style is still "cinematic," with characters moving forward, speaking, dissolving. Their talk is the hard, stiff jabs of seasoned winners who suddenly find themselves slipping and, fearing the slide, strike out at those nearest. With Burt watching and waiting, Harry and Adele repeatedly cut and slash at each other; moving back and forth between them is Fannie Case, loving and hating them both. Tough, generous Fannie is the classic Hollywood first wife, the one discarded when the ambitious husband, finally hitting it big, goes after a younger woman. Pugnacious Harry Case, a Catskills-rackets veteran with a strong resemblance to Philip Hayman's gangster uncle, Papravel, still lusts for Adele. But, at story's end, Adele and Burt decide that together they can better confront their harsh, tinsel world.

For all its vivid, quick-paced truths, *West of the Rockies* is not vintage Fuchs. Shorter than his previous novels, with thoughts and deeds summarized rather than acted out, it seems a condensed version of a much longer work, more screenplay synopsis than novel.

—Ben Siegel

FULLER, Roy (Broadbent). British. Born in Failsworth, Lancashire, 11 February 1912. Educated at Blackpool High School, Lancashire; qualified as a solicitor, 1934. Served in the Royal Navy, 1941–46; Lieutenant, Royal Naval Volunteer Reserve. Married Kathleen Smith in 1936; one son, the writer John Fuller. Assistant solicitor, 1938–58, solicitor, 1958–69, and since 1969, director, Woolwich Equitable Building Society, London. Chairman of the Legal Advisory Panel, 1958–69, and since 1969, a Vice-President, Building Societies Association. Professor of Poetry, Oxford University, 1968–73. Chairman, Poetry Book Society, London, 1960–68; a Governor, BBC, 1972–79; member, Arts Council of Great Britain, and Chairman of the Literature Panel, 1976–77 (resigned). Recipient: Arts Council Poetry Award, 1959; Duff Cooper Memorial Prize, for poetry, 1968; Queen's Gold Medal for Poetry, 1970; Cholmondeley Award, for poetry, 1980. M.A.: Oxford University. Fellow, Royal Society of Literature, 1958. C.B.E. (Commander, Order of the British Empire), 1970. Address: 37 Langton Way, Blackheath, London S.E.3, England.

Publications

Novels

With My Little Eye. London, Lehmann, 1948; New York, Macmillan, 1957.
• *The Second Curtain.* London, Verschoyle, 1953; New York, Macmillan, 1956.
• *Fantasy and Fugue.* London, Verschoyle, 1954; New York, Macmillan, 1956.
Image of a Society. London, Deutsch, 1956; New York, Macmillan, 1957.
• *The Ruined Boys.* London, Deutsch, 1959; as *That Distant Afternoon,* New York, Macmillan, 1959.
The Father's Comedy. London, Deutsch, 1961.
The Perfect Fool. London, Deutsch, 1963.
My Child, My Sister. London, Deutsch, 1965.
The Carnal Island. London, Deutsch, 1970.

Verse

Poems. London, Fortune Press, 1940.

The Middle of a War. London, Hogarth Press, 1942.
A Lost Season. London, Hogarth Press, 1944.
Epitaphs and Occasions. London, Lehmann, 1949.
Counterparts. London, Vershoyle, 1954.
Brutus's Orchard. London, Deutsch, 1957; New York, Macmillan, 1958.
Collected Poems 1936–1961. London, Deutsch, 1962.
Buff. London, Deutsch, 1965.
New Poems. London, Deutsch, 1968.
Pergamon Poets 1, with R.S. Thomas, edited by Evan Owen. Oxford, Pergamon Press, 1968.
Off Course. London, Turret, 1969.
Penguin Modern Poets 18, with A. Alvarez and Anthony Thwaite. London, Penguin, 1970.
To an Unknown Reader. London, Poem-of-the-Month Club, 1970.
Song Cycle from a Record Sleeve. Oxford, Sycamore Press, 1972.
Tiny Tears. London, Deutsch, 1973.
An Old War. Edinburgh, Tragara Press, 1974.
Waiting for the Barbarians: A Poem. Richmond, Surrey, Keepsake Press, 1974.
From the Joke Shop. London, Deutsch, 1975.
The Joke Shop Annexe. Edinburgh, Tragara Press, 1975.
An Ill-Governed Coast. Sunderland, Ceolfrith Press, 1976.
Re-treads. Edinburgh, Tragara Press, 1979.
The Reign of Sparrows. London, London Magazine Editions, 1980.
The Individual and His Times: A Selection of the Poetry of Roy Fuller, edited by V.J. Lee. London, Athlone Press, 1982.
House and Shop. Edinburgh, Tragara Press, 1982.
As from the Thirties. Edinburgh, Tragara Press, 1983.
Mianserin Sonnets. Edinburgh, Tragara Press, 1984.
New and Collected Poems 1934–1984. London, Secker and Warburg, 1985.
Subsequent to Summer. Edinburgh, Salamander Press, 1985.

Other (for children)

Savage Gold London, Lehmann, 1946.
Catspaw. London, Alan Ross, 1966.
Seen Grandpa Lately? London, Deutsch, 1972.
Poor Roy. London, Deutsch, 1977.
The Other Planet and Three Other Fables. Richmond, Surrey, Keepsake Press, 1979.
More about Tompkins and Other Light Verse. Edinburgh, Tragara Press, 1981.
Upright, Downfall, with Barbara Giles and Adrian Rumble. Oxford and New York, Oxford University Press, 1983.

Other

Owls and Artificers: Oxford Lectures on Poetry. London, Deutsch, and New York, Library Press, 1971.
Professors and Gods: Last Oxford Lectures on Poetry. London, Deutsch, 1973; New York, St. Martin's Press, 1974.
Souvenirs (memoirs). London, London Magazine Editions, 1980.
Vamp Till Ready: Further Memoirs. London, London Magazine Editions, 1982.
Home and Dry: Memoirs 3. London, London Magazine Editions, 1984.

Editor, *Byron for Today.* London, Porcupine Press, 1948.

Editor, with Clifford Dyment and Montagu Slater, *New Poems 1952*.   London, Joseph, 1952.

Editor, *The Building Societies Acts 1874–1960: Great Britain and Northern Ireland*, 5th edition.   London, Franey, 1961.

Editor, *Supplement of New Poetry*.   London, Poetry Book Society, 1964.

Editor, *Fellow Mortals: An Anthology of Animal Verse*.   Plymouth, Macdonald and Evans, 1981.

Editor, with John Lehmann, *The Penguin New Writing 1940–1950: An Anthology*.   London, Penguin, 1985.

*

Manuscript Collections: Brotherton Collection, Leeds University; State University of New York, Buffalo; British Library, London.

Critical Study: *Roy Fuller* by Allan E. Austin, Boston, Twayne, 1979.

*   *   *

Roy Fuller is a leading contemporary British poet. He is also a prolific writer of fiction; his production to date includes nine novels, as well as a number of book-length tales for children. For many poets the novel is in a double sense a sport: a *tour de force* in an unaccustomed medium written to pass the time when verse is hard to compose. Fuller has committed himself more seriously to fiction. There is not, in his work, any capricious alternation between verse-writing, and the art of the novel has always held for him a particular fascination. He was, long before he began to publish fiction in the 1950's, an ardent student of Henry James; he was interested in the contributions which the socially conscious crime novelists of the 1930's had made to the wider techniques of fiction; later he was one of a group of English writers, including also Angus Wilson, Walter Allen, and George Woodcock, who critically reinstated William Godwin's great novel, *Caleb Williams*, as the true precursor of the modern novel of pursuit and persecution, with its attendant ambiguities.

All these influences can be found reflected in Fuller's own novels which, like his poetry, proceed by a process of refinement from a concern for man in his relationship to society and its demands, to a preoccupation with the narrowing world of the human being who advances out of youth towards age and death.

If one takes an early Fuller novel, like *The Second Curtain*, the whole Godwinian paradox of the individual and his sense of justice, pitted against a society inevitably inhuman, seems to be re-stated in modern terms. Like Caleb Williams, the solitary writer George Garner finds himself involved in a criminal conspiracy. A friend of his dies mysteriously, and Garner is horrified to discover that the very men who are proposing to establish him as editor of a literary magazine are in fact responsible for his friend's death. Their organization, formed to protect wealthy manufacturers against indiscreet inventors who may render their products obsolete, is to be seen as a microcosm of the unregenerate society we inhabit, and Garner becomes the type of the well-intentioned intellectual, anxious to struggle for what is true, but susceptible to fear if not bribery, and, by a positively Godwinian twist, feeling guilty towards those who are his enemies and whom he knows to be evil.

The equivocal relationship between the individual—particularly the intellectual or the artist—and the collectivity is further developed in Fuller's later novels, one of which is significantly entitled *Image of a Society*, the Building Society whose affairs form the background to the shifting relationships of the characters is in fact a metaphysical substitute for society as a whole, containing all its moral sanctions, all its possibilities for tyranny and injustice. In *The Ruined Boys* the collectivity is a private school on the edge of failure, and the spurious loyalties which the Headmaster tries to induce seem to be merely the emanations of more real loyalties that make tenuous but irresistible demands. A further variation of the social frame occurs in *The Father's Comedy*, where the leading figure, a successful and ambitious civil servant, finds his future in "the Authority" (a mysterious corporation which again is an image of society as a whole) threatened by both the past (his own radical youth) and the present (his son's rebellion against a repressive army). It is only in his late novel, *My Child, My Sister*, that Fuller follows in fiction the move he had made in poetry a decade before, and narrows but at the same time widens his focus to embrace the individual and ageing man grappling with his own nature and by the same token with the generalized horror of the human condition.

Of course, that struggle of the individual with himself and with his human destiny had been present in all the novels, and in a sense the social dimension has acted merely as a frame of the moral core of each book, since what the contest with society shows most clearly is the degree of courage, sensitivity, and adaptability in the individual. It is in the solitude of his own weakness that George Garner in *The Second Curtain* has to consider his defeat by the evil forces of the Power Industries Protection Corporation. And if, at the end of *The Father's Comedy*, Harold Colmore feels—after he has revealed all the secrets of his left-wing past in order to secure his son's acquittal in a court martial—that he must return "to show himself to the Authority and to Dorothy, to find out what his character and his career had become," the significance of the novel to the reader lies not in what will happen to Colmore's career in the future, but in the fact that in the present he has been able to ignore such possibilities and to commit what may well be a sacrifice of his planned future out of love for his son.

For it is ultimately in the validity of human relationships that the characters of Fuller's novels are tested, and here it is—rather than in any stylistic shaping—that the effects of his early Jamesian enthusiasms may be detected. For the rigid forms of society are complemented by the fragile links that bind human beings in a web of indestructible gossamer, and perhaps Fuller's best achievement as a novelist lies in the restraint and sureness with which he establishes this network of relationships. The relationships may be ambiguous: an elderly man, like Albert Shore in *My Child, My Sister*, feeling sexually stirred by his wife's daughter by a second marriage; Harold Colmore in *The Father's Comedy* clandestinely meeting a girl in whom his conscript son had been interested; Gerald Bracher in *The Ruined Boys* sensing all at once the epicene charms of a younger boy who plays a female part in a school play. Nothing happens in a physical sense; Fuller's novels are almost completely lacking in the scenes of sexual action that figure in so many contemporary novels, and even scenes of violence are rare, petty, and dependent on the imperatives of the plot; there is no gratuitous sensationalism of any kind. But the very scantiness of outward action tends to heighten the inward intensity of the relationships.

Almost always, in such relationships, the attraction-repulsion between the young and the ageing is involved, and, as a corollary, the sense in one partner of the loss of a beauty and an innocence that he is trying to regain. It is not merely a sentimental nostalgia that is involved, for often the young seem hardly worthy of the love directed towards them and the person who directs it is at least partly conscious of this fact; the central feeling is rather—less crudely and directly expressed than by the existentialists—of the inexorable progress of every life towards decay.

The tone of Fuller's novels, like the tone of his poetry, is restrained and undramatic; he recognizes that each man to himself is a failure, and it is the inner voice expressing this recognition that he uses. His world is not without fear; indeed, fear pervades it, but it is expressed most often in such forms as anxiety and apprehension. His heroes are of human dimensions, and the whole landscape is that of a normal world which breeds its own terrors, shames, and victories without any need to import disaster or false passion from outside. The consequence is that, while so many novels written out of bogus anger in Britain during the 1950's and early 1960's have become as dated as their years of publication, Fuller's have outlived their time, and if they are too muted to survive in detailed memory, they project, on re-reading, an unblurred freshness of tone and sharpness of outline.

—George Woodcock

* * *

GADDIS, William. American. Born in New York City in 1922. Educated at Harvard University, Cambridge, Massachusetts. Has one son and one daughter. Worked for *The New Yorker*, 1946–47; lived in Latin America, Europe, and North Africa, 1947–55; free-lance speech and filmscript writer, 1956–1970's. Recipient: American Academy grant, 1963; National Endowment for the Arts grant, 1966, 1974; National Book Award, 1976; Guggenheim fellowship, 1981; MacArthur Prize, 1982. Member, American Academy, 1984. Agent: Candida Donadio and Associates, 231 West 22nd Street, New York, New York 10011, U.S.A.

PUBLICATIONS

Novels

The Recognitions. New York, Harcourt Brace, 1955; London, MacGibbon and Kee, 1962.
JR. New York, Knopf, 1975; London, Cape, 1976.
Carpenter's Gothic. New York, Viking, 1985; London, Deutsch, 1986.

*

Critical Studies: *City of Words* by Tony Tanner, London, Cape, and New York, Harper, 1971; *A Reader's Guide to William Gaddis's The Recognitions* by Steven Moore, Lincoln, University of Nebraska Press, 1982, and *In Recognition of William Gaddis* edited by Moore and John Kuehl, Syracuse, New York, Syracuse University Press, 1984; "William Gaddis Issue" of *Review of Contemporary Fiction* (Elmwood Park, Illinois), vol. 2, no. 2, 1982; *American Fictions 1940–1980* by Frederick Karl, New York, Harper, 1983.

*   *   *

John W. Aldridge well describes William Gaddis's *The Recognitions* as an attempt to create "a satirical portrait of no less than the entire modern world ... through a most intricate 956-page exploration of such arcane matters as art forgery, counterfeiting, false religious rhetoric, ambidextrous sexuality,

the fraudulence of political life, and the masquerades of intellectual and artistic society." As one might suspect—given the fact that the novel is dense in style, has little plot, and is encyclopedic in scope (treating in Joycean fashion everything from the origins and varieties of religious belief to every major period in human history)—it was greeted with a mixed reception. Even today, while it is regarded by many as one of the most brilliant works of our century, it has a small reading public. *JR*, Gaddis's second novel, similarly difficult to read and gargantuan in size, has led many of Gaddis's also highly respected critics to question if the effort in reading his books is equal to their rewards. At last, *Carpenter's Gothic*, Gaddis's most recent, shorter, and less dense work has been universally applauded as rich and artful; the two earlier novels have also been reissued.

Throughout, Gaddis focuses his vast erudition and epistemological questions upon the corrupt contemporary world. It is a world overwhelmed by technology and big business—the money and efficiency ethic—and characterized by the demise of human relationship. This he mirrors in the corruption of language and all apparent communicative patterns—from painting to even telephoning. Gaddis focuses upon the human suffering and alienation that exists in a society of hypocrisy, greed, and fraudulence. He searches for redemption with the recurrent question of whether or not the individual can assert some control within such a world, as well as within a universe that may lack design or purpose. Beneath all of society's counterfeit structures, after all, may lie chaos, rather than order and the simplicity of basic form. Although his vision is often grim and his satire black, Gaddis implies the power of human love and the transcending possibilities of artistic creation. The acceptance of self and the *effort* to create or extend towards some fundamental unity may at least set in balance the chaotic and entropic universe.

The Recognitions—with its 50 characters (whose paths cross, and who contrast and parallel one another within a vast number of subplots), and with its echoes from Joyce, Rilke, Dante, Eliot, Augustine, Melville, and dozens more—covers a 30-year period and takes place in New York, New England, Paris, Italy, and Spain. Its central figure is Wyatt Gwyon, the son of an eccentric clergyman, who rejects the ministry to become an artist, and who then rejects his own original work (his aunt had accused him years before of trying to assume God's creative function) to copy the Old Flemish Masters who "found God everywhere." Although he leaves his father and wife to become the counterfeit artist and is exploited by a series of people (like Rectall Brown), his is a pilgrimage to discover the counterfeits of contemporary life. He ultimately arrives at a Spanish monastery and (in blinding insight or madness?) goes beyond copying the "falsifications" of the Masters to arrive at final truth—by erasing their canvases. He departs, presumably having had the ultimate epiphany, having "seen" the simple truth behind all artifice and structure.

The novel is filled with recognitions and failed recognitions—of forgeries on every conceivable level—social, aesthetic, scientific, sexual, religious, and political. There is a sense that man has surrendered all sense of mystery, wonder, feeling, and belief to science, technology, psychology, and commerce. Wyatt tries to get beyond the contemporary disease of ego to original truths, as Gaddis pursues the distinctions between the real and fictional. What lies behind all human enterprise (a forgery), he asks: Is it form, chaos, or God? In the end, it may be that art and reality are, after all, the same—both constructs over and against chaos.

What Wyatt accomplishes, finally, is a spatial, spiritual, and truly creative experience, a "recognition" of the unity of all living and nonliving things. He goes beyond art, which like life (and all human relationships and systems) separates ("afraid of spaces"), to gain even a sense of the intermingling of life and death (in a bizarre scene where he eats bread mistakenly made of his father's ashes).

Although *JR* is vast in scope, its most immediate focus is the corruptive power of money in a society marked by wasted human relationships and aborted creative potentiality. Beneath Gaddis's concentration upon the immediate and topical is once again the sense of cosmic meaninglessness. The novel, moreover, lacks any formal organization: it has no chapter divisions; sentences often do not finish; it utilizes minimum punctuation. The book consists of uninterrupted speeches, in dialogues and monologues. Its minimal plot centers on an 11-year-old boy, rejected by both his family and society, who is a student at a modern (computerized) school on Long Island. An emblem of his society, which teaches wheeling and dealing, rather than thinking and feeling, the illiterate JR—with torn sweater, open sneakers, and running nose—having mastered Wall Street jargon, puts into practice the lessons of his time and place. Horatio Alger magnified (and satirized) a hundred-fold, he builds a paper empire that touches the political, cultural, and social power bases of our society. Gaddis focuses on the decadence of the people involved in all his maneuvering. In their midst, however, is the "hero" Edward Bast, the one-time composer at the school (fired for sneaking some truths about Mozart into his TV lesson). Bast is taken over by JR, who becomes his business agent. At the end, Bast gives up financial security to return to art, and JR, who has never actually realized (i.e., cashed in on) his paper empire, pleads for the respect of personal values. One's worth, it appears, depends upon one's acts—in an existential sense.

Although *JR*'s canvas appears smaller than that of *The Recognitions* and the story takes place in New York and Long Island during a few months, it is even more difficult to read. With little description, narrative, or characterization (which is handled through dialect variations), one has a hard time assigning speeches, even though Gaddis uses a remarkable variety of spoken styles. One has no difficulty, however, focusing upon his predominant image of American life as one of corruption, lovelessness, and easy surrender. This is an insane world where friendship and love, on any level, are betrayed. Language mirrors the separation of the individual from his world and the entropy of that very world. One no longer listens, or if he does, he doesn't hear that is said. Language so studded with bureaucratic and political jargon has lost any "meaning."

Though less dense, *Carpenter's Gothic* retains Gaddis's vision of human corruption and lovelessness. Its bizarre and complex plot revolves around an immoral and scheming veteran, Paul Booth, who works as a media consultant for a fundamentalist preacher, the Reverend Elton Ude. Paul's ambitions are vast: he would transform a local drowning incident into a religious miracle and spread the word as far as Africa. His wife, Elizabeth, is no less ambitious, as she pursues an insurance fraud and, along with her vulgar brother Billy (with whom she has inherited a mining combine), schemes to embrace power and gold in Africa. The backdrop for the ill doings of this family trinity is the rented, gothic house of the geologist-novelist, Mister McCandless. It is a house built in that architectural style noticeably appealing on the outside but inwardly ill-functioning and frequently unseemly. Indeed, it is McCandless, the prince of darkness, the perverse and eternal host, who not only designs several significant plot events—he seduces Liz by falsely claiming discovery of the gold—but he also speaks out the novel's grotesque prophecies of doom. A mad evangelist, it is through his words and house—all tied

to the Gothic—that Gaddis achieves a final statement—a "vision of a disorder which . . . [is] beyond any . . . man to put right"—about the failure of modern faith (irrevocably distorted from that of history's first great Carpenter, Jesus), of contemporary America (whose "grand solutions" inevitably turn to "nightmare"), and, indeed, of all human interaction. The modern world has turned Gothic—decayed, grotesque and violent—in its every dimension, "a patchwork of conceits . . . [and] deceptions," orderly and beautiful on the outside but irreversibly distorted within.

—Lois Gordon

GAINES, Ernest J(ames). American. Born in Oscar, Louisiana, 15 January 1933. Educated at Vallejo Junior College; San Francisco State College, 1955–57, B.A. 1957; Stanford University, California (Stegner Fellow, 1958), 1958–59. Served in the United States Army, 1953–55. Writer-in-Residence, Denison University, Granville, Ohio, 1971, Stanford University, Spring 1981, and Whittier College, California, 1982. Since 1983, Professor of English and Writer-in-Residence, University of Southwestern Louisiana, Lafayette. Recipient: San Francisco Foundation Joseph Henry Jackson Award, 1959; National Endowment for the Arts grant, 1966; Rockefeller grant, 1970; Guggenheim grant, 1970; Black Academy of Arts and Letters award, 1972; San Francisco Art Commission award, 1983. D.Litt.: Denison University, 1980; Brown University, Providence, Rhode Island, 1985; Bard College, Annandale-on-Hudson, New York, 1985. Agent: Dorothea Oppenheimer, 435 East 79th Street, Apartment 4-M, New York, New York 10021. Address: 932 Division Street, San Francisco, California 94115, U.S.A.

PUBLICATIONS

Novels

Catherine Carmier. New York, Atheneum, 1964; London, Secker and Warburg, 1966.
Of Love and Dust. New York, Dial Press, 1967; London, Secker and Warburg, 1968.
The Autobiography of Miss Jane Pittman. New York, Dial Press, 1971; London, Joseph, 1973.
In My Father's House. New York, Knopf, 1978.
A Gathering of Old Men. New York, Knopf, 1983; London, Heinemann, 1984.

Short Stories

Bloodline. New York, Dial Press, 1968.

Uncollected Short Stories

"The Turtles," in *Transfer* (San Francisco), 1956.
"Boy in the Doublebreasted Suit," in *Transfer* (San Francisco), 1957.
"My Grandpa and the Haint," in *New Mexico Quarterly* (Albuquerque), Summer 1966.

Other

A Long Day in November (for children). New York, Dial Press, 1971.

*

Manuscript Collection: Dupree Library, University of Southwestern Louisiana, Lafayette.

Critical Studies: "Human Dignity and Pride in the Novels of Ernest Gaines" by Winifred L. Stoelting, in *CLA Journal* (Baltimore), March 1971; "Ernest J. Gaines: Change, Growth, and History" by Jerry H. Bryant, in *Southern Review* (Baton Rouge, Louisiana), October 1974; "Bayonne ou le Yoknapatawpha d'Ernest Gaines" by Michel Fabre in *Recherches Anglaises et Américaines 9* (Strasbourg), 1976; "To Make These Bones Live: History and Community in Ernest Gaines's Fiction" by Jack Hicks, in *Black American Literature Forum* (Terre Haute, Indiana), Spring 1977; "Ernest Gaines: 'A Long Day in November'" by Nalenz Puschmann, in *The Black American Short Story in the 20th Century* edited by Peter Bruck, Amsterdam, Grüner, 1978; "The Quarters: Ernest J. Gaines and the Sense of Place" by Charles H. Rowell, in *Southern Review* (Baton Rouge, Louisiana), Summer 1985.

Ernest J. Gaines comments:

I have tried to show you a world of my people—the kind of world that I came from.

*   *   *

The fictive world of Ernest J. Gaines, as well as certain technical aspects of his works, might be compared to that of William Faulkner. But useful as such a comparison may be, it should not be pursued to the point of obscuring Gaines's considerable originality, which inheres mainly in the fact that he is Afro-American and very much a spiritual product, if no longer a resident, of the somewhat unique region about which he writes: south Louisiana, culturally distinguishable from the state's Anglo-Saxon north, thus from the nation as a whole, by its French legacy, no small part of which derives from the comparative ease with which its French settlers and their descendants formed sexual alliances with blacks.

Gaines's Afro-American perspective enables him to create, among other notable characters both black and white, a Jane Pittman (*The Autobiography of Miss Jane Pittman*) whose heroic perseverance we experience, rather than a housekeeping Dilsey (*The Sound and the Fury*) for whom we have little more than the narrator's somewhat ambiguous and irrelevant assurance that "She endured." In general, Gaines's peculiar point of view generates a more complex social vision than Faulkner's, an advantage Gaines has utilized with increasing dramatic force and artistic promise. The society of which he writes consists of whites, blacks, and creoles, a traditionally more "favored" class ("shade" is perhaps more appropriate) of Afro-American given to fantasies of racial superiority of the kind Frantz Fanon explores in *Black Skin, White Masks*, in terms of Martinican society.

The Gainesian counterparts of the Sartorises and Snopeses (the moribund aristocracy and parvenu "poor white trash" of Faulkner's mythical Mississippi county) are the south Louisiana plantation owners, mostly of French extraction, and the cajuns, of French extraction but of lesser "quality." The cajuns are inheriting and spoiling the land and displacing the creoles and blacks, the former tragically though not irrevocably doomed by a persistent folly, the latter a people of promise who have never really betrayed their Africanness.

All Gaines's works reflect the inherent socio-economic intricacy of this quadruplex humanity, though we are never allowed to lose sight of its basic element of black and white. In the apprentice first novel *Catherine Carmier*, for instance, we see the sickly proscribed love of Jackson, who is black, and Catherine, daughter of an infernally proud creole farmer, as a perverted issue of the miscegenation that resulted from the white male's sexual exploitation of black people. This mode of victimization assumes metaphoric force in Gaines's works, figuring forth in historical perspective the oppression of black people generally. The fictive plantation world, then, is uniquely microcosmic. It is south Louisiana, the south, the nation as a whole. This aspect is explored, for example, in the title story of *Bloodline*. Copper, a character of mythopoeic proportion, the militant young son of a now deceased white plantation owner and a black woman field hand, stages a heroic return, presumably from his education in school and in the world at large, to claim his heritage: recognition of kinship by an aristocratic white uncle and his rightful share of the land. In *In My Father's House*, and for the first time, Gaines deals with the black father–son relationship, and explores a neglected aspect of Afro-American life: the perplexities of the public vs. private person relative to individual responsibility. The Reverend Phillip Martin, a grass roots Civil Rights leader in the fictional south Louisiana town of St. Adrienne, is forced to confront his wayward past when his estranged son Etienne, reminiscent of Copper, comes to claim paternal recognition and redress of grievances.

In *A Gathering of Old Men* Gaines extends the thematic concerns of his earlier novels into a new South setting, employing a multiple first-person point of view in the manner of Faulkner's *As I Lay Dying*. The conflict between blacks and cajuns comes to a cinematically stylized, somewhat surrealistic climax and resolution as several old black men gather in mutual militant defense of one of their number who has been accused of killing Cajun farmer Beau Boutan, confronting the local sheriff as well as the slain man's avenging father, "retired" nightrider Fix Boutan. The result is a gripping allegorical tale of race relations in the new South resonant with the Gainesian theme of individual responsibility, this time for holding ground in the wake of the civil rights gains of the 1960's and 1970's.

—Alvin Aubert

———

GALLANT, Mavis. Canadian. Born in Montreal, Quebec, 11 August 1922. Reporter, Montreal *Standard*, 1944–50. Writer-in-Residence, University of Toronto, 1983–84. Recipient: *Canadian Fiction* prize, 1978; Governor-General's award, 1982; Canada–Australia Literary Prize, 1984. Honorary degree: Université Sainte-Anne, Pointe-de-Église, Nova Scotia, 1984. Officer, Order of Canada, 1981. Agent: Georges Borchardt Inc., 136 East 57th Street, New York, New York 10022, U.S.A. Address: 14 rue Jean Ferrandi, 75006 Paris, France.

PUBLICATIONS

Novels

Green Water, Green Sky. Boston, Houghton Mifflin, 1959; London, Deutsch, 1960.

A Fairly Good Time.   New York, Random House, and London, Heinemann, 1970.

Short Stories

The Other Paris.   Boston, Houghton Mifflin, 1956; London, Deutsch, 1957.
My Heart Is Broken: Eight Stories and a Short Novel.   New York, Random House, 1964; as *An Unmarried Man's Summer*, London, Heinemann, 1965.
The Pegnitz Junction: A Novella and Five Short Stories.   New York, Random House, 1973; London, Cape, 1974.
The End of the World and Other Stories.   Toronto, McClelland and Stewart, 1974.
From the Fifteenth District: A Novella and Eight Short Stories.   New York, Random House, and London, Cape, 1979.
Home Truths: Selected Canadian Stories.   Toronto, Macmillan, 1981; New York, Random House, and London, Cape, 1985.

Uncollected Short Stories

"Good Morning and Goodbye" and "Three Brick Walls," in *Preview* (Montreal), December 1944.
"A Wonderful Country," in *Standard Magazine* (Montreal), 14 December 1946.
"The Flowers of Spring," in *Northern Review* (Montreal), June–July 1950.
"Madeline's Birthday," in *New Yorker*, 1 September 1951.
"By the Sea," in *New Yorker*, 17 July 1954.
"In Italy," in *New Yorker*, 25 February 1956.
"Thieves and Rascals," in *Esquire* (New York), July 1956.
"An Emergency Case," in *New Yorker*, 16 February 1957.
"A Short Love Story," in *Montrealer*, June 1957.
"Jeux d'Ete," in *New Yorker*, 27 July 1957.
"The Old Place," in *Texas Quarterly* (Austin), Spring 1958.
"When We Were Nearly Young," in *New Yorker*, 15 October 1960.
"Better Times," in *New Yorker*, 3 December 1960.
"Rose," in *New Yorker*, 17 December 1960.
"Crossing France," in *The Critic* (Toronto), December 1960–January 1961.
"Two Questions," in *New Yorker*, 10 June 1961.
"Night and Day," in *New Yorker*, 17 March 1962.
"One Aspect of a Rainy Day," in *New Yorker*, 14 April 1962.
"The Hunter's Waking Thoughts," in *New Yorker*, 29 September 1962.
"Willi," in *New Yorker*, 5 January 1963.
"Careless Talk," in *New Yorker*, 28 September 1963.
"The Circus," in *New Yorker*, 20 June 1964.
"Paolo and Renata," in *Southern Review* (Baton Rouge, Louisiana), Winter 1965.
"In Transit," in *New Yorker*, 14 August 1965.
"The Statues Taken Down," in *New Yorker*, 9 October 1965.
"Questions and Answers," in *New Yorker*, 28 May 1966.
"Vacances Pax," in *New Yorker*, 16 July 1966.
"A Report," in *New Yorker*, 3 December 1966.
"The Sunday after Christmas," *New Yorker*, 30 December 1967.
"April Fish," in *New Yorker*, 10 February 1968.
"The Captive Niece," in *New Yorker*, 4 January 1969.
"Good Deed," in *New Yorker*, 22 February 1969.
"The Rejection," in *New Yorker*, 12 April 1969.
"The Burgundy Weekend," in *Tamarack Review* (Toronto), Winter 1979.

"Speck's Idea," in *The Best American Short Stories 1980*, edited by Stanley Elkin and Shannon Ravenel.   Boston, Houghton Mifflin, 1980.
"A Revised Guide to Paris," in *New Yorker*, 11 February 1980.
"From Sunrise to Daybreak," in *New Yorker*, 17 March 1980.
"Dido Flute, Spouse to Europe," in *New Yorker*, 12 May 1980.
"From Gamut to Yalta," in *New Yorker*, 15 September 1980.
"Europe by Satellite," in *New Yorker*, 3 November 1980.
"Mousse," in *New Yorker*, 22 December 1980.
"The Assembly," in *The Best American Short Stories 1981*, edited by Hortense Calisher and Shannon Ravenel.   Boston, Houghton Mifflin, 1981.
"Mau to Lew: The Maurice Ravel–Lewis Carroll Friendship," in *Exile* (Toronto), vol. 7, nos. 3–4, 1981.
"French Crenellation," in *New Yorker*, 9 February 1981.
"A Painful Affair," in *New Yorker*, 16 March 1981.
"This Space" and "On with the New in France," in *New Yorker*, 16 July 1981.
"La Vie Parisienne," in *New Yorker*, 19 October 1981.
"Larry," in *New Yorker*, 16 November 1981.
"Siegfried's Memoirs," in *New Yorker*, 5 April 1982.
"Treading Water," in *New Yorker*, 24 May 1982.
"A Flying Start," in *New Yorker*, 13 September 1982.
"Luc and His Father," in *New Yorker*, 4 October 1982.
"Grippes and Poche," in *New Yorker*, 29 November 1982.
"A Recollection," in *New Yorker*, 22 August 1983.
"Rue de Lille," in *New Yorker*, 19 September 1983.
"The Colonel's Child," in *New Yorker*, 10 October 1983.
"Lena," in *New Yorker*, 31 October 1983.
"Overhead in a Balloon," in *New Yorker*, 2 July 1984.
"The Chosen Husband," in *New Yorker*, 15 April 1985.

Play

What Is to Be Done? (produced Toronto, 1982).   Montreal, Quadrant, 1984.

Other

The Affair of Gabrielle Russier, with others.   New York, Knopf, 1971; London, Gollancz, 1973.

*

Bibliography: by Judith Skelton Grant and Douglas Malcolm, in *The Annotated Bibliography of Canada's Major Authors 5* edited by Robert Lecker and Jack David, Downsview, Ontario, ECW Press, 1984.

Manuscript Collection: Fisher Library, University of Toronto.

Critical Studies: "Mavis Gallant Issue" of *Canadian Fiction 28* (Prince George, British Columbia), 1978; *Mavis Gallant: Narrative Patterns and Devices* by Grazia Merler, Ottawa, Tecumseh Press, 1978.

Mavis Gallant comments:
    I was born in Montreal. My father was English, my mother German–Rumanian–Breton. My father died when I was still a small child (an only child) and I spent a great deal of time being shifted about here and there and from school to school. I went to seventeen schools in all, beginning with a prison-like French-Canadian convent at the age of four. These schools, are recalled with horror, were in two provinces and two states, Catholic and Protestant, French and English speaking, co-educational and segregated, and this constant shifting and changing

made it virtually impossible for me to obtain any education at all.

I have not had "jobs," but have lived entirely on my writing, except for a few years in my twenties when I worked for a newspaper in Montreal. This paper no longer exists.

I live with writing exactly as an architect lives with design or a doctor with medicine. I knew from the beginning that I was a slow writer and would probably not produce much, and I arranged my life around my work. A girl I knew when we were both fifteen in New York told me recently that I had told her then exactly how and where I would live.

Nothing is as obnoxious to me as a writer talking about himself and his aims and theories. These things should be evident in the work (I am talking about serious writers). I have noticed that what interests people is irrelevant. Whenever I have been interviewed I have been asked if I write on a typewriter, if I work in the morning or the afternoon, and how I first sold a story to *New Yorker*. My answer to the last of these—that I typed a story and sent it in—never seems satisfactory, yet that is all there was to it.

The beginning is easy; what happens next is much harder.

*   *   *

The characters who move through the fiction of Mavis Gallant are unwilling exiles and victims, born or made. Her first collection of short stories, *The Other Paris*, clearly sets the tone of her work: in a series of impersonal, almost clinical sketches the lonely and displaced struggle against an indifferent or hostile world. A naive American girl, engaged to a dull American in Paris, wonders why her colorless days have no connection with the legendary "other Paris" of light and civility; a pathetic American army wife in Germany faces her stale marriage and a rootless future; a bitter, unforgiving set of brothers and sisters gathers after the funeral of their mother, a dingy Romanian shopkeeper in Montreal; a cow-like Canadian girl with Shirley Temple curls is repeatedly deceived by seedy fiancés; a traveler staying in a Madrid tenement watches a petty bureaucrat trying to justify the new order "to which he has devoted his life and in which he must continue to believe." These anti-romantic glimpses of dislocation and despair are rendered in deliberately hard, dry prose, reminiscent, like their subject matter, of Joyce's *Dubliners*. The narrative manner is flat, unadorned, without any relieving touches of wit—or, it seems, compassion (save for the best of the stories, "Going Ashore," in which a sensitive child is dragged from port to port by a desperate, amoral mother). Although there are an admirable consistency of theme and feeling in these stories, and a high degree of professional skill, there is little here to suggest the brilliance of Gallant's later work and her gradual mastery of longer, more demanding fictional forms.

The title of the next collection, *My Heart Is Broken*, reveals a continuation of the same concerns. Yet there is a good deal more vigor here, and an indication as well that the author, if not her characters, may be taking some pleasure in the sharpness of her perceptions. There is also the first clear suggestion of a problem which is to become of major importance in Gallant's later work: the eccentricity and near-madness to which her losers may be driven by want or isolation. Gallant has an appallingly accurate eye for the desperation of the shabby genteel, the Englishwomen who live at the edge of poverty in unfashionable pensions out of season, and a shrewd eye as well for the vulgarities of those who try to keep up the pretense of well being. And there is at least one completely successful story, "An Unmarried Man's Summer" which

manages to combine many of the earlier preoccupations with a degree of wit and energy not present before.

Gallant's first experiment with longer fiction, *Green Water, Green Sky*, despite a vivid central section, suffers from an uncertainty of focus. Three of the four parts of the novella offer peripheral views of the breakdown of a young American wife, raised abroad and now living in Paris. The reasons for her drift into madness are never fully explained, although the blame must in part rest with a vain and foolish mother. Florence remains an intriguing and pathetic puzzle; our questions are unanswered, our sympathies largely unresolved. A second short novel, "Its Image on the Mirror" (*My Heart Is Broken*), is an unqualified success, partly because the point of view is strictly limited to one character—a device which is the source of some ambiguity here as well as consistency. The faintly repressed family hostilities which have appeared in various guises in the earlier work are now given sustained treatment. The narrator, Jean, who has always suffered from a sense of drabness and compromise in contrast to her beautiful younger sister, tries to come to terms with her ambivalent feelings. After years of apparent freedom and romance the spoiled Isobel makes what seems to be an unhappy and confining marriage; looking back, Jean is able to move towards compassion and acceptance. But to what degree is she using the narrative as a kind of revenge for the years she was forced to take second place? Is her sympathy finally untainted by satisfaction? The reader has no means of deciding, precisely because the author makes no comments on Jean's reminiscences. The uncertainty we feel at the end of the work, however, is entirely appropriate: Jean herself is still divided between love, pity and jealousy.

A Fairly Good Time is a splendidly complex full-length novel. Again the plot is familiar and simple in outline: a well-off, still young Canadian woman passes over the borders of sanity as her second marriage, to a Parisian journalist, dissolves. The reasons for her collapse, again, are hinted at rather than developed: an eccentric, domineering mother, a happy first marriage cruelly ended by a freak accident, the frustrating sense of isolation in a foreign world of would-be intellectuals and amoral opportunists—all of these play a partial role. This time, however, Gallant operates directly inside the mind of her heroine, and the result is a spectacular tour de force: the writing is disconcertingly vivid, full of the unmediated poetry of near-hallucination, yet nothing is irrelevant or misplaced. Shirley's madness has a kind of honesty about it which attracts the users and manipulators around her. The sane world of her husband's family and the Maurel family, into whose civil wars she is thrust, seems finally to offer much less integrity than her own world of memories and fantasies. At the conclusion there is just a hint that Shirley may be returning to reality, as she learns to moderate her hopes: "if you make up your mind not to be happy," runs the epigraph from Edith Wharton, "there's no reason why you shouldn't have a fairly good time."

There are no ideas in Gallant's work, no set of theses. The strong and willful may or may not succeed; the sensitive will almost certainly pay for their gifts. And if they endure, as Shirley may, or as Jean does in "Its Image on the Mirror," the only wisdom is a kind of expensive stoicism:

> We woke from dreams of love remembered, a house recovered and lost, a climate imagined, a journey never made. . . . We would waken thinking the earth must stop now, so that we could be shed from it like snow. I knew, that night, we would not be shed, but would remain, because that is the way it was. We would survive, and waking—because there was no help for it—forget our dreams and return to life.

This is not exactly hopeful, but neither is it completely despairing: perhaps if we learned to moderate our hopes we might have a fairly good time. But Gallant's more recent collections *The Pegnitz Junction* and *From the Fifteenth District* seem to deny even this modest possibility. The mood here is that of *The Other Paris*; the effect is considerably more oppressive, however, since Gallant has extended the range of her style. The relatively dry, understated manner of the first books has now been replaced by a highly poetic technique in which feelings are conveyed by sudden, uncanny, and yet astonishingly precise images. Yet as before, her characters do not act, they are acted upon; they suffer, but in the end it hardly seems to matter. Life dwindles away and with it everything which gave pleasure, so perhaps nothing had much substance to begin with. The conclusion of "An Autobiography" (*The Pegnitz Junction*) is typical. A middle-aged woman thinks about her failure to hold onto the love of a shiftless young man called Peter (the cause of the failure is left undefined, these things just "happen"):

These are the indecisions that rot the fabric, if you let them. The shutter slams to in the wind and sways back; the rain begins to slant as the wind increases. This is the season for mountain storms. The wind rises, the season turns; no autumn is quite like another. The autumn children pour out of the train, and the clouds descend upon the mountain slopes, and there we are with walls and a ceiling to the village. Here is the pattern on the carpet where he walked, and the cup he drank from. I have learned to be provident. I do not waste a sheet of writing paper, or a postage stamp, or a tear. The stream outside the window, deep with rain, receives rolled in a pellet the letter to Peter. Actually, it is a blank sheet on which I intended to write a long letter about everything—about Véronique. I have wasted a sheet of paper. There has been such a waste of everything; such a waste.

"The only way to be free," reflects one of the battered characters in *From the Fifteenth District*, "is not to love." This is the freedom of isolation, madness, and death, but perhaps any escape from being is preferable to the pain of living. Thus Piotr, for example, the central figure in the novella "Potter," welcomes the imagined prospect of his death: "Oh, to be told that there were only six weeks to live! To settle scores; leave nothing straggling, to go quietly." Yet even death may offer no release. In "From the Fifteenth District," a truly harrowing prose-poem—it can hardly be called a story—the pathetic ghosts of the dead complain to the "authorities" that the memories of life and the intrusions of the still-living make any final rest impossible.

—Elmer Borklund

GARNER, Helen (née Ford). Australian. Born in Geelong, Victoria, 7 November 1942. Educated at Manifold Heights State School; Ocean Grove State School; The Hermitage, Geelong; Melbourne University, 1961–65, B.A. (honours) 1965. Married 1) William Garner in 1968, one daughter; 2) Jean-Jacques Portail in 1980. Taught at Werribee High School, 1966–67, Upfield High School, 1968–69, and Fitzroy High School, 1971–72, all Victoria. Writer-in-Residence, Griffith University, Nathan, Queensland, 1983, and University of Western Australia, Nedlands, 1984. Melbourne theatre critic,

National Times, Sydney, 1982–83. Since 1981, feature writer, *The Age*, Melbourne. Since 1985, member of the Australia Council Literature Board. Recipient: Australia Council fellowship, 1978, 1979, 1980, 1983; National Book Council award, 1978. Address: 849 Drummond Street, North Carlton, Victoria 3054, Australia.

PUBLICATIONS

Novels

Monkey Grip. Melbourne, McPhee Gribble, 1977; London, Penguin, 1978; New York, Seaview, 1981.
Moving Out (novelization of screenplay), with Jennifer Giles. Melbourne, Nelson, 1983.
The Children's Bach. Melbourne, McPhee Gribble, 1984.

Short Stories

Honour, and Other People's Children: Two Stories. Melbourne, McPhee Gribble, 1980; New York, Seaview, 1982.
Postcards from Surfers. Melbourne, McPhee Gribble, 1985.

Play

The Stranger in the House, adaptation of a play by Raymond Demarcy (produced Melbourne, 1982; London, 1986).

*

Critical Study: "On War and Needlework: The Fiction of Helen Garner" by Peter Craven, in *Meanjin* (Melbourne), no. 2, 1985.

*   *   *

Helen Garner's novels deal with the fractured relationships of "alternative" living in Melbourne. Against a background of communes and shared houses, the drug scene, rock bands, cooperative movies, suburb, and beach her characters try to form relationships and cope with their inevitable failure. Her fiction explores the point at which freedom stops and irresponsibility begins. It is a world in which women with love to spare try to deal with men who have "the attention span of a stick insect" who monopolize them one minute and ignore them the next. There is a sympathetic, fatalistic cast to her writing. Most of her characters could be summed up by the line: "Their mother was dead and they were making a mess of things."

Monkey Grip is Nora's account of her obsessive love for Javo, a junkie. They belong to a subculture where drugs define the real and the tolerable, where there is no tomorrow only today, and therefore where commitments to another person are infinitely redefinable. "I'm not all that worried about futures. I don't want to love anyone forever." Nora's love, her habit of "giving it all away," is as addictive as Javo's heroin habit, and makes her as vulnerable. She supports and is supported by other women, sometimes finding herself consoling or being consoled by a sexual rival. The pain and the jealousy are intense but in the curiously reticent unreticence of this culture, protest about exploitation is limited to declarations as inadequate as, "That makes me feel bad." By the end of the novel Nora has achieved some degree of detachment from Javo, but there is no guarantee that the cycle will not be repeated with another exploitingly helpless male.

Honour, and Other People's Children is a pair of novellas which show characters similar to those in *Monkey Grip* at a later stage in their lives. Each involves separation. In

"Honour" a woman who has been separated for five years from her husband is shocked by his asking for a divorce in order to remarry. Instead of the commune life he now wants "a *real* place to live, with a back yard where I can plant vegies, and a couple of walls to paint, and a dog—not a bloody room in a sort of railway station." Despite their five-year separation Elizabeth still feels a residual bonding which is now threatened. Relationships in this book are much more richly delineated than in the first novel. Here they are products of shared experience, shared jokes and personal rituals, family connections and mutual awareness. When Frank's father is about to die, it is Elizabeth who accompanies him on the visit. Their child stands in the middle of an awkward triangle wanting all to live together and not comprehending the nuances and difficulties of the situation. However her instinct is right, and ex-wife and future wife tentatively feel towards some sort of acquaintance, even friendship, symbolised by the balanced seesaw of the story's conclusion.

"Other People's Children" moves the focus away from heterosexual relationships to the declining friendship between two women who have been the nucleus of a shared house, and have gradually become abrasive towards each other. Over years in the same household Scotty has come to love Ruth's daughter, Laurel, and hers is the greatest loss when the house breaks up. Loving other people's children gives no rights, not even the limited access granted to the non-custodian parent by the divorce court. Ruth's relationship with the self-protective Dennis shows the same sort of male manipulation used by Javo in *Monkey Grip*, while Madigan, to whom Scotty turns for companionship, is so torn between misogyny and the need for acceptance that he ranks as the most destructive of Garner's male characters.

The Children's Bach extends Garner's range of characters, and puts them in a new arrangement. Whereas previous novels concentrated on the isolation of characters and on the failures of bonding, this novel offers at least one couple in a successful relationship: "She loved him. They loved each other. They were friends." Dexter and Athena embody an innocence which characters in the earlier novels seem never to have had. Their marriage is stable and caring despite the strains put on it by their retarded second son who has a musical sense but not speech. Set against them are Dexter's old friend from university days, Elizabeth, her lover Philip, and her younger sister, Vicky. There is a clash of values in this novel, and a sense that characters are redefining their perspectives instead of being depicted at a stage when they are already locked into a fixed way of seeing, and surviving in, the world.

Music has always been an important motif in Garner's books, and here it becomes dominant. In earlier works it offered, like sex or drugs, a way of immersion or escape. It is associated with most of the characters in this novel, and it generally suggests sanity and harmony. While Philip uses music to exploit people, it is a mark of Athena's unglamorous dedication to making life work, and of Dexter's uncomplicated gusto.

Postcards from Surfers is a collection of stories which offers vignettes on the ways people relate and report themselves to others. In the title story a woman holidaying with her parents who have retired to the seaside writes a series of postcards to a former lover which she does not post because it's "too late to change it now." Other stories tell of chance meetings, visits, trips in Europe and Australia. Males in this collection continue to be selfish, manipulative, and arrogant but Garner ends some of the stories more hopefully in the manner of *The Children's Bach*. Women trying to make something of their lives ("The Life of Art") are always going to find males unsatisfactory, but they can support each other. Women are always going to be racked by passion for men who want them less continuously and exclusively, but it is possible to "hang on until the spasm passes."

—Chris Tiffin

GARRETT, George (Palmer, Jr.). American. Born in Orlando, Florida, 11 June 1929. Educated at Sewanee Military Academy; The Hill School, graduated 1947; Princeton University, New Jersey, 1947–48, 1949–52, B.A. 1952, M.A. 1956, Ph.D. 1985; Columbia University, New York, 1948–49. Served in the United States Army Field Artillery, 1952–55. Married Susan Parrish Jackson in 1952; two sons and one daughter. Assistant Professor, Wesleyan University, Middletown, Connecticut, 1957–60; Visiting Lecturer, Rice University, Houston, 1961–62; Associate Professor, University of Virginia, Charlottesville, 1962–67; Writer-in-Residence, Princeton University, 1964–65; Professor of English, Hollins College, Virginia, 1967–71; Professor of English and Writer-in-Residence, University of South Carolina, Columbia, 1971–73; Senior Fellow, Council of the Humanities, Princeton University 1974–77; Adjunct Professor, Columbia University, 1977–78; Writer-in-Residence, Bennington College, Vermont, 1979, and University of Michigan, Ann Arbor, 1979–84. Since 1984, Hoyns Professor of English, University of Virginia, Charlottesville. President of Associated Writing Programs, 1971–73. United States Poetry Editor, *Transatlantic Review*, Rome (later London), 1958–71; Contemporary Poetry Series editor, University of North Carolina Press, Chapel Hill, 1962–68; co-editor, *Hollins Critic*, Virginia, 1965–71; Short Story Series editor, Louisiana State University Press, Baton Rouge, 1966–69. Since 1970, contributing editor, *Contempora*, Atlanta; since 1971, assistant editor, *Film Journal*, Hollins College, Virginia; since 1972, co-editor, *Worksheet*, Columbia, South Carolina; since 1981, editor, with Brendan Galvin, *Poultry: A Magazine of Voice*, Truro, Massachusetts. Recipient: *Sewanee Review* fellowship, 1958; American Academy in Rome fellowship, 1958; Ford grant, for drama, 1960; National Endowment for the Arts grant, 1967; *Contempora* award, 1971; Guggenheim fellowship, 1974. Agent: Jane Gelfman, John Farquharson Ltd., 250 West 57th Street, New York, New York 10107. Address: 1853 Fendall Avenue, Charlottesville, Virginia 22903, U.S.A.

PUBLICATIONS

Novels

The Finished Man. New York, Scribner, 1959; London, Eyre and Spottiswoode, 1960.
Which Ones Are the Enemy? Boston, Little Brown, 1961; London, W.H. Allen, 1962.
Do, Lord, Remember Me. New York, Doubleday, and London, Chapman and Hall, 1965.
Death of the Fox. New York, Doubleday, 1971; London, Barrie and Jenkins, 1972.
The Succession: A Novel of Elizabeth and James. New York, Doubleday, 1983.
Poison Pen. Winston-Salem, North Carolina, Wright, 1986.

Short Stories

King of the Mountain.   New York, Scribner, 1958; London, Eyre and Spottiswoode, 1959.
In the Briar Patch.   Austin, University of Texas Press, 1961.
Cold Ground Was My Bed Last Night.   Columbia, University of Missouri Press, 1964.
A Wreath for Garibaldi and Other Stories.   London, Hart Davis, 1969.
The Magic Striptease.   New York, Doubleday, 1973.
To Recollect a Cloud of Ghosts: Christmas in England.   Winston-Salem, North Carolina, Palaemon Press, 1979.
An Evening Performance: New and Selected Short Stories.   New York, Doubleday, 1985.

Uncollected Short Stories

"The Other Side of the Coin," in *Four Quarters* (Philadelphia), no. 6, 1957.
"The Rare Unicorn," in *Approach* (Wallingford, Pennsylvania), no. 25, 1957.
"The Only Dragon on the Road," in *Approach* (Wallingford, Pennsylvania), no. 31, 1959.
"3 Fabliaux," in *Transatlantic Review* (London), no. 1, 1959.
"The Snowman," in *New Mexico Quarterly* (Albuquerque), no. 29, 1959.
"Two Exemplary Letters," in *Latitudes* (Houston), no. 1, 1967.
"Jane Amor, Space Nurse," in *Fly by Night*, 1970.
"There Are Lions Everywhere," "How Can You Tell What Somebody's Thinking on the Telephone," and "Moon Girl," all in *Mill Mountain Review* (Roanoke, Virginia), Summer 1971.
"Here Comes the Bride," in *Gone Soft* (Salem, Massachusetts), no. 1, 1973.
"Live Now and Pay Later," in *Nassau Literary Magazine* (Princeton, New Jersey), 1974.
"Little Tune for a Steel String Guitar," in *Sandlapper* (Columbia, South Carolina), no. 9, 1976.
"Soldiers," in *Texas Review* (Huntsville), no. 3, 1982.
"Wine Talking," in *Quarterly West* (Salt Lake City), no. 20, 1985.
"Ruthe-Ann," in *Texas Review* (Huntsville), no. 6, 1985.
"Genius Baby," in *Chattahoochie Review* (Dunwoody, Georgia), 1986.
"Dixie Dreamland," in *South Carolina Review* (Clemson), no. 19, 1986.

Plays

Sir Slob and the Princess: A Play for Children.   New York, French, 1962.
Garden Spot, U.S.A. (produced Houston, 1962).
Enchanted Ground.   York, Maine, Old Gaol Museum Press, 1981.

Screenplays: *The Young Lovers*, 1964; *The Playground*, 1965; *Frankenstein Meets the Space Monster*, with R.H.W. Dillard and John Rodenbeck, 1966.

Television Plays: *Suspense* series, 1958.

Verse

The Reverend Ghost.   New York, Scribner, 1957.
The Sleeping Gypsy and Other Poems.   Austin, University of Texas Press, 1958.
Abraham's Knife and Other Poems.   Chapel Hill, University of North Carolina Press, 1961.

For a Bitter Season: New and Selected Poems.   Columbia, University of Missouri Press, 1967.
Welcome to the Medicine Show: Postcards, Flashcards, Snapshots.   Winston-Salem, North Carolina, Palaemon Press, 1978.
Luck's Shining Child: A Miscellany of Poems and Verses.   Winston-Salem, North Carolina, Palaemon Press, 1981.
The Collected Poems of George Garrett.   Fayetteville, University of Arkansas Press, 1984.

Other

James Jones.   New York, Harcourt Brace, 1984.

Editor, *New Writing from Virginia.*   Charlottesville, Virginia, New Writing Associates, 1963.
Editor, *The Girl in the Black Raincoat.*   New York, Duell, 1966.
Editor, with W.R. Robinson, *Man and the Movies.*   Baton Rouge, Louisiana State University Press, 1967.
Editor, with R.H.W. Dillard and John Moore, *The Sounder Few: Essays from "The Hollins Critic."*   Athens, University of Georgia Press, 1971.
Editor, with O.B. Hardison, Jr., and Jane Gelfman, *Film Scripts 1–4.*   New York, Appleton Century Crofts, 4 vols., 1971–72.
Editor, with William Peden, *New Writing in South Carolina.*   Columbia, University of South Carolina Press, 1971.
Editor, with John Graham, *Craft So Hard to Learn.*   New York, Morrow, 1972.
Editor, with John Graham, *The Writer's Voice.*   New York, Morrow, 1973.
Editor, with Walton Beacham, *Intro 5.*   Charlottesville, University Press of Virginia, 1974.
Editor, with Katherine Garrison Biddle, *The Botteghe Oscure Reader.*   Middletown, Connecticut, Wesleyan University Press, 1974.
Editor, *Intro 6: Life As We Know It.*   New York, Doubleday, 1974.
Editor, *Intro 7: All of Us and None of You.*   New York, Doubleday, 1975.
Editor, *Intro 8: The Liar's Craft.*   New York, Doubleday, 1977.
Editor, with Michael Mewshaw, *Intro 9.*   Austin, Texas, Hendel and Reinke, 1979.

*

Bibliography: in *Seven Princeton Poets*, Princeton University Library, 1963; "George Garrett: A Checklist of His Writings" by R.H.W. Dillard, in *Mill Mountain Review* (Roanoke, Virginia), Summer 1971; "George Garrett: A Bibliographical Chronicle 1947–1980" by Stuart Wright, in *Bulletin of Bibliography* (Boston), January–March 1981.

Manuscript Collections: University of Virginia, Charlottesville; Stuart Wright, Winston-Salem, North Carolina.

Critical Studies: by James B. Meriwether, in *Princeton University Library Chronicle* (New Jersey), vol. 25, no. 1, 1963; "George Garrett Issue" of *Mill Mountain Review* (Roanoke, Virginia), Summer 1971; "Imagining the Individual: George Garrett's *Death of the Fox*" by W.R. Robinson, in *Hollins Critic* (Hollins College, Virginia), August 1971; "The Reader Becomes Text: Methods of Experimentation in George Garrett's *The Succession*" by Tom Whalen, in *Texas Review*

(Huntsville), Summer 1983; "George Garrett and the Historical Novel" by Monroe K. Spears, in *Virginia Quarterly Review* (Charlottesville), Spring 1985.

George Garrett comments:

(1972) I feel I am only just beginning, still learning my craft, trying my hand at as many things, as many ways and means of telling as many stories as I'm able to. I hope that this will always be the case, that somehow I'll avoid the slow horror of repeating myself or the blind rigor of an obsession. I can't look back, I'm not ashamed of the work I've done, but it is done. And I am (I hope) moving ahead, growing and changing. Once I've seen something into print I do not re-read it. I have tried always to write out of experience, but that includes imaginative experience which is quite as "real" to me and for me as any other and, indeed, in no way divorces from the outward and visible which we often (and inaccurately) call reality. I only hope to continue to learn and to grow. And to share experience with my imaginary reader. I use the singular because a book is a direct encounter, a conversation between one writer and one reader. Though I couldn't care less how many, in raw numbers, read my work, I have the greatest respect for that one imaginary reader. I hope to manage to please that reader before I'm done, to give as much delight, or some sense of it, as I have received from reading good books by good writers.

(1986) Years and scars, and various and sundry books, later, I would not change much in my earlier statement, innocent as it was. Now that I am in my mid-fifties I would not use the word *hope* so much. Naturally I have less hope for myelf; though I insist on maintaining high hopes for the best of the young writers I teach. And I have every intention, with and without hope, to continue working, trying to learn my craft always (never to *master* it), still seeking, sometimes finding my imaginary reader. I know more than a decade's worth of darker, sadder things than I did in 1972. So does the world. So goes the world. Well, I have learned a full deck of new jokes, also, and never ceased to taste good laughter. If some hopes have faded and been abandoned, faith, which is altogether something else, has replaced them. And the old dog learns new tricks. One: to turn to the light and live on it until it's gone. Another: to be as open as I can until my book is closed.

*   *   *

Directness, seriousness, a Chaucerian comic sense which in no way conflicts with that seriousness, imaginative vigor, sheer intelligence, and a rich variety of matter and manner—these qualities mark the fiction of George Garrett. An American, a southerner, Garrett has published six novels, a collection of short novels, five collections of stories (including the major collection of new and selected stories, *An Evening Performance*), seven books of poems (including *The Collected Poems*), plays and screenplays, and a respectable body of critical work (including the recent biography of James Jones). These figures suggest his energy and the scope of his interests, and they offer some indication of the seriousness with which he pursues his vocation as writer. Garrett approaches his world and his work with an Elizabethan forcefulness and range, directly and with all his strength.

Garrett is a Christian artist—not a pietist, but a writer whose very sense of the living world is infused with an Augustinian Christian understanding. He is a realist and not a fabulist, but, because of his Christian belief, his work is never far from parable, his direct reality always shaped by the enigmas of the spirit. His six novels are very different each from each in subject and texture, but together they form a quest for a narrative structure sufficient to the expression of his increasingly more complex view of the ways of the world. *The Finished Man* is a novel of modern Florida politics; *Which Ones Are the Enemy?* takes place in Trieste during the American occupation following World War II; *Do, Lord, Remember Me* concerns the shattering visit of an evangelist to a small Southern town; *Death of the Fox* is an account of the events, exterior and interior, of the last two days of Sir Walter Ralegh's life; *The Succession* is a synoptic recreation of the events surrounding the succession of James I to the throne of Queen Elizabeth I; *Poison Pen* (a new novel built upon the ruins of a larger, unfinished novel to have been called *Life with Kim Novak Is Hell*) is an acidly satirical examination of American public lives, illusion and reality, and the real and illusory nature of fiction itself. But they are all products of the same central concerns—a blessing of the dark and fallen world, a knowledge of the power of the imagination to create and sustain values in that fallen world, a faith in the possibility of redemption and salvation even in the very process of the fall into sin and death, and a commitment to the individual moment as the sole window on eternity.

Garrett's major works thus far are his Elizabethan historical novels. In *Death of the Fox* all of his major thematic concerns come together in the person of Ralegh, the soldier, the politician, the sailor, and the morally creative man. In his imaginative union with Ralegh, Garrett fuses present and past into an artistic whole which is both truth and lie—the disappointing truth which nevertheless burns ideally in the imagination and dreams of the beholder (as in Garrett's earlier short story, "An Evening Performance") and the saving lie of love (as in his poem "Fig Leaves") which enables us "to live together." *The Succession* both extends and fulfills the stylistic and formal advances of *Death of the Fox* by presenting a thoroughly researched and vividly written account of English and Scottish life in the years succeeding, following and pivoting upon the succession in 1603, and at the same time developing an aesthetic meditation on the creation and revelation of meaning in the succession of moments that make up the nexus of time.

How he will develop as he moves beyond these major milestones of his career (the two historical novels, the collected stories, and the collected poems) is fascinating to contemplate. Garrett has always continued to grow and change in his work while so many of his contemporaries have faltered or simply repeated themselves book after book. His importance becomes clearer year by year as the magnitude of his exploration of reality (outward and inward) reveals itself with each new and startlingly original book.

—R.H.W. Dillard

GASS, William H(oward). American. Born in Fargo, North Dakota, 30 July 1924. Educated at schools in Warren, Ohio; Kenyon College, Gambier, Ohio, 1942–43, 1946–47, A.B. 1947; Ohio Wesleyan University, Delaware, 1943; Cornell University, Ithaca, New York, 1947–50, Ph.D. 1954. Served in the United States Navy, 1943–46: Ensign. Married 1) Mary Pat O'Kelly in 1952; 2) Mary Alice Henderson in 1969; five children. Instructor in Philosophy, College of Wooster, Ohio, 1950–54; Assistant Professor, 1955–58, Associate Professor, 1960–65, and Professor of Philosophy, 1966–69, Purdue

University, Lafayette, Indiana. Since 1969, Professor of Philosophy, now David May Distinguished University Professor in the Humanities, Washington University, St. Louis. Visiting Lecturer in English and Philosophy, University of Illinois, Urbana, 1958–59. Recipient: Longview Foundation award, 1969; Rockefeller fellowship, 1965; Guggenheim fellowship, 1969; American Academy award, 1975, and Award of Merit Medal, 1979. L.H.D.: Kenyon College, 1973. Member, American Academy, 1983. Address: Department of Philosophy, Washington University, St. Louis, Missouri 63130, U.S.A.

PUBLICATIONS

Novels

Omensetter's Luck. New York, New American Library, 1966; London, Collins, 1967.
Willie Masters' Lonesome Wife (essay-novella). New York, Knopf, 1971.

Short Stories

In the Heart of the Heart of the Country and Other Stories. New York, Harper, 1968; London, Cape, 1969.
The First Winter of My Married Life. Northridge, California, Lord John Press, 1979.

Uncollected Short Stories

"The Clairvoyant," in *Location 2* (New York), 1964.
"The Sugar Crock," in *Art and Literature 9* (Paris), 1966.
"We Have Not Lived the Right Life," in *New American Review 6*, edited by Theodore Solotaroff. New York, New American Library, 1969.
"The Cost of Everything," in *Fiction* (New York), vol. 1, no. 3, 1972.
"Mad Meg," in *Iowa Review* (Iowa City), Winter 1976.
"Koh Whistles Up a Wind," in *Tri-Quarterly 38* (Evanston, Illinois), 1977.
"Susu, I Approach You in My Dreams," in *Tri-Quarterly 42* (Evanston, Illinois), 1978.
"August Bees," in *Delta 8* (Montpellier, France), May 1979.
"The Old Folks," in *The Best American Short Stories 1980*, edited by Stanley Elkin and Shannon Ravenel. Boston, Houghton Mifflin, 1980.
"Why Windows Are Important to Me," in *The Best of Tri-Quarterly*, edited by Jonathan Brent. New York, Washington Square Press, 1982.
"Uncle Balt and the Nature of Being," in *The Pushcart Prize 7*, edited by Bill Henderson. Wainscott, New York, Pushcart Press, 1982.

Other

Fiction and the Figures of Life. New York, Knopf, 1970.
On Being Blue. Boston, Godine, 1976; Manchester, Carcanet, 1979.
The World Within the Word: Essays. New York, Knopf, 1978.
The House VI Book, with Peter Eisenman. Boston, Godine, 1980.
Habitations of the Word: Essays. New York, Simon and Schuster, 1985.

*

Bibliography: "A William H. Gass Bibliography" by Larry McCaffery, in *Critique* (Atlanta), August 1976.

Manuscript Collection: Washington University Library, St. Louis.

Critical Studies: "Omensetter's Luck" by Richard Gilman, in *New Republic* (Washington, D.C.), 7 May 1966; "The Stone and the Sermon" by Saun O'Connell, in *Nation* (New York), 9 May 1966; "Nothing But the Truth" by Richard Howard, in *New Republic* (Washington, D.C.), 18 May 1968; interview with Thomas Haas in the *Chicago Daily News*, 1 February 1969; *City of Words* by Tony Tanner, London, Cape, and New York, Harper, 1971; "The Well Spoken Passions of William H. Gass" by Earl Shorris, in *Harper's* (New York), May 1972; "But This Is What It Is Like to Live in Hell," in *Modern Fiction Studies* (Lafayette, Indiana), Autumn 1974; "Against the Grain: Theory and Practice in the Work of William H. Gass" by Ned French, in *Iowa Review* (Iowa City), Winter 1976; *The Metafictional Muse: The Works of Robert Coover, Donald Barthelme, and William H. Gass* by Larry McCaffery, Pittsburgh, University of Pittsburgh Press, 1982.

William H. Gass comments:

I think of myself as a writer of prose rather than a novelist, critic, or story-teller, and I am principally interested in the problems of style. My fictions are, by and large, experimental constructions; that is, I try to make things out of words the way a sculptor might make a statue out of stone. Readers will therefore find very little in the way of character or story in my stories. Working in the tradition of the Symbolist poets, I regard the techniques of fiction (for the contemporary artist) as in no way distinct from the strategies of the long poem.

*   *   *

William H. Gass, a philosopher and literary critic as well as a fiction writer, derives from and is closely allied to the *symbolistes*, Gertrude Stein, Ortega y Gasset, John Crowe Ransom and the New Critics generally, Borges, Robbe-Grillet, Sarraute, and the structuralists. He believes that language is all in all; that words are not agents to instruct or direct us in fiction but that they exist there for their own sake; that the novelist must keep us imprisoned in his language, because there is nothing beyond it; and that the only events in novels are linguistic events. Metaphor is the means by which concepts are expressed in fiction. The writer, furthermore, does not simply render a world; he makes one out of language, creating imaginary objects and imaginary lives. He works toward the purity of prose fiction and the autonomy of art. He works against the concept of mimesis, that is the imitation of "reality," partly because it is futile for the artist to strive for the illusion of life, and partly because he has no obligation to life. His commitment is to aesthetic satisfaction achieved through metaphorical language; it is to writing as process.

Omensetter's Luck is, accordingly, an exercise in the use of language, which in this instance is a prose that strives constantly to be like poetry or music. The words are better than experience, are, indeed, the experience, and the book is intended to be about language and writing. To give himself ample opportunity to exercise his writing capabilities, Gass designed the novel in three sections, each written in a different mode: the first in the narrative, the second in the lyric, and the third in the rhetorical and dramatic modes. The rhythms and images of the Bible, the baroque qualities of Sir Thomas Browne, the technical virtuosity of Flaubert, the stream of consciousness of Joyce all contribute to the writing of the novel in full freedom from the conventional principles of realism and the traditional values of humanism. Nevertheless, lurking behind this dedication to process are narrative and theme, those Gass-identified enemies to the purity of art. The novel dramatizes a conflict between Omensetter, a natural force who represents being-in-nature, and Jethro Furber, a man of religion and thought, obsessed with death and sex. Attractive as he is, Omensetter demonstrates the inadequacies of mindless and spiritless being, while Furber shows us the failure to fuse successfully word, belief, and action in such a way as to elevate the spirit. In short, Gass has drawn, perhaps despite himself, upon the mythological dimensions of Christianity.

While the title story in Gass's *In the Heart of the Heart of the Country* is confessedly modelled on reality, the collection as a whole is experimental. "The Pedersen Kid" is deliberately designed to call into question the nature of reality and the possibility of truth, matters that must live side by side with Gass's concern for the shape of his sentences and the relation of sentence to sentence in the paragraph. In the stories generally, the narrative voice struggles to get inside the characters and with words, magic words, steal their souls away and play with them.

But even more thoroughly committed to experimentalism is *Willie Masters' Lonesome Wife*, in which conventional narrative is largely discarded. The book offers instead a pastiche of various materials: reminiscences of the narrator, little essays on words and the imagination by the author, a variety of typographical play, authorial abuse of the reader, a parody of pornography, and footnotes. All this is designed to destroy the character and form of traditional fiction and to offer opportunities, once the old patterns of linear and logical thought, linear time, and linear print are broken up, for free-wheeling use of the imagination. The book is an experience in art, as Gass tells us at the end, where he inserts a motto: You have fallen into art—return to life. In *Willie Masters' Lonesome Wife* Gass gives himself to self-indulgent play, maximizing the freedom that the author, a god-like figure in Gass's view, justifiably claims in his dedication to the autonomy of art.

—Chester E. Eisinger

GEE, Maggie (Mary). British. Born in Poole, Dorset, 2 November 1948. Educated at Horsham High School for Girls; Somerville College, Oxford (open scholarship), B.A. 1969, M.Litt. 1972, Ph.D. in English 1980. Married Nicholas Rankin in 1983. Editor, Elsevier International Press, Oxford, 1972–74; research assistant, Wolverhampton Polytechnic, 1975–79; Eastern Arts Writing Fellow, University of East Anglia, Norwich, 1982. Lives in London. Agent: Mark Hamilton, A.M. Heath Ltd., 40–42 William IV Street, London WC2N 4DD. Address: c/o Faber and Faber Ltd., 3 Queen Square, London WC1N 3AU, England.

PUBLICATIONS

Novels

Dying, In Other Words. Brighton, Harvester Press, 1981; Boston, Faber, 1984.
The Burning Book. London, Faber, 1983; New York, St. Martin's Press, 1984.
Light Years. London, Faber, 1985; New York, St. Martin's Press, 1986.

Uncollected Short Stories

"Rose on the Broken," in *Granta 7* (Cambridge), 1982.
"Mornington Place," in *London Tales*, edited by Julian Evans. London, Hamish Hamilton, 1983.

Play

Over and Out (broadcast, 1984).   Published in *Literary Review* (London), February 1984.

Radio Play: *Over and Out*, 1984.

Other

Editor, *For Life on Earth.*   Norwich, University of East Anglia, 1982.

*

Maggie Gee comments:

My chief 20th-century models are probably Woolf, Nabokov, and Beckett. But I was also raised on the great 19th-century writers like Dickens and Thackeray. And I loved *stories*: I read and re-read my mother's copy of Hans Christian Andersen. I wanted to write stories myself; and I always felt that the difficulty of much 20th-century "serious" writing must be a problem, not a virtue. If I was difficult, it was despite myself. On the one hand I wanted to write new things, and tell the absolute truth according to my perception of it, which often seems to demand new ways of writing: on the other hand, I've become increasingly aware of the importance of an audience.

My first published novel, *Dying, In Other Words*, is probably the most difficult technically. It is a bizarre kind of thriller. Moira's body is found on the pavement one morning. The police assume it is suicide; yet the milkman who found the body turns out to be a mass-murderer, far too many of Moira's surviving acquaintances start to die in their turn, and increasingly often the sound of typing can be heard in Moira's "empty" room ... is she still alive, and writing the story? The novel is a circle; and when it returns inevitably to the point of Moira's death, we find it was neither suicide nor murder, after all ...

The Burning Book is a variation on the family saga. Two English working families, the Ships and the Lambs, shopkeepers and railway-workers, try to live their own lives, interrupted by two world wars and the threat of a third. One theme of the book is the stupidity of nuclear weapons, which endanger all stories and the continuity embodied in families. There are flashbacks to Hiroshima and Nagasaki. The family itself isn't perfect; violence and frustration inside it counterpoint violence and frustration outside. On a small scale, though, humans can learn to do better. The central couple, Henry and Lorna, finally learn to love each other by the last chapter of the book, when they go for a winter picnic in an earthly Eden, Kew Gardens. By a stupid irony, the public world of war-like headlines breaks in on their "happy ending."

Light Years is an inverted romance, set in 1984. The lovers, Lottie and Harold, split up on the first page of the novel, and are apart through the year (and 52 chapters) that the book lasts, though perhaps things change in the very last chapter ... The longer they are separated, the more they love each other. Meanwhile, the earth turns full circle, and the seasons, the stars, and the planets play their part in the very formal structure of this book. It is my "easiest" book I think—short chapters, short sections within the chapters, with much "lighter"-looking pages: all of which was intended to help express a rather rare commodity in 20th-century literature—happiness.

Retrospectively, I realise that each of my three books has been an attempt to write a new version of a popular genre— thriller, family saga, romance—to appeal to basic emotions, and use basic narrative drives, but to re-work the genre in my own way, and to surprise my readers. All I am conscious of at the time of writing, though, is a desire to show the truth, in ways I never can in speech, and a desire to make structures as beautiful as I can.

*   *   *

In her as yet short career as a novelist Maggie Gee has gained the reputation of an experimentalist. Technically innovative would be the way I would prefer to describe her work, and this is certainly true of her first novel *Dying, In Other Words*. Beginning with the dramatic suicide of a young writer, Moira Penny, *Dying, In Other Words* could have been a brightly written but run-of-the-mill suspense thriller, and in some ways it is. But it is considerably more than that, for Penny's suicide is dropped, as it were, into the pool of lives around her and the ripples spread and impinge on the lives of others and, what makes the novel remarkable, on the continuum of the past and present of those lives. *Dying, In Other Words* has been described as a "Chinese box of a novel" and that is well put. As the novel progresses the implications of Penny's suicide reach further and further into the lives of others. But while the past impinges, the future overshadows, and in *Dying, In Other Words* there are already dark hints of the Armageddon to come. What her characters are unaware of is as important as that of which they are aware: "What Bill didn't know was that the girl he evoked, with her long brown limbs and her full yellow rose bud skirt and her underwear smelling of lemon perfume and seaweed died six months later in a car crash." Gee encourages an awareness that her characters exist in a fiction. She pushes beyond this and writes in her second novel *The Burning Book*: "All of us live in a novel, and none of us do the writing. Just off the stage there are grim old men planning to cut the lighting." Thus Gee can be seen, in spite of (or perhaps because of) her experimentation, to be in the tradition of Fielding and Dickens where the author is ever-present, ready to comment or intervene.

If the ghost of the future is fleetingly glimpsed in *Dying, In Other Words*, it positively haunts *The Burning Book*. Indeed that is its theme and purpose as it explores the loves, joys, frustrations, quarrels, hates, degradations and pettinesses of Lorna and her family. "In an ordinary novel," Gee interpolates, "that would be the whole story," but the shadow cast on the future by Hiroshima and Nagasaki darkens the final episode in this everyday story of ordinary folk. It is to Gee's purpose that they are so ordinary, even petty, in their thoughts and relationships, and it is a tribute to her narrative skills that she carries us with them through their dull and messy lives. Because it is their very dullness and messiness that allow us to identify with them and make their final pointless agonizing destruction so telling and poignantly horrifying. As a nuclear warning the book certainly succeeds; and it succeeds as a work of literature as well.

Nevertheless, *The Burning Book* leaves two largish questions. One is that if Gee wishes her fears and anxieties for our future to be more universally understood, and the passion I sense behind her novels suggests she does, then she may well have to find less sophisticated means to her end. The other question is that having written the terminal novel where does she go?

Where she has gone immediately is to her latest novel *Light Years*. "An oddly simple and old fashioned love story" one reviewer has described it. But all Gee's stories as such are simple and old fashioned: the story of a mysterious suicide in *Dying, In Other Words*, an everyday family saga in *The Burning Book*. It is what she makes of this material that leaves it far from simple and old fashioned. The narrative of Harold and Lottie in *Light Years* can be enjoyed on the story level alone, but Gee's intentions are more involved. She can entertain and does, but she has no wish to entertain alone: her narratives reflect a wider, less immediate, context. Sometimes, in order to do this, she has to rely on her author's interpolations and interventions and there is a danger that these can become digressive or intrusive and defeat their purpose. But there is no danger that Gee will cease to look with a compassionate but unblinking eye at a world in which there are no happy endings.

—John Cotton

GEE, Maurice (Gough). New Zealander. Born in Whakatane, 22 August 1931. Educated at Avondale College, Auckland, 1945–49; University of Auckland, 1950–53, M.A. 1953; Auckland Teachers College, 1954. Married Margaretha Garden in 1970; one son (from previous marriage) and two daughters. Schoolteacher, 1955–57; held various jobs, 1958–66; Assistant Librarian, Alexander Turnbull Library, Wellington, 1967–69; City Librarian, Napier Public Library, 1970–72; Deputy Librarian, Teachers Colleges Library, Auckland, 1974–76. Since 1976, full-time writer. Recipient: New Zealand Literary Fund Scholarship, 1962, 1976, and Award of Achievement, 1967, 1973; University of Otago Robert Burns Fellowship, 1964; Hubert Church Prose Award, 1973; New Zealand Book Award, 1976, 1979, 1982; James Tait Black Memorial Prize, 1979; Sir James Wattie Award, 1979; New Zealand Children's Book of the Year Award, 1983. Agent: Richards Literary Agency, P.O. Box 31240, Milford, Auckland 9, New Zealand.

PUBLICATIONS

Novels

The Big Season. London, Hutchinson, 1962.
A Special Flower. London, Hutchinson, 1965.
In My Father's Den. London, Faber, 1972.
Games of Choice. London, Faber, 1976.
Plumb. London, Faber, 1978.
Meg. London, Faber, 1981; New York, St. Martin's Press, 1982.
Sole Survivor. London, Faber, and New York, St. Martin's Press, 1983.

Short Stories

A Glorious Morning, Comrade. Auckland, Auckland University Press–Oxford University Press, 1975.

Fiction (for children)

Under the Mountain. Wellington, London, and New York, Oxford University Press, 1979.
The World Around the Corner. Wellington, Oxford University Press, 1980; Oxford and New York, Oxford University Press, 1981.

The Halfmen of O.   Auckland and Oxford, Oxford University
Press, 1982; New York, Oxford University Press, 1983.
The Priests of Ferris.   Auckland, Oxford University Press,
1984; New York, Oxford University Press, 1985.
Motherstone.   Auckland, Oxford University Press, 1985.

Plays

Television Series: *Mortimer's Patch*, 1980.

Other

Nelson Central School: A History.   Nelson, Nelson Central
School Centennial Committee, 1978.

*

Critical Studies: "Beginnings" by Gee, in *Islands* (Auckland),
March 1977; *Introducing Maurice Gee* by David Hill, Auck-
land, Longman Paul, 1981; Trevor James, in *World Literature
Written in English* (Guelph, Ontario), vol. 23, no. 1, 1984;
Lawrence Jones, in *Landfall* (Christchurch), September 1984.

*   *   *

With the trilogy of novels comprising *Plumb*, *Meg* and *Sole
Survivor* (published between 1978 and 1983), Maurice Gee
established himself as one of the most distinguished of living
New Zealand writers and indeed as a decidedly prominent
figure in his country's short literary history. Whether this status
makes him a major novelist in the totality of contemporary
literature written in English is less clear and more controversial.

Gee first attracted attention in the mid and late 1950's with
a few stories published in New Zealand's best-known literary
periodical, *Landfall*, and was highly praised by British
reviewers in 1961 for his two stories published in the New
Authors series. For complex reasons characteristic of new
countries founded by colonization, the short story has flourished in New Zealand, and Gee's initial success in the genre
might have encouraged him to adhere to it in the manner of
his great predecessor Katherine Mansfield, rather than turn
to the longer form of the novel, which has taken longer to
acclimatize successfully there than in such countries as Australia and Canada. However, Gee committed himself to the novel
early in his career and his output of stories is small—regrettably
so, because some of his most powerful writing is to be found
in the genre. His best stories, such as the well-known "The
Losers" (1959) and the even more memorable "Eleventh Holiday" (1961), unostentatiously transcend their surface realism
and immediate situations to reverberate with archetypal significance; he possesses the really good story writer's gift of being
able to imply much more than he states, so that the events
described take on a universal, symbolic dimension. Gee concentrates on various aspects of provincial and small-town petit-
bourgeois life in New Zealand, and favourite themes include
isolation, loneliness, the effects of ageing (especially old age),
the conflict between conformity and nonconformity, and the
emotional and spiritual claustrophobia of a middle-class society
in which philistinism and aggression are never far beneath the
respectable veneer. In his stories Gee casts a cold eye on New
Zealand without employing the alienating devices of the dedicated satirist; he therefore achieves a balance between sympathy and criticism.

Gee's first novel, *The Big Season*, is a compressed *bildungsroman* about the central character's quest for selfhood and

identity in a humanly stifling environment, and in this respect
recalls such novels as Joyce's *Portrait of the Artist as a Young
Man* and Lawrence's *Sons and Lovers*. Rob Andrews seems
to be destined to conform to all the expectations of his very
conservative milieu. He is an excellent rugby player (which
probably carries more prestige in New Zealand than anywhere
else), joins his father's small business, becomes engaged to
a nice, wholesome girl, and has the makings of a future pillar
of the blinkered community. Yet Rob also contains within himself the rebellious streak of the outsider. The short Prologue,
set in 1946 and 1947, describes Rob's voyeuristic interest as
a child in a local boarding house considered by his parents
and their circle to be a den of iniquity and vice and therefore
completely out of bounds. The main narrative in 1958 deals
with Rob's crisis of loyalty and responsibility for his own life
when he becomes involved with a small group of social outcasts,
principally the burglar and ex-convict Bill Walters, whom he
had encountered at the boarding house as a child. Torn
between the security of bland conformity and the risks of freedom, Rob eventually rejects the world he knows, repudiating
its values with a public act of defiance, but he also precipitates
a disaster among his new associates. Rob's victory over the
forces of conservatism is heavily qualified, and the conclusion,
as Rob leaves his home town to begin a new life in Auckland,
is open-ended. The strengths of *The Big Season* lie in Gee's
control of the narrative as it builds up to its dramatic showdown
and in the skill with which he invests the particulars of an
individual case-history with symbolic meaning. Gee is less
impressive at dealing with Rob's inner life and psychological
development, but the main reservation—and this is to be a
recurrent one—is that his prose is too flat and unexciting, too
drably realistic, to do justice to the overall imaginative conception.

Structurally and technically Gee's second novel, *A Special
Flower*, is more complex and adventurous than its straightforward predecessor. While adhering to third-person narration, Gee alters the main point of view in every section or
chapter, marking the change by a character's name rather than
orthodox numbering. By means of these shifting perspectives,
Gee achieves narrative relativism as opposed to the omni-
science of *The Big Season*, and his unconventional handling
of time enhances the effect. The first of the two main sections
deals chronologically with the unexpected marriage of a seemingly confirmed bachelor in middle age, the eminently respectable Donald Pinnock, to a woman 20 years his junior and of
a decidedly lower social position, Coralie Marsh. The marriage
soon founders, Coralie leaving her husband for a well-known
footballer, who in turn discards her after making her pregnant
and also after Donald's suicide, triggered off by her demand
for a divorce. In the second section, Gee puts the clock back
to before Donald's death, this time concentrating more on Coralie than on members of the Pinnock family. Only after her
husband's death does Coralie come to a full appreciation of
his love for her, and this eventually leads to a reconciliation
between Coralie and Donald's mother and sister as their hatred
gives way to understanding—understanding that, for Donald,
Coralie provided a gust of fresh air, offering him his one chance
of freedom from the inhibiting confines of New Zealand
middle-class propriety and decorum. The short third section,
describing Coralie's life with the Pinnocks as she awaits the
birth of her baby, gives the novel a more positive and optimistic
conclusion than *The Big Season*, despite the tragedy of
Donald's death.

The mother-son relationship also plays a prominent part in
his third novel, *In My Father's Den*, which opens with a murder,
ends with the identification of the killer, but is only incidentally

a story of mystery and detection. After a Prologue in the form of a newspaper cutting about the killing of Celia Inverarity, a schoolgirl at Wadesville College near Auckland in May 1969, the novel consists of two intercut strands, both narrated by Paul Prior, an unmarried teacher at Celia's school and a prime suspect. One of these is restricted to a few days at the time of the murder, while the other is his life story, told in historical slices such as "1928–1937." The crime prompts Paul to review his entire life, especially in relation to the emotionally and humanly paralysing forces of small-town and suburban New Zealand, embodied in Wadesville. As a literary intellectual who has spent part of his life abroad, Paul is an outsider in his own country. He is strongly contrasted with Celia's father, Charlie, a rough, crude patriarch who marries Paul's former girlfriend and opposes his daughter's educational interests. Charlie represents an ugly, unacceptable face of middle-class New Zealand that manifests itself in the threats, abuse, and violence directed against Paul after Celia's death because, being a Camus-like *étranger*, he is wrongly assumed by the community to be the murderer. In fact, the killer is Paul's conventional and conformist brother, Andrew, a man stunted by his Oedipal relationship with his mother and by the pressures of New Zealand society. *In My Father's Den*, is among other things, a searing indictment of that smug, one-dimensional society.

In *Games of Choice* Gee's examination of a New Zealand family as it virtually disintegrates during a few days over Christmas acquires something of the intensity of Greek tragedy, although the events are much less bloody and extreme, despite the brutal killing of a pet cat with a garden fork. The pressures precipitating catastrophe have built up over many years because the marriage of Kingsley Pratt, a provincial bookseller, and his wife Alison has long been a sham based on empty convention. The departure of their two children from home in pursuit of their own identities is a key factor in dissolving the bonds that have held the family together, often in a mutually enervating, even destructive, configuration. Parents and children are involved in games of choice, quests for freedom. With his wife leaving him for another man, his student daughter having an affair with a much older lecturer, and his son deciding to join the army in defiance of the family's commitment to pacifism, Kingsley is left with his old father Harry, whose memories include his political activities as an idealistic socialist. In one sense the novel is very narrow in its focus, but Gee succeeds in adding an historical and political dimension by giving the Pratt family emblematic as well as realistic status.

In recent years Gee has published work for younger readers, revealing another side of his talent, but his principal imaginative undertaking has been the extremely ambitious trilogy of novels about the Plumb family, *Plumb*, *Meg*, and *Sole Survivor*. Many of the ingredients of the trilogy are present in his earlier novels: the emotional complexity of family life with its blend of loyalty and antagonism, mutual care and incomprehension, love and hate; the relationship between individual and community and between private and public life; conformist acceptance and nonconformist rebellion; relativity of viewpoint. But the scale of trilogy allows Gee to be more expansive and wide-ranging than ever before so that he is able to produce a saga of New Zealand life covering about a hundred years, from the late 19th century to the 1980's, and including six generations while concentrating on three. Because the trilogy incorporates so much of New Zealand's short history since British colonization and includes a number of real-life politicians and major events, it takes on the air of a national epic in the way that a three-generation family saga set in England could not possibly do. Structurally the three novels are similar in that each is

a first-person narrative in which the narrator surveys his or her life from the vantage point of a fictional present, where the immediate action provides a framework for recollecting and reconsidering the past. Roughly 20 years separate the fictional presents of the three novels, *Plumb* being set in the 1940's while *Sole Survivor* brings the cycle to a conclusion in the early 1980's. Gee acknowledges that his family history was an important source of inspiration, especially for the first novel; the eponymous narrator George Plumb is partly based on Gee's maternal grandfather, whose wife was in turn the model for Plumb's wife Edith. In a trilogy containing a number of memorable characters, Plumb is certainly the most extraordinary and interesting. He is a flawed hero, a failed saint, a dedicated idealist of religious and political vision whose moral integrity and over-active conscience blind him to part of the truth about both himself and the world he inhabits. His quest for absolutes and his desire to build a New Jerusalem in New Zealand are undermined by the uncompromising fanaticism that motivates him. Although not a tragic novel, *Plumb* is full of tragic irony.

After the spiritual and ideological crises of *Plumb*, *Meg* seems restrained, but in its own way it is equally panoramic. The narrator, Meg Sole née Plumb, is the youngest of George and Edith's 12 children and very much her father's favourite. A considerable part of her narrative overlaps chronologically with her father's in *Plumb*, but Meg offers her own view of events previously mentioned and introduces a wide range of new material, not only in the later chapters after George's death in 1950. The enormous size of the Plumb family does, of course, mean that there are many parallel strands, only a few of which can be given prominence in any one novel. Towards the end of her memoir, Meg accurately calls it "a tale of deaths," and the novel conveys a characteristically mid- and late 20th-century sense of entropy in contrast to the passionate 19th-century romanticism and utopianism embodied in Plumb in the earlier novel, although that too runs down as the century advances.

Just as George Plumb's death is reported in *Meg*, Meg's horrific death by fire in a domestic accident is related in the punningly titled *Sole Survivor*, narrated by one of her three children, the journalist Raymond Sole, equally punningly known as R. Sole. This is another "tale of deaths," specifically triggered off by the murder of Douglas Plumb, a grandson of George and therefore one of Raymond's numerous cousins, as well as being a cabinet minister. If *Plumb* is the most religious of the three novels and *Meg* the most domestic, *Sole Survivor* is the most political, with fictional and non-fictional elements combined (Douglas is a member of Muldoon's National Government). In *Sole Survivor* Raymond interweaves a selective account of his own life from childhood to middle age with a parallel account of Douglas's career. Even when young, Douglas always put self-interest first, and Raymond recalls his cousin's ruthless pursuit of his own advantage and of power, from the sexual to the political. Douglas's expediency and aggressive opportunism are a total perversion of his grandfather's high-minded dedication to his socialist conception of Man, and the story of Douglas's carefully engineered ascent to prominence, almost to the premiership, is, paradoxically, also a story of decline and fall and entropy—the collapse and disintegration of George Plumb's unrealistic yet noble ideals at both the personal and political levels. The nemesis of Douglas's death does not cancel out what his life represents about the nature of success in the 20th century. The ending of *Sole Survivor* and the trilogy as a whole is open-ended rather than pessimistic, but the emphasis is on the failure to realize the New Zealand dream, the slide from heroic vision to debased materialism. Gee's achievement in encompassing the general through the particular and in sustaining a high level of imaginative input makes the trilogy one of the two or three outstanding works of fiction by a New Zealander in the postwar period.

—Peter Lewis

GELLHORN, Martha (Ellis). American. Born in St. Louis, Missouri, in 1908. Educated at the John Burroughs School, St. Louis; Bryn Mawr College, Pennsylvania. Married 1) the writer Ernest Hemingway in 1940 (divorced, 1945); 2) T.S. Matthews in 1954 (divorced, 1964); one son. Correspondent for *Collier's Weekly* in Spain, 1937–38, Finland, 1939, China, 1940–41, England, Italy, France and Germany, 1943–45, and Java, 1946; for *The Guardian* in Vietnam, 1966, and Israel, 1967; and for *New Statesman* in El Salvador, 1983, and Nicaragua, 1985. Recipient: O. Henry Award, 1958. Lives in London. Agent: Douglas Rae Ltd., 28 Charing Cross Road, London WC2H 0DB, England.

PUBLICATIONS

Novels

What Mad Pursuit.   New York, Stokes, 1934.
A Stricken Field.   New York, Duell, 1940; London, Cape, 1942.
Liana.   New York, Scribner, and London, Home and Van Thal, 1944.
The Wine of Astonishment.   New York, Scribner, 1948.
His Own Man.   New York, Simon and Schuster, 1961.
The Lowest Trees Have Tops.   London, Joseph, 1967; New York, Dodd Mead, 1969.

Short Stories

The Trouble I've Seen.   New York, Morrow, and London, Putnam, 1936.
The Heart of Another.   New York, Scribner, 1941; London, Home and Van Thal, 1946.
The Honeyed Peace.   New York, Doubleday, 1953; London, Deutsch, 1954.
Two by Two.   New York, Simon and Schuster, and London, Longman, 1958.
Pretty Tales for Tired People.   New York, Simon and Schuster, and London, Joseph, 1965.
The Weather in Africa.   London, Allen Lane, 1978; New York, Dodd Mead, 1980.

Plays

Love Goes to Press, with Virginia Cowles (produced London, 1946; New York, 1947).

Television Play: *Venus Ascendant*, 1963.

Other

The Face of War.   New York, Simon and Schuster, and London, Hart Davis, 1959.

Travels with Myself and Another.   London, Allen Lane, 1978; New York, Dodd Mead, 1979.

*

Manuscript Collection: Boston University.

*   *   *

Some novelists are born to their craft. Others are made. Among the latter kind are those who, while possessing no striking originality of gift or of vision, have nonetheless an ability to handle prose, to depict scenes, and to control narrative flow which make them very similar in kind to the good journalist (and the gifts of novelist and journalist do, after all, cross at a great many points). Martha Gellhorn is one of the better "made" writers. None of her novels can be considered a masterpiece, none has pioneered a new kind of fiction and in none do we experience that all-important shock of recognition that comes when we encounter a genuinely original voice. Yet that said it has to be added that if her novels never surprise they rarely disappoint. At the very least there is about them a cool, controlled craftsmanship that rewards our interest in them.

Martha Gellhorn is without doubt remarkable for the utterly candid manner in which she understands and makes the most of her gifts. She does not try to overreach herself; she knows, none better, what she can and what she cannot do, and she keeps her fiction within the scope of her abilities. As a result she is incapable of falling disastrously flat, as is so often the way with would-be "great" writers who lack her sure self-knowledge. On the other hand, it is no good expecting her to take the kind of dangerous risk which is perhaps necessary for the production of major art. Gellhorn is modest, efficient, clever, and above all she is content to move within limits which she knows she can encompass.

Much of her ability as a novelist is bound up with her ability as a journalist, and in this respect it is worth noting that as a journalist she is first-rate. A few years ago, for example, she produced a searingly accurate and moving account of her journey to Vietnam to investigate the effect America's war was having on the unhappy people of that country. And what more than anything else comes across from her reports is her candour, her real feeling for people no matter what the colour of their skins or their political ideologies, and the openness, even perhaps acute vulnerability of her conscience. She did not produce bleeding-heart journalism—and indeed all her writing, fiction especially, is remarkable for the wry toughness of her stance towards life (a kind of controlled stoicism which it would probably be unfair to say she derived from her one-time husband, Ernest Hemingway, but which has striking affinities with his steely self-containment). But for all that, there is in her accounts of life in Vietnam a real tenderness of regard for individuals which shows how easily the novelist and journalist blend into each other. For her fiction is good in its controlled but never dispassionate observation of different people caught up in fates which they can neither control nor ignore.

In this respect *A Stricken Field* and *The Trouble I've Seen* are works in which Gellhorn's powers of judicious, sympathetic, wry, and compassionate observation of human beings are at their best. And although both suffer from what is really a muddled narrative (in neither does she manage to tell the story as well as she might), they succeed admirably in bringing home to us their touching sense of how other people live and suffer privately.

However, her most recent fiction, the collection of stories *The Weather in Africa*, although it makes use of her expected skills is, if compared to the stories of Nadine Gordimer, sadly lacking in political sophistication. Even the best of these tales do not really rise above humdrum reporting supplied by a heart-on-the-sleeve narrator.

Of all her novels it is *Liana* which seems most fully to embody her virtues and which is least marred by her faults. True, there is a suspiciously Hemingway-like handling of the dialogue—Gellhorn is always at her weakest in this area—but for the rest there is a sharpness, a truth of observation in the studies of Liana herself and of Marc that would make the novel worth reading if there were nothing else to commend it. Add to that, however, the keen feeling for atmosphere, emotional as well as environmental, and you have a fine piece of fiction, *Liana* alone assures Martha Gellhorn a respectable place among the order of good if not great novelists.

—John Lucas

GHOSE, Zulfikar. British. Born in Sialkot, Pakistan, 13 March 1935. Educated at Keele University, England, B.A. in English and philosophy 1959. Married in 1964. Cricket correspondent, *The Observer*, London, 1960–65; teacher in London, 1963–69. Since 1969, Professor of English, University of Texas, Austin. Recipient: Arts Council of Great Britain bursary, 1967. Agent: Anthony Sheil Associates Ltd., 43 Doughty Street, London WC1N 2LF, England. Address: Department of English, University of Texas, Austin, Texas 78712, U.S.A.

PUBLICATIONS

Novels

The Contradictions. London, Macmillan, 1966.
The Murder of Aziz Khan. London, Macmillan, 1967; New York, Day, 1969.
The Incredible Brazilian:
  The Native. London, Macmillan, and New York, Holt Rinehart, 1972.
  The Beautiful Empire. London, Macmillan, 1975; Woodstock, New York, Overlook Press, 1984.
  A Different World. London, Macmillan, 1978; Woodstock, New York, Overlook Press, 1985.
Crump's Terms. London, Macmillan, 1975.
The Texas Inheritance (as William Strang). London, Macmillan, 1980.
Hulme's Investigations into the Bogart Script. Austin, Texas, Curbstone Press, 1981.
A New History of Torments. New York, Holt Rinehart, and London, Hutchinson, 1982.
Don Bueno. London, Hutchinson, 1983; New York, Holt Rinehart, 1984.

Short Stories

Statement Against Corpses, with B.S. Johnson. London, Constable, 1964.

Uncollected Short Stories

"The Absences," in *Winter's Tales 14*, edited by Kevin Crossley-Holland. London, Macmillan, and New York, St. Martin's Press, 1968.

"A Translator's Fiction," in *Winter's Tales 1* (new series), edited by David Hughes. London, Constable, 1985.

Verse

The Loss of India. London, Routledge, 1964.
Jets from Orange. London, Macmillan, 1967.
The Violent West. London, Macmillan, 1972.
Penguin Modern Poets 25, with Gavin Ewart and B.S. Johnson. London, Penguin, 1974.
A Memory of Asia. Austin, Texas, Curbstone Press, 1984.

Other

Confessions of a Native-Alien (autobiography). London, Routledge, 1965.
Hamlet, Prufrock, and Language. London, Macmillan, and New York, St. Martin's Press, 1978.
The Fiction of Reality. London, Macmillan, 1983

*

Zulfikar Ghose comments:

My first novel, *The Contradictions*, begins with the words, "The Earth!" I had not thought of that during the 15 years that those words have been in print, but now, writing this in March 1981, a week before my seventh novel, *Hulme's Investigations into the Bogart Script*, is due from the printer, I realise that the earth, or, more precisely, its *landscapes*, is what I've been writing about in my fictions. *Hulme's Investigations into the Bogart Script* begins with the sentence, "Finally we arrived in the desert." And it ends with its principal character, Walt, high among the foothills of the Rockies looking down upon the land and recollecting the landscapes which constitute the idea of America in his mind.

I've tried to do different things in my several novels. In *The Murder of Aziz Khan* I was interested in writing a solid old-fashioned novel, with a strong story, to prove that I could draw so that I could be liberated from the formal constraints of the past and enjoy the freedom of creating new fictions. The next novel I wrote, *Crump's Terms* (which, however, was published eight years after it was written), was what is called "experimental" by those who believe that to give a thing a label is to have arrived at conclusive knowledge. Now, *Crump's Terms* was *about* many things; but, just as in *The Murder of Aziz Khan* I had dwelt upon the landscapes of Pakistan, so in *Crump's Terms* my obsession, in retrospect, had been the landscapes of Europe.

Then I wrote a trilogy, *The Incredible Brazilian*, which takes in 400 years of Brazilian history. But I realize now, long after having written the 1,035 pages of these three books, that it was not Brazil I was writing about so much as the idea of the land to which I myself longed to belong. Indeed, the final volume of the trilogy, *A Different World*, ends with a paragraph which begins, "come, O voyager, the voice of the tribe calls the exile home. . . ."

It is as if I wished to discover that landscape which I could call *home*. The fact is: I was born in Pakistan when Pakistan had not been created but was part of British India; and I left that part of Pakistan-to-be to live in what was India, but ruled then by the British; that my family emigrated from there to England soon after the Empire began to disintegrate; that I emigrated to the U.S.A. from England while developing, by marrying a Brazilian, an interest in South America. In each instance, even when returning to Pakistan for visit, I have remained an alien whose unconscious desire is to attach himself to a land with which he can claim an identity. The poems in my first collection of verse, *The Loss of India*, were written some years before *The Contradictions*; my obsession with landscapes in the subsequent novels is almost an attempt to make up for that *loss*. Of course, while writing the dozen or so books I've so far published I never knew that I was doing anything other than seeking an interesting way of completing the sentence which had somehow been begun by some obscure desire of the imagination.

*   *   *

Zulfikar Ghose's five stories in *Statement Against Corpses* repeatedly concern the metaphysics that unites thought with action, life with death, success with failure, aspirations with accomplishment. "The Zoo People" is the best of these. Thematically complex, linguistically assured, subtle in its evocation of character, delicate in its responses to landscape, provocative in its approach to time, it probes the mind of the English émigré Emily Minns, as she comes to terms with physical and metaphysical perception in an India alien to her upbringing. Is an animal more beautiful in the wild than in a zoo, she asks—and what happens if, taking a cage away, one discovers "primitive wildness' *instead* of beauty? Her ultimate answer arises from her increased sensitivity to Indian paradoxes and her adaptation of them to her "European Enlightenment" patterns of thought:

> Absolute barrenness was a reality with which she now felt a sympathy. There were rocks and rocks: each, whether a pebble or a boulder, was a complete, homogeneous, self-sufficient mass of matter in itself; each stood or lay in the dust at perfect peace with the universe which did no more to it than round its edges; each was there in its established place, a defiant mass of creation, magnificently aloof, without ancestry and without progeny.

Order, in other words, is within her mind's eye.

The Contradictions not only continues the metaphor of barrenness, but also structures itself on East–West logical oppositions. The "assertions" that open the book explore an Englishman's inhibited barriers against India, and India's human fecundity nonetheless. The "contradictions" that close it are set in England and pick up each theme and symbol from the first half of the book—not in order to refute them, but to complete them. The English rationalist philosophers must be blended with India's atemporality; material welfare must be glimpsed concurrently with the numenal importance of the colour of silk squares; Sylvia's English miscarriage must encourage her to appreciate what her experience of India did not directly allow: that an "area of nothingness" might possess "an odd attraction, and in this darkness, a disturbing power."

Attached ambivalently to a landscape of heart as well as a landscape of mind, Sylvia spirals towards a point of balance between antitheses. For Ghose himself, as his autobiography clearly announces, the point of balance is represented by the tenuous hyphen in "native-alien." Pakistan, India, British India, Britain, and the USA are all part of his experience, and all necessary to him, in conjunction. In another short story, "Godbert," the antithesis is conveyed by a different metaphor: "Donald ... looked at horizons whereas John examined the texture of cobblestones." Later in the story, in a similar tense vein, Ghose writes: "One chooses a way of life. Or life imposes its own pattern upon one despite onself." Such a dilemma lies at the core of Ghose's ambitious and moving novel *The Murder of Aziz Khan*, about a peasant farmer's futile effort to preserve his traditional land from industrial expansion, political roguery,

blatant thuggery, and the power of money in other people's hands.

The metaphysics of perception and cultural tension continues to preoccupy Ghose in his later novels. Though *Crump's Terms*, the reflections of a London schoolteacher, is a weak foray into wry social comedy, the three volumes of *The Incredible Brazilian* show the author to be highly imaginative. Influenced by Márquez and others, these three books—*The Native*, *The Beautiful Empire*, and *A Different World*—tell the marvelous, almost picaresque narratives of a single character named Gregório, who in a series of reincarnations is variously native, explorer, soldier, planter, merchant, marketeer, writer, and revolutionary. In writing out the three "lives" of the three books, Gregório confronts various ethical, historical, and mythological claims to both the territory and the idea of Brazil: native land, European colony, and new nation. Beyond the claim to the land lies the claim to the future, he writes, and he asks if cultural contact must necessitate corruption, if power is really man's only motivation, and in a closing and magnificently eloquent irony, if efforts to prevent violence inevitably prove destructive. This knot of abstract ideas gives the work its breadth of vision; its success derives also from Ghose's skill in telling a vivid, concrete narrative.

Even more successful are Ghose's further forays into patterns of imaginative adventure. *A New History of Torments* and *Don Bueno* take prototypical quest cycles and turn them into contemporary adventures of the psyche. *A New History of Torments* follows the life of a young man from his rural South American home to a pleasure-palace island, only to watch him destroy himself after he becomes unwittingly entangled in an incestuous love. With a related setting, *Don Bueno* watches generations of young men grow up to inherit their fate: inevitably they pursue, kill off, and then replace their fathers—secure only in their blindness to the effects of time on their own ambition. By turns poetic, comic, and dramatic, these novels are engaging narratives; they also constitute a continuing analysis of power: of its workings, and of its basis in the economics of ownership and desire.

—W.H. New

GIBBONS, Stella (Dorothea). British. Born in London, 5 January 1902. Educated at North London Collegiate School for Girls; University College, London. Married Allan Bourne Webb in 1933 (died, 1959); one daughter. Cable decoder, British United Press, 1923–25; feature writer, *Evening Standard*, London, 1926–28; drama and literary critic, *The Lady*, London, 1928–31. Recipient: Femina Vie Heureuse Prize, 1934. Fellow, Royal Society of Literature, 1950. Address: 19 Oakeshott Avenue, London N6 6NT, England.

PUBLICATIONS

Novels

Cold Comfort Farm. London, Longman, 1932; New York, Longman, 1933.
Bassett. London and New York, Longman, 1934.
Enbury Heath. London and New York, Longman, 1935.
Miss Linsey and Pa. London and New York, Longman, 1936.
Nightingale Wood. London and New York, Longman, 1938.

My American: A Romance. London, Longman, 1939; New York, Scribner, 1940.
The Rich House. London and New York, Longman, 1941.
Ticky. London and New York, Longman, 1943.
The Bachelor. London, Longman, and New York, Dodd Mead, 1944.
Westwood; or, The Gentle Powers. London, Longman, 1946; as *The Gentle Powers*, New York, Dodd Mead, 1946.
The Matchmaker. London, Longman, 1949.
The Swiss Summer. London, Longman, 1951.
Fort of the Bear. London, Longman, 1953.
The Shadow of a Sorcerer. London, Hodder and Stoughton, 1955.
Here Be Dragons. London, Hodder and Stoughton, 1956.
White Sand and Grey Sand. London, Hodder and Stoughton, 1958.
A Pink Front Door. London, Hodder and Stoughton, 1959.
The Weather at Tregulla. London, Hodder and Stoughton, 1962.
The Wolves Were in the Sledge. London, Hodder and Stoughton, 1964.
The Charmers. London, Hodder and Stoughton, 1965.
Starlight. London, Hodder and Stoughton, 1967.
The Snow-Woman. London, Hodder and Stoughton, 1969.
The Woods in Winter. London, Hodder and Stoughton, 1970.

Short Stories

Roaring Tower and Other Stories. London and New York, Longman, 1937.
Christmas at Cold Comfort Farm and Other Stories. London and New York, Longman, 1940.
Conference at Cold Comfort Farm. London, Longman, 1949.
Beside the Pearly Water. London, Nevill, 1954.

Verse

The Mountain Beast and Other Poems. London, Longman, 1930.
The Priestess and Other Poems. London and New York, Longman, 1934.
The Lowland Venus and Other Poems. London and New York, Longman, 1938.
Collected Poems. London, Longman, 1951.

Other

The Untidy Gnome (for children). London and New York, Longman, 1935.

*

Manuscript Collection: Boston University.

Stella Gibbons comments:

I think of myself as a poet, not a novelist, because I am not deeply interested in human beings, but in ideas and in Nature, and, above all, in the possible existence and nature of God. For what I may call ordinary purposes I think of myself as a moralist and a craftswoman, not as an artist, but I *enjoy* writing. I do not enjoy what may be called the peripheral circumstances attached to being a writer: reputation, literary life, meeting other writers, literary gossip. I love making what is arrogantly called "ordinary people" laugh, and perhaps giving them a happier turn of thought or even some hope. I have a strong distaste for drama and "scenes," which I believe has vitiated my powers as a novelist; my books are really a kind of bitter-sweet fairy story, all of them, though I sometimes flatter myself by calling them poetic realism.

I retired from writing novels in 1970.

*   *   *

Stella Gibbons is a prolific and talented writer whose reputation for wit was immediately established by her first novel, *Cold Comfort Farm.* This is one of the funniest examples of parody ever put into novel form; it takes on the pulp romance, the philosophy of D.H. Lawrence, the pessimism of Thomas Hardy and all those who, in praising the primitive and the rural, devalue the rational and the urbane.

Cold Comfort Farm was published in 1932. It will never date while there are literary critics of more sensibility than sense and a steady annual output of romantic novels. The heroine, Flora, encounters a Lawrence enthusiast who is writing a book to prove that Branwell Brontë is the real author of *Wuthering Heights.* Branwell's sisters, he confides, "were all drunkards, but Anne was the worst of the lot." Reluctantly, Flora accompanies him on a walk. "The stems reminded Mr. Mybug of phallic symbols and the buds made him think of nipples and virgins. Flora used sometimes to ask him the name of a tree, but he never knew." While the source material for this portrait is not known, it seems certain that Gibbons's weekly stint of book reviewing provoked such passages as the following. "Claud, who had served in the Anglo-Nicaraguan war of '46, was at his ease in the comfortable silence in which they sat, and allowed the irony and grief of his natural expression to emerge from beneath the mask of cheerful idiocy with which he usually covered his sallow, charming face."

The story of the Doom Family frequently recalls the more pessimistic episodes from the sagas of Hardy's Wessex but, at a guess, it was a novel by Mary Webb which provided the immediate inspiration. This is *Precious Bane*, a rural tale in which murder, suicide, and infanticide follow each other in quick succession. Thanks to Flora's good sense, none of these misfortunes come to the inhabitants of Cold Comfort Farm. Seth's sexual obsessions are channelled into a career in Hollywood; Elfine is dissuaded from modelling herself on St. Francis of Assisi and groomed for marriage to the local squire, Dick Hawk-Monitor. Even Aunt Ada Doom who as a child "saw something nasty in the woodshed" is restored to health and flies off to Paris in search of a wicked old age.

Since that triumph, Gibbons has sometimes returned to satire but never with such singleness of purpose; her novels are intelligent explorations of the social themes which have always provided the mainstay of English fiction. She writes about love and marriage, class, money, power, and if caricature is still a favourite method of attack, this is usually incidental to her main focus of interest. Her heroines tend to be shy single women with the selfishness that can accompany timidity. They gain self-knowledge and a greater capacity for happiness, often through contact with a group of people from a wider social circle, never without a measure of pain and disillusionment.

Society is as important in these novels as it is in the novels of Jane Austen and for the same reason; both authors believe that the most reliable assessment of character is based on close observation of social behaviour. Gibbons resembles her predecessor in many other ways. She plots her stories skilfully, allowing room for development and surprise; she enjoys putting the cat among the pigeons and confronting one set of social values with another totally opposed to it. She has a good sense of the dramatic. She has chosen one sphere of London life as a natural setting for her comedies of manners: the artistic and literary community centred on the two hills of Hampstead and Highgate. Many of her most successful novels chart this territory and its special charm, although in human terms this is shown to hide an underlying ruthlessness. The houses and streets of the area, on the other hand, provide a continuing source of pleasure. Gibbons may dislike nature worship but her evocations of Hampstead Heath in all its moods reveal her affection for London's largest stretch of countryside.

One of her best novels is *Westwood; or, The Gentle Powers*. This was published in 1946 and contains some fine descriptions of war-time London. "Weeds grew in the City itself; a hawk was seen hovering over the ruins of the Temple, and foxes raided the chicken-roosts in the gardens near Hampstead Heath." It is a dropped ration-book, appropriately enough, which provides the link between the heroine and the glamorous Niland family. Margaret is a young teacher with a great capacity for hero-worship. The ration-book which she finds and returns belongs to Hebe Niland, wife of a famous painter and daughter of a famous playwright. The Nilands exploit Margaret from the first but at the same time they educate her; she loses much of her naivety when she discovers that a distinguished playwright can also be a lecherous old man.

Margaret's story is echoed in a later novel of Hampstead life, *Here Be Dragons*, a study of egoism which shows the author at her most perceptive. Again, the heroine enters a charmed circle, at first dazzled, later disillusioned, and ultimately gains from the experience. This time the artists are poor, young, and struggling and the heroine, Nell, is a natural mother figure for them, a kind, practical girl, not unlike the Flora of *Cold Comfort Farm*. She is fascinated by the leader of the group, a writer of genuine talent and unscrupulous charm who enjoys manipulating people for his own amusement. Nell is in some danger from his influence but is saved by one brutal act of betrayal. A similar theme is handled in *The Charmers*.

Stella Gibbons has never lost her popularity as a writer of traditional, well-constructed novels. Her success is surely based on the two qualities which most characterise her work: a strong sense of moral values and an equally strong sense of fun.

—Judy Cooke

GILCHRIST, Ellen. American. Born in Vicksburg, Mississippi, 20 February 1935. Educated at Vanderbilt University, Nashville; Millsaps College, Jackson, Mississippi, B.A. 1967; University of Arkansas, Fayetteville, 1976. Has three sons. Broadcaster on National Public Radio; also journalist. Recipient: Mississippi Arts Festival poetry award, 1968; *New York Quarterly* award, for poetry, 1978; National Endowment for the Arts grant, 1979; *Prairie Schooner* award, 1981; Mississippi Academy award, 1982, 1985; Saxifrage award, 1983; American Book Award, 1985; University of Arkansas Fulbright Award, 1985. Address: 6295 Old Canton Road, Apartment 2-B, Jackson, Mississippi 39211, U.S.A.

PUBLICATIONS

Novel

The Annunciation. Boston, Little Brown, 1983; London, Faber, 1984.

Short Stories

In the Land of Dreamy Dreams: Short Fiction. Fayetteville, University of Arkansas Press, 1981; London, Faber, 1982.
Victory over Japan. Boston, Little Brown, 1984; London, Faber, 1985.

Play

Television Play: *A Season of Dreams*, from stories by Eudora Welty, 1968.

Verse

The Land Surveyor's Daughter. Fayetteville, Arkansas, Lost Road, 1979.

*   *   *

Ellen Gilchrist is one of America's best contemporary story writers. Her stories usually present a series of scenes through dialogue with relatively little narrative comment, and the stories generally close abruptly after a climactic episode. Narrators are either the main character speaking in the first person or an emotionally detached, critical, or satirical observer. Most of the stories are set in New Orleans, though some feature the rural Louisiana delta or Alabama and Mississippi locales. The presentation of the New Orleans milieu is superficial, despite her use of realistic details such as street names, restaurants, and other landmarks. Her use of stereotyped characters—Jewish lawyers who ignore their wives, country club tennis players, people who separate Jews, Catholics, and Blacks into various caste systems—does not greatly mar her sharp, satirical stories but does lessen the impact of her novel, *The Annunciation*, in which even the main character, Amanda McCamey, has too little depth to sustain a novel. Like most of Gilchrist's women, Amanda is self-centered and often destructive of herself and others, even from childhood.

The novel possesses many of the strengths of the stories: forceful individual scenes; aggressive, stubborn, reckless major characters; interesting eccentrics as minor characters; swiftly sketched scenes; and a heavy balance of dialogue. Amanda's deeply felt, authentic re-creation and revision of childhood experience in Louisiana is more compelling than her adult career at the University of Arkansas as translator of an 18th-century French woman poet, who seems at first to her to be an alter-ego—except for her Catholicism, which Amanda despises. Amanda's affair with a young hippie guitar player, who leaves for Africa after impregnating her and dies at the time his baby is being born, is not fully realized or convincing emotionally. Her dedication for the first time to someone other than herself as she holds her infant son is also unconvincing. One recognizes the intended feminist themes, but they are inadequately developed.

For the time being, then, Gilchrist's reputation rests on her superb stories, collected in two volumes: *In the Land of Dreamy Dreams*, and *Victory over Japan* which won the American Book Award. The stories achieve distinction because of their concentration, intensity, and variety and because of their authentic presentation of feminine protagonists who are aggressive and ambitious to the point of becoming destructive or self-destructive but who are also, to a degree, sympathetic figures, especially as children. Nearly all of the main characters are self-centered, and their egoism can have both positive and negative effects. The harshness of the women and the inflammatory nature of the antagonism they arouse is complicated by their vulnerability and by some feelings of guilt for what they have done.

The swift succession of scenes and the detachment of the narrator in contrast to the violence present in several of the stories are the most distinctive elements in Gilchrist's short fiction. In "Rich" a successful banker shoots through the head his pet dog, then his child, and then himself in a shocking episode. The violence is immediately undercut by the narrator's laconic concluding sentences: "A pair of deputies from the Plaquemines Parish sheriff's office found the bodies ... No one believed that much bad could happen to a nice lady like Letty Dufrechau Wilson, who never hurt a flea ... And no one, not even the district attorney of New Orleans, wanted to believe a man would shoot a $3,000 Labrador retriever sired by Super Chief out of Prestidigitation." Some stories end not in tragedy but in an ecstatic moment, as "There's a Garden in Eden." In this tale a middle-aged woman overcomes momentarily her debilitating depression when an attractive workman arrives to repair her kitchen in a heavy rain, and eventually, in a mock-heroic gesture, sweeps her through the flooded streets of New Orleans in a borrowed canoe to her childhood home and her mother.

Victory over Japan includes two sequences of especially compelling stories. The first focuses on the engaging 19-year-old Nora Jane Whittington, "a self-styled anarchist and a quick-change artist." Nora appeared in Gilchrist's first book in "The Famous Poll at Jody's Bar," where she robbed a New Orleans bar to buy a ticket to join her "fiance" in San Francisco, escaping by changing into a nun's habit and leaving the bar unnoticed. In the stories in *Victory over Japan* ("Jade Buddhas, Red Bridges, Fruits of Love" and "The Double Happiness Bun") Nora arrives in California only to find herself abandoned and broke. She attempts to hold up a music store but is comically foiled as the generous young proprietor instantly falls in love with her, takes her home, and buys her a new car. The old lover re-appears and passion flares briefly; she escapes from him, only to find herself pregnant by one of the men. In a masterful mingling of the poignant and the entertaining, Gilchrist closes the sequence with Nora enjoying her new car and her pregnancy but uncertain about which, if either, of the two men she should choose to be father for her infant.

In the other distinctive sequence, five stories—four by the same narrator—revolve around Crystal Weiss, who "manages to have a good time" while detesting both her wealthy second husband and her brother. Though she is destructive, reckless, and selfish like most of Gilchrist's other women, she attains a more sympathetic dimension by being seen through the eyes of the narrator, Traceleen, Crystal's Black maid. Three of the stories are oral monologues and the fourth, a diary excerpt. As narrator, Traceleen unconsciously reveals herself as well as Crystal and becomes the only fully developed Black person, the only passionately involved narrative observer, and almost the only happily married woman in Gilchrist's fiction. Her accounts meander, chronology becomes confused, extraneous detail sometimes predominates, and asides are frequent ("Her hangin' on every word"); but her interpretation of people and events is convincing because of her simplicity, unguardedness, and tolerance. Her mode of speaking is energetic, and she establishes a mood of authentic excitement.

Although Gilchrist occasionally reveals the influence of her southern predecessors in fiction, such as Carson McCullers, Shirley Ann Grau, Katherine Anne Porter, and Eudora Welty, she is better understood as a "new" southern writer rather than as one who works in the "tradition" of outstanding southern women of the last 50 years. She extends, for example, the subject matter of southern writing by using phenomena associated with the drug culture; she explores the ramifications of marital incompatibility and discordances in contemporary society; and she uses strong-willed and incorrigible children to a greater extent than her immediate predecessors. Among her best presentations of lying, passionate, determined little girls are some forceful stories told in first person. A child named Rhoda appears in several stories in both collections. The most engaging of these girls may be LeLe in "Traveler," who creates herself in the image of Zelda Fitzgerald during a wonderful summer visiting her cousin.

In the fiction related to the drug culture she presents child-pushers ("The President of the Louisiana Live Oak Society"), diet faddists ("The Gauzy Edge of Paradise"), depressed women addicted to multiple prescription drugs ("Crazy, Crazy, Now Showing Everywhere"), and rich and successful persons insidiously addicted to alcohol (in many stories and in *The Annunciation*). In "The Gauzy Edge of Paradise" and "Defender of the Little Falaya" Gilchrist skillfully contrasts the disorientation and hilarity induced by drugs with the dullness of the individuals' lives in their lucid states. Her controlled structure in these stories also contrasts with the erratic nature of the drug experience. Such balancing of formal elements and intensely apprehended subject material is a sign of Ellen Gilchrist's emerging and developing abilities.

—Margaret B. McDowell

GILL, Brendan. American. Born in Hartford, Connecticut, 4 October 1914. Educated at Yale University, New Haven, Connecticut, A.B. 1936. Married Anne Barnard in 1936; five daughters and two sons. Since 1936, regular contributor to *The New Yorker* magazine: film critic, 1961–67; since 1968, drama critic. President, Municipal Art Society, New York; Vice-President, Victorian Society in America, Philadelphia; Member, Board of Directors, Film Society of Lincoln Center, New York. Recipient: American Academy grant, 1951; National Book Award, 1951. Address: c/o The New Yorker, 25 West 43rd Street, New York, New York 10036, U.S.A.

PUBLICATIONS

Novels

The Trouble of One House. New York, Doubleday, 1950; London, Gollancz, 1951.
The Day the Money Stopped. New York, Doubleday, and London, Gollancz, 1957.

Short Stories

The Malcontents. New York, Harcourt Brace, 1973.
Ways of Loving: Two Novellas and Eighteen Stories. New York, Harcourt Brace, 1974; London, Joseph, 1975.

Uncollected Short Stories

"Adriance Prize," in *Saturday Evening Post* (Philadelphia), 22 February 1941.
"Together," in *Saturday Evening Post* (Philadelphia), 8 August 1941.
"Choice," in *New Yorker*, 16 August 1941.

"King Barney the First," and "All the Right People," in *Stories of School and College Life*, edited by Robert J. Cadigan. New York, Appleton, 1942.

"Scientific Mind," in *With a Merry Heart*, edited by Paul J. Phelan. New York, Longman, 1943.

"Interest in Boys," in *New Yorker*, 21 August 1943.

"Grand Old Man," in *Virginia Quarterly Review* (Charlottesville), October 1943.

"Helpmeet," in *New Yorker*, 20 November 1943.

"More Like Home," in *Cross-Section 1944*, edited by Edwin Seaver. New York, Fischer, 1944.

"Privilege," in *World's Great Tales of the Sea*, edited by William McFee. Cleveland, World, 1944.

"Will's Girl," in *Collier's* (Springfield, Ohio), 28 October 1944.

"The Test," in *The Best American Short Stories 1945*, edited by Martha Foley. Boston, Houghton Mifflin, 1945.

"Mother Coakley's Reform," in *Our Father's House*, edited by Mariella Gable. New York, Sheed and Ward, 1945.

"The Guide," in *New Yorker*, 21 April 1945.

"Fall from Grace," in *Collier's* (Springfield, Ohio), 20 December 1945.

"Fine Start," in *Collier's* (Springfield, Ohio), 9 February 1946.

"A Little Rain," in *Fireside Book of Yuletide Tales*, edited by Edward Wagenknecht. Indianapolis, Bobbs Merrill, 1948.

"Night Bus to Atlanta," in *Girls from Esquire*, edited by Frederic A. Birmingham. New York, Random House, 1952.

Play

La Belle (produced Philadelphia, 1962).

Verse

Death in April and Other Poems. Windham, Connecticut, Hawthorn House, 1935.

Wooings: Five Poems. Verona, Italy, Plain Wrapper Press, 1980.

Other

Cole: A Book of Cole Porter Lyrics and Memorabilia, with Robert Kimball. New York, Holt Rinehart, 1971; as *Cole: A Biographical Essay*, London, Joseph, 1972.

Tallulah. New York, Holt Rinehart, 1972; London, Joseph, 1973.

Happy Times, photographs by Jerome Zerbe. New York, Harcourt Brace, 1973; London, Joseph, 1974.

Here at "The New Yorker." New York, Random House, and London, Joseph, 1975.

The U.S. Custom House on Bowling Green. New York, New York Landmarks Conservancy, 1976.

Lindbergh Alone. New York, Harcourt Brace, 1977.

Summer Places, photographs by Dudley Witney. Toronto, McClelland and Stewart, and New York, Methuen, 1978.

The Dream Come True: Great Houses of Los Angeles, photographs by Derry Moore. New York, Harper, and London, Thames and Hudson, 1980.

John F. Kennedy Center for the Performing Arts. New York, Abrams, 1982.

Editor, *States of Grace: Eight Plays*, by Philip Barry. New York, Harcourt Brace, 1975.

*   *   *

A fly mounted a curtain in the sun, and
the fly's shadow mounted the shadow of
lace, like a dream threading a dream.
                    The Trouble of One House

Reversing conventional causation, Brendan Gill's novels and short stories dramatize a present that seems to create, rather than derive from, a densely textured past. Both novels ostensibly focus on immediate problems in upper-middle-class Irish Catholic families—the death of a young mother in *The Trouble of One House*, and the dispute over a father's will in *The Day the Money Stopped*. But the books reveal the past to be as alive and insistent as the present, perhaps more insistent, since in *Money* questions from the past demand solution with an urgency which transcends mere significance for the present, and the dead lawyer father compels greater interest than his son, Charlie Morrow, the protagonist. And in *House*, the nuances of the characters' previous relationships with each other not only explain their responses to Elizabeth's death, but actually seem forced into life for the first time by that death.

This creation by the present of a vital new past does not, however, totally overshadow the more conventional themes of the shaping power of the past, and its continual struggle with the present. Dependent on fragile and illusory human memory, the force of the past can nevertheless guide the present, as does the unlabelled photograph that begins and ends *House*. The last thing the dying Elizabeth sees is this picture of her children, an aid to memory at the moment her memory fades. But the photograph will dominate the father as long as his memory functions: "There was no indication of where the picture had been taken, or when, or by whom. A stranger would have been able to make nothing of it. It was just a picture of three children on a beach. But they were his children; he was theirs. From now on, he was theirs forever." Objects and places redolent with meaning from the past also stimulate conflict in the present: the dead Elizabeth's sister and mother-in-law vie for her chair at the dining table in *House*, and Charlie is intimidated by his father's office chair in *Money*. The cemetery opposite the office window has been a trysting place for as long as Charlie can remember, an image that reinforces the struggle between past and present in his own consciousness. In the story "The Cemetery" a doctor's son confronts the mingled accomplishment and futility of his father's life in a similar office opposite a symbolic cemetery. The American heroine of Gill's recent novella *The Malcontents* redefines herself through the order precariously preserved by an antique mirror, a sign of the 18th-century obsession with the elegance of a remoter past: "In the depths of the intricately carved frame of the mirror, elderly mandarins holding parasols sauntered through latticed pavilions, dreaming that they were butterflies. The mantel and the mirror—all that survived of a red-brick Georgian house in the ferny depths of Sussex—had come up at auction in London, and Claire had outbid the richest magnate in the world in order to make them hers. . . . Claire bowed to her image among the mandarins, and said, 'Well! So I am a nice person, after all!' "

Money is a tour de force creating past and present largely through dialogue during Charlie's brief visit to his father's office. (This abundant dialogue, concentrated time, and a single setting presumably facilitated Maxwell Anderson's dramatic adaptation.) But despite the technical skill of the book, *Money* suffers from Gill's failure to endow Charlie with the charm to which the other characters unvaryingly respond. Though *House* is the better novel, the supporting characters act with a vitality denied Elizabeth, who, like Browning's Pippa, merely stimulates others without herself undergoing much change or awareness. Her sister and undertaker brother-in-law perform with an arresting combination of vulgarity and pathos; Father Degnan and Monsignor Brady are dramatized with a blend of satire and compassion that rivals the best of J.F. Powers; and Elizabeth's daughter awakens to sex on the day of her mother's death in an episode sustaining a complex tone of serious irony. But these brilliant vignettes and characterizations threaten to unbalance the novel, since Elizabeth's character fails to act as a unifying force.

Though *House* is a competent, often moving, work, Gill's major accomplishments are his short stories, which escape the structural problems of the novels. Harry Carter in "Something You Just Don't Do in a Club" is a convincing version of the successful scoundrel, a figure familiar in Gill's fiction, but, like Charlie Morrow in *House*, incapable of sustaining an entire novel. Admittedly, there are some early *Saturday Evening Post* stories, "King Barney the First," "Adriance Prize," and "All the Right People," in which prep school or Yale protagonists manage, through a series of plot contrivances and unmotivated epiphanies, to avoid becoming adult versions of Charlie Morrow. But, contemporary with these works and continuing through the present are a wealth of first-rate *New Yorker* pieces, including Gill's finest, "Triumph," which undercuts, without destroying, an impoverished dowager's distorted reminiscences of an elegant past. The couple in "Helpmeet" provide a grimmer version of the relationship between the undertaker and his wife in *House*; the episode in the novel loses some of its strength to the overall diffuseness of the work, while the story preserves its power intact. "Grand Old Man," the most effective of Gill's clerical stories, dramatizes the same ambivalent struggle between religious innocence and practicality as does *House*. "Interest in Boys" portrays a girl like Elizabeth's daughter, awakening to sexuality and learning that the object of her excitement is a young priest. As in all his best fiction, Gill uses this sudden revelation to illuminate both character and the nature of religious commitment.

Like his biographies *Cole* and *Tallulah*, Gill's story "Fat Girl" and novellas "Last Things" and *The Malcontents* compassionately pursue the new theme of unconventional sexuality, its attendant violence, and its occasional delicate balances: "Jack and Fletcher would go on being lovers, Laura and Harry would go on being man and wife, and Laura and Jack would be lovers in every respect except that of sex" ("Last Things"). A continuity underlies these apparent innovations, however. Although the international theme of *The Malcontents* allows Gill to chart the wanderings of the very rich, and although the protagonists of both novellas finally transcend the family or sexual relationships that dominated their early lives (and much of Gill's early fiction), ultimately these novellas seem secularized versions of "And Holy Ghost" and other religious stories. Harry, having buried his wife, escaped the ministrations of his conventional offspring, and shot his beloved, ailing dog, is apparently ready for "Last Things," while Claire, surviving the death of her antagonist mother, the independence of her son, and the waning of her sexuality "looked forward to enjoying the emptiness for a while. . . . Long ago, she had predicted that she would be coming to the simplest things last."

—Burton Kendle

GILLIATT, Penelope (Ann Douglass, née Conner).   British. Born in London, 25 March 1932. Educated at Queen's College, London, 1942–47; Bennington College, Vermont, 1948–49. Married 1) R.W. Gilliatt in 1954 (marriage dissolved); 2) the playwright John Osborne in 1963 (divorced, 1968), one daughter. Film critic, 1961–65, 1966–67, and theatre critic, 1965–66, *The Observer*, London; film critic, *The New Yorker*, 1967–79. Recipient: American Academy award, 1971; National Society of Film Critics award, 1971; New York Film Critics award, 1971; British Film Academy award, 1972. Fellow, Royal Society of Literature, 1978. Address: c/o The New Yorker, 25 West 43rd Street, New York, New York 10036, U.S.A.

PUBLICATIONS

Novels

One by One.   London, Secker and Warburg, and New York, Atheneum, 1965.
A State of Change.   London, Secker and Warburg, 1967; New York, Random House, 1968.
The Cutting Edge.   London, Secker and Warburg, 1978; New York, Coward McCann, 1979.
Mortal Matters.   London, Macmillan, and New York, Coward McCann, 1983.

Short Stories

What's It Like Out? and Other Stories.   London, Secker and Warburg, 1968; as *Come Back If It Doesn't Get Better*, New York, Random House, 1969.
Penguin Modern Stories 5, with others.   London, Penguin, 1970.
Nobody's Business.   London, Secker and Warburg, and New York, Viking Press, 1972.
Splendid Lives.   London, Secker and Warburg, 1977; New York, Coward McCann, 1978.
Quotations from Other Lives.   London, Secker and Warburg, and New York, Coward McCann, 1982.
They Sleep Without Dreaming.   London, Macmillan, and New York, Dodd Mead, 1985.

Plays

Sunday Bloody Sunday (screenplay).   New York, Bantam, and London, Corgi, 1971.
Property, and Nobody's Business (produced New York, 1980). *Property* published in *The Women's Project: Seven New Plays by Women*, edited by Julia Miles, New York, Performing Arts Journal-American Place Theatre, 1980.
In Trust, in *New Yorker*, 14 January 1980.
Beach of Aurora, music by Tom Eastwood (produced London, 1981).
But When All's Said and Done (3 plays; produced New York, 1981).

Screenplay: *Sunday Bloody Sunday*, 1971.

Radio Play: *In the Unlikely Event of an Emergency*, 1979.

Television Plays: *The Western* (documentary); *The Method* (documentary); *Living on the Box*; *The Flight Fund*, 1975.

Other

Unholy Fools: Wits, Comics, Disturbers of the Peace. London, Secker and Warburg, and New York, Viking Press, 1973.
Jean Renoir: Essays, Conversations, and Reviews. New York, McGraw Hill, 1975.
Jacques Tati. London, Woburn Press, 1976.
Three-Quarter Face: Reports and Reflections. London, Secker and Warburg, and New York, Coward McCann, 1980.

*

Critical Studies: by Vincent Canby, in *New York Times*, 3 October 1971; Anthony Burgess, in *New York Times Book Review*, 10 September 1972; Francis Hope, in *The Observer* (London), 24 September 1972.

*   *   *

Penelope Gilliatt is a writer with impressive talents, though some would argue that she does not possess all the qualities that would entitle her to a place among major modern novelists. She is an alert observer of the modern scene, and more especially the society of the intellectuals and the gifted in the modern age, discovering much that amuses her and also, sometimes, human problems that disturb. For the most part she takes characters who are, in some way, out on the margins of everyday experience, but having created an interest in them by a ready acceptance of their quirkiness, she can then disappoint her readers who have followed a circuitous and elliptical story by declining to provide the sort of conclusion that could round everything off in a satisfactory fashion. Gilliatt seems to enjoy the odd personalities she creates and she certainly shows great virtuosity in placing them in unusual situations, yet, despite many very funny episodes and an engagingly witty way with words, there is in her novels a profound sense of malaise about contemporary life. It is plainly significant that her first novel, *One by One*, depicted the impact of a plague on modern London; not only is the populace as a whole shown as demoralised and resourceless, but Joe Talbot, who sends his pregnant wife away to safety and then endeavours to stem the onset of disaster, becomes alienated from her and eventually kills himself.

A State of Change starts by introducing the character of Kakia, a Polish girl who comes to London shortly after the war. The account of traumatic days in Warsaw in 1939 is a masterpiece of economical narration with every detail counting and nothing wasted on empty heroics, and Gilliatt is equally deft when she tells of Kakia's experiences in Moscow where nobody could understand the sophisticated satire of the cartoons she was always drawing. The chapters about Kakia's early days in London are gripping too, with culture shock neatly encapsulated in discussions between her and the editors to whom she tries unsuccessfully to sell her drawings and in her discovery of the strange world of the offices of a magazine for ladies of a certain age and class. A high point comes with an elaborate and hilarious set-piece; it is an evocation of all the contradictions and embarrassments that make up an English Christmas day when agnosts with advanced opinions find themselves self-consciously conforming to tradition as they kindly invite in a stranger. After that, attention turns to the two men she meets at the party, Don Clancy, a television executive, and Harry Clopton, a doctor. Kakia forms liaisons with each in turn, and all three remain, despite the stresses of the relationships, good friends. Where it all leads to is left as an open question, which is made all the more problematic when Harry takes Kakia up to Northumberland to meet his aunt

and uncle, old-style Socialists who live simple lives of easy domesticity.

The North-East is also the background to the basic stratum of *Mortal Matters*, and Gilliatt is sufficiently interested in the depiction of the area she grew up in to think it worthwhile printing at the end of the novel a list of books on the economic history of the region along with works on female emancipation at the beginning of the century. *Mortal Matters* begins in London with three generations of a curious, well-off family, and their opinionated servants. As usual, Gilliatt creates situations and conflicts by means of uncannily accurate conversations, and the general malaise becomes pervasive. Going back to Northumberland hints at a return to sounder values for Lady Corfe, and vivid flashbacks recall a harder, more bracing lifestyle. Implicit throughout the book is a comparison between the convictions of a former age and the present day when material improvements are discovered to have brought little solace in a world that seems to lack purpose.

Just as *Mortal Matters* juxtaposes generations *The Cutting Edge* explores the lives of two brothers who, though they certainly do not go their ways in parallel, never really part. Peregrine Corbett is a highly articulate journalist who enjoys controversy, while Benedick, of a more reflective nature, is a musician who makes something of a living by playing the harpsichord on ships that take tourists for cruises around the archaeological sights of the Eastern Mediterranean. In this, as in both brothers' dallying in a villa on the shores of the Bosphorus, Penelope Gilliatt displays an almost baroque fancy, and there is some indulgence in rather easy comedy, though they would be stony-hearted readers who did not laugh. As well as containing vintage samples of Gilliatt's brilliant handling of conversation, *The Cutting Edge* makes great play of the exchange of letters, in almost 18th-century style, as a device for portraying characters who, for various reasons, are kept far apart. The link that is gradually formed between them, reinforcing the sympathies of kinship, is Joanna who first marries Benedick and then becomes Peregrine's mistress in a relationship which, so it seems at the end, will be found satisfactory by all concerned. Immensely entertaining, even if sometimes a little too obvious in setting up its jokes, and sharply accurate in its observation of modern manners, despite some liking for the peculiar, *The Cutting Edge* is at one and the same time entertaining and worrying. But, as with Gilliatt's other novels, the problem is to reconcile the apparently disparate elements brought together with such evident intelligence and made vivid and persuasive with such great skill.

—Christopher Smith

GLANVILLE, Brian (Lester). British. Born in London, 24 September 1931. Educated at Newlands School; Charterhouse School, Surrey, 1945–49. Married Pamela De Boer in 1959; two sons and two daughters. Literary Adviser, Bodley Head, publishers, London, 1958–62. Since 1958, sportswriter for *The Sunday Times*, London. Recipient: Berlin Film Festival award, for documentary, 1963; British Film Academy award, for documentary, 1967; Thomas Coward Memorial Award, 1969; Sports Council Reporter of the Year Award, 1982. Agent: John Farquharson Ltd., 162–168 Regent Street, London W1R 5TB. Address: 160 Holland Park Avenue, London W.11, England.

PUBLICATIONS

Novels

The Reluctant Dictator.   London, Laurie, 1952.
Henry Sows the Wind.   London, Secker and Warburg, 1954.
Along the Arno.   London, Secker and Warburg, 1956; New York, Crowell, 1957.
The Bankrupts.   London, Secker and Warburg, and New York, Doubleday, 1958.
After Rome, Africa.   London, Secker and Warburg, 1959.
Diamond.   London, Secker and Warburg, and New York, Farrar Straus, 1962.
The Rise of Gerry Logan.   London, Secker and Warburg, 1963; New York, Delacorte Press, 1965.
A Second Home.   London, Secker and Warburg, 1965; New York, Delacorte Press, 1966.
A Roman Marriage.   London, Joseph, 1966; New York, Coward McCann, 1967.
The Artist Type.   London, Cape, 1967; New York, Coward McCann, 1968.
The Olympian.   New York, Coward McCann, and London, Secker and Warburg, 1969.
A Cry of Crickets.   London, Secker and Warburg, and New York, Coward McCann, 1970.
The Financiers.   London, Secker and Warburg, 1972; as *Money Is Love*, New York, Doubleday, 1972.
The Comic.   London, Secker and Warburg, 1974; New York, Stein and Day, 1975.
The Dying of the Light.   London, Secker and Warburg, 1976.
Never Look Back.   London, Joseph, 1980.
Kissing America.   London, Blond, 1985.

Short Stories

A Bad Streak and Other Stories.   London, Secker and Warburg, 1961.
The Director's Wife and Other Stories.   London, Secker and Warburg, 1963.
Goalkeepers Are Crazy: A Collection of Football Stories.   London, Secker and Warburg, 1964.
The King of Hackney Marshes and Other Stories.   London, Secker and Warburg, 1965.
A Betting Man.   New York, Coward McCann, 1969.
Penguin Modern Stories 10, with others.   London, Penguin, 1972.
The Thing He Loves and Other Stories.   London, Secker and Warburg, 1973.
A Bad Lot and Other Stories.   London, Penguin, 1977.
Love Is Not Love and Other Stories.   London, Blond, 1985.

Plays

A Visit to the Villa (produced Chichester, Sussex, 1981).
Underneath the Arches, with Patrick Garland and Roy Hudd (produced Chichester, Sussex, 1981; London, 1982).

Screenplay (documentary): *Goal!*, 1967.

Television Documentary: *European Centre Forward*, 1963.

Other

Cliff Bastin Remembers, with Cliff Bastin.   London, Ettrick Press, 1950.
Arsenal Football Club.   London, Convoy, 1952.

Soccer Nemesis.   London, Secker and Warburg, 1955.
World Cup, with Jerry Weinstein.   London, Hale, 1958.
Over the Bar, with Jack Kelsey.   London, Paul, 1958.
Soccer round the Globe.   London, Abelard Schuman, 1959.
Know about Football (for children).   London, Blackie, 1963.
World Football Handbook (annual).   London, Hodder and Stoughton, 1964; London, Mayflower, 1966–72; London, Queen Anne Press, 1974.
People in Sport.   London, Secker and Warburg, 1967.
Soccer: A History of the Game, Its Players, and Its Strategy.   New York, Crown, 1968; as *Soccer: A Panorama*, London, Eyre and Spottiswoode, 1969.
The Puffin Book of Football (for children).   London, Penguin, 1970; revised edition, 1984.
Goalkeepers Are Different (for children).   London, Hamish Hamilton, 1971; New York, Crown, 1972.
Brian Glanville's Book of World Football.   London, Dragon, 1972.
The Sunday Times History of the World Cup.   London, Times Newspapers, 1973; as *History of the Soccer World Cup*, New York, Macmillan, 1974; revised edition, as *The History of the World Cup*, London, Faber, 1980, 1984.
Soccer 76.   London, Queen Anne Press, 1975.
Target Man (for children).   London, Macdonald and Jane's, 1978.
The Puffin Book of Footballers.   London, Penguin, 1978; revised edition, as *Brian Glanville's Book of Footballers*, 1982.
A Book of Soccer.   New York, Oxford University Press, 1979.
Kevin Keegan (for children).   London, Hamish Hamilton, 1981.
The Puffin Book of Tennis (for children).   London, Penguin, 1981.
The Puffin Book of the World Cup (for children).   London, Penguin, 1984.
The British Challenge (on the Los Angeles Olympics team), with Kevin Whitney.   London, Muller, 1984.

Editor, *Footballer's Who's Who*.   London, Ettrick Press, 1951.
Editor, *The Footballer's Companion*.   London, Eyre and Spottiswoode, 1962.

*

Critical Study: "Khaki and God the Father" in *A Human Idiom* by William Walsh, London, Chatto and Windus, 1965.

Brian Glanville comments:
    (1972) There has, I suppose, been some tendency to categorise my work under three headings; that which deals with Italy (*Along the Arno, A Cry of Crickets, A Roman Marriage*), that which deals with Jewish life (*The Bankrupts, Diamond*), and that which deals with professional football (*The Rise of Gerry Logan* and many of the short stories). I think I might accept the categorisation of the two Jewish novels, but it scarcely places *The Olympian*, which uses an athlete as its figure, athletics as its theme, or rather as its metaphor; or *A Second Home*, which is narrated in the first person by a Jewish actress—and has been bracketed with *A Roman Marriage*, itself narrated by a young girl. Again, one can, and does, use similar material for widely different purposes.
    A large disenchantment with the conventional novel and its possibilities has, I think, led one gradually away from it, to more experimental methods. Like many novelists of serious intentions, one lives uneasily from one novel to the elusive

next, always questioning and trying to establish the validity of the form.

*   *   *

Brian Glanville has written of his novels that "large disenchantment with the conventional novel ... has, I think, led one gradually away from it, to more experimental methods." Each novel from this prolific writer has demonstrated that impatience; his need to break away from the manners of the traditional novel and from its central narrative line to a more fluid exposition of his thought has meant that the action frequently unfolds through his characterisation instead of through the plot. In *A Roman Marriage* the story is told by the young English girl who has allowed herself to be trapped into a futile, claustrophobic marriage to a handsome young Italian; and through her outraged consciousness we experience, too, the suffocation of her husband's clinging, over-protective mother as the tentacles of family life cut the girl off from reality and draw her in to nightmare. Similarly the tensions and cabalistic integrity of the family are strikingly unfolded in his Jewish novels such as *The Bankrupts*, *Diamond*, and *A Second Home*.

A further strength of the novels in this latter group is Glanville's sure ear for the cadences of everyday speech. The Jewish patois is never forced to gain its effect through comic music-hall over-indulgence but is allowed to expose itself through Glanville's feeling for the poetic possibilities of the spoken language. Although the unforced ease of his dialogue gives it a down-to-earth integrity, Glanville never allows it to become mundane or demeaning, and the simplicity of effect is a structural strength of all his writing.

As a commentator on professional sport Glanville has also written several novels about the stamina and passion that make up the modern athlete. In *The Olympian* a young miler, Ike Low, is torn between his passion for his wife Jill and the almost sexual release that he finds in winning races. Against their uneasy relationship stands the ambiguous figure of Sam Dee, Ike's trainer, who acts as both agent provocateur and chorus over their slowly disintegrating marriage. The narrative is broken up with journalese and taut, film-like dialogue as the drama of Ike's racing career draws to an unexpected climax. *The Dying of the Light* is perhaps Glanville's most profound and satisfying sporting novel to date. Although it is described as "a football novel," it is in effect a parable of contemporary life. Len Rawlings, a footballing hero in the post-war years, slumps gradually to the bottom of the ladder in a world where the aged and the losers are quickly forgotten. In desperation he turns to petty crime but finds salvation in the love of his daughter, so unlike him in character, but the only one to understand the terrifying loneliness of his personal predicament. As in all Glanville's novels, the moralising is made manifest by its absence—Rawlings may have broken the law but it is the law of the jungle that is at fault, the "sporting" code that allows a talented man to be driven to despair through no fault of his own.

Contemporary obsessions of another kind are examined in *Never Look Back*, a novel that explores the world of rock and roll bands and the attitudes of its denizens: the stars, their managers and hangers-on, the agents and the crooks. The documentary detail is impressive but Glanville's mastery of language and skillful handling of dialogue convey subtle shifts of feeling, and they also constantly change his and the reader's focus on this kaleidoscopic world. Above all, Brian Glanville shows that he is one of the few contemporary novelists capable of tackling and expressing the values, or lack of them, in our rapidly changing society.

—Trevor Royle

GLOAG, Julian. British. Born in London, 2 July 1930; son of the writer John Gloag. Educated at Rugby School, Warwickshire; Magdalene College, Cambridge. Served in the British Army, 1949–50. Married Danielle Haase-Dubosc in 1968; one son and one daughter. Researcher, *Chambers's Encyclopaedia*, London, 1954–56; assistant editor, Ronald Press, New York, 1956–59; editor, Hawthorn Books, New York, 1961–63. Fellow, Royal Society of Literature, 1970. Lives in Paris. Agent: Georges Borchardt Inc., 136 East 57th Street, New York, New York 10022, U.S.A.; Richard Scott Simon Ltd., 32 College Cross, London N1 1PR, England; Michelle Lapautre, 6 rue Jean Carriès, 75007 Paris, France.

PUBLICATIONS

Novels

Our Mother's House. New York, Simon and Schuster, and London, Secker and Warburg, 1963.
A Sentence of Life. New York, Simon and Schuster, and London, Secker and Warburg, 1966.
Maundy. New York, Simon and Schuster, and London, Secker and Warburg, 1969.
A Woman of Character. New York, Random House, and London, Weidenfeld and Nicolson, 1973.
Sleeping Dogs Lie. London, Secker and Warburg, and New York, Dutton, 1980.
Lost and Found. New York, Linden Press, and London, Secker and Warburg, 1981.
Blood for Blood. London, Hamish Hamilton, and New York, Holt Rinehart, 1985.

Play

Television Play: *Darley's Folly*, 1986.

Other

The American Nation: A Short History of the United States (revised edition), with John Gloag. London, Cassell, 1955.

*   *   *

Julian Gloag is a writer of diverse talents: he can bring the reader into close contact with a variety of characters through the precise creation of patterns of speech and thought; he has a wit that shows itself not only verbally—"I been livin' in a foolish paradise"—but in the choice of extraordinary incident and the use of ironic juxtaposition; he can handle interweaving threads of narrative skilfully, giving each one room to tug at our moral and emotional sympathies. He keeps us alert and busy, and as a result most of his books are extremely readable.

His first novel, *Our Mother's House*, is in many ways his most successful, having a form of its own, something that the later novels fail to achieve. The book is shaped and dominated by the contrast between the delicate morbidity of its opening chapters, in which a family of children bury their mother's body secretly in the garden, and the subsequent cheerful, only gradually suspicious, homecoming of their long absent father. The book's main impact is in line with this contrast. We are made to see the children as both peculiar and normal, their father as repellent yet, on his own terms, justified. We ourselves are manoeuvred into an ambiguous position by the novel's tone: it encourages us to sympathise yet establishes us as adult and therefore hostile.

A Sentence of Life is given external shape and purpose by its association with the traditional forms of murder enquiry and trial, but the important movement of the book is introspective and fluid as the suspect pursues private definitions of guilt by remembering and reinterpreting his past. Looked at coolly, the lines of the book don't converge as neatly as its final pages, which use the warmth of selected memories to promote an optimistic conclusion, suggest. The novel's discussion of responsibility and its imaginative range are nevertheless good. Again the reader is not permitted to sympathise or dislike too easily and judgment remains uncertain.

Maundy is uncertain in a different way. Maundy is a smooth young banker who goes off the rails: whether this is due to psychological stress or actual devils is one of the things we are left to decide for ourselves. Unfortunately no way of looking at the book makes sense of it. Whereas Gloag's other books present conflicting accounts of reality, this one presents a chaos heavy with sex and violence and lumpy with significance. It's a tale of sound and fury that's not much fun to read.

With *A Woman of Character* Gloag returned to familiar ground. A corpse gets things off to a brisk start and financial negotiations, detective elements and the bereaved fiancée's search for consolation keep up the pace. The book is again concerned with the distribution of sympathy and guilt; it has a sense of some of the ways women feel and a warming portrayal of the rich life. Gloag's work remains interesting, intelligent, and inventive but one cannot see it as important.

—Mary Conroy

GODDEN, (Margaret) Rumer. British. Born in Sussex, 10 December 1907. Educated privately and at Moira House, Eastbourne, Sussex. Married 1) Laurence Sinclair Foster in 1934 (died), two daughters; 2) James Lesley Haynes Dixon in 1949 (died, 1973). Director of a children's ballet school, Calcutta, in the 1930's. Recipient: Whitbread Award, for children's book, 1973. Agent: Curtis Brown, 162–168 Regent Street, London W1R 5TA, England; or, 10 Astor Place, New York, New York 10003, U.S.A. Address: Ardnacloich, Moniaive, Thornhill, Dumfries and Galloway DG3 4HZ, Scotland.

PUBLICATIONS

Novels

Chinese Puzzle. London, Davies, 1936.
The Lady and the Unicorn. London, Davies, 1937.
Black Narcissus. London, Davies, and Boston, Little Brown, 1939.
Gypsy, Gypsy. London, Davies, and Boston, Little Brown, 1940.
Breakfast with the Nikolides. London, Davies, and Boston, Little Brown, 1942.

A Fugue in Time. London, Joseph, 1945; as *Take Three Tenses: A Fugue in Time*, Boston, Little Brown, 1945.
The River. London, Joseph, and Boston, Little Brown, 1946.
A Candle for St. Jude. London, Joseph, and New York, Viking Press, 1948.
A Breath of Air. London, Joseph, 1950; New York, Viking Press, 1951.
Kingfishers Catch Fire. London, Macmillan, and New York, Viking Press, 1953.
An Episode of Sparrows. New York, Viking Press, 1955; London, Macmillan, 1956.
The Greengage Summer. London, Macmillan, and New York, Viking Press, 1958.
China Court: The Hours of a Country House. London, Macmillan, and New York, Viking Press, 1961.
The Battle of the Villa Fiorita. London, Macmillan, and New York, Viking Press, 1963.
In This House of Brede. London, Macmillan, and New York, Viking Press, 1969.
The Peacock Spring. London, Macmillan, 1975; New York, Viking Press, 1976.
Five for Sorrow, Ten for Joy. London, Macmillan, and New York, Viking Press, 1979.
The Dark Horse. London, Macmillan, 1981; New York, Viking Press, 1982.
Thursday's Children. London, Macmillan, and New York, Viking, 1984.

Short Stories

Mooltiki and Other Stories and Poems of India. London, Macmillan, and New York, Viking Press, 1957.
Swans and Turtles: Stories. London, Macmillan, 1968; as *Gone: A Thread of Stories*, New York, Viking Press, 1968.

Fiction (for children)

The Dolls' House, London, Joseph, 1947; New York, Viking Press, 1948; as *Tottie*, London, Penguin, 1983.
The Mousewife. London, Macmillan, and New York, Viking Press, 1951.
Four Dolls. London, Macmillan, 1983; New York, Greenwillow, 1984.
Impunity Jane: The Story of a Pocket Doll. New York, Viking Press, 1954; London, Macmillan, 1955.
The Fairy Doll. London, Macmillan, and New York, Viking Press, 1956.
The Story of Holly and Ivy. London, Macmillan, and New York, Viking Press, 1958.
Candy Floss. London, Macmillan, and New York, Viking Press, 1960.
Mouse House. New York, Viking Press, 1957; London, Macmillan, 1958.
Miss Happiness and Miss Flower. London, Macmillan, and New York, Viking Press, 1961.
Little Plum. London, Macmillan, and New York, Viking Press, 1963.
Home Is the Sailor. London, Macmillan, New York, Viking Press, 1964.
The Kitchen Madonna. London, Macmillan, and New York, Viking Press, 1967.
Operation Sippacik. London, Macmillan, and New York, Viking Press, 1969.
The Old Woman Who Lived in a Vinegar Bottle. London, Macmillan, and New York, Viking Press, 1972.

The Diddakoi. London, Macmillan, and New York, Viking Press, 1972.
Mr. McFadden's Hallowe'en. London, Macmillan, and New York, Viking Press, 1975.
The Rocking Horse Secret. London, Macmillan, 1977; New York, Viking Press, 1978.
A Kindle of Kittens. London, Macmillan, 1978; New York, Viking Press, 1979.
The Dragon of Og. London, Macmillan, and New York, Viking Press, 1981.
The Valiant Chatti-Maker. London, Macmillan, and New York, Viking Press, 1983.

Plays

Screenplays: *The River*, with Jean Renoir, 1951; *Innocent Sinners*, with Neil Patterson, 1958.

Verse (for children)

In Noah's Ark. London, Joseph, and New York, Viking Press, 1949.
St. Jerome and the Lion. London, Macmillan, and New York, Viking Press, 1961.

Other

Rungli-Rungliot (Thus Far and No Further). London, Davies, 1943; as *Rungli-Rungliot Means in Paharia, Thus Far and No Further*, Boston, Little Brown, 1946; as *Thus Far and No Further*, London, Macmillan, 1961.
Bengal Journey: A Story of the Part Played by Women in the Province 1939–1945. London, Longman, 1945.
Hans Christian Andersen: A Great Life in Brief. London, Hutchinson, and New York, Knopf, 1955.
Two under the Indian Sun (autobiography), with Jon Godden. London, Macmillan, and New York, Knopf, 1966.
The Tale of the Tales: The Beatrix Potter Ballet. London, Warne, 1971.
Shiva's Pigeons: An Experience of India, with Jon Godden. London, Chatto and Windus, and New York, Viking Press, 1972.
The Butterfly Lions: The Story of the Pekingese in History, Legend, and Art. London, Macmillan, 1977; New York, Viking Press, 1978.
Gulbadan: Portrait of a Rose Princess at the Mughal Court. London, Macmillan, 1980; New York, Viking Press, 1981.

Editor, *Round the Day, Round the Year, The World Around: Poetry Programmes for Classroom or Library.* London, Macmillan, 6 vols., 1966–67.
Editor, *A Letter to the World: Poems for Young Readers*, by Emily Dickinson. London, Bodley Head, 1968; New York, Macmillan, 1969.
Editor, *Mrs. Manders' Cookbook*, by Olga Manders. London, Macmillan, and New York, Viking Press, 1968.
Editor, *The Raphael Bible.* London, Macmillan, and New York, Viking Press, 1970.

Translator, *Prayers from the Ark* (verse), by Carmen de Gasztold. New York, Viking Press, 1962; London, Macmillan, 1963.
Translator, *The Creatures' Choir* (verse), by Carmen de Gasztold. New York, Viking Press, 1965; as *The Beasts' Choir*, London, Macmillan, 1967.

*

Manuscript Collection: Mugar Memorial Library, Boston University.

Critical Study: *Rumer Godden* by Hassell A. Simpson, New York, Twayne, 1973.

*   *   *

Rumer Godden inherited a love of language from her philologist father. In whatever vein of fiction she writes—and there have been several—her work is informed with a loving sense of the color and shape and rhythm of the words she chooses. It is not surprising that she is also a poet and has published two narratives in verse: *In Noah's Ark* and *St. Jerome and the Lion.*

The traditional novel of individual lives, however, is her natural medium. She thinks as a novelist. When she came to collect some of her short stories (*Swans and Turtles*), she chose to string them together as a "thread," with notes to tell how they had arisen from remembered incidents in her own life. In this sense her novels, too, can be seen to reflect her autobiography.

Three themes, which sometimes interweave, have predominated in the novels and stories: the lives of foreigners in an exotic land (she grew up in India and has often returned there); the religious life (paralleling her own conversion to Roman Catholicism); and the secret lives and thoughts of children viewing their elders through their own fresh eyes. From the latter grows a fourth theme, of imaginative and playful fantasy, which is particularly evident in her many books for children but also occurs in such a novel as *A Breath of Air*, her modern version of *The Tempest.*

In evaluating her novels, one is inclined to give most critical weight, in the Indian group, to *Breakfast with the Nikolides*, a poignantly perceptive study of inter-racial relations, and the beautiful short novel, *The River*, about a childhood tragedy in the mysterious aura of Indian tradition (which she helped Jean Renoir to make into an exceptional motion picture). Experimentally, *China Court*, evoking an English household through several generations with its sense of past and present running concurrently, is perhaps the most interesting. She had earlier tried a similar experiment, less successfully, in *A Fugue in Time*, set in wartime London. Among the books with a religious theme, *In This House of Brede* has the peculiar fascination of a special way of life (a contemporary English Catholic nunnery) show in intimate detail. She completed it in Lamb House at Rye, the long-time home of Henry James where she lived for some years by invitation of its owners, the British National Trust.

The public at large has most loved *Black Narcissus*, about an Anglican sisterhood in India, written before her conversion; *An Episode of Sparrows*, a tender story of street-urchins in London; and *The Greengage Summer*, a mystery involving a family of English children on their own in a French hotel. All three became successful motion pictures.

She writes her adult novels at long intervals, with time for reflection while children's books and lesser writings continue. More recently, *The Peacock Spring* was a shorter work of young love between an English girl and a native boy in India. *Five for Sorrow, Ten for Joy*, came ten years after *Brede*. It renewed the theme of devoted convent life, but in another country, France, and with something quite unexpected added: before the convent came life in a Paris brothel, a murder that might appear as a crime of passion, and years of penitence in a women's prison. In terms of rather ordinary humans, though often in unusual situations, Rumer Godden wins sympathy by dealing thoughtfully and hopefully with some persistent verities.

—Marshall A. Best

GODFREY, Dave. Canadian. Born in Winnipeg, Manitoba, 9 August 1938. Educated at Harvard University, Cambridge, Massachusetts, 1957; University of Toronto, 1957–58; University of Iowa, Iowa City, 1958–60, 1963, 1965–66, B.A. 1960, M.F.A. 1963, Ph.D. 1966; Stanford University, California, 1960–61, M.A. 1963; University of Chicago, 1965. Married Ellen Swartz in 1963; two sons and one daughter. Acting Head of the English Department, Adisadel College, Cape Coast, Ghana, 1963–65; Assistant Professor of English, 1966–68 and 1969–74, and Visiting Professor, 1975–76, Trinity College, Toronto; Writer-in-Residence, Erindale College, Toronto, 1973–74; Visiting Professor, 1974–75, and Associate Professor of English, 1976–77, York University, Toronto. Associate Professor and Head of the Creative Writing Department, 1977–82, and since 1982 Professor of English, University of Victoria, British Columbia. Co-founder, House of Anansi, publishers, Toronto, 1966–70; general editor, Canadian Writers series, McClelland and Stewart, publishers, Toronto, 1968–72; co-founding editor, New Press, Toronto, 1969–73; fiction editor, *Canadian Forum*, Toronto, 1971–72. Since 1972, editor, Press Porcépic, Erin, Ontario, later Victoria, British Columbia; since 1982, Vice-President, Inter-Provincial Association for Telematics and Telidon. President, Association of Canadian Publishers, 1972–73. Recipient: University of Western Ontario President's Medal, 1965; Canada Council award, 1969; Governor-General's award, 1971. Address: Press Porcépic, 235–560 Johnson Street, Victoria, British Columbia V8W 3C6, Canada.

PUBLICATIONS

Novel

The New Ancestors.   Toronto, New Press, 1970.

Short Stories

Death Goes Better with Coca-Cola.   Toronto, Anansi, 1967.
New Canadian Writing 1968, with Clark Blaise and Lewis Stein. Toronto, Clarke Irwin, 1969.
Dark Must Yield.   Erin, Ontario, Press Porcépic, 1978.

Other

I Ching Kanada.   Erin, Ontario, Press Porcépic, 1976.
The Telidon Book.   Victoria, British Columbia, Press Porcépic, 1981; Reston, Virginia, Reston Publishing, 1982.
The Elements of CAL: The How-To Book on Computer-Aided Learning, with Sharon Sterling.   Victoria, British Columbia, Press Porcépic, 1982.
Computer-Aided Learning Using the NATAL Language, with Jack Brahan.   Victoria, British Columbia, Press Porcépic, 1984.

Editor, with Bill McWhinney, *Man Deserves Man.*   Toronto, Ryerson Press, 1967.
Editor, *Gordon to Watkins to You.*   Toronto, New Press, 1970.

Editor, with Robert Fulford and Abraham Rotstein, *Read Canadian: A Book about Canadian Books.*   Toronto, Lorimer, 1972.
Editor, with Douglas Parkhill, *Gutenberg Two.*   Erin, Ontario, Press Porcépic, 1979; 4th edition, 1984.

*

Critical Studies: article by Dorah Hood, in *Oxford Companion to Canadian History and Literature* edited by Norah Story, Toronto, New York, and London, Oxford University Press, 1967; by Margaret Laurence, in *Ellipse* (Quebec), Fall 1970, and in *Mysterious East* (Fredericton, New Brunswick), December 1970; Phyllis Grosskurth, in *Canadian Forum* (Toronto), April 1971; *Sex and Violence in the Canadian Novel* by John Moss, Toronto, McClelland and Stewart, 1977.

Dave Godfrey comments:

I am most interested in that portion of literature where myth meets social realities; literary dogma concerning the purity of fantasy or of realism does not interest me. The Canadian environment has influenced me greatly although I write mainly about people from cultures other than my own. A good part of my twenties was spent travelling about the U.S. and Africa. I strive for great complexity in my writing because that is how I find life; I do not believe the writer has a duty to simplify or interpret life for his readers; his major tasks are to be as intelligent as possible and to take flights of imagination into bodies, minds, and situations other than his own.

*   *   *

In both its form and content Dave Godfrey's fiction reflects the nationalistic political stance that colours his career. As an emerging writer in the 1960's, Godfrey initiated several attempts to define Canadian literary consciousness through policies affecting the publishing industry and through fiction that addressed the issue of foreign influence in Canada. His activities in publishing, including the founding of House of Anansi Press, New Press, and Press Porcépic, as well as the controversial *Gordon to Watkins to You: A Documentary of the Battle for Control of the Canadian Economy*, testified to his early commitment to fostering a national literature by increasing awareness of Canadian writing and culture. More recently, he has become involved in writing about new communication modes, an interest that has prompted him to theorize about the impact of computer and electronic technology on contemporary society.

As this brief description of Godfrey's changing concerns may suggest, he is a writer committed to questioning and to change. In his fiction this commitment makes him an innovator in the best sense of the word. His stories are marked by the characteristics associated with the French *nouveau roman* and with metafictional theories of narrative. Godfrey consistently undermines conventional notions of plot, characterization, and narrative perspective. He juxtaposes time frames, intercuts settings, reveals character through flashback and fantasy, and allows his stories to be told from several points of view which inevitably contradict each other and force the reader to question the narrative act itself. Godfrey's experimentation, however, is not purely formal, since each of his works can be interpreted, implicitly and explicitly, as bearing on his understanding of Canada and what he perceives to be the various predicaments involving the nation.

His experimental, nationalistic stance is suggested by the title of his first collection of stories, *Death Goes Better with*

Coca-Cola, a book that explores the connection between American Coca-Cola culture and death—a death that Godfrey writes against in a series of densely-textured tales about various forms of life-giving liberation. The first of these stories—and certainly the one most widely anthologized—is "The Hard-Headed Collector," an intricate examination of the conflict between a symbolic group of (extinct) Canadian artists attempting to locate themselves in the midst of a pervading American influence on the arts, embodied in the person of an art collector who has sold out to American power and patronage. All of the stories in the collection are subtle and complex, and all rely for their interpretation on an understanding of the murder metaphor that pervades the book: the numerous killers we encounter are Americans or foreigners and therefore threats to an independent and "alive" Canada.

Godfrey's only novel, *The New Ancestors*, is a brilliant Canadian *nouveau roman* set in Ghana. Although the book is set abroad, it is clear that Godfrey saw in an African struggle for independence important parallels with Canada's desire for a similar independence from foreign control. Thus the novel can be read in allegorical terms. But it can also be appreciated for Godfrey's experiments with perspective, in that the story is told from four vastly different viewpoints which must be interpreted individually and collectively before the tragic story can emerge. *The New Ancestors* is not easy reading, but it rewards careful study and demonstrates Godfrey's ability to evoke atmosphere and human emotion with subtlety and power.

I Ching Kanada, which must be doubly read as "I Sing Canada," is a series of prose-poem meditations based on the hexagrams of the *I Ching*, a source that also informs *Death Goes Better with Coca-Cola*. The book presents no final message or overall coherence because Godfrey is interested in exploring the relationship between chance and the movement toward nationhood. If the meditations are also seen as reflections on selfhood, as some commentators have suggested, then *I Ching Kanada* becomes a metafictional text through which Godfrey reveals himself, his fiction, and the relationship he sees between the two.

Dark Must Yield, Godfrey's most recent work of fiction, is also highly experimental, but here he returns to the short story mode familiar to readers of his first collection. The stories, however, are more compressed, less overtly political, and more subtly structured than those in the earlier volume, perhaps because Godfrey chose to emphasize psychological, rather than social processes. In one of the first assessments of Godfrey's work, published in 1974, Frank Davey reached a conclusion that still applies today. He found that Godfrey's involvement with contemporary theories of art and communications has created for him "a deserved reputation as a resourceful and uncompromising prose experimenter."

—Robert Lecker

GODWIN, Gail (Kathleen). American. Born in Birmingham, Alabama, 18 June 1937. Educated at Peace Junior College, Raleigh, North Carolina, 1955–57; University of North Carolina, Chapel Hill, 1957–59, B.A. in journalism 1959; University of Iowa, Iowa City, 1967–71, M.A. 1968, Ph.D. in English 1971. Married 1) Douglas Kennedy in 1960 (divorced); 2) Ian Marshall in 1965 (divorced, 1966). Reporter, Miami *Herald*, 1959–60; consultant, U.S. Travel Service,

United States Embassy, London, 1962–65; researcher, *Saturday Evening Post*, New York, 1966; Instructor in English, 1967–70, and lecturer at the Writers Workshop, 1972–73, University of Iowa; Instructor and Fellow, Center for Advanced Studies, University of Illinois, Urbana, 1971–72; American Specialist, United States Information Service, Brazil, 1976; lecturer, Vassar College, Poughkeepsie, New York, 1977, and Columbia University, New York, 1978, 1981. Recipient: National Endowment for the Arts grant, 1974, and fellowship, for libretto, 1978; Guggenheim fellowship, 1975; St. Lawrence Award, 1976; American Academy award, 1981. Agent: John Hawkins and Associates, 71 West 23rd Street, Suite 1600, New York, New York 10010. Address: R.D. 1, Box 248, Woodstock, New York 12498, U.S.A.

PUBLICATIONS

Novels

The Perfectionists. New York, Harper, 1970; London, Cape, 1971.
Glass People. New York, Knopf, 1972.
The Odd Woman. New York, Knopf, 1974; London, Cape, 1975.
Violet Clay. New York, Knopf, and London, Gollancz, 1978.
A Mother and Two Daughters. New York, Viking Press, and London, Heinemann, 1982.
The Finishing School. New York, Viking, and London, Heinemann, 1985.

Short Stories

Dream Children. New York, Knopf, 1976; London, Gollancz, 1977.
Mr. Bedford and the Muses. New York, Viking Press, 1983; London, Heinemann, 1984.

Uncollected Short Stories

"Fate of Fleeing Maidens," in *Mademoiselle* (New York), May 1978.
"The Unlikely Family," in *Redbook* (New York), August 1979.
"Over the Mountain," in *Antaeus* (New York), 1983.

Plays

The Last Lover, music by Robert Starer (produced Katonah, New York, 1975).
Journals of a Songmaker, music by Robert Starer (produced Philadelphia, 1976).
Apollonia, music by Robert Starer (produced Minneapolis, 1979).

Recording: *Anna Margarita's Will* (song cycle), music by Robert Starer, C.R.I., 1980.

Other

Editor, with Shannon Ravenel, *The Best American Short Stories 1985*. Boston, Houghton Mifflin, 1985.

*

Manuscript Collection: Southern Collection, University of North Carolina Library, Chapel Hill.

Critical Studies: "*The Odd Woman*: Literature and the Retreat from Life" by Susan E. Lorsch, in *Critique* (Atlanta), vol. 20, no. 2, 1978; "Reaching Out: Sensitivity and Order," in *Recent American Fiction by Women* by Anne Z. Mickelson, Metuchen, New Jersey, Scarecrow Press, 1979; interview and "Gail Godwin and Southern Womanhood" by Carolyn Rhodes, both in *Women Writers of the Contemporary South* edited by Peggy Whitman Prenshaw, Jackson, University Press of Mississippi, 1984.

Gail Godwin comments:

Since I began writing fiction I have been most interested in creating characters who operate at a high level of intelligence and feeling as they go about trying to make sense of ther world in which they find themselves, and as they make decisions about how to live their lives.

*   *   *

In her fiction Gail Godwin depicts the choices that modern women make. Whether within marriage or the single life, motherhood or career, these choices necessitate compromise, and none brings complete happiness. Godwin's characters often explore their options through art as they create or analyze images that may reveal or even change reality. A common crisis that precipitates this artistic endeavor or self-exploration is a death in the family, and within renewed family relationships, either nuclear or extended, Godwin's characters defend, dismiss, or display their choices.

Godwin demonstrates the effects of lack of choice in her first two novels, both violent and oppressive tales. In *The Perfectionists* Dane Empson's rage against her stifling marriage erupts when she beats her husband's illegitimate son. Obsessed with sexual acts in which she is either completely powerless or powerful, Dane views any relationship as invasive. Francesca Bolt, a passive princess in *Glass People*, makes not even basic decisions about food and clothes. She may "open out" like a beautiful flower but only if husband Cameron provides the container. Like Dane Empson, Francesca longs for a dark angel to transport her to her "true but unknown destiny." Neither Dane nor Francesca finds the strength to leave her marriage.

In her most insightful novel to date, *The Odd Woman*, Godwin creates Jane Clifford, an academic who researches life in order to control it. Unlike Dane Empson and Francesca Bolt, Jane believes in relationships, in perfect unions, like that of Marian Evans (George Eliot) and George Henry Lewes, in which men and women can communicate but retain separate identities. If she can analyze her married lover's words, Jane believes she can discover his feelings. And to some extent she succeeds, for in a rare moment Jane experiences Gabriel completely. However, she cannot sustain her moment, and her analyses usually lead her away from reality toward melodramas with faceless villains.

The fictive present in *The Odd Woman* begins with Jane's grandmother's death, an event that forces Jane's rediscovery of family relationships. Within her family and in George Gissing's *The Odd Women*, a novel for her next teaching assignment, Jane explores women's choices. Although she hates her aggressive stepfather, the man with whom her mother makes an apparent compromise, Jane still cheers for women who strive for marriage. She destroys the family myth about great-aunt Cleva who ran away with a villain actor in the melodrama *The Fatal Wedding*. Caught between the world of literature in which every plot seems probable and reality in which married lovers seldom leave their wives, Jane struggles with her own

possibilities. She rejects total withdrawal into literature after living in isolation the winter she writes her dissertation. Gerda, her radical feminist *doppelgänger*, cannot convince her to give up on men, but neither will Jane continue to play the role of Understanding Mistress. Jane's insomnia functions as her muse, and keeping herself open to relationships may free the ending of the Jane Clifford Story, with all its Aristotelian requirements. At the end of the novel, back in her apartment, Jane may not have found an Eliot-Lewes union, but she clings to her belief that one can "organize the loneliness and the weather and the long night into something of abiding shape and beauty."

Moving the reader closer to the main character through first-person point of view and less reliance on interior monologue than in *The Odd Woman*, Godwin nevertheless continues her reflections on the thin line between reality and imagination, between art and life in *Violet Clay*. The title character in *Violet Clay* searches idly for her options in "the book of Old Plots" while she projects herself into the romance novels she illustrates for a living. The death of Violet's Uncle Ambrose serves as catalyst for change when he commits suicide in his Adirondack cabin. Ambrose's note to Violet reads: "I'm sorry, there's nothing left." Violet sketches his face and interprets the punctuation in the note until she realizes that the "nothing" is artistic inspiration. When Violet realizes the meaning of Ambrose's note, she takes up serious art again, and the goal in the fictive present becomes the proper artistic subject. Violet finally remembers Ambrose's advice: write about (or create) something you want to happen, rather than postponing it, Violet learns. Art is a way of seeing life rather than postponing it, Violet learns. In her portrait of her neighbor Samantha De Vere, a woman who survives incest and rape, Violet captures the human spirit and earns artistic recognition. Exploring relationships and testing possibilities through artistic expression contribute to Violet's growth; as she states, "Sam put me into proportion, as Ambrose put me into perspective." Godwin continues to explore this connection between art and life in her two short story collections, *Dream Children* and *Mr. Bedford and the Muses*.

Each female character in *A Mother and Two Daughters* represents one choice for women. Cate, the academic who chooses abortion, Lydia, the divorcée who returns to school and career, and Nell, the widow who finds contentment in a second husband, all receive narrative attention in Godwin's longest novel to date. Although Godwin reduces her focus on art to a few comments on *The Scarlet Letter*, the theme of that novel is clearly relevant: "Can the individual spirit survive the society in which it has to live?" The society in *A Mother and Two Daughters* is that of the family, which Cate and Lydia's sibling rivalry threatens to pull apart after their father's death. Although blinded by misunderstanding, Lydia and Cate experience much the same anxiety and desire, as Lydia writes a research paper on Eros, a "striving for what one lacks," and Cate defines hope as "keeping a space ready for what you did want, even though you didn't know what it would be until it came." Neither daughter wants to close off her possibilities, whatever her destiny might bring.

In the most intense scene in the novel, Cate and Lydia explode at each other in anger. They express their resentment of their childhood roles: Cate as rebel, Lydia as dutiful daughter. After the fight, their neglect causes their father's cabin to burn, the fire taking with it not only childhood possessions but much of the sisters' anger. In the peace that follows, Lydia and Cate incorporate each other into their lives, and the connections between Lydia's real family and Cate's extended one allow each to survive as individual spirits. "*Do you remember? ... Does it still hurt here? ... Oh, it all passes, but that's the beauty of it, too.*" Music written by Lydia's son Dickie unites the family in the final scene.

"Your soul craves that constant heightening of reality only art can give you," Ursula DeVane tells Justin Stokes in *The Finishing School* and thus continues Godwin's theme of art affecting life. 14-year-old Justin, grieving for her dead father and grandparents, turns to 44-year-old Ursula for friendship. 26 years later Justin still struggles to understand that tragic summer. Curiosity about that tragedy, Godwin's portrayal of eccentric Ursula, and her sensitive depiction of adolescent Justin propel the reader through *The Finishing School*. Much like Muriel Spark's Jean Brodie, Ursula DeVane serves as muse to the innocent. Always "keep moving forward and making new trysts with life," Ursula advises Justin, and you'll never grow old. However, the time comes when the student becomes independent and sees her teacher as flawed rather than ideal. This inevitability forms the essential part of Ursula's definition of tragedy: the "something terrible" that happens when a person lives out her own "destiny." The intensity of their relationship causes Justin to betray Ursula much as Ursula betrayed her own mother. The adult Justin realizes that now she must use "all the fate" that has happened to her and "make possible what still may happen." Her yearnings and torments strengthen her acting talent: "As long as you can go on creating new roles for yourself, you are not vanquished," Justin concludes much as Ursula would. In Godwin's fictional world, roles for women are artistically created and recreated until they become real.

—Mary M. Lay

GOLD, Herbert. American. Born in Cleveland, Ohio, 9 March 1924. Educated at Columbia University, New York, B.A. 1946, M.A. 1948; the Sorbonne, Paris (Fulbright Scholar), 1949–51. Served in the United States Army, 1943–46. Married 1) Edith Zubrin in 1948 (divorced, 1956), two daughters; 2) Melissa Dilworth in 1968 (divorced, 1975), one daughter and two sons. Lecturer in Philosophy and Literature, Western Reserve University, Cleveland, 1951–53; Lecturer in English, Wayne State University, Detroit, 1954–56. Visiting Professor, Cornell University, Ithaca, New York, 1958, University of California, Berkeley, 1963, Harvard University, Cambridge, Massachusetts, 1964, Stanford University, California, 1967, and University of California, Davis, 1973–79. Recipient: Inter-American Cultural grant, to Haiti, 1950; *Hudson Review* fellowship, 1956; Guggenheim fellowship, 1957; American Academy grant, 1958; Longview Foundation award, 1959; Ford fellowship, for drama, 1960. Address: 1051-A Broadway, San Francisco, California 94133, U.S.A.

PUBLICATIONS

Novels

Birth of a Hero. New York, Viking Press, 1951.
The Prospect Before Us. Cleveland, World, 1954; as *Room Clerk*, New York, New American Library, 1955.
The Man Who Was Not with It. Boston, Little Brown, 1956; London, Secker and Warburg, 1965; as *The Wild Life*, New York, Permabooks, 1957.
The Optimist. Boston, Little Brown, 1959.

Therefore Be Bold. New York, Dial Press, 1960; London, Deutsch, 1962.
Salt. New York, Dial Press, 1963; London, Secker and Warburg, 1964.
Fathers: A Novel in the Form of a Memoir. New York, Random House, and London, Secker and Warburg, 1967.
The Great American Jackpot. New York, Random House, 1970; London, Weidenfeld and Nicolson, 1971.
Swiftie the Magician. New York, McGraw Hill, 1974; London, Hutchinson, 1975.
Waiting for Cordelia. New York, Arbor House, 1977; London, Hutchinson, 1978.
Slave Trade. New York, Arbor House, 1979.
He/She. New York, Arbor House, 1980; London, Severn House, 1982.
Family: A Novel in the Form of a Memoir. New York, Arbor House, 1981; London, Severn House, 1983.
True Love. New York, Arbor House, 1982; London, Severn House, 1984.
Mister White Eyes. New York, Arbor House, 1984.
A Girl of Forty. New York, Fine, 1986.

Short Stories

15 x 3, with R.V. Cassill and James B. Hall. New York, New Directions, 1957.
Love and Like. New York, Dial Press, 1960; London, Deutsch, 1961.
The Magic Will: Stories and Essays of a Decade. New York, Random House, 1971.
Stories of Misbegotten Love. Santa Barbara, California, Capra Press, 1985.
Lovers and Cohorts: Twenty-Seven Stories. New York, Fine, 1986.

Other

The Age of Happy Problems (essays). New York, Dial Press, 1962.
Biafra Goodbye. San Francisco, Twowindows Press, 1970.
My Last Two Thousand Years (autobiography). New York, Random House, 1972; London, Hutchinson, 1973.
The Young Prince and the Magic Cone (for children). New York, Doubleday, 1973.
A Walk on the West Side: California on the Brink (stories and essays). New York, Arbor House, 1981.

Editor, *Fiction of the Fifties: A Decade of American Writing.* New York, Doubleday, 1959.
Editor, with David L. Stevenson, *Stories of Modern America.* New York, St. Martin's Press, 1961; revised edition, 1963.
Editor, *First Person Singular: Essays for the Sixties.* New York, Dial Press, 1963.

*

Herbert Gold comments:
Subjects: Power, money, sex and love, intention in America.
Themes: The same.
Moral: Coming next time.

* * *

In Herbert Gold's introduction to *Fiction of the Fifties*, he makes a distinction between fiction which *avows* and fiction which *controls*. The fiction which avows is a rather faithful transcription of the immediate and personal experience of the writer; such fiction makes use of the writer's own experience of his past and the section of social life where that experience took place. The other sort of fiction makes an attempt to present the experiences of persons who indeed are not the writer; these experiences are given clarity by an effort of the imagination which takes the writer outside himself and immerses him in circumstances that are not his own. All this is done by the exercise of *control*.

These interesting categories can be used to classify Gold's own fiction. A great deal of that fiction falls into the first category, that of avowal, as one can see from an inspection of his autobiographical *My Last Two Thousand Years*. This book is a narrative of Gold's own life, a life that finds its way into several of his novels. It was a life in which, as the son of a Jewish immigrant who settled in Cleveland, Gold experienced a difficult youth, in the shadow of a strong father who had found a place for himself in an alien society. Gold's narrative relates his own struggles to detach himself from his father's ambitions for his son, and to achieve his own goals, in New York and elsewhere, as student, critic, and novelist. All this was a process of self-discovery that demanded acts of will and personal heroism. This self-discovery, as Gold relates it, also involved a succession of painful relationships: marriage, parenthood, divorce, and a second marriage, with various temporary relationships along the way.

These are all matters that various other novelists would regard as private. So are they for Gold. But they are also the stuff of much of his fiction. These are the novels which *avow* (or assert) the essentials of the writer's own life. Such fiction contrasts with other novels in which Gold borrows and reshapes elements of other lives; it is in these latter novels that Gold *controls* the experiences of other persons and also depicts social patterns which the writer does not know directly and immediately.

Gold's frequent adherence to the dictum of Sir Philip Sidney's muse—"Fool . . . look in thy heart and write"—is illustrated by an excellent novel, *Fathers*, which is subtitled "A Novel in the Form of a Memoir." The novel tells of the relation between an immigrant father and his son; it is a vivid recollection of matters that Gold also puts down in *My Last Two Thousand Years*. *Fathers* offers homage to a courageous father and to the equally courageous son who chooses to turn aside from his father. The novel offers a convincing texture of loyalty and enmity. The same section of Gold's life appears in *Therefore Be Bold* which, however, centers attention on "Daniel Berman's" adolescent years in Cleveland: his encounters with poetry and sex and his bitter first experience of anti-Semitism.

Other novels, one can judge, are transcriptions of Gold's own experience of self-assertion and self-discovery in the New York literary world. Thus, *Swiftie the Magician* displays Gold's creative imagination moving onwards from his youth and assessing a man's attempts to find his own way through the jungles of professional and emotional life that surround a person in the second half of the 20th century. The novel relates the involvement of a writer with three women: an East Coast innocent, a West Coast "experienced" young woman, and the hard-bitten Swiftie, a "magician" who knows what the score is in a rough world. *Salt* gives the reader a more complex version of such pursuits of identity. Two men—one a complacent Wasp and the other once more an alter ego for Gold—move from woman to woman, the Wasp learning little and the young Jew from Cleveland a great deal.

Such are the novels in which Gold reworks the stuff of his own life. But there are other novels in which Gold is exercising *control*—is, in more conventional literary language, inventing

persons not himself and following the courses of their experiences. *Birth of a Hero* follows the attempts of a middle-aged business man, Reuben Flair, a faceless cypher, to become a man fully aware of what he has done, in marriage and beyond marriage. As in other novels by Gold, the outlines of Reuben's achievement are cloudy, but a sense of travel and change is conveyed. In *The Prospect Before Us* Gold moves still farther afield. In this novel the chief person is Harry Bowers, manager of a run-down motel in Cleveland. A level of life—low, raunchy, and cruel, and quite different from the world of the novels of avowal—is presented in colors that convince. And there is no touch of the frequent father-son situation; Harry Bowers allows black woman to rent a room in his motel and is hounded for what he has done. *The Man Who Was Not With It* allows us to inhabit the awareness of a carnival worker. Here, however, there is an approach to the themes of the novels of avowal. Bud, the carnie, is saddled with two fathers: one, his real one in Pittsburgh, and the other a carnival barker. The barker delivers Bud from his drug habit (and falls foul of it himself) and hovers like a threatening cloud over the early weeks of Bud's marriage: a relation that links this novel with other work of Gold. In *The Great American Jackpot* the persona is also not Gold's own (the hero is a Berkeley student of the 1960's), but the student's preoccupations are not unfamiliar. Al Dooley loves and hates his teacher, a black sociologist; Dooley tries to find out who he is in the arms of two girls; and, finally, he asserts his identity by breaking out: in this instance, by robbing a bank and experiencing the farce of American justice. Dooley reappears in *Waiting for Cordelia* where he is doing a thesis on prostitution in the San Francisco area. A madam (Cordelia) and Marietta, a woman eager to become a reforming mayor of San Francisco, enrich Dooley's research. In the course of writing his study, Dooley faces Gold's usual questions about the nature of love and the sadness and the loneliness which hamper its realization. Similar preoccupations mark the early novel, *The Optimist*, in which Burr Fuller makes his way through a failed marriage and achieves some mastery of the mysteries of love and career. And similar struggles mark *True Love* where the subject is the uneasiness of middle age; a "respectable" man is harassed by the dreams of his youth and by his fears about his later life. Will the late discovery of "true love" allay these discontents?

In all, a considerable variety. It is a variety bound together by a style that is generally pervasive save for variations that reflect the different social levels reproduced. A certain vigor results from the determined contemporary quality of Gold's references, including commercial products and public diversions, and even turns of speech. What usually holds this variety together is Gold's own sense of the worth of what he is doing. The language of the novels is a considerable support to the portions of wisdom that appear in the novels.

—Harold H. Watts

GOLDING, William (Gerald). British. Born in St. Columb Minor, Cornwall, 19 September 1911. Educated at Marlborough Grammar School; Brasenose College, Oxford, B.A. 1935. Served in the Royal Navy, 1940–45. Married Ann Brookfield in 1939; one son and one daughter. Writer, actor, and producer in small theatre companies, 1934–40; schoolmaster, Bishop Wordsworth's School, Salisbury, Wiltshire, 1945–61;

Visiting Professor, Hollins College, Virginia, 1961–62. Recipient: James Tait Black Memorial Prize, 1980; Booker Prize, 1980; Nobel Prize for Literature, 1983. M.A.: Oxford University, 1961; D.Litt.: University of Sussex, Brighton, 1970; University of Kent, Canterbury, 1974; University of Warwick, Coventry, 1981; the Sorbonne, Paris, 1983; Oxford University, 1983. Honorary Fellow, Brasenose College, 1966. Fellow, 1955, and Companion of Literature, 1984, Royal Society of Literature. C.B.E. (Commander, Order of the British Empire), 1966. Address: Ebble Thatch, Bowerchalke, Wiltshire, England.

PUBLICATIONS

Novels

Lord of the Flies. London, Faber, 1954; New York, Coward McCann, 1955.
The Inheritors. London, Faber, 1955; New York, Harcourt Brace, 1956.
Pincher Martin. London, Faber, 1956; as *The Two Deaths of Christopher Martin*, New York, Harcourt Brace, 1957.
Free Fall. London, Faber, 1959; New York, Harcourt Brace, 1960.
The Spire. London, Faber, and New York, Harcourt Brace, 1964.
The Pyramid. London, Faber, and New York, Harcourt Brace, 1967.
Darkness Visible. London, Faber, and New York, Farrar Straus, 1979.
Rites of Passage. London, Faber, and New York, Farrar Straus, 1980.
The Paper Men. London, Faber, and New York, Farrar Straus, 1984.

Short Stories

The Scorpion God. London, Faber, 1971; New York, Harcourt Brace, 1972.

Uncollected Short Stories

"Miss Pulkinhorn," in *Encounter* (London), August 1960.
"On The Escarpment," in *Kenyon Review* (Gambier, Ohio), June 1967.
"The Anglo-Saxon," in *Winter's Tales 16*, edited by A.D. Maclean. London, Macmillan, 1970; New York, St. Martin's Press, 1971.

Plays

The Brass Butterfly, adaptation of his story "Envoy Extraordinary" (produced London, 1958). London, Faber, 1958; Chicago, Dramatic Publishing Company, n.d.

Radio Plays: *Miss Pulkinhorn*, 1960; *Break My Heart*, 1962.

Verse

Poems. London, Macmillan, 1934; New York, Macmillan, 1935.

Other

The Hot Gates and Other Occasional Pieces. London, Faber, 1965; New York, Harcourt Brace, 1966.

Talk: Conversations with William Golding, with Jack I. Biles. New York, Harcourt Brace, 1970.
A Moving Target (essays). London, Faber, and New York, Farrar Straus, 1982.
An Egyptian Journal. London, Faber, 1985.

*

Critical Studies: (selection): *William Golding* by Samuel Hynes, New York, Columbia University Press, 1964; *William Golding: A Critical Study* by James R. Baker, New York, St. Martin's Press, 1965; *The Art of William Golding* by Bernard S. Oldsey and Stanley Weintraub, New York, Harcourt Brace, 1965; *William Golding* by Bernard F. Dick, New York, Twayne, 1967; *William Golding: A Critical Study* by Mark Kinkead-Weekes and Ian Gregor, London, Faber, 1967, New York, Harcourt Brace, 1968, revised edition, Faber, 1984; *William Golding* by Leighton Hodson, Edinburgh, Oliver and Boyd, 1969, New York, Putnam, 1971; *The Novels of William Golding* by Howard S. Babb, Columbus, Ohio State University Press, 1970; *William Golding: The Dark Fields of Discovery* by Virginia Tiger, London, Calder and Boyars, and Atlantic Highlands, New Jersey, Humanities Press, 1974; *William Golding* by Stephen Medcalf, London, Longman, 1975; *William Golding: Some Critical Considerations* edited by Jack I. Biles and Robert O. Evans, Lexington, University Press of Kentucky, 1978; *Of Earth and Darkness: The Novels of William Golding* by Arnold Johnston, Columbia, University of Missouri Press, 1980; *A View from the Spire: William Golding's Later Novels* by Don Crompton, Oxford, Blackwell, 1985.

*   *   *

In his essay "Crosses" William Golding reveals that one of the things he has regretted in life has been his "inability to write poetry." Instead—besides three volumes of miscellaneous writings—he has produced nine novels and a trio of stories (one of which, "Envoy Extraordinary," he later reworked as a play, *The Brass Butterfly*). Taut, near-allegoric works making much use of myth, symbol, and patterning, these often attain a poetic compression and intensity.

At the heart of all of them is Golding's belief that "man produces evil as a bee produces honey." Books about what he has called "the terrible disease of being human," they aim to make man face "the sad fact of his own cruelty and lust." Behind their wide diversity of tone and setting lies the fixed conviction that "Man is a fallen being. He is gripped by original sin. His nature is sinful and his state perilous." As Golding has recognized, this is an insight that lacks novelty, being "trite, obvious and familiar in theological terms." But, he contends, "what is trite is true, and a truism can become more than a truism when it is a belief passionately held." His fiction could be seen as an attempt to justify this claim. Occasionally, what he calls his "savage grasp on life" appears to be no more than a heavy-handed clutching at standard religious props. More usually, it takes imaginative hold and, in the finest of his clenched fables, his material is moulded into memorably fierce contours.

In subject matter, Golding's fiction is ambitious and diverse. Chronologically, his range is wide, taking in Neanderthal victims of *homo sapiens* at one extreme, and human victims of nuclear war at the other. Intermediate stopping-points include a Pharaoh's court, imperial Rome, a medieval cathedral community, a ship *en route* for Australia in the early 19th century, and a small English town in the 1920's. As might be expected from a devotee of archaeology, Golding reconstructs these little worlds with absorbed precision. Rich in faithfully rendered detail, the physical settings of his books seem as authentic as they are graphic. Energy and ingenuity also go into recreating the social structure of each period, its distinctive rituals, creeds, and assumptions.

But these are far from documentary books. Alongside the archaeologist in Golding—and more dominant—is the moralist. The allegorist makes instructive use of what the anthropologist provides. In Golding's first book, *Lord of the Flies*, for instance, the increasingly tribal-seeming activities of schoolboys wrecked on a desert island are not merely recorded: they also serve to trace harsh diagrams of human history, charting man's social evolution as a grisly decline from fruit-eating commune to totalitarian butchery. Jetsam from a nuclear war, the boys re-enact the process that has brought them to this state; restored to an Eden, they convert it into an abattoir. In Golding's version of the Fall, however, there is no devil. Evil—which the boys hysterically externalize as "The Beast"—turns out to have a human face. The spectre on the mountain that so haunts them is a literal instance of human corruption: the decaying corpse of an airman, victim and perpetrator of military aggression. As the novel concludes, one of the boys, brought to awareness, weeps "for the end of innocence, the darkness of man's heart."

Merging fast-paced narrative into a streamlined, semi-allegoric structure that moves with increasing impetus through scenes of savagery to a terminating pessimism about man, *Lord of the Flies* much resembles Golding's second novel, *The Inheritors*, another myth-like story that can be glossed in both political and religious terms. These two novels, among Golding's most successful, deal with humanity and evil in a generalized, panoramic way. In each, human malevolence shows itself most fearsomely through mob-atrocity and in the arena of power. The subsequent books focus on individuals and private relationships, especially sexual ones. This presents Golding with material of greater emotional and psychological complexity which he doesn't always seem entirely at ease with. Moral intricacies tend to get ironed out under the weight of his didacticism. Character can flatten into stereotype.

Acute when scrutinizing the physical world, Golding's eye usually penetrates less deeply when observing human personality. Able to convey sensory experience with great immediacy—and specializing in capturing hallucinatory, deranged and sub-rational states of mind—he is less adept at portraying thought, speech, or emotional responses. *Free Fall*, *The Pyramid*, and the three stories in *The Scorpion God*, for instance, offer an unusual mix of blur and precision, novelettish cliché and imaginative power. In *Pincher Martin*, Golding's first attempt at focusing on an individual, what is strong and what is weak rather bizarrely polarize. The phantasmagoria sections of the novel—where the efforts of dead Martin's ego to retain its autonomy are depicted as a struggle for survival on a rock in the Atlantic—carry intense physical conviction as exposure and attrition scour at their victim. Paradoxically, though, the "real-life" sections of the book are populated with pasteboard: flash-backs to Martin's past relationships merely light up a lifeless series of crudely-posed moral tableaux demonstrating his selfishness.

Weakness at characterization—something he skilfully bypasses in *Lord of the Flies* and *The Inheritors* by concentrating on protagonists who are not mature human beings—has been one of Golding's most persistent limitations. Repetition is another. Character-types—the selfish sexual predator, the gawky saint, the exploited girl—recur throughout his fiction. So do pieces of plot mechanism and favourite structural devices. *Lord of the Flies*, *The Inheritors*, *Pincher Martin*, *The*

Spire, the story "Clonk Clonk," and *Rites of Passage*, for example, all effect a sudden dramatic shift of viewpoint near their end.

This said, though, it must be added that, throughout a lengthy fictional career, Golding has retained an ability to surprise—by tackling unexpected new material, writing in a fresh vein, or brilliantly refurbishing some of his enduring techniques and preoccupations. The most marked indication of this has been in his return in 1979 to the novel. In style, the trio of novels he has produced since then have been extraordinarily varied, ranging from the surreal myth of *Darkness Visible* to the banality and sarcasms of *The Paper Men*, his parable about the temptations and tribulations of a writer's life. In between these two works came what is perhaps his masterpiece, *Rites of Passage*. Here, Golding's habit of introducing some concluding change of perspective is given its most extended and accomplished use. Penned, for most of the book, into the snobbish, narrow mind of Talbot, a young aristocrat keeping a journal of his voyage out to Australia, the reader is suddenly released from it into a very different account of the journey: that of Colley, an awkward young clergyman, the latest and most convincing of Golding's figures of ungainly virtue. As Colley's receptive consciousness takes over from Talbot's crabbed one, the book burgeons out into an entranced, generous breadth of vision. Colley's responsiveness—rapt, ecstatic, innocent: a Romantic contrast to the Augustan cynicisms and knowing clevernesses that are Talbot's forte—is a reminder that Golding's creativity is happiest when it can slip free of rationality, something unremittingly destructive in his world. His imagination is at its most powerful when occupying consciousnesses—of children, primitives, mystics, obsessives—where logic has least control, allowing him to give inventive scope to his mind's-eye-opening ability to see life from unfamiliar angles.

Rites of Passage concerns itself with some of Golding's most continuing themes: the moral atrophy brought on by being encased in egotism, the way self-centredness cramps perception. But, around them, it constructs a fable of impressive novelty. Restless, experimental, exploratory, Golding's powers of narrative, evocation, and description constantly break new ground. When it comes to getting critical sightings on him, he is still very much, as he says in one of his essays, "a moving target."

—Peter Kemp

GOLDMAN, William. American. Born in Chicago, Illinois, 12 August 1931; brother of the writer James Goldman. Educated at Highland Park High School; Oberlin College, Ohio, 1948–52, B.A. 1952; Columbia University, New York, 1954–56, M.A. 1956. Served in the United States Army, 1952–54: Corporal. Married Ilene Jones in 1961; two daughters. Recipient: Oscar, for screenplay, 1970, 1977. Address: 740 Park Avenue, New York, New York 10021, U.S.A.

PUBLICATIONS

Novels

The Temple of Gold. New York, Knopf, 1957.
Your Turn to Curtsy, My Turn to Bow. New York, Doubleday, 1958.

Soldier in the Rain. New York, Atheneum, and London, Eyre and Spottiswoode, 1960.
Boys and Girls Together. New York, Atheneum, 1964; London, Joseph, 1965.
No Way To Treat a Lady (as Harry Longbaugh). New York, Fawcett, and London, Muller, 1964; as William Goldman, New York, Harcourt Brace, and London, Coronet, 1968.
The Thing of It Is. . . . New York, Harcourt Brace, and London, Joseph, 1967.
Father's Day. New York, Harcourt Brace, and London, Joseph, 1971.
The Princess Bride: S. Morgenstern's Classic Tale of True Love and High Adventure: The "Good Parts" Version, Abridged. New York, Harcourt Brace, 1973; London, Macmillan, 1975.
Marathon Man. New York, Delacorte Press, 1974; London, Macmillan, 1975.
Magic. New York, Delacorte Press, and London, Macmillan, 1976.
Tinsel. New York, Delacorte Press, and London, Macmillan, 1979.
Control. New York, Delacorte Press, and London, Hodder and Stoughton, 1982.
The Color of Light. New York, Warner, and London, Granada, 1984.
The Silent Gondoliers (as S. Morgenstern). New York, Ballantine, 1984.
Heat. New York, Warner, 1985; as *Edged Weapons*, London, Granada, 1985.

Uncollected Short Stories

"Something Blue," in *Rogue* (New York), 1958.
"Da Vinci," in *New World Writing 17.* Philadelphia, Lippincott, 1960.
"Till the Right Girls Come Along," in *Transatlantic Review 8* (London), Winter 1961.
"The Ice Cream Eat," in *Stories from the Transatlantic Review*, edited by Jospeh F. McCrindle. New York, Holt Rinehart, 1970.

Plays

Blood, Sweat and Stanley Poole, with James Goldman (produced New York, 1961). New York, Dramatists Play Service, 1962.
A Family Affair, with James Goldman, music by John Kander (produced New York, 1962).
Butch Cassidy and the Sundance Kid (screenplay). New York, Bantam, and London, Corgi, 1969.
The Great Waldo Pepper (screenplay). New York, Dell, 1975.

Screenplays: *Masquerade*, with Michael Relph, 1964; *Harper* (*The Moving Target*), 1966; *Butch Cassidy and the Sundance Kid*, 1969; *The Hot Rock* (*How to Steal a Diamond in Four Uneasy Lessons*), 1972; *The Stepford Wives*, 1974; *The Great Waldo Pepper*, 1975; *All the President's Men*, 1976; *Marathon Man*, 1976; *A Bridge Too Far*, 1977; *Magic*, 1978.

Television Film: *Mr. Horn*, 1979.

Other

The Season: A Candid Look at Broadway. New York, Harcourt Brace, 1969; revised edition, New York, Limelight, 1984.

Wigger (for children). New York, Harcourt Brace, 1974.
The Story of "A Bridge Too Far." New York, Dell, 1977.
Adventures in the Screen Trade: A Personal View of Hollywood and Screenwriting. New York, Warner, 1983; London, Macdonald, 1984.

*

Critical Study: *William Goldman* by Richard Andersen, Boston, Twayne, 1979.

*   *   *

William Goldman is a successful novelist, film scenarist, playwright, critic, and children's book author who focuses much of his attention on the illusions by which men and women live. These illusions often make existence more miserable than it need be and provide a core from which all of Goldman's protagonists seek to escape. Ironically, what they escape to is more often than not other illusions, which, because of the artificial distinctions society attaches to them, rarely satisfy their human needs.

When Raymond Trevitt's desperate attempts to protect the ideals of his childhood from adult realities in *The Temple of Gold* inadvertently cause the deaths of his closest friends, he leaves his home, but discovers only frustration and intolerance elsewhere. In *Your Turn to Curtsy, My Turn to Bow*, Chad Kimberly is driven by his ambitious illusions into believing he is a new Messiah, whose schizophrenic demands frighten the novel's protagonist, Peter Bell, into a life of escapist daydreaming. Ambition is not the only illusion that drive the characters of *Boys and Girls Together* to New York; most of them are escaping from the unbearable circumstances of their home lives. Nevertheless, their hopes for self-improvement are dashed by unsuccessful love affairs, domineering parents, professional failures, embarrassing social exposures, and suicide. In *Soldier in the Rain*, Eustis Clay and Maxwell Slaughter cannot free themselves from the military-economic complex of which they are so much a part.

The great American illusions about success are the central concerns of *The Thing of It Is . . .* and *Father's Day*, in which the talented, rich, but quirky Amos McCracken spends a tremendous amount of money trying to save his marriage and then his relationship with his daughter. In the end, his guilt-ridden personal failures lead him to create fantasies that enable him to fulfill the images he has of himself but that also pose a serious threat to the safety and well-being of others.

Unlike Amos McCracken or Kit Gil of *No Way to Treat a Lady*, Westley and Buttercup of *The Princess Bride*, Babe Levy of *Marathon Man*, and Corky Withers of *Magic* cannot retreat to a fabulous land to try to make themselves whole; they already live in fabulous land, where they are constantly assaulted by its empirical and psychological facts. Forced to encounter a vast confusion of fact and fiction, to deal with pain and death, and to seek power against forces that are difficult to pinpoint and consequently understand, the protagonists of these three novels must stay rooted in social systems that attempt to deny their vitality while creating illusions that life is what it should be.

Combining the everyday reality of Goldman's early novels with the fabulous reality of his later works, *Tinsel* tells the story of three women who desperately try to escape from the boredom of their daily lives to the fame and fortune of movie stardom, which, like all illusions, eludes them. As he did in *Marathon Man* and *Magic*, Goldman divides this into many chapters, so short and so different from any other in terms of setting and action that they flash by the reader like scenes in a movie. Because of their length, Goldman can keep simultaneously occurring stories running vividly in the reader's imagination without making any significant connections between them. When the individual stories eventually come together, Goldman continues flashing different scenes containing markedly different actions at such a pace that reading Goldman's story about the film industry becomes as close to a cinematic experience as literature can provide.

With the *Color of Light* Goldman returned to the themes of innocence and loss that concerned him in his early novels, only this time around he discusses them as subjects for writing. Unfortunately, this serious book, like some of his early serious novels, wasn't as well received as it should have been, and Goldman returned to the fabulist landscape of *Marathon Man* and *Magic* in *Control* and *Heat*. But he passed through fantasy-land on the way just as he did in 1973 with *The Princess Bride*. *The Silent Gondoliers* tells us why the gondoliers in Venice no longer sing. Even they have lost their innocence in a world from which there is no escape.

Perhaps because of his popularity or the reputation he has established in Hollywood (many of his novels have been adapted to the screen), many critics have misunderstood or underrated Goldman's works. Perhaps these critics have been confused by Goldman's use of multiple modes—novel of manners, confessional journal, psychological novel, social satire, romantic parody, black humor novel, detective story, spy novel, radical protest novel, soap opera, absurdist novel, and more—within a wide frame of genres. Whatever the reason, Goldman is an extraordinarily talented and prolific writer whose incorporation of cinematic techniques with conventional narrative forms mark a significant contribution to the novel tradition.

—Richard Andersen

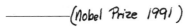

(Nobel Prize 1991)

GORDIMER, Nadine. South African. Born in Springs, Transvaal, 20 November 1923. Educated at a convent school, and the University of the Witwatersrand, Johannesburg. Married 1) G. Gavron in 1949; 2) Reinhold Cassirer in 1954; one son and one daughter. Visiting Lecturer, Institute of Contemporary Arts, Washington, D.C., 1961, Harvard University, Cambridge, Massachusetts, 1969, Princeton University, New Jersey, 1969, Northwestern University, Evanston, Illinois 1969, and University of Michigan, Ann Arbor, 1970; Adjunct Professor of Writing, Columbia University, New York, 1971. Recipient: W.H. Smith Literary Award, 1961; Thomas Pringle Award, 1969; James Tait Black Memorial Prize, 1972; Booker Prize, 1974; Grand Aigle d'Or prize (France), 1975; CNA award, 1975; Scottish Arts Council Neil Gunn Fellowship, 1981; Common Wealth Award, 1981; Modern Language Association award (USA), 1981. D.Lit.: University of Leuven, Belgium, 1980; D.Litt.: Smith College, Northampton, Massachusetts, 1985; City College, New York, 1985; Mount Holyoke College, South Hadley, Massachusetts, 1985. Honorary Member, American Academy of Arts and Sciences, 1980; Honorary Fellow, Modern Language Association (USA), 1985. Agent: A.P. Watt Ltd., 26–28 Bedford Row, London WC1R 4HL, England; or, Russell and Volkening Inc., 50 West 29th Street, New York, New York 10001, U.S.A. Address: 7 Frere Road, Parktown West, Johannesburg 2193, South Africa.

PUBLICATIONS

Novels

The Lying Days. London, Gollancz, and New York, Simon and Schuster, 1953.
A World of Strangers. London, Gollancz, and New York, Simon and Schuster, 1958.
Occasion for Loving. London, Gollancz, and New York, Viking Press, 1963.
The Late Bourgeois World. London, Gollancz, and New York, Viking Press, 1966.
A Guest of Honour. New York, Viking Press, 1970; London, Cape, 1971.
The Conservationist. London, Cape, 1974; New York, Viking Press, 1975.
Burger's Daughter. London, Cape, and New York, Viking Press, 1979.
July's People. London, Cape, and New York, Viking Press, 1981.

Short Stories

Face to Face: Short Stories. Johannesburg, Silver Leaf, 1949.
The Soft Voice of the Serpent and Other Stories. New York, Simon and Schuster, 1952; London, Gollancz, 1953.
Six Feet of the Country. London, Gollancz, and New York, Simon and Schuster, 1956.
Friday's Footprint and Other Stories. London, Gollancz, and New York, Viking Press, 1960.
Not for Publication and Other Stories. London, Gollancz, and New York, Viking Press, 1965.
Penguin Modern Stories 4, with others. London, Penguin, 1970.
Livingstone's Companions. New York, Viking Press, 1971; London, Cape, 1972.
Selected Stories. London, Cape, 1975; New York, Viking Press, 1976; as *No Place Like*, London, Penguin, 1978.
Some Monday for Sure. London, Heinemann, 1976.
A Soldier's Embrace. London, Cape, and New York, Viking Press, 1980.
Town and Country Lovers. Los Angeles, Sylvester and Orphanos, 1980.
Something Out There. London, Cape, and New York, Viking, 1984.

Plays

Television Plays and Documentaries: *A Terrible Chemistry* (*Writers and Places* series), 1981 (UK); *Choosing for Justice: Allan Boesak*, with Hugo Cassirer, 1985 (USA and UK); *Country Lovers, A Chip of Glass Ruby, Praise*, and *Oral History* (all in *The Gordimer Stories* series), 1985 (USA).

Other

African Lit. (lectures). Cape Town, University of Cape Town, 1972.
On the Mines, photographs by David Goldblatt. Cape Town, Struik, 1973.
The Black Interpreters: Notes on African Writing. Johannesburg, Spro-Cas Ravan, 1973.
What Happened to Burger's Daughter; or, How South African Censorship Works, with others. Johannesburg, Taurus, 1980.

Editor, with Lionel Abrahams, *South African Writing Today*. London, Penguin, 1967.

*

Bibliography: *Nadine Gordimer, Novelist and Short Story Writer: A Bibliography of Her Works* by Racilia Jilian Nell, Johannesburg, University of the Witwatersrand, 1964.

Manuscript Collection: University of Texas, Austin.

Critical Studies: *Nadine Gordimer* by Robert F. Haugh, New York, Twayne, 1974; *Nadine Gordimer* by Michael Wade, London, Evans, 1978; *Nadine Gordimer* by Christopher Heywood, Windsor, Berkshire, Profile, 1983.

Theatrical Activities:
Director: **Television**—*Choosing for Justice: Allan Boesak*, with Hugo Cassirer, 1985.

*   *   *

Despite Nadine Gordimer's international status as one of the finest living writers in English, her work is rooted in her native country, South Africa, where she has remained throughout her career. Her social confinement within a white, liberal, English, and middle-class position, in a diverse and divided country, has been a source of strength and weakness in her writing. On the one hand, she has ruthlessly exposed the limitations of Western, liberal humanism as a way of life in apartheid society, yet her characters, and her writing, have for the most part remained located within these very limitations.

Most of Gordimer's main characters are involved in the very serious business of finding suitable moral apparatus to cope with the excruciating *mental* difficulties of living white, with a conscience, in a minority within a greater South African minority. Viewed as a group, Gordimer's male and female protagonists show a parallel development of consciousness towards a point at which most moral options appear to be exhausted (two of her later heroes end up running away, blindly, to nowhere).

In Helen Shaw, Jessie Stilwell, and Liz van den Sandt, the heroines of *The Lying Days*, *Occasion for Loving*, and *The Late Bourgeois World*, respectively, Gordimer charts the development from the racially exclusive confines of a white childhood in South Africa, to the discovery of (and disillusion with) the "freedom" of adult liberal thinking, and from there to the point where personal sacrifice becomes necessary for the sake of political integrity. In *The Lying Days*, Helen Shaw triumphs against the provincial narrowness and racial bigotry of her parents' mining village existence, yet she discovers that she, too, is sealed within her social limitations when she watches, from behind the windscreen of a car, a riot in a black township in which a man is shot dead by the police. As is the case with a number of Gordimer's characters, Helen Shaw's sense of moral failure is realised within and suggested by the failure of a love relationship in which certain moral suppositions function as a way of life. She goes away, to Europe, aware of a need for new sustenance, but essentially disillusioned. She is succeeded by Jessie Stilwell, an older version of Helen, back from Europe, now married and running a family, and committed to a makeshift liberal ideology of being open to one's kind, because the general (white) South African way of life is unacceptable. Yet this ideology is shown to be vulnerable and in danger of hypocrisy by the action of the novel, in which Jessie's world is "invaded" by an illicit love affair between a black artist and a young woman from England

who, with her white musicologist husband, is a guest in the Stilwell home. The liberal idea of openness is belied by Jessie's wish to be left to her own kind of semi-romantic isolation, and all legitimate human reactions to the situation are bedevilled by a factor the Stilwell's profess not to take undue account of—skin colour. In *The Late Bourgeois World* the developments in *The Lying Days* and *Occasion for Loving* find a conclusion. For Liz van den Sandt, the old liberal "way of life" is already dead when the book opens—her liberal-activist former husband has just committed suicide—while her present existence is nothing more than a kind of helpless withdrawal, reflected by a particularly pallid love affair she is conducting. She faces her moment of truth when a black friend, an activist, challenges her to step outside the sealed area of sensibility and conscience, and *do* something to help, at considerable personal risk. Thirteen years later, in *Burger's Daughter*, Rosa Burger appears: she is the daughter of the generation which did in fact take the struggle further from where Liz van den Sandt was poised at the end of *The Late Bourgeois World*. But now the process goes into reverse: Rosa's father dies while in prison for Marxist "subversion," and Rosa finds herself unable simply to go on from where her father and his kind were stopped by politically repressive authority. She is heir to the failure of left-wing activism among whites in South Africa, and she settles for an occupation as a physiotherapist at a black hospital (treating Soweto riot victims), before she too is detained and committed to trial, merely on the basis of her connections with the nether-world of political dissent.

Gordimer's male heroes differ in that they either come in from the outside, or they represent a significantly non-liberal approach to life in South Africa. *A World of Strangers*, in which the new post-1948 apartheid society is anatomised with great clarity, shows the rapid disillusionment of a young Englishman, Toby Hood, who comes to South Africa determined to live a "private life." An altogether different kind of disillusionment faces the more mature and intellectually well-equipped figure of Colonel Evelyn James Bray, hero of *A Guest of Honour*. He returns to the newly independent African state to witness the realisation of ideals of freedom for which, as a colonial civil servant, he was deported. The political situation gradually slips out of control, and Bray is killed as a result of a misunderstanding that underscores the ambiguity of any European's role in Africa.

It is as though all illusions of a meaningful political existence for whites have been stripped bare when Mehring the technologist appears in Gordimer's Booker Prize-winning masterpiece, *The Conservationist*. This is a novel of immense symbolic power and great descriptive beauty. For once, Gordimer's main protagonist is representative of far more than just the white English liberal: he is simply white, South African, of ambiguous European heritage, rich, and politically conservative. His symbolic struggle in the book is a struggle for possession of the land against its black inheritors. Mehring (and by implication the whole of white South Africa) loses the struggle. It is thus not surprising that the protagonists of Gordimer's most recent novel, *July's People*, find themselves being run off the land. They escape revolution by running away with, and becoming captives of, their lifelong black servant, July.

The concerns of Nadine Gordimer's novels are richly amplified in her several collections of short stories.

—Leon de Kock

GORDON, Giles (Alexander Esme). British. Born in Edinburgh, 23 May 1940. Educated at Edinburgh Academy, 1948–57. Married Margaret Anna Eastoe in 1964; two sons and one daughter. Advertising executive, Secker and Warburg, publishers, London, 1962–63; editor, Hutchinson Publishing Group, London, 1963–64, and Penguin Books, London, 1964–66; editorial director, Victor Gollancz, publishers, London, 1967–72. Since 1972, partner, Anthony Sheil Associates, literary agents, London. Lecturer in Creative Writing, in London, for Tufts University, Medford, Massachusetts, 1971–76; C. Day Lewis Fellow in Writing, King's College, London, 1974–75; Lecturer in Drama, in London, for Hollins College, Virginia, 1984–85. Editor, *Drama* magazine, London, 1982–84; theatre critic, *Spectator*, London, 1983–84. Since 1985, theatre critic, *Punch* and *House Magazine*, both London. Member, Arts Council of Great Britain Literature Panel, 1966–69; Member, Society of Authors Committee of Management, 1973–75. Recipient: *Transatlantic Review* prize, 1966; Scottish Arts Council grant, 1976. Address: 9 St. Ann's Gardens, London NW5 4ER, England.

PUBLICATIONS

Novels

The Umbrella Man. London, Allison and Busby, 1971.
About a Marriage. London, Allison and Busby, and New York, Stein and Day, 1972.
Girl with Red Hair. London, Hutchinson, 1974.
100 Scenes from Married Life: A Selection. London, Hutchinson, 1976.
Enemies: A Novel about Friendship. Hassocks, Sussex, Harvester Press, 1977.
Ambrose's Vision: Sketches Towards the Creation of a Cathedral. Brighton, Harvester Press, 1980.

Short Stories

Pictures from an Exhibition. London, Allison and Busby, and New York, Dial Press, 1970.
Penguin Modern Stories 3, with others. London, Penguin, 1970.
Farewell, Fond Dreams. London, Hutchinson, 1975.
The Illusionist and Other Fictions. Hassocks, Sussex, Harvester Press, 1978.
Couple. Knotting, Bedfordshire, Sceptre Press, 1978.

Uncollected Short Stories

"The Line-up on the Shore," in *Mind in Chains*, edited by Christopher Evans. London, Panther, 1970.
"The Partition," in *Triangles*, edited by Alex Hamilton. London, Hutchinson, 1973.
"Crampton Manor," in *The Ninth Ghost Book*, edited by Rosemary Timperley. London, Barrie and Jenkins, 1973.
"Peake," in *The Eleventh Ghost Book*, edited by Aidan Chambers. London, Barrie and Jenkins, 1975.
"Morning Echo," in *The Sixteenth Pan Book of Horror Stories*, edited by Herbert Van Thal. London, Pan, 1975.
"In Spite of Himself," in *The Twelfth Ghost Book*. London, Barrie and Jenkins, 1976.
"Horses of Venice," in *The Thirteenth Ghost Book*, edited by James Hale. London, Barrie and Jenkins, 1977.
"The Necessary Authority," in *The Midnight Ghost Book*, edited by James Hale. London, Barrie and Jenkins, 1978.

"Room, With Woman and Man," in *New Stories 3*, edited by Francis King and Ronald Harwood. London, Hutchinson, 1978.
"Liberated People," in *Modern Scottish Short Stories*, edited by Fred Urquhart and Gordon. London, Hamish Hamilton, 1978.
"The Red-Headed Milkman," in *The Punch Book of Short Stories*, edited by Alan Coren. London, Robson, 1979.
"Screens," in *Labrys 4* (Hayes, Middlesex), 1979.
"Mask," in *The After Midnight Ghost Book*, edited by James Hale. London, Hutchinson, 1980; New York, Watts, 1981.
"Drama in Five Acts," in *New Terrors 2*, edited by Ramsey Campbell. London, Pan, 1980.
"Madame Durand," in *Punch* (London), 19 November 1980.
"The Indian Girl," in *Winter's Tales 27*, edited by Edward Leeson. London, Macmillan, 1981; New York, St. Martin's Press, 1982.
"Three Resolutions to One Kashmiri Encounter," in *Scottish Short Stories 1981*. London, Collins, 1981.
"Your Bedouin," in *Logos* (London), 1982.
"The South African Couple," in *Scottish Short Stories 1983*. London, Collins, 1983.
"A Bloomsbury Kidnapping," in *London Tales*, edited by Julian Evans. London, Hamish Hamilton, 1983.
"Father Christmas, Father Christmases," in *A Christmas Feast*, edited by James Hale. London, Macmillan, 1983.
"The Wheelchair," in *New Edinburgh Review 61*, 1983.
"The Battle of the Blind," in *New Edinburgh Review 65*, 1984.
"Hans Pfeifer," in *Winter's Tales 1* (new series), edited by David Hughes. London, Constable, 1985.

Plays

Radio Plays: *Nineteen Policemen Searching the Sedway Shore*, 1976; *The Jealous One*, 1979; *Birdy*, from the novel by William Wharton, 1980.

Verse

Landscape Any Date. Edinburgh, M. Macdonald, 1963.
Two and Two Make One. Preston, Lancashire, Akros, 1966.
Two Elegies. London, Turret, 1968.
Eight Poems for Gareth. Frensham, Surrey, Sceptre Press, 1970.
Between Appointments. Frensham, Surrey, Sceptre Press, 1971.
Twelve Poems for Callum. Preston, Lancashire, Akros, 1972.
One Man Two Women. London, Sheep Press, 1974.
Egyptian Room, Metropolitan Museum of Art. Rushden, Northamptonshire, Sceptre Press, 1974.
The Oban Poems. Knotting, Bedfordshire, Sceptre Press, 1977.

Other

Book 2000: Some Likely Trends in Publishing. London, Association of Assistant Librarians, 1969.
Walter and the Balloon (for children). London, Heinemann, 1973.

Editor, with Alex Hamilton, *Factions: Eleven Original Stories.* London, Joseph, 1974.
Editor, with Michael Bakewell and B.S. Johnson, *You Always Remember the First Time.* London, Quartet, 1975.
Editor, *Beyond the Words: Eleven Writers in Search of a New Fiction.* London, Hutchinson, 1975.

Editor, with Dulan Barber, *"Members of the Jury—": The Jury Experience.* London, Wildwood House, 1976.

Editor, *Prevailing Spirits: A Book of Scottish Ghost Stories.* London, Hamish Hamilton, 1976.

Editor, *A Book of Contemporary Nightmares.* London, Joseph, 1977.

Editor, with Fred Urquhart, *Modern Scottish Short Stories.* London, Hamish Hamilton, 1978; revised edition, London, Faber, 1982.

Editor, *Shakespeare Stories.* London, Hamish Hamilton, 1982.

Editor, *Modern Short Stories 2: 1940–1980.* London, Dent, 1982.

*

Manuscript Collection: National Library of Scotland, Edinburgh.

*   *   *

Relationships lie at the root of Giles Gordon's novels and short stories, relationships between man and woman, woman and woman, man and man, husband and wife, lover and lover—and also the relationship between the writer and the reader. In his first novel, *The Umbrella Man*, Gordon was content to view the burgeoning affair between Felix and Delia from the outside, using the technique that a film director might bring to bear in building up a scene from different camera angles. This is a device of which Gordon is particularly fond, and its exposition is seen to good effect in his story "Nineteen Policemen Searching the Solent Shore."

About a Marriage is a more straightforward narrative in which the seeming detritus of modern married life assumes a form that the protagonists, the husband and wife, can understand. A reasonably well-off couple. Edward and Ann, move from a bland acceptance of their marriage to a blazing revelation of the strengths of their relationship and of the bond that exists between them. Their love is based not so much on a romantic attachment, although that is also present, as on the many-sided passions and frustrations that ultimately give each partner a vivid insight into their own strengths and weaknesses. Of growing importance in this novel is Gordon's mastery of dialogue and his relaxed ability to enter the minds of his characters who cease to exist as mere cyphers and have grown into stark, living creatures.

Enemies ("A Novel about Friendship") is in the now-familiar Gordon mould of a terse examination of how people relate to each other in familiar and not so familiar circumstances, but its stylistic achievement lies in his ability to strip the central narrative line to a series of scenes which embody sharp dialogue with an internalisation of the characters' thoughts and emotions. The Hiltons live in an unspecified European country, and the action centres on the events of a few days while they are being visited by their parents and friends from England. Events outside their house, which at the beginning of the novel seems to be so secure against outside interference, threaten the fabric of their cosy world as it becomes a microcosm of a beleaguered society with all its concomitant stresses. Faced with the centre falling away, the adults find their relationships shifting uneasy before they reach the triumphant conclusion of the salving power of their own friendships.

100 Scenes from Married Life picks up again the story of Edward and Ann. The intensity of their love for each other is still apparent, but growing self-doubt and encroaching middle age, with its sense of the loss of youth and vitality, gnaw at

Edward's vitals. Interestingly, as if to prove the security of their marriage, Gordon disconcertingly opens the first scene with Edward returning from a week in Venice with his mistress. The novel's title reflects Gordon's debt to Ingmar Bergman's *Scenes from a Marriage*, and in a series of 18 scenes he has captured the warm, womblike, yet claustrophobic story of a close relationship. The inscription is from Philip Roth's *My Life as a Man*: "You want subtlety, then read *The Golden Bowl*. This is life, bozo, not high art." And there are many echoes from Roth's and John Updike's style in Gordon's low-key examination of the matter of middle-class life.

With those two American writers he also shares an interest in language and the economy of its use. At his best he is able to strip his sentences to an almost surreal invisibility which is allied disconcertingly to a lively, sparkling wit. His first collection of what Gordon calls "short fictions," *Pictures from an Exhibition*, was stylistically naive but there was a sense of innovatory excitement as he adopted the attitude of the detached observer in his frequently startling revelations. *Farewell, Fond Dreams* continued many of the same conventions but it showed a surer touch as Gordon risked some breathtaking conceits in his mixture of fact and fantasy, as in the sequence "An attempt to make entertainment out of the war in Vietnam." *The Illusionist and Other Fictions* showed a return to calmer waters, with Gordon seeming to take a fresh interest in the traditional structure of the short story, although he can never lose sight completely of their liquid, three-dimensional possibilities. Critics have been frequently exasperated by the audacious verve of much of Gordon's writing, but he remains one of the few British writers interested in pushing the possibilities of the novel to their outer limits.

—Trevor Royle

GORDON, Mary (Catherine). American. Born on Long Island, New York, 8 December 1949. Educated at Holy Name of Mary School, Valley Stream, New York; Mary Louis Academy; Barnard College, New York, B.A. 1971; Syracuse University, New York, M.A. 1973. Married 1) James Brain in 1974 (marriage dissolved); 2) Arthur Cash in 1979, one daughter and one son. English teacher, Dutchess Community College, Poughkeepsie, New York, 1974–78; lecturer, Amherst College, Massachusetts, 1979. Recipient: Janet Kafka Prize, 1979, 1982. Address: c/o Random House, 201 East 50th Street, New York, New York 10022, U.S.A.

PUBLICATIONS

Novels

Final Payments. New York, Random House, and London, Hamish Hamilton, 1978.

The Company of Women. New York, Random House, and London, Cape, 1981.

Men and Angels. New York, Random House, and London, Cape, 1985.

Uncollected Short Stories

"Now I Am Married," in *Virginia Quarterly Review* (Charlottesville), Summer 1975.

"The Other Woman," in *The Pushcart Prize 1*, edited by Bill
  Henderson.   Yonkers, New York, Pushcart Press, 1976.
"Sisters," in *Ladies Home Journal* (New York), July 1977.
"A Serious Person," in *Redbook* (New York), August 1977.
"Kindness," in *Mademoiselle* (New York), October 1977.
"The Writing Lesson," in *Mademoiselle* (New York), April
  1978.
"Delia," in *Atlantic* (Boston), June 1978.
"Moving," in *Southern Review* (Baton Rouge, Louisiana),
  April 1979.
"Murder," in *Antioch Review* (Yellow Springs, Ohio), Winter
  1979.
"The Thorn," in *Fine Lines*, edited by Ruth Sullivan.   New
  York, Scribner, 1981.
"Murderer Guest," in *Redbook* (New York), November 1981.
"Safe," in *Ms.* (New York), June 1982.
"The Only Son of the Doctor," in *Prize Stories 1983*, edited
  by William Abrahams.   New York, Doubleday, 1983.
"The Neighborhood," in *Ms.* (New York), July 1984.

                    *   *   *

As a Catholic writer of serious fiction, Mary Gordon has
come to seem the natural successor to J.F. Powers, Flannery
O'Connor, and Walker Percy. Like those older writers, she
is steeped in a sense of Roman Catholicism as both high culture
and alma mater, and she conveys vividly a sense of the spiritual
postulates that shape lives distinctively Catholic. Unlike most
writers in the Catholic tradition, however, she reveals little
or no interest in dogma, the quest for salvation, or the demands
of faith. Nor is there any suggestion in her writing that lives
might be touched by grace. Gordon's interest is almost exclusively in religion as mythos—as a pattern of basic values and
ontological assumptions that, once inculcated, prove psychologically inescapable.

Final Payments, Gordon's first novel, treats the situation
of a familiar, now vanishing, type in America: the woman of
Irish descent who gives up her life to nurse an ailing parent.
Isabel Moore has spent eleven years nursing her invalid father,
a conservative Catholic intellectual who prided himself upon
raising a Theresa of Avila rather than a Thérèse of Lisieux.
After his death she sets out on a slow and painful accommodation to the world of the late 1970's, only to discover that her
Catholic erudition is of little help in buying new clothes, searching for a job, and adjusting at the age of thirty to contemporary
sexual mores. In deference to a masochistic impulse, she reverts
to her old role of nurse and takes up the care of her former
housekeeper, but at the end of the book her trained wit and
indomitable intelligence enable her to break free of the old
woman's tyranny. Her final emancipation is linked to the same
matrix of Catholic values that necessitated her "final payments" to father and faith; effectively, Theresa of Avila displaces Thérèse of Lisieux in her person. Complicating this
resolution of the novel, however, is the tentatively feminist
development of a sisterly bond between Isabel and two school
friends. The bond sustains her against the masculine oppressions of father, lover, priest, and God. *Final Payments* is not
a feminist tract, but Gordon seems to feel her way in the ending
to a sense that sisterhood might provide a mythos equal in
power to that of natal Catholicism.

As its title suggests, *The Company of Women* examines in
more detail than *Final Payments* the possibilities of sisterly
bonding. The eponymous "company" in Gordon's second
novel is a group of five women, variously widowed, separated,
and unmarried, united by their devotion to a garrulous and
disaffected Catholic priest named Cyprian. The story revolves
around Felicitas, daughter of the only mother among the
women and depositary of their various kinds of religious faith.
Even more than the women, Cyprian sees Felicitas as his spiritual heir, and the old priest trains her rigorously in his conservative, intellectualized creed. The world proves stronger than
creed: as a college student, Felicitas becomes involved with
a leftist professor, takes up residence in his free-love establishment, and conceives a child whose father she cannot identify.
She is forgiven her trespasses when she returns with her infant
daughter to the company of women, but Cyprian and his devo-
tees transfer to the daughter their hope that Felicitas would
have been their spiritual heir—a fond hope, since the child
is heir to Felicitas's experience of liberation as well as to the
group's conservative Catholicism. The novel ends, like *Final
Payments,* with a tentative hope that women might live on their
own terms, individually and communally. The loosening grasp
of religious fidelities on women's lives is a part of that hope.

The old religious fidelities are largely eclipsed for Anne Foster of Gordon's third novel, *Men and Angels*. Briefly separated
from her husband because of professional obligations, Anne
is an art historian who hires 20-year-old Laura Post as a housekeeper for her two children, not realizing the girl is a religious
fanatic. As Laura wreaks havoc in a warped determination
to "save" her employer, Anne is drawn increasingly into an
absorption with a female painter whom she is researching and
whose life resonates complexly with her own, challenging her
to greater self-determination. She is drawn, too, into seeking
an erotic relationship with a local handyman. What she discovers is both the freedoms and the perils of a self-determined
life. Laura functions as a parody of that life, suggesting that
all such absorptions are religious in form if not in content.
The novel propounds ultimately a double credo: that women
freed from masculine domination face ambiguities in themselves almost irresolvable, and that intelligent women will survive the crisis.

As these three synopses suggest, the intensity of Gordon's
moral imagination is underscored by a tendency of her novels
to drift into melodrama. Intelligence is layered so thickly in
her prose, however, that the problem of sentimentalism does
not arise. Indeed, Gordon's novels are distinctive for their allusive richness, their mordantly ironic tone, their breadth of
human understanding—most distinctive, perhaps, for their precise articulation of delicately shaded awarenesses. Gordon is
not only an able imaginer of affecting situations but an uncommonly thoughtful novelist whose societal and psychological
insights are magisterial.

—Robert F. Kiernan

GOVER, (John) Robert. American. Born in Philadelphia,
Pennsylvania, 2 November 1929. Educated at the University
of Pittsburgh, B.A. in economics 1953. Married 1) Mildred
Vitkovich in 1955 (divorced, 1966); 2) Jeanne-Nell Gement
in 1968; one son. Held a variety of jobs, including that of
reporter on various newspapers, in Pennsylvania and Maryland, until 1961. Address: c/o Ross Erikson Publishers, 223
Via Sevilla, Santa Barbara, California 93105, U.S.A.

PUBLICATIONS

Novels

J.C. Kitten Trilogy.   Santa Barbara, California, Ross Erikson,
  1982.

One Hundred Dollar Misunderstanding. New York, Grove Press, and London, Spearman, 1962.
Here Goes Kitten. New York, Grove Press, 1964; London, Mayflower, 1965.
J.C. Saves. New York, Simon and Schuster, 1968; London, Arrow, 1979.
The Maniac Responsible. New York, Grove Press, 1963; London, MacGibbon and Kee, 1964.
Poorboy at the Party. New York, Simon and Schuster, 1966.
Going for Mr. Big. New York, Bantam, 1973.
To Morrow Now Occurs Again (as O. Govi). Santa Barbara, California, Ross Erikson, 1975.
Getting Pretty on the Table (as O. Govi). Santa Barbara, California, Capra Press, 1975.

Short Story

Bring Me the Head of Rona Barrett. San Francisco, Hargreaves, 1981.

Other

Editor, *The Portable Walter: From the Prose and Poetry of Walter Lowenfels*. New York, Grove Press, 1968.

*

Manuscript Collection: Boston University.

Robert Gover comments:

His trilogy, *One Hundred Dollar Misunderstanding*, *Here Goes Kitten*, and *J.C. Saves*, captures in two characters relations between Black and White in America, especially as it evolved during the 1960's.

J.C. Holland first meets Kitten while he is a university sophomore and she a 13-year-old prostitute. In the second book, J.C. is public relations director of the local political party in power and encounters Kitten as a nightclub singer, or "B-girl." In the third, he finds her ducking police gunfire during a "race riot."

The Maniac Responsible examines the *why* of a rape-murder case. The protagonist, Dean, becomes so involved in the invisible mental process that led to the brutal slaying that he becomes "possessed." Gover uses Joycean techniques to vivify his character's mental world.

Poorboy at the Party mythologizes the split between rich and poor in America. Randy, the main character, goes with his wealthy friend to a party in a large mansion containing art treasures. Conflicting emotions and values plant seeds of frustration and the party erupts into a violent orgy of destruction.

Going for Mr. Big is the tale of a pimp and his two ladies and a millionaire and his wife. Luke Small is a self-styled revolutionary with a lust to pull down the rich and powerful, but his "campaign" to conquer Malcolm McMasters first backfires, then resolves itself in a meaningful togetherness that is outside the prevailing economic system.

To Morrow Now Occurs Again, published under Gover's pen-name O. Govi, is a surrealist romp through a mythical land called all Damnation, which is one big Plantation where Big Money is the Holy Spirit. The protagonist, Big I and little me, soul and ego of one entity, is baffled by the situation he finds himself in. The Rat Doctor, whose experimental maze of millions of rats is periodically studied to show the workings of society and shed light on the religion of Big Money, does not deter Big I from asserting that his currency is eternal.

Victor Versus Mort, a novella published only in Portuguese, pits two archetypal forces against each other in an American social setting. In the end, the main character's wordly successes are eclipsed by death.

Getting Pretty on the Table, also a novella, carries into a suburban orgy a game played by pimps and prostitutes. The game combines psychic therapy and spiritual cleansing.

*   *   *

In the "After Words" to *J.C. Saves* (the last volume of the trilogy begun with *One Hundred Dollar Misunderstanding* and *Here Goes Kitten*), Robert Gover tells us that at the beginning "I had no preconceived idea where these two characters would lead me, their author." Unfortunately, the reader's sharing of that aimlessness is such that he arrives at the last page of the last volume with the sense that the triology is completed only because the author has told him so. There is no reason why the characters might not go on in book after book, *ad infinitum*, like the Rover Boys. When J.C. Holland, the white middle-class protagonist, and Kitten, his black prostitute love, achieve their partial understanding at the end of *J.C. Saves*, it is clear that the slightest alteration provided by another time and other circumstances will be enough to set another story in motion. For the fact is that this is formula fiction: shake up the characters, move them to a new starting point, put them in motion, follow the formula, and you have another book. The other works, form *Poorboy at the Party* through *Getting Pretty on the Table*, play variations on the same basic themes.

Yet there is an honesty in Gover, a vision of the life about him and a quality of writing that raises him above the level of either the pulp pornographer or the slick composer of best sellers. However much he taxes the reader's impatience with shallow characterizations, absurd plot manipulations, gratuitous sex, and moral implications that are occasionally downright silly, he is at times an accomplished satirist. One must only imagine his books in the form of Classic Comics, illustrated by cartoonists for *Mad Magazine*, to be made aware how sure is his touch of the particular grotesque exaggeration that comically, or cruelly, reveals a specific truth. His are not realistic novels, but verbal comic strips, sharing a good many of the virtues and faults of such a paradigm of the genre as Norman Mailer's *An American Dream*.

In large measure he is a moralist—disgusted at times, bitter and angry at others, but always subordinating the matter to the message. And the message is always the same: the Anglo-Saxon American power structure has created a society in which sex and violence are so perversely twisted together that there is no place for honest respect and affection between individuals, classes, or races. Never showing what society might be, he concentrates his attention on the extremes of actuality that he sees as emblematic of the whole. In some respects his most memorable statement is *The Maniac Responsible*, where he parallels the movements of a reporter covering a brutal sex murder with the man's movements while attempting to seduce his teasingly voluptuous neighbor. Finally driven by circumstances (the natural circumstances, the author suggests, of the American way of life) and his own sensitivity, he becomes a suspect in the murder and breaks down into an admission that he, himself, is the maniac responsible (as we all are) for the rape and murder of the girl.

Sex is in the forefront of all Gover's novels. However, the human failures he depicts are not to be blamed on sex, but rather on the failure of its right use, the tendency to treat the other human being as a means rather than an end. Significantly, in the twisted world of Gover's vision the individual who seems best to know how to use her sex is Kitten, the Negro prostitute. Significantly, too, the Kitten trilogy, *Poorboy at the Party*, and *The Maniac Responsible* all end in rejections of the middle-class societies they have portrayed.

—George Perkins

GRACE, Patricia (Frances).   New Zealander.   Born in Wellington, in 1937. Educated at Green Street Convent, Newton, Wellington; St. Mary's College; Wellington Teachers' College. Married; seven children. Has taught in primary and secondary schools in King Country, Northland, and Porirua. Writing Fellow, Victoria University, Wellington, 1985. Recipient: Maori Purposes Fund Board grant, 1974; New Zealand Literature Fund grant, 1975, 1983; Hubert Church Prose Award, 1976; Children's Picture Book of the Year Award, 1982. Address: c/o Longman Paul Ltd., Private Bag, Takapuna, Auckland 9, New Zealand.

PUBLICATIONS

Novels

Mutuwhenua: The Moon Sleeps.   Auckland, Longman Paul, 1978.
Potiki.   Auckland, Penguin, 1986.

Short Stories

Waiariki.   Auckland, Longman Paul, 1975.
The Dream Sleepers and Other Stories.   Auckland, Longman Paul, 1980.

Other (for children)

The Kuia and the Spider.   Auckland, Longman Paul, 1981; London, Penguin, 1982.
Wahine Toa: Women of Maori Myth, paintings by Robyn Kahukiwa.   Auckland, Collins, 1984.
Watercress Tuna and the Children of Champion Street.   Auckland, Longman Paul, 1984.
He aha te mea nui?, Ma wai?, Ko au tenei, Ahakoa he iti (Maori readers).   Auckland, Longman Paul, 4 vols., 1985.

*   *   *

Perhaps it is inevitable that, as a New Zealand writer of short stories whose subject-matter is the intimate, self-sufficient world of the family, Patricia Grace should in her writing suggest certain similarities with Katherine Mansfield. Both treat of themes such as the passing of innocence, the constraints of daily routine and close relationships, and the elusiveness of answers to life's meaning and purpose. Both seek to retrieve the past through a receptive and finely tuned consciousness, and cultivate a narrative style whose modulations extend from haunting lyricism to crisp exposition.

Yet when a reference to Katherine Mansfield actually occurs in one of Grace's short stories, "Letters from Whetu," it signals not their affinity only, but their apartness as well. For Mansfield (as for the little girl in her "How Pearl Button Was Kidnapped"), Maori life could only be, at best, a momentary escape from the pakeha values of time, money, and respectability. For Grace, writing 70-odd years later and from an insider's point of view, the life is binding, vital, and unified, qualities which are figured in the recurring images of the extended family gathered within the home or at some other spot of cherished ground often located by the sea. Their shared activities—feast-making, or gardening, or collecting mussels or diving for *kina*—combine the dual aspects of work and play, and participate in the rhythm of the tides, the seasons, growth, and decay.

Even so, the life Patricia Grace celebrates bears the ineradicable marks of pakeha encroachments and pakeha progress. Old ways and old names are often put aside for the sake of seeming modern; land is abandoned for work in the cities; roads and buildings appear in places which were once held to be *tapu*. In a number of the short stories ("Transition," "And So I Go," "Letters from Whetu"), an awareness that the world is large and that new ways must be learnt is explicitly stated. But running against this, and through all of Grace's writing, is the stronger and more insistent feeling of displacement and loss, and of obligation to keep alive what remains of the old inheritance. The objective correlative of this burden of consciousness is the land, and in the most achieved of her stories, "Journey," the complexity of this symbol, and therefore of the Maori experience, is most fully and imaginatively developed.

At the basis of the story is the very real issue of land ownership, dramatised here as a confrontation between the old Maori who claims the right to leave his land sub-divided among his heirs according to Maori custom, and the government department which has appropriated his land and the entire locality for development. Between the two parties there is no communication possible, a situation underlined by the differences in their language. One argues for people and their need for houses, the other enumerates the engineering problems; one speaks from first-hand experience of the nature of the soil and the vegetables it will produce, the other resorts to maps and plans and the abstractions of "aesthetic aspects."

"Journey" is characteristic of Grace's stories in that the action is sited in the consciousness of the main character, whose claim to the reader's sympathy and serious attention rests upon the author's skilful handling of the interior monologue. As may be expected from the technique, the old man's thoughts and reactions throughout the day provide the reader with insights into his character, which is a mixture of fastidious pride, honesty, stoicism, and imagination. The last quality is demonstrated most vividly in his response to the changes he sees during the train journey to the city. As his memory and observation enter into a dialogue with each other along the way, the journey begins to seem a movement not only across geographical territory but through layers of time also. As past and present overlap, so the reclaimed land over which the train passes is the sea as well where the narrator had once gathered shellfish; suburbia returns to farm land; and great hills loom once more on what is now levelled ground. The old man arrives home at the end of the day disillusioned with a world in which nothing is too sacred or precious to uproot and remove. But, as the reader has been privileged to discover, locked in his memory there survives the record of his own and his country's history.

Not all of Grace's stories have the range and depth of "Journey." Many are concerned with reconstructing a passing mood or an ordinary incident, others with the impingement of the spirit world upon this one. Together however they make clear her strengths as a writer which consist in an energetic and agile prose, a firm and precise and sensitive grasp of the real, and an imagination which mediates with assurance among different dimensions of experience.

Between the appearance of her two volumes of short stories, Grace published her first novel, *Mutuwhenua: The Moon Sleeps*. The story of a Maori girl who falls in love with and marries a pakeha, the action is concerned with the adjustments which each side has to make in order to accommodate the culture of the other. Grace's experiment with the novel form cannot be said to be a success, and the weakness of the work rests chiefly upon her handling of the pakeha. Although the rendering of Maori life and culture by the teenage narrator is lively and poignant, some of the purity which had in the short stories informed the treatment of subjects such as *tapu* is compromised by the presence of an outsider like Graeme. The narrator's attention is naturally divided between her commitment to her own kind and her anxiety concerning his reactions. Yet at the same time, Grace appears unwilling to use the opportunity which the outsider provides for exploring a divergent point of view and to make Graeme's reactions interesting or challenging. The pakeha remains throughout a passive character who, like a male version of the patient Griselda, loves and accepts what he cannot understand. Within the limits of the short story, economy is a virtue and what cannot be developed can often be turned, and effectively, into suggestions and possibilities. But within the more extensive scope of the novel, the reader expects to be told more and to know more. This expectation *Mutuwhenua* does not satisfy and in the end one is left with the suspicion that it is really a short story thinned out into something which in length, at least, answers the name of novel.

—Shirley Chew

GRAHAM, Winston (Mawdsley). British. Born in Victoria Park, Manchester, Lancashire, in 1909(?). Married Jean Mary Williamson in 1939; one son and one daughter. Chairman, Society of Authors, London, 1967–69. Recipient: Crime Writers Association prize, 1956. Fellow, Royal Society of Literature, 1968. O.B.E. (Officer, Order of the British Empire), 1983. Address: Abbotswood House, Buxted, East Sussex, England.

PUBLICATIONS

Novels

The House with the Stained-Glass Windows. London, Ward Lock, 1934.
Into the Fog. London, Ward Lock, 1935.
The Riddle of John Rowe. London, Ward Lock, 1935.
Without Motive. London, Ward Lock, 1936.
The Dangerous Pawn. London, Ward Lock, 1937.
The Giant's Chair. London, Ward Lock, 1938.
Strangers Meeting. London, Ward Lock, 1939.
Keys of Chance. London, Ward Lock, 1939.
No Exit: An Adventure. London, Ward Lock, 1940.
Night Journey. London, Ward Lock, 1941; New York, Doubleday, 1968.

My Turn Next. London, Ward Lock, 1942.
The Merciless Ladies. London, Ward Lock, 1944; revised edition, London, Bodley Head, 1979; New York, Doubleday, 1980.
The Forgotten Story. London, Ward Lock, 1945; as *The Wreck of the Grey Cat*, New York, Doubleday, 1958.
Ross Poldark: A Novel of Cornwall 1783–1787. London, Ward Lock, 1945; as *The Renegade*, New York, Doubleday, 1951.
Demelza: A Novel of Cornwall 1788–1790. London, Ward Lock, 1946; New York, Doubleday, 1953.
Take My Life. London, Ward Lock, 1947; New York, Doubleday, 1967.
Cordelia. London, Ward Lock, 1949; New York, Doubleday, 1950.
Night Without Stars. London, Hodder and Stoughton, and New York, Doubleday, 1950.
Jeremy Poldark: A Novel of Cornwall 1790–1791. London, Ward Lock, 1950; as *Venture Once More*, New York, Doubleday, 1954.
Warleggan: A Novel of Cornwall 1792–1793. London, Ward Lock, 1953; as *The Last Gamble*, New York, Doubleday, 1955.
Fortune Is a Woman. London, Hodder and Stoughton, and New York, Doubleday, 1953.
The Little Walls. London, Hodder and Stoughton, and New York, Doubleday, 1955; abridged edition, as *Bridge to Vengeance*, New York, Spivak, 1957.
The Sleeping Partner. London, Hodder and Stoughton, and New York, Doubleday, 1956.
Greek Fire. London, Hodder and Stoughton, and New York, Doubleday, 1958.
The Tumbled House. London, Hodder and Stoughton, 1959; New York, Doubleday, 1960.
Marnie. London, Hodder and Stoughton, and New York, Doubleday, 1961.
The Grove of Eagles. London, Hodder and Stoughton, 1963; New York, Doubleday, 1964.
After the Act. London, Hodder and Stoughton, 1965; New York, Doubleday, 1966.
The Walking Stick. London, Collins, and New York, Doubleday, 1967.
Angell, Pearl and Little God. London, Collins, and New York, Doubleday, 1970.
The Black Moon: A Novel of Cornwall 1794–1795. London, Collins, 1973; New York, Doubleday, 1974.
Woman in the Mirror. London, Bodley Head, and New York, Doubleday, 1975.
The Four Swans: A Novel of Cornwall 1795–1797. London, Collins, 1976; New York, Doubleday, 1977.
The Angry Tide: A Novel of Cornwall 1798–1799. London, Collins, 1977; New York, Doubleday, 1978.
The Stranger from the Sea: A Novel of Cornwall 1810–1811. London, Collins, 1981; New York, Doubleday, 1982.
The Miller's Dance: A Novel of Cornwall 1812–1813. London, Collins, 1982; New York, Doubleday, 1983.
The Loving Cup: A Novel of Cornwall 1813–1815. London, Collins, 1984; New York, Doubleday, 1985.

Short Stories

The Japanese Girl and Other Stores. London, Collins, 1971; New York, Doubleday, 1972; selection, as *The Cornish Farm*, Bath, Chivers, 1982.

Uncollected Short Story

"The Circus," in *Winter's Crimes 6*, edited by George Hardinge. London, Macmillan, and New York, St. Martin's Press, 1974.

Plays

Shadow Play (produced Salisbury, 1978).
Circumstantial Evidence (produced Guildford, Surrey, 1979).

Screenplays: *Take My Life*, with Valerie Taylor and Margaret Kennedy, 1948; *Night Without Stars*, 1951.

Television Play: *Sleeping Partner*, 1967.

Other

The Spanish Armadas. London, Collins, and New York, Doubleday, 1972.
Poldark's Cornwall, photographs by Simon McBride. London, Bodley Head, 1983.

*

Winston Graham comments:

I look on myself simply as a novelist. I have written—always—what I wanted to write and not what I thought people might want me to write. Reading for me has always been in the first place a matter of enjoyment—otherwise I don't read—and therefore I would expect other people to read my books for the enjoyment they found in them—or not at all. Profit from reading a novel should always be a by-product. The essence to me of style is simplicity, and while I admit there are depths of thought too complex for easy expression, I would despise myself for using complexity of expression where simplicity will do.

If there has been a certain dichotomy in my work, it is simply due to a dichotomy in my own interests. I am deeply interested in history and deeply interested in the present; and I find a stimulus and a refreshment in turning from one subject and one form to another.

I like books of suspense at whatever level they may be written, whether on that of Jane Austen or of Raymond Chandler; so I think all my books of whatever kind contain some of that element which makes a reader want to turn the page—the "and then and then" of which E.M. Forster speaks. This can be a liability if over-indulged in; but so of course can any other preference or attribute.

Although I have always had more to say in a novel than the telling of a story, the story itself has always been the framework on which the rest has depended for its form and shape. I have never been clever enough—or sufficiently self-concerned—to spend 300 pages dipping experimental buckets into the sludge of my own subconscious. I have always been more interested in other people than in myself—though there has to be something of myself in every character created, or he or she will not come to life. I have always been more interested in people than in events, but it is only through events that I have ever been able to illuminate people.

*   *   *

Of the 30-odd novels Winston Graham has published over some 50 years, many of the modern ones are in some way concerned with crime. But they are not, in the usual sense of the term, "crime stories." In them, crime is a kind of catalyst speeding and provoking action, rather than an end in itself or a sufficient reason for the story, as it is in thrillers. It is seen as an aberration in otherwise normal lives, something non-criminal people, generally respectable and middle-class, may slip into or become involved with, gradually, almost imperceptibly, for all kinds of reasons—greed, love, loyalty, even a sudden impulse, but not through a "professional" criminal background. It is not surprising that his novel *Marnie* became one of Hitchcock's most successful films—since Hitchcock too is interested in the way ordinary people may become entangled in the bizarre.

Graham has written straightforward thrillers, and what Michael Gilbert wrote in choosing *The Little Walls* for his "classics of detection and adventure" series applies to the other novels equally well. It was, he says, "the very best of those adventure stories which introduce what has come to be known in critical jargon as the anti-hero ... a useful portmanteau expression to describe someone who undertakes the hero's role, without the hero's normal equipment." The characters in all Graham's novels are, in fact, floundering and all-too-human amateurs, realistically placed in a present-day life that includes jobs and domesticity well observed, and with a normal proneness to fear, indiscretion and lack of nerve; caught in the end by their moral attitudes, by those who love them, by grief, conscience, and the realistic eye of their creator, who knows that their amateur status fails to give them the professional's coolness, his moral indifference.

Graham's sinners are nearly all racked by their sins, and he is fascinated both by the "congenital" liars and outsiders (Marnie, or the crook-lover in *The Walking Stick*), who are conditioned by their past yet devotedly loved in the present, and by their victims, the victims of circumstances, mistakes, impulses, devotions: the narrator of *After the Act*, for instance, who pushes his ailing wife off a balcony, then finds he cannot face the mistress he ostensibly did it for. Graham values suspense; and, for his own fiction, at least, believes in action rather than analysis as the means to bring his characters to life.

His novels can roughly be divided into two, the modern and the historical. To the historical novels he brings the same *kind* of realism that he does to the present day. Through *Cordelia*, the Poldark novels set in 18th-century Cornwall, or *The Forgotten Story*, another tale about ordinary people involved in murder, this time at the turn of the last century, one walks familiarly. Graham has the good historical novelist's ability to suggest, rather than describe, the physical surroundings; above all to avoid gadzookery and picturesqueness. As he can get the feel of an insurance office, a printing works, or an auctioneer's, so he can walk into the past, giving the sense and atmosphere of it rather than the physical detail, making one breathe its air.

—Isabel Quigly

_____

GRAU, Shirley Ann. American. Born in New Orleans, Louisiana, 9 July 1929. Educated at Booth School, Montgomery, Alabama, 1940–45; Ursuline Academy, New Orleans, 1945–46; Sophie Newcomb College, Tulane University, New Orleans (Associate Editor, *Carnival*; Lazarus Memorial Medal, 1949), 1946–50, B.A. 1950 (Phi Beta Kappa); graduate study, Tulane University, 1950–51. Married James Kern Feibleman in 1955; two sons and two daughters. Taught creative writing, University of New Orleans, 1966–67. Recipient: Pulitzer Prize, 1965. Lives in Metairie, Louisiana. Agent:

Brandt and Brandt, 1501 Broadway, New York, New York 10036, U.S.A.

PUBLICATIONS

Novels

The Hard Blue Sky. New York, Knopf, 1958; London. Heinemann, 1959.
The House on Coliseum Street. New York, Knopf, and London, Heinemann, 1961.
The Keepers of the House. New York, Knopf, and London, Longman, 1964.
The Condor Passes. New York, Knopf, 1971; London, Longman, 1972.
Evidence of Love. New York, Knopf, and London, Hamish Hamilton, 1977.

Short Stories

The Black Prince and Other Stories. New York, Knopf, 1955; London, Heinemann, 1956.
The Wind Shifting West. New York, Knopf, 1973; London, Chatto and Windus, 1974.
Nine Women. New York, Knopf, 1986.

Uncollected Short Stories

"The Things You Keep," in *Carnival* (New Orleans), December 1950.
"The Fragile Age," in *Carnival* (New Orleans), October 1951.
"The First Day of School," in *Saturday Evening Post* (Philadelphia), 30 September 1961.
"The Beginning of Summer," in *Story* (New York), November 1961.
"The Empty Night," in *Atlantic* (Boston), May 1962.
"The Loveliest Day," in *Saturday Evening Post* (Philadelphia), 5 May 1962.
"One Night," in *Gentlemen's Quarterly* (New York), February 1966.
"The Young Men," in *Redbook* (New York), April 1968.

*

Critical Study: *Shirley Ann Grau* by Paul Schlueter, Boston, Twayne, 1981.

*   *   *

Shirley Ann Grau may be described as a Southern writer, whose range is sometimes narrowly regional. She may also, therefore, be described as a local colorist whose observations of custom and character suggests an anthropologist at work in a fictional mode. She is a white author who deals with blacks and the black sub-culture, which makes her an anomaly in a period of black militancy. And she is finally a novelist of manners who is sharply aware of the collapse of conventional behavior patterns in modern life. The pervasive style and mood of her work may be summed up best in the terms tough, cold, and realistic. The toughness and the apparent realism seem to reveal a debt to Hemingway. She is never sentimental, and almost always she maintains sufficient distance from her characters to depict them with an objectivity that is sometimes little short of chilling. At her best she displays a kind of cold power. But she is, in general, a limited writer. She lacks originality, especially in her treatment of Negroes and of the South. More seriously, she lacks the complex vision that enables her both to see around and to penetrate deeply into her subject. She is a competent writer who stands at some distance from the center of the Southern Renaissance.

Her best work to date is *The Keepers of the House*, a novel about a southern family. The story concerns Will Howland who inherits a great deal of land and acquires more. After the death of his wife, he brings a Negro girl into his house and has by her three children who survive. Late in the book, it is revealed that Will had secretly married the Negro girl. He is portrayed as a good, compassionate man whose miscegenation arose out of love. His white granddaughter marries a man who enters politics, joins the Klan, runs for governor, and makes anti-Negro speeches. One of Will's children by the Negro woman reveals that his father is related to a racist politician. As a result of the revelation, the latter is ruined and the Howland family estate attacked. The estate endures, and the daughter revenges herself upon the town.

Grau is fully aware that the glamorous past may be a trap, as one of her short stories reveals. But she also knows that family traditions which are rooted in the past may endow life in the present with an illuminating sense of time and a stabilizing sense of place; in these ways the past provides a sense of continuity which enriches life in the present. This novel centers on these conceptions of life, which are characteristically Southern and which mark the work of other contemporary Southern writers as different as Robert Penn Warren and Eudora Welty. The treatment of inter-racial love here, made acceptable by marriage, appears to be an apologia for Southern miscegenation, which is, of course, usually conceived in much harsher terms. The same is true of the manipulation of racial animosities in politics, which in itself is authentic enough in the novel. But in depicting the defeat of the racist, Grau seems to depart from her characteristically objective stance.

That stance she had maintained in *The Hard Blue Sky*, which reveals her talent for local color. The scene is an island in the Gulf of Mexico inhabited by characters of French and Spanish descent. The principal conflict is between them and the inhabitants of another island who are Slavic in descent. A boy from one island marries a girl from another; the marriage precipitates a feud. Added to the violence of men is the violence of nature, displayed when a hurricane sweeps through the Gulf. Grau does not dwell on the quaintness of character or place in her novel, and she does not patronize her characters, although the temptation to do so must have been quite real, since she conceives them as primitives. She looks at them coldly and clearly, dramatizing their attitudes toward life but passing no judgment on their behavior. These are people who recognize no canons of respectability, who admit of no restraints on their passions, and who recognize no guilt. Their sexual attitudes are thus quite free, sex being simply in the natural order of things, and their tendency toward violence is always close to the surface, since they believe that a good fight is healthy. Their life is hard and the hazards of nature, whether snakes or wind, make it harder.

Her treatment of the characters in this novel is the same, generally speaking, as her treatment of Negroes throughout her fiction. Her composite Negro lives an unstructured life in which he obeys appetite and impulse in a naturally selfish movement toward gratification. His morality is virtually nonexistent, but casual if apparent at all. His capacity for violence is like that of the islanders. This Negro does not rise to the level of self-consciousness. Ralph Ellison might say that he is a stereotype, perceived because the white writer suffers from a psychic-social blindness caused by the construction of the inner eye; that is, either Grau is blind or the real Negro is invisible.

Grau's chief contribution to the novel of manners is *The House on Coliseum Street*. Although it is an inferior work, it demonstrates, as some of her short stories have, that she understands the various kinds of moral corruption that mark modern life. She knows that the contemporary world is without values, and she makes divorce and sexual promiscuity the obvious signs, in this novel, of the disintegration of well-to-do society.

The Condor Passes is another family novel, melodramatic in plot but of interest for its method: much of the story is told from the five points of view of the five major characters. *Evidence of Love*, like James Gould Cozzens's *By Love Possessed*, concerns the varieties of love, some a burdensome chore, as Grau shows in the sensitive and effective section on the old mother who, content in her loneliness, awaits the coming of death. The title story of her collection *The Wind Shifting West* displays Grau's feel of water and sky, but only occasionally do the other stories reveal the detachment and power which distinguish her fictional voice at its best.

—Chester E. Eisinger

GRAY, Alasdair (James). Scottish. Born in Glasgow, Lanarkshire, 28 December 1934. Educated at Whitehill Senior Secondary School, 1946–52; Glasgow Art School (Bellahouston travelling scholarship, 1957), 1952–57, diploma in mural painting and design 1957. Married Inge Sørensen in 1962; one son. Art teacher, Lanarkshire and Glasgow, 1958–61; scene painter, Pavilion and Citizens' theatres, Glasgow, 1961–63; free-lance painter and writer, Glasgow, 1963–76; artist recorder, People's Palace Local History Museum, Glasgow, 1976–77; Writer-in-Residence, Glasgow University, 1977–79. Since 1979, free-lance writer and painter. Address: 39 Kersland Street, Glasgow G12 8BP, Scotland.

PUBLICATIONS

Novels

Lanark: A Life in Four Books. Edinburgh, Canongate, and New York, Harper, 1981.
1982, Janine. London, Cape, and New York, Viking, 1984.
The Fall of Kelvin Walker. Edinburgh, Canongate, 1985; New York, Braziller, 1986.

Short Stories

The Comedy of the White Dog. Glasgow, Print Studio Press, 1979.
Unlikely Stories, Mostly. Edinburgh, Canongate, 1983; New York, Penguin, 1984.
Lean Tales, with Agnes Owens and James Kelman. London, Cape, 1985.

Plays

Jonah (puppet play; produced Glasgow, 1956).
The Fall of Kelvin Walker (televised, 1968; produced on tour, 1972).
Dialogue (produced on tour, 1971).
The Loss of the Golden Silence (produced Edinburgh, 1973).

Homeward Bound (produced Edinburgh, 1973).
Tickly Mince (revue), with Tom Leonard and Liz Lochhead (produced Glasgow, 1982).
The Pie of Damocles (revue), with others (produced Glasgow, 1983).

Radio Plays: *Quiet People*, 1968; *The Night Off*, 1969; *Thomas Muir of Huntershill* (documentary), 1970; *The Loss of the Golden Silence*, 1974; *The Harbinger Report*, 1975; *McGrotty and Ludmilla*, 1976; *The Vital Witness* (on Joan Ure), 1979.

Television Plays and Documentaries: *Under the Helmet*, 1965; *The Fall of Kelvin Walker*, 1968; *Triangles*, 1972; *The Man Who Knew about Electricity*, 1973; *Honesty* (for children), 1974; *Today and Yesterday* (3 plays; for children), 1975; *Beloved*, 1976; *The Gadfly*, 1977; *The Story of a Recluse*, 1986.

*

Manuscript Collections: Scottish National Library, Edinburgh; Hunterian Museum, Glasgow University.

Alasdair Gray comments:

Lanark was planned as a whale, *1982, Janine* as an electric eel, *The Fall of Kelvin Walker* as a tasty sprat. Of the short stories I think "A Report to the Trustees" has the most honestly sober prose, "Five Letters from an Eastern Empire" the most inventive fancy, "Prometheus" the greatest scope.

*   *   *

Alasdair Gray came late to the novel and was in middle life when *Lanark*, his first novel was published. Prior to that he had been a painter and scriptwriter and visual influences bear heavily on his work as a consequence. This is especially true of his short stories which were published together under the title *Unlikely Stories, Mostly*. Some stories in this collection are long, such as "Logopandocy" a pastiche on the writing of Sir Thomas Urquhart of Cromartie; others short, and two, "A Likely Story in a Nonmarital Setting" and "A Likely Story in a Domestic Setting," only five lines long. Some are set in modern everyday life, others in a fantastic other world; above all they are rich in imaginative background detail. His story "Five Letters from the Eastern Empire" is set in the time of Marco Polo and the letters are supposedly written by Bohu, the Chinese Emperor's tragic poet, to his parents and they describe the court—"the evergreen garden"—in all its magnificence and in all its cruelty. On the one hand it is an evocative description of the lives led by the divinely justified, and the sharp, cinematic cuts and finely observed detail make it seem an exercise in script writing. On another level it is a parable of power that oppresses, of a backsliding emperor whom Bohu discovers to be an "evil little puppet, and all the cunning, straightfaced, pompous men who use him."

Although Gray makes considerable use of myth and parable in his fiction and delights in creating imaginative worlds and societies, the matter of Scotland is never far away from the heart of his fiction. In *1982, Janine*, the hero, an ageing, divorced, alcoholic, insomniac supervisor of security installations tells his story while sitting in the dingy bedroom of a small Scottish hotel: to him, his native country and his fellow countrymen are subjects of disgust. "The truth is that we are a nation of arselickers, though we disguise it with surfaces: a surface of generous, openhanded manliness, a surface of dour practical integrity, a surface of futile, maudlin defiance like when we break goalposts and windows after football matches on foreign soil and commit suicide on Hogmanay by leaping from fountains in Trafalgar Square." Although this novel is only loosely connected to present-day Scotland, and more concerned with the general human condition as experienced in the narrator's drunken reverie, *1982, Janine* is rich in Scottish literary influences. In one section the narrator meets a pantheon of Scottish poets in an Edinburgh pub; in another Gray's richly lyrical exploration of time and space is reminiscent of Hugh MacDiarmid's long poem, "A Drunk Man Looks at the Thistle."

That Gray should be so concerned with Scotland and yet repelled by it—a classic theme in Scottish fiction—should come as little surprise to readers of *Lanark*, his first and arguably his most inventive novel. In this phantasmagoric exploration of modern city life Gray has an index of plagiarisms—this is a favourite literary device of his—which includes an entry on George Douglas Brown: "Books 1 and 2 owe much to the novel *The House with the Green Shutters* in which heavy paternalism forces a weak-minded youth into dread of existence, hallucination and crime." In Brown's novel Gourlay, a wealthy self-made man is ruined by his monstrous, self-willed nature and his son is castrated both by his malignancy and by the squalid ethics of Barbie, the mean town in which they live. Although Duncan Thaw the narrator of *Lanark* is not subjected to similar pressures he has to cope with a loveless family and the dreary drudgery of growing to maturity in a far-from-idealised city of Glasgow. Gray is at his best in dealing with the realities of modern life and his descriptions of life in post-war Scotland have a sure and naturalistic touch. Elsewhere he descends into fantasy, creating a world which might yet be, and here he is on less secure ground. This is the afterlife to which Thaw is condemned after his death which is half accident and half suicide. Called Unthank it contains echoes of his life on earth in Scotland but it is peopled by strange creatures which have the power of transmogrification. As such Gray seems to be saying that the world of Unthank, and of its hideous, depersonalised city of Provan, is the world which we are creating for tomorrow. Provan, it transpires, is the mirror-image of the worst aspects of Glasgow.

Much of Gray's writing gives an impression of linguistic inventiveness and artistic energy. It is also rich in literary allusions and he delights in using typography to suit his needs. In places that quirkiness can irritate the reader and interrupt the narrative flow, but beneath those occasional self-indulgences lies a novelist of power and imagination, a writer of Rabelaisian exuberance.

—Trevor Royle

----

died April 3, 1991
Geneva, Switz
(1904–1991)   "blood disorder"

GREENE, Graham. British. Born in Berkhamsted, Hertfordshire, 2 October 1904. Educated at Berkhamsted School; Balliol College, Oxford. Served in the Foreign Office, London, 1941–44. Married Vivien Dayrell-Browning in 1927; one son and one daughter. Staff member, *The Times*, London, 1926–30; movie critic, 1937–40, and literary editor, 1940–41, *Spectator*, London. Director, Eyre and Spottiswoode, publishers, London, 1944–48, and The Bodley Head, publishers, London, 1958–68. Member, Panamanian Canal Treaty Delegation to Washington, 1977. Recipient: Hawthornden Prize, 1941; James Tait Black Memorial Prize, 1949; Shakespeare Prize (Hamburg), 1968; Thomas More Medal, 1973; Dos Passos Prize, 1980; City of Madrid Medal, 1980; Jerusalem Prize,

1981. Litt.D.: Cambridge University, 1962; D.Litt.: Edinburgh University, 1967; Oxford University, 1979. Honorary Fellow, Balliol College, 1963. Honorary Citizen, Anacapri, 1978. Companion of Honour, 1966; Chevalier, Legion of Honour (France), 1967; Grand Cross, Order of Balboa (Panama), 1983; Commandant, Order of Arts and Letters (France), 1984; Companion of Literature, Royal Society of Literature, 1984; O.M. (Order of Merit), 1986. Address: c/o The Bodley Head, 9 Bow Street, London WC2E 7AL, England.

PUBLICATIONS

Novels

The Man Within. London, Heinemann, and New York, Doubleday, 1929.
The Name of Action. London, Heinemann, 1930; New York, Doubleday, 1931.
Rumour at Nightfall. London, Heinemann, 1931; New York, Doubleday, 1932.
Stamboul Train. London, Heinemann, 1932; as *Orient Express*, New York, Doubleday, 1933.
It's a Battlefield. London, Heinemann, and New York, Doubleday, 1934; revised edition, London, Heinemann, 1948; New York, Viking Press, 1962.
England Made Me. London, Heinemann, and New York, Doubleday, 1935; as *The Shipwrecked*, New York, Viking Press, 1953.
A Gun for Sale: An Entertainment. London, Heinemann, 1936; as *This Gun for Hire*, New York, Doubleday, 1936.
Brighton Rock. London, Heinemann, 1938; as *Brighton Rock: An Entertainment*, New York, Viking Press, 1938.
The Confidential Agent: An Entertainment. London, Heinemann, and New York, Viking Press, 1939.
The Power and the Glory. London, Heinemann, 1940; as *The Labyrinthine Ways*, New York, Viking Press, 1940.
The Ministry of Fear: An Entertainment. London, Heinemann, and New York, Viking Press, 1943.
The Heart of the Matter. London, Heinemann, and New York, Viking Press, 1948.
The Third Man. New York, Viking Press, 1950.
The Third Man, and The Fallen Idol. London, Heinemann, 1950.
The End of the Affair. London, Heinemann, and New York, Viking Press, 1951.
Loser Takes All. London, Heinemann, 1955; New York, Viking Press, 1957.
The Quiet American. London, Heinemann, 1955; New York, Viking Press, 1956.
Our Man in Havana: An Entertainment. London, Heinemann, and New York, Viking Press, 1958.
A Burnt-Out Case. London, Heinemann, and New York, Viking Press, 1961.
The Comedians. London, Bodley Head, and New York, Viking Press, 1966.
Travels with My Aunt. London, Bodley Head, 1969; New York, Viking Press, 1970.
The Honorary Consul. London, Bodley Head, and New York, Simon and Schuster, 1973.
The Human Factor. London, Bodley Head, and New York, Simon and Schuster, 1978.
Doctor Fischer of Geneva; or, The Bomb Party. London, Bodley Head, and New York, Simon and Schuster, 1980.
Monsignor Quixote. London, Bodley Head, and New York, Simon and Schuster, 1982.

The Tenth Man. London, Bodley Head-Blond, and New York, Simon and Schuster, 1985.

Short Stories

The Basement Room and Other Stories. London, Cresset Press, 1935.
The Bear Fell Free. London, Grayson, 1935.
24 Short Stories, with James Laver and Sylvia Townsend Warner. London, Cresset Press, 1939.
Nineteen Stories. London, Heinemann, 1947; New York, Viking Press, 1949; augmented edition, as *Twenty-One Stories*, London, Heinemann, 1954; New York, Viking Press, 1962; selection, as *Across the Bridge and Other Stories*, Bath, Chivers, 1981.
A Visit to Morin. London, Heinemann, 1959.
A Sense of Reality. London, Bodley Head, and New York, Viking Press, 1963.
May We Borrow Your Husband? and Other Comedies of the Sexual Life. London, Bodley Head, and New York, Viking Press, 1967.
The Collected Stories of Graham Greene. London, Bodley Head–Heinemann, 1972; New York, Viking Press, 1973.
How Father Quixote Became a Monsignor. Los Angeles, Sylvester and Orphanos, 1980.

Uncollected Short Stories

"Church Militant," in *Critic* (Chicago), January 1974.
"On the Way Back," in *Firebird 1*, edited by T.J. Binding. London, Penguin, 1982.

Plays

The Living Room (produced London, 1953; New York, 1954). London, Heinemann, 1953; New York, Viking Press, 1954.
The Potting Shed (produced New York, 1957). New York, Viking Press, 1957; revised version (produced London, 1958), London, Heinemann, 1958.
The Complaisant Lover (produced London, 1959; New York, 1961). London, Heinemann, 1959; New York, Viking Press, 1961.
Carving a Statue (produced London, 1964; New York, 1968). London, Bodley Head, 1964.
The Third Man: A Film, with Carol Reed. London, Lorrimer Films, 1968; New York, Simon and Schuster, 1969.
Alas, Poor Maling, adaptation of his own story (televised, 1975). Published in *Shades of Greene*, London, Bodley Head–Heinemann, 1975.
The Return of A.J. Raffles: An Edwardian Comedy Based Somewhat Loosely on E.W. Hornung's Characters in "The Amateur Cracksman" (produced London, 1975). London, Bodley Head, 1975; New York, Simon and Schuster, 1976.
Yes and No, and For Whom the Bell Chimes (producd Leicester, 1980). London, Bodley Head, 1983.
The Great Jowett (broadcast, 1980). London, Bodley Head, 1981.

Screenplays: *The First and the Last* (*21 Days*), 1937; *The New Britain*, 1940; *Brighton Rock* (*Young Scarface*), with Terence Rattigan, 1947; *The Fallen Idol*, with Lesley Storm and William Templeton, 1948; *The Third Man*, with Carol Reed, 1950; *The Stranger's Hand*, with Guy Elmes and Giorgio Bassani, 1954; *Loser Takes All*, 1956; *Saint Joan*, 1957; *Our Man in Havana*, 1960; *The Comedians*, 1967.

Radio Play: *The Great Jowett*, 1980.

Television Play: *Alas, Poor Maling*, 1975.

Verse

Babbling April. Oxford, Blackwell, 1925.
For Christmas. Privately printed, 1951.

Other

Journey Without Maps. London, Heinemann, and New York, Doubleday, 1936.
The Lawless Roads: A Mexican Journey. London, Longman, 1939; as *Another Mexico*, New York, Viking Press, 1939.
British Dramatists. London, Collins, 1942; included in *The Romance of English Literature*, New York, Hastings House, 1944.
The Little Train (for children; published anonymously). London, Eyre and Spottiswoode, 1946; as Graham Greene, New York, Lothrop, 1958.
Why Do I Write? An Exchange of Views Between Elizabeth Bowen, Graham Greene, and V.S. Pritchett. London, Marshall, and New York, British Book Centre, 1948.
After Two Years. Privately printed, 1949.
The Little Fire Engine (for children). London, Parrish, 1950; as *The Little Red Fire Engine*, New York, Lothrop, 1953.
The Lost Childhood and Other Essays. London, Eyre and Spottiswoode, 1951; New York, Viking Press, 1952.
The Little Horse Bus (for children). London, Parrish, 1952; New York, Lothrop, 1954.
The Little Steamroller: A Story of Adventure, Mystery, and Detection (for children). London, Parrish, 1953; New York, Lothrop, 1955.
Essais Catholiques, translated by Marcelle Sibon. Paris, Editions de Seuil, 1953.
In Search of a Character: Two African Journals. London, Bodley Head, 1961; New York, Viking Press, 1962.
The Revenge: An Autobiographical Fragment. Privately printed, 1963.
Victorian Detective Fiction: A Catalogue of the Collection Made by Dorothy Glover and Graham Greene. London, Bodley Head, 1966.
Collected Essays. London, Bodley Head, and New York, Viking Press, 1969.
A Sort of Life (autobiography). London, Bodley Head, and New York, Simon and Schuster, 1971.
The Virtue of Disloyalty. Privately printed, 1972.
The Pleasure-Dome: The Collected Film Criticism 1935–40, edited by John Russell Taylor. London, Secker and Warburg, 1972; as *Graham Greene on Film: Collected Film Criticism 1935–1940*, New York, Simon and Schuster, 1972.
The Portable Graham Greene, edited by Philip Stratford. New York, Viking Press, 1973; London, Penguin, 1977.
Lord Rochester's Monkey, Being the Life of John Wilmot, Second Earl of Rochester. London, Bodley Head, and New York, Viking Press, 1974.
Ways of Escape. London, Bodley Head, 1980; New York, Simon and Schuster, 1981.
J'Accuse: The Dark Side of Nice (bilingual edition). London, Bodley Head, 1982.
Getting to Know the General: The Story of an Involvement. London, Bodley Head, and New York, Simon and Schuster, 1984.

Editor, *The Old School: Essays by Divers Hands.* London, Cape, 1934.
Editor, *The Best of Saki.* London, Lane, 1950; New York, Viking Press, 1961.

Editor, with Hugh Greene, *The Spy's Bedside Book: An Anthology.* London, Hart Davis, 1957.

Editor, *The Bodley Head Ford Madox Ford.* London, Bodley Head, 4 vols., 1962–63.

Editor, *An Impossible Woman: The Memories of Dottoressa Moor of Capri.* London, Bodley Head, 1975; New York, Viking Press, 1976.

Editor, the Hugh Greene, *Victorian Villainies.* London, Viking, 1984; New York, Viking, 1985.

*

Bibliography: *Graham Greene: A Checklist of Criticism* by J.D. Vann, Kent, Ohio, Kent State University Press, 1970; *Graham Greene: A Descriptive Catalog* by Robert H. Miller, Lexington, University Press of Kentucky, 1978; *Graham Greene: A Bibliography and Guide to Research* by R.A. Wobbe, New York, Garland, 1979; *Graham Greene: An Annotated Bibliography of Criticism* by A.F. Cassis, Metuchen, New Jersey, Scarecrow Press, 1981.

Manuscript Collection: Humanities Research Center, University of Texas, Austin.

Critical Studies (selection): *Graham Greene and the Heart of the Matter* by Marie Mesnet, London, Cresset Press, 1954; *Graham Greene* by Francis Wyndham, London, Longman, 1955, revised edition, 1958; *Graham Greene* by John Atkins, London, Calder, and New York, Roy, 1957, revised edition, London, Calder and Boyars, 1966, New York, Humanities Press, 1967; *The Labyrinthine Ways of Graham Greene* by Francis Leo Kunkel, New York, Sheed and Ward, 1960, revised edition, Mamaroneck, New York, Appel, 1973; *Graham Greene* by David Pryce-Jones, Edinburgh, Oliver and Boyd, 1963, New York, Barnes and Noble, 1968; *Graham Greene: Some Critical Considerations* (includes bibliography by N. Brennan) edited by Robert O. Evans, Lexington, University of Kentucky Press, 1963; *Graham Greene* by A.A. DeVitis, New York, Twayne, 1964; *Graham Greene* by David Lodge, New York, Columbia University Press, 1966; *Graham Greene: A Critical Essay* by Martin Turnell, Grand Rapids, Michigan, Eerdmans, 1967; *Graham Greene: The Aesthetics of Exploration* by Gwenn R. Boardman, Gainesville, University of Florida Press, 1971; *Graham Greene the Entertainer* by Peter Wolfe, Carbondale, Southern Illinois University Press, 1972; *Graham Greene: A Collection of Critical Essays* edited by Samuel Hynes, Englewood Cliffs, New Jersey, Prentice Hall, 1973; *Graham Greene the Novelist* by J.P. Kulshrestha, New Delhi, Macmillan, and Atlantic Highlands, New Jersey, Humanities Press, 1977; *The Other Man: Conversations with Graham Greene* by Marie Françoise Allain, London, Bodley Head, and New York, Simon and Schuster, 1983; *Graham Greene* by John Spurling, London, Methuen, 1983; *Graham Greene* by Richard Kelly, New York, Ungar, 1984; *Saints, Sinners, and Comedians: The Novels of Graham Greene* by Roger Sharrock, Tunbridge Wells, Kent, Burns and Oates, 1984; *The Achievement of Graham Greene* by Grahame Smith, Brighton, Sussex, Harvester Press, 1985.

Theatrical Activities:
Actor: **Film**—*La Nuit americaine* (*Day for Night*), 1973.

*   *   *

The work of Graham Greene represents one of the most considerable achievements of the generation immediately following that of the great masters of earlier 20th-century fiction, James, Conrad, Joyce, Woolf, and Lawrence. Unlike his predecessors, however, Greene has enjoyed a large measure of general popularity as well as critical acclaim and this may help to account for the suspicion in which he is apparently held in some academic circles (his novels rarely appear on the syllabuses of university English Departments) and his failure to win the Nobel Prize for literature. (The frequency with which his work has been adapted for the screen is an indication of his commercial success.)

Greene himself acknowledged this aspect of his gift by labelling some of his fiction "entertainments," as opposed to novels, a distinction he later abandoned. His career really got under way with *Stamboul Train*, his fourth novel; Greene disowned the second and third and they have never been reprinted. *Stamboul Train* is a lively thriller, with political overtones, which depicts the adventures of a cross-section of middle-class English people, including a Jewish businessman and a best-selling novelist in a Europe threatened by Nazism. This vein was continued in *A Gun for Sale* and *The Confidential Agent*, reaching its climax in *The Ministry of Fear*, a masterly combination of the political thriller and the psychological novel which is one of Greene's most under-rated achievements.

Greene's writing style was generally vivid and workmanlike in his earliest novels, but it reached a new level of intensity in *Brighton Rock* which began life as an entertainment only to be transformed into a metaphysical melodrama of good and evil whose conflicts are rendered in language of metaphorical and symbolic complexity. Greene is a Roman Catholic convert who hates to be called a Catholic novelist (he is merely, he insists, a novelists who happens to be a Catholic), but *Brighton Rock* clearly opened a new phase in his work in which questions of faith are dramatized within the tensions of a still popular novelistic form. This realm of spiritual debate was further explored in a remarkable series of novels, *The Power and the Glory*, *The Heart of the Matter*, and *The End of the Affair*, a book which might reasonably be called one of the great love stories of 20th-century fiction. Greene returned to the conflict of faith and doubt in *A Burnt-Out Case*, a novel pared to the bone in its style, plot, characterization, and setting.

The End of the Affair is set in the blitz of war-time London, but these other works have exotic locations (Mexico, West Africa, the Congo), a reflection of Greene's journalism and the fact that he is one of the most widely travelled and politically aware of modern novelists. His fascination with out of the way parts of the world and his ability to re-create them in vivid prose are no doubt two reasons for his continuing popular appeal.

Greene has always been a radical Catholic, a left-wing sympathiser with the underdog, and these preoccupations surface in *It's a Battlefield* and *England Made Me*, the third and fourth novels in the collected edition of his works. He continued these interests in *The Quiet American*, set in Saigon before the American involvement in that part of the world. For some the book is weakened by an indiscriminate anti-Americanism, but there is no denying its political insight, especially when one remembers that it was written long before the general public had become aware of the dangers of western intervention in the Far East.

Up to this point a certain savagery had been evident in Greene's view of the world, his treatment of his characters and, even, his humour. But with *Our Man in Havana* he discovered a vein of genial and tender comedy which seems to have signalled an important shift in his general outlook. An outrageously farcical denunciation of the absurdities and cruelties of espionage, the novel does however reveal a deeply serious purpose in its defence of the ordinariness of decent daily living, and it avoids sentimentality by its examination of the senseless pain caused by bureaucratic institutions.

Greene is still creatively active as two shorter works reveal— *Doctor Fischer of Geneva; or, The Bomb Party* and *Monsignor Quixote*—but the end of his greatest achievement is probably to be found in a trio of very fine novels, *The Comedians*, *The Honorary Consul*, and *The Human Factor*. Greene has complained of a certain short-windedness in his creative output, but with *The Comedians* he discovered an amplitude of style reminiscent of the 19th-century novel. Set in Haiti, the book gives yet new life to Greene's perennial themes of guilt and betrayal unifying, through a metaphor of acting, the horrors of corruption and cruelty in an under-developed country and the faithlessness of love on the personal level. *The Honorary Consul*, set in a viciously repressive South American state, explores the concept of fatherhood, from that of God the father, through the status of society as father to its people, to what it means to be a father in the ordinary sense. The novel combines gripping excitement with an examination of the spiritual, political, social, and personal aspects of human life in a way that deserves to be called profound. With *The Human Factor*, Greene returns to his own birthplace, Berkhamsted, for a novel of apparent simplicity which uses the issues of treason and spying for what is perhaps Greene's most painful enquiry into the perils of ordinariness and the dangers which beset the attempt to live humanly in the contemporary world. Its aging spy-hero's gently depicted marriage to a black South African is evidence of Greene's apparently inexhaustible ability to tap contemporary events in the service of a truly artistic presentation of human life rather than exploit them for mere topicality.

Greene is a man of letters and not simply a novelist. Apart from poetry (he disowns an early volume of verse) he has published in all the major literary forms: short stories, travel books, essays, autobiography and biography, and books for children. His plays have enjoyed success in London, New York, and on the Continent and he was one of the liveliest film reviewers ever (this work was collected in *The Pleasure-Dome*). With some exceptions, Greene's short stories are not among his greatest achievements, but his *Collected Essays* is seriously underrated, containing as it does fine literary criticism, especially on James and Dickens, vivid biographical sketches, and mordant recollections of his involvement with Hollywood. Greene's links with cinema are notably strong for a serious writer. He has written original screenplays (most famously for *The Third Man*), adapted the work of others, been a producer and, even, appeared in a film, Truffaut's *Day for Night*. There seems little doubt that this enthusiasm for cinema has influenced his own work, especially at the level of plot and the choice of subject matter, and to some extent in the detail of his writing. Greene himself has claimed that his descriptions have a quality of movement akin to that of the moving camera.

But it is as a novelist that Greene will be remembered and it seems clear that he is destined to hold an honoured place in the second rank of writers in the 20th century. He regards James and Conrad as giants and, no doubt rightly, rejects his claim to a place with them. But Greene does possess most of the qualities of the first-rate, if not great, writer. His output has been both fertile and varied. He has created a gallery of memorable characters, although very few of them are women. Without his being a great stylist, his writing is strong, supple, and vivid. And the settings of his novels are invariably colourful and detailed. Above all, Greene has marked out his own special

territory as a writer, the anguish created by the guilt of betrayals which are unavoidably a part of the human condition. Greene himself claims that his view of the world pre-dates his conversion and there is little doubt that at his best he has avoided writing novels which merely exemplify a certain system of belief. The spiritual conflicts he has depicted so richly and painfully belong to the experience of living for most people and Greene has given them one of their definitive forms of expression in 20th-century fiction.

—Grahame Smith

GROSSMAN, Alfred. American. Born in New York City, 14 May 1927. Educated at Haverford College, Pennsylvania, 1944–48, B.A. 1948; Harvard University, Cambridge, Massachusetts, 1948–49, M.A. 1949. Served in the United States Navy, 1945–46. Married Althea Eudora Van Boskirk in 1971. Editor, *East Europe Magazine*, New York, 1954–61; after 1968, editor *New York Times Almanac*. Address: c/o Times Books, 201 East 50th Street, New York, New York 10022, U.S.A.

PUBLICATIONS

Novels

Acrobat Admits.   New York, Braziller, 1959; London, Heinemann, 1960.
Many Slippery Errors.   London, Heinemann, 1963; New York, Doubleday, 1964.
Marie Beginning.   London, Heinemann, 1964; New York, Doubleday, 1965.
The Do-Gooders.   New York, Doubleday, and London, Heinemann, 1968.

Uncollected Short Stories

"The Big Girls," in *Rogue* (Evanston, Illinois), 1963.
"The Gobbitch Men," in *Amazing* (New York), February 1965.
"The Beauty Contest," in *Transatlantic Review* (London), Winter 1966–67.

*

Manuscript Collection: Mugar Memorial Library, Boston University.

*   *   *

At his best Alfred Grossman is his own acrobat; putting on disguises, slipping effortlessly from one style to another (the barracks monologue of Sarge, the poor-white-trash dialect of the yokel in *Acrobat Admits*), parodying and punning in a zany show of life's lunacy; at his worst, he is the acrobat tripped, caught in his own trick, unable to disentangle himself, finally resorting to any device to take him off-stage. When his performance is deft, he writes in the ironic mode, exposing man's emotional and spiritual impoverishment, his desperate attempts to make contact through sex, the failure of these attempts to do anything but that. When he flounders, he denies the contradictions which sustain his irony and turns his satire on man's hapless attempts to give life meaning into an insignificant story of the disintegration of a neurotic personality.

New York is Grossman's circus with a publishing house (*Acrobat Admits*), the United Nations Secretariat (*Many Slippery Errors*), or a shoe manufacturing corporation (*Marie Beginning*) as the arena. The time is the 1960's with the radical right and left battling. His theme is that modern, urban life is insupportable—that the only relief from boredom will come from an action. The possibilities for action vary in Grossman's novels, but in no case does Grossman, a comedian of black humor, allow the action to be positive. In *Acrobat Admits* destruction of another is the central action. Kennan attempts self-destruction in both *Marie Beginning* and again in its self-contained sequel, *The Do-Gooders*, and Dicherty succeeds in *Many Slippery Errors*. Finally, in *The Do-Gooders* the act that brings the novel to its conclusion is not murder, or suicide, but the destruction of some part of the System. In Grossman's second novel, Dicherty's dream of blowing-up Con-Ed is only a dream; in *The Do-Gooders* the dream is fulfilled when Marie, Spider, and Kennan blow up the connecting link of a twelve-lane expressway. This reliance on a sophomoric solution diminishes Grossman's art: after sensing the nihilistic vision that lies beneath an often hilarious, but always troubling, surface, the audience expects more from him. Perhaps Grossman's next novel will offer it.

In his arena are his characters: men, imperfectly synchronized with their time—intelligent, restive, bored with the banalities of their jobs and marriages, but always insecure and dependent; and women, of two types, either middle-class and insecure, cloaking that insecurity with the conventions of marriage (Cairo Joy in *Acrobat Admits*, Sally in *Many Slippery Errors*, and Sheila in *Marie Beginning*) or working-class and secure (the typists from Brooklyn: taciturn Pia [*Many Slippery Errors*] or candid Marie [*Marie Beginning*] refreshingly blunt with a flawless sense of the possibilities of moment). The plot revolves around the adventures of these men and women and their constant attempts to couple, which are described in a fashion reminiscent of the rituals in the writings of the Marquis de Sade.

Grossman's strengths lie in his comic voice and his ability to caricature. Few of his characters are deeply motivated; even Marie for whom Grossman has a respect and affection which are lacking in his other portraits, falls short of the mark. But a number of his caricatures are excellent. There are Alexander Forbes, the wealthy playboy who locks women in his padded one-room apartment and subjects them to innumerable indignities as he feeds all his sadistic yearnings and his contempt for his sister; and Dicherty, the aged, wandering lecher who garrulously talks of the vanity of human wishes while he provides a clubhouse for the initiation rites of the toreador-pants set in Brooklyn; and Spider, a mafioso-type with a nice sense of retributive justice; and also Cairo Joy, the embodiment of middle-class consciousness.

His style is often facile, but marred by a self-consciousness which makes much of his dialogue inauthentic. The strained imitations of Hamlet's words in the opening chapter of *Acrobat Admits* provides ample evidence of this defect: "The problem: to start clean, where I am unknown. Self-protection, the bubble that I may burst if needs must, the escape gear of ultimate anonymity, shelter from my own grenades. I intend to complicate, I do not intend to brick myself into a cellar wall. George must not be George."

To complicate life in order to penetrate its banalities is the *raison d'être* of all the antics and pursuits in Grossman's novels. Often the complications are outrageous, occasionally they are hilarious, sometimes, as in his all-too-frequent episodes of amorous impertinences varied with exercises in sadism, they are tedious and without point. A dextrous style saves the superficiality of the characters; a weird but limited imagination creates the lively episodes that carry his art; but until more of Grossman's work emerges, it will not be clear whether he can outgrow his forced service to masters as diverse as Joyce, Shakespeare, and Max Shulman, exercise a care with dialogue which will eliminate the inconsistent images and figures that so often make his parodies inauthentic, and perfect the vehicle which will simultaneously express his moral outrage and convince his readers of the substance and importance of both his characters and themes.

—Carol Simpson Stern

GUERARD, Albert (Joseph). American. Born in Houston, Texas, 2 November 1914. Educated at Stanford University, California, B.A. 1934, Ph.D. 1938; Harvard University, Cambridge, Massachusetts, M.A. 1936. Served in the Psychological Warfare Branch of the United States Army, 1943–45: Technical Sergeant. Married Mary Maclin Bocock in 1941; three daughters. Instructor in English, Amherst College, Massachusetts, 1935–36; Instructor, Assistant Professor, and Associate Professor of English, 1938–54, and Professor of English, 1954–61, Harvard University; Professor of Literature, Stanford University, 1961–85, now emeritus. Recipient: Rockefeller fellowship, 1946; Fulbright fellowship, 1950; Guggenheim fellowship, 1956; Ford fellowship, 1959; *Paris Review* prize, 1963; National Endowment for the Arts grant, 1967, 1974. Member, American Academy of Arts and Sciences. Address: 635 Gerona Road, Stanford, California 94305, U.S.A.

PUBLICATIONS

Novels

The Past Must Alter. London, Longman, 1937; New York, Holt, 1938.
The Hunted. New York, Knopf, 1944; London, Longman, 1947.
Maquisard: A Christmas Tale. New York, Knopf, 1945; London, Longman, 1946.
Night Journey. New York, Knopf, 1950; London, Longman, 1951.
The Bystander. Boston, Little Brown, 1958; London, Faber, 1959.
The Exiles. London, Faber, 1962; New York, Macmillan, 1963.
Christine/Annette. New York, Dutton, 1985.

Uncollected Short Stories

"Davos in Winter," in *Hound and Horn* (Cambridge, Massachusetts), October–December 1933.
"Tragic Autumn," in *The Magazine* (Beverly Hills, California), December 1933.
"Miss Prindle's Lover," in *The Magazine* (Beverly Hills, California), February 1934; revised edition, in *Wake* (Cambridge, Massachusetts), Spring 1948.
"Turista," in *The Best American Short Stories of 1947*, edited by Martha Foley. Boston, Houghton Mifflin, 1947.

"The Incubus," in *The Dial* (New York), vol. 1, no. 2, 1960.
"The Lusts and Gratifications of Andrada," in *Paris Review*, Summer–Fall 1962.
"On the Operating Table," in *Denver Quarterly*, Autumn 1966.
"The Journey," in *Partisan Review* (New Brunswick, New Jersey), Winter 1967.
"The Rabbit and the Tapes," in *Sewanee Review* (Tennessee), Spring 1972.
"The Pillars of Hercules," in *Fiction* (New York), December 1973.
"Bon Papa Reviendra," in *Tri-Quarterly* (Evanston, Illinois), Spring 1975.
"Post Mortem: The Garcia Incident," in *Southern Review* (Baton Rouge, Louisiana), Spring 1978.
"The Poetry of Flight," in *Northwest Magazine* (Portland, Oregon), 22 January 1984.

Other

Robert Bridges: A Study of Traditionalism in Poetry. Cambridge, Massachusetts, Harvard University Press, and London, Oxford University Press, 1942.
Joseph Conrad.   New York, New Directions, 1947.
Thomas Hardy: The Novels and Stories.   Cambridge, Massachusetts, Harvard University Press, 1949; London, Oxford University Press, 1950.
André Gide.   Cambridge, Massachusetts, Harvard University Press, and London, Oxford University Press, 1951; revised edition, 1969.
Conrad the Novelist.   Cambridge, Massachusetts, Harvard University Press, 1958; London, Oxford University Press, 1959.
The Triumph of the Novel: Dickens, Dostoevsky, Faulkner.   New York, Oxford University Press, 1976; London, Oxford University Press, 1977.
The Touch of Time: Myth, Memory, and the Self.   Stanford, California, Stanford Alumni Association, 1980.

Editor, *Prosateurs Américains de XXe Siècle.*   Paris, Laffont, 1947.
Editor, *The Return of the Native*, by Thomas Hardy.   New York, Holt Rinehart, 1961.
Editor, *Hardy: A Collection of Critical Essays.*   Englewood Cliffs, New Jersey, Prentice Hall, 1963.
Editor, *Perspective on the Novel*, special issue of *Daedalus* (Boston), Spring 1963.
Co-Editor, *The Personal Voice: A Contemporary Prose Reader.*   Philadelphia, Lippincott, 1964.
Editor, *Stories of the Double.*   Philadelphia, Lippincott, 1967.
Editor, *Mirror and Mirage.*   Stanford, California, Stanford Alumni Association, 1980.

*

Manuscript Collection: Stanford University Library, California.

Critical Studies: *The Modern Novel in America* by Frederick Hoffman, Chicago, Regnery, 1951; *The Hero with the Private Parts* by Andrew Lytle, Baton Rouge, Louisiana State University Press, 1966; "The Eskimo Motor in the Detention Cell" by Paul West, in *Southern Review* (Baton Rouge, Louisiana), Winter 1979; *The Touch of Time*, 1980, "The Past Unrecaptured: The Two Lives of Lya de Putti," in *Southern Review* (Baton Rouge, Louisiana), Winter 1983, and "Divided Selves," in *Contemporary Authors Autobiography Series 2*

edited by Adele Sarkissian, Detroit, Gale, 1985, all by Guerard.

Albert Guerard comments:

My work has been notably affected by wartime experience (political intelligence work in France) and by the pressures and ambiguities of the subsequent cold war. I have tried without success to put the political subject aside; thousands of unpublished pages, many of them angry, testify to inescapable contemporary pressures.

Maquisard, written immediately after the 1944 events it describes, is an affectionate record of wartime comradeships among men who had been in the underground. Apologetically subtitled *A Christmas Tale*, it is the slightest of my novels and was the most warmly received. *Night Journey*, my most complex and most substantial novel, is more truthful in its picture of the political and moral devastation caused by American–Soviet rivalries in a world as deceptive, and as self-deceptive, as that of *1984*. It was, on publication, repeatedly compared to Orwell's book. The confession of Paul Haldan (wandering and evasive, with his final crime left undescribed, and indeed undetected by most readers) is that of a liberal "innocent" who can accept neither his mother's sexual betrayals nor his country's systematic abuse of power and liberal ideology, nor its threatened use of germ warfare. Haldan's night journey into temporary regression takes him into the middle European city of his childhood, disrupted by the two great powers and betrayed by both. The ambiguities of an undeclared war are internalized by Paul Haldan, and his psycho-sexual anxieties projected onto the screen of public conflict. *The Exiles* (based on a journey to Cuba, Haiti, and Santo Domingo during the turmoil of 1959) explores deception and self-deception in the tragi-comic context of Caribbean propaganda and political intrigue. It dramatizes the conflict of a quixotic Trujillo assassin incorrigibly drawn to the exiled statesman he is supposed to destroy. Manuel Andrada appears to be the most winning of my fictional creations.

In *The Hunted*, an earlier novel and conventionally realistic in technique, psycho-sexual anxieties and monumental vanities reflect public disorders in a small New England college just before World War II. Oedipal conflicts and fantasies, dramatized fairly unconsciously in *The Past Must Alter*, are central to *Night Journey* and to *The Bystander*, another story of romantic love vitiated by immaturity and regression. The technique of *The Bystander* is that of the French *récit*, with the motives either concealed or distorted by the narrator-protagonist. But the story is also of a collision between American "innocence" and European compromise. One of my central aims has been to avoid, while writing fairly complex psychological novels, the deadening burden of explicit and accurate analysis. *The Bystander*—very easy to read, perhaps too easy to read—requires, to be truly understood, the closest attention to hint, to image, to nuance of voice and style.

In *Christine/Annette* I wanted to bring a number of perspectives and narrative methods to bear on the ambiguous case of an actress who changes her name and even her personality several times. We see her through fragments of her own journal, her son's reconstructive memoir, a former lover's screen play, brief oral histories by old friends, a few letters. No two versions entirely agree. A good young writer urged me to simplify my novel in accord with contemporary taste by making it more "linear," with a clear story line and third-person narration. But I kept to my ambiguities and contradictory witnesses, knowing they were true to a past that was irrecoverable and had become mythical. I was much pleased by a reviewer who found in this novel a combination of Proust's impressionism and the post-modern qualities of Italo Calvino.

I was bemused by the turbulent self-destructive life of Louise Brooks, but even more by that of Lya de Putti, a Hungarian star of silent films whom I met when I was ten years old. She left husband and infant daughters to become an actress, and the children were led to believe she was dead. More than 50 years later I met the daughters, and was struck by their loyalty to the lost mother and to the father who had kept them in ignorance. I knew none of this family history when I brought a remembered "Lia" briefly into my first novel of 1937.

*   *   *

Albert Guerard's seven novels, published over a period of nearly fifty years, have shown a steady progression in technique and a constant reconsideration of theme. Nearly all his novels represent a controlled madness, a largely successful attempt to valorize political/psychological issues in a modern world where the center cannot hold. Guerard concentrates on intense moments of introspective terror and possibility for brooding protagonists trapped in futile or apocalyptic situations. The subjects of his major works of literary criticism—Hardy, Conrad, Gide, Dickens, Dostoevsky, Faulkner—and his admiration for the macabre humor and sexual fantasies of anti-realists like Joyce, Kafka, Nabokov, Hawkes, Pynchon, Barthelme lead Guerard to a kind of fiction that refuses linear narration and embraces time distortion, untrustworthy observers, and ambiguous relationships. Dangerously close to the critical praise gained by the academic novelist, with its ensuing commercial failure, Guerard has never wavered from his commitment to the novel as complex experiment. As he states in *The Triumph of the Novel*, the effects he seeks are inventive fantasy, intuitive psychology, solitary obsessions, and political trauma.

Guerard's first novel, *The Past Must Alter*, deals with his major theme, a young man fascinated by his abortive desire for a beautiful older woman and bothered by an implausible relationship with a shadowy father. Drives to gamble and to test himself obsess and threaten the youth. *The Hunted* takes a more traditional fictional approach. The story of a waitress who marries an arrogant college instructor, of her increasing disillusion with his weakness and growing awareness of her own strength, *The Hunted* has a special quality that comes not from this anti-love story, nor from the New England rural college setting, but from a near-Faulknerian treatment of a violent flood and of a hunt for a doomed mythomaniac, the Bomber, who awakens the aggressions of the truly lost "normal" inhabitants and releases the female protagonist. Equally familiar in form is *Maquisard*. Subtitled, deliberately, "A Christmas Tale"—and Guerard's most commercial novel—the short book deals with a group of maquis and an American officer during the last months of the Second World War. Brilliantly compressed, coming close to but ultimately avoiding sentimentality, the novel is Guerard's most positive statement: the personal comradeship, solidarity, and dedication to a cause formed in combat allow the characters to act out their loyalties and sacrifices as well as to discover emotional and political possibilities that can sustain them in the postwar world. The book is warm, dramatic, lyrical.

In *Night Journey* Guerard creates this postwar world as a surreal one that joins varieties of betrayals. Paul Haldan (even the name echoes Conrad) betrays—deserts, literally—his superior officer in a move that re-enacts Haldan's guilt towards

his father's death. Even darker themes of sexual betrayals by a form of projected rape and political betrayal by a military maneuver that alternately liberates and abandons a city qualify *Night Journey* as a work of inward and outer deception and destruction. Certainly Guerard's most imaginative and ambitious book, this novel is intelligent, probing, and yet, like many works of the psycho-political genre, ultimately lacking in human vitality. The madness is too controlled; the passion is too spent.

The Bystander concentrates on personal relations. Anthony, a young man in France, pursues the actress subject of his adolescent dreams. Poor and self-destructive, Anthony does attain his erotic desires, only to discover in Christiane a fundamental pragmatist who can reject passion for financial support from an older man. The book circles back on itself and is as much about loss as about gain. Tormented, sensual, self-lacerating, this anti-hero remains one of Guerard's most fascinating psychological portraits. *The Exiles* returns to the Conrad–Greene political arena that Guerard is drawn to as powerfully as to the psychological realm. (Indeed, sections have appeared during the past decade in magazines of two unpublished political novels, *Suspended Sentence* that concerns an aging middle-European political exile, and *Still Talking*, a post-holocaust vision of wandering armies across a destroyed landscape.) Guerard's most comic effort, *The Exiles* satirizes Central American political refugees and their hangers-on and sympathetically presents a comic/tragic secret agent who combines absolute loyalty to a dictator and emotional commitment to a dissident, quasi-revolutionary poet. The comedy of Manual Andrada's maneuverings in Boston is effective; the tragedy of his self-immolation in his beloved homeland is moving. Guerard's use of an objective, rather colorless narrator, however, mutes both the laughter and the terror.

Constantly dedicated to the writing of fiction despite his careers as professor and critic, Guerard finally achieves his aim of definitively catching his fascination with his earliest subject—the love of an innocent young man for a more experienced lovely actress . . . only for Charles Strickland the actress is in reality his lost mother, and the novel *Christine/Annette* is at once a rewriting of the past and an acceptance of the present. The book is indeed a triumph, easily Guerard's finest. He is lyrical and humorous, wistful and historical, tough-minded and sensitive. Part detective story, part family romance, part *bildungsroman*, part American and European social history, *Christine/Annette* is largely about the mystery of identity. The search for the mother, in all its Freudian and Jungian potentials, takes places in the real, richly evoked worlds of Paris and Berlin, Houston and Los Angeles. The narration is equally sure and varied—autobiography, movie script, objective frame, letters—and the film trope superbly sustained. The novel displays a confidence that comes from years of successful writing, certainly, but the special quality of this final work is its freshness, its variety, its flexibility, its combination of an open, experimental structure, an authentic voice, and a traditional theme of loss, search, and discovery. Like Shakespeare's *The Tempest* or Faulkner's *The Reivers*, Guerard's novel of his mature years recapitulates his earlier conceptions and techniques. The book provides as well a sparkle and energy, an argument with himself rather than with others that in Yeats's formulation leads not to political rhetoric but to lyrical achievement.

—Eric Solomon

GUTHRIE, A(lfred) B(ertram), Jr. American. Born in Bedford, Indiana, 13 January 1901. Educated at schools in Choteau, Montana; University of Washington, Seattle, 1919–20; University of Montana, Missoula, A.B. in journalism 1923. Married 1) Harriet Larson in 1931 (divorced, 1963), one son and one daughter; 2) Carol B. Luthin in 1969. Worked for the Choteau *Acantha*, 1915–19; reporter, 1926–29, city editor and editorial writer, 1929–45, and executive editor, 1945–47, Lexington *Leader*, Kentucky. Fellow, and Lecturer, Bread Loaf Writers Conference, Vermont, 1945–47. Professor of Creative Writing, University of Kentucky, Lexington, 1947–52. Recipient: Nieman fellowship, 1944; Pulitzer Prize, 1950; Boys' Clubs of America Junior Book Award, 1951; National Association of Independent Schools award, 1961; National Cowboy Hall of Fame Wrangler Award, 1970; Western Literature Association award, 1972; Western Writers of America Golden Saddleman Award, 1978. Litt.D.: University of Montana, 1949; Montana State University, Bozeman, 1977; L.H.D.: Indiana State University, Terre Haute, 1975. Agent: Brandt and Brandt, 1501 Broadway, New York, New York 10036. Address: The Barn, Choteau, Montana 59422, U.S.A.

PUBLICATIONS

Novels

Murders at Moon Dance. New York, Dutton, 1943; as *Trouble at Moon Dance*, New York, Popular Library, 1951; London, Long, 1961.
The Big Sky. New York, Sloane, and London, Boardman, 1947.
The Way West. New York, Sloane, 1949; London, Boardman, 1950.
These Thousand Hills. Boston, Houghton Mifflin, 1956; London, Hutchinson, 1957.
Arfive. Boston, Houghton Mifflin, 1971; London, Eyre Methuen, 1972.
Wild Pitch. Boston, Houghton Mifflin, 1973; London, David Bruce and Watson, 1974.
The Last Valley. Boston, Houghton Mifflin, 1975.
No Second Wind. Boston, Houghton Mifflin, 1980.
The Genuine Article. Boston, Houghton Mifflin, 1981.
Fair Land, Fair Land. Boston, Houghton Mifflin, 1982.
Playing Catch-Up. Boston, Houghton Mifflin, 1985.

Short Stories

The Big It and Other Stories. Boston, Houghton Mifflin, 1960; London, Hutchinson, 1961; as *Mountain Medicine*, New York, Pocket Books, 1961.

Uncollected Short Stories

"Newcomer," in *Gunsmoke* (New York), June 1953.
"Loco," in *Esquire* (New York), November 1967.
"Posse on the March," in *Saturday Evening Post* (Philadelphia), September 1976.

Plays

Screenplays: *Shane*, with Jack Sher, 1951; *The Kentuckian*, 1955.

Other

The Blue Hen's Chick (autobiography). New York, McGraw Hill, 1965.

Once upon a Pond (for children). Missoula, Montana, Mountain Press, 1973.

*

Bibliography: in *Western American Literature* (Fort Collins, Colorado), Summer 1969.

Manuscript Collection: University of Kentucky, Lexington.

Critical Studies: *A.B. Guthrie, Jr.*, Austin, Texas, Steck Vaughn, 1968, and *A.B. Guthrie, Jr.*, Boston, Twayne, 1981, both by Thomas W. Ford.

*   *   *

The attempt to create fiction out of one of the central facts of American experience, the existence of the Frontier, is as old as American history. John Smith added a gloss of romance to his geographical and autobiographical ramblings and cast himself as hero of a book that is as much a western as the novel of Zane Grey. Fenimore Cooper set his mark upon the whole future of American mythology by the selection as prime theme for his novels of the conflict between a sophisticated, sometimes decadent but essentially Christian ethos of European culture transplanted and the unsophisticated, sometimes savage, but often wonderfully primitive morality of the wild forests. But just about the time when American historians began to comprehend the influence that the Frontier had exerted upon the whole cultural history of their nation, the Frontier was officially closed, and from the last decade of the 19th century almost until the opening of the Second World War the life of the Frontier was for the American people little more than folk-memory, and even that folk-memory was rapidly perverted by the crude exploitation of the authors of dime novels, Hollywood "B" films, and, finally, television serials.

In the late 1930's and early 1940's a new school of Western authors (Western in both senses of the word) began to emerge, among them two, Walter Van Tilburg Clark and A.B. Guthrie, Jr., outstanding, who put fact back into fiction. Guthrie in particular is a scholarly historian who adds the accuracy of his research to a novelist's power for creating character, to an artist's eye for scenery, and to a Montanan's affection for his home country.

His first novel, *Murders at Moon Dance*, transcends the conventional melodramatic form of the gun-toting Western only insofar as the action explodes with more than ordinary literary force, but his three major novels, *The Big Sky*, *The Way West*, and *These Thousand Hills*, together form a persuasive, sensitive and substantial history of the spirit of the West, free from the stereotypes of the Western.

Arfive, the fourth novel in the sequence, is a more contrived attempt to add a rich cloak of fiction to historical fact—this time the historical facts of the homesteading period—but in the fifth, *The Last Valley*, which takes the story of the West on through the Second World War, Guthrie's miraculous gifts are at work yet again and his sympathy for rural and hitherto isolated communities forced to come to terms with a structured, urbanised and industralised society is as apparent, and almost as vivid, as Faulkner's.

Guthrie insisted that this novel was his last essay in his account of America's westering and he took to writing mystery novels. *Wild Pitch* is adroit if slight and it is only the clarity of the Montana setting which sets it above most books in this genre but his autobiography *The Blue Hen's Chick*, his closely written short stories and his screenplays—above all, that Hollywood classic *Shane*—fill in the interstices in his vast historical reconstruction of the American West.

Even so it remains that the claim that Guthrie be considered in the front rank of contemporary American novelists must rest largely on the achievement of *The Big Sky*, *The Way West*, and *These Thousand Hills*.

—J.E. Morpurgo

HAGGARD, William. Pseudonym for Richard Henry Michael Clayton. British. Born in Croydon, Surrey, 11 August 1907. Educated at Lancing College, Sussex; Christ Church, Oxford, B.A. 1929. Served in the Indian Army, 1939–46: Lieutenant Colonel, General Staff. Married Barbara Myfanwy Sant in 1936; one son and one daughter. Served in the Indian Civil Service, 1931–39; worked for the Board of Trade, 1947–69: Controller of Enemy Property, 1965–69. M.A.: Oxford University, 1947. Agent: John Farquharson Ltd., 162–168 Regent Street, London W1R 5TB; or, 250 West 57th Street, New York, New York 10107, U.S.A. Address: 3 Linkside, Holland Road, Frinton-on-Sea, Essex CO13 9EN, England.

PUBLICATIONS

Novels

Slow Burner. London, Cassell, and Boston, Little Brown, 1958.
The Telemann Touch. London, Cassell, and Boston, Little Brown, 1958.
Venetian Blind. London, Cassell, and New York, Washburn, 1959.
Closed Circuit. London, Cassell, and New York, Washburn, 1960.
The Arena. London, Cassell, and New York, Washburn, 1961.
The Unquiet Sleep. London, Cassell, and New York, Washburn, 1962.
The High Wire. London, Cassell, and New York, Washburn, 1963.
The Antagonists. London, Cassell, and New York, Washburn, 1964.
The Powder Barrel. London, Cassell, and New York, Washburn, 1965.
The Hard Sell. London, Cassell, 1965; New York, Washburn, 1966.
The Power House. London, Cassell, 1966; New York, Washburn, 1967.
The Conspirators. London, Cassell, 1967; New York, Walker, 1968.
A Cool Day for Killing. London, Cassell, and New York, Walker, 1968.
The Doubtful Disciple. London, Cassell, 1969.
The Hardliners. London, Cassell, and New York, Walker, 1970.
The Bitter Harvest. London, Cassell, 1971; as *Too Many Enemies*, New York, Walker, 1972.
The Protectors. London, Cassell, and New York, Walker, 1972.

The Old Masters. London, Cassell, 1973; as *The Notch on the Knife*, New York, Walker, 1973.
The Kinsmen. London, Cassell, and New York, Walker, 1974.
The Scorpion's Tail. London, Cassell, and New York, Walker, 1975.
Yesterday's Enemy. London, Cassell, and New York, Walker, 1976.
The Poison People. London, Cassell, 1978; New York, Walker, 1979.
Visa to Limbo. London, Cassell, 1978; New York, Walker, 1979.
The Median Line. London, Cassell, 1979; New York, Walker, 1981.
The Money Men. London, Hodder and Stoughton, and New York, Walker, 1981.
The Mischief-Makers. London, Hodder and Stoughton, and New York, Walker, 1982.
The Heirloom. London, Hodder and Stoughton, 1983.
The Need to Know. London, Hodder and Stoughton, 1984.
The Meritocrats. London, Hodder and Stoughton, 1985.
The Martello Tower. London, Hodder and Stoughton, 1986.

Uncollected Short Stories

"Night Train to Milan," in *Best Secret Service Stories 2*, edited by John Welcome. London, Faber, 1965.
"Madam," in *Welcome Aboard* (London), 1971.
"Why Beckett Died," in *Blood on My Mind*. London, Macmillan, 1972.
"The Hirelings," in *Winter's Crimes 4*, edited by George Hardinge. London, Macmillan, and New York, St. Martin's Press, 1972.
"Timeo Danaos," in *Winter's Crimes 8*, edited by Hilary Watson. London, Macmillan, and New York, St. Martin's Press, 1976.

Other

The Little Rug Book. London, Cassell, 1972.

*

Critical Studies: in *Sunday Times* (London), 12 May 1963; by Robin W. Winks, in *New Republic* (Washington, D.C.), 30 July 1977.

William Haggard comments:
I write suspense stories with a political background.

*   *   *

William Haggard builds his stories around Colonel Charles Russell, head of the Security Executive. He is about 60, an Anglo-Irishman who looks at the English impersonally. His thoughts are put crisply; what he finds contemptible about the establishment isn't

its power but its inefficiency. The supine respect for precedent, the passion for soldiers in fancy dress. The leathery clubs and the squalid canteens. Industrial bigwigs talking on telly in terms of economics a generation out of date. Pompous trade unionists as startlingly antique. Compromise. Keep it clean. Russell had once told an eminent journalist that he was an old-fashioned radical. The man had blinked then changed the subject. Russell has known he's been misunderstood.

Russell is a gentleman in a tough job which he handles with some intuition and considerable scrupulosity. He has a touch of Edwardian courtesy, a sense of what is proper and becoming.

And so he is hurled into the chessboard puzzles of modern diplomatic, industrial, political struggles. He uncovers and sometimes covers up again the seamier side of public and private life. He has his unofficial contacts with the other side of the curtain, as in *The Antagonists* where his friendship with the "Confederate Republic," an independent satellite, pays off. Again in *The Powder Barrel* he and the (Russian) General share information where their interests are common. Colonel Russell is an individual who appreciates other individuals and his is an unusual, strong character, though paradoxically enough he tends to achieve his ends by inaction rather than action. He waits for others to commit their treacheries, peccadillos, plain mistakes. In Russell's world there are Ministers of the Crown, efficient in some cases, less so in others; there is a crafty Prime Minister, a brilliant study; there is the worried director of a Merchant Bank struggling with diabetes. The range is wide but it is largely drawn from the establishment. There are women who are powerful—and dangerous, such as Sheila Raden in *A Cool Day for Killing* or Madam, the weak Sheik's sister, in *The Powder Barrel*. There are men who are weak and blackmailable, men who are vicious, men who are idealistic. Some become stock types—Mortimer the loyal subordinate, Professor Waserman the German-Jewish refugee now Chairman of Amalgamated Steel, and Lord Normer, a C.P. Snow-like character, who advises Russell on radar matters. There are the classic traitors, and these are often self-deluding, weak left-wing intellectuals, such as Margaret Palfrey in *The Antagonists*. There are also ruthless industrialists or the selfish and sophisticated engineers of whom Gervase Leat in *Venetian Blind* is a good example.

The complicated nexus between characters is well handled. Haggard enjoys the interplay of his characters; his dialogue can be lively and is at its best when sophisticated men and women are engaged in conversations, the serious import of which is lightly conveyed. Colonel Russell himself can be surprising in his unorthodoxies: he is careful not to overstep what he thinks are the proper limits of his difficult, dangerous post. He emerges as very human indeed.

The dangers are given full treatment. The action is crisp; there is suspense in plenty—the waiting after a decision is taken, then the action described with sufficient detail to be convincing, with sufficient speed to remain exciting. The backgrounds are sketched in with small touches of accuracy; the atmosphere of a gulf sheikdom, a Malayan state under British protection, an Italian aircraft factory, a London pub, a country house are all evoked with equal skill. The pattern of modern life evolves in all its complexity: not least in the relationships between men and women, where Russell often throws a cool, tolerant, yet interested eye on intrigues or relationships which affect the action of the characters. In marriages breaking up— the Leggatts' in *The Unquiet Sleep* or the Lowe-Andersons' in *Venetian Blind* are cases in point—Haggard can capture nuances and clashes and the odd mixtures of loyalty and disloyalty with considerable economy. He can show the complexities of racial differences at times as in the Deshmukhs in *The Conspirators*, he Indian, she an Irish nationalist (yet related, way back, to Colonel Russell). *Visa to Limbo* illustrates Haggard's capacity to write a cool account of crisis: the attempted highjack of an Israeli aircraft. He places this in the centre of a story of a coup in a small arab state occurring when Colonel Russell is visiting Israel, though to the distaste of Israeli Intelligence. The threads are neatly tangled and untangled for us, and the violence erupts, though the danger of a large flare-up

is avoided. The terror, the tension, the tightrope walking are conveyed delicately but very convincingly.

The element of chance is something Haggard understands. In *The Median Line*, up-to-date as ever, he explores the Mediterranean Island's relationship with the wealthy Arab Oil State. Irony plays through the account; it is steeped with mellow Mediterranean sunshine, and the clash of human greed and envy, personal and national, echoes in the narrow streets, spreads by the rocky fields and over the distant desert. Russell, on a visit to the island and caught up in his disgust in the quarrel, is wily; he admires the place and its people, but is glad to escape the politicians' blackmail, the pressures and violence of the rulers of both countries.

Perhaps Haggard's chief virtue is that he conveys a sense to the reader of being allowed to know it all works, it being the world as seen by an intelligence service chief. It is not the whole world, but a sophisticatedly stylised one, where an occasional comment—on, say, the reduced role played by a modern head of Mission; or on the restricted options open to a politician, or captain of industry, or chief of police, or diplomat—strikes home with a dash of devastating reality which helps to carry forward the strange doings of Colonel Russell, his helpers and the enemies he often respects. Haggard has shown in *The Need to Know* and *The Meritocrats* that his invention remains fertile, that his capacity to tell a story is as strong as ever, and that he can develop new characters with an easy assurance.

—A. Norman Jeffares

HAILEY, Arthur. Canadian and British. Born in Luton, Bedfordshire, 5 April 1920; emigrated to Canada in 1947: became citizen, 1952. Educated at elementary schools in England. Served as a pilot in the Royal Air Force, 1939–47: Flight Lieutenant. Married 1) Joan Fishwick in 1944 (divorced, 1950), three sons; 2) Sheila Dunlop in 1951, one son and two daughters. Office boy and clerk, London, 1934–39; assistant editor, 1947–49, and editor, 1949–53, *Bus and Truck Transport*, Toronto; sales promotion manager, Trailmobile Canada, Toronto, 1953–56. Since 1956, free-lance writer. Recipient: Canadian Council of Authors and Artists award, 1956; Best Canadian TV Playwright Award, 1957, 1958; Doubleday Prize Novel Award, 1962. Address: Lyford Cay, P.O. Box N.7776, Nassau, Bahamas.

PUBLICATIONS

Novels

Flight into Danger, with John Castle. London, Souvenir Press, 1958; as *Runway Zero-Eight*, New York, Doubleday, 1959.
The Final Diagnosis. New York, Doubleday, 1959; London, Joseph-Souvenir Press, 1960; as *The Young Doctors*, London, Corgi, 1962.
In High Places. New York, Doubleday, and London, Joseph-Souvenir Press, 1962.
Hotel. New York, Doubleday, and London, Joseph-Souvenir Press, 1965.
Airport. New York, Doubleday, and London, Joseph-Souvenir Press, 1968.

Wheels. New York, Doubleday, and London, Joseph-Souvenir Press, 1971.
The Moneychangers. New York, Doubleday, and London, Joseph-Souvenir Press, 1975.
Overload. New York, Doubleday, and London, Joseph-Souvenir Press, 1979.
Strong Medicine. New York, Doubleday, and London, Joseph-Souvenir Press, 1984.

Plays

Flight into Danger (televised, 1956). Published in *Four Plays of Our Time*, London, Macmillan, 1960.
Close-up on Writing for Television. New York, Doubleday, 1960.

Screenplays: *Zero Hour*, with Hall Bartlett and John Champion, 1958; *The Moneychangers*, 1976; *Wheels*, 1978.

Television Plays: *Flight into Danger*, 1956 (USA); *Time Lock*, 1962 (UK); *Course for Collision*, 1962 (UK); and plays for *Westinghouse Studio One*, *Playhouse 90*, *U.S. Steel Hour*, *Goodyear-Philco Playhouse*, and *Kraft Theatre* (USA).

*

Critical Study: *I Married a Best Seller* by Sheila Hailey, New York, Doubleday, and London, Joseph-Souvenir Press, 1978.

Arthur Hailey comments:

My novels are the end product of my work and are widely available. Therefore I see no reason to be analytical about them.

Each novel takes me, usually, three years: a year of continuous research, six months of detailed planning, then a year and a half of steady writing, with many revisions.

My only other comment is that my novels are the work of one who seeks principally to be a storyteller but reflect also, I hope, the excitement of living here and now.

*   *   *

Arthur Hailey has developed and virtually perfected a highly efficient and extremely successful (and profitable) process of novel writing. Whether he is writing about doctors (*The Final Diagnosis*, *Strong Medicine*) or airline pilots (*Flight into Danger*), hotels (*Hotel*) or airports (*Airport*), government (*In High Places*) or industry (*Wheels*), he follows the same formula. Each of his novels is filled with enough information about the subject of his exhaustive research to satisfy the most curious reader; there are enough character types to appeal to the widest possible audience; everything is interwoven into a complex web of plots and sub-plots to satisfy every reader's desire for a good, suspenseful story.

Hailey writes documentary fiction, or what has been called "faction," that is, a mixture of the real and the fictitious. After spending a year of research for each novel, Hailey is prepared to give his reader as much factual information as he can work into the novel. Consequently, only his characters and situations are imaginary, and they are sometimes only slightly fictitious.

To speak of any Hailey novel is to speak of every Hailey novel for there is little to distinguish one from the rest except subject matter. Each novel shares the same characteristic strengths and weaknesses. *Airport* is a typical example. The action of the novel is centered at a fictitious Chicago airport during one of the worst blizzards in the city's history. To give

his reader an inside look at the operations of a major airport and into the lives of the people responsible for its existence, Hailey devises several plots; an airliner is stuck in the snow, blocking a runway and causing emergency situations in the air; an air-traffic controller is planning suicide; a trans-Atlantic airliner is about to take off with a bomb aboard; a stewardess has discovered she is pregnant; a group of local citizens is demonstrating against the excessive noise of the airport. The novel follows each plot to its conclusion, but not before the reader's intellectual curiosity about airports and his emotional curiosity about the characters are satisfied.

The narrative is slick and fast-moving, the information is interesting, the prose is readable, but the seams in Hailey's fabric too often show through. In order to introduce all his researched information into the novel, he is frequently forced to construct irrelevant sub-plots or to break the flow of the narrative for a lecture on such things as the safety records of commercial airlines or the pressures suffered by air-traffic controllers. To manage all his characters, he is forced into a "holding pattern" of his own. The focus of the novel shifts from one character to another as Hailey abandons characters temporarily only to return to them later when their number in the rotation comes up again. Consequently what unity there is in the book is provided only by the subject matter. The characters themselves are paper thin, reduced to simple dimensions; they are so typical that they could be interchanged from one novel to the next with little difficulty.

Wheels is much like *Airport* in its intention and its execution. The main difference is its lack of dramatic suspense; there is less drama to be derived from the introduction of a new car, the primary plot device in the novel, than from the naturally more exciting subjects of the earlier novels.

Hailey is a good popular novelist. He has learned what his audience expects and his audience knows what to expect from him; the reciprocal arrangement ought to ensure a continuing place for Hailey's novels on the best seller lists for years to come.

—David J. Geherin

HALE, Nancy. American. Born in Boston, Massachusetts, 6 May 1908. Educated at Winsor School, Boston, graduated 1926; Boston Museum (Art) School, 1927–28. Married Fredson Bowers in 1942; two sons from previous marriages. Assistant editor, *Vogue*, New York, 1928–32, and *Vanity Fair*, New York, 1932–33; reporter, *New York Times*, 1935. Lecturer, Bread Loaf Writers Conference, Vermont, 1957–62; Phi Beta Kappa Visiting Scholar, 1971–72. Recipient: O. Henry Award, 1933; Benjamin Franklin Citation, 1948; Bellaman Award, 1968; Sarah Josepha Hale Award, 1974. Address: Woodburn, Box 7, Route 14, Charlottesville, Virginia 22901, U.S.A.

PUBLICATIONS

Novels

The Young Die Good. New York, Scribner, 1932.
Never Any More. New York, Scribner, 1934.
The Prodigal Women. New York, Scribner, 1942.
The Sign of Jonah. New York, Scribner, 1950; London, Heinemann, 1952.

Dear Beast.   Boston, Little Brown, 1959; London, Macmillan, 1960.
Black Summer.   Boston, Little Brown, 1963; London, Gollancz, 1964.
Secrets.   New York, Coward McCann, 1971.

Short Stories

The Earliest Dreams.   New York, Scribner, 1936; London, Dickson and Davies, 1937.
Between the Dark and the Daylight.   New York, Scribner, 1943.
The Empress's Ring.   New York, Scribner, 1955.
Heaven and Hardpan Farm.   New York, Scribner, 1957.
The Pattern of Perfection: Thirteen Stories.   Boston, Little Brown, 1960; London, Macmillan, 1961.

Uncollected Short Stories

"Handful of r's," in *Vogue* (New York), 1 November 1961.
"In a Word," in *New Yorker*, 27 July 1963.
"Girl with the Goat-Cart," in *New Yorker*, 30 November 1963.
"An Age for Action," in *Ladies Home Journal* (New York), March 1965.
"The Signorina," in *Transatlantic Review* (London), Autumn 1965.
"Sunday Lunch," in *Prize Stories 1966: The O. Henry Awards*, edited by Richard Poirier and William Abrahams. New York, Doubleday, 1966.
"All Anybody," in *Georgia Review* (Athens), Spring 1966.
"Family Ties," in *Southern Review* (Baton Rouge, Louisiana), April 1966.
"Waiting," in *Virginia Quarterly Review* (Charlottesville), Autumn 1966.
"Animals in the House," in *Harper's* (New York), September 1966.
"The Innocent," in *Virginia Quarterly Review* (Charlottesville), Spring 1967.
"The Most Elegant Drawing Room in Europe," in *Prize Stories 1968: The O. Henry Awards*, edited by William Abrahams. New York, Doubleday, 1968.
"Mr. Hamilton," in *Michigan Quarterly Review* (Ann Arbor), April 1970.
"Dreams of Rich People," in *McCall's* (New York), August 1972.
"The Interior," in *Virginia Quarterly Review* (Charlottesville), Spring 1980.
"Tastes," in *Virginia Quarterly Review* (Charlottesville), Autumn 1982.
"A Past," in *Virginia Quarterly Review* (Charlottesville), Winter 1985.

Plays

The Best of Everything (produced Charlottesville, Virginia, 1951).
Somewhere She Dances (produced Charlottesville, Virginia, 1953).

Other

A New England Girlhood (memoir).   Boston, Little Brown, and London, Gollancz, 1958.
The Realities of Fiction: A Book about Writing.   Boston, Little Brown, 1962; London, Macmillan, 1963.
The Life in the Studio.   Boston, Little Brown, 1969.

Mary Cassatt.   New York, Doubleday, 1975.
The Night of the Hurricane (for children).   New York, Coward McCann, 1977.

Editor, *New England Discovery: A Personal View*.   New York, Coward McCann, 1963.
Editor, *Daughter of Abolitionists*, by Ellen Wright.   Northampton, Massachusetts, Smith College, 1964.
Editor, with Fredson Bowers, *Leon Kroll: A Spoken Memoir*.   Charlottesville, University Press of Virginia, 1983.

*

Manuscript Collections: Smith College Library, Northampton, Massachusetts; Alderman Library, University of Virginia, Charlottesville.

Critical Study: article by Anne Hobson Freeman, in *Dictionary of Literary Biography Yearbook 1980* edited by Karen L. Rood, Jean W. Ross, and Richard Ziegfeld, Detroit, Gale, 1981.

Nancy Hale comments:
    I am averse to making statements on my work because I have found by experience that fiction is so protean that today's aim can be tomorrow's anathema. But I may make the comment that in general I have striven to conceal the purpose underlying my work with "the light touch" since nothing seems to me so self-defeating as overt earnestness. Yet I can assure readers of my work that its purpose is earnest, indeed painful.

*   *   *

    For more than five decades Nancy Hale has depicted varying aspects of the changing American social scene in terms of what for a more precise label must still be called the American upper and upper-middle class. Her fiction—some dozen novels and collections of short stories—ranges from recollections of family life in Massachusetts where she was born and raised to the pseudo-sophisticated intellectual circles of New York City where she lived relatively early in her career and the Virginia Piedmont which has been her home for many years. From the beginnings Hale (who is married to a professor) has been a witty and perceptive observer of individual and societal foibles which she recreates with admirably disciplined craftsmanship.
    Hale's fiction has evoked widely different opinions, although even her least understanding critics have been impressed by the artistry and technical expertise which have been her hallmarks. And as her career progressed Hale's compassion deepened, or perhaps it was the other way around. In either case, *A New England Girlhood*, published rather beyond the midpoint of her career, is described as *An Affectionate Re-creation of Things Past* (some 60 years after her grandfather, Edward Everett Hale, had published his *A New England Boyhood*). And affectionate it is, without slopping into bathos or sentimentality: in her subsequent work the author's concern with stupidity, grossness, absurdity—and their opposites—is constantly alive, constantly keen, but she has learned, as has been observed, to shed the blood without disfiguring the bodies of her subjects.
    Hale's characters fight no great battles to reform society or change the world. Their stories, as is inevitable in the fiction of manners, are extremely personal, involving relations between parents and children, husbands and wives, individuals versus individuals: the growing antagonism between the three teenage girls of *Never Any More* during a summer holiday;

the searing problems of their adult counterparts in Hale's best-known and most commercially successful novel *The Prodigal Women*, a book about the disorders of love and the warfare between men and women which has been aptly described as a depiction of "one kind of Hell ... the Gulf of Self-tormenters"; the experiences of the group of emotionally disturbed women and their psychiatrist of *Heaven and Hardpan Farm*; the situation stories from what is perhaps her best collection, *The Empress's Ring*, which center around incidents no more dramatic than a mother's experiences with a sick child or a quiet day at the beach.

The theater of Nancy Hale's fiction is relatively limited, but she works within it with skill, precision, and a high awareness. And it is in the field of what she has called "Autobiographical Fiction" that she displays a wizardry uniquely her own, manifested in many stories and novels and in such later books as *The Life in the Studio*, recollections of her painter mother, or *Secrets*, an autobiographical memoir. In such work Hale has captured—as she comments in *The Realities of Fiction*—"the atmosphere of the past ... less by remembering than by inventing; less by calling up than by making up. It is as if to capture that atmosphere I have to create it, because in fact it never was on land or sea, least of all in my own childhood."

—William Peden

HALL, James B(yron). American. Born in Midland, Ohio, 21 July 1918. Educated at Miami University, Oxford, Ohio, 1938–39; University of Hawaii, Honolulu, 1938–40; University of Iowa, Iowa City, B.A. 1947, M.A. 1948, Ph.D. 1953; Kenyon College, Gambier, Ohio, summers, 1948, 1949. Served in the United States Army, 1941–46: Chief Warrant Officer. Married Elizabeth Cushman in 1946; four daughters and one son. Instructor, Cornell University, Ithaca, New York, 1952–53; Assistant Professor, 1954–57, Associate Professor, 1958–60, and Professor of English, 1960–65, University of Oregon, Eugene; Director of the Writing Center, and Professor of English, University of California, Irvine, 1965–68; Professor of Literature and Provost of College V (now Porter-Sesnon College), 1968–77, and Writer-in-Residence, 1978–83, University of California, Santa Cruz; now emeritus. Since 1984, full-time writer. Writer-in-Residence, Miami University, 1948–49, University of North Carolina, Greensboro, 1954, University of British Columbia, Vancouver, Summer 1956, Reed College, Portland, Oregon, 1958, University of Colorado, Boulder, 1963, Kansas State University, Manhattan, 1978, University of Missouri, Columbia, 1981, and Eastern Washington University, Cheney, 1982. Co-founding Editor, *Northwest Review*, Eugene, Oregon, 1957–60; founder and director, University of Oregon Summer Academy of Contemporary Arts, Eugene, 1959–64; editorial consultant, Doubleday and Company, publishers (West Coast staff), 1960; cultural specialist, United States Department of State, Washington, 1964; member of the Board of Governors, 1973–76, and President, 1976–77, Associated Writing Programs of America. Recipient: Yaddo grant, 1952; Oregon State Poetry Contest prize, 1958; Chapelbrook fellowship, 1967; Institute of Creative Arts fellowship, 1967; Balch Fiction Prize, 1967. James B. Hall Art Gallery named by University of California Regents, 1984. Agent: Gerald McCauley Agency, P.O. Box AE, Katonah, New York 10536. Address: 31 Hollins Drive, Santa Cruz, California 95060, U.S.A.

PUBLICATIONS

Novels

Not by the Door. New York, Random House, 1954.
TNT for Two. New York, Ace, 1956.
Racers to the Sun. New York, Obolensky, 1960; London, Corgi, 1962.
Mayo Sergeant. New York, New American Library, 1967.

Short Stories

15 × 3, with Herbert Gold and R.V. Cassill. New York, New Directions, 1957.
Us He Devours. New York, New Directions, 1964.
The Short Hall: New and Selected Stories. Denver, Stonehenge, 1980.

Uncollected Short Stories

"By the Distaff's Hot Astonishment," in *Western Review* (Iowa City), Winter 1952.
"Estate and Trespass: A Gothic Story," in *Prize Stories 1954: The O. Henry Awards*, edited by Paul Engle and Hansford Martin. New York, Doubleday, 1954.
"A Session of Summer," in *Western Review* (Iowa City), Spring 1955.
"The Fall and the Twilight," in *Esquire* (New York), September 1957.
"Up in Her Room," in *Gent* (New York), March 1958.
"The Fish Camp under the Snow," in *Accent* (Urbana, Illinois), Summer 1958.
"But Who Gets the Children," in *Esquire* (New York), 1960.
"The World Is a Hubcap Spinning," in *Inland* (Salt Lake City), 1960.
"The Race in the Afternoon," in *Inland* (Salt Lake City), Spring 1960.
"In the Eye of the Storm," in *Western Review* (Iowa City), 1964.
"Letters Never Mailed," in *Gallery of Modern Fiction*, edited by Robie Macauley. New York, Salem Press, 1966.
"Triumph of the Omophagists," in *New Directions 21*. New York, New Directions, 1969.
"I Like It Better Now," in *Atlantic* (Boston), August 1969.
"My Other Kingdom," in *The Best Little Magazine Fiction*, edited by Curt Johnson. New York, New York University Press, 1970.
"The Confessions of Friday," in *New Directions 45*. New York, New Directions, 1983.
"Praeder's Letters," in *Paris Review*, Spring 1983.
"Old Man Finds What Was Lost," in *New Letters* (Kansas City), 1984.
"The Fissure," in *Black Warrior Review* (Birmingham, Alabama), Summer 1984.
"Two Fables: How J.B. Hartley Lost His Father; The Snow Hunters," in *Quarry West* (Santa Cruz, California), Summer 1984.
"Restoring the Mounds," in *Black Warrior Review* (Birmingham, Alabama), Fall 1984.
"A Circle of Friends," in *New Letters* (Kansas City), 1985.

Verse

The Hunt Within. Baton Rouge, Louisiana State University Press, 1973.

Other

Editor, with Joseph Langland, *The Short Story*. New York, Macmillan, 1956.
Editor, *The Realm of Fiction*. New York, McGraw Hill, 1965; revised edition, 1970; with Elizabeth C. Hall, 1977.
Editor, with Barry Ulanov, *Modern Culture and the Arts*. New York, McGraw Hill, 1967; revised edition, 1972.
Editor, *John Barleycorn: Alcoholic Memoirs*, by Jack London. Santa Cruz, California, Western Tanager Press, 1981.

*

Manuscript Collection: Miami University, Oxford, Ohio.

James B. Hall comments:
Although the novels are interesting, the central significance of the work resides largely in the short stories; the poetry is various, and by intention ancillary to the prose.
The novels, short stories, and poetry are thematically inter-related. The re-occurring motifs are the effects of competition on individuals in a system of modified capitalism such as obtains in the United States. Thus acquisitive, frustrated, evasive pro-tagonists re-occur, some of them mad or nearly so. Extreme conduct in a hostile world is not infrequent; the adjustments which protagonists make vary from callous acceptance or the exploitation of others to withdrawal, revenge, and self-destruc-tion. In general, the work shows the difficulty of remaining human in a competitive, non-Darwinian world fashioned in large part by a democratic society. Specifically, *Racers to the Sun* traces the "rise" and fall of a motorcycle racer who builds his own machine; the hero is injured (used up), and then is dropped by those who exploited his talent for machinery and speed. Likewise, in the typical short stories, "Us He Devours" and "The Claims Artist," the protagonists are in some ways laudable, but in the end are victims of their own and of society's demands. A typical poem, "Pay Day Night," treats the counter-productive nature of experience in another bureau-cracy, the Army.
The short stories are experimental, highly compressed, and exploit language poetically for artistic effect. They are con-densed statements that very often extend the possibilities of the genre. Many of the stories are anthologized; because they are complex they apparently "teach well" in classrooms.

*　　　*　　　*

James B. Hall, like Fitzgerald, Lewis, perhaps most of the important American writers of this century, sees the American dream as a combination of an ethic once moral and humane, and a goal of success that inevitably corrupts the ethic and so the dream. This is the theme he began to delineate in 1954 with the publication of *Not by the Door*, and continued to explore in subsequent novels. Howard Marcham, the protagon-ist of the first novel, is an Episcopal clergyman in a middle American town, "an American priest, with no real background of the spirit." Marcham is not an evil man, Hall is saying; but it is difficult for an American to hear a higher call over the rustle of money and the clink of cocktail glasses.
Racers to the Sun is an absorbing novel that examines the almost sexual mystique of machinery and speed—particularly of motorcycle racing—in America. The main character, Harold Hill, is practically raised in an automobile graveyard in Ohio, from where it seems perfectly natural for him to move into the world of the motorcycle track, the world of a worshipper of speed and success named "Gunner," who has transformed

herself into a trophy for winners. He understands his motor-cycle clearly as "a naked force ... a dance step which would take him from Savile, Ohio, to the salt flats of Bonneville or to Daytona Beach where demi-gods in leather riding breeches flashed through the electric timers to the immortality of record books." It is a strength of the novel that Hall causes his spokes-man to recognize the essence of his life and not give way to adolescent bleating about it.
Hall really hit his strike as a novelist in *Mayo Sergeant*. It is clear from the beginning with the appearance of red, white, and blue sails on the sea, that sailing is in some way symbolic of America; sailing vessels and the code the sport imposes (like the hunting code of Hemingway or Faulkner) are a meta-phor of the business ethic and morality in America. The grace-ful old *Indus* is being replaced by the new *Tektra*, even as whatever was human in Industry has yielded to the unfeeling force of Technocracy. Or is the new order in America actually much different, the new businessman less human, or the new real-estate man more rapacious than the old, as Roberte Glous-ter, the easy-going narrator with ties to California history, likes to suppose? The conclusion can only be left in doubt.
The resemblance of Mayo Sergeant to Fitzgerald's Gatsby is unmistakable. Both, for example, come from obscure origins in the Midwest; both depend in part on an awkward personal attractiveness and win material success. But Gatsby never comes into harmony with the American dream, and it destroys him. Mayo Sergeant, who may seem more contemptible than Gatsby because Hall makes him more familiar than Gatsby, succeeds because the dream has become as venal as he is. Hall has more in common with Fitzgerald than character and theme: in one of the most successful broad comic chapters in America fiction, Hall, with a satiric sense no less acute than Fitzgerald's, illuminates the sanctimonious greed of land deve-lopers. If *Mayo Sergeant* falls short of *The Great Gatsby*, it is because Hall does not sustain the satire, and because he scatters the sympathy of the audience among several important characters.

—Alan R. Shucard

HAMMOND INNES, Ralph. See **INNES, (Ralph) Hammond.**

HANLEY, Clifford (Leonard Clark). British. Born in Glas-gow, Scotland, 28 October 1922. Educated at Eastbank School, Glasgow. Conscientious objector in World War II. Married Anna E. Clark in 1948; one son and two daughters. Reporter, Scottish Newspaper Services, Glasgow, 1940–45; sub-editor, *Scottish Daily Record*, Glasgow, 1945–57; feature writer, *TV Guide*, Glasgow, 1957–58; director, Glasgow Films Ltd., 1957–63; columnist, Glasgow *Evening Citizen*, 1958–60; televi-sion critic, *Spectator*, London, 1963. Visiting Professor, Glen-don College, York University, Toronto, 1979–80. Member, Close Theatre Management Committee, Glasgow, 1965–71, Inland Waterways Council, 1967–71, and Scottish Arts Coun-cil, 1967–74; Vice-President, 1966–73, and President, 1974–77, Scottish PEN; Scottish Chairman, Writers Guild of Great Bri-tain, 1968–73. Agent: Curtis Brown, 162–168 Regent Street, London W1R 5TA, England. Address: 36 Munro Road, Glas-gow G13 1SF, Scotland.

PUBLICATIONS

Novels

Love from Everybody. London, Hutchinson, 1959; as *Don't Bother to Knock*, London, Digit, 1961.
The Taste of Too Much. London, Hutchinson, 1960.
Nothing But the Best. London, Hutchinson, 1964; as *Second Time Round*, Boston, Houghton Mifflin, 1964.
The Hot Month. London, Hutchinson, and Boston, Houghton Mifflin, 1967.
The Red-Haired Bitch. London, Hutchinson, and Boston, Houghton Mifflin, 1969.
Prissy. London, Collins, 1978.
Another Street, Another Dance. Edinburgh, Mainstream, 1983; New York, St. Martin's 1984.

Novels as Henry Calvin

The System. London, Hutchinson, 1962.
It's Different Abroad. London, Hutchinson, and New York, Harper, 1963.
The Italian Gadget. London, Hutchinson, 1966.
The DNA Business. London, Hutchinson, 1967.
A Nice Friendly Town. London, Hutchinson, 1967.
Miranda Must Die. London, Hutchinson, 1968; as *Boka Lives*, New York, Harper, 1969.
The Chosen Instrument. London, Hutchinson, 1969.
The Poison Chasers. London, Hutchinson, 1971.
Take Two Popes. London, Hutchinson, 1972.

Plays

The Durable Element (produced Dundee, Scotland, 1961).
Saturmacnalia, music by Ian Gourlay (produced Glasgow, 1965).
Oh for an Island, music by Ian Gourlay (produced Glasgow, 1966).
Dick McWhittie, music by Ian Gourlay (produced Glasgow, 1967).
Jack o' the Cudgel (produced Perth, 1969).
Oh Glorious Jubilee, music by Ian Gourlay (produced Leeds, 1970).
The Clyde Moralities (produced Glasgow, 1972).

Television Plays: *Dear Boss*, 1962; *Down Memory Lane*, 1971; *Alas, Poor Derek*, 1976.

Other

Dancing in the Streets (autobiography). London, Hutchinson, 1958.
A Skinful of Scotch (travel). London, Hutchinson, and Boston, Houghton Mifflin, 1965.
Burns Country: The Travels of Robert Burns. Newport, Isle of Wight, Dixon, 1975.
The Unspeakable Scot. Edinburgh, Blackwood, 1977.
Poems of Ebenezer McIlwham. Edinburgh, Gordon Wright, 1978.
The Biggest Fish in the World (for children). Edinburgh, Chambers, 1979.
A Hypnotic Trance. Edinburgh, BBC Scotland, 1980.
The Scots. Newton Abbot, Devon, David and Charles, and New York, Times, 1980.
Glasgow: A Celebration. Edinburgh, Mainstream, 1984.

*

Clifford Hanley comments:

(1972) *Dancing in the Streets*, my first published book, was written at the suggestion of my publisher, who wanted a book about the city of Glasgow. At the time I thought it a rather pedestrian recital of childhood memories and was taken aback by its critical and commercial success (it is still used as background reading in schools of social studies and urbanology). My first novel, *Love from Everybody*, written previously but published later, was frankly intended as a light entertainment, to make money, and was later filmed as *Don't Bother to Knock*. Having then retired from journalism, I wrote what I considered my first serious work, *The Taste of Too Much*, as a study of "ordinary" adolescence, without crime and adventitious excitement, and it may well be my most successful book in the sense of fully achieving the author's original conception. In the subsequent novels under my own name, I think my intention was to look at some areas of life—a businessman's troubles, the family situation, the agonies of work in the theatre—simply in my own way, without reference to fashionable literary conceptions. I have often been surprised when people found the novels "funny" because their intention was serious; but an author can't help being what he is. I do see the human condition as tragic (since decay and death are the inevitable end), but I don't distinguish between comedy and tragedy. Funerals can be funny too, and life is noble and absurd at the same time. I also insist on distinguishing between seriousness and solemnity, which are opposite rather than similar. On looking back, I realise that the tone of the novels tends to be affirmation rather than despair. This may be a virtue or a fault, or an irrelevance—a novelist should probably leave such judgments to critics and simply get on with what he must do. Maybe they also betray some kind of moral standpoint of which I was unconscious. This was explicit, in fact, in my first professionally produced play, *The Durable Element*, which was a study of the recurrent urge to crucify prophets. It was also deliberate in *The Chosen Instrument*, a pseudonymous Henry Calvin ten years later, in which a contemporary thriller mode was used to do a sort of feasibility study on the New Testament mythology. (The intention was so well disguised that no critic noticed it.)

But I suppose cheerfulness keeps breaking through. I am an entertainer as well as novelist, and the two may be compatible. My first commandment as a writer is not at all highfalutin. It is Thou Shalt Not Bore. *A Skinful of Scotch* is an irreverent guide to one man's Scotland and was written for fun. So, originally, were the Henry Calvin thrillers. I enjoy reading thrillers and I adopted the pen-name simply to feel uninhibited. The thriller too is a morality, but the morality is acceptable only if it has character and pace. These are not intellectual mysteries but tales of conflict between good and evil. My later work for the theatre was exclusively devoted to calculated entertainment and I am glad that people were actually entertained. I find now that I see life in more sombre terms, but whether this will show in future novels is hard to tell. It may even be a temporary condition.

*   *   *

Humour is never far away from the prose writings of Clifford Hanley. Although it is not officially a work of fiction and is based largely on his childhood experiences, his autobiographical study *Dancing in the Streets* gives the best clue to his literary technique. Partly, its success was due to Hanley's ability to realise the sharp and witty cadences of Glasgow patois; partly, too, it was his by no means dispassionate discovery of objective gaiety in a city in which it is not a common commodity. But the main reason for the book's place as Hanley's seminal work was his ability to work himself and his own comic experiences into a punchy and furiously paced narrative. Thus, when he came to write his first novel, *Love from Everybody*, he not only confirmed his competence to write with wit and humour about people and places, but he also gave notice that in his future fiction his persona was never going to be far absent from his writing.

This gift is seen to good advantage in *The Taste of Too Much*, a sensitive study of adolescence clearly based not only on his own experiences in Glasgow but also on his observations of the lives of young people in the city during the late 1950's. (Hanley was then working as a journalist for a Glasgow newspaper.) Once again, as in *Dancing in the Streets*, the central theme is of a clever boy who is about to make good in the world, but in this instance, Peter Haddow, the intelligent and sensitive teenager, has to come face-to-face with a reality that is not always comic. The pinpricks of parental co-existence, an exasperating older sister, a ghoulish younger one, and an outrageous Aunt Sarah make young Peter's life miserable at times, yet shining like a candle in a wicked world is the gleam of his first love for the fabulous Jean Pynne. Although lightly written, *The Taste of Too Much* perceptively records Peter Haddow's adolescent feelings, and its modern council-estate setting marks it as a precursor of the later Scottish school of proletarian romanticism.

In his subsequent novels it became obvious that although Hanley had not lost his comic touch he was striving too hard to achieve his humorous effects. *The Red-Haired Bitch*, with its promising plot combining historical romance and modern reality, is superficially treated, Hanley being unable to sustain the historical motif of Mary Queen of Scots and the *realpolitik* of Glasgow's gangland. An earlier novel, *The Hot Month*, suffered from similar flaws with Hanley treating the Scots Calvinist ethos in comic fashion before plunging on to an attempt at analysis.

Hanley found his touch again in *Another Street, Another Dance* which takes a panoramic view of Glasgow from the troubled years of the Depression and Red Clydeside to the events of the Second World War and the beginning of the end of the city's great industrial supremacy. Much of the action is seen through the eyes of the family of Meg Macrae, a young girl from the western islands of Scotland who has come to terms with the big city and all its associated problems. Through her we come face to face with the reality of spiritual and physical poverty, drunkenness, wretched housing conditions, bad schooling, and furtive sex. Her triumphant ability to rise above those problems and to overcome a series of harrowing domestic disasters without ever losing grasp of her essential femininity gives the book its main theme and provides the backbone to Hanley's narrative, yet it is his sure ear for Glasgow dialogue and his compassion for all of the characters—good and bad—which finally beguile the reader.

Hanley has also written several modest detective novels under the mischievous pseudonym of Henry Calvin; but he is at his most successful when he remains in Glasgow, a city which nourishes his fiction and provides him with a realistic backdrop, and whose people offer unfailingly witty patterns of speech.

—Trevor Royle

HANLEY, Gerald. Irish.   Born 17 February 1916; brother of the writer James Hanley. Served in the Royal Irish Fusiliers, 7 years: Major. Farmer in Kenya before World War II. Lives in Ireland. Member, Irish Academy of Letters. Agent: Gillon Aitken Ltd., 29 Fernshaw Road, London S.W.10, England.

PUBLICATIONS

Novels

Monsoon Victory.   London, Collins, 1946.
The Consul at Sunset.   London, Collins, and New York, Macmillan, 1951.
The Year of the Lion.   London, Collins, 1953; New York, Macmillan, 1954.
Drinkers of Darkness.   London, Collins, and New York, Macmillan, 1955.
Without Love.   London, Collins, and New York, Harper, 1957.
The Journey Homeward.   London, Collins, and Cleveland, World, 1961.
Gilligan's Last Elephant.   London, Collins, and Cleveland, World, 1962.
See You in Yasukuni.   London, Collins, 1969; Cleveland, World, 1970.
Noble Descents.   London, Hamish Hamilton, 1982; New York, St. Martin's Press, 1983.

Plays

Screenplays: *Gandhi*, 1964; *The Blue Max*, with others, 1966.

Radio Play: *A Voice from the Top*, 1962.

Other

Warriors and Strangers.   London, Hamish Hamilton, and New York, Harper, 1971.

*   *   *

The principal themes of Gerald Hanley's novels are the dissolution of the British Empire and the impact of that dissolution on the relationships of individuals of different races, creeds, and cultures. He also explores subsidiary themes to illuminate these main pre-occupations—the nature of courage, the wielding of power, and the public results of personal inadequacy on the part of those responsible for exercising power.

Hanley has lived through these themes and their manifestations himself and writes of what he knows; but although this makes him an interesting and distinctive writer he falls short of outstanding distinction as a novelist. His plots are often resolved rather obviously; his management of authorial point of view, dramatic dialogue, and interior monologue is sometimes uncertain; and in his earlier work the psychological development of his characters is somewhat limited. One can see why he remains in the second rank of contemporary novelists despite the intrinsic interest of his subject-matter and the clarity of his prose.

Before the war Hanley farmed in Kenya, of all the East and Central African colonies the one in which the divisions between the hierarchy of colonial administrators, British settlers, missionaries, Levantine and Indian traders, and the various African tribes were most strongly contrasted. Wartime army service took him through the Somaliland campaign,

India, and Burma, other formative experiences on which his imagination could later draw.

After *Monsoon Victory* he reached a wide public with *The Consul at Sunset*, the best introduction to his work. The novel is set in sun-baked African terrain where there is a tribal dispute over the use of water-holes. Responsibility for maintaining peace and justice rests with a handful of white men whose ability to discharge it successfully demands political realism, understanding of an alien culture, self-confidence, and personal integrity. A political officer dominated by an African mistress, and a well-meaning but weak-willed liberal, both fail in their different ways, while disciplined army officers, a Captain risen from the ranks and a Colonel of the old school, measure up to the situation. But as he stands bare-headed before the Union Jack at sunset the Colonel is uneasy about the adequacy of his kind in the changes that must lie ahead beyond the coming war.

In *The Year of the Lion* again the seeds of racial, social, and political conflict are seen to be germinating in African soil, even though British, Dutch, and African all unite to fight the lions and herds of zebra that threaten their livestock and grazing, while in *Drinkers of Darkness* the slightly odd tensions of the white settlers have been developed into a crazed blindness to political realities as they struggle to assert their prestige.

With *The Journey Homeward* Hanley turned to the setting of a princely state in the Himalayas after partition, portraying in this Indian frame the political failure of leaders whose private lives are tortured, seedy, or corrupt. Twenty years later he returned to this milieu in *Noble Descents*, a novel whose more ambitious twin themes are firstly, the relationships of Western Judaeo-Christian tradition, Islam, and Hindu and Buddhist belief, and secondly, the culture-transcending differentiation of male and female modes of perception and intuitive response. These contrasts and conflicts, in a world dominated by two nuclear superpowers, are explored through the psychological and spiritual crises which affect a princely ruler emotionally atrophied by the death of his European wife, a retired British colonel "staying on" in the India whose multi-faceted culture has nurtured him both as man and as scholar, and two British couples trapped in failed marriages. The crises are precipitated by the intrusion on their collapsing society of an American scriptwriter and film producer on the trail of a pre-Mutiny scandal involving a princess of the royal house and three British officers. *Noble Descents* inevitably begs comparison with Paul Scott's widely acclaimed Indian novels, and in terms of craftsmanship comes off second best. Though philosophically more ambitious than Scott's or indeed Hanley's own earlier work, and psychologically often penetrating, the novel is unevenly realised and verges on melodrama in its final resolutions of its characters' destinies. Hanley's assured milieu remains Africa, revisited in his clear-eyed and thoughtful travel book *Warriors and Strangers*.

—Stewart F. Sanderson

HANNAH, Barry. American. Born in Meridian, Mississippi, 23 April 1942. Educated at Mississippi College, Clinton, B.A. 1964; University of Arkansas, Fayetteville, M.A. 1966, M.F.A. 1967. Divorced; three children. Member of the English Department, Clemson University, South Carolina, 1967–73; Writer-in-Residence, Middlebury College, Vermont, 1974–75; member of the English Department, University of Alabama,

University, 1975–80; writer for Robert Altman, Hollywood, 1980; Writer-in-Residence, University of Iowa, Iowa City, 1981, University of Mississippi, Oxford, 1982, 1984, 1985, and University of Montana, Missoula, 1982–83. Recipient: Bellaman Foundation award, 1970; Bread Loaf Writers Conference Atherton Fellowship, 1971; Gingrich award (*Esquire*), 1978; American Academy award, 1979. Address: Route 2, Box 197, Oxford, Mississippi 38655, U.S.A.

PUBLICATIONS

Novels

Geronimo Rex. New York, Viking Press, 1972.
Nightwatchmen. New York, Viking Press, 1973.
Ray. New York, Knopf, 1980; London, Penguin, 1981.
The Tennis Handsome. New York, Knopf, 1983.
Power and Light. Winston-Salem, North Carolina, Palaemon Press, 1983.

Short Stories

Airships. New York, Knopf, 1978.
Two Stories. Jackson, Mississippi, Nouveau Press, 1982.
Black Butterfly. Winston-Salem, North Carolina, Palaemon Press, 1982.
Captain Maximus. New York, Knopf, 1985.

*   *   *

Barry Hannah's favored form is the monologue, his subject matter the grotesqueries of American life. Hannah's work includes incidents of beheading, a car wreck in the upper branches of an oak tree, a man who saves himself from drowning by balancing on the tip of a car aerial, a walrus's sexual attack on a woman who is having an affair with her nephew, and a drowned man who jump starts himself using a bus battery. "But that's farfetched, and worse than that, poetic, requiring a willing suspension of disbelief along with a willing desire to eat piles of air sausage," complains a character in *Nightwatchmen* while trying to make sense of a senseless death. A reader must bring along this willingness when reading Hannah.

Geronimo Rex, Hannah's first novel, is a long song of remembrance, an ode to southern adolescence, his discoveries of music and women and firearms and, perhaps most importantly, the extra spark style can give to life. Style is very important to Hannah's characters; this and endurance are the virtues they admire and aspire to. Style is also a large element in Hannah's writing: in *Geronimo Rex* impressionistic sentences that at first seem a beginning writer's excesses grate against the coming-of-age context, stylize the bar-stool braggart tone of voice: "I felt very precise in the oily seat; I was a pistol leaking music out of its holster." Far from being excesses the mature Hannah would weed out, sentences such as these (what Thomas McGuane admiringly referred to as Hannah's "moon-landing English") come to dominate the later works, from *Airships* on.

In the stories collected in *Airships* much of the traditional connective tissue of setting and exterior atmosphere is absent, leaving us with thick, nervous monologues by emotionally damaged men and women with a lot of style. Even the Civil War stories (which are enough alike to suggest Hannah may once have planned a Civil War novel) are narrated by characters with a jaded, violent sensibility identical with that of Hannah's characters from a hundred years later—particularly those with some involvement in the Vietnam War in their past. (Vietnam and the Civil War thread through much of Hannah's work.) Sentences such as "Levaster did not dream about himself and French Edward, although the dreams lay on him like the bricks of an hysterical mansion," mix southern gothic with an updated "hardboiled dick" tone, sometimes moving past intelligibility into a private impressionistic flow. At other times this same mix produces beautiful straight-to-the-heart images: "There is a poison in Tuscaloosa that draws souls toward the low middle." Plots are sketchy here, short portraits or sketches of fragmented lives. Characters, as in much of the work that follows, tend to stand or sit around listlessly, or to strike poses that accentuate their stylized speeches.

The title character in the short novel *Ray* is hardly a character at all, serving for the most part as a kind of tuning fork adjusted to the pitches of certain kinds of misery, those that reflect his own. Dr. Ray is a drinker, an adulterer, and perhaps a little too free with his drug prescriptions. Dr. Ray was a pilot during the Vietnam War, and has begun confusing this experience with what he knows of the Civil War. Others living the low middle life around Dr. Ray get ahead or fall, but his yearnings are too huge or too vague, too subject to change, and he remains stalled in a stasis of half-hearted healing, sex, and war memories.

The Tennis Handsome was expanded from a story in *Airships*. The title character, French Edward, sustains brain damage when he is nearly drowned trying either to save or to kill his mother's lover, who is also his old tennis coach. French Edward is still able to continue his career as a tennis pro through the Svengali-like attentions of Levaster, an unsavory old friend who likes to shoot people with a gun loaded with popcorn. The story version ends with everyone admiring, even taking solace in, French Edward's mindless grace and endurance, his perfect second of "blazing" serve. In the novel French Edward phases in and out, sometimes shocking himself into lucidity, writing poetry, finding religion, and generally frustrating everyone around him. Despite its brevity *The Tennis Handsome* seems to sprawl.

Captain Maximus, Hannah's second story collection, is even more spare, more knife-edged than *Airships*. Again these vignettes are filled with people consumed by yearning, but devoid of hope. Only in "Idaho," an ode to the late poet Richard Hugo which captures some of the poet's own style, and in "Power and Light," a reflection on the travails of working women, does Hannah's tone lighten at all, and only marginally.

Standing apart from his other works is Hannah's second novel, *Nightwatchmen*. While the novel's grotesqueries outnumber those of the other novels, it is a much more emotional, caring work. The writing here is much less stylized, and conflicts are not kept at a callous distance. Hannah's other works are plotted concentrically or in parallel lines, with groups of characters having some experience in common rather than sharing some common experience; only in *Nightwatchmen* do lives truly intersect in any significant way. The primary narrator, Thorpe Trove, is open and vulnerable, concerned for the people around him. He spends two years solving the mysteries of who knocked a half dozen people unconscious, and who then beheaded two nightwatchmen. When Thorpe records the stories of the "innocent" parties involved it becomes clear that they care only for their own fears and defenses. In the end the whodunit aspect is overshadowed by the realization of how

much the other characters have in common with The Knocker and The Killer.

—William C. Bamberger

HANRAHAN, Barbara. Australian. Born in Adelaide, South Australia, in 1939. Writer and artist: 24 one-woman exhibitions in Australia, England, and Italy since 1964; prints in the collections of the Australian National Gallery, Canberra, and most Australian state galleries. Address: c/o Chatto and Windus Ltd., 40 William IV Street, London WC2N 4DF, England.

PUBLICATIONS

Novels

The Scent of Eucalyptus.   London, Chatto and Windus, 1973.
Sea-green.   London, Chatto and Windus, 1974.
The Albatross Muff.   London, Chatto and Windus, 1977.
Where the Queens All Strayed.   St. Lucia, University of Queensland Press, 1978.
The Peach Groves.   St. Lucia, University of Queensland Press, 1980.
The Frangipani Gardens.   St. Lucia, University of Queensland Press, 1980.
Dove.   St. Lucia, University of Queensland Press, 1982.
Kewpie Doll.   London, Chatto and Windus, 1984.
Annie Magdalene.   London, Chatto and Windus, 1985; New York, Beaufort, 1986.

*   *   *

Barbara Hanrahan is at least as well known for her prints as her novels; her work is held in most major Australian galleries, and has been exhibited in London, Florence, and Tokyo. There is patent kinship, in both content and technique, between novels and prints. The prints, particularly those used on the covers of her books, can be gaily decorative, but they can also be grotesque, aggressively sexual, the figures menacing, and if not naked dressed in exotic costumes. Flowers, plants, birds, small animals abound. The faces of the human figures show a variety of expressions, but are in the end enigmatic. Most are decorated in minute, delicate detail.

Her first book, *The Scent of Eucalyptus*, is autobiographical, and tells of growing up in suburban Adelaide in the 1950's; a book of great charm and sometimes startling honesty, it contains the seeds of many of the themes, motifs, images, and even characters of the later fiction. Notably, Hanrahan speaks of herself as being at that time divided: "I had always been two," torn between her family's dreams for her of a safe suburban marriage, and her own instinct to pull herself clear of "the mediocrities of the world that sought to claim me," and flee to the dark world of their suburban garden that "came alive only at night." In most of her subsequent novels, major and even minor characters share the sense of being divided, mostly between the desire to conform to social and family expectations, and the instinct, sometimes not consciously realised, that for them conformity is diminution, aridity.

Hanrahan's style is highly individual, and in itself a conjunction of opposites. It accommodates on the one hand a powerful simplicity which can convey important events and motives in a few lines, and, on the other, an image-laden richness, crowded detail, a manner that is both consciously literary and yet earthy, indecorous. Apart from the autobiographical novels (*The Scent of Eucalyptus*, *Kewpie Doll*, and the only partly autobiographical *Sea-green*) Hanrahan's novels are set largely in the past, either the 19th or early 20th century, and usually in Adelaide. She is, as she said in an interview (*Australian Literary Studies*, May 1983) "attracted to the Victorian period. It suits me exactly. There's the weird combination of the spiritual existing side by side with the material." In the novels there is always a piling up of detail, the revealing minutiae of a society: beauty hints, favoured plants in suburban gardens, the butcher's shop, crowds in Adelaide streets on Saturday night, hectic preparations for the visit to Adelaide of the Duke and Duchess of York in 1927. Hanrahan's interest in such detail sprang from listening to her grandmother's stories of her childhood, and from reading old copies of *The Girl's Own Annual* in the midst of Adelaide heatwaves. Her most recent book, *Annie Magdalene*, consists almost entirely of such minutiae, combined with what can only be called gossip about family and friends; astonishingly it grips the attention. The novel has as heroine/narrator one Annie Magdalene McGregor, born 1908, who became a button sewer and then a dressmaker, worked in factories, made wedding gowns for friends who married, tended her garden, fowls, and cat, saw her family and many friends die, and became increasingly incapacitated by arthritis. The bees rest on her arm and do not sting; they come to sit by her when they are dying and she buries them so that the ants will not eat them. The last sentence in the book reads: "But you must never talk loud to the bees, you must talk softly." The epigraph, taken from Virginia Woolf, speaks of "All these infinitely obscure lives" which "remain to be recorded." From all the small events of her life, there emerges in *Annie Magdalene* a totally credible, independent, touching personality.

Annie Magdalene is not, however, wholly typical of Hanrahan's fiction. In the novels which followed *The Scent of Eucalyptus*, she retains "the family" as the social centre, but her view of the family is of a façade of respectability above, turmoil and black emotions below. She retains also the predominantly though not exclusively child's-eye view of the adult world. Hanrahan says that the child's view is clear, direct, "so intense that it takes in all the little details to the side as well"; at the same time the child can be a useful link between the fantasy world and the "earthy, material world" essential to Hanrahan's vision. Fantasy and the possibility of the supernatural in *The Frangipani Gardens* co-exist without tension with the Duke and Duchess of York dancing to "Hi Diddle Diddle" at the Lord Mayor's Ball. Several novels deal with the threat to the child from adults, threats which may be sexual, murderous, or simply an attempt to impose on the child an adult's dream. Typically in a Hanrahan novel, violence is let loose in the world, a festering passion which is sometimes evil, sometimes merely aberrant from social norms; this builds to a climax, usually involving death, and then is dissipated; life goes on as before, normally with a hint, however slight, of optimism.

Opinion would be divided as to which of Hanrahan's novels is "best," but certainly one of the most powerful is *The Frangipani Gardens*, with its overtones of an epic battle of good and evil forces: on the one side the corrupt (and yet still pitiable) Boy and Girlie, and the depraved priest Swells; on the other, Tom and Lou, sheltered by Aunt Doll, and the outcast Charlie, who sends out his mind to do battle with evil on Tom's behalf. Aunt Doll is one of several artist figures in Hanrahan's fiction; by day she paints ladylike, lifeless watercolours; by night, in her locked studio, sensuous paintings which assault the eye and often foretell the future with seemingly supernatural accuracy. Other highly regarded novels are *The Albatross Muff* and *The Peach Groves*.

—Alrene Sykes

HARDWICK, Elizabeth (Bruce). American. Born in Lexington, Kentucky, 27 July 1916. Educated at the University of Kentucky, Lexington, A.B. 1938, M.A. 1939; Columbia University, New York, 1939–41. Married the poet Robert Lowell in 1949 (divorced, 1972); one daughter. Adjunct Associate Professor, Barnard College, New York. Founder and advisory editor, *New York Review of Books*. Recipient: Guggenheim fellowship, 1948; George Jean Nathan Award, for criticism, 1966; American Academy award, 1974. Member, American Academy, 1977. Address: 15 West 67th Street, New York, New York 10023, U.S.A.

PUBLICATIONS

Novels

The Ghostly Lover. New York, Harcourt Brace, 1945.
The Simple Truth. New York, Harcourt Brace, and London, Weidenfeld and Nicolson, 1955.
Sleepless Nights. New York, Random House, and London, Weidenfeld and Nicolson, 1979.

Uncollected Short Stories

"People on the Roller Coaster," in *O. Henry Memorial Award Prize Stories of 1945.* New York, Doubleday, 1945.
"Saint Ursula and Her Eleven Thousand Virgins," in *Yale Review* (New Haven, Connecticut), March 1945.
"The Mysteries of Eleusis," in *The Best American Short Stories 1946*, edited by Martha Foley. Boston, Houghton Mifflin, 1946.
"What We Have Missed," in *O. Henry Memorial Award Prize Stories of 1946.* New York, Doubleday, 1946.
"The Temptations of Dr. Hoffman," in *Partisan Review* (New Brunswick, New Jersey), Fall 1946.
"The Golden Stallion," in *The Best American Short Stories 1947*, edited by Martha Foley. Boston, Houghton Mifflin, 1947.
"Evenings at Home," in *The Best American Short Stories 1949*, edited by Martha Foley. Boston, Houghton Mifflin, 1949.
"The Friendly Witness," in *Partisan Review* (New Brunswick, New Jersey), April 1950.
"A Florentine Conference," in *Partisan Review* (New Brunswick, New Jersey), May–June 1951.
"A Season's Romance," in *New Yorker*, 10 March 1956.
"The Oak and the Axe," in *New Yorker*, 12 May 1956.
"The Classless Society," in *Stories from The New Yorker 1950–1960.* New York, Simon and Schuster, 1960.
"The Purchase," in *The Best American Short Stories 1960*, edited by Martha Foley and David Burnett. Boston, Houghton Mifflin, 1960.
"Two Recent Triumphs," in *Gallery of Modern Fiction*, edited by Robie Macauley. New York, Salem Press, 1966.
"The Faithful," in *The Best American Short Stories 1980*, edited by Stanley Elkin and Shannon Ravenel. Boston, Houghton Mifflin, 1980.

"The Bookseller," in *The Best American Short Stories 1981*, edited by Hortense Calisher and Shannon Ravenel. Boston, Houghton Mifflin, 1981.
"Back Issues," in *New York Review of Books*, 17 December 1981.
"On the Eve," in *New York Review of Books*, 20 December 1983.

Other

A View of My Own: Essays in Literature and Society. New York, Farrar Straus, 1962; London, Heinemann, 1964.
Seduction and Betrayal: Women and Literature. New York, Random House, and London, Weidenfeld and Nicolson, 1974.
Bartleby in Manhattan and Other Essays. New York, Random House, and London, Weidenfeld and Nicolson, 1983.

Editor, *Selected Letters*, by William James. New York, Farrar Straus, 1961.

*   *   *

For over two decades, Elizabeth Hardwick's reputation as a tough-minded, occasionally wry, critic has been secure. Her career as a novelist has been less certain. Her first novel, *The Ghostly Lover*, published in 1945, was promising, but its early feminist slant was not rightly appreciated. A novel about Marian Coleman who learns that she cannot settle for the comforts of a man, it offers telling glimpses into her life, the life of her restless parents, the hot, lazy days in the South, the grubby days studying in New York, and the dreams of the ghostly men who pursue her. Marian knows the value of concealment; the book confirms her suspicion that love is not "the hard, demanding surrender she had imagined." Marian suffers from a peculiar emptiness, one that comes from knowing that what men want from her is not in her, but is "tuned to a certain imaginary pitch in women" that men have invented. The novel closes with Marian's act of independence: she walks unseen away from her lover who has come to the station to meet her. She knows that to accept him would be to accept marriage and not to care about motives. Hardwick's next novel, *The Simple Truth*, appeared a decade later. Tightly plotted, probing the motives behind a frightful act, the novel examines the death of a beautiful college girl, Betty Jane Henderson, who died in her boyfriend's rooming-house, after hours. The trial of the boyfriend, Rudy, dominates the book. It is examined from numerous perspectives, most important those of two curious onlookers, the affable, married Mr. Parks and the middle-aged, married Anita Mitchell who is drawn to the case to investigate the working of the unconscious. The truth about the act, late at night, in a rooming-house where two lovers frolicked and struggled, ultimately emerges, but equally as interesting is the picture of the psyches of the characters who become caught up in the trial. These two early novels were competent—the writing was careful; the characters, ordinary, but true, surprisingly often; the plots were slightly thin.

Sleepless Nights appeared in 1979 and broke a silence of more than 20 years. It should make Hardwick's name. Its form is novel, daringly breaking the strictures of her earlier narrative style. The autobiographical component of the novel is openly confronted, and handled effectively. Roaming like an insomniac from one recollection to another, the book continually surprises us with its fleeting memories of rooms we have all known, feelings we have felt, losses we have never remedied. In retrospect, Hardwick's earlier novels show a niggling regret on the author's part that the story is not a little more important, that life for women is not a little more adventuresome. *Sleepless Nights* reflects a more mature sensibility—one that has learned that ordinary experience needs no apology.

Sleepless Nights offers a record of life's obscenities. The insomniac narrator is identified as "Elizabeth" in the novel. The book is a queer blend of autobiography and fiction. Hardwick's decision to create a persona with her own name heightens our sense of how life informs fiction. The Elizabeth of this book is very nearly the Elizabeth Hardwick who lives, the woman who is a career journalist, writer, reviewer for *Partisan Review* and the *New York Review of Books*, and the ex-wife of the poet Robert Lowell. The memories and imaginings of the persona curl about the lives of deprived souls, of which Elizabeth is one. There is Josette, the Boston cleaning-lady, a victim of "unfair diseases," with her "breasts hacked off by cancer." There is Billie Holiday, self-destructive, haunting, pure style, who died in agony, with the police at her bedside, denied in her last hours the drugs her body craved. Elizabeth wonders at the "sheer enormity" of Holiday's vices. There is Alex A., Elizabeth's bachelor friend, an intellectual and failed academic who does not marry the woman who might have made his life different. There is her other half, the partner of the "we" she alludes to. She complains of his tyranny by the weak, women. He reads and writes all day, drinks quarts of mild, smokes cigarettes, and complains when she plays jazz records. There is her mother, bearer of nine children; childbearing is "what she was always doing, and in the end what she had done." There is the neighborhood prostitute, Juanita, who died of "prodigious pains and sores." This is a bitter, troubling book of memories to keep us all awake. But if the dose is bitter, it is also life. The laundress, the cleaning-lady, the Boston spinster, the middle-aged persona whose divorce has brought her back to her old territory, the talk of a mother, troubled that her son cannot cope and the complaints of a couple too long married are all authentic. The style is often sparse; the details are selected with startling directness and simplicity; yet the whole is very full.

—Carol Simpson Stern

HARDY, Frank (Francis Joseph Hardy). Australian. Born in Southern Cross, Victoria, 21 March 1917. Educated at state schools. Served in the Australian Army, 1941–46. Married Rosslyn Couper in 1939; one son and two daughters. Free-lance writer; President, Realist Writers Group, Melbourne and Sydney, 1945–74; co-founder, Australian Society of Authors, Sydney, 1968–74; President, Carringbush Writers, Melbourne, 1980–83. Recipient: Logic award, for television script, 1972; Television Society award, 1973; 3 Literature Board grants. Agent: Jill Hickson Associates, 137 Regent Street, Chippendale, New South Wales 2008. Address: 9/76 Elizabeth Bay Road, Elizabeth Bay, New South Wales 2011, Australia.

PUBLICATIONS

Novels

Power Without Glory. Melbourne, Realist, 1950; London, Laurie, 1962.
The Four-Legged Lottery. London, Laurie, 1958.

The Outcasts of Foolgarah.   Melbourne, Allara, 1971; London, Panther, 1975.
But the Dead Are Many: A Novel in Fugue Form.   London, Bodley Head, 1975.
Who Shot George Kirkland? A Novel about the Nature of Truth. Melbourne, Arnold, 1981.
Warrant of Distress.   Carlton, Victoria, Pascoe, 1983.
The Obsession of Oscar Oswald.   Carlton, Victoria, Pascoe, 1983.

Short Stories

The Man from Clinkapella and Other Prize-Winning Stories. Melbourne, Realist, 1951.
Legends from Benson's Valley.   London, Laurie, 1963.
The Yarns of Billy Borker.   Sydney, Reed, 1965.
Billy Borker Yarns Again.   Melbourne, Nelson, 1967.
The Great Australian Lover and Other Stories.   Melbourne, Nelson, 1972.
It's Moments Like These.   Melbourne, Gold Star, 1972.
The Loser Now Will Be Later to Win.   Carlton, Victoria, Pascoe, 1985.

Plays

Black Diamonds (produced Sydney, 1956).
The Ringbolter (produced Sydney, 1964).
Who Was Harry Larsen? (produced, 1985).

Other

Journey into the Future (on the Soviet Union).   Melbourne, Australasian Book Society, 1952.
The Hard Way: The Story Behind Power Without Glory.   London, Laurie, 1961.
The Unlucky Australians (on the Gurindji).   Melbourne, Nelson, 1968; revised edition, Melbourne, Gold Star, 1972.
The Needy and the Greedy: Humorous Stories of the Racetrack, with Athol George Mulley.   Canberra, Libra, 1975.
You Nearly Had Him That Time and Other Cricket Stories, with Fred Trueman.   London, Paul, 1978.
A Frank Hardy Swag, edited by Clement Semmler.   Sydney, Harper, 1982.

*

Bibliography: in *A Frank Hardy Swag*, 1982.

Manuscript Collection: Australian National Library, Canberra.

Theatrical Activities:
Actor: **Play**—role in *Black Diamonds*, Sydney, 1956.

*   *   *

Though Frank Hardy has written a number of Australia's best short stories (including the "classic" yarn "The Load of Wood"), he is best known as a novelist. His first novel, *Power Without Glory*, was a long social-realist exposé of corruption in Australian society and political life. The central character, John West, rises above his humble working-class beginnings and amasses wealth, power, and influence; he abandons all concern for the working man, loses all human compassion and decency, and drives his wife to adultery and his children to despair.

Though its prose style is merely workaday and its structure crude (but serviceable), the novel has three enduring strengths. It tells a long story with clarity; it is imbued with a powerful, angry sincerity; and it combines the suspense of fiction with the fascinating factual insights of a journalistic "exposé." The "factuality," however, became the source of controversy when it was alleged that *Power Without Glory* was a disguised portrait of the Melbourne personality John Wren. Hardy was taken to court over the claim that he had defamed Wren's wife by portraying her as having committed adultery. (The story of his trial and acquittal, together with an account of the research-ing and writing of the novel, is told in Hardy's non-fiction book *The Hard Way*.)

Power Without Glory established Hardy's concern with socio-political subjects, but his distinctive handling of structure and narrative point of view does not emerge until his second novel, *The Four-Legged Lottery*. Taking as its epigraph the comment that horse-racing has "ceased to be a valiant sport" and has become "a lottery, with four-legged tickets," Hardy uses the corruption of the Australian horse-racing industry as a metaphor for the injustice and corruption of Australian capi-talism. By an ingenious plot construction, the novel combines a third-person account of race-track life with a first-person analysis of the ills of betting (written from the prison cell of a man who has seen his mate driven to death by punting debts).

In his best novel, *But the Dead Are Many*, Hardy uses a similar but more ambitious structure. Sub-titled "A Novel in Fugue Form," the work concerns the disappearance and appar-ent suicide of John Morel, a leading figure in the Australian Communist Party, and the efforts of Morel's friend, Jack, to retrace Morel's final journey and discover the reasons for his death. Morel's story points to a crisis of confidence in the moral standards of the Communist Party, for Morel has come to see his comrades' ideals as a reflection of Stalinism. But Morel's story becomes the story of another man, the communist intel-lectual Nicolai Buratakov, whose writings converted Morel to communism. Attempting to understand the reasons why Bura-takov was put on trial and executed in Moscow in 1938, Morel's faith in his ideology becomes as weak as the morality of Stalinist practice.

Describing the intentions behind this novel, Hardy claims a desire to speak for the generation of Australian communists born at the time of the Russian revolution and compelled to live through the failure of capitalism (such as the Great Depres-sion) only to witness the collapse of the Utopian dream in the brutality of Stalinism and the Soviet response to events in Hungary. The novel succeeds in this aim, but achieves even more: it is also a study of suicide, an examination of the rela-tionship between the individual and the group, and (less suc-cessfully, perhaps) an attempt to explore the concepts of death and transcendence. The novel also breaks new ground in Aus-tralian fiction, using character and plot to expound themes that are simultaneously social, psychological, and ideological. *But the Dead Are Many* is one of the major works of Australian literature in the 1970's.

Who Shot George Kirkland? (sub-titled "A Novel About the Nature of Truth") is equally ambitious but less successful. The novel clearly draws upon Hardy's own experience in the writing of *Power Without Glory*, for it uses a character named Ross Franklyn, and Hardy has admitted (in the 1971 "Pro-logue" to *The Hard Way*) that Ross Franklyn is his own pseudo-nym. Decades after facing criminal charges over a story of adultery in his novel *Power Corrupts*, Franklyn despairingly wonders whether or not the story was true. His source was a Melbourne underworld figure named Alan Hall, and Frank-lyn recalls that Hall also claimed to have shot the gangster named George Kirkland. If the claim about Kirkland can be shown to be true, presumably the story of the adultery would also be true.

Instead of questioning this spurious logic, the novel proceeds to add complications to its structure and concerns. Ross Franklyn commits suicide without discovering who shot Kirkland, and it is left to a young researcher to retrace Franklyn's final uncertainties and seek to discover the truth. The events which subsequently unfold are used to assert the view that "the truth resides in memory and memory is clouded . . . the recollections of any individual are conditioned by the general truths by which he or she has tried to live." However, the accuracy of such a view is scarcely demonstrated by researchers who fail to take notes, conduct research interviews when drunk, or freely admit they may have "embroidered" their material! Far from being a novel about the nature of truth, *Who Shot George Kirkland?* is merely an indictment of slip-shod research.

Like his comic novel *The Outcasts of Foolgarah*, Hardy's latest novel, *The Obsession of Oscar Oswald*, is disappointingly slight and suffers from the thinness of its characterization. Though published in 1983, the novel purports to be a 1985 manuscript proving that "In *1984*, George Orwell got it all wrong!" Obsessed with the Hire Purchase system (and the capitalist society which supports it), Oscar Oswald sets out to prove that Orwell "ignored the capitalist 'free' market with its built-in cycle of boom, bust and war": "It was not Big Brother but Big Business exploiting the poor . . . not Double Think picking the minds of the intellectuals but Capitalists picking the pockets of the poor."

Hardy has written an accurate literary epitaph for himself, using the words of the young researcher in *Who Shot George Kirkland?*: he "wrote truly of and for the common man. His overall theme is in his concern for the way the ordinary man is cheated by those who manipulate him, and he invests this theme with greater urgency and power than any other writer."

—Van Ikin

HARRIS, Mark. American. Born Mark Finkelstein in Mount Vernon, New York, 19 November 1922. Educated at the University of Denver, B.A. in English 1950, M.A. in English 1951; University of Minnesota, Minneapolis, Ph.D. in American Studies 1956. Served in the United States Army, 1943–44. Married Josephine Horen in 1946; one daughter and two sons. Reporter, *Daily Item*, Port Chester, New York, 1944–45, *PM*, Long Island, New York, 1945, and International News Service, St. Louis, 1945–46; writer for *Negro Digest* and *Ebony*, Chicago, 1946–51. Member of the English Department, San Francisco State College, 1954–68, Purdue University, Lafayette, Indiana, 1967–70, California Institute of the Arts, Valencia, 1970–73, Immaculate Heart College, Los Angeles, 1973–74, and University of Southern California, Los Angeles, 1973–75; Professor of English, University of Pittsburgh, 1975–82. Since 1983, Professor of English, Arizona State University, Tempe. Fulbright Professor, University of Hiroshima, 1957–58; Visiting Professor, Brandeis University, Waltham, Massachusetts, 1963. Member, San Francisco Art Commission, 1961–64; U.S. Delegate, Dartmouth Conference, Kurashiki, Japan, 1974. Recipient: Ford grant, for theatre, 1960; American Academy grant, 1961; Guggeinheim fellowship, 1965, 1974; National Endowment for the Arts grant, 1966. D.H.L.: Illinois Wesleyan University, Bloomington, 1974.

Agent: A.L. Hart, Fox Chase Agency, 401 East 34th Street, New York, New York 10016. Address: P.O. Box 24647, Tempe, Arizona 85282, U.S.A.

PUBLICATIONS

Novels

Trumpet to the World.   New York, Reynal, 1946.
City of Discontent: An Interpretive Biography of Vachel Lindsay, Being Also the Story of Springfield, Illinois, USA, and of the Love of the Poet for That City, That State, and That Nation, by Henry W. Wiggen.   Indianapolis, Bobbs Merrill, 1952.
The Southpaw, by Henry W. Wiggen: Punctuation Inserted and Spelling Greatly Improved.   Indianapolis, Bobbs Merrill, 1953.
Bang the Drum Slowly, by Henry W. Wiggen: Certain of His Enthusiasms Restrained.   New York, Knopf, 1956.
A Ticket for a Seamstitch, by Henry W. Wiggen: But Polished for the Printer.   New York, Knopf, 1957.
Something about a Soldier.   New York, Macmillan, 1957; London, Deutsch, 1958.
Wake Up, Stupid.   New York, Knopf, 1959; London, Deutsch, 1960.
The Goy.   New York, Dial Press, 1970.
Killing Everybody.   New York, Dial Press, 1973.
It Looked Like For Ever.   New York, McGraw Hill, 1979.
Lying in Bed.   New York, McGraw Hill, 1984.

Uncollected Short Stories

"Carmelita's Education for Living," in *Esquire* (New York), October 1957.
"Conversation on Southern Honshu," in *North Dakota Quarterly* (Grand Forks), Summer 1959.
"The Self-Made Brain Surgeon," in *The Best American Short Stories 1961*, edited by Martha Foley and David Burnett. Boston, Houghton Mifflin, 1961.
"La Lumière," in *Denver Quarterly*, Fall 1983.

Plays

Friedman & Son (produced San Francisco, 1962).   New York, Macmillan, 1963.
The Man That Corrupted Hadleyburg, adaptation of the story by Mark Twain (televised, 1980).   Published in *The American Short Story 2*, edited by Calvin Skaggs, New York, Dell, 1980.

Screenplay: *Bang the Drum Slowly*, 1973.

Television Plays: *The Man That Corrupted Hadleyburg*, 1980; *Boswell for the Defence*, 1983 (UK); *Boswell's London Journal*, 1984 (UK).

Other

Mark the Glove Boy; or, The Last Days of Richard Nixon (autobiography).   New York, Macmillan, 1964.
Twentyone Twice: A Journal (autobiography).   Boston, Little Brown, 1966.
Public Television: A Program for Action, with others.   New York, Harper, 1967.
Best Father Ever Invented: The Autobiography of Mark Harris.   New York, Dial Press, 1976.

Short Work of It: Selected Writing. Pittsburgh, University of Pittsburgh Press, 1979.
Saul Bellow, Drumlin Woodchuck. Athens, University of Georgia Press, 1980.

Editor, *Selected Poems*, by Vachel Lindsay. New York, Macmillan, 1963; London, Collier Macmillan, 1965.
Editor, with Josephine and Hester Harris, *The Design of Fiction*. New York, Crowell, 1976.
Editor, *The Heart of Boswell*. New York, McGraw Hill, 1981.

*

Critical Study: *Mark Harris* by Norman Lavers, Boston, Twayne, 1978.

Mark Harris comments:

(1972) I have written eight novels. I think that a constant line travels through them. I didn't know this was happening while it was happening, but I can see it now, looking back after a quarter of a century since my first novel was published.

They are about the writer. That is, if you will, they are about the artist. Which is to say, if you will, they are about the one man against his society and trying to come to terms with his society, and trying to succeed within it without losing his own identity or integrity.

My novels are always very carefully written. Since hard work makes the writing look easy, there exist stupid reviewers and critics who think I (and others) just slam these writings out. My books are all constructed with great care. Nothing is missing from any of them in the way of plot. I forget nothing.

Of course, although I am spiritually at the center of my novels (every novel is mainly about one man), I am disguised as poet or baseball player or professor or historian. I am always a minority person in some sense, either because I am fictionally left-handed or, most recently, Gentile in a Jewish milieu. (My first book was about a black man in a white milieu.) I don't know why this is so. I believe that it is most deeply the result of being a Jew, but it may be attributable to other things I am not fully aware of. Maybe I was just born that way. It is a mystery.

Subject and theme: sometimes these aren't really stated in the works, and people feel disappointed. They want to know what they shouldn't: where does the author stand? In my heart, if not always dogmatically in my books, I stand for human equality and peace and justice.

I also stand for writing well: I don't believe that good ends can come of false or shoddy or hasty means. Books must be beautiful so that the world is put into a mood of beauty. Books mustn't merely *say* but must, on the other hand, *exist* as beauty.

I am opposed to the reduction or paraphrase of works of art. Thus I feel that I may on this page already have written more than I should.

*   *   *

Mark Harris's fiction and autobiography share several themes: the problems of racism and racial justice, the dilemma of violence and pacifism, the price of individualism and the forms of democracy and social justice. His work is dominated by genial comedy, a gently optimistic view of man's possibilities and capacities, and Mark Harris has pursued his own life through his fiction. His journal-autobiographies *Mark the Glove Boy* and *Twentyone Twice* complement fictionalized self-portraits like pitcher-author Henry Wiggen (*The Southpaw, Bang the Drum Slowly, A Ticket for a Seamstitch*), boxer-

novelist-teacher Lee Youngdahl (*Wake Up, Stupid*), soldier-pacifist Jacob Epstein (*Something about a Soldier*) and historian-diarist Westrum (*The Goy*).

Harris's novels depict individuals in pursuit of themselves, discovering through self-analysis, experience, and observation who they are and what their lives mean. His first novel, *Trumpet to the World*, follows a black man through self-discovery and self-education to his rejection of war and violence and his attempts to reach the world through writing. He suffers poverty, hatred, and violence but also discovers friendship and love. Through determination and courage, he overcomes dehumanizing conditions to become fully alive, a fully functioning man. The baseball tetralogy (*The Southpaw, Bang the Drum Slowly, A Ticket for a Seamstitch, It Looked Like For Ever*) describes the career of Henry W. Wiggen, a young man who succeeds in big-league baseball. In a Lardneresque style, Wiggen writes the journal of his maturity as an athlete and a man. Wiggen grapples with the mysteries of love, the problem of hatred and violence, becomes reconciled wth the finality of death. Each story shows Wiggen's growth, mentally and spiritually, and his progress down a road to self-understanding and reconciliation. Overtly a comedy of athletics and folk-hero rambunctiousness, the three books also form a study of pacifism, love and justice.

Something about a Soldier turns explicitly to the problems of violence and nonviolence which appear in the earlier novels. In it Jacob Epp (Epstein) discovers the importance of his identity, the meaning of love and loyalty, and the relationship between violence and justice. A young, very bright, but naive recruit, Jacob rejects the Army and the war (World War II), militantly works for justice and equality for black people and begins to understand love and friendship. He rejects death for life, war for peace, goes AWOL, and through meditation in prison comes to self-reconciliation.

In *Wake Up, Stupid* Harris uses the epistolary form to follow a crisis of insecurity in the life of a man who is successful as an athlete, teacher, and writer. Lee Youngdahl, during a lull in artistic creativity, takes up letter-writing to occupy his imagination. Comic crises of his fantasy life involve all his friends and enemies and lead him to a final understanding of his needs and desires, the sources of his imagination. *Lying in Bed* continues Harris's exploration of marital comedy through the viewpoint of Lee Youngdahl. Older and wiser in the ways of love and literature, Youngdahl extends his imaginative self-analysis and reviews his love affairs, real and fictive, as he tries to defend his virtuous monogamy and his need for varied romance.

The Goy continues the theme of self-discovery. In it, Westrum, a midwestern gentile who has married an eastern Jew, pursues his identity through a massive, life-long journal. He comes to understand, through the journal, his relationship with the Jews in his life, his father's virulent anti-semitism, his own obsession with history, his relationship with his son, his wife and his mistress. The past, through his journal and his study of history, ultimately explains his present.

In *Killing Everybody* Harris explores opposing passions of love and rage, life-giving and death. The novel deals with the madness of the world and of individuals caught up in its madness. It studies revenge and charity, physical love and sexual fantasy, a dialectic skilfully developed as a complex dance between four central minds. The story moves more deeply into the roots of modern psychic life than Harris's earlier fiction, and he confronts a massive theme—civilization and its discontents.

All of Mark Harris's fiction is comic in conception, and sports and games are at the center of the work, especially the social games which are the substance of comedy of manners. Lee

Youngdahl, in *Wake Up, Stupid*, analyzes American literature in a statement epitomizing Harris's own work:

> What is it that thrusts Mark Twain and Sherwood Anderson into one stream, and Henry James into another? . . . It has so much to do with a man's early relationship to the society of boys and games—that miniature of our larger society of men and business, with its codes and rules, its provision for imagination within these rules, with winning, losing, timing, bluffing, feinting, jockeying, with directness of aim and speech and with coming back off the floor again.

Harris's fiction is solidly within this tradition which translates social games into comedy, a comedy which explains our secret lives more clearly than any social or psychological theory.

—William J. Schafer

HARRIS, (Theodore) Wilson. British. Born in New Amsterdam, British Guiana, now Guyana, 24 March 1921. Educated at Queen's College, Georgetown. Married 1) Cecily Carew in 1945; 2) Margaret Whitaker in 1959. Government surveyor in the 1940's, and senior surveyor, 1955–58, Government of British Guiana; moved to London in 1959. Visiting Lecturer, State University of New York, Buffalo, 1970; Writer-in-Residence, University of the West Indies, Kingston, Jamaica, and Scarborough College, University of Toronto, 1970; Commonwealth Fellow in Caribbean Literature, Leeds University, Yorkshire, 1971; Visiting Professor, University of Texas, Austin, 1972, and 1981–82, University of Mysore, 1978, Yale University, New Haven, Connecticut, 1979, and University of Newcastle, New South Wales, 1979; Regents' Lecturer, University of California, Santa Cruz, 1983. Delegate, National Identity Conference, Brisbane, and Unesco Symposium on Caribbean Literature, Cuba, both 1968. Recipient: Arts Council grant, 1968, 1970; Guggenheim fellowship, 1973; Henfield fellowship, 1974; Southern Arts fellowship, 1976. Address: c/o Faber and Faber Ltd., 3 Queen Square, London WC1N 3AU, England.

PUBLICATIONS

Novels

The Guyana Quartet. London, Faber, 1985.
  Palace of the Peacock. London, Faber, 1960.
  The Far Journey of Oudin. London, Faber, 1961.
  The Whole Armour. London, Faber, 1962.
  The Secret Ladder. London, Faber, 1963.
Heartland. London, Faber, 1964.
The Eye of the Scarecrow. London, Faber, 1965.
The Waiting Room. London, Faber, 1967.
Tumatumari. London, Faber, 1968.
Ascent to Omai. London, Faber, 1970.
Black Marsden: A Tabula Rasa Comedy. London, Faber, 1972.
Companions of the Day and Night. London, Faber, 1975.
Da Silva da Silva's Cultivated Wilderness, and Genesis of the Clowns. London, Faber, 1977.
The Tree of the Sun. London, Faber, 1978.

The Angel at the Gate. London, Faber, 1982.
Carnival. London, Faber, 1985.

Short Stories

The Sleepers of Roraima. London, Faber, 1970.
The Age of the Rainmakers. London, Faber, 1971.

Verse

Fetish. Privately printed, 1951.
The Well and the Land. Georgetown, Magnet, 1952.
Eternity to Season. Privately printed, 1954; revised edition, London, New Beacon, 1979.

Other

Tradition, The Writer, and Society: Critical Essays. London, New Beacon, 1967.
History, Fable, and Myth in the Caribbean and Guianas. Georgetown, National History and Arts Council, 1970.
Fossil and Psyche (lecture on Patrick White). Austin, University of Texas, 1974.
Explorations: A Selection of Talks and Articles, edited by Hena Maes-Jelinek. Aarhus, Denmark, Dangaroo Press, 1981.
The Womb of Space: The Cross-Cultural Imagination. Westport, Connecticut, Greenwood Press, 1983.

*

Manuscript Collections: University of the West Indies, Mona, Kingston, Jamaica; University of Texas, Austin; University of Indiana, Bloomington; University of Guyana, Georgetown.

Critical Studies: *Wilson Harris: A Philosophical Approach* by C.L.R. James, Port of Spain, University of the West Indies, 1965; *The Novel Now* by Anthony Burgess, London, Faber, and New York, Norton, 1967, revised edition, Faber, 1971; essay by John Hearne, in *The Islands in Between* edited by Louis James, London, Oxford University Press, 1968; *Wilson Harris and the Caribbean Novel* by Michael Gilkes, Trinidad and London, Longman, 1975; *Enigma of Values* edited by Kirsten Holst Petersen and Anna Rutherford, Aarhus, Denmark, Dangaroo Press, 1975; *The Naked Design: A Reading of Palace of the Peacock*, Aarhus, Denmark, Dangaroo Press, 1976, and *Wilson Harris*, Boston, Twayne, 1982, both by Hena Maes-Jelinek; *West Indian Literature* edited by Bruce King, London, Macmillan, 1979; "The Eternal Present in Wilson Harris's *The Sleepers of Roraima* and *The Age of the Rainmakers*" by Gary Crew, in *World Literature Written in English* (Arlington, Texas), Autumn 1980; "Limbo, Dislocation, Phantom Limb" by Nathaniel Mackey, in *Criticism* (Detroit), Winter 1980.

Wilson Harris comments:
(1972) *Palace of the Peacock* through *The Guyana Quartet* and successive novels up to *The Sleepers of Roraima* and *The Age of the Rainmakers* are related to a symbolic landscape-in-depth—the shock of great rapids, vast forests and savannahs—playing through memory to involve perspectives of imperilled community and creativity reaching back into the Pre-Columbian mists of time.
I believe that the revolution of sensibility in defining community towards which we may now be moving is an extension of the frontiers of the alchemical imagination beyond an *opus*

contra naturam into an *opus contra ritual.* This does not mean the jettisoning of ritual (since ritual belongs in the great ambivalent chain of memory; and the past, in a peculiar sense, as an omen of proportions, shrinking or expanding, never dies); but it means the utilisation of ritual as an ironic bias—the utilisation of ritual, not as something in which we situate ourselves absolutely, but as an unravelling of self-deception with self-revelation as we see through the various dogmatic proprietors of the globe within a play of contrasting structures and anti-structures: a profound drama of consciousness invoking contrasting tones is the variable phenomenon of creativity within which we are prone, nevertheless, to idolise logical continuity or structure and commit ourselves to a conservative bias, or to idolise logical continuity or anti-structure and commit ourselves to a revolutionary bias. Thus we are prone to monumentalise our own biases and to indict as well as misconceive creativity. A capacity to digest as well as liberate contrasting figures is essential to the paradox of community and to the life of the imagination.

*   *   *

Wilson Harris's short experimental novels undoubtedly form one of the major and revolutionary fictional achievements in English in this century. Their visionary character, the terseness and accumulated depths of his language, the progression of the many-layered narratives through significant moments of intuition and the gradual metamorphosis of their metaphorical texture rather than mere plot, his conception of character as a nucleus of selves or "community of being" rather than a sharply defined entity, these are some of the elements that link him with other great novelists in whose fiction form and vision combine into an original work of art. To the realistic novel which, in his eyes, "mimics" reality, consolidates a world view, and presents it as inevitable, Harris opposes the "drama of consciousness" which involves his characters in a process of breaking down of biases and self-deceptions as a preliminary to fulfilment. His work is a focus of cross-cultural traditions (English, South American, Caribbean). Its distinctive character in the first ten novels or so emerges from his confrontation with, and immersion in, the Guyanese landscapes and from his re-interpretation of the basic facts of Caribbean history. Harris is intensely concerned with the future of humanity. He sees the Guyanese (man's) psyche as a "spatial" reality equivalent to the phenomenal world. Both are the receptacle of lost generations of victims. Hence his exploratison of hidden densities in both outer and inner landscapes. Harris's characters develop towards a nameless dimension of being similar to the void-like condition experienced by the Caribbean peoples but seen now as a starting point or a vessel of rebirth out of the hideous polarizations inherited from the colonial past. There are hidden resources, neglected possibilities inherent in any given situation which it is the function of art to redeem in order to transform the consequences of historical catastrophe. These need never be final but offer an occasion for change and renewal when re-lived imaginatively and "digested." Harris's deep faith in the capacity of art to save the world from despair and further catastrophe is paramount in his vision and sets him apart from prevailing trends in contemporary fiction.

Palace of the Peacock, the first novel of *The Guyana Quartet*, is also the first of all Harris's "novels of expedition" and contains in essence all further philosophical and formal developments. The recreation of a journey into the Guyanese interior conveys in startling poetic language the violation of landscape

and people by a multi-racial crew in pursuit of an elusive Amerindian folk. Their leader, Donne (a name that evokes the Renaissance spirit and the creative imagination), is moved by the mixture of idealism, greed, and brutality that usually prompted conquering expeditions. His penetration of the Guyanese jungle and the successive deaths of the crew in the rapids of a nameless river symbolize and initiate a movement to be found in most of Harris's fictions: the disorientation of the characters, the *crumbling* (rather than consolidation) of their personality, which, terrifyingly, shakes them out of their fixed sense of identity but enables them to approach an "otherness," a buried sensibility, in themselves and their opponents and so to alter opposition into an awareness of mutuality. The *Quartet* creates a composite picture of Guyana, its various landscapes and racial communities. In each novel the protagonist is faced with the legacy of a terrible past that must be re-interpreted. Though a sense of social justice may be partly responsible for the change of his attitude towards victimized people, this does not stem from a social or political ideal but rather from a need for individual regeneration prior to a new conception of community. The emphasis is on an underlying unity and interrelatedness, on spiritual freedom and responsibility, all of which are envisaged through the recognition of the alien and weak element in the community as its true roots. The possibility of unlocking a fixed order of things and eroding the certainties in which the characters are self-imprisoned is central. Even their mode of apprehension is shattered and reshaped. Their only hope (the hope of humanity) lies in a regeneration of the creative imagination.

This shattering of rigid ways of being leads to partial and unfinished reconstructions of reality in the protagonist's consciousness, partial because there is no such thing as absolute truth, unfinished because the dynamic tension between dissolution and rebirth is in the very nature of existence and Harris refuses to invest absolutely in one way of being. In his second cycle of novels (from *The Eye of the Scarecrow* to *Ascent to Omai*) there is a double preoccupation with the creation of genuine, though never wholly achieved, community and the art of fiction Harris (and the narrator within the novels) attempts to create. Their subject-matter is, even more specifically, the working of the subjective imagination and of memory in order to transform the accepted view of history and the meaning of individual experience, which is presented as wholly internalized. The protagonist is an "agent of personality" through whom the past re-enacts itself as a free "construction of events." The result is a fragmentation of the surface reality (and of the narrative structure) concomitant with an accumulation of motifs and images, which are so many ways of approaching without ever fully achieving an underlying wholeness. A major impression created by these narratives is of the duality that arises from the sensuous evocation of concrete local environments together with the spiritual, universal dimension pursued by the characters.

In the two ensuing collections of stories, *The Sleepers of Roraima* and *The Age of the Rainmakers*, Harris re-interprets Amerindian myths and shows that they can elicit a new conception of life, for myth, as opposed to history, is shown to be a dynamic force that can convert apparently changeless deprivations. In the enlarged setting of the following novels Harris pursues his tireless search for the vanished "savage" elements (emotions, forms of art, cultures) which have contributed to the shaping of modern civilization or the modern consciousness but which they tend to ignore. *Black Marsden* takes place in Scotland and South America, *Companions of the Day and Night* in Mexico, *Da Silva da Silva's Cultivated Wilderness*,

The Tree of the Sun, and *The Angel at the Gate* in London, while *Carnival* is set in both South America and London. Experience is still largely recreated through the consciousness of the major character who realizes the need to bridge the gap between civilizations and bring to light the mutation by which eclipsed people(s) are beginning to emerge from their buried condition. In these novels Harris's always intensely visual rendering of both outer and psychological landscapes has developed into his use of painting as an exploratory metaphor. Da Silva is a painter who brings together on his visionary canvases models that represent the two faces of tradition, one assertive and oppressive, the other immaterial and hardly perceptible. The need for an imaginative balance between the two inspires his effort to create a "middle ground" between the contrasting figures he paints. The child in all three London novels stands for the renascence or "annunciation of humanity" which Harris keeps presenting through his fiction as a real possibility.

Throughout his work Harris's major concern is with both a "new architecture," a translation of conscience, and the nature, the mystery of creativity itself. This twofold preoccupation comes to a head in *Carnival* which also fuses his exposure of man's incorrigible longing for absolute perfection (usually achieved at the expense of others), with his exploration of the underworld. Once more, Harris *transforms* a traditional form, here the Dantesque allegory through which his characters progress, by modifying the meaning of Inferno, Purgatory, and Paradise. These are not separate or self-sufficient, since, as Harris illustrates it, the inferno of wasted lives runs parallel to and supports the glories of paradise. Through the characters' experience and the partial falling away of the masks they wear in the carnival of history and of existence, 20th-century Inferno, Purgatorio and Paradiso are *altered*. Even Paradise ceases to be an absolute and is envisaged as a revolution of sensibility in modern man, which makes possible a "complex marriage of cultures."

—Hena Maes-Jelinek

HARROWER, Elizabeth. Australian. Born in Sydney, New South Wales, 8 February 1928. Worked for the Australian Broadcasting Commission, Sydney, 1959–60; reviewer, Sydney *Morning Herald*, 1960; worked for Macmillan and Company Ltd., publishers, Sydney, 1961–67. Recipient: Commonwealth Literary Fund fellowship, 1968; Australian Council for the Arts fellowship, 1974. Address: 5 Stanley Avenue, Mosman, New South Wales 2088, Australia.

PUBLICATIONS

Novels

Down in the City. London, Cassell, 1957.
The Long Prospect. London, Cassell, 1958.
The Catherine Wheel. London, Cassell, 1960.
The Watch Tower. London, Macmillan, 1966.

Uncollected Short Stories

"The Cost of Things," in *Summer's Tales 1*, edited by Kylie Tennant. Melbourne and London, Macmillan, and New York, St. Martin's Press, 1964.

"English Lesson," in *Summer's Tales 2*, edited by Kylie Tennant. Melbourne and London, Macmillan, New York, St. Martin's Press, 1965.
"The Beautiful Climate," in *Modern Australian Writing*, edited by Geoffrey Dutton. London, Fontana, 1966.
"Lance Harper, His Story," in *The Vital Decade*, edited by Geoffrey Dutton and Max Harris. Melbourne, Sun, 1968.
"The Retrospective Grandmother," in *The Herald* (Melbourne), 1976.
"A Few Days in the Country," in *Overland* (Melbourne), 1977.

*

Critical Studies: "The Novels of Elizabeth Harrower" by Max Harris, in *Australian Letters* (Adelaide), December 1961; *Forty-Two Faces* by John Hetherington, Melbourne, Cheshire, 1962; "Elizabeth Harrower's Novels: A Survey," in *Southerly* (Sydney), no. 2, 1970, and *Recent Fiction*, Melbourne, Oxford University Press, 1974, both by R.G. Geering; *The Directions of Australian Fiction 1920–1974* by D.R. Burns, Melbourne, Cassell, 1975; "The Novels of Elizabeth Harrower" by Robyn Claremont, in *Quadrant* (Sydney), November 1979; Nola Adams, in *Westerly* (Nedlands, Western Australia), September 1980; "Deep into the Destructive Core" by Frances McInherny, in *Hecate* (St. Lucia, Queensland), vol. 9, nos. 1–2, 1983.

*   *   *

An ideal introduction to Elizabeth Harrower's work is the short story "The Beautiful Climate," since it provides a paradigm of her fictional universe. It is a world in which selfish men manipulate their women and material possessions in a vain attempt to achieve happiness; frustrated by their blind male egotism, they become subject to fits of smouldering violence and frequent relapses into bouts of alcoholism and morbid self-pity. The woman's role is to suffer, to pity, and to provide the innocent seeing eye for the narrative. In "The Beautiful Climate" the paranoiac male is Mr. Shaw, who secretly buys a holiday island, reduces his wife and daughter to domestic slavery there, then sells the place behind their backs. The consciousness that develops from innocent passivity to partial sad wisdom is the daughter's, who reflects her creator in turning from psychology to literature as a guide to truth. The same basic situations and characters recur throughout the novels; and the tormented relationship between father and daughter in this short story might seem to offer a psychological clue to the novelist's preoccupation with male domination.

In *Down in the City*, a very remarkable first novel, Harrower traces the disenchantment that follows when the heroine exchanges the empty security of her wealthy bay-side suburb in Sydney for the puzzling ups and downs of her husband's shady business world. In describing the characteristic claustrophobia of the flat-dwelling city wife, she succeeds wonderfully well in evoking the typical sights and sounds of Sydney and in establishing a connection between climate and states of mind. And the hero, who oscillates between his classy wife and his obliging mistress, reflects the conflicting drives and split personality of many an Australian business man.

What distinguishes Harrower's second novel, *The Long Prospect*, from all her others is that the malevolent main character is a woman not a man. But once again the viewpoint is through an innocent seeing eye; in this case, it is a child's. By the end of the novel, she has plumbed the seedy adult world to its depths. The scene in which four irredeemably corrupt adults spy on the 12-year-old and her middle-aged friend, transferring their own "atmosphere of stealth" onto the innocent pair, is only one of many pieces of superb psychological drama in this accomplished novel.

While the third novel, *The Catherine Wheel*, laudably attempts to extend the range of the fictional world by having its setting in London bed-sitter-land, it is a somewhat disappointing work that hardly prepares the reader for the splendid fourth novel, *The Watch Tower*. The conspicuous success in *The Watch Tower* lies in the creation of Felix Shaw, the Australian business man, who climaxes a series of similar portraits and shares the surname of the father in "The Beautiful Climate." But equally subtle is the analysis of pity, through the contrasted characters of Shaw's two victims, who show that pity may enslave as well as ennoble (this a continuous preoccupation in the novels). Shaw's capriciousness, his bursts of petty pique and rage, his resentment at others' success, his dark nihilism, brutal aggression, unrecognised homosexuality and alcoholism, all point to a profound psychic disorder. But it is the novelist's triumph to suggest that this disorder is at least partly the product of a society that worships materialism and masculinity.

In most of her work, Elizabeth Harrower combines sharp observation of individual life with a searching critique of Australian society. Although she lacks the resilient vitality of such English novelists as Margaret Drabble, her vision of a male-dominated society is depressingly authentic. She has been highly praised and compared favourably with Patrick White, but her unflattering, somewhat drab and disenchanted view of Australian life is unlikely to win her the wide local readership her work certainly deserves.

—John Colmer

HASLUCK, Nicholas. Australian. Born in Canberra, 17 October 1942. Educated at the University of Western Australia, Nedlands, 1960–63, LL.B. 1963; Oxford University, 1964–66, B.C.L. 1966. Married Sally Anne Bolton in 1966; two sons. Lawyer: admitted to Supreme Court of Western Australia as barrister and solicitor, 1968. Deputy Chairman, Australia Council, 1978–82. Recipient: *The Age* Book of the Year Award, 1984. Agent: Murray Pollinger, 4 Garrick Street, London WC2E 9BH, England. Address: 14 Reserve Street, Claremont, Western Australia 6010, Australia.

PUBLICATIONS

Novels

Quarantine. Melbourne and London, Macmillan, 1978; New York, Holt Rinehart, 1979.
The Blue Guitar. Melbourne and London, Macmillan, and New York, Holt Rinehart, 1980.
The Hand That Feeds You: A Satiric Nightmare, photographs by the author. Fremantle, Western Australia, Fremantle Arts Centre Press, 1982.
The Bellarmine Jug. Ringwood, Victoria, Penguin, 1984.

Short Stories

The Hat on the Letter O and Other Stories. Fremantle, Western Australia, Fremantle Arts Centre Press, 1978.

Verse

Anchor and Other Poems. Fremantle, Western Australia, Fremantle Arts Centre Press, 1976.
On the Edge, with William Grono. Claremont, Western Australia, Freshwater Bay Press, 1980.
Chinese Journey, with C.J. Koch. Fremantle, Western Australia, Fremantle Arts Centre Press, 1985.

*

Critical Studies: review by Martin Seymour-Smith, in *Financial Times* (London), 15 June 1978; article by Helen Daniel, in *The Age Monthly Review* (Melbourne), December 1984.

*   *   *

Nicholas Hasluck is a novelist, short-story writer, poet, and amateur photographer as well as a lawyer. He brings to his work unusual versatility allied to a legally honed sense of moral issues. His first novel, *Quarantine*, was set in an ominous, run-down hotel on the banks of the Suez Canal where the passengers of a cruise ship are unaccountably held in isolation under the charge of Shewfik Arud, the corrupt proprietor, and the enigmatic, dipsomaniac Dr. Magro. The exiles are soon dominated by Burgess, an inept social bully, and a gang of menacing louts. They are eventually saved by the engaging David Shears, who pays for his independent stand with his life, and the story is told through the memory of the morally crippled don whose jealous cowardice betrays David. The allegorical levels—which led the novel to be compared to Camus's—are explicit when Magroo says the pain of the human condition is better than its cure—acceptance—but the nerve of the novel is a taut handling of narrative and atmosphere, that constantly edges towards the comic absurd, and a vivid range of characterisation.

The Blue Guitar, as exuberant as *Quarantine* was restrained, is an urban-picaresque account of Dyson Garrick's quest through the commercial jungles of a city recognisably Sydney, seeking financial backing for a guitar that will play music "automatically." The reference to Wallace Stevens's poem ("Things as they are are changed upon the blue guitar") points to an idealism implicit in Dyson's search, but the guitar itself is ambiguously commercial, and, in another metaphor in the book, parachuting, free falling may be exhilarating but you can't fall upwards. The final casualty is Dyson's own integrity as he betrays his inventor friend in a scene finely set among images of a shattered city where the old man and a boy sit making kites.

The Hand That Feeds You, set in an Australia of the near-future, has elements of science fiction, although the often hilarious satire relates it more to Heller's *Catch-22* than to Huxley's *Brave New World*. Dee, a typical Hasluck hero, naive and morally vulnerable, finds himself caught in a world where paid work is taboo, tax evasion and social handouts the new morality, mediocrity directed by the amalgamated unions and the mass media. Pushed into standing as political leader, Dee, lacking all qualifications, wins—disastrously. In this novel any plot has to be an anti-plot, and Dee's quest for the founder of the social order, Meynard (Keynes?), is a structure to hold together a sequence of satiric sketches. Itself a satire on contemporary fashions in fiction, the book includes a "kit" of standard reviews for the intending critic.

The Bellarmine Jug is Hasluck's most complex and artistically assured novel to date. The story is told by a successful barrister in the 1980's looking back on his involvement in student agitation in 1948 when he was a student at the Grotius Institute in Amsterdam. The expulsion of a student uncovers an attempt to cover evidence of the 1629 Batavia mutiny and the subsequent violent attempt to create a Rosicrucian community on the Abrolhos Islands. One apparent concealment could be explained by the Institution's anxiety to hide the fact that the son of Huig de Groot, codifier of international law and the Grotius of their title, was leader of the mutiny. But the tense labyrinthine plot reveals a web of concealment stretching from the possible first white colonisation of Australia to British nuclear tests in the South China Sea. The novel combines the method of an espionage novel with those of Socratic dialogue and an examination paper in legal history, leading to the ultimate question—what are the meanings of "truth" and "right" in the context of the social order?

Hasluck's range is further confirmed by his collection *The Hat on the Letter O*. However, his versatility comes not from an interest in literary form for its own sake so much as a poet's instinct for an idea or theme which then dictates its own evolving structure. It is this that gives his work a particular sense of artistic integrity, and makes him a continuously interesting writer.

—Louis James

HAU'OFA, Epeli. Tongan. Born in Papua New Guinea, 7 December 1939, to missionary parents. Educated at Tupou College, Tonga, 1951–55; Lelean Memorial School, Fiji, 1956–59; Armidale High School, New South Wales, 1960; University of New South Wales, Kensington, 1961–64; McGill University, Montreal, 1965–68; Australian National University, Canberra, 1970–75, Ph.D. in social anthropology 1975. Married Barbara Hau'ofa in 1966; two children. Senior Tutor, University of Papua New Guinea, Port Moresby, 1968–70; Research Fellow, University of the South Pacific, Suva, Fiji, 1975–77; Visiting Fellow, University of New South Wales, 1977; deputy private secretary to the King of Tonga, in Nuku'alofa, 1978–81; director, University of the South Pacific Rural Development Centre, Nuku'alofa, Tonga, 1981–83. Since 1983, Reader in Sociology, University of the South Pacific. Visiting Fellow, Centre for Pacific Studies, University of Auckland, 1985. Consultant to the Asian Development Bank, 1979, and the World Bank, 1980. Co-founder and co-editor, *Faikava*, a Tongan literary journal. Address: School of Social and Economic Development, University of the South Pacific, P.O. Box 1168, Suva, Fiji.

PUBLICATIONS

Short Stories

Tales of the Tikongs. Auckland, Longman Paul, 1983.

Other

Our Crowded Islands, photographs by Randy Thaman. Suva, Fiji, Institute of Pacific Studies, 1977.
Corned Beef and Tapioca: A Report on the Food Distribution Systems in Tonga. Canberra, Australian National University Development Studies Centre, 1979.

Mekeo: Inequality and Ambivalence in a Village Society. Canberra, Australian National University Press, 1981.

*　　　*　　　*

Comic writers are always welcome. Epeli Hau'ofa's humorous *Tales of the Tikongs* consists of linked short stories about a South Pacific island so small that it is left off maps owing to the difficulty of finding "a dot sufficiently small to represent it faithfully and at the same time big enough to be seen without the aid of a microscope." The Tikongs have become Christians and work so hard praying on Sunday that it takes a six-day rest to recover. They practise the Christian virtue of forgiveness: "when five very, very important men discovered that they had together helped themselves to half a million dollars of public money to which they had no right to help themselves, they prayed for God's forgiveness, they forgave each other, and they neither had to resign from their very important jobs nor return any money to anyone." They are also "expert tellers of half-truths, quarter-truths, and one-percent truths." When Inoke forges and cashes a cheque for $100 and is caught, he swears on the Bible that it was the fault of the cashier who supposedly misread a $1.00 cheque.

While Hau'ofa's stories often have a satiric relationship to actual events and persons in the South Pacific, they show an amused appreciation of the trickster and swindler. At times satire is blended with a tolerance of extravagance, outrageousness, and absurdity which approaches moral anarchy and fun for its own sake. His Holiness Bopeep Dr. Toki Tumu, "a descendent of one of the thieves of Captain Cook's chamber pot," comes from Chamber Island. Seeing that the Tikongs are "thoroughly conditioned" by the many church bells on the island, he conditions them to his bell-ringing and sets up his own church, "based on the Doctrine of the Infallibility of the Bopeep"; "The Bopeep can do anything he wants, for his decisions and actions are spotless in the eyes of the Lord." Besides gaining absolute control of church finances ("all financial transactions of the Church shall, unless otherwise decreed by His Holiness, remain forevermore Unwritten"), and "taking his cue from benighted Melanesian cargo cult leaders," he assembles a harem as "it is a necessity that he experience the suffering and agony of sin in order to transcend earthly pleasures." While Hau'ofa, for the sake of his art, appears amused at the comedy of human relations, including the ways people use and exploit each other, the *Tales* are explicitly satiric of institutionalized injustice: "organized religion was the most effective instrument, in Tiko at least, for the attainment of wealth, power and renown"; "White lambs abound in Australia ... because no sheep of tinted fleece is ever allowed into that spotless land."

These are more than tales of charming, roguish, eccentric natives and the foibles of foreign-aid experts. Although satire at its best can appear self-contradictory and anarchistic, the *Tales* have many of the same concerns as writing after national independence in other parts of the Third World. The stories show the various ways European culture and politics have affected the South Pacific, leaving a conformist middle class and a corrupt elite, a legacy of church dominance, inappropriate forms of education and educational qualifications, and subservience to and dependence on foreigners. Although the islanders' way of life was not destroyed despite Christianity and colonialism, national independence led to increased dependence. At Independence the local rulers and their relatives change their English clothes for a melange of "Afro-shirts and other Third World clothes" and take over from the colonial administration positions for which they are not trained or qualified. Mistrusting and feeling threatened by their own new university graduates, so that the skilled and talented flee the country, they fill the resulting vacancies with foreign experts, technical advisers, youthful volunteers, and the well-paid employees of United Nations organizations.

Manu, the character closest to the author's sympathies, wears a shirt lettered with "Over Influenced" on the front and "Religion and Education Destroy Original Wisdom" on the back. There is the obvious symbolism of Ole Pasifikiwei who during his spare time collects oral traditions which he records in school exercise books until he attracts the attention of an Australian cultural aid official. Now supported by an annual grant, trips abroad, duty-free goods, and a committee, he progresses to forming the National Council for Social, Economic, and Cultural Research, which is placed by "the Great International Organization on the list of the Two Hundred Least Developed Committees—those in need of urgent, generous aid." Within six years Ole applies for fourteen million dollars for his organization, is given honorary doctorates, and loses his old exercise books with the oral records. "He has since shelved his original sense of self-respect and has assumed another, more attuned to his new, permanent role as a first-rate, expert beggar."

If at times *Tales of the Tikongs* seems artless, that can be an art. Four of the stories were revised from previous publication and show improvements along with expansion. One of the additions is an example of an Australian expert attempting to communicate in pidgin:

> "Me big brother, you little brother. You me help Tiko come up all same big fela rich country. Plenty plenty ice cream, sweet sweet all same lollies from Heaven. All right?"
> "Me doan know."
> "You no can savvy? Gawd! Me talk talk all same simple something na you no can savvy! Whassamatter? Me think think head belong you too much dumdum na full up shit something no good true! All right, me all same try one more time yet, na you try savvy good or I'll bloody well bash your coon head in, O.K.?"

That is from "The Tower of Babel." The book starts with allusions to Genesis in "The Seventh and Other Days" and works its way through "The Second Coming" to its final revelation, the corruption of Ole by an organization with the acronym MERCY in "The Glorious Pacific Way," the title of which is itself a reference to the way nationalist values are manipulated by the rulers and elite. Manu says, "the Pacific Way belongs to regional Elites, Experts, Wheeler-dealers, and Crooks!" Even when not being so explicit, Hau'ofa provides social comment through the ludicrous, mocking parody, topical allusions, and witty malice.

—Bruce King

HAWKES, John (Clendennin Burne, Jr.). American. Born in Stamford, Connecticut, 17 August 1925. Educated at Trinity School, 1940–41; Pawling High School, 1941–43; Harvard University, Cambridge, Massachusetts, 1943–49, A.B. 1949. Served as an ambulance driver with the American Field Service in Italy and Germany, 1944–45. Married Sophie Goode Tazewell in 1947; three sons and one daughter. Assistant to the production manager, Harvard University Press, 1949–55; Visiting Lecturer, 1955–56, and Instructor in English, 1956–58, Harvard University. Assistant Professor, 1958–62, Associate Professor, 1962–67, Professor of English, 1967–73, and since 1973, T.B. Stowell University Professor, Brown University, Providence, Rhode Island. Visiting Assistant Professor, Massachusetts Institute of Technology, 1959; special guest, Aspen Institute for Humanistic Studies, Colarado, 1962; staff member, Utah Writers Conference, summer 1962, and Bread Loaf Writers Conference, Vermont, summer 1963; Visiting Professor of Creative Writing, Stanford University, California, 1966–67; Visiting Distinguished Professor of Creative Writing, City College of the City University of New York, 1971–72. Member, Panel on Educational Innovation, Washington, D.C., 1966–67. Recipient: American Academy grant, 1962; Guggenheim fellowship, 1962; Ford fellowship, 1964; Rockefeller fellowship, 1968; Foreign Book Prize (France), 1974. Member, American Academy of Arts and Sciences, 1973; Member, American Academy, 1980. A.M.: Brown University, 1962. Agent: Lynn Nesbit, International Creative Management, 40 West 57th Street, New York, New York 10019. Address: 18 Everett Avenue, Providence, Rhode Island 02906, U.S.A.

PUBLICATIONS

Novels

The Cannibal. New York, New Directions, 1949; London, Spearman, 1962.
The Beetle Leg. New York, New Directions, 1951; London, Chatto and Windus, 1967.
The Lime Twig. New York, New Directions, 1961; London, Spearman, 1962.
Second Skin. New York, New Directions, 1964; London, Chatto and Windus, 1966.
The Blood Oranges. New York, New Directions, and London, Chatto and Windus, 1971.
Death, Sleep, and the Traveler. New York, New Directions, 1974; London, Chatto and Windus, 1975.
Travesty. New York, New Directions, and London, Chatto and Windus, 1976.
The Passion Artist. New York, Harper, 1979.
Virginie: Her Two Lives. New York, Harper, 1982; London, Chatto and Windus, 1983.
Adventures in the Alaskan Skin Trade. New York, Simon and Schuster, 1985.

Short Stories

The Goose on the Grave, and The Owl: Two Short Novels. New York, New Directions, 1954; *The Owl* published separately, 1977.
Lunar Landscapes: Stories and Short Novels 1949–1963. New York, New Directions, 1969; London, Chatto and Windus, 1970.
The Universal Fears. Northridge, California, Lord John Press, 1978.
Innocence in Extremis. Providence, Rhode Island, Burning Deck, 1985.

Uncollected Short Stories

"The Heart Demands Satisfaction," in *Vogue* (New York), 15 January 1964.

"Island Fire," in *Hellcoal Annual* (Providence, Rhode Island), Spring 1979.
"Two Shoes for One Foot," in *The Best of Tri-Quarterly*, edited by Jonathan Brent.   New York, Washington Square Press, 1982.

Plays

The Wax Museum (produced Boston, 1966; New York, 1977).   Included in *The Innocent Party*, 1966.
The Questions (produced Stanford, California, 1966).   Included in *The Innocent Party*, 1966.
The Innocent Party: Four Short Plays.   New York, New Directions, 1966; London, Chatto and Windus, 1967.
The Undertaker (produced Boston, 1967).   Included in *The Innocent Party*, 1966.
The Innocent Party (produced Boston, 1968).   Included in *The Innocent Party*, 1966.

Verse

Fiasco Hall.   Privately printed, 1943.

Other

Humors of Blood and Skin: A John Hawkes Reader.   New York, New Directions, 1984.

Editor, with others, *The Personal Voice: A Contemporary Prose Reader.*   Philadelphia, Lippincott, 1964.
Editor, with others, *The American Literary Anthology 1: The 1st Annual Collection of the Best from the Literary Magazines.*   New York, Farrar Straus, 1968.

*

Bibliography: *Three Contemporary Novelists: An Annotated Bibliography* by Robert M. Scotto, New York, Garland, 1977; *John Hawkes: An Annotated Bibliography* by Carol A. Hryciw, Metuchen, New Jersey, Scarecrow Press, 1977, revised edition, as *John Hawkes: A Research Guide*, New York, Garland, 1986.

Manuscript Collection: Houghton Library, Harvard University, Cambridge, Massachusetts.

Critical Studies: *The Fabulators* by Robert Scholes, New York, Oxford University Press, 1967; *Hawkes: A Guide to His Fictions* by Frederick Busch, Syracuse, New York, Syracuse University Press, 1973; *Comic Terror: The Novels of John Hawkes* by Donald J. Greiner, Memphis, Memphis State University Press, 1973, revised edition, 1978; *John Hawkes and the Craft of Conflict* by John Kuehl, New Brunswick, New Jersey, Rutgers University Press, 1975; *A John Hawkes Symposium* edited by Anthony C. Santore and Michael N. Pocalyko, New York, New Directions, 1977; *A Poetry of Force and Darkness: The Fiction of John Hawkes* by Eliot Berry, San Bernardino, California, Borgo Press, 1979; *John Fowles, John Hawkes, Claude Simon: Problems of Self and Form in the Post-Modernist Novel* by Robert Burden, Würzberg, Königshausen & Neumann, and Atlantic Highlands, New Jersey, Humanities Press, 1980; *John Hawkes* by Patrick O'Donnell, Boston, Twayne, 1982; "John Hawkes Issue" of *Review of Contemporary Fiction* (Elmwood Park, Illinois), vol. 3, no. 3, 1983.

*   *   *

John Hawkes, perhaps the most original American novelist since Faulkner, bears only superficial resemblances to other contemporary innovators. His work is distinctly less philosophical and less parodic than that of Barth, Nabokov, Pynchon, Durrell, Borges. And if he chooses to create fictional worlds, rather than represent ours—fictional worlds in which one man on a motorcycle may occupy a third of Germany, or a Caribbean island wander in space and time—these visionary landscapes yet seem genuine dynamic projections of our real underground lives. Childhood terror, oral fantasies and castration fears, fears of regression and violence, profound sexual disturbances—these (rather than the spatial inventions of science fiction or of Nabokov's *Ada*) are the components of Hawkes's myths and of the "places" he calls Germany or America or England.

Hawkes claims to have recognized at the outset of his career four enemies: plot, character, setting, theme. Haunting chordal insistences and recurring images replace plot; the symbols of nightmare and neurosis and of the preconscious serve for character; a general vision of deterioration and collapse offers a semblance of theme. All these, and the dark hallucinatory landscapes, are redeemed by humor and by what Tony Tanner calls the "complicated and wrought fabric of his style." To a degree rare even in contemporary literature ugly materials—violence, suffering, deliberately reversed sympathies, magnified obscenities of landscape or human form—become things of beauty. Are the visions of violence and collapse prompted, as the author has occasionally insisted, by a belief in order and love? These stylized, distanced enormities maintain a very powerful hold on us, even as we enjoy them aesthetically, in part because they are rarely explained. This is the one thing Hawkes has in common with Robbe-Grillet; his world is unexplained. Hawkes's fictional world simply and dynamically, even magically, *is*.

Such originality and uncompromising difficulty long restricted Hawkes to an underground audience. *The Cannibal*, written as a Harvard undergraduate, drew some attention because it appeared to be a powerful symbolic commentary on the American occupation of a diseased, deteriorated Germany. The ruined landscape of 1945 is juxtaposed against a Germany of 1914, already doomed; there is a vision of history as fated yet inconsecutive and absurd. But at least a few readers were drawn rather by powerful scenes of grotesque transformation and psychic substitution (as cannibalism for homosexual assault) and by the nervous, exceptionally brilliant phrasing. *The Cannibal* is, for some readers, the masterpiece of American avant-garde fiction.

The Beetle Leg is a cooler vision, at times parodic, often comic, of a mythical American west and sexless wasteland in which helpless persons somnambulistically wander. This excellent novel had few readers at first; *The Goose and the Grave* (a volume containing also *The Owl*) was also almost completely ignored. It has been reissued, with several stories added, as *Lunar Landscapes*. These darkly playful short novels are laid in 20th-century Italy and in a fictionalized San Marino locked in medieval legend and ritual: "two sides of a single dream," Tony Tanner has remarked, "centering on human violence in a hostile terrain—sudden deaths in still squares." (Tanner's essay in *City of Words* is one of the best brief introductions to Hawkes's work.)

By 1961, with *The Lime Twig*, a number of major writers and critics had discovered Hawkes, and this novel has become a favorite in American college classrooms. Moreover, Hawkes had by now moved to a more conscious understanding of his own materials and methods, and even some distance toward realism and narrative suspense. Parody of the detective novel form is merely the thin surface or pretext, in *The Lime Twig*, for another powerful vision of violence and tormented sexuality, this time laid in a bleakly plausible wartime and post-war England. Freudian substitutions and displacements are clearly evident as such, and are therefore oddly comic (an injection in the place of sexual penetration, or beating by a truncheon as rape). Yet the writing is so powerful that we continue to experience fascination and terror, even as we coolly watch the author's game. Few novels have dramatized so powerfully ultimate threats to identity.

With *Second Skin*, which lost the National Book Award to Saul Bellow's *Herzog* by one vote, Hawkes reached a much larger audience. And now for the first time the concealed affirmations and sympathies of the earlier books come to the surface in a vision of death and disaster (in America and on a north Atlantic island) succeeded by pastoral bliss on a wandering southern island. The narrator has survived the suicide of father, wife, daughter, and, escaped from a world of impotence, has become an artificial inseminator of cows. He is also, possibly, the father of the child of the black Catalina Kate, whom he shares with his messboy Sonny. Some of the dark materials of Hawkes's earlier fiction are present, even on that lush tropical island—a monstrous iguana, for instance, clinging to Catalina Kate's back. But the final vision of equanimity is genuine, reinforced by a conversational style of Nabokovian loveliness.

Hawkes has clearly moved from the brilliant groping of a wholly original, half-conscious, at times primitive visionary to the wholly conscious artistry and calculated rhetoric of a novelist who is also a gifted literary critic and professor of English (at Brown University). The writing of several tightly constructed plays, collected as *The Innocent Party*, may have contributed to Hawkes's development toward a more open and public art. *The Blood Oranges* has only a few scenes of wildly antirealist invention, though it has many moments of original and exquisite writing. Its comic treatment of two couples who have exchanged partners, yet still live together, often seems both to parody Ford's *The Good Soldier* and to satirize the gravity with which middle-class Americans, in the 1960's, contemplated their sexual anxieties. In one respect *The Blood Oranges* is like its predecessors. The Mediterranean world of "Illyria"—recalling *Twelfth Night* as *Second Skin* evoked *The Tempest*—is absolutely plausible, and absolutely Hawkes's own.

Hawkes's later fictions reveal a more and more conscious and suave art. *Death, Sleep, and the Traveler* is perhaps the slightest of the later novels, and in its ambiguities and comic sexuality is even closer than *The Blood Oranges* to Nabokovian fictional games. In place of a quaternion of lovers there are now three sexual triangles, with the pleasures of "sharing" and complicity, and those of fellatio, even more overt than before. *Travesty*, on the other hand, is a masterpiece of first-person narration, though the very existence of the narrator's interlocutors remains problematic. The *données* of the fiction, while superficially melodramatic, invite a teasing, speculative, even philosophical voice reminiscent of Clamence's voice in Albert Camus's *The Fall*: the narrator and only speaker driving fast toward a deliberate murder and suicide that will crash the car against an already designated wall far ahead; beside him "Henri," who has been the lover of both the narrator's wife and his daughter, who is riding in the back seat. In a statement of cosmic skepticism as absolute as Camus's the car's journey becomes, metaphorically, that of the earth's "progress through the fortress of space." Between the Creation (the mechanic's last adjustments) and "the life of the mind that holds the moving car to the road there is

nothing, nothing at all"; or there is only "design and debris."

With *The Passion Artist* Hawkes returned deliberately to the fictional world of *The Cannibal*, its bleak city and devastated landscape reflecting the psychic impotence of its protagonist, its gratuitous violence stemming from a revolt in a penal institution for women. The misogynous imagination evident in powerful pages throughout Hawkes's fiction is now allowed altogether free play; the familiar sexual materials (castration fear and fear of engulfment, Oedipal configurations, etc.) are wholly unrepressed and virtually undisplaced. The first 50 or 60 pages of *The Passion Artist* may seem disappointingly methodical and realistic to the lover of the audacities of *The Cannibal*. But the later portions of the novel, energized by a remarkable dream sequence, recover the tension and terror, the dynamic fantasies and stylistic beauties of the best earlier work. The circumstance is virtually unique in modern literature: that of a suave, immensely skilled conscious artist remanipulating the powerful dreams and atavistic energies of 30 years before.

An increasing sophistication and poetic delicacy, but also an increasing serenity, is evident in three of the four books Hawkes published between 1982 and 1985. *Virginie* could well mark the culmination of a love affair with France, where Hawkes spends some of his years freed from teaching, and with French literature. In 1980 in Provence "we knew we had come to the end of the line in a long search for vineyards, rude beams, red tiles, Picasso's dancing goats, literary voluptuousness" (*Humors of Blood and Skin*). Hawkes hoped to write a novel based on the life of the Marquis de Sade, but could not. In *Virginie* he did capture the calm, suave, graceful, highly formal manner in which Sade recites his itany of horrors.

The *tour de force*, entirely credible within its enclosed world, has a nine-year-old girl tell her two complementary lives—one as the innocent student of an artist in the erotic education of women, a man known only as Seigneur; the other as the still innocent inhabitant of a Paris brothel. The first life is lived in 1740, the second in 1945. Even more striking than this Nabokovian game with time is the successful combination of the child's fresh wondering vision of things, even the most depraved things, and her rich suave voice capable of expressing the author's gnomic wit and philosophical insight. *Virginie*, like the pornography it occasionally parodies, establishes fiction's autonomy from the "real" real world. Sexual manipulation, misogynous fantasies of omnipotence, real erotic bliss— all exist in a realm of poetic artifice.

Humors of Blood and Skin, subtitled *A John Hawkes Reader*, offers a not entirely fortunate selection of four short stories and extracts from ten novels. The selections were not made by Hawkes, but presumably had his approval. The stories, placed at the beginning of the volume, would put a new reader on the wrong track, and the pages from *The Cannibal*, *Second Skin*, and *Travesty* are far from the best. On the cover is a reclining Bacchic Hawkes, nude to the waist and about to address a listener, with a demure young woman (his daughter) in the background. The genial but not complacent serenity of the later Hawkes is evident in the eleven autobiographical notes, prefatory musings rather, that introduce the selections. The author looks back on past turmoil as quietly as Conrad did in his prefaces, but much less evasively than Conrad. He examines good-humoredly the fears and obsessions behind his fiction, the psychic sources as well as the sources in lands visited, books read, anecdotes heard, traumatic experiences remembered. An Alaskan childhood, from ages ten to fifteen, and nine months as a driver with the American Field Service ("not so much horrific as bizarre") have left obvious marks on the fiction. But earlier still were "nightly asthma attacks and listening to the thumping and snorting of the horses in the riding stable that adjoined our back yard then in Old Greenwich, Connecticut," also a "trim young girl" contemplated at the age of six. "I think that my writing has always depended in one way or another on those first configurations of suffocation, faint stirrings of desire, and horses."

Horses are ancient and terrifying in *The Cannibal* and *The Lime Twig* and explicitly sexual in *The Passion Artist*, where they are associated with initiation by powerful women and with fears of castration. But it is the horse who suffers and is overcome in *Virginie*, where Seigneur organizes the ceremonial extraction of a horse's tooth. (The tooth becomes the fragment of a glacier in *Adventures in the Alaskan Skin Trade*!) In *Innocence in Extremis* are has totally prevailed. Both dressage and the carefully staged mounting of a mare are emblematic of the artist who exerts power by subduing violence. *Innocence in Extremis*, though nominally an offshoot of the Alaskan novel, is more closely allied to *Virginie*: a stately saraband danced by an American family visiting their French aristocratic connection, and witnessing both the mounting of the mare and the ritualized treading of grapes by village virgins. This long story or very short novel is a flawless exercise in style.

Adventures in the Alaskan Skin Trade, much the longest of the novels, and the most realistic in method, represents a surprising departure from the dark intensities of *The Passion Artist* and the cameo perfection of *Virginie*. Hawkes's wife, he says, urged him to "try relaxing into the pleasures of autobiographical fiction"—autobiographical though the narrator Sunny is a disillusioned 39-year-old proprietress of a Juneau brothel, thinking back on her childhood discovery of Alaska and on the legendary exploits of her father "Uncle Jake," a reckless, improvident, sentimentally meddling heroic adventurer and chronic failure. The novel is very nearly as warm and un-neurotic as Faulkner's *The Reivers*, and the inhabitants of the two brothels are similarly good-natured. Hawkes's Gallicized imagination has here allowed itself to expand into the most traditional of American modes: the tomboy childhood on the last frontier, with a wily and garrulous father to cope with bears, Indians, glaciers and steep cliffs, a leaking boat, a small smashed plane. The father's disappearances and hairbreadth escapes and abrupt returns seem to parody the tall tales of 19th-century southwest humor and even the serialized movies of the 1920's. Each escape introduces a new yarn.

Adventures in the Alaskan Skin Trade is perhaps the one "big novel," sprawling and vigorous, that a number of American writers attempt at some late moment in their careers. There is far more realistic detail of landscape, weather, flora, clothing, furniture than in any earlier book. And Alaska is a real place, though mythical exploits occur there. Sunny recreates her childhood vision of things—innocent yet probing, vivid, at times unmoral—with the authenticity of *Great Expectations* and *David Copperfield*. By contrast the gloomy present and recent past of the brothel, with some attention to Sunny's own sexual history, seem contrived and unimportant. A few archetypal dreams echo powerful dreams in the earlier books, and in these the author's true voice is dominant. But Sunny's waking voice, and the yarn-spinning voice of her father, are wandering and diffuse, colloquially slack of syntax. The conversational ease is "in character," a further realism. But something is lost for the reader committed to the beautiful rhythms, great compression, and metaphorical intensity of the earlier books.

As a poetic novelist, caring most about language and the imagination, Hawkes has wanted "to try everything" (to use Joyce's comment on himself), and he has gone very far. There will probably be further unpredictable movements in the career of this great writer.

—Albert Guerard

HAZZARD, Shirley. Australian. Born in Sydney, New South Wales, 30 January 1931. Educated at Queenwood School, Sydney. Married the writer Francis Steegmuller in 1963. Worked in Combined Services Intelligence, Hong Kong, 1947–48; United Kingdom High Commissioner's Office, Wellington, New Zealand, 1949–50; United Nations Headquarters, New York (General Service Category), 1951–61. Recipient: American Academy award, 1966; Guggenheim fellowship, 1974; O. Henry Award, 1977; National Book Critics Circle award, 1981. Address: 200 East 66th Street, New York, New York 10021, U.S.A.

PUBLICATIONS

Novels

The Evening of the Holiday. New York, Knopf, and London, Macmillan, 1966.
People in Glass Houses: Portraits from Organization Life. New York, Knopf, and London, Macmillan, 1967.
The Bay of Noon. Boston, Little Brown, and London, Macmillan, 1970.
The Transit of Venus. New York, Viking Press, and London, Macmillan, 1980.

Short Stories

Cliffs of Fall and Other Stories. New York, Knopf, and London, Macmillan, 1963.

Uncollected Short Stories

"The Flowers of Sorrow," in *Winter's Tales 10*, edited by A.D. Maclean. London, Macmillan, and New York, St. Martin's Press, 1964.
"Forgiving," in *Ladies Home Journal* (New York), August 1964.
"Comfort," in *New Yorker*, 24 October 1964.
"The Evening of the Holiday," in *New Yorker*, 17 April 1965.
"Out of Itea," in *New Yorker*, 1 May 1965.
"Nothing in Excess," in *New Yorker*, 26 March 1966.
"The Meeting," in *New Yorker*, 23 July 1966.
"A Sense of Mission," in *New Yorker*, 4 March 1967.
"Swoboda's Tragedy," in *New Yorker*, 20 May 1967.
"Story of Miss Sadie Graine," in *New Yorker*, 10 June 1967.
"Official Life," in *New Yorker*, 24 June 1967.
"The Separation of Dinah Delbanco," in *New Yorker*, 22 July 1967.
"The Everlasting Delight," in *New Yorker*, 19 August 1967.
"Statue and the Bust," in *McCall's* (New York), August 1971.
"Sir Cecil's Ride," in *Winter's Tales 21*, edited by A.D. Maclean. London, Macmillan, 1975; New York, St. Martin's Press, 1976.
"A Long Story Short," in *Prize Stories 1977: The O. Henry Awards*, edited by William Abrahams. New York, Doubleday, 1977.

"A Crush on Doctor Dance," in *Winter's Tales 24*, edited by A.D. Maclean. London, Macmillan, 1978; New York, St. Martin's Press, 1979.
"Something You'll Remember Always," in *New Yorker*, 17 September 1979.
"She Will Make You Very Happy," in *New Yorker*, 26 November 1979.

Other

Defeat of an Ideal: A Study of the Self-Destruction of the United Nations. Boston, Little Brown, 1972; London, Macmillan, 1973.
Coming of Age in Australia (lectures). Sydney, Australian Broadcasting Corporation, 1985.

*

Critical Studies: "Patterns and Preoccupations of Love: The Novels of Shirley Hazzard" by John Colmer, in *Meanjin* (Melbourne), December 1970; *Recent Fiction* by R.G. Geering, Melbourne, Oxford University Press, 1974; "Shirley Hazzard: Dislocation and Continuity" by Robert Sellick, in *Australian Literary Studies* (Hobart), October 1979; "Shirley Hazzard Issue" of *Texas Studies in Literature and Language* (Austin), vol. 25, no. 2, 1983.

*   *   *

Shirley Hazzard was born and spent her early years in Australia, but she is essentially an expatriate cosmopolitan writer, deeply rooted in the European literary tradition, much travelled, acutely sensitive to the spirit of place, with a keen eye for national differences, and an acute ear for the words that express and unconsciously betray human values. So far she has drawn mainly on experiences gained from foreign travel, ten years employment in UNO, and residence in America for the material of her fiction. However, the brilliant short story "Woollahra Road," which holds in poignant juxtaposition a child's eye and an adult's eye view of Australia during the Depression, suggests that there is a store of memories belonging to the first 15 years of her life that has only partly found fictional expression. And the portrait in *People in Glass Houses* of the Australian UNO official, Mervyn, protected alike from disenchantment and beauty by his "defensive scepticism," establishes her skill in getting under the skin of certain Australian types.

The publication of *Cliffs of Fall*, a collection of short stories that had already appeared in *The New Yorker*, drew enthusiastic and discriminating praise from reviewers in America and Britain. It did not require the photograph of the author holding a copy of *Madame Bovary* on the dust-jacket to establish her admiration for Flaubert and other continental masters: Maupassant, Chekhov, and Turgenev, for example. Her insight into the paradoxes of love, her power to render moments of unspoken anguish (as in "The Worst Moment of the Day"), the combination of reticent suggestion and poetic resonance, the extraordinary economy of means in creating character and situation, and the unerring feel for the *mot juste*, all these qualities link her writing to the continental masters. In several of the stories, especially those set in an Italian pensione, the contrast between true and false values and the concern with sudden moments of illumination is reminiscent of E.M. Forster, without in any way being derivative. Of all the stories, the longest, called "A Place in the Country," is the best and foreshadows the author's later work. And the fact that "The

Picnic" deals with the same characters suggests that the material might once have been intended for a novel. The central character in each, Nettie, come to realise that there is balance but no fairness in life and that the claims of humanity are prior to the demands of reason. These two ideas inform and control Hazzard's fictional universe.

In *The Evening of the Holiday* the promise of the Italian short stories is fulfilled, but the work is still only a novella rather than a full length novel. For the experience explored, the form is perfect. Each situation is exactly placed; the relationship between the half-English half-Italian heroine, Sophie, and the Italian architect Tancredi slowly unfolds towards its moment of piercing illumination and sad climax. It is not only Tancredi's married state that stands in the way of happiness; masculine pride and Sophie's reluctance to commit herself play their part. Sophie, like many of Hazzard's heroines, is an expatriate of the heart, in search of her spiritual home abroad, but forced to look for it within herself. In some respects *The Bay of Noon* is the natural extension and development of that search, but in between come the dazzlingly witty portraits from organization life called *People in Glass Houses*.

The "Portraits," like the short stories in *Cliffs of Fall*, first appeared in *The New Yorker*. Each could be read as a separate study, but because similar characters recur and a single controlling vision illuminates each, they cohere into an amusing but highly serious work of satirical fiction. Two related paradoxes bring the portraits into a single focus. The first is that the attempt to bring new life to the peoples of the undeveloped countries often destroys not only them but the bureaucrats and technologists themselves, who become the maimed and inhuman servants of a great impersonal machine. The second is that language and reason, the two great sources of truth and reality, become translated into the instruments of power, self-deception, and unreality. The irony which in the other works controls and profoundly modifies the poetic vision, bites deeper here, producing an astringent but still deeply compassionate view of life. And the sensitivity to language, the source of the marvellous evocation of person and place in *Cliffs of Fall* and *The Evening of the Holiday*, becomes one of the main weapons in the author's satiric armoury. What gives *People in Glass Houses* its special power is the author's perception that the debasement of language and the dehumanising of man are but different aspects of a single process. Because the cast of characters is representatively cosmopolitan and because even love affairs are moulded by the great administrative machine, no corner of life seems untouched; the political and social implications of this for the whole world are startlingly revealed in Hazzard's historical study of the United Nations, *Defeat of an Ideal*.

Although *The Bay of Noon* develops naturally from *The Evening of the Holiday*, it is much more of a Proustian exercise in fiction than the earlier novella. The story is simple, but the pattern of relationships is intricate and subtle. In essence it deals with the experiences of a young girl, Jenny, a secretary-translator at a NATO base at Naples. In seeking to escape from a triangular affair involving her brother and her brother's wife, she finds herself enmeshed within an intricate web spun by a beautiful Italian novelist and her film-producer lover. The novel seems to suggest that one escapes from one pattern of relationships only to recreate a similar pattern elsewhere. It is centrally concerned with two themes: the achievement of happiness and the search for one's true home. Jenny finds momentary happiness in her flat at Naples, where as a convalescent she looks out on the tranquil bay, but the quest remains. At the end of the novel, Jenny revisits Italy. Whereas once she had expected to find the object of her pilgrimage in people and places, she has come to realize that the pilgrims of the heart must learn to take their inward bearings if they are to know the meanings of the outward journeys. Memory supplies the signposts. But which point home and which point elsewhere? Through its superbly controlled composition, *The Bay of Noon* invites the reader to bring Jenny's remembered images into final focus. For her, as for the reader, the images, so tinted by sadness and irradiated by hope, serve "not to direct, but to solace us; not to fix our positions, but show us how we came." This is a wise and beautiful novel that shows equal understanding of male pride and female need.

The Transit of Venus marks a striking expansion and deepening of the novelist's vision. Concerned with the lives of two Australian sisters who go to England after the death of their parents, the novel evokes an acute sense of time and place, as it moves, through action and through Proustian flights of memory, from country to country and from past to present, covering the period from World War I to the present. In this first full-length novel, the minor characters are as firmly and memorably created as the major ones and contribute as significantly to the thematic pattern, which is woven out of the threads of loyalty and abnegation. The moral issues affect public and private life and involve the consciences of scientists, artists, and lovers. Appropriately, the novelist's prose acquires a deeper resonance than in earlier works as she condenses her mature, George Eliot-like, reflections on chance and human fallibility. Yet for all the sudden shocks and disasters that befall the characters, the novel finally affirms that in spite of the malignities of fate truth has a life of its own.

In Shirley Hazzard's fiction, as in the mind of one of her fictional characters, "poetry and reason meet without the customary signs of struggle." This accounts for her classic beauty of form. With exquisite delicacy and restraint, she reveals the coexistence of happiness and sorrow in love, the poignancy of misunderstanding and regret, and the consolations of memory. Through the eyes of her very different heroines, all of whom combine intellectual toughness and extreme vulnerability, she presents a world that immediately strikes the reader as both beautiful and true.

—John Colmer

HEAD, Bessie. Citizen of Botswana. Born in Pietermaritzburg, South Africa, 6 July 1937. Educated at Umbilo Road High School. Married Harold Head in 1961; one son. Teacher in primary schools in South Africa and Botswana, for four years; journalist, Drum Publications, Johannesburg, for two years. Private and unpaid agricultural worker in Botswana. Address: P.O. Box 15, Serowe, Botswana.

PUBLICATIONS

Novels

When Rain Clouds Gather. New York, Simon and Schuster, and London, Gollancz, 1969.
Maru. London, Gollancz, and New York, McCall, 1971.
A Question of Power. London, Davis Poynter, 1973; New York, Pantheon, 1974.
A Bewitched Crossroad: An African Saga. Johannesburg, Donker, 1984.

Short Stories

The Collector of Treasures and Other Botswana Village Tales. Cape Town, Philip, and London, Heinemann, 1977.

Other

Serowe, Village of the Rainwind.   London, Heinemann, 1981.

*

Manuscript Collection: Mugar Memorial Library, Boston University.

Critical Studies: "The Novels of Bessie Head" by Arthur Ravenscroft, in *Aspects of South African Literature* edited by Christopher Heywood, London, Heinemann, 1976.

Bessie Head comments:

I call myself—The New African. It is an extremely painful title full of sudden and disastrous changes of fortune and a sort of mental tight-rope walk with an abyss beneath. The abyss seems to be un-African and to belong to my soul. It is an almost violent urge to make gigantic moral abdications for the sake of mankind. What is African in the urge is the process of learning how to make these abdications in the face of human weakness. I do not believe African society caters for the superman. Other societies do and that is why their Gods are clothed in so much mumbo jumbo and hazy mysticism and dubious holiness. (People in India were angered by a biography about Gandhi which stated that he found celibacy extremely difficult. Gandhi was their God and presumably a superman and they did not care to examine *his* abyss, his humanity, though he clearly stated that celibacy was a mistake for him, I think in a letter to Tolstoy.)

Now, in Africa you have to be pretty clear about what you are thinking and feeling. NO ONE is going to set you up as a God. People are too human, too deep in their understanding of human nature. Therefore, my men—Makhaya and Maru—I first created majestic, with vast, straddling personalities and set them on a tightrope of my own abyss. It is always touch and go. There is really no God in Africa or a feeling of assurance that one would make it to the end of the tightrope and find eternal salvation and perfection, like Buddha, Gandhi and Jesus. The devil is equally paramount but his thought processes can be explained just as much as God's can. This means they are equals here and forced to think things over together. These themes are the basis of my preoccupations, the equality of man, the equality of God and the devil in Africa.

*   *   *

Bessie Head's first three novels are set in Botswana and form a cohesive treatment of the experience of national, racial, and religious displacement leading to a delicate equilibrium between scepticism and a humanist faith. Despite similarity of setting and, superficially, of narrative, these novels chart different psychological and moral landscapes. But their cohesion is revealed in the frequent, perhaps not entirely conscious, use of words, phrases, and images connoting "control" and "prison." The former usually convey the idea of necessary restraint upon an individual's own disruptive appetites no less than upon those with which people exercising political power mangle the lives of others. "Prison" tends to be applied to a state of escape from the pressures of reality, but more often in order to find refreshment before a more vital engagement in communal affairs. The action in Bessie Head's novels takes place against a vivid rendering of Botswana landscape and climate; nevertheless, the issues, worked out unobtrusively, are not merely regional but radiate, politically and morally, right across Africa.

The central character in *When Rain Clouds Gather* is Makhaya, a black South African who enters Botswana on the run from apartheid and his own inner "jumble of chaotic discord." In the village of Golema Mmidi he joins other exiles from past pain in a co-operative farming venture under the guidance of an expatriate expert, himself in flight from a middle-class English background. Through back-breaking labour in reluctant soil the characters learn how to intermesh their raw, damaged personalities in the attainment of a restorative communal self-sufficiency, both economic and human. This creative process is under constant threat from self-indulgent traditional chiefs and from new demogogic politicians. Golema Mmidi is no pastoral retreat, for it makes insatiable demands upon their physical energy and wrenches away their tightly clutched individualism. Gradually they take on new shared responsibilities of the very kind they had fled from in seeking the seclusion of Golema Mmidi.

The second novel, *Maru*, is more complex and adventurous in technique. That the opening projects two of the characters into a situation timed after the events of the story is no mere clever quirk but a necessary mechanism to provide insight into the humane motives behind Maru's seemingly selfish use of power. He is a paramount-chief elect who manipulates his sister's marriage with his friend Moleka so that he himself can marry the racially outcast Masarwa woman, Margaret, whom Moleka also loves. Maru's methods seem unscrupulous, but he knows that his kingdom is of love and that, because Moleka's is of power, Moleka would be unable to live with the social consequences of marrying a Masarwa. Maru renounces his chieftaincy when he marries Margaret, and, although he loves her dearly, the marriage to a Masarwa has also a symbolic meaning for the status of the Masarwa people in Botswana.

Much more than *When Rain Clouds Gather*, *Maru* is about interior experience, though that experience is closely related to political behaviour. *A Question of Power* moves even more deeply and disturbingly into the recesses of personality. From the engagement, there emerges a clearly shaped integration of the personal and social levels of experience. Like Makhaya, Elizabeth, the heroine of *A Question of Power*, has sought political refuge from apartheid, and, like Margaret, has endured the ignominy of being regarded as a half-caste. Even in Botswana she feels so racially alienated that she suffers nightmares of mental torture which later affect her waking life, where, in a co-operative gardening enterprise she is, ironically, being fully accepted as a member of the community. The frighteningly vivid, cinema-like world of her nightmares is dominated by Sello who enacts her lust for moral powers and Dan who exhibits the full propensities of her carnal appetites. The tussle for her allegiance constitutes also a debate about the present and future of Africa, so that it is no mere personal agony that we witness. The novel is a profoundly honest, courageous confrontation of the horrors of 20th-century existence that every news bulletin gives us a glimpse of.

The Collector of Treasures is a volume of village tales that Head collected and re-fashioned, *Serowe, Village of the Rainwind* a history of the Bamangwato capital in Botswana, based on interviews with its older inhabitants. These books led to the novel, *A Bewitched Crossroad*, which draws heavily upon oral tradition, though also upon written sources. It reaches back to the Mfecane (the early 19th-century "Wars of Calamity" in Southern Africa), presenting the personality and experience of a minor chieftain and clan, who, after their Mfecane uprooting (c.1837–1882), find peace under the hospitable and benevolent rule of the Bamangwato King, Khama III (1875–1923). Fiction, then, as in Achebe's *Things Fall Apart*, to record oral versions of African history and celebrate a great African ruler who protected his people from full-blooded European colonialism, but fiction to irradiate history by creating the daily tensions that individuals experienced as Khama grafted European religion (with monogamy) and education (including literacy) upon traditional African ways.

—Arthur Ravenscroft

HEARNE, John. Jamaican. Born in Montreal, Canada, 4 February 1926. Educated at Edinburgh University, 1947–49; M.A. 1949; London University, 1949–50, T.D. 1950. Served in the Royal Air Force, 1943–46: air gunner. Married 1) Joyce Veitch in 1947; 2) Leeta Hopkinson in 1955; two children. Teacher in London and Jamaica, 1950–59; information officer, Government of Jamaica, 1962; resident tutor, Department of Extra-Mural Studies, 1962–67, and since 1968, head of the Creative Arts Centre, University of the West Indies, Kingston. Visiting Fellow in Commonwealth Literature, University of Leeds, Yorkshire, 1967; O'Connor Professor in Literature, Colgate University, Hamilton, New York, 1969–70. Recipient: Rhys Memorial Prize, 1956; Institute of Jamaica Silver Musgrave Medal, 1964. Address: c/o Creative Arts Centre, University of the West Indies, Kingston 7, Jamaica.

PUBLICATIONS

Novels

Voices under the Window. London, Faber, 1955.
Stranger at the Gate. London, Faber, 1956.
The Faces of Love. London, Faber, 1957; as *The Eye of the Storm*, Boston, Little Brown, 1958.
Autumn Equinox. London, Faber, 1959; New York, Vanguard Press, 1961.
Land of the Living. London, Faber, 1961; New York, Harper, 1962.
Fever Grass (as John Morris, with Morris Cargill). London, Collins, and New York, Putnam, 1969.
The Candywine Development (as John Morris, with Morris Cargill). London, Collins, 1970; New York, Stuart, 1971.
The Sure Salvation. London, Faber, 1981; New York, St. Martin's Press, 1982.

Uncollected Short Stories

"The Wind in This Corner" and "At the Stelling," in *West Indian Stories*, edited by Andrew Salkey. London, Faber, 1960.
"A Village Tragedy" and "The Lost Country," in *Stories from the Caribbean*, edited by Andrew Salkey. London, Elek, 1965; as *Island Voices*, New York, Liveright, 1970.

Plays

Soldier in the Snow, with James Mitchell (televised, 1960). Published in *New Granada Plays*, London, Faber, 1960.

The Golden Savage (produced London, 1965).

Television Plays: *Soldier in the Snow*, with James Mitchell, 1960 (UK); *A World Inside*, 1962 (UK).

Other

Our Heritage, with Rex Nettleford.   Mona, University of the West Indies, 1963.

Editor, *Carifesta Forum: An Anthology of 20 Caribbean Voices*.   Kingston, Carifesta 76, 1976.

*

John Hearne comments:

My first concern has been to try to say something about the way we live now that could not be said except by the use of fiction.

When I first started to write I had the feeling that the novel and the short story are the forms that keep the individual most alive in the necessary but increasing synonymity of the industrial and post-industrial world.

Themes, as such, don't interest me much—only a gesture, made by some unsolicited person, that suddenly seizes the imagination and which must be finally explained.

Style and technique are very important, but if the gesture that comes to you when you're not looking for it really needs explanation, then you'll find the style and technique to work it out.

*   *   *

John Hearne is essentially a West Indian novelist: at the same time he lies outside the main stream of the Caribbean novel. Where this has focussed characteristically on the peasant experience, Hearne has explored the predicament of the middle-class intellectual, who can be twice an exile in the largely black developing nations. In *Voices under the Window* it is Mark Lattimer, a "white" Jamaican lawyer, who has devoted himself to the people, but is cut down pointlessly by a marijuana-smoking peasant in a city riot. In *Stranger at the Gate* the hero is Roy McKenzie, again a lawyer who becomes a communist and dies ramming a police car to allow a communist ex-president of a neighbouring island to escape. In *Autumn Equinox* Jim Diver, a young American of Cuban origin, attempts to run a communist paper on a noncommunist island.

These novels do not suggest political solutions; indeed the sketchy treatment of political themes only suggests their irrelevance to his real concern, which is with the difficulty and importance of individual relationships, in particular between men and women. This emerges overtly in *The Faces of Love* and his best novel to date, *Land of the Living*. In the latter the love theme is related to recognisable Caribbean social issues through the involvement of Mahler, a German Jew lecturing at a Caribbean university, with Joan Culpepper, a middle-class "white," and Brysie, a "black" bar servant with paternal links with a politico-religious cult.

Hearne's third concern is with the physical experience of the Caribbean, showing a gift for description and narrative put to vivid use also in his "James Bond" type thrillers (with Morris Cargill) *Fever Grass* and *The Candywine Development*. They have helped him create a fictional world, Cayuna, an island closely resembling Jamaica.

Twenty years after his last "serious" novel, Hearne published *The Sure Salvation*. On a slave ship becalmed in mid-

Atlantic a conflict develops between the white Captain Hogarth and the leader of the Blacks, Delafosse. With echoes of Melville and Conrad, but original in its exploration of the roots of historical conflict in the Caribbean, the novel shows an impressive development in Hearne's art, and confirms his place among the small group of significant West Indian novelists.

—Louis James

HEATH, Roy A(ubrey) K(elvin).   Guyanese.   Born in British Guiana, now Guyana, 13 August 1926. Educated at Central High School, Georgetown; University of London, 1952–56, B.A. (honours) in French 1956; called to the bar, Lincoln's Inn, 1963. Married to Aemilia Oberli; three children. Treasury clerk, Georgetown, 1944-51; clerical worker, London, 1951–58; primary school teacher, Inner London Education Authority, 1959–68. Since 1968, French and German teacher, Barnet Borough Council, London. Recipient: Guyana Theatre Guild award, 1972; *Guardian* Fiction Prize, 1978. Agent: Bill Hamilton, A.M. Heath, 40–42 William IV Street, London WC2N 4DD. Address: c/o Allison and Busby Ltd., 6-A Noel Street, London W1V 3RB, England.

PUBLICATIONS

Novels

A Man Come Home.   London, Longman, 1974.
The Murderer.   London, Allison and Busby, 1978.
Georgetown Trilogy:
   From the Heat of the Day.   London, Allison and Busby, 1979.
   One Generation.   London, Allison and Busby, 1981.
   Genetha.   London, Allison and Busby, 1981.
Kwaku; or, The Man Who Could Not Keep His Mouth Shut.   London, Allison and Busby, 1982.
Orealla.   London, Allison and Busby, 1984.

Uncollected Short Stories

"Miss Mabel's Burial," in *Kaie* (Georgetown, Guyana), 1972.
"The Wind and the Sun," in *Savacou* (Kingston, Jamaica), 1974.
"The Writer of Anonymous Letters," in *Firebird 2*, edited by T.J. Binding.   London, Penguin, 1983.

Play

Inez Combray (produced Georgetown, Guyana, 1972).

Other

Art and History (lectures).   Georgetown, Guyana, Ministry of Education, 1984.

*

Roy A.K. Heath comments:

A Man Come Home relates the story of a large working-class Guyanese family whose mores provide a striking contrast to those of their middle-class brethren. *From the Heat of the Day* and *One Generation* are the first two parts of a trilogy treating the condition of the middle classes in Guyana in the 20th century. *Genetha* completes the trilogy and shows the heroine faced with the choice of joining the Catholic church, returning to a life of prostitution, or living with her aunts in a stifling middle-class atmosphere. *Kwaku* is the tale of a trickster figure. Orealla, the unseen haven for the main character in the novel of that title, is real, yet imagined.

I see myself as a chronicler of Guyanese life in this century.

*   *   *

Roy A.K. Heath's seven novels, beginning with *A Man Come Home* and concluding with the most recent, *Orealla*, represent a distinctive body of fictive insights into contemporary Guyanese society. It blends traditional social realism with local folklore and myths to dramatize the everyday lives of the poor and the lower middle class in the capital, Georgetown, and, occasionally, in the rural hinterlands. Indeed, it is this kind of blending, or interweaving, that makes for one of Heath's distinctive strengths as a novelist. The folk myths of "obeah" or voudun ("voodoo"), the strict orthodoxies of biblical morality, local legends drawn from Amerindian or East Indian sources—these all co-exist with the empirical "realities" of everyday village life, the familiar routine of middle-class home life, or the rough-and-tumble of the streets and slum-yards of Georgetown's impoverished districts. Heath's is a world of popular beliefs and customs which determine the perceptions and choices of his characters; and the very diversity of values and viewpoints, not only within the community but also within any single individual, dramatizes the discrete complexities of the social milieu, complicates the very notion of moral judgement or social choices in the recurrent tensions between classes, religious traditions, and cultural backgrounds, and, finally, challenges conventional assumptions about "social realism" in prose fiction.

This discreteness also goes hand in hand with Heaths other strength—his ability to evoke a given environment and its social milieu (urban slum, middle-class neighbourhood, rural village, and so forth), bringing to life the sights and sounds of a family dining room or a Georgetown whorehouse in vivid, richly suggestive vignettes. In his more recent fiction, especially in the impressively crafted *Kwaku*, he has shown signs of developing a flair for a lively, effective prose style as well as for credible characterization; but even in the previous novels where thinness of characterization and of style is often a problem, Heath's reader is always aware of a provocative intelligence perpetually raising questions about the nature of social reality and of moral judgements in a vividly realized world. These questions are integrated with recurrent themes which typify all of Heath's fiction: the inevitable obsession with material success in a society dominated by poverty, and the price of success as well as of failure; the conflict between the needs and desires of the private self and the restrictive conventions of a world in which ideals of family responsibility, social respectability, and moral conventions are paramount; and that unending war between the sexes in which mutual exploitiveness and shared dependency, hostility and desire all seem to mirror tensions and contradictions in human society as a whole. In turn all of these conflicts center on a fundamental dilemma which links all the novels, the dilemma of freedom: for whether the quest be freedom from poverty or from some intolerable marriage, Heath's rebel-protagonists must always wrestle, usually inconclusively, with certain unresolved contradictions—it seems all but impossible to flee from poverty without losing a part of one's basic humanity in the process of amassing wealth; the

despised spouse (Heath's marriages are invariably wretched) is also an integral, indispensable part of one's self; and the young rebels against family and conventional morality soon discover that the target of their rebellion is also an ineradicable part of themselves.

In *A Man Come Home* the chief rebel is Archie "Bird" Foster who tries to escape from the poverty of Georgetown's slum-yards by entering into a liaison with one of the legendary "Water People" of Guyanese folklore, a "Fair Maid," or witch. She gives him unlimited wealth on condition that he returns regularly to her bed at her bidding. Now wealthy, he quickly collects the usual trappings of middle-class affluence—an ostentatious house in the suburbs, expensive habits, and a wife (in the person of his long-suffering girlfriend from the slum-yard). The legendary materials provide Heath with a rather obvious and ready-made allegory on the middle-class aspirations of the poor, and the moral cost of acquiring wealth in exchange for one's humanity—for the contract with the Fair Maid is, in effect, a Faustian pact. His marriage, his ties with the rest of his family and with his old friends all conflict with that pact, and when he reneges on his agreement with the Fair Maid in order to re-establish the "normal" relationships and "respectable" conventions of his society, she exacts the inevitable price: he dies in a car accident which also claims the life of his sister's children.

Bird's tragedy is not isolated, for even the most isolated of Heath's characters are bound up with their families and the rest of society. The deaths of the children therefore emphasize that Bird's tragedy has become a family disaster. His sister never recovers from her loss, and her marriage eventually collapses. At the same time his father's household continues the steady decline which actually started before Bird's misadventures. Egbert Foster, the father, tries, unsuccessfully, to establish peace in a home in which his mistress envies the social life and sexual activity of her young daughter Melda. She administers a savage beating from which Melda never recovers fully, spending the rest of her life as an idiot. In the meanwhile the older woman enters upon an affair with one of Bird's slum-yard friends (who is also Melda's lover), than betrays him to her husband's inevitable violence. Viewed in the context of the Foster family as a whole, then, it becomes clear that Bird's liaison with the Fair Maid is not only an allegory on the moral dilemmas of poverty and materialism; it is also a mythological re-enactment of sexual conflicts and contradictions. The weakness and domination, the mutual exploitation, the futile obsession with escape and freedom—these are not only the patterns of Bird's ill-fated liaison with the Fair Maid, but also the familiar, repetitive patterns in his family and among his friends.

This grim vision of sexual relationships dominates *The Murderer* where the waste and mutual destructiveness of many conventional relationships are explored through the experiences of abnormal psychology—a narrative strategy which allows Heath to juxtapose images of the "normal" or "conventional" with patterns of "abnormality" in order to challenge settled assumptions about these terms. The murderer is an archetypal psychotic: Galton Flood has been scarred by a wretched childhood in which his sexuality and social instincts were repressed or warped by the ridicule and harshness of a domineering mother who also made life miserable for her husband. His parents' marriage is a model of the shared resentment and contempt which characterize sexual unions in Galton's world, and when he becomes an adult he is deeply suspicious of women, a suspiciousness that is aggravated by his general inability to socialize. When he does marry, he chooses a wife whose prior experience (with an older lover and a dependent but unloving father) has convinced her that men are unreliable and weak beneath the usual male bravado. The marriage quickly fails because of Galton's jealousy and because of the unsociability which prevents him from developing a stable career. His jealousy is the first symptom of criminal insanity. He kills his wife, and although he confesses the murder to both her family and to his own, he is never brought to justice. He ends up, instead, as a street derelict, a relatively harmless idiot who is supported by his kind-hearted brother. Galton's inability to function as part of the family unit or in society at large is partly counteracted by the generosity and family loyalties of his older brother; but Heath's main achievement is to evoke ironic parallels between Galton's "abnormal" obsessions and those familiar habits of possessiveness and abusiveness which characterize the sexual relationships of "normal" people. "Abnormal" psychology is as much an allegory of the "real" world here, as "supernatural" events are in *A Man Come Home*.

Heath's other family tragedy, the tragedy of the Armstrong family, is the subject of his Georgetown trilogy, *From the Heat of the Day*, *One Generation*, and *Genetha*. The first work traces the history of the parents' marriage (Sonny Armstrong, from a poor, relatively uneducated background, resents his wife's middle-class family even before he marries her). It is a history of failing affections and growing isolation on both sides, a growing misery which inevitably affects the two children, Genetha and Rohan, and which concludes with the death of Mrs. Armstrong. *Her* misery, at least, ends with her death. He drowns his in drink, until he dies as a derelict pensioner, early in *One Generation*. The second novel describes Rohan's flight from the Georgetown family home, away from the possessive caring of his sister, to a Civil Service job in rural Guyana where he falls in love with a married woman while living with her sister. He is killed by his impoverished East Indian assistant who envies him his social standing and relative prosperity. His murderer is never discovered, and his impunity reinforces the grim realities which lend an air of inevitability and repetition to the trilogy as a whole: Rohan's personal life has been as wasted as his parents'; his sexual relationships have been equally fraught with betrayals and exploitation; and he, too, leaves behind him a legacy of hurt. The inheritors of that legacy are Dada, the mother of his unborn child, who has been victimized by his duplicity with her sister, and his own sister, Genetha, whom he has abandoned to face life alone as a single, inexperienced girl in Georgetown. Finally, in the third part of the trilogy, Genetha recalls her late mother by virtue of her loneliness and isolation, her inability to develop satisfactory relationships with men, and the perpetual tension between her need for the middle-class respectability of her mother's family and her dislike of the family's suffocating propriety. She ends as a total dependent on the family's former maid, now a very successful "madam" of a Georgetown whorehouse (another "success" acquired at the cost of one's humanity). Esther, like Mr. Armstrong before her, despises the middle-class attitudes of Genetha and the late Mrs. Armstrong, but the eventual bond between Genetha and Esther transcends the barriers, for it has been strengthened by their common experiences as women in a world of weak, bullying men.

Kwaku, the hero of the novel of the same name, is no bully, but he is another weak, insecure male whose dependency on his wife (Gwendoline) and his close, lifelong friend (Blossom) has been intensified by the fact that as a social misfit he has never made friends among the villagers with whom he has grown up. Like the other figures of poverty in Heath's fiction, he tries to make money, succeeding for a while as a "healer" in the small town of New Amsterdam. But his insecurity, his need to brag and command respect, leads to his downfall: he

runs afoul of the village fisherman when he fails to "cure" the latter's family problems. The fisherman retaliates by resorting to obeah: Gwendoline becomes blind and the family sinks into utter destitution. Kwaku's children rebel or are forced to leave home for sheer survival, and both Kwaku and Gwendoline end up as a drunken pair of derelicts in New Amsterdam. It is worth noting that, to his credit, Kwaku never deserts his family in order to resuscitate his business as "healer"—despite the fact that the expenses of supporting a blind wife and eight children make it impossible for him to start up his business again. But the familiar irony with which Heath handles family and love remains the final judgement here. Kwaku is loyal to his family because he needs them. As he himself recognizes, his love for his wife is a kind of possessiveness—a possessiveness which we can easily recognize, in some of its most repulsive forms, in Gwendoline. Unlike Gwendoline, Blossom is fiercely independent—but her own marriage survives, after a fashion, because she has bullied her own husband into his (accepting) place, even manipulating him into "accepting" a child which, he himself knows, he never fathered. In the uncompromising realism of Heath's 20th-century vision, Wilfred's marital happiness with Blossom is the happiness of the Swiftian fool in *A Tale of a Tub*—the state of being well deceived. It is the kind of "happiness" which exemplifies the solid achievements and rich possibilities of Heath's narrative irony.

—Lloyd W. Brown

HEINLEIN, Robert A(nson). American.   Born in Butler, Missouri, 7 July 1907. Educated at Central High School, Kansas City, graduated 1924; University of Missouri, Columbia, 1924–25; United States Naval Academy, Annapolis, Maryland, B.S. 1929; University of California, Los Angeles, 1934–35. Served in the United States Navy, 1929 until retirement because of physical disability, 1934. Married 1) Leslyn McDonald (divorced); 2) Virginia Gerstenfeld in 1948. Owned a silver mine, Silver Plume, Colorado, 1934-35; worked in mining and real estate, 1936–39; civilian engineer, Philadelphia Navy Yard, 1942–45. Forrestal Lecturer, United States Naval Academy, 1973. Recipient: Hugo Award, 1956, 1960, 1962, 1967; Boys' Clubs of America award, 1959; Grand Master Nebula Award, 1974. Guest of Honor, World Science Fiction Convention, 1941, 1961, 1976. L.H.D.: Eastern Michigan University, Ypsilanti, 1977. Agent: Spectrum Literary Agency, 432 Park Avenue South, Suite 1205, New York, New York 10016. Address: 6000 Bonny Doon Road, Santa Cruz, California 95060, U.S.A.

PUBLICATIONS

Novels

Beyond This Horizon. Reading, Pennsylvania, Fantasy Press, 1948; London, Panther, 1967.
Sixth Column. New York, Gnome Press, 1949; as *The Day after Tomorrow*, New York, New American Library, 1951; London, Mayflower, 1962.
Waldo, and Magic Inc. New York, Doubleday, 1950; as *Waldo, Genius in Orbit*, New York, Avon, 1958.
The Puppet Masters. New York, Doubleday, 1951; London, Museum Press, 1953.

Double Star.   New York, Doubleday, 1956; London, Joseph, 1958.

The Door into Summer.   New York, Doubleday, 1957; London, Panther, 1960.

Methuselah's Children.   New York, Gnome Press, 1958; London, Gollancz, 1963.

The Robert Heinlein Omnibus.   London, Sidgwick and Jackson, 1958.

Stranger in a Strange Land.   New York, Putnam, 1961; London, New English Library, 1965.

Glory Road.   New York, Putnam, 1963; London, New English Library, 1965.

Farnham's Freehold.   New York, Putnam, 1964; London, Dobson, 1965.

Three by Heinlein (includes *The Puppet Masters*, *Waldo*, *Magic Inc.*).   New York, Doubleday, 1965; as *A Heinlein Triad*, London, Gollancz, 1966.

A Robert Heinlein Omnibus.   London, Sidgwick and Jackson, 1966.

The Moon Is a Harsh Mistress.   New York, Putnam, 1966; London, Dobson, 1967.

I Will Fear No Evil.   New York, Putnam, 1970; London, New English Library, 1972.

Time Enough for Love: The Lives of Lazarus Long.   New York, Putnam, 1973; London, New English Library, 1974.

The Number of the Beast.   New York, Fawcett, and London, New English Library, 1980.

Friday.   New York, Holt Rinehart, and London, New English Library, 1982.

Job: A Comedy of Justice.   New York, Ballantine, and London, New English Library, 1984.

The Cat Who Walks Through Walls: A Comedy of Manners. New York, Putnam, 1985; London, New English Library, 1986.

Short Stories

The Man Who Sold the Moon.   Chicago, Shasta, 1950; London, Sidgwick and Jackson, 1953.

Universe.   New York, Dell, 1951.

The Green Hills of Earth.   Chicago, Shasta, 1951; London, Sidgwick and Jackson, 1954.

Revolt in 2100.   Chicago, Shasta, 1953; London, Digit, 1959.

Assignment in Eternity.   Reading, Pennsylvania, Fantasy Press, 1953; London, Museum Press, 1955; abridged edition, as *Lost Legacy*, London, Digit, 1960.

The Menace from Earth.   New York, Gnome Press, 1959; London, Dobson, 1966.

The Unpleasant Profession of Jonathan Hoag.   New York, Gnome Press, 1959; London, Dobson, 1964; as *6 x H: Six Stories*, New York, Pyramid, 1961.

Orphans of the Sky.   London, Gollancz, 1963; New York, Putnam, 1964.

The Worlds of Robert A. Heinlein.   New York, Ace, 1966; London, New English Library, 1970.

The Past Through Tomorrow: Future History Stories.   New York, Putnam, 1967; abridged edition, London, New English Library, 2 vols., 1977.

The Best of Robert Heinlein 1939–1959, edited by Angus Wells, London, Sidgwick and Jackson, 1973.

Destination Moon.   Boston, Gregg Press, 1979.

Expanded Universe.   New York, Grosset and Dunlap, 1980.

Fiction (for children)

Rocket Ship Galileo.   New York, Scribner, 1947; London, New English Library, 1971.

Space Cadet.   New York, Scribner, 1948; London, Gollancz, 1966.

Red Planet.   New York, Scribner, 1949; London, Gollancz, 1963.

Farmer in the Sky.   New York, Scribner, 1950; London, Gollancz, 1962.

Between Planets.   New York, Scribner, 1951; London, Gollancz, 1968.

The Rolling Stones.   New York, Scribner, 1952; as *Space Family Stone*, London, Gollancz, 1969.

Starman Jones.   New York, Scribner, 1953; London, Sidgwick and Jackson, 1954.

The Star Beast.   New York, Scribner, 1954; London, New English Library, 1971.

Tunnel in the Sky.   New York, Scribner, 1955; London, Gollancz, 1965.

Time for the Stars.   New York, Scribner, 1956; London, Gollancz, 1963.

Citizen of the Galaxy.   New York, Scribner, 1957; London, Gollancz, 1969.

Have Space Suit—Will Travel.   New York, Scribner, 1958; London, Gollancz, 1970.

Starship Troopers.   New York, Putnam, 1959; London, New English Library, 1961.

Podkayne of Mars: Her Life and Times.   New York, Putnam, 1963; London, New English Library, 1969.

Plays

Screenplays: *Destination Moon*, with Rip Van Ronkel and James O'Hanlon, 1950; *Project Moonbase*, with Jack Seaman, 1953.

Other

The Discovery of the Future (address).   Los Angeles, Novacious, 1941.

Of Worlds Beyond: The Science of Science-Fiction Writing, with others, edited by Lloyd Arthur Eshbach.   Reading, Pennsylvania, Fantasy Press, 1947; London, Dobson, 1965.

The Science Fiction Novel, with others, edited by Basil Davenport.   Chicago, Advent, 1959.

The Notebooks of Lazarus Long.   New York, Putnam, 1978.

Editor, *Tomorrow, The Stars: A Science Fiction Anthology*. New York, Doubleday, 1952.

*

Bibliography: *Robert A. Heinlein: A Bibliography* by Mark Owings, Baltimore, Croatan House, 1973.

Manuscript Collection: University of California Library, Santa Cruz.

Critical Studies: *Seekers of Tomorrow* by Sam Moskowitz, Cleveland, World, 1966; *Heinlein in Dimension: A Critical Analysis* (includes bibliography) by Alexei Panshin, Chicago, Advent, 1968; *Robert A. Heinlein, Stranger in His Own Land*, San Bernardino, California, Borgo Press, 1976, and *The Classic Years of Robert A. Heinlein*, Borgo Press, 1977, both by George Edgar Slusser; *Robert A. Heinlein* edited by Martin H. Greenberg and Joseph D. Olander, New York, Taplinger, and Edinburgh, Harris, 1978; *Robert A. Heinlein: America as Science Fiction* by H. Bruce Franklin, New York, Oxford University Press, 1980, Oxford, Oxford University Press, 1981; *Yesterday or Tomorrow? The Work of Robert A. Heinlein* by R. Reginald, San Bernardino, California, Borgo Press, 1984.

Robert A. Heinlein comments:

I got into writing because I was unexpectedly disabled and retired from my chosen profession, the Navy. Like many others in precarious health I turned to what I was physically able to do. Writing is, and has been for 45 years, my only profession and my livelihood. But I have never devoted as much as half my time to it: Mrs. Heinlein and I have traveled much of the time—three times around the world and to about 80 countries, in long, leisurely trips. (I have a smattering of several languages; she speaks eight—no, she's not a linguist, she's a chemist and engineer—and a Fellow of the British Royal Horticulturist Society; she experiments in plant genetics.) I am a member of many scientific, engineering, and military associations, plus the Authors League of America, but am not very active in them, as we prefer a quiet life and avoid publicity as much as we can. We are country people, living 15 miles from the nearest town, almost 100 miles from a city. My study faces the Pacific Ocean, past a heated pool and through some of my wife's gardens—I don't work very hard when the weather is good; life is too short and too sweet.

My stories have been mostly speculations about the future and what mankind may make of it. I am hopelessly old-fashioned in many of my opinions and this annoys some people. My writing has been strongly affected by Rudyard Kipling, Winston Churchill, H.G. Wells, et al. My interests and hobbies are catholic, ranging from stone masonry, cats, sculpture, ballistics, fiscal theory, figure skating, to figure drawing. I enjoy life and believe that Man will live forever and spread out through the universe.

*   *   *

At any one time there have never been more than a dozen or so writers working at the very core of the science-fiction field, a handful of innovators who to greater or lesser extent influence all other practitioners. It is a measure of Robert A. Heinlein's success that he has been among the leaders of this select band almost since the publication of his first story in 1939.

"Innovator" is the key word if we wish to measure Heinlein's contributions to science-fiction writing. His innovations have been in ideas, in storytelling techniques, but most importantly of all in *attitudes*. In this respect he is responsible more than any other for establishing the methods and traditions of modern science fiction.

To understand fully his achievement we must look at science fiction as it was, an ingrown species of category fiction confined almost entirely to the American pulp magazines. The vitality and literacy of earlier pioneers such as Wells had been lost, and science fiction was, quite simply, fiction *about* science, with the occasional space operatics for good measure. Heinlein picked up the field and shook it until it rattled. By his example he changed that definition to mean instead "fiction written according to the scientific method," and there is a vast difference between the two. Almost for the first time there began to appear stories in which the marvel of technology was a beginning rather than an end in itself.

Once this bridge had been crossed science fiction could take a large stride towards maturity, and others besides Heinlein started to stress characterisation and the treatment of human responses to new situations. In the three years between 1939

and 1942 Heinlein himself wrote 22 stories for the leading magazine, *Astounding*, including most of his "Future History" series and three major novels, *Sixth Column, Beyond This Horizon*, and *Methuselah's Children*. Had he stopped then his name would have been one of the "greats" of the science-fiction field. But after the Second World War Heinlein returned with stories which concentrated even more upon human values than on science for science's sake. Quite deliberately he wrote to "make the American public think about the future," and the medium he chose was the *Saturday Evening Post*. Stories such as "Columbus Was a Dope" and "It's Great to Be Back" are skilfully written and topical today, and the complete series is available in the collection *The Green Hills of Earth*. He also commenced the famous juvenile series which eventually was to amount to 13 novels in 13 years. Here again the aim was similar—to "educate" the growing generation, although the books have tremendous appeal to all ages. Several, such as *Have Space Suit—Will Travel* and *Citizen of the Galaxy*, were initially published in adult magazines.

During the 1950's Heinlein produced few short stories and only four adult novels, of which three—*The Puppet Masters, Double Star*, and *The Door into Summer*—may prove to be among his most well-rounded work. The fourth, *Starship Troopers*, marked the beginning of Heinlein's final period. This and four subsequent long novels (*Stranger in a Strange Land, Glory Road, Farnham's Freehold, The Moon Is a Harsh Mistress*) provoked more controversy than any of Heinlein's earlier work. *Stranger* became a "hippie" cult-book, much to the author's dismay, one imagines, and all have showed some flaws in construction, in particular the loss of Heinlein's former economy of words.

Nonetheless they have a fascination of their own, through the inventiveness and narrative power of the writer. The same cannot be said of *I Will Fear No Evil* and *Time Enough for Love*, which have almost no redeeming virtues and can only be regarded as over-wordy and fatuous. They mark a sad development in a truly great writing career.

So perhaps they and other more recent books should be ignored when considering the splendid record from 1939 to 1969 (and fittingly the anniversary coincided with the landing of Apollo 11 upon the moon)—30 years in which the name of Robert Heinlein dominated the entire field of science fiction. His gift has been to combine a truly compulsive storytelling power with a disciplined, brilliant imagination.

—Peter R. Weston

HELLER, Joseph. American. Born in Brooklyn, New York, 1 May 1923. Educated at Abraham Lincoln High School, New York; New York University, B.A. 1948 (Phi Beta Kappa); Columbia University, New York, M.A. 1949; Oxford University (Fulbright Scholar), 1949–50. Served in the United States Army Air Force in World War II: Lieutenant. Married Shirley Held in 1945; one son and one daughter. Instructor in English, Pennsylvania State University, University Park, 1950–52; advertising writer, *Time* magazine, New York, 1952–56, and *Look* magazine, New York, 1956–58; promotion manager, *McCall's* magazine, New York, 1958–61. Recipient: American Academy grant, 1963; Prix Médicis Etranger (France), 1985. Member, American Academy, 1977. Address: c/o Knopf Inc., 201 East 50th Street, New York, New York 10022, U.S.A.

PUBLICATIONS

Novels

Catch-22. New York, Simon and Schuster, 1961; London, Cape, 1962.
Something Happened. New York, Knopf, and London, Cape, 1974.
Good as Gold. New York, Simon and Schuster, and London, Cape, 1979.
God Knows. New York, Knopf, and London, Cape, 1984.

Uncollected Short Stories

"I Don't Love You Anymore," in *Story* (New York), September–October 1945.
"Castle of Snow," in *Atlantic* (Boston), May 1947.
"Bookies, Beware!," in *Esquire* (New York), March 1948.
"Girl from Greenwich," in *Esquire* (New York), June 1948.
"A Man Named Flute," in *Atlantic* (Boston), August 1948.
"Nothing to Be Done," in *Esquire* (New York), August 1948.
"MacAdam's Log," in *Gentlemen's Quarterly* (New York), December 1959.
"World Full of Great Cities," in *Nelson Algren's Own Book of Lonesome Monsters*, edited by Algren. New York, Lancer, 1962; London, Panther, 1964.
"Love, Dad," in *Playboy* (Chicago), December 1969.

Plays

We Bombed in New Haven (produced New Haven, Connecticut, 1967; New York, 1969; London, 1971). New York, Knopf, 1968; London, Cape, 1969.
Catch-22, adaptation of his own novel. New York, Delacorte Press, and London, French, 1973.
Clevinger's Trial, adaptation of chapter 8 of his novel *Catch-22* (produced London, 1974). New York, French 1973; London, French, 1974.

Screenplays: *Sex and the Single Girl*, with David R. Schwartz, 1964; *Casino Royale* (uncredited), 1967; *Dirty Dingus Magee*, with Tom and Frank Waldman, 1970.

Other

No Laughing Matter (autobiographical), with Speed Vogel. New York, Putnam, 1986.

*

Bibliography: *Three Contemporary Novelists: An Annotated Bibliography* by Robert M. Scotto, New York, Garland, 1977; *Joseph Heller: A Reference Guide* by Brenda M. Keegan, Boston Hall, 1978.

Critical Studies: "Joseph Heller's *Catch-22*" by Burr Dodd, in *Approaches to the Novel* edited by John Colmer, Edinburgh, Oliver and Boyd, 1967; "The Sanity of *Catch-22*" by Robert Protherough, in *Human World* (Swansea), May 1971; *A Catch-22 Casebook* edited by Frederick T. Kiley and Walter McDonald, New York, Crowell, 1973; *Critical Essays on Catch-22* edited by James Nagel, Encino, California, Dickinson Seminar Series, 1974; "Something Happened: A New Direction" by George J. Searles, in *Critique* (Atlanta), vol. 18, no. 3, 1977; *From Here to Absurdity: The Moral Battlefields of Joseph Heller* by Stephen W. Potts, San Bernardino, California, Borgo Press, 1982.

*   *   *

Joseph Heller has a better claim than any other American writer to having written the definitive novel of modern war—if universal response to his definition of that war is any measure. People now know as "catch-22" the circular bureaucratic formula they had learned from experience. In Heller's book the "catch" works simply. Anyone who is crazy can be grounded; all he has to do is ask. If he asks, he can't possibly be crazy. The unyielding absurdity of Heller's routine could be observed as easily in Flanders and Vietnam as in the air war over Europe that was the setting of his novel.

Catch-22 is a burlesque epic built upon the "catch-22" routine. Vaudeville, comic strips, and animated cartoons provide its basic structure and pace, which is not to say that Heller is flippant or callous. Far from it. It is his special talent to render the war in the formats of popular culture, then juxtaposing it with the feelings it provokes in such men as his hero, Yossarian—feelings also bordered in film frames and comic strip panels. Yossarian is determined to "live forever or die in the attempt." Almost as often as assorted characters perform the catch-22 routine, he relives the moment in the air over Avignon when the wounded gunner, Snowden, lay "spilling his secret all over the back of the plane." "Ou sont les neigedens . . ." Yossarian murmurs over his crewman's body, touching the secret with a wisecrack.

Yossarian struggles to survive against a system in which a Lieutenant Scheisskopf necessarily moves through the ranks to become a general. Another name from the folklore of humor is Captain Aardvark, "Good Old Arfie," who can ignore the suffering he sees because he can't quite hear it. The chaplain is an Anabaptist. The Soldier in white is a plaster-cast embodiment of the system with a circuitry of tubes running into and out of what is supposed to be his body. There is the Unknown Soldier killed on his first mission before he has a chance to unpack his bags and get to meet anyone. His name is Mudd. In the world of *Catch-22*, a conversation begins with someone inventing the rumor that the Germans are now using the Le Page anti-aircraft gun to spray webs of mucilage over formations of Allied bombers and ends with official confirmation that Le Page guns at Bologna have inflicted losses on the squadron by shooting webs of mucilage over formations of its planes. *Catch-22* is a brilliant, if exhausting, mosaic of comic invention.

Something Happened seems to be the effort to write as complicated a book as *Catch-22* about the mean, narrow life of a New York corporation executive. Bob Slocum is an insensitive man who knows himself quite well. "A friend in need is no friend of mine," he says. His "Snowden" is the older girl who teased him when he was an office boy and left the rest of his agitated sex life short of fulfillment. Slocum is a mimic and an echolalic who cannot resist imitating the defects of those who suffer at his hands. One recognizes the comic techniques of *Catch-22* grimly transformed in *Something Happened*, which is deadlier and more polished than Heller's undoubted masterpiece.

After these two extraordinarily ambitious books, critics were harsh with *Good as Gold*. This novel is often funnier than *Catch-22* and always funnier than *Something Happened*, but it is also an uneasy mixture of two comic inspirations. One was to have Bruce Gold try to write about "The Jewish Experience in America," despite his headlong efforts to reject that experience for every token of assimilation. The other was to burlesque the career of Henry Kissinger. Accordingly, Gold is a plodding intellectual who even-handedly covets power in Washington and tall gentile girls. His father bullies him and his prospective father-in-law addresses him with anti-Semitic epithets; his closest gentile friend admits that if worst came to worst he wouldn't hide him. The Washington fantasies are less effective than the bitter comedy involving Gold and his father, which is a little surprising given the similarities between Heller's top brass in government and the military of *Catch-22*.

Heller sets himself his greatest challenge by retelling the story of David in *God Knows*. His narrator is the psalmist, the King of Israel, and the archetypal Jewish ironist, wit, and standup comic. His narration is a torrent of anachronism that flows brilliantly as when, for example, David's modernisms give the reader a precise notion of the scruffy little town that he handed on to Solomon as Jerusalem, site for the temple God has forbidden him to build. The middling or rapid-fire anachronisms are such as David's view of another town: "The city of Hebron is not Versailles, you know." The richest language Heller has ever used rests on his anachronisms as when the psalmist proclaims his place among all the poets ("How the mighty have fallen. Proud of that line. That *goneff*, William Shakespeare . . .") and when the king laments one son ("Absalom, my son" . . .) and disparages plodding Solomon ("You're a hard man, Shlomo"). Of course, Heller is no more restrained than he was in *Catch-22*, unable to resist describing Michal as the first Jewish American Princess and exploiting David's reputation as elegist by having him proclaim Abner as "the noblest Israelite of them all."

—David Sanders

HELWIG, David (Gordon). Canadian. Born in Toronto, Ontario, 5 April 1938. Educated at Stamford Collegiate Institute; University of Toronto, B.A. 1960; University of Liverpool, 1960–62, M.A. 1962. Married Nancy Keeling in 1959; two daughters. Member of the Department of English, Queen's University, Kingston, Ontario, 1962–80; literary manager, CBC television drama, 1974–76. Address: 106 Montreal Street, Kingston, Ontario K7K 3E8, Canada.

PUBLICATIONS

Novels

The Day Before Tomorrow.   Ottawa, Oberon Press, 1971; as *Message from a Spy*, Don Mills, Ontario, PaperJacks, 1975.
The Glass Knight.   Ottawa, Oberon Press, 1976.
Jennifer.   Ottawa, Oberon Press, 1979; New York, Beaufort, 1983.
The King's Evil.   Ottawa, Oberon Press, 1981; New York, Beaufort, 1984.
It Is Always Summer.   Toronto, Stoddart, and New York, Beaufort, 1982.
A Sound Like Laughter.   Toronto, Stoddart, and New York, Beaufort, 1983.
The Only Son.   Toronto, Stoddart, and New York, Beaufort, 1984.
The Bishop.   New York, Viking, and London, Penguin, 1986.

Short Stories

The Streets of Summer.   Ottawa, Oberon Press, 1969.

Uncollected Short Stories

"Presences" and "Things That Happened Before You Were Born," in *The Narrative Voice*, edited by John Metcalf. Toronto, McGraw Hill Ryerson, 1972.
"Avia da Capo," in *80: Best Canadian Stories*, edited by Clark Blaise and John Metcalf.   Ottawa, Oberon Press, 1980.

Plays

A Time in Winter (produced Kingston, Ontario, 1967). Included in *Figures in a Landscape*, 1967.
The Hanging of William O'Donnell (produced Toronto, 1970).
Barnardo Boy (opera libretto), music by Clifford Crawley (produced Kingston, Ontario, 1981).

Verse

Figures in a Landscape.   Ottawa, Oberon Press, 1967.
The Sign of the Gunman.   Ottawa, Oberon Press, 1969.
The Best Name of Silence.   Ottawa, Oberon Press, 1972.
Atlantic Crossings.   Ottawa, Oberon Press, 1974.
A Book of the Hours.   Ottawa, Oberon Press, 1979.
The Rain Falls Like Rain.   Ottawa, Oberon Press, 1982.
Catchpenny Poems.   Ottawa, Oberon Press, 1983.

Other

A Book about Billie (documentary on Billie Miller).   Ottawa, Oberon Press, 1972; as *Inside and Out: The Story of Billie, Junkie, Pimp, Booster, Robber, and Conman*, Don Mills, Ontario, PaperJacks, 1975.

Editor, with Tom Marshall, *Fourteen Stories High: Best Canadian Stories of 71*.   Ottawa, Oberon Press, 1971.
Editor, with Joan Harcourt, *72, 73, 74* and *75: New Canadian Stories*.   Ottawa, Oberon Press, 4 vols, 1972–75.
Editor, *Words from Inside*.   Kingston, Ontario, Prison Arts, 1972(?).
Editor, *The Human Elements: Critical Essays* (and *Second Series*).   Ottawa, Oberon Press, 2 vols, 1978–81.
Editor, *Love and Money: The Politics of Culture*.   Ottawa, Oberon Press, 1980.
Editor, with Sandra Martin, *83* and *84: Best Canadian Stories*. Ottawa, Oberon Press, 2 vols, 1983–84.
Editor, with Sandra Martin, *Coming Attractions 1–2*. Ottawa, Oberon Press, 2 vols., 1983–84.

*

Manuscript Collection: McMaster University, Hamilton, Ontario.

Critical Studies: "Bourgeois and Arsonist," in *Harsh and Lovely Land* by Tom Marshall, Vancouver, University of British Columbia Press, 1979; "David Helwig's Kingston Novels: This Random Dance of Atoms" by Diana Brydon, in *Present Tense* edited by John Moss, Toronto, NC Press, 1985.

*   *   *

David Helwig's novels, in particular the Kingston tetralogy (*The Glass Knight, Jennifer, It Is Always Summer, A Sound Like Laughter*), give universal, humane enigmas a local habitation. The setting, Kingston, is chosen for definite reasons. Founded by United Empire Loyalists and former capital of Canada, the city epitomized values and traditions which somehow by the 1970's were in shards. From Kingston, with its proximity to Montreal, Ottawa, and Toronto, there is the added awareness of the English and French centres of politics, economics, and culture.

At another level the books may be read as a commentary on Book IV especially of Plato's *Republic*. Helwig wrestles with the disparity between the modern city and modern civilisation and the ideal symbol of the city as the expression of the virtues of justice, wisdom, courage, and temperance. Plato's words, "We must not pursue complexity nor great variety in the basic movements, but must observe what are the rhythms of a life that is orderly and brave . . ." form the epigraph of *The Glass Knight* and *Jennifer*. Here, though the ideal is tarnished and debased, the characters are at least haunted by intimations of a lost order. The final two novels, *A Sound Like Laughter* and *It Is Always Summer* are without epigraphs, implying that the opposites of the ideal, injustice, madness, cowardice, violent licence, and sensual excess, are paramount.

A brief reading of character and event in each book supports such assertions. Helwig takes major images of control from Western cultural history and associates his characters with them. Plato is always important, but in *The King's Evil* it is the saintly figure of Edward the Confessor and his ability (handed down to future monarchs) to cure the ills of humankind, who is pervasive. In *The Glass Knight*, chivalric ideals and Freudian explanation are associated with the central character Robert Mallon poring over *Civilization and Its Discontents*. Likewise, Robert's ex-wife Jennifer is absorbed in questions of responsibility and moral choice raised by George Eliot's *Middlemarch* and Elizabeth his mistress is drawn to the unworldly romanticism of Saint-Denys-Garneau.

Helwig forces his readers to see beyond the pragmatic and material glue of a society which in actuality is in ruins. Moral, and therefore legal and political, consensus is gone. Thus the sensitive and intelligent, like Robert and Jennifer, are driven to suicide, and the shallow, unscrupulous, and morally reprehensible, like Charlie or Remnant or Anne, survive. Helwig's vision of contemporary Ontario is a more despairing *Wasteland*, for if there is an approximation to the Fisher King here it is the suicidal Mallon whose name suggests (he planned a book on the F.L.Q. crisis) the French for corruption and dishonesty.

—Barrie Davies

HERLIHY, James Leo. American. Born in Detroit, Michigan, 27 February 1927. Educated at Black Mountain College, North Carolina, 1947–48; Pasadena Playhouse, California, 1948–50; Yale University Drama School, New Haven, Connecticut (RCA Fellow), 1956–57. Served in the United States Navy, 1945–46: petty officer. Taught playwriting at City College of New York 1967–68; Distinguished Visiting Professor, University of Arkansas, Fayetteville, 1983. Lives in Los Angeles. Agent: Jay Garon-Brooke Associates Inc., 415 Central Park West, New York, New York 10025, U.S.A.

PUBLICATIONS

Novels

All Fall Down.   New York, Dutton, 1960; London, Faber, 1961.

Midnight Cowboy.   New York, Simon and Schuster, 1965; London, Cape, 1966.
The Season of the Witch.   New York, Simon and Schuster, and London, W.H. Allen, 1971.

Short Stories

The Sleep of Baby Filbertson and Other Stories.   New York, Dutton, and London, Faber, 1959.
A Story That Ends with a Scream and Eight Others.   New York, Simon and Schuster, 1967; London, Cape, 1968.

Plays

Streetlight Sonata (produced Pasadena, California, 1950).
Moon in Capricorn (produced New York, 1953).
Blue Denim, with William Noble (produced New York, 1958; Swansea, Wales, 1970).   New York, Random House, 1958.
Crazy October, adaptation of his story "The Sleep of Baby Filbertson" (also director: produced New Haven, Connecticut, 1958).
Terrible Jim Fitch (produced Chicago, 1965; London, 1973).
Stop, You're Killing Me (includes *Terrible Jim Fitch; Bad Bad Jo-Jo; Laughs, Etc.*) (produced Boston, 1968; New York, 1969; *Bad Bad Jo-Jo* produced London, 1970; *Laughs, Etc.* produced London, 1973).   New York, Simon and Schuster, 1970.

*

Manuscript Collection: Boston University.

Theatrical Activities:
Director: **Play**—*Crazy October*, New Haven, Connecticut, 1958.
Actor: **Plays**—roles at the Pasadena Playhouse, California; in *The Zoo Story* by Edward Albee, Boston and Paris, 1961; title role in *Terrible Jim Fitch*, Chicago, 1965. **Films**—*In the French Style*, 1963; *Four Friends* (*Georgia's Friends*), 1981.

*   *   *

In the seven bizarre stories which comprise *The Sleep of Baby Filbertson* James Leo Herlihy first made clear his interest in the themes of loneliness, crippled emotions, and physical debility. The themes converge in his work to create a picture of the modern urban world as a purgatory, but a purgatory lightened somewhat by the pathos and respect with which the author presents his twisted characters. Readers of this collection frequently linked Herlihy's name with such gifted contemporaries as Truman Capote, James Purdy, and Flannery O'Connor.

All Fall Down, Herlihy's remarkable first novel, widely extended the dimensions of his ironic humor in chronicling the misadventures and the disintegration of a middle-class family. The father, a disillusioned socialist, declines into alcoholism and the mother into helpless inaction. One son has become a vagabond and petty criminal, and the other is a 16-year-old drop-out who imagines his older brother a great romantic rebel against bourgeois convention. Clinton, the younger son, eventually frees himself not only from his family but also from the projections of his own imagination, a process recorded in graphic detail in lengthy extracts from his journal. The very commonplace nature of Herlihy's characters lends an air of authenticity to the novel and intensifies the horror of their dilemmas by making them seem so constant and unavoidable.

This sense of horror was more intensely explored in *Midnight Cowboy*, the story of a simple-minded cowboy, Joe Buck, who travels to New York in the hope of making his fortune as a hustler. Instead, he is cast adrift on a sea of grotesques, eventually casting his lot with that of a crippled pickpocket, with whom he creates a community of love and grudging respect against the hostile world outside. When Ratso becomes ill, Joe cares for him, steals for him, and undertakes a quixotic journey to Florida in the hope that his friend may recover. *Midnight Cowboy* is a grim novel in which the author repeatedly exploits his own talent for depicting the grotesque. Nonetheless, because the central characters' needs are so basic and so human, they rise above the fashions of alienation, urban malaise, and sexual degeneracy which are often the gratuitous complements of contemporary fiction.

Gloria Random, the heroine of Herlihy's third novel, *The Season of the Witch*, runs away from home with a friend, a homosexual draft-evader. The novel records their adventures in New York City, Gloria's reunion with her father, and her eventual return to her mother. As a study of the geography of the generation gap, the novel oversimplifies and glamorizes the essential cultural schism which that term loosely designates. Nonetheless, *The Season of the Witch* is a memorable exploration of the growth of a sensitive, troubled consciousness as it struggles to find some correlation beween revolutionary hope and quotidian realities.

Herlihy is fascinated by society's rejects, by men and women whose lives seem doomed by their emotional needs and their longing, but who struggle to maintain some shred of human dignity in a world which seems remorseless in its devices for destroying the self. Such themes are also explored in Herlihy's plays, where the raucous spirit of black humor is even more pervasive than in the novels.

—David Galloway

HERSEY, John (Richard). American. Born in Tientsin, China, 17 June 1914. Educated at Hotchkiss School; Yale University, New Haven, Connecticut, B.A. 1936; Clare College, Cambridge (Mellon Fellow), 1936–37. Married 1) Frances Ann Cannon in 1940 (divorced, 1958), three sons and one daughter; 2) Barbara Day Kaufman in 1958, one daughter. Secretary to Sinclair Lewis, 1937; writer and correspondent, in China, Japan, the South Pacific, the Mediterranean and Russia, for *Time*, New York, 1937–45, *Life*, New York, 1944–46, and *The New Yorker*, 1945–46; editor and director of the writers' cooperative magazine *'47*, 1947–48. Fellow of Berkeley College, 1950–65, Master of Pierson College, 1965–70, Lecturer, 1971–76, Visiting Professor, 1976–77, and Adjunct Professor, 1977–84, now emeritus, Yale University; member of the Yale University Council Committee on the Humanities, 1951–56, and member, 1959–64, and Chairman, 1964–69, Yale University Council Committee on Yale College. Writer-in-Residence, American Academy in Rome, 1970–71. Member, National Citizens' Commission for the Public Schools, 1954–56; consultant, Fund for the Advancement of Education, 1954–56; Chairman, Connecticut Committee for the Gifted, 1954–57; delegate, White House Conference on Education, 1955; trustee, National Citizens' Council for the Public Schools, 1956–58; trustee, National Committee for Support of the Public Schools, 1962–68. Chairman, Connecticut Volunteers for Stevenson, 1952; member, Stevenson campaign staff, 1956. Member of the Council, 1946–71, and Vice-President, 1949–55, Authors League of America; delegate, P.E.N. Congress, Tokyo, 1958. Since 1946, member of the Council, and President, 1975–80, Authors League. Recipient: Pulitzer Prize, 1945; Anisfield-Wolf Award, 1950; Daroff Memorial Award, 1950; Sidney Hillman Foundation award, 1950; Yale University Howland Medal, 1952; Tuition Plan award, 1961; Sarah Josepha Hale Award, 1963. LL.D.: Washington and Jefferson College, Washington, Pennsylvania, 1946; University of New Haven, West Haven, Connecticut, 1975; M.A.: Yale University, 1947; L.H.D.: New School for Social Research, New York, 1950; D.H.L.: Dropsie College, Philadelphia, 1950; Litt.D.: Wesleyan University, Middletown, Connecticut, 1957; Bridgeport University, Connecticut, 1959; Clarkson College of Technology, Potsdam, New York, 1972; Syracuse University, New York, 1983; Yale University, 1984. Member, 1953, Secretary, 1961–76, and Chancellor, 1981–84, American Academy. Honorary Fellow, Clare College, Cambridge, 1967. Address: 420 Humphrey Street, New Haven, Connecticut 06511, U.S.A.

PUBLICATIONS

Novels

A Bell for Adano. New York, Knopf, 1944; London, Gollancz, 1945.
The Wall. New York, Knopf, and London, Hamish Hamilton, 1950.
The Marmot Drive. New York, Knopf, and London, Hamish Hamilton, 1953.
A Single Pebble. New York, Knopf, and London, Hamish Hamilton, 1956.
The War Lover. New York, Knopf, and London, Hamish Hamilton, 1959.
The Child Buyer. New York, Knopf, 1960; London, Hamish Hamilton, 1961.
White Lotus. New York, Knopf, and London, Hamish Hamilton, 1965.
Too Far to Walk. New York, Knopf, and London, Hamish Hamilton, 1966.
Under the Eye of the Storm. New York, Knopf, and London, Hamish Hamilton, 1967.
The Conspiracy. New York, Knopf, and London, Hamish Hamilton, 1972.
My Petition for More Space. New York, Knopf, 1974; London, Hamish Hamilton, 1975.
The Walnut Door. New York, Knopf, 1977; London, Macmillan, 1978.
The Call. New York, Knopf, 1985; London, Weidenfeld and Nicolson, 1986.

Uncollected Short Stories

"Joe Is Home Now," in *Life* (New York), 3 July 1944.
"The Breadline," in *Taken at the Flood*, edited by Ann Watkins. New York, Harper, 1946.
"The Death of Buchan Walsh," in *Atlantic* (Boston), April 1946.
"Pen," in *Atlantic* (Boston), June 1946.
"The Woman Who Took Gold Intravenously," in *Cosmopolitan* (New York), 1947.
"In Touch," in *Cosmopolitan* (New York), 1947.
"Short Wait," in *New Yorker*, 14 June 1947.
"Why Were You Sent Here?," in *The Best American Short Stories 1948*, edited by Martha Foley. Boston, Houghton Mifflin, 1948.

"Moment of Judgment," in *World's Best*, edited by Whit Burnett. New York, Dial Press, 1950.
"Peggety's Parcel of Shortcomings," in *Prize Stories 1951: The O. Henry Awards*, edited by Herschel Brickell. New York, Doubleday, 1951.
"Bridge over Dry Creek Bed," in *Sports Illustrated* (New York), 1972.

Other

Men on Bataan. New York, Knopf, 1942.
Into the Valley: A Skirmish of the Marines. New York, Knopf, 1943.
Hiroshima. New York, Knopf, and London, Penguin, 1946.
Here to Stay: Studies in Human Tenacity. London, Hamish Hamilton, 1962; New York, Knopf, 1963.
The Algiers Motel Incident. New York, Knopf, and London, Hamish Hamilton, 1968.
Robert Capa, with others. New York, Paragraphic, 1969.
Letter to the Alumni. New York, Knopf, 1970.
The President. New York, Knopf, 1975.
Aspects of the Presidency: Truman and Ford in Office. New Haven, Connecticut, Ticknor and Fields, 1980.

Editor, *Ralph Ellison: A Collection of Critical Essays*. Englewood Cliffs, New Jersey, Prentice Hall, 1973.
Editor, *The Writer's Craft*. New York, Knopf, 1974.

*

Bibliography: *John Hersey and James Agee: A Reference Guide* by Nancy Lyman Huse, Boston, Hall, and London, Prior, 1978.

Manuscript Collection: Yale University Library, New Haven, Connecticut.

Critical Studies: *John Hersey* by David Sanders, New York, Twayne, 1967; *The Survival Tales of John Hersey* by Nancy Lyman Huse, Troy, New York, Whitston, 1983.

John Hersey comments:

I believe that a writer should be reticent about himself and his work. Ideally he should, I feel, appear in his books and nowhere else in public. Each of his works entails a double act of creation: he makes one part of the finished work, but until the reader brings his imagination and experience to bear on it, the book does not come to life, does not even *exist* as a book. I do not think that the writer should attempt to influence the second half of this partnership of makers by stating intentions, his "meaning." The writing process is a mysterious one; the writer works within a magic circle—and his intentions, if indeed he understands them himself, may not have much to do with the effect he produces. If he is honest and at all able, the work speaks his deepest self, its themes derive from his view of humanity, its style comes from the cadences and vibrations of his innermost voice. The work interprets him better than he can interpret the work.

*   *   *

John Hersey, who once described himself as a novelist of contemporary history, began his writing career as a reporter for *Time* and *Life* with his earliest dispatches collected as *Men on Bataan* and *Into the Valley*. His first novel, *A Bell for Adano*, was a simple, vivid story based on incidents he had seen while reporting American military government in Sicily. It became

widely read and won Hersey a Pulitzer Prize on V-E Day. In 1946 he visited Hiroshima, interviewed survivors of the first atomic bomb attack, and wrote the *New Yorker* article that had an extraordinary impact as the first personal—and, therefore, comprehensible—account of the event.

In *Hiroshima* and later in his great novel *The Wall*, Hersey drew from the victims themselves the understanding of history that neither he nor anyone else had gained in reporting the war. The six Hiroshima residents told him how they had lived before the bomb struck, why they were not killed, and precisely how illness, exhaustion, and sorrow had accompanied their survival. He had no comparable opportunity to interview participants in the Warsaw ghetto uprising, but this holocaust obsessed him as much as the other. He read such documentary evidence as *The Black Book of the Polish Jewry*, listened to victims' eyewitness accounts as sight-translated by Polish Jews who had escaped to America, and created a story in the form of Noach Levinson's archive. This fictional scholar records not merely the events leading through four years to the uprisings, but also every occurrence that he feels may help to explain the culture under attack. The result is an achievement that defines the novel of contemporary history: the narrative of an event with its full historic implications and without any melodramatic action or a single sentimental cliché.

Hersey's novels since *The Wall* have in common the author's constant attention to large social issues. In most of these books he attempts some experiment in narrative form as appropriate as Noach Levinson's archive was to *The Wall*. He failed in *The Marmot Drive*, a dim allegory about witch-hunting in the heyday of Joseph McCarthy. *A Single Pebble*, a short novel reaching into his Chinese background, beautifully illuminates the limitations of technology as the way to happiness. In *The War Lover* Hersey's narrator, an American bombardier, fights psychotic changes in his war-loving pilot, yearns for his own survival, and contradicts Hersey's earlier accounts in *Life* of the necessarily impersonal perspective that flyers developed through their bombsights.

The Child Buyer is Hersey's extended irony on an educational system that neglects the bright child. A whole town acquiesces in selling ten-year-old Barry Rudd to a "defense" firm, which, by tying off his senses, will try to turn him into a human computer capable of reaching an I.Q. of 1000. The story, told in the form of the record of a legislative committee hearing, is often awkward, but it is luminous at the moment when the child himself joins the conspiracy "because life at U Lympho might at least be *interesting*." In *White Lotus* Hersey's intention was nothing less than to make white readers feel what it would be like if they were an oppressed minority taken as slaves from America after a late 20th-century conquest by the Chinese. The author's admiration for Ralph Ellison is apparent, but, unfortunately, his story cannot, like Ellison's, encompass the whole history of a culture. With less poetry or humor than Ellison's narrator, White Lotus, still a young woman as she ends her story, must account for the full outline of parallels from her capture as a teenager up to her celebrity as a civil rights leader.

Too Far to Walk employs the Faust legend to describe college unrest of the late 1960's and perhaps is a further ironic reflection on themes from *The Child Buyer*. *Under the Eye of the Storm* opposes the behavior of two yachtsmen, a technologist and a humanist, struggling to bring their boat in from the sea. These comparatively slight books were followed in the 1970's by three remarkable allegories that recall *The Single Pebble* and *The Child Buyer* in lucidity and feeling. *The Conspiracy*, an account of a plot to overthrow Nero, states not only that a writer's duty is to write, but that he most nearly overcomes his enemies when he is lost to anything but his writing. Lucan, the poet, and Tigellinus, the secret policeman, are among Hersey's strongest and subtlest characters. The narrator of *My Petition for More Space* tells his story in the time that it takes him to move in a line of human beings, four abreast, three-quarters of a mile long to the window where he will have his only chance to tell authorities why he should be granted more than his allotted cubicle. The credibility that had eluded Hersey in *White Lotus* is immediate and painful in this novel, although he is again almost trapped by his ingenuity with this story as bleak and cramped as its premise. The hero and heroine of *The Walnut Door* are isolated drop-outs who meet after years of drifting through the wreckage of the student revolution. Without denying sympathies he had expressed as a college master at Yale, Hersey develops a plot in which erotic discoveries rescue his characters from the empty failure of their early ideals.

Revisiting China in the early 1980's, Hersey strayed from his observations of a new nation to seek traces of the missionary world of his Tientsin childhood. "One of the things I was most interested in ...," he wrote in his *New Yorker* report of the trip, "was whether my parents' lives had been worth living." That curiosity led to *The Call*, which rivals *The Wall* as a novel of contemporary history and, in accounting for his parents' mission, goes deeper than any of Hersey's work into the meaning of his own existence. *The Call* is the story of the career of an imaginary American YMCA secretary (not Roscoe Hersey) from 1905 to the chaos after the end of Japanese internment. The man is so "stupefied by his work" that when he is cut off from it and compelled to read and think, he disbelieves in the God he has served. It is a measure of this novel's power that the question of whether the Herseys' lives were worth living cannot be answered easily—not even by praising their son's art which has inscribed their lives so memorably on the roll of a lost endeavor.

—David Sanders

HIGGINS, Aidan. Irish. Born in Celbridge, County Kildare, 3 March 1927. Educated at Celbridge Covent; Killashee Preparatory School; Clongowes Wood College. Married Jill Damaris Anders in 1955; three sons. Copywriter, Domas Advertising, Dublin, in the early 1950's; factory hand, extrusion moulder, and storeman, London, in the mid-1950's; puppet-operator, John Wright's marionettes, in Europe, South Africa and Rhodesia, 1958–60; script-writer, Filmlets (advertising films), Johannesburg, 1960–61. Recipient: British Arts Council grants; James Tait Black Memorial Prize, 1967; DAAD grant (Berlin), 1969; Irish Academy of Letters award, 1970; American-Irish Foundation grant, 1977. Lives in London. Address: c/o Allison and Busby Ltd., 6-A Noel Street, London W1V 3RB, England.

PUBLICATIONS

Novels

Langrishe, Go Down.   London, Calder and Boyars, and New York, Grove Press, 1966.
Balcony of Europe.   London, Calder and Boyars, and New York, Delacorte Press, 1972.

Scenes from a Receding Past.   London, Calder, and New York, Riverrun Press, 1977.
Bornholm Night-Ferry.   Dingle, County Kerry, Brandon, and London, Allison and Busby, 1983.

Short Stories

Felo de Se.   London, Calder, 1960; as *Killachter Meadow*, New York, Grove Press, 1961; revised edition, as *Asylum and Other Stories*, Calder, 1978; New York, Riverrun Press, 1979.

Plays

Radio Plays (UK): *Assassination*, 1973; *Imperfect Sympathies*, 1977; *Discords of Good Humour*, 1982; *Vanishing Heroes*, 1983; *Texts for the Air*, 1983; *Winter Is Coming*, 1983; *Tomb of Dreams*, 1984 (Ireland); *Zoo Station*, 1985.

Other

Images of Africa: Diary 1956–60.   London, Calder and Boyars, 1971.

Editor, *A Century of Short Stories.*   London, Cape, 1977.
Editor, *Colossal Gongorr and the Turkes of Mars*, by Carl, Julien, and Elwin Higgins.   London, Cape, 1979.

*

Manuscript Collection: University of Victoria, British Columbia.

Critical Studies: by David Holloway, in *The Bookman* (London), December 1965; "Maker's Language" by Vernon Scannell, in *Spectator* (London), 11 February 1966; in *New Leader* (London), 25 September 1967; Morris Beja, in *Irish University Review* (Dublin), Autumn 1973; "Aidan Higgins Issue" of *Review of Contemporary Fiction* (Elmwood Park, Illinois), Spring 1983.

*   *   *

In his attempt to escape the traditional constraints of Irish fiction, Aidan Higgins has emerged as an Irish internationalist, firmly grounded in his Irish experience and yet devoted to an extensive view. In *Asylum and Other Stories* he drifts from the delapidated Irish big house of "Killaghter Meadow" through the seedy England of "Asylum" and the decadent German cosmopolitanism of "Winter Offensive" to the stultifying South Africa of "Southfall on Cape Piscator." The collection displays an amalgam of literary sources—Higgins's answer to Frank O'Connor's "lonely voice." Among his characters are Beckettian down-outs such as Eddy Brazill in "Asylum," whose rise from hopelessness to mindlessness is synchronised with the fall to lunacy of his Anglo-Irish alcoholic benefactor. There is Borges's fascination with doubles and mirrors, and Proust's with time and space. And Higgins's scenery is as barren as Eliot's waste land. Yet the collection is dominated by the influence of Joyce's *Dubliners*. Higgins's "leaded windows" also have "blind views," and his inert characters are also unable to share in any form of intercourse. Like Joyce, Higgins enlivens morbidity with flashes of—mostly verbal—irony, as when he has "an angelic line of chorus girls" in "Asylum" sing "*Coming over Jordan* out of key." In "Winter Offensive," irony gives way to a sarcastic depiction of Herr Bausch's "sole preoccupation," "venery not so pure not so simple."

Langrishe, Go Down details the sinking of the languid inhabitants of the big house that in "Killaghter Meadow" was "flooded unsolicited on a mixed bag of male and female gentry come to pay ... their last respects." The novel is Higgins's dismissal of Irish regional fiction in the light of major international events. As the Langrishe sisters, vestiges of the big house, prepare for their dying fall, Germany is rising to war. The novel is framed by political events; when, at the start, Helen Langrishe suffers the nausea of her marvellously detailed bus-ride home, the paper on her lap reports the Spanish Civil War, and when she dies in the end a chapter factually reports Germany's invasion of Austria. The main part of the book is set in 1932 and skilfully combines Irishism and internationalism in the love affair of Imogen Langrishe, the only big house maiden with a trace of sexuality, and the German Otto Beck, a toned-down version of Herr Bausch, and Higgins's least constrained character. The German hunter's invasion of Springfield and Imogen, his poaching on the estate and his indifferent departure parallel the factual framework of the novel.

Although *Balcony of Europe* begins and ends in grey Ireland, it is not concerned with the tensions between Irish fiction and world events. The only reminders of the external reality are the bombers that continually contour the sky over Andalusia, where the main part of the book, the adulterous affair between Dan Ruttle, passionate Irish artist, and the American Jewess, Charlotte Bayless, is set. Instead, Ruttle's experiences are probed in an almost continuous first-person narrative which attempts to do for fiction what Husserl did for philosophy. In *Langrishe*, Higgins's interest in phenomenology remained subservient to the narrative, but it determines the shape of *Balcony*. Higgins tries to coalesce the moment of experience and expression. Plot is largely sacrificed for a number of cognitive tableaux, held together by cross-references and a distinctively idiosyncratic voice. As a result, the novel is dominated by a technique of Beckettian repetitions, ellipses, and grammatical distortions to which are added spices of Sterne and numerous quotations from Yeats. Rather than drawing us to Dan Ruttle's point of view, Higgins's technique emphasises his laboured and insistent symbolism. Higgins, for example, transforms the eagles from *A Portrait of the Artist* into the bombers that in turn are associated with the ghost of Ruttle's mother flying to heaven and with a football that is kicked in the air on a Spanish beach.

Scenes from a Receding Past adds further scraps to the memory of Dan Ruttle from his early childhood and adolescence to his early maturity. The book is set in Sligo, but we are told in a note that Sligo stands for Celbridge, the author's birthplace and the parish near the big house in *Langrishe*, which bears out Higgins's contention that most of his books follow his life "like slug-trails." Again, Joyce is very much in evidence in verbal reminiscences. Young Ruttle's *bildung* is quite similar to young Stephen's. The pangs of growing up are projected unto Ruttle's brother, the inflexible and intransigent Wally, who ends up in a lunatic asylum. Interleaved are records, and records of records, including a—faulty—Dutch Mass Card, a clothes list for La Sainte Union Convent, and two pages from the score book for the Fifth Oval, August 20–23, 1938. In the final part, Ruttle meets and woos Olivia Orr, a girl from New Zealand who hovers in the background of *Balcony of Europe* as his unhappy wife; present and glimpses of their past intermingle in a mixture of mawkish poetry and matter-of-fact prose that is disrupted by a page-long list of names for the baby which Olivia loses in her fifth month.

The epistolary form of *Bornholm Night-Ferry* is a logical follow-up to the snap-shot technique of *Scenes from a Receding Past*. It enables Higgins to combine successfully post-modernism and his timeless gift for detail. The novel is as full of linguistic distortions, chronological jumps, and occasional lyricism as any of his works, but they are sustained by the form and add to the tension of the extra-marital affair of a Danish girl with poor English and an Irish writer with poor commonsense. And between Elin Marstrander's tell-tale errors in English and Finn Fitzgerald's passionate errors in decorum, Higgins introduces an implied narrator-as-archivist who identifies letters and diaries as they come to him, far more in charge than his camouflaged counterpart who emerged on the last page of *Balcony of Europe* to ask us if we "are still awake."

—Peter G.W. van de Kamp

HIGGINS, George V(incent). American. Born in Brockton, Massachusetts, 13 November 1939. Educated at Rockland High School, Massachusetts; Boston College, A.B. in English 1961; Stanford University, California, 1961–62, M.A. 1965; Boston College Law School, Brighton, Massachusetts, J.D. 1967; admitted to the Massachusetts Bar, 1967. Married 1) Elizabeth Mulkerin in 1965 (divorced, 1979), one daughter and one son; 2) Loretta Lucas Cubberley in 1979. Reporter, *Journal* and *Evening Bulletin*, Providence, Rhode Island, 1962–63; bureau correspondent, Springfield, Massachusetts, 1963–64, and newsman, Boston, 1964, Associated Press; researcher, Guterman Horvitz and Rubin, attorneys, Boston, 1966–67; legal assistant, Administrative Division and Organized Crime Section, 1967, Deputy Assistant Attorney General, 1967–69, and Assistant Attorney General, 1969–70, Commonwealth of Massachusetts; Assistant U.S. Attorney for the District of Massachusetts, 1970–73, and Special Assistant U.S. Attorney, 1973–74; President, George V. Higgins, Inc., Boston, 1973–78; partner, Griffin and Higgins, Boston, 1978–82. Consultant, National Institute of Law Enforcement and Criminal Law, Washington, D.C., 1970–71; Instructor in Trial Practice, Boston College Law School, 1973–74 and 1978–79; columnist, Boston *Herald American*, 1977–79, Boston *Globe*, 1979–85, and *Wall Street Journal*, since 1984. Address: 15 Brush Hill Lane, Milton, Massachusetts 02186, U.S.A.

PUBLICATIONS

Novels

The Friends of Eddie Coyle. New York, Knopf, and London, Secker and Warburg, 1972.
The Digger's Game. New York, Knopf, and London, Secker and Warburg, 1973.
Cogan's Trade. New York, Knopf, and London, Secker and Warburg, 1974.
A City on a Hill. New York, Knopf, and London, Secker and Warburg, 1975.
The Judgment of Deke Hunter. Boston, Little Brown, and London, Secker and Warburg, 1976.
Dreamland. Boston, Little Brown, and London, Secker and Warburg, 1977.
A Year or So with Edgar. New York, Harper, and London, Secker and Warburg, 1979.
Kennedy for the Defense. New York, Knopf, and London, Secker and Warburg, 1980.

The Rat on Fire. New York, Knopf, and London, Secker and Warburg, 1981.
The Patriot Game. New York, Knopf, and London, Secker and Warburg, 1982.
A Choice of Enemies. New York, Knopf, and London, Secker and Warburg, 1984.
Penance for Jerry Kennedy. New York, Knopf, and London, Deutsch, 1985.
Impostors. New York, Holt Rinehart, and London, Deutsch, 1986.

Short Story

Old Earl Died Pulling Traps. Columbia, South Carolina, Bruccoli Clark, 1984.

Uncollected Short Stories

"All Day Was All There Was," in *Arizona Quarterly* (Tucson), Spring 1963.
"Mass in Time of War," in *Cimarron Review* (Stillwater, Oklahoma), September 1969.
"Something Dirty You Could Keep," in *Massachusetts Review* (Amherst), Autumn 1969.
"Dillon Explained That He Was Frightened," in *North American Review* (Cedar Falls, Iowa), Fall 1970.
"The Habits of Animals, The Progress of the Seasons," in *The Best American Short Stories 1973*, edited by Martha Foley. Boston, Houghton Mifflin, 1973.
"Two Cautionary Tales: Donnelly's Uncle and The Original Watercourse," in *North American Review* (Cedar Falls, Iowa), Winter 1974.
"Warm for September" and "A Place of Comfort, Light, and Hope," in *North American Review* (Cedar Falls, Iowa), Spring 1977.
"Dublin Coat," in *Harper's* (New York), August 1980.
"Adults," in *Playboy* (Chicago), December 1982.
"Devlin's Wake," in *Playboy* (Chicago), December 1983.
"Ducks and Other Citizens," in *Hudson Review* (New York), Winter 1983–84.
"A Case of Chivas Regal," in *Black Mask Quarterly 1* (Orlando, Florida), 1985.
"Mother's Day," in *Playboy* (Chicago), March 1985.
"The Balance of the Day," in *Gentlemen's Quarterly* (New York), November 1985.
"The Devil Is Real," in *Playboy* (Chicago), March 1986.

Other

The Friends of Richard Nixon. Boston, Little Brown, 1975.
Style Versus Substance: Boston, Kevin White, and the Politics of Illusion. New York, Macmillan, 1984.

*

George V. Higgins comments:

In retrospect I think *A Choice of Enemies* represented some sort of watershed in my development as a writer. At the time I was not aware that I was doing things that I had not done before, but it seems to me now that that book was the fruition of an evolutionary development I began with *The Friends of Eddie Coyle* twelve years before. *Coyle* although the first published was the fifteenth book I had written. I did not plan to write it almost entirely in dialogue; that just seemed the most efficient way of telling the story. Similarly, with *Enemies*, I did not intentionally strive to combine storytelling with trial practice, but as it turned out that was what I did.

Trial lawyers, though lacking the liberties of novelists to usher witnesses back and forth to lend chronological order to the presentation, nevertheless employ those summoned as surrogate narrators, each adding his or her piece to make the puzzle whole. Trial lawyers—barristers, if you like—depend upon the triers of fact (whether jurors or judges) to inspect the testimony laid before them and arrive at their own conclusions. And trial lawyers are uncomfortably aware, as they go about their tasks, that those judgments of what happened may disagree with their own.

It distresses me when slothful or stupid readers declare that my books have no plots. Such reactions indicate that the readers have not been paying attention. The characters do not appear to provide cheap yucks; they appear when they do because they are telling their own stories. When it works right, I am replacing the omniscient author with the omniscient reader. That reader for the money gets what amounts to a valid warrant to observe and to eavesdrop upon all the actions and conversations material to the unfolding story. At the end, the reader should be able to judge whether their conduct was morally and ethically good. I won't do it for him.

I realize this demands a good deal of the reader. I recognize that not all readers desire quite so much exercise. Nevertheless, the books that I have most enjoyed have been those by writers who made me partner in their schemes, and since I am the first reader as well as the scribbler, those are the kind I try to write. After all, if we're not going to have any fun doing this, why bother?

*   *   *

George V. Higgins has a marvelous ear for cadence and verbal tone, so his talky novels appeal to us first of all because they promise to satisfy our inherent interest in story-telling. But promoters of Higgins's fiction cannot rest content with mere story-telling. Read Higgins, they say, for a picture of criminal life as it really is. Meanwhile his critics glance away from the undoubted accomplishment of style in the novels to wonder if it makes sense to consider them some sort of answer to Raymond Chandler's call in "The Simple Art of Murder" for realistic fiction of the mean streets, a demonstration that the crime story can be important writing too.

Certainly the talk in Higgins's stories goes beyond titillation to disclose the culture of the underworld. In *The Digger's Game* and *Cogan's Trade* we discover the system of specialization and division of labor in the contemporary criminal world. Loan sharking, fraudulent travel agencies, robbery, and fencing of stolen goods from dogs to TV's have their peculiar principles of operation and their particular practitioners. Similarly, conversation among these specialists reveals the violent means by which a scheme of order is enforced in the predatory criminal environment. On a more subtle level the manner of talk communicates a pattern of values. *The Friends of Eddie Coyle* adumbrates criminal activity as a distorted mirror image of American social mobility, and like the other novels focused on criminals, demonstrates the fact that a desire for commodity-based living and sensual gratification is as central to underworld life as it is to respectable bourgeois culture.

It might be expected that amoral frankness about the ways of the underworld might appear attractive in contrast to the hypocrisy in the legitimate world, but Higgins does nothing to suggest that. Neither do we find that the amusing passages of sarcastic or wise-guy dialogue endear the characters to us. On the other hand, Higgins makes no effort to represent hoods as social victims either. Nearly all have spent time in prison, lost opportunities, and experienced failure in personal relationships. Absent any other explanation, they have chosen to live as they do. Their desires and mistakes, bigotry and predaciousness are traits of character. That's all.

With *A City on a Hill* and *A Choice of Enemies* Higgins tries his narrative technique in a new area, the realm of political insiders, and in the process reveals a limitation. The connecting thread among the dialogues in the first book is the entirely legitimate effort to advance the candidacy of a politician who might restore credibility to national government after Watergate. The effort fails for lack of interest among potential supporters of the candidate, but the whole attempt would seem to be doomed by the failure of character Higgins reveals in his leading figures' speech. Like their counterparts in the previous novels, they too live deracinated lives waiting for the big hit. *A Choice of Enemies* presents the last days of Bernie Morgan as Speaker of the Massachusetts lower legislative house. The attorneys in a labor racketeer's trial, a contractor learning the ways of the pay-off in the big time, the principals in an investigative commission, and Morgan's right hand man providing the angles to view Morgan's machine expose themselves motivated by greed, typified by cynicism and bigotry, and not significantly different from violent thugs. In both novels the convoluted dialogue reminds us how one-dimensional stylized conversation really is. The illusion of overheard speech permits us to consider characters as human while they speak, but the milieu created by the mingling of characters in the plot has the quality of caricature. Something important has been left out.

The same charges can be leveled against *Dreamland, A Year or So with Edgar*, and *The Rat on Fire*. In the book about Edgar the narrator is an alcoholic newspaper reporter whose rambling tale cannot conceal the stereotype, while the story of a building torched by an arsonist who sends a burning rat up inside its walls repeats the structure of unvaried chapters of overheard dialogue without intrusion of interpretive statement either by the author or by a normative character.

In writing so committed to exclusion of an evaluative perspective or the provision of information beyond what can be given through basic physical descriptions or the voices of characters in conversation, the only way to get beyond the caricature of a naturalistic world is by selection of narrators who will take a sidelong look at ethical issues. So, *The Judgment of Deke Hunter*, a novel concerning the career of a plainclothes officer in the Massachusetts State Police, involves an exploration of Deke's discovery of the will to become the best cop he can be, regardless of personal disappointments and without exceptional compromise with a frustratingly imperfect criminal justice system. *Kennedy for the Defense* continues in this direction by introducing as narrator a man characterized by his wife as Boston's "classiest, sleazy criminal lawyer." Kennedy handles the cases of such small time criminals as populate Higgins's first novels, so there is plenty of opportunity for the talk of hoodlums. But there is in addition Kennedy himself who is without illusion rather than incapable of it. He knows what sort of people he has to talk to, and his own aggressive talk is his means of sustaining control over the situations he finds himself in so that he can accomplish the not inconsiderable task of providing clients their Constitutional right to the best possible defense. The new Kennedy novel, *Penance for Jerry Kennedy*, presents the counsellor with a mid-life crisis in career and marriage as his antagonism for an incompetent judge makes him the object of attacks on TV and by the IRS and his feeling of a loss of control over his life results in hostility to his family. The ultimate problem for Kennedy is the world he works in, and as Raymond Chandler said, "it is not a very

fragrant world, but it is the world you live in." But the attempt to reconcile the demands of reality and integrity can be the stuff of ethical drama, as it is in Higgins's novels about Hunter and Kennedy.

As for the other novels, it is questionable if they deserve the reputation for telling "the real story," because, odd as it may seem, they are not complete stories. Lacking explanation of why and how the characters became the figures they present in their wonderfully rendered speech, and lacking implied statement of what significance those characters hold for the society reading about them, the narratives are materials not yet shaped by an intelligence that sees beyond their surface.

—John M. Reilly

HIGHSMITH, (Mary) Patricia (née Plangman). American. Born in Fort Worth, Texas, 19 January 1921; grew up in New York. Educated at Barnard College, New York, B.A. 1942. Has lived in Europe since 1963. Recipient: Grand Prix de Littérature Policière, 1957; Crime Writers Association Silver Dagger, 1964. Agent: Diogenes Verlag, Sprecherstrasse 8, CH-8032 Zurich, Switzerland.

PUBLICATIONS

Novels

Strangers on a Train. New York, Harper, and London, Cresset Press, 1950.
The Price of Salt (as Claire Morgan). New York, Coward McCann, 1952.
The Blunderer. New York, Coward McCann, 1954; London, Cresset Press, 1956; as *Lament for a Lover*, New York, Popular Library, 1956.
The Talented Mr. Ripley. New York, Coward McCann, 1955; London, Cresset Press, 1957.
Deep Water. New York, Harper, 1957; London, Heinemann, 1958.
A Game for the Living. New York, Harper, 1958; London, Heinemann, 1959.
This Sweet Sickness. New York, Harper, 1960; London, Heinemann, 1961.
The Cry of the Owl. New York, Harper, 1962; London, Heinemann, 1963.
The Two Faces of January. New York, Doubleday, and London, Heinemann, 1964.
The Glass Cell. New York, Doubleday, 1964; London, Heinemann, 1965.
The Story-Teller. New York, Doubleday, 1965; as *A Suspension of Mercy*, London, Heinemann, 1965.
Those Who Walk Away. New York, Doubleday, and London, Heinemann, 1967.
The Tremor of Forgery. New York, Doubleday, and London, Heinemann, 1969.
Ripley under Ground. New York, Doubleday, 1970; London, Heinemann, 1971.
A Dog's Ransom. New York, Knopf, and London, Heinemann, 1972.
Ripley's Game. New York, Knopf, and London, Heinemann, 1974.
Edith's Diary. New York, Simon and Schuster, and London, Heinemann, 1977.

The Boy Who Followed Ripley. New York, Lippincott, and London, Heinemann, 1980.
People Who Knock on the Door. London, Heinemann, 1983; New York, Penzler, 1985.
Found in the Street. London, Heinemann, 1986.

Short Stories

The Snail-Watcher and Other Stories. New York, Doubleday, 1970; as *Eleven*, London, Heinemann, 1970.
Kleine Geschichten für Weiberfeinde. Zurich, Diogenes, 1974; as *Little Tales of Misogyny*, London, Heinemann, 1977.
The Animal-Lover's Book of Beastly Murder. London, Heinemann, 1975.
Slowly, Slowly in the Wind. London, Heinemann, 1979.
The Black House. London, Heinemann, 1981.
Mermaids on the Golf Course and Other Stories. London, Heinemann, 1985.

Other

Miranda the Panda Is on the Veranda (for children), with Doris Sanders. New York, Coward McCann, 1958.
Plotting and Writing Suspense Fiction. Boston, The Writer, 1966; revised edition, 1981; London, Poplar Press, 1983.

*

Critical Studies: by Julian Symons, in *London Magazine*, June 1969; *Über Patricia Highsmith* edited by Franz Cavigelli and Fritz Senn, Zurich, Diogenes, 1980.

Patricia Highsmith comments:

I am said to write stories of psychological terror and suspense, but as I think all novels are psychological I cannot understand why this quality is so often singled out in my writing. My main characters, or heroes, are often the culprits, and murderers, and so my books have never any element of mystery. On the contrary, my chief goal is clarity, and if possible an explanation of criminal behaviour.

*   *   *

A profound moral ambivalence is evoked by the four Ripley novels which Patricia Highsmith has so far published. An American living in France, Tom Ripley is polite, sophisticated, intelligent, and charming, a considerate husband to his comfort-loving wife. He has a connoisseur's taste and, though an embezzler, might easily pass as the best type of gentleman crook. The only trouble is, he is also a resourceful, ruthless killer. Ripley's character is his destiny and, confronted by it, we want—and do not want—him to be caught. However we may disapprove of him, we are entranced by permutations of an evil which transcend the environmental circumstances which have shaped him.

Highsmith's finest creation, Ripley is no ordinary psychopath. He prefers not to kill and does so reluctantly and not always with premeditation. He is a complex character, and that complexity is most evident in the fourth novel, *The Boy Who Followed Ripley*, in which Ripley takes under his wayward protection a patricidal and deeply troubled adolescent.

As Highsmith remarks in *Plotting and Writing Suspense Fiction* (for all its practicality, less a how-to book than an invaluable guide to the author's imaginative sources and narrative methods), the theme "used over and over again in my novels is the relationship between two men, usually quite different in make-up, sometimes an obvious contrast in good and evil, sometimes merely ill-matched friends." (This doubleness—and the villain's complicated charm—was brilliantly rendered in *Strangers on a Train*, the film which Alfred Hitchcock made from Highsmith's first novel.) By the author's own count, such pairing occurs in seven novels. Besides Charley Bruno/Guy Haines in *Strangers on a Train*, and Tom Ripley/Frank Pierson in *The Boy Who Followed Ripley*, other conspicuous examples include Gawill and Carter in *The Glass Cell*, Sydney and Alex in *The Story-Teller*, Ripley and Dickie Greenleaf in *The Talented Mr. Ripley*, Rydal and Chester in *The Two Faces of January*, and Ray and Coleman in *Those Who Walk Away*. These men often exchange alibis and aliases, and share various degrees of complicity and guilt. An interesting variation occurs in *This Sweet Sickness*: here the protagonist splits into David and his alias, Neumeister. In any case, Highsmith's use of a dual point of view lends itself to incremental tension.

Like Graham Greene, a novelist whom she much admires, Highsmith makes her novels very much of a piece in mood and atmosphere. Certain themes and characters recur as masterful variations on a central key. The kindly older woman perhaps modeled on the grandmother who raised the author; the emotionally constricted young man fixed on an iconic female figure; the older, outwardly dapper, inwardly sleazy con-man; the vain, pretty, amoral young woman—all come into frequent play.

The ruses of psychic defenses, of consistent self-delusion, are typical interests. Characteristically, Highsmith sends her characters down a path toward doom, and the fact that they sometimes do not deserve their fate can make for *almost* unbearable reading. The unjustly convicted Philip Carter in *The Glass Cell* is savagely tortured by prison guards and becomes a morphine addict. Paroled, he is driven to a crime and this time it is not swindling, but murder. Edith in *Edith's Diary* has her husband desert her for another woman, leaving his aged uncle in her unwilling care; her son grows up to become a self-obsessed blimp. With calm, almost icy care, Highsmith plots Edith's disintegration through the pages of her wish-fulfilling diary.

Rightly, Highsmith does not care to be labeled merely a genre-author; in fact, respectful British and European critics have not aped their American counterparts in doing so. She is a crime novelist who rejects puzzles, gimmicks, and gratuitous violence. A recent novel, *People Who Knock on the Door*, has a teenage protagonist who is not a murderer, though Arthur Alderman does benefit from the murder in that he is simultaneously rid of his troublesome younger brother Robbie, the murderer, and the victim, their tyrannical father Richard. But wider social preoccupations are present: the story-line is based on Richard's involvement in the conservative fundamentalist revival in America.

It should be added that Highsmith's extreme authorial detachment, spare, incisive descriptions, and shrewd pacing work best in more narrowly focussed novels like *This Sweet Sickness* and *The Cry of the Owl*. On the other hand, Highsmith's short fiction collected in books like *Slowly, Slowly in the Wind* and much of it first published in periodicals like *Ellery Queen's Mystery Magazine*, though skilfully devised, is inferior to her novels. In fact, her work is least impressive in gatherings of extremely short fiction like *Little Tales of Misogyny*, the mordancy of that book becoming intrusive and even arch. With more space but a limited number of characters, the author is able superbly to unravel her sequence of deadly events.

—Fraser Sutherland

HILL, Carol (née Dechellis). American. Born in New Jersey, 20 January 1942. Educated at Chatham College, Pittsburgh, 1957–61, B.A. 1961. Publicist, Crown Publishers, 1965–67, and Bernard Geis Associates, 1967–69, both New York; publicist, 1969–71, and editor, 1971–73, Pantheon Books, New York; publicity manager, Random House, New York, 1973–74; senior editor, William Morrow, publishers, New York, 1974–76; senior editor, editor-in-chief, Vice-President, and Publisher, Harcourt Brace Jovanovich, New York, 1976–79. Since 1980, full-time writer. Formerly, actress at Judson Poets Theatre, New York, and in summer stock, Gateway Playhouse, New Jersey. Agent: Liz Darhansoff Literary Agency, 1220 Park Avenue, New York, New York 10128. Address: 2 Fifth Avenue, Apartment 19-U, New York, New York 10011, U.S.A.

PUBLICATIONS

Novels

Jeremiah 8:20. New York, Random House, 1970.
Let's Fall in Love. New York, Random House, 1974; London, Quartet, 1975.
An Unmarried Woman (novelization of screenplay). New York, Avon, and London, Coronet, 1978.
The Eleven Million Mile High Dancer. New York, Holt Rinehart, 1985.

Uncollected Short Stories

"The Shameless Shiksa," in *Playboy* (Chicago), September 1969.
"Gone," in *Viva* (New York), November 1974.
"Lovers," in *Viva* (New York), April 1975.

Play

Mother Loves (produced New York, 1967).

Other

Subsistence U.S.A., photographs by Bruce Davidson, edited by Jamie Shalleck. New York, Holt Rinehart, 1973.

*

Critical Studies: by Christopher Ricks, in *New York Review of Books*, July 1970; Annie Gottleib, in *New York Times Book Review*, 14 April 1975; Emily Prager, in *New York Times Book Review*, 31 March 1985; Carolyn See, in *Los Angeles Times Book Review*, 5 May 1985.

*   *   *

Carol Hill writes with a wit and sense of the absurd that some critics have likened to the bizarre humor found in the novels of Tom Robbins. Her characters are varied, genuine,

and somewhat offbeat. The protagonists usually find themselves in absurd situations sometimes of their own making, but often coming as a surprise. Contemporary issues are interwoven in the plots, although they are not necessarily central to the stories.

In her first novel, *Jeremiah 8:20*, peace marchers protesting the war in Vietnam and problems of racial integration affect the rather unusual hero of this novel. Jeremiah Francis Scanlon, fat, balding, and 39, is a bookkeeper of mediocre abilities who has worked for the same company for almost 20 years. After years of living in the protective environment of his parents' suburban home he has taken the plunge and moved to New York City, not far from his place of employment. He rents a room in a boarding house that comes complete with a cast of strange and unusual characters. Hill's talent for delineating a varied array of individuals is evident in her description of Jeremiah, the social misfit; Miles, a part-time actor who specializes in female roles and is often seen prancing around the house in full costume and makeup; his friend Jocko, a pseudo-revolutionary and a cynic who excels in debate and delights in flustering his opponent. There are also two ladies: a prim old maid, and a wasp-tongued librarian who secretly yearns for Jocko. Although Jeremiah seems the most unlikely sort of protagonist to carry a novel, Hill makes us care for this pathetic, befuddled man who suffers great loneliness and depair. He does not, however, give up on life, but in a strangely courageous way keeps seeking an answer to his misery. Admittedly the answer he comes up with—that there is a secret held by Negroes that will end all his problems—seems absurd, but we have come to know Jeremiah so well that we can believe he would believe such nonsense.

The humor in *Jeremiah* is dark, though not oppressive. In Hill's next two novels the tone is lighter. *Let's Fall in Love* has a $10,000-a-shot hooker caught up in a web of murder and intrigue. This book has plenty of sex, including some very strange forms of coupling, a considerable departure from her first novel (about which, she says, people complained because there was not enough sex). *Let's Fall in Love* offers Hill's usual humor, and satire that some readers may find shocking, others erotic. Although this novel sold well, in the author's own estimation it lacked the power of her first. With her most recent book, *The Eleven Million Mile High Dancer*, Hill is back on form although writing in a very different vein from *Jeremiah*. She combines her flare for the comic with a layman's knowledge of physics, a concern for the environment, and a natural penchant for fantasy. And here again is a multitude of characters.

The heroine is Amanda Jaworski, pilot, particle physicist, ardent feminist (most of the time), America's leading lady astronaut, and free spirit who roller skates through the NASA complex in red and white striped nonregulation shorts. She lives with a cat named Schrodinger who spends 23 out of 24 hours in a catatonic state that Amanda believes must be a form of narcolepsy. Meanwhile Amanda, a champion of female rights, finds herself wildly in love with the ultimate macho man, Bronco McCloud. He was "devastating in the most literal sense of the word. It was quite exciting to be devastated by McCloud, and he knew it. His business was devastation not love. And this was why women adored him." Fortunately for Amanda there is another man in her life, Donald Hotchkiss, who is as masculine as Bronco, but capable of loving Amanda in a way she deserves to be loved. Love is an important theme in Hill's works: Jeremiah spent an entire novel in a desperate, futile search for it, while Amanda not only receives love in its many guises but returns it in abundance.

Bringing everything together is an intricate plot in which Amanda is selected to make an 18-month journey to Mars, but is diverted from this mission by the Great Cosmic Brain who kidnaps Schrodinger. The GCB is a disgustingly huge, bloated snake-like creature that discharges a foul odor with every exhalation. He is earth's creator and he is angry that humankind seems so ready to destroy itself either with nuclear weapons or pollution of the air and water. Amanda is helped in her search for Schrodinger by a tough-talking subatomic particle named Oozie. Their adventure in another dimension brings all Hill's imaginative skills to the fore. She amazes the reader with ever more exotic creatures and situations, culminating in a starry spin through space with the Dancer of the title. Throughout the story she intersperses quotes from scientists writing on the new physics which show how strange our world of reality can be (Paul Davies: "One of the more bizarre consequences of quantum uncertainty is that matter can appear more or less out of nowhere"). So perhaps the wild imaginings of Hill are not so farfetched after all.

Her literary style is often blunt, filled with contemporary jargon, and always to the point. She demonstrates the feelings of her characters by letting the reader eavesdrop on internal conversations. In this way she shows the desperate unhappiness and bewilderment suffered by Jeremiah as well as the gutsy determination and deep-felt love that drive Amanda to the ends of the universe to save Schrodinger. Although the themes of her books have varied greatly, there is one element that permeates them all—her ability to portray the human condition in all of its terrible and wonderful ways, and to portray even the darkest moments with plenty of wit.

—Patricia Altner

HILL, Susan (Elizabeth). British. Born in Scarborough, Yorkshire, 5 February 1942. Educated at grammar schools in Scarborough and Coventry; King's College, University of London, B.A. (honours) in English 1963. Married Stanley Wells in 1975; two daughters (one deceased). Since 1963, full-time writer: since 1977, monthly columnist, *Daily Telegraph*, London. Recipient: Maugham Award, 1971; Whitbread Award, 1972; Rhys Memorial Prize, 1972. Fellow, King's College, 1978. Fellow, Royal Society of Literature, 1972. Lives in Beckley, Oxfordshire. Address: c/o Hamish Hamilton Ltd., 57–59 Long Acre, London WC2E 9JZ, England.

PUBLICATIONS

Novels

The Enclosure. London, Hutchinson, 1961.
Do Me a Favour. London, Hutchinson, 1963.
Gentleman and Ladies. London, Hamish Hamilton, 1968; New York, Walker, 1969.
A Change for the Better. London, Hamish Hamilton, 1969.
I'm the King of the Castle. London, Hamish Hamilton, and New York, Viking Press, 1970.
Strange Meeting. London, Hamish Hamilton, 1971; New York, Saturday Review Press, 1972.
The Bird of Night. London, Hamish Hamilton, 1972; New York, Saturday Review Press, 1973.
In the Springtime of the Year. London, Hamish Hamilton, and New York, Saturday Review Press, 1974.
The Woman in Black: A Ghost Story. London, Hamish Hamilton, 1983.

Short Stories

The Albatross and Other Stories. London, Hamish Hamilton, 1971; New York, Saturday Review Press, 1975.
The Custodian. London, Covent Garden Press, 1972.
A Bit of Singing and Dancing. London, Hamish Hamilton, 1973.

Uncollected Short Story

"Kielty's," in *Winter's Tales 20*, edited by A.D. Maclean. London, Macmillan, 1974; New York, St. Martin's Press, 1975.

Plays

The Cold Country and Other Plays for Radio (includes *The End of Summer, Lizard in the Grass, Consider the Lilies, Strip Jack Naked*). London, BBC Publications, 1975.
On the Face of It (broadcast, 1975). Published in *Act 1*, edited by David Self and Ray Speakman, London, Hutchinson, 1979.
The Ramshackle Company (for children; produced London, 1981).
Chances (broadcast, 1981; produced London, 1983).

Radio Plays: *Taking Leave*, 1971; *The End of Summer*, 1971; *Lizard in the Grass*, 1971; *The Cold Country*, 1972; *Winter Elegy*, 1973; *Consider the Lilies*, 1973; *A Window on the World*, 1974; *Strip Jack Naked*, 1974; *Mr. Proudham and Mr. Sleight*, 1974; *On the Face of It*, 1975; *The Summer of the Giant Sunflower*, 1977; *The Sound That Time Makes*, 1980; *Here Comes the Bride*, 1980; *Chances*, 1981; *Out in the Cold*, 1982; *Autumn*, 1985; *Winter*, 1985.

Television Play: *The Badness Within Him*, 1980.

Other

The Magic Apple Tree: A Country Year. London, Hamish Hamilton, 1982; New York, Holt Rinehart, 1983.
Through the Kitchen Window. London, Hamish Hamilton, 1984.
One Night at a Time (for children). London, Hamish Hamilton, 1984.

Editor, *The Distracted Preacher and Other Tales*, by Thomas Hardy. London, Penguin, 1979.
Editor, with Isabel Quigly, *New Stories 5*. London, Hutchinson, 1980.
Editor, *People: Essays and Poems*. London, Chatto and Windus, 1983.
Editor, *Ghost Stories*. London, Hamish Hamilton, 1983.

*

Manuscript Collection: Eton College Library, Windsor, Berkshire.

*   *   *

One striking feature of Susan Hill's novels is the wide-ranging diversity of the experience they depict; and another, a maturity of understanding remarkable in so young a writer, who began publishing her work at the age of only 19.

From the first she has shown a painful awareness of the dark abysses of the spirit—fear, grief, loneliness, and loss. A recurring early theme is that of lives warped and ruined by the selfishness of maternal domination. In *A Change for the Better* Deirdre Fount struggles in vain to break the shackles of dependence forged by her overbearing mother. The boy Duncan in the short story "The Albatross" is the impotent victim of a similar situation, dogged by the mother-created image of his own inadequacy. Driven finally over the brink of desperation, he does achieve his desired freedom, however brief, through a climactic act of violence.

Hill has always been especially perceptive in her portrayal of children. One of her most memorable novels, *I'm the King of the Castle*, is a penetrating study of mounting tensions in a bitter conflict between two 11-year-old boys. This arises when a widower engages a new housekeeper, who brings with her a son the same age as his own. The peevish weakling already in possession is outraged at this invasion of his cherished territory, and in a subtle campaign of persecution, relentlessly hounds the hapless intruder towards an inevitably tragic denouement.

Hill's sensitive insight into the behaviour and motivations of the young is matched by equal acuteness in delineating the problems and attitudes of those at the opposite end of the human life-span. *Gentleman and Ladies*, a novel simultaneously funny and sad, observes with a shrewdly amused yet compassionate eye the daily life and personalities of the inmates of an old people's home. The same intuitive sympathy informs the short story called "Missy." Through a dying woman's fragmentary memories—frustratingly interrupted by the ministrations of brisk nurse and single visitor—the author intimately identifies with the thought-processes of extreme age.

Hill's gift of imaginative projection into worlds of experience far removed from her own is nowhere more apparent than in *Strange Meeting*. Probably her most notable *tour de force*, this is set in the trenches of Flanders during the 1914–18 war, and depicts with power, and at times almost intolerable poignancy, the doomed friendship of two young officers drawn together by their mutual daily contact with destruction and imminent death. There is also an irresistible attraction between opposite temperaments and family backgrounds: the reserved, introspective Hilliard finding inhibition magically thawed in the warmth of his companion Barton's easy, outgoing generosity.

Not only is the impact of actuality in this novel, both in its factual detail and the immediacy of involvement in the responses of combatants, an astonishing achievement for a young woman. *Strange Meeting* also exemplifies Susan Hill's capacity —comparatively rare among women novelists either past or present—for the convincing depiction of life from a male viewpoint. *The Bird of Night* is another highly original novel of great intensity which surveys a close relationship between two men. The central character is a poet, Francis Croft, whose tormented struggle against intermittent but increasing insanity is chronicled by the withdrawn scholar Lawson, whose life becomes devoted to care of his friend. The first-person masculine narrative of *The Woman in Black*, published after a silence of some years in her career as a novelist, provides a further instance of this aspect of Susan Hill's talent. An atmospherically charged ghost story, it is related in a formal, rather stately past idiom, although carefully unlocated in any particular time. Full of Jamesian echoes and undercurrents, it traces with chilling compulsiveness the progress of a mysterious and sinister haunting.

Her adventurous charting of such varied areas of experience —childhood and old age, loyalties between men, the horrors of war and of insanity—demonstrates this versatile writer's ability to participate truthfully in many states of mind and conditions of life. But this does not preclude her treatment of the more conventionally "feminine" subject. Perhaps more than any of her books, *In the Springtime of the Year* has a direct appeal for a readership of women. Its heroine is a young widow cruelly bereaved after a short and happy marriage; and it movingly explores the successive stages of her grief, from initial angry refusal to accept the fact of loss through a gradual coming to terms and adjustment to her changed situation. The surrounding countryside, evoked with poetic precision, plays a key role in Ruth's final renewal of hope. This echoes the author's own belief in the restoring influence of rural rhythms and simplicities, reflected in her recent volumes of essays, *The Magic Apple Tree* and *Through the Kitchen Window*.

—Margaret Willy

HILLIARD, Noel (Harvey). New Zealander. Born in Napier, Hawke's Bay, 6 February 1929. Educated at Gisborne High School, 1942–45; Victoria University, Wellington, 1946–50; Wellington Teachers College, 1954–55. Married Kiriwai Mete in 1954; four children. Journalist, *Southern Cross*, Wellington, 1946–50; teacher, Khandallah School, Wellington, 1955–56, and District High School, Mangakino, 1956–64; chief sub-editor, *New Zealand Listener*, Wellington, 1965–70; sub-editor, *New Zealand's Heritage* and *New Zealand Today*, 1972–73; deputy editor, *New Zealand's Nature Heritage*, 1973–74; full-time writer, 1974–77. Since 1977, sub-editor, Wellington *Evening Post*. Chairman, Mangakino-Pouakani Maori Executive Committee, and Delegate to the Waiariki District Council of Maori Executive Committees, 1962–64. Recipient: Hubert Church Prose Award, 1961; New Zealand Literary Fund Scholarship, 1963, 1975; University of Otago Robert Burns Fellowship, 1981. Address: 28 Richard Street, Titahi Bay, Wellington, New Zealand.

PUBLICATIONS

Novels

Maori Girl. London, Heinemann, 1960.
Power of Joy. Christchurch, Whitcombe and Tombs, and London, Joseph, 1965; Chicago, Regnery, 1966.
A Night at Green River. Christchurch, Whitcombe and Tombs, and London, Hale, 1969.
Maori Woman. Christchurch, Whitcombe and Tombs, and London, Hale, 1974.
The Glory and the Dream. London, Heinemann, 1978.

Short Stories

A Piece of Land: Stories and Sketches. Christchurch, Whitcombe and Tombs, and London, Hale, 1963.
Send Somebody Nice: Stories and Sketches. Christchurch, Whitcombe and Tombs, and London, Hale, 1976.
Selected Stories. Dunedin, McIndoe, 1977.

Other

We Live by a Lake (for children), photographs by Ans Westra. Auckland, Heinemann, 1972.
Wellington: City Alive, photographs by Ans Westra. Christchurch, Whitcoulls, 1976.

*

Bibliography: *Noel Hilliard: A Preliminary Bibliography* by Jeffrey Downs, Wellington, National Library of New Zealand, 1976.

Critical Studies: *The New Zealand Novel 1860–1965*, Wellington, Reed, 1966, and *New Zealand Short Stories*, Wellington, Price Milburn, 1968, both by Joan Stevens; *New Zealand Fiction since 1945*, Dunedin, McIndoe, 1968, and *New Zealand Novels*, Wellington, New Zealand University Press, 1969, both by H. Winston Rhodes; "The Maori and Literature 1938–65" by Bill Pearson, in *The Maori People in the Nineteen-Sixties*, Auckland, Paul, 1968; *A Descriptive Account of Social Attitudes in the Fiction of Noel Hilliard* by T.J. Mullinder, Christchurch, University of Canterbury, 1974; "The Persistence of Realism: Dan Davin, Noel Hilliard, and Recent New Zealand Short Stories" by Lawrence Jones, in *Islands 20* (Auckland), December 1977; *The New Zealand Novel* by Kevin Cunningham, Wellington, Department of Education, 1980; *Noel Hilliard: La tetralogia di Netta Samuel* by Tiziana Nisini, Rome, University of Rome, 1985.

Noel Hilliard comments:

My principal area of interest has been life in New Zealand today, and particularly how Maori and Pakeha view and behave towards each other. All my writing has been about working people. Since 1978 my work has been mainly in journalism, most recently in a collection of impressions of Bulgaria and the Soviet Union.

*   *   *

Maori Girl, Noel Hilliard's first novel, made an immediate impact on its readers. It appeared at a time when many New Zealanders were becoming uncomfortably aware that all was not well with race relations in their country; and the story of Netta Samuel's early life in a Maori farming community, together with her painful experiences when she arrived alone in the city, were as disturbing as they were impressive. The competence and sincerity of the author could hardly be questioned. Yet the realistic portrayal and unrelenting exposure of discriminatory practices caused some to disparage the novel as mere documentary and to complain that Hilliard was too obviously writing to a thesis.

Although complete in itself, *Maori Girl* proved to be the prelude to a theme. It was the first of a series of novels that can be said to be without parallel in New Zealand fiction. When *Power of Joy* appeared and was followed at intervals by *Maori Woman* and *The Glory and the Dream*, it became apparent that the whole tetralogy had been devised and orchestrated to give life and form to a much more complex theme than had been surmised. If the first novel had evoked the childhood and youth of a Maori girl, forced to endure the pressures of a bi-racial society, *Power of Joy* followed the development of a Pakeha or European boy who almost unconsciously discovers his sense of identity in the spirit of earth, in tree and river and hill, in all his natural New Zealand surroundings, and is forced to resist the traditional pressure of his conventional but poverty-stricken family background. Both are significant variations of the theme of growing up in New Zealand. With *Maori Woman* the lives of these two become interwoven and entangled in a harsh city-world of dominant pakehas and under-privileged Maoris. In the final book of the tetralogy Maori girl and Pakeha boy have come together, to find unity through a process of adjustment, to discover harmony in difference.

Hilliard has certainly been intent on exploring relations between Maoris and Pakehas, and unmasking discriminatory practices, but his aim has been far more comprehensive. He has been even more intent on revealing the human implications of cultural diversity, on identifying his leading characters with the spirit of place and with their inherited but distinctive traditions. He has attempted to reveal and dramatise the tensions that are produced in the community at large and in the unitary family of mixed race from the different ways of life of Maori and Pakeha. However, the major difficulty in such an ambitious undertaking is that of achieving both individuality and typicality, of avoiding the special case and of refraining from the temptation to stereotype characters and their responses to particular situations. This must always be a daunting task for any writer whose aim is not confined to entertainment of a trivial kind. The measure of Hilliard's achievement is that he succeeds not only in establishing his leading characters in an authentic setting and involves the reader in their problems of adjustment, but also in introducing subsidiary themes and characters to illuminate and give further meaning to his many-sided treatment of human relations in a bi-racial community.

In the midst of writing this quartet of novels Hilliard produced a number of short stories. A group of these shorter pieces contains episodes in the lives of two Maori children, and the involvement of the whole family in the simple rhythms of work, play, and ceremonial occasions; but other stories touch on Maori–Pakeha relations and on aspects of the ordinary life of ordinary New Zealanders, generally with implications that have some social significance. Hilliard has always shown his preference for dealing with subjects and people that are of the earth.

Besides these stories Hilliard has written *A Night at Green River*, a novel with the very simple theme of a Pakeha farmer's need for assistance in stacking his hay. Its patterned development emphasises the different values of Pakeha and Maori, especially in relation to material wealth and possessions, to the gospel of work and to human dignity. *A Night at Green River* becomes a comic parable that has relevance to the human predicaments caused when two races with different life-styles and aspirations attempt to mingle. As a lively parable it achieves a rare distinction and enhances Hilliard's reputation for providing valuable insights to the mental and emotional processes that collide when European and Polynesian come together.

—H. Winston Rhodes

HINDE, Thomas. Pseudonym for Sir Thomas Willes Chitty, Baronet. British. Born in Felixstowe, Suffolk, 2 March 1926; succeeded father to the baronetcy, 1955. Educated at Winchester School, Hampshire; University College, Oxford. Served in the Royal Navy, 1944–47. Married Susan Elspeth (i.e., the writer Susan Chitty) in 1951; one son and three daughters. Worked for Inland Revenue, London, 1951–53; staff member, Shell Petroleum Company, in England, 1953–58, and in Nairobi, Kenya, 1958–60. Granada Arts Fellow, University of York, 1964–65; Visiting Lecturer, University of Illinois, Urbana, 1965–67; Visiting Professor, Boston University, 1969–70. Fellow, Royal Society of Literature. Address: Bow Cottage, West Hoathly, near East Grinstead, Sussex RH19 4QF, England.

PUBLICATIONS

Novels

Mr. Nicholas. London, MacGibbon and Kee, 1952; New
York, Farrar Straus, 1953.
Happy as Larry. London, MacGibbon and Kee, 1957; New
York, Criterion, 1958.
For the Good of the Company. London, Hutchinson, 1961.
A Place Like Home. London, Hodder and Stoughton, 1962.
The Cage. London, Hodder and Stoughton, 1962.
Ninety Double Martinis. London, Hodder and Stoughton,
1963.
The Day the Call Came. London, Hodder and Stoughton,
1964; New York, Vanguard Press, 1965.
Games of Chance: The Interviewer, The Investigator. Lon-
don, Hodder and Stoughton, 1965; New York, Vanguard
Press, 1967.
The Village. London, Hodder and Stoughton, 1966.
High. London, Hodder and Stoughton, 1968; New York,
Walker, 1969.
Bird. London, Hodder and Stoughton, 1970.
Generally a Virgin. London, Hodder and Stoughton, 1972.
Agent. London, Hodder and Stoughton, 1974.
Our Father. London, Hodder and Stoughton, 1975; New
York, Braziller, 1976.
Daymare. London, Macmillan, 1980.

Other

Do Next to Nothing: A Guide to Survival Today, with Susan
Chitty. London, Weidenfeld and Nicolson, 1976.
The Great Donkey Walk, with Susan Chitty. London, Hodder
and Stoughton, 1977.
*The Cottage Book: A Manual of Maintenance, Repair, and
Construction.* London, Davies, 1979.
Sir Henry and Sons: A Memoir. London, Macmillan, 1980.
A Field Guide to the English Country Parson. London,
Heinemann, 1983.
Stately Gardens of Britain, photographs by Dmitri Kasterine.
London, Ebury Press, and New York, Norton, 1983.
Forests of Britain. London, Gollancz, 1985.
Just Chicken, with Cordelia Chitty. Woodbury, New York,
Barron's, 1985; London, Bantam Press, 1986.

Editor, *Spain: A Personal Anthology.* London, Newnes,
1963.
Editor, *The Domesday Book: England's Heritage, Then and
Now.* London, Hutchinson, 1985.

*

Manuscript Collection: University of Texas, Austin.

Critical Studies: in *New York Herald Tribune*, 24 May 1953;
The Angry Decade by Kenneth Allsop, London, Owen, 1958;
Times Literary Supplement (London), 26 May 1961, 27 October
1966, 7 November 1968, 11 September 1970; *The Observer*
(London), 7 June 1964; *New York Times*, 9 August 1967; *Books
and Bookmen* (London), September 1974.

Thomas Hinde comments:

I write novels because I like novels and I like trying to make
my own. These aim to be—but unfortunately hardly ever succeed in being—the novels I will like best of all. Just as my
taste in novels changes, so the sort of novel I try to write
changes. I also believe in the importance of the novel—one
of the few places where individual art as opposed to script-

conference art can still flourish. I believe that it can and will
change and develop, however fully explored it seems at present. I believe that people will go on wanting to read novels.
But however much I am convinced by these logical arguments
of the vitality, value, and survival of the form, the real reason
why I go on writing novels remains personal: despite its anxiety
and difficulties, I like the process, and, despite disappointments, I am still excited by the results which I aim for.

*   *   *

When, in 1957, American popular journalism first discovered
the "Angry Young Men," Thomas Hinde was listed, in articles
in *Time* and *Life*, along with Kingsley Amis, John Wain, and
John Braine, as one of the principal progenitors of the "Movement." *Happy as Larry*, Hinde's second novel, had just been
published and the novel's protagonist was a rather feckless
young man who lost menial jobs, was vaguely trying to write,
and irresponsibly drifted away from his wife. Yet the designation of "Angry Young Men," over-generalized and inappropriate as it was for all the writers to whom it was applied,
was particularly inappropriate for Hinde. Far from "angry"
or defiantly rebellious, Hinde's protagonist wanders about apologetically, full of guilt, trying to help a friend recover a lost
photograph that might be used for blackmail. His indecision,
inhibitions, and constant self-punishment characterize him far
more consistently than do any articulate attitudes toward
society. In addition, Hinde's point of view in the novel is far
from an unqualified endorsement of his protagonist's actions
and attitudes. The ending, like the endings of most of Hinde's
novels, is left open, without any definitive or summarizable
statement. And the kind of judgment frequently assumed in
popular accounts of novelists, the clarion call for a new way
of life or the castigation of depraved contemporary morality,
is entirely absent.

At the same time, however, in other terms, *Happy as Larry*
is a novel of the 1950's. The protagonist's wandering, his lack
of certainty, his allegiance only to close personal friends, his
inhibitions and apologies, his insistence on self as a starting
point for value, are all characteristic of much of the serious
fiction of the decade. London, too, shrouded in rain, and
gloom, spotted with crowded pubs that provide the only refuge,
is also made the grim post-war city. In addition, Hinde uses
a frequent symbol in fiction, the photograph, as central to the
plot of his novel. In a world in which identity was regarded
as shifting, unreliable, unknowable, only the photograph, the
fixed and permanent image, could give identity any meaning,
although that meaning, far more often than not, was itself a
distortion, an over-simplification, occasion for blackmail. In
fact, Hinde's novels most characteristically begin with categories definable in terms of other novels and novelists, with genres
to which the reader is accustomed.

His first novel, *Mr. Nicholas*, chronicles the struggles of a
young Oxonian, home on holidays, to define himself against
his domineering and insensitive father. Another novel, *For
the Good of the Company*, deals with the struggles for definition
and power within the business combine, the complex organization that seemed a microcosm to depict human efforts to maintain a sense of rational control. *The Cage* and *A Place Like
Home* are Hinde's African novels, *The Cage* a particularly
sensitive and effective treatment of a young British colonial
girl in Kenya attempting to retain her ties to the world of her
parents while simultaneously understanding sympathetically
the emerging black society. *The Village* establishes, without
sentimentality or nostalgia, the world of the small English village about to be levelled by bulldozers and flooded for a new

reservoir. *High* is Hinde's American visit novel, an account of the 40-year-old British writer teaching at an American university, including the familiar device of a novelist character writing a novel which is itself partly reproduced within the novel. In other words, the themes, techniques, concerns, and atmosphere of Hinde's novels are all familiar, all representative of their time and place—the heroine of *The Cage* often sounds like a more restrained Doris Lessing heroine, the protagonist of *High* is well established in a lineage that stretches back to Eric Linklater—yet Hinde is also an individual novelist of great skill with an individual sense of texture and intelligence.

Hinde is frequently at his best in describing the sensitivities of his young characters—their introspections, their naivety, their commitments to attitudes and to people they cannot entirely understand. The heroine of *The Cage*, unable to untangle the racial antagonisms she does not entirely understand, thinks her young colonial boyfriend will kill the black man he thinks she's been sleeping with, over-dramatizing a conflict she cannot solve. The young budding capitalist in *For the Good of the Company* makes love to the boss's daughter but cannot really fathom all the perplexities of her emotions. He is loyal to the enigma he has partially observed and partially constructed, always wondering how much he has made up himself. A similarly intelligent sensitivity characterizes the love affair in *The Village* between the harassed local doctor and the opportunistic young stockbroker's wife, and affair in which love is created out of mutual desperation. Hinde's sensitivity is applied not only to personal relationships, but to exterior atmospheres as well. Each novel contains many descriptions of weather, rich and subtle evocations of different climates and seasons—equally acute whether England, America or Africa—that are shaped carefully to suit the emotions or the problems of the characters. Weather is both the material for physical description and a principal means of controlling the atmosphere of the novel.

Hinde's novels are also full of action, concerned with plot. Yet the plots never reach definitive conclusions, never entirely resolve the issues they present. The protagonist of *Happy as Larry* finally finds the photograph, but may or may not become a solid citizen and create a home for his faithful wife. The young capitalist in *For the Good of the Company* is enmeshed in the system and, at the end, like his boss, is about to live his past over again. But whether or not he will be any wiser is an open question. *The Village* ends with the feeling that the old English village is probably doomed, as much from its own hypocrisies and inadequacies as from an insensitive "urban bureaucracy," but the fight to save the village is not completely finished. Hinde's novels are, in a way, slices of recognizable contemporary life, a life in which people live and react, in which things happen although those things are not irremediably conclusive, and in which judgment is superficial or irrelevant. And these slices, communicated with a rich sense of personal and historical atmosphere, are never distorted by conversion into an object lesson or part of a message. In fact, Hinde, as author, keeps his distance. He can use familiar themes effectively because he treats them from a distance, stands far enough away to demonstrate a compassionate irony or an intelligent sympathy with his fictional world, a world effectively communicated because, like our larger world, it is one not easily reduced to understandable principles or judgments.

—James Gindin

HINES, (Melvin) Barry. British. Born in Barnsley, South Yorkshire, 30 June 1939. Educated at Ecclesfield Grammar School, 1950–57; Loughborough College of Education, Leicestershire, 1958–60, 1962–63, teaching certificate. Divorced; one daughter and one son. Taught physical education in secondary schools in London, 1960–62, Barnsley, 1963–68, and South Yorkshire, 1968–72; Yorkshire Arts Fellow in Creative Writing, University of Sheffield, 1972–74; East Midlands Arts Fellow in Creative Writing, Matlock College of Further Education, Derbyshire, 1975–77; Fellow in Creative Writing, University of Wollongong, New South Wales, 1979; Arts Council Fellow, Sheffield City Polytechnic, 1982–84. Recipient: Writers Guild award, for screenplay, 1970. Fellow, Royal Society of Literature, 1977; Honorary Fellow, Sheffield City Polytechnic, 1985. Agent: Curtis Brown, 162–168 Regent Street, London W1R 5TA; or, Sheila Lemon Ltd., 24 Pottery Lane, London W11 4LZ. Address: 717 Ecclesall Road, Sheffield S11 8TG, England.

PUBLICATIONS

Novels

The Blinder. London, Joseph, 1966.
A Kestrel for a Knave. London, Joseph, 1968; as *Kes*, 1974.
First Signs. London, Joseph, 1972.
The Gamekeeper. London, Joseph, 1975.
The Price of Coal. London, Joseph, 1979.
Looks and Smiles. London, Joseph, 1981.
Unfinished Business. London, Joseph, 1983.

Uncollected Short Stories

"First Reserve," in *Argosy*, 1967.
"Another Jimmy Dance," in *Dandelion Clocks*, edited by Alfred Bradley and Kay Jamieson. London, Joseph, 1978.
"Christmas Afternoon," in *The Northern Drift*, edited by Alfred Bradley. London, Blackie, 1980.

Plays

Billy's Last Stand (televised, 1970; produced London, 1985).
Two Men from Derby (televised, 1976). Published in *Act Two*, edited by David Self and Ray Speakman, London, Hutchinson, 1979.
Kes, with Allan Stronach, adaptation of the novel by Hines. London, Heinemann, 1976.
The Price of Coal (includes *Meet the People* and *Back to Reality*) (televised, 1977). London, Hutchinson, 1979.

Screenplays: *Kes*, with Ken Loach and Tony Garnett, 1970; *Looks and Smiles*, 1981.

Television Plays: *Billy's Last Stand*, 1970; *Speech Day*, 1973; *Two Men from Derby*, 1976; *The Price of Coal* (*Meet the People* and *Back to Reality*), 1977; *The Gamekeeper*, 1979; *A Question of Leadership* (documentary), with Ken Loach, 1981; *Threads*, 1984.

*

Critical Studies: *The Silent Majority: A Study of the Working Class in Post-War British Fiction* by Nigel Gray, London, Vision Press, and New York, Barnes and Noble, 1973; *Fire in Our Hearts* by Ronald Paul, Gothenburg, Sweden, Gothenburg Studies in English, 1982; "Miners and the Novel" by Graham Holderness, in *The British Working-Class Novel in the*

Twentieth Century edited by Jeremy Hawthorn, London, Arnold, 1984.

Barry Hines comments:

My novels are mainly about working-class life. They are about people who live on council estates or in small terraced houses. The men work in mines and steelworks, the women in underpaid menial jobs—or, increasingly, are on the dole. I feel a strong sense of social injustice on behalf of these people which stems from my own mining background. The hardness and danger of that life (my grandfather was killed down the pit, my father was injured several times) formed my attitudes and made me a socialist.

My political viewpoint is the mainspring of my work. It fuels my energy; which is fine, as long as the characters remain believable and do not degenerate into dummies merely mouthing my own beliefs. However, I would rather risk being didactic than lapsing into blandness—or end up writing novels about writers writing novels. If that happens it will be time to hang up the biro.

My books are all conventional in form. They have a beginning, a middle, and a sort of ending (mainly in that order), with the occasional flashback thrown in. I think, after seven novels, I've now probably exhausted this form and need to explore different ways of telling a story, using some of the more fractured techniques I employ in writing film scripts.

*   *   *

The setting of all Barry Hines's novels is the working-class community of his native West Riding of Yorkshire. But every new work has dealt with another section or facet of this community, a new experience or dilemma as encountered by a representative, if highly individualised, figure from this class.

The author began his writing career in the wake of the late 1950's and 1960's movement in which a whole generation of northern working-class novelists had come to the fore, imprinting themselves on the map of English literary history through an unblinking representation of their native milieu and its language. Like Alan Sillitoe, Keith Waterhouse, Brendan Behan, or Sid Chaplin, Hines is initially concerned with the problems of young people. Like David Storey's *This Sporting Life*, Hines's first novel *The Blinder* considers professional football as an escape route from the working class, and Lenny Hawk is clearly akin to Arthur Seaton or Arthur Machin in his unbounded confidence, ready wit, and aggressiveness, though his gifts—intellectual as well as physical—reach far beyond the football pitch.

However, almost from the outset, certainly from *A Kestrel for a Knave* onward, Hines has found his own voice. It is not only an angry voice denouncing class prejudice and class privilege, and attacking the shortcomings of the once celebrated affluent society. It has also a cautiously hopeful ring emanating from the creative, defiant, and ultimately invincible qualities which his working-class characters display, often against overwhelming opposition. Thus *The Blinder* ends with Lenny publicly throwing torn-up sterling notes in the face of the powerful mill owner and football club director Leary who has sought to take revenge on the young soccer star by aiming to destroy his brilliant career through ugly intrigue. And even Billy Casper, despite being more isolated than ever after the violent death of the hawk which he has reared and looked after with the care and devotion that he has never himself received from

any human being, will, we feel, somehow carry on unsubdued, a victim but also an Artful Dodger of the ways of the adults.

A Kestrel for a Knave, better known by the title of the acclaimed film adaptation *Kes*, remains Hines's best-known and best-selling novel to date. It is technically an accomplished work, breaking up the story of a day in the life of an undersized lad from a one-parent family through a series of skilfully interwoven flashbacks. It has a number of memorable scenes (e.g., Billy before the careers officer), some of which have entered textbooks. What they convey is not only a sense of the complete breakdown of communication between adults and the adolescent but also his consequent negative perception of social relations and institutions—the family, school, law, work. Significantly, his one point of succour and fulfilment in an otherwise hostile and crippling environment lies outside society—the hawk, trained but not tamed, embodying strength, pride, and independence.

The author pursues this theme in *The Gamekeeper* just as the previous novel had developed the school subject from *The Blinder*. If *A Kestrel for a Knave* could be read as an affirmation of the Lawrentian opposition between an alienating and degrading urban-industrial world and a fuller, more aware natural life, *The Gamekeeper* demonstrates that the author has either emancipated himself from this view or has never fully endorsed it. For the life of George Purse, who works on a ducal estate rearing and protecting pheasants from predators and poachers alike, is unspectacular and bare of romanticism. It is true that he has chosen this ill-paid job precisely in order to get away from the heat and dust of shiftwork in a steel mill. But the contentment and pride that he finds in his occupation are questioned and subverted by its inherent contradictions: the game is preserved for no other reason than to provide the Duke and his shooting party with the maximum bag; the gamekeeper's family suffers from the isolation imposed by living in a far-off cottage; chasing the poachers implies turning against members of his own class. Gamekeeping may thus be a personal alternative to industrial labour, but this form of living in direct contact with natural processes cannot shed capitalist relations of property and domination.

With *The Price of Coal* Hines returns to the industrial working class, this time confronting squarely such central issues as the nature of the work underground, the relationship between management and workforce, and the exigencies of an industrial policy to which, despite nationalisation, the interests of the men remain firmly subordinated. The miners of this novel—the author has here visibly widened his cast even though he retains a central working-class family—are a singularly class-conscious and humorous breed; the way they poke fun at the absurdly exaggerated preparations for the impending Royal Visit to the colliery shows them drawing upon unfailing sources of resilience.

The militant spirit and satirical perspective of *The Price of Coal* clearly owe something to the 1972 and 1974 strikes in the industry, which goes to show how close to the thoughts and feelings of ordinary working people Hines has remained over the years, how loyal to his roots and faithful to his socialist humanist creed. The episodic structure of this terse narrative, its revealing juxtaposition of contrasting scenes and parts, and the dominance of dialogue derive in part from cinematographic techniques. The film version of *The Price of Coal* did, in fact, precede the novel by two years, and it is important to remember that Hines is a television playwright and filmscript writer as well as a novelist. He has been lucky to find a congenial interpreter of his material in the film director Ken Loach, whose documentary realist approach successfully transposed *Kes*, *The Gamekeeper*, *The Price of Coal*, and *Looks and Smiles* onto the screen, and has thus enabled the author to reach new audiences at home and abroad.

—H. Gustav Klaus

HOAGLAND, Edward (Morley). American. Born in New York City, 21 December 1932. Educated at Deerfield Academy; Harvard University, Cambridge, Massachusetts, 1950–54, A.B. 1954. Served in the United States Army, 1955–57. Married 1) Amy Ferrara in 1960 (divorced, 1964); 2) Marion Magid in 1968; one daughter. Taught at the New School for Social Research, New York, 1963–64, Rutgers University, New Brunswick, New Jersey, 1966, Sarah Lawrence College, Bronxville, New York, 1967 and 1971, City College, New York, 1967–68, University of Iowa, Iowa City, 1978 and 1982, and Columbia University, New York, 1980–81. Recipient: Houghton Mifflin Literary Fellowship, 1956; Longview Foundation award, 1961; Guggenheim fellowship, 1964, 1975; American Academy traveling fellowship, 1964, and Vursell Memorial Award, 1981; O. Henry Award, 1971; New York State Council on the Arts fellowship, 1972; Brandeis University Citation in Literature, 1972. Member, American Academy, 1982. Agent: Robert Lescher, Lescher and Lescher Ltd., 155 East 71st Street, New York, New York 10021. Address: c/o Random House Inc., 201 East 50th Street, New York, New York 10022, U.S.A.

PUBLICATIONS

Novels

Cat Man.   Boston, Houghton Mifflin, 1956.
The Circle Home.   New York, Crowell, 1960.
The Peacock's Tail.   New York, McGraw Hill, 1965.

Short Stories

City Stories.   Santa Barbara, California, Capra Press, 1986.

Uncollected Short Stories

"Cowboys," in *Noble Savage 1* (New York), 1960.
"The Last Irish Fighter," in *Esquire* (New York), August 1960.
"The Colonel's Power," in *New American Review 2*, edited by Theodore Solotaroff. New York, New American Library, 1967.
"A Fable of Mammas," in *Transatlantic Review* (London), Summer 1969.

Other

Notes from the Century Before: A Journal from British Columbia.   New York, Random House, 1969.
The Courage of Turtles: Fifteen Essays about Compassion, Pain, and Love.   New York, Random House, 1970.
Walking the Dead Diamond River (essays).   New York, Random House, 1973.
The Moose on the Wall: Field Notes from the Vermont Wilderness.   London, Barrie and Jenkins, 1974.
Red Wolves and Black Bears (essays).   New York, Random House, 1976.

African Calliope: A Journey to the Sudan.   New York, Random House, 1979; London, Penguin, 1981.
The Edward Hoagland Reader, edited by Geoffrey Wolff. New York, Random House, 1979.
The Tugman's Passage (essays).   New York, Random House, 1982.

Editor, *The Mountains of California*, by John Muir.   New York and London, Penguin, 1985.

*

Critical Studies: by R.W. Flint, in *New York Review of Books*, 11 September 1969; Alfred Kazin, 25 March 1973, and Diane Johnson, 16 September 1979, both in *New York Times Book Review*.

*   *   *

So far Edward Hoagland has not achieved through his novels and non-fiction a secure or influential place as an important American writer, even though his circus and boxing novels have been labelled required reading for those interested in these activities, and his prose style is distinctively his own. It is perhaps this distinctiveness that may disappoint readers who expect an author to be a virtuoso. Hoagland enjoys travelling in relatively primitive areas of North America and detailing life in occupations where brawn or physical skills are more important than intellect. His essay, "Big Cats," is a deft description of the cat family; *Cat Man* is a novel of circus life that contains sordid but not unrealistic detail about the human struggles unseen by the spectators; and *The Circle Home* is a novel full of information about the training of boxers and life among the destitute. In his third but not best novel, *The Peacock's Tail*, he still shows an interest in the lower classes, for the protagonist is a young white man who gradually loses cultural and racial prejudice as he works among the urban poor.

Throughout his works there is a uniformity of prose style. He is fond of an unembellished, staccato prose that at times is reminiscent of Hemingway, yet because his narrators and protagonists are usually lower-class men, relatively uneducated and inarticulate, the direct, colloquial, often simple, prose is not inappropriate. In its direct, deflationary tone, the beginning of his short story, "The Final Fate of the Alligators," is a succinct introduction to most of his main characters: "In such a crowded, busy world the service each man performs is necessarily a small one. Arnie Bush's was no exception." Yet the lack of subtle, intellectual prose does not mean that the author offers no insights. A description of leopards in motion ends, for example, with a deft comment: "Really, leopards are like machines. They move in a sort of perpetual motion. Their faces don't change; they eat the same way, sleep the same way, pace much the same as each other. Their bodies are constructed as ideally as a fish's for moving and doing, for action, and not much room is left for personality." Regrettably, the final clause may aptly be applied to his characters, for many of them are so busy learning survival techniques in an uncaring world that their personalities are never fully developed. We may believe in them, but we are not always interested in them. The lack of interest sometimes results from the brevity of a character's role or the analysis devoted to it. Thus when characters fall back into self-destructive habits such as self-pity or alcoholism, we feel little sympathy. We impatiently dismiss them as born losers.

An accurate and just sense of Hoagland's strengths and weaknesses in prose style, narrative technique, characterization, and thought may be obtained from *The Circle Home*, the story of Denny Kelly, an irresponsible 29-year-old who has failed and continues to fail as a prize fighter and husband. In prose direct and at times colourful, the author demonstrates a close knowledge of the world of third-rate boxers.

A lively fight: One-hand found occasion to manoeuver into every foot the ring provided. He'd be close, mining in the belly, and spring back with a lithe light antelope-type movement. Often when his left returned from thrusts his arms dropped by his sides to balance him. Those leaps, narrow body straight upright and turning in the air to face the way he wanted, were the essence of his style. . . .

The author seems intent, not upon muckraking, but upon having readers understand the world of boxers and boxing. The reader comes to know Denny through the straight chronological flow of his attempted comeback, and through a series of flashbacks that chronicle his irresponsible and immature behaviour as a husband and father. In re-creating the flow of events Hoagland shows a keen ear for dialogue. The end of the novel, however, is weak: Denny, contrite yet once more, phones to inform his wife that he is determined (because of *his* miseries) to return and to be henceforth a good family man. The title, *The Circle Home*, suggests that at last he will be truly home, but because he has failed so often before and has shown no true deep reformation, the reader may prophesy further backsliding. If we are meant to view Denny's future optimistically, the author's compassion for the dwellers in the "lower depths" has led him to a sentimental conclusion.

From his works as a whole, Hoagland appears as a careful writer who, steeped in firsthand knowledge of his material, attempts with some humour and considerable compassion to show us men and women struggling first to survive and then to improve themselves or the world. Because life embraces much that is sordid, he uses sordidness in his works; but he is neither a muckraker nor a sensationalist.

—James A. Hart

HOBAN, Russell (Conwell). American. Born in Lansdale, Pennsylvania, 4 February 1925. Educated at Lansdale High School; Philadelphia Museum School of Industrial Art, 1941–43. Served in the United States Army Infantry, 1943–45: Bronze Star. Married 1) Lillian Aberman (i.e., the illustrator Lillian Hoban) in 1944 (divorced, 1975), one son and three daughters; 2) Gundula Ahl in 1975, three sons. Magazine and advertising agency artist and illustrator; story board artist, Fletcher Smith Film Studio, New York, 1951; television art director, Batten Barton Durstine and Osborn, 1951–56, and J. Walter Thompson, 1956, both in New York; advertising copywriter, Doyle Dane Bernbach, New York, 1965–67. Since 1967, full-time writer; since 1969 has lived in London. Recipient: Christopher Award, for children's book, 1972; Whitbread Award, for children's book, 1974; George G. Stone Center for Children's Books award, 1982; Ditmar Award (Australia), 1982; John W. Campbell Memorial Award, 1982. Agent: David Higham Associates Ltd., 5–8 Lower John Street, London W1R 4HA, England.

PUBLICATIONS

Novels

The Lion of Boaz-Jachin and Jachin-Boaz.   New York, Stein and Day, and London, Cape, 1973.
Kleinzeit.   London, Cape, and New York, Viking Press, 1974.
Turtle Diary.   London, Cape, 1975; New York, Random House, 1976.
Riddley Walker.   London, Cape, and New York, Summit, 1980.
Pilgermann.   London, Cape, and New York, Summit, 1983.

Fiction (for children)

Bedtime for Frances.   New York, Harper, 1960; London, Faber, 1963.
Herman the Loser.   New York, Harper, 1961; Kingswood, Surrey, World's Work, 1972.
The Song in My Drum.   New York, Harper, 1962.
London Men and English Men.   New York, Harper, 1962.
Some Snow Said Hello.   New York, Harper, 1963.
The Sorely Trying Day.   New York, Harper, 1964; Kingswood, Surrey, World's Work, 1965.
A Baby Sister for Frances.   New York, Harper, 1964; London, Faber, 1965.
Bread and Jam for Frances.   New York, Harper, 1964; London, Faber, 1966.
Nothing to Do.   New York, Harper, 1964.
Tom and the Two Handles.   New York, Harper, 1965; Kingswood, Surrey, World's Work, 1969.
The Story of Hester Mouse Who Became a Writer.   New York, Norton, 1965; Kingswood, Surrey, World's Work, 1969.
What Happened When Jack and Daisy Tried to Fool the Tooth Fairies.   New York, Four Winds Press, 1965.
Henry and the Monstrous Din.   New York, Harper, 1966; Kingswood, Surrey, World's Work, 1967.
The Little Brute Family.   New York, Macmillan, 1966.
Save My Place.   New York, Norton, 1967.
Charlie the Tramp.   New York, Four Winds Press, 1967.
The Mouse and His Child.   New York, Harper, 1967; London, Faber, 1969.
A Birthday for Frances.   New York, Harper, 1968; London, Faber, 1970.
The Stone Doll of Sister Brute.   New York, Macmillan, and London, Collier Macmillan, 1968.
Harvey's Hideout.   New York, Parents' Magazine Press, 1969; London, Cape, 1973.
Best Friends for Frances.   New York, Harper, 1969; London, Faber, 1971.
The Mole Family's Christmas.   New York, Parents' Magazine Press, 1969; London, Cape, 1973.
Ugly Bird.   New York, Macmillan, 1969.
A Bargain for Frances.   New York, Harper, 1970; Kingswood, Surrey, World's Work, 1971.
Emmet Otter's Jug-Band Christmas.   New York, Parents' Magazine Press, and Kingswood, Surrey, World's Work, 1971.
The Sea-Thing Child.   New York, Harper, and London, Gollancz, 1972.
Letitia Rabbit's String Song.   New York, Coward McCann, 1973.
How Tom Beat Captain Najork and His Hired Sportsmen.   New York, Atheneum, and London, Cape, 1974.
Ten What? A Mystery Counting Book.   London, Cape, 1974; New York, Scribner, 1975.

Dinner at Alberta's. New York, Crowell, 1975; London, Cape, 1977.
Crocodile and Pierrot, with Sylvie Selig. London, Cape, 1975; New York, Scribner, 1977.
A Near Thing for Captain Najork. London, Cape, 1975; New York, Atheneum, 1976.
Arthur's New Power. New York, Crowell, 1978; London, Gollancz, 1980.
The Twenty-Elephant Restaurant. New York, Atheneum, 1978; London, Cape, 1980.
The Dancing Tigers. London, Cape, 1979.
La Corona and the Tin Frog. London, Cape, 1979.
Flat Cat. London, Methuen, and New York, Philomel, 1980.
Ace Dragon Ltd. London, Cape, 1980.
The Serpent Tower. London, Methuen, 1981.
The Great Fruit Gum Robbery. London, Methuen, 1981; as *The Great Gumdrop Robbery*, New York, Philomel, 1982.
They Came from Aargh! London, Methuen, and New York, Philomel, 1981.
The Battle of Zormla. London, Methuen, and New York, Philomel, 1982.
The Flight of Bembel Rudzuk. London, Methuen, and New York, Philomel, 1982.
Ponders (*Jim Frog, Big John Turkle, Charlie Meadows, Lavinia Bat*). London, Walker, and New York, Holt Rinehart, 4 vols., 1983–84.

Play

Riddley Walker, adaptation of his own novel (produced Manchester, 1986).

Verse (for children)

Goodnight. New York, Norton, 1966; Kingswood, Surrey, World's Work, 1969.
The Pedaling Man and Other Poems. New York, Norton, 1968; Kingswood, Surrey, World's Work, 1969.
Egg Thoughts and Other Frances Songs. New York, Harper, 1972; London, Faber, 1973.

Other (for children)

What Does It Do and How Does It Work? Power Shovel, Dump Truck, and Other Heavy Machines. New York, Harper, 1959.
The Atomic Submarine: A Practice Combat Patrol under the Sea. New York, Harper, 1960.

*   *   *

Russell Hoban wrote nearly fifty books for children before he turned to adult fiction. The longest and most mature of these children's books, *The Mouse and His Child*, with its theatrical rooks who work for the Caws of Art, displays the love of word-play and punning which runs through all his work, and which finds its fullest and most serious expression in Riddley Walker. Six years before that novel was published he was having macabre fun with mathematical terms in a medical context in *Kleinzeit*, whose hero (of that name) is in hospital with a slipped hypotoneuse. A copy writer who has been sacked for the irrelevance of his slogans, Kleinzeit's case is complicated by his mental distress. He is constantly haunted by sheets of yellow paper demanding words.

Had *Kleinzeit* been produced by a less original writer it could have been written off as "experimental." Hoban, however, cannot be fitted into any classification. He is in fact always experimenting in the sense that although his signature is unmistakeable he never repeats himself in form or content. The year after *Kleinzeit* he published a completely straightforward work. *Turtle Diary* is related by two characters, William, a bookseller, and Neaera, a children's writer and illustrator. These two set out to abduct some turtles from the London Zoo and return them to their native element. They choose the Cornish holiday village of Polperro as a suitable place to launch the creatures. On the whole this is a gentle, sympathetic story, but the threads of violence which appear in his later work begin to be apparent in William's uncontrollable hatred of one of his fellow lodgers and the suicide of the other.

Riddley Walker is set 2,000 years after the greatest violence of all: the nuclear holocaust. Hoban imagines that some sort of organised life has become possible again, and the novel centres on a group of hunter gatherers slowly moving into an iron age as they dig up long-buried scrap metal. They have settled in Kent and speak a contrived language which bears a loose resemblance to English as we know it, although words and syntax are built up in ways that manifest new ways of thinking. Riddley Walker, the narrator, is already a man at 12, for nobody can expect to live to any great age. His name comes from his status in this rudimentary society. After the death of his father his role is to walk around asking riddles. In fact he is a sort of priest whose function is to reveal connections between man and his puzzling universe.

That novel, set in some horrific future, in which man, beset by packs of wild dogs which epitomize the hostility of nature, is complemented by Hoban's fifth novel, *Pilgermann*, in which he goes back to a precise past: the years of the First Crusade (1096–98), and the siege of Antioch by the Franks. Pilgermann is Everyman. He is also a Jew, castrated for making love to a tax collector's wife. The main part of the novel takes place after he has been captured by pirates and sold as a slave to the Muslims while making a pilgrimage from Germany to Jerusalem. He tells his story long after his death, by which time he has become a fluctuation of waves and particles that can materialize as an owl. The metaphor of that bird is important, for *Pilgermann* is an exploration of man's search for wisdom and a vision of the religions that he has devised to give meaning to life and death.

So the story starts with Everyman/Pilgermann climbing a ladder to the arms of the beautiful and aptly named Sophia and ends with his death at the hands of the Frankish giant, Bohemond, who is likened to Elijah, the "enemy as messenger of God." Between these two events Pilgermann is directed by his inner voice, which can assume the person of Christ, and he is accompanied by the figure of Death and by the mangled body of the man he has cuckolded. From time to time he has a vision of his own personal death slowly growing to maturity.

A thread of optimism runs through the macabre violence of his journey, for Pilgermann, like his creator, is a pattern maker and his *post mortem* vision is enriched by knowledge of the tortured paintings of Hieronymus Bosch, the detached tranquility of Vermeer, and the sculpture in Naumberg Cathedral. In his lifetime, at the request of his benign Muslim master, he designs a mosaic floor, an arrangement of red, black, and tawny triangles, from which the emblem of a lion emerges. These floor tiles form the place of the Hidden Lion, a centre of human hopes and meetings, until broken and bloodstained they become the place of his death. Then another pattern immediately emerges, as with his dying eyes he sees a "drifting meditation of storks" making their seasonal return.

Pilgermann's perceptions reflect Hoban's own imaginative use of intricate patterns made out of unusual intellectual concepts and so designed that a spontaneous life suddenly emerges from the contrived form. It is significant that Russell Hoban, whose novels are worthy of the most serious attention, should have been an illustrator before he became a writer. His books convey indelible visual images.

—Shirley Toulson

HOBSON, Laura Z(ametkin). American. Born in New York City, 18 June 1900. Educated at Cornell University, Ithaca, New York, B.A. 1921. Married Thayer Hobson in 1930 (divorced, 1935); two adopted sons. Advertising copywriter until 1934, except for one year as a reporter for the *New York Post*; promotion writer, later copy chief of all magazine promotion, Time Inc., then director of promotion for *Time* magazine, New York, 1934–40. Since 1941, full-time writer: columnist ("Trade Winds"), *Saturday Review of Literature*, 1952–56, and for International News Service, 1953–54, and *Good Housekeeping* ("Thumbing Through"), 1953–56; consultant, Time Inc., 1956–62; since 1960, consultant, as puzzle editor, *Saturday Review*. Member of the National Council, Authors League of America, 1947–75. *Died 28 February 1986.*

PUBLICATIONS

Novels

Outlaws Three (as Peter Field, with Thayer Hobson). New York, Morrow, 1933.
Dry-Gulch Adams (as Peter Field, with Thayer Hobson). New York, Morrow, 1934.
The Trespassers. New York, Simon and Schuster, 1943; London, Gollancz, 1944.
Gentleman's Agreement. New York, Simon and Schuster, 1947; London, Cassell, 1948.
The Other Father. New York, Simon and Schuster, and London, Cassell, 1950.
The Celebrity. New York, Simon and Schuster, 1951; London, Cresset Press, 1953.
First Papers. New York, Random House, 1964; London, Heinemann, 1965.
The Tenth Month. New York, Simon and Schuster, and London, Heinemann, 1971.
Consenting Adult. New York, Doubleday, and London, Heinemann, 1975.
Over and Above. New York, Doubleday, 1979.
Untold Millions. New York, Harper, 1982.

Play

Screenplay: *Her Twelve Men*, with William S. Roberts, 1954.

Other

A Dog of His Own (for children). New York, Viking Press, and London, Hamish Hamilton, 1941.

"I'm Going to Have a Baby" (for children). New York, Day, and London, Heinemann, 1967.
Laura Z: A Life. New York, Arbor House, 1983; vol. 2, New York, Fine, 1986.

*

Manuscript Collection: Butler Library, Columbia University, New York.

*   *   *

Laura Z. Hobson is best known for her competent thesis fiction on current social problems. Her most singular success was her 1947 bestseller, *Gentleman's Agreement*. The film version received the Academy Award for best picture of the year.

Gentleman's Agreement details the experience of a New York journalist who pretends to be Jewish for several months in order to gain inside information for a series on anti-semitism for his magazine. Hobson's target in this novel is not the professional bigot, but those well-meaning people who acquiesce in prejudice not realizing how deeply it exists in daily life. Her protagonist finds anti-semitism in the employment practices of his own liberal magazine and in his fiancée, who had suggested the series to him. Although the novel was criticized for its cardboard characters and contrived plot, most critics agreed that it performed a needed service in alerting readers to the existence of widespread prejudice in American life.

Hobson has frequently been ahead of the public debate in her choice of unpopular and emotional issues. Her first novel, published during World War II, is a well-documented indictment of the United States' failure to help European refugees before the war. *The Tenth Month* is about a 40-year-old unwed mother who wants to keep her baby. *Consenting Adult* details the internal struggle of a mother whose son admits he is a homosexual. Always, Hobson takes a liberal view of the issue, researches it well, and dramatizes it in a form accessible to readers of light fiction. Many reviewers have criticized Hobson's writing style and her didacticism, but most have approved of her commitments and ideals; and many have praised her for daring fictional treatment of subjects other authors prefer to ignore.

—Kay J. Mussell

HODGINS, Jack (John Stanley Hodgins). Canadian. Born in Comox Valley, Vancouver Island, British Columbia, 3 October 1938. Educated at Tsolum School, Courtenay, British Columbia; University of British Columbia, Vancouver, 1956–61, B.Ed. 1961. Married Dianne Child in 1960; one daughter and two sons. Teacher, Nanaimo District Senior Secondary School, British Columbia, 1961–80; Visiting Professor, University of Ottawa, 1981–83. Visiting Professor, 1983–85, and since 1985, Associate Professor of Creative Writing, University of Victoria, British Columbia. Writer-in-Residence, Simon Fraser University, Burnaby, British Columbia, 1977, and University of Ottawa, 1979; Canadian Department of External Affairs Lecturer, Japan, 1979. Recipient: University of Western Ontario President's Medal, for short story, 1973; Canada Council award, 1980; Governor-General's award, 1980. Agent: Gloria Stern, 1230 Park Avenue, New York, New York 10128, U.S.A.; or, Herta Ryder, c/o Toby

Eady Associates, 55 Great Ormond Street, London WC1N 3HZ, England. Address: Creative Writing Department, University of Victoria, Box 1700, Victoria, British Columbia V8W 2Y2, Canada.

PUBLICATIONS

Novels

The Invention of the World.   Toronto, Macmillan, 1977; New York, Harcourt Brace, 1978.
The Resurrection of Joseph Bourne; or, A Word or Two on Those Port Annie Miracles.   Toronto, Macmillan, 1979.

Short Stories

Spit Delaney's Island: Selected Stories.   Toronto, Macmillan, 1976.
The Barclay Family Theatre.   Toronto, Macmillan, 1981.
Beginnings: Samplings from a Long Apprenticeship: Novels Which Were Imagined, Written, Re-Written, Submitted, Rejected, Abandoned and Supplanted.   Toronto, Grand Union, 1983.

Uncollected Short Stories

"Change of Scenery," in *Small Wonders*, edited by Robert Weaver.   Toronto, CBC, 1982.
"The Crossing," in *Vancouver Magazine*, February 1985.

Other

Teachers' Resource Book to Transition II: Short Fiction, with Bruce Nesbitt.   Vancouver, CommCept, 1978.
Teaching Short Fiction, with Bruce Nesbitt.   Vancouver, CommCept, 1981.

Editor, with W.H. New, *Voice and Vision.*   Toronto, McClelland and Stewart, 1972.
Editor, *The Frontier Experience.*   Toronto, Macmillan, 1975.
Editor, *The West Coast Experience.*   Toronto, Macmillan, 1976.

*

Manuscript Collection: National Library of Canada, Ottawa.

Critical Studies: "Jack Hodgins and the Island Mind," in *Book Forum* (Rhinecliff, New York), 1978, and "The Resurrection of the World," in *Canadian Literature* (Vancouver), 1980, both by David Jeffrey; "Setting Out into the Unknown" by R. Schieder, in *Canadian Forum* (Toronto), December 1979–January 1980; "The Invention of Hodgins' World" by Alan Twigg, in *Quill and Quire* (Toronto), December 1979; "Jack Hodgins, Story-Teller" by Viveca Ohm, in *University of British Columbia Chronicle* (Vancouver), December 1980.

Jack Hodgins comments:

(1981) I write fiction in order to free myself of those shadowy creatures that walk briefly across the back of my mind and then return to grow into living breathing people who aren't satisfied to live in my skull: Spit Delaney, the engineer who falls apart when his steam locomotive is sold to a museum; Maggie Kyle, the gorgeous "loggers' whore" who sets herself up a new life in the ruins of a failed utopian colony; Joseph

Bourne, the famous poet who dies and returns to life in a tiny town on the edge of the world; Jacob Weins, the small-town mayor never seen without a different costume on, who after his town has slid off the mountain and into the sea has to search for a new role for himself, and a new costume. Writing them down is a way of getting rid of them. It is also, I hope, a way of sharing them—of allowing other people to love them too, as I must do myself before I'm through with them. I write fiction in order to explain their mysteries to myself—what makes them tick?—but always in the process of writing uncover more mystery than I solve. I write fiction in order to nail down a place before it disappears. If much has been made of the fact that most of my stories are set on Vancouver Island, it is not just that there is some excitement in introducing a part of the world seldom represented before in fiction. The place is changing while I look at it and I want to get the trees, the rocks, the beaches down right before they disappear. I also feel that if I nail the place down right, the people who walk around in it will be just that much more convincing to the reader, wherever he is in the world. I write fiction, finally, for the same reason the magician creates *his* illusions—in order to start something magical happening in the audience's (reader's) mind. If the critics insist on calling me a "magic realist" it isn't because I distort reality or indulge in fantasy but because I see the magic that's already there.

*   *   *

Jack Hodgins is a strongly regional writer in the sense that up to now, though he had lived elsewhere, he had never departed in his fiction from the fairly closely circumscribed region where he was born and spent his childhood and young manhood. Yet, in common with the best of regional writers, he finds the local a staging point for the universal, and his novels and short stories owe their appeal largely to his recurrent theme that—as Frank Davey put it in the *Oxford Companion to Canadian Literature*—"imagination can redeem or transcend the physical," a theme exemplified in the title as well as in the action of his most considerable book, *The Invention of the World.* Given such a vision, his work is necessarily comic in character, and its humour seems to spring from a temperamental inability on the author's part to see life as other than good, prospects as other than expansive, human nature as other than extravagant in its potentialities.

Hodgins was reared in an area of Canada that runs to excess, the rural north of Vancouver Island which represents the country's westernmost edge of settlement, and which until recently still counted as a frontier area, attracting with its fine scenery and its good winters a rich variety of eccentrics who populated its fishing villages, stump farms, and logging camps. The present writer inhabited the same area for a period, and can give a certificate of authenticity to the rustic society with its peculiar behaviour patterns that Hodgins makes the setting of his fictions. Imagine the oddities of Erskine Caldwell's deep southern villages transferred to the green wilderness of far western Canada, and one gets an image of the kind of world Hodgins portrays, except that his optimistic vision lacks Caldwell's darker shadows.

Hodgins's first book was a group of loosely linked stories, *Spit Delaney's Island*; Spit Delaney himself, wild and often shocking in the unconventionality of his behaviour, is the first of Hodgins's roguish and exuberant heroes who live by their dreams and in the process expose the futilely limited lives of the literal-minded.

Hodgins in fact practices a latter-day picaresque fiction. His central characters are often variants on the classic picaro, the ultimately redeemable rogue; his novels take on the loose structure of the picaresque romance, and in the process, as his evident master Cervantes did in *Don Quixote*, he constantly intertwines parable with realism.

The Invention of the World, his first novel, is to date the most satisfying of Hodgins's novels and the most representative of his writing at its best. It is a mingling, which does not always blend well, of the eccentrically regional and the extravagantly parabolical. A larger-than-life evangelist (based on an actual confidence trickster who once operated in the same area under the name of Brother Twelve) persuades an entire Irish village to follow him to Vancouver Island and form a community subservient to his wishes. In a way the evangelist thus invents a world, but it is a false one; the real heroine and creative spirit of the book is the exuberant and promiscuous Maggie Kyle, eventual bride in an epic and Brueghelesque wedding in which the island loggers break out into ferocious battle. Maggie is not only a splendidly complex personality; she also spans the literary genres and approaches, from Joycean interior monologue to vitalist action.

His broad grasp of literary approaches and his intent to use them in comic affirmation have given Hodgins short-term advantages but they may offer long-term perils, for his second novel, the *The Resurrection of Joseph Bourne*, though it is even more emphatically vitalist than *The Invention of the World* in its insistence on the power of the human imagination to make its own terms with existence, is not merely less plausible mimetically, but also less satisfying on the parabolic level, since Hodgins fails to reinvigorate his "resurrected" poet Joseph Bourne into a convincing personification of the life principle.

Most recent among Hodgins's fictions, *The Barclay Family Theatre* is also the most shallow and facile of his books, a series of stories concerning the daughters of a single backwoods family and their disconcerting impact on the world. The stories all seem to suffer from the strain of surprising the reader with ever greater extravagance, and the authenticity of characterization is correspondingly diminished. Hodgins has clearly come to the point when the possibility of his existing material and his current methods are almost exhausted. Speaking in his own terms, he will have to invent a new world for himself if he is to continue the process of creative change that is needed for any writer to outlive his early promise.

—George Woodcock

HOFFMAN, Alice. American. Born in New York City, 16 March 1952. Educated at Adelphi University, Garden City, New York, B.A. 1973; Stanford University, California (Mirelles Fellow), M.A. 1975. Married to Tom Martin; one son. Recipient: Bread Loaf Writers Conference Atherton Scholarship, 1976. Lives in Brookline, Massachusetts. Address: c/o Putnam, 200 Madison Avenue, New York, New York 10016, U.S.A.

PUBLICATIONS

Novels

Property Of. New York, Farrar Straus, 1977; London, Hutchinson, 1978.
The Drowning Season. New York, Dutton, and London, Hutchinson, 1979.

Angel Landing. New York, Putnam, 1980; London, Severn House, 1982.
White Horses. New York, Putnam, 1982; London, Collins, 1983.
Fortune's Daughter. New York, Putnam, and London, Collins, 1985.

Uncollected Short Stories

"Blue Tea," in *Redbook* (New York), June 1982.
"Sweet Young Things," in *Mademoiselle* (New York), June 1983.

*   *   *

Alice Hoffman's female protagonists have much in common. They are all drawn to dangerous men: a saboteur, a gang leader, a drug-dealing older brother, a nihilistic singer. They are all estranged from their parents, though most have strong relationships with their grandparents or someone of their grandparents' age. These older people are often fortunetellers of some kind. There is a strong undercurrent of magic in Hoffman's work.

In Hoffman's first novel, *Property Of*, the unnamed narrator attaches herself to McKay, a gang leader whose life is dedicated to the notion of honor as the gang had adapted it to the violent world of The Avenue, gang territory on the edge of New York City. When she leaves McKay it is because his glittering image and his honor have both crumbled. Hoffman brings almost nothing new to this old-hat situation, and only in the scattered passages where the narrator meditates on deeper things does her language come alive. The neo-hardboiled style dialogue is undermined by an unrealistic candor between characters who hardly know one another. Hoffman tries to pass this off as cool detachment, but it is clearly narrative strategy; a way to delineate character without much development. Hoffman's interest in ceremonial or ritual behavior, and in personal mythmaking that will continue to be a part of all her work is present here, though muffled by the screen of toughness. There is also the first of many magic charms and talismans: a locket with a human tooth inside given the narrator by Monty, an older man who tries to look out for her.

Property Of's narrator, like many of Hoffman's women, seeks a life of magic. She contrasts the "little magic" of herbs and that nature that fights its way up through the concrete with the "big magic" of alcohol and drugs. "Difficult to categorize, until, of course, the consequences are seen. The little magic only causes a smile, but the big magic always seems to end up in the slammer or at a wake." In the last sentence of the novel she smiles.

The Drowning Season is the story of Esther the White and her granddaughter Esther the Black. The generation between these two women, Esther the Black's parents, are both lost: her father to his compulsion to drown himself every summer, and her mother to drink and dreams of escape to the desert. Esther the White and the caretaker who loves her try to help the younger Esther come to grips with the emptiness of her life.

Like *The Drowning Season*, *Angel Landing* is set on the shore of a large cove. Two women live in a nearly empty boarding house across the bay from a nuclear plant under construction. When the plant is sabotaged the younger of the women, Natalie, discovers who "the bomber" is and finds herself falling in love with him. This "dangerous" man works his way through his feelings of alienation through his commitment to Natalie. Aunt Minnie, the older woman and owner of the boarding house, encourages Natalie in the relationship, even when she knows the man is "the bomber." As in *Property Of* the parts of this novel that are timely—the protesting over the nuclear plant, the struggle for better conditions in an old age home—clutter the story and add little. And again there is the unbelieveable openness: Finn, the "bomber," who had been completely closed up, speaks his first emotionally committed words to Natalie in front of five strangers at a Thanksgiving dinner. After a *deus ex machina* helps Finn escape prosecution, he and Natalie run off to Florida, ending the novel on a hopeful but vague note.

White Horses is a difficult novel. The writing is as emotional and poetic as Hoffman's best work, but there is no character with which a reader might comfortably identify, or even sympathize. Aversion or pity are the likely responses. Young Teresa spends her life waiting for an "Aria," a mythical kind of outlaw lover, whose image has been passed down to her from her mother. The mother passes up real love while she waits, surrendering the myth only as she is dying. Both Teresa and her mother believe Teresa's brother Silver is an Aria, and Teresa enters into an incestuous relationship with him. Mother and daughter are both caught between the romance of the wild outlaw lover and the harsh life of attachment to the self-centered cruel Silver. Teresa breaks away from this destructive love only in the last pages.

Fortune's Daughter is a story of nurturing, and of "female mythology" as the jacket copy reads. Rae Perry is pregnant by a cruel and dangerous man, Jessup. Here the older woman Rae (who has cut herself off from her parents) turns to is Lila, a fortune-telling woman whose illegitimate daughter was given up at birth. She helps Rae, though her tea-leaf reading turns up the image of a dead baby. The dead child, however, turns out to be Lila's daughter, and Lila has to choose between isolating herself with the ("actual") ghost of her dead child, or giving it up and accepting her childless life with her supportive husband—who had a dangerous reputation when she met him. (In all Hoffman's novels women are the real movers, the instigators. The men run in circles raising dust, but accomplish little.) Lila chooses the living. Rae does not cut herself off completely from Jessup, and their relationship is left an open question at the novel's end.

Alice Hoffman seems content to rework her favored themes and ideas again and again, but manages to keep them fresh. Of the five tellings of the Alice Hoffman story, *Fortune's Daughter* is surely the finest, with *The Drowning Season* not far behind.

—William C. Bamberger

HOGAN, Desmond. Irish. Born in Ballinasloe, County Galway, 10 December 1950. Educated at Garbally College, Ballinasloe, 1964–69; University College, Dublin, 1969–73, B.A. 1972, M.A. 1973. Writer and actor with Children's T. Company theatre group, Dublin, 1975–77; moved to London, 1977: teacher, 1978–79. Recipient: Hennessy Award, 1971; Irish Arts Council grant, 1977; Rooney Prize (USA), 1977; Rhys Memorial Prize, 1980; *Irish Post* award, 1985. Agent: Deborah Rogers Ltd., 49 Blenheim Crescent, London W11 2EF; or, Maggie Curran, International Creative Management, 40 West 57th Street, New York, New York 10019, U.S.A. Address: 6 Stanstead Grove, London S.E.6, England.

PUBLICATIONS

Novels

The Ikon Maker. Dublin, Co-op, 1976; London, Writers and Readers, and New York, Braziller, 1979.
The Leaves on Grey. London, Hamish Hamilton, and New York, Braziller, 1980.
A Curious Street. London, Hamish Hamilton, and New York, Braziller, 1984.

Short Stories

The Diamonds at the Bottom of the Sea and Other Stories. London, Hamish Hamilton, 1979.
Children of Lir: Stories from Ireland. London, Hamish Hamilton, and New York, Braziller, 1981.
Stories. London, Pan, 1982.

Uncollected Short Stories

"Elysium," in *London Tales*, edited by Julian Evans. London, Hamish Hamilton, 1983.
"The Airedale," in *Literary Review* (London), October 1983.
"Ties," in *PEN New Fiction*, edited by Peter Ackroyd. London, Quartet, 1984.
"Recovery," in *Irish Times* (Dublin), August 1984.
"Martyrs," in *Irish Times* (Dublin), August 1985.

Plays

A Short Walk to the Sea (produced Dublin, 1975). Dublin, Co-op, 1979.
Sanctified Distances (produced Dublin, 1976).
The Ikon Maker, adaptation of his own novel (produced Bracknell, Berkshire, 1980).

Radio Play: *Jimmy*, 1978 (UK).

Television Play: *The Mourning Thief*, 1984 (UK).

*

Desmond Hogan comments:
Looking at my work now I'd like to return to my first four books and insert commas, correct certain grammatical errors, etc. From my first two collections of stories I'd like to get rid of certain stories and reshuffle the order.

*   *   *

The writings of Desmond Hogan testify to the strength of the creative impulse, and the fragility of those who carry it within them. In his novels and stories he depicts the struggles of isolated individuals to assert and define themselves in the face of social pressures. The tragedies he explores—whether set in rural Ireland or urban Britain—present a vision of human frailty, with characters unable to withstand the force of their own destructive passions and the smothering proprieties of the world. They are rendered vulnerable to attack by their fellows, succumbing to a collective psychological violence whose inevitable outcome is madness and suicide. The mental hospital and the dark depths of the river are images that recur constantly in Hogan's fiction. Equally common to his work are other images, the ikon objects used by his characters to give meaning to their lives.

The Ikon Maker, Hogan's first novel, describes the close, obsessional relationship between a mother and son in a remote part of Galway. Charting its growth from the boy's childhood, through the trauma of a friend's early death, and later through his travels among hippies, homosexuals, and IRA activists in England, Hogan portrays compellingly the son's desire for freedom and the fierce, all-consuming need of the mother who pursues him in a doomed effort to re-establish the original bond between them. Building up his narrative from a pattern of terse, fragmented sentences, the author draws the threads of plot neatly together, his style at once jagged and poetic. Diarmaid, the quiet, self-contained youth creating his own inner world through "ikons" of collage, and the mother struggling to suppress her rampant life-force, are both memorable. Here too, as elsewhere in his works, Hogan reveals the bleak, stultifying nature of life in rural Ireland, and its gradual change under the impact of the modern world with its television and terrorism.

The Leaves on Grey has as its central point the friendship, ripening into love, of three privileged youngsters in 1950's Dublin. Growing up in a world where the ideals of the Easter Rising have already been betrayed, forming an elite distinct from their fellows, the three friends see themselves as being chosen for a noble destiny, prospective arbiters of their country's regeneration. Liam the mystic intellectual, Sarah with her religiously charged sexuality, and the narrator Sean together experience the varieties of love and loss, pursuing in their different ways the search for fulfilment. The suicide of Liam's mother, a beautiful Russian émigré, binds them closer, and shadows the course of their future lives. Hogan evokes with subtlety the characters and their shifting perceptions, and once more employs his "splintered" technique of short, sharp sentences to good effect. He also uses a device not unlike Joyce's "epiphany," fixing on moments of revelation and insight which bridge chronological time and emphasize the continuity of human experience. (This device, as well as the fragmented style, is used later in the more ambitious *A Curious Street*.) *The Leaves on Grey* contains the symbol which most appropriately sums up the nature of Hogan's art: the stained glass window, here the last act of creation by a dying artist, in which broken shards are fitted together and transformed by light into a vision of beauty, perfectly encapsulates the method—and the achievement—of this writer.

Most complex of all Hogan's novels, *A Curious Street* is also his most impressive. Taking as its beginning the suicide of Alan Mulvanney, a teacher and unpublished writer, in Athlone in 1977, the story is presented in the form of a memoir by its half-English narrator, son of the woman with whom Mulvanney enjoyed a brief, frustrating affair. Scanning these two lives and the lives of those closest to them, the narrative glides freely in and out of time, going back to explore previous generations, returning to touch on an intense threefold friendship involving the narrator himself. The novel appears to expand outward, branching through families and friends, delving by way of Mulvanney's unpublished writings into the traumas of the past—the Cromwellian invasion, the devastating famine of the 1840's, the 1916 revolution. Hogan's treatment of his subject is nothing less than inspired. As ever, he constructs from broken splinters of sentences, adroitly marshalling his devices—potted "biographies" of his numerous characters, spreading outward from the novel's core, dream-vision passages from history and legend that still strike echoes in the modern Irish consciousness, the transcendent moment linking the experience of successive generations. *A Curious Street* probes at the purity and the loss of innocence, the brutal violence that lurks in family relationships, the destructive power of creativity. Images of the quest, of constant journeyings in search of peace through a wartorn land, and of the ever-present threat of death and madness haunt the reader. Hogan has created his own literary ikon, light shining through a sequence of moments seized from the passage of time.

—Geoff Sadler

HOLMES, John Clellon. American. Born in Holyoke, Massachusetts, 12 March 1926. Educated at Columbia University, New York, 1943, 1945–46; New School for Social Research, New York, 1949–50. Served in the Hospital Corps of the United States Navy, 1944–45. Married 1) Marian Miliambro in 1944; 2) Shirley Allen in 1953. Lecturer, Yale University, New Haven, Connecticut, 1959; Visiting Lecturer, Writers Workshop, University of Iowa, Iowa City, 1963–64; Writer-in-Residence, University of Arkansas, Fayetteville, 1966; Visiting Professor, Bowling Green State University, Ohio, 1968, and Brown University, Providence, Rhode Island, 1971–72. Associate Professor, 1976–80, and since 1980, Professor of English, University of Arkansas. Member of the Executive Board, Associated Writing Programs of America. Recipient: *Playboy* award, for non-fiction, 1964, 1970, 1971, 1972, 1973; Guggenheim fellowship, 1976; Alexander Cappon Prize (*New Letters*, Kansas City), 1978. Agent: Sterling Lord Agency Inc., 660 Madison Avenue, New York, New York 10021. Address: Box 75, Old Saybrook, Connecticut 06475, U.S.A.

PUBLICATIONS

Novels

Go. New York, Scribner, 1952; as *The Beat Boys*, London, Ace, 1959.
The Horn. New York, Random House, 1958; London, Deutsch, 1959.
Get Home Free. New York, Dutton, 1964; London, Corgi, 1966.

Uncollected Short Stories

"Tea for Two," in *Neurotica* (St. Louis), Spring 1948.
"A Length of Chain," in *Nugget* (New York), August 1960.
"The Next to the Last Time," in *Escapade* (New York), September 1967.
"The Manifest Destiny of Mrs. Polk's Sudie," in *Penthouse* (New York), February 1977.
"Night-Blooming Cereus," in *Black Warrior Review* (Birmingham, Alabama), Spring 1978.
"At Pompeii," in *Black Warrior Review* (Birmingham, Alabama), Spring 1981.

Verse

The Bowling Green Poems. California, Pennsylvania, Unspeakable Visions, 1977.
Death Drag: Selected Poems 1948–1979. Pocatello, Idaho, Limberlost Press, 1979.

Other

Nothing More to Declare. New York, Dutton, 1967; London, Deutsch, 1968.

Visitor: Jack Kerouac in Old Saybrook.   California, Pennsylvania, Unspeakable Visions, 1981.
Interior Geographies.   Warren, Ohio, Literary Denim, 1981.
Gone in October.   Pocatello, Idaho, Limberlost Press, 1985.
Break the Black Heart.   Racine, Wisconsin, Still Night, 1986.

*

Bibliography: *An Annotated Bibliography of the Works of John Clellon Holmes* by Richard Kirk Ardinger, Pocatello, University of Idaho Press, 1979.

Manuscript Collection: Boston University Library.

Critical Studies: *Radical Innocence* by Ihab Hassan, Princeton, New Jersey, Princeton University Press, 1961; *The Erotic Revolution* by Lawrence Lipton, Los Angeles, Sherbourne Press, 1965; *Voices from the Love Generation* by Leonard Wolf, Boston, Little, Brown, 1968; *Naked Angels* by John Tytell, New York, McGraw Hill, 1976; interview with Tim Hunt, in *Quarterly West* (Salt Lake City), 1978; *Jack's Book* by Barry Gifford, New York, St. Martin's Press, 1979; article by Richard Kirk Ardinger, in *The Beats* edited by Ann Charters, Detroit, Gale, 1983.

John Clellon Holmes comments:

I take as my working-rule D.H. Lawrence's statement: "Man is a great venture in consciousness." To me, this venture into new areas of awareness is the underlying theme of most important 20th-century work.

The rebel, the outcast, the artist, the young—all those whose extremes of consciousness match their extremes of experience—are my subjects. The single recurring theme of my work so far has been a concern with the origins and effects of contemporary uprootedness—particularly its psychological and spiritual aspects. The search for new continuities to replace those of the family, religious faith, and social idealism—continuities in comradeship, passional love, and artistic creation—occurs again and again in my work.

As a novelist, I find myself wedded to the idea that the building of living characters is the first essential for enduring fiction, and so I tend to work outward, from character toward events, instead of vice versa. The power of the novel to illuminate our lives lies precisely in its ability to convince us that others live as intensely as ourselves.

*   *   *

John Clellon Holmes writes novels that one would find easy to praise extravagantly if they were written by a friend. He is an alert and intelligent observer of the public and private life about him. His prose is precise, his images clearly etched and accurate in detail, his novels carefully structured. Whenever he sits down to write he has a subject squarely in front of him, and for the most part he gives every evidence of knowing precisely what he wants to do with it. Yet his novels are good primarily in the sense that they are pedestrian, workmanlike, and completely serious. He has not yet broken through to the BIG novel he might one day write.

Much of his later performance is an extension of what was begun in his first novel, *Go*, where he recorded the life style of his friends in the late 1940's in New York, and because two of those friends were Jack Kerouac and Allen Ginsberg (fictionalized as Gene Pasternak and David Stofsky) the novel has acquired an interest for literary historians that it did not have on its initial appearance. Firmly entrenched as a chronicler of his times after the appearance of *Go* and the fine essay "This Is the Beat Generation," he turned to the world of jazz—told from the perspective of its Negro performers—in *The Horn*. Again the interest is not solely novelistic; the reader's affection for such musicians as Lester Young and Billie Holiday adds a dimension not generally present in the fictional characters who serve as their surrogates. Only in *Get Home Free*, where the life of Holmes himself seems more central than it does in the earlier novels, does he begin to create characters who are asked to exist firmly on their own, without the support of the reader's outside knowledge and interest. (This last statement must be qualified by the recognition that when Holmes began *Go* he could not have known of the fame later to be attained by Kerouac and Ginsberg and when he got into the last hundred pages of *The Horn* he did much to lift his horn player out of the world of fact and into the world of fictional reality.)

One thinks in terms of a BIG novel for Holmes primarily because he has tried to force bigness upon each one that he has thus far written. In *Go* he spread the action north to Connecticut and south to Louisiana in search of a geographic definition for the rootlessness of Americans making it in Manhattan. An old-fashioned novelist in some ways, he displays an old-fashioned desire to write the Great American Novel. One of his most annoying traits is his habit of assigning SIGNIFICANCE to the actions of his characters, so that it comes as a relief when an individual scratches his nose without the author informing us that the action is a peculiarly American one, with Freudian overtones, dating from Cotton Mather's investigations of the psychology of the invisible world. His structure, too, can be burdensome, as it is in *The Horn*, where he selects an American literary figure to associate, for reasons not usually clear, with each of his characters.

In *Nothing More to Declare* he informs us that he has less desire now than he once had to classify, to generalize. Whether that also means that he has less urge to write novels is not clear; perhaps it means that if he does write them he will allow the meanings to grow from within rather than imposing them from without. If he does that he may yet write a better book than those he has given us to date.

—George Perkins

HOOD, Hugh (**John Blagdon**).   Canadian.   Born in Toronto, Ontario, 30 April 1928. Educated at De La Salle College, Toronto; University of Toronto, 1947–55, B.A. 1950, M.A. 1952, Ph.D. 1955. Married Ruth Noreen Mallory in 1957; two sons and two daughters. Teaching Fellow, University of Toronto, 1951–55; Associate Professor, St. Joseph College, West Hartford, Connecticut, 1955–61. Since 1961, Professeur titulaire, University of Montreal. Recipient: University of Western Ontario President's Medal, for story, 1963, for article, 1968; Beta Sigma Phi prize, 1965; Canada Council grant, 1968, award, 1971, 1974, and Senior Arts grant, 1977; Province of Ontario award, 1974; City of Toronto award, 1976; Queen's Jubilee Medal, 1977. Address: 4242 Hampton Avenue, Montreal, Quebec H4A 2K9, Canada.

PUBLICATIONS

Novels

White Figure, White Ground.   New York, Dutton, 1964.

The Camera Always Lies. New York, Harcourt Brace, 1967.
A Game of Touch. Toronto, Longman, 1970.
You Cant Get There from Here. Ottawa, Oberon Press, 1972;
   New York, Beaufort, 1984.
The New Age:
   The Swing in the Garden. Ottawa, Oberon Press, 1975.
   A New Athens. Ottawa, Oberon Press, 1977.
   Reservoir Ravine. Ottawa, Oberon Press, 1979.
   Black and White Keys. Downsview, Ontario, ECW Press,
     1982.
   The Scenic Art. Toronto, Stoddart, 1984.
   The Motor Boys in Ottawa. Toronto, Stoddart, 1986.

Short Stories

Flying a Red Kite. Toronto, Ryerson Press, 1962.
Around the Mountain: Scenes from Montreal Life (sketches).
   Toronto, Peter Martin, 1967.
The Fruit Man, The Meat Man, and The Manager. Ottawa,
   Oberon Press, 1971.
Dark Glasses. Ottawa, Oberon Press, 1976.
Selected Stories. Ottawa, Oberon Press, 1978.
None Genuine Without This Signature. Downsview, Ontario,
   ECW Press, 1980.
August Nights. Toronto, Stoddart, 1985.

Uncollected Short Stories

"The Isolation Booth," in *Tamarack Review* (Toronto), Fall
   1958.
"I'm Not Desperate!," in *Exchange* (Montreal), November
   1961.
"The Changeling," in *Canadian Forum* (Toronto), March
   1962.
"The Ingenue I Should Have Kissed But Didn't," in *Tamarack
   Review* (Toronto), Fall 1962.
"A Season of Calm Weather," in *Queen's Quarterly* (Kingston,
   Ontario), Spring 1963.
"The Perfect Night," in *Story* (New York), July–August 1963.
"The Fable of the Ant and the Grasshopper," in *Yes 13* (Mon-
   treal), December 1964.
"Educating Mary," in *Montrealer*, September 1965.
"The Granite Club," in *Journal of Canadian Fiction* (Mon-
   treal), Winter 1972.
"Suites and Single Rooms, with Bath," in *Queen's Quarterly*
   (Kingston, Ontario), Fall 1972.
"The Winter," in *Jubilee 3*, Spring 1976.

Play

Friends and Relations, in *The Play's the Thing: Four Original
   Television Dramas*, edited by Tony Gifford. Toronto, Macmillan, 1976.

Other

Strength Down Centre: The Jean Béliveau Story. Toronto,
   Prentice Hall, 1970.
*The Governor's Bridge Is Closed: Twelve Essays on the Cana-
   dian Scene.* Ottawa, Oberon Press, 1973.
Scoring: The Art of Hockey, illustrated by Seymour Segal.
   Ottawa, Oberon Press, 1979.
Trusting the Tale (essays). Downsview, Ontario, ECW Press,
   1983.

*

Bibliography: by J.R. Struthers, in *The Annotated Bibliography of Canada's Major Authors 5* edited by Robert Lecker
and Jack David, Downsview, Ontario, ECW Press, 1984.

Manuscript Collection: University of Calgary Library,
Alberta.

Critical Studies: "Line and Form" by Dave Godfrey, in *Tama-
rack Review* (Toronto), Spring 1965; "Grace: The Novels of
Hugh Hood" by Dennis Duffy, in *Canadian Literature* (Van-
couver), Winter 1971; *The Comedians: Hugh Hood and Rudy
Wiebe* by Patricia A. Morley, Toronto, Clarke Irwin, 1977;
Before the Flood: Hugh Hood's Work in Progress by J.R.
Struthers, Downsview, Ontario, ECW Press, 1979; *On the Line*
by Robert Lecker, Downsview, Ontario, ECW Press, 1982;
Hugh Hood, Boston, Twayne, 1983, and *Hugh Hood*, Downs-
view, Ontario, ECW Press, 1984, both by Keith Garebian.

Hugh Hood comments:
(1972) An interviewer recently asked me why all my fiction
began with an appearance of realism and then almost always
merged into a dream or reverie or fantasy. I thought that this
was a very astute question, because this is exactly how I design
my work. I consider it as both realist and super-realist, somewhat like the movies of Fellini or the paintings of Stanley
Spencer or Alex Colville—where a pertinacious imitation of
the appearance of social reality turns without much warning
into a very curious and private vision. I couldn't answer the
interviewer's question "why?" I just know that this is how
I do it. I might add that I do not think that the Romantic
Movement failed, nor do I think that it is over. It seems to
me that I, at least, am still in the middle of it.

*   *   *

Hugh Hood is a writer in whom pedantry wars with creative
gifts of a high order. His best work so far occurs in his short
stories which demonstrate his mastery at revealing what is
immense through what is small. He is an indefatigable explorer
of human aspiration, conveying much of its mystery, heroism,
and comedy. An impassioned drive towards some symbolic
victory is celebrated seriously or gaily in such stories as "Silver
Bugles, Cymbals, Golden Silks" (*Flying a Red Kite*), "The
Pitcher" (*Dark Glasses*), and "Le Grand Déménagement"
(*Around the Mountain*). His art is at its finest in "Looking
Down from Above" (*Around the Mountain*), where separate
characters connect in a visionary moment of great beauty,
crowded like a medieval tapestry with life: "inscrutable but
undeniable."
Hood's earlier novels have something of this imaginative
intensity, as in the burning warehouse scene (*A Game of
Touch*), an incident pivotal to the hero's fate and a keystone
in the novel's structure. However, Hood is unable to control
the tone of his prose over the long course of a novel. When
the painter in *White Figure, White Ground* retreats to the safety
of his old manner and family life, Hood's point of view is
unclear. Although the hard urbanity and narrow sympathies
of the wife offend, it is uncertain whether the artist's glorification of her is to be received with irony or approval. In *The
Camera Always Lies*, a romance, Hood's continuing problem
with creating likeable characters re-emerges. A romance
requires archetypal figures on whom fantasies can be projected:
yet "virtuous" Rose Leclair, suffering through near-death and

rebirth, is a bore, the hero who saves her an overbearing prig. Precise detail of film financing, production, and costume design merely throws into relief Hood's difficulty with his characters. *You Cant Get There from Here*, set in an imaginary African nation, is both a study of struggle in a new society and "Christological [except] ... that the Christ figure does not rise again...." Because he is writing satire and allegory, Hood must be excused for missing opportunities of further defining the two tribes, and of describing the personal history of his sketchy hero; but his Cabinet villains need sharper outlines to succeed either as allegory or satire.

When Hood attempts in *The New Age*, a serial novel in twelve volumes of which six have been completed, to work on the scale of "Coleridge, Joyce, Tolstoy, and Proust," his inadequacies become obvious. He is striving for "a very wide range of reference without apparent connection on the surface which nonetheless will yield connections and networks and links and unities if you wait and allow them to appear." Moving back and forth through time, the huge project includes passages of philosophy, social history, topography, and lectures on a broad variety of topics, as well as the fictionalized incidents of his own life.

As a simultaneous "realist and transcendental allegorist" (his admitted aim), Hood falls short in these novels, for although characters and events have a formal importance, they rarely achieve emotive significance. The marriage in *A New Athens*, for instance, is never felt as the redemptive force intended, because Edie is no more than a shadow, and Matt Goderich remains, as one character observes, "a pompous ass." Too often Hood offers neither psychological nor pictorial realism, but the factuality of an encyclopaedia or a catalogue. Obsessive lists of, for example, baseball players (*The Swing in the Garden*) suggest an inability to select. Local history and neighbourhood cartography too often supply the substance rather than the raw material of these fictions. Pedantic tenacity in description cannot of itself invest places or objects with meaning, nor is Hood's style sufficiently adept, usually, to produce this result by its own power. He even slips into bathos with the showpiece engagement scenes in *A New Athens* and *Reservoir Ravine*. His uninspired prose has created a bland, provincial world where values do not develop organically, but are imposed from without. Only when he writes of marvels does the reader's interest freshen, as with the appearance of the visionary painter (*A New Athens*). Striving to write a masterpiece, Hood is so concerned with large patterns and themes that he fails to breathe life into the material of which these patterns are composed. Heterogeneity can succeed only for the writer gifted enough to consume disparate material in the unifying fire of his art; but, with half the sequence still to come, Hood may yet produce work on a level comparable to that of the short stories.

—Margaret Keith

HOOPER, Peter. Pseudonym for Hedley Colwill Hooper. British and New Zealander. Born in London, 19 May 1919. Educated at the University of New Zealand, B.A. 1946. Served in the Royal New Zealand Air Force, 1942–45. Worked as teacher and bookseller; Deputy-principal, Westland High School, Hokitika, 1966–77. Recipient: PEN Prose award, 1980; New Zealand Literary Fund bursary, 1981. Address: 369 Milton Road, Paroa, Greymouth, New Zealand.

PUBLICATIONS

Novels

A Song in the Forest.   Dunedin, McIndoe, 1979.
People of the Long Water.   Dunedin, McIndoe, 1985.

Short Stories

The Goat Paddock and Other Stories.   Dunedin, McIndoe, 1981.

Play

The Heritage of Westland (pageant; produced Greymouth, 1960).   Published in *Grey River Argus*, May 1960.

Verse

A Map of Morning and Other Poems.   Christchurch, Pegasus Press, 1964.
Journey Towards an Elegy and Other Poems.   Christchurch, Nag's Head Press, 1969.
The Mind of Bones.   Wellington, Inter-Media, 1971.
Earth Marriage.   Christchurch, Young and Waddington, 1972.
Profiles in Monochrome.   Titahi Bay, Aspect Press, 1974.
Selected Poems.   Dunedin, McIndoe, 1977.

Other

Our Forests Ourselves (essay on environment).   Dunedin, McIndoe, 1981.

Editor (as Hedley Colwill Hooper), with Barry J. Smithson, *Greymouth High School Golden Jubilee 1923–1973.*   Greymouth, Golden Jubilee Committee, 1973.
Editor, *Winter Skies.*   Hokitika, West Coast Writers Group, 1983.
Editor, *Saturday Afternoons.*   Greymouth, Longacres Press, 1984.

*

Peter Hooper comments:

The first two volumes of the trilogy *Time and the Forest*, set several centuries ahead in a post-holocaust New Zealand, examine issues of religious and secular authority in remnant tribal groups of hunters and fishermen. Modern knowledge has been lost to myth and legend in a culture where the young priest Tama discovers evidence of the lost civilization, and gradually develops a written language. Between the Stag and the Shepherd peoples cultural differences provoke hostilities, which change the lives of both peoples.

The fiction of a holocaust is the mechanism by which I distance my characters from topical irrelevances to the main theme, which is that in spite of all threats to survival, in spite of humanity's errors and repeated self-betrayals, with no guarantees of the ultimate just society, human beings do go on working and hoping. Sometimes they even express in some measure unlikely virtues of self-sacrifice, heroism, and intellectual daring, or bring back from artistic and spiritual explorations gifts for their fellows.

*   *   *

Like his better-known compatriot Keri Hulme, Peter Hooper is associated with the west coast of New Zealand's

South Island. "The Coast" (as it is always called) is regarded by New Zealanders in much the same way as Irishmen regard Connemara or the Aran Islands. It is seen as the essential New Zealand—a sparsely populated area of great natural beauty, where one can still pursue the energetic outdoor life-style which lies at the heart of the great New Zealand dream. Hulme and Hooper share a reverence for the Coast's beauty and freedom, and in the case of Hooper (but not Hulme, whose work is more eclectic) this reverence seems to be the principal impulse behind almost everything he has written.

Our Forests Ourselves—his most impassioned work to date—is more than just a conservationist tract; it is an eloquent defence of animism which insists that "these forests have . . . a spiritual significance . . ., they afford us a path back to a natural wholeness of being." What this means in practice is indicated by the following passage:

> The young Coaster who grows up with the forest at his back door, who traps possums in it as a boy, hunts deer as a young man, curses its tangled profusion, climbs its ridges and emerges into vast expanses of light, is not afraid of the forest. It holds no evil for him. Difficulty, yes; danger, certainly, but measuring up to these are the tests of his manhood.

With the partial exception of "Girls and Boys Come Out to Play" (a diffuse "slice-of-life" study of adolescence), all the stories in *The Goat Paddock* can be seen as illustrations of the philosophy expounded in *Our Forests Ourselves*. In "There Was This Joker," "Something to Think About," "A Breath of Fresh Air," "Landscape with Two Figures," and "The Hut" Hooper shows how urban life inhibits natural impulses. Encroaching industrialization shatters a pastoral idyll in "The Goat Paddock," and suburban values (always attributed to women) conflict with romantic (and usually pastoral) dreams in "The Fountains of Rome," "Too Wide the World," and "The End of the Road."

Some of the simpler stories come close to sentimentality. Others (notably "The Hut") are saved by their frank confrontation of the "difficulty," the "danger," and indeed the cruelty of the country life which is recommended to us. The dark side of Hooper's forest Arcadia comes under even closer scrutiny in the two novels which he has published to date, *A Song in the Forest* and *People of the Long Water*.

Both novels are part of a projected trilogy about life in New Zealand many generations after the destruction of our civilization in a nuclear holocaust. A small percentage of the population of Christchurch (on the South Island's east coast) evidently survived the devastation. Part of this percentage made its way through the mountains to the west coast and settled there. Another part moved over the hills to the east and settled beside what is now Akaroa Harbour. *A Song in the Forest* focusses on the west coast tribe (the Stag people), and especially on Tama, a young orphan who, fleeing from the tribe's harsh initiation rites, passes through the mountains and rediscovers the land to the east. He returns and is severely punished for his truancy, but when an extraordinarily harsh winter threatens the very survival of the tribe he comes to the rescue by leading them across to the milder climate of the east coast. By the end of the book he has redeemed his lost stature and is set to succeed the Old Wise as the tribe's high priest. In the east the Stag people quickly encounter the Shepherd people who live beside the Long Water (an English translation of the Maori word Akaroa). *People of the Long Water* depicts the relations between the two tribes, which begin cordially enough but deteriorate markedly before the end of the book. The indications

are that in the third and final volume of the trilogy things will get worse before they get better.

This in brief is the plot of the trilogy so far. Both the novels are thoroughly good yarns. *A Song in the Forest* is built around the classic progression from prosperity to adversity (Tama's punishment) and back to prosperity. *People of the Long Water* is more episodic, but it is held together not only by a louring sense of doom but also by the ever effective motif of unrequited love (Tama's for Gilda, one of the Shepherd women). In the third novel the tension between the doom and the love will have to be resolved, and other lesser motifs (notably Tama's attempt to reinvent printing) rounded off.

More interesting than the details of the narrative, however, is the sociological theme which emerges from the juxtaposition of cultures in *People of the Long Water*. Stag culture and Shepherd culture approximate roughly to what A.D. Lovejoy once called "hard primitivism" and "soft primitivism." Stag society is disciplined, hierarchical, patriarchal, devout, and rather dour. The Stags are meat-eaters and therefore attach great importance to the prowess of their hunters. The Shepherds, on the other hand, are vegetarians. Their society inclines towards communism and hedonism, and women have at least an equal say in their affairs.

Of the two the Shepherds are superficially the more attractive, and it is dispiriting to see them developing a taste for meat and for violence under the influence of their neighbours. Ultimately, however, the Stags have three important factors in their favour. Their religion works (notably in Tama's remarkable vision which concludes *People of the Long Water*). Their forest origins and their love of hunting correspond to Hooper's own predilections. And Hooper has given them a whole book (*A Song in the Forest*) to themselves. The indications are, then, that the disciplined Stag culture—probably modified to allow women more influence (Hooper atoning for his own misogyny in *The Goat Paddock*?)—will eventually stand as a bulwark against the sort of *hubris* which is supposed to have caused the destruction of the old civilization.

As science fiction goes, Hooper's two novels are conservative in style. There are few exotic neologisms. Indeed, Hooper makes no real attempt to evoke the predicament of primitive people groping after new concepts. He does not seek to capture the different idioms of the two cultures (whose languages are supposed to be similar—being both derived from a common source—but far from identical). And no individual character has a truly idiosyncratic mode of speech. The stories in *The Goat Paddock* indicate that Hooper can work subtle variations on the New Zealand vernacular, and *Our Forests Ourselves* shows that he is capable of real passion, but with the exception of a few purple passages (notably the concluding section of *People of the Long Water*) the novels are written in an even, workmanlike style.

—Richard Corballis

HOPE, Christopher (David Tully). South African. Born in Johannesburg, 26 February 1944; moved to Europe in 1975. Educated at Christian Brothers College, Pretoria, 1952–60; University of the Witwatersrand, Johannesburg, 1963–65, B.A. 1965, M.A. 1970; University of Natal, Durban, 1968–69, B.A. (honours) 1969. Served in the South African Navy, 1962. Married Eleanor Marilyn Klein in 1967; two sons. Underwriter,

South British Insurance, Johannesburg, 1966; editor, Nasionale Pers, publishers, Cape Town, 1966–67; reviewer, Durban *Sunday Tribune*, 1968–69; copywriter, Lintas, Durban, 1967–69 and Durban and Johannesburg, 1973–75; copywriter, Lindsay Smithers, Durban, 1971; English teacher, Halesowen Secondary Modern School, 1972. Editor, *Bolt*, Durban, 1972–73; Writer-in-Residence, Gordonstoun School, Elgin, Morayshire, 1978. Recipient: English Academy of Southern Africa Pringle Award, 1974; Cholmondeley Award, for poetry, 1978; David Higham Prize, 1981; Natal University Petrie Arts Award, 1981; Silver Pen Award, 1982; Whitbread Award, 1985. Lives in London. Agent: A.P. Watt Ltd., 26–28 Bedford Row, London WC1R 4HL, England.

PUBLICATIONS

Novels

A Separate Development.   Johannesburg, Ravan Press, 1980; London, Routledge, and New York, Scribner, 1981.
Kruger's Alp.   London, Heinemann, 1984; New York, Viking, 1985.

Short Stories

Private Parts and Other Tales.   Johannesburg, Bateleur Press, 1981; London, Routledge, 1982.

Uncollected Short Story

"Carnation Butterfly," in *London Magazine*, April–May 1985.

Plays

Television Plays: *Ducktails*, 1976; *Bye-Bye Booysens*, 1979; *An Entirely New Concept in Packaging*, 1983.

Verse

Whitewashes, with Mike Kirkwood.   Privately printed, 1971.
Cape Drives.   London, London Magazine Editions, 1974.
In the Country of the Black Pig and Other Poems.   Johannesburg, Ravan Press, and London, London Magazine Editions, 1981.
Englishmen.   London, Heinemann, 1985.

Other (for children)

The King, The Cat, and the Fiddle, with Yehudi Menuhin. Tonbridge, Kent, Benn, and New York, Holt Rinehart, 1983.
The Dragon Wore Pink.   London, A. and C. Black, and New York, Atheneum, 1985.

*

Christopher Hope comments:
I grew up in Pretoria, capital of South Africa and a fiercely Calvinist city. Early on I became aware that, as an Irish Catholic, I was a member of an unpopular minority. This was followed by the discovery that my minority was itself part of another minority, the English-speaking community, who were locked in the iron embrace of the Afrikaner nationalists who controlled the country and ruled the Black majority with ambitious and enthusiastic policies of racial division and dominance.

Faced with bizarre and disagreeable race laws, the English-speaking whites might complain but they would comply. I discovered to my dismay that my minority was politically impotent. The Afrikaner government, for its part, was regarded as mad but sincere.

My first novel, *A Separate Development*, is set in the 1950's and describes what might be called the era of apartheid rampant, as it is experienced by a boy who cannot decide what colour he is in a society which thinks of little else. The South African censors were quick to ban this novel.

In the following decades the priests of apartheid, while losing none of their fervour for racial purity and separation, became rather more worldly and talked of "realism" and "reform." People who opposed their policies continued to regard them as mad—but doubts began to grow over their sincerity. My second novel, *Kruger's Alp*, considers this later stage; it is an allegorical work about power and its counterfeiters. My poems and stories, written between these novels, as it were, also consider the fearful comedy of those dedicated to taking charge.

*   *   *

Christopher Hope is a leading example of an important new group of white South African writers who have broken free of the traditional mould of liberal realism in South African fiction. These writers have cast off the predictable and often sterile tones of superior intellectual humanism or impassioned but helpless outrage against apartheid. Seen against the seriousness and moral sanctimony of the liberal idiom, Hope's writing is positively liberating. His vision is black, wicked, and surreal, and his satire and humour have a measure of viciousness which seems peculiarly appropriate to South Africa. In the case of both his fairly recent novels, *A Separate Development* and *Kruger's Alp*, one feels that here, at last, is a writer who has the measure of the system; who, indeed, has found a language of fiction which matches the system point by point for ruthlessness, power, subtlety, and the ability to knock down targets.

Hope, who has been living in voluntary exile in London since 1976, has also published several volumes of poetry and a collection of short stories, *Private Parts*. In the stories, as in the novels, Hope's unusual blend of familiar reality and bizarre, surreal inventiveness is apparent. Increasingly in his fiction, Hope has created a special space for himself halfway between the real and the bizarre, showing how interchangeable these categories are and establishing newly capacious and flexible fictional conventions for himself.

Like Herman Charles Bosman and Tom Sharpe before him, Hope demonstrates how endlessly funny South African life is when seen from a great and merciless distance. In *A Separate Development* the notions of mixed blood and miscegenation, so tragically dealt with by such South African heavyweights as Sarah Gertrude Millin and Alan Paton, not to mention André Brink, become a mainspring for blackish and farce-filled comedy. The novel's young first-person narrator, Harry Moto, thrives on irony and absurdity. He has little choice, having grown up as a white South African and then being forced to take refuge as a "black" denizen of Johannesburg. Moto scrambles the categories: his darkish skin and somewhat frizzy hair suggest certain irregularities in his ancestry, and through no fault of his own he becomes a comic victim. In Harry Moto, Hope achieves what has always remained impossible for South African writers in their more serious efforts: to combine or unify black and white experience in a country which reduces such unification to a fictional pipe-dream. By discarding the heavy mantle of serious liberalism, Hope happily indulges in that pipe-dream. Moto, who has grown up spending idle hours around swimming pools and ruminating about sex, finally goes "black" under the weight of neurotic moral condemnation because he was caught in an advanced state of intimacy with a wealthy white girl at a school-leaving dance. Given Harry's hue of skin, this situation is humiliatingly close to sexual immorality, and Harry faces absolute disapproval from his parents, who see in him tangible evidence of their deep psychological fears about mixed blood. Harry disappears to become a black, working first as a runner for an Indian clothing merchant, and later as a "living proof" assistant to a man who sells skin-lightening creams to infinitely deluded blacks. He ends up as the invisible "boy" collecting trays from cars at a roadhouse, and finally as a detainee writing his story to stay alive.

If *A Separate Development* is an unusually deft first novel, then *Kruger's Alp* is a truly remarkable effort for a second novel. More "serious" in effect, the novel demonstrates literary artifice and fictional inventiveness of masterful proportions. Hope combines modern political mystery with historical myth, revelatory allegorical structure with acid-strength satire. This amalgam is based on a wide vision of present and past South African experience, in which social and historical myth is reformulated and given new meaning. Hope's principal point of reference in this novel is John Bunyan's *The Pilgrim's Progress*. As in Bunyan's allegory, there is a dream of revelation as a narrative vehicle, a physical journey of discovery and a mythic destination. Like Bunyan's Christian, Hope's main protagonist, Blanchaille (white-bait), is obsessed with the idea of escape. Whereas Christian is filled with a sense of doom because he realises that "our city will be burned with fire from heaven," Blanchaille is envisioned as experiencing the acute anxiety of a "despised sub-group within a detested minority [waiting] for the long-expected wrath to fall on them and destroy them." Blanchaille's anxiety is fuelled by the news that a former friend of his, a top fiscal official, has been murdered, apparently by his own government for political reasons.

As boys, Blanchaille and the murdered official, Tony Ferreira, both served under a prophesying and idiosyncratic Irish priest, Father Lynch. Lynch was obsessed with and preached the truth of the missing Kruger millions, a great hoard of gold which the Boer War president of the Transvaal republic, Paul Kruger, is reputed to have taken away with him into exile in Switzerland. As interpreted in this novel, Kruger is supposed to have established a "shining city" ("celestial city" in *The Pilgrim's Progress*) for white South Africans seeking an ultimate haven after lifetimes of *trekking*. Ferreira was killed because he uncovered massive irregular spending on huge projects to buy world opinon (the situation is closely modelled on the Information Scandal which rocked South Africa in the late 1970's), and these efforts to find a haven in world opinion constitute only one of several equivalents of the Kruger myth. Blanchaille is set off by Father Lynch on an allegorical journey of revelation to Kruger's "white location in the sky" in Switzerland. It is a journey which goes backwards and forwards at the same time, into the heart of the mythic secrets of white South African existence. The Kruger refuge is recognisable as the mythic basis of an escape syndrome cutting across all periods and categories in white South African history. The notion of pilgrims seeking a promised land remains a key interpretation of this history, today as much as in earlier times.

Given his mythical/allegorical structure, Hope uses the wide freedom of a dream-narrative to pattern and shape each stop on the journey, its revelations, people, and stories, according to the needs of his satirical and revelatory vision, yet at the same time the author manages to stay very close to recent and familiar characters and events. Ultimately, he fulfills the larger promises of his dream of revelation with admirable neatness. *Kruger's Alp* must be counted as one of the most telling novels to be produced by a South African writer in recent times. Certainly, Hope is a writer to watch.

—Leon de Kock

HORGAN, Paul. American. Born in Buffalo, New York, 1 August 1903. Educated at Nardin Academy, Buffalo; Albuquerque public schools; New Mexico Military Institute, Roswell, 1920–23. Served in the United States Army as Chief of the Army Information Branch, 1942–46: Lieutenant Colonel; Legion of Merit; recalled to active duty, General Staff, 1952. Member of the production staff, Eastman Theatre, Rochester, New York, 1923–26; librarian, 1926–42, and assistant to the President, 1947–49, New Mexico Military Institute (the Institute library is named for him); Lecturer, University of Iowa, Iowa City, 1946. Senior Fellow, 1959–61, and Director, 1962–67, Center for Advanced Studies, Adjunct Professor of English and Author-in-Residence, 1967–71, and since 1971, Professor Emeritus and permanent Author-in-Residence, Wesleyan University, Middletown, Connecticut. Hoyt Fellow, 1965, and since 1967, Associate Fellow, Saybrook College, Yale University, New Haven, Connecticut. President, Roswell Museum, 1946–52; member of the Board, Roswell Public Library, 1958–62; Chairman of the Board, Santa Fe Opera, New Mexico, 1958–62. President, American Catholic Historical Association, 1960. Member, National Council on the Humanities, 1966–71. Scholar-in-Residence, 1968, 1970, 1972, 1973, and since 1974, Fellow, Aspen Institute, Colorado. Member of the Editorial Board, 1969–72, Book of the Month Club, New York. Recipient: Harper Prize Novel Award, 1933; Guggenheim fellowship, 1945, 1958; Pulitzer Prize, for history, 1955, 1976; Bancroft Prize, for history, 1955; Catholic Book Club Campion Award, 1957; Catholic Book Award, 1965, 1969; Christopher Award, 1976; Western Writers of America Spur Award, for non-fiction, 1976; University of Notre Dame Laetare Medal, 1976; Wesleyan University Baldwin Medal, 1982; Washington College award, 1985. D.Litt.: Wesleyan University, 1956; Southern Methodist University, Dallas, 1957; University of Notre Dame, Indiana, 1958; Boston College, 1958; New Mexico State University, Las Cruces, 1961; College of the Holy Cross, Worcester, Massachusetts, 1962; University of New Mexico, Albuquerque, 1963; Fairfield University, Connecticut, 1964; D'Youville College, Buffalo, New York, 1965; Pace College, New York, 1968; Loyola College, Baltimore, 1968; Lincoln College, Illinois, 1969; St. Bonaventure University, New York, 1969; LaSalle College, Philadelphia, 1971; Catholic University, Washington, D.C., 1973; St. Mary's College, 1976; Yale University, 1978; D.H.L.: Canisius College, Buffalo, 1960; Georgetown University, Washington, D.C., 1963. Member, American Academy, and American Academy of Arts and Sciences. Knight of St. Gregory, 1957. Address: 77 Pearl Street, Middletown, Connecticut 06457, U.S.A.

PUBLICATIONS

Novels

The Fault of Angels. New York, Harper, 1933; London, Hamish Hamilton, 1934.

No Quarter Given. New York, Harper, and London, Constable, 1935.
Mountain Standard Time (trilogy). New York, Farrar Straus, and London, Macmillan, 1962.
Main Line West. New York, Harper, and London, Constable, 1936.
Far from Cibola. New York, Harper, and London, Constable, 1938.
The Common Heart. New York, Harper, 1942.
A Lamp on the Plains. New York, Harper, and London, Constable, 1937.
The Devil in the Desert: A Legend of Life and Death in the Rio Grande. New York, Longman, 1952.
The Saintmaker's Christmas Eve. New York, Farrar Straus, 1955; London, Macmillan, 1956.
Give Me Possession. New York, Farrar Straus, 1957; London, Macmillan, 1958.
A Distant Trumpet. New York, Farrar Straus, and London, Macmillan, 1960.
Things as They Are. New York, Farrar Straus, 1964; London, Bodley Head, 1965.
Everything to Live For. New York, Farrar Straus, 1968; London, Bodley Head, 1969.
Whitewater. New York, Farrar Straus, 1970; London, Bodley Head, 1971.
The Thin Mountain Air. New York, Farrar Straus, 1977; London, Bodley Head, 1978.
Mexico Bay. New York, Farrar Straus, and Henley-on-Thames, Oxfordshire, Ellis, 1982.

Short Stories

The Return of the Weed. New York, Harper, 1936; as *Lingering Walls*, London, Constable, 1936.
Figures in a Landscape. New York, Harper, 1940.
One Red Rose for Christmas (novella). New York, Longman, 1952.
Humble Powers: 3 Novelettes. London, Macmillan, 1954; New York, Doubleday, 1956.
The Peach Stone: Stories from Four Decades. New York, Farrar Straus, 1967; London, Bodley Head, 1968.

Plays

A Tree on the Plains: A Music Play for Americans, music by Ernst Bacon (produced Spartanburg, South Carolina). Published in *Southwest Review* (Dallas), Summer 1943.
Yours, A. Lincoln (produced New York, 1942).

Verse

Lamb of God. Privately printed, 1927.
Songs after Lincoln. New York, Farrar Straus, 1965.
The Clerihews of Paul Horgan. Middletown, Connecticut, Wesleyan University Press, 1985.

Other

Men of Arms (for children). Philadelphia, McKay, 1931.
From the Royal City of the Holy Faith of Saint Francis of Assisi, Being Five Accounts of Life in That Place. Santa Fe, Villagra Bookshop, 1936.
The Habit of Empire. Santa Fe, Rydal Press, and New York, Harper, 1938.
Look at America: The Southwest, with the editors of Look. Boston, Houghton Mifflin, 1947.

Great River: The Rio Grande in North American History. New York, Rinehart, 2 vols., 1954; revised edition, Austin, Texas Monthly Press, 1 vol., 1984.
The Centuries of Santa Fe. New York, Dutton, 1956; London, Macmillan, 1957.
Rome Eternal. New York, Farrar Straus, 1957.
One of the Quietest Things (address). Los Angeles, University of California School of Library Service, 1960.
Citizen of New Salem. New York, Farrar Straus, 1961; as *Abraham Lincoln: Citizen of New Salem*, London, Macmillan, 1961.
Toby and the Nighttime (for children). New York, Farrar Straus, and London, Macmillan, 1963.
Conquistadors in North American History. New York, Farrar Straus, 1963; as *Conquistadors in North America*, London, Macmillan, 1963.
Peter Hurd: A Portrait Sketch from Life. Austin, University of Texas Press, 1965.
Memories of the Future. New York, Farrar Straus, and London, Bodley Head, 1966.
The Heroic Triad: Essays in the Social Energies of Three Southwestern Cultures. New York, Holt Rinehart, 1970; London, Heinemann, 1971.
Encounters with Stravinsky: A Personal Record. New York, Farrar Straus, and London, Bodley Head, 1972.
Approaches to Writing. New York, Farrar Straus, 1973; London, Bodley Head, 1974.
Lamy of Santa Fé: His Life and Times. New York, Farrar Straus, 1975; London, Faber, 1977.
Josiah Gregg and His Vision of the Early West. New York, Farrar Straus, 1979.
Of America East and West: Selections. New York, Farrar Straus, 1984.
Under the Sangre de Cristo. Santa Fe, Rydal Press, 1985.

Editor, with M.G. Fulton, *New Mexico's Own Chronicle: Three Races in the Writings of Four Hundred Years.* Dallas, Upshaw, 1937.
Editor, *Maurice Baring Restored: Selections from His Work.* New York, Farrar Straus, and London, Heinemann, 1970.

*

Manuscript Collection: Beinecke Library, Yale University, New Haven, Connecticut.

Critical Study: *Paul Horgan* by Robert Gish, Boston, Twayne, 1983.

Paul Horgan comments:

In my fiction I hope to enclose in a precisely appropriate and thus beautiful form a story which rises from the interaction of characters brought alive through understanding of human life, in settings which are evocative in atmosphere, set forth in language interesting for its own sake as well as for its suitability to the subject matter.

In my non-fiction—history, biography, other forms—I hope to tell the truth of actual events while retelling them in such a manner that the resources of the novelist in presenting scene and character allow the reader a sense of experiencing the past rather than simply hearing about it.

*　　　*　　　*

One literary legend has it that as an orphan Paul Horgan was standing on a Buffalo, New York, street corner singing to passersby; by chance, and attracted by the quality of the song, a wealthy gentleman befriended the waif and among other things later sponsored professional vocal training at a conservatory. Precisely true or not, this legend gives certain insights into Horgan's life and work.

The Horatio Alger implication of Horgan's career is manifest in steady production and wide variety; novels, short stories, plays, opera, biography, cultural reportage, national, regional, and church history. Among other things, he is an acknowledged national authority on Lincoln, Beethoven, the conquistadors, the cultures and history of the Great Southwest in America, most notably the regions of the Rio Grande River. Horgan brings to all his work an artistic integrity of a very high order. The style is supple and clean; the attitude towards all subjects is broadly humanistic. The history and the cultural reportage are remarkable for the visual quality, scrupulous attention to detail, and the exploitation of symbolic incident or encounter. Horgan's talent is fully dramatic in nature; his responses to his subject matter are symphonic in scale. Industry for its own sake, however, is not implied, for the author's concept of work is of an order which in fact tends to enrich the writer's life. Thus Horgan's well-known gift for friendship is another facet of a productive, well-integrated personality of great warmth and charm. These things are even more remarkable when it is understood that Horgan taught himself to write while serving as a librarian in a boy's school in the Southwest; only after a long literary apprenticeship of frustration and isolation was his talent recognized when he won a major American literary prize for his novel *The Fault of Angels*.

Horgan is a deeply committed Catholic and is America's foremost writer of that conviction at the present time. This fact has several literary implications. Although *Rome Eternal* may suggest a thoroughly Catholic point of view, Horgan is much too deeply committed as an artist to become merely a "spokesman" for the Church. Doubtless he would concur with the suggestion that he is an artist who happens to be a Catholic; yet, presumably, he would not seriously imagine writing to greater advantage from any other viewpoint. Actually the weight of his very personal kind of commitment varies a great deal. When handling church-connected subject matter he treats the theme sympathetically, urbanely, and with great delicacy; when writing on materials less specifically Catholic he displays a characteristic optimism, a charity, a softening of certain re-occurring realities of life. In turn this softening of the hard edge of reality is not so much sentiment as it is an awareness of spiritual forces in the world which may be registered as ultimately harmonious. Whether or not these fundamentally optimistic attitudes are to be equated with either the more fortuitous aspects of his own life and/or his spiritual training is a question too complex for brief analysis.

Ultimately, Horgan's literary significance will rest less with a commitment to Catholicism and much more with his stature as a regional writer. America's literature is a regional literature, and Horgan already is the Master of the Great Southwest. In comparison with Faulkner (of the same literary generation) Horgan's clarity, objectivity, and consistency are the greater; on the other hand, Horgan is the less experimental and is less inclined to focus on the more pervasive, sordid aspects of modernity. Unlike Faulkner, Horgan probably makes more concessions to the genteel audience, the literary passersby of America. In any event, the comparison as regionalists of the two talents reflects no discredit on either artist.

Horgan continues to be vital and productive. His life itself is a meaningful, artistic statement of what a gifted writer in America may accomplish even though the odds were great beyond calculation.

—James B. Hall

HOUSEHOLD, Geoffrey (Edward West). British. Born in Bristol, 30 November 1900. Educated at Clifton College, Bristol, 1914–19; Magdalen College, Oxford, 1919–22, B.A. (honours) in English 1922. Served in the Intelligence Corps, 1939–45: Lieutenant Colonel; Territorial Decoration; mentioned in despatches. Married Ilona M.J. Zsoldos-Gutmán in 1942; one son and two daughters. Engaged in commerce abroad, 1922–35: worked for Bank of Romania, Bucharest; Elders and Fyffes, importers, in Spain; sold children's encyclopedias in the U.S.A., and printing ink for John Kidd in Europe and South America. Address: Chatterwell, Charlton, Banbury, Oxfordshire OX17 3DL, England.

PUBLICATIONS

Novels

The Third Hour.   London, Chatto and Windus, 1937; Boston, Little Brown, 1938.
Rogue Male.   London, Chatto and Windus, and Boston, Little Brown, 1939; as *Man Hunt*, New York, Triangle, 1942.
Arabesque.   London; Chatto and Windus, and Boston, Little Brown, 1948.
The High Place.   London, Joseph, and Boston, Little Brown, 1950.
A Rough Shoot.   London, Joseph, and Boston, Little Brown, 1951.
A Time to Kill.   Boston, Little Brown, 1951; London, Joseph, 1952.
Fellow Passenger.   London, Joseph, and Boston, Little Brown, 1955; as *Hang the Man High*, New York, Spivak, 1957.
Watcher in the Shadows.   London, Joseph, and Boston, Little Brown, 1960.
Thing to Love.   London, Joseph, and Boston, Little Brown, 1963.
Olura.   London, Joseph, and Boston, Little Brown, 1965.
The Courtesy of Death.   London, Joseph, and Boston, Little Brown, 1967.
Dance of the Dwarfs.   London, Joseph, and Boston, Little Brown, 1968.
Doom's Caravan.   London, Joseph, and Boston, Little Brown, 1971.
The Three Sentinels.   London, Joseph, and Boston, Little Brown, 1972.
The Lives and Times of Bernardo Brown.   London, Joseph, 1973; Boston, Little Brown, 1974.
Red Anger.   London, Joseph, and Boston, Little Brown, 1975.
Hostage—London: The Diary of Julian Despard.   London, Joseph, and Boston, Little Brown, 1977.
The Last Two Weeks of Georges Rivac.   London, Joseph, and Boston, Little Brown, 1978.
The Sending.   London, Joseph, and Boston, Little Brown, 1980.
Summon the Bright Water.   London, Joseph, and Boston, Little Brown, 1981.

Rogue Justice.   London, Joseph, 1982; Boston, Little Brown, 1983.
Arrows of Desire.   London, Joseph, 1985.

Short Stories

The Salvation of Pisco Gabar and Other Stories.   London, Chatto and Windus, 1938; augmented edition, Boston, Little Brown, 1940.
Tales of Adventurers.   London, Joseph, and Boston, Little Brown, 1952.
The Brides of Solomon and Other Stories.   London, Joseph, and Boston, Little Brown, 1958.
Sabres on the Sand and Other Stories.   London, Joseph, and Boston, Little Brown, 1966.
The Cats to Come.   London, Joseph, 1975.
The Europe That Was.   Newton Abbot, Devon, David and Charles, and New York, St. Martin's Press, 1979.
Capricorn and Cancer.   London, Joseph, 1981.

Other

The Terror of Villadonga (for children).   London, Hutchinson, 1936; revised edition, as *The Spanish Cave*, Boston, Little Brown, 1936; London, Chatto and Windus, 1940.
The Exploits of Xenophon (for children).   New York, Random House, 1955; as *Xenophon's Adventure*, London, Bodley Head, 1961.
Against the Wind (autobiography).   London, Joseph, 1958; Boston, Little Brown, 1959.
Prisoner of the Indies (for children).   London, Bodley Head, and Boston, Little Brown, 1967.
Escape into Daylight (for children).   London, Bodley Head, and Boston, Little Brown, 1976.

*

Manuscript Collection: Lilly Library, Indiana University, Bloomington.

Critical Studies: "The Governance of Geoffrey Household" by L.E. Sissman, in *New Yorker*, 1 May 1971; "The Lives and Times of Geoffrey Household" by Michael Barber, in *Books and Bookmen* (London), January 1974.

Geoffrey Household comments:

My first concern is with the English I write, simple, evocative, and therefore enabling me to produce the required impact on the reader without any obscurity. I cannot estimate its literary worth, but I suggest that if there is any permanent value in my work it is to be found in my short stories.

My novels are all suspense novels and deal with the individual trapped in an unwelcome or thoroughly dangerous environment. Only one is a "spy" story and none is a "crime" story. I am told that they seem to be written on two levels—which may mean that in order to create the illusion of reality I have to examine the political, ethical, or religious motives of the characters.

By and large the books fall into two classes. *The Third Hour, Arabesque, The High Place, Thing to Love,* and *The Three Sentinels* are fairly straight novels, though certainly depending on action and the development of plot. The rest are unashamed "thrillers" with the possible exception of *Olura, Dance of the Dwarfs,* and *Doom's Caravan,* which are less conventional in form or subject or both and may be defined as the reader likes.

Pedigree: a good, working strain directly descended from Defoe, with a dash of thoroughbred blood from Stevenson and Conrad.

*   *   *

Geoffrey Household came slowly to prominence as a novelist by way of banking, business, and war-time Intelligence service. His first notable success, *Rogue Male,* was published in 1939. He had already placed a number of short stories in the upper reaches of the magazine market, written radio plays for children, and published one novel; with *Rogue Male* his career as a professional author was finally consolidated though the war years were to interrupt his output.

He specialised at first in what used to be called "thrillers" or "suspense stories"—action stories with a strong narrative line, unexpected turns and checks of plot, and on the whole rather slight attention to the portrayal and development of character. Probably the best known of his books in this genre, after *Rogue Male,* are *A Rough Shoot, Watcher in the Shadows,* and *Sabres on the Sand,* set in John Buchan/Richard Hannay territory, complete with officers and gentlemen, foreign agents and manhunts, sketchily realised and subordinate female characters, tweeds, shotguns and sporting rifles, whose telescopic sights are suddenly put to use on more sinister targets than red deer. Many of the social assumptions of Buchan's Hannay novels seem strangely dated today; but one can never fault the author's sure-footed narrative pace. It is a mark of Geoffrey Household's excellence that his Buchanesque novels stand comparison with his master's in this latter respect and do much better in the former.

The main themes he explores are courage and endurance in extreme danger and at the limits of human survival; the discharge of obligation and duty; loyalty; and personal honour. The best of his man-hunts take place in the English West Country, about which he writes with affection and the kind of knowledge which comes only to those who stalk wild life with fieldglasses and camera or gun. The rogue male's survival in his hideout in a thicket-choked lane, the hunt through the Cotswolds by the shadowy watcher, the hero's frenzied tunnelings in the Mendips in *The Courtesy of Death,* and the dirty work in the hedgerows and rabbit warrens of *A Rough Shoot* are stamped with authenticity.

There is a change of milieu to South America in *Thing to Love,* which portrays the conflict between technologically based progress and romantic attachment to the traditional way of life, but which continues to examine the theme of divided loyalty and an officer's personal honour. This was followed by novels which exploited a vein of fantasy less familiar to Household's established readership, until he returned once more to the pursuit thriller with *The Lives and Times of Bernardo Brown,* in which he successfully extended the earlier conventions of the genre. The period is just before the time of Hitler and Franco, the hero-on-the-run a young shipping agent in Bilbao who is suspected by international racketeers of knowing more than is good for him or for them. Abducted to the Balkans, he escapes and goes to ground in Romania, hiding in the underworlds of the ghetto and a travelling fair, the victim of an unjust hunt and a refugee from official investigation. This fast-moving novel with its brilliantly exotic settings is matched in quality by *The Last Two Weeks of Georges Rivac.* A French-based businessman of mixed Latin and British descent, Rivac innocently takes to London a couple of Czechoslovakian brochures, only to find himself caught up in international espionage; accompanied by a dashing Hungarian girl, he goes on the run from both foreign agents and the British police, in an example of a well-known variation of the thriller genre which consistently maintains freshness and excitement.

The vein of fantasy was mined again in *The Sending*, a strange novel whose protagonist, scion of an ancient Somerset family who has seen service in India, becomes aware of the mediumistic communicatory power of a tame polecat which places him in contact with the mental world of Neolithic hunters and the hunted.

Geoffrey Household has also published children's fiction which exhibits a characteristically swift pace, while his collections of beautifully crafted short stories, *The Europe That Was* and *Capricorn and Cancer*, display a wide range of themes, tone, and narrative techniques.

—Stewart F. Sanderson

HOWARD, Elizabeth Jane. British. Born in London, 26 March 1923. Educated privately; trained as an actress at the London Mask Theatre School and with the Scott Thorndyke Student Repertory; played at Stratford-upon-Avon, and in repertory theatre in Devon. Served as an Air Raid Warden in London during World War II. Married 1) Peter M. Scott in 1942 (divorced), one daughter; 2) James Douglas-Henry in 1959 (divorced); 3) Kingsley Amis, *q.v.*, in 1965 (divorced, 1983). Worked as a model, and in radio and television broadcasting, 1939–46; secretary, Inland Waterways Association, London, 1947–50; editor, Chatto and Windus Ltd., London, 1953–56, and Weidenfeld and Nicolson Ltd., London, 1957; book critic, *Queen* magazine, London, 1957–60. Honorary Artistic Director, Cheltenham Literary Festival, 1962; Co-Artistic Director, Salisbury Festival, 1973. Recipient: Rhys Memorial Prize, 1951; *Yorkshire Post* award, 1983. Lives in London. Agent: Jonathan Clowes Ltd., 22 Prince Albert Road, London NW1 7ST, England.

PUBLICATIONS

Novels

The Beautiful Visit. London, Cape, and New York, Random House, 1950.
The Long View. London, Cape, and New York, Reynal, 1956.
The Sea Change. London, Cape 1959; New York, Harper, 1960.
After Julius. London, Cape, 1965; New York, Viking Press, 1966.
Something in Disguise. London, Cape, 1969; New York, Viking Press, 1970.
Odd Girl Out. London, Cape, and New York, Viking Press, 1972.
Getting It Right. London, Hamish Hamilton, and New York, Viking Press, 1982.

Short Stories

We Are for the Dark: Six Ghost Stories, with Robert Aickman. London, Cape, 1951.
Mr. Wrong. London, Cape, 1975; New York, Viking Press, 1976.

Plays

Screenplay: *The Very Edge*, 1963.

Radio Plays: *Make Thee an Ark*, 1969; *Wife Swapping 7–10:30 P.M.*, 1970.

Television Plays: *The Glorious Dead* (*Upstairs, Downstairs* series), 1974; *Skittles* (*Victorian Scandals* series), 1976; *Sight Unseen* (*She* series), 1977; *After Julius*, from her own novel, 1979; *Something in Disguise*, from her own novel, 1980.

Other

Bettina: A Portrait, with Arthur Helps. London, Chatto and Windus, and New York, Reynal, 1957.

Editor, *The Lover's Companion: The Pleasure, Joys, and Anguish of Love.* Newton Abbot, Devon, David and Charles, 1978.

*

Elizabeth Jane Howard comments:

I consider myself to be in the straight tradition of English novelists. I do not write about "social issues or values"—I write simply about people, by themselves and in relation to one another. The first aim of a novel should be readability. I do not write (consciously, at least) about people whom I know or have met.

My methods are to be able to write in one sentence what my novel is to be about, to test this idea for several months, and then to invent situations that will fit the theme. I make the people last—to suit the situations. I write only one draught and rarely make any alterations to it. Occasional cutting has sometimes seemed necessary. I write about 300 words a day with luck and when I am free to do so. I do it chiefly because it is the most difficult thing that I have ever tried to do.

I began by writing plays when I was 14. Before that I wrote 400 immensely dull pages (since destroyed) about a horse. I have also written a film script of *The Sea Change* with Peter Yates, but this has not yet been produced. I would very much like to write a good play, and, indeed, come to that, a first rate novel.

*   *   *

All Elizabeth Jane Howard's novels are distinguished by sharp and sensitive perceptions about people—their loves, their guilts, the damage they wittingly or unwittingly do to others. Sometimes, the perceptions are worked into satirical set pieces, like the treatment of a group of feckless post-Oxford young people sponging in London in *Something in Disguise*. Often the satire is more gentle and generous, like that of the patriotic major in *After Julius* who combines long, boring speeches about the past with silent sensitivity to the human dramas around him. Howard's protagonists, often simple, gentle young girls from a variety of backgrounds, are treated with a great deal of sympathy, with respect for their quiet intelligence and their capacity to feel for others. Any tendency toward the mawkish or sentimental is carefully controlled by a prose that works on sharp and often comic juxtapositions of images: the heavy-handed Colonel, trying to appear sympathetic to others in *Something in Disguise*, is "about as jocular and useless as the Metro-Goldwyn-Mayer Lion", in *The Sea Change* a young actress tries desperately to impress a playwright by showing a knowledge of his plays, "broadcasting her innocuous opinions like weed killer on a well kept lawn", the repressed and deferential hairdresser who is the central character in *Getting It Right* begins by noticing a wealthy and demanding client whose face has the "apoplectic bloom of unpeeled beetroot" and eyes "the shade of well-used washing-up water," and then proceeds, in a moment of personal conflict, to discover his mind like a "partially disused branch railway line."

The careful control visible in Howard's prose is also apparent in the structure of her novels. Sometimes, as in all of *The Sea Change* and most of *After Julius*, the novel consists of alternate narrations from the point of view of a small number of closely connected characters. Each episode is seen from at least two points of view, started by one character, taken up by the next who then moves the narrative on a little further until a third character takes it up. In *After Julius* the action of the novel is confined to a three-day week-end, although most of the characters are engaged in sorting out casual connections of current problems to the heroic death of Julius at Dunkerque 20 years earlier. *Something in Disguise* compresses action into three segments: April, August, and December of a single year. *The Long View* begins with a marriage breaking up in 1950 and its consequences for the couple's children, then traces the marriage back, through several precisely dated stages of problem and uneasy reconciliation, to its desperate origin in 1926. The past invariably leads to the present in Howard's fictional world, and the structural control often indicates both a working out of causation in human affairs and a kind of moral control, an insistence on a combination of awareness, responsibility, and refusal to hurt others in order to end the painful isolation of contemporary dilemmas.

More tightly controlled, and showing characters able to resolve their dilemmas more positively than do some other novels, *After Julius* depends, to some extent, on a rather striking coincidence. A young woman, visiting her mother for the week-end, finds her London lover, whom she had thought in Rome, arriving, with his wife, for dinner, and the affair explodes in a scene where fireworks are literal as well as symbolic. The structured plot shapes a novel in which moral or immoral actions eventually reveal themselves, in which moral judgment insists that characters take publicly visible responsibility for their actions. Similarly, in *Odd Girl Out* the young girl, amoral from a conventional point of view, who visits a young couple who have established a self-sufficient "island" in ten years of marriage and, in turn, sleeps with each of the partners, refuses to lie and insists on confronting both together to try to establish the "truth" of a three-way love that could nourish a child. Although the *ménage à trois*, full of ironic parallels and other forms of structural compression, cannot work for these three characters, the young girl who proposes it is seen as more moral, more willing to face the consequences of her actions and her emotions, than is the superficially more respectable couple. Virtue, in Howard's world, is not fragmented or buried, never the private gesture of an alienated sensibility; rather, actions have consequences, visible and direct, on the people closest to one.

Knowing and facing the past allows all three of the central women in *After Julius* some kind of resolution of their current dilemmas, but Howard's endings are not always so positive. In *The Sea Change* an aging playwright, who has longed for a renewal of youth in loving a young girl brought up in a village parsonage, and his wife, who has lost her only child, can understand and forgive each other in an acknowledgment of mutual pain and loss. The acknowledgment, the assumption of responsibility, allows them to survive, although it is far from a triumphant resolution. In *Something in Disguise* the resolution is melodramatic. The mother, a war widow who has raised her children alone, finally marries a retired army colonel to whom both her children object. Underneath the colonel's blunt, dull, insensitive exterior, the author slowly reveals, is the criminal heart of a man who tries gradually to poison his wife for her money, as he has poisoned two previous wives. And the daughter, who unpredictably marries a man who is both exciting and considerate, both a successful man of the world and a paragon of simple understanding and virtue, is desolate when the man is killed in an auto accident, having been sent on a fool's errand by one of the inconsiderate. Although moral judgment on each of the characters is clear enough, the plot punishes with an intensity that seems, somewhat sensationally, to detract from the emphasis on moral choice in some of the other novels. In the most recent novel, *Getting It Right*, melodrama and sensationalism recede into the background, useful for the hairdresser's discovery of sex, but not finally relevant to his moral choices that require the careful adjustment of both his concern for others' pain and his need to establish a satisfying life for himself.

Howard's carefully shaped moral tales are also dense with descriptions and references that convey the social texture of the times. *The Long View* is skillful in recreating both the sense of the wealthy English in southern France between the wars and the austerely genteel dinner party of 1950. *The Sea Change* contrasts the conventional life in the village parsonage with that of the 1950's playwright conveying a young girl to London, New York, and a Greek island. *After Julius* is brilliant with settings: the tiny attic office of the editorial staff of an old, respectable publishing firm; the spacious, chintzy Tudor of the mother's house in Sussex; the cheerful chaos of a young doctor's and his family's crowded flat. *Something in Disguise* contains a terrifying portrait of daily life in the pseudo-Spanish surroundings of the "distinguished" house on a new suburban housing estate. Within these tartly observed and wholly recognizable environments, certain types appear in novel after novel. The apparently dull retired Army officer, either basically sensitive and kindly or basically cruel and criminal, represents an older England, an irrelevant survival. The confident man of the world, playwright in *The Sea Change*, doctor in *After Julius*, international business-man in *Something in Disguise* (though quickly parodied in *Getting It Right*), generally has not allowed charm, success, or the modern world to distort his basically simple sense of responsibility. But all these men are seen from the point of view of women, and the novels reiterate a constant sense that women are more responsible, more affectionate, more genuinely concerned with others than men are. After the dinner party that opens *The Long View*, the men rejoin the women "having discussed the fundamentals as superficially as the women in the drawing room discussed the superficialities fundamentally." *Getting It Right* switches the emphasis to the young lower-middle class male hairdresser discovering his need for risking conflict and responsibility, his recognition that one "can't take out a kind of emotional insurance policy with people." The three principal women in the novel have known this all along.

Howard's intelligent and sensitive heroines are, however, far from independent. They often regret or seek to rediscover the wise father lost. The benign and revered village parson father in *The Sea Change* is killed in a bicycle accident; fathers in other novels are killed in the Second World War; still other fathers, like the one in *The Long View*, are remote and indifferent or, like the actor who deserts his family in a melodramatic sub-plot in *Odd Girl Out*, completely irresponsible. The heroines seek protection, look for the man who might replace the absent father and make smoothly decisive all the hard and complex edges of a difficult world. They want to be safe and cosseted, a desire that can lead to the aridity of *The Long View*, the self-discovery of *After Julius*, or the impossible fantasies of *Something in Disguise* and *Odd Girl Out*. The complexities of the search for protection are stated explicitly near the end of *Odd Girl Out*, when the couple turns the amoral young girl who proposed it into a scapegoat who can be exorcised. Yet they cannot return to their "island": "Each thought of what he had to do to sustain life for the other; each considered his efforts and translated them into nobility and unselfish determination." The roles are not equivalent, for, a few pages later, at the very end of the novel, the wife realizes that she, who had thought herself protected originally, must now become the principal protector. And they will not have a child. In Howard's fictional world sympathetic and competent mothers, who abound, are not enough. Heroines need the wisdom, the control, and the safety of the responsible and caring father, a safety dimly seen, always lost, and invariably over-compensated for. Looking for safety, always precarious in a world of airplanes and betrayals, requires a great deal of risk, sensitivity, and control. Elizabeth Jane Howard's great distinction is that the search for safety is presented with such rare and intelligent discrimination.

—James Gindin

HOWARD, Maureen (née Keans). American. Born in Bridgeport, Connecticut, 28 June 1930. Educated at Smith College, Nrthampton, Massachusetts, B.A. 1952. Married 1) Daniel F. Howard in 1954 (divorced, 1967), one daughter; 2) David J. Gordon in 1968; 3) third marriage. Worked in publishing and advertising, 1952–54; Lecturer in English, New School for Social Research, New York, 1967–68, 1970–71, and since 1974, and at University of California, Santa Barbara, 1968–69, Amherst College, Massachusetts, and Brooklyn College. Currently, Member of the English Department, Columbia University, New York. Recipient: Guggenheim fellowship, 1967; Radcliffe Institute fellowship, 1967; National Book Critics Circle award, 1979. Address: c/o Summit Books, Simon and Schuster, 1230 Avenue of the Americas, New York, New York 10020, U.S.A.

PUBLICATIONS

Novels

Not a Word about Nightingales. London, Secker and Warburg, 1960; New York, Atheneum, 1962.
Bridgeport Bus. New York, Harcourt Brace, 1965.
Before My Time. Boston, Little Brown, 1975.
Grace Abounding. Boston, Little Brown, 1982; London, Abacus, 1984.
Expensive Habits. New York, Summit, 1986.

Uncollected Short Stories

"Bed and Breakfast," in *Yale Review* (New Haven, Connecticut), March 1961.
"Sherry," in *The Best American Short Stories 1965*, edited by Martha Foley and David Burnett. Boston, Houghton Mifflin, 1965.
"Three Pigs of Krishna Nura," in *Partisan Review* (New Brunswick, New Jersey), Winter 1971–72.

"Sweet Memories," in *Statements*, edited by Jonathan Baumbach. New York, Braziller, 1975.

Other

Facts of Life (autobiography). Boston, Little Brown, 1978.

Editor, *Seven American Women Writers of the Twentieth Century.* Minneapolis, University of Minnesota Press, 1977.
Editor, *The Penguin Book of Contemporary American Essays.* New York, Viking, 1984.

*   *   *

In her award-winning autobiography, *Facts of Life*, Maureen Howard explains the conflict between her goals and her father's hopes for her: "I think because I loved him, coarse and unlettered as he pretended to be, that he would have known from experience that our lives do not admit the fictional luxury of alternate endings." Howard's fiction reflects this view that alternate endings are illusive. As her characters attempt to recreate their stories, they discover that the past has predetermined their lives. One cannot alter personality; one can only understand, accept, and grow within the frame of individual talent. At the end of *Facts of Life*, Howard describes herself at 23: "I am beginning. My life is beginning which cannot be true." Her life began long ago, her character determined years before that moment. That the majority of Howard's fictional characters are female seems coincidental; in her introduction to *Seven American Women Writers of the Twentieth Century*, Howard asserts her preference for universal concerns: "To my mind this is the most egalitarian manner in which to study women's literature—to presume that these women are artists first and do not have to be unduly praised or their reputations justified on grounds of sex." In Howard's novels, discovery and acceptance of one's own character challenge both genders.

When Professor Albert Sedgely, in *Not a Word about Nightingales*, prolongs his sabbatical in Italy, he wants "to take his life as it was and alter its limits as though he lived in a theatrical set, movable flats—and having created a new scene, then he could shift his tastes, his emotions, even his appearance." To create this illusive possibility, Howard emphasizes Albert's daughter Rosemary's reaction. As with Henry James's Strether in *The Ambassadors*, Rosemary, sent to bring Albert back, is so charmed by his new personality and environment that she ignores her pledge until she discovers Albert's affair with Carlotta Manzini. Sexual awakening so threatens Rosemary, her mother Anne, and even Albert that all three retreat to narrow and confined lives. Is this the novel that Howard alludes to in *Facts of Life* as her "mannered academic novel," that displays a "sense of order as I knew it in the late fifties and early sixties with all the forms that I accepted and even enjoyed: that was the enormous joke about life—that our passion must be contained if we were not to be fools"? If so, at least Albert's final decision rests on acknowledgement of his own character; that his love for Carlotta is "incomplete" and his business with Anne "unfinished" brings Albert home.

With humor Howard tackles the same questions in *Bridgeport Bus*. Although Howard shifts point of view frequently between her protagonist Mary Agnes Keely and other characters, the central question belongs to Mary Agnes: is "the mutually destructive love of mother and daughter more substantial than tidy freedom"? Howard's readers view Mary Agnes's attempts as recorded in her journals. When Mary Agnes begins her affair with Stanley Sarnicki, she records the event twice: first as "a thirty-five-year-old virgin would write it—the easy dodge and genteel fade-out," and then "done by a thirty-five-year-old lady *writer* who fancies herself a woman of experience when really there will always be something too delicate about her sensibility." Mary Agnes cannot escape her own nature, despite the different journal entries. As in her play, "The Cheese Stands Alone," one of several creative interludes in her journal, Mary Agnes recognizes that her fate is "inextricably woven" to her mother's. She returns, pregnant and unmarried, to help her mother die. Truth and fiction are not always discernible in Mary Agnes's journal, but as her friend Lydia comments, "she has in fact got at us in every meaningful respect." Mary Agnes's "triumph" is that she knows that "it was not a great sin to be, at last, alone." She has grown within her limits.

By sharing personal histories, Laura Quinn in *Before My Time* exchanges spirits with her cousin's son, Jim Cogan. At the end of the novel, a more responsible Jim returns to face drug charges while Laura writes of personal rather than public feelings. However, Howard states clearly, "Whoever compares the present and the past will soon perceive that there prevail and always have prevailed the same desires and passions." Although beneficial, this ending reflects an awakening, not a creation, of character. To develop the pedagogy to instruct young Jim, Laura resees her brother Robert's failed relationship with their father; silently to Jim, Laura urges, "Think that this story is your answer: Robert and all my honesty and self-knowledge are here for you at last. Think before you run." Howard also offers histories of other family members. The most successful story, that of Jim's twin siblings Cormac and Siobhan, parallels Jim and Laura's as the twins have similar desires but are out of step with each other. Mary Agnes Keely may have had "triumph" in *Bridgeport Bus*, but at the end of *Before My Time*, Laura Quinn's new doubt is as "sweet"; the confines of her personality contain newly tapped emotion.

Because Howard's characters in *Grace Abounding* remain isolated from each other, the reader senses little more than ongoing struggle at the end of this novel. Within shifts of point of view and time frame, each character attempts to discern what in the past enlightens the present. The reader first meets Maude and Elizabeth Dowd in shock after Frank Dowd's death; widow Maude and daughter Elizabeth, "unable to speak of their abandonment," "have drawn off into private desolation." Maude's mother, lost in the world of senility, and her nurse die soon after. Years later, neither Maude's nor Elizabeth's husbands know their wives' true natures. In a disturbing scene, three-year-old Warren, a victim of child abuse who is locked within himself, dies before Maude, now a psychologist, can reach him. Only the mad poet Mattie appears to have a whole life, but, after her death, her heir inadvertently burns all her poems. After the first two sections of the novel, "Sin" and "Sorrow," the reader expects in the final "Grace Note" some resolution but encounters instead Theodore Lasser, Maude's husband's son, a priest more concerned with public relations than spiritual needs. Where then is that "grace abounding"? The last line holds some answer: "The young priest stumbles back and forth from bush to lemon tree, brushing and brushing at cold cobwebs that will fade with the morning dew." The reader knows that Theodore's ghostly cobwebs stem from unresolved conflicts with his father. *Grace Abounding* may well serve as Howard's warning rather than model: to accept limits, one must discover, know, and then share one's nature.

—Mary M. Lay

HUGHES, David (John). British. Born in Alton, Hampshire, 27 July 1930. Educated at Eggar's Grammar School, Alton; King's College School, Wimbledon; Christ Church, Oxford (Editor, *Isis*), B.A. in English 1953, M.A. 1965. Served in the Royal Air Force, 1949–50. Married 1) the actress and director Mai Zetterling in 1958 (divorced, 1976); 2) Elizabeth Westoll in 1980; one daughter and one son. Assistant editor, *London Magazine*, 1953–54; editor, *Town* magazine, London, 1960–61; documentary and feature film writer in Sweden, 1961–68; lived in France, 1970–74; editor, New Fiction Society, 1975–77, 1981–82; film critic, *Sunday Times*, London, 1982–83. Recipient: W.H. Smith Literary Award, 1985; Welsh Arts Council prize, 1985. Lives in London and South Wales. Agent: Anthony Sheil Associates, 43 Doughty Street, London WC1N 2LF, England.

PUBLICATIONS

Novels

A Feeling in the Air. London, Deutsch, 1957; as *Man Off Beat*, New York, Reynal, 1957.
Sealed with a Loving Kiss. London, Hart Davies, 1959.
The Horsehair Sofa. London, Hart Davis, 1961.
The Major. London, Blond, 1964; New York, Coward McCann, 1965.
The Man Who Invented Tomorrow. London, Constable, 1968.
Memories of Dying. London, Constable, 1976.
A Genoese Fancy. London, Constable, 1979.
The Imperial German Dinner Service. London, Constable, 1983.
The Pork Butcher. London, Constable, 1984; New York, Schocken, 1985.
But for Bunter. London, Heinemann, 1985.

Uncollected Short Stories

"The Coloured Cliffs," in *Transatlantic Review* (London), Spring 1961.
"Rough Magic," in *Shakespeare Stories*, edited by Giles Gordon. London, Hamish Hamilton, 1982.

Plays

Flickorna (screenplay). Stockholm, PAN/Norstedt, 1968.

Screenplays (with Mai Zetterling): *Loving Couples*, 1964; *Night Games*, 1966; *Dr. Glas*, 1967; *The Girls*, 1968.

Other

J.B. Priestley: An Informal Study of His Work. London, Hart Davis, 1958; Freeport, New York, Books for Libraries, 1970.
The Road to Stockholm and Lapland. London, Eyre and Spottiswoode, 1964.
The Cat's Tale (for children), with Mai Zetterling. London, Cape, 1965.
The Seven Ages of England. Stockholm, Swedish Radio, 1966.
The Rosewater Revolution: Notes on a Change of Attitude. London, Constable, 1971.

Editor, *Memoirs of the Comte de Gramont*, translated by Horace Walpole. London, Folio Society, 1965.
Editor, *Sound of Protest, Sound of Love: Protest-Songs from America and England.* Stockholm, Swedish Radio, 1968.

Editor, *Evergreens.*   Stockholm, Swedish Radio, 1977.
Editor, *Winter's Tales 1* (new series).   London, Constable, 1985.
Editor, *The Stories of Ernest Hemingway.*   London, Folio Society, 1986.

*   *   *

David Hughes takes war for his subject, but he is certainly not concerned to make stirring adventures out of the sordid tragedies, mass killings, and crowd emotions of armed conflict, nor to contrive intellectual puzzles out of the intrigues of international enmity. His business is with individuals and the way that their lives have been shaped (and frequently grossly distorted) by the wars of this century.

His skilful control of his subject matter, his ingenuity as a story teller, and his subtle and powerful delineation of character enable him to create unforgettable novels out of his chosen material. He seldom makes overt judgements. His characters may condemn themselves out of their obsessions and stored guilt, but their creator insists that, whatever they may have done to other people, they are themselves frail and vulnerable, and therefore, in some respects at least, loveable. However much the readers are kept at a distance by the way Hughes structures his novels, they are never allowed to forget that he is dealing with people not ciphers.

The history of the war-torn first half of this century is epitomised in *Memories of Dying*, in which Flaxman, a prosperous business man on the brink of a nervous breakdown is suddenly caught up into the consciousness of his old history teacher, Hunter. As Flaxman flies to the south of France, in a vain attempt to escape from the pressures of work and family, he finds his mind invaded by thoughts of his home town and the aged lonely man who once taught him, now engaged in the impossible task of writing a history of the world that will present the facts honestly to future generations of schoolchildren. It is an act of penitence, for in the first world war Hunter through accident and panic shot one of his fellow officers. For years thereafter he carried the man's wallet around with him, vowing that he would marry the widow whose photograph it contained. He achieved his aim. He located the woman, who had turned into a lonely alcoholic, married her, and had one son. At the outbreak of World War II he insisted that she should leave their home for a more remote cottage. In that place, of his choosing, she was killed by a random air raid. History had not finished with Hunter. Sometime in the years of unsteady peace, his son was found dead of drugs and alcohol in an Oxford college.

Like Hunter, the narrator of *The Imperial German Dinner Service* tries to make some reparative and creative response to the war-torn century into which he has been born. In his case, his task takes the symbolic form of collecting the scattered pieces of a dinner service made in Edwardian England as a gift for the Kaiser. Many threads are drawn into his search, for Hughes is determined to show, yet again, how individual needs are woven into public events. As his obsessed narrator journeys to meet his unlikely contacts in the countries of western Europe and Scandinavia, and ultimately reaches the precarious geology of Iceland in his search for the fragile pieces of china, he is reconstructing his own life as well as searching for the innocence of an impossible golden age. Each bit of the dinner service is adorned with an English scene, which he has visited at some time with his estranged wife. So, as Europe is torn, so is he, both by the torments of his marriage to an ambitious Sunday columnist (who discovered the first plate of the dinner service and so set him off on his quest) and the futility of his own work as a free-lance journalist.

Ernst Kestner, the protagonist of *The Pork Butcher*, Hughes's most important and serious novel so far, is also on a quest. A widower from Thomas Mann's town of Lubeck, he is dying of lung cancer and determined that his final act shall be a confrontation with the guilt of his war-time past. So he goes to Paris to take his coldly neurotic, self-obsessed daughter (who has married a Frenchman) on a weekend trip to the village where he had been stationed in the 1940's. In that village, Kestner had met Jannie and become so infatuated with her that he wrote home to his German fiancée breaking off the engagement. The letter never arrived, for the day he posted it, the order came that the village was to be "punished," the inhabitants were to be lured to the central square and shot, and the whole place was to be abandoned. In the numbed brutality of that act, Kestner killed the girl he loved. Now, like Hunter, he is determined to make some amends, even if all he can do is to give himself up to the mayor of the restored village. Beating the usual intransigence of local bureaucracy, he manages to talk to the mayor and gradually realises that the man is Jannie's brother. When the mayor also recognises to whom he is talking, he drives the car in which he is conveying Kestner with such wild fury that it is involved in a fatal accident. The mayor is killed; and Kestner, now badly injured, has to end his life with a double guilt on his shoulders. This irony underlines the impossibility of making amends either internationally or personally for the obscenities of war.

But for Bunter takes up the same theme in a strangely light-hearted vein. Hughes imagines that Billy Bunter (the fat boy of Greyfriars, who entertained generations of schoolboys) has survived into the 1980's, and is now ready to confess his own responsibility for the horrors of the century he has lived through. Once again Hughes makes his point: none of us, not even the most unlikely, can shelve responsibility for the times we live in.

—Shirley Toulson

———————

HUIE, William Bradford.   American.   Born in Hartselle, Alabama, 13 November 1910. Educated at the University of Alabama, A.B. 1930 (Phi Beta Kappa). Served in the United States Navy, 1943–45: Lieutenant. Married 1) Ruth Puckett in 1934 (died, 1973); 2) Martha Hunt Robertson in 1977. Reporter, Birmingham *Post*, Alabama, 1932–36; associate editor, 1942–43, and editor and publisher, 1945–52, *American Mercury*, New York. Agent: Ned Brown, P.O. Box 5020, Beverly Hills, California 90210. Address: P.O. Box 1567, Scottsboro, Alabama 35768, U.S.A.

PUBLICATIONS

Novels

Mud on the Stars.   New York, Fischer, 1942; London, Hutchinson, 1944.
The Revolt of Mamie Stover.   New York, Duell, 1951; London, W.H. Allen, 1953.
The Americanization of Emily.   New York, Dutton, 1959; London, W.H. Allen, 1960.
Hotel Mamie Stover.   London, W.H. Allen, 1962; New York, Potter, 1963.

The Klansman.   New York, Delacorte Press, 1967; London, W.H. Allen, 1968.
In the Hours of the Night.   New York, Delacorte Press, 1975.

Short Stories

Wolf Whistle and Other Stories.   New York, New American Library, 1959.
The Hero of Iwo Jima and Other Stories.   New York, New American Library, 1962.

Other

The Fight for Air Power.   New York, Fischer, 1942.
Seabee Roads to Victory.   New York, Dutton, 1944.
Can Do! The Story of the Seabees.   New York, Dutton, 1944.
From Omaha to Okinawa: The Story of the Seabees.   New York, Dutton, 1946.
The Case Against the Admirals: Why We Must Have a Unified Command.   New York, Dutton, 1946.
The Execution of Private Slovik: The Hitherto Secret Story of the Only American Soldier since 1864 to Be Shot for Desertion.   New York, Duell, and London, Jarrolds, 1954.
Ruby McCollum: Woman in the Suwannee Jail.   New York, Dutton, 1956; revised edition, New York, New American Library, 1964; as *The Crime of Ruby McCollum*, London, Jarrolds, 1957.
The Hiroshima Pilot.   New York, Putnam, and London, Heinemann, 1964.
Three Lives for Mississippi.   New York, Whitney Communication Corporation, and London, Heinemann, 1965.
He Slew the Dreamer: My Search with James Earl Ray for the Truth about the Murder of Martin Luther King.   New York, Delacorte Press, and London, W.H. Allen, 1970; revised edition, as *Did the FBI Kill Martin Luther King?*, Nashville, Nelson, 1977.
It's Me, O Lord! (on Dan Ronsisvalle).   Nashville, Nelson, 1979.

*   *   *

William Bradford Huie is primarily a journalist, and his fiction shows that in two ways—by his being able to turn out a light, popular novel, and by his recourse to fiction to present a situation of controversy which he could not prove well enough to present as fact. His non-fiction, however, can be read as a novel, for his books are always structured well, and the subjects he chooses are dramatic to the point of being shocking. Only once has he failed to build horrendous suspense in a story, and that was when he was let down in his interviews with James Earl Ray, the convicted murderer of Martin Luther King, by Ray's persisting that he had no accomplices. *The Revolt of Mamie Stover* and *Hotel Mamie Stover* are lusty stories carried by the character of the title figure. *The Americanization of Emily* is a sentimental story of a love affair between an English girl and an American soldier during the war. Although highly popular, these are ephemeral works, and if Huie had written nothing but this kind of thing and his short stories he would not be the important figure that he is in American writing.

Huie soon became interested in lost, forgotten, or obscured causes. He came across the fact that only one American soldier had been executed for desertion during the Second World War; and in *The Execution of Private Slovik* he not only presented a thorough and understanding biography and analysis of that pathetic slum boy, who was chosen out of many deserters as

an example because he seemed worthless to the reviewing officers, but made the point of view of all such people come clear. Huie's book is essential to the understanding of a book like Nelson Algren's *The Man with the Golden Arm.*

The Hiroshima Pilot blasts the myth that the man who dropped the first atom bomb was consumed by conscience over it—this man wasn't the pilot who carried the bomb out but one who flew a weather plane. Huie is a native Southerner, and lives in Alabama, so he has written extensively about the injustices of his region, especially toward Blacks. When three young civil rights workers were murdered in Mississippi in 1964, with at least the connivance of the county sheriff, he investigated deeply and produced *Three Lives for Mississippi.*

Unable to tell all he knew, not only about this atrocity, Huie produced a novel, *The Klansman*, that although too melodramatic and journalistic to be considered a fine novel, is certainly more polished than that earlier polemic, *Uncle Tom's Cabin.* His villain is the system, not people. His sheriff, although a racist, is above the average. His hero, a descendent of the old southern aristocracy, and his victim, a Negro girl with a good job in Chicago, back in Mississippi, are too good to be true. Huie uses fiction, but he uses it to good effect.

—William Bittner

HULME, Keri.   New Zealander. Born in Christchurch, 9 March 1947. Educated at North Beach primary school; Aranui High School; Canterbury University, Christchurch. Formerly, senior postwoman, Greymouth, and director for New Zealand television; Writer-in-Residence, Canterbury University, 1985. Recipient: New Zealand Literary Fund grant, 1975, 1977, 1979; Katherine Mansfield Memorial Award, for short story, 1975; Maori Trust Fund prize, 1978; East-West Centre award, 1979; ICI bursary, 1982; New Zealand writing bursary, 1984; Book of the Year Award, 1984; Mobil Pegasus Prize, 1984; Booker Prize, 1985. Address: Okarito, Westland, New Zealand.

Publications

Novels

The Bone People.   Wellington, Spiral, 1983; London, Hodder and Stoughton, and Baton Rouge, Louisiana State University Press, 1985.
Lost Possessions (novella).   Wellington, Victoria University Press, 1985.

Short Stories

The Windeater/Te Kaihau.   Wellington, Victoria University Press, 1986.

Uncollected Short Stories

"One Whale Singing," in *Broadsheet 39* (Auckland), May 1976.
"King Bait," in *New Zealand Listener* (Wellington), 13 April 1977.
"Kiteflying at Doctor's Point," in *Islands* (Auckland), Autumn 1977.
"Stations on the Way to Avalon," in *Islands* (Auckland), Spring 1978.

"Nightsong for the Shining Cuckoo" (as Kai Tainui), in *Landfall 137* (Christchurch), March 1981.
"Hooks and Feelers" and "The Kaumatua and the Broken Man," in *Into the World of Light*, edited by Witi Ihimaera and D.S. Long. Auckland, Heinemann, 1982.
"See Me, I Am Kei," in *Spiral 5* (Wellington), 1982.
"He Tauwere Kawa," in *Manawatu Evening Standard*, 1984.

Verse

The Silences Between (Moeraki Conversations). Auckland, Auckland University Press-Oxford University Press, 1982.

*

Critical Studies: "In My Spiral Fashion" by Peter Simpson, in *Australian Book Review* (Kensington Park), August 1984; "Spiralling to Success" by Elizabeth Webby, in *Meanjin* (Melbourne), January 1985; "Keri Hulme: Breaking Ground" by Shona Smith, in *Untold 2* (Christchurch).

Keri Hulme comments:
    I have a grave suspicion that Life is a vast joke: we are unwitting elements of the joke.
    It is not a nice or kind joke, either.
    I write about people who are in pain because they cant see the joke, see the point of the joke.
    What I write is fantasy-solidly-based-in-Reality, everyday myths.
    I rarely write out of a New Zealand context and, because I am lucky enough to be a mongrel, draw extensively from my ancestral cultural heritages—Maori (Kai Tahu, the South Island tribe), Scots (the Orkneys), and English (Lancashire). (Remember that the Pakeha elements of my ancestry predominate, but they have been well-sieved by Aotearoa.)
    I want to touch the raw nerves in NZ—the violence we largely cover up; the racism we dont acknowledge; the spoliation of land & sea that has been smiled at for the past 150 years—and explore *why* we (Maori & Pakeha) have developed a very curious type of humour which not many other people in the world understand, like, or appreciate and which is a steel-sheathed nerve I want to hide inside.
    I'm not particularly serious about anything except whitebaiting. (Whitebait are the fry of NZ galaxids: they are a greatly relished and *very* expensive—about $50NZ a kilo—delicacy. I whitebait every season.)

*   *   *

    Keri Hulme comes from the heartland of New Zealand—the South Island's west coast—and, perhaps as a consequence, she has developed an idiom which remains distinctively New Zealand even when it is feeding on the great traditions of English, Irish, American, and other (notably sufic) literature. This New Zealandness is the most immediately striking feature of the work for which she is best known, *The Bone People*.
    The Maori phrases which permeate the text immediately proclaim its provenance. But the texture of the English which she writes is also unmistakably New Zealand. Many writers before her have managed a passable imitation of Kiwi pub argot, but Hulme is one of the first to have succeeded in giving a characteristic account of the speech and thoughts of New Zealanders as educated and intelligent as her protagonist, Kerewin Holmes. In passages like the following one can sense the typical rhythms and accents ("thunk"), the half-suppressed obscenities ("whateffers"), the gentle ironies and not-so-gentle prejudices ("Poms" are Englishmen) of New Zealand's more

articulate denizens. (Kerewin has just discovered that her young protégé, Simon Gillayley, may have aristocratic Irish blood):

    Ah hell, urchin, it doesn't matter, you can't help who your forbears were, and I realized as I thunk it, that I was revelling in the knowledge of my whakapapa and solid Lancashire and Hebridean ancestry. Stout commoners on the left side, and real rangatira on the right distaff side. A New Zealander through and through. Moanawhenua bones and heart and blood and brain. None of your (retch) import Poms or whateffers.

    The uncovering of Simon's background constitutes one strand of the plot of *The Bone People*, but ultimately it turns out to be an inconclusive strand. All we can be sure of is that he comes from a background of violence and drug-dealing. The more detailed clues lead nowhere, and it seems that Hulme intended merely to tease her readers with these elements of a "well-made" plot, and that her real interest lay elsewhere. As Kerewin begins to check out Simon's Irish background she apologizes for "dragging" the reader "out of the cobweb pile, self-odyssey." The phrase highlights not only the book's principal concern (Kerewin's mental and spiritual progress) but also one of its dominant images (the spider's web, which at different times represents entanglement and intricate harmony).
    Even more prominent than the spider and its web is the traditional Maori (and sufic) motif of the spiral. Kerewin lives in a tower full of spirals, notably a spiral staircase and a double spiral engraved on the floor: "one of the kind that wound your eyes round and round into the centre where surprise you found the beginning of another spiral that led your eyes out again to the nothingness of the outside ... it was an old symbol of rebirth, and the outward-inward nature of things ...." At the beginning of the book Kerewin has clearly begun a downward spiral into "nothingness." Her Tower, conceived as a "hermitage," "a glimmering retreat," has become an "abyss," a "prison." She is entangled in a web of self-absorption and materialism.
    Into her life walks Simon, who is her opposite in almost every respect. She is dark (though only one-eighth Maori); he is fair. She is "heavy shouldered, heavy-hammered, heavy-haired"; he is lithe, almost skeletal. She is wonderfully articulate; he is a mute. (Again Hulme teases our expectations of a "well-made" plot by holding out the promise that he will eventually learn to speak. He does not.) She is obsessed by her possessions, and fears as a consequence that she has "lost the main part" of life; he is "rough on possessions," but has a sense of the deeper aura of things. She shrinks from touching others; he and his adoptive father (Joe) are, as Hulme subsequently put it, "huggers and kissers deluxe." She is clever; he is trusting—two terms which are juxtaposed in the book. She is associated with the moon; he is a "sunchild." She is an introvert; he and Joe are extroverts.
    Symbol-hunters have been quick to latch on to Simon's character, but they have so far been baffled by the diffuseness of the portrait. Hulme herself claims that she writes "from a visual base and a gut base rather than sieving it through the mind," and so it is probably futile to search for any conscious allegorical design in the book. A psycho-analytical approach offers greater rewards. Many aspects of *The Bone People*—notably the dreams (which often foretell the future) the paintings, the search for "wholeness" (and the dance imagery which accompanies it), the emphasis on myth, the eclectic attitude to religion, the disdainful attitude towards sex, and the mandala-like

tricephalos which anticipates the asexual harmony ("commensalism") achieved by the principal characters at the end—suggest the influence of Jung. Jung also provides as good an explanation as any of Simon's relationship with Kerewin.

The book is full of projections and personifications of deviant aspects of the characters' personalities. Kerewin's more cynical thoughts are attributed to an inner voice labelled "the snark"; her violent tendencies turn at length into a palpable cancer; and the mysterious character who helps her to grapple with this cancer ("a thin wiry person of indeterminate age. Of indeterminate sex. Of indeterminate race") appears to be a projection of her own enfeebled self. Similarly Simon (who was originally conceived as a figment of Kerewin's dreams and not as an independent character) may be seen as her "shadow"—the embodiment of everything she has lost by withdrawing from society. This includes not only positive factors like trust and responsiveness to touch but also negative ones, especially violence.

Simon brings with him a long history of violence, culminating in the savage beatings inflicted on him by Joe. Kerewin's spiralling descent is accompanied and to a large extent occasioned by her recognition of this violence, and the nadir of her "self-odyssey" comes when she gives way to violence herself. At the same time an orgy of violence (effectively amplified by the recurrent images of knives and splintered glass) erupts among the other characters, so that at the end of the third part of the novel Simon is hospitalized, Joe (wounded) is in jail, one minor character is dead, another seriously ill, and Kerewin's Tower has been reduced to a single storey. Many readers feel that Hulme should have left the book there—that, as in much of her other fiction (of which the fine story "Hooks and Feelers" and the novella *Lost Possessions* are the most accessible examples) it is the violence, and especially the violence that wells out of love, which is the most compelling element. But Hulme added a fourth section and an epilogue in which the principals, aided by a set of unorthodox assistants and (except in Simon's case) by a deep draught of Maori culture, spiral back towards "rebirth," "wholeness," and harmony.

In a recent interview Hulme has acknowledged that the ending owes something to Jung, which encourages the notion advanced here that the whole novel is susceptible to a Jungian interpretation. Just who is really the focus of this interpretation—Kerewin Holmes or her virtual namesake, Keri Hulme—is a question difficult to resolve. Hulme concedes that the three protagonists emerged from her dreams. (She keeps a dream diary, and at least one of the dreams in *The Bone People*—Kerewin's at Moerangi—is lifted straight from it.) Much of the material also seems quasi-autobiographical. Time will tell if she can write effectively on less personal subjects.

—Richard Corballis

HUMPHREY, William. American. Born in Clarkesville, Texas, 18 June 1924. Educated at Southern Methodist University, Dallas; University of Texas, Austin. Married to Dorothy Humphrey. Recipient: American Academy award, 1962. Lives in Lexington, Virginia. Address: c/o Delacorte Press, 1 Dag Hammarskjold Plaza, New York, New York, 10017, U.S.A.

PUBLICATIONS

Novels

Home from the Hill. New York, Knopf, and London, Chatto and Windus, 1958.
The Ordways. New York, Knopf, and London, Chatto and Windus, 1965.
Proud Flesh. New York, Knopf, and London, Chatto and Windus, 1973.
Hostages to Fortune. New York, Delacorte Press, 1984; London, Secker and Warburg, 1985.

Short Stories

The Last Husband and Other Stories. New York, Morrow, and London, Chatto and Windus, 1953.
A Time and a Place: Stories. New York, Knopf, 1968; as *A Time and a Place: Stories of the Red River Country*, London, Chatto and Windus, 1969.

The Collected Stories. New York, Delacorte Press, 1985.

Other

The Spawning Run: A Fable. New York, Knopf, and London, Chatto and Windus, 1970.
Ah, Wilderness! The Frontier in American Literature. El Paso, Texas Western Press, 1977.
Farther Off from Heaven. New York, Knopf, and London, Chatto and Windus, 1977.
My Moby Dick. New York, Doubleday, 1978; London, Chatto and Windus, 1979.

*

Critical Study: *William Humphrey* by James W. Lee, Austin, Texas, Steck Vaughn, 1967.

*   *   *

Locale is a potent force in most of William Humphrey's best work. Three of his four novels and nearly all of his successful short stories are set in the Red River country of northeast Texas. Humphrey should not, however, be dismissed as nothing more than a regionalist. Like Faulkner, with whom he is often compared, Humphrey uses locale as a framework for the discussion of universal issues.

Home from the Hill, Humphrey's first and certainly his best novel, is both a first-class *Bildungsroman* and a family tragedy of mythic dimensions. Much of the novel concerns young Theron Hunnicutt's passage to manhood, a journey largely related to his hunting experiences. The most powerful force in the novel, however, is Theron's father, Captain Wade—wealthy cotton planter, legendary hunter, notorious philanderer—more an embodiment of Texas myth than an actual flesh-and-blood man. The House of Hunnicutt is destined to have the father's sins visited upon it. The captain is murdered by the crazed father of a pregnant teenage girl in a highly ironic case of mistaken identity. Following the primitive code of manhood learned from his father and other hunting men, Theron pursues the murderer and eventually kills him. Theron then retreats to the recesses of Sulphur Bottom, an almost impenetrable swamp, presumably to die alone. Hannah Hunnicutt, the long-suffering wife, is taken away to a Dallas asylum where she spends the last 15 years of her life. Though often compelling, *Home from the Hill* contains more than a touch of melodrama, and the last third of the novel is too much a series of coincidences.

While Humphrey's first novel is a melodramatic tragedy, his second is a mock epic. *The Ordways* is a panoramic novel spanning four generations. Its first section largely concerns the journey of the wounded blinded Civil War veteran, Thomas Ordway, and his wife, Ella, along with both the remains and the tombstones of their kindred from eastern Tennessee to northeast Texas. Most of the rest of the novel concerns the 1898 journey of Sam Ordway, who traverses much of Texas in an attempt to find his kidnapped son. Despite his solemn oath to search to the ends of the earth if necessary, Sam Ordway is no avenging western hero, no believer in the primitive code of manhood that governs the life of Theron Hunnicutt and, for that matter, the lives of Sam's own Texas neighbors. His quest becomes picaresque and includes such events as a political rally in the small town of Paris, Texas, a jailing in Dallas on charges of intent to commit murder, and a stint with a traveling circus. In the best picaresque tradition, *The Ordways* ends happily, though in this case the hero fails in his quest. The reunion of father and son takes place some 30 years after Sam's journey. The strength of the novel is in its evocation of late 19th-century Texas. The author also includes an enlightening discourse on the relationship of the Southerner to his past. The book's major weakness is in the extent of the episodic account of Sam's travels. Though highly entertaining at points, this segment often seems like nothing more than a collection of incidents. One wishes for an end to the sequence long before it comes.

Humphrey has written of the Southerner: "Clannishness was and is the key to his temperament." *Proud Flesh*, his third novel, is about clannishness gone berserk. Centering on the death of matriarch Edwina "Ma" Renshaw, the novel is highly grotesque and often hilarious. Grotesquerie piles upon grotesquerie. When the family physician pronounces Edwina dead, he is forced to spend an additional three-day vigil at her bedside, just to make sure that his judgment has not been premature. An irrationally guilt-ridden oldest daughter entombs herself in the storm cellar, vowing never to emerge, an event which leads to the formation of a new religious cult. Finally, the dead matriarch's body is stored in a local cold storage plant while two Renshaws are dispatched to New York City to search for the family "black sheep," Edwina's favorite, who must return home before the funeral takes place. The novel's weakness is the same as that of *The Ordways* and even more apparent. More a collection of incidents than a coherent novel, *Proud Flesh* is allowed to continue far too long.

Humphrey's fourth novel, *Hostages to Fortune*, differs markedly from his first three in setting, theme, and tone. Set in the northeast, the novel concerns the agonized struggle of Ben Curtis, a 50-year-old writer and onetime avid fly-fisherman, to rebuild his life after a series of personal tragedies—the suicides of both his beloved god-daughter and his teenage son, the supposedly accidental death of his best friend, and the break-up of his marriage of 20 years. Having barely failed in a suicide attempt, the convalescing writer, hoping to regain the desire to go on living, journeys to a fishing lodge where he has spent some of his happiest moments. The novel consists largely of flashbacks which cover most of the significant events of Curtis's adult life. Curtis's tormented attempts to understand both his son's suicide and the demise of his once-happy marriage constitute some of the most poignant passages in Humphrey's fiction. Though *Hostages to Fortune* lacks the mythic dimension of *Home from the Hill*, Humphrey's tortured writer is among his most sympathetic creations.

Most of Humphrey's short stories are competent, and some are first-rate. Among the best are "The Shell," an account of a young man's growth to self-awareness as he struggles to

free himself from the shadow of his deceased father, a legendary hunter; "A Fresh Snow," a sensitive sketch of a lonely southern girl in a northern industrial city; "The Ballad of Jesse Neighbors," a tale of an ill-fated "poreboy" in Depression-era Red River Country who, as a victim of society and circumstance, recalls Hardy's Tess; and "Mouth of Brass," perhaps Humphrey's best story, a sensitive young narrator's recounting of his first experience with racial prejudice and small-town cowardice.

In addition to his fiction, Humphrey has written two slender volumes on fishing, *The Spawning Run* and *My Moby Dick*, a critical study, *Ah, Wilderness! The Frontier in American Literature*, and a poignant autobiographical work, *Farther Off from Heaven*. Though uneven, his work is quite readable. In his ability to evoke his native region, Humphrey has few if any equals.

—Craig Hudziak

HUMPHREYS, Emyr (Owen). British. Born in Prestatyn, Clwyd, Wales, 15 April 1919. Educated at University College of Wales, Aberystwyth, 1937–39; University College of North Wales, Bangor, 1946–47. Served as a relief worker in the Middle East and the Mediterranean during World War II. Married Elinor Myfanwy Jones in 1946; three sons and one daughter. Teacher, Wimbledon Technical College, London, 1948–50, and Pwllheli Grammar School, North Wales, 1951–54; producer, BBC Radio, Cardiff, 1955–58; drama producer, BBC Television, 1958–62; free-lance writer and director, 1962–65; Lecturer in Drama, University College of North Wales, 1965–72. Since 1972, free-lance writer. Recipient: Maugham Award, 1953; Hawthornden Prize, 1959; Welsh Arts Council award, 1972, 1975, 1979, for non-fiction, 1984; Gregynog Fellowship, 1974; Society of Authors travelling scholarship, 1979. Agent: Richard Scott Simon Ltd., 32 College Cross, London N1 1PR, England. Address: Llinon, Pwllgwyngyll, Gwynedd LL61 5YT, Wales.

PUBLICATIONS

Novels

The Little Kingdom. London, Eyre and Spottiswoode, 1946.
The Voice of a Stranger. London, Eyre and Spottiswoode, 1949.
A Change of Heart. London, Eyre and Spottiswoode, 1951.
Hear and Forgive. London, Gollancz, 1952; New York, Putnam, 1953.
A Man's Estate. London, Eyre and Spottiswoode, 1955; New York, McGraw Hill, 1956.
The Italian Wife. London, Eyre and Spottiswoode, 1957; New York, McGraw Hill, 1958.
Y Tri Llais (in Welsh). Llandybie, Dyfed, Llyfrau'r Dryw, 1958.
A Toy Epic. London, Eyre and Spottiswoode, 1958.
The Gift. London, Eyre and Spottiswoode, 1963.
Outside the House of Baal. London, Eyre and Spottiswoode, 1965.
National Winner. London, Macdonald, 1971.
Flesh and Blood. London, Hodder and Stoughton, 1974.
The Best of Friends. London, Hodder and Stoughton, 1978.

The Anchor Tree. London, Hodder and Stoughton, 1980.
Jones. London, Dent, 1984.
Salt of the Earth. London, Dent, 1985.
An Absolute Hero. London, Dent, 1986.

Short Stories

Natives. London, Secker and Warburg, 1968.
Miscellany Two. Bridgend, Glamorgan, Poetry Wales Press, 1981.

Uncollected Short Stories

"Down in the Heel on Duty," in *New English Review* (London), 1947.
"Michael Edwards," in *Wales* (London), vol. 7, nos. 26–27, 1947.
"A Girl in the Ice" and "The Obstinate Bottle," in *New Statesman* (London), 1953.
"Mrs. Armitage," in *Welsh Short Stories.* London, Faber, 1959.
"The Arrest," in *Madog 3* (Barry), 1977.

Plays

King's Daughter, adaptation of a play by Saunders Lewis (produced London, 1959; as *Siwan*, televised, 1960). Published, as *Siwan*, in *Plays of the Year 1959–60*, London, Elek, 1960.
Dinas, with W.S. Jones. Llandybie, Dyfed, Llyfrau'r Dryw, 1970.

Radio Plays: *A Girl in a Garden*, 1963; *Reg*, 1964; *The Manipulator*, 1970; *Etifedd y Glyn*, 1984; *The Arrest*, 1985.

Television Plays and Films: *Siwan*, 1960; *The Shining Pyramid*, from a story by Arthur Machen, 1979; *Y Gosb* (The Penalty), 1983; *Wŷn ir Lladdfa* (Lambs to the Slaughter), 1984; *Hualau* (Fetters), 1984; *Bwy yn Rhydd* (Living Free), 1984; *Angel o'r Nef* (An Angel from Heaven), 1985; *Teulu Helga* (Helga's Family), 1985.

Verse

Roman Dream, music by Alun Hoddinott. London, Oxford University Press, 1968.
An Apple Tree and a Pig, music by Alun Hoddinott. London, Oxford University Press, 1969.
Ancestor Worship: A Cycle of 18 Poems. Denbigh, Gee, 1970.
Landscapes, music by Alun Hoddinott. London, Oxford University Press, 1975.
Penguin Modern Poets 27, with John Ormond and John Tripp. London, Penguin, 1979.
The Kingdom of Bran. London, Holmes, 1979.
Pwyll a Riannon. London, Holmes, 1979.

Other

The Taliesin Tradition: A Quest for the Welsh Identity. London, Black Raven Press, 1983.

*

Bibliography: in *A Bibliography of Anglo-Welsh Literature 1900–1965* by Brynmor Jones, Swansea, Library Association, 1970.

Critical Studies: *The Novel 1945–1950* by P.H. Newby, London, Longman, 1951; *Y llenor a'i Gymdeithas* by A. Llewelyn Williams, London, BBC, 1966; *The Dragon Has Two Tongues* by Glyn Jones, London, Dent, 1968; *Ysgrifau Beirniadol VII* by Derec Llwyd Morgan, Denbigh, Gee, 1972; Jeremy Hooker and André Morgan, in *Planet 39* (Llangeitho Tregaron, Dyfed), 1977; *Emyr Humphreys*, Cardiff, University of Wales Press, 1980, and "Land of the Living," in *Planet 52* (Llangeitho Tregaron, Dyfed), 1985, both by Ioan Williams; "Channels of Grace: A View of the Earlier Novels of Emyr Humphreys," in *Anglo-Welsh Review 70* (Tenby, Dyfed), 1982, and article in *British Novelists 1930–1959* edited by Bernard Oldsey, Detroit, Gale, 1983, both by Roland Mathias.

*   *   *

The preoccupations of Emyr Humphreys are peculiarly Welsh, and since there are very few Welsh novelists writing in English who spring from or have assimilated the Welsh Nonconformist heritage, his work has few parallels in that of his contemporaries. Humphreys manifests in his novels a Puritan seriousness about the purpose of living, about the need for tradition and the understanding of it, and about the future of the community (usually seen as Wales) as well as the good of the individual. Welsh Nationalist as well as Christian, he re-emphasised in 1953 that "personal responsibility is a Protestant principle" and saw himself as engaged in writing the *Protestant novel*. His interest in the non-realist novel is minimal and his technical experimentation is limited to the use, in *A Man's Estate*, of a number of narrators and, in *Outside the House of Baal*, to an interleaving of narratives in which the past rapidly catches up with the present.

His first two novels, *The Little Kingdom* and *The Voice of a Stranger*, are concerned respectively with idealism betrayed by false leadership and idealism bludgeoned by knavery. Their conclusions are pessimistic. The earlier of those themes appears again in *A Toy Epic*. But with *A Change of Heart* begins Humphreys's concern with the Christian belief in the gradual progress of society towards *the good* and the means by which *good* is transmitted from generation to generation. Heredity is soon discarded in favour of answers more complex. Perhaps the finest of the earlier novels which pursue this theme is *Hear and Forgive*, and of the later, *Outside the House of Baal*. In this book Humphreys faces the apparently total defeat of his Calvinistic Methodist minister, leaving the reader only with the silence which might make room for faith. Since the problems involved plainly need the longest time-scale possible, Humphreys's more recent novels (with the exception of *The Anchor Tree*, which is a digression, with the same preoccupations, into his Welsh-American experience) were intended as a quartet, the fourth of which, *National Winner*, he wrote first. The appearance of the first and second, *Flesh and Blood* and *The Best of Friends*, has, however, been accompanied by the intimation that the quartet is now to be a sextet, so that *Salt of the Earth* still leaves two gaps in the sequence. *Jones* is a single-volume study of the refusal of responsibility.

—Roland Mathias

HUNTER, Evan. American. Born Salvatore A. Lombino in New York City, 15 October 1926. Educated at Evander Childs High School, New York; Cooper Union, New York,

Eighty Million Eyes. New York, Delacorte Press, and London, Hamish Hamilton, 1966.

Fuzz. New York, Doubleday, and London, Hamish Hamilton, 1968.

Shotgun. New York, Doubleday, and London, Hamish Hamilton, 1969.

Jigsaw. New York, Doubleday, and London, Hamish Hamilton, 1970.

Hail, Hail, The Gang's All Here! New York, Doubleday, and London, Hamish Hamilton, 1971.

Sadie When She Died. New York, Doubleday, and London, Hamish Hamilton, 1972.

Let's Hear It for the Deaf Man. New York, Doubleday, and London, Hamish Hamilton, 1973.

Hail to the Chief. New York, Random House, and London, Hamish Hamilton, 1973.

Bread. New York, Random House, and London, Hamish Hamilton, 1974.

Where There's Smoke. New York, Random House, and London, Hamish Hamilton, 1975.

Blood Relatives. New York, Random House, 1975; London, Hamish Hamilton, 1976.

Guns. New York, Random House, 1976; London, Hamish Hamilton, 1977.

So Long as You Both Shall Live. New York, Random House, and London, Hamish Hamilton, 1976.

Long Time No See. New York, Random House, and London, Hamish Hamilton, 1977.

Goldilocks. New York, Arbor House, 1977; London, Hamish Hamilton, 1978.

Calypso. New York, Viking Press, and London, Hamish Hamilton, 1979.

Ghosts. New York, Viking Press, and London, Hamish Hamilton, 1980.

Rumpelstiltskin. New York, Viking Press, and London, Hamish Hamilton, 1981.

Heat. New York, Viking Press, and London, Hamish Hamilton, 1981.

Beauty and the Beast. London, Hamish Hamilton, 1982; New York, Holt Rinehart, 1983.

Ice. New York, Arbor House, and London, Hamish Hamilton, 1983.

Jack and the Beanstalk. New York, Holt Rinehart, and London, Hamish Hamilton, 1984.

Lightning. New York, Arbor House, and London, Hamish Hamilton, 1984.

Snow White and Rose Red. New York, Holt Rinehart, and London, Hamish Hamilton, 1985.

Eight Black Horses. New York, Arbor House, and London, Hamish Hamilton, 1985.

Short Stories

The Jungle Kids. New York, Pocket Books, 1956.

I Like 'em Tough (as Curt Cannon). New York, Fawcett, 1958.

The Last Spin and Other Stories. London, Constable, 1960.

The Empty Hours (as Ed McBain). New York, Simon and Schuster, 1962; London, Boardman, 1963.

Happy New Year, Herbie, and Other Stories. New York, Simon and Schuster, 1963; London, Constable, 1965.

The Beheading and Other Stories. London, Constable, 1971.

The Easter Man (a Play) and Six Stories. New York, Doubleday, 1972; as *Seven*, London, Constable, 1972.

The McBain Brief (as Ed McBain). London, Hamish Hamilton, 1982; New York, Arbor House, 1983.

Uncollected Short Stories

"Classification: Dead" (as Richard Marsten), in *Dames, Danger, and Death*, edited by Leo Margulies. New York, Pyramid, 1960.

"Easy Money," in *Ellery Queen's Mystery Magazine* (New York), September 1960.

"Nightshade" (as Ed McBain) in *Ellery Queen's Mystery Magazine* (New York), August 1970.

"Someone at the Door," in *Ellery Queen's Mystery Magazine* (New York), October 1971.

"Sympathy for the Devil," in *Seventeen* (New York), July 1972.

"Weeping for Dustin," in *Seventeen* (New York), July 1973.

"The Analyst," in *Playboy* (Chicago), December 1974.

"Dangerous Affair," in *Good Housekeeping* (New York), March 1975.

"Eighty Million Eyes" (as Ed McBain), in *Ellery Queen's Giants of Mystery*. New York, Davis, 1976.

"Stepfather," in *Ladies Home Journal* (New York), June 1976.

Plays

The Easter Man (produced Birmingham and London, 1964; as *A Race of Hairy Men*, produced New York, 1965). Included in *The Easter Man (a Play) and Six Stories*, 1972.

The Conjuror (produced Ann Arbor, Michigan, 1969).

Screenplays: *Strangers When We Meet*, 1960; *The Birds*, 1963; *Fuzz*, 1972; *Walk Proud*, 1979.

Television Plays: *Appointment at Eleven* (*Alfred Hitchcock Presents* series), 1955–61; *The Chisholms* series, from his own novel, 1978–79; *The Legend of Walks Far Woman*, 1983.

Other (for children)

Find the Feathered Serpent. Philadelphia, Winston, 1952.

Rocket to Luna (as Richard Marsten). Philadelphia, Winston, 1952; London, Hutchinson, 1954.

Danger: Dinosaurs! (as Richard Marsten). Philadelphia, Winston, 1953.

The Remarkable Harry. New York and London, Abelard Schuman, 1961.

The Wonderful Button. New York, Abelard Schuman, 1961; London, Abelard Schuman, 1962.

Me and Mr. Stenner. Philadelphia, Lippincott, 1976; London, Hamish Hamilton, 1977.

Other (as Ed McBain)

Editor, *Crime Squad*. London, New English Library, 1968.

Editor, *Homicide Department*. London, New English Library, 1968.

Editor, *Downpour*. London, New English Library, 1969.

Editor, *Ticket to Death*. London, New English Library, 1969.

*

Manuscript Collection: Mugar Memorial Library, Boston University.

Evan Hunter comments:

(1972) The novels I write under my own name are concerned mostly with identity, or at least they have been until the most recent book. (I cannot now predict what will interest or concern me most in the future.) I change my style with each novel, to fit the tone, the mood, and the narrative voice. I have always considered a strong story to be the foundation of any good novel, and I also apply this rule to the mysteries I write under the Ed McBain pseudonym. Unlike my "serious" novels, however, the style here is unvaried. The series characters are essentially the same throughout (although new detectives appear or old ones disappear from time to time, and each new case involves a new criminal or criminals), the setting is the same (the precinct and the city), and the theme is the same—crime and punishment. (I look upon these mysteries, in fact, as one *long* novel about crime and punishment, with each separate book in the series serving as a chapter.) I enjoy writing both types of novels, and consider each equally representative of my work.

*　　*　　*

The vividness and immediacy of the author's prose, coupled with the timeliness of his subject, drew considerable attention to Evan Hunter's novel *The Blackboard Jungle*. This story of a young teacher confronting the brutal realities of a big city vocational high school was praised for its realism and for opening to fiction an area of public concern that had begun to attract national attention in the United States. *Second Ending* was an even more aggressively topical novel, tracing the effects of drugs on four young New Yorkers. The central character, a young trumpet player who has been addicted for two years, draws the other characters together, and they are all altered in some way by his descent toward death. Some of the novel's episodes, which were termed "sensational" at the time of publication, now no longer seem so unique, and despite the awkwardness with which portions of the novel are narrated. Hunter's power as a storyteller moved his characters unerringly toward the slough of mutual desparation.

In *Strangers When We Meet* Hunter elected to describe a more muted kind of action in which a young architect, happily married and the father of two children, drifts into an affair with a suburban neighbor. Hunter showed a keen eye for the minute details which slowly gather round the illicit relationship, creating a highly realistic impression of a young man unable to cope with conflicting loyalties. Nonetheless, his characters finally seem insignificant—certainly not sufficiently strong to carry the philosophical baggage which the author gives them in an improbable conclusion.

A Matter of Conviction was a return to the mode of social protest which Hunter had developed so successfully in his two earlier novels. A polemic against the forces in society that make young men into killers, it was too contrived to offer more than passing interest. *Mother and Daughters*, which chronicles the youth and maturity of four middle-class women—their dreams and their loves—is a more substantial work, despite its occasional melodrama.

Much of Hunter's fiction is over-written: striving for a realistic thickness, it bogs down in minutiae, and while the author writes with a high and consistent degree of professionalism, his vision rarely penetrates beneath the elaborate surfaces which his prose projects. *Last Summer* is a major exception to this adroit verbosity. It is told with an unforgettable simplicity and directness which nonetheless conveys the author's own highly sophisticated point of view. During a summer holiday two teenage boys and a girl explore an Atlantic island, tell each other the "truth," and dominate a shy young girl. Their experiences end in violence which vividly symbolizes the moral degeneracy of their society.

Few contemporary writers can match the versatility and consummate professionalism of Evan Hunter. His work includes a highly successful series of detective novels published under the pseudonym of Ed McBain, a science-fiction novel for children; a comic cops-and-robbers novel, *A Horse's Head*, written with great inventiveness and wit; and a spirited children's book in verse, illustrated by his own sons. *Sons* tells the story of three generations of a Wisconsin family, powerfully challenging some of the basic presumptions of the American Dream; *The Paper Dragon* is a densely plotted, intriguing story of a five-day plagiarism trial; and *Buddwing* plunges its amnesiac hero into the heart of a Washington Square riot, a hold-up, and a crap game. *Nobody Knew They Were There* takes a futuristic look at the innate forces of violence that assail man's attempt to achieve world peace. Throughout a varied and highly prolific career, Hunter has produced a body of work distinguished for its sound craftsmanship, although only one of his novels, *Last Summer*, clearly demonstrates the art which such craft should sustain.

—David Galloway

———————

HUNTER, Kristin (Elaine, née Eggleston). American. Born in Philadelphia, Pennsylvania, 12 September 1931. Educated at Haddon Heights High School, New Jersey, graduated 1947; University of Pennsylvania, Philadelphia, 1947–51, B.S. in education 1951. Married John I. Lattany in 1968. Philadelphia columnist and feature writer, Pittsburgh *Courier*, 1946–52; teacher, Camden, New Jersey, 1951; copywriter, Lavenson Bureau of Advertising, Philadelphia, 1952–59; research assistant, School of Social Work, University of Pennsylvania, 1961–62; copywriter, Wermen and Schorr, Philadelphia, 1962–63; information officer, City of Philadelphia, 1963–64, 1965–66; director of health services, Temple University, Philadelphia, 1971–72; director, Walt Whitman Poetry Center, Camden, 1978–79. Lecturer in Creative Writing, 1972–79, Adjunct Professor of English, 1980–83, and since 1983, Senior Lecturer in English, University of Pennsylvania. Writer-in-Residence, Emory University, Atlanta, 1979. Recipient: Fund for the Republic prize, for television documentary, 1955; Whitney fellowship, 1959; Bread Loaf Writers Conference De Voto Fellowship, 1965; Sigma Delta Chi award, for reporting, 1968; National Council on Interracial Books for Children award, 1968; National Conference of Christians and Jews Brotherhood Award, 1969; *Book World* Festival award, for children's book, 1973; Christopher Award, for children's book, 1974; Drexel Citation, for children's book, 1981; New Jersey Council on the Arts fellowship, 1982, 1985; Pennsylvania Council on the Arts fellowship, 1983. Agent: Don Congdon Associates, 177 East 70th Street, New York, New York 10021. Address: 721 Warwick Road, Magnolia, New Jersey 08049, U.S.A.

PUBLICATIONS

Novels

God Bless the Child. New York, Scribner, 1964; London, Muller, 1965.
The Landlord. New York, Scribner, 1966; London, Pan, 1970.
The Survivors. New York, Scribner, 1975.

The Lakestown Rebellion.   New York, Scribner, 1978.

Uncollected Short Stories

"To Walk in Beauty," in *Sub-Deb Scoop* (Philadelphia), 1953.
"Supersonic," in *Mandala* (Philadelphia), vol. 1, no. 1, 1956.
"There Was a Little Girl," in *Rogue* (New York), 1959.
"An Interesting Social Study," in *The Best Short Stories by Negro Writers*, edited by Langston Hughes.   Boston, Little Brown, 1967.
"Debut," in *Negro Digest* (Chicago), June 1968.
"Honor among Thieves," in *Essence* (New York), April 1971.
"The Tenant," in *Pennsylvania Gazette* (Philadelphia).
"Bleeding Berries," in *Callaloo* (Lexington, Kentucky), vol. 2, no. 2, 1979.
"The Jewel in the Lotus," in *Quilt 1* (Berkeley, California), 1981.
"Bleeding Heart," in *Hambone* (Santa Cruz, California), 1983.
"Perennial Daisy," in *Nightsun* (Frostburg, Maryland), 1984.

Fiction (for children)

The Soul-Brothers and Sister Lou.   New York, Scribner, 1968; London, Macdonald, 1971.
Boss Cat.   New York, Scribner, 1971.
The Pool Table War.   Boston, Houghton Mifflin, 1972.
Uncle Daniel and the Raccoon.   Boston, Houghton Mifflin, 1972.
Guests in the Promised Land: Stories.   New York, Scribner, 1973.
Lou in the Limelight.   New York, Scribner, 1981.

Plays

The Double Edge (produced Philadelphia, 1965).

Television Play: *Minority of One*, 1956.

*

Critical Studies: *From Mammies to Militants: Domestics in Black American Literature* by Trudier Harris, Philadelphia, Temple University Press, 1982, and article by Sondra O'Neale, in *Afro-American Fiction Writers after 1955* edited by Harris and Thadious M. Davis, Detroit, Gale, 1984.

Kristin Hunter comments:

The bulk of my work has dealt—imaginatively, I hope—with relations between the white and black races in America. My early work was "objective," that is, sympathetic to both whites and blacks, and seeing members of both groups from a perspective of irony and humor against the wider backdrop of human experience as a whole. Since about 1968 my subjective anger has been emerging, along with my grasp of the real situation in this society, though my sense of humor and my basic optimism keep cropping up like uncontrollable weeds.

*   *   *

In her first two novels Kristin Hunter played upon the contradictions between reality as it is experienced by the black urban poor and the false optimism of popular story. *God Bless the Child* parodies the tale of the enterprising but low-born youngster who, since the origins of middle-class fiction, has set out to achieve a place in society by the application of nerve and energy. In the case of Rosie Fleming, however, her vitality leads to failure, for by setting up as a small entrepreneur in the numbers game she earns the enmity of the white men who manage the poor people's version of finance capitalism. Despite her portrayal of the relentless power that destroys Rosie, Hunter is not resigned to a sense of human powerlessness. A sympathetic and complex portrayal of three generations of black women conveys an intensely humanistic conception of character, which in her second novel, *The Landlord*, becomes the basis for an optimistic theme. The formal foundation of this book is the novel of maturation. Its main character, determined to "become a man" by exercising mastery over his tenants, is frustrated and tricked at every turn as they disabuse him of the mythology of white male dominance. Against his will, and contrary to the assumptions of middle-class convention the landlord forms an admiration and appreciation for the diverse styles by which blacks cope with life's troubles, large and small.

Following publication of *The Landlord* Hunter occupied herself with stories of ghetto life directed toward "younger readers." Like the adult novels that preceded them these children's books reject the idealizations of popular genres while preserving a belief in the capacity of the black underclass to transform their lives by the power of their spirit. In both the adult and children's books the message has been that society's "victims" refuse the dehumanization which either social relations or a literature of pity would assign them.

This insider's view, informed by Hunter's commitment to the verve and quality of black life, led her to write two additional adult novels that must be termed celebrations. The first signifies by its title, *The Survivors*, its author's devotion to the rendition of character traits that enable a middle-aged dressmaker and a street kid to form an emotional and practical alliance that enables them both to overcome the predacious circumstances of the neighborhood. There are more than enough coincidence and pathos in the plot, but that is a small price to pay for the vibrancy of humor and characterization.

It is with *The Lakestown Rebellion*, however, that Hunter achieves the fulfillment of her craft. This story of a small black township, originally settled by fugitive slaves, battling against plans to build a highway that will destroy their homes, renews the tradition of the folk tricksters. A range of ingenious, zany, and simply unusual characters play the entire repertory of stereotypical roles popularly assumed to be black in order to stop the encroachment of "progress" upon their lives. The wit of the novel's conception perfectly suits Hunter's optimistic humanism. The book is so enjoyable one is almost unaware that it is also a symbolic reenactment of cultural history, but there can be no missing the fact that it places Kristin Hunter squarely in the tradition of Afro-American fiction at one of its best moments.

—John M. Reilly

IHIMAERA, Witi (Tame). New Zealander. Born in Gisborne, 7 February 1944. Educated at Te Karaka District High School, 1957–59; Church College of New Zealand, 1960–61; Gisborne Boys High School, 1962; University of Auckland, 1963–66; Victoria University, Wellington, 1968–72; B.A. 1972. Married Jane Cleghorn in 1970. Cadet reporter, Gisborne *Herald*, 1967; journalist, Post Office Headquarters, Wellington, 1968–72; information officer, 1973–74, Third Secretary, Wellington, 1975–78, and Second Secretary, Canberra, 1978–81, New Zealand Ministry of Foreign Affairs. Recipient: Freda Buckland Literary Award, 1973; James Wattie Award, 1974; University of Otago Robert Burns Fellowship, 1974. Address: 11 Hungerford Road, Wellington 3, New Zealand.

PUBLICATIONS

Novels

Tangi. Auckland and London, Heinemann, 1973.
Whanau. Auckland, Heinemann, 1974; London, Heinemann, 1975.

Short Stories

Pounamu, Pounamu. Auckland, Heinemann, 1972; London, Heinemann, 1973.
The New Net Goes Fishing. Auckland, Heinemann, 1977; London, Heinemann, 1978.

Other

Maori. Wellington, Government Printers, 1975.
New Zealand Through the Arts: Past and Present, with Sir Tosswill Woollaston and Allen Curnow. Wellington, Friends of the Turnbull Library, 1982.

Editor, with D.S. Long, *Into the World of Light: An Anthology of Maori Writing.* Auckland, Heinemann, 1982.

*

Critical Studies: "Participating" by Ray Grover, in *Islands* (Auckland), Winter 1973; "Tangi" by H. Winston Rhodes, in *Landfall* (Christchurch), December 1973; "Maori Writers," in *Fretful Sleepers and Other Essays* by Bill Pearson, Auckland, Heinemann, 1974; *The Maoris of New Zealand* by Joan Metge, London, Routledge, 1977; *Introducing Witi Ihimaera* by Richard Corballis and Simon Garrett, Auckland, Longman Paul, 1984.

Witi Ihimaera comments:

There are two cultural landscapes in my country, the Maori and the Pakeha (European), and although all people, including Maori, inhabit the Pakeha landscape, very few know the Maori one. It is important to both Maori and Pakeha that they realize their dual cultural heritage, and that is why I began to write. Not to become the first Maori novelist but to render my people into words as honestly and as candidly as I could; to present a picture of Maoritanga which is our word for the way we feel and are, in the hope that our values will be maintained. I like to think that I write with both love—aroha—and anger in the hope that the values of Maori life will never be lost. So far I have written about exclusively Maori people within an exclusively Maori framework, using our own oral tradition of Maori literature, our own mythology, as my inspiration. Cultural difference is not a bad thing, it can be very exciting, and it can offer a different view of the world, value system, and interpretation of events. This is what I would like to offer: a personal vision of Maori life as I see it, the Maori side of New Zealand's dual heritage of culture.

*   *   *

With Ihimaera's collection of short stories, *Pounamu, Pounamu*, together with his novels, *Tangi* and *Whanau*, each with its appropriate Maori title, have given shape and significance to his people's traditional but rapidly disappearing life in village and rural settings. He has written "both with anger and with love"; but although as the first Maori novelist he is proudly conscious that he is conducting what amounts to a crusade, he has not allowed any missionary zeal to corrupt his artistic integrity.

In his unusual narratives human experience is not distorted. Maori characters act, feel and speak as authentic human beings, not as the formalised or picturesque figures of some romantic tale. They do not become inverted stereotypes, nor is their behaviour marred by false emotionalism. As author, Ihimaera does not pretend to be superior to his creations but, without a trace of irony, he joins in the their gaiety, shares in their sorrows, accepts their shortcomings and participates in their traditional ceremonies. He identifies himself with old and young: laments with his elders because so many of a later generation have gone the Pakeha way, and sympathises with those who cannot resist the attraction of the city lights and are forgetful of their Maoritanga. Yet such sympathy and such authorial fellowship cannot conceal that a serious purpose lies behind his artistic endeavours or that he is deeply concerned with those values which too often have been ignored or derided.

If there is a central theme running through his short stories and novels, it is one related to the title of his third book. "Whanau" refers to the enlarged family community of the Maori village, held together not only by tradition but by bonds of relationship and love that are not easily comprehended by the sophisticated Pakeha. "Aroha" is used to imply something more than individual love; it includes that warmth of human affection that subsists within and through the whole whanau. Both relationship and love are vitally important elements of Maoritanga, a word that suggests all those customs and qualities regarded as specifically Maori. The conception of the enlarged family community therefore gives a very different flavour to the narratives of Ihimaera because, even in many of his short stories, the reader is continually aware of a complex pattern of relationships uniting the whanau and of an indescribable warmth of feeling that should not be confused with sexual love. His central characters are not and cannot be isolated. However different their personalities may be, however far they may roam, they remain members of the extended family, and sooner or later they will return, for the deep sense of belonging to the whanau is part of their heritage. The literary consequence of this is that each of Ihimaera's narratives may be recognised as a fragment of a contemporary saga, and "character in action" becomes less than an adequate description of his dramatic method.

Although at times the reader of *Whanau* may be disconcerted by the number of village people that together constitute the whole group, by their interconnections and by the variety of their fortunes and aspirations, it would be wrong to suggest that the novel is merely episodic or that it is a series of loosely linked short stories. With remarkable success the author has devised a form suitable to his dominant theme and, without loss of individuality or neglect of personal drama, has given life, substance, and meaning to the whanau itself. *Tangi*, as its name implies, is concerned with death, the death of a father, and its effect on the son and all the members of the extensive Maori family. It is a journey of self-discovery in which the present reality of the funeral rites and the expression of uninhibited grief are intertwined with personal memories, with the life of the whanau and the beginning of a journey to the future. In his less ambitious and more accessible short stories, Ihimaera demonstrates his talent for finding and moulding those significant incidents that reveal the life-style and attitudes of the Maori people. His lightness of touch and his ability to alternate between humour, tenderness, and pathos are more effective and more powerful as a commentary on race-relations than undue emphasis or stridency of tone could possibly be.

Pounamu, Pounamu and the two novels are not linked together, but they, nevertheless, form something in the nature of a trilogy. An ancient mythology, time-honoured traditions, and the values inherent in Maoritanga are woven into the texture of narratives that record the community life and rural setting of the older generation of Maoris. Even here, the whanau, the family, and the aroha which binds them are being increasingly disrupted by the alien culture, by the pale stranger with his "you got to get on" way of living. The younger people in particular are departing from their villages, lured by the bright lights of the city and the attractions of a pakeha world.

Ihimaera began a second trilogy with *The New Net Goes Fishing*—a title borrowed from a Maori proverb which implies that a new generation takes the place of the old. The short stories contained in this volume should be regarded as a prelude to the urban novels which will follow; and the published collection has its own prelude in "Yellow Brick Road," and its own envoy, "Return from Oz." The former is concerned with the hopes and expectations of a Maori family as adults and children travel from their ancestral home to the Emerald City; and the latter with the return of the grandfather to Waituhi in the hope that he will draw his descendants back there again. Between Prelude and Envoy are 15 short stories that recount episodes in the lives of those who in the city environment still retain some of the values of Maoritanga, of those who are lost and discarded, of those who succeed or fail or rebel. Without enhancing or typifying his Maori characters Ihimaera reveals the mental and emotional turmoil experienced by so many of his people. He has said, "Te taha Maori [the Maori side] belongs to us all," and in this conviction he has written from a point of view that with insight interprets the meaning of Maoritanga and the meaning of its loss to Maori and Pakeha alike.

—H. Winston Rhodes

INNES, (Ralph) Hammond. British. Born in Horsham, Sussex, 15 July 1913. Educated at Cranbook School, Kent, graduated 1931. Served in the Royal Artillery, 1940–46: Major. Married Dorothy Mary Lang in 1937. Staff member, *Financial News*, London, 1934–40. C.B.E. (Commander, Order of the British Empire), 1978. D.Litt.: Bristol University, 1985. Agent: Curtis Brown, 162–168 Regent Street, London W1R 5TA. Address: Ayres End, Kersey, Suffolk IP7 6EB, England.

PUBLICATIONS

Novels

The Doppelganger. London, Jenkins, 1937.
Air Disaster. London, Jenkins, 1937.
Sabotage Broadcast. London, Jenkins, 1938.
All Roads Lead to Friday. London, Jenkins, 1939.
Wreckers Must Breathe. London, Collins, 1940; as *Trapped*, New York, Putnam, 1940.
The Trojan Horse. London, Collins, 1940.
Attack Alarm. London, Collins, 1941; New York, Macmillan, 1942.
Dead and Alive. London, Collins, 1946.
The Killer Mine. London, Collins, and New York, Harper, 1947; as *Run by Night*, New York, Bantam, 1951.
The Lonely Skier. London, Collins, 1947; as *Fire in the Snow*, New York, Harper, 1947.
Maddon's Rock. London, Collins, 1948; as *Gale Warning*, New York, Harper, 1948.

The Blue Ice. London, Collins, and New York, Harper, 1948.
The White South. London, Collins, 1949; as *The Survivors*, New York, Harper, 1950.
The Angry Mountain. London, Collins, 1950; New York, Harper, 1951.
Air Bridge. London, Collins, 1951; New York, Knopf, 1952.
Campbell's Kingdom. London, Collins, and New York, Knopf, 1952.
The Strange Land. London, Collins, 1954; as *The Naked Land*, New York, Knopf, 1954.
The Mary Deare. London, Collins, 1956; as *The Wreck of the Mary Deare*, New York, Knopf, 1956.
The Land God Gave to Cain. London, Collins, and New York, Knopf, 1958.
The Doomed Oasis. London, Collins, and New York, Knopf, 1960.
Atlantic Fury. London, Collins, and New York, Knopf, 1962.
The Strode Venturer. London, Collins, and New York, Knopf, 1965.
Levkas Man. London, Collins, and New York, Knopf, 1971.
Golden Soak. London, Collins, and New York, Knopf, 1973.
North Star. London, Collins, 1974; New York, Knopf, 1975.
The Big Footprints. London, Collins, and New York, Knopf, 1977.
Solomons Seal. London, Collins, and New York, Knopf, 1980.
The Black Tide. London, Collins, 1982; New York, Doubleday, 1983.
High Stand. London, Collins, 1985; New York, Atheneum, 1986.

Plays

Screenplay: *Campbell's Kingdom*, with Robin Estridge, 1957.

Television Play: *The Story of Captain James Cook*, 1975.

Other (for children) as Ralph Hammond

Cocos Gold. London, Collins, and New York, Harper, 1950.
Isle of Strangers. London, Collins, 1951; as *Island of Peril*, Philadelphia, Westminster Press, 1953.
Saracen's Tower. London, Collins, 1952; as *Cruise of Danger*, Philadelphia, Westminster Press, 1954.
Black Gold on the Double Diamond. London, Collins, 1953.

Other

Harvest of Journeys. London, Collins, and New York, Knopf, 1960.
Scandinavia, with editors of Life. New York, Time, 1963.
Sea and Islands. London, Collins, and New York, Knopf, 1967.
The Conquistadors. London, Collins, and New York, Knopf, 1969.
Hammond Innes Introduces Australia, edited by Clive Turnbull. London, Deutsch, and New York, McGraw Hill, 1971.
The Last Voyage: Captain Cook's Lost Diary. London, Collins, 1978; New York, Knopf, 1979.
Hammond Innes' East Anglia. London, Hodder and Stoughton, 1986.

Editor, *Tales of Old Inns*, by Richard Keverne, revised edition. London, Collins, 1947.

*

Critical Study: in *Sunday Telegraph Magazine* (London), 10 August 1980.

Hammond Innes comments:

Writing and travelling can be kept in separate compartments of time. But the organisation and preparation for journeys and voyages cannot. And this is a major problem, for I need the familiarity of my own home and the peace of the country in order to write. I need my books and my maps and charts around me. I also need to live with it seven days a week, for I am a painfully slow writer, usually discarding far more than appears in the final work.

I find it very difficult to be certain at what point I became conscious of the role travel was to play in my writing. I think probably after the war. I had cut my writing teeth in the great depression of the early 1930's, a particularly insular period that I believe to have been the result of the mud and blood of Flanders. To earn my living, however, I worked as a journalist on a London daily. My starting wage was a now unbelievable 17s. 6d. a week, and at the time I counted myself fortunate to get the job, for most newspapers were firing, not hiring, staff. All through the 1930's I had to be content to discover my own country, so that when I finally did go abroad it was at H.M.'s expense—a voyage round the Cape, my destination the Western desert.

I was 27 when I joined the services. I felt the best years of my life were being wasted. It was only when I was demobilised, and had taken the plunge and abandoned journalism for full-time writing, that I realised what a wealth of experience I had been soaking up.

As a youngster, my imagination had been fired by geography almost as much as by literature. On my return to England after the war, I was made strongly aware that, whilst I had been absorbing the atmosphere of the old world of the Mediterranean, the vast majority of the British people had been locked up in their island fortress for six long years. I had characters and backgrounds that seemed to interest them. There is always an element of luck in everything, and in writing the luck is to find that what you want to write, and therefore what you write best, is what people happen to want to read.

I wanted to write about far-off places and people. Because of that I determined to plough back as much of my royalties as possible into travel. And looking back now, how glad I am that I did. A writer has no business, no land, no factory that he can call his own. His capital assets are all in his head, and one of the very few things that can't be taxed, expropriated, or in any way filched by others, is personal experience.

This was a conscious decision, the only one I have ever made about my writing. The rest has developed in the normal haphazard way of things. I cannot even say what it is that draws me at a certain period of time to a certain part of the world. The choice would appear to be intuitive. But I can say that, as with the voyages under sail, a lot of preparation is necessary. The research, the books, the maps, the visits to London to seek out the right contacts. This is all necessary, so that when one arrives in the country itself there is a sense of familiarity; by which I mean that the people and their way of life are at least within one's comprehension. And the journey itself needs to be planned—meetings with ministers, industrialists, writers to get the overall picture, and then, with the country's problems clear in mind, a prolonged stay in one area so that one gets to grips with the people themselves.

Returning, one begins a long, slow process of rendering down. The mind is too often overflowing with all that one has absorbed, and the only way I know to rid oneself of this embarrassment of riches is to write a travel piece—hence my two books in search of background. Even then, it may be two or three years before I am ready to start on the novel, for if it is to be real, the story has to grow out of the background. And in the case of remote areas like the Labrador, or Addu Atoll in the Indian Ocean, there is probably only one real story line that will achieve my purpose and show what the country and the people are really like.

It may appear from this that I am a highly organised writer. I wish this were so. It would make my life a lot easier if it were. But at least by building on a background of very personal travel I know what I am trying to achieve. And whether I succeed or not, it is at least a start to have the goal clear in mind.

* * *

Hammond Innes is one of the foremost thriller writers of his day. Like John Buchan—a writer whom he much resembles—he believes that there is only a thin dividing line between the claims of civilisation and the slide into anarchy, between the warm room and the savage out-of-doors. For that reason Innes's characters often find themselves in conflict as much with their environment—the sea, the polar regions, the desert—as with other men. *Maddon's Rock*, one of his earliest sea tales, is ostensibly about a ghost ship which never sank during the Second World War, but that is only an undercurrent to his main theme of the crew's defiance of the gale-swept ocean. The theme of man against the sea is also central to *The Mary Deare* and *Atlantic Fury*, both of which contain excellent and moving descriptions of man's age-old battle with the elements. Innes is equally at home in the services—he served as a Royal Artillery officer during the Second World War—and his novels *Attack Alarm* and *The Trojan Horse* both deal with infiltration of enemy agents into Britain's defence establishment. His strong clear prose makes for compulsive reading, and his attention to detail—essential to the writer of thrillers—enables readers to feel that they are actually involved in the action at the height of any crisis.

These abilities are not confined to his books about the sea. *The White South* is set in the Antarctic and *Campbell's Kingdom* and *The Land God Gave to Cain* in Canada, yet the sense of place and his concern with background detail remain constant factors. Like all his novels these are excellent entertainments, and his hard-hitting action always flows along at a great pace. At the back of each adventure, too, lies the theme of redemption, with each hero having to pass through a necessary ordeal before good is allowed to triumph. Thus, in *Dead and Alive* the central character, David Cunningham, has to endure many trials before the feels again the "strange contentment" of being once more in command of his own ship. This early Innes adventure story acts as a pointer to much of his later fiction. Cunningham, scarred by his wartime experiences, becomes a partner in a dubious trading enterprise, using a landing craft in the Mediterranean: part of his mission is to discover the whereabouts of a young Anglo-French girl who has gone missing in Italy. While in Naples, Cunningham and his partners become drawn into the post-war black market and are forced to fight their way through the garish haunts of petty criminals and racketeers before the girl, Monique, is found and all obstacles have been overcome.

Critics of Innes's style have claimed that because his adventures tend to follow a pattern he only writes to a proven formula. This is to miss both the point of many of his plots and also his concern with morality. His belief that his heroes must face a necessary ordeal before virtue can triumph is no idle bow to the basic convention of the thriller plot. Innes is frequently at pains to point out that by enduring danger and risking his life the hero not only becomes a better person but also enriches the lives of those around him. In *The Strode Venturer*, for example, the Englishman in the central role might be a typical post-colonial adventurer interested only in exploiting a market for manganese in the Maldive Islands, but through his actions the primitive islanders are also enabled to establish their own claims. In this case, the hero is neither a paragon nor a superman but an ordinary man caught up in a dangerous position from which he can escape only by virtue of his own quick-thinking.

Characterisation is another strong point of Innes's fiction, even though he does tend to rely on the stock figure of the clean-limbed young Englishman as his central character. His villains excite neither fear nor pity: they are usually ruthless men motivated by greed, envy, or politics. In most novels the most telling opponent is the environment, and in addition to his concern with natural detail, Innes also has the ability to draw natural adversaries almost as if they were human beings. An avalanche, volcanic explosion, or gale at sea in an Innes novel can often be possessed of stealth, cunning, or strength, attributes which one normally associates with the human race. His prose is conventional, but his sense of place and his ability to evoke it manages to transport his readers to the far-flung regions of the world.

—Trevor Royle

IRELAND, David. Australian. Born in Lakemba, New South Wales, 24 August 1927. Married Elizabeth Ruth Morris in 1955; two sons and two daughters. Recipient: *Adelaide Advertiser* award, 1966; Miles Franklin Award, 1972, 1977, 1980; *The Age* Book of the Year Award, 1980. Agent: Curtis Brown (Australia) Pty. Ltd., 27 Union Street, Paddington, New South Wales 2021, Australia.

PUBLICATIONS

Novels

The Chantic Bird. London, Heinemann, and New York, Scribner, 1968.
The Unknown Industrial Prisoner. Sydney and London, Angus and Robertson, 1971.
The Flesheaters. Sydney and London, Angus and Robertson, 1972.
Burn. Sydney and London, Angus and Robertson, 1975.
The Glass Canoe. Melbourne and London, Macmillan, 1976.
A Woman of the Future. Ringwood, Victoria, Allen Lane, and New York, Braziller, 1979; London, Penguin, 1980.
City of Women. Ringwood, Victoria, Allen Lane, 1981.
Archimedes and the Seagle. Ringwood, Victoria, Viking, 1984; London, Viking, 1985.

Uncollected Short Story

"The Wild Colonial Boy," in *Winter's Tales 25*, edited by Caroline Hobhouse. London, Macmillan, 1979; New York, St. Martin's Press, 1980.

Play

Image in the Clay (produced Sydney, 1962). Brisbane, University of Queensland Press, 1964.

*   *   *

David Ireland is Australia's most mature and astute political novelist, and one of the nation's most innovative prose stylists.

Ireland's first three novels depict a world that is in its "industrial adolescence," obsessed with profit and production to the point where those who do not contribute to industry (the poor, the aged, the unemployed) are treated as failures and misfits—as social lepers. Written in the absurdist-surrealist mode, *The Flesheaters* is set in a boarding-house for the poor and unemployed. These "terminal cases" of industrial uselessness are forced to live in trees, tin sheds, or dog kennels. (Old Granny Upjohn is the one in the kennel: an emblem of society's treatment of the aged, she is fitted with collar and chain and kept under sedation.) Ireland attempts to counter this "functional" mentality (which insists that all human activity must have a public and profit-making purpose) by insisting upon the value to the individual of such "useless" activities as day-dreaming, fantasizing, and self-expression.

Arguably the best of Ireland's novels, *The Unknown Industrial Prisoner* develops this concern with greater insight and complexity, sketching the life of workers in a foreign-owned Sydney oil refinery, examining their plight piece by piece and layer by layer until the fragmented mosaic builds into a microcosm of Australian industrial society. Ireland himself worked for a time in such a refinery, and the novel provides an absurdist (but acutely authentic) record of the dehumanisation of the workforce, the emasculation of management, and the laziness and inefficiency of both employer and employee.

The Unknown Industrial Prisoner is an angry and rigorous account of the absurdities of industrialism. But Ireland is Australia's most intensely *analytical* writer, and it should therefore come as no surprise that he is prepared to question the assumptions behind his own angry sense of injustice. This analytic quality is seen in frequent bitter references to the workers as "the soil" in which the "money tree" of industry is growing. This is primarily an image of protest at exploitation and degradation—but it can also be seen as a wholly natural organic image (for if there is to be a "money tree" there must be "soil" to sustain it). Instead of accepting social realities at face value, Ireland digs for underlying assumptions and implications.

Monotonous conformity is the keynote of Ireland's vision of Australian society. He sees Australians as tame and insipid, bowed in philistine worship to the god of materialism. *The Chantic Bird* portrays the people of Sydney sitting at home at night, "filling in insurance policies on their fowls, their wrought-iron railings, concrete paths, light globes, their health, funeral expenses, borers, carpets," and so on. *The Glass Canoe* deals with characters who escape this monotony by drowning their woes in "amber fluid" (beer). A bawdy and violent celebration of life in a Sydney pub, the novel portrays the urban drinkers as the last of a colourful "tribe" which preserves values (such as mateship and "macho" brawniness) from Australia's mythic past.

Though the writer of this essay would strongly defend Ireland's earlier novels, most critical opinion favours the works of his "second phase." These recent novels have moved more clearly in the direction of fable, the prose style has become remarkably agile and witty, and the author's earlier concern with specific political issues has broadened into a preoccupation with the inner world of the imagination.

A Woman of the Future is Ireland's first attempt to create a full-scale female character, but—more importantly—it is an attempt to confront Australia's dauntingly masculine national self-image. By setting the novel some years in the future, Ireland allows himself to extrapolate the effects of current social problems (especially unemployment), but the novel's chief concern is to draw a parallel between the young heroine stepping out into life, and her country—Australia—stepping out into nationhood. Ireland has argued in an interview that "women seem more open [than men] to experience and to new things," and *A Woman of the Future* attempts to redefine the national consciousness in these terms.

City of Women pursues these preoccupaions, but often by questioning them. Ostensibly, the novel is set in the city of Sydney after all males have been expelled, and tells the story of an ageing mother's loneliness after her daughter has joined an engineering project in the heart of the continent. Challenging his earlier novel's premise that women have an outlook different to that of men, Ireland portrays the city of women as being no different from the former city of men. The functions of bully or criminal or whinger are still fulfilled—but by women, not men (which suggests that the basic humanity of the sexes is more important than their differences). But this judgement in turn is questioned when the novel's ending reveals that the City of Women exists only in the mind of the central character. Though frequently criticized as a "cop out," this unexpected denouement is an effective means of insisting upon the value of individual viewpoint and perception.

As if having had enough of women, Ireland's most recent novel takes a dog as its central character. *Archimedes and the Seagle* is the memoir of a dog in the city of Sydney ... but it is also a deliberately (and successfully) "upbeat" novel, celebrating the joys of life and the beauties of nature even in the midst of a huge city's urban sprawl. The novel asserts Ireland's optimism about the world, re-affirming his preoccupation with fantasy and individual perception. Ireland's novels not only reflect man's yearning for a free a more joyous way of life, they also assert the cautious belief that this is possible.

—Van Ikin

IRVING, John (Winslow). American. Born in Exeter, New Hampshire, 2 March 1942. Educated at Phillips Exeter Academy, Exeter, graduated 1962; University of Pittsburgh, 1961–62; University of Vienna, 1963–64; University of New Hampshire, Durham, B.A. (cum laude), 1965; University of Iowa, Iowa City, M.F.A. 1967. Married Shyla Leary in 1964; two sons. Taught at Windham College, Putney, Vermont, 1967–69; lived in Vienna, 1969–71; Writer-in-Residence, University of Iowa, 1972–75; Assistant Professor of English, Mount Holyoke College, South Hadley, Massachusetts, 1975–78. Recipient: Rockefeller grant, 1972; National Endowment for the Arts grant, 1974; Guggenheim grant, 1976; American Book Award, for paperback, 1980. Agent: Literistic Ltd., 264 Fifth Avenue, New York, New York 10001. Address: c/o William Morrow Inc., 105 Madison Avenue, New York, New York 10016, U.S.A.

PUBLICATIONS

Novels

Setting Free the Bears. New York, Random House, 1969; London, Corgi, 1979.

The Water-Method Man. New York, Random House, 1972; London, Corgi, 1980.
The 158-Pound Marriage. New York, Random House, 1974; London, Corgi, 1980.
The World According to Garp. New York, Dutton, and London, Gollancz, 1978.
The Hotel New Hampshire. New York, Dutton, and London, Cape, 1981.
The Cider House Rules. New York, Morrow, and London, Cape, 1985.

Uncollected Short Stories

"A Winter Branch," in *Redbook* (New York), November 1965.
"Weary Kingdom," in *Boston Review*, Spring-Summer 1968.
"Almost in Iowa," in *The Secret Life of Our Times*, edited by Gordon Lish. New York, Doubleday, 1973.
"Lost in New York," in *Esquire* (New York), March 1973.
"Brennbar's Rant," in *Playboy* (Chicago), December 1974.
"Students: These Are Your Teachers!," in *Esquire* (New York), September 1975.
"Vigilance," in *Ploughshares* (Cambridge, Massachusetts), no. 4, 1977.
"Dog in the Alley, Child in the Sky," in *Esquire* (New York), June 1977.
"Interior Space," in *Fiction* (New York), No. 6, 1980.

*

Manuscript Collection: Phillips Exeter Academy, Exeter, New Hampshire.

Critical Studies: introduction by Terrence DuPres to *3 by Irving* (omnibus), New York, Random House, 1980; *Fowles, Irving, Barthes: Canonical Variations on an Apocryphal Theme* by Randolph Runyon, Columbus, Ohio State University Press, 1982; *John Irving* by Gabriel Miller, New York, Ungar, 1982.

Theatrical Activities:
Actor: **Film**—*The World According to Garp*, 1982.

*   *   *

The publication of *The World According to Garp* was an important event in contemporary American literature. For John Irving himself, of course, the novel's reception must have been extremely gratifying; the book neatly divided his career forever into the pre- and post-*Garp* periods. Initially a little-known academic writer whose first three books—*Setting Free the Bears, The Water-Method Man,* and *The 158-Pound Marriage*—rapidly sought the remainder lists, he suddenly found himself inundated by critical superlatives and, no doubt, positively drenched in money. He achieved that rare combination of literary acclaim and wide readership that every writer dreams of. The success of *Garp*, along with the previous popularity of E.L. Doctorow's *Ragtime*, indicated that fiction after more than a decade of stifling academicism, may have finally graduated from college and ventured out into the arena of ordinary life. Because many professors seem to believe that literature was written to be studied in their courses and because probably far too many writers receive their training at their hands, a great deal of American writing has been marked by a sterile obsession with technique for its own sake, a conscious avoidance of traditional subjects, and a perverse desire to appeal only to a coterie of initiates.

Irving's works in general, and *Garp* most spectacularly, signal the return of fiction to its proper and honorable concerns—a close engagement with the stuff of real life, a profound compassion for humanity, and—inextricably and possibly even causally connected to these qualities—great dedication to the narrative process, to storytelling itself. Irving cares very much about his characters and their stories and makes his readers care about them as well; in doing so he places his work in the greatest traditions of the novel. Only a bold and innovative writer could venture so daringly backward into the literary past.

In addition to his refreshingly old-fashioned qualities, Irving also demonstrates his appropriateness to his own time and place. His novels are in many ways as contemporary as those of any of his peers. They possess all the familiar elements we have come to recognize as landmarks of the American literary countryside: violence, grotesquerie, a certain craziness, a racey energetic style, a powerful interest in the fiction-making process. All of his works differ from one another in manner, matter, and merit—*The 158-Pound Marriage* seems his weakest performance—but they also share certain peculiarly Irvingesque subjects that help to give them their special zany charm. Until *The Cider House Rules* his books all dealt with such matters as academia, art, children, marital triangles and quadrangles, wrestlers, writers, sexual mutilation, Vienna, and bears. The last named occurs in his first book, in the long story "The Pension Grillparzer," that appears in *The World According to Garp*, and in *The Hotel New Hampshire*.

The pre-*Garp* Irving is lively, comic, whimsical, a writer whose works display confidence, a kind of assured easiness unusual in a young beginner, beyond the usual condescending critical clichés about promise. *Setting Free the Bears* is a kind of revitalized American picaresque improbably set against the landscape of Austria; the goal of its protagonist's lunatic quest is suggested in its title and works out to be as unusual and improbable as its setting. *The Water-Method Man* deals with the sexual escapades, personal failures, and professional problems of a more or less lovable rogue wonderfully named Bogus Trumper; it explores, with rich glee, some fascinating notions about the creation of art from the chaos of Trumper's life, through the medium of *avant garde* film making and Trumper's absurd doctoral dissertation.

Whatever the value of his earlier work, however, in retrospect it now seems a preliminary for the main event, *The World According to Garp*, which would change the author's career forever. The novel is written with enormous energy and strength, clearly the work of a writer in full command of his material and his method. Although its style presents no particular problems and its plot moves in a leisurely, straightforward manner, the novel seems radically experimental for its complicated narrative progress. Its generally simple story of the life of T.S. Garp from conception to death is interrupted by a number of other fictions from "The Pension Grillparzer" to a horribly violent account of rape, murder, and despair, Garp's novel, *The World According to Bensenhaver*; the book also includes bits from Garp's mother's autobiography, *A Sexual Suspect*, other short stories, and parts of the biography of Garp that will only be written after his life and the book are over. In an action that must have called for some courage, Irving even includes an epilogue, detailing the lives of his characters after the main events of his major fiction have concluded; once again, in reverting to the methods of the past the author seems daringly innovative.

The actual subjects and events of *Garp*, as unusual as its narrative archaism, come to dominate all of Irving's works. Although the novel itself was almost universally regarded as comic and, in Irving's words, "life affirming," it is also a book

haunted by violence, savagery, fear, horror, and despair, an immensely sad and troubling work. From beginning to end a bleeding wound of mutilation gapes across the book: Garp's mother slashes a soldier in a theater; his father dies of a terrible war wound; his wife bites her lover's penis off in the same automobile accident that kills one of Garp's sons and half-blinds the other; and Garp's own strange novel, *The World According to Bensenhaver*, presents one of the most vivid rape scenes in all of literature. The relationship between sexuality and violence is emphasized in virtually every character—from Roberta Muldoon, the transsexual former football player to the man-hating feminists who cut out their own tongues to commemorate the similar maiming of a rape victim; Garp himself is assassinated by a cult member, the sister of the girl who was responsible for his sexual initiation.

Along with the bizarre and horrific narrative and the close attention to the character and life of the artist, the theme of sexual mutilation suggests something about the creative act itself. Throughout the novel, art is generated out of fear, pain, blood, and guilt; experiencing all these, Garp creates his fictions, which also make up a large part of the book about him. Art, life, and the interpretation of both provide the novel's rich and often puzzling structure, sometimes causing it to roam far off its initially simple narrative line into a region of horror, grotesquerie, insanity, and myth.

The post-*Garp* Irving, no longer the obscure academic writer, was rapidly transformed into the celebrity author, attentive to sales, publicity, and movie rights. He soon began to appear on the TV talks shows, demonstrating his recipes for breaded veal cutlet; dressed in wrestling togs and flexing his wrestler's muscles, he brooded in full color for the readers of slick magazines. His good looks, his popularity, and his willingness to publicize his books and films earned him a more than literary fame and no doubt a more than literary fortune—his post-*Garp* novels are copyrighted by something called Garp Enterprises Ltd.

Those books, *The Hotel New Hampshire* and *The Cider House Rules*, demonstrate the pernicious influence of success. The former continues the themes and ideas of its predecessor, boiling over with violence and whimsy, with such matters as a gang rape, a plane crash, suicide, terrorism, a lesbian who dresses in a bear suit, and a flatulent dog named Sorrow. All the obsessions are intact, but by now they seem mechanical and perfunctory in substance and style; the laborious drollery and the easy cynicism, along with the specious profundities of the repeated catch phrases and verbal tags, read like warmed-over Vonnegut.

Although it is probably only a mixed success, *The Cider House Rules* shows Irving moving away from self-imitation towards slightly newer materials. With the sureness of *Garp* but without the obsessive violence of most of his work, the book tells a Dickensian story of a peculiarly Irvingesque place, an orphanage where abortions are performed; though heavily dependent on the kind of academic research that few authors handle gracefully, *The Cider House Rules* recaptures and increases the compassion of *Garp*. The quirkiness of style and the fascination with genital wounds and sexual pain remain, but they are mixed with less labored touches of lightness and a good deal of love. The hip wiseguy in Irving has been replaced by a warmer, more loving speaker who avoids those familiar occasions for gratuitous pain that have so richly preoccupied him in the past.

It seems likely that John Irving has reached the point, in a relatively brief span of time, at which he can be considered a major contemporary novelist. The body of work he has created, however uneven, shows originality, development, and breadth. His startling mixture of humor and sorrow, of accessibility and complexity, of clarity and confusion, of strong narrative with humane vision, of horrified despair and life-affirming comedy, seems perfectly suited to the present state of our culture and literature. The chord he struck in a large and varied public with *Garp* continues to resonate; his works still appeal to a readership that encompasses many levels of literacy, an indication of their timeliness and power.

—George Grella

JACOBSON, Dan. British. Born in Johannesburg, South Africa, 7 March 1929. Educated at the University of the Witwatersrand, Johannesburg, 1946–49, B.A. 1949. Married Margaret Pye in 1954; three sons and one daughter. Public relations assistant, South African Jewish Board of Deputies, Johannesburg, 1951–52; correspondence secretary, Mills and Feeds Ltd., Kimberley, South Africa, 1952–54. Fellow in Creative Writing, Stanford University, California, 1956–57; Visiting Professor, Syracuse University, New York, 1965–66; Visiting Fellow, State University of New York, Buffalo, 1971, and Australian National University, Canberra, 1980; Lecturer, 1976–80, and since 1980, Reader in English, University College, London. Vice-Chairman of the Literature Panel, Arts Council of Great Britain, 1974–76. Recipient: Rhys Memorial Prize, 1959; Maugham Award, 1964; H.H. Wingate Award (*Jewish Chronicle*, London), 1978. Fellow, Royal Society of Literature, 1974. Agent: A.M. Heath, 40–42 William IV Street, London WC2N 4DD, England; or, Russell and Volkening Inc., 50 West 29th Street, New York, New York 10001, U.S.A.

PUBLICATIONS

Novels

The Trap. London, Weidenfeld and Nicolson, and New York, Harcourt Brace, 1955.
A Dance in the Sun. London, Weidenfeld and Nicolson, and New York, Harcourt Brace, 1956.
The Price of Diamonds. London, Weidenfeld and Nicolson, 1957; New York, Knopf, 1958.
The Evidence of Love. London, Weidenfeld and Nicolson, and Boston, Little Brown, 1960.
The Beginners. London, Weidenfeld and Nicolson, and New York, Macmillan, 1966.
The Rape of Tamar. London, Weidenfeld and Nicolson, and New York, Macmillan, 1970.
The Wonder-Worker. London, Weidenfeld and Nicolson, 1973; Boston, Little Brown, 1974.
The Confessions of Josef Baisz. London, Secker and Warburg, 1977; New York, Harper, 1979.

Short Stories

A Long Way from London. London, Weidenfeld and Nicolson, 1958.
The Zulu and the Zeide. Boston, Little Brown, 1959.
Beggar My Neighbour. London, Weidenfeld and Nicolson, 1964.
Through the Wilderness. New York, Macmillan, 1968.

Penguin Modern Stories 6, with others. London, Penguin, 1970.
A Way of Life and Other Stories, edited by Alix Pirani. London, Longman, 1971.
Inklings: Selected Stories. London, Weidenfeld and Nicolson, 1973; as *Through the Wilderness*, London, Penguin, 1977.

Uncollected Short Story

"Brian," in *New Yorker*, 13 August 1984.

Play

Radio Play: *The Caves of Adullan*, 1972.

Other

No Further West: California Visited. London, Weidenfeld and Nicolson, 1959; New York, Macmillan, 1961.
Time of Arrival and Other Essays. London, Weidenfeld and Nicolson, and New York, Macmillan, 1963.
The Story of the Stories: The Chosen People and Its God. London, Secker and Warburg, and New York, Harper, 1982.
Time and Time Again: Autobiographies. London, Deutsch, and Boston, Atlantic Monthly Press, 1985.

*

Bibliography: *Dan Jacobson: A Bibliography* by Myra Yudelman, Johannesburg, University of the Witwatersrand, 1967.

Critical Studies: "The Novels of Dan Jacobson" by Renee Winegarten, in *Midstream* (New York), May 1966; "Novelist of South Africa," in *The Liberated Woman and Other Americans* by Midge Decter, New York, Coward McCann, 1971; "The Gift of Metamorphosis" by Pearl K. Bell, in *New Leader* (New York), April 1974; "Apollo, Dionysus, and Other Performers in Dan Jacobson's Circus" by Michael Wade, in *World Literature Written in English* (Arlington, Texas), April 1974; "A Somewhere Place" by C.J. Driver, in *New Review* (London), October 1977; *Dan Jacobson* by Sheila Roberts, Boston, Twayne, 1984.

Dan Jacobson comments:

My novels and stories up to and including *The Beginners* were naturalistic in manner and were written almost entirely about life in South Africa. This is not true of the novels I have written subsequently.

*   *   *

Dan Jacobson's first two novels, *The Trap* and *A Dance in the Sun*, marked him as a writer of considerable ability, with an interest in typically South African "problems." Since then, he has developed rapidly to become one of South Africa's best known and most interesting novelists.

The two early novels are both concerned with the tensions inherent in the extremely close, almost familial, relationships between white employer and black employee, which tend to develop in the particular kind of farm community Jacobson describes. Both embody what might be described as allegorical statements about the South African situation. Jacobson implies that the inhabitants of the country are trapped in their own environment and condemned to perform a ritualistic "dance in the sun." To an outsider this can only appear to be a form of insanity. This vision of South Africa leaves out of account, or, at best, finds irrelevant, the group (English speaking, liberal, white) to which Jacobson himself belongs, and it is, therefore, not surprising that he should have chosen to live and work abroad.

For some years, however, his novels continued to deal with South African subjects. *The Evidence of Love* tells the story of a black man and a white woman who fall in love and attempt to defy South African law and custom by living together. The novel treats the theme of interracial love in a more relaxed and naturalistic way than is usual in South African fiction, and also highlights aspects of the individual struggle for freedom and the achievement of self-identity. *The Price of Diamonds* focusses on shady dealings and financial corruption in a small town in South Africa, and reveals Jacobson's quite considerable gift for comedy.

The Beginners, which, together with the collection of stories *A Long Way from London*, established Jacobson's position as a writer of stature, is an ambitious and substantial novel. The story of three generations of an immigrant Jewish family, it offers a penetrating, subtle, and complex analysis of what it means to be a "demi-European at the foot of Africa" and a "demi-Jew" in the modern world. The novels which follow *The Beginners* are not concerned with South Africa directly, nor are they naturalistic in manner. But two of the three later novels deal with political tensions and power struggles, and in so doing appear to have deliberate parallels with the contemporary situation in South Africa. Jacobson's continuing interest in South Africa is also reflected in his recent collection of autobiographical pieces, *Time and Time Again*, in which he reflects, among other things, on the way in which his perceptions of the country have changed since the days when he could see it only as a place from which he had to escape.

The Rape of Tamar is a witty and sophisticated reconstruction of an episode at the court of the biblical King David, focussing on a power struggle between the ageing king and his politically ambitious sons. *The Wonder-Worker*, set in contemporary London, explores the world of a sensitive and lonely character whose inability to establish meaningful relationships leads inevitably to his complete alienation from the world around him, but, paradoxically, also to his ability to understand people completely. Jacobson's most recent novel, *The Confessions of Joseph Baisz*, is a brilliantly inventive and deeply disturbing fantasy: the "extraordinary autobiography" of an emotionally stunted individual who discovers very early in his bleak life that he is capable of loving only those people whom he has first betrayed. Set in an imaginary country with a nightmarish but distinctly recognisable resemblance of South Africa, the novel is wholly convincing in its portrayal of a society whose members illustrate what Baisz calls "the iron law: the wider their horizons, the narrower their minds."

Like other contemporary South African novelists, Jacobson has written some excellent short stories. Many of them probe the guilts and fears of white South Africans living in the midst of what they regard as an alien and hostile black culture. Two stories which are among the best things he has done are "The Zulu and the Zeide" and "Beggar My Neighbour." The former contrasts the small-minded meanness of a wealthy Jewish businessman with the unaffected humanity of the black servant he employs to care for his ailing father; while "Beggar My Neighbour" movingly evokes the world of a young white boy forced to come to terms with the cruel realities of a racist society through his chance meeting with two black children. In these stories, as in all his work, Jacobson's special skills are displayed: detailed observation, economic presentation,

and a compassionate but objective analysis of the varieties of human behaviour.

—Ursula Edmands

JAMES, C(yril) L(ionel) R(obert). Trinidadian. Born in Trinidad, 4 January 1901. Educated at Queen's Royal College, Port of Spain, Trinidad, 1911–18. Married Selma Weinstein in 1955; one child by a previous marriage. Journalist and teacher in the West Indies until 1932, when he moved to England; press correspondent, chiefly on cricket, in England, until 1938; went to the United States in 1938, and remained there, lecturing on politics and literature, until 1953; has lived in England since 1953, except for two years in the West Indies, 1958–60, when he worked as Secretary of the West Indian Federal Labour Party. Editor or co-editor, *Trinidad* literary magazine, 1929–30, *Fight* (later *Workers Fight*), London, late 1930's, *The Nation*, Trinidad, 1958–60, and *We the People*, Port of Spain, 1965. Address: c/o Allison and Busby, 6-A Noel Street, London W1V 3RB, England.

PUBLICATIONS

Novels

Minty Alley.   London, Secker and Warburg, 1936.

Uncollected Short Stories

"La Divina Pastora," in *The Best Short Stories of 1928*, edited by Edward J. O'Brien.   London, Cape, 1928.
"Triumph," in *Stories from the Caribbean*, edited by Andrew Salkey.   London, Elek, 1965; as *Island Voices*, New York, Liveright, 1970.

Play

Toussaint L'Ouverture (produced London, 1936).   One scene published in *Life and Letters* (London), Spring 1936; revised version, as *The Black Jacobins* (produced Ibadan, Nigeria, 1967; London, 1986), published in *A Time and a Season: 8 Caribbean Plays*, edited by Errol Hill, Port of Spain, Trinidad, University of the West Indies, 1976.

Other

The Life of Captain Cipriani: An Account of British Government in the West Indies.   Nelson, Lancashire, Coulton, 1932; abridged edition, as *The Case for West-Indian Self-Government*, London, Hogarth Press, 1933; New York, University Place Book Shop, 1967.
World Revolution 1917–1936: The Rise and Fall of the Communist International.   London, Secker and Warburg, and New York, Pioneer, 1937.
A History of Negro Revolt.   London, Fact, 1938; New York, Haskell House, 1967; revised edition, as *A History of Pan-African Revolt*, Washington, D.C., Drum and Spear Press, 1969.
The Black Jacobins: Toussaint L'Ouverture and the San Domingo Revolution.   London, Secker and Warburg, and New York, Dial Press, 1938; revised edition, New York, Random House, 1963; London, Allison and Busby, 1980.
Why Negroes Should Oppose the War (as J.R. Johnson).   New York, Pioneer, 1939.

My Friends: A Fireside Chat on the War. Privately printed, 1940.

Down with Starvation Wages in South-East Missouri. St. Louis, UCAPAWA-CIO, 1942.

The Invading Socialist Society, with F. Forest and Ria Stone. New York, Johnson Forest Tendency, 1947.

The Balance Sheet: Trotskyism in the United States 1940–47 (as J.R. Johnson), with F. Forest and Martin Glaberman. New York, Johnson Forest Tendency, 1947.

World Revolutionary Perspectives and the Russian Question. New York, Johnson Forest Tendency, 1947.

State Capitalism and World Revolution (published anonymously). Privately printed, 1950; as C.L.R. James, Detroit, Facing Reality, 1969.

The Balance Sheet Completed: Ten Years of American Trotskyism, with F. Forest. New York, Johnson Forest Tendency, 1951.

Mariners, Renegades, and Castaways: The Story of Herman Melville and the World We Live In. Privately printed, 1953; London, Allison and Busby, 1984.

Every Cook Can Govern: A Study of Democracy in Ancient Greece, and Negro Americans and American Politics. Detroit, Correspondence, 1956.

Facing Reality. Detroit, Correspondence, 1958.

Lecture on Federation (West Indies and British Guiana). N.p., British Guiana Argosy, 1959.

Dr. Eric Williams, First Premier of Trinidad and Tobago: A Biographical Sketch. Port of Spain, PNM, 1960.

Modern Politics (lectures). Port of Spain, PNM, 1960.

Federation: We Failed Miserably—How and Why. San Juan, Trinidad, Vedic, 1961.

Party Politics in the West Indies. Privately printed, 1962.

Marxism and the Intellectuals (as J.R. Johnson). Detroit, Facing Reality, 1962.

Kwame Nkrumah and the West Indies. Privately printed, 1962.

Beyond a Boundary. London, Hutchinson, 1963; New York, Pantheon, 1984.

Letters on Organization (as J.R. Johnson). Detroit, Facing Reality, 1963.

Leon Trotsky and the Vanguard Party. Detroit, Facing Reality, 1964.

Negro Americans Take the Lead: A Statement on the Crisis in American Civilization. Detroit, Facing Reality, 1964.

Marxism for the Sixties. Detroit, Facing Reality, 1965.

West Indians of East Indian Descent. Trinidad, IBIS, 1965.

Wilson Harris: A Philosophical Approach. Port of Spain, University of the West Indies, 1965.

Perspectives and Proposals. Detroit, Facing Reality, 1966.

Towards a Caribbean Nation. N.p., Caribbean Conference, 1967.

The Gathering Forces. Detroit, Facing Reality, 1967.

Education, Propaganda, and Agitation. Detroit, Facing Reality, 1968.

Black Studies and the Contemporary Student. Detroit, Facing Reality, 1969.

The Hegelian Dialectic and Modern Politics. Detroit, Facing Reality, 1970; revised edition, as *Notes on Dialectics: Hegel, Marx, Lenin*, London, Allison and Busby, and Westport, Connecticut, Hill, 1980.

Dialectic and History: An Introduction. Cambridge, Massachusetts, Radical America, 1972.

Nkrumah and the Ghana Revolution. London, Allison and Busby, and Westport, Connecticut, Hill, 1977; revised edition, Allison and Busby, 1982.

Selected Writings:
1. *The Future in the Present.* London, Allison and Busby, and Westport, Connecticut, Hill, 1977.
2. *Spheres of Existence.* London, Allison and Busby, and Westport, Connecticut, Hill, 1980.
3. *At the Rendezvous of Victory.* London, Allison and Busby, 1984; Westport, Connecticut, Hill, 1985.

Black Nationalism and Socialism, with Tony Bogues and Kim Gordon. London, Socialists Unlimited, 1979.

Walter Rodney and the Question of Power. London, Race Today, 1983.

80th Birthday Lectures. London, Race Today, 1983.

Translator, *Stalin: A Critical Survey of Socialism*, by Boris Souvarine. London, Secker and Warburg, and New York, Longman, 1939.

*

Bibliography: in *At the Rendezvous of Victory*, 1984.

Critical Studies: "C.L.R. James Issue" of *Radical America* (Cambridge, Massachusetts), May 1970, and *Urgent Tasks* (Chicago), 1981.

Theatrical Activities:
Actor: **Play**—role in *Toussaint L'Ouverture*, London, 1936.

*   *   *

C.L.R. James shocked the middle-class Trinidadian readers of the late 1920's and early 1930's with short stories that explored the manners and morals of the indigenous population. For while everyone knew of them, this central area of Caribbean experience was kept out of "respectable" literature. Today levels of moral acceptance, not only in Trinidad, have drastically changed, and the work of writers such as V.S. Naipaul and Samuel Selvon in the same area makes part of James's explorations of lower-class Caribbean life colourless; nevertheless James's qualities of human compassion in an area landmined with prejudices of class and colour have not been superseded, and will never be irrelevant.

Minty Alley, James's only full-length novel, tells how a young office-worker, Haynes, is forced by poverty to live in the unfamiliar surroundings of a lower-class tenement. It is run by a Mrs. Rouse and her man Benoit, who is also carrying on an affair with a powerful and somewhat sinister woman known only as "the nurse." The community is violent and unstable in its relationships, lit with sudden moments of tenderness, and Haynes quickly becomes involved in it, in particular through his liaison with the servant Maisie, Mrs. Rouse's niece. Although at first Haynes appears a "superior" figure by class and education, by the end he can begin to realise that he came as an immature person, and has been mothered into manhood by the little community. Benoit dies, and, although he has deserted Mrs. Rouse for the nurse, Mrs. Rouse loses all desire to run the house, and Haynes leaves as its inhabitants disperse.

James hoped that a second novel would be his major work, but this never appeared. *Minty Alley*, however, assures him a place in Caribbean fiction.

—Louis James

JAMES, P(hyllis) D(orothy). British. Born in Oxford, 3 August 1920. Educated at Cambridge Girls' High School,

1931–37. During World War II worked as a Red Cross nurse and at the Ministry of Food. Married Ernest C.B. White in 1941 (died, 1964); two daughters. Prior to World War II, assistant stage manager, Festival Theatre, Cambridge; Principal Administrative Assistant, North West Regional Hospital Board, London, 1949–68; Principal, Home Office, in police department, 1968–72, and criminal policy department, 1972–79. Justice of the Peace, Willesden, London, 1979. Fellow, Institute of Hospital Administrators; Chairman, Society of Authors, 1985. Recipient: Crime Writers Association prize, 1967. O.B.E. (Officer, Order of the British Empire), 1983. Agent: Elaine Greene Ltd., 31 Newington Green, London N16 9PU, England.

Publications

Novels

Cover Her Face.   London, Faber, 1962; New York, Scribner, 1966.
A Mind to Murder.   London, Faber, 1963; New York, Scribner, 1967.
Unnatural Causes.   London, Faber, and New York, Scribner, 1967.
Shroud for a Nightingale.   London, Faber, and New York, Scribner, 1971.
An Unsuitable Job for a Woman.   London, Faber, 1972; New York, Scribner, 1973.
The Black Tower.   London, Faber, and New York, Scribner, 1975.
Death of an Expert Witness.   London, Faber, and New York, Scribner, 1977.
Innocent Blood.   London, Faber, and New York, Scribner, 1980.
The Skull Beneath the Skin.   London, Faber, and New York, Scribner, 1982.

Uncollected Short Stories

"Moment of Power," in *Ellery Queen's Murder Menu.*   Cleveland, World, 1969.
"The Victim," in *Winter's Crimes 5*, edited by Virginia Whitaker.   London, Macmillan, 1973.
"Murder, 1986," in *Ellery Queen's Masters of Mystery.*   New York, Davis, 1975.
"A Very Desirable Residence," in *Winter's Crimes 8*, edited by Hilary Watson.   London, Macmillan, 1976.
"Great-Aunt Ellie's Flypapers," in *Verdict of Thirteen*, edited by Julian Symons.   London, Faber, and New York, Harper, 1979.
"The Girl Who Loved Graveyards," in *Winter's Crimes 15*, edited by George Hardinge.   London, Macmillan, and New York, St. Martin's Press, 1983.

Play

A Private Treason (produced Watford, Hertfordshire, 1985).

Other

The Maul and the Pear Tree: The Ratcliffe Highway Murders, 1811, with Thomas A. Critchley.   London, Constable, 1971.

*

Critical Study: *P.D. James* by Norma Siebenheller, New York, Ungar, 1982.

*   *   *

Moving from the well-crafted but thin detective story (*Cover Her Face*) to the almost fully realised novel (*Innocent Blood*), P.D. James has rapidly increased her command of character and tone and has learned how to give substance to the worlds of her fiction. The crimes she writes about are usually committed in closely knit, sometimes isolated communities, no doubt suggested by her own administrative experience: a home for the disabled, a psychiatric clinic, a teaching hospital, a forensic laboratory, the routines of which, interesting in themselves, form a continuum which gives a sense of extended reality.

James's characters likewise suggest duration, often having more detailed off-stage lives than their immediate plot functions require. For instance, when a painted hag co-opts Sergeant Masterson into dancing an exhibition tango, James explains his success by inventing an off-stage affair with a randy blonde, who taught him ballroom dancing and with whom he won medals until her dull husband became suspicious and Masterson prudent. Sometimes, however, James establishes character so substantially in the present that unexpected revelations crucial to her plots seem arbitrary, the shock of disbelief temporarily superseding the shock of recognition that the new piece fits the puzzle—as in the discovery that Stella Mawson was briefly Dr. Lorrimer's wife and that Matron Mary Taylor had been Irmgard Grobel, an untrained nurse at a Nazi death camp. Occasionally, too, James withholds information by censoring the long interior monologues she uses for characterization. Motivations obviously interest her more than plot does. Although her puzzles are ingenious, she is content in *The Skull Beneath the Skin* to use such archetypal situations as Agatha Christie's houseparty-on-an-island, Eugene Sue's locked trapdoor with water rising below, and Ann Radcliffe's confrontation with a *memento mori*.

In James's best works, on the other hand, delicate webs of relationship are constantly being spun, broken, or unravelled. The touch of his pupil's inner forearm as they sit together in their wheel chairs gives Henry Carwardine "the sudden realisation of joy." The young private detective, Cordelia Gray, wraps the strap that hanged Mark Callender around her waist as her own talisman. Filaments of personal and spiritual nostalgia connect Commander Adam Dalgliesh to the dead Father Baddeley. Other, unbreakable gossamers stretch between Cordelia and Adam after their brief passage, and elsewhere Dalgliesh thinks that the strangest part of a detective's work is to build up a relationship with the victim.

Dalgliesh is sensitive enough to be both a superior detective and a good minor poet, yet he is often detached; even his subordinates change from case to case. Sometimes he feels an ineffable, but almost impersonal sadness for his dead wife. He and Cordelia are each essentially alone, although Cordelia is more vulnerable to pity. It is characteristic of them both that the bouquet she sends him in hospital contains honesty.

The tone of these novels is often autumnal, the most frequent imagery that of the sea and its cliffs. In a recent interview (*Dial*, September 1985), James described herself as born with a sense "that every moment is lived, really, not under the shadow of death but in the knowledge that this is how it's going to end." She believes that detective fiction may ease that fear for some people, although her works contain moments of psychological brutality which intensify rather than mitigate the sense of mortality. Sergeant Maskell, for instance, thrusts a photograph of Mark's hanging body at Cordelia—neck elongated, head lolling, tongue protruding; or a pathologist inserts his pudgy fingers into the "tender orifices" of a warm female corpse. Yet there is a certain compassion in these works which is less present in *Innocent Blood*, a novel about truth and "the wasteland between imagination and reality already too nebulous" in the mind of an embryonic writer, Philippa, adopted daughter of the sociologist Maurice Palfrey and his negligible second wife.

Philippa has constructed a romantic history about her unknown natural parents, only to learn that they are rapist and child-murderess, Martin and Mary Ducton. Leaving the Palfreys, Philippa furnishes a cheap flat for herself and her newly released mother, and works out a new scenario in which her mother gave her up selflessly through love. This, too, proves wrong. Mary was an abusive mother, and Philippa's adoption completed before her parents' crimes. Crying, "I wish you were dead," she rushes into the dreadful night. When she returns, prepared to love, Mary has committed suicide. Intercut with this plot is Norman Scase's methodical preparation to kill Mary for having strangled his daughter. But he is too late; his knife enters a dead throat. In an epilogue, Philippa is at Cambridge, has written a harsh, brilliant novel, and sometimes tries to be kind.

As always, James seeks out the nuances of relationship from the invisible thread of sexuality running between Philippa and Maurice to the joy Norman feels when a sparrow lights on his palm. Mary Ducton, however, is left deliberately enigmatic. She has written a third-person narrative of the rape and murder for Philippa to read, but is it an artful fabrication like the jumper she knits for her daughter in a variety of stitches and subtle shades, using yarn unravelled from others' garments? Significantly, Philippa throws this jumper into the canal, where it stretches out like a dying child.

These constant themes of truth and reality, together with the central character's progress from private fictions to literary control, from pleasure in wounding to some "small accession of grace," identify *Innocent Blood* as a violent *Lehrjahre*, a little thin at times for James's new genre, but uncommonly full for her old one.

—Jane W. Stedman

JAMESON, (Margaret) Storm. British. Born in Whitby, Yorkshire, 8 January 1891. Educated at Leeds University, Yorkshire, 1909–12, B.A. (1st class honours) in English language and literature 1912; King's College, London, 1912–13, M.A. 1914. Married Guy Patterson Chapman in 1924 (second marriage; died, 1972); one son from first marriage. Formerly copywriter, Carlton Agency, advertising firm, London; editor, *New Commonwealth*, London, 1919–21; English representative, and later London co-manager, Alfred A. Knopf, publishers, New York, 1925–28; reviewer, *New English Weekly*, London, 1934. President, PEN English Centre, 1938–45. Recipient: Calabrian International Prize, 1972; PEN Award, 1974. D.Litt.: Leeds University, 1943. Honorary Member, American Academy, 1978. Address: c/o C.C. Storm-Clark, Department of Economics and Related Studies, University of York, York YO1 5DD, England.

PUBLICATIONS

Novels

The Pot Boils. London, Constable, 1919.
The Happy Highways. London, Heinemann, and New York, Century, 1920.
The Clash. London, Heinemann, and Boston, Little Brown, 1922.
Lady Susan and Life: An Indiscretion. London, Chapman and Hall, and New York, Dodd Mead, 1923.
The Pitiful Wife. London, Constable, 1923; New York, Knopf, 1924.
Three Kingdoms. London, Constable, and New York, Knopf, 1926.
The Triumph of Time: A Trilogy. London, Heinemann, 1932.
  The Lovely Ship. London, Heinemann, and New York, Knopf, 1927.
  The Voyage Home. London, Heinemann, and New York, Knopf, 1930.
  A Richer Dust. London, Heinemann, and New York, Knopf, 1931.
Farewell to Youth. London, Heinemann, and New York, Knopf, 1928.
That Was Yesterday. London, Heinemann, and New York, Knopf, 1932.
The Single Heart. London, Benn, 1932.
A Day Off. London, Nicholson and Watson, 1933.
Women Against Men (includes *A Day Off*, *The Delicate Monster*, and *The Single Heart*). New York, Knopf, 1933.
The Mirror in Darkness:
  Company Parade. London, Cassell, and New York, Knopf, 1934.
  Love in Winter. London, Cassell, and New York, Knopf, 1935.
  None Turn Back. London, Cassell, 1936.
In the Second Year. London, Cassell, and New York, Macmillan, 1936.
Delicate Monster. London, Nicholson and Watson, 1937.
The Moon Is Making. London, Cassell, 1937; New York, Macmillan, 1938.
The World Ends (as William Lamb). London, Dent, 1937.
Loving Memory (as James Hill). London, Collins, 1937.
No Victory for the Soldier (as James Hill). London, Collins, 1938.
Here Comes a Candle. London, Cassell, 1938; New York, Macmillan, 1939.
Farewell, Night: Welcome Day. London, Cassell, 1939; as *The Captain's Wife*, New York, Macmillan, 1939.
Europe to Let: The Memoirs of an Obscure Man. London, Macmillan, and New York, Macmillan, 1940.
Cousin Honoré. London, Cassell, 1940; New York, Macmillan, 1941.
The Fort. London, Cassell, and New York, Macmillan, 1941.
Then We Shall Hear Singing: A Fantasy in C Major. London, Cassell, and New York, Macmillan, 1942.
Cloudless May. London, Macmillan, 1943; New York, Macmillan, 1944.
The Journal of Mary Hervey Russell. London, Macmillan, and New York, Macmillan, 1945.
The Other Side. London, Macmillan, and New York, Macmillan, 1946.
Before the Crossing. London, Macmillan, and New York, Macmillan, 1947.
The Black Laurel. London, Macmillan, 1947; New York, Macmillan, 1948.

The Moment of Truth. London, Macmillan, and New York, Macmillan, 1949.

The Green Man. London, Macmillan, 1952; New York, Harper, 1953.

The Hidden River. London, Macmillan, and New York, Harper, 1955.

The Intruder. London, Macmillan, and New York, Macmillan, 1956.

A Cup of Tea for Mr. Thorgill. London, Macmillan, and New York, Harper, 1957.

A Ulysses Too Many. London, Macmillan, 1958; as *One Ulysses Too Many*, New York, Harper, 1958.

Last Score; or, The Private Life of Sir Richard Ormston. London, Macmillan, and New York, Harper, 1961.

The Road from the Monument. London, Macmillan, and New York, Harper, 1962.

A Month Soon Goes. London, Macmillan, and New York, Harper, 1963.

The Aristide Case. London, Macmillan, 1964; as *The Blind Heart*, New York, Harper, 1964.

The Early Life of Stephen Hind. London, Macmillan, and New York, Harper, 1966.

The White Crow. London, Macmillan, and New York, Harper, 1968.

There Will Be a Short Interval. London, Harvill Press, and New York, Harper, 1973.

Short Stories

A Day Off: Two Short Novels and Some Stories. London, Macmillan, 1959.

Plays

Full Circle (produced Liverpool, 1928). Oxford, Blackwell, 1928.

William the Defeated (televised). Published in *The Book of the P.E.N.*, edited by Hermon Ould, London, Barker, 1950.

Television Plays: *William the Defeated*; *The Commonplace Heart*, 1953.

Other

Modern Drama in Europe. London, Collins, and New York, Harcourt Brace, 1920.

The Georgian Novel and Mr. Robinson. London, Heinemann, and New York, Morrow, 1929.

The Decline of Merry England. London, Cassell, and Indianapolis, Bobbs Merrill, 1930.

No Time Like the Present (autobiography). London, Cassell, and New York, Knopf, 1933.

The Soul of Man in the Age of Leisure. London, Nott, 1935.

The Novel in Contemporary Life. Boston, The Writer, 1938.

Civil Journey. London, Cassell, 1939.

The End of This War. London, Allen and Unwin, 1941.

The Writer's Situation and Other Essays. London, Macmillan, and New York, Macmillan, 1950.

Morley Roberts: The Last Eminent Victorian. London, Unicorn Press, 1961.

Journey from the North (autobiography). London, Collins-Harvill Press, 2 vols., 1969–70; New York, Harper, 1 vol., 1971.

Parthian Words. London, Collins-Harvill Press, 1970; New York, Harper, 1971.

Speaking of Stendhal. London, Gollancz, 1979.

Editor, *Challenge to Death.* London, Constable, 1934; New York, Dutton, 1935.

Editor, *London Calling.* London, Harper, 1942.

Editor, *A Kind of Survivor: The Autobiography of Guy Chapman.* London, Gollancz, 1975.

Translator, *Mont-Oriol*, by Maupassant. New York, Knopf, 1924.

Translator, *Horla and Other Stories*, by Maupassant. New York, Knopf, 1925.

Translator, with Ernest Boyd, *88 Short Stories*, by Maupassant. London, Cassell, and New York, Knopf, 1930.

*

Manuscript Collections: University of Texas, Austin; Wellesley College, Massachusetts.

Storm Jameson comments:

(1981) My earliest novels are not worth reading. Nor are all of the later ones. It took me some years to learn how to write. A short list of those novels worth looking at might run: *That Was Yesterday*; *A Day Off*; *Company Parade*, *Love in Winter*, *None Turn Back*—three novels of an unfinished series; *Farewell*, *Night: Welcome*, *Day*; *Europe to Let*; *Cousin Honoré*; *Cloudless May*; *The Journal of Mary Hervey Russell*; *Before the Crossing* and *The Black Laurel*—two novels which are really one; *The Green Man*; *The Hidden River*; *A Cup of Tea for Mr. Thorgill*; *The Road from the Monument*; *The Early Life of Stephen Hind*; *The White Crow*; *There Will Be a Short Interval*.

Of more lasting value is my autobiography: *Journey from the North*. It says all that needs to be said about my novels, myself and my life.

My last but one book, *Parthian Words*, contains my declaration of faith as a writer.

Readers of *Journey from the North* will discover that I have written three novels under other names. One of these, *The World Ends*, by William Lamb, is good, I think.

*   *   *

Storm Jameson was born in Whitby, Yorkshire, into a family of shipbuilders in 1891; and these basic facts are relevant for both her outlook and writing. Three of her novels—*The Lovely Ship*, *The Voyage Home*, and *A Richer Dust*—form a trilogy in which the author chronicles the fortunes of a shipbuilding family and its Victorian matriarch. Some of her later novels have continued the story of Mary Hervey's descendants, and one may suppose that James drew freely on personal contacts and memories, as well as on records, of her own family.

Jameson has told us much—and told it memorably—about her own life in her autobiography, *Journey from the North*, so it is clear that her own life and her family background have provided a great deal of her subject matter. After reading English at Leeds University she did post-graduate research for her M.A. degree at King's College, London, and her thesis appeared in book form as *Modern Drama in Europe*. Already, then, one notes her interest in European literary art and ideas. Despite her consciousness of and pride in her Yorkshire roots, she is the least insular of writers. As President of the English Centre of P.E.N. she revealed herself as an outspoken liberal and anti-Nazi, and a hard-working friend to refugee writers.

"I have every talent of the good businessman," Jameson has said of herself, "shrewdness, persistence, a talent for strategy—except a talent for enjoying business." More pertinent, perhaps, in considering her fiction is her statement, "My mother was a Congregationalist and what religion I got in youth was coloured by that stiff, self-regarding faith. It would be no use for me to deny to myself my Nonconformist upbringing." There one finds both her strength and her limitation, for she appears to have retained the Nonconformist "narrow ideas of right and wrong, its distrust of enjoyment." Few writers can have been so honest as to declare bluntly: "I am not what you may call a born writer, and I should have been much happier as an engineer."

Born writer or not, Jameson has proved herself a prolific writer. She has been candid enough to admit that her earliest novels are not very good; and few critics would wish to dispute the author's own judgment. Out of a great mass of fiction only a handful of novels are worth attention. Those that may be singled out for scrutiny and some praise are *Cousin Honoré*, *The Road from the Monument*, *The White Crow*, and *A Cup of Tea for Mr. Thorgill*.

Cousin Honoré, possibly the most satisfying novel Jameson has written, draws the portrait not only of Honoré Burckheim but of the province of Alsace. She brings out splendidly the flavour of an area which is partly French in character and partly German, but yet remains stubbornly itself. Burckheim is the owner of the family ironworks in the village that bears their name but his real interest—almost to the point of obsession—is his vineyards and the fine Alsatian wine they produce. He likes to turn over in his mind the old rhyme: "Burckheim, Burckheim, A little town, a great wine." The "Nonconformist" Storm Jameson appears to have been fascinated by her own creation: a wily, yet fundamentally sound, old sensualist. The period of time covered runs from 1918 to 1939, and this gives Jameson the opportunity to reveal her love of France and her contempt for the aggressive, boorish aspect of the German national character that found its ultimate expression in Nazi brutality and hysteria. She also flays those Frenchmen whose corruption and inertia led to the defeat of France in 1940.

Burckheim is studied in depth. A self-willed not to say selfish man, a greedy, self-indulgent man, he nevertheless represents much that is good in the French tradition. But it is Berthelin who stands for the true élite of France: intelligent, honourable, responsible. Siguenau, a schemer and liar, stops short of treachery to his country if not to his friends. Eschelmer, the son of Burckheim's illegitimate daughter and a half-German, works as a German agent; he is hysterical in nature, driven by self-pity and vanity, and ends up as a murderer. Reuss, while not pro-German, does not appreciate that saving Alsace from destruction is too narrow an objective when the West is faced with the destruction of its values.

But *Cousin Honoré* does not consist simply of men and ideas. Jameson explores—and with great sensitivity—the feminine world. She brings to life for us Caroline, Burckheim's second wife, who comes from Boston and assesses her husband as being "as naturally honest as a child and completely unmanageable"; the English Blanche Siguenau who "rode, gardened, dried herbs for the different teas"; and eager young Fanny Siguenau who watches her fiancé go off to fight the incorrigible Boche from across the Rhine.

Cousin Honoré is an Englishwoman's tribute to French civilisation. It can also be enjoyed for the skilful way in which Jameson builds up her situations and characters. Perceptive, witty, generous, it is vintage Jameson.

A question Jameson often tries to answer is this: are people really, at bottom, what they seem to others or even to themselves? This theme runs through *The Road from the Monument* and *The White Crow*. In the first of these Gregory Mott comes under the microscope. On the surface his life seems happy and assured; but religious faith and the support of friends fail him when he comes face to face with his real self. Reality is also explored in *The White Crow*. Here, the setting runs from 1890 to 1942, so Jameson takes the opportunity not only to probe into her main character but to underline the social changes of that half-century.

A Cup of Tea for Mr. Thorgill satirises the self-consciously clever academic world. She lashes the "profound frivolity—frivolity at a deep level, below whatever you like of scholarship, sophistication, wit" that can be found in the inbred society of an Oxford college. She brings to her task delicacy and irony and not a little feminine malice. Yet, as in all her work, she is a committed writer: one to whom the integrity of the human personality and freedom of individual action are of supreme importance. Had she been less prolific, Storm Jameson's reputation on the literary stock exchange would undoubtedly be quoted as a much higher figure than it is today. Her best work assures her a place among the significant English novelists of our time.

—Robert Greacen

JENKINS, (John) Robin. British. Born in Cambuslang, Lanarkshire, Scotland, 11 September 1912. Educated at Hamilton Academy; Glasgow University, 1931–35, B.A. (honours) in English 1935, M.A. 1936. Married Mary McIntyre Wyllie in 1937; one son and two daughters. Taught at Dunoon Grammar School; Ghazi College, Kabul, Afghanistan, 1957–59; British Institute, Barcelona, 1959–61; Gaya School, Sabah, Malaysia, 1963–68. Recipient: Frederick Niven Award, 1956. Address: Fairhaven, Toward, by Dunoon, Argyll, Scotland.

PUBLICATIONS

Novels

So Gaily Sings the Lark. Glasgow, Maclellan, 1951.
Happy for the Child. London, Lehmann, 1953.
The Thistle and the Grail. London, Macdonald, 1954.
The Cone-Gatherers. London, Macdonald, 1955; New York, Taplinger, 1981.
Guests of War. London, Macdonald, 1956.
The Missionaries. London, Macdonald, 1957.
The Changeling. London, Macdonald, 1958.
Love Is a Fervent Fire. London, Macdonald, 1959.
Some Kind of Grace. London, Macdonald, 1960.
Dust on the Paw. London, Macdonald, and New York, Putnam, 1961.
The Tiger of Gold. London, Macdonald, 1962.
A Love of Innocence. London, Cape, 1963.
The Sardana Dancers. London, Cape, 1964.
A Very Scotch Affair. London, Gollancz, 1968.
The Holy Tree. London, Gollancz, 1969.
The Expatriates. London, Gollancz, 1971.
A Toast to the Lord. London, Gollancz, 1972.
A Figure of Fun. London, Gollancz, 1974.
A Would-Be Saint. London, Gollancz, 1978; New York, Taplinger, 1980.
Fergus Lamont. Edinburgh, Canongate, and New York, Taplinger, 1979.
The Awakening of George Darroch. Edinburgh, Harris, 1985.

Short Stories

A Far Cry from Bowmore and Other Stories.   London, Gollancz, 1973.

Uncollected Short Story

"Exile," in *Modern Scottish Short Stories*, edited by Fred Urquhart and Giles Gordon.   London, Hamish Hamilton, 1978.

*   *   *

Scotland, Spain, Afghanistan—the countries in which he has lived—have provided the backdrops for much of Robin Jenkins's writing, and it is his uncanny ability to realise those settings and the people who inhabit them which has given so much immediate strength to his fictional output. "You must write about people you know best," Jenkins has written, "and they are the ones you were born and brought up with."

His Scottish novels—*So Gaily Sings the Lark*, *Happy for the Child*, *The Thistle and the Grail*, *The Cone-Gatherers*, *Guests of War*, *The Missionaries*, *The Changeling*, *Love Is a Fervent Fire*, *A Love of Innocence*, *The Sardana Dancers*, *A Toast to the Lord*, *A Would-Be Saint*, *Fergus Lamont*, and *The Awakening of George Darroch*—tend to focus on the sterner aspects of Calvinism. The best of the early novels, *The Cone-Gatherers*, set on the patrician country estate of Lady Runcie-Campbell, follows to its bitter conclusion the enmity between Duror the gamekeeper and Calum, a simple-minded hunchback who gathers pine cones for their seeds. The contrast between the Christ-like figure of Calum and the forces of evil ranged against him is pointed up by a religious symbolism which suffuses the novel with a timeless, poetic quality as the story unfolds like a fable. Loss of innocence is also a central theme of *The Changeling* and *Guests of War*, and is transformed in Jenkins's later novels to a yearning for the level of grace that transcends human frailty.

In all his work Jenkins's writing is characterised by his probing insights into the paradox that makes human relationships both loving and self-destructive, and by his skilful delineation of character and psychological make-up. Poverty, too, is a central issue, whether it be the spiritual poverty which disfigures men like Mungo Niven, the self-deluding hero of *A Very Scotch Affair*, or the physical poverty of the slums of Drumsagart in *The Thistle and the Grail*. Yet, despite his moral stance and his round condemnation of a society which breeds those twin evils, Jenkins is not without mercy. The reader is invited to examine the reasons which make Niven such an unattractive character and to understand how other factors, such as religion, upbringing, and heredity have helped to warp his life. Even when Niven commits adultery, sympathy for his stupidity is never far away from Jenkins's narrative. Similarly, the citizens of the mean town of Drumsagart experience a moment of grace when their football team wins a cup competition. Irony is never far away from Jenkins's literary style.

Nowhere is this virtue seen to better advantage than in his most recent novel, *The Awakening of George Darroch*. Set in 1843, the year of the Disruption (the schism in the Church of Scotland over livings and privileges which led to the foundation of the Free Church of Scotland), it follows the crisis of conscience which affects George Darroch, a minister of the church whose parish is in a typically grim and Jenkinsian small Scottish town. On one level Darroch's dilemma is political in origin. Should he follow the dictates of his conscience and side with the Free Church reformers, or should he allow himself to be tempted into staying with the established church? At that level the arguments for following the first option are his engrained beliefs in the necessity for change, beliefs which he wishes to make manifest; balanced against these is his brother-in-law's promise of a rich living in a decent country area. On another level, Darroch is besieged by a moral problem. To throw in his lot with the reformers means that he will have to sacrifice his family and their well-being.

As time passes and the day of the "Disruption" meeting comes closer, Darroch sways from one direction to the other, much to the dismay of his family who expect him not only to remain constant to the established church but also to have the good sense to accept the offer of a new and more agreeable parish. When he eventually makes the fateful decision to join the reformers it seems, superficially, that Darroch is doing so to expiate past sins, in the full knowledge that he is of the Elect. But Jenkins is too clever a writer and too committed a critic of the effects of extreme Calvinism to allow Darroch such a simple exit. It is not religious faith which carries Darroch forward but simple hypocrisy: the important motive for him is not the action itself but the view which others will have of his part in it. The central narrative line of *The Awakening of George Darroch* has a rich historical texture and the central hero is a flawed lost soul unable either to come to terms with reality or to understand the emotions of those who occupy his world.

Although Jenkins is capable of ranging easily and fluently over a wide range of social backgrounds, his vision of the demonic state of the world and the salving balm of love remain the central motifs. Anger, sexual disappointments, the betrayal of innocence are emotions never far from the surface, and like Edwin Muir (1887–1959) Jenkins is aware of the fall from grace and the widening gulf between man and Eden.

—Trevor Royle

JHABVALA, Ruth Prawer.   British.   Born in Cologne, Germany, of Polish parents, 7 May 1927; emigrated to England, as a refugee, 1939; became citizen, 1948. Educated at Hendon County School, London; Queen Mary College, University of London, 1945–51, M.A. in English literature 1951. Married the architect C.S.H. Jhabvala in 1951; three daughters. Lived in India, 1951–75. Since 1975 has lived in New York City. Recipient: Booker Prize, 1975; Guggenheim fellowship, 1976; Neil Gunn International Fellowship, 1978; MacArthur Fellowship, 1984. Agent: Harriet Wasserman, 137 East 36th Street, New York, New York 10016. Address: 400 East 52nd Street, New York, New York 10022, U.S.A.

PUBLICATIONS

Novels

To Whom She Will.   London, Allen and Unwin, 1955; as *Amrita*, New York, Norton, 1956.
The Nature of Passion.   London, Allen and Unwin, 1956; New York, Norton, 1957.
Esmond in India.   London, Allen and Unwin, and New York, Norton, 1958.
The Householder.   London, Murray, and New York, Norton, 1960.
Get Ready for Battle.   London, Murray, 1962; New York, Norton, 1963.
A Backward Place.   London, Murray, and New York, Norton, 1965.

A New Dominion. London, Murray, 1972; as *Travelers*, New York, Harper, 1973.
Heat and Dust. London, Murray, 1975; New York, Harper, 1976.
In Search of Love and Beauty. London, Murray, and New York, Morrow, 1983.

Short Stories

Like Birds, Like Fishes and Other Stories. London, Murray, 1963; New York, Norton, 1964.
A Stronger Climate: Nine Stories. London, Murray, 1968; New York, Norton, 1969.
An Experience of India. London, Murray, 1971; New York, Norton, 1972.
Penguin Modern Stories 11, with others. London, Penguin, 1972.
How I Became a Holy Mother and Other Stories. London, Murray, and New York, Harper, 1976.

Uncollected Short Stories

"Parasites," in *New Yorker,* 13 March 1978.
"A Summer by the Sea," in *New Yorker,* 7 August 1978.
"Commensurate Happiness," in *Encounter* (London), January 1980.
"Grandmother," in *New Yorker,* 17 November 1980.
"Expiation," in *New Yorker,* 11 October 1982.
"Farid and Farida," in *New Yorker,* 15 October 1984.

Plays

Shakespeare Wallah: A Film, with James Ivory, with *Savages,* by James Ivory. London, Plexus, and New York, Grove Press, 1973.
Autobiography of a Princess, Also Being the Adventures of an American Film Director in the Land of the Maharajas, with James Ivory and John Swope. London, Murray, and New York, Harper, 1975.
A Call from the East (produced New York, 1981).

Screenplays: *The Householder,* 1963; *Shakespeare Wallah,* with James Ivory, 1965; *The Guru,* 1968; *Bombay Talkie,* 1970; *Autobiography of a Princess,* with James Ivory and John Swope, 1975; *Roseland,* 1976; *Hullabaloo over Georgie and Bonnie's Pictures,* 1978; *The Europeans,* 1979; *Quartet,* 1981; *Heat and Dust,* 1983; *The Bostonians,* 1984; *A Room with a View,* 1986.

Television Plays and Films: *The Place of Peace,* 1975; *Jane Austen in Manhattan,* 1980.

Other

Meet Yourself at the Doctor (published anonymously). London, Naldrett Press, 1949.

*

Critical Studies: *The Fiction of Ruth Prawer Jhabvala* by H.M. Williams, Calcutta, Writer's Workshop, 1973; "A Jewish Passage to India" by Renee Winegarten, in *Midstream* (New York), March 1974; *Ruth Prawer Jhabvala* by Vasant A. Shahane, New Delhi, Arnold-Heinemann, 1976; *Silence, Exile and Cunning: The Fiction of Ruth Prawer Jhabvala* by Yasmine Gooneratne, New Delhi, Orient Longman, and London, Sangam, 1983.

Ruth Prawer Jhabvala comments:

(1972) The central fact of all my work, as I see it, is that I am a European living permanently in India. I have lived here for most of my adult life and have an Indian family. This makes me not quite an insider but it does not leave me entirely an outsider either. I feel my position to be at a point in space where I have quite a good view of both sides but am myself left stranded in the middle. My work is an attempt to charter this unchartered territory for myself. Sometimes I write about Europeans in India, sometimes about Indians in India, sometimes about both, but always attempting to present India to myself in the hope of giving myself some kind of foothold. My books may appear objective but really I think they are the opposite: for I describe the Indian scene not for its own sake but for mine. This excludes me from all interest in all those Indian problems one is supposed to be interested in (the extent of Westernisation, modernity vs. tradition, etc! etc!). My work can never claim to be a balanced or authoritative view of India but is only one individual European's attempt to compound the puzzling process of living in it.

(1981) In 1975 I left India, and am now living in and writing about America—but not for long enough to be able to make any kind of comment about either of these activities.

(1986) I have now lived in the U.S. for ten years and have written one novel, several stories, and several film scripts about the experience. I cannot claim that India has disappeared out of—synonymously—myself and my work; even when not overtly figuring there, its influence is always present. But influence is too weak a word—it is more like a restructuring process: of one's ways of thinking and being. So I would say that, while I never became Indian, I didn't stay totally European either.

*   *   *

Ruth Prawer Jhabvala has lived in New York since leaving India in 1975, having gone there in 1951 as the wife of a young Indian architect. Although she has published only one novel and some short stories since taking up residence in the U.S., her film output has increased considerably, and the screenplays she has contributed to the film-making partnership of James Ivory and Ismail Merchant has led to one of the most remarkable creative collaborations to emerge in recent years.

It is still true to say that most of Jhabvala's fiction relates to India and to the unusual position which she adopted as an outsider able to take an inside view of Indian society. The unique character of the eight novels and numerous short stories published during the 24 years she spent in India arises from the insight she is able to bring to bear on the stresses of contemporary Indian society. At the same time she retained the background of a European, particularly rootless as a Polish/German émigré educated in Britain, and this deep sense of alienation from society is explored in several characters in her novels. The position of Westerners confronting Indian culture is also developed in her early screenplays such as *Shakespeare Wallah,* *Autobiography of a Princess,* and *The Guru.* Her short stories, widely published in American and English magazines as well as in collections, also reveal her preoccupations with the tensions and complexities of Indian life.

The term "comedy of manners" is often used in connection with Jhabvala because of her domestic settings and her witty observation of the social interplay of New Delhi. There is, however, much more of her than that; the corruption, snobbery, and hypocrisy of the upper and middle classes in Delhi are certainly very efficiently exposed but there is also a deep understanding of the unhappiness of men and women who find themselves locked in a role, whether of concubine or clerk or wealthy princess, and are unable to escape from its restrictions.

Her first two novels, *To Whom She Will* and *The Nature of Passion*, remain narrow in scope, dealing with marriage and the pressures in a society that is torn between ancient customs and modern western ideas. *Esmond in India* develops themes that are to become typical of the author, examining as it does the Englishman Esmond whose love/hate relationship with India is clearly revealed. His Indian wife represents the sensual side of India; its smells, its relaxed lifestyle, its passion that once made Esmond decide to stay in India and to delight in his dark son. Now he is disgusted with these very features, and wants to leave India which he now sees as representing only "boredom and futility." Another strand in the novel is concerned with a restless, educated Indian girl who aspires to a life beyond the confines of her well-run, luxurious home, with an arranged marriage in the offing; yet she is unable to define her dissatisfaction or her ideals. She drifts, as do her father's old friends, middle-aged idealists who battled for Indian independence and now feel out of place in the prosperous consumer society that engulfs them.

The Householder is a deceptively simple tale using almost entirely Indian characters, and in its restricted canvas it develops several themes that are to recur in Jhabvala's work: the difficulties of arranged marriages, the gap between westernized Indians and those who refuse to change, the attractions of the swami, the ludicrous enthusiasms of the Europeans who peck at the surface of Indian life. The early married days of Prem and Indu, and Prem's not very successful experience as a young teacher in his first post, are treated with considerable warmth and sympathy, and although many of the problems of the young couple are particularly Indian, many are also universal, such as the visit of the disapproving mother-in-law, and the hideously awkward tea-party given by the headmaster for his staff and their wives.

The chief character in *Esmond in India* resembles another Englishman, Raymond, who is central to *A New Dominion*, a much more profound novel that again explores the effect that India has on the European visitor. The figure of the swami has by now become a familiar satirical target for Ruth Prawer Jhabvala; obviously she has observed many examples of young Europeans seeking the world of Hindu transcendentalism who attach themselves to a mystic, usually an avaricious sham, and mislead themselves into becoming dedicated disciples. Her long story "How I Became a Holy Mother" deals humorously with such a situation, but in *A New Dominion* the exploitation of three young English girls by a swami ends in tragedy. Raymond, like Esmond, retains his essential English attitudes; although fascinated by India he cannot bear Indian food and prefers to stay in air-conditioned hotels. This novel employs a form of omniscient narration, but shifts the viewpoint from one character to another until gradually, as the plot develops, all the characters are linked together.

Technical innovation is also notable in *Heat and Dust* (Booker Prize, 1975). Although it is a short novel, the historical dimension adds considerably to the rather enclosed interiors that characterised much of her early work. Structurally, *Heat and Dust* is a brilliant inter-weaving of contemporary observations by a young English visitor, juxtaposed with the events of 1923 when Olivia, the young wife of a District Officer, falls in love with an Indian prince and runs away with him. Using Olivia's letters as a basis for her own journal, the contemporary traveller who is in fact grand-daughter of the deserted District Officer, visits the town and even the bungalow where Olivia used to live. By filtering the past through the present we are able to share the complicated attitudes held by the English civilian and military staff in 1923, and although background details are suggested rather than described, the reactions of the two races are totally convincing, even as cameo studies.

Since changing the focus of her world to New York, Jhabvala has ceased to write directly about India, although she continues to be preoccupied with the themes of exile, alienation, and loneliness that emerged strongly in her last three Indian novels. Her latest novel, *In Search of Love and Beauty*, is a major work, coolly ironic yet not unsympathetic in its treatment of German Jewish émigrés to New York in the 1930's and the relationships which have evolved since then. Three generations are portrayed, and these wealthy, indulgent, and rootless New Yorkers search desperately for "love and beauty," clinging to a guru who can teach them the point of their own existence. The gross and rapacious Leo is the latest in a line of suspect spiritual leaders who appear in Jhabvala's fiction, and whose credibility is sharply questioned. Sharp cutting between scenes dealing with different decades and different generations is clearly a result of Jhabvala's increased interest in film techniques, and enhances the sense of contrast between young and old, although such abrupt cutting can sometimes be disorientating to the reader. India remains an indefinable presence, almost a metaphor rather than a concrete evocation, providing the only brief period of happiness for Marietta, a brittle and possessive mother of a selfish homosexual property dealer. In this novel, Jhabvala is adding to the growing number of fictional works by writers who take their strength from their position as aliens, and recognise their creative world from the viewpoint of the outsider.

Jhabvala's most recent work for films includes screenplays for *The Europeans*, *Roseland*, *Jane Austen in Manhattan*, *Quartet*, *The Bostonians*, and *A Room with a View*, revealing a further shift away from Indian themes but an increasing engagement with the rootless individual in America and Europe.

—Margaret B. Lewis

JOHNSON, Colin. Australian. Born in 1938. Address: c/o Hyland House Publishing, 23 Bray Street, South Yarra, Victoria 3141, Australia.

PUBLICATIONS

Novels

Wild Cat Falling. Sydney and London, Angus and Robertson, 1965.
Long Live Sandawara. Melbourne, Quartet, 1979; London, Quartet, 1980.
Doctor Wooreddy's Prescription for Enduring the Ending of the World. Melbourne, Hyland House, 1983.

Other

Before the Invasion: Aboriginal Life to 1788, with Colin Bourke and Isobel White. Melbourne, Oxford University Press, 1980.

*   *   *

Colin Johnson's three novels deal with the displacement of modern Aborigines and their inability either to find a place in white society or to hold to the traditional ways. His first novel was concerned with the world he knew growing up in Perth—a world of the bodgie subculture often in trouble with the law—while subsequent novels confront events from the Australian past and their implications for Aborigines today.

Wild Cat Falling portrays a cynical young Aborigine on his release after a prison sentence. One *leitmotif* of the novel is Beckett's *Waiting for Godot*. It is the absurdist view of a pointless world which appeals to the principal character as he moves among various groups in Perth, reticent and detached. He becomes involved in a burglary during which he shoots a policeman. Fleeing, he encounters an old Aborigine who represents both the lore of the Aboriginal and the moral centre which he is seeking even while he thinks he is impervious to it. The conclusion sees him showing concern for the man he shot, and finding a glimmer of humanity even in the policeman who is arresting him.

A number of motifs in this novel reappear in the next, in particular the opposition between a directionless "modern" Aborigine and a decayed though still integral Elder. *Long Live Sandawara* is the story of a group of young Perth Aborigines whose 16-year-old leader, Alan, is keen to organise them to improve their opportunities, but his attempts to do so through the local Aboriginal leader get nowhere. Alan eventually leads the gang in a farcial raid on a bank during which all except himself are killed. Throughout the novel he has visited Noorak who as a child saw the clash between an Aboriginal resistance fighter, Sandawara, and the whites. Noorak recounts the adventures of the past, and it is in emulation of these that Alan leads his ill-fated raid. Johnson treats the freedom fighters of the past with seriousness and dignity as true spiritual products of the soil. The sort of holistic integrity in Sandawara and his fighters contrasts strongly with the rootlessness of the modern characters. This is marked by different narrative styles, a sort of biblical cadence being used for the past events, while the modern story is told in a sometimes awkward historical present using a good deal of dialogue. Johnson has attempted to render in the one novel the ethos of two quite different genres, the epic past, and the problem drama present. In this novel, the past offers to the present a model of what may be done to correct injustice. However, Johnson argues that more than Western guerrilla resistance is required—that to make anything of their lives modern Aborigines must re-establish contact with the centres of their cultural heritage. At the conclusion of the novel Alan leads the old man, Noorak, to the airport to fly north to their tribal country where he, Alan, will undergo initiation and Noorak will die contented.

The past in this novel is a time of glorious and inspiring resistance to the whites, invariably referred to as "invaders." In Johnson's most recent novel, history becomes less a source of political instruction than a crucible within which a philosophy of survival must be forged. *Doctor Wooreddy's Prescription for Enduring the Ending of the World* is concerned with the annihilation of the Tasmanian Aborigines in the first half of the 19th century. The controlling viewpoint is that of a learned man of the Bruny Island tribe who sees his land polluted by the aggressive practices of the whites. The focus of the novel is on Wooreddy's attempts to understand the processes of change where there had been no change before. Wooreddy is obsessed with the belief that he has been chosen to survive to see the imminent end of the world. This insight comes to him as a child when he sees his first sailing ship which he takes to be a floating island drawn by clouds from the domain of the evil spirit, *Ria Warawah*. Wooreddy's sense of being elect enables him to avoid the worst pangs of outrage and regret as the dispossession of the Aborigines proceeds. He retreats

into a fatalistic numbness which cannot be termed cowardice, for bravery and cowardice are no longer meaningful concepts.

Wooreddy's initial vision of the ship is balanced by a second vision which collapses the Manichean world-view which the Aborigines have held. In a sea cave to which he is led by a Port Phillip Aborigine he comes to see that instead of the traditional binary cosmology of a good spirit, *Great Ancestor*, and an opposing evil spirit, *Ria Warawah*, there is but one force which is primal and that all things are a manifestation of it. Johnson uses historical events and characters in this novel to investigate the state of doomed suspension in which the Aborigines found themselves after the arrival of the white man. Since there never was any chance of the Tasmanian Aborigines resisting the invaders, their world effectively ended from the appearance of the whites. From early in the novel the invading and polluting whites are seen as the embodiment of the evil spirit, *Ria Warawah*, but when the disjunction between him and the benevolent creator, *Great Ancestor*, is rejected by Wooreddy's second major vision the processes of history no longer allow the assignment of guilt. The whites are a force of history as much as a manifestation of the evil of man. Wooreddy is denied even the satisfaction of having someone to blame.

—Chris Tiffin

JOHNSON, Denis. American. Born in 1949. Recipient: American Academy Kaufman prize, 1984. Address: c/o Knopf Inc., 201 East 50th Street, New York, New York 10022, U.S.A.

PUBLICATIONS

Novels

Angels. New York, Knopf, 1983; London, Chatto and Windus, 1984.
Fiskadoro. New York, Knopf, and London, Chatto and Windus, 1985.

Uncollected Short Stories

"The Taking of Our Own Lives," in *Three Stances of Modern Fiction*, edited by Stephen Minot and Robley Wilson, Jr. Cambridge, Massachusetts, Winthrop, 1972.
"There Comes after Here," in *Atlantic* (Boston), April 1972.
"Tattoos and Music," in *North American Review* (Cedar Falls, Iowa), Spring 1977.

Verse

The Man among the Seals. Iowa City, Stone Wall Press, 1969.
Inner Weather. Port Townsend, Washington, Graywolf Press, 1976.
The Incognito Lounge and Other Poems. New York, Random House, 1982.

*   *   *

Denis Johnson's two novels, *Angels* and *Fiskadoro*, delineate the lives of outcasts on the fringes of their societies. The first is a contemporary urban novel whose characters drift into tragedy and moral and physical decline; still, it is a novel of hope. In the second, though the landscape is bleaker, an even deeper, more elemental hope for human survival is posited. Johnson brings his considerable gifts as a poet to help explore the possibilities of persistence and redemption in two separate worlds, one in decline, the other struggling to be born.

The surface of *Angels* is sensational, melodramatic, and even savage at times. Occasionally the characters are presented as cartoon-like as Johnson depicts the contemporary world in ways that bring this work close to the absurdist novel; however, *Angels* is finally a novel more in the realistic mode, and the self-conscious gothicism is meant as a comment on the irrationalism and hysteria that have become commonplace in descriptions of contemporary urban life in the United States.

The two lower-class characters, Jamie Mays and Bill Houston, an ex-sailor and ex-convict, are losers who travel across America in a state of radical drift. What we see is a society spiritually blighted by vacuous radio, movies, and TV, and superstitious cults that function as ersatz religions; all these derive from the human need for moral purpose and personal transcendence that have everywhere been lost and which only serve to disguise the destructive forces that lay just beneath the surface, often represented in images of self-immolation: "Scarlet light and white heat awoke her. She was in flames. ... It was not her clothing, but her flesh itself that was burning." The setting of this hallucination is a mental ward where Jamie is taken after a psychotic break precipitated by a rape that is motivated by an almost indifferent sadism, itself the amoral outcome of a society spiritually lost, one in which self-identity is always at risk: "For a second standing in line behind a half dozen people, she felt as if no one part of herself was connected to any other."

Bill Houston becomes involved in a bank robbery during which he kills a bank guard, but given the circumstances of his life, it is difficult to determine moral culpability. Mainly for political reasons, he is sentenced to die in the gas chamber, but the angel of light finally prevails and Bill's life is at the end given moral dimension in his epiphany at the moment of death: "He got it right in the dark between heartbeats, and rested there. And then he saw that another one wasn't going to come. That's it. That's the last. He looked at the dark. I would like to take this opportunity, he said, to pray for another human being." This is the angel of light, corresponding to Jamie's return to sanity and wholeness, and is the hope that infuses the end of the novel. However, no such hope is held out for a social healing.

Fiskadoro, Johnson's second novel, set in the Florida Keys two generations after the nuclear holocaust, is also a novel about survival, this time removed from an urban environment and put in the larger social context of the entirety of human society.

The question posed at the center of the novel is "What must be done to ensure the rebirth of civilization?" Several alternate societies coexist, and it is their clash and intermingling that provide the answer. Mr. Cheung represents the old pre-nuclear society built on art and rationalism; members of his group meet to try and reconstruct the Western (and to some extent, the Eastern) tradition from the bits and pieces of it that have survived: various artifacts, a book on nuclear war, a clarinet, spent radiation-sensitive buttons that declare the wearers believers in reason and science. The anti-culture, represented by Fiskadoro, a young teen, clashes with the defunct culture when Fiskadoro comes to Mr. Cheung (who is manager of the bedraggled Miami Symphony Orchestra) for clarinet lessons, as if asking Cheung to integrate him into the old cultural tradition. However, Fiskadoro has no talent for music and fails to master the instrument until at the end of the novel when he is transformed.

Fiskadoro becomes the leader of the new order, but only after he spends days among the jungle savages who destroy his memory through drugs and primitive ritual, which includes self-inflicted circumcision. This memory loss fits Fiskadoro as the harbinger, and perhaps founder, of the new world struggling to be born because, Johnson says, memory is the faculty through which history lives and culture is transmitted; memory severed makes rebirth possible. After the cleansing, the historical cycle will again be put in motion: "Everything we have, all we are, will meet its end, will be overcome, taken up, washed away. But everything came to an end before. Now it will happen again. Many times. Again and again."

Alternating action at the end of the novel juxtaposes Fiskadoro's rebirth with that of Cheung's grandmother, a shipwrecked Vietnamese refugee who is the offspring of a Western Father and Asian mother. She spends 20 hours in the sea awaiting rescue: "The shock of finding herself here where she'd always been was like a birth." She has obvious parallels with Fiskadoro: "... saved not because she hadn't given up, because she had, and in fact she possessed no memory of the second night...." Thus Johnson integrates within this complex poetic novel the themes of social and individual regeneration. The work at times strains to keep these and other elements in balance and manages often enough to make this ambitious work succeed.

—Peter Desy

JOHNSON, Diane (née Lain).   American.   Born in Moline, Illinois, 28 April 1934. Educated at Stephens College, Columbia, Missouri, 1951–53; A.A. 1953; University of Utah, Salt Lake City, B.A. 1957; University of California, Los Angeles (Woodrow Wilson Fellow), M.A. 1966, Ph.D. 1968. Married 1) B. Lamar Johnson, Jr., in 1953, two sons and two daughters; 2) John Frederic Murray in 1968. Member of the English Department since 1968, currently Professor of English, University of California, Davis. Recipient: American Association of University Women fellowship, 1968; Guggenheim fellowship, 1977; American Academy Rosenthal Award, 1979. Agent: Helen Brann Agency, 157 West 57th Street, New York, New York 10019. Address: 26 Edith Street, San Francisco, California 94133, U.S.A.

PUBLICATIONS

Novels

Fair Game.   New York, Harcourt Brace, 1965.
Loving Hands at Home.   New York, Harcourt Brace, 1968; London, Heinemann, 1969.
Burning.   New York, Harcourt Brace, and London, Heinemann, 1971.
The Shadow Knows.   New York, Knopf, 1974; London, Bodley Head, 1975.
Lying Low.   New York, Knopf, 1978; London, Bodley Head, 1979.

Uncollected Short Story

"An Apple, An Orange," in *Prize Stories 1973,* edited by William Abrahams.   New York, Doubleday, 1973.

Play

Screenplay: *The Shining*, with Stanley Kubrick, 1980.

Other

The True History of the First Mrs. Meredith and Other Lesser Lives. New York, Knopf, 1972; London, Heinemann, 1973.
Terrorists and Novelists. New York, Knopf, 1982.
Dashiell Hammett. New York, Random House, 1983; as *The Life of Dashiell Hammett,* London, Chatto and Windus, 1984.

*

Critical Studies: article by Judith S. Baughman, in *Dictionary of Literary Biography Yearbook 1980* edited by Karen L. Rood, Jean W. Ross, and Richard Ziegfeld, Detroit, Gale, 1981; *Women Writers of the West Coast: Speaking of Their Lives and Careers* edited by Marilyn Yalom, Santa Barbara, California, Capra Press, 1983.

Diane Johnson comments:

I try not to think about my novels in sum too directly; but I guess I think of them as serious comic novels on subjects of contemporary concern. At the moment I'm writing a novel (set in Iran) about being American, and about political meddling, being a woman, relationships and ideas. I think these are pretty much the subjects of my other novels too. This is the first one not set in California.

*   *   *

In *Fair Game*, Diane Johnson's first novel, the characters' movement is toward pairing off and finding stability, despite some outward denials that this is what they want. The characters here are "types": the frustrated virgin, the ambitious executive, the frustrated executive, the ambitious writer, and the libidinous eccentric writer (clearly modeled on Henry Miller). Only in some of the matchmaking and in making the woman writer the author of a children's book taken up by intellectuals, does Johnson show much originality in dealing with the clichéd material.

Beginning with *Loving Hands at Home* the momentum of the characters' lives tends toward the splitting of bonds between people; man-woman love relationships in particular require heroic efforts to sustain them. In Johnson's two most recent novels the women characters stand almost completely alone.

On the first page of *Fair Game* a man is said to have a knack for finding "moments of truth" in the course of any experience. Most of Johnson's protagonists are sensitized—at times to an obsessive degree—to this search for epiphanies. In *The Shadow Knows* N. Hexam is haunted by her premonition of evil and probes every occurrence for significance; Ouida in *Lying Low* believes in "old" magic, and watches for signs. And, as Karen fry says in *Loving Hands at Home*, "It is odd how events follow suspicions, as if, by wondering about things, you cause them to happen." This is often the case in Johnson's work, though the characters are never prepared for the form these conjured-up events ultimately take. Despite this hunger for signs (and, in the early novels, a glut of psychiatrists) Johnson's characters are not particularly inward-looking; the outside world has to nudge or shake them. Karen Fry, for example, discovers she is unhappy with her life only after she impulsively accepts a motor-cycle ride from a stranger and falls off: "A pratfall in the middle of Santa Monica Boulevard is too large

a symbol to be overlooked." Karen, married into a tradition-bound Mormon family, longs to be like a shiftless girl she knew when she was younger; a girl who, in Karen's mind, directed her own fate in defiance of convention. Karen finally does free herself, becomes "shiftless," and takes up residence on the sand at the Pacific beach. There she creates her own symbol: a huge baroque sandcastle she contentedly lets the waves destroy because she knows she has done her work on it well.

In *Burning* the jolt that forces Barney and Bingo Edwards to look at themselves is the removal of high hedge that kept out the sight of the disturbing, passionate lives of their psychiatrist neighbor and his patients. Bingo is a perfect wife, "infinitely erudite … witty when she wasn't depressed," and the mother of two. But when she stands-in for a junkie mother whose children are about to be taken by the state her truthful answers to a bank of psychological tests classify her as an unfit mother. Here, as in all Johnson's novels except *Fair Game*, the main female character encounters women who personify hidden aspects of her own makeup: in Bingo's case, the unfit mother and promiscuous women. With their protective hedge gone, Bingo and Barney are infected with the neighbor's passions and the neighborhood burns—literally.

If the problem in these first three novels is how to attain and manage a passion-filled, self-determinate life, the problem in *Lying Low* and *The Shadow Knows* is not one of escaping the clichéd life, but how to be protected from slipping out of such a life into something truly horrible. In *Lying Low* Marybeth lives "underground," in fear of imprisonment for her part in a political bombing that took a life. Her life of passionate commitment has led her to a decade of the most mundane, restricted kind of life. Marybeth's landlady, Theo, is a dancer who chose the unsung life rather than risk failure trying to become a prima ballerina. Marybeth and Ouida, a Brazilian girl who is hiding from officials who want to have her deported, hide and live in fear of discovery, but when tragedy comes it comes not to them but to Theo while she is trying to move out of her mundane life and do something worthwhile for others.

The Shadow Knows is Johnson's most complex novel, partly because its subject is the indeterminate, lurking nature of evil. N. Hexam begins the new year with a prophetic dread she interprets as a premonition that she will be murdered. As in *Loving Hands at Home*, the root of her fear is "the realization that life can change on you, can darken like a rainy day; wretchedness and dread can overtake the lightest heart." It is this dread that is N. Hexam's worst enemy. For her evil is a closing circle with its center nowhere and its circumference all around her. (Johnson has said that *The Shadow Knows* was in part intended to show how race relations stood at the time of its writing, 1974, but the blackness of the two women that figure most prominently in N. Hexam's life is not their most important attribute: what is important about these women is that they live out two of N. Hexam's own possible fates: life drives one mad, while the other is killed by a violent man.)

All through *The Shadow Knows* N. Hexam tries to solve the puzzle of how and from where the anticipated evil will strike. The method she uses is to conceive an ideal Famous Inspector, someone part lover and part Sherlock Holmes, to whom she compares her own efforts at finding the answers she seeks. (Still, she knows such a Famous Inspector would be unable to understand her fears, because he would be male. Here, more clearly than in her other novels, Johnson insists there is a basic irreconcilable difference between women and men based in their different fears.) When a real life counterpart of this Famous Inspector appears, his name is Dyce, "suggesting the tincture of chance." He tells her many mysteries are insoluble, and so is the voice not of reason but of reality. As in *Lying Low* the anticipated evil does manifest itself, though in a form N. Hexam never anticipates. Her reaction is one of relief: now that she truly knows evil (I ... have taken on the thinness and the lightness of a shadow ...") she can live with it.

—William C. Bamberger

JOHNSON, Josephine (Winslow). American. Born in Kirkwood, Missouri, 20 June 1910. Educated at Washington University, St. Louis. Married Grant G. Cannon in 1941 (died); three children. Taught at the University of Iowa, Iowa City, 1942–45. Recipient: O. Henry Award, 1934, 1935, 1942–45; Pulitzer Prize, 1935; Alumnae Citation, Washington University, 1955; Cincinnati Institute of Fine Arts award, 1964; American Academy award, 1974. D.H.L.: Washington University, 1970. Address: 4907 Klatte Road, Cincinnati, Ohio 45244, U.S.A.

PUBLICATIONS

Novels

Now in November. New York, Simon and Schuster, 1934; London, Gollancz, 1935.
Jordanstown. New York, Simon and Schuster, and London, Gollancz, 1937.
Wildwood. New York, Harper, 1946; London, Gollancz, 1947.
The Dark Traveler. New York, Simon and Schuster, 1963.

Short Stories

Winter Orchard and Other Stories. New York, Simon and Schuster, 1935.
The Sorcerer's Son and Other Stories. New York, Simon and Schuster, 1965.

Verse

Unwilling Gypsy. Dallas, Kaleidograph, 1936.
Year's End. New York, Simon and Schuster, 1937.

Other

Paulina: The Story of an Apple-Butter Pot. New York, Simon and Schuster, 1939.
The Inland Island (essays). New York, Simon and Schuster, 1969.
Seven House: A Memoir of Time and Places. New York, Simon and Schuster, 1973.
Circle of Seasons, photographs by Dennis Stock. New York, Viking Press, and London, Secker and Warburg, 1974.
Florence Farr: Bernard Shaw's "New Woman." Totowa, New Jersey, Rowman and Littlefield, and Gerrards Cross, Buckinghamshire, Smythe, 1975.

*   *   *

The world of Josephine Johnson's fiction is circumscribed and quiet, but not untroubled and not without echoes of the wider and more troubled outer world. The affairs in her books are affairs of jealousy, rejection, disappointment, and frustration, relieved on every page by the beauty of nature and the music of breath and blood. Larger affairs are not so much shut out as reflected and symbolized. "Salamanders and fungus seem more exciting to me than war or politics," she wrote early in her career, "but it is cowardly and impossible to ignore them or try to escape."

She was prodigious enough to receive the Pulitzer Prize for her first novel, *Now in November*, published when she was 24 years old. It came out of a time when the whole of the economy of the United States was in crisis, and when the agricultural economy was still in the throes of an even older crisis. It tells the story of small farmers in Missouri. A pall of doom is made to hang over every turn of every season, culminating in disastrous fire. And the emotional patterns within the family she depicts are far from idyllic. Yet somehow it is more a celebration of rural life than a denunciation. It has more bitterness than anger, more resignation than protest. It is certainly not the masterpiece some eager reviewers proclaimed it. But the significant view it gave of a part of American life was odd at the time and is still almost entirely unique.

Jordanstown was an attempt to increase the proportion of anger and protest in her fiction, in step with the movement for the "proletarian novel" of that time. It was by far less successful than her initial effort, and bears the marks of having been nurtured in a publisher's office rather than in an author's heart.

Wildwood and *The Dark Traveler* are novels of terror and disturbance in the young, followed by some degree of resolution and hope. Neither has the unity of conception and execution to be found in *Now in November*; indeed, these later books have the exploratory and tentative qualities which are usually found in a novelist's earliest projects. Furthermore, there are a preoccupation with neurosis and phantasm, and an absence of real harshness and deprivation, that deny to these works the steadiness and balance to be found in the earliest book. She shows that only perfect love casteth out fear, but in showing it she somehow makes the flavor of fear stronger than the flavor of love.

Like many American writers who have turned away from fiction to journalism, memoirs, and diaries as a means of expression, Johnson has tried to give her vision through a calendar of rural life. *The Inland Island* is divided into twelve sections for the months of the year, and records not only the naturalist's findings in the field but the philosopher's accompanying thoughts, in a tradition that goes back to Thoreau's *Walden*. The book came at the beginning of the ecology movement. Here again, her pessimism seems to have outlasted her love of life: "democracy becomes less and less capable to cope as the numbers increase. If we want to save law, we shall have to stop our lawless, fertile sprawl." She has given up, it would seem, any hope that man can order his affairs in such a way as to accommodate more and more human life upon the planet Earth.

—Richard Greenleaf

JOHNSTON, Jennifer (Prudence). Irish. Born in Ireland, 12 January 1930; daughter of the dramatist Denis Johnston. Educated at Park House School, Dublin; Trinity College, Dublin. Married 1) Ian Smyth in 1951, two sons and two daughters;

2) David Gilliland in 1976. Recipient: Pitman award, 1972; *Yorkshire Post* award, 1973, 1980; Whitbread Award, 1979. Fellow, Royal Society of Literature, 1979; Member, Aosdana. D.Litt.: University of Ulster, Coleraine, 1984. Address: Brook Hall, Culmore Road, Derry BT48 8JE, Northern Ireland.

PUBLICATIONS

Novels

The Captains and the Kings. London, Hamish Hamilton, 1972.
The Gates. London, Hamish Hamilton, 1973.
How Many Miles to Babylon? London, Hamish Hamilton, and New York, Doubleday, 1974.
Shadows on Our Skin. London, Hamish Hamilton, 1977; New York, Doubleday, 1978.
The Old Jest. London, Hamish Hamilton, 1979; New York, Doubleday, 1980.
The Christmas Tree. London, Hamish Hamilton, 1981; New York, Morrow, 1982.
The Railway Station Man. London, Hamish Hamilton, 1984; New York, Viking, 1985.

Uncollected Short Stories

"Trio," in *Best Irish Short Stories 2*, edited by David Marcus. London, Elek, 1977.
"The Theft," in *Irish Ghost Stories*, edited by Joseph Hone. London, Hamish Hamilton, 1977.

Plays

The Nightingale and Not the Lark (produced Dublin, 1979). London, French, 1981.
Indian Summer (produced Belfast, 1983).

*   *   *

All Jennifer Johnston's novels deal in different ways with aspects of life in her native Ireland. The countryside is depicted with a loving delicacy of detail which vividly communicates its elusive, mysterious quality, colours the thoughts and feelings of the characters, and generates the distinctive mood and atmosphere of the period in which each story is set. A sense of place, and of the past, is pervasive, combining with the living landscape to form a presence as active and potent as any of the human protagonists in the changing social structures of this century.

A lonely relic of Anglo-Irish society run to seed is the central character in *The Captains and the Kings*, which won instant critical acclaim for a poise and technical expertise rare in any first novel. Mr. Prendergast, a fastidious, testy old gentleman seeking solace for his weary disillusion in church music and drink, by chance discovers an unlikely imaginative affinity with a sharp, gauche lad from the village, whom he befriends. Inevitably his encouragement of an untutored intelligence and aspirations is misinterpreted by malicious gossip, and the ensuing situation steadily accelerates towards its inexorable conclusion.

How Many Miles to Babylon? again portrays an unconventional alliance. During the First World War the English ascendancy still seems securely entrenched, and social barriers rigid between the landed gentry and the peasantry they employ. This poignant and powerful novel, haunted by the poetic shades of Yeats and Sassoon, depicts the bridging of that apparently unbridgeable gulf, in the childhood comradeship of squire's son and stable-boy. Strong enough to defy social taboos at home in Ireland, and later on the battlefields of France to survive and transcend the great divide between the officer class and "other ranks," this profoundly moving loyalty ends only with death.

Passing on a few years to the period just after that war, *The Old Jest* portrays an Ireland with the ascendancy already on the wane, riven by rumours of unrest and rebellion. These barely impinge upon the consciousness of the 18-year-old heroine, Nancy, an orphan living with her aunt and aged grandfather in a village on the east coast. The peace and freshness of the place, idyllically evoked, echo the girl's unsuspecting innocence in her growing secret involvement with a cryptic stranger she meets on the beach, watching and waiting for some unspecified event. Predictable disenchantment awaits her, when this potentially explosive situation finally erupts into violence and bloodshed.

An innocent forced into reluctant contact with the harshness of political reality is again the main protagonist in *Shadows on Our Skin*. The friendship between a dreamy, sensitive boy and his school-teacher, secretly engaged to marry a British soldier, introduces a new, exciting dimension into his life; and their excursions into the wild, surrounding countryside, untouched by human conflict, release his imagination from the greyness, tensions, and danger of the Belfast streets. But this story too ends in disillusion, with the boy's unwitting betrayal of his teacher's trust to an I.R.A. elder brother, and the inevitable retribution.

Present-day "troubles" also form the background of *The Railway Station Man*, whose middle-aged heroine is in retreat in a bleak coastal village after the senseless savagery of her husband's killing in the city. Here she finds late fulfilment and a sense of personal identity as a painter, followed by a tentative reawakening to love for a man as crippled as she has been by past violence. Her precarious happiness again proves short-lived, with a denouement of further bereavement in the double loss of both lover and only son—futile sacrifices to the temper of the time.

The woman in *The Christmas Tree* is beset by a different problem: another confrontation with death, not this time of those she loves but her own from a terminal illness. Coming home to Dublin to die, she painfully struggles with regret over past failures, and emerges finally into a triumphant reassertion of the individuality so often challenged by her disapproving family, who are now shocked anew by the austerity of the path she has chosen to follow towards her approaching end.

Shadowed by such a sense of the vulnerability and transience of human relationships, the elusiveness of any permanent happiness, the prevailing mood of Jennifer Johnston's work is that of an elegiac melancholy. Yet there is no softness of sentimentality either in her attitudes towards her characters or in the taut vigour of her style, whose keynote is economy. Tightly knit, at times almost laconic in the telling, all her novels are short ones: consistently employing the restraint of understatement to communicate strong emotions and shocking events whose starkness is subtly intensified by the contrast. With William Trevor, this writer shares the distinction of being the most powerful and perceptive delineator of the Irish scene in the latter half of this century.

—Margaret Willy

JOLLEY, (Monica) Elizabeth. Australian. Born in Birmingham, England, 4 June 1923; moved to Australia, 1959; became citizen, 1978. Educated at Friends' School, Sibford, Oxfordshire, 1934–40; St. Thomas' Hospital, London (orthopaedic nursing training), 1940–43; Queen Elizabeth Hospital, Birmingham (general training), 1943–46. Nurse, domestic, and salesperson after moving to Australia. Since 1974, part-time tutor in English, Fremantle Arts Centre, Western Australia; since 1982, Writer-in-Residence, Western Australian Institute of Technology, Bentley. Writer-in-Residence, Western Australian College of Advanced Education, Nedlands, 1983. Recipient: State of Victoria Prize, for short story, 1966, 1981, 1982; Australian Writers Guild prize, for radio play, 1982; *West Australia Week* prize, 1983; *The Age* Book of the Year Award, 1983; New South Wales Premier's Award, 1985. Agent: Caroline Lurie, Australian Literary Management, 26 Yarraford Avenue, Alphington, Victoria 3078. Address: 28 Agett Road, Claremont, Western Australia 6010, Australia.

PUBLICATIONS

Novels

Palomino. Collingwood, Victoria, Outback Press, and London, Melbourne House, 1980.
The Newspaper of Claremont Street. Fremantle, Western Australia, Fremantle Arts Centre Press, 1981.
Mr. Scobie's Riddle. Ringwood, Victoria, Penguin, 1983; New York, Penguin, 1984; London, Penguin, 1985.
Miss Peabody's Inheritance. St. Lucia, University of Queensland Press, 1983; New York, Viking, 1984; London, Viking, 1985.
Milk and Honey. Fremantle, Western Australia, Fremantle Arts Centre Press, 1984.
Foxybaby. St. Lucia, University of Queensland Press, and New York, Viking, 1985; London, Viking, 1986.

Short Stories

Five Acre Virgin and Other Stories. Fremantle, Western Australia, Fremantle Arts Centre Press, 1976.
The Travelling Entertainer and Other Stories. Fremantle, Western Australia, Fremantle Arts Centre Press, 1979.
Woman in a Lampshade. Ringwood, Victoria, Penguin, 1983.
Stories. Fremantle, Western Australia, Fremantle Arts Centre Press, 1984.

Uncollected Short Stories

"The Well-Bred Thief," in *South Pacific Stories*, edited by Chris and Helen Tiffin. St. Lucia, Queensland, SPACLALS, 1980.
"Mark F," in *The True Life Story of ...*, edited by Jan Craney and Esther Caldwell. St. Lucia, University of Queensland Press, 1981.
"Night Report: It's about Your Daughter Miss Page" and "Poppy Seed and Sesame Rings," in *Frictions*, edited by Anna Gibbs and Alison Tilson. Fitzroy, Victoria, Sybylla, 1983.
"Bathroom Dance," in *Overland* (Melbourne), August 1983.
"Night Runner," in *Room to Move*, edited by Suzanne Falkiner. Sydney, Unwin, 1985.
"Fairfields," in *New Yorker*, 22 July 1985.

Plays

Woman in a Lampshade (broadcast, 1979). Published in *Radio Quartet*, Fremantle, Western Australia, Fremantle Arts Centre Press, 1980.

Radio Plays: *Night Report*, 1975; *The Performance*, 1976; *The Shepherd on the Roof*, 1977; *The Well-Bred Thief*, 1977; *Woman in a Lampshade*, 1979; *Two Men Running*, 1981.

*

Critical Studies: articles by Jolley and by Laurie Clancy, in *Australian Book Review* (Melbourne), November 1983; Helen Garner, in *Meanjin* (Melbourne), no. 2, 1983; "Between Two Worlds" by A.P. Riemer, in *Southerly* (Sydney), 1983; "The Goddess, The Artist, and the Spinster" by Dorothy Jones, in *Westerly* (Nedlands, Western Australia), no. 4, 1984; Joan Kirkby, in *Meanjin* (Melbourne), no. 4, 1984; Martin Harrison, in *The Age Monthly Review* (Melbourne), May 1985.

*   *   *

Elizabeth Jolley has had a more meteoric rise in fame than any recent Australian novelist. Born in Birmingham in 1923, of mixed English and Austrian parentage, she came to Western Australia in 1959, and has lived there ever since. She worked at an extraordinary variety of jobs throughout the 1960's and early 1970's while continuing to write assiduously but publishing little, except in anthologies and journals. Then in 1976 her first collection *Five Acre Virgin* was published. Since then her rate of publication has been phenomenal, and it is perhaps no accident that it coincided with the rise of an indigenous Western Australian press. The exact chronology of her books is extremely difficult to determine as, like Nabokov, she intersperses new works with heavily revised and rewritten versions of old ones.

The stories in *Five Acre Virgin* were written over the 16 years prior to publication and show already her peculiar combination of unsentimental realism and original, often bizarre humour. The title itself suggests one of the most pervasive themes in Jolley's work, especially that of the earlier period. "There's nothing like having a piece of land," the central character in several of the stories says. "It makes a man feel better to clear the scrub and have a good burning off." "Having a piece of land" is crucial to the characters in these books. Many of them are dispossessed or migrants or both. They have come from Vienna where the author's father grew up, or the Black Country of England where she herself lived, or Holland, from where the recurring figure of Uncle Bernard migrated. They struggle all their lives to buy the talismanic five acres, only to find out that they cannot live off them. They lie and blackmail in order to stay on other people's land. Adam in "Adam's Wife," one of the most powerful and sombre stories that Jolley has written, even marries a retarded woman in order to gain possession of her miserable shack and few acres.

Jolley's second collection, *The Travelling Entertainer*, contains her longer stories from much the same period as the first book and reveals for the first time the extent to which her work is a continuum. She tends to go back again and again, revising and reworking the same material—themes, characters, landscapes, situations, motifs, even names. The stories contain many elements that appear throughout her work: the preoccupation with land again, the allusions to music (especially Beethoven) and literature (especially Tolstoy), the nursing homes and hospitals, the defeated salesmen, the migrants from Holland and the Black Country including Uncle Bernard again, the first of Jolley's many treatments of lesbian relationships, and of women offering themselves to other women as a form of comfort or consolation or even occasionally as a means of achieving power.

Jolley's third book and first novel, *Palomino*, was written partly in the late 1950's, partly in 1962, and then re-written in the early 1970's before finally appearing in 1980. Her least typical book and the one that most divides her critics, it is a lyrical, rhapsodic, even reverential account of a love affair between a 60-year-old deregistered doctor and another woman barely half her age. It is totally devoid of Jolley's usual humour and sense of the incongruous, and despite the potentially explosive subject matter the two women behave with such relentless nobility towards one another that at times they seem rather dull.

The Newspaper of Claremont Street is vintage Jolley, not the most profound book she has written but a delightfully amusing and sometimes moving one. The heroine of this novella is a cleaning woman known as Newspaper, or Weekly, because she gathers gossip from her rich clients and passes it on to the rest of her community.

Mr. Scobie's Riddle is unquestionably Jolley's finest achievement, and made her instantly one of Australia's most important fiction writers; it was inexplicably passed over by the judges of the Miles Franklin prize, who declined to give the award in that year. Set in the appalling nursing home of St. Christopher and St. Jude, the novel gives full vent for the first time to Jolley's penchant for mordant and grotesque humour; it is both hilarious and horrifying and yet its triumph is that it avoids the extremes of seeing the aged people of the home as either the victims of society's cruelty and indifference on the one hand or merely comic and eccentric figures, devoid of depth or identity, on the other.

Woman in a Lampshade is an assured collection of stories, though there is little in it to surprise readers of the earlier work, and *Miss Peabody's Inheritance*, which appeared in the same extraordinarily productive year of 1983, is an earlier novella rewritten, which cuts back and forth between two separate but inter-related stories. At the end of the novel the two stories, the real and the imagined, England and Australia, converge in an unexpected way to make a comment on a theme that increasingly concerns Jolley in her later work, the relationships between life and art and between reality and fantasy.

Jolley's most recent works are the fairly short novel *Milk and Honey*, a strange parable, and a darkly disturbing, sombre book that seems to belong in tone and mood with earlier novels like *Palomino*, and the recent novel *Foxybaby*, which returns to the bizarrely comic and almost surreal mode of *Mr. Scobie's Riddle*. With its novel-within-a-novel plot of a writer attempting to conduct a summer school at the isolated and imprisoning Trinity College, it again examines in a compassionate but blackly humorous way the question of the relationship between life and art.

Elizabeth Jolley has introduced a comic note into Australian writing that is both new and individual; it is difficult to find any other writer who has influenced her and she is probably most admired of Australia's contemporary women novel-

—Laurie Clancy

———————

, Gayl. American. Born in Lexington, Kentucky, 23 ber 1949. Educated at Connecticut College, New London. A. in English 1971; Brown University, Providence, Rhode Island, M.A. 1973, D.A. 1975. Member of the English Department, University of Michigan, Ann Arbor, 1975–83. Recipient: Howard Foundation award, 1975; National Endowment for the Arts grant, 1976. Address: c/o Lotus Press, P.O. Box 21607, Detroit, Michigan 48221, U.S.A.

PUBLICATIONS

Novels

Corregidora.   New York, Random House, 1975.
Eva's Man.   New York, Random House, 1976.

Short Stories

White Rat.   New York, Random House, 1977.

Uncollected Short Stories

"Almeyda," in *Massachusetts Review* (Amherst), Winter 1977.
"Ensinança," in *Confirmation*, edited by Amiri and Amina Baraka.   New York, Morrow, 1983.

Play

Chile Woman.   New York, Shubert Foundation, 1975.

Verse

Song for Anninho.   Detroit, Lotus Press, 1981.
The Hermit-Woman.   Detroit, Lotus Press, 1983.
Xarque.   Detroit, Lotus Press, 1985.

*   *   *

Gayl Jones's first novel, *Corregidora*, focuses on the lingering effects of slavery in black America—specifically on its sexual and psychological manifestations in the life of Ursa Corregidora, a Kentucky blues singer. The great granddaughter of a Portuguese plantation owner who fathered not only her grandmother but also her mother, and who used his progeny both in the fields and in his own whorehouse, Ursa is unable to free herself of painful and obsessive family memories. In each personal relationship she finds yet again the sickness of the master-slave dynamic. Her short-lived first marriage is convulsive with desire, possessiveness, humiliation, and violence; her second, safer, marriage fails as she cannot forget the first. In relating Ursa's story, Jones shows the difficulty of loving when abusive relationships have been naturalized by cultural continuity, when so much has been taken that one's only dignity is in withholding. Her taut and explicit idiom, sometimes plainly narrative, sometimes wildly stream-of-consciousness, captures the nuances of a tormented sexuality that is both specific to black experience and symptomatic of our troubled gender system. "I knew what I still felt. I knew that I still hated him. Not as bad as then, not with the first feeling, but an after feeling, an aftertaste, or like an odor still in a room when you come back to it, and it's your own." The book's ending, almost unbearably intense but strangely hopeful, suggests that we may begin to heal ourselves only as we confront the deep sexual hatred that pervades our lives.

Whereas *Corregidora* allows us to perceive the construction of personality as historical process, *Eva's Man* offers a very different kind of experience, one that many readers have found profoundly disturbing. Eva Canada, the main character of the novel, tells her tale from an institution for the criminally insane, where she has been imprisoned for a hideous sexual crime of murder and dental castration. Like Ursa, Eva has been damaged by abuse and by a legacy of violence; unlike the protagonist of *Corregidora*, she has no sense of how her past motivates her present. As she speaks her disjointed narrative, an ugly story disrupted by flashes of recalled nastiness, she remains alien to us, a personality beyond promise or repair.

> I put my hand on his hand. I kissed his hand, his neck. I put my fingers in the space above his eyes, but didn't close them. They'd come and put copper coins over them. That's why they told you not to suck pennies. I put my forehead under his chin. He was warm. The glass had spilled from his hand. I put my tongue between his parted lips. I kissed his teeth.

In *Eva's Man*, Jones takes us into the pathological mind, and we do not find ourselves before us. As the tidy reader-protagonist identification is denied us, we are left with the horror of what we can't sympathetically imagine. Jones's unflinching violation of our strongest taboos—made all the more chilling by her starkly controlled prose—raises a number of questions about the roles of writers, readers, and cultural conventions. Beyond shock value, what does a writer achieve in presenting the truly sordid? Is our understanding necessarily dependent upon the protagonist's understanding? What do disturbing books demand of us that comforting ones do not? How must we see the world in order to change it?

The stories that make up *White Rat* suggest that Jones is intent on keeping those questions before us. The majority of these pieces ("Legend," "Asylum," "The Coke Factory," "The Return," "Version 2," "Your Poems Have Very Little Color in Them") are about madness or extreme psychic alienation. Some ("The Women," "Jevata") address the painful complications of desperate sexual arrangements. The most attractive, of course, are those few ("White Rat," "Persona," "The Roundhouse") that hint of successful human connection despite overwhelming odds. Like *Eva's Man*, most of the stories in *White Rat* challenge our notions of what fiction should do. What we make of Gayl Jones's work depends largely on what we are willing to perceive as the function of art—on how, as readers, we enter into the dialogue.

—Janis Butler Holm

JONES, (Morgan) Glyn. Welsh. Born in Merthyr Tydfil, Glamorgan, 28 February 1905. Educated at Castle Grammar School, Merthyr Tydfil; St. Paul's College, Cheltenham. Married Phyllis Doreen Jones in 1935. Formerly a schoolmaster in Glamorgan; now retired. Former Vice-President, Yr Academi Gymreig (English Section). Recipient: Welsh Arts Council prize, for non-fiction, 1969, and Premier Award, 1972. D.Litt.: University of Wales, Cardiff, 1974. Agent: Laurence Pollinger Ltd., 18 Maddox Street, London W1R 0EU, England. Address: 158 Manor Way, Whitchurch, Cardiff CF4 1RN, Wales.

PUBLICATIONS

Novels

The Valley, The City, The Village.   London, Dent, 1956.

The Learning Lark.   London, Dent, 1960.
The Island of Apples.   London, Dent, and New York, Day, 1965.

Short Stories

The Blue Bed.   London, Cape, 1937; New York, Dutton, 1938.
The Water Music.   London, Routledge, 1944.
Selected Short Stories.   London, Dent, 1971.
Welsh Heirs.   Llandysul, Dyfed, Gomer, 1977.

Play

The Beach of Falesá (verse libretto), music by Alun Hoddinott (produced Cardiff, 1974). London, Oxford University Press, 1974.

Verse

Poems.   London, Fortune Press, 1939.
The Dream of Jake Hopkins.   London, Fortune Press, 1954.
Selected Poems.   Llandysul, Dyfed, Gomer, 1975.

Other

The Dragon Has Two Tongues: Essays on Anglo-Welsh Writers and Writing.   London, Dent, 1968.
Profiles: A Visitor's Guide to Writing in Twentieth Century Wales, with John Rowlands.   Llandysul, Dyfed, Gomer, 1980.
Setting Out: A Memoir of Literary Life in Wales (lecture).   Cardiff, University College Department of Extra Mural Studies, 1982.
Random Entrances to Gwyn Thomas (lecture).   Cardiff, University College Press, 1982.

Editor, *Poems '76.*   Llandysul, Dyfed, Gomer, 1976.

Translator, with T.J. Morgan, *The Saga of Llywarch the Old.*   London, Golden Cockerel Press, 1955.
Translator, *What Is Worship?*, by E. Stanley John.   Swansea, Wales for Christ Movement, 1978.
Translator, *When the Rose-bush Brings Forth Apples* (Welsh folk poetry).   Gregynog, Powys, Gregynog Press, 1980.
Translator, *Honeydew on the Wormwood* (Welsh folk poetry).   Gregynog, Powys, Gregynog Press, 1984.

*

Bibliography: by John and Sylvia Harris, in *Poetry Wales 19* (Bridgend, Glamorgan), nos. 3–4, 1984.

Manuscript Collection: National Library of Wales, Aberystwyth.

Critical Studies: article by Iolo Llwyd, in *South Wales Magazine* (Cardiff), Autumn 1970; *Glyn Jones* by Leslie Norris, Cardiff, University of Wales Press, 1973, and article by Norris in *British Novelists 1930–1959* edited by Bernard Oldsey, Detroit, Gale, 1983; Harri Pritchard-Jones, in *Welsh Books and Writers* (Cardiff), Autumn 1981; David Smith, in *Arcade* (Cardiff), February 1982.

Glyn Jones comments:

I began my literary life as a poet. In 1934 I first became friendly with Dylan Thomas, who suggested I should write short stories, as he himself was doing then. My first published book was a volume of short stories, *The Blue Bed*. This was written when the great industrial depression was at its most intense in South Wales and the longest story in the book takes this for its subject. South Wales, industrial and agricultural—this is the theme in all the stories in *The Blue Bed*. Indeed, all my prose, and much of my poetry, is concerned with this region. The novel *The Valley, The City, The Village*, which is partly autobiographical, tries to convey what it was like to grow up in South Wales; *The Learning Lark* deals with learning and teaching in the area; *The Island of Apples* describes childhood and its fantasies in a closely knit community in the Welsh valleys.

The Water Music has stories about both the industrial east of South Wales (Glamorgan) and the agricultural west (Carmarthen, Pembroke, Cardigan). To quote my publisher—I have "carried the medium [i.e., the imaginative short story] to an unexcelled synthesis of realism and fantasy, magic and humour. From the regional contrasts of industrialism and pastoralism, modernity and tradition, he builds up a world of convincing beauty, and expresses himself in a prose style of unusual poetic vitality." I would accept this as a statement of what I have *tried* to do in my short stories. Whether I've done it is of course quite another question.

*   *   *

"While using cheerfully enough the English language, I have never written in it a word about any country other than Wales, or any people other than Welsh people," wrote Glyn Jones in *The Dragon Has Two Tongues*. This deliberate limitation of his material is the only reason I can suggest for any kind of restriction to the general recognition his gifts deserve.

Certainly his stories and novels, although they share a Welsh background, are set in widely separate countries of the mind, pose different problems, and offer to us recognisable human situations. His prose, too, is very much more than the "cheerful use" of the English language. Always exuberant and seemingly spendthrift ("I fancy words," he says in his poem, "Merthyr"), it is also exact, muscular, very energetic. He can range from elegant and mannered writing—and the use of a vocabulary so exotic that it upset some reviewers of his first novel, *The Valley, The City, The Village*—to the direct, racy, almost physical style, the true, idiosyncratic speaking voice we find in some of the stories and in the two later novels.

His Wales commonly has two contrasting faces, that of the idyllic land of country happiness opposing the suppurating mining towns where the ugly, comical people are unfailingly kindly. But it also exists as a metaphysical universe, and the young people who are to be found in almost everything Jones writes are given early experience of both Heaven and Hell. To some extent this duality reflects Jones's own early life; during his impressionable boyhood he lived in the grimy steel and coal town of Merthyr Tydfil, but spent significant periods in Llanstephan, a beautiful Carmarthenshire village.

His identification with the scenes and characters of his imagination is absolutely complete, and it is noticeable that many of these stories and all three of his novels are told in the first person. Many critics, indeed, thought *The Valley, The City, The Village* largely autobiographical, although this story of a young painter, aware of his vocation but forced by the obstinate love of his grandmother to go to university to train as a preacher, has only tenuous links with Jones's own life. It is

the quality of Jones's visual imagination and the unjudging tolerance that lies behind his observation that make his young artist credible.

For in the end Jones's love of his people is the illuminating quality of his work. He has created a whole gallery of memorable characters, some of them fully realised, some of whom enter his pages but once. He sees their blemishes, particularly their physical shortcomings, as clearly as their virtues, but to him they are loveable because their faults are the faults of human beings. Even in *The Learning Lark*, that picaresque send-up of the state of education in a corrupt mining valley where teachers have to bribe their way to headships, there is no scalding satire. Both bribed and bribers are seen as only too human and the book is full of gargantuan laughter.

The world of childhood and adolescence, that magical period when the real and the imagined are hardly to be distinguished, has been a particularly fertile area of Jones's concern. *The Water Music*, for example, is a collection of stories about young people: of his three novels only one is set entirely in the world of adults, and even that one has some very realistic schoolboys in it.

The Island of Apples is a full-scale exploration of the world of adolescence, seen through the eyes of the boy Dewi. It is a remarkable novel, using a prose which is obviously the boy's voice, yet flexible and powerful enough to describe an enormous range of events and emotions. Its sensitivity, its combination of dreamlike confusion and the clear, unsentimental observation which is the adolescent state of mind, the excitement with which the boy invests the commonplace with the exotic, are perfectly balanced attributes of a work which is as individual and complete as *Le Grand Meaulnes*, that other evocation of vanishing youth.

Perhaps the greatest of Jones's qualities is that of delight in the created world and the people who inhabit it. If he writes of a small and often shabby corner of that world—the first story in *The Blue Bed* is called "I Was Born in the Ystrad Valley" and it is to Ystrad that he returns for *The Island of Apples*—yet his writing is a celebration, an act of praise. To this end he has shaped his craftsmanship and inspiration, and his achievement is permanent and real.

—Leslie Norris

* * *

JONES, Gwyn. British. Born in Blackwood, Monmouthshire, 24 May 1907. Educated at Tredegar Grammar School; University College, Cardiff, 1924–29, B.A. 1927, M.A. 1929. Married 1) Alice Rees in 1928 (died, 1979); 2) Mair Sivell in 1979. Schoolmaster, 1929–35; Lecturer, University College, Cardiff, 1935–40; Professor of English Language and Literature, University College of Wales, Aberystwyth, 1940–65, and University College, Cardiff, 1965–75. Ida Beam Visiting Professor, University of Iowa, Iowa City, 1982. Editor, *Welsh Review*, Cardiff and Aberystwyth, 1939, 1944–48; director, Penmark Press, Cardiff, 1939–60. President, Viking Society for Northern Research, 1951–52; Chairman, Welsh Arts Council, 1957–67. Recipient: Welsh Arts Council award, 1973; Christian Gauss Award, for non-fiction, 1973. D.Litt.: University of Wales, Cardiff, 1977; University of Nottingham, 1978; University of Southampton, Hampshire, 1983. Fellow, University College, 1980. Knight of the Order of the Falcon, Iceland, 1963. C.B.E. (Commander, Order of the British Empire), 1965. Address: Castle Cottage, Sea View Place, Aberystwyth, Dyfed, Wales.

PUBLICATIONS

Novels

Richard Savage.   London, Gollancz, and New York, Viking
   Press, 1935.
Times Like These.   London, Gollancz, 1936.
The Nine-Days' Wonder.   London, Gollancz, 1937.
Garland of Bays.   London, Gollancz, and New York, Macmil-
   lan, 1938.
The Green Island.   London, Golden Cockerel Press, 1946.
The Flowers Beneath the Scythe.   London, Dent, 1952.
The Walk Home.   London, Dent, 1962; New York, Norton,
   1963.

Short Stories

The Buttercup Field and Other Stories.   Cardiff, Penmark
   Press, 1945.
The Still Waters and Other Stories.   London, Davies, 1948.
Shepherd's Hey and Other Stories.   London, Staples Press,
   1953.
Selected Short Stories.   London, Oxford University Press,
   1974.

Other

A Prospect of Wales.   London, Penguin, 1948.
Welsh [and *Scandinavian*] *Legends and Folk-Tales Retold* (for
   children).   London, Oxford University Press, 2 vols.,
   1955–56; New York, Walck, 2 vols., 1965.
The First Forty Years: Some Notes on Anglo-Welsh Literature
   (lecture).   Cardiff, University of Wales Press, 1957.
*The Norse Atlantic Saga, Being the Norse Voyages of Discovery
   and Settlement to Iceland, Greenland, America.*   London
   and New York, Oxford University Press, 1964; revised edi-
   tion, Oxford, Oxford University Press, 1986.
The Legendary History of Olaf Tryggvason (lecture). Glasgow,
   Jackson, 1968.
A History of the Vikings.   London and New York, Oxford
   University Press, 1968; revised edition, Oxford, Oxford
   University Press, 1984.
Kings, Beasts, and Heroes.   London and New York, Oxford
   University Press, 1972.
Babel and the Dragon's Tongue (lecture).   Southampton,
   Hampshire, University of Southampton, 1981.
The Novel and Society (lecture; in Welsh and English).   Ban-
   gor, North Wales Arts Association, 1981.

Editor, with E.M. Silvanus, *Narrative Poems for Schools.*
   London, Rivingtons, 3 vols., 1935.
Editor, *Prose* [and *Poems*] *of Six Centuries.*   London, Riving-
   tons, 2 vols., 1935–36.
Editor, *Welsh Short Stories.*   London, Penguin, 1940.
Editor, with Gweno Lewis, *Letters from India,* by Alun Lewis.
   Cardiff, Penmark Press, 1946.
Editor, *Salmacus and Hermaphroditus.*   London, Golden
   Cockerel Press, 1951.
Editor, *Circe and Ulysses: The Inner Temple Masque,* by Wil-
   liam Browne.   London, Golden Cockerel Press, 1954.
Editor, *Welsh Short Stories.*   London, Oxford University
   Press, 1956.
Editor, *Songs and Poems of John Dryden.*   London, Golden
   Cockerel Press, 1957.
Editor, *The Metamorphosis of Publius Ovidius Naso.*   Lon-
   don, Golden Cockerel Press, 1958.

Editor, *The Poems and Sonnets of Shakespeare.*   London,
   Golden Cockerel Press, 1960.
Editor, with Islwyn Ffowc Elis, *Twenty-Five Welsh Short Stories.*
   London, Oxford University Press, 1971.
Editor, *The Oxford Book of Welsh Verse in English.*   London
   and New York, Oxford University Press, 1977.
Editor, with Michael Quinn, *Fountains of Praise: University
   College, Cardiff, 1883–1983.*   Cardiff, University College
   Cardiff Press, 1983.

Translator, *Four Icelandic Sagas.*   London, Allen and Unwin,
   and Princeton, New Jersey, Princeton University Press,
   1935.
Translator, *The Vatnsdalers' Saga.*   London, Oxford Univer-
   sity Press, and Princeton, New Jersey, Princeton University
   Press, 1944.
Translator, with Thomas Jones, *The Mabinogion.*   London,
   Golden Cockerel Press, 1948; New York, Dutton, 1950;
   revised edition, London, Dent, 1975.
Translator, *Sir Gawain and the Green Knight.*   London, Gol-
   den Cockerel Press, 1952.
Translator, *Egil's Saga.*   Syracuse, New York, Syracuse
   University Press, 1960.
Translator, *Eirik the Red and Other Icelandic Sagas.*   London
   and New York, Oxford University Press, 1961.

*

Bibliography: in *A Bibliography of Anglo-Welsh Literature,
1900–1965* by Brynmor Jones, Swansea, Library Association,
1970.

Critical Study: *Gwyn Jones* by Cecil Price, Cardiff, University
of Wales Press, 1976.

*   *   *

Gwyn Jones did not begin as an "Anglo-Welsh" writer—that
is, as a Welshman writing in English about Wales; his first
book was a weighty historical novel, *Richard Savage*, in which
he traced the decline of the 18th-century poet against a richly
described background peopled with a large number of real
and imaginary characters. The same ability to conjure up the
very smell of a bygone age is apparent in his *Garland of Bays*,
an even longer, picaresque, novel in which the story of Robert
Greene is used to link striking pictures of Elizabethan life—in
country and city, in university and prison, at home and abroad.
In between these considerable undertakings he produced a
Manchester novel—*The Nine-Days' Wonder*—in which there
is an attempt to depict part-time criminals living otherwise
ordinary lives, and his first book with a Welsh background—
Times Like These, a novel of the General Strike of 1926 as
it affected life in a South Wales mining valley.
   All Jones's fiction after 1938 is set in Wales, but he seems
to have largely avoided the themes most immediately associated with Anglo-Welsh writers from South Wales. It is true
that a part of *The Flowers Beneath the Scythe* recalls pit disasters, unemployment, and poverty in the Welsh valleys between
the wars, but the filter is the middle-class guilt-feelings of the
hero, and the novel is equally concerned with the horrors of
trench warfare, the rise of the dictators, the debate about pacifism, the challenge of the Second World War—in short, it looks
retrospectively at some of the major preoccupations of the
period covered. *The Walk Home*, too, reaches out to more
general themes; here Jones returns to the historical novel,
though this time the place is 19th-century Wales and the hero

the victim not of his own folly and weakness but of Evil incarnate in experienced, ruthless men.

Of the volumes of short stories, *The Buttercup Field* is the most conventionally "Anglo-Welsh" and it sounds notes of comedy and whimsy heard more rarely in the two later collections. The dominant features of the more impressive stories in this and the later volumes are strong story-lines, dramatic—even melodramatic—situations, and that acceptance of the importance and dignity of ordinary people which so often informs serious regional fiction. The characters and settings are Welsh, certainly, but the Welshness is taken for granted as the elemental situations take hold of the author's imagination.

Orthodox in structure, Jones's fiction has been notable for the energy of its narrative style, the vividness of its descriptive passages, and the boldness of its characterisation; it has been most successful when the material has been sufficiently distanced in the exercise of an outstanding talent for research, whether historical or cultural. Many readers will find it interesting to note the tensions between the writer's fascination with crime and violence and his tacit acceptance of the most humane standards of his time, between the shrewdness of his even-toned reflections on human nature and a strain of romanticism not always held in check, between occasional self-indulgence and a strong, versatile prose style rooted in detailed observation and firm self-discipline.

—Roy Thomas

JONES, Madison (Percy, Jr.). American. Born in Nashville, Tennessee, 21 March 1925. Educated at Vanderbilt University, Nashville, A.B. 1949; University of Florida, Gainesville, 1950–53, A.M. 1951. Served in the United States Army in the Corps of Military Police, Korea, 1945–46. Married Shailah McEvilley in 1951; two daughters and three sons. Farmer in Cheatham County, Tennessee, in the 1940's; Instructor in English, Miami University, Oxford, Ohio, 1953–54, and University of Tennessee, Knoxville, 1955–56. Since 1956, Member of the English Department, since 1967, Writer-in-Residence, and since 1968, Professor of English, Auburn University, Alabama. Recipient: *Sewanee Review* fellowship, 1954; Rockefeller fellowship, 1968; Guggenheim fellowship, 1973. Agent: McIntosh McKee and Dodds Inc., 276 Fifth Avenue, New York, New York 10001. Address: 800 Kuderna Acres, Auburn, Alabama 36830, U.S.A.

PUBLICATIONS

Novels

The Innocent. New York, Harcourt Brace, and London, Secker and Warburg, 1957.
Forest of the Night. New York, Harcourt Brace, 1960; London, Eyre and Spottiswoode, 1961.
A Buried Land. New York, Viking Press, and London, Bodley Head, 1963.
An Exile. New York, Viking Press, 1967; London, Deutsch, 1970; as *I Walk the Line*, New York, Popular Library, 1970.
A Cry of Absence. New York, Crown, 1971; London, Deutsch, 1972.
Passage Through Gehenna. Baton Rouge, Louisiana State University Press, 1978.

Season of the Strangler. New York, Doubleday, 1982.

Uncollected Short Stories

"The Homecoming," in *Perspective* (St. Louis), Spring 1952.
"Dog Days," in *Perspective* (St. Louis), Fall 1952.
"The Cave," in *Perspective* (St. Louis), Winter 1955.
"Home Is Where the Heart Is," in *Arlington Quarterly* (Texas), Spring 1968.
"A Modern Case," in *Delta Review* (Memphis, Tennessee), August 1969.
"The Fugitives," in *Craft and Vision*, edited by Andrew Lytle. New York, Delacorte Press, 1971.
"The Family That Prays Together Stays Together," in *Chattahoochee Review* (Dunwoody, Georgia), Winter 1983.
"A New Beginning," in *Chattahoochee Review* (Dunwoody, Georgia), Spring 1985.

Other

History of the Tennessee State Dental Association. Nashville, Tennessee Dental Association, 1958.

*

Manuscript Collection: Auburn University, Alabama.

Critical Studies: by Ovid Pierce, in *New York Times Book Review*, 4 July 1971; Joseph Cantinella, in *Saturday Review* (New York), 9 July 1971; Reed Whittemore, in *New Republic* (Washington, D.C.), July 1971; *Separate Country* by Paul Binding, London and New York, Paddington Press, 1979; interview, in *Southern Quarterly* (Hattiesburg, Mississippi), Spring 1983.

Madison Jones comments:

Generally, on a more obvious level, my fiction is concerned with the drama of collision between past and present, with emphasis upon the destructive elements involved. More deeply, it deals with the failure, or refusal, of individuals to recognize and submit themselves to inevitable limits of the human condition.

*   *   *

There is a homogeneity of theme which links together into a coherent body the published fiction of Madison Jones. The setting of these books is invariably Jones's native South. But whether their time be late 18th-century settlement days or the region's more recent past, his unvarying song is abstraction, ideology, and its consequences. *The Innocent*, his first novel, set in rural Tennessee immediately after the coming of modernity, treats of the attempts by a young Southerner, Duncan Welsh, to repent of earlier impiety and reestablished himself upon inherited lands in inherited ways. The enterprise is a failure because of Duncan's deracinated preconception of it. Welsh "sets up a grave in his house." Soon he and his hopes are buried in another.

A Cry of Absence again focuses on a fatal archaist, a middle-aged gentlewoman of the 1960's who is anything but innocent. Hester Glenn finds an excuse for her failures as wife, mother and person in a self-protective devotion to the tradition of her family. But when her example proves, in part, responsible for her son's sadistic murder of a Negro agitator, Hester is driven to know herself and, after confession, to pay for her sins with suicide.

A kind of Puritanism distorts Mrs. Glenn. In *The Innocent* the error is a perversion of the Agrarianism of Jones's mentors

(Lytle, Davidson). But in his other novels the informing abstractions are not so identifiably Southern. Jones's best, *A Buried Land*, is set in the valley of the Tennessee River during the season of its transformation. Percy Youngblood, the heir of a stern hill farmer (and a central character who could be any young person of our century), embraces all of the nostrums we associate with the futurist dispensation. He attempts to bury the old world (represented by a girl who dies aborting his child) under the waters of the TVA; but its truths (and their symbol) rise to haunt him back into abandoned modes of thought and feeling. In *An Exile* Hank Tawes, a rural sheriff, is unmanned by a belated explosion of passion for a bootlegger's daughter. His error has no date or nationality, but almost acquires the force of ideology once Tawes recognizes that, because he followed an impulse to recover his youth, his "occupation's gone." *Forest of the Night* tests out an assumption almost as generic, the notion that man is inherently good. An interval in the Tennessee "outback" is sufficient to the disabusement of Jonathan Cannon. There is no more telling exposé of the New Eden mythology.

In all of Jones's fiction there operates an allusive envelope embodied in a concrete action and supported by an evocative texture. That action is as spare as it is archetypal; and in every case its objective is to render consciousness. Jones is among the most gifted of contemporary American novelists, a craftsman of tragedy in the great tradition of his art.

—M.E. Bradford

JONES, Marion Patrick.   Citizen of Trinidad and Tobago. Born in Trinidad. Married. Librarian and social anthropologist. A founder of Campaign Against Racial Discrimination, London. Address: c/o Columbus Publishers, 64 Independence Square, Port of Spain, Trinidad.

PUBLICATIONS

Novels

Pan Beat.   Port of Spain, Columbus, 1973.
J'Ouvert Morning.   Port of Spain, Columbus, 1976.

*   *   *

The relatively limited contributions of women writers to Caribbean literature has been one of the long-standing curiosities about the region. In the area of prose fiction there has been a small handful of women novelists, and from the English-language Caribbean in particular there have only been Sylvia Wynter of Jamaica, the Barbados-born Paule Marshall of the United States, and Merle Hodges and Marion Patrick Jones of Trinidad. Jones therefore belongs to a rather small circle in Caribbean literature, one that has unfortunately been slow—with the exception of Paule Marshall—to attract significant attention from students and teachers of the literature. And on the basis of her published works it is clear that Jones has already carved out a distinctive niche for herself within that small circle.

Thus far, at any rate, she has chosen to concentrate on domestic drama as the main staple of her novels. For example, both *Pan Beat* and *J'Ouvert Morning* center on middle-class marriages in Port of Spain, Trinidad, each work concentrating on not one but several couples, on the quality of the marriages (invariably bad and getting worse), on the circle within which the couples move (usually since their childhood), and on a social background that is experiencing the growing pains of new nationhood. And in the case of *J'Ouvert Morning* this all spans three generations. As this synopsis is intended to imply, Jones's fiction usually borders on soap opera. Her plots are endless strands of unrelieved misery that are interwoven in a pattern of endless conflicts and unmitigated wretchedness.

In *Pan Beat*, for example, the narrative events are sparked by Earline MacCardie's return home to Trinidad for a holiday visit. As a high-schooler she was associated with the Flamingoes steel band. After high-school she and David Chow, a member of the band, emigrated to England. He committed suicide after their estrangement, and she promptly turned to prostitution to assuage her grief—and to express her resentment at his suicide. Then she had subsequently married a British homosexual in New York (where she has been "passing" as a white Brazilian). Now that she is in Trinidad her husband breaks off the marriage, and she discovers that her former friends have been just as unhappy as she has been abroad: another old boyfriend, Louis Jenkins, is a futile, left-wing radical who is eventually killed in a gang war during Earline's visit; Louis's wife, Denise, enjoys some success, but merely as an insipid, commercially popular artist; Alan Hastings is a highly paid oil refinery worker who divides his time between a disastrous marriage and an affair with Earline herself. Of the two persons who have managed to avoid the endemic miseries of marriage, Tony Joseph is a desperately lonely prude of a civil servant, while Leslie Oliver, a Roman Catholic priest, is tormented by his sexual passion for Denise Jenkins.

The middle-class miseries of *J'Ouvert Morning* are less convoluted, largely because Jones mercifully concentrates on a smaller, more tightly knit group of sufferers in this novel—the Grant family. But their collective wretchedness is no less acute. Helen and Mervyn Grant have worked hard to secure a good education and middle-class affluence for their children. But one daughter, Elizabeth, is a well-known city drunk whom everyone knows as "Stinking Fur Liz." Their son, John, is a wealthy Port-of-Spain doctor with an unhappy marriage and a rebellious son, John Jr. Eventually John Jr.'s rebelliousness leads to an anti-government, left-wing plot that ends in his death at the hands of the police. The novel itself ends with the abortive suicide attempt by John Jr.'s distraught mother.

In spite of the soap operatic quality of her narrative materials, Jones's novels succeed as riveting documents of a troubled society in a state of transition. Jones's Trinidad has left official colonialism behind, but it has not yet discovered a vital sense of its own direction and purpose. It is soulless, without a driving motive, except the predictable trappings of neo-colonial values and the second-hand middle-class aspirations that have been handed down from Europe and the United States. The present tragedies and failures of her characters therefore reflect the unfulfilled promise of a generation that grew up in the years before independence. The empty successes of her achievers demonstrate the limitations of the neocolonial imitativeness that too often thwarts the growth of a healthy national consciousness. The radical dissidents like Louis Jenkins or John Jr. are equally failures in their own way: their radicalism is too often a self-destructive aimlessness that merely underscores their irrelevance in a society which is completely indifferent to them and their revolutionary messages.

Moreover, all of this remains convincing in the long run, because, despite Jones's melodramatic tendencies, the characters are vividly drawn and the language—especially in

J'Ouvert Morning—is original and invigorating. Thus far she has demonstrated considerable promise, one that should be fulfilled to a significant degree if she continues to integrate an engaging narrative language with both disturbing social insights and a formidable grasp of the human personality.

—Lloyd W. Brown

———————

JONES, Mervyn. British. Born in London, 27 February 1922. Educated at Abbotsholme School, Derbyshire; New York University, 1939–41. Served in the British Army, 1942–47: Captain. Married Jeanne Urquhart in 1948; one son and two daughters. Assistant editor, 1955–60, and dramatic critic, 1958–66, *Tribune*, London; assistant editor, *New Statesman*, London, 1966–68. Recipient: Society of Authors travelling scholarship, 1982. Agent: Christine Bernard, 7 Well Road, London N.W.3. Address: 10 Waterside Place, Princess Road, London N.W.1, England.

PUBLICATIONS

Novels

No Time to Be Young. London, Cape, 1952.
The New Town. London, Cape, 1953.
The Last Barricade. London, Cape, 1953.
Helen Blake. London, Cape, 1955.
On the Last Day. London, Cape, 1958.
A Set of Wives. London, Cape, 1965.
John and Mary. London, Cape, 1966; New York, Atheneum, 1967.
A Survivor. London, Cape, and New York, Atheneum, 1968.
Joseph. London, Cape, and New York, Atheneum, 1970.
Mr. Armitage Isn't Back Yet. London, Cape, 1971.
Holding On. London, Quartet, 1973; as *Twilight of the Day*, New York, Simon and Schuster, 1974.
The Revolving Door. London, Quartet, 1973.
Strangers. London, Quartet, 1974.
Lord Richard's Passion. London, Quartet, and New York, Knopf, 1974.
The Pursuit of Happiness. London, Quartet, 1975; New York, Mason Charter, 1976.
Nobody's Fault. London, Quartet, and New York, Mason Charter, 1977.
Today the Struggle. London, Quartet, 1978.
The Beautiful Words. London, Deutsch, 1979.
A Short Time to Live. London, Deutsch, 1980; New York, St. Martin's Press, 1981.
Two Women and Their Man. London, Deutsch, and New York, St. Martin's Press, 1982.
Joanna's Luck. London, Piatkus, 1984.
Coming Home. London, Piatkus, 1986.

Short Stories

Scenes from Bourgeois Life. London, Quartet, 1976.

Uncollected Short Stories

"The Foot," in *English Story 8*, edited by Woodrow Wyatt. London, Collins, 1948.

"The Bee-Keeper," in *English Story 10*, edited by Woodrow Wyatt. London, Collins, 1950.
"Discrete Lives," in *Bananas* (London), 1978.
"Five Days by Moonlight," in *Encounter* (London), November 1978.
"Living Together," in *Woman* (London), 1979.

Plays

The Shelter (produced London, 1982).

Radio Plays: *Anna*, 1982; *Taking Over*, 1984; *Lisa*, 1984; *Generations*, 1986.

Other

Guilty Men, 1957: Suez and Cyprus, with Michael Foot. London, Gollancz, and New York, Rinehart, 1957.
Potbank (documentary). London, Secker and Warburg, 1961.
Big Two: Life in America and Russia. London, Cape, 1962; as *The Antagonists*, New York, Potter, 1962.
Two Ears of Corn: Oxfam in Action. London, Hodder and Stoughton, 1965; as *In Famine's Shadow: A Private War on Hunger*, Boston, Beacon Press, 1967.
Life on the Dole. London, Davis Poynter, 1972.
Rhodesia: The White Judge's Burden. London, Christian Action, 1972.
The Oil Rush, photographs by Fay Godwin. London, Quartet, 1976.
The Sami of Lapland. London, Minority Rights Group, 1982.

Editor, *Kingsley Martin: Portrait and Self-Portrait.* London, Barrie and Rockliff, and New York, Humanities Press, 1969.
Editor, *Privacy.* Newton Abbot, Devon, David and Charles, 1974.

Translator, *The Second Chinese Revolution*, by K.S. Karol. New York, Hill and Wang, 1974.

*

Critical Study: chapter by Kiernan Ryan, in *The Socialist Novel in Britain* edited by H. Gustav Klaus, Brighton, Harvester Press, 1982.

Mervyn Jones comments:

(1981) I have become known as a political novelist, although only two of my books—*Joseph* and *Today the Struggle*—could be defined strictly as political novels, and some others are deliberately limited to the study of personal relationships. Probably, this reveals how rarely most British novelists concern themselves with the political framework of life. Taking account of that framework does, I think, extend the novel's range. But I also think, decidedly, that a novel ceases to be a novel when it does not have human character and human experience at its centre. Those interested in my views on the matter are referred to a *Guardian* interview, 9 July 1979.

I have never planned a recurrent theme in my writing, but when I consider it I believe that there is one: the nobility and irony of idealism. I take both the nobility and the irony to be realities. This is the subject of *Strangers*, the novel with which I am least dissatisfied and by which I should wish to be judged.

*   *   *

Mervyn Jones is a fine storyteller whose skill continues to improve after more than 30 years of writing. While some of his novels are about a broad variety of characters, and tend to be built on his journalistic experience, his specialty seems to be the problems of those people who have enough time and money to enable them to reflect on life. The conflicts between their ideals and their experiences, or between values related to ideals, are the themes of *The New Town, Mr. Armitage Isn't Back Yet, Strangers, Joanna's Luck*, and the short stories "The Syndrome" and "Happiness Is. . . ." How these people reconcile themselves to reality while retaining their ideals or, more often, how they retain ideals that have less and less to do with their actions and decisions is of primary interest to Jones. He has said that the theme of the nobility and irony of idealism is a recurrent one in his writing, and crucial to his depiction of this theme is his calculated distance from his characters. They are intellectual rather than emotional; their thoughts are clear, their emotions suppressed; and if they seem to lack depth, it may be because this lack is an aspect of the modern middle-class idealist.

Strangers, the novel by which Jones has said he would like to be judged, is the best example of his study of the problems of idealism. Andrew Stanton is a pacifist who refuses to live in his native South Africa, and whose refusal to fight in the Second World War has alienated him from his conservative family. He has devoted himself to the ideal of fighting the pure evil in the world with the pure good of compensatory charitable actions. His first wife was a frail survivor of a concentration camp, who was killed by a sniper in Israel. His young second wife, Val, marries him out of her own idealism and faith in him. When Andrew leaves to work with refugees in Uganda, Val is left with a house full of charity cases: a pregnant teenager on the run from her parents, an American on the run from the draft, and a foreign student who runs off with a local schoolgirl. As Andrew and Val struggle in their separate situations, both are confronted with the futility of charity, but while Val sheds specific failures to become more hopeful, Andrew, after a major success, is cruelly struck by the failure of his ideals.

A Short Time to Live is a more cynical view of the idealist. A charismatic journalist with a conscience, Michael Kellet, dies mysteriously on a Pacific island. Each of the old schoolfriends, teacher, ex-wife, and widow who attend his funeral is carefully examined, as the solution to the mystery gradually becomes apparent. None of them cherishes much of any ideal, except the old teacher, secure in his faith in education, and each is laid bare with a cold, journalistic precision that could have been that of the dead Kellet.

Joanna's Luck is a study of one of the children of the idealists of the 1960's. Joanna's mother and father are ex-hippies, described with the snide acceptance of a disillusioned young woman of the 1980's: the one is still smoking dope and wearing beads at 48, the other has shed it all to become a prosperous businessman. Locked in the thoughts of their era, they cannot comprehend why Joanna cares so much about finding a rewarding job or about wanting to feel close to a man before she goes to bed with him. Joanna is bright, but muddled in her emotions, lonely and drifting. It is not until she drifts into situations that force decisions that she begins to analyse her own emotions and beliefs with the same clarity that she had applied to her work in social research. Jones has always written sympathetically about women, but here he extends that to a deeper, fuller portrayal of a character.

The Beautiful Words is probably Jones's finest book to date, combining his excellent storytelling with interesting characterisation. Here he contrasts a sensitive, full description of his main character, Tommy, with flatter, colder perceptions of the many people Tommy encounters but cannot understand. Tommy is a handsome boy of 17 with the mind of a very small child. After a life of being shunted among relatives, he becomes a homeless drifter. All that his confused mind can offer for consolation in times of loneliness, fear, and despair are the "beautiful words" his one kind aunt taught him to memorise. He wanders into the home of a prostitute, who cares for him and has him do her cleaning, but her pimp uses him for a robbery and he gets beat up by the police. Lost, he lives with the dossers and drunks on London's Embankment until he finds an empty house and becomes a squatter. Others move in and care for him in a haphazard way, finally dumping him on Belle, a rich and greedy old woman who uses him as a watchdog. The story is about how all of these people deal with the responsibility of innocence as much as what it is like for poor Tommy to be an innocent, and Jones tells the sad story with compassion.

Because of their topical nature, some of Jones's novels date quickly, but not those which delve deeply into the effort of modern people trying to find something to believe and to live by it. For the craft of his storytelling alone, Mervyn Jones continues to be well worth reading.

—Anne Morddel

JONG, Erica (née Mann).   American.   Born in New York City, 26 March 1942. Educated at the High School of Music and Art, New York; Barnard College, New York (George Weldwood Murray Fellow, 1963), 1959–63, B.A. 1963 (Phi Beta Kappa); Columbia University, New York (Woodrow Wilson Fellow, 1964), M.A. 1965; Columbia School of Fine Arts, 1969–70. Married 1) Michael Werthman; 2) Allan Jong in 1966 (divorced, 1975); 3) the writer Jonathan Fast in 1977 (divorced, 1983), one daughter. Lecturer in English, City College of New York, 1964–66, 1969–70, and University of Maryland European Division, Heidelberg, Germany, 1967–68; Instructor in English, Manhattan Community College, New York, 1969–70. Since 1971, Instructor in Poetry, YM-YWHA Poetry Center, New York. Recipient: Bess Hokin Prize (*Poetry*, Chicago), 1971; New York State Council on the Arts grant, 1971; Madeline Sadin Award (*New York Quarterly*), 1972; Alice Fay di Castagnola Award, 1972; National Endowment for the Arts grant, 1973. Agent: Morton Janklow Associates, 598 Madison Avenue, New York, New York 10022. Address: P.O. Box 6395, New York, New York 10128, U.S.A.

PUBLICATIONS

Novels

Fear of Flying.   New York, Holt Rinehart, 1973; London, Secker and Warburg, 1974.
How to Save Your Own Life.   New York, Holt Rinehart, and London, Secker and Warburg, 1977.
Fanny, Being the True History of the Adventures of Fanny Hackabout-Jones.   New York, New American Library, and London, Granada, 1980.
Parachutes and Kisses.   New York, New American Library, and London, Granada, 1984.

Uncollected Short Stories

"From the Country of Regrets," in *Paris Review*, Spring 1973.
"Take a Lover," in *Vogue* (New York), April 1977.

Verse

Fruits and Vegetables. New York, Holt Rinehart, 1971; London, Secker and Warburg, 1973.
Half-Lives. New York, Holt Rinehart, 1973; London, Secker and Warburg, 1974.
Here Comes and Other Poems. New York, New American Library, 1975.
Loveroot. New York, Holt Rinehart, 1975; London, Secker and Warburg, 1977.
The Poetry of Erica Jong. New York, Holt Rinehart, 1976.
Selected Poems 1–2. London, Panther, 2 vols., 1977–80.
At the Edge of the Body. New York, Holt Rinehart, 1979; London, Granada, 1981.
Ordinary Miracles: New Poems. New York, New American Library, 1983; London, Granada, 1984.

Other

Four Visions of America, with others. Santa Barbara, California, Capra Press, 1977.
Witches (miscellany). New York, Abrams, 1981; London, Granada, 1982.
Megan's Book of Divorce: A Kid's Book for Adults. New York, New American Library, 1984; London, Granada, 1985.

*

Critical Studies: interviews in *New York Quarterly 16*, 1974, *Playboy* (Chicago), September 1975, and *Viva* (New York), September 1977; article by Emily Toth, in *Twentieth-Century American-Jewish Fiction Writers* edited by Daniel Walden, Detroit, Gale, 1984.

*   *   *

Erica Jong is an impressive poet of the confessional school (Anne Sexton, Robert Lowell, Sylvia Plath, John Berryman) who writes an energetic, garrulous, witty, and tender verse, both erudite and earthy, about the conflict between sexuality and inhibiting intelligence, about death (and one's impulse to and away from suicide), the problems of sexual and creative energy (both consuming and propelling), and the hunger for love, knowledge, and connecting. Although she has aligned herself with the Feminist movement, her poetry goes beyond the dilemma of being a woman in a male-dominated world, or for that matter, a Jew in an urban culture to the ubiquitous need for human completeness in a fiercely hostile social and cosmic world.

Jong distinguishes her poetic and fictional forms: "In poetry I could be pared down, honed, minimal. In the novel what I wanted was excess, digression, rollicking language, energy, and poetry." Her stated preference was always for the novel that made one believe "it was all spilled truth." To be sure, "excess," "energy," and "rollicking language" are terms that well describe her fiction, along with its absolute quest for truth.

Fear of Flying is a funny, moving, and deeply serious book. "Nothing human was worth denying," her heroine, Isadora Wing, says, "and even if it was unspeakably ugly, we could learn from it, couldn't we?" Isadora, a picaresque creation, is a bright, pretty, Jewish, guilt-ridden writer who accompanies her Chinese-American, child psychiatrist husband, Bennett

Wing, to a psychoanalytic congress in Vienna. Torn between the stability of marriage and her sexual fantasies for the "zipless fuck," she abandons Bennett for Adrian Goodlove, a rather illiterate, sadistic, but very sexy London psychiatrist. Adrian is a selfish and pompous bully, whose words arouse her as much as his sexual promise. (Bennett, though "often wordless," is a far better lover.) Her excursions into the past, where we meet her family and childhood world, her brilliant but sad and mad first husband, and her various sexual partners, are drawn in an earthy and ebullient fashion. But beneath all the bravura is Isadora's basic unfulfilment. Sex is only the apparent means toward connecting and feeling alive, an outlet that confounds desperation and freedom. It is only a temporary departure from guilt, an illusory means of "flying." Isadora's life remains tortured. The end of the book only half-heartedly suggests some sort of insight and the half-believed "People don't complete us. We complete ourselves." Isadora has struggled to write as a means of self-discovery and as a sublimated but illusory fulfillment for the frustrations of the real world. She retains an unremitting sense of guilt, vulnerability, childish impulsiveness, and romanticism.

The less successful sequel, *How to Save Your Own Life*, focuses on Isadora's literary success, her divorce from Bennett, and her subsequent move to Hollywood with its virtually limitless number of disappointments, sexual and otherwise. As Jong again portrays it, the plight of the woman is to be torn between her own restlessness and the bourgeois virtues of marriage. She illustrates poignantly and powerfully how a woman's greatest fear is of being alone, and yet her deepest wish is to break free as "hostage" to her own "fantasies," her "fears," and "false definitions."

Fanny, Being the True History of the Adventures of Fanny Hackabout-Jones is an extraordinary *tour de force*. In the style (with careful modifications) and ebullient spirit of the 18th century, it tells of the tragic and comic fortunes of the beautiful and brilliant young Fanny, whose picaresque adventures en route to becoming a writer and member of the gentry include everything from membership in a witches' coven (really a modern sisterhood), a brothel, and a pirate ship to a series of sexual adventures with the likes of Alexander Pope, Jonathan Swift, and Theophilus Cibber. It is a rich, racy, and enormously funny and serious book—moving, at times to the extreme, in its focus on love, friendship, motherhood, and courage. It is filled with serious, playful, and frequently ironic references to an enormous body of literature (Fanny is conversant with Homer, Virgil, Horace, Boileau, Le Rochefoucauld, Voltaire, Locke, and Pascal). Although, as a character, Fanny speaks with a 1980's consciousness, the kind of woman she represents might have lived during any age, for, to quote Jong's stated intention in creating her, Fanny transcends her own time. *Fanny*, as a character and novel, embodies, above all, an unflagging and uncompromising search for truth.

"A Woman is made of Sweets and Bitters. . . . She is both Reason and Rump, both Wit and Wantonness," Fanny remarks, in an observation that is applicable to all of Jong's females, including her most recent Isadora Wing character in *Parachutes and Kisses*. Here Jong portrays the famous, rich, brilliant, and beautiful writer, now nearly forty and separated from her husband. Isadora once again possesses a prodigious sexuality, but it is now accompanied by a purposive loneliness. Although she would seem to have reconciled her sexuality with her personal and professional responsibilities—mainly as mother and writer—it is the quest for love that remains her driving force. Isadora relates her experiences with a series of lovers—including a real estate developer, rabbi, antiques dealer, plastic surgeon and medical student—but the need for love and security remain insatiable. Isadora may long ago have given up the fear of flying, but she remains, in many ways, the woman she described herself as in the earlier works: "My life had been a constant struggle to get attention, not to be ignored, to be the favored child, the brightest, the best, the most precocious, the most outrageous, the most adored." Such is her relationship with parents, lovers, and not least of all, the world.

—Lois Gordon

JORDAN, Neil. Irish. Born in Sligo, in 1950. Co-founder, Irish Writers Co-operative, 1974. Recipient: *Guardian* Fiction Prize, 1979. Address: c/o Palace Productions, 16–17 Wardour Mews, London W.1, England.

PUBLICATIONS

Novels

The Past. London, Cape, and New York, Braziller, 1980.
The Dream of a Beast. London, Chatto and Windus, 1983.

Short Stories

Night in Tunisia and Other Stories. Dublin, Co-op, 1976; London, Writers and Readers, 1979.

Uncollected Short Stories

"A Bus, a Bridge, a Beach" and "The Old-Fashioned Lift," in *Paddy No More.* Nantucket, Massachusetts, Longship Press, 1978.
"The Artist" and "The Photographer," in *New Writing and Writers 16.* Atlantic Highlands, New Jersey, Humanities Press, 1979.

Plays

Screenplays: *Angel,* 1982; *The Company of Wolves,* with Angela Carter, 1984.

*

Theatrical Activities:
Director: **Film**—*Angel,* 1982.

*   *   *

Neil Jordan is one of the most talented of the new generation of Irish writers. His book of short stories, *Night in Tunisia,* put his name on the map and this was quickly followed by his novel *The Past.* He scripted and directed the film *Angel* in 1982, and says that for him the disciplines of film-making and written fiction have never been mutually exclusive. "I don't know any novelists, particularly the younger ones, who aren't working in film. In the fifties, people used to talk about the death of the novel and saw television as a threat to writing. Now the writers have pushed their way in."
Born in Sligo in 1950, Jordan has lived for some time in Dublin, a city which he made the setting for his second novel,

The Dream of a Beast. In this book Dublin is a place of heightened intensity, where opposing forces of beauty and ugliness hold an uneasy balance and the mood can shift quickly from vision into nightmare. Jordan says of his home town: "It's in a strange state these days. It's become a very small city. The economic recession hit much faster there than in larger places; the poverty there is more extreme, the wreckage is so visible." In *Beast*—as in *Angel*—Jordan's comment on, and portrayal of, the situation is conveyed in a narrative that juxtaposes lyricism and squalor, love and death. The effect is often baffling and disturbing but never essentially pessimistic. He writes so well, sentence by sentence, that it is the clarity and energy of his work which remain in the mind. In *Dream of a Beast* a man loses every previously held point of reference; he becomes "beastly," non-rational, lost to his wife and child and to his work, lost to his own perception of himself transformed physically. This is a journey into grief and confusion, even madness, but at the same time an initiation into mystery: "I walked forward. There were doors off the corridor, with rooms leading to more doors. What I had assumed to be devoid of life I soon found to be a bestiary. A deep-piled room seethed with mice. A moth watched me from a filing-cabinet. His eyes, full of the wisdom of the ages and the fierceness of his few hours here, seemed to require my attention."
There are two strong complementary elements in Jordan's work: an ability to pull the reader into the narrative, the subjective dream, and an equally forceful sense of good old-fashioned storytelling. The situations he describes are dramatic, the characters easily recognisable. He says of his "beast" that "it wasn't really Kafka, more the B Movie feature, the Creature from the Black Lagoon, the sort of fabulous monster you find in children's fiction." He has made good use of his own work in children's theatre and his close involvement with the world of music. Jazz and rhythm and blues played a great part in *Angel.*
Not surprisingly, Angela Carter's fables have a great appeal for Jordan and his adaptation of her story "The Company of Wolves" made another successful film. His description of Carter's "highly visual and dramatic imagination, her ability to combine this with a sense of ironic perspective on what she describes" could as well be related to his own work. While continuing to direct and script films, Jordan remains committed to the novel form.

—Judy Cooke

JOSE, F. Sionil. See **SIONIL JOSE, F.**

JOSIPOVICI, Gabriel (David). British. Born in Nice, France, 8 October 1940. Educated at Victoria College, Cairo, 1950–56; Cheltenham College, Gloucestershire, 1956–57; St. Edmund Hall, Oxford, 1958–61, B.A. 1961. Married in 1963. Lecturer, 1963–74, Reader, 1974–80, part-time Reader, 1981–84, and since 1984 Professor of English, University of Sussex, Brighton. Northcliffe Lecturer, University College, London, 1981. Recipient: *Sunday Times* award, for play, 1970; South East Arts prize, 1978. Agent: John Johnson, 45–47 Clerkenwell Green, London EC1R 0HT. Address: Department of English, University of Sussex, Falmer, Brighton, Sussex BN1 9RH, England.

PUBLICATIONS

Novels

The Inventory.   London, Joseph, 1968.
Words.   London, Gollancz, 1971.
The Present.   London, Gollancz, 1975.
Migrations.   Hassocks, Sussex, Harvester Press, 1977.
The Echo Chamber.   Brighton, Harvester Press, 1980.
The Air We Breathe.   Brighton, Harvester Press, 1981.
Conversations in Another Room.   London, Methuen, 1984.
Contre-Jour: A Triptych after Pierre Bonnard.   Manchester, Carcanet, 1986.

Short Stories

Mobius the Stripper: Stories and Short Plays (includes the plays *One*, *Dreams of Mrs. Fraser*, *Flow*).   London, Gollancz, 1974.
Four Stories.   London, Menard Press, 1977.

Uncollected Short Stories

"Children's Voices," in *Stand* (Newcastle-upon-Tyne), 1979.
"In the Fertile Land," in *PN Review* (Manchester), 1979.
"Memories of a Mirrored Room in Hamburg," in *New Stories 5*, edited by Susan Hill and Isabel Quigly. London, Hutchinson, 1980.
"Absence and Echo," in *Jewish Perspectives*, edited by Jacob Sontag.   London, Secker and Warburg, 1980.
"A Changeable Report," in *Shakespeare Stories*, edited by Giles Gordon.   London, Hamish Hamilton, 1982.
"Waiting," in *Quarto* (London), 1982.
"That Which Is Hidden Is That Which Is Shown; That Which Is Shown Is That Which Is Hidden," in *London Review of Books*, 1982.
"Vol. IV, pp. 167–9" and "Exiles," in *Comparative Criticism* (Cambridge), 1984.
"Brothers," in *Jewish Quarterly* (London), 1984.
"The Bitter End," in *Twenty Stories*, edited by Francis King. London, Secker and Warburg, 1985.

Plays

Dreams of Mrs. Fraser (produced London, 1972).   Included in *Mobius the Stripper*, 1974.
Evidence of Intimacy (produced London, 1972).
Flow (produced Edinburgh and London, 1973).   Included in *Mobius the Stripper*, 1974.
Echo (produced London, 1975).   Published in *Proteus 3*, 1978.
Marathon (produced London, 1977).   Published in *Adam* (London), 1980.
A Moment (produced London, 1979).
Vergil Dying (broadcast, 1979).   Windsor, SPAN, 1981.

Radio Plays: *Playback*, 1973; *A Life*, 1974; *Ag*, 1976; *Vergil Dying*, 1979; *Majorana: Disappearance of a Physicist*, with Sacha Rabinovitch, 1981; *The Seven*, with Jonathan Harvey, 1983; *Metamorphosis*, from the story by Kafka, 1985.

Other

The World and the Book: A Study of Modern Fiction.   London, Macmillan, and Stanford, California, Stanford University Press, 1971; revised edition, Macmillan, 1979.

The Lessons of Modernism and Other Essays.   London, Macmillan, and Totowa, New Jersey, Rowman and Littlefield, 1977.
Writing and the Body: The Northcliffe Lectures 1981.   Brighton, Harvester Press, 1982; Princeton, New Jersey, Princeton University Press, 1983.
The Mirror of Criticism: Selected Reviews 1977–1982.   Brighton, Harvester Press, and New York, Barnes and Noble, 1983.

Editor, *The Modern English Novel: The Reader, The Writer, and the Work.*   London, Open Books, and New York, Barnes and Noble, 1976.
Editor, *The Sirens' Song: Selected Essays*, by Maurice Blanchot.   Brighton, Harvester Press, and Bloomington, Indiana University Press, 1982.

*

Critical Studies: interview with Bernard Sharratt, in *Orbit* (Tunbridge Wells, Kent), December 1975; "True Confessions of an Experimentalist" by Josipovici, and interview with Maurice Kapitanchik, in *Books and Bookmen* (London), 1982; article by Linda Canon and Jay L. Halio, in *British Novelists since 1960* edited by Halio, Detroit, Gale, 1983; interview with Timothy Hyman, in *Jewish Quarterly* (London), 1985; James Hansford, in *Prospice* (Portree, Isle of Skye), 1985.

*   *   *

"Modern art," says Gabriel Josipovici in *The Lessons of Modernism*, "moves between two poles, silence and game." In his own novels the game is that of verbal art; the silence is that of unanswered questions. Conversations abound, explanations are sought, inquiries are pursued, but answers are always lacking. Characters experience an overwhelming pressure to speak, like a weight on the chest. But there is no narrator with authority to pronounce on the truth. The reader is drawn into puzzled involvement, impotent attentiveness, and pleasure in the play of the text.

In *The Inventory* a young man is constructing a list of the contents of a flat in which an old man and his son Sam used to live. They are both now dead. The precision of the inventory contrasts with the uncertainty of what he hears about their lives from Susan who tells him stories about her experiences of the two men. Why did Sam suddenly leave? Was he in love with Susan? Did she love him? Are her stories based on memory or invention? The novel is almost entirely in dialogue form and its effect depends on the author's precise control of rhythm, pace, and tone. It demonstrates his fascination with the musical, kinaesthetic, and dramatic aspects of speech which he has explored primarily in his work for radio and theatre.

In *Words* Louis and his wife Helen are visited by Jo, who was once Louis's girlfriend and who may or may not also have had an affair with his brother Peter. The reader learns about the characters only through what they say to each other. Conversations return again and again to certain nagging questions. What happened years ago when Louis and Jo separated? Are either of them in earnest now when they talk about going away together? Are they serious or are they playing games? We only have their words to go on and words always leave open a variety of possible interpretations: cheerful banter or wounding aggression, flirtation or contempt, honesty or evasion?

The Present represents a change in fictional technique, for in this novel even the basic narrative situation is left undecided. The narrative, in the present tense, simultaneously develops stories in a number of different possible directions. The present leaves the future open. Reg and Minna share a flat with Alex; Minna is in hospital after a breakdown and dreams or imagines her life with Reg; Minna is married to Alex and they live with their two daughters in the country; Alex is dead having thrown himself from the window of Reg and Minna's flat. The stories interweave, each compelling but inconclusive.

Since 1977 Josipovici has written his most ambitious and accomplished work, including the major radio play *Vergil Dying* and the novels *Migrations* and *The Air We Breathe*. In these novels he moves further away from the conventions of realist narrative. Whereas the early novels (and *The Echo Chamber*) are constructed around inconclusive stories and are primarily in dialogue form the later novels are constructed around multiple repetitions of fragmentary scenes and haunting images.

In *Migrations* a man lies on a bed in an empty room; a man collapses in an urban street; an autistic child fails to communicate with uncomprehending adults; a man talks in an over-furnished room with an unsympathetic woman, and so on. The text migrates restlessly from scene to scene: "You try to find a place to stop, roots ... attempt to find a resting place for the imagination." "A series of places. Each must be visited. In turn. Then it will be finished. Then they will disappear." Temporary stillness and a disturbing sense of the physicality of speech, of words in the mouth, are achieved as the narrative voice repeats certain rhythms, images, and sound patterns and occasionally settles on certain sensuous sentences: "The black sky presses on his face like a blanket." "The sun streams in through the closed panes." "Silence drains away from him in dark streams." There is a poetic preoccupation with certain elemental forces, water and light, motion and rest, air and breath, which are to become an explicit theme of inquiry in *The Air We Breathe*.

In *Conversations in Another Room* an old woman, Phoebe, lies in bed. She shares her flat with a companion and is visited regularly by her niece. The narration is in the present tense and is mostly dialogue, at times very funny. The conversations circle around unanswered questions about Phoebe's husband who vanished without trace, and her son David whose marriage has broken up. In the hall the niece's boyfriend sits under a convex mirror, occasionally jotting in a notebook. To the reader's surprise, towards the end of the book there is suddenly a section in an unfamiliar and unidentified voice, in the first person. We do not know what the relationship is between this voice and the characters in Phoebe's flat. The voice says: "Perhaps we cannot write about our real selves, our real lives, the lives we have really lived. They are not there to be written about. The conversation always goes on in another room."

Josipovici's new novel, *Contre-Jour*, is his most substantial since *The Air We Breathe*. It derives from a fascination with the French painter Pierre Bonnard. The first half of the novel is in the voice of his daughter, who has left home. The second half is in the voice of his wife. She compulsively bathes as her husband sits and sketches her. She voices her complaints and her unhappiness about her daughter's behaviour. She writes odd notes and pins them around the house. We begin to realise that she is seriously disturbed. Perhaps the daughter does not exist at all but is made up as a consolation or a demented irritant by the painter's wife. We hear only short fragments of the painter's own speech as they are quoted by the women. Through all of his wife's miseries he continues, apparently serenely, to paint. Is his absorption in his work immensely cruel or is it that he has extraordinary patience? At the end we read a short, formal letter from the painter to a friend announcing the death of his wife. It has come to

seem that the main subject of the work is the painter himself even though we scarcely hear his own voice directly. We view him only in the negative shapes he makes against the background of those who surround him, against the light.

One central image from *Migrations* can serve as an index of Gabriel Josipovici's concerns as a novelist. The friends and relations of Lazarus wait outside the tomb, excited, anticipating a miracle. Lazarus emerges and slowly unwinds the linen cloth. He unwinds and unwinds and when he is finished there is nothing there, nothing but a little mound of dust. There is nothing in the centre. There is no central meaning. As Josipovici says in *The Lessons of Modernism* the modern writer, like Eliot's Prufrock, rejects the role of Lazarus, "come back from the dead, come back to tell you all."

—John Mepham

KAPLAN, Johanna. American. Born in New York City, 29 December 1942. Educated at the High School of Music and Art, New York; University of Wisconsin, Madison; New York University, B.A. 1964; Columbia University Teachers College, M.A. in special education 1965. Since 1966, teacher of emotionally disturbed children in New York public schools and at Mount Sinai Hospital, New York. Recipient: Creative Artists Public Service grant, 1973; National Endowment for the Arts grant, 1973; Jewish Book Council Epstein Award, 1976; Wallant Award, 1981; Jewish Book award, 1981; Smilen-*Present Tense* award, 1981. Agent: Georges Borchardt Inc., 136 East 57th Street, New York, New York 10022. Address: 411 West End Avenue, New York, New York 10024, U.S.A.

PUBLICATIONS

Novel

O My America! New York, Harper, 1980.

Short Stories

Other People's Lives. New York, Knopf, 1975.

Uncollected Short Stories

"Not All Jewish Families Are Alike," in *Commentary* (New York), January 1976.
"Family Obligations," in *Forthcoming* (New York), March 1983.

*   *   *

By all the laws of literary logic, Johanna Kaplan should not have a career at all, much less an increasingly successful one. She began publishing short fiction about American-Jewish life in the early 1970's, at a time when the tapestry of American-Jewish life seemed threadbare, when sheer exhaustion had taken its toll on imaginative transformations of American-Jewish material, when critics and reviewers alike outraced themselves to say "Enough already!"

Other People's Lives proved just how wrong the nay-sayers had been. In this collection of five short stories and a novella, Kaplan made us aware, once again, of how vital, how dynamically alive, renderings of the American-Jewish milieu could be—especially if one had Kaplan's ear for speech rhythms and an instinctive grasp of our time, our place. Here, for example, is a snippet from the title story:

> When your mother wrote that book [a character hectors a disaffected daughter], it was the Age of Conformity. And I'm not just talking about gray flannel suits! What I'm talking about is all those people who got caught up—they couldn't help themselves—in the whole trend and sway and spirit of the times. Not that I got trapped into it even then. Because it always seemed escapist and reactionary to me. And that's all that was going on—the flight to the suburbs! Your own *lawn*. Your own *house*. Your own *psyche*. Your own little *garden*—and for some people, not so little! And *that*, Julia darling, was what your mother was up against! Forget the city and live in the trees! And these were genuinely progressive people, not just ordinary *shtunks*!

Kaplan's congenial turf is the ordinariness of ordinary New York Jewish life. You walk into her stories as if through a crowded living room—never as an invited, "formal" guest, but, rather, as some distant cousin catching up on family gossip. It is a world where one's childhood is fixed forever in the mind of an aunt, even when that "child" is now an adult, and a psychiatrist to boot:

> "Naomi!" the aunt said, jumping up from a green plastic chair that could easily have come from the office of a dentist with no eye for the future.
> "I know," Naomi said. "My panti-hose are crooked. I'll go to the ladies' room and fix them."
> "*When* did I—"
> "All right, then, I'll go to the *men's* room and fix them. . . ."

But that much said about the comic ironies, the delicately shaded satire of Kaplan's stories, what *lasts* in these fictions are the complex privacies that simmer just beneath the surface. In "Sour or Suntanned, It Makes No Difference," for example, a ten-year-old protagonist who hates, absolutely *hates*, the regimen and artificiality of a summer camp ("at flag lowering you joined hands and swayed . . . in swimming you had to jump for someone else's dripping hand. . . . There was no reason to spend a whole summer hugging them"), is confused, and frightened, by the part she must play in a camp production directed by a visiting Hebrew playwright. The story's concluding sentence, brilliantly written and hauntingly evocative, might stand for many of the stories in *Other People's Lives*: "standing there on the stage, a little girl in braids and a too-long dress who would end up not dead, Miriam promised herself that never again in her life would anyone look at her face and see in it what Amnon did, but just like the girl who could fake being dead, she would keep all her aliveness a secret."

O My America! extended the range and depth of Kaplan's fiction. It is, on one level, the story of Ezra Slavin, a crusty, unremitting social critic who dies at an anti-war rally in 1972. As an obituary puts it:

> From very early in his career, Mr. Slavin was harshly critical of the anomic trends of urban, mechanized American life, yet his vision of the city as a place of "limitless, tumultuous possibility" was a lyrical, even celebratory one. "I have had a lifelong affair with the idea of America," Mr. Slavin once said. "And when people find that difficult to believe, I remind them of that flintier vision which is bound to result when love is unrequited."

That, one might say, is the "official," the pundit's, version of Ezra Slavin and what he stood for. *O My America!*, on the other hand, is that life told in flashback by his daughter Merry, one of his six children and part of what can only be called a complicated, free-form and exasperatingly extended "family."

The result is a canvas large enough for Kaplan to pour in a satiric history of immigrant Jewish life, to sketch minor characters by the dozen and to deepen the connections between American Jews and contemporary versions of the American Dream. Even more impressive, *O My America!* opened new possibilities for American-Jewish fiction, at a time when its dimensions seemed limited to pale re-tellings of Borsht Belt jokes or to pale imitations of major writers like Bernard Malamud, Saul Bellow, and Philip Roth. Even the most skeptical reviewers admitted that if Kaplan's fiction were the norm, there would be plenty of American-Jewish novels to kick around, for some time to come.

—Sanford Pinsker

KATZ, Steve. American. Born in New York City, 14 May 1935. Educated at Cornell University, Ithaca, New York, 1952–56, A.B. (honors) 1956; University of Oregon, Eugene, M.A. in English 1959. Married Patricia Bell in 1956 (divorced, 1979); three sons. Staff member, English Language Institute, 1960, and faculty member, University of Maryland Overseas, 1961–62, both Lecce, Italy; Assistant Professor of English, Cornell University, 1962–67; Lecturer in Fiction, University of Iowa, Iowa City, 1969–70; Writer-in-Residence, Brooklyn College, New York, 1970–71; Assistant Professor of English, Queens College, New York, 1971–75; Associate Professor of English, Notre Dame University, Indiana, 1976–78. Since 1978, Associate Professor of English, and Director of Creative Writing, 1978–81, Univeristy of Colorado, Boulder. Has also worked for the Forest Service in Idaho, in a quicksilver mine in Nevada, and on dairy farms in New York State; since 1971, teacher of Tai Chi Chuan. Recipient: National Endowment for the Arts grant, 1976, 1981; Creative Artists Public Service grant, 1976. Agent: Georges Borchardt Inc., 136 East 57th Street, New York, New York 10022. Address: 3060 8th Street, Boulder, Colorado 80302, U.S.A.

PUBLICATIONS

Novels

The Lestriad. Lecce, Italy, Milella, 1962.
The Exaggerations of Peter Prince. New York, Holt Rinehart, 1968.
Posh (as Stephanie Gatos). New York, Grove Press, 1971.
Saw. New York, Knopf, 1972.
Moving Parts. New York, Fiction Collective, 1977.
Wier and Pouce. College Park, Maryland, Sun and Moon, 1984.

Short Stories

Creamy and Delicious: Eat My Words (in Other Words). New York, Random House, 1970.

Stolen Stories.   New York, Fiction Collective, 1984.

Play

Screenplay: *Grassland* (*Hex*), with Leo Garen, 1972.

Verse

The Weight of Antony.   Ithaca, New York, Eibe Press, 1964.
Cheyenne River Wild Track.   Ithaca, New York, Ithaca
House, 1973.

*

Critical Studies: *The Life of Fiction* by Jerome Klinkowitz,
Urbana, University of Illinois Press, 1977; "Fiction and the
Facts of Life" by J.K. Grant, in *Critique* (Atlanta), Summer
1983; article by Sinda J. Gregory and Larry McCaffery, in *Dic-
tionary of Literary Biography Yearbook 1983* edited by Mary
Bruccoli and Jean W. Ross, Detroit, Gale, 1984.

Steve Katz comments:

   The nature of our work is determined by our peculiar collaborative procedures. There are nine Steve Katz and each
of us makes a contribution to each piece. Three of the Steve
Katz are women, putting them in a minority, but allowing,
at least, for some female input into all of the work, which
sometimes invokes misogyny, but because of the female component in its composition transcends that inference. We break
down into three groups of three, each one with a woman at
its pivot most of the time, though sometimes the women col-
laborate as a separate cadre. Three of us live in New York
City, three travel all over North America, and sometimes to
South America, and are stationed in Boulder, Colorado, and
the third three never rest as travelers of the remaining world.
Sometimes for variety one Steve Katz from the New York
triumvirate will replace one Steve Katz from the world travelers
and etc., generally without disruption or conflict. Some of the
works can be written by only five of us (this blurb, for instance),
and some by seven. In these instances we arbitrarily eliminate
the four Steve Katz, or the two, by a process we call "blister-
ing." For more information about this process please contact
our agent. We have never before revealed our method of composition because we had expected great financial gain from
this unique procedure. Since this has not been forthcoming,
voilà!

*   *   *

   Steve Katz's fictions are woven from two distinct strands:
from playful fable-like tales, often of serious intent, and from
disruptive watch-the-writer-writing materials. The proportions
in which these two narrative impulses are mixed varies from
book to book, and give each its individual character.
   Experiments in textual disruption dominate and shape *The
Exagggerations of Peter Prince.* Devices used include crossed-
out pages, notices of deleted passages, partially whited-out
ads, and authorial injunctions to the characters and to the
author himself. Despite the emphasis on technical manipulations, the emotional contour of a caring young man's struggles
to do the right thing comes through—both from Peter Prince
and from Katz. Katz's hope here, as in most of his quasi-
autobiographical fiction, is that by writing *Peter Prince* he will
invent for himself a better life. It is an admission of uncertainty
about the future that the novel has no ending, that the planned
ending is lost in the "archives of the unwritten." (The ending

was to have been "America, with a rock and roll band at the
castle, and all the new dances, formal and primitive ..." This
scene does appear, 16 years later, as "The Death of Bobby
Kennedy" in *Wier and Pouce.*) Between disruptive passages
Katz also shows himself to be a visually oriented writer, with
a gift for evoking realistic detail: "... trees like candelabra,
holding vultures, their gray and carmine heads flickering, and
the small dark kites circling the umbrella crowned acacias."
   With the stories in *Creamy and Delicious* Katz's neo-fable
style hits its stride. This book collects the "Mythologies," satirical reworkings and defacings of the stories and images of
Wonder Woman, Nancy and Sluggo, Dickens, and Greek
mythology. The writing here shares with *Peter Prince* a tense
feel, and a need to discomfit or shock the reader: "Wonder
Woman was a dike, but she was nice." The plain speech style
is in places extended and stylized, with results not unlike some
of Gertrude Stein's work: "A man there was called Thomas
who in the aged long ago time before I was a boy was the
man of many creatures, a many-creatured man in the hills
before my youth. ..." Katz's disruptive side is here confined
to two short, comparatively unsuccessful pieces, and some
short poems. Katz followed this collection with the erotic novel
Posh, which he wrote in six weeks.
   With *Saw* Katz finds his mature voice. The disruptive and
the fabulous are blended in a much more confident and relaxed,
even whimsical, way. Characters in the novel include Eileen,
who feeds a puppy to a hawk; a sphere from the center of
the earth; a cylinder; a talking fly; and an astronaut from a
distant galaxy—who, as Katz confesses midway through the
book, is really the author. The Astronaut has come to Earth
seeking a substance which can revitalize his world, a substance
which is an amalgam of "ambition, greed, bullshit, pride, envy,
bourbon, and smut." If we can credit the authorial interruptions in *Saw,* this is identical with Katz's idea of the substance
of fiction. So in some ways *Saw* is about, not the process,
but the experience of creating fiction. The final chapter (titled
"The First Chapter") is a detailed account of a long hot day
filled with poets and worries, and concludes with Katz getting
away from it all in the more genial company of The Astronaut;
leaving his everyday life behind and going off to explore his
fictional world.
   Beginning with "Female Skin" in *Moving Parts* Katz's fables
move into new territory, become more deeply reflective of
modern life and concerns than was possible through the more
conventionally satirical characters of the earlier "Mythologies." "Female Skin" takes literally the metaphorical idea of
getting inside another's skin. Called a novel, *Moving Parts*
contains stories, diary entries, photographs, and a log of
encounters with the number 43. Katz's playful side is evident
everywhere: a photograph of Katz with a beard is followed
by one of a barber shop, then one of a clean-shaven Katz.
The author's face is one more "moving part" employed in the
process of creating his fiction.
   In *Stolen Stories* the literary experimentalist and the fable-
wright once again speak separately. Half the pieces here are
disembodied monologues, which are disruptive not in the sense
of any authorial intrusion, but through their staccato, Bur-
roughs-like use of language ("come in: this is my tent: you
carry the sickness:"). These monologues succeed only in evoking the sounds of the experiences and states Katz deals with,
with little of the emotional depth of his best work. The fabulous
stories here are Katz's best. "Friendship" makes a convincing
case for cannibalism being the logical and loving end towards
which all friendships should move. "Death of the Band" crosses
John Cage-style compositional ideas with psychotic urban violence to prophesy a new musical form.

Wier and Pouce is Katz's masterpiece, an encapsulation of the spiritual/ideological crisis in America since the 1950's. (*Wier and Pouce* is a very American novel: it begins and ends with ball games.) The writing style varies to mirror the temper of the times, from the Horatio Algerish first chapter, through anagramic and alphabetical sections (covering roughly the years of Katz's early literary experiments), before settling into the mature Katz voice.

Dusty Wier is clearly Katz's stand-in here, but he is also representative of everyone who grew up in those times hoping for a better American Way to manifest itself. E. Pouce embodies the arrogance and ambition of the dark side of that Way: among his other deeds he drops napalm on his own party—this in the wake of "The Death of Bobby Kennedy," that is, of the death of 1960's idealism. Episodes and images subtly mirror one another from scene to scene and country to country, reinforcing the universal feel Katz is striving to establish. Fiction's role here is spelled out for the reader: "When the day gets short people must make up stories just to get through the nights." As at the end of *Peter Prince*, Katz here is uncertain about what is to come: an impossibly high fly ball is falling toward a long-dormant giant's glove as the novel closes.

—William C. Bamberger

KELLEY, William Melvin. American. Born in Bronx, New York, 1 November 1937. Educated at Fieldston School, New York; Harvard University, Cambridge, Massachusetts (Reed Prize, 1960). Married Karen Gibson in 1962; two children. Writer-in-Residence, State University College, Geneseo, New York, Spring 1965; taught at New School for Social Research, New York, 1965–67. Recipient: Bread Loaf Writers Conference grant, 1962; Whitney Foundation award, 1963; Rosenthal Foundation award, 1963; *Transatlantic Review* award, 1964. Address: The Wisdom Shop, P.O. Box 2658, New York, New York 10027, U.S.A.

PUBLICATIONS

Novels

A Different Drummer. New York, Doubleday, 1962; London, Hutchinson, 1963.
A Drop of Patience. New York, Doubleday, 1965; London, Hutchinson, 1966.
Dem. New York, Doubleday, 1967.
Dunfords Travels Everywheres. New York, Doubleday, 1970.

Short Stories

Dancers on the Shore. New York, Doubleday, 1964; London, Hutchinson, 1965.

Uncollected Short Stories

"Jest, Like Sam," in *Negro Digest* (Chicago), October 1969.
"The Dentist's Wife," in *Women and Men, Men and Women,* edited by William Smart. New York, St. Martin's Press, 1975.

*   *   *

William Melvin Kelley's novels to date have dealt with interracial conflict, but the emphasis has been on the examination of characters, black and white, and the myths with which they delude themselves. His novels pose no "solutions" to the conflict but the solution of self-understanding, and his depiction of the relationships—loving and competitive—between men and women and blacks and whites combines compassion, objectivity, and humor.

His first novel, *A Different Drummer*, set realistically rendered characters in a fantasy plot. From multiple points of view he displayed the reactions of the whites of a fictional Southern state to the spontaneous grass-roots emigration of the state's blacks. A minor incident in *A Different Drummer* concerns Wallace Bedlow, who is waiting for a bus to take him to New York City, where he plans to live with his brother, Carlyle. Bedlow appears only that one time, but he surfaces again in "Cry for Me," probably the best short story in *Dancers on the Shore*, in which he becomes a famous folk singer. In that story the themes of one's public image versus the true self and commercialism versus art are explored.

These themes are developed further in Kelley's second novel, *A Drop of Patience*. The protagonist is a blind, black jazz musician, whose intuitive experimentation is contrasted to the intellectualization of critics, and whose love of music comes into conflict with the commercialization of music. More important than these themes, however, is the development of the character himself, who passes through various rites of passage as he learns to deal with sex, love, racism, and fame.

Carlyle Bedlow, who appeared in several of the stories in *Dancers on the Shore*, reappears in *Dem*, Kelley's third novel. "Lemme tellya how dem folks live," the novel begins. It goes on to show dem white folks living out their myths of white superiority, masculine prerogative, and soap-opera escapism. They are such victims of the pernicious myths of their culture that they are no longer even a threat to black people.

Racial conflict nearly disappears amidst the experimentation and fantasy of *Dunfords Travels Everywheres*, Kelley's own clever and original permutation of *Finnegans Wake*, A tryptich in plot, style, and character. *Dunfords Travels Everywheres* is an ambitious short novel; it succeeds in being clever, but as an exploration into character it's less satisfying that his earlier novels.

Kelley has shown himself a skillful craftsman in a variety of styles and approaches. In his stories and in his first three novels his exploration of character develops as the character seeks—or refuses to seek—a unity between the person he feels he is and the personality he or society thinks he should be. This is true also in one of the three interwoven stories of *Dunfords Travels Everywheres*. In the other two stories a playful fantasy dominates. If Kelley's fiction has a direction, it's one that moves from seriousness and psychological probing to fantasy, playfulness, and comedy.

—William Borden

KENEALLY, Thomas (Michael). Australian. Born in Sydney, New South Wales, 7 October 1935. Educated at St. Patrick's College, Strathfield, New South Wales; studied for the priesthood and studied law. Served in the Australian Citizens Military Forces. Married Judith Martin in 1965; two daughters. High school teacher in Sydney, 1960–64; Lecturer in Drama, University of New England, Armidale, New South

Wales, 1968–69. Recipient: Commonwealth Literary Fund fellowship, 1966, 1968, 1972; Miles Franklin Award, 1968, 1969; Captain Cook Bi-Centenary Prize, 1970; Royal Society of Literature Heinemann Award, 1973; Booker Prize, 1982; *Los Angeles Times* award, 1983. Fellow, Royal Society of Literature, 1973; Officer, Order of Australia, 1983. Agent: Tessa Sayle Agency, 11 Jubilee Place, London SW3 3TE, England. Address: P.O. Box 237, Avalon Beach, New South Wales 2107, Australia.

PUBLICATIONS

Novels

The Place at Whitton.   Melbourne and London, Cassell, 1964; New York, Walker, 1965.
The Fear.   Melbourne and London, Cassell, 1965.
Bring Larks and Heroes.   Melbourne, Cassell, 1967; London, Cassell, and New York, Viking Press, 1968.
Three Cheers for the Paraclete.   Sydney, Angus and Robertson, 1968; London, Angus and Robertson, and New York, Viking Press, 1969.
The Survivor.   Sydney, Angus and Robertson, 1969; London, Angus and Robertson, and New York, Viking Press, 1970.
A Dutiful Daughter.   Sydney and London, Angus and Robertson, and New York, Viking Press, 1971.
The Chant of Jimmie Blacksmith.   Sydney and London, Angus and Robertson, and New York, Viking Press, 1972.
Blood Red, Sister Rose.   London, Collins, and New York, Viking Press, 1974.
Moses the Lawgiver (novelization of TV play).   London, Collins-ATV, and New York, Harper, 1975.
Gossip from the Forest.   London, Collins, 1975; New York, Harcourt Brace, 1976.
Season in Purgatory.   London, Collins, 1976; New York, Harcourt Brace, 1977.
A Victim of the Aurora.   London, Collins, 1977; New York, Harcourt Brace, 1978.
Passenger.   London, Collins, and New York, Harcourt Brace, 1979.
Confederates.   London, Collins, 1979; New York, Harper, 1980.
The Cut-Rate Kingdom.   Sydney, Wildcat Press, 1980; London, Allen Lane, 1984.
Schindler's Ark.   London, Hodder and Stoughton, 1982; as *Schindler's List*, New York, Simon and Schuster, 1982.
A Family Madness.   London, Hodder and Stoughton, 1985; New York, Simon and Schuster, 1986.

Uncollected Short Story

"The Performing Blind Boy," in *Festival and Other Stories*, edited by Brian Buckley and Jim Hamilton.   Melbourne, Wren, 1974; Newton Abbot, Devon, David and Charles, 1975.

Plays

Halloran's Little Boat, adaptation of his novel *Bring Larks and Heroes* (produced Sydney, 1966).   Published in *Penguin Australian Drama 2*, Melbourne, Penguin, 1975.
Childermass (produced Sydney, 1968).
An Awful Rose (produced Sydney, 1972).
Bullie's House (produced Sydney 1980).   Sydney, Currency Press, 1981.

Screenplay: *The Priest* (episode in *Libido*), 1973.

Television Plays (UK): *Essington*, 1974; *The World's Wrong End* (documentary; *Writers and Places* series), 1981.

Other

Ned Kelly and the City of Bees (for children).   London, Cape, 1978; Boston, Godine, 1981.
Outback, photographs by Gary Hansen and Mark Lang.   Sydney and London, Hodder and Stoughton, 1983.

*

Manuscript Collections: Mitchell Library, Sydney; Australian National Library, Canberra.

Theatrical Activities:
Actor: **Films**—*The Devil's Playground*, 1976; *The Chant of Jimmie Blacksmith*, 1978.

Thomas Keneally comments:

(1972) I would like to be able to disown my first two novels, the second of which was the obligatory account of one's childhood—the book then that all novelists think seriously of writing.

I see my third novel as an attempt to follow out an epic theme in terms of a young soldier's exile to Australia.

The fourth and fifth were attempts at urbane writing in the traditional mode of the English novel: confrontations between characters whose behaviour shows layers of irony and humour, in which all that is epic is rather played down.

For *A Dutiful Daughter*, the best novel I have written (not that I claim that matters much), I have turned to myth and fable, as many a novelist is doing, for the simple reason that other media have moved into the traditional areas of the novel.

(1986) I can see now that a great deal of my work has been concerned with the contrast between the new world—in particular Australia—and the old; the counterpoint between the fairly innocent politics of the new world and the fatal politics of Europe. One of the most remarkable phenomena of my lifetime has been the decline of both the British Empire and the European dominance in the world. As a colonial, I was just getting used to these two phenomena and adjusting my soul to them when they vanished, throwing into doubt the idea that artists from the remote antipodes must go into the northern hemisphere to find their spiritual source and forcing me to reassess my place in the world as an Australian.

Blood Red, Sister Rose, for example, concerned a European aboriginal, a potent maker of magic, Joan of Arc. *Gossip from the Forest* concerned the war, World War I, by which Europe began its own self destruction. These books are characteristic of my middle period, the historical phase, when in a way, coming from a fairly innocent and unbloodied society, I was trying to work Europe out. There was some of this too in *Schindler's Ark*. In my last book, *A Family Madness*, you have Australian ingenuousness and the ancient, complicated and malicious politics of Eastern Europe standing cheek by jowl.

I feel it is significant that *A Family Madness* is set in 1985. I believe the historic phase is nearly over for me and was merely a preparation for the understanding of the present. Time—and future work—will tell.

*   *   *

Thomas Keneally's prodigious literary output since he first started publishing in 1964 is remarkable not only for its scope but for its clear and sustained concern for moral issues. Moral imperatives emerge from everyday life, but their significance is best understood in the continuum of history, and Keneally is one of very few contemporary novelists who is able to handle these difficult themes.

There is much in Keneally's background to explain the characteristic savour of his novels. Like many Australian writers, he is unable to forget his Irish Catholic ancestry, and it is surely no coincidence that his central characters are invariably those who function outside the official channels and whose strong moral sense does not usually sit easily within the Establishment. One of his characters refers to "the lies of history," and these lies have continued to engross Keneally, together with a fascination for the nature of leadership and those whose charisma and vision inspire other men to action.

A writer who deals with such large issues as good and evil and the nature of the historical process has many options open to him in the way he handles his material. Paul Scott in *The Raj Quartet* and J.G. Farrell in *The Singapore Grip* have also dealt with recent history, successfully creating vast canvases of individuals caught up in the complexities of the 20th century. But Keneally's historical imagination is more daring and more crude. He forces his way into the railway carriage where the armistice was signed at the end of World War I, convincing his readers of the veracity of the dialogue between the pompous French, the superior British, and the defeated Germans. He sits his readers comfortably in Abe Lincoln's office (*Confederates*) and under the cut-glass chandeliers of the Minsk Opera House for the first session of the Belorussian Central Congress (*A Family Madness*).

Keneally's grasp of historical pressures is indivisible from a profound moral questioning of human motives. As someone who trained for the Catholic priesthood and then abandoned his calling, Keneally is still searching, like Camus or Patrick White, for the secular saints. Oskar Schindler's story is described as "the pragmatic triumph of good over evil," although the writer is well aware that "it is a risky enterprise to have to write of virtue." Unlike White, Keneally has continued to pursue his moral absolutes through the actual events of history, eschewing the realms of psychological and religious quest. By concentrating his narrative in this way, Keneally firmly delineates the responsibility of the individual for the course of history.

Keneally first found his characteristic voice as a novelist in his third novel, *Bring Larks and Heroes*, which deals with early convict days in Australia. But this remains a slight and even mannered work in comparison with his much admired novel *The Chant of Jimmie Blacksmith*, which marks the beginning of his mature fiction. It is hardly surprising that an Australian writer with Keneally's concern for the underdog, the outcast, should choose to write a novel based on an event which shocked the nation in 1900; the slaughter of a white family by a hitherto docile Aboriginal employee. Keneally the storyteller is at his best in this novel, but the actual characterisation of Jimmie Blacksmith has been criticised. The tendency in his early novels to use character to make moral points rather than to explore them as individuals still lingers here, making it hard to explain Jimmie except in the most obvious terms. The novel needs a stronger symbolic dimension to allow Jimmie's predicament to become clearer as he uneasily straddles two worlds, "lost somewhere between the Lord God of Hosts and the shrunken cosmogony of his people."

Nevertheless, *The Chant of Jimmie Blacksmith* and the successful film made from it brought Keneally world-wide attention, and his next novel, *Blood Red, Sister Rose*, was awaited with interest. This novel could hardly have contrasted more with the previous work, dealing as it does with Joan of Arc and her impact on the French nobility of the time. Keneally seems on firmer ground in *Gossip from the Forest*, a dry, ironic, and questioning account of the conference in a railway carriage that led to the surrender of Germany at the end of the First World War. Typically, the character who most interests Keneally is the hard-pressed German negotiator Matthias Erzberger, a civilian politician of peasant origins. The aristocratic pride of the French and British representatives is skilfully revealed through imaginary dialogue over drinks and meals, while Erzberger's growing distaste for all representatives of European militarism gives the novel an interesting dimension in terms of the pattern of history that was to unfold. The assassination of Erzberger by right-wing elements in Germany a year later prefigures the fate of German liberalism in the two decades before the Second World War.

The three novels following *Gossip from the Forest* again differ widely in subject matter but not in the underlying concerns. *Season in Purgatory* captures a small slice of history, evoking the desperate state of Tito's partisans during World War Two on the islands off the Yugoslav coast. David Pelham, a young British army doctor who sets up a field hospital for the partisans, soon turns into another of Keneally's outsiders, challenging his upper-class superiors, and, while working frenziedly to save badly wounded partisans, realising that "even the bland ideology of democracy . . . was blood crazed." A similar realisation of the nature of heroism and the manipulative forces that protect a nation's ideals comes to the narrator of *A Victim of the Aurora*, who, as a 92-year-old man, recalls an expedition to the Antarctic in 1909. The small group of British heroes is soon revealed as riddled with conflicts: sexual, racial, and class. These culminate in the murder of a ruthless journalist who threatens to expose the weaknesses of all who have taken part in the expedition. The journey at the heart of *Passenger* must be Keneally's strangest creation, taking the viewpoint of a foetus who tenaciously resists all threats to his well-being and is finally born with a hole in his heart during a flashback to his convict ancestry. The effrontery of Keneally's masculine bias undermines this work, despite the novelty of its viewpoint.

In Keneally's expansive novel of the American Civil War, *Confederates*, the defeated are again chosen as his heroes. General Stonewall Jackson and the Southern Army are fighting for an unjust cause, but they are all just men, a moral conundrum that Keneally dramatizes but makes no attempt to explain. What makes this novel memorable, and justly praised, is the detailed description of battle and bivouac, of long marches and the comradely conversation of simple men.

In comparison to his other novels dealing with the Second World War, *The Cut-Rate Kingdom* seems flat and lacking in interest. The spare, clipped style is characteristic of the detached, ironic narrator, "Paper" Tyson, a crippled veteran of Gallipoli, now a journalist and confidant of the Prime Minister of Australia. Despite the understatement of the narrative, the blend of fictitious characters and actual events such as the bombing of Darwin does convey something of the edginess of Australian political life after 1942, when an invasion from Japan seemed imminent.

Schindler's Ark, which won the Booker Prize in 1982, reveals narrative power and technical sophistication present but not always sustained in earlier work. The story of Oskar Schindler, the German industrialist who by sheer audacity and cunning managed to employ and eventually bring through the war a group of about 1100 Jewish prisoners, is dazzling in its insights. Keneally hastens to show us that Oskar was a womanizer, a heavy drinker, and an opportunist, but his automatic antagonism to the system in control makes him, like other Keneally heroes, an unexpected supporter of a doomed race: "behind the playboy exterior, an implacable judge." Accounts by survivors provided Keneally with most of the raw material he needed for this narrative, but the gripping detail, the acrid air of the cattle trucks, the shared experience of desperation, despair, and tremulous hope centred on one individual are all the product of Keneally's rich imagination. Official documentation relating to the destruction of the Jewish Ghetto in Cracow and details of camps and transports become vitally important to the reader as he traces the fortunes of the "Schindlerjuden," Schindler's Jews. Against the horror of the holocaust is placed the stubbornness of one individual, a gambler with the lives of others at stake. Ultimately, for all the horrors described, this is not a pessimistic novel, because it demonstrates clearly the positive role that an exceptional individual can play in altering the course of history.

Paradoxically, Keneally's latest novel, *A Family Madness*, is much more sombre in tone, even though it is set in contemporary Sydney. Considerable structural ingenuity has produced an interplay of narrative which draws together the world of a naive, rugby-playing Australian and a family of Belorussian exiles. Like Paul Scott, Keneally makes use of intercutting between letters, rugby match reports, police journals from wartime Poland and a family journal from the viewpoint of a young boy. Again the destruction of Europe's Jews haunts the novel, and this time the complicity of the aspiring Belorussian State with Nazi Germany casts a shadow over the second and third generation of the Kabbel family, even in the commercial wasteland of the western suburbs. The self-slaughter of the Kabbel family was based on an actual event that took place in Sydney in 1984, revealing again that Keneally's chief source of inspiration continues to be the individual and his relation to the historical process.

—Margaret B. Lewis

KENNEDY, William (Joseph). American. Born in Albany, New York, 16 January 1928. Educated at Siena College, Loudonville, New York, B.A. 1949. Served in the United States Army, 1950–52: sports editor and columnist for Army newspapers. Married Ana Daisy Dana Segarra in 1957; two daughters and one son. Assistant sports editor and columnist, Glens Falls *Post Star*, New York, 1949–50; reporter, Albany *Times-Union*, 1952–56; assistant managing editor and columnist, *Puerto Rico World Journal*, San Juan, 1956; reporter, Miami *Herald*, 1957; Puerto Rico correspondent for Time-Life publications, and reporter for Dorvillier business newsletter and Knight newspapers, 1957–59; founding managing editor, San Juan *Star*, 1959–61; full-time writer, 1961–63; special writer, 1963–70, and film critic, 1968–70, Albany *Times-Union*; book editor, *Look*, New York, 1971. Lecturer, 1974–82, and since 1983, Professor of English, State University of New York,

Albany. Visiting Professor of English, Cornell University, Ithaca, New York, 1982–83. Since 1957, free-lance magazine writer and critic; brochure and special project writer for New York State Department of Education and State University system, New York Governor's Conference on Libraries, and other organizations. Director, New York State Writers Institute. Recipient: Puerto Rican Civic Association of Miami award, 1957, NAACP award, 1965, Newspaper Guild Page One Award, 1965, and New York State Publishers award, 1965, all for reporting; National Endowment for the Arts fellowship, 1981; Siena College Career Achievement award, 1983; MacArthur Foundation fellowship, 1983; National Book Critics Circle award, 1984; Celtic Foundation Frank O'Connor Award, 1984; Before Columbus Foundation award, 1984; New York Public Library award, 1984; Pulitzer Prize, 1984; Governor's Arts award, 1984. L.H.D.: Russell Sage College, Troy, New York, 1980; Siena College, 1984; D.Litt.: College of St. Rose, Albany, 1985. Agent: Liz Darhansoff Literary Agency, 1220 Park Avenue, New York, New York 10128. Address: R.D. 3, Box 508, Averill Park, New York 12018, U.S.A.

PUBLICATIONS

Novels

- *The Ink Truck*. New York, Dial Press, 1969; London, Macdonald, 1970.
- *Legs*. New York, Coward McCann, 1975; London, Cape, 1976.
- *Billy Phelan's Greatest Game*. New York, Viking Press, 1978; London, Penguin, 1983.
- *Ironweed*. New York, Viking Press, 1983; London, Penguin, 1984.

Uncollected Short Stories

"The Secrets of Creative Love," in *Harper's* (New York), July 1983.
"An Exchange of Gifts," in *Glens Falls Review* (Glens Falls, New York), no. 3, 1985–86.

Play

Screenplay: *The Cotton Club*, with Francis Ford Coppola, 1984.

Other

Getting It All, Saving It All: Some Notes by an Extremist. Albany, New York State Governor's Conference on Libraries, 1978.
- *O Albany! Improbable City of Political Wizards, Fearless Ethnics, Spectacular Aristocrats, Splendid Nobodies, and Underrated Scoundrels*. Albany and New York, Washington Park Press-Viking Press, 1983.
Albany and the Capitol (photographs). New York, Aperture, 1986.
Charley Malarkey and the Belly Button Machine (for children), with Brendan Kennedy. Boston, Atlantic Monthly Press, 1986.

*

Manuscript Collection: Houghton Library, Harvard University, Cambridge, Massachusetts.

Critical Study: "The Sudden Fame of William Kennedy" by Margaret Croyden, in *New York Times Magazine*, 26 August 1984.

*   *   *

The emergence of William Kennedy's distinctive fictional voice corresponds to his discovery of his native Albany, New York, as home ground to his imagination. All Kennedy's novels have a lyric quality with a narrative voice that ranges in tone and mood: sometimes meditative or brooding; other times playful, exuberant, or mocking. What changes is Kennedy's increasing use of Albany townscape as vehicle for this voice. Much like Faulkner, Kennedy makes place the subject of his fiction. His characters cannot be detached from their Albany setting—their speech, memories, and peculiarities are as thoroughly localized as those of Faulkner's characters. Evoking the rich particularities of Albany's landscape, Kennedy expresses himself as novelist, for, as he says, "my imagination has become fused with a single place, and in that place finds all the elements that a man ever needs for the life of the soul."

Style is another distinguishing feature of Kennedy's fiction. Kennedy loves language, loves it in the way that Irish-American descendants of James Joyce do. To Kennedy, language offers countless variations of style, diction, and expression. His favorite stylistic modes include the language of memory, the prose poetry in which narrative aspires to lyric expressiveness, and the gritty dialogue of the down and out (always a source of energy in Kennedy's novels). Kennedy weaves these and many other styles together, until his books have the variousness of March weather. But whatever stylistic manner Kennedy chooses, he is always sure-handed.

Like many first novels, *The Ink Truck* is imitative. With Joyce's *Ulysses* providing him a loose model, Kennedy casts the story of a failed newspaper strike as a prose excursion. The excursion includes playlets, title pages designed as newspaper banner headlines, a surrealistic account of a 19th-century Albany cholera epidemic, a Walpurgis-like description of a party at the strike-breaker Stanley's house, and an imitation of spoken Spanish heard by someone who does not know Spanish. While many of these moments are highly energized, too often Kennedy does not join his stylistic play to the story. Moreover, Kennedy does not use actual Albany townscape, with the result that his fictional voice does not have the natural authenticity that it does in his later novels.

Legs, the first novel in Kennedy's Albany cycle, mixes fact and fiction in recounting the career of the gangster Legs Diamond, Kennedy frames the novel the way F. Scott Fitzgerald does *The Great Gatsby*: the life of the gangster presented through the memories of a confidant who has a more traditional moral outlook. In each novel, he narrator-confidant becomes apologist for the gangster, preferring his purity of aspiration to society's hypocrisies. This framework serves Fitzgerald better than it does Kennedy, because Kennedy fails to interest the reader in his narrator-rememberer Marcus Gorman, to establish Gorman's claims about Diamond's ethical worth, and to create as tight a tale as Fitzgerald does. *Legs*, however, does have considerable merit. Kennedy renders gangster life—the speak-easies, stills, and gangster molls—with the fidelity of a Mathew Brady photograph. He experiments with narrative form, most notably closing the novel with the point of view of the now-dead Legs Diamond, and anchors his language in the lawyerish prose of Marcus Gorman.

In *Billy Phelan's Greatest Game* Albany becomes for the first time the subject of Kennedy's fiction. Kennedy tells about the gamester Billy Phelan and the journalist Martin Daugherty and their efforts as middlemen in securing the release of a kidnap victim, Charlie Boy McCall. McCall is the sole heir to the McCall brothers, the party bosses of Albany's Democratic machine—not that either Phelan or Daugherty is interested in politics or in aiding the politically well-placed. Kennedy pays less attention to the mechanics of this plot than he does to the opportunity it affords to explore night-time Albany of the 1930's. The scenes are presented with evocative and painstaking detail—as, for instance, the scenes in Becker's bar with its huge photograph of its patron's 30th anniversary outing. Kennedy cannot have his characters enter Becker's without lingering to tell what happened to the people in the photograph. Like the anniversary photograph, *Billy Phelan* memorializes a past recoverable only in memory.

The Pulitzer Prize-winner *Ironweed* is clearly Kennedy's best novel. The story concerns the return to Albany of Francis Phelan (Billy's father)—former big-league baseball player, now bum, lush, and sentimentalist. During his two-day return, Francis roams the streets of memory, confronting often for the first time the events that prompted him to flee his family and to live the life of the open road. The Albany landscape awakens Francis to his past—"They walked on to the end of North Pearl Street, where it entered Menands. . . . They walked past the place where the old Bull's Head Tavern used to be. Francis was a kid when he saw Gus Ruhlan come out of the corner in bare knuckles. The bum he was fighting stuck out a hand to shake, Gus give him a shot and that was all she wrote"—and enables him to map his future—"So they sat there and looked down the hill toward Broadway and over the hills of Rensselaer and Troy. . . . Francis decided this would be a fine place to be buried. The hill had a nice flow to it that carried you down the grass and out onto the river. . . . Being dead here would situate a man in place and time."

Kennedy's narrative method fuses Francis's memories and hallucinatory fantasies. We see this when, working as a day laborer, Francis communes with his dead ancestors: "Francis's mother twitched nervously in her grave . . . and Francis's father lit his pipe, smiled at his wife's discomfort." Haunted by these and other ghosts, Francis grows restless, visits his family, and flees once again. At novel's end, he is riding a freight train away from Albany. His mind, however, remains anchored in Albany, wandering the old neighborhoods: "watch[ing] Jake Becker lettin' his pigeons loose" and asking his wife Annie "about setting up the cot in Danny's room." At such moments, William Carlos Williams might say of each Phelan and Kennedy: "the city,/the man, an identity, it cannot be/ otherwise."

—David M. Craig

KESEY, Ken (Elton). American. Born in La Junta, Colorado, 17 September 1935. Educated at a high school in Springfield, Oregon; University of Oregon, Eugene, B.A. 1957; Stanford University, California (Woodrow Wilson Fellow), 1958–59. Married Faye Haxby in 1956; four children. Ward attendant in mental hospital, Menlo Park, California; president, Intrepid Trips film company, 1964. Since 1974, publisher, *Spit in the Ocean* magazine, Pleasant Hill, Oregon. Served prison term for marijuana possession, 1967. Recipient: Saxton Memorial Trust award, 1959. Address: 85829 Ridgeway Road, Pleasant Hill, Oregon 97401, U.S.A.

PUBLICATIONS

Novels

One Flew over the Cuckoo's Nest.   New York, Viking Press, 1962; London, Methuen, 1963.
Sometimes a Great Notion.   New York, Viking Press, 1964; London, Methuen, 1966.

Short Story

The Day Superman Died.   Northridge, California, Lord John Press, 1980.

Uncollected Short Stories

"The First Sunday in October," in *Northwest Review* (Seattle), Fall 1957.
"McMurphy and the Machine," in *Stanford Short Stories 1962*, edited by Wallace Stegner and Richard Scowcroft.   Stanford, California, Stanford University Press, 1962.
"Letters from Mexico," in *Ararat* (New York), Autumn 1967.
"Excerpts from Kesey's Jail Diary," in *Ramparts* (Berkeley, California), November 1967.
"Correspondence," in *Tri-Quarterly* (Evanston, Illinois), Spring 1970.
"Once a Great Nation," in *Argus* (College Park, Maryland), April 1970.
"Dear Good Dr. Timothy," in *Augur* (Eugene, Oregon), 19 November 1970.
"Cut the Motherfuckers Loose," in *The Last Whole Earth Catalog*.   San Francisco, Straight Arrow, 1971.
"The Bible," "Dawgs," "The I Ching," "Mantras," "Tools from My Chest," in *The Last Supplement to the Whole Earth Catalog-The Realist* (New York), March–April 1971.
"Over the Border," in *Oui* (Chicago), April 1973.
"'Seven Prayers' by Grandma Whittier," in *Spit in the Ocean 1–5* (Pleasant Hill, Oregon), 1974–79.

Other

Kesey's Garage Sale (miscellany; includes screenplay *Over the Border*).   New York, Viking Press, 1973.

*

Manuscript Collection: University of Oregon, Eugene.

Critical Studies: *The Electric Kool-Aid Acid Test* by Tom Wolfe, New York, Farrar Straus, 1968, London, Weidenfeld and Nicolson, 1969; *Ken Kesey* by Bruce Carnes, Boise, Idaho, Boise State College, 1974; "Ken Kesey Issue" of *Northwest Review* (Eugene, Oregon), vol. 16, nos. 1-2, 1977; *Ken Kesey* by Barry H. Leeds, New York, Ungar, 1981; *Ken Kesey* by Stephen L. Tanner, Boston, Twayne, 1983.

*   *   *

Ken Kesey's critical reputation rests for the time being on his two novels. The first, *One Flew over the Cuckoo's Nest*, was a widely popular success which has been adapted as a play and a film. The second novel, *Sometimes a Great Notion*, has received relatively little attention. Since finishing it, Kesey has announced a shift from "literature" to "life," and has achieved a great deal of public notoriety in the process of making the change. He was public news during the late 1960's forming a band of "Merry Pranksters" (reported on at length in Tom Wolfe's *Electric Kool-Aid Acid Test*) who attempted to live life as a work of comic fiction. Stray pieces of notebooks have been published, suggesting that eventually a new work, perhaps a new kind of work, will emerge. Until then Kesey followers will have to content themselves with *The Last Supplement to the Whole Earth Catalog.* This volume has more of Kesey's writing in it (mostly reviews and articles) than anything published since his second novel.

Both of Kesey's novels are richly northwestern and regional in quality, with a strong sense of the impingement of the white man on the Indian's land and way of life. The emphasis is a bit one-sided in *Cuckoo's Nest*, which has for its stream-of-consciousness center and narrator-observer an Indian named Chief, whose father was in fact the last chief of his tribe. The novel could be read as an allegory of how the white man is driven to subjugate and eliminate the Indian because he is a reminder to him of those parts of himself he has lost through a conquest of the will over the passions. More basically, however, the novel reveals the power struggle between man's desire to be free and his fears of the consequence of that freedom. Most of the characters in the mental institution could leave if they wished; but their fear of the outside is more intense than their hatred of the inside. The novel tempts one to allegorical generalities because the institution in which it is set becomes increasingly recognizable as a microcosm of the world we all live in. Recognizable, but comically exaggerated, as are the main characters who represent general qualities and attitudes towards life and humanity. The book captures and reflects the reality of a "Walt Disney world," as perceived by the "Big Chief" who used to be on our childhood writing tablet covers but is now pretending to be a vegetable in a nut house. What he sees is "Like a cartoon world, where the figures are flat and outlined in black, jerking through some kind of goofy story that might be real funny if it weren't for the cartoon figures being real guys. ..." The comic-book quality has lent itself nicely to dramatic production, as have the compactness and wild humor of the novel. These qualities also tempt one to allegorize, but at the same time mock the attempt as absurd. For the work is not itself allegorical; it is a report or presentation of the way people see themselves and their world in allegorical or comic-book fashion, yet without being able to laugh at what they see. The reality of the villain, "Big Nurse," is as exaggerated by the characters who fear and hate her as it is by the novelist. The institution, with its equipment and routines, is a focus for sociological and psychological myths and techniques pushed to an illogical but all-too-plausible extreme. The prefrontal lobotomy performed on McMurphy at the end is *any* operation on or treatment of or way of seeing a man, that decides to limit and dehumanize him for his own sake. The Big Nurse is that spirit which loves the "idea" of man so much it can't allow individual men to exist.

Sometimes a Great Notion deserves more attention than *Cuckoo's Nest*, and much more than I can give it here. I can indicate its ambition, by pointing out that it is in considerable part an *Absalom, Absalom!* set in Oregon. I pick this example not only to suggest the intense regionalism of the book, but to indicate the intricate complexities of the narrative structure which Kesey has attempted. After the second reading, what at first seem like gratuitous confusions and exploitations of "the miracle of modern narrative technique," begin to emerge as the necessary supports for a novelistic structure which doesn't quite get brought into finished shape. In this novel Kesey has aimed higher than many of his contemporaries, and he came impressively close to his target.

—Thomas A. Vogler

KHAN, Ismith (Mohamed). American. Born in Port of Spain, Trinidad, 16 March 1925; became American citizen, 1958. Educated at Queen's Royal College, Port of Spain; Michigan State University, East Lansing, 1948–51; New School for Social Research, New York, 1951–54, B.A. in social sciences 1954; Johns Hopkins University, Baltimore, 1969–70, M.A. in creative writing 1970. Married 1) Mariam Ghose in 1949 (marriage dissolved, 1966); 2) Vera Simon in 1966; two children. Research assistant, Department of Far Eastern Studies, Cornell University, Ithaca, New York, 1955–56; library assistant, New York Public Library, 1956–61; Instructor in Creative Writing, New School for Social Research, 1959–69, and Great Neck public schools, Long Island, New York, 1963; Visiting Professor of English, University of California, Berkeley, 1970–71; Assistant Professor of Caribbean and Comparative Literature, University of California, San Diego, 1971–74; Senior Lecturer, University of Southern California, Los Angeles, 1977, and California State University, Long Beach, 1978, 1980. Agent: John Schaffner Associates, 114 East 28th Street, New York, New York 10016, U.S.A.

PUBLICATIONS

Novels

The Jumbie Bird. London, MacGibbon and Kee, 1961; New York, Obolensky, 1963.
The Obeah Man. London, Hutchinson, 1964.

Uncollected Short Stories

"In the Subway," in *New Voices 2*, edited by Don M. Wolfe. New York, Hendricks House, 1955.
"A Day in the Country," in *From the Green Antilles*, edited by Barbara Howes. New York, Macmillan, 1966; London, Souvenir Press, 1967.
"The Red Ball," in *New Writing in the Caribbean*, edited by A.J. Seymour. Georgetown, Government of Guyana, 1972.
"The Village Shop," in *Lambailey*, edited by Ron Heapy and Anne Garside. Oxford, Oxford University Press, 1980.
"Shadows Move in the Bratania Bar," in *Sunlight and Shadows*. London, Cassell, 1980.

*

Ismith Khan comments:

All of my novels and short stories are set in the Caribbean. This has necessitated certain choices, questions, and considerations: 1) what language to write in, pidgin or Standard English; 2) how well can an expatriate writer, despite frequent visits to his area, speak for and about its times; 3) which audience to write for, local or international, bearing in mind the size and literacy of the local audience, and the prohibitive cost of books.

Despite the drawbacks, I have opted to write for a local audience in an attempt to revivify the cultural milieu from which my work derives its inspiration, because the writer from the Caribbean has to assume the responsibility of "teacher" and "historian" in order to record periods of history not normally found in history books. It is the long view, the long term that is of importance. There should be a body of literature written by Caribbean authors that will fill the literary vacuum for the younger generation, and other generations to come, so that they will be able to come to grips with their "identity"

in what has become a world of rapid change where the sense of intrinsic values and the importance of traditions are lost, swallowed up by international values that seem to mitigate the breakdown of culture and human personality. This is the material from which the "drama" of the Caribbean and its people is made.

My work is an attempt to confront "culture shock," to resurrect a sense of self, to look at values and traditions in the period of bewildering change that our independence has brought with it, changes not necessarily of our own making but which nonetheless affect out lives directly.

*   *   *

Ismith Khan's fiction takes the Indian community of Trinidad as its starting point, analyzing the special features of that community at the same time that the writer explores the Indian experience as a microcosm of the West Indian experience as a whole. In his two published novels this exploration centers on the theme of exile and isolation: the historical exile of Indians, Africans, and Europeans to the Caribbean has resulted in a culture that is simultaneously linked with and isolated from its original sources.

In the first novel, *The Jumbie Bird*, the narrative plot centers on three generations of the Khan family—Kale, his son Rahmin, and his grandson Jamini. Kale is one of the original migrants from India, those who first came to Trinidad and other islands in the British Caribbean colonies as contract labourers. But he is a lifelong malcontent, always busy with plans to return to India from a world in which he has never really felt at home. Rahmin shares some of his father's revulsion at Trinidad, but having grown up in the Caribbean he does not identify as strongly with the Indian homeland or with Kale's perennial back-to-India schemes. And in the third generation Jamini is even further removed from the Indian memories of his grandfather, even though he is very fond of old Kale himself.

The theme of isolation in the novel—especially Kale's isolation—is therefore integrated with the migrant's sense of dislocation and cultural exile. The fact that the old man lives alone, in a separate room of the Khan house, emphasizes the degree to which he is alienated from the family while belonging to it. Similarly, he belongs to Trinidad to the extent that, willy-nilly, it is his permanent home; but he is wholly alienated from the society—its colonial heritage, its Western trappings, and, quite simply, the fact that it is not India. But although he is a prime mover of local repatriation politics, he really hates India itself—it is the place that forced him into exile in the first place because it had nothing to offer him by way of socio-economic survival.

The tragedy of Kale's isolation is that it is so complete. His profound dissatisfaction with the world around him leads to a deep-seated revulsion at people in general. His alienation is not just the migrant's usual nostalgia: it is also a form of isolation from the human condition in general. And in fact his involvement with the repatriation movement is really a desperate attempt to provide himself with a sense of belonging. When the movement fails, when the official representative from India makes its futility quite clear, Kate literally has nothing to live for, and he dies shortly afterwards. His grandson is left to carry the burden of isolation, but when the novel ends the reader is left with the assurance that Jamini can cope. He recognizes that isolation is not simply a cultural condition imposed by the circumstances of (West Indian) history: it is also an integral part of the human condition. His early, and abortive, sexual experience demonstrates to him that even in moments of intimacy human beings usually manage to remain "locked up within themselves and quite alone." And paradoxically enough this recognition of the nature of isolation prepares him to deal with people, and with his culture, on a much more substantial basis than his grandfather ever could.

In *Obeah Man* Khan returns to the theme of individual loneliness, by emphasizing once again that individual feelings and identity are often "locked up" from others as a normal course of events, and that this prevailing human tendency usually thwarts or dilutes attempts to formulate patterns of cultural solidarity or sexual intimacy. In the first novel Jamini learns that even in intimate relationships we see only the "outer surfaces" of others. In this second novel the hero, Zampi the obeah man, sees the masks of carnival as symbols of those outer surfaces. Thus when he removes a grinning mask from a carnival reveller's face he discovers a face that's sweaty, tearful, and pathetic.

Zampi himself is a mixture of several races on the island, and to this degree he represents the history of synthesis and fusion that has been characteristic of Caribbean culture. And on another level his role as obeah man, or healer, represents a certain commitment to the well-being of his community. But at the same time that role requires a certain distance from others—hence he lives as a hermit, away from the city and—except for this carnival—away from its festivals and flesh-pots. And this isolation reflects his scepticism about the possibility of maintaining really enduring relationships based on complete knowledge of the other. In turn this scepticism has led to his estrangement from his girlfriend Zolda. Finally, his private estrangement, and the jealousies and social divisions that he discovers underneath the joyous masks of carnival, all counteract the sense of cultural and social fusion that his own ethnic heritage represents. As in *Jumbie Bird* Khan offers no sweeping, transcendental solutions to all of this. At best we are left with Zampi's ability to survive, emotionally and physically, precisely because he refuses to take the "outer surfaces" of human behaviour at face value. And this is the lesson that Zolda is beginning to learn at the end of the novel when she agrees to join him in his hermit's exile from the city.

It is a central paradox of Ismith Khan's fiction, and one of its major achievements, that he is able to explore the social milieu of his characters in convincing detail—at the same time that he insists on the prevailing isolation of individuals from each other and from their social milieu as a whole. The world of the Indian in Trinidad is painted in painstaking detail in *Jumbie Bird*; and in *Obeah Man* the carnival is not only a picturesque celebration as such, it is also a microcosm of Trinidad society as the novelist envisions it. As a result Khan's fiction occupies a rather special, though too often neglected niche in Caribbean literature: it celebrates the special vitality of the region's culture without romanticizing it, allowing writer and reader alike to remain painfully aware of the degree to which a sense of social or ethnocultural belonging is often counter-balanced, even thwarted, by persistent isolation and divisiveness between individuals.

—Lloyd W. Brown

KIELY, Benedict. Irish.   Born in Dromore, County Tyrone, 15 August 1919. Educated at Christian Brothers' schools, Omagh; National University of Ireland, Dublin, B.A. (honours) 1943. Married Maureen O'Connell in 1944; two daughters and two sons. Journalist in Dublin, 1939–64. Writer-in-Residence, Hollins College, Virginia, 1964–65; Visiting Professor, University of Oregon, Eugene, 1965–66; Writer-in-Residence, Emory University, Atlanta, 1966–68. Since 1970, Visiting Lecturer, University College, Dublin. Recipient: American-Irish Foundation award, 1980; Irish Academy of Letters award, 1980. Member of the Council, and President, Irish Academy of Letters. Address: c/o The Irish Times, Westmoreland Street, Dublin, Ireland.

PUBLICATIONS

Novels

Land Without Stars.   London, Johnson, 1946.
In a Harbour Green.   London, Cape, 1949; New York, Dutton, 1950.
Call for a Miracle.   London, Cape, 1950; New York, Dutton, 1951.
Honey Seems Bitter.   New York, Dutton, 1952; London, Methuen, 1954.
The Cards of the Gambler: A Folktale.   London, Methuen, 1953.
There Was an Ancient House.   London, Methuen, 1955.
The Captain with the Whiskers.   London, Methuen, 1960; New York, Criterion, 1961.
Dogs Enjoy the Morning.   London, Gollancz, 1968.
Proxopera.   London, Gollancz, 1977.
Nothing Happens in Carmincross.   London, Gollancz, and Boston, Godine, 1985.

Short Stories

A Journey to the Seven Streams: Seventeen Stories.   London, Methuen, 1963.
Penguin Modern Stories 5, with others.   London, Penguin, 1970.
A Ball of Malt and Madame Butterfly: A Dozen Stories.   London, Gollancz, 1973.
A Cow in the House and Nine Other Stories.   London, Gollancz, 1978.
The State of Ireland: A Novella and Seventeen Stories.   Boston, Godine, 1980; London, Penguin, 1982.

Uncollected Short Stories

"Fionn in the Valley," in *The Pushcart Prize 6*, edited by Bill Henderson.   Wainscott, New York, Pushcart Press, 1981.
"Oh Dear, What Can the Matter Be?," in *Tri-Quarterly* (Evanston, Illinois), Winter 1981.

Other

Counties of Contention: A Study of the Origins and Implication of the Partition of Ireland.   Cork, Mercier Press, 1945.
Poor Scholar: A Study of the Works and Days of William Carleton 1794–1869.   London, Sheed and Ward, 1947; New York, Sheed and Ward, 1948.
Modern Irish Fiction: A Critique.   Dublin, Golden Eagle, 1950.
All the Way to Bantry Bay and Other Irish Journeys.   London, Gollancz, 1978.
Ireland from the Air.   London, Weidenfeld and Nicolson, and New York, Crown, 1985.

Editor, *The Various Lives of Keats and Chapman and The Brother*, by Flann O'Brien. London, Hart Davis MacGibbon, 1976.
Editor, *The Penguin Book of Irish Short Stories*. London, Penguin, 1981.
Editor, *Dublin*. Oxford and New York, Oxford University Press, 1983.

*

Critical Studies: *Benedict Kiely* by Daniel J. Casey, Lewisburg, Pennsylvania, Bucknell University Press, 1974; *Benedict Kiely* by Grace Eckley, New York, Twayne, 1974.

*   *   *

Myth and legend, the heroic and the mock-heroic, form the central strands to the short stories of Benedict Kiely. He relies heavily on the Irish genius for creating epic myths about man, his heroic deeds and his human frailties. Although his fiction is largely set in the County Tyrone of his boyhood, a landscape that he knows intimately and with a sense of delight, it is transformed in a story like "A Journey to the Seven Streams" to a land of eternal and universal childhood. The trip to the stone-fiddle beside Lough Erne in Hookey Baxter's whimsical motor car takes on the aspect of a pilgrimage to a shrine or the tale of travellers in a magic, dreamlike land who have to face numerous adventures and dangers. And Kiely's language, too, is finely honed to a mock-serious note, with elegy never far away, reflecting both the absurdity of the journey and its underlying comic pathos: "White cottages far away on the lower slopes of Dooish could have been in another country."

Kiely's reputation has been somewhat retarded by what many critics dismiss as a narrow provincialism but what is also a source of joy to his readers. In a second collection, *A Ball of Malt and Madame Butterfly*, Kiely confirmed that although his work continues to be rooted in the Ireland that he knows so well, it has a breadth of vision and humanity in its subject matter and literary style that raises it above the merely provincial. The Tyrone of his childhood and the Dublin of his formative years are favourite backdrops for his novels where the mood changes from the mock-epic to the mock-gothic romance in a work like *The Captain with the Whiskers* with its memorable scene of the mad captain drilling his three sons in Boer War uniforms in the doomed big house; and in *Dogs Enjoy the Morning* with its satirical mixture of pub gossip and idle anecdote in the grotesque, but finely drawn, village of Cosmona where a newspaper reporter remarks, aptly enough, that "all human life is here."

A new note in Kiely's work was struck with the publication of *Proxopera* in 1977, a savagely indignant novel with its anger directed against all men of violence in Ireland. The title comes from an "operation proxy" when an elderly grandfather, Binchey, is forced by three terrorists holding his family ransom to take a bomb into the neighbouring town. The background is again Tyrone, but the mood is at once savage in Binchey's outrage at the terrorism that Ireland has helped to spawn, and at once an elegy for the non-sectarian, chivalrous past of his own childhood. Everything is seen through the enraged consciousness of Binchey and his sense of loss that nothing, his past, his family, the countryside and his relationship to them, will ever be the same again.

The same theme is continued—although this time on a larger canvas—in *Nothing Happens in Carmincross*, a novel which is constructed with enormous skill, layer upon layer, until its final and devastating act of violence. Mervyn Kavanagh, the central character, has a career as an academic in America, but has retained a great love for his native Ireland. Unlike many Irish-Americans, though, he has no love for terrorism; this cannot save him from the reality he has to face when, on a visit to Ireland, he is brought face to face with the violence of his country's past and present history. Just as in *Proxopera* Kiely kept sentimentality and bathos at bay, so too does he manage to view terrorism dispassionately yet shockingly in *Nothing Happens in Carmincross*. At the novel's end the reader is left with the certainty that another meaningless act of horror is about to become just another memory, part of the historical process: in that sense Kiely has faced up courageously to the peculiar tragedy of the Irish situation. In contrast to his morbid theme Kiely writes with zest and grace, humour and irony, in a style which is totally individual, the cadences of his language pointing and counterpointing feelings and ideas.

—Trevor Royle

KILLENS, John Oliver. American. Born in Macon, Georgia, 14 January 1916. Educated at Edward Waters College, Jacksonville, Florida; Morris Brown College, Atlanta; Terrel Law School, Washington, D.C.; Columbia University, New York; New York University. Served in the United States Army during World War II. Married to Grace Killens; one son and one daughter. Worked for the National Labor Relations Board, Washington, D.C., 1936–42 and after 1946; taught creative writing at New School for Social Research, New York, Fisk University, Nashville, 3 years, Columbia University, 3 years, Trinity College, Hartford, Connecticut, Howard University, Washington, D.C., 7 years, and Bronx Community College, New York. Currently, Distinguished Professor, Medgar Evers College, Brooklyn. Former Vice-President, Black Academy of Arts and Letters. Recipient: Afro-Arts award, for theatre, 1955; Rabinowitz Foundation grant, 1964; Harlem Writers Guild award, 1978; National Endowment for the Arts fellowship, 1980. Lives in Brooklyn, New York. Agent: Laurence Jordan Associates, 2067 Broadway, Suite 4, New York, New York 10023, U.S.A.

PUBLICATIONS

Novels

Youngblood. New York, Dial Press, 1954; London, Bodley Head, 1956.
And Then We Heard the Thunder. New York, Knopf, 1963; London, Cape, 1964.
'Sippi. New York, Simon and Schuster, 1967.
Slaves. New York, Pyramid, 1969.
The Cotillion; or, One Good Bull Is Half the Herd. New York, Simon and Schuster, 1971.
Great Gittin' Up Morning. New York, Doubleday, 1972.

Uncollected Short Stories

"God Bless America," in *American Negro Short Stories*, edited by John Henrik Clarke. New York, Hill and Wang, 1966.
"The Stick Up," in *The Best Short Stories by Negro Writers*, edited by Langston Hughes. Boston, Little Brown, 1967.

Plays

Lower than the Angels (produced New York, 1965).
Cotillion, adaptation of his own novel (produced New York, 1975).

Screenplays: *Odds Against Tomorrow*, with Nelson Gidding, 1959; *Slaves*, with Herbert J. Biberman and Alida Sherman, 1969.

Other

Black Man's Burden (essays).   New York, Simon and Schuster, 1966.
A Man Ain't Nothin' But a Man (for children).   Boston, Little Brown, 1975.

                    *   *   *

The career of John Oliver Killens now spans over 30 years, during which he has continued to shape the Afro-American novel as an instrument in the black struggle for equality and recognition. His left-wing convictions and his conception of literature as embattled make him an immediate heir to Richard Wright whose concern for truth, for relevance, for focussing the reader's attention on timely issues, for contributing to change he undoubtedly shares, together with his Southern origins.

Killens is not only a productive novelist but a social critic and an organizer. In the late 1940's, he helped found the Harlem Writers Guild with like-minded colleagues like Rosa Guy and John Henrik Clarke; that organisation was the training ground for many younger playwrights and novelists who produced significant work in the 1960's. Later as a member of the executive council of the National Center of Afro-American Artists, and as Vice-President of the Black Academy of Arts and Letters, Killens was involved in setting up conferences and literary events. He has written inspirational books for younger readers: *Great Gittin' Up Morning* is a fictionalized biography of Denmark Vesey, who led the 1802 insurrection in Charleston, South Carolina; *A Man Ain't Nothin' But a Man* celebrates the life of John Henry, a giant among American laborers who laid the railroad tracks in the 19th century. Significantly, Killens stresses interracial unity in the working class by giving Henry a poor white and a Chinese as companions. He clearly does not shun propaganda in his non-fiction volumes; his novels, likewise, are often laden with explicit social criticism and racial protest but Killens's sense of humor and, especially, his recourse to the popular forms of folklore aesthetically sustain his affirmation of cultural identity as well as his crusade for justice.

His first novel is the saga of a southern black family whose name serves as a title, *Youngblood*. Set in the symbolical Crossroads community in Killens's native Georgia, the novel explores the four protagonists and demonstrates the stifling, oppressive impact of their environment. Joe Youngblood is compelled to flee North; involved in the Civil Rights movement, he dies a victim of racism, though the Ku Klux Klan is routed by his friends. His mother has to whip young Robby in front of the sheriff because he has fought white schoolboys who insulted his sister. The police stop Richard Nyles and his fiancée on the road, symbolically castrating him. Nyles is a fascinating character who serves as a guide and a mentor to his pupil, Robby; he persuades his friend, Dr. Riley, to have the wounded Joe Youngblood admitted into the all-white hospital just as he had convinced him to tend to his missionary work among the whites, not the blacks. One of the protagonists is a white man, Oscar, a destitute laborer who befriends "Little Jim," the proud black who refuses to accept Jim Crow's unwritten laws. When Joe is wounded, Oscar's son gives his blood to try to save him. The forthright message is that the struggle must be conducted within the ranks of organized labor, and the unions are seen as a means towards racial equality. Much like Richard Wright's novella "Bright and Morning Star," *Youngblood* stresses both the spontaneous allegiance to the race and the ideological choice in favor of the working class which leads to accepting whites of good will as allies.

Killens drew heavily from his army experiences (he served in the South Pacific) to document *And Then We Heard the Thunder*, his second novel. Despite similarities to Mailer's *The Naked and the Dead*, it stands as a stringent protest against segregation and discrimination in the U.S. Army. Only Lieutenant Samuels, a liberal New York Jew, behaves decently to the blacks, and he serves as a worthy interlocutor to disillusioned Solly Saunders, a law student who enlisted, at his wife Millie's prompting, to take advantage of the Officer's Training School. Millie is a rich Brooklyn girl with middle-class expectations who urges her husband to make good after the war. Solly has a girl friend, Annie Mae, while in the army, but it takes still a third woman, an Australian, to boost his consciousness. Solly's buddies are numerous, from the ever-joking Joe "Bookworm" Taylor to the company cook. The novel is no *Catch-22*, but it deals with the growing realization that the Army is a sort of tyranny, although the stakes are greater than individual freedom. The hypocrisy, racial prejudice, and pretense of democracy in the American system are exposed, and little is left to support the hero except his own resolve: a necessary stage of self-acceptance must precede allegiance to the group, even if it be the human race. *And Then We Heard the Thunder* sounds a new proud note which heralds the Black Power ideology in a prose that is openly at the service of the novel's message.

'Sippi continues in the militant vein but is a lesser achievement as fiction. Set during the Civil Rights period of the 1960's, it concerns two Mississippi families—one white, one black—which provide contrapuntal examples of the conditioning of youngsters. Carrie, the white Wakefields' daughter, has a black roommate, Cheryl Kingsley, at college; unlike her puritanical parents, she tries to adapt to social changes but she is dismayed at encountering repudiation from blacks at a party. Jesse Chaney is a black sharecropper whose son Charles is attracted by the new militancy. The plot teems with violent incidents, from the bombing of churches to marches and sit-ins, and actual heroic characters of the Freedom Now campaign, from Martin Luther King to Malcolm X. The title itself alludes to a joke, according to which a proud black man refuses to use "Miss" in front of any white name. The novel, however, remains more a chronicle of those troubled times than a truly alive, imaginative creation.

By comparison, *The Cotillion* marks a new, more interesting departure for Killens. It resorts more substantially to the folk tradition, namely to verbal contests in the style of the "dirty dozens" but it is closer to, say, Chester Himes's *Pinktoes* than the yarns of Zora Neale Hurston. The satire of Negro high society focusses upon its assimilationist tendencies, its snobbery, its shallowness and lack of authentic ethnic culture. "The Cotillion" is the annual ball of the Femmes Fatales, a black women's club in the fashionable Crowning Heights suburbs. Fun-loving and West Indian-born Daphne Lovejoy will eventually be rescued by good sense from the "oreo" imitation of white high society devised by the likes of Mrs. Prissy Patterson. But it takes scratching the whitewashed Negro to reveal the authentic black beneath, and this can only be achieved by the earthy, ethnic humor of Matthew "Man" Lovejoy, Daphne's husband, a porter who relishes soul food and barbershop talk. Their daughter Yoruba is confronted with the choice between assimilation and nationalism, while Ernest Billings, who renames himself Lumumba, sports militant black nationalism and a dashiki. He succeeds in turning the cotillion into a celebration of blackness. The novel advocates racial unity, pride in one's people's culture, and a return to African values, but, in this case, the parody, humor, and freewheeling fantasy create a convincing, jubilant fiction far from the mimetic plodding of social realism. John Oliver Killens's works thus register not only the changes in black ideology and sensibility, but they move towards a more contemporary style of writing as he finds new ways of remaining committed to the struggle.

—Michel Fabre

KIM, Richard E(unkook). American. Born in Hamhung City, Korea, 13 March 1932; became United States citizen, 1964. Educated at primary and secondary schools in Korea; Middlebury College, Vermont, 1955–59; Johns Hopkins University, Baltimore, 1959–60, M.A. in writing 1960; University of Iowa, Iowa City, 1960–62, M.F.A. in writing 1962; Harvard University, Cambridge, Massachusetts, 1962–63, M.A. in Far Eastern literature 1963. Served in the Korean Army and Marines, 1950–54: First Lieutenant. Married Penelope Anne Groll in 1960; one son and one daughter. Instructor in English, California State College, Long Beach, 1963–64; Assistant Professor, 1964–68, and Associate Professor of English, 1968–69, University of Massachusetts, Amherst; also, Director, University of Massachusetts Imaginative Writers' Workshop, Nantucket, summers 1967–69. Visiting Writer, Mediterranean Institute, Mallorca, 1969; Visiting Professor of English, Syracuse University, New York, 1970–71, and San Diego State University, California, 1975–77; Fulbright Scholar, Seoul National University, South Korea, 1981–83. Columnist, *Korea Herald*, 1982–84. Recipient: Mary Roberts Rinehart Foundation fellowship, 1961; Ford Foreign Area Fellowship, 1962; Guggenheim fellowship, 1965; National Endowment for the Arts grant, 1977. Address: Leverett Road, Shutesbury, Massachusetts 01072, U.S.A.

PUBLICATIONS

Novels

The Martyred. New York, Braziller, and London, Hutchinson, 1964.
The Innocent. Boston, Houghton Mifflin, 1968; London, Hutchinson, 1969.

Short Stories

Lost Names: Scenes from a Korean Boyhood. New York, Praeger, 1970; London, Deutsch, 1971.

Uncollected Short Stories

"Crossing" and "An Empire for Rubber Balls," in *Asian-American Heritage*, edited by David Hsin-Fu Wang. New York, Washington Square Press, 1974

Other

In Search of Lost Years (essays). Seoul, Korea, Suhmoon-Dang, 1985.

Translator, *Arrow to the Sun* (for children). Seoul, Korea, Omun-Gak, 1982.
Translator, *Picture World 100* (for children). Seoul, Korea, Dong-Hwa, 1983.
Translator, *A Blue Bird* (for children). Seoul, Korea, Dong-Hwa, 1983.
Translator, *Touch the Earth.* Seoul, Korea, Pumyang, 1983.

*

Critical Studies: "The Love Stance: Richard E. Kim's *The Martyred*" by David Galloway, in *Critique* (Atlanta), Winter 1964–65; article by Robert W. French, in *Massachusetts Review* (Amherst), Fall 1970; "A Study of Richard E. Kim" by Dae Sung Lee, unpublished thesis, Korea University, Seoul, 1975.

*   *   *

Richard E. Kim's fiction deals with war's effect on private morality. Using an inexperienced first-person narrator—an unnamed child in *Lost Names* and a young officer named Lee in *The Martyred* and *The Innocent*—he sensitively delineates questions of bravery, patriotism, humaneness, and even the nature of truth as they are clouded by violence and made more complex by despair.

Periods of national crisis in recent Korean history provide a background against which are focused the moral crises of individuals. Love of country, despair over the suffering of its people, and pride in their resilience are recurring themes. The forbidding Korean countryside, especially the winter scenery of North Korea, is used to underscore the characters' anguish. At the end of each book, the narrator's education—though incomplete—leads him to hope for Korea's future despite the suffering and death he has seen.

Lost Names is a collection of stories dealing with the ordeal of a single family during the last 13 years of the 36-year Japanese occupation. The book is thematically unified by the child's growing awareness that the mere survival of his father is significant heroism. Although the stories vary in weight, the best of them, such as the title story, are taut and powerful. Natural imagery is skillfully used, and the maturation process of a child is well suited to the thematic development.

The Innocent treats a compelling question; how much bloodshed can an individual justify by patriotism? The focal character, Colonel Min, is struggling for his soul while leading a *coup d'état*. There is some fine descriptive writing in this book, too, and characters such as Min and Chaplain Koh are strikingly alive, but it does not have the solid power one might wish for. The complexity of the plot detracts from the moral drama, and the large cast of conspirators requires too much sorting out, especially when they are all men designated by military titles and similar monosyllabic Korean names. There is special difficulty with the three characters opposing the coup: General Mah, General Ahn and General Ham.

Kim's best book, *The Martyred*, is uniformly fine. It is tightly plotted, austere in style, and moving in subject matter. The tone of passion never approaches bathos; the people are believable and their struggles compelling. Economy of incident and explication heightens the drama. The writing is smooth and strong; necessary information about the movement of armies is worked in unobtrusively and does not detract from the focus on a single moral drama and the half dozen characters intimately concerned with its unfolding. Brutality and helplessness are effectively portrayed without sensational description. *The Martyred* deserves a wide readership.

Though each of these books draws heavily upon the tragic history of Korea, the reader feels that Kim is equipped to deal sensitively with the human condition wherever he finds it. These are not ethnic novels; they simply use the compelling historical situation with which the novelist is familiar.

—Barbara M. Perkins

KINCAID, Jamaica. American. Born in St. John's, Antigua, 25 May 1949. Educated at a girls' school in Antigua, and a college in New Hampshire. Married Allen Evan Shawn; one daughter. Since 1974 contributor, and currently staff writer, *The New Yorker*. Recipient: American Academy Morton Dauwen Zabel Award, 1984. Address: The New Yorker, 25 West 43rd Street, New York, New York 10036, U.S.A.

PUBLICATIONS

Novel

Annie John. New York, Farrar Straus, and London, Pan, 1985.

Short Stories

At the Bottom of the River. New York, Farrar Straus, 1983; London, Pan, 1984.

*   *   *

Jamaica Kincaid is a greatly talented writer who has so far written two arresting books, *At the Bottom of the River* and *Annie John*. In both books Kincaid uses the voice of a girl preoccupied with love and hate for her mother, a woman who caresses her only child one moment and then berates her as "the slut you are about to become." In the ten episodic and meditative sections of *At the Bottom of the River*, neither the child nor her homeland (Antigua in the West Indies) have names; in *Annie John*, both do. Because in *Annie John* the girl's age changes from ten to 17, this second book offers more specific chronology and somewhat greater continuity; however, the narrator still presents her experiences, and her reflections upon them, in monologues which complement one another but could stand separately. Critics refer to *At the Bottom of the River* variously as a novel, a collection of stories, and even as "ten pieces," but its characteristics so closely parallel *Annie John* that both books can be considered similar episodic novels offering insight into the psychological nature of a girl's growth into maturity. In spite of the relative autonomy of chapters in these books, Kincaid achieves in both works an aesthetic unity through a careful and sparse selection of characters, an emphasis on the relative isolation of the child, a preoccupation with the child's relationship with her mother, and the use of a distinctive narrative voice. Kincaid reflects the childlike simplicity and apparent naivety of the youthful speaker, even while she conveys through the child's voice a sophisticated vision

of her cultural milieu, her sexual awakening, her responses to nature, and her sensitivity to events, persons, and influences possessing symbolic overtones. Hypnotically talking to herself, the girl in both books speaks with directness and specificity and often makes use of parallel phrases reminiscent of Biblical poetry. The narrator is keenly receptive to sense impressions—sounds, scents, and colors—and seems to be endowed with a poet's sensibility.

In these books, transitions from everyday school and home life into the psychic are lacking as Kincaid changes abruptly from depicting realistically the Caribbean milieu to an extraordinary geography and groups of personages that fill a child's dreams and fantasies. Kincaid at the most intense crises of her protagonists' experiences approaches the mythic and archetypal in depicting the unusual and timeless aspects of the mother–daughter conflict as a continuous merging and separating of two spirits. The child in both books grows by breaking the rules dictated by her mother—rules that define the girl's role in household routines and social behavior. Some of the memorized rules which she chants are ominous: "this is how to make a good medicine for a cold; this is how to make a good medicine to throw away a child before it even becomes a child . . . this is how to bully a man; this is how a man bullies you." The young narrator in *At the Bottom of the River* parodies some of the commandments as she mischievously recites, "this is how to spit up in the air if you feel like it, and this is how to move quick so that it doesn't fall on you."

Whether she is talking to herself or to a perceived listener, the girl learns by verbalizing certain truths that she had intuitively sensed but previously could not articulate. In the first book more than in the second, the protagonist moves into the disordered and the surreal as in dreams she walks with her mother through caves, empty houses, and along the shores of the sea. She dreams of happy marriage to a red woman (her mother) who wears "skirts big enough to bury your head in" and who will always make her happy with tales that begin, "Before you were born...." In *At the Bottom of the River* the most notable explorations of the visionary and contemplative mind of the child occur in the sections entitled "Wingless," "Blackness" and "My Mother." But the child does not always drift into fantasy. At the bottom of the river of her mind, truth appears as cold, hard, and uncompromising as the rocks embedded there below the moving water. As she moves into the surreal or unconscious, she does not abandon her world of household routine, the rigors of her life at school, or her sensitivity to the details of external nature. In the midst of a visionary passage, she startles the reader with a meditative statement based upon her observation of concrete realities: "I covet the rocks and the mountains their silence."

On the closing page of *At the Bottom of the River*, the girl finds direction and substance, not as much in her visionary flights as in familiar objects: books, a chair, a table, a bowl of fruit, a bottle of milk, a flute made of wood. As she names these objects, she finds them to be reminders of human endeavor, past and present, though in themselves they are transient. She identifies herself as part of this endeavor as it betokens a never-ending flow of aspiration and creativity. That kinship determines her identity in the last analysis as a human being and as a part of nature: "I claim these things then—mine—and now feel myself grow solid and complete, my name filling up my mouth." Similarly, at the close of *Annie John*, as Annie leaves for England to become a nurse (simply because she wants to leave home and time-worn experiences), she also achieves a sense of her identity from familiar reality. She wakes the morning of her departure to see her own name written large on all her luggage and later she stands quietly on the ship and watches her mother become for her a mere dot in the distance.

—Margaret B. McDowell

* * *

KING, Francis (Henry). British. Born in Adelboden, Switzerland, 4 March 1923. Educated at Shrewsbury School; Balliol College, Oxford, B.A. 1949, M.A. 1951. Poetry reviewer, *The Listener*, London, 1945–50; worked for the British Council, 1949–63: lecturer in Florence, 1949–50, Salonika, 1950–52, and Athens 1953–57; assistant representative, Helsinki, 1957–58; regional director, Kyoto, 1959–63. Literary reviewer, 1964–78, and since 1978, theatre reviewer, *Sunday Telegraph*, London; since 1978, fiction reviewer, *Spectator*, London. Member of the Executive Committee, 1969–73, Vice-President, 1977, and President, 1978–85, English PEN; since 1986, International President, PEN. Chairman, Society of Authors, 1975–77; member of the Executive Committee, National Book League, 1980–81. Since 1977, member of the Royal Literary Fund Committee. Recipient: Maugham Award, 1952; Katherine Mansfield-Menton Prize, 1965; Arts Council bursary, 1966; *Yorkshire Post* award, 1983. Fellow, Royal Society of Literature, 1952; resigned, then re-elected, 1967. O.B.E. (Officer, Order of the British Empire), 1979; C.B.E. (Commander, Order of the British Empire), 1985. Agent: A.M. Heath, 40–42 William IV Street, London WC2N 4DD. Address: 19 Gordon Place, London W8 4JE, England.

PUBLICATIONS

Novels

To the Dark Tower. London, Home and Van Thal, 1946.
Never Again. London, Home and Van Thal, 1948.
An Air That Kills. London, Home and Van Thal, 1948.
The Dividing Stream. London, Longman, and New York, Morrow, 1951.
The Dark Glasses. London, Longman, 1954; New York, Pantheon, 1956.
The Firewalkers: A Memoir (as Frank Cauldwell). London, Murray, 1956.
The Widow. London, Longman, 1957.
The Man on the Rock. London, Longman, and New York, Pantheon, 1958.
The Custom House. London, Longman, 1961; New York, Doubleday, 1962.
The Last of the Pleasure Gardens. London, Longman, 1965.
The Waves Behind the Boat. London, Longman, 1967.
A Domestic Animal. London, Longman, 1970.
Flights (2 novellas). London, Hutchinson, 1973.
A Game of Patience. London, Hutchinson, 1974.
The Needle. London, Hutchinson, 1975; New York, Mason Charter, 1976.
Danny Hill: Memoirs of a Prominent Gentleman. London, Hutchinson, 1977.
The Action. London, Hutchinson, 1978.
Act of Darkness. London, Hutchinson, and Boston, Little Brown, 1983.
Voices in an Empty Room. London, Hutchinson, and Boston, Little Brown, 1984.

Short Stories

So Hurt and Humiliated and Other Stories. London, Longman, 1959.
The Japanese Umbrella and Other Stories. London, Longman, 1964.
The Brighton Belle and Other Stories. London, Longman, 1968.
Penguin Modern Stories 12, with others. London, Penguin, 1972.
Hard Feelings and Other Stories. London, Hutchinson, 1976.
Indirect Method and Other Stories. London, Hutchinson, 1980.
One Is a Wanderer: Selected Stories. London, Hutchinson, 1985; Boston, Little Brown, 1986.

Plays

Far East (produced Coventry, 1980).

Radio Plays: *The Prisoner*, 1967; *Corner of a Foreign Field*, 1969; *A Short Walk in Williams Park*, from a story by C.H.B. Kitchin, 1972; *Death of My Aunt*, from the novel by C.H.B. Kitchin, 1973; *Desperate Cases*, 1975.

Verse

Rod of Incantation. London, Longman, 1952.

Other

Japan, photographs by Martin Hürlimann. London, Thames and Hudson, and New York, Viking Press, 1970.
Christopher Isherwood. London, Longman, 1976.
E.M. Forster and His World. London, Thames and Hudson, and New York, Scribner, 1978.
Florence, photographs by Nicolas Sapieha. New York, Newsweek, 1982.

Editor, *Introducing Greece.* London, Methuen, 1956; revised edition, 1968.
Editor, *Collected Short Stories*, by Osbert Sitwell. London, Duckworth, 1974.
Editor, with Ronald Harwood, *New Stories 3.* London, Hutchinson, 1978.
Editor, *Prokofiev by Prokofiev: A Composer's Memoir*, translated by Guy Daniels. London, Macdonald and Jane's, 1979.
Editor, *My Sister and Myself: The Diaries of J.R. Ackerley.* London, Hutchinson, 1982.
Editor, *Writings from Japan*, by Lafcadio Hearn. London, Penguin, 1984.
Editor, *Twenty Stories: A South East Arts Collection.* London, Secker and Warburg, 1985.

*

Manuscript Collection: Humanities Research Center, University of Texas, Austin.

Critical Studies: essay by King, in *Leaving School*, London, Phoenix House, 1957; "Waves and Echoes: The Novels of Francis King" by John Mellors, in *London Magazine*, December 1975–January 1976.

Francis King comments:
Except for the period of my schooling and the war, mine has, until the last decade, always been an itinerant life. As

a child, I was brought up alternately in India and Switzerland (the country of my birth); subsequently I worked for the British Council in Italy, Greece, Egypt, Finland and Japan. This desire always to set off for another destination is reflected in my novels. Of course, certain themes in them are constant; but I have never wished to be identified with only one type of fiction. Perhaps this has harmed me in popular esteem; the public tends to like its novelists to write the same novel over and over again.

Foreign places have always provided me with imaginative stimulation and the majority of my books have foreign settings. Most English novelists, like the society from which they derive, seem to me to be too much preoccupied with differences of class, which obscure for them differences more profound between human beings. In choosing so often to write about "abroad," I have, perhaps subconsciously, attempted to avoid this class-obsession.

I believe strongly in national character, and a recurrent theme of my books is the way in which people struggle to break out of the patterns of national behaviour in which they have been imprisoned since birth.

Critics sometimes say that they find my work "depressing" and my readers sometimes ask why I never write about "nice" people or "normal" people—not surprisingly perhaps, since mine is an attitude of profound, if resigned, pessimism about the world. I do not expect people to behave consistently well, and my observation is that few of them do. But I should like to think that the tolerance and compassion that I genuinely feel are also reflected in my writing.

I have always been preoccupied with style and form. I feel that I am most successful in achieving both if the reader is unconscious of any straining for them.

In my early books, written at a period of loneliness in my own life, isolation is a recurrent theme; in my later books I see now that envy and jealousy—to my mind the least attractive of human traits—have taken over.

My biggest and most successful novels were *The Custom House* and *Act of Darkness*. The novel that comes nearest to saying what I wanted to say—and that cost me most—was *A Domestic Animal*.

*   *   *

Francis King's first novel, *To the Dark Tower*, is his most experimental. In some of the stories in *The Japanese Umbrella* he adopts Isherwood's trick of using a narrator to whom he gives his own name, and *The Firewalkers*, subtitled "a memoir," was first published under the pseudonym of Frank Cauldwell, who is also the narrator, and who first appeared as a novelist in *To the Dark Tower*. King's stress on the plurality of truth, as formulated in the early story "A True Story" (*So Hurt and Humiliated*), led him to write from both first- and third-person angles in *The Custom House* and *The Last of the Pleasure Gardens*. *The Action*, actually about a novel, seems redolent with echoes from King's previous work. The bawdy *Danny Hill*, with much linguistic humour, purports to be an 18th-century text by John Cleland and is written by King in that idiom, modernized. The very structure of *Voices in an Empty Room*, linking three separate stories of attempts at communication with the dead, mirrors death's arbitrary cut-off and residual loose ends.

The themes of separation and loss recurring throughout King's work may be traced to his second novel, *Never Again*, a moving evocation of childhood and adolescence in India and at an English prep school. In his third novel, *An Air That Kills*, there is a rare lyricism, often negated, in the spirit of

Housman's poem whence the title comes. *The Dividing Stream*, a complex novel set in Florence, is imbued with a sense of decay and the melancholy that pervades much of King's world. These moods are articulated in the stark ending of *The Dark Glasses*, as Patrick recognizes "the terrible, morbid beauty of this world." Yet the Greek setting seems to make for an easier sensual acceptance; in *The Dark Glasses* King evokes the natural beauty of Corfu, while *The Firewalkers* is a mainly happy reminiscence of a group of friends in Athens centred on the dilettante and metaphorical firewalker, Colonel Grecos. In *The Man on the Rock* King succeeds in impersonating as narrator the parasitic Spiro, a character utterly removed from the self-effacing King/Cauldwell persona. King is as skilful with the short story form as the novel, and some of the stories in his first collection, *So Hurt and Humiliated*, are set in Greece. So is the second short novel in *Flights*, "The Cure," which like the other, "The Infection," set in Hungary, has political overtones.

King's most ambitious book to date, *The Custom House*, also has political implications. In this long, complex novel he focuses on a cross-section of Japanese society, both from within and through Western eyes. King's writing is always rich in ambivalence; he found congenial material in Japanese formalism, recording "the echoes which surround events, not merely after they have taken place but also before them." Yet the novel has his characteristic intense sensualism hedged with negatives. Like the collection of short stories, *The Japanese Umbrella*, *The Waves Behind the Boat* is set in Japan, though its theme of incest and dishonesty concerns expatriates, who include the woman narrator.

Christine Cornwell in *The Widow* is outstanding among King's female portraits. The novel's opening illustrates his skill in manipulating the reader's sympathy in a few pages as he highlights alternately her unlikeable and likeable traits. His evocation of wartime London in Part II of *The Widow* is complemented by his account of civilian rural experience, chiefly through the eyes of a 17-year-old land-girl, in *A Game of Patience*. In *The Last of the Pleasure Gardens* King shows how an idiot child exacerbates beyond endurance the weaknesses in a marriage. Most of the short stories in *The Brighton Belle* are studies in decay, symbolized in the town itself. *A Domestic Animal*, about unreciprocated homosexual love, is a poignant and powerful study of sexual jealousy; the narrator's attitude to Pam recalls the narrator's attitude to Anne in *An Air That Kills*, although the novels are different in tone.

The darkness of *The Needle*, about a doctor's love for her weak brother, is expressed too in some of the stories in *Hard Feelings*. The stories in *Indirect Method* are either set abroad or involve foreigners in Britain. *The Action*, about the libel action threatened against Hazel's novel on the eve of publication, incidentally reveals much about King's understanding of the novel form; the ending, as Hazel begins a new story, is something of a writer's credo. *Act of Darkness*, set mainly in 1930's India, focuses on a child's murder apparently by someone in his family circle; it is a major novel of suspense with powerful psychological depths. *Voices in an Empty Room* shows para-normal communication as mainly fraudulent, though the only certainty is doubt.

Francis King is a master of implication, in the Forsterian tradition, and writes with unnerving precision, strength, and sensitivity.

—Val Warner

KINSELLA, W(illiam) P(atrick). Canadian. Born in Edmonton, Alberta, 25 May 1935. Educated at Eastwood High School, Edmonton, graduated 1953; University of Victoria, British Columbia, B.A. 1974; University of Iowa, Iowa City, 1976–78, M.F.A. 1978. Married 1) Myrna Salls in 1957, two children; 2) Mildred Clay in 1965 (divorced, 1978); 3) Ann Knight in 1978. Clerk, Government of Alberta, 1954–56, and manager, Retail Credit Co., 1956–61, both Edmonton; account executive, City of Edmonton, 1961–67; owner, Caesar's Italian Village restaurant, 1967–72, editor, *Martlet*, 1973–74, and cab driver, 1974–76, all Victoria, British Columbia; Assistant Professor of English, University of Calgary, Alberta, 1978–83. Since 1983, full-time writer. Recipient: *Edmonton Journal* prize, 1966; *Canadian Fiction* award, 1976; Alberta Achievement award, 1982; Houghton Mifflin Literary Fellowship, 1982; *Books in Canada* prize, 1982; Canadian Authors Association prize, 1983. Agent: Nancy Colbert, 303 Davenport Road, Toronto, Ontario M5R 1K5. Address: Box 400, White Rock, British Columbia V4B 5G3, Canada.

PUBLICATIONS

Novels

Shoeless Joe.   Boston, Houghton Mifflin, 1982.
The Iowa Baseball Confederacy.   Boston, Houghton Mifflin, 1986.

Short Stories

Dance Me Outside.   Ottawa, Oberon Press, 1977; Boston, Godine, 1985.
Scars.   Ottawa, Oberon Press, 1978.
Shoeless Joe Jackson Comes to Iowa.   Ottawa, Oberon Press, 1980.
Born Indian.   Ottawa, Oberon Press, 1981.
The Ballad of the Public Trustee.   Vancouver, Standard, 1982.
The Moccasin Telegraph and Other Indian Tales.   Toronto, Penguin, 1983; Boston, Godine, 1984; London, Arrow, 1985.
The Thrill of the Grass.   Toronto and London, Penguin, 1984; New York, Viking, 1985.
The Alligator Report.   Minneapolis, Coffee House Press, 1985.
The Fencepost Chronicles.   Toronto, Collins, 1986.

Uncollected Short Stories

"These Changing Times" (as Felicien Belzile), in *Civil Service Bulletin* (Edmonton), vol. 35, no. 9, October 1955.
"I Walk Through the Valley" (as Felicien Belzile), in *Civil Service Bulletin* (Edmonton), vol. 36, no. 1, January 1956.
"I Was a Teen-age Slumlord," in *Edmonton Journal*, 27 May 1966.
"Hofstadt's Cabin," in *Edmonton Journal*, 14 June 1966.
"The Jackhammer," in *Edmonton Journal*, 24 June 1966.
"Something Evil This Way Comes," in *Edmonton Journal*, September 1966.
"Night People Never Come Back," in *Martlet* (Victoria, British Columbia), 10 February 1972.
"White Running Shoes," in *View from the Silver Bridge*, vol. 2, no. 1, May 1972.

"Children of the Cartomancy," in *Martlet* (Victoria, British Columbia), November 1972.
"Does Anyone Know How They Make Campaign Buttons?," in *Karaki* (Victoria, British Columbia), January 1973.
"Broken Dolls" (as Leslie Smith), in *Martlet* (Victoria, British Columbia), Fall 1973.
"The Snow Leprechaun," in *This Week* (Coquitlam, British Columbia), 9 March 1974.
"Famines," (as Angie Jean Jerome), in *Martlet* (Victoria, British Columbia), Spring 1974.
"A Literary Passage at Arms; or, TX vs. BK," in *Iowa City Creative Reading Series Magazine*, Spring–Summer 1977.
"The Sundog Society," in *Wisconsin Review* (Oshkosh), vol. 14, no. 4, 1980.
"The Elevator," in *Canadian Fiction* (Vancouver), nos. 40–41, 1981.
"Something to Think About," in *Saturday Night* (Toronto), May 1981.
"Intermediaries," in *Scrivener* (Montreal), Spring 1982.
"Mother Tucker's Yellow Duck," in *Rainshadow*, edited by Ron Smith and Stephen Guppy.   Vancouver, Oolichan, 1983.
"The Bear Went over the Mountain," in *Vancouver Magazine*, March 1984.
"Indian Joe," in *Prism International* (Vancouver), Fall 1984.
"Dancing," in *West Coast Review* (Burnaby, British Columbia), October 1984.
"Real Indians," in *Waves* (Downsview, Ontario), vol. 13, no. 4, 1985.
"The Performance," in *Descant* (Toronto), Summer 1985.
"Being Invisible," in *Western Living* (Vancouver), August 1985.
"The Truck," in *Matrix* (Lennoxville, Quebec), Fall 1985.

*

Bibliography: *W.P. Kinsella: A Partially-Annotated Bibliographic Checklist (1953–1983)* by Ann Knight, Iowa City, Across, 1983.

Manuscript Collection: National Library of Canada, Ottawa.

Critical Studies: "Down and Out in Montreal, Windsor, and Wetaskiwin" by Anthony Brennan, in *Fiddlehead* (Fredericton, New Brunswick), Fall 1977; "Don't Freeze Off Your Leg" Spring 1979, and "Say It Ain't So, Joe" Spring–Summer 1981, both by Frances W. Kaye, in *Prairie Schooner* (Lincoln, Nebraska); article by Brian E. Burtch, in *Canadian Journal of Sociology* (Edmonton), Winter 1980; essay by Anne Blott, in *Fiddlehead* (Fredericton, New Brunswick), July 1982; Marjorie Retzleff, in *NeWest Review* (Edmonton), October 1984; "Search for the Unflawed Diamond" by Don Murray, in *NeWest Review* (Edmonton), January 1985.

*   *   *

Before the publication of his only novel, W. P. Kinsella had already written extensively about baseball in four short story collections. *Shoeless Joe* is preeminently a paean to baseball as it was once played when it was the national pastime, before inflated salaries, players disputes, and artificial turf. The novel is almost studiously old-fashioned in its unabashed lyricism and unmitigated affirmation of life and love. *Shoeless Joe* has nothing in common with either the modernist or postmodernist traditions, and very little with the realist tradition. It posits the possibility of achieving the Whitmanesque dream, but denies that *Democratic Vistas* had ever been written. Its antecedent is J. D. Salinger's *The Catcher in the Rye*, but only Holden Caulfield's vision of a world redeemed through his sister Phoebe's innocence. *Shoeless Joe* is, in many ways, a plea for a return to the Edenic dream in which the serpent appears only to be crushed. Although Kinsella's novel often seems to be all surface, it can be read on the levels of love story, tall tale, and myth.

Shoeless Joe affirms the absolute redemptive power of human love. Ray Kinsella, the narrator and main character, makes love to his wife Annie who "sings to me, love songs in tongues, bird songs thrilling and brilliant as morning," and he marvels that he "can love her so much ... that [their] love puts other things in perspective." (The reader may suspect that Kinsella owes more to E.E. Cummings's views of love and his detestation of technology than he does to any novelist.) Above all, baseball has the power to unite in love those estranged by time and emotional distance. Eddie Scissons, an old player, advises Ray that to be reconciled with his dead father he must realize that they "both love the game. Make that your common ground, and nothing else will matter."

But it is baseball mythologized and raised to the levels of magic and religion that has the transcendent power. As a Moses of the midwest, Ray hears a voice tell him "If you build it, he will come"; the "he" is Shoeless Joe Jackson, a member of the infamous 1919 Black Sox team that fixed the World Series. So bidden, Ray erects a baseball stadium, replete with bleachers and lights, on his Iowa farm, which is soon peopled with the entire Chicago team that nightly play their opponents on a field of planted grass, undefiled by the artificial turf of modern playing fields. But only those who firmly believe in magic and love the game can see the players or the action, when "all the cosmic tumblers have clicked into place and the universe appears for a few seconds, or hours, and shows you what is possible." Ray's twin brother, Richard, is not privy to the shades because his "eyes are blind to the magic," and he must ask Ray to "teach me how to see."

At times Kinsella puts too great a burden on baseball's redemptive power by giving it too many of the trappings of religion and myth. J. D. Salinger (whom Ray, obeying the voice, has kidnapped from his home in New Hampshire, and who soon becomes Ray's mythic accomplice) eulogizes that people will "watch the game, and it will be as if they have knelt in front of a faith healer, or dipped themselves in magic waters where a saint once rose like a serpent and cast benedictions to the wind like peach petals." Playing baseball is like being "engaged in a pagan ceremony," and as Eddie "Kid" Scissons says, "I know there are many who are troubled, anxious, worried, insecure. What is the cure? ... The answer is in the word, and baseball is the word," and those who heed the message "will be changed by the power of the living word." The game becomes too freighted with symbolism to survive the attributions. Then there is the question of evil, which in this Garden takes two forms. One is Ray's wife's brother who contrives to buy Ray's land and plans to turn it into part of a vast computerized farm, destroying the stadium and playing field. Needless to say, his brother-in-law is foiled; technology cannot prevail against the pastoral ideal. The second is Eddie Scissons who has lied about his baseball triumphs and is punished by striking out in a game he is allowed to play as a returned youth; the serpent head cane he fondles is too intrusive and obvious a symbol.

But *Shoeless Joe* has a great many strengths, in particular its sustained lyricism and Kinsella's love for the literal game and its authentic rituals. It is worth noting that in his recent short story collection *The Thrill of the Grass* Kinsella continues to write about baseball; his lyricism is unabated, but he usually avoids the excesses that mar *Shoeless Joe.*

—Peter Desy

KNEBEL, Fletcher. American. Born in Dayton, Ohio, 1 October 1911. Educated at Miami University, Oxford, Ohio, B.A. 1934 (Phi Beta Kappa). Served in the United States Navy, 1942–45: Lieutenant. Married Laura Bergquist in 1965; Constance Wood in 1985; one son and one daughter from earlier marriage. Reporter, Coatesville *Record*, Pennsylvania, 1934, Chattanooga *News*, Tennessee, 1934–35, and Toledo *News-Bee*, Ohio, 1935; reporter, 1936, and Washington correspondent, 1937–50, Cleveland *Plain Dealer*; Washington correspondent, 1950–64, and columnist ("Potomac Fever"), 1951–64, Cowles Publications; writer for *Look* magazine, New York, 1950–71. Recipient: Sigma Delta Chi award, for reporting, 1955. D.L.: Miami University, 1964; D.LL.: Drake University, Des Moines, Iowa, 1968. Address: 1070 Oilipuu Place, Honolulu, Hawaii 96825, U.S.A.

PUBLICATIONS

Novels

Seven Days in May, with Charles W. Bailey II. New York, Harper, and London, Weidenfeld and Nicolson, 1962.
Convention, with Charles W. Bailey II. New York, Harper, and London, Weidenfeld and Nicolson, 1964.
Night of Camp David. New York, Harper, and London, Weidenfeld and Nicolson, 1965.
The Zinzin Road. New York, Doubleday, 1966; London, W.H. Allen, 1967.
Vanished. New York, Doubleday, and London, W.H. Allen, 1968.
Trespass. New York, Doubleday, and London, W.H. Allen, 1969.
Dark Horse. New York, Doubleday, 1972; London, Hodder and Stoughton, 1973.
The Bottom Line. New York, Doubleday, 1974; London, Hodder and Stoughton, 1975.
Dave Sulkin Cares! New York, Doubleday, 1978.
Crossing in Berlin. New York, Doubleday, 1981; London, Deutsch, 1982.
Poker Game. New York, Doubleday, 1983; London, Hale, 1984.

Other

No High Ground, with Charles W. Bailey II. New York, Harper, and London, Weidenfeld and Nicolson, 1960.

*

Manuscript Collection: Mugar Memorial Library, Boston University.

Critical Study: in *New York Times Book Review*, January 1968.

Fletcher Knebel comments:

My novels are basically suspense stories with a major social or political theme in the background. The first aim is always to tell a good story, but I hope the message comes through.

*   *   *

Fletcher Knebel, a former Washington, D.C., journalist, has written several political novels since 1962, the first two written with Charles W. Bailey, a former colleague. He is recognized as one of the foremost writers of the political suspense thriller, combining his journalistic skill with well-constructed plots to produce popular and entertaining accounts of fictionalized but plausible crises in American politics. Knebel is at his best in the depiction of behind-the-scenes action, and the vivid immediacy of his plots must be accounted as a main element of appeal to his audience. His extensive knowledge of the Washington scene gives him the ability to delineate the surface details of his stories with verisimilitude, and his journalistic experience has aided him in developing a direct descriptive prose style. His characters are often vividly drawn, particularly members of the press or professional politicians, although some reviewers have criticized him for over-dependence upon the stock characters or for caricaturing those characters, such as military or intelligence chiefs, that he does not like.

Knebel's plots consistently portray his liberal political views, particularly in his protagonists' dependence upon rational problem-solving and his antagonists' Machiavellian disregard for democratic procedures. His books are concerned with such problems as a projected military takeover of the government, a utopian Presidential plan for peace, mental illness as a Presidential disability, black terrorism, and the political nomination process. He is consistently interested in such issues as the acquisition and maintenance of power, the Presidency as an institution, and conspiracy as a political tool. In his books both protagonists and antagonists conspire secretly to accomplish their aims, indicating to the reader that this is the way goals are reached in American politics.

The major shortcomings of his novels are inherent in their conception. If Knebel sincerely believes in the dangers that he warns against and desires to alert his readers to possible pitfalls in the present system, as he has indicated he does, then his choice of the political thriller as the vehicle for his jeremiads renders those warnings, to some extent, hollow. Because he relies, somewhat simplistically, upon the rationality and good will of his main characters to solve the significant and overwhelming problems with which they are faced, he runs the risk of trivializing those problems for the purpose of fictional excitement. Ultimately, it is difficult to see the seriousness of the threats when the books ritually exorcise them in the resolution of the action, reassuring the reader of the essential soundness of his political system. Knebel does well in reporting the events of his stories; he is too competent a journalist to do otherwise. But in his attempts to explore the dilemma of the sensitive man of good will in the face of political apocalypse, he succumbs to the essential optimism of popular fiction, and, in so doing, succeeds in entertaining but fails to develop the ultimate implications of the messages he professes to deliver.

—Kay J. Mussell

———————

KNOWLES, John. American. Born in Fairmont, West Virginia, 16 September 1926. Educated at Phillips Exeter Academy, Exeter, New Hampshire, graduated 1945; Yale University, New Haven, Connecticut, B.A. 1949. Reporter, Hartford *Courant*, Connecticut, 1950–52; free-lance writer, 1952–56; associate editor, *Holiday* magazine, Philadelphia, 1956–60. Writer-in-Residence, University of North Carolina, Chapel Hill, 1963–64, and Princeton University, New Jersey, 1968–69. Recipient: Rosenthal Foundation award, 1961; Faulkner Foundation award, 1961; National Association of Independent Schools award, 1961. Address: P.O. Box 939, Southampton, New York 11968, U.S.A.

PUBLICATIONS

Novels

A Separate Peace. London, Secker and Warburg, 1959; New York, Macmillan, 1960.
Morning in Antibes. New York, Macmillan, and London, Secker and Warburg, 1962.
Indian Summer. New York, Random House, and London, Secker and Warburg, 1966.
The Paragon. New York, Random House, 1971.
Spreading Fires. New York, Random House, 1974.
Vein of Riches. Boston, Little Brown, 1978.
Peace Breaks Out. New York, Holt Rinehart, 1981.
A Stolen Past. New York, Holt Rinehart, 1983; London, Constable, 1984.

Short Stories

Phineas: Six Stories. New York, Random House, 1968.

Other

Double Vision: American Thoughts Abroad. New York, Macmillan, and London, Secker and Warburg, 1964.

*

Manuscript Collection: Beinecke Library, Yale University, New Haven, Connecticut.

*   *   *

John Knowles writes, in general, not about his home turf but about New England or Europe. Only one novel, *Vein of Riches*, and that not his best, is about West Virginia, his childhood home. His fictional world is a cultivated, cosmopolitan, somewhat jaded world. He is a fine craftsman, a fine stylist, alert to the infinite resources and nuances of language. Yet, as he says, he is one of the live-around-the-world people, rootless, nomadic, and making a virtue of that rootlessness. He is a connoisseur of different cultures but master of none—or perhaps of one only, the sub-culture of the New England prep school. One defect of this very cosmopolitanism is the feeling of alienation that Knowles feels from his fictional world. As a veteran of many cultures he finds this trait an advantage when he writes graceful travel essays for *Holiday* magazine. He finds it a disadvantage when he wishes to create for *Vein of Riches* a thoroughly credible fictional character.

A Separate Peace, his first novel, is also by far his most important novel. It is a prep school novel about Gene Forrester and his close friend, Finney, and the studied set of ambiguities and ambivalences arising from the intense and complex relationship between the two. Gene, beset by a love-hate attitude toward Finney, causes Finney to suffer a serious injury and still later is the putative cause of his death from a second injury. But Finney's death is preceded by Gene's reconciliation with him, a redemptive act which to some degree assuages his feeling of guilt. Thus, the novel recounts Gene's initiation into manhood and into both worldly and moral maturity. Fifteen years after Finney's death, Gene returns to Devon to conclude the novel by thinking—"Nothing endures, not a tree, not love, not even a death by violence." What does endure is the extraordinary popularity of this novel with prep school and college students.

Knowles's later books display his writing grace but not the inner strength of *A Separate Peace*. His second novel, *Morning in Antibes*, has a pot-pourri of comatose characters revolving about the deracinated Nicholas Petrovich Bodine in a kind of latter day *The Sun Also Rises*; it lacks, however, the Hemingway tone, atmosphere, and taut dialogue. The people are phony and maybe the novel is too. The long passivity of Nick makes him seem to move under water. The novel fails in characterization.

Indian Summer follows Cleet Kinsolving, World War II vet, in his jousting with his friend, Neil Reardon, Irish Catholic and heir to multi-millions (seemingly modelled on John Kennedy). Cleet's conviction, which he shares with T.S. Eliot's Sweeney, is that each man needs to do someone in. A good deal of cultural primitivism is spread about, but again the characters are unconvincing. *The Paragon* describes Lou Colfax, a brilliant, handsome sophomore in love with a beautiful actress four years older than he. In spite of the Yale ambience and a plethora of cocktail parties and beautiful people the intended "Gatsby glamour" never comes to this novel. Perhaps because we miss the "yellow cocktail music" of *Gatsby*, perhaps because the characters remain partially developed. *Spreading Fires*, a brief novel of decadence and homosexual vagaries set in the south of France, deals with madness, potential madness, and the low life of the upper class.

Vein of Riches is a study of the great coal boom of 1910–1924 in a West Virginia town. Knowles shows a house, a family, and an industry, and the interactions of the three; he employs one of the central themes of American fiction, money versus land. It is a pleasant novel but the characters again are given perfunctory treatment. We do not have the empathy and zest that bubbled up from *A Separate Peace*. Coal does not interest Knowles the way New England prep school life did.

Peace Breaks Out is set in Devon School, New Hampshire, and is an attempt by Knowles to revisit the scene of his greatest fictional success, *A Separate Peace*. The parallels between the two novels are very strong: the place is the same school, the time is five years later and the crux of the plot is the wrongful death of a disliked schoolmate, Hochschwender, who dies of heart failure after being tortured by four of his classmates. Again, as in *A Separate Peace*, there is a legacy of guilt suffered by the four survivors. Knowles is much at home in the world of the private school and depicts it with grace and clarity. But it has all been done before in his earlier and better novel and thus lacks freshness and spontaneity. Many readers will find the excessive hypocrisy of Wexford, the ringleader of the torturers, a little unrealistic. This novel will not achieve the status of *A Separate Peace*, although it is well crafted and knowledgeably written.

In summary, Knowles is intelligent, highly literate, a skilled and sensitive craftsman and stylist. He is knowledgeable of the world, tolerant, a connoisseur of many cultures. He possesses in his own person that bifocal vision which he praises in *Double Vision*. He has created one extraordinary novel, *A Separate Peace*, which for many young people has truly caught the *zeitgeist*. There is also a negative side. Every novel but his first suffers from one fundamental defect—the characters are not plausible. There is not a single memorable woman character in his fiction and only two male characters—Gene Forrester and Phineas—that stay in our memory. The result is an imperfect empathy and a resultant lack of reader interest. In general his male protagonists are inert, deracinated, ambivalent, depersonalized, dehumanized. Why does Knowles create such types? Only he can answer this definitively, but perhaps he gives us the answer in his book *Double Vision* where he argues *against roots* and for rootlessness, the new form of nomadism. "We need to be nomadic and uprooted today," he maintains. As he says, he is not regional, does not come from a town or a city. He is one of the live-around-the-world people. So he is and so are the characters in his books. This is his fundamental failure and it is a major one. He may yet overcome this and give us again a convincing, brilliant novel as was *A Separate Peace*.

—Ruel E. Foster

KOCH, C(hristopher) J(ohn). Australian. Born in Hobart, Tasmania, 16 July 1932. Educated at Clemes College; St. Virgil's Christian Brothers College; Hobart State High School, 1946–50; University of Tasmania, Hobart, 1951–54, B.A. 1954. Has one son. Until 1972, radio producer, Australian Broadcasting Commission, Sydney. Recipient: *The Age* Book of the Year Award, 1978; Australian National Book Award, 1979. Agent: Curtis Brown, 162–168 Regent Street, London W1R 5TA, England. Address: 7 Jersey Street, Turramurra, Sydney, New South Wales 2074, Australia.

PUBLICATIONS

Novels

The Boys in the Island. London, Hamish Hamilton, 1958; revised edition, Sydney, Angus and Robertson, 1974.
Across the Sea Wall. London, Heinemann, 1965; revised edition, Sydney and London, Angus and Robertson, 1982.
The Year of Living Dangerously. Melbourne, Nelson, and London, Joseph, 1978; New York, St. Martin's Press, 1979.
The Doubleman. London, Chatto and Windus, 1985; New York, McGraw-Hill, 1986.

Other

Chinese Journey, with Nicholas Hasluck. Fremantle, Western Australia, Fremantle Arts Centre Press, 1985.

*

Critical Studies: "In the Shadow of Patrick White" by Vincent Buckley, in *Meanjin* (Melbourne), no. 2, 1961; "The Novels of C.J. Koch" by Robyn Claremont, in *Quadrant* (Sydney), 1980; "Asia, Europe and Australian Identity: The Novels of Christopher Koch," May 1982, and "Asia and the Contemporary Australian Novel," October 1984, both by Helen Tiffin, in *Australian Literary Studies* (St. Lucia, Queensland); "*Pour mieux sauter*: Christopher Koch's Novels in Relation to White, Stow and the Quest for a Post-colonial Fiction," in *World Literature Written in English* (Guelph, Ontario), 1983, and "Living

Dangerously: Christopher Koch and Cultural Tradition," in *Quadrant* (Sydney), September 1985, both by Paul Sharrad; "Oedipus in the Tropics: A Psychoanalytical Interpretation of C.J. Koch's *The Year of Living Dangerously*" by Xavier Pons, in *Colonisations* (Toulouse), 1985; "Expanding Otherworld: The Achievement of C.J. Koch" by Andrew Sant, in *The Age Monthly Review* (Melbourne), June 1985; "The Envenomed Dreams of C.J. Koch" by Laurie Clancy, in *Island* (Hobart, Tasmania), Winter 1985.

C.J. Koch comments:

I began by writing verse, but gave my main attention to the novel from the age of 19. I believe that the novel can be a poetic vehicle, and that it has taken over the function of narrative poetry in this century. By this I do not mean that it uses the techniques of verse; nor do I mean that it can replace the lyric. But I would place such works as *Heart of Darkness*, *A Passage to India*, and *The Alexandria Quartet* in a class of their own—what I am forced to call "poetic novels"—is that they work through metaphor as much as through narrative: their metaphor and symbolism being more extended than that of verse. To such novels the same amount of time and reworking must be given as a poet gives to verse. Where a poet concentrates on metre, the poetic novelist concentrates on cadence and resonance. To me this is the summit of the novelist's art, the only goal worth aiming for.

My first two novels were youthful and over-written. I have cut and revised both, and am now more satisfied with them. I don't expect to do this again, since I feel that I reached the stage of mastering my craft with *The Year of Living Dangerously*. Poets and some novelists have reserved the right to revise youthful work, and I see no reason why a novelist should not do the same, if he thinks the work worth preserving. I admire John Fowles for doing this with *The Magus*.

Two things preoccupy me as a novelist: the way in which many people search for a world just outside normal reality; and dualities: the dualities that run through both the human spirit and the world itself. It is the effort to reconcile these contradictions that makes for the pathos and drama I am interested in. Perhaps an Australian is attuned to duality more than some other writers, since he comes from a country born of Europe, but lying below Asia.

*   *   *

C.J. Koch (who originally signed himself Christopher Koch) had his first poem accepted when he was 17 and still at school and began his first novel when he was only 19. He wrote two novels which were well received commercially and critically but was then silent until, at the age of 40, he left his senior position at the Australian Broadcasting Commission to devote himself full-time to writing. Since then, he has published two novels and substantially revised his first two books; he sees his earlier work as being marred by over-writing, and the changes are mostly in the direction of cutting and making the prose more spare. These second versions are the only ones the author wishes to survive.

Koch's concerns in all four novels remain remarkably unified, as does the imagery and symbolism through which he explores them. He is especially preoccupied with the nature of reality and illusion and the relationship between them. Subordinate to this, but also important, is the Conradian question of whether it is not, after all, necessary to live by illusion if one is to live at all: waking up and growing up are, for

Koch's earlier and younger characters, especially, painful experiences. Adulthood is a condition to be feared: "They were growing up. It was what Shane had seen, before any of them. It was a thing that happened when you did not want it, and sooner than you expected," the protagonist of *The Boys in the Island* thinks, as he ponders on a fellow adolescent who is driven to suicide by exactly that realisation.

Whatever the changes made to *The Boys in the Island*, the novel still retains very much the feel of a young man's book. It tells the story of a sensitive young boy from the age of six (in 1936) through his school days and adolescence to his final, reluctant initiation into early manhood. Francis falls in love with a young girl who suddenly, heartbreakingly, abandons him. He fails his exams and travels from Tasmania to Melbourne, where he becomes involved in a meaningless life of petty crime. Then the suicide of a friend and his own near-death in a car crash send him back to his home to reassess his life and accept unprotestingly what the author calls "the iron bonds of his imminent adulthood." Despite the familiarity of the material, Koch's keen ear for colloquial speech, his sensuous command of natural detail, and the delicate restraint with which his understated prose conveys the boy's confusion and distress give the novel a fresh and poignant flavour.

Across the Sea Wall opens with Robert O'Brien, a 29-year-old journalist, looking back over an affair he had had six years ago. Fleeing from an imminent marriage and the terrors of the life of a staid suburbanite working for his future father-in-law, O'Brien and a schoolhood friend take a boat to Naples. En route he falls in love with Ilsa Kalnins and they skip the boat at Ceylon. But eventually O'Brien discovers that he is a suburbanite after all. He cannot accept the challenge of Ilsa's love or believe in its sincerity against the facts which his friends bring against Ilsa's character and returns to Australia. Two years later she turns up in Sydney and they make plans to marry but once again O'Brien abandons her. In its original form *Across the Sea Wall* is over-written—the descriptions of India in particular, finely done though they are, go on much too long. But the novel has many shrewd touches of characterisation and the same sensitivity in dealing with the impact of love on the uninitiated that marked Koch's first novel.

The Year of Living Dangerously is set in Indonesia in 1965, the last year of Sukarno's regime. The Sukarno of this novel is a man who seemed originally to embody the hopes and dreams of his people (as well as in particular an Australian-Chinese dwarf named Billy Kwan who is in the country as a press photographer) but who now has lost himself in grandiose schemes and the pursuit of private gratification. Unknowingly, a coup is being prepared against him and it is this that provides the spectacular climax to the novel. Slowly, as Billy begins to see through Sukarno, his idealistic allegiance to and hope in a saviour begin to switch towards Guy Hamilton, the journalist who has been sent out to replace Billy's previous boss. Once again, the novel is told in the first person, this time by a narrator identified only as "Cookie" or by the initials he supplies to his occasional footnotes, R.J.C. Through the use of diaries, speaking through the voices of various characters, using purloined documents from Billy Kwan's private files, speculating and inventing when he cannot know for certain, the narrator builds up layer upon layer of texture upon the basic structure of the narrative. At the end Koch tries, unfashionably and audaciously, to suggest Hamilton's final redemption and capacity to love as he ascends into insight via partial blindness.

The central character in *The Doubleman* is Richard Miller, a thoughtful complex man, an observer rather than a participant in life. His tendency to retreat into himself is exacerbated by the fact that he contracts poliomyelitis as a child, is dependent on crutches for a long time, and develops a heavy psychological dependence on worlds of fantasy and illusion. Although barred from an active physical life he is drawn towards his athletic cousin Brian Brady, who is both simpler and more adventurous than himself. Miller leaves his native Tasmania and follows Brady and his friend Darcy Burr to the Mainland where he pursues a career as a radio actor (illusion again) and the other two form a musical group. When the three men come together again, it is in Sydney several years later. Miller is now a successful radio producer, moving into television, Burr, Brady, and eventually Miller's émigré wife Katrin form a folk group called Thomas and the Rymers and it is inevitable that he will become entangled in the complex moral and ethical choices that confront Koch's protagonists sooner or later.

Like *The Year of Living Dangerously*, the novel is compelling reading; its narrative power is intense and firmly sustained. Koch's finely sensuous imagination can conjure up the burning, windless atmosphere of a Sydney summer as skilfully as the cold, haunted isolation of the Tasmania of his boyhood and adolescence. As with his previous novel, comparisons with Graham Greene come to mind—the superb sense of place and atmosphere, the conviction of the ambiguous and double-edged nature of the quality of innocence—and in fact Greene has expressed his admiration for the novel. Koch is a writer who has something fundamentally serious to say and who brings his characters subtly but remorselessly to the point where they have to question the basis on which they have constructed their lives.

—Laurie Clancy

KOPS, Bernard. British. Born in London, 28 November 1926. Educated in London elementary schools to age 13. Married Erica Gordon in 1956; four children. Has worked as a docker, chef, salesman, waiter, lift man, and barrow boy. Writer-in-Residence, London Borough of Hounslow, 1980–82; Lecturer in Drama, Spiro Institute, 1984–85. Recipient: Arts Council bursary 1957, 1975; C. Day Lewis Fellowship, 1980. Agent: David Higham Associates, 5–8 Lower John Street, London W1R 4HA. Address: Flat 1, 35 Canfield Gardens, London N.W.6, England.

PUBLICATIONS

Novels

Awake for Mourning. London, MacGibbon and Kee, 1958.
Motorbike. London, New English Library, 1962.
Yes from No-Man's Land. London, MacGibbon and Kee, 1965; New York, Coward McCann, 1966.
The Dissent of Dominick Shapiro. London, MacGibbon and Kee, 1966; New York, Coward McCann, 1967.
By the Waters of Whitechapel. London, Bodley Head, 1969; New York, Norton, 1970.
The Passionate Past of Gloria Gaye. London, Secker and Warburg, 1971; New York, Norton, 1972.
Settle Down Simon Katz. London, Secker and Warburg, 1973.
Partners. London, Secker and Warburg, 1975.
On Margate Sands. London, Secker and Warburg, 1978.

Plays

The Hamlet of Stepney Green (produced Oxford, 1957; London and New York, 1958). London, Evans, 1959.
Goodbye World (produced Guildford, Surrey, 1959).
Change for the Angel (produced London, 1960).
The Dream of Peter Mann (produced Edinburgh, 1960). London, Penguin, 1960.
Enter Solly Gold, music by Stanley Myers (produced Wellingborough, Northamptonshire, and Los Angeles, 1962; London, 1970). Published in *Satan, Socialites, and Solly Gold: Three New Plays from England*, New York, Coward McCann, 1961; in *Four Plays*, 1964.
Home Sweet Honeycomb (broadcast, 1962). Included in *Four Plays*, 1964.
The Lemmings (broadcast, 1963). Included in *Four Plays*, 1964.
Stray Cats and Empty Bottles (televised, 1964; produced London, 1967).
Four Plays (includes *The Hamlet of Stepney Green, Enter Solly Gold, Home Sweet Honeycomb, The Lemmings*). London, MacGibbon and Kee, 1964.
The Boy Who Wouldn't Play Jesus (for children; produced London, 1965). Published in *Eight Plays: Book 1*, edited by Malcolm Stuart Fellows, London, Cassell, 1965; Chicago, Dramatic Publishing Company, n.d.
David, It Is Getting Dark (produced Rennes, France, 1970). Paris, Gallimard, 1970.
It's a Lovely Day Tomorrow, with John Goldschmidt (televised, 1975; produced London, 1976).
More Out Than In (produced on tour and London, 1980).
Ezra (produced London, 1981).
Simon at Midnight (broadcast, 1982; produced London, 1985).

Radio Plays: *Home Sweet Honeycomb*, 1962; *The Lemmings*, 1963; *Born in Israel*, 1963; *The Dark Ages*, 1964; *Israel: The Immigrant*, 1964; *Bournemouth Nights*, 1979; *I Grow Old, I Grow Old*, 1979; *Over the Rainbow*, 1980; *Simon at Midnight*, 1982; *Trotsky Was My Father*, 1984.

Television Plays: *I Want to Go Home*, 1963; *Stray Cats and Empty Bottles*, 1964; *The Lost Years of Brian Hooper*, 1967; *Alexander the Greatest*, 1971; *Just One Kid*, 1974; *Why the Geese Shrieked*, and *The Boy Philosopher*, from stories by Isaac Bashevis Singer, 1974; *It's a Lovely Day Tomorrow*, 1975; *Moss*, 1975; *Rocky Marciano Is Dead*, 1976; *Night Kids*, 1983.

Verse

Poems. London, Bell and Baker Press, 1955.
Poems and Songs. Northwood, Middlesex, Scorpion Press, 1958.
An Anemone for Antigone. Lowestoft, Suffolk, Scorpion Press, 1959.
Erica, I Want to Read You Something. Lowestoft, Suffolk, Scorpion Press, and New York, Walker, 1967.
For the Record. London, Secker and Warburg, 1971.

Other

The World Is a Wedding (autobiography). London, MacGibbon and Kee, 1963; New York, Coward McCann, 1964.
Neither Your Honey nor Your Sting: An Offbeat History of the Jews. London, Robson, 1985.

Editor, *Poetry Hounslow*.   London, Hounslow Civic Centre, 1981.

*

Manuscript Collections: University of Texas, Austin; Indiana University, Bloomington.

*   *   *

The novels of Bernard Kops are an extension of his work as poet and playwright. His prose is rhythmic, almost ritualistic, and his plots unfold through dialogue. He is concerned with Jewishness, with the Jew as outsider to the world at large, and as a trapped insider in the claustrophobic atmosphere of the tightly knit Jewish family in which a child can find it almost impossible to grow up. So 16-year-old Dominick in *The Dissent of Dominick Shapiro* is driven to run away from home and join a collection of drop-outs protesting against established society; and in *By the Waters of Whitechapel* Aubrey, at 35, can only free himself from his financial and emotional dependency on his mother by indulging in far-fetched fantasies of a prospective career which will bring him wealth and fame.

These goals have indeed been realised by the successful Jewish businessman, Daniel Klayman, in *Partners*, but his achievement leads to madness. At the very height of his powers, while the house-warming celebrations for his new St. John's Wood home are in progress, he goes crazy. Lionel is his partner in lunacy, a projected *doppelgänger*, who pushes him into killing his new neighbour's dog, and which eventually engineers the situation which makes him responsible for the death of his beloved son, Zachary. Until that moment, despite the disastrous party, Daniel manages to disguise his madness by running away from his wife and family, and by pretending that Lionel is a real person, who is going to become a partner in his business and so relieve him of the stress and strain which has caused his strange behaviour.

The lengths that the mad will go to in attempts to hide their condition is the theme of Kops's most mature novel, *On Margate Sands*. Here he abandons his Jewish concern for one which affects the whole of society, and which is even more urgent in Britain now than it was eight years ago when this novel was published. He wrote his study of five former patients of a psychiatric hospital in the light of the 1975 Parliamentary White Paper on the revised services to the mentally ill as a result of new drug treatments. Because their sickness can be more or less controlled by "Happy tabs" as their warden landlady calls them, Brian, Larry, Dolores, Buzz, and Michelle can exist in sheltered accommodation outside the hospital.

On Margate Sands should be compulsory reading for any planners concerned with the present widespread closure of psychiatric hospitals, who still believe that "Community care" is anything more than a socially acceptable phrase. Kops's confused characters experience the reality of being "post-mad" in a society that is both fearful and uncaring. The owners of the run-down seaside hotel in which they are housed are clearly on to a money-making enterprise, squeezing their sick lodgers into cramped rooms, and kicking them out of the house during the daylight hours. The five of them walk the streets and lounge on the beach, and the "pre-mad" citizens of Margate and the frenzied holidaymakers do their best to ignore them.

Yet this is not simply a novel of social concern. It is one which could only have been written by a poet, for it demands that the reader experience the simultaneous levels of rational thought and irrational emotional response that lead to the bizarre and anti-social behaviour of the insane. Like most of Kops's characters, Brian, the most integrated of the quintet, is a middle-aged man still in thrall to his parents, even though they are long dead. His emotional life stopped at the age of seven; and although he is both intellectually aware and well-read (the novel's title comes from a quotation from T.S. Eliot with which he is familiar—"On Margate Sands/I can connect/Nothing with nothing") he is incapable of controlling the violent impulses that push him back into his past. Yet he is capable of a real, non-sexual affection for the adolescent boy, Buzz, and is seriously concerned when the lad runs off with a group of drop-outs, who can be compared with the hippies that Dominick linked up with in the previous novel. In Brian's estimation, and in that of his creator, the Alternative Society offers its "ragged and self-indulgent" adherents a life that is no better than the killing waste of time experienced by former psychiatric patients at the mercy of the community.

Despite his wretched and crazy behaviour, Brian has courage, determination and an ability to appreciate reality and the cruelty of the machine age. In a lyrical, rural passage, the old man Larry recalls family holidays in the Kent hop fields; so all five go off in search of the farm where he spent those childhood, summer days. Of course it has been mechanised, and this abrupt encounter with present reality is the fulcrum of the novel. His companions return to Margate, but Brian goes off on his own, tablet-less, on a quest for his lost sister and a sane and normal life. It cannot be achieved. In a state far worse than the one in which he set out he returns to Margate beach. His story of tragic waste is repeated in thousands of case studies, but it takes a poet to enable the "pre-mad" to enter the turbulent, sad world of the "post-mad."

—Shirley Toulson

KOSINSKI, Jerzy (Nikodem). American. Born in Lodz, Poland, 14 June 1933; emigrated to the United States in 1957; became citizen, 1965. Educated at the University of Lodz, 1950–55, M.A. in political science 1953, M.A. in history 1955; Columbia University, New York (Ford Foundation Fellow), 1958–64; New School for Social Research, New York, 1962–65. Married Mary Hayward Weir in 1962 (died, 1968). Ski instructor, Zakopane, Poland, winters 1950–56; Aspirant (graduate assistant), Polish Academy of Science, Warsaw, 1955–57; visiting researcher, Lomosov University, Moscow, 1957; laborer, truck driver, chauffeur, and projectionist on arriving in U.S.A.; Fellow, Center for Advanced Studies, Wesleyan University, Middletown, Connecticut, 1968–69; Senior Fellow, Council for the Humanities, and Visiting Lecturer, Princeton University, New Jersey, 1969–70; Professor of English Prose and Criticism, School of Drama, and Resident Fellow, Davenport College, Yale University, New Haven, Connecticut, 1970–73. Photographer: individual show—Crooked Circle Gallery, Warsaw, 1957. President, PEN American Center, 1973–75. Member of the Executive Board, National Writers Club; Director, International League for Human Rights, 1973–79. Recipient: Polish Academy of Science grant, 1955; Foreign Book Prize (France), 1966; Guggenheim fellowship, 1967; National Book Award, 1969; American Academy award, 1970; Yale University John Golden Fellowship in Playwriting, 1970; Brith Sholom Humanitarian Freedom Award, 1974; American Civil Liberties Union First Amendment Award, 1978; Writers Guild of America award, for screenplay, 1979; Polonia Media award, 1980;

BAFTA award, for screenplay, 1981; Spertus College Humanitarian Award, 1982. Doctor of Hebrew Letters: Spertus College, 1982. Address: Scientia-Factum, 60 West 57th Street, New York, New York 10019, U.S.A.

PUBLICATIONS

Novels

The Painted Bird.   Boston, Houghton Mifflin, 1965; London, W.H. Allen, 1966; revised edition, New York, Modern Library, 1970.
Steps.   New York, Random House, 1968; London, Bodley Head, 1969.
Being There.   New York, Harcourt Brace, and London, Bodley Head, 1971.
The Devil Tree.   New York, Harcourt Brace, and London, Hart Davis MacGibbon, 1973; revised edition, New York, St. Martin's Press, 1981; London, Arrow, 1982.
Cockpit.   Boston, Houghton Mifflin, and London, Hutchinson, 1975.
Blind Date.   Boston, Houghton Mifflin, 1977; London, Hutchinson, 1978.
Passion Play.   New York, St. Martin's Press, 1979; London, Joseph, 1980.
Pinball.   New York, Bantam, and London, Joseph, 1982.
The Hermit.   New York, Bantam, 1986.

Plays (screenplays)

Being There.   New York, Scientia Factum, 1973; revised edition, Los Angeles, Lorimar, 1980.
Passion Play.   New York, Scientia Factum, 1982.

Screenplay: *Being There*, 1980.

Other

Dokumenty walki o czlowieka (Documents of the Struggle for Man).   Lodz, Scientific Society of Lodz, 1955.
Program rewolucji Ludowej Jakoba Jaworskiego (Jakob Jaworski's Program of People's Revolution).   Lodz, Scientific Society of Lodz, 1955.
The Future is Ours, Comrade: Conversations with the Russians (as Joseph Novak).   New York, Doubleday, and London, Bodley Head, 1960.
No Third Path (as Joseph Novak).   New York, Doubleday, 1962.
Notes of the Author on "The Painted Bird" 1965.   New York, Scientia Factum, 1965.
The Art of the Self: Essays à propos "Steps."   New York, Scientia Factum, 1968.

Editor, *Socjologia Amerykánska* (American Sociology).   New York, Polish Institute of Arts and Sciences in America, 1962.

*

Bibliography: *John Barth, Jerzy Kosinski, and Thomas Pynchon: A Reference Guide* by Thomas P. Walsh and Cameron Northouse, Boston, Hall, 1977.

Critical Studies: "The End of Humanism" by Don Anderson, in *Quadrant* (New York), December 1976; "Horatio Algers of the Nightmare" by Elizabeth Stone, in *Psychology Today* (New York), December 1977; "Life at a Gallop" by Daniel J. Cahill, in *Washington Post*, 16 September 1978; "The Moral Universe of Jerzy Kosinski" by Lawrence S. Cunningham in *America* (New York), 11 November 1978; *Jerzy Kosinski: Literary Alarm Clock* by Byron L. Sherwin, Chicago, Cabala Press, 1981; "The Romance and Terror of Jerzy Kosinski," in *In the Singer's Temple* by Jack Hicks, Chapel Hill, University of North Carolina Press, 1981; "Kosinski's Early Fiction: The Problem of Language," in *Victims: Textual Strategies in Recent American Fiction* by Paul Bruss, Lewisburg, Pennsylvania, Bucknell University Press, 1981; interview in *Writers at Work 5* edited by George Plimpton, New York, Viking Press, and London, Secker and Warburg, 1981; *Jerzy Kosinski* by Norman Lavers, Boston, Twayne, 1982; "Being Jerzy Kosinski" by Barbara Gelb, in *New York Times Magazine*, 21 February 1982; Ron Base, in *Washington Post*, 21 February 1982; "Talking with the Novelist Jerzy Kosinski," in *Newsday* (Melville, New York), 14 March 1982; "Seventeen Years of Ideological Attack on a Cultural Target" by John Cory, in *New York Times*, 7 November 1982; "Betrayed by Jerzy Kosinski" by Jerome Klinkowitz, in *Missouri Review* (Columbia), Summer 1983.

Theatrical Activities:
Actor: **Film**—*Reds*, 1981.

*   *   *

Trained as a sociologist and the author of two studies of collective behavior (*The Future Is Ours, Comrade* and *No Third Path*), Jerzy Kosinski turned to fiction as the most appropriate form to express his ideas about individuality and the human imagination.

His first novel, *The Painted Bird*, is an imaginative response to his childhood in Poland during and immediately following the Second World War. Its protagonist, simply called "The Boy," is separated from his parents in Warsaw, and wanders the war-torn countryside for five years as an orphan. Brutalized by all factions, who by reason of their superstition or ideology see him as a threatening outsider, The Boy learns that the power of his own imagination is all that can protect him from the ravages of these collectivized herds. He admires models of superior power and especially of silent revenge, of which he becomes a master. After the war, he is unable to adapt himself to the collectivized order of the new social world; the scenes of unmatched brutality he has survived by his own ingenuity and daring have shaped him as a superior individual, who by the greater power (and freedom) of his imagination transcends society. In 1975, for a new edition of *The Painted Bird*, Kosinski prepared a revealing foreword, clarifying his own relationship to the fictional events his novel describes.

Kosinski's subsequent novels expand and explore the theme of the individual versus society, and the imagination as pitted against the quotidian reality of social life. *Steps*, the author's most experimental work, consists of fragmentary independent narratives linked together by brief italicized conversations, usually of two lovers discussing the themes emerging from these narrative sections. The predominant topic is that of love—how one is most attracted to the reflection of one's self, and how fear, rivalry, and the inclination to dominate often destroys any chance for a full relationship. "Meet me within your own self," the true lover urges; only in this way can there be a true union of selves.

Being There is a short parable illustrating just how dangerous this fascination with self-image can be. Chance, a retarded gardener whose only contact with the world has been through television, is suddenly shoved out into the social mainstream.

Unable to communicate except by repeating the tag ends of his listener's conversation and speaking in utterly bland metaphors (for which references can be supplied at will), Chance becomes an instantaneous media celebrity and likely Vice-Presidential candidate. He succeeds as everyone's favorite person simply by reflecting back a flattering image of themselves.

This third novel is Kosinski's first work set entirely in the United States (to which he emigrated from Poland in 1957), and reflects his own fear that mass media and commercialization have created a collectivism no less oppressive than in the Communist countries. His subsequent novels describe the attempts of various protagonists to overcome this collective impulse by asserting their singular imaginative wills. In *The Devil Tree* the young man Jonathan Whalen struggles to assert his own identity within the strangling branches of his family tree; he survives only by drowning his godparents. Tarden, the retired secret agent of *Cockpit*, finds full security only by isolating himself from human relations within his manipulative "cockpit" of intellectual and emotional controls. A God who variously rewards or punishes individuals for their actions, he succeeds only in alienating himself from life. *Blind Date* and *Passion Play* construct elaborate parallels to Kosinski's own life as a novelist: Levanter, the speculative investor, and Fabian, the professional polo player, live by their wits—more specifically, by constructing lives of fiction around themselves so that nothing and nobody can penetrate to their personal beings. Their virtues are a professional facility; but in the process they, like Tarden, isolate themselves from life and love.

The extreme state of isolation is found in *Pinball*. Here Kosinski's anti-democratic fascination with the very rich, which was a distracting element in *Passion Play*, controls the narrative itself, as the composer Patrick Domostroy pursues the elusive rock performer Goddard in hopes of reinvigorating his own life and career. Sexuality, as provided by Patrick's girlfriend Andrea Gwynplaine, eclipses even the kinky chicness of Kosinski's previous novel, in which the lovers seemed to step forth from the steamier television dramas such as *Dallas* and *Dynasty*. *Pinball* is X-rated, with the obligatory scenes in sex clubs and the combination of sadistic sex with outright murder. In the end, Kosinski's characters have little depth. His writing works best when evoking the desolation of New York's South Bronx, a devastated landscape which provides mute moral judgment on the lives his characters live around it.

As a writer of fiction, Jerzy Kosinski has been most widely praised for the clear and lucid quality of his prose. Writing in an adopted language learned in adulthood, free from the traumatizing obstacles of his native Polish and Russian, Kosinski claims he is in full rational control of the words he uses, immune to any conditional response or phobia. His success is evident in *The Painted Bird* and in certain grisly passages from *Blind Date*, where the most exceptional violence is described in unrelenting, spellbinding detail, with no lapses into the all-too-possible titillation or farce. A peasant is eaten alive in a cistern literally boiling with voracious rats; a band of mass murderers slaughter a group of the narrator's closest friends (an incident recalling the Sharon Tate/Charles Manson murders, to which Kosinski was a tardy guest). In each case his precise and unrelenting prose fastens the reader's attention to a reality our culture has otherwise found to be unimaginable—Kosinski's own measure of the writer's greatest success.

—Jerome Klinkowitz

KOSTELANETZ, Richard (Cory). American. Born in New York City, 14 May 1940. Educated at Brown University, Providence, Rhode Island, A.B. (honors) in American civilization 1962 (Phi Beta Kappa); Columbia University, New York (Woodrow Wilson Fellow), M.A. 1966; King's College, London (Fulbright Fellow, 1964–65). Program Associate, John Jay College, New York, 1972–73; Visiting Professor, University of Texas, Austin, 1977; artist-in-residence, Mishkenot Sha'ananim, Jerusalem, 1979, and DAAD Kunstlerprogramm, Berlin, 1981–83. Co-founder, Assembling Press, 1970–82; contributing editor, *Lotta Poetica*, Villa Nuova, Italy, 1970–71, *Arts in Society*, Madison, Wisconsin, 1970–75, *The Humanist*, Buffalo, 1970–78, *New York Arts Journal*, 1980–82, and *Menu*, 1982. Since 1976, proprietor, Future Press; since 1977, co-editor and publisher, *Precisely*, New York. Visual poetry and related language art exhibited at galleries and universities since 1975. Recipient: Pulitzer fellowship, 1965; Guggenheim fellowship, 1967; National Endowment for the Arts grant, 1976, 1978, 1979, 1980, 1981; Vogelstein Foundation fellowship, 1980; Fund for Investigative Journalism grant, 1980; CCLM Editor's Fellowship, 1981; ASCAP Standard Award, 1983, 1984, 1985; American Public Radio Fund grant, 1984. Address: P.O. Box 444, Prince Street Station, New York, New York 10012, U.S.A.

PUBLICATIONS

Novels

One Night Stood. New York, Future Press, 1977.
Tabula Rasa: A Constructivist Novel. New York, RK Editions, 1978.
Exhaustive Parallel Intervals. New York, Future Press, 1979.

Short Stories and Novellas

In the Beginning. Somerville, Massachusetts, Abyss, 1971.
Accounting. Brescia, Italy, Amodulo, 1972; Sacramento, California, Poetry Newsletter, 1973.
Ad Infinitum: A Fiction. Friedrichsfehn, Germany, International Artists' Cooperation, 1973.
Metamorphosis. Milwaukee, Membrane, 1974.
Obliterate. Sacramento, California, Ironhorsebook, 1974.
Openings and Closings. New York, D'Arc, 1975.
Constructs. Reno, Nevada, West Coast Poetry Review, 1975.
Come Here. New York, Assembling Press, 1975.
Extrapolate. New York, Assembling Press, 1975.
Modulations. New York, Assembling Press, 1975.
Three Places in New Inkland, with others. New York, Zartscorp, 1977.
Milestones in a Life. Lethbridge, Alberta, Lethbridge Herald, 1978; Pittsburgh, Carnegie-Mellon University Press, 1979.
Constructs Two. Milwaukee, Membrane, 1978.
Foreshortenings and Other Stories. Willits, California, Tuumba Press, 1978.
Inexistences: Constructivist Fictions. New York, RK Editions, 1978.
And So Forth. New York, Future Press, 1979.
More Short Fictions. New York, Assembling Press, 1980.
Reincarnations. New York, Future Press, 1981.
Epiphanies. Berlin, Literarisches Colloquium, 1983.

Audiotapes: *Experimental Prose*, 1976; *Openings and Closings*, 1977; *Audio Art*, 1977; *Foreshortenings and Other Stories*,

1977; *Monotapes*, 1978; *Seductions*, 1981; *Conversations/Dialogues*, 1983; *Audio Writing*, 1984.

Play

Epiphanies (produced Grand Forks, North Dakota, 1980).

Verse

Visual Language.   New York, Assembling Press, 1970.
I Articulations, with *Short Fictions*.   New York, Kulchur, 1974.
Portraits from Memory.   Ann Arbor, Michigan, Ardis, 1975.
Word Prints.   Privately printed, 1975.
Rain Rains Rain.   New York, Assembling Press, 1976.
Numbers: Poems and Stories.   New York, Assembling Press, 1976.
Illuminations.   Woodinville, Washington, and New York, Laughing Bear-Future Press, 1977.
Arenas Fields Pitches Turfs.   Kansas City, BkMk-University of Missouri, 1982.

Other

The Theatre of Mixed-Means: An Introduction to Happenings, Kinetic Environments, and Other Mixed-Means Performances.   New York, Dial Press, 1968; London, Pitman, 1970.
Master Minds: Portraits of Contemporary American Artists and Intellectuals.   New York, Macmillan, 1969.
The End of Intelligent Writing: Literary Politics in America.   New York, Sheed and Ward, 1974.
Recyclings: A Literary Autobiography.   New York, Assembling Press, 1974; augmented edition, New York, Future Press, 1984.
Grants and the Future of Literature.   New York, RK Editions, 1978.
Wordsand.   Burnaby, British Columbia, Simon Fraser Gallery, 1978.
Twenties in the Sixties: Previously Uncollected Critical Essays.   Westport, Connecticut, Greenwood Press, 1979.
"The End" Essentials, "The End" Appendix.   Metuchen, New Jersey, Scarecrow Press, 1979.
Metamorphosis in the Arts.   New York, Assembling Press, 1980.
Autobiographies.   Santa Barbara, California, Mudborn, 1981.
The Old Poetics and the New.   Ann Arbor, University of Michigan Press, 1981.
American Imaginations.   Berlin, Merve, 1983.
Prose Pieces/Aftertexts.   Calexico, California, Atticus, 1986.
The Old Fictions and the New.   Jefferson, North Carolina, McFarland, 1986.

Editor, *On Contemporary Literature: An Anthology of Critical Essays on Major Movements and Writers of Contemporary Literature*.   New York, Avon, 1964; revised edition, 1969.
Editor, *The New American Arts*.   New York, Horizon Press, 1965.
Editor, *Twelve from the Sixties*.   New York, Dell, 1967.
Editor, *The Young American Writers: Fiction, Poetry, Drama, and Criticism*.   New York, Funk and Wagnalls, 1967.
Editor, *Beyond Left and Right: Radical Thought for Our Time*.   New York, Morrow, 1968.
Editor, *Imaged Words and Worded Images*.   New York, Outerbridge and Dienstfrey, 1970.
Editor, *Possibilities of Poetry: An Anthology of American Contemporaries*.   New York, Dell, 1970.

Editor, *John Cage*.   New York, Praeger, 1970; London, Allen Lane, 1971.
Editor, *Moholy-Nagy*.   New York, Praeger, 1970; London, Allen Lane, 1972.
Editor, *Assembling*, and *Second* through *Eleventh Assembling*.   New York, Assembling Press, 12 vols., 1970–81.
Editor, *Future's Fiction*.   New York, Panache, 1971.
Editor, *Human Alternatives: Visions for Our Time*.   New York, Morrow, 1971.
Editor, *Social Speculations: Visions for Us Now*.   New York, Morrow, 1971.
Editor, *In Youth*.   New York, Ballantine, 1972.
Editor, *Seeing Through Shuck*.   New York, Ballantine, 1972.
Editor, *Breakthrough Fictioneers: An Anthology*.   New York, Something Else Press, 1973.
Editor, *The Edge of Adaptation: Man and the Emerging Society*.   Englewood Cliffs, New Jersey, Prentice Hall, 1973.
Editor, *Essaying Essays*.   New York, OOLP, 1975.
Editor, *Language and Structure*.   New York, Kensington Arts, 1975.
Editor, *Younger Critics of North America: Essays on Literature and the Arts*.   Fairwater, Wisconsin, Margins, 1977.
Editor, *Esthetics Contemporary*.   New York, Prometheus, 1977.
Editor, *Assembling Assembling*.   New York, Assembling Press, 1978.
Editor, *Visual Literature Criticism: A New Collection*.   Carbondale, Southern Illinois University Press, 1979.
Editor, *Text-Sound Texts*.   New York, Morrow, 1980.
Editor, *The Yale Gertrude Stein* (selection).   New Haven, Connecticut, Yale University Press, 1980.
Editor, *Scenarios*.   New York, Assembling Press, 1980.
Editor, *Aural Literature Criticism*.   New York, Precisely-RK Editions, 1981.
Editor, *The Avant-Garde Tradition in Literature*.   Buffalo, Prometheus, 1982.

*

Richard Kostelanetz comments:

In 17 years' exploration of fiction writing, I have produced 1) a novella with no more than two words to a paragraph (and then, in one published form, no more than two words to a book page); 2) a story with only single-word paragraphs; 3) stories that are narrated through a series of shapes that are composed exclusively of words or letters; 4) stories consisting exclusively of words whose meaning changes with the introduction not of other words but of different shapes or nonverbal imagery; 5) stories composed entirely of nonrepresentational line-drawings that metamorphose so systematically that each image in the sequence belongs only to its particular place; 6) stories composed of just cut-up photographs whose chips move symmetrically through narrative cycles; 7) individual sentences that are either the openings or the closings of otherwise unwritten stories; 8) separate modular fictions of photographs that can be read in any order, of line-drawings whose positions in a sequence are interchangeable (and thus can be shuffled), of sentences that are reordered in systemic ways to produce different emphases of the same words and gestures, if not radically different stories; 9) circular stories that flow from point to point but lack beginnings or ends; 10) narratives, one as long as a book, composed exclusively of numerals; 11) a story composed of 16 different (but complementary) stories interwoven in print in 16 different typefaces and on audiotape told in 16 purposefully different amplifications of a single voice; 12) a modular fiction whose sentences are reordered in systemic ways to produce different emphases of the same words and gestures, if not radically different stories; 13) over two thousand single-sentence fictions representing the epiphanies of over two thousand otherwise unwritten stories; 14) manuscripts of stories (*Epiphanies*) that have been offered to periodical editors not to publish *in toto* but for them to make their own selections that can then be ordered and designed to their particular tastes; 15) fiction books published in formats ranging from conventional spine-bound volumes to such alternatives as tabloid-sized newsprint books, loose-leaf books (whose pages are gathered in an envelope), and accordion books that are 4 inches high and several feet long; 16) a film and a videotape whose imagery is nothing other than words telling stories; 17) a film with symmetrical abstract fictions (described in #5 above) that metamorphose in systemic sequence; 18) fictions that exist primarily on audiotape—that cannot be performed live, whose printed version is no more than a score for its realization; 19) a film composed of verbal and visual epiphanies that have no connection to each other, either vertically or horizontally, other than common fictional structure; 20) perhaps a few other departures whose character cannot yet, for better or worse, be neatly encapsulated; 21) the purest *oeuvre* of fiction, as fiction, uncompromised by vulgar considerations, that anyone has ever done; 22) no conventional fiction—absolutely none—which is to say nothing that could pass a university course/workshop in "fiction writing" (and get me a job teaching such), and no familiar milestone from which simpleminded critics could then measure my "departure."

Even though these fictions of mine have appear in over three dozen literary magazines, and over a dozen volumes of these fictions have appeared in print, there have been few reviews of individual books, no commercial contracts, no offers from small presses to do a second book, no grants for fiction writing, no inclusion in surveys of contemporary fiction, no public acknowledgement of my alternative purposes in creating and publishing fiction; only one story was ever anthologized by someone else (Eugene Wildman, in his *Experiments in Prose* [1969]). Does anyone care? Should anyone care (other than me)? (Should I care? If so, how? Should I have written this?) What should be made of the fact that no one else—absolutely no one else visible to us—is making fiction in these ways?

*   *   *

Richard Kostelanetz's experimental fiction reflects a formalist program that he has elaborated in his writings as a critic, anthologist, and memoirist. He takes as his "principal assumption . . . that the foundation of experimental literature is a history of formal innovation." On the basis of this assumption, he asserts that "the canon of modernist fiction—Kafka, Stein, Faulkner, Joyce, Beckett, Borges—establishes a tradition of the new" and comprises the only "relevant succession of precedents for the present"; but he adds that several subsequent "post-realist, post-symbolist 'avant-gardes'" now have extended that succession. On the basis of this extended succession, he founds his own experimentalist practice. He has intended "to extend poetry and fiction into other media and, conversely, to discover how other media could best be used for publishing poetry and fiction"; and he has devised a "constructivism" that, in his words, "represents an extreme, perhaps ultimate, development of formalism in fiction."

Kostelanetz's program commits him to a particular polemics. He assails publishing conventions that virtually proscribe "pronounced stylistic originality" and, especially, "predominantly visual fiction"; and he argues that "only a philistine would

dare dismiss an unfamiliar creation as 'not-fiction' " and characterizes as such critics who accept the abstract and the non-representational in painting but not in fiction. Kostelanetz's defense of such fictional practice, however, does not entirely satisfy. He argues that even the most non-representational fictions are mimetics of the "constructive process" itself; that formally experimental fictions can sensitize the reader to "unfamiliar forms in everyday experience"; that such fictions tend to emphasize "kinds of information and perceptions that were previously foreign to literature"; and that such fictions are "culturally progressive" *because* they are "formally progressive." But he also tends to strip these classical avant-garde arguments from their specific ideological bases and ends up appealing generally to what Meyer Schapiro has characterized as a modernist ideology of individual accomplishment in which "artistic integrity required a permanent concern with self-development and the evolution of art." This appeal is implicit in Kostelanetz's assertion that "the sum of my artworks is ultimately about the discovery of possibilities—not only in the exploitation of media but in art and, by extension, in oneself as a creative initiator."

Because he is a polemicist, Kostelanetz has sought to isolate the definition of fiction on which his program rests. He begins with negative propositions. He asserts that "words need not be the building blocks of fiction, or sentences the frame, or human beings the 'characters' "; and he asserts that statement in fiction is neither the referential statement he identifies with such expository prose forms as history and journalism nor the "concise, static, generally formalized statement" he identifies with poetry. He then proceeds to his positive definition. Fiction is "a frame filled with a circumscribed world of cohesively self-relating activity," the frame necessarily containing "some kind of movement from one point to another," some internal "diversity and change," some form of "sequential[ity]" or "internal event." Fiction, then, might be made of any material and might therefore exist in any medium; it might be referential but need not be; it need be only dynamic and, for reasons unexplained but locatable in his formalist assumptions, framed. One inclined to challenge Kostelanetz's premises and his reasoning might conclude that they have led him to mistake necessary conditions for sufficient conditions.

It should be obvious that the radically minimalist fiction predicated on Kostelanetz's definition does not resemble fiction in any usual acceptation, and no more so when he is exploring the possibilities of the print medium than when he is exploring those of audiotape, videotape, or film. His annotated "Inventory of My Fictions" lists forty-one works. They include visual fictions, such as the "alphabet novellas" *In the Beginning* and *Ad Infinitum: A Fiction*, in each of which Kostelanetz explored how "images in sequence could tell a story by themselves, apart from any additional language." They include numerical fictions, ranging from early concretist pieces such as *Accounting* to more sophisticated mathematical variations such as *Exhaustive Parallel Intervals*, "a book-length narrative, perhaps a novel," in which Kostelanetz attempted "to see whether I could create a Literature composed of numbers alone." They include his "constructivist" works *Constructs* and *Constructs Two*, each comprising "sequential four-sided symmetrical line-drawings that metamorphose in systemic sequence; the accordian books *Modulations* and *Extrapolate*, "constructivist novella(s) that can be read from one end to the other and back again"; *Tabula Rasa: A Constructivist Novel*, comprising approximately 1,000 pages, "blank with exception of the title page from which subsequent content can be inferred," and *Inexistences: Constructivist Fictions*, "a collection of stories, likewise blank with the exception of the title page from which subsequent contents can be inferred." And they include sophisticated verbal pieces: "One Night Stood," an early "story" comprising two-word paragraphs on the theme of "boy meets girl," becomes *One Night Stood*, printed "in two radically different book formats," in one of which each two-word phrase "take(s) up the entire page of a book, thereby expanding the 'story' into a minimal *novel*"; *Openings and Closings*, comprising "single sentence fictions" that "were meant to be either the *opening* sentences of hypothetical stories that might have followed or the *closing* sentences of stories that might have come before," finds its companion piece in *Epiphanies*, comprising single-sentence fictions "that are meant to be . . . the key lines in the middle—the epiphany that, in James Joyce's theory, jells the narrative and reveals everything around it." Whether new works or new realizations of printed works, his explorations in other media are equally provocative, at once exuberantly audacious and fastidiously formalistic.

—Charles Caramello

KRIGE, Uys. South African. Born in Swellendam, Cape Province, 4 February 1910. Educated at Paul Roos Gymnasium; Stellenbosch University, 1927–29, B.A. in law 1929. Married Lydia Pindeque in 1937; two children. Reporter, *Rand Daily Mail*, Johannesburg, 1930; lived in France and Spain, 1931–36; correspondent, *Die Suiderstem*, Cape Town, 1936; broadcaster, Bureau of Information, 1939; war correspondent in Egypt and Abyssinia during World War II: prisoner of war in Italy, 1941–43; founding editor, *Vandag* (Today), Johannesburg, 1949. Recipient: French government bursary, 1952; Carnegie grant, 1959; Hertzog Prize, for poetry, 1974, for drama, 1985. Honorary doctorate: University of Natal, 1958. Address: P.O. Box 25, Onrust, Cape Province 7201, South Africa.

PUBLICATIONS

Short Stories

Die Palmboom (The Palm Tree). Pretoria, Van Schaik, 1940.
The Dream and the Desert. London, Collins, 1953; Boston, Houghton Mifflin, 1954.
Rooi, with others. Cape Town, Malherbe, 1965.
Orphan of the Desert. Cape Town, Malherbe, 1967.

Plays

Binnenshuis, adaptation of a play by Maeterlinck, in *Huiggenoot*, 14 August 1931.
Magdalena Retief (in Afrikaans). Cape Town, Unie Volkspers, 1938; revised edition, 1948.
Die Wit Muur (includes *Die Wit Muur* [The White Wall], *Die Skaapwagters van Bethlehem* [The Shepherds of Bethlehem], *Die Arrestasie* [The Arrest]). Cape Town, Unie Volkspers, 1940.
All Paaie Gaan na Rome (All Roads Go to Rome). Cape Town, Unie Volkspers, 1949.
Die Twee Lampe (The Two Lamps), adaptation of a story by Sannie Uys. Johannesburg, Afrikaanse Pers, 1951.
Die Sluipskutter (The Sniper) (includes *Die Gees van die Water* [The Spirit of the Water]). Johannesburg, Afrikaanse Pers, 1951.

Die Ryk Weduwee (The Rich Widow) (produced 1950). Johannesburg, Afrikaanse Pers, 1953.
Die Goue Kring (The Golden Circle) (produced Johannesburg, 1950's). Cape Town, Balkema, 1956.
The Sniper and Other One-Act Plays (includes *The Arrest, Fuente Sagrada, All Roads Lead to Rome*). Cape Town, Hollands-Afrikaanse Uitwegers Maatskappy, 1962.
Yerma (in Afrikaans), adaptation of the play by Lorca. Cape Town, Hollands-Afrikaanse Uitwegers Maatskappy, 1963.
The Two Lamps, and The Big Shots. Cape Town, Hollands-Afrikaanse Uitwegers Maatskappy, 1964.
Twaalfde Nag, adaptation of the play *Twelfth Night* by Shakespeare (produced Transvaal, 1965[?]).
Muur van die Dood (Wall of Death). Cape Town, Constantia, 1968.
Die Grootkanonne (The Big Shots). Johannesburg, Dramatiese Artistieke en Letterkundige Regte Organisasie, 1969.
Die Ongeskrewe Stuk (The Unwritten Play). Johannesburg, Dramatiese Artistieke en Letterkundige Regte Organisasie, 1970.
Die Huis van Bernarda Alba, from a play by Lorca. Cape Town, Tafelberg, 1980.
Vier Eenbedrywe. Pretoria, Van Schaik, 1980.
Die Wit Muur en ader Eenbedrywe. Pretoria, Van Schaik, 1983.
Die Lewe is Alleen Draaglik as Mens bietjie Dronk is (Life Is Bearable Only While One Is a Little Drunk) (produced Cape Town, 1985). Cape Town, Tafelberg, 1985.

Television Play: *Die Apie* (The Little Monkey), 1985.

Verse

Kentering (Turning Point). Pretoria, Van Schaik, 1935.
Rooidag (Daybreak). Pretoria, Van Schaik, 1940.
Ooclogsgedigte. Pretoria, Van Schaik, 1942.
Die Einde van die Pad (The End of the Road). Pretoria, Van Schaik, 1947.
Hart Sonder Hawe (Heart Without Haven). Cape Town, Unie Volkspers, 1949.
Vir die Luit en die Kitaar (For the Lute and the Guitar). Johannesburg, Afrikaanse Pers, 1950.
Ballade van die Groot Begeer (Ballad of the Great Desiring). Cape Town, Balkema, 1960.
Gedigte 1927–1940 (Poems). Pretoria, Van Schaik, 1961.
Eluard en die Surrealisme (Eluard and Surrealism). Cape Town, Hollands-Afrikaanse Uitwegers Maatskappy, 1962.
Vooraand (Eve). Johannesburg, Afrikaanse Pers, 1964.
Versamelde Gedigte (Collected Poems). Cape Town, Human & Rousseau, 1985.

Other

Vanguard of Victory: A Short Review of the South African Victories in East Africa 1940–1941, with Conrad Norton. Pretoria, Bureau of Information, 1941.
The Way Out: Italian Intermezzo. London, Collins, 1946; revised edition, Cape Town, Maskew Miller, 1955.
Sol y Sombra (in Afrikaans). Pretoria, Unie Volkspers, 1948; revised edition, Pretoria, Van Schaik, 1955.
Ver in die Wereld (Far in the World). Johannesburg, Afrikaanse Pers, 1951.
Sout van die Aarde (Salt of the Earth). Cape Town, Hollands-Afrikaanse Uitwegers Maatskappy, 1961.

Editor, *Poems of Roy Campbell.* Cape Town, Maskew Miller, 1960.

Editor, *Olive Schreiner: A Selection.* Cape Town and London, Oxford University Press, 1968; New York, Oxford University Press, 1969.

Editor, with Jack Cope, *The Penguin Book of South African Verse.* London, Penguin, 1968.

Editor and Translator, *Spaans-Amerikaanse Keuse* (Spanish-American Verse). Cape Town, Human & Rousseau, 1969.

*

Critical Study: *Uys Krige* by Christina Van Heyningen and Jacques Berthoud, New York, Twayne, 1966.

*   *   *

Uys Krige is one of the very few white South African writers who have established a literary reputation in both the official languages of the country: English and Afrikaans. Of Afrikaner descent, and brought up in an Afrikaans environment, Krige's first allegiance is, naturally, to Afrikaans; and his contribution to its rapidly growing literature is considerable, comprising poetry, plays and criticism. Characteristic of his work is an obvious delight in exploring the nuances of a relatively new and constantly changing language. His linguistic facility is seen to good advantage in his successful comedy, *Die Ryk Weduwee,* in much of his recent poetry, and in his translations from Spanish, notably Lorca's play *Yerma.* He has also successfully translated *Twelfth Night,* adapting Shakespeare's verse patterns into idiomatic and colourful Afrikaans.

Krige's interest in English, consciously developed throughout his writing career, was stimulated by his extensive pre-war travels in Europe, and by his experience during the Second World War, first as a war correspondent in Africa, later as a prisoner of war in Italy. Contact with Europe sharpened his awareness of European civilization, and contact with Englishmen stimulated his desire to write for an English audience. On his return to South Africa in 1946, he began not only to write in English, but to translate some of his own work, in an attempt to bridge the language barrier which, traditionally, separates the white races in South Africa. His work has thus become available to a much wider audience than that reached by most Afrikaans authors, and has opened hitherto largely inaccessible areas of experience to the non-Afrikaans reader. Krige, that is, writes as an Afrikaner, about Afrikaners, and his work is valuable for its patently honest, consistently realistic account of a people who, more often than not, have been portrayed as conscienceless, narrow-minded white supremacists. Krige's Afrikaners are ordinary people, involved in the common human experiences of birth, love, and death. He is particularly conscious of Afrikaner traditions, which both link the people with, and separate them from their European ancestors. He is aware, too, of their limitations, as well as justly proud of their achievements. His poetic sensibility enables him to see his characters in a close and living relationship with the peculiar South African landscape, which has always had a strong fascination for him, and which he presents with accuracy and deep feeling, disguising neither its harshness nor its great beauty.

"The Coffin" and "The Dream," both of which appear in *The Dream and the Desert,* demonstrate one side of Krige's awareness. "The Coffin" is a story about a kindly Afrikaner patriarch, living life to the full though always conscious of death, and prepared to meet it, with his coffin standing ready in the loft. "The Dream" is a delightful evocation of a half-rural South African childhood, in which humorous irony controls but does not destroy the deliberately romantic nostalgia for a way of life which is rapidly disappearing. *The Two Lamps* displays another facet of the Afrikaner personality, and of Krige's talent. This play, which has received much critical acclaim in America as well as in South Africa, dramatises, in a typically South Africa version, the conflict between father and sons. It presents an uncompromising study of the Calvinist conscience, which is powerless, finally, to avert overwhelming tragedy. Set against a haunting background of mist, marsh and farmland, *The Two Lamps* is possibly Krige's finest achievement.

An important part of Krige's work is not confined exclusively to South Africa. Much of this is criticism, translation (from French and Spanish), and a popular genre in South Africa, travel literature. In addition however, there is some fine war writing, in which Krige's talent for objective reportage is seen to good advantage. *The Way Out* is an account of Krige's escape from an Italian prison camp, but it is more than a simple escape story. The narrative develops into a penetrating psychological study of men under stress, and at the same time celebrates the loyalty and courage of the impoverished Italian partisans who risked their lives to help the escapers. "The Death of the Zulu," also based on his war experiences, is one of the few stories in which Krige attempts to deal with black characters. Although it is very slight, being hardly more than the description of a single incident (one man's death in the desert), the story shows Krige's ability to present all his characters, whatever their race, with genuine sympathy.

Where many South African writers succumb to a self-conscious humanitarianism, understandable in the present political context, but often destructive of literary merit, it is Krige's distinctive achievement to write without any obvious bias: his work thus reflects the reality of the South Africa he knows, and of which he is part. Although this reality is limited (to the extent that it virtually excludes black South Africa, and includes "non-whites" only as servants and inferiors), it is a reality which is a living part of the South African experience, and deserves recognition as such.

—Ursula Edmands

KROETSCH, Robert (Paul). Canadian. Born in Heisler, Alberta, 26 June 1927. Educated at schools in Heisler and Red Deer, Alberta; University of Alberta, Edmonton, B.A. 1948; McGill University, Montreal, 1954–55; Middlebury College, Vermont, M.A. 1956; University of Iowa, Iowa City, Ph.D. 1961. Married 1) Mary Jane Lewis in 1956 (divorced, 1979), two daughters; 2) Smaro Kamboureli in 1982. Laborer and purser, Yellowknife Transportation Company, Northwest Territories, 1948–50; information specialist (civilian), United States Air Force Base, Goose Bay, Labrador, 1951–54; Assistant Professor, 1961–65, Associate Professor, 1965–68, and Professor of English, 1968–78, State University of New York, Binghamton. Professor of English, 1978–85, and since 1985 Distinguished Professor, University of Manitoba, Winnipeg. Artist-in-Residence, Calgary University, Alberta, Fall 1975, University of Lethbridge, Alberta, Spring 1976, and University of Manitoba, 1976–78. Recipient: Bread Loaf Writers Conference grant, 1966; Governor-General's Award, 1970. Agent: Ed Carson, General Publishing, 30 Lesmill Road, Don Mills, Ontario M3B 2T6. Address: Department of English, University of Manitoba, Winnipeg, Manitoba R3T 2N2, Canada.

PUBLICATIONS

Novels

But We Are Exiles. Toronto, Macmillan, 1965; London, Macmillan, and New York, St. Martin's Press, 1966.
The Words of My Roaring. Toronto and London, Macmillan, and New York, St. Martin's Press, 1966.
The Studhorse Man. Toronto, Macmillan, and London, Macdonald, 1969; New York, Simon and Schuster, 1970.
Gone Indian. Toronto, New Press, 1973.
Badlands. Toronto, New Press, 1975; New York, Beaufort, 1983.
What the Crow Said. Toronto, General, 1978.
Alibi. Toronto, Stoddart, and New York, Beaufort, 1983.

Play

The Studhorse Man, adaptation of his own novel (produced Toronto, 1981).

Verse

The Stone Hammer: Poems 1960–1975. Nanaimo, British Columbia, Oolichan, 1975.
The Ledger. London, Ontario, Applegarth Follies, 1975.
Seed Catalogue. Winnipeg, Turnstone Press, 1977.
The Sad Phoenician. Toronto, Coach House Press, 1979.
The Criminal Intensities of Love as Paradise. Lantzville, British Columbia, Oolichan, 1981.
Field Notes: Collected Poems. Toronto, General, and New York, Beaufort, 1981.
Advice to My Friends. Toronto, Stoddart, 1985.

Other

Alberta. Toronto, Macmillan, and New York, St. Martin's Press, 1968.
The Crow Journals. Edmonton, Alberta, NeWest Press, 1980.
Labyrinths of Voice: Conversations with Robert Kroetsch, with Shirley Neuman and Robert Wilson. Edmonton, Alberta, NeWest Press, 1982.
Letters to Salonika. Toronto, Grand Union, 1983.

Editor, with James Bacque and Pierre Gravel, *Creation* (interviews). Toronto, New Press, 1970.
Editor, *Sundogs: Stories from Saskatchewan.* Moose Jaw, Saskatchewan, Thunder Creek, 1980.
Editor, with Smaro Kamboureli, *Visible Visions: The Selected Poems of Douglas Barbour.* Edmonton, Alberta, NeWest Press, 1984.

*

Bibliography: "An Annotated Bibliography of Works by and about Robert Kroetsch" by Robert Lecker, in *Essays on Canadian Writing* (Toronto), Fall 1977.

Manuscript Collection: University of Calgary Library, Alberta.

Critical Studies: *Robert Kroetsch* by Peter Thomas, Vancouver, Douglas and McIntyre, 1980; "Robert Kroetsch Issue" of *Open Letter* (Toronto), Spring 1983 and Summer-Fall 1984; *Robert Kroetsch* by Robert Lecker, Boston, Twayne, 1986.

*   *   *

From his first novel, *But We Are Exiles*, to his latest one, *Alibi*, Robert Kroetsch has consistently attempted to reconcile two of his abiding passions: his personal attraction to the literal realities of Canada's rural west, and his artistic desire to transform those realities into various myths, to redefine them by the mere process of telling about them. If our fictions make *us* real, as he has said on many occasions, then everything in our world is transformed by those fictions, too, as long as the fictions last, as it were. And this is the central problem about realistic fiction as he sees it: since it has a beginning, a middle, and an end, it does not last, and the process of transformation is both limited and finite. But if we don't have to worry about beginnings and endings, or if they remain confused for us, then we are continually involved in the process of re-creation ourselves, and the realities we once were so sure of take on new and forever changing shapes.

Inevitably, there will be a gap between the intellectualizing of such ideas and their workings out in fiction, and to many readers Kroetsch is more convincing in a critical work like *Labyrinths of Voice* than in his novels that try to dramatize these theories, like his surrealistic *What the Crow Said*. Reality keeps intruding itself in his fiction, and so passionate is Kroetsch about these realities that they, and not the theories, carry the weight of his fiction. The day-to-day activities aboard the *Nahanni Jane* in his first novel, the politics, the beer parlours, and the funeral parlours of *The Words of My Roaring*, the conjoining evidences of man's past and present along the Red Deer River in *Badlands*, the erotic fantasies and realities in spas around the world in *Alibi*: these are the components that give substance and credibility to his novels. *The Studhorse Man* and *Gone Indian* succeed, too, where *What the Crow Said* does not, because they do have tangible landscapes across which we can precisely trace the wanderings of Hazard Lepage and Jeremy Sadness, and their mythical increments assume conviction because of that. *What the Crow Said* is unique amongst Kroetsch's novels in that all its components violate the criteria of empirical reality, and in a sense we have to allow ourselves to be carried along by words that have no tangible referents. It is Kroetsch at his best as a post-modernist, but not at his best as a novelist, for it lacks that fusion of imagination and reality that give his other six novels their power.

As a novelist, Kroetsch is shaped by his belief in a prevailing duality, that finds its mythical manifestations in such patterns as the death/rebirth cycle, the quest for identity, the *doppelgänger* motif, the narcissus theme. All of these informed even his first novel which is essentially his most realistic one; Peter Guy's literal role there as a pilot on a riverboat on the MacKenzie allowed Kroetsch to use these mythical accretions as natural extensions of Guy's situation. The novel derives much of its power from Kroetsch's exploitation of the element of water, deriving in turn from his familiarity with his landscape: the absence of water on the dry prairies, where Peter and Mike first meet; the hot springs in the Rockies, where their immersion constitutes a re-birth; the wide expanse of the MacKenzie, in effect all water and no land, where Peter and Mike achieve their final death/rebirth resolution.

In this respect, this first novel anticipates many water-related events of his later works: the drowning of Jonah Bledd in *The Words of My Roaring* and the coming of the apocalyptic rain; Hazard Lepage's and Eugene Utter's trial by flood in *The Studhorse Man*; Dawe and his crew floating towards the past on the Red Deer River in *Badlands*; and, most obviously, Dorf's uncontrollable obsession with spas in *Alibi*. In one sense, this latest novel can be seen to constitute an obligatory conclusion to the quest for water first launched in *But We Are Exiles*, though in tone or vision, Kroetsch has moved from the tragic to the comic in the process. River valleys, spring floods, rains, spas, ingredients of the realities and dreams of rural westerners, have become for Kroetsch brilliantly workable symbols in his creation of his fictional worlds.

The male quest, whether for identity, sexuality, power, or death and resurrection, constitutes another recurring motif in Kroetsch's fiction, particularly in what is called his *Out West* trilogy. Built on a fusion of the myth of Genesis and the reality of Alberta's 1935 election, *The Words of My Roaring* chronicles the ascension of the undertaker, Johnnie Judas Backstrom, as he not only defeats the old party incumbent, Doc Murdoch (who had brought Johnnie into the world), but also sexually captures his daughter. The comic tone of this novel camouflages some of its grim realities, like poverty, drought, suicide, auction sales, but the novel's conclusion, like the election itself, can be seen as either the end or the beginning, and within this perspective, its picaresque hero represents the triumph of a new form of chaos over an old, outdated order.

The action of *The Studhorse Man* takes place some ten years later, just as World War II comes to an end, which helps to transform Hazard Lepage's literal quest into a comic odyssey. The realistic narrative, with its precise times, places, and events moves quite readily into surrealistic and mythological dimensions, and Kroetsch's startling achievement here is how easily he makes us believe that Hazard and Poseidon belong in all three worlds, done in part through his manipulation of the sexual quest. Hazard's earthy sexuality, his lust for Martha kept active by numerous women he encounters on his odyssey, is balanced against his need to reserve Poiseidon's rampant sexuality for the right mare to ensure the survival of his breed. It is the studhorse *man* who triumphs here, for his last sexual act bestows life upon Martha, while the studhorse is pressed into service to provide ingredients for the artificial controlling of life.

Formally, *The Studhorse Man* reflects a number of postmodernist tendencies, from its sense of discontinuity, its fusion of the biographical and autobiographical forms, to the story shaping itself without the traditional rules of narration. It points in these respects to the third work of the trilogy, *Gone Indian*, with its stichomythic structure, its simultaneous narration and narrative revision as Jeremy Sadness exchanges his messages with his graduate professor back in Binghamton. Kroetsch here reflects a novel treatment of the duality pattern, as he structures Sadness's quest in the form of a total identity change, to transform himself into another Grey Owl. The novel lacks the sustaining humour of *The Studhorse Man*, depending unduly on extravagant incidents that do not rise organically out of the fictional ingredients that always made the earlier work plausible, despite its outrageous scenes. Some of the familiar academic games in *Gone Indian*, the infidelities and in-jokes add at best only minor complications to Jeremy's situation, but that he has only one sentence of his dissertation written after nine years, and that he is sexually impotent in a prone position, obviously give him good reason to come to this "far, last edge of our civilization" to start over again. Like Hazard, he is resurrected into death by his final sexual success, and thus can follow his idol, Grey Owl, who also "died into a new life."

The resurrective powers that Bea Sunderman and Martha Proudfoot demonstrated in these last two novels suggests amongst other things their ability, like Faulkner's Dilsey, to survive time, and Kroetsch's next two novels put even more weight on the female adaptability. *Badlands* in effect is a chronicle of distortions and obsessive ambition transformed into truth by the two women who survived this folly, Anna Dawe and Anna Yellowbird, both of whom have been twisted by the actions of William Dawe and his crew. Dawe's daughter at 45 has been denied love and life; Anna Yellowbird has given of her body and life to those men, and then was discarded, much like the bones and the relics they dug up and left behind. Now in league with one another, they make the reverse trip up the river to its source in the Rockies, undoing, as it were, and unrecording all of Dawe's achievements.

In *What the Crow Said* the opposition between the male and female worlds is firmly entrenched—only men are allowed in the beer parlour and in the card game—but the female world gets even with a vengeance. In the more than a dozen marriages in this novel, all the husbands die, except for Liebhaber, some in most gruesome ways, while all the wives survive. This expendability of husbands fulfills, too, the sexual message of Vera's orgasmic cry at the outset, that no mortal man can ever satisfy her after her seduction by the swarm of bees. But it is an extravagant way to make a point, and reflects the fact that the novel's many interplays of cosmic jokes, silences, overlappings of time, and circumstantial exaggerations do not sufficiently come together to create a consistent success.

With *Alibi* Kroetsch has in a sense come full circle from his earlier serious concerns with the quest myths that characteristically had as their goals such respectable revelations as identity, sexuality, or a death/rebirth possibility. But the quest order here—"Find me a spa, Dorf"—is not so much a comment on Deemer's greed or stupidity as it is on the hero's eagerness to continue playing the ritual of the games even when its realization is impossible. It gives Kroetsch the excuse (the alibi) to poke fun at himself, and as a result he has written one of his richest and bawdiest works to date. He is back in a credible, realistic world again, much as he was in *Exiles*, but in that he takes a rest here from the word games of his previous novel, *Alibi* is informed by a refreshing spontaneity. It may well mark the end (or the beginning) of a significant stage in Kroetsch's fictional development.

—Hallvard Dahlie

LAMMING, George (Eric). Barbadian. Born in Carrington Village, 8 June 1927. Educated at Roebuck Boys' School; Combermere School. Teacher in Trinidad, 1946–50; moved to England, 1950; host of book review programme, BBC West Indian Service, London, 1951. Writer-in-Residence, University of the West Indies, Kingston, 1967–68. Co-editor of Barbados and Guyana independence issues of *New World Quarterly*, Kingston, 1965 and 1967. Recipient: Guggenheim fellowship, 1954; *Kenyon Review* fellowship, 1954; Maugham Award, 1957; Canada Council fellowship, 1962. D.Litt.: University of the West Indies, Cave Hill, Barbados, 1980. Address: 14-A Highbury Place, London N.5, England.

PUBLICATIONS

Novels

In the Castle of My Skin. London, Joseph, and New York, McGraw Hill, 1953.
The Emigrants. London, Joseph, 1954; New York, McGraw Hill, 1955.
Of Age and Innocence. London, Joseph, 1958; New York, Schocken, 1981.

Season of Adventure.   London, Joseph, 1960.
Water with Berries.   London, Longman, 1971; New York, Holt Rinehart, 1972.
Natives of My Person.   London, Longman, and New York, Holt Rinehart, 1972.

Uncollected Short Stories

"David's Walk," in *Life and Letters* (London), November 1948.
"Of Thorns and Thistles" and "A Wedding in Spring," in *West Indian Stories*, edited by Andrew Salkey.   London, Faber, 1960.
"Birds of a Feather," in *Stories from the Caribbean*, edited by Andrew Salkey.   London, Elek, 1965; as *Island Voices*, New York, Liveright, 1970.
"Birthday Weather," in *Caribbean Literature*, edited by G.R. Coulthard.   London, University of London Press, 1966.

Other

The Pleasures of Exile.   London, Joseph, 1960.
Influencia del África en las literaturas antillanas, with Henry Bangou and René Depestre.   Montevideo, Uruguay, I.L.A.C., 1972.

Editor, *Cannon Shot and Glass Beads: Modern Black Writing.*   London, Pan, 1974.

*

Bibliography: *George Lamming: A Select Bibliography*, Cave Hill, Barbados, University of the West Indies Main Library, 1980.

Critical Study: *The Novels of George Lamming* by Sandra Pouchet Paquet, London, Heinemann, 1982.

Theatrical Activities:
Director: **Play**—*Meet Me at Golden Hill*, Barbados, 1974.

*   *   *

The critical reception of George Lamming's first four novels fell short of their real merits and originality. It is often said that Lamming demands too much of the reader; it might be truer to say that the reader demands too little of Lamming. West Indian fiction has often been distinguished by a certain energy and rhetorical glow but not, except in the work of Lamming and Wilson Harris, by much complexity of form or texture. Right from his first book, *In the Castle of My Skin*, Lamming made it clear that the real complexity of West Indian experience demanded some adequate response of its writers. He has since elaborated this view in an important essay called "The Negro Writer and His World," where he wrote: "To speak of his [the Negro Writer's] situation is to speak of a general need to find a centre as well as a circumference which embraces some reality whose meaning satisfies his intellect and may prove pleasing to his senses. But a man's life assumes meaning first in relation to other men. ..."

In the Castle of My Skin may at first appear to be an autobiography of childhood, but it soon becomes apparent that the book is also the collective autobiography of a Barbadian village moving through the break-up of the old plantation system dominated by the Great House and into the new age of nationalism, industrial unrest and colonial repression. The four boys who stand at the centre of the book are given a more or less equal importance though it is "George" who ultimately registers the meaning of their disparate experiences as they are driven asunder by education, travel, and emerging social distinctions.

The collective quality already evident in this, the most personal of all Lamming's books, is more strongly present in *The Emigrants*. Here the portrait is of one boatload of the black emigrants (the title is significant, for it stresses what they leave as well as what they find) who flocked from the Caribbean to Britain between 1950 and 1962. On the boat the emigrants discover a new identity as "West Indians," only to lose it again as they fly centrifugally apart under the stresses of life in an alien culture.

The Emigrants is the saddest of all Lamming's books, because there is almost no focus of hope amid so much disillusionment and despair. By contrast both *Of Age and Innocence* and *Season of Adventure* are powerfully positive books in which what is shed is a set of values adhering to the older generation, those who are unable to match the pace and tendency of the times. *Of Age and Innocence* is set in San Cristobal, a fictional Caribbean island colony rapidly approaching independence. The dominant generation of islanders is unable to break away from its class and racial identities to work together for a new society which will redeem the past of slavery and colonialism, but it is throughout juxtaposed to the generation of its children, who struggle towards that meaning which the nationalist leader Shepherd has glimpsed and then lost again:

> I had always lived in the shadow of a meaning which others had placed on my presence in the world, and I had played no part at all in making that meaning, like a chair which is wholly at the mercy of the idea guiding the hand of the man who builds it. ... But like the chair, I have played no part at all in making that meaning which others use to define me completely.

Shepherd is destroyed by the forces of the past, but the children look out through the flames of destruction which end the novel towards a future they have already presaged in their games. At the centre of *Season of Adventure* stands another unawakened character, the "big-shot coloured" girl Fola, whose father is a West Indian police officer imbued with all the old ideas of order, dominance, and segregation. A visit to a Voduñ ceremony awakens her to the real capacity of her nature for self-discovery and self-renewal. This awakening by ancestral drums is in itself a cliché of Caribbean literature, but here it escapes banality by the intensity of Lamming's lyrical style and the bizarre violence of much of the action. *Season of Adventure* is in some ways the finest of his novels, just as *The Emigrants* is certainly the weakest. Yet the hesitancy which overtakes the drums at the end of the novel, in the very moment of their triumph as the expression of popular values, is analogous to the problem of language Lamming faces in projecting a West Indian culture which will be truly united, consistent and free: "But remember the order of the drums ... for it is the language which every nation needs if its promises and its myths are to become a fact."

After a silence of more than ten years, Lamming published two new novels within a year. These were powerfully contrasted in style and theme. *Water with Berries* is superficially a naturalistic novel about three West Indian artists living difficult and ever more lonely lives in modern London. Gradually, however (and the quotation of Caliban in the title gives a clue), the reader becomes aware that this is a study of what happens when Caliban comes to Prospero's original home. The revenges of history work themselves out through characters who are helpless to prevent completing the bizarre and violent patterns of the past. Each of the friends is an aspect of Caliban and each passes through an extreme personal crisis at the novel's end. But Derek, erect upon the stage before a howling audience, having completed the rape of Miranda at last, or Teeton, erect upon a northern island after destroying his last links with the racial past, have at least sketched the possibilities of freedom from these tyrannies of history.

Natives of My Person is more of an extended reverie upon certain dominant themes in Atlantic mythology—the demonic captain, the slave-ship, the imprisoned Amerindian prince, the crew variously haunted by tragedy and terror—which are treated like themes in music. The style is deliberately wrought from the timbers of 17th-century maritime prose, in which this mythology finds its roots. Hence the novel voyages freely in the dimension of space-time, deriving its structure simply from the musical resolution of its dominant themes. This is a work of great beauty, originality, and difficulty, which may finally prove to be Lamming's most important achievement.

—Gerald Moore

LAURENCE, (Jean) Margaret (née Wemyss). Canadian. Born in Neepawa, Manitoba, 18 July 1926. Educated at the University of Manitoba, Winnipeg, B.A. 1947. Married John F. Laurence in 1947 (divorced, 1969); one son and one daughter. Lived in Somali and Ghana, 1950–57, and in England; Writer-in-Residence, University of Toronto, 1969–70, University of Western Ontario, London, 1973, and Trent University, Peterborough, Ontario, 1974. Chancellor, Trent University, 1981–83. Recipient: Beta Sigma Phi award, 1961; University of Western Ontario President's Medal, 1961, 1962, 1964; Governor-General's Award, 1967, 1975; Canada Council Senior Fellowship, 1967, 1971; Molson Prize, 1975; B'nai B'rith award, 1976; Periodical Distributors award, 1977; City of Toronto award, 1978; Canadian Booksellers Association Writer of the Year Award, 1981; Banff Centre award, 1983. Honorary Fellow, United College, University of Winnipeg, 1967. D.Litt.: McMaster University, Hamilton, Ontario, 1970; University of Toronto, 1972; Carleton University, Ottawa, 1974; Brandon University, Manitoba, 1975; Mount Allison University, Sackville, New Brunswick, 1975; University of Western Ontario, 1975; Simon Fraser University, Burnaby, British Columbia, 1977; LL.D.: Dalhousie University, Halifax, Nova Scotia, 1972; Trent University, 1972; Queen's University, Kingston, Ontario, 1975. Companion, Order of Canada, 1971; Fellow, Royal Society of Canada, 1977. Address: P.O. Box 609, Lakefield, Ontario K0L 2H0, Canada.

PUBLICATIONS

Novels

This Side Jordan. Toronto, McClelland and Stewart, London, Macmillan, and New York, St. Martin's Press, 1960.
The Stone Angel. Toronto, McClelland and Stewart, London, Macmillan, and New York, Knopf, 1964.
A Jest of God. Toronto, McClelland and Stewart, London, Macmillan, and New York, Knopf, 1966; as *Rachel, Rachel*, New York, Popular Library, 1968; as *Now I Lay Me Down*, London, Panther, 1968.

The Fire-Dwellers. Toronto, McClelland and Stewart, London, Macmillan, and New York, Knopf, 1969.
The Diviners. Toronto, McClelland and Stewart, London, Macmillan, and New York, Knopf, 1974.

Short Stories

The Tomorrow-Tamer. Toronto, McClelland and Stewart, and London, Macmillan, 1963; New York, Knopf, 1964.
A Bird in the House. Toronto, McClelland and Stewart, London, Macmillan, and New York, Knopf, 1970.

Other

The Prophet's Camel Bell (travel). Toronto, McClelland and Stewart, and London, Macmillan, 1963; as *New Wind in a Dry Land*, New York, Knopf, 1964.
Long Drums and Cannons: Nigerian Novelists and Dramatists 1952–1966. London, Macmillan, and New York, Praeger, 1968.
Jason's Quest (for children). Toronto, McClelland and Stewart, London, Macmillan, and New York, Knopf, 1970.
Heart of a Stranger (essays). Toronto, McClelland and Stewart, 1976; Philadelphia, Lippincott, 1977.
Six Darn Cows (for children). Toronto, Lorimer, 1979.
The Olden-Days Coat (for children). Toronto, McClelland and Stewart, 1979.
The Christmas Birthday Story (for children). New York, Knopf, 1980.

Editor and Translator, *A Tree of Poverty: Somali Poetry and Prose.* Nairobi, Eagle Press, 1954.

*

Bibliography: by Susan J. Warwick, in *The Annotated Bibliography of Canada's Major Authors 1* edited by Robert Lecker and Jack David, Downsview, Ontario, ECW Press, 1979.

Manuscript Collections: McMaster University, Hamilton, Ontario; York University, Toronto.

Critical Studies: "The Maze of Life" by S.E. Read, in *Canadian Literature* (Vancouver), Winter 1966; "Geographer of Human Identities" by Walter Swayze, in *A.C.U.T.E.* (Ottawa), 1967; *Margaret Laurence*, Toronto, McClelland and Stewart, 1969, and *The Manawaka World of Margaret Laurence*, McClelland and Stewart, 1975, both by Clara Thomas; "Ten Years' Sentences," in *Canadian Literature* (Vancouver), Summer 1969, and "Sources," in *Mosaic* (Winnipeg), April 1970, both by Laurence; *Three Voices: The Lives of Margaret Laurence, Gabrielle Roy, and Frederick Philip Grove* by Joan Hind-Smith, Toronto, Clarke Irwin, 1975; *Margaret Laurence: The Writer and Her Critics* edited by W.H. New, Toronto, McGraw Hill Ryerson, 1977; "Margaret Laurence Issue" of *Journal of Canadian Studies* (Peterborough, Ontario), vol. 13, no. 3, 1978, and *Journal of Canadian Fiction* (Montreal), no. 27, 1980; *Margaret Laurence* by Patricia Morley, Boston, Twayne, 1981; *A Place to Stand On: Essays by and about Margaret Laurence* edited by George Woodcock, Edmonton, Alberta, NeWest Press, 1983.

*   *   *

Margaret Laurence's first novel, *This Side Jordan*, is set in the Gold Coast, some months before it became Ghana, the first British colony in Africa to gain independence. The novel deals with conflicting pulls of tribal and urban ways, misunderstandings between Europeans and Africans, and between Africans and Africans. Nathaniel Amegbe, a schoolmaster, experiences many of these pressures; he rejects the older pattern of life, yet he constantly feels its influence on him, finally deciding, despite severe setbacks, that his work must be undertaken in the new life of the city. This novel is fundamentally concerned with change; its texture is sufficiently complex to give depth to its picture of rapidly altering Ghananian life. The characters emerge convincingly, and the novel has a pulsating sense of immediacy about it.

Laurence's collection of Somali folk tales and poetry, *A Tree for Poverty*, was followed by an account of her life in British Somaliland, *The Prophet's Camel Bell*; and her study of Nigerian literature, *Long Drums and Cannons*, rounds off the picture we form of an author who is sensitive to oral and written literature, but, above all, to human beings.

A rich pattern of African life was exhibited in her early stories, published in book form in *The Tomorrow-Tamer*. In these, too, we see her preoccupation with people rather than background, however successful her portrayal of the contrasts of the African scene. For her characters have humour and pathos, strength and weakness, and a capacity for increasing self knowledge which involves the reader in their fortunes, in their development as human beings. Her further volume, *A Bird in the House*, reinforced the success of *The Tomorrow-Tamer*; Hagar in *The Stone Angel* is a character who reveals herself freely, and continues to hold the reader's attention. In *A Jest of God* Laurence developed further a capacity to invest an introspective character's account of her own life with increasing interest as the story develops. In this case it is the sterile life of Rachel Cameron, a spinster schoolteacher of 34 living with her mother in a small provincial Canadian town. The story of sudden awakening and incautious love is unfolded with skill and great sensitivity. The crippling conventionalism of a small community is a suitable background for this study, which is ultimately focussed on Rachel Cameron's escape from this stifling environment into a new and freer life, away from the pain of her past experience. Rachel's relationships with her colleagues, with her friend, and with neighbours, are the punctuation in her story, the pauses for breath in her long monologue with herself.

Laurence has a capacity for conveying the intensity of emotion which racks her characters; she chooses detail illuminatingly and economically; and she develops her human sympathies steadily from book to book. The reader is left with a comforting sense of architectonic control at work, however uncontrolled the actions of the characters may seem at some crucial point of story or novel.

—A. Norman Jeffares

LAVIN, Mary. Irish. Born in East Walpole, Massachusetts, United States, 11 June 1912; moved with her family to Ireland as a child. Educated at East Walpole schools; Loreto Convent, Dublin; University College, Dublin, B.A. (honours) in English 1934; National University of Ireland, Dublin, M.A. (honours) 1938. Married 1) William Walsh in 1942 (died, 1954), three daughters; 2) Michael MacDonald Scott in 1969. President, Irish PEN, 1964–65. Recipient: James Tait Black Memorial

Prize, 1944; Guggenheim fellowship, 1959, 1962, 1972; Katherine Mansfield-Menton Prize, 1962; Ella Lynam Cabot Fellowship, 1971; Eire Society Gold Medal (USA), 1974; Gregory Medal, 1974; American Irish Foundation award, 1979; Allied Irish Bank award, 1981. D.Litt.: National University of Ireland, 1968. President, Irish Academy of Letters, 1971–73. Address: The Abbey Farm, Bective, Navan, County Meath; or, Apartment 5, Gilford Pines, Gilford Road, Sandymount, Dublin 4, Ireland.

PUBLICATIONS

Novels

The House in Clewe Street.   Boston, Little Brown, and London, Joseph, 1945.
Mary O'Grady.   Boston, Little Brown, and London, Joseph, 1950.

Short Stories

Tales from Bective Bridge.   Boston, Little Brown, 1942; London, Joseph, 1943.
The Long Ago and Other Stories.   London, Joseph, 1944.
The Becker Wives and Other Stories.   London, Joseph, 1946; as *At Sallygap and Other Stories*, Boston, Little Brown, 1947.
A Single Lady and Other Stories.   London, Joseph, 1951.
The Patriot Son and Other Stories.   London, Joseph, 1956.
Selected Stories.   New York, Macmillan, 1959.
The Great Wave and Other Stories.   London, Macmillan, and New York, Macmillan, 1961.
The Stories of Mary Lavin.   London, Constable, 3 vols., 1964–85.
In the Middle of the Fields and Other Stories.   London, Constable, 1967; New York, Macmillan, 1969.
Happiness and Other Stories.   London, Constable, 1969; Boston, Houghton Mifflin, 1970.
Collected Stories.   Boston, Houghton Mifflin, 1971.
A Memory and Other Stories.   London, Constable, 1972; Boston, Houghton Mifflin, 1973.
The Shrine and Other Stories.   London, Constable, and Boston, Houghton Mifflin, 1977.
Selected Stories.   London, Penguin, 1981; New York, Penguin, 1984.
A Family Likeness.   London, Constable, 1985.

Other (for children)

A Likely Story.   New York, Macmillan, 1957.
The Second-Best Children in the World.   London, Longman, and Boston, Houghton Mifflin, 1972.

*

Bibliography: by Paul A. Doyle, in *Papers of the Bibliography Society of America 63* (New York), 1969; *Mary Lavin: A Check List* by Ruth Krawschak, Berlin, Krawschak, 1979.

Manuscript Collections: Southern Illinois University, Carbondale; Mugar Memorial Library, Boston University.

Critical Studies: preface by Lavin to *Selected Stories*, 1959, and by V.S. Pritchett to *Collected Stories*, 1971; *Mary Lavin* by Zack Bowen, Lewisburg, Pennsylvania, Bucknell University Press, 1975; *Mary Lavin* by Richard Peterson, Boston,

Twayne, 1978; "Mary Lavin Issue" of *Irish University Review* (Dublin), Autumn 1979; *Mary Lavin, Quiet Rebel: A Study of Her Short Stories* by A.A. Kelly, Dublin, Wolfhound Press, and New York, Barnes and Noble, 1980.

*   *   *

Mary Lavin has obvious gifts for fiction: she can tell a story, invent characters and give them vivid speech, a life of their own, settings described economically yet evocatively. But she has more also, a capacity for selecting those moments of crisis when the world passes by but time stops still as the meaning of life is suddenly crystalised for some person. She first showed this gift in her short stories, which are Chekhovian in scope. *Tales from Bective Bridge* contained "Love Is for Lovers" where Mathew, an elderly bachelor, is attracted and then repelled by Mrs. Cooligan, a widow. His sudden nausea at the thought of her, of her love of warmth, of her dog, of cushions, of her orange dress, occurs one summer day in her garden. She tips a half dead fly out of her tea: the fly shakes the liquid out of his wings, as though celebrating his release. But the lazy fat dog swallows him. The whole Saturday afternoon's lesson is there, and we are prepared for Mathew's thoughts that evening: he had been trying to go back, to his dreams of a slender girl, a sweet cool fragrant marriage: "But you couldn't go back, ever."

These sudden moments of perception enrich her stories, which also explore the differences between dream and reality. The story "Magenta," for instance, in *The Becker Wives* builds slowly and remorselessly up to a climax where the girl's quickly invented stories about the supposed actress who employs her, lending her her clothes, are punctured by the small mistake of her being 20 minutes too late for the train back, so that she cannot replace the clothes she has stolen.

There is a remorseless quality about Lavin's fiction which marks her two novels, *The House in Clewe Street* and *Mary O'Grady*. In both she displays an impressive skill in handling different ages in family groupings. *The House in Clewe Street* explores a boy's growing up under the care of two aunts, and his sudden rebellion and running away with the servant girl. In this story Lavin explores the tyranny given by the possession of both money and ruthless self-confidence and shows its crippling effect upon Gabriel, the protagonist. The story is, in essence, about the gradual undermining of his innocence. He does not question or rebel, without the outside stimulus given by his friend Sylvester. The exploration of his school, his growing interest in Onny the servant, his jealousy of her friendships in Dublin are all unfolded with the precision of a surgeon's skill. Yet this is no clinical novel, for we are aware of a compassionate attitude on the part of the authoress towards her characters. They have choice, they even enjoy the after effects of making a wrong choice. They are indeed children to whom Yeats's lines might well apply: "young/We loved each other and were ignorant."

In *Mary O'Grady* we are given the history of a family living in a Dublin suburb: a devoted husband and wife, their children growing up, and becoming adults, one going to America and eventually returning, one studying to become a priest, the girls finding husbands. The emotional content is rich and varied, the mother's strength impressive, the children's development into adults charted with convincing knowledge.

If the reader were to concentrate upon one specific aspect of Lavin's story-telling capacity and the subtle human understanding which informs all her fiction it might well be upon that delicate stage where adolescence asserts independence, is critical of parents while half ashamed of being so, yet determined to escape from the round of accustomed family life. In *Mary O'Grady*, for instance, there is the brilliantly evoked evening when the daughters are visited for the first time by the two engineering students who fall in love with them. The shyness, the gaucherie, the gradually developing friendliness of the family are handled with an assurance which not only encourages the reader to accept the narrator's unobtrusive, tactful guidance, but reinforces the sympathetic interest created from the beginning of the novel.

The secret of Lavin's success is, perhaps, to be found in that ability she possesses of taking her readers into her confidence, sharing with them her panoptic survey of those characters whom she regards in a kindly yet detached fashion. She has an awareness of the comedy as well as the tragedy of human life. She relishes its absurdities, weaves them into the tapestry, and keeps her proportions right. Her stories are set in Ireland, but her characters are universal. They may speak with the accents of the Irish countryside or of the city of Dublin, their particular modes of tact or forthrightness may be Irish in emphasis or accent, but these are people who exist anywhere in the world, given the author's ability to see them with insight, and, like Lavin, to portray them with realistic compassion, in their actions and in their self-revealing speech. She believes a writer distills the essence of his thought in a short story, that this kind of writing is only looking closer into the human heart. Her themes are loneliness, despair, escape, paralysis, and frustration: her strength comes from the impersonal objectivity with which she depicts unhappy characters. Ultimately she is an enduring writer, because the irony which is the mainstay of her technique is matched by penetrating insight into human thought and its effect on behaviour.

—A. Norman Jeffares

le CARRÉ, John. Pseudonym for David John Moore Cornwell. British. Born in Poole, Dorset, 19 October 1931. Educated at Sherborne School, Dorset; St. Andrew's Preparatory School; Bern University, Switzerland, 1948–49; Lincoln College, Oxford, B.A. (honours) in modern languages 1956. Married 1) Alison Ann Veronica Sharp in 1954 (divorced, 1971), three sons; 2) Valerie Jane Eustace in 1972, one son. Tutor at Eton College, 1956–58; member of the British Foreign Service, 1959–64: Second Secretary, Bonn Embassy, 1961–64; Consul, Hamburg, 1963–64. Recipient: British Crime Novel Award, 1963; Maugham Award, 1964; Mystery Writers of America Edgar Allan Poe Award, 1965, and Grand Master Award, 1984; Crime Writers Association Gold Dagger, 1978; James Tait Black Memorial Prize, 1978. Honorary Fellow, Lincoln College, 1984. Agent: John Farquharson Ltd., 162–168 Regent Street, London W1R 5TB, England.

PUBLICATIONS

Novels

Call for the Dead. London, Gollancz, 1961; New York, Walker, 1962; as *The Deadly Affair*, London, Penguin, 1966.
A Murder of Quality. London, Gollancz, 1962; New York, Walker, 1963.
The Spy Who Came In from the Cold. London, Gollancz, 1963; New York, Coward McCann, 1964.

The Looking-Glass War. London, Heinemann, and New York, Coward McCann, 1965.
A Small Town in Germany. London, Heinemann, and New York, Coward McCann, 1968.
The Naive and Sentimental Lover. London, Hodder and Stoughton, 1971; New York, Knopf, 1972.
The Quest for Karla. London, Hodder and Stoughton, and New York, Knopf, 1982.

   Tinker, Tailor, Soldier, Spy. London, Hodder and Stoughton, and New York, Knopf, 1974.
   The Honourable Schoolboy. London, Hodder and Stoughton, and New York, Knopf, 1977.
   Smiley's People. London, Hodder and Stoughton, and New York, Knopf, 1980.

The Little Drummer Girl. London, Hodder and Stoughton, and New York, Knopf, 1983.
A Perfect Spy. London, Hodder and Stoughton, 1986.

Uncollected Short Stories

"Dare I Weep, Dare I Mourn," in *Saturday Evening Post* (Philadelphia), 28 January 1967.
"What Ritual Is Being Observed Tonight?," in *Saturday Evening Post* (Philadelphia), 2 November 1968.

Play

Television Play: *Smiley's People*, with John Hopkins, from the novel by le Carré, 1982.

*

Critical Studies: *John le Carré* by Peter Lewis, New York, Ungar, 1984; *The Novels of John le Carré: The Art of Survival* by David Monaghan, Oxford, Blackwell, 1985; *Taking Sides: The Fiction of John le Carré* by T. Barley, Milton Keynes, Buckinghamshire, Open University Press, 1986.

*   *   *

Though John le Carré had written two thrillers, *Call for the Dead* and *A Murder of Quality*, it was when *The Spy Who Came In from the Cold* was published that it became obvious that a new talent for writing a different kind of spy story had emerged. Le Carré caught a new mood of chilling horror in this picture of the beastliness underlying the espionage of the cold war, for this is a novel which shows how man's capacity for inhumanity to man and woman is heightened through the process of espionage. The style matches the material. The moods evoked are of grey despair. The tone is cold, almost clinical. The conversations convince; they have the authentic texture of contemporary speech. And the details of the British, Dutch and German background are painted in with a casual assurance. The story is unfolded, given fresh twists, until the reality of life itself becomes warped. Leamas, the British agent, is created convincingly; he carries out his role of defector only to find that his own people have framed him, in order to frame Fiedler, an East German who has discovered the truth about Mundt, his chief.

This is a world of intellectual skills applied arbitrarily, of brilliance without scruple, of brutality without restraint. The inexorable march of the story continues: its destiny is disaster, the same kind of disaster which opens its account of the effects of treason and betrayal. And yet in the final moment Leamas returns for Liz, the English communist party member who

befriended him in London, who has been brought to East Germany to testify against him. Before their final moments, before they attempt to cross the Berlin wall, he makes his apology to her. To him it seems the world has gone mad. His life and hers, their dignity, are a tiny price to pay. They are, ultimately, the victims of a temporary alliance of expediency. His people save Mundt because they need him, "so that," he says to her, "the great moronic mass that you admire can sleep soundly in their beds at night. They need him for the safety of ordinary crummy people like you and me." He sees the loss of Fiedler's life as part of the small-scale war which is being waged, with a wastage of innocent life sometimes, though it is still smaller than other wars. Leamas doesn't believe in anything, but he sees people cheated, misled, lives thrown away, "people shot and in prison, whole groups and classes of men written off for nothing." Her party, he remarks, was built on the bodies of ordinary people, and she remembers the German prison wardress describing the prison as one for those who slow down the march, "for those who think they have the right to err."

Le Carré's next book, *The Looking-Glass War*, carries his exploration of the work of intelligence services further. This story opens impressively, with the death of a courier who has gone to Finland to pick up films made by the pilot of a commercial flight apparently off course over Eastern Germany. An unconfirmed report indicates the likelihood of a rocket site there. Then a small intelligence unit is authorized to put an agent into the area. The preparations are described in detail: the recruiting and training of the agent, the ineptitude involved, and the rivalry among the different agencies—and ultimately the schooled indifference with which the older professionals see their scheme fail abysmally. They are already planning the future, disowning the agent whose slow broadcasting on single frequencies on an obsolete radio has doomed him to capture. The story is well told; it explores the stresses and the vanities, the dangerous risks, even delusions, which beset the world of intelligence; it has a curious pathos, accentuated by the naivety and decency of the young man Avery which is opposed in fury by Haldane, who has become a technician: "We sent him because we needed to; we abandon him because we must."

In *A Small Town in Germany* there is an enlarging of scope. Here is a story of the British Embassy in Bonn, from which secret files—and Leo Harting—have vanished. Turner comes from London to investigate. His interrogations of some of the Embassy staff are brilliant. The pattern of thieving, of treachery, of insinuation, of making himself indispensable, of using others, emerges slowly as Turner tries to build up his picture of Leo Harting. The contrasts of personalities as Turner painstakingly pursues his enquiries give this picture depth, and yet the nature of the vanished man remains elusive. The complications of the British negotiations in Brussels where German support is necessary, the student riots, and the ugly neo-nazism give the man-hunt an extreme urgency. The attitude of the German authorities, and that of the Head of Chancery, surprise Turner. And the events he unravels surprise the reader.

The novel has a continuous tension; the discoveries of the investigator are cumulative; and finally his aggressive desire to hunt out the missing man turns to a sympathetic understanding of just what Harting has been doing. At this point his attitude differs markedly from that of the Head of Chancery. To a certain extent his reactions are parallel to those of Avery in *The Looking-Glass War*. Both are younger men, outside the orthodoxies of their elders, possessed ultimately of more humanity, though they have no capacity to influence the final stages of the story. The difference lies between the character who professes to control the processes of his own mind and the character who believes we are born free, we are not automatons and cannot control the processes of our minds. The novel is, in fact, about the problems of forgetting, and about the problems of idealism, innocence, and practical politics; and the incidental picture it gives of the complex working life of an Embassy provides a very suitable background against which political issues can be spotlit.

The Naive and Sentimental Lover lacks the punch and energy of his earlier works. In them the tendency of the characters to be warped, maimed, frustrated men and women mattered little because the action backed by skilful description carried the plot forward at such headlong speed that analysis of character *per se* was less important than the actions taken by the participants. In this novel there is a need for a deeper analysis of character, and this does not seem to have been fully achieved, while the story does not move with the same sureness. However, it is likely that le Carré was experimenting with a new genre, and just as *The Spy Who Came In from the Cold* needed preliminary studies this may herald a development in character depiction similar to his earlier advances in technique and architectonic power in *The Spy Who Came In from the Cold*, which will remain as a chilling exposé of the continuous underground battle of intelligence services.

Tinker, Tailor, Soldier, Spy and *The Honourable Schoolboy* are both surpassed by *Smiley's People*, the narrative art of which is combined with a sympathetic compassion for its characters. Here le Carré shows Smiley torn by loyalties, uncovering instead of covering up the murder of an ex-agent, and in the process peeling layer after layer from the mystery of betrayal, getting steadily closer to his old enemy the Russian Karla. The story moves deliberately, the details are amassed, but the tension is maintained right to the climax. This is a *tour de force* because its present action demands an understanding of the past, and that past is revealed so skilfully that its actions live as a pressing part of the present. The reader is involved in the characters' memories, their evasions and searchings.

In *The Little Drummer Girl* le Carré portrays the violent conflicts of Arab and Israeli, moving his characters freely about Europe as he tightens the tense atmosphere created by terrorism. His characters are meticulous in their attention to detail; he conveys the concentration, the ruthlessness, the tyranny of abstract concepts made utterly inhuman. This is a story in which several ways of looking at life—and the deaths of victims—are juxtaposed convincingly; the effect is achieved through le Carré's capacity to create confidence in his readers through an inside knowledge of how terrorists and counterterrorists operate.

—A. Norman Jeffares

LE GUIN, Ursula K(roeber). American. Born in Berkeley, California, 21 October 1929; daughter of the anthropologist Alfred L. Kroeber. Educated at Radcliffe College, Cambridge, Massachusetts, A.B. 1951 (Phi Beta Kappa); Columbia University, New York, (Faculty Fellow; Fulbright Fellow, 1953), M.A. 1952. Married Charles A. Le Guin in 1953; two daughters and one son. Instructor in French, Mercer University, Macon, Georgia, 1954, and University of Idaho, Moscow, 1956; department secretary, Emory University, Atlanta 1955; taught writing workshops at Pacific University, Forest Grove, Oregon, 1971, University of Washington, Seattle, 1971–73,

Portland State University, Oregon, 1974, 1977, 1979, in Melbourne, Australia, 1975, at the University of Reading, England, 1976, Indiana Writers Conference, Bloomington, 1978 and 1983, and University of California, San Diego, 1979. Recipient: Boston *Globe-Horn Book* Award, for children's book, 1969; Nebula Award, 1969, 1974 (twice); Hugo Award, 1970, 1973, 1974, 1975; National Book Award, for children's book, 1972; Jupiter Award, 1974 (twice), 1976; Gandalf Award, 1979; University of Oregon Distinguished Service award, 1981; *Locus* award 1983 (twice). Guest of Honor, World Science Fiction Convention, 1975. D.Litt.: Bucknell University, Lewisburg, Pennsylvania, 1978; Lawrence University, Appleton, Wisconsin, 1979; D.H.L.: Lewis and Clark College, Portland, Oregon, 1983; Occidental College, Los Angeles, 1985. Lives in Portland, Oregon. Agent: Virginia Kidd, Box 278, Milford, Pennsylvania 18337, U.S.A.

PUBLICATIONS

Novels

Rocannon's World. New York, Ace, 1966; London, Tandem, 1972.
Planet of Exile. New York, Ace, 1966; London, Tandem, 1972.
City of Illusions. New York, Ace, 1967; London, Gollancz, 1971.
The Left Hand of Darkness. New York, and London, Macdonald, 1969.
The Lathe of Heaven. New York, Scribner, 1971; London, Gollancz, 1972.
The Dispossessed: An Ambiguous Utopia. New York, Harper, and London, Gollancz, 1974.
The Word for World Is Forest. New York, Putnam, 1976; London, Gollancz, 1977.
Malafrena. New York, Putnam, 1979; London, Gollancz, 1980.
The Eye of the Heron. London, Gollancz, 1982; New York, Harper, 1983.
Always Coming Home. New York, Harper, 1985.

Short Stories

The Wind's Twelve Quarters. New York, Harper, 1975; London, Gollancz, 1976.
Orsinian Tales. New York, Harper, 1976; London, Gollancz, 1977.
The Water Is Wide. Portland, Oregon, Pendragon Press, 1976.
Gwilan's Harp. Northridge, California, Lord John Press, 1981.
The Compass Rose. New York, Harper, 1982; London, Gollancz, 1983.
The Visionary: The Life Story of Flicker of the Serpentine, with *Wonders Hidden,* by Scott Russell Sanders. Santa Barbara, California, Capra Press, 1984.

Uncollected Short Stories

"Two Delays on the Northern Line," in *New Yorker,* 12 November 1979.
"The Word of Unbinding," in *Basilisk,* edited by Ellen Kushner. New York, Ace, 1980.
"The Spoons in the Basement," in *New Yorker,* 2 August 1982.
"The Professor's Houses," in *New Yorker,* 1 November 1982.

"The Ascent of the North Face," in *Isaac Asimov's Space of Her Own*, edited by Shawna McCarthy. New York, Davis, 1983.
"She Unnames Them," in *New Yorker*, 21 January 1985.

Fiction (for children)

Earthsea. London, Gollancz, 1977; as *The Earthsea Trilogy*, London, Penguin, 1979.
> *A Wizard of Earthsea*. Berkeley, California, Parnassus Press, 1968; London, Gollancz, 1971.
> *The Tombs of Atuan*. New York, Atheneum, 1971; London, Gollancz, 1972.
> *The Farthest Shore*. New York, Atheneum, 1972; London, Gollancz, 1973.
Very Far Away from Anywhere Else. New York, Atheneum, 1976; as *A Very Long Way from Anywhere Else*, London, Gollancz, 1976.
Leese Webster. New York, Atheneum, 1979; London, Gollancz, 1981.
The Beginning Place. New York, Harper, 1980; as *Threshold*, London, Gollancz, 1980.
The Adventure of Cobbler's Rune. New Castle, Virginia, Cheap Street, 1982.

Plays

No Use to Talk to Me, in *The Altered Eye*, edited by Lee Harding. Melbourne, Norstrilia Press, 1976; New York, Berkley, 1980.
King Dog (screenplay), with *Dostoevsky* by Raymond Carver and Tess Gallagher. Santa Barbara, California, Capra Press, 1985.

Verse

Wild Angels. Santa Barbara, California, Capra Press, 1975.
Hard Words and Other Poems. New York, Harper, 1981.
In the Red Zone. Northridge, California, Lord John Press, 1983.

Other

From Elfland to Poughkeepsie (lecture). Portland, Oregon, Pendragon Press, 1973.
Dreams Must Explain Themselves. New York, Algol Press, 1975.
The Language of the Night: Essays on Fantasy and Science Fiction, edited by Susan Wood. New York, Putnam, 1979.

Editor, *Nebula Award Stories 11*. London, Gollancz, 1976; New York, Harper, 1977.
Editor, with Virginia Kidd, *Interfaces*. New York, Ace, 1980.
Editor, with Virginia Kidd, *Edges*. New York, Pocket Books, 1980.

*

Bibliography: *Ursula K. Le Guin: A Primary and Secondary Bibliography* by Elizabeth Cummins Cogell, Boston, Hall, 1983.

Manuscript Collection: University of Oregon Library, Eugene.

Critical Studies: "Wholeness and Balance" by Douglas Barbour, in *Science-Fiction Studies* (Terre Haute, Indiana), Spring 1974; "The Good Witch of the West" by Robert Scholes, in *Hollins Critic* (Hollins College, Virginia), April 1974; *The Farthest Shores of Ursula K. Le Guin* by George Edgar Slusser, San Bernardino, California, Borgo Press, 1976; "Ursula Le Guin Issue" of *Science-Fiction Studies* (Terre Haute, Indiana), March 1976; *Ursula Le Guin* by Joseph D. Olander and Martin H. Greenberg, New York, Taplinger, and Edinburgh, Harris, 1979; *Ursula K. Le Guin: Voyager to Inner Lands and to Outer Space* edited by Joseph W. De Bolt, Port Washington, New York, Kennikat Press, 1979; *Ursula K. Le Guin* by Barbara J. Bucknall, New York, Ungar, 1981; *Ursula K. Le Guin* by Charlotte Spivack, Boston, Twayne, 1984; *Approaches to the Fiction of Ursula K. Le Guin* by James Bittner, Ann Arbor, Michigan, UMI Research Press, 1984.

*   *   *

Ursula K. Le Guin's earliest works attracted, almost exclusively, the devoted audience of science-fiction readers. *Rocannon's World*, *Planet of Exile*, and *City of Illusions* are interconnected novels which depict a situation entirely familiar to such readers. Earth and other planets of a far-future "League of All Worlds" are peopled by "human" races which must struggle to recognize one another as such. The League prepares to meet a rather vaguely defined invasion from afar. Heroes out of touch with lost civilization undertake quests of self-discovery, or get the enemy's location through to headquarters just in time to repel the invasion. In short, Le Guin offers us space opera, although the delicate tone, the theme of communication, and the imagery of light and darkness suggest her future development.

With *The Left Hand of Darkness*, "The Word for World Is Forest," her "Earthsea" fantasy trilogy, and *The Dispossessed*, Le Guin has moved to another level, and has begun, deservedly, to attract an audience outside the science-fiction ghetto. The treatment of androgyny in *The Left Hand of Darkness* has made the book into a minor classic. The League of All Worlds has been succeeded by a non-imperialistic "Ekumen," which sends a lone envoy, Genly Ai, to make an alliance with the isolated planet Winter (Gethen). The Ekumen has no wish to subdue Winter but to extend "the evolutionary tendency inherent in Being; one manifestation of which is exploration." Subverting the stock situation of civilization brought to the savages, Le Guin has Ai learn at least as much from the relatively primitive Gethenians as they from him. Gethenians mate only once a month, and they may adopt alternatively male and female roles. We heart at one point that "the King is pregnant." Ai, a male chauvinist, learns how difficult it is to think of our fellow humans as people rather than as men and women. When he forms an alliance with a Gethenian called Estraven, Ai learns how close together the words "patriot" and "traitor" can be. Ai's loyalty begins to shift from the Ekumen to Gethen, but this shift is a precondition of his mission's success. Conversely, Estraven's loyalty shifts to Ai, but only because he loves his country well enough to want Ai to succeed.

Although Ai and Estraven grow closer to one another, a vast distance also remains between them. Humans are alienated from one another in a wintry universe. But hope springs from the melancholy. The universe is dark but young, and spring will follow winter. The book reverberates with a nontheistic prayer: "Praise then darkness and Creation unfinished."

Although they meet as equal individuals, Ai and Estraven are members of differing societies. Le Guin would insist on Aristotle's definition of people as social animals. In her ambivalent utopia *The Dispossessed*, Le Guin preserves this insistence—while making it equally clear that anarchism is one of her centers of value. The book is an important break in science fiction's anti-utopian trend. A scientist, Shevek, moves to and fro between an anarchist utopia which is becoming middle-aged, and a world—obviously analogous to our own—that is divided between propertarian (capitalist) and statist (communist) countries. Nowhere does he find full self-expression; conversely, full self-expression requires one's participation in a society. In alternating chapters which disrupt sequential chronology, Shevek moves both away from the anarchist utopia and back toward it. Le Guin identifies herself both as a stylistic artist and as a thinker. Her stark, wintry worlds are philosophically rich with dialectic Taoism and the co-reality of such opposites as light and darkness, religion and politics, and language and power. In *A Wizard of Earthsea* the magician has power over things when he knows their true names, so that his power is the artist's power. Le Guin plays with the notion, in "The Author of the Acacia Seeds and Other Extracts from *The Journal of the Association of Therolinguistics*," that ants, penguins, and even plants might be producing what could be called language and art.

Since writing *The Dispossessed*, Le Guin has been turning in the direction of fantasy. *Malafrena* is a compelling mixture of fantasy and historical fiction. Le Guin sets the imaginary country of Orsinia into central Europe in the 19th century. It is Itale Sorde's story: he rejects the ease of an inherited landed estate (Malafrena) to work for revolution against Orsinia's domination by the Austrian Empire. After being jailed for several years and after a failed insurrection in 1830, he returns to Malafrena, but there are hints that he will leave again. True voyage is return, and structure and theme coalesce, as in *The Dispossessed*.

In her recent works Le Guin often presents us with the ambiguity of revolution, once again the theme of a long short story, "The Eye of the Heron." A colony of young counter-culturalists attempts to break away from their elders, with typically ambiguous results. A central paradox in Le Guin's fiction is her simultaneous recognition of the need for harmony and the need for revolt.

Praise for Le Guin has been high—too uniformly high. Her style is unexceptional and her desire for peace and harmony borders on sentimentality at times. But she has taken important steps toward blending politics and art in her novels, and she is still experimenting with both form and content. Thus *Always Coming Home* both returns to the anthropological format of *The Left Hand of Darkness* and greatly expands that format. Le Guin has gathered together stories, folklore, histories, and other materials into what she calls "an archaeology" of primitive people living in a far-future northern California. The central story (occupying only a small part of the book) is of the coming of age of the woman "Stone Telling," whose mother lives in the peaceful Valley, which is integrated with nature, and whose father is of the war-like Condor people. Stone Telling leaves her valley to join her father for a while, but she becomes "woman always coming home" when she returns, her to-and-fro motion reminding us of *The Dispossessed*. When we discover that the Condor can build bridges and that they have electric lights, we may wonder how their traditional culture is supposed to have survived. But Le Guin's ability to capture the language, culture, and thought of primitive people is, despite some lapses, generally remarkable.

—Curtis C. Smith

LEHMANN, Rosamond (Nina). British. Born in Bourne End, Buckinghamshire, 3 February 1901; sister of the writer John Lehmann and the actress Beatrix Lehmann. Educated at home and at Girton College, Cambridge (scholar), 1919–22. Married 1) Leslie Runciman in 1924 (marriage dissolved, 1927); 2) the Honorable Wogan Philipps, later Lord Milford, in 1928 (marriage dissolved, 1942), one son, and one daughter (deceased). Co-director, John Lehmann Ltd., publishers, London, 1946–53. Past President, PEN English Centre, and International Vice-President, PEN; council member, Society of Authors; Vice-President, College of Psychic Studies. Recipient: Denyse Clairouin Prize, for translation, 1948. Commandant, Order of Arts and Letters (France), 1968; C.B.E. (Commander, Order of the British Empire), 1982. Address: 30 Clareville Grove, London SW7 5AS, England.

PUBLICATIONS

Novels

Dusty Answer. London, Chatto and Windus, and New York, Holt, 1927.
A Note in Music. London, Chatto and Windus, and New York, Holt, 1930.
Invitation to the Waltz. London, Chatto and Windus, and New York, Holt, 1932.
The Weather in the Streets. London, Collins, and New York, Reynal, 1936.
The Ballad and the Source. London, Collins, 1944; New York, Reynal, 1945.
The Echoing Grove. London, Collins, and New York, Harcourt Brace, 1953.
The Sea-Grape Tree. London, Collins, 1976; New York, Harcourt Brace, 1977.

Short Stories

The Gipsy's Baby and Other Stories. London, Collins, 1946; New York, Reynal, 1947.

Play

No More Music (produced London, 1939). London, Collins, 1939.

Other

A Letter to a Sister. London, Hogarth Press, 1931; New York, Harcourt Brace, 1932.
A Man Seen Afar, with W. Tudor Pole. London, Spearman, 1965.
The Swan in the Evening: Fragments of an Inner Life. London, Collins, 1967; New York, Harcourt Brace, 1968.
Letters from Our Daughters, with Cynthia Sandys. London, College of Psychic Studies, 2 vols., 1972.
Rosamond Lehmann's Album. London, Chatto and Windus, 1985.

Editor, with others, *Orion: A Miscellany 1–3.* London, Nicholson and Watson, 3 vols., 1945–46.
Editor, with Cynthia Sandys, *The Awakening Letters.* London, Spearman, 1978.

Translator, *Geneviève*, by Jacques Lemarchand. London, Lehmann, 1947.

Translator, *Children of the Game*, by Jean Cocteau. London, Harvill Press, 1955; as *The Holy Terrors*, New York, New Directions, 1957; as *Les Enfants terribles*, London, Folio Society, 1976.

*

Bibliography: "Rosamond Lehmann: A Bibliography" by M.T. Gustafson, in *Twentieth Century Literature 4* (Hempstead, New York), 1959.

Manuscript Collections: King's College, Cambridge; University of Texas, Austin.

Critical Studies: *Rosamond Lehmann* by Diana E. Le Stourgeon, New York, Twayne, 1965; *Rosamond Lehmann: An Appreciation* by Gillian Tindall, London, Chatto and Windus, 1985.

*   *   *

Rosamond Lehmann's distinctive gift as a novelist lies in her sympathetically realistic depiction of the intimate psychology of young girls. This won her instant critical recognition in her first novel, *Dusty Answer*, a portrayal of childhood and adolescence, set partly in Cambridge, which anticipates several of her favourite later themes. *Invitation to the Waltz* explores, with a delicacy of perception reminiscent of Elizabeth Bowen's *The Death of the Heart*, a girl's growth in insight and understanding—during a single evening, that of her first dance—of the hitherto unintelligible and intimidating adult world. Eighteen-year-old Olivia, gauche, naive, and pitifully over-exposed to the chill of unconscious or imagined snubs which cause her "to bleed in her self-esteem," is shown gradually turning her gaze outward from the adolescent agonies of self to participate in the problems and perplexities of others. In this process of quickening comprehension, she achieves a new confidence and readiness for the future adventures of living related in the book's sequel, *The Weather in the Streets*. Here experience has replaced innocence, but beneath superficial sophistication the old, painful vulnerability remains. Ten years later *The Ballad and the Source* was also presented through the awakening consciousness of a girl, fascinated by the personality of a dominating old woman whose story powerfully compels her imagination. The characters of girls likewise play an important part in the collection of short stories entitled *The Gipsy's Baby*.

The complex narrative structure of *The Ballad and the Source*, as the listening child comments and questions, sometimes only half understanding what she hears, is handled with a Jamesian subtlety of technique. So, too, is the unfolding of relationships in *The Echoing Grove*, Lehmann's most intricately constructed, accomplished, and perhaps most satisfying novel, which skilfully interweaves the experience of three characters helplessly embroiled in a mutually tormenting passion. The conflict of emotions suffered by two sisters, divided yet finally united by their love for the same man—a character whose charm and weakness are presented with relentless feminine penetration—evoked the tribute from Marghanita Laski that "no English writer has told of the pains of women in love more truly or movingly .. of what it felt like to be a woman." It is probably this novel, more than any other, which reveals a strong affinity between Lehmann's deliberately wrought prose and finely attuned sensibility and those of Virginia Woolf.

But *The Echoing Grove* is not only a tale of personal exaltations and miseries: it is also a vivid portrait of the era immediately preceding and during the last war. The restless turbulence of private lives, chronicled with such intensity and compassion, is mirrored and echoed in the upheavals of the social and political scene. The characters are firmly established as recognizable products of their generation, class, and background; and the disintegration of the old order and of the stability of its values is acutely anatomized through the musings of the Marxist daughter, Dinah, on "the contemporary situation, the crack-up." Lehmann has, in fact, a keen eye for the detail of a period, particularly in the life of the upper middle classes. *The Ballad and the Source* communicates an indefinable sense of "a defeat somewhere, a failure of the vital impulse" undermining comfortable patrician security in the years leading into the First World War. *Invitation to the Waltz* recreates with nostalgic precision the atmosphere—old family servants, the rituals of nursery tea, "finishing" in Paris, and country-house balls—of a safe and sheltered childhood between the wars. The self-consciously cynical stance of the older, bohemian Olivia of *The Weather in the Streets* conveys something of the disenchanted climate of living—adultery, backstreet abortion, divorce—among the fashionable young during the mid-1930's.

For all the accuracy of her social observation, however, it is finally as a delineator of the inner world of feeling, and in her subtle investigation of the nuances of personal relationship, that Rosamond Lehmann excels, and for which she will be remembered.

—Margaret Willy

LEIBER, Fritz (Reuter, Jr.). American. Born in Chicago, Illinois, 25 December 1910. Educated at the University of Chicago, Ph.B. 1932; Episcopal General Theological Seminary, Washington, D.C. Married Jonquil Stephens in 1936 (died, 1969); one son. Episcopal minister at two churches in New Jersey, 1932–33; actor, 1934–36; editor, Consolidated Book Publishers, Chicago, 1937–41; Instructor in Speech and Drama, Occidental College, Los Angeles, 1941–42; precision inspector, Douglas Aircraft, Santa Monica, California, 1942–44; associate editor, *Science Digest*, Chicago, 1944–56. Lecturer, Clarion State College, Pennsylvania, summers 1968–70. Recipient: Hugo Award, 1958, 1965, 1968, 1970, 1971, 1976; Nebula Award, 1967, 1970, 1975, and Grand Master Nebula Award, 1981; Ann Radcliffe Award, 1970; Gandalf Award, 1975; Derleth Award, 1976; World Fantasy Award, 1976, 1978. Guest of Honor, World Science Fiction Convention, 1951. Address: 565 Geary Street, Apartment 604, San Francisco, California 94102, U.S.A.

PUBLICATIONS

Novels

Gather, Darkness! New York, Pellegrini and Cudahy, 1950; London, New English Library, 1966.
Conjure Wife. New York, Twayne, 1953; London, Penguin, 1969.
The Green Millennium. New York, Abelard Press, 1953; London, Abelard Schuman, 1959.
Destiny Times Three. New York, Galaxy, 1957.
The Big Time. New York, Ace, 1961; London, New English Library, 1965.

The Silver Eggheads.   New York, Ballantine, 1962; London, New English Library, 1966.
The Wanderer.   New York, Ballantine, 1964; London, Dobson, 1967.
Tarzan and the Valley of Gold.   New York, Ballantine, 1966.
The Swords of Lankhmar.   New York, Ace, 1968; London, Hart Davis, 1969.
A Specter Is Haunting Texas.   New York, Walker, and London, Gollancz, 1969.
Swords and Deviltry.   New York, Ace, 1970; London, New English Library, 1971.
Our Lady of Darkness.   New York, Berkley, 1977; London, Millington, 1978.

Short Stories

Night's Black Agents.   Sauk City, Wisconsin, Arkham House, 1947; London, Spearman, 1975.
The Sinful Ones.   New York, Universal, 1953; as *You're All Alone*, New York, Ace, 1972.
Two Sought Adventure: Exploits of Fafhrd and the Gray Mouser.   New York, Gnome Press, 1957.
The Mind Spider and Other Stories.   New York, Ace, 1961.
Shadows with Eyes.   New York, Ballantine, 1962.
A Pail of Air.   New York, Ballantine, 1964.
Ships to the Stars.   New York, Ace, 1964.
The Night of the Wolf.   New York, Ballantine, 1966; London, Sphere, 1976.
The Secret Songs.   London, Hart Davis, 1968.
Swords Against Wizardry.   New York, Ace, 1968; London, Prior, 1977.
Swords in the Mist.   New York, Ace, 1968; London, Prior, 1977.
Night Monsters.   New York, Ace, 1969; revised edition, London, Gollancz, 1974.
Swords Against Death.   New York, Ace, 1970; London, New English Library, 1972.
The Best of Fritz Leiber, edited by Angus Wells.   London, Sphere, and New York, Doubleday, 1974.
The Book [and *Second Book*] *of Fritz Leiber.*   New York, DAW, 2 vols., 1974–75.
The Worlds of Fritz Leiber.   New York, Ace, 1976.
Swords and Ice Magic.   New York, Ace, and London, Prior, 1977.
Rime Isle.   Chapel Hill, North Carolina, Whispers Press, 1977.
Bazaar of the Bizarre.   West Kingston, Rhode Island, Grant, 1978.
Heroes and Horrors.   Browns Mills, New Jersey, Whispers Press, 1978.
The Change War.   Boston, Gregg Press, 1978.
Ship of Shadows.   London, Gollancz, 1979.
The Ghost Light (includes essay).   New York, Berkley, 1984.

Verse

The Demons of the Upper Air.   Glendale, California, Squires, 1969.
Sonnets to Jonquil and All.   Glendale, California, Squires, 1978.

Other

The Mystery of the Japanese Clock.   Santa Monica, California, Montgolfier Press, 1982.
Quicks Around the Zodiac: A Farce.   New Castle, Virginia, Cheap Street, 1983.

Editor, with Stuart David Schiff, *The World Fantasy Awards 2.*   New York, Doubleday, 1980.

*

Bibliography: *Fritz Leiber: A Bibliography 1934–1979* by Chris Morgan, Birmingham, Morgenstern, 1979.

Critical Studies: "Fritz Leiber Issue" of *Fantasy and Science Fiction* (New York), July 1969; *Fritz Leiber* by Tom Staicar, New York, Ungar, 1983.

*   *   *

Uncommonly elegant, rich in wit and ideas, Fritz Leiber's fiction is unusual in its appeal to lovers of science fiction and fantasy alike. Arguably he is the field's finest stylist; certainly a man who has played every part. One can almost imagine the anguish of historians in years to come as they try to classify the unclassifiable: "Primarily a fantasy writer"; "no, a great satirist"; "far more concerned with serious social and technological extrapolation." For Leiber has done the lot, and done it superbly.

His very first sales in 1939 introduced Fafhrd the Barbarian and his cosmopolitan colleague the Gray Mouser, two of the most unusual swashbucklers ever to emerge from the realms of swordplay and sorcery. Over the years he has woven a tangled web of the adventures of these two fine rogues in the fabled land of Nehwon, and recently the author has put them into chronological order in the five books of the "Swords of Lankhmar" series. Many readers seem to enjoy these stories while generally disliking most other heroic fantasies. Probably the reason is that Leiber never lets his heroes take themselves too seriously; the sardonic humour and writing skill are entirely above the level of usual epics of blood and gore or supernatural mystery.

This first active period from 1939–43 culminated in two novels, *Gather, Darkness!* and *Conjure Wife* (later filmed as *Burn, Witch, Burn!*), both juxtaposing the trappings of witchcraft against technological or contemporary settings to produce original and memorable results. Then came a dry spell, and Leiber did not return to science fiction until the early 1950's. his new work was mostly in a biting, satiric vein, almost more so than the market dared to handle in the age of McCarthyism. The novelette "Coming Attraction" is a frightening glimpse of a psychotic America, and the two stories "The Night He Cried" and "Poor Superman" are superb take-offs of Mickey Spillane and L. Ron Hubbard respectively. *The Green Millennium* is similarly outrageous but equally ingenious and soundly constructed.

Once again Leiber stopped writing, this time until 1958 when he made a triumphant return with *The Big Time*, one of the most unusual of all science-fiction novels and which won him his first Hugo Award. With this story something became apparent which had been there all along if anyone had looked for it; Leiber writes *plays* rather than stories, even in his fantasies. His works are scripts, acted out by characters in settings suited to a restricted theatrical stage (in *Big Time*, one room throughout). There are some superb lines, superbly delivered; one whole chunk of this particular novel is delivered by a girl of Bronze Age Crete in perfectly-scanning iambic pentameter.

Another novel, *The Silver Eggheads*, was not well received; in 1963 the author decided to try something different, and after a year of effort the result was *The Wanderer*, a long, incredible "catastrophe" novel which simultaneously does more things than can easily be recounted. It won a Hugo for 1965, and

Leiber never looked back. He has at last been recognised as one of the truly major talents in science fiction, while publishers too have suddenly woken up and are issuing his stories in new form for the enjoyment of an entirely new generation of readers.

Perhaps the most revealing test of all is this. Science fiction nearly always dates very rapidly, and yet Leiber's earliest stories are in print alongside his most recent work, and they read as well as ever. His fiction has a timeless quality that will endure long after the arbitrary divisions between "literature" and "science fiction" have disappeared.

—Peter R. Weston

LELCHUK, Alan. American. Born in Brooklyn, New York, 15 September 1938. Educated at Brooklyn College, B.A. 1960; University College, London, 1962–63; Stanford University, California, M.A. 1963, Ph.D. in English 1965. Married Barbara Kreiger in 1979. Assistant Professor of English, 1966–75, and Writer-in-Residence, 1975–81, Brandeis University, Waltham, Massachusetts; Visiting Writer, Amherst College, Massachusetts, 1982–84. Associate editor, *Modern Occasions* quarterly, Cambridge, Massachusetts, 1970–72. Guest, Mishkenot Sha'Ananim, Jerusalem, 1976–77. Recipient: Yaddo Foundation grant, 1968, 1971, 1973; MacDowell Colony fellowship, 1969; Guggenheim fellowship, 1976. Agent: Georges Borchardt, 136 East 57th Street, New York, New York 10022. Address: RFD 2, Canaan, New Hampshire 03741, U.S.A.

PUBLICATIONS

Novels

American Mischief. New York, Farrar Straus, and London, Cape, 1973.
Miriam at Thirty-Four. New York, Farrar Straus, 1974; London, Cape, 1975.
Shrinking: The Beginning of My Own Ending. Boston, Little Brown, 1978.
Miriam in Her Forties. Boston, Houghton Mifflin, 1985.

Uncollected Short Stories

"Sundays," in *Transatlantic Review 21* (London), Summer 1966.
"Of Our Time," in *New American Review 4*, edited by Theodore Solotaroff. New York, New American Library, 1968.
"Winter Image," in *Transatlantic Review 32* (London), Summer 1969.
"Cambridge Talk," in *Modern Occasions 1* (Cambridge, Massachusetts), Fall 1970.
"Hallie of the Sixties," in *Works in Progress 6* (New York), 1972.
"Doctor's Holiday," in *Atlantic* (Boston), March 1981.

Play

Screenplay: *Tippy*, with Jiri Weiss, 1978.

Other

Editor, with Gerson Shaked, *Eight Great Hebrew Short Stories.* New York, New American Library, 1983.

*

Manuscript Collection: Mugar Memorial Library, Boston University.

Critical Studies: by Philip Roth in *Esquire* (New York), September 1972; "Lelchuk's Inferno" by Wilfrid Sheed, in *Book-of-the-Month Club News* (New York), March 1973; "The Significant Self" by Benjamin DeMott, in *Atlantic* (Boston), October 1974; "Faculty in Fiction: Images of the Professor in Recent Novels" by Frances Barasch, in *Clarion* (New York), June 1982.

Alan Lelchuk comments:
Some points about my fiction:
A realism of extreme sensibilities and modernism of content . . . the intensity and ambiguity of the sensual life . . . a blurring of the line between the comic and the serious . . . vibrating the odd strings of obsession . . . character through sexuality, and sexuality as (native) social gesture . . . a mingling of lofty thought and contemporary vulgarity . . . playing out the deep comic disorders of our culture . . . some unnerving fables and sweet myths of our time camouflaged by realistic garb and inhabited by real souls. . . .

*   *   *

Alan Lelchuk's novels recreate that rich American intellectual life which synthesizes John Garfield with Bakunin. These cautionary tales dramatize the self-destructiveness inherent in political, artistic, and sexual revolt, and are frequently fused, as an academician (*American Mischief*), a woman photographer (*Miriam at Thirty-Four*), and a novelist (*Shrinking*) painfully test the boundaries of contemporary experience. *American Mischief*, Lelchuk's version of *The Possessed*, explores 1960's campus upheaval through the contrapuntal voices of a radical student, Lenny Pincus ("Not the son of Harry and Rose Pincus of Brooklyn, but a boy with fathers like Reston and Cronkite, mothers such as Mary McCarthy and Diana Trilling"), and a liberal dean, Bernard Kovell ("a kind of Americanized version of Romanov-Quixote, a European Liberal-Idealist turned Massachusetts sensualist, tilting simultaneously at foolish theories and female bodies"). A wealth of political and literary theories and allusions threatens to overwhelm the novel, as the protagonists share both their private agonies and extensive bibliographies with the reader. But the novel impresses with its vivid style, ultimately sane perspective, and frequently brilliant imagination: the notorious episode detailing Norman Mailer's symbolically appropriate bloody end manages to outdo an already bizarre reality (Lelchuk often seems to be challenging such contemporaries as Mailer and Roth). Like Lelchuk's other novels, *American Mischief* attempts narrative complexity by telling its story through a variety of "documents": Lenny's preface; Kovell's journal focusing on his six mistresses; his lengthy speech during a campus uprising, interlarded with Lenny's comments; Lenny's "Gorilla Talk," his account of radical activities that occupies more than half the book. This attempt to heighten the dialectical tension between the two men fails because their voices sound so alike from the beginning that the fusion of their ideologies into a compassionate, ultimately victimized, humanity seems predictable.

Victimization goes even further in *Miriam at Thirty-Four*. The heroine's sexual experimentation (three lovers with a variety of tastes) parallels her exploration of the Cambridge setting, which was "a male with secrets . . ., one whom she could arouse by uncovering different parts of his anatomy and photographing them." This obsession with exposing truth leads Miriam to take sexually revealing pictures of herself and exhibit them at a prestigious gallery to the sound of "early Dylan, trio sonatas (Tartini? Bach?), the Beatles." Miriam's final breakdown results from the uncomprehending responses of her audience: "they were cannibals who had just feasted on human flesh with no time yet for digestion. And the flesh was herself, Miriam." To provide multiple views of Miriam, Lelchuk supplements the narrative with her letters, and notebook ("her self-therapy kit, her doctor-between-covers, her book of reason, reflection, questions . . ."). Shorter and less ambitious than *American Mischief*, the novel conveys merely Miriam's pathos and leaves the sources of her disaster uncertain: a society that simultaneously seeks and savages the new, or the destructive urges that accompany Miriam's authentic artistry?

A similar uncertainty pervades *Shrinking*, which chronicles the breakdown of novelist/academician Lionel Solomon, victimized by both inner doubts and a hostile world epitomized by Tippy, a predatory young woman who humiliates him sexually, reveals his inadequacies in an *Esquire* exposé, and leads him on a strange journey into Hopi country. Elaborately narrated, *Shrinking* includes a foreword and afterword by Solomon's psychiatrist, letters from other characters, and the text of Tippy's article with Solomon's comments and marginalia. The article forces a comparison of Tippy's version with the "real" experience, a contrast that underscores the novel's obsession with truth: "what happens in life, when put into fiction, can sound 'in poor taste' and be near impossible to write about." This apologia and Lelchuk's witty parodies of foolish reviewers almost disarm criticism, but do not blind the reader to the catch-all quality of the book: essays on Hopi culture and Melville, however they reflect the workings of Solomon's mind, are too long for the effects they achieve, and Lelchuk's wit seems more forced, less outrageous than in *American Mischief*. Despite these weaknesses, *Shrinking*, like Lelchuk's other fiction, conveys a real voice that is often brilliant, often loquaciously irrelevant, and more often suggests an underlying despair that the writing can only imperfectly duplicate.

—Burton Kendle

LESSING, Doris (May, née Tayler). British. Born in Kermansha, Persia, 22 October 1919; moved with her family to Southern Rhodesia, 1924. Educated at Girls High School, Salisbury. Married 1) Frank Charles Wisdom in 1939 (divorced, 1943), one son and one daughter; 2) Gottfried Lessing in 1945 (divorced, 1949), one son. Lived in Southern Rhodesia, 1924–49, then settled in London. Recipient: Maugham Award, 1954; Médicis Prize (France), 1976; Austrian State Prize, 1982; Shakespeare Prize (Hamburg), 1982; W. H. Smith Literary Award, 1986. Associate Member, American Academy, 1974; Honorary Fellow, Modern Language Association (USA), 1974. Agent: Jonathan Clowes Ltd., 22 Prince Albert Road, London NW1 7ST, England.

PUBLICATIONS

Novels

The Grass Is Singing. London, Joseph, and New York, Crowell, 1950.
Children of Violence:
  Martha Quest. London, Joseph, 1952.
  A Proper Marriage. London, Joseph, 1954; with *Martha Quest*, New York, Simon and Schuster, 1964.
  A Ripple from the Storm. London, Joseph, 1958.
  Landlocked. London, MacGibbon and Kee, 1965; with *A Ripple from the Storm*, New York, Simon and Schuster, 1966.
  The Four-Gated City. London, MacGibbon and Kee, and New York, Knopf, 1969.
Retreat to Innocence. London, Joseph, 1956; New York, Prometheus, 1959.
The Golden Notebook. London, Joseph, and New York, Simon and Schuster, 1962.
Briefing for a Descent into Hell. London, Cape, and New York, Knopf, 1971.
The Summer Before the Dark. London, Cape, and New York, Knopf, 1973.
The Memoirs of a Survivor. London, Octagon Press, and New York, Knopf, 1975.
Canopus in Argos: Archives:
  Shikasta. London, Cape, and New York, Knopf, 1979.
  The Marriages Between Zones Three, Four, and Five. London, Cape, and New York, Knopf, 1980.
  The Sirian Experiments. London, Cape, and New York, Knopf, 1981.
  The Making of the Representative for Planet 8. London, Cape, and New York, Knopf, 1982.
  The Sentimental Agents. London, Cape, and New York, Knopf, 1983.
The Diaries of Jane Somers. New York, Vintage, 1984; London, Joseph, 1985.
  The Diary of a Good Neighbour (as Jane Somers). London, Joseph, and New York, Knopf, 1983.
  If the Old Could— (as Jane Somers). London, Joseph, and New York, Knopf, 1984.
The Good Terrorist. London, Cape, and New York, Knopf, 1985.

Short Stories

This Was the Old Chief's Country. London, Joseph, 1951; New York, Crowell, 1952.
Five: Short Novels. London, Joseph, 1953.
No Witchcraft for Sale: Stories and Short Novels. Moscow, Foreign Language Publishing House, 1956.
The Habit of Loving. London, MacGibbon and Kee, and New York, Crowell, 1957.
A Man and Two Women. London, MacGibbon and Kee, and New York, Simon and Schuster, 1963.
African Stories. London, Joseph, 1964; New York, Simon and Schuster, 1965.
Winter in July. London, Panther, 1966.
The Black Madonna. London, Panther, 1966.
Nine African Stories, edited by Michael Marland. London, Longman, 1968.
The Story of a Non-Marrying Man and Other Stories. London, Cape, 1972; as *The Temptation of Jack Orkney and Other Stories*, New York, Knopf, 1972.
Collected African Stories. New York, Simon and Schuster, 1981.

1. *This Was the Old Chief's Country.* London, Joseph, 1973.
2. *The Sun Between Their Feet.* London, Joseph, 1973.
(Stories), edited by Alan Cattell. London, Harrap, 1976.
Collected Stories: To Room Nineteen and *The Temptation of Jack Orkney.* London, Cape, 2 vols., 1978; as *Stories*, New York, Knopf, 1 vol., 1978.

Plays

Before the Deluge (produced London, 1953).
Mr. Dollinger (produced Oxford, 1958).
Each His Own Wilderness (produced London, 1958). Published in *New English Dramatists*, London, Penguin, 1959.
The Truth about Billy Newton (produced Salisbury, Wiltshire, 1960).
Play with a Tiger (produced London, 1962; New York, 1964). London, Joseph, 1962; in *Plays by and about Women*, edited by Victoria Sullivan and J.V. Hatch, New York, Random House, 1973.
The Storm, adaptation of a play by Alexander Ostrowsky (produced London, 1966).
The Singing Door, in *Second Playbill 2*, edited by Alan Durband. London, Hutchinson, 1973.

Television Plays: *The Grass Is Singing*, from her own novel, 1962; *Please Do Not Disturb*, 1966; *Care and Protection*, 1966; *Between Men*, 1967.

Verse

Fourteen Poems. Northwood, Middlesex, Scorpion Press, 1959.

Other

Going Home. London, Joseph, 1957; revised edition, London, Panther, and New York, Ballantine, 1968.
In Pursuit of the English: A Documentary. London, MacGibbon and Kee, 1960; New York, Simon and Schuster, 1961.
Particularly Cats. London, Joseph, and New York, Simon and Schuster, 1967.
A Small Personal Voice: Essays, Reviews, Interviews, edited by Paul Schlueter. New York, Knopf, 1974.

*

Bibliography: *Doris Lessing: A Bibliography* by Catharina Ipp, Johannesburg, University of the Witwatersrand Department of Bibliography, 1967; *Doris Lessing: A Checklist of Primary and Secondary Sources* by Selma R. Burkom and Margaret Williams, Troy, New York, Whitston, 1973; *Doris Lessing: An Annotated Bibliography of Criticism* by Dee Seligman, Westport, Connecticut, Greenwood Press, 1981; *Doris Lessing: A Descriptive Bibliography of Her First Editions* by Eric T. Brueck, London, Metropolis, 1984.

Critical Studies (selection): *Doris Lessing* by Dorothy Brewster, New York, Twayne, 1965; *The Novels of Doris Lessing* by Paul Schlueter, Carbondale, Southern Illinois University Press, 1973; *Doris Lessing*, London, Longman, 1973, and *Doris Lessing's Africa*, London, Evans, 1978, New York, Holmes and Meier, 1979, both by Michael Thorpe; *Doris Lessing: Critical Studies* edited by Annis Pratt and L.S. Dembo, Madison, University of Wisconsin Press, 1974; *The City and the Veld: The Fiction of Doris Lessing* by Mary Ann Singleton, Lewisburg, Pennsylvania, Bucknell University Press, 1976; *The Tree*

Outside the Window: Doris Lessing's Children of Violence by Ellen Cronan Rose, Hanover, New Hampshire, University Press of New England, 1976; *The Novelistic Vision of Doris Lessing: Breaking the Forms of Consciousness* by Roberta Rubenstein, Urbana, University of Illinois Press, 1979; *From Society to Nature: A Study of Doris Lessing's Children of Violence* by Ingrid Holmquist, Gothenburg, Studies in English, and Atlantic Highlands, New Jersey, Humanities Press, 1980; *Notebooks/Memoirs/Archives: Reading and Re-reading Doris Lessing* edited by Jenny Taylor, London and Boston, Routledge, 1982; *Substance under Pressure: Artistic Coherence and Evolving Form in the Novels of Doris Lessing* by Betsy Draine, Madison, University of Wisconsin Press, 1983; *Doris Lessing* by Lorna Sage, London, Methuen, 1983; *Doris Lessing* by Mona Knapp, New York, Ungar, 1984.

*   *   *

Doris Lessing's writings extend the boundaries of fiction, experiment with different genres, explore the worlds of Africa, Britain, and Space, and offer a socio-political and cultural commentary of the post-modern world. She is a descendant of those 19th-century women writers who made poverty, class conflict, women's suffrage, and slavery the subjects of their novels. She is a writer of epic scope and startling surprises. In her more than 35 books she ranges from social realism to science fiction with brief forays into speculative mysticism. After completing five books in her science-fiction sequence, *Canopus in Argos*, in 1983, Lessing startled her public by turning away from the Antarctic cold of two of her planetary realms and returning to novels of post-war London with its welfare state, terrorists, and aging population. Two of these recent books, *The Diary of a Good Neighbour* and *If the Old Could—* were written under the name of Jane Somers; the third, *The Good Terrorist*, offers a detailed psychological and political portrait of a group of radicals-turned-terrorists living in London in a dilapidated council flat.

The Antarctic expeditions of Britain's once revered, now tarnished hero, Robert Falcon Scott, profoundly influenced Lessing's *The Sirian Experiments* and *The Making of the Representative for Planet 8*, not only by providing her with an understanding of the landscape of paralyzing ice and snow, but by offering her insights into the social processes of Scott's time— the Edwardian era of fierce nationalistic pride and Imperial longings—and of ours. Her three most recent books, a complete departure from her science-fiction vein, nonetheless continue her preoccupation with human behavior and social processes. Two depict, with graphic psychological realism and rich naturalistic detail, the ordinary day-to-day life of an unmarried, middle-aged career woman living in London and tending society's outcast aged, and belatedly trying to love and give—something she was always too busy to do. The third recounts the life of a group of squatters whose radical spirits transform them into revolutionaries. Many greeted *The Golden Notebook*, written in 1962, as Lessing's feminist manifesto, underestimating its critique of the twin gods, Communism and Freud. Almost two decades later, Lessing is pioneering in writing novels of aging and dying, making us confront the pressing social problems they entail, but more important, making us know intimately that world we try so hard to ignore and repress. Her fierce reformist spirit pervades her writings; her anger and indignation at society's mishandling of its concerns is still very much with her, but her disillusionment is tempered by a wisdom learned through living. Her uncanny gift for knowing characters deeply is very much in evidence.

Lessing's books have always articulated her ideas, whether they be about women's orgasms, Armageddon, or utopia.

More often than one would expect from so prolific a writer, she is sufficiently imaginative to integrate smoothly her ideas into her narrative. Even more to her credit is that her writing is continually evolving and is unusual in its breadth. Her plunge into science fiction seemed entirely unexpected. In its incipient stages, in *Briefing for a Descent into Hell*, it was startling and seemed to mark a change as radical as Picasso's when he moved from the Blue Period to Abstract Cubism. With more reflection, one can discover the thread that connects *The Golden Notebook* to her science-fiction sequence, *Canopus in Argos*; but it is hard to think of a writer of her stature in the past half-century who has demonstrated such range.

Her career began with *The Grass Is Singing*, a gem of a book. Set in Rhodesia, it charts with an economy rare in Lessing's works the dissolution of a couple's relationship. After Lessing left Africa in 1949, she devoted ten years to the *Children of Violence* series which explored exhaustively the theme of the "free woman" long before it was fashionable. It also displayed Lessing's preoccupation with politics which many have criticized as tedious. *The Golden Notebook* is the best of her works from this period despite its obvious flaws. It is as much a book about writing as it is an exploration of women's relationships with each other and men. In many ways it ought to be compared to Gide's *The Counterfeiters*—the writer's quest to capture the self intended in fiction, not a different, diminished, or enhanced self; the journey through madness that this task requires—the visions of violence it calls up are integral to both books. Both descend from Joyce; both require a sophisticated audience which enjoys unravelling puzzles; both mirror an age when the Heisenberg Uncertainty Principle threatens the reliability of all narrators and estranges the artist from world and self.

In the 1970's came the unexpected turn to science fiction. Lessing's interest in extra-sensory perception first emerged in *Landlocked*. Madness had been seen as a state offering Anna Wulf a respite from the obsessional insistence upon the self that Saul Green spattered out like machine-gun bullets in *The Golden Notebook*. In *Briefing for a Descent into Hell* Lessing took her interest in madness a step further. Calling the book a work of "inner space fiction," she built a story around Charles Watkins, a 50-year-old classics professor who is found wandering on Waterloo Bridge and is confined for a stay in a psychiatric hospital. Two doctors, of conflicting views, struggle to bring back his memory while he follows a visionary journey in which he enjoys a different, higher identity—one conferred upon him by the Crystal—and one that ordained that he enter earth, hell, as part of a Descent Team whose mission is to show the mad, ego-obsessed humans that they are part of a larger harmony. Lessing, following R.D. Laing, explores the possibility that only the mad are sane. But much more intriguing than this idea is Lessing's decision to fashion the language and metaphors of madness from the idiom of science fiction and the visions experienced through ESP. The inner journey of this modern Odysseus is travelled on the space-time warp of science fiction. The regions he visits are vividly depicted. The language which attempts to capture the visions Watkins is experiencing is one where words are understood by their sounds, not their connotative meanings. "I" glides into "aye" and "eye" as Watkins's mind seems to float in limbo, carrying his body through an unfamiliar medium, revealing images from the visionary realm. Lessing sustains this style, interrupted by only the curt notations of the two psychiatrists, for over a hundred pages. The effect is startling. At times one almost drowns in verbiage, but the flow of the vision is interrupted with the banal observations of the doctors, or the staccato questioning of the patient. Undoubtedly, Lessing's style will cost her some readers, but

those who bear with her will find themselves caught up in this bizarre account and caring very much whether this amnesiac will tenaciously hang on to his visionary self or succumb to the pressures of the doctors and society and return to the ordinary realm where he is merely a slightly eccentric don. Watkins's hold on the link between the two ways of seeing is most precarious. The reader must try to decide whether Felicity, Constancia, and Nancy, creatures in his visions, correspond with his wife, Felicity, his mistress, Constance, and the wife of his friend. We are also left puzzling whether Miles and Watkins are at some level identical, and whether the loss of Watkins's higher self is total, or whether it matters at all since others in the Descent Team seem still to be around. Also, of course, there is the possibility that Watkins is nothing more than temporarily schizophrenic, though the weight of the story seems to negate this alternative. This book introduces all the ideas and the paraphernalia of science fiction that dominate the *Canopus in Argos* sequence.

Shikasta and *The Marriages Between Zones Three, Four, and Five* are the first works in the sequence. In the first a compilation of reports, historical documents, letters, and psychiatric diagnoses is used to unfold the story of Johor's three visits to Shikasta (Earth), the last taking place in the final phase just following the Third World War. Johor is an emissary from the galactic Empire of Canopus, sent to Shikasta to report on the colony. It is Johor's task to educate those who survive the Third World War to their true place in a larger planetary System, where cosmological accidents have heavily contributed to the blighted human condition, and where Shammat, the criminal planet of another galactic empire, has temporarily obstructed the Lock that will connect Shikasta to Canopus. A Chronicler from Zone Three is the narrator of the second book. He tells one of the myths that accounts for man's fallen state and reveals the will of the Powers that the potentates of three hitherto separate zones are to marry and so hasten the evolutionary design that governs the six zones encircling Earth. The myth he tells is of the marriage of Al·Ith, Queen of Zone Three, to Ben Ata, ruler of Zone Four, and, later, the marriage of Ben Ata to Vahshi, ruler of Zone Five. Two births follow. The marriages alter the Zones, estrange their monarchs from the old dispensation, and bring about alterations which enable all the peoples to move between the Zones and fulfill the will of the Powers. Both books allow Lessing to explore again, in new metaphors, the human qualities responsible for the catastrophic happenings in this century, and the nature of the kinds of relationships men and women must make and the kinds of societies that must be constructed to move humans to a higher consciousness. *The Marriages Between Zones Three, Four, and Five* is far more lyrical than *Shikasta*. The Chronicler uses songs and pictures to capture the mythic dimension of the story he tells. *The Sirian Experiments* recounts the colonial experiments practised upon Shikasta, leading its people into their 20th century of Destruction. *The Making of the Representative for Planet 8* tells of Johor's journeys to the planet and the ordeal that he and Doeg, the narrator of the novel, along with other representatives, encounter when the planet begins to freeze to death. Doeg comes to understand his part in the Canopean grand design and recognizes finally the mystical transformation which makes him both many and one and enables him to transcend time and space, entering the realm of all possibility under the tutelage of the Canopean Agents. The most recent book in the series, *The Sentimental Agents*, is the most disappointing. The history of invasions and conquests of the Volyen Empire enables Lessing to reflect on Klorathy's educational process and his attempts to free the Volyens from the power of words, rhetoric, and teach them the power of thought. The book aspires to place itself in the tradition of Plato, Rousseau, Mill, and Orwell as a novel about an educational project, but it is over-written and the ideas seem tedious. Her old concerns abound—how a revolutionary is made; why man has created a world he cannot manage; that history is a repetition of invasion and conquest with the oppressors of one age the oppressed of the next—but the narrative frame is predictable and the ideas simplistic.

Lessing's two books as Jane Somers and *The Good Terrorist* return her to the kind of fiction she was writing before she tackled science fiction. *The Summer Before the Dark, The Memoirs of a Survivor*, and the ambitious *The Golden Notebook* are of a piece with her recent writing. *The Summer Before the Dark* is one of Lessing's most perfectly crafted novels. Compact, tightly constructed, it tells the moving story of a woman's coming to terms with aging. Kate Brown, the 45-year-old mother of four children, all grown, and the wife of a neurologist of some standing, is a woman who has lived her married years making accommodations, to her husband's choices, to the needs of her children. In the summer of the story, events unexpectedly leave Kate Brown without family responsibilities and alone in London for the first time since her marriage. She holds a job briefly, depending again on the talents that the sympathetic understanding of mothering taught her. Then she has a brief affair with a young man on the continent. Both fall sick; Kate returns to London where she lies ill, preoccupied with a recurring dream of a seal which she must complete. She loses weight; her brightly tinted red hair becomes brassy, then banded in grey. In the last phase of the story, she shares quarters with a young woman who is struggling with her own coming of age. The two women work upon each other; Kate's dream is completed; both separate to enter another stage of their lives—the young woman choosing marriage, children, even respectability; Kate, returning to her husband, with her hair grey, as a woman who acts for her own reasons, not merely to please others.

The Memoirs of a Survivor is an even more remarkable book, and equally as mature. It is the memoirs of a nameless woman who has survived "it," a nameless war that has left the cities of England empty shells, with conclaves of people living barricaded in their apartments while gangs of youths roam the streets and the air is so polluted that hand-driven machines are necessary to purify it. The narrator retells how she lived through this period; how she came by a child, Emily, who was entrusted to her care; how she entered a space behind the white walls of her living-room, and inhabited other rooms, from earlier times, and witnessed the traumatic moments of Emily's youth spent with her real parents. She struggles to tell in words how the two worlds, at first so different, began to impinge upon one another. She contrasts what she calls "personal" moments of experience with others that she labels "impersonal." Both reside in the world behind the wall. The story blends the dreamy, prophetic, timeless moments behind the wall where some heightened consciousness, some visionary powers, exist, with a dispassionate, often chilling, realistic account of "ordinary" life in a ravaged London apartment. Always, when the narrator goes behind the wall, she seeks, with a sense of urgency, the inhabitant of that other house, those other gardens. The protagonist's memoirs end with her account of how they somehow came through the darkest times, and realized that the worst was over, that something new would be built. The final paragraphs describe the moment when the walls opened again, and she saw the face she had sought so long, the inhabitant of that hidden world. And that presence takes the hands of Emily, her boyfriend, and the evil child

who had terrorized the London streets and leads them into the garden. It is a mystical moment, transfiguring, mysterious, and a consummate end for this exquisitely crafted book.

In *The Diary of a Good Neighbour* Jane Somers, like Kate Brown, is a middle-aged, seemingly successful woman, but, unlike Kate, she is childless and recently widowed with only a career to give her definition. To compensate for her lack of relationships and to try to come to terms with cancer and dying—she had faced neither when her husband was terminally ill—she befriends an elderly woman, Maudie, whom she has met in a corner store. The book offers an extraordinarily moving, also frightening, story of this stubborn old woman's final years, living in a council flat, tended to by Meals on Wheels, day nursing, a cadre of Home Helpers, and the volunteer Good Neighbours. Lessing diligently details the life of the 90-year-old woman, alone in London, too ill to care for herself, too proud to let others help her, and too angry to let friendship or death come easily to her. Soiled in her own clothing, almost too weak and brittle to walk to the unheated lavatory in the hall outside her flat, or to light her meagre fire, far beyond any ability to clean her rooms or even dress or bathe, Maudie fiercely clings to her independence, refusing to be put in a home or a hospital which she knows will only mark her end. This is a novel about our time, aging, and society's refusal to differentiate between growing old and dying. It calls forth Lessing's gifts—a precise eye for detail, an absorption in the quotidian, a psychological understanding of people, and the ability to tell a story. The book is full of stories—Maudie's, the elderly Anne's, another of the women Jane comes to help, and, of course, Jane's. The second book in the series is less successful. *If the Old Could*— tells a triter story of Jane's affair with a married man whose unhappy daughter shadows them and whose son baffles her with his unexpected declaration of love. The portions that deal with the elderly, however, are again excellent. Lessing, in both these books, forces the reader to see the elderly. After reading the books, I found myself looking searchingly at the solitary old people sitting on benches, or queuing in the grocery store, or shuffling to a bus, and more important, I looked forward and within.

The Good Terrorist is absorbing, so apt is its portrait of Alice Mellings, a 36-year-old over-aged adolescent, and her "family" of squatters. Alice's instincts are motherly; her zeal to save council flats from being condemned makes her a valuable friend for other, younger, motley members of the Communist Centre Union who join her as a squatter. Her rages are instantaneous and inexplicable to her. Immersed in her day-to-day life, we witness her transformation into a terrorist.

It is too early to assess Lessing's place in literary history. Her imagination is too rich. What can be said is that she is deeply concerned with the human condition, and hungry to explore new dimensions, to redefine relationships. Her writings reflect a nearly obsessive effort to find a way through the historical ravages of this century to a condition beyond the one of personal unhappiness that plagues so many human relationships. Her novels try to teach us how better to manage our world; they expose a world out of control.

—Carol Simpson Stern

LEVIN, Ira. American. Born in New York City, 27 August 1929. Educated at Drake University, Des Moines, Iowa, 1946–48; New York University, 1948–50, A.B. 1950. Served in the United States Army Signal Corps, 1953–55. Married 1) Gabrielle Aronsohn in 1960 (divorced, 1968), three sons; 2) Phyllis Finkel in 1979 (divorced, 1982). Recipient: Mystery Writers of America Edgar Allan Poe Award, 1954, and Special Award, 1980. Agent: Harold Ober Associates, 40 East 49th Street, New York, New York 10017, U.S.A.

PUBLICATIONS

Novels

A Kiss Before Dying. New York, Simon and Schuster, 1953; London, Joseph, 1954.
Rosemary's Baby. New York, Random House, and London, Joseph, 1967.
This Perfect Day. New York, Random House, and London, Joseph, 1970.
The Stepford Wives. New York, Random House, and London, Joseph, 1972.
The Boys from Brazil. New York, Random House, and London, Joseph, 1976.

Plays

No Time for Sergeants, adaptation of the novel by Mac Hyman (produced New York, 1955; London, 1956). New York, Random House, 1956.
Interlock (produced New York, 1958). New York, Dramatists Play Service, 1958.
Critic's Choice (produced New York, 1960; London, 1961). New York, Random House, 1961; London, Evans, 1963.
General Seeger (produced New York, 1962). New York, Dramatists Play Service, 1962.
Drat! The Cat!, music by Milton Schafer (produced New York, 1965).
Dr. Cook's Garden (also director; produced New York, 1967). New York, Dramatists Play Service, 1968.
Veronica's Room (produced New York, 1973; Watford, Hertfordshire, 1982). New York, Random House, 1974; London, Joseph, 1975.
Deathtrap (produced New York and London, 1978). New York, Random House, 1979.
Break a Leg (produced New York, 1979). New York, French, 1981.

*

Theatrical Activities:
Director: **Play**—*Dr. Cook's Garden*, New York, 1967.

*   *   *

The heroine of *Rosemary's Baby* is overwhelmed by the "elaborate ... evil" of the witches' coven through whose agency she has unknowingly borne Satan's child, which now lies in a black bassinet with an inverted crucifix for a crib toy. Elaborateness is, indeed, the chief characteristic of both evil and good in Ira Levin's novels. Bud Corliss of *A Kiss Before Dying* makes neat lists of ways to arrange his pregnant girlfriend's "suicide" and to win his eldest sister's love. In *This Perfect Day* all human actions are ostensibly directed by a world computer and everyone must touch his identification bracelet to scanners before he can do anything, go anywhere, or receive any supplies. The novel's hero, Chip (or Li RM35M4419, to give him his "nameber") fights system with system in a complicated expedition to disable UniComp's memory banks. The

first dozen pages of *The Boys from Brazil* describe, course by course, Dr. Mengele's dinner party-*cum*-briefing for the assassination of 94 retired civil servants, each of whom has unwittingly adopted a clone of Hitler, produced by the Doctor, who now intends to recreate Hitler's family environment.

Such procedures provide the sustaining interest and suspense of Levin's novels, combining neatness and system with Satanism, secrets, universal surveillance, violence, and death. Rosemary uses a scrabble set to work out the anagram which identifies her friendly neighbor Roman Castevet as devil-worshipping Steven Marcato. In *A Kiss Before Dying* Dorothy's provision of "Something old, Something new, Something borrowed, And something blue" enables her sister to deduce that Dorothy intended marriage, not suicide. The husbands of *The Stepford Wives* make speaking, moving replicas of their spouses. They begin with seemingly innocuous sketches of each real wife and tape recordings of her voice; they end by killing her off-stage. Levin increases the "reality" of such sinister processes by mingling them with ordinary routines of eating, pregnancy, moving to a new house, etc.

Both good and bad characters must, at times, revise their elaborate plans on the spur of the crisis. Their expedients are ingenious, often complex, and the pleasure of following Levin's details is enough to make some of his novels re-readable when their surprise is over.

The forward movement and acceleration of the plots are further complicated by sudden reversals, single or double, overt or psychological, in which characters (and often readers) are temporarily disoriented. For example, Rosemary, arriving at the logical conclusion that her husband had joined the coven, "didn't know if she was going mad or going sane." Joanna cannot tell if her best friend is still a person or has become an automaton. (She *is* an automaton, and stabs Joanna.) Although the reader is sometimes prepared for these discoveries, there are also unexpected shocks as when Rosemary, thinking herself safe, sees her witch-obstetrician enter, or when Chip, suddenly taken prisoner by a trusted team-member, discovers that betrayal is really recruitment by the elite subterranean programmers. The effect on the reader of such continual reversals and realignments is a constant uneasiness as to his personal safety and moral identity, which produces horror very successfully in *Rosemary's Baby*, but rather mechanically in *This Perfect Day* and *The Stepford Wives*. No doubt Levin's constant readers now anticipate his surprises, which may account for his increasing detail of violence as excitement in *The Boys from Brazil*.

Occasionally, and chiefly in *This Perfect Day*, Levin's literary antecedents are apparent. His shock techniques are essentially those of Ambrose Bierce and Villiers de l'Isle Adam. Bud's slow plunge into a vat of molten copper recalls H.G. Wells's "The Cone" with its archetypal death by blast furnace. The world of UniComp is essentially a Brave New World with a Big Brother mentality, but controlled by a mad scientist out of Edgar Rice Burroughs, who rejuvenates through body transference. In short, Levin has drawn upon the almost inescapable traditional materials of his genre, but he uses them intelligently and individually.

Increasingly, Levin's novels imply larger significances. Looking at the copper smelter, the murderer says seriously, "It makes you realize what a great country this is." Rosemary's subtly evil apartment house is owned by the church next door, and there are seemingly casual references to the Death of God. An ideal universe of "the gentle, the helpful, the loving, the unselfish" is the vision of a power-joyful egoist. Even the intelligent Stepford husbands in a strange feminist fable want only big-breasted, floor-waxing, mindless wives. A wise old Nazi-hunter, clashing with a radical rabbi, refuses to let 94 teenage Hitlers be exterminated for the sake of future Jewish safety, saying, "This was *Mengele's* business, killing children. Should it be ours?" These moral paradoxes, undeveloped though they are, both extend and intensify the disquieting uncertainty which is Levin's chief characteristic.

—Jane W. Stedman

LEVINE, (Albert) Norman. Canadian. Born in Ottawa, Ontario, 22 October 1923. Educated at York Street School and High School of Commerce, Ottawa; Carleton College, Ottawa, 1945; McGill University, Montreal, 1946–49, B.A. 1948, M.A. 1949; King's College, London, 1949–50. Served in the Royal Canadian Air Force, 1942–45: Flying Officer. Married 1) Margaret Payne in 1952 (died, 1978), three daughters; 2) Anne Sarginson in 1983. Employed by the Department of National Defence, Ottawa, 1940–42; Head of the English Department, Barnstaple Boys Grammar School, Devon, 1953–54; Resident Writer, University of New Brunswick, Fredericton, 1965–66. Recipient: Canada Council fellowship, 1959, and Arts Award, 1969, 1971, 1974. Has lived in England since 1949. Address: 45 Bedford Road, St. Ives, Cornwall, England; or, 103 Summerhill Avenue, Toronto, Ontario M4T 1B1, Canada.

PUBLICATIONS

Novels

The Angled Road. London, Laurie, 1952.
From a Seaside Town. London, Macmillan, 1970; as *She'll Only Drag You Down*, Toronto, PaperJacks, 1975.

Short Stories

One Way Ticket. London, Secker and Warburg, 1961.
I Don't Want to Know Anyone Too Well: 15 Stories. London, Macmillan, 1971.
Selected Stories. Ottawa, Oberon Press, 1975.
In Lower Town, photographs by Johanne McDuff. Ottawa, Commoners', 1977.
Thin Ice. Ottawa, Deneau, and London, Wildwood House, 1980.
Why Do You Live So Far Away? A Novella and Six Stories. Ottawa, Deneau, 1984.
Champagne Barn. Toronto and London, Penguin, 1984; New York, Penguin, 1985.

Uncollected Short Story

"Django, Karfunkelstein, and Roses," in *Encounter* (London), December 1985.

Verse

Myssium. Toronto, Ryerson Press, 1948.
The Tight-Rope Walker. London, Totem Press, 1950.
I Walk by the Harbour. Fredericton, New Brunswick, Fiddlehead, 1976.

Other

Canada Made Me. London, Putnam, 1958.

Editor, *Canadian Winter's Tales.* Toronto and London, Macmillan, 1968.

*

Manuscript Collections: University of Texas, Austin; York University, Toronto.

Critical Studies: "The Girl in the Drugstore" by Levine, in *Canadian Literature 41* (Vancouver), 1969; interview in *Canadian Literature 45* (Vancouver), 1970; Philip Oakes, in *Sunday Times* (London), 19 July 1970; Alan Heuser, in *Montreal Star*, 26 September 1970; *Times Literary Supplement* (London), 3 December 1971; Maurice Capitanchik, in *Books and Bookmen* (London), September 1972; George Galt, in *Saturday Night* (Toronto), June 1984.

Norman Levine comments:

For anyone who wants to know where to begin, I suggest that the start would be *Canada Made Me, From a Seaside Town*, then *Champagne Barn*.

I wrote in the *Atlantic Advocate*: "When you go to a writer's work—it is into his personal world that you enter. What he is doing is paying, in his own way, an elaborate tribute to people and places he has known."

*   *   *

Norman Levine has always been remarkable for the reserve of his writing; but it took him some years to learn what best to withhold and what to reveal. In his early autobiographical stories and novel, *The Angled Road*, he was "trying to cut out [his] past, to cover . . . up" his origins as the Canadian-bred son of a Jewish street-peddler. As if to compensate for this leaching of colour from his material, he was also experimenting with patches of vulgar prose-poetry. While teaching himself to write simply and directly, he came to terms with his personal history. Now, in *Thin Ice*, although his range is narrow, he shapes his stories with the unmistakable authority of a writer who has found his subject and style.

Speaking for the most part in the first person, Levine relates in neutral prose incidents from his Canadian upbringing and his years in England. Certain worlds are revealed which he leaves and is drawn back to: Jewish society, life at McGill University summer cottages by the Richelieu, the tourist villages of Cornwall, poverty in a small town. He has achieved the outsider's vantage point from which he turns a telephoto lens on ordinary people and events. The danger of his method is that when it miscarries, as sometimes it does, the reader is left with a commonplace, colourless anecdote that adds up to nothing. His later stories and novel do not differ greatly from his travel-narrative, *Canada Made Me*, except in being increasingly crafted, concise, and superficially detached. Although he has escaped the heavy cold of Montreal and the intimate squalor of lower Ottawa, he takes with him wherever he goes his Canadian melancholy and taste for failure.

In drawing on his personal past, Levine often returns to the same scenes, characters, and even fragments of conversation, as if he were unable to invent afresh or to leave behind any of his life. An Englishman awaiting the flowering of a large cactus, a woman without a nose, a prowling man whom a couple nicknames "the house detective," are only a few of many recurrent elements in the work of this man who mines his own writings, word for word, as well as his past. The friction of repeated use has polished his memories until all that is inessential has worn away, leaving a smooth pebble of experience.

Levine consistently avoids evocative vocabulary, choosing instead to make a plain statement of fact in language so empty of implication that it becomes mysterious. It is as if he is trying to create prose as objective as the reality he perceives. Yet, in his best work, when everything possible has been jettisoned, a core of emotion remains. He writes in short, often broken, sentences that correspond to the fragmentary moments of human contact in his tales. Sometimes an ugly expression such as "less worse" (*Canada Made Me*) has been selected as the only way of expressing what he means, but at other times a sentence muddles into ambiguity that adds nothing, or an angularity almost illiterate. Except for brief periods, Levine has lived in England since 1949; so it is not surprising that he has somewhat lost his grasp of Canadian idiom and fact. His use of such expressions as "the School of Seven," "motorways," "left luggage." and "do some walks" is evidence of the distance he has travelled from his native speech. Even his distinguished German translator, Heinrich Böll, the Nobel prize-winner, must have felt it a hopeless task to convey in all its aspects Levine's continual shuttling between England and Canada.

Although Levine says little about his feelings, one cannot miss the passion that concentrates his prose and sends him back to places and people he cannot forget. His journeys are the counterpart of the sexual hunger that runs through *From a Seaside Town*. His appetite for experience and his enjoyment of the grotesque have so far saved him from the sterility that threatens autobiographical writers in middle age. In his low-keyed world even tiny incidents stand out like figures against a landscape of snow. They may mean nothing or anything, but to him they have an importance which the reader feels, but never entirely understands.

—Margaret Keith

LEWIS, Janet. American. Born in Chicago, Illinois, 17 August 1899. Educated at the Lewis Institute, Chicago, A.A. 1918; University of Chicago, Ph.B. 1920. Married the writer Yvor Winters in 1926 (died, 1968); one daughter and one son. Passport Bureau clerk, American Consulate, Paris, 1920; proof reader, *Redbook* magazine, Chicago, 1921; English teacher, Lewis Institute, 1921–22; Editor, with Howard Baker and Yvor Winters, *Gyroscope*, Palo Alto, California, 1929–30. Lecturer, Writers Workshop, University of Missouri, Columbia, 1952, and University of Denver, 1956; Visiting Lecturer, then Lecturer in English, Stanford University, California, 1960, 1966, 1969, 1970. Recipient: Friends of American Literature award, 1932; Shelley Memorial Award, for poetry, 1948; Guggenheim fellowship, 1950. Address: 143 West Portola Avenue, Los Altos, California 94022, U.S.A.

PUBLICATIONS

Novels

The Invasion: A Narrative of Events Concerning the Johnston Family of St. Mary's. New York, Harcourt Brace, 1932.
The Wife of Martin Guerre. San Francisco, Colt Press, 1941; London, Rapp and Carroll, 1967.
Against a Darkening Sky. New York, Doubleday, 1943.

The Trial of Sören Qvist. New York, Doubleday, 1947; London, Gollancz, 1967.
The Ghost of Monsieur Scarron. New York, Doubleday, and London, Gollancz, 1959.

Short Stories

Goodbye, Son, and Other Stories. New York, Doubleday, 1946.

Uncollected Short Stories

"At the Swamp," in *The Best Short Stories of 1930*, edited by Edward J. O'Brien. Boston, Houghton Mifflin, 1930.
"La Pointe Chegiomegon," in *Hound and Horn* (Portland, Maine), October-December 1931.
"A Still Small Voice," in *McCall's* (New York), 1946.
"The Breakable Cup," in *Saturday Evening Post* (Philadelphia), 27 February 1965.

Plays (opera libretti)

The Wife of Martin Guerre, music by William Bergsma, adaptation of the novel by Lewis (produced New York, 1956). Denver, Swallow, 1958.
The Last of the Mohicans, adaptation of the novel by Cooper, music by Alva Henderson (produced Wilmington, Delaware, 1976).
A Birthday of the Infanta, adaptation of the story by Wilde, music by Malcolm Seagrave (produced Carmel, California, 1977). Los Angeles, Symposium Press, 1979.
Mulberry Street, music by Alva Henderson. Onset, Massachusetts, Dermont, 1981.

Verse

The Indians in the Woods. Bonn, Germany, Monroe Wheeler, 1922; Palo Alto, California, Matrix Press, 1980.
The Wheel in Midsummer. Lynn, Massachusetts, Lone Gull Press, 1927.
The Earth-Bound 1924–1944. Aurora, New York, Wells College, 1946.
The Hangar at Sunnyvale 1937. San Francisco, Book Club of California, 1947.
Poems 1924–1944. Denver, Swallow, 1950.
The Ancient Ones. Portola Valley, California, No Dead Lines, 1979.
Poems Old and New 1918–1978. Athens, Ohio University Press-Swallow Press, 1981.

Other

The Friendly Adventure of Ollie Ostrich (for children). New York, Doubleday, 1923.
Keiko's Bubble (for children). New York, Doubleday, 1961; Kingswood, Surrey, World's Work, 1963.
The U.S. and Canada, with others. Green Bay, University of Wisconsin Press, 1970.

*

Manuscript Collection: Stanford University Library, California.

Critical Studies: by Richard F. Goldman, in *Musical Quarterly* (New York), July 1956; "The Legacy of Fenimore Cooper," in *Essays in Criticism* (Brill, Buckinghamshire), July 1959, and

"The Historical Novels of Janet Lewis," in *Southern Review* (Baton Rouge, Louisiana), January 1966, both by Donald Davie; "Genius Unobserved" by Evan S. Connell, Jr., in *Atlantic* (Boston), December 1969; "Patriarchal Women: A Study of Three Novels by Janet Lewis" by Ellen Killoh, in *Southern Review* (Baton Rouge, Louisiana), Spring 1974.

Janet Lewis comments:

It is difficult to know what to say about my own work. Most of it needs little if any explanation. In regard to *The Invasion* I can state that I meant to write history as if I were writing fiction. It is in every way, in so far as I could manage, faithful to the facts and the events. When it comes to the three novels based on the famous cases of circumstantial evidence, I can only state again that I intended to write history as if it were fiction. I remained in each case as faithful to the facts as I could, but I was so far from them in time and space that I needed to invent rather freely, in order to clothe the facts with life. In the case of *Martin Guerre* I began with a very brief account of the events, and have learned bit by bit since the day the book was first published more and more about the truth of the matter, so that now, thirty years later, I have at hand the ultimate source for the story, the account by one of the judges, Jean de Coras. My story of Martin Guerre is fiction, but it is very close indeed to the known facts.

*   *   *

Janet Lewis is admired as one of the purest stylists in contemporary fiction, and as a novelist who continued to write quietly probing dramas of psycho-moral ambiguity with almost total disregard for the changing fashions of American fiction. She is to be compared, in the quiet integrity of her art, with Willa Cather, Caroline Gordon, and her friend Elizabeth Madox Roberts. Only her modest volume of short stories (*Goodbye, Son*) and the slowpaced, intelligent, at times dreary *Against a Darkening Sky* are contemporary in scene. Her reputation rests instead on her four historical novels, one related to her own part-Indian background, the others laid in remote European times.

The Invasion occupies a surprisingly satisfying border region between fiction and history, and contains some of the loveliest prose in modern American literature. Its singular achievement is to present without pretentiousness or strain an Indian culture from within (the Ojibway of the Lake Superior area), and its gradual change and slow obliteration over a century and a half. The family chronicle extends from 1791, when we meet the 14-year-old Woman of the Glade, who married the trader John Johnston, to the death in 1944 of Anna Maria Johnston, the Red Leaf. The novel is the work of a poet recording delicate nuances of landscape and mood, and of a scrupulous historian contemplating with equanimity the inevitable outrages of human passion and eroding time. It combines with remarkable success an intimate immersion in scene (a succession of lived moments) and a flow of time that is calm as well as swift. The chronicle's exceptional authenticity is strengthened by the fact that the famous ethnologist, linguist, and Indian agent Henry Rowe Schoolcraft is a central figure in the family history.

Three very different historical novels are based on incidents recorded in Phillips's *Famous Cases of Circumstantial Evidence*, an early 19th-century work. *The Trial of Sören Qvist*, laid in 17th-century Denmark, is the story of a saintly pastor executed for a crime he did not commit. This is a spare and dramatic novel, but meditative too, like everything Lewis has written. *The Ghost of Monsieur Scarron* is the product of years of research, some of it in a part of Paris that has not greatly

changed since 1694. It is the minutely realistic story of a bookbinder falsely accused of authoring a libelous pamphlet directed against Louis XIV and Madame de Maintenon. The evocation of the Paris of that time is remarkable.

The best of these novels, one of the greatest short novels in American literature, is *The Wife of Martin Guerre*, a quietly authentic, immaculately written story of a man whose physical "double" (but far more considerate and more loving than the original) returns to claim the wife of a soldier supposed dead in the wars of 16th-century France. Here as in her other two novels of ambiguous crime and punishment Janet Lewis dramatizes, always calmly, situations exerting extreme pressure on her characters. The marriage of Martin Guerre and Bertrande de Rols, at 11, is of its time, and so too the execution 21 years later. A sentence from Janet Lewis's "Foreword" suggests the human understanding underlying all her work. "The rules of evidence vary from century to century, and the morality which compels many of the actions of men and women varies also, but the capacities of the human soul for suffering and for joy remain very much the same."

—Albert Guerard

LINDSAY, Jack. Australian. Born in Melbourne, Victoria, 20 October 1900; son of the writer and artist Norman Lindsay. Educated at Brisbane Grammar School; University of Queensland, Brisbane, 1918–21, B.A. (honours) in classics 1921. Served in the British Army, 1941–45, in the Royal Corps of Signals, 1941–43, and as a scriptwriter in the War Office, 1943–45. Married Meta Waterdrinker in 1956; one son and one daughter. Editor, with Kenneth Slessor and F. Johnson, *Vision*, Sydney, 1923–24; settled in England, 1926; proprietor and director, Fanfrolico Press, London, 1927–30; editor, with P.R. Stephensen, *London Aphrodite*, 1928–29; editor, *Poetry and the People*, London, 1938–39; editor, *Anvil*, London, 1947; editor, with John Davenport and Randall Swingler, *Arena*, London, 1949–51. Recipient: Australian Literature Society Couch Gold Medal, 1960; Order of Merit (USSR), 1968. D.Litt.: University of Queensland. Fellow, Royal Society of Literature, 1945, and Ancient Monuments Society, 1961; Member, Order of Australia, 1981. Agent: Murray Pollinger, 4 Garrick Street, London WC2E 9BH. Address: 25 Clarendon Street, Cambridge, England.

PUBLICATIONS

Novels

Cressida's First Lover: A Tale of Ancient Greece. London, Lane, 1931; New York, Long and Smith, 1932.
Rome for Sale. London, Mathews and Marrot, and New York, Harper, 1934.
Caesar Is Dead. London, Nicholson and Watson, 1934.
Last Days with Cleopatra. London, Nicholson and Watson, 1935.
Despoiling Venus. London, Nicholson and Watson, 1935.
Storm at Sea. London, Golden Cockerel Press, 1935.
The Wanderings of Wenamen: 1115–1114 B.C. London, Nicholson and Watson, 1936.
Shadow and Flame (as Richard Preston). London, Chapman and Hall, 1936.

Adam of a New World. London, Nicholson and Watson, 1936.

Sue Verney. London, Nicholson and Watson, 1937.

End of Cornwall (as Richard Preston). London, Cape, 1937.

1649: A Novel of a Year. London, Methuen, 1938.

Brief Light: A Novel of Catullus. London, Methuen, 1939.

Lost Birthright. London, Methuen, 1939.

Giuliano the Magnificent, adapted from a work by D. Johnson. London, Dakers, 1940.

Light in Italy. London, Gollancz, 1941.

Hannibal Takes a Hand. London, Dakers, 1941.

The Stormy Violence. London, Dakers, 1941.

We Shall Return: A Novel of Dunkirk and the French Campaign. London, Dakers, 1942.

Beyond Terror: A Novel of the Battle of Crete. London, Dakers, 1943.

The Barriers Are Down: A Tale of the Collapse of a Civilisation. London, Gollancz, 1945.

Hullo Stranger. London, Dakers, 1945.

Time to Live. London, Dakers, 1946.

The Subtle Knot. London, Dakers, 1947.

Men of Forty-Eight. London, Methuen, 1948.

Fires in Smithfield. London, Lane, 1950.

The Passionate Pastoral. London, Lane, 1951.

Betrayed Spring: A Novel of the British Way. London, Lane, 1953.

Rising Tide. London, Lane, 1953.

The Moment of Choice. London, Lane, 1955.

A Local Habitation: A Novel of the British Way. London, Bodley Head, 1957.

The Great Oak: A Story of 1549. London, Bodley Head, 1957.

The Revolt of the Sons. London, Muller, 1960.

All on the Never-Never: A Novel of the British Way of Life. London, Muller, 1961.

The Way the Ball Bounces. London, Muller, 1962.

Masks and Faces. London, Muller, 1963.

Choice of Times. London, Muller, 1964.

Thunder Underground: A Story of Nero's Rome. London, Muller, 1965.

The Blood-Vote. St. Lucia, University of Queensland Press, 1985.

Short Stories

Come Home at Last and Other Stories. London, Nicholson and Watson, 1936.

Death of a Spartan King and Two Other Stories of the Ancient World. London, Inca Books, 1974.

Plays

Marino Faliero: A Verse-Play. London, Fanfrolico Press, 1927.

Helen Comes of Age: Three Original Plays in Verse (includes *Ragnild* and *Bussy d'Amboise*). London, Fanfrolico Press, 1927.

Hereward: A Verse Drama, music by J. Gough. London, Fanfrolico Press, 1930.

The Whole Armour of God (produced London, 1944).

Robin of England (produced London, 1945).

The Face of Coal, with B. Coombes (produced London, 1946).

Iphigeneia in Aulis, adaptation of a play by Euripides (produced London, 1967).

Hecuba, adaptation of a play by Euripides (produced London, 1967).

Electra, adaptation of a play by Euripides (produced London, 1967).

Orestes, adaptation of a play by Euripides (produced London, 1967).

Nathan the Wise, adaptation of a play by Lessing (produced London, 1967).

Verse

Fauns and Ladies. Sydney, Kirtley, 1923.

The Pleasante Conceited Narrative of Panurge's Fantastic Ally Brocaded Codpiece. Sydney, Panurgean Society, 1924.

The Spanish Main and Tavern. Sydney, Panurgean Society, 1924.

The Passionate Neatherd. London, Fanfrolico Press, 1926.

Into Action: The Battle of Dieppe. London, Dakers, 1942.

Second Front. London, Dakers, 1944.

Clue of Darkness. London, Dakers, 1949.

Peace Is Our Answer. London, Collet, 1950.

Three Letters to Nikolai Tikhonov. London, Fore, 1951.

Three Elegies. Sudbury, Suffolk, Myriad Press, 1957.

Faces and Places. Toronto, Basilike, 1974.

Collected Poems. Lake Forest, Illinois, Cheiron, 1981.

Other

William Blake: Creative Will and the Poetic Image. London, Fanfrolico Press, 1927; revised edition, 1929; New York, Haskell House, 1971.

Dionysos; or, Nietzsche contra Nietzsche: An Essay in Lyrical Philosophy. London, Fanfrolico Press, 1928.

The Romans. London, Black, 1935.

Runaway (for children). London, Oxford University Press, 1935.

Rebels of the Goldfields (for children). London, Lawrence and Wishart, 1936.

Marc Antony: His World and His Contemporaries. London, Routledge, 1936; New York, Dutton, 1937.

John Bunyan: Maker of Myths. London, Methuen, 1937; New York, Kelley, 1969.

The Anatomy of Spirit: An Enquiry into the Origins of Religious Emotions. London, Methuen, 1937.

To Arms! A Story of Ancient Gaul (for children). London, Oxford University Press, 1938.

England, My England. London, Fore, 1939.

A Short History of Culture. London, Gollancz, 1939; revised edition, London, Studio Books, 1962; New York, Citadel Press, 1964.

The Dons Sight Devon: A Story of the Defeat of the Invincible Armada (for children). London, Oxford University Press, 1942.

Perspective for Poetry. London, Fore, 1944.

British Achievement in Art and Music. London, Pilot Press, 1945.

Mulk Raj Anand: A Critical Essay. Bombay, Hind Kitabs, 1948; revised edition, as *The Elephant and the Lotus*, Bombay, Kutub Popular, 1954.

Song of a Falling World: Culture During the Break-up of the Roman Empire (A.D. 350-600). London, Dakers, 1948; Westport, Connecticut, Hyperion Press, 1979.

Marxism and Contemporary Science; or, The Fulness of Life. London, Dobson, 1949.

A World Ahead: Journal of a Soviet Journey. London, Fore, 1950.

Charles Dickens: A Biographical and Critical Study. London, Dakers, and New York, Philosophical Library, 1950.

Byzantium into Europe: The Story of Byzantium as the First Europe (362-1204 A.D.) and Its Further Contribution till 1453 A.D. London, Lane, 1952.

Rumanian Summer, with M. Cornforth. London, Lawrence and Wishart, 1953.

Civil War in England: The Cromwellian Revolution. London, Muller, 1954; New York, Barnes and Noble, 1967.

George Meredith: His Life and Work. London, Lane, 1956; New York, Kraus, 1973.

The Romans Were Here: The Roman Period in Britain and Its Place in Our History. London, Muller, 1956; New York, Barnes and Noble, 1969.

After the Thirties: The Novel in Britain and Its Future. London, Lawrence and Wishart, 1956.

Life Rarely Tells (autobiography). Ringwood, Victoria, Penguin, 1982.

>*Life Rarely Tells: An Autobiographical Account Ending in the Year 1921 and Situated Mostly in Brisbane, Queensland.* London, Bodley Head, 1958.

>*The Roaring Twenties: Literary Life in Sydney, New South Wales, in the Years 1921–26.* London, Bodley Head, 1960.

>*Fanfrolico and After.* London, Bodley Head, 1962.

Arthur and His Times: Britain in the Dark Ages. London, Muller, 1958; New York, Barnes and Noble, 1966.

The Discovery of Britain: A Guide to Archaeology. London, Merlin Press, 1958.

1764: The Hurly-Burly of Daily Life Exemplified in One Year of the 18th Century. London, Muller, 1959.

The Writing on the Wall: An Account of Pompeii in Its Last Days. London, Muller, 1960.

Death of the Hero: French Painting from David to Delacroix. London, Studio, 1960.

William Morris: Writer. London, William Morris Society, 1961.

Our Celtic Heritage. London, Weidenfeld and Nicolson, 1962.

Daily Life in Roman Egypt. London, Muller, 1963; New York, Barnes and Noble, 1964.

Nine Days' Hero: Wat Tyler. London, Dobson, 1964.

The Clashing Rocks: A Study of Early Greek Religion and Culture, and the Origins of Drama. London, Chapman and Hall, 1965.

Leisure and Pleasure in Roman Egypt. London, Muller, 1965; New York, Barnes and Noble, 1966.

Our Anglo-Saxon Heritage. London, Weidenfeld and Nicolson, 1965.

J.M.W. Turner: His Life and Work: A Critical Biography. London, Adams and MacKay, and Greenwich, Connecticut, New York Graphic Society, 1966.

Our Roman Heritage. London, Weidenfeld and Nicolson, 1967.

Meetings with Poets: Memories of Dylan Thomas, Edith Sitwell, Louis Aragon, Paul Eluard, Tristan Tzara. London, Muller, 1968; New York, Ungar, 1969.

Men and Gods on the Roman Nile. London, Muller, and New York, Barnes and Noble, 1968.

The Ancient World: Manners and Morals. London, Weidenfeld and Nicolson, and New York, Putnam, 1968.

Cézanne: His Life and Art. London, Adams and MacKay, and Greenwich, Connecticut, New York Graphic Society, 1969.

The Origins of Alchemy in Graeco-Roman Egypt. London, Muller, and New York, Barnes and Noble, 1970.

Cleopatra. London, Constable, and New York, Coward McCann, 1971.

Origins of Astrology. London, Muller, and New York, Barnes and Noble, 1971.

Gustave Courbet: His Life and Work. Bath, Adams and Dart, 1973; New York, Harper, 1974.

Helen of Troy: Woman and Goddess. London, Constable, and Totowa, New Jersey, Rowman and Littlefield, 1974.

Blast-Power and Ballistics: Concepts of Force and Energy in the Ancient World. London, Muller, and New York, Barnes and Noble, 1974.

The Normans and Their World. London, Hart Davis MacGibbon, 1974; New York, St. Martin's Press, 1975.

William Morris: His Life and Work. London, Constable, 1975; New York, Taplinger, 1979.

Decay and Renewal: Critical Essays on Twentieth Century Writing. Sydney, Wild and Woolley, 1976; London, Lawrence and Wishart, 1977.

The Troubadours and Their World of the Twelfth and Thirteenth Centuries. London, Muller, 1976.

Hogarth: His Art and World. London, Hart Davis MacGibbon, 1977; New York, Taplinger, 1979.

William Blake: His Life and Work. London, Constable, 1978; New York, Braziller, 1979.

The Monster City: Defoe's London 1688–1730. London, Hart Davis MacGibbon, and New York, St. Martin's Press, 1978.

Thomas Gainsborough: His Life and Art. London, Granada, and New York, Universe, 1981.

The Crisis in Marxism. Bradford on Avon, Wiltshire, Moonraker Press, and New York, Barnes and Noble, 1981.

Turner: The Man and His Art. London, Granada, and New York, Watts, 1985.

Editor, with Kenneth Slessor, *Poetry in Australia.* Sydney, Vision Press, 1923.

Editor, with P. Warlock, *Loving Mad Tom: Bedlamite Verses of the XVI and XVII Centuries.* London, Fanfrolico Press, 1927; New York, Kelley, 1970.

Editor, *The Metamorphosis of Aiax,* by Sir John Harington. New York, McKee, 1928.

Editor, *The Parlement of Pratlers.* London, Fanfrolico Press, 1928.

Editor (as Peter Meadows), *Delighted Earth,* by Robert Herrick. London, Fanfrolico Press, 1928.

Editor, *Inspiration.* London, Fanfrolico Press, 1928.

Editor, *Letters of Philip Stanhope, Second Earl of Chesterfield.* London, Fanfrolico Press, 1930.

Editor, with Edgell Rickword, *A Handbook of Freedom: A Record of English Democracy Through Twelve Centuries.* London, Lawrence and Wishart, and New York, International Publishers, 1939.

Editor, with Maurice Carpenter and Honor Arundel, *New Lyrical Ballads.* London, Editions Poetry, 1945.

Editor, *Anvil: Life and the Arts: A Miscellany.* London, Meridian, and New York, Universal Distributors, 1947.

Editor, *New Development Series.* London, Lane, 1947–48.

Editor, *Herrick: A Selection.* London, Grey Walls Press, 1948.

Editor, *William Morris: A Selection.* London, Grey Walls Press, 1948.

Editor, with Randall Swingler, *Key Poets.* London, Fore, 1950.

Editor, *Barefoot,* by Z. Stancu. London, Fore 1950.

Editor, *Paintings and Drawings of Leslie Hurry.* London, Grey Walls Press, 1952.

Editor, *The Sunset Ship: Poems of J.M.W. Turner.* Lowestoft, Suffolk, Scorpion Press, 1966.

Editor, *The Autobiography of Joseph Priestley*.   Bath, Adams and Dart, 1970; Teaneck, New Jersey, Fairleigh Dickinson University Press, 1971.

Translator, *Lysistrata*, by Aristophanes.   Sydney, Kirtley, 1925; London, Fanfrolico Press, 1926.

Translator, *Propertius in Love*.   London, Fanfrolico Press, 1927.

Translator, *Satyricon and Poems*, by Petronius.   London, Fanfrolico Press, 1927; revised edition, London, Elek, 1960.

Translator, *Homage to Sappho*.   London, Fanfrolico Press, 1928.

Translator, *Complete Poems of Theocritus*.   London, Fanfrolico Press, 1929.

Translator, *Hymns to Aphrodite*, by Homer. London, Fanfrolico Press, 1929.

Translator, *Women in Parliament*, by Aristophanes.   London, Fanfrolico Press, 1929.

Translator, *The Mimiambs of Herondas*.   London, Fanfrolico Press, 1929.

Translator, *The Complete Poetry of Gaius Catullus*.   London, Fanfrolico Press, 1930; revised edition, London, Sylvan Press, 1948.

Translator, *Sulpicia's Garland: Roman Poems*.   New York, McKee, 1930.

Translator, *Patchwork Quilt: Poems by Ausonius*.   London, Fanfrolico Press, 1930.

Translator, *The Golden Ass*, by Apuleius.   New York, Limited Editions Club, 1931; revised edition, London, Elek, and Bloomington, Indiana University Press, 1960.

Translator, *I Am a Roman*.   London, Mathews and Marrot, 1934.

Translator, *Medieval Latin Poets*.   London, Mathews and Marrot, 1934.

Translator, *Daphnis and Chloe*, by Longus.   London, Daimon Press, 1948.

Translator, with S. Jolly, *Song of Peace*, by V. Nezval.   London, Fore, 1951.

Translator, *Poems of Adam Mickiewicz*.   London, Sylvan Press, and New York, Transatlantic Arts, 1957.

Translator, *Russian Poetry 1917–1955*.   London, Lane, 1957; Chester Springs, Pennsylvania, Dufour, 1961.

Translator, *Asklepiades in Love*.   Twinstead, Essex, Myriad Press, 1960.

Translator, *Modern Russian Poetry*.   London, Vista, 1960.

Translator, *Cause, Principle, and Unity: 5 Dialogues*, by Giordano Bruno.   London, Daimon Press, 1962; New York, International Publishers, 1964.

Translator, *Ribaldry of Ancient Greece*.   London, Elek, and New York, Ungar, 1965.

Translator, *Ribaldry of Ancient Rome*.   London, Elek, and New York, Ungar, 1965.

Translator, *The Elegy of Haido*, by Tefcros Anthias.   London, Anthias Publications, 1966.

Translator, *The Age of Akhenaten*, by Eleonore Bille-de-Mot.   London, Adams and MacKay, 1967; New York, McGraw Hill, 1968.

Translator, *Greece, I Keep My Vigil for You*, by Tefcros Anthias.   London, Anthias Publications, 1968.

Translator, *The Twelve, and The Scythians*, by Alexander Blok.   London, Journeyman Press, 1982.

*

Manuscript Collection: University of Queensland, St. Lucia.

Critical Studies: *Mountain in the Sunlight* by Alick West, London, Lawrence and Wishart, 1958; *A Garland for Jack Lindsay*, St. Albans, Hertfordshire, Piccolo Press, 1980 (?); *Culture and History: Essays Presented to Jack Lindsay* edited by Bernard Smith, Sydney, Hale and Iremonger, 1984.

Jack Lindsay comments:

I began as a poet and feel that my devotion to poetry has determined my writing career in all its aspects. First as poet and classical scholar I turned to translating Greek and Latin poetry; then as critic seeking to understand the ancient poets I worked at history, needing to grasp their world and find out how far the poems were linked with that world's workings; out of concern for the nature of poetry I turned to philosophy, especially Plato and Nietzsche though also to poet-philosophers like Blake; later the same interests drew me to cultural anthropology and to psychoanalysis. Thus out of various disciplines, which I approached always from the angle of poetry and its nature, I expanded my interests and the range of my work.

A friend and I hand-printed my *Lysistrata* in Sydney, Australia, 1924–25, with illustrations by my father Norman Lindsay. The book was well received and he asked me to come to London to start a fine press, the Fanfrolico (a name devised by my father in *contes drolatiques* he had written for an Abbey of Thelema): we used that name to express the aesthetic we had devised in Australia. The friend handed the press over to me, as he wanted to return to Australia; I was thus involved in much typographical, editing, translating work, and did much literary research at the B.M. Reading Room, as well as writing poetry. When the press ended in 1930 I went to Cornwall in an effort to find a new basis for work, and lived in extreme hardship till 1934 when I managed to synthesise my interests (as outlined above) in the historical novel. I had translated and annotated Catullus, and I now developed a picture of his world in a Roman trilogy.

My method was thus derived wholly from poetry and my quest into its nature as the highest point of human consciousness. It sought to bring together the following elements: (a) the element of sensuous immediacy in experience, the timeless present of the poetic image; (b) the tragic pattern of conflict, breakdown, recognition, triumph as I had learned it from the Greeks, Nietzsche, and Freudian technique, and from my broodings over Shakespeare and Dostoevsky; (c) the related pattern of death-rebirth which was revealed in tribal ritual (especially of the initiation-ceremony) and carried on by the mystery-religions of the ancient world and by Christianity. I then attempted to make a dynamic synthesis of all these elements in an interpretation of the structure of development in history and of the dialectical relation of individual and social whole. I was (and have continued to go on) seeking to grasp in a single conception or image a largescale moment of life, especially a moment of revolutionary change when all the issues come together in full force, and at the same time to realise the situation at a multiple series of levels (personal, social, aesthetic, philosophic, legal, religious, etc.).

This has continued to be my method, with varying emphases—though I soon turned to English history as well as to ancient, and then moved on to the contemporary situation. I have tried to grasp the particular forms of death-rebirth in every period, to grasp both the total movement and the individual refractions. In turn I have expanded this method to deal directly with many periods of history (especially Graeco-Roman Egypt), with problems of anthropology, with the biographies of writers and artists, and so on. I think I can then claim a definite unity in all my work despite its very multifarious nature. The novels have been especially recognized in the Soviet Union, where over a million copies have been sold in translation and *Betrayed Spring* has been printed in its English form as a textbook. Versions have also appeared in Chinese and Mongolian, as well as in German, Polish, Hungarian, Czech, Romanian, Bulgarian. I believe that this wide interest has been because of the fusion I have attempted of a poetic and an historical vision—the way in which my method seeks to grasp the patterns of change in a perspective of all that constitutes the human universal.

*   *   *

Jack Lindsay divides his many novels into two groups: "Historical Novels" and "Contemporary Novels of the British Way." These two groups are closely linked by an overwhelming concern for the socialist ideal in its purist form. What interests this writer primarily is the moment of revolutionary struggle when the forces working for the good life for every human being rise up against the apathy and de-humanisation caused by an out-of-control capitalist system. This moment of change may take place in Rome in 63 B.C., as it does in the early novel *Rome for Sale*, or in the formation of a branch of the Campaign for Nuclear Disarmament in a small midland town, as it does nearly 30 years later in *The Way the Ball Bounces*.

It is no doubt because of this strong political bias that Lindsay's novels are so widely read in the Soviet Union and the Eastern bloc. But political propaganda and the art of the novelist are two separate activities. One must look beyond the unvarying message, however much one may agree or disagree with it, to discover how these novels take shape and live. The first thing one notices after reading several of them from any period is how strongly they are influenced by Elizabethan drama. These novels are structured as plays, the reader being given a list of the main characters. The plot is almost invariably of a strong and definite nature involving events of life and death; and the action is divided into contrasting scenes, with comic relief supplied in an almost Shakespearean manner in the Roman novels by the most bawdy of the common soldiers and their prostitutes.

As for love, as distinct from lust, that is an emotion that for Lindsay is very strongly linked with political ideals. Catalina in *Rome for Sale* owes the deep love he has for his wife Orestilla to the knowledge that they are both working for the same cause, the prosperity of the common citizens of Rome. In a much later novel, *The Revolt of the Sons*, Chris, the youngest of Samuel Todd's five sons, realises his love for his cousin Rebecca at the same time that he becomes convinced of the need to break free of the tyranny of private family capitalism in which he and his brothers are locked. The case of Alan Horton, the young solicitor in *The Way the Ball Bounces*, is somewhat different. A withdrawn young man, he was so emotionally shattered by his experiences in the Korean war that he successfully inured himself against any form of feeling apart from a mild delight in the verbal logic of the law. It takes a short, sincere, and slightly desperate affair with a young West Indian girl to batter these defences down.

Lindsay is above all a very conscious novelist. He does not expect the reader totally to suspend disbelief. So in the historical novels he keeps very closely to the actual recorded events, and in the contemporary novels in imagined settings he often lets the reader observe how the characters are being handled. Francis Musgrave, one of the main characters in *A Local Habitation*, acts as a sort of chorus in *The Revolt of the Sons*. He and his friend Roland have been discussing old Todd, his five sons and the wives of the three older ones. He reports "You

might say that family represents our world in miniscule. . . . I said it was a Balzacian theme: the power of money and its ubiquitous tendrils of distortion. He said it was Dostoevskian: the fascination and hatred of authority, the jealous sons surrounding the father-god." In fact, as in so many of these novels, it is both.

—Shirley Toulson

LITVINOFF, Emanuel. British. Born in London, 30 June 1915. Served in the Royal West African Frontier Force, 1940–46: Major. Married Cherry Marshall in 1942 (divorced); three children. Before World War II, worked in tailoring, cabinet-making, and the fur trade; after the war worked as a journalist and broadcaster, and founded the journal, *Jews in Eastern Europe*, London. Since 1958, director of the Contemporary Jewish Library, London. Recipient: Wingate Award (*Jewish Chronicle*, London), 1979. Address: c/o David Higham Associates, 5–8 Lower John Street, London W1R 4HA, England.

<small>PUBLICATIONS</small>

Novels

The Lost Europeans. New York, Vanguard Press, 1959; London, Heinemann, 1960.
The Man Next Door. London, Hodder and Stoughton, 1968; New York, Norton, 1969.
A Death Out of Season. London, Joseph, 1973; New York, Scribner, 1974.
Blood on the Snow. London, Joseph, 1975.
The Face of Terror. London, Joseph, and New York, Morrow, 1978.
Falls the Shadow. London, Joseph, and New York, Stein and Day, 1983.

Short Stories

Penguin Modern Stories 2, with others. London, Penguin, 1969.
Journey Through a Small Planet. London, Joseph, 1972.

Uncollected Short Stories

"The God I Failed," in *The Guardian* (London), 1966.
"Call Me Uncle Solly," in *The Listener* (London), 1967.

Plays

Magnolia Street Story, adaptation of a novel by Louis Golding (produced London, 1951).

Television Plays: *Another Branch of the Family*, 1967; *Marriage and Henry Sunday*, 1967; *A Dream in the Afternoon*, 1967; *A Foot in the Door*, 1969; *The World Is a Room*, 1970; *Warm Feet, Warm Heart*, 1970.

Verse

Conscripts: A Symphonic Declaration. London, Favil Press, 1941.

The Untried Soldier. London, Routledge, 1942.
A Crown for Cain. London, Falcon Press, 1948.
Notes for a Survivor. Newcastle upon Tyne, Northern House, 1973.

Other

Editor, *Soviet Anti-Semitism: The Paris Trial.* London, Wildwood House, 1974.
Editor, *The Penguin Book of Jewish Short Stories.* London, Penguin, 1979.

*

Emanuel Litvinoff comments:
My novel *The Lost Europeans* is haunted by the Holocaust. It describes the morbid psychological obsessions of victim and persecutor in a situation where former German Jews return to Germany after the war and confront their erstwhile neighbours.
The Man Next Door is, in a sense, related to this theme. Its central character is a conventional suburban Englishman of the middle-class whose personality begins to disintegrate under the encroachments of middle-age, accompanied by a sense of social and sexual failure. In the process, a mild and commonplace xenophobia turns to rabid hatred of Jews and Negroes of the kind so hideously expressed by the Nazis.
A Death Out of Season, *Blood on the Snow* and *The Face of Terror* comprise a trilogy following the fortunes of a group of young revolutionaries in the early years of the century, through the Russian Revolution, civil war and famine, to their final disillusion and bitterness in the Stalinist purges of the mid-1930's.
Falls the Shadow, written in thriller form, shows how the Nazi holocaust intertwines with modern life in Israel, raising moral issues that Israel must still some to terms with.
My short stories, set in the milieu of the London Jewish East End, celebrate the idealism, pain, and promise of adolescence.

*   *   *

Emanuel Litvinoff's short stories describe the atmosphere of a close Jewish community in London's East End where he grew up between the wars. The stories contain some poignant and sometimes verbose semi-autobiographical sketches of adolescence, as in "A View from the Seventh Floor":

"What do you do on week-ends?" I stammered.
"On Saturday," she whispered, without lifting her head, "I go to the synagogue with my aunt."
Soft black hair curled on the nape of her slender neck and I was tormented by her narrow, sleepy Russian eyes. I wanted to say something miraculous and unforgettable, or so sharp, cruel and eloquent it would remain a fresh wound all of her life. But instead I said: "Does your aunt shave on Shabbos?"

In the same story, Litvinoff mentions his early feelings of rootlessness which inform much of his later work: "In those days I had the shadowy premonition that unless my life was shattered to pieces and I could put it together differently, I'd never, never be myself."
As Litvinoff approaches maturity, he becomes increasingly aware of his "ancestry of misfortune." He regards it as mere chance that he was born in Whitechapel. His home could as

easily have been in Hitler's Germany or Stalin's Russia. Litvinoff's first novel, *The Lost Europeans*, develops this idea and examines the restless lives of a few World War II survivors. The novel is set in post-war Berlin, where ex-nazis and communists, hedonistic young Aryans, whores, and a few Jews live in awkward peace. Martin Stone, a London accountant, takes time off to visit the city of his childhood and claim the legal restitution of his family's fortune. The war-blighted Berliners whom Martin meets involuntarily inflame his smouldering bitterness. There is Hugo Krantz, a fellow Jew, once the witty doyen of Berlin's theatre circles, now a fat businessman in relentless pursuit of sensual pleasures, and the friend who betrayed him to the SS. Hugo arranges accommodation for Martin in the guesthouse of his oldest friend, Frau Goetz. Her gothic hair-do and bird-like charm cannot conceal the marks of Auschwitz. Every Berliner is a victim. In the parks and pastryshops and honky tonk bars, Martin feels once more "the poisons moving in the bloodstream, the familiar throbbing of the diseased night." But it is in this city that Martin meets Karin, a docile factory worker from the eastern sector. She too is a victim—raped in childhood by conquering Russian soldiers. In order to offer her his love, Martin must expiate Karin's years of numbness and resolve his own haunting resentments.
Litvinoff's descriptions of the strange personal lives of Hugo and Frau Goetz are especially good, and Hugo's foray into the ambiguous and dangerous world of intelligence agents has all the atmosphere of a first-rate spy thriller. But just as the pace is getting really hot, we are back with the dour, curiously faceless Martin. The impact of each story—Martin's and Hugo's—is reduced rather than enhanced by its entanglement with the other. Nevertheless, *The Lost Europeans* is a very readable and frequently compelling account of the obsessions of German Jews and their former persecutors.
The Man Next Door focuses on Harold Bollam, a man who blossomed early in life. Boarding school, the army, and a spell as a store manager in West Africa supported and strengthened his hawkish sentiments on class and race. Back in England he finds life somewhat bewildering:

The country had gone mad for gimmicks. Young smart alecks were getting in everywhere. Long-haired popsingers bought up the stately homes, public opinion media were in the hands of queers and sensation-mongers who made England look cheap in the eyes of the world. Cheap, indeed, when black college boys became prime ministers of ridiculous "independent" states, dined with the Queen and lectured the British on the what's-what of democracy.

Middle-age does not mellow a man like Bollam; failures and frustrations pile upon him. Relations with his fretful wife Edna are bleak; prospects for promotion at International Utilities dwindle daily; sex is a combat between flesh and despair; his children, away at boarding school, are strangers. When the Winstons (born Weinsteins) move in next door, Bollam's resentments and fears become obsessions. His wife, his colleagues, the Blacks, the Jews, and especially the Jews next door, are all conspiring to degrade and defeat him. Obsession turns to paranoia and Bollam seeks insane revenge. ". . . as soon as the Winstons arrived he'd guessed it would end badly. They didn't fit. Apart from being Jews, there was something alien and disruptive about them. They were the kind who carried the germ of misfortune wherever they went, like spores of an invisible cancer . . ."
The Man Next Door has a certain morbid fascination, but it lacks the authenticity of Litvinoff's first novel. Most of the

characters are incredibly stereotyped, and his portrayal of Bollam's grim, neurotic life is often glib. The analogy between Bollam's retrogression and the rise of nazism is obvious but rarely effective.

Litvinoff's obsession with Jewish persecution has further opened out in recent work. *A Death Out of Season*, *Blood on the Snow*, and *The Face of Terror* constitute a trilogy of historical novels which seek to portray the experience of revolutionary and Stalinist Russia, and have been highly praised by reviewers. Though these novels have complicated and dazzling plots, the double agents, summaries of Russian history, and rather conventional iconography lack real conviction. Much more original is *Falls the Shadow*. The plot is genuinely unusual (a SS torturer masquerading as a Jewish victim, complete with concentration camp tattoo, and an obsessed police investigator). The moral problems (does living the life of an orthodox Jew for 40 years balance having been an SS torturer?) and the convincing description of suburban life in Tel Aviv give strength to the work, though the messages are rather thumped home, the reader continually nudged into historical awareness.

Litvinoff writes about people whose painful history has left them bitter, tormented, and potentially destructive. But he does not have the sheer grasp or the calm incisiveness that characterizes the best writing of this kind.

—Roland Turner

LODGE, David (John). British. Born in London, 28 January 1935. Educated at St. Joseph's Academy, London; University College, London, 1952–55, 1957–59, B.A. (honours) in English 1955, M.A. 1959; University of Birmingham, Ph.D. 1967. Served in the Royal Armoured Corps, 1955–57. Married Mary Frances Jacob in 1959; two sons and one daughter. Assistant, British Council, London, 1959–60. Assistant Lecturer, 1960–62, Lecturer, 1963–71, Senior Lecturer, 1971–73, Reader, 1973–76, and since 1976, Professor of Modern English Literature, University of Birmingham. Visiting Associate Professor, University of California, Berkeley, 1969; Henfield Writing Fellow, University of East Anglia, Norwich, 1977. Recipient: Harkness Commonwealth Fellowship, 1964; *Yorkshire Post* award, 1975; Hawthornden Prize, 1976; Whitbread Award, for fiction and for book of the year, 1980. Fellow, Royal Society of Literature, 1976, and University College, London, 1982. Address: Department of English, P.O. Box 363, University of Birmingham, Birmingham B15 2TT, England.

PUBLICATIONS

Novels

The Picturegoers.   London, MacGibbon and Kee, 1960.
Ginger, You're Barmy.   London, MacGibbon and Kee, 1962; New York, Doubleday, 1965.
The British Museum Is Falling Down.   London, MacGibbon and Kee, 1965; New York, Holt Rinehart, 1967.
Out of the Shelter.   London, Macmillan, 1970; revised edition, London, Secker and Warburg, 1985.
Changing Places: A Tale of Two Campuses.   London, Secker and Warburg, 1975; New York, Penguin, 1979.
How Far Can You Go?   London, Secker and Warburg, 1980; as *Souls and Bodies*, New York, Morrow, 1982.

Small World: An Academic Romance.   London, Secker and Warburg, 1984; New York, Macmillan, 1985.

Uncollected Short Stories

"The Man Who Couldn't Get Up," in *Weekend Telegraph* (London), 6 May 1966.
"By the Waters of Disneyland," in *Commonweal* (New York), 7 November 1980.

Plays

Between These Four Walls (revue), with Malcolm Bradbury and James Duckett (produced Birmingham, 1963).
Slap in the Middle (revue), with others (produced Birmingham, 1965).

Other

About Catholic Authors (for children).   London, St. Paul Publications, 1958.
Language of Fiction.   London, Routledge, and New York, Columbia University Press, 1966; revised edition, Routledge, 1984.
Graham Greene.   New York, Columbia University Press, 1966.
The Novelist at the Crossroads and Other Essays on Fiction and Criticism.   London, Routledge, and Ithaca, New York, Cornell University Press, 1971.
Evelyn Waugh.   New York, Columbia University Press, 1971.
The Modes of Modern Writing: Metaphor, Metonymy, and the Typology of Modern Literature.   London, Arnold, and Ithaca, New York, Cornell University Press, 1977.
Modernism, Antimodernism, and Postmodernism (lecture).   Birmingham, University of Birmingham, 1977.
Working with Structuralism: Essays and Reviews on Nineteenth- and Twentieth-Century Literature.   London, Routledge, 1981.

Editor, *Jane Austen: "Emma": A Casebook.*   London, Macmillan, 1968; Nashville, Aurora, 1970(?).
Editor, with James Kinsley, *Emma*, by Jane Austen.   London, Oxford University Press, 1971.
Editor, *Twentieth Century Literary Criticism: A Reader.*   London, Longman, 1972.
Editor, *Scenes of Clerical Life*, by George Eliot.   London, Penguin, 1973.
Editor, *The Woodlanders*, by Thomas Hardy.   London, Macmillan, 1974.
Editor, *The Best of Ring Lardner.*   London, Dent, 1984.

*

Critical Studies: interview with Bernard Bergonzi, in *The Month* (London), February 1970, and "The Decline and Fall of the Catholic Novel," in *The Myth of Modernism and Twentieth-Century Literature* by Bergonzi, Brighton, Harvester Press, 1986; "The Novels of David Lodge" by Michael Parnell, in *Madog* (Barry, Wales), Summer 1979; article by Dennis Jackson, in *British Novelists since 1960* edited by Jay L. Halio, Detroit, Gale, 1983; interview with John Haffenden, in *Literary Review* (London), April 1984.

David Lodge comments:

(1972) My novels belong to a tradition of realistic fiction (especially associated with England) that tries to find an appropriate form for, and a public significance in, what the writer has himself experienced and observed. In my case this experience and observation include such things as: lower-middle-class life in the inner suburbs of South East London; a wartime childhood and a post-war "austerity" adolescence; Catholicism; education and the social and physical mobility it brings; military service, marriage, travel, etc. My first, second, and fourth novels are "serious" realistic novels about such themes, the last of them, *Out of the Shelter*, which is a kind of *Bildungsroman*, being, as far as I am concerned, the most inclusive and most fully achieved.

My third novel, *The British Museum Is Falling Down*, was something of a departure in being a comic novel, incorporating elements of farce and good deal of parody. I plan to write more fiction in the comic mode, as I enjoy the freedom for invention and stylistic effect it affords. On the other hand, I have not (like many contemporary writers) lost faith in traditional realism as a vehicle for serious fiction. The writer I admire above all others, I suppose, is James Joyce, and the combination one finds in his early work of realistic truthtelling and poetic intensity seems to me an aim still worth pursuing.

As an academic critic and teacher of literature with a special interest in prose fiction, I am inevitably self-conscious about matters of narrative technique, and I believe this is a help rather than a hindrance. I certainly think that my criticism of fiction gains from my experience of writing it.

(1981) Since writing the above I have come to have less faith in the viability of the traditional realistic novel of the kind that seeks, by suppressing the signs that it is written, and narrated, to give the illusion of being a transparent window upon the real. This shift of attitude does not entail abandoning the novel's traditional function of engaging with, organizing, and interpreting social-historical experience—merely being open about the necessarily conventional and artificial ways in which it does so. My last two works of fiction, therefore, have a prominent "metafictional" thread running through them, through which the self-consciousness about fictional technique referred to above is allowed some play in the texts themselves—licenced by comedy in *Changing Places*, but with more serious thematic intent in *How Far Can You Go?*

*   *   *

David Lodge combines the writing of fiction with a keen interest in its theory, as is shown in his books of criticism *Language of Fiction* and *The Modes of Modern Writing*. As a critic he is sympathetic to literary experiment and the kind of fiction that probes the problematical relations between art and reality, though as a novelist he still finds the realistic tradition viable and continues to write within it, drawing in large measure on autobiographical material.

Lodge is a Roman Catholic by birth and upbringing. His basic milieu is shabby-genteel Catholic family life in South London, whose nearest literary equivalent lies in the domestic scenes of Joyce's *Portrait of the Artist*. His first novel, *The Picturegoers*, was set against this background, which was treated in a warm and even sentimental manner; he returned to it ten years later in *Out of the Shelter*, where it was regarded with a cool but not contemptuous eye, and with a much greater sense of its narrowness and limitations.

The Picturegoers was an ambitious novel, focused on a suburban cinema and showing a broad range of contrasted characters, though it was rather lacking in dramatic movement and interplay. It suggested that despite a speculative interest in the hero's religious struggles, Lodge's basic talent was as a comic novelist. It was followed by *Ginger, You're Barmy*, an obsessively realistic story of army life that was clearly a working-off of unassimilated resentments about the author's military service. *The British Museum Is Falling Down* represented a real development. It was a comic novel on a serious topic, the Roman Catholic ban on contraception. The central character is an anxious Catholic graduate student, married with three children and the nagging possibility that a fourth might be on the way; he spends his days working on a literary thesis at the British Museum, which Lodge presents as an area for farcical happenings of all kinds. The hero's professional interest in literary style is worked into the fabric of the novel in recurring passages of accomplished parody of distinguished modern novelists.

Out of the Shelter is, in all senses, a serious novel, though often showing its author's humorous bias. It is a *Bildungsroman* that traces its hero's childhood in wartime London up to a point in his mid-teens when he spends a holiday with his sister who is a secretary with the American army of occupation in Germany. After the deprivations of English life the boy is overwhelmed by the riches of the American Way of Life: the story, as Lodge tells it, is both an account of individual sensibility, and a representative treatment of a significant Anglo-American cultural encounter. Clashes between English and American attitudes are further exploited in *Changing Places*, an unreserved and satisfying return to comic fiction. It traces the fortunes of two university teachers of English, one from the English Midlands, one from the American West Coast, who exchange jobs and, eventually, wives. It is both a compellingly funny story and an intelligent expression of Lodge's interests in the nature of fictional form.

How Far Can You Go? follows the lives of a group of English Catholics, from their student days in the early 1950's to the crises of impending middle age in the late 1970's. It shows their personal and professional struggles, the successes or failures of their marriages, and their problems with contraception (by the end of the novel most of them have rejected the continuing official Catholic ban on it). Lodge registers the rapid changes in English society over a quarter of a century in an excellent novel that, though sometimes unconvincing in characterization, is faultlessly observant and readable.

Small World is an exuberant and inventive novel which follows the later fortunes of some of the principal characters of *Changing Places*. Whereas that novel had restricted itself to a contrast between two representative American and British academic settings, *Small World* ranges over the whole world as its performers tirelessly follow the global conference circuit; the campus as a physical setting has now become obsolete, replaced by the telephone, the jet airliner, and the photocopier. Lodge uses as his model the Italian romance epic, where knights and ladies are continually and rapidly moving from one adventure to the next. It contains much good-humoured satire on academic life and some informative disquisitions on structuralism and other late 20th-century cults. It is also full of puns and jokes, whether sophisticated or low, and is loaded with parodies and allusions. It is splendidly comic and extraordinarily ingenious. With *Small World* Lodge emerged as one of the leading English novelists of his generation.

—Bernard Bergonzi

LOVELACE, Earl. Trinidadian. Born in Trinidad in 1935. Married. Civil servant: agricultural assistant in Jamaica. Recipient: B.P. Independence Award, 1965. Address: c/o Heinemann Ltd., 10 Upper Grosvenor Street, London W1X 9PA, England.

PUBLICATIONS

Novels

While Gods Are Falling. London, Collins, 1965; Chicago, Regnery, 1966.
The Schoolmaster. London, Collins, and Chicago, Regnery, 1968.
The Dragon Can't Dance. London, Deutsch, 1979; Washington, D.C., Three Continents Press, 1981.
The Wine of Astonishment. London, Deutsch, 1982; New York, Vintage, 1984.

Plays

The New Hardware Store (produced London, 1985). Included in *Jestina's Calypso and Other Plays*, 1984.
Jestina's Calypso and Other Plays (includes *The New Hardware Store* and *My Name Is Village*). London, Heinemann, 1984.

*   *   *

Earl Lovelace is primarily a wonderful storyteller. He holds one's interest whether through exciting dialogue which rings true, or by his descriptive ability and his portrayal of the inner conflicts which puzzle his characters.

To say that he is an excellent storyteller is in no way to belittle his work; nor is it to deny that his work embodies values and has its serious moral concerns. But his great ability as a writer of fiction, i.e., as a writer who through images works at a deeper level than that of the preacher or "social scientist," is much downgraded by the kind of statement made by one reviewer about two of Lovelace's novels: "This tension between the ideal and the reality (of Trinidad and Tobago's 'national motto' 'all o' wi is one") creates the chief interest of both *The Wine of Astonishment* and *The Dragon Can't Dance.*" Thank heavens there is much more to both novels than that! There is, for one thing, Lovelace's control of the Trinidadian language, and his constant concern with the ambiguous relationship between change and progress. The arrival of the Schoolmaster, the behaviour of Ivan Morton (the new "Independence" politician), the coming of "good behaviour" and sponsorship to the Steel Bands, the passing of the stick fighters and stick fighting—all these are developed, in different novels, subtly, and at a subconscious level, as signs and images of the profit and loss of change, and also of the inevitability of some of the changes and of the disturbance that they necessarily bring in their wake.

One of the changes occurs in the relationship between the rural and urban styles of living. At the beginning of *While Gods Are Falling* Walter, much to the distress of his wife, wishes to leave the confusion, "scuffling," and sycophancy of Port of Spain. He wishes to return to the country, where he grew up—none too happily—but where he feels he can be "a man," full of spunk and independence. The concern with being

one's own person—with "being a man"—to use the old formulation—constantly appears in Lovelace's work.

But then again one must not forget that Lovelace is mainly a storyteller. A story uses and recounts disparate elements which create a pattern and make sense and give satisfaction only when they come together in a certain way under the master's hand. Lovelace holds our attention without being trivial or facile. He not only pleases by verisimilitude, he also enables aspects of the significance of the life of a people, and of individual persons, to dawn upon us. When, for instance, in *The Schoolmaster*, Christiana confesses to the priest that she is with child by the Schoolmaster, who has seduced her, the priest is dismayed, and we read, as she stares at his face turned sideways in the confessional: "And now the priest's ear gazed at her, and she saw now that it was a pool, a deep pool and her mother was sitting on the bank there, waiting for her in her long white dress . . . waiting for her." In this way Lovelace begins to prepare us for the only solution which Christiana, betrothed to Pedro, can find to her predicament, a predicament —be it noted—which has risen out of the fact that it was part of progress to set up a school and to bring a schoolmaster to the "backward", "illiterate" village. Those who helped with this necessary and progressive step are the ones who suffer most from the unfortunate consequences of the move!

This paradoxical, non-linear relationship between change and progress is often made palpable in Lovelace's fiction. In *The Dragon Can't Dance* those who would have been, in the old days, ornaments of the village as stick fighters become nuisances in the city as "Bad Johns," and the old struggles of would-be warriors become competitions between sponsored bands; it is no longer the warrior as musician, but the musician as would-be competitor.

In *The Wine of Astonishment* a son goes off from the restrictions of the village to the wider opportunities of the city—never to be heard from again. And Ivan Morton, the people's man, moves from his more than adequate home to the vacated "great house" without even taking a "favourite" chair along. For a long time he seems to do nothing for the bell-ringing Baptists who have worked to vote him in, and when he does help to remove the ban from their mode of worship, it seems too late. The old Spirit deserts them. And yet at the end, as Ma, the wonderful narrator of the tale, turns the corner "where Miss Hilda living," she says, as she passes the carnival tent, "I listening to the music; for the music that those boys playing on the steelband have in it that same Spirit that we miss in our church: the same Spirit; and listening to them, my heart swell and it is like resurrection morning. I watch Bee, Bee watch me, the both of us bow, nod, as if, yes, God is great, and like if we passing in front of something holy." So ends the book which 145 pages before had started: "God don't give you more than you can bear, I say . . ." One has a slight feeling of uneasiness about Ma's firm feeling that "the steelband have in it the same Spirit that we miss in our church." But then *she* should know!

Lovelace is a great storyteller. He often has a dramatic way of presenting his characters and images. Think of the opening dialogue in *While Gods Are Falling.* He has a very good feeling for, and ability to bring to life, the complicated reality of Trinidad society—"everybody wanted to see Mr. Ramroop dance because he danced in the awkward East Indian fashion, a waltz, a castilliane or a calypso." There we have Vienna, Spain, Afro-Trinidad, and the Asian as perceived by others! Lovelace's ability to handle the English and Trinidadian languages recommend him strongly to our attention. But particularly in England he should be read because his excellent fiction is a good antidote to the limited view often touted by many, including Caribbean

Heritage people, of the rich variety and mixture that is Caribbean culture.

—John J. Figueroa

LUDWIG, Jack (Barry). Canadian. Born in Winnipeg, Manitoba, 30 August 1922. Educated at St. John's High School, Winnipeg; University of Manitoba, Winnipeg, B.A. 1944; University of California, Los Angeles, Ph.D. 1953. Married Leya Lauer in 1946; two daughters. Instructor, Williams College, Williamstown, Massachusetts, 1949–53; Assistant and Associate Professor, Bard College, Annandale-on-Hudson, New York, 1953–58, and University of Minnesota, Minneapolis, 1958–61. Since 1961, Professor of English, State University of New York, Stony Brook. Co-editor, *Noble Savage*, New York, then Cleveland, 1960–62. Chairman, Humanities Group, International Seminar, Harvard University, Cambridge, Massachusetts, summers 1963–66. Writer-in-Residence, University of Toronto, 1968–69; Playwright-in-Residence, Stratford Shakespearean Festival Workshop, Ontario, 1970; Writer-in-Residence, Banff Centre, Alberta, Summer 1974; Visiting Professor, University of California, Los Angeles, Summer 1976. Recipient: Longview Foundation award, 1960; *Atlantic* "Firsts" Award, 1960; O. Henry Award, 1961, 1965; Canada Council award, 1962, and Senior Arts Fellowship, 1967, 1975. Address: Department of English, State University of New York, Stony Brook, New York 11794, U.S.A.

PUBLICATIONS

Novels

Confusions. Greenwich, Connecticut, New York Graphic Society, and London, Secker and Warburg, 1963.
Above Ground. Toronto and Boston, Little Brown, 1968.
A Woman of Her Age. Toronto, McClelland and Stewart, 1973.

Short Story

Requiem for Bibul. Agincourt, Ontario, Book Society of Canada, 1967.

Uncollected Short Stories

"Orlick Miller and Company," in *Commentary* (New York), January 1960.
"Thoreau in California," in *Noble Savage 1* (New York), April 1960.
"Meesh," in *Tamarack Review* (Toronto), Autumn 1961.
"Death Was the Glass," in *Midstream* (New York), Winter 1961.
"Celebration on East Houston Street," in *Tamarack Review* (Toronto), Spring 1963.
"Einstein and This Admirer," in *London Magazine*, September 1965.
"A Death of One's Own," in *Tamarack Review* (Toronto), Winter 1968.
"Shirley," in *Tamarack Review* (Toronto), Spring 1969.

Plays

The Alchemist, adaptation of the play by Ben Jonson (produced Stratford, Ontario, 1969).
Bustout, with Peter Scupham (produced Stratford, Ontario, 1969).
Ubu Rex, adaptation of a play by Alfred Jarry (produced Stratford, Ontario, 1970).

Television Play: *Hedda Gabler*, from the play by Ibsen, 1979.

Verse

Homage to Zolotova. Banff, Alberta, Banff Centre Press, 1974.

Other

Recent American Novelists. Minneapolis, University of Minnesota Press, 1962.
Hockey Night in Moscow. Toronto, McClelland and Stewart, 1972; revised edition, as *The Great Hockey Thaw; or, The Russians Are Here!*, New York, Doubleday, 1974.
Games of Fear and Winning: Sports with an Inside View. New York, Doubleday, 1976.
The Great American Spectaculars: The Kentucky Derby, Mardi Gras, and Other Days of Celebration. New York, Doubleday, 1976.
Five-Ring Circus: The Montreal Olympics. New York, Doubleday, 1977.

Editor, with Richard Poirier, *Stories: British and American.* Boston, Houghton Mifflin, 1953.
Editor, with Andy Wainwright, *Soundings: New Canadian Poets.* Toronto, Anansi, 1970.

*

Jack Ludwig comments:

Winnipeg, Los Angeles, New York, London were for me never centres of abstraction. Doubtless each city had its moral paralytics; doubtless I didn't run into them often. A liar and a truth-teller have always been equally fascinating to me. The imagination's scale of values is not easily coerced. When I look at Brueghel's paintings I see life without categories, without underlined morals, without tilting: the paltry and exalted, the sleazy and the grand are great challenges to the image that alone makes for realization. Comedy and tragedy are different, but, to the imagination, equal. I reject the Eliot and Pound notions about the past giving shape to the formless present. Whether literature rises out of Dublin or Rome, New York or London, it begins, as Yeats finally recognized, in "A mound of refuse or the sweepings of a street."

*   *   *

Taken together, all of Jack Ludwig's several voices are the voice of a civilized North American; also the voice of a cultured man. His culture, a culture he wears with ease, comes more from the roots of things genuine than from the academy alone. It comes from underground. Ludwig was born into the Jewish community of Winnipeg. He knows it in North America and in its European roots; his own, in Odessa; he knows much of its rich Yiddish and Hasidic backgrounds. In reading him one may think of Mordecai Richler or Philip Roth or I.B. Singer.

To a degree all his writing voices one central, pervasive concern. With his emphasis included, it reads: "... *re-educate*

which linked them almost irrevocably to the substantial tradition of London, by geography, which set them virtually inescapably in the suburbs of New York, by language which gave them two giant brothers, and by economics which committed them to a minuscule circulation unless they were prepared to commit the treason of making themselves comprehensible and acceptable in the huge market-places of Britain and the United States.

The analogy between Canada in the 50 years since the end of the First World War and the United States a century earlier is, of course, both incomplete and deceptive, the more so because Canada has produced no unquestionable masters of the order of Melville or Whitman who could transpose national characteristics into the magnificence of universality, nor a Canadian Emerson who could lead rebellion against the courtly and uncourtly muses of the greater literary nations while borrowing the philosophical inheritance that they provided, nor even a Canadian Fenimore Cooper who could create an intrinsically Canadian mythology.

Some Canadian writers, Mazo de la Roche, Thomas B. Costain, even, in more subtle, less popular, and more truly artistic manner, Morley Callaghan, Malcolm Lowry, and John Glassco, have on occasion solved the problem of their Canadianism by ignoring it, by writing as if the world is their country. Others of a meaner sort have been persistently parochial and are in consequence acceptable only in the tiny confines of the parish or else, outside it, as folklorish curiosities. Only one Canadian novelist, Hugh MacLennan, has been consistent in his efforts to represent the Canadian character both as something quintessentially idiosyncratic and as a parable to the human condition.

It is no paradox but in itself typical of the Canadian ethos that MacLennan is himself in so many ways an untypical Canadian. For all that he is a fourth generation Nova Scotian, MacLennan is the son of a man who spoke Gaelic or a lilting Highland English and who held to the Calvinist ways of the Scots and their superstition. His son has inherited the religiosity, something of the fatalism, and much of the Scotsman's not unjustified conceit in the pioneering achievements of his race, so that several of his novels—and above all *Each Man's Son* and *Return of the Sphinx*—can be regarded as transatlantic epilogues to the history of Scottish literature, as the records of a pastoral people battered and bewildered by urban society, rather than as the opening chapters of the glorious literary enterprise of an ebullient new nation.

Yet for all his urgent Canadianism and for all his inescapable Scottishness the most obvious influences on MacLennan are cosmopolitan and urbane. True, when he moves outside the Canadian setting, as in parts of *The Precipice* and *Return of the Sphinx*, his novelist's confidence falters, but in everything that he writes, whether fiction or non-fiction, his style is overtly the product of the two great civilised institutions (some would say over-civilised) in which he was educated. His literary manners are set to the precepts of Oxford and Princeton, and fashioned by communities that are centuries and worlds away from the Canada he describes. A classical scholar of repute, he creates characters who move to patterns that were fashioned long ago by Greek mythology.

To argue that an author's first novel is also his most successful would seem to imply a lack of development, and in one sense this claim for *Barometer Rising* does reduce the stature of all that has come from MacLennan since 1941. Certainly never again has MacLennan achieved an equivalent synthesis of theme and narrative without that constant interruption of didactic exposition which is the prime fault in most of MacLennan's books. But the entire success of *Barometer Rising* is

almost an accident; it could hardly be repeated for MacLennan is deliberately both chronicler and creator of parables and there have been few other incidents in Canadian history so significant to Canadian development as the First World War and no event so open to translation into parable as the Halifax explosion of 1917. The First World War, the foreground and the background of *Barometer Rising*, was the time when Canada discovered its identity, and the explosion is at once a moment from history and an inescapable symbol of the end of the colonial era and the true beginning of nationhood.

Almost all of MacLennan's later work attempts in one form or another a similar fusion of realism and symbolism and always he is concerned not so much with narrative, plot, or setting (though with all these elements in the writing of novels MacLennan is a master) as with laying bare one or the other of the major impulses that lie behind the peculiarly Canadian nature of Canada. In *Two Solitudes*, for example, it is the schism between French and English Canadians. In *The Precipice* and *Each Man's Son* the puritanical sense of guilt that Puritanism has inflicted upon Canadian life, "the belief that man has inherited from Adam a nature so sinful that there is no hope for him and that, furthermore, he lives and dies under the wrath of an arbitrary God who will forgive only a handful of his elect on the Day of Judgment."

Archie MacNeil, the shabby decaying boxer of *Each Man's Son*, is the most complete character in all MacLennan's work, and the book as a whole contrives well two seemingly disparate themes, the gentleness of a man who lives by violence, and a threnody for the rural culture of Highlanders condemned by a cynical society to live by coal-mining.

The Watch That Ends the Night shows MacLennan as superb craftsman, handling with extraordinary skill a complicated time-sequence and with remarkable vividness the life of English Montreal, but because it is constructed on a grand scale it reveals in broad terms weaknesses which are less palpable in most of the other novels. MacLennan in all his books, but in *The Watch That Ends the Night* (and in *Return of the Sphinx*) more than in the others, is oppressively didactic. He is also an essayist almost more than he is a novelist. His expository asides and his descriptive vignettes though in themselves powerful and often elegant give to the book a stammering indecisiveness in which the hesitations become more compelling and sometimes more substantial than the fiction itself.

With courage beyond that of any other Canadian author, and to-day rare in all literatures, MacLennan writes on a grand scale. *Barometer Rising* and *The Watch That Ends the Night* are not masterpieces of the order of *War and Peace* but MacLennan has attempted to be Canada's Tolstoy and in doing so has disgraced neither himself nor Canada.

—J.E. Morpurgo

MADDEN, (Jerry) David. American. Born in Knoxville, Tennessee, 25 July 1933. Educated at Knox High School, Knoxville; Iowa State Teachers College (now University of Northern Iowa), Cedar Falls, 1956; University of Tennessee, Knoxville, B.S. 1957; San Francisco State College, M.A. 1958; Yale Drama School (John Golden Fellow), New Haven, Connecticut, 1959–60. Served in the United States Army, 1955–56. Married Roberta Margaret Young in 1956; one son. Instructor in English, Appalachian State Teachers College, Boone, North Carolina, 1958–59, and Centre College, Danville, Kentucky,

1960–62; Lecturer in Creative Writing, University of Louisville, Kentucky, 1962–64; Member of the English Department, Kenyon College, Gambier, Ohio, and assistant editor, *Kenyon Review*, 1964–66; Lecturer in Creative Writing, Ohio University, Athens, 1966–68. Since 1968, Writer-in-Residence, Louisiana State University, Baton Rouge. Recipient: Rockefeller grant, 1969; National Endowment for the Arts prize, 1970; Bread Loaf Writers Conference William Raney Fellowship, 1972. Agent: Georges Borchardt Inc., 136 East 57th Street, New York, New York 10022. Address: 614 Park Boulevard, Baton Rouge, Louisiana 70806, U.S.A.

PUBLICATIONS

Novels

The Beautiful Greed.   New York, Random House, 1961.
Cassandra Singing.   New York, Crown, 1969.
Brothers in Confidence.   New York, Avon, 1972.
Bijou.   New York, Crown, 1974.
The Suicide's Wife.   Indianapolis, Bobbs Merrill, 1978.
Pleasure-Dome.   Indianapolis, Bobbs Merrill, 1979.
On the Big Wind.   New York, Holt Rinehart, 1980.

Short Stories

The Shadow Knows.   Baton Rouge, Louisiana State University Press, 1970.
The New Orleans of Possibilities.   Baton Rouge, Louisiana State University Press, 1982.

Uncollected Short Stories

"My Name Is Not Antonio," in *Yale Literary Magazine* (New Haven, Connecticut), March 1960.
"Hair of the Dog," in *Adam* (Los Angeles), April–November 1967.
"The Master's Thesis," in *Fantasy and Science Fiction* (New York), July 1967.
"Nothing Dies But Something Mourns," in *Carleton Miscellany* (Northfield, Minnesota), Fall 1968.
"The Day the Flowers Came," in *The Best American Short Stories 1969*, edited by Martha Foley and David Burnett. Boston, Houghton Mifflin, 1969.
"A Voice in the Garden," in *English Record* (Oneonta, New York), October 1969.
"Traven," in *Short Stories from the Little Magazines*, edited by Jarvis Thurston and Curt Johnson. Chicago, Scott Foresman, 1970.
"Home Comfort," in *Jeopardy* (Bellingham, Washington), March 1970.
"No Trace," in *The Best American Short Stories 1971*, edited by Martha Foley and David Burnett. Boston, Houghton Mifflin, 1971.
"Night Shift," in *Playboy's Ribald Classics 3*. Chicago, Playboy Press, 1972.
"A Secondary Character," in *Cimarron Review* (Stillwater, Oklahoma), July 1972.
"The Spread-Legged Girl" (as Jack Travis), in *Knight* (Los Angeles), October 1972.
"The Singer," in *Scenes from American Life: Contemporary Short Fiction*, edited by Joyce Carol Oates. New York, Vanguard Press, 1973.
"Here He Comes! There He Goes!," in *Contempora* (Atlanta, Georgia), Summer 1973.

"Wanted: Ghost Writer," in *Epoch* (Ithaca, New York), Fall 1973.
"The World's One Breathing," in *Appalachian Heritage* (Pippa Passes, Kentucky), Winter 1973.
"Hurry Up Please, It's Time," in *The Botteghe Oscure Reader*, edited by George Garrett and Katherine Garrison Biddle. Middletown, Connecticut, Wesleyan University Press, 1974.
"The Hero and the Witness," in *New Orleans Review*, vol. 4, no. 3, 1974.
"On the Big Wind," in *The Pushcart Prize 5*, edited by Bill Henderson.   Yonkers, New York, Pushcart Press, 1980.
"Putting an Act Together," in *Southern Review* (Baton Rouge, Louisiana), Winter 1980.
"Code-a-Phone," in *Crescent Review* (Winston-Salem, North Carolina), vol. 1, no. 1, 1983.
"Lights," in *New Letters* (Kansas City), Winter 1984–85.
"Willis Carr at Bleak House," in *Southern Review* (Baton Rouge, Louisiana), Spring 1985.
"Rosanna," in *South Dakota Review* (Vermillion), Summer 1985.

Plays

Call Herman in to Supper (produced Knoxville, Tennessee, 1949).
They Shall Endure (produced Knoxville, Tennessee, 1953).
Cassandra Singing (produced Knoxville, Tennessee, 1955). Published in *New Campus Writing 2*, edited by Nolan Miller, New York, Putnam, 1957; (expanded version, produced Albuquerque, New Mexico, 1964).
From Rome to Damascus (produced Chapel Hill, North Carolina, 1959).
Casina, music by Robert Rogers, lyrics by Joseph Matthewson (produced New Haven, Connecticut, 1960).
In My Father's House, in *First Stage* (Lafayette, Indiana), Summer 1966.
Fugitive Masks (produced Abingdon, Virginia, 1966).
The Day the Flowers Came (produced Baton Rouge, Louisiana, 1974).   Chicago, Dramatic Publishing Company, 1975.

Other

Wright Morris.   New York, Twayne, 1965.
The Poetic Image in Six Genres.   Carbondale, Southern Illinois University Press, 1969.
James M. Cain.   New York, Twayne, 1970.
Harlequin's Stick, Charlie's Cane: A Comparative Study of Commedia dell'Arte and Silent Slapstick Comedy.   Bowling Green, Ohio, Popular Press, 1975.
A Primer of the Novel, For Readers and Writers.   Metuchen, New Jersey, Scarecrow Press, 1980.
Writers' Revisions: An Annotated Bibliography of Articles and Books about Writers' Revisions and Their Comments on the Creative Process, with Richard Powers. Metuchen, New Jersey, Scarecrow Press, 1981.
Cain's Craft.   Metuchen, New Jersey, Scarecrow Press, 1985.

Editor, *Tough Guy Writers of the Thirties.*   Carbondale Southern Illinois University Press, 1968.
Editor, *Proletarian Writers of the Thirties.*   Carbondale Southern Illinois University Press, 1968.
Editor, *American Dreams, American Nightmares.*   Carbondale, Southern Illinois University Press, 1970.
Editor, *Rediscoveries: Informal Essays in Which Well-Known Novelists Rediscover Neglected Works of Fiction by One of Their Favorite Authors.*   New York, Crown, 1971.

Editor, with Ray B. Browne, *The Popular Cultural Explosion: Experiencing Mass Media*. Dubuque, Iowa, William Brown, 2 vols., 1972.

Editor, *Nathanael West: The Cheaters and the Cheated*. Deland, Florida, Everett Edwards, 1973.

Editor, *Remembering James Agee*. Baton Rouge, Louisiana State University Press, 1974.

Editor, *Creative Choices: A Spectrum of Quality and Technique in Fiction*. Chicago, Scott Foresman, 1975.

Editor, with Virgil Scott, *Studies in the Short Story*. New York, Holt Rinehart, 1975; 6th edition, 1984.

*

Bibliography: "A David Madden Bibliography 1952–1981" by Anna H. Perrault, in *Bulletin of Bibliography* (Westport, Connecticut), September 1982.

Manuscript Collection: University of Tennessee Library, Knoxville.

Critical Studies: "A Conversation with David Madden," and "The Mixed Chords of David Madden's *Cassandra Singing*" by Sanford Pinsker, in *Critique* (Atlanta), vol. 15, no. 2, 1973; "An Interview with David Madden," in *The Penny Dreadful* (Bowling Green, Ohio), vol. 3, no. 3, 1974; "The Story Teller as Benevolent Con Man" by Madden, in *Appalachian Heritage* (Pippa Passes, Kentucky), Summer 1974; interviews in *Southern Review* (Baton Rouge, Louisiana), vol. 11, no. 1, 1975, *New Orleans Review*, Spring 1982, and *Louisiana Literature* (Hammond), Fall 1984.

David Madden comments:

I've been trying all my life to pass the test F. Scott Fitzgerald set for himself. "The test of a first-rate intelligence is the ability to hold two opposed ideas in the mind at the same time and still retain the ability to function." Camus's concept of the absurd helped clarify Fitzgerald's: one's life should be a self-created contradiction of the fact that life is basically absurd. A similar polarity has given some form to my art as well as my life. It was not books but my grandmother's story-telling and the movies' charged images that inspired me to write. My first literary hero was the Dionysican Thomas Wolfe; then came the Apollonian James Joyce. In the tensions between those two extremes I have tried to shape my own work. I have practiced for a long time now the concept that it is between the limitations externally imposed by the form I'm working in and limitations I imposed on myself in the writing of a specific work that I experience genuine and productive freedom. Two metaphors of the artist (and the teacher) are useful for me: the magician and the con man. As with the magician's techniques of illusion, art works by a phantom circuit; and the relationship between writer and reader is like that between the con man and his mark, except that the climax (the sting) is beneficial for both. For me, the function of fiction is to create imaginary worlds; discipline and technique enable me to cause that to happen. And in that process I consider my reader as an active collaborator.

*   *   *

Much of David Madden's fiction is autobiographical. Like Lucius Hutchfield in *Bijou*, Madden goes over his personal history again and again, remolding details. Incidents appear in more than one work; short stories are absorbed into novels;

the short novel *Brothers in Confidence* becomes the first half of the longer novel *Pleasure-Dome*, as Madden works at perfecting the tale of his life. Arranged in chronological order Madden's fictional autobiography would begin with two stories from *The Shadow Knows*, "The Pale Horse of Fear" and the title story, then continue on through *Bijou*, *The Beautiful Greed*, *Pleasure-Dome*, to the elegiac story "The World's One Breathing."

Madden's goal is to transport his readers into "the Pleasure-Dome." As Lucius says in the novel of that name, "Everyday life is an effort to disentangle facts and illusions. There are rare moments in our lives when we transcend captivity in fact-and-illusion through pure imagination and dwell in the Pleasure-Dome, a luminous limbo between everyday experience and a work of art." Lucius knows well the value of a good story. He is an aspiring writer, and his older brother is a con man—which for Madden is nearly the same thing: "The relationship between the storyteller and the listener is like that between the con man and his mark," Madden has said. Madden himself is at his best when emulating the oral storytelling style he learned from his grandmother when he was growing up in the Tennessee hills, the setting of much of his fiction.

In the stories collected in *The Shadow Knows* the characters are caught between the knowledge that their old lives—in many cases rural or small town lives—are disappearing, and that the new lives available to them are spiritually unsatisfying. Madden's world here is primarily one of moonshiners and county fairs, motorcycles and coalmines, but a few of these stories are set outside the mountains. "Love Makes Nothing Happen," set in Alaska, is the best of these, while "The Day the Flowers Came," set in some faceless suburb, is maudlin and unbelievable. Two of the mountain stories here turn up as Lucius's memories in *Bijou*.

Bijou picks up Lucius's story in early adolescence, when he becomes an usher in a movie theater. Lucius tries to reinvent his life in the image of the films he sees. The Bijou itself is a symbol of the exotic mysteries of adulthood: ". . . the Bijou . . . seemed foreign, beyond his life, as if he were entering a special Bijou experience prematurely. The Bijou was somehow for other people, people who were superior to him because they'd had Bijou experiences he hadn't had." The promising framework of the theater as Lucius's doorway into adulthood is unfortunately overloaded with page after page of movie synopses, and undercut by the repetitive nature of his experiences with the other characters. We last see Lucius lurking about Thomas Wolfe's house, ready to give up films for the idea of the writer's life.

The Beautiful Greed relates the adventures of a young man named Alvin (who is just a little older than Lucius at the end of *Bijou*) on a merchant marine voyage to South America. This novel was Madden's first, and it seems thin in almost all regards when compared to his later works, though the plot here is unusually straight for Madden.

Pleasure-Dome is perhaps Madden's finest novel to date, despite a structure of two clumsily hinged together story lines. Lucius Hutchfield is once again the main character. He has been in the merchant marine and has become a writer since the events of *Bijou*. Lucius spends the first half of the novel trying to free his younger brother from jail by using his storytelling gifts. But it is the eldest brother, the con man, who succeeds in this—by telling taller tales than those Lucius tells. The second half is a cautionary tale about the responsibilities of being a storyteller. A boy's outlaw side lies dormant until Lucius awakens it with a story about Jesse James. The boy tries to emulate the outlaw's success with a young woman, with disastrous results. Though the boy goes to prison he is happy: he has on some small scale entered the world of legendary figures.

Cassandra Singing, the story of a wild boy and his invalid sister, is generally considered one of Madden's least autobiographical works, but it would be more accurate to say that Madden's character is here split between Lone and his sister Cassie. Lone is the motorcycle rider, the one with the need to escape the small world of the hills, while bedridden Cassie's life is in touch with the country's oral tradition, through the songs and stories she knows. That these two lie down together at the novel's end may be more of a self-portrait than a suggestion of incest. *On the Big Wind* is a loose string of satiric sketches with obvious targets, tied together by the voice of Big Bob Travis, nomadic radio announcer. The most telling thing here is "The World's One Breathing," spliced in from *The Shadow Knows*.

The Suicide's Wife stands apart from the rest of Madden's work. It is the story of a woman, and a story of the city. The language and plot are very spare and straightforward. Ann Harrington's husband kills himself, leaving "a vacuum into which *things* rushed." The novel is the story of Ann's struggle to gain a command over these "things," which is also the struggle to open herself to possibilities: "*Before, I had never really imagined possibilities. Since she never caused events, they just happened, and she took them as they came.*" Ann's triumph over the forboding world of "things" is symbolized by her successful quest to earn a driver's license, an officiahad never really imagined possibilities. Since she never caused events, they just happened, and she took them as they came." Ann's triumph over the forboding world of "things" is symbolized by her successful quest to earn a driver's license, an official recognition of her right to take herself where she wants to go.

—William C. Bamberger

MAILER, Norman (Kingsley). American. Born in Long Branch, New Jersey, 31 January 1923. Educated at Boys' High School, Brooklyn, New York, graduated 1939; Harvard University, Cambridge, Massachusetts (Associate Editor, *Harvard Advocate*), 1939–43, S.B. (cum laude) in aeronautical engineering 1943; the Sorbonne, Paris, 1947. Served in the United States Army, 1944–46: Sergeant. Married 1) Beatrice Silverman in 1944 (divorced, 1951), one daughter; 2) Adèle Morales in 1954 (divorced, 1961), two daughters; 3) Lady Jeanne Campbell in 1962 (divorced, 1963), one daughter; 4) Beverly Bentley in 1963 (divorced, 1979), two sons; 5) Carol Stevens in 1980 (divorced, 1980); 6) Norris Church in 1980, one son. Co-founder, 1955, and columnist, 1956, *Village Voice*, New York; columnist ("Big Bite"), *Esquire*, New York, 1962–63, and *Commentary*, New York, 1962–63. Member of the Executive Board, 1968–73, and since 1984, President, PEN American Center. Independent Candidate for Mayor of New York City, 1969. Recipient: *Story* prize, 1941; American Academy grant, 1960; George Polk Award; National Book Award, for non-fiction, 1969; Pulitzer Prize, for non-fiction, 1969, 1980; MacDowell Medal, 1973; National Arts Club Gold Medal, 1976. D.Litt.: Rutgers University, New Brunswick, New Jersey, 1969. Member, American Academy, 1985. Lives in Brooklyn, New York. Agent: Scott Meredith Literary Agency, 845 Third Avenue, New York, New York 10022, U.S.A.

PUBLICATIONS

Novels

The Naked and the Dead. New York, Rinehart, 1948; London, Wingate, 1949.
Barbary Shore. New York, Rinehart, 1951; London, Cape, 1952.
The Deer Park. New York, Putnam, 1955; London, Wingate, 1957.
An American Dream. New York, Dial Press, and London, Deutsch, 1965.
Why Are We in Vietnam? New York, Putnam, 1967; London, Weidenfeld and Nicolson, 1969.
A Transit to Narcissus: A Facsimile of the Original Typescript, edited by Howard Fertig. New York, Fertig, 1978.
Ancient Evenings. Boston, Little Brown, and London, Macmillan, 1983.
Tough Guys Don't Dance. New York, Random House, and London, Joseph, 1984.

Short Stories

New Short Novels 2, with others. New York, Ballantine, 1956.
Advertisements for Myself (includes essays and verse). New York, Putnam, 1959; London, Deutsch, 1961.
The Short Fiction of Norman Mailer. New York, Dell, 1967.
The Short Fiction of Norman Mailer (not same as 1967 book). New York, Pinnacle, 1981; London, New English Library, 1982.

Plays

The Deer Park, adaptation of his own novel (produced New York, 1960; revised version, produced New York, 1967). New York, Dial Press, 1967; London, Weidenfeld and Nicolson, 1970.
A Fragment from Vietnam (as *D.J.*, produced Provincetown, Massachusetts, 1967). Included in *Existential Errands*, 1972.
Maidstone: A Mystery (screenplay and essay). New York, New American Library, 1971.

Screenplays: *Wild 90*, 1968; *Beyond the Law*, 1968; *Maidstone*, 1971; *The Executioner's Song*, 1982.

Verse

Deaths for the Ladies and Other Disasters. New York, Putnam, and London, Deutsch, 1962.

Other

The White Negro. San Francisco, City Lights, 1957.
The Presidential Papers. New York, Putnam, 1963; London, Deutsch, 1964.
Cannibals and Christians. New York, Dial Press, 1966; London, Deutsch, 1967.
The Bullfight. New York, Macmillan, 1967.
The Armies of the Night: The Novel as History, History as a Novel. New York, New American Library, and London, Weidenfeld and Nicolson, 1968.
Miami and the Siege of Chicago: An Informal History of the Republican and Democratic Conventions of 1968. New York, New American Library, and London, Weidenfeld and Nicolson, 1968.
The Idol and the Octopus: Political Writings on the Kennedy and Johnson Administrations. New York, Dell, 1968.
Of a Fire on the Moon. Boston, Little Brown, 1971; as *A Fire on the Moon*, London, Weidenfeld and Nicolson, 1971.

The Prisoner of Sex. Boston, Little Brown, and London, Weidenfeld and Nicolson, 1971.

The Long Patrol: 25 Years of Writing from the Works of Norman Mailer, edited by Robert F. Lucid. Cleveland, World, 1971.

King of the Hill: On the Fight of the Century. New York, New American Library, 1971.

Existential Errands. Boston, Little Brown, 1972; included in *The Essential Mailer,* 1982.

St. George and the Godfather. New York, New American Library, 1972.

Marilyn: A Novel Biography. New York, Grosset and Dunlap, and London, Hodder and Stoughton, 1973.

The Faith of Graffiti, with Mervyn Kurlansky and Jon Naar. New York, Praeger, 1974; as *Watching My Name Go By,* London, Mathews Miller Dunbar, 1975.

The Fight. Boston, Little Brown, 1975; London, Hart Davis MacGibbon, 1976.

Some Honorable Men: Political Conventions 1960–1972. Boston, Little Brown, 1976.

Genius and Lust: A Journey Through the Major Writings of Henry Miller, with Henry Miller. New York, Grove Press, 1976.

The Executioner's Song: A True Life Novel (on Gary Gilmore). Boston, Little Brown, and London, Hutchinson, 1979.

Of Women and Their Elegance, photographs by Milton H. Greene. New York, Simon and Schuster, and London, Hodder and Stoughton, 1980.

The Essential Mailer. London, New English Library, 1982.

Pieces and Pontifications (essays and interviews). Boston, Little Brown, 1982; London, New English Library, 1983.

*

Bibliography: *Norman Mailer: A Comprehensive Bibliography* by Laura Adams, Metuchen, New Jersey, Scarecrow Press, 1974.

Critical Studies (selection): *Norman Mailer* by Richard Foster, Minneapolis, University of Minnesota Press, 1968; *The Structured Vision of Normal Mailer* by Barry H. Leeds, New York, New York University Press, 1969; *Sexual Politics* by Kate Millett, New York, Doubleday, 1970, London, Hart Davis, 1971; *Norman Mailer: The Man and His Work* edited by Robert F. Lucid, Boston, Little Brown, 1971; *Norman Mailer* by Richard Poirier, London, Collins, and New York, Viking Press, 1972; *Norman Mailer: A Collection of Critical Essays* edited by Leo Braudy, Englewood Cliffs, New Jersey, Prentice Hall, 1972; *Down Mailer's Way* by Robert Solotaroff, Urbana, University of Illinois Press, 1974; *Norman Mailer: A Critical Study* by Jean Radford, London, Macmillan, and New York, Barnes and Noble, 1975; *Existential Battles: The Growth of Norman Mailer* by Laura Adams, Athens, Ohio University Press, 1976; *Mankind in Barbary: The Individual and Society in the Novels of Norman Mailer* by Stanley T. Gutman, Hanover, New Hampshire, University Press of New England, 1976; *Norman Mailer* by Philip Bufithis, New York, Ungar, 1978; *Norman Mailer* by Robert Merrill, Boston, Twayne, 1978; *Norman Mailer's Novels* by Sandy Cohen, Amsterdam, Rodopi, 1979; *Norman Mailer, Quick-Change Artist* by Jennifer Bailey, London, Macmillan, 1979, New York, Barnes and Noble, 1980; *Acts of Regeneration: Allegory and Archetype in the Work of Norman Mailer* by Robert J. Begiebing, Columbia, University of Missouri Press, 1980; *An American Dreamer: A Psychoanalytic Study of the Fiction of Norman Mailer* by Andrew M. Gordon, Rutherford, New Jersey, Fairleigh Dickinson University Press, 1980; *Mailer: A Biography* by Hilary Mills, New York, Empire, 1982, London, New English Library, 1983; *Mailer: His Life and Times* by Peter Manso, New York, Simon and Schuster, and London, Viking, 1985.

Theatrical Activities:
Director: **Films**—*Wild 90,* 1968; *Beyond the Law,* 1968; *Maidstone,* 1971.
Actor: **Films**—his own films, and *Ragtime,* 1981.

*   *   *

A formal distinction between fiction and non-fiction, or between fiction and journalism, is not the most helpful way to approach either the direction or the value of Norman Mailer's work. Involving himself directly with public events as well as private concerns, reporting on activities as diverse as protest marches, prizefights, the moon landing, political conventions, and the life of the first man executed for murder in America in more than ten years, Mailer characteristically blurs, argues about, and plays with the conventional categories of fiction and non-fiction. The public events he reports become metaphors that clarify and demonstrate the issues he sees as significant, apocalyptic, or destructive about contemporary America. This combination of reporting with a personal fictive vision underlies some of Mailer's best and most searching prose, like *The Armies of the Night* or much of *The Executioner's Song.* Mailer began his career with a much more conventional idea of the difference between fiction and non-fiction, for, in the early novel *The Deer Park,* he had Sergius O'Shaughnessy, the young Air Force veteran trying to become a writer in the "new" Hollywood off-shoot of Desert D'Or, smugly certain that "a newspaperman is obsessed with finding the facts in order to tell a lie, and a novelist is a galley-slave to his imagination so he can look for the truth." More central to Mailer's later, more complicated, fiction and reporting is another statement from the same novel, the remark by Charles Eitel, the failed and (in the 1950's) politically suspect Hollywood writer and director, musing that "the artist was always divided between his desire for power in the world and his desire for power over his work." This emphasis on power, on the capacity to change both public and private circumstances, is never far from the center of Mailer's consciousness.

Rather than using any formal means of distinguishing one example of Mailer from another, the reader recognizes that a problem of selectivity, of what to include and what to exclude, is always visible. At times, Mailer seems to concentrate too repetitiously for too long on the relatively trivial or excessively personal, as in the rather stereotyped and remote satire of Hollywood in *The Deer Park,* all the legalisms of the last third or so of *The Executioner's Song,* or the defense of his own part in literary squabbles at the beginning of *The Prisoner of Sex.* Frequently, as he recognized himself in *The Presidential Papers,* he lacks a sense of proportion, is not sure about "how to handicap the odds."

Mailer's considerable literary ambition and the popular success of his first novel, *The Naked and the Dead,* published when he was just 25, placed his own development as a writer in a highly public focus. In spite of all the claims (many of them not from Mailer himself) about the "new" voice of his generation, his first three novels were somewhat literary and derivative. *The Naked and the Dead,* the novel about the platoon fighting both the Japanese and its own army on a Pacific island during World War II, shows considerable allegiance to the fiction of Hemingway and Dos Passos, as well as deference to the ethnic mix visible in Hollywood films made during the war. *Barbary Shore*, probably the best of the three novels, taking place in a Brooklyn rooming house after the war, using characters to debate all the various perspectives of radical politics in the 1930's, and ending with no resolution for the young alienated writer, is reminiscent of James T. Farrell. And *The Deer Park*, depicting the Hollywood world of drugs, pimps, mate-swapping, and politics, contains echoes of Fitzgerald and Nathanael West without the force or originality of either, all seen at a great distance, as if the chronicle of events could shock with nothing of the feelings rendered. Although interesting, often competent, and (particularly *Barbary Shore*) full of excellent description, this fiction was more distinctive in aim than in achievement. Mailer's perspective, however, changed considerably in the middle and late 1950's, a change first visible in the 1957 essay *The White Negro*, a recognition of the clash of cultures and the violence endemic in American life. In that essay, as well as in the work that followed, Mailer began to associate imagination and creativity with the position of a sociological minority, a potentially healthy underside of American life. As he later, in *The Presidential Papers*, explained, he had not earlier acknowledged his own secret admiration for his violent characters in *The Naked and the Dead*, his own obsession with violence. From *The White Negro* on, although still disapproving strongly of the "inhuman" or abstract violence of technology, Mailer recognized the possibilities of creative change through violence, both in himself and in others. He also began to probe himself more consciously as a metaphor for the larger world he described.

Mailer regards his central characters, whether in the persona of himself in works like *The Armies of the Night* or *Miami and the Siege of Chicago* or through fictional personae in the novels *An American Dream*, *Why Are We in Vietnam?*, or *Ancient Evenings*, as "existential" heroes who constantly test the possible edges of human experience. Always in conflict, within themselves and with others, they dare, like Rojack walking around the parapet of the terrace high above New York, possible destruction in order to live all the possibilities of the self. Through action, they create the self, as Rojack does through murder, varieties of sexual experience, escape, criminality, and understanding. The self-creation involves a good deal of fear, as well as overcoming fear, for the hero must break away from the safe and familiar, acknowledging violence and destruction within himself. In *Why Are We in Vietnam?*, the novel of Texans on a bear hunt in Alaska, a metaphor that coalesces all those attitudes, tests, totems, and taboos that explain the American presence in Vietnam, the young voice, D.J., must create himself by recognizing and overcoming his own fear of the bear. The most frequent action in Mailer's work, which overcomes stasis and safety, is sex, the direct relationship with another being. In *Ancient Evenings* sexuality extends to procreation and lineage, speculations about new means of explaining human continuity and change. Each sexual encounter is a victory over isolation and abstraction, and, as Mailer explains in *The Prisoner of Sex*, he objects to masturbation and contraception because, in different ways, they prevent the fullest exploration of direct physical relationship. Mailer has always implicitly thought of sex in these terms, ending *The Deer Park* with a God-like voice intoning "think of Sex as Time, and time as the connection of new circuits." Yet the full development of self-creation through sexual experience, the sense of the orgasm as "the inescapable existential moment," detailed variously and explicitly, is in the work that follows *The White Negro*.

Mailer's "existentialism" is not simply private self-definition. In the first place, he frequently argues that existentialism is

rootless unless one hypothesizes death as an "existential continuation of life," so that how one dies, how one faces destruction, matters. In addition, and emphasized much more frequently, Mailer's "existential" values are also social, the public consequences of definitions at the edges of experience. Social conflict is always visible, men defining themselves through the active public and social metaphors of parties, prizefights, and wars. War (and Mailer frequently distinguishes "good" wars from "bad") has the possibility, seldom actually achieved, of changing the consciousness of a sufficient number of people to alter the whole society. Mailer began his definition of "existential politics" in 1960, with his essay called "Superman Comes to the Supermarket," on the nomination of John Kennedy for president at the convention in Los Angeles. He called Kennedy an "existential" leader because he displayed the capacity to commit himself to the "new" when "the end is unknown," a contrast to the safety and the public predictability of the Eisenhower years, although Mailer doubted that Kennedy had the "imagination" to create a wholly beneficial revolution. Yet, for Mailer, the potentiality for change and revolution, for self-creation on a public scale, is always there, a human impulse that if repressed or thwarted causes "cancer" on either the individual or social level. In these terms, Mailer, through subsequent "reports" on protests, political conventions, and public events, propounds both a vision and an analysis of contemporary American society.

In rather undiscerning popular terms, Mailer is often accused of a monstrous ego. Yet, the persona of "Norman Mailer," as it develops through many of the "journalistic" works, is highly complicated and self-critical, a metaphor for all the possibilities in contemporary man that the author can visualize and understand. As he explains in *The Armies of the Night*, he can accept the ambivalences of all the personae he adopts, "warrior, presumptive general, ex-political candidate, embattled aging enfant terrible of the literary world, wise father of six children, radical intellectual, existential philosopher, hard-working author, champion of obscenity, husband of four battling sweet wives, amiable bar drinker, and much exaggerated street fighter, party giver, hostess insulter." But the one persona he finds "insupportable" is that of "the nice Jewish boy from Brooklyn," the one with which he began, which would deny his possibility to change and create himself. The personae of his later fiction are also complicated and carefully structured voices: the violent explosions, sensitivities, challenges, and social concerns of Rojack in *An American Dream* (still, to some extent, literary, as one critic, Richard Poirier, has explained, "both a throwback to Christopher Marlowe and . . . a figure out of Dashiell Hammett"); the scatology, sensitivity, fear, bravery, and self-recognition of D.J. in *Why Are We in Vietnam?* These voices, rhetorical and linguistic creations of a point of view, effectively express much of Mailer's complexity, although they lack something of the arch self-criticism (though not the humor) and the multiplicity of the persona of Norman Mailer which enriches *The Armies of the Night* and *Of a Fire on the Moon*, and whose implicit and more self-abnegating presence created *The Executioner's Song*. As personae, creative and capacious as they are, Rojack and D.J. can sound slightly more insistent, missing something of the "Norman Mailer" acknowledged incapacity to represent immediately all of America.

More recent examples of Mailer's fiction extend the personae into different forms. *Ancient Evenings*, an ambitious novel on which he worked for more than a decade, magnifies Mailer's scope as cultural historian. Set in Egypt over two centuries more than a thousand years before Christ, the novel locates the historical genesis and implications of many of Mailer's ideas concerning sexuality, lineage, violence, public power, society, and religion. Critically regarded as either the most probing or most pretentious of Mailer's fictions, *Ancient Evenings* manifests the enormous intellectual risks which the persona confronts. A much more limited and comic side of Mailer is visible in *Tough Guys Don't Dance*, his contemporary extension of Dashiell Hammett's world. The form, the multiple killings and suicides, as well as their discovery by the "macho" narrator who could have but, in fact, did not commit them, leaves room for many characteristic digressions. In addition to the central charting of the "tough guy" lineage, Mailer includes pages on topics such as the geological and historical topography of Provincetown, the implications of different uses of adjectives in the prose of Hemingway and Updike, the horrors for an addict of giving up smoking, and the inverse relationship between cancer and schizophrenia—all done with a sharp infusion of the comic that fits both the style and substance of Mailer's personae.

As a writer, Norman Mailer is variously talented. He is a superb journalist, always aware of the differences between what an observer sees directly and what he creates. He is an excellent literary critic, as in his attack on Kate Millett and his defenses of Henry Miller and D.H. Lawrence in *The Prisoner of Sex*. He can describe pictorially and movingly, as in *Of a Fire on the Moon*, or select brilliantly to chronicle American life, as in most of *The Executioner's Song*. More than any of these, he is consciously, seriously, humorously, and often convincingly the heir to a tradition of American visionaries, the writer who can create, in terms of the imagination, a new consciousness for his time and his country. In spite of his prolixity, his repetition, his occasional tendency to simplify polarities (his arguments against "technology" can become rant that denies his own understanding of science), and his occasional insistence on the literal applications of his own metaphors (as in parts of *The Prisoner of Sex*), Mailer has achieved something of his own revolutionary form in transforming the consciousness of others.

—James Gindin

MAJOR, Clarence. American. Born in Atlanta, Georgia, 31 December 1936. Educated at the Art Institute, Chicago (James Nelson Raymond Scholar), 1952–54; Armed Forces Institute, 1955–56; New School for Social Research, New York, 1972; State University of New York, Albany, B.S.; Union Graduate School, Ph.D. Served in the United States Air Force, 1955–57. Married 1) Joyce Sparrow in 1958 (divorced 1964); 2) Pamela Jane Ritter. Research analyst, Simulmatics, New York, 1967. Taught in the Harlem Education Program Writers Workshop, New York, 1967, and the Teachers and Writers Collaborative, New York, 1967–72; Member of the Faculty, Sarah Lawrence College, Bronxville, New York, 1972–75; Assistant Professor of English, Howard University, Washington, D.C., 1974–75, and University of Washington, Seattle, 1976–77. Associate Professor, 1977–81, and since 1981, Professor of English, University of Colorado, Boulder. Visiting Professor, University of Maryland, College Park, 1976, State University of New York, Buffalo, 1976, and University of Nice, France, 1981–82, 1983. Editor, *Coercion Review*, Chicago, 1958–60; associate editor, *Anagogic and Paideumic Review*, San Francisco, *Proof*, Chicago, 1961–63, and *Caw!*, 1967–68, and *Journal of Black Poetry*, 1967–70, both San Francisco.

Recipient: New York Cultural Foundation grant, 1971. Address: Department of English, University of Colorado, Boulder, Colorado 80309, U.S.A.

PUBLICATIONS

Novels

All-Night Visitors.   New York, Olympia Press, 1969.
NO.   New York, Emerson Hall, 1973.
Reflex and Bone Structure.   New York, Fiction Collective, 1975.
Emergency Exit.   New York, Fiction Collective, 1979.
My Amputations.   New York, Fiction Collective, 1986.

Uncollected Short Stories

"Church Girl," in *Human Voices 3* (Homestead, Florida), Summer-Fall 1967.
"An Area in the Cerebral Hemisphere," in *Statements*, edited by Jonathan Baumbach.   New York, Braziller, 1975.
"Dossy O," in *Writing under Fire*, edited by Jerome Klinkowitz and John Somer.   New York, Dell, 1978.
"Tattoo," in *Massachusetts Review* (Amherst), vol. 22, no. 4, 1981.

Verse

The Fires That Burn in Heaven.   Privately printed, 1954.
Love Poems of a Black Man.   Omaha, Nebraska, Coercion Press, 1965.
Human Juices.   Omaha, Nebraska, Coercion Press, 1965.
Swallow the Lake.   Middletown, Connecticut, Wesleyan University Press, 1970.
Symptoms and Madness.   New York, Corinth, 1971.
Private Line.   London, Paul Breman, 1971.
The Cotton Club: New Poems.   Detroit, Broadside Press, 1972.
The Syncopated Cakewalk.   New York, Barlenmir House, 1974.
Inside Diameter: The France Poems. London, Permanent Press, 1985.

Other

Dictionary of Afro-American Slang.   New York, International, 1970; as *Black Slang: A Dictionary of Afro-American Talk*, London, Routledge, 1971.
The Dark and Feeling: Black American Writers and Their Work.   New York, Third Press, 1974.
The Other Side of the Wall.   San Francisco, Black Scholar Press, 1982.

Editor, *Writers Workshop Anthology*.   New York, Harlem Education Project, 1967.
Editor, *Man Is Like a Child: An Anthology of Creative Writing by Students*.   New York, Macomb's Junior High School, 1968.
Editor, *The New Black Poetry*.   New York, International, 1969.

*

Bibliography: "Clarence Major: A Checklist of Criticism" by Joe Weixlmann, in *Obsidian* (Fredonia, New York), vol. 4, no. 2, 1978; "Toward a Primary Bibliography of Clarence Major" by Joe Weixlmann and Major, in *Black American Literature Forum* (Terre Haute, Indiana), Summer 1979.

Critical Studies: in *Interviews with Black Writers* edited by John O'Brien, New York, Liveright, 1973; "La Problematique de la communication" by Muriel Lacotte, unpublished dissertation, University of Nice, 1984.

*   *   *

"In a novel, the only thing you have is words," Clarence Major told the interviewer John O'Brien. "You begin with words and you end with words. The content exists in our minds. I don't think it has to be a reflection of anything. It is a reality that has been created inside of a book." Clarence Major's fiction exists as a rebellion against the stereotype of mimetic fiction—that telling a story, one of the things fiction can do, is the only thing fiction can do.

His first novel, *All-Night Visitors*, is an exercise in the imaginative powers of male sexuality. Major takes the most physical theme—the pleasure of the orgasm—and lyricizes it, working his imagination upon the bedrock world of sense not customarily indulged by poetry. The pre-eminence of the imagination is shown by blending Chicago street scenes with fighting in Vietnam—in terms of the writing itself, Major claims that there is no difference. His second novel, *NO*, alternates narrative scenes of rural Georgia life with a more disembodied voice of fiction, and the action advances as it is passed back and forth, almost conversationally, between these two fictive voices. In both books, language itself is the true locus of action, as even the most random and routine development is seized as the occasion for raptures of prose (a fellatio scene, for example, soon outstrips itself as pornography and turns into an excuse for twelve pages of exuberant prose).

Major's best work is represented in his third and fourth novels, *Reflex and Bone Structure* and *Emergency Exit*. In the former, he describes an action which takes place legitimately within the characters' minds, as formed by images from television and film. "We're in bed watching the late movie. It's 1938. *A Slight Case of Murder*. Edward G. Robinson and Jane Bryan. I go into the bathroom to pee. Finished, I look at my aging face. Little Caesar. I wink at him in the mirror. He winks back./I'm back in bed. The late show comes on. It's 1923. *The Bright Shawl*. Dorothy Gish. Mary Astor. I'm taking Mary Astor home in a yellow taxi. Dorothy Gish is jealous." Throughout this novel, which treats stimuli from social life and the output of a television set as equally informative, Major insists that the realm of all these happenings is in language itself. "I am standing behind Cora," he writes. "She is wearing a thin black nightgown. The backs of her legs are lovely. I love her. The word standing allows me to watch like this. The word nightgown is what she is wearing. The nightgown itself is in her drawer with her panties. The word Cora is wearing the word nightgown. I watch the sentence: the backs of her legs are lovely."

Emergency Exit is Major's most emphatic gesture toward pure writing, accomplished by making the words of his story refer inward to his own creative act, rather than outward toward the panoramic landscape of the socially real. The novel's structure makes this strategy possible. *Emergency Exit* consists of elementary units of discourse; words, sentences, paragraphs, vignettes, and serial narratives. The novel is composed of equal blocks of each, spread out and mixed with the others. At first, simple sentences are presented to the reader. Then elements from these same sentences (which have stood in reference-free isolation) recur in paragraphs, but still free of narrative meaning. The plan is to fix a word, as word, in the reader's mind, apart from any personal conceptual reference—just as an abstract expressionist painter will present a line, or a swirl of color, without any reference to figure. Then come a number of narratives, coalescing into a story of lovers and family. When enough sections of the serial narrative have accumulated to form a recognizable story, we find that the independent and fragmentary scenes of the sentences and paragraphs have been animated by characters with whom we can now empathize. Forestalling any attempt to rush off the page into incidental gossip is the memory and further repetition of these words—whether they be of black mythology, snatches of popular song, or simply brilliant writing—all within Major's arresting sentences and paragraphs. A word, an image, or scene which occurs within the narrative leads the reader directly back to the substance of Major's writing. All attention is confined within the pages of the book.

Silent as a writer for the better part of a decade, though actively engaged in teaching, speaking, and world travel, Major takes the occasion of his fifth novel, *My Amputations*, to comment on his own identity as a writer and person. His protagonist, named Mason Ellis, has a biography which matches Major's own, and his responsiveness to black music and folklore recalls the techniques of *Emergency Exit*. Mason's writing is like a closet he steps into in a recurring dream: a "door to darkness, closed-off mystery" through which his muse leads him in search of his personal and literary identities, both of which have been assumed by an "Impostor" nearly a decade ago (when Major's last novel was written). Mason's personal struggle has been with "the unmistakable separation of Church and State," which for him produces an unbearable polarity between spirit and body, mentality and sexuality, and eventually a contradiction between "clean" and "dirty" which he refuses to accept. His muse must guide him away from this middle ground of separation where he languishes; imprisoned in various forms of life (which correspond to Major's background growing up in Chicago and serving in the Air Force), he must literally "write his way out" by constructing a different paradigm for God's interests and Caesar's. Falsely jailed while "the Impostor" continues his career, Mason joins a group of urban terrorists who rob a bank to finance their dreams—in his case, the recovery of his role as novelist. To do this, Mason adopts the pose of the black American writer abroad, living in Nice and speaking at various universities across Europe. But at every stage the concerns of State intervene, as each country's particular style of political insurgency disrupts his visit. Even his idealistic goal of Africa is torn by conflicts of body and spirit, and he finds himself either caught in the crossfire of terrorists or imprisoned as a political suspect. These circumstances, while being complications in the narrative, prompt some of the novel's finest writing, as Major couches Mason's behavior in a linguistic responsiveness to the terroristic nature of our times. The achievement of *My Amputations* is its conception of Mason Ellis as a creature of the world's signs and symbols. He moves in a world of poetic constructions, where even crossing the street is an artistic adventure: "Mason Ellis sang 'Diddie Wa Diddie' like Blind Blake, crossed the street at Fifth Avenue and Forty-Second like the Beatles on the cover of *Abbey Road* and reaching the curb leaped into the air and coming down did a couple of steps of the Flat Foot Floogie." Not surprisingly, Major points his character toward a tribal sense of unity in Africa, pre-colonial and hence pre-political, where the separations of "Church" and "State" do not exist.

—Jerome Klinkowitz

————————

MALAMUD, Bernard.   American.   Born in Brooklyn, New York, 26 April 1914. Educated at Erasmus Hall High School, New York; City College of New York, 1932–36, B.A. 1936; Columbia University, New York, 1937–38, M.A. 1942. Married Ann de Chiara in 1945; one son and one daughter. Teacher, New York high schools, evenings 1940–49; Instructor to Associate Professor of English, Oregon State University, Corvallis, 1949–61. Since 1961, Member of the Division of Languages and Literature, Bennington College, Vermont. Visiting Lecturer, Harvard University, Cambridge, Massachusetts, 1966–68. President, PEN American Center, 1979–81. Recipient: *Partisan Review* fellowship, 1956; Rosenthal Award, 1958; Daroff Memorial Award, 1958; Ford fellowship, 1959, 1960; National Book Award, 1959, 1967; Pulitzer Prize, 1967; O. Henry Award, 1969, 1973; Jewish Heritage Award, 1977; Vermont Council on the Arts award, 1979; Brandeis University Creative Arts Award, 1981; American Academy Gold Medal, 1983; Bobst Award, 1983; Mondello prize (Italy), 1985. Member, American Academy, 1964, and American Academy of Arts and Sciences, 1967. *Died 18 March 1986.*

PUBLICATIONS

Novels

The Natural.   New York, Harcourt Brace, 1952; London, Eyre and Spottiswoode, 1963.
The Assistant.   New York, Farrar Straus, 1957; London, Eyre and Spottiswoode, 1959.
A New Life.   New York, Farrar Straus, 1961; London, Eyre and Spottiswoode, 1962.
The Fixer.   New York, Farrar Straus, 1966; London, Eyre and Spottiswoode, 1967.
Pictures of Fidelman: An Exhibition.   New York, Farrar Straus, and London, Eyre and Spottiswoode, 1969.
The Tenants.   New York, Farrar Straus, 1971; London, Eyre Methuen, 1972.
Dubin's Lives.   New York, Farrar Straus, and London, Chatto and Windus, 1979.
God's Grace.   New York, Farrar Straus, and London, Chatto and Windus, 1982.

Short Stories

The Magic Barrel.   New York, Farrar Straus, 1958; London, Eyre and Spottiswoode, 1960.
Idiots First.   New York, Farrar Straus, 1963; London, Eyre and Spottiswoode, 1964.
Penguin Modern Stories 1, with others.   London, Penguin, 1969.
Rembrandt's Hat.   New York, Farrar Straus, and London, Eyre Methuen, 1973.
Two Fables.   Bennington, Vermont, Bennington College, 1978.

The Stories of Bernard Malamud.   New York, Farrar Straus, 1983; London, Chatto and Windus, 1984.

Uncollected Short Stories

"An Exorcism," in *Harper's* (New York), December 1968.
"Home Is the Hero," in *The Best American Short Stories 1979*, edited by Joyce Carol Oates and Shannon Ravenel.   Boston, Houghton Mifflin, 1979.
"A Wig," in *Atlantic* (Boston), January 1980.
"The Flood," in *Esquire* (New York), August 1982.
"Alma Redeemed," in *Commentary* (New York), July 1984.
"A Lost Grave," in *Esquire* (New York), May 1985.

Other

A Malamud Reader.   New York, Farrar Straus, 1967.

*

Bibliography: *Bernard Malamud: An Annotated Checklist* by Rita N. Kosofsky, Kent, Ohio, Kent State University Press, 1969; *Bernard Malamud: A Reference Guide* by Joel Salzburg, Boston, Hall, 1985.

Manuscript Collection: Library of Congress, Washington, D.C.

Critical Studies: *Bernard Malamud* by Sidney Richman, New York, Twayne, 1967; *Bernard Malamud and Philip Roth: A Critical Essay* by Glenn Meeter, Grand Rapids, Michigan, Eerdmans, 1968; *Bernard Malamud and the Critics*, New York, New York University Press, and London, University of London Press, 1970, and *Bernard Malamud: A Collection of Critical Essays*, Englewood Cliffs, New Jersey, Prentice Hall, 1975, both edited by Leslie A. and Joyce W. Field; *Art and Idea in the Novels of Bernard Malamud* by Robert Ducharme, The Hague, Mouton, 1974; *Bernard Malamud and the Trial by Love* by Sandy Cohen, Amsterdam, Rodopi, 1974; *The Fiction of Bernard Malamud* edited by Richard Astro and Jackson J. Benson, Corvallis, Oregon State University Press, 1977 (includes bibliography); *Rebels and Victims: The Fiction of Richard Wright and Bernard Malamud* by Evelyn Gross Avery, Port Washington, New York, Kennikat Press, 1979; *Bernard Malamud* by Sheldon J. Hershinow, New York, Ungar, 1980; *The Good Man's Dilemma: Social Criticism in the Fiction of Bernard Malamud* by Iska Alter, New York, AMS Press, 1981; article by Malamud, in *New York Times*, 28 August 1983.

Bernard Malamud comments:
   My work revolves around the values of human life seen in the perspective of an assortment of souls. It is, above all, a work of imagination: I invent what is happening and it often happens.

*   *   *

   Since *The Assistant* in 1957, Bernard Malamud has easily maintained his rank with Bellow as one of the leading novelists of contemporary America and especially of his generation of "urban Jewish-American writers." Since the 1970's, readers of Malamud, Bellow, Roth, Salinger, Mailer, have been less attentive to the ethnic hyphen that links them and more concerned with their wide divergence as literary artists. Benefiting from this enlarged focus, Malamud's work is seen as that of "an American novelist in the tradition of Hawthorne," drawing upon Jewish material as component elements of his larger design and achievement. Malamud himself has said that "as a writer, I've been influenced by Hawthorne, James, Mark Twain, Hemingway, more than I have by Sholem Aleichem and I.L. Peretz." Malamud's self-mocking irony, comic caricatures redolent of Yiddish folktales, his urban ghetto heroes struggling for maturity in the shadow of immigrant families, indeed his whole fictional populace of characters and motifs familiar from Aleichem and Peretz, interweave in fictions superficially resembling much naturalistic work of the hyphenated school but profoundly kindred to symbolic moral romance in the Hawthorne manner.

Concerning pursuit of the American dream of money and fame as played out in the national sport of baseball, Malamud's first novel *The Natural* is clearly the work of a moral fabulist. In the extended metaphor of life-as-game, Roy Hobbs's baseball career would have been spectacular were it not for the moral concerns that intrude onto the playing field and destroy him, a disgraced failure who—partly from desire for his rival's mistress—throws a playoff game and ends sobbing in the street. Hobbs was a "natural," naturally gifted in the physical skills of the game, but those are insufficient to Malamud. Whatever its exterior form, the elemental contest in Malamud's people is played out in narrated monologues, in the long haunted questionings and discoveries of self. Hobbs is the first and least adroit of these auto-interrogators, whom readers variously describe as Jewish self-examiners tracking their own mysterious inadequacy and guilt, or existential solitaries in quest of self-knowledge and certitude, and who are undoubtedly both. To themselves they are all qualified failures, failing to attain the norm of human dignity that they either discern in the social world or unwittingly inherit from lineage or (in the late works) literature. As in Hobbs's disgrace, many adverse elements come into the play (bad luck, flawed friends, pressure of debts) but the failure is a personal one, a flaw in the moral character of the protagonist who is seen to be weak or fearful, paralyzed in the face of what he knows to be a right action. In later novels the pained intensity of the moral struggle transcends the hero's own negative assessment of himself, and affirms value in his small, contingent victories. Though *The Natural* inaugurates this pattern of self-confrontation, discovery, and judgement, it is not satisfying, primarily because of the simplicity of the ethical failure as "the champ" degenerates into crime. After *The Natural* Malamud modifies the proportions, locating the climax of his drama in emotional rather than public events and focusing in finer detail upon subtle shifts of mood and nuance that constitute emotion, as well as concentrating exclusively on characters signifying Jew-Gentile interrelations.

The Assistant brought Malamud national acclaim and introduced his claustral immigrant world of dark tenement houses and dim shops. Deft caricatural figures such as Breitbart the lightbulb peddler flesh out Malamud's symbolic society, whose primary figures are an old grocer, Morris Bober, and his young assistant Frank Alpine. Frank is a thieving drifter and anti-Semite whom the good-hearted Morris rescues and employs in his shop, only to discover him rifling the till and insulting his daughter. Malamud traces the emergent self of the youth against the diminishing powers of the old man. Frank works his way from cynicism through uncertainties to grace, which in Malamud always means moral commitment to others, and after Bober's death stays on to run the store. In the bleak misery to which these lives are bound, small objects have a grotesque edge to them, and large ones seem like open mouths or tombs devouring the living ("the blood-sucking store"). But with misery comes the clarity won through great suffering and the frail victory of "a little peace, a little order" won in common

struggle. Just as the Bober characterization threatens to dissolve in sentimentality but does not because subsumed into the contest with the cynical youth, so the events of plot threaten to collapse into simplistic fable but do not because of the fabulist's subtle orchestration of symbolic narrative, daring even to end on the youth's conversion to the old man's religion.

In setting and tone, each of Malamud's novels is an abrupt *volte-face* away from the last one, recasting the moral quest and menaced values in wholly new ways. *A New Life* opens far from the ghetto in mountainous western America, where Seymour Levin arrives at a small college to take up teaching duties and seek happiness. Levin's comic rounds of ecstasy and despair, as he discards one romantic and humanist ideal after the other, are often amusing, and it is a measure of the novel's density that it has been called both an academic satire and a mock pastoral. Counterpointed in comic grotesque with the public events of the 1950's (Korea, the Cold War, McCarthyism), Levin's personal crisis of humanism seems ended in dismal defeat when he is dismissed from the college. But as the novel ends, in startling reversal Levin offers to marry a woman he no longer loves and to adopt her whining children. Malamud protagonists must fail the social tests of success (solid employment, marriage, income) in order to reach the rockbed of solitude, self-discovery, candor, and courage from which they can accede to the moral heights of true manhood and humanism (elements and process impacted in the name Frank Alpine) through commitment of self to others similarly deprived. The comical sufferings of Levin the zany idealist cannot bear such moral weight, and *A New Life* reveals Malamud's satirical skills without transposing the moral quest onto a new or greater scale. Like *Pictures of Fidelman* five years later, and many of the short stories of the 1950's and 1960's, *A New Life* is light metaphysical fiction, often wondrously funny as the comic loser reaches for infinity (a great love to Levin, a great painting to Fidelman) only to fall back into mortal finitude, sympathetic to human frailties.

The Fixer is a somber historical fiction set in Tsarist Russia, where persecution of the Jews echoes Biblical events and foreshadows modern genocide. Yakov Bok is a "fixer," a repairman, and what he fixes—as well as how—are the paramount concerns of the novel. This gentle bookish idealist is falsely imprisoned as a scapegoat, and the moral dilemma is clear; sign a false confession, freeing oneself while contributing to the historical scapegoating of the Jews, or refuse, accept persecution as an innocent man suddenly swept out of books into the bigoted cruelty of the historical moment. In the end he does "fix" (in the dual sense of to mend and to set firmly in the mind) his identity as Yakov and as a Jew though anguished analysis of himself as Everyman. Freed when another Jew is arrested, Yakov knows that "the purpose of freedom is to create it for others," and that no one is ever free of history and ethical imperatives. It is a searing novel, constructed with self-deprecating humor and some of the finest narrated monologues Malamud has ever crafted.

Without literary pretensions, both Yakov and Levin record their "insights," in a diaristic mode of self-exploration. In *The Tenants* and *Dubin's Lives* Malamud's protagonists are professional writers, novelist and biographer respectively. Harry Lesser writes his novel in a crumbling tenement he thinks abandoned, only to discover the presence of another novelist also completing a manuscript. Harry seems to be a modernist in the tradition of Flaubert and Joyce ("Once I hit it right—it's a matter of stating the truth in unimpeachable form"), but Willie Spearmint is a militant Black writing appalling social truths in jived prose. In irritation, then fear, then terror for his life and above all his manuscript, each writer stalks the other and by night accelerates the writing, in the belief that whichever novel is finished first effectively slays the other. The prose art of two New York City generations collides in these last tenants of a crumbling building. Though they slowly understand that as writers they both falsify the "self" expressed, and that as men they are more alike than different in experience, neither will yield to the other. They kill each other with ax and razor ("Each, thought the writer, feels the anguish of the other") as the novel ends on the slumlord's scream "mercy," the word repeated over eighty times until the reader sees it as mere ink on the page. The moral fable moves from light farce into bloody grotesque, and any humorous nostalgia for the 1950's heyday of Jewish-American art dies in the apocalyptic damning of all such ethnic hyphens in art as in life.

One of the unanswered questions in *The Tenants* was whether art does indeed help people to be free. The answer appears in *Dubin's Lives* and, though qualified, is positive. A prominent biographer of literary lives (Thoreau, Emerson), William Dubin knows the vicarious nature of his craft ("One writes lives he can't live") but does not know why he is drawn to a life of D.H. Lawrence. His own life becomes a Lawrentian odyssey through various liberations, not always his: his affair with a sexually liberated woman half his age causes him untold confusion and pain, while his wife finds satisfaction in her first job, his daughter finds fulfillment in having an illegitimate child, and even his son as a Vietnam deserter in Sweden finally achieves personal peace, while Dubin the self-appointed center of their lives disintegrates in self-discovery ("My God, what else am I capable of that I didn't know? How many more hollows will I uncover in myself?") His manuscript at a standstill, Dubin must learn to live the truths that art discovers. He is Malamud's most articulate self-interrogator, as a literary man in full command of verbal expression, and one of the most amusing. He is astonished to find that his Lawrentian liberation seems only to free his three women from their orbit round him. Once he learns what an unstructured muddle real life and true emotion actually are, and appreciates that "one's essential loneliness" is more than a literary cliché, Malamud seems fondly to rescue him: his mistress suddenly reappears to buy a farm near his and he is saved, as wife and mistress agree to share him, in an ending that suggests Lawrentian fantasia.

Dubin's Lives and *The Tenants* are as distinct in their handling of similar themes as are all of Malamud's works from one another. His canon spans not only a remarkable variety of settings and modes, but one of the most diverse assortments of literary heroes in modern fiction. Moving through their moral odysseys, they suggest prismatic reflections of one essential odyssey through self-discovery to the humanistic life.

For 30 years Malamud varied only the modes and settings for this quintessential moral tale. Then in 1982 he startled readers with *God's Grace*, an apocalyptic allegory in beast-fable: God destroys humanity because they have defiled his work with depravity and pollution, but one Jewish scientist escapes to an island where he teaches the animals speech and as much as he can remember of all human learning, even mating with the chimpanzee Mary Madelyn to create posterity for this Eden; after some amusing parodies and beast-dialogues, Malamud's tone shifts abruptly to gloom, as the animals viciously destroy themselves and this last hope of earth. Even Malamud's most disappointed readers recognized that *God's Grace* sought to be a cry in the moral wilderness of modern times, a now angry novelist's warning that time is running out for the humanistic life.

—Jan Hokenson

MALGONKAR, Manohar (Dattatray). Indian. Born in Bombay, 12 July 1913. Educated at Karnatak College, Dharwar; Bombay University, B.A. (honours) in English and Sanskrit 1936. Served in the Maratha Light Infantry, 1942–52: Lieutenant Colonel. Married Manorama Somdutt in 1947; one daughter. Professional big-game hunter, 1935–37; cantonment executive officer, Government of India, 1937–42. Owner, Jagalbet Mining Syndicate, 1953–59. Since 1959, self-employed farmer in Jagalbet. Independent candidate for Parliament, 1957, and Swatantra Party candidate, 1962. Address: P.O. Jagalbet, Londa, Belgaum District, India.

PUBLICATIONS

Novels

Distant Drum. Bombay, Asia Publishing House, 1960; London and New York, Asia Publishing House, 1961.
Combat of Shadows. London, Hamish Hamilton, 1962; Thompson, Connecticut, InterCulture, 1968.
The Princes. London, Hamish Hamilton, and New York, Viking Press, 1963.
A Bend in the Ganges. London, Hamish Hamilton, 1964; New York, Viking Press, 1965.
The Devil's Wind: Nana Saheb's Story. New York, Viking Press, and London, Hamish Hamilton, 1972.
Shalimar. New Delhi, Vikas, 1978.
The Garland Keepers. New Delhi, Vision, 1980.
Bandicoot Run. New Delhi, Vision, 1982.

Short Stories

A Toast in Warm Wine. New Delhi, Hind, 1974.
In Uniform. New Delhi, Hind, 1975.
Bombay Beware. New Delhi, Orient, 1975.
Rumble-Tumble. New Delhi, Orient, 1977.

Play

Spy in Amber (screenplay). New Delhi, Hind, 1971.

Other

Kanhoji Angrey, Maratha Admiral: An Account of His Life and His Battles with the English. Bombay, London, and New York, Asia Publishing House, 1959; as *The Sea Hawk*, New Delhi, Vision, 1978.
The Puars of Dewas Senior. Bombay, Orient Longman, 1963.
Chhatrapatis of Kolhapur. Bombay, Popular Prakashan, 1971.
Dead and Living Cities. New Delhi, Hind, 1978.
The Men Who Killed Gandhi. Madras, Macmillan, 1978; London, Macmillan, 1979.
Cue from the Inner Voice: The Choice Before Big Business. New Delhi, Vikas, 1980.
Inside Goa (travel). Panaji, Government of Goa, 1982.
Princess. London, Century Hutchinson, 1985.

*

Critical Studies: *An Area of Darkness* by V.S. Naipaul, London, Deutsch, 1964, New York, Macmillan, 1965; "Purdah and Caste Marks" by Malgonkar, in *Times Literary Supplement* (London), 4 June 1964; *Eating the Indian Air* by John Morris, London, Hamish Hamilton, 1968; *Manohar Malgonkar* by G.S. Amur, New Delhi, Arnold-Heinemann, and New York, Humanities Press, 1973; *Manohar Malgonkar* by James Y. Dayananda, New York, Twayne, 1974.

Manohar Malgonkar comments:

Praise can embarrass but it does not call for a rejoinder. Censure often does, so here goes. Those who disparage my work think that (1) I write with one eye on Hollywood, (2) my writing is "withdrawn" from the reality of my country's poverty as well as the reality of the four-letter word, and (3) I inject my values and politics and prejudices into my writings.

Well, I do strive to write the sort of novel I also like to read, full of meat, exciting, well-constructed, plausible and with a lot of action—in short, to tell a good story. If this is what Hollywood also likes, good for Hollywood and, I hope, some day for me too. I know one admits this rather shame-facedly, as one might say "I'm afraid I do chew paan," or "Yes, I do use a night shirt." At the same time, I often think of myself as belonging to the advance guard in the swing back of the romantic novel. The pedlars of erotica and drug dreams may churn out best sellers, but these are not novels; and the interminable ramblings about a day in the life of somebody or the other are like dissecting the veins in every single leaf of a cabbage. All this was a phase and it has had too long a run, but you cannot go on playing with a cabbage forever. The novel will be back, plot, action and all; the signs are already there.

Withdrawn? I maintain that my novels are close enough to the ground to pass off for straight history. The withdrawal is seen in my refusal to be trapped in the dirt and misery of India. The social life of millions of Indians centres around the dustbins of cities. Granted. But mine doesn't, and for me to write about it would be as insincere as a white man writing about Harlem life. And this is perhaps related to my other "withdrawal"—the disrelish for the language of graffiti. For two years during my army service, I was in daily contact with British and other ranks and can thus claim to have acquired a fairly full vocabulary of raw words which I can use far more naturally than those who discovered a handful of them since *Fanny Hill* came out as a paperback. I don't use them for the same reason that I don't have my characters talking in local accents: they would show up as being utterly false to my style.

But the third point of criticism I accept as a kind of compliment. I believe that it is the thinking man's business to influence. In a country such as ours, where democracy itself is threatening to throttle individual freedom, it is the duty of every writer to do so.

*   *   *

Essentially a romantic novelist of action, Manohar Malgonkar adds the freshness of an exotic scene and the novelty of a bi-focal viewpoint to an expert use of tried and true Western techniques. English is his own first language and his life style is westernized (unlike his compatriot R.K. Narayan, for example). He had a university education and is a man of cosmopolitan culture, widely read; but he has lived for the past many years on a remote estate in the heart of India. He commands a lively and colloquial English, full of vivid metaphors. He uses dialogue fluently. One thinks of affinities to Conrad on the one hand and John Masters on the other.

In the earliest of his novels first published in the West, *Combat of Shadows*, he writes of British tea planters in the last years of the British Raj, somewhat in the vein of a disillusioned Kipling; he is able to mock the pukka-sahib Establishment by letting the reader see it through the eyes of its own cynics and outcasts. But it is primarily a story of love and derring-do rather than social comment. *The Princes*, on the other hand, deals with the old Indian aristocracy before the Princely States were absorbed in the new India, and with the painful transition. This has been his most widely read, most thoughtful, and perhaps most distinguished work. Here E.M. Forster comes to mind.

A Bend in the Ganges, though politically objective, echoes recent history in its personal love story set against the cruelty of a great civil disaster—the Indian-Pakistani split of 1947. Two other novels of post-Independence days, still unpublished in the West, reflect his involvement with current Indian politics, in which he has participated from a minority position to the right of the dominant Congress Party. One is an adventure story of the Indian take-over of Goa; the other a character study of a land-owning politician in a country district.

The Devil's Wind goes back a century to the so-called "Indian Mutiny," never before presented from the Indian point of view. He narrates it in the person of Nana Saheb, an actual princely leader of the rebellion and a notorious villain in British eyes. Neither a hero nor an anti-hero, he is the kind of ambiguous character that Malgonkar delights in. In being an historical novel, and in its marked change of sympathy toward the British, this is a new departure; but in style and in story-telling qualities, particularly its violence, it has the characteristics of his other best novels.

While Malgonkar's books all have thoughtful overtones, he is first of all the storyteller. He enjoys heroic characters fighting the odds and struggling with inner conflicts. He understands how to stretch the reader's willing suspension of disbelief for the sake of a dramatic confrontation. He makes graphic the hunt for a rogue elephant or a tiger; the crude violence of a human massacre; the tragic dislocations of civil war, from the burning of a single house to bombers over a great city. He bridges the nostalgia of India's past with the turbulence of her present.

—Marshall A. Best

MALOUF, David. Australian. Born in Brisbane, Queensland, 20 March 1934. Educated at Brisbane Grammar School, 1947–50; University of Queensland, Brisbane, 1951–54, B.A. (honours) in English 1954. Lecturer, University of Sydney, 1968–77. Recipient: Australian Literature Society Gold Medal, 1974, 1983; Grace Leven Prize, 1975; James Cook Award, 1975; Australia Council fellowship, 1978; New South Wales Premier's Prize, for fiction, 1979; *The Age* Book of the Year Award, 1982. Agent: Curtis Brown (Australia) Pty. Ltd., 27 Union Street, Paddington, New South Wales 2021; or, Curtis Brown, 162–168 Regent Street, London W1R 5TA, England. Address: 242 Kingsford Smith Drive, Hamilton, Brisbane, Queensland 4007, Australia.

PUBLICATIONS

Novels

Johnno. St. Lucia, University of Queensland Press, 1975;
  New York, Braziller, 1978; London, Penguin, 1984.
An Imaginary Life. New York, Braziller, and London,
  Chatto and Windus, 1978.
Child's Play, with Eustace and the Prowler. London, Chatto
  and Windus, 1982; as *Child's Play, The Bread of Time to
  Come: Two Novellas*, New York, Braziller, 1982.
Fly Away Peter. London, Chatto and Windus, 1982.
Harland's Half Acre. London, Chatto and Windus, and New
  York, Knopf, 1984.

Short Stories

Antipodes. London, Chatto and Windus, 1985.

Verse

Four Poets, with others. Melbourne, Cheshire, 1962.
Bicycle and Other Poems. St. Lucia, University of Queens-
  land Press, 1970; as *The Year of the Foxes and Other Poems*,
  New York, Braziller, 1979.
Neighbours in a Thicket. St. Lucia, University of Queensland
  Press, 1974.
Poems 1975–76. Sydney, Prism, 1976.
Selected Poems. Sydney, Angus and Robertson, 1980.
Wild Lemons. Sydney, Angus and Robertson, 1980.
First Things Last. St. Lucia, University of Queensland Press,
  1980; London, Chatto and Windus, 1981.

Other

New Currents in Australian Writing, with Katharine Brisbane
  and R.F. Brissenden. Sydney and London, Angus and
  Robertson, 1978.
12 Edmondstone Street (essays). London, Chatto and Windus, 1985.

Editor, with others, *We Took Their Orders and Are Dead:
  An Anti-War Anthology*. Sydney, Ure Smith, 1971.
Editor, *Gesture of a Hand* (anthology of Australian
  poetry). Artarmon, New South Wales, Holt Rinehart,
  1975.

*

Manuscript Collections: University of Queensland, Brisbane;
Australian National University Library, Canberra.

Critical Studies: interviews in *Commonwealth 4* (Rodez,
France), 1979–80, *Meanjin 39* (Melbourne), and *Australian
Literary Studies* (Hobart), October 1982.

*   *   *

David Malouf was already an established and well-regarded
poet when he published his first novel in 1975. His career seems
to have taken a decisive turn for it is primarily prose works
that he has published since 1980, including two major novels,
some novellas, a book of short stories, and one of autobiographical essays. Malouf writes the prose one might expect
from a poet, rich in precise and elaborated metaphor, intensely
lyrical, symbolic, almost visionary at times, and at others built
on passages of powerfully realised concrete detail.

His novels show a continuous interest in certain themes and
images. He is fascinated by opposites, for example by Australia
and Europe which are not only at opposite ends of the earth
but also make possible contrary forms of experience. He often
returns to images of life on the periphery; in *An Imaginary
Life* Ovid is exiled to the limits of the known world, and in
Harland's Half Acre Frank Harland lives in a tent by the Pacific
Ocean. At the margins there can still just about be a certain
innocence, an intensity of relationship with nature, a way of
being relatively at ease with time and death. In each of Malouf's
novels there is a main pair of male characters who embody
these opposites (in the centre/on the periphery of society and
culture) whose tense, ambivalent relationship is the central
theme of the novel. Through them Malouf creates a view which
is simultaneously "from both sides," as though he needed to
come back again and again to these fundamentally different
forms of life and to create a space in which a choice between
them can be avoided.

In other respects his novels show very little continuity, for
in overt subject matter they are extraordinarily diverse.
Malouf's first novel, *Johnno*, is about growing up in suburban
Brisbane during and after the Second World War. It contains
much autobiographical material, to some of which Malouf has
recently returned in the essays in *12 Edmondstone Street*. The
hero, Johnno, is like a character from the Paris of Sartre or
Cortazar, a 1950's existentialist but stranded in a subtropical
suburb at the wrong end of the earth, full of angst and the
wildness of an untamed spirit. The narrator is nick-named
Dante, and he tells the tale of Johnno's life without ever resolving his ambivalence towards him. On the one hand Johnno
seems to be an authentic fresh wind blowing away the suffocating, humid atmosphere of Brisbane life; on the other he is
irresponsible, reckless, and ultimately self-destructive (he dies
in a swimming incident that was quite probably suicide). The
narrator maintains an affectionate though ironic distance from
this wild hero, and uses him as a way of exploring his own
youthful indecisions about family, about Europe, and about
work. A strength of the novel is its convincing and moving
depiction of life in Brisbane, but its interest by far transcends
this particularity.

On the face of it Malouf's next novel, *An Imaginary Life*,
could hardly be more different. It tells the imaginary story
of the Roman poet Ovid, living in exile in a village on the
edge of the known world in the most appallingly harsh conditions and entirely cut off from his own family and culture.
The novel vividly realises the harshness of the very long
winters, the bleakness of the landscape, but also the power
of the symbolic life of the village community (its shamanistic
rituals, its burial ground, its hunting expeditions). Ovid
becomes obsessed with a child who is discovered living wild
among wolves in the forest. He is captured and brought into
the village where the poet begins to teach him to speak. Ovid
gradually realises, however, that it is the boy who is the teacher.
Ovid increasingly identifies him with a mysterious child of
whom he had visions when he was himself very young. Forced
to flee the village together, Ovid is led by the boy through
vast grasslands and is taught to observe insects, plants and
the earth. At last he finds the place where he will die. His
exile and journey have been an education. He has put behind
him the frivolity of his life as an urban poet and has been
forced into regions of experience beyond the limits of his imagination. There, on the margins, he has found peace and truth.
It is a novel of rather grand themes and enigmatic visions.

Fly Away Peter contains some of Malouf's most powerful
writing. It is again a story of exile, only in this case it turns
out to be catastrophic. Jim, a young Queenslander, has a strong
sense of having found his place when he becomes the warden
of a bird sanctuary on the Queensland coast. He is a silent

young man, at ease when observing with endless, meticulous patience the markings and migrations of the birds. His life is marginal, since world history does not pass through this remote region, but it is harmless, innocent, and rich in detailed experience of nature. The migrating birds, however, remind him that it is possible to span the immense distances that separate him from Europe. His friend and employer, Ashley Crowther, is a sophisticated and educated man who has recently returned from the heartlands of European culture in Cambridge and Germany. They could not be more different. But these differences and distances are to count for nothing, for it is 1914 and in that other hemisphere a war begins. Jim and Ashley migrate to Europe and to that horrific negation of all landscape, the trenches and mud of the First World War. Jim's life, and eventual death, in the trenches are written with great intensity. It is perhaps Malouf's most symbolic novel, built around a series of collapsing opposites (Europe and Australia, innocence and cruelty, history and nature). Little episodes and images come to carry a great weight of meaning. As in all of his novels, and here particularly successfully, Malouf constructs a perspective that allows life to be seen "from both sides." He brings together the opposite poles of human capacity, the patient and loving receptiveness to nature, and the obliterating cruelty of war, each described with visionary intensity.

The novella *Child's Play* may be the oddest and least successful of Malouf's attempts to write "from both sides." On the one hand, he creates a man of great learning, an immensely important author with a central role in modern Italian culture. On the other, there is a terrorist who is to assassinate him. We are shown a strange office where a group of terrorists work with the discipline and industry of a community of scholars in a library, studying their victims and plotting murder. The story is told in the first person by the killer, who becomes obsessed with his victim and with his reflections on the role of meaningless coincidence and brute accident in human affairs. But this personification of metaphysical themes does not convince.

A similar problem affects at least some of the short stories in *Antipodes*. It is as if they strain to be about matters of too great significance. Many of the stories are about particularly crucial or traumatic episodes in the lives of the characters (first sex, death of loved ones, and so on). The events are so weighty that the attempt to encompass them within the short story format does not allow that expansion of metaphor and slow preparation of the more visionary moments which Malouf achieves in his novels. As a consequence the writing is uneven and sometimes hovers dangerously close to cliché.

In *Harland's Half Acre* Malouf successfully returns to a more ambitious format. It is his longest novel since *Johnno*, and tells the long life stories of an eccentric Queensland painter, Frank Harland, and of the narrator, a Brisbane lawyer, Phil Vernon. As in all of his novels, the characters form a pair of opposites. Harland is the son of an impoverished farmer and always lives on the margins of society, sometimes as a swagman roaming the state jobless during the Great Depression, at another period painting in an abandoned cinema on a pier in the coastal town of Southport. In the last period of his life, even though he is by then celebrated and wealthy, he lives in a tent in the bush near the ocean. Phil Vernon, who helps to sort out his affairs and to protect him and his brother, has an utterly different life trajectory. He comes from a small business family who are always struggling against possible disasters. He chooses the safe and orderly life of a lawyer. Both of their lives are shaped by significant family deaths. Europe and its wars have an indirect impact on this peripheral

society. Scenes of concentration camps are shown at the newsreel cinemas in Brisbane. A slave camp of derelict tramps and winos is discovered on the outskirts of the city. The tidal wave of cruelty and inhumanity which has swept across Europe has reached these remote shores. As in all of Malouf's work, we get in this novel a strong sense of the power of family attachments and loyalties and of the memories of childhood experience. The novel celebrates endless small acts of kindness and of anger that shape our lives. It is the quality of Malouf's writing that is, here as in all of his novels, the most notable feature of his work.

—John Mepham

MANFRED, Frederick (Feikema). Also wrote as Feike Feikema. American. Born near Doon, Rock Township, Iowa, 6 January 1912. Educated at Western Academy, Hull, Iowa; Calvin College, Grand Rapids, Michigan, 1930–34, B.A. 1934; Nettleton Commercial College, Sioux Falls, South Dakota, 1937; correspondence courses, University of Minnesota, Minneapolis, 1941–42. Married Maryanna Shorba in 1942 (divorced 1978); two daughters and one son. Worked as a filling-station attendant, harvest and factory hand, salesman, etc., 1934–37; reporter, Minneapolis *Journal*, 1937–39; interviewer, Minnesota Opinion Poll, St. Paul, 1939–40; patient in a tuberculosis sanitarium, 1940–42; abstract writer, *Modern Medicine*, Minneapolis, 1942–43; reporter, *East Side Argus*, Minneapolis, 1943–44; Writer-in-Residence, Macalester College, St. Paul, Minnesota, 1949–52, and University of South Dakota, Vermillion, 1968–82. Since 1983, chair in regional heritage, Augustana College, Sioux Falls, South Dakota. Recipient: Rockefeller fellowship, 1944, 1945; American Academy grant, 1945; Field fellowship, 1948; Andreas fellowship, 1949, 1952; McKnight fellowship, 1959; Huntington Hartford fellowship, 1963, 1964; National Endowment for the Arts grant, 1976, 1983. D.Litt.: Augustana College, 1977; D.H.L.: Morningside College, Sioux City, Iowa, 1981; Buena Vista College, Storm Lake, Iowa, 1984. Address: Roundwind, R.R. 3, Luverne, Minnesota 56156, U.S.A.

PUBLICATIONS

Novels as Feike Feikema

The Golden Bowl. St. Paul, Minnesota, Webb, 1944; London, Dobson, 1947.
Boy Almighty. St. Paul, Minnesota, Itasca Press, 1945; London, Dobson, 1950.
This Is the Year. New York, Doubleday, 1947.
The Chokecherry Tree. New York, Doubleday, 1948; London, Dobson, 1950; revised edition, Denver, Swallow, 1961.
World's Wanderer, revised edition, as *Wanderlust*, Denver, Swallow, 1962.
   The Primitive. New York, Doubleday, 1949.
   The Brother. New York, Doubleday, 1950.
   The Giant. New York, Doubleday, 1951.

Novels as Frederick Manfred

The Buckskin Man Tales
   Lord Grizzly. New York, McGraw Hill, 1954; London, Corgi, 1957.

Riders of Judgment.   New York, Random House, 1957.
Conquering Horse.   New York, McDowell Obolensky, 1959.
Scarlet Plume.   New York, Simon and Schuster, 1964.
King of Spades.   New York, Simon and Schuster, 1966.
Morning Red: A Romance.   Denver, Swallow, 1956.
The Man Who Looked Like the Prince of Wales.   New York, Simon and Schuster, 1965; as *The Secret Place*, New York, Pocket Books, 1967.
Eden Prairie.   New York, Simon and Schuster, 1968.
Milk of Wolves.   Boston, Avenue Victor Hugo, 1976.
The Manly-Hearted Woman.   New York, Crown, 1976.
Green Earth.   New York, Crown, 1977.
Sons of Adam.   New York, Crown, 1980.

Short Stories

Arrow of Love.   Denver, Swallow, 1961.
Apples of Paradise and Other Stories.   New York, Simon and Schuster, 1968.

Uncollected Short Stories

"Sleeping Dogs," in *Fiction 8* (New York), 1974.
"The Founding of the Rock River Church," in *The Far Side of the Storm*, edited by Gary Elder.   Los Cerillos, New Mexico, San Marcos Press, 1975.
"Splinters," in *Dakota Arts Quarterly* (Fargo, North Dakota), Summer 1977.
"Going to Town with Ma," in *Great River Review* (Winona, Minnesota), vol. 5, no. 1, 1984.

Verse

Winter Count: Poems 1934–1965.   Minneapolis, Thueson, 1966.
Winter Count II.   Minneapolis, Thueson, 1985.

Other

Conversations with Frederick Manfred, edited by John R. Milton.   Salt Lake City, University of Utah Press, 1974.
The Wind Blows Free: A Reminiscence.   Sioux Falls, South Dakota, Augustana College Center for Western Studies, 1979.
Dinkytown.   Minneapolis, Dinkytown Antiquarian Bookstore, 1984.
Prime Fathers (biographical portraits).   Salt Lake City, Howe, 1985.

*

Bibliography: *Frederick Manfred: A Bibliography* by George Kellogg, Denver, Swallow, 1965; *Frederick Manfred: A Bibliography and Publishing History* by Rodney J. Mulder and John H. Timmerman, Sioux Falls, South Dakota, Augustana College Center for Western Studies, 1981.

Manuscript Collection: University of Minnesota, Minneapolis.

Critical Studies: "Writing in the West and Midwest Issue" of *Critique* (Minneapolis), Winter 1959; "The Novel in the American West" by John R. Milton, in *South Dakota Review* (Vermillion), Autumn 1964; "Sinclair Lewis-Frederick Manfred Issue" of *South Dakota Review* (Vermillion), Winter 1969–70; *The Literature of the American West* by J. Golden Taylor, Boston,

Houghton Mifflin, 1971; *Frederick Manfred* by Joseph M. Flora, Boise, Idaho, Boise State College 1973; "An Interview in Minnesota with Frederick Manfred" by James W. Lee, in *Studies in the Novel* (Denton, Texas), Fall 1973; *Frederick Manfred* by Robert C. Wright, Boston, Twayne, 1979.

Frederick Manfred comments:

It has been my dream for many years to be able to finish a long hallway of pictures in fiction dealing with the country I call Siouxland (located in the center of the Upper Midlands, USA) from 1800 and on to the day I die. Not only must the history be fairly accurate, and the description of the flora and fauna fairly precise, and the use of the language of the place and time beautiful, but the delineation of the people by way of characterization living and illuminating. It has long been my thought that a "place" finally selects the people who best reflect it, give it voice, and allow it to make a cultural contribution to the sum of all world culture under the sun. In fact, it is the sun beating on a certain place in a certain time that at last causes that place to flower into literature, the highest expression of intelligence (and not necessarily human intelligence).

It has been my feeling for some time that Middle America is more apt to speak with a clear voice from this continent than are either of the two American seaboards, the East with New York as the center and the West with Los Angeles as the center. The East in New York (and Boston and Washington, etc.) still speaks in part with an alien voice. It is not clear. It is muddy. It is as polluted with foreign sounds as is the air with foreign particles. And the West in Los Angeles (and all other California points) speaks with a most artificial voice, that of Hollywood, of the sudden uncultured rich. Only the Upper Midlands (and in my case, only my Siouxland) has a chance to speak with as clear a separate voice within the whole Western Culture complex as say Madrid for Spain and Paris for France and London for England.

The final test of good fiction rests with how well the characters come through, their reality, their meaning, their stature, their durability, no matter what the situation may be. The characters should be so well done that the reader should not be aware of plot or the unraveling of time in the work. The reader should be lost in the story. The plot should be hidden like a skeleton is in a flying eagle.

If a "place" truly finds voice at last the ultimate sacred force speaks.

And in the USA, Western American literature does this the best.

*   *   *

The author was born Frederick Feikema; later as Feike Feikema he changed his name again (1951) and thereafter is Frederick Feikema Manfred. The final name-taking is apparently of literary impulse, for in the most characteristic early novels the main protagonist is Thurs Manfred Wrâldsoan, an orphan, a wanderer, a reader of Lord Byron. Thus an invented character's name becomes in fact the author's name. This literary anomaly, with its strong implication of continuing self-analysis, indicates that questions of identity indeed are central to a full appreciation of the most significant prose fiction.

For example, *The Primitive*, *The Brother*, and *The Giant* constitute a trilogy wherein the main protagonist embarks on a journey of dual intention: a literary journey from a "Siouxland" college of fundamentalist persuasion to New York City and return. This is a quest for identity, for a viable past, for meaningful human relationships; by parallel, although not always comprehended by Wrâldsoan, himself, there is an inner quest for spiritual enlightenment, psychic resolutions, for means of artistic expression, for adulthood, for wisdom. In *Conquering Horse*, a characteristic later work of considerably higher literary quality, the quest for identity is dramatized in the emergence from adolescence of an American Indian. A comparison and contrast of the supportive institutions shown in the midwestern trilogy in contrast to parallel institutions in an Indian culture is instructive and—incidentally—suggests one measure of Manfred's artistic growth.

The breadth of the subject matter of the novels is greater than the reoccurring thematic concerns might suggest. The early *Golden Bowl* dramatizes the conflict between two generations of midwest "Siouxland" farmers; *Boy Almighty* is the semi-autobiographical tale of a writer's life as a patient in a midwestern tuberculosis sanitarium; *This Is the Year* concerns a wilful Frisian-American farmer; *Morning Red* treats politics and journalism in a small Minnesota town; "Arrow of Love" and *Scarlet Plume* are best described as Romance; *Lord Grizzly* and *Riders of Judgment* exploit materials of the American past, the mountain men, and the cattle wars in Wyoming in the 1890's. The poetry in *Winter Count* is of little technical interest and suffers from a rhetoric which is often inappropriate for the subject matter; the two irregular short story collections command discerning approval. On balance, possibly because of his unswerving commitment to midwestern, American region "Siouxland" where the literary audience is notoriously few and unfit, Manfred's work remains not much appreciated at the present time.

By no means, however, can it be said that Manfred's work is an example of isolated literary genius. Far from it. The novels are very much a part of a little explored sub-genre of American literature: those works of "epic" vision, of great vigor and industry by writers who value a direct rendering of their own life-experience; from one point-of-view those writers may be seen in contrast to the more cloistered, the merely "literary" artists who rely on the received virtues of consistency, of well-wrought structure, the "fully dramatic" posture. Aside from the controversial implications of the suggested sub-genre of American literature, Manfred's materials, themes, scope, "giantism," reliance on autobiography—and an inevitable redundancy of effect—suggest a close alignment with the novels of Thomas Wolfe. In the use of dialect, "down-home folks" protagonists, and a stubborn, at times anti-intellectual concern with "Truth," Manfred's work also suggests the tone and the strengths of Sherwood Anderson. In Manfred's intensity of attitude towards materials—though not always in erudition—the work also suggests the novels of Vardis Fisher. All of these writers, including possibly Upton Sinclair, are to be distinguished from the American naturalistic school. Manfred and the others are more consciously democratic, in the Whitman-esque sense of that word; more empirical in their methods. As a matter of literary principle they remain unreconstructed by continental or British literary conventions. The price paid for this fierce, regional independence is high: critical acclaim comes slowly, if at all; the weakest fictions teeter on the edge of literary disaster. Yet the best novels, by force of authorial energy alone, appear to sweep all merely literary reservations aside.

Presently this sub-genre of American literature is insufficiently explored possibly because it represents an old-fashioned, limited concept of the novel form. Understandably, the present age does not much approve of a reoccurring, implied didacticism, or of authorial voices behind the works which freely elected the novel form and then declined to assume the full obligations of the totally aware literary artist.

There is an overall unity in Manfred's novels, stories, letters, and poems that becomes each year more apparent. The authorial voice behind the work remains unchanged: energetic, widely referential, optimistic, quiet—until aroused—not overwhelmingly intellectual, but of a very wide, resourceful imagination. The common denominator of consistent voice gives substance to the large concepts, such as "Siouxland." Without consistent voice, such a concept will be only an imposition of pattern not fictionally "earned."

—James B. Hall

MANGIONE, Jerre (Gerlando Mangione). American. Born in Rochester, New York, 20 March 1909. Educated at Syracuse University, New York, B.A. 1931. Married Patricia Anthony in 1957. Staff writer, *Time* magazine, New York, 1931; book reviewer, New York *Herald Tribune*, 1931–35, and the *New Republic*, New York, 1931–37; book editor, Robert M. McBride Company, New York, 1934–37; national coordinating editor, Federal Writers' Project, 1937–39; information specialist, 1940–42, special assistant to the United States Commissioner, 1942–48, and editor-in-chief of the *Monthly Review*, 1944–48, Immigration and Naturalization Services of the United States Department of Justice; advertising and public relations writer for various firms in New York and Philadelphia, 1948–61. Lecturer, 1961–63, Associate Professor, 1963–68, Professor of English and Director of the Writing Program, 1968–78, Acting Director, Italian Studies Center, 1978–80, and since 1978, Emeritus Professor of American Literature, University of Pennsylvania, Philadelphia. Visiting Lecturer, Bryn Mawr College, Pennsylvania, 1967–68; Visiting Professor, Trinity College, Rome, Summer 1973, and Queens College, City University of New York, 1980. Editor-in-chief, *WFLN Philadelphia Guide*, 1959–61; advisory editor, *Humanist*, 1979. National President, Friends of Danilo Dolci Inc., New York, 1969–71; member of the Executive Council, American-Italian Historical Association, 1980. Recipient: Guggenheim fellowship, 1946; Fulbright fellowship, 1965; Rockefeller grant, 1968; American Philosophical Society grant, 1971; Philadelphia Athenaeum award, 1973; American Institute for Italian Culture award, 1979; National Endowment for the Arts grant, 1980, 1984; American-Italian Historical Association special award, 1983; Empedocles prize (Italy), 1984. M.A. 1971, and D.Lit. 1980, University of Pennsylvania. Commander, Order of the Star of Italian Solidarity, 1971; Fellow, Society of American Historians, 1974. Address: 1901 Kennedy Boulevard, No. 2404, Philadelphia, Pennsylvania 19103, U.S.A.

PUBLICATIONS

Novels

Mount Allegro.   Boston, Houghton Mifflin, 1943; revised (non-fiction) edition, New York, Columbia University Press, 1981.
The Ship and the Flame.   New York, Wyn-Current, 1948.
Night Search.   New York, Crown, 1965; as *To Walk the Night*, London, Muller, 1967.

Short Stories

Life Sentences for Everybody (fables).   New York and London, Abelard Schuman, 1966.

for each narrative Marshall sets up a relationship with a woman more vital than the man to develop the point of the Yeatsian epigraph, that the older man has become "a paltry thing." Thus, the geographic breadth given to the condition of modern rootlessness by the range of settings is accompanied in each story by evidence of Marshall's continuing interest in the distinctive roles women can assume in society. A later story, "Reena" (1962), returns the theme of the unique concerns of female identity to the center of the narrative, where it remains for all of Marshall's later work. "Reena" investigates the matrimonial and political choices made by an educated black woman, using the occasion of a wake for Reena's aunt as opportunity to frame the matter of self-definition within consideration of the continuities and differences between two generations of women. "Reena" together with "To Da-duh, in Memoriam," the story of a nine-year-old girl exchanging boasts about the size and energy of New York City for an introduction to the flora and fauna of Barbados from her grandmother, establish the focus for Marshall's mature fiction: the importance of lineage in the lives of women on the cusp of historical change.

Her first major novel, *The Chosen Place, The Timeless People*, reveals that focus to be profoundly political as well as intensely personal. The book records the encounter of an American research team with the "backward" people inhabiting Bournehills, the wasted corner of an island resembling perhaps Barbados but signifying the entire Caribbean. Marshall sympathetically portrays both aliens and natives in terms of the motives of guilt and frustration by which they characterize their own lives. As Merle Kinbona, a woman of Bournehills whose residence in England included schooling in painfully exploitive relationships along with professional training, assumes predominance in the narrative personal drama is translated into general social meaning. A native of the island despite her "modernization," Merle shares the timelessness of the people to whom the experience of slavery and particularly the momentary success of the rebellion of Cuffee Ned remain palpably present. On a level as deep as culture and as unavailable to measurement as the subconscious, they know that technological change is nothing compared to the redemption presaged in Cuffee's rebellion, and in their integrity they will settle for nothing less. The politics of the novel are conservative in a way that is unknown in parliaments or organized parties. This conservative politics grows from knowledge that the configurations of character and the complex relationships of love or resentment gain their shape from historical cultures.

With *Praisesong for the Widow* Marshall tentatively completes the exploration of black women's relationship to their history. Having begun with Selina Boyce, a young adult intent on gaining personal independence before all else, and then continuing with the narrative of Merle Kinbona, who seeks a viable cause beyond herself in middle age, Marshall carries her study forward with Avey Johnson, the 64-year-old widow who leaves her friends on a cruise ship for reasons she cannot articulate though they are as compelling as a subconscious drive. Juxtaposing memory of the past with present setting, the narrative recalls Avey's relationship to her great aunt who brought alive the tale of slaves who had left Ibo Landing, South Carolina, to walk home across the sea to Africa, and traces the course of Avey's marriage to Jay, who with respectability assumed the proper name of Jerome and the distant manner of a man mistaking status for integrity. Avey understood the value of middle-class security, but the loss of joy and spontaneity subsequent to its attainment has left her bereft in age. The sense of loss originates as an individual's trouble, its remedy lies in regaining a sense of collectivity; therefore, the later sections of the novel are structured around the symbolic rituals of a journey to Carriacou and the ceremonies of the blacks who annually return to the island to "beg pardon" to their ancestors and to dance the "nation dances" that survive from their African origins. By these means *Praisesong for the Widow* leads Avey through her crisis of integrity so that she can re-experience the connection to collective history she once felt as a child, reclaim her original name of Avatara (for which Avey is the diminutive), and join the movements of traditional dance that link her in body and spirit to her heritage.

Unquestionably more deliberate in its aesthetic form than the talk of the West Indian women in her childhood kitchen, Paule Marshall's stories share qualities with that speech while also distinguishing itself as markedly literary. Full of rich detail, the best of her writing brings character and incident alive in the vivid manner of popular tale telling. Informed, however, by a reflexivity that is absent from the creations of "unknown bards," the tales Marshall makes into novels reach beyond simulation of folk art, beyond the surface realism, nostalgia, or elementary denunciations of modernization that would constitute the easy and simple responses to historical transformation of traditional culture. Instead Marshall makes complex literature of the proposition that every woman needs to gain the power to speak the language of her elder kinswomen.

—John M. Reilly

MASSIE, Allan. British. Born in Singapore in 1938. Educated at Glenalmond College, Perthshire; Trinity College, Cambridge. Married; three children. Recipient: Niven Award, 1981; Scottish Arts Council award, 1982. Fellow, Royal Society of Literature. Address: c/o Bodley Head Ltd., 9 Bow Street, London WC2E 7AL, England.

PUBLICATIONS

Novels

Change and Decay in All Around I See. London, Bodley Head, 1978.
The Last Peacock. London, Bodley Head, 1980.
The Death of Men. London, Bodley Head, 1981; Boston, Houghton Mifflin, 1982.
One Night in Winter. London, Bodley Head, 1984.

Uncollected Short Story

"In the Bare Lands," in *Modern Scottish Short Stories*, edited by Fred Urquhart and Giles Gordon. London, Hamish Hamilton, 1978.

Other

Muriel Spark. Edinburgh, Ramsay Head Press, 1979.
Ill Met by Gaslight: Five Edinburgh Murders. Edinburgh, Harris, 1980.
The Caesars. London, Secker and Warburg, 1983; New York, Watts, 1984.
Portrait of Scottish Rugby. Edinburgh, Polygon, 1984.

Editor, *Edinburgh and the Borders: In Verse.* London, Secker and Warburg, 1983.

*   *   *

When Allan Massie's first novel, *Change and Decay in All Around I See*, was first published, immediate comparisons were made with the young Evelyn Waugh. The analogies were not fanciful. Atwater, the flawed central character, would feel equally at home in the world of Waugh's *Decline and Fall*, and the 1950's wasteland of London created by Massie is a timeless city in which social and spiritual life has slumped to a low ebb. As he cuts his path through a jungle of Turkish baths, pubs, betting shops, and seedy restaurants, Atwater comes to the sad realisation that perfection is not to be found on God's earth, that his world will be forever peopled by a sad collection of drunks, failures, and poseurs. Nevertheless—and Massie subscribes to Muriel Spark's theory of contrasts—the novel is not without its humour. Atwater's insights and asides are witty and sharp and his upside-down world is cleverly brought alive by Massie's shrewd powers of observation and by his delight in describing life's foibles, such as the scene in an Indian restaurant in which Atwater and his party drunkenly ponder the wisdom of mixing champagne and curry.

The sense of change and decay was taken a stage further in *The Last Peacock*, a sensitive comedy of manners set against the background of the landed gentry and reminiscent in style and tone of James Kennaway's novel *Household Ghosts* (1961). Once again, the central characters, in this case, Colin and his sister Belinda, are disillusioned people, divorced from the main thrust of life, yet cocooned from reality by their private language and creation of a childhood world. The death of their grandmother and their subsequent confrontation with the other members of their family bring them face to face with some uncomfortable truths and the aftermath heralds Colin's imminent destruction. Despite the sombre theme and the autumnal mood which Massie has brought to the damp Perthshire manse in which most of the action takes place, *The Last Peacock* showed that the author had not lost his comic skills. In many respects Colin's cleverly contrived asides are as cutting and witty as anything uttered by Atwater in Massie's previous novel.

In his third novel, *The Death of Men*, Massie discovered his true voice. Whereas literary artefact, a certain prosiness, and a desire to please intellectually had slowed down the rhythm of his earlier fiction, he discovered a new urgency in this modern parable of terrorism and Italian politics. The scene is set in Rome during the summer of 1978, a period of political instability in the country. Corrado Dusa, Senior Minister in the ruling Christian Democrat Party and a leading proponent of resolving the crisis of dissent and violence permeating Italy, is mysteriously kidnapped, and a tangled series of political trails leads to the involvement of his son in the kidnap. The action is based loosely on the events surrounding the real-life kidnap and murder in 1978 of the Italian politician Aldo Moro, but it would be wrong to draw too many parallels between *The Death of Men* and those real events; neither would it be accurate to describe Massie's novel as a *roman à clef*. Writing with great assurance, Massie's novel transforms itself into a fast-moving political thriller, building up to a conclusion which, however expected it might be, is still cleverly handled. His gallery of characters all play their expected roles and the Italian background is expertly and lovingly described: there are few better pictures of life in the inner city of modern Rome. And in the background Massie keeps open his moral options. Terrorism is roundly condemned, but he never loses sight of the question which is central to its occurrence: what are the political conditions which bring it into existence?

Massie returned to Scotland for his fourth novel, *One Night in Winter*, but it is a very different kind of Scotland from the place he portrayed in *The Last Peacock*. Whereas his earlier preoccupations were social, Massie keeps to the political line which served him so well in *The Death of Men*. Dallas Graham, an Atwater-figure with substance, looks back from his middle-class London middle age to the years of his young manhood in Scotland when he found himself drawn into a bizarre coterie of Scottish Nationalists and their camp followers. A murder lies at the heart of the novel, but Massie's theme is the tragedy of overweening ambition and flawed motives. Fraser Donnelly, the self-made man who espouses political nationalism, has his career ruined when fantasy overcomes his sense of reality, but Massie's concern seems to be less with the murder which Donnelly commits than with the effect it has on the young Graham. In that sense, Donnelly's rise and fall seems to mirror the imperfect political ambitions of those who take up the cause of nationalism. It is an assured and handsomely written novel which fully justifies Massie's reputation as one of the most inventive of the younger generation of Scottish novelists.

—Trevor Royle

MATHERS, Peter. Australian. Born in England in 1931; brought to Australia as an infant. Educated at Sydney Technical College. Married in 1961 (divorced); two daughters. Recipient: Miles Franklin Award, 1967. Address: 4 Fordham Court, Richmond, Victoria 3121, Australia.

PUBLICATIONS

Novels

Trap. Melbourne, Cassell, 1966; London, Sphere, 1970.
The Wort Papers. Melbourne, Cassell, 1972; London, Penguin, 1973.

Short Stories

A Change for the Better. Adelaide, WAV, 1984.

*   *   *

Peter Mathers is the author of only three books of fiction, yet he is undoubtedly one of the best of the generation of Australian fiction writers that followed in the wake of White, Stead, and Xavier Herbert. Though he was born in England, his work is marked by a deep strain of Australian nationalism, a conscious attempt at mythologising Australian experience.

His first novel, for instance, begins as the story of the eponymous Jack Trap, a part-Aboriginal, but as it continues its concerns steadily widen until finally it takes in, with the discussion of Trap's forebears, the whole savage history of the Aboriginal race over the last two hundred years: its shooting down and poisoning by white settlers, exploitation by businessmen and missionaries, abuse and mistreatment by foremen and fellow workers, and, finally, assaults by police and jailing by magistrates. If the novel is dominated by the angry, ebullient presence of its central character, the author makes it clear nevertheless that Jack is in part the product of a whole history of exploitation, cruelty, and contemptuous indifference on the part of white people. Trap is a misfit—neither craven nor surly, neither in society nor wholly out of it. Although he schools himself to patience, he is prone to violent eruptions at periodic intervals, and the result is always "six months from an understanding magistrate." He is resentful of his Aboriginal features and hopes they will not be recognized but at the same time he "marries" an Aboriginal woman and his final scheme is to lead a party of followers across the continent to the Narakis Mission.

Despite its subject matter, *Trap* is essentially a comic novel with its author much given to word play, puns, and episodes of slap-stick. In *The Wort Papers* Mathers takes both his concerns and his experiments with language a good deal further, virtually out of the realm of social realism altogether. Style in *The Wort Papers* is not merely the means of recording the rebellious and independent freedom to which the protagonist aspires, but it is also the means of achieving it. The last word in the novel is MATTERS, the name of the protagonist's alter ego and the mysterious writer who has hovered on its outskirts throughout the narrative.

Although it is concerned with a smaller period of time than *Trap*—roughly from the 1930's onwards—*The Wort Papers* is similarly involved with questions of identity and mythic journeys inland; there are two series of journeys which are described in comic and even parodic terms. The first third of the novel is taken up with the various expeditions of William Wort, and his attempt to define himself in terms of sense of Englishness. Like his son later, William is constantly "In Flight." Mathers's awareness that William's peregrinations carry him over territory already covered by other Australian writers such as Patrick White is shown by the heading of one section: "Journey and Employers (& obligatory bushfire)."

William's son Percy is an explorer, but whereas earlier explorers and even his father had travelled on foot or on horseback, Percy mounts a 500 c.c. Norton motor-bike. Whereas they had travelled into the heart of the inland, he sticks mostly to the cities, and his predicaments are urban ones, often taking a farcical form. Where their enemies were droughts or hostile natives, Percy's are figures of bureaucratic authority—policemen, mysterious representatives of A.S.I.O. (the Australian equivalent of the C.I.A.), and recalcitrant bosses and bar-keepers.

Percy's acts of insurrection are embodied in the language of the novel itself. Wort's words are exuberant, very funny, and finally surreal weapons fired by his "sturdy, 350 shot Remington." At the end of the novel Percy dies but his doppelgänger Matters is still around. It is the artist, the word-maker, who in Mathers's view survives.

A gap of 12 years separates *The Wort Papers* from Mathers's third book of fiction, a collection of short stories titled *A Change for the Better*, and when it did appear it was greeted by sympathetic reviewers with no more than respectful disappointment. The distinguishing elements of Mathers's writing—the compression, density, and self-conscious linguistic play—have been taken as far as they can possibly go, to the point where the style is cryptic, rather than merely compressed, not so much self-conscious as hermetic. The title story is both witty and accessible. It tells of a young boy with homosexual inclinations who is therefore the scandal of his country district. Eventually he is discovered peering through the bathroom at a girl bathing. The outraged parents send for his father but are deeply chagrined at his reaction of delight: at least his sexual proclivities indicate "a change for the better." Another story that works well is "Like a Maori Prince," which returns the reader to the territory of the novels: a black man poses as a Maori Prince in order to escape the tag of "Lairy Boong" and is treated with fawning respect by the whites of the town. For the most part, though, the stories are marked by long exchanges of almost indecipherable puns and one-liners. One of the characters in "Like a Maori Prince" comments of one pun that "People have been run out of town for better jokes." There are enough bad ones in this collection to cause a mass exodus.

Mathers continues to write constantly but like Malcolm Lowry is never able to consider a work finished and is deeply reluctant to relinquish it to a publisher. Like Lowry, also, it is probable that much of his writing will be published posthumously, a suggestion that delights the author when it is put to him.

—Laurie Clancy

MATTHEWS, Jack (John Harold Matthews).   American. Born in Columbus, Ohio, 22 July 1925. Educated at Ohio State University, Columbus, 1945–49, 1952–54, B.A. in classics and English 1949, M.A. in English 1954. Served in the United States Coast Guard, 1943–45. Married Barbara Jane Reese in 1947; two daughters and one son. Post office clerk, Columbus, 1950–59; Associate Professor, 1959–62, and Professor of English, 1962–64, Urbana College, Ohio. Associate Professor, 1964–70, Professor of English, 1971–77, and since 1978 Distinguished Professor, Ohio University, Athens. Distinguished Writer-in-Residence, Wichita State University, Kansas, 1970–71. Recipient: Florence Roberts Head Award, 1967; Quill Award (*Massachusetts Review*, Amherst), 1967; Guggenheim grant, 1974. Agent: Ann Elmo Agency, 60 East 42nd Street, New York, New York 10165. Address: 24 Briarwood Drive, Athens, Ohio 45701, U.S.A.

PUBLICATIONS

Novels

Hanger Stout, Awake!   New York, Harcourt Brace, 1967.
Beyond the Bridge.   New York, Harcourt Brace, 1970.
The Tale of Asa Bean.   New York, Harcourt Brace, 1971.
The Charisma Campaigns.   New York, Harcourt Brace, 1972.
Pictures of the Journey Back.   New York, Harcourt Brace, 1973.
Sassafras.   Boston, Houghton Mifflin, 1983.

Short Stories

Bitter Knowledge.   New York, Scribner, 1964.
Tales of the Ohio Land.   Columbus, Ohio Historical Society, 1978.
Dubious Persuasions.   Baltimore, Johns Hopkins University Press, 1981.
Crazy Women.   Baltimore, Johns Hopkins University Press, 1985.

Uncollected Short Stories

"'When the Shark, Babe,'" in *North American Review* (Mt. Vernon, Iowa), January 1966.
"The Names of My Brothers," in *Georgia Review* (Athens), Spring 1966.
"My Son," in *Prairie Schooner* (Lincoln, Nebraska), Spring 1966.
"Night" and "A Fire on the Hill," in *North American Review* (Mt. Vernon, Iowa), May 1966.

"Inviolate on Shawnee Street," in *North American Review* (Mt. Vernon, Iowa), July 1966.
"The Strong One," in *University Review* (Kansas City, Missouri), Autumn 1966.
"Schlachner, The Hero," in *December 9* (Western Springs, Illinois), 1967.
"A Slightly Different World," in *North American Review* (Mt. Vernon, Iowa), March 1967.
"The Hotel," in *Massachusetts Review* (Amherst), Autumn 1967.
"In the Neighborhood of Dark," in *North American Review* (Mt. Vernon, Iowa), September 1967.
"The Knife," in *Yale Review* (New Haven, Connecticut), December 1968.
"The Betrayal," in *Malahat Review* (Victoria, British Columbia), April 1969.
"A Geneaology of Trees and Flesh," in *Iowa Review* (Iowa City), Spring 1971.
"On Chad Creek," in *Prize Stories 1972: The O. Henry Awards*, edited by William Abrahams. New York, Doubleday, 1972.
"The Colonel's Birthday Party," in *Ohio Review* (Athens), Spring 1972.
"The Stone in the Path," in *Sewanee Review* (Tennessee), Summer 1972.
"A Questionnaire for Emilio Roszas," in *Malahat Review* (Victoria, British Columbia), July 1972.
"Questionnaire for T.M. Connolly," in *Salmagundi* (Flushing, New York), Spring 1974.
"Muerte, Nada, and Bradley Jones," in *Malahat Review* (Victoria, British Columbia), July 1979.
"Tableau with Three Ghostly Women," in *Chariton Review* (Kirksville, Missouri), Fall 1979.
"Trophy for an Earnest Boy," in *Western Humanities Review* (Salt Lake City), Autumn 1980.
"Philo's Calling," in *Western Humanities Review* (Salt Lake City), Autumn 1981.
"Critical Decisions of Early Years," in *Kenyon Review* (Gambier, Ohio), Fall 1985.

Verse

An Almanac for Twilight. Chapel Hill, University of North Carolina Press, 1966.
In a Theater of Buildings. Marshall, Minnesota, Ox Head Press, 1970.

Other

Collecting Rare Books for Pleasure and Profit. New York, Putnam, 1977.

Editor, with Elaine Gottlieb Hemley, *The Writer's Signature: Idea in Story and Essay*. Chicago, Scott Foresman, 1972.
Editor, *Archetypal Themes in the Modern Story* (anthology). New York, St. Martin's Press, 1973.

*

Manuscript Collection: Ohioana Library, Ohio Departments Building, Columbus.

Critical Studies: "That Appetite for Life So Ravenous" by Dave Smith, in *Shenandoah* (Lexington, Virginia), Summer 1974; "One Alternative to Black Humor: The Satire of Jack Matthews" by Stanley W. Lindberg, in *Studies in Contemporary Satire* (Cambridge Springs, Pennsylvania), vol. 1, no. 1, 1977; "Jack Matthews and the Shape of Human Feelings" by Elmer F. Suderman, in *Critique* (Atlanta), vol. 21, no. 1, 1979.

Jack Matthews comments:

I think of every literary work as a place where three classes of people come together: the author, the reader, and the characters. The work is importantly, if not solely, definable in terms of these three classes and their relationships to one another and to the story (or poem) which is the arena of their convention. Thus, every story can be viewed as, in varying degrees, an occasion and ceremony of passionate learning.

All stories are philosophical probes, hypotheses, heuristic journeys, maps of powerful and conceivable realities, speculations, ceremonies of discovery. All these, every one. Some attempts to write a good story work beautifully; others prove sadly unworthy, false, flat, silly. Nevertheless, an author should have the courage and energy to experiment constantly and knowledgeably (i.e., remembering and adding to his craft), even in his awareness that he will often miss whatever mark is there, and knowing also that whatever can conceivably happen to him and come out of him will ultimately be found to have taken place within his signature.

Man's character is his fate, but he should never let this fact inhibit his real freedom of the real moment. I celebrate this truth in my stories, as well as in the act of writing them.

* * *

Many contemporary fiction writers—especially in America—are displaced persons: they don't really live *in* any particular location, they merely reside there. But Jack Matthews's mature imagination lives in the American heartland where it was shaped. In fact, Matthews is at his best when he is taking the pulse of Middle America (not merely a geographical area, of course, but a state of consciousness extending far beyond Matthews's native Ohio). In his six novels (and in many of his remarkable short stories) the reader can sense the wide-open spaces of the midwest, the often-closed minds of its inhabitants, the limitless possibilities of success and failure, the comic and the tragic in ironic balance. Like Sinclair Lewis, Matthews captures the essence of Middle America. He does so, however, without the didacticism of Lewis and with more of the comic and a surer control of the dramatic.

Matthews's early novels are all rather short, though they are richly developed and populated with memorable characters —originals with much more than just literary validity, ranging from gas-station attendants and warehouse laborers to used-car salesmen and battered cowboys. Most of them are essentially innocents, viewed with unsentimental compassion as they try to cope with what they see of the confusion around them; but they carry their innocence in interestingly differing ways.

The most openly naive of his characters is "Hanger" Stout, the narrator of Matthews's first novel, who relates a poignant but truly funny account of how he was tricked into competing for the championship of a nonexistent sport ("free-hanging" by one's hands). Genuinely unaware of how much others are using him, and often unaware of the refreshing comedy in his tale, "Hanger" emerges from his experiences relatively untouched, still kind and trusting, a most convincing original.

Less convincing is the self-conscious narrator of *Beyond the Bridge*, a middle-aged man who narrowly escapes death when the Silver Bridge collapses, plunging a number of people into the Ohio River. Knowing that his family expects him to be crossing the bridge at that hour, he seizes this unique chance to shed all his responsibilities, to disappear and begin a new life elsewhere. Such a break with one's past is not that easy,

Matthews demonstrates, and the novel offers some nicely detailed moments in the mind of the neurotic narrator. When compared to Matthews's other fiction, however, the action here seems excessively internalized, and the symbolism often too overt.

Matthews's ironic sense of humor surfaces as witty sexual satire in *The Tale of Asa Bean*, where the innocent is a former Ph.D. candidate in philosophy now working in an A & P grocery warehouse. Asa, burdened with an IQ of more than 170 and an over-active libido, is a compulsive verbalist with a tendency to drop recondite phrases (often in Latin) at inappropriate moments—a habit that regularly scares off the women he so desperately wants. "What ironic man can make love?" Asa agonizes, "And yet, how can man achieve truth, understanding, humor, manhood, without irony?" But Asa's hilarious misadventures end triumphantly—despite himself—in a brilliant demonstration of wit and verbal precision, a winning performance.

In *The Charisma Campaigns* Matthews takes a calculated risk in creating a character who is announced as possessing magnetic charisma—and, indeed, convincingly projects it on the page. A used-car dealer in a small Ohio town, Rex McCoy plays with a full deck of corny sales slogans and gimmicks, but like nearly all of Matthews's characters, he moves far beyond any stereotyped model. His cunning machinations and energetic naivety, his success in selling cars and his failures in other aspects of life, all blend into a fascinating portrait. It is easy to agree with Anthony Burgess, who proclaimed it "an American classic." This is a superb novel—Matthews's finest accomplishment to date.

In *Pictures of the Journey Back*, set in the early 1970's, Matthews portrays a trip from Kansas to Colorado by three disparate characters: a weathered ex-rodeo hand, a confused college girl estranged from her mother, and the girl's hippie lover, an aspiring filmmaker. The cowboy insists upon returning the girl to her dying mother because, he argues, it is "only right," and the boy friend accompanies them to make a film of the total experience. Here is the vehicle for the unending dialectics of youth *vs.* age, freedom *vs.* tradition, appearance *vs.* reality, etc. More ambitious technically than his earlier work, *Pictures* employs a shifting point of view to examine a concern that occupies much of Matthews's fiction—a sense that something is slowly being lost: "the sacred ideals of one's family and culture," as Matthews sees it, "what the Romans termed *Pietas*."

In his most recent (and longest) novel, Matthews sets the action in 1840 on the American frontier. The protagonist/narrator of *Sassafras* is Thad Burke, a young phrenologist who takes his show from village to village, lecturing and "reading" the heads of a wild assortment of soldiers, Indians, settlers, and whores. Thad's Candide-like journey is not without its moving and painful lessons, but Matthews infuses a marvelous comic energy into this picaresque novel, and the dominant tone is that of a boisterous tall tale. Like Huck Finn, Thad is a splendid innocent—despite his natural "sass" and the sophistication he thinks he has acquired.

A fiction writer's achievement is usually determined primarily by assessing his novels, and those of Jack Matthews certainly merit serious consideration. Yet it has been through his mastery of short fiction that Matthews has attracted many of his readers. More than two hundred of his stories have been published—in all the major American quarterlies and magazines (and regularly in the prize anthologies). Of the several splendid collections now available, the most thematically integrated are *Tales of the Ohio Land*, rich in its blend of history and myth, and his latest gathering, *Crazy Women*, "dedicated to all those

who will understand how negotiable and variously ironic the title is." But even in these two, Matthews displays a wide range of telling effects, and his other collections, *Bitter Knowledge* and *Dubious Persuasions*, provide further evidence of his engaging versatility, his sure powers of observation, his compassionate understanding of the human comedy. Without question, he has established himself as one of America's finest short-story writers.

Much more significant than the impressive quantity of fiction produced by Jack Matthews is the remarkably high percentage of it that seems likely to endure, inviting and sustaining additional readings and reflection. Moreover, as his audience has grown and as his distinctive fusion of the regional and the archetypal has become more widely recognized and appreciated, solid critical acclaim has begun to accumulate. It is well earned.

—Stanley W. Lindberg

MATTHIESSEN, Peter. American. Born in New York City, 22 May 1927. Educated at Hotchkiss School, Connecticut; Yale University, New Haven, Connecticut, B.A. 1950; the Sorbonne, Paris, 1948–49. Married 1) Patricia Southgate in 1951 (divorced); 2) Deborah Love in 1963 (died, 1972), four children; 3) Maria Eckhart in 1980. Commercial fisherman, 1954–56. Has made anthropological and natural history expeditions to Alaska, the Canadian Northwest Territories, Peru, New Guinea (Harvard-Peabody Expedition, 1961), Africa, Nicaragua, and Nepal. Founder, 1952, and editor, *Paris Review*. Trustee, New York Zoological Society, 1965–79. Recipient: *Atlantic* "Firsts" Award, 1951; American Academy award, 1963; National Book Award, for non-fiction, 1979; Brandeis University Creative Arts Award, 1979; American Book Award, for non-fiction, 1980; John Burroughs Medal, 1982; National Academy of Sciences Gold Medal, 1984. Member, American Academy, 1974. Address: Bridge Lane, Sagaponack, Long Island, New York 11962, U.S.A.

PUBLICATIONS

Novels

Race Rock. New York, Harper, 1954; London, Secker and Warburg, 1955.
Partisans. New York, Viking Press, 1955; London, Secker and Warburg, 1956; as *The Passionate Seekers*, New York, Avon, 1957.
Raditzer. New York, Viking Press, 1961; London, Heinemann, 1962.
At Play in the Fields of the Lord. New York, Random House, 1965; London, Heinemann, 1966.
Far Tortuga. New York, Random House, 1975.

Short Story

Midnight Turning Gray. Bristol, Rhode Island, Ampersand Press, 1984.

Uncollected Short Stories

"Sadie," in *Atlantic* (Boston), January 1951.

"Fifth Day," in *Atlantic* (Boston), September 1951.
"A Replacement," in *Paris Review 1*, Spring 1953.
"Lina," in *Cornhill* (London), Fall 1956.
"Travelin' Man," in *Prize Stories 1958: The O. Henry Awards*, edited by Paul Engle.   New York, Doubleday, 1958.

Play

Screenplay (documentary): *The Dead Birds*, 1965.

Other

Wildlife in America.   New York, Viking Press, 1959; London, Deutsch, 1960.
The Cloud Forest: A Chronicle of the South American Wilderness.   New York, Viking Press, 1961; London, Deutsch, 1962.
Under the Mountain Wall: A Chronicle of Two Seasons in the Stone Age.   New York, Viking Press, 1962; London, Heinemann, 1963.
The Shorebirds of North America.   New York, Viking Press, 1967; as *The Wind Birds*, 1973.
Oomingmak: The Expedition to the Musk Ox Island in the Bering Sea.   New York, Hastings House, 1967.
Sal Si Puedes: Cesar Chavez and the New American Revolution.   New York, Random House, 1970.
Blue Meridian: The Search for the Great White Shark.   New York, Random House, 1971.
Everglades: Selections from the Writings of Peter Matthiessen, edited by Patricia Caulfield.   New York, Ballantine, 1971.
Seal Pool (for children).   New York, Doubleday, 1972; as *The Great Auk Escape*, London, Angus and Robertson, 1974.
The Tree Where Man Was Born: The African Experience, photographs by Eliot Porter.   New York, Dutton, and London, Collins, 1972.
The Snow Leopard.   New York, Viking Press, 1978; London, Chatto and Windus, 1979.
Sand Rivers (on the Selous Game Reserve), photographs by Hugo van Lawick.   New York, Viking Press, and London, Aurum Press, 1981.
In the Spirit of Crazy Horse.   New York, Viking Press, 1983.
Indian Country.   New York, Viking, 1984; London, Collins, 1985.

*

Bibliography: *Peter Matthiessen: A Bibliography 1952–1979* by D. Nicholas, Canoga Park, California, Orirama Press, 1980.

*   *   *

Peter Matthiessen has a dream of mankind living gracefully in the world, one species of many in an organic relationship. Unlike earlier American authors given to a version of this dream, Matthiessen can have no illusions. He writes with our contemporary knowledge that the "natural man," whose free application of energy to the environment was for earlier Americans to be the means of achieving a paradise, has wrought ecological disaster. Materially that disaster derives from the rapacious application of technology to the subjugation of nature, and Matthiessen's works of non-fiction are its historical record reporting the extinction and threatened destruction of animal species, the fateful meetings of representatives of industrial society with people yet to experience even the agricultural revolution, and the desperate resistance of American farm workers to the culminating stage of exploitation. Philosophically, the disastrous consequences of the traditional American dream result from the theoretical separation of society, usually conceived of as oppressive, and the individual, always assumed to be noble; thus, people celebrating individualism but nonetheless required to construct a social system find that their rejection of the claims of fraternity does not foster sturdy independence but merely produces anomie. The counterpart of his historical record of the destruction of the natural environment, Matthiessen's first novels are a representation of this disabled American character.

Writing evocatively of his own generation and social class in *Race Rock*, he links four young Americans in exploring the directions their lives have taken since their adolescence in the same seacoast setting. The shifting viewpoint and intermingling of recollection and present event provide the sense of movement we associate with growth, but it is ironic since there has been no growth. Two of the male characters—George and Sam —are the ineffectual products of middle-class culture: uncertain of vocation, implausible in deeds, in short unable to complete the arc between thought and action because they doubt the efficacy of their thought. Providing the apex of a triangle is a woman who, though female and, therefore, less intensively drawn by the romance of achievement, is herself ungratified. Her fulfillment must come through the ineffectual males to one of whom she has been married and with the second of whom she is involved in a love affair. The point of reference for all three is Cady, a man whose natural capacity to act let him bully them in childhood. As adults these four are bound as they were in adolescence into personally destructive relationships. Cady's irresponsible brutishness has merely become more lethal. He still seeks to get what he wants according to a base code of individual force, while George, Sam, and Eve ambivalently resent and admire his dominance. For Matthiessen the behavior of the characters has explanation, but no excuse. Carefully avoiding extenuating circumstances that would lift their personal responsibility, he shows that they have neither the direction nor the will to exist in other than an unjustifiably predatory arrangement.

In *Partisans* Matthiessen again focuses upon an ineffectual son of the American bourgeoisie. Barney Sand, alienated from family and culture, proceeds on a search for a revolutionary who had befriended him as a child. By means of a descent into Parisian working class life on which Barney is led by a Stalinist Party functionary named Marat, Matthiessen parallels the physical search with an inquiry into the motives for revolutionary action. The Brechtian portrayal of proletarian conditions denies Barney the clarity available to those who think in the abstract. The bestial lives of the poor make sympathy, or even the belief in their natural rectitude, impossible for Barney, and a politics without idealism is beneath his consideration. All that Matthiessen permits Barney to grasp is that revolutionaries have strong convictions for which they will sacrifice everything—the man for whom he searches gives life and reputation. But since there can be no doubt that revolutionary forces are in motion, the failure to comprehend must lie in Barney. Matthiessen seems to be suggesting that so long as thought and action are held to be categorically separate, as they are in Barney's mind, no motive will be sufficient for action and no action entirely justifiable. It is integration of both in practice that makes a revolutionary and comprehension of that fact that is necessary for modern men to make their lives adequately human.

Technically Matthiessen's neatest explication of character occurs in *Raditzer*. The figure who gives his name to the book is a passive-aggressive, physically weak and socially a parasite, yet able to strike through the mask of civilized respectability and mastery to reveal in those he victimizes a deep-seated guilt and bewildering remorse. The kinship Raditzer insists he shares with the respectable Navy men whose tenuous security he undermines conveys, as in *Race Rock*, Matthiessen's perception of the split between thought and action that manifests itself in the indecisiveness of American men. The tight narrative construction enforcing psychological parallels goes beyond the earlier novel, however, making it evident in *Raditzer* through the substance of style that the leading characters of the book amalgamate into a general type.

Successful though he has been in the manner of psychological realism, Matthiessen's developing vision has required that he exceed the form of his first three novels, and in *At Play in the Fields of the Lord* he introduces to fiction the comprehensiveness of philosophical anthropology. Carrying the ineffectual civilized types he has previously described into the jungle of South America, Matthiessen strips away the protective coloration they gain from their native culture; thus, they are as exposed as the jungle Indians to the test of survival. As the narrative increasingly centers upon the grand attempt of a reservation trained North American Indian to reclaim his past by immersing himself in the natural and cultural world of the primitive South American Indians, three levels of meaning emerge. The first concerns the historical conflict between modern technological civilization and the less developed societies whose destruction is only a matter of time. Through imaginative sympathy with both Indians and whites Matthiessen, then, establishes a second theme of the unity of desire to humanize the world. For the Indians this involves a balanced relationship to nature that yet allows a sense of transcendence. For the North Americans sharing the same impulse the desire is domination. Certainly their technology will eventually dominate but for the time being they are alone with only personal resources inadequate to sustain their sanity. Finally, on a third level of meaning he reveals both Indians and whites to be lonely beings who must find salvation through development of community that embraces the total material and social world.

Thematically more spare than the previous novels, *Far Tortuga* embodies in literary technique itself the forces of the natural and human world that might make community. The crew of a Grand Cayman fishing boat going about the business of sailing to the turtle banks off Nicaragua communicates in dialogue detached from expository context. Their speech, afloat as they are, concerns the specifics of job and personality but is imbued with the sense that fishing has come upon hard times. Tales of past voyages, former captains, and historical events imply the decline their way of life has suffered because excessive fishing has depleted marine life. Impressionistic description of sea and weather and time dominates the narrative just as natural forces dominate the watery world. There is no significant plot to the narrative, for at sea the men cannot be a cause of their destiny, and, for the same reason, narrative movement is simply temporal. Human purpose appears in the novel's title, which refers to a legendary cay where fishing is eternally good, but that very purpose has sustained material nature as the ultimate force in human life.

Peter Matthiessen's fiction and non-fiction are one. As he writes in *Sal Si Puedes*: "In a damaged human habitat, all problems merge." The good life will be achieved, if at all,

only when man and society and nature are equally nurtured and cherished.

—John M. Reilly

MAVOR, Elizabeth (Osborne). British. Born in Glasgow, Lanarkshire, 17 December 1927. Educated at St. Leonard's School, St. Andrews, Scotland; St. Anne's College, Oxford (Editor, *Cherwell*), 1947–50, B.A. in history, M.A. Married Haro Hodson in 1953; two sons. Address: Home Close, Garsington, Oxfordshire, England.

PUBLICATIONS

Novels

Summer in the Greenhouse.   London, Hutchinson, 1959; New York, Morrow, 1960.
The Temple of Flora.   London, Hutchinson, 1961.
The Redoubt.   London, Hutchinson, 1967.
A Green Equinox.   London, Joseph, 1973.

Other

The Virgin Mistress: A Study in Survival: The Life of the Duchess of Kingston.   London, Chatto and Windus, and New York, Doubleday, 1964.
The Ladies of Llangollen: A Study in Romantic Friendship. London, Joseph, 1971; New York, Penguin, 1984.

Editor, *Life with the Ladies of Llangollen.*   London, Viking, 1984.

*   *   *

Elizabeth Mavor's forte is the combination of different— often incongruous—tones in a single novel. Each of her four novels centres on a woman in love, around whom revolve questions of the justification of adultery, and who pits herself against time, past or future.

In Mavor's first novel, *Summer in the Greenhouse*, the predominant mood of lyrical reminiscence contrasts with the stylized and fantastic plotting on which it is hinged. The middle-aged Claire Peachey recounts the sad love-affair of her youth to a child and a young man who see "not so much Mrs. Peachey's house and the walks and flower-beds about it as the buildings and monuments of Florence beneath an identical burning sky in that June of 1895." Mrs. Peachey is observed through the grand-daughter of her old admirer; the child's quest for the Fra Angelico painting of "the face," which she has seen reproduced, brings the adults together after 45 years. Though anticipated throughout the book, this encounter remains a *tour de force*, upstaged by the radio announcement of Britain's entry into the Second World War.

Mavor boldly extends the range of broad comedy in *The Temple of Flora*, which switches from rural fun reminiscent of *Cold Comfort Farm* to sometimes serious theology. Dinah Gage's aspirations to reform the semi-pagan village of Thrussel are complicated by her tangling with a local youth. In a heavily symbolic but hilarious climax, a bull disrupts the harvest festival, which has already transformed the church into the temple of the title. The novel shifts to a consideration of the eternal triangle in which Dinah now involves herself. In the closing farewell scenes, as she decides to renounce her married lover, Mavor successfully treads a dizzy tightrope between poignance and ridicule, with Dinah's wish for "a sacramental relationship between him and me so that I could live apart from him with courage and a belief that I was doing something true and creative."

In *The Redoubt* Mavor broke away from the third-person narration of her two previous novels for a mixture of first- and third-person narration which she retained in *A Green Equinox*, though in both books the potentialities of this freedom are left unexplored. In *The Redoubt*, too, she extended her range of characterization with the publican Lil, who is her only fullscale lower-class portrait. The novel is set over the weekend of the 1953 East Coast floods, as Eve gives birth to a child. Through flashbacks grafted on to the chaos of the floods and the proverbial reliving of the past before drowning, the flickering validity of a childhood friendship comes across, "a kind of marriage in that childhood moment." But the book's ending is facile as Eve, who wishes that the father of her child were not her abandoned husband, but Faber, her rediscovered— married—and now drowned childhood friend, resolves that "it is out of his death that my own life must be remade somehow."

A Green Equinox ranges even wider than *The Temple of Flora*, and fuses its diverse material better in an ironical circular structure. It follows Hero Kinoull's search for "Heaven now" in her successive loves for Hugh Shafto, the Rococo expert, his wife and his mother, in Beaudesert—to be found on the same allegorical map as Thrussel. The novel partially resolves itself into a meditation on age, as Hero's third love is seen as the most lyrical; old Mrs Shafto's gardens and model boats— "a love for the miniature"—recall Faber's in *The Redoubt*. *A Green Equinox* combines the bathetic comedy of saving the Bunyan Elm with a plethora of dramatic disasters—car accident, typhoid epidemic, near-drowning, drowning, and fire. Complete with metaphysical overtones, all this is crammed into six months which culminate in Hero's defiance of time; the reader has been initially forewarned to her "love affair, sexual almost, with the lost past." The Rococo, "the worst and most provocative of all styles," subsumes all the ramifications of this tale under its imagery.

In *The Virgin Mistress*, the first of her two historical biographies, Mavor affirmed that "a human personality is not mewed up in its own life-span." She has an antiquarian fascination with objects, just as Imogen in *Summer in the Greenhouse* listening to Mrs. Peachey's story was spellbound by "all the props of the play that had been." *A Green Equinox* is Elizabeth Mavor's most ambitious and best novel because the extended metaphor of Rococo frivoloty permits her even greater licence for lyricism and satire.

—Val Warner

MAXWELL, William (Keepers). American. Born in Lincoln, Illinois, 16 August 1908. Educated at the University of Illinois, Urbana, B.A. 1930; Harvard University, Cambridge, Massachusetts, M.A. 1931. Married Emily Gilman Noyes in 1945; two daughters. Member of the English Department, University of Illinois, 1931–33. Since 1936, in the art department, then fiction editor, *New Yorker*; retired 1976. Recipient: Friends of American Writers award, 1938; American Academy award, 1958, and Howells Medal, 1980; American Book Award, for paperback, 1982. D.Litt.: University of Illinois, 1973. President, National Institute of Arts and Letters, 1969–72. Address: 544 East 86th Street, New York, New York 10028, U.S.A.

PUBLICATIONS

Novels

Bright Center of Heaven. New York, Harper, 1934.
They Came like Swallows. New York, Harper, and London, Joseph, 1937.
The Folded Leaf. New York, Harper, 1945; London, Faber, 1946.
Time Will Darken It. New York, Harper, 1948; London, Faber, 1949.
The Château. New York, Knopf, 1961.
So Long, See You Tomorrow. New York, Knopf, 1980.

Short Stories

Stories, with others. New York, Farrar Straus, 1956; as *A Book of Stories*, London, Gollancz, 1957.
The Old Man at the Railroad Crossing and Other Tales. New York, Knopf, 1966.
Over by the River and Other Stories. New York, Knopf, 1977.

Uncollected Short Stories

"Love," in *New Yorker*, 14 November 1983.
"My Father's Friends," in *New Yorker*, 30 January 1984.
"The Man in the Moon," in *New Yorker*, 12 November 1984.

Other

The Heavenly Tenants (for children). New York, Harper, 1946.
The Writer as Illusionist (lecture). New York, Unitelum Press, 1955.
Ancestors. New York, Knopf, 1971.

Editor, *The Garden and the Wilderness*, by Charles Pratt. New York, Horizon Press, 1980.
Editor, *The Letters of Sylvia Townsend Warner*. London, Chatto and Windus, 1982; New York, Viking Press, 1983.

*   *   *

The subjects of William Maxwell's major novels vary, but the sensibility that informs them is a midwestern one. In both *They Came like Swallows* and *The Folded Leaf*, for example, the novelist is reworking and focusing his recollections of an Illinois boyhood and college experience. The materials he draws on in these novels he thus shares with somewhat older writers like Sinclair Lewis and Sherwood Anderson. But these novelists were involved in labors of repudiation; their work was marked by what has been called the "revolt from the village," by a keen sense that the midwestern setting was a stultifying one from which the writer, by a satirical and unflattering report, had to separate himself. This accent of mockery and dismissal is absent from Maxwell's novels, which render the texture of midwestern life in the early decades of this century. It is an accent which is absent from Maxwell's *Ancestors*, a work of non-fiction which gives an attentive account of the writer's forbears.

In general, then, there is a cherishing of the provincial limitations that other writers have found galling. There is, in most of the novels, a precise if not loving recollection of the diversions and the limited esthetic taste that created upper-class, prosperous sensibility in "downstate" Illinois towns. *They Came like Swallows*, for example, tells of the impact of a mother's death on a decent and conventional Illinois household. *Time Will Darken It* is an account of a protracted visit which Southern relatives pay and the disruption that the visitors bring to what was a moderately happy family. *The Folded Leaf*, which the French critic Maurice Coindreau has referred to as the best novel about college experience, tells of the adolescent and college experiences of two young midwestern men; it leaves them on the threshold of an uneasy maturity, a maturity far short of ideal, but the only maturity that is open to them under midwestern conditions.

The clearest indications of Maxwell's attitude toward his American materials appears in two novels: *The Folded Leaf* and *So Long, See You Tomorrow*. *The Folded Leaf* is about the "coming of age" of two boys; the author draws explicit parallels between the boys' rather casual passage from youth to maturity and the "rites of passage" that anthropologists and students of comparative religion describe in the tradition-oriented societies they study. *So Long, See You Tomorrow* also deals with the friendship of two boys. It is friendship terminated by the sensational crime and death of the father of one of the boys. Here also Maxwell deals with studious attention to matters that other writers handle sensationally or ironically. Maxwell even allows us to see how he has collected his materials—old newspapers—as a first step to his imaginative reconstruction. Both novels contain controlled attention, free of animus.

The same sort of attention is offered adult experience in *The Château*. The American travellers at the center of this novel undergo contacts with an enigmatic culture—that of the French—which are a series of challenges that are neither mockingly presented, as in Sinclair Lewis's *Dodsworth*, nor offered as proof of American superiority, as in Booth Tarkington's *The Plutocrat*. Rather is Maxwell's prevailing note that of detached comprehension, the same sort of comprehension that the anthropologist offers the alien culture that he wishes to grasp. The anthropologist does not question the values of his "informants"; he reports those values. Such is also the attitude of Maxwell toward the aspirations of the characters he creates.

—Harold H. Watts

McCARTHY, Mary (Therese). American. Born in Seattle, Washington, 21 June 1912; sister of the actor Kevin McCarthy. Educated at Forest Ridge Convent, Seattle; Annie Wright Seminary, Tacoma, Washington; Vassar College, Poughkeepsie, New York, A.B. 1933 (Phi Beta Kappa). Married 1) Harold Johnsrud in 1933; 2) the writer Edmund Wilson in 1938, one son; 3) Bowden Broadwater in 1946; 4) James Raymond West in 1961. Editor, Covici Friede, publishers, New York, 1936–38; editor, 1937–38, and drama critic, 1937–62, *Partisan Review*, New York, and New Brunswick, New Jersey; Instructor, Bard College, Annandale-on-Hudson, New York, 1945–46, and Sarah Lawrence College, Bronxville, New York, 1948; Northcliffe Lecturer, University College, London, 1980; President's Distinguished Visitor, Vassar College, 1982. Recipient: Guggenheim fellowship, 1949, 1959; *Horizon* prize,

1949; American Academy grant, 1957; National Medal for Literature, 1984; MacDowell Medal, 1984. D.Let.: Syracuse University, New York, 1973; Bard College, 1976; D.Litt.: University of Hull, Yorkshire, 1974; Bowdoin College, Brunswick, Maine, 1981; University of Maine, Orono, 1982. Member, American Academy. Agent: A.M. Heath, 40–42 William IV Street, London WC2N 4DD, England. Address: Box 5, Castine, Maine 04421, U.S.A.

PUBLICATIONS

Novels

The Company She Keeps. New York, Simon and Schuster, 1942; London, Nicholson and Watson, 1943.
The Oasis. New York, Random House, 1949; as *A Source of Embarrassment*, London, Heinemann, 1950.
The Groves of Academe. New York, Harcourt Brace, 1952; London, Heinemann, 1953.
A Charmed Life. New York, Harcourt Brace, 1955; London, Weidenfeld and Nicolson, 1956.
The Group. New York, Harcourt Brace, and London, Weidenfeld and Nicolson, 1963.
Birds of America. New York, Harcourt Brace, and London, Weidenfeld and Nicolson, 1971.
Cannibals and Missionaries. New York, Harcourt Brace, and London, Weidenfeld and Nicolson, 1979.

Short Stories

Cast a Cold Eye. New York, Harcourt Brace, 1950; London, Heinemann, 1952.
The Hounds of Summer and Other Stories. New York, Avon, 1981.

Uncollected Short Stories

"The Company Is Not Responsible," in *New Yorker*, 22 April 1944.
"The Unspoiled Reaction," in *Modern Short Stories*, edited by Marvin Felheim and others. New York, Oxford University Press, 1951.

Other

Sights and Spectacles 1937–1956. New York, Farrar Straus, 1956; as *Sights and Spectacles: Theatre Chronicles 1937–1958*, London, Heinemann, 1959; augmented edition, as *Theatre Chronicles 1937–1962*, Farrar Straus, 1963.
Venice Observed: Comments on Venetian Civilization. Paris, Bernier, and New York, Reynal, 1956; London, Heinemann, 1961.
Memories of a Catholic Girlhood. New York, Harcourt Brace, and London, Heinemann, 1957.
The Stones of Florence. New York, Harcourt Brace, and London, Heinemann, 1959.
On the Contrary (essays). New York, Farrar Straus, 1961; London, Heinemann, 1962.
The Humanist in the Bathtub (essays). New York, New American Library, 1964.
Vietnam. New York, Harcourt Brace, and London, Weidenfeld and Nicolson, 1967.
Hanoi. New York, Harcourt Brace, and London, Weidenfeld and Nicolson, 1968.
The Writing on the Wall and Other Literary Essays. New York, Harcourt Brace, and London, Weidenfeld and Nicolson, 1970.

Medina. New York, Harcourt Brace, 1972; London, Wildwood House, 1973.
The Mask of State: Watergate Portraits. New York, Harcourt Brace, 1974.
The Seventeenth Degree. New York, Harcourt Brace, 1974; London, Weidenfeld and Nicolson, 1975.
Can There Be a Gothic Literature? (lecture). Amsterdam, Harmonie, 1975.
Ideas and the Novel. New York, Harcourt Brace, 1980; London, Weidenfeld and Nicolson, 1981.
La Traviata (story adaptation), music by Verdi. Boston, Little Brown, 1983.
Occasional Prose. New York, Harcourt Brace, and London, Weidenfeld and Nicolson, 1985.

Translator, *The Iliad; or, the Poem of Force*, by Simone Weil. New York, Politics, 1948.
Translator, *On the Iliad*, by Rachel Bespaloff. New York, Pantheon, 1948.

*

Bibliography: *Mary McCarthy: A Bibliography* by Sherli Goldman, New York, Harcourt Brace, 1968.

Manuscript Collection: Vassar College, Poughkeepsie, New York.

Critical Studies: "Mary McCarthy," in *A View of My Own* by Elizabeth Hardwick, New York, Farrar Straus, 1962, London, Heinemann, 1964; interview with Elisabeth Niebuhr, in *Paris Review*, Winter–Spring 1962; *Mary McCarthy* by Barbara McKenzie, New York, Twayne, 1966; *The Company She Kept* by Doris Grumbach, New York, Coward McCann, and London, Bodley Head, 1967; *Mary McCarthy*, Minneapolis, University of Minnesota Press, 1968, and *Fiction as Wisdom: From Goethe to Bellow*, University Park, Pennsylvania State University Press, 1980, both by Irvin Stock; *Mary McCarthy* by Willene Schaefer Hardy, New York, Ungar, 1981; interview with Carol Brightman, in *The Nation* (New York), Autumn 1984.

*   *   *

Mary McCarthy's America is a remarkably small country, inhabited by that equally small group of people she considers worth describing, or, since it amounts to the same thing, worth ridiculing. Her young women never seem to go further north than Wellfleet or further south than Washington Square. They come from well-off families, have been expensively educated in the east, and now live in New York or the Connecticut suburbs. They came of age—it would be misleading to say they "grew up"—during the middle years of the Depression, and were married young (and often unhappily) to men whose schools, professions, and attitudes are generally as predictable as their own. Of course a severely limited range of persons and places is not necessarily a handicap; but if a writer is to win anything like the respect and success Mary McCarthy has been enjoying for over 40 years, he needs some collateral virtues. In McCarthy's case, as everyone recognized from the start, the strength comes from her unerring gift for social satire, that species of comedy which thrives on recording the follies of groups rather than stray individuals. This placing of McCarthy works well enough—up to a certain point.

McCarthy's comments about the "comic" are useful here. In "Characters in Fiction" (*On the Contrary*) she asks, "Who

would deny that Stephen Dedalus ... seems less 'real' than Mr. Bloom and Molly, less 'real' than his father? In what does this 'reality' consist?" Her answer is as curious as it is revealing: Leopold and Molly Bloom, Falstaff and Mr. Micawber are "real" because of their "incorrigibility and changelessness." By some extraordinary sleight-of-hand McCarthy then makes the "real" and the "comic" synonymous. Heroes and heroines, she maintains, can learn their lessons and change, but "the comic element is the incorrigible element in every human being; the capacity to learn, from experience or instruction, is what is forbidden to all comic creations and to what is comic in you and me." This comic inability to learn and grow is thus more "real," more typical of the way the world is, than any heroic capacity to develop. What is involved here, then, is not simply a literary distinction but a whole set of assumptions about human nature itself. When we do encounter a hero in fiction, we "identify" with him and

> follow him with all our hopes, i.e., with our subjective conviction of human freedom; on the comic characters we look with despair, in which, though, there is a queer kind of admiration—we really, I believe, admire the comic characters *more* than we do the hero or the heroine, because of their obstinate power to do-it-again, combined with a total lack of self-consciousness and shame.

The comic mode is thus "the subjective as opposed to the objective"; but "subjective," for McCarthy, comes perilously close to meaning simply "egotistical," and as she soon suggests, we are left with an all too familiar paradox: we are subjects to ourselves, objects to others. Moreover, we are subjects to ourselves because of our own vanity; we need to *feel* we are free and able to change, whereas in fact we are largely what others see us as being, fixed comic "objects."

An important part of McCarthy's aim as a writer has always been to demonstrate that however free her characters may think they are, they are not free at all, and especially not free of that "subjective" self-love—here she is as obsessed as La Rochefoucauld—which makes them, in their own eyes, capable of growth and therefore some dignity. In passing she concedes that "the principle of growth is as real, of course (though possibly not so common), as the principle of eternity or inertia represented by the comic," but the concession is purely theoretical. No one in her world is free; and her claim that we "admire" the "power" of such characters to "do-it-again" could hardly be more deceptive. We are amused, as she means us to be, by, for example, the pathetic inability of Margaret Sargent, Henry Mulcahy, and Martha Sinnott, *not* to lie (and come to believe the lies), *not* to cheat, and *not* to pick, once again, the fatally wrong lover. Finally McCarthy's conception of comedy seems to have a firm classical basis; it is essentially the revelation of human failings, though not failings so extreme that they arouse in us complete disgust or contempt.

It is easy enough to list the comic objects in McCarthy's fiction. In *The Company She Keeps* and *Cast a Cold Eye* they are the bright young New Yorkers mentioned before; in *A Charmed Life* "creative" upper-Bohemians; in *The Oasis* self-righteous liberals and leftists; in *Cannibals and Missionaries* a deluded group of do-gooders hijacked en route to a futile humanitarian enterprise in Iran. The satire is all the more intriguing when McCarthy lets us glimpse, behind these figures, "real" people—Edmund Wilson, Dwight Macdonald, Philip Rahv, Eugene McCarthy, a good many others, and, always, McCarthy herself. *The Group*, which remains her best-known novel, is no different in kind. It is, she has explained, "a kind of mock-chronicle novel ... about the idea of progress ...

seen in the female sphere": "home economics, architecture, domestic technology, contraception, child-bearing, the study of technology in the home, in the play-pen, in the bed. It's supposed to be the history of the loss of faith in progress, in the idea of progress, during that twenty-year period." "Idea of progress" is perhaps too resounding a phrase: loss of faith in the possibility of fulfillment and, once again, growth would be more accurate. Even so, it is the author and her readers and not the characters themselves who come to realize what has become, on the verge of World War II, of the hopeful, energetic young Vassar graduates, Class of '33.

There is a good deal of cruelty in *The Group*, possibly more than McCarthy intended. And by this time attentive readers should have recognized that "satire" was no longer a very precise label for her art. Traditionally, or at least academically, satire has always been regarded as a kind of comedy which has as its goal the amendment of human folly. By definition, then, the satirist believes he has a remedy, some way of correcting the vices he records, either by urging a return to old values or by proposing a new set of standards. And it is precisely here that McCarthy is silent. She never suggests that things could be changed, never offers any prescriptions for amendment; the alternatives are no better than things she mocks. The fact that she fails to conform to an academic definition is of course irrelevant; but her unwillingness or inability to imagine something better makes her a writer considerably more despairing than readers seem to have realized. In this respect *Birds of America* is her most moving and revealing novel. An engaging young American, Peter Levi, intent on living by the Kantian ethic (treat others as ends in themselves, not as objects or means), encounters a series of rebuffs and disappointments during his junior year abroad. At the close of the novel he is recovering from one of these adventures when he sees a "tiny man" with "something to tell him" by his hospital bed:

He spoke in a low thin voice. "God is dead," Peter understood him to say. "I *know* that," he protested. "And you didn't say that anyway. Nietzsche did." He felt put upon, as though by an imposter. Kant smiled. "Yes, Nietzsche said that. And even when Nietzsche said it, the news was not new, and maybe not so tragic after all. Mankind can live without God." "I agree," said Peter. "I've always lived without him." "No, what I say to you is something important. You did not hear me correctly. Listen now, carefully and remember." Again he looked Peter steadily and searchingly in the eyes. "Perhaps you have guessed it. Nature is dead, *mein kind*."

There is muted anger in *Birds of America*, and despair, but eloquence as well, and no gratuitous cruelty. For the first time McCarthy has created a completely believable male character and given him the kind of humane sympathy she has always withheld from her central figures and the company they keep.

—Elmer Borklund

* * *

McELROY, Joseph (Prince). American. Born in Brooklyn, New York, 21 August 1930. Educated at Williams College, Williamstown, Massachusetts, 1947–51, B.A. 1951; Columbia University, New York, 1951–52, 1954–56, M.A. 1952, Ph.D. in English 1961. Served in the United States Coast Guard 1952–54. Married Joan Leftwich in 1961; one daughter. Instructor and Assistant Professor of English, University of New Hampshire, Durham, 1956–61. Since 1964, Professor of English, Queens College, City University of New York. Visiting Professor, Johns Hopkins University, Baltimore, 1976, Columbia University, 1978, and University of Paris, 1981. Writer-in-Residence, Northwestern University, Evanston, Illinois, 1977; Hurst Professor, Washington University, St. Louis, 1979. Recipient: Rockefeller grant, 1968; Ingram Merrill Foundation grant, 1970; Creative Artists Public Service grant, 1973; National Endowment for the Arts fellowship, 1973; Guggenheim fellowship, 1976; American Academy award, 1977. Agent: Georges Borchardt, 136 East 57th Street, New York, New York 10022, U.S.A.

PUBLICATIONS

Novels

A Smuggler's Bible. New York, Harcourt Brace, 1966; London, Deutsch, 1968.
Hind's Kidnap: A Pastoral on Familiar Airs. New York, Harper, 1969; London, Blond, 1970.
Ancient History. New York, Knopf, 1971.
Lookout Cartridge. New York, Knopf, 1974.
Plus. New York, Knopf, 1977.
Ship Rock, A Place: From Women and Men, A Novel in Progress. Concord, New Hampshire, Ewert, 1980.

Uncollected Short Stories

"The Accident," in *New American Review 2*, edited by Theodore Solotaroff. New York, New American Library, 1967.
"The Future," in *The Best American Short Stories 1981*, edited by Hortense Calisher and Shannon Ravenel. Boston, Houghton Mifflin, 1981.
"Departed Tenant," in *New Yorker*, 23 November 1981.

* * *

I hope that I am writing for readers who would be willing to commit themselves to a strenuous, adventurous fiction, but I don't write fiction of deliberate difficulty. What I believe I am doing is being, possibly in some new way I'm not sure about, a realist. In the collaboration between the syntax of my sentences and the observation of phenomena that is contained in my sentences, I think that I am being faithful as much as I can be to the world that I find with my senses and feel in the forms that are in my mind. I have a choice between going on as I have been or leavening and loosening and to some extent dissolving the surface obstacles that a reader finds reading me. I am trying to write easier prose because I don't think people have time for long books and I am not even sure the human race has a great deal of time. So I want to write easier prose, but what comes out continues to be a sentence which is packed and convoluted (interview with Thomas LeClair, in *Chicago Review*, Spring 1979).

From Melville and James to Faulkner and Pynchon, the most important American novelists have practiced the art of excess, have used mass and multiplicity to present new versions of complexity. Joseph McElroy has extended this tradition to bring into fiction the Age of Information, the world of cybernetics, computers, and space technology. McElroy loads, even overloads, his books with information and techniques that resist the reader to create what he calls "models," fictions that offer systems of relation more congruent with contemporary science than with the mechanism that one finds in most fiction. This description of McElroy's ambition—and achievement—is rather abstract, but the novels are specifically located in recent American life, rich in character and memory, feeling and concern for human survival. Information is used to provide new metaphors, microscopic and macroscopic ways of measuring family experience. While McElroy's originality and intelligence have unfortunately intimidated some readers, his is the kind of work, a fiction of the true leading edge, that seems bound to be valued as more readers come to know what McElroy knows and reflects in his five books.

The complexities of McElroy's first three novels, which lead up to the major achievement of *Lookout Cartridge*, can be suggested by comparing them with the works of writers McElroy discusses in his remarkable autobiographical/critical essay "Neural Neighborhoods and Other Concrete Abstracts" (*Tri-Quarterly 34*, 1975). *A Smuggler's Bible* is an exhaustive novel, similar to Gaddis's *The Recognitions*, about recovering and avoiding the past. McElroy's writer-hero attempts to smuggle himself across boundaries of time and temperament to his dead father, whom he both loves and fears. Like the Bible, the novel is composed of different books and styles; it is an imitative form of continuities and discontinuities, authentic acts and apocryphal gestures. In *Hind's Kidnap* McElroy returns to the search-for-a-father theme, this time using extreme Nabokovian word play to express the difficulty of connecting with the past. The novel's hero, Jack Hind, is a pastoral figure in an urban landscape who realizes, as he attempts to find a kidnapped boy and his own father, that the duplicity of language disallows him a detective's certainty. The languages of city and country, which Hind has used as clues, interpenetrate, foiling both separation and simple unity.

A Smuggler's Bible and *Hind's Kidnap* are ambitious and sophisticated, yet finally exploratory, books. *Ancient History* is less derivative and literary, more confident in the uses to which scientific language and abstract structures can be put. As the anthropologist Cy meditates on his relationship with the polymath Dom, Cy also considers his childhood friends Al and Bob. These A, B, C, D characters are presented as points in space, figures in a field composition influenced by physics. The various languages of space McElroy employs—historical, mathematical, astronomical—give vitality to the familiar materials of friendship and childhood.

Lookout Cartridge is, I think, one of the most underrated books of the decade. It does not humor the reader as Pynchon's *Gravity's Rainbow* does, but McElroy's novel equals that book in its awareness of power and "the great multiple field of impinging informations" in which we make our lives. The novel begins as a linear detective pursuit—the hero Cartwright's trying to locate a stolen film he has shot—and turns into a circling model of collaborating systems as Cartwright has to find his way through natural, political, technological, and spiritual networks of relation. Several dozen British and American characters, pipelines and capillaries of plot, Stonehenge, liquid crystals, cartography, cartridges, and much more combine for a new planetary realism, the plenitude of a fine-linked chain of being. Because McElroy seems to find the world's intricate connections—rather than arbitrarily invent them—*Lookout Cartridge* has the force of fact and the economy of fiction. The style of impacted homologies that McElroy has created is both illustrated and commented on in the following passage: "So much more: not only the idea of the sun cutting across the eyeball as if its vitreous arc were a gate giving a million alignments to that other energy the brain—oh not only the hot god or mere star or grid-fixed force passing from parallel

to parallel across that useful fiction the celestial sphere . . . each day each year each 26,000-year cycle of the whole solar system."

McElroy's most recent novel, *Plus*, is a short *tour de force* that brings together a stock science-fiction situation—a disembodied brain sent into space—and a radical experiment with language. As the brain, called Imp Plus, begins to grow, it develops its own singular consciousness, a hybrid of neurophysiology and Gertrude Stein. A moving story of recovery, *Plus* is also a coda to McElroy's career, for this orbiting consciousness Plus, like McElroy, sends back to earth original and large visions of human possibility few other minds have ventured. Plus means positive, and plus means more, and these two meanings also apply to McElroy's art of excess.

—Thomas LeClair

McEWAN, Ian (Russell). British. Born in Aldershot, Hampshire, 21 June 1948. Educated at Woolverstone Hall School; University of Sussex, Brighton, B.A. (honours) in English 1970; University of East Anglia, Norwich, M.A. in English 1971. Married Penny Allen in 1982; one son and two daughters. Recipient: Maugham Award, 1976; *Standard* award, for screenplay, 1983. Fellow, Royal Society of Literature, 1984. Address: c/o Jonathan Cape Ltd., 32 Bedford Square, London WC1B 3EL, England.

PUBLICATIONS

Novels

The Cement Garden. London, Cape, and New York, Simon and Schuster, 1978.
The Comfort of Strangers. London, Cape, and New York, Simon and Schuster, 1981.

Short Stories

First Love, Last Rites. New York, Random House, and London, Cape, 1975.
In Between the Sheets. London, Cape, 1978; New York, Simon and Schuster, 1979.

Uncollected Short Stories

"Intersection," in *Tri-Quarterly* (Evanston, Illinois), Fall 1975.
"Untitled," in *Tri-Quarterly* (Evanston, Illinois), Winter 1976.
"Deep Sleep, Light Sleeper," in *Harpers and Queen* (London), 1978.

Plays

The Imitation Game: Three Plays for Television (includes *Solid Geometry* and *Jack Flea's Birthday Celebration*). London, Cape, 1981; Boston, Houghton Mifflin, 1982.
Or Shall We Die? (oratorio), music by Michael Berkeley (produced London, 1983; New York, 1985). London, Cape, 1983.
The Ploughman's Lunch (screenplay). London, Methuen, 1985.

Screenplay: *The Ploughman's Lunch*, 1983.

Radio Play: *Conversation with a Cupboardman*, 1975.

Television Plays and Films: *Jack Flea's Birthday Celebration*, 1976; *The Imitation Game*, 1980; *The Last Day of Summer*, from his own short story, 1983.

*

Critical Studies: "*The Cement Garden* d'Ian McEwan" by Max Duperray, in *Études Anglaises* (Paris), vol. 35, no. 4, 1982; "McEwan/Barthes" by David Sampson, in *Southern Review* (Adelaide), March 1984.

*   *   *

With the publication of three books between 1975 and 1978, Ian McEwan was promoted during the late 1970's as one of the most exciting new talents in English fiction for many years, but he has not published a novel or collection of stories since 1981. Instant fame and excessive media hype are seldom propitious for the development of a gifted young writer because they arouse absurdly high expectations that he or she finds it impossible to fulfil. To some extent McEwan's recent silence may be the price he is paying for being over-praised and over-publicized too soon. Like Martin Amis, the other literary *enfant terrible* of the 1970's, McEwan won the Somerset Maugham Award for his first book, a collection of stories called *First Love, Last Rites*, which also achieved a *succès de scandale*. McEwan, like Amis, immediately acquired notoriety as a "shocking sensationalist" on the basis of work neither shocking nor sensational—except, it appears, in England. Admittedly, McEwan's subject matter is often potentially lurid and pornographic, with sex, perversion, and bodily functions featuring frequently, but his actual treatment of these is highly controlled and even reticent. It is easy to damn McEwan as obscene or praise him as liberated by isolating the "dirty" bits, but both responses reveal more about the commentators than about McEwan since they are based on misrepresentation.

Nevertheless, there is something obsessional in his early work, a quality not evident when his stories are read separately, but conspicuous enough when encountered in a collection. Several stories in *First Love, Last Rites* include scenes of male masturbation, and the title story involves copulation during menstruation. "Homemade" is about a teenage boy, determined to lose his virginity, who seduces his ten-year-old sister during a game of Mummies and Daddies; "Disguises" treats a teenage boy forced to dress as a girl; "Solid Geometry" features a pickled penis; "Butterflies" concerns a lonely man who almost inadvertently becomes the sex killer of a nine-year-old girl. McEwan's second collection, *In Between the Sheets*, is similar in this respect, featuring bondage, bestiality, a sex doll, and teenage lesbianism, while the first story, actually called "Pornography," culminates in a penis amputation performed as an act of revenge. Although *The Cement Garden*, his third book but first novel, is less replete with the more bizarre and deviant aspects of sexuality, it still contains incest, adolescent sex games, and childhood transvestism. Again there is a considerable emphasis on the sexually confused world of adolescents and teenagers, one of McEwan's favourite subjects and the impulse behind some of his best work.

Yet obsessional as he is, McEwan is no more a pornographer than T.S. Eliot is in that poem full of gloomy sexuality, *The Waste Land*. In a number of his stories, McEwan, too, is depicting an existential void, an emotional and spiritual waste land of frustration, lovelessness, non-communication, isolation, and *la nausée*, and he finds some of his objective correlatives in sexual behaviour. His reputation as a "shocking" writer has probably arisen not because he writes about sex and perversion but because he deals with them in such an anti-romantic and unerotic way. When he focuses on masturbation, or love-making with non-human substitutes, or the link between disease and sex, McEwan severs the connection between sex and meaningful fulfilment and is therefore radically undermining the importance sex has assumed in Western society as a substitute for religion, with orgasm replacing God. One thing McEwan most decidedly is not is titillating.

Sex is an important source of objective correlatives for McEwan, as it was for Eliot, but it is far from being the only one. It is significant that in the first paragraph of *First Love, Last Rites* the narrator of "Homemade" says, "this story is about Raymond and not about virginity, coitus, incest and self-abuse," suggesting that the sex, prominent though it is, is not there just for its own sake. In the ironically entitled "Butterflies" the images of widespread industrial decay, the "brown stinking water" of the canal, and the boys torturing a cat in a scrap yard, all correspond to the emotional sterility, stifled passion, and inner waste land of the narrator himself. The futuristic and dystopian "Two Fragments: March 199—" (*In Between the Sheets*), which is strongly reminiscent of Doris Lessing's *The Memoirs of a Survivor* in its prophetic portrayal of a disintegrating civilization, employs similar imagery to convey McEwan's bleak, joyless vision of the human condition. The house occupied by the orphaned children in *The Cement Garden*, a fable about the fallen and apparently irredeemable world of adolescence and therefore bearing some resemblance to Golding's *Lord of the Flies*, is an island in a sea of demolition and desolation, and the symbolism of this urban wilderness, like that of the nature-destroying cement garden itself, is as clear as those of the polluted Thames and the dust heaps in Dickens's *Our Mutual Friend*, to take an example other than *The Waste Land*.

McEwan's mastery of the short story is unquestionable. The outstanding example in his first collection is the title story, "First Love, Last Rites," a complex study of adolescence on the verge of adulthood, awakening to the potency of sexual love, the possibility of parenthood, and the reality of death. This compact and electrifying story builds up to a horrific climax with the brutal killing of a pregnant rat, an event that has a profound effect on the narrator. The title story of *In Between the Sheets* is also very memorable, but not perhaps as stunning as the longest and only American one in the collection, "Psychopolis," a word summing up the city where it is set, Los Angeles, the symbolic "unreal city" of many writers' waste land. While containing an abundance of the "outrageous" ingredients for which he is famous, this story is really about dislocation, incoherence, futility, and the impossibility of achieving wholeness in the pluralist, multi-faceted psychopolis we have created for ourselves where truth is so ambiguous and uncertain. The admirable technical control of his stories is not so evident in *The Cement Garden*, where the first-person narration by a teenager is less consistently sustained than it might be, the adolescent consciousness sometimes appearing to have an adult awareness of the situation. McEwan appears to have approached the writing of the longer form with some trepidation, and *The Cement Garden* might have been more satisfactory had it been concentrated into a long story rather than extended into a novel, short though it is.

With *The Cement Garden* McEwan exhausted one particular creative vein. This first phase has been much admired for the stylish power with which he conveys his own variant of the grotesque, but is not altogether immune to the charge that there is something intellectually modish in his underlying nihilism, morbidity, and gothicism. The first sign of an important and unexpected change of direction in his work was one of the best British television plays in recent years, *The Imitation Game*, which differs from his fiction of the 1970's in being conventionally realistic and commitedly polemical. Dealing with British intelligence during World War II, the play cogently yet subtly articulates an anti-war, pro-feminist argument about male hegemony and patriarchal values, especially the threat they pose to the future of civilization. McEwan's libretto for a television oratorio, *Or Shall We Die?*, specifically about the danger of a nuclear holocaust, presents similar ideas in a more overtly propagandist way. His only work of fiction since *The Cement Garden*, another short novel, *The Comfort of Strangers*, introduces related themes but much more obliquely and without the element of doctrinaire provocation appropriate to the mass medium of television but undesirable in the one-to-one author-reader relationship of fiction. Set in Venice, although neither the city nor its sights are ever mentioned by name, *The Comfort of Strangers* is an impressionistic, dream-like narrative that finally bursts into violent nightmare. By describing the encounter between an almost androgynous English couple on holiday in the city and a totally different couple they meet there, McEwan explores the nature of human relationships, especially between the sexes, and how patriarchal societies implicitly endorse domination and brutality. After the publication of *The Comfort of Strangers* John Fletcher said of McEwan that he might "turn out to be a mere nine-days'-wonder in the British literary scene"; having shed one skin, he still seems to be in pursuit of another.

—Peter Lewis

McGAHERN, John. Irish. Born in Dublin, 12 November 1934. Educated at St. Patrick's Training College, Dublin; University College, Dublin. Married Madeline Green in 1973. Primary school teacher, St. John the Baptist Boys School, Clontarf, 1963–70; Research Fellow, University of Reading, Berkshire, 1968–71; Visiting O'Connor Professor of Literature, Colgate University, Hamilton, New York, 1969, 1972, 1978, 1980; Northern Arts Fellow, University of Newcastle, 1974–76. Recipient: AE Memorial Award, 1962; Macauley fellowship, 1964; Arts Council award, 1966, 1968, 1971, 1978; Society of Authors travelling scholarship, 1975. Address: c/o Faber and Faber Ltd., 3 Queen Square, London WC1N 3AU, England.

PUBLICATIONS

Novels

The Barracks. London, Faber, 1963; New York, Macmillan, 1964.
The Dark. London, Faber, 1965; New York, Knopf, 1966.
The Leavetaking. London, Faber, 1974; Boston, Little Brown, 1975; revised edition, Faber, 1984.
The Pornographer. London, Faber, and New York, Harper, 1979.

Short Stories

Nightlines. London, Faber, 1970; Boston, Little Brown, 1971.

Getting Through. London, Faber, 1978; New York, Harper, 1980.
High Ground and Other Stories. London, Faber, 1985.

Plays

Sinclair (broadcast, 1971; produced London, 1972).

Radio Play: *Sinclair*, 1971.

Television Play: *Swallows*, 1975.

*   *   *

John McGahern achieved immediate fame with his first novel, *The Barracks*. The opening scene—a kitchen interior with a woman darning in the dying twilight, surrounded by her stepchildren—seemed as comfortable as the first act of an old Abbey play. What was new and startling was the quality of the writing; Irish provincial life had never been transcribed with such exactness before. Lovingly recorded, the details are yet presented without any protective sentimentality. Regionalists like Francis MacManus and Michael MacLaverty had evoked the details of Irish country life as part of a pattern, a way of belief, suggesting that unhurriedness was all. But McGahern rips all this away, showing that man, as well as nature, was as "red in tooth and claw" in Ireland as elsewhere: "They all lived on each other and devoured each other as they themselves were devoured, who would devour whom the first was the one question."

So Elizabeth Regan reflects at the end of her life, the end of the book. This brilliant study (especially for a young writer in his mid-twenties) of the mind of a dying woman inevitably recalls *Madame Bovary*, both in its subject-matter and the poetic detail of its style. But if McGahern's work is technically anachronistic there is a dimension of sympathy which is absent in Flaubert. Emma Bovary's death is recorded with clinical distaste; although there is a brief look of peace on her face when she receives the Last Sacraments, she never breaks through to the almost mystical acceptance of Elizabeth Regan: "All real seeing grew into smiling and if it moved to speech it must be praise."

The other main character in *The Barracks* is not a seducer but a police sergeant, more pathetic even than his sick wife in his baffled, male violence. This dominant figure appears again in *The Dark* where the ebb and flow of his struggle with his eldest son provide most of the structure of the book. Now all feminine gentleness has disappeared, and McGahern's keening rage against the emptiness of life takes over. Like the adolescent hero we are soiled and insulted by the ordeal of growing up under the double pressures of poverty and piety. Short chapters and flowing, often punctuationless sentences, leave no escape: we have moved from the calm detail of Flaubert to the involving claustrophobia of a Mauriac. But we are not allowed the grim consolations of Jansenism: it is not evil which rules the world but the hopeless clash of our needs: "It seemed that the whole world must turn over in the night and howl in its boredom. . . ."

There is no alleviation of this vision in his collection of stories, *Nightlines*, but there are some extensions of theme and background. "Summer in Strandhill," "Bomb Box," "Korea," still focus on the narrow world of childhood, with its humiliations and adult enforced boredom. There is, however, a more varied treatment of sex; the stories move from the familiar initiation theme of "Coming into His Kingdom," through the youthful frustration of "My Love, My Umbrella," to the analysis of a disintegrating marriage in "Peaches." The latter is set in Spain, but neither travel nor love can finally dissolve childhood patterns of guilt and conflict, and we are left with the crude message of the story about building site labourers in London, "Lungs of Oak and Bellies of Brass": "pork chops, pints of bitter and a good old ride before you sleep, that's fukken ambition." McGahern's stripped style, his emotional honesty, and his ear for dialogue make him a harrowing witness of the void which underlies a good deal of Irish, and perhaps modern, life.

To redeem that void there is only the meaning which memory can draw from the past, and the search for love in the present. "If I was lucky I'd find someone I liked as well as loved, the dream of a friend and a beloved in one, a person as well as a body." In *The Leavetaking* the protagonist has suffered a great hurt in his youth, the death by cancer of his beloved mother. Years later he discovers a love to redeem the old but because she is a divorcée he will have to leave his job as a teacher in a Catholic school. The book is structured around the ebb and flow of his thoughts, which later join or parallel those of his beloved. Only those who have been hurt, the implication is, can solace each other; she is guarded by a gigolo father whom, like the school authorities, the main character has to face down. It is a relatively slight novel, and the international world of the divorcée and her parasite father are more exhibited than felt, but there are tenderness and honesty in the love scenes—a new note in McGahern.

Getting Through again shows that McGahern can ring changes on the traditional Irish short story, but it is *The Pornographer*, a novel which seems to guy his twin obsessions with death and sex, which represents a real advance. "Write it like a life, but with none of life's unseemly infirmities," prescribes his editor, a failed poet, to the pornographer narrator. Meanwhile the latter's aunt is dying of cancer, and he gets involved with a woman, who gets pregnant and flees to London. This tragicomedy of "life's unseemly infirmities" ends with a funeral, like *The Barracks*, but the wild dance of opposites, country and town, love and death, Dublin and London, makes for a harsher, more ironic statement.

—John Montague

McGUANE, Thomas (Francis, III). American. Born in Wyandotte, Michigan, 11 December 1939. Educated at the University of Michigan, Ann Arbor; Olivet College, Michigan; Michigan State University, East Lansing, 1958–62, B.A. 1962; Yale University School of Drama, New Haven, Connecticut, 1962–65, M.F.A. 1965; Stanford University, California (Stegner Fellow), 1966–67. Married 1) Portia Rebecca Crockett in 1962 (divorced, 1975), one son; 2) the actress Margot Kidder in 1976 (divorced, 1977), one daughter; 3) Laurie Buffet in 1977, two daughters. Since 1968, free-lance writer and film director. Recipient: Rosenthal Foundation award, 1972. Agent: John Hawkins and Associates, 71 West 23rd Street, Suite 1600, New York, New York 10010. Address: c/o Random House Inc., 201 East 50th Street, New York, New York 10022, U.S.A.

PUBLICATIONS

Novels

The Sporting Club. New York, Simon and Schuster, 1968; London, Deutsch, 1969.

The Bushwhacked Piano. New York, Simon and Schuster, 1971.
Ninety-Two in the Shade. New York, Farrar Straus, 1973; London, Collins, 1974.
Panama. New York, Farrar Straus, 1978.
Nobody's Angel. New York, Random House, 1982.
Something to Be Desired. New York, Random House, 1984; London, Secker and Warburg, 1985.

Uncollected Short Stories

"Another Horse," in *Atlantic* (Boston), October 1974.
"To Skin a Cat," in *Tri-Quarterly* (Evanston, Illinois), Winter 1981.

Plays

The Missouri Breaks (screenplay). New York, Ballantine, 1976.

Screenplays: *The Bushwhacked Piano*, 1970; *Rancho Deluxe*, 1973; *The Missouri Breaks*, 1975; *Ninety-Two in the Shade*, 1975; *Tom Horn*, with Bud Shrake, 1980.

Other

An Outside Chance: Essays on Sport. New York, Farrar Straus, 1980.

*

Manuscript Collection: University of Rochester, New York.

Theatrical Activities:
Director: **Film**—*Ninety-Two in the Shade*, 1975.

Thomas McGuane comments:
I write fiction in the hope of astounding myself. I am seldom successful, and have long ago lost interest in the rest of my audience.

*   *   *

Thomas McGuane writes a new style novel of manners, crafted for an age in which the signs of behavior have become a self-conscious medium with the name of *semiotics*. We cannot know characters until we understand the codes by which they function—Henry James established that truth in his own mastery of the novel of manners. But in McGuane's world manners have become a topic themselves, and as his characters posture in a display of cultural signs the novelist is challenged to sort out the active from the reflexive. It is the drama between these two poles which creates the energy of McGuane's fiction.

His first novel, *The Sporting Club*, adapts the Hemingway code of sportsmanship and grace under pressure to contemporary times. There has been an apparent generational decline, as the descendants of a hundred-year-old sporting club destroy themselves and the camp in an atavistic fury. Two main characters, Stanton and Quinn, emerge as the contrary tendencies within the club's tribal framework: the spokesman for order, and the shamanistic "fiend" who by exaggerating all tendencies to disorder provides the tension which holds the group intact even as it threatens to fly apart. As in all of McGuane's novels, there is "a readiness for calamity . . . in the air," and expressing this sense allows the author scope for his best writing. Stanton "thrusts" rather than "steps," and transforms the club's civil practice of sport into a primeval combat. When Quinn himself reverts to Stanton's beliefs, the cycle is nearly complete, and is rounded off when a time-capsule reveals that the founders' genteel standards have been a sham all this time.

From the northern Michigan woods McGuane moves the action of his next three novels to the Florida Keys, "America's land's end" as he calls it, and within this context of intermingled exoticness and shabbiness he conducts his most thorough survey of manners. In *The Bushwhacked Piano* it is the region to which young Nicholas Payne flees with his girlfriend (who has decided to adopt "floozihood" with the ambition other girls her age would look forward to a prestigious woman's college). Payne has rejected the bland "Waring blender" world of his parents' suburbia, choosing instead to embrace the raw aspects of his country and its people with a sensuosity that infuses his prose. A motorcycle ride through a valley and out onto a beach is described with a heady sense of smell and sound; even an inventory of his girlfriend's room becomes a riot of unconnected materiality celebrated for its sense of being. "I am at large" is Payne's testimony to his role in life, and in his vision the extremes of America are created.

Ninety-Two in the Shade finds another drop-out, Thomas Skelton, leaving college for a life of guide-fishing in the Keys. Here he finds two alternative models of conduct, and even though he knows one is a sure road to destruction, he embraces it with a sense of destiny. "He had long since learned that the general view was tragic, but he had simultaneously learned that the trick was to become interested in something else. Look askance and it all shines on," which is Skelton's method for feasting on the manners of Key West while his own life rushes toward its destructive end. *Panama* transforms the typical McGuane hero into a rock star whose career and sanity are on the skids. Because of his inability to control his own poetic vision, he has destroyed everything of value around him. As a performer he is "paid to sum up civilization or to act it out in a glimmer," and as his rock theatrics become more bizarre the culture rushes ahead of him. One of contemporary fiction's best insights into drug use, *Panama* shows its central character walking a tightrope between life and death. In lucid moments between the effect of drugs one can appreciate "memory," which is "the only thing which keeps us from being murderers." Yet destruction predominates. "Something about our republic makes it go armed," the narrator confesses. "I myself am happier having a piece within reach, knowing that if some goblin humps into the path, it's away with him." In this subtle rhythm of cultural malevolence lies the novel's fascination.

Key West proved to be a burn-out for McGuane himself as well as for his characters, and his recent novels have been set in the harsher country of Montana, where nature conspires to enforce an isolated sense of stability and self-reliance on the characters McGuane now considers. *Nobody's Angel* finds an Army officer returning to his family's ranch, where he serves as the reflector of a narrative action whose language expresses his feelings of change and loss—from an empty water sluice which cooled milkcans before the supermarket days to a friend's Cadillac which is parked nose-up to the straw outside the barn. A devotee of lost causes, McGuane's protagonist invites danger and failure by falling in love with a married woman, largely because she is as unobtainable as the fantasy girlfriend he used to keep life at bay as a teenager. But as his barren west is peopled, he must flee it for a more pure legend of himself, living alone in Seville, Spain, from whence his old friends can concoct their own off-base fantasies of what his life is like.

With *Something to Be Desired* McGuane shows the ability to synthesize his work, using a Montana setting for the enactment of a carnival equal to any of the excesses of his previous novels. His protagonists have always gravitated toward living at the edge, and in this case Lucien Taylor withdraws from a conventional career and marriage in order to tempt fate by romancing the much wilder woman timidity kept him from years before. Yet even on the edge in Montana, where he begins an outlandish tourist resort attracting all types of crazies, he still finds that life is shrouded in a protective textuality. People relate via lines of dialogue instead of with meaningful statements, and roles are played more often than lives are lived. Yet Lucien is also a painter, and his artistic eye relates to nature better than to the thin, superficial social types around him, which gives him a higher goal.

McGuane's progress has been to celebrate the materiality of his fiction—the lilting song of his characters' language, especially the minor ones; the mad fandango of their behavior, especially when it counterpoints the narrator's more inquisitive action; and the special atmospheres of the regions about which he writes. Like his protagonists, these regions are always on the edge: in the northernmost woods of Michigan, at the extreme tip of Florida, and at America's virtual disappearance into perspective in the foothills of the Rocky Mountains. Finding the right words for each makes his fiction a success of language and image, providing readers with an aural picture of life in these places and times.

—Jerome Klinkowitz

McMURTRY, Larry (Jeff). American. Born in Wichita Falls, Texas, 3 June 1936. Educated at Archer City High School, Texas, graduated 1954; North Texas State College, Denton, B.A. 1958; Rice University, Houston, 1954, 1958–60, M.A. 1960; Stanford University, California (Stegner Fellow), 1960–61. Married Josephine Scott in 1959 (divorced, 1966); one son. Taught at Texas Christian University, Fort Worth, 1961–62, Rice University, 1963–64 and 1965, George Mason College, Fairfax, Virginia, 1970, and American University, Washington, D.C., 1970–71. Since 1971, owner, Booked Up Inc., antiquarian booksellers, Washington, D.C. Regular reviewer, Houston *Post* in 1960's, and Washington *Post* in 1970's; contributing editor, *American Film*, New York, 1975. Recipient: Guggenheim grant, 1964. Address: Booked Up Inc., 1209 31st Street N.W., Washington, D.C. 20007, U.S.A.

PUBLICATIONS

Novels

Horseman, Pass By. New York, Harper, 1961; as *Hud*, New York, Popular Library, 1963; London, Sphere, 1971.
Leaving Cheyenne. New York, Harper, 1963; London, Sphere, 1972.
The Last Picture Show. New York, Dial Press, 1966; London, Sphere, 1972.
Moving On. New York, Simon and Schuster, 1970; London, Weidenfeld and Nicolson, 1971.
All My Friends Are Going to Be Strangers. New York, Simon and Schuster, 1972; London, Secker and Warburg, 1973.
Terms of Endearment. New York, Simon and Schuster, 1975; London, W.H. Allen, 1977.

Somebody's Darling. New York, Simon and Schuster, 1978.
Cadillac Jack. New York, Simon and Schuster, 1982.
The Desert Rose. New York, Simon and Schuster, 1983; London, W.H. Allen, 1985.
Lonesome Dove. New York, Simon and Schuster, 1985; London, Pan, 1986.

Uncollected Short Stories

"The Best Day Since," in *Avesta* (Denton, Texas), Fall 1956.
"Cowman," in *Avesta* (Denton, Texas), Spring 1957.
"Roll, Jordan, Roll," in *Avesta* (Denton, Texas), Fall 1957.
"A Fragment from Scarlet Ribbons," in *Coexistence Review* (Denton, Texas), vol. 1, no. 2, 1958(?).
"There Will Be Peace in Korea," in *Texas Quarterly* (Austin), Winter 1964.
"Dunlop Crashes In," in *Playboy* (Chicago), July 1975.

Play

Screenplay: *The Last Picture Show*, with Peter Bogdanovich, 1971.

Other

In a Narrow Grave: Essays on Texas. Austin, Texas, Encino Press, 1968.
It's Always We Rambled: An Essay on Rodeo. New York, Hallman, 1974.
Larry McMurtry: Unredeemed Dreams, edited by Dorey Schmidt. Edinburgh, Texas, Pan American University, 1980.

*

Manuscript Collection: University of Houston Library.

Critical Studies: *Larry McMurtry* by Thomas Landess, Austin, Texas, Steck Vaughn, 1969; *The Ghost Country: A Study of the Novels of Larry McMurtry* by Raymond L. Neinstein, Berkeley, California, Creative Arts, 1976; *Larry McMurtry* by Charles D. Peavy, Boston, Twayne, 1977.

*   *   *

The literature of the American west forming the popular genre freezes the brief period when the cowboy roved the plains and peace officers and outlaws contended over the wealth of new settlements. Disregarding the process of historical change and contriving character on an heroic frame, the western projects a disconnected myth, a picture of the American past in the service of ideology. Larry McMurtry's grand accomplishment is a reconstruction of the story of the west that emplots the moment of the cowboy as a reference point in a saga of continuing change.

His first two novels dramatize past and present through contrast between the distinctive lives of cowboys and ranchers, the anachronism of the one and the increasingly business-like practice of the other. In *Horseman, Pass By* McMurtry uses the perspective of a 17-year-old boy to record the calamitous season when disease infects his grandfather's herd of cattle. The boy does not reflect upon events, but it is clear their theme is the passing of a way of ranching that had begun in the previous century. The cattle are destroyed by order of government agents acting to protect the commercial investment of the region, and Homer Bannon, too old to start anew, can do nothing but retreat mentally into his past. Arrogant, amoral

"Hud," Homer's stepson, speaks of resistance to the government as if he were a plains anarchist. Calamity, however, is simply an opportunity he grasps for gaining control of the ranch. Hud is a man of the future despite his cowboy's style.

Leaving Cheyenne pairs a genuine cowboy, Johnny, with another rancher, Gid, in a tale of the way their lives from boyhood to old age interweave through work and their mutual devotion to the spontaneous Molly. Johnny, the free worker, moves as he wishes, always content to be the hired hand, while Gid, despite unusual skills as a bronc buster, cannot help but be entranced by the thought of the money to be made dealing in cattle and land. Each man lives as a unique personality; yet, the casual joy experienced by the one and the guilt felt by the other in loving Molly urge the reader to understand them also as psycho-historical types. The rancher loves the land, but the desire to be its respectable master foreshadows eventual conversion to big business ranching. The cowboy acts as the complete individualist but however attractive that may be in myth, the cowboy's individualism is misplaced in a present where his craft is no longer essential.

In the novels he published during the 1970's McMurtry moved forward into the present that once was the future for Hud and Johnny. As regional life no longer provides definition he relates the tales of people in the medium of cities and mass culture. Restless characters pair briefly until they change their lives by acquiring new sexual partners and irresolutely devote themselves to role after role. Passing through the concretely realized settings of the rodeo circuit and the graduate student community Pete and Patsy Carpenter of *Moving On* speak a language reminiscent of the source of their affluence in an older Texas, but each of the cultural orbits into which they veer is a second-hand interpretation of reality. The rodeo, which Pete wishes to capture in a book of photographs, is a ritualization of cowboy skill; a motion picture he works on idealizes a rodeo celebrity; and the graduate study of literature consists of boning up on criticism and making fetishes of first editions. The memorialized past no longer has use; it has become currency of exchange among the alienated.

A character named Danny Deck who is briefly introduced in *Moving On* as a sort of tragic hero for the rootless young people becomes the main figure in *All My Friends Are Going to Be Strangers*. His story presents the dilemma of the new free-floating culture. Deck, as restless as his contemporaries, nevertheless attains the control to complete a novel, but the achievement is insufficient to give him security. He wades into a river, like a land-locked Martin Eden, destroying his work and himself. The act is both an assertion of residual individualism and evidence of hopelessness before the task of discovering what values might be created in the new America.

It would be an error to see the themes of these works as solemn or mordant, for each of McMurtry's novels is located in the range of comic distance, and the compelling expressions of particularity in character behavior keep our attention upon immediate events. Thus, *The Last Picture Show*, an early work, evokes first of all recognition of the foolish-serious ways high-school-age boys center their lives upon gratification of their sexual needs. The lives of adults appearing also in terms of instincts enter the story first as backdrop then gradually become future options. And, though integrity eludes the characters of the 1970's fiction, it is present in the author's striking portrayal of such characters as Aurora Greenway who dominates the narrative in *Terms of Endearment* or in the shifting perspectives on Jill Peel's advancement as a film artist in *Somebody's Darling*.

The cross-references among McMurtry's 1970's novels, and their portrayal of a loosely acquainted cast of contemporary figures surfacing in each others' picaresque lives give the impression of a chronicle of the times. In his most recent work, however, the scope has broadened as McMurtry's imagination moves into additional corners of life that may be seen as part of a narrative history in which the west is central. *Cadillac Jack* relates the story of a wanderer whose trade as a scout for antiques gives him a role as practical historian. A cast of Washington, D.C. eccentrics in supporting positions and a set of adventures that includes discovery of a plan to sell off the plundered treasures of the Smithsonian Institution gives this keeper of the material records of society a stage on which he performs as though a cowboy with historical consciousness.

McMurtry is deservedly acclaimed for his representation of women, and to the list of fine portrayals that includes Molly of *Leaving Cheyenne*, Aurora of *Terms of Endearment*, and the woman and girls of *Cadillac Jack* can be added the central character of *The Desert Rose*. The showgirl who simply displays her glamour but neither sings nor dances is a figure from an earlier period in Las Vegas, so Harmony who was nearly legendary as the most beautiful showgirl in town will be replaced as she reaches the advanced age of 39. Survivor that she is, Harmony comes through the personal exploitation by husbands, lovers, and employers and the larger social exploitation imaged in the glamour world of Vegas with cheer and humanity that must be McMurtry's testament to female resilience.

With *Lonesome Dove* McMurtry has produced the foundation for all of his previous work. This long novel about a cattle drive from Texas to Montana is set in the year of the national centennial, which is also the date of Custer's last stand and the beginning of the cowboy's heyday. As though to supplant the myths surrounding those events, *Lonesome Dove* builds upon detail of foreground landscape, vascular spoken language, vital character description, and the specifics of hardship. The result is an authenticity of narrative that works like realism at its best. Yet as the story progresses, taking the cowhands and their herd into new lands and returning with the body of one of the dead protagonists to the starting place on the Rio Grande, the reader realizes that here is a novel rendering the origin of the culture of the American west. Divested of myth and informed by an understanding that our history is continuous, *Lonesome Dove* shows us the source of the characters who people McMurtry's fiction and tells us also much about the framework of contemporary America.

—John M. Reilly

McPHERSON, James A(lan). American. Born in Savannah, Georgia, 16 September 1943. Educated at Morris Brown College, Atlanta, 1961–63, 1965, B.A. 1965; Morgan State College, Baltimore, 1963–64; Harvard University, Cambridge, Massachusetts, LL.B. 1968; University of Iowa, Iowa City, M.F.A. 1971. Married in 1973 (divorced); one daughter. Instructor, University of Iowa Law School, 1968–69; Lecturer in English, University of California, Santa Cruz, 1969–70; Assistant Professor of English, Morgan State University, 1975–76; Associate Professor of English, University of Virginia, Charlottesville, 1976–81. Since 1981, Professor of English, University of Iowa. Guest editor of fiction issues of *Iowa Review*, Iowa City, 1984, and *Ploughshares*, Cambridge, Massachusetts, 1985. Since 1969, contributing editor, *Atlantic Monthly*, Boston. Recipient: *Atlantic* "Firsts" Award, 1968;

American Academy award, 1970; Guggenheim fellowship, 1972; Pulitzer Prize, 1978; MacArthur Foundation award, 1981. Agent: Brandt and Brandt, 1501 Broadway, New York, New York 10036. Address: 711 Rundell Street, Iowa City, Iowa 52240, U.S.A.

PUBLICATIONS

Short Stories

Hue and Cry.   Boston, Little Brown, and London, Macmillan, 1969.
Elbow Room.   Boston, Little Brown, 1977.

Uncollected Short Story

"There Was Once a State Called Franklin," in *Callaloo* (Lexington, Kentucky), May 1979.

Other

Railroad: Trains and Train People in American Culture, with Miller Williams.   New York, Random House, 1976.

*   *   *

In two collections of brilliant short fiction, James A. McPherson has surveyed contemporary black American culture and defined its sensibility. His work, sharply realistic and dramatic, focuses on the connections and abrasions of black and white individuals in our time. The insights accumulated in the stories form a comprehensive mosaic of U.S. life as viewed by black citizens.

Hue and Cry, McPherson's first collection, revolves around the world of work and black positions in it. The stories deal with "traditional" black occupations—waiter, Pullman porter, stockboy, janitor—from the inside, where each position is a window on the white world. McPherson's controlled, incisive style offers shrewdly defined character-types almost mythic in proportion. Stories like "A Solo Song: For Doc," which describes the end of a man's lifelong career as a railroad waiter, offer important illuminations on daily life for black people in America. "Gold Coast" and "Hue and Cry," two of the best-known stories of the book, deal directly with the tensions and tragic ironies of black-white sexual relationships.

The stories in *Elbow Room* are more complex extensions of McPherson's concerns. His narrative style is often dense and subtle, but his focus is still on archetypal characters and situations. "The Story of a Dead Man," for example, is a kind of bad-man ballad contrasting a near-mythic "bad nigger" with his educated, upwardly mobile nephew. This "Railroad Bill" character is a fighting, lying wanderer whose existence embarrasses blacks aspiring to gentility in white middle-class terms. The same theme emerges in "Elbow Room," which describes the marriage of a young white draft-resister to a sharp, urbane black woman. It is narrated by a black consciousness tormented with problems of definition. The young white man is obsessed with the question "What is a nigger?" He finally bursts out:

> "At *least* I tried! At *least* I'm *fighting!* And I know what a *nigger* is, too. It's what you are when you begin thinking of yourself as a work of art!"
>
> I did not turn to answer, although I heard him clearly. I am certain there was no arrogance at all left in his voice.

James McPherson has used the medium of the short story to extend the intense meditations on black Americans begun by

Ralph Ellison in *Invisible Man.* McPherson's stories are carefully crafted, subtle and penetrating observations of the range and variety of the contemporary black experience. His characters are vivid storytellers, too, and he captures their inflections and idioms precisely. His people—black and white—struggle to know themselves and each other, to penetrate the barriers of appearances to the central mysteries of being. As the narrator of "Just Enough for the City" expresses it:

> I think love must be the ability to suspend one's intelligence for the sake of something. At the basis of love therefore must be imagination. Instead of thinking always "*I am I,*" to love one must be able to feelingly conjugate the verb *to be.* Intuition must be part of the circuitous pathway leading ultimately to love.

This seeking for love and identity, love for self and others, the world itself, is at the center of McPherson's stories. His people become visible to others because they learn to see themselves.

—William J. Schafer

METCALF, John (Wesley). Canadian. Born in Carlisle, Cumberland, England, 12 November 1938. Educated at Bristol University, 1957–61, B.A. (honours) in English 1960, Cert. Ed. 1961. Married 1) Gail Courey in 1965 (marriage dissolved, 1972), one daughter; 2) Myrna Teitelbaum in 1975, one stepson and two adopted children. Taught at a secondary school and a boys' borstal, Bristol, 1961, Rosemount High School, Montreal, 1962–63, Royal Canadian Air Force Base, Cold Lake, Alberta, 1964–65, at a Catholic comprehensive school in England, 1965, and at schools and universities in Montreal, part-time, 1966–71. Writer-in-Residence, University of New Brunswick, Fredericton, 1972–73, Loyola College, Montreal, 1976, University of Ottawa, 1977, Concordia University, Montreal, 1980–81, and University of Bologna, Italy, 1985. Recipient: Canada Council award, 1968, 1969, 1971, 1974, 1976, 1978, 1980, 1983; University of Western Ontario President's Medal, for short story, 1969. Address: P.O. Box 2700, Station D, Ottawa, Ontario K1P 5W7, Canada.

PUBLICATIONS

Novels

Going Down Slow. Toronto, McClelland and Stewart, 1972.
Girl in Gingham. Ottawa, Oberon Press, 1978; as *Private Parts: A Memoir*, Scarborough, Ontario, Macmillan–New American Library of Canada, 1980.
General Ludd. Downsview, Ontario, ECW Press, 1980.

Short Stories

New Canadian Writing 1969, with C.J. Newman and D.O. Spettigue. Toronto, Clarke Irwin, 1969.
The Lady Who Sold Furniture. Toronto, Clarke Irwin, 1970.
The Teeth of My Father. Ottawa, Oberon Press, 1975.
Dreams Surround Us: Fiction and Poetry, with John Newlove. Delta, Ontario, Bastard Press, 1977.
Selected Stories. Toronto, McClelland and Stewart, 1982.

Other

Kicking Against the Pricks (essays). Downsview, Ontario, ECW Press, 1982.

Editor, with others, *Wordcraft 1–5* (textbooks). Toronto, Dent, 5 vols., 1967–77.
Editor, *Razor's Edge*, by Somerset Maugham. Richmond Hill, Ontario, Irwin, 1967.
Editor, *The Flight of the Phoenix*, by Elleston Trevor. Scarborough, Ontario, Bellhaven House, 1968.
Editor, *Daughter of Time*, by Josephine Tey. Richmond Hill, Ontario, Irwin, 1968.
Editor, with Gordon Callaghan, *Rhyme and Reason.* Toronto, Ryerson Press, 1969.
Editor, with Gordon Callaghan, *Salutation.* Toronto, Ryerson Press, 1970.
Editor, *Sixteen by Twelve: Short Stories by Canadian Writers.* Toronto, Ryerson Press, and New York, McGraw Hill, 1970.
Editor, *The Narrative Voice: Short Stories and Reflections by Canadian Authors.* Toronto, McGraw Hill Ryerson, 1972.
Editor, *Kaleidoscope: Canadian Stories.* Toronto, Van Nostrand, 1972.
Editor, *The Speaking Earth: Canadian Poetry.* Toronto, Van Nostrand, 1973.
Editor, with Joan Harcourt, *76 [77]: Best Canadian Stories.* Ottawa, Oberon Press, 2 vols., 1976–77.
Editor, with Clark Blaise, *Here and Now.* Ottawa, Oberon Press, 1977.
Editor, with Clark Blaise, *78 [79, 80]: Best Canadian Stories.* Ottawa, Oberon Press, 3 vols., 1978–80.
Editor, *Stories Plus: Canadian Stories with Authors' Commentaries.* Toronto, McGraw Hill Ryerson, 1979.
Editor, *New Worlds: A Canadian Collection of Stories.* Toronto, McGraw Hill Ryerson, 1980.
Editor, *First [Second, Third] Impressions.* Ottawa, Oberon Press, 3 vols., 1980–82.
Editor, with Leon Rooke, *81 [82]: Best Canadian Stories.* Ottawa, Oberon Press, 2 vols., 1981–82.
Editor, *Making It New: Contemporary Canadian Stories.* Toronto, Methuen, 1982.
Editor, with Leon Rooke, *The New Press Anthology 1–2: Best Canadian Short Fiction.* Toronto, General, 2 vols., 1984–85.

*

Manuscript Collections: Special Collections, University of Calgary, Alberta; University of Maine, Orono.

Critical Studies: *On the Line* by Robert Lecker, Downsview, Ontario, ECW Press, 1982, and article by Douglas Rollins, in *Canadian Writers and Their Works 7* edited by Lecker, Jack David, and Ellen Quigley, ECW Press, 1985; "John Metcalf Issue" of *Malahat Review 70* (Victoria, British Columbia).

*   *   *

When one realizes why so little commentary has been devoted to John Metcalf's fiction, one also understands the unique quality of his work: his prose is so chaste, so uncompromisingly direct, that exegesis often seems to be redundant.

But to be seduced by this directness is to ignore the extraordinary narrative compression which multiplies the weight of Metcalf's words and to miss the ideas he develops through his concentration on things. As a mature writer, Metcalf advises the novice to "avoid literary criticism which moves away from the word on the printed page" and to "stick to the study of the placement of commas." Only through this study, and by knowing "the weight, colour, and texture of *things*" will the writer create "the distillation of experience" that makes fiction valid.

The terminology here suggests that Metcalf is a traditionalist, and he is. He believes that a plot should be interesting, mysterious, and constructed in such a way that it will endure. He is concerned with the morality of his characters and their culture. His stories are generally realistic in their emphasis on the details of time and place. Above all, he is preoccupied with a traditional theme: the relationship between art and human experience. Consequently his stories explore the nature of the aesthetic process and the ingredients from which his own art is composed.

The Lady Who Sold Furniture contains several stories in which the nature of art and the nature of learning about art are explored through a central character who is sensitive, intelligent, and in the process of learning about himself as he learns about his world. In the title novella, Peter's encounter with Jeanne forces him to examine his own values and his responsibility as a teacher. "The Tide Line" presents a younger protagonist, but one who must also define his future—here explicitly connected with art—against the influence of his parents and the various forms of tradition their presence implies. "Keys and Watercress," one of Metcalf's most anthologized stories (along with "Early Morning Rabbits" from the same collection), again focuses on the initiation of a young boy into a world of symbols, and, by extension, into a new world that can be transformed through imagination. If the stories seem self conscious it is because they are actually self critical. Here, as in his later fiction, Metcalf uses the story to explore the value of storytelling itself.

This self-critical stance is certainly revealed in his first novel, *Going Down Slow*, through the character of David Appelby, a teacher who is obviously involved with the conflict between his ideals—both aesthetic and political—and those held by a provincial social order that would stifle all forms of personal expression, be they social, sexual, or cerebral. The novel's episodic form suggests that it is the first long work of a writer who really feels most at home in the short-story mode. Nevertheless, it provides a strong sense of Metcalf's finicky attention to detail, and to the linguistic precision that is the hallmark of all his writing.

The Teeth of My Father, a second short-story collection, revealed a much more mature writer than the earlier works. Metcalf's language is tighter than before; his attention to structure is more sophisticated and complex; and the stories are increasingly autobiographical and overtly concerned with the implications of story-telling. Five of the stories focus explicitly on art and artists, often in allegorical terms. Metcalf is most successful in "Gentle As Flowers Make the Stones," a bitter, complex, and ultimately poignant record of one day in the life of the poet Jim Haine; in "The Years in Exile," a moving record of a senescent, displaced writer's thoughts; and in the title story, in which the antiphonal structure suggests an implicit exchange between writer and critic, significant because it allows Metcalf to assume the role of self-commentator, the role his fiction seems to seek from its inception.

In *Girl in Gingham* his commentary is expressed through Peter Thornton, whom we meet after the divorce that isolates him, shakes his sense of identity, and forces him to attempt some form of personal recovery by finding a new, ideal woman. The juxtaposition of Peter's educated sensibility with the tastelessness and frequently grotesque lifestyles of successive CompuMate dates invests the novella with a sustained level of comedy that tends to mask Peter's tragic desperation. Peter's encounters with the CompuMate women provide a fertile ground for Metcalf to satirize the debased values of contemporary society. But Peter's failure in those encounters, and Anna's fate, are connected with a death of taste that Metcalf increasingly mourns. As the story develops it becomes clear that for Peter the pursuit of true art is inseparable from the pursuit of true love. Because the search for an ideal girl in gingham is part of Peter's quest for aesthetic fulfillment, he becomes more and more preoccupied with art as his relationship with Anna takes form.

This preoccupation is even more obvious in *Private Parts*, Metcalf's third published novella. Here the narrator is all-too-conscious of the aesthetic implications arising from the autobiographical fragments he presents. "Life," as T.D. Moore sees it, is "mainly lies." In short, life in *Private Parts* is private art. It comes as no surprise to discover that Moore is himself a writer dedicated to mythologizing those autobiographical fragments which constitute the private parts of memory. In him we find the qualities and frustrations that define all of Metcalf's highly articulate first-person narrators: an ability to fashion life through meaning; a rejection of contemporary taste and the threat it poses to genuine creativity; an involvement in others' art; and a consciousness of being involved in the narrative structure of his tale.

Metcalf's second novel makes his criticism of contemporary society hard to ignore. *General Ludd* takes its name from the 19th-century Luddite movement's radical opposition to so-called "progress" through technology and mechanization. Metcalf's Jim Wells is a contemporary Luddite, and a poet, who takes exception to the debased forms of communication—be they audio-visual, sartorial, or verbal—that seem ever-present in his world. No summary of this kind can do justice to the range of Metcalf's ferocious satire, or to his exposition of a host of characters through powerful vignettes, or to the continual purity of his language. Although the success of *Ludd* as a novel is still in debate, what cannot be questioned is Metcalf's dedication to his craft, or his reputation as one of Canada's most accomplished fiction writers.

—Robert Lecker

MICHAELS, Leonard. American. Born in New York City, 2 January 1933. Educated at the High School for Music and Art, New York, graduated 1949; New York University, 1949–53, B.A. 1953; University of Michigan, Ann Arbor, M.A. 1956, PhD. 1967. Married 1) Priscilla Older in 1966 (divorced), two sons; 2) Brenda Hillman in 1976, one daughter. Taught at Paterson State College, New Jersey, 1961–62; Assistant Professor of English, University of California, Davis, 1967–69. Since 1970, Professor of English, University of California, Berkeley. Since 1977, editor, *University Publishing* review, Berkeley. Recipient: National Endowment for the Arts grant, 1967; *Massachusetts Review* award, 1969, 1970; Guggenheim fellowship, 1970; American Academy Award, 1971. Agent: Lynn Nesbit, International Creative Management, 40 West 57th Street, New York, New York 10019. Address: Department of English, University of California, Berkeley, California 94720, U.S.A.

PUBLICATIONS

Novel

The Men's Club. New York, Farrar Straus, and London, Cape, 1981.

Short Stories

Going Places. New York, Farrar Straus, 1969; London, Weidenfeld and Nicolson, 1970.
I Would Have Saved Them If I Could. New York, Farrar Straus, 1975.

Uncollected Short Stories

"Words for Penis," in *Tri-Quarterly* (Evanston, Illinois), Winter 1976.
"Pretty Women," "Imagine a Man," and "You," in *American Review 26*, edited by Theodore Solotaroff. New York, Bantam, 1977.
"Toiler," in *Partisan Review* (Boston), vol. 51, 1984.
"The Statue of John Wayne," in *Antaeus* (New York), Spring 1984.
"The Abandoned Farmhouse," in *Grand Street* (New York), Summer 1984.

Other

Editor, with Christopher Ricks, *The State of the Language.* Berkeley, University of California Press, 1980.

*

Leonard Michaels comments:

My writing tends to be terse and quick, usually about urban types and the kinds of psychological violence they inflict upon one another. I have no philosophical or political messages. My work depends on traditional beliefs.

*   *   *

Leonard Michaels's fiction is not easily described—it resists categories. It is realistic, but its dominant feature is irrationality of plot, sometimes comic, sometimes tragic, sometimes both at once. It is symbolic in its depiction of urban life, but its meanings are never reducible to messages, never allegorical. It is surreal and fragmented, but there is a consistency of viewpoint which can tie stories together and make for an overall coherence not to be found in the individual pieces. It reflects, sometimes self-consciously, the influence of such writers as Kafka, Roth, Malamud, Barthelme, and Borges, but it is nevertheless distinctive and compelling. At their best, Michaels's stories are intense, active, and imaginative; they can also be vague and even incomprehensible.

Michaels's fiction has been published in two thin volumes of stories, *Going Places* and *I Would Have Saved Them If I Could*, and one short novel, *The Men's Club*, which is also really a collection of stories. Most of the earlier pieces consist of brief glimpses of contemporary urban existence, full of bizarre incidents meant to suggest the unnatural condition of city life: a naked boy is denied entrance to the subway for lack of a token; a couple maim each other in a fight and then decide to marry; a Talmudic scholar slips on an icy street and is assumed to be a drunken derelict; by never speaking in class, a professor of philosophy wins a reputation for profundity; an honors graduate preferring to make a living by driving a cab is beaten gratuitously; a boy spying on his rabbi making love falls to his death; a telephone call to a friend's apartment reaches the burglar there. Usually some form of intense, though often anonymous, sexual encounter begins or ends the story. In all of this there is the recognition of the craziness of things and yet of their plausibility—at least so long as the setting is New York City.

The element that provides continuity in both volumes is the "central intelligence" of a recurring character, Phillip Liebowitz. Identified in many stories, present as unnamed narrator in others, he is a self-proclaimed, street-wise "city boy." In story after story he experiences strange twists of fate, absurd reversals of normal expectations, but being a New Yorker he takes all in his stride.

Michaels's stories are full of plot, but except for Phillip Liebowitz there are no real persons, and even Phillip emerges as a character not in any particular story but only in the collection as a whole. His contact with others is almost entirely in a sexual context: the women in the stories are merely objects of his lust, the other men his rivals for their favors. Through sexual conquest, Phillip asserts his existence and a degree of control over the hostile urban environment. But none of this is explicit; there are no explanations, only actions.

Although novelistic in form, *The Men's Club* is strongly reminiscent of Michaels's story collections. A group of men get together to form what might be called a consciousness-raising group. They decide that each will tell the story of his life, but what we get instead are fragments of stories, not biographical data but moments of intense self-awareness. As in a group of Chaucer tales (one of the characters is named Canterbury), there is a recurring theme: the fascinating power of women over men. These husbands who come together this evening specifically to be free of women can speak of nothing but their wives and lovers, women they have lived with for many years, women they spent a few moments with many years before. The anecdotes, like all Michaels's stories, lack endings. When one character complains that he did not get the point of another's story, the narrator expresses views which apply to all Michaels's fiction: "Doesn't matter ... I don't get it either. I could tell other stories that have no point. This often happens to me. I start to talk, thinking there is a point, and then it never arrives. What is it, anyhow, this point? Things happen. You remember. That's all. If you take a large perspective, you'll realize there never is a point."

—Robert E. Lynch

———

MICHENER, James A(lbert). American. Born in 1907(?); brought up by foster parents. Educated at Doylestown High School, Pennsylvania; Swarthmore College, Pennsylvania, A.B. (summa cum laude) 1929 (Phi Beta Kappa); University of Northern Colorado, Greeley, A.M. 1936; University of St. Andrews, Scotland. Served in the United States Navy, 1944–45: Lieutenant Commander. Married 1) Patti Koon in 1935 (divorced, 1948); 2) Vange Nord in 1948 (divorced, 1955); 3) Mari Yoriko Sabusawa in 1955. Master, Hill School, Pottstown, Pennsylvania, 1929–31, and George School, Newtown,

Pennsylvania, 1934–36; Professor, University of Northern Colorado, 1936–40; Visiting Professor, Harvard University, Cambridge, Massachusetts, 1940–41; associate editor, Macmillan Company, New York, 1941–49. Since 1949, free-lance writer. Member, Advisory Committee on the Arts, United States Department of State, 1957; Chairman, President Kennedy's Food for Peace Program, 1961; Secretary, Pennsylvania Constitution Convention, 1967–68; member of the Advisory Committee, United States Information Agency, 1970–76, and NASA, 1980–83. Since 1983, member of the Board, International Broadcasting. Recipient: Pulitzer Prize, 1948; National Association of Independent Schools award, 1954, 1958; Einstein Award, 1967; National Medal of Freedom, 1971. D.H.L.: Rider College, Lawrenceville, New Jersey, 1950; Swarthmore College, 1954; LL.D.: Temple University, Philadelphia, 1957; Litt.D.: Washington University, St. Louis, 1967; Yeshiva University, New York, 1974; D.Sc.: Jefferson Medical College, Philadelphia, 1979. Address: c/o Random House Inc., 201 East 50th Street, New York, New York 10022, U.S.A.

PUBLICATIONS

Novels

The Fires of Spring. New York, Random House, 1949; London, Corgi, 1960.
The Bridges at Toko-Ri. New York, Random House, and London, Secker and Warburg, 1953.
Sayonara. New York, Random House, and London, Secker and Warburg, 1954.
The Bridge at Andau. New York, Random House, and London, Secker and Warburg, 1957.
Hawaii. New York, Random House, 1959; London, Secker and Warburg, 1960.
Caravans. New York, Random House, 1963; London, Secker and Warburg, 1964.
The Source. New York, Random House, and London, Secker and Warburg, 1965.
The Drifters. New York, Random House, and London, Secker and Warburg, 1971.
Centennial. New York, Random House, and London, Secker and Warburg, 1974.
Chesapeake. New York, Random House, and London, Secker and Warburg, 1978; selections published as *The Watermen*, Random House, 1979.
The Covenant. New York, Random House, and London, Secker and Warburg, 1980.
Space. New York, Random House, and London, Secker and Warburg, 1982.
Poland. New York, Random House, 1983; London, Secker and Warburg, 1984.
Texas. New York, Random House, and London, Secker and Warburg, 1985.

Short Stories

Tales of the South Pacific. New York, Macmillan, 1947; London, Collins, 1951.
Return to Paradise. New York, Random House, and London, Secker and Warburg, 1951.

Other

The Unit in the Social Studies, with Harold M. Long. Cambridge, Massachusetts, Harvard University Graduate School of Education, 1940.

The Voice of Asia. New York, Random House, 1951; as *Voices of Asia*, London, Secker and Warburg, 1952.
The Floating World (on Japanese art). New York, Random House, 1954; London, Secker and Warburg, 1955.
Rascals in Paradise, with A. Grove Day. New York, Random House, and London, Secker and Warburg, 1957.
Selected Writings. New York, Modern Library, 1957.
Japanese Prints from the Early Masters to the Modern. Rutland, Vermont, Tuttle, and London, Paterson, 1959.
Report of the County Chairman. New York, Random House, and London, Secker and Warburg, 1961.
The Modern Japanese Print: An Introduction. Rutland, Vermont, Tuttle, 1962.
Iberia: Spanish Travels and Reflections. New York, Random House, and London, Secker and Warburg, 1968.
Presidential Lottery: The Reckless Gamble in Our Electoral System. New York, Random House, and London, Secker and Warburg, 1969.
The Quality of Life. Philadelphia, Lippincott, 1970; London, Secker and Warburg, 1971.
Facing East: A Study of the Art of Jack Levine. New York, Random House, 1970.
Kent State: What Happened and Why. New York, Random House, and London, Secker and Warburg, 1971.
A Michener Miscellany 1950–1970, edited by Ben Hibbs. New York, Random House, 1973; London, Corgi, 1975.
About "Centennial": Some Notes on the Novel. New York, Random House, 1974.
Sports in America. New York, Random House, 1976; as *Michener on Sport*, London, Secker and Warburg, 1976.
In Search of Centennial: A Journey. New York, Random House, 1978.
Testimony. Honolulu, White Knight, 1983.
Collectors, Forgers—and a Writer: A Memoir. New York, Targ, 1983.

Editor, *The Future of the Social Studies: Proposals for an Experimental Social-Studies Curriculum.* New York, National Council for the Social Studies, 1939.
Editor, *The Hokusai Sketch Books: Selections from the Manga.* Rutland, Vermont, Tuttle, 1958.
Editor, *Firstfruits: A Harvest of 25 Years of Israeli Writing.* Philadelphia, Jewish Publication Society of America, 1973.

*

Manuscript Collection: Library of Congress, Washington, D.C.

Critical Studies: *James Michener* by A. Grove Day, New York, Twayne, 1964, revised edition, 1977; *James Michener* by George J. Becker, New York, Ungar, 1983; *James A. Michener: A Biography* by John P. Hayes, Indianapolis, Bobbs Merrill, 1984.

James A. Michener comments:
I had the good fortune to arrive on the scene when America was broadening its intellectual horizons to include the entire world. Millions of our men would experience the South Pacific; millions of families would live in Japan or Germany, and countries like Great Britain and Italy became commonplace adventures. Had I written as I did twenty years earlier, I doubt seriously that I would have enjoyed much of a readership. America was not only prepared for what I had to say, but apparently eager to hear it.
Also, I came along when the television set was about to command the attention of the middle American family to the

exclusion of almost all else, and I made a conscious decision: "If they look at television long enough, they will grow hungry for the more substantial experience they can get only through books," and it became evident to me that instead of abandoning reading, the people I was aiming at would demand more of it, and would be prepared to accept long and difficult books, would indeed seek them out. In this judgment I was confirmed.

I am sometimes thought of, for these reasons, as an exotic writer. On the contrary, I have worked in an unusually wide spectrum of human experience, from politics to ecology to education to Asian art to the fine arts. I have also worked in these fields, having been an active politician and a connoisseur of the arts. My life has been therefore a vain attempt to keep many interests in balance, and my books have been proof of how one or the other of those interests has run away with me from time to time.

My style has always been deceptively simple, and I have worked assiduously to keep it that way. This requires not only careful writing, but endless rewriting, redrafting, rejection, and final polishing. I find that I work principally in a Latinized vocabulary, in fairly long sentences; revision consists of going back to simpler Anglo-Saxon words and shorter sentences. My ideals have been Henry James, Gustave Flaubert and Ivan Turgenev, whom I have never tried to ape, and William Thackeray, Honoré Balzac, Leo Tolstoy and Samuel Butler, whom I have. My influences have thus been almost exclusively European rather than American, a consequence of my education, and I have always felt this to have been a pity.

*   *   *

No one could ever justifiably accuse James A. Michener of being intellectually stagnant or lazy. Few, if any, other contemporary American writers have dared to explore the vast territories he has covered in so much depth. No period of history or topic of social concern, it would seem, has escaped Michener's pen. From the ancient Middle East to modern-day Texas, Michener has written the histories of places and their inhabitants, always with a sharp, clear eye for detail and description. His non-fiction work is perhaps even more impressive in scope and bulk; his subjects range from the Kent State killings and ensuing investigation to the world of Japanese art.

Michener began his writing career in 1947 with the publication of *Tales of the South Pacific*, a collection of loosely connected stories concerning the lives and loves of American soldiers stationed in that area during World War II. The book, an immediate success which was hailed as one of the most significant books to emerge from a war-time experience in decades, won the Pulitzer Prize. Against the backdrop of the lush islands and sensuous natives, Michener places a group of American military personnel. The lives and cultures of the two disparate peoples become entwined, the first of many such juxtapositions of cultures to be found in Michener's works. (A later novel, *Sayonara*, displays even more of this clash as it chronicles the tragic love affair of an American GI and his Japanese mistress.) Although a definite flair for story-telling is evident, the author does have a tendency to go into rather too much detail, causing some of the weaker stories to fall flat.

An attempt at an autobiographical novel, *The Fires of Spring*, followed. The story of a poor boy from Pennsylvania who, through academic success and help from a Quaker family, travels to New York to try his luck at writing has all the marks of a too-autobiographical work. It comes off as hastily written and lacking in perspective.

Depending upon the reader's taste, Michener is at either his best or his worst in his long historical novels. After *Sayonara* was published in 1954, Michener allowed his love of place and history to overtake his fiction. Whereas in his earlier novels he paid careful consideration to characterization and dialogue, in his later novels, he seems to believe that the sweeping historical plots will interest his readers enough to carry them through books that even his most avid fans must find too often long and sometimes dull.

Hawaii, perhaps the most famous of the historical novels, is a panoramic book that depicts the formation, development, and settlement of the islands. While rich in historical and cultural description, the book is flawed in that the characters are not well-drawn or expanded. Still, the novel is a masterful example of the genre. *Centennial* and *Chesapeake* both rival *Hawaii* as Michener's historical masterpieces, but, again, the books suffer from length, lack of characterization, and descriptive overkill. Even less successful are *Caravans* and *The Source*, in which the background and sense of history play a larger part than do essential fictional elements.

That Michener is an important and popular novelist there is no denying. He would prove himself a more capable novelist, however, if he developed his characters more fully and kept a tighter rein on his rather unwieldy historical descriptions.

—Sally H. Bennett

MIDDLETON, O(sman) E(dward Gordon). New Zealander. Born in Christchurch, 25 March 1925. Educated at New Plymouth Boys High School, 1939–41; Auckland University, 1946, 1948; the Sorbonne, Paris (New Zealand Government bursary), 1955–56. Served in the Royal New Zealand Air Force, 1944–45. Married Maida Edith Middleton (marriage dissolved, 1970), two children. Resident, Károlyi Memorial Foundation, Vence, France, Summer 1983; lectured at several European universities, 1983. Recipient: New Zealand Award for Achievement, 1960, and Scholarship in Letters, 1965; Hubert Church Prose Award, 1964; University of Otago Robert Burns Fellowship, 1970; New Zealand Prose Fiction award, 1976. Address: 20 Clifford Street, Dunedin, New Zealand.

PUBLICATIONS

Short Stories

Short Stories. Wellington, Handcraft Press, 1954.
The Stone and Other Stories. Auckland, Pilgrim Press, 1959.
A Walk on the Beach. London, Joseph, 1964.
The Loners. Wellington, Square and Circle, 1972.
Selected Stories. Dunedin, McIndoe, 1975.
Confessions of an Ocelot, Not for a Seagull. Dunedin, McIndoe, 1978.

Verse

Six Poems. Wellington, Handcraft Press, 1951.

Other

From the River to the Tide (for children). Wellington, School Publications Branch, 1964.

*

Manuscript Collections: Auckland Public Library; Hocken Library, Dunedin.

Critical Studies: *New Zealand Fiction since 1945* by H. Winston Rhodes, Dunedin, McIndoe, 1968; "O.E. Middleton: Not Just a Realist" by Jim Williamson, in *Islands* (Auckland), Winter 1973; *O.E. Middleton: The Sympathetic Imagination and the Right Judgements*, Dunedin, Pilgrims South Press, 1980, and "Out from Under My Uncle's Hat: Gaskell, Middleton and the Sargeson Tradition," in *Critical Essays on the New Zealand Short Story* edited by Cherry Hankin, Auckland, Heinemann, 1982, both by Lawrence Jones.

O.E. Middleton comments:

My published fiction comprises two novellas, several dozen short stories and a work for children. Unpublished material includes two novels and numerous stories.

It is not my wish to explain, analyse, or otherwise obscure what I have sought to render in fictional terms. I should feel that I had failed as a writer if my work did not speak for itself.

*   *   *

As a short story writer primarily devoted to the New Zealand scene, O.E. Middleton remains faithful to the tradition of unsophisticated realism. He is less interested in technical innovation than in his wide experience of people and places at home and abroad, less attracted to ironic or symbolic patterns than to the rhythms of the spoken language and the texture of the workaday world. The titles of his best-known collections, *The Stone and Other Stories* and *A Walk on the Beach*, are symptomatic of an unpretentious manner and direct approach to subject matter that is rarely remote from the commonplace, but is raised to a level of significance by its truth of substance.

Unlike some writers held in greater esteem he never adopts an authorial position from which he finds it convenient to look down on the antics of his characters with fastidious disapproval or superior sensibility. On the contrary he is always democratically at ease in the scene and among the people he has created. The narrators of "The Corporal's Story" and "The Greaser's Story" are familiar with their occupations and in harmony with their backgrounds.

Middleton populates his fictional world with labourers and seamen, farmers and city-dwellers, Europeans and Maoris, children and adolescents. They are ordinary people, generally unremarkable for subtlety of thought or emotion; and the incidents related are associated with their normal activities during work and leisure. Their understanding is limited and their conversation borders on the banal; but what must be lost in felicity of expression is gained in authenticity and restraint. "A Married Man" concludes tritely with " 'Never mind,' she said, smiling and friendly, 'It will come right in the end.' " The narrator of "A Day by Itself" observes "It had been a funny day really, and there were things about it which I still didn't understand." Even when stories are based on episodes derived from the eventful years of the writer's wanderings, both language and character become absorbed into the raw material of life.

Despite the absence of any guide-lines which can be attributed to the author, a moral sensibility is distinctly present in choice of theme, development of action, and establishment of character. A particular kind of neo-colonial egalitarian humanism informs every aspect of his writing and is readily detected in what he has called "sorties into the No-man's-land of inter-racial relations." The most substantial of these stories is found in the novella *Not for a Seagull*, told by a young Maori who is continually made aware that goodfellowship often masks attitudes of racial discrimination. This has recently been republished with the addition of a later and more sophisticated work, *Confessions of an Ocelot*, which relates the experiences of a human victim innocently trapped in a city-jungle. The narrator is a withdrawn and sensitive youth whose "confessions" are intended to reveal "to any who may share a like sensibility the perils that can await its flowering." With characteristic thoroughness Middleton enters into the interior world of his guideless recorder and at the same time uncovers the external world in which he moves uncomprehendingly. Yet, surprisingly enough, the didacticism latent in this and other themes does not often obtrude. Middleton is too honest a craftsman to allow strongly held opinions to falsify his representation of the life he has both experienced and observed. His characters play their parts in the diverse activities of the communities in which they find themselves, with the result that any temptation to over-emphasise private perplexities is checked by the recognition of otherness, and Middleton is able both to explore his chosen terrain and disclose rather than publish his humane attitudes.

The measure of his work is to be found not in terms of quantity, for his output has not been large, but in the success he has achieved in responding to the epigraph from Dryden which he attached to his *Selected Stories*—"For the spirit of man cannot be satisfied but with truth or at least verisimility...." It is also to be found in the range and variety of scene, character, and situation. He moves easily from land to sea, from the Americas to Europe and back again to New Zealand, distilling fragments of his wide experiences and activity into imaginative work that attains significance from the authenticity of its treatment. Such stories as "The Crows," "For Once in Your Life," "The Doss-House and the Duchess," and "The Collector" (all in *Selected Stories*) are characterised by the same concern with variations of the human predicament as is to be found in his more frequent New Zealand narratives.

—H. Winston Rhodes

MIDDLETON, Stanley. British. Born in Bulwell, Nottingham, 1 August 1919. Educated at High Pavement School, Nottingham; University College of Nottingham, now Nottingham University, 1938–40, 1946–47, B.A. (London) 1940; M.Ed. (Nottingham) 1952. Served in the Royal Artillery and the Army Education Corps, 1940–46. Married Margaret Shirley Welch in 1951; two daughters. English Master, 1947–81, and Head of the English Department, 1958–81, High Pavement College, Nottingham. Judith E. Wilson Visiting Fellow, Emmanuel College, Cambridge, 1982–83. Recipient: Booker Prize, 1974. M.A.: Nottingham University, 1975. Address: 42 Caledon Road, Sherwood, Nottingham NG5 2NG, England.

PUBLICATIONS

Novels

A Short Answer. London, Hutchinson, 1958.
Harris's Requiem. London, Hutchinson, 1960.
A Serious Woman. London, Hutchinson, 1961.
The Just Exchange. London, Hutchinson, 1962.
Two's Company. London, Hutchinson, 1963.
Him They Compelled. London, Hutchinson, 1964.

Terms of Reference.   London, Hutchinson, 1966.
The Golden Evening.   London, Hutchinson, 1968.
Wages of Virtue.   London, Hutchinson, 1969.
Apple of the Eye.   London, Hutchinson, 1970.
Brazen Prison.   London, Hutchinson, 1971.
Cold Gradations.   London, Hutchinson, 1972.
A Man Made of Smoke.   London, Hutchinson, 1973.
Holiday.   London, Hutchinson, 1974.
Distractions.   London, Hutchinson, 1975.
Still Waters.   London, Hutchinson, 1976.
Ends and Means.   London, Hutchinson, 1977.
Two Brothers.   London, Hutchinson, 1978.
In a Strange Land.   London, Hutchinson, 1979.
The Other Side.   London, Hutchinson, 1980.
Blind Understanding.   London, Hutchinson, 1982.
Entry into Jerusalem.   London, Hutchinson, 1983.
The Daysman.   London, Hutchinson, 1984.
Valley of Decision.   London, Hutchinson, 1985.
An After Dinner's Sleep.   London, Century Hutchinson, 1986.

Plays

Radio Plays: *The Captain from Nottingham*, 1972; *Harris's Requiem*, 1972; *A Little Music at Night*, 1972; *Cold Gradations*, from his own novel, 1973.

*

Manuscript Collection: Central Library, Nottingham.

Critical Studies: "Stanley Middleton and the Provincial Novel" by John Lucas, in *Nottingham Quarterly*, 1978; article by June Sturrock, in *British Novelists since 1960* edited by Jay L. Halio, Detroit Gale, 1983; "The Art of Stanley Middleton" by A.S. Byatt, in *Fiction Magazine* (London), 1985.

Stanley Middleton comments:
(1972) I put down a few obvious points about my novels.

They are set mainly in the English midlands with characters drawn from the professional middle-classes (students, teachers, actors, writers, architects), though one will find labourers and factory-workers as well as businessmen of real affluence.

The action usually occupies a short period of some months only (*Wages of Virtue* is an exception), and the plot deals with people in a state of crisis or perplexity caused by illness and death, or a breakdown of personal relationships, or the difficulties of creating a work of art (which may be music, *Harris's Requiem*, or poetry, *Him They Compelled*, or a novel in *Brazen Prison*). At this time of dilemmas, friends or relatives intervene, and thus learn their own inadequacies and, sometimes, strengths. No perfect characters or solutions exist; all is difficult, compromising, but a bonus of success or joy is occasionally found.

My idea is not only to tell an interesting story but to demonstrate the complexity of human character and motive. One must not only describe what has happened to people, or what they are like; one must make the characters live out what they are said to be, and this must include deviations from normality and actions "out of character." I find this most difficult, but when I am charged, sometimes, with "mere reportage," I can see no sense at all in the accusation. My novels are imaginative attempts to write down illuminating actions and talk from the lives of fictional people, and not transcriptions of tape-recordings of real conversations or blow-by-blow commentaries on events which have really taken place. I am sometimes praised for the "realism" of my dialogue, and this makes me wonder

if these critics, who may of course be using a "shorthand" dictated by the small space at their disposal, know how different my sort of dialogue is from that of real life.

This preoccupation leads to a choice of different levels of writing. A novel cannot always be intense; both by the shape of my work and my use of language I try constantly to interfere with the reader, to rest him as well as violently assault him. Therefore it is galling when I find critics who apparently subscribe to the notion that contemporary novels are either "well-written" (i.e. in "mandarin") or dashed down without care. Mine are usually dumped by such people in the second category. Shifts on my part from the point-of-view of one character to that of another also seem to pass unnoticed. I enjoy putting obstacles in my own way to find out if I can surmount them.

I am often asked if my novels are didactic. I wouldn't object to that word since the greatest work of art I know—Bach's *St. Matthew Passion*—could be so described. But unless a novel is complex, memorable, capable of holding a reader and moving him deeply, I've not much time for it.

I can't think these notes very helpful. General exegesis as opposed to critical discussion of precise points in specific books has little attraction for me as a writer. A novel should be its own defence; if it does not speak for itself to a well-equipped reader, call out echoes in him, it's not properly written.

*   *   *

Middle-class, middle-aged, midland dwellers provide most of the material for Stanley Middleton's novels from 1960 to the 1980's. His remarkable achievement in producing such lively work from such an unpromising source lies in his ability to make most of his characters both unlikeable and interesting at the same time. His women for the most part are tormented frigid tormentors, while his affluent men are generally mediocrities in their professions and indecisive shamblers in their personal lives, if they are not driven by an ugly and ruthless streak of ambition or obsessed by the demands of art.

He makes his readers understand that people at the end of their tether do not become heroic and loveable through their suffering, and that emotional snarl-ups render the participants selfish, irritable, and dull. The skill of Middleton's handling of dialogue is that although the first two qualities are caught, the third is avoided. The reader is held by the way the seemingly pointless remarks of the speakers can grate against each other. This is especially true when there is any attempt to bridge gaps of generation, social class, or economic status. In *Terms of Reference* the two late middle-aged couples are perplexed and powerless when confronted by the failure of the marriage between the son of the very wealthy pair and the daughter of the academics. Yet although they can do nothing to hold their wayward children together, and are by no means certain that it would be a good thing to do so, all four are too fascinated by the situation to leave it alone.

Edward Tenby, the architect hero of *Apple of the Eye*, is not only the sole moderately creative and productive character in the novel, he is also the only man. He becomes involved with three neurotic women, each young enough to be his daughter. One of them has enough money to indulge her sickness to its limit, while the other two are poor enough to be flattered and astounded at making any contact so high in the social scale. In *Brazen Prison* Charles Stead, the ex-grammar school novelist, has to cope with the social nuances of relating to his wealthy socialite wife and the company she keeps, while at the same time involving himself with the husband and family of the local girl he had picked up in the dance hall as a youth.

Many novelists use the device of seeing their created world through the eyes of a fellow-writer, and it is one that Middleton is fond of. As well as Charles Stead, there is the best-selling novelist Eric Chamberlain in *Ends and Means*. His obsession with success make him almost insensitive to the fatal distress of his son and mistress, who both kill themselves. His detachment is matched by that of Frank, the modest, doomed, and isolated poet in *Two Brothers*.

Middleton is at his best, however, when he uses music or the visual arts to convey the excitement and compulsion of creation, and to give an added dimension to the construction of a novel. There are marvellous passages of musical analysis in *In a Strange Land*, which is an unusual Middleton novel in that the protagonist, James Murren, organist and composer, leaves the midlands to further his career in London. In *Valley of Decision*, which concerns a young music teacher married to an ambitious singer, the stages of the novel almost correspond to musical movements which are heightened by the analysis of the performances of an amateur quartet with whom the husband is invited to play.

Entry into Jerusalem explores the way a man can be driven to create a visual image. Like Middleton's novelists and musicians, John Worth, the 30-year-old painter of this novel, successfully harnesses his imagination by living a life somewhat detached from his fellows, however many disasters take place around him. His work is barely touched when his former teaching colleague has a breakdown and kills himself.

Suicides of minor characters are frequent in Middleton's later novels, throwing the main events into a sharper focus. Death is ever-present, lurking in the background of everyday life, or accepted as a concomitant of age as it is in *Blind Understanding*. That novel follows the ruminations of a retired small-town solicitor as he lives out a day between attending a funeral in the morning and hearing of the heart attack suffered by a member of his wife's bridge party in the evening.

In these later novels, Middleton makes little use of his experience as a school teacher, the main exception being his sensitive exploration in *The Daysman* of the character of John Richardson, headmaster of a comprehensive school in a middle-class area and general friend and counsellor to pupils and staff alike. He is a man who lets ambition and the lure of the media gradually rot his integrity and understanding. In this he is contrasted with his practical, capable wife, and the working out of their marriage is the main point of that novel. Indeed Middleton's preoccupation with the shifting adjustments of marriages enables him to make full use of his remarkable gift for describing the minute nuances of human interaction from the merest twitchings of "body language" to full-scale emotional and physical outbursts.

—Shirley Toulson

MILLAR, Margaret (Ellis, née Sturm). American. Born in Kitchener, Ontario, Canada, 5 February 1915. Educated at Kitchener-Waterloo Collegiate Institute, 1929–33; University of Toronto, 1933–36. Married Kenneth Millar, i.e., Ross Macdonald, *q.v.*, in 1938 (died, 1983); one daughter (deceased). Screenwriter, Warner Brothers, Hollywood, 1945–46. President, Mystery Writers of America, 1957–58. Recipient: Mystery Writers of America Edgar Allan Poe Award, 1956, and Grand Master Award, 1983; Los Angeles *Times* Woman of the Year Award, 1965. Agent: Harold Ober Associates, 40

East 49th Street, New York, New York 10017. Address: 87 Seaview Drive, Santa Barbara, California 93108, U.S.A.

PUBLICATIONS

Novels

The Invisible Worm. New York, Doubleday, 1941; London, Long, 1943.
The Weak-Eyed Bat. New York, Doubleday, 1942.
The Devil Loves Me. New York, Doubleday, 1942.
Wall of Eyes. New York, Random House, 1943; London, Lancer, 1966.
Fire Will Freeze. New York, Random House, 1944.
The Iron Gates. New York, Random House, 1945; as *Taste of Fears*, London, Hale, 1950.
Experiment in Springtime. New York, Random House, 1947.
It's All in the Family. New York, Random House, 1948.
The Cannibal Heart. New York, Random House, 1949; London, Hamish Hamilton, 1950.
Do Evil in Return. New York, Random House, 1950; London, Museum Press, 1952.
Rose's Last Summer. New York, Random House, 1952; London, Museum Press, 1954; as *The Lively Corpse*, New York, Dell, 1956.
Vanish in an Instant. New York, Random House, 1952; London, Museum Press, 1953.
Wives and Lovers. New York, Random House, 1954.
Beast in View. New York, Random House, and London, Gollancz, 1955.
An Air That Kills. New York, Random House, 1957; as *The Soft Talkers*, London, Gollancz, 1957.
The Listening Walls. New York, Random House, and London, Gollancz, 1959.
A Stranger in My Grave. New York, Random House, and London, Gollancz, 1960.
How Like an Angel. New York, Random House, and London, Gollancz, 1962.
The Fiend. New York, Random House, and London, Gollancz, 1964.
Beyond This Point Are Monsters. New York, Random House, 1970; London, Gollancz, 1971.
Ask for Me Tomorrow. New York, Random House, 1976; London, Gollancz, 1977.
The Murder of Miranda. New York, Random House, 1979; London, Gollancz, 1980.
Mermaid. New York, Morrow, and London, Gollancz, 1982.
Banshee. New York, Morrow, and London, Gollancz, 1983.

Uncollected Short Stories

"Last Day in Lisbon," in *Five Novels* (New York), February 1943.
"The Couple Next Door," in *Ellery Queen's Awards: Ninth Series.* Boston, Little Brown, 1954; London, Collins, 1956.
"The People Across the Canyon," in *Ellery Queen's Mystery Magazine* (New York), October 1962.
"McGowney's Miracle," in *Every Crime in the Book.* New York, Putnam, 1975.

Other

The Birds and Beasts Were There (autobiography). New York, Random House, 1968.

*

Critical Study: article by John M. Reilly, in *Ten Women of Mystery* edited by Earl F. Bargainnier, Bowling Green, Ohio, Popular Press, 1981.

*   *   *

Margaret Millar began her career with an effort to create a series of detection stories presided over by the comically named Dr. Paul Prye. His vocation as a consulting psychiatrist suggested that he might become the modern version of the scientists Sherlock Holmes and Dr. Thorndyke whose stories provided the basic conventions of the detection novel that Millar employed in *The Invisible Worm* and *The Weak-Eyed Bat*. As it turned out, the conventional emphasis in the classic detection story upon ratiocination was misplaced for Millar's purposes. In structuring her later novels she began to shift attention from the agent who clears up a mystery to the source of the mystery itself, in the process reducing detection to a narrative device for laying bare the causes of criminal behavior in the submerged realm of the irrational.

The effect is to produce what Julian Symons terms her "art of bamboozlement." Writing in *Mortal Consequences*, he says that Millar "presents us with a plausible criminal situation, builds it up to a climax of excitement, and then in the last few pages shakes the kaleidoscope and shows us an entirely different pattern from the one we have been so busily interpreting." Symons's comment is an accurate enough description of the shape of Millar's plots. In *Do Evil in Return* the logic of circumstantial evidence points to the guilt of Lewis Ballard for the murder of a young woman he has made pregnant, until it is revealed that in a mad attempt to keep her home intact Lewis's wife had killed the woman; and in the remarkable *Beast in View* Millar develops readers' sympathetic participation in Helen Clarvoe's terror as she is persecuted by Evelyn Merrick, who is finally revealed as the malignant dimension of Helen's own split personality.

Yet it is insufficient to comment on plot manipulation in Millar's narratives as though she were mainly concerned with creating a better puzzle for detection stories. As her career has developed she has become a fundamental revisionist of the genre, going beyond alteration of narrative focus to provide her adopted form with a new premise. In their consistent centering on the family circle, detection narratives offer an insight Millar believes to be profoundly true: the family as the individual's most immediate social environment generates criminal psychology. In revising the detection story so that the psychology of minds under the stress of guilt, sexual desire, or jealousy (and their issue in hatred) become the substance of her fictional reality, Millar creates the post-Freudian mystery. The problems that demand explanation are those that typify human experience within the mind, so her plots bamboozle with twists and reverses in order to represent movement within the novels from external circumstances amenable to rational ordering to the irrational inner life. Discovery of cause and effect in external circumstances could establish socially defined guilt and lead to reconstruction of social order, but revelation of the sequence of internal occurrences leads only to knowledge, gratifying in single cases but leaving a residue of uncertainty rather than optimism.

In *The Iron Gates*, *How Like an Angel*, and *Beyond This Point Are Monsters* events arising from experiences long past determine present life. In books such as *Vanish in an Instant*, *A Stranger in My Grave*, and *Wives and Lovers* the intensity of family relationships is portrayed as inevitably damaging for characters working their ways through patterns of submission and dominance. The evidence of distorted behavior and the harm done in the most personal relationships is fascinating when we read it in psychiatric anecdote, but related in fiction with its means of dramatization it is unsettling. Relieved as we may be by a story's apparent resolution, we are shocked by its revelation and carry away with us a nagging sense of kinship with desperate characters.

The full significance of the new premise Millar establishes for the received form of classic detection fiction becomes even clearer in her two recent novels. In *Mermaid* Tom Aragon, a character employed as investigator also in *Ask for Me Tomorrow* and *The Murder of Miranda*, works on the case of a young retarded woman who has been encouraged by a concerned counselor to demand her rights as a citizen, the right to vote, for example. The perfectly reasonable demand, however, creates circumstances resulting in suicide for the counselor, the shooting of the woman's cousin, the breakup of her brother's marriage, and disgrace for the headmistress of the home where she resides. In the reader's native region of commonsense life such linkage of consequences would be implausible, just as it would be merely ingenious in a simple puzzle story, but as the psychology of the characters is brought to the surface of the story by Millar's narration, the reader enters a reality beyond protective commonsense or diverting puzzles, a reality where reason does not control events, and belief that it can may be irresponsible. In *Banshee* the bereaved father of a child who died of probable foul play joins with a friend to interrogate the list of likely suspects. And considering the evidence, they are certainly likely. Only it turns out that the evidence of crime is misleading because an eyewitness has been so traumatized she cannot help the investigators understand their evidence. Once again rationality from the well-lit daily world is powerless to control the consequences.

Margaret Millar writes out of the conviction that fate originates in the conflicts between an individual's needs or desires and the repressive controls exercised upon them by the social environment. In her chosen literary form these conflicts usually have been a submerged story, perhaps sensed by readers but unacknowledged in the structure of plot or narration. Displaying a mastery of technique, including the conventions of realistic setting and characterization, Millar creates narrative means to bring the story of pre-rational psychology to the surface where it must be seen not as alien, or maybe not even as aberrational, but as determinant in the circumstances of ordinary life.

—John M. Reilly

MIRSKY, Mark (Jay). American. Born in Boston, Massachusetts, 11 August 1939. Educated at Harvard University, Cambridge, Massachusetts, B.A. (magna cum laude) 1961 (Phi Beta Kappa); Stanford University, California (Woodrow Wilson Fellow), M.A. 1962. Served in the United States Air Force Reserve, 1962–68. Married Kinger Channah Grytting in 1980; two children. School teacher, Boston, 1962; staff writer, *American Heritage*, New York, 1964; Lecturer in English, Stanford University, 1966. Lecturer, 1967–70, Assistant Professor, 1970–74, Associate Professor, 1975–80, director of the M.A. program, 1978–84, and since 1980, Professor of English, City College, New York. Founding Member of the Board, Teachers-Writers Collaborative, 1967, and Fiction Collective, 1974, both New York; Editor, *Fiction*, New York, 1972–84. Recipient: Bread Loaf Writers Conference grant; National

Endowment for the Arts award, for editing, 1980, and Senior Fellowship, 1981; Creative Artists Public Service grant, 1982. Address: Department of English, City College of New York, New York, New York 10031, U.S.A.

Publications

Novels

Thou Worm, Jacob. New York, Macmillan, and London, Collier Macmillan, 1967.
Proceedings of the Rabble. Indianapolis, Bobbs Merrill, 1970.
Blue Hill Avenue. Indianapolis, Bobbs Merrill, 1972.

Short Stories

The Secret Table. New York, Fiction Collective, 1975.

Uncollected Short Stories

"Swapping," in *Statements 1*, edited by Jonathan Baumbach. New York, Braziller, 1975.
"The Last Lecture," in *Tri-Quarterly* (Evanston, Illinois), Spring 1976.
"Last Boat to America," in *Massachusetts Review* (Amherst), Summer 1981.
"Child's Alphabet," in *Literary Review* (Madison, New Jersey), Summer 1982.

Other

My Search for the Messiah: Studies and Wanderings in Israel and America. New York, Macmillan, 1977.

*   *   *

A catalogue of Mark Mirsky's fictional liabilities in his early work is short and bittersweet: he reworks worn material; he cannot resist dreamworld and fantasyland scenes; he is too delighted with royal-purple prose and "experimentalism"; finally he breaks himself up with broad ethnic humor that often offends. Yet he has such large talent that he skillfully turns each of these faults to advantage even when he does not transcend them.

His first volume of fiction seemed partly to be a parodic mélange of Aleichem, Singer, and Malamud. The inversions of Yiddish, the barrage of exclamation and interrogation points, the spread-finger resignation of the Jewish immigrant, all knotted and clotted the young writer's style and suggested the bar mitzvah school of cheap Catskill entertainment. Thus, the "Introduction" begins:

> "I've got the whole state of Jewish affairs right between my fingers!
> "What? You don't understand? Take a seat. Don't worry, it won't break. A bit cracked but it's had a rest. Watch out! Watch out for that pile of books. Knock one over, my whole place is on your head. Pages, dust, dirty yarmulkes. Eh! Let it fall."

In spite of such false starts, Mirsky knows and loves his "material" and manages to move us to both laughter and pity in this collection of tales about East European immigrants struggling to remain Jews in their new homeland. The familiar figure of the schlemiel hero is brilliantly renewed in the collection's finest story, "The Shammos from Aroostook County."

Five years later, Mirsky returned to the struggling Jews of the old towns near Boston with *Blue Hill Avenue*. Although he labeled his tale "vaudeville," he writes here with more control, except for an inappropriate slapstick ending. Four of the characters are superbly drawn: Rabbi Lux, who is "a little too good, too pious for much of Dorchester"; the rabbi's wife, once timid and passionate, now a loving, lunatic protectress; Simcha Tanzenn, a canny, lisping politician who collects on favors rarely delivered; and a demented Jewish mother, who uses the telephone like a mortar and wills her war-lost (and worthless) son back to safety. Mirsky's latest treatment of Jewish traditions, *The Secret Table*, is more serious in tone and, despite some obscurity of form, marks another fictional advance for the author in portraying his fierce bookish forebears. The first novella depicts the search through memory of 30-year-old Maishe for the womb-security now lacking in the decayed streets of Blue Hill Avenue: the companion novella, "Onan's Child," builds upon Genesis to explore, through Jacob, Isaac, Joseph, and Onan, the terrible contradictions of man's nature and Jewish history. In both stories, past and present, subjective and objective worlds, the Jew and the universal man, are blended into a believable, densely-textured reality.

Mirsky's second novel, *Proceedings of the Rabble*, may be his most ambitious to date. Anticipating Robert Altman's film, *Nashville*, in an urban locale, Mirsky uses the evangelical right-wing political crusade of William Starr to portray the murderous impotence moving American democracy toward rage, outrage, and self-destruction. Despite the straining interior-cinema technique employed, Mirsky's apocalyptic ending matches the final upheaval of West's *The Day of the Locust*. Indeed, in all four "novels," Mirsky renews such staple items of contemporary American fiction as violence, sexual sickness, and the Jew as representative sufferer, so that they still serve to tell us about ourselves.

—Frank Campenni

* * * * *

MITCHELL, Joseph (Quincy). American. Born in Fairmont, North Carolina, 27 July 1908. Educated at the University of North Carolina, Chapel Hill, 1925–29. Married Therese Dagny Jacobsen in 1931; two daughters. Reporter, New York *World*, 1929–30, New York *Herald Tribune*, 1929–31, and New York *World Telegram*, 1931–38. Since 1938, staff writer, *The New Yorker* magazine. Since 1982, commissioner, New York City Landmarks Preservation Commission. Recipient: American Academy award, 1965; State of North Carolina Gold Medal for Literature, 1983. Vice-President, 1971, and Secretary, 1972–74, National Institute of Arts and Letters. Address: c/o The New Yorker, 25 West 43rd Street, New York, New York 10036, U.S.A.

Publications

Short Stories

McSorley's Wonderful Saloon. New York, Duell, 1943; London, Porcupine Press, 1946.
Old Mr. Flood. New York, Duell, 1948.
The Bottom of the Harbor. Boston, Little Brown, 1959; London, Chatto and Windus, 1961.

Joe Gould's Secret.   New York, Viking Press, 1965.

Other

My Ears Are Bent (collection of newspaper articles).   New
   York, Sheridan House, 1938.

                                      *

Critical Studies: "The Grammar of Facts" by Malcolm Cowley,
in *New Republic* (New York), 26 July 1943; "The Art of Joseph
Mitchell" by Stanley Edgar Hyman, in *New Leader* (New
York), 6 December 1965; "Paragon of Reporters: Joseph
Mitchell" by Noel Perrin, in *Sewanee Review* (Sewanee, Ten-
nessee), Spring 1983.

                        *   *   *

   Throughout his works Joseph Mitchell places himself in the
tradition of the tall tale in America and reveals why he can
say in *McSorley's Wonderful Saloon* to the "Gifted Child" that
Mark Twain's *Life on the Mississippi* is the one book he likes
above all others. He walks in wonder and records what he
sees. All of his central figures emerge as larger-than-life people,
yet there is almost always a quality of reflection and tone-setting
that makes them believable as well as memorable.
   In an author's note to *McSorley's Wonderful Saloon* Mitchell
concludes with, "There are no little people in this book. They
are as big as you are, whoever you are." And he then works
with a fine eye, ear, and hand to give profile to such "little"
people as John McSorley, president of "an organization of
gluttons called the Honorable John McSorley Pickle, Beefsteak, Baseball Nine and Chowder Club"; Mazie P. Gordon,
owner of, ticket seller, and bouncer at the Venice theater in
the Bowery; King Cockeye Johnny Nikanov, a Russian and
King of the Gypsies in New York; Lady Olga Jane Bardwell,
the freak show bearded lady, with a fourteen-and-a-half inch
beard, mustache, and her fourth husband; and various others.
His favorite setting is lower Manhattan, and his stories become
urban pastorals, strongest when he focuses with care on his
people: Mr. Hugh G. Flood, in *Old Mr. Flood*, and Joe Gould,
in *Joe Gould's Secret*, exemplify best Mitchell's role as profilist-
story teller.
   Mr. Flood, age 93 to 95, wants to live to be 115, is a "seafood-
etarian," and can eat bushels of clams and consume large quantities of whiskey. From the many scenes and wild anecdotes
of "Old Mr. Flood," "The Black Clams," and "Mr. Flood's
Party" comes a man whom the narrator obviously loves, one
who, as Mr. Mitchell says, is not one man but "several old
men, who work or hang out in Fulton Fish Market." He's
too big to exist, but he is nonetheless there, and the *I* of the
story penetrates his moods—from extreme loneliness to convi-
vial joy—with touching sensitivity. One feels that Mr. Flood
will indeed live to age 115.
   Joe Gould, on the other hand, is, as the author says in a
note, "a lost soul." As Professor Sea Gull in *McSorley's Wonderful Saloon*, he is a tall-tale character too—a blithe and ema-
ciated little man who has been a notable in the cafeterias,
diners, barrooms, and dumps of Greenwich Village for a
quarter of a century. A Harvard alumnus, class of 1911, he
sometimes brags that he is the last of the bohemians. Of chief
interest to Mitchell is Gould's *An Oral History of Our Time*—a
document eleven times as long as the Bible, over 9,000,000
words in longhand and still unfinished. As a solitary nocturnal
wanderer he talks much of his *Oral History* and of his ability,
among other things, to translate Longfellow's "Hiawatha" into

sea gull. Here he shouts to a Village waitress: "I'm Joe Gould,
the poet; I'm Joe Gould, the historian; I'm Joe Gould, the
wild Chippewa Indian dancer; and I'm Joe Gould, the greatest
authority in the world on the language of the sea gull."
   Joe Gould's secret, however, discovered by Mitchell years
later, is that there is no *Oral History*. Gould has not only duped
Mitchell and the people but has duped himself. He can recite
it but cannot put it down. Mitchell keeps the secret until he
writes it down in his story, stepping out of, as he says, "the
role I had stepped into the afternoon I discovered that the
Oral History did not exist."
   My Ears Are Bent and *The Bottom of the Harbor* show
Mitchell's consistency throughout his career in reporting on
but also building on the people and places of his world, from
Sloppy Louie's, the old Fulton Ferry Hotel, and the "Baymen"
to the rats on the waterfront. When he writes of his home
country in rural North Carolina he uses his same profilist's
eye and feeling for his "people" to bring to life such characters
as Mrs. Copenhagen Calhoun in "I Blame It All on Mama,"
Uncle Dockery in "Uncle Dockery and the Independent Bull"
and Mr. Catfish Giddy in "The Downfall of Fascism in Black
Ankle County." Mitchell is the country boy who went to the
city to find his way—and found it in *The New Yorker* where
he perfected the urban tall-tale pastoral.

                                                —Frank T. Phipps

                        ———————

MITCHELL, (Charles) Julian (Humphrey).   British.   Born
in Epping, Essex, 1 May 1935. Educated at Winchester Col-
lege, 1948–53; Wadham College, Oxford, B.A. 1958; St.
Antony's College, Oxford, M.A. 1962. Served in the Royal
Naval Volunteer Reserve, 1953–55: Midshipman. Member,
Arts Council Literature Panel, 1966–69; formerly, Governor,
Chelsea School of Art, London. Recipient: Harkness fellow-
ship, 1959; Rhys Memorial Prize, 1965; Maugham Award,
1966; International Critics Prize, for television play, 1977;
Christopher Award, for television play, 1977 (USA); Florio
Prize, for translation, 1980; Society of West End Theatre
award, 1982. Address: 2 Castle Rise, Llanvaches, Newport,
Gwent NP6 3BS, Wales.

PUBLICATIONS

Novels

Imaginary Toys.   London, Hutchinson, 1961.
A Disturbing Influence.   London, Hutchinson, 1962.
As Far as You Can Go.   London, Constable, 1963.
The White Father.   London, Constable, 1964; New York, Far-
   rar Straus, 1965.
A Circle of Friends.   London, Constable, 1966; New York,
   McGraw Hill, 1967.
The Undiscovered Country.   London, Constable, 1968; New
   York, Grove Press, 1970.

Short Stories

Introduction, with others.   London, Faber, 1960.

Plays

A Heritage and Its History, adaptation of the novel by Ivy Compton-Burnett (produced London, 1965). London, Evans, 1966.
Shadow in the Sun (televised, 1971). Published in *Elizabeth R*, edited by J.C. Trewin, London, Elek, 1972.
A Family and a Fortune, adaptation of the novel by Ivy Compton-Burnett (produced Seattle, 1974; Bath and London, 1975). London, French, 1976.
Half-Life (produced London, 1977; New York, 1981). London, Heinemann, 1977.
Henry IV, adaptation of the play by Pirandello. London, Eyre Methuen, 1979.
The Enemy Within (produced Leatherhead, Surrey, 1980).
Another Country (produced London, 1982; New Haven, Connecticut, 1983). Ambergate, Derbyshire, Amber Lane Press, 1982; New York, Limelight, 1984.
Francis (produced London, 1983). Ambergate, Derbyshire, Amber Lane Press, 1984.

Screenplays: *Arabesque*, with Stanley Price and Pierre Marton, 1966; *Another Country*, 1984.

Radio Documentary: *Life and Deaths of Dr. John Donne*, 1972.

Television Plays: *Persuasion*, from the novel by Jane Austen, 1971; *Shadow in the Sun*, 1971; *The Man Who Never Was*, 1972; *A Perfect Day*, 1972; *Fly in the Ointment*, 1972; *A Question of Degree*, 1972; *Rust*, 1973; *Jennie*, 1974; *Abide with Me*, from the book *A Child in the Forest* by Winifred Foley, 1976; *Staying On*, from the novel by Paul Scott, 1980; *The Good Soldier*, from the novel by Ford Madox Ford, 1981; *The Weather in the Streets*, from the novel by Rosamond Lehmann, 1984; and other adaptations.

Other

Truth and Fiction (lecture). London, Covent Garden Press, 1972.
Jennie, Lady Randolph Churchill: A Portrait with Letters, with Peregrine Churchill. London, Collins, 1974; New York, St. Martin's Press, 1975.

Editor, with others, *Light Blue, Dark Blue: An Anthology of Recent Writing from Oxford and Cambridge Universities*. London, Macdonald, 1960.

*   *   *

Julian Mitchell's books reveal a remarkably talented writer, whose work is consistently fluent, witty and ingenious. But they do leave a doubt in the mind whether his literary gifts are, in the last analysis, those of a natural novelist. He began his career precociously early, and published four novels before he was thirty. The first of them, *Imaginary Toys*, is, like many other first novels, a partly sentimental, partly satirical recreation of university life. It covers a small group of young people during a few days in one summer term at Oxford; the story is of the slightest, but Mitchell uses it as the vehicle for some serious disquisitions on sexual and social problems. The novel is at its most engaging, though, in its fanciful, essay-like speculations, which make it a little reminiscent of the early Aldous Huxley. Mitchell is like Huxley, too, in his acute sense of period; *Imaginary Toys* effectively catches the feel of the late 1950's, though this responsiveness to contemporary atmosphere inevitably made the book seem dated after a few years. His next novel, *A Disturbing Influence*, was not a particularly exciting development, though it was a smoothly written narrative. It described the impact on a complacent, even sleepy Berkshire village of a strange, destructive, amoral young man, the "disturbing influence" of the title. Such types evidently have a particular fascination for Mitchell, for they tend to recur in his fiction. This book was followed by a more substantial and interesting work, *As Far as You Can Go*, in which Mitchell drew on some of his own recent experience to write the kind of novel that was to become increasingly common in England in the 1960's—the account of a peripatetic Englishman's adventures in America. Harold Barlow, the central character, is a typical Mitchell hero—intelligent, amiable, rather inept—and he conveys a tourist's eye view of life in the hipster sub-culture of California.

The White Father, which won Mitchell the Somerset Maugham Award, was a more determinedly ambitious novel than its predecessors. The narrative is divided between London and a remote African territory, and Mitchell shows much of the action through the eyes of Hugh Shrieve, a district officer in Africa who has come to London to plead for his tribe at a conference to arrange independence for the territory. Shrieve has been out of England for years, and he is unprepared for what he finds when he arrives: the frenetic beginnings of the "Swinging London" cult. Mitchell looks satirically though tolerantly at the world of pop music, and there is a powerful imaginative touch in his portrayal of the megalomaniac Mr. Brachs, head of a vast commercial empire catering to the youth cult, who is going steadily mad in his inaccessible penthouse on top of the London skyscraper that houses all his many enterprises. *The White Father* is one of Mitchell's best novels, which makes some sharp observations about life in a high-consumption society, as well as telling an entertaining story. The novelist and the essayist are more closely fused than is usual in his fiction. Two years later Mitchell published an extremely thin novel, *A Circle of Friends*, which moves between New York and the English Home Counties, showing how one of his characteristically weak young men gets unhappily entangled with a wealthy Anglo-American family, culminating in a wholly undeserved position as co-respondent in a divorce action.

All these novels present, at varying levels of literary achievement, some recurring characteristics: a tendency to draw fairly directly on personal experience and to use the novel as a vehicle for airing ideas, a taste for likeable but weak central characters, and a generally relaxed and good-humoured tone. In *The Undiscovered Country*, Mitchell's most striking fiction, all these qualities are present in a new combination. Unlike his previous novels, it is a deliberately experimental work, which plays with the conventions of fiction writing, and the relations between art and reality, in the manner of Nabokov or Borges. The first part is, on the face of it, undisguised autobiography, where Mitchell writes in his own person about his friendship with an enigmatically attractive young man, Charles Humphries, who dies at an early age. He leaves behind the fragmentary manuscript of a novel called "The New Satyricon," which Mitchell edits with introduction and commentary, and presents as the second part of *The Undiscovered Country*. Undoubtedly "Humphries" is an alter ego for "Mitchell" (whose full Christian names are Charles Julian Humphrey), though the relation between them remains teasing. *The Undiscovered Country* is a generally entertaining novel, and the second part is full of pleasant literary jokes, where Mitchell engages to the full his essayistic tendencies. It is also a watershed in his development as a novelist, and marks his dissatisfaction with his more conventional earlier novels. Indeed, at the end of part one, before he introduces "The New Satyricon," Mitchell observes, "I think it unlikely that I shall write another book of my own for a long time, with the fact of this one before me. Charles said that all art comes from an inner need. He said that I began to write because I wanted to be a writer, and that was the wrong kind of need."

—Bernard Bergonzi

MITCHELL, W(illiam) O(rmond). Canadian. Born in Weyburn, Saskatchewan, 13 March 1914. Educated at St. Petersburg High School, Florida; University of Manitoba, Winnipeg (Gold Medal for Philosophy, 1934), 1932–34; University of Alberta, Edmonton, B.A. 1942. Married Merna Lynne Hirtle in 1942; two sons and one daughter. Has worked as a seaman, salesman, teacher, and high school principal. Writer-in-Residence, University of Calgary, Alberta, 1969–71; University of Toronto, 1973–74; York University, Downsview, Ontario, 1977–78; University of Windsor, Ontario, 1979–81. Recipient: *Maclean's* award, 1953; University of Western Ontario President's Medal, 1953; CCAA award, for drama, 1956; Leacock Medal, 1962; Drainie award, 1968; Actra award, for drama, 1975; Chalmers award, for drama, 1976; Banff School of Fine Arts award, 1980; Canadian Authors Association award, for drama, 1983. D.Litt.: University of Ottawa, 1972; LL.D.: University of Saskatchewan, Saskatoon, 1972. Officer, Order of Canada, 1973. Lives in Calgary, Alberta. Address: c/o Macmillan of Canada, 146 Front Street West, Suite 685, Toronto, Ontario M5J 1G2, Canada.

PUBLICATIONS

Novels

Who Has Seen the Wind.   Boston, Little Brown, 1947; Edinburgh, Canongate, 1980.
The Kite.   Toronto, Macmillan, 1962.
The Vanishing Point.   Toronto, Macmillan, 1973.
How I Spent My Summer Holidays.   Toronto, Macmillan, 1981.
Since Daisy Creek.   Toronto, Macmillan, 1984; New York, Beaufort, 1985.

Short Stories

Jake and the Kid.   Toronto, Macmillan, 1961.

Uncollected Short Stories

"But as Yesterday," in *Queen's Quarterly* (Kingston, Ontario), Summer 1942.
"Elbow Room," in *Maclean's* (Toronto), 15 September 1942.
"Gettin' Born," in *Maclean's* (Toronto), 1 May 1943.
"Something's Gotta Go," in *Maclean's* (Toronto), 1 July 1945.
"Shoparoon for Maggie," in *Maclean's* (Toronto), 15 May 1948.
"Air-Nest and the Child Harold," in *Maclean's* (Toronto), 1 August 1948.
"Air-Nest and La Belle Dame," in *Maclean's* (Toronto), 1 November 1948.
"Crocus at Coronation," in *Maclean's* (Toronto), 1 June 1953.
"The Alien" (serial), in *Maclean's* (Toronto), 15 September 1953–15 January 1954.

"Princess and the Wild Ones," in *Cavalcade of the North*, edited by George F. Nelson.   New York, Doubleday, 1958.
"How Crocus Got Its Seaway," in *Maclean's* (Toronto), 20 June 1959.
"Patterns," in *Ten for Wednesday Night*, edited by Robert Weaver.   Toronto, McClelland and Stewart, 1961.
"Melvin Arbuckle's First Course in Shock Therapy," in *Singing under Ice*, edited by Grace Merserau.   Toronto, Macmillan, 1974.
"A Tree of Feathers," in *Globe and Mail* (Toronto), 25 December 1975.

Plays

The Devil's Instrument (broadcast, 1949; produced Ottawa, 1972).   Toronto, Simon and Pierre, 1973.
The Black Bonspiel of Wullie MacCrimmon, adaptation of his own story (broadcast, 1951; produced Calgary, Alberta, 1979).   Calgary, Alberta, Frontiers Unlimited, 1965.
Ladybug, Ladybug (radio play), in *Edge 5* (Edmonton, Alberta), Fall 1966.
Centennial Play, with others (produced Lindsay, Ontario, 1967).   Ottawa, Centennial Commission, 1967.
The White Christmas of Archie Nicotine (televised, 1971).   Published in *Prairie Performance*, edited by Diane Bessai, Edmonton, Alberta, NeWest Press, 1980.
Back to Beulah (broadcast, 1974; produced Vancouver, 1976).
The Day Jake Made 'er Rain (produced Winnipeg, 1979).
The Kite, adaptation of his own novel (produced Calgary, Alberta, 1981).
The Dramatic W.O. Mitchell.   Toronto, Macmillan, 1984.

Screenplays (documentaries): *Face of Saskatchewan*, 1955; *Fires of Envy*, 1957; *Political Dynamite*, 1958; *Alien Thunder*, 1976.

Radio Plays: *The Devil's Instrument*, 1949; *Jake and the Kid* series, 1950–56; *The Black Bonspiel of Wullie MacCrimmon*, 1951; *Foothill Fables* series, 1963–64; *Ladybug, Ladybug; Back to Beulah*, 1974; and other plays for CBC since 1947.

Television Plays: *The Devil's Instrument*, 1956; *The White Christmas of Archie Nicotine*, 1971; and other plays for CBC.

*

Bibliography: by Sheila Latham, in *The Annotated Bibliography of Canada's Major Authors 3* edited by Robert Lecker and Jack David, Downsview, Ontario, ECW Press, 1981.

Manuscript Collection: University of Calgary Library, Alberta.

*   *   *

W.O. Mitchell, generally considered a "regional humourist," perhaps himself encourages such a reputation. In the guise of the homespun philosopher he finds a traditional folk identity with which to meet contemporary life and a literary format which matches his penchant for the humour of understatement, wise saws, tall tales, and home truths. But this is not to say that he spurns sophistication, progress, or the 20th century. His stories constantly ask blunt questions about reality and values, probing "sophistication" to see if it isn't hypocrisy by a different name, and reducing contemporary problems to domestic proportions in order to reveal the lineage of human foible which the present has inherited.

Most clearly illustrative of such a technique are the wry though somewhat dated stories of Jake and the Kid, which were written first as dramas and were performed on the Canadian Broadcasting Corporation as a continuing radio series in the 1940's. Set in the ranching country of the Alberta foothills which Mitchell knows well, they detail the laconic education in the vagaries of life which Jake, a hired hand, gives to the young son of his employers—and incidentally, always ironically, to himself. They seldom directly invoke contentious social issues—indeed, when Mitchell does contend head-on with such matters as race relations, as in his serialized novel *The Alien*, the result is more melodramatic than provocative. In rewritten form, *The Alien* was published as *The Vanishing Point* in 1973, but the radical structural changes do not alter its central weakness. Despite Mitchell's wit, his capacity for creating lively scenes and clever caricatures, his central characters here do not develop. Accordingly, their reflections on life seem to lack substance.

One of Mitchell's most successful uses of anecdote occurs in his novel *The Kite*, when the centenarian central character, Daddy Sherry, irrepressibly individual (particularly when officialdom dictates prudence to him), accepts a flooding river as an invitation to a South Seas cruise and sails his uprooted house matter-of-factly away, at dark of night, across the American border. The wit is paramount, but incidentally Mitchell manages bemused swipes at customs regulations and bureaucratic nervousness, and builds up the engagingly exaggerated personalities of his cast. The book as a whole celebrates the virtue of living life fully, of engaging oneself in the *process* of living, of which the cruise incident is merely a genial sign.

The developing spiritual affinity between Daddy and a young boy varies the Jake-Kid relationship, and adds a Wordsworthian dimension to Mitchell's world that is more readily seen in his best book, *Who Has Seen the Wind*. In it, the young Brian O'Connal is broken out of his innocent childhood oneness with the world (into the imperfect loves and prejudices of ordinary humanity) by his increasingly adaptive encounters with death and disorder. The "sleep and forgetting" that marks his growth are accompanied by a developing social conscience, however, revealed ultimately in his "mature" child's commitment to agricultural science, and counter-pointed by the novel's subplots. Their exploration of institutional hypocrisy, educational rigidity, race prejudice, and religious intemperance tends sometimes towards the maudlin, but in the characters of Saint Sammy and the Young Ben, "naturals" whose oneness with the prairie and the wind serves as a kind of true spiritual example to Brian, Mitchell has created unforgettable animated forces. With Brian's renegade Uncle Sean, they together fill the "Jake" role to Brian's "kid" and widen rather than reduce the intensity of the effect Jake was meant to exert. For a generation of radio listeners Jake was a shrewd observer of daily life; Brian's relationship with the world of the Young Ben appeals to rather more, for the imaginative experience it represents transcends place and time. Tracing the loss of a child's self and the gain of a man's, the book probes the many dimensions of reality—raising Berkeleyan dilemmas, countering them with Wordsworthian intuitions—and covering all with the gentle humour of a man in love with life whose acute eyes remind him constantly of the failings of mankind as well as of its humane possibilities.

Mitchell's subsequent novels—*How I Spent My Summer Holidays* and *Since Daisy Creek*—probe the dark counterpoint to the young Brian's summer hopes. The world of childhood, in the first of these, ends abruptly when the central character's pretend-adventure runs into real violence instead, when the small town's geniality is discovered to be riddled with bitterness and vice. *Since Daisy Creek* reaches for greater equanimity, but more by indirection than by grasp: the aging narrator, recovering from a grizzly attack, reflects sardonically on staid expectations and professorial criticism. The moments of tenderness are those when he admits to his own infirmities, and accepts his opportunities for love.

—W.H. New

MITCHISON, Naomi (Margaret, née Haldane). British. Born in Edinburgh, Scotland, 1 November 1897; daughter of the scientist John Scott Haldane; sister of the writer J.B.S. Haldane. Educated at Lynam's School, Oxford; St. Anne's College, Oxford. Served as a volunteer nurse, 1915. Married G.R. Mitchison (who became Lord Mitchison, 1964) in 1916 (died, 1970); three sons and two daughters. Labour candidate for Parliament, Scottish Universities constituency, 1935; member, Argyll County Council, 1945–66; member, Highland Panel, 1947–64, and Highlands and Islands Development Council, 1966–76. Tribal adviser, and Mmarona (Mother), to the Bakgatla of Botswana, 1963–73. D.Univ.: University of Stirling, Scotland, 1976; D.Litt.: University of Strathclyde, Glasgow, 1983; D.Law: University of Dundee, Scotland. Honorary Fellow, St. Anne's College, 1980, and Wolfson College, 1983, Oxford. Officer, French Academy, 1924. C.B.E. (Commander, Order of the British Empire), 1985. Address: Carradale House, Campbeltown, Argyll, Scotland.

PUBLICATIONS

Novels

The Conquered. London, Cape, and New York, Harcourt Brace, 1923.
Cloud Cuckoo Land. London, Cape, 1925; New York, Harcourt Brace, 1926.
The Corn King and the Spring Queen. London, Cape, and New York, Harcourt Brace, 1931; as *The Barbarian*, New York, Cameron, 1961.
The Powers of Light. London, Cape, and New York, Peter Smith, 1932.
Beyond This Limit. London, Cape, 1935.
We Have Been Warned. London, Constable, 1935; New York, Vanguard Press, 1936.
The Blood of the Martyrs. London, Constable, 1939; New York, McGraw Hill, 1948.
The Bull Calves. London, Cape, 1947.
Lobsters on the Agenda. London, Gollancz, 1952.
Travel Light. London, Faber, 1952.
To the Chapel Perilous. London, Allen and Unwin, 1955.
Behold Your King. London, Muller, 1957.
Memoirs of a Spacewoman. London, Gollancz, 1962.
When We Become Men. London, Collins, 1965.
Cleopatra's People. London, Heinemann, 1972.
Solution Three. London, Dobson, and New York, Warner, 1975.
Not by Bread Alone. London, Boyars, 1983.

Short Stories

When the Bough Breaks and Other Stories. London, Cape, and New York, Harcourt Brace, 1924.

Black Sparta: Greek Stories.   London, Cape, and New York, Harcourt Brace, 1928.
Barbarian Stories.   London, Cape, and New York, Harcourt Brace, 1929.
The Delicate Fire: Short Stories and Poems.   London, Cape, and New York, Harcourt Brace, 1933.
The Fourth Pig: Stories and Verses.   London, Constable, 1936.
Five Men and a Swan: Short Stories and Poems.   London, Allen and Unwin, 1958.
Images of Africa.   Edinburgh, Canongate, 1980.
What Do You Think Yourself? Scottish Short Stories.   Edinburgh, Harris, 1982.

Uncollected Short Stories

"After the Accident," in *The Year 2000*, edited by Harry Harrison.   New York, Doubleday, 1970; London, Faber, 1971.
"Mary and Joe," in *Nova 1*, edited by Harry Harrison.   New York, Delacorte Press, 1970; London, Sphere, 1975.
"Death of a Peculiar Boar," in *Worlds of Fantasy* (New York), Winter 1970.
"Miss Omega Raven," in *Nova 2*, edited by Harry Harrison.   New York, Walker, 1972; London, Sphere, 1975.
"The Factory," in *Nova 3*, edited by Harry Harrison.   New York, Walker, 1973; London, Sphere, 1975.
"Out of the Waters," in *Nova 4*, edited by Harry Harrison.   New York, Walker, 1974; London, Sphere, 1976.
"Valley of the Bushes," in *Andromeda 1*, edited by Peter Weston.   London, Futura, 1976; New York, St. Martin's Press, 1979.
"The Finger," in *Best Science Fiction Stories of the Year 10*, edited by Gardner Dozois.   New York, Dutton, 1981.
"Was It So," in *A Christmas Feast*.   London, Macmillan, 1983.
"Words," in *Despatches from the Frontiers of the Female Mind*, edited by Jen Green and Sarah Lefanu.   London, Women's Press, 1985.

Plays

Nix-Nought-Nothing: Four Plays for Children (includes *My Ain Sel'*, *Hobyah! Hobyah!*, *Elfen Hill*).   London, Cape, 1928; New York, Harcourt Brace, 1929.
Kate Crackernuts: A Fairy Play.   Oxford, Alden Press, 1931.
The Price of Freedom, with L.E. Gielgud (produced Cheltenham, 1949).   London, Cape, 1931.
Full Fathom Five, with L.E. Gielgud (produced London, 1932).
An End and a Beginning and Other Plays (includes *The City and the Citizens*, *For This Man Is a Roman*, *In the Time of Constantine*, *Wild Men Invade the Roman Empire*, *Charlemagne and His Court*, *The Thing That Is Plain*, *Cortez in Mexico*, *Akbar*, *But Still It Moves*, *The New Calendar*, *American Britons*).   London, Constable, 1937; as *Historical Plays for Schools*, 2 vols., 1939.
As It Was in the Beginning, with L.E. Gielgud.   London, Cape, 1939.
The Corn King, music by Brian Easdale, adaptation of the novel by Mitchison (produced Glasgow, 1951).   London, French, 1951.

Verse

The Laburnum Branch.   London, Cape, 1926.
The Alban Goes Out.   Harrow, Middlesex, Raven Press, 1939.
The Cleansing of the Knife and Other Poems.   Edinburgh, Canongate, 1978.

Other (for children)

The Hostages and Other Stories for Boys and Girls.   London, Cape, 1930; New York, Harcourt Brace, 1931.
Boys and Girls and Gods.   London, Watts, 1931.
The Big House.   London, Faber, 1950.
Graeme and the Dragon.   London, Faber, 1954.
The Swan's Road.   London, Naldrett Press, 1954.
The Land the Ravens Found.   London, Collins, 1955.
Little Boxes.   London, Faber, 1956.
The Far Harbour.   London, Collins, 1957.
Judy and Lakshmi.   London, Collins, 1959.
The Rib of the Green Umbrella.   London, Collins, 1960.
The Young Alexander the Great.   London, Parrish, 1960; New York, Roy, 1961.
Karensgaard: The Story of a Danish Farm.   London, Collins, 1961.
The Young Alfred the Great.   London, Parrish, 1962; New York, Roy, 1963.
The Fairy Who Couldn't Tell a Lie.   London, Collins, 1963.
Alexander the Great.   London, Longman, 1964.
Henny and Crispies.   Wellington, New Zealand, Department of Education, 1964.
Ketse and the Chief.   London, Nelson, 1965; New York, Nelson, 1967.
A Mochudi Family.   Wellington, New Zealand, Department of Education, 1965.
Friends and Enemies.   London, Collins, 1966; New York, Day, 1968.
The Big Surprise.   London, Kaye and Ward, 1967.
Highland Holiday.   Wellington, New Zealand, Department of Education, 1967.
African Heroes.   London, Bodley Head, 1968; New York, Farrar Straus, 1969.
Don't Look Back.   London, Kaye and Ward, 1969.
The Family at Ditlabeng.   London, Collins, 1969; New York, Farrar Straus, 1970.
Sun and Moon.   London, Bodley Head, 1970; Nashville, Nelson, 1973.
Sunrise Tomorrow.   London, Collins, and New York, Farrar Straus, 1973.
The Danish Teapot.   London, Kaye and Ward, 1973.
Snake!   London, Collins, 1976.
The Little Sister, with works by Ian Kirby and Keetla Masogo.   Cape Town, Oxford University Press, 1976.
The Wild Dogs, with works by Megan Biesele.   Cape Town, Oxford University Press, 1977.
The Brave Nurse and Other Stories.   Cape Town, Oxford University Press, 1977.
The Two Magicians, with Dick Mitchison.   London, Dobson, 1978.
The Vegetable War.   London, Hamish Hamilton, 1980.

Other

Anna Comnena.   London, Howe, 1928.
Comments on Birth Control.   London, Faber, 1930.
The Home and a Changing Civilisation.   London, Lane, 1934.
Vienna Diary.   London, Gollancz, and New York, Smith and Haas, 1934.
Socrates, with Richard Crossman.   London, Hogarth Press, 1937; Harrisburg, Pennsylvania, Stackpole, 1938.
The Moral Basis of Politics.   London, Constable, 1938; Port Washington, New York, Kennikat Press, 1971.
The Kingdom of Heaven.   London, Heinemann, 1939.

Men and Herring: A Documentary, with Denis Macintosh. Edinburgh, Serif, 1949.

Other People's Worlds (travel). London, Secker and Warburg, 1958.

A Fishing Village on the Clyde, with G.W.L. Paterson. London, Oxford University Press, 1960.

Presenting Other People's Children. London, Hamlyn, 1961.

Return to the Fairy Hill (autobiography and sociology). London, Heinemann, and New York, Day, 1966.

The Africans: A History. London, Blond, 1970.

Small Talk: Memories of an Edwardian Childhood. London, Bodley Head, 1973.

A Life for Africa: The Story of Bram Fischer. London, Merlin Press, and Boston, Carrier Pigeon, 1973.

Oil for the Highlands? London, Fabian Society, 1974.

All Change Here: Girlhood and Marriage (autobiography). London, Bodley Head, 1975.

Sittlichkeit (lecture). London, Birkbeck College, 1975.

You May Well Ask: A Memoir 1920–1940. London, Gollancz, 1979.

Mucking Around: Five Continents over Fifty Years. London, Gollancz, 1981.

Margaret Cole 1893–1980. London, Fabian Society, 1982.

Among You, Taking Notes: The Wartime Diary of Naomi Mitchison 1939–1945, edited by Dorothy Sheridan. London, Gollancz, 1985.

Editor, *An Outline for Boys and Girls and Their Parents.* London, Gollancz, 1932.

Editor, with Robert Britton and George Kilgour, *Re-Educating Scotland.* Glasgow, Scoop, 1944.

Editor, *What the Human Race Is Up To.* London, Gollancz, 1962.

*

Manuscript Collections: National Library of Scotland, Edinburgh; University of Texas, Austin.

Naomi Mitchison comments:

I write a number of different kinds of books, as you see. When I began writing this was possible because at that time books were written because the authors had something they wanted to say; today books are a commodity like other commodities. What is important is whether publishers think they can sell them. Most publishers have definite selling plans and if a given book does not fit into this, the author has little chance of getting it published. Today, if one wants to write about something special, one has to try and persuade a publisher that this was something he had already thought of. I like writing children's books because one has to write absolutely straight, without playing any of the stylistic or literary tricks which will take in an adult audience. I like digging out the facts of history and seeing what they will add up to. I like thinking what people do in strange situations, for instance in the past, in Africa or India, or in imaginary but possible situations in science fiction. This may enable one—or other people—to make some contribution towards a happier world.

*   *   *

In Naomi Mitchison's historical novels and short stories, with which she established her earliest reputation, an essential theme is conflict of loyalties, whether in Gaul at the time of Caesar's conquest, as in her first novel, *The Conquered*, or among the people of a small Aegean island who are dragged willy-nilly, on one side or another, into the bitter fratricidal battle between Athens and Sparta in the 4th century B.C.—the subject of her ironically entitled *Cloud Cuckoo Land*. Her major work in this genre is *The Corn King and the Spring Queen*, a study in the relationships between the people of three different societies—an agricultural community in the Crimea where the old fertility religion still remains strong enough to provide the folk with purposive unity; a decadent Greece where religious belief has broken down and the struggle to create a just society is conducted—and fails—on a secular basis; and an imperial Egypt where despotism has led to political apathy, disillusion, cynical hedonism, and a frantic search for religious consolation. At once a presentation of personal breakdown and reintegration, a picture of the stresses between idealism and expediency involved in the rise and fall of a revolutionary movement, and an exploration of the relationship between religious conviction and communal solidarity, between scepticism and the loosening of social cohesion, this novel is unsurpassed in 20th-century British historical fiction for range and variety of scene and characterisation, for political awareness, and for religious depth.

On Scottish subjects, Mitchison is at her best in *The Big House*, a children's fairytale which is also a tragi-comedy expressing a profound understanding of the intermingled light and darkness of the human situation, a book where the natural magic of childhood, the terrible charm of the supernatural, the dark power of history, and a vision of life as at once dreadful and sublime, are all woven together. From the fairytale she has gone on to a science-fiction fantasy with *Memoirs of a Spacewoman*, where she shows—in three related chapters about a world inhabited by butterflies and their larvae—a deep imaginative comprehension of extra-terrestrial modes of existence, and a compassionate reverence for life, even at its most remote and mysterious, which lift her work out of the category of the merely inventive and fanciful to give it something of the universality of legend. A poet as well as a prose-writer, Mitchison has written a futuristic story about the exploration of space which is itself a myth, a concentrated symbolical expression of generations of experience.

Alongside fantasy, Mitchison has also written "documentary" novels on contemporary social experience, some with a Scottish location and some set in Africa, where she has worked in Botswana. In these, characterisation tends to be subordinated to background detail. Perhaps the finest of her contemporary studies is the title-story of her collection *Five Men and a Swan*, a modern Scottish folk-tale which combines tenderness, brutality, humour, beauty, and sheer magic in a parable on the theme of human greed and stupidity. While the detail of this story is exactly in period, the writing has a quality of timelessness before which criticism must needs be silent.

—Alexander Scott

MOMADAY, N(avarre) Scott. American. Born in Lawton, Oklahoma, 27 February 1934. Educated at the University of New Mexico, Albuquerque, A.B. 1958; Stanford University, California (Creative Writing Fellow, 1959), A.M. 1960, Ph.D. 1963. Married 1) Gaye Mangold in 1959 (divorced), three daughters; 2) Regina Heitzer in 1978, one daughter. Assistant Professor, 1963–67, and Associate Professor, 1967–69, University of California, Santa Barbara; Professor of English and

Comparative Literature, University of California, Berkeley, 1969–72; Professor of English, Stanford University, 1972–80. Since 1980, Professor of English and Comparative Literature, University of Arizona, Tucson. Professor, University of California Institute for the Humanities, 1970; Whittall Lecturer, Library of Congress, Washington, D.C., 1971; Visiting Professor, New Mexico State University, Las Cruces, 1972–73, State University of Moscow, Spring 1974, Columbia University, New York, 1979, and Princeton University, New Jersey, 1979. Since 1978, member of the Board of Trustees, Museum of the American Indian, New York. Recipient: Guggenheim grant, 1966; Pulitzer Prize, 1969; American Academy award, 1970; Western Heritage Award, 1974; Western Literature Association award, 1983. D.H.L.: Central Michigan University, Mt. Pleasant, 1970; University of Massachusetts, Amherst, 1975; Yale University, New Haven, Connecticut, 1980; Hobart and William Smith Colleges, Geneva, New York, 1980; College of Santa Fe, 1982; D.Litt.: Lawrence University, Appleton, Wisconsin, 1971; University of Wisconsin, Milwaukee, 1976; College of Ganado, 1979; D.F.A.: Morningside College, Sioux City, Iowa, 1980. Address: 1041 Roller Coaster Road, Tucson, Arizona 85704, U.S.A.

PUBLICATIONS

Novel

House Made of Dawn.   New York, Harper, 1968; London, Gollancz, 1969.

Verse

Angle of Geese and Other Poems.   Boston, Godine, 1974.
The Gourd Dancer.   New York, Harper, 1976.

Other

The Journey of Tai-me (Kiowa Indian tales).   Privately printed, 1967; revised edition, as *The Way to Rainy Mountain*, Albuquerque, University of New Mexico Press, 1969.
Colorado: Summer, Fall, Winter, Spring, photographs by David Muench.   Chicago, Rand McNally, 1973.
The Names: A Memoir.   New York, Harper, 1976.

Editor, *The Complete Poems of Frederick Goddard Tuckerman.*   New York, Oxford University Press, 1965.

*

Manuscript Collection: Bancroft Library, University of California, Berkeley.

Critical Study: *Four American Indian Literary Masters* by Alan R. Velie, Norman, University of Oklahoma Press, 1982.

*   *   *

The Rainy Mountain that is central to both of N. Scott Momaday's major works is the lost Eden of the Kiowa Indians. In *The Way to Rainy Mountain* it haunts the narrator's memory and is the still point around which the complex chronology of myth, telling, and recollection is woven. Like a piece of Renaissance typography the text is differentiated by typefaces into the myth, the history of the tribe that the narrator's grandmother remembers, and the more lyrical Wordsworthian recollections of a land of lost content that are the narrator's own

observations. And in this fiction Momaday gives us the American equivalent of a whole tradition of English writing that runs from Hardy and Jefferies and Hudson to Ronald Blythe and Peter Laslett.

What is strikingly different in Momaday is the central symbolic myth—the Tai-me image of the human in white feathers, for instance. The government's prohibition of the ritual of the Sun-Dance, to which this image of the tribe's ancient power of survival was central, spelled the end of the Kiowa as a people who knew who they were and why. No one knows better than Momaday that "a people without history is not redeemed from time, for history is a pattern of timeless moments." And it is that pattern that his triads of myth, history, and recollection present again and again, almost musically, the significance of the myth finding itself felt upon the narrator's pulses as uncorrupted spectator.

In this sense Momaday becomes the voice of the past but in no merely nostalgic way, rather its literal discoverer in the present world of drab that looks for roots. "What the dead had no speech for when living, they can tell you, being dead," might also be his text, for the world of myth and history belongs to an oral culture that had no need for the dead letters of the printed page and is written down only when it has been forgotten.

So the Abel of Momaday's *House Made of Dawn* is paradoxically Cain—the outcast, the man running forever to find the world that was lost almost before he began. There are echoes of Fitzgerald in him—perhaps he might run a little faster, and one fine day . . . , as there are echoes of Faulkner's Christmas in the outcast who runs out in a circle never breaking out or being understood. And like the figures in Faulkner's landscapes the distance seems never to diminish. In the prologue Abel, running against the wintry sky and the long, light landscape of the valley at dawn, "seemed almost to be standing still, very little and alone." Above all the landscape is important in a way that a post-ecology generation has only begun to discover—the Indians' incomprehension of the white man's desire to possess the land that, like the air, is everyone's legacy.

Abel's experience is increasingly of the starvation of that life in the sterility of Los Angeles. Perhaps partly because Momaday is less effective writing about the white demi-monde into which Abel stumbles—his momentary stasis of love is never satisfactory and curiously third-hand—the images of his dissolution are the more telling—broken like a bird against a fence, his hands swollen useless under the violence of meaningless attack.

One sees him at this moment close-up as if the runner were passing. Increasingly he recedes as a figure in a landscape, running—the sound of the feet and the breathless runner. But one's sense is also of a rhythm in that, the beat of the heart that measures terror, loneliness, and hope—always winning near the goal, never achieving. The land of lost content is lost even though Abel has to come home to find it so. But even in his dying there is a hauntingly eloquent evocation of myths that are truer than those of Faulkner's Sartorises, felt at last, wordlessly, only at the moment of death.

—D.D.C. Chambers

d. 1999 (Jan.

MOORE, Brian.   Canadian.   Born in Belfast, Northern Ireland, 25 August 1921; moved to Canada in 1948 and to the United States in 1959. Educated at Saint Malachy's College,

Lies of Silence (199)

No Other Life (1993)

Belfast. Served in the Belfast Fire Service, 1942–43, and with the British Ministry of War Transport, in North Africa, Italy, and France, 1943–45. Married 1) Jacqueline Sirois in 1951; 2) Jean Denney in 1967; one son. Served with United Nations Relief and Rehabilitation Administration (UNRRA) Mission to Poland, 1946–47; reporter, Montreal *Gazette*, 1948–52. Regents' Professor, 1974–75, and since 1976, Professor, University of California, Los Angeles. Recipient: Authors Club of Great Britain award, 1956; Beta Sigma Phi award, 1956; Quebec Literary Prize, 1958; Guggenheim fellowship, 1959; Governor-General's award, 1961, 1975; American Academy grant, 1961; Canada Council fellowship, 1962; W.H. Smith Literary Award, 1973; National Catholic Book Award, 1973; James Tait Black Memorial Prize, 1976; Scottish Arts Council senior fellowship, 1983. Lives in Malibu, California. Agent: Curtis Brown, 10 Astor Place, New York, New York 10003, U.S.A.

PUBLICATIONS

Novels

The Executioners (as Michael Bryan).   Toronto, Harlequin, 1951.
Wreath for a Redhead (as Michael Bryan).   Toronto, Harlequin, 1951.
Judith Hearne.   Toronto, Collins, and London, Deutsch, 1955; as *The Lonely Passion of Judith Hearne*, Boston, Little Brown, 1956.
Intent to Kill (as Michael Bryan).   New York, Dell, and London, Eyre and Spottiswoode, 1956.
Murder in Majorca (as Michael Bryan).   New York, Dell, 1957; London, Eyre and Spottiswoode, 1958.
The Feast of Lupercal.   Boston, Little Brown, 1957; London, Deutsch, 1958; as *A Moment of Love*, London, Panther, 1965.
The Luck of Ginger Coffey.   Boston, Little Brown, and London, Deutsch, 1960.
An Answer from Limbo.   Boston, Little Brown, 1962; London, Deutsch, 1963.
The Emperor of Ice-Cream.   New York, Viking Press, 1965; London, Deutsch, 1966.
I Am Mary Dunne.   New York, Viking Press, and London, Cape, 1968.
Fergus.   New York, Holt Rinehart, 1970; London, Cape, 1971.
Catholics.   London, Cape, 1972; New York, Harcourt Brace, 1973.
The Great Victorian Collection.   New York, Farrar Straus, and London, Cape, 1975.
The Doctor's Wife.   New York, Farrar Straus, and London, Cape, 1976.
The Mangan Inheritance.   New York, Farrar Straus, and London, Cape, 1979.
The Temptation of Eileen Hughes.   New York, Farrar Straus, and London, Cape, 1981.
Cold Heaven.   New York, Holt Rinehart, and London, Cape, 1983.
Black Robe.   New York, Dutton, and London, Cape, 1985.

Short Stories

Two Stories.   Northridge, California, Santa Susana Press, 1978.

Plays

Catholics, adaptation of his own novel (televised, 1973; produced Seattle, 1980; Belfast, 1985).

Screenplays: *The Luck of Ginger Coffey*, 1964; *Torn Curtain*, 1966; *The Slave*, 1967; *Catholics*, 1973; *The Blood of Others*, 1984; *The Sight*, 1985.

Television Play: *Catholics*, 1973.

Other

Canada, with the editors of Life.   New York, Time, 1963.
The Revolution Script.   New York, Holt Rinehart, 1971; London, Cape, 1972.

*

Critical Studies: "The Simple Excellence of Brian Moore" by Christopher Ricks, in *New Statesman* (London), 18 February 1966; "Crisis and Ritual in Brian Moore's Belfast Novels" by John Wilson Foster, in *Eire-Ireland* (St. Paul, Minnesota), Autumn 1968; *Brian Moore*, Toronto, Copp Clark, 1969, and *Brian Moore*, Boston, Twayne, 1981, both by Hallvard Dahlie; *Odysseus Ever Returning* by George Woodcock, Toronto, McClelland and Stewart, 1970; "The Novels of Brian Moore" by Michael Paul Gallagher, S.J., in *Studies (Ireland)* (Dublin), Summer 1971; "The Crisis of Identity in the Novels of Brian Moore" by Murry Prosky, in *Eire-Ireland* (St. Paul, Minnesota), Summer 1971; *Brian Moore* by Jeanne Flood, Lewisburg, Pennsylvania, Bucknell University Press, 1974; "Brian Moore: Private Person" by Bruce Cook, in *Commonweal* (New York), 23 August 1974; "The Novels of Brian Moore: A Retrospective" by De Witt Henry, in *Ploughshares* (Cambridge, Massachusetts), Fall 1974; "Webs of Artifice" by Derek Mahon, in *New Review* (London), October 1975; "Brian Moore: Past and Present" in *Critical Quarterly* (Manchester), 1976, and *Four Contemporary Novelists*, Montreal, McGill-Queen's University Press, 1982, London, Scolar Press, 1983, both by Kerry McSweeney; "Portrait of the Artist as Émigré" by Philip French, in *Observer* (London), October 1977; "The Calligraphy of Pain" by Hubert de Santana, in *Maclean's* (Toronto), September 1979.

*   *   *

Highly praised by reviewers and critics, Brian Moore's compressed and effective fiction has not always achieved the wide popular acclaim it merits. His subjects indicate an extraordinary diversity of interest and sympathy: the lonely spinster who drinks while she longs for contacts with others she cannot sustain in *Judith Hearne*; the young Canadian newspaperman who returns to the Ireland his grandfather migrated from to try to find whether or not he is descended from the famous Irish poet, James Clarence Mangan, in *The Mangan Inheritance*; the contemporary women uneasy about their sexuality and their marriages, in America in *I Am Mary Dunne* and in Northern Ireland in *The Doctor's Wife*; different forms of religious obsession, both sought after and struggled against in *The Temptation of Eileen Hughes* and *Cold Heaven*; the impingement, disastrous for all, of 17th-century Jesuits on various tribes of North American Indians in *Black Robe*. Moore doesn't repeat themes, metaphors, and subjects from novel to novel. Similarly, his settings (often immediately contemporary, but with frequent reference to the past) vary from Belfast to Montreal to California to New York to southern Ireland and England, paralleling Moore's own migration from Belfast to Canada to California.

Moore's best-known novel, made into a popular film, and the one that can be most easily attached to a popular genre of fiction, is *The Luck of Ginger Coffey*. An Irish immigrant to Canada whose dreams of business success are at odds with his shabby reality, as his small green feathered fedora is out of place in Montreal in the late 1950's, Ginger is forced to accept jobs as a night-shift proof-reader for a newspaper and a driver for a diaper service rather than the entrepreneurial positions of his imagination. In the difference between Ginger's vision of himself and reality, Moore manages a brisk and highly comic version of the contemporary picaresque, the estranged hero wandering about the modern world. But, unlike some of his contemporaries, Moore combines satirical distance with a respect for Ginger, a sympathy with this aging displaced man who would do anything to give his wife and daughter the kind of life he assumes they ought to have. Finally, when arrested for drunkenness and indecent exposure, Ginger gives the police a false name and is willing to accept further punishment just to protect his family. His wife recognizes, in a moving and understated conclusion, the humane concern for others that propels Ginger's feeble self-deceptions.

In Moore's fiction, the alienation of the central characters is often, in part, the result of internalized clashes between cultures dramatized with considerable sensitivity. Young Gavin Burke in *The Emperor of Ice-Cream* is growing up as a Catholic in Belfast at the beginning of the Second World War, experiencing all the religious and national divisions involved, and rebelling from his family by working for the Home Guard instead of following his brother to the university. When the Germans bomb Belfast, Gavin is publicly vindicated, but vindication is less the issue than Gavin's realization of his own identity, his capacity to resolve the dualisms of his childhood, in which he had always a "white" angel contending with a "black," and recognize his own responsibility for what he is. In a later novel, *The Doctor's Wife*, the "troubles" of Northern Ireland are also visible as constantly present background, handled with skill and subtlety, in the story of Sheila Redden, married to a Belfast doctor for 16 years, who runs off with a young American she meets in Paris. Again, the issue is self-definition far more than cultural conflict or victimization. Frequently, the conflict is presented in religious terms, as in *Cold Heaven* where Marie Davenport's fears that her rejection of her convent education may have combined with her guilt concerning her adultery to create her vision of the Virgin Mary on a rock near Carmel, California—a vision she can finally exorcise by reporting it to others. *Catholics* deals with a young American priest of Irish descent who is sent by Rome to gain the obedience of a remote abbey on the rocky west coast of Ireland to the new order for the secular mass. He is successful, yet the novel concludes with a powerful and understated sense that the remote community, which had resisted despoliation by Henry VIII and by Cromwell, will never be the same again, an inevitable sacrifice to the historical process in which "yesterday's orthodoxy is today's heresy." *Black Robe* grounds its clash of cultures in historical fact, using Francis Parkman's journals and other sources in a prefatory note stating that the novel shows "that each of these beliefs inspired in the others fear, hostility, and despair," which led to both the abandonment of the Jesuit missions and the destruction of the Hurons.

Always treating his central characters with considerable respect, no matter how comic or ludicrous the dilemmas in which they involve themselves, Moore sometimes writes from the point of view of female characters. He is, in his own way, sensitive to changes in the general perception of female consciousness. In his 1960's novel from the female point of view, *Mary Dunne*, presented on the single day that recalls all her other days and her two earlier marriages as well as her present successful one, marriages that parallel her migration from the Canadian maritimes to Montreal to New York, is likely to attribute too much of her uneasiness to pre-menstrual tension. In his 1970's novel, *The Doctor's Wife*, such an explanation is part of the impercipient doctor's point of view, and Sheila Redden, finally, must work out what she is independently, not through marriage or an affair. Similarly, in the 1980's version of a woman coming to understand herself and her world, *The Temptation of Eileen Hughes*, the initially innocent Eileen must recognize that, in her connection with the strangely spiritually obsessed Bernard, she is both temptress and tempted and must finally achieve independence by rejecting both roles, leaving Bernard to commit suicide for which Eileen is not responsible. All these novels maintain a combination of sympathy and distance, and convincingly show a character coming to terms with both her past and her present, as, in Mary Dunne's terms, "Memento ergo sum" ("I remember, therefore I am").

Moore's prose is always effective, often sharply referential, as in describing the California nuns in *Cold Heaven* who grow lettuce in the convent garden as "peasants at harvest in a Brueghel painting" stacking the lettuce in "yellow plastic containers." His plots often contain inventive fantasy that incorporates past visions or history. *The Great Victorian Collection* begins with a young history professor from Montreal temporarily in Carmel who wakes to find that a full collection of Victoriana he has just dreamed really exists in a motel parking lot. The complications of his strange creation are comically fascinating, although the novel, perhaps Moore's least effective, does not sustain the interest initially generated by the metaphor and the fantasy. The search for the Irish poetic past in *The Mangan Inheritance* is also highly inventive, propelled by young Jamie Mangan's resemblance to a photograph he finds of his famous ancestor, a physical similarity as well as a similarity in poetic talent and a tendency toward self-destruction. The novel proceeds through a gradual revelation of mystery, sometimes with touches of the macabre. Yet, in this novel, revelation of the past yields some similarities and some differences for the central character. Identity is a complicated mixture of acting out what one has inherited and consciously working out what one wants to be. In this kind of complexity, in depicting characters living both what of themselves they can change and what of themselves they must accept, Brian Moore, writing always with economy and understatement, is at his very best.

—James Gindin

MOORHOUSE, Frank. Australian. Born in Nowra, New South Wales, 21 December 1938. Educated at the University of Queensland, Brisbane. Served in the Australian Army and Reserves, 1957–59. Divorced. Journalist, Sydney *Telegraph*, 1956–59; editor, *Lockhart Review*, New South Wales, 1960, and *Australian Worker*, Sydney, 1962; assistant secretary, Workers' Educational Association, Sydney, 1963–65; union organiser, Australian Journalists' Association, 1966; contributor and columnist, 1970–79, and night club writer, 1980, *Bulletin*, Sydney; co-founding editor, *Tabloid Story*, Sydney, 1972–74. Vice-President, 1978–80, and President, 1979–82, Australian Society of Authors; Chairman, Copyright Council of Australia, 1985. Recipient: Lawson Short Story Prize, 1970; National Award for Fiction, 1975; Senior Literary Fellowship,

1976. Member, Order of Australia, 1985. Address: G.P.O. Box 4430, Sydney, New South Wales 2001, Australia.

PUBLICATIONS

Short Stories

Futility and Other Animals. Sydney, Powell, 1969.
The Americans, Baby. Sydney and London, Angus and Robertson, 1972.
The Electrical Experience. Sydney, Angus and Robertson, 1974.
Conference-ville. Sydney, Angus and Robertson, 1976.
Tales of Mystery and Romance. London, Angus and Robertson, 1977.
The Everlasting Secret Family and Other Secrets. Sydney and London, Angus and Robertson, 1980.
Selected Stories. Sydney and London, Angus and Robertson, 1982.
Room Service. Ringwood, Victoria, Penguin, 1985.

Plays

Screenplays: *Between Wars*, 1974; *The Disappearance of Azaria Chamberlain*, 1984; *Conference-ville*, 1984; *The Coca Cola Kid*, 1985.

Other

Editor, *Coast to Coast.* Sydney, Angus and Robertson, 1973.
Editor, *Days of Wine and Rage.* Ringwood, Victoria, Penguin, 1980.
Editor, *The State of the Art: The Mood of Contemporary Australia in Short Stories.* Ringwood, Victoria, Penguin, 1983.

*

Manuscript Collections: Fryer Library, University of Queensland, Brisbane; National Library of Australia, Canberra.

Critical Studies: "The Short Stories of Wilding and Moorhouse" by Carl Harrison-Ford, in *Southerly* (Sydney), vol. 33, 1974; "Frank Moorhouse's Discontinuities" by D. Anderson, in *Southerly* (Sydney), vol. 35, 1975; "Some Developments in Short Fiction 1969–80" by Bruce Clunies Ross, in *Australian Literary Studies* (Hobart, Tasmania), vol. 10, no. 2, 1981; interview in *Sideways from the Page* edited by J. Davidson, Melbourne, Fontana, 1983; "The Thinker from the Bush" by Humphrey McQueen, in *Gallipoli to Petrov*, Sydney, Hale and Iremonger, 1984.

Frank Moorhouse comments:

Futility and Other Animals, *The Americans, Baby*, *The Electrical Experience*, and *The Everlasting Secret Family* are described as "discontinuous narratives" and are experiments with interlocked and overlapped short stories. The individual books also overlap and characters recur.

*   *   *

In the stories of Frank Moorhouse Australian life has nothing to do with Jackeroos, kangaroos, or desert places. The Australians of whom he writes are a "modern, urban tribe which does not recognize itself as a tribe," he says in introductory comments for the first collection, *Futility and Other Animals*.

The tribe in *Futility* weave love affairs around knives, walk "vehicle-stewing" streets, are lectured in pubs and tutored in beds. Whatever their niche in the city, they share in the common futility. Moorhouse doesn't seem to like these animals, this tribe, and after a while the limited emotional range of the stories begins to pall. This doesn't happen in *The Electrical Experience*. Here Moorhouse is at his best, still lucidly satirical but this time with some affection, playful and inventive. The stories centre around George McDowell, who grows and ages with the century. George is an earnest manufacturer of aerated waters, a Rotarian *par excellence* (nothing thrills him like the 1923 Rotary Convention in St. Louis), an inveterate talker and sometimes bully who worries about being shy (but manages to "diminish" his shyness when he burns down Charles Crowhurst's house—legally, of course). Detail by detail, McDowell's life and mind accrue mythological stature. Moorhouse has created with wit and intelligence the Australian companion to that American archetype, Sinclair Lewis's Babbitt. Through McDowell, Moorhouse dramatizes his country's political conservatism and its 20th-century subservience to American ideas and products.

In *The Americans, Baby* the milieu is a Sydney confused by the enervating enthusiasm and precarious sexuality of the 1960's. Here are the under-40's who hope that by being either earnest or outrageous, they will turn out to be real. Demonstrations provide religious training mixed with summer camp. They seem more self-conscious than self-fulfilling. If there should happen to be a moment of ease, something will quickly ruin it. Carl will move "of his own free volition" into the arms of the American journalist, Paul Jonson, but afterwards will feel guilty and humiliated and trapped—and will return to the flat again. Throughout these stories dramatic tension develops between impulse, which is associated with sex in various avatars, and an egregiously cerebral approach to life, an approach which suffocates physicality and seems to offer nothing much more appealing than baked potatoes with lemon for dinner, even though the potatoes are served in "a beautiful dark wooden bowl" with "a pile of coarse black bread." The virtue of it all scarcely seems worth the trouble.

Both *The Electrical Experience* and *The Americans, Baby* are sub-titled "a discontinuous narrative." The phrase suggests that each collection is held together as a definable fictional world but that the world is created episodically through an accretion of incident rather than linearly through the chronological narrative traditional to novels. When Moorhouse began publishing his collections, Australian fiction was still heavily bound to the conventions of realism. Few writers had experimented with altering forms to enact experience. Moorhouse did. There was nothing formalistic or sterile about his experiments. He needed a notion of narrative which would suit his vision of what life has become in an Australia where almost a quarter of the country's population was born overseas. As he has said in an interview, "The discontinuous narrative and the fragmented view that come out in the structure of my books" is "a map of how the world—Australia—seems to appear to me. I don't see any underlying harmonies. . . . That old homogeneity through Anglo-Saxon dominance has gone."

The later collections are further evidence of this view but none of them is quite as satisfying as *The Electrical Experience* and *The Americans, Baby*. *Tales of Mystery and Romance* circles around the intricacies of a relationship between two men, the writer-narrator and an academic named Milton. The social vision has contracted to the literary-bohemian life which swirled around the Libertarian Society in the Sydney suburb of Balmain. The stories don't overcome the claustrophobia of that world. The same is true of *Conference-ville*. There

Moorhouse uses the conference as a social ritual which detaches people from their ordinary life and makes them vulnerable to the pressures of ideas and personalities. As in *Tales of Mystery and Romance* the narrator is so given to ironic detachment, self-deprecation, and world-weariness that the stories lack vividness and energy. Aridity spreads from the conference to the prose. The most recent collection, *The Everlasting Secret Family*, contains four separate story sequences. The first, "Pacific City," returns to George McDowell's world but this time focuses on the much shadier, gloomier Irving Bow, proprietor of the Odeon Cinema and of a world of darkness where he entertains and seduces children, where illusion is reality and fantasy, where the imagination incurs guilt and runs a business. The second and third sequences are again conference stories in a quasi-documentary vein, but the final section, which gives the collection its title, is something rather different. Political allegory is fused with pornography in the story of a politician who seduces a schoolboy to whom years later he brings his own son for initiation into a secret and unrecognized family with full membership in that urban Australian tribe whose lives are the stories in Moorhouse's fiction.

Since *The Everlasting Secret Family*, there has been no new collection of stories, although individual stories continue to appear and selections have also been published. The major recent work has been in film. Moorhouse's most ambitious scripts have been for a documentary based on the disappearance of a baby in the Australian outback, and for a feature directed by Dusan Makavejev and released in 1985 as *The Coca Cola Kid*. A decade earlier, the Yugoslav director had talked with Moorhouse about developing a filmscript from the stories about Becker in *The Americans, Baby*, and during the years that followed, Moorhouse wrote and re-wrote scripts before the film was eventually shot in Australia in 1984, an international endeavour with some of its battle-scars still visible on screen.

—Lucy Frost

MORRIS, Wright (Marion). American. Born in Central City, Nebraska, 6 January 1910. Educated at Lakeview High School, Chicago; Crane College, Chicago; Pomona College, Claremont, California, 1930–33. Married 1) Mary Ellen Finfrock in 1934 (divorced, 1961); 2) Josephine Kantor in 1961. Has lectured at Haverford College, Pennsylvania, Sarah Lawrence College, Bronxville, New York, and Swarthmore College, Pennsylvania; Professor of English, California State University, San Francisco, 1962–75. Also a photographer. Recipient: Guggenheim fellowship, 1942, 1946, 1954; National Book Award, 1957; American Academy grant, 1960; Rockefeller grant, 1967; American Book Award, 1981; Los Angeles *Times* Kirsch Award, 1981; Common Wealth award, 1982; Whiting Award, 1985. Honorary degrees: Westminster College, Fulton, Missouri, 1968; University of Nebraska, Lincoln, 1968; Pomona College, 1973. Member, American Academy, 1970. Address: 341 Laurel Way, Mill Valley, California 94941, U.S.A.

PUBLICATIONS

Novels

My Uncle Dudley. New York, Harcourt Brace, 1942.

The Man Who Was There. New York, Scribner, 1945.
The World in the Attic. New York, Scribner, 1949.
Man and Boy. New York, Knopf, 1951; London, Gollancz, 1952.
The Works of Love. New York, Knopf, 1952.
The Deep Sleep. New York, Scribner, 1953; London, Eyre and Spottiswoode, 1954.
The Huge Season. New York, Viking Press, 1954; London, Secker and Warburg, 1955.
The Field of Vision. New York, Harcourt Brace, 1956; London, Weidenfeld and Nicolson, 1957.
Love among the Cannibals. New York, Harcourt Brace, 1957; London, Weidenfeld and Nicolson, 1958.
Ceremony in Lone Tree. New York, Atheneum, 1960; London, Weidenfeld and Nicolson, 1961.
What a Way to Go. New York, Atheneum, 1962.
Cause for Wonder. New York, Atheneum, 1963.
One Day. New York, Atheneum, 1965.
In Orbit. New York, New American Library, 1967.
Fire Sermon. New York, Harper, 1971.
War Games. Los Angeles, Black Sparrow Press, 1972.
A Life. New York, Harper, 1973.
The Fork River Space Project. New York, Harper, 1977.
Plains Song: For Female Voices. New York, Harper, 1980.

Short Stories

Green Grass, Blue Sky, White House. Los Angeles, Black Sparrow Press, 1970.
Here Is Einbaum. Los Angeles, Black Sparrow Press, 1973.
The Cat's Meow. Los Angeles, Black Sparrow Press, 1975.
Real Losses, Imaginary Gains. New York, Harper, 1976.

Uncollected Short Stories

"Lover and the Beloved," in *New Yorker*, 13 July 1981.
"Victoria," in *The Best American Short Stories 1983*, edited by Anne Tyler and Shannon Ravenel. Boston, Houghton Mifflin, 1983.
"Glimpse into Another Country," in *New Yorker*, 26 September 1983.
"Going into Exile," in *New Yorker*, 6 February 1984.
"To Calabria," in *New Yorker*, 23 July 1984.
"Fellow-Creatures," in *New Yorker*, 31 December 1984.
"Country Music," in *New Yorker*, 11 March 1985.

Other

The Inhabitants (photo-text). New York, Scribner, 1946.
The Home Place (photo-text). New York, Scribner, 1948.
The Territory Ahead (essays). New York, Harcourt Brace, 1958; London, Peter Smith, 1964.
A Bill of Rites, A Bill of Wrongs, A Bill of Goods (essays). New York, New American Library, 1968.
God's Country and My People (photo-text). New York, Harper, 1968.
Wright Morris: A Reader. New York, Harper, 1970.
Love Affair: A Venetian Journal (photo-text). New York, Harper, 1972.
About Fiction: Reverent Reflections on the Nature of Fiction with Irreverent Observations on Writers, Readers, and Other Abuses. New York, Harper, 1975.
Structure and Artifacts: Photographs 1933–1954. Lincoln, Nebraska, Sheldon Memorial Art Gallery, 1975.
Conversations with Wright Morris: Critical Views and Responses, edited by Robert E. Knoll. Lincoln, University of Nebraska Press, 1977.

Earthly Delights, Unearthly Adornments: American Writers as Image Makers. New York, Harper, 1978.
Will's Boy: A Memoir. New York, Harper, 1981.
Wright Morris (portfolio of photographs). Roslyn Heights, New York, Witkin Berley, 1981.
Picture America, photographs by Jim Alinder. Boston, New York Graphic Society, 1982.
Wright Morris: Photographs and Words, edited by Jim Alinder. Carmel, California, Friends of Photography, 1982.
The Writing of My Uncle Dudley (address). Berkeley, California, Friends of the Bancroft Library, 1982.
Solo: An American Dreamer in Europe 1933–34. New York, Harper, 1983; London, Penguin, 1984.
Time Pieces: The Photographs and Words of Wright Morris (exhibition catalogue). Washington, D.C., Corcoran Gallery, 1983.
A Cloak of Light: Writing My Life. New York, Harper, 1985.

Editor, *The Mississippi River Reader.* New York, Doubleday, 1962.

*

Manuscript Collection: Bancroft Library, University of California, Berkeley.

Critical Studies: *Wright Morris* by David Madden, New York, Twayne, 1965; *Wright Morris* by Leon Howard, Minneapolis, University of Minnesota Press, 1968; *The Novels of Wright Morris: A Critical Interpretation* (includes bibliography) by G.B. Crump, Lincoln, University of Nebraska Press, 1978.

*   *   *

No contemporary American novelist has managed to be so persistently unfashionable as Wright Morris. Despite his many books, and despite both occasional public honors and a continuous critical assent to his talents, intelligence, integrity, and seriousness, he has never commanded a general attention. His work has resisted categories and obvious affiliations, while in its uniqueness it has prevented imitation. Morris is now an undeniable literary fact, without ever having been an event.

It is in part strange that this should be the case, because no other contemporary American novelist has been so diligently or sensitively in touch with the manners, voices, and things of American civilization. Morris's knowledge has led him, however, to an effort which prohibits ideological assertion for the reason that it prevents final judgements. Narrative line in Morris's fiction is seldom forthright. Thematic development is always subject to new doubts and allurements. The prose is elliptical, allusive, punning, to so great an extent as to seem sometimes incapable of statement. Indeed, language itself seems to be for Morris one more of those mysterious objects produced by the American civilization, which is to be explored for the hint of a revelation rather than be exploited. And the individual novels are not even discrete episodes of realization. Morris borrows freely from himself from book to book, reusing not only characters and events but lengthy passages of narration and reflection. He seems to have been long engaged in thinking through a single work—consisting of fiction, photographs, and an amount of literary and cultural criticism—the end of which is not yet in sight.

He has been so engaged for more than 40 years and through more than 35 books. In this time his single subject has been American nativity, and, if he has been influenced by any literary or cultural movement, it is that new nationalism which was being predicated in the 1910's and 1920's by Van Wyck Brooks, Lewis Mumford, Waldo Frank, Sherwood Anderson, the photographer Alfred Stieglitz, and others. Brooks had made a case for what he called the "usable past." More particularly, he had called upon American writers and critics to seek their own—American—literary past in such a way as to discover a cultural coherence, in which they then might participate. The invitation had itself become a part of the past by the time that Morris began to write, but he seems to have been impressed by some of the later nationalists, notably James Agee and Walker Evans. In any event, quite like those artists who participated in Brooks's enterprise, Morris has made his field of endeavor the American folk past and its relationship to the American present. The subject is the continuity of the American character, sought in its typicality and in its everydayness.

Despite the continuousness—indeed, the circularity—of effort proposed to Morris by his subject, the subject has also commanded a distinguishable progress in his thinking. He began with a commitment to discovery of the past, and he repeated that commitment without qualification, though with varying kinds of cunning, in the five books which he published in the 1940's. In the first, *My Uncle Dudley*, he composed a narrative which would ironically recapitulate the American past of the early middle 19th century. The time present of the novel is the 1920's. Uncle Dudley and his sidekick, the boy who tells the story, do a stint of vagabondage, which secures its significance because it simulates pioneering. In this day and age, the pursuit of the frontier must go from west to east, from Los Angeles to Chicago, and the pretence of the vagabonds to a covered wagon is an ancient touring car. They are assaulted on all sides by contemporary materialism, timidity, and restrictiveness, but they thereby are able to prove the older ways and virtues. And they succeed in their pretence until, just like Huckleberry Finn before them, they are incarcerated in a small town in Missouri. In the succeeding books in this period, Morris reversed his strategy for recovery of the past. *My Uncle Dudley* accepts a conventional myth of the older America and imposes it upon the present. The next books—a volume of novellas, two photo-texts, and a novel—have protagonists who, from their vantage in the present, come upon ambiguous, buried, and ambiguous mementos of the past. As is usually the case in Morris's work, the locus of the past is the rural or small-town midwest. The protagonists of these books find a beckoning but elusive vitalism in occasional survivors from the past, and in such artifacts as peeling Mail Pouch signs on old barns, the fading pages of the old mail order catalogue, or an old and sputtering Model T. The process of apprehension is the area of Morris's concern.

This process seems finally, however, to have borne malign implications for Morris. With *The World in the Attic* he began to explore another realization, to the effect that the past was also potentially imprisoning, and the books thereafter become progressively less retrospective. The protagonists are not at home in the present, which is seen to be a spiritual wasteland, but they avoid regressive nostalgia. The intent of the books of the 1950's—novels and one volume of literary criticism—is recovery into the present not of the past but of a native American character, which is seen to be at once conservative, practical, desperate for spiritual liberation, and audacious. Salvation, if there is to be any, is in the occasional gesture on the part of the protagonists which combines past and present, transcending both.

In these books there was an implication of an astonishing persistence of the rural, frontiering American past, symbolized perhaps most aptly by a character who appeared first in *The*

World in the Attic and who becomes the protagonist of *Ceremony in Lone Tree*. Tom Scanlon is the one remaining inhabitant of the town of Lone Tree, Nebraska. Lone Tree is a ghost town in which there is a life, which if solitary and ancient is yet imperative.

In likely response to a more anarchic climate in American society, in recent novels Morris has begun to explore still another realization within his general subject. That audacity which had been proposed as one of the resources of heroism in the American character, might well be criminal in this time. In *One Day* he speculates on the native American character as it emerges in the American boy who killed President Kennedy. The novel *In Orbit* speculates, not quite so harshly, on the nativity of those randomly violent American boys who are to be seen crossing the landscape on their motorcycles, in perpetual flight. In still more recent novels, stories, and phototexts the area of discovery has again been broadened, now to include speculation on the qualities of resiliency or merely quirky defiance that may be the secret direction of seemingly feckless lives in America. In the title story of the collection *Here Is Einbaum* the protagonist survives wars and insults by the strategem of refusing usual commitments. (In this instance the protagonist, for once, is not a midwestern American. He is an Austrian-Jewish refugee living in New York, but he is nonetheless clearly related to Morris's usual characters, as may be indicated by the fact that a credible translation of "Einbaum" would be "Lone Tree.") In the paired novels *Fire Sermon* and *A Life*, Morris repeats the plot lineaments of his first novel, *My Uncle Dudley*, but now both the mode and the objects of the defiance which is the old man's legacy to the young boy are more complex and more desperate. Defying God, Heaven, and progress, the old man manages to be murdered by a surviving American Indian. In such seemingly topical novels as *The Fork River Space Project* and *Plains Song: For Female Voices*, which find their subject matters alternately in space landings and in the women's movement, Morris's protagonists again discover the true sources of their defiant knowledge in their inheritance of the rural American past. In the severity and loneliness of that past is the origin of the imaginative independence with which they can confront a crowded and demanding contemporary civilization.

These later novels, too, fail to make final assertions. Like all of Morris's novels, they are populated by characters who confess themselves to be frustrated and bewildered, thereby providing opportunity for other and continuous reaches of realization.

—Marcus Klein

MORRISON, Toni (Chloe Anthony Morrison, née Wofford). American. Born in Lorain, Ohio, 18 February 1931. Educated at Howard University, Washington, D.C., B.A. 1953; Cornell University, Ithaca, New York, M.A. 1955. Married Harold Morrison (separated, 1964); two sons. Instructor in English, Texas Southern University, Houston, 1955–57, and Howard University, 1957–64. Since 1965, Senior Editor, Random House, publishers, New York. Visiting Lecturer, Yale University, New Haven, Connecticut, 1976–77, Bard College, Annandale-on-Hudson, New York, and State University of New York, Albany. Recipient: American Academy award,

1979. Agent: Lynn Nesbit, International Creative Management, 40 West 57th Street, New York, New York 10019. Address: c/o Random House, 201 East 50th Street, New York, New York 10022, U.S.A.

PUBLICATIONS

Novels

The Bluest Eye. New York, Holt Rinehart, 1970; London, Chatto and Windus, 1980.
Sula. New York, Knopf, and London, Allen Lane, 1974.
Song of Solomon. New York, Knopf, 1977; London, Chatto and Windus, 1978.
Tar Baby. New York, Knopf, and London, Chatto and Windus, 1981.

* * *

A comparison of Toni Morrison with Joyce and Faulkner is irresistible. One dominant aspect of her work is an exhaustive, mythical exploration of place. Another is the search for the nexus of past and present. She is to the black milieu of Lorain what Joyce and Faulkner are to Dublin and Oxford, and her Medallion is as curiously fascinating as Anderson's Winesburg. Her stories translate a multiplicity of places, often superficially tawdry, into a rich cultural matrix. Likewise, the times of her forbears and herself in Ohio are a duration, not a chronology. She thus makes the legendary altogether new, and discovers in colloquial habit and naming the altogether legendary. Legend includes not only the tales of her black folk, but the myths of world literature. She has excluded Caucasians from her fiction more than Joyce and Faulkner have excluded ethnic "others" from theirs. But her focus on personality and character (in the moral sense) is indisputably universal. Her pervasive irony and paradox are not merely adroit but ethically motivated. At times they accentuate an erosion of the dignified, reliable courtliness of ancestral blacks, the more profound because it was maintained through the grossest depredations in American history. She is able to say of her contemporaries: "We raised our children and reared our crops; we let infants grow, and property develop." It is a deep regard for craft—for verbal nuance, metaphor, image, point of view—that enables Toni Morrison not merely to discourse upon but to animate social process and existential crisis.

The Bluest Eye tells of the incestuous rape of 11-year-old Pecola Breedlove by her father. The girl's need to be loved (pushed to the extreme when she observes her mother, a "domestic," heaping upon a little white girl affections Pecola has only dreamed of) takes the doomed form of a yearning for blue eyes. The insanity of this flight from reality comes to fruition after the death of the baby, when she actually believes herself to have acquired them. With her ubiquitous metaphor of flight, Morrison sums up this personal fate and the novel's powerful theme:

> The damage done was total. She spent her days . . . walking up and down, up and down, her head jerking to the beat of a drummer so distant only she could hear. Elbows bent, hands on shoulders, she flailed her arms like a bird in an eternal, grotesquely futile effort to fly. Beating the air, a winged but grounded bird, intent on the blue void it could not reach—could not even see—but which filled the valleys of the mind.

We are led to conclude that the narrator, Claudia Macteer, and her sister Frieda probably dodged this perversion by directing an ordinate malice at their Shirley Temple dolls and by being born to a family that, though rough and austere, did know how to breed love.

Sula explores equally an extraordinary consciousness and the gap between generations. Sula Mae Peace and her grandmother, Eva, share a great deal in common. Both left the same home in Medallion's "Bottom" only to return and inhabit it in willful isolation. Both shun tender expressions of love. Both have authored another's death. But in her indifference to family bonds, Sula is her grandmother's opposite. Where Eva left to save her family, Sula left to indulge her fancy. Where Eva returned for her children (though only content alone on the second floor), Sula returned from boredom and put her grandmother in a home. Where Eva, with tragic awareness, ignited her son's drug-addicted body, Sula dropped the little boy "Chicken" to his death with a weird inadvertence. And where Eva maimed herself trying to save her flaming daughter Hannah, Sula watched her mother's immolation with distant curiosity.

Yet this portrait is not simply a paean to the old ways. There is sympathy for Sula because as a child she had misconceived Hannah's remark about her, "I love her, I just don't like her," and because of her vain effort to save "Chicken." Of that the narrator remarks that it has exorcised "her one major feeling of responsibility." Moreover, her temperament blends "Eva's arrogance and Hannah's self indulgence" in an "experimental life" which itself seems a precondition for seeing and acting upon hard social truths. And finally, she seems like Pecola Breedlove, whose "guilt" mysteriously sanctified those around her. Sula performs the original Eve's purpose; as a community "witch," she provides others with a scapegoat, a model of such evil conduct that their own is actually elevated thereby.

Song of Solomon is a work of enormous breadth. Macon and Ruth Dead complete an often devastating characterization of genteel blacks begun with Geraldine and Helene in the earlier novels. Self-serving and cool, their son "Milkman" has given full life to the family name. Burdened by his parents' merciless marriage and prompted by his saintly aunt, Pilate, he sets out for Virginia and the skeletons in his family closet. But lore steadily leads and yields to more interesting truth, in the form of persons who correct his myopic view. He discovers his dead grandmother, Sing, so called because she was half Indian, Singing Bird, but also the daughter of a white Virginian named Byrd. And he discovers his great grandfather, Solomon, who once proudly flew the coop of slavery and about whom the country black kids still sing: "O Solomon don't leave me." Song and flight make life endurable and beautiful in Morrison's world. Having discovered these true ancestors, Milkman forgets the mundane, taking his best friend Guitar's advice to heart: "[If you] wanna fly, you got to give up the shit that weighs you down." The murderous conflict that had developed between the two (Guitar is a consummate study of an extremist racial approach toward which the novel displays both sympathy and disgust) is ended: "For now [Milkman] knew what Shalimar knew: If you surrendered to the air, you could *ride* it."

The design of *Tar Baby*, so allegorical and symbolic, probably overextends the mythic note of *Song of Solomon*. Folk legend is provided by the title, but elsewhere little is quite so down to earth and the supporting realism is undercut by both the fabulous Haitian settings and Morrison's anthropomorphizing of them. The key figures are Jadine and Son. Their union and divorce embody a black man's search for an authentic, natural past and a black woman's estrangement from it.

Committed to materialistic white values, she ends by fondling her sealskin coat. She ends, more unbelievably than the airborne Milkman, by entering a jungle so humanoid that it "make[s] the way easier for a certain kind of man," Morrison's archetype.

—David M. Heaton

MORTIMER, Penelope (Ruth, née Fletcher). British. Born in Rhyl, Flint, 19 September 1918. Educated at Croydon High School; New School, Streatham; Blencathra, Rhyl; Garden School, London; St. Elphin's Clergy Daughters School; Central Educational Bureau for Women; University College, London. Married 1) Charles Dimont in 1937 (divorced, 1949), four daughters; 2) the writer John Mortimer in 1949 (divorced, 1971), one son and one daughter. Free-lance writer and journalist: movie critic, *The Observer*, London, 1967–70. Recipient: Whitbread Award, for non-fiction, 1979. Fellow, Royal Society of Literature. Address: The Old Post Office, Chastleton, Moreton-in-Marsh, Gloucestershire, England.

PUBLICATIONS

Novels

Johanna (as Penelope Dimont). London, Secker and Warburg, 1947.
A Villa in Summer. London, Joseph, 1954; New York, Harcourt Brace, 1955.
The Bright Prison. London, Joseph, 1956; New York, Harcourt Brace, 1957.
Daddy's Gone A-Hunting. London, Joseph, 1958; as *Cave of Ice*, New York, Harcourt Brace, 1959.
The Pumpkin Eater. London, Hutchinson, 1962; New York, McGraw Hill, 1963.
My Friend Says It's Bullet-Proof. London, Hutchinson, 1967; New York, Random House, 1968.
The Home. London, Hutchinson, 1971; New York, Random House, 1972.
Long Distance. London, Allen Lane, and New York, Doubleday, 1974.
The Handyman. London, Allen Lane, 1983; New York, St. Martin's Press, 1985.

Short Stories

Saturday Lunch with the Brownings. London, Hutchinson, 1960; New York, McGraw Hill, 1961.

Uncollected Short Stories

"Philpot," in *New Yorker*, 25 August 1962.
"The Skylight," in *Tales of Unease*, edited by John Burke. London, Pan, 1966; New York, Doubleday, 1969.
"Love Story," in *New Yorker*, 15 July 1974.
"Curriculum Vitae," in *New Yorker*, 26 May 1975.
"In the First Place," in *New Yorker*, 22 December 1975.
"Granger's Life So Far," in *New Yorker*, 22 March 1976.
"Diver," in *Encounter* (London), February 1978.

Plays

Screenplay: *Bunny Lake Is Missing*, with John Mortimer, 1965.

Television Plays: *The Renegade*, from her own story, 1961; *Ain't Afraid to Dance*, 1966; *Three's One*, 1973.

Other

With Love and Lizards (travel), with John Mortimer. London, Joseph, 1957.
About Time: An Aspect of Autobiography. London, Allen Lane, and New York, Doubleday, 1979.
Queen Elizabeth: A Life of the Queen Mother. London, Viking, 1986.

*

Penelope Mortimer comments:

(1972) My father was a C. of E. clergyman and I was brought up in Buckinghamshire, Thornton Heath, and Belper in Derbyshire. For various reasons (my father's changing theories as well as residences) I went to seven schools, ending up at a School for the Daughters of the Clergy (disaster). Did a secretarial course in London at the age of 17, hated it, went to London University, left after a year because my father said he was broke, took a job as a secretary to the Publicity Manager of Butlins Holiday Camp, decided after three weeks that marriage was preferable, married, had four children, wrote the odd piece for the *New Statesman* and *Our Time* and spent four years writing *Johanna*, which sank like a stone in 1947.

As well as the 8 books and 2 Mortimer children, I wrote a lot for the *New Yorker*, did fiction reviews for the *Sunday Times*, wrote a Lonely Hearts column under the pseudonym of Ann Temple for the *Daily Mail* (2 ghastly years), and did a considerable amount of other journalism.

The canvas of my fiction is narrow—domestic, mainly concerned with sexual and parental relationships—but I hope makes up in depth what it lacks in breadth. So far, I am almost entirely concerned with individuals, motives (i.e. what "makes them tick") and the development of their personalities from an early age (*Pumpkin Eater* and *The Home* particularly). Rather obviously (though not necessarily) I write through the eyes and ears of a woman. My men, I think, are getting better, and maybe I will someday venture to try to put myself inside a man's head and write from there. I believe that comedy is absolutely essential to tragedy, and I hope my books are almost as funny as they are (I'm told) sad or depressing. I would like to enlarge my scope, but not if it's at the expense of depth. Once my characters are established psychologically—heredity, environment, the lot—they take over their own growth and perform their own actions; I have very little to do with it.

*   *   *

The themes of popular fiction remain what they have always been: sex and marriage, class, money, and power. What has changed is the writer's attitude towards this material. A Victorian novel in this genre ended with a wedding; nowadays the plot tends to begin with an unhappy marriage, trace the course of the more or less unhappy affairs and end where it began, in sexual stalemate.

Of the many English novelists who have explored this territory, none has more sheer ability to write than Penelope Mortimer. She catalogues the debris of failure: the repetitive rows, the broken resolutions, the betrayals which would exact revenge had they not paralysed their victim. In each book the central relationship is destructive; only the children survive "sitting in a patient row on the sofa ... their eyes restless as maggots, expecting us to bring them up." This description from *The Pumpkin Eater* is an example of her writing at its best, candid and original.

A Villa in Summer is an accomplished study of corruption, a portrait of a couple who cling together out of habit as much as out of love. Emily has drifted so far from her husband that he feels "there were two species: Emily and women." Their marriage is vulnerable enough and easily shaken by a predatory pair of adulterers, teachers from the local progressive school.

Emily is the first in a string of lost innocents, heroines who are aware of the truth but unable to act on it. The central character in *Daddy's Gone A-Hunting* is shut off from potential pleasure, experiencing life in waves of guilt and pain. She cannot use her suffering to change her own situation but is able to protect her daughter against their common enemy, Rex, the unfaithful husband and callous father. Rex is typical of the men in Mortimer's fiction, drifting in and out of the story, excluded, pacified, accused. Only occasionally does the implicit violence break through into an open declaration of war. "A man has to be drunk, insane or unbalanced by talent before he'll behave like a woman," comments the heroine of *The Pumpkin Eater*, begging an awful lot of questions.

It is ironic that Penelope Mortimer has been both praised and criticised for her analysis of modern marriage. She keeps a witty and compassionate eye on that institution, it is true, but her observations do not set out to be objective. She is not a satirist, nor does her writing reflect the struggles of that old phenomenon, the new woman. Society is of secondary importance in her novels, which are intense, imaginative explorations of an inner world. It is an enclosed world, dominated by fear, in which physical experiences such as sterilisation and abortion isolate her characters from their fellow beings and are metaphors for a deeper spiritual isolation. More recent work shows an intensification of this mood. *My Friend Says It's Bullet-Proof* and *The Home* are about women at the edge, held from destruction by an obsessive need to record and understand their own despair.

—Judy Cooke

MOSLEY, Nicholas (Lord Ravensdale). British. Born in London, 25 June 1923; eldest son of Sir Oswald Mosley; became 3rd Baron Ravensdale on the death of his aunt, Baroness Ravensdale, 1966; succeeded to the baronetcy of his father, 1980. Educated at Eton College, 1937–42; Balliol College, Oxford, 1946–47. Served in the Rifle Brigade, 1942–46: Captain; Military Cross, 1944. Married 1) Rosemary Laura Salmond in 1947 (marriage dissolved, 1974), three sons and one daughter; 2) Verity Elizabeth Bailey in 1974, one son. Address: Church Row Studios, 21-A Heath Street, London N.W.3, England.

PUBLICATIONS

Novels

Spaces of the Dark. London, Hart Davis, 1951.
The Rainbearers. London, Weidenfeld and Nicolson, 1955.
Corruption. London, Weidenfeld and Nicolson, 1957; Boston, Little Brown, 1958.

Meeting Place. London, Weidenfeld and Nicolson, 1962.

Accident. London, Hodder and Stoughton, 1965; New York, Coward McCann, 1966.

Assassins. London, Hodder and Stoughton, 1966; New York, Coward McCann, 1967.

Impossible Object. London, Hodder and Stoughton, 1968; New York, Coward McCann, 1969.

Natalie Natalia. London, Hodder and Stoughton, and New York, Coward McCann, 1971.

Catastrophe Practice: Plays for Not Acting, and Cypher: A Novel (includes *Skylight, Landfall, Cell*). London, Secker and Warburg, 1979.

Imago Bird. London, Secker and Warburg, 1980.

Serpent. London, Secker and Warburg, 1981.

Plays

Screenplays: *The Assassination of Trotsky*, with Masolini d'Amico, 1973; *Impossible Object*, 1975.

Other

Life Drawing, with John Napper. London, Studio, 1954.

African Switchback (travel). London, Weidenfeld and Nicolson, 1958.

The Life of Raymond Raynes. London, Faith Press, 1961.

Experience and Religion: A Lay Essay in Theology. London, Hodder and Stoughton, 1965; Philadelphia, United Church Press, 1967.

The Assassination of Trotsky. London, Joseph, 1972.

Julian Grenfell: His Life and the Times of His Death 1888–1915. London, Weidenfeld and Nicolson, and New York, Holt Rinehart, 1976.

Rules of the Game: Sir Oswald and Lady Cynthia Mosley 1896–1933. London, Secker and Warburg, 1982.

Beyond the Pale: Sir Oswald Mosley and Family 1933–1980. London, Secker and Warburg, 1983.

Editor, *The Faith: Instructions on the Christian Faith*, by Raymond Raynes. London, Faith Press, 1961.

*

Critical Studies: "Nicholas Mosley Issue" of *Review of Contemporary Fiction* (Elmwood Park, Illinois), vol. 2, no. 2, 1982.

*   *   *

Since 1951 Nicholas Mosley has published 11 novels as well as a miscellaneous assortment of other books, notably biographies, and although his fiction has not won widespread popularity or much academic recognition, he is acknowledged in the literary world to be one of the most individual and innovative English novelists of his generation. What is most striking about his *oeuvre* as a whole is his ability to break free from one mode of writing and to experiment with something very different in his constant quest for appropriate forms and authentic expression.

The four novels he wrote during the 1950's—the second, *A Garden of Trees*, has not been published—form a distinct group and can be considered as the first phase in his growth as a writer. The three published novels of this decade, *Spaces of the Dark*, *The Rainbearers*, and *Corruption*, are essentially realistic in mode, although they explore beneath the level of character and society to locate a metaphysical or spiritual malaise in modern Western civilization. All three novels are mainly set in the post-war world, although they look back both directly and indirectly to the war itself, and not surprisingly

they reveal the influence of the dominant European philosophical movement of the 1940's and 1950's, Existentialism. *Spaces of the Dark* (a phrase from T.S. Eliot's "Rhapsody on a Windy Night") is an ambitious attempt at a tragic novel whose protagonist, Paul Shaun, is torn apart by guilt and angst as a result of a wartime incident in which he killed a close friend and fellow-officer. The past again casts its shadow on the present in *The Rainbearers*, and although this novel lacks the tragic intensity of his first novel, the emphasis is on unrealized potential, lost possibilities, and failure. *Corruption*, in which the Venetian setting plays an important part, is structurally and stylistically more complex than *Spaces of the Dark* and *The Rainbearers*, and differs from them in being a first-person narrative. The title could be that of a medieval Morality play, and the characters in this analysis of modern decadence and corruption function symbolically as well as realistically. Until its later stages, *Corruption* emanates a similar type of doom-laden fatalism and pessimism as the earlier novels, but then there is a crucial episode in which the oppression and bleakness lift to produce an unexpectedly open ending rather than a tragic denouement. This shift, marked by the adoption of a simpler idiom, may be inconsistent but it dramatizes Mosley's subversion of his own tragic pretensions as he discovers light at the end of the existential tunnel his fiction had been probing in the 1950's.

Five years separate *Corruption* from his next novel, *Meeting Place*, a transitional novel inaugurating the second phase of his development, ending with *Natalie Natalia* in 1971. Mosley now discards many of the features of his previous novels, which had been long, exhaustively analytical, densely written (Henry James and William Faulkner are important influences), and sometimes convoluted to the point of turgidity. The prose is simpler, sentences and paragraphs shorter, and the style more visually immediate, indeed cinematic. Furthermore, the narrative method is elliptical, selective, and discontinuous, and involves intercutting between the various strands of the plot with its Murdochian network of relationships. Comedy, conspicuous by its absence from the earlier novels, plays an important part in *Meeting Place*, which also features a broader range of characters than its predecessors and is remarkable for its positive conclusion, embodying Mosley's new commitment to the possibilities of renewal, growth, and creativity. With *Meeting Place* Mosley liberated himself from his preoccupations of the 1950's and therefore prepared the way for his first major achievement, *Accident*, subsequently turned into a distinguished film by Joseph Losey using a screenplay by Harold Pinter. The story in *Accident* is very simple: a version of the eternal triangle narrated by an Oxford philosophy don, Stephen Jervis, who knows the three people involved. Mosley's way of telling the story, however, is highly original because the unorthodox style enacts both the indeterminacy of reality and the inevitable tentativeness of human attempts to apprehend it. By using verbal fragments and staccato rhythms, Mosley captures the disjointed, ambiguous, even contradictory nature of experience in a way that may owe something to the French *nouveau roman* and its underlying phenomenology. Yet although *Accident* begins with a death and incorporates disintegration and severed relationships, it is not pessimistic; the end, with the birth of a baby to the narrator's wife, looks forward, not back, and emphasizes continuity, not finality.

In *Assassins* Mosley applies the methods of *Accident* to the world of public affairs and politics by narrating the attempted assassination of an Eastern bloc leader in England. The subject matter is that of the political thriller, but Mosley completely transforms and revitalizes that genre without, however, achieving such subtlety and profundity as he did in *Accident*. The most difficult of the novels belonging to his second phase is *Impossible Object*, which at first sight seems to be a collection of short stories about love and marriage but proves to be a complex study in multiple viewpoint. By means of certain repetitions and patterns, Mosley provides his readers with a key to decode his collage of narratives and reassemble the fragments, but the reflexivity of the novel, as in *Accident*, draws attention to the impossibility of ever being able to fix or represent something as fluid and relativistic as reality. *Natalie Natalia*, probably Mosley's finest achievement, is less consciously experimental and more accessible than *Impossible Object*, but again displays his willingness to take risks with both language and narrative technique. The story line about a politician, Anthony Greville, and involving love, adultery, shame, and breakdown is unexceptional, but Mosley's way of treating familiar material is, as usual, startlingly different, and illuminates it in unexpected, mind-opening ways. The title, providing two names for the same woman, Greville's mistress, epitomizes Mosley's preoccupation with the enigmatic inconsistencies of life, because she is a living contradiction, both ravenous Natalie and angelic Natalia.

After *Natalie Natalia* Mosley published no fiction for eight years, and then in 1979 he launched by far his most ambitious project with *Catastrophe Practice*, intended to be the first of a group of seven novels, two more of which, *Imago Bird* and *Serpent*, have so far appeared. *Catastrophe Practice*, a compilation of three "plays not for acting" (with prefaces and a concluding essay) and a novella-length piece of fiction, is much more abstract than any of his other work. Catastrophe Theory is a mathematical attempt to account for discontinuities in the natural world: *Catastrophe Practice* is Mosley's attempt to create a literary form capable of encompassing and articulating the discontinuities of human experience. Superficially, the book is fragmented and dislocated, but by means of a complicated arrangement of correspondences and cross-references, including the appearance of the six principal characters in various guises in different sections, Mosley creates a form of unity out of apparent disunity and chaos. Running through *Catastrophe Practice* is a strain of polemic about the need to free consciousness, language, and art from the confines of convention, and also to rescue modern art from its devotion to versions of negativity—failure, disillusionment, pessimism, despair. Mosley intends the six subsequent novels in the sequence to be self-contained yet inter-related books, each centering on one of the main figures in *Catastrophe Practice* itself. After the complexities of the very demanding *Catastrophe Practice*, *Imago Bird* is an immediately engaging and relatively straightforward novel, which presents a wide spectrum of contemporary life through the innocent eyes of its 18-year-old narrator, Bert. In trying to come to terms with the randomness of experience and to reconcile inner and outer reality, Bert apprehends the essential theatricality of adult life—how human beings allocate stereotyped parts to themselves and then proceed to act these out in a fictional illusion they mistake for reality. While believing themselves to be free, people, whether establishment politicians, media personalities, or dedicated revolutionaries, have imprisoned themselves in linguistic and behavioural conventions. *Imago Bird*, like its predecessor, is about the need to break out of the cage of false consciousness. *Serpent* is more intricate and less satisfactory than *Imago Bird*. Mosley interweaves a screenplay about the Jewish revolt against the Romans at Masada with contemporary events involving its writer, Jason, and a crisis in Israel. Parallels emerge between past and present, especially concerning the polarities of devotion and reason and of the individual and society. After *Serpent* Mosley temporarily shelved work on his large-scale project

in order to write two books about his father, Sir Oswald Mosley, who died at this time leaving all his papers to his son, but now that these are finished it is to be hoped that he will return to fiction.

—Peter Lewis

MPHAHLELE, Es'kia (Ezekiel Mphahlele).   South African. Born in Pretoria, 17 December 1919. Educated at St. Peter's Secondary School, Johannesburg; Adam's College, Natal, 1939–40; University of South Africa, Pretoria, 1946–49, 1953–54, 1956, B.A. (honours) 1949, M.A. in English 1956; University of Denver, 1966–68, Ph.D. in English 1968. Married Rebecca Mochadibane in 1945; five children. Clerk in institution for the blind, 1941–45; English and Afrikaans teacher, Orlando High School, Johannesburg, 1945–52; Lecturer in English Literature, University of Ibadan, Nigeria, 1957–61; Director of African Programmes, International Association for Cultural Freedom, Paris, 1961–63; Director, Chemchemi Creative Centre, Nairobi, Kenya, 1963–65; Lecturer, University College, Nairobi, 1965–66; Senior Lecturer in English, University of Zambia, Lusaka, 1968–70; Associate Professor of English, University of Denver, 1970–74; Professor of English, University of Pennsylvania, Philadelphia, 1974–77; Inspector of Education, Lebowa, Transvaal, 1978–79. Since 1979, Professor of African Literature, University of the Witwatersrand, Johannesburg. Fiction editor, *Drum*, Johannesburg, 1955–57; editor, *Black Orpheus*, Ibadan, 1960–66, and *Journal of New African Literature and the Arts*. Address: African Studies Institute, University of the Witwatersrand, Jan Smuts Avenue, Johannesburg 2001, South Africa.

PUBLICATIONS

Novels

The Wanderers.   New York, Macmillan, 1971; London, Macmillan, 1972.
Chirundu.   Johannesburg, Ravan Press, 1979; Walton-on-Thames, Surrey, Nelson, 1980; Westport, Connecticut, Hill, 1981.

Short Stories

Man Must Live and Other Stories.   Cape Town, African Bookman, 1947.
The Living and Dead and Other Stories.   Ibadan, Black Orpheus, 1961.
In Corner B and Other Stories.   Nairobi, East African Publishing House, 1967.

Other

Down Second Avenue (autobiography).   London, Faber, 1959; New York, Doubleday, 1971.
The African Image (essays).   London, Faber, and New York, Praeger, 1962; revised edition, Faber and Praeger, 1974.
The Role of Education and Culture in Developing African Countries.   Tel Aviv, Afro-Asian Institute for Labor Studies and Co-operation in Israel, 1965.
A Guide to Creative Writing.   Nairobi, East African Literature Bureau, 1966.

Voices in the Whirlwind and Other Essays. New York, Hill and Wang, 1972; London, Macmillan, 1973.
The Unbroken Song: Selected Writings of Es'kia Mphahlele. Johannesburg, Ravan Press, 1981.
Let's Write a Novel. Cape Town, Maskew Miller, 1981.
Afrika My Music: An Autobiography 1957–1983. Johannesburg, Ravan Press, 1984.
Bury Me at the Marketplace: Selected Letters of Es'kia Mphahlele 1943–1980, edited by N. Chabani Manganyi. Johannesburg, Skotaville, 1984.
Father Come Home (for children). Johannesburg, Ravan Press, 1984.

Editor, with Ellis Komey, *Modern African Stories.* London, Faber, 1964.
Editor, *African Writing Today.* London, Penguin, 1967.

*

Critical Studies: *Seven African Writers,* London, Oxford University Press, 1962, and *The Chosen Tongue,* London, Longman, 1969, both by Gerald Moore; "The South African Short Story," by Mphahlele in *Kenyon Review* (Gambier, Ohio), 1969; *Ezekiel Mphahlele* by Ursula A. Barnett, Boston, Twayne, 1976; *Exiles and Homecomings: A Biography of Es'kia Mphahlele* by N. Chabani Manganyi, Johannesburg, Ravan Press, 1983.

Es'kia Mphahlele comments:
(1972) I began my writing career as a short-story writer during World War II. I wrote for *Drum* magazine in Johannesburg, *Fighting Talk* and *New Age* in Johannesburg, and *Africa South* in Cape Town (the last 3 journals since banned by the South African Government). My earliest stories, i.e., *Man Must Live,* were escapist stuff which came spontaneously. I moved on to vitriolic protest fiction. I left South Africa as an exile in September 1957 to teach in Nigeria where I finished the second half of *Down Second Avenue,* my autobiography. Even in exile my fictional themes have always been South Africa. But *In Corner B,* which I wrote in Paris in 1963, has two stories set in Nigeria: "The Barber of Bariga" and "The Ballad of Oyo." The rest are set in South Africa. I wrote these Nigerian stories and "Mrs. Plum" in Paris. The rest had appeared in Johannesburg journals. "Mrs. Plum" in that volume was my first attempt at the long short-story. I have often thought of fiction as my specific commitment; when I am still composing such a work in my mind, I write critical essays—such as *The African Image* and *Voices in the Whirlwind. The Wanderers* has an autobiographical outline but the incidents are fictional. I am planning a novel set in Zambia. I am trying to come to terms with the greater Africa as a setting, but I know the South African in me will accompany me to the grave.

*   *   *

Es'kia Mphahlele has been one of the most versatile and influential of African authors. As literary critic, autobiographer, journalist, short story writer, novelist, dramatist, and poet, he has probably contributed more than any other individual to the growth and development of an African literature in English. Since leaving South Africa he has travelled widely, stopping to teach for a year or two in at least five different countries—Nigeria, Kenya, Zambia, France and the United States.

In South Africa Mphahlele wrote mainly short stories about life in the urban black ghettos where he had grown up and

spent most of his adult years. The events in these stories were based on his personal experiences and reflected a wide variety of responses to the people and places he knew best. There were humorous sketches and satirical vignettes as well as more serious stories about human or social problems. Later, as stringent apartheid legislation made life more difficult for urban blacks, Mphahlele began to write angry protest fiction. By the mid-1950's he felt stifled in his home country and applied for an "exit permit," a document allowing him to leave South Africa on the condition that he never return. The South African government granted his request in 1957, and he lived in exile for the next 20 years, finally returning to South Africa in 1977.

His first major piece of writing abroad was an autobiography, *Down Second Avenue,* in which he tried to work off the emotional steam and creative energy that had been building up inside him during his last years in South Africa. It is a moving story, told with candour and compassion for his people. In 1962 he published a pioneering work of literary criticism, *The African Image,* part of which had been written in South Africa as an M.A. thesis. He also brought out two collections of his short stories and produced a manual for aspiring fiction writers. His first novel, *The Wanderers,* examined the plight of the black South African intellectual in exile, a depressing tale constructed out of the debris of his own personal life. A second novel, *Chirundu,* which appears to have been inspired by his years in Zambia, dealt with postcolonial power politics in an independent African state. In 1972 he published another volume of perceptive literary criticism.

During his years in exile Mphahlele was able to arrive at the kind of emotional balance and aesthetic distance from his subject matter that he found impossible to achieve as a young man living in South Africa. But after a time he began to feel increasingly restless, angry, and politically impotent abroad, so he elected to return to his homeland, despite the hazards and frustrations he knew would confront him there. In recent years he has been extremely prolific, producing a sequel to his autobiography, a children's book, another manual for writers, and a new selection of his writings, including short stories and poems. These books have contained forthright protest, yet he has managed to get them all published in South Africa. In addition, a volume of his letters has appeared, and he has been the subject of a locally written biography. Repatriation, like exile, has obviously served as an intense creative stimulus for him, releasing pent-up energies of passionate self-expression. Instead of aiming for aesthetic distance, he now seeks close emotional engagement with the people and places that serve as primary sources of his inspiration. After decades of wandering, he has rediscovered his roots as a South African writer.

—Bernth Lindfors

MUNONYE, John (Okechukwu). Nigerian. Born in Akokwa, 28 April 1929. Educated at Christ the King College, Onitsha, 1943–47; University College, Ibadan, 1948–52, B.A. in classics and history 1952; Institute of Education, University of London, 1952–53, Cert. Ed. 1953. Married Regina Nwokeji in 1957; one daughter and one son. Education Officer, 1954–57, and Provincial Education Officer and Inspector of Education, 1958–70, Nigerian Ministry of Education; Principal, Advanced Teachers College, Owerri, 1970–73; Chief Inspector of Education, East Central State, 1973–76, and Imo State, 1976–77.

Columnist, *Catholic Life* magazine, Lagos, and *Nigerian Statesman*, Owerri. Member of the Board of Directors, East Central State Broadcasting Service, Enugu, 1974–76. Member, Order of the Niger, 1980. Agent: David Higham Associates Ltd., 5–8 Lower John Street, London W1R 4HA, England. Address: P.O. Box 23, Akokwa, Orlu, Imo State, Nigeria.

PUBLICATIONS

Novels

The Only Son.   London, Heinemann, 1966.
Obi.   London, Heinemann, 1969.
Oil Man of Obange.   London, Heinemann, 1971.
A Wreath for Maidens.   London, Heinemann, 1973.
A Dancer of Fortune.   London, Heinemann, 1974.
Bridge to a Wedding.   London, Heinemann, 1978.

Uncollected Short Stories

"Silent Child," in *Okike 4* (Amherst, Massachusetts), December 1973.
"Pack Pack Pack," in *Festac Anthology of Nigerian New Writing.* Lagos, Ministry of Information, 1977.
"Man of Wealth," in *Catholic Life* (Lagos), 1981.
"On a Sunday Morning," in *Catholic Life* (Lagos), 1982.
"Rogues," in *Catholic Life* (Lagos), 1985.

Other

Drills and Practice in English Language (textbook), with J. Cairns.   Lagos, African Universities Press, 1966.

*

John Munonye comments:

All six of my novels are children of the land. Set in the Igbo area of Nigeria, they draw from the experiences of ordinary men and women, children too. The motif is the processes of change that started with the arrival of Christian missionaries some 60 years ago. Culture ("all the arts, beliefs, social institutions . . . characteristic of a community") had to shift ground. And the environment, sensitive in its own way, was transformed too. How did our ordinary men and women fare in it all? Is there anything of their authentic nature that could be said to have survived the stress? The earliest experiences, which are depicted in *The Only Son* and *Obi*, were severe and traumatic. Later, people came to live with the new state of things, and the result is *Bridge to a Wedding*, a novel of accommodation and reconciliation between traditional and modern. We do indeed need the bridge.

Oil Man of Obange is a relentless tragedy, a novel of confrontation on an individual scale. The Oil Man musters all his energy, zeal, optimism, and integrity towards improving his low social status. But did he consult the god of success? *A Wreath for Maidens* also deals with moral issues—on a wider canvas. The blood shed in the end is not, unfortunately, that of the protagonists: it is a novel of futility. *A Dancer of Fortune* proceeds on much lighter feet.

What next? The beautyful ones are not yet born—yes. But hope is one of man's sustaining gifts, a gift of the spirit. With it goes vision (without which a people perish) and commitment. Nothing shrill or didactic; no sermons; no protest.

*   *   *

Though he wrote six novels in one 12-year period, John Munonye has attracted surprisingly little critical attention. The reason is not far to seek: despite the intrinsically interesting material he works on, his craftsmanship and command of English have flagged noticeably since his earliest books. Yet, as a compassionate chronicler of the ways in which ordinary Eastern Nigerian people have been affected by historical and social change, he is a writer well worth reading. In his first and third novels, *The Only Son* and *Oil Man of Obange*, theme and treatment interlock admirably and reveal his competence at its best. Jeri, the petty trader in palm oil of *Oil Man of Obange*, pits his own elemental resources of courage, devotion, and physical strength against fate, accident, and malice to raise money for his children's schooling; Munonye subdues the narration rigorously to a stark recording of the everyday hardships of bare human existence that is still the lot of most Nigerians, indeed of the peoples of the Third World in general. With similar, though slightly less stringent, narrative austerity, *The Only Son* presents the privations of a self-reliant widow whose humble, sparse life is touched into tragic proportions by her simple courage and steadfastness: the relationship between Chiaku and her son is tenderly but unsentimentally handled, and, in their estrangement, when he seeks western and Christian education, Munonye achieves a sympathetic insight into both sides of an irreconcilable clash of aspirations.

The Only Son is the first novel in Munonye's trilogy about the fortunes of one family, the 20th-century descendants of the legendary Udemezue of Burning Eyes in the community of Umudiobia of ten villages and two. In *Obi* the fully Christianized son and his Christian wife return to Umudiobia to re-establish his father's *obi* or homestead, but the tensions between traditional custom and their new faith culminate in their flight into exile in a distant town. *Bridge to a Wedding* introduces them as the materially prosperous parents of six children and traces the patient and successful efforts of a highly respected Umudiobian to heal the feud between them and their village kinsfolk so that his son can marry their daughter. While these two novels share the attractive unifying theme of how African custom still operates upon the lives of ordinary Nigerians, for good and for ill, Munonye's very concern with this theme, especially in *Bridge to a Wedding*, leads him into an often irritating discursiveness.

The virtue of Munonye's civil-war novel, *A Wreath for the Maidens*, rests upon his intimate knowledge of how the common people are affected for the worse by large historical events, despite the public rhetoric that accompanies them. Poor characterization and a tendency to wordiness do not vitiate the sombre moral concern at the heart of this book. That it could so soon be followed by *A Dancer of Fortune*, with its apparent endorsement of mere individualist opportunism, is a disturbing measure of Munonye's increasing lack of self-criticism as a writer.

—Arthur Ravenscroft

MUNRO, Alice (née Laidlaw). Canadian. Born in Wingham, Ontario, 10 July 1931. Educated in Wingham public schools; University of Western Ontario, London, 1949–51. Married 1) James Armstrong Munro in 1951 (divorced, 1976), three children; 2) Gerald Fremlin in 1976. Artist-in-Residence, University of Western Ontario, 1974–75, and University of British Columbia, Vancouver, 1980. Recipient: Governor-

General's Award, 1969, 1978; Great Lakes Colleges Association award, 1974; Province of Ontario award, 1974; Canada–Australia Literary Prize, 1978. D.Litt.: University of Western Ontario, 1976. Lives in Clinton, Ontario. Address: c/o Writers Union of Canada, 24 Ryerson Street, Toronto, Ontario M5T 2P4, Canada.

PUBLICATIONS

Novel

Lives of Girls and Women. Toronto, McGraw Hill Ryerson, 1971; New York, McGraw Hill, 1972; London, Allen Lane, 1973.

Short Stories

Dance of the Happy Shades. Toronto, Ryerson Press, 1968; New York, McGraw Hill, 1973; London, Allen Lane, 1974.
Something I've Been Meaning to Tell You: Thirteen Stories. New York, McGraw Hill, 1974.
Personal Fictions, with others, edited by Michael Ondaatje. Toronto, Oxford University Press, 1977.
Who Do You Think You Are? Toronto, Macmillan, 1978; as *The Beggar Maid: Stories of Flo and Rose*, New York, Knopf, 1979; London, Allen Lane, 1980.
The Moons of Jupiter. Toronto, Macmillan, 1982; New York, Knopf, and London, Allen Lane, 1983.

Uncollected Short Stories

"The Dimensions of a Shadow" April 1950, "Story for Sunday" December 1950, and "The Widower" April 1951 (as Alice Laidlaw), all in *Folio* (London, Ontario).
"A Basket of Strawberries," in *Mayfair* (Toronto), November 1953.
"The Idyllic Summer" (as Alice Laidlaw), in *Canadian Forum* (Toronto), August 1954.
"At the Other Place" (as Alice Laidlaw), in *Canadian Forum* (Toronto), August 1955.
"The Edge of Town," in *Queen's Quarterly* (Kingston, Ontario), Autumn 1955.
"How Could I Do That?," in *Chatelaine* (Montreal), March 1956.
"The Dangerous One," in *Chatelaine* (Montreal), July 1957.
"Home," in *74: New Canadian Stories*, edited by David Helwig and Joan Harcourt. Ottawa, Oberon Press, 1974.
"Characters," in *Ploughshares* (Cambridge, Massachusetts), vol. 4, no. 3, Summer 1978.
"A Better Place Than Home," in *The Newcomers*, edited by Charles E. Israel. Toronto, McClelland and Stewart, 1979.
"Wood," in *The Best American Short Stories 1981*, edited by Hortense Calisher and Shannon Ravenel. Boston, Houghton Mifflin, 1981.
"The Ferguson Girls Must Never Marry," in *Grand Street* (New York), Spring 1982.
"Miles City, Montana," in *New Yorker*, 14 January 1985.

Plays

How I Met My Husband (televised, 1974). Published in *The Play's the Thing*, edited by Tony Gifford, Toronto, Macmillan, 1976.

Television Plays: *A Trip to the Coast*, 1973; *How I Met My Husband*, 1974; *1847: The Irish* (*The Newcomers* series), 1978.

*

Bibliography: by Robert Thacker, in *The Annotated Bibliography of Canada's Major Authors 5* edited by Robert Lecker and Jack David, Downsview, Ontario, ECW Press, 1984.

Manuscript Collection: University of Calgary Library, Alberta.

Critical Studies: *Probable Fictions: Alice Munro's Narrative Acts* edited by Louis K. MacKendrick, Downsview, Ontario, ECW Press, 1984; *Alice Munro and Her Works* by Hallvard Dahlie, Downsview, Ontario, ECW Press, 1985.

*   *   *

In the area of contemporary Canadian fiction, reflecting as it does the traditions of literary realism and the intrusions of various forms of anti-realism, Alice Munro occupies a particularly prominent position. Her fiction to date—one novel and four collections of short stories—is firmly rooted in the tangible realities of the rural and urban worlds of her own experiences in southwestern Ontario and the Pacific coast, but it characteristically probes those undefined areas that lie beyond the empirical. "I am very excited by what you might call the surface of life," she has stated, but her fiction makes it clear that it is what that surface conceals rather than what it reveals that is of real interest to her. She has not attempted the kind of formal experimentation that characterizes writers like Mavis Gallant or Audrey Thomas, but her fiction nevertheless gives rise to similar metaphysical and psychological uncertainties. Stylistically, it is the more traditional writers like Ethel Wilson whom she evokes, whose fiction, too, is deceptively simple in form, but disturbing in its implications.

Formally, Munro's explorations of the various conjunctions and contradictions between appearance and reality have been manifested more in the short story than in the novel, but there are many who see *Lives of Girls and Women*, with its episodic structure, as being somewhat distinct from the traditional novel form. What seems to attract Munro here, as it does in her short stories, are those moments of intensity or illumination that mark stages in the life of her protagonist, rather than any desire to work out fully the implications or resolutions of these moments. In this respect there is a formal parallel between *Lives* and here third collection of stories, *Who Do You Think You Are?*, whose ten separate glimpses of Rose create just as complex a portrait of her as the more unified earlier work does for Del Jordan. It can be argued, too, that the other three collections of stories, each of which deals with a wide cast of characters, reflect a recognizable thematic unity, though any such simplification ignores the subtle complexity of her stories. But many of the 15 stories of *Dance of the Happy Shades* explore the fractured and incomplete relationships that keep people in isolation; the 13 stories of *Something I've Been Meaning to Tell You* constitute variations on the theme of silence, of the inability to communicate; and the 12 stories of *The Moons of Jupiter* dramatize the importance and simultaneous dangers of the many connections we inherit or create in our lives.

That first collection of stories dramatizes the dilemmas of youthful, female protagonists in positions of isolation and rejection, as they try to understand the signals that come through to them from unfamiliar worlds. Marital and extra-marital relationships ("Walker Brothers Cowboy"), adolescent sexual experiences ("Postcard," "Thanks for the Ride"), family misunderstandings ("Boys and Girls"), constitute the bases for some of these dilemmas, whose resolution does not come easily or automatically with maturity. There are different areas of consciousness, of understanding, that will create a more or less permanent existential aloneness, and the term "unconsummated relationships" from "The Peace of Utrecht" suggests the normal situation these protagonists experience. The title story of this collection is powerful in its juxtaposing of areas of reality: as Miss Marsalles parades a group of retarded children through their music recital, the narrator recognizes that all the mothers and daughters—i.e., the "normal" people—have lost their previous sense of superiority, for the music that Miss Marsalles understands is "that one communiqué from the other country where she lives," that cannot be understood by "other people, people who live in the world."

Something I've Been Meaning to Tell You shifts this kind of fear to older protagonists: a grandmother trying to understand her granddaughter ("Marrakesh"), an elderly man confused by the selfishness of youth ("Walking in Water"), or, as in the title story, elderly sisters striving to understand their present lives that in turn are distorted by their memories of the past. Modulations of the title words constitute disturbing notes throughout the collection: "What is here that is not being told?" ("Marrakesh"), "This is a message, but I don't see how I can deliver it" ("The Spanish Lady"), "I must believe . . . that we have connections that cannot be investigated" ("Winter Wind"), and the title words of "Tell Me Yes or No." In many of these stories, the protagonists move from positions of certainty about their moral or rational superiority, to increasing doubts and frustrations, and very quickly the sense of complete control can turn to bitter desperation. By exploiting the devices of irony and ambiguity, by dramatizing the interplay of reality and fantasy, Munro turns seemingly simple and straightforward events into complex and somewhat terrifying consequences.

Similar ambiguities and distortions inform the stories of *The Moons of Jupiter*, most of which deal with the various connections between people, whether deriving from forms of love or from forms of necessity. Whether between daughter and father, as in the title story, between elderly ladies in a nursing home ("Mrs. Cross and Mrs. Kidd"), between adulterous teachers and their community ("Accident"), or between generations of nieces, cousins, and aunts ("Chaddeleys and Flemings"), these connections are never stable or easily accepted. "Connection. That was what it was all about," says one narrator. "A connection with the real, and prodigal, and dangerous, world," and though these three kinds of world can be separate, they not infrequently overlap with each other. The real world becomes a dangerous one in "Labor Day Dinner," as a family barely misses certain death when a speeding car plunges across their road, and it becomes a prodigal one in "Hard-Luck Stories," which turns on a series of sexual experiences narrated by three people returning to Toronto. As the story ends, the narrator realizes that a mild sexual advance preferred by a male companion, "with no promise about it, could admonish and comfort me. Something unresolved could become permanent." It is the fact that these worlds are full of what the narrator of the title story calls "various knowns and unknowns and horrific immensities" that leads the protagonists of these stories into desperate rationalizations at times, and at other times to give vent to irrational manifestations of self-justification.

The process of "remembering" that Munro on one occasion defined as the equivalent of "fictional invention" operates in many stories from these three collections, but it is of particular importance in her two more formally unified works, *Lives of Girls and Women* and *Who Do You Think You Are?* It is in fact the very resolution that Del and Rose arrive at near the end of their experiences, but Munro adds a strong note of ambiguity to these resolutions by juxtaposing the protagonists against characters, Bobby Sheriff and Ralph Gillespie, who inhabit both the normal world and the irrational world. The latter book is on the whole more despairing than *Lives*, its contradictions and ambiguities more threatening; Rose wasn't always able to "shuck off" what she didn't want, as Del could do, who in a sense lucks her way through many experiences whose equivalents always seem to confuse Rose. The third-person point of view undoubtedly allowed Munro to remain more objective about Rose's dilemmas, and it also gave her more freedom in structural experimentation: the overlapping of experiences allows us to observe Rose from different perspectives simultaneously, and as a result she frequently seems pathetic or trapped or deluded. Del, on the other hand, as we see her progressively mature, from her initial exposure to Uncle Benny's tabloid world through to her sexual initiation by Garnet French, remains in control of her worlds, suffering only momentary doubts as she pursues the different ways of being "endangered and desired."

Throughout her fiction, Munro maintains a disciplined control between the demands of the various forms of reality and the formal requirements of her art. Sometimes there is an uneasy striving between her use of the conventional fictional elements and her seeming belief that moral chaos is never far away, and one impact of this upon the reader is the requirement constantly to reassess motive and character. Like Rose in "Simon's Luck," the reader is disturbed by "those shifts of emphasis that throw the story line open to question, the disarrangements which demand new judgements and solutions." Munro does not provide easy or comfortable ways out of these dilemmas; her art resides in the honest manner in which she analyzes ordinary characters and their motives, and in her ability to make an unremarkable world quite remarkable.

—Hallvard Dahlie

MURDOCH, (Jean) Iris. British. Born in Dublin, Ireland, 15 July 1919. Educated at the Froebel Education Institute, London; Badminton School, Bristol; Somerville College, Oxford, 1938–42, B.A. (first class honours) 1942; Newnham College, Cambridge (Sarah Smithson Student in philosophy), 1947–48. Married the writer John Bayley in 1956. Assistant Principal in the Treasury, London, 1942–44; administrative officer with the United Nations Relief and Rehabilitation Administration (UNRRA) in London, Belgium, and Austria, 1944–46; Fellow, St. Anne's College, Oxford, and University Lecturer in Philosophy, Oxford University, 1948–63: Honorary Fellow of St. Anne's College since 1963; Lecturer, Royal College of Art, London, 1963–67. Recipient: James Tait Black Memorial Prize, 1974; Whitbread Award, 1974; Booker Prize, 1978. D.Litt.: University of London, 1985. Member, Irish Academy, 1970; Honorary Member, American Academy, 1975, and American Academy of Arts and Sciences, 1982; Honorary Fellow, Somerville College, Oxford, 1977. C.B.E. (Commander, Order of the British Empire), 1976. Lives in Oxfordshire. Agent: Ed Victor Ltd., 162 Wardour Street, London W1V 4AT, England.

PUBLICATIONS

Novels

Under the Net. London, Chatto and Windus, and New York, Viking Press, 1954.
The Flight from the Enchanter. London, Chatto and Windus, and New York, Viking Press, 1956.
The Sandcastle. London, Chatto and Windus, and New York, Viking Press, 1957.
The Bell. London, Chatto and Windus, and New York, Viking Press, 1958.
A Severed Head. London, Chatto and Windus, and New York, Viking Press, 1961.
An Unofficial Rose. London, Chatto and Windus, and New York, Viking Press, 1962.
The Unicorn. London, Chatto and Windus, and New York, Viking Press, 1963.
The Italian Girl. London, Chatto and Windus, and New York, Viking Press, 1964.
The Red and the Green. London, Chatto and Windus, and New York, Viking Press, 1965.
The Time of the Angels. London, Chatto and Windus, and New York, Viking Press, 1966.
The Nice and the Good. London, Chatto and Windus, and New York, Viking Press, 1968.
Bruno's Dream. London, Chatto and Windus, and New York, Viking Press, 1969.
A Fairly Honourable Defeat. London, Chatto and Windus, and New York, Viking Press, 1970.
An Accidental Man. London, Chatto and Windus, 1971; New York, Viking Press, 1972.
The Black Prince. London, Chatto and Windus, and New York, Viking Press, 1973.
The Sacred and Profane Love Machine. London, Chatto and Windus, and New York, Viking Press, 1974.
A Word Child. London, Chatto and Windus, and New York, Viking Press, 1975.
Henry and Cato. London, Chatto and Windus, 1976; New York, Viking Press, 1977.
The Sea, The Sea. London, Chatto and Windus, and New York, Viking Press, 1978.
Nuns and Soldiers. London, Chatto and Windus, 1980; New York, Viking Press, 1981.
The Philosopher's Pupil. London, Chatto and Windus, and New York, Viking Press, 1983.
The Good Apprentice. London, Chatto and Windus, 1985; New York, Viking, 1986.

Uncollected Short Story

"Something Special," in *Winter's Tales 3.* London, Macmillan, and New York, St. Martin's Press, 1957.

Plays

A Severed Head, with J.B. Priestley, adaptation of the novel by Murdoch (produced Bristol and London, 1963; New York, 1964). London, Chatto and Windus, 1964.
The Italian Girl, with James Saunders, adaptation of the novel by Murdoch (produced Bristol, 1967; London, 1968). London, French, 1969.
The Servants and the Snow (produced London, 1970). Included in *The Three Arrows, and The Servants and the Snow,* 1973.
The Three Arrows (produced Cambridge, 1972). Included in *The Three Arrows, and The Servants and the Snow,* 1973.
The Three Arrows, and The Servants and the Snow: Two Plays. London, Chatto and Windus, 1973; New York, Viking Press, 1974.
Art and Eros (produced London, 1980).
The Servants (opera libretto), adaptation of her play *The Servants and the Snow,* music by William Mathias (produced Cardiff, 1980).

Verse

A Year of Birds. Tisbury, Wiltshire, Compton Press, 1978.

Other

Sartre, Romantic Rationalist. Cambridge, Bowes, and New Haven, Connecticut, Yale University Press, 1953.
The Sovereignty of Good over Other Concepts (lecture). Cambridge, University Press, 1967.
The Sovereignty of Good (essays). London, Routledge, 1970; New York, Schocken, 1971.
The Fire and the Sun: Why Plato Banished the Artists. London and New York, Oxford University Press, 1977.
Reynolds Stone (address). London, Warren, 1981.
Acastos: Two Platonic Dialogues. London, Chatto and Windus, 1986.

*

Bibliography: *Iris Murdoch and Muriel Spark: A Bibliography* by Thomas T. Tominaga and Wilma Schneidermeyer, Metuchen, New Jersey, Scarecrow Press, 1976.

Manuscript Collection: University of Iowa, Iowa City.

Critical Studies: *Degrees of Freedom: The Novels of Iris Murdoch,* London, Chatto and Windus, and New York, Barnes and Noble, 1965, and *Iris Murdoch,* London, Longman, 1976, both by A.S. Byatt; *The Disciplined Heart: Iris Murdoch and Her Novels* by Peter Wolfe, Columbia, University of Missouri Press, 1966; *Iris Murdoch* by Rubin Rabinovitz, New York, Columbia University Press, 1968; *Iris Murdoch* by Frank Baldanza, New York, Twayne, 1974; *Iris Murdoch* by Donna Gerstenberger, Lewisburg, Pennsylvania, Bucknell University Press, 1974; *Iris Murdoch: The Shakespearian Interest,* New York, Barnes and Noble, and London, Vision Press, 1979, and *Iris Murdoch,* London, Methuen, 1984, both by Richard Todd; *Iris Murdoch: Work for the Spirit* by Elizabeth Dipple, Chicago, University of Chicago Press, 1981, London, Methuen, 1982; *Iris Murdoch's Comic Vision* by Angela Hague, Cranbury, New Jersey, Susquehanna University Press, 1983; *Iris Murdoch: The Saint and the Artist* by P.J. Conradi, London, Macmillan, 1985.

*   *   *

Having written more than 20 novels in just over 30 years, Iris Murdoch has established a prodigious body of reflective and philosophical work, a wide-ranging, discursive, often metaphorically conveyed commentary on the contemporary world. She began with *Under the Net,* with what seems in retrospect a novel in the avant-garde mode of the 1950's, following a group of rootless characters in picaresque adventures around London as they try to develop some semblance of individual identities. Two of the characters are actresses, sisters, able to switch and create roles, although far less certain of what the self is behind the various selves they create. These and other characters manage to avoid or slip through the "nets" of conventional or exterior definition, to preserve their independence and existential freedom by reducing their scale or function to little more than the amorphous identity of the living creature. With her second novel, *The Flight from the Enchanter*, Murdoch began to assert more explicitly her difference from Sartrean existentialism (about which she wrote a book entitled *Sartre, Romantic Rationalist*). In *The Flight from the Enchanter* some of the characters are less free than others, conditioned to a point of incapacity to choose by circumstance, nation, psyche, or history. Even among those for whom meaningful choice is possible, Murdoch maintains a difference between those who choose to exercise power over others, to "enchant," and those who build their identities, however trivial, to preserve the creature in resistance to various contemporary "enchantments." The novels that followed, like *The Sandcastle* and *The Bell*, detailed similarly elaborate constructions of human identity, presented with striking drama in metaphors like scaling towers and dredging sunken bells from lakes, in which the creature was visible despite the impossibility of his or her project. Identities were always in flux, related in different combinations, a texture of constantly shifting relationship nowhere more visible than in *A Severed Head*, in which each of the three principal males, at some point in the novel, has an affair with each of the three principal females. The sudden and unpredictable coupling is not, however, the sign of a solipsistic world, for, through these changes, the central character learns to value relationships that depend on his risks and his wine-tasting abilities, his instincts, not those carefully calibrated by the various conventions of the "head."

Subsequent novels expanded the range of experience Murdoch treated and began to question the value of the simple creature, the sanction of unconsciousness. *An Unofficial Rose*, for example, uses the cultivation of roses as a central metaphor and values "unofficial" forms that can give rich, floral, yet individual and ethical shapes to human experience. The novel is also distinguished by the careful and moving treatment of a love affair between an elderly couple. *The Unicorn* adds dimensions of mystery and myth to Murdoch's treatment of human identity, and this novel, along with *The Time of the Angels*, begins to probe the meaning and value of religious experience (religion had appeared earlier, in *The Bell*, although its complexities were more those of the religious community as social entity, less the significance of the religious experience itself). History and politics are apparent in a novel like *The Red and the Green*, transferring the issues of individual and social identity to a group of characters in Dublin just before the Easter uprising of 1916. Murdoch's England has never been insular or self-enclosed; it is always, metaphorically, an England after the Second World War, conscious of its good fortune in surviving and sympathetic with various displaced persons. Acute sympathy for Poles, for example, is important to novels as far apart in time and as dissimilar in theme as *The Flight from the Enchanter* and *Nuns and Soldiers*.

In the late 1960's Murdoch's fiction became more directly and coherently ethical in focus. In novels such as *The Nice and the Good*, *Bruno's Dream*, *A Fairly Honourable Defeat*, and *An Accidental Man*, the ethical framework provides a fairly consistent structure, a central debate and resolution worked through the usual Murdoch world of bizarre incident and predictably unpredictable encounters. In two of these novels, *The Nice and the Good* and *A Fairly Honourable Defeat*, the debate contrasts a false morality with a genuine one by establishing a married couple who think their relationship a model for others. In one novel, Murdoch satirizes their hollowness; in the other, she introduces an agent of evil, impelled by his own

isolation and pain, who destroys them. In these novels, characters seen as false, smug, or self-righteous are articulate about their pretended virtues; they theorize and erect structures that delude themselves and others. But those posed against them, the genuinely good, are not the unconscious creatures of the earlier novels; rather, more quietly, less grandiosely, they both articulate and act out their ethics, their concern for others, and their respect for the boundaries between the self and others. The unconscious characters, in these novels, are often seen as "accidental," just following random personal impulse and living as harmful parasites. God figures, too, are not simply the deluding myths of the earlier novels, but can choose whether to involve themselves in human concerns or retain the mystery of their own power and remoteness. In these novels, too, interference in the lives of others is a complex ethical issue, reflecting all the possibilities of human connection. Sometimes interference is cruel and brutal, an immoral imposition; at other times, it is incompetent but warmhearted, leading to the ludicrous rather than to disaster. Some who theorize too much and too consistently, interfere in the wrong way at the wrong time, violate, in their inconsistent attempts at consistency, both themselves and others; some interfere only as a projection of themselves, with no recognition of the other. Yet some interference is genuinely relevant and helpful to others, as one of the characters says, in *An Accidental Man*, "separated" help is possible. In Murdoch's world, characters reveal themselves through the quality of their impositions, their deliberate and conscious connections with other people.

Murdoch also sees her fiction as itself a form of interference that engages. The bizarre plots, the elaborate structures overturned, the human pretensions made comic—all interfere with settled abstract versions of experience. In a May 1972 speech before the American Academy of Arts and Letters, Murdoch defended both this moral role of serious literature in the modern world and the moral function of language itself: "Words constitute the ultimate texture and stuff of our moral being, since they are the most refined and delicate and detailed, as well as the most universally used and understood of the symbolisms whereby we express ourselves into existence. We became spiritual animals when we became verbal animals. The *fundamental* distinctions can only be made in words. Words are spirit. Of course eloquence is no guarantee of goodness, and an inarticulate man can be virtuous. But the quality of a civilization depends upon its ability to discern and reveal truth, and this depends on the scope and the purity of its language."

Murdoch's fiction continues to suggest the range of human thought, the classically philosophical as well as the linguistic and ethical. In addition to her novels, she has published a book on ethics, *The Sovereignty of Good*, and a more recent consideration of Plato, *The Fire and the Sun*. The fiction expands and elaborates, or converts to metaphor, the abstract inquiry. *The Sacred and Profane Love Machine* explores various versions of human passion and commitment, both conscious and unconscious. *A Word Child* treats the kind of linguistic analysis common in academic philosophy since the days of the Logical Positivists; Wittgenstein, both as cultural tag and as representing questions that cannot be avoided, is a frequent reference point in a number of the novels. Often, the later fiction, like *The Sea, The Sea*, is mystical and visionary. *The Black Prince* considers possible justifications for murder, as well as an entire artistic career based on imposition. Death and its effects on survivors are metaphorically central in novels like *Bruno's Dream* and *Nuns and Soldiers*. *The Good Apprentice* establishes the civilized great house in the center of the wilderness and examines both the religious and the artistic forms that emanate from the house into the wider and more chaotic world of the fiction. In all Murdoch's novels, existence is precarious and difficult: plot consists of unexpected assaults on any certainty and unexpected changes in allegiance or emotion; most characters' backgrounds, increasingly in more recent novels, include the sudden deaths or desertion of parents and the early deaths of siblings or close friends. The existence of God, of some pattern or meaning, or of faith in something beyond the knowable, is always a question, considered, debated, treated with indifference or anguish, yet never resolved. Myth and metaphor suggest a world outside the self: the generalization of particular human dilemmas into all of history, or the externalization of particular issues in a given novel, like the crucible of heat in which *The Nice and the Good* takes place or the isolating frost or dissolving rain that surrounds some of the other novels. In all these novels, the human being is tested by her or his response to or possible recovery from pain and deprivation. The forms of response are various and imaginative; as one of the characters in *Nuns and Soldiers* concludes, "We are all the judges and the judged, victims of the casual malice and fantasy of others, and ready sources of fantasy and malice in our turn." Yet, in Murdoch's world, despite all the pain of existence, most people (and all of those seen as worthy) resist the safety and stasis of the enclosures of the incompletely knowable self.

—James Gindin

NAHAL, Chaman (Lal). Indian. Born in Sialkot (now in Pakistan), 2 August 1927. Educated at the University of Delhi, M.A. in English 1948; University of Nottingham (British Council scholar), 1959–61, Ph.D. in English 1961. Married Sudarshna Rani in 1955; two daughters. Lecturer at universities in India, 1949–62; Reader in English, Rajasthan University, Jaipur, 1962–63. Reader in English, 1963–80, and since 1980 Professor of English, Delhi University. Visiting Fulbright Fellow, Princeton University, New Jersey, 1967–70; since 1971 has been visiting lecturer at several universities in the U.S.A., Malaysia, Japan, Singapore, Canada, and North Korea. Columnist ("Talking about Books"), *Indian Express*, New Delhi, 1966–73. Recipient: Sahitya Academy Award, 1977; Federation of Indian Publishers award, 1977, 1979. Agent: John Farquharson Ltd., 162–168 Regent Street, London W1R 5TB, England. Address: 2/1 Kalkaji Extension, New Delhi 110 019, India.

PUBLICATIONS

Novels

My True Faces. New Delhi, Orient, 1973.
Azadi (Freedom). New Delhi, Arnold-Heinemann, and Boston, Houghton Mifflin, 1975; London, Deutsch, 1977.
Into Another Dawn. New Delhi, Sterling, 1977.
The English Queens. New Delhi, Vision, 1979.
The Crown and the Loincloth. New Delhi, Vikas, 1981.

Short Stories

The Weird Dance and Other Stories. New Delhi, Arya, 1965.

Uncollected Short Stories

"Tons," in *The Statesman* (New Delhi), 12 June 1977.
"The Light on the Lake," in *Illustrated Weekly of India* (Bombay), 22 July 1984.

"The Take Over," in *Debonair* (Bombay), August 1985.

Other

Moby Dick (for children), adaptation of the novel by Melville. New Delhi, Eurasia, 1965.
A Conversation with J. Krishnamurti. New Delhi, Arya, 1965.
D.H. Lawrence: An Eastern View. South Brunswick, New Jersey, A.S. Barnes, and London, Yoseloff, 1971.
The Narrative Pattern in Ernest Hemingway's Fiction. New Delhi, Vikas, and Rutherford, New Jersey, Fairleigh Dickinson University Press, 1971.
The New Literatures in English. New Delhi, Allied, 1985.

Editor, *Drugs and the Other Self: An Anthology of Spiritual Transformations*. New York, Harper, 1971.

*

Bibliography: in *The New Literatures in English*, 1985.

Critical Studies: *Commonwealth Literature in the Curriculum* edited by K.L. Goodwin, St. Lucia, University of Queensland Press, 1980; introduction by A. Komarov to *The Crown and the Loincloth*, Moscow, Raduga, 1984; *Three Contemporary Novelists* edited by R.K. Dhawan, New Delhi, Classical, 1985.

Chaman Nahal comments:
I have largely concerned myself with two themes in my novels; the individual vs. the joint family system in India, and my historical identity as an individual, as an Indian. For the latter theme I have drawn extensively on history, especially our freedom movement, 1915–47. *The Crown and the Loincloth* is part of a trilogy on that theme. I use Gandhi as the ultimate symbol of that identity.

*   *   *

Chaman Nahal's distinction lies in writing about India without any touch of exoticism; he scrupulously avoids the stereotyped "East" of maharajahs, tigers, and snake-charmers. The actual town of Delhi (in *My True Faces* and *The English Queens*) and the typical Punjabi town of Sialkot are presented vividly, and we get a good idea of middle-class life in India. *Azadi* is the best of the Indian-English novels written about the traumatic partition which accompanied Indian Independence in 1947. *The Crown and the Loincloth* portrays Mahatma Gandhi as a character in fiction. *The English Queens* breaks new ground by using the comic mode to treat a problem which has concerned all Indians—the tendency of the educated elite in India to ape the West.

Nahal's first novel, *My True Faces*, adequately portrays the agony of a sensitive young man when he finds his wife and baby son missing. But the crisis seems to be too minor to warrant the heavy philosophical treatment, with the hero realizing at the end of the novel that all earthly manifestations are but faces of Krishna, and they are all his "true faces." The involved language occasionally betrays the fact that it is the work of a scholarly professor of English.

Azadi ("Freedom"), which won the Sahitya Akademi (the national academy of letters) award, employs an entirely different style. In *My True Faces* the action is confined to three days, the rest being recounted in flashbacks; in *Azadi* the action is spread over several months. It is a straightforward account of a rich Hindu grain merchant and his family. The novel begins with the people of Sialkot hearing the announcement regarding partition, but they refuse to believe that they now have to move. Nahal shows how Kanshi Ram the Hindu, Barkat Ali the Mohammedan, and Teja Singh the Sikh share the same Punjabi culture and language, and consider Sialkot their homeland. Meticulous attention to details and a first hand knowledge of the life of the characters enable Nahal to make the plight of the refugees real to the reader. The novel ends with a sadly depleted family trying to begin life anew in Delhi. *Azadi* has none of the sensationalism of other novels about India's partition, such as Khushwant Singh's *Train to Pakistan* or Manohar Malgonkar's *A Bend in the Ganges*. Nahal shows the cruelty as well as the humanity of both sides. The novel also shows the maturing of Arun, Kanshi Ram's only son, but the account of his love, first for Nur, the Muslim girl left behind in Pakistan, and then for Chandni, a low-caste girl who is abducted on the way to India, is not as gripping as the rest of the novel.

Nahal's next novel, *Into Another Dawn*, is basically an East–West love story, set chiefly in the U.S.A. *The English Queens* shifts back to New Delhi and deals with post-Independence India; it is a very funny but hard-hitting satire against the elitism of the English-speaking groups in India, such as the officers of the defence forces, the *nouveau riche*, the highly placed civil servants, or Indians having foreign wives. Nahal unfolds a fantastic plot hatched by Lord Mountbatten, the last British Viceroy of India, to ensure India's subjugation to Britain. On the eve of handing over political power he prepares a charter for the "safe transfer of linguistic power" by which he gives the English language to India. To "preserve, propagate and spread" English in India he appoints six women to "The Order of the Queens." Rekha, the daughter of one of these queens, horrifies them by wanting to marry a young man from a working-class slum; worse still, he wears Indian clothes and is an expert in Indian classical music. The novel takes a further fantastic turn when the bridegroom reveals himself as an avatar of Vishnu, who has come to remove this pernicious second-hand English culture. He flies back to heaven with the charter, but it drops out of his hand accidentally, and comes back to continue its destructive work; perhaps even God cannot help India! Of course, Nahal is not against the English language as such; his satire is against the kind of Indian who thinks that it is shameful to know anything about his own culture. One wonders whether non-Indian readers would enjoy the book as much as Indians do, because much of the humour rests on topical allusions.

The Crown and the Loincloth is the first novel in a projected trilogy dealing with the struggle for Indian Independence. The central figure is Mahatma Gandhi, and Nahal presents him directly as well as in terms of the effect he has on the family of Thakur Shanti Nath, a landowner in a Punjabi village. The novel is set in the period 1915–22, and deals with many historical events, such as Gandhi's return to India from South Africa, the Jallianwala Bagh massacre, the terrorists in the Punjab and Bengal who wanted to gain independence through violence, and the birth of the Muslim League. But the novel is long and unwieldy; undue importance is given to the love affairs of Sunil, the Thakur's freedom-fighter son. In places, the writing is hurried and lacks distinction, and the novel lacks the unity and simplicity of *Azadi*. One hopes that the remaining novels of this trilogy (yet to be published) live up to the achievement of *Azadi*.

—Shyamala A. Narayan

NAIPAUL, V(idiadhar) S(urajprasad). Trinidadian. Born in Trinidad, 17 August 1932; brother of the writer Shiva Naipaul. Educated at Queen's Royal College, Port of Spain, Trinidad, 1943–48; University College, Oxford, 1950–54, B.A. (honours) in English 1953. Married Patricia Ann Hale in 1955. Settled in England, 1950; editor, "Caribbean Voices," BBC, London, 1954–56; fiction reviewer, *New Statesman*, London, 1957–61. Recipient: Rhys Memorial Prize, 1958; Maugham Award 1961; Phoenix Trust Award, 1962; Hawthornden Prize, 1964; W.H. Smith Literary Award, 1968; Arts Council grant, 1969; Booker Prize, 1971; Bennett Award (*Hudson Review*, New York), 1980; Jerusalem Prize, 1983. D.Litt.: Columbia University, New York, 1981; Litt.D.: Cambridge University, 1983. Fellow, Royal Society of Literature; Honorary Fellow, University College, Oxford, 1983. Address: c/o André Deutsch Ltd., 105 Great Russell Street, London WC1B 3LJ, England.

PUBLICATIONS

Novels

The Mystic Masseur. London, Deutsch, 1957; New York, Vanguard Press, 1959.
The Suffrage of Elvira. London, Deutsch, 1958; in *Three Novels*, New York, Knopf, 1982.
Miguel Street. London, Deutsch, 1959; New York, Vanguard Press, 1960.
A House for Mr. Biswas. London, Deutsch, 1961; New York, McGraw Hill, 1962.
Mr. Stone and the Knights Companion. London, Deutsch, 1963; New York, Macmillan, 1964.
The Mimic Men. London, Deutsch, and New York, Macmillan, 1967.
In a Free State. London, Deutsch, and New York, Knopf, 1971.
Guerrillas. London, Deutsch, and New York, Knopf, 1975.
A Bend in the River. London, Deutsch, and New York, Knopf, 1979.

Short Stories

A Flag on the Island. London, Deutsch, 1967; New York, Macmillan, 1968.

Other

The Middle Passage: Impressions of Five Societies—British, French and Dutch—in the West Indies and South America. London, Deutsch, 1962; New York, Macmillan, 1963.
An Area of Darkness: An Experience of India. London, Deutsch, 1964; New York, Macmillan, 1965.
The Loss of El Dorado: A History. London, Deutsch, 1969; New York, Knopf, 1970; revised edition, London, Penguin, 1973.
The Overcrowded Barracoon and Other Articles. London, Deutsch, 1972; New York, Knopf, 1973.
India: A Wounded Civilization. London, Deutsch, and New York, Knopf, 1977.
The Return of Eva Perón, with The Killings in Trinidad (essays). London, Deutsch, and New York, Knopf, 1980.
A Congo Diary. Los Angeles, Sylvester and Orphanos, 1980.
Among the Believers: An Islamic Journey. London, Deutsch, and New York, Knopf, 1981.
Finding the Centre: Two Narratives. London, Deutsch, and New York, Knopf, 1984.

Critical Studies: by David Pryce-Jones, in *London Magazine*, May 1967; Karl Miller, in *Kenyon Review* (Gambier, Ohio), November 1967; *The West Indian Novel* by Kenneth Ramchand, London, Faber, and New York, Barnes and Noble, 1970; *V.S. Naipaul: An Introduction to His Work* by Paul Theroux, London, Deutsch, and New York, Africana, 1972; *V.S. Naipaul* by Robert D. Hamner, New York, Twayne, 1973, and *Critical Perspectives on V.S. Naipaul* edited by Hamner, Washington, D.C., Three Continents, 1977, London, Heinemann, 1979; *V.S. Naipaul* by William Walsh, Edinburgh, Oliver and Boyd, and New York, Barnes and Noble, 1973; *V.S. Naipaul: A Critical Introduction* by Landeg White, London, Macmillan, and New York, Barnes and Noble, 1975; *Paradoxes of Order: Some Perspectives on the Fiction of V.S. Naipaul* by Robert K. Morris, Columbia, University of Missouri Press, 1975; *V.S. Naipaul* by Michael Thorpe, London, Longman, 1976; *Four Contemporary Novelists* by Kerry McSweeney, Montreal, McGill-Queen's University Press, 1982, London, Scolar Press, 1983; *V.S. Naipaul: A Study in Expatriate Sensibility* by Sudha Rai, New Delhi, Arnold-Heinemann, 1982.

V.S. Naipaul comments:

I feel that any statement I make about my own work would be misleading. The work is there: the reader must see what meaning, if any, the work has for him. All I would like to say is that I consider my non-fiction an integral part of my work.

*   *   *

V.S. Naipaul is the most accomplished novelist yet to emerge from the English-speaking Caribbean. This definition, however, can limit his achievement, which stands in the main stream of the modern English novel. Similarly, although it is impossible to discuss his work without seeing it as a progressive exploration of an awareness based in the Caribbean, his concern is with the universal human predicament.

His work to date falls into three phases. His first-written (though third-published) work is *Miguel Street*. It consists of sketches of life in a lower-class area of Trinidad. The focus is that of a child, but although this changes as the boy grows older and more comprehending, Naipaul omitted the story intended to show the boy's own involvement in its frustrated and inherently tragic world. (Reprinted as "The Enemy" in *A Flag on the Island*.) The child's point of view can therefore avoid adult implications: in spite of the plots of the stories—which include a prostitute Laura driving her daughter to commit suicide when in her time she also has an illegitimate child, and Man Man, who wants to be crucified as Christ until the villagers throw too large rocks—the tone is one of delicately balanced humour. This is both its achievement and its limitation.

The Mystic Masseur achieves a greater complexity. On one hand there is the narrator who views the story from a changing perspective as he grows up; on the other there is use of the main protagonist's own suppressed autobiography, significantly called "The Years of Guilt." The hero moves from humble beginnings as Pundit Ganesh Ramsummair, an incompetent Trinidad masseur, through assumption of powers as a mystic and writer, to the position of G. Ramsay Muir, Esq., M.B.E., member of the Legislative Council. It is at once a satire on the roots of power that lie in popular superstition and apparent education, and of a figure driven by the forces he himself

exploits. Ganesh provides a human centre lacking in *The Suffrage of Elvira*, another satire on popular political power in the Caribbean.

These three novels led George Lamming in *The Pleasures of Exile* (1960) to attack Naipaul's work as "castrated satire," an attempt to take a superior ironic stance avoiding full involvement in the Caribbean predicament. Whatever truth lies behind Lamming's criticism, it is not applicable to *A House for Mr. Biswas*, a major novel spanning three generations of life in Trinidad. There is satire on Caribbean ways of life, from the West Indian social structure to such facets as popular journalism. But the satire itself is mediated through the particular sensibility of the ever-present Mohun Biswas. Biswas, born with an extra finger which shows both his endemic bad luck and the effects of malnutrition, reacts to his world with an artist's fastidious consciousness, although in Trinidad the only outlets he can find for his creative imagination are sign-writing and the reporting of sensational episodes for the Trinidad *Sentinel*. Of Brahmin caste, he is seized in marriage by the merchant family of Tulsis, who are hungry for every bit of status they can get, to bolster up their own immigrant insecurity. Everything in the commercial vulgarity and oppressive clannishness revolts Biswas, who struggles to get free of them, while needing (and taking) the home they offer. Mr. Biswas's quest for a house of his own is an attempt to find both independence and some place that he can imbue with meaning. Surrounding this overt theme is Naipaul's sense of the inherent loneliness of man himself—the darkness both physical and spiritual that Biswas faces when a hurricane blows his house from around him causing him a nervous breakdown. But by the end Biswas has his own precarious house, while the Tulsi family is disintegrating. A tender tragi-comedy, in scope and theme the book approaches epic proportions.

With *Mr. Stone and the Knights Companion*—about a middle-class Englishman coming to terms with old age—Naipaul's work begins to look more deliberately outward from the Caribbean. *The Mimic Men* is set largely on the fictional West Indian Island of Isabella, and explores the rise to power of Ralph Kriplesingh, building on fortunes from Coca Cola and real estate. It follows up many of the questions *Elvira* poses about the roots of political power in the Caribbean, brought up to date with the advent of Black Power. One possibility for a meaningful society is offered in Ralph's father who becomes a *sunyasi* (holy man), but the novel questions whether any actions in the contemporary island predicament can have meaning. Partly because he too is a "mimic man," Ralph cannot see any. The novel opens and closes in England, and Ralph's vision comes in a moment of existential desolation at the end.

In a Free State is a thematically united trio of stories, set between two factual diary entries of a Middle East tour. They concern an Indian servant in the United States, West Indians in England, and an Englishman in an African state at time of revolution. Action and description are stripped to the nerve, and slight actions, such as an image in a television set, or a blank stare, take on momentous impact. The cutting away of the rich detail that characterised *Miguel Street* to elements of consciousness, here reaches a brilliant stage of development. It is the logical progression of both Naipaul's style and themes.

Naipaul has noted above that his non-fiction and fiction form an integral whole. As *The Middle Passage* is essential background to *A House for Mr. Biswas* and *The Mimic Men*, other journalistic work, including *The Killings in Trinidad*, has laid the groundwork for his more recent novels. *Guerrillas* is set on a Caribbean island smouldering on the brink of revolution. Jimmy Ahmed, Afro-Chinese, Muslim, and English educated, attempts to organise a socialist commune, but is defeated by his own illusions and the futile racial and social conflicts of the island. So also is Roche, a hero of the South African freedom struggle, who is finally trapped into confessing his political disillusionment. Jane, an English girl, pays for her shallow attempts to relate to both Roche and Ahmed by being brutally murdered. As objective analysis, the novel is sharper than *The Mimic Men*, but the cold despair impairs the book's imaginative impact. Focused through the character of Selim, an East African merchant, *A Bend in the River* is a more emphatic work. It masterfully recreates the experience of living in a contemporary central African state under dictatorship, where the political struggle is complicated by race, education, and modern ideologies awkwardly coexisting with traditional society. Those in power one day may be prey to others the next, while, underlying all, the jungle, river, and forest people remain impervious to the vagaries of history. Complex, objective, yet emotively powerful, the novel is arguably Naipaul's finest since *A House for Mr. Biswas*.

—Louis James

NARAYAN, R(asipuram) K(rishnaswamy). Indian. Born in Madras, 10 October 1906. Educated at Maharaja's College, Mysore, graduated 1930. Owner, Indian Thought Publications, Mysore. Recipient: Sahitya Academy Award, 1961; Padma Bhushan, India, 1964; National Association of Independent Schools award (USA), 1965; English-Speaking Union award, 1975; Royal Society of Literature Benson Medal, 1980. Litt. D.: University of Leeds, Yorkshire, 1967; D.Litt.: University of Delhi; Sri Venkateswara University, Tirupati; University of Mysore. Fellow, Royal Society of Literature, 1980; Honorary Member, American Academy, 1982. Agent: Anthony Sheil Associates Ltd., 43 Doughty Street, London WC1N 2LF, England. Address: 15 Vivekananda Road, Yadavagiri, Mysore 2, India.

PUBLICATIONS

Novels

Swami and Friends: A Novel of Malgudi. London, Hamish Hamilton, 1935; with *The Bachelor of Arts*, East Lansing, Michigan State College Press, 1954.
The Bachelor of Arts. London, Nelson, 1937; with *Swami and Friends*, East Lansing, Michigan State College Press, 1954.
The Dark Room. London, Macmillan, 1938.
The English Teacher. London, Eyre and Spottiswoode, 1945; as *Grateful to Life and Death*, East Lansing, Michigan State College Press, 1953.
Mr. Sampath. London, Eyre and Spottiswoode, 1949; as *The Printer of Malgudi*, East Lansing, Michigan State University Press, 1957.
The Financial Expert. London, Methuen, 1952; East Lansing, Michigan State College Press, 1953.
Waiting for the Mahatma. London, Methuen, and East Lansing, Michigan State College Press, 1955.
The Guide. Madras, Higginbothams, London, Methuen, and New York, Viking Press, 1958.
The Man-Eater of Malgudi. New York, Viking Press, 1961; London, Heinemann, 1962.

The Vendor of Sweets. New York, Viking Press, 1967; as *The Sweet-Vendor*, London, Bodley Head, 1967.
The Painter of Signs. New York, Viking Press, 1976; London, Heinemann, 1977.
A Tiger for Malgudi. London, Heinemann, and New York, Viking Press, 1983.

Short Stories

Malgudi Days. Mysore, Indian Thought, 1943.
Dodu and Other Stories. Mysore, Indian Thought, 1943.
Cyclone and Other Stories. Mysore, Indian Thought, 1944.
An Astrologer's Day and Other Stories. Mysore, Indian Thought, and London, Eyre and Spottiswoode, 1947.
Lawley Road. Mysore, Indian Thought, 1956.
A Horse and Two Goats. London, Bodley Head, and New York, Viking Press, 1970.
Old and New. Mysore, Indian Thought, 1981.
Malgudi Days (not same as 1943 book). London, Heinemann, and New York, Viking Press, 1982.
Under the Banyan Tree and Other Stories. London, Heinemann, and New York, Viking, 1985.

Uncollected Short Story

"The Cobbler and the God," in *Playboy* (Chicago), 1975.

Other

Mysore. Mysore, Government Branch Press, 1939.
Next Sunday: Sketches and Essays. Mysore, Indian Thought, 1956.
My Dateless Diary (travel in America). Mysore, Indian Thought Publications, 1960.
Gods, Demons, and Others. New York, Viking Press, 1964; London, Heinemann, 1965.
The Ramayana: A Shortened Modern Prose Version of the Indian Epic. New York, Viking Press, 1972; London, Chatto and Windus, 1973.
Reluctant Guru (essays). New Delhi, Hind, 1974.
My Days: A Memoir. New York, Viking Press, 1974; London, Chatto and Windus, 1975.
The Emerald Route (includes play *The Watchman of the Lake*). Bangalore, Government of Karnataka, 1977.
The Mahabharata: A Shortened Modern Prose Version of the Indian Epic. New York, Viking Press, and London, Heinemann, 1978.

*

Manuscript Collection: Mugar Memorial Library, Boston University.

Critical Studies: *R.K. Narayan: A Critical Study of His Works* by Harish Raizada, New Delhi, Young Asia, 1969; *R.K. Narayan*, London, Longman, 1971, and *R.K. Narayan: A Critical Appreciation*, London, Heinemann, and Chicago, University of Chicago Press, 1982, both by William Walsh; *The Novels of R.K. Narayan* by Lakshmi Holmstrom, Calcutta, Writers Workshop, 1973; *R.K. Narayan* by P.S. Sundaram, New Delhi, Arnold-Heinemann, 1973; *Perspectives on R.K. Narayan* edited by Atma Ram, Ghaziabad, Vimal, 1981; *R.K. Narayan: A Critical Spectrum* edited by Bhagwat S. Goyal, Meerut, Shalabh Book House, 1983; *The Ironic Vision: A Study of the Fiction of R.K. Narayan* by M.K. Naik, New Delhi, Sterling, 1983.

* * *

No other 20th-century novelist besides William Faulkner has so well succeeded in creating through a succession of novels an imagined community that microcosmically reflects the physical, intellectual, and spiritual qualities of a whole culture as has R.K. Narayan in his tales of the South Indian community of Malgudi. His stories have made a naive, highly emotional society half a world away as much a part of a reader's experience as Faulkner's novels have made the mad, decadent world of the red hills of Mississippi.

Narayan took longer than Faulkner to discover his metier, though all the Indian writer's novels have been largely set in Malgudi. With his third novel, *Sartoris* (1929), published when he was 32, Faulkner laid the cornerstone for his Yoknapatawpha saga of pride-doomed families. Narayan published four apprentice works based largely on reminiscences before producing, at the age of 43, *Mr. Sampath*, the first of the five most remarkable studies of flamboyant characters who electrified the sleepy city of Malgudi.

It is unlikely that anyone would have guessed that Narayan's first two novels were the work of a major artist. *Swami and Friends* is a kind of charming Indian *Penrod and Sam*, an episodic account of the adventures of two cricket-playing chums as they start high school. *The Bachelor of Arts* is another episodic account of a young man's graduating from college, experiencing a frustrating love affair, wandering about the country disconsolately, returning home to become agent for a big city newspaper, and finally marrying under family auspices. His third novel, *The Dark Room*, he describes as dealing with a Hindu wife who submitted passively to an overbearing husband.

His work changed drastically with *The English Teacher*, a thinly veiled account of his own marriage and the event that most matured and shaped his character, the early death of his beloved wife. This novel begins like Narayan's earlier ones with episodic sketches of a young preparatory school teacher's relationships with his students, colleagues, and family. After the tragic death of the wife while househunting, however, the novel becomes a much deeper and more tightly unified work.

With his next novel, Narayan settled upon the kind of characters and narrative patterns that he was to employ in his five remarkable explorations of the fantastic agitations beneath the enervating surface of the life of Malgudi. Near the end of *Mr. Sampath*, Narayan observes of Srinivas, the principal character, that "he felt he had been involved in a chaos of human relationships and activities."

Nearly all of Narayan's subsequent novels involve characters and readers in such chaos. Srinivas is a rather aimless young man who has finally been driven by his family to choose a profession and who comes to Malgudi in 1938—when war clouds hang over the whole world—to found a newspaper that has "nothing special to note about any war, past or future," but is "only concerned with that war that is always going on—between man's inside and outside." He falls into the hands of a printer, Mr. Sampath, who takes a proprietary interest in the success of the paper, but who is lured from his printing trade into a film-producing venture. Even Srinivas is briefly tempted to abandon his paper and take up script writing. Despite frantic activity and great expenditures, however, the movie-making venture collapses. Only Srinivas emerges unscathed. He finds another printer and returns to publishing his paper, reflecting on one of the men involved in the catastrophe he has witnessed:

> throughout the centuries . . . this group was always there: Ravi with his madness, his well-wishers with their panaceas and their apparatus of cure. Half the madness was his

own doing, his lack of self-knowledge, his treachery to his own instincts as an artist, which had made him a battleground. Sooner or later he shook off his madness and realized his true identity—though not in one birth, at least in a series of them.

The passage is a key to understanding Narayan's major works and their relationship to Hindu philosophy; for the characters he focuses upon are those who are "mad" as a result of their lack of self-knowledge. Some must await another reincarnation; but some manage to shake off the madness and find their true identities.

One who must wait is the title character of *The Financial Expert*, Margayya, whom we meet sitting under a banyan tree assisting peasants in obtaining loans from a co-operative banking institution. The society's officers resent Margayya's activities, but his business flourishes until his spoiled young son throws into a sewer the book in which all accounts are kept. During a trip to collect a red lotus needed for a penitential ritual, Margayya meets Dr. Pal, a self-styled sociologist, who has written a pornographic manuscript based on the *Kama Sutra*. Margayya recoups his fortune by publishing it under the title *Domestic Harmony*; then, embarrassed by the source of his new wealth, he goes back into a money-lending business that is based on withholding the interest from the first installment on the loan. He becomes so successful that he achieves an honored position in the community and recruits Dr. Pal to attract investors. The scheme collapses, however, when the son, who has been gambling with Dr. Pal, demands a share in the business; Margayya assaults Dr. Pal, who in turn discredits the money-lender with his investors. When investors demand their money back, both Margayya and his son are ruined and driven back into dealings with the peasants beneath the banyan tree.

Narayan's next novel, *Waiting for the Mahatma*, is one of his most noble-minded, but least successful. It tells, in the episodic manner of his earlier books, of the misadventures of two young disciples of Mahatma Gandhi during the master's long effort to free his native land. Written after Gandhi's assassination, the book is an admirable tribute, but the fictional characters are too sketchily developed to make it of more than historical interest.

Narayan next turned to the work that has generally been recognized as his most outstanding, *The Guide*, an extremely complicated tale of a confidence man turned saint. In flashbacks, we learn of the rise of Raju from food-seller in the Malgudi railroad station to manager and apparent husband of Rose, who becomes an extremely popular dancer, and his quick fall when he is jailed for forging her signature to a package of jewels. We meet him first, however, when he has installed himself in an abandoned temple after his release from jail and has begun to play the role of spiritual advisor to a peasant community that accepts him as a Mahatma. Gradually he comes to believe in the role he has created, and to relieve a drought he feels compelled to make a 15-day fast that he has suggested as an appropriate penance. As a great crowd gathers, he gains "a peculiar strength" from, for the first time in his life, "learning the thrill of full application, outside money and love." Despite grave peril to his health he continues to fast until he feels that the rain is falling in the hills. The ending of this novel like that of *The English Teacher* is ambiguous: does Swami Raju die? do the rains come? Narayan tells us only, "He sagged down"; but he has transcended the madness that once affected him and found a fulfillment denied the printer of Malgudi and the financial expert.

Such fulfillment is denied also Vasu, the fanatical taxidermist of *The Man-Eater of Malgudi*, Narayan's greatest picture of the madness that leads to self-destruction. After successfully flaunting his great strength about the community unchecked through a series of outrageous incidents, he finally devises a plot against Malgudi's beloved temple elephant. The beast seems doomed, but Vasu dies instead; and in one of the most spectacular conclusions to any of Narayan's works, the almost incredible but carefully foreshadowed way in which he destroyed himself is disclosed. In the complementary *The Vendor of Sweets* Narayan portrays a man who discovers his true identity. Jagan had been freed from patriarchal thralldom when he broke with his orthodox family and followed Mahatma Gandhi. His example, however, proves of no value to a son who prefers American "get-rich-quick" ideas to the self-sacrificial life Gandhi recommended. Jagan indulges the boy by selling sweetmeats to the luxury-loving community; but when the son gets into serious trouble, Jagan feels helpless. He abandons his business and retires to a decrepit garden of meditation. Having freed himself from successive bondages to parents, hero, and child, he finds a tranquility unique to this point in Narayan's tales.

Only confusion, however, awaits the protagonist of *The Painter of Signs*, in which Narayan also deals boldly with a new India's urgent and controversial problem of population control. Raman, a highly traditional 30-year-old bachelor, who took up signboard painting because he "loved calligraphy," is cared for selflessly by his aunt until he meets Daisy, a dynamic propagandizer for birth control. When Raman induces Daisy to marry him, the aunt departs on a religious pilgrimage from which she does not expect to return. Then when Daisy discovers that she cannot give up her missionary work for marriage, Raman finds that he has destroyed his old life without creating a new one.

Reviewers accustomed to the down-to-earth manner of Narayan's ironic fictions were as disconcerted by *A Tiger for Malgudi* as the frantic villagers who are confronted by Raja, the tiger. Since Raja is the hero-narrator of the novel, Narayan seems to be abandoning reality for fantasy; but *A Tiger for Malgudi* is no traditional anthropomorphic beast fable. Drawing delicately on Hindu doctrines of reincarnation, Narayan depicts Raja as a creature with a soul, who lacks only the faculty of conversing with humans. His tale is told by those who learn to read his mind: the fictional master that saves Raja from the rest of the wryly depicted human community and the master of fiction who has conjured him up. The tale is of the overcoming of "the potential of violence," with which, Raja's master observes, "every creature is born." The seemingly whimsical history of a talking tiger thus expands into an ironic fable and prophecy about not just the recent troubled history of Narayan's own country, but of mankind generally. A wise and witty message from one who has aged serenely without missing the significance of a moment of his experiences, this novel should take its place among the most beatific visions of a century that has produced far more diabolical ones. It climaxes the achievement of the major Malgudi novels in depicting the soul's erratic progress from fanaticism toward the tranquil transcendence of the dusty streets of Malgudi.

—Warren French

NAUGHTON, Bill (William John Francis Naughton).   British.   Born in Ballyhaunis, County Mayo, Ireland, 12 June 1910; grew up in Lancashire, England. Educated at St. Peter and St. Paul School, Bolton, Lancashire. Civil Defence driver in London during World War II. Married to Ernestine Pirolt. Has worked as a lorry driver, weaver, and coal-bagger. Recipient: Screenwriters Guild award, 1967, 1968; Prix Italia, for radio play, 1974; Children's Rights Workshop Other Award, 1978. Agent: Michael Imison Playwrights Ltd., 28 Almeida Street, London N1 1TD, England. Address: Kempis, Orrisdale Road, Ballasalla, Isle of Man, United Kingdom.

PUBLICATIONS

Novels

Rafe Granite.   London, Pilot Press, 1947.
One Small Boy.   London, MacGibbon amd Kee, 1957.
Alfie.   London, MacGibbon and Kee, and New York, Ballantine, 1966.
Alfie, Darling.   London, MacGibbon and Kee, 1970; New York, Simon and Schuster, 1971.

Short Stories

Late Night on Watling Street and Other Stories.   London, MacGibbon and Kee, 1959; New York, Ballantine, 1966.
The Goalkeeper's Revenge and Other Stories.   London, Harrap, 1961.
The Goalkeeper's Revenge, and Spit Nolan.   London, Macmillan, 1974.
The Bees Have Stopped Working and Other Stories.   Exeter, Wheaton, 1976.

Plays

My Flesh, My Blood (broadcast, 1957).   London, French, 1959; revised version, as *Spring and Port Wine* (produced Birmingham, 1964; London, 1965; as *Keep It in the Family*, produced New York, 1967), London, French, 1967.
She'll Make Trouble (broadcast, 1958).   Published in *Worth a Hearing: A Collection of Radio Plays*, edited by Alfred Bradley, London, Blackie, 1967.
June Evening (broadcast, 1958; produced Birmingham, 1966).   London, French, 1973.
All in Good Time (as *Honeymoon Postponed*, televised, 1961; as *All in Good Time*, produced London, 1963; New York, 1965).   London, French, 1964.
Alfie (as *Alfie Elkins and His Little Life*, broadcast, 1962; as *Alfie*, produced London, 1963).   London, French, 1964.
He Was Gone When We Got There, music by Leonard Salzedo (produced London, 1966).
Annie and Fanny (produced Bolton, Lancashire, 1967).
Lighthearted Intercourse (produced Liverpool, 1971).

Screenplays: *Alfie*, 1966; *The Family Way*, with Roy Boulting and Jeffrey Dell, 1966; *Spring and Port Wine*, 1970.

Radio Plays: *Timothy*, 1956; *My Flesh, My Blood*, 1957; *She'll Make Trouble*, 1958; *June Evening*, 1958; *Late Night on Watling Street*, 1959; *The Long Carry*, 1959; *Seeing a Beauty Queen Home*, 1960; *On the Run*, 1960; *Wigan to Rome*, 1960; *'30–'60*, 1960; *Jackie Crowe*, 1962; *Alfie Elkins and His Little Life*, 1962; *November Day*, 1963; *The Mystery*, 1973; *A Special Occasion*, 1982.

Television Plays: *Nathaniel Titlark* series, 1957; *Starr and Company* series 1958; *Yorky* series, with Allan Prior, 1960–61;

Looking for Frankie, 1961; *Honeymoon Postponed*, 1961; *Somewhere for the Night*, 1962; *It's Your Move*, 1967.

Other

A Roof over Your Head (autobiography). London, Pilot Press, 1945.
Pony Boy (for children). London, Pilot Press, 1946.
A Dog Called Nelson (for children). London, Dent, 1976.
My Pal Spadger (for children). London, Dent, 1977.

*   *   *

Bill Naughton's first book, *A Roof over Your Head*, was written while he was working as a Civil Defence driver in London during the War. This book, a blend of fiction and autobiography, deals with working-class life in Lancashire where Naughton, the son of Irish immigrants, grew up. For background, there is the unplanned industrial jungle of the 1920's and 1930's, the grimy, crumbling factories and the monotonous rows of brick houses that L.S. Lowry has so accurately depicted.

A Roof over Your Head is artlessly constructed as a series of short sketches: a naive yet oddly moving and direct account of what life was like under the shadow of the dole queue. Childhood, elopement, married life, a first baby, efforts to find work, a job as a coalman, and finally, extracts from a war-time diary: these form the subject matter that is narrated unsentimentally and without self-pity. Naughton writes frankly but undepressingly about poverty and hardship, and shows how these were made more endurable by the good-hearted camaraderie of Lancashire's ordinary people.

Pony Boy is a novel for boys. In it, two Pony Boys—Corky and Ginger—set out to discover "the world." Here is a rollicking, picaresque tale that indicates how well Naughton remembers what boyhood was like. In the 1940's and 1950's Naughton was busy writing short stories for magazines, the best of which were collected in *Late Night on Watling Street*. In these stories, descriptive writing is kept to a minimum and Naughton reveals his gift for dialogue that explains situation and illuminates character. He keeps the narrative on the move like a true storyteller. His title story emphasises the solidarity of lorry-drivers, especially in their dealings with bosses and the police, and brings out their sense of right and wrong. They ostracise a man who has committed murder but will not "split" on him: "He might have got one across the law, but he hadn't got one across Watling Street." Of this collection Naughton has said: "This book includes stories I heard people tell and I just 'put together,' as they say. . . . I write mostly about the life I have known."

More cross-sections of the life Naughton actually experienced may be found in *The Goalkeeper's Revenge*, a collection of stories mainly about but not written specifically for boys. One of these stories, "Gift of the Gab," tells the reader what can happen when a deaf-and-dumb boy is taught to speak. The result is both prosaic and humorous. The boy returns to his home town and at first seems as silent as ever. But he readily bursts into speech when questioned about food in the "institution": "Cold suet pud! Morning, noon and ruddy night—nothing but cold suet pud!"

One Small Boy is a novel in which a family—like Naughton's own—leave the West of Ireland for Lancashire's milltowns. A boy grows up and the author explores his relationship with parents and girls. *Alfie*—and Alf is a recurrent name in Naughton's work—was first a radio play called "Alfie Elkins and His Little Life," then a stage play, a film, and a novel. Here,

too, one finds the usual understated humor, the eye for detail, and the tolerant good humour. Yet *Alfie*, despite its sophisticated finish, lacks the urgency and freshness of *A Roof over Your Head* and the best of the short stories.

—Robert Greacen

*

NAYLOR, Gloria. American. Born in New York City, 25 January 1950. Educated at Brooklyn College, New York, B.A. in English 1981; Yale University, New Haven, Connecticut, 1981–83, M.A. in Afro-American Studies 1983. Missionary for the Jehovah's Witnesses, New York, North Carolina, and Florida, 1968–75; telephone operator, New York City hotels, 1975–81. Writer-in-Residence, Cummington Community of the Arts, Massachusetts, Summer 1983; Visiting Professor, George Washington University, Washington, D.C., 1983–84; United States Information Agency Cultural Exchange Lecturer, India, Fall 1985; Visiting Writer, New York University, Spring 1986. Columnist, *New York Times*, 1986. Recipient: American Book Award, 1983; National Endowment for the Arts fellowship, 1985. Address: c/o Ticknor and Fields, 52 Vanderbilt Avenue, New York, New York 10017, U.S.A.

PUBLICATIONS

Novels

The Women of Brewster Place: A Novel in Seven Stories. New York, Viking Press, 1982; London, Hodder and Stoughton, 1983.
Linden Hills. New York, Ticknor and Fields, and London, Hodder and Stoughton, 1985.

Uncollected Short Story

"Life on Beekman Place," in *Essence* (New York), March 1980.

*

Gloria Naylor comments:

I think of *The Women of Brewster Place* as a love letter to the black women of America—a celebration of their strength and endurance. *Linden Hills* is a cautionary tale—an example of the drastic results if a people forsake their ethnocentric identity under the pressure to assimilate into a mainstream society and seek its rewards.

*   *   *

Gloria Naylor has written two original and absorbing novels, *The Women of Brewster Place: A Novel in Seven Stories* (which won the American Book Award for best first writing in 1983) and *Linden Hills*. Naylor's success lies, in part, in the intensity of her presentation of such social issues as poverty, racism, discrimination against homosexuals, the unequal treatment of women, the value of a sense of community among blacks, and the failure of some upper middle-class educated blacks to address racial problems and social injustice.

The Women of Brewster Place has a simple structure. Most of the scenes take place in the decaying apartment complex,

Brewster Place. The dwellers expect to go nowhere else. The brick wall that closed their street several years earlier now separates them from the rest of the city and symbolizes their psychological and spiritual isolation. In the closing pages of the novel, one woman removes a brick that she thinks is stained with the blood of a resident recently gang-raped and left to die. Impulsively, the other women join her and collectively they tear down the wall, experiencing as they do so an inner regeneration, a sense of community and solidarity, and a re-birth of hope.

The novel includes seven narratives, each focusing on a woman and illuminating her present situation while abundant flashbacks recapitulate her earlier experience. The dominant woman in one chapter appears as a less important figure in several others, so that the entire book, consisting of related though not always consecutive episodes, emerges as a novel rather than as a collection of stories only. While each of the narratives has its own climax, the book builds toward the most threatening crises faced by the Brewster Place community: Ciel's starving herself almost to death in grief for her lost child, the antagonism that builds against two lesbian tenants, and the rape-murder of Lorraine, the lesbian elementary school teacher who has tried to help Kiswana (an idealistic radical) establish a closely organized community among the tenants. Through the suffering of Ciel and that of Lorraine, the other women achieve a new understanding of one another and deep-ened insight into the problems that confront them individually and collectively. The work considered as a novel gains unity through Naylor's use of a single setting, her concentration upon a small number of women in each narrative, her analysis of the major threats to the community in the tragedies of Ciel and Lorraine, and her resort to rituals of healing in which the characters join each other in expressing their human con-cern in acts rather than in words.

In *Linden Hills* Naylor again confines her scenes to one loca-tion, but her tone and outlook are more sardonic and pessimis-tic. In her castigation of middle-class black society, Naylor here finds little hope for renewal of spiritual values or for a development of communal responsibility or identity among the residents. Linden Hills blacks are ambitious and selfish; the richer ones live close to the bottom of the hillside; and richest of all is Luther Nedeed. For five generations Luther Nedeed has controlled Linden Hills real estate and also been the local mortician. Next to the Nedeed home and morgue lies the ceme-tery. The Nedeed wives in each generation have been so deprived of affection and companionship by their "frog-eyed" husbands that they looked forward finally only to death.

Linden Hills has a far more intricate narrative structure than Naylor's first novel. Two young poets, Willie and Lester, in the six days before Christmas earn gift money doing odd jobs. Most of the action is seen through their eyes, except for flash-backs related to past experience of householders who employ them. As they journey further down the hillside each day, they encounter death, suicide, hypocrisy, exploitation, and treachery. The poets agonize and rage over the people who are living a meaningless, deathlike existence.

An additional narrative line appears in "inserts" in the text that interrupt the narration of the experiences of Willie and Lester during this week. The lines addressed directly to the reader reveal secret horrors unknown to Willie and Lester. Luther Nedeed, dissatisfied with the light skin of his infant son, has banished his wife, Willa, and their infant to his aban-doned basement morgue, and he begins lowering food and water to her only after the infant has starved to death. In her desperate isolation, Willa searches for any sign of humanity. From day to day she discovers—and furtively reads—the secret notes recorded in diaries, letters, Bibles, and recipe books by the wives of Nedeed men since 1837. Sharing their tales of abuse, she feels their presence with her and gains strength to climb the stairs on Christmas Eve, carrying her dead son, and to confront her husband. At that moment the decorated tree bursts into flame and in the inferno that follows all traces of the Nedeeds disappear. No neighbor bothers to assist them or even to sound an alarm.

Naylor uses Dante's journey through the lower world in the symbolism that gives additional coherence and depth to the multiple plots. The powerful in Linden Hills resist spiritual illumination and prefer a life in Hell to a life in Paradise. They illustrate the principle underlying Dante's vision of those who inhabit the nether world, "Abandon hope, all ye who enter here." Naylor's work demonstrates that in hell all malefactors are concerned only with their own suffering, rather than with their guilt. Blacks in Linden Hills have the wealth and resources to attain self-awareness, love, and grace, but they are actually far less receptive to the promptings of the spirit than the poor women in Brewster Place, who are capable of spiritual illumina-tion and conversion to a regenerate existence.

—Margaret B. McDowell

NEUGEBOREN, Jay.   American.   Born in Brooklyn, New York, 30 May 1938. Educated at Columbia University, New York, B.A. 1959 (Phi Beta Kappa); Indiana University, Bloomington, M.A. 1963. Married 1) Betsy Bendorf in 1964, three children; 2) Judy Karasik in 1985. Junior executive trainee, General Motors Corporation, Indianapolis, 1960; Eng-lish teacher, Saddle River Country Day School, New Jersey, 1961–62; teacher, New York City public high and junior high schools, 1963–66; Preceptor in English, Columbia University, 1964–66; Lecturer, Stanford University, California, 1966–67; Assistant Professor, State University of New York, Old West-bury, 1968–69. Since 1971, Writer-in-Residence, University of Massachusetts, Amherst. Recipient: Bread Loaf Writers Con-ference De Voto Fellowship, 1966; *Transatlantic Review* novella award, 1969; National Endowment for the Arts grant, 1973; Guggenheim fellowship, 1977; Massachusetts Council on the Arts fellowship, 1978; Smilen-*Present Tense* award, 1982; PEN-National Endowment for the Arts prize, 1982. Address: Department of English, University of Massachusetts, Amherst, Massachusetts 01002, U.S.A.

PUBLICATIONS

Novels

Big Man.   Boston, Houghton Mifflin, 1966.
Listen Ruben Fontanez.   Boston, Houghton Mifflin, and Lon-don, Gollancz, 1968.
Sam's Legacy.   New York, Holt Rinehart, 1974.
An Orphan's Tale.   New York, Holt Rinehart, 1976.
The Stolen Jew.   New York, Holt Rinehart, 1981.
Before My Life Began.   New York, Simon and Schuster, 1985.

Short Stories

Corky's Brother and Other Stories.   New York, Farrar Straus, 1969; London, Gollancz, 1970.
Penguin Modern Stories 3, with others.   London, Penguin, 1970.

Uncollected Short Stories

"My Son, The Freedom Rider," in *Colorado Quarterly* (Boulder), Summer 1964.

"Connorsville, Virginia," in *Transatlantic Review* (London), Winter 1969.

"My Life and Death in the Negro American Baseball League: A Slave Narrative," in *Massachusetts Review* (Amherst), Summer 1973.

"The Place Kicking Specialist," in *Transatlantic Review* (London), Fall-Winter 1974.

"Monkeys and Cowboys," in *Present Tense* (New York), Summer 1976.

"A Worthy Cause," in *Willmore City 6–7* (Carlsbad, California), 1978.

"Uncle Nathan," in *Ploughshares* (Cambridge, Massachusetts), vol. 4, no. 4, 1978.

"His Violin," in *Atlantic* (Boston), November 1978.

"Kehilla," in *Present Tense* (New York), Winter 1978.

"Star of David," in *Tri-Quarterly* (Evanston, Illinois), Spring 1979.

"The St. Dominick's Game," in *Atlantic* (Boston), December 1979.

"On a Beach near Herzlia," in *Ploughshares* (Cambridge, Massachusetts), vol. 6, no. 3, 1980.

"Poppa's Books," in *Atlantic* (Boston), July 1980.

"Bonus Baby," in *John O'Hara Journal* (Pottsville, Pennsylvania), Fall 1980.

"Visiting Hour," in *Shenandoah* (Lexington, Virginia), Fall 1980.

"Noah's Song," in *Present Tense* (New York), Winter 1980.

"Daughter," in *Confrontation* (New York), Spring 1981.

"When the Cheering Turned to Sorrow," in *Inside Sports* (Evanston, Illinois), May 1981.

"Death and the Schoolyard," in *Boston Globe Magazine*, 3 May 1981.

"The 7th Room," in *Rendezvous* (Pocatello, Idaho), Summer 1981.

"Leaving Brooklyn," in *Literary Review* (Madison, New Jersey), Fall 1981.

"Jonathan," in *Tri-Quarterly* (Evanston, Illinois), Winter 1981.

"The Imported Man," in *Midstream* (New York), February 1982.

"The Golden Years," in *New England Review* (Hanover, New Hampshire), Spring 1982.

"Before the Camps," in *Congress Monthly* (New York), April 1982.

"Lev Kogan's Journey," in *Boston Globe Magazine*, 6 June 1982.

"The Year Between," in *Boston Review*, January 1983.

"Fix," in *Denver Quarterly*, Spring 1985.

"Stairs," in *Present Tense* (New York), Fall 1985.

"Abe's Room," in *Confrontation* (New York), Fall 1985.

Plays

The Edict (produced New York, 1981).

Radio Play: *The Stolen Jew*, 1980.

Other

Parentheses: *An Autobiographical Journey*.   New York, Dutton, 1970.

Editor, *The Story of "Story" Magazine: A Memoir*, by Martha Foley.   New York, Norton, 1980.

*

Critical Studies: statement by Ian Watt, in *Listen Ruben Fontanez*, London, Gollancz, 1968; "Parentheses" by Charles Moran, in *Massachusetts Review* (Amherst), Fall 1970; "From Kerouac to Koch" by Michael Willis, in *Columbia College Today* (New York), Winter-Spring 1971; "A Decade of the Ethnic Fiction of Jay Neugeboren," in *Melus* (Los Angeles), Winter 1978 and article in *Twentieth-Century American-Jewish Fiction Writers* edited by Daniel Walden, Detroit, Gale, 1984, both by Cordelia Candelaria; interview with Steven Goldleaf, in *Columbia College Today* (New York), December 1979, and "A Jew Without Portfolio" by Goldleaf, in *Partisan Review* (Boston), Summer 1983; interview in *Literary Review* (Madison, New Jersey), Fall 1981; "Wonderful Lies That Tell the Truth: Neugeboren Reviewed" by Peter Spackman in *Columbia* (New York), November 1981.

*   *   *

It is easy, perhaps too easy, to dismiss all American-Jewish novelists as confirmed self-haters, as "know-nothings" bent on turning Jewish life into a vulgar joke. In this respect, the Jack Portnoy of Philip Roth's *Portnoy's Complaint* (1969) speaks up for those who have grown impatient with their impatient, belligerent sons: "Tell me something, do you know Talmud? Do you know history? ... Do you know a single thing about the wonderful history and heritage of the saga of your people?" And while such charges are true enough about the likes of Alexander Portnoy—and his wise-cracking creator—they are no longer an accurate assessment of contemporary Jewish-American fiction. Writers like Cynthia Ozick, Arthur Cohen, and Hugh Nissenson have made mighty efforts on behalf of a Jewish aesthetic, one that would draw its sustenance from Jewish sources both wider and deeper than suburban assimilation. With *The Stolen Jew* Jay Neugeboren—a journeyman writer with a half dozen volumes to his credit—adds himself to their number.

The Stolen Jew is a thick, complicated novel, but at bottom it is about the inextricable connections between personal memory and Jewish history, between the patterning that Art makes possible and the insistencies of Life, between an aging ex-writer named Nathan Malkin and his obligations to those, living and dead, who comprise his "family." The result is a novel-within-a-novel, as Nathan rewrites "The Stolen Jew," hoping to sell the manuscript at a high price on the Russian black market and, thus, to raise money to aid the refusniks. Whole chapters of Nathan's novel are interspersed with Neugeboren's; each refracts upon the other. As Nathan puts it, in what I take to be a significant reading direction: "A true mosaic was made by shattering the original picture—and putting it together again."

The Stolen Jew was selected as best novel of 1981 by the American Jewish committee and, suddenly, Neugeboren became a writer to reckon with. As he himself suggests in a recent interview:

In my early books [e.g. *Big Man* or *Listen Ruben Fontanez*], I used to pride myself on their "objective" quality. I mean, I don't think I'd ever done an autobiographical novel in a way that even anyone who knew me could feel. My books always seemed to be very much about other things. I think that was one way, in my own life, of not dealing with certain materials, potentially very rich materials, things that I do know about, but also material that I was afraid of, and felt I couldn't handle. . . . [Now, with *The Stolen Jew*] I've found a *subject*, a subject that comes from deep personal wells with me.

Before My Life Began is another installment in Neugeboren's continuing effect to combine aspects of traditional fiction (character, plot, naturalistic surface) with experimentation. As Neugeboren would have it, describing his new aesthetic manifesto, "I'd like to raise some of the questions some of the innovative writers are raising about the relation to art to life, but I would like to do it without losing the nineteenth-century novel—without losing character, history, story, the love of these things." In *The Stolen Jew* the result was as compelling as it was densely textured; with *Before My Life Began* one feels Neugeboren's ambition insisting too much.

"Oh you are so good *inside*, David, don't you know that? You're a truly good *and* strong person, and there aren't many of your kind left. It's just so hard for me to watch you walking through the world, pulled on from so many sides, without my being able to help. I keep wanting to run in front of you—the court Jester, yes?—so I can steer you away from Evil and Hate and Anger and Cruelty and all the forces of Darkness—so I can point you to the true path—to righteousness and to light and to happiness. . . ."

For an author who can capture speech rhythms so accurately, who can reduplicate the Brooklyn streets of his doomed protagonist, David Voloshin, so well, such flights through airy abstraction strike us as embarrassing. But Neugeboren is out for nothing short of Big Stuff. *Before My Life Began* is the story of a man forced by circumstances to live "two" lives—one as the David Voloshin who grows up in Brooklyn during the years immediately after World War II; the other as Aaron Levin, a civil rights activist during the mid-1960's.

The rub with Neugeboren's ever-thickening plot is that David, as a character, gets lost in the process. Somewhere, despite the rich texture and the patches of lyrical prose, there is no "David" one can grab hold of. He reappears as Aaron Levin, Freedom School teacher and civil rights activist, a man out to do dangerously good work in the Deep South. Once again, Neugeboren has an admirable feel for that time, that place, but he cannot quite resist those moments when David/ Aaron speculates abstractly about his situation: "Sometimes, as now, he feels that his second life—all the years that have passed since he left Brooklyn, along with all the years to come—will only prove to be a rumination on his first life. . . . Why is it so, he wonders—that truth sometimes has the potential to destroy, while lies can save?"

Given the displacement and wrenching dislocations of Neugeboren's protagonist, we are hardly surprised that he seeks pockets of respite. Unfortunately, Neugeboren protests too much about the happiness Voloshin/Levin presumably achieves. *Before My Life Began* ends in a litany of future tenses, of those movements back to a Brooklyn that will bring the novel—and David's life—full circle: "He will take his boys to his old neighborhood and show them his street and his house and the courtyards and the alleyways. He can see the four small rooms of his apartment, can see himself walking through them with his boys, room by room. The rooms are clean and

white and empty, freshly painted and full of pale morning light—the way they might have been, he thinks, before his life began." Evidently one *can* go home again, at least in the final vision of *Before My Life Began*. But as Hemingway, a tougher, wiser American novelist knew full well: "Isn't it pretty to think so?"

Nonetheless, Neugeboren's last novels have established him as an important—rather than as simply a "talented"—writer. And if his most recent novel looks fondly "backward," his growing readership is, I suspect, much more interested in those Neugeboren novels that lie ahead.

—Sanford Pinsker

NEWBY, P(ercy) H(oward). British. Born in Crowborough, Sussex, 25 June 1918. Educated at Hanley Castle Grammar School, Worcester; St. Paul's College, Cheltenham, 1936–38. Served in the Royal Army Medical Corps, in France and Egypt, 1939–42. Married Joan Thompson in 1945; two daughters. Lecturer in English Language and Literature, Fouad I University, Cairo, 1942–46; free-lance writer and journalist, 1946–49; joined the BBC, London, 1949: producer, Talks Department, 1949–58; controller of the Third Programme, subsequently Radio 3, 1958–71; Director of Programmes, Radio, 1971–75; Managing Director of Radio, 1975–78; Chairman, English Stage Company, 1978–84. Recipient: Atlantic Award, 1946; Maugham Award, 1958; Smith-Mundt fellowship, 1952; Booker Prize, 1969. C.B.E. (Commander, Order of the British Empire), 1972. Address: Garsington House, Garsington, Oxfordshire OX9 9AB, England.

PUBLICATIONS

Novels

A Journey to the Interior. London, Cape, 1945; New York, Doubleday, 1946.
Agents and Witnesses. London, Cape, and New York, Doubleday, 1947.
Mariner Dances. London, Cape, 1948.
The Snow Pasture. London, Cape, 1949.
The Young May Moon. London, Cape, 1950; New York, Knopf, 1951.
A Season in England. London, Cape, 1951; New York, Knopf, 1952.
A Step to Silence. London, Cape, 1952.
The Retreat. London, Cape, and New York, Knopf, 1953.
The Picnic at Sakkara. London, Cape, and New York, Knopf, 1955.
Revolution and Roses. London, Cape, and New York, Knopf, 1957.
A Guest and His Going. London, Cape, 1959; New York, Knopf, 1960.
The Barbary Light. London, Faber, 1962; Philadelphia, Lippincott, 1964.
One of the Founders. London, Faber, and Philadelphia, Lippincott, 1965.
Something to Answer For. London, Faber, 1968; Philadelphia, Lippincott, 1969.
A Lot to Ask. London, Faber, 1973.
Kith. London, Faber, and Boston, Little Brown, 1977.

Feelings Have Changed.   London, Faber, 1981.

Short Stories

Ten Miles from Anywhere and Other Stories.   London, Cape, 1958.

Other

The Spirit of Jem (for children).   London, Lehmann, 1947; New York, Delacorte Press, 1967.
The Loot Runners (for children).   London, Lehmann, 1949.
Maria Edgeworth.   London, Barker, and Denver, Swallow, 1950.
The Novel 1945–1950.   London, Longman, 1951.
The Third Programme.   London, BBC Publications, 1965.
The Egypt Story: Its Art, Its Monuments, Its People, photographs by Fred J. Maroon.   London, Deutsch, and New York, Abbeville Press, 1979.
Warrior Pharaohs: The Rise and Fall of the Egyptian Empire.   London, Faber, 1980.
Saladin in His Time.   London, Faber, 1983.

Editor, *A Plain and Literal Translation of the Arabian Nights' Entertainments*, by Sir Richard Burton.   London, Barker, 1950; as *Tales from the Arabian Nights*, New York, Pocket Books, 1951(?).

*

Critical Studies: "Portrait of the Artist as a Jung Man" by Lucia Dickerson, in *Kenyon Review* (Gambier, Ohio), Winter 1959; "A Novelist on His Own," in *Times Literary Supplement* (London), 6 April 1962; *The Fiction of P.H. Newby* by F.X. Mathews, Madison, University of Wisconsin Press, 1964; *Identity in Four of P.H. Newby's Novels* by M.G. St. Leger, unpublished master's thesis, American University, Beirut, 1969; *P.H. Newby* by G.S. Fraser, London, Longman, 1974; *P.H. Newby* by E.C. Bufkin, Boston, Twayne, 1975.

P.H. Newby comments:
In common with many English novelists my preoccupations have always been with what seems and what is. Many of my novels have been set in the Middle East but that is only because I spent some years there; it does not mean that I regard myself as particularly knowledgeable about that part of the world, only that I used this part of my experience to say what I would otherwise have said out of my English background—that the most interesting problem is the relationship between innocence and knowledge.

*   *   *

The lengthy series of novels by P.H. Newby can, with some justice, be assigned to two categories. There are novels which represent Newby's assessment of the contacts of two cultures; *Revolution and Roses*, *The Picnic at Sakkara*, and *Something to Answer For* are examples of these. And there are novels like *A Season in England*, *The Barbary Light*, and *One of the Founders* which abandon the fascinating game of assessing sharp cultural differences and that instead take up an analysis of a single culture: the texture of middle- and lower-class British life. The center of awareness in the novels which specialize in cultural clash is always that of some British traveller or teacher who has been thrust into an alien world, usually Arab but in one instance—*Revolution and Roses*—Greek. The center

of awareness in novels that take up a specifically British theme is usually that of a fairly well-educated person who can assess the clash and diversity inherent in a society that, to the careless viewer, is or should be homogeneous.

Both varieties of subject matter have long been worked on by writers of British fiction. Alien cultural contacts experienced in the course of Britain's bearing "the white man's burden" are the stock-in-trade of writers as various as Kipling, E.M. Forster, and Joyce Cary. And novels which relate the maturing of an English hero in his own environment abound. But it is not just to Newby to suggest that he works in two traditions only loosely related to each other. For he brings to either tradition a variation that is his own. Moreover, this variation appears in almost every novel and effects a unity of tone that pervades the novels despite the variety of subject-matter. That tone is the tone of farce.

It is a tone that separates the novels that represent contact with an alien culture from Forster's *A Passage to India* in which the English characters achieve some kind of understanding of the world they visit. Newby's English visitors begin in incomprehension and end there; at certain moments they indeed think they grasp the mystery of Arab or Greek temperament, but later turns of event and later deeds of the "natives" indicate that the comprehension of the English visitor rests on an insecure basis or no basis at all. Thus, in as late a novel as *Kith*, the young Englishman who becomes involved with his uncle's Coptic wife never "has a clue" when he tries to understand his aunt who is also his mistress. He has, instead, a series of encounters with her that are isolated rather than interdependent.

Newby's tone of farce also separates his novels with an English setting from the "coming of age" category they may seem to belong to. For in novels like *The Barbary Light* the characters only seem to "come of age"; new events and new potentialities within the hero's own nature give the lie to stances that had seemed final. Only in *A Season in England* and *One of the Founders* do the heroes finally transcend the texture of farce and achieve positions that are crypto-Christian. More usually, the heroes of the English novels just move through a succession of attitudes—attitudes that are related to each other only in that they flow in upon the same person. They do not come to compose a character, a fixed personality, a settled body of convictions. The attitudes simply overtake the hero, temporarily overwhelm him, and presently give way to other emotions and impressions thrust upon him by new events or by discovery of new potentialities within himself. The character lives in a society which is far from unified; this being so, how can he arrive at any consistency of gesture and aspiration? He has no more chance to arrive at a consistent view of his own motives than does the English visitor in *The Picnic at Sakkara*. He will fall in and out of love, will alter his purposes from year to year. Just as will the travelling Englishmen impose one revision after another on their impressions about "natives."

If a discrimination can indeed be made between the two groups of novels, it is this one. The farce of *The Picnic at Sakkara* and *Revolution and Roses* is overt and often violent. The farce of the British novels—which on the surface seem to be more serious—is covert. If one defines farce as existence seen under the sign of radical inconsequence, the definition is easily applied to the non-British novels, which despite the acuteness of Newby's notations on foreign customs and sensibilities are rich in the traditional pleasures of farce: the pleasures that come to us from events that are unpredictable and utterly disconcerting. A "native" who has seemed to be a friend, in *The Picnic at Sakkara*, turns into a bitter foe—and yet gives the English visitor a farewell gift. A man spits in an English woman's face (*Revolution and Roses*) and yet later turns up in London as a suitor. The pleasures of such foreign contacts are not much more predictable than entrance into a lion's cage; docility or murderous assault is equally likely. Such experience cannot be expected to yield a steady meaning; in its presence the visitor can brace himself to offer resignation and, at the worst, amused contempt. The safest course, in such farcically operating worlds, is to keep one's distance and expect very little in the way of fixed and dependable certainties.

One might expect a diminution of these farcical inconsequences when the hero of a novel is living in a world that is culturally his own. But this is not so of Newby's novels that represent the English world. The farcical texture of that world is simply more difficult to bear just because it is indeed one's own world. Gestures of kindness that ought to yield happy results beget unforeseen consequences—consequences that disconcert because of the unpredictable choices of other characters and, most painfully, because of changes in one's own wishes. For the British world of Newby is, in large part, that of Kingsley Amis's *Lucky Jim*, where farce is the product of an endemic British hypocrisy and, still worse, of a lack of any fixed values that could support social consensus. Farce experienced at one remove, in a visit to a foreign country, has become, in novels like *One of the Founders* and *The Barbary Light*, farce experienced at the very center of the culture one belongs to and, indeed, at the very center of one's own nature. Both tragedy and comedy, in varying ways, presuppose a society of shared values. Farce, instead, invites one to the fashioning of a detached, self-protective monologue that celebrates, as do the novels of Newby, the lack of consequence and coherence. It is a lack that just as strongly marks one's own culture and, if sharply inspected, one's own nature. If farce is to be left behind, this must be done by religious gesture (as in *One of the Founders*) which is private and quite incommunicable. Or by religious gesture, as in *A Lot to Ask*, that when it comes to the surface finally reveals itself as not notably unlike hopes for identity and meaning that are both commonplace and important in our time.

—Harold H. Watts

NEWMAN, (Jerry) C(oleman) J(oseph). Canadian. Born in Montreal, Quebec, 17 February 1935. Educated at Sir George Williams University, Montreal (Woodrow Wilson Fellow), 1954–59, B.A. in English 1959; University of Toronto, 1959–60; Marianopolis College, Montreal, 1967–68. Married Frances Margaret Newman in 1962 (separated, 1977); two sons and one daughter. Lecturer, 1960–66, and Assistant Professor of English, 1971–72, Sir George Williams University; Assistant Professor, Macdonald College, McGill University, Montreal, 1966–71. Assistant Professor, 1972–77, and since 1977, Associate Professor of Creative Writing, University of British Columbia, Vancouver. Recipient: Canada Council bursary, 1966, and grant, 1968, 1969. Agent: Russell and Volkening Inc., 50 West 29th Street, New York, New York 10001, U.S.A. Address: Department of Creative Writing, University of British Columbia, Vancouver, British Columbia V6T 1W5, Canada.

PUBLICATIONS

Novels

We Always Take Care of Our Own. Toronto, McClelland and Stewart, and London, Gollancz, 1965.
A Russian Novel. Toronto, New Press, and London, Gollancz, 1973.

Short Stories

New Canadian Writing 1969, with John Metcalf and D.O. Spettigue. Toronto, Clarke Irwin, 1969.

Uncollected Short Stories

"A Time To Heal," in *Canadian Genesis* (Toronto), 1971.
"Your Green Coast," in *Malahat Review* (Victoria, British Columbia), 1973.
"That Old David Copperfield Kind of Crap," in *Canadian Fiction* (Prince George, British Columbia), Winter 1973.
"The Best Lay I Ever Had," in *Journal of Canadian Fiction* (Fredericton, New Brunswick), vol. 3, no. 3, 1974.
"Falling in Love, Again," in *Fiddlehead* (Fredericton, New Brunswick), Fall 1974.
"The Game of Limping," in *Prairie Schooner* (Lincoln, Nebraska), Winter 1974–75.
"The Last Beginning. The Last! The Last!" in *Canadian Fiction* (Prince George, British Columbia), Winter 1975.

Plays

Radio Plays: *All the State Children Got Shoes*, *The Jam on Gerry's Rocks*, *A Work of Art*, *The Last Potato*, and *The Haunted House of Capuscins*, 1959–63.

Television Plays: *The Birth of a Salesman*; *A Bottle of Milk for Mother*.

*   *   *

C.J. Newman's first novel, *We Always Take Care of Our Own*, is a *bildungsroman* in which the protagonist Meyer Rabinovitch seeks an identity independent of the series of roles offered him by his parents, his rich relatives, and the Jewish community of Montreal as a whole. The family and the community, dedicated to the North American ideal of material success, are self-enclosing and self-absorbed. Meyer, in such an atmosphere, suffocates, but he is primarily motivated by a need to replace the deadening material conformity with values he believes to be essentially spiritual and peculiarly Jewish, values which derive from a Jewish past of suffering and humility. Hence his decision to be the only Jewish beggar in Montreal. Much of the novel is devoted to Meyer's droll and sometimes grotesque attempts to remain a beggar in face of the family's and the Jewish community's attempts to return him to a conformity more North American than Jewish; or more exactly because the Jewish community strives neurotically to be accepted, even more North American than the North Americans themselves. The simple plot is complicated by Meyer's disturbance at his father's business inability, by his socialistic uncle's approval which becomes disapproval, and his love for Rachel, the daughter of the crass *nouveau riche* Eli Echenberg. During the latter's decline and eventual death Meyer becomes indispensable to the family and almost weds the pregnant Rachel. She, however, marries into an even richer Jewish family and the abandoned and disillusioned Meyer is left at the end of the book contemplating the image of his earlier self, this time in the form of another young man who has also decided to be the only Jewish beggar in Montreal. Reflecting on the young man's triumphant hopelessness and smug humility Meyer decides that it is not enough to be Jewish, that the self-definition he seeks must lie in areas beyond the mere inversion of the acceptable patterns of the Jewish and North American community.

Newman's short stories have appeared in many Canadian and American little magazines. Only three so far have been collected, in *New Canadian Writing 1969*. The first two, "Yenteh" and "Everything Must Be Sold," are set in contemporary Montreal and the third, "An Arab Up North," though set in the Canadian Arctic is paradoxically intensely aware of the international situation in the Middle East. The first two stories have in common a strong sense of an urban setting in transition from the small, intimate, and dilapidated to the large, impersonal, and modern. These settings are important inasmuch as they emphasize Newman's apparent theme of the loss of humane warmth in face of a world increasingly materialistic, insecure, and either suspicious of, or hostile to, the idiosyncrasies of being. Mrs. Klein may well be a *yenteh*, but energetic vulgarity is preferable to the deadly gentility of the ironically named Wisemans and the dis-ease of the Schachters who trail after the Wisemans of this world. Likewise the aged owner of the store which is about to be demolished so that the neighbourhood may be "renewed" arouses the malice of the two young men—a malice obscurely motivated by the rootlessness and depersonalization which such renewal seems to breed. Again in the third story it is the claims of history, race, religion, or class which blind the central characters, Arab and Jew, to the important realization that they have more in common with each other than with the rest of the men in the camp. It is because the recognition of each other's humanity is finally less important than a situation seemingly so remote from the Canadian Arctic that the story ends in death and desperate isolation.

A Russian Novel is a much more ambitious book than Newman's first one, and also a less successful one. The protagonist, David Miller, like Meyer Rabinovitch, is Jewish-Canadian and this novel too, appears to be concerned with an identity quest. Miller's mother emigrated many years ago from Russia, and after her death he decides to go there. It is only at the beginning, however, that the quest theme is emphasized. Much of the book is concerned with the love affair between Miller and the wife of the Russian novelist he is supposed to be studying, and with the political complexities surrounding Mikhali Ratin. It is especially in these areas that the novel becomes more of a tract than anything else and the didactic and documentary interests which have always been present in Newman's work usurp narrative, dramatic, and character emphases. One's final impression is of a novel which lacks both direction and linguistic vigour.

—Barrie Davies

NEWMAN, Charles (Hamilton). American. Born in St. Louis, Missouri, 27 May 1938. Educated at North Shore Country Day School, Winnetka, Illinois, graduated 1956; Yale University, New Haven, Connecticut (Editor, *Criterion* magazine), B.A. (summa cum laude) in American Studies 1960 (Phi Beta Kappa); Balliol College, Oxford (Woodrow Wilson Fellow, Fulbright Fellow), 1960–62. Served in the United States Air Force Reserve. Administrative assistant to Congressman

Sidney R. Yates (Democrat, Illinois), 1962–63. Instructor, 1964–65, Assistant Professor, 1965–68, Associate Professor, 1968–73, and Professor of English, 1974–75, Northwestern University, Evanston, Illinois; Professor of English, and Chairman of the Writing Seminars, Johns Hopkins University, Baltimore, 1975–77. Founding editor, 1964–75, and since 1975, advisory editor, *Tri-Quarterly*, Evanston, Illinois. Director, Coordinating Council of Literary Magazines, National Endowment for the Arts, Washington, D.C., 1968–74. Since 1976, Director, PEN American Center. Recipient: National Endowment for the Arts grant, for editing, 1966, and fellowship, 1973; Rockefeller grant, 1967; Bread Loaf Writers Conference Atherton Fellowship, 1969; Ingram Merrill Foundation grant, 1974; Guggenheim grant, 1974; American Academy Morton Dauwen Zabel Award, 1975. Agent: Georges Borchardt Inc., 136 East 57th Street, New York, New York 10022, U.S.A.

PUBLICATIONS

Novels

New Axis; or, The Little Ed Stories: An Exhibition. Boston, Houghton Mifflin, 1966; London, Calder and Boyars, 1968.
The Promisekeeper: A Tephromancy. New York, Simon and Schuster, 1971.
White Jazz. New York, Dial Press, 1984.

Short Stories

There Must Be More to Love Than Death: Three Short Novels. Chicago, Swallow Press, 1976.

Uncollected Short Stories

"That's the Way the American People Like to Do," in *Tri-Quarterly* (Evanston, Illinois), Spring 1964.
"The Scavengers," in *Vogue* (London), 1968.
"Eclipse, Etc.," in *Chicago Review*, Spring 1971.
"Comprehensive Development Project for These United States ...," in *Tri-Quarterly* (Evanston, Illinois), Winter 1976.
"Age of Art," in *Paris Review*, Winter 1976.
"The Woman Who Thought Like a Man," in *The Best American Short Stories 1977*, edited by Martha Foley. Boston, Houghton Mifflin, 1977.

Other

A Child's History of America: Some Ribs and Riffs for the Sixties. Chicago, Swallow Press, 1973.
The Post-Modern Aura: The Act of Fiction in an Age of Inflation. Evanston, Illinois, Northwestern University Press, 1985.

Editor, with George Gömöri, *New Writing from East Europe.* Chicago, Quadrangle, 1968.
Editor, *The Art of Sylvia Plath: A Symposium.* Bloomington, Indiana University Press, and London, Faber, 1970.
Editor, with William A. Henkin, Jr., *Under 30: Fiction, Poetry, and Criticism of the New American Writers.* Bloomington, Indiana University Press, 1970.
Editor, *For Edward Dahlberg.* Evanston, Illinois, Northwestern University Press, 1970.
Editor, with Alfred Appel, Jr., *Nabokov: Criticism and Reminiscences, Translations and Tributes.* Evanston, Illinois, Northwestern University Press, 1970; London, Weidenfeld and Nicolson, 1971.

Editor, with George Abbott White, *Literature in Revolution*. New York, Holt Rinehart, 1972.

Editor, with Mary Kinzie, *Prose for Borges*. Evanston, Illinois, Northwestern University Press, 1974.

*   *   *

Charles Newman is one of America's better experimental writers. Writing in the tradition of Burgess, Barth, Pynchon, and Vonnegut, Newman employs his verbal pyrotechnics and Derridean deconstructions to create the fictive world of post-modern man threatened by obsolescence in a high-tech age.

From 1964 to 1975 Newman served as founding editor of *Tri-Quarterly* and forged the magazine in his own style, attracting the works of the best experimental writers of this continent and abroad. Later, he edited several volumes of criticism on Plath, Borges, and the literature of revolution. 1985 saw the publication of *The Post-Modern Aura: The Act of Fiction in an Age of Inflation*. Dissecting the underlying principles of post-modern literature, he exposes a literature that is as debased as our money supply, and he dates the swings in post-modernism to coincide with the periodicity of the velocity of the money supply from 1946 when it first started rising, through the 1950's when it accelerated, to 1968 when it peaked at the height of the Great Society and the Vietnam War, on through the 1970's when it was out of control, and ending in 1981 when it subsided as one by one the myths of inflation were dismantled. Paralleling the collapse in value of our money is the collapse of the house of fiction and its replacement with the growth of metafiction and a banal poetry which comes near to being prose or primitive speech. Newman charts the course of fiction and criticism, launching a scathing attack on the fallacy of the indeterminists, and exposing the false dichotomy created by William Gass and Donald Barthelme of the avant garde on the one hand, and Saul Bellow of the realist revival on the other. In Gass, we find the absolutist aesthetic: he takes formalism to its affirmative extreme and asserts that the novel is all technique with no mimetic obligations; it is a cultural object that transcends and transforms history. Bellow responds by insisting that mimesis and an audience be restored to art, that art and the artist recover the centrality they once held in an integrated society that privileged each, and that art seek again to find that "lost something" which once inhabited it and gave it meaning and value beyond its own literary confines. Newman's credo is to reject all binary classifications as misguided and to draw upon the methods of science, of the wave/particle theories of light, to give him direction. Refusing to partake of the formalist/realist debate, he argues that what is needed is a method that permits one to hold simultaneously irreconcilable ideas—to entertain a wave/particle theory of reality. Newman asks that the artist rededicate himself to literature's peculiar generic constitution, "its lack of an ontology, and the consequent cross-processing which defies autonomy—a practical energy which can never be systematic, but cannot fail to be inclusive." He concludes that "Fiction, in short, is modern man's method by which antinomies can be unlearned; a process in which oppositions are neither resolved nor transcended but made reciprocally evocative. ... And the truth of fiction is not indeterminate—only a set of facts which cannot be presumptively inferred from other facts, which is thus unlikely to find expression as a coherent theory." Newman's imaginative writing, like his books of criticism, is unpredictable, verbally adroit, and utterly committed to the task of describing minutely the consciousness industry—our society as a massive communications industry, an information system of extraordinary technical sophistication tied to a kinetic media and operating like a planetary system of "increasingly merged bodies which conform to an increasingly inexorable set of mundane laws." The artist's task is still the one Forster wrote about: "only connect," and this connection must relate art to its audience and its world. Art to survive must serve an ethical function. *White Jazz*, Newman's latest novel, travels the farthest in fulfilling the credo Newman writes about in *The Post-Modern Aura*. It is marked by his zany imagination, a fine intelligence, an inquiring mind, a genius with words, and a stubborn humanistic craving for meaning in a world where future shock threatens to reduce life to a computer game.

An examination of Newman's novels and satirical history since 1966 is usefully informed by reference to the periods of inflation that he describes in *The Post-Modern Aura*. In the period of the Great Society and the Vietnam War when the modernist idea of salvation through aesthetics seemed sorely wanting, and when fiction revelled in egalitarianism and filled its margins in a search for a new point of view, Newman wrote *New Axis* and *A Child's History of America*. In *New Axis*, Little Ed narrates a series of stories about the life of the affluent D family and their neighbors in a wealthy suburb located in middle America. Little Ed's world is one of diminished, ordinary, well-meaning affection. It is also a world of inflation and automation: Vibrolators restore the circulation and make plump, curved women slim. In *A Child's History of America* Newman recounts with colloquial ease his travels through Haight-Ashbury when the Hippies were confronting the "pigs," on to Paris during the May revolt of the students, and ending in Czechoslovakia during the Russian invasion. The margins of his book are cluttered with aptly chosen quotes from such notables as Trotsky and Marx, Bergson and Merleau-Ponty, Locke and Thoreau, and a gentleman who left graffiti on a lavatory wall. The book offers a disarming and refreshingly original portrait of the confusion of 1968.

In 1971 Newman wrote *The Promisekeeper*, his "tephromancy." Auguries of the future are found by reading the ashes of Chicago. Super-elegant, suave, executive Sam Hooper climbs the ladder of success at Management Concerns. Hooper, the technocrat's dream of efficiency and success, is a promise-keeper who only pledges what he can deliver; he is only victor when he relinquishes his limited powers and lets himself be killed. Hooper's relaxation takes the form of reading the journal of Captain Fuess, a millionaire mariner who voyages around the world in ever smaller ships crafted by his own hands. The narrative, in the manner of meta-fiction, is interspersed with Captain Fuess's tale, relics of Sam's past, his report cards, his Christmas market analysis, and other diverse odds and ends. In *There Must Be More to Love Than Death* Newman presents three novelettes. The first tells the story of Gee Patek of the 112st Air Dispensary Unit. Never seeing active duty, Patek manages to be accused of sexual deviancy and of attacking Commander Pompillo with a hypodermic needle filled with morphine. The story recounts the events that lie behind these accusations. The second short novel, a masque, is a "hopelessly confused affair in which everyone feels neglected." The third short novel is the narrative of a 13-year-old boy who possesses a photographic memory and perfect recall of all that he hears. He admonishes the reader to "please remember that what I'm saying is what other people said—something I've read or heard somewhere—and a lot of the time I honestly don't understand myself." The story is allegorical. With the advantage of hindsight and anachronism, one could say that the story is Newman's answer to Harold Bloom's idea of the anxiety of influence. The story tells of a trip the narrator takes with his imaginary brother into the forest and back home. It is not the entrance into the forest that matters, nor the discovery that at the heart of the forest is a broken-down machine. What matters, and what is difficult to tell, is the story of how one comes out of the forest and survives. Newman's latest novel is exploring the same question but the forest is replaced by Yuppie highrises and strobe-lit discos.

White Jazz is Newman's novel of the 1980's; the myth of inflation is in ruins; the hype of the information age is bust; the protagonist's dream of discovering the Great Computer is shattered; and the protagonist's need to make human contact in an age where the consciousness industry has almost emptied man of meaning is poignantly expressed in the final pages of the novel. Newman's novel insists that we register the textures of the media age. He fashions the Nowspeak of computers and videogames; he is the architect of the urban metropolis surrounded by eight-laned Interstate highways, looping around retirement parks that face upscale young-adult communities, all built by the same architect out of the same mindless mold. His novel is lit by the artificial orb light of the expressways, or the bombarding rays of electrons projected from a television screen or computer terminal, or the hot and cool strobe lights of a jazz disco. The novel charts a week in the life of the protagonist, Sandy—Sandman to his CB-radio cronies—who probes the circuitry of his computer terminal at Human Resources by day and unwinds by night at el Cielito Lindo. His book is liberally laced with quotations from Bishop Berkeley, Albert Einstein, and the latest self-help moral inventory generated by the computer.

Newman is an accomplished writer who delights in language and its deceptions and who forges stories that force us to confront our technological age and consider what can give us meaning in this minimalist, mediocritizing world.

—Carol Simpson Stern

NGUGI wa Thiong'o. Formerly wrote as James T. Ngugi. Kenyan. Born in Kamiriithu, near Limuru, Kiambu District, 5 January 1938. Educated at Kamaandūra School, Limuru; Karing'a School, Maanguū; Alliance High School, Kikuyu; University College, Kampala, Uganda (Editor, *Penpoint*), 1959–63, B.A. 1963; Leeds University, Yorkshire, 1964–67, B.A. 1964. Married Nyambura in 1961; two sons and three daughters. Columnist ("As I See It"), in early 1960's, and reporter, 1964, Nairobi *Daily Nation*; Lecturer in English, University College, Nairobi, 1967–69; Fellow in Creative Writing, Makerere University, Kampala, 1969–70; Visiting Lecturer, Northwestern University, Evanston, Illinois, 1970–71; Senior Lecturer, Associate Professor, and Chairman of the Department of Literature, University of Nairobi, 1972–77. Imprisoned under Public Security Act, 1977–78. Editor, *Zuka*, Nairobi, 1965–70. Recipient: East African Literature Bureau award, 1964. Address: c/o Heinemann Educational Books, 22 Bedford Square, London WC1B 3HH, England.

PUBLICATIONS

Novels

Weep Not, Child. London, Heinemann, 1964; New York, Collier, 1969.

The River Between. London, Heinemann, 1965.
A Grain of Wheat. London, Heinemann, 1967.
Petals of Blood. London, Heinemann, 1977; New York, Dutton, 1978.
Caitaani Mutharaba-ini (in Kikuyu). Nairobi, Heinemann, 1980; as *Devil on the Cross*, London, Heinemann, 1982.

Short Stories

Secret Lives and Other Stories. London, Heinemann, and New York, Hill, 1975.

Plays

The Black Hermit (produced Kampala, 1962). London, Heinemann, 1968.
This Time Tomorrow (broadcast, 1967). Included in *This Time Tomorrow*, 1970.
This Time Tomorrow (includes *The Rebels* and *The Wound in the Heart*). Nairobi, East African Literature Bureau, 1970.
The Trial of Dedan Kimathi, with Micere Mugo (produced London, 1984). Nairobi, Heinemann, 1976; London, Heinemann, 1977.
Ngaahika Ndeenda (in Kikuyu), with Ngugi wa Mirii (produced Limuru, 1977). Nairobi, Heinemann, 1980; as *I Will Marry When I Want*, London, Heinemann, 1982.

Radio Play: *This Time Tomorrow*, 1967.

Other

Homecoming: Essays on African and Caribbean Literature, Culture, and Politics. London, Heinemann, 1972; New York, Hill, 1973.
The Education of Africa and Cultural Decolonisation. Lagos, Afrografika, 1977.
Writers in Politics: Essays. London, Heinemann, 1981.
Detained: A Writer's Prison Diary. London, Heinemann, 1981.
Education for a National Culture. Harare, Zimbabwe Publishing House, 1981.
Barrel of a Pen: Resistance to Repression in Neo-Colonial Kenya. London, New Beacon, and Trenton, New Jersey, Africa World Press, 1983.

*

Critical Studies: *Ngugi wa Thiong'o* by Clifford Robson, London, Macmillan, 1979; *An Introduction to the Writings of Ngugi* by G.D. Killam, London, Heinemann, 1980; *Ngugi wa Thiong'o: An Exploration of His Writings* by David Cook and Michael Okenimkpe, London, Heinemann, 1983.

*   *   *

Ngugi wa Thiong'o was a Gikuyu adolescent in Kenya during the Mau Mau Rebellion, and the events of those years, of the larger issues of Black dispossession by white settlers, and of the history of the Gikuyu from pre-colonial times to the present, lie at the centre of his novels and most of his short stories. He was the first Anglophone African writer to give in fiction a Gikuyu view of the bitter colonial war that the British called the Mau Mau Emergency—a healthy corrective to other fictional accounts, like Robert Ruark's, from a white man's point of view. Ngugi's attitudes to larger political questions are by no means unambiguous in his first two novels (hence some considerable uncertainty of craftsmanship in them) but what emerges clearly from *The River Between* (the first to be written, but the second published) is a deep sense of African deprivation and of the desire to win back a lost heritage. It is expressed in *Weep Not, Child* through Ngotho's religious attachment to the land of his ancestors taken from him by Mr. Howlands, and through his older sons' determination to fight for their lands by joining the Mau Mau. But Ngugi is also aware of another part of the African heritage diminished by white colonialism—the Gikuyu religion and tribal culture; it is this aspect of their disinheritance that figures particularly in *The River Between*.

The river is a symbol of sustenance and growth, but it also divides the christianized half of the tribe from the adherents of the traditional tribal ways, soon after the advent of colonialism. Waiyaki, the hero, is an idealistic youth, who dreams with messianic fervour of leading his people out of colonial tutelage, peacefully, by acquiring the white man's education. He would also reconcile the two religiously divided villages; though associated with the traditionalists, he loves a daughter of the fanatical Christian Gikuyu pastor. But Waiyaki's enthusiasm for western education blinds him to political methods, and he is rejected by his people. The weakness of the novel is that Ngugi romanticizes and glamorizes Waiyaki: his tribal opponents are presented as vindictive personal enemies; their different political approach is not seriously considered.

Njoroge in *Weep Not, Child* is another self-centred youth with mission-school education and messianic ambitions, whose hopes are destroyed when his brothers' involvement in Mau Mau forces him out of school, but again self-centredness is not part of any ironic regarding of the hero by the novelist. Yet *Weep Not, Child* is a better novel, for Ngugi develops some complexity of structure. There are ironic parallels between the African devotion to ancestral lands and the white settler's love of the soil he has acquired, with the opposed characters oblivious to their common human suffering. Such ironical treatment is a great advance in Ngugi's technique, as are the convincing portraits of subsidiary characters who betray the very values they struggle to achieve, or who suffer constant frustration.

A Grain of Wheat is a novel of mature outlook and much subtler technique. Ostensibly about the Uhuru celebrations of Kenya's independence in 1963, it keeps flashing back to individual sufferings in Mau Mau days. There is no single, central hero this time, but four major characters, each guilty of betraying himself and others when sorely tried in the Rebellion. Mugo, regarded by his people as a Mau Mau hero, has messianic visions before the Rebellion, but his jealousy of the real leader led him to betray him to the British. At last Ngugi is able to treat a messianic figure with detachment, but also with humane sympathy: the years of Mugo's lonely, conscience-ridden life are movingly conveyed. Other characters who also committed acts of betrayal painfully learn, first, the depths of utter disillusion, and then, the harrowing experience of coming to terms with their own limitations. Mugo's public confession brings *him* peace of mind, and helps *them* to face the future with some hope. A great strength of this finely orchestrated novel is Ngugi's skilful use of disrupted time sequence to indicate the inter-relatedness of the characters' behaviour in the Rebellion and the state of their lives (and of the nation) at Independence. Ngugi's maturity appears also in his sober attitude both to the struggle for, and attainment of, Independence; there are signs of the new African politicians already betraying the ordinary people who suffered under colonialism. Though a disturbing novel, it proclaims hope for the regenerative capabilities of ordinary human nature.

In his critical essays in *Homecoming*, Ngugi argues the vital social function of literature in Africa, and the Third World generally. In *Petals of Blood* he impressively puts this belief into practice. A convincing attack, often Marxist in language, upon neo-colonialism in Independent Africa is achieved fictionally by indicating powerfully and effectively how the lives of dispossessed little people are all but broken by an imported capitalist system. The four major characters, each a misfit in Independent Kenyan society, have come to the distant village of Ilmorog to seek personal peace and modest new beginnings. Long associated with heroic Gikuyu legends, Ilmorog becomes a living presence in the novel. In the grip of prolonged drought, and ignored by the M.P. who had begged their votes, the desperate villagers undertake an epic march to the capital to lay their troubles before the authorities. Subsequently religious, political, and economic exploiters swarm upon Ilmorog to "develop" it, and using such devices as foreclosed loans eventually dispossess the local inhabitants and establish New Ilmorog. The ample detail with which Ngugi conveys the ruthless stripping of already deprived ordinary people gains power from a sophisticated narrative technique that enables Kenya's history since 1963 to be felt through the consciousness of its social victims. *Petals of Blood* is an angry novel but it does affirm the potentialities of native communality for a just, humane African polity.

With greater fervour of feeling and rhetoric, Ngugi renews in *Devil on the Cross* his attack upon neo-colonial exploiters of ordinary Kenyan people. The story of the economically and sexually exploited young woman, Warĩĩnga, is given some of the drama of fantasy by being told by "Gĩcaandĩ Player, Prophet of Justice," a figure drawn from the oral tradition, who uses language emotively and didactically in ways reminiscent of Armah's novel *Two Thousand Seasons* (1973). While the device allows Ngugi to employ a variety of highly charged rhetorical modes, it is questionable whether he deploys them as convincingly as he might have. Would such a narrator use not only songs, incantations, the very idiom of oral tradition, but also echoes and parodies of Bible stories and Biblical English, together with Marxist analysis and denunciation of capitalism? Ngugi doesn't seem to have tried very hard to disguise his authorial voice, or perhaps it is the effect of translating from his own original Gikuyu. While in *Devil on the Cross* he combines the biblical linguistic and moral flavour of his first two novels with the acerbic political tones of *Petals of Blood*, the cost is much wordy reiteration. Nevertheless, the catastrophic effects of the western economic stranglehold on many African nations is starkly revealed in the misery of the destitute and starving and the monstrosity of the new Kenyan affluent class.

—Arthur Ravenscroft

NICOL, Abioseh. Pseudonym for Davidson Sylvester Hector Willoughby Nicol. Sierra Leonean. Born in Freetown, 14 September 1924. Educated at schools in Nigeria and Sierra Leone; Christ's College, Cambridge, 1943–50, B.A. 1946, M.A., M.D., Ph.D. Married Marjorie Esme Johnston in 1950; three sons and two daughters. Science master, Prince of Wales School, Freetown, 1941–43; house physician and research assistant, London Hospital Medical College, University of London, 1950–52; University Lecturer, Medical School, Ibadan,

1952–54; Beit Memorial Fellow, 1954, and Benn Levy University Student, 1956, Cambridge University; Fellow and Supervisor in Natural Sciences and Medicine, Christ's College, Cambridge, 1957–59; Senior Pathologist, Sierra Leone Government, 1958–60; Visiting Lecturer, University of California, Berkeley, and Mayo Clinic, Rochester, Minnesota, 1958; Principal, Fourah Bay College, 1960–67, and Vice-Chancellor, 1966–68, University of Sierra Leone, Freetown; Aggrey-Fraser-Guggisberg Lecturer, University of Ghana, Accra, 1963; Danforth Lecturer, Association of American Colleges, 1968–70. Ambassador of Sierra Leone to the United Nations, 1968–71; High Commissioner of the Republic of Sierra Leone to the United Kingdom, and Ambassador of Sierra Leone to Denmark, Norway, Sweden, and Finland, 1971–72; Executive Director, United Nations Institute for Training and Research (UNITAR), and Under-Secretary-General, United Nations, New York, 1972–82; Guest Scholar, Woodrow Wilson International Center, Washington, D.C., and Hoover Institution, Stanford, California, 1983; Visiting Fellow, Johns Hopkins School of Advanced International Studies, Washington, D.C., 1984. Since 1985, Lecturer, Cambridge University. Member, West African Council for Medical Research, 1959–62; Chairman, Sierra Leone National Library Board, 1959–65; member, Public Service Commission of Sierra Leone, 1960–68; President, Sierra Leone Red Cross Society, 1962–66; delegate, Unesco Higher Education Conference, Tananarive, 1963; President, West African Science Association, 1964–66; delegate, Commonwealth Prime Ministers Conference, London, 1965, 1969, 1971. Director, Sierra Leone Selection Trust Ltd., 1961–71, Central Bank of Sierra Leone, 1963–68, and since 1961, Consolidated African Selection Trust Ltd., London. Since 1983, President, World Federation of United Nations Associations. Recipient: Margaret Wrong Prize, 1951; Independence Medal (Sierra Leone), 1961. D.Sc.: University of Newcastle-upon-Tyne, 1964; Kalamazoo College, Michigan, 1964; Laurentian University, Sudbury, Ontario, 1984; LL.D.: University of Leeds, 1968; Barat College, Lake Forest, Illinois, 1978; University of the West Indies, St. Augustine, 1981; Tuskegee Institute, Alabama, 1981; D.Litt.: Davis-Elkins College, Elkins, West Virginia, 1971. Honorary Fellow, Ghana Academy of Sciences, Christ's College, Cambridge, 1972, and UNITAR, 1983. C.M.G. (Companion, Order of St. Michael and St. George), 1964; Grand Commander, Order of Rokel, Sierra Leone, 1974; Star of Africa, Liberia, 1974. Address: Christ's College, Cambridge University, Cambridge CB2 3BU, England.

PUBLICATIONS

Short Stories

The Truly Married Woman and Other Stories. London, Oxford University Press, 1965.
Two African Tales. London, Cambridge University Press, 1965.

Other (as Davidson Nicol)

On Not Being a West African (lecture). Ibadan, Ibadan University Press, 1955.
Alienation, with others, edited by Timothy O'Keefe. London, MacGibbon and Kee, 1960.
Africa: A Subjective View. London, Longman, 1964.
New and Modern Roles for the Empire and Commonwealth (lecture). London, Cambridge University Press, 1976.

The United Nations and Decision Making: The Role of Women, with others. New York, UNITAR, 1978.
The United Nations Security Council: Towards Greater Effectiveness. New York, UNITAR, 1982.

Editor, *Africanus Horton: The Dawn of Nationalism in Modern Africa*. London, Longman, 1969; as *Black Nationalism in Africa 1867*, New York, Africana, 1969.
Editor, *Paths to Peace: Essays on the United Nations Security Council and Its Presidency*. Elmsford, New York, Pergamon Press, 1981.
Editor, with Luis Echeverria, *Regionalism and the New International Economic Order*. Elmsford, New York, Pergamon Press, 1981.
Editor, with Pamela D'Onofrio-Flores, *Scientific-Technological Change and the Role of Women in Its Development*. Boulder, Colorado, Westview Press, 1981.
Editor, with others, *Creative Women in Changing Societies: A Quest for Alternatives*. Dobbs Ferry, New York, Creative Publishers, 1982; Epping, Essex, Bowker, 1984.

*

Bibliography: in *A Bibliography of Sierra Leone, 1925–1969* edited by G.J. Williams, New York, Africana, 1970.

Manuscript Collections: Royal Commonwealth Society Library, London; Yale University, New Haven, Connecticut.

Critical Studies: *The African Image* by Es'kia Mphahlele, London, Faber, and New York, Praeger, 1962, revised edition, Faber and Praeger, 1974; *African-English Literature* by Anne Tibble, London, Owen, 1965; *Mother Is Gold: A Study in West African Literature* by Adrian Roscoe, London, Cambridge University Press, 1971; *Commonwealth Literature* by William Walsh, London and New York, Oxford University Press, 1973; *Cowries and Kobos: The West African Oral Tale and Short Story* edited by Kirsten Holst Petersen and Anna Rutherford, Aarhus, Denmark, Dangaroo Press, 1981.

Abioseh Nicol comments:
(1972) My short stories and poetry have predominantly an African background although a few are set in Europe and America. Their characters are drawn from all levels of black and white society in Africa, and are based on observations gained by me during my work as a teacher, administrator, and doctor, plus the insight gained as a black African patriot engaged in plans towards our independence. I tried to keep an independent and non-racist outlook.

My appearance in print owes itself to the encouragement of the late Langston Hughes, the black American writer, who first included me in his anthology of African verse, and to Stephen Spender, the English poet, and Irving Kristol, the American writer, both of whom, as former editors of *Encounter*, gave me the unprecedented encouragement of publishing three of my short stories within a year in their magazine. My literary criticism was encouraged and fostered in that excellent weekly *West Africa* by its Editor, David Williams, and by Walter Allen, former Literary Editor of the *New Statesman and Nation*. Without the advice and encouragement of these writers, my publications would still have been in manuscript form, at the bottom of a drawer.

All this, of course, refers to creative writing. I have written a considerable amount also on higher education and politics over the past twenty years and have also published in professional journals the results of research carried out in Europe and Africa on medical and scientific subjects such as malnutrition, tropical diseases, endocrinology, and biochemistry.

(1986) I am now teaching a postgraduate course on international organizations at Cambridge University, and working on my autobiography. I am also working on a novel set in the 19th century and based on West African society and slavery. My retirement from active duty at the UN has freed my mind for more creative writing.

*   *   *

Abioseh Nicol, one of Africa's most talented short story writers, belongs to the older generation of living African authors who wrote in the twilight of the colonial era, when Africa was still under the political thumb of Europe. Unlike many of his contemporaries, he did not write militant protest fiction but chose instead to deal with the cultural problems and moral dilemmas of Africans and Europeans who lived in this era "with its emphasis on pensionable jobs in Government service, official decorations, and black and white keeping their distance." Nicol has stated that he started writing

partly because I wanted to and partly because I found that most of those who wrote about us seldom gave any nobility to their African characters unless they were savages or servants or faced impending destruction. I knew differently. I saw all around me worthy Africans who lived and worked with varying degrees of success, distinction, and happiness. I began to write about them.

Nicol's stories are usually set in the part of Africa under British rule and frequently describe situations in which British colonial administrators and Africans strain against each other and toward each other. Nicol, who admits he owes much to E.M. Forster, Joyce Cary, Graham Greene, and Evelyn Waugh, pictures the mutual misunderstandings, the problems of communication, the gropings toward friendship, the lapses into anger and hostility, the hopes and the fears that characterize the relationships between the colonizers and the colonized, between white and black in Africa. It is a credit to Nicol's sensitivity and literary skill that these stories paint both sides of the racial fence accurately and compassionately.

In other stories Nicol investigates the plight of westernized Africans who still cling to traditional beliefs and customs. Victims of internal culture conflict, these men and women have to struggle to maintain their equilibrium in a changing world. Sometimes their difficulties are resolved in hilarious comedy, sometimes in tender pathos. Nicol's sharp eye for human foibles and tolerance for individual eccentricities make these stories a delight to read. He is an urbane humorist with a talent for gently poking fun at some of Africa's most entertaining absurdities.

—Bernth Lindfors

NYE, Robert. British. Born in London, 15 March 1939. Educated at Dormans Land, Sussex; Hamlet Court, Westcliff, Essex; Southend High School. Married 1) Judith Pratt in 1959 (divorced, 1967), three sons; 2) Aileen Campbell in 1968, one daughter, one stepdaughter, and one stepson. Since 1961, freelance writer: since 1967, poetry editor, *The Scotsman*; since 1971, poetry critic, *The Times*. Writer-in-Residence, University of Edinburgh, 1976–77. Recipient: Eric Gregory Award, 1963; Scottish Arts Council bursary, 1970, 1973, and publication award, 1970, 1976; James Kennaway Memorial Award, 1970; *Guardian* Fiction Prize, 1976; Hawthornden Prize, 1977. Fellow, Royal Society of Literature, 1977. Agent: Anthony Sheil Associates, 43 Doughty Street, London WC1N 2LF, England; or, Wallace and Sheil Inc., 177 East 70th Street, New York, New York 10021, U.S.A. Address: 2 Westbury Crescent, Wilton, Cork, Ireland.

PUBLICATIONS

Novels

Doubtfire.   London, Calder and Boyars, and New York, Hill and Wang, 1968.
Falstaff.   London, Hamish Hamilton, and Boston, Little Brown, 1976.
Merlin.   London, Hamish Hamilton, 1978; New York, Putnam, 1979.
➤ *Faust*.   London, Hamish Hamilton, 1980; New York, Putnam, 1981.
The Voyage of the Destiny.   London, Hamish Hamilton, and New York, Putnam, 1982.

Short Stories

Tales I Told My Mother.   London, Calder and Boyars, 1969; New York, Hill and Wang, 1970.
Penguin Modern Stories 6, with others.   London, Penguin, 1970.
The Facts of Life and Other Fictions.   London, Hamish Hamilton, 1983.

Uncollected Short Stories

Lines Review 38 (includes 4 stories, verse, and a film script) (Edinburgh), 1971.

Plays

Sawney Bean, with Bill Watson (produced Edinburgh, 1969; London, 1972; New York, 1982).   London, Calder and Boyars, 1970.
Sisters (broadcast, 1969; produced Edinburgh, 1973).   Included in *Penthesilea, Fugue, and Sisters*, 1976.
Penthesilea, adaptation of a play by Heinrich von Kleist (broadcast, 1971; produced London, 1983).   Included in *Penthesilea, Fugue, and Sisters*, 1976.
The Seven Deadly Sins: A Mask, music by James Douglas (produced Stirling, 1973).   Rushden, Northamptonshire, Omphalos Press, 1974.
Mr. Poe (produced Edinburgh and London, 1974).
Penthesilea, Fugue, and Sisters.   London, Calder and Boyars, 1976.

Radio Plays: *Sisters*, 1969; *A Bloody Stupit Hole*, 1970; *Reynolds, Reynolds*, 1971; *Penthesilea*, 1971; *The Devil's Jig*, with Humphrey Searle, from a work by Thomas Mann, 1980.

Verse

Juvenilia 1.   Northwood, Middlesex, Scorpion Press, 1961.
Juvenilia 2.   Lowestoft, Suffolk, Scorpion Press, 1963.
Darker Ends.   London, Calder and Boyars, and New York, Hill and Wang, 1969.

Agnus Dei. Rushden, Northamptonshire, Sceptre Press, 1973.
Two Prayers. Richmond, Surrey, Keepsake Press, 1974.
Five Dreams. Rushden, Northamptonshire, Sceptre Press, 1974.
Divisions on a Ground. Manchester, Carcanet, 1976.

Other (for children)

Taliesin. London, Faber, 1966; New York, Hill and Wang, 1967.
March Has Horse's Ears. London, Faber, 1966; New York, Hill and Wang, 1967.
Bee Hunter: Adventures of Beowulf. London, Faber, 1968; as *Beowulf: A New Telling*, New York, Hill and Wang, 1968; as *Beowulf, The Bee Hunter*, Faber, 1972.
Wishing Gold. London, Macmillan, 1970; New York, Hill and Wang, 1971.
Poor Pumpkin. London, Macmillan, 1971; as *The Mathematical Princess and Other Stories*, New York, Hill and Wang, 1972.
Cricket: Three Stories. Indianapolis, Bobbs Merrill, 1975; as *Once upon Three Times*, London, Benn, 1978.
Out of the World and Back Again. London, Collins, 1977; as *Out of This World and Back Again*, Indianapolis, Bobbs Merrill, 1978.
The Bird of the Golden Land. London, Hamish Hamilton, 1980.
Harry Pay the Pirate. London, Hamish Hamilton, 1981.
Three Tales. London, Hamish Hamilton, 1983.

Other

Editor, *A Choice of Sir Walter Ralegh's Verse*. London, Faber, 1972.
Editor, *William Barnes: A Selection of His Poems*. Oxford, Carcanet, 1972.
Editor, *A Choice of Swinburne's Verse*. London, Faber, 1973.
Editor, *The Faber Book of Sonnets*. London, Faber, 1976; as *A Book of Sonnets*, New York, Oxford University Press, 1976.
Editor, *The English Sermon 1750–1850*. Cheadle, Cheshire, Carcanet, 1976.

*

Manuscript Collections: University of Texas, Austin; National Library of Scotland, Edinburgh; University of Edinburgh.

*   *   *

A hallmark of Robert Nye's fiction has been his ability to harness the imagination to his will, to take the facts of everyday history and to transform them into fantastic happenings so that myth and reality become as one. The stories in *Tales I Told My Mother* rework the lives of literary personalities, and his first novel, *Doubtfire*, ranges in time and space between different worlds with remarkable ease and fluidity of style. Equally fantastic have been his children's novels which have followed faithfully C.S. Lewis's dictum that children's stories should be equally enjoyed by adults.

In his four most recent novels, *Falstaff*, *Merlin*, *Faust*, and *The Voyage of the Destiny*, Nye has created a quartet of loosely-related myths from characters, real or imaginary, who exist in our collective pasts. The worlds that they people are dream-like and fabulous, half-caught, half-forgotten by the subconscious mind. And yet their darksome existence is lightened by Nye's ability to steer away from allegory by making their worlds new again and instantly recognisable: Falstaff lives in an England that is demonstrably 14th-century, Merlin's world is one of medieval chivalry, and Faust knows a Europe shared by Luther and Calvin.

Falstaff, a novel of 100 chapters, tells the story of Sir John Fastolf—his relationship to the English aristocracy and to the giant of Cerne Abbas, his conduct at the siege of Kildare, his friendship with Prince Hal, and his prowess at the Battle of Agincourt. Much of the story is recognisable from the Falstaff of Shakespeare's plays, but Nye takes in the whole panorama of life in England at a time of cultural and economic transition. Falstaff's adventures, often unlikely and scabrous, unfold before the reader's eyes like a medieval tapestry, and by the end of the novel he has been consumed by myth, the eternal John Bull, both patriot and buffoon.

Myth of another kind lies at the heart of *Merlin* whose central character is at once the unmistakable Merlin of Sir Thomas Malory's *Le Morte Darthur* and at the same time an older, more cunning figure from Welsh vernacular literature and from the poetry of the 12th-century French poet Robert de Boron, who created a Merlin capable of seeing both past and future and thus able to connect the ancient history of the Grail with the court of King Arthur. Nye's Merlin is a nebulous figure, sired by the Devil and a virgin in an attempt to create the Anti-Christ, and a man whose sexual ambiguity is a source of good and of evil. The veiled eroticism of medieval courtly love is torn open in Nye's version of a world in which sexual deviation is more potent than chivalry and black magic more powerful than religious faith. Throughout the novel, which keeps more or less faithfully to the facts of the medieval romance, runs the seminal myth of the Quest for the Holy Grail and man's striving for the eternal.

Faust follows many of the same themes and expands on them: a delight in mixing myth with reality, an earthy eroticism, and a fast-moving dialogue that is both funny and deeply serious. The story of Faust's final 40 days on earth, having sold his soul to the devil, is seen through the excited reaction of his servant, Kit Wagner. For, unlike Marlowe's Faust, Dr. John Faust is not content to wait meekly for his damnation in the company of Helen of Troy, Mephistopheles, and his monkey Akercocke; rather he sets out with his entourage on a pilgrimage to Rome in hot pursuit of a dog called Satan. The story of the chase takes on the aspect of a thriller with supernatural overtones as the inevitable conclusion is reached in Rome during Holy Week and the outcome of Faust's pact.

The mythical strain is continued in *The Voyage of the Destiny* which tells the story of Sir Walter Ralegh, explorer, poet, adventurer, and favourite of Queen Elizabeth I. Ralegh himself is the central narrator and his voice leads us through the three great voyages of his life: his return from the Americas, his journey through life, and the impending transition from life to death which gives the book its title. Although the voice of Ralegh is central to the novel's purpose, its insistent tones cannot ignore the historical background of Elizabethan England which is touchingly and faithfully brought to life. At the end, though, Nye offers no solutions to the puzzle of this enigmatic man's life: a sailor who hated the sea, a family man who could not abide his family, a hero with a soft centre. With Ralegh's untimely execution we are left with the remains of a human being who is more man than the demi-god created by historical myth. As in all Nye's novels the writing is crisp and lucid, a mixture of scholarly anecdotes racily told and erudite low comedy.

Robert Nye is one of the most inventive and adventurous of contemporary novelists with an imagination of Rabelaisian proportions, capable of encapsulating different worlds so that the reader is presented not so much with a mirror image as a crystallisation of them.

—Trevor Royle

OATES, Joyce Carol. American. Born in Millersport, New York, 16 June 1938. Educated at Syracuse University, New York, 1956–60, B.A. in English 1960 (Phi Beta Kappa); University of Wisconsin, Madison, M.A. in English 1961; Rice University, Houston, 1961. Married Raymond J. Smith in 1961. Instructor, 1961–65, and Assistant Professor of English, 1965–67, University of Detroit; Member of the Department of English, University of Windsor, Ontario, 1967–78. Since 1978, Writer-in-Residence, Princeton University, New Jersey. Since 1974, publisher, with Raymond J. Smith, *Ontario Review*, Windsor, later Princeton. Recipient: National Endowment for the Arts grant, 1966, 1968; Guggenheim fellowship, 1967; O. Henry Award, 1967, and Special Award for Continuing Achievement, 1970; Rosenthal Award, 1968; National Book Award, 1970. Member, American Academy, 1978. Address: c/o Dutton Inc., 2 Park Avenue, New York, New York 10016, U.S.A.

PUBLICATIONS

Novels

With Shuddering Fall. New York, Vanguard Press, 1964; London, Cape, 1965.
A Garden of Earthly Delights. New York, Vanguard Press, 1967; London, Gollancz, 1970.
Expensive People. New York, Vanguard Press, 1968; London, Gollancz, 1969.
Them. New York, Vanguard Press, 1969; London, Gollancz, 1971.
Wonderland. New York, Vanguard Press, 1971; London, Gollancz, 1972.
Do with Me What You Will. New York, Vanguard Press, 1973; London, Gollancz, 1974.
The Assassins: A Book of Hours. New York, Vanguard Press, 1975.
Childwold. New York, Vanguard Press, 1976; London, Gollancz, 1977.
Son of the Morning. New York, Vanguard Press, 1978; London, Gollancz, 1979.
Unholy Loves. New York, Vanguard Press, 1979; London, Gollancz, 1980.
Cybele. Santa Barbara, California, Black Sparrow Press, 1979.
Bellefleur. New York, Dutton, 1980; London, Cape, 1981.
Angel of Light. New York, Dutton, and London, Cape, 1981.
A Bloodsmoor Romance. New York, Dutton, 1982; London, Cape, 1983.
Mysteries of Winterthurn. New York, Dutton, and London, Cape, 1984.
Solstice. New York, Dutton, and London, Cape, 1985.
Marya: A Life. New York, Dutton, 1986.

Short Stories

By the North Gate. New York, Vanguard Press, 1963.

Upon the Sweeping Flood and Other Stories. New York, Vanguard Press, 1966; London, Gollancz, 1973.
The Wheel of Love. New York, Vanguard Press, 1970; London, Gollancz, 1971.
Cupid and Psyche. New York, Albondocani Press, 1970.
Marriages and Infidelities. New York, Vanguard Press, 1972; London, Gollancz, 1974.
A Posthumous Sketch. Los Angeles, Black Sparrow Press, 1973.
The Girl. Cambridge, Massachusetts, Pomegranate Press, 1974.
Plagiarized Material (as Fernandes/Oates). Los Angeles, Black Sparrow Press, 1974.
The Goddess and Other Women. New York, Vanguard Press, 1974; London, Gollancz, 1975.
Where Are You Going, Where Have You Been? Stories of Young America. Greenwich, Connecticut, Fawcett, 1974.
The Hungry Ghosts: Seven Allusive Comedies. Los Angeles, Black Sparrow Press, 1974; Solihull, Warwickshire, Aquila, 1975.
The Seduction and Other Stories. Los Angeles, Black Sparrow Press, 1975.
The Poisoned Kiss and Other Stories from the Portuguese (as Fernandes/Oates). New York, Vanguard Press, 1975; London, Gollancz, 1976.
The Triumph of the Spider Monkey. Santa Barbara, California, Black Sparrow Press, 1976.
Crossing the Border. New York, Vanguard Press, 1976; London, Gollancz, 1978.
Night-Side. New York, Vanguard Press, 1977; London, Gollancz, 1979.
A Sentimental Education (single story). Los Angeles, Sylvester and Orphanos, 1978.
All the Good People I've Left Behind. Santa Barbara, California, Black Sparrow Press, 1979.
The Step-Father. Northridge, California, Lord John Press, 1979.
Queen of the Night. Northridge, California, Lord John Press, 1979.
The Lamb of Abyssalia. Cambridge, Massachusetts, Pomegranate Press, 1979.
A Middle-Class Education. New York, Albondocani Press, 1980.
A Sentimental Education (collection). New York, Dutton, and London, Cape, 1981.
Last Days. New York, Dutton, 1984; London, Cape, 1985.
Wild Saturday and Other Stories. London, Dent, 1984.

Uncollected Short Story

"The Raven's Wing," in *The Best American Short Stories 1985*, edited by Gail Godwin and Shannon Ravenel. Boston, Houghton Mifflin, 1985.

Plays

The Sweet Enemy (produced New York, 1965).
Sunday Dinner (produced New York, 1970).
Ontological Proof of My Existence, music by George Prideaux (produced New York, 1972). Included in *Three Plays*, 1980.
Miracle Play (produced New York, 1974). Los Angeles, Black Sparrow Press, 1974.
Daisy (produced New York, 1980).

Three Plays (includes *Ontological Proof of My Existence, Miracle Play, The Triumph of the Spider Monkey*).   Windsor, Ontario Review Press, 1980.
Presque Isle (produced New York, 1982).

Verse

Women in Love and Other Poems.   New York, Albondocani Press, 1968.
Anonymous Sins and Other Poems.   Baton Rouge, Louisiana State University Press, 1969.
Love and Its Derangements.   Baton Rouge, Louisiana State University Press, 1970.
Wooded Forms.   New York, Albondocani Press, 1972.
Angel Fire.   Baton Rouge, Louisiana State University Press, 1973.
Dreaming America and Other Poems.   New York, Aloe Editions, 1973.
The Fabulous Beasts.   Baton Rouge, Louisiana State University Press, 1975.
Women Whose Lives Are Food, Men Whose Lives Are Money.   Baton Rouge, Louisiana State University Press, 1978.
Celestial Timepiece.   Dallas, Pressworks, 1980.
Nightless Nights: Nine Poems.   Concord, New Hampshire, Ewert, 1981.
Invisible Woman: New and Selected Poems 1970–1982.   Princeton, New Jersey, Ontario Review Press, 1982.

Other

The Edge of Impossibility: Tragic Forms in Literature.   New York, Vanguard Press, 1972; London, Gollancz, 1976.
The Hostile Sun: The Poetry of D.H. Lawrence.   Los Angeles, Black Sparrow Press, 1973; Solihull, Warwickshire, Aquila, 1975.
New Heaven, New Earth: The Visionary Experience in Literature.   New York, Vanguard Press, 1974; London, Gollancz, 1976.
Contraries: Essays.   New York, Oxford University Press, 1981.
The Profane Art: Essays and Reviews.   New York, Dutton, 1983.

Editor, *Scenes from American Life: Contemporary Short Fiction.*   New York, Vanguard Press, 1973.
Editor, with Shannon Ravenel, *The Best American Short Stories 1979.*   Boston, Houghton Mifflin, 1979.
Editor, *Night Walks: A Bedside Companion.*   Princeton, New Jersey, Ontario Review Press, 1982.
Editor, *First Person Singular: Writers on Their Craft.*   Princeton, New Jersey, Ontario Review Press, 1983.

*

Critical Studies: *The Tragic Vision of Joyce Carol Oates* by Mary Kathryn Grant, Durham, North Carolina, Duke University Press, 1978; *Joyce Carol Oates* by Joanne V. Creighton, Boston, Twayne, 1979; *Critical Essays on Joyce Carol Oates* edited by Linda W. Wagner, Boston, Hall, 1979; *Dreaming America: Obsession and Transcendence in the Fiction of Joyce Carol Oates* by G.F. Waller, Baton Rouge, Louisiana State University Press, 1979; *Joyce Carol Oates* by Ellen G. Friedman, New York, Ungar, 1980; *Joyce Carol Oates's Short Stories: Between Tradition and Innovation* by Katherine Bastian, Bern, Switzerland, Lang, 1983; *Isolation and Contact: A Study of Character Relationships in Joyce Carol Oates's Short Stories 1963–1980* by Torborg Norman, Gothenburg, Studies in English, 1984.

*   *   *

The sheer quantity of Joyce Carol Oates's writing is impressive: 16 novels since her first, *With Shuddering Fall*, in 1964, in addition to numerous volumes of short stories, verse, plays, and criticism. Often she writes about extraordinary people, people whose will to dominate their lives, to compel life to conform to their vision of it, is all-consuming, and finally destructive. In these books, she relentlessly charts the disintegration of the self in what appears to be her protest against the solipsistic view that underlies most of modern fiction. *Son of the Morning* offers perhaps her most shocking and gripping exploration of this theme. Here it is a pentecostal preacher, Nathanael Vickery, who witnesses seven visitations from the Lord, each more terrifying than the last. The last shows him that God had withdrawn himself and left him, Nathanael, to sink back into oblivion and write the book of himself. Oates's appetite as a writer is as voracious as the will of her most willful protagonists. She consumes and disgorges experience, her own and that of others. She has recast the visions and stories of numerous writers. She has imaginatively entered into the lives of pentecostal preachers, children of the Detroit slums, a 19th-century detective, professors in academia, schoolteachers, artists, and countless others. Her writing is thoroughly American, after the manner of Fitzgerald and Faulkner, Dreiser and Farrell. Her Yoknapatawpha County is Eden County, set near Millersport, New York where she lived as a child. Farrell's Chicago is her Detroit: Studs Lonigan is made over into Jules and Maureen Wendall in *Them*. Fitzgerald's Gatsby is her Jules, a man in love with the aloofness money brings, crazily hungry for Nadine, Daisy's counterpart in *Them*. Like her American ancestors, Oates is fascinated with property and the violence it engenders in those obsessed with it. She searches for the American epic, built around a dynastic family, which will place American history and American appetites, each in its true perspective. *Bellefleur* is her ambitious attempt at such an epic, an attempt which eluded the grasp of writers whose talents dwarf hers—Melville and Twain, Faulkner and Bellow. *A Bloodsmoor Romance* and *Mysteries of Winterthurn* continue Oates's treatment of 19th-century and early 20th-century America. Each imitates brilliantly the genre of the gothic saga, the romance, and the detective novel respectively. Oates is a storyteller of considerable gifts. She is also a writer's writer. Although she claims to write with a social purpose, out of concerns that are moral and political, recently she is turning more and more towards myth, and she is searching for new forms to capture her vision. Her literary borrowings are becoming more functional as they are increasingly more integrated into her works.

Childwold and *Cybele* offer the first real evidence of Oates's shift away from naturalism, with *The Assassins* figuring as a transitional, experimental work in her evolution as a writer. The assassin who stalks Andrew Petrie, the one-time State Senator, is Andrew. The murderer in this book is monistic thinking, the willful fixation upon one idea, be it religious, philosophic, or literary, which severs the individual from the community of man, isolates him, and destroys him. The monism encases its believer in an isolation as total as that which Hugh experiences as a paralytic, breathing with the aid of an iron lung, without his sight. *Bellefleur* and *Unholy Loves*—few books could be less alike—testify to Oates's skill and range.

Bellefleur is vast, sprawling, weirdly welding the natural and supernatural together to create a psychologically and imaginatively plausible history of six generations of the Bellefleur family, from 1744 to the present. The book belongs in the tradition of American Gothic, but it has stretched the genre, bringing history into its domain. *Unholy Loves* is a tightly constructed, unified book: five chapters, five parties, it lays bare the soul of Birgit Stott, a recent divorcée, member of the English Department, and writer in a university modelled after Syracuse University where Oates earned her B.A. Oates's writings are usually humorless, but *Unholy Loves* belongs with Amis's *Lucky Jim* and Murdoch's *A Severed Head*. It still contains scenes of erupting violence, but the general atmosphere is one of forced conviviality. Oates knows intimately the scandals of the university, the ambitions, bitchiness, pomposity, petty jealousy, and colossal loneliness that are endemic to modern university life. *Marya: A Life* and *Solstice* each extend Oates's treatments of teachers and academics. *Marya: A Life*, in some ways an autobiographical book, treats in eleven disconnected episodes the life of a woman from her squalid origins to her rapid success as a writer. *Solstice* offers an absorbing study of an obsessive relationship between Monica Jensen, a thirtyish divorcée and teacher in a private school in the wilds of Pennsylvania and a much older, widowed, eccentric artist, Sheila Trask, whose self-dramatization and self-destructiveness ensnare Monica, binding her in a relationship as passionate and all-consuming as any Oates has hitherto delineated. *Cybele* and *Childwold* are the books that mark Oates's movement away from her quasi-naturalistic fiction, preoccupied with America from the 1930's through the 1960's, and committed to a narrative line that reveals the violence-filled lives of her protagonists. The style of *Childwold* is lyrical. It is set back in Eden County, but nature is more mysterious and erotic, and, in a Faulknerian way, Oates celebrates the survivors. *Cybele* is more disturbing. Edwin Locke is the luckless victim of *Cybele*, the great goddess of nature who asks for nothing less than the life of this man who falls under her enchantment during his mid-life crisis. She is a demanding goddess; he pays her the ultimate sacrifice when he allows himself to be consumed by his own passions. He confuses eros with love and falls. The action of *Cybele* is typical of the action in portions of *Do with Me What You Will*; however, love redeems Elena in *Do with Me What You Will*, whereas Edwin never experiences love. The narrative angle of *Cybele* shifts, reflecting Oates's desire to move more overtly into the realm of the demonic and the unconscious. She embraces such terrain in *Bellefleur*, *A Bloodsmoor Romance*, and *Mysteries of Winterthurn*.

Much has been written about Oates's obsession with violence. Rape, incest, patricide, infanticide, self-mutilation, animal mutilation, suicide, and child-abuse abound in her fiction, shocking and numbing her readers, often occasioning a shudder of recognition of the acts we want to deny. Sometimes the violence is gratuitous; too often, it is sensational; but more often than one wants to admit it demands to be confronted. Conceptions are violent in her fiction, blighting the children born of them. In *Them* Jules is conceived in a coupling that leaves his father murdered by his mother's brother, and leaves his mother bathed in the blood of her dead lover and hostage to the policemen whose help she seeks. The violence that marked his conception doggedly pursues him. Hopelessly drawn to Nadine, he finds himself the target of her gun after a night of love-making in which he could not satisfy her. Later, caught up in the chaos of the Detroit fires, he kills a man and paradoxically recovers himself. Nathanael Vickery, the pentecostal preacher of *Son of the Morning*, is a child born of his mother's rape. Lacking a father, he grows up believing he is God's child and that his will is not his own. The initiation that rids him of this delusion, leaving him a nullity, is a terrifying one. When God withdraws from this man he has inhabited for 35 years, Nathanael is left without words or gestures. He

crawls off the platform where he had been preaching before thousands, numbering himself among the damned. Stephen in *The Assassins* and Jebediah in *Bellefleur* are similarly abandoned by the god of their willful self-creation. In *Bellefleur* Oates is not satisfied to stop with only two or three of these familiar scenes of sensational violence. Every one of the violent acts numbered above and many more plague the lives of six generations of Bellefleurs. And this violence is not enough. Germaine is one of the Bellefleurs who survives. Her father, Gideon, wreaks his vengeance on his past and his wife when he dive-bombs his plane into the Bellefleur Mansion, destroying it, and killing himself, his wife, and her numerous followers. The special child he saves is the child whose birth chills us in the opening of the book. She is born a biological freak, with the genitalia of her male twin protruding from her abdomen to be sliced-off by her quick-thinking mother. (I could not read this without thinking that Judith Rossner's *Attachments* had had an unfortunate influence upon the already sufficiently grotesque imagination of Oates.)

A Bloodsmoor Romance is a 19th-century romance, narrated by a young virgin and chronicling the "ignominious" history of the five marriageable daughters of the Zinn family settled in the Bloodsmoor Valley of Pennsylvania. More overtly feminist than Oates's early naturalistic writing, this book has been described as the other side of *Little Women*, the tale it did not dare to tell. The style is turgid; the tale is replete with the trademarks of the historical romance—fainting virgins, a sudden abduction, ghosts, and the unspeakable evils of drink and dissipation. An odd mingling of myth and history, *A Bloodsmoor Romance*, and its successor, *Mysteries of Winterthurn*, indulge Oates's excursions into Victoriana and humor, the latter often absent from her writing.

Mysteries of Winterthurn disguises itself as a detective story told by an orotund, male connoisseur of criminal investigations, while it probes the mystery of personality and religion. The detective-hero, Xavier Kilgarvan, confronts three bizarre cases, each separated by twelve years. The first begins when he is but a twelve-year-old boy, besmitten with his wayward cousin, and caught up in a bizarre series of bedchamber murders, the first being the vampirish murder of a child. The second mystery, "Devil's Half-Acre; or the Mystery of the 'Cruel Suitor,'" occurs twelve years later and involves a succession of butchered factory girls. The third case, "The Bloodstained Bridal Groom" involves an outbreak of frenzy in a disbeliever resulting in the death of a clergyman, his mother, and a female parishioner. The detective finally surrenders to brain-fever and forgetfulness rather than know what Perdita, his wayward cousin, has done, and the story dissolves into one of radical ambiguity in which guilt and innocence cannot be distinguished. All three of these sagas of 19th-century America are full of ghastly circumstances, authorial asides, quaint, baroque descriptions, extravagances and morbid preoccupations. All three are pointedly feminist. All are stylistically self-indulgent.

At this stage in Oates's career it is difficult to know what finally to say about her reliance on violence. It is integral to her vision. It rivets her action and often constellates her characters. And it does not go away. Often it seems to mar her characterization, leaving motives ill-defined or murky. The tensions unleashed by the violence threaten the boundaries of her art. But the violence is often believable and it does not let us forget. It stuns us; makes us wonder how the imagination that so clear-sightedly depicts it can remain intact. Some would say that Oates is monstrously consumed with self-hatred; that it is her imagination that is the nightmare. I think not. She is touching something little understood, but now that she is tunnelling behind it, letting us glimpse its mainsprings more fully, I think she may in the end justify the experience she forces us to endure.

—Carol Simpson Stern

O'BRIEN, Edna. Irish. Born in Tuamgraney, County Clare, 15 December 1932. Attended National School, Scariff; Convent of Mercy, Loughrea; Pharmaceutical College of Dublin: Licentiate, Pharmaceutical Society of Ireland; practiced pharmacy briefly. Married Ernest Gébler in 1952 (marriage dissolved, 1967); two sons. Recipient: Kingsley Amis Award, 1962; *Yorkshire Post* award, 1971. Agent: Douglas Rae Ltd., 28 Charing Cross Road, London WC2H 0DB, England; or, Robert Lescher, Lescher and Lescher Ltd., 155 East 71st Street, New York, New York 10021, U.S.A.

PUBLICATIONS

Novels

The Country Girls. London, Hutchinson, and New York, Knopf, 1960.
The Lonely Girl. London, Cape, and New York, Random House, 1962; as *Girl with Green Eyes*, London, Penguin, 1964.
Girls in Their Married Bliss. London, Cape, 1964; New York, Simon and Schuster, 1968.
August Is a Wicked Month. London, Cape, and New York, Simon and Schuster, 1965.
Casualties of Peace. London, Cape, 1966; New York, Simon and Schuster, 1967.
A Pagan Place. London, Weidenfeld and Nicolson, and New York, Knopf, 1970.
Night. London, Weidenfeld and Nicolson, 1972; New York, Knopf, 1973.
Johnny I Hardly Knew You. London, Weidenfeld and Nicolson, 1977; as *I Hardly Knew You*, New York, Doubleday, 1978.

Short Stories

The Love Object. London, Cape, 1968; New York, Knopf, 1969.
A Scandalous Woman and Other Stories. London, Weidenfeld and Nicolson, and New York, Harcourt Brace, 1974.
Mrs. Reinhardt and Other Stories. London, Weidenfeld and Nicolson, 1978; as *A Rose in the Heart*, New York, Doubleday, 1979.
Returning. London, Weidenfeld and Nicolson, 1982.
A Fanatic Heart: Selected Stories. New York, Farrar Straus, 1984; London, Weidenfeld and Nicolson, 1985.

Uncollected Short Story

"A Long Way from Home," in *Redbook* (New York), May 1985.

Plays

A Cheap Bunch of Nice Flowers (produced London, 1962). Published in *Plays of the Year 1962–1963*, London, Elek, 1963.

Zee and Co. (screenplay). London, Weidenfeld and Nicolson, 1971.
A Pagan Place, adaptation of her own novel (produced London, 1972; New Haven, Connecticut, 1974). London, Faber, 1973; Port Townsend, Washington, Graywolf Press, 1984.
The Gathering (produced Dublin, 1974; New York, 1977).
The Ladies (produced London, 1975).
Virginia (produced Stratford, Ontario, 1980; London and New York, 1981). London, Hogarth Press, and New York, Harcourt Brace, 1981.
Flesh and Blood (produced Bath, 1985; New York, 1986).

Screenplays: *Girl with Green Eyes*, 1964; *I Was Happy There* (*Time Lost and Time Remembered*), with Desmond Davis, 1965; *Three into Two Won't Go*, 1969; *Zee and Co.*, 1971; *The Country Girls*, 1984.

Television Plays: *The Wedding Dress*, 1963; *The Keys of the Cafe*, 1965; *Give My Love to the Pilchards*, 1965; *Which of These Two Ladies Is He Married To?*, 1967; *Nothing's Ever Over*, 1968; *Mrs. Reinhardt*, from her own story, 1981.

Other

Mother Ireland. London, Weidenfeld and Nicolson, and New York, Harcourt Brace, 1976.
Arabian Days, photographs by Gerard Klijn. New York, Horizon Press, and London, Quartet, 1977.
The Collected Edna O'Brien (miscellany). London, Collins, 1978.
The Dazzle (for children). London, Hodder and Stoughton, 1981.
James and Nora: A Portrait of Joyce's Marriage. Northridge, California, Lord John Press, 1981.
A Christmas Treat (for children). London, Hodder and Stoughton, 1982.
The Rescue (for children). London, Hodder and Stoughton, 1983.

Editor, *Some Irish Loving: A Selection.* London, Weidenfeld and Nicolson, and New York, Harper, 1979.

*

Critical Study: *Edna O'Brien* by Grace Eckley, Lewisburg, Pennsylvania, Bucknell University Press, 1974.

Edna O'Brien comments:

I quote from two critics: William Trevor and John Berger.

A Pagan Place: "Constitutes a reconstruction of a childhood experience which so far as I know, is unique in the English language. In this respect, though otherwise it is different, it invites comparison with Proust; a book whose genius is memory" (Berger).

The Love Object: "Rarely has a woman protested as eloquently as Edna O'Brien. In sorrow and compassion she keens over the living. More obviously now, despair is her province" (Trevor).

My aim is to write books that in some way celebrate life and do justice to my emotions as well as form a connection with the reader, the unknown one.

* * *

The major theme of Edna O'Brien's fiction is the ineffable pain of loneliness, guilt, and loss. Her works record a bleak odyssey from naive optimism, through rancour, bitterness, and hatred, to a resigned but nonetheless content nostalgia. Her insights into the conflicting forces experienced by women today have won her international acclaim.

Her fiction grows out of the trilogy which follows Caithleen and Baba from their initiation into life and love to their chilling disillusionment with both. At the outset, innocent and intelligent Caithleen Brady (Kate) wants every story to have a happy ending. Baba is so brazen that even her father, Mr. Brennan, prefers Kate: "Poor Caithleen, you've always been Baba's tool." *The Country Girls* and its sequel represent a woman's version of a traditionally masculine motif: that of an ego tempted by an alter-ego to enjoy forbidden fruit (cf. Faust/Mephistopheles). The entire trilogy operates around this theme. Kate has "one mad eye," but her softness, daftness, and wantonness are not her essential nature. They come to her from an alter-ego whose influence she is unable to resist. Baba promotes Kate's decisions, and the story follows their consequence: their expulsion from the convent-school and Kate's affair with Mr. Gentleman in *The Country Girls*; and her affair with Eugene Gaillard in *The Lonely Girl*. Because she is so influenced by her friend, she is always restless. She feels "lonely" without the weight of Eugene's body, but she cannot commit herself to him: "Before she left Eugene she had often thought of being with other men—strange distant men who would beckon to her. ..." She recognizes that she is disloyal to anyone who is "real" for her, and that what she yearns for is a "shadow"—but she cannot stop herself. This weakness is reflected in the shift in narrative perspective. In *Girls in Their Married Bliss* Baba, the temptress, has become the narrator and Kate, the ego, is correspondingly unable to determine her actions. She becomes increasingly introverted, afraid of giving herself: "Life was a secret with the Self. The more one gave out the less there remained for the centre." The novel ends with Baba regretting the loss of "some important region that they both knew nothing about."

The sense of being divided also lies at the heart of her next novel. "This is not me, I am not doing this" thinks Ellen, the heroine of *August Is a Wicked Month*. While the "Not-I" has her "jaunt into iniquity"—a holiday in France following her separation—her son, on holiday with his father, is killed. Unable to discover an adequate reaction to the loss of part of her essential self, she returns to England, anxious only about whether she has contracted gonorrhoea. Worry about the "Not-I"—which proves needless—replaces concern about the "I." This mechanism anticipates the next novel, *Casualties of Peace*, in which the insubstantial ego (Willa) is accidentally killed in place of the alter-ego figure (Patsy). The motif is further explored in *Zee and Co.*, the only work in which it achieves even a tentative, though unstable, resolution.

The humour, so intrinsic to the early work, is gradually replaced by sharp and sometimes acid observations. But the most notable tendency in O'Brien's fiction is the progress from the "realism" of the trilogy to the introverted monologues, reminiscences, and reconstructions of her later work. The author has declared that her favourite is *A Pagan Place*, which tells the problems of a young girl very similar to Kate. Its second-person narrative voice is a bold but sometimes disconcerting device. *Night*, a disturbing and impressive novel, traces Mary Hooligan's reconstruction of her past. In *Johnny I Hardly Knew You* bitterness and invective detract from its technical merits.

All these works rest on the assumption that there is an inevitable conflict between men's and women's needs, and that the only way for a woman to come to terms with this is to learn to be independent. At the end of *Girls in Their Married Bliss*,

Kate says: "What Baba doesn't know is that I'm finding my feet, and when I'm able to talk I imagine that I won't be alone." The subsequent novels represent ever bolder experiments in talking—that is, in narrative technique. They lean on words to ward off an increasingly desperate inner loneliness.

O'Brien has been accused of having an obsession with sex. This is not so. If she has an obsession, it is with the problem posed for a woman by the conflict between a craving to be with "a certain kind of man that controlled her and bewitched her" and a fear that commitment is phoney. The first reflects the emotional immaturity characteristic of all her heroines—an inordinate amount of her work deliberately seeks to recapture the "essence" of childhood; the second is a dubious proposition. But the experiences she records, and the reactions and reflections of her female characters, are entirely authentic. Indeed, perhaps no other contemporary novelist has captured the agony of separation, guilt, and disappointment as vividly and as poignantly as has O'Brien.

Her strength is a lyricism which is always evocative and often haunting. Her weakness is that the characters, particularly in the more experimental novels, are never quite strongly enough drawn to counter the weakness of her plots. The short story is therefore an ideal vehicle for her. She has published five volumes of short stories. Although they cover much the same ground as her novels—her 1982 collection is aptly titled *Returning*—they reverberate more freely in the reader's imagination.

—Terence Dawson

O'FAOLAIN, Julia. Irish. Born in London, England, 6 June 1932; daughter of Sean O'Faolain, *q.v.* Educated at the Sacred Heart Convent, Dublin; University College, Dublin, B.A. and M.A.; University of Rome; the Sorbonne, Paris. Married Lauro Martines; one son. Has worked as a language teacher and translator. Recipient: Arts Council of Great Britain bursary, 1981. Agent: Deborah Rogers Ltd., 49 Blenheim Crescent, London W11 2EF, England; or, International Creative Management, 40 West 57th Street, New York, New York 10019, U.S.A.

PUBLICATIONS

Novels

Godded and Codded. London, Faber, 1970; as *Three Lovers*, New York, Coward McCann, 1971.
Women in the Wall. London, Faber, and New York, Viking Press, 1975.
No Country for Young Men. London, Allen Lane, 1980.
The Obedient Wife. London, Allen Lane, 1982; New York, Carroll and Graf, 1985.
The Irish Signorina. London, Viking, 1984.

Short Stories

We Might See Sights! and Other Stories. London, Faber, 1968.
Man in the Cellar. London, Faber, 1974.
Melancholy Baby and Other Stories. Dublin, Poolbeg Press, 1978.
Daughters of Passion. London, Penguin, 1982.

Other

Editor, with Lauro Martines, *Not in God's Image: Women in History from the Greeks to the Victorians*. London, Temple Smith, and New York, Harper, 1973.

Translator (as Julia Martines), *Two Memoirs of Renaissance Florence: The Diaries of Buonaccorso Pitti and Gregorio Dati*, edited by Gene Brucker. New York, Harper, 1967.
Translator, *A Man of Parts*, by Piero Chiara. Boston, Little Brown, 1968.

*

Critical Studies: *Two Decades of Irish Writing* edited by Douglas Dunn, Manchester, Carcanet, and Philadelphia, Dufour, 1975; "The Irish Novel in Our Time" edited by Patrick Rafroidi and Maurice Harmon, in *Publications de l'Université de Lille 3*, 1975–76; by O'Faolain, in *Contemporary Authors Autobiography Series 2* edited by Adele Sarkissian, Detroit, Gale, 1985.

Julia O'Faolain comments:

I like fiction to be a Trojan horse. It can seem to be engineering an escape from alien realities but its true aim is to slip inside them and get their measure. Sly and demystificatory, it dismantles myths. This can arouse mixed feelings, for myths, though more interesting when taken apart, are grander while intact. But then ambivalence, it seems, is the nerve of narrative. Regret plus pleasure moves more than either can alone. Moreover, having grown up in a place where myth ran rampant, my native impulse is to cut through and past it.

*   *   *

There is something *déjà vu* about Julia O'Faolain's first novel, *Godded and Codded*, centring on the innocent Irish Sally's further education—in several senses—in Paris, not wholly redeemed by the book's uproarious comedy. The inevitably pregnant Sally's equally inevitable Christmas visit to her parents in Ireland covers even more familiar ground, as we are shown the circumstances that have made Sally what she is—that is, what she must react against. O'Faolain's earlier story "A Pot of Soothing Herbs" encapsulated this—the archetypal Irish virginal dilemma; the later story "Lots of Ghastlies" more adroitly transplants to an English bourgeois setting the theme of a return visit to the parental home. More interesting in *Godded and Codded* than the "innocents abroad" theme is the peripheral description of the underground activities of a group of Algerian students in Paris shortly before Independence. Irish expatriates provide much of the novel's burlesque comedy.

Her first collection, *We Might See Sights!*, are divided by O'Faolain into Irish and Italian stories. The outstanding story is "Dies Irae," set in an Italian hairdresser's salon and perhaps influenced by Colette; to pacify an elderly Russian princess, the hairdresser points out signs of decay in the narrator, for whom a normally pleasant occasion becomes her *dies irae*. There is black comedy in the plight of the husband chained in the cellar by his wife, in the title story of *Man in the Cellar*; the story is told in letters and the final surprisingly affectionate letter from the decamped and mentally disturbed wife reveals how securely *invisible* chains are fastened on her. The didactic element is stronger in this later collection of stories, but is offset by the use of out-of-the-way situations; "This is My Body," for instance, set in a 6th-century convent, handles the female Irish writer's stock-in-trade of convent material from a new angle, which *Women in the Wall* also exploits.

In *Women in the Wall*, set in 6th-century Gaul, O'Faolain breathes life into a group of characters who—except two—existed in history, though as the author explains in her introduction, she departed from history in plotting. The monologue of the anchoress in the convent wall alternates with an account of the darkening political situation, bringing barbarism to the very convent walls; the two threads finally merge in the denouement. But even behind the convent walls, the nuns' lives are shown as often far from quiet, as O'Faolain probes the stresses of celibacy, its occasional abandonment and its link to mystical experience. Her description of nature is always vivid, especially here where she relies heavily on natural imagery to avoid anachronism.

O'Faolain also interweaves different narrative threads to provide explosive connections in *No Country for Young Men*: the death of an American Republican fund-raiser in Ulster in 1922 casts a long shadow as an American ex-academic arrives in Ireland in 1979 to interview survivors of the 1920's Troubles for a film and so crosses paths with an old half-insane nun through his romantic entanglement with her married great-niece. This novel, shortlisted for the Booker Prize, is O'Faolain's best novel to date, enabling her to deploy all her skills of allusively connecting social, cultural, historical, and economic insights. These electric interconnections are often wittily achieved, sometimes pivoting on linguistic humour. O'Faolain's style is so exciting that the reader may overlook the fact that her characters tend to share a similar wide-ranging, ironic perception, imposed by the style.

An outstanding illustration of the disadvantage of O'Faolain's brilliant style, notwithstanding that it provides a vivid impression of whatever society she's writing about, comes in *The Obedient Wife*; Carla is endowed by the author with witty dialogue and far-ranging ironic thought that seem too dazzling for the character as otherwise presented. An Italian living in California from where her husband has returned, supposedly temporarily, to Italy, Carla despite her paganism believes in the traditional role of the wife—or has been culturally brainwashed into believing in it. Yet, she becomes emotionally involved with a Catholic priest. Carla's relationship with her teenage son is especially well drawn, with empathy for both sides.

In *The Irish Signorina*, as in earlier books, the plot is engendered by the criss-crossing of inter-generational threads. A young Irish girl is invited by the dying Italian Marchesa Cavalcanti to stay in the villa where her mother had worked for the marchesa as a girl. Against the background of the Cavalcanti family's roots in the land and modern terrorism, complex webs of personal relationships, old and new, emerge. Though a shorter novel than O'Faolain's previous novels, the economy and restraint that she here shows in dealing with her always interesting material illustrate her extraordinary stylistic development since her early writing and ensure this book is by no means slight but the work of a major novelist.

—Val Warner

O'FAOLAIN, Sean. Irish. Born John Francis Whelan in Cork, 22 February 1900. Educated at University College, Dublin, B.A. in English 1921, M.A. in Irish 1924, M.A. in English 1926; Harvard University, Cambridge, Massachusetts (Commonwealth Fellow, 1926–28; John Harvard Fellow, 1928–29), 1926–29, M.A. 1929. Served in the Irish Republican Army, 1918–21: director of publicity, 1923. Married Eileen Gould in 1928; one daughter (Julia O'Faolain, *q.v.*) and one son. Taught at Christian Brothers School, Ennis, 1924; Lecturer in English, Boston College and Princeton University, New Jersey, 1929, and St. Mary's College, Strawberry Hill, Twickenham, Middlesex, 1929–33. Full-time writer from 1933: editor, *The Bell*, Dublin, 1940–46. Director, Arts Council of Ireland, 1957–59. D. Litt.: Trinity College, Dublin, 1957. Address: 17 Rosmeen Park, Dunlaoire, County Dublin, Ireland.

PUBLICATIONS

Novels

A Nest of Simple Folk.   London, Cape, 1933; New York, Viking Press, 1934.
Bird Alone.   London, Cape, and New York, Viking Press, 1936.
Come Back to Erin.   London, Cape, and New York, Viking Press, 1940.
And Again?   London, Constable, 1979.

Short Stories

Midsummer Night Madness and Other Stories.   London, Cape, and New York, Viking Press, 1932; as *Stories of Sean O'Faolain*, London, Penguin, 1970.
There's a Birdie in the Cage.   London, Grayson, 1935.
A Born Genius.   Detroit, Schuman's, 1936.
A Purse of Coppers: Short Stories.   London, Cape, 1937; New York, Viking Press, 1938.
Teresa and Other Stories.   London, Cape, 1947; as *The Man Who Invented Sin and Other Stories*, New York, Devin Adair, 1948.
The Finest Stories of Sean O'Faolain.   Boston, Little Brown, 1957; as *The Stories of Sean O'Faolain*, London, Hart Davis, 1958.
I Remember! I Remember!   Boston, Little Brown, 1961; London, Hart Davis, 1962.
The Heat of the Sun: Stories and Tales.   Boston, Little Brown, and London, Hart Davis, 1966.
The Talking Trees.   Boston, Little Brown, 1970; London, Cape, 1971.
Foreign Affairs and Other Stories.   Boston, Little Brown, and London, Constable, 1976.
Selected Stories.   Boston, Little Brown, and London, Constable, 1978.
The Collected Stories of Sean O'Faolain 1–3.   London, Constable, 3 vols., 1980–82; Boston, Little Brown, 1 vol., 1983.

Plays

She Had to Do Something (produced Dublin, 1937; London, 1954).   London, Cape, 1938.
The Train to Banbury (broadcast, 1947).   Published in *Imaginary Conversations*, edited by Rayner Heppenstall, London, Secker and Warburg, 1948.

Radio Play: *The Train to Banbury*, 1947.

Other

The Life Story of Eamon De Valera.   Dublin, Talbot Press, 1933.
Constance Markievicz; or, The Average Revolutionary: A Biography.   London, Cape, 1934; revised edition, London, Sphere, 1968.

King of the Beggars: A Life of Daniel O'Connell.   London, Nelson, and New York, Viking Press, 1938.
De Valera: A Biography.   London, Penguin, 1939.
An Irish Journey.   London and New York, Longman, 1940.
The Great O'Neill: A Biography of Hugh O'Neill, Earl of Tyrone 1550–1616.   London, Longman, and New York, Duell, 1942.
The Story of Ireland.   London, Collins, 1943.
The Irish: A Character Study.   London, Penguin, 1947; New York, Devin Adair, 1949; revised edition, Penguin, 1969.
The Short Story.   London, Collins, 1948; New York, Devin Adair, 1951.
A Summer in Italy.   London, Eyre and Spottiswoode, 1949; New York, Devin Adair, 1950.
Newman's Way: The Odyssey of John Henry Newman.   London, Longman, and New York, Devin Adair, 1952.
South to Sicily.   London, Collins, 1953; as *An Autumn in Italy*, New York, Devin Adair, 1953.
The Vanishing Hero: Studies in Novelists of the Twenties.   London, Eyre and Spottiswoode, 1956; Boston, Little Brown, 1957.
Vive Moi! (autobiography).   Boston, Little Brown, 1964; London, Hart Davis, 1965.

Editor, *Lyrics and Satires from Tom Moore.*   Dublin, Cuala Press, 1929.
Editor, *The Autobiography of Theobald Wolfe Tone.*   New York and London, Nelson, 1937.
Editor, *The Silver Branch: A Collection of the Best Old Irish Lyrics.*   London, Cape, and New York, Viking Press, 1938.
Editor, *Short Stories: A Study in Pleasure.*   Boston, Little Brown, 1961.

*

Manuscript Collection: Bancroft Library, University of California, Berkeley.

Critical Studies: *Sean O'Faolain: A Critical Introduction* by Maurice Harmon, Notre Dame, Indiana, University of Notre Dame Press, 1966, revised edition, Dublin, Wolfhound Press, 1985; *Sean O'Faolain* by Paul A. Doyle, New York, Twayne, 1968; *The Short Stories of Sean O'Faolain: A Study in Descriptive Techniques* by Joseph Storey Rippier, Gerrards Cross, Buckinghamshire, Smythe, and New York, Barnes and Noble, 1976; "Sean at Eighty" by Julia O'Faolain, in *Fathers: Reflections by Daughters* edited by Ursula Owen, London, Virago Press, 1983.

*   *   *

Emerging at a period in Irish history when the passionate man cannot identify with any particular group, Sean O'Faolain remains in fundamental discord with society and has to work out his own destiny by relying on his own intense demand for a rich and varied existence, and for a background appropriate to his imagination's image of life. Each of his first three novels contains a central figure who abides at first the canons of respectability that govern the lower middle class to which he belongs, but rebels in favour of more liberal, less restrictive ways and in search of a more desirable vision of life than is available to him in his own class. That rebellion affects all of his subsequent life, cutting him off from the familiar moral and social patterns of his childhood and early life and propelling him in quest of a more congenial and more satisfying adult existence. It is his fate however to be forever denied a happy solution to his search for fulfillment. *And Again?*, a playful treatment of memory and of human nature, is free of social problems.

O'Faolain's short stories reflect a similar concern. It is through them that his development as a writer may be most fully seen. Beginning with romantic stories that try to deal objectively with his experience as a revolutionary, he moved on to stories that reveal the emergence of a distinctive, pessimistic point of view. The central issue is the plight of the individual in a stagnant, post-revolutionary society. In his second collection, *A Purse of Coppers*, his characters experience an alienation so complete that it becomes an impasse beyond which there seems to be no accessible line of development. But gradually O'Faolain discovered a less rigid response. Instead of portraying the sensitive, intelligent man, struggling against insurmountable social conditions, he treats, gently and humorously, of the ambivalent man, who is not particularly concerned with social or moral issues. In this figure he wanted to express the contradictory forces in Irish life at a time when the country was emerging into a modern civilisation but was moulded instinctively by forces from the past. In the process of describing the contradictory nature of the modern Irishman, O'Faolain came to appreciate the power and the value of the various influences on thought and behaviour that lie beneath the conscious or rational part of the individual. With his greater respect for the deeper psychological experiences, he began to concentrate on the universal themes of time and change, the impermanence of youth and age, and the accommodations of middle age.

No account of O'Faolain's fiction should ignore his other prose, in particular his historical biographies which also study the relation of the individual to his society. Each attempts to understand how a great figure emerges from his background, to calculate to what degree he personifies his people's needs, and to determine the nature of the heritage he created for subsequent Irishmen. Nor should one ignore his work as editor of *The Bell*, in which he sought to stimulate Irish writers and in which he spoke out clearly in favour of liberal values. His many articles in Irish, English, and American journals, his literary criticism, and even his travel books are all part of the picture of a man of letters, and one who was deeply engaged as an intellectual and creative writer with the whole range of Irish life. "There is," he said, "only one admirable form of the imagination—the imagination that is so intense that it creates a new reality, that it makes things happen, whether it be a political thing, or a social thing, or a work of art."

—Maurice Harmon

OLSEN, Tillie (née Lerner). American. Born in Omaha, Nebraska, 14 January 1913. High school education. Married Jack Olsen in 1936; four daughters. Has worked in the service, warehouse, and food processing industries, and as an office typist. Visiting Professor, Amherst College, Massachusetts, 1969–70; Visiting Instructor, Stanford University, California, Spring 1971; Writer-in-Residence, Massachusetts Institute of Technology, Cambridge, 1973; Visiting Professor, University of Massachusetts, Boston, 1974; Visiting Lecturer, University of California, San Diego, 1978; International Visiting Scholar, Norway, 1980. Creative Writing Fellow, Stanford University, 1956–57; Fellow, Radcliffe Institute for Independent Study,

Cambridge, Massachusetts, 1962–64. Recipient: Ford grant, 1959; O. Henry Award, 1961; National Endowment for the Arts grant, 1966; American Academy award, 1975; Guggenheim fellowship, 1975; Unitarian Women's Federation award, 1980. Doctor of Arts and Letters: University of Nebraska, Lincoln, 1979; Litt.D.: Knox College, Galesburg, Illinois, 1982. Address: 1435 Laguna, No. 6, San Francisco, California 94115, U.S.A.

PUBLICATIONS

Novel

Yonnondio: From the Thirties.   New York, Delacorte Press, 1974; London, Faber, 1975.

Short Stories

Tell Me a Riddle: A Collection.   Philadelphia, Lippincott, 1961; enlarged edition, London, Faber, 1964.

Uncollected Short Story

"Requa: Part One," in *The Best American Short Stories 1971*, edited by Martha Foley and David Burnett. Boston, Houghton Mifflin, 1971.

Play

I Stand Here Ironing (produced New York, 1981).

Other

Silences.   New York, Delacorte Press, 1978; London, Virago Press, 1980.

Editor, *Mother to Daughter, Daughter to Mother: Mothers on Mothering.*   Old Westbury, New York, Feminist Press, 1984; London, Virago Press, 1985.

*

Manuscript Collection: Berg Collection, New York Public Library.

Critical Studies: "The Short Stories of Tillie Olsen" by William Van O'Connor, in *Studies in Short Fiction* (Newberry, South Carolina), Fall 1963; Annie Gottlieb, in *New York Times Book Review*, 31 March 1974; "Fragments of Time Lost" by Jack Salzman, in *Washington Post Book World*, 7 April 1974; "Tillie Olsen: The Weight of Things Unsaid" by Sandy Boucher, in *Ms.* (New York) September 1974; "De-Riddling Tillie Olsen's Writings" by Selma Burkom and Margaret Williams, in *San Jose Studies 2* (California), 1976.

*   *   *

Tillie Olsen repeatedly expresses her conviction that literature is impoverished to the degree that creativity is not nourished and sustained in women and in people of the working class. Her speeches and essays on the waste of talent and on periods of aridity in the lives of authors, her long treatise on Rebecca Harding Davis's thwarted career following marriage, and her notes and quotations on this theme—collected over a period of 15 years—constitute *Silences*. Her own artistic recognition was postponed by the exigencies of making a living for herself and her children. She "mislaid" a novel for 35 years and wrote no story she thought worthy of publication until she was 43.

Tell Me a Riddle includes the three stories and the novella published between 1956 and 1960. "Tell Me a Riddle" centers on the antagonism which arises between two Jewish immigrants after their 37 years of marriage. In this novella Olsen reflects also upon the embarrassment and bewilderment of their married children as the "gnarled roots" of this marriage split apart. The wife's slow death from cancer greatly intensifies the conflict, but also dramatizes the love that remains only because it has become a habit. The wife returns in her delirium to their 1905 revolutionary activism, as her husband sighs, "how we believed, how we belonged." Almost without plot, this novella demonstraters Olsen's artistry in characterization, dialogue, and sensory appeal, and it fully displays, as does all her fiction, her highly rhythmic and metaphorical use of language. In the monologue "I Stand Here Ironing" a woman reviews the 19 years of her daughter's life and mourns those days which blighted the daughter's full "flowering." Most intense are the mother's memories of being torn away from her infant in order to support her after they were abandoned. In "Hey Sailor, What Ship?" Whitey, a sailor, is given to drink and to buying admiration from the children of Lennie and Helen by giving them expensive gifts. Here he endures his last visit with his adopted family, with whom he has spent San Francisco shore leaves for years. The oldest daughter, embarrassed before her friends, turns in judgment upon the man who has brought a sense of adventure and romance to the family, while they have provided him some understanding and security over the years. In the elegiac close, Whitey pauses at the top of the third of seven hills to look back through the fog to the house with "its eyes unshaded." In the story "O Yes" a 12-year-old black girl invites her white friend to her baptism. As the throb of voices and clapping and the swaying of bodies intensifies the congregation's religious fervor, the white child feels her senses assailed and faints. The next year in junior high, as rigid social patterns separate the two friends, she mourns the warmth and openness she felt momentarily at the baptism.

The novel *Yonnondio: From the Thirties*, which Olsen began at the age of 19 (when she was already a mother), she abandoned five years later, a few pages short of its close. The manuscript was found 35 years later, and in 1973, in "arduous partnership" with her younger self, Olsen selected, edited, and organized the fragments, but she could not write the ending or rewrite sections. The novel significantly adds to American fiction of the Depression years, and it provides remarkable evidence of Olsen's artistry in her early youth. Greatly impressive are the imagery, the use of smells and sounds, the rhythms which shift notably between the first two sections written from the view of the child Mazie, and the third section which emerges from the narrative consciousness of the mother, Mary Holbrook, dying gradually of exhaustion, childbearing, and malnutrition. The title of this novel is taken from Walt Whitman's "Yonnondio" and in Iroquois means a lament for the aborigines—the authors mourn the common folk who suffered greatly but left "No picture, poem, statement, passing them to the future." During the course of the novel, Jim Holbrook moves from a Wyoming mine to a North Dakota tenant farm and finally to a Chicago or Omaha meat-packing plant with his wife and family. The zestful and imaginative Mazie in the early months of their life on the farm becomes ecstatically pantheistic in the style of Whitman's nature poetry, but in the city, in section three, she has lost her aspiration and much of her sensitivity and moves into the background in her bewilderment at her mother's illness and her father's increasing bad temper and dependence on alcohol. Critics generally acclaimed the novel, but several complained that Olsen gives her readers no mercy and that her work may be too painful for sustained reading and too unrelenting in its despair to allow characters to triumph through suffering.

—Margaret B. McDowell

OZICK, Cynthia. American. Born in New York City, 17 April 1928. Educated at New York University, B.A. (cum laude) in English 1949 (Phi Beta Kappa); Ohio State University, Columbus, M.A. 1951. Married Bernard Hallote in 1952; one daughter. Instructor in English, New York University, 1964–65. Stolnitz Lecturer, Indiana University, Bloomington, 1972; Distinguished Artist-in-Residence, City University, New York, 1982; Phi Beta Kappa Orator, Harvard University, Cambridge, Massachusetts, 1985. Recipient: National Endowment for the Arts fellowship, 1968; Wallant Award, 1972; B'nai B'rith award, 1972; Jewish Book Council Epstein Award, 1972, 1977; American Academy award, 1973; Hadassah Myrtle Wreath Award, 1974; O. Henry Award, 1975, 1981, 1984; Lamport Prize, 1980; Guggenheim fellowship, 1982; Strauss Living Award, 1983; Jewish Theological Seminary Distinguished Service Award, 1984; New York University Distinguished Alumnus Award, 1984. Honorary degree: Yeshiva University, New York, 1984; Hebrew Union College, Cincinnati, 1984. Lives in New Rochelle, New York. Agent: Theron Raines, Raines and Raines, 71 Park Avenue, New York, New York 10016, U.S.A.

PUBLICATIONS

Novels

Trust. New York, New American Library, 1966; London, MacGibbon and Kee, 1967.
The Cannibal Galaxy. New York, Knopf, 1983; London, Secker and Warburg, 1984.

Short Stories

The Pagan Rabbi and Other Stories. New York, Knopf, 1971; London, Secker and Warburg, 1972.
Bloodshed and Three Novellas. New York, Knopf, and London, Secker and Warburg, 1976.
Levitation: Five Fictions. New York, Knopf, and London, Secker and Warburg, 1982.

Uncollected Short Stories

"The Sense of Europe," in *Prairie Schooner* (Lincoln, Nebraska), June 1956.
"Stone," in *Botteghe Oscure* (Rome), Autumn 1957.
"The Laughter of Akiva," in *New Yorker*, 10 November 1980.
"The Shawl," in *The Best American Short Stories 1981*, edited by Hortense Calisher and Shannon Ravenel. Boston, Houghton Mifflin, 1981.
"Rosa," in *The Best American Short Stories 1984*, edited by John Updike and Shannon Ravenel. Boston, Houghton Mifflin, 1984.

"At Fumicaro," in *New Yorker*, 6 August 1984.

Other

Art and Ardor (essays).   New York, Knopf, 1983.

*

Bibliography: "A Bibliography of Writings by Cynthia Ozick" by Susan Currier and Daniel J. Cahill, in *Texas Studies in Literature and Language* (Austin), Summer 1983.

Critical Study: "The Art of Cynthia Ozick" by Victor Strandberg, in *Texas Studies in Literature and Language* (Austin), Summer 1983.

*   *   *

Cynthia Ozick has said that she began her first novel as an American writer and ended it six and a half years later as a Jewish writer. Overarching this book, *Trust*, is a third cultural presence made manifest in the seductive appeal of the pagan earth-gods, who have maintained their potency under various names from old Greek and Canaanite times to our own. Ozick's conviction regarding this insight is attested by her view of "the issue of Hellenism-versus-Hebraism as the central quarrel of the West."

As that phrase implies, during her formative years as an artist Ozick was strongly attracted to British writers with a Hellenic cast of mind: Gibbon, Matthew Arnold, and E. M. Forster (whose "Greeky heroes" enticed her to read *The Longest Journey* every year). Nevertheless, it was the American writer Henry James who most deeply stamped his image upon her youthful imagination. She wrote her master's thesis on parable in James's fiction, and spent seven apprentice years writing a never-published novel in the Jamesian manner, followed by almost as long a period working on the neo-Jamesian *Trust.*

Completed on the day President Kennedy was murdered, *Trust* was published in 1966 to a thin but highly favorable chorus of reviews. Its Jamesian elements are immediately evident in its style ("both mandarin and lapidary," Ozick calls it), its social milieu (a wealthy American family), its masking of greed and duplicity under an elegant surface of manners, and its international theme (half the book is set in Europe, half in America). The title itself is ironic to a Jamesian degree of complexity in that lack of trust affects every relationship from the familial (husband-wife, mother-daughter) to the theological (God's covenant having been broken in the Holocaust). What revives trust in the end is the young heroine's disavowal of her decaying cultural heritage (epitomized in her mother's crassly misspent trust fund) in favor of the spontaneous gods of nature—which is to say, her reversion to the ancient pagan ethos. Her discovery of that ethos in her lost father (who had sired her as his "illegitimate issue" and then was succeeded by unsatisfactory Christian and Jewish father figures) makes up the central plot line of this immense and densely written novel. In the end, her father's apotheosis as a fertility god (which she witnesses) occasions one of the most vividly imagined sexual encounters in American literature—an imagistic rendering of sensation that is perhaps Ozick's finest (and most difficult) artistic achievement.

Even while she was working on *Trust*, Ozick's fascination with the Pan versus Moses theme (as a character in *Trust* calls it) gathered such force as to promulgate her next book, the collection of stories titled *The Pagan Rabbi*. Within the title story, Pan overcomes Moses when the rabbi couples with a dryad—in another vividly imagined sexual encounter—and then hangs himself from her tree, not in guilt but in pantheistic ecstasy. "The molecules dance within all forms ... and within the atoms dance still profounder sources of divine vitality. There is nothing that is Dead," says the rabbi's last testament. Behind this heretical hunger for the world's beauty lies the chief paradox, for Ozick, of the Jewish artist. "The single most serviceable description of a Jew—as defined 'theologically'— ... is someone who shuns idols," she has written; yet to create literature is to put oneself "in competition, like a god, with the Creator," so that "[art] too is turned into an idol."

Ozick memorably transmutes this theme into fiction in her next book, *Bloodshed*, where the artist-as-idolator appears triumphant in "Usurpation (Other People's Stories)." Here the Jewish poet, so apostate as to have published a hymn to Apollo, ascends to the Olympic rather than Jewish afterworld in the end, totally rejecting his Jewish heritage. But though the God of Israel permits him to espouse this new identity, the Gentile gods do not: "Then the taciturn little Canaanite idols call him, in the language of the spheres, kike." Flight from and coerced movement back toward Jewish identity is thus the unifying theme of the four tales in *Bloodshed*, with the Holocaust exerting the most powerful such coercive force. In "A Mercenary" a Polish Jew who survived the Holocaust tries to expunge his Jewishness by becoming United Nations ambassador for a black African nation, but he is subtly called Jew by his black aide and even by inanimate objects: his cigarette reminds him of Holocaust smoke; his "white villa on the blue coast," of the "bluish snow" and "snow-white hanging stars of Poland" during his Holocaust period. Conversely, in the title story, "Bloodshed," despair over the Holocaust prompts its Jewish protagonist to contemplate suicide, until he is rescued by a Holocaust survivor's powerful lesson that "despair must be earned."

Among Ozick's latest three books, *The Cannibal Galaxy* is rather disappointing compared with the grand scope and power of *Trust* and the stories; its title uses the image of a black hole sucking in surrounding stars to oblivion as a metaphor for the Holocaust. *Levitation: Five Fictions* uses its title as a three-part pun for one of its stories: levitation, levity, and the tribe of Levi. It portrays the Holocaust as an identity-defining device, levitating genuine Jews away from pseudo- or de-Judaized Jews who remain below on ground level. The most ambitious thing in this collection of stories is the Puttermesser-Xanthippe series, a new version of Pan versus Moses. In this instance, the Pan figure (Xanthippe) is a female golem chanted into existence by Puttermesser to save New York City, but in the end the Jewish lawgiver (Puttermesser has become mayor) must regretfully chant her charming friend back to a pile of mud ater Xanthippe begins to inflame the whole city with illicit sexual hunger.

Although Ozick's Jewish materials—including a sprinkling of Yiddish words on many pages—can create an initial impression of opacity, her general reading audience should not find Ozick's cultural heritage more difficult to apprehend than Faulkner's or LeRoi Jones's Southern and ethnic materials. Through her greatly original and powerful expression of the Jewish ethos, Ozick contributes importantly to the larger American literary tradition.

—Victor Strandberg

PALEY, Grace (née Goodside). American. Born in New York City, 11 December 1922. Educated at Evander Childs High School, New York; Hunter College, New York, 1938–39. Married 1) Jess Paley in 1942, one daughter and one son; 2) Robert Nichols in 1972. Has taught at Columbia University, New York, and Syracuse University, New York. Since 1966 has taught at Sarah Lawrence College, Bronxville, New York, and since 1983 at City College, New York. Recipient: Guggenheim grant, 1961; National Endowment for the Arts grant, 1966; American Academy award, 1970. Member, American Academy, 1980. Address: 126 West 11th Street, New York, New York 10011, U.S.A.

PUBLICATIONS

Short Stories

The Little Disturbances of Man: Stories of Men and Women in Love. New York, Doubleday, 1959; London, Weidenfeld and Nicolson, 1960.
Enormous Changes at the Last Minute. New York, Farrar Straus, 1974; London, Deutsch, 1975.
Later the Same Day. New York, Farrar Straus, and London, Virago Press, 1985.

*   *   *

The individuality of Grace Paley's voice—warm, comic, defensive, and without illusions—and the sophistication of her technique led to the reissue of her first collection of short stories, *The Little Disturbances of Man*, ten years after it first appeared. Her stories, invariably set in New York and often with a Jewish background, depend especially on her ear for dialogue. Her realism, with a concision sometimes deliberately telescoped into the absurd, admits sudden surrealistic perceptions: "A Subject of Childhood" ends as the sun comes out above a woman being comforted by her child for the desertion of her lover: "Then through the short fat fingers of my son, interred forever, like a black and white barred king in Alcatraz, my heart lit up in stripes."

According to one character, who has risen above the slums of his childhood, the difficulties of a woman bringing up four children on her own in the New York slums are merely "the little disturbances of man" beside the real cataclysms of existence. All the stories in *Enormous Changes at the Last Minute* are set in these slums, but in *The Little Disturbances of Man* Paley ranges over the wider social strata, probing similar preoccupations of loneliness, lust, and escapism. "An Irrevocable Diameter" relates the forced marriage of Charles C. Charley to a rich teenager, less than half his age, who claimed to have seduced him. "The Pale Pink Roast" swings between farce and lyricism in a picture of a woman going to bed with her ex-husband immediately after her new marriage to a richer man.

Paley's concern in *The Little Disturbances of Man* with broken and shifting relationships where the women are dominant is even more important in *Enormous Changes*. For each of the unmarried or separated mothers, it is a question of whether her "capacity for survival has not been overwhelmed by her susceptibility to abuse." There is also a new sense of commitment in *Enormous Changes*, where the key story is "Faith in a Tree"; when the police break up a tiny demonstration against napalm-bombing in Vietnam, Faith's son defiantly writes up the demonstrators' slogan again. The story concludes: "And I think that is exactly when events turned me around ... directed ... by my children's heartfelt brains, I thought more and more and every day about the world."

Earlier in that story, Faith says of some of her neighbours, "our four family units, as people are now called, are doomed to stand culturally still as this society moves on its caterpillar treads from ordinary affluent to absolute empire." These tenants crop up in other stories, some reappearing from *The Little Disturbances of Man*. "An Interest in Life" in the earlier book is retold from another character's angle as "Distance" in the later one: "There is a long time in me between knowing and telling."

The subject of "Dreamer in a Dead Language" in *Later the Same Day*, a father-daughter relationship is important in several stories in *Enormous Changes*, where in an introductory note the author states: "Everyone in this book is imagined into life except the father. No matter what story he has to live in, he's my father. ...." *Enormous Changes at the Last Minute* is altogether darker in tone than *The Little Disturbances of Man*: the interplay of two generations is used to show the long shadow of "the cruel history of Europe" continuing to darken second-generation immigrant lives, while the "last minute" of the title refers to the nuclear threat. As the title suggests, *Later the Same Day* picks up these concerns where *Enormous Changes at the Last Minute* left off.

These later stories are set against a backcloth of the grassroots political struggle of the peace movement, although this is never intrusive in the stories but indissolubly meshed, as it must be, with the everyday concerns of semi-adult and adult children, ageing parents, and the sickness and death of middle-aged friends. The "day" of *Later the Same Day* is the dangerous contemporary moment in the life of the planet as the "poor, dense, defenseless thing—rolls round and round. Living and dying are fastened to its surface and stuffed into its softer parts" and also in Paley's life as she approaches old age. A striking example of her habitual criss-crossing of perceptions is the story "Zagrowsky Tells," where the first-person narrater, an old Jew, tells Faith how his mentally handicapped daughter came to bear a black baby. Faith, the woman who continues to appear centrally in the stories, often in the first person, in this book is old enough to be "remembering babies, those round, staring, day-in day-out companions of her youth"; now, her son and his step-father are equal companions, in "Listening." Celebrating precarious human relationships in a society, and a world, of dangerous inequalities, Grace Paley's voice is comically appalled and positive.

—Val Warner

⸻

PATON, Alan (Stewart). South African. Born in Pietermaritzburg, Natal, 11 January 1903. Educated at Maritzburg College, University of Natal, B.Sc. 1923, B.Ed. 1966. Married 1) Doris Francis in 1928 (died, 1967), two sons; 2) Anne Hopkins in 1969. Schoolteacher, Ixopo, Natal, and at Maritzburg College, 1925–35; Principal, Diepkloof Reformatory, Johannesburg, 1935–48; full-time writer since 1948. Honorary Commissioner, Toc H Southern Africa, 1949–58; President of the Convocation, University of Natal, 1951–55, 1957–59; founder and President, Liberal Party of South Africa, 1958–68 (party made an illegal organisation in 1968). Chubb Fellow, Yale University, New Haven, Connecticut, 1973. Since 1969, Honorary President, South African National Union of Students. Recipient: Anisfield-Wolf Award, 1948; Newspaper

Guild of New York award, 1949; Freedom House award, 1960; Free Academy of Arts Medal (Hamburg), 1960; National Conference of Christians and Jews Brotherhood Award, 1962; CNA award, 1964, 1974; International League for Human Rights prize, 1977. L.H.D.: Yale University, 1954; D.Litt.: Kenyon College, Gambier, Ohio, 1962; University of Natal, 1968; Harvard University, Cambridge, Massachusetts, 1971; Trent University, Peterborough, Ontario, 1971; Rhodes University, Grahamstown, South Africa, 1972; Willamette University, Salem, Oregon, 1974; University of Michigan, Flint, 1977; D.D.: University of Edinburgh, 1971; LL.D.: University of the Witwatersrand, Johannesburg, 1975. Fellow, Royal Society of Literature, 1961; Honorary Member, Free Academy of Arts, Hamburg, 1961. Address: P.O. Box 278, Hillcrest, Natal 3650, South Africa.

PUBLICATIONS

Novels

Cry, The Beloved Country. London, Cape, and New York, Scribner, 1948.
Too Late the Phalarope. London, Cape, and New York, Scribner, 1953.

Short Stories

Meditation for a Young Boy Confirmed. London, National Society-S.P.C.K., 1944; Cincinnati, Forward Movement, 1954.
Debbie Go Home. London, Cape, 1961; as *Tales from a Troubled Land*, New York, Scribner, 1961.

Plays

Sponono, with Krishna Shah, adaptation of stories by Paton (produced New York, 1964). New York, Scribner, 1965.

Screenplay: *Cry, The Beloved Country (African Fury)*, 1952.

Other

Freedom as a Reformatory Instrument. Pretoria, Penal Reform League of South Africa, 1948.
Christian Unity: A South African View. Grahamstown, Rhodes University, 1951.
South Africa Today. New York, Public Affairs Committee, 1951; London, Lutterworth Press, 1953.
Salute to My Great Grandchildren. Johannesburg, St. Benedict's House, 1954.
The Land and People of South Africa. Philadelphia, Lippincott, 1955; as *South Africa and Her People*, London, Lutterworth Press, 1957; revised edition, Lippincott, 1965, 1972; Lutterworth Press, 1970.
South Africa in Transition. New York, Scribner, 1956.
Hope for South Africa. London, Pall Mall Press, 1958; New York, Praeger, 1959.
The People Wept. Privately printed, 1959(?).
The Charlestown Story. Pietermaritzburg, Liberal Party of South Africa, 1961(?).
Hofmeyr. Cape Town, Oxford University Press, 1964; London, Oxford University Press, 1965; abridged edition, as *South African Tragedy: The Life and Times of Jan Hofmeyr*, New York, Scribner, 1965.
The Long View, edited by Edward Callan. New York, Praeger, and London, Pall Mall Press, 1968.

Instrument of Thy Peace: The Prayer of St. Francis. New York, Seabury Press, 1968; London, Collins, 1970; revised edition, New York, Seabury Press, 1982.
Civil Rights and Present Wrongs. Johannesburg, South African Institute of Race Relations, 1968.
Kontakion for You Departed. London, Cape, 1969; as *For You Departed*, New York, Scribner, 1969.
Case History of a Pinky. Johannesburg, South African Institute of Race Relations, 1972.
Apartheid and the Archbishop: The Life and Times of Geoffrey Clayton, Archbishop of Cape Town. Cape Town, Philip, 1973; New York, Scribner, and London, Cape, 1974.
Knocking on the Door: Shorter Writings, edited by Colin Gardner. Cape Town, Philip, and London, Collings, 1975; New York, Scribner, 1976.
Towards the Mountain: An Autobiography. Cape Town, Philip, and New York, Scribner, 1980; Oxford, Oxford University Press, 1981.
Ah, But Your Land Is Beautiful. Cape Town, Philip, and London, Cape, 1981; New York, Scribner, 1982.

*

Critical Studies: introduction by Lewis Gannet to *Cry, The Beloved Country*, New York, Scribner, 1950; *Alan Paton* by Edward Callan, New York, Twayne, 1968, revised edition, 1982 (includes bibliography).

Alan Paton comments:
(1981) I would not really regard myself as a contemporary novelist. In the fifties I turned to the writing of biography, and at the moment I am engaged on my autobiography.

*   *   *

Alan Paton's growing concern with enlightened penology and his personal harassment by compatriots resentful of his unflattering picture of his native South Africa have limited the production of one of the most gifted and compassionate 20th-century fiction writers to two novels and a slender collection of short stories. In *Cry, The Beloved Country* and *Too Late the Phalarope*, however, Paton succeeds in baring to the world the tragic effects and deeprooted causes of his country's repressive racist policies. Paton's writings are powerful modern renderings of one of the great tragic themes of art through the ages—the contrast between the beauty of the natural world as man found it and the ugly place that his greed and narrow mindedness have made of it.

Cry, The Beloved Country begins "There is a lovely road that runs from Ixopo into the hills. These hills are grass-covered and rolling, and they are lovely beyond any singing of it." From them, "if there is no mist, you look down on one of the fairest valleys in Africa." But this affectionate note cannot be sustained, for all is not well in the valley. Paton himself speaks of the novel as describing "a process of deterioration" and identifies its theme as the change in the black natives' characters as, envious of the white man's world, they leave their tribal lands and discipline to huddle in the slums of the white man's cities.

The novel follows the Reverend Stephen Kumalo of Ndotsheni, Natal, as he searches in "the great city," Johannesburg, for his son Absalom. He discovers that the boy—who has been in a reformatory—has shot and killed during a robbery attempt a white man, Arthur Jarvis, the son of a wealthy landowner who lives in the hills above Ndotsheni. Ironically, Arthur Jarvis has been one of the most courageous white fighters for justice for the African blacks. At the time of his death, he had been working on a paper called "The Truth about Native Crime."

Although Absalom pleads that he shot in fear and did not intend to kill Jarvis, he is sentenced to be hanged. His father takes home the pregnant girl that the boy marries after he is condemned; but the preacher is unsuccessful in bringing home also his errant sister Gertrude. As a result of Arthur Jarvis's young son's visiting Kumalo's church, the elder Jarvis and the black minister are brought together and measures are taken to rehabilitate the black farming community. Thus Jarvis helps realize his dead son's dream of setting up "another system of order and tradition and convention" to replace the old tribal system that the white man has thoughtlessly destroyed, so that at last out of the evil spawned by fear comes a promise of good for the community.

Although he has turned from fiction to biography and autobiography, Paton includes in the first volume of the autobiography, *Towards the Mountain*, a moving account of his inspiration to write *Cry, The Beloved Country* while visiting the cathedral in Trondheim, Norway, in 1946, and of his subsequent vision of the work as he composed it.

Too Late the Phalarope deals only secondarily with racial problems and focuses primarily on the tragic consequences of the austere, loveless way of life of the Afrikaans-speaking descendants of the Dutch settlers in South Africa. Pieter van Vlaanderen has been a heroic soldier in World War II and is a police lieutenant and rugby player whom both black and white communities hold in almost god-like respect. Yet there is a dark, secret side to the young man that is revealed by the distraught, sympathetic aunt who tells his story. Although always respectful, Pieter has been alienated from his father since the boy at the age of 14 was deprived of his stamp collection for failing to be at the top of his class. When at 17 he received first-class marks in his Matriculation Examination, the collection was restored, but the boy did not thank the father nor would he ever speak about the stamps again. He has also become alienated from his shy, fearful wife because she cannot respond adequately to his demands for love. A dispute over the identification of a bird called the *phalarope* in a book of South African birds that Pieter gives his father promises to bring the two men into the kind of joyous relationship that they had lost long ago; but the novel's title stresses that the older man's overture comes too late. Pieter has already been driven by his strong passions into an illicit affair with a black woman. Terror assails Pieter as he begins to receive anonymous messages intimating that his liaison has been observed and as the black girl—out of work—begins to beg for money. Pieter is entrapped by a jealous, self-righteous police sergeant; and the news of his crime results in his father's death, his family's ostracism, and the termination of his sister's engagement. The aunt prophesies that after Pieter is released from jail, he and his family will be obliged to leave the country that he has served with such distinction. *Too Late the Phalarope* is not simply a South African tragedy, however. While Pieter van Vlaanderen is a victim of the fear and ignorance of his fellow countrymen, he symbolizes all those extraordinary men everywhere who demand a more dynamic life than their pusillanimous societies can provide and thus must suffer for their honesty, enlightenment, and irrepressible human desires.

The title of *Tales from a Troubled Land*, Paton's collection of short stories, suggests the contents. Perhaps the most memorable, "The Waste Land," epitomizes Paton's ironic view of the South African situation and relates it—through the use of the title of T.S. Eliot's famous poem—to the condition of 20th-century man generally. The brief tale tells of a frightened black man killing one of three young robbers who are pursuing him across a junkyard and then discovering when the boy's companions shove his body under the same truck chassis that hides the man that the boy is his own son.

—Warren French

PATTERSON, (Horace) Orlando (Lloyd). American. Born in Jamaica, 5 June 1940. Educated at the University of the West Indies, Kingston, 1959–62 (Jamaica Government Exhibition Scholar), B.Sc. in economics 1962; London School of Economics (Commonwealth Scholar), 1962–65, Ph.D. in sociology 1965. Married Nerys Wyn in 1963; two children. Assistant Lecturer in Sociology, London School of Economics, 1965–67; Lecturer in Sociology, University of the West Indies, 1967–70. Visiting Associate Professor, 1970–71, Allston Burr Senior Tutor, 1971–73, and since 1971, Professor of Sociology, Harvard University, Cambridge, Massachusetts. Special Advisor to the Prime Minister of Jamaica, 1972–79; member of the Technical Advisory Council, Government of Jamaica, 1972–74; Visiting Member, Institute for Advanced Study, Princeton University, New Jersey, 1975–76; Visiting Fellow, Wolfson College, Cambridge, 1978–79. Member of the Editorial Board, *New Left Review*, London, 1965–66. Recipient: Dakar Festival prize, 1966; National Endowment for the Humanities grant, 1973, 1978, 1981, 1983; Guggenheim fellowship, 1978; Ralph Bunche Award, 1983; Harvard University Cabot Fellowship, 1984. A.M.: Harvard University, 1971. Address: 15 Shepard Street, Cambridge, Massachusetts 02138, U.S.A.

PUBLICATIONS

Novels

The Children of Sisyphus. London, Hutchinson, 1964; Boston, Houghton Mifflin, 1965; as *Dinah*, New York, Pyramid, 1968.
An Absence of Ruins. London, Hutchinson, 1967.
Die the Long Day. New York, Morrow, 1972; London, Mayflower, 1973.

Uncollected Short Stories

"The Very Funny Man: A Tale in Two Moods" and "One for a Penny," in *Stories from the Caribbean*, edited by Andrew Salkey. London, Elek, 1965; as *Island Voices*, New York, Liveright, 1970.
"The Alien," in *New Left Review* (London), September-October 1965.
"Into the Dark," in *Jamaica Journal* (Kingston), vol. 1, no. 2, 1968.

Other

The Sociology of Slavery: An Analysis of the Origins, Development, and Structure of Negro Slave Society in Jamaica. London, MacGibbon and Kee, 1967; Rutherford, New Jersey, Fairleigh Dickinson University Press, 1969.
Ethnic Chauvinism: The Reactionary Impulse. New York, Stein and Day, 1977.

Slavery and Social Death: A Comparative Study. Cambridge, Massachusetts, Harvard University Press, 1982.

*

Manuscript Collection: University of the West Indies, Kingston.

Orlando Patterson comments:

My main concern is with the theme of survival on all levels—physical, emotional, moral. Also concerned with related themes of isolation and exile.

*   *   *

Jamaican fiction is marked by its "realistic" examination of the local social scene. Though this reduces neither its technical range nor its emotional potency—the prose tone poems of Roger Mais, the imaginative adventures of Andrew Salkey, and the mythmaking of Vic Reid and Lindsay Barrett offer ready evidence to the contrary—it does mean that its central concern for the sociological exigencies of daily life often overcomes the urge to use words to build worlds rather than to analyze them. Of the contemporary analytic writers, three stand out as particularly shrewd observers/participators: John Hearne, whose austere novels explore the political impact of race and class; Sylvia Wynter, whose Marxist economic observations underlie her interpretation of Jamaican history; and Orlando Patterson, the sociologist, whose sense of individual potential is informed and guided always by his understanding of class structure and slave heritage.

Patterson's treatise *The Sociology of Slavery*, an analysis of the patterns of negro slave society in Jamaica, supplies an intelligent background to his novels, considering both the subservient and the resistant responses of the slave population to white society, and the social institutions—sorcery, religion, folk song and story, and so on—that provided some way of contending with life. To Patterson's mind, those responses and institutions continue to exert their effect, and in his novels he has attempted to demonstrate the inhibition that such a history casts over the lives of people today. Freedom in such a world is a watchword and a dream, always urging individuals into open acts of defiance, and always thwarted by the dead weight of the past.

The Children of Sisyphus is set in the slum world of Kingston, and traces the attempts that the prostitute Dinah makes to break out of the Dungle, to flee her surroundings and the course of life that circumstance has forced her into, and to find happiness, order, peace. Paralleling her search is the back-to-Africa quest of the Rastafarian movement, seeking its heritage and home in Ethiopia—"the soil . . . so fertile with everything that's joy back home in Zion"—and a different dream of freedom. But just as that dream is denied by deceit within Rastafarian ranks, so inside Dinah's experience is the Dungle that she cannot altogether leave. Drawn back to it and destroyed, she is typical of not only *her* world, but in Patterson's view *the* world. The suicide that closes the novel, the "soul-consuming" mockery of the shanty surroundings and the universal void, and the attempt thus to reach paradise wilfully supply an ironic perspective towards man's lot. The human ritual of striving for order appears as nothing so much as flight from uncertainty—a negative rather than a positive action—and because it is founded in emptiness and need, it lacks the self-possession that might make it anything but futile. Hence the circle back to the Dungle, like Dinah's, is closed, and absurd. For Alexander Blackman, in *An Absence of Ruins*, the discovery of such a relationship with futility voids his attempts not only to enunciate his identity but also to believe in his possession of one. Walking in London at the end, he recognizes himself only as an absence, the nothingness that a cipher concretely and phenomenally represents: "I cannot say whether I am civilized or savage, standing as I do outside of race, outside of culture, outside of history, outside of any value that could make your question meaningful. I am busy going nowhere, but I must keep up the appearance of going in order to forget that I am not." Thus the dilemma of existentiality—the conflict involved between intention, desire, history, and circumstance—is taken from Camus and given Caribbean voice. As Patterson realized, freeing the mind from slavery is a greater task than freeing the body, for it cannot be enacted by law. When people do not even believe in their capacity to attain freedom, however, the knowledge of the absurdity of their actions offers little comfort and no cure, and becomes their only reality.

—W.H. New

PEARSON, Bill (William Harrison Pearson). New Zealander. Born in Greymouth, 18 January 1922. Educated at Greymouth Technical High School; Canterbury University College, Christchurch, 1939, 1947–48; University of Otago, Dunedin, 1940–41, B.A., M.A.; King's College, London, 1949–51, Ph.D. 1952. Served in the New Zealand forces, in Fiji, Egypt, Italy, and Japan, 1942–46. Student teacher, Dunedin Teachers Training College, 1940–41; teacher, Blackball School, 1942, Oxford District High School, 1949, and in London County Council schools, 1952–53; Lecturer in English, University of Auckland, 1954–66; Senior Research Fellow, Department of Pacific History, Australian National University, Canberra, 1967–69. Since 1970, Associate Professor of English, University of Auckland. Closely associated with Maori students at the University of Auckland, 1956–66, and was patron of their club for some of those years; internal rapporteur at several Maori Leadership Conferences, 1959–63. Recipient: *Landfall* Readers' Award, for non-fiction, 1960; Hubert Church Prose Award, for non-fiction, 1975. Address: Department of English, University of Auckland, Private Bag, Auckland, New Zealand.

PUBLICATIONS

Novel

Coal Flat. Hamilton, Paul's Book Arcade, and London, Angus and Robertson, 1963; revised edition, Auckland, Longman Paul, 1970.

Uncollected Short Stories

"The Sins of the Fathers," in *Canterbury University College Review* (Christchurch), 1947.
"Indemnity," in *Canterbury Lambs* (Christchurch), 1947.
"Social Catharsis," in *Landfall* (Christchurch), December 1947; as "Purge," in *New-Story* (Paris), January 1952.
"At the Leicesters'," in *Canterbury Lambs* (Christchurch), 1948.
"Babes in the Bush," in *New-Story* (Paris), May 1951.

Other

Henry Lawson among Maoris. Canberra, Australian National University Press, and Wellington, Reed, 1968.
Fretful Sleepers and Other Essays. Auckland, Heinemann, 1974.
Rifled Sanctuaries: Some Views of the Pacific Islands in Western Literature to 1900. Auckland, Oxford University Press, 1984.

Editor, *Collected Stories, 1935–63*, by Frank Sargeson. Auckland, Blackwood and Janet Paul, 1964; London, MacGibbon and Kee, 1965.
Editor, *Brown Man's Burden and Later Stories*, by Roderick Finlayson. Auckland, Auckland University Press-Oxford University Press, 1973.

*

Critical Studies: "*Coal Flat*: The Major Scale, The Fine Excess," in *Comment* (Wellington), October 1963, and "*Coal Flat* Revisited," in *Critical Essays on the New Zealand Novel* edited by Cherry Hankin, Auckland, Heinemann, 1976, both by Allen Curnow; *The New Zealand Novel 1860–1965* by Joan Stevens, Wellington, Reed, 1966; "Conversation on a Train" by Frank Sargeson, in *Landfall* (Christchurch), December 1967; *New Zealand Fiction since 1945* by H. Winston Rhodes, Dunedin, McIndoe, 1968.

Bill Pearson comments:
Some commentators have seen a correspondence between my aims in *Coal Flat* and my analysis of the motifs of New Zealand behaviour and the implications for the artist which I wrote in 1951, "Fretful Sleepers."

While it has been said that a traditional structure, with sub-plots and a wide range of characters, is appropriate to a social novel set in a community whose attitudes and aspirations and social relations were rooted in 19th-century Britain, it has sometimes been a matter of objection that I chose a structure and style that appeared to take no cognisance of the developments in the form of the novel since Joyce. Yet I think that those commentators who stress the social realism or what they miscall "sociology" have been thrown off by a distaste for what they mistake for an outmoded technique, appropriate to *New Writing* reportage. The writers in the light of whose practice my aspirations as a writer developed were those that in common with young men of my time I read with sympathy and a deep respect, Lawrence, Joyce, Forster, Faulkner, Hemingway, Koestler; and I had a series of passions for the novels of Virginia Woolf and John Dos Passos and Thomas Hardy. At the time of my novel's first conception in 1946, the novelist who most excited me was Graham Greene. What I hoped to do when I was writing it (mostly in 1952 and 1953) was to devise a traditional structure that would be large enough to comprehend a community and sensitive enough to reflect the crises of feeling and conscience that might come to a man who was out of sympathy with the materialist values of the community. The plot would grow easily from the initial situation and by its own logic would reach a satisfying outcome without recourse to any of the tricks and evasions or improbabilities by which some of the 19th-century English novelists reached their answers. I had found, I thought, theoretical justification in Aristotle's conception of the plot as the probable and necessary consequence of certain initial acts and I conceived it as having the shape of the noble symmetrical curve that I saw in the plots of *Troilus and Criseyde* and *Wuthering Heights* and the great

19th-century Russian novels. This was not a scale that I pretended my ability or the comparatively pedestrian quality of New Zealand life would allow me to reach. But my concern for probability was necessary as a check against the rhetorical falsification that would be the risk of writing in the awareness of such examples, created from other communities and other times. My hope was to achieve an imaginative authenticity that my countrymen would immediately recognise as true, and which at the same time would be sufficiently clear of the accidents of parochiality to translate into human experience recognisable to readers from other societies. Whether I succeeded in this I cannot tell; but no one but an expatriate knows the pleasure of imaginatively recreating one's country in its detail, without sentimentality. It has often surprised me that some New Zealand commentators have seen sourness and "unappeased resentment" in a work that was written with love.

Since the moral meaning of the novel was to be in the sequence or consequence of events and their outcome, it was this rather than diction or characters or setting that demanded most thought. In its 13 years between conception and the last version, the novel survived a number of re-thinkings and radical overhauls, by which I think it gained. The last major revision was the discarding of a superficially optimistic ending, in keeping with a broadly Marxist literary theory hardly tenable after the events of 1956.

When I am moved to write fiction again, however, it is likely to be different in treatment.

*   *   *

Bill Pearson, essayist, critic, and scholar, has edited Frank Sargeson's *Collected Stories*, written about the impact of Western society on the Polynesian as reflected in literature, investigated in *Henry Lawson among Maoris* a little known area of the Australian writer's life, and produced a number of short stories together with a long novel, *Coal Flat*. Novels are sometimes written with a thesis. This may be religious or sociological but, whichever it is, the thesis may too easily destroy those qualities we have a right to expect in any attempt to create a life-like representation.

Coal Flat contains a thesis but survives as a novel. In "Fretful Sleepers," described as "a sketch of New Zealand behaviour and its implications for the artist," Pearson suggested that "our job is to penetrate the torpor and out of meaninglessness make a pattern that means something." *Coal Flat*, with its depressing but significant title, became not only a demonstration of the difficulties involved in such an attempt, but also as a novel partially fulfilled the aim that had been proposed for at least some artists.

Without allowing it to turn into satire or degenerate into a sociological survey, Pearson chose a small coal-mining and gold-dredging settlement on the West Coast of New Zealand in order to chart the course of family and community life; and by close attention to naturalistic detail evoked its oppressive narrowness, puritanism, and smugness. At one level the reader is introduced to a wide range of provincial characters, including the publican, parson, policeman, and visiting politicians, to miners, dredgers and their officials, to schoolteachers and children, to the doctor and priest, all firmly established in their local setting that combines natural grandeur with human inadequacy. The shriek of the dredge echoes and re-echoes through the book and acts as an inhuman accompaniment to the bitter animosities, perverted affections, and destructive behaviour of the people of Coal Flat. At another and perhaps more significant level these become signs and portents of a wider deterioration in the quality of life, extending well beyond its confines. Nevertheless, Coal Flat is by no means an inferno of lost souls. There are kindness, comradeship, and loyalty in abundance; there is not even a complete absence of sweetness and light; there are moments of idyllic charm and many good intentions. It is New Zealand, the world, reduced to Coal Flat.

Because its pitfalls cannot always be avoided, a close adherence to the slightly outmoded method of naturalism is liable to provoke criticism that is seldom without justification. *Coal Flat* is not a faultless novel, but it is a valuable one and especially for New Zealand. By the accumulation of detail relevant to the settlement and its inhabitants, by involving the central character, a young teacher of liberal instincts, in a mesh of conflicting loyalties, Pearson is able to dramatise the struggle between the individual conscience and the collective will, explore personal and family relationships in the broader context of the community and reveal distortions of sexual, parental, and social love. *Coal Flat* is neither a blueprint for future novels about New Zealand, nor is it an imitation of earlier novels in the naturalistic mode; but its achievement is such that it becomes an anatomy of social and spiritual decline, an exploration of the impoverishment of life, and a melancholy comment on thwarted but confused idealism unable to make headway against the conventional attitudes and mental lethargy of the majority.

—H. Winston Rhodes

PERCY, Walker. American. Born in Birmingham, Alabama, 28 May 1916. Educated at the University of North Carolina, Chapel Hill, B.A. 1937; Columbia University, New York, M.D. 1941; intern at Bellevue Hospital, New York, 1942. Married Mary Bernice Townsend in 1946; two daughters. Contracted tuberculosis, gave up medicine, and became a full-time writer, 1943. Recipient: National Book Award, 1962; American Academy grant, 1967; National Catholic Book Award, 1972; Los Angeles *Times* award, for non-fiction, 1983. Fellow, American Academy of Arts and Sciences; Member, American Academy. Agent: McIntosh and Otis Inc., 475 Fifth Avenue, New York, New York 10017. Address: P.O. Box 510, Covington, Louisiana 70433, U.S.A.

PUBLICATIONS

Novels

The Moviegoer. New York, Knopf, 1961; London, Eyre and Spottiswoode, 1963.
The Last Gentleman. New York, Farrar Straus, 1966; London, Eyre and Spottiswoode, 1967.
Love in the Ruins: The Adventures of a Bad Catholic at a Time Near the End of the World. New York, Farrar Straus, and London, Eyre and Spottiswoode, 1971.
Lancelot. New York, Farrar Straus, and London, Secker and Warburg, 1977.
The Second Coming. New York, Farrar Straus, 1980; London, Secker and Warburg, 1981.

Other

The Message in the Bottle: How Queer Man Is, How Queer Language Is, and What One Has to Do with the Other. New York, Farrar Straus, 1975.

Lost in the Cosmos: The Last Self-Help Book. New York, Farrar Straus, 1983.
Novel-Writing in an Apocalyptic Time. New Orleans, Faust, 1984.
Conversations with Walker Percy, edited by Lewis A. Lawson and Victor A. Kramer. Jackson, University Press of Mississippi, 1985.

*

Bibliography: *Andrew Lytle, Walker Percy, Peter Taylor: A Reference Guide* by Victor A. Kramer, Boston, Hall, 1983.

Manuscript Collection: University of North Carolina, Chapel Hill.

Critical Studies: *The Sovereign Wayfarer: Walker Percy's Diagnosis of the Malaise* by Martin Luschei, Baton Rouge, Louisiana State University Press, 1972; *Walker Percy: An American Search* by Robert Coles, Boston, Little Brown, 1978; *The Art of Walker Percy: Stratagems for Being* edited by Panthea Reid Broughton, Baton Rouge, Louisiana State University Press, 1979; *Walker Percy: Art and Ethics* edited by Jac Tharpe, Jackson, University Press of Mississippi, 1980, and *Walker Percy* by Tharpe, Boston, Twayne, 1983; *Walker Percy's Heroes: A Kierkegaardian Self* by L. Jerome Taylor, New York, Seabury Press, 1984; *Walker Percy and the Old Modern Age: Reflections on Language, Argument, and the Telling of Stories* by Patricia Lewis Poteat, Baton Rouge, Louisiana State University Press, 1985.

*   *   *

Walker Percy is that rare phenomenon of American letters: a philosophical novelist. He is a Catholic and a Southerner and his novels, firmly grounded in social observation, are a working out of his own special version of the problem of being. Percy finds the modern world in a state of moral confusion; the values of the past no longer hold, and the majority of men are spiritually dead, abstracted, cut off from life outside themselves. Percy's protagonists to some extent share in this confusion but are set apart by their awareness of the problem and, especially, by their ability to love. While that ability raises them above the general spiritual deadness, it also creates a special kind of problem which, simply stated, is: How can a man find his way in a world that regards love as a mechanical act, particularly when the traditional view he has to fall back on treats love as a set of grand ideals having little to do with physical reality? Each novel explores this dilemma.

The Moviegoer concludes with the protagonist, a lusty 30-year-old bachelor, failing in his latest sexual escapade and marrying a neurotic young woman of his own class, apparently out of affection, a feeling of kinship, and a sense of *experienced* responsibility. In *The Last Gentleman* the hero, who suffers from abstraction and the modern malaise of detachment, cures himself through his personal devotion to a dying youth and, in turn, helps cure a confused and beautiful young woman and her older brother, a cynical, corrupt doctor. *Love in the Ruins*, which is set in the future ("at a time near the end of the world") deals with the collapse of modern technology and concludes with the responsible marriage of the protagonist who had tried to save his mad world but, failing at that, had given himself up to whisky and lust for three beautiful women. Significantly he marries the most responsible and moral of the three and begins to live a simple, natural, and properly lustful life. *Lancelot* considers the problem from the point of view of a self-deceived moralist, a kind of latter-day gnostic who demands perfection of everyone but himself and ends by committing murder and arson. In *The Second Coming* Percy takes up again the story of Will Barrett of *The Last Gentleman* and shows how his hero's love for the fugitive from a mental asylum becomes the means of combatting alienation and despair.

While the philosophical and moral bases of Percy's novels are familiar enough, his rendering of characters and scenes is strikingly fresh, vivid, and bitingly satirical. He is a moral and, ultimately, a religious writer, but he is also a novelist of manners who can delineate with remarkable skill the contrast between certain kinds of Northerners, Southerners, and Midwesterners. Also, though he confines himself for the most part to the region around New Orleans, Percy is able to extend the implications of his material by creating characters and events obviously derived from the national scene, such as the white man who, some time back, went about the country masquerading as a Negro, and the Masters-Johnson studies in sexual response. Percy's style, which is sensitive and poetic, elevates material that less subtly treated might have seemed contrived and even moralistic.

—W.J. Stuckey

PERUTZ, Kathrin. American. Born in New York City, 1 July 1939. Educated at Barnard College, New York, B.A. 1960; New York University, M.A. 1966. Married Michael Studdert-Kennedy in 1966; one son. Lived in London, 1960–64. Executive Director, Contact Programs Inc., New York. Address: 16 Avalon Road, Great Neck, Long Island, New York 11021, U.S.A.

PUBLICATIONS

Novels

The Garden. London, Heinemann, and New York, Atheneum, 1962.
A House on the Sound. London, Heinemann, 1964; New York, Coward McCann, 1965.
The Ghosts. London, Heinemann, 1966.
Mother Is a Country: A Popular Fantasy. New York, Harcourt Brace, and London, Heinemann, 1968.
Reigning Passions: Leopold von Sacher-Masoch and the Hapsburg Empire. Philadelphia, Lippincott, and London, Weidenfeld and Nicolson, 1978.
Scents (as Johanna Kingsley). New York, Bantam, and London, Corgi, 1985.

Uncollected Short Story

"An American Success," in *Voices 2*, edited by Michael Ratcliffe. London, Joseph, 1965.

Other

Beyond the Looking Glass: America's Beauty Culture. New York, Morrow, 1970; as *Beyond the Looking Glass: Life in the Beauty Culture*, London, Hodder and Stoughton, 1970.
Marriage Is Hell: It's Better to Burn Than to Marry. New York, Morrow, 1972; as *The Marriage Fallacy: It's Better to Burn Than to Marry*, London, Hodder and Stoughton, 1972; as *Liberated Marriage*, New York, Pyramid, 1973.
I'd Love To, But What'll I Wear?, with Polly Bergen. New York, Wyden, 1977.

*

Critical Studies: *Don't Never Forget* by Brigid Brophy, London, Cape, 1966, New York, Holt Rinehart, 1967; "The Truth about Fiction" by George P. Elliott, in *Holiday* (New York), March 1966.

Kathrin Perutz comments:

(1972) The only general theme (or background) of my books is America. *Mother Is a Country* is a direct parody of certain American dreams (the acquisition of power and the desire to become a commodity); *A House on the Sound* charts the distance from reality to where rich liberals have their camp. *Beyond the Looking Glass*, a non-fiction book often fictionalized, examines preoccupation with appearance in America, where people have the hope of seeming what they have not yet become, and where self-knowledge is replaced by concern over minutiae of deception.

My first three novels also concern sub-rosa relationships, the area of self that is undeveloped or suppressed. *The Garden* presents a love affair between two girls, not Lesbian (both girls are young and boy-crazy), but of an essential intensity to contradict fears of not existing. *A House on the Sound* shows different manifestations of embryonic love—homosexuality, incest, masochism—never acknowledged by the characters. The two main characters of *The Ghosts* have not reconciled themselves to the sexual roles, male and female, they are supposed to play, and often parody or pervert these roles.

But mainly, each book has been my attempt to learn more of the craft. The first was a simple diary; the second tried, in six hours, to cut through time past and present, more similar to movie techniques than traditional flashbacks. The third book tried to give a sense of development, over the space of a year. The fourth, a satire, was deliberately "surface," a board game played over true but generalized emotions. My fifth book presented problems of journalism, in organization of material, tone, pace, and the creation of a personal, but abstracted, narrator.

(1976) My last book, *Marriage Is Hell*, is an essay on the institution of marriage as it exists today in the West, particularly in America. It deals with the anachronism of marriage, its false expectations, its imprisonment of personality and distortion of both privacy and personal liberty. The book, which is strongly opinionated, attacks marriage from many perspectives—legal, historical, anthropological, sexual—and then goes on to suggest reform and finally a turning that will make marriage possible again. I consciously tried to keep the style loose and colloquial, the better to let readers argue with me, and literary experiment is superseded in this book by political, or pragmatic, aims.

*   *   *

Kathrin Perutz has a baroque spider-web sensibility; it is as exquisite as it is tough, and permits her to explore such matters as incest, sadomasochism, homosexuality, suicide, and murder with the delicacy of an appropriate dinner wine. It is the most pervasive force in her novels and the one that diminishes the importance of whatever flaws may appear in them as a consequence of her experimentation with form and theme.

The first novel, *The Garden*, is a straightforward first-person narrative of life at a small women's college in Massachusetts.

Its treatment of the urge to put aside the burden of virginity becomes tedious, and the book is marked with jejune expressions ("O.K., Pats, shoot") that may be true to dormitory life but are vexatious in a novel. Perutz handles the garden symbolism of the novel well, however; describes a memorably tender, vivacious relationship between Kath and the Blossom, the two principal characters; and, with perfect briskness of pace and lightness of tone, captures the banal essence of a party weekend at an American men's college probably better than any other writer has.

The Ghosts, Perutz's third novel, walks the maze of a love affair in which the participants—or combatants—Luke, an excessively cerebral writer, and Judith, an undercerebral but sensitive hairdresser, are haunted chiefly by Luke's dead father and an assortment of cast-off lovers. The deficiency of the volume is that there is no one with whom an audience would much care to identify. Luke is insatiably clinical toward the involvement, and he and Panda, a deep platonic love of his who befriends Judith, are sometimes mouthpieces discussing their actions and Judith's, and examining one of the immediate themes of the novel, abortion, and, of more general metaphysical interest, the nature of human action. The conception of the characters is acute; their mechanism, however, is too much exposed and not enough is left for the reader to infer. They are often pieces of an essay rather than people in a work of fiction. Judith is too pliable, too much prop for Luke, until the end, when she takes control of herself and Luke becomes more human. But that occurs too late to place the novel in balance.

Mother Is a Country is a satiric fantasy that strikes at the mass-produced, antiseptic, Saran-wrapped materialism in American life. That quality accounts for the death of the three main characters, and the most palpable reaction in the cosmically unfeeling nation is that "a mother eagle in her nest flapped powerful wings and laid another egg." Though the book has been criticized for its superficiality of characterization, it can be argued that since superficial consumerism is primarily what the satire is about, John Scudely (a hero with much of the feeling of a Bellow character, but without the profundity) and the other characters are properly shallow. *Reigning Passions*, Perutz's latest novel, has done nothing to enhance her reputation. It is a fictionalized account of the complex man who gave his name to masochism, and so flat are the nuances of his life made to seem that to get through the book it helps to have a fair dose of the affliction.

It was Perutz's second novel, *A House on the Sound*, that proved her excellence. She paints a dinner party of sham liberals on a small canvas with precise detail, probing through the word, the facial expression, the gesture, the nuance of conversation the variety of characters present and their secret relationships. In this and in her control of time through brief, illuminating flashbacks and staging of the moments of her characters, there is the clear echo—but just the echo—of Virginia Woolf. When the experimentation ends, as far as it ever does, it is to be hoped that Perutz will return to a place like the house on the Sound and give full voice to her sensibility.

—Alan R. Shucard

PETERKIEWICZ, Jerzy (Michal). British. Born in Fabianki, Poland, 29 September 1916; emigrated to England in 1940. Educated at Dlugosz School, Wloclawek; University of Warsaw; University of St. Andrews, Scotland, M.A. 1944; King's College, London, Ph.D. 1947. Married Christine Brooke-Rose, *q.v.*, in 1948 (divorced, 1975). Lecturer, 1950–64, Reader, 1964–72, and Professor of Polish Language and Literature, 1972–79, School of Slavonic and East European Studies, University of London. Address: 7 Lyndhurst Terrace, London N.W.3, England.

PUBLICATIONS

Novels

Umarli nie są bezbronni. Glasgow, Książnica, 1943.
The Knotted Cord. London, Heinemann, 1953; New York, Roy, 1954.
Loot and Loyalty. London, Heinemann, 1955.
Future to Let. London, Heinemann, 1958; Philadelphia, Lippincott, 1959.
Isolation: A Novel in Five Acts. London, Heinemann, 1959; New York, Holt Rinehart, 1960.
The Quick and the Dead. London, Macmillan, 1961.
That Angel Burning at My Left Side. London, Macmillan, 1963.
Inner Circle. London, Macmillan, 1966.
Green Flows the Bile. London, Joseph, 1969.

Plays

Sami Swoi (produced London, 1949).
Scena ma trzy sciany. London, Wiadomości, 1974.
Three Walls to a Stage (produced Wimbledon, 1978).

Verse

Prowincja. Warsaw, 1936.
Wiersze i poematy. Warsaw, Prosto z Mostu, 1938.
Pokarm cierpki. London, Myśl Polska, 1943.
Piaty poemat. Paris, Instytut Literacki, 1950.
Poematy Londynskie i wiersze przedwojenne. Paris, Kultura, 1965.
Kula magiczna (Selected Poems). Warsaw, Ludowa Spoldzielnia Wydawnicza, 1980.

Other

Znaki na niebie. London, Mildner, 1940.
Po chlopsku: Powieść. London, Mildner, 2 vols., 1941.
Pogrzeb Europy. London, Mildner, 1946.
The Other Side of Silence: The Poet at the Limits of Language. London and New York, Oxford University Press, 1970.
The Third Adam. London, Oxford University Press, 1975.

Editor, *Polish Prose and Verse*. London, Athlone Press, 1956.
Editor and Translator, *Antologia liryki angielskiej 1300–1950*. London, Veritas, 1958.
Editor and Translator, with Burns Singer, *Five Centuries of Polish Poetry 1450–1950*. London, Secker and Warburg, 1960; Philadelphia, Dufour, 1962; revised edition, with Jon Stallworthy, as *Five Centuries of Polish Poetry 1450–1970*, London and New York, Oxford University Press, 1970.

Translator, *Easter Vigil and Other Poems*, by Karol Wojtyla. London, Hutchinson, and New York, Random House, 1979.
Translator, *Collected Poems*, by Karol Wojtyla. London, Hutchinson, and New York, Random House, 1982.

*

Critical Studies: in *New Statesman* (London), 10 October 1959; *Sunday Times Magazine* (London), 10 June 1962; "Speaking of Writing" by Peterkiewicz, in *The Times* (London), 9 January 1964; *Le Monde* (Paris), 28 June 1967; *The Novel Now* by Anthony Burgess, London, Faber, and New York, Norton, 1967, revised edition, Faber, 1971; by Peterkiewicz, in *Times Literary Supplement* (London), 30 July 1971; "Three Conversations," in *New Literary History* (Charlottesville, Virginia), vol. 15, 1984.

Jerzy Peterkiewicz comments:

If titles are significant, *Isolation* and *Inner Circle* seem to be my representative novels, both structurally and thematically.

*   *   *

Three of Jerzy Peterkiewicz's last six novels are comic entertainments of a high order of literary craftsmanship; three others show a marked falling-off of standards. His first novels have little bearing on the later work. *The Knotted Cord* is a genuinely moving account of a peasant boyhood in Poland; its hero has to escape from many things, but particularly from the "cord" of the scratchy brown cassock that his pious mother has thrust him into, and from all that cord represents. The work is a "first novel" of promise, and it is a pity the Peterkiewicz has chosen not to develop or integrate into his later work a mode which might have provided a carbohydrate counterbalance to the sometimes too frothy champagne of the books which follow. *Loot and Loyalty* is a trivial and poorly constructed historical novel about a 17th-century Scots soldier of fortune exiled in Poland, and his connection with the "false Dmitri."

Future to Let, the first of the really successful books, is less "mannerist" by far than its successors. It is a very funny roman à clef on the tortured loves, English, plots, and politics of contemporary Polish emigrés, chief among them Julian Atrament ("ink" in Polish), quite unidentifiable, of course, but almost recognizable, whose "escape to freedom" by means of his St. Bernard dog is Peterkiewicz's finest comic turn. *Isolation*, probably his best book, parodies the erotic mystifications of a modern spy story with a skill that even the suggestions of deep meanings about the mutual isolation of sexuality, etc., cannot spoil. The Powell-esque (or Waugh-like) Commander Shrimp (alias Pennyworthing), faded semi-spy and bathetic con-man, is a great comic creation. *That Angel Burning at My Left Side* has some of the virtues of *The Knotted Cord*; it is realism with a light touch, of a boy growing up through the Second World War and post-war refugeehood, looking for father, country, and self. The gimmick of the "angels" grows tiresome, but descriptions of place and event and the hero himself are vivid and concrete—until the hero gets to England, and everything, including him, suddenly (and apparently inadvertently on the author's part) becomes less real.

The three unsuccessful works include *The Quick and the Dead*, a spoof ghost-story and fantasy of serio-comic realism, involving among other things the amorous relations of the dead in Limbo, the suffering and repentance of ghosts (a somewhat Golding-like concept), with significance, apparently, but the coy handling of its basic situation makes for heavy reading. Still harder to read, but even more significant, is *Inner Circle*, in which a three-layered story of Surface (the far future), Underground (present-day sub-Firbankian London), and Sky (a version of the Eden story), is held together by repeated "circle" and "underground" image patterns, and by analogous destinies. The themes and point-of-view games again make it seem almost like a collaboration between Golding, Burgess,

and Arthur C. Clarke. Peterkiewicz's most recent novel, *Green Flows the Bile*, is as tastelessly affected a social satire as its title would suggest. It recounts the last journey together of two "fellow-travellers" (in all senses), the Secretary, a "political gigolo," and his employer, the "senior prophet of the age ... the travelling peace salesman." The comic travelogue is passable in places, but the political satire is either painfully obvious or intensely private; the two pitfalls that await the topical roman à clef have caught Peterkiewicz this time.

Peterkiewicz's heroes are almost all coyly hollow semi-comic shadow-men, pretending to contain abysses and seeking with morose jocularity for an "identity" to which they are fundamentally indifferent. Their human relationships are sketched with equal shallowness. Even the intrigues are lower Greeneland, territory more powerfully explored by Burgess, though at times Peterkiewicz is clearly aiming for the playful, complex "meanings" of a Chesterton, or a Woolf (*Orlando*), or a Nabokov, or for the light, horrid satire of a Waugh (*Scott-King's Modern Europe*). Stage-metaphors, mirrors, masks, costumes, photographs, cute but pallid versions of Nabokovian artifices, crowd the pages of *Isolation*, in which mock-pornography and reciprocal voyeuristic spyings, slowly building up a posthumous portrait, bring to mind *Lolita* (courteously, or perhaps coincidentally, acknowledged in a parrot of that name) or *The Real Life of Sebastian Knight*. These are samples of tone, not assertions of source; but even the best of Peterkiewicz's work is marred by hearing continually whispered chords made up of the murmurs of other men's voices, almost as if he were unwilling to hear his own voice. His real talent for language and comedy is almost swamped by his need to be terribly à la mode in these six novels, and it is a pity, for, to paraphrase a comment he makes on one of his characters, "his anonymous extraterritorial aura predicts at every step a possible eruption of personality."

It may be that, for all the polished virtues and assurance of his better novels, Peterkiewicz will be remembered longest and known most widely for his critical essays and anthologies, and for his book *The Other Side of Silence*, in which he sensitively discusses some intricacies of modern literature and places Polish literature in their context. One would like, however, to have as well his views on his own Polish contemporaries, who are giving us one of the most flourishing of modern minor literatures. Perhaps in his criticism he has more truly earned the right than he has in his fiction, to the inevitable, and specious, comparison with Conrad, that other Polish man of letters who turned himself, in adult life, and not without success, into an English writer.

—Patricia Merivale

PETRAKIS, Harry Mark. American. Born in St. Louis, Missouri, 5 June 1923. Educated at the University of Illinois, Urbana, 1940–41. Married Diane Perparos in 1945; three sons. Has worked in steelmills, and as a real-estate salesman, truck driver, and sales correspondent. Since 1960, free-lance writer and lecturer. Taught at the Indiana University Writers Conference, Bloomington, 1964–65, 1970, 1974; McGuffey Visiting Lecturer, Ohio University, Athens, 1971; Writer-in-Residence, Chicago Public Library, 1976–77, and for the Chicago Board of Education, 1978–80; taught at Illinois Wesleyan University, Bloomington, 1978–79, Ball State University,

Muncie, Indiana, 1978 and 1980, University of Wisconsin, Rhinelander, 1978–80, and University of Rochester, New York, 1979–80. Recipient: *Atlantic* "Firsts" Award, 1957; Benjamin Franklin Citation, 1957; Friends of American Writers award, 1964; Friends of Literature award, 1964; Carl Sandburg Award, 1983. D.H.L.: University of Illinois, 1971; Governors State University, Park Forest South, Illinois, 1980; Hellenic College, Brookline, Massachusetts, 1984. Address: 80 East Road, Dune Acres, Chesterton, Indiana 46304, U.S.A.

PUBLICATIONS

Novels

Lion at My Heart. Boston, Little Brown, and London, Gollancz, 1959.
The Odyssey of Kostas Volakis. New York, McKay, 1963.
A Dream of Kings. New York, McKay, 1966; London, Barker, 1967.
In the Land of Morning. New York, McKay, 1973.
The Hour of the Bell. New York, Doubleday, 1976; London, Severn House, 1986.
Nick the Greek. New York, Doubleday, 1979; London, New English Library, 1980.
Days of Vengeance. New York, Doubleday, 1983; London, Sphere, 1985.

Short Stories

Pericles on 31st Street. Chicago, Quadrangle, 1965.
The Waves of Night and Other Stories. New York, McKay, 1969.
A Petrakis Reader. New York, Doubleday, 1978.

Plays

Screenplays: *A Dream of Kings*, with Ian Hunter, 1969; *In the Land of Morning*, 1974.

Television Plays: *Pericles on 31st Street*, with Sam Peckinpah, from the story by Petrakis, and *The Judge*, with Bruce Geller (both in *Dick Powell Show*), 1961–62; *The Blue Hotel*, from the story by Stephen Crane, 1978.

Other

The Founder's Touch: The Life of Paul Galvin of Motorola. New York, McGraw Hill, 1965.
Stelmark: A Family Recollection (autobiography). New York, McKay, 1970.
Reflections: A Writer's Life, A Writer's Work. Chicago, Lake View Press, 1983.

*

Critical Studies: in *Old Northwest* (Oxford, Ohio), December 1976; interview in *Chicago Review*, Winter 1977.

Harry Mark Petrakis comments:

(1972) Reaching the half-century point in my life, I am grateful for having survived this long to write my stories and novels. An immense amount of work ahead that grows harder to accomplish each year, because the spirit demands new challenges and because time diminishes the reserves of energy and health. Yet I cannot conceive of living without writing. On writing as a profession, one might aptly quote Thucydides writing of the Athenians captured in war and set to labor in the stone quarries of Syracuse. "Having done what men could, they suffered what men must."

*   *   *

In a book of personal recollections, *Stelmark*, Harry Mark Petrakis confirms what the reader of his novels would guess; that Petrakis is the son of Greek immigrants to the United States. He is in fact a second generation man who is intent on estimating the meaning of his presence in a country that is far from the Crete of his ancestors. To the territory of South Chicago, Petrakis's father, a Greek Orthodox priest, brought the recollections of a strange and noble sort of life where poverty was the foreground of an existence lived in an awesome setting of mountains and an equally demanding texture of ancient custom and suffering. As a young man, Petrakis was impressed by the interplay of his inheritance and the sections of American culture that he came into contact with in the land of promise: the narrow opportunities of a great and indifferent city, the materialism of midwestern life as the immigrants encountered it and the continuation of the pride and violence that crossed the Atlantic with the Greek immigrants. It is this basic contrast between America as dreamed in the Cretan valleys and America as experienced by an ethnic minority that gives Petrakis his subject.

It is a subject full of challenges to Petrakis's novelistic imagination. And that imagination is equal to the passions, the disappointments, and the envies of the newcomers among whom, as a meditator and creator, Petrakis has lived his artistic life. He has created a striking company of persons who are, as Kurt Vonnegut has observed, at least 14 feet tall. These persons are swept by passions that are awesome when they are compared with the feebler desires and lesser dignities of men and women who have had several generations to adapt to the conditions of American life. The male figures still know the Greek versions of omertà, the Sicilian code of honor. These men act on the basis of personal pride and have loyalties that bind them less to American society than to family and a few close acquaintances. They have a sentimental vision of the cruel and impoverished land they—or their parents—fled. There is a dual center to their lives. One center is the church, whose ministers they respect, but whose teachings they put aside as having little to do with the lives of Greeks in South Chicago. The other center, more compulsive for them, is the world of cheap restaurants, backroom gambling dens that are full of con men and bookies, and seedy offices above grocery stores where, as in *A Dream of Kings*, palms are read and advice is given to clients who do not know where to turn in a society that has scant tolerance for new arrivals. This male world has, in large part, a cold indifference for wives and mistresses; women are tolerated because men must have sons or because sexual desires must find expression. Sincere and deep affection is known to some of the men, as in *The Odyssey of Kostas Volakis*. But even so, the hopes of women remain alien to male concerns and are seldom respected or shared.

Mention of particular novels fills out this general description. *Lion at My Heart*, Petrakis's first novel, rehearses the fortunes of an immigrant household made up of a father and two sons. The father, with pride and suspicion, watches over the education and the marriages of his two sons, esteeming the son who takes a Greek wife and repudiating the son who marries "outside." A priest, a familiar figure in the novels, intervenes to mollify the father's harshness. *The Odyssey of Kostas Volakis* tells a similar story. Kostas is a young Cretan man who married a slightly older woman for her dowry, which pays for the passage to America. The novel traces stages in Kostas's adjustment to his new land: his struggle as a restaurant owner, his overcoming of his illiteracy, and—most important—his final forgiveness of his murderer-son who has disgraced his family.

A Dream of Kings explores a slightly higher social level and tells of the life of Masoukas the palm-reader and consultant, half charlatan and half concerned adviser, by turns a compulsive gambler and adulterer. But Masoukas's dreams are fixed on an ailing son, for whose cure everything must be sacrificed. A journey to the sacred land of Greece will restore the health of the child and, perhaps, of the father. In another novel with a Chicago setting, *In the Land of Morning*, Petrakis moves into the post-Vietnam American world where the shock of a veteran's return is gradually merged with the on-going tumult of life in the community. All this is a passionate and sad human encounter which the reader can find elsewhere in Petrakis, as in the collections of short stories, *Pericles on 31st Street* and *The Waves of Night*. Petrakis circles back to such themes—Greeks in a strange land—in *Nick the Greek*. Here the hero, Nick Dandalos, comes to the United States in the 1920's and allows himself to be drawn into the gambling life of Chicago, all at the cost of a sound future and a happy love affair. Particularly strong are the gambling scenes which take readers back to a distant time in the Greek community.

A bit to one side is *The Hour of the Bell*. This novel is an account of the revolution that commenced in Greece in 1820 when a confused but finally successful revolt against Turkish power began. Instead of finding the usual cultural enclave in South Chicago, the reader moves back and forth over the tumultuous Greek landscape, which is seen through various eyes: those of military leaders, some savage, some resigned to years of violence; those of a priest who respects the humanity of the slaughtered Turks; and those of an educated young man who is trying to write the history of the confusion that surrounds him. With his usual power, Petrakis, as it were, adds the completing piece to the Greek-American puzzle that is his concern. *The Hour of the Bell* is the "explanation" of the pride and the harsh tauntings and the intermittent tenderness that the novels about South Chicago record.

It is a record that is made up of prose of varying textures: realistic and poetically fierce by turns. The result is an indispensable report and also an imaginative world that takes its place along with the works of fiction—Chekhov's and others—that, Petrakis tells us, used to make him weep as a youth.

—Harold H. Watts

PETRY, Ann (Lane). American. Born in Old Saybrook, Connecticut, 12 October 1908. Educated at Connecticut College of Pharmacy, now University of Connecticut School of Pharmacy, 1928–31, Ph.G. 1931; Columbia University, New York, 1943–44. Married George D. Petry in 1938; one daughter. Pharmacist, James Pharmacy, Old Saybrook and Old Lyme, Connecticut, 1931–38; writer and reporter, *Amsterdam News*, New York, 1938–41; women's editor, *People's Voice*, New York, 1941–44; Visiting Professor of English, University of Hawaii, Honolulu, 1974–75. Secretary, Authors League of America, 1960. Recipient: Houghton Mifflin Literary Fellowship, 1946; National Endowment for the Arts grant, 1977. D.Litt.: Suffolk University, Boston, 1983. Agent: Russell and Volkening Inc., 50 West 29th Street, New York, New York

10001. Address: 113 Old Boston Post Road, Old Saybrook, Connecticut 06475, U.S.A.

PUBLICATIONS

Novels

The Street. Boston, Houghton Mifflin, 1946; London, Joseph, 1947.
Country Place. Boston, Houghton Mifflin, 1947; London, Joseph, 1948.
The Narrows. Boston, Houghton Mifflin, 1953; London, Gollancz, 1954.

Short Stories

Miss Muriel and Other Stories. Boston, Houghton Mifflin, 1971.

Other (for children)

The Drugstore Cat. New York, Crowell, 1949.
Harriet Tubman, Conductor on the Underground Railroad. New York, Crowell, 1955; as *The Girl Called Moses: The Story of Harriet Tubman*, London, Methuen, 1960.
Tituba of Salem Village. New York, Crowell, 1964.
Legends of the Saints. New York, Crowell, 1970.

*

Manuscript Collection: Mugar Memorial Library, Boston University.

Critical Studies: *Black on White: A Critical Study of Writing by American Negroes* by David Littlejohn, New York, Grossman, 1966; *Interviews with Black Writers* edited by John O'Brien, New York, Liveright, 1973.

Ann Petry comments:
I write short stories, novels, books for children and young people. I vary what I write, even the style, but the underlying theme deals with race relations in the U.S.A.

*   *   *

Ann Petry has written three novels for adults, *The Street, Country Place*, and *The Narrows*. Her short stories of the early 1940's in *The Crisis* and *Phylon*, as well as more recent fiction in *Redbook* and *The New Yorker*, also merit attention. "On Saturday the Siren Sounds at Noon" began her career: its reception encouraged her to write *The Street*. "Like a Winding Sheet" was chosen for *The Best American Short Stories of 1946*. "Solo on the Drums," appearing in *'47 Magazine of the Year*, has a lyrical anguish that reflects her novels in theme and style.

The Street offers more than just another example of environmental determinism overshadowed by its precursor, *Native Son*. True, it opens with "a cold November wind" on 116th Street in Harlem that "did everything it could to discourage the people walking along the street" and closes with "the grime and the garbage and the ugliness" of that street as the defeated, pretty heroine-turned-murderess flees by train. Boots Smith, unscrupulous in avoiding a return to "a life of saying 'yes sir' to every white bastard who had the price of a Pullman ticket," is an older Bigger Thomas, with cash, a luxurious car, and political connections. Authorial digressions that rationalize

Lutie Johnson's fear of the street—"an evil father and a vicious mother" to Black children like her Bub—replace Boris Max's 16-page courtroom speech that blames a racist environment for Bigger's dilemma. Ann Petry's own life had verified the glum details of *The Street*, but her feminine and racial perceptions of those domestic tragedies that cluster in Black slums gave psychological sharpness to passages still alive with meaning. The Connecticut middle class with its insulting generalizations about Black women, the unemployed Harlem men reduced to loitering and philandering and desertion, the Black man with a resentment of his oppressors "so bad and so deep that I wouldn't lift a finger to help 'em stop Germans or nobody else," the tenement radios blaring to kill the feel of unbearable misery, "carrying pain and a shrinking from pain"—all these are realistic types that advance the author's theme of entrapment and resignation. The sometimes excessive description and the rather contrived plights of Lutie and Bub are redeemed by a sympathy that humanizes even the maniacally obsessed William Jones and the repulsively scarred Mrs. Hedges.

The ugliness of a small-town New England white environment, personified early by the scandalmongering cab driver "the Weasel," permeates *Country Place*. The conflict sustained between past and present is moral in the frustrations of returning war veteran Johnnie Roane and his faithless wife Glory, and philosophical in the insistence of Mrs. Gramby that her middle-aged son Mearns uphold a gracious tradition beyond his powers and desires. Sensitive to fusions of imagery, metaphor, and symbol, the author has Johnnie struggle past storm-felled trees to reach Ed Barrell's cabin and suffer disillusion in Glory's infidelity. The long storm, like the rain in which Johnnie walks after his first doubts about his wife, is emblematic of the turbulence of climactic changes forced upon the main characters. The thematic absorption of disenchantment into thinner but stronger life is presaged in Johnnie's decision not to strangle his wife and, later not to kill her lover; it is advanced—through an equally distressing decision by Mrs. Gramby—by his opportunity to become an artist in New York. *Country Place*, marred like *The Street* by seemingly thesis-conjured death at the end, continues Ann Petry's attack against a cash-and-carry society hostile to moral beauty.

The Narrows, titled after its setting, the Black neighbourhood in Monmouth, Connecticut, not only has a conscience-gripping theme, but is remarkable for its vivid array of minor characters. Sexually radiant, blues-singing Mamie Powther; the frightful amputee, Cat Jimmie, who speeds on his homemade cart to peer under the dresses of women; Cesar the Writing Man, who records his sonorous prophecies on the side-walk with colored chalk; and Weak Knees, with his collapsible limbs and innumerable gestures and mutterings ("Get away, Eddie, get away!") at the ghost of his best friend—these and others unforgettably enliven Dumble Street and the foggy dock of the River Wye. The novel is about love and its betrayal. Abbie Crunch lets puritanical snobbishness fatally betray her love for her husband, then lets grief betray her love for their adopted child, Link. Later, Link sacrifices his love for rich, white Camilo Treadway to Black pride, while she gives in to jealousy and racism. And mistakenly jealous little Malcolm Powther, having no manhood himself, betrays that of Link. "All of us," Abbie concludes, "had a hand in [Link's death], we all reacted violently ... because he was coloured and she was white." Almost every character applies to himself the author's repeated refrain: "I, executioner." *The Narrows* is attuned to the 1970's in other racial themes, and it thoughtfully views the responsibilities that attend power and artistic talent. Flashbacks are excessive, sometimes confusing; but stream-of-consciousness passages are skillfully written, and the leaven of humor appears.

The craftsmanship, social truth, and humanity of Ann Petry's fiction deserve wider recognition. Her basically tragic vision, linked in some way with themes of Lorraine Hansberry and Ralph Ellison, could culminate, if she produces more, in a distinguished, comprehensive novel.

—James A. Emanuel

PHELPS, Gilbert (Henry). British. Born in Gloucester, 23 January 1915. Educated at the Crypt School, Gloucester; Fitzwilliam College, Cambridge, B.A. (honours) in English 1937; St. John's College, Cambridge (Strathcona Research Student), 1937–39, M.A. 1941. Served in the Royal Air Force, 1940–43. Married 1) Dorothy Elizabeth Coad in 1939 (divorced), one son and one daughter; 2) Kay Batchelor in 1972, three stepsons. Assistant Supervisor of English Studies, St. John's College, 1937–40; Lecturer and Tutor, Cambridge University Board of Extra-Mural Studies, 1938–40; Lecturer in English, British Council British Institute, Lisbon, 1940–42; Senior English Master, Blundell's School, Tiverton, Devon, 1943–45; talks producer, BBC, Bristol, 1945–50; supervisor, Educational Talks, 1950–52, producer, Third Programme, 1950–53, and general instructor, 1953–56, and chief instructor, 1956–60, Staff Training Department, all for BBC, London. Since 1960, free-lance writer, broadcaster, and lecturer. Recipient: Arts Council award, 1965, and bursary, 1968. Fellow, Royal Society of Literature, 1979. Address: The Cottage, School Road, Finstock, Oxford OX7 3DJ, England.

PUBLICATIONS

Novels

The Dry Stone. London, Barker, 1953; earlier version, as *The Heart in the Desert*, New York, Day, 1954.
A Man in His Prime. London, Barker, and New York, Day, 1955.
The Centenarians: A Fable. London, Heinemann, 1958.
The Love Before the First. London, Heinemann, 1960.
The Winter People. London, Bodley Head, 1963; New York, Simon and Schuster, 1964.
Tenants of the House. London, Barrie and Jenkins, 1971.
The Old Believer. London, Barrie and Jenkins-Wildwood House, 1973; as *Mortal Flesh*, New York, Random House, 1974.
The Low Roads. London, Barrie and Jenkins, 1975.

Uncollected Short Stories

"I Have Lived a Hundred Years," in *The Pleasureground*, edited by Malcolm Elwin. London, Macdonald, 1947.
"The Guv'nor," in *Countryman* (London), 1948.
"The Corner Ghost," in *West Country Magazine* (London), 1949.
"Playing Dead," in *Cornhill* (London), 1950.
"The Loft," in *World Review* (London), 1951.
"A Body for Amsterdam," in *Cornhill* (London), 1953.
"Hide and Seek," in *The Listener* (London), 1958.
"Who Were You with Last Night?," in *The Ninth Ghost Book*, edited by Rosemary Timperley. London, Barrie and Jenkins, 1973.

"Call a Spade a Spade," in *The Twelfth Ghost Book*, edited by Rosemary Timperley. London, Barrie and Jenkins, 1976.

Plays

Radio Plays: *The Tide Comes In*, 1960; *The Spanish Cave*, from the novel by Geoffrey Household, 1960; *The Tankerdown Skull*, 1962; *The Winter People*, from his own novel, 1964; *Deliberate Adventure*, 1968.

Other

The Russian Novel in English Fiction. London, Hutchinson, 1956; St. Clair Shores, Michigan, Scholarly Press, 1971.
A Short History of English Literature. London, Folio Society, 1962; revised edition, as *A Survey of English Literature: Some of the Main Themes and Developments from Beowulf to 1939*, London, Pan, 1965.
The Last Horizon: Travels in Brazil. London, Bodley Head, 1964; as *The Green Horizons: Travels in Brazil*, New York, Simon and Schuster, 1964; revised edition, London, Charles Knight, 1971.
Latin America. London, BBC Publications, 1965.
Latin America. London, Bank of London and South America, 1970.
Romeo and Juliet. Petersfield, Hampshire, Studytapes, 1973.
Arnold Bennett: The Old Wives' Tale. London, British Council, 1973.
Tragedy of Paraguay. London, Charles Knight, and New York, St. Martin's Press, 1975.
Squire Waterton of Walton Hall. Wakefield, Yorkshire, EP, 1976.
Story of the British Monarchy. London, Nile and Mackenzie, 1977.
An Introduction to Fifty British Novels 1650–1900. London, Pan, 1979; as *A Reader's Guide to Fifty British Novels 1650–1900*, London, Heinemann, and New York, Barnes and Noble, 1979.

Editor, *Living Writers.* London, Sylvan Press, 1947.
Editor, *Vanity Fair*, by Thackeray. London, Pan, 1967.
Editor, *Question and Response: A Critical Anthology of English and American Poetry.* London, Cambridge University Press, 1969.
Editor, *The Byronic Byron: A Selection from the Poems of Lord Byron.* London, Longman, 1971.
Editor, *Villette*, by Charlotte Brontë. London, Pan, 1973.
Editor, *Wanderings in South America, the North-West of the United States, and the Antilles in the Years 1812, 1816, 1820, 1824*, by Charles Waterton. London, Charles Knight, 1973.
Editor, *The Rare Adventures and Painful Peregrinations of William Lithgow.* London, Folio Society, 1974.
Editor, *Henry Esmond*, by Thackeray. London, Pan, 1974.
Editor, *Arlott and Trueman on Cricket.* London, BBC Publications, 1977.
Editor, with John Phelps, *Animals Tame and Wild.* London, Angus and Robertson, and New York, Sterling, 1979.

*

Gilbert Phelps comments:
(1976) The age-old theme in which I am most interested in my fiction is that of the intellect versus the heart and the imagination. I have attempted to explore this in two types of story: first, close studies of family life in a West Country context, especially figuring children—as in my *The Love Before*
the First, which is about a boy and girl who "love" each other at a pre-adolescent stage; and second, in fables or allegories, sometimes with a Science Fiction element, as in *The Centenarians* and *The Winter People*. I have also experimented with the "realistic fable" in *Tenants of the House*, a story about a lodging house in London which might also be either the state of man or the layers of personality and the varying *personae* of the individual; and in *The Old Believer* I have tried the imaginary autobiography, in this case that of an old man on his death-bed who recreates the duality of sensuality and spirit in his past. *The Low Roads* seeks to explore the life of an educated man who cuts away all his old intellectual and cultural props—in order to become a tramp—and who receives "intimations" which may possibly be described as "religious."

*   *   *

Gilbert Phelps's work is characterized by its vitality, both in its vigorous narrative style and in the belief in "life and love" engendering basic optimism. This affirmative tone is common to the two genres of his earlier work, family studies and fantasies, and to his later attempts at their synthesis. All his novels end on a positive note.

Phelps's first novel, *The Dry Stone*, takes the form of a first-person account by Martin Crystal of a poor childhood in a West-country town, from which he wins through to Cambridge, and his subsequent career leading to success as a writer. The early part of the book is the best, and wisely Phelps returned to the theme of childhood in Cranwyck in *The Love Before the First*. In the context of what becomes in *The Dry Stone* an almost melodramatic plot, Phelps's treatment of Vera Crystal's mental breakdown and Martin's later happiness with his first love, Patricia, induces the sense of uneasiness of much of his work, as his strong narrative binds together willy-nilly different levels of perception.

A Man in His Prime, written in the third person, is less ambitious and more successful; the protagonist's rhetorical questions are redeemed by a humour absent in Crystal's turgid soul-searchings. This novel deals with the affair of William Corrie, the middle-aged man of the title, with an American girl, whom he renounces, in the context of his enduring marriage. In the lyrical family holiday scene closing the book, Corrie remains, realistically, "still rebellious at the losses."

While in *A Man in His Prime* Phelps gave affectionate thumbnail sketches of Corrie's children, in his fourth novel, *The Love Before the First*, he approached childhood subjectively, though writing in the third person. He focuses on the "no-man's-land" inhabited by Alan, "where he had to endure both the pangs of regret and those of foreboding," as he grows up and away from his constant companion and cousin, Meg, but yet remains excluded from the adults, whose preoccupations are highlighted by the arrival of debonair Uncle Hector.

The Love Before the First was written between Phelps's two fantasies. The first, the "fable" *The Centenarians*, posits a group of especially distinguished old men preserved in the future in a "beautiful retreat," while the rest of the world destroys itself. Two unprepossessing survivors reach the mountain plateau to be fêted foolishly by the old men. The tale is told by Jerrould, "court jester" to the leader, Chard, with whose wife he had been in love. In *The Old Believer* Phelps explores more fully meaning latent in lyrical memory, but here Jerrould's personal memories do not form an integral part of the fable, which by a sparing use of science-fiction props translates to laboratory conditions predominantly vain human attitudes.

In *The Winter People* "mad" Colonel John Parr's belief in his discovery of a gracious, peaceable people in an uninhabitable altitude of the Andes serves to condemn by contrast the tribe of "respectable Parrs" who are merely "slowly dying." His journal, describing this people's annual winter hibernation and their "retrospective amnesia," is introduced by the lawyer, David Parr. Though he explains the Winter People in terms of his great-uncle's thwarted early love, he himself comes to believe in the discovery as one of "the miracles of Nature and of Love", his own life will be fertilized by his great-uncle's madness, which is presented as less pernicious than the respectable Parrs' sanity.

Tenants of the House is an extended metaphor for the workings of a man's mind—perhaps at different periods in his life—into which the reader is plunged direct. Written in the third person, it is ostensibly a description of Hugo's house, inhabited by a multitude of conventional and subversive tenants, for "if the house chose to admit them, there was nothing he could do about it." The characters seem further intended to represent schizophrenia and other derangements, though the introduction of a stock "Doctor" figure to comment on Hugo's "house of many mansions" seems superfluous. The basic mental metaphor accommodates some amusing word-play, while the tenants' and squatters' antics provide the full-blooded—and sometimes black—comedy characteristic of Phelps's later work.

An integral part of Phelps's celebration of "life and love" is the recognition of death as their natural completion; the old man in *The Old Believer* becomes "proud to be dying of 'natural causes,' by the simple wearing away of time and experience." Yet his belief in the instinctive testimony of the senses, which he fully comprehends as he remembers in his hospital bed the experiences which nurtured it, seems facile. The pattern of his love for Tanya recalls *The Dry Stone*, and Phelps retains from his first novel the self-defeating trick of writing about superficial experience superficially.

In *The Low Roads* a successful cartoonist abandons his home to take to the road as a tramp, dying to his family. Coincidence, a favourite device of Phelps, comes into its own in this picaresque novel of "the episodic life" in a sub-culture of squatters, drop-outs, social workers, and the gentlemen of the road themselves. His success as a pavement artist nearly leads to his integration in "society" again, but he breaks down and undergoes electric shock treatment. Ironically, he is then overtaken by so-called fantasies of widespread pollution. The Joycean echo in the ending seems pretentious, but helps Gilbert Phelps to make even his tramps affirm ultimately.

—Val Warner

PHILLIPS, Jayne Anne. American. Born in Buckhannon, West Virginia, 19 July 1952. Educated at West Virginia University, Morgantown, B.A. 1974; University of Iowa, Iowa City, M.F.A. 1978. Married; one son. Has taught at Humboldt State University, Arcata, California, Boston University, and Williams College, Williamstown, Massachusetts. Recipient: National Endowment for the Arts grant, 1977, 1984; St. Lawrence award, 1978; American Academy Kaufman Award, 1980. Agent: Lynn Nesbit, International Creative Management, 40 West 57th Street, New York, New York 10019, U.S.A.

PUBLICATIONS

Novel

Machine Dreams.   New York, Dutton, and London, Faber, 1984.

Short Stories

Sweethearts.   Carrboro, North Carolina, Truck Press, 1976.
Counting.   New York, Vehicle, 1978.
Black Tickets.   New York, Delacorte Press, 1979; London, Allen Lane, 1980.
How Mickey Made It.   St. Paul, Bookslinger Press, 1981.
Fast Lanes.   New York, Vehicle, 1984.

Uncollected Short Stories

"Something That Happened," in *The Best American Short Stories 1979*, edited by Joyce Carol Oates and Shannon Ravenel.   Boston, Houghton Mifflin, 1979.
"Bess," in *Esquire* (New York), August, 1984.

*   *   *

Black Tickets, Jayne Anne Phillips's first major collection of short fiction, is a curious anthology, both irritating and impressive. Many of the stories end too quickly to permit a conventional readerly engagement. 16 of the 27 pieces are really sketches rather than stories—a few paragraphs of intensely wrought language and emphatic image. Primarily about love, alienated sexuality, and the street worlds of destitution, prostitution, and drug addiction, these are best understood as exercises in voice. They suggest a remarkable invention and a drive to articulate what is usually muted or unsaid. In places, they are truly dazzling. (See, for example, "Stripper," "Cheers," and "Happy.") But too often these compositions leave us with an impression of authorial self-consciousness, grotesqueness for its own sake. Phillips's more substantial achievements lie in some of the longer stories, where she seems less anxious to be poetic and more at ease with the rhythms of the lives she explores.

The best piece in the collection is "Home," a perfectly told story of complex family relationships. This wistful but pungent tale of mother-daughter empathy and disjunction focuses on the impasse at the heart of generational difference, as experienced by a rather ordinary but perceptive protagonist. In its telling, Phillips uses language that is modest and spare, appropriate to the commonplaces of familial suffering. Relations are drawn with a subtle counterpart, as when a daughter remarks, "It upsets my mother to see me naked; she looks at me so curiously, as though she didn't recognize my body," then later observes her mother: "She is so fragile, standing there, naked, with her small shoulders. Suddenly I am horribly frightened."

In the most effective stories (in addition to "Home," see "Souvenir" and "The Heavenly Animal"), Phillips slowly draws us down into the undertow of middle-class trauma—filial sexuality, divorce, gradual psychosis. The prose succeeds as we are pulled in by something beneath its surface.

With *Machine Dreams*, a full-length family chronicle, Phillips combines depth and resonance with the interest of alternating voices. The novel develops through a succession of storytellers whose narrative choices at first seem casual and unrelated. Autobiography, letters, and omniscient narration recount major and minor events in the history of the Hampson family through two generations, from the Depression to the early 1970's. The Hampsons, who live in a small town in West Virginia, lead apparently undistinguished lives—Jean and Mitch are unhappily married and just scraping by, Danner and her brother Billy share the usual childhood adventures and the indignities of adolescence. As representatives of any lower-middle-class American family of their time, these characters are familiar and conventional. But the varying inflections and mundane details of their stories, as they accumulate, suggest human experience that is profoundly troubling. What the story-tellers reveal are affiliated tragedies of powerlessness, the psychic wounds of post-war American culture.

Throughout the narrative, Phillips contrasts the promise of fulfillment with the insufficient lives of people whose most powerful experiences are in some way tied to machines. Mitch's fascination with things mechanical, with the technological possibilities of his time, leads him to open a concrete plant which the local economy cannot support. Jean realizes her dream of higher education, but her schooling is joyless, prompted by the failure of her husband's factory and the subsequent misery of their family life. Longing for connection, both Billy and Danner learn a makeshift sexuality in the cramped, confined quarters of automobiles. Cars, trucks, planes, trains, televisions, and radios punctuate the most significant events in this novel—but subtly, so that their presence signifies without disruption. Technology is a means for marking frustrated human desire: "Fuck was the word written all over basement walls of the old school; it was scrawled even on the big round pipes that were too hot to touch. Scrawled with crayon that melted and left a bright wax thickness, then a pale stain after the janitor scraped the texture off. There were ghostly fucks every few feet along the round steaming pipes; an angry, clinched word, wild." Phillips's skillful meshing of the mechanical and the human culminates in her final, devastating chapters on Viet Nam, in which she shows us the shattering of both machines and dreams and the awful impotence of what survives.

Machine Dreams is not a flawless work. The first half of the book moves slowly, and one chapter repeats information unnecessarily. But the varying voices of the Hampson family, rich with what cannot be spoken, are moving and provide an effective commentary on our most destructive cultural myths. Jayne Anne Phillips's first novel is a good one.

—Janis Butler Holm

PIERCY, Marge. American. Born in Detroit, Michigan, 31 March 1936. Educated at the University of Michigan, Ann Arbor (Hopwood Award, 1956, 1957), A.B. 1957; Northwestern University, Evanston, Illinois, M.A. 1958. Married Ira Wood (third marriage) in 1982. Instructor, Indiana University, Gary, 1960–62; Poet-in-Residence, University of Kansas, Lawrence, 1971; Visiting Lecturer, Thomas Jefferson College, Grand Valley State Colleges, Allendale, Michigan, 1975; staff member, Fine Arts Work Center, Provincetown, Massachusetts, 1976–77; Writer-in-Residence, College of the Holy Cross, Worcester, Massachusetts, 1976; Butler Professor of Letters, State University of New York, Buffalo, 1977; Elliston Professor of Poetry, University of Cincinnati, 1986. Member of the Board of Directors, 1982–85 and of the Advisory Board since 1985, Coordinating Council of Literary Magazines.

Recipient: Borestone Mountain award, 1968, 1974; National Endowment for the Arts grant, 1977; Rhode Island School of Design Faculty Association Medal, 1985. Agent: Lois Wallace, Wallace and Sheil Agency, 177 East 70th Street, New York, New York 10021. Address: Box 943, Wellfleet, Massachusetts 02667, U.S.A.

PUBLICATIONS

Novels

Going Down Fast. New York, Simon and Schuster, 1969.
Dance the Eagle to Sleep. New York, Doubleday, 1970; London, W.H. Allen, 1971.
Small Changes. New York, Doubleday, 1973.
Woman on the Edge of Time. New York, Knopf, 1976; London, Women's Press, 1979.
The High Cost of Living. New York, Harper, 1978; London, Women's Press, 1979.
Vida. New York, Summit, and London, Women's Press, 1980.
Braided Lives. New York, Summit, and London, Allen Lane, 1982.
Fly Away Home. New York, Summit, and London, Chatto and Windus, 1984.

Uncollected Short Stories

"Crossing over Jordan," in *Transatlantic Review* (London), Fall 1966.
"Love Me Tonight, God," in *Paris Review*, Summer 1968.
"A Dynastic Encounter," in *Aphra* (New York), Spring 1970.
"And I Went into the Garden of Love," in *Off Our Backs* (Washington, D.C.), Summer 1971.
"Do You Love Me?," in *Second Wave* (Cambridge, Massachusetts), vol. 1, no. 4, 1972.
"The Happiest Day of a Woman's Life," in *Works in Progress 7* (New York), 1972.
"Somebody Who Understands You," in *Moving Out* (Detroit), vol. 2, no. 2, 1972.
"Marriage Is a Matter of Give and Take," in *Boston Phoenix*, 3 July and 10 July 1973.
"Little Sister, Cat and Mouse," in *Second Wave* (Cambridge, Massachusetts), Fall 1973.
"God's Blood," in *Anon*, no. 8, 1974.
"Like a Great Door Closing Suddenly," in *Detroit Discovery*, March-April 1974.
"The Retreat," in *Provincetown Poets* (Provincetown, Massachusetts), vol. 2, nos. 2–3, 1976.
"What Can Be Had," in *Chrysalis 4* (San Diego, California), 1977.
"The Cowbird in the Eagles' Nest," in *Maenad*, Fall 1980.
"I Will Not Describe What I Did," in *Mother Jones* (San Francisco), February-March 1982.
"Spring in the Arboretum," in *Michigan Quarterly Review* (Ann Arbor), Winter 1982.
"Of Chilblains and Rotten Rutabagas," in *Lilith* (New York), Winter-Spring 1985.

Play

The Last White Class: A Play about Neighborhood Terror, with Ira Wood (produced Northampton, Massachusetts, 1978). Trumansburg, New York, Crossing Press, 1980.

Verse

Breaking Camp. Middletown, Connecticut, Wesleyan University Press, 1968.
Hard Loving. Middletown, Connecticut, Wesleyan University Press, 1969.
A Work of Artifice. Detroit, Red Hanrahan Press, 1970.
4-Telling, with others. Trumansburg, New York, Crossing Press, 1971.
When the Drought Broke. Santa Barbara, California, Unicorn Press, 1971.
To Be of Use. New York, Doubleday, 1973.
Living in the Open. New York, Knopf, 1976.
The Twelve-Spoked Wheel Flashing. New York, Knopf, 1978.
The Moon Is Always Female. New York, Knopf, 1980.
Circles on the Water: Selected Poems. New York, Knopf, 1982.
Stone, Paper, Knife. New York, Knopf, and London, Pandora Press, 1983.
My Mother's Body. New York, Knopf, and London, Pandora Press, 1985.

Recordings: *Laying Down the Tower*, Black Box, 1973; *Reading and Thoughts*, Everett Edwards, 1976; *At the Core*, Watershed, 1978.

Other

The Grand Coolie Damn. Boston, New England Free Press, 1970.
Parti-Colored Blocks for a Quilt. Ann Arbor, University of Michigan Press, 1982.

*

Bibliography: in *Contemporary American Women Writers: Narrative Strategies* edited by Catherine Rainwater and William J. Scheick, Lexington, University Press of Kentucky, 1985.

Critical Studies: "Marge Piercy: A Collage" by Nancy Scholar Zee, in *Oyez Review* (Berkeley, California), vol. 9, no. 1, 1975; *Ways of Knowing: Critical Essays on Marge Piercy* edited by Sue Walker and Eugenie Hamner, Mobile, Alabama, Negative Capability Press, 1986.

Marge Piercy comments:

Each of my novels appears to me a different miniature world, in which the style, the language appropriate to the characters, is worked out of my understanding of them and their universe of action and discourse. My intention is always appropriateness, and when I do what is usually seen as "fine writing," I do my best to strike it out. My impulse to autobiography is given ample play in my poetry, and thus has little reason to shape my novels. My novels divide into those which are placed in the present; those which are placed in speculative time; and those which occur entirely, or largely, in the past. My interest is always centered on the results of choice through time.

I start with a theme, and then work through character. Fiction is as old a habit of our species as poetry. It goes back to telling a tale, the first perceptions of pattern, and fiction is still about pattern in human life. For me, writing fiction issues from the impulse to tell the story of people who deserve to have their lives revealed, examined, clarified, to people who deserve to read good stories. To find ourselves spoken for in art gives dignity to our pain, our anger, our lust, our losses. I have been particularly although not exclusively concerned with the choices open to—or perceived to be open to—women

of various eras, races, and classes. I am one of the few contemporary American novelists consciously and constantly preoccupied with social class and the economic underpinnings of decision and consequence.

In the end, I suspect my novels find readers because they create full characters easy to enter, no matter how hard they might be for the reader to identify within actuality, and because I try to tell a good story.

*   *   *

Not satisfied to be only a chronicler of social revolution in the late 1960's and 1970's, though her facts about these times are compellingly accurate, too much an artist to write the domestic melodramas that infest newsstands, Marge Piercy is first of all interested in character and the relation of the individual to society. Her fiction is a tough, courageous, yet tender representation of individuals confronting oppression. What makes Piercy a fine writer, one of the best to use the contemporary as her milieu, is her understanding that the external world, society, is not the only oppressor. Oppression can be chosen by an act of will.

Piercy identifies the external oppressors: capitalism with its emphasis on possession of objects sets up institutions that foster objectness. For example, in marriage women are possessions to serve male needs, nuclear families are closed to sustenance from others; love is thus defined in this society as the cement that binds. Individuals in this system are powerless. Yet people can choose to be oppressed because they fear the freedom that other ways of living can bring.

Those who choose not to be oppressed in Piercy's work pay a tremendous price in relation to the society they reject. Piercy's main character is the outcast, who rejects her bonds, but who then must suffer the consequences. The lesbian lovers Beth and Wanda in *Small Changes*, both fugitives from exploitative marriages, must hide from the law. Connie in *Woman on the Edge of Time* is placed in a mental hospital, as is Joanna in *Dance the Eagle to Sleep*. In *Vida* the vibrant, charismatic title character, one of Piercy's most splendid creations, has been underground for ten years. Jill in *Braided Lives* faces illegal abortion alone. But this is not to say that Piercy's works are gloomy, naturalistic stories of defeated lives. Her novels sparkle with humor and shock with recognition; they show paths—and alley ways—to fulfillment; their intent is to give the reader the courage to try to throw off at least a small oppression or two.

Several aspects of Piercy's fiction are especially noteworthy. Her handling of contemporary settings is deft: parties bristle with the intrigue of subtle connections and betrayals; offices oppress with their hierarchies of bosses and secretaries; bedrooms too often are battlegrounds; homes are sometimes prisons where children hold moms prisoner. The utopian impulse to suggest alternative societies is strong in her work, most notably in *Woman on the Edge of Time* and *Dance the Eagle to Sleep*; in these experiments with science fiction, Piercy shows an idyllic utopia and harsh dystopia. Moreover, as a poet, Piercy reveals a sensitivity to the creative process and its ability to heal the problems she is decrying, to make "feelings real and articulate" as a character says in *Dance the Eagle*. In *Fly Away Home* Daria discovers a family of activists who are more loving than her biological family.

But it is her characterizations of men and women the reader remembers. Unlike some feminist writers, Piercy draws men who are as multi-dimensional, appealing, or odious as her women—that is, they are not stereotypes. Even her establishment men—bosses like George in *The High Cost of Living* or husbands like Leigh in *Vida*, Neil in *Small Changes*, and Ross in *Fly Away Home*—are not entirely wicked. Three other types of men recur in her novels. One is the man whose charismatic, brooding silences attract women, such as Rowley in *Going Down Fast*, Corey in *Dance the Eagle to Sleep*, Jackson in *Small Changes*, and Jackrabbit in *Woman on the Edge of Time*. The second is the counterculture activist who sells out to materialism, such as Asher in *Going Down Fast* and Leigh in *Vida*. Third is the marginal man who cannot function at all, such as Leon in *Going Down Fast* and Bernard in *The High Cost of Living*. In *Fly Away Home*, activist Tom Silver is Piercy's first truly liberated male—strong, tender, and masculine.

Her women are superb; few other contemporary novelists have presented the range of women Piercy has. And no one has given us a Miriam Berg or a Vida, outcasts yet free. Her other women characters are of three types. First, the victims of domesticity whose self-sacrifice for the comfort of men threatens to destroy them, such as Dorine and on occasion Miriam and Beth in *Small Changes* and Daria in *Fly Away Home*. Second, the victims of the plastic media-image of women, such as Gildina in *Woman on the Edge of Time*, Caroline in *Going Down Fast*, and Honor in *The High Cost of Living*. Finally, the alternative women Beth in *Small Changes*, Luciente in *Woman on the Edge of Time* and Jill in *Braided Lives* show new ways of being female.

What alternatives does Piercy offer to cultural oppression and demeaning human relationships? Her work suggests that people must make their own culture, through communal living away from the nuclear family and through work that does not add to human misery. Her most recent novel, *Fly Away Home*, states emphatically that the means to these ends are as various as there are people, but the end is the same: good love and good work.

—Kathryn Lee Seidel

PLANTE, David (Robert). American. Born in Providence, Rhode Island, 4 March 1940. Educated at Boston College, 1957–59, 1960–61, B.A. in French 1961; University of Louvain, Belgium, 1959–60. Teacher, English School, Rome, 1961–62; guide book writer, New York, 1962–64; teacher, Boston School of Modern Languages, 1964–65, and St. John's Preparatory School, Massachusetts, 1965–66; moved to England in 1966. Henfield Writing Fellow, University of East Anglia, Norwich, 1977; Writer-in-Residence, University of Tulsa, Oklahoma, 1979–82; Visiting Fellow, Cambridge University, 1984–85. Recipient: Arts Council bursary, 1977; American Academy award, 1983; Guggenheim grant, 1983. Lives in London. Agent: Deborah Rogers Ltd., 49 Blenheim Crescent, London W11 2EF, England; or, Georges Borchardt Inc., 136 East 57th Street, New York, New York 10022, U.S.A.

PUBLICATIONS

Novels

The Ghost of Henry James.   London, Macdonald, and Boston, Gambit, 1970.
Slides.   London, Macdonald, and Boston, Gambit, 1971.
Relatives.   London, Cape, 1972; New York, Avon, 1974.

The Darkness of the Body.   London, Cape, 1974.
Figures in Bright Air.   London, Gollancz, 1976.
The Francoeur Family.   London, Chatto and Windus, 1984.
  The Family.   London, Gollancz, and New York, Farrar Straus, 1978.
  The Country.   London, Gollancz, and New York, Atheneum, 1981.
  The Woods.   London, Gollancz, and New York, Atheneum, 1982.
The Foreigner.   London, Chatto and Windus, and New York, Atheneum, 1984.
The Catholic.   London, Chatto and Windus, 1985; New York, Atheneum, 1986.

Short Stories

Penguin Modern Stories 1, with others.   London, Penguin, 1969.

Uncollected Short Stories

"The Buried City," in *Transatlantic Review* (London), Spring 1967.
"The Tangled Centre," in *Modern Occasions* (Cambridge, Massachusetts), Spring 1971.
"Mr. Bonito," in *New Yorker*, 7 July 1980.
"The Accident," in *New Yorker*, 9 August 1982.
"The Student," in *Tri-Quarterly* (Evanston, Illinois), Fall 1982.
"Work," in *Prize Stories 1983: The O. Henry Awards*, edited by William Abrahams.   New York, Doubleday, 1983.
"Paris, 1959," in *New Yorker*, 4 June 1984.

Other

Difficult Women: A Memoir of Three.   London, Gollancz, and New York, Atheneum, 1983.

*

Bibliography: in *American Book Collector* (New York), November-December 1984.

Manuscript Collection: University of Tulsa, Oklahoma.

David Plante comments:

One of course always writes with an intention in mind, but it is what one cannot intend that is my fascination in writing. I know, all the while I am choosing my words, making as vivid as possible my descriptions, that there is something floating beneath my words and descriptions which has a will of its own, which sometimes rises up to meet my words and most often sinks away, and one can no more intend it than one can (to borrow an image from William James) turn up a bright light to see the darkness. The best one can do is allow it to well up, to give it space.

One is or isn't in touch with this sense, and one knows one is or isn't as matter of factly, as unmysteriously, as one knows one is happy or depressed. In touch with it, one writes "Mr. Stein woke to a room of shadows," and the sentence comes to life, evokes a deep world of associations, while out of touch with it the same sentence, "Mr. Stein woke to a room of shadows," is banal, dull, dead. The difference between good and bad writing is quite as simple as that.

How does one know one is in touch or not? One knows the signs, particular enough to be recognizable. For example, walking down a street most often I am unaware of the litter that's around me, or I am aware of it only to wish it weren't there. This past afternoon, however, walking along a sidewalk, I found myself studying, on the cement, a small printed target with three or four bullet holes blown through it, a match book printed with three spades, a page torn from a magazine, a parking lot ticket, an addressed envelope, and it seemed to me that everything I saw was indicative of much more than what it was—after all, just litter—was, because of its rich suggestiveness, beyond my imaginative grasp. I wanted to *write* about that target, match book, page, ticket, letter, and I wanted to with the similarly recognizable, similarly matter of fact urge one has when one wants to sneeze. *I was in touch with something.*

One is, at various times, *aware* that one has to sneeze, one is aware that one is sexually attracted to someone, one is aware that one must work and eat and sleep, and one is aware that there is a sense, informing things yet capable of being abstracted from them, which one hopes to be the essence of one's writing, which one hopes will bring one's words and one's world to life.

Sneezing is important, and making love is important, and working and eating and sleeping are important, and something else is also important, something longed for, something which is the whole purpose of my work. William James said: "It is, the reader will see, the reinstatement of the vague and inarticulate to its proper place in our mental life which I am so anxious to press on the attention."

*   *   *

Separateness and tension distinguish the writing of David Plante, his novels containing within themselves a complex balance of ambiguities. Beneath its unremarkable surface, his fiction seethes with an inner life sensed rather than observed, the books seeming to vibrate with half-heard resonances. The outer skin of the novels, crowded as they are with a succession of apparently trivial incidents, serves merely to mask the hidden conflicts waiting to explode, whose pulses travel upward to meet the consciousness of the reader.

The Ghost of Henry James explores the group identity of a family in New England, following through a series of abrupt transitions the subtle alteration in attitudes, the shifts of understanding that bind the members one to another despite their differences, and the trauma that ensues when the central character tries to break free of the rest. Lost without the family, he finds only madness and death, but from it comes a transformation and a re-ordering of the other lives as his ghostly presence pervades the final scenes. Plante pays homage to the author of *The Turn of the Screw*, both in his evocation of sinister New England landscapes and in a style which distinguishes the text as a separate entity from what it describes. *Slides* pursues the same theme, the group this time consisting of adolescent friends, and the violent climax an attempted suicide. The shade of Hawthorne is summoned here, the gothic aspect of his writings recreated as Plante hints subtly at the conflict between freedom and unity, the sexuality repressed beneath an innate puritanism, in a carefully weighted language that throbs behind the matter-of-fact conversations and weekend outings that make up the action of the book.

The Darkness of the Body and *Figures in Bright Air* reveal a deeper probing beneath the surface. In them, Plante undertakes a detailed portrayal of obsessive states of mind, presenting through the charged love-hate relationships of his characters the destructive force of physical love, the body's threat to the innerness of the beloved, the need for the personality to retain separateness and distance. Lovemaking is shown

as a death-struggle, a falling into a black pit. The world itself is broken down to intensely potent fragments, individuals perceived as geometric shapes that clash against each other. Elements of air and stone are balanced in opposition, mirrors of the narrator's inward struggle where art, like life, is set the incompatible tasks of all-embracing vision and the reduction of everything to nothing. Plante's finely poised language, his matching of stillness with explosive action, invest the surface with its necessary undercurrents of tension and release. In these works in particular, he appears to be striving towards the ideal of Flaubert, and later of Robbe-Grillet, of the perfect irreducible text as a self-sufficient entity from which nothing can be removed.

In his trilogy on the Francoeur family—*The Family*, *The Country*, and *The Woods*—Plante's expression is less elusive than before, drawing directly from his personal experience. *The Country* especially veers close to documentary at times, representing the author's sense of himself as a native of two countries, his French-speaking birthplace on Rhode Island, and the rest of the United States. His central character, Daniel Francoeur, discovers through the contact of the last days with his dying father an affinity between them, and beyond it a kinship with the father's long-dead Indian ancestors: "My father was born, as I was, among the ghosts of a small community of people of strange blood. They were people who saw that they were born in darkness and would die in darkness, and who accepted that. They spoke, in their old French, in whispers, in the churchyard, among the gravestones, in the snow, and with them, silent, were squaws with papooses on their backs, and the woods began beyond the last row of gravestones. They were strange to me, and yet they were not strange."

Daniel's transformation, the slow change that takes place in him as he witnesses the death of his father and cares for his ageing mother, is movingly and simply described. Plante builds up through meetings and casual conversation the relationship between parents and brothers, the feuds and differences that strain the underlying unity. The brooding presence of the forest permeates the novel, but *The Country* is among the clearest of its author's works. Daniel's mother above all, with her hatred of sex and childbirth, explains much of the meaning behind the "destructive love" theme in previous writings.

With *The Woods* Plante forsakes documentary techniques, returning to a third-person narrative that explores Daniel's inner world, culminating in his adolescent lovemaking, again visualized as a violation. This approach is continued with *The Foreigner* and *The Catholic*. More "fictionalized" than some of the Francoeur trilogy, these novels contain a greater degree of violence and erotic force which blasts more often to the surface. Here, as in earlier works, the core of the book lies almost out of sight beneath the text, a white-hot magma that simmers under the skin.

—Geoff Sadler

PLUNKETT, James. Irish. Born James Plunkett Kelly in Dublin, 21 May 1920. Educated at Synge Street Christian Brothers School, Dublin; Dublin College of Music. Married Valerie Koblitz in 1945; one daughter and three sons. Branch secretary, Workers Union of Ireland, 1946–55; assistant head of drama, Radio Eireann, Dublin, 1955–60; producer-director 1961–68, head of features, 1969–71, and senior producer

1974–85, Radio Telefís Eireann (Irish Television), Dublin. Council member, Society of Irish Playwrights, 1984–85. Recipient: Irish Television award, 1964, 1966; *Yorkshire Post* award, 1969. Member, 1970, and President, 1980–82, Irish Academy of Letters; Toscaire (council member), Aosdana, 1981–85. Agent: A.D. Peters, 10 Buckingham Street, London WC2N 6BU, England. Address: Collakeagh, Old Long Hill, Kilmacanogue, County Wicklow, Ireland.

PUBLICATIONS

Novels

Strumpet City. London, Hutchinson, and New York, Delacorte Press, 1969.
The Gems She Wore: A Book of Irish Places. London, Hutchinson, 1972; New York, Holt Rinehart, 1973.
Farewell Companions. London, Hutchinson, 1977; New York, Coward McCann, 1978.

Short Stories

The Trusting and the Maimed, and Other Irish Stories. New York, Devin Adair, 1955; London, Hutchinson, 1959.
Collected Short Stories. Dublin, Poolbeg Press, 1977.

Plays

Homecoming (broadcast, 1954). Published in *The Bell* (Dublin), June 1954.
Big Jim (broadcast, 1954). Dublin, O'Donnell, 1955.
The Risen People (produced Dublin, 1958; London, 1959; New York, 1978). Dublin, Co-op, 1978.

Radio Plays: *Dublin Fusilier*, 1952; *Mercy*, 1953; *Homecoming*, 1954; *Big Jim*, 1954; *Farewell Harper*, 1956.

Television Plays and Programs: *Memory Harbour*, 1963; *The Life and Times of Jimmy O'Dea*, 1964; *Portrait of a Poet*, 1965; *When Do You Die, Friend?*, 1966; *The Great O'Neill*, 1966; *Inis Fail*, 1971; *The State of the Nation*, 1972; *A Dash of Genius*, 1979; *That Solitary Man*, 1979; *The Wicklow Way*, 1980; *I Hear You Calling Me* (on John McCormack), 1984; *The Eagles and the Trumpets*, 1984; *One Man in His Time* (on Cyril Cusack), 1985.

*

Critical Studies: *Dublin and the Drama of Larkinism* by Godeleine Carpentier, Lille, France, Université de Lille, 1975; *Great Hatred, Little Room: The Irish Historical Novel* by James Cahalan, Dublin, Gill and Macmillan, 1984.

*   *   *

Of his native Dublin, the city which forms the backdrop to his historical novel *Strumpet City*, James Plunkett has written: "Despite its tensions and its tragedies, Dublin was a good city to grow up in. The sea was at its feet, its Georgian buildings gave it nobility, its squares and its expanses of water made it a place of openness and light and air." Something of that affection is immediately apparent in this first novel—and, indeed, Dublin appears as a character in its own right in just about everything he has written—for unlike James Joyce Plunkett did not feel compelled to leave his native city in order to put it into perspective.

Set in the angry years leading to the First World War, *Strumpet City*'s first concern is with the down-trodden working classes; in particular Plunkett deals with the attempts of the trades union movement to win better conditions for its members. Standing like a colossus above his fellow men is the figure of Barney Mulhall, a trades union leader whom Plunkett based upon Barney Conway, in real life the right-hand man of the political activist Jim Larkin. The other characters are no less firmly drawn and each is created in the likeness of men whom Plunkett, himself once a trades union official, had known in Dublin: Fitz, the idealistic foreman who joins the strike, Pat his friend and sage adviser, Keever who turns traitor, and perhaps the most colourful of them all, "Rashers" Tierney, the poorest of the poor.

Although *Strumpet City* finds its truest voice in Plunkett's vivid creation of Dublin working-class life, it does not ignore other strata of society. The middle-class world of the Bradshaws is faithfully reproduced, as is the claustrophobic life led by the priests Fathers Giffley and O'Connor, but the reader senses that although the facts of their existences are carefully enough drawn, Plunkett's heart is not in these creations. It is only when he returns to the grit and the grime of the workers' tenements that Plunkett is on sure ground. But for all that his sympathies are with the meek and the down-trodden, and for all that he writes about their lives with humanity and compassion, *Strumpet City* offers no easy answers. As each character's story draws to its conclusion, all we are left with is Plunkett's faith in the essential decency of people if only they can escape from the snare of the human condition.

In *Farewell Companions* Plunkett moves ahead in time to the inter-war years. A younger generation has arrived to come to terms with a country which has broken its shackles with Britain: they have to face up to, and come to terms with, a different set of rules. As in its predecessor, politics are never far away from the main narrative line but here the arguments are polarised between the demands of sentimental nationalism and the airier ideals of international socialism. Tim McDonagh, the novel's central character, is based loosely on Plunkett himself, and his story plots the journey from the old world occupied by his parent's generation to the hopes and fears of an independent Ireland. Once again, the description of Dublin and the delineation of Irish working-class life is faultless, equalled only by Plunkett's uncanny ability to create a gallery of vivid characters, each with a story to tell. Given such a broad tapestry it is not surprising perhaps to discover some loose threads, and for many readers the novel's ending will come as an anticlimax. Unable to come to terms with the demands of industrial life, McDonagh opts out of the real world and takes holy orders, a limp conclusion that is out of keeping with the speculative intent of the first half of the novel.

No understanding of the fictional world created by James Plunkett is complete without reading his collection of short stories, *The Trusting and the Maimed*, the title story in particular giving a clue to the success of Plunkett's technique: the use of multiple voices and film-like scenes as he cuts from one character, one situation, one time, to another.

—Trevor Royle

POHL, Frederik. American. Born in New York City, 26 November 1919. Served in the United States Air Force, in the USA and Italy, 1943–45: Sergeant. Married 1) Doris Baumgardt in 1940 (divorced, 1944); 2) Dorothy LesTina in 1945 (divorced, 1947); 3) the writer Judith Merril in 1949 (divorced, 1953), one daughter; 4) Carol Metcalf Ulf in 1952 (divorced, 1981), two sons (one deceased) and one daughter; 5) Elizabeth Anne Hull in 1984. Editor, Popular Publications, New York, 1939–43; copywriter, Thwing and Altman, New York, 1946; book editor and associate circulation manager, Popular Science Publication Company, New York, 1946–49; literary agent, New York, 1949–53; features editor, later editor, *If*, New York, 1959–70; editor, Galaxy Publishing Company, New York, 1961–69; executive editor, Ace Books, New York, 1971–72; science fiction editor, Bantam Books, New York, 1973–79. Since 1976, contributing editor, *Algol*, New York. President, Science Fiction Writers of America, 1974–76; President, World SF, 1980–82 and current Vice-President (West); Mid-West Area Chair, Authors Guild of America. Recipient: Edward E. Smith Memorial Award, 1966; Hugo Award, for editing, 1966, 1967, 1968, for fiction, 1973, 1978; *Locus* award, 1973, 1978; Nebula Award, 1976, 1977; John W. Campbell Memorial Award, 1978, 1985; Prix Apollo (France), 1979; American Book Award, 1980. Guest of Honor, World Science Fiction Convention, 1972; Fellow, American Association for the Advancement of Science. Agent: Curtis Brown, 10 Astor Place, New York, New York 10003; or, Leslie Flood, Carnell Literary Agency, Rowneybury Bungalow, near Old Harlow, Essex CM20 2EX, England. Address: 855 South Harvard Drive, Palatine, Illinois 60067, U.S.A.

PUBLICATIONS

Novels

The Space Merchants, with C.M. Kornbluth.   New York, Ballantine, 1953; London, Heinemann, 1955.
Search the Sky, with C.M. Kornbluth.   New York, Ballantine, 1954; London, Digit, 1960; revised edition (by Pohl only), New York, Baen, 1985.
Preferred Risk (as Edson McCann, with Lester del Rey).   New York, Simon and Schuster, 1955; London, Methuen, 1983.
Gladiator-at-Law, with C.M. Kornbluth.   New York, Ballantine, 1955; London, Digit, 1958.
A Town Is Drowning, with C.M. Kornbluth.   New York, Ballantine, 1955; London, Digit, 1960.
Presidential Year, with C.M. Kornbluth.   New York, Ballantine, 1956.
Sorority House (as Jordan Park, with C.M. Kornbluth).   New York, Lion, 1956.
The God of Channel 1 (as Donald Stacy).   New York, Ballantine, 1956.
Turn the Tigers Loose, with Walter Lasly.   New York, Ballantine, 1956.
Edge of the City (novelization of screenplay).   New York, Ballantine, 1957.
Slave Ship.   New York, Ballantine, 1957; London, Dobson, 1961.
Wolfbane, with C.M. Kornbluth.   New York, Ballantine, 1959; London, Gollancz, 1961.
Drunkard's Walk.   New York, Ballantine, 1960; revised edition, London, Gollancz, 1961.
The Starchild Trilogy, with Jack Williamson.   New York, Doubleday, 1977; London, Penguin, 1980.
   The Reefs of Space.   New York, Ballantine, 1964; London, Dobson, 1965.

Starchild.   New York, Ballantine, 1965; London, Dobson, 1966.
Rogue Star.   New York, Ballantine, 1969; London, Dobson, 1972.
A Plague of Pythons.   New York, Ballantine, 1965; London, Gollancz, 1966; revised edition, as *Demon in the Skull*, New York, DAW, 1984.
The Age of the Pussyfoot.   New York, Trident Press, 1969; London, Gollancz, 1970.
Farthest Star, with Jack Williamson.   New York, Ballantine, 1975; London, Pan, 1976.
Man Plus.   New York, Random House, and London, Gollancz, 1976.
Gateway.   New York, St. Martin's Press, and London, Gollancz, 1977.
Jem: The Making of a Utopia.   New York, St. Martin's Press, and London, Gollancz, 1979.
Beyond the Blue Event Horizon.   New York, Ballantine, and London, Gollancz, 1980.
The Cool War.   New York, Ballantine, and London, Gollancz, 1981.
Starburst.   New York, Ballantine, and London, Gollancz, 1982.
Syzygy.   New York, Bantam, 1982.
Wall Around a Star, with Jack Williamson.   New York, Ballantine, 1983.
Midas World.   New York, St. Martin's Press, and London, Gollancz, 1983.
Heechee Rendezvous.   New York, Ballantine, and London, Gollancz, 1984.
The Years of the City.   New York, Simon and Schuster, 1984; London, Gollancz, 1985.
The Merchants' War.   New York, St. Martin's Press, 1984; London, Gollancz, 1985.
Black Star Rising.   New York, Ballantine, 1985.

Short Stories

Danger Moon (as James MacCreigh).   Sydney, American Science Fiction, 1953.
Alternating Currents.   New York, Ballantine, 1956; London, Penguin, 1966.
The Case Against Tomorrow.   New York, Ballantine, 1957.
Tomorrow Times Seven.   New York, Ballantine, 1959.
The Man Who Ate the World.   New York, Ballantine, 1960; London, Panther, 1979.
Turn Left at Thursday.   New York, Ballantine, 1961.
The Wonder Effect, with C.M. Kornbluth.   New York, Ballantine, 1962; London, Gollancz, 1967; revised edition, as *Critical Mass*, New York, Bantam, 1977.
The Abominable Earthman.   New York, Ballantine, 1963.
The Frederik Pohl Omnibus.   London, Gollancz, 1966; selection, as *Survival Kit*, London, Panther, 1979.
Digits and Dastards (includes essays).   New York, Ballantine, 1966; London, Dobson, 1968.
Day Million.   New York, Ballantine, 1970; London, Gollancz, 1971.
The Gold at Starbow's End.   New York, Ballantine, 1972; London, Gollancz, 1973.
The Best of Frederik Pohl, edited by Lester del Rey.   New York, Doubleday, 1975; London, Sidgwick and Jackson, 1977.
In the Problem Pit.   New York, Bantam, and London, Corgi, 1976.
The Early Pohl.   New York, Doubleday, 1976; London, Dobson, 1980.

Planets Three.   New York, Berkley, 1982.
Pohlstars.   New York, Ballantine, 1984; London, Gollancz, 1986.

Uncollected Short Stories

"The Kindly Isle," in *Isaac Asimov's Science Fiction Magazine* (New York), November 1984.
"Criticality," in *Analog* (New York), December 1984.
"The Saved," in *Playboy* (Chicago), February 1985.

Other

Undersea Quest [*Fleet, City*] (for children), with Jack Williamson.   New York, Gnome Press, 3 vols., 1954–58; London, Dobson, 3 vols., 1966–68.
Tiberius (biography; as Ernst Mason).   New York, Ballantine, 1960.
Practical Politics 1972.   New York, Ballantine, 1971.
The Way the Future Was: A Memoir.   New York, Ballantine, 1978; London, Gollancz, 1979.
Science Fiction: Studies in Film, with Frederik Pohl IV.   New York, Ace, 1981.

Editor, *Beyond the End of Time*.   New York, Permabooks, 1952.
Editor, *Shadow of Tomorrow*.   New York, Permabooks, 1953.
Editor, *Star Science Fiction Stories 1–6*.   New York, Ballantine, 6 vols., 1953–59; vols. 1 and 2, London, Boardman, 1954–55.
Editor, *Assignment in Tomorrow*.   New York, Hanover House, 1954.
Editor, *Star Short Novels*.   New York, Ballantine, 1954.
Editor, *Star of Stars*.   New York, Doubleday, 1960; as *Star Fourteen*, London, Whiting and Wheaton, 1966.
Editor, *The Expert Dreamers*.   New York, Doubleday, 1962; London, Gollancz, 1963.
Editor, *Time Waits for Winthrop and Four Other Short Novels from Galaxy*.   New York, Doubleday, 1962.
Editor, *The Seventh* [through *Eleventh*] *Galaxy Reader*.   New York, Doubleday, 5 vols., 1964–69; *Seventh* through *Tenth*, London, Gollancz, 4 vols., 1965–68; *Eighth*, as *Final Encounter*, New York, Curtis, 1970; *Tenth*, as *Door to Anywhere*, New York, Curtis, 1970.
Editor, *The If Reader of Science Fiction*.   New York, Doubleday, 1966; London, Whiting and Wheaton, 1967; second volume, New York, Doubleday, 1968.
Editor, *Nightmare Age*.   New York, Ballantine, 1970.
Editor, *The Best Science Fiction for 1972*.   New York, Ace, 1972.
Editor, with Carol Pohl, *Science Fiction: The Great Years*.   New York, Ace, 1973; London, Gollancz, 1974; 2nd volume, Ace, 1976.
Editor, with Carol Pohl, *Jupiter*.   New York, Ballantine, 1973.
Editor, *The Science Fiction Roll of Honor*. New York, Random House, 1975.
Editor, with Carol Pohl, *Science Fiction Discoveries*.   New York, Bantam, 1976.
Editor, *The Best of C.M. Kornbluth*.   New York, Doubleday, 1976.
Editor, with Martin H. Greenberg and Joseph D. Olander, *Science Fiction of the 40's*.   New York, Avon, 1978.
Editor, with Martin H. Greenberg and Joseph D. Olander, *Galaxy: Thirty Years of Innovative Science Fiction*.

Chicago, Playboy Press, 1980; 2nd volume, New York, Ace, 1981.
Editor, *Nebula Winners 14*.   New York, Harper, 1980; London, W.H. Allen, 1981.
Editor, with Martin H. Greenberg and Joseph D. Olander, *The Great Science Fiction Series*.   New York, Harper, 1980.
Editor, *Yesterday's Tomorrows: Favorite Stories from Forty Years as a Science Fiction Editor*.   New York, Berkley, 1982.

*

Manuscript Collection: Syracuse University Library, New York.

Critical Study: *New Maps of Hell* by Kingsley Amis. New York, Harcourt Brace, 1960; London, Gollancz, 1961.

Frederik Pohl comments:

My principal work has been in science fiction, and within that field in the special kind of science fiction best described as cautionary literature. Now that the world has been well alerted to such problems as pollution, overpopulation, and so on—largely, in the first instance, by science-fiction stories—it is old hat to say that we must look to the long-range consequences of our society and technology. My stories have often touched on such themes long before they were fashionable.

Apart from argument, I have been interested in exploring all the possible range of alternate futures for the human race. Some of the work in which I take most pride—short stories like *Day Million*, novels like *Wolfbane*—are not at all cautionary in the sense that they call attention to dangerous current trends; instead, they attempt to show some of the stranger, but quite possible, directions the human world-line may take.

However, no writer, myself least of all, writes very attractively when he writes according to a coldblooded plan. I don't set out to write either political agitprop or think-tank scenarios; I only attempt to think out the consequences of what seem to me to be interesting developments, to set living characters in such worlds and then to let them live their lives.

*   *   *

Frederik Pohl has distinguished himself both as one of the most prolific writers of science fiction and as one of its most explicit promoters. The two distinctions seem to stem from his firm didactic concern with science fiction as a social early warning system. To write science fiction, he says, "is to try to look ahead to see not only what is likely to fall upon us by way of science and technology, but to see what the side effects and the consequences and the second and third order derivatives of these things will be" (MLA Forum on Science Fiction, December 1968). In a Shavian catalogue of prefaces and postscripts, Pohl repeats and amplifies his fictional purpose "to question everything . . . in the light of what Harlow Shepley calls the 'View from a distant star.'"

The explicit didactic purpose is borne out by his fiction, which historically falls in line with that of Wells, Huxley, and Hoyle as a kind of allegorical social satire, earth-bound rather than space-speculative. His major novels are concerned with both the special consequences of particular trends in the 20th-century and the general effects of our current population expansion and waste of natural resources. Thus, *Space Merchants* and *Gladiator-at-Law* are, respectively, biting denunciations of 20th-century commercial advertising and corporation monopoly; unrestricted expansion of advertising agencies and super-corporations permits them to become the new power blocs of the 21st century, perverting the democratic process and lowering the quality of life by pandering to society's greed for immediate physical gratification.

In *Reefs of Space* and *Starchild* Pohl looks further ahead. The earth is teeming with 13 billion human beings necessarily organised under an entire totalitarian, computer-directed Plan of Man which has the sole aim of keeping a balance of resources. Private liberty has vanished because previous centuries have wasted natural resources only to turn the earth into a closed-system in which there still "isn't enough to go round." *The Age of the Pussyfoot* takes the same distant view but focuses more closely on the quality of personal life in a society so dependent on computers that it is, in fact, symbiotic with them. Instant information and immediate self-indulgence are possible, yet no attempt has been made to solve the problems of poverty, war, and cultural triviality.

Throughout Pohl's work runs the paradoxical theme that, while we progress technologically, we don't improve the quality of living, we don't remove the inequalities of material possession, and we don't improve the prospects of human creativity and fulfilment. The only answer is the choice also expounded by Hoyle: we either stay in an entirely closed, programmed system or we evolve to another level.

Although most of Pohl's novels are written with collaborators, there is no discernible difference in the quality of writing of the collaborated and independent work. What emerges is a profoundly disturbing sense of reality, truth, and honesty which is Swiftian in its impact. In Pohl's hands, science fiction is a weapon to be used vigorously in defence of humanity. As a social critic, Pohl must rank high. In addition, however, as his *Underseas* novels indicate, he is a first-rate storyteller who never lets the message wholly take over the medium.

—Frederick Bowers

POTOK, Chaim. American. Born Herman Harold Potok in the Bronx, New York, 17 February 1929. Educated at orthodox Jewish schools; Yeshiva University, New York, 1946–50, B.A. (summa cum laude), 1950; Jewish Theological Seminary, New York, 1950–54, M.H.L. and rabbinic ordination 1954; University of Pennsylvania, Philadelphia, 1959–65, Ph.D. in philosophy 1965. Served as a chaplain in the United States Army in Korea, 1955–56: Lieutenant. Married Adena Sara Mosevitsky in 1958; two daughters and one son. National director of Leaders Training Fellowship, Jewish Theological Seminary, 1954–55; director, Camp Ramah, Ojai, California, 1957–59; Instructor, University of Judaism, Los Angeles, 1957–59; Scholar-in-Residence, Har Zion Temple, Philadelphia, 1959–63; member of the Teachers' Institute faculty, Jewish Theological Seminary, 1964–65; managing editor, *Conservative Judaism*, New York, 1964–65. Associate editor, 1965, editor-in-chief, 1966–74, and since 1974, special projects editor, Jewish Publication Society, Philadelphia. Lived in Israel, 1973–77. Visiting Professor of Philosophy, University of Pennsylvania, 1983, and Bryn Mawr College, Pennsylvania, 1985. Recipient: Wallant Award, 1968. Address: 20 Berwick Street, Merion, Pennsylvania 19131, U.S.A.

PUBLICATIONS

Novels

The Chosen. New York, Simon and Schuster, and London, Heinemann, 1967.

The Promise. New York, Knopf, 1969; London, Heinemann, 1970.
My Name Is Asher Lev. New York, Knopf, and London, Heinemann, 1972.
In the Beginning. New York, Knopf, 1975; London, Heinemann, 1976.
The Book of Lights. New York, Knopf, 1981; London, Heinemann, 1982.
Davita's Harp. New York, Knopf, 1985.

Uncollected Short Stories

"The Dark Place Inside," in *Dimensions in American Judaism* (New York), Fall 1964.
"The Cats of 37 Alfasi Street," in *American Judaism* (New York), Fall 1966.
"Miracles for a Broken Planet," in *McCall's* (New York), December 1972.
"The Fallen," in *Hadassah* (New York), December 1973.
"Reflections on a Bronx Street," in *May My Words Feed Others*, edited by Chayym Zeldis. Cranbury, New Jersey, A.S. Barnes, 1974.
"A Tale of Two Soldiers," in *Ladies Home Journal* (New York), December 1981.
"The Gifts of Andrea," in *Seventeen* (New York), October 1982.

Other

Jewish Ethics (pamphlet series). New York, Leaders Training Fellowship, 14 vols., 1964–69.
The Jew Confronts Himself in American Literature. Hales Corners, Wisconsin, Sacred Heart School of Theology, 1975.
Wanderings: Chaim Potok's History of the Jews. New York, Knopf, and London, Hutchinson, 1978.
Ethical Living for a Modern World. New York, Jewish Theological Seminary of America, 1985.

*

Critical Studies: "Culture Confrontation in Urban America: A Writer's Beginnings" by Potok, in *Literature and the Urban Experience* edited by Michael C. Jaye and Ann C. Watts, New Brunswick, New Jersey, Rutgers University Press, 1981; article by S. Lillian Kremer, in *Twentieth-Century American-Jewish Fiction Writers* edited by Daniel Walden, Detroit, Gale, 1984.

*   *   *

In the crowded field of Jewish-American fiction, the novelist Chaim Potok is remarkable for his persistent, intense analysis of contemporary Jews and Judaism. The question underlying virtually everything he publishes is how traditional Judaism in all its forms relates to the modern world, and each of his young male protagonists struggles to make his Jewish heritage somehow fit the reality of his own life and circumstances. In his latest book, a young female protagonist is involved in a similar conflict.

The Chosen is his first novel and perhaps still his best. The plot charts the relationship between Reuven Malter, the teenage son of a progressive or scientific Talmudic scholar at a Brooklyn yeshiva, and Danny Saunders, the son of a Hassidic rabbi, which begins in hate and ends in close friendship. Reuven, who narrates the story, slowly comes to understand the somewhat alien Hassidic world of his friend and, in particular, the gulf of silence which has been deliberately imposed by the rabbi between himself and his son. Ironically, Danny, a remarkably gifted Talmudic scholar and heir to his father's position of *tzaddik* (spiritual leader) to his people, eventually chooses to study psychology in a secular graduate school while Reuven, the secularist, studies to be a rabbi.

A sequel entitled *The Promise* continues with the story of Reuven's yeshiva training and further develops Potok's interest in Hassidism, as Reuven attempts to formulate his own identity as a Jew somewhere between intolerant Hassidic zealots and secular humanists such as Abraham Gordon, who treasures ritual but cannot accept theology. The plot centers on the evolving case of Gordon's son Michael, who is treated by Danny Saunders, now a clinical psychologist, and once again involves intense father-son relationships.

In *My Name Is Asher Lev* the protagonist himself is Hassidic, the son of a Brooklyn-based emissary of a Landovian Rebbe. Asher must break away from his roots in order to become an artist—whose masterpieces turn out to be two Crucifixions. Potok returns to his favorite subject of theological scholarship in *In the Beginning*. David Lurie is the son of a successful real estate broker and militant Zionist leader (once again, in Brooklyn), who organizes the immigration of friends and family from Poland but who loses his fortune in the Depression. Just as the Hassidic Danny Saunders had shifted his awesome intellectual powers from the study of Talmud to the secular field of psychology, David, another child prodigy and extraordinary yeshiva student, develops an interest in "secular" Bible study. David's is an even more shocking and scandalous shift, since the field was pioneered by German, Gentile scholars and since he announces his intention to pursue this line when the horrors of the Holocaust (which has claimed members of his own family in Europe) are fresh on everyone's mind.

In his works Potok continually relates Jewish sacred texts to contemporary experience in a variety of ways, and *The Book of Lights* provides the most striking example. In this novel, Gershon Loran, who grows up in the midst of family tragedy, turns from the terror of World War II to the study of the Kabbalah (Jewish mysticism). His roommate turns out to be the guilt-ridden son of a Jewish physicist who helped to develop the atomic bomb. In contrasting the "light" of the Kabbalah with that of the bomb, Potok strives to develop universal moral concerns in this most ambitious novel. Finally, the protagonist of *Davita's Harp*, the daughter of Communist parents, after considerable suffering and confusion, reclaims her Jewish heritage (but then, ironically, finds sexual discrimination in the yeshiva she attends).

Obviously Potok's concerns are consistently philosophical (or theological) and consistently ethnic. It is as though he has set out to analyze and explain every aspect of Judaism both to society at large and to American Jews themselves, always moving from the traditional and narrowly defined aspects of Jewish religion and culture to their broad implications for the modern world. His enormous ambition in carrying out this task is also evident in his monumental but flawed popular history of the Jews entitled *Wanderings*.

Potok's novels from first to last are hampered by a mediocre writing style, and they deal with a relatively narrow range of human experience. Dialogue sounds unnatural, hopelessly "academic." Plots unravel tediously. Potok's "good students" sometimes seem too good to be true. For example, David Lurie (*In the Beginning*) is almost unbearably earnest and solemn, a more extreme version of the studious Reuven Malter introduced in *The Chosen*. Potok is capable of portraying interesting human relationships, as in the Reuven-Danny friendship and

the parallel father-son relationships in his first novel. However, his continuing popularity with a certain dedicated readership is probably not attributable to his skill at creating characters, plots, or dialogue. Sometimes Potok creates characters that seem flat and uninteresting, but in working with ideas and cultural traditions, he confronts those ambiguities and internal conflicts that most engage the mind of the reader. The controlling consciousness in a typical Potok novel may be described as ascetic, generous, intellectually uncompromising.

Potok has been accused of presenting a sentimentalized version of Judaism in his works, but this criticism is misleading. He does not shy away from factionalism and doctrinal disputes, or from the misunderstanding and even hatred that they generate. The problem is that Potok seems fully at ease with his narrative art only when he is describing the lesson in a yeshiva classroom or a philosophical dialogue. The further he drifts away from the lesson, the less convincing he becomes, and he practically ignores some areas of human experience that have least to do with intellectual or religious perceptions. Potok is not for everyone, but it is heartening that such a novelist can maintain a certain popularity in contemporary American fiction.

—Clinton Machann

POWELL, Anthony (Dymoke). British. Born in London, 21 December 1905. Educated at Eton College; Balliol College, Oxford, M.A. Served in the Welch Regiment, 1939–41, and in the Army Intelligence Corps, 1941–45: Major; Order of the White Lion, Czechoslovakia; Order of Leopold II, Belgium; Oaken Crown and Croix de Guerre, Luxembourg. Married the writer Lady Violet Pakenham in 1934; two sons. Worked for Duckworth, publishers, London, 1926–35; scriptwriter for Warner Brothers of Great Britain, 1936; full-time writer from 1936; literary editor, *Punch*, London, 1953–58; reviewer for the *Daily Telegraph*, *Times Literary Supplement*, and other London papers. Trustee, National Portrait Gallery, London, 1962–76. Recipient: James Tait Black Memorial Prize, 1958; W.H. Smith Literary Award, 1974; *Hudson Review* Bennett Prize, 1984; Ingersoll Foundation Eliot Award, 1984. D.Litt.: University of Sussex, Brighton, 1971; University of Leicester, 1976; University of Kent, Canterbury, 1976; Oxford University, 1980; Bristol University, 1982. Honorary Fellow, Balliol College, 1974, and Modern Language Association (USA), 1981; Honorary Member, American Academy, 1977. C.B.E. (Commander, Order of the British Empire), 1956. Address: The Chantry, near Frome, Somerset, England.

PUBLICATIONS

Novels

Afternoon Men. London, Duckworth, 1931; New York, Holt, 1932.
Venusberg. London, Duckworth, 1932; with *Agents and Patients*, New York, Periscope Holliday, 1952.
From a View to a Death. London, Duckworth, 1933; as *Mr. Zouch: Superman: From a View to a Death*, New York, Vanguard Press, 1934.
Agents and Patients. London, Duckworth, 1936; with *Venusberg*, New York, Periscope Holliday, 1952.

What's Become of Waring. London, Cassell, 1939; Boston, Little Brown, 1963.
A Dance to the Music of Time:
  A Question of Upbringing. London, Heinemann, and New York, Scribner, 1951.
  A Buyer's Market. London, Heinemann, 1952; New York, Scribner, 1953.
  The Acceptance World. London, Heinemann, 1955; New York, Farrar Straus, 1956.
  At Lady Molly's. London, Heinemann, 1957; Boston, Little Brown, 1958.
  Casanova's Chinese Restaurant. London, Heinemann, and Boston, Little Brown, 1960.
  The Kindly Ones. London, Heinemann, and Boston, Little Brown, 1962.
  The Valley of Bones. London, Heinemann, and Boston, Little Brown, 1964.
  The Soldier's Art. London, Heinemann, and Boston, Little Brown, 1966.
  The Military Philosophers. London, Heinemann, 1968; Boston, Little Brown, 1969.
  Books Do Furnish a Room. London, Heinemann, and Boston, Little Brown, 1971.
  Temporary Kings. London, Heinemann, and Boston, Little Brown, 1973.
  Hearing Secret Harmonies. London, Heinemann, 1975; Boston, Little Brown, 1976.
O, How the Wheel Becomes It! London, Heinemann, and New York, Holt Rinehart, 1983.
The Fisher King. London, Heinemann, 1986.

Uncollected Short Story

"A Reference for Mellors," in *Winter's Tales 12*, edited by A.D. Maclean. London, Macmillan, and New York, St. Martin's Press, 1966.

Plays

Two Plays: The Garden God, and The Rest I'll Whistle. London, Heinemann, 1971; Boston, Little Brown, 1972.

Verse

Caledonia: A Fragment. Privately printed, 1934.

Other

John Aubrey and His Friends. London, Heinemann, and New York, Scribner, 1948; revised edition, Heinemann, and New York, Barnes and Noble, 1963.
To Keep the Ball Rolling: The Memoirs of Anthony Powell (abridged edition). London, Penguin, 1983; New York, Penguin, 1984.
  Infants of the Spring. London, Heinemann, 1976; New York, Holt Rinehart, 1977.
  Messengers of Day. London, Heinemann, and New York, Holt Rinehart, 1978.
  Faces in My Time. London, Heinemann, 1980; New York, Holt Rinehart, 1981.
  The Strangers All Are Gone. London, Heinemann, 1982; New York, Holt Rinehart, 1983.

Editor, *Barnard Letters 1778–1884.* London, Duckworth, 1928.
Editor, *Novels of High Society from the Victorian Age.* London, Pilot Press, 1947.

Editor, *Brief Lives and Other Selected Writings of John Aubrey.* London, Cresset Press, and New York, Scribner, 1949.

*

Critical Studies: *Anthony Powell* by Bernard Bergonzi, London, Longman, 1962, revised edition, 1971; *The Novels of Anthony Powell* by Robert K. Morris, Pittsburgh, University of Pittsburgh Press, 1968; *Anthony Powell: A Quintet, Sextet and War* by John Russell, Bloomington, Indiana University Press, 1970; "Anthony Powell Issue" of *Summary* (London) Autumn 1970; "Sisyphus Descending: Mythical Patterns in the Novels of Anthony Powell" by Frederick Karl, in *Mosaic* (Winnipeg), vol. 4, no. 3, 1971; *Anthony Powell* by Neil Brennan, New York, Twayne, 1974; *The Novels of Anthony Powell* by James Tucker, London, Macmillan, and New York, Columbia University Press, 1976; *Handbook to Anthony Powell's Music of Time* by Hilary Spurling, London, Heinemann, 1977, and *Invitation to the Dance: A Guide to Anthony Powell's Dance to the Music of Time*, Boston, Little Brown, 1978; *Anthony Powell's "Music of Time" as a Cyclic Novel of Generation* by Rudolf Bader, Bern, Switzerland, Francke, 1980.

*   *   *

Anthony Powell has been writing books for more than 50 years, though it is only in the last 20 that he has emerged as one of a small handful of contemporary British novelists who can reasonably be considered major. His reputation rests almost exclusively on *A Dance to the Music of Time*, a panoramic sequence of extraordinary scope and complexity. A work that has never relinquished its surface brilliance at portraying the insular, private, self-contained, snobbish world of the British upper and middle classes has more latterly become a vast canvas of all English life between the wars and afterwards and in the profoundest way no less than a comic epic on time, history, and change.

Powell's novelistic career falls into two parts with World War II as the convenient dividing line. The five novels written in the 1930's are wittily structured and skillfully textured, still of some critical interest, but hinting only imperceptibly at the great achievement to come. *Afternoon Men* is perhaps most representative of the 1930's ethos and Powell's early style. Its atmosphere is charged with the insouciance and paralysis of "the lost generation," and resonates with echoes of Waugh and Huxley, though Waugh's bright young things have become older and tarnished, some even rusty, while Huxley's windy intellectuals and poseurs have declined into frustrated, bored, laconic, loveless drifters. Powell's nine-year tenure with Duckworth as reader and editor no doubt inspired the most skillfully plotted of the early novels, *What's Become of Waring*; it is the only one of them to use the first-person narrator that Powell was to employ with increasing complexity in *The Music of Time*. The novel tells of the attempt of a handful of persons to reconstruct the biography of a best-selling author who has remained incognito even up to his death. As the ambiguities of his character unfold, so do those of the characters charged with the quest. Nearly half a century later, Powell—a classic recycler of themes, characters and situations—was to return to Grub Street and the quasi-mystery story with *O, How the Wheel Becomes It!*, and to recapture some of the comic brilliance of the 1930's novels that had decidedly darkened with the final volume of *The Music of Time*. *O, How the Wheel Becomes It!* moves back and forth between the late 1920's and the present as a dull, elderly, third-rate author and literary hack, invited to edit the diary of a deceased acquaintance, uncovers in its pages the reasons for his own failure in love and letters. If, in light of *O, How the Wheel Becomes It!*, *What's Become of Waring* has taken on a new status as perhaps the most interesting of Powell's pre-war books, *From a View to a Death* still remains the best of them; retrospectively it is certainly the most important, anticipating in its several character sketches the more fully realized and rounded portraits of eccentrics in *The Music of Time*, and thematically introducing a dualism of human nature that has become peculiarly associated with Powell's artistic vision and with the thrust and core of his sequence: the opposition of the man of will and the man of imagination, the power-hungry and the sensualist.

Powell began *The Music of Time* shortly after the war, projecting it initially as six volumes, then expanding the plan to twelve. In a rare aside on his work, Powell stated in 1961 that the series "is concerned with the inter-relations of individuals, their lives and love affairs, and is intended to illustrate and bring up to date considerations of the way in which the middle and upper classes live in England." This confidence proved something of a false scent to his early critics, who tended to read the series as biography or sociology with fiction as mere overlay; nor (in all fairness to them) were its intricacies and formidable design apparent even after the first trilogy: *A Question of Upbringing*, set at Eton and Oxford during the 1920's; *A Buyer's Market*, centered in a party-going ambience similar to that of *Afternoon Men*; and *The Acceptance World*, dealing with various gambits to make it both sexually and professionally in the London of the 1930's. Narrated unhurriedly, coolly, and at times in a way that seems maddeningly pointless by Nicholas Jenkins—the hero-narrator of the entire sequence—the first three volumes interweave his life with the lives of a growing nucleus of acquaintances, introduce almost gratuitously several amiable eccentrics, and turn potentially dramatic confrontations into low-keyed comedy of manners.

Looking back over volumes of the series, however, one realizes that Powell, from the beginning, remained consistent to his title and controlling metaphor, both inspired by the painting of Poussin in which "the seasons, hand in hand and facing outward, tread in rhythm to the notes of the lyre that the winged and naked greybeard plays." Like the Seasons, Powell's dancers step "slowly, methodically, sometimes a trifle awkwardly, in evolutions that take recognizable shape: or [break] into seemingly meaningless gyrations, while partners disappear only to reappear again, once more giving pattern to the spectacle." The world of *The Music of Time*, then, is generated through continuing change, though what Powell does with the notion is unique. By seeing all possible, shifting, interchangeable patterns, but by placing the burden of interpreting them squarely on his narrator, he makes the present the center of the novel, enlarges the most underplayed actions or contracts overblown ones without focusing on their immediate significance, integrates individual steps of the dance into the greater flux, and charts necessarily changing sensibilities against the continuum of human history.

Such is the linear movement *in* time, but there is also the vertical movement of *time*: its qualitative rather than quantitative function, the thing-in-itself that makes one "unable . . . to control the steps of the dance." As Nick says in *The Kindly Ones*, "Time can play within its own folds tricks that emphasize the insecurity of those who trust themselves over much to that treacherous concept." The prime mover that does not ostensibly move, does—in a sequence continually reshaping the dance—move, itself become a part of a "kaleidoscope, the colours of which are always changing, always the same." Sheer, protean, fluid, spatial, time is the backdrop for posing and transporting character, theme and plot, but also the dominating archetype embracing all of life and art and of those who would take part in them.

A dozen or more archetypal patterns throughout the sequence would confirm it as the work of a mythopoeicist rather than realist. Nevertheless, Powell has created a remarkable gallery of "real" characters: originals like Giles Jenkins, General Conyers, Lady Molly Jeavons, Lord Erridge, tinged with the harmless grotesqueries of human behaviour; men of imagination like Edgar Deacon, Hugh Moreland, Captain Rowland Gwatkin, Charles Stringham and Peter Templer, romantic transplants from another age who suffer "the strain of living simultaneously in two different historical periods"; and of men of will, cold, mechanical, disciplined, controlling the times and harmonizing with them, of which Kenneth Widmerpool is the most notorious and vital. He is certainly one of the great contemporary comic villains as well. Son of a liquid manure manufacturer, and fat-boy butt of his school fellows at Eton, Widmerpool ascends with astonishing persistence and phoenixlike regularity to positions of status and power. From a highly competent businessman to army colonel and Labour M.P., from peer of the realm to university chancellor to near-divine guru, he has moved uninterruptedly and unfeelingly toward success. Yet though Widmerpool is a super-competent, specious, insensitive, self-aggrandizing, and dangerous egomaniac, one cannot dislike him. In the dance he occupies a pivotal position; and being but one more partner in the just and harmonious evolutions of time, he, like the several hundred other characters, is treated comically, not satirically. Powell accepts Widmerpool as a phenomenon of the ethos without attempting to correct the failings of either.

More importantly, perhaps, Widmerpool becomes the perfect foil for Nick Jenkins's emergent decency, dignity, and probity. Proper, fashionable, sincere, innocent, self-reliant, Nick is the above average, upper-class all-right-guy wanting to fit in and keep from becoming defeated, excessively eccentric, too ostentatiously successful, or too scandalously simple. Nick operates through a comic stoicism that one feels is Powell's as well. He witnesses dissolution about him and charts a course between extremes—measuring the smallest signs or gestures against contemporary standards and holding fast to sensible and humane values. From his shadowy beginnings as narrator and his often obvious role as author-surrogate, he has blossomed into a full-blown hero; for above and beyond other things, he has learned how a student of history and society should confront the uses of the past and of men. It is the Nick of *At Lady Molly's* who finally understands that excess of either power or sensuality may become the principal destroyer of society; the Nick of *Casanova's Chinese Restaurant*, thrust into a world of decaying marriages, infidelity, frustration, failure, and suicide, whose faith in morals and ethics is shaken, but not annihilated; and the Nick of the war trilogy (*The Valley of Bones*, *The Soldier's Art*, *The Military Philosophers*) who, above all the others, remains human in the face of impersonal and fatal dehumanizing processes. It is the Nick, too, of *Temporary Kings*, who finally grasps how *The Music of Time*'s decelerating dance of death approaches the inevitable statement to which the series has long been tending. Powell's preoccupation throughout the volumes with the artist's death, and with art in general as being representative of mutability, has been transferred to the imminent death of one work of art in particular. *Temporary Kings* does not merely view the passing of friends, family, society and culture; it looks to the passing of Powell's great multi-layered novel itself that comes with *Hearing Secret Harmonies*, wherein Powell's *danse macabre* and antic hay are finally "suspended in the wintry silence" in which the dance of the Seasons first began and to which (one sees at last) it was always tending. As a conclusion, the suspension is esthetically perfect; for clearly Powell never meant his sequence to "end": mourning the lost past (like Galsworthy) or (like Proust) recapturing it. The gyrations and patterns of his dancers—Poussin's painting and Powell's description of it must ever be kept in mind—though drawn from life by a master ironist and comedian, were inspired by art to be turned back into art. Thus, *The Music of Time* has proven itself to be less a fictional history about 60 years of English society than a mythical delineation of it. Powell's plan, it seems, was to create a world where life and art, time and space spiraled on synchronously and parallel, a world in which his characters "disappear" at the vanishing point, "only to reappear again."

Such is the world of myth. From the seasonal dance on page two of the first volume, Powell has gone about invoking myths of the seven deadly sins, the Furies, Childe Roland and *Orlando Furioso*, Casanova and Ezekiel—to name but a trickle of the torrent of allusions. He has used these archetypes to heighten his comedy, force ironies, and swell the dimensions of the half-dozen or so recurring characters who loom larger than life. One may have long recognized how truly important the shaping power of myth has been to the sequence, but only with *Hearing Secret Harmonies* does it become crystal-clear that the force behind Powell's mythic vision has all the while been Nietzsche: another writer who fashioned his art out of the apparently contradictory materials of myth and history. What Nietzsche ultimately does for *The Music of Time* is to give it a novelistic, as well as philosophic order. For Poussin/Powell's dancers, reappearing again and again to weave the great comic tapestry of this splendid sequence, are none other than Nietzsche's timeless actors, caught up in the myth of recurrence and eternal return. Earlier writers (Spengler for one; Toynbee for another) have chosen to treat the myth tragically; Powell goes about treating it comically, balancing life and death, reality and art, accepting them and not expecting to change them; even as Nick himself, now in his late sixties, greets the news of the death of his oldest friend-antagonist-bête noire, Kenneth Widmerpool, as merely a temporary suspension of life for those, like himself, still caught up in time's dance.

Nick, a survivor, survives, endures.

—Robert K. Morris

POWERS, J(ames) F(arl). American. Born in Jacksonville, Illinois, 8 July 1917. Educated at Quincy College Academy, Illinois; Northwestern University, Chicago campus, 1938–40. Married the writer Betty Wahl in 1946; three daughters and two sons. Worked in Chicago, 1935–41; editor, Illinois Historical Records Survey, 1938; worked as a hospital orderly during World War II; taught at St. John's University, Collegeville, Minnesota, 1947 and after 1975, Marquette University, Milwaukee, 1949–51, and University of Michigan, Ann Arbor, 1956–57; Writer-in-Residence, Smith College, Northampton, Massachusetts, 1965–66. Recipient: American Academy grant, 1948; Guggenheim fellowship, 1948; Rockefeller fellowship, 1954, 1957, 1967; National Book Award, 1963. Member, American Academy. Address: c/o Alfred A. Knopf Inc., 201 East 50th Street, New York, New York 10022, U.S.A.

PUBLICATIONS

Novel

Morte d'Urban. New York, Doubleday, and London, Gollancz, 1962.

Short Stories

Prince of Darkness and Other Stories. New York, Doubleday, 1947; London, Lehmann, 1948.
The Presence of Grace. New York, Doubleday, and London, Gollancz, 1956.
Look How the Fish Live. New York, Knopf, 1975.

Uncollected Short Stories

"Sailing Against the Wind," in *Gallery of Modern Fiction*, edited by Robie Macauley. New York, Salem Press, 1966.
"Hair Shirt," in *New Yorker*, 30 January 1978.
"Warm Sand," in *New Yorker*, 26 March 1979.

*

Critical Studies: *J.F. Powers* by John F. Hagopian, New York, Twayne, 1968; *J.F. Powers* edited by Fallon Evans, St. Louis, Herder, 1968.

*   *   *

When the stories of J.F. Powers first appeared in American literary magazines during the 1940's, they were welcomed by many readers with an enthusiasm perhaps even greater than their own merits would otherwise have generated, for here was a new writer—a northern writer, a midwestern writer—whose stories carried as much creative authority as did the southern writing that had dominated American fiction for three decades. Here were the same structural finesse and verbal sensitivity, but now applied to northern materials. And here was the same concern for ultimate value, now transplanted to a milieu in which some southern critics had contended it could never flourish.

In short, Powers wrote about Chicago and the small towns of Illinois and Wisconsin with skills learned essentially from such writers as Caroline Gordon, Eudora Welty, Robert Penn Warren, and other southern fictionists, and thus brought to his materials a more sensitive fictional approach than that of earlier midwestern writers, such as Sinclair Lewis, James T. Farrell, or Nelson Algren. To put it another way, a native metaphysical storywriter, using the term perhaps somewhat loosely, had appeared in the very home of American naturalism and had taken at least some of naturalism's themes for his own, with results that were stimulating to say the least.

Powers had a remarkable ear for the dialects and idioms of midwestern speech, and could put together pages of dialogue with perfect fluency, realism, and economy. At the same time he could construct stories of great significance from the smallest episodes, using reticence of symbol and event to suggest meaning and feeling. As a stylist, he was plain rather than fancy, with a classical instinct for concision and a lively sense of prose rhythm. In general, his early stories centered on two main areas of experience: social conflict in Chicago, especially between whites and blacks, and the lives of the Roman Catholic clergy in America. Both these themes appeared powerfully in his first book, *Prince of Darkness*.

The first, that of racial conflict and the misery of Negroes in northern American cities, is best developed in the story entitled "He Don't Plant Cotton," which tells about three black jazz musicians, two men and a woman, who are fired from their job in a third-rate Chicago night club after a disagreement with drunken white customers. The story is memorable on several counts. For one, Powers wrote about jazz and its place in Negro sensibility without any of the mawkishness or plain musical stupidity that has characterized most other white and even much black writing on the subject. For another, without resorting to violence of either speech or event, he conveyed the real violence of feeling that dominates the black community's response to its predicament in America, and it is worth noting that this was done a full decade before the beginning of the modern civil rights movement. Nothing since then has surpassed Powers's story in seriousness, integrity, and artistic relevance, though much recent writing has been more turbulent.

The second theme, that of Catholic religious life in America, is perhaps best exemplified in the early story called "Lions, Harts, Leaping Does," in which Powers wrote about an elderly Franciscan friar plagued by intellectual self-doubt and spiritual anxiety. As he approaches his own death, his small shortcomings seem more and more ominous to him, until in a state of demoralization he cannot experience the least impulse toward good without questioning it and reversing his motives. Very subtly Powers contrasts this spiritual finicality with the real crassness and brutishness of modern commercial civilization, showing the true value of spiritual discipline even in its own weakest condition.

These two stories, "Lions, Harts, Leaping Does" and "He Don't Plant Cotton," belong among the best short stories written in America during the years of mid-century.

In Powers's second book, *The Presence of Grace*, the religious theme became dominant, and the mood turned from that of spiritual anguish to something more objective and satirical. Some stories in the collection moved toward whimsy, including several narrated by a rectory cat, but though they won much popularity for Powers when they were first published in *The New Yorker*, in retrospect they seem comparatively insubstantial. Other stories dealt more toughly with subversion in the Church and with the restlessness of modern clerics who are drawn from true priestliness by ideas of status, power, and popular success; and these were the stories which culminated in Powers's third and most important book, the satirical novel entitled *Morte d'Urban*.

Father Urban is a proselytizing priest attached to the (fictional) Clementine Order. Beginning with the purest motives, desire to bring renewed strength and spiritual influence to his Order, he moves more and more in the direction of a manipulator, a spiritual wheeler-and-dealer, in the most degraded American commercial tradition. In other words, he is progressively subverted by the methods and ideals of the wealthy businessmen whom he parasitizes, and though for a time his efforts, like theirs, succeed remarkably, in the end they lead to catastrophe. The novel is perfectly controlled, perfectly articulated in its elaboration of the levels of religious and lay sensibility. What saves it from being merely an "in" novel for Catholic intellectuals is its clear if indirect exposure of the broad social forces at work behind the dereliction of certain elements in the Church. *Morte d'Urban* is the best American satire of any kind in recent decades.

—Hayden Carruth

POWNALL, David. British. Born in Liverpool, Lancashire, 19 May 1938. Educated at Lord Wandsworth College, Long Sutton, Hampshire, 1949–56; University of Keele, Staffordshire, 1956–60, B.A. (honours) 1960. Married 1) Glenys Pownall in 1961 (divorced, 1971); 2) Mary Ellen Pownall in 1972; two sons. Personnel officer, Ford Motor Co., Dagenham, Essex, 1960–63; personnel manager, Anglo-American, Zambia, 1963–69; resident writer, Century Theatre touring group, 1970–72, and Duke's Playhouse, Lancaster, 1972–75; founder and resident writer, Paines Plough Theatre, London, 1975–80. Recipient (for drama): John Whiting Award, 1982; Giles Cooper Award, 1982, 1986. Agent: Andrew Hewson, John Johnson Ltd., 45–47 Clerkenwell Green, London EC1R 0HT. Address: 136 Cranley Gardens, London N10 3AH, England.

PUBLICATIONS

Novels

The Raining Tree War. London, Faber, 1974.
African Horse. London, Faber, 1975.
God Perkins. London, Faber, 1977.
Light on a Honeycomb. London, Faber, 1978.
Beloved Latitudes. London, Gollancz, 1981.

Short Stories

My Organic Uncle and Other Stories. London, Faber, 1976.

Plays

As We Lie. Zambia, Nkana-Kitwe, 1969.
How Does the Cuckoo Learn to Fly? (produced on tour, 1970).
How to Grow a Guerrilla (produced Preston, Lancashire, 1971).
All the World Should Be Taxed (produced Lancaster, 1971).
The Last of the Wizards (for children; produced Windermere, Cumbria, and London, 1972).
Gaunt (produced Lancaster, 1973).
Lions and Lambs (produced on Lancashire tour, 1973).
The Dream of Chief Crazy Horse (for children; produced Fleetwood, Lancashire, 1973). London, Faber, 1975.
As We Lie (produced Cheltenham, 1973).
Beauty and the Beast (produced Lancaster, 1973).
The Human Cartoon Show (produced Lancaster, 1974).
Crates on Barrels (produced on tour, 1974; London, 1984).
The Pro (produced London, 1975).
Lile Jimmy Williamson (produced Lancaster, 1975).
Buck Ruxton (produced Lancaster, 1975).
Ladybird, Ladybird (produced Edinburgh and London, 1976).
Music to Murder By (produced Canterbury, 1976; Miami, 1984). London, Faber, 1978.
A Tale of Two Town Halls (produced Lancaster, 1976).
Motocar, and Richard III, Part Two, music by Stephen Boxer (produced Edinburgh and London, 1977). London, Faber, 1979.
An Audience Called Édouard (produced London, 1978). London, Faber, 1979.
Seconds at the Fight for Madrid (produced Bristol, 1978).
Livingstone and Sechele (produced Edinburgh, 1978; London and New York, 1980).
Barricade (produced on tour, 1979).
Later (produced London, 1979).
Choice of the Caucasus (produced London, 1979).
The Hot Hello (produced Edinburgh, 1981).

Beef (produced London, 1981; New York, 1986).
Master Class (produced Leicester and London, 1983). London, Faber, 1983.
Pride and Prejudice, adaptation of the novel by Jane Austen (produced Leicester, 1983; New Haven, Connecticut, 1985; London, 1986).

Radio Plays: *Free Ferry*, 1972; *Free House*, 1973; *A Place in the Country*, 1974; *An Old Year*, 1974; *Fences*, 1976; *Under the Wool*, 1976; *Back Stop*, 1977; *Butterfingers*, 1981; *The Mist People*, 1981; *Flies*, 1982; *Ploughboy Monday*, 1985.

Television Plays: *High Tides*, 1976; *Mackerel Sky*, 1976; *Return Fare*, 1978; *Follow the River Down*, 1979; *Room for an Inward Light*, 1980; *The Sack Judies*, 1981; *Love's Labour* (*Maybury* series), 1983.

Verse

An Eagle Each: Poems of the Lakes and Elsewhere, with Jack Hill. Carlisle, Cumbria, Arena, 1972.
Another Country. Liskeard, Cornwall, Harry Chambers/Peterloo Poets, 1978.

Other

Between Ribble and Lune: Scenes from the North-West, photographs by Arthur Thompson. London, Gollancz, 1980.
The Bunch from Bananas (for children). London, Gollancz, 1980; New York, Macmillan, 1981.

Editor, with Gareth Pownall, *The Fisherman's Bedside Book*. London, Windward, 1980.

*   *   *

David Pownall's vision reveals and satirises a world of microcosm. His favoured territory is the crammed, seething canvas peopled with grotesques, whose collective idiocy he lampoons in a style at once comic and macabre. Several of his novels have African locations, and it is here—where technology rubs shoulders uneasily with tribal magic—that he appears most at home. Pownall utilises a variety of literary techniques, subordinating them to a single individual utterance. His wit is caustic and pitiless, sparing no one, yet at times he shows glimpses of a touching faith in humanity.

The Raining Tree War depicts a power struggle between the ruthless president Mulombe and the Muntu religious cult under their prophetess Maud, an archetypal earth-mother figure who claims to be the "Wife of God." Maud embodies the strength of older African traditions, and constitutes a challenge to Mulombe's authority. Into their gradually intensifying conflict Pownall weaves the threads of other lives, following his eccentric characters through the turmoil of a comic-opera war. The ridiculous, mock-heroic climax of the government's attack on Maud's capital in the Bengweulu swamp is a tour de force, Pownall expertly juxtaposing the broadest slapstick with the most stygian of black humour. In the aftermath of this "main event," where dozens of lives are drawn together and not a few abruptly snuffed out, the novel's conclusion is strangely poignant and moving. *The Raining Tree War* is an excellent work, skilfully handled in its action sequences, the thumbnail character sketches capably achieved.

African Horse uses the same location and several characters from the previous novel, but the main plot is devoted to the

Englishman Hurl Halfcock and his search for an imagined animal ancestor. Hurl's odyssey through the bars, brothels, and house-parties of the newly independent Zonkendavo provides a mixture of picaresque adventure and potent symbolism which Pownall continually ridicules en route. Confrontations abound, whether Hurl's battle with an Afrikaner rugby 15, or the more deeply layered duel between a power shovel operator and a crocodile in a colliery sump. The narrative is crowded with memorable individuals—Pyper the hard-drinking journalist, Hammerkop the Afrikaner pit manager, and the anarchistic group of black mine workers known as the Bucket Wheel Excavator Gang—and Pownall highlights each in turn. His presentation of Hurl's weird metamorphosis into his "animalself," for instance, is both absurd and convincing. *African Horse* amuses, but lacks the coherence of *The Raining Tree War*, which is the more satisfying novel of the two.

More impressive is *Light on a Honeycomb*, set in a fictional English town where for centuries insane people have been settled and rehabilitated, and which is now ruled by madmen. Pownall recreates the Biblical concept of an upper and lower world, the "honeycomb" of limestone caverns with its shadowy dream-population of slaves, Irish labourers, and ancestral tribes overset by its modern counterpart run by lunatic businessmen and gangsters, typified by the spray-on carpet foam they use to hide the universe beneath their feet. The "light" is cast by Kevin, inmate of the mental hospital, who invokes the dormant ancestors to overthrow the world above as its rulers succumb to death and madness. *Light on a Honeycomb* is a striking success, Pownall's skills marshalled to full effect. Characterisation is sure, with contrasting and symbolic portrayals, and the blending of scenes is ably rendered. The author's keen eye for the ridiculous touches coldly on landowner and ineffectual revolutionaries alike, both being shown as deluded simpletons unaware of the reality about to burst from the ground beneath them. Pownall compels the reader's attention, drawing him through a complex network of scenes to the light above, where a new world waits to be made. Perhaps the most controlled of his works, *Light on a Honeycomb* must be ranked among his best.

Beloved Latitudes is a new departure for Pownall. Outwardly the most "serious" of his books, it also has the smallest cast. Presented in the form of a spoken autobiography, the story follows the career of an overthrown African dictator, recounted in prison to his English "advisor" and friend. Central to the novel is the close, lover-like relationship between the two men and the tension of their conflicting personalities. Touches of humour brighten the work, but for once Pownall's mood is unusually sombre, as when Sebusia reads his fate in the flying ants on the cell window: "In the squirming translucence there was no solidity, no firm wall, floor or ceiling: everything slipped and trembled. This was the future for the name of a man of destiny. The paper would shake. The words would tumble off the page and the truth would be forgotten." *Beloved Latitudes* is a powerful, thought-provoking novel, whose visual strength is matched by the author's careful under-statement.

A rich amalgam of subtlety, slapstick, horror, and pathos, Pownall's style is perfectly adapted to the novels he writes. Comparisons have been made with Evelyn Waugh, and certainly similarities may be found in the barbed, waspish humour of the early works, but Pownall comes over as more caring and humane, his writing containing an idealism, a love of innocence quite at odds with that of Waugh. In a world of brutality and fake ideologies, he appears to find virtue in "primitive" societies and backward states of mind. Maud and Kevin prevail against the armies and corporations, and they alone offer any future hope. Though even this, where unseen, may not be comprehended: "But it is the last story that the lowland tribes cannot believe./It tells of a people who are black and white and live as one."

—Geoff Sadler

PRICE, (Edward) Reynolds. American. Born in Macon, North Carolina, 1 February 1933. Educated at Duke University, Durham, North Carolina, 1951–55 (Angier Duke Scholar), A.B. (summa cum laude) 1955 (Phi Beta Kappa); Merton College, Oxford, 1955–58 (Rhodes Scholar), B.Litt. 1958. Member of the Faculty since 1958, Assistant Professor, 1961–68, Associate Professor, 1968–72, Professor of English, 1972–77, and since 1977, James B. Duke Professor, Duke University. Writer-in-Residence, University of North Carolina, Chapel Hill, 1965, and Greensboro, 1971, and University of Kansas, Lawrence, 1967, 1969, 1980; Glasgow Professor, Washington and Lee University, Lexington, Virginia, 1971; member of the Faculty, Salzburg Seminar on American Studies, 1977. Editor, *The Archive*, Durham, 1954–55. Since 1964, advisory editor, *Shenandoah*, Lexington, Virginia. Chairman, National Endowment for the Arts Literature Advisory Panel, 1976. Recipient: Faulkner Foundation prize, 1963; Guggenheim fellowship, 1964; National Association of Independent Schools award, 1964; National Endowment for the Arts fellowship, 1967; American Academy award, 1971; Bellamann Foundation award, 1976; Lillian Smith award, 1976. Litt.D.: St. Andrews Presbyterian College, Laurinburg, North Carolina, 1978; Wake Forest University, Winston-Salem, North Carolina, 1979. Agent: Russell and Volkening Inc., 50 West 29th Street, New York, New York 10001. Address: 4813 Duke Station, Durham, North Carolina 27706, U.S.A.

PUBLICATIONS

Novels

A Long and Happy Life. New York, Atheneum, and London, Chatto and Windus, 1962.
A Generous Man. New York, Atheneum, 1966; London, Chatto and Windus, 1967.
Love and Work. New York, Atheneum, and London, Chatto and Windus, 1968.
The Surface of Earth. New York, Atheneum, 1975; London, Arlington, 1977.
The Source of Light. New York, Atheneum, 1981.
Mustian (2 novels and a story). New York, Atheneum, 1983.

Short Stories

The Names and Faces of Heroes. New York, Atheneum, and London, Chatto and Windus, 1963.
Permanent Errors. New York, Atheneum, 1970; London, Chatto and Windus, 1971.

Uncollected Short Stories

"Night and Day at Panacea," in *Harper's* (New York), August 1974.
"Commencing," in *Virginia Quarterly Review* (Charlottesville), Spring 1975.

Plays

Early Dark (produced New York, 1978). New York, Atheneum, 1977.
Private Contentment. New York, Atheneum, 1984.

Verse

Late Warning: Four Poems. New York, Albondocani Press, 1968.
Torso of an Archaic Apollo—after Rilke. New York, Albondocani Press, 1969.
Lessons Learned: Seven Poems. New York, Albondocani Press, 1977.
Christ Child's Song at the End of the Night. Privately printed, 1978.
Nine Mysteries (Four Joyful, Four Sorrowful, One Glorious). Winston-Salem, North Carolina, Palaemon Press, 1979.
Vital Provisions. New York, Atheneum, 1982.

Other

Two Theophanies: Genesis 32 and John 21. Privately printed, 1971.
Things Themselves: Essays and Scenes. New York, Atheneum, 1972.
Presence and Absence: Versions from the Bible. Bloomfield Hills, Michigan, Bruccoli Clark, 1973.
Conversations, with William Ray. Memphis, Memphis State University, 1976.
The Good News According to Mark. Privately printed, 1976.
Oracles: Six Versions from the Bible. Durham, North Carolina, Friends of the Duke University Library, 1977.
A Palpable God: Thirty Stories Translated from the Bible with an Essay on the Origins and Life of Narrative. New York, Atheneum, 1978.
Country Mouse, City Mouse (essay). Rocky Mount, North Carolina, Friends of the Wesleyan College Library, 1981.
A Start (miscellany of early work). Winston-Salem, North Carolina, Palaemon Press, 1981.

*

Critical Studies: "A Conversation with Reynolds Price" by Wallace Kaufman, in *Shenandoah* (Lexington, Virginia), Summer 1966; "The Reynolds Price Who Outgrew the Southern Pastoral" by Theodore Solotaroff, in *Saturday Review* (New York), 26 September 1970; "Love (and Marriage) in *A Long and Happy Life*," in *Twentieth Century Studies* (Los Angeles), January 1971.

*   *   *

Reynolds Price has moved from detailed examination of North Carolina rural life to an intense concern with the artist's vision of reality. Beginning with the tragicomic saga of the Mustian family (the novels *A Long and Happy Life* and *A Generous Man* and the story "A Chain of Love," now collected in *Mustian*), he has come in *Love and Work* and *Permanent Errors* to wrestle with narrative forms closer to the bone. In the preface to *Permanent Errors* Price described his work as "the attempt to isolate in a number of lives the central error of act, will, understanding which, once made, has been permanent, incurable, but whose diagnosis and palliation are the hopes of continuance."

This applies to all Price's fiction. *A Long and Happy Life* is the inside story of Rosacoke Mustian, a country girl seeking a conventional life with an unconventional young man, Wesley Beavers. Her error is that she conceives "a long and happy life" only in the clichéd terms of romance, of settled-wedded-bliss tradition. She reviews her life, her family's life, is discontent, becomes pregnant by Wesley and finally comes to see him and herself in larger terms, terms of myth, in a Christmas pageant which shows her the complete (and divine) meanings of motherhood, birth, and love.

Myth becomes the vehicle of self-understanding more overtly in *A Generous Man*, which shows the Mustian family several years earlier. It describes an allegorical search for an escaped circus python, a giant serpent named Death, and the discovery of a lost treasure. Milo Mustian describes the stifling forces of convention which circumscribe their lives: "it's what nine-tenths of the humans born since God said 'Adam!' have thought was a life, planned out for themselves—all my people, my Mama, my Daddy (it was what strangled him), Rosacoke . . ." Only by transcending the everyday, by seeing human life in larger terms, can the individual escape the slow strangulation of "permanent errors" and find direction and meaning in existence.

Price's fiction has become increasingly abstract and complex as he has moved to a more inward vision. From the first he has used sets of images and metaphors to suggest a mysterious or magical reality beyond his pastoral settings. He has deepened this metaphorical (and psychological) interest in *Love and Work* and *Permanent Errors*, where the protagonists are no longer the eccentric pastoral figures of the Mustian clan but are closer to Price's own viewpoint. Price's fiction has always dealt with confusion of the heart and alienation of the mind, but the recent work draws its images and symbols from Price's own experience—his family, a visit to Dachau prison camp, the writer's situation. The grotesqueness and unfamiliarity of the Mustian clan are replaced by more familiar and universal facts of contemporary life.

In two large novels, *The Surface of Earth* and *The Source of Light*, Price is most ambitious. The narratives deal with a family saga encompassing the first half of our century and drawing from Price's own experience. The novels detail through letters, conversations, and lyrical soliloquies the Mayfield family and its cycle of birth, maturity and death as viewed by Rob Mayfield, who focuses the narratives. The family is more genteel than the Mustians, and these novels detail a world of important things and social valences. The search by Rob Mayfield for a sense of himself and for a peaceful reconciliation with his father's memory is an important mirror image of Rosacoke Mustian's growth into adulthood.

Love and death are polarities in Price's work—how to save life from death, how to prevent life from becoming deathly, stale, void of myth and magic? The theme appears most clearly in *A Generous Man*, when the Mustians set out to find and kill Death, the great serpent, and when they are finally told, "Death is dead." In the course of this magical hunt, Milo Mustian comes to understand what he must do to save himself from the slow death of a clichéd life; Rato Mustian, the wise fool, grapples with Death and escapes its coils through his cunning folly; Rosacoke moves from complete innocence to the dawn of maturity. In his later fiction Price has moved from symbols of external life to more internalized ones: sleep, dreams, a writer seeking a relationship between love and work, self and others, private life and shared life. Price's fiction describes the individual's perceptions of himself and of the realities around him, the uses of imagination. His characters travel on a quest for the potency of myth and the ability to transcend a closed vision of everyday reality. They move toward permanent truths through "permanent errors."

—William J. Schafer

PRITCHETT, (Sir) V(ictor) S(awdon). British. Born in Ipswich, Suffolk, 16 December 1900. Educated at Alleyn's School, Dulwich, London. Married Dorothy Rudge Roberts in 1936; one son and one daughter. Worked in the leather trade in London, 1916–20, and in the shellac, glue, and photographic trade in Paris, 1920–32; correspondent in Ireland and Spain for the *Christian Science Monitor*, Boston, 1923–26; critic from 1926, permanent critic from 1937, and director, 1946–78, *New Statesman*, London; Christian Gauss Lecturer, Princeton University, New Jersey, 1953; Beckman Professor, University of California, Berkeley, 1962; Writer-in-Residence, Smith College, Northampton, Massachusetts, 1966, 1970–72; Visiting Professor, Brandeis University, Waltham, Massachusetts, 1968; Clark Lecturer, Cambridge University, 1969; Visiting Professor, Columbia University, New York, 1972; Writer-in-Residence, Vanderbilt University, Nashville, 1981. President, PEN English Centre, 1970, and President of International PEN, 1974–76. Since 1977, President, Society of Authors. Recipient: Heinemann Award, for non-fiction, 1969; PEN award, for non-fiction, 1974. D.Litt.: University of Leeds, 1972; Columbia University, 1978; University of Sussex, Brighton, 1980; Harvard University, Cambridge, Massachusetts. Fellow, Royal Society of Literature, 1969. Honorary Member, American Academy, 1971, and American Academy of Arts and Sciences, 1971. C.B.E. (Commander, Order of the British Empire), 1968. Knighted, 1975. Address: 12 Regent's Park Terrace, London N.W.1, England.

PUBLICATIONS

Novels

Clare Drummer.   London, Benn, 1929.
Shirley Sanz.   London, Gollancz, 1932; as *Elopement into Exile*, Boston, Little Brown, 1932.
Nothing like Leather.   London, Chatto and Windus, and New York, Macmillan, 1935.
Dead Man Leading.   London, Chatto and Windus, and New York, Macmillan, 1937.
Mr. Beluncle.   London, Chatto and Windus, and New York, Harcourt Brace, 1951.

Short Stories

The Spanish Virgin and Other Stories.   London, Benn, 1930.
You Make Your Own Life.   London, Chatto and Windus, 1938.
It May Never Happen and Other Stories.   London, Chatto and Windus, 1945; New York, Reynal, 1947.
Collected Stories.   London, Chatto and Windus, 1956.
The Sailor, The Sense of Humour, and Other Stories.   New York, Knopf, 1956.
When My Girl Comes Home.   London, Chatto and Windus, and New York, Knopf, 1961.
The Key to My Heart.   London, Chatto and Windus, 1963; New York, Random House, 1964.

The Saint and Other Stories.   London, Penguin, 1966.
Blind Love and Other Stories.   London, Chatto and Windus, 1969; New York, Random House, 1970.
Penguin Modern Stories 9, with others.   London, Penguin, 1971.
The Camberwell Beauty and Other Stories.   London, Chatto and Windus, and New York, Random House, 1974.
Selected Stories.   London, Chatto and Windus, and New York, Random House, 1978.
On the Edge of the Cliff.   New York, Random House, 1979; London, Chatto and Windus, 1980.
Collected Stories.   New York, Random House, and London, Chatto and Windus, 1982.
More Collected Stories.   New York, Random House, and London, Chatto and Windus, 1983.

Uncollected Short Stories

"Trip to the Seaside," in *Atlantic* (Boston), February 1981.
"Writer's Tale," in *Vogue* (New York), March 1981.
"Neighbors," in *New Yorker*, 5 July 1982.
"Just Friends," in *Seventeen* (New York), August 1983.

Plays

The Gambler (broadcast, 1947).   Published in *Imaginary Conversations*, edited by Rayner Heppenstall, London, Secker and Warburg, 1948.
La Bohème, adaptation of the libretto by Giuseppe Giacosa and Luigi Illica, music by Puccini.   Boston, Little Brown, and London, Joseph, 1983.

Screenplays: *Essential Jobs* (documentary), 1942; *The Two Feathers*, with Anthony Asquith, 1944.

Radio Play: *The Gambler*, 1947.

Other

Marching Spain.   London, Benn, 1928.
In My Good Books.   London, Chatto and Windus, 1942; Port Washington, New York, Kennikat Press, 1977.
Build the Ships: The Official Story of the Shipyards in War-Time.   London, His Majesty's Stationery Office, 1946.
The Living Novel.   London, Chatto and Windus, 1946; New York, Reynal, 1947; revised edition, New York, Random House, 1964.
Why Do I Write: An Exchange of Views Between Elizabeth Bowen, Graham Greene, and V.S. Pritchett.   London, Marshall, 1948; New York, Haskell House, 1976.
Books in General.   London, Chatto and Windus, and New York, Harcourt Brace, 1953.
The Spanish Temper.   London, Chatto and Windus, and New York, Knopf, 1954.
London Perceived.   London, Chatto and Windus, and New York, Harcourt Brace, 1962.
Foreign Faces.   London, Chatto and Windus, 1964; as *The Offensive Traveller*, New York, Knopf, 1964.
New York Proclaimed.   London, Chatto and Windus, and New York, Harcourt Brace, 1965.
The Working Novelist.   London, Chatto and Windus, 1965.
Dublin: A Portrait.   London, Bodley Head, and New York, Harper, 1967.
A Cab at the Door: Childhood and Youth 1900–1920.   London, Chatto and Windus, and New York, Random House, 1968.

George Meredith and English Comedy.   London, Chatto and Windus, and New York, Random House, 1970.
Midnight Oil (autobiography).   London, Chatto and Windus, 1971; New York, Random House, 1972.
Balzac: A Biography.   London, Chatto and Windus, and New York, Knopf, 1973.
The Gentle Barbarian: The Life and Work of Turgenev.   London, Chatto and Windus, and New York, Random House, 1977.
Autobiography (address).   London, English Association, 1977.
The Myth Makers: Essays on European, Russian, and South American Novelists.   London, Chatto and Windus, and New York, Random House, 1979.
The Tale Bearers: Essays on English, American, and Other Writers.   London, Chatto and Windus, and New York, Random House, 1980.
The Turn of the Years, with Reynolds Stone.   Salisbury, Russell, and New York, Random House, 1982.
The Other Side of a Frontier: A V.S. Pritchett Reader.   London, Clark, 1984.
A Man of Letters.   London, Chatto and Windus, 1985; New York, Random House, 1986.

Editor, *This England.*   London, New Statesman and Nation, 1938.
Editor, *Novels and Stories*, by Robert Louis Stevenson.   London, Pilot Press, 1945; New York, Duell, 1946.
Editor, *Turnstile One: A Literary Miscellany from the New Statesman.*   London, Turnstile Press, 1948.
Editor, *The Oxford Book of Short Stories.*   Oxford and New York, Oxford University Press, 1981.

*

V.S. Pritchett comments:
My chief interests have been: travel, specially Spanish; short stories, which I value most; literary criticism over the years for the *New Statesman*.

*   *   *

V.S. Pritchett is one of the most richly endowed of living men of letters and has written with equal distinction as literary critic, travel-writer, autobiographer, novelist, and short-story-writer. In whatever field he writes the work bears his thumb-print and is marked by his unfailing curiosity about the oddities and vagaries of human nature and by his exceedingly close observation of the human scene, and these are allied to a darting, idiosyncratic prose akin to brilliant talk.

If there is one subject that Pritchett has made his own and that, in one way or another, informs his writings, it is puritanism. He is, so to say, the connoisseur of puritanism in its characteristically English manifestations, which are generally lower-middle-class. As he writes in his essay on Gosse's *Father and Son*:

Extreme puritanism gives purpose, drama and intensity to private life. . . . Outwardly, the extreme puritan appears narrow, crabbed, fanatical, gloomy and dull; but from the inside—what a series of dramatic climaxes his life is, what a fascinating casuistry beguiles him, how he is bemused by the comedies of duplicity, sharpened by the ingenious puzzles of the conscience, and carried away by the eloquence of hypocrisy.

Such a character is described in Matthew Burkle, the central figure in Pritchett's early novel, *Nothing like Leather*. As the title indicates, the novel is set against the background of the leather trade: though it may not be its main interest, Pritchett's fiction is always saturated in the actual.

Burkle is a man who, hating sex, channels his energies to making money. To the extent that one feels Pritchett to be moved in his delineation by intellectual curiosity rather than by sympathy, Burkle is still a more or less conventional representation of the puritan. This is true also of the representation of Harry Johnson in *Dead Man Leading*, an explorer who deserts the scientific expedition he is with in Brazil in order to search for his father, who has disappeared in the interior. The background—the heat, damp, and squalor of the Amazon forests—is most brilliantly rendered; and so, too, is the tortured mind of Johnson, who goes up the river "with the speechless fear of a son guiltily approaching his father."

But something appears in *Dead Man Leading* that is not present in the earlier novel. Intermittently, Pritchett displays himself as a comic writer, which is how one now thinks of him, and there is, in these comic passages, a sense of liberation, of ease, a delight in human oddity for its own sake.

In Pritchett's major novel, *Mr. Beluncle*, comedy takes over completely, and comedy here is an aspect of sympathy; Beluncle is accepted totally. Beluncle, a furniture manufacturer on a small scale, during the course of life has been in turn Congregationalist, Methodist, Plymouth Brother, Baptist, Unitarian, Theosophist, Christian Scientist. All these changes are related in some way to his economic situation. When the novel begins, he is a member of an American sect called The Church of the Last Purification, Toronto, a sect that denies the objective existence of evil.

Beluncle may seem and is indeed a self-deceiver, a liar, a cheat, a hypocrite, and a domestic tyrant. But all this is not so important as the fact that he is a man who is as it were lived by a dream, the victim of a compulsive fantasy that rules his life and turns everything and everyone he meets into its accomplices, a fantasy that renders his life and those of his children who must suffer under him always dramatic. He is a character, in the tradition and even the mode of Dickens, on whom Pritchett, as literary critic, has written with such intuitive understanding. And the novel is extraordinarily faithful to and revealing of one section, which seems to be permanent, of English lower-middle-class life.

Pritchett's novels are intellectually exciting and wonderfully well-written. But they are less satisfying aesthetically. *Mr. Beluncle*, for instance, is curiously static. He is there all the time but does not develop or change in his being. The same could be said of Pecksniff, but Pecksniff, great creation though he is, is, in *Martin Chuzzlewit*, only one character among many. One feels, indeed, that for all his great knowledge of it Pritchett is not wholly at home or comfortable in the novel form. In the short story, on the other hand, he is completely at home, and it is in the short story, for which he seems to have abandoned the novel, that he has done his finest work in fiction.

Settings and characters are much the same as in the novels. Very often the scene is the south-east of England, with London and the City not far away; the characters again from the lower-middle-class, clerks and commercial travellers. It is a world closely akin to Wells's in his early novels; the characters might be the children or grandchildren of Wells's. One thinks of a story like "Many Are Disappointed," with its four characters, office-workers, on a cycling tour dreaming of beer in an inn and, in the end, settling for tea. At times, too, the matter is much the same, as in "The Saint," which might almost be an episode in *Mr. Beluncle*. The difference, however, is that

in his short stories Pritchett's touch is absolutely sure; he is the complete master of the form. There are also, of course, the qualities one takes for granted in him: the swift economical language, racy, colloquial, the Dickensian eye for detail, the unerring instinct for idiosyncrasy that reveals character. There is the sense, too, that the stories are not abstractions; one feels that behind them there is a whole actual observable world which in some mysterious way they sum up in themselves. Pritchett is not a writer easily classified; his stories are his own and like no one else's. They seem very English. But each one of them, like Joyce's in *Dubliners*, is the rendering of what Joyce called an "epiphany," an incident or a sudden glimpse of a happening in which a moment of reality is made manifest. This is indeed the modern story-writer's art, and among contemporary writers no one is a greater master of it than Pritchett.

—Walter Allen

PROKOSCH, Frederic. American. Born in Madison, Wisconsin, 17 May 1908. Educated at Haverford College, Pennsylvania, 1922–25, M.A. 1926; Yale University, New Haven, Connecticut, 1930–31, Ph.D. 1933; King's College, Cambridge, 1935–37, M.A. 1937. Instructor in English, Yale University, 1932–34, and New York University, 1936–37; printer, of modern poetry, in Bryn Mawr, Pennsylvania, Cambridge, Florence, Venice, and Lisbon, 1933–40; Cultural Attaché, American Legation, Stockholm, 1943–45; Visiting Lecturer, University of Rome, 1950–51. Squash-racquets champion of France, 1933–39, and of Sweden, 1944. Recipient: Guggenheim fellowship, 1937; Harper prize, 1937; Harriet Monroe Memorial Prize (*Poetry*, Chicago), 1941; Fulbright fellowship, 1951; National Endowment for the Arts grant, 1977; Prix Médicis (France), 1984. Address: Ma Trouvaille, 06 Plan de Grasse, Alpes Maritimes, France.

PUBLICATIONS

Novels

The Asiatics. New York, Harper, and London, Chatto and Windus, 1935.
The Seven Who Fled. New York, Harper, and London, Chatto and Windus, 1937.
Night of the Poor. New York, Harper, and London, Chatto and Windus, 1939.
The Skies of Europe. New York, Harper, 1941; London, Chatto and Windus, 1942.
The Conspirators. New York, Harper, and London, Chatto and Windus, 1943.
Age of Thunder. New York, Harper, and London, Chatto and Windus, 1945.
The Idols of the Cave. New York, Doubleday, 1946; London Chatto and Windus, 1947.
Storm and Echo. New York, Doubleday, 1948; London Faber, 1949.
Nine Days to Mukalla. New York, Viking Press, and London Secker and Warburg, 1953.
A Tale for Midnight. Boston, Little Brown, 1955; London Secker and Warburg, 1956.

A Ballad of Love. New York, Farrar Straus, 1960; London, Secker and Warburg, 1961.
The Seven Sisters. New York, Farrar Straus, 1962; London, Secker and Warburg, 1963.
The Dark Dancer. New York, Farrar Straus, 1964; London, W.H. Allen, 1965.
The Wreck of the Cassandra. New York, Farrar Straus, and London, W.H. Allen, 1966.
The Missolonghi Manuscript. New York, Farrar Straus, and London, W.H. Allen, 1968.
America, My Wilderness. New York, Farrar Straus, and London, W.H. Allen, 1971.

Verse

Three Mysteries. New Haven, Connecticut, privately printed, 1932.
Three Sorrows. New Haven, Connecticut, privately printed, 1932.
Three Deaths. New Haven, Connecticut, privately printed, 1932.
Three Images. New Haven, Connecticut, privately printed, 1932.
The Voyage. Bryn Mawr, Pennsylvania, privately printed, 1933.
The Dolls. Bryn Mawr, Pennsylvania, privately printed, 1933.
The Grotto. Bryn Mawr, Pennsylvania, privately printed, 1933.
The Enemies. Bryn Mawr, Pennsylvania, privately printed, 1933.
The Survivors. Bryn Mawr, Pennsylvania, privately printed, 1934.
Going Southward. Bryn Mawr, Pennsylvania, privately printed, 1935.
The Red Sea. Cambridge, privately printed, 1935.
Andromeda. Cambridge, privately printed, 1935.
The Assassins. Cambridge, privately printed, 1936.
The Assassins (collection). New York, Harper, and London, Chatto and Windus, 1936.
The Sacred Wood. Cambridge, privately printed, 1936.
The Carnival. New York, Harper, and London, Chatto and Windus, 1938.
Death at Sea. New York, Harper, and London, Chatto and Windus, 1940.
Sunburned Ulysses. Lisbon, privately printed, 1941.
Among the Caves. Lisbon, privately printed, 1941.
Song. New York, privately printed, 1941.
Song. Stockholm, privately printed, 1943.
Fable. New York, privately printed, 1944.
Chosen Poems. London, Chatto and Windus, 1944; New York, Doubleday, 1947.
The Flamingoes. Rome, privately printed, 1948.
Snow Song. Paris, privately printed, 1949.
Boat Song. Venice, privately printed, 1950.
Wood Song. Florence, privately printed, 1951.
Phantom Song. Naples, privately printed, 1952.
Banquet Song. Barcelona, privately printed, 1953.
Temple Song. Stuttgart, privately printed, 1954.
Fire Song. Zurich, privately printed, 1955.
Island Song. Hong Kong, privately printed, 1956.
Jungle Song. Bangkok, privately printed, 1957.
The Death Ship. Singapore, privately printed, 1958.
The Ghost City. Antwerp, privately printed, 1959.
The Mirror. Vienna, privately printed, 1960.

Other

Voices: A Memoir. New York, Farrar Straus, and London, Faber, 1983.

Translator, *Some Poems of Friedrich Hölderlin.* New York, New Directions, 1943; London, Grey Walls Press, 1947.
Translator, *Love Sonnets of Louise Labé.* New York, New Directions, 1947; London, Grey Walls Press, 1948.
Translator, *The Medea of Euripides.* New York, Dial Press, 1949.

*

Manuscript Collection: University of Texas, Austin.

Critical Study: *Frederic Prokosch* by Radcliffe Squires, New York, Twayne, 1964.

Frederic Prokosch comments:

It has always, it appears, been difficult, almost impossible, for English and American critics to classify or label or categorize my novels. Perhaps because an element of poetry has been infused into their themes, style, and structure; or perhaps they fall more naturally into the genre of Slavic, German, or even French styles of fiction. My influences, I should say at random, were Grimm, Cervantes, Chekov, Conrad, possibly Thomas Mann among the moderns, even Céline, in the employment of a kind of dream-picaresque form to embody certain basic themes of perpetual search, perpetual flight, multiple identities, ambiguities of destiny, and geographical symbolisms. These themes have permeated my work all the way from *The Asiatics* and *The Seven Who Fled* up through *The Missolonghi Manuscript* and *America, My Wilderness.* Thus, my commentaries on "contemporary crises" have been covert, subtle, indirect. In this aversion to purely naturalistic or overtly sociological observation I find, I suppose, a certain kinship in the work of Borges, Nabokov, I.B. Singer, Hermann Hesse, and certain Japanese writers. I pity those poor critics who might try to disentangle the Gordian knot of my obsessive symbols and images.

*   *   *

When Frederic Prokosch's first novel, *The Asiatics*, appeared in 1935 it immediately became clear that here was an important novelist with unique gifts. The metaphoric style touched the reader as does an intimate dream whose intensity leaves the dreamer lonely for the dream when he wakes. The tolerant, sensuous, yet ultimately mysterious young narrator who wanders through the beautifully detailed landscapes of Asia, encountering characters who are in turn vicious and virtuous, neurotic and heroic, mad and wise, enthralled a large audience. Translated into seventeen languages, the book claimed the attention of André Gide who called *The Asiatics* "an authentic masterpiece"; of Thomas Mann who wrote, "I was unable to tear myself away from this astonishing, picaresque romance, flashing with talent and an audacious, adventurous spirit. I count it among the most brilliant and original achievements of the young literary generation."

Prokosch's second novel, *The Seven Who Fled*, published as the Harper prize novel in 1937, affirmed these impressions, and high praise continued to greet his work for the next decade. Yet it was praise that tended to dwell with the surfaces rather than the recesses of his talent. In this respect the response of Albert Camus is typical: "He has invented what might be called the geographical novel, in which he mingles sensuality with irony, lucidity with mystery. He conveys a fatalistic sense of life half-hidden beneath a rich animal energy. He is a master of moods and undertones, a virtuoso in the feeling of place, and he writes in a style of supple elegance." These words are true enough, but they neither ask nor tell the purposes of "the geographic novel."

While Prokosch's popularity as a novelist has declined, especially in America, since the end of World War II, his stature as a serious novelist, particularly in Europe, has increased. That stature rests upon stubborn teleological strengths that buttress the protean shimmer of his designs. For no aspect of Prokosch's fiction is merely what at first glance it appears to be. The vagrant drift of such novels as *Storm and Echo* contains a symbolic anthropology. The "naturalistic" or "realistic" qualities of such novels as *The Skies of Europe* contain a symbolic history. The historical aspects of such novels as *A Tale for Midnight* contains a symbolic psychology. The biographical qualities of such novels as *The Dark Dancer* or *The Missolonghi Manuscript* contain a symbolic philosophy of art.

In an anagogic sense, the nomadic novels—*The Asiatics, The Seven Who Fled, Storm and Echo, Nine Days to Mukalla*—contemplate man as an evolving, but not an evolved, being. Africa, vibrant with treachery and violence, chthonian gods and Promethean vision, is seen as the amoral but innocent beginning of man's emergence from the moronic babble of Nature. Asia, tricked by its own shrewdness, staggering under the burden of its exquisite civilization, is seen as decadent denouement. However, this extensive symbology is less important than the intensive symbology. The journey-novels—like the journey-poems of the Romantic poets—employ the fortuitous encounter as a means of fixing the fluctuant portrait of man's psychic being. Landscape, natural hardship—whether in Asia or Africa, Europe or America—act upon the characters as an "X-ray" to reveal what is hidden beneath the surface. The hidden self comes forth, the characters come to terms with it or else are destroyed by their fear of it.

But what does it mean, this coming to terms with the submerged atomies of self. It means at least a little more than the simple integration of personality advocated by Carl Jung, for the purpose of such integration involves for Prokosch a liberal yet austere morality. In the late novel *The Seven Sisters* Prokosch pursues the mythic rehearsals of archetypal themes in the careers of seven daughters. Ultimately one sees that these careers embody the conflicting or unmeshed elements of the hero's personality. Until he understands these elements he feels he is "dangling" in life, and his painting is a vagary of discrete daubs. Until he understands and thus reconciles these elements, he cannot love, though he is tyrannized by love; nor can he "create."

The word "create," as it involves the artist, takes us into the core of Prokosch's work. His villains (as his brief portrait of Hitler in *The Skies of Europe* makes evident) are failed artists. His ruined characters are those who, pursuing, like Rimbaud, a fanatical ideal of art, burn out and fail. But that is only the dark side of the problem. Toward the end of *The Asiatics* the narrator admonishes himself not to be

strong; don't be alone; don't be proud; it's your only chance ever to understand anything at all. Be fragile, be tender, humiliate yourself, and let the discoloration of dream close in on you. Do that, and oddly enough, you'll remain healthy; you'll be yourself; you'll discover the best way to live in this particular most fruitless and tantalizing of possible worlds. The reality becomes a cruel dream while the dream fades into a tender man-made reality.

That rejection of strength and pride is at base a rejection of the imbalance of idealism; it parallels and equals the theme

of awareness and integration of personality. Hence, from the fickle and promiscuous can come, as in *The Dark Dancer*, an eternal praise of love, the Taj Mahal. So also in *The Missolonghi Manuscript* (a novel which contains too many witty anachronisms and discrepancies for the careful reader to suppose its intent is simply a biography of Lord Byron) the Romantic ideal of "eternity" can only be attained by acceptance of decay. A susurrus of paradox articulates the resolution: to abandon idealism in life permits life to become an ideal art.

—Radcliffe Squires

PURDY, James (Otis). American. Born near Fremont, Ohio, 14 July 1923. Educated at the University of Chicago, 1941, 1946; University of Puebla, Mexico. Worked as an interpreter in Latin America, France, and Spain; taught at Lawrence College, Appleton, Wisconsin, 1949–53. Since 1953, full-time writer. Visiting Professor, University of Tulsa, Oklahoma, 1977. Recipient: American Academy award, 1958; Guggenheim fellowship, 1958, 1962; Ford fellowship, for drama, 1961. Address: 236 Henry Street, Brooklyn, New York 11201, U.S.A.

PUBLICATIONS

Novels

Malcolm. New York, Farrar Straus, 1959; London, Secker and Warburg, 1960.
The Nephew. New York, Farrar Straus, 1960; London, Secker and Warburg, 1961.
Cabot Wright Begins. New York, Farrar Straus, 1964; London, Secker and Warburg, 1965.
Eustace Chisholm and the Works. New York, Farrar Straus, 1967; London, Cape, 1968.
Sleepers in Moon-Crowned Valleys:
   Jeremy's Version. New York, Doubleday, 1970; London, Cape, 1971.
   The House of the Solitary Maggot. New York, Doubleday, 1974.
I Am Elijah Thrush. New York, Doubleday, and London, Cape, 1972.
In a Shallow Grave. New York, Arbor House, 1976; London, W.H. Allen, 1978.
Narrow Rooms. New York, Arbor House, 1978; Godalming, Surrey, Black Sheep, 1980.
Mourners Below. New York, Viking Press, 1981; London, Owen, 1984.
On Glory's Course. New York, Viking, 1984; London, Owen, 1985.

Short Stories

Don't Call Me by My Right Name and Other Stories. New York, William Frederick Press, 1956.
63: Dream Palace. New York, William Frederick Press, 1956; London, Gollancz, 1957.
Color of Darkness: Eleven Stories and a Novella. New York, New Directions, 1957; London, Secker and Warburg, 1961.
Children Is All (stories and plays). New York, New Directions, 1961; London, Secker and Warburg, 1963.

An Oyster Is a Wealthy Beast (story and poems).   Los Angeles, Black Sparrow Press, 1967.
Mr. Evening: A Story and Nine Poems.   Los Angeles, Black Sparrow Press, 1968.
On the Rebound: A Story and Nine Poems.   Los Angeles, Black Sparrow Press, 1970.
A Day after the Fair: A Collection of Plays and Stories.   New York, Note of Hand, 1977.
Lessons and Complaints.   New York, Nadja, 1978.
Sleep Tight.   New York, Nadja, 1979.
The Candles of Your Eyes.   New York, Nadja, 1985.

Uncollected Short Stories

"Lily's Party," in *New Directions 29.*   New York, New Directions, 1974.
"The Anonymous/Anomalous Letters of Passion," in *New Directions 38.*   New York, New Directions, 1979.

Plays

Mr. Cough Syrup and the Phantom Sex, in *December* (Western Springs, Illinois), vol. 8, no. 1, 1960.
Cracks (produced New York, 1963).
Wedding Finger, in *New Directions 28.*   New York, New Directions, 1974.
Two Plays (includes *A Day after the Fair* and *True*).   Dallas, New London Press, 1979.
Scrap of Paper, and The Berry-Picker: Two Plays.   Los Angeles, Sylvester and Orphanos, 1981.

Verse

The Running Sun.   New York, Paul Waner Press, 1971.
Sunshine Is an Only Child.   New York, Aloe, 1973.

*

Manuscript Collection: Yale University, New Haven, Connecticut.

Critical Studies: introduction by David Daiches to *Malcolm*, 1959, by Edith Sitwell to *Colour of Darkness*, London, Secker and Warburg, 1961, and by Tony Tanner to *Color of Darkness, and Malcolm*, New York, Doubleday, 1974; *The Not-Right House: Essays on James Purdy* by Bettina Schwarzchild, Columbia, University of Missouri Press, 1968; *City of Words*, London, Cape, and New York, Harper, 1971, and "Birdsong," in *Partisan Review* (New Brunswick, New Jersey), Fall 1972, both by Tony Tanner; "James Purdy on the Corruption of Innocents" by Frank Baldanza, in *Contemporary Literature* (Madison, Wisconsin), 1974; interview with Fred Barron, in *Penthouse* (New York), July 1974; *James Purdy* by Henry Chupack, Boston, Twayne, 1975; *James Purdy* by Stephen D. Adams, London, Vision Press, and New York, Barnes and Noble, 1976; James Purdy and the Black Mask of Humanity" by Joseph T. Skerrett, Jr., in *Melus* (Los Angeles), 1979.

James Purdy comments:

(1972) As I see it, my work is an exploration of the American soul conveyed in a style based on the rhythms and accents of American speech. From the beginning my work has been greeted with a persistent and even passionate hostility on the part of the New York literary establishment which tries to rule America's literary taste—and the world's. My early work was privately printed by friends. Dame Edith Sitwell read these works, and persuaded Victor Gollancz to publish the book in England. Without her help I would never have been published in America and never heard of. The mediocrity of the American literary scene, as is evidenced in the *New York Times* and the creatures of the vast New York establishment, has tried to reduce me to starvation and silence. Yet as a matter of fact I believe my work is the most American of any writer writing today. My subject, as I said, is the exploration of the inside of my characters, or as John Cowper Powys put it, "under the skin." The theme of American culture, American commercial culture, that is, is that man can be adjusted, that loudness and numbers are reality, and that to be "in" is to exist. My work is the furthest from this definition of "reality." All individual thought and feeling have been silenced or "doped" in America today, and to be oneself is tantamount to non-existence. I see no difference between Russia and America; both are hideous failures, both enemies of the soul, both devourers of nature, and undisciplined disciplinarians who wallow in the unnatural. Anything in America is sacred which brings in money, and the consumers can easily be persuaded to move from their old crumbling Puritan ethic to belief in things like sexual deviation and coprophilia, provided and only provided these bring in money and notoriety. The one crime is to be oneself, unless it is a "self" approved and created by the commercial forces. Beneath this vast structure of madness, money, and anaesthetic prostitution, is my own body of work.

I prefer not to give a biography since my biography is in my work, and I do not wish to communicate with anybody but individuals, for whom my work was written in the first place. I began writing completely in the dark, and so continue. Were I in a financial position to do so, I would never publish anything commercially, since the literary establishment can promote only lies, and the critics, newspapers, and public having been fed on poison so long are incapable of reading anything that is not an advertisement for their own destruction. The most applauded writers in America are those who have had no contact with native American speech, but who seem to have been born in a television studio, where words are hourly produced from baking tins. In New York City, where American speech is unknown, a writer such as myself is considered a foreigner. Clarity and idiomatic language are considered in fact mad, while the language of dope addicts and coprophiliacs is now standard "American," approved for use by the dowagers who make best-sellers.

*   *   *

James Purdy is fascinated by the "color of darkness." His stories and novels deal with consuming narcissism and they assume, consequently, the "normal" love is, for the most part, cruel and nightmarish.

In *Color of Darkness* he gives us many heroes who are confused, lonely, and freakish. They do not know how to love (or to be loved). They are afraid to commit themselves. We see them sitting in dark rooms or roaming city streets; we hear their silent screams. Fenton Riddleway is so tormented by love for Claire, his dying brother, in "63: Dream Palace," the most impressive story in the collection, that he must kill him. The murder is the culmination of perverse love; it is perfectly in keeping with the "not-rightness" and rot of their dream palace.

In another collection, *Children Is All*, Purdy returns to the conflicts in family relationships. Often his heroes are orphans or bachelors. The narrator of "Daddy Wolf," for example, has seen his wife and child leave him; he turns for solace to the invisible "daddy." He calls him on the "trouble phone"; he rants, confesses, and rambles. But he is, finally, alone—

except for the rats which crawl near him. "Goodnight, Sweetheart," like all of the best stories, fuses the realistic (or cliché) dialogue and the fantastic incident. It begins with Pearl Miranda walking "stark naked from her class-room in the George Washington" to the house of Winston, a former pupil. Both are victims of love (or "rape"); both cannot exist in the wolfish world. Unfortunately, they cannot even live with each other. As the story ends, they "both muttered to themselves in the darkness as if they were separated by different rooms from one another." They pray for help.

Purdy's novels are more varied than his stories. (It is questionable whether they surpass the great achievement of the stories.) The hero of his first novel, *Malcolm*, searches for his father, hoping thereby to affirm his own identity and *name*. But, like Fenton Riddleway, he cannot exist as a "person"—he becomes another shadow in the rotten city. He is manipulated by others; he is never understood completely, except as a mere reflection of their selfish demands. Malcolm is, to quote his lusty wife, "a little bit of this and that," and when he dies—has he ever lived?—he apparently vanishes into thin air. *Malcolm* is a wonderfully strange mixture of comedy and pathos, and it alone asserts Purdy's impressive gifts as a novelist. Although it deals with the lack of substance in relationships—between men and women; between men and men; between human beings and the cosmos—it creates its own substantial texture largely as a result of Purdy's mixed, "transformational" style.

The Nephew is set in Rainbow Center, a small American town. (It is a change from the "fairy-tale" *Malcolm*.) It delights in clichés, minor scandals, and popular holidays; it is, at least superficially, a realistic picture of the middle Americans. But it represents Boyd and Alma (and Cliff, their missing nephew) in such a deceptive, complex way that "local color" changes subtly to universal darkness. When Alma discovers that she has never known Cliff (despite having lived with him for many years) and, consequently, realizes her own needs and dreams, she is depressed *and* exalted. She grasps the hard truth; she understands that we are all "missing" shadows; we live briefly and secretly. She accepts the significance of memorial days—the novel begins and ends on this holiday—and the "faint delicious perfume" of our lives before the court house clock strikes again. Thus *The Nephew*, like all of Purdy's novels, must be read closely (as Alma reads her nephew's life)—it presents two worlds and demands the recognition that only art can reconcile their differences.

Cabot Wright Begins is a savage satire on American life. It attacks the automatic, false, and empty values which make us treat people as *valuable objects*. Cabot Wright becomes a rapist because he can assert his identity only as a vital, pumping being. Later he runs away from the others—Bernie, Zoe, and Princeton—who want to trap and use his exotic past for their narcissistic ends. Cabot Wright begins to laugh and write; he rises from the "deadly monotony of the human continuity" when he lies on the ground, "weeping a little from the pain of his laughter, a thread of drivel coming down from his mouth onto his pointed dimpled chin." Despite the cluttered sermons, this novel is brilliantly effective when it says "HA!" to the boredom of our daily routines. It is Purdy's blackest comedy.

Eustace Chisholm and the Works details the various strategies of lovers who refuse to acknowledge their own potentialities. The homosexuality which colored *Malcolm*, *The Nephew*, and "63: Dream Place" flourishes here. Daniel Haws, for example, cannot accept his love for Amos (except at the end); he flees from it into the Army. There he is "satisfied" by sadistic Captain Stadger in a powerfully detailed execution (or embrace?). These Army scenes are perhaps the most brutal ones in all of Purdy's fiction.

Eustace Chisholm is a writer. He resembles Alma, Cabot Wright, and Bernie of *Cabot Wright Begins* in trying to solve the mysteries of love and will in the community; and, like them, he discovers that he cannot get to the heart of the matter. He *abdicates*—unlike Purdy himself—and turns instead to his wife for incredible love. He warms her with "a kind of ravening love," knowing that they will probably "consume" each other in the future. He is saved only momentarily.

Jeremy's Version is the first part of an uncompleted trilogy called *Sleepers in Moon-Crowned Valleys*, but it stands alone. Jeremy is an adolescent who writes down the sermons, tales, and histories of Matthew Lacy. He is, therefore, the familiar character we have met before, but unlike the other earlier writers, he is more open, innocent and *human* than they are. He learns as he listens and transcribes.

Jeremy moves into the past. He becomes so involved with the family conflicts of the 19th-century Fergises—he identifies especially with Jethro, another adolescent writer—that at times he becomes a free-floating *spirit*. Thus he forces us to recognize that only by giving oneself to others can we survive and create. He offers hope. His "version" is finally a mellow, full, and sunny account which indicates some new directions for Purdy's forthcoming novels.

The House of the Solitary Maggot, the second volume of the trilogy, presents different characters—Lady Bythwaite and her illegitimate sons—but it also assumes that love is a bloody mixture. The "family" is, again, a maggot-ridden, melodramatic structure. Thus this novel, a discontinuous part of the trilogy, parallels the first, implying a mythic, disturbing, general design; it offers few solutions and little hope for American society.

—Irving Malin

PUZO, Mario. American. Born in New York City, 15 October 1920. Educated at the New School for Social Research, New York; Columbia University, New York. Served in the United States Army Air Force during World War II. Married Erika Lina Broske in 1946; three sons and two daughters. Administrative assistant in U.S. Government offices, in New York and overseas, for 20 years; assistant editor of a magazine in late 1960's. Recipient: Oscar, for screenplay, 1972, 1974. Lives on Long Island, New York. Address: c/o Linden Press, Simon and Schuster, 1230 Avenue of the Americas, New York, New York 10020, U.S.A.

PUBLICATIONS

Novels

The Dark Arena. New York, Random House, 1955; London, Heinemann, 1971.
The Fortunate Pilgrim. New York, Atheneum, 1965; London, Heinemann, 1966.
The Godfather. New York, Putnam, and London, Heinemann, 1969.
Fools Die. New York, Putnam, and London, Heinemann, 1978.
The Sicilian. New York, Linden Press, 1984; London, Bantam Press, 1985.

Uncollected Short Stories

"Last Christmas," in *American Vanguard 1950*, edited by
 Charles I. Glicksberg.   New York, Cambridge, 1950.
"First Sundays," in *Redbook* (New York), February 1968.

Plays

Screenplays: *The Godfather*, with Francis Ford Coppola, 1972;
The Godfather, Part 2, with Francis Ford Coppola, 1974; *Earth-
quake*, with George Fox, 1974; *Superman*, with others, 1978;
Superman II, with David Newman and Leslie Newman, 1981.

Other

The Runaway Summer of Davie Shaw (for children).   New
 York, Platt and Munk, 1966; Kingswood, Surrey, World's
 Work, 1976.
The Godfather Papers and Other Confessions.   New York,
 Putnam, and London, Heinemann, 1972.
Inside Las Vegas.   New York, Grosset and Dunlap, 1977.

*

Manuscript Collection: Boston University.

*   *   *

Mario Puzo has developed through his novels a close examination of the social and psychological bases of power and authority in human affairs. Beginning with *The Dark Arena*, a study
of law, justice, compassion, and corruption in occupied Germany, and continuing through *The Godfather* and *The Sicilian*,
close studies of organized crime and its operation in Sicily and
the U.S., Puzo has reiterated variations on the root idea that
power corrupts.

Using his observations of Italo-American culture and a
strong mythopoeic imagination, Puzo has created a saga-his-
tory of the "American dream" as it has been played out in
the 20th century. In *The Dark Arena* we follow Mosca, an
ex-G.I. of Italian descent, who adapts himself to the complex
moral-psychological drama of Germany rising from the ashes
of World War II. *The Fortunate Pilgrim* traces in a parallel
fashion the adaptation of an Italian woman to America after
emigration. The same theme emerges in *The Godfather* and
The Sicilian, where we follow the Corleone clan, their family
connections in Sicily and the tangled web of the Mafia and
its ancient codes and rules. The collision of "official" law and
the laws of the family, of honor, and of social reality forms
a major focus of Puzo's imagination.

In *The Godfather* the immigrant saga is epitomized by Don
Corleone, a self-named, self-made "businessman" who has
become the ultimate entrepreneur-controller in New York
City, a "crime boss" whose operation is a close parody of legitimate corporate America. A profound ambivalence colors the
Corleone saga, a realization by the Don, his wife, and his sons
that the chivalric-baronial role they uphold operates at once
for good and for evil. The novel traces the development of
the Corleones as modern-day Borgias, *condottieri* who impose
their code of self-interested "honor" by brutal force and terror.

The Sicilian turns from the American version of the Mafia
rule to that of Sicily, where we follow the parallel careers of
Michael Corleone, heir to the U.S. family empire, and Turi
Giuliano, his counterpart in the Old World. Puzo dexterously
reveals how the "family" structure of both empires creates
a powerful, repressive society. The paralleling allows Puzo to
fill in details of the Corleone saga omitted in the first large

novel and to reinforce his theme of the corruption that accompanies power-by-terror.

In *Fools Die* Puzo develops some of these themes in a more
complex setting—the interconnecting worlds of bigtime gambling, the film industry, and publishing. The book strains in
developing the chivalric theme so natural in *The Godfather*
and *The Sicilian* by following the lines of brothers Arthur and
(John) Merlyn through a "new Camelot" of contemporary
America. The themes of personal honor and seduction to corruption are blurred by the large cast of characters and shifting
scenes and made too obvious in the allegorizing parallels with
the Arthurian romances.

Puzo's strongest gifts lie with a powerful, simple, and direct
naturalistic style, with a grasp on the historical experience of
adaptation to 20th-century America by the dispossessed immigrant and with a matter-of-fact examination of the moral,
social, and psychological issues surrounding organized crime
as an important U.S. subculture. His mythmaking powers are
best displayed in the Corleone story, in which a Machiavellian
ethos is created by the conditions and limitations of U.S. culture, so that the Sicilian codes and mores can be transferred
and amplified in the economic ferment of America. The basic
questions of ethics and justice are significant ones, and Puzo
shows how the bootstrap philosophy of material success can
operate effectively as "crime," even when it is defined as "law."
The figures he creates in the Corleone family reflect important
images of the American, as self-defined.

—William J. Schafer

PYNCHON, Thomas.   American.   Born in Glen Cove, New
York, 8 May 1937. Educated at Cornell University, Ithaca,
New York, 1954–58, B.A. 1958. Served in the United States
Naval Reserve. Former editorial writer, Boeing Aircraft, Seat-
tle. Recipient: Faulkner Award, 1964; Rosenthal Memorial
Award, 1967; National Book Award, 1974; American Acad-
emy Howells Medal, 1975. Agent: Candida Donadio and As-
sociates, 231 West 22nd Street, New York, New York 10011.
Address: c/o Little Brown, 34 Beacon Street, Boston, Massa-
chusetts 02106, U.S.A.

PUBLICATIONS

Novels

V.   Philadelphia, Lippincott, and London, Cape, 1963.
The Crying of Lot 49.   Philadelphia, Lippincott, 1966; Lon-
 don, Cape, 1967.
Gravity's Rainbow.   New York, Viking Press, and London,
 Cape, 1973.

Short Stories

Mortality and Mercy in Vienna.   London, Aloes, 1976.
Low-lands.   London, Aloes, 1978.
The Secret Integration.   London, Aloes, 1980.
The Small Rain.   London, Aloes, 1980(?).
Slow Learner: Early Stories.   Boston, Little Brown, 1984;
 London, Cape, 1985.

*

Bibliography: *Three Contemporary Novelists: An Annotated
Bibliography* by Robert M. Scotto, New York, Garland, 1977;

John Barth, Jerzy Kosinski, and Thomas Pynchon: A Reference Guide by Thomas P. Walsh and Cameron Northouse, Boston, Hall, 1977.

Critical Studies: *Thomas Pynchon* by Joseph V. Slade, New York, Warner, 1974; *Mindful Pleasures: Essays on Thomas Pynchon* edited by George Levine and David Leverenz, Boston, Little Brown, 1976; *The Grim Phoenix: Reconstructing Thomas Pynchon* by William M. Plater, Bloomington, Indiana University Press, 1978; *Pynchon: A Collection of Critical Essays* edited by Edward Mendelson, Englewood Cliffs, New Jersey, Prentice Hall, 1978; *Pynchon: Creative Paranoia in Gravity's Rainbow* by Mark Richard Siegel, Port Washington, New York, Kennikat Press, 1978; *Thomas Pynchon: The Art of Allusion* by David Cowart, Carbondale, Southern Illinois University Press, 1980; *The Rainbow Quest of Thomas Pynchon* by Douglas A. Mackey, San Bernardino, California, Borgo Press, 1980; *Pynchon's Fictions: Thomas Pynchon and the Literature of Information* by John O. Stark, Athens, Ohio University Press, 1980; *A Reader's Guide to Gravity's Rainbow* by Douglas Fowler, Ann Arbor, Michigan, Ardis, 1980; *Critical Essays on Thomas Pynchon* edited by Richard Pearce, Boston, Hall, 1981; *Thomas Pynchon* by Tony Tanner, London, Methuen, 1982; *Signs and Symptoms: Thomas Pynchon and the Contemporary World* by Peter L. Cooper, Berkeley, University of California Press, 1983.

*   *   *

Early in *V*, Thomas Pynchon's first novel, the character named Benny Profane is hunting alligators in the sewers of New York. He is hunting them on the city payroll, for a great number of baby alligators, bought as pets for children, have been flushed down toilets all over the city and are now breeding in the drainage tunnels. And as he hunts, Profane remembers the legend of Father Fairing, a Catholic priest who, during the Great Depression, decided that the rats were going to inherit the earth and went to live in the sewers, in order to convert the new chosen race to the one true faith. "At no point," Profane realized, "in the twenty or so years the legend had been handed on did it occur to anyone to question the old priest's sanity. It is this way with sewer stories. They just are. Truth or falsity don't apply."

It is a passage which says a great deal, not only about the dark and manic world of *V*, but about Pynchon's highly individual comic talent, and about the decade of the 1960's in which that talent flourished. Upon his first appearance, Pynchon was grouped by most critics with the other so-called "black humorists" of the decade: with writers like Bruce Jay Friedman, Kurt Vonnegut, and John Barth, whose satirical vision of contemporary America, with roots as diverse as Petronius, Nathanael West, and Lenny Bruce, suggested something like a new "movement" in literature, a turning away from the realistic conventions of 1950's fiction (e.g. Saul Bellow, J.D. Salinger), and from the political passivism associated with the Eisenhower era. This grouping had, indeed, some polemical point to it, in establishing the major talent and importance of some of its members. But like most other prematurely named "movements," it tended to obscure the vast differences between the writers involved, and finally to obscure even the structure of the works themselves. *V* has finally made it: reprinted as a Modern Library "Classic," it is taught in Modern Novel surveys across the country as an example of "black humor." But *V*, like *The Crying of Lot 49*, and especially the staggering *Gravity's Rainbow*, is not an example of anything, except of its

creator's unique vision. For if the "black humor" of Vonnegut consists of a series of simple, bitter parables about man's terrible need of charity, and that of Barth of an immense, baroque fantasia upon solipsism and nihilism, Pynchon's genius, neither allegorical nor epic, remains that of the teller of "sewer stories"; tales of the psychotic underground of the modern imagination, where "truth or falsity don't apply."

The image of the sewer, of the underground labyrinth, the secret network, the hidden "plot," is central to all of Pynchon's novels. But his use of this very common metaphor for modern life (one thinks of Gide, Norman Mailer, and Alain Robbe-Grillet) is a unique one. For Pynchon's labyrinths hold no mystery, and his deep dark secrets are, if anything, overillumined. Their terror, that is, is not the terror of the unknown, but precisely that of the *too well* known, of the twisted underbrush of the modern mind which has become so much our daily bread that we can never hope to see it in the full, unfamiliarized ghastliness of its reality. Another name for sewer stories, then, is perhaps "anti-Gothic romances." For Pynchon gives us an America, a world so inured to the unspeakable that one can, actually, speak about it. And his characters are somnambulists inhabiting ghost stories where their distinctive curse is to be incapacitated for horror itself.

Pynchon, while an undergraduate at Cornell, majored in English literature, but with a heavy helping of courses in modern physics: one of his former teachers still wonderingly remembers his apparently voracious appetite for the complexities of elementary particle theory. And physics, along with the myth of the labyrinth, has proved to be crucial to Pynchon's imagination. For if the modern condition may be imagined as a city honeycombed with secret subterranean passages, mind-boggling in their darkness and extensiveness, it may also be imagined as a cosmic version of that most critical quandary of contemporary physics, the so-called "Uncertainty Principle." This principle, in its baldest form, simply states that the complete description of *any* physical event is impossible—not because of the complexity of the event, but because *consciousness itself*, in attempting to examine the event, also alters the event from its "true" form into an impossible maze of self-reflexiveness. It is difficult, indeed, not to think of this principle when, in *The Crying of Lot 49*, the heroine Oedipa Maas faces the difficulty of ever discovering what, in its entirety, the mysterious "Trystero System" might mean: "Now here was Oedipa, faced with a metaphor of God knew how many parts; more than two, anyway. With coincidences blossoming these days wherever she looked, she had nothing but a sound, a word, Trystero, to hold them together." A word, a sound to resolve a metaphor which, like the "many body" problem of physics, consists of too many parts and is therefore *intrinsically* insoluble: truth and falsity don't, cannot apply in a world where those fundamentally moral values of the reason have been reduced to the dead level of infinitely extensive "facts."

Pynchon's three novels to date are concerned, in their different ways, with the great and urgent difficulty of finding a human truth within the manifold, labyrinthine coincidences of the modern experience. In *V* the labyrinth is the gigantic one of European history since the First World War. Herbert Stencil, seeking the truth about the death of his father in 1919, is led on a crazy quest for the identity of "V," a mysterious female—seductress, hag, secret agent—who appears to have been present at every disaster which has contributed to the making of modern Europe and America. The quest for V leads to a kind of terminal despair of history, a sense that the "Plot Which Has No Name," the master diabolical plot of the Twentieth Century, is necessarily unknowable to any of its victims. (Stencil himself, who refers to himself only in the third person, is literally a "stencil," a recording instrument incapable of passing moral judgment on that which he records.) But not before Stencil and the "whole sick crew" of existential bums he gathers around him have explored what is literally an underground history of the age, from Sarajevo through the Great Depression and Nazism to the formation of "Yoyodyne," the massive munitions industry which is Pynchon's chief image of the super-industrialized death factories of modern technology. V herself, though of course ultimately unknowable, appears in one of the book's most apocalyptic moments, the bombing of Malta during World War II, as a seductress who has been systematically replacing her living organs with pieces of precision machinery: the *femme fatale* become a shuddering *fatalité feminisée*.

After the sprawling genius of *V*, the classically spare economy of *Lot 49* seemed, in 1966, rather a terminal refinement and articulation of Pynchon's despair. Oedipa Maas searches for the clue which will reveal the meaning of "Trystero"—it is either an underground mail system which threatens the end of all civilization or an underground conspiracy which will build a new, more humane civilization—and finds the clue ungraspable. Nearly a short story compared to the length and range of *V*, *Lot 49* is nevertheless one of the most elegantly crafted nightmares of recent American fiction. And in the long, six year silence which followed its publication, many (including the present writer) felt that Pynchon's vision had grown so unrelievedly dark that there was nothing else to say. But then came *Gravity's Rainbow*.

Of *Gravity's Rainbow*, the most efficient thing that can be said is that it is one of the few truly great novels of the century, and at the same time one of the most disappointing, disturbing, maddening. Generally (and only "generally" may we summarize this immense book, nearly twice as long as *all* Pynchon's previous work), it is the story of Tyrone Slothrop, an American officer hounded into desertion at the end of the Second World War and wandering, ever losing more and more of his personality, in the area of post-War occupied Germany called "the Zone"—the greatest and most surreal of Pynchon's labyrinths. Slothrop is both archetypal man and archetypal machine—he is nearly turned into a guinea pig by British and American scientists because it is found that his erections correspond exactly and predictively to the sites of V-2 explosions in London. And as he wanders through the Zone he discovers, in the arthritic psyches of the victims of the War, the unprocreative seeds of the modern world at their most ghastly—including, of course, his own fragmented soul. A paradigm of modern man as literally in love with his own death, Slothrop's fate is complexly linked to the fate of the V-2 rockets themselves, those first mechanized versions of the Great Bombs which still terrify us, and whose graceful, deadly arc from launch to target is the "rainbow of gravity," the negative covenant of damnation, which gives the book its title. Pynchon narrates Slothrop's fate, moreover, in a language which is one of the most original fictive styles to have been developed since Joyce: a mélange of scientific jargon, Gothic lyricism, and comic-book pop dialect whose range of tone and fundamental irreverence perfectly catches—with almost Swiftean efficiency—its creator's horror of and fascination with the contemporary nightmare.

Pynchon is a fanatically private man: his photograph has not been taken in years, and no one knows where he lives or what he is doing at this moment. And, for a man of such deep and dark imagination, the wonder is that he has written so much: he may never write another word. But even if he does not, he has created two major novels and one incomparable one; and the strange, scandalous, absurd urge to create may overcome even a perfectly rational despair. For Pynchon's heroism, more than even his talent, is to be a matchless writer *against* the darkness, so that we might better, by talking aloud, see each other.

—Frank D. McConnell

RADDALL, Thomas Head. Canadian. Born in Hythe, Kent, England, 13 November 1903; emigrated to Canada in 1913. Educated at St. Leonard's School, Hythe; Chebucto School, Halifax, Nova Scotia; Halifax Academy. Wireless operator, Canadian Merchant Marine, 1918–22; served in the 2nd (Reserve) Battalion, West Nova Scotia Regiment, 1942–43: Lieutenant. Married Edith Margaret Freeman in 1927 (died); two children. Accountant in the wood pulp and paper industries in Nova Scotia, 1923–38. Full-time writer since 1938. Recipient: Governor-General's Award, 1944, for non-fiction, 1949, 1958; Boys' Clubs of America Junior Book Award, 1951; Lorne Pierce Medal, 1956. LL.D.: Dalhousie University, Halifax, 1949; St. Francis Xavier University, Antigonish, Nova Scotia, 1973; D.Litt.: St. Mary's University, Halifax, 1969; D.C.L.: King's College, Halifax, 1972. Fellow, Royal Society of Canada, 1953. Officer, Order of Canada, 1970. Address: 44 Park Street, Liverpool, Nova Scotia, BOT 1KO, Canada.

PUBLICATIONS

Novels

Saga of the "Rover," with C.H.L. Jones. Halifax, Nova Scotia, Royal, 1931.
His Majesty's Yankees. Toronto, McClelland and Stewart, and New York, Doubleday, 1942; Edinburgh, Blackwood, 1944.
Roger Sudden. Toronto, McClelland and Stewart, and New York, Doubleday, 1944; London, Hurst and Blackett, 1946.
Pride's Fancy. Toronto, McClelland and Stewart, and New York, Doubleday, 1946; London, Hurst and Blackett, 1948.
The Nymph and the Lamp. Toronto, McClelland and Stewart, and Boston, Little Brown, 1950; London, Hutchinson, 1951.
Son of the Hawk. Philadelphia, Winston, 1950.
Tidefall. Toronto, McClelland and Stewart, and Boston, Little Brown, 1953; London, Hutchinson, 1954; as *Give and Take*, New York, Popular Library, 1954.
The Wings of Night. New York, Doubleday, 1956; London, Macmillan, 1957.
The Governor's Lady. New York, Doubleday, 1960; London, Collins, 1961.
Hangman's Beach. New York, Doubleday, 1966.

Short Stories

Pied Piper of Dipper Creek and Other Tales. Edinburgh, Blackwood, 1939.
Tambour and Other Stories. Toronto, McClelland and Stewart, 1945.
The Wedding Gift and Other Stories. Toronto, McClelland and Stewart, 1947.
A Muster of Arms and Other Stories. Toronto, McClelland and Stewart, 1954.
At the Tide's Turn and Other Stories. Toronto, McClelland and Stewart, 1959.

Uncollected Short Stories

"The Singing Frenchman," in *Sunday Leader* (Halifax, Nova Scotia), 11 December 1921.
"Three Wise Men," in *Maclean's* (Toronto), 1 April 1928.
"The Little Red Gods," in *Sea Stories*, 1929.
"Maxim Gun McCuish," in *War Stories*, 1929.
"The Ghost of Sable Island," in *Sea Stories*, January 1929.
"Pounding Brass," in *Sea Stories*, August 1929.
"The Pressing of Bowline," in *Sea Stories*, October 1929.
"Admiral Togo's Remark," in *Sea Stories*, December 1929.
"Captain Moonlight," in *Excitement*, July 1930.
"The Pay-Off at Duncan's," in *Blackwood's* (Edinburgh), September 1934.
"A Matter of History," in *Blackwood's* (Edinburgh), May 1937.
"Between the Lines," in *Blackwood's* (Edinburgh), September 1938.
"The Lower Learning," in *Blackwood's* (Edinburgh), October 1938.
"Lupita," in *Maclean's* (Toronto), 1 June 1940.
"Mr. Embury's Hat," in *Maclean's* (Toronto), 1 July 1940.
"O'Shannaigh's Wooden House," in *Star Weekly* (Toronto), 28 January 1941.
"Swan Dance," in *Maclean's* (Toronto), 15 April 1941.
"Once upon a Time," in *Chatelaine* (Montreal), December 1941.
"Action at Sea," in *Collier's* (Springfield, Ohio), 11 April 1942.
"The Drumlin of Joe Tom," in *Adventure Magazine*, June 1942.
"The Miracle," in *Saturday Evening Post* (Philadelphia), 9 January 1943.
"G" (serial), in *Halifax Chronicle* (Nova Scotia), 1944.
"For Beginners Only," in *The Writer* (Boston), September 1944.
"Brooms for Sale," in *Wide Open Windows*, edited by Franklin L. Barrett. Toronto, Copp Clark, 1947.
"The Credit Shall Be Yours," in *Montreal Standard Weekend Magazine*, 16 October 1954.
"The Dreamers," in *Evening Telegram Weekend Magazine* (St. John's, Newfoundland), 30 July 1955.

Other

A Souvenir from the Land of Maple. Liverpool, Nova Scotia, Mersey Paper Company, n.d.
The Markland Sagas, with C.H.L. Jones. Montreal, Gazette Printing, 1934.
Ogomkegea: The Story of Liverpool, Nova Scotia. Liverpool, Nova Scotia, Liverpool Advance, 1934.
Canada's Deep Sea Fighters. Halifax, Government of Nova Scotia, 1936; revised edition, 1937.
West Novas: A History of the West Nova Scotia Regiment. Montreal, Provincial, 1948.
Halifax, Warden of the North. Toronto, McClelland and Stewart, 1948; London, Dent, 1950; revised edition, New York, Doubleday, 1965; McClelland and Stewart, 1971.
The Path of Destiny: Canada from the British Conquest to Home Rule 1763–1850. New York, Doubleday, 1957.
The Rover: The Story of a Canadian Privateer (for children). London, Macmillan, 1958; New York, St. Martin's Press, 1959.
Halifax and the World in 1809 and 1959. Halifax, Nova Scotia, Halifax Insurance Company, 1959.

Footsteps on Old Floors: True Tales of Mystery. New York, Doubleday, 1968.
This Is Nova Scotia, Canada's Ocean Playground. Halifax, Nova Scotia, Book Room, 1970.
In My Time: A Memoir. Toronto, McClelland and Stewart, 1976.
The Mersey Story. Liverpool, Nova Scotia, Bowater-Mersey Paper Company, 1979.

*

Bibliography: *Thomas Head Raddall: A Bibliography* by Alan R. Young, Kingston, Ontario, Loyal Colonies Press, 1982.

Manuscript Collection: Killam Memorial Library, Dalhousie University, Halifax.

Critical Studies: "Thomas H. Raddall: The Man and His Work" by W.J. Hawkins, in *Queen's Quarterly* (Kingston, Ontario), Spring 1968; "Thomas Raddall: The Art of Historical Fiction" by Donald Cameron, in *Dalhousie Review* (Halifax), Winter 1970; *Thomas Head Raddall* by Alan R. Young, Boston, Twayne, 1983.

Thomas Head Raddall comments:

As a youth I went to sea in Canadian ships, served in the North Atlantic for three years, and then a year as wireless operator on Sable Island, "The Graveyard of the Atlantic." Subsequently these experiences and observations gave me material for short stories and a novel, *The Nymph and the Lamp*. When I left the sea I took a job as book-keeper for a wood-pulp mill in the Nova Scotia forest. This gave me many interesting years of friendship with mill hands, loggers, river-drivers, hunters, and a band of Micmac Indians. I spent most of my spare time in the woods, exploring the Mersey River and its lakes, on foot and by canoe. On the indoor side I had a deep interest in Canadian, and especially Nova Scotian, history, and my experience of the sea and the forest gave me light on many of the old documents I found in the archives at Halifax and elsewhere. Hence, a dozen novels, many short stories of colonial times, and three books of plain history.

In all my fiction, whether historical or contemporary, I sought to inform as well as to give intelligent entertainment, and to convey in words and style my own delight in the English language.

*   *   *

Despite a long and distinguished career as a professional novelist, Thomas Head Raddall is curiously ignored by criticism. In part this neglect may be the result of his conservatism; he is no experimenter in either form or choice of material, he is personally retiring, and he unabashedly seeks a wide audience.

More unusually, he has achieved one. Raddall is deeply Nova Scotian, and though his novels sell well elsewhere and have been translated into several languages, perhaps the most unusual feature of his career has been his relationship with his native province. In Nova Scotia the most astonishing spectrum of people reads Raddall, from cabbies to the Cabinet. Nothing remotely parallel exists elsewhere in English Canada, and it is an inspiring example of the public uses to which the novel may still be put.

All Raddall's novels are set in Nova Scotia. Some of them are contemporary— notably *Tidefall* and *The Nymph and the Lamp*, the story of a strange love affair beween a radio operator and a frustrated, lonely typist who comes to live with him amidst the collection of isolated men on thinly disguised Sable Island. Though it has done well in the bookstores, however, the novel has never found much critical favour.

Raddall points out—quite correctly—that he is not just an historical novelist, but historical fiction has yielded his greatest success. The historical passion is strong in Raddall, and his work includes a volume of Canadian history, *The Path of Destiny*, as well as perhaps the finest work of local history ever written in Canada, *Halifax, Warden of the North*.

Raddall's historical fiction includes *Roger Sudden*, *Pride's Fancy*, *The Governor's Lady*, and *Hangman's Beach*, as well as numerous short stories. Perhaps the best, however, is Raddall's first novel, *His Majesty's Yankees*, an account of the changing loyalties and fortunes of David Strang, a young Nova Scotian fired with revolutionary zeal during the American War of Independence who finally comes to accept the forces which keep his colony British. The change in David is the change in the mood of Nova Scotia itself, and the understanding he achieves of the reasons for the colony's fate is the objective of the novel.

Such a story demands precisely the gifts Raddall possesses: a strong sense of story and a flair for the description of action, a clear and muscular style, an astute awareness of the interrelation between such private concerns as sex and such public concerns as revolution. The political division separates David from part of his family and his girl, and throws him into the centre of great events. Though he is not an extraordinary young man, he is intelligent, observant, and honest, an easy man for the reader to trust.

In conversation, Raddall describes his books not as novels, but as "tales" or "romances." The terms are not ill-chosen. Northrop Frye suggests that in a romance we know at the beginning how the work will end, and in this sense historical fiction is necessarily romantic. Moreover our interest in the hero is not centred in his uniqueness, but in his typicality; he stands not for an individual ideal or value, but for a communal mode of experience.

The hero's experience, says Lukács, is the necessary prehistory of the present; understanding it, we understand our own condition. At his best, Raddall conveys just such an understanding. Because of Nova Scotia's pivotal position in both the great French-English conflict in North America and the American Revolution, his work is relevant to an audience far beyond his beloved native province.

—Silver Donald Cameron

RAO, Raja. Indian. Born in Hassan, Mysore, 5 November 1908. Educated at Madarasa-e-Aliya School, Hyderabad, 1915–25; Aligarh Muslim University, 1926–27; Nizam College, Hyderabad (University of Madras), B.A. in English 1929; University of Montpellier, France, 1929–30; the Sorbonne, Paris, 1930–33. Married 1) Camille Mouly in 1931; 2) Katherine Jones in 1965, one son. Editor, *Tomorrow*, Bombay, 1943–44. Lived in France for many years; now lives half the year in India and half in Europe and the United States. Since 1965, Professor of Philosophy, teaching one semester a year, University of Texas, Austin. Recipient: Sahitya Academy Award, 1964; Padma Bhushan, 1969. Address: Department of Philosophy, University of Texas, Austin, Texas 78712, U.S.A.

PUBLICATIONS

Novels

Kanthapura.   London, Allen and Unwin, 1938; New York, New Directions, 1963.
The Serpent and the Rope.   London, Murray, 1960; New York, Pantheon, 1963.
The Cat and Shakespeare: A Tale of India.   New York, Macmillan, 1965.
Comrade Kirillov.   New Delhi, Orient, 1976.

Short Stories

The Cow of the Barricades and Other Stories.   Madras and London, Oxford University Press, 1947.
The Policeman and the Rose.   New Delhi and London, Oxford University Press, 1978.

Uncollected Short Story

"Jupiter and Mars," in *Pacific Spectator* (Stanford, California), vol. 8, no. 4, 1954.

Other

The Chess Master and His Moves.   New Delhi, Vision, 1978.

Editor, with Iqbal Singh, *Changing India*.   London, Allen and Unwin, 1939.
Editor, with Iqbal Singh, *Whither India?*   Baroda, Padmaja, 1948.
Editor, *Soviet Russia: Some Random Sketches and Impressions*, by Jawaharlal Nehru.   Bombay, Chetana, 1949.

*

Critical Studies: *Raja Rao* by M.K. Naik, New York, Twayne, 1972; *Raja Rao: A Critical Study of His Work* (includes bibliography) by C.D. Narasimhaiah, New Delhi and London, Heinemann, 1973; *The Fiction of Raja Rao* by K.R. Rao, Aurangabad, Parimal, 1980; *Perspectives on Raja Rao* edited by K.K. Sharma, Ghaziabad, Vimal, 1980.

Raja Rao comments:

(1972) Starting from the humanitarian and romantic perspective of man in *Kanthapura* and *The Cow of the Barricades*—both deeply influenced by Mahatma Gandhi's philosophy of non-violence—I soon came to the metaphysical novel, *The Serpent and the Rope*, and *The Cat and Shakespeare*, based on the Vedantic conception of illusion and reality. My main interest increasingly is in showing the complexity of the human condition (that is, the reality of man is beyond his person), and in showing the symbolic construct of any human expression. All words are hierarchic symbols, almost mathematical in precision, on and of the unknown.

*   *   *

Raja Rao has published two volumes of short fiction. One, *The Cow of the Barricades*, reveals its author's dedication to Indian independence. The second, *The Policeman and the Rose*, contains stories from the previous volume plus three others which are more metaphysical and more difficult in their symbolism than the earlier ones. But Rao is best known and most successful as a novelist. A South Indian Brahmin, he is chiefly concerned with religion and philosophy, not only of

India but also of the West, which he has come to know through many years of residence and study in France and, more recently, in the United States. During his youth he was deeply influenced by Mahatma Gandhi; and his first novel, *Kanthapura*, testifies unmistakably to its author's intellectual involvement in the Gandhian drive for national independence—to Rao as much a religious as a political movement.

E.M. Forster considered *Kanthapura* to be the best novel ever written in English by an Indian, and indeed it has great literary strength. Not the least of its merits is the picture it gives of life in one of the innumerable villages that are the repositories of India's ancient but living culture. In vivid detail, Rao describes the daily activities, the religious observances, and the social structure of the community, and he brings to life in his pages a dozen or more unforgettable individual villagers. The novel is political on a superficial level in that it chronicles a revolt against an exploitative plantation manager and the police who support him. But more profoundly it traces the origins of the revolt more to an awakening of the long-dormant Indian soul than to the activities of the Congress party. One of the young men of the village, while away, undergoes a mystical conversion to Satyagraha, and returns to incite his fellow villagers to civil disobedience. He arouses in them not only a sense of social wrong but, more importantly, a religious fervor which proves to be the true source of their strength against the oppressors.

Kanthapura is a novel in which the reader's interest is held mainly by its action and characters. *The Serpent and the Rope* and *The Cat and Shakespeare* are unabashedly metaphysical novels in which plot, setting and even characters are of secondary interest. Semiautobiographical, *The Serpent and the Rope* records the disintegration of a marriage, mainly on philosophical grounds, of a very scholarly Indian Brahmin and a French woman professor. The union founders on the incompatibility of the Brahmin's vedantic conviction that "reality is my Self" and the wife's Western belief—even though she has become a Buddhist—that the evidence of our senses is based on an objective reality outside ourselves. "The world is either unreal or real—the serpent or the rope," the Brahmin assures his wife. "There is no in-between-the-two. . . ." The intellectual demands that Raja Rao, roaming at large through world history and among the religions, philosophies, and literatures of Europe and Asia, makes upon his readers are unequalled in any modern novel since Thomas Mann's *The Magic Mountain*. Though he quotes at length from a bewildering assortment of languages, he provides translations in the case of only one—Sanskrit. The reader is flatteringly assumed to be fluent in Latin, Provençal, Italian, Old French, and other tongues.

The Cat and Shakespeare is much shorter and lighter in tone, though scarcely less metaphysical. The subject of its probings is the problem of individual destiny, and the solution is conveyed in an odd analogy stated by a government clerk: "Learn the way of the kitten. Then you are saved. Allow the mother cat, sir, to carry you." Critics disagree as to what the mother cat symbolizes. The most likely suggestion, made by Uma Parameswaran, is that the cat is karma, the inevitable results of our actions.

Rao's most recent novel, *Comrade Kirillov*, was first written in the late 1940's and underwent much revision and rewriting in the years that followed. Scarcely more than a novella in length, it recounts the efforts of a westernized Indian to interpret and advance the Indian independence movement in accord with Marxist theory and practice. The efforts come to nought, because, as Rao made clear in *Kanthapura*, the movement's strength and hope of success reside in the Indian soul and the Hindu religion. Attempted infusions of alien ideologies

are not only bound to fail but are irrelevant and doomed to be ignored by the Indian populace.

All of Rao's work is notable for seriousness of purpose, profundity of thought, a flair for vivid presentation of detail and distinctive and vigorous English prose. He asserts: "We cannot write like the English. We should not. We cannot write only as Indians. We have grown to look at the large world as part of us. Our method of expression therefore has to be a dialect which will some day prove to be as distinctive and colorful as the Irish or the American. Time alone will justify it." We might add that Raja Rao's books have gone far to justify it.

—Perry D. Westbrook

* * *

RAPHAEL, Frederic (Michael). American. Born in Chicago, Illinois, 14 August 1931. Educated at Charterhouse School, Surrey; St. John's College, Cambridge, 1950–54 (Major Classics Scholar, 1950; Harper Wood Studentship, 1954), M.A. (honours) 1954. Married Sylvia Betty Glatt in 1955; two sons and one daughter. Since 1962, contributor, and fiction critic, 1962–65, *Sunday Times*, London. Recipient: British Screen Writers award, 1965, 1966, 1967; British Academy award, 1965; Oscar, for screenplay, 1966; Royal Television Society Writer of the Year Award, 1976. Fellow, Royal Society of Literature, 1964. Agent: Hilary Rubinstein, A.P. Watt Ltd., 26–28 Bedford Row, London WC1R 4HL. Address: The Wick, Langham, near Colchester, Essex CO4 5PE, England; or, Largardelle, St. Laurent-la-Vallée, 24170 Belvès, France.

PUBLICATIONS

Novels

Obbligato. London, Macmillan, 1956.
The Earlsdon Way. London, Cassell, 1958.
The Limits of Love. London, Cassell, 1960; Philadelphia, Lippincott, 1961.
A Wild Surmise. London, Cassell, 1961; Philadelphia, Lippincott, 1962.
The Graduate Wife. London, Cassell, 1962.
The Trouble with England. London, Cassell, 1962.
Lindmann. London, Cassell, 1963; New York, Holt Rinehart, 1964.
Darling. New York, New American Library, 1965.
Orchestra and Beginners. London, Cape, 1967; New York, Viking Press, 1968.
Like Men Betrayed. London, Cape, 1970; New York, Viking Press, 1971.
Who Were You with Last Night? London, Cape, 1971.
April, June, and November. London, Cape, 1972; Indianapolis, Bobbs Merrill, 1976.
Richard's Things. London, Cape, 1973; Indianapolis, Bobbs Merrill, 1975.
California Time. London, Cape, 1975; New York, Holt Rinehart, 1976.
The Glittering Prizes. London, Allen Lane, 1976; New York, St. Martin's Press, 1978.
Heaven and Earth. London, Cape, and New York, Beaufort, 1985.

Short Stories

Sleeps Six. London, Cape, 1979.
Oxbridge Blues and Other Stories. London, Cape, 1980; Fayetteville, University of Arkansas Press, 1984.
Oxbridge Blues (includes *Sleeps Six* and *Oxbridge Blues and Other Stories*). London, Penguin, 1984.
Think of England. London, Cape, 1986.

Plays

Lady at the Wheel, with Lucienne Hill, music and lyrics by Leslie Bricusse and Robin Beaumont (produced London, 1958).
A Man on the Bridge (produced Hornchurch, Essex, 1961).
The Island (for children), in *Eight Plays 2*, edited by Malcolm Fellows. London,Cassell, 1965.
Two for the Road (screenplay). London, Cape, and New York, Holt Rinehart, 1967.
An Early Life (produced Leicester, 1979).
The Serpent Son: Aeschylus: Oresteia, with Kenneth McLeish (televised, 1979). London, Cambridge University Press, 1979.
From the Greek (produced Cambridge, 1979).

Screenplays: *Bachelor of Hearts*, with Leslie Bricusse, 1958; *Don't Bother to Knock* (*Why Bother to Knock*), with Denis Cannan and Frederic Gotfurt, 1961; *Nothing But the Best*, 1963; *Darling*, 1965; *Two for the Road*, 1967; *Far from the Madding Crowd*, 1967; *A Severed Head*, 1970; *Daisy Miller*, 1974; *Richard's Things*, 1981.

Radio Documentaries: *The Daedalus Dimension*, 1979; *Death in Trieste*, 1981.

Television Plays: *The Executioners*, 1961; *Image of a Society*, from the novel by Roy Fuller, 1963; *The Trouble with England*, from his own novel, 1964; *The Glittering Prizes*, 1976; *Rogue Male*, from the novel by Geoffrey Household, 1976; *Something's Wrong*, 1978; *The Serpent Son*, with Kenneth McLeish, 1979; *Of Mycenae and Men*, with Kenneth McLeish, 1979; *School Play*, 1979; *The Best of Friends*, 1980; *Byron: A Personal Tour* (documentary; also narrator), 1981; *Oxbridge Blues*, 1984.

Other

W. Somerset Maugham and His World. London, Thames and Hudson, and New York, Scribner, 1977.
Cracks in the Ice: Views and Reviews. London, W.H. Allen, 1979.
The List of Books: An Imaginary Library, with Kenneth McLeish. London, Mitchell Beazley, and New York, Harmony, 1981.
Byron. London, Thames and Hudson, 1982.

Editor, *Bookmarks*. London, Cape, 1975.

Translator, with Kenneth McLeish, *The Poems of Catullus*. London, Cape, 1978; Boston, Godine, 1979.

*

Critical Study: "The Varied Universe of Frederic Raphael" by Frederick P.W. McDowell, in *Critique* (Minneapolis), Fall 1965.

Theatrical Activities:
Director: **Television**—*Something's Wrong*, 1978; *He'll See You Now*, 1984.

Frederic Raphael comments:

Although in many ways I am the most marginal of Jews (I am agnostic in religion and wary of communities), I suppose it is honest to say that I would not be a novelist if it were not for the singular experiences of the Jewish people and for my sense of being, if not a direct participant, at least a witness, of them. My themes, if I have themes, are scarcely Jewish since I lack intimate knowledge of the practices and habits of those who live in so-called Jewish society. When I do come in contact with them I do not necessarily find them congenial. Yet, the Final Solution—its vulgarity no less than its brutality, its greedy malice no less than its murderous factories—lies always at the back of my mind even if I myself, as a child growing up in England, suffered nothing more than its bad breath blowing in my face from across the Channel. It may be an indulgence for anyone who did not have closer experience to claim personal acquaintance with the holocaust; it is equally frivolous to ignore it. It is too convenient a conclusion to dispose of the Jewish experience under the Germans (and the Austrians and the Poles and the Hungarians and the Ukrainians and the Russians, and the English and the Americans) as a sort of freakish explosion, a San Francisco earthquake of an event, a once-and-for-all catastrophe after which, in the comforter's cliché, one has to "go on living." And yet, of course, one does.

For me, the novelist is, above all, the historian of conscience. How does the individual conscience—in other words, how do I—go on living in a world which gives the clearest possible testimony of the cruelty and indifference of man? How does one continue to worry about the nuances of personal life, about love, friendship, taste, and responsibility when all the signs are that man is essentially rapacious, vindictive, and stupid? I have no answers to these questions, nor do I pretend they are in themselves new; they have been asked often enough and yet one does live at a particular time and, despite all the elegant suggestions to the contrary, it seems to me that our time is still linear. Certain things are beyond change, others lie ahead.

The problem is, in a sense, of language. Only in language is it possible to assimilate horrors and yet to achieve something which is both clear and, in a sense, pure. The way in which man remembers meaningfully is by not refusing sense in his language to those things which most profoundly influence or instruct him. This might be an argument for writing either history or philosophy and in a way I tried to do this, but I am not an historian or a philosopher. An obsession with a particular instance of the human character and a desire no less than a tendency—to show the futility of generalisation in the face of the fatuous and magnanimous individuality of human beings, lead me to examine the world through dramatic and emotional states rather than through a study of documents or the analysis of trends. Beyond and through the tragic comes the comic—the comic which does not explode the tragic but defines it—and this interpenetration is only one example of the sort of ambiguities in which the novelist finds himself at home. These ambiguities reveal themselves in drama and I have always found that, in spite of the attractions of both the theatre and the cinema, the drama can be worked out at its most personal and in the most piercing fashion in fiction. Truth may be stranger than fiction but fiction is truer.

How loftily one speaks in such generalising terms as these. The actual impulses which start a book are, of course, less grand. They spring as much from a sense of one's own contradictions as from any perception of human inadequacy or follies. When one begins to speak in the first person it sounds like conceit but it is more often confession, at least at my age.

I am conscious above all of being equipped to be a novelist because it is only in a multiplicity of characters that I can reconcile my own ragbag personality. When people speak of a crisis of identity, I remind them that we know very well who we are, where we are having dinner and with whom we are sleeping, yet when I consider myself I am less commonsensical.

I was born in Chicago of a British father and an American mother. Beyond them, my grandparents and great-grandparents branched off across the world like an airline network. I was educated at Charterhouse which, I am told, is a great English Public School, and at Cambridge. I was readily influenced both by the ethos of the English middle class and by the intellectual habits of a classical education. Although I now regret much of what I was told and some of what I learned, I cannot shrug off the influence of these places, nor am I certain that I would wish to do so. The conflict of values reveals itself in fiction in the conflict of characters. I am conscious of being foreign in England and I find myself at home to some extent in many other places, yet I cannot sever myself entirely from the country where I live or from the language in which I write. I am sickened by xenophobia and yet in many ways I fear what lies beyond me. I believe that reason is better than unreason and that intelligence is better than instinct but I have not always been impressed by the decency of those who are most intelligent or by the capacity for affection and love of those who are most reasonable.

Within the nooks and crannies of the great edifices of generalisation and judgement, the innocently guilty and the guiltily innocent scurry about carrying nuts to their families, seeking their pleasures, snapping at their enemies, and providing, for those who have eyes to see, the proof of the impossibility of final solutions to the human condition.

*   *   *

Frederic Raphael began with a slight novel, *Obbligato*, a satiric and mock-heroic account of the rise to fame of an improvising pop-singer. Literary merit is abundant, however, in Raphael's second book, *The Earlsdon Way*, a realistic novel about the futility of British suburban life and the ineffectual revolt against its mores undertaken by Edward Keggin and his daughter Karen.

The Limits of Love gained for Raphael wide and deserved recognition. Its protagonist, Paul Riesman, is a Jew divorced by his training and inclinations from his race. Because he will not recognize what is necessity for him, his Jewishness, he becomes a selfish, life-destroying man despite his continuing efforts to achieve identity. But Paul increasingly sees that love is a defeating force if it is limited to the personal sphere and if it rejects the community; and he finds in his mother-in-law, Hannah Adler, stability that he lacks and in her daughter Julia, his wife, flexibility and depth.

In *A Wild Surmise* Raphael used a technique of montage to reveal his protagonist, Robert Carn, gradually. Carn hopes to escape British conventions in San Roque and to find genuine value through the spontaneous, impassioned, disinterested self. Ultimately, he supplements his introspective endeavors with a commitment to others in his efforts, ostensibly unsuccessful, to save some Indians from being poisoned. The novel is powerful and evocative, especially as it charts the processes of Carn's mind and the subtleties of his psychic life.

Raphael has written a number of brief novels, ironically executed, which concentrate upon a moral problem and its significance for the chief characters. *The Trouble with England* develops the moral contrasts between two vacationing couples on the French Riviera; *The Graduate Wife* focuses upon the forward development of a priggish heroine to inner stability. *Who Were You with Last Night?* has, as first-person narrator, the disenchanted Charles Hanson who is amusing as he deflates bourgeois values (sometimes his own), recounts his satisfactions and frustrations with wife and mistress, and analyzes the delicate balance existing between love and hate in intimate relationships. *Richard's Things* is a *tour de force*, suggesting the impermanence not only of the marital relationship but of life itself, as the piquant relationship between the wife of the now dead Richard and his mistress diminishes from its first ardor to something near hatred. More recently, *The Glittering Prizes* reveals Raphael's remarkable technical expertise and depth of emotional insight as he traces the unfolding lives, after their graduation, of a group of Cambridge contemporaries. The chief of these, Adam Morris, is a novelist similar in temperament to Raphael himself. He is an ironically minded but aesthetically talented Jew whose temporary foray into the world of the mass media is engaging farce, meant also to define the difficulties that the serious artist encounters in holding fast to his genuine impulses.

The peak of Raphael's achievement in writing the experimental novel is *Lindmann*. A British civil servant, James Shepherd, connived in 1942 to prevent the *SS Broda* from landing in Turkey with its Jewish refugees. Shepherd, to expiate his guilt and to achieve self-definition, assumes the identity of Jacob Lindmann, one of the two survivors from the ship who later died from exposure. A certain chastity gives Shepherd as Lindmann his moral force, since he forgoes any kind of fulfillment for himself; and he is, by his spiritual tenacity, something more than the failure he judges himself to be. Through patience and love he tries to influence others to a course of moderation, toleration, consideration, and affection.

Orchestra and Beginners, *Like Men Betrayed*, *April, June, and November*, and *California Time* are also works of considerable scope. In *Orchestra and Beginners* Raphael analyzes the ineffectual decency and the effete decay which characterized British upper-middle-class society just prior to World War II. Linda Strauss suffers from the moral paralysis of the class into which as an American she has married but is sympathetically seen, even if she fails her husband at his military enlistment because of her intensely personal reactions to experience. Leonard, in turn, is too impersonal toward Linda. Paradoxically, Linda's passion and Leonard's critical intelligence are both needed in confronting the complexities of modern life.

Like Men Betrayed is about Greek and, by implication, English politics, and it is remarkable for penetrating the relationships between the individual's psyche and social institutions. Three main points in time contrapuntally organize the book: the Greece of the 1930's under the Marshal's moderate dictatorship; Greece during the Second World War when factional jealousies are only less intense than hatred for the Italians and Germans; and postwar Greece when a power struggle develops between the corrupt royalist regime and the leftist insurgents. Artemis Theodoros defects from the Royalists when government troops fail in World War II to support the leftist General Papavastrou against the Germans. The novel is subtle and complex as it traces Artemis's endeavors to reach spiritual and political truth. As the novel opens he is fleeing north to the frontier where supposedly his forces will reach asylum. Instead, he learns that they will be betrayed. He remains faithful to his inner standards, however, despite misunderstanding, violence, betrayal, imprisonment, and exile. In Artemis a deplorable waste of genius occurs. The integrity inherent in such a heroic man, however, is the resource which we will have to learn how to use to insure a revitalized polity, Raphael would seem to be saying.

April, June, and November, California Time, and *Heaven and Earth* are also novels about talented men whose creative energies are deflected either by weakness of will or by circumstances. In *April, June, and November* the liberal and magnetic Daniel Meyer is, in fact, capable of a heroism which he can never display to any purpose in his hedonistic, effete milieu. The football field rather than the political arena claims his intelligence and genius. In *California Time* Victor England is likewise a victim, but could he have ever achieved distinction in the cutthroat and standardless world of the motion picture studios, a world which needs his creativity but which also humiliates him to the greatest possible extent? Raphael is frankly experimental in this novel, collapsing all of Victor's experience into the ongoing present and creating doubts in him as to the reality of his perceptions of the given moment, in a milieu in which the reality and the hallucination become barely distinguishable. In *Heaven and Earth* Gideon Shand is a good man whose happiness, prosperity, and integrity seem unassailable. Underneath, the irrational forces in himself and others lead, unexpectedly to him (and to the reader), to destruction and self-destruction. Life is at once tougher and more fragile than he had at first realized; and the implicit question raised in this novel, but not decisively answered, is whether a man like Gideon can survive the violent effects of these unconscious forces. In these three novels Raphael develops the tragedy of the man who cannot actualize his good intentions and give free expression to his genius, with the same density, elusiveness, and complication that characterize his fiction as a whole.

—Frederick P.W. McDowell

RAVEN, Simon (Arthur Noël). British. Born in London, 28 December 1927. Educated at Charterhouse School, Surrey, 1941–45; King's College, Cambridge, 1948–52, B.A. 1951, M.A. 1955. Served in the British Army, 1946–48 (commissioned in India, 1947), and 1953–57 (Captain, King's Shropshire Light Infantry). Married Susan Mandeville Kilner in 1951 (divorced, 1957); one son. Agent: Curtis Brown, 162–168 Regent Street, London W1R 5TA, England.

PUBLICATIONS

Novels

The Feathers of Death.   London, Blond, 1959; New York, Simon and Schuster, 1960.
Brother Cain.   London, Blond, 1959; New York, Simon and Schuster, 1960.
Doctors Wear Scarlet.   London, Blond, 1960; New York, Simon and Schuster, 1961
Close of Play.   London, Blond, 1962.
Alms for Oblivion:
   The Rich Pay Late.   London, Blond, 1964; New York, Putnam, 1965.
   Friends in Low Places.   London, Blond, 1965; New York, Putnam, 1966.
   The Sabre Squadron.   London, Blond, 1966; New York, Harper, 1967.
   Fielding Gray.   London, Blond, 1967; New York, Beaufort, 1985.
   The Judas Boy.   London, Blond, 1968.
   Places Where They Sing.   London, Blond, 1970.

Sound the Retreat.   London, Blond, 1971.
Come like Shadows.   London, Blond and Briggs, 1972.
Bring Forth the Body.   London, Blond and Briggs, 1974.
The Survivors.   London, Blond and Briggs, 1975.
The Roses of Picardie: A Romance.   London, Blond and Briggs, 1980.
An Inch of Fortune.   London, Blond and Briggs, 1980.
September Castle.   London, Blond and Briggs, 1983.
The First-Born of Egypt:
   Morning Star.   London, Muller Blond and White, 1984.
   The Face of the Waters.   London, Muller Blond and White, 1985.

Short Stories

The Fortunes of Fingel.   London, Blond and Briggs, 1976.

Plays

The Scouncing Stoup (broadcast, 1964).   Published in *New Radio Drama*, London, BBC Publications, 1966.
Royal Foundation and Other Plays (radio and television plays: *The Move Up Country; The Doomsday School; The Scapegoat; Panther Larkin; The High King's Tomb; The Gaming Book; Sir Jocelyn, The Minister Would Like a Word*). London, Blond, 1966.
The Case of Father Brendan (produced London, 1968).

Screenplays: *On Her Majesty's Secret Service*, with Richard Maibaum, 1969; *Unman, Wittering, and Zigo*, 1971.

Radio Plays: *Loser Pays All*, 1961; *A Present from Venice*, 1961; *The Gate of Learning*, 1962; *A Friend in Need*, 1962; *The Doomsday School*, 1963; *The High King's Tomb*, 1964; *The Scouncing Stoup*, 1964; *Panther Larkin*, 1964; *The Melos Affair*, 1965; *The Last Expedition*, 1967; *The Tutor*, 1967; *The Prisoners in the Cave*, 1968; *Salvation*, 1974; *In Transit*, 1978.

Television Plays: *The Scapegoat*, 1964; *The Gaming Book*, 1964; *Advise and Dissent*, 1965; *Sir Jocelyn, The Minister Would Like a Word*, 1965; *A Soirée at Bossom's Hotel*, 1966; *A Pyre for Private James*, 1966; *Point Counter Point*, from the novel by Aldous Huxley, 1968; *The Way We Live Now*, from the novel by Trollope, 1969; *The Human Element*, from the novel by Somerset Maugham, 1970; *The Pallisers*, from novels by Trollope, 1974; *An Unofficial Rose*, from the novel by Iris Murdoch, 1974; *Red Sky at Night* (*The Brothers* series), 1976; *Edward and Mrs. Simpson*, from a work by Frances Donaldson, 1978; *Sexton Blake* series, 1978; *Love in a Cold Climate*, from the novels *Love in a Cold Climate* and *The Pursuit of Love* by Nancy Mitford, 1980; *The Search for Alexander the Great*, with George Lefferts, 1981.

Other

The English Gentleman: An Essay In Attitudes.   London, Blond, 1961; as *The Decline of the Gentleman*, New York, Simon and Schuster, 1962.
Boys Will Be Boys and Other Essays.   London, Blond, 1963.
Shadows on the Grass (on cricket).   London, Blond and Briggs, 1982.

Editor, *The Best of Gerald Kersh.*   London, Heinemann, 1960.

*

Critical Study: "The Novels of Simon Raven" by Kerry McSweeney, in *Queen's Quarterly* (Kingston, Ontario), Spring 1971.

Simon Raven comments:
My theme is the vanity of human wishes.
My object is to make money by presenting this theme in such a way as to interest and amuse intelligent readers of the upper and upper-middle classes.

*   *   *

A prolific and thoroughly professional writer, Simon Raven has delivered himself of a steady stream of novels for over a quarter of a century. Ten of these form the sequence *Alms for Oblivion* (1964–75); he has since embarked on a second novel sequence under the general title *The First-Born of Egypt*; and some of the persons, places, and institutions which figure in both these sequences appear also in his other tales.

The cumulative impact of his fiction tends therefore to be essentially restricted and concentrated rather than wide-ranging and expansive. We have here an author who works, and works brilliantly, within the confines of his chosen territory, but who runs the risk of leaving his readers with the sense that they have been all over that particular ground before. The risk in the longer term, one might ask, of boring his readers? Certainly not, for he is always entertaining; but there is bound to be some danger of the reader's appetite becoming sated by the constant repetition of Raven's spicy line of literary cuisine.

It is on the merits of the two novel sequences that he will no doubt mainly be judged. The society they depict is that of the English upper middle classes since the end of the second world war, the loosely (and in Raven's book often louchely) knit society of politicians and businessmen, soldiers and civil servants, journalists and dons, crooks, nice men and out-and-out shits whose overlapping interests and influence comprise the English establishment. In Raven's fiction even the nice men tend to become embroiled in crooked or squalid behaviour, while the nastier men and women are nasty indeed.

Alms for Oblivion was planned by the author as a loosely organised series of novels, each of which would present an independent story and be assimilable on its own. The cohesive element which holds the series together is the fact that the principal characters are related by ties of birth, education, and professional interests. The plan allowed Raven to move backwards as well as forwards in time, with the earliest novel in the fictional chronology, *Fielding Gray*, appearing as the fourth in the sequence. Here he introduced the younger members of the cast as schoolboys in the process of initiation into the conflicts of adult life in which he had already portrayed them. The themes of self-advancement and self-preservation, of personal and group loyalty, of sexual adventure and emotional betrayal (both homosexual and heterosexual), examined here within the social microcosm of an English public school, recur throughout the series with different complications and in different settings.

"If there is one theme which will dominate the series," wrote the author in an epigraph to *Alms for Oblivion*, "it is that human effort and goodwill are persistently vulnerable to the malice of time, chance, and the rest of the human race." This sounds like a blueprint for farce; and farcical events certainly abound in his novels, many of them blue enough in print. But there is more to Raven than pure—or even impure—farce. He sets out deliberately to contrive violent and macabre accidents and incidents, drawing aside the curtain on scenes of debauchment and corruption, blackmail and double-dealing, malpractice and malversation. In particular, he beckons the reader to witness, through the voyeurism of his fictions, extraordinary facts of life in the way of sexual practices and perversions.

The aim, no doubt, is partly to titillate and thus to amuse; it is also no doubt partly to shock, in the bounderish tradition of shocking the bourgeois. But there is a darker distance in these scabrous perspectives. The reader senses some kind of underlying resentment, perhaps a desire to revenge lost innocence or to offload a burden of guilt or regret. Such undertones may be found even in those novels which stand outside the major sequences, while the same themes, milieux, and persons are immediately recognisable there also.

In his variation on the Oxbridge murder story, *Doctors Wear Scarlet*, for instance, the college and its dons are clearly the Lancaster College and its Fellows of *Alms for Oblivion*; the detective work and unravelling of clues are cast from the same mould as the quests for lost manuscripts and the scholarly decipherments and decodings met with in the sequence's last volume and in the "free-standing" novels, *The Roses of Picardie* and *September Castle*.

It is probably too soon to pass judgment on *The First-Born of Egypt*, which is designed to show "the purposes, beliefs and ways of life of the growing young as observed, deplored, or encouraged by their elders." The first volume, *Morning Star*, deploys a long cast list and establishes a number of subplots for potential exploitation, while *The Face of the Waters* is less crowded with people and incidents. But if there seems so far to be little new in the way of character, theme, or novelistic technique, the author's energy and ability to create entertainingly scandalous comedy is as evident as ever. One looks forward eagerly to the subsequent instalments.

—Stewart F. Sanderson

READ, Piers Paul. British. Born in Beaconsfield, Buckinghamshire, 7 March 1941; son of the writer Herbert Read. Educated at Ampleforth College; St. John's College, Cambridge, B.A. 1961, M.A. 1962. Married Emily Boothby in 1967; two sons and two daughters. Sub-editor, *Times Literary Supplement*, London, 1964–65. Artist-in-Residence, Ford Foundation, Berlin, 1963–64; Adjunct Professor of Writing, Columbia University, New York, 1980. Recipient: Commonwealth Fund Harkness Fellowship, 1967; Faber Memorial Award, 1968; Hawthornden Prize, 1969; Maugham Award, 1970; Thomas More Association Medal, 1974. Fellow, Royal Society of Literature. Agent: Deborah Rogers Ltd., 49 Blenheim Crescent, London W11 2EF. Address: 50 Portland Road, London W11 4LG, England.

PUBLICATIONS

Novels

Game in Heaven with Tussy Marx. London, Weidenfeld and Nicolson, and New York, McGraw Hill, 1966.
The Junkers. London, Secker and Warburg, 1968; New York, Knopf, 1969.
Monk Dawson. London, Secker and Warburg, 1969; Philadelphia, Lippincott, 1970.
The Professor's Daughter. London, Secker and Warburg-Alison Press, and Philadelphia, Lippincott, 1971.

The Upstart. London, Alison Press, and Philadelphia, Lippincott, 1973.
Polonaise. London, Alison Press, and Philadelphia, Lippincott, 1976.
A Married Man. London, Secker and Warburg, 1979; Philadelphia, Lippincott, 1980.
The Villa Golitsyn. London, Secker and Warburg, 1981; New York, Harper, 1982.

Plays

The Class War, in *Colloquialisms* (produced London, 1964).

Radio Plays: *The Family Firm*, 1970; *The House on Highbury Hill*, music by Julian Slade, 1971.

Television Plays: *Coincidence*, 1968; *The Childhood Friend*, 1974; *Margaret Clitheroe* (*Here I Stand* series), 1977.

Other

Alive! The Story of the Andes Survivors. London, Secker and Warburg, and Philadelphia, Lippincott, 1974.
The Train Robbers. London, Allen and Unwin-Alison Press, and Philadelphia, Lippincott, 1978.

*   *   *

Piers Paul Read is intensely concerned with moral issues. Many of his main themes are epitomized in *Monk Dawson*, the best novel he has yet written. Dissatisfied with his monastic existence, Edward Dawson enters the main stream of contemporary society—a society that is decadent, sex-obsessed, hedonistic, bored, and exceedingly materialistic. Despite sports, gambling, relaxing in the sun, and similar pleasures, Dawson finds sybaritic activities empty; life becomes painful and without meaning. Dawson's woman companion, to whom he is deeply devoted, deserts him for another lover, and qualities such as basic kindness, integrity, and good character are out of fashion. Dawson's return to monasticism is a recognition that man should possess spiritual purpose, exalt solidity in his life, and give service to moral values, which are an individual's and the world's only hope for at least partial betterment.

In Read's first novel, an extravagant fantasy in which Karl Marx's youngest daughter, Tussy, views life from an anteroom of heaven, the reader perceives that well-intentioned philosophies are marred by people who are, by their very nature, corrupt and amoral and allow the whims and blandishments of love to dominate even when love is found to be usually unstable, impermanent, and fraudulent.

Read's interest in various political theories is pervasive. In *The Professor's Daughter* Henry Rutledge is a distinguished Harvard master of political theory. Handsome, intelligent, and rich, he champions liberal and progressive ideas. His death, which results from militant revolutionary activity carried out by some of his graduate students, exposes the sharp contrast between idealistic theory and reality. Politically, Rutledge may be on the side of the angels, but has made a wreck of his family relationships. His wife is continuously unfaithful and an alcoholic, while his oldest daughter is, successively, hippie, prostitute, and revolutionary. She is saved from suicide by the merest of accidents. She is seen not only as a casualty of a rotten society, but also as the sad victim of the breakdown of family life. Since Read stresses that the family is society's fundamental stabilizing unit, this institution must first be put in order before any significant success can be achieved outside the home.

The vicious degeneracy and animalistic cruelty of the Nazis, so expertly exposed in *The Junkers*, demonstrate anew the desperate need for moral standards in a world of treachery, SS, concentration camps, and genocide. *The Upstart* also emphasizes this theme as Hilary Fletcher commits almost every evil of which a person is capable; yet ultimately, for Fletcher, there is hope achieved by genuine repentance and atonement. Even the Communist can be applauded if morality and genuine humanitarian concerns can overcome the dominance of evil and cruelty which constantly plagues individuals.

At one point Read quotes from Julien Green's *Diary* to the effect that within each of us there is a sinner and a saint. Even though one phase dominates, the other aspect makes progress on the imaginative plane so that this mixture and conflict will cause constant turmoil, and the yearning for betterment will continue to torment. In the fiction of Read we are reminded that all too often "the devil is prince of the world. ... He has powers too."

Both *Polonaise* and *A Married Man* are notable examples of an increasing mastery of style and plotting. Read's earlier novels suffered from occasional stretches of pedestrian prose and a tendency to melodrama and contrived happenings. Read now demonstrates a definite growth in craftsmanship. This artistry and his perceptive and penetrating probing into crucial 20th-century moral issues demonstrate that he is a still young novelist of a considerable significance.

—Paul A. Doyle

———

RECHY, John (Francisco). American. Born in El Paso, Texas, 10 March 1934. Educated at Texas Western College, El Paso, B.A.; New School for Social Research, New York. Served in the United States Army. Has taught creative writing at University of California, Occidental College, and University of Southern California, all Los Angeles. Recipient: Longview Foundation prize, 1961; National Endowment for the Arts grant, 1976. Lives in Los Angeles. Address: c/o Carroll and Graf, 260 Fifth Avenue, New York, New York 10001, U.S.A.

PUBLICATIONS

Novels

City of Night. New York, Grove Press, 1963; London, MacGibbon and Kee, 1964.
Numbers. New York, Grove Press, 1967.
This Day's Death. New York, Grove Press, and London, MacGibbon and Kee, 1970.
The Vampires. New York, Grove Press, 1971.
The Fourth Angel. New York, Viking Press, and London, W.H. Allen, 1972.
Rushes. New York, Grove Press, 1979.
Bodies and Souls. New York, Carroll and Graf, 1983; London, W.H. Allen, 1984.

Play

Momma As She Became—Not As She Was (produced New York, 1978).

Other

The Sexual Outlaw: A Documentary ... of Three Days and Nights in the Sexual Underground. New York, Grove Press, 1977; London, W.H. Allen, 1978.

*

Manuscript Collection: Boston University.

*   *   *

John Rechy's world is the heir of Hawthorne's. His characters inhabit a moral universe whose codes are as rigorous as Calvin's and whose cops are the vigilantes of a new unmerciful Salem. The "youngmen" of *City of Night* and *Numbers* are the fallen angels of an eternally inaccessible paradise and their lives are characterised by a search for the *eros* that will at last become *agape*. That the search is frenetic is scarcely surprising; it has all the desperate urgency that characterises the role of the sensitive American—the anguish of exile within one's own country. And although in *City of Night* Rechy never quite succeeds in conveying Francis Thompson's added sense of "dreadful," it is plain that the implication is there. New York, from the first page, is a metaphor city, a fairy city—in a sense like the London of Stevenson—where anything might happen. That is not to say that Rechy's urban fantasy has the calibre of Purdy's. It is more limited in its focus. Its world is a moral world turned upside down, where the *Deus abscondi-tus* is Priapus. The quest for that god is a never-ending and insatiable one and one in which the tyrants of the old moral order have all the destructive vindictiveness of Diocletian against the Christians.

Having said all that, one should also say that neither *City of Night* nor *Numbers* (in spite of the deliberate "allegorical" pretensions of the former) often rises above what seem to be the masturbatory fantasies of an aging queen—bad Genet. Only with his third and by far his best novel, *This Day's Death*, does Rechy get beyond the unfortunate dualisms of his earlier novels—a catalogue of well-equipped muscleboys on the one hand and a labored novelistic artifice to contain it on the other. That is not to say that *This Day's Death* does not suffer from a somewhat contrivedly concealed central event and a time scheme that is sometimes confusing and tedious. Its *à la récherche de la virginité perdue*, however, is convincing in a way that is true of neither of the earliest novels. Rechy's New Mexico, like Steinbeck's Oklahoma, is a small-town world of poverty and pain, the anguish of growth and the desire to break out. His California is the nightmare inversion of that desire—a world where the law is a monster devouring the innocents who nonetheless have a Genet-like fascination with its devious iniquities. And together these worlds, as commentaries on one another, form a larger moral universe than any Rechy has created before.

It is disenchanting then to find that in *The Vampires*, the novel that succeeds *This Day's Death*, he returns to the world of gothic fiction with an overlay of baroque Satanism—a parody of scenarios for Heliogabalus as rewritten by Albee. *The Fourth Angel* suffers less from this, being set once again in the southwest. But if its teenage characters are more "real," their problems are too much the stereotypes of the late 1960's to remain interesting, and the sentimentality of their presentation—"and so, suddenly, they're gentle children playing gentle children's games"—sounds like the worst of the Woodstock inheritance.

Rechy discovered earlier than most what Tom Wolfe drew attention to—the new reporting style of the 1960's. His first

two pieces appeared in *Evergreen Review* and from one of them came *City of Night*. But journalists are as prone as anyone else to being taken over by easy "rhetoric," and the mode of confession that fascinates Rechy easily becomes trite. As Ruskin said of the first painting by Leighton, the Victorian painter, "if he does not do much better he will do worse."

—D.D.C. Chambers

REED, Ishmael (Scott). American. Born in Chattanooga, Tennessee, 22 February 1938. Educated at Buffalo Technical High School; East High School, Buffalo, graduated 1956; University of Buffalo, 1956–60. Married 1) Priscilla Rose in 1960 (separated 1963, divorced 1970), one daughter; 2) Carla Blank-Reed in 1970, one daughter. Staff writer, *Empire Star Weekly*, Buffalo, 1960–62; free-lance writer, New York, 1962–67: co-founder, *East Village Other*, New York, and *Advance*, Newark, New Jersey, 1965. Since 1971, Chairman and President, Yardbird Publishing Company, and since 1973, Director, Reed Cannon and Johnson Communications, both Berkeley, California. Since 1967, Lecturer, University of California, Berkeley. Lecturer, University of Washington, Seattle, 1969–70; and State University of New York, Buffalo, 1975; Visiting Professor, Fall 1979, and since 1983 Associate Fellow of Calhoun House, Yale University, New Haven, Connecticut; Visiting Professor, Dartmouth College, Hanover, New Hampshire, 1980. President, Before Columbus Foundation. Recipient: National Endowment for the Arts grant, 1974; Rosenthal Foundation award, 1975; Guggenheim fellowship, 1975; American Academy award, 1975; Michaux Award, 1978. Address: c/o St. Martin's Press, 175 Fifth Avenue, New York, New York 10010, U.S.A.

PUBLICATIONS

Novels

The Free-Lance Pallbearers. New York, Doubleday, 1967; London, MacGibbon and Kee, 1968.
Yellow Back Radio Broke-Down. New York, Doubleday, 1969; London, Allison and Busby, 1971.
Mumbo-Jumbo. New York, Doubleday, 1972.
The Last Days of Louisiana Red. New York, Random House, 1974.
Flight to Canada. New York, Random House, 1976.
The Terrible Twos. New York, St. Martin's Press—Marek, 1982.

Verse

Catechism of d neoamerican hoodoo church. London, Paul Breman, 1970.
Conjure: Selected Poems 1963–1970. Amherst, University of Massachusetts Press, 1972.
Chattanooga. New York, Random House, 1973.
A Secretary to the Spirits. New York, NOK, 1978.

Other

The Rise, Fall and ...? of Adam Clayton Powell (as Emmett Coleman), with others. New York, Bee-Line, 1967.
Shrovetide in Old New Orleans (essays). New York, Doubleday, 1978.

God Made Alaska for the Indians. New York, Garland, 1982.

Editor, *19 Necromancers from Now*. New York, Doubleday, 1970.
Editor, *Yardbird Reader* (annual). Berkeley, California, Yardbird, 5 vols., 1971–77.
Editor, with Al Young, *Yardbird Lives!* New York, Grove Press, 1978.
Editor, *Calafia: The California Poetry*. Berkeley, California, Yardbird, 1979.
Editor, *Quilt 2–3*. Berkeley, California, Reed and Young's Quilt, 2 vols., 1981–82.

*

Bibliography: "Mapping Out the Gumbo Works: An Ishmael Reed Bibliography" by Joe Weixlmann, Robert Fikes, Jr., and Ishmael Reed, in *Black American Literature Forum* (Terre Haute, Indiana), Spring 1978.

Critical Studies: "Robin the Cock & Doopeyduk Doing the Boogaloo in Harry Sam with Rusty Jethroe and Letterhead America . . ." by Lawrence Lipton, in *Cavalier* (Greenwich, Connecticut), no. 70, 1967; review by Tam Fiofori, in *Negro Digest* (Chicago), December 1969; "Blood of the Lamb" by Calvin Hernton, in *Amistad 1*, New York, Knopf, 1970; "Ishmael Reed Issue" of *Review of Contemporary Fiction* (Elmwood Park, Illinois), vol. 4, no. 2, 1984.

*   *   *

In an introduction to an essay collection, *Shrovetide in Old New Orleans*, Ishmael Reed says: "Many people here called my fiction muddled, crazy, incoherent, because I've attempted in fiction the techniques and forms painters, dancers, film makers, musicians in the West have taken for granted for at least fifty years, and the artists of many other cultures, for thousands of years." Reed's strengths are enunciated here: flexible, vivid language ranging from street argot to lofty estheticism, experimentation with materials and means, and a deep awareness of the mythic roots of all cultures. Reed is an Afro-American ironist, but his gifts and insights are multicultural, multimedia.

Reed's early novels, *The Free-Lance Pallbearers* and *Yellow Back Radio Broke-Down*, are musical and mythical in conception and development. Using "hoodoo" as a system both of ideas and of language, Reed describes our world in terms of the hero and the prison of society. In *The Free-Lance Pallbearers* Bukka Doopeyduk is the epigonous hero fighting against HARRY SAM, which is the nation-state transformed into a monstrous personification, a dragon. In similar fashion, the Loop Garoo Kid of *Yellow Back Radio Broke-Down* is a shaman-hero (Loupe Garou = werewolf in Creole-French folklore) of a cowboy saga, in which the town of Yellow Back Radio is threatened by Drag Gibson, the stultifying force of the square world. The vaudevillian jokes, surrealism, and wordplays flow at *allegro* tempo.

In *Mumbo Jumbo* Reed concentrates on a mythic time (the 1920's) and magic places (New Orleans and Harlem) in U.S. culture. The ideas of hoodoo/voodoo and other Afro-American magic-religious cults figure in Reed's tapestry of the Jazz Age and the Harlem Renaissance. Reed describes the epic struggle between Jes Grew, the black cultural impulse, and the Atonists, i.e., the monotheistic Western tradition. In the narrative, Reed incorporates drawings, photographs, collages, and handwritten texts, along with many scholarly references.

The Last Days of Louisiana Red extends this mythology, bringing many of the same characters and ideas to Berkeley in the 1970's. "Louisiana Red" is the plague of modern technocratic-industrial culture:

Louisiana Red was the way they related to one another, oppressed one another, maimed and murdered one another, carving one another while above their heads, fifty thousand feet, billionaires flew in custom-made jet planes equipped with saunas tennis courts swimming pools discotheques and meeting rooms decorated like the Merv Griffin show set.

In *Flight to Canada* Reed moves back to the mythos of slavery and the Civil War, applying the same wild, anachronistic expressionism to the central tragedy of the black American culture. In ironic, dramatic terms, Reed answers the "cliometric" revisors of history: "Revisionists. Quantitative historians. What does a computer know? Can a computer feel? Make love? Can a computer feel passion?" Quickskill tears off his shirt. "Look at these scars. Look at them! All you see is their fruit, but their roots run deep. The roots are in my soul."

The Terrible Twos is a comic-mythological tour de force, uniting elements of our culture's Christmas story—Dickens's "A Christmas Carol," the legend of St. Nicholas, the commercial street-corner Santa Claus—into a bizarre satire on greed, racism and inhumanity. Reed chides the U.S. of the 1980's as a mindless, grasping two-year-old, an infant-giant draining the world of resources, hope, and compassion, hiding behind a phony costume of charity and concern.

Ishmael Reed's brilliant comic vision of American history brings together the basic ingredients of black culture in a rich musical-dramatic form. His expansion of language into a radically personal style points to the richness of that culture as a storytelling source. Reed's wide interests in traditions outside the received mainstream of "Western Culture" courses, in magic, myth, and ritual, make him one of the most forceful and persuasive novelists of the past 20 years.

—William J. Schafer

REID, Vic(tor Stafford). Jamaican. Born in Jamaica, 1 May 1913. Educated in Jamaica. Married; four children. Reporter, editor, and foreign correspondent for various newspapers; worked in advertising; currently, managing director and chairman of a printing and publishing company in Kingston, Jamaica; has travelled extensively in the Americas, Africa, Europe, and the Middle East. Recipient: Guggenheim fellowship, 1959; Canada Council fellowship; Mexican Writers fellowship. Address: c/o Institute of Jamaica Publications, 2-A Suthermere Road, Kingston 10, Jamaica.

PUBLICATIONS

Novels

New Day. New York, Knopf, 1949; London, Heinemann, 1950.
The Leopard. New York, Viking Press, and London, Heinemann, 1958.

Short Stories

The Jamaicans. Kingston, Institute of Jamaica, 1976.

Other (for children)

Sixty-Five.   London, Longman, 1960.
The Young Warriors.   London, Longman, 1967.
Buildings in Jamaica (for adults).   Kingston, Jamaica Information Service, 1970.
Peter of Mount Ephraim.   Kingston, Jamaica Publishing House, 1971.
The Sun and Juan de Bolas.   Kingston, Institute of Jamaica, 1974.
Nanny-Town.   Kingston, Jamaica Publishing House, 1983.

*   *   *

Vic Reid gives the impression of being a "loner," a man of few words. His literary out-put has not been large, but he has been an innovative and unusual novelist.

When *New Day* appeared in 1949, it proved to be innovative in two ways: in its use of a formalised Jamaican English, and in its concerns—for national growth, for the resumption and expansion of responsible government, for the role of a local family in national growth. *The Leopard*, set as it is in Kikuyu land, does not use a distinctive form of Jamaican speech, but it is structurally more interesting than *New Day*, and its concerns are not as unconnected with West Indian experience as they might seem. In fact, Reid's life as a Jamaican would have prepared him well to work out such a combination of gentleness and violence, in fact a fugue and coda, which could also be a prelude to a "new day" in Africa, and in the world.

New Day, using the flashback technique, has structural weaknesses, and from time to time its special formalised Jamaican language does not ring absolutely true. (To give two small examples: "Duppy-ghost," "congo-pea soup".) Was Reid too concerned with the fact that his Jamaican characters had to speak not only to each other, but also to a wider audience?

His historical grasp of the political and power situation in 1865 has been criticised both on ideological and historical grounds. In this connection, it should not be forgotten that Reid was very careful to say in the last paragraph of the "Author's Note" prefaced to the first edition of *New Day*: "I have not by any means attempted a history of the period from 1865 to 1944. ... What I have attempted is to transfer to paper some of the beauty, kindness, and humor of my people, ... creating a tale that will offer as true an impression as fiction can of the way by which Jamaica and its people come to today."

There are many remarkable things in *New Day*; one notable section deals with Pastor Humphrey's sermon on "constituted authority." It starts, "Whenever we go to church ... Naomi and me sit side-and-side ... but when the sermon begins we close our knees tight, and then there is good space for crab-race. You know how to play crab-race?" That very Jamaican question sets the aspect of the children's presence at the service, while as Humphrey warms to his theme—"Mouth came down *snap* on authority, long neck shot out, then drew back into his cassock like iguana in stonehole"—the Stoney Gut men are about to create a groaning objection to Paul's text on obedience and the pastor's interpretation of it. The chapter ends with "'Let us pray for rain,' says Pastor Humphrey." But we know that it is blood that will soon be quenching the long drought which had intensified, and symbolised, the disillusion and deterioration in St. Thomas Parish.

Often old John Campbell (as narrator) slips delightfully into the skin of the young boy, he had been when "in media res": "Good it is to hear her laugh but when mother says *Heh!* like that, all of your manhood is gone. ... Is funny how your breeches drop off anytime Mother says *heh!*" But the ably-used device of having a sleepless narrator recall his family's role in the dawning of the "new day" has its disadvantages. For one thing, John Campbell has to rush a few sequences to help us suspend, willingly, our disbelief, and it might well be this technical difficulty that tends to exaggerate a falsely Romantic view (even in Campbell's mouth) of the fighting years of Jamaican men.

The Leopard is in some ways, particularly in structure, even more noteworthy. The clean juxta-positioning of the few personae, the untransitioned switching from group to group of those concerned and then converging for the final point of the story—and meanwhile the leopard alone understands Kenya "for he avoids the strong and eats the wounded, and the weak is stalking the stalked"—all these build up into an image of sick, hunting and hunted man, not unlike Derek Walcott's in "A Far Cry from Africa." In the end the lieutenant ("robbed me of my first Kike") becomes the leopard, whom he has just deprecatingly, but more truthfully than he realises, called "Brother Leopard," and the fate long since planned for that animal becomes the lieutenant's at the hands of Nebu ("one of the loyal bucks").

Vic Reid is a flexible and varied writer, with, at times, a fist of mail beneath that gauntlet of silk. An innovator on the West Indian literary scene, he has written, besides the novels mentioned, a variety of short stories and books for young people. His work shows forth his gifts and care, and underlines our need for more from him.

—John J. Figueroa

REID BANKS, Lynne.   See **BANKS, Lynne Reid.**

RICHLER, Mordecai.   Canadian.   Born in Montreal, Quebec, 27 January 1931. Educated at the Montreal Hebrew Academy; Baron Byng High School, Montreal, 1944–49; Sir George Williams University, Montreal, 1949–51. Married Florence Wood in 1959; three sons and two daughters. Lived in Europe, 1951, 1954–72; worked for CBC, 1952–53; Writer-in-Residence, Sir George Williams University, 1968–69; Visiting Professor, Carleton University, Ottawa, 1972–74. Since 1972, member of the Editorial Board, Book-of-the-Month Club. Recipient: University of Western Ontario President's Medal, for non-fiction, 1959; Canada Council junior arts fellowship, 1959, 1960, and senior arts fellowship, 1966; Guggenheim fellowship, 1961; *Paris Review* award, 1968; Governor-General's Award, 1969, 1971; Writers Guild of America award, for screenplay, 1974; Berlin Film Festival Golden Bear, for screenplay, 1974; Schwartz Award, for children's book, 1976; *Jewish Chronicle*-Wingate Award, 1981. Address: 1321 Sherbrooke Street, Apartment 80-C, Montreal, Quebec H3G 1J4, Canada.

PUBLICATIONS

Novels

The Acrobats.   Toronto, Ambassador, London, Deutsch, and New York, Putnam, 1954; as *Wicked We Love*, New York, Popular Library, 1955.

Son of a Smaller Hero.   London, Deutsch, 1955; New York,
    Paperback Library, 1965.
A Choice of Enemies.   London, Deutsch, 1957.
The Apprenticeship of Duddy Kravitz.   London, Deutsch, and
    Boston, Little Brown, 1959.
The Incomparable Atuk.   London, Deutsch, 1963; as *Stick
    Your Neck Out*, New York, Simon and Schuster, 1963.
Cocksure.   London, Weidenfeld and Nicolson, and New
    York, Simon and Schuster, 1968.
St. Urbain's Horseman.   London, Weidenfeld and Nicolson,
    and New York, Knopf, 1971.
Joshua Then and Now.   London, Macmillan, and New York,
    Knopf, 1980.

Short Stories

The Street.   Toronto, McClelland and Stewart, 1969; London,
    Weidenfeld and Nicolson, 1972; Washington, D.C., New
    Republic, 1975.

Uncollected Short Story

"Manny Moves to Westmount," in *Saturday Night* (Toronto),
    January–February, 1977.

Plays

Duddy, adaptation of his own novel (produced Edmonton,
    Alberta, 1981).

Screenplays: *Dearth of a Salesman*, 1957; *Insomnia Is Good
for You*, 1957; *No Love for Johnnie*, with Nicholas Phipps,
1961; *Tiara Tahiti*, with Geoffrey Cotterell and Ivan Foxwell,
1962; *The Wild and the Willing* (*Young and Willing*), with
Nicholas Phipps, 1962; *Life at the Top*, 1965; *The Apprenticeship of Duddy Kravitz*, with Lionel Chetwynd, 1974; *Fun with
Dick and Jane*, with David Giler and Jerry Belson, 1976; *Joshua
Then and Now*, 1985.

Radio Play: *It's Harder to Be Anybody*, 1961 (UK).

Television Plays (UK): *Paid in Full*, 1958; *The Trouble with
Benny*, 1959; *The Apprenticeship of Duddy Kravitz*, from his
own novel, 1961; *The Fall of Mendel Crick*, from a story by
Isaak Babel, 1963.

Other

Hunting Tigers under Glass: Essays and Reports.   Toronto,
    McClelland and Stewart, 1968; London, Weidenfeld and
    Nicolson, 1969.
Shovelling Trouble (essays).   Toronto, McClelland and Stew-
    art, 1972; London, Quartet, 1973.
Notes on an Endangered Species and Others.   New York,
    Knopf, 1974.
Jacob Two-Two Meets the Hooded Fang (for children).   Lon-
    don, Deutsch, and New York, Knopf, 1975.
Creativity and the University, with André Fortier and Rollo
    May.   Toronto, York University, 1975.
Images of Spain, photographs by Peter Christopher.   New
    York, Norton, 1977; London, Thames and Hudson, 1978.
The Great Comic Book Heroes and Other Essays, edited by
    Robert Fulford.   Toronto, McClelland and Stewart, 1978.

Home Sweet Home: My Canadian Album.   Toronto, McClel-
    land and Stewart, New York, Knopf, and London, Chatto
    and Windus, 1984.

Editor, *Canadian Writing Today*.   London, Penguin, 1970.
Editor, *The Best of Modern Humor*.   Toronto, McClelland
    and Stewart, and New York, Knopf, 1983; London, Allen
    Lane, 1984.

*

Bibliography: "Mordecai Richler: An Annotated Bibliogra-
phy" by Michael Darling, in *The Annotated Bibliography of
Canada's Major Authors 1* edited by Robert Lecker and Jack
David, Downsview, Ontario, ECW Press, 1979.

Manuscript Collection: University of Calgary, Alberta.

Critical Studies: *Mordecai Richler* by George Woodcock, Toronto, McClelland and Stewart, 1970; *Mordecai Richler* edited
by G. David Sheps, Toronto, McGraw Hill Ryerson, 1971;
Mordecai Richler by Arnold E. Davidson, New York, Ungar,
1983.

*   *   *

Mordecai Richler exemplifies one of the difficulties Canadian
critics have always experienced—defining a Canadian novelist.
Many of those who have found their ways into histories of
Canadian writing have in fact been passing visitors like Brian
Moore and Malcolm Lowry. To an extent—in Lowry's case
to a great extent—their fiction has been affected in content
and even attitude by their residence in Canada. Yet their
"Canadian works" constitute a phase in lives whose inspiration
has remained largely elsewhere.

On the other side, following the nomadic pattern of life in
a great and loosely populated country, some Canadians have
left their homeland and spent much of their writing lives
abroad. Of these, Mordecai Richler is one of the most important. Richler left Canada in 1951, when he was 20; it would
be a quarter of a century before he would return from Europe
to live again in Montreal. All his novels but one, and most
of his stories, have been written abroad. And yet, as Richler
said in 1957, "All my attitudes are Canadian. I'm a Canadian;
there's nothing to be done about it." Not merely are his attitudes Canadian; so are the leading figures in all his novels,
whether they are shown in his native Montreal, or abroad,
as unassimilable exiles.

Even as a Canadian writer, Richler is extremely localized
in his frame of reference, largely celebrating a vanished way
of life in a part of Montreal that has changed completely since
he knew it. It is the old Jewish ghetto, the region centred
on St. Urbain Street, where most of Richler's heroes were
born into the expatriate community of Jews who had fled from
Eastern Europe under the Tsarist regime and who had brought
with them a religion and a way of life which were gradually
eroded by the social pressures of a city divided between English
and French.

If one can isolate a theme from Richler's novels it is that
of the Jew who is powerfully conscious of his people's past,
and deeply nostalgic for a childhood spent in the chaotic and
colourful background of the ghetto, yet who understands that
in the modern world traditional Jewish attitudes have become
irrelevant. Yet also, for Richler, the Jew is only one exemplifi-
cation of the human individual set against the impersonal forces
of the modern world. Three of his novels—*The Acrobats*, *A*

Choice of Enemies, and *Cocksure*—are based on a deliberate inversion of the pattern of the persecuted Jew. In these books the hero (or anti-hero if it seems more fitting) is a Gentile, and Jews reveal in their actions towards him that they too can be persecutors if the circumstances permit. At the end of one of these novels—*Cocksure*—we find a clue which illuminates this central Richlerian preoccupation. When Mortimer Griffin is pursued and about to be destroyed by his enemies, a Jewish intellectual remarks to him: "A Jew is an idea. Today you're my idea of a Jew."

It would be an over-simplification to suggest that embedded on Richler's fiction is the idea that the Jew has an exemplary role in the modern world. It is more accurate to say that Richler believes any writer should draw from his own experience whatever has universal experience, and shape that meaning into a form of social as well as aesthetic significance. His own experience has been his childhood on St. Urbain Street and his expatriate life which echoes that of his grandparents. This has resulted in an alternating pattern between the early background and the land of exile.

The Acrobats, his first novel, was set in Spain; its young Canadian hero was murdered by a psychopathic ex-Nazi. *Son of a Smaller Hero*, set in Montreal, was Richler's portrait of the artist as a young man—a story of the Montreal ghetto and the trauma of self-liberation from its moral pressures. *A Choice of Enemies*—the hero again is a Canadian exile—is set in the world of film producers (expatriate from the radical America of the 1930's) with which Richler's need to earn a living as a script writer had made him familiar. Next followed what may well be Richler's best novel, *The Apprenticeship of Duddy Kravitz*, telling of the ruthless rise to wealth of a poor boy of St. Urbain Street, followed by *The Incomparable Atuk*, a fable in the manner of Voltaire on Canadian cultural pretensions. The England of the exile is again the setting of *Cocksure*, a satirical fantasy filled with monsters and hollow men in the manner of Wyndham Lewis. A collection of sketches and short stories, *The Street*, devoted entirely to the vanished past of the Montreal ghetto, completes the pattern of alternations and prepares the way for *St. Urbain's Horseman*.

In Richler's work up to the early 1970's *St. Urbain's Horseman* is the key novel, combining satire and nostalgia, and bringing the world of the exile and the world of the ghetto together in their proper and intimate relationship. Jake Hersh, a minor character in *The Apprenticeship of Duddy Kravitz*, and a film man like the victim-heroes of *Cocksure* and *A Choice of Enemies*, has reached the final stage in the classic ordeal of the pursued man; he is on trial on a morals charge, a situation brought about by police inventiveness combined with his own foolishness in associating with a blackmailing misanthrope, Harry Stein. As the trial unfolds its sinister background action, we are shown, in parallel streams of memory, Jake's life in England where a marriage that should be happy is marred by his guilts and fears, and his past life in the dense atmosphere of the Jewish family and the noisy streets of Montreal. The two lives are united by Jake's abiding obsession with his cousin, Joey Hersh, the wandering ne'er-do-well whom Jake fantasizes into an avenger seeking to destroy the destroyers of the Jews. As Jake escapes without honour at his trial, the news arrives that Joey has died as a smuggler in Paraguay. Jake is released from perils and obsessions alike, and the novel has an ending of happiness neither unthreatened nor inappropriate.

Richler's most recent novel, *Joshua Then and Now*, was nine years in the writing. It shows less the painstaking skills of a careful and deliberate writer (for often it is stylistically awkward) than the indecisions of a writer who had really used up his material. For in *Joshua Then and Now* Richler constantly

repeats and parodies himself. There is a familiar pattern of a bright and ruthless Jewish intellectual married to a beautiful gentile girl from Montreal's WASP elite and trying to find his way in her alien world whose values he both despises and envies. There are familiar Richler lessons: the past cannot be rectified; youthful amoralism provides no foundation for a happy old or even middle age. After heavily comic misunderstandings and passages where tragedy seems all too obviously looming, the novel flows into the smooth reaches of a sententious ending in which the values of personal commitment and familial love are reasserted. *Joshua Then and Now* shows Richler a dogged literary workman; it adds nothing to his achievement.

In retrospect, the novels by Richler that stand most securely are *Son of a Smaller Hero*, *The Apprenticeship of Duddy Kravitz*, and *St. Urbain's Horseman*. Taken together, they form a triptych representing the difficulty of escaping from the mental chains laid on a young Jew by the rigours of his own traditions and the hostility of other traditions. Central to these novels, and indeed to all of Richler's books, is the sexual encounter between Jew and Gentile. It is the steering of Jake's mixed marriage through its rapids to final and convincing success that distinguishes *St. Urbain's Horseman* and suggests that this novel might be the basis for a critical summation of his work.

If *St. Urbain's Horseman*, indeed, represents a thematic reconciliation, it also represented a reconciliation of the two manners that are in conflict or at least in competition in Richler's earlier writings—the fantastic and the realistic. In the vividly remembered scenes of Montreal life it is realism (not naturalism) that prevails. In the foreign scenes, the tendency is to create grotesque and implausible hollow figures of satiric fantasy, beginning with Kraus, the unlikely Nazi of *The Acrobats*, and reaching an apogee in the Starmaker, the monstrous gangster-tycoon of *Cocksure*. In *St. Urbain's Horseman* the fantasy indeed persists, but it is in Jake's mind only, where Joey the Horseman rides on his unlikely quests, and what the novel mainly explores is the fantastic nature of much that happens in the actual world, particularly if one sees with the eyes of a stranger.

For Richler is still the exile, the essential Canadian, unable to render except in caricature anything outside that hypnotic circle of locality which creates what Northrop Frye has called "the garrison mentality" among Canadian writers. What his novels suggest is that "the idea of a Jew" is very much like the idea of a Canadian, for Canada is a land of minorities, regions, disguised ghettoes. In that lies Richler's appeal to his countrymen, and the reason why he is never considered as other than a Canadian writer.

—George Woodcock

ROBBINS, Tom (Thomas Eugene Robbins). American. Born in Blowing Rock, North Carolina, 22 July 1936. Educated at high school in Warsaw, Virginia; Hargarve Military Academy; Washington and Lee University, Lexington, Virginia; Richmond Professional Institute (now Virginia Commonwealth University), graduated 1960. Served in the United States Air Force in Korea. Married Terrie Robbins (second marriage; divorced); one child. Copy editor, Richmond *Times-Dispatch*, 1960–62, and Seattle *Times* and *Post-Intelligencer*, 1962–63; reviewer and art columnist, *Seattle Magazine*, and radio host, 1964–68. Address: c/o Bantam Books, 666 Fifth Avenue, New York, New York 10103, U.S.A.

PUBLICATIONS

Novels

Another Roadside Attraction.   New York, Doubleday, 1971; London, W.H. Allen, 1973.
Even Cowgirls Get the Blues.   Boston, Houghton Mifflin, 1976; London, Corgi, 1977.
Still Life with Woodpecker.   New York, Bantam, and London, Sidgwick and Jackson, 1980.
Jitterbug Perfume.   New York, Bantam, 1984.

Uncollected Short Story

"The Chink and the Clock People," in *The Best American Short Stories 1977,* edited by Martha Foley. Boston, Houghton Mifflin, 1977.

Other

Guy Anderson.   Seattle, Gear Works Press, 1965.

*

Critical Study: *Tom Robbins* by Mark Siegel, Boise, Idaho, Boise State University, 1980.

*   *   *

Although practically ignored by academic critics, except as an eccentric regionalist, Tom Robbins with his first two novels became the only American novelist since J.D. Salinger and Jack Kerouac in the 1950's to become a cult hero among disaffected college undergraduates.

Like Salinger—and the even more elusive Thomas Pynchon, who has uncharacteristically publicly praised Robbins's second novel—the author lives in seclusion. He allows himself to be described only as "a student of art and religion" who "dropped out" to write fiction in a Washington state fishing village. Although Kerouac is the only author Robbins mentions in his novels, these more nearly resemble Salinger's Glass Family stories. The ostensible "author" frequently interrupts the stories; and, although the characters are more bizarre than Salinger's, they tend like his to be highly talkative, much given to self-analysis, lengthy confessions, and populist philosophical speculation.

Robbins's writing is even more bitterly anti-Establishment than Salinger's or Kerouac's; FBI and CIA violence and treachery and the conspiratorial practices of the Roman Catholic Church are his most frequent targets. Much of the action of *Another Roadside Attraction,* for example, deals with the involvement of Plucky Purcell (a renegade football player) in a secret order of monks that leads to his discovery during an earthquake of the mummified body of Jesus hidden in the Vatican catacombs. He brings his grotesque find to the "roadside attraction," a giant West Coast hot-dog stand operated by drop-out artist John Paul Ziller and his wife Amanda, an archetypal matriarchal figure. The principal movement of the story narrated by Marx Marvelous, a skeptical scientific dropout from an East Coast think tank, is toward "light," toward a physical dissolution of the individual in his reunion with the sun, which Ziller describes to Marvelous as "the source of

all biological energy, and ultimately . . . the source of you." While Plucky debates how to use Christ's corpse to expose the hoax of Christian culture, Ziller steals it and sets off with it and his pet baboon on a space balloon for the "return to sunlight," which he had said was an "inevitability" he'd been "reckoning with." "Let Amanda be your pine cone," the novel concludes as a joyous tribute to her survival.

Even Cowgirls Get the Blues is longer, talkier, and more self-consciously whimsical than its predecessor. The first half of the novel dwells upon the picaresque adventures of Sissy Hankshaw, a born hitch-hiker with monstrous thumbs. Most of the second half is dominated by the "clock people," Indian refugees from the San Francisco earthquake, who have substituted rigid individual rituals for societal rituals. The two fantasies are united by events at the Rubber Rose Ranch, a wealthy women's retreat that is seized by insurgent cowgirls. Their brush with the government culminates in the Whooping Crane war, after the cowgirls disrupt the endangered species' migration by feeding them peyote. The convoluted story, which is related by an offbeat psychiatrist curiously named Robbins, winds up with the cranes circling the globe while Sissy is envisioned as the mother of a tribe of big-thumbed people in the "postcatastrophe" world.

Whimsy predominates in Robbins's third book, the short and relatively uncomplicated *Still Life with Woodpecker,* which counterpoints such trendy topics of the early 1980's as deposed royalty, red-headed bombers, and pyramid power to ask the plaintive question, "Who knows how to make love stay?" Robbins despairs of an answer during an era of distrust between the sexes, but an almost *Aida*-like ending hints at a way out of the dilemma.

Heavy-handed whimsy turns into sheer fantasy in *Jitterbug Perfume.* The action of this fourth novel focuses on Alobar, tribal king of a tiny, barbarous medieval city-state, who escapes the customary execution of the ruler at his first sign of aging to become for a thousand years a wanderer to exotic places who has learned the Bandaloop principles of immortal life. Interpolated into this bizarre pilgrimage are brief glimpses of life among the perfume-makers in contemporary Seattle, New Orleans, and Paris. This fable simply lays the groundwork for the climactic proclamation of Wiggs Dannyboy (a character reminiscent of Timothy Leary) that man is on the verge of leaving behind his reptilian and mammalian consciousness to enter the phase of "floral consciousness," during which the production of sensorily stimulating perfumes will be his highest good. It is hard to tell how seriously to take this preachment; but if it isn't serious, there seems no point at all to long stretches of Robbins's increasingly self-indulgent prose. As the title suggests the whole production has the dated air of celebrating the culture of the flower children of the 1960's. These two recent works have done little to sustain Robbins's position as guru to an underground cult.

—Warren French

_____

ROBINSON, Marilynne. American. Born in Sandpoint, Idaho, in 1943. Educated at Brown University, Providence, Rhode Island, B.A. in American literature; University of Washington, Seattle, M.A. and Ph.D. in English. Married;

two sons. Lives in Massachusetts. Recipient: American Academy Rosenthal Foundation award, 1982; Hemingway Foundation award, 1982. Address: c/o Farrar Straus and Giroux Inc., 19 Union Square West, New York, New York 10003, U.S.A.

PUBLICATIONS

Novel

Housekeeping. New York, Farrar Straus, 1980; London, Faber, 1981.

Uncollected Short Story

"Orphans," in *Harper's* (New York), February 1981.

*   *   *

Housekeeping is, for most people, a basic requirement, if only on the simplest level of maintaining shelter. Little chores become so routine that they are done without thinking: washing the dishes or clothes, sweeping, dusting, all take up time and energy that we disregard, write off. Not many of us can or would bother to total the hours spent in such minor labors, any more than we could tally up the hours spent in the bath; they are just necessary losses. Those hours are acceptably, if boringly, spent in the small acts that give our lives some structure, some normality. Changing the linens on Mondays, shopping on Thursdays, church on Sundays, accumulate to keep our lives from flapping loose out into the chaos, like a dress blown off the laundry line and clean away.

Marilynne Robinson's novel *Housekeeping* is about the collapse and abandonment of housekeeping and of the frail structure it provides. For Ruth, who tells the story, housekeeping is a phase of the past, disintegrated in a childhood of isolated women and the constant presence of a lake. Ruth and Lucille were little girls when their mother drove them to her home town on a mountain lake in Idaho. The town, with the macabre and ludicrous name of Fingerbone, is small, completely surrounded, with the lake on one side, and the mountains and forest on the others. As in all remote towns, the people know one another too well, and the closeness is oppressive: "The people of Fingerbone and its environs were very much given to murder. And it seemed that for every pitiable crime there was an appalling accident. What with the lake and the railroads, and what with blizzards and floods and barn fires and forest fires and the general availability of shotguns and bear traps and homemade liquor and dynamite, what with the prevalence of loneliness and religion and the rages and ecstasies they induce, and the closeness of families, violence was inevitable." With long, slow sentences, Ruth tells how the mountains shut out light and the rest of the world, the forest holds darkness and danger, and the lake is a bowl of death. Never once is there any mention of "natural beauty."

The lake, the reason for the town's location, sits by, always in one's awareness, passive, a relentless presence. Ruth's first experience of the lake comes when, after dropping the girls off at the house of a grandmother they had never met, her mother drives her car off the cliffs and into the lake, drowning herself. Years earlier, a train had derailed and, plunging into the lake, drowned all aboard, including Ruth's grandfather. All of the dead remain in their underwater capsules. When the lake freezes, people go ice-skating. During the summer, Ruth and her sister play by it, fish in it. Slowly and undramatically, its importance grows. One winter, the snows melt but

the lake does not, leaving the water to back up and flood the town. In Ruth's house, they move upstairs, letting the water take the downstairs, soaking furniture and curtains and sloshing against the walls. The whole town sits and waits, sodden, for the ice on the lake to melt so the water can flow home. "The clashes and groans from the lake continued unabated, dreadful at night, and the sound of the night wind in the mountains was like one long indrawn breath. Downstairs the flood bumped and fumbled like a blind man in a strange house, but outside it hissed and trickled, like the pressure of water against your eardrums, and like the sounds you hear in the moment before you faint."

There are no men in this story, no sweet romance, no subtle sexuality, and the women are quiet, solitary, odd. Ruth's mother rarely spoke to her children. After her suicide, the girls are cared for by a very old grandmother living in her memories. When the girls find her dead, two elderly aunts are summoned from Spokane, but they then track down another aunt, Sylvie, to take over. Desertions and deaths are recounted in Ruth's helpless, rarely angry tone of acceptance in the same way that she tells of a fishing trip with Lucille, or of Sylvie's strange, transient ways. Sylvie rummages in rubbish bins, eats only in the dark, saves all tins, never cleans anything, plays crazy eights during the flood. She does her best to care for the girls, but housekeeping and structure left her life long ago.

As they reach adolescence, Ruth begins to acquiesce to her fate, while Lucille begins to fight it. Lucille wants to dress cleanly, to have friends, be normal, learn housekeeping. In a final desertion, she moves in with her Home Economics teacher. Ruth is left to drift, having decided "it is better to have nothing."

Robinson's style itself is evocative of drifting and drifters' tales, with long, often poetic descriptions that suddenly snap back to the original point or deflect to a new, unrelated one. At times, Ruth's anger appears in harsher narrative: a cold realisation about Lucille, snide comments about Fingerbone's church ladies, or one long tirade about Cain's betrayal of Abel, which seems slightly inappropriate in a book without men: betrayal exists among sisters as well. At times, too, the sneering is so rough as to seem more than could be felt by this bland girl who cannot tell the difference between what she has dreamed and what she has imagined. These are small flaws in a book that is so rich with thought and feeling that it compels the reader to slow down and truly read.

—Anne Morddel

ROBISON, Mary. American. Born in 1950. Educated at Johns Hopkins University, Baltimore, B.A. Taught at Ohio University, Athens. Currently member of the English Department, Harvard University, Cambridge, Massachusetts. Recipient: Guggenheim fellowship, 1980. Address: Department of English, Harvard University, Cambridge, Massachusetts 02138, U.S.A.

PUBLICATIONS

Novel

Oh! New York, Knopf, 1981.

Short Stories

Days.   New York, Knopf, 1979.
An Amateur's Guide to the Night.   New York, Knopf, 1983.

Uncollected Short Stories

"Help," in *New Yorker*, 9 July 1979.
"Happy Boy," in *The Pushcart Prize 7*, edited by Bill Henderson.   Wainscott, New York, Pushcart Press, 1982.
"In the Woods," in *New Yorker*, 26 March 1984.
"While Home," in *New Yorker*, 21 May 1984.

*   *   *

Mary Robison has published one novel, *Oh!*, and two collections of short stories, *Days* and *An Amateur's Guide to the Night.* Many readers have been introduced to her writing through the appearance of her short stories in the prestigious pages of the *New Yorker*. She writes of people caught in a web of alienation and living amid the trivia of contemporary suburban America. Her characters seem cut off from events in their lives and their own innermost feelings. For example, in *Oh!* Maureen and Howdy, the two adult children of Mr. Cleveland, a self-made, semi-retired millionaire, still live at home, passing the time drinking, complaining, watching TV, and vaguely trying to figure out what to do with their lives. At one point Maureen says, "I love this house .... I've never lived any place else. I couldn't be comfortable or feel safe anywhere else .... Yet I don't want to be stuck here the rest of my life .... Except I'm scared of going anywhere else. Of living out my days being poor." The narrator of the short story "Smart" is an unmarried, pregnant, 36-year-old woman living alone in a seedy apartment. She spends her hours sitting, or getting up "just to change a record or twist my spine, or to nibble some of the food my neighbor, Mrs. Sally Dixon, brought me."

Robison's characters are rootless and without ambition. They have difficulty making connections with anyone or anything. They live their lives in a holding pattern. Like Maureen and Howdy, few find anything that motivates them to improve their lives. One exception to this, however, is the 17-year-old protagonist of the title story in *An Amateur's Guide to the Night.* Lindy lives with her divorced mother and her maternal grandfather. She works as a waitress, goes to school and watches *Fright Night* with the family. But beyond that, Lindy has discovered and learned on her own the beauty of the night sky, and armed with her star charts and telescope she explores the splendor of one of nature's most spectacular shows.

The narrative voice of Robison contains a stark, unmelodic poetry devoid of frills, usually brushing only the surface, describing rather than exploring. Although much can be learned in this way, the author's detachment from her characters has been the persistent criticism leveled at her work. A scene in a Robison story is like a snapshot. She has an eye for detail and tends to focus on mundane, ordinary events—a woman ironing a blouse while her husband sits nearby attempting to give himself a haircut; a couple spending an evening carving pumpkins for Halloween. The author's voice throughout is cool and meticulous. The reader watches along with the author as the story unfolds, slowly at times, just the same as it does in life. Sometimes the insight gleaned from this approach is no more discerning than when we observe strangers. Often, though, we catch a clear, penetrating glimpse into a person's heart and mind. At these times, despite the usual meticulous distancing, something quite profound is achieved. For example, in "I Am Twenty-one" a college student struggles with an essay question on an exam, watching the time pass, unable to answer all the questions. The young narrator is obviously under severe strain, something more than worry over a test, but only later do we understand the depth of her struggle to just keep going. She describes her apartment, a spartan arrangement, except for one photograph, an eight-by-ten glossy of her parents in their youth. "My folks [are] two and a half years gone," she says flatly yet meaningfully, and then talks of her visits to the scene of the accident.

Robison has a playwright's ear for dialogue. Her characters speak the way people really do, in fits and starts with half-formed thoughts and sentences. Their conversations center on common events. In *Oh!* Mr. Cleveland and Virginia, his born-again-Christian fiancée, become involved with Maureen and Howdy in a prolonged discussion about which restaurant they should dine in. Cleveland votes for the Steak Warehouse, where the waiters wear roller skates. Virginia prefers the French cuisine of Rue de Lenoire, which Cleveland vetoes as too expensive. Howdy suggests a college hangout named Bacon and Maureen calls it a dive. At times, it might seem that these conversations go nowhere, but such is not truly the case because through these snippets of talk the essence of the characters evolve and their values are revealed. Sometimes that revelation comes very suddenly as the meaningless chitchat abruptly becomes substantive. At one point Maureen and her 7-year-old daughter Violet are splashing in the child's pool. They are talking about the maid, Lola, when suddenly the conversation shifts to the topic of Maureen's mother. Maureen's resentment of her father and anguish over her mother's abandonment are poignantly revealed. She wants only to remember the good things about this woman and tells her daughter, "You just remember when your grandpa talks about your grandma, no matter what he's saying, he's making it all up. Everything about drinking or about ranting and raving? That's all rubbish."

Robison gives her readers vignettes of life that have a great deal of power in their very sparseness. Her scenes begin in the middle and stop as if a TV were being switched on and off with the program in progress. The characters are talking, dreaming, or moving about when the reader arrives and they continue as the reader exits. It is this ability to convince us that we are observing living, breathing people who proceed with their lives whether observed by the reader or not that gives such strength and power to the writings of Mary Robison.

—Patricia Altner

———————

ROOKE, Daphne (Marie, née Pizzey).   British and South African.   Born in Boksburg, Transvaal, South Africa, 6 March 1914. Educated at Durban Girls' High School. Married Irvin Rooke in 1937; one daughter. Has lived in Australia, 1946–53, and since 1965. Recipient: Afrikaanse Pers Beperk novel prize, 1946. Address: 34 Bent Street, Fingal Bay, New South Wales 2315, Australia.

PUBLICATIONS

Novels

The Sea Hath Bounds.   Johannesburg, A.P.B. Bookstore, 1946; as *A Grove of Fever Trees*, Boston, Houghton Mifflin, 1950; London, Cape, 1951.

Mittee. London, Gollancz, 1951; Boston, Houghton Mifflin, 1952.

Ratoons. London, Gollancz, and Boston, Houghton Mifflin, 1953.

Wizards' Country. London, Gollancz, and Boston, Houghton Mifflin, 1957.

Beti. London, Gollancz, and Boston, Houghton Mifflin, 1959.

A Lover for Estelle. London, Gollancz, and Boston, Houghton Mifflin, 1961.

The Greyling. London, Gollancz, 1962; New York, Reynal, 1963.

Diamond Jo. London, Gollancz, and New York, Reynal, 1965.

Boy on the Mountain. London, Gollancz, 1969.

Margaretha de la Porte. London, Gollancz, 1974.

Uncollected Short Stories

"The Deal," in *Woman* (Sydney), 26 June 1950.

"Emily," in *John Bull* (London), 1952.

"The Boundary Dog," in *John Bull* (London), 1957.

"The Friends," in *South African Stories*, edited by David Wright. London, Faber, and New York, Duell, 1960.

"Fikizolo," in *Over the Horizon*. London, Gollancz, 1960.

"There Lies Hidden ...," in *Optima* (Johannesburg), 1963.

Other (for children)

The South African Twins. London, Cape, 1953; as *Twins in South Africa*, Boston, Houghton Mifflin, 1955.

The Australian Twins. London, Cape, 1954; as *Twins in Australia*, Boston, Houghton Mifflin, 1956.

New Zealand Twins. London, Cape, 1957.

Double Ex! London, Gollancz, 1971.

A Horse of His Own. London, Gollancz, 1976.

*

Bibliography: *Daphne Rooke: Her Works and Selected Criticism: A Bibliography* by Helen Camburg, Johannesburg, University of the Witwatersrand, 1969.

Manuscript Collections: Mugar Memorial Library, Boston University; National English Literary Museum, Grahamstown, South Africa.

Critical Studies: by Orville Prescott, in *New York Times*, 1 March 1950; Dorothy Canfield Fisher, in *Book-of-the-Month News* (New York), January 1952; Sylvia Stallings, in *New York Herald Tribune*, 20 December 1953; *Illustrated London News*, 21 December 1957; *Saturday Review of Literature* (New York), 7 March 1959; *Chicago Tribune*, 26 February 1961; Paul Scott, in *Country Life* (London), 24 May 1962.

Daphne Rooke comments:

The places where I have lived have been most important to my writing. My early memories of the Transvaal are reflected in *Mittee. Ratoons* has for background the South Coast of Natal where I lived for many years on a sugar plantation. Zululand made a most profound impression on me: I lived there for years as a girl: *A Grove of Fever Trees, A Lover for Estelle,* and *Wizards' Country* all have Zululand for background. *Beti* is set in India and East Africa, and *Boy on the Mountain* in New Zealand. All are written in the first person.

There is a pattern of sorts in some of the South African works: the race of the narrator has an important bearing on the story. In *Mittee* the whole story hinges on the fact that the narrator Selina is a Coloured girl; in *Ratoons* the narrator is an English-speaking South African girl who falls in love with an Afrikaner; in *Wizards' Country* the narrator is a Zulu; in *A Lover for Estelle* the narrator is an Afrikaans girl whose life is influenced by a sophisticated English-woman. I did not consciously set out to create this pattern; it was pointed out to me after I had written *Wizards' Country.*

All the stories, including those for children, are imaginative works but have a basis in fact. In *Wizards' Country* when writing about superstition I attempted to avoid the supernatural; for example, Benge is a hunchback and masquerades as a magic dwarf (the tokoloshi). In my short story for children, "Fikizolo," the ingredients of a fairytale were actually present in Zululand: the two children were called a prince and princess, there was a real old witch, and Fikizolo himself was like a fabled beast, a cross between a donkey and a zebra!

*   *   *

Recently the common verdict has been that Africa is to be written about by Africans, which has implicitly been taken to mean black male writers. And as often as not to mean black male writers preoccupied with violence and politics. Daphne Rooke, therefore, presents the critic with an interesting and not yet fashionable problem. She is a native born South African, white and female.

Racial identity and conflict do not provide the emotional power of Rooke's work. Her interests and point of view are those of a frontier woman. Set mostly on the South African frontier of the past two centuries, her works share with American fiction that sense of space, violence, and sheer physical vitality that attends the north European appetite for quest and contest. Characteristically, she writes what is commonly called women's fiction, a melodramatic form, the roots of which are firmly in the 18th-century English novels of sensibility and of gothic terror and suspense.

Rooke does not probe the past. She does not trouble to explain the present. Her narrators, secure in the present, simply recall their past. Its violence is distanced and the lessons learned do not now seem too pressing. Her narrators are each in some way oppressed, being either crippled, insane, female, or coloured. Yet social customs and institutions seem almost immaterial. Her narrators are alive. They have felt and assimilated their experience. Ideological assessment has not intervened. This is women's fiction in the very fundamental sense that the highly touted male faculties of abstraction and rationality are absent—and more ingenuously so than in the works of males who are spoken of as having a feminine sensibility.

Female culture is rich and complex. And it has been described almost exclusively in the works of women novelists because male historians and anthropologists have either been oblivious to its existence or have not deemed it of adequate importance to record. It has been left for such writers as Rooke to reveal the circumscribed but complex ambitions of women and to show how pregnancy, birth, and the management of the domestic realm are as exciting and heroic as war and politics. The richness of *The Sea Hath Bounds, Ratoons,* and *A Lover for Estelle* derive from her intimate awareness of the South Africa that women have experienced.

There is nothing soft and protected about the life Rooke describes. Her best effects invariably involve danger or the threat of it as when the farmer's widow and her children try to make a little egg money hatching pythons in an abandoned front bedroom. Such moments have the economy and immediacy of a treasured snapshot. Rooke has not the stature of

Doris Lessing or Nadine Gordimer, but her success as a popular writer is justified. In retrospect a Rooke work is more haunting than it ought to be—an effect which depends on the part rather than the whole. When the oppressive density of events and the relentless heightening of plot and situation have faded from mind, there remain solid characters and sharp, arresting vignettes.

—Cynthia Secor

ROSS, Sinclair. Canadian. Born in Shellbrook, Saskatchewan, 22 January 1908. Served in the Canadian Army, 1942–45. With the Royal Bank of Canada: in country branches, 1924–31, in Winnipeg, 1931–42, and in Montreal, 1946–68. Lived in Greece and Spain, 1968–80; now lives in Vancouver. Address: c/o McClelland and Stewart Ltd., 25 Hollinger Road, Toronto, Ontario M4B 3G2, Canada.

PUBLICATIONS

Novels

As for Me and My House.   New York, Reynal, 1941.
The Well.   Toronto, Macmillan, 1958.
Whir of Gold.   Toronto, McClelland and Stewart, 1970.
Sawbones Memorial.   Toronto, McClelland and Stewart, 1974.

Short Stories

The Lamp at Noon and Other Stories.   Toronto, McClelland and Stewart, 1968.
The Race and Other Stories, edited by Lorraine McMullen. Ottawa, University of Ottawa Press, 1982.

*

Bibliography: by David Latham, in *The Annotated Bibliography of Canada's Major Authors 3* edited by Robert Lecker and Jack David, Downsview, Ontario, ECW Press, 1981.

Critical Studies: introduction by Roy Daniells to *As for Me and My House*, Toronto, McClelland and Stewart, 1957; "Wolf in the Snow" by Warren Tallman, in *A Choice of Critics* edited by George Woodcock, Toronto, Oxford University Press, 1966; introduction by Margaret Laurence to *The Lamp at Noon*, 1968; "Sinclair Ross's Ambivalent World" by W.H. New, in *Canadian Literature* (Vancouver), Spring 1969; "No Other Way: Sinclair Ross's Stories and Novels" by Sandra Djwa, in *Canadian Literature* (Vancouver), Winter 1971; *Patterns of Isolation in English–Canadian Fiction* by John G. Moss, Toronto, McClelland and Stewart, 1974; "The Mirror and the Lamp in Sinclair Ross's *As for Me and My House*" by David Stouck, in *Mosaic* (Winnipeg, Manitoba), Winter 1974; *Sinclair Ross and Ernest Buckler* by Robert D. Chambers, Vancouver, Copp Clark, 1975; introduction to *Sawbones Memorial*, Toronto, McClelland and Stewart, 1978, and *Sinclair Ross*, Boston, Twayne, 1979, both by Lorraine McMullen; *Sinclair Ross: A Reader's Guide* by Ken Mitchell, Regina, Saskatchewan, Thunder Creek, 1981; essay in *Canadian Literature* (Vancouver), Autumn 1984.

Sinclair Ross comments:

The little I have done has been spread over so many years that there is no outstanding or unifying theme. Man and nature, perhaps—especially in *The Lamp at Noon* and to some degree in *As for Me and My House*. *The Well* is a bad novel: an attempt, unsuccessful, to stretch a little the prairie and small town world of which I had been writing. *Whir of Gold* is, I suppose, another break-away attempt—or stretch; better, with some fairly good things in it, but small in range.

*   *   *

Sinclair Ross is primarily a chronicler of life on the Canadian prairies, and his first novel, *As for Me and My House*, seems destined to become established as a classic of prairie realism, along with the novels of Frederick Philip Grove and Margaret Laurence. Even better than his first novel are some of his short stories, such as "The Lamp at Noon," "The Painted Door," and "One's a Heifer." Ross's later novels, *The Well* and *Whir of Gold*, have some traces of the subdued intensity which makes his early work so memorable, but as wholes they are disappointing. Ross's career seems to bear out the theory that Herbert Read advanced about Wordsworth: that as his memories of his boyhood faded, his art too lost its strength. Ross lived on the prairies as a boy and young man, but his adult life has been lived mainly in Montreal, and in his later work he was too far removed from the life he once knew to write of it with continuous conviction and accuracy.

It is, then, on the early fiction that Sinclair Ross's reputation is almost certain to rest. The qualities of this early work are quite remarkable. Perhaps most remarkable of all is Ross's gift for empathy, for full identification of himself with the character he is portraying. For the boys who are the central figures of several of his short stories this is not surprising, since one is able to assume that the hero is Ross himself slightly disguised, and that he is drawing heavily upon the memories of his own boyhood. The feat is more surprising when it is applied to Philip Bentley, the clergyman and amateur artist of *As for Me and My House*, particularly since much of the tension in the novel springs from Philip's relationship with his wife: Ross is a bachelor. But what is really remarkable is that Ross is able to enter with apparently equal facility into the minds of women, as in the powerful story of a prairie dust storm, "The Lamp at Noon," and in the portrayal of Mrs. Bentley in the novel.

The special quality in the human situation which seems to attract Ross as an artist and which he treats with consummate skill is the sense of isolation and of alienation, the feeling of being trapped in a set of circumstances from which there is no apparent escape. Thus Philip Bentley finds himself trapped in a profession for which he no longer feels a vocation, in a small prairie town which seems to have no sympathy for the values he cherishes, and in a marriage which has come to be an irritant rather than an unguent. In "The Lamp at Noon" the prairie farm-wife finds herself trapped in an isolated farmhouse when she would like to be in a city, and the dust storm in which she goes mad and her baby dies becomes a symbol of the inexorable doom which is closing in upon her. Only her husband's fidelity and love stand between her and total defeat.

This use of the prairie climate and landscape both as a realistic setting and as a symbolic obbligato to the human situation is another of Ross's strengths as a writer of fiction. In words which are carefully chosen to achieve the maximum of accuracy in description, he makes vivid to us the reality of the prairie landscape with its vast distances and its overwhelming sky, and the fierce extremes of heat and cold, the long harsh winters and brief, brilliant, but often explosive summers, that mark the climate of that region. Beyond the accuracy of the descriptions, however, lie the powerful atmospheric effects which Ross achieves by relating the fluctuations of the weather to the moods and aspirations of his characters, and the way in which snow-storms and wind-storms are made to seem symbolic of the malevolence of the universe in which man finds himself a victim.

The sombreness of Ross's fiction is to some extent relieved, however, by the positive way in which he records the efforts of his characters to overcome or transcend the forbidding environment in which fate has placed them. The wife in "The Lamp at Noon" is broken, but her husband perseveres until he sees the storm go down; for all the tribulations to which the Bentleys are subjected, it is their human will which finally prevails: the last words of the novel are "I want it so." Philip's art is his means of transcending the environment: by portraying the prairie in all its harsh power he reduces it to form, transforms it by the power of the human imagination, asserts his human will in the face of its vast indifference.

Ross's own art as a novelist and writer of short stories represents a similar triumph of the human imagination. By his unremitting honesty in portraying human beings living in a physical environment which presents the maximum challenge to the instinct for survival, he has produced a small but significant volume of work which will endure.

—Desmond Pacey

* * *

ROSSNER, Judith (née Perelman). American. Born in New York City, 31 March 1935. Educated at City College of New York, 1952–55. Married 1) Robert Rossner in 1954 (divorced, 1972), one daughter and one son; 2) Mort Persky (divorced, 1983). Lives in New York City. Agent: Wendy Weil, Julian Bach Literary Agency, 747 Third Avenue, New York, New York 10017, U.S.A.

PUBLICATIONS

Novels

To the Precipice. New York, Morrow, 1966; London, Barker, 1977.
Nine Months in the Life of an Old Maid. New York, Dial Press, 1969; London, Weidenfeld and Nicolson, 1977.
Any Minute I Can Split. New York, McGraw Hill, 1972; London, Weidenfeld and Nicolson, 1977.
Looking for Mr. Goodbar. New York, Simon and Schuster, and London, Cape, 1975.
Attachments. New York, Simon and Schuster, and London, Cape, 1977.
Emmeline. New York, Simon and Schuster, and London, Cape, 1980.
August. Boston, Houghton Mifflin, and London, Cape, 1983.

Uncollected Short Stories

"Please Think of Me as a Friend," in *Ararat* (New York), Winter 1967.
"Voyage of the Earth Maiden," in *Cosmopolitan* (New York), May 1968.

Other

What Kind of Feet Does a Bear Have? (for children). Indianapolis, Bobbs Merrill, 1963.

*

Manuscript Collection: Mugar Memorial Library, Boston University.

* * *

Judith Rossner's novels are concerned with women and relationships. In almost all of them, starting with *To the Precipice* in 1966 and continuing through *August* in 1983, the story opens with the protagonist's admission that the choices she has made, or not made, in life have been painfully wrong. In most cases, Rossner employs a first-person narrative to chronicle her protagonist's journey to self-discovery. The self-discovery never comes easily and it usually requires hard choices. Rossner's women are often outrageously self-indulgent and needy. They take pride in thinking of themselves as hysterical types; they bemoan their maimed childhoods; they dwell upon their dreams and daydreams; and most have woken up one day to discover that their marriage of many years is hopelessly inadequate and must be abandoned if they are ever to have a chance to live as complete women with a self of their own. In the hands of a less able and inventive writer, this theme could quickly become banal. It is Rossner's interest in character and her flair for the grotesque and extravagant that carry her narratives. Many of her novels offer a clinical dissection of America's failed marriages and of a culture that has not permitted women to have a life apart from their children and husband. Almost all her books deal with women and their children, women and their sexual hunger, and women and their men. It is difficult to read her novels without keenly appreciating the depth of the psychological disorders which plague our era. Her novels travel from the quiescence and affluence of the 1950's, through the turbulence of the sexual and political upheavals in the mid-60's, to the more mature feminism of the 1970's and early 1980's when women began to reassess their cry for independence and the house father and judge anew another set of sacrifices they have made in the pursuit of balancing the rival claims of mate, children, and work. Even in *Emmeline*, a novel which ostensibly takes the cotton-mills in Lowell, Massachusetts in the early 19th century as its subject, Rossner makes the reader feel a 20th-century feminist's outrage at the status of women and the plight of her heroine, a 14-year-old girl seduced by the mill foreman and later luckless enough to marry unwittingly her own son, the child she had given up for adoption some 19 years earlier.

Rossner is intimately knowledgeable about women's dependency and her novels examine it with an often witty and ironic lens. She is thoroughly conversant with the world of what she calls her "off-the-wall" women and details in a most convincing way the world of the commune or the New York singles bar or the 19th-century mill town. She is immensely indebted to Freud, to the point that one entire novel, *August*, devotes itself to the month when psychiatrists vacation and patients struggle with the pains of withdrawal and transference while the analysts try to resist the tugs of counter-transference. She is heavily influenced by the writings of Doris Lessing, most particularly, *The Golden Notebook* and *The Children of Violence* series, as well as by Erica Jong's ribald *Fear of Flying*. Her writing is often sexually explicit, reveling in its own creation of women's fantasies, quick to celebrate multiple orgasms, and candid in its study of impotence and sexual indifference between married couples. She is savvy about the novel and its readership, exploiting her feminist subject and catering to the tastes of the New York/California sophisticate with an insatiable appetite for novels about neurotic women, free sex, and identity. She has also capitalized on the vogue for non-fiction, drawing on Truman Capote's *In Cold Blood* in her own clinical dissection of a rapist-murderer in *Looking for Mr. Goodbar* and upon the oral telling of Nettie Mitchell, a 94-year-old woman who knew Emmeline when she herself was a child and Emmeline was an old woman. Whether she is exploring the victimization of Emmeline or Terry Dunne, the attractive, educated young schoolteacher of *Looking for Mr. Goodbar* whose sex with a stranger costs her her life, or whether she is analyzing the self-destructiveness of Ruth Kossoff in *To the Precipice*, or Nadine in *Attachments*, or Margaret in *Any Minute I Can Split*, or Dawn Henley in *August*, Rossner manages to make her reader recognize a part of themselves in her confused protagonists. Even when she is depicting with Rabelaisian humor some of the most grotesque scenes—the four-way orgy of Nadine and Dianne and the two joined Siamese twins Amos and Eddie in *Attachments*, or the scene where a 250-pound pregnant naked Margaret prances about her house, hardly raising an eyebrow among her husband's friends in *Any Minute I Can Split*—she is able to make her scene credible, illuminating its psychological underpinnings, and arousing our compassion. Understanding women in psychological *extremis*, Rossner can write ably about them.

In Rossner's early novels the women chose men for the wrong reasons and had their children, or a child not by their husbands, also for wrong reasons. A goodly portion of the novels charted the women's bewildered emotional state in which they were afraid to leave the man whom they had married but never loved, afraid to leave their children although often they were in such despair that they did their children no good, and afraid to accept responsibility for the lives they had chosen and for the actions they have belatedly recognized they must take. *To the Precipice* ends with the protagonist pregnant with her lover's child contemplating the difficult decisions she is going to have to confront when she finally acknowledges to her husband that this new child is not his. Knowing she may risk losing custody of her other children, knowing that she has already lost any chance of marrying her childhood lover, knowing that in all probability she might be simply a single mother, she has come to know that no matter what the pain and suffering she fears, she must not slip back into the depression-unto-death that she has previously succumbed to, but rather must face the difficulties ahead. Margaret, in *Any Minute I Can Split*, also learns self-respect. This woman who flees her husband when she is nine months pregnant at the opening of the book and bears his children in a commune where he does not bother to visit her for many months, and who flirts with the notion of loving either the young hippie who has befriended her on the road, or the married guru of the commune, finally comes to terms with herself, her father, and her husband. Again, the novel leaves us uncertain whether Margaret will, in fact, remain with her husband. He, like the male protagonist in most of Rossner's novels, knows himself most imperfectly, but Margaret has come to recognize some of her own delusions and is determined to grow up herself, even if her husband cannot. In *Attachments*, Nadine's needs and capacity for anomie are seemingly without limits. Marrying one of the freakish Siamese twins, and coercing her friend to marry the other so that the two women can remain together, Nadine lives in the circus atmosphere of her own making for more than 13 years—through the birth of several children, through

the operation which separates the twins, through the trials of her adolescent daughter, to her final decision to leave Amos and accept the guilt of knowing she had neither loved him when he was a freak, nor when he became normal. She has to go because she had now learned limits and it has become intolerable to live with the image of her own twisted, hopelessly vulnerable adolescent self. But in this novel, unlike the other two, the reader feels a terrible pity for the male protagonist and much more ambivalent about the decision that Nadine makes. In *August* Rossner finally offers a full portrait of a divorced psychiatrist's life with her children and her lovers, not to mention her patients. In the other novels we see much of the moral confusion of broken households and much of the weight of despair alternating with boredom of the households which remain intact. *August*, although it traces the torturous childhood of Lulu Shinefeld's patient, Dawn, is a more compassionate and healing novel than any of the others. Dawn's life has more than its share of aberrations—after the tragic death of her parents, she has been raised by two lesbians, her surrogate parents, whose "divorce" when the novel opens drives Dawn into the arms of the analyst and many lovers. Nonetheless, despite the lurid details of Dawn's past which are recounted upon the analyst's couch as Dawn tries to recover her past, the novel itself is full of comic and affecting moments and the subplot about Dr. Shinefeld's private life is handled with humor and warmth. Ultimately, in this novel, both women mend, and, in the case of Dr. Shinefeld, we witness how life feels after she has mended and what life without a husband and with a career and children is actually like. The more affirmative character of this novel marks a greater maturity in its author.

Emmeline is a poignant book. It is written simply, capturing life in the industrial city of Lowell, and making us see how Emmeline's deprivations and innocence lead to her ruin. There is a sentimentality in the tale, but it is also simple and affecting. When the incest theme completes itself, there is a darkness reminiscent of Edith Wharton's *Ethan Frome*.

Rossner is an accomplished writer. She can spin a good tale; she can write a chilling, taut novel of suspense and murder or a raucous, bawdy tale of attachments. She writes mostly about women and her writing has further broken the silence that has shrouded so much of women's lives. Her accounts of pregnancy, sex with a stranger, the introduction of another man into a single household with child, and women's needs all put into language areas of experience that have traditionally been ignored in the novel.

—Carol Simpson Stern

ROSTEN, Leo (Calvin). American. Born in Lodz, Poland, 11 April 1908; emigrated to the United States in 1910. Educated at the University of Chicago, Ph.B. 1930 (Phi Beta Kappa), Ph.D. 1937 (research assistant, Political Science Department, 1933–35; Fellow, Social Science Research Council, 1934–36); London School of Economics, 1934. Married 1) Priscilla Ann Mead in 1935 (died), one son and two daughters; 2) Gertrude Zimmerman in 1960. English teacher in Chicago, 1930–32; motion picture writer, 1937–38; special consultant to the National Defense Commission, 1939–40; director, Motion Picture Research Project (Carnegie Foundation grant), 1939–41; chief, Motion Picture Division, Office of Facts and Figures, Washington, D.C., 1941–42; deputy director, Office of War Information, Washington, 1942–43; special consultant to the United States Secretary of War, 1945 (Colonel, United States Army, 1945); member, Senior Staff, RAND Corporation,

Santa Monica, California, 1947–49; editorial adviser, *Look* magazine, New York, 1949–71. Since 1955, Lecturer, Columbia University, New York. Ford Visiting Professor of Political Science, University of California, Berkeley, 1960–61. Member of the National Board of the Authors League of America. Recipient: Rockefeller grant, 1940; George Polk Memorial Award, 1955; Freedoms Foundation Award, 1955; Professional Achievement Award, University of Chicago, 1969. D.H.L.: University of Rochester, New York, 1973; Hebrew Union College, Cincinnati, 1980. Honorary Fellow, London School of Economics, 1975; Member, American Academy of Arts and Sciences. Address: 36 Sutton Place South, New York, New York 10022, U.S.A.

PUBLICATIONS

Novels

The Education of Hyman Kaplan (as Leonard Q. Ross). New York, Harcourt Brace, and London, Constable, 1937.
Dateline: Europe (as Leonard Ross). New York, Harcourt Brace, 1939; as *Balkan Express*, London, Heinemann, 1939.
Adventure in Washington (as Leonard Ross). New York, Harcourt Brace, 1940.
The Dark Corner. New York, Century, 1945; London, Edward, 1946.
Sleep, My Love. New York, Triangle, 1946.
The Return of Hyman Kaplan. New York, Harper, and London, Gollancz, 1959.
Captain Newman, M.D. London, Gollancz, 1961; New York, Harper, 1962.
A Most Private Intrigue. New York, Atheneum, and London, Gollancz, 1967.
Dear "Herm"—With a Cast of Dozens. New York, McGraw Hill, 1974; London, W.H. Allen, 1975.
O Kaplan! My Kaplan! New York, Harper, 1976; London, Constable, 1979.
Silky: A Detective Story. New York, Harper, 1979.
King Silky! New York, Harper, 1980.

Uncollected Short Stories

"Happy Was the Soldier!," in *Saturday Evening Post Stories 1956.* New York, Random House, 1956.
"Medal in the Sky," in *Atlantic* (Boston), February 1956.
"Lonely Pursuit," in *Cosmopolitan* (New York), September 1956.
"The Guy in Ward 4," in *The Best American Short Stories 1959*, edited by Martha Foley and David Burnett. Boston, Houghton Mifflin, 1959.
"The 'P' Party," "The Chaos Club," "The Happiest Couple in the World," "Freud and Monte O.," "I, The Count of Monte Cristo," and "The Cigar: A Fervent Footnote to History," in *Saturday Review/World* (New York), 1973–74.

Plays

Screenplays: *All Through the Night*, with Leonard Spigelgass and Edward Gilbert, 1942; *The Conspirators*, with Vladimir Pozner and Jack Moffitt, 1944; *Lured*, 1947; *Sleep, My Love*, with others, 1947; *The Velvet Touch*, with others, 1948; *Where Danger Lives*, with Charles Bennett, 1950; *Whistle at Eaton Falls*, with others, 1951; *Double Dynamite*, with Mel Shavelson and Harry Crane, 1952; *Walk East on Beacon*, with others, 1952.

Other

The Washington Correspondents. New York, Harcourt Brace, 1937.
The Strangest Places (as Leonard Ross). New York, Harcourt Brace, and London, Constable, 1939.
Hollywood: The Movie Colony, The Movie Makers. New York, Harcourt Brace, 1941.
112 Gripes about the French. Washington, D.C., United States War Department, 1944.
The Story Behind the Painting. New York, Doubleday-Cowles, 1962.
The Many Worlds of Leo Rosten. New York, Harper, 1964; as *The Leo Rosten Bedside Book*, London, Gollancz, 1965.
The Joys of Yiddish. New York, McGraw Hill, 1968; London, W.H. Allen, 1970.
A Trumpet for Reason. New York, Doubleday, 1970; London, W.H. Allen, 1971.
People I Have Loved, Known, or Admired. New York, McGraw Hill, 1970; London, W.H. Allen, 1971.
Rome Wasn't Burned in a Day: The Mischief of Language. New York, Doubleday, 1972; London, W.H. Allen, 1973.
Leo Rosten's Treasury of Jewish Quotations. New York, McGraw Hill, 1972; London, W.H. Allen, 1973.
The 3:10 to Anywhere. New York, McGraw Hill, 1976.
The Power of Positive Nonsense. New York, McGraw Hill, 1977.
Passions and Prejudices; or, Some of My Best Friends Are People. New York, McGraw Hill, 1978.
Hooray for Yiddish: A Book about English. New York, Simon and Schuster, 1982; London, Elm Tree, 1983.
Leo Rosten's Giant Book of Laughter. New York, Crown, 1985.

Editor, *A Guide to the Religions of America.* New York, Simon and Schuster, 1955; as *Religions of America*, London, Heinemann, 1957; revised edition, as *Religions in America*, Simon and Schuster, 1963, 1975.
Editor, *The "Look" Book.* New York, Abrams, 1975.
Editor, *Infinite Riches: Gems from a Lifetime of Reading.* New York, McGraw Hill, 1979.

*

Manuscript Collection: Brandeis University, Waltham, Massachusetts.

Leo Rosten comments:
I write as my interests guide and seduce me: see the preface to *The Many Worlds of Leo Rosten*. My work ranges from political analysis to humor, from social comment to art to movie screenplays, from inquiries about science and theology to biographical vignettes of Churchill, Freud, Groucho Marx, Adam Smith—and a juicy assortment of wits, half-wits, sages, psychiatrists, and trail-blazers.
People I Have Loved, Known, or Admired suggests the range of my susceptibilities—and the varieties of techniques to which I resort. I write melodrama for pleasure, as some men play chess or go fishing. The titles of my works indicate the range of the nets I have cast into the sea of my fancies. I find writing an indescribably complex, difficult, frustrating, challenging,

exhilarating, unyielding, exciting, depressing, and joyous calling, to which I commit the resources of the self. I also enjoy the play and elusiveness of my fantasies.

The only reason for being a professional writer is that you just can't help it.

*   *   *

Leo Rosten earned a permanent place (as Leonard Q. Ross) on the rolls of ethnic-humorists with the publication in 1937 of *The Education of Hyman Kaplan*. The title is a parody of the autobiographical "study of failure" of the patrician Henry Adams; Rosten's collection of his *New Yorker* short-stories chronicles the sharply contrasting efforts of European immigrants to learn "good English" in night school and thereby succeed in America. The brash hero of these episodes is the determined, cagey and warmly likable Kaplan, who signs his name in red crayon capitals, outlined in blue and punctuated with green stars. Kaplan innocently torments his fusspot teacher, Mr. Parkhill, with bold syntax, dazzling malapropisms, and creative mispronunciations, whereby the plural of "sandwich" is "delicatessen" and the Chinese premier becomes "Shanghai Jack." In 1959, Rosten offered a revival of the popular Kaplan-Parkhill duels, complete with familiar minor characters, but critics agreed that Rosten was too distant from the early years when he had actually taught garment workers in a Chicago night school.

Although his reputation rests on Kaplan's eager shoulders, Rosten's work has been varied, as suggested by one anthology. *The Many Worlds of Leo Rosten*. His Ph.D thesis in sociology at the University of Chicago became *The Washington Correspondents*, followed by a Carnegie Foundation-supported study entitled *Hollywood: The Movie Colony, The Movie Makers*. Both studies are methodically sound, thorough and readable. Among his potboilers, his best is *A Most Private Intrigue*, an old-fashioned spy thriller which eschews James Bond-like violence, sex, and technology in favor of romance, plot twists, and breath-holding escapes.

Rosten's best-selling novel *Captain Newman, M.D.* illustrates his major strengths and weaknesses. As chief of the mental ward of an Air Force base in wartime, psychiatrist Newman is superhumanly insightful, while the ranking officers are as predictably arrogant as the G.I.'s are cute in their shenanigans. If the comic ethnic stereotypes in the Hyman Kaplan stories seemed embarrassing upon re-issue, Rosten nevertheless repeats them all here: the simple-minded Negro private is lovable and humble, the Italian P.O.W.'s roll their eyes and mutter "Mama Mia," the Jewish Laibowitz schemes shrewdly and parries questions with questions. The author skillfully alternates chapters of situation comedy and melodrama to suggest emotional range, but all sequences are as neatly rounded out as in television series.

Rosten handles many genres with professional competence and intelligence but clearly prefers a light, superficial touch. *The Joys of Yiddish* displayed Rosten's impressive knowledge of the impact of English and Yiddish upon each other, as well as his familiarity with Jewish humor and history. *People I Have Loved, Known, or Admired* offers facile interpretations of public figures but is deeply moving in the author's splendid portrait of his own father. *A Trumpet for Reason* resonantly sounds off on contemporary militancy, but the author seems much more attuned to the status quo than he cares to admit. At his best, Rosten writes smooth, witty prose and wears his layers of learning with grace. At worst, he succumbs to the easy appeal of the stock character or belief and reveals the slick writer's affinity for the heart-warming cliché.

—Frank Campenni

———

ROTH, Henry. American. Born in Tysmenica, Austria-Hungary, 8 February 1906; brought to New York City, 1908. Educated at DeWitt Clinton High School, New York, graduated 1924; City College of New York, B.S. 1928. Married Muriel Parker in 1939; two sons. Worked for the Works Progress Administration (WPA), 1939; teacher, Roosevelt High School, New York, 1939–41; precision metal grinder in New York, Providence, Rhode Island, and Boston, 1941–46; teacher in Montville, Maine, 1947–48; attendant, Maine State Hospital, 1949–53; waterfowl farmer, 1953–62; private tutor, 1956–65. Recipient: American Academy grant, 1965; City College of New York Townsend Harris Medal, 1965; University of New Mexico D.H. Lawrence Fellowship, 1968. Agent: Roslyn Targ Literary Agency, 105 West 13th Street, New York, New York 10011. Address: 2600 New York Avenue N.W., Albuquerque, New Mexico 87104, U.S.A.

PUBLICATIONS

Novel

Call It Sleep.   New York, Ballou, 1934; London, Joseph, 1963.

Uncollected Short Stories

"Broker," in *New Yorker*, 18 November 1938.
"Somebody Always Grabs the Purple," in *New Yorker*, 23 March 1940.
"Petey and Yorsee and Mario," in *New Yorker*, 14 July 1956.
"At Times in Flight," in *Commentary* (New York), July 1959.
"The Dun Dakotas," in *Commentary* (New York), August 1960.
"The Surveyor," in *The Best American Short Stories 1967*, edited by Martha Foley and David Burnett. Boston, Houghton Mifflin, 1967.
"Final Dwarf," in *Atlantic* (Boston), July 1969.

Other

Nature's First Green (memoir).   New York, Targ, 1979.

*

Manuscript Collections: Mugar Memorial Library, Boston University; New York Public Library.

Critical Studies: *Bilingual Markers of a Culture in Translation* by Frances Kleederman, unpublished dissertation, New York University, 1974; *World of Our Fathers* by Irving Howe, New York, Harcourt Brace, 1976, as *The Immigrant Jews of New York 1881 to the Present*, London, Routledge, 1976; *Henry Roth* by Bonnie Lyons, New York, Cooper Square, 1977; "Weekends in New York: A Memoir" by Roth, in *Commentary* (New York), September 1984.

Henry Roth comments:

(1972) The writing of the novel, I feel, was too long ago for me to have anything cogent to say about it now, which is not to imply that I ever did have a clear notion of what I was doing. I recall the ambience and the sensation—the affect—of the writing more than I do the "ideas" connected with it. However, one of these does persist in the memory, a kind of guide or credo: That I had no thesis whatever to advance (that I was aware of), only to convey what it felt to be alive, in my time.

I have a strong suspicion that the reason I wrote no more than I did was that I failed of maturity, lost the will to force the next stage in development at the opportune moment.

(1986) As afterthought, I would add that separation from source, or the abandonment of the parochial in favor of the cosmopolitan, could also serve to explain my failure, as well as that of others, to develop and mature as a writer. The separation, which gives the writer a vantage point at first, opposes return—if anything is left to return to—and leaves him stranded in the new world with nothing like the same degree of imaginative and emotional certainty he felt in the old.

*   *   *

Although Henry Roth's only novel, *Call It Sleep*, received favorable reviews and sold tolerably well when it first appeared in 1934, it was known to relatively few readers until its republication in 1960. Its first paperback reprinting in 1964 was a turn in the public reception of the book. *Call It Sleep* is now recognized as one of the finest American novels of this century, perhaps the best novel about childhood ever written by an American, rivalling Dickens's Dostoevsky's sense of the pathos of childhood.

The popularity of *Call It Sleep* during the 1960's can be explained on a number of levels. The interest in Jewish writers and the rediscovery of "ethnic identity," along with increasing curiosity about the life of the Jews in the lower East Side of New York around the turn of the century, are some of the explanations for the book's increasing readership. Also, the concern for urban experience and a renewed interest in the writers of the 1930's contributed toward a rediscovery of Roth's novel.

The vitality of the novel can be felt in the fact that it relates to and yet escapes convenient literary and social categories. A product of the 1930's, and a reflection of some of that decade's concerns, the book can hardly be categorized as a proletarian novel. A description of a Jewish family in New York City during the years preceding World War I, the book cannot be fixed by the term "Jewish novel." A keen portrayal of the mind of a boy, the book cannot quite be called a psychological novel. Yet all of these elements are vibrantly part of the novel.

Call It Sleep begins with the child David Schearl slightly less than two years old and continues to the time he is eight, concentrating on his life in the family and in the streets from his sixth to eighth year. His troubled relationships with his mother and father are keenly portrayed by Roth who describes an oedipal situation with the force of actual life and with no factitious clinical details. The novel resembles D.H. Lawrence's *Sons and Lovers* in its ability to evoke that conflict as a literary and not just a clinical event.

The image of the morose, physically powerful, and stern father is counterpointed by the characterization of the sympathetic, loving mother. The child is torn between his affection for his mother (his only security in the novel) and his secret desire to emulate and challenge the powerful and threatening stance of his father.

The scenes both in the apartment and in the street, among the family and among other children, are overwhelming experiences for David. He struggles to gain some kind of foothold by means of which he can withstand the onslaught of both his father and the gangs and friends of the street. The terrors of the family life eventually relate to the terrors and the testing of experience outside the family.

There are three levels of language in the book which Roth sometimes interweaves. First of all there is the language of narration; then there is the Yiddish spoken at home, rendered through an intelligible and confident English, unlike the broken and noisy English of the street, the third level. There is even a fourth level of language in one scene when Roth also brings into play the Hebrew of the Bible during a Hebrew class the boy attends. In that scene (in chapter IV of Book III), Roth intersperses the Biblical-ritual Hebrew of the rabbi-teacher; the angry Yiddish of that teacher as he curses his recalcitrant pupils; the puzzled, exploratory thoughts of David; and the whining, aggressive remarks of the children. It is a passage that shows to good effect Roth's absorption of Joyce and Eliot.

In an effort to match the power of his father, to meet the frustrations of his family life, to escape the puzzlements of street life, and to emulate the rabbi's description of Isaiah and the burning coal that purified his soul and burned away his sins, as well as to recover a vision he once had when staring into the light of the East River, David slips a metal milk ladle into a slot of a third rail from a trolley car line. He causes a blinding flash (the light of salvation and of authority that he longs for). He is also knocked unconscious and causes a temporary power failure in the neighborhood. In an unsuccessful effort to bring together many persons from different backgrounds in response to that power failure, Roth is forced to leave the consciousness of the child for the first time in the book and tries an unsuccessful collage of "proletarian voices" around the unconscious child in his search for light. Roth's poetic prose becomes forced at this point but regains its regular force when the novel returns to the now awakened boy who back home thinks of rest and self-possession before he falls again into sleep.

Henry Roth has not written another novel since *Call It Sleep*. A few stories have appeared over the years as Roth destroyed a second novel, imperfectly started a third, and went on to hold a number of jobs, finally becoming a raiser of waterfowl in Maine. Probably the best of those stories are "At Times in Flight" and "The Dun Dakotas." Both tales reflect Roth's difficulty in returning to writing. But whether or not Roth will be able to write again at the level of *Call It Sleep*, he has accomplished in that novel one of the finest works of imagination by an American novelist in this century.

—Richard J. Fein

ROTH, Philip (Milton). American. Born in Newark, New Jersey, 19 March 1933. Educated at Weequahic High School, New Jersey; Newark College, Rutgers University, 1950–51; Bucknell University, Lewisburg, Pennsylvania, 1951–54, A.B. 1954 (Phi Beta Kappa); University of Chicago, 1954–55, M.A. 1955. Served in the United States Army, 1955–56. Married Margaret Martinson in 1959 (separated, 1962; died, 1968). Instructor in English, University of Chicago, 1956–58; Visiting Writer, University of Iowa, Iowa City, 1960–62; Writer-in-

Residence, Princeton University, New Jersey, 1962–64; Visiting Writer, State University of New York, Stony Brook, 1966, 1967, and University of Pennsylvania, Philadelphia, 1967–80. General Editor, Writers from the Other Europe series, Penguin, publishers, London, 1975–80. Member of the Corporation of Yaddo, Saratoga Springs, New York. Recipient: Houghton Mifflin Literary Fellowship, 1959; Guggenheim fellowship, 1959; National Book Award, 1960; Daroff Award, 1960; American Academy grant, 1960; O. Henry Award, 1960; Ford Foundation grant, for drama, 1965; Rockefeller fellowship, 1966. Member, American Academy, 1970. Address: c/o Farrar Straus and Giroux, 19 Union Square West, New York, New York 10003, U.S.A.

PUBLICATIONS

Novels

Letting Go. New York, Random House, and London, Deutsch, 1962.
When She Was Good. New York, Random House, and London, Cape, 1967.
Portnoy's Complaint. New York, Random House, and London, Cape, 1969.
Our Gang (Starring Tricky and His Friends). New York, Random House, and London, Cape, 1971.
The Breast. New York, Holt Rinehart, 1972; London, Cape, 1973; revised edition in *A Philip Roth Reader,* 1980.
The Great American Novel. New York, Holt Rinehart, and London, Cape, 1973.
My Life As a Man. New York, Holt Rinehart, and London, Cape, 1974.
The Professor of Desire. New York, Farrar Straus, 1977; London, Cape, 1978.
Zuckerman Bound (includes *The Prague Orgy*). New York, Farrar Straus, 1985.
    The Ghost Writer. New York, Farrar Straus, and London, Cape, 1979.
    Zuckerman Unbound. New York, Farrar Straus, and London, Cape, 1981.
    The Anatomy Lesson. New York, Farrar Straus, 1983; London, Cape, 1984.
The Prague Orgy. London, Cape, 1985.

Short Stories

Goodbye, Columbus, and Five Short Stories. Boston, Houghton Mifflin, and London, Deutsch, 1959.
Penguin Modern Stories 3, with others. London, Penguin, 1969.
Novotny's Pain. Los Angeles, Sylvester and Orphanos, 1980.

Uncollected Short Stories

"Philosophy, or Something Like That" May 1952, "The Box of Truths" October 1952, "The Fence" May 1953, "Armando and the Frauds" October 1953, and "The Final Delivery of Mr. Thorn" May 1954, all in *Et Cetera* (Lewisburg, Pennsylvania).
"The Day It Snowed," in *Chicago Review,* Fall 1954.
"The Contest for Aaron Gold," in *Epoch* (Ithaca, New York), Fall 1955.
"Heard Melodies Are Sweeter," in *Esquire* (New York), August 1958.
"Expect the Vandals," in *Esquire* (New York), December 1958.

"The Love Vessel," in *Dial* (New York), Fall 1959.
"Good Girl," in *Cosmopolitan* (New York), May 1960.
"The Mistaken," in *American Judaism* (New York), Fall 1960.
"Psychoanalytic Special," in *Esquire* (New York), November 1963.
"On the Air," in *New American Review 10,* edited by Theodore Solotaroff.   New York, New American Library, 1970.
"Smart Money," in *New Yorker,* 2 February 1981.

Play

Television Play: *The Ghost Writer,* with Tristram Powell, from the novel by Roth, 1983.

Other

Reading Myself and Others. New York, Farrar Straus, and London, Cape, 1975.
A Philip Roth Reader. New York, Farrar Straus, 1980; London, Cape, 1981.

*

Bibliography: *Philip Roth: A Bibliography* by Bernard F. Rodgers, Jr., Metuchen, New Jersey, Scarecrow Press, 1974; revised edition, 1984.

Manuscript Collection: Library of Congress, Washington, D.C.

Critical Studies: *Bernard Malamud and Philip Roth: A Critical Essay* by Glenn Meeter, Grand Rapids, Michigan, Eerdmans, 1968; "The Journey of Philip Roth" by Theodore Solotaroff, in *The Red Hot Vacuum,* New York, Atheneum, 1970; *The Fiction of Philip Roth* by John N. McDaniel, Haddonfield, New Jersey, Haddonfield House, 1974; *The Comedy That "Hoits": An Essay on the Fiction of Philip Roth* by Sanford Pinsker, Columbia, University of Missouri Press, 1975, and *Critical Essays on Philip Roth* edited by Pinsker, Boston, Twayne, 1982; *Philip Roth* by Bernard F. Rodgers, Jr., Boston, Twayne, 1978; "Jewish Writers" by Mark Shechner, in *The Harvard Guide to Contemporary American Writing* edited by Daniel Hoffman, Cambridge, Massachusetts, Harvard University Press, 1979; introduction by Martin Green to *A Philip Roth Reader,* New York, Farrar Straus, 1980, London, Cape, 1981; *Philip Roth* by Judith Paterson Jones and Guinevera A. Nance, New York, Ungar, 1981; *Philip Roth* by Hermione Lee, London, Methuen, 1982.

*   *   *

In the title of one of the best essays on Philip Roth, Alfred Kazin used the word "toughminded." This quality pervades his novels, stories, and essays. Roth's unsparing portraits of Jews too adept at scheming and compromise have upset rabbis and Jewish organizations. His frank acknowledgment of such unmentionables as abortion, masturbation, and sexual calisthenics has alarmed the blue-noses. These irate—usually unliterary—responses have fortunately failed to unsettle him.

Until now Roth has seemed most at ease with Jewish characters and settings. His ear is especially sensitive to the verbal rhythm and pulse beat of the second-generation American Jew who has recently abandoned the inner city for the suburbs. The stories in Roth's first book, *Goodbye, Columbus,* are almost all concerned with confrontations between Jews of radically different persuasions and temperaments. Thus Neil Klugman, in the title story, confronts the Jewish society of Short

Hills, as represented by Brenda Patimkin and her family, where "fruit grew in their refrigerator and sporting goods dropped from their trees!" Neil's wrong-side-of-the-track Judaism fails to make the proper concessions and adjustments. In "Eli, The Fanatic" the assimilated Jews of another suburban community, Woodenton, employ the lawyer Eli Peck to force a Yeshivah to move elsewhere or at least to "modernize." We see a skillful confrontation between the Talmudic logic of the Yeshivah's headmaster and the more worldly logic of Eli. Eli ends by donning the Hasidic garb of one of the Yeshivah instructors—which suggests to his fellow Jews of Woodenton the return of an earlier nervous breakdown. Jew is also pitted against Jew in "The Conversion of the Jews." This time the questioning Jewish schoolboy Ozzie Freedman forces embarrassing ideological concessions from Rabbi Binder and the Jewish establishment when he threatens to jump from the roof of the synagogue. The stories in Goodbye, Columbus are brilliantly irreverent.

Roth's heterodoxy continues into his first novel, Letting Go. He enlarges the focus here to include not only the idiosyncrasies of the Jewish community but also of university faculties, charlatan abortionists, and ill-suited love relationships. Very little is left out. Gabe Wallach's "I" controls the early parts of the novel; then it recedes into a kind of background first-person and finally turns into a more respectably detached third-person. Wallach is the intruder who keeps moving in and out of delicate situations—always avoiding complete involvement—and so this changing of narrative focus is especially apt. He defines his position early in the novel: "It was beginning to seem that toward those for whom I felt no strong sentiment, I gravitated; where sentiment existed, I ran." Wallach's years as a graduate student at the University of Iowa and as an instructor at the University of Chicago offer a rejection of his eastern seaboard Jewish background (born in New York, educated at Harvard). The first words of the novel are the deathbed letter of Gabe Wallach's mother. This letter, inadvertently tucked between the pages of his copy of James's Portrait of a Lady, starts Gabe off on the midwestern pilgrimage which involves the series of precarious relationships with Libby and Paul Herz and with Martha Reganhart. The terribly flawed Herz marriage somehow survives Gabe's "meddling"; in fact, it is strengthened by the adoption of a child and by a spirited assertion of Judaism. Gabe Wallach's love affair with Martha Reganhart fares less well. Gabe speaks of himself in a final letter to Libby as an "indecisive man" who had had but "one decisive moment."

Roth also places his next novel, When She Was Good, in the midwest—this time a midwest without Jews. The texture of his writing changes markedly; it seems to flatten out, to become, as Theodore Solotaroff suggests, "a language of scrupulous banality." The midwestern Protestantism which underlies the novel is threatened only by an adolescent flirtation with the Catholic Church by the heroine Lucy Nelson; this is lightly dismissed as "all that Catholic hocus-pocus." Lucy's intolerance and uncomfortable moral provincialism manage to get in the way of her own marriage and that of her parents. She cannot put up with her husband's rather puerile brashness and incompetence or with her father's alcoholism.

Just as Roth was able to capture the special quality of the conversation of both first and second generation American Jews in Goodbye, Columbus and Letting Go, so in When She Was Good he manages handsomely with the cliché-ridden language of Main Street.

Portnoy's Complaint is a return, with a vengeance, to Roth's earlier manner. It seems to come out of the best pages of Goodbye, Columbus and Letting Go. Roth has settled here on all the things he knows how to do best, especially in his creation of the urban Jewish family with the mother at its moral center. Portnoy's Complaint is the staccato confession of Alexander Portnoy to his psychiatrist Dr. Spielvogel (who makes another appearance in My Life As a Man) in heavily free associative prose.

The novel begins with a section entitled "The Most Unforgettable Character I've Met"; the reference is to Sophie Portnoy who dominates not only the family but also the "confessions" of her son. (She is in part anticipated by Aunt Gladys in "Goodbye, Columbus" and Paul Herz's mother in Letting Go.) She characteristically pushes to the background her perpetually constipated and henpecked husband and her pathetically unendowed daughter. The confrontation is between mother and son. The fiercely aggressive, domineering mother seems to win out since it is the son who does the confessing from the analyst's couch. Alex, however, gains some measure of revenge through seiges of masturbation in his youth and through affairs with gentiles (shiksas) in his more mature years. He masterfully uncovers chinks in his Jewish mother's armor by taunting her with his conquest of Christian girls and by abusing the family rabbi, but always at the expense of his own too active feelings of guilt. Everything in this novel, it would seem, "can be traced to the bonds obtaining in the mother-child relationship." Jewish mothers, in the past few years, have presented a challenge to some of the best American Jewish novelists, like Wallace Markfield, Bruce Jay Friedman, and Herbert Gold. Probably the most realized and convincing of all is Sophie Portnoy.

Roth's versatility is very much in evidence in Our Gang (Starring Tricky and His Friends); he seems able to manage the rhetoric of political corruption quite as easily as the language of the Jewish urban dweller who has recently retreated to the suburbs. In Our Gang Roth takes on a formidable adversary, the Nixon administration: he carries a certain Trick E. Dixon from a press conference, an underground meeting with his "coaches," an address to his "fellow Americans," to an election speech—following his assassination—to his "fellow Fallen" in Hell. This speech ends with the revealing sentence: "And let there be no mistake about it: if I am elected Devil, I intend to see Evil triumph in the end; I intend to see that our children, and our children's children, need never know the terrible scourge of Righteousness and Peace." Passages from Swift and Orwell appropriately serve as epigraphs for this novel.

The Breast, in certain ways, marks a return to Portnoy's Complaint. One might think of this novella—with its college professor narrator, David Alan Kepesh, who turns into a female breast—as a working out of certain fantasies suggested by Portnoy with some help from Kafka, Gogol, and Swift. The bookish hero cannot resist likening his peculiar condition to that of Kafka's Gregor Samsa who awakens to discover that he has turned into a huge bug or to that of Gogol's Kovalyov who awakens to find that he is missing his nose; he makes reference also to Swift's "self-satisfied Houyhnhnms" and to "Gulliver among the Brobdingnags," in which country "the king's maidservants had him walk out on their nipples for the fun of it."

The Great American Novel seems to have little in common with the previous fiction. This baseball novel is Roth's contribution to a genre which has already attracted several other American Jewish writers, including Bernard Malamud and Mark Harris. It is filled with oblique references to a wide variety of literary works. Thus it begins with the sentence, "Call me Smitty." A sensational pitcher goes under the name Gil Gamesh. American literature and baseball are occasionally brought together in uneasy confrontation; they make for strange bedfellows. This mock-heroic tone reinforces the sense of caricature and pastiche which runs through the novel. Roth holds up the myth of the Great American Novel to the same ridicule as the myth of the Great American Pastime.

My Life As a Man fits snugly into place in the main line of Philip Roth's development. The Jewish ingredients are less pronounced here than in *Goodbye, Columbus, Letting Go,* and *Portnoy's Complaint,* yet the ambience is unmistakably the same. The writer-hero of the novel, Peter Tarnopol, has much in common with Gabe Wallach, Alexander Portnoy, and David Alan Kepesh. Indeed he has the same bookish tendencies as Kepesh. Roth offers a clever variation on the novel-within-the-novel device as he prefaces the main part of his latest work, "My True Story" (Tarnopol's sustained confessional), with two of his protagonist's short stories. The "useful fictions," as Roth calls these stories, have a great deal to do with Tarnopol's "true story"; truth and fiction, it would seem, are ultimately interchangeable. *My Life As a Man* reveals Roth in his dual roles as novelist and critic. The narrative strategy allows for a good deal of theorizing about the nature of novel-writing and a certain amount of literary criticism.

The Professor of Desire and *The Ghost Writer*, both first-person novels, borrow as narrators characters who appeared in the earlier fiction. *The Professor of Desire*, like *The Breast,* is told by David Kepesh while Nathan Zuckerman, the central presence in the "Useful Fictions" section of *My Life As a Man,* narrates *The Ghost Writer. The Professor of Desire* offers an elaborate unfolding of Kepesh's *wanderjahre* in the years preceding his metamorphosis. The restless narrative starts and ends in the Catskills—the Jewish still point of the novel. The itinerary is dotted with literary and amorous "excavations." Since his graduate school days at Stanford, Kepesh has been working intermittently on a book about romantic disillusionment in Chekhov's stories. A real and imagined Kafka occupies a central position in the Prague interlude. The amorous is even more in evidence than the literary, as Kepesh makes his way from a succession of girl friends, to a marriage and divorce, finally to a rather idyllic relationship with Claire Ovington.

The literary and the amorous are also strongly in evidence in *The Ghost Writer*. The novel turns about an odd triangular relationship, involving the narrator, Zuckerman, the renowned writer E.I. Lonoff, and a young lady who has served a kind of apprenticeship (literary and perhaps also sexual) at Lonoff's feet, Amy Bellette. Zuckerman, a youthful author, arrives at Lonoff's house at the beginning of this short novel, in retreat from his cloying Jewish parents and his Newark childhood. He is an onlooker, in much the same way as Styron's narrator in *Sophie's Choice,* as he tries to unravel the complications of a situation which couples the erotic with the literary. With some help from Henry James's *The Middle Years* and other literary texts, Zuckerman weaves a complex mosaic which turns Amy Bellette into the author of *The Diary of Anne Frank.* The mythological machinery he invents here is in a sense his work of art: the gesture which will make him worthy of becoming Lonoff's "spiritual son" and perhaps eventually Amy's sexual partner. In *The Ghost Writer* Roth seems to have moved his familiar literary baggage to a new setting, rural New England; with the change has come a minimizing of the ethnically Jewish world of the early fiction in favor of a broader Judaeo-Christian canvas.

The Ghost Writer can probably be read, as several reviewers have suggested, as being something of a *roman à clef*: with Zuckerman taking on many aspects of the young Roth, halfway through his first book, *Goodbye, Columbus,* looking for a Jewish literary patron and finding him in Lonoff, who is probably a composite figure with a heady dose of Bernard Malamud and a suspicion of Isaac Bashevis Singer and Isaac Babel. One

can continue this kind of reading with *Zuckerman Unbound,* which takes place in 1969, 13 years after the events of *The Ghost Writer.* Nathan Zuckerman, who has abdicated his role as narrator in this third-person novel, has just published a controversial best-seller, *Carnovsky,* which bears an uncanny resemblance to Roth's 1969 *Portnoy's Complaint.* (This title may offer an oblique reminder of I.J. Singer's *The Family Carnovsky* which, in its translation from the Yiddish, also appeared in 1969.)

Zuckerman Unbound concerns the aftermath of this event as Zuckerman spends much of his time coping with the bitter-sweet smell of post-*Carnovsky* success, disentangling himself from his creature Gilbert Carnovsky, picking up the pieces of his most recent broken marriage. We see him during a variety of encounters: with his agent, his answering service, a beautiful Irish actress, members of his family, and a curious interloper named Alvin Pepler (who takes on the role of his "double" or "secret sharer"). If the novel has an epiphany it occurs toward the end when Zuckerman flies to Miami to witness the death of his father, only to hear him pronounce, as his dying word, "bastard"—unmistakenly directed at his author son. Nathan's desperate litany in the final paragraph sums up the futility: "You are no longer any man's son, you are no longer some good woman's husband, you are no longer your brother's brother, and you don't come from anywhere anymore, either."

The Anatomy Lesson sounds an even more wrenching note of despair. Zuckerman, now 40 years old, is unable to write and is forced to wear an orthopedic collar to support his neck; psychic pain combines with physical pain to make his life unbearable. The only reprieve is offered by the visits of four women who "exercise" (also exorcise) him on a "playmat." The central text in *The Anatomy Lesson* is probably Mann's *The Magic Mountain,* which one of the women reads to him; it serves something of the same purpose as *The Middle Years* did in *The Ghost Writer.* Alvin Pepler was a haunting presence throughout *Zuckerman Unbound,* but nothing quite as terrifying and obsessive as the literary critic Milton Appel proves to be here. (In another flirtation with the possibilities of *roman à clef,* Roth has modeled Appel after Irving Howe who had singularly harsh things to say about his work, including the devastating comment, in a December 1972 *Commentary* article, "Philip Roth Reconsidered," that the cruelest thing would be to read *Portnoy's Complaint* twice.)

Zuckerman finally decides to renegotiate the circumstances of his life, as he leaves New York for Chicago: "By nightfall his career as a writer would be officially over and the future as a physician underway." The closest he gets to a medical career is a long stay at a university hospital, first as patient, then as patient accompanying interns on their monotonous rounds.

Zuckerman Bound contains the three Zuckerman novels, now declared to be a trilogy, and an epilogue, the novella-length *The Prague Orgy.* This postlude offers segments from Zuckerman's notebooks, one from New York, dated 11 January 1976, the other two from Prague, dated February 4 and 5 of the same year. A seemingly revitalized Zuckerman leaves New York for Prague to recover the unpublished Yiddish stories of a certain Sisovsky, the father of a Czech writer he meets in New York; we are told that "this is not the Yiddish of Sholem Aleichem. This is the Yiddish of Flaubert." Zuckerman does finally gain possession of this material only to have it confiscated before he leaves Prague. This failed mission seems to be linked to Kafka at every turn. The author of "The Metamorphosis," for example, makes an intriguing appearance: "*As Nathan Zuckerman awoke one morning from uneasy dreams he found himself transformed in his bed into a sweeper of floors in a railway café*" (Roth's italics). This is not only the 20th-century Prague of Kafka revisited but also perhaps the 16th-century Prague of the golem—the creation of the Maharal, Rabbi Jehuda Loew—who was to save the Jews from Czech atrocities. One can agree with Harold Bloom who sees *The Prague Orgy* as something of a summa, "a kind of coda to all his [Roth's] fiction so far."

—Melvin J. Friedman

RUBENS, Bernice (Ruth). British. Born in Cardiff, Wales, 26 July 1928. Educated at Cardiff High School for Girls; University College of South Wales and Monmouthshire, Cardiff, 1944–47, B.A. (honours) in English 1947. Married Rudi Nassauer in 1947; two daughters. English teacher, Handsworth Grammar School for Boys, Birmingham, 1948–49. Since 1950, documentary film writer and director, for the United Nations and others. Recipient: American Blue Ribbon Award, for filmmaking, 1968; Booker Prize, 1970; Welsh Arts Council award, 1976. Fellow, University of Wales, Cardiff, 1982. Address: 89 Greencroft Gardens, London NW6 3LJ, England.

PUBLICATIONS

Novels

Set on Edge.   London, Eyre and Spottiswoode, 1960.
Madame Sousatzka.   London, Eyre and Spottiswoode, 1962.
Mate in Three.   London, Eyre and Spottiswoode, 1965.
The Elected Member.   London, Eyre and Spottiswoode, 1969; as *Chosen People*, New York, Atheneum, 1969.
Sunday Best.   London, Eyre and Spottiswoode, 1971; New York, Summit, 1980.
Go Tell the Lemming.   London, Cape, 1973; New York, Washington Square Press, 1984.
I Sent a Letter to My Love.   London, W.H. Allen, 1975; New York, St. Martin's Press, 1978.
The Ponsonby Post.   London, W.H. Allen, 1977; New York, St. Martin's Press, 1978.
A Five Year Sentence.   London, W.H. Allen, 1978; as *Favours*, New York, Summit, 1979.
Spring Sonata.   London, W.H. Allen, 1979.
Birds of Passage.   London, Hamish Hamilton, 1981; New York, Summit, 1982.
Brothers.   London, Hamish Hamilton, 1983; New York, Delacorte Press, 1984.
Mr. Wakefield's Crusade.   London, Hamish Hamilton, and New York, Delacorte Press, 1985.

Plays

I Sent a Letter to My Love, adaptation of her own novel (produced New Haven, Connecticut, 1978; London, 1979).

Screenplays (documentaries; also director): *One of the Family*, 1964; *Call Us by Name*, 1968; *Out of the Mouths*, 1970.

Television Play: *Third Party*, 1972.

*

Bernice Rubens comments:

(1972) I am never consciously aware of the actual matter of my work and never think about it unless the question is directly raised. There seems to be a terrible finality about assessing one's own work, because such an assessment might bind you to that evaluation forever. I am open to the most radical changes in my thinking and outlook. I hope it will be reflected in my work. My first four novels were essentially on Jewish themes in a Jewish environment, for in that environment I felt secure. My fifth novel, *Sunday Best*, was an attempt to challenge myself to step outside that familiarity. I noticed that my radical change of location did not involve as radical a change of style, which seems to remain simple, direct, always empty of what in school is called "descriptive passages," for these frighten me. As to the matter of what I write about, I can only be general. I am concerned with the communication, or non-communication as is more often the case, between people and families. A general enough statement, and in this general sense my books will always be about that theme.

*   *   *

The salient feature of Bernice Rubens's writing is her maddening refusal to fit neatly into any single category, while proffering the same unchanging, unmistakably individual vision of humanity. Some of her novels approach sheer slapstick (*Set on Edge*), others a Hitchcockian murder story (*Mr. Wakefield's Crusade*, *Sunday Best*), others a case study of the strains of family life (*The Elected Member*, *Set on Edge*, *Spring Sonata*, *Brothers*), others again a comedy of manners (the expatriate set in *The Ponsonby Post*, a cruise in *Birds of Passage*, eccentric lodgers in *Madame Sousatzka*). The variety is considerable, but they all present the same picture of human misery, miscomprehension, of loneliness slipping into madness.

Her earlier novels pillory the claustrophobic closeness of Jewish family life, pointing an accusing finger at the Jewish matriarch with her devouring, ambitious mother love. Her first novel, *Set on Edge*, takes its title from the words of the prophet Ezekiel ("The fathers have eaten sour grapes, and the children's teeth are set on edge") which ought to hang as a motto over any analyst's couch. Mrs. Sperber burdens her daughter Gladys with guilt, and at the close of the novel we watch Gladys taking over her mother's role as the accuser as well as the provider. Mrs. Crominski in *Madame Sousatzka*, Mrs. Zweck in *The Elected Member*, Sheila's mother and grandmother in *Spring Sonata* all provide good Laingian material, parading their maternal guilt. Indeed Bernice Rubens shows her *romans* to be very much *à thèse* here, particularly in her Booker prize winner, *The Elected Member*, with its epigraph from R.D. Laing himself ("If patients are *disturbed*, their families are *disturbing*").

Her novelist's imagination, however, refuses to be circumscribed, and she turns away from the familiarity of Jewish life in North London to find the same tragicomedies of emotional crippling played out against a gentile background. The transvestite George Verrey Smith in *Sunday Best*, the lonely spinster Jean Hawkins in *A Five Year Sentence*, the sad homosexual Luke in *Mr. Wakefield's Crusade* are all walking wounded on the battlefield of life, maimed by a loveless childhood, free of guilt because they are the victims, the sinned against rather than the sinning.

Faced with such unspeakable misery, Rubens chooses to laugh, and her echoing laughter is truly shocking. She is a witty writer, with a brilliant sense of comedy: Jenny's client in *Madame Sousatzka*, in his shirtsleeves, masquerading as a carpenter; Mrs. Sperber in *Set on Edge* taking her rolled-up corset to bed with her like a child with a teddy bear; the parade of too many Hitlers at the fancy dress party in *Birds of Passage* (like "the Hall of Mirrors in Berchtesgaden"), all these are very funny set pieces. There are many such moments of high comedy in Rubens's novels, but she is equally skilled in the use of sly verbal wit (Luke's comment on the "posh deaths" in *The Times*, Betty Knox in *Birds of Passage* asking her husband how many people had witnessed her humiliation "as if he were responsible for the gate").

Like all witty writers she uses language with great care—if a single right word (like "gate" in the quotation above) is enough to make a reader laugh then words must be treated with proper respect. Her writing is spare, as befits the bleak landscape of her vision. Her sombre, plain sentences can be very moving (the chilling prayer that closes *The Elected Member*, "Dear God, look after us cold and chosen ones," has such power). There is a striking absence of description. Although she provides those recognisable authentic touches that mark present-day novels—Alice's silk dungarees in *Birds of Passage*, the shuffling post office queue in *Mr. Wakefield's Crusade*—her characters move against a blank background, almost faceless themselves. This technique, particularly remarkable in *Birds of Passage* where full descriptions are provided of the supporting cast and yet we never see the two protagonists, Ellen and Alice, is obviously deliberate. By blurring the faces she is calling our attention to the turmoil behind. It is the human mind and the human heart that interest her, and if her interest strikes us at times as chillingly clinical (as, again in *Birds of Passage*, in the description of the two women's reaction to rape: "The women were reacting in diametrically opposed fashion to exactly the same agent, though neither knew of the other's connection") then our shocked reaction is exactly what the author intended. Her purpose is to shock, as well as to amuse, and to achieve this dual purpose she will stop at nothing. Such deliberate excesses (as the episode of Betty Knox's soiled skirt in *Birds of Passage*) are of course all the more startling in a writer so much in control of her material.

To dwell only on her attention to her craft, however, is to present a false picture, for she is a writer of imagination, with a penchant for the bizarre, the grotesque. The foetus which refuses to be born, playing the fiddle and writing his diary in his mother's womb (*Spring Sonata*) is the product of no ordinary imagination, and comparisons with Gogol's *Nose* are not entirely out of place. The same rich imagination is at work on the plot of *Mr. Wakefield's Crusade* (over which the plump shadow of Alfred Hitchcock seems to hover) and on the domesticated madness of *A Five Year Sentence*. These are excesses of imagination, shocking and frightening as they are fully intended to be, for they are a part of Bernice Rubens's world in which the dullness of pain can only be broken by a loud laugh or a scream of terror.

—Hana Sambrook

RULE, Jane (Vance). Canadian. Born in Plainfield, New Jersey, United States, 28 March 1931. Educated at Palo Alto High School, California; Mills College, Oakland, California (Ardella Mills Award, 1952), 1948–52, B.A. 1952 (Phi Beta Kappa); University of London, 1952–53; Stanford University, California, 1953. Teacher of English and biology, Concord Academy, Massachusetts, 1954–56; assistant director of International House, 1958–59, intermittent lecturer in English, 1959–72, and guest lecturer in creative writing, 1972–73, University of British Columbia, Vancouver. Since 1974, full-time writer. Recipient: Canada Council award, 1969, 1970; Canadian Authors Association prize, for short story, 1978, for novel, 1978; Gay Academic Union (USA) award, 1978; Fund for Human Dignity (USA) award, 1983. Agent: Georges Borchardt Inc., 136 East 57th Street, New York, New York 10022, U.S.A. Address: The Fork, Route 1, Galiano, British Columbia V0N 1PO, Canada.

PUBLICATIONS

Novels

Desert of the Heart.   Toronto, Macmillan, and London, Secker and Warburg, 1964; Cleveland, World, 1965.
This Is Not for You.   New York, McCall, 1970.
Against the Season.   New York, McCall, 1971; London, Davies, 1972.
The Young in One Another's Arms.   New York, Doubleday, 1977.
Contract with the World.   New York, Harcourt Brace, 1980.

Short Stories

Theme for Diverse Instruments.   Vancouver, Talonbooks, 1975.
Outlander (includes essays).   Tallahassee, Florida, Naiad Press, 1981.
Inland Passage.   Tallahassee, Florida, Naiad Press, 1985.

Uncollected Short Stories

"Your Father and I," in *Housewife* (London), vol. 23, no. 8, 1961.
"No More Bargains," in *Redbook* (New York), September 1963.
"Three Letters to a Poet," in *Ladder* (Reno, Nevada), May-June 1968.
"Moving On," in *Redbook* (New York), June 1968.
"Houseguest," in *Ladder* (Reno, Nevada), January 1969.
"The List," in *Chatelaine* (Toronto), April 1969.
"Not an Ordinary Wife," in *Redbook* (New York), August 1969.
"Anyone Will Do," in *Redbook* (New York), October 1969.
"The Secretary Bird," in *Chatelaine* (Toronto), August 1972.
"The Bosom of the Family," in *75: New Canadian Stories*, edited by David Helwig and Joan Harcourt. Ottawa, Oberon Press, 1975.
"This Gathering," in *Canadian Fiction* (Vancouver), Autumn 1976.
"Pictures," in *Body Politic* (Toronto), December 1976–January 1977.
"The Sandwich Generation," in *Small Wonders*, edited by Robert Weaver. Toronto, CBC, 1982.
"Ashes, Ashes," in *New: West Coast Fiction*. Vancouver, Pulp Press, 1984.
"Blessed Are the Dead," in *The Vancouver Fiction Book*, edited by David Watmough. Winlaw, British Columbia, Polestar Press, 1985.

Other

Lesbian Images (history and criticism).   New York, Doubleday, 1975; London, Davies, 1976.

A Hot-Eyed Moderate. Tallahassee, Florida, Naiad Press, 1985.

*

Critical Studies: "Jane Rule and the Reviewers" by Judith Niemi, in *Margins* (Milwaukee), vol. 8, no. 23, 1975; "Jane Rule Issue" of *Canadian Fiction* (Vancouver), Autumn 1976; interview with Michele Kort, in *rara avis* (Los Angeles), Summer-Fall 1981.

*　　*　　*

Jane Rule's writing is best known for its open exploration of unconventional human relationships, particularly lesbianism. Her first two novels contrast two different types of relations between women. *Desert of the Heart* traces, in alternating chapters, the lives of two women, widely separated by age and background, as they overcome their initial fear and prejudice and risk living together. *This Is Not for You*, the only one of Rule's novels to be narrated from a single perspective (it takes the form of an unmailed letter) follows the development of two women, friends from their California college days, who fail to break free of convention, so that their love for each other remains unfulfilled.

Rule's third novel branches out to embrace a larger cross-section of the human community. Set in a small American town, *Against the Season* explores the intersecting lives of a wider range of female and male characters, including a lame 72-year-old spinster, two pregnant teenage girls from a home for "unwed mothers," and a lesbian businesswoman of Greek descent. Although kinship, habit, and professional functions link some of the townspeople, Rule highlights the element of free choice in their social interactions, and her work extends the usual boundaries of romantic love to include the longings and desires of the elderly.

The tyranny of conventional morality, which marginalizes the handicapped and nonconforming, set against a more generous and innovative concept of community, which values human differences, is explored further in Rule's fourth and fifth novels, where multiple points of view again are used to reflect a non-hierarchical vision of society. *The Young in One Another's Arms* describes how the residents of a Vancouver boarding house—slated for demolition in a program of urban renewal—regroup around the owner, a crippled 50-year-old woman, to form a voluntary four-generation "family," related by bonds of affection rather than by legal or blood ties. They seek shelter from urban politics and an intrusive social order by working together to establish a restaurant as an experiment in communal living. *Contract with the World* describes the life and work of six different Vancouver artists or art dealers, all friends, who must confront philistinism, prejudice, and failure, and who suffer existential crises over their sexual and artistic identities, being homosexuals in a homophobic culture or artists in a barbarous climate.

Rule's short stories, collected in three books—*Theme for Diverse Instruments, Outlander*, and *Inland Passage*—present a similar diversity of emotional and sexual relationships. Again, despite her primary interest in female sexuality and identity, especially lesbianism, Rule does not ignore male and heterosexual perspectives. The characters' attempts at self-definition are sometimes frustrated, resulting in feelings of weakness, vulnerability, alienation, and even madness. However, most of the characters, in the end, manage to discover some means of integrating personal and social realities. The stories are set variously in England, the U.S., and West Coast Canada; but more significant than geographic location are the smaller domestic spaces or psychic "houses" which the characters inhabit, construct, or deconstruct. Arguably her best stories, "Theme for Diverse Instruments" and "Outlander" celebrate woman's vitality and emphasize a recurring theme—that tolerance for a variety of lifestyles engenders a sense of community, thereby extending the creative potential of the group and of each of its members.

Rule's essays, many written for her column in the controversial paper *The Body Politic*, deal with various aspects of sexuality, morality, and literature, and are particularly valuable on the subject of lesbianism. Twelve essays appear alongside the short stories in *Outlander*; others have been collected in *Lesbian Images* and *A Hot-Eyed Moderate*. The former begins with an essay surveying attitudes to female sexuality over the centuries, condemning the prejudices fostered by churchmen and psychologists, and it contains searching studies of individual women writers such as Radclyffe Hall, May Sarton, and Vita Sackville-West, and of the veiled forms through which they projected their love for other women. The latter is a collection of Rule's reflections, courageously honest and deeply personal, on her own life as a lesbian and a writer; in addition there are miscellaneous reviews and articles on topics such as pornography, censorship, morality in literature, homosexuals and children, and caring for the elderly.

In all her writing, Rule says, she has tried "to speak the truth as I saw it," to present lesbians and homosexuals as "not heroic or saintly but *real*." Refusing the strategies of evasion of many earlier women's texts, but equally resisting the separatist and utopian tendencies of some contemporary lesbian literature, Rule has been criticized recently by the gay community for not being political enough; she maintains, however, that "literature is the citadel of the individual spirit which inspires rather than serves the body politic."

—Wendy Robbins Keitner

———

RUMAKER, Michael. American. Born in Philadelphia, Pennsylvania, 5 March 1932. Educated at Rider College, Trenton, New Jersey; Black Mountain College, North Carolina, graduated 1955; Columbia University, New York, M.F.A. 1970. Visiting Writer-in-Residence, State University of New York, Buffalo, 1967; Lecturer in Creative Writing, New School for Social Research, New York, 1967–71; Writer-in-Residence and Lecturer, City College of New York, 1969–71, 1985. Recipient: Dell Publishing Foundation award, 1970. Agent: Harold Ober Associates, 40 East 49th Street, New York, New York 10017. Address: 139 South Broadway, South Nyack, New York 10960, U.S.A.

PUBLICATIONS

Novels

The Butterfly. New York, Scribner, 1962; London, Macdonald, 1968.
A Day and a Night at the Baths. Bolinas, California, Grey Fox Press, 1979.
My First Satyrnalia. San Francisco, Grey Fox Press, 1981.

Short Stories

The Bar.   San Francisco, Four Seasons, 1964.
Exit 3 and Other Stories.   London, Penguin, 1966; as *Gringos and Other Stories*, New York, Grove Press, 1967.

Play

Schwul (Queers), translated by Wylf Teichmann and Dirk Mülder.   Frankfurt, März, 1970.

Other

Prose 1, with Ed Dorn and Warren Tallman.   San Francisco, Four Seasons, 1964.

*

Bibliography: by George F. Butterick, in *Athanor 6* (Clarkson, New York), Spring 1975.

Manuscript Collection: University of Connecticut, Storrs.

Critical Studies: "The Use of the Unconscious in Writing" by Rumaker, in *New American Story* edited by Donald Allen and Robert Creeley, New York, Grove Press, 1965; article by George F. Butterick, in *The Beats* edited by Ann Charters, Detroit, Gale, 1983.

*   *   *

Michael Rumaker's coterie reputation rests upon an astonishingly small output, none of it very recent and virtually all completed by his thirtieth birthday. Yet he demonstrates virtuosity, versatility, and sophistication, all traits which normally suggest the maturity of experience. Rumaker must be counted among the new breed of writers who deliberately call attention to the artifice of their writing: with these fellow-writers he achieves his effects mostly through style, especially in the brilliantly clear rendering of the world of objects, his created milieu regressing to primal states of being and manifestations of the unconscious. What sets him off from his counterparts is his willingness to work within the apparent constraints of traditional fiction, so that his stories may be mass-read (and perhaps misread) as easily as those of Stephen Crane or Mark Twain.

Rumaker is best within the short story form, particularly when writing of "natural" men in raw settings. His three best stories, "Gringos," "The Pipe," and "The Desert," depict intuitive men—misfits, cast-offs, wanderers—who create temporary "societies" with each other which threaten imminently to explode. They fight, lust, drink, and sometimes kill each other, yet at their most bizarre or violent they remain intensely human and, for that reason, are interesting, even likable, though grotesque. In "Gringos" a young American named Jim teams up with a friendly, blustering sailor in a small Mexican town. Jim agrees to share the sailor's room and hospitality; they saunter through the streets, dodge the aggressive prostitutes, drink, turn down a young male prostitute and finally "purchase" a girl (sailor's treat). At the night's end, they are attacked by Mexicans with knives, but they beat them off and return home. Simply as experience, this account is brilliantly realized, but from the start the mutual hostility of the intruding Americans and the impoverished Mexicans, the sink-hole quality of the squalid town, the oppressive atmosphere of cripples, pornography, exploitation, and homosexuality all point a descent into the hells of our own making. "The Pipe" is even

more vividly a landscape of the unconscious, projecting myth and symbol without obtruding upon the bare narrative. Five men wait by the mouth of a huge pipe. A dredgeboat anchored in mid-river will soon blow submerged waste into their midst; these scavengers will then extract the pig-iron and other "valuables" in which they trade for a livelihood. Waiting, they tease and brag, swap stories, talk sex; the idiot-boy Billy amuses his companions with an elaborate re-enactment of finding an infant's legless corpse within the muck. The "blow" comes, the men scramble among tons of oozy waste and Sam and Alex (who had found the dead baby) quarrel over a disputed find. A sudden burst of violence and Sam is dead. Bunk, who was earlier denied a drink from the common bottle because of mouth-sores, brushes the swirling flies from Sam's wound and covers his head with a sack. As the men leave, the circling chicken hawks land near the pipe and strut among the slime toward the body. Two other impressive stories, entirely different in locale and plot, deal with a group of young thieves in Camden, and suggest an incipient novel which never materialized.

In *The Butterfly*, a 28-year-old man (emotionally, a 17-year-old boy) fearfully re-enters society after two years in a mental institution. Different again from Rumaker's other fiction, the novel's cloistered atmosphere and simple story line hazard the risk on each page of descending from pathos to bathos yet rarely do so. Jim moves from the loving protection of a sensitive doctor to his love affair with a Japanese girl; the love affair fails, but only because Eiko, too, is disturbed and, unlike Jim, is fearful of loving someone. His courage in risking further disappointment is rewarded when he meets Alice and their love develops without mishap. There are perhaps too many significant, detailed dream-sequences, and the novel abounds with symbols—yellow balloons rising to the sun, birds hunted by thoughtless boys, flat rocks skipping across streams—but the sensitivity of the protagonist and the aptness of the imagery sustain a novel as delicate as haiku. Rumaker here avoids dramatizing a subject intrinsically pregnant with drama and, as with his stories, invents the form and language necessary to his ends.

—Frank Campenni

———————

RUSHDIE, (Ahmed) Salman.   British.   Born in Bombay, India, 19 June 1947. Educated at Cathedral School, Bombay; King's College, Cambridge, M.A. (honours) in history 1968. Married Clarissa Luard in 1976; one son. Actor in London, 1968–69; free-lance advertising copywriter, London, 1970–80. Since 1983, member of the Executive Committee, National Book League. Recipient: Arts Council bursary; Booker Prize, 1981; English-Speaking Union award, 1981; James Tait Black Memorial Prize, 1982; Foreign Book Prize (France), 1985. Fellow, Royal Society of Literature, 1983. Address: c/o Jonathan Cape Ltd., 32 Bedford Square, London WC1B 3EL, England.

PUBLICATIONS

Novels

Grimus.   London, Gollancz, 1975; New York, Overlook Press, 1979.
Midnight's Children.   London, Cape, and New York, Knopf, 1981.

Shame. London, Cape, and New York, Knopf, 1983.

Uncollected Short Stories

"Prophet's Hair," in *Atlantic* (Boston), September 1981.
"The Free Radio," in *Firebird 1*, edited by T.J. Binding. London, Penguin, 1982.

*   *   *

A curious and not very pleasant story by Kipling called "His Chance in Life" relates how Michele D'Cruz, a Telegraph Signaller, put down almost single-handedly a small band of Hindu and Mohammedan rioters. Later, when Michele tried to report the incident to the Assistant Collector, "the tale of the Tibasu Riots ended, with the strain on the teller . . . and childish anger that his tongue could not do justice to his great deeds." Michele's predicament—the absence of a language—is located in his mixed descent. He was one of the "Borderline folk," neither Black nor White, a victim of two cultures.

Since Kipling, the silence which defeated Michele has been filled by Commonwealth writers writing in English, and perhaps by no one writer so inventively and richly as Salman Rushdie. Rushdie's background seems to incline him naturally towards characters who inhabit the Borderline. One thinks of Omar Khayyam in *Shame*, "a peripheral man"; of that novel's narrator who, like Rushdie himself, is "an emigrant from one country" and "a newcomer in two"; of Adam Aziz in *Midnight's Children*; and above all, of Saleem Sinai, born at the stroke of midnight on 15 August 1947, an Anglo-Indian, a changeling. In each of these novels, however, by centering the Borderline character as the "I" narrator, the perspective is remade and Borderline territory is transformed into "a strange middle country," a position of vantage from which the narrator tells his story, or, more accurately, his "so many stories."

Not surprisingly, bearing in mind meaningful wholes have to be created out of fragments of individual lives and isolated memories, formal strategies are a central concern in the novels. They are talked about openly, or covertly by means of metaphors and symbols, and they are enacted in the advances and retreats, the stresses and strains, the swoops and swerves of the narrative itself. In a work as voluminous as *Midnight's Children*, for example, plot and character are often of secondary interest when placed beside the action and excitement generated by Saleem's attempts to shape and order his irrepressible material. From the first, choices are open to him—to write autobiography or history; to use the once-upon-a-time formula and exploit the "fantastic heart" of the tale or to "spell it out" in realistic fashion; to recite his story to the devoted Padma or to write it out for the shadowy reader waiting behind her. But, repeatedly, no sooner is a narrative genre or convention fixed upon than it is subverted so that the *Bildungsroman* uncovers a baby swap which is the property of melodrama; science fiction shares the same space as the language of comic strips and American English; and a realistic account of the events surrounding the murder of a politician spills over into horror story and the romance of the Bombay-talkie. If India is a land divided by "walls of words," then Rushdie's "strange middle country" becomes the site of a variety of competing languages and discourse which Saleem manipulates with flair and gusto even while they continually threaten to overwhelm him.

This idea of multiplicity is also foregrounded in the uneasy relationship between fiction and history depicted in the novel. The period it covers—from World War I to the end of Indira Gandhi's Emergency in 1977—is one of momentous events, the earliest of which are still recoverable by living memory. And "memory's truth" is the argument Saleem uses to quell Padma's scepticism regarding his narrative. Yet ironically, for someone whose life is meant to mirror India's, his own memory is often unreliable. On two occasions, its fallibility astounds even Saleem himself. He misdates the assassination of Mahatma Gandhi in 1948 and the elections of 1957. "In my India, Gandhi will continue to die at the wrong time," because to dismantle the structure he has built up of private and public events would be to destroy the meaning and purpose he has given to his life and to deny the centrality of his role. By highlighting the arbitrary and distorting nature of Saleem's history, the novelist draws attention to the possibility of other versions of the same events. Among midnight's children, Shiva's story remains to be told, and that still leaves another 579. To be mindful of multiplicity is, however, the means by which one extricates oneself from the imperialist view of history according to which the West "discovered" India and eludes also the absolutism of the Widow "who was not only Prime Minister of India but also aspired to be Devi, the Mother-goddess in her most terrible aspect."

Rushdie's weaknesses are in a sense inseparable from his strengths. Fertile invention spills over into excess, linguistic versatility into overwriting. *Shame* does not always avoid the self-indulgence of *Midnight's Children* but on the whole is more tightly constructed, its imagination more controlled. In telling the story of the rivalry between Iskander Harappa and Raza Hyder, and the marriage between Omar Khayyam and Sufiya Zinobia, it also harks back to the allegorical mode of *Grimus*. It cannot be accidental that Omar Khayyam comes from the town of Q., the location of the Impossible Mountains, and that one of the heirlooms his three mothers sell off is "an exquisitely carved walnut screen on which was portrayed the mythical circular mountain of Qaf, complete with the thirty birds playing God thereupon." Unlike the first novel, however, the fiction in *Shame* is planted in history, though "at a slight angle to reality."

The "slight" must appear less than ingenuous on the part of the "I" narrator when characters like Raza Hyder and Iskander Harappa are compared with their parallels in real life, the present president of Pakistan, Zia ul-Haq, and the late prime minister, Zulfikar Ali Bhutto, whom Zia's government executed in 1977. The deliberate exaggerations suggest the techniques of black comedy but perhaps this is the only way of rendering the extreme situation in a country where silence, concealment, and violence are the pervading realities, and where language is either impotent or duplicitous since, like everything else, it has been severed from its roots in history.

One of the ideas which *Shame* explores, then, is that of translation whereby a work is "borne across" from one language to another; a person from one reality to another; and, since talking about art is Rushdie's way of talking about history and politics, a country from one layer of time to another. In the process it is likely that much is deliberately or inadvertently suppressed. To put across the image of itself as a new country, it is necessary for Pakistan "to cover up Indian history"; in the fictitious character Sufiya Zinobia, a great deal of the murdered Pakistani girl from the East End of London has to be stripped away; Fitzgerald's version of *The Rubáiyát* is in content and spirit often very different from its original.

One problem with literary translation is that certain concepts refuse to cross linguistic frontiers. In *Shame*, "takallouf" is cited as an extreme example. But there is also "sharam" whose subtle cluster of connotations cannot be fully carried by the

English word "shame." What Rushdie's writing enacts brilliantly is the process by which "shame" is de-colonised and remade in the context of the experiences rendered in the novel until the name and the thing become one and the same, and like the perforated sheet in *Midnight's Children*, shame is transformed into a rich and multiple symbol. If one of the controlling themes of the novel is Pakistan's incapacity to transform itself, the other is the resourcefulness of the country of the imagination.

Rushdie has often been compared to Sterne, Cervantes, Rabelais. Perhaps his real significance lies in his intimate knowledge of the Indian sub-continent, his strong and sensitive grasp of the political and social realities in the modern world, and his ability to transmute these realities into fictional works which may leave the reader exhausted but never indifferent.

—Shirley Chew

RUSS, Joanna. American. Born in New York City, 22 February 1937. Educated at Cornell University, Ithaca, New York, B.A. 1957; Yale University School of Drama, New Haven, Connecticut, M.F.A. 1960. Married Albert Amateau in 1963 (divorced, 1967). Lecturer in Speech, Queensborough Community College, New York, 1966–67; Instructor, 1967–70, and Assistant Professor of English, 1970–72, Cornell University; Assistant Professor of English, State University of New York, Binghamton, 1972–73, 1974–75, and University of Colorado, Boulder, 1975–77. Associate Professor 1977–84, and since 1984 Professor of English, University of Washington, Seattle. Occasional book reviewer, *Fantasy and Science Fiction*, 1966–79. Recipient: Nebula Award, 1972, 1983; O. Henry Award, 1977; National Endowment for the Humanities fellowship, 1974; Hugo Award, 1983; *Locus* award, 1983; *Science Fiction Chronicle* award, 1983. Agent: Ellen Levine Literary Agency, 432 Park Avenue South, New York, New York 10016. Address: Department of English, University of Washington, Seattle, Washington 98195, U.S.A.

PUBLICATIONS

Novels

Picnic on Paradise. New York, Ace, 1968; London, Macdonald, 1969.
And Chaos Died. New York, Ace, 1970.
The Female Man. New York, Bantam, 1975; London, Star, 1977.
We Who Are About to . . . . New York, Dell, 1977.
The Two of Them. New York, Berkley, 1978.
On Strike Against God. New York, Out and Out, 1980.
Extra(Ordinary) People. New York, St. Martin's Press, 1984; London, Women's Press, 1985.

Short Stories

Alyx. Boston, Gregg Press, 1976.
The Adventures of Alyx. New York, Pocket Books, 1983.
The Zanzibar Cat. Sauk City, Wisconsin, Arkham House, 1983.

Uncollected Short Stories

"Nor Custom Stale," in *Fantasy and Science Fiction* (New York), September 1959.
"I Had Vacantly Crumpled It into My Pocket," in *Fantasy and Science Fiction* (New York), August 1964.
"Life in a Furniture Store," in *Epoch* (Ithaca, New York), Fall 1965.
"Visiting," in *Manhattan Review* (New York), Fall 1966.
"Mr. Wilde's Second Chance," in *Fantasy and Science Fiction* (New York), September 1966.
"This Night at My Fire," in *Epoch* (Ithaca, New York), Winter 1966.
"Harry Longshanks," in *Fiction as Process*, edited by Carl Hartman and Hazard Adams. New York, Dodd Mead, 1968.
"Scenes from Domestic Life," in *Consumption* (Seattle), Fall 1968.
"This Afternoon," in *Cimarron Review* (Stillwater, Oklahoma), December 1968.
"Oh! She Has a Lover," in *Kinesis 1* (Carbondale, Illinois), February 1969.
"The Throaways," in *Consumption* (Seattle), Spring 1969.
"What Really Happened," in *Just Friends 1*, October 1969.
"Window Dressing," in *New Worlds of Fantasy 2*, edited by Terry Carr. New York, Ace, 1970.
"The View from This Window," in *Quark 1*, edited by Samuel R. Delany and Marilyn Hacker. New York, Paperback Library, 1970.
"The Man Who Could Not See Devils," in *Alchemy and Academe*, edited by Anne McCaffrey. New York, Doubleday, 1970.
"Visiting Day," in *South* (Deland, Florida), Spring 1970.
"Cap and Bells," in *Discourse* (Moorhead, Minnesota), Summer 1970.
"Suffer a Sea-Change," in *William and Mary Review* (Williamsburg, Virginia), Fall 1970.
"Not for Love," in *Arlington Quarterly* (Arlington, Texas), Fall 1970.
"The Wise Man," in *Cimarron Review* (Stillwater, Oklahoma), October 1970.
"The Precious Object," in *Red Clay Reader 7* (Charlotte, North Carolina), November 1970.
"Foul Fowl," in *Little Magazine* (New York), Spring 1971.
"Dear Diary," in *Northwest Review* (Eugene, Oregon), Fall 1972.
"Laura, The Camp, and That Terrible Thing," in *Monmouth Review*, Spring 1973.
"Old Pictures," in *Little Magazine* (New York), Winter 1973.
"Reasonable People," in *Orbit 14*, edited by Damon Knight. New York, Harper, 1974.
"An Old Fashioned Girl," in *Final Stage*, edited by Edward L. Ferman and Barry N. Malzberg. New York, Charterhouse, 1974.
"Passages," in *Galaxy* (New York), January 1974.
"A Few Things I Know about Whileaway," in *The New Improved Sun*, edited by Thomas M. Disch. New York, Harper, 1975; London, Hutchinson, 1976.
"The Experimenter," in *Galaxy* (New York), October 1975.
"Dragons and Dimwits or . . . Lord of the Royalties," in *Fantasy and Science Fiction* (New York), December 1979.
"Little Tales from Nature," in *Woman Space*, edited by Claudia Laperti. Lebanon, New Hampshire, New Victoria, 1981.
"The Little Dirty Girl," in *Elsewhere 2*, edited by Terri Windling and Mark Alan Arnold. New York, Ace, 1982.

"Elf Hill," in *Fantasy and Science Fiction* (New York), November 1982.
"Sword Blades and Poppy Seed with Homage to (Who Else?) Amy Lowell," in *Heroic Visions*, edited by Jessica Amanda Salmonson.   New York, Ace, 1983.
"Main Street: 1953," in *Sinister Wisdom* (Lincoln, Nebraska), Fall 1983.

Play

Window Dressing, in *The New Women's Theatre*, edited by Honor Moore.   New York, Random House, 1977.

Other

Kittatinny: A Tale of Magic (for children).   New York, Daughters, 1978.
How to Suppress Women's Writing.   Austin, University of Texas Press, 1983; London, Women's Press, 1984.
Magic Mommas, Trembling Sisters, Puritans and Perverts: Feminist Essays.   Trumansburg, New York, Crossing Press, 1985.

*   *   *

The work of Joanna Russ is thematically unified and formally, generically, and stylistically diverse. She has written six fine novels that fall under the rubric of speculative fiction; she has written brilliant short stories; she has written what's called mainstream fiction (*On Strike Against God*). She has written in the genre of thematically related tales such as Mary McCarthy's *The Company She Keeps* and John Horne Burns's *The Gallery* (*Extra[Ordinary] People*); she has written a children's fantasy, verging on lush fairy tale (*Kittatinny: A Tale of Magic*); she has written a closely reasoned and scholarly book, *How to Suppress Women's Writing*, and the very personal, peppery, and opinionated essays of *Magic Mommas, Trembling Sisters, Puritans and Perverts.*

Her underlying theme in all these works is empowerment: empowerment and powerlessness; aggression and negation. Other concerns that run through the body of her work include survival, alienation, loneliness, community, violence, sex roles, the nature of oppression both external and internal, the necessity and the nature of further civilization and what is gained and what is lost by its progress.

One advantage of working in a genre is that the plot must move along, and that discipline keeps Russ's springy intelligence anchored. If she resembles another writer, it is Swift. She is as angry, as disgusted, as playful, as often didactic, as airy at times and at times as crude, as intellectual. The quality of outraged, clear-sighted pained intelligence at once incandescent and exacerbated is one of the major experiences in reading her work. Her critical essays are often witty and savage. She has started frequent controversies with her criticism, partly because of her habit of saying what others may think but will not dare publish.

Russ gives a sense of speed in her narration. She is a master of pacing and often eliminates intermediate steps and decisions. She has the habit of starting *in medias res* and in a place and time the reader will simply have to deduce, whether we are on earth or elsewhere and what essentially is going on among all these articulate people. Sometimes she uses a jazzy style that gives a feeling of clever and controlled improvisation. I am in no way suggesting that the novels are, in fact, improvisations, for they are put together intricately in all their parts.

Another characteristic of her style is the combination of serious, even dark concerns with wit. *The Female Man* is studded with jokes, vaudeville routines, addresses to the reader, instructive vignettes, catalogues. Her short piece "Useful Phrases for the Tourist" is a stand-up comic routine. At the core of her humor is the perception of incongruity, absurdity.

She is precise in her characterization. In a sense, the four protagonists of *The Female Man*, Jeannine, Joanna, Jael and Janet, are the same woman in four social contexts. Jeannine lives in a New York City where World War II never happened and which is only slowly emerging from a generations-long depression. Joanna lives here and now. Janet lives in Whileaway, an all-female society far in the future after a plague has carried off the men. Jael is an agent and assassin from the near future, part of the "plague" that gives birth to bucolic Whileaway. They are all "the same woman," yet each (with the exception of Joanna) is sharply flavored and unmistakable in habits of thought, words, and movement. Alyx, a Greek thief from Alexandrian times, is the heroine of *Picnic on Paradise* and a number of short stories, extremely sharply etched. From the sexually ambiguous Victorian traveller of *Extra (Ordinary) People* to the brave and pragmatic young girl of *Kittatinny*, Russ's works present a gallery of fully fleshed-out women of great diversity.

Russ is one of our best novelists of ideas because she possesses the traditional fictional virtues. She creates characters full of quirks, odd memories, hot little sexual nodes that make them believable. She embodies ideas in a fast-moving arc of action. Finally, she has wide emotional range, from savage indignation to broad humor, from the bleak to the lush, from extreme alienation (as in *We Who Are About to ...*, where the protagonist fights and kills for the right to die) to a warm and powerful projection of community (as in "Nobody's Home").

What Russ does not create is a world where love conquers all, certainly not her women. The push toward freedom, appetite, curiosity both intellectual and sensual, the desire to control and expand their own existence, figure far more importantly in the lives of her female characters than does traditional romance. In *The Two of Them* her protagonist Irene enjoys a long and satisfying emotional and sexual bond with her mentor Ernst. However, Ernst, besides being Irene's lover, is her limiting factor. As their goals diverge, he begins to use his power not to free but to confine her. Ultimately in order to save a young girl she has rescued and to preserve her own ability to act in accordance with her own values, she kills Ernst. A theme that Russ identifies in her own work and that of other contemporary feminist writers is the quest for the lost daughter, or the quest to save the daughter or young woman who will be true posterity.

One aspect of Russ's work that sometimes shocks is the place that violence holds in her fiction, particularly violence not against women—a commonplace of our fiction as of our society—but violence by women. Russ is concerned with what price freedom and autonomy may exact. In her works, violence is never glorified and never without consequence, but neither is it for long absent. Her women are as apt as her men to consider the full range of alternatives open to them in carrying out their will or their duty as they see it. Certainly nobody saves them unless they save themselves, which is often not possible. Hers are worlds in which there is frequently a wide range of nasty consequence to action, as to inaction.

Russ is a writer equally serious and entertaining. Although themes recur, she never repeats herself. Each book represents a new intellectual and literary voyage into darkness and light.

—Marge Piercy

SAHGAL, Nayantara (Pandit). Indian. Born in Allahabad, 10 May 1927. Educated at Wellesley College, Massachusetts, 1943–47, B.A. in history 1947. Married 1) Gautam Sahgal in 1949 (divorced, 1967), three children; 2) E.N. Mangat Rai in 1979. Scholar-in-Residence, Southern Methodist University, Dallas, 1973, 1977; research scholar, Radcliffe Institute, Cambridge, Massachusetts, 1976; lecturer, University of Colorado semester-at-sea, 1979; Fellow, Woodrow Wilson International Center, Washington, D.C., 1981, and National Humanities Center, North Carolina, 1983. Political journalist for Indian, American, and British newspapers; columnist, *Sunday Express*, New Delhi. Member, United Nations Indian Delegation, New York, 1978. Recipient: Sinclair Prize, 1985. Address: 181-B Rajpur Road, Dehra Dun 248 009, Uttar Pradesh, India.

PUBLICATIONS

Novels

A Time to Be Happy. New York, Knopf, and London, Gollancz, 1958.
This Time of Morning. London, Gollancz, 1965; New York, Norton, 1966.
Storm in Chandigarh. New York, Norton, and London, Chatto and Windus, 1969.
The Day in Shadow. New Delhi, Vikas, 1971; New York, Norton, 1972; London, London Magazine Editions, 1975.
A Situation in New Delhi. London, London Magazine Editions, 1977.
Rich Like Us. London, Heinemann, 1985; New York, Norton, 1986.
Plans for Departure. New York, Norton, 1985; London, Heinemann, 1986.

Uncollected Short Stories

"The Promising Young Woman," in *Illustrated Weekly of India* (Bombay), January 1959.
"The Golden Afternoon," in *Illustrated Weekly of India* (Bombay), February 1959.
"The Trials of Siru," in *Triveni* (Madras), January 1967.
"Crucify Me," in *Indian Horizons* (New Delhi), October 1979.

Other

Prison and Chocolate Cake (autobiography). New York, Knopf, and London, Gollancz, 1954.
From Fear Set Free (autobiography). London, Gollancz, 1962; New York, Norton, 1963.
The Freedom Movement in India. New Delhi, National Council of Educational Research and Training, 1970.
Sunlight Surround You, with Chandralekha Mehta and Rita Dar. Privately printed, 1970.
A Voice of Freedom. New Delhi, Hind, 1977.
Indira Gandhi's Emergence and Style. New Delhi, Vikas, and Durham, North Carolina, Academic Press, 1978.
Indira Gandhi: Her Road to Power. New York, Ungar, 1982; London, Macdonald, 1983.

*

Bibliography: *Bibliography of Indian Writing in English 2* by Hilda Pontes, New Delhi, Concept, 1985.

Critical Studies: *Bridges of Literature* by M.L. Malhotra, Ajmer, Sunanda, 1971; essay by Sahgal, in *Adam* (London),

August 1971; *Nayantara Sahgal and the Craft of Fiction* by Suresh Kohli, New Delhi, Vikas, 1972; *Nayantara Sahgal: A Study of Her Fiction and Non-Fiction 1954–1974* by A.V. Krishna Rao, Madras, Seshachalam, 1976; *Nayantara Sahgal* by Jasbir Jain, New Delhi, Arnold-Heinemann, 1978; interview with Nergis Dalal, in *Times of India Sunday Review* (New Delhi), 30 June 1985.

Nayantara Sahgal comments:
  I am a novelist and a political journalist. My novels have a political background or political ambience. I didn't plan it that way—I was dealing with people and situations—but looking back, each one seems to reflect the hopes and fears the political scene held out to us at the time.
  I have a very strong emotional as well as intellectual attachment to my roots ... I have certainly been plagued with wondering from time to time why I was born and what I'm doing here and why I haven't had to worry about my next meal when millions live lives of anxiety and drudgery. And then there is the problem of evil and pain. At times all that abstract conjecture has become very personal, with the need to atone for the terrible things people do to each other. Some of these matters fell into place for me when I gave up the struggle to be an atheist. Atheism—or agnosticism—is my general family background, but I am a believer to the marrow of my bones, and much has become clearer to me since I faced the fact.
  I see myself as both novelist and journalist. In the course of a lifetime one is many things, fiction is my abiding love, but I need to express myself on vital political issues. Political and social forces shape our lives. How can we be unaware of them? I believe there is a "poetics of engagement" where commitment and aesthetics meet and give each other beauty and power.

*   *   *

Most of Nayantara Sahgal's characters belong to the affluent upper class of Indian society. Sahgal scrupulously sticks to the people she knows intimately; she does not try to write about the caste-ridden middle class or the poor Indian villager just to conform with the accepted image of India. Her range of characters simplifies her technique; she does not have to struggle to present Indian conversation in English (a problem which bedevils many other Indian novelists writing in English) as most of her characters are the kind of people who would talk and think in English in real life.
  Sahgal has a first-hand knowledge of politics and political figures in India, for she spent most of her childhood in Anand Bhawan, the ancestral home of the Nehrus in Allahabad. One could say that politics is in her blood—Jawaharlal Nehru was her mother's brother, while her father died because of an illness he suffered in prison when he was jailed for participating in India's freedom struggle. An important political event forms the background for each of her novels. Her first novel, *A Time to Be Happy*, presents the dawn of Indian independence. *This Time of Morning* comes later, when the initial euphoria has worn off, and things no longer look rosy. *Storm in Chandigarh* deals with the partition of the Punjab on linguistic lines just when the state had recovered from the trauma of the 1947 partition. *A Situation in New Delhi* presents the Indian capital faced with the After-Nehru-Who question; established politicians have given up all moral values, and the frustrated youth are becoming Naxalites (Communist extremists). But sometimes this political consciousness is not transmuted fully in artistic terms. Some of her characters are easily recognizable public

figures: Kailash Sinha (Krishna Menon) in *This Time of Morning* or Shivraj (Jawaharlal Nehru) in *A Situation in New Delhi* are two examples. Her autobiographies, *Prison and Chocolate Cake* and *From Fear Set Free* are more satisfying than her earlier novels. An outstanding novel is *The Day in Shadow*; here personal concerns take precedence over politics. The Heroine, Simrit Raman, a writer, is a divorcée (like Sahgal herself), and the novel shows the prejudice she faces in male-dominated Indian society. She grows close to Raj, an idealistic Member of Parliament, who shares her values, unlike her husband, who believes in money-making above all. Sahgal gives an authentic picture of high-level politicians and bureaucrats, wrapped up in their cocktail parties, worried more about themselves than about the problems which face the country. The mutual attraction between Simrit and Raj is not primarily sexual. As in her other novels, Sahgal suggests that marriage is not just a sexual relationship, it means companionship on equal terms. She pleads for a basic honesty in human relationships, whether they are between man and woman or the ruler and the ruled.

Because of her birth and upbringing, Sahgal makes an ideal spokesman for the western-educated Indian who finds it difficult to come to terms with India. As her character Sanad in *A Time to Be Happy* confesses, "I don't belong entirely to India. I can't. My education, my upbringing, and my sense of values have all combined to make me unIndian. ... Of course there can be no question of my belonging to any other country." Jawaharlal Nehru, too, had articulated the same problem when he wrote in his autobiography, "I have become a queer mixture of the East and the West, out of place everywhere, at home nowhere. Perhaps my thoughts and approach to life are more akin to what is called Western than Eastern, but India clings to me as she does to all her children, in innumerable ways." This realization leads to a passionate concern with the Indian heritage and its meaning in the modern age; all of Sahgal's novels are concerned with the present decadence of India, and how creative use can be made of its past. It is this concern with the country which led her openly to protest against the Emergency imposed by her cousin Indira Gandhi when the majority of Indian writers preferred to keep silent. Her political acumen had led her to anticipate Mrs. Gandhi's action, and she had cautioned against it in her weekly newspaper column. Her recent book, *Indira Gandhi: Her Road to Power*, shows that Sahgal deserves attention as a political commentator, not only as a novelist.

Rich Like Us, Sahgal's novel about the Emergency, is her best so far. Sahgal's searching look at India reveals that democracy and spirituality are only skin-deep. The murder of the narrator's great-grandmother in the name of *Suttee*, the mutilation of the sharecropper because he asks for his due, the rape of the village women by the police because their menfolk dare to resist the landlord, and the murder of Rose, the large-hearted Englishwoman, in New Delhi just because her frank talk is an embarrassment to her stepson Dev, are all described in an entirely credible manner. The narrative technique is interesting; the narrator is Sonali, but alternate chapters deal (in the third person) with her father Keshav's friend Ram, a businessman who marries Rose, so we get a dual perspective on events. The novel ends on a note of hope; in the midst of sycophancy, there are persons like Kishori Lal, a petty shopkeeper, who have the courage to protest against tyranny.

—Shyamala A. Narayan

ST. OMER, Garth. St. Lucian. Born in Castries, St. Lucia. Educated at the University of the West Indies, Kingston, Jamaica, degree in French. Has lived in France, Ghana, and England. Address: c/o Heinemann Educational Books, 22 Bedford Square, London WC1B 3HH, England.

PUBLICATIONS

Novels

A Room on the Hill. London, Faber, 1968.
Nor Any Country. London, Faber, 1969.
J—, Black Bam and the Masqueraders. London, Faber, 1972.

Short Stories

Shades of Grey. London, Faber, 1968.

Uncollected Short Story

"Syrop," in *Introduction 2*. London, Faber, 1968.

*   *   *

Garth St. Omer creates in his fiction characters filled with an unrest which they themselves cannot define or explain. It is a *malaise* of the islands which makes them hesitate even before opportunities which are apparently dazzling, which makes them hurt and abandon those they love, or turn aside from courses of action they have embarked on with every sign of conviction. The immediacy of his writing springs from the fact that he is so involved himself with this unrest that he is not yet able to distance or judge his heroes. The passion and the pain of these young island lives are fully conveyed, but it is perhaps this very lack of distance that makes his writing, at present, ideally suited to the novella form. His reputation was first made with "Syrop," and the fact that he followed his first novel with a volume comprising two more novellas demonstrates his addiction to the form.

"Syrop" is a harsh, tragic story of a family blighted by inexplicable misfortune, as well as by the poverty they share with their neighbours. Syrop, the young hero, differs from other St. Omer protagonists in that he doesn't live to carry his anguish and restlessness into adult life. He is smashed by a ship's propellers, diving for pennies on the very day he has been chosen to join the fishing crews, and on the eve of his much-loved brother's return from prison. John Lestrade, in St. Omer's first novel, *A Room on the Hill*, is older and tougher, but still haunted by intimate misfortunes and early deaths in his little island circle of relatives, friends and lovers. This book ends with a hard gesture towards departure, for it is increasingly obvious that all who stay in the island are doomed or lost, and Lestrade is determined to survive and transmute grief into action.

Of the two stories in *Shades of Grey* the first, "The Lights on the Hill," is the more tightly organised. It starts at a moment of crisis in the hero's relationship with Thea, the beautiful and original girl whom he has long desired and who now loves him. Neither can explain the nature of this crisis and it can only cause pain to them both, yet Stephenson knows in his being that he must now leave her. The madman's cry from the asylum which punctuates this realisation begins and ends the story. In between these cries (or are they the same?) St. Omer cross-cuts a number of short scenes from the hero's past in Jamaica and in his native St. Lucia. We see him charcoal-burning with his father and his illiterate brother Carl in the mountains, or seeking refuge with his mother in the empty barracks on the Morne after the Castries fire of 1948, or drifting into corruption, trial and dismissal as a petty official in the Civil Service. And we see the other affairs, some furtive and bourgeois, others casual and earthy, which have preceded all the phases of his rich relationship with Thea. Through it all we are conscious of the two lovers sitting on the hillside, smoking and talking in the darkness, numbed by their awareness that some force within him is sweeping them apart. The writing is full of sharp, perfectly registered dialogue. His narrative and descriptive passages are rendered throughout in short, rather spikey paragraphs and staccato sentences, which carry the same burden of unease as the lives they describe. The effect can occasionally be irritating for the reader who longs for a deeper and more measured breath. Again, it is a style for the novella rather than the novel, but it perfectly fits the peculiar and sustained tension of this story in which jobs, lives and love affairs are all snapped off before fruition.

The second story, "Another Place Another Time," adopts a more chronological approach to a short period in the boyhood of its hero, Derek Charles. It lacks the originality and power of the first, but is full of a distinctive pain of its own. This pain stems largely from the sheer unlikeableness of this boy. He is priggish, snobbish, and jumpy, difficult to reach. He behaves brutally to Berthe, the simple girl whom he seduces and throws over. Yet we see in this society of few and roving males, of unfathered children, abortions, poverty and abandonment, how difficult it is for the growing child to find models by which to climb to maturity. It is as though leaving the island were an indispensable part of growing up, a *rite de passage* from which most of the initiates never return. The story is a cry from the forest of exile, a cry to which St. Omer fits the words of Shakespeare: "How like a winter has my absence been/From thee."

St. Omer is particularly good at rendering the speech of those who, though educated elsewhere, are still very close to the islands and unable to relate their living satisfactorily to any other place. The uncertainty of their position is registered in the groping movement of the sentences with which they seek to explain their lives. The handling of dialogue is less successful where it derives from the *patois* of St. Lucia, a dialect largely of French derivation for which St. Omer tries to find an English dialect equivalent. The shape and rhythm of this dialect are necessarily very different from those of *patois*, and the effect, despite an occasional "oui" or "non" at the end of a sentence, is vaguely West Indian rather than specifically St. Lucian. Yet it is hard to think of any more faithful alternative which would not leave most readers struggling.

To Peter Breville in *Nor Any Country*, as to all St. Omer's heroes, the memories of St. Lucia are the sore tooth which mars his enjoyment of more exotic pleasures and experiences. That nagging pain draws him at last to revisit the island in which he has left for eight years a scarcely-known wife, married only because of her pregnancy. Yet the return, which perhaps he hoped would be purgative, leads to a partial acceptance of what he is and has ever been. Phyllis is still there, still young, still open to his love and still able to awaken his lust. Peter's long-standing resentment of her existence is modified by what he sees of other lives forgotten during his absence. His brother Paul, who likewise impregnated a local girl, has become a special kind of island failure because of his refusal to marry her. The girl herself has committed suicide but her neglected son Michael has survived, whereas Peter's marriage has produced the mirror image of twins born and dead in his absence but a neglected wife who survives to challenge his egotism by her

presence. At the end of his week-long visit Peter knows that he must take both Phyllis and Michael with him now. By this single gesture he will attempt to redeem the past. *Nor Any Country* thus ends on a more positive note than any of St. Omer's earlier writing. It stints nothing of the narrow fate attending those who stay in the islands. The failures lie steeped in rum and self-pity, whilst the few successes grow flashy and Americanised in their loud insecurity. Yet, when all this is said, it was the long-postponed return to the island which brought Peter Breville to his late maturity. For the last *rite de passage* is the reunification with one's origins, without which the cycle of exile can never be complete.

J—, Black Bam and the Masqueraders is a return to the themes and situations of *Nor Any Country*, with the same actors. The approach in this short novel is less naturalistic, intermingling long epistles from Paul (in St. Lucia) to Peter (in Europe), which snatches from the life of Peter in exile. There is far less memorable descriptive writing than in any of St. Omer's earlier work. The anguish of personal failure is as strong as ever, but this book gives off a powerful odour of decay. The actions, motives, and lost possibilities of the past are being raked over and examined yet again, but the novelist himself impresses us as a talent desperately in need of an entirely new subject.

—Gerald Moore

SALINGER, J(erome) D(avid). American. Born in New York City, 1 January 1919. Educated at McBurney School, New York; Valley Forge Military Academy, Pennsylvania (editor, *Crossed Sabres*), graduated 1936; New York University, 1937; Ursinus College, Collegetown, Pennsylvania, 1938; Columbia University, New York, 1939. Served in the 4th Infantry Division of the United States Army, 1942–45: Staff Sergeant. Married Claire Douglas in 1955 (divorced, 1967); one daughter and one son. Has lived in New Hampshire since 1953. Agent: Harold Ober Associates, 40 East 49th Street, New York, New York 10017, U.S.A.

PUBLICATIONS

Novel

The Catcher in the Rye. Boston, Little Brown, and London, Hamish Hamilton, 1951.

Short Stories

Nine Stories. Boston, Little Brown, 1953; as *For Esmé—With Love and Squalor and Other Stories*, London, Hamish Hamilton, 1953.
Franny and Zooey. Boston, Little Brown, 1961; London, Heinemann, 1962.
Raise High the Roof Beam, Carpenters, and Seymour: An Introduction. Boston, Little Brown, and London, Heinemann, 1963.

Uncollected Short Stories

"The Young Folks," in *Story* (New York), March-April 1940.
"The Hang of It," in *Collier's* (Springfield, Ohio), 12 July 1941.

"The Heart of a Broken Story," in *Esquire* (New York), September 1941.

"Personal Notes on an Infantryman," in *Collier's* (Springfield, Ohio), 12 December 1942.

"The Varioni Brothers," in *Saturday Evening Post* (Philadelphia), 17 July 1943.

"Both Parties Concerned," in *Saturday Evening Post* (Philadelphia), 26 February 1944.

"Soft-Boiled Sergeant," in *Saturday Evening Post* (Philadelphia), 15 April 1944.

"Last Day of the Last Furlough," in *Saturday Evening Post* (Philadelphia), 15 July 1944.

"Once a Week Won't Kill You," in *Story* (New York), November-December 1944.

"A Boy in France," in *The Saturday Evening Post Stories 1942–1945*, edited by Ben Hibbs. New York, Random House, 1945.

"Elaine," in *Story* (New York), March-April 1945.

"The Stranger," in *Collier's* (Springfield, Ohio), 1 December 1945.

"I'm Crazy," in *Collier's* (Springfield, Ohio), 22 December 1945.

"Slight Rebellion Off Madison," in *New Yorker*, 21 December 1946.

"A Young Girl in 1941 with No Waist at All," in *Mademoiselle* (New York), May 1947.

"The Inverted Forest," in *Cosmopolitan* (New York), December 1947.

"Blue Melody," in *Cosmopolitan* (New York), September 1948.

"The Long Debut of Lois Taggett," in *Story: The Fiction of the Forties*, edited by Whit and Hallie Burnett. New York, Dutton, 1949.

"A Girl I Knew," in *The Best American Short Stories 1949*, edited by Martha Foley. Boston, Houghton Mifflin, 1949.

"This Sandwich Has No Mayonnaise," in *The Armchair Esquire*, edited by Arnold Gingrich and L. Rust Hills. New York, Putnam, 1958.

"Hapworth 16, 1924," in *New Yorker*, 19 June 1965.

"Go See Eddie," in *Fiction: Form and Experience*, edited by William M. Jones. Lexington, Massachusetts, Heath, 1969.

*

Bibliography: *J.D. Salinger: A Thirty Year Bibliography 1938–1968* by Kenneth Starosciak, privately printed, 1971; *J.D. Salinger: An Annotated Bibliography 1938–1981* by Jack R. Sublette, New York, Garland, 1984.

Critical Studies (selection): *The Fiction of J.D. Salinger* by Frederick L. Gwynn and Joseph L. Blotner, Pittsburgh, University of Pittsburgh Press, 1958, London, Spearman, 1960; *Salinger: A Critical and Personal Portrait* edited by Henry Anatole Grunwald, New York, Harper, 1962, London, Owen, 1964; *J.D. Salinger and the Critics* edited by William F. Belcher and James W. Lee, Belmont, California, Wadsworth, 1962; *J.D. Salinger* by Warren French, New York, Twayne, 1963, revised edition, 1976; *Studies in J.D. Salinger* edited by Marvin Laser and Norman Fruman, New York, Odyssey Press, 1963; *J.D. Salinger* by James E. Miller, Jr., Minneapolis, University of Minnesota Press, 1965; *J.D. Salinger: A Critical Essay* by Kenneth Hamilton, Grand Rapids, Michigan, Eerdmans, 1967; *Zen in the Art of J.D. Salinger* by Gerald Rosen, Berkeley, California, Creative Arts, 1977; *J.D. Salinger* by James Lundquist, New York, Ungar, 1979; *Salinger's Glass Stories as a Composite Novel* by Eberhard Alsen, Troy, New York, Whitston, 1984; *J.D. Salinger: A Writing Life* by Ian Hamilton, London, Heinemann, 1986.

*   *   *

In terms of subject matter, the fiction of J.D. Salinger falls into two groups. His most celebrated work, *The Catcher in the Rye*, tells of several days in the life of a young man, Holden Caulfield, after he has left the school from which he has been expelled; he wanders around New York City in a late-adolescent pursuit of contacts that will have meaning for him. The novel itself is Holden's meditation on these days some months later when he is confined to a West Coast clinic. The rest of Salinger's work, with the exception of some of the stories in *Nine Stories*, has for its subject elements drawn from the experience of the Glass family who live in New York. The parents, Less and Bessie, are retired vaudeville dancers; Les is Jewish in origin, Bessie Catholic—a fact that announces the merging of religious traditions effected in the lives of their children. The children, begotten over a considerable period of time, are seven in number. There are Seymour, a gifted poet; Buddy, a writer; Walker and Wake, twins—one killed in war, the other finally a priest; Boo Boo, a happily married daughter; and two much younger children, Franny and Zooey.

The diverse subject matter of Salinger's fiction tends, in retrospect, to coalesce. Holden Caulfield's parents, less loving and concerned than the Glass couple, have also begotten several children. But in Holden's case, there is only one child—a ten-year-old girl—to whom Holden can turn in his desperation.

But it is not just the mirror-image of subject matter that binds the Caulfied narrative together with the tales of the Glass family. There are a unity of tone and a prevailing interest that inform all of Salinger's narratives and that have made them appeal deeply to readers for two decades. The tone and interest combine to produce a sad, often ironic meditation on the plight of young persons who are coming to maturity in a society where precise and guiding values are absent. This recurrent meditation, concealed in wrappings that are usually grotesque and farcical, has drawn readers to Salinger. His characters move through a "world they never made"; they address questions to that world and receive, for the most part, only a "dusty answer." Casual social contacts so nauseate Holden Caulfield, for example, that he is frequently at the point of vomiting. His quest for love is harassed by the sexual basis of love, and he is repelled. The only good relation in his life rests on the affection he feels for his younger sister; she is the one light in a wilderness of adult hypocrisy, lust, and perversion. In contrast, affection takes in a larger area in the Glass family chronicles; mutual esteem and concern bind the family together and somewhat offset the dreary vision of human relations in *The Catcher in the Rye*.

Perhaps one reason for this contrast is that, in *The Catcher in the Rye*, the narrative is presented from the point of view of Holden, a malleable, only half-conscious person. He moves in many directions, but none leads him toward the goals he aspires to. His teachers are "phonies"; the one in whom he puts some trust turns out to be a homosexual. His encounter with a prostitute gives him nothing, and his relations with girls of his class do not offer him the gift of comprehension. His parents are as deceived as he is about the proper use of the gift of life. As indicated, only his younger sister can offer him the love he needs, and she is too immature to counterbalance the panorama of insincerity that unfolds before Holden's eyes.

So for Holden, all is in suspense—an effect that appealed strongly to Salinger's readers.

But for members of the Glass family, all is not fully in suspense. That gifted group of young people has indeed been badly shaken by the suicide of Seymour, their most gifted sibling. Thus, the central "mystery" which they must come to terms with is not Holden's general panorama of hypocrisy; the death and even more the remembered life of Seymour contain a secret that they are haunted by. The actual death of Seymour is briefly narrated in the story, "A Perfect Day for Bananafish," in *Nine Stories*. Later work, told from various points of view, relates the efforts of members of the Glass family to grasp and apply the eclectic religious truths that the memory of Seymour reminds them of. In none of these tales is there an effort to explain the suicide; this is a fact which the brothers and sisters accept rather than assess. What they do assess, in terms of their own later experience, is the teaching presence of Seymour as they recall it. In the two sections of *Franny and Zooey*, the two youngest members of the family reach out in directions that Seymour, in effect, has already pointed out. In "Franny" the heroine is obsessed by the "Jesus prayer" which she has come across in the memoirs of a Russian monk; she does not know how to pray the prayer and is only aware that, until she does, all her other relations will be without meaning. In "Zooey" her charming brother helps her and himself to come to a grasp of what Seymour's existence had announced: repetition of the Jesus prayer transforms life that is contemptible into a constant act of love and reveals that a "fat lady" is indeed Christ—the "fat lady" and every other human being one encounters. In "Raise High the Roof Beam, Carpenters"—told from the point of view of Buddy, the writing brother—the ridiculous circumstances of Seymour's wedding day are related: Seymour and his fiancée finally elope rather than endure an elaborate and empty wedding ceremony. Finally, in "Seymour: An Introduction"—also told from the point of view of Buddy—all that can be recalled of Seymour is put down. Recalled are his mastery of the allusive oriental haiku and his even more important mastery of the process of extorting the greatest significance from trivial event (e.g., a game of marbles becomes a vehicle of Zen instruction).

It is undoubtedly the merging of Eastern and Western religious wisdom—the solution of the "mystery" of existence—that gives the work of Salinger its particular élan. In pursuit of what might be called the Seymour effect, the other Glasses consume innumerable packs of cigarettes and break out into perspiration when they find themselves in blind alleys. But the alleys occasionally open up, and fleeting vistas of human unity flash before the eyes. One can but hope that Holden Caulfield, in his later years, will meet one of the younger Glasses whose personal destinies swell to the proportions of regulative myth.

—Harold H. Watts

SALKEY, (Felix) Andrew (Alexander). Jamaican. Born in Colon, Panama, 30 January 1928. Educated at St. George's College, Kingston, Jamaica; Munro College, St. Elizabeth, Jamaica; University of London (Thomas Helmore Poetry Prize, 1955), B.A. in English 1955. Married Patricia Verden in 1957; two sons. English teacher in a London comprehensive school, 1957–59; interviewer and scriptwriter, BBC External Services (Radio), London, 1952–76. Since 1976, Professor of Creative Writing, Hampshire College, Amherst, Massachusetts. Recipient: Guggenheim fellowship, 1960; Casa de las Américas Poetry Prize, 1979. Address: Flat 8, Windsor Court, Moscow Road, London W.2, England; or, Department of English, Hampshire College, Amherst, Massachusetts 01002, U.S.A.

PUBLICATIONS

Novels

A Quality of Violence.   London, Hutchinson, 1959.
Escape to an Autumn Pavement.   London, Hutchinson, 1960.
The Late Emancipation of Jerry Stover.   London, Hutchinson, 1968.
The Adventures of Catullus Kelly.   London, Hutchinson, 1969.
Come Home, Malcolm Heartland.   London, Hutchinson, 1976.

Short Stories

Anancy's Score.   London, Bogle L'Ouverture, 1973.

Fiction (for children)

Hurricane.   London, Oxford University Press, 1964; New York, Oxford University Press, 1979.
Earthquake.   London, Oxford University Press, 1965; New York, Roy, 1969.
Drought.   London, Oxford University Press, 1966.
Riot.   London, Oxford University Press, 1967.
Jonah Simpson.   London, Oxford University Press, 1969; New York, Roy, 1970.
Joey Tyson.   London, Bogle L'Ouverture, 1974.
The River That Disappeared.   London, Bogle L'Ouverture, 1980.
Danny Jones.   London, Bogle L'Ouverture, 1980.

Verse

Jamaica.   London, Hutchinson, 1973.
Land.   London, Readers and Writers, 1976.
In the Hills Where Her Dreams Live: Poems for Chile 1973–1978.   Havana, Casa de las Américas, 1979; Sausalito, California, Black Scholar Press, 1981.
Away.   London, Allison and Busby, 1980.

Other

The Shark Hunters (school reader).   London, Nelson, 1966.
Havana Journal.   London, Penguin, 1971.
Georgetown Journal: A Caribbean Writer's Journey from London via Port of Spain to Georgetown, Guyana, 1970.   London, New Beacon, 1972.

Editor, *West Indian Stories.*   London, Faber, 1960.
Editor, *Stories from the Caribbean.*   London, Elek, 1965; as *Island Voices: Stories from the West Indies*, New York, Liveright, 1970.
Editor, Caribbean Section, *Young Commonwealth Poets '65.*   London, Heinemann, 1965.
Editor, *Caribbean Prose: An Anthology for Secondary Schools.*   London, Evans, 1967.
Editor, *Breaklight: An Anthology of Caribbean Poetry.*   London, Hamish Hamilton, 1971; as *Breaklight: The Poetry of the Caribbean*, New York, Doubleday, 1972.

Editor, with others, *Savacou 3–4.* Kingston, Jamaica, and London, Caribbean Artists Movement, 2 vols., 1972.
Editor, *Caribbean Essays.* London, Evans, 1973.
Editor, *Writing in Cuba since the Revolution: An Anthology.* London, Bogle L'Ouverture, 1977.
Editor, *Caribbean Folk Tales and Legends.* London, Bogle L'Ouverture, 1980.

*

Theatrical Activities:
Actor: **Film**—*Reggae* (narrator), 1978.

*   *   *

Andrew Salkey's novels deal with the situation of the brown-skinned Jamaican, a man whose social origins lie between the black masses and the white elite, whose tongue is divided between standard and dialect, who is driven towards exile and then caught by "a double lock-out," who has missed his role in history and is caught between attraction to women and flight from the "tender snare." There is a yet bigger ambivalence in the novels which subsumes all these, between the hope that the Salkey hero can hold these divisions in complementary creative tension, and the fear that they will destroy him.

A Quality of Violence, set in 1900 in a remote rural parish in Jamaica during a drought which is driving the villagers off the land, explores the antagonisms between the wealthier brown-skinned planters and the black villagers. Both groups are divided in their response to the drought, the brown families, the Marshalls and the Parkins, between the rational solution of emigration and the millenarian hope of divine providence, and the blacks between incipient class consciousness and lingering African beliefs in the redemptive power of ritual sacrifice. Salkey's response to the vestiges of Africa in the pocomania cult is ambivalent. He describes the rites dismissively, emphasising their "primitive," exotic features, and the fact that Dada Johnson, the leader, abuses the credulity of the villagers to enrich himself. And yet, what Johnson represents cannot be dismissed. The culture he keeps alive is one of the few things that actually belongs to the people, and when he and his chief acolyte flog each other to death as a sacrifice to end the drought, the image of shallow confidence trickster is undermined. After Johnson's death, Brother Parkin, the archetypal Salkey figure, a "man who always finding himself in the middle of things," tries to bridge the gulf between the Marshalls with their view of pocomania as savage nastiness and Mother Johnson's persuasive plea for holding onto Africa in the heart. Parkin fears that if his class does not assert leadership and stand for the "slow, thoughtful process of salvation and decency," that once the dreams of Africa turn sour, all that will be left will be nihilistic rage. At the end of the novel Mother Johnson has sacrificed herself to keep the African dream alive, an ugly nihilism has surfaced, and the brown group begins its journey away.

That flight is continued by Johny Sobart in *Escape to an Autumn Pavement*, a "rather white-washed nig with lots of coolth" as he describes himself. Johny has escaped from middle-class Jamaica, and from the "slave-class skeletons-in-the-cupboard," but only to wondering what "happened to me between African bondage and British hypocrisy" and trying on and rejecting various roles. His most serious bid is to find the human beneath the skin, but he discovers that he can't shed his history and relationships can't be separated from issues of race and identity. However, *Escape to an Autumn Pavement*

is not a pessimistic novel; it is often very funny, though Johny's relentless, self-protective wise-cracking sometimes becomes wearisome. At the end, nothing has been resolved, but Sobart has learned that the choices he must make require patience, courage, and the honesty to "learn the truth about myself."

In *The Late Emancipation of Jerry Stover* Salkey returns to the Jamaica of his early adulthood to portray the middle class from which Jerry Stover will at some point flee into exile. It is a novel full of energy and despair, memories of a "halcyon time" of sybaritic youth and the painful recognition of the waste and futility which the hell-raising of the Termites cannot disguise. The Termites are Jerry's civil service friends, a group with vitality, ritual loyalty, and an illusion of freedom but no sense of creative responsibility. They see themselves gnawing away at the fabric of hypocritical middle-class Jamaica, but Jerry comes to recognise that they are part of the problem, merely shadow-boxing. He makes the gesture of leaving his comfortable home and going to live amongst the Rastafarians of the Dung'll, teaching them and fighting for their cause like a Felix Holt among the unwashed Victoria working class. In his relationship with the Rastas, the children of Dada Johnson, Jerry plays a Brother Parkin role. He is sceptical of their mystical beliefs and hostile to their dream of returning to Africa, seeing them mainly as the foot soldiers for his idea of protest politics. The Dung'll gives Jerry a confessional where he can pour out his middle-class guilt, but his political gestures are naive failures and he is forced to recognise that he is what his mother says, a do-gooder without a plan, playing at social reform. All that is left for Jerry is either burial on the island, as the other Termites are literally buried under a landslide, or flight. The only other force for change in the island are the Blood and Thunder Brethren who despise gentle mysticism and promise the fire next time. They are the descendants of the ganga addicts in *A Quality of Violence*, who lead the attack on both Brother Parkin and Mother Johnson. Jerry's emancipation from his illusions is both belated and too late. What is left is an honest examination of the reasons for failure.

Both *The Adventures of Catullus Kelly* and *Come Home, Malcolm Heartland* deal with the position of the exiled middle-class Jamaican contemplating return. Neither, in their different ways, is a very satisfactory novel. *The Adventures of Catullus Kelly* uses the form of a Voltairian innocent's journey through London. Much of the writing is entertaining, particularly its exploration of Catullus's "two-way Weltanschauung: his Kingston dialect mood, and his Standard English mood," but the emphasis on language and satirical social vignettes makes it a rather wordy and static novel. Underlying the satire is a black comedy whose seriousness is not fully integrated into the novel as a whole. Catullus's experiences of racism in London make him "blacker an' blacker wit' the days," and he begins to lose his ability to celebrate his "split allegiance, schizophrenic delight, synthesis through analysis and fracture." As a result he decides to return to Jamaica but fails to grasp that exile has changed his heart. Back home, the schizophrenic delight becomes real schizophrenia, and Catullus is incarcerated when having first appeared as Churchill's representative on the island, and then as a matted-haired rasta, he then sheds these false skins and parades himself naked.

In *Come Home, Malcolm Heartland*, Salkey's least successful novel, the hero never reaches home. Its theme is once more the inability of the middle-class Caribbean man to make commitments, in this instance either to the British "Black Power" movement or to home. Return to Jamaica is no more than another escape, from racism and from the guilt he feels over his casual and exploitative use of relationships. However, just before his return, Heartland becomes involved with an absurd but dangerously paranoid group of conspiratorial pseudo-revolutionaries, whom, unfortunately, Salkey fails to bring alive as characters. Finally, the nihilistic retribution which Salkey has warned of in his earlier novels is exacted on Malcolm as a punishment for the sins of his class, when Clovis, a Jamaican migrant, "ravaged by Kingston poverty" and "spiritual desolation," stabs him to death on the order of the conspirators.

One suspects that Salkey's novels have reached a point of exhaustion. However, his collection of short stories, *Anancy's Score*, reworkings of the traditional tales of the trickster spider which explore their contemporary social and political resonances, suggests that he has found a form more appropriate to the kind of preaching he is tempted into in the later novels. Here the use of a poetic, literary Creolese and the form of the fable provides an engaging and serious vehicle for Salkey's perceptiveness, honesty, and aphoristic wit.

—Jeremy Poynting

SARTON, (Eleanor) May.   American.   Born in Wondelgem, Belgium, 3 May 1912, daughter of the historian of science George Sarton; brought to the United States in 1916; became citizen, 1924. Educated at the Institut Belge de Culture Française, Brussels, 1924–25; Shady Hill School and the High and Latin School, both in Cambridge, Massachusetts. Apprentice, then member, and director of the Apprentice Group, Eva Le Gallienne's Civic Repertory Theatre, New York, 1930–33; founder and director, Apprentice Theatre, New York, and Associated Actors Inc., Hartford, Connecticut, 1933–36. Taught creative writing and choral speech, Stuart School, Boston, 1937–40. Documentary scriptwriter, Office of War Information, 1944–45. Poet-in-Residence, Southern Illinois University, Carbondale, Summer 1946; Briggs-Copeland Instructor in English Composition, Harvard University, Cambridge, Massachusetts, 1950–53; Lecturer, Bread Loaf Writers Conference, Middlebury, Vermont, 1951–52, Boulder Writers Conference, Colorado, 1953–54, and Radcliffe College, Cambridge, Massachusetts, 1956–58; Phi Beta Kappa Visiting Scholar, 1959–60; Danforth Lecturer, 1960–61; Lecturer in Creative Writing, Wellesley College, Massachusetts, 1960–63; Poet-in-Residence, Lindenwood College, St. Charles, Missouri, 1964, 1965; Visiting Lecturer, Agnes Scott College, Decatur, Georgia, Spring 1972. Recipient: New England Poetry Club Golden Rose, 1945; Bland Memorial Prize, 1945 (*Poetry*, Chicago); American Poetry Society Reynolds Prize, 1953; Bryn Mawr College Lucy Martin Donnelly Fellowship, 1953; Guggenheim fellowship, 1954; Johns Hopkins University Poetry Festival Award, 1961; National Endowment for the Arts grant, 1967; Sarah Josepha Hale Award, 1972; College of St. Catherine Alexandrine Medal, 1975. Litt.D.: Russell Sage College, Troy, New York, 1959; New England College, Henniker, New Hampshire, 1971; Clark University, Worcester, Massachusetts, 1975; Bates College, Lewiston, Maine, 1976; Colby College, Waterville, Maine, 1976; University of New Hampshire, Durham, 1976; King School of the Ministry, Berkeley, California, 1976; Nasson College, Springvale, Maine, 1980; University of Maine, Orono, 1981; Bowdoin College, Brunswick, Maine, 1983. Fellow, American Academy of Arts and Sciences. Agent: Russell and Volkening Inc., 50 West 29th Street, New York, New York 10001. Address: Box 99, York, Maine 03909, U.S.A.

PUBLICATIONS

Novels

The Single Hound.   Boston, Houghton Mifflin, and London, Cresset Press, 1938.
The Bridge of Years.   New York, Doubleday, 1946.
Shadow of a Man.   New York, Rinehart, 1950; London, Cresset Press, 1952.
A Shower of Summer Days.   New York, Rinehart, 1952; London, Hutchinson, 1954.
Faithful Are the Wounds.   New York, Rinehart, and London, Gollancz, 1955.
The Birth of a Grandfather.   New York, Rinehart, 1957; London, Gollancz, 1958.
The Small Room.   New York, Norton, 1961; London, Gollancz, 1962.
Joanna and Ulysses.   New York, Norton, 1963; London, Murray, 1964.
Mrs. Stevens Hears the Mermaids Singing.   New York, Norton, 1965; London, Owen, 1966.
Miss Pickthorn and Mr. Hare: A Fable.   New York, Norton, 1966; London, Dent, 1968.
The Poet and the Donkey.   New York, Norton, 1969.
Kinds of Love.   New York, Norton, 1970.
As We Are Now.   New York, Norton, 1973; London, Gollancz, 1974.
Crucial Conversations.   New York, Norton, 1975; London, Gollancz, 1976.
A Reckoning.   New York, Norton, 1978; London, Gollancz, 1980.
Anger.   New York, Norton, 1982.
The Magnificent Spinster.   New York, Norton, 1985.

Uncollected Short Stories

"Old-Fashioned Snow," in *Collier's* (Springfield, Ohio), 23 March 1946.
"The Return of Corporal Greene," in *American Mercury* (New York), June 1946.
"The Contest Winner," in *Liberty* (New York), 10 August 1946.
"Mrs. Christiansen's Harvest," in *Ladies Home Journal* (New York), March 1947.
"The Town Will Talk," in *Ladies Home Journal* (New York), June 1947.
"The Miracle in the Museum," in *Church and Home* (London), March 1948.
"The Paris Hat," in *Cosmopolitan* (New York), March 1948.
"Mr. Pomeroy's Battle," in *Better Homes and Gardens* (Des Moines, Iowa), November 1948.
"If This Isn't Love," in *Woman's Home Companion* (Springfield, Ohio), April 1949.
"The Little Purse," in *Redbook* (New York), June 1949.
"Alyosha and His Horse," in *World Review* (London), September 1949–February 1950.
"The Last Gardener," in *Woman's Day* (New York), April 1953.
"The Screen," in *Harper's Bazaar* (New York), October 1953.
"Aunt Emily and Me," in *Woman's Day* (New York), April 1960.

Plays

The Underground River.   New York, Play Club, 1947.

Screenplays (documentaries): *Valley of the Tennessee*, 1945; *A Better Tomorrow*, with Irving Jacoby, 1945; *The Hymn of the Nation*, 1946.

Verse

Encounter in April.   Boston, Houghton Mifflin, 1937.
Inner Landscape.   Boston, Houghton Mifflin, 1939; with a selection from *Encounter in April*, London, Cresset Press, 1939.
The Lion and the Rose.   New York, Rinehart, 1948.
The Leaves of the Tree.   Mount Vernon, Iowa, Cornell College, 1950.
Land of Silence and Other Poems.   New York, Rinehart, 1953.
In Time like Air.   New York, Rinehart, 1957.
Cloud, Stone, Sun, Vine: Poems, Selected and New.   New York, Norton, 1961.
A Private Mythology: New Poems.   New York, Norton, 1966.
As Does New Hampshire and Other Poems.   Peterborough, New Hampshire, Richard R. Smith, 1967.
A Grain of Mustard Seed: New Poems.   New York, Norton, 1971.
A Durable Fire: New Poems.   New York, Norton, 1972.
Collected Poems 1930–1973.   New York, Norton, 1974.
Selected Poems, edited by Serena Sue Hilsinger and Lois Brynes.   New York, Norton, 1978.
Halfway to Silence: New Poems.   New York, Norton, 1980.
Letters from Maine: New Poems.   New York, Norton, 1984.

Other

The Fur Person: The Story of a Cat.   New York, Rinehart, 1957; London, Muller, 1958.
I Knew a Phoenix: Sketches for an Autobiography.   New York, Holt Rinehart, 1959; London, Owen, 1963.
Plant Dreaming Deep (autobiography).   New York, Norton, 1968.
Journal of a Solitude.   New York, Norton, 1973; London, Women's Press, 1985.
Punch's Secret (for children).   New York, Harper, 1974.
A World of Light: Portraits and Celebrations.   New York, Norton, 1976.
A Walk Through the Woods (for children).   New York, Harper, 1976.
The House by the Sea: A Journal.   New York, Norton, 1977; London, Prior, 1978.
Recovering: A Journal 1978–1979.   New York, Norton, 1980.
Writings on Writing.   Orono, Maine, Puckerbrush Press, 1980.
At Seventy: A Journal.   New York, Norton, 1984.

*

Bibliography: *May Sarton: A Bibliography* by Lenora P. Blouin, Metuchen, New Jersey, Scarecrow Press, 1978.

Manuscript Collections: Berg Collection, New York Public Library; Houghton Library, Harvard University, Cambridge, Massachusetts; Amherst College, Massachusetts (letters); Westbrook College, Maine.

Critical Studies: *May Sarton* by Agnes Sibley, New York, Twayne, 1972; *May Sarton: Woman and Poet* edited by Constance Hunting, Orono, Maine, National Poetry Foundation, 1982; interview with Karen Saum, in *Paris Review*, October 1983.

May Sarton comments:

The novelists of the moderate human voice, from Trollope through Tchekov and Forster, are not in fashion, but I like to believe that I am in their line of descent, for what has interested me always is ordinary human relations, the heroism, despair, and rich complex fibre of day to day living among the middle class. European as I am by birth, it was natural that my first four novels should be laid in Europe, Belgium and England—my father was Belgian and my mother English—though the important thing has never been the setting but the intimate relationships explored. Five of the novels are centered in a marriage, from the coming of age through marriage of a young man (*Shadow of a Man*), to a marriage in its middle years (*The Bridge of Years*), to late middle age (*The Birth of a Grandfather*), and old age (*Kinds of Love*). The other major theme of my novels has been how the singular man or woman may find his identity and/or fulfillment through an art or profession. In two cases the protagonist is homosexual, a male professor in *Faithful Are the Wounds*, and a female poet in *Mrs. Stevens Hears the Mermaids Singing*. The former is a relentless exploration of the effect of a suicide (a political suicide) on the protagonist's colleagues at Harvard University. The latter is a study of the woman as artist. And the theme of the value of the single woman to society is touched on again in a novel, *The Small Room*, laid in a woman's college. Finally there is a group of slighter short novels, humorous or poetic accounts of how solitary individuals—a woman painter, a male poet—have dealt with kinds of deprivation, and triumphed.

It is my hope that all the novels, the books of poems, and the autobiographical works may come to be seen as a whole, the communication of a vision of life that is unsentimental, humorous, passionate, and, in the end, timeless. We can bear any Hell if we can "break through" to each other and come to understand ourselves.

*   *   *

May Sarton (also a poet and memoirist) is particularly skillful at character development and the examination of the pleasures and difficulties of important human relationships, steadily analyzing her characters' simultaneous needs for independence from and union with others.

She is also very able in the evocation of place, and setting is often central to her novels. The physical and intellectual milieu of Boston and Harvard in *Faithful Are the Wounds*, for example, symbolizes the characters' habits of introspection and self-analysis which generate the action. *Kinds of Love* is set in Willard, New Hampshire, during its bicentennial, and several characters have important responsibilities for the celebration. Their researches into the village's changes and consistencies parallel their serious consideration of the stable and the unstable patterns of their own lives, resulting in a splendid unification of action and theme. *Kinds of Love* is also a sound portrait of modern New England village life, and, when contrasted with the equally vivid European settings of such earlier works as *The Single Hound, The Bridge of Years*, and *A Shower of Summer Days*, reveals Sarton's deep love for her adopted homeland as well as her appreciation of her European heritage and roots. *Joanna and Ulysses* is set on Santorini. The Aegean island's well-rendered atmosphere, its isolation, and its distance from Joanna's home all dramatize her growing understanding of her obligations to herself as opposed to her obligations to her father. This wedding of theme and setting is one of Sarton's greatest strengths.

One of the author's most significant themes is her protagonists' professional commitment. *Mrs. Stevens Hears the Mermaids Singing* is a portrait of an elderly writer, based on Sarton herself, reflecting upon her life and work. She reconfirms the worth of her writing, recognizing and accepting the fact that professional dedication often impinges upon a love and friendship. In contrast, Lucy Winter, protagonist of *The Small Room*, is depicted at the outset of her career as a professor. Having undertaken her job almost accidentally, Lucy falls in love with her work even as she achieves a realistic understanding of it. The demands of original research are delineated in the portrayal of a highly revered senior professor, and those of the classroom are conveyed through the characterization of a brilliant but deeply troubled student. *The Small Room* offers a remarkably fair and moving analysis of the joys as well as the responsibilities of academe.

Like *Mrs. Stevens Hears the Mermaids Singing* and *Joanna and Ulysses*, *The Small Room* presents useful insights into modes of balancing human relationships against professional drive, always stressing the fact that honorable commitment to one's talent demands sacrifice and self-discipline. Sarton's belief that this level of dedication is particularly taxing for women is clearly evident in these three important works.

Some novels explore major social problems. The powerful *Faithful Are the Wounds* depicts anti-communist witch hunts while it examines the effect of Edward Cavan's suicide upon his circle of friends. *Crucial Conversations*, a somewhat weaker novel, incorporates insights about the Viet Nam War and the Watergate scandal into the account of Poppy Whitelaw's late decision to abandon marriage to attempt a career as a sculptor. The brilliant *As We Are Now* denounces substandard care for the infirm through Caro Spencer's struggle to control her own destiny as well as to preserve her very sense of self within the debasing atmosphere of the "home" into which she has been remanded. Plot and social commentary are always firmly united, translating sweeping issues into human terms.

With Keats, Sarton believes that the fruitful life is a continuing process of "soul-making"; this theme, particularly well conveyed in *The Birth of a Grandfather*, which recounts Sprig Wyeth's development as husband, father, and friend, is almost invariably present in the author's work. Used as a positive motivation in that novel and in *A Reckoning*, the effective story of Laura Spelman's responses to cancer and approaching death, it also lends biting irony to *As We Are Now*.

Willing to confront challenging issues and basic human problems, Sarton has also experimented with form; her works range from the panoramic *Kinds of Love* through the slender, delicate *Joanna and Ulysses* to *As We Are Now*, spare and incisive. She has won deserved respect and wide popularity.

—Jane S. Bakerman

SCHAEFFER, Susan Fromberg. American. Born in Brooklyn, New York, 25 March 1941. Educated at Simmons College, Boston; University of Chicago, 1958–66, B.A. 1961, M.A. 1963, Ph.D. 1966. Married Neil J. Schaeffer in 1970; one son and one daughter. Instructor in English, Wright Junior College, Chicago, 1964–65; Instructor, 1965–66, and Assistant Professor of English, 1966–67, Illinois Institute of Technology, Chicago. Assistant Professor, 1967–71, Associate Professor, 1972–74, since 1974 Professor of English, and since 1985 Broeklundian Professor, Brooklyn College. Recipient: Wallant Award, 1975; O. Henry Award, 1980; St. Lawrence award, 1984; Guggenheim fellowship, 1984; *Centennial Review* award, for poetry, 1985. Agent: Timothy Seldes, Russell and Volkening Inc., 50 West 29th Street, New York, New York 10001.

Address: 783 East 21st Street, Brooklyn, New York 11210, U.S.A.

PUBLICATIONS

Novels

Falling. New York, Macmillan, 1973.
Anya. New York, Macmillan, 1974; London, Cassell, 1976.
Time in Its Flight. New York, Doubleday, 1978.
Love. New York, Dutton, 1981.
The Madness of a Seduced Woman. New York, Dutton, 1983; London, Hamish Hamilton, 1984.
Mainland. New York, Simon and Schuster, and London, Hamish Hamilton, 1985.

Short Stories

The Queen of Egypt. New York, Dutton, 1980.

Uncollected Short Stories

"In the Hospital and Elsewhere," in *Prairie Schooner* (Lincoln, Nebraska), Winter 1981–82.
"Virginia; or, A Single Girl," in *Prairie Schooner* (Lincoln, Nebraska), Fall 1983.

Verse

The Witch and the Weather Report. New York, Seven Woods Press, 1972.
Granite Lady. New York, Macmillan, 1974.
The Rhymes and Runes of the Toad. New York, Macmillan, 1975.
Alphabet for the Lost Years. San Francisco, Gallimaufry, 1976.
The Red, White, and Blue Poem. Denver, The Ally, 1977.
The Bible of the Beasts of the Little Field. New York, Dutton, 1980.

*   *   *

Susan Fromberg Schaeffer's novels, spanning 12 years, are basically mainstream fictions that employ stream of consciousness, radical time shifts, and other modernist techniques, but only incidentally. Apparently she believes that the traditional form is adequate to her purposes, and she is right in so thinking. Schaeffer is mainly interested in exploring and illuminating the shapes of her characters' lives through presentation of the mundane details of their existences. Although she sometimes has her characters move through the larger contexts of historical times, and although she often offers elaborate explanations for behavior, her main strengths as a novelist are her ability to evoke the real quality of quotidian life and the particularities of emotional states.

Falling, Schaeffer's first novel, contains all her strengths and weaknesses as a writer. It is the story of Elizabeth Kamen, a graduate-school Jewish intellectual who suffers several near mental breakdowns, who has unfailingly bad judgment about the men in her life, and whose life is largely determined by her family background. In this and subsequent novels, the lives of characters are traced through their often harrowing childhoods which permanently stamp their personalities. As a child, Elizabeth had stolen a quarter to buy a doll, which her mother and grandmother demolished then hung on the wall to remind

Elizabeth of her "crime." This and other accounts, including events from her present life, are woven together in sessions with her psychiatrist. The aim is to arrest her falling and to get control of her life which, like others characters' lives, suffers from various kinds of slippage. But the human condition is to fall because, as Elizabeth's mother says in Elizabeth's dream. "There is no bottom, there is only this falling," only motion and journey, as opposed to stasis and goal. Elizabeth's mother also asks, "Can you swim, Elizabeth?" "Yes, Mother, if you hold, I'll kick."

However, as a narrative *Falling* suffers from a peculiar stasis. The story is a series of vignettes or anecdotes that do not make up a single, satisfying narrative framework. This is not principally due to Schaeffer's abandoning traditional narrative technique; rather, the episodes are disjointed and without flow. As in other novels, characters are introduced only to show up later, after the reader has forgotten them; adding to the diffuseness that characterizes the entire novel. Yet the strengths of *Falling* remain. Schaeffer's skill as a poet saves many of the scenes; vivid images and descriptions help give the novel a heightened sense of life.

In *Anya* Schaeffer again concentrates on the incidental, even minute aspects of dailiness that are presented with the quality of a personal diary. The novel chronicles the life of Anya, a young Jewish woman in Poland, from the mid-1930's up to the present. Though the novel is partly set during the holocaust years, it is not really about the holocaust (descriptions of life before the Hitler years are among the most compelling in the novel), but about Anya whose life intersects, but is not principally affected by, social events of the time. Schaeffer almost always selects family history as more determinative of character and personality than culture or history. Again, life is the accretion of small things. Anya says, "If you are going to learn a person's life, then, like learning a language, you must start with the little things, the little pictures, the tiny, square images, like rooms, that will grow into a film." To this must be added all of Anya's personal history, from naive, happy student to tough survivor in contemporary America. And Anya always draws on her former lives for strength, so the reader—more so than in *Falling*—experiences a more multi-dimensional character. It should be added that at the time Schaeffer was writing *Anya*, American-born Jewish novelists were more concerned with American social history than with the formation of a "Jewishness" as a response to the death camps and the World War II years. One thinks immediately of Bellow, say, as opposed to a writer like Cynthia Ozick. Now, of course, the holocaust has become an almost fashionable subject.

Love again details the potent, permanent effects of family and married lives, as opposed to culture and history. Esheal Luria is abandoned at ten by his widowed mother after he has been rejected by his stepfather. He is rescued by a mysterious "zenshima" (witch) whose memory haunts him through adulthood and is in part responsible for his wanting, from childhood, "to find an American woman and take care of her." Despite the fact that the novel is a saga of two Jewish immigrant families, the ultimate determinant is, as Luria's wife Emily puts it, the fact that we are "only a new step in the continuing dance . . . of the genes." Resembling at times an Isaac Bashevis Singer tale, *Anya* gains its strength through evocative detail, even the oddities of life lived away from the sweep of events. Emily's mother speaks for Schaeffer: "I remember all those things, but now I don't like to save odd things. They take you over, all those books, cards, litter and pictures. They keep accumulating and it becomes a chore to sort them out and they pile up until they overwhelm you and then you get rid of them all."

As though trying to escape the influence of Emily's mother's words, *The Madness of a Seduced Woman* is Schaeffer's attempt to understand a single life as compounded of personal history, woman's biology, psychiatry, and community standards. The novel is based on an actual murder trial in Vermont early in the century in which Agnes Dempster is tried for the murder of her rival and pronounced insane, largely on psychiatric testimony that Agnes's insanity resulted from "the madness of a seduced woman." However, Schaeffer does not accept this judgment and painstakingly examines her motives (reminiscent of Joyce Carol Oates) as seen through the speculations of lawyers, friends, and her father. No firm conclusions are reached, except that no life may be understood exclusively by objective or subjective means. This process of examination is often numbing, especially since Agnes's life is more complicated than understood. Schaeffer, in this novel, does not allow the character's life to speak for itself; analyses and comment are often substituted for dramatization and the tale itself as an adequate vehicle for meaning.

Mainland, Schaeffer's most recent novel, is in many ways a return to her more lighthearted first novel and to a less complex tale, whose theme is maturity. Eleanor, the main character, is a famous writer and professor, basically happy but almost obsessed by the moralistic voices of her dead grandmother and mother. The novel, comically delightful, avoids the difuseness of much of her earlier work. The theme is expertly handled and the characterization fully realized. Before the novel's end Elizabeth realizes that her adulterous affair was necessary, so she forgives herself, realizing along the way that the dialogues in her head are only carry-overs from childhood and that "maturity" is a false ideal. Schaeffer demonstrates here that a less ambitious theme does not necessarily preclude a higher art.

—Peter Desy

SCHULBERG, Budd (Wilson). American. Born in New York City, 27 March 1914; son of the Hollywood film pioneer, B.P. Schulberg. Educated at Los Angeles High School, 1928–31; Deerfield Academy, 1931–32; Dartmouth College, Hanover, New Hampshire, 1932–36, A.B. (cum laude) 1936 (Phi Beta Kappa). Served in the United States Navy, 1943–46: Lieutenant. Married 1) Virginia Ray in 1936 (divorced, 1942); 2) Victoria Anderson in 1943 (divorced, 1964); 3) the actress Geraldine Brooks in 1964 (died, 1977); 4) Betsy Anne Langman in 1979; five children. Screenwriter, Hollywood, 1936–39; in charge of photographic evidence for the Nuremberg Trials; boxing editor, *Sports Illustrated*, New York, 1954. Has taught writing at Columbia University, New York, Phoenixville Veterans Hospital, University of the Streets, New York, Southampton College, New York, Dartmouth College, and Hofstra University, Hempstead, New York; founder, Watts Writers Workshop, Los Angeles, 1965. Since 1958, president, Schulberg Productions, New York; since 1970, Founding Chairman, Frederick Douglass Creative Arts Center, New York. Member of the New York Council, Authors' Guild, 1958–60; since 1983, council member, Writers Guild. Recipient: American Library Association award, New York Critics award, Foreign Correspondents award, Screen Writers Guild award, and Oscar, all for screenplay, 1955; Christopher Award, 1956; German Film Critics award, for screenplay, 1958. D.Litt.: Dartmouth College, 1960; Long Island University, Greenvale, New York,

1983; Hofstra University, 1985. Lives in Westhampton Beach, New York. Address: c/o Alyss Dorese, 41 West 82nd Street, New York, New York 10024, U.S.A.

PUBLICATIONS

Novels

What Makes Sammy Run? New York, Random House, and London, Jarrolds, 1941.
The Harder They Fall. New York, Random House, and London, Lane, 1947.
The Disenchanted. New York, Random House, 1950; London, Lane, 1951.
Waterfront. New York, Random House, 1955; London, Lane, 1956; as *On the Waterfront*, London, Corgi, 1959.
Sanctuary V. Cleveland, World, 1969; London, W.H. Allen, 1970.
Everything That Moves. New York, Doubleday, 1980; London, Robson, 1981.

Short Stories

Some Faces in the Crowd. New York, Random House, 1953; London, Lane, 1954.

Uncollected Short Stories

"Road to Recovery," in *New Stories for Men*, edited by Charles Grayson. New York, Doubleday, 1941.
"Somebody Has to Be Nobody," in *Post Stories 1941.* New York, Random House, 1941.
"The Real Viennese Schmaltz," in *The Best American Short Stories 1942*, edited by Martha Foley. Boston, Houghton Mifflin, 1942.
"Great South Sea Story," in *Continent's End*, edited by Joseph Henry Jackson. New York, McGraw Hill, 1944.
"Passport to Nowhere," in *These Your Children*, edited by Harold U. Ribalow. New York, Beechhurst Press, 1952.
"All the Town's Talking," in *This Week's Short-Short Stories*, edited by Stewart Beach. New York, Random House, 1953.
"The Barracudas," in *Playboy* (Chicago), 1958.
"A Second Father," in *Playboy* (Chicago), 1961.
"Say Goodnight to Owl," in *Redbook* (New York), August 1965.
"Señor Discretion Himself," in *Playboy* (Chicago), January 1966.
"Spotlight," in *Famous Short Stories 1*, edited by Kurt Singer. Minneapolis, Denison, 1968.
"A Latin from Killarney," in *Playboy* (Chicago), January 1968.
"10th Avenue of the Banks of the Jumna," in *American Rag* (New York), 1980.

Plays

Hollywood Doctor (broadcast, 1941). Published in *The Writer's Radio Theatre*, edited by Norman Weiser, New York, Harper, 1941.
Tomorrow (radio play), in *Free World Theatre*, edited by Arch Oboler and Stephen Longstreet. New York, Random House, 1944.
The Pharmacist's Mate, in *The Best Television Plays 1950–1951*, edited by William I. Kauffman. New York, Merlin Press, 1952.

A Face in the Crowd: A Play for the Screen. New York, Random House, 1957.
Across the Everglades: A Play for the Screen. New York, Random House, 1958.
The Disenchanted, with Harvey Breit, adaptation of the novel by Schulberg (produced New York, 1958). New York, Random House, 1959.
What Makes Sammy Run?, with Stuart Schulberg, music by Ervin Drake, adaptation of the novel by Budd Schulberg (produced New York, 1964).
On the Waterfront: Original Story and Screenplay, edited by Matthew J. Bruccoli. Carbondale, Southern Illinois University Press, 1980.

Screenplays: *Little Orphan Annie*, with Samuel Ornitz and Endre Bohem, 1938; *Winter Carnival*, with Maurice Rapf and Lester Cole, 1939; *Weekend for Three*, with Dorothy Parker and Alan Campbell, 1941; *Government Girl*, with Dudley Nichols, 1943; *City Without Men*, with Martin Berkeley and W.L. River, 1943; *On the Waterfront*, 1954; *A Face in the Crowd*, 1957; *Wind Across the Everglades*, 1958; *Joe Louis—For All Time*, 1984.

Radio Play: *Hollywood Doctor*, 1941.

Television Play: *A Question of Honor*, 1982.

Other

Loser and Still Champion: Muhammad Ali. New York, Doubleday, and London, New English Library, 1972.
The Four Seasons of Success. New York, Doubleday, 1972; London, Robson, 1974; revised edition, as *Writers in America*, New York, Stein and Day, 1983.
Swan Watch, photographs by Geraldine Brooks. New York, Delacorte Press, and London, Robson, 1975.
Moving Pictures: Memories of a Hollywood Prince. New York, Stein and Day, 1981; London, Souvenir Press, 1982.

Editor, *From the Ashes: The Voices of Watts.* New York, New American Library, 1967.

*

Manuscript Collections: Princeton University, New Jersey; Dartmouth College, Hanover, New Hampshire.

Critical Study: interview in *Cineaste* (New York), 1981.

Budd Schulberg comments:
(1972) I was raised in Hollywood, in the middle of the film capital, and had an early education in the vicissitudes of success and failure. I became convinced, before I was out of high school, that the dynamics of success and failure were of earthquake proportions in America, and that Hollywood was only an exaggerated version of the American success drive. Undoubtedly this influenced my first novel, *What Makes Sammy Run?*, as it did *The Harder They Fall*, *The Disenchanted*, and many other things I have tried to write. I believe it is the prime American theme, prompting my essays on Sinclair Lewis, Scott Fitzgerald, William Saroyan, Nathanael West, Thomas Heggen, and John Steinbeck, all writers I knew well. I believe that the seasons of success and failure are more violent in America than anywhere else on earth. Witness only Herman Meville and Jack London, to name two of the victims.
I have been influenced by Mark Twain, by Frank Norris, Jack London, Upton Sinclair, John Steinbeck, and the social

novelists. I believe in art, but I don't believe in art for art's sake; while despising the Soviet official societal writing, I believe in art for people's sake. I believe the novelist should be an artist cum sociologist. I think he should see his characters in social perspective. I think that is one of his obligations. At the same time, I think he also has an obligation to entertain. I think the novel should run on a double track. I am proud of the fact that *Uncle Tom's Cabin* and *The Jungle* and *The Grapes of Wrath* helped to change or at least alarm society. I am proud of the fact that books of mine, *Sammy*, or *On the Waterfront*, caught the public attention but also made it more aware of social sores, the corruption that springs from the original Adam Smith ideal of individuality. I think Ayn Rand tries to apply 18th-century ideals to 20th-century problems—and I'm not sure they worked that well then. My flags are down: I believe in neither Smith nor Marx, in neither Nixon nor Mao nor the Soviet bureaucrats who persecute my fellow writers. There was a time when I was young when I sang the "International." Who would have guessed that the "International" would result in the two largest countries in the world, both "Socialist," brandishing lethal weapons at each other? As long as we can wonder and remember, speculate and (perhaps vainly) hope, we are not dead. The non- or anti-communist humanist writer of novels may be slightly out of style, but there are miles and decades and many books to go before he sleeps.

*   *   *

Budd Schulberg earned fame with his first and best novel, *What Makes Sammy Run?*, published in 1941 on the author's 27th birthday. This narrative of an obnoxious office boy's quick rise to head of a major motion picture studio threatened to become the author's type story for all his novels. *The Harder They Fall* told the pathetic story of the rise of Toro Molina to heavy-weight boxing champion, although "El Toro" is actually the victim of an ambitious, unscrupulous fight promoter named Nick Latka. Schulberg's *The Disenchanted* traced the doomed comeback attempt of Manley Halliday, a novelist and culture-hero of the 1920's now reduced to writing movie scenarios when sober. In these three early novels and many of the collected short stories of *Some Faces in the Crowd*, Schulberg is absorbed with the theme of rapid success and the psychic losses of public winners: compromise with self, betrayal by or of others, doubt, guilt, isolation, and fear haunt and shame his restless characters.

Schulberg's plots have frequently reflected the author's background as screenwriter and son of a Hollywood producer. Not surprisingly, many of his novels have been produced as movies, but his fourth novel, *Waterfront*, was a successful movie first, with the novel version a distinct improvement over the author's own scenario. After a 15 year lapse, Schulberg returned to the novel with *Sanctuary V*, a melodramatic study of a failed revolution and the ruinous effects of sudden power. In this least successful novel, Justo Suarez, the provisional president of what is obviously Cuba, has fled from the corrupted revolutionary Angel Bello to take sanctuary in a corrupt embassy among corrupt or perverted refugees and jailer-hosts.

Not only is Angel Bello clearly Fidel Castro, earlier novels just as recognizably modeled their protagonists on real-life counterparts: the hapless, peasant-fighter Toro Molina is Primo Carnera, while Manley Halliday is Scott Fitzgerald, with whom Schulberg ("Shep" in the book) had once worked on a Dartmouth winter carnival scenario. When Schulberg is not "exposing" Hollywood through memories of real-life counterparts or composites, he utilizes journalistic skill and thorough research

for fictional exposés of the fight game (*Harder They Fall*) and the brutal life around New York harbor (*Waterfront*). Like most exposés, the novels exploit the most sensational elements, though Schulberg reveals an un-Hollywoodian preference for the seamy over the sexy. He does commit many other major "Hollywood" faults, employing gimmicks, stereotyped characters, sentimentality, and mechanical, reflex responses to life-situations in place of serious ideas or a personal vision.

With *Sammy*, however, even the faults seem appropriate. The snappy repartee and artificial dialogue brilliantly sum up the brittle, superficial world of 1930's Hollywood. The novel's fast pace, the picaresque audacity of the almost likable, conscienceless heel-hero, the predictable ending of the betrayer betrayed (and, implicitly, of the hunter about to be hunted) still add up, after 40 years, to one of the best Hollywood novels ever written. Like many other commercial writers, Schulberg knows that first-person is the easiest way to tell a story; he uses this form often and well, and in *What Makes Sammy Run?* he created a minor classic of this form and the Hollywood sub-genre.

—Frank Campenni

SELBY, Hubert, Jr. American. Born in Brooklyn, New York, 23 July 1928. Educated in New York City public schools, including Peter Stuyvesant High School. Served in the United States Merchant Marine, 1944–46. Married 1) Inez Taylor in 1953; 2) Judith Lumino in 1964; 3) Suzanne Shaw in 1969; four children. Hospital patient, with tuberculosis, 1946–50; held various jobs, including seaman and insurance clerk, 1950–64. Lives in Los Angeles. Address: c/o Grove Press, 196 West Houston Street, New York, New York 10014, U.S.A.

Publications

Novels

Last Exit to Brooklyn. New York, Grove Press, 1964; London, Calder and Boyars, 1966.
The Room. New York, Grove Press, 1971; London, Calder and Boyars, 1972.
The Demon. New York, Playboy Press, 1976; London, Boyars, 1977.
Requiem for a Dream. New York, Playboy Press, 1978; London, Boyars, 1979.

Short Stories

Song of the Silent Snow. New York, Grove Press, and London, Boyars, 1986.

Uncollected Short Stories

"Home for Christmas," in *Neon 2* (New York), 1956.
"Love/s Labour/s Lost," in *Black Mountain Review* (Black Mountain, North Carolina), Autumn 1957.
"Double Feature," in *Neon 4* (New York), 1959.
"Another Day, Another Dollar," in *New Directions 17.* New York, New Directions, 1961.
"A Penny for Your Thoughts," in *The Moderns*, edited by LeRoi Jones. New York, Corinth, 1963; London, MacGibbon and Kee, 1965.

"And Baby Makes Three," in *New American Story*, edited by Robert Creeley and Donald Allen. New York, Grove Press, 1965.
"Fat Phil's Day," in *Evergreen Review* (New York), August 1967.
"Happy Birthday," in *Evergreen Review* (New York), August 1969.

*

Critical Studies: "Hubert Selby Issue" of *Review of Contemporary Fiction* (Elmwood Park, Illinois), vol. 1, no. 2, 1981.

Hubert Selby, Jr., comments:
I write by ear. Music of line important. Want to put reader through emotional experience.

*   *   *

If *Last Exit to Brooklyn* and its ludicrous obscenity trial hadn't exhausted moralistic disgust, Hubert Selby, Jr.'s work could probably stand at the bench in perpetuity. The Seventh Circle of the Violent in Dante's *Inferno*; Gulliver upon the cancerous Brobdignagian breast; Genet's onanist reveries. These suggest Selby's fictive world. He is our eye-witness on the dead-ends of the daily. Stuck in the sick gut of the city, his camera fixes the disaffected masses and completes a picture begun with Crane's *Maggie*. On the other hand, his biblical epigraphs are both ironically and straightforwardly applicable. He is, then, at once a determinist and a moralist whose narratives are naturalistic fables. Consequently, his psychological landscape is more than social realism or a Hogarth satire could accommodate. It is a Bosch and Francis Bacon triptych. As the witness for the damned, Selby *is* mired in America's slime. But given a populace which could nod off on the Viet Nam War, his ability to shock may be remarkable, even morally so.

The title of his first novel is taken from an expressway sign that overlooks a cemetery of solid concrete. The work thematically connects six tales of hopeless human isolation. Its people delude themselves with faith in family and ideal dreams of profound sexual communion. But Abraham's infidelity, angry remoteness, and, finally, sleep are domesticity. Tralala's rape is heterosexuality. "Georgette's" and Vinnie's bestiality is homosexuality. Casual and sadistic, the violent are little Eichmanns and Mengeles. In the background Selby works with a timeless symbology of darkness overwhelming light. This is conveyed to us by depth associations with *Ecclesiastes*, Poe's *Raven*, and our own disillusioned black "Bird," Charlie Parker. It is only by viewing Selby in this context that we can grasp his preoccupation with drugs. He knows unequivocally the life renouncing and futile lie at the heart of "kind nepenthe."

The Room shifts our focus from the sick social to the sick individual organism. Its sole province is the mind of a nameless paranoid schizophrenic, though Selby might resist terminology. The "room" is both a cell and the disconnected consciousness of the single character. Locked within each, he constructs antithetically lofty and brutal fantasies, but always out of a single-minded hatred of authority. Thus his imaginary revenges include delusions of magnanimity in which he self-sacrificially fights social injustice with the help of liberal lawyers. Conversely, they include totally dehumanizing tortures of police officers, sadistic acts which reduce his adversaries to canines. These are rendered with nauseating detail. Selby seems unwilling to attribute this state of mind to a sick society, an indifferent family, or a bad character. It is simply a *donnée*, and Selby's

forte is neither sociological nor psychological reductionism but graphic presentation. The novel's unsavory force and its interest are considerably enhanced by the author's tactic of gliding constantly between an omniscient and a first person perspective.

The "demon" of Selby's third novel is sexual obsession and its mutations. It begins as womanizing so unalleviated that Harry White can sustain no connection, except tenuously to his career, with any other activity. (He cannot last out a softball game with friends or a party for his grandparents.) It ends with his murdering, on Palm Sunday, a Christlike Cardinal and his subsequent suicide. So the demoniacal obsession is larger than carnality, passing through debauchery and theft toward this ultimately exciting destructiveness which seems proof for Selby that "The wages of sin is death." The novel's complementary epigraph is from *James* 1:15. At all times, whether White is fornicating or thieving, the demon exists as a physical tension so great that Harry hates whatever stands between himself and a feeling of exhausting gratification. But all respite from enslavement, including his marriage to Linda (the healthiest person Selby has drawn), is stop-gap. Only death does the job. As a study of the connection between sex and violence in the obsessive person, the book has merit. But the conclusion is unfortunately mystical in part, especially because the only psychological perspective is provided by an arrogant neo-Freudian simpleton. This straw man certainly doesn't exhaust more modestly agnostic interpretations of the events.

Requiem for a Dream is about hope ruined by narcotic habit. It sees America in terms of a pervasive dependence upon metaphorical and literal drugs. The widow Sara Goldfarb eats compulsively and lives a stuporously vicarious life through soap operas and TV game shows. Thinking she has a chance to appear in one and wanting to be appropriately svelte, she sees a physician who addicts her to dexedrine. She ends up a skeletal and slavering schizoid in a mental hospital. Concurrently, her son Harry, his friend Tyrone Love, and Harry's lover, Marion, plot their own dreams' fulfillments. All are sad clichés. And the trio are heroin addicts. From drug profits, Harry will build a coffeehouse for sensitive artists and writers where Marion's drawings will be admired; the black Tyrone will buy into the bliss of a modest suburb. But their endeavors only increase their addiction. Marion winds up in a sort of bisexual freak show working for her portion of bliss. Harry loses his arm from an infection and sinks into oblivion in a Miami hospital. Having gone south with Harry for a big pay-off, Tyrone gets to be brutalized by rednecks and thrown in prison. By now we have to ask if Hubert Selby Jr. has anything more to tell us along these lines.

—David M. Heaton

SELVON, Samuel (Dickson). Trinidadian. Born in Trinidad, 20 May 1923. Educated at Naparima College, Trinidad, 1935–39. Served as a wireless operator in the Trinidad Royal Naval Volunteer Reserve, 1940–45. Married 1) Draupadi Persaud in 1947, one daughter; 2) Althea Nesta Daroux in 1963, two sons and one daughter. Journalist, *Trinidad Guardian*, 1946–50; civil servant, in the High Commission, London, 1950–53. Since 1954, full-time writer. Recipient: Guggenheim fellowship, 1954, 1968; Society of Authors travelling scholarship, 1958; Trinidad Government scholarship, 1962; Arts

Council of Great Britain grant, 1967, 1968; Humming Bird Medal (Trinidad), 1969. D.Litt.: University of the West Indies, Kingston, Jamaica, 1985. Lives in Canada. Address: c/o Williams-Wallace Publishers, 2 Silver Avenue, Toronto, Ontario M6R 3A2, Canada.

PUBLICATIONS

Novels

A Brighter Sun.   London, Wingate, 1952; New York, Viking Press, 1953.
An Island Is a World.   London, Wingate, 1955.
The Lonely Londoners.   London, Wingate, 1956; New York, St. Martin's Press, 1957; as *The Lonely Ones*, London, Digit, 1959.
Turn Again Tiger.   London, MacGibbon and Kee, 1958; New York, St. Martin's Press, 1959.
I Hear Thunder.   London, MacGibbon and Kee, and New York, St. Martin's Press, 1963.
The Housing Lark.   London, MacGibbon and Kee, 1965.
The Plains of Caroni.   London, MacGibbon and Kee, 1970.
Those Who Eat the Cascadura.   London, Davis Poynter, 1972.
Moses Ascending.   London, Davis Poynter, 1975.
Moses Migrating.   London, Longman, 1983.

Short Stories

Ways of Sunlight.   London, MacGibbon and Kee, and New York, St. Martin's Press, 1958.

Uncollected Short Story

"Ralphie at the Races," in *Ariel* (Calgary, Alberta), October 1982.

Plays

Screenplay: *Pressure*, with Horace Ové, 1975.

Radio Plays: *Lost Property*, 1965; *A House for Tenna*, 1965; *A Highway in the Sun*, 1967; *Rain Stop Play*, 1967; *You Right in the Smoke*, 1968; *Worse Than Their Bite*, 1968; *Bringing in the Sheaves*, 1969; *Perchance to Dream*, 1969; *Eldorado West One*, 1969; *Home Sweet India*, 1970; *Mary Mary Shut Your Gate*, 1971; *The Magic Stick*, from work by Ismith Khan, 1971; *Voyage to Trinidad*, 1971; *Those Who Eat the Cascadura*, 1971; *Water for Veronica*, 1972; *Cry Baby Brackley*, 1972; *The Harvest in Wilderness*, 1972; *Milk in the Coffee*, 1975; *Zeppi's Machine*, 1977.

*   *   *

"...choose one, choose a time, a place, any time or any place, and take off, as if this were interrupted conversation, as if you and I were earnest friends and there is no need for preliminary remark." These words, taken from *Ways of Sunlight*, offer a valuable insight into the work of Samuel Selvon. Mastery of the casual, conversational narrative, frequently using the creole speech patterns of his native Trinidad, is an important facet of his style. His one collection of short stories, *Ways of Sunlight*, rewards closer examination, not least in the way that several stories—while excellent in themselves—contain themes which are explored more fully in later novels. For example, the conflict of generations in "Cane Is Bitter" brings *Turn Again Tiger* to mind, while the humorous accounts

of West Indians in London prefigure the works of the Moses canon.

Selvon was born and raised in Trinidad, and has recently returned there after living for 30 years in London. The two locations of Trinidad and Britain's metropolis are the focal points of all his major fiction. From the former come the "Tiger" novels, while London provides the background for Selvon's Caribbean exile, notably "the old Moses." The shorter pieces in *Ways of Sunlight* are divided between the two geographical settings.

In *A Brighter Sun* and its sequel, *Turn Again Tiger*, Selvon describes the adventures of a young East Indian labourer, tracing his growth to manhood and eventual self-fulfilment. Tiger's experiences in suburban Barataria, his integration into the mixed "creolize" community there, and his relationship with his child-bride Urmilla, are ably evoked in the first novel, while in *Turn Again Tiger* Selvon has him endure a humiliating, though ultimately strengthening "return to the roots" in the old-fashioned cane plantation village of Five Rivers. In these works, both of them outstanding novels, Selvon makes use of a conventional narrative style, albeit rich with symbol and allusion. The creole language is reserved mainly for dialogue between the characters, where it is skilfully exploited by the author.

Foremost among the novels of exile is *The Lonely Londoners*, which must be ranked a masterpiece of its kind. Here Selvon takes the imaginative step of adopting Trinidad creole speech as the means of narration, the book coming over to the reader as conversational fragments uttered by a friend. It depicts vividly the tragi-comic adventures of Caribbean exiles in a bleak, smog-laden 1950's London. There are a number of memorable characters, the most important being the worldly wise veteran Moses, who, as his name implies, has the task of guiding his fellows through the white man's inhospitable wilderness. All the same, care is taken to ensure that he does not dominate at the expense of the rest, so that a communal experience is presented. *The Housing Lark*, written in the same basic style, is equally poignant and amusing, though it lacks the scope of its predecessor.

Moses returns as the central figure of Selvon's two most recent novels. In *Moses Ascending* and *Moses Migrating* he stars as the narrator, his language mingling creole with an archaic and inflated English which symbolizes both his literary pretensions and his absurd British patriotism: "When it come to opening the door when opportunity knock, or make hay when the sun shine, or beat the iron when the fire hot, my brain become nimble and pellucid." Both novels display sly under-layers of meaning, and Selvon, speaking from behind his character, allows his satire a free rein. Black Power and white racism are continually ridiculed, together with the ignorance and hypocrisy of their adherents. The Crusoe myth is lampooned in the white man Bob, Moses's "man Friday," an illiterate, lecherous, untrustworthy drunkard who fulfils most of the "savage" stereotypes. Bod, a tedious but necessary figure, appears in both novels. *Moses Ascending* charts the hero's rise from basement to penthouse as a slum landlord, only to be brought down again by his "friends," while in *Moses Migrating* he returns to Trinidad. Regarding himself as England's representative abroad, Moses takes part in the Carnival, where as "Britannia" he wins a prize, but his triumph proves hollow and the book ends with him heading back to England again. These novels are accomplished works, amusing and thought-provoking. If they lack some of the spontaneity of *The Lonely Londoners*, it is perhaps not surprising. Similarly, the Moses of the later books appears a naive simpleton alongside his man-of-the-world namesake in *Londoners*, but this obviously suits the author's purpose, presenting the hero as a source of amusement himself even as he mocks the pretensions of others. No good author remains the same, and it is to Selvon's credit that his work continues to develop beyond his early successes.

Selvon celebrates the folk experience. His writing utilises oral traditions, notably the calypso story-form and the speech patterns of his native island. He does not romanticize his heroes or the nature of their lives, and takes a long, hard look at the antagonism between the races. Yet at the same time he makes us identify with Tiger and Moses, and his work shows a clear commitment to the mixed creole society emerging in Trinidad, and to a multi-racial community in Britain, Selvon does not glorify his origins, but unlike Naipaul he sees no reason to be ashamed of them. One need not accept George Lamming's estimate of him as "the most important folk poet the British Caribbean has yet produced" to believe that he is a significant and innovative novelist whose work has too often been undervalued.

—Geoff Sadler

SHADBOLT, Maurice (Francis Richard). New Zealander. Born in Auckland, 4 June 1932. Educated at Te Kuiti High School; Avondale College; University of Auckland. Married 1) Gillian Heming in 1953, three sons and two daughters; 2) Barbara Magner in 1971; 3) Bridget Armstrong in 1978. Journalist for various New Zealand publications, 1952–54; documentary scriptwriter and director for the New Zealand National Film Unit, 1954–57; full-time writer from 1957; lived in London and Spain, 1957–60, then returned to New Zealand. Recipient: New Zealand Scholarship in Letters, 1959, 1970, 1982; Hubert Church Prose Award, 1960; Katherine Mansfield Award, 1963, 1967; Otago University Robert Burns Fellowship, 1963; National Association of Independent Schools award (USA), 1966; Freda Buckland Award, 1969; Pacific Area Travel Association award, for non-fiction, 1971; James Wattie Award, 1973, 1981; New Zealand Book Award, 1981. Agent: Curtis Brown, 162–168 Regent Street, London W1R 5TA, England. Address: Box 60028, Titirangi, Auckland 7, New Zealand.

PUBLICATIONS

Novels

Among the Cinders. London, Eyre and Spottiswoode, and New York, Atheneum, 1965; revised edition, Auckland, Hodder and Stoughton, 1984.
This Summer's Dolphin. London, Cassell, and New York, Atheneum, 1969.
An Ear of the Dragon. London, Cassell, 1971.
Strangers and Journeys. London, Hodder and Stoughton, and New York, St. Martin's Press, 1972.
A Touch of Clay. London, Hodder and Stoughton, 1974.
Danger Zone. Auckland, Hodder and Stoughton, 1975; London, Hodder and Stoughton, 1976.
The Lovelock Version. Auckland and London, Hodder and Stoughton, 1980; New York, St. Martin's Press, 1981.

Short Stories

The New Zealanders: A Sequence of Stories. Christchurch, Whitcombe and Tombs, and London, Gollancz, 1959; New York, Atheneum, 1961.
Summer Fires and Winter Country. London, Eyre and Spottiswoode, 1963; New York, Atheneum, 1966.
The Presence of Music: Three Novellas. London, Cassell, 1967.
Figures in Light: Selected Stories. London, Hodder and Stoughton, 1979.

Play

Once on Chunuk Bair. Auckland, Hodder and Stoughton, 1982.

Other

New Zealand: Gift of the Sea, photographs by Brian Brake. Christchurch, Whitcombe and Tombs, 1963; revised edition, 1973.
The Shell Guide to New Zealand. Christchurch, Whitcombe and Tombs, 1968; London, Joseph, 1969; revised edition, Whitcombe and Tombs, 1973; Joseph, 1976.
Isles of the South Pacific, with Olaf Ruhen. Washington, D.C., National Geographic Society, 1968.
Love and Legend: Some Twentieth Century New Zealanders. Auckland, Hodder and Stoughton, 1976.

*

Critical Study: by the author, in *Islands* (Auckland), June 1981.

Theatrical Activities:
Actor: **Film**—*Among the Cinders*, 1983.

Maurice Shadbolt comments:
I should like to say only that, as a man of my time and place, I have simply tried to make sense of both, in the course of a journey which allows no satisfying destination; my books might thus be seen as bottled messages tossed out at points along that journey. I know I might have been otherwise: I am frequently unsure why I write at all. But then I look from my study window out upon a bruised Eden, my country, and I begin again; there is no escape. My equivocal feeling for the country in which I happened to be born admits of no easy realease in either a physical or literary sense. So I make, in diverse shapes, in stories and novels, my not always unhappy best of it. As a New Zealander, resident at the ragged edge of Western civilization, upon the last land of substance to be claimed by mankind, I often feel my involvement with the rest of the human race rather peripheral—as if upon a lonely floating raft. Yet fires lit upon the periphery may still illuminate the central and abiding concerns of man—the fires, I mean, which everywhere the human spirit ignites, and which everywhere shape the artist. So I make no apology. I might envy a Russian or an American—a Solzhenitsyn or a Mailer—his capacity to approach the giant themes of the 20th century. But I would not wish, really, to be otherwise. For I have tried, beyond the particularities of time and place, to observe and examine those hungers and thirsts which remain constant in man; those hungers and thirsts which, in my peripheral position, may sometimes be more evident than elsewhere.

*   *   *

Maurice Shadbolt is one of New Zealand's most prolific and popular writers of fiction. His first book, the collection of stories boldly entitled *The New Zealanders*, brought him almost immediate recognition. With their emphasis on the often uneasy relationship of New Zealanders in the first half of this century with their environment, these first stories foreshadow the themes of Shadbolt's subsequent writing.

A personal identification with the landscape has continued to inform his fiction. The exploration of New Zealand in terms of its history, its topographical characteristics, and its people is not, however, a mere exercise in nationalism: it exemplifies the imaginative writer's search, in a rapidly changing world, for the inner permanence afforded by conscious recognition and acceptance of one's roots.

For Shadbolt, these roots derive chiefly from a near-emotional involvement with the land. If this preoccupation with the "spirit of place" has been remarked upon frequently, it is because the visually intense depiction of his characters' relationships with their physical surroundings is one of his major strengths. There is a suggestion, in this "painterly" approach to writing, of an affinity with New Zealand's school of landscape artists and with the similar concern of the Australian novelist Patrick White to delineate in words the actual appearance as well as the feeling of life in his own country.

Following *The Presence of Music*, where he used the form of the novella to examine in three complementary pieces the position of the artist in New Zealand society, Shadbolt wrote his first novel, *Among the Cinders*. Structurally loose and with a somewhat contrived ending, this light-hearted account of a run-away boy's adventures with his unconventional grandfather remains one of his most popular books.

The most typical characters in Shadbolt's earlier fiction are aimless young adults. Torn between a desire for escape from binding commitment on the one hand and for emotional security on the other, they seek but rarely find solace in personal relationships. In *This Summer's Dolphin* a variety of narrative techniques is used to investigate the troubled inner lives of several such isolated individuals. Unifying their essentially separate stories is the novel's island setting and the appearance of a friendly dolphin who, through his temporary transcendence of the characters' self-absorption, becomes a symbol with Christlike overtones.

The incorporation of easily traceable biographical material in *An Ear of the Dragon* aroused some local criticism. Nevertheless, the skilful manipulation of flashbacks to illuminate the link between an immigrant writer's adolescent experiences in wartime Italy and his difficult adjustment to new Zealand life and people makes this a compelling narrative.

Strangers and Journeys, written over a period of ten years, is a long and ambitious book. Gathering together many of the themes and characters of his previous fiction, Shadbolt details in a complex pattern of social realism the contrasting lives and aspirations of two generations of fathers and sons. There is an epic sweep to the first part of the novel with its masterly evocation of the two separate working men who, in an economically harsh era, pitted themselves against their environment and survived. This is not sustained, partly because Shadbolt himself is too close to the sons. For them, external battle against the land has given way to an even more debilitating, internal struggle to find meaning in the city.

Two shorter novels, *A Touch of Clay* and *Danger Zone*, chronicle aspects of New Zealand society in the 1970's. The former, centering on the unsatisfactory relationship between an ex-lawyer turned potter and a drug-addicted girl from a neighbouring hippy commune, is emotionally unconvincing. *Danger Zone* takes as its subject New Zealand opposition to French nuclear testing in the Pacific. The work derives its force from Shadbolt's exploration of the differing motives and attitudes of the four men who crew a small protest yacht into the Mururoa danger zone.

Generally recognised as Shadbolt's finest (and longest) novel to date is *The Lovelock Version*. Set amid the rugged conditions of life in 19th-century New Zealand, this is an exuberant, near-epic saga of three pioneering brothers, their families, lovers, friends, and enemies. In terms of time, place, events, and people, the scope of the narrative is vast while its form is innovative. The reader is presented with an exciting, if sometimes outrageous, mixture of realism and melodrama, fact and fantasy, history and myth. Narrated in the present tense, the work is sustained by a detached, ironic style that balances the tragedies of human existence with the comedies.

—Cherry A. Hankin

SHARP, Margery. British. Born in 1905. Educated at Streatham Hill High School, London; Bedford College, University of London, B.A. (honours) in French. Married Major Geoffrey Castle in 1938. Army Education Lecturer in World War II. Lives in London. Address: c/o Heinemann Ltd., 10 Upper Grosvenor Street, London W1X 9PA, England.

PUBLICATIONS

Novels

Rhododendron Pie. London, Chatto and Windus, and New York, Appleton, 1930.
Fanfare for Tin Trumpets. London, Barker, 1932; New York, Putnam, 1933.
The Nymph and the Nobleman. London, Barker, 1932.
The Flowering Thorn. London, Barker, 1933; New York, Putnam, 1934.
Sophy Cassmajor. London, Barker, and New York, Putnam, 1934.
Four Gardens. London, Barker, and New York, Putnam, 1935.
The Nutmeg Tree. London, Barker, and Boston, Little Brown, 1937.
Harlequin House. London, Collins, and Boston, Little Brown, 1939.
The Stone of Chastity. London, Collins, and Boston, Little Brown, 1940.
Three Companion Pieces: Sophy Cassmajor, The Tigress on the Hearth, and The Nymph and the Nobleman. Boston, Little, Brown, 1941; *The Tigress on the Hearth* published separately, London, Collins, 1955.
Cluny Brown. London, Collins, and Boston, Little Brown, 1944.
Britannia Mews. London, Collins, and Boston, Little Brown, 1946.
The Foolish Gentlewoman. London, Collins, and Boston, Little Brown, 1948.
Lise Lillywhite. London, Collins, and Boston, Little Brown, 1951.
The Gipsy in the Parlour. London, Collins, 1953; Boston, Little Brown, 1954.

The Eye of Love. London, Collins, and Boston, Little Brown, 1957; as *Martha and the Eye of Love*, London, New English Library, 1969.

Something Light. London, Collins, 1960; Boston, Little Brown, 1961.

Martha in Paris. London, Collins, 1962; Boston, Little Brown, 1963.

Martha, Eric, and George. London, Collins, and Boston, Little Brown, 1964.

The Sun in Scorpio. London, Heinemann, and Boston, Little Brown, 1965.

In Pious Memory. Boston, Little Brown, 1967; London, Heinemann, 1968.

Rosa. London, Heinemann, 1969; Boston, Little Brown, 1970.

The Innocents. London, Heinemann, 1971; Boston, Little Brown, 1972.

The Faithful Servants. London, Heinemann, and Boston, Little Brown, 1975.

Summer Visits. London, Heinemann, 1977; Boston, Little Brown, 1978.

Short Stories

The Lost Chapel Picnic and Other Stories. London, Heinemann, and Boston, Little Brown, 1973.

Fiction (for children)

The Rescuers. London, Collins, and Boston, Little Brown, 1959.

Miss Bianca. London, Collins, and Boston, Little Brown, 1962.

The Turret. Boston, Little Brown, 1963; London, Collins, 1964.

Lost at the Fair. Boston, Little Brown, 1965; London, Heinemann, 1967.

Miss Bianca in the Salt Mines. London, Heinemann, and Boston, Little Brown, 1966.

Miss Bianca in the Orient. London, Heinemann, and Boston, Little Brown, 1970.

Miss Bianca in the Antarctic. London, Heinemann, 1970; Boston, Little Brown, 1971.

Miss Bianca and the Bridesmaid. London, Heinemann, and Boston, Little Brown, 1972.

The Magical Cockatoo. London, Heinemann, 1974.

The Children Next Door. London, Heinemann, 1974.

Bernard the Brave. London, Heinemann, 1976; Boston, Little Brown, 1977.

Bernard into Battle. London, Heinemann, and Boston, Little Brown, 1979.

Plays

Meeting at Night (produced London, 1934).

Lady in Waiting, adaptation of her novel *The Nutmeg Tree* (produced New York, 1940; as *The Nutmeg Tree*, produced London, 1941). New York, French, 1941.

The Foolish Gentlewoman, adaptation of her own novel (produced London, 1949). London, French, 1950.

Television Play: *The Birdcage Room*, 1954.

Other (for children)

Mélisande. London, Collins, and Boston, Little Brown, 1960.

*

Manuscript Collection: Houghton Library, Harvard University, Cambridge, Massachusetts.

*   *   *

The genre for which Margery Sharp is best known is light entertainment involving the incongruity of unclassifiable or even zany characters operating in the most conventional of settings. These off-beat characters, however, are basically sound, and the conventional persons are basically kind; all turns out well, and the satire of social assumptions lacks bitterness. Some of the books are very slightly plotted, depending for their effect on amusing conversation, while others lead the reader rapidly along a zigzag path through well-planted, but not unexpected, surprises.

The novel which best realizes her comic potentialities is her seventh, *The Nutmeg Tree.* Julia, a minor vaudeville personage, plump and glowing at 39, is discovered in her usual plight of warding off bailiffs and looking for financial succor from some male source. Technically, she is also Mrs. Packett, the daughter-in-law of a conservative county family, widowed in her teens after a necessary wartime marriage. After a year with the kindly Packetts, she had fled back to the theatre. Now a letter has arrived from her daughter asking her to come to the south of France to persuade the older Mrs. Packett to assent to her marriage. Julia genuinely tries to fill her maternal, ladylike role, but since she is without resources she must use an adventuress's means. Her off-beat nature is immediately recognized by the young suitor, and a tug-of-war results, for Julia has seen that his essentially picaresque tastes, so like her own, would prove disastrous in a union with her prim, idealistic daughter. The price of the young man's renunciation is Julia's refusal, in turn, of the hand of another guest, the distinguished, elderly Sir William. Julia accepts the sacrifice, but after a paper-chase all ends well.

As an entertainer Sharp aims at readers who bring a literary background—though this is not essential—and a familiarity with the expected social niceties. These last she values, seeing their utility in easing life's relationships; but she jettisons meaningless social impositions. Of the heroine of *Cluny Brown*, a plumber's niece, everyone keeps saying, "The trouble with young Cluny is she don't know her place." For tall, loping Cluny, with her unmanageable dark hair and large features that distract the imperceptive from her fine eyes and attentive gaze, is a restless explorer, disconcertingly far from the stereotype of clerk, typist, or servant, and her class has no place for such a girl. Neither has the class of county families, but the author sends her as a parlor-maid to such a family in Devon who are harboring also a refugee Polish professor.

Of her less purely comic novels, *The Flowering Thorn* is an unsentimental account of a young London sophisticate's adoption of a little boy and her gradual acceptance of village life. Sharp has written three historical novels. The synoptic, overly thin *Britannia Mews* presents the social changes from 1865 to 1945 in a West End mews and the courageous life of a woman who, as a young girl, had naively declassed herself.

—Alice Bensen

SHARPE, Tom (Thomas Ridley Sharpe). British. Born in London, 30 March 1928. Educated at Lancing College, Sussex, 1942–46; Pembroke College, Cambridge, 1948–51, M.A.;

teacher's training, Cambridge University, 1962–63, P.C.G.E. 1963. Served in the Royal Marines, 1946–48. Married Nancy Anne Looper in 1969; three daughters. Social worker, 1951–52, and teacher, 1952–56, Natal, South Africa; photographer, Pietermaritzburg, South Africa, 1956–61; deported from South Africa on political grounds, 1961; teacher, Aylesbury Secondary Modern School, Buckinghamshire, 1961; Lecturer in History, Cambridge College of Arts and Technology, 1963–71. Since 1971, full-time writer. Lives in Cambridge. Agent: Richard Scott Simon Ltd., 32 College Cross, London N1 1PR. Address: c/o Secker and Warburg Ltd., 54 Poland Street, London W1V 3DF, England.

PUBLICATIONS

Novels

Riotous Assembly. London, Secker and Warburg, 1971; New York, Viking Press, 1972.
Indecent Exposure. London, Secker and Warburg, 1973.
Porterhouse Blue. London, Secker and Warburg, and Englewood Cliffs, New Jersey, Prentice Hall, 1974.
Blott on the Landscape. London, Secker and Warburg, 1975; New York, Vintage, 1984.
Wilt. London, Secker and Warburg, 1976; New York, Vintage, 1984.
The Great Pursuit. London, Secker and Warburg, 1977; New York, Harper, 1978.
The Throwback. London, Secker and Warburg, 1978; New York, Vintage, 1984.
The Wilt Alternative. London, Secker and Warburg, 1979; New York, St. Martin's Press, 1981(?).
Ancestral Vices. London, Secker and Warburg, 1980.
Vintage Stuff. London, Secker and Warburg, 1982; New York, Vintage, 1984.
Wilt on High. London, Secker and Warburg, 1984; New York, Random House, 1985.

Plays

The South African (produced London, 1961).

Television Play: *She Fell among Thieves,* from the novel by Dornford Yates, 1978.

*   *   *

Tom Sharpe's comic vision was formed under the pressure of state persecution strong enough to infuriate but not crush him. His initial satires on South Africa set the pattern for all his subsequent fiction. These early works draw their energy from the seditious author's deportation from South Africa in 1961.

Sharpe's first published novel, *Riotous Assembly*, is as funny as anything he has written. It has as its hero the tormented Anglophile policeman Kommandant Van Heerden. Van Heerden's feud with his scheming subordinate Verkramp (a fanatic Boer) and the murderous blunderings of Konstabel Els are one source of black merriment. Another is the degenerate world of the upper-class English colonials. Bungling authoritarian institutions and the English ruling class reappear as black

beasts in all Sharpe's later novels. *Indecent Exposure* is a straight sequel, with the same principal characters as *Riotous Assembly* and the same "Piemburg" setting. Its comedy, however, is even broader. (At one point in the narrative the whole of Van Heerden's police force is subjected to electric shock therapy and converted to rampant homosexuality.)

After this novel, Sharpe evidently felt his South African vein was exhausted. *Porterhouse Blue* is set in a Cambridge college. Most of the plot revolves around the manoeuvrings of a reform and a reactionary faction. There is the usual play with comic ruthlessness and sexual perversions. (One comic climax has the quad full of inflated condoms.) In the largest sense, *Porterhouse Blue* can be read as a satire on English life, and its resistance to change. *Blott on the Landscape* is more straightforwardly funny. The central joke of the narrative is the modernisation of Handyman Hall from stately home to theme park. The vivaciously homicidal lady of the house, Maude Lynchwood, is particularly well done.

With his next novel, *Wilt*, Sharpe created his most durable hero. The first in the series presents Henry Wilt as a henpecked and downtrodden lecturer at "Fenland College" (based transparently on the polytechnic where Sharpe himself taught). There is some effective incidental comedy on Wilt's futile attempts to educate a day release class of butchers ("Meat One"). But the main plot concerns Henry's involvement in suspected murder, following his witnessed disposal of a life-size sex doll which he accidentally came by. This leads to an epic struggle of will with the long-suffering Inspector Flint. Flint and Wilt reappear in *The Wilt Alternative*, which embroils the hero with international terrorists who mount a siege in his house. Wilt's murderously maternal wife Eva makes a notable comic appearance in this novel. *Wilt on High* (which brings in Greenham Common-style peace protesters) suggests that a whole saga may evolve around the misadventures of Sharpe's most likeable hero.

The Great Pursuit returns to the high Cambridge of *Porterhouse Blue*. The title plays on the titles of Cambridge critic F.R. Leavis's best known works. And Sharpe's novel is a jaundiced burlesque on the Leavisite disdain for merely popular literature. The story has a female don of austere critical rectitude who clandestinely writes pulp romance. An ingenuous acolyte, Peter Piper, is manipulated into fronting for her and undertakes an American promotional tour. Cantabrigian snobbishness and transatlantic vulgarity are comically opposed, with the usual fiendish plot complications.

The Throwback is a routine Sharpe comedy on the British rural gentry, and their inextinguishable capacity for survival even among the persecutions of a democratic age and modern world. *Ancestral Vices* has much the same theme. Walden Yapp, an American professor of demotic historiography, is hired to write the family history of the Petrefacts. In their native Vale of Bushampton, he discovers unspeakable sexual horrors underlying their prosperity. *Ancestral Vices* is probably the nastiest of Sharpe's novels, with some incredibly tasteless comedy on the subject of dwarves. But the rule of his fiction is that the more offensive to common decency, the funnier it is. *Vintage Stuff* finds Sharpe in the territory of the English public school. The novel climaxes in a chase across France and a chateau siege. (Chases and sieges recur in many of Sharpe's narratives.) Again, the novel comically testifies to the indestructibility and the simultaneous awfulness of England's upper classes.

The main influence on Sharpe's fiction is clearly early Evelyn Waugh. Unlike the mature Waugh, Sharpe seems still to be waiting for something to believe in, to ballast the otherwise increasingly brittle negativities of his fiction. But for his admirers (they remain almost exclusively cis-Atlantic, incidentally) it is probably enough that he is consistently the most amusing novelist writing.

—John Sutherland

SHEED, Wilfrid (John Joseph). American. Born in London, England, 27 December 1930; emigrated to the United States in 1940. Educated at Downside Academy, Bath; Lincoln College, Oxford, B.A. 1954, M.A. 1957. Married Maria Bullitt Darlington in 1957; three children. Film critic, 1957–61, and associate editor, 1959–66, *Jubilee* magazine, New York; drama critic and book editor, *Commonweal* magazine, New York, 1964–67; film critic, *Esquire* magazine, New York, 1967–69; Visiting Lecturer in Creative Arts, Princeton University, New Jersey, 1970–71; columnist, *New York Times Book Review*, 1971–75. Since 1972, judge, Book-of-the-Month Club. Agent: Lynn Nesbit, International Creative Management, 40 West 57th Street, New York, New York 10019. Address: Rysam and High Streets, Sag Harbor, New York 11963, U.S.A.

PUBLICATIONS

Novels

A Middle Class Education. Boston, Houghton Mifflin, 1960; London, Cassell, 1961.
The Hack. New York, Macmillan, and London, Cassell, 1963.
Square's Progress. New York, Farrar Straus, and London, Cassell, 1965.
Office Politics. New York, Farrar Straus, 1966; London, Cassell, 1967.
Max Jamison. New York, Farrar Straus, 1970; as *The Critic*, London, Weidenfeld and Nicolson, 1970.
People Will Always Be Kind. New York, Farrar Straus, 1973; London, Weidenfeld and Nicolson, 1974.
Transatlantic Blues. New York, Dutton, 1978; London, Sidgwick and Jackson, 1979.

Short Stories

The Blacking Factory, and Pennsylvania Gothic: A Short Novel and a Long Story. New York, Farrar Straus, 1968; London, Weidenfeld and Nicolson, 1969.

Other

Joseph. New York, Sheed and Ward, 1958.
The Morning After (essays). New York, Farrar Straus, 1971.
Three Mobs: Labor, Church and Mafia. New York, Sheed and Ward, 1974.
Muhammad Ali. New York, Crowell, and London, Weidenfeld and Nicolson, 1975.
The Good Word and Other Words (essays). New York, Dutton, 1978; London, Sidgwick and Jackson, 1979.
Clare Boothe Luce. New York, Dutton, and London, Weidenfeld and Nicolson, 1982.
Frank and Maisie: A Memoir with Parents. New York, Simon and Schuster, 1985; London, Chatto and Windus, 1986.

Editor, *Essays and Poems*, by G.K. Chesterton. London, Penguin, 1958.
Editor, *Sixteen Short Novels.* New York, Dutton, 1985.

*   *   *

Wilfrid Sheed is an acute cultural historian, critic, and satirist who has mapped out a special province of Anglo-American life as his own. His novels are polished comedies of manners on highly serious topics: the degeneracy of the "communications industry" in all its forms, the anxiety of Roman Catholics in a secularized society, the profound alienation of individuals who find themselves trapped between two cultures.

Beginning with *A Middle Class Education*, Sheed deals with the failure of both schooling and learning, especially the vaunted British public school and university system, a major target of satire recurring in *The Blacking Factory* and *Transatlantic Blues*. In *The Hack* Sheed combines two favorite subjects—the failure of the Roman Catholic church in the modern world and the variegated follies of modern communications media. The story tracks hapless Bert Flax, a freelance writer grinding out theological pulp for popular religious magazines. *Office Politics* focuses half of this theme on Gilbert Twining, a writer for a struggling popular magazine, in an extended study of self-deception in life and literature.

Behind the vaudevillian comic turns Sheed constructs are serious investigations of alienated, self-divided individuals in a world with little solace or aid. Fred and Alison Cope (who, of course, *can't* cope) in *Square's Progress* try to flee the confines of their middle-class educations and marriage for beat-bohemian-hippy freedoms, only to find the hip life as empty and sharp-cornered as suburbia. *Max Jamison* charts another hack writer's attempts to understand his own unravelling life. Max, a magazine critic, finds himself unable to reconcile his vocation with his desires, although writing criticism has been his life's goal: "The difference between a critic and a reviewer is, I forget. . . . I've always wanted to be a critic. Yes, really. Like wanting to be a dentist or an undertaker. Some kids are funny that way. No, ma'am, I have never wanted to write creatively. I was an unnatural little boy in many ways. The rumor that I used to torture flies probably contains some truth. I did write a poem once, in alexandrines, but I didn't much care for it. Yes, it's in my wallet now."

People Will Always Be Kind observes the anomalies and aberrations of American politics in the early 1970's through a journalistic point of view, a mock-biography of an Irish Catholic presidential candidate feeling profound conflicts between religious, moral, and political realities. The novel is divided between a view of Brian Casey's personal and political life and the ruminations of a political hack writer, Sam Perkins, so Sheed again analyzes the failure of journalism, of writing, to capture the subtleties of life.

In *Transatlantic Blues* Sheed pulls together many early satiric themes. In some ways, the novel inverts and expands the brilliant short novel *The Blacking Factory*, detailing the schizophrenic development of Pendrid "Monty" Chatworth, a TV talk-show host educated in Britain and working in the U.S. Chatworth, a Roman Catholic, dictates the novel in the form of a sprawling mock-confession, a litany of the sins and disasters of his life. The conflicts between a British identity (Pendrid) and an American one (Monty), between high British culture (Oxford) and U.S. popular culture (TV ratings), between Catholicism and secular fame, makes the novel painful as well as comic. Pendrid is another version of the "hack writer," the "office politician," the Anglo-American accepted in neither world, the Catholic who finds no solace in the church and who is rejected by the secular-Protestant culture in which he is immersed.

Sheed's acute ear for both British and American speech (and thought), his ability to parody popular idioms in journalism, his serious questions about education, the content of popular culture, the role of the Roman Catholic church in a secularized society all make him one of the most penetrating satirists of our day. His specific view of the world in which rootlessness, divorce, and flamboyant failure are imposed against the old values of work, stability, marriage, and modest success gives his novels a sharp edge and clarity, the bite of classic satire.

—William J. Schafer

SIGAL, Clancy. American. Born in Chicago, Illinois, 6 September 1926. Educated at the University of California, Los Angeles, B.A. in English 1950. Served in the United States Army Infantry, 1944–46: Staff Sergeant. Assistant to the Wage Coordinator, United Auto Workers, Detroit, 1946–47; story analyst, Columbia Pictures, Hollywood, 1952–54; agent, Jaffe Agency, Los Angeles, 1954–56. Member, Citizens Committee to Defend American Freedoms, Los Angeles, 1953–56, and Group 68, Americans in Britain Against the Indo-China War. Has lived in England since 1957. Recipient: Houghton Mifflin Literary Fellowship, 1962. Agent: Elaine Greene Ltd., 31 Newington Green, London N16 9PU. Address: 58 Willes Road, London N.W.5, England.

PUBLICATIONS

Novels

Weekend in Dinlock. Boston, Houghton Mifflin, and London, Secker and Warburg, 1960.
Going Away: A Report, A Memoir. Boston, Houghton Mifflin, 1962; London, Cape, 1963.
Zone of the Interior. New York, Crowell, 1976.

Uncollected Short Story

"Doctor Marfa," in *Paris Review 35*, Fall 1965.

Play

Radio Play: *A Visit with Rose*, 1983.

*   *   *

Two documentary novels, *Weekend in Dinlock* and *Going Away*, have given Clancy Sigal a large reputation. These novels, imaginative fusions of autobiography, social history and fiction, convey a strong sense of time and place, a powerful feeling of reality.

Going Away (Sigal's first novel, though revised and published after *Weekend in Dinlock*) is subtitled "A Report, A Memoir." It is a compendium of significant social and political observations, an "American Studies" novel answering the question, *"What's it like in America these days?"* The time is 1956, the opening days of the Hungarian Revolt, and the autobiographical narrator drives from Los Angeles to New York with the manuscript of a confessional novel, experiencing a nervous breakdown as he passes through America and

reviews his past. It is an "on-the-road" novel, a pursuit of lost time, a gathering of the narrator's experiences and a diagnosis of America's spiritual and political malaise: "for years, possibly since adolescence, I have dryly and studiously examined the indications of my own life as a clue to the country at large, as though reading a psychic thermometer."

The narrator is half-Irish, half-Jewish, a radical ex-union-organizer, an ex-Hollywood-agent, an ex-soldier in Occupied Germany; by age 29 he has led half a dozen full, complex lives and reached the end of his road in America. He realizes he must leave America in order to find it. He visits old friends and enemies, sees them in despair and collapse, so he flees his dead past encapsulated in an America of brutalizing forces—billboards, highways, movies, the blank, alienating face of capitalist culture.

Once in England, where he finished *Going Away*, Sigal also wrote a much smaller but beautifully articulated study of Yorkshire mines and miners, *Weekend in Dinlock*. A documentary study of a composite mining village in the midlands, the book compares favorably with George Orwell's classic *The Road to Wigan Pier*. It chronicles the miner's life in the nationalized mines and draws almost the same conclusion Orwell made a generation earlier—that mining is an atrocity, a deadening, dehumanizing torment on which all industrial civilization rests. The novel is also the story of Davie, a Lawrence-like young man who is both a gifted painter and a miner, caught between the need to paint, to escape Dinlock, and the powerful *machismo* ethic of the miners which demands that he stay on the job and prove himself at the coal face. Finally, the narrator leaves Davie wrestling with his irresolvable conflict, still trapped by Dinlock.

This brilliant small study is a logical extension of *Going Away*. The narrator has fled America and found in England's coal country yet another world of dehumanizing technology and alienated individuals. The wide-open feeling of crossing America (the loneliness of the land itself) is replaced by the paranoid claustrophobia of the mine shaft and the paranoid closed society of the provincial village. Both novels chronicle the pressures of modern life on the individual, both reflect Sigal's own history: "I was a member, in good standing, of the Double Feature Generation: nothing new was startling to me." Sigal, in *Going Away*, gives the intense, confessional view of the 1950's in the backwash of McCarthyism, the collapse of the old left, and draws conclusions about his own sense of self: "I see no salvation in personal relationships, in political action, or in any job I might undertake in society. Everything in me cries out that we are meaningless pieces of paste; everything in me hopes this is not the end of the story."

Zone of the Interior carries forward Sigal's odyssey into the 1960's, exploring a subculture of artists and dropouts. An R.D. Laing-like protagonist observes the disintegration of culture and personality in British society of the time. The world has gone thoroughly mad, and the personal experience of insanity, first encountered in *Going Away*, seems less scarifying against a background of general disillusionment, drugs, and the cornucopia of therapeutic theories that promise personal salvation in the face of apocalypse.

—William J. Schafer

SILKO, Leslie Marmon. American. Born in 1948. Educated at Board of Indian Affairs schools, Laguna, New Mexico, and a Catholic school in Albuquerque; University of New Mexico, Albuquerque, B.A. in English 1969; studied law briefly. Taught for 2 years at Navajo Community College, Tsaile, Arizona; lived in Ketchikan, Alaska, for 2 years; taught at University of New Mexico. Since 1978, Professor of English, University of Arizona, Tucson. Recipient: National Endowment for the Arts award, 1974. Address: Department of English, University of Arizona, Tucson, Arizona 85721, U.S.A.

PUBLICATIONS

Novel

Ceremony. New York, Viking Press, 1977.

Short Stories

Storyteller (includes verse). New York, Seaver, 1981.

Uncollected Short Stories

"Bravura" and "Humaweepi, The Warrior Priest," in *The Man to Send Rain Clouds: Contemporary Stories by American Indians*, edited by Kenneth Rosen. New York, Viking Press, 1974.
"Laughing and Loving," in *Come to Power*, edited by Dick Lourie. Trumansburg, New York, Crossing Press, 1974.

Play

Lullaby, with Frank Chin, adaptation of the story by Silko (produced San Francisco, 1976).

Verse

Laguna Woman. Greenfield Center, New York, Greenfield Review Press, 1974.

Other

With the Delicacy and Strength of Lace: Letters Between Leslie Marmon Silko and James A. Wright, edited by Annie Wright. St. Paul, Graywolf Press, 1985.

*

Manuscript Collection: University of Arizona, Tucson.

Critical Studies: *Leslie Marmon Silko* by Per Seyersted, Boise, Idaho, Boise State University, 1980; *Four American Indian Literary Masters* by Alan R. Velie, Norman, University of Oklahoma Press, 1982.

*   *   *

Through her works Leslie Marmon Silko has defined herself as an American Indian writer, concentrating on ethnic themes, motifs, and genres. She had already established a minor reputation as a short story writer when she published her novel *Ceremony*, which, along with N. Scott Momaday's *House Made of Dawn*, is one of the two most important novels in modern American Indian literature.

Like the earlier novel, *Ceremony* focuses on a young Indian who, under somewhat similar circumstances, struggles to realign himself with traditional Indian culture and reservation

life after having been torn away. Tayo, Silko's half-Laguna, half-Anglo protagonist, returns to his New Mexico reservation just after World War II. The horrors of the war against the Japanese in the Philippine jungles have led him to the brink of insanity and the mental ward of a veterans hospital. Back home, he is in constant danger of succumbing to mental illness as he faces a sad, apparently hopeless life. His half-breed status among his own people and the legacy of shame from his promiscuous mother, now dead, exacerbate the pain of living among a dispossessed people who are constantly reminded of their lost heritage. He associates with fellow veterans who fill their meaningless lives with alcohol and anecdotes about their sexual exploits among white women during the war, and he observes Indian prostitutes and winos in scenes of skid-row squalor that remind him of his own ruined mother. Guided by Betonie, an old medicine man, Tayo finds a helpmeet in a sort of Indian earth-goddess figure and gradually proceeds through the mystical ceremonies—or rather series of ceremonies or rituals—that will make him whole again, and in the process he outwits the witchcraft of his evil antagonist Emo.

As an American Indian writer, Silko deals with the usual dichotomies: in general, white culture is cruel, artificial, dead, cut off from nature, based on greed; traditional Indian culture is holistic, natural, communal. Silko is by no means simple-minded in working within this framework of values. She is a close observer of both nature and human nature, and, in particular, she handles her male protagonist well. She is also a craftsman who writes her novel with the same meticulous care that she takes with her short stories.

Aside from providing her with distinctive materials for her fiction, her particular cultural heritage is useful in an important way. Like many contemporary writers, Silko experiments with the narrative line, weaving in and out of chronological time as she explores the consciousness of her protagonist. However, her habitual use of what she takes to be the Indian concept of reality—or at least one's experience of reality—as narrative (or myth) helps her to avoid the morbid extremes of self-consciousness that can result from an analysis of the narrative process. She begins *Ceremony* with a description of Thought-Woman, the spider, "sitting in her room/thinking of a story now/I'm telling you the story she is thinking."

Storyteller, an anthology of tribal folk tales, short stories, family anecdotes, photographs, and poems, continues her fascination with storytelling. It also reminds the reader of her slender output, since it contains poems and bits of prose which had been incorporated into *Ceremony*, just as materials from her earlier short stories had been worked into the novel. *Storyteller*, as a family photo album, is self-indulgent. Several of the Laguna fables inherited from her family are charming, however, and in a manner that does not rely on sentimentality or mere picturesqueness. Some of the verse forms that she employs in her narratives lack the artistry of her prose, although they may be intended to capture something of the rhythms of the Indian originals. Interestingly, the title story, which is probably the most successful prose piece in the collection, is set not in her native southwest, as is most of her other work, but in Alaska, where she lived and worked for a time. It is about a girl who lives with an old Eskimo man, a storyteller who seems to live only to extend his extraordinary, seemingly endless narrative, and it illustrates the destructive effects of the Gussucks (whites) on the native society.

This last work reinforces the impression that Silko is interested in developing more than a personal, tribal, or even regional identity as a writer. She is an *Indian* writer, and although she is not particularly prolific, she has already established herself as an important figure in American Indian literature. As such, she writes for two audiences: the small group of readers who identify with her ethnic background and share her Indian sensibilities, and the general readers who, regardless of their sympathy for Indian problems and concerns, find her works somewhat exotic. Indeed, their exoticness provides a large part of their appeal. Since the image of the Indian has always been problematic in American culture—with strong tendencies toward the mythic, either "Devil" or "Noble Savage"—Silko, like other writers in her position, must be wary of appealing to easy sentimentality or other conventional responses. Her success as a writer has been largely due to her ability to deal convincingly with Indian traditions and myth while recognizing the demands of psychological realism and exercising a strict control over her narrative art.

—Clinton Machann

SILLITOE, Alan. British. Born in Nottingham, 4 March 1928. Educated in Nottingham schools until 1942. Served as a wireless operator in the Royal Air Force, 1946–49. Married the writer Ruth Fainlight in 1959; one son and one daughter. Factory worker, 1942–45; air control assistant, Langar Aerodrome, Nottinghamshire, 1945–46; lived in France and Spain, 1952–58. Recipient: Authors Club prize, 1958; Hawthornden Prize, 1960. Fellow, Royal Geographical Society, 1975; Honorary Fellow, Manchester Polytechnic, 1977. Agent: Tessa Sayle Agency, 11 Jubilee Place, London SW3 3TE. Address: 21 The Street, Wittersham, Kent, England.

PUBLICATIONS

Novels

Saturday Night and Sunday Morning. London, W.H. Allen, 1958; New York, Knopf, 1959.
The General. London, W.H. Allen, 1960; New York, Knopf, 1961; as *Counterpoint*, New York, Avon, 1968.
Key to the Door. London, W.H. Allen, 1961; New York, Knopf, 1962.
The Death of William Posters. London, W.H. Allen, and New York, Knopf, 1965.
A Tree on Fire. London, Macmillan, 1967; New York, Doubleday, 1968.
A Start in Life. London, W.H. Allen, 1970; New York, Scribner, 1971.
Travels in Nihilon. London, W.H. Allen, 1971; New York, Scribner, 1972.
Raw Material. London, W.H. Allen, 1972; New York, Scribner, 1973; revised edition, W.H. Allen, 1978.
The Flame of Life. London, W.H. Allen, 1974.
The Widower's Son. London, W.H. Allen, 1976; New York, Harper, 1977.
The Storyteller. London, W.H. Allen, 1979; New York, Simon and Schuster, 1980.
Her Victory. London, Granada, and New York, Watts, 1982.
The Lost Flying Boat. London, Granada, 1983; Boston, Little Brown, 1984.
Down from the Hill. London, Granada, 1984.
Life Goes On. London, Grafton, 1985.

Short Stories

The Loneliness of the Long-Distance Runner. London, W.H. Allen, 1959; New York, Knopf, 1960.
The Ragman's Daughter. London, W.H. Allen, 1963; New York, Knopf, 1964.
A Sillitoe Selection, edited by Michael Marland. London, Longman, 1968.
Guzman Go Home. London, Macmillan, 1968; New York, Doubleday, 1969.
Men, Women, and Children. London, W.H. Allen, 1973; New York, Scribner, 1974.
Down to the Bone (selection). Exeter, Wheaton, 1976.
The Second Chance and Other Stories. London, Cape, and New York, Simon and Schuster, 1981.

Uncollected Short Story

"The Insider," in *New Departures* (Oxford), 1960.

Plays

The Ragman's Daughter (produced Felixstowe, Suffolk, 1966).
All Citizens Are Soldiers, with Ruth Fainlight, adaptation of a play by Lope de Vega (produced Stratford upon Avon and London, 1967). London, Macmillan, and Chester Springs, Pennsylvania, Dufour, 1969.
The Slot Machine (as *This Foreign Field*, produced London, 1970). Included in *Three Plays*, 1978.
Pit Strike (televised, 1977). Included in *Three Plays*, 1978.
The Interview (produced London, 1978). Included in *Three Plays*, 1978.
Three Plays. London, W.H. Allen, 1978.

Screenplays: *Saturday Night and Sunday Morning*, 1960; *The Loneliness of the Long Distance Runner*, 1961; *The Ragman's Daughter*, 1974.

Radio Play: *The General*, from his own novel, 1984.

Television Play: *Pit Strike*, 1977.

Verse

Without Beer or Bread. London, Outposts, 1957.
The Rats and Other Poems. London, W.H. Allen, 1960.
A Falling Out of Love and Other Poems. London, W.H. Allen, 1964.
Love in the Environs of Voronezh and Other Poems. London, Macmillan, 1968; New York, Doubleday, 1970.
Shaman and Other Poems. London, Turret, 1968.
Poems, with Ted Hughes and Ruth Fainlight. London, Rainbow Press, 1971.
Barbarians and Other Poems. London, Turret, 1974.
Storm: New Poems. London, W.H. Allen, 1974.
Day-Dream Communiqué. Knotting, Bedfordshire, Sceptre Press, 1977.
From "Snow on the North Side of Lucifer." Knotting, Bedfordshire, Sceptre Press, 1979.
Snow on the North Side of Lucifer. London, W.H. Allen, 1979.
More Lucifer. Knotting, Bedfordshire, Booth, 1980.
Sun Before Departure: Poems 1974 to 1982. London, Granada, 1984.
Tides and Stone Walls, photographs by Victor Bowley. London, Grafton, 1986.

Other

Road to Volgograd (travel).   London, W.H. Allen, and New York, Knopf, 1964.
The City Adventures of Marmalade Jim (for children).   London, Macmillan, 1967; revised edition, London, Robson, 1977.
Mountains and Caverns: Selected Essays.   London, W.H. Allen, 1975.
Big John and the Stars (for children).   London, Robson, 1977.
The Incredible Fencing Fleas (for children).   London, Robson, 1978.
Marmalade Jim at the Farm (for children).   London, Robson, 1980.
The Saxon Shore Way: From Gravesend to Rye, photographs by Fay Godwin.   London, Hutchinson, 1983.
Marmalade Jim and the Fox (for children).   London, Robson, 1985.
Nottinghamshire, photographs by David Sillitoe.   London, Grafton, 1986.

Editor, *Poems for Shakespeare 7.*   London, Bear Gardens Museum and Arts Centre, 1979.

*

Critical Studies: *Alan Sillitoe* edited by Michael Marland, London, Times Authors Series, 1970; *Alan Sillitoe* by Allen Richard Penner, New York, Twayne, 1972; *Alan Sillitoe: A Critical Assessment* by Stanley S. Atherton, London, W.H. Allen, 1979.

Alan Sillitoe comments:

As one gets older there is less to say about why one writes, but at the same time there is more to write. The writing also gets more difficult, which is as it should be.

*   *   *

As Alan Sillitoe's fiction developed beyond the self-contained and brilliantly presented world of *Saturday Night and Sunday Morning*, the point of view changed from that of Arthur Seaton, the energetic, unsentimental, and superficially satisfied protagonist of the first novel, to that of his elder brother, Brian, the central figure of *Key to the Door*. Arthur, grateful for the luck involved in the contrast between his current well-paid job at the capstan lathe and his father's life on the dole before the Second World War, is relatively content so long as he can find a plentiful supply of beer and women. Sillitoe, emphasizing his perceptive intransigence in a world that is both hypocritical and hostile, makes him an attractive force. Brian, however, is more intellectual, a man who questions and feels strongly, who, like Frank Dawley, the Midlands working-man in a later trilogy, searches for a more complete life he cannot easily find. Brian is given more background, more development from childhood, than Arthur was, seen in incidents like that in which he saves pennies to buy a copy of *The Count of Monte Cristo*, his impoverished parents furious that he could waste his hard-scrounged money on a book. Part of the difference in these points of view is apparent in the treatment of politics. For Arthur, all political systems are fraudulent rhetoric to cheat the working-man, although he has some sympathy with the Communists because, in England in the 1950's, they are so universally despised or ignored. Brian is interested in Communism as an idea, a possible transformation of the society of privilege. When conscripted after the war and sent to Malaya, Brian considers helping a Communist revolution against the establishment he now inadvertently

represents. Frank Dawley, in *The Death of William Posters* and *A Tree on Fire*, running guns to the FLN in Algeria, aids the Communists directly by ideological choice, although back in England in *The Flame of Life*, the final novel of the trilogy, concerning the death of a comrade in Algeria, he questions the value of his revolutionary commitment.

Although these presentations of the working-class intellectual developing against strong pressures of class and society are more vulnerable to sentimentality or rhetorical rant than is Arthur Seaton's tightly controlled perspective, they are deeper both intellectually and emotionally. Sillitoe's interest in abstract ideas has been evident since his early novel, *The General*, in which the symbols of music (in the form of a symphony orchestra) and mathematics (in the form of the general's focus on precise maps) contrast contradictory attitudes toward the best way of controlling the "primeval slime" of men involved in war. Many later novels are similarly constructed around an idea: *Travels in Nihilon* recounts the adventures of five travelers who go into the corrupt world of nihilism to write a guide-book; *A Start in Life*, in which the metaphors are more literary, follows the picaresque account of a contemporary bastard looking for a social locus; a later novel, *The Lost Flying Boat*, chronicles the disastrous journey of eight former military crewmen to retrieve treasure from the island of Kerguelen in the Indian Ocean near the Antarctic, a metaphor for the actions of a small group of the dedicated and accomplished defeated by the larger, greedier, more amorphous social forces outside. Sillitoe is not always at his best in the novels totally dependent on a single idea or metaphor. *Travels in Nihilon* degenerates into a kind of farcical violence, as if characters from a Marx brothers film are suddenly caught in a James Bond world taken seriously, and *A Start in Life* blends the comic and picaresque techniques of the early John Wain with those of Henry Fielding, without the sense of humor of either. Rather, Sillitoe is most probing and effective in fiction, like *Key to the Door*, *The Death of William Posters*, *The Flame of Life*, *The Widower's Son*, and *Her Victory*, in which the struggle to become intelligent and independent is part of a developing perspective and the ideas part of the attitude toward experience.

In *Key to the Door* Sillitoe depicts effectively the lives of Brian's parents: his mother's childhood as the daughter of a rural blacksmith, his father as the craftsman who slowly decays in an economy of continuous slump between the two World Wars, and the origins of the constant emotional violence and alternations between love and hatred. The background is close to that which Sillitoe gives himself in *Raw Material*, a volume of memoirs that he calls fiction design to get at the truth since "everything written is fiction." *Raw Material* details his family background, the contrast between the simple, explosive blacksmiths, "the poetry," the Burtons, his mother's family, and the dark, sallow, complex, politically rebellious Sillitoes, "the force that pushes" the poetry. Accounts of the personal past are interspersed with and connected to an argument that the social fabric of England was destroyed by the disaster of the First World War, the needless struggle in which the upper classes sent millions to their deaths in order to preserve their own mindless kind of privilege: "Before 1914 a unity could have been possible, and the men might then have tried it. Joining up to fight was, in a sense, their way of saying yes, but the old men used this affirmation to try and finish them off." This view of history provides a combination of intensity and a social dimension that are consistent and cogently argued in all Sillitoe's fiction. This sense of a social past, behind descriptions like that of the Nottingham Goose Fair in *Saturday Night and Sunday Morning*, the grubby night lights and

Nottingham music hall in the 1920's in *Key to the Door*, the 1972 miner's strike in "Pit Strike" (as well as descriptions in "Before Snow Comes" and "The Chiker," other stories published in *Men, Women, and Children*), and the rural Lincolnshire where Albert Handley, Frank Dawley's friend, begins, the proletarian painter, begins, gives Sillitoe's prose a violent energy, a hard explosive quality. His speculations about the complicated nature of fiction are also dramatized in *The Storyteller*, a novel in which a poor Nottingham boy escapes schoolyard beatings by telling stories, an art he develops into a career as storyteller in pubs. As his stories increasingly mix with his own life, the art of fiction is seen reflexively as both destroying and creating its maker.

In all Sillitoe's fiction, the world is seen as a jungle. Yet the nature of the jungle changes. In the earliest fiction, like *Saturday Night and Sunday Morning* and "The Loneliness of the Long Distance Runner," society and the exterior world are jungles in which the protagonist, himself neutral, must survive through a combination of luck and shrewd skill. But, starting with *Key to the Door*, the jungle is both the exterior worlds of Nottingham and Malaya and the questions, uncertainties, false starts, and violence within the protagonist himself. Brian has internalized all the casual violence in his background, and, unlike Arthur, cannot relegate it to a cheerful acceptance of a Saturday night punch-up. Brian begins the recognition that brutality, although endemic, can be overcome, that violence is not the "key to the door," a recognition developed further in the character of Frank Dawley through the three novels of the trilogy. In *The Death of William Posters*, chronicling Frank's movement away from his stifling Nottingham world, William Posters is the fictional image of the working-class man, defiant, persecuted, always hounded by society but never finally caught, using violence against others and himself indiscriminately and self-destructively. Frank derives his name from the notices that read "Bill posters will be prosecuted." As Frank tries to move out of Nottingham, then out of England, directing his sense of violence appropriately outward and politically, he attempts to exorcise the image of Posters, leaving it moribund in Nottingham. Yet, in Sillitoe's world, Posters is never finally exorcised. Appearing as a casualty in the First World War and as a figure who casually beats his wife or his children, he is even reincarnated in *The Flame of Life* as an itinerant, pot-smoking youth of the 1970's, Dean William Posters, who runs off with Albert Handley's wife, just one of the gestures of irrationality and violence that destroys the community Albert and Frank Dawley have tried to establish. The theme of brutality, in Sillitoe's world, is also treated in its rationalized and institutionalized version, the military. Although many of the working-class characters deride the military and none is patriotic, Sillitoe demonstrates, particularly in an excellent novel, *The Widower's Son*, the use of the military career as the conscious focus for working out all the stresses of the individual and social jungles within modern man. Although unable finally to justify his interest in gunnery or the parallel war of his marriage to a general's daughter, the career soldier, heroic back at Dunkerque, an analogue for an attempted assimilation of class in England, is treated with complexity and sympathy. In the best and most comprehensive of the later novels, *Her Victory*, a Nottingham woman, after twenty years of marriage, leaves her crass, newly successful husband and his three brutal, parasitic brothers. Alone in London, she attempts suicide and is rescued by a former naval man who lives by maps, routines, and carefully calibrated assertions against the jungle and chaos of human emotions. Although their ensuing relationship is stormy, even violent, and is not seen as conclusive or permanent (she is also strongly attracted to a bisexual woman who lives with them), he teaches her some capacity to give her life conscious direction and control while she helps him discover a hitherto unknown partial Jewish identity that leads him to Israel. The military and cartographic are partial measures of human and civilized control.

Although his most effectively articulated details are often those of geography and class, Sillitoe has always felt that the majority of any class is unintelligent and unresponsive. In all his fiction, he frequently refers to "rats," a term that in his long poem called "The Rats," he uses to refer to all the agents of organized religious, political, or industrial society, a category that includes most people. Increasingly in the later fiction, he concentrates attention on the non-rat, the special person (even, as in *The Widower's Son*, the special person within an institution of "rats"), the man who attempts to challenge experience, to achieve something more than might have been expected. The special person is devoted to work, to human dignity, and to exorcising his own brutality and that of others. Yet contemporary society rewards futile, parasitic, or soul-destroying work; England remains, for the most part, the land of William Posters, or that of the greedy capitalist or advertising agency. The special person is always posed against the society, burns with energy, and has roots in a meaningful past. He is, imagistically, "a tree on fire" or "the flame of life," needing to test his specialness in some kind of vital connection with the modern world (the terms of that connection were more political in the 1960's than later). The similarity between Sillitoe's fiction and that of D.H. Lawrence goes deeper than a common origin in the working-classes in and near Nottingham, a capacity to describe the area physically and acutely, and possible imitation in a particular novel, as *The Death of William Posters* particularly resembles *Aaron's Rod*. As Sillitoe's concerns have widened, he has, with similar themes and attitudes, developed an authentically Lawrentian perspective of his own. The two writers are alike in their representation of the complexity of working-class characters (Albert Handley, for example, had a portrait of the Queen in his front hall when he was poor and replaced it with one of Mao Tse-tung when he became rich), in their insistence on the need to recognize violence and brutality in human experience, in their incipient romanticism, in their essays about work, in their constantly restless thoughtfulness, in their slow recognition of the need for the special person to get away from England (although this is never, finally, a panacea), and even in their occasional reduction of and lack of sympathy for middle-class characters. Sillitoe lacks Lawrence's ease with theoretical and metaphysical argument, for which he is likely to substitute charts, calibrations, and equations. But both writers share a restless energy, probing and serious, as well as a social and historical range, that make possible the creation of unique and effective fiction.

—James Gindin

SINCLAIR, Andrew (Annandale). British. Born in Oxford, 21 January 1935. Educated at the Dragon School, Oxford; Eton College (King's Scholar), 1948–53; Trinity College, Cambridge, 1955–58, B.A. (double 1st) in history, 1958; Churchill College, Cambridge, Ph.D. in American history 1962. Served in the Coldstream Guards, 1953–55: Ensign. Married 1) Marianne Alexandre in 1960 (divorced), one son; 2) Miranda Seymour in 1972 (divorced, 1984), one son; 3) Sonia Lady Melchett in 1984. Harkness Fellow, Harvard University, Cambridge, Massachusetts, and Columbia University, New York, 1959–61;

Fellow and Director of Historical Studies, Churchill College, Cambridge, 1961–63; Fellow, American Council of Learned Societies, 1963–64; Lecturer in American History, University College, London, 1965–67; Managing Director, Lorrimer Publishing Ltd., London, 1967–84, and Timon Films, 1969–84. Recipient: Maugham Award, 1967. Fellow, Royal Society of Literature, 1973; Fellow, Society of American Historians, 1973. Address: 16 Tite Street, London SW3 4HZ, England.

PUBLICATIONS

Novels

The Breaking of Bumbo. London, Faber, and New York, Simon and Schuster, 1959.
My Friend Judas. London, Faber, 1959; New York, Simon and Schuster, 1961.
The Project. London, Faber, and New York, Simon and Schuster, 1960.
The Hallelujah Bum. London, Faber, 1963; as *The Paradise Bum*, New York, Atheneum, 1963.
The Raker. London, Cape, and New York, Atheneum, 1964.
Gog. London, Weidenfeld and Nicolson, and New York, Macmillan, 1967.
Magog. London, Weidenfeld and Nicolson, and New York, Harper, 1972.
The Surrey Cat. London, Joseph, 1976; as *Cat*, London, Sphere, 1977.
A Patriot for Hire. London, Joseph, 1978.
The Facts in the Case of E.A. Poe. London, Weidenfeld and Nicolson, 1979; New York, Holt Rinehart, 1980.
Beau Bumbo. London, Weidenfeld and Nicolson, 1985.

Uncollected Short Stories

"To Kill a Loris," in *Texas Quarterly* (Austin), Autumn 1961.
"A Head for Monsieur Dimanche," in *Atlantic* (Boston), September 1962.
"The Atomic Band," in *Transatlantic Review 21* (London), Summer 1966.
"Twin," in *The Best of Granta*. London, Secker and Warburg, 1967.

Plays

My Friend Judas (produced London, 1959).
Adventures in the Skin Trade, adaptation of the work by Dylan Thomas (produced London, 1966; Washington, D.C., 1970). London, Dent, 1967; New York, New Directions, 1968.
Under Milk Wood (screenplay). London, Lorrimer, and New York, Simon and Schuster, 1972.
The Blue Angel, adaptation of the screenplay by Josef von Sternberg (produced Liverpool, 1983).

Screenplays: *Before Winter Comes*, 1969; *The Breaking of Bumbo*, 1970; *Under Milk Wood*, 1971.

Television Plays: *The Chocolate Tree*, 1963; *Old Soldiers*, 1964; *Martin Eden*, from the novel by Jack London, 1980.

Other

Prohibition: The Era of Excess. London, Faber, and Boston, Little Brown, 1962; as *Era of Excess*, New York, Harper, 1964.

The Available Man: The Life Behind the Masks of Warren Gamaliel Harding. New York, Macmillan, 1965.
The Better Half: The Emancipation of the American Woman. New York, Harper, 1965; London, Cape, 1966.
A Concise History of the United States. London, Thames and Hudson, and New York, Viking Press, 1967; revised edition, Thames and Hudson, 1970.
The Last of the Best: The Aristocracy of Europe in the Twentieth Century. London, Weidenfeld and Nicolson, and New York, Macmillan, 1969.
Guevara. London, Fontana, and New York, Viking Press, 1970.
Dylan Thomas: Poet of His People. London, Joseph, 1975; as *Dylan Thomas: No Man More Magical*, New York, Holt Rinehart, 1975.
Inkydoo, The Wild Boy (for children). London, Abelard Schuman, 1976; as *Carina and the Wild Boy*, London, Beaver, 1977.
Jack: A Biography of Jack London. New York, Harper, 1977; London, Weidenfeld and Nicolson, 1978.
The Savage: A History of Misunderstanding. London, Weidenfeld and Nicolson, 1977.
John Ford: A Biography. London, Allen and Unwin, and New York, Dial Press, 1979.
Corsair: The Life of J. Pierpont Morgan. London, Weidenfeld and Nicolson, and Boston, Little Brown, 1981.
The Other Victoria: The Princess Royal and the Great Game of Europe. London, Weidenfeld and Nicolson, 1981; as *Royal Web*, New York, McGraw Hill, 1982.
Sir Walter Raleigh and the Age of Discovery. London, Penguin, 1984.

Editor, *GWTW* [Gone with the Wind]*: The Screenplay*, by Sidney Howard. London, Lorrimer, 1979.
Editor, *The Call of the Wild, White Fang, and Other Stories*, by Jack London. London, Penguin, 1981.

Translator, *Selections from the Greek Anthology*. London, Weidenfeld and Nicolson, 1967; New York, Macmillan, 1968.
Translator, with Carlos P. Hansen, *Bolivian Diary: Ernesto "Che" Guevara*. London, Lorrimer, 1968.
Translator, with Marianne Alexandre, *La Grande Illusion* (scenario), by Jean Renoir. London, Lorrimer, 1968.

*

Critical Study: *Old Lines, New Forces* edited by Robert K. Morris, Rutherford, New Jersey, Fairleigh Dickinson University Press, 1976.

Theatrical Activities:
Director: **Films**—*The Breaking of Bumbo*, 1970; *Under Milk Wood*, 1971.

Andrew Sinclair comments:
    I work between fact and fiction: history and biography, the novel and film. The one informs the other without confusion, I hope. Aging, I find myself admiring professionals, not philosophers. Like the Victorians I have found liberty in writing and in not working for wages. Freedom is having four jobs—and only on hire. Before I die I would like to make one more good film, complete *Gog* and *Magog* with *King Ludd*, and write a trilogy on my Scots roots. That would be quite enough.

*   *   *

From the beginning Andrew Sinclair established himself as a writer of extraordinary fluency and copiousness, whether in fiction or in American social history. His early novels were light-hearted attempts to capture significant moments in the life of the 1950's: the misadventures of a young National Service officer in the Brigade of Guards in *The Breaking of Bumbo* (later adventures are recounted in *Beau Bumbo*), or life in Cambridge when traditional academic forms were coming apart at the seams in *My Friend Judas*. Sinclair's awareness of social nuance and his ready ear for changing forms of speech made him an effective observer, though at the cost of making these novels soon seem dated. *The Project* was a deliberate attempt to move to new ground—the moral fable and apocalyptic science fiction—but the result was wooden and contrived. In *The Hallelujah Bum* Sinclair returned to Ben Birt, the cheerfully iconoclastic hero of *My Friend Judas*, and thrust him into a thin but fast-moving narrative about driving across the United States in a stolen car. The book was partly a loving evocation of American landscape, and partly an example of a new fictional genre that emerged in the 1960's which showed the impact of America on a visiting Englishman.

Sinclair's next novel, *The Raker*, was a fresh endeavour to get away from the fictional recreation of personal experience, though it was still a projection of personal obsession, in this case what Sinclair has described as a preoccupation with death. *The Raker* is, if anything, too nakedly allegorical, with a strong flavour of Gothic fantasy about it. But it brings together the separate vision of the novelist and the historian, and it is most powerful in its superimposition of the plague-ridden London of the 17th century on the modern metropolis. The preoccupation with history and myth in *The Raker* was fully worked out in *Gog*, which is Sinclair's one outstanding contribution so far to contemporary fiction, compared with which he dismisses his previous five novels as no more than "experiments in style." "Gog" is a legendary giant of British mythology, personified in the novel by an enormous naked man washed up on the Scottish coast in the summer of 1945. The book is essentially a long picaresque account of his walk to London to claim his inheritance as a representative of the British people. On the way he has many fantastic adventures, some comic, some cruel, but all reflecting Sinclair's extraordinary imaginative exuberance. The journey takes him to many sacred places, such as York Minster, Glastonbury, and Stonehenge, and on one level the story is an exploration of the multi-layered past of England, almost like the excavation of an archaeological site. The richness of content is matched by a great variety of formal device: *Gog* draws on the techniques of the comic strip and the cinema, as well as those of the novel. It may, though, be an isolated achievement. *Magog*, its sequel, which describes the life and times of Gog's villainous brother in postwar England, is much less interesting. Although an intelligent, inventive and entertaining piece of social satire, it has little of *Gog*'s mythic power.

—Bernard Bergonzi

SINCLAIR, Jo. Pseudonym for Ruth Seid. American. Born in Brooklyn, New York, 1 July 1913. Educated at John Hay High School, Cleveland; attended night classes in playwriting, Western Reserve University, Cleveland. Has worked in a factory, in advertising, as a ghost-writer and trade magazine writer, and for the Works Progress Administration (WPA).

Assistant Director, Publicity and Promotion, American Red Cross, Cleveland, 1942–46. Since 1946, free-lance writer. Recipient: Harper prize, 1946; Daroff Memorial Award, 1956; National Conference of Christians and Jews Brotherhood Award, 1956; Fund for the Republic prize, 1956; Wolpaw playwriting grant, 1969. Address: 1021 Wellington Road, Jenkintown, Pennsylvania 19046, U.S.A.

PUBLICATIONS

Novels

Wasteland. New York, Harper, 1946; London, Macmillan, 1948.
Sing at My Wake. New York, McGraw Hill, 1951.
The Changelings. New York, McGraw Hill, 1955.
Anna Teller. New York, McKay, 1960; London, W.H. Allen, 1961.

Uncollected Short Stories

"Children at Play," in *Theme and Variation in the Short Story*, edited by John de Lancey Ferguson and others. New York, Cordon, 1938.
"Red Necktie," in *America in Literature*, edited by Termaine McDowell. New York, Crofts, 1944.
"I Was on Relief," in *Social Insight Through Short Stories*, edited by Josephine Strode. New York, Harper, 1946.
"The Brothers," in *Cross Section 1947*, edited by Edwin Seaver. New York, Fischer, 1947.
"Listen to My Heart," in *Common Ground* (New York), vol. 8, no. 3, 1948.
"Night Time," in *Accent* (Urbana, Illinois), vol. 10, no. 4, 1950.
"The Family," in *Accent* (Urbana, Illinois), vol. 12, no. 2, 1952.
"Night and the General," in *Epoch* (Ithaca, New York), vol. 4, no. 2, 1952.
"Curtain at Midnight," in *Saturday Evening Post* (Philadelphia), 15 November 1952.
"The Boy Who Stole Pennies," in *American Magazine* (Springfield, Ohio), December 1953.
"I Choose You," in *Collier's* (Springfield, Ohio), 23 July 1954.
"Night Club Baby," in *Cosmopolitan* (New York), February 1957.
"The Medal," in *The American Judaism Reader*, edited by Paul Kresh. New York, Abelard Schuman, 1967.

Play

The Long Moment (produced Cleveland, 1951; New York, 1952).

*

Manuscript Collection: Mugar Memorial Library, Boston University.

Jo Sinclair comments:

I write because I have to; it's the only meaning I have discovered for my life. Writing is extremely hard for me, and yet nothing else draws me as a profession. I am particularly interested in the psychological aspects of man, woman, and child; in the impact of race and religion on people; and the enormous influence of love and hope on anybody and everybody.

I'd add this: Writer, get yourself a trade, profession, or job—and write, if you must, weekends and holidays. It's no fun to earn little or no money—even on what you consider in your heart a good book. The writer, at least in the United States, needs either a weekly salary or a patron of the arts!

*   *   *

It's not easy to remember when even enlightened people were fearful of consulting a psychiatrist lest they be considered insane or immoral. Now that seeing a "shrink" is almost as casual as going to a dentist, most of the novels which aided and abetted the shift in public opinion toward psychotherapy seem dated. The struggle to survive as reflected in contemporary fiction subsumes without fanfare psychic conflicts that were once daringly controversial.

Jo Sinclair's early fame and fortune were functions of her talent, tenacity, and timing. Back in 1946, alienated by fear and shyness from sources of help, we were ready for *Wasteland*, Jo Sinclair's first and still best-known novel. Winner of the Harper Prize, as well as enthusiastic critical notices, *Wasteland* gained its author a permanent place in that sometimes fickle sun which shines on successful novelists. It is good to be able to report that Jo Sinclair survived the dangerous aspects of these events. The three novels which followed at intervals of approximately five years were spaced far enough apart clearly to imply the kind of deliberation and concern which results in much revising. Unlike the first work, however, they never caught the same public fancy that boomed *Wasteland*.

From the first flash success in 1946 through *Sing at My Wake*, *The Changelings*, and *Anna Teller*, Sinclair's writing certainly did not deteriorate, but readers' interests moved faster toward more violent resolutions than her reasonable humanity allowed for. Sinclair continues to exhort human beings not to be afraid, urging them to scrutinize their wastelands and to cultivate them if possible. She unflinchingly insisted on noting ghetto problems long before aggressive defenses of minorities had become fashionable. In a real sense she pioneered the so-called Jewish novel, breaking ground for the more sophisticated—but not necessarily more honest—works of Bellow, Malamud, and Roth. Furthermore, Sinclair was virtually the first to focus on the inner conflict in minority identification as amenable to treatment.

Jake, the protagonist of *Wasteland*, was a weakling. He was uncertain of what it meant to be a Jew, anxious and under-potentiated as a man. Supported by his sister's enthusiasm for psychotherapy he finally agreed to consult her psychiatrist. The account of his therapy includes flashbacks and relevant digressions, emphasizing particularly the role played in his life by his sister, Debbie. Jake's progress toward understanding is simply and clearly delineated, and the novel possesses a classical unity that Sinclair's later works perforce lack—as her objectives became more complex. Jake's therapy-trip, piloted by a good and wise doctor, was a bold adventure into an unknown which has only since then been charted—*ad nauseam*.

Sinclair's second novel grew out of the author's concern with another kind of alienation. An insecure woman, trying to adjust to an inadequate marriage, finally settled for the mature love of a son she had helped liberate. The problem is personal, but it takes on meaning in the context of Sinclair's championing of all outsiders. If *Wasteland* is a better novel, it is only because the problem is there limited by the structure implicit in the therapeutic process.

The Changelings is packed with desperate young people—Jews, blacks, and deviants—each of whom feels as if he were "left in a place secretly, instead of the person who's supposed to be there." The one we care most about is an outrageous tomboy, resembling Debbie in the first novel, whose experiments with sex, race relations, and other existential realities, anticipate contemporary liberation movements.

Finally, in *Anna Teller* Sinclair engaged a big subject in the life-story of a 74-year-old woman, who, after fighting in the Hungarian uprisings, fled to America, putative land of freedom. At once bewildered by those aspects of freedom that seemed to her childish, extravagant, and insincere, she eventually, like all Sinclair's protagonists, helped others to transcend the sterility of their wastelands and the bigotries of their ghettos.

—John A. Weigel

SINGER, Isaac Bashevis. American. Born in Radzymin, Poland, 14 July 1904; emigrated to the United States in 1935; became citizen, 1943. Educated at the Tachkemoni Rabbinical Seminary, Warsaw, 1920–22. Married Alma Haimann in 1940; one son from earlier marriage. Proofreader and translator for *Literarishe Bleter*, Warsaw, 1923–33; journalist for the *Jewish Daily Forward*, New York, from 1935. Recipient: Louis Lamed Prize, 1950, 1956; American Academy grant, 1959; Daroff Memorial Award, 1963; Foreign Book Prize (France), 1965; two National Endowment for the Arts grants, 1966; Bancarella Prize, 1968; Brandeis University Creative Arts Award, 1969; National Book Award, for children's literature, 1970, and for fiction, 1974; Nobel Prize for Literature, 1978. D.H.L.: Hebrew Union College, Los Angeles, 1963; D.Lit.: Colgate University, Hamilton, New York, 1972; D.Litt.: Texas Christian University, Fort Worth, 1972; Ph.D.: Hebrew University, Jerusalem, 1973; Litt.D.: Bard College, Annandale-on-Hudson, New York, 1974; Long Island University, Greenvale, New York, 1979. Member, American Academy, 1965; American Academy of Arts and Sciences, 1969; Jewish Academy of Arts and Sciences; Polish Institute of Arts and Sciences. Address: 209 West 86th Street, New York, New York 10024, U.S.A.

PUBLICATIONS

Novels

The Family Moskat, translated by A.H. Gross.   New York, Knopf, 1950; London, Secker and Warburg, 1966.
Satan in Goray, translated by Jacob Sloan.   New York, Farrar Straus, 1955; London, Owen, 1958.
The Magician of Lublin, translated by Elaine Gottlieb and Joseph Singer.   New York, Farrar Straus, 1960; London, Secker and Warburg, 1961.
The Slave, translated by the author and Cecil Hemley.   New York, Farrar Straus, 1962; London, Secker and Warburg, 1963.
The Manor, translated by Elaine Gottlieb and Joseph Singer.   New York, Farrar Straus, 1967; London, Secker and Warburg, 1968.
The Estate, translated by Joseph Singer, Elaine Gottlieb, and Elizabeth Shub.   New York, Farrar Straus, 1969; London, Cape, 1970.
Enemies: A Love Story, translated by Aliza Shevrin and Elizabeth Shub.   New York, Farrar Straus, and London, Cape, 1972.

Shosha, translated by Joseph Singer. New York, Farrar Straus, 1978; London, Cape, 1979.
Reaches of Heaven. New York, Farrar Straus, 1980; London, Faber, 1982.
The Penitent. New York, Farrar Straus, 1983; London, Cape, 1984.

Short Stories

Gimpel the Fool and Other Stories, translated by Saul Bellow and others. New York, Farrar Straus, 1957; London, Owen, 1958.
The Spinoza of Market Street and Other Stories, translated by Elaine Gottlieb and others. New York, Farrar Straus, 1961; London, Secker and Warburg, 1962.
Short Friday and Other Stories, translated by Ruth Whitman and others. New York, Farrar Straus, 1964; London, Secker and Warburg, 1967.
Selected Short Stories, edited by Irving Howe. New York, Modern Library, 1966.
The Séance and Other Stories, translated by Ruth Whitman and others. New York, Farrar Straus, 1968; London, Cape, 1970.
A Friend of Kafka and Other Stories, translated by the author and others. New York, Farrar Straus, 1970; London, Cape, 1972.
A Crown of Feathers and Other Stories, translated by the author and others. New York, Farrar Straus, 1973; London, Cape, 1974.
Passions and Other Stories. New York, Farrar Straus, 1975; London, Cape, 1976.
Old Love. New York, Farrar Straus, 1979; London, Cape, 1980.
The Collected Stories. New York, Farrar Straus, and London, Cape, 1982.
The Image and Other Stories. New York, Farrar Straus, 1985.

Fiction (for children; translated by the author and Elizabeth Shub)

Zlateh the Goat and Other Stories. New York, Harper, 1966; London, Longman, 1970.
Mazel and Shlimazel; or, The Milk of a Lioness. New York, Farrar Straus, 1967; London, Cape, 1979.
The Fearsome Inn. New York, Scribner, 1967; London, Collins, 1970.
When Shlemiel Went to Warsaw and Other Stories, translated by Channah Kleinerman-Goldstein and others. New York, Farrar Straus, 1968; London, Longman, 1974.
Joseph and Koza; or, The Sacrifice to the Vistula. New York, Farrar Straus, 1970; London, Hamish Hamilton, 1984.
Alone in the Wild Forest. New York, Farrar Straus, 1971; Edinburgh, Canongate, 1980.
The Topsy-Turvy Emperor of China. New York, Harper, 1971.
The Fools of Chelm and Their History. New York, Farrar Straus, 1973.
A Tale of Three Wishes. New York, Farrar Straus, 1976.
Naftali the Storyteller and His Horse, Sus, and Other Stories, translated by the author and others. New York, Farrar Straus, 1976; London, Oxford University Press, 1977.
The Power of Light: Eight Stories for Hanukkah. New York, Farrar Straus, 1980; London, Robson, 1983.
The Golem. New York, Farrar Straus, 1982; London, Deutsch, 1983.
Stories for Children. New York, Farrar Straus, 1985.

Plays

The Mirror (produced New Haven, Connecticut, 1973).
Shlemiel the First (produced New Haven, Connecticut, 1974).
Yentl, The Yeshiva Boy, with Leah Napolin, adaptation of a story by Singer (produced New York, 1974). New York, French, 1979.
Teibele and Her Demon, with Eve Friedman (produced Minneapolis, 1978; New York, 1979).

Other (for children; translated by the author and Elizabeth Shub)

A Day of Pleasure: Stories of a Boy Growing Up in Warsaw (autobiographical), translated by Channah Kleinerman-Goldstein and others, photographs by Roman Vishniac. New York, Farrar Straus, 1969; London, MacRae, 1980.
Elijah the Slave: A Hebrew Legend Retold. New York, Farrar Straus, 1970.
The Wicked City. New York, Farrar Straus, 1972.
Why Noah Chose the Dove. New York, Farrar Straus, 1974.

Other

In My Father's Court (autobiography), translated by Channah Kleinerman-Goldstein and others. New York, Farrar Straus, 1966; London, Secker and Warburg, 1967.
An Isaac Bashevis Singer Reader. New York, Farrar Straus, 1971.
The Hasidim: Paintings, Drawings, and Etchings, with Ira Moskowitz. New York, Crown, 1973.
Love and Exile: The Early Years: A Memoir. New York, Doubleday, 1984; London, Cape, 1985.
 A Little Boy in Search of God: Mysticism in a Personal Light, illustrated by Ira Moskowitz. New York, Doubleday, 1976.
 A Young Man in Search of Love, translated by Joseph Singer. New York, Doubleday, 1978.
Lost in America, translated by Joseph Singer. New York, Doubleday, 1981.
Nobel Lecture. New York, Farrar Straus, and London, Cape, 1979.
Isaac Bashevis Singer on Literature and Life: An Interview, with Paul Rosenblatt and Gene Koppel. Tucson, University of Arizona Press, 1979.
Conversations with Isaac Bashevis Singer, with Richard Burgin. New York, Doubleday, 1985.

Editor, with Elaine Gottlieb, *Prism 2.* New York, Twayne, 1965.

Translator, *Roman Rolland*, by Stefan Zweig. Vilna, Kletzkian, 1927.
Translator, *Die Vogler*, by Knut Hamsun. Vilna, Kletzkian, 1929.
Translator, *Victoria*, by Knut Hamsun. Vilna, Kletzkian, 1929.
Translator, *All Quiet on the Western Front*, by Erich Maria Remarque. Vilna, Kletzkian, 1930.
Translator, *Pan*, by Knut Hamsun. Vilna, Kletzkian, 1931.
Translator, *The Way Back*, by Erich Maria Remarque. Vilna, Kletzkian, 1931.
Translator, *The Magic Mountain*, by Thomas Mann. Vilna, Kletzkian, 4 vols., 1932.

Translator, *From Moscow to Jerusalem*, by Leon S. Glaser. New York, Kankowitz, 1938.

*

Bibliography: in *Bulletin of Bibliography* (Boston), January–March, 1969; *A Bibliography of Isaac Bashevis Singer 1924–1949* by David N. Miller, Bern, Switzerland, Lang, 1984.

Manuscript Collection: Butler Library, Columbia University, New York.

Critical Studies (selection): *Isaac Bashevis Singer and the Eternal Past* by Irving Buchen, New York, New York University Press, 1968; *The Achievement of Isaac Bashevis Singer* edited by Marcia Allentuck, Carbondale, Southern Illinois University Press, 1969; *Critical Views of Isaac Bashevis Singer* edited by Irving Malin, New York, New York University Press, 1969, and *Isaac Bashevis Singer* by Malin, New York, Ungar, 1972; *Isaac Bashevis Singer* by Ben Siegel, Minneapolis, University of Minnesota Press, 1969; *Isaac Bashevis Singer and His Art* by Askel Schiotz, New York, Harper, 1970; *Isaac Bashevis Singer, The Magician of the West 86th Street* by Paul Kresh, New York, Dial Press, 1979; *Isaac Bashevis Singer* by Edward Alexander, Boston, Twayne, 1980; *The Brothers Singer* by Clive Sinclair, London, Allison and Busby, 1983; *Fear of Fiction: Narrative Strategies in the Works of Isaac Bashevis Singer* by David N. Miller, Albany, State University of New York Press, 1985.

Isaac Bashevis Singer comments:

I believe in story telling and dislike commentary by the author. The events must speak for themselves. A fiction writer who tries to explain his story from a psychological or sociological point of view destroys his chances to endure. I expressed this idea with the words: Events never become stale; commentary is stale from the very beginning. Commentary has almost destroyed the literature of our present century.

*   *   *

Better known for his short stories and tales than for his longer fiction, Isaac Bashevis Singer's novels nevertheless represent his most considerable accomplishment as a writer. He began writing in Yiddish before he left Warsaw, where *Satan in Goray* and his earliest stories were written, but although he has lived in the United States for fifty years, he still composes in his native language, which is then translated into English. Even in English the rhythms and pungency of the original come through, and he has taken an increasingly greater role in the translations himself. Similarly, though many of his characters are Polish Jews living within the Pale, in recent years he has turned more and more to those Jews and others who have left Europe and found a home—if it can be called that—in New York City or elsewhere.

For many of his major characters are in a radical sense displaced, deracinated. This is clearest, perhaps, in the situation of Herman Broder, the protagonist of *Enemies: A Love Story*. A survivor of the Holocaust, he lives in Brooklyn with Yadwiga, the Polish peasant woman who saved his life by hiding him in a barn for three years during the Nazi occupation. His

wife and children, from whom he had already been separated, were killed, he believes, and in gratitude for saving him he took Yadwiga along to the States. He pretends to be a book salesman who needs to travel to distant cities (actually, he is the ghostwriter for a busy American rabbi); the subterfuge is to help him spend several days a week with his mistress, Masha Tortshiner, another victim of the Holocaust, and her pious mother, Shifrah Puah. Masha has long lived apart from her husband Leon, who refuses to give her a divorce until, believing herself pregnant by Herman, she finally gets his consent. She pays a price for this concession, and when Leon seeks Herman out to tell him about it, Herman refuses for a while to have anything more to do with Masha. Meanwhile, Herman's first wife, the still beautiful but embittered Tamara, turns up. Shot by the Nazis, she managed to escape death and eventually make her way to America after years of turmoil and deprivation.

This plot outline appears almost like the ingredients of a bedroom farce, but *Enemies: A Love Story* is far removed from that genre. The three women in Herman Broder's life are manifestations, rather, of the complex entanglements human beings fall into when they are unable to reconcile the conflicting claims of their moral sensibilities and passionate desires. Broder feels a different obligation to each one of the women he loves or has loved, and a different kind of attraction. To Yadwiga, he owes his life; despite her growing suspicions of his infidelity, she remains absolutely devoted to him, wants to become Jewish and bear his child. Masha, for all her neuroses, holds a powerful fascination that is more than sexual for Broder—it is partly masochistic and partly, through her mother, an attachment to the old ways he has not entirely renounced. Tamara is the women who has been and, after their poignant reunion, is closest to him and understands him best. But none of these women is finally able to assuage the torments that beset someone who, having long ago lost his faith, is unable to find anything in the modern world to take its place.

That is the predicament of many of Singer's major characters. Brought up in an environment of strict religious observation, typically the offspring of devout rabbis or Hassidim, their belief in the deity has been weakened or abandoned but not so completely that they cannot remember what it was or remains for others near or dear to them. This, for example, is Ezriel Babad's problem in *The Manor*, Singer's sprawling, two-part historical novel set in late 19th-century Russian Poland. Son of a rabbi, he chooses to become a doctor, no longer retains the faith of his fathers, and—as an enlightened Jew—scorns many of the religious practices and superstitions of his wife, Shaindel. When he falls in love with Olga, a widow with two children who becomes his mistress, he finds he cannot leave his wife, who has borne his children, is utterly dependent upon him, and whose father has supported his studies and helped him to become what he is. Others in the novel, like Ezriel's sister, Mirale, seek in radical socialism or in human relationships alternatives to the traditions of their forebears, but with little or no success. Calman Jacoby, the patriarchal figure who dominates the first volume of the novel, becomes very wealthy and respected as an entrepreneur and businessman, only to find everything turning to ashes in his mouth, first when one of his daughters elopes with Count Lucian Jampolski and becomes an apostate, and later when his wife dies and he remarries the attractive but immoral Clara Kaminer.

Even before the Enlightenment, Jews had their problems with faith. Singer dramatizes some of these in his first novel (and one of his best), *Satan in Goray*, which centers on the advent of the false Messiah, Sabbatai Zevi, and his impact upon Jews living within the Polish Pale during the mid-17th century. Victims of Chmielnicki's depredations, these Jews living in the remoter parts of Poland, in small towns or villages like Goray, are ready for the kind of hope a Messiah offers. Singer vividly portrays the customs and folkways of the poor, superstitious people, as they fall prey first to the ravings of Reb Mordecai Joseph, who drives the skeptical Rabbi Benish from Goray, then more disastrously to Reb Gedaliya who, together with the prophetess Rechele, captivates the townspeople and leads them into all manner of depravity. At the end, after the apostasy of Sabbatai Zevi, Reb Gedaliya is exposed for what he truly is, and a *dybbuk* enters Rechele's body and torments her until it is finally exorcised by the now repentant and reformed Reb Mordecai Joseph.

By the eve of World War II, many of the beliefs and customs of an earlier time persisted, and many Polish Jews remained devout despite the increasing threat of a virulent anti-Semitism that would surpass even Chmielnicki's depredations. Some, like Aaron Greidinger in *Shosha*, had given up the Orthodox observances in which, as a rabbi's son, he had been reared and sought in contemporary life and literature (Aaron is an aspiring writer) to find an alternative kind of life. But despite close ties to people like the intellectual Morris Feitelzohn or Haiml and Celia Chentshiner, Aaron, or "Tsutsik," as they affectionately nickname him, cannot utterly forget or forsake his traditions. These are intimately bound up in the person of his childhood playmate, Shosha, whom he has not seen in many years. He rediscovers her, however, while in the company of an alluring but troubled actress, Betty Slonim, for whom he has been commissioned to write a play by her patron and lover, the wealthy American, Sam Dreiman. At one point, Sam and Betty make Aaron an offer it seems impossible for him to refuse—not only money and a career, but a chance to escape from Poland and come to America with them. Despite grave doubts about the wisdom of his choice, Aaron finds his ties to innocent and adoring Shosha—and to what she represents—are stronger than ever. Remaining with her, he alone survives the Holocaust that engulfs the rest, except Haiml, whom Aaron meets after the war in Israel. In their different ways, they have found a kind of peace. But others, like Betty, who had left with Sam before the invasion of Poland and inherited a fortune after he died, cannot find happiness. Suicide, as for Masha, her counterpart in *Enemies*, is her destiny.

Singer is at his best, many critics assert, when he is telling stories about Jews locked in the traditions of their fathers, living lives barely touched (if at all) by contemporary civilization. Without doubt, the stories collected in *Gimpel the Fool*, *Short Friday*, or *The Spinoza of Market Street* are superb. In them Singer's imagination seems to take flight more readily and quickly, soaring to realms where fantasy and mundane reality meet and intermingle in ways that astonish earth-bound literalmindedness. In "The Gentleman from Cracow," for example, Singer tells a tale that can be interpreted allegorically on the theme of the wages of sin and the value of repentance. But its power derives much more directly from the striking representations of the Devil (in his ancient disguise of evil-seeming-fair) and of his consort, Lilith. In Singer's hands, these characterizations seize the reader's own imagination swiftly and surely, compelling assent before the rational intellect has a chance to challenge their validity. If Singer excels in such short "bursts and flares" of imagination, his less extravagant tales, like "Teibele and Her Demon" or "Guests on a Winter Night," also successfully mingle the ordinary and the wonderful, though in more homely and poignant fashion. But Singer's other achievements, especially those in the novel, must not be slighted. They as much as his stories earned him the well-deserved Nobel Prize for literature in 1978.

—Jay L. Halio

SINGH, Khushwant. Indian. Born in Hadali, India (now Pakistan) 2 February 1915. Educated at the Modern School, New Delhi; St. Stephen's College, New Delhi; Government College, Lahore, B.A. 1934; King's College, London, LL.B. 1938; called to the Bar, Inner Temple, London, 1938. Married Kaval Malik in 1939; one son and one daughter. Practising lawyer, High Court, Lahore, 1939–47; press attaché, Indian Foreign Service, in London and Ottawa, 1947–51; member of the staff of the Department of Mass Communications, Unesco, Paris, 1954–56; editor, *Yejna*, an Indian government publication, New Delhi, 1956–58; Visiting Lecturer, Oxford University, 1965, University of Rochester, New York, 1965, Princeton University, New Jersey, 1967, University of Hawaii, Honolulu, 1967, and Swarthmore College, Pennsylvania, 1969; editor, *Illustrated Weekly of India*, Bombay, 1969–78; editor-in-chief, *National Herald*, New Delhi, 1978–79; chief editor, *New Delhi*, 1979–80; editor-in-chief, *Hindustan Times* and *Contour*, both New Delhi, 1980–83. Since 1980, Member of the Indian Parliament. Head of the Indian Delegation, Manila Writers Conference, 1965. Recipient: Rockefeller grant, 1966; Punjab Government grant, 1970; Mohan Singh award. Padma Bhushan, India, 1974. Address: 49-E Sujan Singh Park, New Delhi 110 003, India.

PUBLICATIONS

Novels

Train to Pakistan. London, Chatto and Windus, 1956; New York, Grove Press, 1961; as *Mano Majra*, Grove Press, 1956.
I Shall Not Hear the Nightingale. New York, Grove Press, 1959; London, Calder, 1961.

Short Stories

The Mark of Vishnu and Other Stories. London, Saturn Press, 1950.
The Voice of God and Other Stories. Bombay, Jaico, 1957.
A Bride for the Sahib and Other Stories. New Delhi, Hind, 1967.
Black Jasmine. Bombay, Jaico, 1971.

Play

Television Documentary: *Third World—Free Press* (also presenter; *Third Eye* series), 1982 (UK).

Other

The Sikhs. London, Allen and Unwin, and New York, Macmillan, 1953.
The Unending Trail. New Delhi, Rajkamal, 1957.
The Sikhs Today: Their Religion, History, Culture, Customs, and Way of Life. Bombay, Orient Longman, 1959; revised edition, 1964; revised edition, New Delhi, Sangam, 1976.
Fall of the Kingdom of the Punjab. Bombay, Orient Longman, 1962.

A History of the Sikhs 1469–1964.   Princeton, New Jersey, Princeton University Press, and London, Oxford University Press, 2 vols., 1963–66.

Ranjit Singh: Maharajah of the Punjab 1780–1839.   London, Allen and Unwin, 1963.

Not Wanted in Pakistan.   New Delhi, Rajkamal, 1965.

Ghadar, 1915: India's First Armed Revolution, with Satindra Singh.   New Delhi, R and K, 1966.

Homage to Guru Gobind Singh, with Suneet Veer Singh.   Bombay, Jaico, 1966.

Shri Ram: A Biography, with Arun Joshi.   London, Asia Publishing, 1968.

Religion of the Sikhs (lecture).   Madras, University of Madras, 1968.

Khushwant Singh's India: A Mirror for Its Monsters and Monstrosities.   Bombay, India Book House, 1969.

Khushwant Singh's View of India (lectures), edited by Rahul Singh.   Bombay, India Book House, 1974.

Khushwant Singh on War and Peace in India, Pakistan, and Bangladesh, edited by Mala Singh.   New Delhi, Hind, 1976.

Good People, Bad People, edited by Rahul Singh.   New Delhi, Orient, 1977.

Khushwant Singh's India Without Humbug, edited by Rahul Singh.   Bombay, India Book House, 1977.

Around the World with Khushwant Singh, edited by Rahul Singh.   New Delhi, Orient, 1978.

Indira Gandhi Returns.   New Delhi, Vision, 1979.

Editor's Page, edited by Rahul Singh.   Bombay, India Book House, 1981.

We Indians.   New Delhi, Orient, 1982.

Delhi: A Portrait.   New Delhi and Oxford, Oxford University Press, 1983.

The Sikhs, photographs by Raghu Rai.   Benares, Lustre Press, 1984.

Punjab Tragedy, with Kuldip Nayar.   New Delhi, Vision, 1984.

Editor, with Peter Russell, *A Note . . . on G.V. Desani's "All about H. Hatterr" and "Hali."*   London and Amsterdam, Szeben, 1952.

Editor, with Jaya Thadani, *Land of the Five Rivers: Stories of the Punjab*.   Bombay, Jaico, 1965.

Editor, *Sunset of the Sikh Empire*, by Sita Ram Kohli.   Bombay, Orient Longman, 1967.

Editor, *I Believe*.   New Delhi, Hind, 1971.

Editor, *Love and Friendship*.   New Delhi, Sterling, 1974.

Editor, with Qurratulain Hyder, *Stories from India*.   New Delhi, Sterling, 1974.

Editor, *Gurus, Godmen, and Good People*.   Bombay, Orient Longman, 1975.

Translator, *Jupji: The Sikh Morning Prayer*.   London, Probsthain, 1959.

Translator, with M.A. Husain, *Umrao Jan Ada: Courtesan of Lucknow*, by Mohammed Ruswa.   Bombay, Orient Longman, 1961.

Translator, *The Skeleton and Other Writings*, by Amrita Pritam.   Bombay, Jaico, 1964.

Translator, *I Take This Woman*, by Rajinder Singh Bedi.   New Delhi, Hind, 1967.

Translator, *Hymns of Guru Nanak*.   Bombay, Orient Longman, 1969.

Translator, *Dreams in Debris: A Collection of Punjabi Short Stories*, by Satindra Singh.   Bombay, Jaico, 1972.

Translator, with others, *Sacred Writings of the Sikhs*.   London, Allen and Unwin, 1974.

Translator, with others, *Come Back, My Master, and Other Stories*, by K.S. Duggal.   New Delhi, Bell, 1978.

Translator, *Shikwa and Jawab-i-Shikwa/Complaint and Answer: Iqbal's Dialogue with Allah*.   New Delhi and Oxford, Oxford University Press, 1981.

*

Critical Study: *Khushwant Singh* by V.A. Shahane, New York, Twayne, 1972.

*   *   *

Although Khushwant Singh is a distinguished Sikh historian, his reputation as a fiction writer rests solely upon *Train to Pakistan*, a harrowing tale of events along the borders of the newly divided nations of India and Pakistan in the summer of 1947.

The atrocities that accompanied the division of these nations had an enormously depressing effect on a world that had just fought a long, bitter war to defeat practitioners of genocide. The somewhat artificial division of the subcontinent (the boundaries remain in dispute) had been strictly along religious lines: Pakistan was to be a nation of Moslems; India, of Hindus, Sikhs, and what Singh calls "pseudo Christians." There were, however, colonies of non-coreligionists left within each nation. Rather than settle down to peaceful coexistence or permit a passive exchange of populations, partisans on both sides set out on a violent campaign of annihilating the communities that were trapped on their ancestral lands beyond friendly borders.

Train to Pakistan is set against a background of this ruthless and senseless mass destruction. This powerful novel derives its title from a squalid border town, where a rail line crosses from India to Pakistan. At first this mixed community of Sikhs and Moslems is undisturbed by the violence that is breaking out elsewhere on the frontier, but inevitably it, too, is caught up in the mass hysteria as ominous "ghost trains" of slain Sikhs begin to arrive in town from across the border. Agitation for reprisals follows when the Moslems of the town are at last rounded up and fanatics urge the Sikhs of the community to kill their former neighbors as the train carrying them to Pakistan passes through town.

Singh's story contrasts the ineffectualness of the educated and ruling classes with the power of the violent and irrational peasants. Early in the story the town's only educated citizen, a Hindu moneylender, is gruesomely murdered by a band of Dacoity (professional bandits). Juggut Singh, a passionate Sikh farmer with a bad record, is suspected of the crime—though he played no part in it—and imprisoned; at the same time, an educated young former Sikh, Iqbal, comes to the community to agitate for a radical cause and is also imprisoned on suspicion of being a Moslem League agent. While these two are off the scene, the unlighted trains with their cargoes of dead begin to roll into town, and the agitation for reprisals begins. Both the young radical and a government commissioner, Hukum Chand, are unable to prevent the vicious plot against the fleeing Moslems from being carried out, and collapse emotionally; but in an extraordinary gesture of self-sacrifice, Juggut Singh—who had been in love with a Moslem girl—foils the plotters and allows the train to roll over his body "on to Pakistan."

Singh's terse fable suggests a profound disillusionment with the power of law, reason, and intellect in the face of elemental human passions. The philosophy that sparked his tale seems to be expressed through the thoughts of Iqbal, the young radical, as he realizes his helplessness and drifts off into a drugged sleep the night of the climactic incident of the train's passing:

"If you look at things as they are ... there does not seem to be a code either of man or God on which one can pattern one's conduct. ... In such circumstances what can you do but cultivate an utter indifference to all values? Nothing matters."

The same disillusioned tone characterizes Singh's second novel, *I Shall Not Hear the Nightingale*, but the rather wooden tale is almost overwhelmed by heavy-handed ironies. The action occurs about five years before that of the earlier novel, at a time when the British are expressing a willingness to get out of India once the Axis nations have been defeated in World War II. Sher Singh, the ambitious but lazy son of a Sikh senior magistrate, cannot decide between two worlds, "the one of security provided by his father ... and the other full of applause that would come to him as the heroic leader of a band of terrorists." His dabblings in terrorism—actually abetted by a cynical young British civil servant—end in the pointless killing of a village leader, who has also been a political spy. Sher is suspected of the murder and imprisoned, but on the advice of his mother (when his father will not speak to him) he refuses to betray his companions. The British release him for lack of evidence, and he is honored as a kind of local hero—seemingly his political future is assured. His father is even honored by the British.

The novel takes a much dimmer view of the human capacity for compassion and self-sacrifice than *Train to Pakistan* (at one point Sher Singh reflects that "for him loyalties were not as important as the ability to get away with the impression of having them"), so that the novel ends not with the kind of thrilling gesture that its predecessor did, but with the obsequious magistrate, Sher Singh's father, sitting in the Britisher's garden observing, "As a famous English poet has said, 'All's well that ends well.'" The title of the book comes from Sher Singh's reply to his mother when she asks, "What will you get if the English leave this country?" He replies lyrically, "Spring will come to our barren land once more ... once more the nightingales will sing." Khushwant Singh evidently thinks not, if the land is to fall into such self-serving hands as Sher Singh's.

His ironic short stories resemble Angus Wilson's and express a similar disillusionment about man's rationality. Singh is a brilliant, sardonic observer of a world undergoing convulsive changes; and his novels provide a unique insight into one of the major political catastrophes of this century. His difficulties in fusing his editorial comments with the action in his stories, however, cause his novels to remain principally dramatized essays.

—Warren French

SIONIL JOSE, F(rancisco). Filipino. Born in Rosales, Pangasinan, 3 December 1924. Educated at the University of Santo Tomas, Manila, Litt.B. 1949. Married Teresita G. Jovellanos in 1949; five sons and two daughters. Staff member, *Commonweal*, Manila, 1947–48; assistant editor, United States Information Agency, U.S. Embassy, Manila, 1948–49; associate editor, 1949–57, and managing editor, 1957–60, Manila *Times Sunday Magazine*, and editor of Manila *Times* annual *Progress*, 1958–60; editor, *Comment* quarterly, Manila, 1956–62; managing editor, *Asia Magazine*, Hong Kong, 1961–62; information officer, Colombo Plan Headquarters, Ceylon, 1962–64; correspondent, *Economist*, London, 1968–69. Since 1965 publisher,

Solidaridad Publishing House, and general manager, Solidaridad Bookshop, since 1966 publisher and editor, *Solidarity* magazine, and since 1967 manager, Solidaridad Galleries, all Manila. Lecturer, Arellano University, 1962, University of the East graduate school, 1968, and De La Salle University, 1984–86, all Manila. Consultant, Department of Agrarian Reform, 1968–79. Founder and National Secretary, PEN Philippine Center, 1958. Recipient: U.S. Department of State Smith-Mundt grant, 1955; Asia Foundation grant, 1960; National Press Club Award, for journalism, 3 times; British Council grant, 1967; Palanca Award, for journalism, 3 times, and for novel, 1981; ASPAC fellowship, 1971; Rockefeller Foundation Bellagio Award, 1979; Cultural Center of the Philippines award, 1979; City of Manila award, 1979; Magsaysay Award, 1980; East–West Center fellowship (Honolulu), 1981; International House of Japan fellowship, 1983. Address: Solidaridad Publishing House, 531 Padre Faura Street, Ermita P.O. Box 3959, Manila, Philippines.

PUBLICATIONS

Novels

The Pretenders. Manila, Solidaridad, 1962.
Tree. Manila, Solidaridad, 1978.
My Brother, My Executioner. Manila, New Day, 1979.
Mass. Amsterdam, Wereldvenster, 1982; Sydney, Allen and Unwin, 1985; as *Mis*, Manila, Solidaridad, 1983.
Po-on. Manila, Solidaridad, 1985.

Short Stories

The Pretenders and Eight Short Stories. Manila, Regal, 1962.
The God Stealer and Other Stories. Manila, Solidaridad, 1968.
Waywaya and Other Short Stories from the Philippines. Hong Kong, Heinemann, 1980.
Two Filipino Women (novellas). Manila, New Day, 1982.
Platinum and Other Stories. Manila, Solidaridad, 1983.

Uncollected Short Stories

"The Chief Mourner" (serial), in *Women's Weekly* (Manila), 11 May–10 July 1953.
"The Balete Tree" (serial), in *Women's Weekly* (Manila), 4 March 1954–6 July 1956.

Other

(*Selected Works*). Moscow, 1977.

Editor, *Equinox 1.* Manila, Solidaridad, 1965.
Editor, *Asian PEN Anthology 1.* Manila, Solidaridad, 1966; New York, Taplinger, 1967.

*   *   *

F. Sionil Jose holds two distinctions in Philippine writing in English, indeed in Philippine writing in general. He is the only writer who has produced a series of novels that constitute an epic imaginative creation of a century of Philippine life, and he is perhaps the most widely known abroad, his writings having been translated into more foreign languages than those of any other Filipino writer.

We are introduced to the early world of Sionil Jose in *Po-on*. The earliest novel in terms of chronology, it is set in the later decades of the 19th century during the decaying years of the Spanish Empire, which still retained some struggling remnants of its colonial civil services, including some manorial lords in the plains of Central Luzon, descendants of the Basque and Spanish–Catalan settlers, served by immigrants from the deep Ilocano country up north. In one scene a Basque grandee comes to the town of Rosales, when the settlement is still unorganized, and designates the limits of his domain with his whip.

After the Philippine revolution, which saw the change of colonial masters from Spanish to American, no significant change occurred in the feudal relations of the agrarian economy. In fact, free trade was instituted between the Philippines and the United States, benefiting the native landowners and their hirelings and the leaders of industry and their subalterns while impoverishing the tenants of the land and the laborers in small-scale industries. Such relationships are examined in *Tree*. Despite all the injustices they suffered during the American colonial regime, when war came in December 1941, the tenants and their leaders decided to fight the Japanese invaders as guerrillas, hoping that at the end of the war they would be afforded improved living conditions.

My Brother, My Executioner occurs at this point in Sionil Jose's epic narrative. It deals with the activities of two half-brothers, one a dispossessed guerrilla. With more than enough property to keep his family in comfort, the bourgeois half-brother can afford to entertain liberal ideas and even consider embracing progressive ways, but his dispossessed half-brother avenges himself by destroying the more fortunate.

The master-servant, lord-slave relationship may also be found in the industrial world in Manila. One specific case is Antonio Samson in *The Pretenders*. Overcoming the disadvantages of rural birth, Samson manages to earn a doctorate at a prestigious New England university, afterwards planning to return to his hometown sweetheart whom he had impregnated. Instead, he is snatched away by a powerful agro-industrial baron and married off to his socialite daughter. Samson is now made to move in elevated social circles and do work he had not prepared himself to do. He has frequent spats with his wife who, he discovers to his dismay, has been conducting affairs. Determined to end his shame, Samson throws himself under a train.

We are afforded a rich composite picture of events of the contemporary Philippines in the last novel, *Mass*, covering the years before and after the proclamation of martial rule. A few of the old names reappear, but new characters emerge—student activists, women's liberation movement followers, drug addicts, intellectuals. The major character is the bastard son of Antonio Samson, Pepe Samson, now living in the slums of Tondo. He is a faithful follower of a former anti-Japanese Huk commander now devoted to local affairs, and a student leader at a university in Manila. A reform movement that started with protest at the increase in oil prices becomes a struggle for human rights, student rights, tenant's rights, women's liberation, and eventually a heterogeneous mass of protests manipulated by fraudulent leaders. After the failure of the intended uprising, one of the dedicated characters decides to return to Central Luzon to seek his roots and build anew.

The Philippines has been under colonial rule for some four centuries, one fourth of which has been portrayed in this epic. We are shown all kinds of people, from the moral cowards to the fiercely heroic, from the ferociously greedy to the selflessly philanthropic. In the face of all the tragic events in their lives, many of the people in Sionil Jose's epic are still able to say "We shall overcome."

—Leopoldo Y. Yabes

SMART, Elizabeth. Canadian. Born in Ottawa, Ontario, 27 December 1913. Educated at Elmwood School, Ottawa; Hatfield Hall, Cobourg, Ontario; King's College, University of London. Had two daughters and two sons. Worked for *House and Garden* and *Queen*, both London, and as advertising copywriter. Writer-in-Residence, University of Alberta, Edmonton, 1982–83. Recipient: Arts Council of Great Britain grant, 1966; Canada Council grant, 1983. *Died 4 March 1986.*

PUBLICATIONS

Novels

By Grand Central Station I Sat Down and Wept.   London, Editions Poetry London, 1945; New York, Popular Library, 1975.
The Assumption of the Rogues and Rascals.   London, Cape-Polytantric Press, 1978.

Verse

A Bonus.   London, Polytantric Press, 1977.
Eleven Poems.   Bracknell, Berkshire, Kirton, 1982.
In the Meantime (includes prose).   Ottawa, Deneau, 1984.

*

Manuscript Collection: National Library of Canada, Ottawa.

*   *   *

When *By Grand Central Station I Sat Down and Wept*, Elizabeth Smart's first novel, was published in 1945, its appearance went largely un-noticed—"to the shame of those professing to practise criticism at the time," according to Brigid Brophy who supplied an introduction to the 1966 edition.

The reasons for its comparative lack of attention, though, may be due more to the novel's form than to any prevailing literary taste. *By Grand Central Station I Sat Down and Wept* belongs to a genre which has not always found favour in English letters—the poetic novel. On the one hand it is the banal story of a young woman who falls in love with a married man, of their attempted elopement, of her subsequent pregnancy, and of his return to his wife; but those are the bare bones of the novel. On another level, the flesh is Smart's eloquent and poetic prose which tells the story in terms of classical imagery. Thus the woman's doomed love is seen as the story of Tristan and Isolde; at other times she wishes she were Daphne turned motionless and green to avoid the touch of a god. Metamorphosis is also central to the novel. The woman wishes that she could be transformed into a boy because her lover has told that "a boy with green eyes and long lashes" once made love to him in a print shop. Her womanly shape begins to offend her and she desires to be transfigured into another being, into a boy "with armpits like chalices." At other times she wishes only to be a hermaphrodite, that she and her lover can be fused into one, without the attendant need of physical sex. "But again and again when I peer into the mirror to find a distortion of my own image which would make my pain into a bearable legend, that form bends over me in embrace forever, like the persistent neon lights, or I remember the night it turned him into an Assyrian girl, casting down his lashes under a blossoming turban. Then we were two sisters and I the protive." As the girl's feelings progress towards the novel's terrible conclusion, her love becomes the final reality, triumphant over the pain and misery of her desertion.

Beckett, Auden, and Joyce are all perceptible influences on Smart's writing. Like Beckett she creates an unrealistic world filled with repugnant and pointless details and which make the point that the real world is repugnant and pointless. She also shares with him a quality of prose which, phrase by phrase, and sentence by sentence, has an utterly charming simplicity and clarity. Although her first novel is largely autobiographical and derived in a large measure from her own experience, it has the distance and integrity of art, a virtue she shares with Joyce's prose-poetry.

Above all, it is her ability to encompass the whole modern female reaction to the male-ordered world that has impressed most modern critics of her work. *The Assumption of the Rogues and Rascals* is a howl of anguish, a distillation of one woman's struggle to survive in a world of faithless lovers and boring office jobs while she has the added burden of bringing up her own children alone. Her grim wit is perhaps better with the agonies visited upon the woman than with her occasional ecstasies, and the blessings of her so-called survival appear vague and unfocused, but this is a largely successful attempt to come to terms with the position of women in the world today. As notice of her intentions, most of her section headings have combative titles—"After the War," "Signed On for the Duration," "On, On," "Pacification"—but the enduring quality of this short novel is the luminosity of her prose.

—Trevor Royle

SMITH, Emma. British. Born in Newquay, Cornwall, 21 August 1923. Married R.L. Stewart-Jones in 1951 (died, 1957); one son and one daughter. Recipient: Atlantic Award, 1947; Rhys Memorial Prize, 1949; James Tait Black Memorial Prize, 1950. Agent: Curtis Brown, 162–168 Regent Street, London W1R 5TA, England.

PUBLICATIONS

Novels

Maidens' Trip. London, Putnam, 1948.
The Far Cry. London, MacGibbon and Kee, 1949; New York, Random House, 1950.
The Opportunity of a Lifetime. London, Hamish Hamilton, 1978; New York, Doubleday, 1980.

Uncollected Short Stories

"A Surplus of Lettuces," in *The Real Thing*, edited by Peggy Woodford. London, Bodley Head, 1977.
"Mackerel," in *Misfits*, edited by Peggy Woodford. London, Bodley Head, 1984.

Fiction (for children)

Emily: The Story of a Traveller. London, Nelson, 1959; as *Emily: The Travelling Guinea Pig*, New York, McDowell Obolensky, 1959.
Out of Hand. London, Macmillan, 1963; New York, Harcourt Brace, 1964.
Emily's Voyage. London, Macmillan, and New York, Harcourt Brace, 1966.
No Way of Telling. London, Bodley Head, and New York, Atheneum, 1972.

Other

Village Children: A Soviet Experience. Moscow, Progress, 1982.

*

Emma Smith comments:
What one writes for children is quite as important as what one writes for adults, and I'm not at all sure it isn't more important; because what children read can colour their feelings, and affect their behaviour, for the rest of their lives. If they are sufficiently impressed, what they read is absorbed into themselves and becomes part of their own experience to an extent that can't be so after they've grown up. Consequently, everything I write for children is really full of secret messages and exhortations and warnings of what I think the whole of life, which lies ahead waiting for them, is all about, and what I think they're going to need in the way of equipment.

*   *   *

Emma Smith has published three novels and several books designed for the young. In all her work there are a precise creation of character, a sensitive response to setting, and a careful attention to detail.

Her first book, *Maidens' Trip*, set in England during the Second World War, is the story of three girls, Emma, Charity, and Nanette, who, during the manpower shortage, become "boaters" and guide their motorboat *Venus* and its "butty" *Adrane* over the network of locks and canals running through the heartland of the English countryside. Their adventures, observations, and problems make up the substance of the story as, without formal plot or characterizations, Smith manages to create a forward-moving, frequently suspenseful narrative. The adventures become misadventures as awkwardly at first, and later with more skill, the girls make the trip for supplies from London to Birmingham and back again. There are the physical hardships of rain and cold, blistered hands and aching backs; the hazards of machinery broken down, accidents with other boats, mud that sticks and locks that refuse to open. Charity is the housewife; Nanette, the coquette; Emma, the steady "professional" who directs the whole operation. The reality of the constant rain and cold with the contrasted coziness of the little cabin on the *Venus*, the ubiquitous steaming cups of tea, the hearty flavor of the cooking stew, and the sights and sounds of the loading docks form a background for the most memorable feature of the book—the characterization of the girls and their realization of the world of the "boaters," a world completely apart from that of a great nation at war. Even the brief appearance of a young soldier on leave is no more than a vague reminder of the danger and death in the world beyond. The other notable feature of the book is Smith's understanding of the three young girls forced by circumstances to deal with people and situations totally foreign to them. Each is a real person; not one of the three a stereotype of the adolescent. Each, however, at the same time is realized as young and immature.

Smith's second book, *The Far Cry*, is even more distinguished than *Maidens' Trip*. It is the story of an eccentric schoolmaster, Mr. Digby, who flees with his 14-year-old daughter, Teresa, to India and the sanctuary of his elder daughter, Ruth, to escape his estranged second wife, Teresa's mother. Their departure and trip across the ocean make up the first two sections of the book; the trip across India by train, the third. The fourth section is Ruth's as the reader discovers that she and her husband Edwin have not succeeded in resolving all the differences of their marriage. The last section is a kind of summary for Teresa when, confronted by the sudden horror of her father's death from a heart attack and Ruth's accidental death in Calcutta, she is obliged to become more mature than seems possible for her to be. Even at the end she "had yet to learn that the relationships of people are never established, are ever mutable. . . ." All the principal characters are skilfully drawn: Mr. Digby, a failure as husband, father, and schoolmaster; Ruth, an exotic beauty without confidence in herself or her role as wife; Teresa, sensitive and perceptive, escaping from the repression of her unimaginative Aunt May; and Edwin, the young English tea planter who understands India and his tea workers far more than he does his beautiful wife Ruth.

The journey from England to India, the introduction of India itself, and the daily life of the tea plantation make up the chronology of the story. There is hardly a plot in the conventional definition of the term since there is little doubt from the beginning that Teresa and her father will escape her American mother. The real focus of the novel is on Teresa and her varying responses to the people she meets and the constantly shifting scenery she observes. Smith is especially good in realizing the detail of setting—the crowded life on ship board; the arresting picture of camels and their drivers at Port Suez, a kind of point in time for Teresa; the arrival at Bombay and the acquisition of their bearer, Sam; the long uncertain train trip in dirty cramped quarters; the English way of life Ruth has created in the midst of a tea plantation. The book is as full of the multitude of details as is reality itself, but each so skillfully chosen that it seems precisely right for the observation of the characters to whom it is assigned. *The Far Cry* is a beautifully sensitive novel of time, place, and character.

The Opportunity of a Lifetime was Smith's first adult novel for almost 30 years. It again centers on a young girl. In this case the heroine is a 15-year-old on a summer holiday in Cornwall in 1937. And again there are many finely wrought characters, a nice sense of time and place, and moving contrasts between innocence and betrayal. If Emma Smith has chosen a rather limited range, her virtue is that she has done well what she set out to do, and her work shows an unusual sensitivity to people and a real artist's eye for detail.

—Annibel Jenkins

SMITH, Iain Crichton. Gaelic name: Iain Mac A'Ghobainn. British. Born on the Isle of Lewis, Outer Hebrides, Scotland, 1 January 1928. Educated at the University of Aberdeen, M.A. (honours) in English 1949. Served in the British Army Education Corps, 1950–52: Sergeant. Married. Secondary school teacher, Clydebank, 1952–55; teacher of English, Oban High School, 1955–77. Recipient: Scottish Arts Council award, 1966, 1968, 1974, 1977, and prize, 1968; BBC award, for television play, 1970; Book Council award, 1970; Silver Pen Award, 1971; Queen's Silver Jubilee Medal. LL.D.: Dundee University, 1983; D.Litt.: Glasgow University, 1984. Fellow, Royal Society of Literature. O.B.E. (Officer, Order of the British Empire), 1980. Address: Tigh na Fuaran, Taynuilt, Argyll PA35 1JW, Scotland.

PUBLICATIONS

Novels

Consider the Lilies. London, Gollancz, 1968; as *The Alien Light*, Boston, Houghton Mifflin, 1969.
The Last Summer. London, Gollancz, 1969.
My Last Duchess. London, Gollancz, 1971.
Goodbye, Mr. Dixon. London, Gollancz, 1974.
An t-Aonaran (The Hermit). Glasgow, University of Glasgow Celtic Department, 1976.
An End to Autumn. London, Gollancz, 1978.
On the Island. London, Gollancz, 1979.
A Field Full of Folk. London, Gollancz, 1982.
The Search. London, Gollancz, 1983.
The Tenement. London, Gollancz, 1985.

Short Stories

Burn is Aran (Bread and Water; includes verse). Glasgow, Gairm, 1960.
An Dubh is an Gorm (The Black and the Blue). Aberdeen, Aberdeen University, 1963.
Maighstirean is Ministearan (Schoolmasters and Ministers). Inverness, Club Leabhar, 1970.
Survival Without Error and Other Stories. London, Gollancz, 1970.
The Black and the Red. London, Gollancz, 1973.
An t-Adhar Ameireaganach (The American Sky). Inverness, Club Leabhar, 1973.
The Village. Inverness, Club Leabhar, 1976.
The Hermit and Other Stories. London, Gollancz, 1977.
Murdo and Other Stories. London, Gollancz, 1981.
Mr. Trill in Hades and Other Stories. London, Gollancz, 1984.

Plays

An Coileach (The Cockerel; produced Glasgow, 1966). Glasgow. An Comunn Gaidhealach, 1966.
A'Chuirt (The Trial; produced Glasgow, 1966). Glasgow, An Comunn Gaidhealach, 1966.
A Kind of Play (produced Mull, 1975).
Two by the Sea (produced Mull, 1975).
The Happily Married Couple (produced Mull, 1977).

Radio Play: *Goodman and Death Mahoney*, 1980.

Verse

The Long River. Edinburgh, M. Macdonald, 1955.
New Poets 1959, with Karen Gershon and Christopher Levenson. London, Eyre and Spottiswoode, 1959.
Deer on the High Hills: A Poem. Edinburgh, Giles Gordon, 1960.

Thistles and Roses. London, Eyre and Spottiswoode, 1961.
The Law and the Grace. London, Eyre and Spottiswoode, 1965.
Biobuill is Sanasan Reice (Bibles and Advertisements). Glasgow, Gairm, 1965.
Three Regional Voices, with Michael Longley and Barry Tebb. London, Poet and Printer, 1968.
At Helensburgh. Belfast, Festival, 1968.
From Bourgeois Land. London, Gollancz, 1969.
Selected Poems. London, Gollancz, and Chester Springs, Pennsylvania, Dufour, 1970.
Penguin Modern Poets 21, with George Mackay Brown and Norman MacCaig. London, Penguin, 1972.
Love Poems and Elegies. London, Gollancz, 1972.
Hamlet in Autumn. Edinburgh, M. Macdonald, 1972.
Rabhdan is rudan (Verses and Things). Glasgow, Gairm, 1973.
Eadar Fealla-dhà is Glaschu (Between Comedy and Glasgow). Glasgow, University of Glasgow Celtic Department, 1974.
Orpheus and Other Poems. Preston, Lancashire, Akros, 1974.
Poems for Donalda. Belfast, Ulsterman, 1974.
The Permanent Island: Gaelic Poems, translated by the author. Edinburgh, M. Macdonald, 1975.
The Notebooks of Robinson Crusoe and Other Poems. London, Gollancz, 1975.
In the Middle—. London, Gollancz, 1977.
Selected Poems 1955–1980, edited by Robin Fulton. Edinburgh, M. Macdonald, 1982.
The Exiles. Manchester, Carcanet, 1984.
Selected Poems. Manchester, Carcanet, 1985.
A Life. Manchester, Carcanet, 1986.

Other

The Golden Lyric: An Essay on the Poetry of Hugh MacDiarmid. Preston, Lancashire, Akros, 1967.
Iain Am Measg nan Reultan (Iain among the Stars; for children). Glasgow, Gairm, 1970.
River, River: Poems for Children. Edinburgh, M. Macdonald, 1978.
Na h-Ainmhidhean (The Animals; verse for children). Aberfeldy, Perthshire, Clo Chailleann, 1979.

Editor, *Scottish Highland Tales*. London, Ward Lock, 1982.

Translator, *Ben Dorain*, by Duncan Ban Macintyre. Preston, Lancashire, Akros, 1969.
Translator, *Poems to Eimhir*, by Sorley Maclean. London and Newcastle upon Tyne, Gollancz-Northern House, 1971.

*

Bibliography: in *Lines Review 29* (Edinburgh), 1969.

Critical Studies: interview in *Scottish International* (Edinburgh), 1971; *Iain Crichton Smith*, Glasgow, National Book League, 1979; *Literature of the North* edited by David Hewitt and M.R.G. Spiller, Aberdeen, Aberdeen University Press, 1983; *New Edinburgh Review*, Summer 1984.

Iain Crichton Smith comments:

(1972) There is no real connection between my first two novels; one is about old age, the other about youth. However, I would like to write novels which have imagistic content, like poetry, but not "poetic" novels. I like them if possible to be generated from some kind of image or "given" imaginative fact.

*   *   *

One of Iain Crichton Smith's greatest abilities as a writer of fiction is the uncanny way in which he can get inside his characters' heads and create not the places of everyday reality but worlds as perceived by his characters. He gave early notice of that deftness of touch in his first novel, *Consider the Lilies*, a tautly written evocation of the period of 19th-century Scottish history known as the Clearances, when the people of the Highlands were evicted from their traditional lands to make way for the cultivation of sheep. In this novel the world was seen through the eyes of an old woman, Mrs. Scott, whose own life had been wasted by the catastrophe of the Clearances which had broken up the community in which she lived. In that sense the story of the old woman and her hardships—both spiritual and physical—is inseparable from an interpretation of her cultural situation. Another typical Smith hero-narrator who acts as a cypher for our better understanding of a cultural or social problem is Mark Simmons, the diffident Scottish intellectual of *My Last Duchess* who loses his faith in literature and in the ability of human beings to communicate. His detachment from the modern world and all its ills leaves him with little chance of survival until he comes to the realisation that life can be made more acceptable when coarser and more worldly values are taken for granted instead of being despised.

Both characters provide a key for a better understanding of one of Smith's more durable characters, Mr. Trill, the hero of "Mr Trill in Hades" from the collection of short stories of the same title. As he lies dying, Mr. Trill, a schoolmaster—as so many of Smith's heroes are—sees himself being ferried across the Styx to the country of the shades. What he sees and hears of his heroes and heroines in that awful landscape is deeply disillusioning: Agamemnon and Achilles, "those marvellous heroes," are revealed as simple boasters; Hector has no nobility and only lusts after Helen; Ulysses is treacherous and false. When he discovers the duplicity of the classical figures who fuelled his imagination while he was in the land of the living, Mr. Trill escapes instead into the world of his childhood. But this provides no comfort with memories of bullies and violence returning to terrorise him. Given the choice of returning to his earlier life as a teacher, a disillusioned Mr. Trill elects to become a streetcorner seller of newspapers and to eschew the dubious delights of academe. Beneath his character's ironic stance Smith seems to be questioning false values and to viewing the world of his creation in a far from happy light. Intellectual ability and delight in imagination are as naught in comparison to the triumph of the senses.

Mr. Trill is a fictional cousin to the Revd. Donald Black of Smith's short story "The Missionary" (from *Murdo and Other Stories*). Here, he is inside the mind and world of a Christian minister who goes out to Africa to convert the heathen but is overpowered by the strange and hostile environment in which he has to live. At first he is only mildly dismayed by the conditions and by the smallness of his half-naked flock, but gradually he becomes discomfited by the warped idea of Christianity held by his congregation who profess to the Christians but in name only. Even the fate of his predecessor is uncertain and returns in idle moments to haunt him. Gradually, though, he is drawn into the life of the tribe, and when his well-meant Christian interference results in the massacre of a family he begins to crack. Suddenly he realises how thin is the dividing line between naked aggression and the ability to live in harmony, and it is only a new-found grace which gives him the humanity to survive his personal crisis. As with Mr. Trill, Smith is at his most convincing when he deals with the intellectual torment undergone by the missionary and with his eventual and unexpected salvation.

In recent years Smith has shown himself to be at his happiest in short fiction where he has created his best work through a sustained exploration of the insular worlds inhabited by his main characters. His work may be timeless or rooted in history, as in *Consider the Lilies*, but it is difficult not to believe that environmental factors have played a part in his literary development. He was born and brought up in the Outer Hebridean Island of Lewis and he writes both in English and his native Gaelic; both have affected his work. This is certainly true of his novel *A Field Full of Folk* in which a small Highland village becomes a microcosm for the world and all its ills. A minister wrestles with his loss of faith while his parishioners harbour their own loves and hates, doubts and certainties. In other words, the village is like any other, but the transformation comes when the minister views his flock on the green during the annual sports and realises that he and everyone else is part of "this supremely imperfect and perfect earth." Like all of Smith's heroes, he has been transformed by the grace of common humanity.

—Trevor Royle

SONTAG, Susan. American. Born in New York City, 16 January 1933. Educated at the University of California, Berkeley, 1948-49; University of Chicago, 1949–51, B.A. 1951; Harvard University, Cambridge, Massachusetts, 1954–57, M.A. 1955; St. Anne's College, Oxford, 1957. Has one son. Instructor in English, University of Connecticut, Storrs, 1953–54; Teaching Fellow in Philosophy, Harvard University, 1955–57; editor, *Commentary*, New York, 1959; Lecturer in Philosophy, City College of New York, and Sarah Lawrence College, Bronxville, New York, 1959–60; Instructor in Religion, Columbia University, New York, 1960–64; Writer-in-Residence, Rutgers University, New Brunswick, New Jersey, 1964–65. Recipient: American Association of University Women fellowship, 1957; Rockefeller fellowship, 1965, 1974; Guggenheim fellowship, 1966, 1975; American Academy award, 1976; Brandeis University Creative Arts Award, 1976; Ingram Merrill Foundation award, 1976; National Book Critics Circle award, 1977; Academy of Sciences and Literature award (Mainz, Germany), 1979. Member, American Academy, 1979; Officer, Order of Arts and Letters (France), 1984. Lives in New York City. Address: c/o Farrar Straus and Giroux, 19 Union Square West, New York, New York 10003, U.S.A.

PUBLICATIONS

Novels

The Benefactor. New York, Farrar Straus, 1963; London, Eyre and Spottiswoode, 1964.
Death Kit. New York, Farrar Straus, 1967; London, Secker and Warburg, 1968.

Short Stories

, *etcetera*. New York, Farrar Straus, 1978; London, Gollancz, 1979.

Uncollected Short Stories

"Man with a Pain," in *Harper's* (New York), April 1964.
"Description (of a Description)," in *Antaeus* (New York), Autumn 1984.

Plays (screenplays)

Duet for Cannibals. New York, Farrar Straus, 1970; London, Allen Lane, 1974.
Brother Carl. New York, Farrar Straus, 1974.

Screenplays: *Duet for Cannibals*, 1969; *Brother Carl*, 1971.

Other

Against Interpretation and Other Essays. New York, Farrar Straus, 1966; London, Eyre and Spottiswoode, 1967.
Trip to Hanoi. New York, Farrar Straus, and London, Panther, 1969.
Styles of Radical Will (essays). New York, Farrar Straus, and London, Secker and Warburg, 1969.
On Photography. New York, Farrar Straus, 1977; London, Allen Lane, 1978.
Illness as Metaphor. New York, Farrar Straus, 1978; London, Allen Lane, 1979.
Under the Sign of Saturn (essays). New York, Farrar Straus, 1980; London, Writers and Readers, 1983.
A Susan Sontag Reader. New York, Farrar Straus, 1982; London, Penguin, 1983.

Editor, *Selected Writings of Artaud*, translated by Helen Weaver. New York, Farrar Straus, 1976.
Editor, *A Barthes Reader*. New York, Hill and Wang, and London, Cape, 1982; as *Barthes: Selected Writings*, London, Fontana, 1983.

*

Theatrical Activities:
Director: Plays—*As You Desire Me* by Pirandello, Turin and Italian tour, 1979–80; *Jacques and His Master* by Milan Kundera, Cambridge, Massachusetts, 1985. Films—*Duet for Cannibals*, 1969; *Brother Carl*, 1971; *Promised Lands* (documentary), 1974; *Unguided Tour*, 1983.

*   *   *

Traditionally readers have approached works of fiction as verbal structures which reveal and generally make statements about a pre-existing "real" subject. The writer may represent his subject directly, "imitating" in accordance with conventional understandings about the probable behavior of the human and the natural order; or he may render his subject indirectly by presenting a metaphor which stands for and usually implies a generalization about that same reality. Thus traditional criticism was designed to judge the verisimilitude of fiction and to provide a way of understanding metaphor, allegory, and parable as symbolic statements. It is impossible, however, to discuss the fiction of Susan Sontag in critical terms derived from this essentially naturalistic tradition, just as Sontag herself has attempted to construct a new critical approach to do justice to those works of *avant-garde* artists whose rendering of the modern world she finds significant.

The tough, polemical essays collected in *Against Interpretation* and *Styles of Radical Will* are more impressive than Sontag's fiction thus far, which too often seems contrived to illustrate a doctrine. For Sontag, the final "most liberating value of art" is "transparency," which means experiencing "the luminousness of the thing in itself, of things being what they are." Interpretation, which seeks to replace the work with something else—usually historical, ethical or psychological paraphrase—is essentially "revenge which the intellect takes upon art." To interpret is "to impoverish, to deplete." Sontag's chief interest as a critic is the work of artists (especially film makers) whose work is misunderstood because it resists "being reduced to a story." Thus Sontag observes that in his film *Persona* Bergman presents not a story, but "something that is, in one sense, cruder, and, in another, more abstract: a body of material, a subject. The function of the subject or material may be as much its opacity, its multiplicity, as the ease with which it yields itself to being incarnated by a determinate plot or action." Deliberately frustrating any conventional attempt to determine "what happens," the new novels and films are able, she maintains, to involve the audience "more directly in other matters, for instance in the very processes of seeing and knowing. . . . The material presented can then be treated as a thematic resource, from which different (and perhaps concurrent) narrative structures can be derived as variations." The artist intends his work to remain "partly encoded": the truly modern consciousness challenges the supremacy of naturalism and univocal symbolism.

While vestiges of naturalistic situations remain in Sontag's fiction (her story "The Will and the Way," for example, seems to be an allegory concerning the image of women in modern life), "interpretation" is by definition more or less irrelevant. *The Benefactor* is in its general outline a dream novel; its "thematic resource" is the problem of attaining selfhood and genuine freedom. Just as Sontag sees Montaigne's essays as "dispassionate, varied explorations of the innumerable ways of being a self," the hero of *The Benefactor* uses his dreams as a means of achieving freedom. "It seemed to me," Hippolyte concludes, that "all my life had been converging on the state of mind . . . in which I would finally be reconciled to myself— myself as I really am, the self of my dreams. That reconciliation is what I take to be freedom." The device which keeps the reader from treating the novel as paraphrasable allegory is the deliberate ambiguity of the narrative frame: we are left to decide whether the narrative is an account of what happened or an account which is at least in part the construction of a mad Hippolyte whose dreams are symbolic transformations, in the usual Freudian sense, of "what happened." Sontag owes a good deal to Sartre and Camus, but even more to the *auteurs* of *Last Year at Marienbad* and *L'Avventura*. *Death Kit* has as its concern the failure of a man who has no true self. "Diddy, not really alive, had a life. Not really the same. Some people are their lives. Others, like Diddy, merely inhabit their lives." Diddy commits a murder, or thinks he commits a murder; there is no way of determining this, but what matters is how Diddy handles the possibility that he is a murderer, and how he tries to appropriate the self of a blind girl whom he selfishly "loves." Out of the materials of his life Diddy assembles his death; out of his failure the reader may assemble an understanding of vanity, inauthenticity, and death. Wholly successful or not, *The Benefactor* and *Death Kit* are haunting works, effective to the degree to which the reader can accept Sontag's powerful arguments elsewhere about the exhaustion of the naturalistic tradition. As the American critic E.D. Hirsch puts it, "Knowledge of ambiguity is not necessarily ambiguous knowledge."

—Elmer Borklund

SORRENTINO, Gilbert. American. Born in Brooklyn, New York, 27 April 1929. Educated in New York public schools; Brooklyn College, 1950–51, 1955–57. Served in the United States Army Medical Corps, 1951–53. Married 1) Elsene Wiessner (divorced); 2) Vivian Victoria Ortiz; two sons and one daughter. Re-insurance clerk, Fidelity and Casualty Company, New York, 1947–48; messenger, American Houses Inc., 1948–49; freight checker, Ace Assembly Agency, New York, 1954–56; packer, Bennett Brothers, New York, 1956–57; shipping room supervisor, Thermo-fax Sales, 1957–60. Editor, *Neon* magazine, 1956–60, and Grove Press, 1965–70, both New York; book editor, *Kulchur*, New York, 1961–63; taught at Columbia University, New York, 1965; Aspen Writers Workshop, Colorado, 1967; Sarah Lawrence College, Bronxville, New York, 1971–72; New School for Social Research, New York, 1976–79, 1980–82; Edwin S. Quain Professor of Literature, University of Scranton, Pennsylvania, 1979. Since 1982, Professor of English, Stanford Univeristy, California. Recipient: Guggenheim fellowship, 1973; National Endowment for the Arts grant, 1974, 1978; Fels Award, 1975; Ariadne Foundation grant, 1975; Creative Artists Public Service grant, 1975; John Dos Passos Prize, 1981; American Academy award, 1985. Agent: Mel Berger, William Morris Agency, 1350 Avenue of the Americas, New York, New York 10019. Address: Department of English, Stanford University, Stanford, California 94305, U.S.A.

PUBLICATIONS

Novels

The Sky Changes. New York, Hill and Wang, 1966.
Steelwork. New York, Pantheon, 1970.
Imaginative Qualities of Actual Things. New York, Pantheon, 1971.
Splendide-Hôtel. New York, New Directions, 1973.
Mulligan Stew. New York, Grove Press, 1979; London, Boyars, 1980.
Aberration of Starlight. New York, Random House, 1980; London, Boyars, 1981.
Crystal Vision. Berkeley, California, North Point Press, 1981; London, Boyars, 1982.
Blue Pastoral. Berkeley, California, North Point Press, 1983; London, Boyars, 1985.
Odd Number. Berkeley, California, North Point Press, 1985.

Uncollected Short Stories

"The Moon in Its Flight," in *New American Review 13*, edited by Theodore Solotaroff. New York, Simon and Schuster, 1971.
"Land of Cotton," in *Harper's* (New York), November 1977.
"Decades," in *The Best American Short Stories 1978*, edited by Theodore Solotaroff and Shannon Ravenel. Boston, Houghton Mifflin, 1978.
"Chats with the Real McCoy," in *Atlantic* (Boston), March 1979.
"A Beehive Arranged on Humane Principles," in *Conjunctions* (New York), Fall 1985.

Play

Flawless Play Restored: The Masque of Fungo. Los Angeles, Black Sparrow Press, 1974.

Verse

The Darkness Surrounds Us.   Highlands, North Carolina, Jargon, 1960.
Black and White.   New York, Totem, 1964.
The Perfect Fiction.   New York, Norton, 1968.
Corrosive Sublimate.   Los Angeles, Black Sparrow Press, 1971.
A Dozen Oranges.   Santa Barbara, California, Black Sparrow Press, 1976.
White Sail.   Santa Barbara, California, Black Sparrow Press, 1977.
The Orangery.   Austin, University of Texas Press, 1978.
Selected Poems 1958–1980.   Santa Barbara, California, Black Sparrow Press, 1981.

Other

Something Said (essays).   Berkeley, California, North Point Press, 1984.

Translator, *Sulpiciae Elegidia / Elegiacs of Sulpicia.*   Mount Horeb, Wisconsin, Perishable Press, 1977.

*

Manuscript Collection: University of Delaware, Newark.

Critical Studies: "Gilbert Sorrentino Issue" of *Vort* (Silver Spring, Maryland), Fall 1974, and *Review of Contemporary Fiction* (Elmwood Park, Illinois), Fall 1981.

Gilbert Sorrentino comments:
   My writing is the act of solving self-imposed problems.

                    *   *   *

   Gilbert Sorrentino's novels are dedicated to several anti-traditional propositions; that space, rather than time, is the most revealing principle for narrative structure; that the physical texture of language, rather than its semantic properties, are the key to communication between a novelist and the reader; and that an awareness of the author's act of writing, rather than the willing suspension of disbelief, yields the greatest pleasure in experiencing a novel.
   The Sky Changes and *Steelwork*, Sorrentino's earliest novels (from the days when he was still best known as a poet), are demonstrations of spatial order. The first is the record (told in block sections of separate narrative) of a protagonist's dis-solving marriage, framed by an auto trip across the United States. Both the relationship and the journey would seem to imply a temporal order; but at several points Sorrentino self-consciously violates that order to show that the human imagina-tion transcends simple chronology—the trip's emotional reso-lution comes as early as two-thirds through the cross-country journey. *Steelwork* is the spatial portrait of a Brooklyn neigh-borhood over two decades of human experience. On one street-corner, for example, the events of several years' distance are imaginatively rehearsed; and characters' lives are studied in a simultaneity of presence, although by the clock they have lived through much of their lives. Because space—the neigh-borhood—is the organizing principle, the chronology is deliber-ately scrambled, so that we move back and forth from 1951 to 1942 to 1949. As a result, the reader experiences the neigh-borhood as the spatial whole it would be for anyone who lived there all those years. Emotions and the imagination outstrip time.
   Imaginative Qualities of Actual Things is Sorrentino's wildly comic exercise of his most self-apparent writing techniques.

Ostensibly a *roman à clef* exposing the petty jealousies and seductions of the 1950's and 1960's New York art world, the book is in fact a demonstration of Sorrentino's pleasure in writing a novel. Characters' statements are undercut by rudely sarcastic footnotes; midway through a piece of exposition the author will stop and berate the reader for making him supply such petty details; and when the author hates a character, ludi-crous scenes are devised for the unfortunate soul's humiliation and punishment. Throughout, the reader is aware that the real subject of this novel is not its mimicry of a projected real world, but is instead the process of its own composition, which the reader witnesses firsthand.
   Making fiction its own subject—not a representation of an illusionary world but instead its own artifice as added to the world, an aesthetic Sorrentino learned from his mentor, Wil-liam Carlos Williams—is the achievement of *Splendide-Hôtel.* Its brief chapters are named after the successive letters of the alphabet, which provide the topics for composition—the capital letter A's on the page looking like flies on a wall, breeding in decay; the letter K reminding Sorrentino the baseball score-card symbol for strike-out, and of a headline which spoke volumes just by saying "K-K-K-Koufax!!!!"
   In his fifth and most commercially successful work of fiction, *Mulligan Stew*, Sorrentino offers a full display of novelistic talents at work. Indeed, he wishes to surpass his previous efforts by showing all aspects of fiction writing, from the novelist's act of composition to his notebooks, letters, and even the perso-nal thoughts of his characters. Borrowing his structure from Flann O'Brien's novel *At Swim-Two-Birds* (1939), Sorrentino invents an imaginary novelist named Anthony Lamont who is struggling to shore up a sagging career with an experimental novel, a piece of "surfiction" (Sorrentino despises the term) titled *Guinea Red.* A murder mystery, it features unabashedly miserable writing; Lamont keeps losing the murdered body and forgetting where he's placed the fatal wound, and the prose itself is dreadfully overwritten in a parody of low-brow style. The reader is also given access to Lamont's letters, notebooks, and journal entries. Midway through, his characters mutiny and seek ways to escape Lamont's leaden narrative and find work in a more promising repertoire. A massive novel which by its very bulk and meticulous range of styles immerses the reader in its own subject, *Mulligan Stew* is Sorrentino's fullest repertoire of writing talent.
   Mulligan Stew exhausts the innovative techniques of 1960's fiction, and also clears the way for a new lyricism in Sorrentino's work. Whereas his earlier novels turned to poetic devices as a way of eclipsing the quotidian, his recent works *Aberration of Starlight*, *Crystal Vision*, and *Blue Pastoral* are able to con-front both experience and the act of writing directly.
   Aberration of Starlight explains experience as a matter of point of view, fragmenting a summer's experience at a New Jersey vacation lodge into four narratives, much in the manner of William Faulkner's *The Sound and the Fury.* Sorrentino uses these distinct modes of vision in order to highlight lan-guage, especially how essentially stupid world views are, in the manner of Flaubert's *Dictionnaire des idées reçues*, created by and not just expressed through banalities of language. *Crys-tal Vision* embraces language directly, transcribing streetcorner conversations from the verbally rich Brooklyn of Sorrentino's youth, as the characters of his earlier *Steelwork* re-emerge from their "world of light" to speak directly. Their language expands the author's previous vision, showing how they have the vitality to survive on their own in fiction, without narrative's customary supporting devices. *Blue Pastoral* celebrates the stylistics of Blue Serge Gavotte as he creates a pastoral accompanying his journey from New York to San Francisco (a less lyrical trip

once made west by the protagonist of *The Sky Changes*). Sorrentino takes the occasion to parody pastoral forms and satirize stock characters; much of his play consists in delighting with obviously bad writing. But with all conventions demolished by his earlier works, and with unconventionality itself made a sham by the achievement of *Mulligan Stew*, there seems little else for Sorrentino to do with the novel than continue to write it, even poorly.

Sorrentino's inward turn of narrative is confirmed by his practice in *Odd Number*, a brief (159-page) reinvestigation of how his earlier novel, *Imaginative Qualities of Actual Things*, might have been assembled. In the earlier work Sorrentino had used the well-established formal device of the *roman à clef* to structure his narrative; his use of footnotes and intrusively parenthetical remarks indicates that the form is barely able to contain his rage against some of these characters drawn from a lifestyle he was now rejecting. *Odd Number* transposes this volatility to the novel's form itself. Like *Aberration of Starlight*, the tale is told several times, but here the emphasis is even more on the uncertainty of events. The first time through the reader is given a question-and-answer dialogue, as in detective fashion the voice of the novel interrogates its own resources to discover exactly what has happened. This section's awkward and uncertain rhythm yields to a more fluently conversational account of the book's events—all of which originally transpired in *Imaginative Qualities of Actual Things*, now supplemented with coy references to Sorrentino's other novels. But the authority of part two yields to a cross examination of the documents themselves: the contents of dresser drawers, photographs, and other possessions which contradict certain assertions of both previous sections, virtually unmaking the novel which has been read. The novel, therefore, is no more reliable a report on the world than the self-conscious rage of Sorrentino's earlier version, a reminder that truth, if one cares for it, must be found beyond the fiction writer's practice no matter how it might be structured.

—Jerome Klinkowitz

SOUTHERN, Terry. American. Born in Alvarado, Texas, 1 May 1924. Educated at Southern Methodist University, Dallas; University of Chicago; Northwestern University, Evanston, Illinois, B.A. 1948; the Sorbonne, Paris, 1948–50. Served in the United States Army, 1943–45. Married Carol Kauffman in 1956; one son. Recipient: British Screen Writers award, 1965; Writers Guild of America West award, 1965. Agent: Sterling Lord Agency, 600 Madison Avenue, New York, New York 10021. Address: c/o Arbor House, 235 East 45th Street, New York, New York 10017, U.S.A.

PUBLICATIONS

Novels

Flash and Filigree. London, Deutsch, and New York, Coward McCann, 1958.
Candy (as Maxwell Kenton, with Mason Hoffenberg). Paris, Olympia Press, 1958; as Terry Southern and Mason Hoffenberg, New York, Putnam, 1964; London, Geis, 1968.
The Magic Christian. London, Deutsch, 1959; New York, Random House, 1960.
Lollipop (as Maxwell Kenton). Paris, Olympia Press, 1962.

Blue Movie. Cleveland, World, 1970; London, Calder and Boyars, 1973.

Short Stories

Red-Dirt Marijuana and Other Tastes. New York, New American Library, 1967; London, Cape, 1971.

Uncollected Short Story

"Heavey Put-Away," in *Paris Review*, Spring 1981.

Plays

Easy Rider (screenplay), with Peter Fonda and Dennis Hopper. New York, New American Library, 1969.

Screenplays: *Candy Kisses*, with David Burnett, 1955; *Dr. Strangelove*, with Stanley Kubrick and Peter George, 1964; *The Loved One*, with Christopher Isherwood, 1965; *The Cincinnati Kid*, with Ring Lardner, Jr., 1966; *Casino Royale* (uncredited), with others, 1967; *Barbarella*, with others, 1968; *Easy Rider*, with Peter Fonda and Dennis Hopper, 1969; *The End of the Road*, with Aram Avakian, 1969; *The Magic Christian*, with others, 1969; *Meetings with Remarkable Men*, 1979.

Other

The Journal of "The Loved One": The Production Log of a Motion Picture. New York, Random House, 1965.
The Rolling Stones on Tour. New York, Dragon's Dream, 1978.

Editor, with Richard Seaver and Alexander Trocchi, *Writers in Revolt*. New York, Fell, 1963.

*   *   *

Terry Southern has baffled American reviewers and annoyed critics since the appearance in 1958 of *Flash and Filigree*, which had been well received in England. This novel and subsequent efforts have variously been labeled "pointless," "pornographic," and "sick" for their thematic content or apparent lack of it. The form of Southern's fiction similarly defies easy classification: part put-on, part satire, part parody, with occasional stretches of "straight," well-written prose. Plotting is rarely conventional: *Flash and Filigree* is really two completely separate plots, while *The Magic Christian* and *Candy* are disjointedly picaresque. *Blue Movie* is straightforwardly told, but conventional style and plotting seem strange indeed when used to chronicle (in living detail) the filming, and subsequent seizure by a Vatican Army, of a Hollywood-produced stag movie.

The main plot in *Flash and Filigree* centers on a dermatologist-sports car buff named Dr. Frederick Eichner, who is haunted by a prank-playing transvestite named Felix Treevly. Eichner kills his weird nemesis and is tried for murder and acquitted. Dr. Eichner is too aloofly repulsive to sustain interest, but the heroine of the sub-plot, Nurse Babs of Eichner's clinic, is just "darling," Southern's satirical tip-off word about the pretty, puerile, American Dream Girl he loves to parody. Objects of satire also include television shows ("What's My Disease?"), the medical profession, law courts, the drug scene, the American mania for gadgetry and technical data, and the crazy-culture of California. But the best scene is the seduction in a taxicab of "darling" Babs the button-nosed beauty.

Candy (co-authored with Mason Hoffenberg) was originally published pseudonymously in Paris in 1958, then published in America in 1964, by which time its shocking pornography had lost some sting. The titular heroine, a female, saccharine Candide, is reminiscent also of De Sade's Justine, Harold Gray's Little Orphan Annie, and Southern's own Nurse Babs. The book may be read equally as a satire on cherished American institutions and current delusions, or as a geography of pornography; in Southern's mind the two areas obviously blend, perhaps in their common language of cant and cliché. Candy encounters faddists and fakes in the stronghold of western culture: in academia, the mad bi-sexual Professor Mephisto; in science, the mother-ridden Irving Krankheit, author of *Masturbation Now!*; in religion, Guru Grindle, who convinces Candy of matter's unreality even as he enjoys her body. The most successful scene evolves as a psychotic, witless hunchback—whom sentimental Candy re-names Derek—copulates with the heroine ("he needs me") while he struggles to keep his half-mind on his real goal—money.

Whatever social targets the earlier works neglected, *The Magic Christian* shoots for. Guy Grand, a rich practical joker, spends ten million a year "making it hot for them": he builds superlong autos that jam up intersections; publishes a newspaper cluttered with foreign language phrases; enters a cannibalistic panther in a dog show; and goes on safari with a 75 mm. howitzer. He also inserts short pornographic scenes into film classics; in *The Best Years of Our Lives*, the war hero's hook-hands grapple under his sweetheart's skirt. Guy also opens grocery stores with preposterously low prices—then closes them the same night, to re-locate in mysterious places.

Southern's collected short stories, *Red-Dirt Marijuana and Other Tastes*, revealed greater range and sympathy than the novels. Southern writes well of boys and men, of poor southern whites, of razor fights between Negro brothers, of an American in Paris who is "too hip," and of a surrealistic auto trip through Mexico. The writing is uneven and Southern's questionable taste prevails, but style and mood in the successful stories are superbly lyrical. *Blue Movie* explores sexual boundaries never visited by Candy, but boredom is defeated only by Southern's fine ear for trade talk and some brilliantly awful Hollywood types. Southern is familiar with movie argot and technique, having written scenarios for *Dr. Strangelove*, *The Loved One*, and *Barbarella*. In his movies he employed the same shock therapy by indecency and dehumanization which dominates his novelistic black comedies.

—Frank Campenni

SPARK, Muriel (Sarah, née Camberg). British. Born in Edinburgh, Scotland. Educated at James Gillespie's School for Girls and Heriot Watt College, both Edinburgh. Married S.O. Spark in 1937 (marriage dissolved); one son. Worked in the Political Intelligence Department of the British Foreign Office during World War II. General Secretary of the Poetry Society, and editor of the *Poetry Review*, London, 1947–49. Recipient: *The Observer* story prize, 1951; Italia Prize, for radio drama, 1962; James Tait Black Memorial Prize, 1966. D.Litt.: University of Strathclyde, Glasgow, 1971. Fellow, Royal Society of Literature, 1963; Honorary Member, American Academy, 1978. O.B.E. (Officer, Order of the British Empire), 1967. Lives in Rome. Address: c/o Macmillan London Ltd., 4 Little Essex Street, London WC2R 3LF, England.

PUBLICATIONS

Novels

The Comforters. London, Macmillan, and Philadelphia, Lippincott, 1957.
Robinson. London, Macmillan, and Philadelphia, Lippincott, 1958.
Memento Mori. London, Macmillan, and Philadelphia, Lippincott, 1959.
The Ballad of Peckham Rye. London, Macmillan, and Philadelphia, Lippincott, 1960.
The Bachelors. London, Macmillan, 1960; Philadelphia, Lippincott, 1961.
The Prime of Miss Jean Brodie. London, Macmillan, 1961; Philadelphia, Lippincott, 1962.
The Girls of Slender Means. London, Macmillan, and New York, Knopf, 1963.
The Mandelbaum Gate. London, Macmillan, and New York, Knopf, 1965.
The Public Image. London, Macmillan, and New York, Knopf, 1968.
The Driver's Seat. London, Macmillan, and New York, Knopf, 1970.
Not to Disturb. London, Macmillan, 1971; New York, Viking Press, 1972.
The Hothouse by the East River. London, Macmillan, and New York, Viking Press, 1973.
The Abbess of Crewe. London, Macmillan, and New York, Viking Press, 1974.
The Takeover. London, Macmillan, and New York, Viking Press, 1976.
Territorial Rights. London, Macmillan, and New York, Coward McCann, 1979.
Loitering with Intent. London, Bodley Head, and New York, Coward McCann, 1981.
The Only Problem. London, Bodley Head, and New York, Coward McCann, 1984.

Short Stories

The Go-Away Bird and Other Stories. London, Macmillan, 1958; Philadelphia, Lippincott, 1960.
Voices at Play (includes the radio plays *The Party Through the Wall*, *The Interview*, *The Dry River Bed*, *Danger Zone*). London, Macmillan, 1961; Philadelphia, Lippincott, 1962.
Collected Stories I. London, Macmillan, 1967; New York, Knopf, 1968.
Bang-Bang You're Dead and Other Stories. London, Granada, 1982.
The Stories of Muriel Spark. New York, Dutton, 1985.

Plays

Doctors of Philosophy (produced London, 1962). London, Macmillan, 1963; New York, Knopf, 1966.

Radio Plays: *The Party Through the Wall*, 1957; *The Interview*, 1958; *The Dry River Bed*, 1959; *The Ballad of Peckham Rye*, 1960; *Danger Zone*, 1961.

Verse

Out of a Book (as Muriel Camberg). Leith, Midlothian, Millar and Burden, 1933(?).
The Fanfarlo and Other Verse. Aldington, Kent, Hand and Flower Press, 1952.

Collected Poems I. London, Macmillan, 1967; New York, Knopf, 1968.
Going Up to Sotheby's and Other Poems. London, Granada, 1982.

Other

Child of Light: A Reassessment of Mary Wollstonecraft Shelley. London, Tower Bridge, 1951.
Emily Brontë: Her Life and Work, with Derek Stanford. London, Owen, 1953; New York, British Book Centre, 1960.
John Masefield. London, Nevill, 1953.
The Very Fine Clock (for children). New York, Knopf, 1968; London, Macmillan, 1969.

Editor, with Derek Stanford, *Tribute to Wordsworth.* London, Wingate, 1950.
Editor, *A Selection of Poems*, by Emily Brontë. London, Grey Walls Press, 1952.
Editor, with Derek Stanford, *My Best Mary: The Letters of Mary Shelley.* London, Wingate, 1953.
Editor, *The Brontë Letters.* London, Nevill, 1954; as *The Letters of the Brontës: A Selection*, Norman, University of Oklahoma Press, 1954.
Editor, with Derek Stanford, *Letters of John Henry Newman.* London, Owen, 1957.

*

Bibliography: *Iris Murdoch and Muriel Spark: A Bibliography* by Thomas T. Tominaga and Wilma Schneidermeyer, Metuchen, New Jersey, Scarecrow Press, 1976.

Critical Studies: *Muriel Spark: A Biographical and Critical Study* by Derek Stanford, Fontwell, Sussex, Centaur Press, 1963; *Muriel Spark* by Karl Malkoff, New York, Columbia University Press, 1968; *Muriel Spark* by Patricia Stubbs, London, Longman, 1973; *Muriel Spark* by Peter Kemp, London, Elek, 1974, New York, Barnes and Noble, 1975; *Muriel Spark* by Allan Massie, Edinburgh, Ramsay Head Press, 1979; *The Faith and Fiction of Muriel Spark* by Ruth Whittaker, London, Macmillan, 1982, New York, St. Martin's Press, 1983; *Muriel Spark* by Velma B. Richmond, New York, Ungar, 1983; *Comedy and the Woman Writer: Woolf, Spark, and Feminism* by Judy Little, Lincoln, University of Nebraska Press, 1983; *Muriel Spark: An Odd Capacity for Vision* edited by Alan Bold, London, Vision Press, and New York, Barnes and Noble, 1984.

*   *   *

"Her prose is like a bird, darting from place to place, palpitating with nervous energy; but a bird with a bright beady eye and a sharp beak as well." Francis Hope's description crystallizes one important aspect of Muriel Spark's highly idiosyncratic talent. A late starter in the field of fiction, she had until early middle age published only conventional criticism and verse which gave little hint of her real gifts and future development. These were triumphantly released with the publication of *The Comforters* in 1957, and the spate of creative activity which followed: speedily establishing her reputation as a genuine original with a style and slant on life uniquely her own.

Spark spoke in an interview of her mind "crowded with ideas, all teeming in disorder." In 1954 she had become a convert to Roman Catholicism; and she regards her religion primarily as a discipline for this prodigal fertility—"something to measure

from," as she says, rather than a direct source of its inspiration. Yet her Catholicism pervasively colours a vision of life seen, in her own phrase, "from a slight angle to the universe." For all her inventive energy, verve and panache, and glittering malice, this writer is profoundly preoccupied with metaphysical questions of good and evil. Like Angus Wilson, she is a moral fabulist of the contemporary scene who works through the medium of comedy, and like him, she is often most in earnest when at her most entertaining.

Her novels abound in Catholic characters, but these are by no means always on the side of the angels. In *The Comforters* they teeter on the brink of delusion, retreating from orthodoxy into eccentric extremes of quasi-religious experience satirized with the wicked acuteness with which she later pillories spiritualism in *The Bachelors*, focussing upon the trial of a medium for fraud. Religious hypocrites such as the self-consciously progressive couple in "The Black Madonna" are quite as likely to be her targets as rationalist unbelievers. Her awareness of the powers of darkness as a palpable force at work in the world is most effectively embodied in her study of satanism in the suburbs, *The Ballad of Peckham Rye*, in the diabolic person and activities of an industrial welfare worker born with horns on his head.

Such manifestations of the supernatural in the midst of prosaic actuality are a central element in Spark's novels. Her fantasy, earthed in the everyday, is presented not as illusion but natural extension of the material scene: the product of "that sort of mental squint," as she calls it, which perceives the credible co-existence of the uncanny with the most rational aspects of experience. Those who attempt to ignore or reject its reality—like the cynics staging their tawdry Nativity play and confounded by the avenging intervention of a real angel in "The Seraph and the Zambesi," or the sceptical George trying to explain away the flying saucer of "Miss Pinkerton's Apocalypse"—do so at their peril. Another short story, "The Portobello Road," is narrated by the ghost of a girl who materializes to her murderer in the Saturday morning street market; while *Memento Mori*, in which a number of old people are the victims of a sinister anonymous telephone caller, is a mordant exercise in the macabre. It is subtly suggested that these events might well, for those who choose to believe so, have a straightforward psychological explanation. The ghostly visitant need be no more than an externalization of the murderer's guilty conscience belatedly returned to plague him; the grim practical joker of *Memento* (never finally traced by the police) may embody the insistent reminder of imminent mortality already present within each aged subconscious mind.

Spark's work was highly prized by Evelyn Waugh, whose influence is detectable in the quickfire satirical wit of what one critic called her "machine-gun dialogue." The savage grotesqueries of early Waugh comedy are strongly recalled, too, by the chilling vein of heartlessness, even cruelty, in the violent ends to which so many Spark characters are remorselessly doomed: Needle, smothered in a haystack; the octogenarian Dame Letty, battered in her bed; Joanna Childe, bizarrely chanting passages from the Anglican liturgy as she burns to death; and the bored and loveless office worker of *The Driver's Seat* obsessively resolved to get herself killed in the most brutal possible fashion.

Yet if disaster and death haunt the pages of Spark's novels, her piquant humours are still more abundant. Although *The Girls of Slender Means* ends in tragedy, its portrayal of the impoverished inmates of a war-time hostel for young women of good family is as delectably funny as the depiction, in *The Bachelors*, of their gossipy male counterparts in London bedsitterland; or as the intrigues among nuns at a convent besieged by the media avid for ecclesiastical scandal in *The Abbess of Crewe*. Perhaps Spark's greatest comic triumph is her creation of the exuberant Edinburgh schoolmistress Jean Brodie, grooming her girls for living through an educationally unorthodox but headily exhilarating curriculum ranging from her heroes, Franco and Mussolini, to the love-lives of remarkable women of history, including her own.

Spark's narrative expertise is best exemplified in shorter forms, where her stylistic economy so often achieves a riveting intensity of impact. By contrast a longer, more ambitious book like *The Mandelbaum Gate*, about the adventures of a half-Jewish Catholic convert caught up in the divisions of warring Jerusalem, seems laboured and diffuse. Two later novels, *The Takeover*, set during the 1970's but rooted in classical mythology, and *Territorial Rights*, have the Italian background which the author clearly finds a fruitful imaginative climate for exploring such themes as the exploitation of bogus religion and excessive wealth.

Loitering with Intent returns to her earlier London scene, and a time just after the Second World War. The composition of a struggling author's first novel is skilfully interwoven with her experiences in the employ of a bizarre society of pseudo-writers, whose grotesque fantasies, deceptions, and intrigues entertainingly reveal the possibilities of confusion between life and art. In *The Only Problem* the central character is a hapless scholar vainly seeking peace and seclusion in order to wrestle with interpreting the Book of Job. The daily problems of his own life increasingly impinge upon this task—not least the procession of modern counterparts of his biblical subject's comforters, or persecutors.

All these later works wryly illustrate those characteristic qualities of sly, deadly wit in observing human oddity and weakness, the ingenious fusion of fact with fantasy and unpredictable surprise, and the underlying moral seriousness, which make Muriel Spark one of our most stimulating and quirkily individual novelists.

—Margaret Willy

SPENCER, Colin. British. Born in London, 17 July 1933. Educated at Brighton Grammar School, Selhurst; Brighton College of Art. Served in the Royal Army Medical Corps, 1950–52. Married Gillian Chapman in 1959 (divorced, 1969); one son. Paintings exhibited in Cambridge and London; costume designer. Chairman, Writers Guild of Great Britain, 1982–83. Agent: (plays) Margaret Ramsay Ltd., 14a Goodwin's Court, London WC2N 4LL; (novels) Richard Scott Simon, 32 College Cross, London N1 1PR. Address: 2 Heath Cottages, Tunstall, near Woodbridge, Suffolk IP12 2HQ, England.

PUBLICATIONS

Novels

An Absurd Affair.   London, Longman, 1961.
Generation:
    Anarchists in Love.   London, Eyre and Spottiswoode, 1963; as *The Anarchy of Love*, New York, Weybright and Talley, 1967.
    The Tyranny of Love.   London, Blond, and New York, Weybright and Talley, 1967.

Lovers in War.   London, Blond, 1969.
    The Victims of Love.   London, Quartet, 1978.
Asylum.   London, Blond, 1966.
Poppy, Mandragora, and the New Sex.   London, Blond, 1966.
Panic.   London, Secker and Warburg, 1971.
How the Greeks Kidnapped Mrs. Nixon.   London, Quartet, 1974.

Uncollected Short Stories

"Nightworkers," in *London Magazine*, vol. 2, no. 12, 1955.
"An Alien World," in *London Magazine*, vol. 3, no. 6, 1956.
"Nymph and Shepherd," in *London Magazine*, vol. 6, no. 8, 1959.
"It's Anemones for Mabel," in *Transatlantic Review* (London), Spring 1963.
"The Room," in *Transatlantic Review* (London), Summer 1966.
"Carpaccio's Dream," in *Harpers and Queen* (London), December 1985.

Plays

The Ballad of the False Barman, music by Clifton Parker (produced London, 1966).
Spitting Image (produced London, 1968; New York, 1969). Published in *Plays and Players* (London), September 1968.
The Trial of St. George (produced London, 1972).
The Sphinx Mother (produced Salzburg, Austria, 1972).
Why Mrs. Neustadter Always Loses (produced London, 1972).
Keep It in the Family (also director: produced London, 1978).
Lilith (produced Vienna, 1979).

Television Plays: *Flossie*, 1975; *Vandal Rule OK?* (documentary), 1977.

Other

Gourmet Cooking for Vegetarians.   London, Deutsch, 1978.
Good and Healthy.   London, Robson, 1983; as *Vegetarian Wholefood Cookbook*, London, Panther, 1985.
Reports from Behind, with Chris Barlas.   London, Enigma, 1984.
Cordon Vert.   Wellingborough, Northamptonshire, Thorsons, 1985.

*

Critical Study: interview with Peter Burton, in *Transatlantic Review 35* (London), 1970.

Theatrical Activities:
Director: **Play**—*Keep It in the Family*, London, 1978.

Colin Spencer comments:
    I have the impression that my work taken as a whole can be confusing to a critic or a reader. Both the novels and the plays appear to be written in too many various styles; if this is true I make no apologies but will attempt an explanation. The main core of my work as a writer is found in the four volumes of the unfinished sequence of novels: *Generation*. This, in its simplest form is nothing but fictionalised autobiography—the line where fiction begins and reality ends is a philosophical enigma that continually fascinates me. The volumes are sagas of various families, their children and grand-

children, their marriages and relationships; their social context is firmly middle-class though in later volumes some of the characters move into the upper-middle stratas while others remain socially rootless. I have struggled in these books to make the characters and their backgrounds as true to what I have observed and experienced as my perception and recollection allow. For I believe that the novel form is unique in being as exact a mirror to our experience as is afforded in the whole range of art forms. For not only can the novel communicate the great obsessive passions, frustrations, and longings of individuals, but it can also conjure up a picture of all the myriad details—quite trivial in themselves—which at certain times affect major actions. In form I based these interrelating novels on the 19th-century tradition (it is a complicated story with many characters) but I have allowed myself within that framework to use all the literary experiments forged in the first half of this century. The characters that I have created from my experience and observation are not puppets; I cannot control and guide them into some preconceived aesthetic pattern, for they exist in life and in the narration I have to pursue and relate as truthfully as possible their own tragic mistakes, their comic failures and triumphs, their self-deceit and affirmation of life.

But in my plays there is no direct autobiographical experience: they are, like some of the other novels, satires on social problems that oppress individuals. I like to entertain in the theatre, to make an audience laugh but at the same time debate at the core of the work a serious and unresolved problem. The novels *Poppy, Mandragora, and the New Sex* and *How the Greeks Kidnapped Mrs. Nixon* also use comedy to expose gross injustice. *Panic* treats another subject, that of child assault, on the surface as a murder mystery, yet its main intention was to induce the reader to understand the psychological nature of the killer. I would dismiss my first novel, *An Absurd Affair*, as merely a public rehearsal in the craft of fiction. But there is one novel that falls outside any of the above categories —*Asylum*. The Oedipus myth has always fascinated me. (The play *The Sphinx Mother* is a contemporary account of the Jocasta figure refusing to commit suicide and struggling for final and complete possession of her son/husband.) Another myth, the Fall of Man, with its pervasive sense of original sin corroding free will seems for me with the Oedipus myth to have influenced the compulsive aspirations in Western culture for over two thousand years. In *Asylum* I created a plot, loosely based on a 19th-century American scandal, where I united both myths in the same family and set it in a hierarchic social commune, almost a science-fiction Asylum. I then tried to imply how our religious and judicial structure worked through arbitrary indifference and cruel repression. I might add that for large passages of the book I allowed myself the indulgence of writing in a style akin to poetic prose.

If I may sum up I would say that I feel my job as a writer is to state the truth in as vivid a manner as is possible and to involve the reader in a celebration of life, while uncovering the injustices that as individuals and as society we impose upon each other.

                              *   *   *

Colin Spencer's novels revel in the eccentric, the bizarre, and the grotesque while tending toward social commentary. His event-filled books treat of human relationships buffeted by sexual antagonisms of various, extreme types. In depicting his frequently polymorphously perverse characters, Spencer plays a recurrent theme of protest against conventional mores

and morality, although, perhaps unintentionally, the alternatives he presents hardly seem more satisfactory. With casts of almost Dickensian proportions and curiosity, he runs the gamut of sexual expression, particularly homosexual. Sympathetic understanding, graphic detail, and a fine talent for low comedy do not often, however, extend his narratives beyond the superficial or raise them from mere sensationalism to genuine significance. Nor does his tendency to have protagonist-spokesmen speechify make his arguments more appealing.

In *An Absurd Affair* Spencer sketches some telling scenes of marital dependence and oppression, but soon gives way to improbable melodrama. Conceited, petty, and dull, James dominates his immature, thoughtless child-wife, Sarah. Though he is undereducated and boring, James finds his wife inferior and her love of art beyond his comprehension. By accident, Sarah finds the negative of a "dirty" picture, and, to the prudish James's shock, she is fascinated. Undue influence by this "art," along with romantic infatuation and huge amounts of alcohol, leads the insecure woman into a ludicrous pursuit of a sadistic schoolteacher and finally into a delusory affair with a Sicilian gigolo. Though James rescues her, she finds she no longer loves him and declares her independence. For all Spencer's obvious and overdrawn psychologizing, both characters remain rather implausible caricatures in what is, indeed, an absurd affair, unredeemed by the crude poetic justice—or ladies' magazine moralizing—of its pat ending.

Of considerably more merit and interest are the volumes of the projected series *Generation*, a sizeable contribution to the large corpus of English novels examining life in reaction to post-World War II conditions, in this case a sprawling saga of the Simpson family from World War I through the 1960's. Shifting back and forth over the years, Spencer draws vivid, well-rounded portraits of several characteristic types, some of which develop into unique personalities; the ever more complicated alliances and misalliances of the heterogeneous Simpsons reveal a fascinating panorama of several social milieus. While realistic scenes are well-executed, the more emotional confrontations take on the unfortunate tone of a soap opera. And though characters occasionally mention and blame the War for their uncertain, disjointed worlds, its significance for their individual struggles is implied more than clearly stated.

Weaving in and out of the separate stories of the factional family members, friends, and lovers, Eddy Simpson's raunchy career, depicted in short, often raucous vignettes, becomes a central focus for understanding the wayward, amusing, and sometimes pathetic journeys in the novels. Crude and conscious only of his own desires, paterfamilias Eddy jokes, drinks, and womanizes. His Rabelaisian zest for life can be hilarious, but it is also ruinous for the rest of the Simpsons. Long-suffering wife hester turns to religion, whose comforts are of little use to her artistic and volatile children Sundy and Matthew. The major portions of the novels are devoted to their painful growing up and tortured adulthood.

Hetero-, homo-, and bi-sexual roles are played out in several combinations; in the convoluted course of the interconnected plots there is more changing of partners than in a country square dance. Sundy is most original. After dallying with lesbianism, she is caught briefly in an incestuous bond. She takes up with Reg, a handsome liar, self-proclaimed anarchist, and sometimes rent-boy, aborts their illegitimate child, and finally, confusedly, marries him. After losing Reg to her brother Matthew, she leads a bohemian life with an unreliable publisher. Through tumultuous years, Matthews's reactions to his father's boorishness and cruelty alternate between dejection and desire for revenge, religious fanaticism and self-hatred.

His homosexuality comes slowly to consciousness but not acceptance, and his ambivalence ends in a disastrous and mutually destructive marriage to a priggish, unstable shrew.

Along the way he portrays lower-, middle-, and upper-class life, as well as the more baroque aspects of the homosexual world, with deftness and insight. Sometimes his prose sags, but generally Spencer's humor, irony, and use of contrast are skillful, allowing his themes to reveal themselves by inference. Perhaps his strongest points are made by the self-inflicted wounds of the "anarchists" whose intellectual poses ineffectually mask their adolescent, mixed-up libertinism.

Constructed in a fantastic mode, *Asylum* displays Spencer's penchant for the macabre. The patients in the ultra-modern insane asylum are prompted to act out their twisted pasts and perverse imaginings by the equally but scientifically demented psychiatrists (who are, in turn, directed by monstrous computers), before they are hunted and left to die. Spencer's surrealistic vision combines and curiously reworks *Oedipus* and the Book of Genesis through phantasmagoric permutations. In the confused dimension of illusion-reality, Cleo-Jocasta tries to work her incestuous vindicative will upon her priest-husband Max (Addams) through their dark-skinned son Carl, but Carl prefers the charms of his fair-skinned brother Angelo. While the inversions and embroidery of the Greek and Judaic myths are imaginative, their point is often as obscure as Cleo's mad history.

Perhaps Spencer's most mature work is his probing analysis of the mentality of the child molester in *Panic*. With the seamy Brighton underworld as a backdrop, the novel unfolds the wretched life of Woody and his mother Saffron May and their increasingly perverted relationship, culminating in the tragic child-murders. Spencer tells the gripping story through the voices of the major characters, carefully controlling the tensions to the last climactic moments. What was once used largely for shock value in earlier books, now is integral to theme and structure. Both killer and victims are revealed with sympathy from the inside, and even the freakish characters of the lesbian burglar Trigger and the wretched dwarf Jumbo emerge as strange but human beings.

—Joseph Parisi

SPENCER, Elizabeth. American. Born in Carrollton, Mississippi, 19 July 1921. Educated at Belhaven College, Jackson, Mississippi, 1938–42, A.B. 1942; Vanderbilt University, Nashville, 1942–43, M.A. 1943. Married John Rusher in 1956. Instructor, Northwest Mississippi Junior College, Senatobia, 1943–44, and Ward-Belmont College, Nashville, 1944–45; reporter, Nashville *Tennessean*, 1945–46; Instructor, 1948–49, and Instructor in Creative Writing, 1949–51, 1952–53, University of Mississippi, Oxford; Donnelly Fellow, Bryn Mawr College, Pennsylvania, 1962; Creative Writing Fellow, University of North Carolina, Chapel Hill, 1969; Writer-in-Residence, Hollins College, Virginia, 1973. Member of the creative writing faculty, 1976–81, and since 1981, Adjunct Professor, Concordia University, Montreal. Recipient: American Academy Recognition Award, 1952, Rosenthal Award, 1957, and Award of Merit Medal, 1983; Guggenheim fellowship, 1953; *Kenyon Review* fellowship, 1957; McGraw-Hill fiction award, 1960; Bellaman Award, 1968; National Endowment for the Arts grant, 1982. D.L.: Southwestern (now Rhodes) University, Memphis, 1968. Member, American Academy, 1985. Agent:

Virginia Barber, 353 West 21st Street, New York, New York 10011, U.S.A. Address: 2300 St. Matthew, Apartment 610, Montreal, Quebec H3H 2J8, Canada.

PUBLICATIONS

Novels

Fire in the Morning.   New York, Dodd Mead, 1948.
This Crooked Way.   New York, Dodd Mead, and London, Gollancz, 1952.
The Voice at the Back Door.   New York, McGraw Hill, 1956; London, Gollancz, 1957.
The Light in the Piazza.   New York, McGraw Hill, 1960; London, Heinemann, 1961.
Knights and Dragons.   New York, McGraw Hill, 1965; London, Heinemann, 1966.
No Place for an Angel.   New York, McGraw Hill, 1967; London, Weidenfeld and Nicolson, 1968.
The Snare.   New York, McGraw Hill, 1972.
The Salt Line.   New York, Doubleday, 1984; London, Penguin, 1985.

Short Stories

Ship Island and Other Stories.   New York, McGraw Hill, 1968; London, Weidenfeld and Nicolson, 1969.
The Stories of Elizabeth Spencer.   New York, Doubleday, 1981; London, Penguin, 1983.
Marilee: Three Stories.   Jackson, University Press of Mississippi, 1981.
The Mules.   Winston-Salem, North Carolina, Palaemon Press, 1982.

Uncollected Short Stories

"To the Watchers While Walking Home," in *Ontario Review* (Princeton, New Jersey), 1982.
"Jean-Pierre," in *Prize Stories 1983: The O. Henry Awards*, edited by William Abrahams. New York, Doubleday, 1983.
"Madonna" and "Puzzle Poem," in *Hudson Review* (New York), Summer 1983.
"The Cousins," in *Southern Review* (Baton Rouge, Louisiana), Summer 1985.

*

Manuscript Collections: National Library of Canada, Ottawa; University of Kentucky, Lexington.

Critical Study: *Elizabeth Spencer* by Peggy Whitman Prenshaw, Boston, Twayne, 1985.

Elizabeth Spencer comments:

I began writing down stories as soon as I learned how to write; that is, at about age six; before that, I made them up anyway and told them to anybody who was handy and would listen. Being a rural Southerner, a Mississippian, had a lot to do with it, I have been told, with this impulse and with the peculiar mystique, importance, which attached itself naturally thereto and enhanced it. We had been brought up on stories, those about local people, living and dead, and Bible narratives, believed also to be literally true, so that other stories read aloud—the Greek myths, for instance—while indicated as "just" stories, were only one slight remove from the "real" stories of the local scene and the Bible. So it was with history, for local event spilled into the history of the textbooks; my grandfather could remember the close of the Civil War, and my elder brother's nurse had been a slave. The whole world, then, was either entirely in the nature of stories or partook so deeply of stories as to be at every point inseparable from them. Even the novels we came later to read were mainly English 19th-century works which dealt with a culture similar to our own—we learned with no surprise that we had sprung from it.

Though I left the South in 1953, I still see the world and its primal motions as story, since story charts in time the heart's assertions and gives central place to the great human relationships. My first three novels, written or projected before I left the South, deal with people in that society who must as the true measure of themselves either alter it or come to terms with it. Years I spent in Italy and more recently in Canada have made me see the world in other than this fixed geography. The challenge to wring its stories from it became to me more difficult at the same time that it became more urgent that I and other writers should do so. A story may not be the only wrench one can hurl into the giant machine that seems bent on devouring us all, but is one of them. A story which has been tooled, shaped, and slicked up is neither real nor true—we know its nature and its straw insides. Only the real creature can satisfy, the one that is touchy and alive, dangerous to fool with. The search for such as these goes on with me continually, and I think for all real writers as well.

*   *   *

Elizabeth Spencer's first three novels portray the upper middle class of her native Mississippi trapped between the decadent planter aristocrats and politically ambitious "redneck" bigots who were William Faulkner's special province. *Fire in the Morning* (titled from Djuna Barnes's *Nightwood*) grimly depicts the effectiveness of petty greed in stifling a small community's vitality. The Gerrard family moved into Tarsus in the wake of Civil War disruptions and made themselves leading citizens through perjury and blackmail. Their machinations result, however, only in the destruction of almost everyone involved except one Gerrard son and a former schoolmate, son of one of the family's principal victims. These young men achieve a reconciliation when the Gerrard follows the many other people driven from the community and the other, Kinloch Armstrong, learns that his strength is the very "strangeness" he has always felt that allows him to transcend the squalor that engulfs the others. *This Crooked Way* is a less complex and more cynical tale about an opportunist who comes down from the hills to become a Delta planter. Amos Dudley has always dreamed of seeing a ladder of angels, but his inability to face reality results only in the wreckage of the lives of his family and most of those around him.

Spencer's most powerful novel, *The Voice at the Back Door*, bares the history of a well-educated and inherently decent young lawyer, Kerney Woolbright, who must sacrifice his integrity to win political preferment in his community. The novel contrasts Kerney's lying about his knowledge of an explosive situation involving a Negro in order to assure his victory at the polls with the behavior of Duncan Harper, a truculently honest athelete—once idol of the community—who sacrifices a comfortable career to protect the Negro from ignorant bigotry.

After this chilling revelation of the corruption of competence and the persecution of decency, Spencer abandoned Mississippi

for Italy, which inspired two brief novels about women who escape abroad to victory, *The Light in the Piazza*, source of an unusually tasteful and subtle film, tensely relates an American mother's risky effort to marry her mentally retarded daughter to an attractive young Florentine despite her husband's misgivings and the Italian family's efforts to profit by the match. *Knights and Dragons* studies an American woman who has fled to Rome after her marriage collapse and who finds at last that human love demands too much of the individual to be worth the struggle, so that she frees herself—like Frederico Fellini's Juliet of the Spirits—to become "a companion to cloud and sky."

After these short, intense international novels, Spencer returned by stages to the United States and, at last, Mississippi. *No Place for an Angel* chronicles against an international background (Washington–Florida, Rome–Sicily and elsewhere) the intricate interrelationships of two married couples and their sprawling families and a young American sculptor, who dreams like Amos Dudley of angels. One wife says of her husband, "Jerry had to be great, and he almost made it." The novel is a mature, unsentimental account of characters that almost make it, only to find—as one put it—that "life keeps turning into a vacuum," though the author tempers the bleakness by suggesting that these people's children may find happiness by wanting less. *The Snare* concentrates on a woman who does at last "make it" by never seeking greatness. Julia Garrett's life in a New Orleans that the novelist pictures with special skill has been a search on "a many-branched road" for an identity from the time that her aimless father abandons her in the arms of better-placed relatives. Frustrated in efforts to achieve mature relationships, Julia realizes herself at last not through the vision of an angel, but the person of her own very real child.

After a long period during which she experimented with a variety of short stories, Spencer returned to Mississippi's Gulf Coast in *The Salt Line*; but the region is no longer Faulkner's gothic south nor the transitory plastic America that materialized after World War II. *The Salt Line* occurs after Hurricane Camille, which in 1969 devastated the modernizing region. We witness efforts to rebuild principally through three survivors—two of whom were former friends as college professors, the other a petty gangster—through whose own lives hurricanes have passed. While they blame "bad luck," they are what Scott Fitzgerald called "careless people." Just as residents of the hurricane-prone areas return to waiting out seasons nervously, these leading characters return to their old ways. At the end of the novel, Spencer holds out the possibility of "the bright redemption of love"; but the vision illuminating the novel is that love helps people endure, but not prevail. As Peggy Prenshaw points out, the Byronic central figure of *The Salt Line* faces the future asking the same question as Robert Frost's oven-bird—what to make of "a diminished thing."

—Warren French

STEGNER, Wallace (Earle). American. Born in Lake Mills, Iowa, 18 February 1909. Educated at the University of Utah, Salt Lake City, A.B. 1930; University of Iowa, Iowa City, A.M. 1932, Ph.D. 1935; University of California, Berkeley, 1932–33. Married Mary Stuart Page in 1934; one son. Instructor, Augustana College, Rock Island, Illinois, 1933–34, University of Utah, 1934–37, and University of Wisconsin,

Madison, 1937–39; Faculty Instructor, Harvard University, Cambridge, Massachusetts, 1939–45; Professor of English, 1945–69, and Jackson Eli Reynolds Professor of Humanities, 1969–71, Stanford University, California. Writer-in-Residence, American Academy in Rome, 1960; Phi Beta Kappa Visiting Scholar, 1960. West Coast Editor, Houghton Mifflin Company, publishers, Boston, 1945–53. Assistant to the United States Secretary of the Interior, Washington, D.C., 1961. Member, 1962–66, and Chairman, 1965–66, National Parks Advisory Board, Washington, D.C. Editor-in-Chief, *American West* magazine, Palo Alto, California, 1966–68. Recipient: Little Brown Prize, 1937; O. Henry Award, 1942, 1950, 1954; Houghton Mifflin Life-in-America Award, 1945; Anisfield-Wolf Award, 1945; Guggenheim fellowship, 1949–51, 1959; Rockefeller fellowship, 1950; Wenner-Gren grant, 1953; Center for Advanced Studies in the Behavioral Sciences fellowship, 1955; National Endowment for the Humanities senior fellowship, 1972; Pulitzer Prize, 1972; Western Literature Association award, 1974; National Book Award, 1977; *Los Angeles Times* Kirsch Award, 1980. D.Litt.: University of Utah, 1968; Utah State University, Logan, 1972; D.F.A.: University of California, 1969; D.L.: University of Saskatchewan, Saskatoon, 1973; D.H.L.: University of Santa Clara, California, 1979. Member, American Academy, and American Academy of Arts and Sciences. Agent: Brandt and Brandt, 1501 Broadway, New York, New York 10036. Address: 13456 South Fork Lane, Los Altos Hills, California 94022, U.S.A.

PUBLICATIONS

Novels

Remembering Laughter.   Boston, Little Brown, and London, Heinemann, 1937.
The Potter's House.   Muscatine, Iowa, Prairie Press, 1938.
On a Darkling Plain.   New York, Harcourt Brace, 1940.
Fire and Ice.   New York, Duell, 1941.
The Big Rock Candy Mountain.   New York, Duell, 1943; London, Hammond, 1950.
Second Growth.   Boston, Houghton Mifflin, 1947; London, Hammond, 1948.
The Preacher and the Slave.   Boston, Houghton Mifflin, 1950; London, Hammond, 1951; as *Joe Hill: A Biographical Novel*, New York, Doubleday, 1969.
A Shooting Star.   New York, Viking Press, and London, Heinemann, 1961.
All the Little Live Things.   New York, Viking Press, 1967; London, Heinemann, 1968.
Angle of Repose.   New York, Doubleday, and London, Heinemann, 1971.
The Spectator Bird.   New York, Doubleday, 1976; London, Prior, 1977.
Recapitulation.   New York, Doubleday, 1979.

Short Stories

The Women on the Wall.   Boston, Houghton Mifflin, 1950; London, Hammond, 1952.
The City of the Living.   Boston, Houghton Mifflin, 1956; London, Hammond, 1957.
New Short Novels 2, with others.   New York, Ballantine, 1956.

Uncollected Short Stories

"He Who Spits at the Sky," in *Esquire* (New York), March 1958.
"Something Spurious from the Mindanao Deep," in *Harper's* (New York), August 1958.
"The Wolfer," in *Harper's* (New York), October 1959.
"Carrion Spring," in *Prize Stories 1964: The O. Henry Awards*, edited by Richard Poirier.   New York, Doubleday, 1964.

Other

Mormon Country.   New York, Duell, 1942.
One Nation, with editors of *Look*.   Boston, Houghton Mifflin, 1945.
Look at America: The Central Northwest, with others.   Boston, Houghton Mifflin, 1947.
The Writer in America (lectures).   Tokyo, Hokuseido Press, 1952; South Pasadena, California, Perkins and Hutchins, 1953.
Beyond the Hundredth Meridian: John Wesley Powell and the Second Opening of the West.   Boston, Houghton Mifflin, 1954.
Wolf Willow: A History, A Story, and A Memory of the Last Plains Frontier.   New York, Viking Press, 1962; London, Heinemann, 1963.
The Gathering of Zion: The Story of the Mormon Trail.   New York, McGraw Hill, 1964; London, Eyre and Spottiswoode, 1966.
The Sound of Mountain Water: The Changing American West.   New York, Doubleday, 1969.
The Uneasy Chair: A Biography of Bernard DeVoto.   New York, Doubleday, 1974.
Ansel Adams: Images 1923–1974.   Greenwich, Connecticut, New York Graphic Society, 1974.
American Places, with Page Stegner, photographs by Eliot Porter, edited by John Macrae II.   New York, Dutton, and London, Aurum Press, 1981.
One Way to Spell Man (essays).   New York, Doubleday, 1982.
Conversations with Wallace Stegner on Western History and Literature, with Richard W. Etulain.   Salt Lake City, University of Utah Press, 1983.

Editor, with others, *An Exposition Workshop*.   Boston, Little Brown, 1939.
Editor, with others, *Readings for Citizens at War*.   New York, Harper, 1941.
Editor, with Richard Scowcroft, *Stanford Short Stories 1946*.   Stanford, California, Stanford University Press, 1947 (and later volumes).
Editor, with Richard Scowcroft and Boris Ilyin, *The Writer's Art: A Collection of Short Stories*.   Boston, Heath, 1950.
Editor, *This Is Dinosaur: Echo Park Country and Its Magic Rivers*.   New York, Knopf, 1955.
Editor, *The Exploration of the Colorado River of the West*, by J.W. Powell.   Chicago, University of Chicago Press, 1957.
Editor, with Mary Stegner, *Great American Short Stories*.   New York, Dell, 1957.
Editor, *Selected American Prose: The Realistic Movement*.   New York, Rinehart, 1958; London, Owen, 1963.
Editor, *The Adventures of Huckleberry Finn*, by Mark Twain.   New York, Dell, 1960.
Editor, *The Outcasts of Poker Flat*, by Bret Harte.   New York, New American Library, 1961.

Editor, *Report on the Lands of the Arid Region of the United States*, by J.W. Powell. Cambridge, Massachusetts, Harvard University Press, and London, Oxford University Press, 1962.

Editor, with others, *Modern Composition*. New York, Holt Rinehart, 4 vols., 1964.

Editor, *The American Novel: From Cooper to Faulkner*. New York, Basic Books, 1965.

Editor, *The Big Sky*, by A.B. Guthrie, Jr. Boston, Houghton Mifflin, 1965.

Editor, with Richard Scowcroft, *Twenty Years of Stanford Short Stories*. Stanford, California, Stanford University Press, 1966.

Editor, *Twice-Told Tales*, by Nathaniel Hawthorne. New York, Heritage Press, 1967.

Editor, *The Letters of Bernard DeVoto*. New York, Doubleday, 1975.

*

Manuscript Collections: University of Iowa, Iowa City; Stanford University, California.

Critical Studies: *Wallace Stegner* by Merrill and Lorene Lewis, Boise, Idaho, Boise State College, 1972; "Wallace Stegner: Trial by Existence" by Robert Canzoneri, in *Southern Review* (Baton Rouge, Louisiana), Autumn 1973; *Wallace Stegner* by Forrest G. and Margaret G. Robinson, Boston, Twayne, 1977.

Wallace Stegner comments:

My subjects and themes are mainly out of the American West, in which I grew up. Because I grew up without history, in a place where human occupation had left fewer traces than the passage of buffalo and antelope herds, I early acquired the desire to find some history in which I myself belonged, and some tradition within which I might have a self-respecting part. For that reason, I suppose, I have never been a rebel against tradition in general, however much I may have resisted specific and rigid aspects of it. I have written fiction whose impulse was at least as much social as psychological. I do not think any individual, in fiction or in life, is defined except within the group life that formed him. Even *The Big Rock Candy Mountain*, which deals with a wandering, asteroid-like family on the western frontiers, is a search for a place and a stability. Even *Angle of Repose*, which likewise deals with a pioneering family of a kind, is a study in continuity.

*　　*　　*

Wallace Stegner is a writer whose sizable body of work includes not only novels and volumes of short stories but also historical works such as *Mormon Country*, *Beyond the Hundredth Meridian*, and *The Gathering of Zion: The Story of the Mormon Trail*. These latter works indicate a mind and a temperament which are profoundly stirred by elements in the American past. It is a past that has great usefulness to a writer who, in many of his works of fiction, tries to see that past as a permanent element in present American experience. This past has its beginnings in Eastern, "cultivated" experience and extends westward, in time and space, across plains and mountains, until it reaches the rich promises and frustrating ambiguities of modern California.

In his novels Stegner singles out various stages of this westward movement and attempts to assess the partial meanings that each stage offers an attentive novelist who brings to his reading of chosen subject-matter insights which he shares with social historians. Stegner's subject-matter is marked by a richness and complexity that are not easily reduced to simple patterns. Yet a kind of constant can be isolated as cropping up again and again as the novels move from New England experience of the present in *Second Growth* to various Western times and places. *On a Darkling Plain* tells of the experiment in isolation made by a young veteran of World War I in Western Canada; the young man, rather significantly in relation to Stegner's later work, feels a need to detach himself from a modern world that has distorted human promise. *The Big Rock Candy Mountain* has for its subject the wanderings of a family in Western lands: lands that offer the group a mixture of promise and defeat. In *The Preacher and the Slave* Stegner offers a fictionalized account of the IWW movement of the first decades of this century. Three later novels—*A Shooting Star*, *All the Little Live Things*, and *The Spectator Bird*—move to the California of the present; they measure the sad realization of the promise inherent in the great westward movement. It is a promise badly betrayed in the experience of the neurotic heroine of *A Shooting Star*. It is a promise that is in part realized by the ability of the retired academic in *All the Little Live Things* to be a stern judge of the course that American civilization is taking. The retired academic reappears—in essence if not in fact—as the historian-hero of *Angle of Repose*, a man confined to a wheel-chair where he passes his time writing a work, part-history, part-fiction, that recreates the Western experience of his grandmother: a Western life more charged with promise than the heroes—men of the arts, one and all—find in the California present. Certainly the retired literary agent, "writer" of *The Spectator Bird* blends his personal meditation on his coming death with strictures of the emptiness of current life and literature, and meditation on a transient affair hardly offsets these. Another late novel, *Recapitulation*, is set in Utah rather than California, but its effect is much the same; once more an elderly man—in this instance a diplomat—is forced by circumstance to make a reckoning of his life, its betrayals and its small triumphs.

These brief summaries give one some idea of what one will encounter in the novels of Stegner. The subject-matter is, within the limits indicated, various. But the style and the writer's attention to his material create an effect of considerable unity in the entire body of work. The style is sober and expresses the desire of the author to reproduce the persons and the settings of their experience as, supposedly, they actually existed. The novels plainly rest at many points on careful research, as Stegner notes in prefatory remarks to *Second Growth*: "The making of fiction entails the creation of places and persons with all the seeming of reality, and these places and persons, no matter how a writer tries to invent them, must be made up piece-meal from sublimations of his own experience and his own acquaintance. There is no other material out of which fiction can be made." This is an observation that is supplemented—but not contradicted by—the "Foreword" to the IWW novel, *The Preacher and the Slave*, where Stegner defends the novelist's right to reshape what has come to him not from direct experience but from research. This is a set of remarks that express and justify the boldness with which the historian-novelist of *Angle of Repose* handles and supplements the letters, articles, and drawings out of which he reconstructs his grandmother's Western life. If there is indeed a "seeming of reality" in Stegner's fiction, it is a reality constructed by a prose that is exhaustive and faithful; there are no turns of language that, as in much modern fiction, mock the reality that the author has created only to put in question.

This style is, of course, an expression of the unfolding assessment of experience in Stegner's novels. It is an assessment that moves toward precision and some bitterness in the most recent novels. But the main outlines of this assessment are already apparent in an early work like *On a Darkling Plain*. When desperate laughter sweeps a roomful of persons suffering from influenza, Stegner indicates that there are two ways to view miserable humanity. The world may indeed be the work of a "malevolent torturer—a reference to a dark power that is the nearest Stegner comes to the theological reference, for he is the most non-theological of novelists. This "torturer" may indeed have peopled the earth with "cannibal apes." Yet Stegner qualifies this vision. "At its worst the world had that face, but at its best, in its stricken hours, one saw the reserves of nobility and endurance and high-hearted courage that kept the race alive." Stegner's hero "knew, as he had always known since Ypres, that in the comradeship of ruin there was a tempering of the spirit; the resiliency of humanity under the whip was justification for all its meannesses."

In his reading of human behaviour Stegner tends to separate the "cannibal apes" from those who display "reserves of nobility and endurance and high-hearted courage." In contrast to the resilient in *On a Darkling Plain* is a low-minded, lecherous Cockney who introduces the influenza virus to his betters. *Second Growth* offers us a New England Eden—or comparative Eden—corrupted by the presence of a Lesbian. Stegner's dichotomy becomes intense in *All the Little Live Things* and *Angle of Repose*. Both novels, as noted, are told from the point of view of a meditative, scholarly, and elderly man who is able to remember and reconstruct the hopes of earlier generations. Against these hopes, both men put the current reality. It is a reality in which the privileged have lost the sense that privilege imposes obligations. It is a reality in which the underprivileged have detached themselves from the "comradeship of ruin" and seek the instant salvation that drugs and "meditation" offer. The grandmother of *Angle of Repose* accepted the "comradeship of ruin"; those who have come after her try to evade it. So doing, they turn their backs on the sort of experience that Stegner finds in the Western past. It is this keen sense of wilful modern betrayal, wilful evasion of the harsh conditions under which all men exist, that accounts for the bitter and prophetic ire that now marks Stegner's work.

—Harold H. Watts

STERN, James (Andrew). British. Born in Kilcairne, County Meath, Ireland, 26 December 1904. Educated at Eton College; Royal Military College, Sandhurst. Married Tania Kurella in 1935. Farmer in Rhodesia, 1925–26; bank clerk in London and Germany, 1927–29. Assistant editor, *London Mercury*, 1929–31; free-lance journalist throughout Europe; lived for 16 years in the United States. Recipient: American Academy grant, 1949; Arts Council grant, 1966. Fellow, Royal Society of Literature, 1953. Address: Hatch Manor, Tisbury, Wiltshire, England.

PUBLICATIONS

Short Stories

The Heartless Land. London, Macmillan, and New York, Macmillan, 1932.
Something Wrong. London, Secker and Warburg, 1938.

The Man Who Was Loved. New York, Harcourt Brace, 1951; London, Secker and Warburg, 1952.
The Stories of James Stern. London, Secker and Warburg, 1968; New York, Harcourt Brace, 1969.

Uncollected Short Stories

"The Dunce," in *London Mercury*, July 1931.
"Strangers Defeated," in *London Mercury*, August 1933.
"The Man from Montparnasse," in *Penguin Parade 1.* London, Penguin, 1937.
"The Young Lady," in *Penguin Parade 7.* London, Penguin, 1940.
"The Thief," in *New Statesman and Nation* (London), 14 September 1940.
"The Ebbing Tide," in *Penguin New Writing.* London, Penguin, 1942.
"The Pauper's Grave," in *Harper's Bazaar* (New York), 1946.
"Allergies," in *London Magazine*, June 1970.
"A Day at the Races," in *Dublin Magazine*, Winter 1970–71.
"Bloody Monday," in *London Magazine*, June-July 1972.
"The Facts of Life," in *Winter's Tales 23*, edited by Peter Collinette. London, Macmillan, 1977; New York, St. Martin's Press, 1978.
"The Terriers' Treat," in *Irish Press* (Dublin), February 1979.

Play

The Caucasian Chalk Circle, with W.H. Auden and Tania Stern, adaptation of the play by Brecht (produced London, 1962). Published in *Plays*, London, Methuen, 1960.

Other

The Hidden Damage (autobiographical). New York, Harcourt Brace, 1947.

Editor and Translator, *Grimm's Fairy Tales.* New York, Pantheon, 1944; London, Routledge, 1948; as *The Complete Grimm's Fairy Tales*, Pantheon, 1974; Routledge, 1975.

Translator (as Andrew St. James), *Brazil: Land of the Future*, by Stefan Zweig. New York, Viking Press, 1941; London, Cassell, 1942.

Translator (as Andrew St. James), *Amerigo: A Comedy of Errors in History*, by Stefan Zweig. New York, Viking Press, 1942.

Translator, *The Rise and Fall of the House of Ullstein*, by Herman Ullstein. New York, Simon and Schuster, 1943; London, Nicholson and Watson, 1944.

Translator (as Andrew St. James, with E.B. Ashton), *The Twins of Nuremberg*, by Hermann Kesten. New York, Fischer, 1946.

Translator, *Spark of Life*, by Erich Maria Remarque. New York, Appleton Century Crofts, and London, Hutchinson, 1952.

Translator, with Tania Stern, *Selected Prose*, by Hugo von Hofmannsthal. New York, Pantheon, and London, Routledge, 1952.

Translator, with Tania Stern, *Letters to Milena*, by Kafka. London, Secker and Warburg, 1953; New York, Schocken, 1954.

Translator, *A Woman in Berlin* (anonymous). New York, Harcourt Brace, and London, Secker and Warburg, 1954.

Translator, with Robert Pick, *Casanova's Memoirs.* New York, Harper, 1955.

Translator, *The Foreign Minister*, by Leo Lania. Boston, Houghton Mifflin, and London, Davies, 1956.

Translator, with Tania Stern, *Description of a Struggle and Other Stories*, by Kafka. New York, Schocken and London, Secker and Warburg, 1960.

Translator, with Tania Stern, *Letters of Sigmund Freud 1873–1939*. New York, Basic Books, 1960; London, Hogarth Press, 1961.

Translator, with Elisabeth Duckworth, *Letters to Felice*, by Kafka, edited by Erich Heller and Jurgen Born. New York, Schocken, 1973; London, Secker and Warburg, 1974.

*

Critical Studies: by William Plomer, in *London Magazine*, April 1968; *The Short Story in English* by Walter Allen, Oxford, Clarendon Press, and New York, Oxford University Press, 1981; "Highdown," in *London Magazine*, April-May 1981, "Revelations," in *Quarto* (London), August 1981, and "Disbeliefs," in *London Magazine*, November 1982, all by Stern.

James Stern comments:

The main comment I feel like making about my fiction is that it is *short*. The difference between a short story writer and a novelist is similar to that between a sprinter and a miler. Unfortunately the short story form has never been popular in England. As a result the writer of stories is frowned upon by publishers. Unless he will consent to write a novel.

*   *   *

The settings of James Stern's stories are as varied as the parts of the world in which he has travelled and lived. The Irish stories reflect the memories of his youth; those set in South Africa (most of which were collected in his first volume, *The Heartless Land*) his life there as a farmer; there are stories from his years in France, Germany, and the United States; there are even several set in the South Pacific.

His best work, however, is more concerned with a special time of life than a particular place. Certainly his stories of boyhood ("Our Father," "The Beginning and the End," "Under the Beech Tree," and "The Broken Leg," for instance) must be ranked high. Most of these ("The Broken Leg" is an exception) are narrated in the first person. Whether or not, therefore, they represent artistically arranged versions of events in the author's life, these stories have the mark of truth. One knows, in "The Beginning and the End," that this is exactly how a ten-year-old boy would react to the news of the death of his first "love."

The early South African stories have a special flavor quite their own—possibly because to most readers, even now, Africa is still the "mysterious continent." And, indeed, Stern catches something of the primeval force of that land in stories such as "The Cloud." Long before the racial problems of South Africa became matters of world interest, his stories were dealing with them. In fact, "The Force," a story from the 1932 collection, anticipates Alan Paton's use of the theme of miscegenation in *Too Late the Phalarope*.

Several good uncollected stories, e.g., "The Dunce" (which must be one of the earliest) and "The Thief," deal with boyhood. But it is a story with an African background, "Strangers Defeated," that one most regrets not finding in any of Stern's collections. This is the story of a spirited horse and its owner, neither of whom is accepted by the natives until their spirits are broken; the horse's by sickness and the master's by his inability to deal with the stubbornness of his workers. Seeing what happens to the horse and his owner, we are able better to understand a land and its people.

And indeed, this is what makes James Stern the fine writer that he is. It is not simply that the incidents on which his stories are based are interesting, as they surely must be for success, or that his settings give us a sense of place, or even that his characters are real and, in today's cant term, "psychologically sound." It is, rather, the fact that, in his best stories, because of what his characters do and say as they act out their little dramas in whatever setting Stern has chosen for them, we, as readers, are able to catch a momentary vision of the truth that shimmers under the surface of life. And if a storyteller can help us to do this, he has done much.

—Norman T. Gates

STERN, Richard G(ustave). American. Born in New York City, 25 February 1928. Educated at the University of North Carolina, Chapel Hill, B.A. 1947 (Phi Beta Kappa); Harvard University, Cambridge, Massachusetts, M.A. 1949; University of Iowa, Iowa City, Ph.D. 1954. Served as an educational adviser, United States Army, 1951–52. Married Gay Clark in 1950 (divorced, 1972); three sons and one daughter. Lecturer, Jules Ferry College, Versailles, France, 1949–50; Lektor, University of Heidelberg, 1950–51; Instructor, Connecticut College, New London, 1954–55. Assistant Professor, 1956–61, Associate Professor, 1962–64, and since 1965, Professor of English, University of Chicago. Visiting Lecturer, University of Venice, 1962–63; University of California, Santa Barbara, 1964; State University of New York, Buffalo, 1966; Harvard University, 1969; University of Nice, 1970; University of Urbino, 1977. Recipient: Longwood fellowship, 1960; Friends of Literature award, 1963; Rockefeller fellowship, 1965; American Academy grant, 1968, and Award of Merit Medal, 1985; National Endowment for the Arts grant, 1969; Guggenheim fellowship, 1977; Sandburg Award, 1979. Address: Department of English, University of Chicago, 1050 East 59th Street, Chicago, Illinois 60637, U.S.A.

PUBLICATIONS

Novels

Golk. New York, Criterion, and London, MacGibbon and Kee, 1960.

Europe; or, Up and Down with Schreiber and Baggish. New York, McGraw Hill, 1961; as *Europe; or Up and Down with Baggish and Schreiber*, London, MacGibbon and Kee, 1962.

In Any Case. New York, McGraw Hill, 1962; London, MacGibbon and Kee, 1963; as *The Chaleur Network*, Sagaponack, New York, Second Chance Press, and London, Sidgwick and Jackson, 1981.

Stitch. New York, Harper, 1965; London, Hodder and Stoughton, 1967.

Other Men's Daughters. New York, Dutton, 1973; London, Hamish Hamilton, 1974.

Natural Shocks. New York, Coward McCann, and London, Sidgwick and Jackson, 1978.

A Father's Words. New York, Arbor House, 1986.

Short Stories

Teeth, Dying, and Other Matters, and The Gamesman's Island:
A Play. New York, Harper, and London, MacGibbon and
Kee, 1964.
1968: A Short Novel, An Urban Idyll, Five Stories, and Two
Trade Notes. New York, Holt Rinehart, 1970; London,
Gollancz, 1971.
Packages. New York, Coward McCann, and London, Sidg-
wick and Jackson, 1980.

Uncollected Short Story

"In the Dock," in *Tri-Quarterly* (Evanston, Illinois), Summer
1984.

Other

The Books in Fred Hampton's Apartment (essays). New
York, Dutton, 1973; London, Hamish Hamilton, 1974.
The Invention of the Real. Athens, University of Georgia
Press, 1982.

Editor, *Honey and Wax: Pleasures and Powers of Narrative:*
An Anthology. Chicago, University of Chicago Press, 1966.

*

Manuscript Collection: Regenstein Library, University of
Chicago.

Critical Studies: by Marcus Klein, in *Reporter* (Washington,
D.C.), 1966; article by Hugh Kenner and interview with Robert
Raeder, in *Chicago Review*, Summer 1966; "Conversation with
Richard Stern" by Elliott Anderson and Milton Rosenberg,
in *Chicago Review*, Winter 1980; "On Richard Stern's Fiction"
by G. Murray and Mary Anne Tapp, in *StoryQuarterly* (North-
brook, Illinois), Winter 1980; M. Harris, in *New Republic*
(Washington, D.C.), March 1981; David Kubal, in *Hudson
Review* (New York), Summer 1981; John Blades, in *Wash-
ington Post Book World*, November 1982; J. Spencer, in
Chicago Tribune, 25 April 1985.

*   *   *

In a time when serious American fiction has tended towards
extreme personal assertion and extravagance of manner,
Richard G. Stern has been composing a body of work which
is notable for its detailed craftsmanship, its intricacy, and its
reticences. His novels and stories are neither lyrically confessional nor abstractly experimental. They are processes quite
in the mode of an older tradition, in which character and event
discover theme. In one and another incidental observation
within his fiction, Stern has rejected both the idea of the novel
as "a roller coaster of distress and sympathy, love and desire,"
and the idea of the novel as a deliberate attack on formal
expectations *(Europe)*; he has addressed qualification to the
view that a story is fully autonomous (see the sketch called
"Introductory" in *1968*), but he has also rejected the idea of
the author as solipsist (see "Story-Making" in *1968*). His own
fiction accepts no extremities of technique and form. Its characteristic tone as well as its strategy of development is created
by ironic modulations.

The tone and the technique are, moreover, exact functions
of Stern's characteristic subject. The broad theme is the adjustment of private lives with public events. Typically, Stern's protagonist has been a passive, sensitive fellow, who is a little
too old for adventuring, or a little too fat, or a little too fine-

grained, but nonetheless possessing romantic inclinations. His
latent disposition is tested when public event of one sort and
another seeks him out. He is now forced to regard his own
actions and the actions of others as moral events. And, typically, this protagonist has found himself engaged in a drama
of betrayals, which have the effect of chastening his new ambitions as a public man. The end is his rather baffled, nonetheless
scrupulous assessment of personal adventure. Between the
beginning and the end, his motives are subjected to more and
more contingencies. He has been lured from his innocent privacy into life, defined as public action which by its nature is
dangerous and ambiguous. At the end he has sacrificed the
self-protectedness with which he began, and he has also failed
to discover an easy ground of general participation in life. His
modest success is that he has become potentially moral.

Stern's first novel, *Golk*, is somewhat more spare and blatant
in its actions than the fictions which follow, but it is otherwise
exemplary. The hero is a 37-year-old boy, Herbert Hondorp,
who lives alone with his widowed father in New York City.
As he has done for most of the days of his life, he now spends
his days wandering in and near Central Park, until on an occasion, abruptly, he is snared into public view and public occupation. The agent is a television program—"Golk"—which is
created, precisely, by making public revelation of privacy.
Ordinary, unwary people are caught by the television camera
in prearranged, embarrassing situations. Stern's hero discovers
that he likes not only the being caught, as do most of the
Golk victims, but he also likes the catching. He takes a job
with the television program, and not fortuitously at the same
time he secures his first romance. Within this new situation
there are moral implications, of course, but both "Golk" and
Hondorp's romance are tentative and jesting. The novel then
proceeds to raise the stakes of involvement: the program is
transformed by its ambitious director into a device for political
exposé, and Hondorp's romance becomes a marriage. This
newer situation beckons and perhaps necessitates treacheries,
which make it morally imperative that public involvement be
terminated. Hondorp betrays the director of the program, in
order to save the program—so he believes—from the fury of
the political powers, and he thereby reduces it to vapidity.
In a consequent narrative movement, his wife leaves him. Hondorp goes home at the end, "all trace of his ambition, and
all desire for change gone absolutely and forever."

In his subsequent fictions, Stern has avoided such metaphorical ingenuity as the television program in *Golk*, and the lure
to public action has been carefully limited to a matter of background or accident, but the area of his concerns has remained
constant. In *Europe; or, Up and Down with Schreiber and
Baggish*, the two protagonists are American civil employees
in post-war occupied Germany. The pattern of their
adventuring—despite the comic suggestion in the title of the
novel—allows nothing implausible, and there are no sudden
reversals. Realization is to be achieved, rather, through implied
contrasts and comparisons. Schreiber is an aging sensitive
gentleman who tries for intimate understanding of the ancient,
bitter, guilty, and conquered people. Baggish is a shrewd young
opportunist, who exploits the populace. Baggish succeeds, and
Schreiber fails. *In Any Case* is the story of another aging American in post-war Europe, who is innocent for the reason that
he has never sufficiently risked anything, his affections
included. His testing comes when he is told that his son, dead
in the war, was a traitor. In a belated and ironic act of love,
he tries to prove that his son was really innocent, and he discovers that treachery is a vital ingredient of all social living.
Although his son was indeed not guilty in the way supposed,
everyone is a double agent.

His acceptance of that discovery provides the hero with the possibility of a modest participation in other people's lives. In his more recent fiction, Stern has apparently wanted to make that possibility more emphatic, by bringing historical and aesthetic confirmations to it. *Stitch* is in large part a *roman à clef* about one of the great modern traitors, Ezra Pound. The would-be discile in the novel receives from the aged master, Stitch, lessons in the fusion of personality with civilization, and the consequence of expression in art. The background of the novel is Venice, which, from the muck of its history, raises its beauties. In the short novel *Veni, Vidi... Wendt* (included in *1968*), the protagonist is a composer who is writing an opera about modern love. The opera will extend backwards to include great love affairs of the past, which are founded on adulteries. The composer himself, meanwhile, realizes both his composition and his domestic love for wife and children only after experiments in romantic duplicity. The chief adventurer in *Other Men's Daughters* is a middle-aged professor of biology at Harvard. His life heretofore has been completely defined by such seeming ineluctabilities as filial ties, domestic habits, and the concretion of compromises, and the stern decencies of his New England ancestry. He betrays everything when he falls in love with a girl not much older than the eldest of his own children, and hopefully discovers, in nature, the justification for this treachery to nurture. In *Natural Shocks* Stern writes about a talented and successful journalist, which in this case is to say a man who with all decent goodwill has made a career of transforming private lives into public knowledge. The protagonist is now forced to confront the fact of death, alternately as a subject for journalism and as a domestic event, and he is thereby invited to learn the necessary treachery that is involved in his calling and also its ethical insufficiency. A true participation in life will require more strenuous sympathies, which he may or may not achieve.

The endings of Stern's fictions record an acquiescence at the most, and always something less than the assertion of a principle. The kind of realization that is in the novels makes it necessary that they be probationary and open-ended. They are by that, as well as by their detailed, persistent, and moderate account of human motives, in the great tradition of moral realism.

—Marcus Klein

STEWART, J(ohn) I(nnes) M(ackintosh). Pseudonym: Michael Innes. British. Born in Edinburgh, Scotland, 30 September 1906. Educated at Edinburgh Academy; Oriel College, Oxford (Matthew Arnold Memorial Prize, 1929; Bishop Fraser's Scholar, 1930), B.A. (honours) in English 1928. Married Margaret Hardwick in 1932 (died, 1979); three sons and two daughters. Lecturer in English, University of Leeds, Yorkshire, 1930–35; Jury Professor of English, University of Adelaide, South Australia, 1935–45; Lecturer, Queen's University, Belfast, 1946–48; Student (i.e., Fellow) of Christ Church, Oxford, 1949–73, now Emeritus; Reader in English Literature, Oxford University, 1969–73. Walker-Ames Professor, University of Washington, Seattle, 1961. D.Litt.: University of New Brunswick, Fredericton, 1962; University of Leicester, 1979; University of St. Andrews, Scotland, 1980. Address: Fawler Copse, Fawler, Wantage, Oxfordshire, England.

PUBLICATIONS

Novels

Mark Lambert's Supper. London, Gollancz, 1954.
The Guardians. London, Gollancz, 1955; New York, Norton, 1957.
A Use of Riches. London, Gollancz, and New York, Norton, 1957.
The Man Who Won the Pools. London, Gollancz, and New York, Norton, 1961.
The Last Tresilians. London, Gollancz, and New York, Norton, 1963.
An Acre of Grass. London, Gollancz, 1965; New York, Norton, 1966.
The Aylwins. London, Gollancz, 1966; New York, Norton, 1967.
Vanderlyn's Kingdom. London, Gollancz, 1967; New York, Norton, 1968.
Avery's Mission. London, Gollancz, and New York, Norton, 1971.
A Palace of Art. London, Gollancz, and New York, Norton, 1972.
Mungo's Dream. London, Gollancz, and New York, Norton, 1973.
A Staircase in Surrey:
  The Gaudy. London, Gollancz, 1974; New York, Norton, 1975.
  Young Pattullo. London, Gollancz, 1975; New York, Norton, 1976.
  A Memorial Service. London, Gollancz, and New York, Norton, 1976.
  The Madonna of the Astrolabe. London, Gollancz, and New York, Norton, 1977
Full Term. London, Gollancz, 1978; New York, Norton, 1979.
Andrew and Tobias. New York, Norton, 1980; London, Gollancz, 1981.
A Villa in France. London, Gollancz, 1982; New York, Norton, 1983.
An Open Prison. London, Gollancz, and New York, Norton, 1984.
The Naylors. London, Gollancz, and New York, Norton, 1985.

Novels as Michael Innes

Death at the President's Lodging. London, Gollancz, 1936; as *Seven Suspects*, New York, Dodd Mead, 1937.
Hamlet, Revenge! London, Gollancz, and New York, Dodd Mead, 1937.
Lament for a Maker. London, Gollancz, and New York, Dodd Mead, 1938.
Stop Press. London, Gollancz, 1939; as *The Spider Strikes*, New York, Dodd Mead, 1939.
The Secret Vanguard. London, Gollancz, 1940; New York, Dodd Mead, 1941.
There Came Both Mist and Snow. London, Gollancz, 1940; as *Comedy of Terrors*, New York, Dodd Mead, 1940.
Appleby on Ararat. London, Gollancz, and New York, Dodd Mead, 1941.
The Daffodil Affair. London, Gollancz, and New York, Dodd Mead, 1942.
The Weight of the Evidence. New York, Dodd Mead, 1943; London, Gollancz, 1944.
Appleby's End. London, Gollancz, and New York, Dodd Mead, 1945.

From London Far. London, Gollancz, 1946; as *The Unsuspected Chasm*, New York, Dodd Mead, 1946.

What Happened at Hazelwood? London, Gollancz, and New York, Dodd Mead, 1946.

A Night of Errors. New York, Dodd Mead, 1947; London, Gollancz, 1948.

The Journeying Boy. London, Gollancz, 1949; as *The Case of the Journeying Boy*, New York, Dodd Mead, 1949.

Operation Pax. London, Gollancz, 1951; as *The Paper Thunderbolt*, New York, Dodd Mead, 1951.

A Private View. London, Gollancz, 1952; as *One-Man Show*, New York, Dodd Mead, 1952; as *Murder Is an Art*, New York, Avon, 1959.

Christmas at Candleshoe. London, Gollancz, and New York, Dodd Mead, 1953; as *Candleshoe*, London, Penguin, 1978.

The Man from the Sea. London, Gollancz, and New York, Dodd Mead, 1955; as *Death by Moonlight*, New York, Avon, 1957.

Old Hall, New Hall. London, Gollancz, 1956; as *A Question of Queens*, New York, Dodd Mead, 1956.

Appleby Plays Chicken. London, Gollancz, 1957; as *Death on a Quiet Day*, New York, Dodd Mead, 1957.

The Long Farewell. London, Gollancz, and New York, Dodd Mead, 1958.

Hare Sitting Up. London, Gollancz, and New York, Dodd Mead, 1959.

The New Sonia Wayward. London, Gollancz, 1960; as *The Case of Sonia Wayward*, New York, Dodd Mead, 1960.

Silence Observed. London, Gollancz, and New York, Dodd Mead, 1961.

A Connoisseur's Case. London, Gollancz, 1962; as *The Crabtree Affair*, New York, Dodd Mead, 1962.

Money from Holme. London, Gollancz, 1964; New York, Dodd Mead, 1965.

The Bloody Wood. London, Gollancz, and New York, Dodd Mead, 1966.

A Change of Heir. London, Gollancz, and New York, Dodd Mead, 1966.

Appleby at Allington. London, Gollancz, 1968; as *Death by Water*, New York, Dodd Mead, 1968.

A Family Affair. London, Gollancz, 1969; as *Picture of Guilt*, New York, Dodd Mead, 1969.

Death at the Chase. London, Gollancz, and New York, Dodd Mead, 1970.

An Awkward Lie. London, Gollancz, and New York, Dodd Mead, 1971.

The Open House. London, Gollancz, and New York, Dodd Mead, 1972.

Appleby's Answer. London, Gollancz, and New York, Dodd Mead, 1973.

Appleby's Other Story. London, Gollancz, and New York, Dodd Mead, 1974.

The Mysterious Commission. London, Gollancz, 1974; New York, Dodd Mead, 1975.

The "Gay Phoenix." London, Gollancz, 1976; New York, Dodd Mead, 1977.

Honeybath's Haven. London, Gollancz, 1977; New York, Dodd Mead, 1978.

The Ampersand Papers. London, Gollancz, 1978; New York, Dodd Mead, 1979.

Going It Alone. London, Gollancz, and New York, Dodd Mead, 1980.

Lord Mullion's Secret. London, Gollancz, and New York, Dodd Mead, 1981.

Sheiks and Adders. London, Gollancz, and New York, Dodd Mead, 1982.

Appleby and Honeybath. London, and New York, Dodd Mead, 1983.

Carson's Conspiracy. London, Gollancz, and New York, Dodd Mead, 1984.

Short Stories

The Man Who Wrote Detective Stories and Other Stories. London, Gollancz, and New York, Norton, 1959.

Cucumber Sandwiches and Other Stories. London, Gollancz, and New York, Norton, 1969.

Our England Is a Garden and Other Stories. London, Gollancz, 1979.

The Bridge at Arta and Other Stories. London, Gollancz, 1981; New York, Norton, 1982.

My Aunt Christina and Other Stories. London, Gollancz, and New York, Norton, 1983.

Parlour 4 and Other Stories. London, Gollancz, 1986.

Short Stories as Michael Innes

Three Tales of Hamlet, with Rayner Heppenstall. London, Gollancz, 1950.

Appleby Talking: Twenty-Three Detective Stories. London, Gollancz, 1954; as *Dead Man's Shoes*, New York, Dodd Mead, 1954.

Appleby Talks Again: Eighteen Detective Stories. London, Gollancz, 1956; New York, Dodd Mead, 1957.

The Appleby File. London, Gollancz, 1975; New York, Dodd Mead, 1976.

Play as Michael Innes

Strange Intelligence (broadcast, 1947). Published in *Imaginary Conversations*, edited by Rayner Heppenstall, London, Secker and Warburg, 1948.

Radio Play: *Strange Intelligence*, 1947.

Other

Educating the Emotions. Adelaide, New Education Fellowship, 1944.

Character and Motive in Shakespeare: Some Recent Appraisals Examined. London, Longman, 1949; New York, Barnes and Noble, 1966.

James Joyce. London, Longman, 1957; revised edition, 1960.

Thomas Love Peacock. London, Longman, 1963.

Eight Modern Writers. London and New York, Oxford University Press, 1963.

Rudyard Kipling. London, Gollancz, and New York, Dodd Mead, 1966.

Joseph Conrad. London, Longman, and New York, Dodd Mead, 1968.

Thomas Hardy: A Critical Biography. London, Longman, and New York, Dodd Mead, 1971.

Shakespeare's Lofty Scene (lecture). London, Oxford University Press, 1971.

Editor, *Montaigne's Essays: John Florio's Translation.* London, Nonesuch Press, and New York, Random House, 1931.

Editor, *The Moonstone*, by Wilkie Collins. London, Penguin, 1966.

Editor, *Vanity Fair*, by Thackeray. London, Penguin, 1968.

*

Critical Study: *Michael Innes* by George L. Scheper, New York, Ungar, 1985.

*   *   *

Michael Innes, undoubtedly a grand-master of crime fiction, is remarkable for his wide range which extends from intricate closed-group murder cases (*The Weight of the Evidence* and *The Bloody Wood*) to fights against large-scale criminal operators (*From London Far*) and organised madness as a global menace (*Hare Sitting Up*). John Appleby, the gentleman turned policeman and rising from plain inspector to knighted commissioner until his (active) retirement, is the main detective figure. At times he is replaced by the formidable Inspector Cadover (*What Happened at Hazelwood?*), and other books manage without a detective altogether: psychological studies like *The New Sonia Wayward*, or the puzzling *Money from Holme*, or frolics like *Going It Alone*. Also the narrative technique varies. A detached third-person narrator dominates (sometimes rather obtrusively), but some stories are told by involved, highly self-conscious, and unreliable figures like Arthur Ferryman (*There Came Both Mist and Snow*).

Basic characteristics are the academic, professional, and aristocratic background, an inexhaustible knowledge of literature and the arts in most characters, which not only forms a large contents element but is frequently also functional to the plot (*The Secret Vanguard*); the skilful distribution of suspense and surprise throughout the stories, but sometimes concentrated in long, enthralling accounts of flight and pursuit (*The Journeying Boy*, *Operation Pax*, and *The Man from the Sea*); a strain of the fantastic, indeed the fairly tale (very strong in *The Daffodil Affair* and *Appleby's End*); finally, a penchant for wild comedy, manifesting itself in innumerable jokes, in prank-like interludes, in stock characters such as Hildebert Braunkopf with his "voonderable voorlt of art" as well as entire stories (*A Change of Heir*). The late works, while suggesting some fatigue (*A Family Affair*, *Appleby's Answer*, *Sheiks and Adders*), continue to provide cultured, intelligent, and interesting—if no longer gripping—entertainment (*The "Gay Phoenix"* and *Appleby and Honeybath*) and evince a persistent refusal to join the remorseless, bleak, and insecure world of modern British thrillers where the integrity of the police has crumbled alongside that of everybody else, where Piero, Keats, and Raeburn are totally irrelevant.

The novels and stories written as J.I.M. Stewart, by now a sizeable corpus, are set in the same academic and artistic, middle- and upper-class milieu, and show the same apt sense of people, places, of dramatic and—more recently—comic effects as well as an increasing interest in senescence, resulting in a gallery of astute portraits of old age (Lampriere, the Mannerings), balanced by lively sketches of rather young people (Gilbert Pillman and Francis Gethin), the grandchildren generation, as it were. If the crime stories often turn on *objets d'art*, many of the novels concentrate on the creative process, on the artist and his relations to other people. The most obvious link is the quest for posthumous works of writers or painters—developing a theme from Henry James's "The Aspern Papers" (*Mark Lambert's Supper*, *The Guardians*, *An Acre of Grass*, and, as a grim if farcical climax, *A Villa in France*); James also provides some technical inspiration ("reflectors"—notably *The Aylwins*, *Vanderlyn's Kingdom*, *Avery's Mission*). When he makes university life the main subject—particularly in the massive Pattullo sequence—Stewart is truly covering home ground. But whereas the refined world of the Oxford don adds (along with social and intellectual snob appeal) a brilliant, strange, and often hilarious light to the world of crime, it does not easily stand up on its own. The mild perplexities and irregularities of an old college, though in themselves a pleasant variant to most, more earthy and strident "campus" literature, and though nicely presented and spiced up with modern phenomena like bed-sitters, demonstrations, and patchily educated freshmen, often seems somewhat pale.

Stewart's most important contributions to the mainstream of English fiction so far are probably *A Use of Riches* and *The Last Tresilians*. With his thrillers becoming tamer and his "serious" fiction more relaxed, this author's large and varied creative powers have of late produced interesting things in the middle ground between the two (where should one place *Lord Mullion's Secret* or *The Naylors?*). One notes in particular short, incisive sketches like "The Men," "George," and "The Little Duffer," the long story "Our England Is a Garden" (a *roman fleuve* in outline which shows the pull of Trollope and Hardy rather than James), and *Andrew and Tobias*, a compact and striking novel sure to engage attention for a long time to come.

—H.M. Klein

STONE, Irving. American. Born Irving Tannenbaum in San Francisco, California, 14 July 1903; adopted in 1912. Educated at Lowell High School, San Francisco; Manual Arts High School, Los Angeles; University of California, Berkeley, A.B. 1923, graduate study, 1924–26; University of Southern California, Los Angeles, M.A. 1924. Married Jean Factor in 1934; one daughter and one son. Teaching Fellow in Economics, University of Southern California, 1923–24, and University of California, Berkeley, 1924–26. Visiting Lecturer in Creative Writing, University of Indiana, Bloomington, 1948, and University of Washington, Seattle, 1961; lecturer on the writing of biography and the biographical novel, University of Southern California, 1966; Lecturer, California State Colleges, 1966. Since 1984, Regents' Professor, University of California, Los Angeles. Art critic, Los Angeles *Mirror-News*, 1959–60. United States Department of State Cultural Exchange Specialist, in the Soviet Union, Poland, and Yugoslavia, 1962. President, California Writers Guild, 1960–61; founder, Academy of American Poets, 1962; founder, California State Colleges Committee for the Arts, 1967; trustee, Douglass House Foundation, Watts, Los Angeles, 1967–74; President, Dante Alighieri Society, Los Angeles, 1968–69. Since 1955, founder and President, Fellows for Schweitzer, Southern California; since 1963, Vice-President, Eugene V. Debs Foundation, Terre Haute, Indiana, and member, Advisory Board, University of California Institute for the Creative Arts; since 1969, President, Affiliates of the Department of English, University of California, Los Angeles. "Irving Stone Day" observed in Los Angeles, 1983. Recipient: Christopher Award, 1957; Western Writers of America Spur Award, 1957. D.L.: University of Southern California, 1965; D.Litt.: Coe College, Cedar Rapids, Iowa, 1967; California State Colleges, 1971; LL.D.: University of California, Berkeley, 1968; D.H.L.: Hebrew Union College, Cincinnati, 1978. Commendatore (Knight Commander), Republic of Italy, 1962; Grande Ufficiale (Italy), 1982; Commandant, Order of Arts and Letters (France), 1984. Lives in Beverly Hills, California. Address: c/o Doubleday and Company, 245 Park Avenue, New York, New York 10167, U.S.A.

PUBLICATIONS

Novels

Pageant of Youth. New York, King, 1933.
Lust for Life. New York, Longman, and London, Lane, 1934.
Sailor on Horseback. Boston, Houghton Mifflin, and London, Collins, 1938; as *Jack London, Sailor on Horseback*, New York, Doubleday, 1947.
False Witness. New York, Doubleday, 1940.
Immortal Wife. New York, Doubleday, 1944; London, Falcon Press, 1950.
Adversary in the House. New York, Doubleday, 1947; London, Falcon Press, 1950.
The Passionate Journey. New York, Doubleday, 1949; London, Falcon Press, 1950.
The President's Lady. New York, Doubleday, 1951; London, Lane, 1952.
Love Is Eternal. New York, Doubleday, 1954; London, Collins, 1955.
The Agony and the Ecstasy. New York, Doubleday, and London, Collins, 1961.
Those Who Love. New York, Doubleday, 1965; London, Cassell, 1966.
The Passions of the Mind. New York, Doubleday, and London, Cassell, 1971.
The Greek Treasure. New York, Doubleday, and London, Cassell, 1975.
The Origin. New York, Doubleday, 1980; London, Cassell, 1981.
Depths of Glory. New York, Doubleday, and London, Bodley Head, 1985.

Plays

The Dark Mirror (produced New York, 1928).
The White Life: A Play Based on the Life of Baruch Spinoza (produced Jersey City, New Jersey, 1929). New York, League of Jewish Community Associations, 1932.
Truly Valiant (produced New York, 1936).

Screenplay: *The Magnificent Doll*, 1946.

Other

Clarence Darrow for the Defense. New York, Doubleday, 1941; as *Darrow for the Defence*, London, Lane, 1950.
They Also Ran: The Story of the Men Who Were Defeated for the Presidency. New York, Doubleday, 1943; revised edition, 1945.
The Evolution of an Idea. Privately printed, 1945.
Earl Warren. New York, Prentice Hall, 1948.
Men to Match My Mountains: The Opening of the Far West 1840–1900. New York, Doubleday, 1956; London, Cassell, 1967.
Three Views of the Novel, with John O'Hara and MacKinlay Kantor. Washington, D.C., Library of Congress, 1957.
The Irving Stone Reader. New York, Doubleday, 1963.
The Story of Michelangelo's Pietà. New York, Doubleday, 1964.
The Great Adventure of Michelangelo (for children). New York, Doubleday, 1965.
There Was Light: Autobiography of a University, Berkeley 1868–1968. New York, Doubleday, 1970.
Mary Todd Lincoln: A Final Judgement? Springfield, Illinois, Abraham Lincoln Association, 1973.

Editor, *Dear Theo: The Autobiography of Vincent van Gogh.* Boston, Houghton Mifflin, and London, Constable, 1937.
Editor, with Richard Kennedy, *We Speak for Ourselves: Self Portrait of America.* New York, Doubleday, 1950.
Editor, with Allan Nevins, *Lincoln: A Contemporary Portrait.* New York, Doubleday, 1962.
Editor, with Jean Stone, *I, Michelangelo, Sculptor: An Autobiography Through Letters.* New York, Doubleday, 1962; London, Collins, 1963.
Editor, *Irving Stone's Jack London.* New York, Doubleday, 1977.

*

Bibliography: *Irving Stone: A Bibliography* by Lewis F. Stieg, Los Angeles, Friends of the Libraries of the University of Southern California, 1973.

Manuscript Collection: Special Collections, University of California Library, Los Angeles.

Irving Stone comments:
The biographical novel is a true and documented story of one human being's journey across the face of the years, transmuted from the raw material into the delight and purity of an authentic art form. The research must be honest and far reaching, but the result must stand as a compelling novel.

*   *   *

The historian in Irving Stone has cohabited with the artist through a dozen or so novels now, and although the public sanctions the arrangement by purchasing and reading the offspring books, the union is neither literarily nor historically holy. The novels that come of it suffer congenital defects; for all their broad appeal, there are problems with historical novels that are inescapable. Stone is an astute novelist, insofar as he recognizes a compelling story and can control the reader's attention for the most part, and he is a willing historian who researches his material copiously. But in the novels, the historian tends to inhibit the inventive imagination, embalming the dialogue and losing the plot for long periods in thickets of detail, while the artist always opens the history to a doubt that the most impressive bibliographical lists cannot still. This is, of course, true of all historical novelists, to an extent, but, paradoxically, the generic difficulty is more acute in the case of more serious ones, such as Stone, than in the case of slighter ones, such as Frank G. Slaughter, whose concern is entertainment and not authenticity, and whose works may be consumed like popcorn.

The point may be illustrated by any of Stone's novels. *Love Is Eternal*, for example, which treats the relationship between Mary Todd and Abraham Lincoln to the time of Lincoln's assassination, demonstrates Stone's characteristic use of the most minute details to evoke a sense of historical place. But while the setting and circumstances in which the main characters play are without doubt essentially correct, there remains the question of whether or not the conception of the characters is accurate as well. Stone is unconvincing in his attempt to restore the reputation of Mary Todd Lincoln, who has been excoriated by history. He may be right in his judgment of her, or his vindication of her may be simply an act of sentimental gallantry. There is no way to be certain; if the novel is an unfounded interpretation of her, Stone has misrepresented, and if there is historical evidence for his view, she would have been far better served by a documented history.

Stone is apparently aware, consciously or unconsciously, of the dilemma created by writing fiction that purports to echo fact, for, as in *Passionate Journey* a fictional biography of the American painter John Noble, he is usually better when his characters act and react with each other according to the scenario provided by historical fact than when he seeks to interpret motivation. Perhaps the use of detail to the point of tediousness is an attempt to bring the problem that is imposed by the *genre* under control—an attempt to overwhelm it. *Those Who Love*, for instance, a treatment of the life and times of John and Abigail Adams, is not only lumbered with wooden dialogue, but overburdened with historical minutiae. The Michelangelo study, *The Agony and the Ecstasy*, as if to counter the effect of a great deal of love interest that smacks of modern interpolation, contains endless description of stone cutting and of anatomy, in a way that is reminiscent of Melville's whaling chapters but is less easily justifiable.

But the biographical novel does exist, of course, and Stone is undeniably one of its ablest practitioners. The history he spoonfeeds is far more palatable and interesting than popcorn, and it is no wonder that an enormous public should devour it.

—Alan R. Shucard

* * *

STONE, Robert (Anthony). American. Born in Brooklyn, New York, 21 August 1937. Educated at New York University, 1958–59; Stanford University, California (Stegner Fellow, 1962). Served in the United States Navy, 1955–58. Married Janice G. Burr in 1959; one daughter and one son. Editorial assistant, New York *Daily News*, 1958–60; Writer-in-Residence, Princeton University, New Jersey, 1971–72; taught at Amherst College, Massachusetts, 1972–75, 1977–78, Stanford University, 1979, University of Hawaii, Manoa, 1979–80, Harvard University, Cambridge, Massachusetts, 1981, University of California, Irvine, 1982, and San Diego, 1985, New York University, 1983, and Princeton University, 1985. Recipient: Houghton Mifflin Literary Fellowship, 1967; Faulkner Foundation award, 1967; Guggenheim grant, 1968; National Book Award, 1975; Dos Passos Prize, 1982; American Academy award, 1982; National Endowment for the Arts fellowship, 1983. Agent: Candida Donadio and Associates, 231 West 22nd Street, New York, New York 10011, U.S.A.

PUBLICATIONS

Novels

A Hall of Mirrors. Boston, Houghton Mifflin, 1967; London, Bodley Head, 1968.
Dog Soldiers. Boston, Houghton Mifflin, 1974; London, Secker and Warburg, 1975.
A Flag for Sunrise. New York, Knopf, and London, Secker and Warburg, 1981.
Children of Light. New York, Knopf, and London, Deutsch, 1986.

Uncollected Short Stories

"Geraldine," in *Twenty Years of Stanford Short Stories*, edited by Wallace Stegner and Richard Scowcroft. Stanford, California, Stanford University Press, 1966.

"Farley the Sailor," in *Saturday Evening Post* (Philadelphia), 14 January 1967.
"Thunderbolts in Red, White, and Blue," in *Saturday Evening Post* (Philadelphia), 28 January 1967.
"Porque no tiene, porq le falta," in *The Best American Short Stories 1970*, edited by Martha Foley and David Burnett. Boston, Houghton Mifflin, 1970.
"Aquarius Observed," in *American Review 22*, edited by Theodore Solotaroff. New York, Bantam, 1975.
"A Hunter in the Morning," in *American Review 26*, edited by Theodore Solotaroff. New York, Bantam, 1977.
"WUSA," in *On the Job*, edited by William O'Rourke. New York, Vintage, 1977.
"War Stories," in *Harper's* (New York), May 1977.

Plays

Screenplays: *WUSA*, 1970; *Who'll Stop the Rain*, with Judith Roscoe, 1978.

* * *

Robert Stone combines old-fashioned concerns—the morality of human behavior, the responsibility of choice, the relationship between the individual and history—with topical interests—racism in the U.S., the war in Vietnam, American involvement in Latin-American revolutions—to produce fiction that is both emotionally engaging and thought provoking.

A Hall of Mirrors, Stone's first novel, tells the story of three rootless drifters whose paths converge in New Orleans: Rheinhardt, an alcoholic ex-musician; Geraldine, a battered woman; and Morgan Rainey, an idealistic social worker. Victims of both circumstance and of their own self-destructiveness, the trio is eventually caught up in an orgy of violence touched off by a patriotic rally sponsored by the owner of right-wing radio station WUSA, where Rheinhardt works. The final third of the novel is devoted to a nightmarish description of the rally and the ensuing riot (portrayed in almost hallucinatory language), which leaves 19 persons dead. The apocalyptic conclusion is reminiscent of the movie premiere riot that ends Nathanael West's *The Day of the Locust*, but Stone's version of Armageddon has its roots not so much in the unrealized longings of the alienated outsider as in the racism and fanatical right-wing extremism he sees poisoning American society in the 1960's.

Dog Soldiers centers on the desperate flight of Ray Hicks, an ex-marine, and Marge Converse, wife of Hicks's friend John Converse, a journalist on assignment in Vietnam, to escape the narcotics agents who are after the three kilos of heroin Hicks smuggled into California from Vietnam. Exciting as the narrative is, *Dog Soldiers* is much more than an adventure thriller, for by showing that the action is set into motion by events which have their origin in Vietnam where the novel begins, Stone links the madness of the war depicted in the early sections with the tragic fallout it has at home.

The novel begins with a quotation from Joseph Conrad's *Heart of Darkness*, a work which has strongly influenced *Dog Soldiers*. Like Conrad, who saw in Kurtz's ivory a symbol of man's "rapacious and pitiless folly," Stone uses heroin as a symbol of his characters' obsessions and of the war's tragic cost. In Vietnam Converse finds himself, as Kurtz did in the African jungle, torn loose from all the conventional supports of civilized society. Afloat emotionally and morally, he turns to heroin as a way of asserting himself ("This is the first real thing I ever did in my life," he declares), but his decision will soon prove to have costly consequences as the heroin's deadly poison begins to spread.

Like *Hall of Mirrors, Dog Soldiers* concludes with an apocalyptic finale, a shootout between Hicks and the federal agents pursuing him, the action punctuated by the recorded sounds of combat amplified over loudspeakers set up around the mountain compound where the scene occurs. By reminding the reader of the actual battle taking place in Vietnam, Stone underscores the relationship between the war in Asia and its consequences at home. Also, he makes the point that here, as in Vietnam, it is difficult to tell the good guys from the bad guys: Antheil, the government agent who ends up with the heroin at the end, decides to keep it and use it for his own profit. In Stone's view, there are no victors; everyone is corrupted by the poison.

A Flag for Sunrise is Stone's most ambitious and successful novel to date. Set in the fictional Central American country of Tecan, it features the stories of three Americans, each with his own reason for coming to the country: Sister Justin Feeney, a devoted young Roman Catholic nun who runs a local mission; Frank Holliwell, an anthropologist who declines the request of a CIA buddy to look into the situation at the mission, but whose curiosity compels him to go anyway; and Pablo Tabor, a paranoid, pill-popping soldier of fortune whose thirst for excitement leads to his involvement in the dangerous business of gun-running to the Tecanecan revolutionaries. Inexorably, the fates of all three Americans become intertwined, just as, Stone suggests, America itself has gotten itself involved in the fate of this ravaged little country.

The novel represents Stone's most effective attempt at incorporating political issues—here the economic, military, political, and cultural roles the U.S. is playing in Latin American countries—and personal ones—individual commitment and responsibility for one's actions. By examining a variety of motives ranging from the simple purity of Sr. Justin's desire to help the poor, a commitment for which she is willing to die, to Holliwell's feckless drifting, to the combination of "circumstance, coincidence, impulse, and urging" that has driven a host of other characters (e.g., whiskey priests, journalists, CIA agents, resort developers, soldiers of fortune) to Tecan, Stone exposes the reasons which have led the U.S. itself to an active involvement in the affairs of undeveloped countries like Tecan.

Stone's ambitious thematic concerns are matched by his artistic skills in the novel, which deftly weaves together elements of the murder mystery, love story, adventure thriller, spiritual drama, and political satire. Stone displays mastery of both the broad canvas of action and incident as well as the carefully observed telling detail and the subtle nuances of character. In theme and setting, *A Flag for Sunrise* once again recalls Conrad, here *Nostromo* more than *Heart of Darkness*. Such a comparison, however, in no way disparages Stone's accomplishment, for in scope, seriousness of purpose, and artistic vision, *A Flag for Sunrise* deserves to be included among the classic novels of moral and political seriousness.

A Flag for Sunrise concludes with the statement, "A man has nothing to fear ...who understands history." All of Stone's fiction offers both a penetrating examination of our recent history and a serious warning about the price one pays for acting irresponsibly in light of that history.

—David J. Geherin

STOREY, David (Malcolm). British. Born in Wakefield, Yorkshire, 13 July 1933; brother of the writer Anthony Storey. Educated at Queen Elizabeth Grammar School, Wakefield, 1943–51; Wakefield College of Art, 1951–53; Slade School of Fine Art, London, 1953–56, diploma in fine arts 1956. Married Barbara Rudd Hamilton in 1956; two sons and two daughters. Played professionally for the Leeds Rugby League Club, 1952–56. Associate Artistic Director, Royal Court Theatre, London, 1972–74. Fellow, University College, London, 1974. Recipient: Rhys Memorial Award, 1961; Maugham Award, 1963; *Evening Standard* award, for drama, 1967, 1970; New York Drama Critics Circle award, 1971, 1973, 1974; Faber Memorial Prize, 1973; Obie Award, for drama, 1974; Booker Prize, 1976. Lives in London. Address: c/o Jonathan Cape Ltd., 32 Bedford Square, London WC1B 3EL, England.

PUBLICATIONS

Novels

This Sporting Life. London, Longman, and New York, Macmillan, 1960.
Flight into Camden. London, Longman, 1960; New York, Macmillan, 1961.
Radcliffe. London, Longman, 1963; New York, Coward McCann, 1964.
Pasmore. London, Longman, 1972; New York, Dutton, 1974.
A Temporary Life. London, Allen Lane, 1973; New York, Dutton, 1974.
Saville. London, Cape, 1976; New York, Harper, 1977.
A Prodigal Child. London, Cape, 1982; New York, Dutton, 1983.
Present Times. London, Cape, 1984.

Plays

The Restoration of Arnold Middleton (produced Edinburgh, 1966; London, 1967). London, Cape, 1967; New York, French, 1968.
In Celebration (produced London, 1969; Los Angeles, 1973). London, Cape, 1969; New York, Grove Press, 1975.
The Contractor (produced London, 1969; New Haven, Connecticut, 1970; New York, 1973). London, Cape, 1970; New York, Random House, 1971.
Home (produced London and New York, 1970). London, Cape, 1970; New York, Random House, 1971.
The Changing Room (produced London, 1971; New Haven, Connecticut, 1972; New York, 1973). London, Cape, and New York, Random House, 1972.
The Farm (produced London, 1973; Washington, D.C., 1974; New York, 1976). London, Cape, 1973; New York, French, 1974.
Cromwell (produced London, 1973; Sarasota, Florida, 1977; New York, 1978). London, Cape, 1973.
Life Class (produced London, 1974; New York, 1975). London, Cape, 1975.
Mother's Day (produced London, 1976). London, Cape, 1977.
Sisters (produced Manchester, 1978).
Early Days (produced Brighton and London, 1980).
Phoenix (produced London, 1984).

Screenplays: *This Sporting Life*, 1963; *In Celebration*, 1974.

Television Play: *Grace*, from the story by James Joyce, 1974.

*

Critical Study: *David Storey* by John Russell Taylor, London, Longman, 1974.

Theatrical Activities:
Director: **Television**—*Portrait of Margaret Evans*, 1963; *Death of My Mother* (D. H. Lawrence documentary), 1963.

*   *   *

David Storey's first three novels were organized around a concept. In *This Sporting Life* he attempted to show the world of the body, the atmosphere of physicality in both players and spectators, in the account of a young man from the lower middle classes who plays professional rugby. His second novel, *Flight into Camden*, is the novel depicting soul, the description of the hard spiritual independence of a miner's daughter who defies family to live with her married lover in London. *Radcliffe*, the third and most ambitious novel, portraying the troubled and violent relationship between Leonard Radcliffe, the sensitive descendant of impoverished gentility and aestheticism, and Victor Tolson, the powerful representative of the working classes, demonstrates the incompatibility of body and soul. In all the religious discussions and images in the novel, as well as in the epigraph from Yeats's "Vacillation VII," this irreconcilability between body and soul is regarded as original sin. A projected fourth novel in which body and soul were to be reconciled, never appeared after the 1963 publication of *Radcliffe*, and more recent novels are not dependent on the concept.

Explicitly apparent in *Radcliffe*, the body-soul conflict is reflected in the conflict between the working classes and the remnants of the aristocracy in northern English society. Beaumont, the place where Leonard's family lives, his father as caretaker and restorer, represents an aesthetically and historically valuable past that cannot survive in current industrial society without special and privileged attention. Similarly, Leonard himself needs the vital and sexual connection to Tolson's physicality in order to feel "whole." Storey combines the religious, social, and personal dimensions of the body-soul controversy, keeps his metaphors consistent, and presents the issues with a fierce emotional intensity, but he also pushes his characters to the point where the intense, narrow focus and the representational quality explodes into melodrama. Leonard kills Tolson and soon dies himself; another central character, a buffoon who also wanted Tolson, kills his family and himself. The melodrama simplifies the questions of class and religion presented, yet the power of the presentation itself, the intensity, invites the melodrama.

In spite of the limitations implicit in working out his concept, Storey's early fiction has considerable power, especially in dramatic scenes that come to life apart from their function as demonstrations of an idea. Characters in revolt from working-class origins, like Arthur Machin in *This Sporting Life* and Margaret Thorpe and her brother in *Flight into Camden*, are seen with a strong sympathy and complexity, described as partially entering a new world alien to their backgrounds and partially tied to the values and attitudes of their parents. Relationships between parents and children, the unique combinations of love and hatred bred in tidy, self-contained working-class kitchens, are particularly well done. The children, like

Margaret Thorpe and her brother, or like Colin, the college teacher who deserts his wife and children in *Pasmore*, or another Colin who is a central figure in *Saville*, have been educated because of their parents' self-sacrifice, yet the process of education has moved them further from their parents, produced a difficult combination of independence, stubborn freedom, and guilt. For the parents, educating children had seemed the passport to the good life, a release from the grinding physicality of survival in the pits, and the parents, like those in *Pasmore* or the baffled mother of Yvonne, a young wife whose incapacity to handle the strains of her life and education cause mental breakdown in *A Temporary Life*, cannot understand the complications of their educated childrens' lives. The children, too, like almost all Storey's characters, are characterized by a defensive intensity, an inability to release themselves into the flux of contemporary classless experience, still carry something of the working-man's bitter intransigence and self-protective isolation. Women, like the defensively unyielding Mrs. Hammond in *This Sporting Life* or the remote and incommunicative mistress of the central characters in both *Pasmore* and *A Temporary Life*, sometimes display this intransigence more fully than men do in Storey's world; as the author comments on a character in *Pasmore*, the woman reveals "a determination, in effect, not to deny herself the pleasure as well as the security which came from holding herself apart." Relationship, in Storey's world, is difficult and dangerous, likely to lead to breakdown or dissolution, and this quality is seen as part of a social and historical inheritance. This inheritance is still manifest in the recent novel *Present Times*, in which Attercliffe, a former rugby professional, demonstrates Job-like endurance under the assaults of his wife leaving him, his five children immured in one form or another of contemporary inanity, his lost job, and his best friend's death.

In a nine-year gap between novels, Storey turned toward drama, writing highly praised and effective plays. Often, characters and situations in the plays are similar, sometimes even identical, to those in the novels. Both *In Celebration* and *The Farm* reveal the highly charged familial emotions involved when educated children return to visit their parents in the mining or the farming village where they grew up. The parents are reminiscent of those in *Pasmore* or the Thorpes in *Flight into Camden*. *The Contractor* divides attention between the workmen setting up a large tent for a wedding and the family of the tenting company's owner, also the father of the bride. Again, family and class issues dominate the play. A similar group of workmen setting up tents is detailed in *Radcliffe*, although the dramatic version is more comic; even the name of the company's owner—Ewbank—is the same. *Life Class* depicts a simplified version of some of the events, those centering around the life model in a class in a northern art school, of *A Temporary Life*, although a full characterization of the teacher, his background, and his connection to other characters, is omitted in the play. Generally, the dramatic version of each character or incident is simpler and more immediately communicable than is the novelistic version. Yet Storey's parallel working of themes, incidents, and characters has also given his novelistic treatments an immediacy and force, perhaps contributed by his work in drama, that make his later novels, especially *Pasmore* and *A Prodigal Child*, particularly effective and compelling.

Storey is also trained and talented in drawing and painting. His writing has always been characterized by an acute sense of visual imagery, apparent in descriptions of the industrial town or the rugby crowd in *This Sporting Life*. The later fiction, particularly *A Temporary Life*, in which the first-person narrator is a painter and a teacher of painting, and *A Prodigal Child*, which describes the development of the artist, exploits this sense of visual imagery even more effectively, creating descriptions that are precisely detailed and representative of the character's or observer's state of mind or emotion simultaneously. Color, shape, and landscape become terse yet complex metaphors. Later novels also use sharply observed short dramatic scenes to portray changing psychological patterns within characters. *Pasmore* depicts a dissolving marriage, the changes from dependence to almost comatose shock and neglect to a nervous, tenuous independence in the deserted wife, as well as changes between concerned indifference, an artificial sense of jolly control, passivity, guilt, jealousy, explosive fury, and, finally, near breakdown before ultimate recovery, in the erring husband. Yvonne's breakdown in *A Temporary Life* is also carefully portrayed, the alternations between withdrawal and the desperate efforts to make life and relationships around her seem "whole." *Saville*, although like its principal character evolving more slowly, carefully constructs the miner's environment and complicates the pressures of differing representations of parents, brothers, and potential wives from which Colin emerges as educated, sensitive, and finally independent. In *A Prodigal Child*, Storey's most deeply and convincingly realized fiction, the background through and against which the artist gains consciousness is agricultural as well as industrial, sophisticated as well as simple, middle-class as well as working-class, and destructively as well as creatively sexual. Here, as in the other fiction, breakdown, loss of control, is always at the edge of Storey's fictional world.

All the novels since 1972 show little of the generalized concept about experience that restricted the earlier fiction, particularly *Radcliffe*. Rather, the reliance on theories about life is satirized in the treatment of theories about art in *A Temporary Life*. Both the radical art students, who refuse to learn technique and justify work that is both slovenly and unimaginative in the name of free expression and an "empirical" point of view, and the principal of the art school, who spends his time campaigning against smoking, madly collecting excreta in his locked bathroom, and painting pseudo-realistic advertising posters that proclaim the "old values," are made ludicrous. Teachers and their theories, variously made brutal, self-preening, or insensitive, are more often than not barriers to genuine education in *Saville* and *A Prodigal Child*. The human being, isolated, attempting to unify the world around him, searches for his own intellectual and emotional forms of control. The fiction expresses this with a packed, potentially explosive prose, a form that dramatically conveys the pressure of experience. At its best, the fiction itself, steadily gaining range as Storey continues to develop, is a strong and intensely human achievement, a bastion, just on the edge of chaos.

—James Gindin

STOW, (Julian) Randolph. Australian. Born in Geraldton, Western Australia, 28 November 1935. Educated at Guildford Grammar School, Western Australia; University of Western Australia, Nedlands, B.A. 1956. Formerly, anthropological assistant, working in Northwest Australia and Papua New Guinea. Taught at the University of Adelaide, 1957; Lecturer in English, University of Leeds, Yorkshire, 1962 and 1968–69, and University of Western Australia, 1963–64. Recipient: Australian Literature Society Gold Medal, 1957, 1958; Miles Franklin Award, 1959; Commonwealth Fund Harkness Travelling Fellowship, 1964–66; Britannica-Australia Award, 1966; Grace Leven Prize, 1970; Australia Council grant, 1973; Patrick White Prize, 1979. Agent: Richard Scott Simon Ltd., 32 College Cross, London N1 1PR, England.

PUBLICATIONS

Novels

A Haunted Land. London, Macdonald, 1956; New York, Macmillan, 1957.
The Bystander. London, Macdonald, 1957.
To the Islands. London, Macdonald, 1958; Boston, Little Brown, 1959; revised edition, Sydney, Angus and Robertson, 1981; London, Secker and Warburg, and New York, Taplinger, 1982.
Tourmaline. London, Macdonald, 1963; New York, Taplinger, 1983.
The Merry-Go-Round in the Sea. London, Macdonald, 1965; New York, Morrow, 1966.
Visitants. London, Secker and Warburg, 1979; New York, Taplinger, 1981.
The Girl Green as Elderflower. London, Secker and Warburg, and New York, Viking Press, 1980.
The Suburbs of Hell. London, Secker and Warburg, and New York, Taplinger, 1984.

Plays

Eight Songs for a Mad King, music by Peter Maxwell Davies. London, Boosey and Hawkes, 1969.
Miss Donnithorne's Maggot, music by Peter Maxwell Davies (produced 1974). London, Boosey and Hawkes, 1977.

Verse

Act One. London, Macdonald, 1957.
Outrider: Poems 1956–1962. London, Macdonald, 1962.
A Counterfeit Silence: Selected Poems. Sydney and London, Angus and Robertson, 1969.
Poetry from Australia: Pergamon Poets 6, with Judith Wright and William Hart-Smith, edited by Howard Sergeant. Oxford, Pergamon Press, 1969.

Recording: *Poets on Record 11*, University of Queensland, 1974.

Other

Midnite: The Story of a Wild Colonial Boy (for children). Melbourne, Cheshire, and London, Macdonald, 1967; Englewood Cliffs, New Jersey, Prentice Hall, 1968.

Editor, *Australian Poetry 1964.* Sydney, Angus and Robertson, 1964.

*

Bibliography: *Randolph Stow: A Bibliography* by P.A. O'Brien, Adelaide, Libraries Board of South Australia, 1968; "A Randolph Stow Bibliography" by Rose Marie Beston, in *Literary Half-Yearly* (Mysore), July 1975.

Manuscript Collection: National Library of Australia, Canberra.

Critical Studies: "Raw Material" by Stow, in *Westerly* (Nedlands, Western Australia), 1961; "The Quest for Permanence" by Geoffrey Dutton, in *Journal of Commonwealth Literature* (Leeds, Yorkshire), September 1965; "Outsider Looking Out" by W.H. New, in *Critique* (Minneapolis), vol. 9, no. 1, 1967; "Waste Places, Dry Souls" by Jennifer Wightman, in *Meanjin* (Melbourne), June 1969; "Voyager from Eden" by Brandon Conron, in *Ariel (Canada)* (Calgary, Alberta), October 1970; *The Merry-Go-Round in the Sea* by Edriss Noall, Sydney, Scoutline, 1971; "The Family Background and Literary Career of Randolph Stow" by John B. Beston, in *Literary Half-Yearly* (Mysore), July 1975; *Randolph Stow* by Ray Willbanks, Boston, Twayne, 1978; "Randolph Stow's *Visitants*," in *Australian Literary Studies* (Brisbane), October 1980, and *Strange Country*, St. Lucia, University of Queensland Press, 1986, both by Anthony J. Hassall.

*   *   *

The contrast between *The Merry-Go-Round in the Sea*, with its local "realism," and *Tourmaline*, which makes a symbolic landscape out of Randolph Stow's native land, indicates the initial range of his fiction. *Merry-Go-Round* by no means eschews symbolic patterns, but it emerges more directly from Australian national sensibilities. Stow's novel links the isolating impact that World War II had on the country with the older traditions of convict settlement and South Pacific paradise. (Stow is careful to debunk the easy myths which see convict and bushranger mateyness as the *sole* generative character trait *throughout* Australia; his comic children's book *Midnite*, about the triumphant adventures of a native bushranger and his gang—a cockatoo and a cat—delightfully overturns assorted local archetypes. Yet with linguistic playfulness it celebrates the spirit of the country as well, which serves as a reminder of the ambivalent blend of prison and paradise which has always provoked the Australian imagination.) For Rick Maplestead, in *Merry-Go-Round*, imprisoned in Changi and then freed only to discover his bonds to history, family, mates, and mediocrity, there is no escape but flight. But as he and his young cousin Rob Coram (whose offshore vision gives the book its title) know, glimpses of paradise are illusory and attempts to inhabit them are fraught with disappointment.

By focussing ultimately on the quests of the mind, the book recapitulates many of Stow's earlier themes. His first books, full of mad characters and melodramatic incidents, are the Gothic attempts of a young novelist to record his knowledge of power and passion, of the relation between man and landscape and the impact of belief on action. Not till these sensibilities were controlled by Stow's anthropological and historical commitments did they exert a powerful literary effect. *To the Islands* reduced the reliance on incident and traced instead the wanderings of a man through the desert of his belief, in search of the afterworld islands of aboriginal dream order. His soul, he discovers, "is a strange country"—which seems at first to be no advance on what he began by knowing. Increasingly, however, that very state of suspended apprehension becomes the world that Stow tries to explore. *Tourmaline*, about a wasteland of that name, which welcomes a stranger as a water-diviner (who begins to clothe himself in such a role), only to be desolated and turn to another authority when he fails, provides an even more archetypal canvas. Consciously symbolic and heavily mannered in style, the book tries to evoke the world of symbol, the fleeting perceptions that symbols try to convey, rather than the realities of everyday event. The reiteration on the part of The Law, the narrator, that to describe a heritage as "bitter" is "not to condemn it," urges

readers also to consider what it is that he does not say: what it is that he cannot say.

Tarot, Tao, and Jungian commentary become means to fathom the deep intuitive communications of silence: but wordless understandings present problems for a writer to communicate. Later novels pursue the imaginative reaches of the reflective mind. *Visitants* explores Melanesian tribal life and traces its impact on Australians of different sensibilities; the novel is cast as a series of depositions at a legal enquiry, which prove unable entirely to explain the cultural other-worldliness. *The Girl Green as Elderflower* turns imaginative threat—the pressures of tropical disease and a foreign tongue upon a sensitive young man—into imaginative renewal; the young man, in Suffolk, reconciles himself with his heritage and his experience, and in a series of fables he writes out his recognition of the ways in which the unusual has always permeated the everyday. To admit to such flights of mind, he discovers, is to admit to a kind of health and a kind of love, and to win a "paradise" of a different, more fluid, perhaps freer, certainly more comic nature.

But in *The Suburbs of Hell* Stow's vision is once again more problematic. The novel tells of a series of murders among both insiders and outsiders in an isolated East Anglia village. Who is the culprit? Adapting the forms of popular fiction, the narrative contrives to suggest a number of possibilities—but settles on none. The novelist here is interested more in the nature of motive and interpretive response than he is in simply bringing a story to a conclusion. He probes what the pressure of fear and uncertainty does to an apparently stable society—an interest not without its sociological import. But he fastens particularly on the power of narrative, and on the sometimes insidious capacity that the impulse to create narrative has on the way people (readers included) encode and therefore enclose all human behaviour around them.

—W.H. New

STUART, (Henry) Francis (Montgomery). Irish. Born in Townsville, Queensland, Australia, 29 April 1902. Educated at Rugby School, Warwickshire. Married 1) Iseult Gonne in 1920 (died), one son and one daughter; 2) Gertrude Meiszner in 1954. Fought on the side of the Irish Nationalists in the Civil War; imprisoned by the British, 1922. Lecturer in English and Irish Literature, University of Berlin, 1940. Imprisoned by the Allied forces, 1945–46. Founding member, Irish Academy of Letters. Recipient: Young Poet's Prize (*Poetry*, Chicago), 1921; Royal Irish Academy award, 1924; Northern Ireland Arts Council bursary, 1974. Address: 2 Highfield Park, Dublin 14, Ireland.

PUBLICATIONS

Novels

Women and God. London, Cape, 1931.
Pigeon Irish. London, Gollancz, and New York, Macmillan, 1932.
The Coloured Dome. London, Gollancz, 1932; New York, Macmillan, 1933.
Try the Sky. London, Gollancz, and New York, Macmillan, 1933.

Glory. London, Gollancz, and New York, Macmillan, 1933.
In Search of Love. London, Collins, and New York, Macmillan, 1935.
The Angel of Pity. London, Grayson, 1935.
The White Hare. London, Collins, and New York, Macmillan, 1936.
The Bridge. London, Collins, 1937.
Julie. New York, Knopf, and London, Collins, 1938.
The Great Squire. London, Collins, 1939.
The Pillar of Cloud. London, Gollancz, 1948.
Redemption. London, Gollancz, 1949; New York, Devin Adair, 1950.
The Flowering Cross. London, Gollancz, 1950.
Good Friday's Daughter. London, Gollancz, 1952.
The Chariot. London, Gollancz, 1953.
The Pilgrimage. London, Gollancz, 1955.
Victors and Vanquished. London, Gollancz, 1958; Cleveland, Pennington Press, 1959.
Angels of Providence. London, Gollancz, 1959.
Black List, Section H. Carbondale, Southern Illinois University Press, 1971; London, Martin Brian and O'Keeffe, 1975.
Memorial. London, Martin Brian and O'Keeffe, 1973.
A Hole in the Head. London, Martin Brian and O'Keeffe, and Nantucket, Massachusetts, Longship Press, 1977.
The High Consistory. London, Martin Brian and O'Keeffe, 1981.
Faillandia. Dublin, Raven Arts Press, 1985.

Uncollected Short Stories

"Relativity," in *Lovat Dickson's Magazine* (London), November 1934.
"Isles of the Blest," in *English Review* (London), December 1934.
"Bandit," in *Cornhill* (London), February 1938.
"The Stormy Petrel," in *Paddy No More*, edited by William Vorm. Nantucket, Massachusetts, Longship Press, 1978.
"The Heart That Melted," in *Irish Times* (Dublin), August 1985.

Plays

Men Crowd Me Round (produced Dublin, 1933).
Glory, adaptation of his own novel (produced London, 1936).
Strange Guest (produced Dublin, 1940).
Flynn's Last Dive (produced Croydon, Surrey, 1962).
Who Fears to Speak? (produced Dublin, 1970).

Verse

We Have Kept the Faith (as H. Stuart). Dublin, Oak Leaf Press, 1923.

Other

Nationality and Culture (lecture). Dublin, Sinn Fein Ardchomahairle, 1924.
Mystics and Mysticism. Dublin, Catholic Truth Society of Ireland, 1929.
Things to Live For: Notes for an Autobiography. London, Cape, 1934; New York, Macmillan, 1935.
Racing for Pleasure and Profit in Ireland and Elsewhere. Dublin, Talbot Press, 1937.
Der Fall Casement: Das Leben Sir Roger Casement und der Verleumdungsfeldzug des Secret Service, translated by Ruth Weiland. Hamburg, Hanseatische, 1940.

States of Mind: Selected Short Prose 1936–1983. Dublin, Raven Arts Press, and London, Martin Brian and O'Keeffe, 1984.

Translator, *The Captive Dreamer*, by Christian de La Mazière. New York, Saturday Review Press, 1974; as *Ashes of Honour*, London, Wingate, 1975.

*

Manuscript Collections: Southern Illinois University Library, Carbondale; National Library of Ireland, Dublin.

Critical Studies: *A Festschrift for Francis Stuart on His Seventieth Birthday 29 April 1972*, Dublin, Dolmen Press, 1972 (includes bibliography); *Francis Stuart* by J.H. Natterstad, Lewisburg, Pennsylvania, Bucknell University Press, 1974.

Francis Stuart comments:

(1976) I consider myself a dissident writer, someone who is keeping flowing a countercurrent to many of the assumptions and attitudes of contemporary society. For this reason I have been called a Ghetto novelist, and several of my books have been black-listed not only in Ireland but elsewhere. For instance, *Black List, Section H*. has taken five years since its appearance in America to considerable acclaim (Lawrence Durrell in *The New York Times*, etc.) to find a publisher in England.

*   *   *

In the middle 1930's Francis Stuart said he was "interested in life where it is most intense," a condition he often found in races or in football matches rather than among writers and artists "with their narrow limits of the studio and library," and indeed Stuart was a practising athlete through his youth and middle years, as well as a breeder of horses and an airplane pilot. His imaginative writing reflects these activities, yet it is often introspective and psychologically motivated. And it is often, in the best sense of the word, poetic.

Stuart has published more than 20 novels, but has never been so highly praised for them as for his one book of verse, *We Have Kept the Faith*, which won an award from the Royal Irish Academy, with William Butler Yeats as presiding judge. Yeats was consistent in his admiration of Stuart's work, and once said in a letter, "If luck comes to his aid he will be our great writer." Elsewhere he stated that Stuart's novel *The Coloured Dome* was "strange and exciting in theme and perhaps more personally and beautifully written than any book of our generation," and that it would work towards an understanding of "the strange Ireland that is rising up here." But not much luck came to Stuart's aid, and the new "strange Ireland" failed, for the most part, to recognise his gifts.

In marrying Iseult Gonne, he was in a sense marrying into the Irish Renaissance, and at the time of the Civil War he smuggled guns into Ireland from the Continent and was later imprisoned. Even the production of two of his plays at the Abbey Theatre did not bring him the widespread acceptance that might have been anticipated; neither did the British and American publication of his novels, which are among the finest fiction in modern Irish literature.

The second of them, *Pigeon Irish*, projects a war in the future, with the pigeons, in the best Celtic manner, somewhat symbolic creatures who in carrying messages from country to country speak slang (Pigeon Irish) and carry on love affairs and sometimes meet a grim fate. His next story, the one which won Yeats's strong admiration—*The Coloured Dome*—is another picture of war, perhaps based partly on Stuart's own 16-months' imprisonment. It was not until after the Second World War that Stuart was to write so well again, though his middle-period work won acclaim outside Ireland, by such authors as Compton Mackenzie.

Early in 1939, Stuart was invited to lecture in Berlin, and the next year he returned there to remain throughout the war, teaching modern English and Irish literature at the University of Berlin until that institution was destroyed by bombs. After the war he was imprisoned by the French forces and, after his release, lived in Paris and London, and in 1958 moved to Ireland.

Such facts are necessary in any considerations of Stuart's work, for they explain much about his work and about the response to it in Ireland. His residence in Nazi Germany was that of a neutral Irish author who, like P.G. Wodehouse, made some harmless broadcasts from Berlin; Stuart ceased this activity, however, when he discovered that he was expected to deliver Nazi propaganda. His life during those years has been examined elsewhere, and it has been established that he was never a Hitlerite or in any way antisemitic. But his willingness to stay on in Germany has been criticised, though readers must acknowledge the skilfulness of his superb (necessarily grim and appalling) pictures of a country being smashed into defeat. In *The Pillar of Cloud*, for example, he forcefully tells the story of an Irish poet in wartime Germany, and *Redemption* is the tale of a similar figure who, after the conflict, returns to his native Ireland. These are powerful books in which some critics have found almost a Dostoyevskian intensity.

These novels lead towards Stuart's twentieth, the massive and elaborate *Black List, Section H.*, an example of autobiography transformed into effective imaginative work. It deals not only with the Irish experiences of the central character H (that unused initial of Francis Stuart), but also of those connected with his travels on the Continent, before, during, and after the Second World War. It deals candidly with H's marriage and his wartime love affair in Germany, as well as with his subsequent imprisonment. The story is at once complicated and profound; and it is vividly written. It is one of the imaginative masterpieces of modern Ireland.

—Harry T. Moore

STYRON, William. American. Born in Newport News, Virginia, 11 June 1925. Educated at Christchurch School, Virginia; Davidson College, North Carolina, 1942–43; Duke University, Durham, North Carolina, 1943–44, 1946–47, B.A. 1947 (Phi Beta Kappa). Served in the United States Marine Corps, 1944–45, 1951: 1st Lieutenant. Married Rose Burgunder in 1953; three daughters and one son. Associate editor, McGraw Hill, publishers, New York, 1947. Since 1952, advisory editor, *Paris Review*, Paris and New York; member of the Editorial Board, *American Scholar*, Washington, D.C., 1970–76. Since 1964, Fellow, Silliman College, Yale University, New Haven, Connecticut; Honorary Consultant in American Letters, Library of Congress, Washington, D.C. Recipient: American Academy Prix de Rome, 1952; Pulitzer Prize, 1968; Howells Medal, 1970; American Book Award, 1980; Connecticut Arts Award, 1984; Cino del Duca Prize, 1985. Litt.D.: Duke University 1968. Member, American Academy, and American Academy of Arts and Sciences; Commandant,

Order of Arts and Letters (France). Address: R.F.D., Roxbury, Connecticut 06783, U.S.A.

PUBLICATIONS

Novels

Lie Down in Darkness. Indianapolis, Bobbs Merrill, 1951; London, Hamish Hamilton, 1952.
The Long March. New York, Random House, 1956; London, Hamish Hamilton, 1962.
Set This House on Fire. New York, Random House, 1960; London, Hamish Hamilton, 1961.
The Confessions of Nat Turner. New York, Random House, 1967; London, Cape, 1968.
Sophie's Choice. New York, Random House, and London, Cape, 1979.

Short Story

Shadrach. Los Angeles, Sylvester and Orphanos, 1979.

Uncollected Short Stories

"Autumn," and "Long Dark Road," in *One and Twenty*, edited by W.M. Blackburn. Durham, North Carolina, Duke University Press, 1945.
"Moments in Trieste," in *American Vanguard 1948*, edited by Charles I. Glicksburg. New York, Cambridge, 1948.
"The Enormous Window," in *American Vanguard 1950*, edited by Charles I. Glicksburg. New York, Cambridge, 1950.
"The McCabes," in *Paris Review 22*, Autumn-Winter 1959–60.
"Pie in the Sky," in *The Vintage Anthology of Science Fantasy*, edited by Christopher Cerf. New York, Random House, 1966.

Play

In the Clap Shack (produced New Haven, Connecticut, 1972). New York, Random House, 1973.

Other

The Four Seasons, illustrated by Harold Altman. University Park, Pennsylvania State University Press, 1965.
Admiral Robert Penn Warren and the Snows of Winter: A Tribute. Winston-Salem, North Carolina, Palaemon Press, 1978.
The Message of Auschwitz. Blacksburg, Virginia, Press de la Warr, 1979.
Against Fear. Winston-Salem, North Carolina, Palaemon Press, 1981.
As He Lay Dead, A Bitter Grief (on William Faulkner). New York, Albondocani Press, 1981.
This Quiet Dust and Other Writings. New York, Random House, 1982; London, Cape, 1983.
Conversations with William Styron (interviews), edited by James L. W. West III. Jackson, University Press of Mississippi, 1985.

Editor, *Best Short Stories from the Paris Review.* New York, Dutton, 1959.

*

Bibliography: *William Styron: A Descriptive Bibliography* by James L.W. West III, Boston, Hall, 1977; *William Styron: A*

Reference Guide by Jackson R. Bryer and Mary B. Hatem, Boston, Hall, 1978; *William Styron: An Annotated Bibliography of Criticism* by Philip W. Leon, Westport, Connecticut, Greenwood Press, 1978.

Manuscript Collections: Library of Congress, Washington, D.C.; Duke University, Durham, North Carolina.

Critical Studies: *William Styron* by Robert H. Fossum, Grand Rapids, Michigan, Eerdmans, 1968; *William Styron* by Cooper R. Mackin, Austin, Texas, Steck Vaughn, 1969; *William Styron* by Richard Pearce, Minneapolis, University of Minnesota Press, 1971; *William Styron* by Marc L. Ratner, New York, Twayne, 1972; *William Styron* by Melvin J. Friedman, Bowling Green, Ohio, Popular Press, 1974; *The Achievement of William Styron* edited by Irving Malin and Robert K. Morris, Athens, University of Georgia Press, 1975, revised edition, 1981; *Critical Essays on William Styron* edited by Arthur D. Casciato and James L. W. West III, Boston, Hall, 1982; *The Root of All Evil: The Novels of William Styron* by John K. Crane, Columbia, University of South Carolina Press, 1984.

*   *   *

Of the American novelists who have come onto the literary scene since the end of the Second World War, William Styron would seem to have worked most directly in the traditional ways of story-telling. As a writer from the American South, he was heir to a mode of fiction writing most notably developed by William Faulkner and practiced to striking effect by such fellow Southerners as Robert Penn Warren, Thomas Wolfe, Eudora Welty, and Katherine Anne Porter. It involved—as the mode of Hemingway did not involve—a reliance upon the resources of a sounding rhetoric rather than upon understatement, a dependence upon the old religious universals ("love and honor and pity and pride and compassion and sacrifice," as Faulkner once termed them) rather than a suspicion of all such external moral formulations, and a profound belief in the reality of the past as importantly affecting present behavior—an "historical sense," as contrasted with the dismissal of history as irrelevant and meaningless.

His first novel, *Lie Down in Darkness*, was strongly indebted to the example of Faulkner; Styron began it, he said, after reading Faulkner night and day for several weeks. Yet though Styron portrayed a young Southern woman, Peyton Loftis, as she battled for love and sanity in a dreary family situation, doomed to defeat by her father's weak, self-pitying ineffectuality and her mother's hypocrisy and sadistic jealousy, and though the setting was a tidewater Virginia city among an effete upper-class society, what resulted was not finally Faulknerian. At bottom the causes of Styron's tragedy were familial, not dynastic; the deficiencies of Milton and Helen Loftis were not importantly those of decadent aristocracy whose concept of honor and pride has become empty posturing and self-indulgence, as they would have been for a writer such as Faulkner, but rather personal and psychological. When Peyton flees Virginia for New York City, there is little sense of her plight as representing isolation from the order and definition of a time and place that are no longer available. Instead, hers was a break for freedom, and the failure to make good the break is the result of the crippling conflict within her mind and heart imposed by the example of her parents, and which symbolizes the hatreds engendered by a society that does not know how to love. The suicide of Peyton Loftis represents a plunge into the moral abyss of a self-destructive modern world. Styron, in other words, wrote out of a tradition that taught him to measure his people and their society against the traditional values, and to see the absence of those values in their lives as tragic; but he did not depict that absence as a falling away from a more honorable, more ordered Southern historical past.

The success of *Lie Down in Darkness* was considerable, perhaps in part because a novel that could depict the modern situation as tragic, rather than merely pathetic, and could thus make use of the High Style of language to chronicle it, was all too rare. Styron followed in with *The Long March,* a novella set in a Marine Corps camp during the Korean War period (Styron himself was briefly recalled to active duty in 1951). Depicting the irrationality of war and the military mentality, it demonstrates the dignity, and also the absurdity, of an individual's effort to achieve nobility amid chaos.

Eight years elapsed before Styron's second full-length novel, *Set This House on Fire.* The story of a Southern-born artist, Cass Kinsolving, who is unable to paint, and is married and living in Europe, it involved a man in spiritual bondage, undergoing a terrifying stay in the lower depths before winning his way back to sanity and creativity. In Paris, Rome, and the Italian town of Sambucco, Cass Kinsolving lives in an alcoholic daze, tortured by his inability to create, wandering about, drinking, pitying himself, doing everything except confronting his talent. The struggle is on existential terms. Kinsolving has sought to find a form for his art outside of himself, looking to the society and the people surrounding him for what could only be located within himself: the remorseless requirement of discovering how to love and be loved, and so to create.

Set This House on Fire encountered a generally hostile critical reception, to some extent because it was sprawling and untidy, occasionally overwritten, and therefore so very different from his well-made first novel. It seemed, too, even further removed than *Lie Down in Darkness* from the customary Southern milieu: not only were there no decaying families, no faithful black retainers, no blood-guilt, and no oversexed Southern matrons, but we are told very little about the protagonist's past, either familial or personal, that might explain how he got the way he was. Yet there *was* a past; but Styron gives it to a friend of Kinsolving's, Peter Leverett, who tells the story. The fact is that Leverett's failure to find definition in his Southern origins is what really accounts for Kinsolving's present-day plight. Styron apparently could not avoid grounding his tragedy in history one way or the other. And after Kinsolving has fought his way back to personal responsibility and creativity, he leaves Europe and returns to the South. There is thus a kind of circular movement involved in the first two novels. Peyton Loftis finds the Southern community impossible to live within and love within, and she goes to New York. Cass Kinsolving, equally at loose ends, goes abroad and conducts his struggle for identity and definition there, and then comes home to the South. He has had in effect to ratify the individual and social worth of his attitudes and values away from the place and the institutions of their origins, and make them his own, not something merely bequeathed automatically to him.

If so, it was not surprising that Styron's next and most controversial novel, *The Confessions of Nat Turner*, once again was set in the South—in Southside Virginia, no more than an hour's automobile drive from Port Warwick where Peyton Loftis grew up and Newport News, Virginia, where Styron was born and raised—and that it concerned itself squarely with the Southern past, as exemplified in the presence and the role of the black man. For though *The Confessions of Nat Turner* is based upon a famous slave insurrection that took place in 1831, its implications involve race and racism, integration and separatism, and the use of violent means in order to achieve political and social ends. Styron's strategy, for what he termed his "meditation upon history," was to tell his story from the viewpoint of the slave leader Nat Turner, of whose actual life almost nothing is known. Rather than restrict his protagonist's language, however, to that which a plantation slave in the early 19th-century might be expected to have used, Styron decided that the range and complexity of such a man's mind could not be adequately represented in any such primitive fashion, and he cast Nat Turner's reflections in the rich, allusive, polysyllabic mode of the early Victorian novel. Styron was thus able to have his slave leader utilize the resources of a sounding rhetoric in order to look beyond his immediate circumstance into the moral and ethical implications of his actions.

The initial critical verdict on *The Confessions of Nat Turner* was highly favorable, with such critics as Alfred Kazin, Philip Rahv, C. Vann Woodward, and others declaring it an impressive contribution both to contemporary American fiction and to the knowledge of slavery. Almost immediately, however, the book became embroiled in a controversy, not so much literary as sociological, which made both novel and novelist into a *cause célèbre*. For in presuming, as a white man, to portray the consciousness of a black revolutionist of a century-and-a-half ago, Styron came into collision with the impetus of the black separatist movement. His novel appeared at a time when the black American was straining as never before to assert his identity and his independence of white paternalism, and the result was that numerous black critics, together with some white sympathizers, began heaping abuse on Styron for his alleged racism, his alleged unwarranted liberties with historical "fact," and his alleged projection of "white liberal neuroses" onto a revolutionary black leader's personality. A host of reviews and essays and even a book appeared in denunciation of Styron. Other critics rose to the rebuttal, and historians joined in to certify the authenticity of Styron's historical portrayal. The outcome has been a voluminous literature of controversy that may well interest future social historians almost as much as the Nat Turner insurrection itself.

In 1979 Styron entered the lists again with a lengthy novel on another controversial subject. *Sophie's Choice* involved the confrontation of a young and very autobiographically-clued Virginian with a Polish refugee who has undergone the horrors of concentration camp existence, and her lover, a young New York Jew who is a brilliant conversationalist but turns out to be quite mad. Written very much in the mode of Thomas Wolfe's fiction of encounter with the metropolis, Styron's novel records the growing helplessness of a youthful American in the face of a developing acquaintance with the enormity of human evil and irrationality. The novel drew much criticism for its excesses of rhetoric and the apparent irrelevance of much of its sexual material; in effect it would seem to imitate the author's own difficulties in coming to terms with the subject matter described. Yet it contains powerful sequences, and as always represents Styron's unwillingness to seek easy ways out or avoid central human problems.

—Louis D. Rubin, Jr.

SUKENICK, Ronald. American. Born in Brooklyn, New York, 14 July 1932. Educated at Cornell University, Ithaca, New York, B.A. 1955; Brandeis University, Waltham, Massachusetts, M.A. 1957, Ph.D. in English 1962. Married Lynn Luria in 1961. Lecturer, Brandeis University, 1956–57, and Hofstra University, Hempstead, New York, 1961–62; part-time teacher, 1963–66; Assistant Professor of English, City College, New York, 1966–67, and Sarah Lawrence College, Bronxville, New York, 1968–69; Writer-in-Residence, Cornell University, 1969–70, and University of California, Irvine, 1970–72. Since 1975, Professor of English, and director of the creative writing program, 1975–77, University of Colorado, Boulder. Taught at Université Paul Valéry, Montpellier, France, Fall 1979; Butler Professor of English, State University of New York, Buffalo, Spring 1981. Contributing editor, *Fiction International*, Canton, New York, 1970–84; chairman, Coordinating Council of Literary Magazines, 1975–77. Since 1974, founding member and co-director, Fiction Collective, New York; since 1977, founding publisher, *American Book Review*, New York. Recipient: Fulbright fellowship, 1958, 1984; Guggenheim fellowship, 1977; National Endowment for the Arts fellowship, 1980; Faculty fellowship, 1982; Coordinating Council of Literary Magazines award, for editing, 1985. Address: Department of English, University of Colorado, Boulder, Colorado 80309, U.S.A.

PUBLICATIONS

Novels

Up. New York, Dial Press, 1968.
Out. Chicago, Swallow Press, 1973.
98.6. New York, Fiction Collective, 1975.
Long Talking Bad Conditions Blues. New York, Fiction Collective, 1979.

Short Stories

The Death of the Novel and Other Stories. New York, Dial Press, 1969.
A Postcard from "The Endless Short Story." Austin, Texas, Cold Mountain Press, 1974.
The Endless Short Story. New York, Fiction Collective, 1986.

Uncollected Short Stories

"One Every Minute," in *Carolina Quarterly* (Chapel Hill, North Carolina), Spring 1961.
"A Long Way from Nowhere," in *Epoch* (Ithaca, New York), Fall 1964.
"Extract from *The Fortune Teller*," in *Trema* (Paris), no. 2, 1977.

Other

Wallace Stevens: Musing the Obscure. New York, New York University Press, 1967.
In Form: Digressions Towards a Study of Composition. Carbondale, Southern Illinois University Press, 1985.

*

Critical Studies: "Getting Real: Making It (Up) with Ronald Sukenick," in *Chicago Review*, Winter 1972, and "Persuasive Account: Working It Out with Ronald Sukenick," in *Seeing Castaneda*, edited by Daniel Noel, New York, Putnam, 1976, both by Jerome Klinkowitz; "Reading *Out*" by Melvin J. Friedman, in *Fiction International 1* (Canton, New York), Fall 1973; "Imagination and Perception" (interview), in *The New Fiction: Interviews with Innovative American Writers* by Joe David Bellamy, Urbana, University of Illinois Press, 1974; "Tales of Fictive Power: Dreaming and Imagining in Ronald Sukenick's

Postmodern Fiction" by Daniel Noel, in *Boundary 2* (Binghamton, New York), Fall 1976; "Obscuring the Muse: The Mock-Autobiographies of Ronald Sukenick" by Timothy Dow Adams, in *Critique* (Atlanta), vol. 20, no. 1, 1978; "Way Out West: The Exploratory Fiction of Ronald Sukenick" by Alan Cheuse, in *Itinerary Criticism 7* edited by Charles Crow, Bowling Green, Ohio, Bowling Green State University Press, 1978.

Ronald Sukenick comments:
  My fiction is not "experimental."

*   *   *

Ronald Sukenick's four novels together exemplify the quest for "a world elsewhere" that Richard Poirier has identified with classic American literature and that extends to contemporary American fiction; they do so, however, with a high degree of self-consciousness. They chart an archetypal American odyssey from East Coast (*Up*), through the midwest to the West Coast (*Out*), from the West Coast to an imaginary social and mental state called Palestine (*98.6*), and then to an even more abstracted state beyond that (*Long Talking Bad Conditions Blues*). This odyssey serves as the exponent of Sukenick's parallel odyssey from conventional fiction through experimental writing toward the overtly mystified poetic speech he seeks. And this latter is the odyssey of a reflexive novelist who recognizes his problem. He knows that he is a post-modern formalist and that he is a romantic vitalist and primitivist; but he does not know whether his formalism enables or ultimately constrains his vitalism and primitivism.

Sukenick's odyssey begins with *Up*, whose protagonist, "Ronald Sukenick," rejects conventional assumptions about fiction but encounters difficulties writing his novel *The Adventures of Strop Banally*. Defending this novel against a friend's criticism of its lack of chronological structure and lack of verisimilitude, "Suckenick" counters: "It's just a sequence of words. The only thing that matters is the order of revelation in print"; and asks, "Why should we have to suspend disbelief? It's all words and nothing but words." This is the doctrine that Sukenick would soon after express in his own voice in "The New Tradition in Fiction." He would characterize his "Bossa Nova" writing as having "no plot, no story, no character, no chronological sequence, no verisimilitude, no imitation, no allegory, no symbolism, no subject matter, no 'meaning.' ... The Bossa Nova is non-representational—it represents itself. Its main qualities are abstraction, improvisation, and opacity." This is the doctrine of post-modern formalism, and Sukenick would next consider its problems.

A narrative that diminishes itself incrementally toward blank pages, *Out* represents Sukenick's desire to escape the autonomous reality he had claimed fiction to be. In a crucial passage, its protagonist announces his intention to write a Bossa Nova fiction: "I want to write a book like a cloud that changes as it goes." His native-American interlocutor counters: "I want to erase all books. ... I want to unlearn and unlearn till I get to the place where the ocean of the unknown begins. ... Then I want to ... bring my people to live beside that ocean where they can be whole again as they were before the [whites] came." This dialogue marks the center of Sukenick's quest and defines the terms of an ambivalence that he then renders concrete. *Out* parallels movement westward across America to movement out of itself. At the appropriate point in these two movements, *Out* reaches "a huge absence in the middle of the country," locates in the Great Divide Basin "a drainhole in the middle emptying into the void," and identifies that drainhole as "the source." One must pass through the waste of language to reach the purity of silence, this rather noxious, vaginal metaphor suggests; and *Out*, indeed, eventually relocates the "way out"—relocates that drainhole, that source—on itself as an O centered on a final page of text that precedes eleven blank ones.

But Sukenick sees the impossibility, if not the fatuity, of this quest. The first section of *98.6*, "Frankenstein," implants a collage of references documenting violence and dehumanization in American society within a narrative that tries to make sense of the American "Monster." The second section, "The Children of Frankenstein," tells the story of a commune on the California coast, on the edge of the ocean of the unknown. "Ron," or "Cloud," has founded this commune in order to make a novel from it. "Cloud has tried up and he has tried out. Neither of them works." Nor, however, does the commune, and its dispersal leads to the third section, "Palestine," a delirious and powerful monologue based on "The Mosaic Law the law of mosaics or how to deal with parts in the absence of wholes." Its speaker tries to attain "A Moment of Luminous Coincidence." He begins with a reference to the blues musician Jesse Lonecat Fuller, who settled in California and became "AONEMANBAND playing all the instruments AT THE SAME TIME"; he then refers to "an article by Ihab Hassan on Prometheus Frankenstein Orpheus" and laments that "when you try to sew Orpheus back together what you get is Frankenstein"; and he concludes his monologue and *98.6* still trying to "stitch together" the "bungled fragments" of his novel "but AT THE SAME TIME playing the blues letting it go it is as it is. Another failure."

As its title suggests, *Long Talking Bad Conditions Blues* represents Sukenick's attempt to play the blues successfully, to attain through an unpunctuated experimental writing an expressive wail he hopes will tap into the source. Geography and the page are now collapsed into an abstracted "this world" that is again connected by "holes" to "that one." A central character, Victor, proposes that "more and more would disappear through the gaping hole ... till people learned how to control the hole to go through it and find out what was on the other side." This requires prediction, "and the medium of prediction was the written word ... all written words comprise a vast and growing coincidence ... not so with spoken words which disappear ... into the gaping hole." Victor also proposes that "the first thing to do is decontrol the language ... by breaking the language code when you break the language code you get a new language like the tongue of the peasant crazies which they simply call tongue." The way to control the hole, then, and thereby reach the Territory beyond, is to locate a writing that is also a primitivistic speech. Huckleberry Finn meets Jack Kerouac and William S. Burroughs in a conceptual universe borrowed from *Finnegans Wake*. But Sukenick, again, is no naif: in his neat reversal, the Monster America creates a Victor (Frankenstein) who tries through his blues to remember Orpheus but who becomes just another Prometheus in the attempt.

—Charles Caramello

SWARTHOUT, Glendon (Fred).   American.   Born in Pinckney, Michigan, 8 April 1918. Educated at the University of Michigan, Ann Arbor, 1935–39, A.B. 1939, A.M. 1946; Michigan State University, East Lansing, 1952–55, Ph.D. 1955. Served in the United States Army Infantry, 1943–45: Sergeant.

Married Kathryn Blair Vaughn in 1940; one son. Teaching fellow, University of Michigan, 1946–48; Instructor, University of Maryland, College Park, 1948–51; Associate Professor of English, Michigan State University, 1951–59; Lecturer in English, Arizona State University, Tempe, 1959–62. Recipient: Theatre Guild award, 1947; Hopwood Award, 1948; O. Henry Award, 1960; Western Writers of America Spur Award, 1976. Agent: William Morris Agency, 1350 Avenue of the Americas, New York, New York 10019. Address: 5045 Tamanar Way, Scottsdale, Arizona 85253, U.S.A.

PUBLICATIONS

Novels

Willow Run. New York, Crowell, 1943.
They Came to Cordura. New York, Random House, and London, Heinemann, 1958.
Where the Boys Are. New York, Random House, and London, Heinemann, 1960.
Welcome to Thebes. New York, Random House, 1962; London, Heinemann, 1963.
The Cadillac Cowboys. New York, Random House, 1964.
The Eagle and the Iron Cross. New York, New American Library, 1966; London, Heinemann, 1967.
Loveland. New York, Doubleday, 1968.
Bless the Beasts and Children. New York, Doubleday, and London, Secker and Warburg, 1970.
The Tin Lizzie Troop. New York, Doubleday, and London, Secker and Warburg, 1972.
Luck and Pluck. New York, Doubleday, and London, Secker and Warburg, 1973.
The Shootist. New York, Doubleday, and London, Secker and Warburg, 1975.
The Melodeon. New York, Doubleday, and London, Secker and Warburg, 1977.
Skeletons. New York, Doubleday, and London, Secker and Warburg, 1979.
The Old Colts. New York, Fine, and London, Secker and Warburg, 1985.

Uncollected Short Stories

"Pancho Villa's One-Man War," in *Cosmopolitan* (New York), February 1953.
"A Horse for Mrs. Custer," in *New World Writing 5.* New York, New American Library, 1954.
"What Every Man Knows," in *Collier's* (Springfield, Ohio), 17 February 1956.
"Ixion," in *New World Writing 13.* New York, New American Library, 1958.
"A Glass of Blessings," in *Esquire* (New York), January 1959.
"Attack on the Mountain," in *Saturday Evening Post* (Philadelphia), 4 July 1959.
"Going to See George," in *Esquire* (New York), August 1965.
"The Ball Really Carries in the Cactus League Because the Air Is Dry," in *Esquire* (New York), March 1978.

Play

The Shootist, adaptation of his own novel (produced London, 1984).

Other (for children) with Kathryn Swarthout

The Ghost and the Magic Saber. New York, Random House, 1963.

Whichaway. New York, Random House, 1966; London, Heinemann, 1967.
The Button Boat. New York, Doubleday, 1969; London, Heinemann, 1971.
TV Thompson. New York, Doubleday, 1972.
Whales to See the. New York, Doubleday, 1975.
Cadbury's Coffin. New York, Doubleday, 1982.

*

Manuscript Collection: Hayden Memorial Library, Arizona State University, Tempe.

*   *   *

Of the novels Glendon Swarthout has published since 1943, all are eminently readable; two—*They Came to Cordura* and *Bless the Beasts and Children*—are outstanding. Whether set in a World War II bomber plant in Michigan, or in a present-day boy's camp in Arizona, each reflects the author's intense involvement with the persons and places he writes of.

Willow Run, a novel about blue-collar workers in a World War II defense plant, is somewhat heavy on win-the-war speeches and lacks story and character development. And while the book is rhapsodic on the details of building airplanes and a bit obvious in the symbolism, it does give us a glimpse into the mind of the factory worker under stress.

Some 15 years later, Swarthout published his finest novel: *They Came to Cordura.* The tantalizing glance into a factory worker's psyche is explored with a probe—this time using the peace-time soldier as the object. Preparing for World War I, the country needed heroes. The time is 1916, and the place, the Mexican border, where the punitive forces of the U.S. Cavalry are trying to route the rebels of Villa. Five men are chosen to receive the Congressional Medal of Honor, and it is Major Thorn's duty to keep them alive to receive it. The story concerns their six-day journey to Cordura, during which the men are revealed to be pathetic, corrupt, hypocritical, cowardly, and degenerate. It is a remarkable book for its creation of tension and its probing into the motives which make men behave courageously and selflessly on the battlefield. A gripping novel in every respect, it demonstrates Swarthout's power as a writer of major dimensions.

Where the Boys Are, a commercial success, is the story of the annual student spring trek to Florida. Although there is some attempt to inject a serious note into the proceedings by pointing out the possible tragic consequences of sexual indiscretion, it is largely a novel about youth with an appeal to youth—somewhat dated in the light of the freedoms demanded by youth in the years since its publication.

After the huge commercial and critical success of *They Came to Cordura,* Swarthout and his family moved to southern Arizona. It is here that *The Cadillac Cowboys* is set. This work satirically depicts the pitfalls an Easterner faces in fitting into the not-so-wild West. Basically farcical, this novel nevertheless has elements of sentiment, poignancy, adventure, and nostalgia. Its main appeal, however, is its wild and often outrageous humor, bordering frequently on slapstick.

The same southern Arizona scene provides the background for *The Eagle and the Iron Cross.* The place is a prisoner-of-war camp; the time, 1945; the protagonists, two young German soldiers. They escape and ultimately find refuge with a bedraggled tribe of Indians. Despite the Indians' help, the soldiers meet violent death. Swarthout does not mask his bitterness in this novel: it is a tale of intolerable, misplaced faith, and wanton brutality. There are no winners and no heroes. The young Germans retain their dignity, even in death; the Indians retain theirs and endure life. Our villains are the American super patriots who, under the guise of retaliation, practice atrocities equal to those of the Nazis. It is not a pretty story.

Returning to his native Michigan, Swarthout in *Loveland* depicts the growing-up adventures of a young musician struggling with both adolescence and the depression of the 1930's. This story is told with warmth and humor, and captures the frantic era of a waning opulent society and a dying way of life. Heavily larded with the slang and idiom of the 1930's, the humor is occasionally strained; essentially though the lighter side of the era is handled tastefully and knowingly. Swarthout has been through this, we feel, and writes lovingly about those innocent days.

Bless the Beasts and Children brings the reader back to Arizona. Six sensitive boys from a summer camp witness a buffalo kill. Misfits and castoffs all their lives, their obsession leads them to free the remaining animals. Their nocturnal adventures and ultimate victory are interspersed with delicately handled flashbacks which probe to the core of each boy's personality problem. In the course of the adventure, there are humor, courage, suspense, and tragedy.

In *The Old Colts* Bat Masterson and Wyatt Earp, now well past their prime, meet again in New York City. Bat, now thoroughly urbanized, a columnist for the *Telegraph*, and compulsive horse play, owes several thousand dollars to the mob. Earp, also destitute, has ironically come to New York to ask Bat for a stake. After several abortive and hilarious attempts to raise cash, they return to Dodge City, scene of their earlier heroic exploits, to rob the bank there. Through a series of bizarre and slapstick mishaps, they instead kill bankrobbers who had beaten them to the heist, receive a generous reward, and return to their respective homes—Earp to California, Bat to New York. The tone throughout is tongue-in-cheek and light, and Swarthout displays a reverence for his subjects. He purports to have been given a hitherto unknown manuscript of Masterson's, outlining this unknown escapade of the two frontier legends.

—Martin L. Kornbluth

SWIFT, Graham. British. Born in London, 4 May 1949. Educated at Dulwich College, 1960–67; Queens' College, Cambridge, 1967–70, B.A., M.A.; York University, 1970–73. Recipient: Geoffrey Faber Memorial Prize, 1983; *Guardian* Fiction Prize, 1983; Royal Society of Literature Winifred Holtby Award, 1984. Fellow, Royal Society of Literature, 1984. Lives in London. Agent: A.P. Watt Ltd., 26–28 Bedford Row, London WC1R 4HL, England.

PUBLICATIONS

Novels

The Sweet Shop Owner. London, Allen Lane, 1980; New York, Washington Square Press, 1985.
Shuttlecock. London, Allen Lane, 1981; New York, Washington Square Press, 1984.
Waterland. London, Heinemann, 1983; New York, Poseidon Press, 1984.

Short Stories

Learning to Swim and Other Stories. London, London Magazine Editions, 1982; New York, Poseidon Press, 1985.

Other

Editor, with David Profumo, *The Magic Wheel: An Anthology of Fishing in Literature.* London, Heinemann, 1985.

*   *   *

When there is a narrator speaking in the first person, there is an author manipulating the narrator for purposes of his own, which may or may not coincide with the narrator's. There may be things the author wishes to show the reader of which the narrator himself will be unaware: that is why the first-person narrative is the most ambitious and the one that requires most skill. In *The Sweet Shop Owner* Graham Swift moves from third-person to first-person narrative and makes it a little easy for himself. The novel is good but carries none of the reverberations of *Waterland*. *Shuttlecock* is more ambitious: the themes of guilt and atonement, of personal and "objective" history, of nature and the nature of cruelty and love are already present. But author and narrator are perhaps too closely identified, the reader does not feel a contrary pull, a kind of sub-text from which the central issue will emerge. Too much of what the narrator says is said by the author; too much of what the author wants to say is said by the narrator.

In *Waterland*, on the other hand, although not completely successful in the device of a history teacher talking to a class, narrator and author are separate, and the narrator reveals things about himself that he does not realise he is revealing. The most explicit and reiterated themes are the linked histories of man and nature. The narrator of a tale of teenage love in the war years is a history teacher who, more than 30 years later, is about to be retired because his wife has caused a scandal by snatching a baby and being committed to a mental health institute—although the Head proffers a more rational reason: the growing conviction that History as a separate subject is redundant and should be integrated into General Studies. And Tom, the teacher, in a sense proves the Head right when he begins to tell his pupils his own story, fitting it into the context of two centuries of a History that centres on the industrialisation of the Fenlands and the development and decline of a brewery. This local history is carefully placed and dated in relation to European History, and the narrator insists in pointing out the part the larger movement played in the smaller but no less momentous changes in his own area up to 1947.

Interspersed with these tracts of History are descriptions of the Fens and the eel, viewed by the narrator as examples of Natural History, that "which cleaves to itself. Which perpetually travels back to where it came from." The eel migrates to the Sargasso Sea to reproduce and die, and returns to the Fenlands to live, in a perennial movement that has no history, no dates except those which mark man's discovery of the habits of eels, thereby transforming a state into a progression, just as man imposed on the Fenlands, whose natural state is to be waterland, the constant changes of a "reclaimed" land. Both the Fens and the eels become metaphors in the mind of the narrator, the one for History, man's ambition to reclaim the past by giving it a shape it may not have had originally, and the other for the curiosity which in the person of Mary brings about the three deaths for which Tom is also responsible.

Underlying the explicit, reiterated themes Tom propounds and insists in elaborating, is the network of compulsions, guilts, and cruelties that are the author's main comment on his narrator. Actions and consequences are clearly observed as a counterpoint to History: it would be impossible to say, for example, that if only the First World War hadn't happened, Tom's mother would not have become her father's lover and given birth to Dick. The affair between father and daughter has other roots, which the narrator avoids exploring, just as he avoids exploring his own peculiar role in the events during the Second World War: a pimp to Mary's sexual curiosity, encouraging her to "educate" Dick beyond Dick's comprehension; a sly observer, noting cold-bloodedly Dick's bewilderment after the murder of Freddy, and yet manipulating his retarded brother, wanting not to know *why* although that is what he says he wants to know 30 years on, but wanting to see what Dick is going to do, wanting to find out what's in the locked box in the attic. His is a curiosity parallel to Mary's, but it would be difficult to accept that it is equally instinctive (yet by the end of the novel, we are forced to accept precisely that).

Tom commits the only gratuitous act in the whole book, setting up the scenario for Dick's death. Dick does not die out of guilt for killing Freddy, he dies because he discovers, as a consequence of Tom's interference, that he is the "bungled" result of an inherently unnatural relationship. What reason for Tom's action? None. And 30 years on, when his wife suffers a breakdown as a direct result of her self-inflicted abortion (the most powerful piece of writing in the book), Tom elaborates a whole novel of History to avoid confrontation with himself.

The final twist and central paradox, however, is that it is Tom's very ability to make story out of facts, to change reality to fit into his theories, his ability to invent excuses for himself, that is shown by the author to be the only way out of the despair that would follow an honest confrontation (it drove Dick to kill himself, it drives Mary mad). It is the other side of the coin of the reader's dislike of Tom: there is no way out except by fictionalising ourselves, by elaborating an historical novel around our actions and their consequences, be it psychoanalytic history, sociological history, religious history. We dislike in Tom what we dislike in ourselves: the fundamental, necessary dishonesty that allows us to go on living, reclaims us from Waterland (Wasteland?) by dredging and redredging. But not to move forward, not to achieve anything, simply as "a struggle to make things not seem meaningless." Swift seems to be saying that we have to accept, as Tom accepts, that we are not part of a progressive History nurtured by reason, but of a natural history which "doesn't go anywhere," that all the particular complexities of human endeavour and curiosity are nothing more than dredging machines, and the only important thing is to have "tried and so prevented things slipping," not to have "let the world get any worse." In fact, the important thing is to write the historical novel that the narrator is engaged in telling his pupils, in the hope that the readers and the pupils will see through the smokescreen to the truth the smokescreen is, after all, revealing.

—M.J. Fitzgerald

SYMONS, Julian (Gustave). British. Born in London, 30 May 1912. Educated in various state schools. Married Kathleen Clark in 1941; one son and one daughter (deceased). Shorthand typist and secretary for an engineering company, 1929–41; advertising copywriter, 1944–47. Founding editor, *Twentieth Century Verse*, London, 1937–39; reviewer, Manchester *Evening News*, 1947–56; editor, Penguin Mystery Series, 1974–79. Since 1958, reviewer for the *Sunday Times*, London. Visiting Professor, Amherst College, Massachusetts, 1975–76. Co-founder, 1953, and Chairman, 1958–59, Crime Writers Association; Chairman, Committee of Management, Society of Authors, 1969–71; council member, Westfield College, University of London, 1972–75; President, Detection Club, 1976–85. Recipient: Crime Writers Association Award, 1957, 1966; Mystery Writers of America Edgar Allan Poe Award, 1961, 1973, and Grand Master Award, 1982; Swedish Academy of Detection Grand Master Diploma, 1977. Fellow, Royal Society of Literature, 1975. Agent: Curtis Brown, 162–168 Regent Street, London W1R 5TA. Address: Groton House, 330 Dover Road, Walmer, Deal, Kent CT14 7NX, England.

PUBLICATIONS

Novels

The Immaterial Murder Case. London, Gollancz, 1945; New York, Macmillan, 1957.
A Man Called Jones. London, Gollancz, 1947.
Bland Beginning. London, Gollancz, and New York, Harper, 1949.
The Thirty-First of February. London, Gollancz, and New York, Harper, 1950.
The Broken Penny. London, Gollancz, and New York, Harper, 1953.
The Narrowing Circle. London, Gollancz, and New York, Harper, 1954.
The Paper Chase. London, Collins, 1956; as *Bogue's Fortune*, New York, Harper, 1957.
The Colour of Murder. London, Collins, and New York, Harper, 1957.
The Gigantic Shadow. London, Collins, 1958; as *The Pipe Dream*, New York, Harper, 1959.
The Progress of a Crime. London, Collins, and New York, Harper, 1960.
The Killing of Francie Lake. London, Collins, 1962; as *The Plain Man*, New York, Harper, 1962.
The End of Solomon Grundy. London, Collins, and New York, Harper, 1964.
The Belting Inheritance. London, Collins, and New York, Harper, 1965.
The Man Who Killed Himself. London, Collins, and New York, Harper, 1967.
The Man Whose Dreams Came True. London, Collins, 1968; New York, Harper, 1969.
The Man Who Lost His Wife. London, Collins, 1970; New York, Harper, 1971.
The Players and the Game. London, Collins, and New York, Harper, 1972.
The Plot Against Roger Rider. London, Collins, and New York, Harper, 1973.
A Three-Pipe Problem. London, Collins, and New York, Harper, 1975.
The Blackheath Poisonings. London, Collins, and New York, Harper, 1978.
Sweet Adelaide. London, Collins, and New York, Harper, 1980.
The Detling Murders. London, Macmillan, 1982; as *The Detling Secret*, New York, Viking Press, 1983.
The Name of Annabel Lee. London, Macmillan, and New York, Viking Press, 1983.

The Criminal Comedy of the Contented Couple.   London, Macmillan, 1985; as *A Criminal Comedy*, New York, Viking, 1986.

Short Stories

Murder! Murder!   London, Fontana, 1961.
Francis Quarles Investigates.   London, Panther, 1965.
Ellery Queen Presents Julian Symons' How to Trap a Crook and Twelve Other Mysteries.   New York, Davis, 1977.
The Great Detectives: Seven Original Investigations.   London, Orbis, and New York, Abrams, 1981.
The Tigers of Subtopia and Other Stories.   London, Macmillan, 1982; New York, Viking Press, 1983.

Plays

Radio Plays: *Affection Unlimited*, 1968; *Night Ride to Dover*, 1969.

Television Plays: *I Can't Bear Violence*, 1963; *Miranda and a Salesman*, 1963; *The Witnesses*, 1964; *The Finishing Touch*, 1965; *Curtains for Sheila*, 1965; *Tigers of Subtopia*, 1968; *The Pretenders*, 1970; *Whatever's Peter Playing At*, 1974.

Verse

Confusions about X.   London, Fortune Press, 1939.
The Second Man.   London, Routledge, 1943.
A Reflection on Auden.   London, Poem-of-the-Month Club, 1973.
The Object of an Affair and Other Poems.   Edinburgh, Tragara Press, 1974.
Seven Poems for Sarah.   Edinburgh, Tragara Press, 1979.

Other

A.J.A. Symons: His Life and Speculations.   London, Eyre and Spottiswoode, 1950.
Charles Dickens.   London, Barker, and New York, Roy, 1951.
Thomas Carlyle: The Life and Ideas of a Prophet.   London, Gollancz, and New York, Oxford University Press, 1952.
Horatio Bottomley.   London, Cresset Press, 1955.
The General Strike: A Historical Portrait.   London, Cresset Press, 1957.
The Thirties: A Dream Revolved.   London, Cresset Press, 1960; revised edition, London, Faber, 1975.
A Reasonable Doubt: Some Criminal Cases Re-examined.   London, Cresset Press, 1960.
The Detective Story in Britain.   London, Longman, 1962.
Buller's Campaign.   London, Cresset Press, 1963.
England's Pride: The Story of the Gordon Relief Expedition.   London, Hamish Hamilton, 1965.
Crime and Detection: An Illustrated History from 1840.   London, Studio Vista, 1966; as *A Pictorial History of Crime*, New York, Crown, 1966.
Critical Occasions.   London, Hamish Hamilton, 1966.
Bloody Murder.   London, Faber, 1972; as *Mortal Consequences*, New York, Harper, 1972; revised edition, as *Bloody Murder*, London and New York, Viking, 1985.
Between the Wars: Britain in Photographs.   London, Batsford, 1972.
Notes from Another Country.   London, London Magazine Editions, 1972.
The Tell-Tale Heart: The Life and Works of Edgar Allan Poe.   London, Faber, and New York, Harper, 1978.

Conan Doyle: Portrait of an Artist.   London, G. Whizzard, 1979.
The Modern Crime Story.   Edinburgh, Tragara Press, 1980.
Critical Observations.   London, Faber, and New Haven, Connecticut, Ticknor and Fields, 1981.
Tom Adams' Agatha Christie Cover Story (paintings by Tom Adams).   Limpsfield, Surrey, Dragon's World, 1981; as *Agatha Christie: The Art of Her Crimes*, New York, Everest House, 1982.
Crime and Detection Quiz.   London, Weidenfeld and Nicolson, 1983.
Dashiell Hammett.   New York, Harcourt Brace, 1985.

Editor, *An Anthology of War Poetry.*   London, Penguin, 1942.
Editor, *Selected Writings of Samuel Johnson.*   London, Grey Walls Press, 1949.
Editor, *Selected Works, Reminiscences and Letters*, by Thomas Carlyle.   London, Hart Davis, 1956; Cambridge, Massachusetts, Harvard University Press, 1957.
Editor, *Essays and Biographies*, by A.J.A. Symons.   London, Cassell, 1969.
Editor, *The Woman in White*, by Wilkie Collins.   London, Penguin, 1974.
Editor, *The Angry 30's.*   London, Eyre Methuen, 1976.
Editor, *Selected Tales*, by Poe.   London and New York, Oxford University Press, 1976; revised edition, 1980.
Editor, *Verdict of Thirteen: A Detection Club Anthology.*   London, Faber, and New York, Harper, 1979.
Editor, *The Complete Sherlock Holmes*, by Arthur Conan Doyle.   London, Secker and Warburg, and New York, Abrams, 1981.
Editor, *A.J.A. Symons to Wyndham Lewis: Twenty-Four Letters.*   Edinburgh, Tragara Press, 1982.
Editor, *New Poetry 9.*   London, Hutchinson, 1983.
Editor, *Classic Crime Omnibus.*   London, Penguin, 1984.

*

Manuscript Collection: Humanities Research Center, University of Texas, Austin.

Critical Studies: in *Auden and After: The Liberation of Poetry 1930–1941* by Francis Scarfe, London, Routledge, 1942; "Julian Symons and Civilization's Discontents" by Steven R. Carter, in *Armchair Detective* (White Bear Lake, Minnesota), January 1979; Larry E. Grimes, in *Thirteen English Gentlemen of Mystery* edited by Earl F. Bargainnier, Bowling Green, Ohio, Popular Press, 1985.

Julian Symons comments:
   I think the reason—well, one reason apart from money—for writing crime stories may be of interest. The quotation comes from the introduction to my Omnibus volume (Collins, 1967):

   Why put such ideas (as those in my books) into the form of crime stories, rather than "straight" novels? The thing that absorbs me most in our age is the violence behind respectable faces, the civil servant planning how to kill Jews most efficiently, the judge speaking with passion about the need for capital punishment, the quiet obedient boy who kills for fun. These are extreme cases, but if you want to show the violence that lives behind the bland faces most of us present to the world, what better vehicle can you have than the crime novel?

*   *   *

Julian Symons, a leading poet of the 1930's and later a distinguished literary critic (with books to his credit on Dickens, Carlyle, and Poe) and social historian (author of *The Thirties* and *The General Strike*), took to writing crime novels as a sideline to his main literary interests, almost as a game, and when his first book of this kind, *The Immaterial Murder Case*, appeared in 1945, he hardly envisaged that stories of detection would assume such importance as they later did in his career. But gradually such fiction became not merely a means of entertaining his public, but also a vehicle for his criticism of the world he lived in, a world he saw as exploitative and corrupted by power. In this context the literary critic has joined the social critic, and Symons has discussed in depth the role of the crime novel in presenting an examination of social motives, and become one of its most prolific writers.

In his novels (such as *The Narrowing Circle*, *The Colour of Murder*, *The Progress of a Crime*, *The End of Solomon Grundy*, *The Man Who Killed Himself*, etc.) Symons has used the necessary structure of the thriller—the presence and explanation of a crime or an apparent crime—for many more purposes than those exploited by the writer of the ordinary neatly contrived detective story which depends on the solution of a complex puzzle. Symons's plots are often, by comparison, loose and even obvious, and his denouements are sometimes deliberately anti-climactic; there is a distinctly ironic element in his attitude towards such matters. What he injects into his deliberately disjointed version of the classic crime plot is the kind of content that comes from his own wider interests.

He is concerned with the decay of a society, with cultural pretences, with politics as a corrupting element, with the manners of a world he had made his own: the Bohemian borderland where failed artists and hack writers, advertisement men and broadcasters, and their lesser hangers-on, come together to create a setting whose very alienation from moral stability tends to encourage the emergence of crime. It is a setting where the murderer and the victim seem to attract each other, a world of hollow men which suggests that as a novelist Symons learnt lessons from Wyndham Lewis, whom he knew in his early days as a writer.

But it is not merely the landscape of a rotting society that is recreated. Within it there is likely to be enacted a pursuit in which the ambiguous guilt of unjustly accused men play their part. These novels, indeed, are often psychologically quite complex, and it is such inner drama that in the end seems more important than the solution of the crime, or even the crime itself.

In *The Thirty-First of February*, for example, there is no crime at all, and a man is grimly hunted to insanity by a detective with a megalomaniac sense of being an agent of divine justice, for a death that was after all not a murder. This novel illustrates the ambiguity of Symons's attitude towards the policeman as a fictional type. Even when the police turn out in the end to be on the side of right, they are still menacing and unpredictable figures, and upon them Symons seems to focus the criticism of society that permeates his novels, and especially the dilemma of self-defeating authority and its semblances of justice which are hollow because they lack the core of true justice which rests on mercy.

Lately, and perhaps inevitably, given the preoccupations with literary form that become evident in his critical essays, Symons has shown an inclination to challenge not merely the moral pretensions of the conventional detective novel, but also its formal conventions. He has found his own use for literary devices like parody and palimpsest, and one of his most interesting recent novels, *Sweet Adelaide*, is an experiment in reconstructing earlier attitudes towards crime and giving them expression in a novel whose structure and linguistic pattern are those of the turning century, as Victorian mores slipped over into Edwardian social accommodations. In such a novel literary skills and social insights are balanced in the distance of history, and we recognize the extraordinary versatility of Symons's literary craftsmanship.

—George Woodcock

TAYLOR, Peter (Hillsman). American. Born in Trenton, Tennessee, 8 January 1917. Educated at Vanderbilt University, Nashville, 1936–37; Southwestern College, Memphis, Tennessee, 1937–38; Kenyon College, Gambier, Ohio, 1938–40, A.B. 1940. Served in the United States Army, 1941–45. Married Eleanor Lilly Ross in 1943; two children. Taught at the University of North Carolina, Chapel Hill, 1946–67. Since 1967, Professor of English, University of Virginia, Charlottesville. Visiting Lecturer, Indiana University, Bloomington, 1949, University of Chicago, 1951, Kenyon College, 1952–57, Seminar in American Studies, Oxford University, 1955, Ohio State University, Columbus, 1957–63, and Harvard University, Cambridge, Massachusetts, 1964. Recipient: Guggenheim fellowship, 1950; American Academy grant, 1952, and Gold Medal, 1979; Fulbright fellowship, to France, 1955; O. Henry Award, 1959; Ford fellowship, for drama, 1960. Member, American Academy, 1969. Address: 1841 Wayside Place, Charlottesville, Virginia 22903, U.S.A.

PUBLICATIONS

Novel

A Woman of Means. New York, Harcourt Brace, and London, Routledge, 1950.

Short Stories

A Long Fourth and Other Stories. New York, Harcourt Brace, 1948; London, Routledge, 1949.
The Widows of Thornton. New York, Harcourt Brace, 1954.
Happy Families Are All Alike: A Collection of Stories. New York, McDowell Obolensky, 1959; London, Macmillan, 1960.
Miss Leonora When Last Seen and 15 Other Stories. New York, Obolensky, 1963.
The Collected Stories of Peter Taylor. New York, Farrar Straus, 1969.
In the Miro District and Other Stories. New York, Knopf, and London, Chatto and Windus, 1977.
The Old Forest and Other Stories. New York, Doubleday, and London, Chatto and Windus, 1985.

Plays

Tennessee Day in St. Louis (produced Gambier, Ohio, 1956). New York, Random House, 1957.
A Stand in the Mountains (produced Abingdon, Virginia, 1971). Published in *Kenyon Review* (Gambier, Ohio), 1965.
Presences: Seven Dramatic Pieces. Boston, Houghton Mifflin, 1973.

Other

Editor, with Robert Penn Warren and Robert Lowell, *Randall Jarrell 1914–1965*.   New York, Farrar Straus, 1967.

*

Bibliography: *Andrew Lytle, Walker Percy, Peter Taylor: A Reference Guide* by Victor A. Kramer, Boston, Hall, 1983.

Critical Study: *Peter Taylor* by Albert J. Griffith, New York, Twayne, 1970.

*   *   *

Robert Penn Warren's laudatory introduction to Peter Taylor's first collection of short stories, *A Long Fourth*, has accurately oriented much subsequent criticism of Taylor's work on two counts. First, Warren identifies Taylor's primary material as the smaller crises and collisions of urban, middle-class life in the contemporary, upper south. Taylor has explored this world for some 45 years in his fiction, and his work often centers around a breakdown of either family or social relationships. Thus, although most of Taylor's characters are southern, his fiction consists of variations on a broad theme: the difficulties that change causes human beings. Second, Warren describes Taylor's "skeptical, ironic cast of mind" with which he treats his material. Taylor has never seriously deviated from either of these features of his work, and readers quickly become familiar with the characteristic slant of Taylor's vision.

This vision differs significantly from that of many other well-known Southern writers. Taylor's vision of the south is, as Alfred J. Griffith terms it, a "peculiar mixture of sentiment and irony" which simultaneously enables him to view tradition sympathetically and change realistically. Certainly Taylor's life has not only offered him the material on which he has chosen to focus his artistry, but also has helped determine this orientation. Born in a small, rural Tennessee town, Taylor grew up in such southern cities as Memphis, St. Louis, and Nashville, and he has lived in urban areas outside the south. In fact, Griffith suggests that it is this background which has made Taylor, more than any of his southern contemporaries, "the one most capable of seeing Southern culture simultaneously both as insider and as outsider." These personal experiences have made him acutely aware of how older patterns of behavior disintegrate and how, sometimes, newer ones replace them. The central issues of his fiction are, then, the difficulties, problems, and opportunities which people face as a result of changes in time and place. Some works which provide a representative view of Taylor's vision are "A Wife of Nashville," "The Scoutmaster," "The Old Forest," "The Throughway," "The Dark Walk," "Allegiance," "What You Hear from 'em?," "The Death of a Kinsman," "A Long Fourth," and *A Woman of Means*.

Still, he displays an ability to understand the value once present in the "old ways." This derives from Taylor's comprehension of the southern, agrarian mythos; he understands and is able to view that heritage, so centered on manners, tradition, and identity, with a full appreciation of what positive things that mythos offered many southerners. Not the least important of these positive aspects were clearly defined family and social roles. For example, characters as diverse as Aunt Muncie, a black mother of a white family, in "What You Hear from 'em?" and Major Basil Manley, a civil war veteran who had ridden with Bedford Forrest, from "In the Miro District," continue to play their roles with dignity. In other words, they struggle

to retain the identity they would have if they still lived in a relatively static society. While their attempts are admirable and Taylor presents them as such, he is not willing to validate their naïve illusions about the world. Muncie and Manley are doomed to failure by time—and Taylor will not condone their being out of step.

For Taylor, time is change. Understandably, many of his characters try to deny that. Some are reasonably successful for a while, as Margie and Lida Wade, transplanted southerners living in Detroit, in "The Death of a Kinsman"; some are less so, as Harry in "The Throughway." At some point though, most of Taylor's characters are forced either to confront the effects of change or to resort to acting out parodies of their former roles. It is a truism with Taylor that traditional roles and patterns of behavior tend to become less effective and more limiting. If one continues to play a role which is no longer functional within a society, one becomes isolated. Frequently, without any valid models on which to pattern their behavior, Taylor's characters can only fall back on stereotyped parodies which reduce their worth even further. So it is with Aunt Muncie when she finally confronts the fact that the Tolliver family will never return to Thornton and realizes she has lost her relationship with the "quality." Outside the old system, Aunt Muncie's actions become meaningless and initiate her descent into caricature. And in Major Manley's case, he becomes an anachronism, an antique which his children and grandson are pleased to have in the house as a conversation piece. Manley's grandson, the narrator of the story, only imperfectly senses the loss of his grandfather's independent personality, which, of course, reflects his own lack of individuality.

Some of Taylor's characters are capable of throwing off the burden of the past and adopting new, purposeful roles, but it is difficult and requires a good deal of flexibility. In "The Old Forest," for example, the narrator's wife displays the love and flexibility necessary to win both herself and her husband a new, purposeful life. Sylvia Harrison, in "The Dark Walk," may be the best individual example. A widow, Sylvia must decide whether to remain and begin a new life in Chicago, or to take her family back to Tennessee, which had always been her plan. In anticipation of this final trip, Sylvia had, for years, kept all her furniture and moved this burden all over the country. In a symbolic gesture, she sends all the furniture back to Tennessee and remains in Chicago having learned that she needed "to dispense with all that was old and useless and inherited."

Even a passing acquaintance with some of Taylor's work will convince a reader that he deserves close attention. Certainly his fiction will not suffer the same fate as Sylvia's furniture.

—William M. Karis

TENNANT, Emma (Christina).   British.   Born in London, 20 October 1937. Educated at St. Paul's Girls' School, London. Has one son and two daughters. Travel correspondent, *Queen*, London, 1963; features editor, *Vogue*, London, 1966; editor, *Bananas*, London, 1975–78. Since 1982, general editor, *In Verse*, London; since 1985, editor, Lives of Modern Women series, Viking, publishers, London. Fellow, Royal Society of Literature, 1982. Address: 146 Kensington Park Road, London W.11, England.

PUBLICATIONS

Novels

The Colour of Rain (as Catherine Aydy). London, Weidenfeld and Nicolson, 1964.
The Time of the Crack. London, Cape, 1973; as *The Crack*, London, Penguin, 1978.
The Last of the Country House Murders. London, Cape, 1974; New York, Nelson, 1976.
Hotel de Dream. London, Gollancz, 1976.
The Bad Sister. London, Gollancz, and New York, Coward McCann, 1978.
Wild Nights. London, Cape, 1979; New York, Harcourt Brace, 1980.
Alice Fell. London, Cape, 1980.
Queen of Stones. London, Cape, 1982.
Woman Beware Woman. London, Cape, 1983; as *The Half-Mother*, Boston, Little Brown, 1985.
Black Marina. London, Faber, 1985.
The Adventures of Robina, by Herself. London, Faber, 1986.

Uncollected Short Stories

"Mrs. Ragley," in *Listener* (London), 1973.
"Mrs. Barratt's Ghost," in *New Statesman* (London), 28 December 1973.
"Philomela," in *Bananas*, edited by Tennant. London Quartet-Blond and Briggs, 1977.
"The Bed That Mick Built," in *New Stories 2*, edited by Derwent May and Alexis Lykiard. London, Arts Council, 1977.
"Cupboard Love," in *New Stories 4*, edited by Elaine Feinstein and Fay Weldon. London, Hutchinson, 1979.
"Tortoise-Shell Endpapers," in *Time Out* (London), 21 December 1979.
"The Frog Prints," in *London Tales*, edited by Julian Evans. London, Hamish Hamilton, 1983.
"The German in the Wood," in *London Review of Books*, 1984.

Other (for children)

The Boggart. London, Granada, 1980.
The Search for Treasure Island. London, Penguin, 1981.
The Ghost Child. London, Heinemann, 1984.

Other

Editor, *Bananas*. London, Quartet-Blond and Briggs, 1977.
Editor, *Saturday Night Reader*. London, W.H. Allen, 1979.

*   *   *

With nine novels published in rapid succession since 1973, Emma Tennant has established herself as one of the leading British exponents of "new fiction." This does not mean that she is an imitator of either the French *nouveaux romanciers* or the American post-modernists, although her work reveals an indebtedness to the methods and preoccupations of some of the latter. Like them, she employs parody and rewriting, is interested in the fictiveness of fiction, appropriates some science-fiction conventions, and exploits the possibilities of generic dislocation and mutation, especially the blending of realism and fantasy. Yet, although parallels can be cited and influences suggested, her work is strongly individual, the product of an intensely personal, even idiosyncratic, attempt to create an original type of highly imaginative fiction.

The first novel she published under her own name is *The Time of the Crack*. This futuristic fable about an ever-widening crack in the riverbed of the Thames, leading to the partial destruction of London and eventually to the breaking-off of the entire south of England and its Atlantis-like disappearance under the sea, is a fusion of black farce, wide-ranging satire, and apocalyptic vision. One reviewer described it as "Lewis Carroll technique applied to H.G. Wells material," but other names suggest themselves even more strongly, notably Orwell and Waugh. Like *Nineteen Eighty-Four*, *The Time of the Crack* is, in its bizarre way, a "condition of England" novel, projecting onto the immediate future current obsessions with decline and fall, and literalizing the metaphor of national disintegration. Stylistically, the book is characterized by a satirical panache recalling Waugh's early period, as Tennant mercilessly caricatures many aspects of contemporary society.

In 1973 *The Time of the Crack* seemed an original novel of great promise. Since then, with the changes in direction and emphasis of her work, critics have disagreed about whether these developments represent a fulfilment of that potential or a regrettable misuse of considerable talent. The comedy and satire of *The Time of the Crack*, together with its panoramic sweep and its visionary quality, have gradually given way to work narrower in focus, more intense, more introspective, more explicitly serious. There has been a gain in the sheer virtuosity of her writing, but there has also been a loss—especially of elements that made *The Time of the Crack* so immediately enjoyable and impressive.

Her next novel, *The Last of the Country House Murders*, is also set in the near future—Britain after the Revolution—and in its oblique way is another "condition of England" novel. Again like Orwell, Tennant extrapolates from the present a possible picture of the future, but what makes this novel so different from other dystopias is her ingenious fusion of the novel of pessimistic prophecy with an amusing parodistic reworking of the country-house brand of detective fiction. Indeed, the book increasingly focuses on the small group of peculiar, virtually caricature figures who arrive at Woodiscombe Manor to participate in the murder mystery planned by the government as a tourist attraction; the wider social and national issues become more marginal than in *The Time of the Crack*. The result is bizarre comedy, replete with the eccentricities, foibles, and oddities that recur throughout her *oeuvre*.

Eccentricity also pervades the small hotel that provides the setting for *Hotel de Dream*, in which the dreams and fantasies of the few residents, one of whom is a romantic novelist, play a much more important part than the framework of waking reality. Reality itself dissolves into fantasy and vice versa, and the various dreams and fictions merge with one another to create a super-reality of the collective unconscious, in which the dreamers acquire new identities and the romantic novelist's imaginary characters become as real as their creator. While the book is certainly not lacking in the weird humour of her two previous books, and actually abounds in the grotesque, there is a shift away from satirical comedy in favour of psychological fantasy, from a broad perspective to a closed world. Even so, Tennant still provides a tangentially symbolic comment on the "condition of England" issue through her characters and their dream-selves.

In both *The Last of the Country House Murders* and *Hotel de Dream*, Tennant plays self-consciously with novelistic conventions, but in *The Bad Sister*, another futuristic novel (it opens and ends in 1986), she attempts something much more daring and ambitious—some would say foolhardy. She models the entire book very closely on a literary masterpiece, Hogg's *Confessions of a Justified Sinner*. While setting her novel in the present and locating only part of it in Scotland, she adheres to Hogg's highly original structure, adopts some of the main features of his plot, and retains his embodiment of the Devil, Gil-Martin, though in a peripheral role. However, she does alter the sex of the main characters, the equivalent of the Justified Sinner being Jane Wild and her evil genius being Meg rather than Gil-Martin. This change allows Tennant to introduce the subject of feminism and the contemporary phenomenon of female urban guerrillas, but the main focus is not social or political but psychological—the split personality of Jane under the influence of the obsessional Meg. Like Hogg, Tennant is concerned with human duality, fanaticism, the subjectivity of reality, and the possibility of possession, but she interprets these in a contemporary context, developing the theme of the schizoid nature of modern woman.

If *The Bad Sister* is imaginatively claustrophobic, her two subsequent novels, *Wild Nights* and *Alice Fell*, are even more so, the dividing line between reality and fantasy being increasingly blurred and ambiguous. In *Wild Nights*, for example, the child-narrator presents a vision of the world controlled by the imagination rather than reason, in which magic and enchantment are an integral part of nature. Seasonal symbolism and archetypal images play a vital part, and the action seems timeless and placeless despite being located in postwar Scotland and England. For the most part, the relatively few characters in this closed world are strange, eccentric beings, more mythical than social. *Alice Fell* is strikingly similar to *Wild Nights* in a number of these respects, despite the differences that arise from it being a third-person narration. Tennant sustains the obsessive visionary quality of both novels by brilliant and evocative writing, but she does so at a price. In moving so far from *The Time of the Crack*, she sacrifices some of her most attractive qualities as a novelist. Nevertheless, *Alice Fell*, reworking of the myth of Persephone in terms of contemporary British society in a state of upheaval, is a most ambitious imaginative feat, even if the symbolism and archetypal characterization tend to be too intrusive.

Queen of Stones represents a move away from the cul-de-sac of poetic fiction into which Tennant was in danger of becoming trapped. Like *The Bad Sister* this novel has a specific literary model, *Lord of the Flies* (itself an antidote to Ballantyne's *The Coral Island*), but Tennant does not provide such close parallels to Golding's novel as she does to Hogg's in her earlier book. The most striking resemblance between *Queen of Stones* and *The Bad Sister* is Tennant's use of sex-reversal, substituting females for their male equivalents in her sources. A sponsored walk in Dorset goes terribly wrong when a group of girls are lost in appalling fog; cut off from their normal everyday surroundings and the adult world, like Golding's schoolboys, they create their own imaginative reality involving ritual and sacrifice. Tennant arrives at a conclusion not dissimilar from Golding's. In her next novel, *Woman Beware Woman*, Tennant again investigates the deeper mythic reality behind the appearances of social reality, the subconscious drives that shape reality itself, especially as they manifest themselves in women and their behaviour. The literary roots of *Woman Beware Woman* are less obvious than in *The Bad Sister* and *Queen of Stones*, but the close similarity to the title of Middleton's Jacobean revenge tragedy *Women Beware Women* suggests that Tennant is creating her own highly imaginative equivalent of a drama of thwarted love, resentment, suppressed passion, hatred and revenge as various people assemble in a quiet part of Ireland following the death of a distinguished literary man.

Political undercurrents are present in a number of Tennant's novels, but *Black Marina* is the most explicitly political. The setting is the imaginary island of St. James, adjacent to Grenada in the Caribbean; the time, Christmas Eve 1983, not long after the murderous real-life coup against Maurice Bishop's government in Grenada which precipitated American military intervention. During the day of the novel, St. James is expected to be the target of a similar Marxist-Leninist coup by a group of those involved in the attempt to seize power in Grenada. The subject-matter is topical and journalistic, but Tennant's handling of it is characteristically complex and far removed from orthodox social realism. The principal narrator, Holly Baker, an English woman who came to the island in the 1960's and stayed, gradually unfolds in piecemeal fashion the network of human relationships in St. James and England that has eventually precipitated the happenings of Christmas Eve 1983. As usual in Tennant's fiction, mythic elements lie just beneath the contemporary surface, and the title itself, alluding to Shakespeare's *Pericles* (Marina is the King's long-lost daughter) and Eliot's related Ariel poem "Marina," points towards the most important of these, a daughter's quest for her father. Even so, *Black Marina* is something of a new departure for Tennant in setting and theme, and it confirms her ability to go on regenerating herself as a novelist.

—Peter Lewis

TENNANT, Kylie. Australian.   Born in Manly, New South Wales, 12 March 1912. Educated at Brighton College, Manly; University of Sydney, 1931. Married Lewis C. Rodd in 1932 (died, 1979); one daughter and one son (deceased). Full-time writer, 1935–59; journalist, publisher's reader, literary adviser, and editor, 1959–69; resumed full-time writing career, 1969. Life Patron, Fellowship of Australian Writers; member, Commonwealth Literary Fund Advisory Board, 1961–73. Recipient: S.H. Prior Memorial Prize, 1936, 1940; Australian Literature Society Gold Medal, 1941; Commonwealth Jubilee Stage Prize, 1951. Officer, Order of Australia, 1980. Agent: Judy Barry, 25 Yarranabbe Road, Darling Point, New South Wales. Address: Cliff View, via Shipley, Blackheath, New South Wales 2785, Australia.

PUBLICATIONS

Novels

Tiburon.   Sydney, Bulletin Press, 1935.
Foveaux.   London, Gollancz, 1939.
The Battlers.   London, Gollancz, and New York, Macmillan, 1941.
Ride on Stranger.   New York, Macmillan, and London, Gollancz, 1943.
Time Enough Later.   New York, Macmillan, 1943; London, Macmillan, 1945.
Lost Haven.   New York, Macmillan, 1946; London, Macmillan, 1947.
The Joyful Condemned.   New York, St. Martin's Press, and London, Macmillan, 1953; complete version, as *Tell Morning This*, Sydney and London, Angus and Robertson, 1968.
The Honey Flow.   London, Macmillan, and New York, St. Martin's Press, 1956.

Tantavallon. Melbourne and London, Macmillan, 1983.

Short Stories

Ma Jones and the Little White Cannibals. London, Macmillan, 1967.

Uncollected Short Stories

"A Bargain," in *Coast to Coast 1941*, edited by Cecil Mann. Sydney, Angus and Robertson, 1941.
"Foster Child," in *Tales by Australians*, edited by Edith M. Fry. London, British Authors' Press, n.d.
"The Face of Despair," in *Australia Writes*, edited by T. Inglis Moore. Melbourne, Cheshire, 1953.
"Eight-Hour Day," in *Australian Idiom*, edited by H.P. Heseltine. Melbourne, Cheshire, 1963.
"The Antagonist," in *Summer's Tales 1*, edited by Tennant. Melbourne and London, Macmillan, 1964.
"The Cool Man," in *The Cool Man and Other Contemporary Stories by Australian Authors*. Sydney and London, Angus and Robertson, 1973.

Plays (for children)

John o' the Forest and Other Plays. London, Macmillan, 1950.
Tether a Dragon (for adults). Sydney, Associated General Publications, 1952.
The Bells of the City and Other Plays. London, Macmillan, 1955.
The Bushrangers' Christmas Eve and Other Plays. Melbourne, Macmillan, 1959.

Other

Australia: Her Story: Notes on a Nation. London, Macmillan, and New York, St. Martin's Press, 1953; revised edition, London, Pan, 1964, 1971.
Long John Silver: The Story of the Film. Sydney, Associated General Publications, 1953; London, Robertson and Mullens, 1954.
The Development of the Australian Novel. Canberra, Commonwealth Literary Fund, 1958.
All the Proud Tribesmen (for children). London, Macmillan, 1959; New York, St. Martin's Press, 1960.
Speak You So Gently (travel). London, Gollancz, 1959.
Trail Blazers of the Air. Melbourne, Macmillan, 1965; London, Macmillan, and New York, St. Martin's Press, 1966.
The Australian Essay, with L.C. Rodd. Melbourne, Cheshire, 1968.
Evatt: Politics and Justice (biography). Sydney and London, Angus and Robertson, 1970.
The Man on the Headland (biography). Sydney, Angus and Robertson, 1971; London, Angus and Robertson, 1973.
The Missing Heir (autobiography). Melbourne, Macmillan, 1986.

Editor, *Great Stories of Australia 1–7*. London, Macmillan, and New York, St. Martin's Press, 1963–66.
Editor, *Summer's Tales 1–2*. Melbourne and London, Macmillan, and New York, St. Martin's Press, 1964–65.

*

Manuscript Collection: Australian National Library, Canberra.

Critical Studies: *An Introduction to Australian Fiction* by Colin Roderick, Sydney, Angus and Robertson, 1950; "The Novels of Kylie Tennant" by Dorothy Auchterlonie, in *Meanjin 4* (Melbourne), 1953; "The Tragi-Comedies of Kylie Tennant," in *Southerly 1* (Sydney), 1957, and *Social Patterns in Australian Literature*, Sydney, Angus and Robertson, 1971, both by T. Inglis Moore; *The Novels of Kylie Tennant* by Margaret Dick, Adelaide, Rigby, 1966 (includes bibliography).

*   *   *

Kylie Tennant is an outstanding figure in the Australian literary scene. Versatile, original, with a strong creative flow, she has produced plays, history, biography, poetry, travel, and criticism, but primarily she is a novelist.

Her range is wide, her view of existence complex. High-spirited, humorous, with a pervading sense of the comic cross-purposes of the way life is lived, she combines a delighted appreciation of human idiosyncrasy with an open-eyed acceptance of man's innate destructiveness; affirms the value of life in the face of an ironic perception of the basic futility of the human predicament; uses the imagination of a poet to praise the prosaic and celebrate the commonplace.

When her first book, *Tiburon*, appeared she was hailed in some quarters as a social realist and it is true that there is an element of social challenge in all her work: politics, bureaucracy, education, law are derided with a good humour that did not in her early days as a writer save her from considerable backlash of indignation. Yet her sense of the intractability of human nature prevents her from supposing that a change in society would eradicate human perversity. Kylie Tennant, in fact, refuses to be pigeon-holed.

Certain themes recur—the instinctive against the civilised, the value of the outcast and the reject, the country against the city. The country has always been a refuge for her. Her spirits rise to the sights and sounds and smells of the bush, and her evocation of the Australian landscape in *The Battlers*, *Lost Haven*, and *The Honey Flow* are unsurpassed. Yet her feeling for the time she lives in insists that for good or ill our age is centred in cities. A line joining the one with the other is the axis on which her writing turns, preserving an almost perfect balance between the two.

Foveaux, *Ride on Stranger*, *Tell Morning This* together create a sense of Sydney that reflects the corruption of city life, the raffishness, crime, struggle, and despair that underlie the fine edifices of law and respectable custom. Only the gay comedy *Time Enough Later* adds a wholesome, softer note to the grim and grimy city symphony.

Each of Kylie Tennant's books is an exploration of an aspect of reality—a search for meaning and significance in life; yet her approach is pragmatic, her immediate attention directed outwards: her imagination needs firm roots in the actual. Before beginning a novel, she spends long periods immersed in the kind of life she means to represent—travelling for months with the unemployed along the long roads of Australia before writing *The Battlers*, living in a slum in Surry Hills before *Foveaux*, working on boat-building before *Lost Haven*, even contriving to be sent to gaol before *Tell Morning This*.

Her implication in many different ways of life gives her books a generously varied texture, but the effect is far from documentary. Each is a living world, seen in a tragi-comic perspective that is this writer's peculiar stamp: her mode is comedy, but her strength lies in the breadth of her vision and in her ability to handle a dynamic and complex system of relationships with vitality and freedom.

—Margaret Dick

THEROUX, Alexander (Louis). American. Born in Medford, Massachusetts, in 1939; brother of Paul Theroux, *q.v.* Educated at St. Francis College, Biddeford, Maine; University of Virginia, Charlottesville, Ph.D. Taught at Longwood College, Farmville, Virginia, Harvard University, Cambridge, Massachusetts, and Phillips Academy, Andover, Massachusetts, after 1978. Recipient: Fulbright fellowship; Guggenheim grant, 1974. Address: c/o Doubleday, 245 Park Avenue, New York, New York 10167, U.S.A.

PUBLICATIONS

Novel

Darconville's Cat.   New York, Doubleday, 1981; London, Hamish Hamilton, 1983.

Short Stories

Three Wogs.   Boston, Gambit, 1972; London, Chatto and Windus-Wildwood House, 1973.

Uncollected Short Stories

'Fark Pooks," in *Esquire* (New York), August 1973.
'Scugnizzo's Pasta Co.," in *Encounter* (London), September 1974.
'Lynda Van Cats," in *The Pushcart Prize 1*, edited by Bill Henderson.   Yonkers, New York, Pushcart Press, 1976.
'Finocchio; or, The Tale of a Man with a Long Nose," in *Massachusetts Review* (Amherst), Summer 1976.

Other

Theroux Metaphrastes: An Essay on Literature.   Boston, Godine, 1975.
The Great Wheadle Tragedy (for children).   Boston, Godine, 1975.
The Schinocephalic Waif (for children).   Boston, Godine, 1975.
Master Snickup's Cloak (for children).   New York, Harper, and Limpsfield, Surrey, Dragon's World, 1979.

*   *   *

Unlike his prolific brother Paul, whose travel books and novels supply readers the here and now with journalistic directness, Alexander Theroux is the soul of anachronism, a backwards literary history: unconcerned with modern markets, romantic in sensibility, neo-classical in aesthetic judgments, renaissance in learning and style, medieval in spirit. His line of descent recedes from game-playing Nabokov to the late-Victorian romance writer Baron Corvo, satirists Swift and Sterne, and encyclopedist Thomas Browne. For Alexander, observation of the present, whether the London of *Three Wogs* or the American eastern seaboard of *Darconville's Cat*, is the occasion for, not the purpose of, writing, an activity generated by a long memory of other writing. And yet, despite or, perhaps, because of his hyperliteracy—his esoteric allusions, archaic lexicon, elegant inversions, and orotund voice—the here and now are somehow defamiliarized, his artificial characters made curiously human, by his hermetic eccentricities.

Theroux's first book, *Three Wogs*, collects three long stories, each featuring an immigrant from the Empire clashing with a representative 1960's Londoner. In "Mrs. Proby Gets Hers" a widowed middle-class matron develops a paranoid and ultimately killing fear of an old shopkeeper from Hong Kong. "Childe Roland" exercises a stupid laborer's hatred for an educated Indian student. In "The Wife of God" an epicene Anglican priest selfishly attempts to stop his African choirmaster's marriage. The Britishers' pride and racism mask feelings of inferiority to and envy of the more energetic and even better-mannered "wogs." While Theroux has innocent fun with his foreigners' malapropisms and misinformation, the English are savaged by their own smugly expressed pretensions and by the ironic punishments Theroux gives them at stories' ends. Wholly appropriate for the dilettante Reverend Which Therefore (sic) of "The Wife of God," Theroux's stylistic contrivances sometimes overwhelm their satiric targets in the first two stories, manufacturing sentence to sentence wit but risking a reversal of sympathies for his characters from the present "Age of Shoddy."

Three Wogs was a startling debut, sufficiently noticed to be read by a character in *Darconville's Cat*; but it's this later book that earns Theroux prominent shelfspace in the Library of Literary Extravagance, the "A" range of alphabetical amusements, anomalies, anatomies, and artificial autobiographies. Theroux's predilections struggled within the constraints of the short story; here they are freed to create a 704-page, densely printed story of courtly love gone sour. A crazed character named Crucifer slightly scrambles the novel's strategy and achievement: "Nothing exceeds like excess."

According to an essay on the Theroux family by James Atlas (*New York Times Magazine*, 30 April 1978), Alexander was once engaged to and then jilted by one of his students at Longwood College. He vowed literary revenge, and she said "Do your worst." *Darconville's Cat* is his best and worst, a very funny send-up of young love and a compendium of misogyny in which, says Atlas, Theroux doesn't change the name of the girl who disappointed him. The novel's writer-protagonist, Alaric Darconville, was, like Theroux, in and out of monasteries as a youth and taught at Harvard and a Virginia college for women. But as the very simple plot inches from first meeting through courtship to betrayal and bitterness, the parallels between life and art increasingly feel like literary hoaxing, a way to draw life-minded readers into worlds made of words. Once again, Crucifer seems to speak for Theroux, "Love was the invention of the Provencal knight-poets to justify their verse."

What's best about *Darconville's Cat* is the advantage Theroux takes of the tradition of The Book, the large storehouse of knowledge such as The Bible, *Gargantua*, or *Moby-Dick*. Elaboration is all. The reader who doesn't care for a chapter on college girls' late-night rap sessions or the dialogue in verse between Alaric and his beloved Isabel or a classical oration by Crucifer can skip ahead or back without losing essential continuity. There are learned disquisitions on love, hate, and the human ear; wonderful odd-lot lists; Shandyian japes such as a one-word chapter and a page of asterisks; and Swiftian renderings of small-town southern life, ranting religionists, academic foolery, and much more. The parts are all related but don't disappear into a whole, into an illusion of reality.

Darconville's Cat is boring and brilliant, both puerile and profound, self-indulgent and often cruel. Theroux lacks Pynchon's interest in this century and the popular humor of Gilbert Sorrentino's *Mulligan Stew*, the recent novel Theroux's most closely resembles. "Madness," Darconville says of a book very like the one in which he is a character. But like that excessive anomaly of the 1950's, William Gaddis's *The Recognitions*, *Darconville's Cat* should find a dedicated following, readers with an appetite for ambition and literary aberration, for a prodigal art that, in Darconville's world, "declassifies."

—Thomas LeClair

THEROUX, Paul (Edward). American. Born in Medford, Massachusetts, 10 April 1941; brother of Alexander Theroux, *q.v.* Educated at Medford High School; University of Maine, Orono, 1959–60; University of Massachusetts, Amherst, B.A. in English 1963. Married Anne Castle in 1967; two sons. Lecturer, University of Urbino, 1963; Peace Corps lecturer, Soche Hill College, Limbe, Malawi, 1963–65; Lecturer, Makerere University, Kampala, Uganda, 1965–68, and University of Singapore, 1968–71; Writer-in-Residence, University of Virginia, Charlottesville, 1972. Recipient: *Playboy* award, 1971, 1977, 1979; American Academy award, 1977; Whitbread Award, 1978; *Yorkshire Post* award, 1982; James Tait Black Memorial Prize, 1982. D.Litt.: Tufts University, Medford, Massachusetts, 1980; Trinity College, Washington, D.C., 1980. Fellow, Royal Society of Literature, and Royal Geographical Society; Member, American Academy, 1984. Lives in London. Address: c/o Hamish Hamilton Ltd., 57–59 Long Acre, London WC2E 9JZ, England.

PUBLICATIONS

Novels

Waldo. Boston, Houghton Mifflin, 1967; London, Bodley Head, 1968.
Fong and the Indians. Boston, Houghton Mifflin, 1968; London, Hamish Hamilton, 1976.
Girls at Play. Boston, Houghton Mifflin, and London, Bodley Head, 1969.
Murder in Mount Holly. London, Ross, 1969.
Jungle Lovers. Boston, Houghton Mifflin, and London, Bodley Head, 1971.
Saint Jack. London, Bodley Head, and Boston, Houghton Mifflin, 1973.
The Black House. London, Hamish Hamilton, and Boston, Houghton Mifflin, 1974.
The Family Arsenal. London, Hamish Hamilton, and Boston, Houghton Mifflin, 1976.
Picture Place. London, Hamish Hamilton, and Boston, Houghton Mifflin, 1978.
The Mosquito Coast. London, Hamish Hamilton, 1981; Boston, Houghton Mifflin, 1982.
Doctor Slaughter. London, Hamish Hamilton, 1984.
Half Moon Street: Two Short Novels (includes *Doctor Slaughter* and *Doctor DeMarr*). Boston, Houghton Mifflin, 1984.

Short Stories

Sinning with Annie and Other Stories. Boston, Houghton Mifflin, 1972; London, Hamish Hamilton, 1975.

The Consul's File. London, Hamish Hamilton, and Boston, Houghton Mifflin, 1977.
World's End and Other Stories. London, Hamish Hamilton, and Boston, Houghton Mifflin, 1980.
The London Embassy. London, Hamish Hamilton, 1982; Boston, Houghton Mifflin, 1983.

Plays

The Autumn Dog (produced New York, 1981).

Screenplay: *Saint Jack*, with Peter Bogdanovich and Howard Sackler, 1979.

Other

V.S. Naipaul: An Introduction to His Work. London, Deutsch, and New York, Africana, 1972.
The Great Railway Bazaar: By Train Through Asia. London, Hamish Hamilton, and Boston, Houghton Mifflin, 1975.
A Christmas Card (for children). London, Hamish Hamilton, and Boston, Houghton Mifflin, 1978.
The Old Patagonian Express: By Train Through the Americas. London, Hamish Hamilton, and Boston, Houghton Mifflin, 1979.
London Snow (for children). Salisbury, Wiltshire, Russell, 1979; Boston, Houghton Mifflin, 1980.
Sailing Through China. Salisbury, Wiltshire, Russell, 1983; Boston, Houghton Mifflin, 1984.
The Kingdom by the Sea: A Journey Around the Coast of Great Britain. London, Hamish Hamilton, and Boston, Houghton Mifflin, 1983.
Sunrise with Seamonsters: Travels and Discoveries 1964–1984. London, Hamish Hamilton, and Boston, Houghton Mifflin, 1985.
The Imperial Way: Making Tracks from Peshawar to Chittagong, photographs by Steve McCurry. London, Hamish Hamilton, and Boston, Houghton Mifflin, 1985.
Patagonia Revisited, with Bruce Chatwin. Salisbury, Wiltshire, Russell, 1985; Boston, Houghton Mifflin, 1986.

*

Paul Theroux comments:
Both in my fiction and non-fiction I have tried to write about the times in which I have lived. Although I have been resident in various countries for the past 25 years, and these countries have been the settings for my books, I consider myself an American writer. I have a strong homing instinct.

*   *   *

Paul Theroux has emerged as a major writer of novels, short fiction, and travel reportage. His fiction ranges over England, America, and many foreign settings, and it focuses on complex relationships between people and places. His travel books (*The Great Railway Bazaar, The Old Patagonia Express*) are vivid, minutely detailed, and ironically elegant. Theroux's fiction reflects the same qualities.

Some of the novels echo Joseph Conrad and V.S. Naipaul, centering on Westerners caught in remote and alien settings— *Girls at Play*, *Jungle Lovers*, *Saint Jack*, and the short stories in *The Consul's File*. An important theme is the stranger who can discover himself only in the strangeness of alien society. This appears also in *Fong and the Indians* but is most elaborately developed in *Saint Jack*. It recurs in the macabre *The Black House*, in which an Englishman must come home to discover a ghostly "foreigner." It appears in transmuted form in *The Family Arsenal*, in which IRA terrorists (led by an American) are the strangers, and London is the "foreign land." If Jack in *Saint Jack* is a Dostoevskian hoodlum-saint, a pander peddling material salvation, the bombers of *The Family Arsenal* are a parody of close community, offering not love and comfort but violence and death to the unsaved world of London.

Theroux has mastered the art of exact observation and cultivated his memory for sights, voices, and sensations. As Maude Coffin Pratt, the central character in *Picture Palace*, says of her photography: "art should require no instrument but memory, the pleasurable fear of hunching in a dark room and feeling the day's hot beauty lingering in the house." The drama in Theroux's fiction often arises in the complexity of his characters' sensibilities and in the sexual and spiritual desires they are driven to express.

Theroux's novels often revolve around physical violence— revolutions or civil wars in Africa or Asia, terrorism, casual assault—but also involve the violence of suppressed, warped, or mistaken desires. Frustrated desires lead to sadism, which leads inexorably to masochism. The colonialist who beats his servant keeps a closetful of chains and whips to be used on himself. Theroux opens these closets in England and America as well as in Malaysia. Maude Coffin Pratt of *Picture Palace* prepares for a 50-year retrospective photography show and reveals the single image that has warped her life—her thwarted incestuous desire for her brother, who preferred their sister. Alfred Munday of *The Black House* returns from haunted Africa to find a succubus in an English country house.

The Mosquito Coast is a large and important novel on the theme of American ideals and energies, echoing Melville and Twain. It details the suicidal odyssey of a brilliant but crazed inventor, Allie Fox, and his family, who flee an imagined nuclear holocaust to set up an ideal community in the jungles of Honduras. It is a complex meditation on technology, belief, and the values of the 1980's and an arresting study of the basic American character.

In *Half Moon Street* Theroux combines two novellas on the theme of double identity, *Doctor Slaughter* (set in England) and *Doctor DeMarr* (set in the U.S.). The complementary tales recall Poe's "William Wilson" or Conrad's "The Secret Sharer" and other tales of the *doppelgänger* or magic double. Theroux develops the mystery of identity in contrasting ways but shows how self-deception and delusion erode character and lead to final dissolution of the true self.

The characters Theroux depicts most sharply are complexly folded. His fiction shows us the disguises and distractions which shield them from the world. Hood, the sharply observant, ironic American terrorist of *The Family Arsenal*, sees his world turn alien:

For every one who used the city as an occasion to perform, a thousand chose it as a place of concealment. In its depths bombs were stifled. His own was local, personal, a family matter; it had not been heard here. ... He had thought the world was his to move in, an extension of his own world. But he had seen it grow unfamiliar, and smaller, and he was not moving at will.

Theroux's novels are urbane, paradoxical, and often comic. They also probe tragic fractures in the modern world and sensibility, in brightly evocative snapshots of foreign places—at home and abroad.

—William J. Schafer

THOMAS, Audrey (Grace, née Callahan).   American; Canadian Landed Immigrant.   Born in Binghamton, New York, 17 November 1935. Educated at Smith College, Northampton, Massachusetts, B.A. 1957; University of British Columbia, Vancouver, M.A. in English 1963. Married Ian Thomas in 1958 (divorced); three daughters. Lived in Kumasi, Ghana, 1964–66. Scottish–Canadian Exchange Fellow, Edinburgh, 1985–86. Recipient: *Atlantic* "Firsts" Award, 1965; Canada Council grant, 1969, 1971, 1972, 1974, Senior Arts grant, 1974, 1977, 1979. Address: 3305 West 11th Avenue, Vancouver, British Columbia V6R 2J7, Canada.

PUBLICATIONS

Novels

Mrs. Blood.   Indianapolis, Bobbs Merrill, 1967.
Munchmeyer, and Prospero on the Island.   Indianapolis, Bobbs Merrill, 1972.
Songs My Mother Taught Me.   Indianapolis, Bobbs Merrill, 1973.
Blown Figures.   Vancouver, Talonbooks, 1974; New York, Knopf, 1975.
Latakia.   Vancouver, Talonbooks, 1979.
Intertidal Life.   Toronto, Stoddart, 1984; New York, Beaufort, 1985.

Short Stories

Ten Green Bottles.   Indianapolis, Bobbs Merrill, 1967.
Ladies and Escorts.   Ottawa, Oberon Press, 1977.
Personal Fictions, with others, edited by Michael Ondaatje. Toronto, Oxford University Press, 1977.
Real Mothers.   Vancouver, Talonbooks, 1981.
Two in the Bush and Other Stories.   Toronto, McClelland and Stewart, 1981.

Plays

Radio Plays: *Once Your Submarine Cable Is Gone* ..., 1973; *Mrs. Blood*, from her own novel, 1975.

*

Manuscript Collection: University of British Columbia Library, Vancouver.

Audrey Thomas comments:
I write primarily about women—modern women with their particular dreams, delights, despairs. Also how these women relate to men and the terrible things we do to one another in the name of love. I am also interested in what happens to a person set down in a strange city or country, without a familiar environment, friends, or job to define him, when

he must ask serious questions. Madness, too, interests me, and the delicate balance between sanity and madness.

I like to tell a good tale, and at the same time I like to make the reader work. I assume my readers will want to run a bit for their money.

*   *   *

Audrey Thomas has demonstrated in her quasi-autobiographical fictions how small the territory of incident need be in order for the writer to create a continent of psychological complexity. Such categories as novel, novella, and short story are not easy to apply in Thomas's work, for continuities are always present, within and between works. The short stories in her first book, *Ten Green Bottles*, for example, are very closely inter-related, for all of them are told by an unhappy female who, whether as a girl or a woman, appears to be the same persona, so that in the end the book takes on in one's mind the character of a sequence of psychologically linked incidents. More loosely, the later collections appear as real organic unities in their representation respectively of the pain and sadness in sexual relations and the reality of generational links.

Similarly, the two novellas published in a single volume, *Munchmeyer* and *Prospero on the Island*, are not in reality separate works; they are linked by the fact that *Munchmeyer* (itself a kind of mirror work in which it is hard to tell what is meant as plot and what is the novelist-hero's fantasizing) is presented as the novel that had been written by Miranda, the narrator in *Prospero on the Island*, and is being discussed by her with "Prospero," an elderly painter friend who lives in retreat on the same British Columbian island. And the novels *Mrs. Blood*, *Songs My Mother Taught Me*, *Latakia*, and *Intertidal Life* are in turn constructed within loose frameworks, so that structurally there are considerable resemblances between the groups of inter-related stories and the highly episodic novels.

It soon becomes evident that the structural principle of Thomas's fictions is one in which the psychological patterns take precedence over the aesthetic or self-consciously formal. The experience in them is, in merely physical terms, limited and largely repetitious; it also runs fairly closely parallel to Thomas's own life. She was born and brought up in upper New York state, spent some time in England and in Ghana, travelled in the Levant and in recent years has been dividing her life between Vancouver and the nearby islands of the Gulf of Georgia, with their mixed population of frontier eccentrics, ageing English expatriates, writers, and artists.

In fictional terms it is equally interesting to observe the fact that the central persona of the books appears to be the same, yet treated unchronologically, since a middle period book, *Songs My Mother Taught Me*, deals in a rather shapelessly flowing narrative with the childhood memories that already occur as memories in earlier stories. *Mrs. Blood*, which harrowingly evokes a somewhat perilous pregnancy in West Africa, also incorporates the persona's sentimental journeys in England, while in the novella *Prospero on the Island* creation and memory meld together with the persona-now-turned-novelist reflecting on the creative present to which all these pasts contribute. As in the case of the novella *Munchmeyer* (the one item presented as totally fictional), it is hard to tell when the actuality of the author's life merges into the invented narration.

An added complication arises from Thomas's acute sense of place, whose expression she has developed from book to book so that in her most recent novels, *Latakia* and *Intertidal Life*, the evocations of the Levantine background and of the Pacific coast, respectively, become almost as important as the

always frustrated and pathetic relationships between human beings.

Constant throughout Thomas's fictions is the fact of suffering, and an acute awareness of suffering's psychological results —its power to distort our perceptions and our memories. A recurrent situation takes us to the appalling borderland between sanity and madness; on that knife edge of mental anguish appears the terror that haunts all Thomas's fiction. Yet the essential quality of her work does not lie in the nightmare that shadows her psychologically complex characters and loosens their grasp of experience, but rather in the precarious equilibrium between the fear and the joy of existence which so intermittently they achieve.

—George Woodcock

THOMAS, D(onald) M(ichael). British. Born in Redruth, Cornwall, 27 January 1935. Educated at Redruth Grammar School; University High School, Melbourne; New College, Oxford, B.A. (honours) in English 1958, M.A. Served in the British Army (national service), 1953–54. Has two sons and one daughter. Teacher, Teignmouth Grammar School, Devon, 1959–63; Senior Lecturer in English, Hereford College of Education, 1964–78. Visiting Lecturer in English, Hamline University, St. Paul, Minnesota, 1967; Lecturer in Creative Writing, American University, Washington, D.C., 1982. Recipient: Richard Hillary Memorial Prize, 1960; Cholmondeley award, for poetry, 1978; *Guardian*—Gollancz Fantasy Novel prize, 1979; *Los Angeles Times* prize, 1981; Silver Pen Award, 1982. Address: 10 Greyfriars Avenue, Hereford HR4 0BE, England.

PUBLICATIONS

Novels

The Flute-Player.   London, Gollancz, and New York, Dutton, 1979.
Birthstone.   London, Gollancz, 1980.
The White Hotel.   London, Gollancz, and New York, Viking Press, 1981.
Ararat.   London, Gollancz, and New York, Viking Press, 1983.
Swallow.   London, Gollancz, and New York, Viking, 1984.

Uncollected Short Stories

"Seeking a Suitable Donor," in *The New SF*, edited by Langdon Jones.   London, Hutchinson, 1969.
"Labyrinth," in *New Worlds* (London), April 1969.

Plays

The White Hotel, adaptation of his own novel (produced Edinburgh, 1984).

Radio Plays: *You Will Hear Thunder*, 1981; *Boris Godunov*, from play by Pushkin, 1984.

Verse

Personal and Possessive.   London, Outposts, 1964.

Penguin Modern Poets 11, with D.M. Black and Peter Redgrove.   London, Penguin, 1968.

Two Voices.   London, Cape Goliard Press, and New York, Grossman, 1968.

The Lover's Horoscope: Kinetic Poem.   Laramie, Wyoming, Purple Sage, 1970.

Logan Stone.   London, Cape Goliard Press, and New York, Grossman, 1971.

The Shaft.   Gillingham, Kent, Arc, 1973.

Lilith-Prints.   Cardiff, Second Aeon, 1974.

Symphony in Moscow.   Richmond, Surrey, Keepsake Press, 1974.

Love and Other Deaths.   London, Elek, 1975.

The Rock.   Knotting, Bedfordshire, Sceptre Press, 1975.

Orpheus in Hell.   Knotting, Bedfordshire, Sceptre Press 1977.

The Honeymoon Voyage.   London, Secker and Warburg, 1978.

Protest: A Poem after a Medieval Armenian Poem by Frik.   Privately printed, 1980.

Dreaming in Bronze.   London, Secker and Warburg, 1981.

Selected Poems.   London, Secker and Warburg, and New York, Viking Press, 1983.

News from the Front, with Sylvia Kantaris.   Todmorden, Lancashire, Arc, 1983.

Other

The Devil and the Floral Dance (for children).   London, Robson, 1978.

Editor, *The Granite Kingdom: Poems of Cornwall.*   Truro, Cornwall, Barton, 1970.

Editor, *Poetry in Crosslight.*   London, Longman, 1975.

Editor, *Songs from the Earth: Selected Poems of John Harris, Cornish Miner, 1820–84.*   Padstow, Cornwall, Lodenek Press, 1977.

Translator, *Requiem, and Poem Without a Hero*, by Anna Akhmatova.   London, Elek, and Athens, Ohio University Press, 1979.

Translator, *Way of All the Earth*, by Anna Akhmatova.   London, Secker and Warburg, and Athens, Ohio University Press, 1979.

Translator, *Invisible Threads*, by Evtushenko.   New York, Macmillan, 1981.

Translator, *The Bronze Horseman and Other Poems*, by Pushkin.   London, Secker and Warburg, and New York, Viking Press, 1982.

Translator, *A Dove in Santiago*, by Evtushenko.   London, Secker and Warburg, 1982; New York, Viking Press, 1983.

Translator, *You Will Hear Thunder: Poems*, by Anna Akhmatova.   London, Secker and Warburg, and Athens, Ohio University Press-Swallow Press, 1985.

*   *   *

D.M. Thomas began his writing career as a poet, and his early work in this medium was notable for the way it ranged across the heights of the fantasy worlds of science fiction and the stocking-topped suspender-belt of sensuality. Both of these clearly demonstrated Thomas's obvious narrative ability and his gifts for imaginative fantasy which have been developed and extended in his novels, and it is not surprising that eventually the poet and the novelist came together in his later writing.

Thomas's first novel, *The Flute-Player*, is set in an unnamed city of chaos. There are strong suggestions it is in Russia, and the dedication of the book to the Russian poets Mandlestam, Pasternak, Akhmatova, and Tsvetayeva tends to underline this, as do the glimpses of Leningrad which appear from time to time. But the city is deliberately undefined and left mysteriously so. Indeed, it would not be out of place in one of Thomas's science-fiction narratives. It is an amalgam of cities which Thomas populates with his own imagined phantasmagoria, the chief of which is Elena, the flute-player, who embodies the persecuted creative spirit which is endangered and threatened with destruction by the city's totalitarian regime. The purport of the dedication can now be seen. But in a sense Thomas is too successful in depicting the chaos of the city with its plethora of characters, fast-moving incidents, and changes of mood, in that the theme of the novel itself becomes obscured while Thomas's fecund imagination is always in danger of going over the top. It is as if the engine of Thomas's powerful imagination has not quite engaged with the vehicle it is to drive, as if it is running de-clutched and that all the time Thomas is searching for a theme with which his creative energies can mesh. He found this theme in *The White Hotel*.

The terrain of *The White Hotel* is that of hysteria. On the title page Thomas quotes from W.B. Yeats's "Meditations in Time of Civil War:" "We have fed the heart on fantasies," which could be a description of Thomas's earlier novels; now the fantasies were to be the theme of the novel itself. It was a daring enough enterprise to enter the world of hysteria; to begin the novel with an extended poem, "Don Giovanni," in which Lisa Erdman, an imagined patient of Sigmund Freud, expresses her hysterical sexual fantasies in all their exaggerated and crudely masochistic sensuality was daring indeed: "Am I too sexual? I sometimes think/I am obsessed by it,—". Had Thomas gone over the top this time in a self-indulgent orgy of sexual fantasy? It could well have daunted and proved an initial obstacle to anyone coming to Thomas's writing for the first time. But the poem is followed by Thomas at his narrative best, with brilliant displays of his remarkable skills in pastiche when he catches convincingly the tenor and style of Freud's case studies. For sheer skill in writing the book is remarkable in itself; but there are a human warmth and concern informing *The White Hotel* which distinguish it from the earlier novels. In those it was as if Thomas's penchant for fantasy had distanced him from his characters. In *The White Hotel*, because he is writing of the fantasies of others, he is able to empathize the better with his characters.

This is evident especially in the Babi Yar sequence towards the end of *The White Hotel*, which while relying heavily on Anatoli Kuznetsov's book of that name for the factual information, is informed by Thomas's own imaginative response: "The soul of man is a far country, which cannot be approached or explored. Most of the dead were poor and illiterate. But every single one of them had dreamed dreams, seen visions and had amazing experiences. —If a Sigmund Freud had been listening and taking notes from the time of Adam, he would still not fully have explored even a single group, even a single person." And it is to the horrors of Babi Yar to which the novel relentlessly progresses, and it is its theme. The hysteria of Lisa Erdman, with its perverted masochistic brutality, is paralleled by the perverted mass hysteria of a world in which a Babi Yar can take place. Thus *The White Hotel* moves from a particular to the general in a convincing, overwhelmingly forceful way.

Since *The White Hotel* Thomas has published two more novels, *Ararat* and *Swallow*, which are the first of a sequence of three novels in which he has returned to his imagined world of free-wheeling fantasy. In both novels published so far there are involved a number of "improvisatores." In *Swallow* there is an actual Olympiad of these extempore storytellers whose rhyming narratives take up a large proportion of the novel: so we see Thomas the poet and Thomas the novelist. All the improvisatores' stories in *Swallow* are paralleled in their own lives and those of the people they encounter. So the reader is never quite sure, nor is meant to be sure, where the frontiers of reality and fantasy lie, if indeed there are any frontiers. Which comes first, the fiction or the actuality? Or are they, in fact, both fictions where we cannot be sure if life is imitating art or vice versa. It is all brilliantly done and there are some fine narrative passages; but it tends towards an abstract juggling and juxtapositioning of ideas and themes which distances itself from the direct and telling humanity we encounter in *The White Hotel*. This is emphasised when in *Swallow* Thomas includes episodes from his own childhood; while they are ingeniously interlaced with adapted passages from *King Solomon's Mines*, the episodes themselves stand out from the rest of the novel because of their warmth and human feeling. It is as if Thomas's remarkable gifts are beginning to mesh again and that he could be working towards another novel as humanly relevant as *The White Hotel*. Let's hope so.

—John Cotton

TINDALL, Gillian (Elizabeth). British. Born in London, 4 May 1938. Educated at Lady Margaret Hall, Oxford, B.A. (honours) in English, M.A. Married Richard Lansdown in 1963; one son. Free-lance journalist since 1960. Recipient: Mary Elgin Prize, 1970; Maugham Award, 1972. Agent: Curtis Brown, 162–168 Regent Street, London W1R 5TA, England.

PUBLICATIONS

Novels

No Name in the Street. London, Cassell, 1959; as *When We Had Other Names*, New York, Morrow, 1960.
The Water and the Sound. London, Cassell, 1961; New York, Morrow, 1962.
The Edge of the Paper. London, Cassell, 1963.
The Youngest. London, Secker and Warburg, 1967; New York, Walker, 1968.
Someone Else. London, Hodder and Stoughton, and New York, Walker, 1969.
Fly Away Home. London, Hodder and Stoughton, and New York, Walker, 1971.
The Traveller and His Child. London, Hodder and Stoughton, 1975.
The Intruder. London, Hodder and Stoughton, 1979.
Looking Forward. London, Hodder and Stoughton, 1983; New York, Arbor House, 1985.

Short Stories

Dances of Death: Short Stories on a Theme. London, Hodder and Stoughton, and New York, Walker, 1973.
The China Egg and Other Stories. London, Hodder and Stoughton, 1981.

Play

Radio Play: *A Little Touch of Death*, 1985.

Other

The Israeli Twins (for children). London, Cape, 1963.
A Handbook on Witches. London, Barker, 1965; New York, Atheneum, 1966.
The Born Exile: George Gissing. London, Temple Smith, and New York, Harcourt Brace, 1974.
The Fields Beneath: The History of One London Village (on Kentish Town). London, Temple Smith, 1977; Chicago, Academy, 1982.
City of Gold: A Biography of Bombay. London, Temple Smith, 1982.
Rosamond Lehmann: An Appreciation. London, Chatto and Windus, 1985.

Translator, *Number One*, by René Masson. London, Hutchinson, 1964.

*   *   *

Gillian Tindall's first novel, *No Name in the Street*, was published soon after she graduated from Oxford, and its heroine, Jane, is 19 years old. However, it was not just another autobiographical first novel about teenagers, jazz, and ennui. Though concerned with bohemian life on the Left Bank in Paris, it is written in a lucid and formal prose, and the novel is straightforward, if unexpected in its movement and denouement.

Jane is a half-French visitor from England who falls in love with Vincent Lebert, a painter much older than herself. She lives happily with him till she discovers that Vincent is having a homosexual affair with an English boy, and finds herself pregnant. Up to this point, the novel is merely pleasant, chiefly because of its somewhat naive, but innocent and thorough, romanticism; from this point on, it develops a dramatic power which Tindall handles with striking maturity and dexterity. The contrast between the everyday materials she chooses to use, and the depth of the uses to which she puts them, marks all of Tindall's most successful work.

Her second novel, *The Water and the Sound*, was also about a young girl, Nadia, and about Bohemian life in Paris. Nadia hopes to find out the truth about her parents, both of whom died young. She has been told that her father was a poetic genius, wild in his private life; and that her mother had misguidedly attempted to save him from himself, having loved him so much that she had committed suicide the day after he died. Nadia interviews every person she can find who had known her parents: friends, enemies, literary critics, servants, doctors, gossips, all. Tindall's sketches of these people are memorable, and her allusive descriptions bring the atmosphere of Paris, with its night clubs and trendies, to vivid life. There is nothing notable about the story itself: it is interesting because of Tindall's delineation of her characters, her compassionate insight into their psychology. She masters her wealth of material by the sheer quality of her writing, welding together the similar but historically separate worlds of Nadia and her parents with unhurried aplomb.

The Youngest, too, is a kind of psychological detective story of the soul. Elizabeth, intelligent, sensitive, educated, articulate, gives birth to a deformed baby, whom she smothers. Tindall's novel explores the question of what sort of woman Elizabeth is. Increasingly disturbed, Elizabeth undergoes a hard journey of self-discovery, realizing that her response to her deformed baby has typified her response to life as a whole: she has consistently rejected her responsibility towards others in her absorption with herself and her towering effort to become "independent," and she has, without earlier realizing it or putting it in these terms, actually sacrificed her mother, sister, and husband to her own views and desires. Written in the mid-1960's, this implicit condemnation of the attitudes of the "me-generation" was highly unusual in the fiction of the time, and remains unusual in contemporary fiction. Possibly for this reason, the virtues of this novel were not as widely appreciated as they might have been. Tindall has always been keen to use symbolism, but it had not been wholly integrated into her earlier novels; here, however, the deformed baby provides a powerful symbol of Elizabeth herself, with her own character and actions triggering her self-discovery. The book was variously received; some people perceived it as a complex and insightful work, her best book so far; others thought of it as "intelligent but limited," as failing to subjugate a social problem to the art of fiction, and as a fictionalised documentary rather than a novel.

In *Fly Away Home* Antonia is a fairly sensitive, but not particularly intelligent woman nearing 30 and going through an emotional crisis. She is married to Marc, as well-to-do and thoroughly assimilated Parisian Jew; her two daughters are growing up and needing her less than they did. We share Antonia's journey of self-discovery through the diary she keeps from 1966 to 1968. This diary is one of Tindall's best achievements, revealing the pattern of Antonia's life with something of the surprising-but-inevitable quality of reality. Events that are outwardly dramatic (deaths, births, violent quarrels) rub shoulders with more internal, emotional dramas "which prepare themselves for years and then are abruptly revealed." Antonia is excited by the Israeli victories, and she cannot understand why Marc remains unelated, putting it down to his Jewish fear of involvement. However, when students take over the Sorbonne, Marc's youthful revolutionary romanticism is stirred and he does become enthusiastically involved; Antonia, on the other hand, finds herself unmoved by the excitement of the times, perceiving the events as obscure and senseless. Such moments come rarely in fiction, moments in which people who think they know each other discover, by their unexpected reactions to events, how little they know each other in reality. Such moments occur repeatedly in this novel—for example, in the different way that people regard Marc's brother Jean-Luc after his accidental death in Israel; or in Antonia's deepening understanding of her mother whom she had earlier regarded as a typical do-gooder, always rushing after the latest thing which might be considered progressive, without her activities actually making much positive impact; or in the change in Marc's attitude to his parents, from dutiful politeness to anger when they condemn the students as gangsters or, worse, as anarchists. Like all of Tindall's best novels, this is moving and tender in its portrayal of human relationships, exquisitely written, and packed with insights. These qualities are even more in evidence in the short stories in *Dances of Death* and *The China Egg and Other Stories*.

The Traveller and His Child concerns the unusual theme of the paternal instinct. Robert, divorced by his appalling American wife for his inability to adjust to her orgasmic sexuality, finds that he misses his son Robbie terribly; so much, in fact, that he decides to kidnap another boy, the 7-year-old son of old friends. This is apparently done on impulse, though Tindall shows how his character and situation have been leading up to this moment through the years of his miserable childhood and unfortunate marriage. Robert's longing for his own son, now in America, and the way in which that unexpressed love and longing are focused on the boy, Pip, are convincingly narrated. In showing us Robert's heart, Tindall is showing us too the heart of the woman who steals someone else's baby

from a pram. Robert is selfish as much as he is self-deceived but, on a desperate journey through France with the boy, he experiences fear and shame, and slowly gains insight. He realizes that he has caused overwhelming anguish, and that he has caused this anguish to people who have trusted him and for whom he cares. He sees that his action is unforgivable. Yet, miraculously, he is forgiven, by the child, by his friends, and—it is hinted—by himself.

In her most recent novel, *Looking Forward*, Tindall's protagonist is a childless gynaecologist concerned with finding ways of overcoming infertility; and the book typifies the qualities of Tindall's less successful novels. The infertility is emblematic of the book itself: good intentions struggle against creative deficiency. Earnest, professional, and well researched, it lacks the germ of imaginative vitality which might be warmed to life by Tindall's brooding. This is partly, perhaps, due to an over-concern with formal cleverness. The characters—families and friends whose careers are charted through the first seven decades of this century—are relatively inert, but arranged in tableaux characteristic of the various periods in which the narrative is set.

What really interests Tindall and brings her characters to life are the emotional cores of people. Where she is content to let her heart lead her, Tindall's work comes alive; where she allows her considerable intellectual gifts too much play, she has not yet shown that she can embody her strong and subtle moral sense to produce impressive fictional work. This is not to deride her intellectual gifts, which are best evidenced by her non-fictional books. In all her books she has a highly accomplished style, and her fictional examination of current shibboleths is cool and penetrating. Unpretentious and unusual, she has an impeccable sense of the nuances of life.

—Prabhu S. Guptara

TINNISWOOD, Peter. British. Born in Liverpool, Lancashire, 21 December 1936. Educated at Sale County Grammar School, 1947–54; University of Manchester, 1954–57, B.A. 1957. Married Patricia Mallen in 1966; three children. Insurance clerk, Vienna, 1957; journalist, Sheffield *Star*, 1958–63, Cardiff *Western Mail*, 1966–69, and Liverpool *Echo*, 1967. Recipient: Authors Club award, 1969; Winifred Holtby Prize, 1974; Welsh Arts Council bursary, 1974, and prize, 1975. Fellow, Royal Society of Literature, 1974. Agent: Anthony Sheil Associates Ltd., 43 Doughty Street, London WC1N 2LF, England.

PUBLICATIONS

Novels

A Touch of Daniel. London, Hodder and Stoughton, and New York, Doubleday, 1969.
Mog. London, Hodder and Stoughton, 1970.
I Didn't Know You Cared. London, Hodder and Stoughton, 1973.
Except You're a Bird. London, Hodder and Stoughton, 1974.
The Stirk of Stirk. London, Macmillan, 1974.
Shemerelda. London, Hodder and Stoughton, 1981.
The Home Front (novelization of TV series). London, Granada, 1982.

The Brigadier Down Under. London, Macmillan, 1983.
The Brigadier in Season. London, Macmillan, 1984.
Call It a Canary. London, Macmillan, 1985.

Short Stories

Collected Tales from a Long Room. London, Hutchinson, 1982.
Tales from a Long Room. London, Arrow, 1981.
More Tales from a Long Room. London, Arrow, 1982.

Uncollected Short Story

"Summer, New York, 1978—That's All," in *The After Midnight Ghost Book*, edited by James Hale. London, Hutchinson, 1980; New York, Watts, 1981.

Plays

The Investiture (produced Bristol, 1971).
Wilfred (produced London, 1979).
The Day the War Broke Out (produced London, 1981).
You Should See Us Now (produced Scarborough, Yorkshire, 1981; London, 1983). London, French, 1983.
Steafel Variations (songs and sketches), with Keith Waterhouse and Dick Vosburgh (produced London, 1982).

Radio Plays: *Hardluck Hall* series, with David Nobbs, 1964; *Sam's Wedding*, 1973; *The Bargeman's Comfort*, 1977; *A Touch of Daniel*, from his own novel, 1977; *The Umpire's Thoughts Regarding a Certain Murder*, 1979; *Jake and Myself*, 1979; *The Siege*, 1979; *A Gifted Child*, 1980; *Home Again* series, 1980; *An Occasional Day*, 1981; *Crossing the Frontier*, 1985.

Television Plays: scripts for *That Was the Week That Was* and *Not So Much a Programme* series, with David Nobbs; *Lance at Large* series, with David Nobbs, 1964; *The Signal Box of Grandpa Hudson*, with David Nobbs, 1966; *Never Say Die* series, 1970; *The Rule Book*, 1971; *The Diaries of Stoker Leishman*, 1972; *I Didn't Know You Cared*, 4 series, 1975–79; *Tales from a Long Room* series, 1980; *More Tales from a Long Room* series, 1982; *A Gifted Adult* and *At the Grammar* (*The Home Front* series), 1983; *South of the Border*, 1985.

Other

The Brigadier's Brief Lives. London, Pan, 1984.

*

Critical Study: in *The New Review* (London), November 1974.

Peter Tinniswood comments:

I write very short sentences.
And very short paragraphs.
I try to make people laugh. I am a very serious writer, who has a gloomily optimistic outlook on life.
My books about the Brandon family contain all the above qualities.

*   *   *

Peter Tinniswood's reputation as the funniest novelist of his generation is founded on *A Touch of Daniel, I Didn't Know You Cared*, and *Except You're a Bird*, three interlinked but self-contained novels about the Brandon Family. The Brandons live in the North of England.

The characters in these novels exist, according to their lights, in noisy or muted desperation. Some want to be left alone, some want to chivvy away to get affairs moving. Whether terse or garrulous, their words rise from various mutations of what passes for the working-class heart to register comment on, or frustration at, life's endless capacity for being ordinary. Of course, whether the Brandons, Uncle Mort, Mrs. Partington *et alia* are prepared to accept things as they relentlessly persist, or whether they want them changed, the results are identical. When personalities are stubbed against the protruding end of life's sharp bedstead, when situations get so stultifyingly bad that people cannot see through their own blind and laughable prejudices, they are sometimes driven to dark outposts of expression and go to the kitchen to splash heavily under the cold tap. Sometimes they are driven even further and, in ultimate siberias of being badgered or misunderstood, can only rattle the knife-drawer. It is a crucial part of Tinniswood's invention that his central character, the Brandons' son Carter, caught as he is between his lusty zest for life and his bafflement, between love and the eager pernicketiness of Pat the loved one, gives out as comment on most circumstances an almost invariable "Mm." Tinniswood is a Lancastrian.

His characters don't realise it but what they want (given a fair ration of, say, fried tripe in batter and potato scallops, their bridge rolls and a pickled beetroot or two to go with their black-and-tan beer) is to be spirit. Mr. Brandon once ran away, but came back having got as far as Kensal Green. Mrs. Brandon wants a second honeymoon:

"Do you fancy a second honeymoon, Les?"
"No thank you," said Mr. Brandon.
"Why not?" said Mrs. Brandon.
"Well, I didn't reckon on much on the first one," said Mr. Brandon. "The breakfasts were a bloody disgrace."
"There's no use skulking off, Les. I want a definite answer from you. Do you or do you not want a second honeymoon?"
"No," said Mr. Brandon.
"Don't prevaricate," said Mrs. Brandon.

Their daughter-in-law Pat gets badly injured in a car accident and Mr. Brandon assesses reality:

Reality? It's all a bloody cod is reality. If there were such a thing as reality, you wouldn't have that poor lass fighting for her life with tubes sticking out of her. . . . If there was such a thing as reality, she'd be sitting in a garden with flowering peaches in full bloom and a fountain tinkling into a pond full of lilies and there'd be the buzz of bees and the song of nightingales and beer would only cost fivepence a pint. . . . If there were such a thing as reality, we'd turn into birds when unpleasantness cropped up and fly off to the sun until it all blew over.

Daniel is the baby begat by Uncle Mort and Auntie Lil when all Uncle Mort was doing was trying to keep warm. The infant is doomed to die, but not before it turns out that to touch him is to have some part of lost life restored. It is here that Tinniswood reaches a controlled audacity of imagination. For Daniel's spirit, moving through all the marvellous laughter, is the spirit of life itself. If that sounds too earnest it is not so in the texts. Carter Brandon carries on conversations with the dead Daniel who becomes his conscience and his goad:

"What the hell's she on about, Daniel? What's this union she's talking about?"

"The Amalgamated Society of Unborn Babies and Allied Trades. I'm the general secretary. . . . We held an emergency meeting in Pat's womb on account of a complaint received by one of our members—to wit, your baby. He said he had information to hand that led him to conclude that he was to be born with less than the agreed rate of grandfathers for the job—to wit, two."

Tinniswood has created for himself a form in which the precisely observed and fantastic can live side by side and feed off each other. Because of his humour some have failed to see his poetic meaning. His invention is combined with a capacity delicately to amplify the ridiculous in ordinary speech. He has a savouring and loving eye for people's foibles. His knowledge of nature, especially ornithology, permits him to set his action against a changing cyclorama of vividly seen and stated details. Working at language with a fine chisel, he believes in telling a story; and it is obvious that he does not go along with those who think the novel is in crisis. Reading his work, one is on his side.

—John Ormond

TRACY, Honor (Lilbush Wingfield).   British.   Born in Bury St. Edmunds, Suffolk, 19 October 1913. Educated at the Grove School, Highgate, London, 1925–29. General assistant, Simpkin Marshall, publishers, London, 1934–37. Served in the Women's Auxiliary Air Force, 1939–41: Sergeant; Ministry of Information Specialist, Political Warfare (Japan), London, 1942–45. Assistant editor, *The Bell*, Dublin, 1946; Paris, Eastern Europe and Japan correspondent, *The Observer*, London, 1947–48; Dublin correspondent, *Sunday Times*, London, 1950. Recipient: Writers Guild award, 1968. Address: 1 Mead House, Heathfield Lane, Chislehurst, Kent, England.

PUBLICATIONS

Novels

The Deserters.   London, Methuen, 1954.
The Straight and Narrow Path.   London, Methuen, and New York, Random House, 1956.
The Prospects Are Pleasing.   London, Methuen, and New York, Random House, 1958.
A Number of Things.   London, Methuen, and New York, Random House, 1960.
A Season of Mists.   London, Methuen, and New York, Random House, 1961.
The First Day of Friday.   London, Methuen, and New York, Random House, 1963.
Men at Work.   London, Methuen, 1966; New York, Random House, 1967.
The Beauty of the World.   London, Methuen, 1967; as *Settled in Chambers*, New York, Random House, 1968.
The Butterflies of the Province.   London, Methuen, and New York, Random House, 1970.
The Quiet End of Evening.   London, Eyre Methuen, and New York, Random House, 1972.
In a Year of Grace.   London, Eyre Methuen, and New York, Random House, 1975.

The Man from Next Door.   London, Hamish Hamilton, and New York, Random House, 1977.
The Ballad of Castle Reef.   London, Hamish Hamilton, 1979; New York, Random House, 1980.

Uncollected Short Stories

"A Question of Minority," in *Horizon* (London), March 1944.
"Mr. Solomon Wastes a Rosebud," "Papa Is Dying," "The Ever Rolling Stream," "My Aunt and Ernest Hemingway," "I Am Peter," "A Strange Encounter," "The Connoisseur," in *Lilliput, Queen*, and *Punch* (all in London), and *Harper's Bazaar* (New York), 1944–56.
"The Behavior of Mr. Frumkin," in *Atlantic* (Boston), March 1953.
"Please Respect Our Grief," in *Mademoiselle* (New York), June 1961.
"Via Dolorosa," in *Winter's Tales 22*, edited by James Wright. London, Macmillan, 1976; New York, St. Martin's Press, 1977.

Plays

Radio Plays: *De l'Angleterre; or, Miss Austen Provides a Footnote; The Sorrows of Ireland*, 1967.

Other

Kakemono: A Sketch Book of Post-War Japan.   London, Methuen, 1950; New York, Coward McCann, 1951.
Mind You, I've Said Nothing: Forays in the Irish Republic.   London, Methuen, 1953; Boston, Little Brown, 1955.
Silk Hats and No Breakfast: Notes on a Spanish Journey.   London, Methuen, 1957; New York, Random House, 1958.
Spanish Leaves.   London, Methuen, and New York, Random House, 1964.
Winter in Castille.   London, Eyre Methuen, 1973; New York, Random House, 1974.
The Heart of England.   London, Hamish Hamilton, 1983.

Translator, *The Conquest of Violence: An Essay on War and Revolution*, by Barthélemy de Light.   London, Routledge, 1937; New York, Dutton, 1938.

*

Honor Tracy comments:
I haven't thought about my work in a general way. Roughly, if something interests, pleases, or amuses me I imagine it may do the same for other people and I try to pass it on. Also, I have an orderly mind, and writing is a sort of tidying up and clarifying of life.

*   *   *

Toward the end of *A Number of Things* appears a passage that casts light not only on this novel of Honor Tracy's. With necessary modifications it offers illumination that extends its light to most of the other novels of this writer—work intensely comic and, in its own way, intensely sensible. The hero of this novel, a young man named Henry Lamb, has had great success with his first novel; on the basis of this novel, he wins the appointment of roving correspondent for a new liberal publication entitled *Torch*. He is sent to a Caribbean island, to report on the flowering of new black political consciousness; his reports are expected to gratify the liberal prejudices of the magazine he serves. But Henry finds only nonsense rather than wisdom in the island he visits. After a series of farcical adventures, reports of which are deeply disturbing to his enlightened editor, he is deported under humiliating circumstances. He is finally allowed to pay a shore visit to the island of Madeira. He suddenly feels a sense of relief after the exotic nightmare of his Caribbean weeks. Henry's impression of deliverance takes this form: "I am in Europe! he thought. He had, suddenly, a quite vivid new sense of Europe, not as a place for holidays where the people behaved like foreigners, but of something wonderfully precious, that he had had to go all the way to the mindless tropics to discover, something as old as the hills and young as the flowers in the women's baskets." Something—Europe—that Henry had been too ready to discard is kindly restored to him, and Henry is beatifically grateful—grateful even for the prospect of once more having back a job for which he once had had contempt.

Henry Lamb's experience is one that is often retraced in the novels of Tracy. Her books are a celebration of the nonsense in which human beings allow themselves to be immersed and, by indirection at least, a celebration of the sense—dull, tedious, but as reliable as anything human can be—which exists as a criticism of nonsense. But if Tracy is a kind of moralist, she is one who tips her hand very delicately; the bulk of her fictional texture is indeed a reproduction of the follies that seduce persons from the relatively dull life of sense and rationality. Thus, the observer—if not the hero—of *The Straight and Narrow Path* is a dispassionate anthropologist who has come from labors in the Congo for a rest in an Irish village. To his English eyes—English rather than more generally "European" in this novel—the religious customs of the Irish village are no less strange than the primitivism he has been observing in Africa. The visitor observes and reports for the London press the behavior of nuns jumping over fires and assimilates the spectacle to ancient fertility rites practiced the world over. Unwittingly, he has affronted Catholic self-respect, becomes involved in a law-suit, and escapes the consequences of his imprudence only when a simple-minded Irish boy offers the distraction of an apparition of the Virgin. At the end of the novel, the visitor observes a pious procession that includes the only sensible Irishman he has met. Tracy's comment on her hero's discomfiture points up his confusion. "What he had just seen had bereft him of power to think. ... Now he saw that the joke was far more complex and ramified than he had supposed, and that it was on him." The hero has been, throughout the novel, an apostle of prudent common sense in a world that is determined to lose itself in the superstition, puritanism, and deference to authority that are—as Tracy usually sees it—the mark of Irishry.

The common note of all Tracy's work, it should be plain, is to shoot folly where it flies. She is the tart enemy of all simplifying 20th-century expectations, and her powers of invention, as she pursues this task, are considerable. In addition to the themes already inspected—which come to the glorification of the wisdom of simple folk, whether in Ireland or the Caribbean—other modern expectations receive lethal arrows from Tracy. The cult of self-realization receives its just due in *A Season of Mists* and *The Butterflies of the Province*; satirical plotting and the juxtaposition of a raree-show of odd persons demonstrate that there are limits to the pursuit of pleasure and self-esteem. The delusions of the literary life receive their lashing in *Men at Work*; the book tells of the misfortunes of a successful novelist whose vanity and lack of personal scruple make him a sitting target for the sycophants that gather around him. *Settled in Chambers* brings to the English legal profession the same stringent regard that, in *Men at Work*, strips away

the pleasing outer integuments of the literary career. There is, in all the novels, a kind of center—a kind of "Europe"—which amounts to a pervasive and yet unobtrusive judgment on the fretful ignorance of human limits that is the self-indulgence of the characters who move through the fiction.

In all the novels there is an electric vitality; the novels never run down. As in following novels, the unending inter-play of Irish fecklessness and English propriety produces rich and charmingly unexpected contrasts. Thus, in *The Prospects Are Pleasing*, the central plot concerns the efforts of a light-headed Irish youth to steal from the English a painting that "morally" should hang in an Irish gallery. Irish madness and English self-righteousness compose a ballet of opposed ideas and manners. This ballet surfaces again in *The Man from Next Door*: a dull English woman allows herself a brief dalliance with an Irish scoundrel who, without any sense of guilt, sees to it that the English woman lands in jail for handling counterfeit money. And *The Ballad of Castle Reef* pits the fox-hunting British resident in Ireland against vacillating Irish constabulary and mindless Irish terrorists. In such novels sense is on the side of neither the Irish nor the staid, habit-encrusted British. Sense, as always, is the possession of a small and select group: Tracy and her understanding readers. One might say that the novels are designed to be read with a glass of sherry in the hand, preferably in the company of persons as basically sensible as Honor Tracy herself.

—Harold H. Watts

TREMAIN, Rose (née Thomson).   British.   Born in London, 2 August 1943. Educated at Frances Holland School, 1949–54; Crofton Grange School, 1954–60; the Sorbonne, Paris, 1960–61, diploma in literature 1962; University of East Anglia, Norwich, 1964–67, B.A. (honours) 1967. Married 1) Jon Tremain in 1971 (divorced, 1978), one daughter; 2) Jonathan Dudley in 1982. Teacher, Lynhurst House School, London, 1968–70; assistant editor, British Printing Corporation, London, 1970–72; part-time research jobs, 1972–79; Creative Writing Fellow, University of Essex, Wivenhoe, 1979–80. Since 1980, full-time writer and part-time lecturer in creative writing, University of East Anglia. Recipient: Dylan Thomas Prize, for short story, 1984; Giles Cooper Award, for radio play, 1985; Angel Literary Award, 1985. Fellow, Royal Society of Literature, 1983. Agent: Richard Scott Simon, 32 College Cross, London N1 1PR. Address: 23 Cambridge Street, Norwich, Norfolk NR2 2BA, England.

PUBLICATIONS

Novels

Sadler's Birthday.   London, Macdonald, 1976; New York, St. Martin's Press, 1977.
Letter to Sister Benedicta.   London, Macdonald, 1978; New York, St. Martin's Press, 1979.
The Cupboard.   London, Macdonald, 1981; New York, St. Martin's Press, 1982.
The Swimming Pool Season.   London, Hamish Hamilton, and New York, Summit, 1985.

Short Stories

The Colonel's Daughter and Other Stories.   London, Hamish
   Hamilton, and New York, Summit, 1984.

Uncollected Short Stories

"Will and Lou's Boy," in *Paris Review*, Summer 1985.
"Tropical Fish," in *Listener* (London), 25 July 1985.

Plays

Mother's Day (produced London, 1980).
Yoga Class (produced Liverpool, 1981).

Radio Plays: *The Wisest Fool*, 1976; *Dark Green*, 1977; *Blossom*, 1977; *Don't Be Cruel*, 1978; *Leavings*, 1978; *Down the Hill*, 1979; *Half Time*, 1980; *Hell and McLafferty*, 1982; *Temporary Shelter*, 1984; *The Birdcage*, 1984.

Television Plays: *Halleluiah, Mary Plum*, 1978; *Findings on a Late Afternoon*, 1980; *A Room for the Winter*, 1981; *Moving on the Edge*, 1983; *Daylight Robbery*, 1986.

Other

The Fight for Freedom for Women.   New York, Ballantine,
   1973.
Stalin: An Illustrated Biography.   New York, Ballantine,
   1975.
Journey to the Volcano (for children).   London, Hamish
   Hamilton, 1985.

                                *

Rose Tremain comments:
   Most interesting to me is my attempt to communicate ideas through many different forms of writing; this is allied to my belief that a writer who stays working in one form only risks becoming repetitive and stale. Hence, the large output of plays for radio and, lately, a first attempt to write for children.
   I have strenuously resisted categorisation as a "woman's writer" and the notion that women should address themselves only to women's problems, as this strikes me as limiting and inhibiting, a kind of literary sexism in itself.
   Themes that recur in my work are: dispossession, the effect of religious and exclusive "clubs" of all kinds on the individual's compassion, class antagonisms, solitariness, sexual bereavement, emotional bravery, and, above all, love.

                    *   *   *

   The writings of Rose Tremain reveal an author with a hard, unsentimental vision. Her novels probe the essence of the human tragedy in studies of loneliness, old age, and failure, an exploration of lives that touch but cannot fit together. Adroit, often poignantly sad, these works avoid mawkishness and self-pity, the author's skill enlivening the procession of tragic events with deft touches of humour, and memorable dialogue and characterisation.
   Sadler's Birthday, her first novel, is perhaps the most stark of her portrayals, depicting as it does the bleak desert of old age. Sadler, a former butler living in the stately home willed to him by the gentry he once served, moves alone and friendless

through the maze of empty rooms. A decrepit old man, betrayed by his body and its humiliations, he looks back over the existence that has shaped him for a life apart. In a carefully mustered sequence which mingles recollections with the routine visits of the day—the vicar, the cleaning lady, a prying estate agent—the reader is acquainted with the course of Sadler's past life. Parted from his mother as a boy, finding love only to have it taken from him, Sadler has spent the years imprisoned in the strait-jacket of domestic service, his feelings hidden behind a polite, dehumanising reserve. His unacknowledged emotions, the longings of a lonely man for love and friendship, move by their presentation, which is shorn of all sentiment. As a first novel, *Sadler's Birthday* is a remarkably accomplished work. Characters and conversations have the ring of authenticity, and the blend of incidents is capably achieved.
   Letter to Sister Benedicta centres on the struggle of the heroine, Ruby Constad, to survive the crises of those about her. Fat and unattractive, a middle-aged woman passed over by life, Ruby exists in the shadow of her successful lawyer husband and their beautiful children. When her husband succumbs to a stroke, and her son and daughter embark upon an incestuous relationship, Ruby's character is tested to the utmost. Her battle for self-preservation, written in the form of a letter to the nun who raised her at a convent school in India, reveals her personality gradually and subtly, showing not only her inner turmoil but her innate warmth, strength, and self-deprecating humour. Ruby's emergence from the family traumas to begin living her own life is ably portrayed, the interest sustained through a succession of quiet, perfectly constructed scenes.
   The Cupboard is more ambitious in scope, embodying as it does one woman's vision of the 20th century and its two world wars. At its core is the life of Erica March, a major but neglected novelist, now old and nearing death. The work is balanced between the polar characters of Erica herself and Ralph, the failed hack journalist who is sent to interview her. Erica's past and her innermost feelings unfold slowly in a series of conversations, interspersed with quotations from her books. A forerunner of the modern radical feminists, she has managed with difficulty to shape her existence to her own desires. Her ability to act for herself is contrasted with the impotence of Ralph, who mirrors the modern age in his willingness to conform to the rules imposed upon him. Tired of being the faceless member of a team, Ralph seizes on the interview as an act of rebellion, hoping to draw from Erica's life some meaning that will infuse his own. Erica, meanwhile, knows her time is running out and prepares for death. A powerful, complex, and intriguing novel, *The Cupboard* is perhaps the least accessible of Tremain's books, but the richness of its content rewards a careful reading.
   With the stories of *The Colonel's Daughter* and the novel *The Swimming Pool Season* Tremain broadens her vision still further, moving beyond single central characters to encompass a network of lives. The title story and her most ambitious novel to date share strong similarities. Written in a strong, direct present tense, they build to climax through a series of brief, sharply visualized incidents, showing the differing perceptions, the unforeseen ways in which lives touch and affect one another. Whether the criminal act of "The Colonel's Daughter," or the ill-fated venture to build a swimming pool in a remote French village, each plot serves as a focus around which the author connects the interwoven lives of her characters, the events unfolding almost imperceptibly and with deceptive stillness as crisis and tragedy reveal themselves. Dialogue, as ever, is strong and assured, the characters gradually and meticulously developed. Here as nowhere else, Tremain

captures the multi-faceted nature of her men and women, presenting them by turns as comic, tragic, and profound.

—Geoff Sadler

TREVOR, William. Pseudonym for William Trevor Cox. Irish. Born in Mitchelstown, County Cork, 24 May 1928. Educated at St. Columba's College, Dublin, 1942–46; Trinity College, Dublin, B.A. 1950. Married Jane Ryan in 1952; two sons. History teacher, Armagh, Northern Ireland, 1951–53; art teacher, Rugby, England, 1953–55; sculptor, in Somerset, 1955–60; advertising copywriter, London, 1960–64. Recipient: *Transatlantic Review* prize, 1964; Hawthornden Prize, 1965; Society of Authors travelling fellowship, 1972; Allied Irish Banks prize, 1976; Heinemann Award, 1976; Whitbread Award, 1976, 1983; Irish Community Prize, 1979; Giles Cooper Award, for radio play, 1981, 1983; British Academy award, for television play, 1983. D.Litt.: University of Exeter, 1984; Trinity College, Dublin, 1986. Member, Irish Academy of Letters. C.B.E. (Commander, Order of the British Empire), 1977. Lives in Devon, England. Agent: A.D. Peters, 10 Buckingham Street, London WC2N 6BU; or, Literistic Ltd., 264 Fifth Avenue, New York, New York 10001, U.S.A. Address: c/o Bodley Head Ltd., 30 Bedford Square, London WC1B 3RP, England.

PUBLICATIONS

Novels

A Standard of Behaviour. London, Hutchinson, 1958.
The Old Boys. London, Bodley Head, and New York, Viking Press, 1964.
The Boarding-House. London, Bodley Head, and New York, Viking Press, 1965.
The Love Department. London, Bodley Head, 1966; New York, Viking Press, 1967.
Mrs. Eckdorf in O'Neill's Hotel. London, Bodley Head, 1969; New York, Viking Press, 1970.
Miss Gomez and the Brethren. London, Bodley Head, 1971.
Elizabeth Alone. London, Bodley Head, 1973; New York, Viking Press, 1974.
The Children of Dynmouth. London, Bodley Head, 1976; New York, Viking Press, 1977.
Other People's Worlds. London, Bodley Head, 1980; New York, Viking Press, 1981.
Fools of Fortune. London, Bodley Head, and New York, Viking Press, 1983.

Short Stories

The Day We Got Drunk on Cake and Other Stories. London, Bodley Head, 1967; New York, Viking Press, 1968.
Penguin Modern Stories 8, with others. London, Penguin, 1971.
The Ballroom of Romance and Other Stories. London, Bodley Head, and New York, Viking Press, 1972.
The Last Lunch of the Season. London, Covent Garden Press, 1973.
Angels at the Ritz and Other Stories. London, Bodley Head, 1975; New York, Viking Press, 1976.
Lovers of Their Time and Other Stories. London, Bodley Head, 1978; New York, Viking Press, 1979.
The Distant Past. Dublin, Poolbeg Press, 1979.

Beyond the Pale and Other Stories. London, Bodley Head, 1981; New York, Viking Press, 1982.
The Stories of William Trevor. London and New York, Penguin, 1983.
The News from Ireland and Other Stories. London, Bodley Head, 1986.

Uncollected Short Stories

"The Nicest Man in the World," in *Transatlantic Review* (London), Winter 1962.
"Memories of Youghal," in *Transatlantic Review* (London), Summer 1969.
"On Christmas Day," in *The Times* (London), 25 December 1969.
"The Only Story," "The Love of a Good Woman," and "Alice and George and Isabel," in *The Seventh, Eighth*, and *Ninth Ghost Book*, edited by Rosemary Timperley. London, Barrie and Jenkins, 1971–73.
"Poppy and Alice," in *Encounter* (London), April 1974.
"Autumn Sunshine," in *Winter's Tales 26*, edited by A.D. Maclean. London, Macmillan, 1980; New York, St. Martin's Press, 1981.
"Saints," in *Atlantic* (Boston), January 1981.
"Sinned Against and Sinning," in *Firebird 1*, edited by T.J. Binding. London, Penguin, 1982.

Plays

The Elephant's Foot (produced Nottingham, 1965).
The Girl (televised, 1967; produced London, 1968). London, French, 1968.
A Night with Mrs. da Tanka (televised, 1968; produced London, 1972). London, French, 1972.
Going Home (broadcast, 1970; produced London, 1972). London, French, 1972.
The Old Boys, adaptation of his own novel (produced London, 1971). London, Davis Poynter, 1971.
A Perfect Relationship (broadcast, 1973; produced London, 1973). London, Burnham House, 1976.
The 57th Saturday (produced London, 1973).
Marriages (produced London, 1973). London, French, 1973.
Scenes from an Album (broadcast, 1975; produced Dublin, 1981). Dublin, Co-op, 1981.
Beyond the Pale (broadcast, 1980). Published in *Best Radio Plays of 1980*, London, Eyre Methuen, 1981.

Radio Plays: *The Penthouse Apartment*, 1968; *Going Home*, 1970; *The Boarding House*, from his own novel, 1971; *A Perfect Relationship*, 1973; *Scenes from an Album*, 1975; *Attracta*, 1977; *Beyond the Pale*, 1980; *The Blue Dress*, 1981; *Travellers*, 1982.

Television Plays: *The Baby-Sitter*, 1965; *Walk's End*, 1966; *The Girl*, 1967; *A Night with Mrs. da Tanka*, 1968; *The Mark-2 Wife*, 1969; *The Italian Table*, 1970; *The Grass Widows*, 1971; *O Fat White Woman*, 1972; *The Schoolroom*, 1972; *Access to the Children*, 1973; *The General's Day*, 1973; *Miss Fanshawe's Story*, 1973; *An Imaginative Woman*, from story by Thomas Hardy, 1973; *Love Affair*, 1974; *Eleanor*, 1974; *Mrs. Acland's Ghosts*, 1975; *The Statue and the Rose*, 1975; *Two Gentle People*, from story by Graham Greene, 1975; *The Nicest Man in the World*, 1976; *Afternoon Dancing*, 1976; *Voices from the Past*, 1976; *Newcomers*, 1976; *The Love of a Good Woman*, from his own story, 1976; *The Girl Who Saw a Tiger*, 1976; *Last Wishes*, 1978; *Another Weekend*, 1978; *Memories*, 1978;

Matilda's England, 1979; *The Old Curiosity Shop*, from the novel by Dickens, 1979; *Secret Orchards*, from works by J.R. Ackerley and Diana Petre, 1980; *The Happy Autumn Fields*, from story by Elizabeth Bowen, 1980; *Elizabeth Alone*, from his own novel, 1981; *Autumn Sunshine*, from his own story, 1981; *The Ballroom of Romance*, from his own story, 1982; *Mrs. Silly* (*All for Love* series), 1983; *One of Ourselves*, 1983; *Aunt Suzanne*, 1984; *Broken Homes*, from his own story, 1985.

Other

Old School Ties (miscellany). London, Lemon Tree Press, 1976.
A Writer's Ireland: Landscape in Literature. London, Thames and Hudson, and New York, Viking, 1984.

*

Manuscript Collection: University of Tulsa, Oklahoma.

*   *   *

Readers of William Trevor's early novels, *The Old Boys* and *The Boarding-House*, will at once understand why some critics refer to his fiction as "Dickensian." Filled with colorful characters drawn from London life, they display not only a fascination with eccentricity but, more profoundly, the motives that set characters against one another in wicked and often comical fashion. The comedy, in fact, tends to overlay and thus disguise the kinds of evil that ultimately show through and that Trevor becomes more concerned with in his later fiction. Mr. Jaraby's ambition to become president of the Old Boys Association of his school is hardly diabolical, and the extent to which he is willing to go to insure his election is as funny as it is outlandish. But as we learn more and more about him and his ambition, aspects of his private life—particularly his attitude towards his wife and son—reveal a sinister side to his nature that even his worst enemy, Mr. Nox, does not suspect. At the end, defeated in ways he had not anticipated, Mr. Jaraby is left alone with his wife who, though she counsels hope, rightly questions, "Has hell begun, is that it?" and urges, "Come now, how shall we prove we are not dead?"

William Wagner Bird's death at the beginning of *The Boarding-House* provides one answer to Mrs. Jaraby's question. He leaves a will that bequeaths his boarding-house, occupied by an odd assortment of individuals of both sexes, to two of its most vigorous enemies, Studdy and Nurse Clock, both of them senior residents. Studdy is a petty con artist whose success in stealing one of Nurse Clock's elderly patients away from her has heightened the rivalry and ugliness between the pair. The specific condition of the bequest—that they make no changes in the residents or staff—puts them in an awkward position, but not for long. Like many of Trevor's less reputable characters, they are extremely acquisitive and quickly see that they have more to gain by working together than by working against each other. Unholy alliance though it may be, it seems to be succeeding, as they systematically try to rid themselves of those strange and solitary inmates in whose hearts Mr. Bird believed he had kindled some comfort by bringing them together in his "great institution in the south-western suburbs of London." Studdy and Nurse Clock intend to convert the boarding-house into a home for old folks, easy targets for their different skills. But they have not reckoned sufficiently with the nature of those already within the premises, about whom Mr. Bird had much greater understanding, as his "Notes on Residents" show. By attempting to disrupt the careful arrangement Bird had created and cultivated, they finally destroy

everything else, as from his grave Mr. Bird takes his revenge—in the person of a deranged and dispossessed resident who believes he is taking revenge on *him*.

Timothy Gedge in *The Children of Dynmouth* is a younger version of Mr. Studdy, and, being younger, displays the causes of his behavior more clearly. An unwanted child, neglected at home by his working mother and sister and abandoned by his father, Gedge finds in others' lives not so much vicarious pleasures as sources of information and feelings that feed his diseased imagination. These help him to blackmail various townspeople, even those once kindly disposed towards him. While his demands are seemingly innocuous—a wedding dress, a dog's-tooth suit, a discarded tin bath—his means to secure those ends are entirely vicious, masked by a false heartiness and cheer that belie his true feelings. Ironically—and Trevor is a master of irony—what he invents to piece out his knowledge often comes close to the truth, close enough in any case to cause considerable anguish and hurt, for example, to Commander and Mrs. Abigail, who for years—ever since they first got married—have been living a lie; or to Stephen and Kate, whose parents—Stephen's father and Kate's mother—have just been married and are off on a honeymoon, leaving their children to begin a difficult adjustment to a new family life. In these and other relationships, Gedge pretends to a friendship that none of the others feels, and that tends to drive him into greater fantasies—and greater invasions of their privacy. His worse invasions, however, are those of the human heart—until he is stopped by someone who recognizes what he is doing and whose wife, through understanding Gedge's plight, puts away her own discontents and concerns herself more fully with her family's future—and his, too.

This somewhat upbeat ending should not be overemphasized, for though subsequent novels also show an effort to overcome despair and pathos, optimism is always very qualified in Trevor's fiction and very hard-won, as his many short stories also reveal. His most recent novels, *Other People's Worlds* and *Fools of Fortune*, give a good idea of just how high the costs can be. Francis Tyte, another descendant of Studdy in Trevor's own rogue's gallery, is a very attractive young man who works as an actor in bit parts and in making commercials. Even more than Timothy Gedge, he has been victimized in his youth by a male boarder in his parents' home, a debt-collector who draws Francis into what one of his later benefactors aptly describes as a "bitter world." Since that time, Francis has also turned into a debt-collector of sorts, like Studdy and Gedge reaping from others what he regards as his due. Already married to an elderly dressmaker in Folkstone who has thrown him out, he later meets Julia, 14 years his senior, who becomes infatuated with him and agrees to marry him and give him her jewelry. Their Italian honeymoon lasts a single day, during which Francis tells Julia everything, including the daughter he has fathered with Doris Smith, a poor shopgirl in Fulham, 12 years earlier. He absconds with the jewels and is not heard from again. But Julia is drawn into Dorrie Smith's world as well as Francis's other circles, including that of the aged parents he has long since abandoned in a retirement home. Despite the humiliation and despondency she naturally suffers because of her folly, Julia becomes more and more deeply involved in the shambles of others' lives Francis has left behind him. Once a devout Catholic, she nearly loses her faith altogether. But Francis's and Dorrie's Joy in more than one sense finally becomes her own, as Gedge becomes Lavinia Featherston's. Drawn into other people's worlds and the messes they contain, she learns to value more her own, but not with smugness. The pain she has experienced has made her invulnerable to that and more truly compassionate than she had ever been before.

Fools of Fortune deepens the focus and the tone displayed in all of these novels, as Trevor resorts to first-person narrative and tells a story of revenge and retribution from several points of view. His eccentrics are still present, but here subordinated to their proper functions in a novel that spans the present century and deals with the perennial conflict between the Irish and their erstwhile British masters. Actually, the narrative goes back to the 19th century, when Irish Protestant William Quinton married English Anna Woodcombe and brought her to live in Kilneagh, County Cork. Two generations later, when for the third time a Quinton had taken a Woodcombe for his bride, Kilneagh is burned down by Black and Tans under the leadership of a Liverpool sergeant named Rudnick. Young Willie and his widowed mother survive the ordeal, but when years afterward Eve Quinton commits suicide—an alcoholic, she has never recovered from the disaster—Willie decides to exact his revenge upon Rudnick. Just before he does so, he falls in love with yet another Woodcombe, Marianne, and fathers a child. But he is forced to spend most of the rest of his life in lonely exile, while Marianne and their daughter Imelda are taken in by Willie's aging aunts at what is left of Kilneagh.

Anglo-Irish himself, William Trevor has for many years lived in England and only occasionally attempted to treat the people and the landscapes of his native land in his fiction. In his short story "Attracta," about an elderly Protestant schoolteacher in a village near Cork, he sketched out some of the same themes he developed more fully in *Fools of Fortune*. But in "Matilda's England" he shows how the atrocities of the past and their impact upon the present are by no means limited to a single time or place or series of events. If *Fools of Fortune* is any indication, his growth and development as a novelist are stronger than ever, and he is an heir along with Iris Murdoch to the Anglo-Irish tradition in fiction that has given us the superb novelist and short-story writer Elizabeth Bowen.

—Jay L. Halio

TRICKETT, (Mabel) Rachel. British. Born in Lathom, Lancashire, 20 December 1923. Educated at the High School for Girls, Wigan, Lancashire; Lady Margaret Hall, Oxford, 1942–45, B.A. (honours) in English 1945, M.A. 1949. Assistant to the Curator, Manchester City Art Galleries, 1945–46; Assistant Lecturer, 1946–49, and Lecturer, 1950–54, University College of Hull, Yorkshire; Fellow and Tutor, 1954–73, and since 1973, Principal, St. Hugh's College, Oxford. Visiting Lecturer, 1962–63, and Drew Professor, 1971, Smith College, Northampton, Massachusetts; Lecturer, Bread Loaf School of English, Middlebury, Vermont, 1967, 1969. Recipient: Commonwealth Fund fellowship, 1949; Rhys Memorial Prize, 1953. Honorary Fellow, Lady Margaret Hall, 1978. Address: St. Hugh's College, Oxford OX1 3BD, England.

PUBLICATIONS

Novels

The Return Home.   London, Constable, 1952.
The Course of Love.   London, Constable, 1954.
Point of Honour.   London, Constable, 1958.
A Changing Place.   London, Constable, 1962.

The Elders.   London, Constable, 1966.
A Visit to Timon.   London, Constable, 1970.

Uncollected Short Story

"The Schoolmasters," in *Cornhill* (London), Summer 1965.

Plays

Antigone, music by John Joubert (broadcast, 1954).   London, Novello, 1954.
Silas Marner, music by John Joubert (produced Cape Town and London, 1960).   London, Novello, 1960.

Radio Play: *Antigone*, 1954.

Other

The Honest Muse: A Study in Augustan Verse.   Oxford, Clarendon Press, 1967.
Browning's Lyricism (lecture).   London, Oxford University Press, 1971.
Tennyson's Craft.   Lincoln, Tennyson Society, 1981.

*

Rachel Trickett comments:

I have always been particularly interested in my novels in the relationships between people, and between people and their environment. Place plays an important part in all my books. I have also grown increasingly interested in the essential solitude and uniqueness of my characters. This is not the same as the popular idea of alienation or isolation; it is rather the individual differentiating principle which identifies character and is most obviously exhibited in love where so often those who love each other are, consciously or not, learning to recognise their differences, their separateness. The passing of time has become an important element in my novels from *A Changing Place* to *A Visit to Timon*. My works are often retrospective in tone and mood as I am particularly interested in the way in which the imagination plays over the past and relates it to the present.

*   *   *

In one of Rachel Trickett's novels, *The Elders*, a character is asked, "And what is your contribution to the war effort?" to which she replies quite simply, "Literature." The ironic implications of this exchange are best understood in the context of the novel, but we see here one of the rare moments in this writer's work where the relation between the inner and outer worlds is given direct critical presentation. Her chosen territory appears to be the private world of personal relationships, often among highly cultivated people. Nevertheless her presentation of it is such that her work reflects very clearly the changing public world of her time. A tough searching out of the responses of individual sensibilities to private experience, given in language of unfailing clarity, inevitably leads to an accurate recording of how the inner world is affected by the outer. In *A Changing Place* a working-class hero's attachment to a girl from the upper middle class follows a course in which private emotions are seen as subtly bound up with the wider social circumstances of pre-war hardship, the war, and the disorientating effects of the war on people's private lives. A more recent novel, *A Visit to Timon*, shows a different reaction to experience on the part of a man whose retreat from public life is complicated by his relationship with a friend who works in television. Similarly, Trickett's ability to evoke a sense of place and of time passing is partly a matter of vividly realised landscape and a rare gift for the delineation of nostalgia, but also rests in a strong sense of the community, a recognition of the relations and tensions in a social structure. This may range in different novels from the non-conformist community of a small town in Yorkshire, to the life of industrial quarry workers in Lancashire, and again to the quite different structures of life in Oxford University.

A common theme is the confrontation between worlds, the invasion of one set of values by another. Often the clash is between spontaneity of feeling and the more sophisticated attitude to experience cultivated by certain artistic, literary, and academic circles. In *The Return Home* the simple and passionate young innocent, Christiana, becomes the victim of more sophisticated beings, but in *The Elders* there is a comic reversal of this theme when the return from abroad of a spontaneous, romantic poet disturbs the existing pattern of relationships in an academic community and causes a reassessment of values by both old and young alike. These confrontations, too, are subject to the processes of time, and one of Rachel Trickett's gifts as a moralist is the careful account she takes of change and the complexity of the moral life in relation to it. Do civilised rituals of friendship really preserve love, or do they cause it to become atrophied, or do they perhaps simply come to disguise a lack of true commitment? In her work, this is a question that becomes increasingly important. It would be difficult to show by quotation the way in which she uses small acts, remarks, and gestures to build gradually a strong sense of the distinctive atmosphere peculiar to a relationship; but this extract from *A Changing Place*, in which she describes the refusal to envisage love, shows another important gift, the ability to describe emotional states with both elegance and accuracy:

> Love of the kind Sarah no longer envisaged is rare after all, because it is so seldom wanted. It seems dangerous in the dependence it creates, and some would rather have less than be threatened with the demand for this surrender. As they grow older the urge to protect themselves from it grows stronger and appears disguised as a sort of wisdom and settled maturity that can afford to smile at excesses of the heart and the imagination. But it is not emotion as such they fear; it is commitment, the loss of any part of themselves. The desire to conserve what remains of the self becomes so strong with age that it grows harder to believe that only he who loses his life shall save it. Superficially we become more generous with time and with new acquaintances and new responsibilities, all those things which have a touch of virtue in them and so often cover up for the lack of any real surrender of the self. It is like a religion that consists entirely of thinking and doing, of the theological arguments and pious duties and refuses to take into account feeling, because it is dangerous.

—Bridget O'Toole

TUCCI, Niccolò. American. Born in Lugano, Switzerland, 1 May 1908; emigrated to the United States in 1938; became citizen, 1953. Educated in Florence, Italy, Dr. in law and political sciences 1933. Married Laura Rusconi in 1936; two children.

Writes in Italian and English. Correspondent, *Politics Magazine*, New York, 1943–46; co-founder, 1954, and columnist ("The Press of Freedom"), *Village Voice*, New York; columnist ("Offhand"), *Saturday Review*, New York, 1961–62. Writer-in-Residence, Columbia University, New York, 1965–66. Co-founder, The Wide Embrace theatre company, New York, 1973. Recipient: Viareggio prize, 1956; Ford grant, 1959; Bagutta Prize, 1969. Address: 25 East 67th Street, New York, New York 10021, U.S.A.

PUBLICATIONS

Novels

Il Segreto. Milan, Garzanti, 1956.
Those of the Lost Continent (in Italian: *Gli Atlantici*):
    Before My Time. New York, Simon and Schuster, 1962; London, Cape, 1963.
    Unfinished Funeral. New York, Simon and Schuster, 1964; London, Cape, 1965.
    Gli Atlantici. Milan, Garzanti, 1968.
Confessioni involontarie. Milan, Mondadori, 1975.
The Sun and the Moon. New York, Knopf, 1977; London, Allen Lane, 1979.

Uncollected Short Stories

"Where Anarchy Begins," in *Partisan Review* (New Brunswick, New Jersey), Spring 1944.
"Hey!," in *Twice a Year* (New York), Fall-Winter 1946–47.
"Excellency," in *Partisan Review* (New Brunswick, New Jersey), Winter 1946.
"The Siege," in *The Best American Short Stories 1947*, edited by Martha Foley. Boston, Houghton Mifflin, 1947.
"The Truce," in *New Yorker*, 5 July 1947.
"The Assignment," in *New Yorker*, 10 April 1948.
"Military Intelligence," in *New Yorker*, 29 May 1948.
"The Prisoner," in *New Yorker*, 23 October 1948.
"The Evolution of Knowledge," in *55 Stories from the New Yorker*. New York, Simon and Schuster, 1949.
"Tronco," in *Harper's* (New York), November 1949.
"History Comes C.O.D.," in *New Yorker*, 14 January 1950.
"Brother Lenin," in *New Yorker*, 1 April 1950.
"The Lonely Song," in *New Directions 13*. New York, New Directions, 1951.
"The Long Shadows," in *Botteghe Oscure* (Rome), 1951.
"The Underground Settlers," in *New Yorker*, 4 August 1951.
"Stolen Dream," in *New Yorker*, 19 January 1952.
"The Queen and I," in *New Yorker*, 3 May 1952.
"The Death of the Maid," in *Harper's* (New York), October 1952.
"Last Stand," in *New Yorker*, 17 April 1954.
"Those Long Shadows," in *Mademoiselle* (New York), September 1955.
"Morte di Scarandogi," in *Botteghe Oscure* (Rome), 1956.
"Special Ambassador," in *Mademoiselle* (New York), April 1956.
"Dollmaker," in *Atlantic* (Boston), September 1956.
"The Beautiful Blue Horse," in *New Yorker*, 13 April 1957.
"This Particular Rich Lady," in *Botteghe Oscure* (Rome), 1959.
"Terror and Grief," in *Stories from the New Yorker 1950–1960*. New York, Simon and Schuster, 1960.
"Death of the Professor," in *New Yorker*, 27 February 1960.
"The Trigger," in *New Yorker*, 10 June 1961.
"Fragments," in *Encounter* (London), August 1961.

"Four Dialogues," in *New Yorker*, 18 August 1962.
"The Announcement," in *New Yorker*, 29 December 1962.
"The Desert in the Oasis," in *The Best American Short Stories 1963*, edited by Martha Foley and David Burnett.   Boston, Houghton Mifflin, 1963.
"The Worst," in *Esquire* (New York), August 1965.
"Strong Man," in *Insights*.   New York, Aronson, 1973.

Play

Posterity for Sale (produced New York, 1967).

*

Niccolò Tucci comments:

The reason I have never allowed anyone to translate me from one of my two present languages into the other is that I consider myself alive, and these two languages are the two parts of me into which my experiences are split, so that my daily effort is to weld them together again. Perhaps I am another Humpty-Dumpty who sees himself as a new Lazarus. I don't know but I see no great danger of self-delusion in this: Lazarus was not a great man and certainly not a writer, he was a poor guinea-pig, and we have never been told how he climbed back into life after his place was taken by his Absence. I only know that no one in the world is worth his absence, and *as a writer*, I feel this very intensely, for I associate with words more than with people. I still don't know how to write a good thank-you letter in English, French, or German, even in my native Italian, but the *word-population* of all languages is still at my orders for nonsense, fairy tales, plays, stories, polemical articles and even love letters, in spite of my venerable age. In fact I find it hard to limit myself to English and Italian, and none of the king's jet-planes and supermen, let alone his horses and men, could put me together again as well as I do every time I jump back into Italian or into English from that terrible wall. In the process of doing this almost daily repair-work I have learned a great deal about languages, and I know how to avoid the Temptations of the Writing Devil, namely hot-water and wind in the place of blood and soul to fill your characters with. It is an interesting life, but it dooms me to poverty as long as it lasts, because I can't let anyone bury me under *his* words while I am away from one of my two homes. But then this arrangement has its advantages too: the temptations of Success are far more sinister than those of habit, laziness or fatigue, in fact they are the *real* tools of the Devil.

*   *   *

The privileged deserve their literary investigators, as much as do the disadvantaged. Niccolò Tucci has devoted generous attention to an interesting minority group, the continental aristocracy and their heirs. Time and democracy have reduced their numbers and influence, but their fascination remains, less because of what they are than what they represent: the confluence of wealth, education, tradition, power, and social *élan* evidenced in a life style where eccentricity and self-will are not fatal flaws but the identifying stripes of their breed.

Like jet travel or new money, the clash of conflicting moral or social values is not Tucci's ostensible concern. Yet it is there, under the Tucci characters' public show of conservatism and propriety. A young Spanish woman in *Unfinished Funeral*, the author's second novel in English, is reminded that she is "a girl of 26" and that her honor may have to be avenged, not because she may or may not have been compromised by an elderly gentleman met on a train, but because all will assume she has been. "The defense of your honor is my business, not yours," her brother insists. To liberate woman is to deprive man of his protector image, and, always, appearances count. Yet paradoxically, the strongest characters in Tucci's English novels are women—not the equals of men, but their proven superiors in the art of tyranny.

Tucci's reputation as a short story writer was already established before his first English novel, *Before My Time*, appeared in 1962. The long novel, in part an autobiographical nod to the author's own Russian–Italian parentage, is not merely dominated, but overwhelmed, by the idiosyncratic widow, Mamachen. A rich Russian matriarch at the turn of the century, she plays czarina to the large, elegant, and slavish family entourage she pilots from Italy to Switzerland to France to Germany—and to despair at times. Yet there is no family revolution, least of all by the daughter, Mary, who verges on treason by falling in love with a humble Italian doctor, and then in turn makes him a family thrall. The possible rebels are really defectors, the daughter Ludmilla and the son Pierre, who find lives of their own elsewhere. Mamachen's eventual death, with tragi-comic dividing of the spoils by her heirs, changes nothing, but merely hands on the matriarchal torch to Mary. Aristocracy persists, Tucci suggests, because its leaders are equal to those they succeed. And why not? They have been handpicked and rigorously trained.

Unfinished Funeral is another investigation of tyranny, this time very compressed in length and told in symbols (largely Freudian) so obvious that they themselves invite questions. Ermelinda, the widowed Duchess of Combon de Triton, is "the acrobat of pain" who has survived 36 major operations and innumerable heart attacks, having found that physical crises are the handles by which she can grasp and hold power. Her funeral cortege is always on call, yet she nevers dies—and so her son, Bernandrasse, and daughter, Eloise, never really live. The book states and restates a proposition rather than treating a question; hence those who seek ready answers are doomed to disappointment.

In all of Tucci's work the style is witty, clever, polished—appropriate to the worldy figures he illuminates but never dissects.

—Marian Pehowski

TUOHY, Frank (John Francis Tuohy).   British.   Born in Uckfield, Sussex, 2 May 1925. Educated at Stowe School; King's College, Cambridge, 1943–46, B.A. (honours) 1946. Lecturer, Turku University, Finland, 1947–48; Professor of English Language and Literature, University of Sao Paulo, Brazil, 1950–56; Contract Professor, Jagiellonian University, Krakow, Poland, 1958–60; Visiting Professor, Waseda University, Tokyo, 1964–67; Visiting Professor and Writer-in-Residence, Purdue University, Lafayette, Indiana, 1970–71, 1976, 1980. Since 1983, Visiting Professor, Rikkyo University, Tokyo. Recipient: Katherine Mansfield-Menton Prize, 1959; Society of Authors Travelling Fellowship, 1963; James Tait Black Memorial Prize, 1965; Faber Memorial Prize, 1965; E.M. Forster Award (USA), 1972; Heinemann Award, 1979. Fellow, Royal Society of Literature, 1965. Agent: A.D. Peters Ltd., 10 Buckingham Street, London WC2N 6BU, England. Address: 5-15-21 Mejiro, Toshima-ku, Tokyo 171, Japan.

PUBLICATIONS

Novels

The Animal Game. London, Macmillan, and New York, Scribner, 1957.
The Warm Nights of January. London, Macmillan, 1960.
The Ice Saints. London, Macmillan, and New York, Scribner, 1964.

Short Stories

The Admiral and the Nuns with Other Stories. London, Macmillan, 1962; New York, Scribner, 1963.
Fingers in the Door. London, Macmillan, and New York, Scribner, 1970.
Live Bait and Other Stories. London, Macmillan, 1978; New York, Holt Rinehart, 1979.
The Collected Stories. London, Macmillan, and New York, Holt Rinehart, 1984.

Play

Television Play: *The Japanese Student*, 1973.

Other

Portugal. London, Thames and Hudson, and New York, Viking Press, 1970.
Yeats (biography). London, Macmillan, and New York, Macmillan, 1976.

*

Frank Tuohy comments:

Most of what I write seems to start off with the interaction between two cultures, modes of behaviour, ways of living, etc. Sometimes this confrontation is between a foreigner and an alien environment, sometimes between groups in that environment itself. For me, the sense of displacement, loss, anxiety which happens to people derives from the world outside them, in their relationships with that world. If I thought of it as starting inside, as being a part of the Self, I probably would not write at all.

*   *   *

The novels and short stories of Frank Tuohy are marked by a strong sense of social reality. They are set in various places —England, Brazil, Poland—and give one a vivid sense of the physical place: the climate, landscape, local customs. Against the backdrop of special place, the drama of the characters' lives unfolds. In the short stories interest focuses usually on intense personal encounters in which the protagonist is made to face some unpleasant decision or harsh truth about himself or people close to him. These stories, sharply etched and intensely though quietly dramatic, have no apparent underlying theme. It is the revelation itself, the exquisitely rendered but "painful bite down on the rotten tooth of fact," to borrow a phrase from Tuohy, that one is meant to savor.

In his novels and longer stories there are the same sharp awareness of external reality and savoring of unpleasant fact, but there is also clearly a discernible moral structure. The writer's sympathies are with those who suffer and respond, who are capable of loyalty and self-abnegation. His dislike is for characters who, protected by money, indulge their appetites at the expense of those socially or culturally inferior or morally more sensitive.

The protagonist of Tuohy's first novel, *The Animal Game*, is Robin Morris, a young Englishman working in Sao Paulo, who encounters the beautiful corrupt daughter of a Brazilian aristocrat. Morris is attracted to this woman but is saved at the end of the novel from a relationship which, one sees, would have been sterile, self-indulgent, and ultimately destructive. Tuohy's moral sense is even more fully involved in his second novel about Brazil, *The Warm Nights of January*, which also deals with self-indulgence and sexual corruption. *The Ice Saints* takes place in Poland, some time after the Stalinist "thaw." Here the protagonist, an attractive, pleasant, but inexperienced and pampered young English woman visits her married sister and Polish brother-in-law with the idea of rescuing their son from what she regards as a grim and depressing existence, and taking him back to England to live. Although we are at first allowed to identify with the young woman's point of view (the horrors of Polish life are vividly presented), we are made to see, finally, the moral superiority of the Polish brother-in-law whose human qualities outweigh his lack of polish and urbanity.

Tuohy's stories and novels are written in a style that is compressed and economical yet remarkably evocative. One has the immediate sense of a physical world vividly and objectively presented and yet one also feels, but unobtrusively, the authorial presence choosing and arranging for judgmental effect.

—W.J. Stuckey

TURNER, George (Reginald). Australian. Born in Melbourne, Victoria, 8 October 1916. Educated in Victoria state schools; at University High School, Melbourne. Served in the Australian Imperial Forces, 1939–45. Employment officer, Commonwealth Employment Service, Melbourne, 1945–49, and Wangaratta, Victoria, 1949–50; textile technician, Bruck Mills, Wangaratta, 1951–64; senior employment officer, Volkswagen Ltd., Melbourne, 1964–67; beer transferrer, Carlton and United Breweries, Melbourne, 1970–77. Since 1970, science fiction reviewer, Melbourne *Age*. Recipient: Miles Franklin Award, 1963; Commonwealth Literary Fund award, 1968; Ditmar award, 1984. Agent: Carl Routledge, 22 Knoll House, Carlton Hill, London N.W.8, England. Address: 87 Westbury Street, Balaclava, Victoria 3183, Australia.

PUBLICATIONS

Novels

Young Man of Talent. London, Cassell, 1959; as *Scobie*, New York, Simon and Schuster, 1959.
A Stranger and Afraid. London, Cassell, 1961.
The Cupboard under the Stairs. London, Cassell, 1962.
A Waste of Shame. Melbourne and London, Cassell, 1965.
The Lame Dog Man. Melbourne, Cassell, 1967; London, Cassell, 1968.
Beloved Son. London, Faber, 1978; New York, Pocket Books, 1979.
Transit of Cassidy. Melbourne, Nelson, 1978; London, Hamish Hamilton, 1979.
Vaneglory. London, Faber, 1981.
Yesterday's Men. London, Faber, 1983.

Uncollected Short Stories

"In a Petri Dish Upstairs," in *Rooms of Paradise*, edited by
Lee Harding. Melbourne, Quartet, 1978; New York, St.
Martin's Press, 1979.
"A Pursuit of Miracles," in *Universe 12*, edited by Terry Carr.
New York, Doubleday, 1982.
"Feedback," in *Dreamworks*, edited by David King. Mel-
bourne, Norstrilia Press, 1984.
"The Fittest," in *Urban Fantasies*, edited by David King and
Russell Blackford. Melbourne, Ebony Press, 1985.
"On the Nursery Floor," in *Strange Attractors*, edited by
Damien Broderick. Sydney, Hale and Iremonger, 1985.

Other

In the Heart or in the Head (autobiography). Melbourne,
Norstrilia Press, 1984.

Editor, *View from the Edge*. Melbourne, Norstrilia Press,
1977.

*

George Turner comments:

I make few specific statements in my novels, and don't consider it my business to do so since the themes are usually such
as bedevil the experts as much as they do the man in the street—
insanity, alcoholism, the urge to meddle, the habit of making
moral judgments and so on. I try to examine these themes
under reasonably familiar circumstances, with no more of the
exotic than is to be found in an average life, in the hope that
some useful insight or recognition will emerge. The intention
is that the reader will be able to identify with the problem
as well as the characters.

To eliminate personal point of view as much as possible,
I do not plan a novel in detail in advance of writing it. I select
my general theme on no better ground than that I find it interesting and challenging, conceive a few characters who could
reasonably become involved in such a matter, and set them
in motion. Since plot is very literally character in action, something useful usually emerges in 20 or 30 thousand words, and
I know in which direction I am going.

Only at this point do I begin to shape the work as a whole
(and it generally means scrapping everything so far written)
but rarely have more than a generalised idea of what the climax
and resolution will be. These must be decided by the interactions of the characters: authorial manipulation is restricted
to the minimum necessary to give shape and balance to the
work.

One personally useful by-product of this method is that I
find that such concentration on a problem for many months
often changes my original points of view about it, and the
outcome is commonly rather far from what I had in mind during
the shaping phase.

I am sufficiently old-fashioned to prefer a story with a beginning, a development, and a resolution (though not to the point
of tying up every loose end in sight) but sufficiently of my
time to avoid moral or ethical attitudes. Those of my characters
who display them are apt to come to grief as the theme tests
and retests them.

For this reason I have been termed "existentialist," which
is probably true, and have also been said to have no moral
or ethical views at all, which is not. I merely condemn rigidity
of attitude and I suppose that in the final summation that is
what my novels so far have been about.

*   *   *

George Turner has managed the remarkable feat of becoming a critical, if hardly commercial success in the two very
different genres of naturalism and science fiction. His first and
arguably best novel, *Young Man of Talent*, is set in New Guinea
in 1943, with the Japanese in retreat, although as both author
and publisher rushed to assure us, it is not a "war novel."
Then Turner wrote four novels all set in the fictitious Victorian
country town of Treelake, 120 miles north of Melbourne, followed by a straightforward novel about a teenage boy's search
for his ex-boxer father, *Transit of Cassidy*: this was actually
written before *Beloved Son* but published after it. That novel
was the first part of a trilogy dealing with the Earth in, respectively, AD 2032, 2037, and 2087. Only in retrospect does the
reader come to understand that Turner's concerns—
psychological, moral, often didactic—are the same in the SF
novels as they are in the Treelake ones and *Young Man of
Talent*, and that the two sequences of books are linked by
much more than their habit of employing the same characters,
locales, and situations, viewed from a multitude of different
perspectives.

Turner is concerned first of all with the outsider, the misfit,
a man like Payne in *Young Man of Talent*, or Ted Johnson
in *The Lame Dog Man* or the eponymous Cassidy. As the
Australian critic and novelist Frank Kellaway has perceptively
pointed out, his stance towards these figures is the opposite
of Patrick White's. Where White glories in the special insight
or wisdom of the reject of society Turner sees him as a man
usually driven by obsessions of a destructive and anti-social
kind; the misfit frequently suffers from some form of delusion.
Sometimes, the symbol of it is alcoholism, a phenomenon
which, his frank and fascinating autobiography makes clear,
is not unknown to Turner himself.

In *A Waste of Shame*, for instance, Joe Bryen's refusal to
acknowledge his own alcoholism, or the support of his loyal
but self-deluded wife, results eventually in his own destruction
and the suicide of the ex-alcoholic he oddly befriends and leads
back to drinking. Unfortunately, Turner insists on his point
with such heavy-handedness that the novel finally becomes
tedious.

There is a second side, however, to the notion of the misfit—
that of the person who takes it upon himself to assist him,
and the complexity of the "helper's" motives. This situation
is explored in *Young Man of Talent*. Andrew Payne (the novel
specifically disdains the possibility of symbolism in the name)
is a man manifestly unsuited to belonging in the army, or anywhere else for that matter. His commanding officer Peter Scobie is warned against him but in his boredom finds the challenge
irresistible and sets out to convert the man to a creature of
his own making. What seems on the face of it to be an altruistic
gesture is slowly shown to proceed out of corruption, out of
vanity and egotism in Scobie and his delight in the brilliance
of his exploitation of Payne. Something similar happens with
Jimmy Carlyon, "the lame dog man" and his protégé Ted Johnson. Although Turner remains more guarded or reticent in
his view of Carlyon, other characters constantly point to the
elements of vanity in the assistance he feels obliged to provide
to characters weaker than himself. Jimmy is forced finally to
reject Verna Craig, the woman he wants to marry, because
she makes a stand on the issue: "The vanity, she thought,
the gargantuan vanity masquerading as pity! He was lost, fated
to wander among the corridors of the ego, collecting human
beings and tailoring their destinies until each one could be
finally boxed and labelled 'Healed, possessed and absorbed,'
and placed in his showcase of success." The charge is not wholly

fair or justified but there is enough truth in it to make Jimmy feel uncomfortable. Even the unlikely relationship between Joe Bryen and Arthur Craig, the man he beats violently and then befriends, contains many of the same elements, although Bryen has not the manipulative intelligence of a Jimmy Carlyon or Peter Scobie. (Like many Australian novelists, Turner is in general stronger in depicting male relationships than female.)

In the later novels, which may be of more interest to SF fans than the general reader, the qualities of unruliness and disorderliness of personality have not merely personal but cosmic consequences. Turner sees man's impulse to order as inherently fragile and delicately preserved and maintained. Even the leaders in *Yesterday's Men*, for instance, are as driven by unsound personal motivations as the enemies they affect to despise. A firm although by no means rigid or uncharitable moralist, Turner believes that human beings must always seek to explore and examine the motives of their own behaviour as rigorously as they do that of others. Most of his work is marked by a tone of almost Conradian pessimism and scepticism.

—Laurie Clancy

TUTUOLA, Amos. Nigerian. Born in Abeokuta, Western Nigeria, in June 1920. Educated at the Salvation Army School and the Anglican Central School, Abeokuta. Served as a blacksmith in the Royal Air Force, Lagos, 1943–46. Married Victoria Alake in 1947; four sons and four daughters. From 1956, stores officer, Nigerian (later, Federal) Broadcasting Corporation, Ibadan; now retired. Visiting Research Fellow, University of Ife, 1979. Founder, Mbari Club of Nigerian Writers. Address: Box 2251, Ibadan, Nigeria.

d. 1997 (June)

PUBLICATIONS

Novels

The Palm-Wine Drinkard and His Dead Palm-Wine Tapster in the Deads' Town. London, Faber, 1952; New York, Grove Press, 1953.
My Life in the Bush of Ghosts. London, Faber, and New York, Grove Press, 1954.
Simbi and the Satyr of the Dark Jungle. London, Faber, 1955; New York, Grove Press, 1962.
The Brave African Huntress. London, Faber, and New York, Grove Press, 1958.
Feather Woman of the Jungle. London, Faber, 1962.
Ajaiyi and His Inherited Poverty. London, Faber, 1967.
The Witch-Herbalist of the Remote Town. London, Faber, 1981.
The Wild Hunter in the Bush of the Ghosts, edited by Bernth Lindfors. Washington, D.C., Three Continents, 1982.

Play

The Palm-Wine Drinkard, with Professor Collis, adaptation of the novel by Tutuola (produced Ibadan, 1962).

*

Critical Studies: *Amos Tutuola* by Harold R. Collins, New York, Twayne, 1969; *Critical Perspectives on Amos Tutuola* edited by Bernth Lindfors, Washington, D.C., Three Continents, 1975, London, Heinemann, 1980.

*   *   *

Amos Tutuola's eight books follow the same basic narrative pattern. A hero (or heroine) with supernatural powers or access to supernatural assistance sets out on a journey in quest of something important and suffers incredible hardships before successfully accomplishing his mission. He ventures into unearthly realms, performs arduous tasks, fights with fearsome monsters, endures cruel tortures, and narrowly escapes death. Sometimes he is accompanied by a relative or by loyal companions; sometimes he wanders alone. But he always survives his ordeals, attains his objective, and usually emerges from his nightmarish experiences a wiser, wealthier man. The cycle of his adventures—involving a Departure, Initiation, and Return—resembles that found in myths and folktales the world over.

Tutuola's first and most famous book, *The Palm-Wine Drinkard and His Dead Palm-Wine Tapster in the Deads' Town*, which describes a hero's descent into an African underworld in search of a dead companion, was greatly influenced by oral tradition. Tutuola made use of common Yoruba tales and motifs, stringing them together like a fireside reconteur. As a consequence, the book's neat cyclical narrative pattern rests on a very loosely coordinated inner structure. The hero is involved in one adventure after another but these adventures are not well integrated. Like boxcars on a freight train, they are independent units joined with a minimum of apparatus and set in a seemingly random and interchangeable order. There is no foreshadowing of events, no dramatic irony, no evidence of any kind that the sequence of events was carefully thought out. Tutuola appears to be improvising as he goes along and employing the techniques and materials of oral narrative art in his improvisations. This is true of his other writings too, especially *The Wild Hunter in the Bush of the Ghosts*, a recently discovered manuscript that antedates *The Palm-Wine Drinkard*. All these fantastic tales have been inspired and shaped by indigenous storytelling traditions.

However, research has shown that none of Tutuola's works is entirely innocent of literary influence either. He clearly owes his greatest debt to D.O. Fagunwa, who began to publish folkloric "novels" in Yoruba in 1938. In his earliest fiction Tutuola tried to imitate Fagunwa's method of weaving a number of old stories into an elastic narrative pattern that could be stretched into a book. Both Fagunwa and Tutuola appear to have been stimulated by John Bunyan's *The Pilgrim's Progress* and *The Arabian Nights*, which were widely used in Nigerian elementary schools. Later Tutuola turned to other foreign sources of inspiration; Edith Hamilton's *Mythology* may have been responsible for the nymphs, satyrs, myrmidons, and phoenixes which started to infiltrate his African jungles. Goblins, imps, and gnomes also turned up regularly. Tutuola, like a great syncretic sponge, easily absorbed these alien creatures into his exotic imaginative universe.

This is not to say, of course, that all his writings is derivative or that it lacks originality or accomplishment. In descriptive ability and sheer visionary power Tutuola far surpasses most of his contemporaries. His fertile imagination, never fettered by reason or common sense, constantly begets the surprising, the unorthodox, the incongruous, the bizarre. Events are recounted with a hallucinatory energy that swiftly transports the reader into realms of fantasy. Characters are painted in the most vivid and memorable colors. Whatever Tutuola borrows from oral or literary tradition he immediately makes his own, enlarging it with details of his own invention. He is a master storyteller.

Tutuola's most conspicuous idiosyncrasy as a writer, and perhaps his most controversial, is his style, which Dylan Thomas once termed "naive English." Because he grew up speaking Yoruba and had only six years of formal schooling, Tutuola tends to make spectacular grammatical and spelling blunders on every page he writes. Some critics hold that this fractured idiom is one of his greatest assets for it adds extra tang to the primitive flavor of his works; his language is just as weird and unpredictable as the adventures he describes. Others argue that it is an unfortunate liability for it quickly tires the average reader who is not conditioned to jumping unfamiliar linguistic hurdles. It is unlikely that this critical debate will have any appreciable effect on Tutuola's writing, for he is not a conscious stylist experimenting with language. He is simply trying to do the best he can in a foreign tongue he has not adequately mastered.

The initial reaction to Tutuola's first books was mixed. Readers in Europe and America were enthusiastic for they had never seen anything quite like them before, and they were convinced that Tutuola was a marvellous "original," a diamond in the rough with rich and dazzling creative powers. Reviewers hailed him as an uncouth genius unspoiled by civilization, a mute, inglorious Milton who had suddenly found his voice, albeit a curiously cracked one. Many educated Nigerians, however, were extremely angry that such an unschooled author should receive so much praise and publicity abroad, for they recognized his borrowings, disapproved of his bad grammar, and suspected he was being lionized by condescending racists who had a clear political motive for choosing to continue to regard Africans as backward and childlike primitives. Since Nigeria was struggling to free itself from colonial rule at the time, Tutuola was more than merely an embarrassment; he was a disgrace, a setback, a national calamity. Later, after Nigeria had achieved its independence, Tutuola was no longer an explosive literary or political issue, and his works began to receive more intelligent critical attention. Today his reputation is secure both at home and abroad, for he has come to be accepted as a unique phenomenon in world literature, a writer who bridges two narrative traditions and two cultures by translating oral art into literary art.

—Bernth Lindfors

TYLER, Anne. American. Born in Minneapolis, Minnesota, 25 October 1941. Educated at Duke University, Durham, North Carolina, 1958–61, B.A. 1961; Columbia University, New York, 1961–62. Married Taghi Modarressi in 1963; two daughters. Russian bibliographer, Duke University Library, 1962–63; assistant to the librarian, McGill University Law Library, Montreal, 1964–65. Recipient: American Academy award, 1977; Janet Kafka Prize, 1981; PEN Faulkner Award, 1983. Agent: Russell and Volkening Inc., 50 West 29th Street, New York, New York 10001. Address: 222 Tunbridge Road, Baltimore, Maryland 21212, U.S.A.

PUBLICATIONS

Novels

If Morning Ever Comes. New York, Knopf, 1964; London, Chatto and Windus, 1965.
The Tin Can Tree. New York, Knopf, 1965; London, Macmillan, 1966.
A Slipping-Down Life. New York, Knopf, 1970.
The Clock Winder. New York, Knopf, 1972; London, Chatto and Windus, 1973.
Celestial Navigation. New York, Knopf, 1974; London, Chatto and Windus, 1975.
Searching for Caleb. New York, Knopf, and London, Chatto and Windus, 1976.
Earthly Possessions. New York, Knopf, and London, Chatto and Windus, 1977.
Morgan's Passing. New York, Knopf, and London, Chatto and Windus, 1980.
Dinner at the Homesick Restaurant. New York, Knopf, and London, Chatto and Windus, 1982.
The Accidental Tourist. New York, Knopf, and London, Chatto and Windus, 1985.

Uncollected Short Stories

"I Play Kings," in *Seventeen* (New York), August 1963.
"Street of Bugles," in *Saturday Evening Post* (Philadelphia), 30 November 1963.
"Nobody Answers the Door," in *Antioch Review* (Yellow Springs, Ohio), Fall 1964.
"I'm Not Going to Ask You Again," in *Harper's* (New York), September 1965.
"Everything But Roses," in *Reporter* (New York), 23 September 1965.
"As the Earth Gets Old," in *New Yorker*, 29 October 1966.
"Feather Behind the Rock," in *New Yorker*, 12 August 1967.
"Flaw in the Crust of the Earth," in *Reporter* (New York), 2 November 1967.
"Common Courtesies," in *McCall's* (New York), June 1968.
"With All Flags Flying," in *Redbook* (New York), June 1971.
"Bride in the Boatyard," in *McCall's* (New York), June 1972.
"Respect," in *Mademoiselle* (New York), June 1972.
"Misstep of the Mind," in *Seventeen* (New York), October 1972.
"Knack for Languages," in *New Yorker*, 13 January 1975.
"Some Sign That I Ever Made You Happy," in *McCall's* (New York), October 1975.
"Your Place Is Empty," in *New Yorker*, 22 November 1976.
"Holding Things Together," in *New Yorker*, 24 January 1977.
"Average Waves in Unprotected Waters," in *New Yorker*, 28 February 1977.
"Foot-Footing On," in *Mademoiselle* (New York), November 1977.
"The Geologist's Maid," in *Stories of the Modern South*, edited by Ben Forkner and Patrick Samway. New York, Penguin, 1981.
"Laps," in *Parents' Magazine* (New York), August 1981.
"The Country Cook," in *Harper's* (New York), March 1982.
"Teenage Wasteland," in *Seventeen* (New York), November 1983.

Other

Editor, with Shannon Ravenel, *The Best American Short Stories 1983*. Boston, Houghton Mifflin, 1983; as *The Year's Best American Short Stories*, London, Severn House, 1984.

*   *   *

Anne Tyler writes principally of life in Baltimore or in Southern small towns and is basically concerned with the theme of loneliness and human isolation and the difficulties people have both in understanding and in communicating with one another. When Ben Joe Hawkes, the protagonist of *If Morning Ever Comes*, returns for a visit to his home town of Sandhill, North Carolina, he ponders the gap which separates him from his family, although they are as friendly and as affectionate to him as their natures will allow. There is family unity at the same moment that there is family disunity. Ben Joe can reach his mother and sisters only half-heartedly, for within them and within himself mysterious factors in the human heart lure and yet resist complete harmony and understanding. Ben Joe comes to realize that his condition is life itself; he will never fully understand his wife or even his own children when they are eventually born. Parts of every human being and of life itself are forever closed to understanding. Such parts are sadly "unreachable."

This melancholy presentation of existence is related with a painfully sensitive awareness of the tragedy of things as they are. In *The Tin Can Tree* the parents of a six year old girl become exceedingly distraught over the child's accidental death. The mother, in particular, attempts to shut out any further life and light. But her only son suffers so intensely from her neglect that she finally comprehends that life even with its heartbreak and lack of fulfillment is all one has; and, as a consequence, the best should be made of it. Half-fulfilled relationships are better than no relationships at all. The ideal or even the semi-ideal cannot be reached in this life, and no matter how unhappy or disappointing life may be, it is life and not death. People are exalted most of all in Tyler's philosophy when they love other mortals although they consciously know that death awaits both themselves and the ones they love. And a further burden is added because the tin can tree is always rattling, never allowing anyone to forget the dead.

Individuals must arrive at deliberate choices on the relative scales of possibility and degree of bittersweetness. For example, one has a choice of imperfect love or no love at all. Tyler's protagonists generally prefer the former, or at least settle for what their consciousness informs them will be the most appropriate degree for them—although outsiders and even close friends continually insist that their selection is both incomprehensible and foolish. A "belonging to" someone else becomes necessary while life starts slipping away from everyone. Only the artist can really bear almost total loneliness; and despite intense dedication to his calling, even he is drawn by the needs of human love.

The search for belonging is just as pronounced in *Earthly Possessions* and *Morgan's Passing*. The characters sadly come to realize that they cannot "step inside" another's life. Nevertheless, individual barriers and inadequate relationships are juxtaposed with wry touches of humor and Tyler's delight in the contradictions and whimsies which accompany existence.

Dinner at the Homesick Restaurant represents a new breakthrough for Tyler. She is now able to develop fully not just the central characters, but also the cameo-role figures come fully alive. A wider probing of the ambivalence of family relationships dominates, and now several generations are probed.

An even more vivid wryness underscores the tragic-comic varieties of existence. Thematic motifs are broadened, and her innate storytelling skills constantly mesmerize.

These aspects show no decline in *The Accidental Tourist*. Her ability to document her material down to the most convincing minute particulars grows with each novel. While ostensibly delineating a small geographical area of America, she has now extended her portraits and given them a universal recognition and scope.

—Paul A. Doyle

———

UPDIKE, John (Hoyer). American. Born in Shillington, Pennsylvania, 18 March 1932. Educated in Shillington public schools; Harvard University, Cambridge, Massachusetts, A.B. (summa cum laude) 1954; Ruskin School of Drawing and Fine Arts, Oxford, 1954–55. Married 1) Mary Pennington in 1953 (marriage dissolved), two daughters and two sons; 2) Martha Bernhard in 1977. Staff reporter, *New Yorker*, 1955–57. Recipient: Guggenheim fellowship, 1959; Rosenthal Award, 1960; National Book Award, 1964; O. Henry Award, 1966; Foreign Book Prize (France), 1966; New England Poetry Club Golden Rose, 1979; MacDowell Medal, 1981; Pulitzer Prize, 1982; American Book Award, 1982; National Book Critics Circle award, for fiction, 1982, for criticism, 1984; Union League Club Abraham Lincoln Award, 1982; National Arts Club Medal of Honor, 1984. Member, American Academy, 1976. Address: 675 Hale Street, Beverly Farms, Massachusetts 01915, U.S.A.

PUBLICATIONS

Novels

The Poorhouse Fair. New York, Knopf, and London, Gollancz, 1959.
Rabbit, Run. New York, Knopf, 1960; London, Deutsch, 1961.
The Centaur. New York, Knopf, and London, Deutsch, 1963.
Of the Farm. New York, Knopf, 1965.
Couples. New York, Knopf, and London, Deutsch, 1968.
Rabbit Redux. New York, Knopf, 1971; London, Deutsch, 1972.
A Month of Sundays. New York, Knopf, and London, Deutsch, 1975.
Marry Me: A Romance. New York, Knopf, 1976; London, Deutsch, 1977.
The Coup. New York, Knopf, 1978; London, Deutsch, 1979.
Rabbit Is Rich. New York, Knopf, 1981; London, Deutsch, 1982.
The Witches of Eastwick. New York, Knopf, and London, Deutsch, 1984,

Short Stories

The Same Door. New York, Knopf, 1959; London, Deutsch, 1962.
Pigeon Feathers and Other Stories. New York, Knopf, and London, Deutsch, 1962.
Olinger Stories: A Selection. New York, Knopf, 1964.
The Music School. New York, Knopf, 1966; London, Deutsch, 1967.

Penguin Modern Stories 2, with others. London, Penguin, 1969.

Bech: A Book. New York, Knopf, and London, Deutsch, 1970.

The Indian. Marvin, South Dakota, Blue Cloud Abbey, 1971.

Museums and Women and Other Stories. New York, Knopf, 1972; London, Deutsch, 1973.

Warm Wine: An Idyll. New York, Albondocani Press, 1973.

Couples: A Short Story. Cambridge, Massachusetts, Halty Ferguson, 1976.

Too Far to Go: The Maples Stories. New York, Fawcett, 1979; as *Your Lover Just Called: Stories of Joan and Richard Maple*, London, Penguin, 1980.

Problems and Other Stories. New York, Knopf, 1979; London, Deutsch, 1980.

Three Illuminations in the Life of an American Author. New York, Targ, 1979.

The Chaste Planet. Worcester, Massachusetts, Metacom Press, 1980.

The Beloved. Northridge, California, Lord John Press, 1982.

Bech Is Back. New York, Knopf, 1982; London, Deutsch, 1983.

Uncollected Short Stories

"Trust Me," in *New Yorker*, 16 July 1979.

"Morocco," in *Atlantic* (Boston), November 1979.

"Still of Some Use," in *The Best American Short Stories 1981*, edited by Hortense Calisher and Shannon Ravenel. Boston, Houghton Mifflin, 1981.

"Pygmalion," in *Atlantic* (Boston), July 1981.

"Learn a Trade," in *New Yorker*, 28 December 1981.

"First Wives and Trolley Cars," in *New Yorker*, 27 December 1982.

"The City," in *Prize Stories 1983: The O. Henry Awards*, edited by William Abrahams. New York, Doubleday, 1983.

"Deaths of Distant Friends," in *The Best American Short Stories 1983*, edited by Anne Tyler and Shannon Ravenel. Boston, Houghton Mifflin, 1983.

"More Stately Mansions," in *Great Esquire Fiction*, edited by L. Rust Hills. New York, Viking Press, 1983.

"One More Interview," in *New Yorker*, 4 July 1983.

"The Other," in *New Yorker*, 15 August 1983.

"Slippage," in *New Yorker*, 20 February 1984.

"Poker Night," in *Esquire* (New York), August 1984.

"A Constellation of Events," in *New Yorker*, 25 February 1985.

"Made in Heaven," in *Atlantic* (Boston), April 1985.

"The Wallet," in *Yankee* (Durham, New Hampshire), September 1985.

"The Other Woman," in *New Yorker*, 23 December 1985.

Plays

Three Texts from Early Ipswich: A Pageant. Ipswich, Massachusetts, 17th Century Day Committee, 1968.

Buchanan Dying. New York, Knopf, and London, Deutsch, 1974.

Verse

The Carpentered Hen and Other Tame Creatures. New York, Harper, 1958; as *Hoping for a Hoopoe*, London, Gollancz, 1959.

Telephone Poles and Other Poems. New York, Knopf, and London, Deutsch, 1963.

Verse. New York, Fawcett, 1965.

Dog's Death. Cambridge, Massachusetts, Lowell House, 1965.

The Angels. Pensacola, Florida, King and Queen Press, 1968.

Bath after Sailing. Monroe, Connecticut, Pendulum Press, 1968.

Midpoint and Other Poems. New York, Knopf, and London, Deutsch, 1969.

Seventy Poems. London, Penguin, 1972.

Six Poems. New York, Aloe, 1973.

Query. New York, Albondocani Press, 1974.

Cunts (Upon Receiving the Swingers Life Club Membership Solicitation). New York, Hallman, 1974.

Tossing and Turning. New York, Knopf, and London, Deutsch, 1977.

Sixteen Sonnets. Cambridge, Massachusetts, Halty Ferguson, 1979.

An Oddly Lovely Day Alone. Richmond, Virginia, Waves Press, 1979.

Five Poems. Cleveland, Bits Press, 1980.

Jester's Dozen. Northridge, California, Lord John Press, 1984.

Facing Nature. New York, Knopf, 1985; London, Deutsch, 1986.

Other

The Magic Flute (for children), with Warren Chappell. New York, Knopf, 1962.

The Ring (for children), with Warren Chappell. New York, Knopf, 1964.

Assorted Prose. New York, Knopf, and London, Deutsch, 1965.

A Child's Calendar. New York, Knopf, 1965.

On Meeting Authors. Newburyport, Massachusetts, Wickford Press, 1968.

Bottom's Dream: Adapted from William Shakespeare's "A Midsummer Night's Dream" (for children). New York, Knopf, 1969.

A Good Place. New York, Aloe, 1973.

Picked-Up Pieces. New York, Knopf, 1975; London, Deutsch, 1976.

Hub Fans Bid Kid Adieu. Northridge, California, Lord John Press, 1977.

Talk from the Fifties. Northridge, California, Lord John Press, 1979.

Ego and Art in Walt Whitman. New York, Targ, 1980.

People One Knows: Interviews with Insufficiently Famous Americans. Northridge, California, Lord John Press, 1980.

Invasion of the Book Envelopes. Concord, New Hampshire, Ewert, 1981.

Hawthorne's Creed. New York, Targ, 1981.

Hugging the Shore: Essays and Criticism. New York, Knopf, 1983; London, Deutsch, 1984.

Editor, *Pens and Needles*, by David Levine. Boston, Gambit, 1970.

Editor, with Shannon Ravenel, *The Best American Short Stories 1984.* Boston, Houghton Mifflin, 1984; as *The Year's Best American Short Stories*, London, Severn House, 1985.

*

Bibliography: *John Updike: A Bibliography* by C. Clarke Taylor, Kent, Ohio, Kent State University Press, 1968; *An Annotated Bibliography of John Updike Criticism 1967–1973, and a Checklist of His Works* by Michael A. Olivas, New York,

Garland, 1975; *John Updike: A Comprehensive Bibliography with Selected Annotations* by Elizabeth A. Gearhart, Norwood, Pennsylvania, Norwood Editions, 1978.

Manuscript Collection: Harvard University, Cambridge, Massachusetts.

Critical Studies: interviews in *Life* (New York), 4 November 1966, *Paris Review*, Winter 1968, and *New York Times Book Review*, 10 April 1977; *John Updike* by Charles T. Samuels, Minneapolis, University of Minnesota Press, 1969; *The Elements of John Updike* by Alice and Kenneth Hamilton, Grand Rapids, Michigan, Eerdmans, 1970; *Pastoral and Anti-Pastoral Elements in John Updike's Fiction* by Larry E. Taylor, Carbondale, Southern Illinois University Press, 1971; *John Updike: Yea Sayings* by Rachael C. Burchard, Carbondale, Southern Illinois University Press, 1971; *John Updike* by Robert Detweiler, New York, Twayne, 1972, revised edition, 1984; *Rainstorms and Fire: Ritual in the Novels of John Updike* by Edward P. Vargo, Port Washington, New York, Kennikat Press, 1973; *Fighters and Lovers: Theme in the Novels of John Updike* by Joyce B. Markle, New York, New York University Press, 1973; *John Updike: A Collection of Critical Essays* edited by David Thorburn and Howard Eiland, Englewood Cliffs, New Jersey, Prentice Hall, 1979; *John Updike* by Suzanne H. Uphaus, New York, Ungar, 1980; *The Other John Updike: Poems/Short Stories/Prose/Play*, 1981, and *John Updike's Novels*, 1984, both by Donald J. Greiner, Athens, Ohio University Press; *John Updike's Images of America* by Philip H. Vaughan, Reseda, California, Mojave, 1981; *Married Men and Magic Tricks: John Updike's Erotic Heroes* by Elizabeth Tallent, Berkeley, California, Creative Arts, 1982; *Critical Essays on John Updike* edited by William R. Macnaughton, Boston, Hall, 1982.

John Updike comments:

In over thirty years as a professional writer I have tried to give my experience of life imaginative embodiment in novels, short stories, and poems. Art is, as I understand it, reality passed through a human mind, and this secondary creation remains for me unfailingly interesting and challenging.

*   *   *

John Updike takes his place as a major figure in contemporary fiction not only by virtue of his steady production of praiseworthy novels and short stories since 1959, when both *The Poorhouse Fair* and *The Same Door* appeared, but also because he devotes a blessed gift for language to the process and dimensions of dissolution in religion, morality, and society that have characterized our culture in the post-Christian world. Updike is a traditional novelist whose literary mode is essentially although not always realist and whose literary values derive from a mythic and Christian past; the destruction of belief in that past and in those values is the theme in almost everything he has written.

Updike has said that good works of art direct us back outward to reality again, and that good writers focus on the excitements of normal, everyday life. He believes that contemporary fiction is thin in showing how the world operates and that it is an obligation for fiction to be factually right; he therefore tries to give convincing, accurate detail. If he succeeds, he believes that he can, as a writer, deliver the truth. The two assumptions that an apprehensible reality is available to the artist and that truth may be ascertained and grasped by the writer mark Updike as a legitimate swimmer in the traditional stream of fiction. These allegiances explain his admiration for Vermeer, a painter to whom he alludes frequently and whose verisimilitude he happily imitates. He has, like the masters of the Dutch school, the power to see precisely. When he looks at the world of nature, it is an act of discovery. When he shows us a girl biting into an apple, it is like Nabokov showing us Lolita at play on the tennis court—a self-contained thing of beauty. When he shows us the houses on the street where Rabbit and Janice live in *Rabbit, Run*, we can taste the grime and feel in our stomach the gray dreariness. He gives us the details of the linotype machine that Rabbit operates in *Rabbit Redux* or of architecture and construction as Piet practices these in *Couples*. Building on the capacity for sharp observation and the command of knowledgeable detail, Updike writes the kind of social comedy that reports on and analyzes the world around him. He is, among other things, a novelist of manners; his characters are often sophisticated metropolitan or suburban people, and his concerns are often marriage, divorce, and sex, *Marry Me* is a prime example of Updike's capacity for a carefully articulated anatomy of marriage, adultery, and divorce in suburbia. It is this talent for realism that makes Updike an indispensable observer of middle-class life in America.

He is, furthermore, an observer with a point of view. He has said that he does not wish to pronounce on great matters and that he disapproves of writers who have made a full commitment to ideas or social issues. Agreeing with John Cage, he has claimed that not judgments, but openness and curiosity are the artist's proper business. Yet he finds that he cannot altogether refrain from opinion, or even judgment. He does speak out, as he himself indicates when he describes his work as saying, "yes, but." Yes in *Rabbit, Run*, to urgent whispers, but the social fabric collapses; yes in *The Centaur* to self-sacrifice and duty, but what of private agony and dwindling? No in *The Poorhouse Fair* to homogenization and loss of faith, but listen to the voices speaking about the joy of persistent existence; no in *Couples* to a religious community founded on physical and psychical interpretations, but what else shall we do as God destroys our churches?

This dialectic, these fruitful tensions, arise in part from Updike's perception of the world in which he lives. Our century is celebrated for the breakdown of communication, he has said, resorting deliberately to the cliché; we live in an Age of Unconsummation in which we enjoy only solipsistic ecstasies. He had begun his career with a belief in the relevance of art; and he was concerned to forestall apocalypse, but some 25 years later he observes an interest on the part of some writers in bringing it on. When T.S. Eliot died in 1965, Updike has said, we were deprived of a cultural presence that extended the tradition of the presiding poet-critic into our time; as long as he was alive our literature seemed restrained from the apocalyptic formlessness and obscenity that it now seeks.

Updike's dilemma, which is both the subject and the generating force of his fiction, is to understand that his culture is in serious if not fatal disarray, moving inexorably toward the dissolutions of entropy. The stay against this drift into formlessness and anarchy is faith in some mythic or Christian structure of values. But the evidence is everywhere around us that the vitality has been sucked out of what were once life-giving myths. Recognizing that Christianity is an anachronism, Updike cannot commit himself to it. Yet he is unwilling to surrender altogether the attitudes and values that it represents to him and that he learned in his Lutheran boyhood. His fiction, therefore, cannot affirm anything, except a sense of loss. All is sullied o'er with hesitancy and skepticism and the nostalgic but forlorn hope that what we so confidently knew and had in the past might be in the present. He is the traditional novelist who celebrates the decay of tradition, recording its dissolution with meticulous accuracy.

In his first novel, the anti-Utopian *Poorhouse Fair*, Updike confronts the crisis of Christianity in the clash between a social scientist as a dehumanized humanitarian who would rationalize human behaviour and an old man who asserts that there is no goodness without a belief in God. On one side are progress and egalitarianism, on the other, awe, ceremony, mystery, reverence for the past and for the spirit. But these latter qualities belong to the old and are fading into the past. In *Rabbit, Run* a half-articulated quest for Edenic nature fails, and a search for a sustaining religious faith fails, shattered in good part by a minister who himself has no faith. The consequences of failure in this novel are flight, escape, loss, as they are in other work. Updike's most pessimistic comment on the state of religion is in his portrayal of the Negro pusher in *Rabbit Redux* who, in a bitter parody, is made to see himself as the Christ of the Second Coming.

Updike's treatment of religion frequently involves a sexual dimension. Fornication in his fiction is accompanied by feelings of guilt and knowledge of sin, but the relationship between sex—love and passion—and Christianity goes well beyond these matters to speculation that sex may replace religion or that sexual vitality is an expression of the Christian life or that sexual passion destroys Christianity. In "Lifeguard" a divinity student recognizes the relation between concupiscence and piety. He sees the assault on heaven as a kind of lust. To desire a woman is to desire to save her. Every seduction is a conversion and every copulation is a rescue in Christ's name. In *A Month of Sundays* the bad priest whose belief in God has made his life a feast of inconvenience and unreason argues that sex is the exterior sign of interior grace. The fullest development of these ideas is in *Couples*, which asks the question, after Christianity, what? and tests the proposition that sexual vitality may defy death and lead to Christian fulfillment. The protagonist, who believes in the sovereignty of God, takes many women to bed as a way of serving his God and thinks that total sexual satiation, including fellatio and cunnilingus, is a celebration of the holiness of the flesh: to eat another is sacred, he decides. This man fails the test, but it is not altogether clear that Updike has rejected the notion that the unity of two in one during sex is like being one with God. Updike's ambiguity here avoids didacticism but does not rescue Christianity.

If Christianity cannot be made to work, then perhaps some other myth can. Updike has made two different extended explorations of myth. *The Centaur* is an effort to blend the lives of gods and men, using the Chiron variant of the Hercules myth, because it is one of the few classical examples of self-sacrifice, and it affords an opportunity to exploit the closeness of the name Chiron to that of Christ, as Updike has said. Unfortunately, it is precisely this intention that gives the key to the flaw in the novel: Updike does not fully commit himself to the classical myth, that is to the structure of belief in ancient Greece to which the myth belongs. Not only does he dilute the Greek world with the Christian, but also he fails to develop the Prometheus character, the son for whom the sacrifice is made. Ancient myth, in short, treated tentatively and incompletely, does not sustain Updike any more than Christian myth can. In *The Coup* Updike quite deliberately rejects myth. The dictator protagonist of a Third World country in this novel undertakes a perilous journey to the most fearsome corner of his country in order to destroy the spirit of the tyrannical king he has deposed and killed. In accomplishing his mission he will purify his own life, redeem the land, and bring fertility, i.e. rain, to it. But when he reaches the cave which contains the mystery—the deposed king's talking head—he finds that it has been wired for sound by his Russian allies; the cave, full of electronic equipment, has become a tourist attraction. Myth can exist only as parody in a world dominated by high technology and imperialism.

In Updike's fiction generally, it is contemporary culture that debases belief—in Christianity or myth—and values and renders them well-nigh impossible. His characters struggle to be moral, to take responsibility for others, but they find no acceptable authority, divine or human, to define for them a "good" life, and they cannot struggle successfully against a culture hostile to the genuine needs of human beings. Thus the vision of loss and disintegration pervades Updike's fiction. Everything decays: sexual and political morality, the family, patriotism, food (it is synthetic, plastic), sport, craftsmanship, language itself. In *Bech: A Book*, Updike comes, he says, to confess sterility, and he writes about how authors themselves betray literature and about the impotency of literature. A subtle writer and a master of paradox, Updike acts out in his own career an astonishing paradox: the survival of a writer who wishes, needs, to believe while demonstrating that belief is impossible.

New work continues to appear. *The Witches of Eastwick* is a tentative exploration of evil in which Updike uses witchcraft as a metaphor for the presence of evil in American life, for something corrupt, degenerate, even fatal lurking beneath the surface of a culture that feeds on the air-brushed commercial photograph and the banalities of the television screen. The three witches of the title live in a Rhode Island village, a part of the country where witches had flourished and been punished three hundred years earlier. These women also flourish, using their diabolical powers for mischief both whimsical and damaging as well as for murder most foul. But although each is deprived of one of her desires—marriage to an apparently wealthy newcomer in town who may be the devil—they suffer no appropriate punishment. It is not clear, therefore, what Updike is doing in this novel, in which he obviously raises questions about good and evil, crime and punishment, and then lamely skips away from them.

Bech Is Back returns to Updike's non-productive Jewish writer who is living on his reputation. Updike is ill at ease with Jews, and this volume reflects his discomfort in its many ethnic clichés. But the brief, final episode summons the presence of dark forces (especially as associated with sex, women, and mud—a combination that has sickened Updike since childhood) with a power rarely glimpsed in Updike's fiction.

Rabbit Is Rich is the most successful social chronicle of the three novels dealing with Rabbit and Janice Angstrom. In this fully detailed account of how the consumer society flowers in America, Updike unfolds the classic American success story in its 1970's version. Rabbit, the son of a working-class father, and Janice, the daughter of a marginal second-hand automobile dealer, act out the drama of upward mobility in their time. A lazy and sloppy businessman, Rabbit enjoys a success that is essentially unearned; it is not the fruit of the Protestant work ethic that had guided earlier generations of successful men. It is achieved in a setting of urban sprawl that has at once assaulted the natural world and destroyed the center of town and thus the binding ideas of community and order. The new order of this homogeneous society is imposed by plastics. The unleashed acquisitive spirit displaces the order of traditional values and religion. Without a foundation for discipline and morality in their lives, the children are confused and disillusioned and their middle-aged parents willingly move toward sloth, prejudice, and the chaos of the sexual revolution. Updike imparts a flavor and dynamism to this dreary but scrupulously honest profile of American culture by giving his ignorant anti-hero some redeeming features: Rabbit feels guilt; he has an atavistic sense of God's presence in the world; and he comes to terms with death by understanding that his granddaughter represents the miracle of birth, life out of death, the continuity of humankind. *Rabbit Is Rich*, as a species of the examined life, is rewarding realism of a high order.

—Chester E. Eisinger

UPWARD, Edward (Falaise). British. Born in Romford, Essex, 9 September 1903. Educated at Repton School, 1917–21; Corpus Christi College, Cambridge (Chancellor's Medal for Verse), 1922–24, M.A. 1925. Married to Hilda Maude Percival; one son and one daughter. Schoolmaster, 1928–62. Member of the Editorial Board, *The Ploughshare*, London, 1936–39. Address: c/o Heinemann Ltd., 10 Upper Grosvenor Street, London W1X 9PA, England.

PUBLICATIONS

Novels

Journey to the Border.   London, Hogarth Press, 1938.
The Spiral Ascent (includes *No Home But the Struggle*).   London, Heinemann, 1977.
   In the Thirties.   London, Heinemann, 1962.
   The Rotten Elements.   London, Heinemann, 1969.

Short Stories

The Railway Accident and Other Stories.   London, Heinemann, 1969.

Uncollected Short Stories

"An Old-Established School" May 1981, "The Interview" May 1984, and "At the Ferry Inn" July 1985, all in *London Magazine.*

Verse

Buddha.   London, Cambridge University Press, 1924.

*

Manuscript Collection: British Library, London.

Critical Studies: introduction by W.H. Sellers to *The Railway Accident and Other Stories*, 1969; article by Upward, in *London Magazine*, June 1969.

*   *   *

Edward Upward as a young writer in the 1930's achieved a great reputation, was indeed something of a legend, among a number of writers of his own age and younger. Christopher Isherwood told in *Lions and Shadows* how he and Upward (called Chalmers in Isherwood's book) at Cambridge invented a fantasy world they called Mortmere which paralleled and parodied the world about them. Mortmere seems to have been at once sinister and comic, partly surrealist and partly Gothic. That it had affinities with Auden's early poetry, influenced as it was by Freud, seems clear, and something of it seems to emerge in the plays Isherwood wrote in collaboration with Auden, notably *The Dog Beneath the Skin.* Upward, however, overtly pursued the vein of fantasy in his fiction, but, even then politically committed, in the cause of Marxism. The central character of *Journey to the Border* is a middle-class young man employed as a tutor in the house of a rich man; he is constantly struggling against the implications and ignominies of his position but is unable to resolve them. He is persuaded against his will to accompany his employer to a race-meeting. On the way, and while there, he experiences a series of hallucinations that mount in intensity and are the counterparts of the debate going on in his mind. By the end of the novel he is forced to realise that the only solution to this problem, the only way to reality, is for him to identify himself with the working-class struggle.

When the novel was first published, reviewers read the influence of Kafka into it. This is not much apparent now, if it ever existed. Upward's novel is much less complex than those of Kafka, and what begins as a work of symbolism peters out in simple allegory. Nevertheless, the voltage of imaginative excitement generated is high, and the dreamlike quality of the work is admirably sustained. It remains a brilliant experimental novel of a very unusual kind.

Upward published nothing for 25 years, and then in 1962 appeared *In the Thirties* (followed by *The Rotten Elements* and, as a complete trilogy incorporating *No Home But the Struggle*, *The Spiral Ascent*). These novels are based, it is impossible not to think, on the author's own life. *In the Thirties* describes the stages by which a young middle-class man comes to Communism. In a sense, the theme is that of *Journey to the Border*, but the treatment is entirely different. Fantasy has been replaced by literal realism, which is also the vein of the later volumes of the trilogy. In *The Rotten Elements* the hero of the earlier novel, a school teacher now married, finds himself compelled in the years immediately after the war to leave the Communist Party, not because he has lost his political faith but because for him and his wife the British Communist Party, under the influence of Moscow, has deviated from Marxism-Leninism. *No Home But the Struggle* shows them recommitted to the campaign for nuclear disarmament. The trilogy lacks the literary interest of *Journey to the Border*, but it has an anguish of its own and a documentary quality which suggests that, though it may not be read in the future for its artistic value, it will be essential reading for scholars concerned with the role of the Communist party in Britain.

—Walter Allen

URIS, Leon (Marcus). American. Born in Baltimore, Maryland, 3 August 1924. Educated at schools in Baltimore. Served in the United States Marine Corps, 1942–45. Married 1) Betty Beck in 1945 (divorced, 1965); 2) Margery Edwards in 1968 (died, 1969); 3) Jill Peabody in 1970; three children. Newspaper driver for the San Francisco *Call-Bulletin* in the late 1940's. Full-time writer since 1950. Recipient: Daroff Memorial Award, 1959; American Academy grant, 1959. Lives in Aspen, Colorado. Address: c/o Doubleday, 245 Park Avenue, New York, New York 10167, U.S.A.

PUBLICATIONS

Novels

Battle Cry. New York, Putnam, and London, Wingate, 1953.
The Angry Hills. New York, Random House, 1955; London, Wingate, 1956.
Exodus. New York, Doubleday, 1958; London, Wingate, 1959.
Mila 18. New York, Doubleday, and London, Heinemann, 1961.
Armageddon: A Novel of Berlin. New York, Doubleday, and London, Kimber, 1964.
Topaz. New York, McGraw Hill, 1967; London, Kimber, 1968.
Q.B. VII. New York, Doubleday, 1970; London, Kimber, 1971.
Trinity. New York, Doubleday, and London, Deutsch, 1976.
The Haj. New York, Doubleday, and London, Deutsch, 1984.

Plays

Ari, music by Walt Smith and William Fisher, adaptation of the novel *Exodus* by Uris (produced New York, 1971).

Screenplays: *Battle Cry*, 1955; *Gunfight at the OK Corral*, 1957; *Israel* (documentary), 1959.

Other

Exodus Revisited. New York, Doubleday, 1960; as *In the Steps of Exodus*, London, Heinemann, 1962.
The Third Temple, with *Strike Zion*, by William Stevenson. New York, Bantam, 1967.
Ireland, A Terrible Beauty: The Story of Ireland Today, with Jill Uris. New York, Doubleday, 1975; London, Deutsch, 1976.
Jerusalem: Song of Songs, with Jill Uris. New York, Doubleday, and London, Deutsch, 1981.

*   *   *

Critics were willing to be charitable to Leon Uris's popular novel, *Battle Cry*, when it appeared in 1953. While it is a war novel not as psychologically complex as Wouk's *The Caine Mutiny*, nor as deeply probing into the nature of man and war as Mailer's *The Naked and the Dead* or Jones's *From Here to Eternity*, it is a good, straightforward, blood-and-guts adventure of the U.S. Marine Corps in which dialogue and action are matched well to characters. Though Uris's treatment by professional critics has generally been much harsher for the novels that have been published since, their disparagement of his work is, in an important sense, not entirely fair. There is no reason to suppose that the present is different from earlier periods in literary history when there has been a popular, ephemeral literature as distinct from a smaller body of serious and lasting literature with limited public appeal. Uris makes no pretense of contributing to an enduring *corpus* of American literature. He bulls his way forward on the sheer strength of his narrative ability, which was acknowledged at the beginning of his career, and though he may stumble over literary matters of characterisation, plot detail, dialogue, or theme, his handling of the story line unfailingly carries him through, and the book-buying public acclaims him over the grumbling of critics.

Yet the faults are real and cannot be overlooked; they are in evidence in all of the novels. *The Angry Hills*, a romantic war adventure of Greek resistance to the Nazi occupation, contains obtrusively contrived circumstances. The invention of the love sub-plot of *Exodus*, between the Zionist hero Ari Ben Canaan and the gentile nurse Kitty Fremont, often seems gratuitous, and its execution pre-Cinemascope. *Armageddon*, like *Exodus* and Uris's other works, has its plot in large measure constructed by history, in this case Russian-American relations in Berlin after World War II, and especially the American airlift. And, like *Exodus*, it is plagued by a love affair that seems, at times, to be arbitrarily appended to the progression of historical events. It suffers, too, from a weakness of dialogue that is not unusual in Uris, and from the trite response of the main character, an American occupation officer, to the German and Russian nations in turn. *Mila 18* does an injustice to the Jews of the Warsaw ghetto, whose resolute defiance of the Nazis it chronicles, by transforming them into a series of stock characters. Here, as elsewhere in his novels, Uris seems to be best when he is recounting the history he has researched and at his worst when he requires one of the obviously indispensable attributes of the novelist—the power to weave the plot line into a smooth integument of all the elements of fiction.

Yet there is the brute force of the narrative in all of the novels that compels the reader through to the finish despite all imperfections, even through the too-lengthy trial and concentration camp horrors of *Q.B. VII*. And, though it would be wrong to assume that Uris has begun to compose deathless prose at this late date, in pitting the American novelist Abraham Cady against the former camp inmate Adam Kelno, he demonstrates an increased ability to create characters of interest and depth.

—Alan R. Shucard

———————

URQUHART, Fred(erick Burrows). British. Born in Edinburgh, Scotland, 12 July 1912. Educated at village schools in Scotland; Stranraer High School, Wigtownshire; Broughton Secondary School, Edinburgh. Worked in an Edinburgh bookshop, 1927–34; reader for a London literary agency, 1947–51, and for MGM, 1951–54; London scout for Walt Disney Productions, 1959–60; reader for Cassell and Company, London, 1951–74, and for J.M. Dent and Sons, London, 1967–71. Recipient: Tom-Gallon Trust award, 1951; Arts Council of Great Britain grant, 1966, bursary, 1978, 1985; Scottish Arts Council grant, 1975. Agent: Herta Ryder, c/o Toby Eady Associates, 55 Great Ormond Street, London WC1N 3HZ. Address: Spring Garden Cottage, Fairwarp, Uckfield, Sussex TN22 3BG, England.

PUBLICATIONS

Novels

Time Will Knit. London, Duckworth, 1938.
The Ferret Was Abraham's Daughter. London, Methuen, 1949.
Jezebel's Dust. London, Methuen, 1951.
Palace of Green Days. London, Quartet, 1979.

Short Stories

I Fell for a Sailor and Other Stories. London, Duckworth, 1940.

The Clouds Are Big with Mercy.   Glasgow, Maclellan, 1946.
Selected Stories.   Dublin, Fridberg, 1946.
*The Last GI Bride Wore Tartan: A Novella and Some Short
   Stories.*   Edinburgh, Serif, 1948.
The Year of the Short Corn and Other Stories.   London, Meth-
   uen, 1949.
The Last Sister and Other Stories.   London, Methuen, 1950.
The Laundry Girl and the Pole: Selected Stories.   London,
   Arco, 1955.
Collected Stories:
   1. *The Dying Stallion and Other Stories.*   London, Hart
      Davis, 1967.
   2. *The Ploughing Match and Other Stories.*   London, Hart
      Davis, 1968.
Proud Lady in a Cage: Six Historical Stories.   Edinburgh, Har-
   ris, 1980.
A Diver in China Seas.   London, Quartet, 1980.
Seven Ghosts in Search.   London, Kimber, 1983.

Uncollected Short Stories

"Hector's Hectic Hogmanay," in *Scottish Hogmanay Annual*
   (Edinburgh), 1950–51.
"Charlie Calling," in *Modern Reading* (London), Summer
   1952.
"The Gay Gush Girls," in *Thy Neighbour's Wife*, edited by
   James Turner.   London, Cassell, 1964.
"Two Lives: 1914," in *Texas Quarterly* (Austin), Autumn 1974.

Other

Scotland in Colour.   London, Batsford, and New York, Viking Press, 1961.

Editor, with Maurice Lindsay, *No Scottish Twilight: New Scot-
   tish Stories.*   Glasgow, Maclellan, 1947.
Editor, *W.S.C.: A Cartoon Biography* (on Winston Churchill).
   London, Cassell, 1955.
Editor, *Great True War Adventures.*   London, Arco, 1956;
   New York, Arco, 1957.
Editor, *Scottish Short Stories.*   London, Faber, 1957.
Editor, *Men at War: The Best War Stories of All Time.*   Lon-
   don, Arco, 1957.
Editor, *Great True Escape Stories.*   London, Arco, 1958.
Editor, *The Cassell Miscellany 1848–1958.*   London, Cassell,
   1958.
Editor, *Everyman's Dictionary of Fictional Characters*, by Wil-
   liam Freeman, revised edition.   London, Dent, and New
   York, Dutton, 1973.
Editor, with Giles Gordon, *Modern Scottish Short Stories.*
   London, Hamish Hamilton, 1978; revised edition, London,
   Faber, 1982.
Editor, *The Book of Horses: The Horse Through the Ages
   in Art and Literature.*   London, Secker and Warburg, and
   New York, Morrow, 1981.

                              *

Manuscript Collections: National Library of Scotland, Edinburgh; University of Texas Library, Austin; Edinburgh University Library.

Critical Studies: review by Janet Adam Smith, in *New York
Times Book Review*, 31 July 1938; Alexander Reid, in *Scot-
land's Magazine* (Edinburgh), February 1958; Iain Crichton
Smith in *The Spectator* (London), 24 May 1968; *History of*

Scottish Literature by Maurice Lindsay, London, Hale, 1977;
A Companion to Scottish Culture edited by David Daiches,
London, Arnold, 1981; *Modern Scottish Literature* by Alan
Bold, London, Longman, 1983; *The Macmillan Companion
to Scottish Literature* by Trevor Royle, London, Macmillan,
1983, as *Companion to Scottish Literature*, Detroit, Gale, 1983;
Guide to Modern World Literature by Martin Seymour-Smith,
London, Macmillan, and New York, Bedrick, 1985.

Fred Urquhart comments:
   I never talk to people about my work. When I'm writing
a story or novel I don't want anybody to see it or know anything
about it until it is completely finished and it satisfies me. I
can't understand the habit of some authors of reading their
work aloud to their friends as the work progresses. It is only
after I've written a story that I show it to friends, inviting
criticism.

                 *   *   *

   Fred Urquhart is a wonderful listener. He gets the exact
lilt of Clydeside or the Mearns or Leith or Scots dialect modified by the army or navy. He seems to be fascinated by the
corruption of language: how Glasgow speech adds an embroi-
dering diminutive "ie"—flashie, steamie—but is itself a corrupted English from what was the Clyde ditch into which the
fleeing Gaelic speakers piled themselves hoping for a puckle
siller and a wee housie or roomie to live and love in. Those
are his backgrounds. But his tongue or maybe his pen is as
skilled as his deeply interested ear. He gets it all down often
with a minimal plot but with such liveliness and such involvement of characters that the story line hardly matters. Indeed
there are times when he has a good heart-throb ending but
he usually gets away with it because of the way it is told. This
is why his work is so successful on radio.
   These writings of his are too artful and delicate to be in
fact the kind of stories which have been told into the unsympathetic ear of a tape recorder. Thus always another human
but invisible listener may be asking the odd question that stirs
the story up and this invisible other is infinitely aware of the
fine points of dialogue and the hidden feelings of the characters,
which only appear between the lines, making tensions which
are never underlined. Oddly enough Urquhart is best with his
women characters, his schoolmistresses and farmers' wives or
daughters; his Glasgow lassies on the make or his dirty old
wifies. He really gets into the skin of the "Last G.I. Bride."
Why? Maybe he finds the toughness of the average male Scot
a bit of a bore—as so many women also find it! But he is
sensitive to other second class citizens, for instance the Italian
prisoners working on a lowland farm in one of his World War
II stories.
   He is not a quick writer. Perhaps that is why his novels
are really longer short stories, though *Palace of Green Days*
is the kind of long novel that takes us right into the lowland
heartland. On the whole he spends little time on the background unless it is farm detail, and here he is often away back
to the days of splendid Clydeside mares and comparatively
unhygienic byres and dairies. Most comes through conversation
or the fleeting thoughts which are near to speech. He is also
very much interested in what other writers are doing, especially
in Scotland. He must often have been sorely tempted to do
a bit of quick slick writing for the "popular" family magazines.
But he believes that writers have a certain duty to tell the
truth, even when it is displeasing to the audience they would
most like—their own folk. This audience of course is what
all writers want but few if any get, because of the corruption

of the chosen hearers. It is hard luck to have to wait till you are dead before you are appreciated. One hopes this won't have to happen to Fred Urquhart.

—Naomi Mitchison

---

van der POST, (Sir) Laurens (Jan). South African. Born in Philippolis, 13 December 1906. Educated at Grey College, Bloemfontein. Served in the British Army, in the Western Desert and the Far East, in World War II; prisoner of war in Java, 1943–45; Military Attaché to the British Minister, Batavia, 1945–47; C.B.E. (Commander, Order of the British Empire), 1947. Married 1) Marjorie Wendt in 1929 (divorced, 1947), one son (deceased) and one daughter; 2) the writer Ingaret Giffard in 1949. Reporter, *Natal Advertiser*, Durban, 1925–26; leader writer, *Cape Times*, Cape Town, 1930; editor, *Natal Daily News*. Durban, 1948; farmer in the Orange Free State, South Africa, 1948–65. Explorer: several missions in Africa for the Colonial Development Corporation and the British Government, including a mission to Kalahari, 1952. Since 1974, Trustee, World Wilderness Fund. Recipient: Anisfield-Wolf award, 1951; National Association of Independent Schools award (USA), 1959; CNA award, 1964, 1968. D.Litt.: University of Natal, Pietermaritzburg, 1964; University of Liverpool, 1976; Rhodes University, Grahamstown, 1978; St. Andrews University, Scotland, 1980; D. Univ.: University of Surrey, Guildford, 1971. Fellow, Royal Society of Literature, 1955. Knighted, 1981. Address: c/o Viking, 536 King's Road, London SW10 0UH, England.

PUBLICATIONS

Novels

In a Province. London, Hogarth Press, 1934; New York, Coward McCann, 1935.
The Face Beside the Fire. London, Hogarth Press, and New York, Morrow, 1953.
A Bar of Shadow. London, Hogarth Press, 1954; New York, Morrow, 1956.
Flamingo Feather. London, Hogarth Press, and New York, Morrow, 1955.
The Seed and the Sower (includes *A Bar of Shadow* and *The Sword and the Doll*). London, Hogarth Press, and New York, Morrow, 1963.
The Hunter and the Whale: A Tale of Africa. London, Hogarth Press, and New York, Morrow, 1967.
A Story like the Wind. London, Hogarth Press, and New York, Morrow, 1972.
A Far-Off Place. London, Hogarth Press, and New York, Morrow, 1974.
A Mantis Carol. London, Hogarth Press, 1975; New York, Morrow, 1976.

Plays

Screenplays: *The Lost World of the Kalahari*, 1956; *A Region of Shadow*, 1971; *The Story of Carl Gustav Jung*, 1971; *All Africa Within Us*, 1975; *Zulu Wilderness: Black Umfolozi Rediscovered*, 1979.

Other

Venture to the Interior. New York, Morrow, 1951; London, Hogarth Press, 1952.

The Dark Eye in Africa. London, Hogarth Press, and New York, Morrow, 1955.
Race Prejudice as Self-Rejection. New York, Workshop for Cultural Democracy, 1957.
The Lost World of the Kalahari. London, Hogarth Press, and New York, Morrow, 1958.
The Heart of the Hunter. London, Hogarth Press, and New York, Morrow, 1961.
Patterns of Renewal. Wallingford, Pennsylvania, Pendle Hill, 1962.
Intuition, Intellect, and the Racial Question. New York, Myrin Institute, 1964.
Journey into Russia. London, Hogarth Press, 1964; as *A View of All the Russias*, New York, Morrow, 1964.
A Portrait of All the Russias. London, Hogarth Press, and New York, Morrow, 1967.
A Portrait of Japan. London, Hogarth Press, and New York, Morrow, 1968.
The Night of the New Moon: August 6, 1945 . . . Hiroshima. London, Hogarth Press, 1970; as *The Prisoner and the Bomb*, New York, Morrow, 1971.
African Cooking, with the editors of Time-Life. New York, Time 1970.
Man and the Shadow. London, South Place Ethical Society, 1971.
Jung and the Story of Our Time: A Personal Experience. New York, Pantheon, 1975; London, Hogarth Press, 1976.
First Catch Your Eland: A Taste of Africa. London, Hogarth Press, 1977; New York, Morrow, 1978.
Yet Being Someone Other. London, Hogarth Press, 1982; New York, Morrow, 1983.
Testament to the Bushmen, with Jane Taylor. London, Viking, 1984; New York, Viking, 1985.

*

Critical Study: *Laurens van der Post* by Frederic I. Carpenter, New York, Twayne, 1969.

*   *   *

All the novels of Laurens van der Post have dealt, at least in part, with the life and problems of his native South Africa. All draw upon the author's actual life, which his most famous books of non-fiction (such as *Venture to the Interior*) have described autobiographically. All are distinguished by vivid descriptions of the natural scene, and by psychological depth. But each has been written from a different point of view, and has used a different technique.

In a Province is narrated in the first person by a young, white South African whose black friend runs afoul of the law. Both become involved with a communist agitator, and are finally killed by a posse of self-appointed commandos. The novel is realistic in technique, and is distinguished both by its wealth of incidents involving race relations, and by its balance between the theme of racial injustice on the one hand, and communist exploitation on the other. Although the author has opposed apartheid all his life, he has equally opposed communist subversion.

Nineteen years elapsed between the author's first and second novels—years including his move to England and his distinguished service in World War II, ending with his capture and imprisonment by the Japanese. *The Face Beside the Fire* deals with the problems of an expatriate South African artist in London. Narrated by a life-long friend of the hero, the novel covers a period of many years, and moves from Africa to

England and back. Its many episodes find unity in the psychological theme of alienation. Its technique is that of the psychological novel pioneered by Thomas Mann.

Flamingo Feather is a fast-paced tale of mystery and adventure set in war-time South Africa. Narrated in the first person by a young anthropologist, the plot concerns a communist attempt to subvert a native tribe in the interior. The action includes a vividly narrated trek through tropical jungles. A mystery-melodrama, the novel is distinguished both by its fast action and its vivid description of the wild country of Africa.

The Seed and the Sower consists of three "novellas" describing warfare in Africa and Asia, but focusing on the life of the prisoner-of-war. The first novella, *A Bar of Shadow* (published separately in 1956), centers upon the narrator's attempt to understand his Japanese captors. The second (and longest) returns to South Africa to narrate the early experiences of another officer, and ends with his capture and execution by the Japanese. The third narrates a brief wartime romance. All focus upon the author's experiences as prisoner-of-war, which also shadow much of his autobiographical writing.

The Hunter and the Whale, subtitled *A Tale of Africa*, is narrated by a 17-year-old boy who serves as lookout on a whaling ship working out of Durban. The novel is richer and more complex than the others, and combines realistic with symbolic techniques. Its unusual subject matter and unusual techniques both suggest comparison with Melville's *Moby-Dick*, and help to explain both the fascination and the occasional difficulty of the novel.

A Story like the Wind narrates the adventures of a white boy whose ancestral farm in the interior of South Africa is attacked and captured by communist-led guerillas, and of his escape with the help of a Bushman friend of his own age. *A Far-Off Place* is a continuation of *A Story like the Wind*, though self-contained. The second novel tells of the long journey of these two across the southwest African desert to the coast, and their rescue. Both novels are fastpaced, and filled with adventure and the lore of the Africa which the author knows so well.

—Frederic I. Carpenter

VANSITTART, Peter. British. Born in Bedford, 27 August 1920. Educated at Marlborough House School; Haileybury College, Hertford; Worcester College, Oxford (major scholar in modern history). Director, Burgess School, London, 1947–59; formerly, publisher, Park Editions, London. Recipient: Society of Authors travelling scholarship, 1969; Arts Council bursary, 1981, 1984. Fellow, Royal Society of Literature, 1985. Agent: Anthony Sheil Associates Ltd., 43 Doughty Street, London WC1N 2LF. Address: 9 Upper Park Road, London N.W.3, England.

PUBLICATIONS

Novels

I Am the World.   London, Chatto and Windus, 1942.
Enemies.   London, Chapman and Hall, 1947.
The Overseer.   London, Chapman and Hall, 1949.
Broken Canes.   London, Lane 1950.
A Verdict of Treason.   London, Lane 1952.
A Little Madness.   London, Lane 1953.

The Game and the Ground.   London, Reinhardt, 1956; New York, Abelard Schuman, 1957.
Orders of Chivalry.   London, Bodley Head, 1958; New York, Abelard Schuman, 1959.
The Tournament.   London, Bodley Head, 1959; New York, Walker, 1961.
A Sort of Forgetting.   London, Bodley Head, 1960.
Carolina.   London, New English Library, 1961.
Sources of Unrest.   London, Bodley Head, 1962.
The Friends of God.   London, Macmillan, 1963; as *The Siege*, New York, Walker, 1963.
The Lost Lands.   London, Macmillan, and New York, Walker, 1964.
The Story Teller.   London, Owen, 1968.
Pastimes of a Red Summer.   London, Owen, 1969.
Landlord.   London, Owen, 1970.
Quintet.   London, Owen, 1976.
Lancelot.   London, Owen, 1978.
The Death of Robin Hood.   London, Owen, 1981.
Harry.   London, Park, 1981.
Three Six Seven.   London, Owen, 1983.
Aspects of Feeling.   London, Owen, 1986.

Other

The Dark Tower: Tales from the Past (for children).   London, Macdonald, 1965; New York, Crowell, 1969.
The Shadow Land: More Stories from the Past (for children).   London, Macdonald, 1967.
Green Knights, Black Angels: The Mosaic of History (for children).   London, Macmillan, 1969.
Vladivostok (essay).   London, Covent Garden Press, 1972.
Dictators.   London, Studio Vista, 1973.
Worlds and Underworlds: Anglo-European History Through the Centuries.   London, Owen, 1974.
Flakes of History.   London, Park, 1978.
The Ancient Mariner and the Old Sailor: Delights and Uses of Words.   London, Centre for Policy Studies, 1985.
Paths from a White Horse: A Writer's Memoir.   London, Quartet, 1985.

Editor, *Voices from the Great War.*   London, Cape, 1981; New York, Watts, 1984.
Editor, *Voices: 1870–1914.*   London, Cape, 1984; New York, Watts, 1985.
Editor, *John Masefield's Letters from the Front 1915–1917.*   London, Constable, 1984; New York, Watts, 1985.

*

Peter Vansittart comments:

Though I have published non-fiction, novels alone excite my ambitions; not plays, short stories, poems, manifestos, sermons. My novels have been appreciated, if not always enjoyed, more by critics than the reading public, which shows no sign of enjoying them at all. This must be partly due to my obsession with language and speculation at the expense of narrative, however much I relish narrative in others. Today I take narrative more seriously, though still relying, perhaps over-relying, on descriptive colour, unexpected imagery, the bizarre and curious, no formula for popular success. *The Game and the Ground*, *The Tournament*, *Lancelot*, and *Quintet*, have succeeded the most in expressing initial vision and valid situation in fairly accessible terms. Others—*A Verdict of Treason*, *A Sort of Forgetting*—had interesting and provocative material, clumsily handled. *The Story Teller*, my own favourite, failed through excess of ambition, *A Little Madness* and *Sources of Unrest*, through too little.

My novels range in time from the 2nd millennium BC, to AD 1986. They share the effect of time, and the apparently forgotten or exterminated on the present, time transmuting, distorting, travestying, ridiculing facts and ideas, loves and hates, generous institutions and renowned reputations. I was long impressed by the woeful distinction between the historical Macbeth and Shakespeare's: by the swift transformation of E.M. Forster's very English Mrs. Moore into an Indian goddess. Such phenomena relate very immediately to my own work, in which myth can be all too real, and the real degenerate into fantasy.

* * *

In his memoirs, *Paths from a White Horse*, Peter Vansittart comments enlighteningly on the genre with which he is most closely associated, the historical novel. He knows that it has come to be disdained by many readers because of its long tradition of crude sentimentality and easy picturesqueness, with language that is either over-spiced with random archaism in vocabulary and syntax or else bled white for the sake of coining a supposedly timeless idiom. Worst of all, the desire to present the "facts" is too often allowed to come between the novelist and his primary duty of creating significant fictions. Though Vansittart is uncommonly well informed about history, it has never been his intention to attempt to rehabilitate the historical novel by basing his work on a sounder foundation of scholarship. Instead, appreciating that the objects and methods of history and fiction are distinct, for all that the starting point in both enterprises is a serious contemplation of the past, he is content to leave research and verification to the historians and claims for novelists the right to speculate over the facts that are available. He argues that he is entitled to let his imagination brood over events, situations, and characters, discovering by poetic insight mythic continuities that would be too daring for academic minds. This can happen in especially interesting ways when the past is reflected through the personalities of highly individualised characters whose outlook necessarily colours every interpretation of what is related. For Vansittart, the historical novel is, moreover, not exclusively concerned with the depiction of the past. Far more excitingly, he always presents past and present as a continuity, and while relishing the otherness of remote ages and of the people who lived through them, he makes his historical fiction a vehicle for an alert commentary on our present discontents.

The Death of Robin Hood, for instance, is an ambitious attempt to unify experiences by portraying a huge tract of time, with fantasy and realism mingled to create myth. First comes a spell-binding evocation of the forest in primal times when strange rites are already seen as failing to arrest the processes of change and decay. The second part of the novel, "John in the Castle," depicts the paranoid terrors of a tyrant who cowers behind stone walls, dreading the prospect of conflict with the unruly bands that have taken refuge in the forest. Here there is fine descriptive writing, but it is John's state of mind that is the centre of attention. Next, not pausing to make the linkage explicit, Vansittart moves on to the Luddite riots of 1811 when Nottinghamshire workers rose up and smashed the new machines that were taking away their livelihood and then, as the forces of repression gathered, ran off in droves into the forest. Finally, reverting to the environment he had portrayed with satiric verve in *Broken Canes*, Vansittart shows the old values under attack in the closed world of an independent school just before the outbreak of the Second

World War. With its abrupt transitions, *The Death of Robin Hood* can be puzzling, but the immediacy of the emotions and the vividness of the scenes carry the reader along. *Lancelot* is more straightforward. It takes as its starting point Field-Marshal Wavell's observation that "Arthur was probably a grim figure in a grim, un-romantic struggle in a dark period of history," and, once again, it presents within a framework of exciting events an enquiry into the meaning of change and apparent decay. *Three Six Seven* is set in A.D. 367, a year of cataclysm for Roman Britain.

Vansittart is by no means only an historical novelist, and his gift for description and his disabused insight into human motivations are equally well revealed in the portrayal of the life of the bourgeoisie in modern times in such novels as *Quintet*. The first of its five parts is set in Africa in the immediate post-war era when Britain was shedding its colonial responsibilities, and institutional decay is generally the framework within which flawed human beings pursue their complex ways.

As well as presenting a personal vision of man's lot and exploring the possibilities of narrative technique in challenging fashion, Vansittart possesses a most distinguished prose style. Provided every thought of complacent exuberance and lush imagery is banished, it might well be called poetic, for here there is a rare regard for the communicative power of the exact word in precisely the right place. Nouns in particular he values, not cluttering them with adjectives but letting them stand stark and unmodified to convey meaning. This gives an impression of elemental vigour which is apt in *Lancelot*, for example, and the tight-lipped statements suggest pressures that can be held in check only with difficulty just as dark hints leave us to draw dire conclusions for ourselves. In *The Death of Robin Hood* the prose, which is very stylised at first, becomes more and more relaxed as we move towards modern times, though Vansittart continues to use words with scrupulous care for their effect. In his novels there is humour too, but usually the laughter is uneasy, in situations that are becoming uncomfortable. Quite a prolific novelist, Vansittart has kept a voice that is distinctively his own.

—Christopher Smith

VIDAL, Gore (Eugene Luther Vidal, Jr.). American. Born in West Point, New York, 3 October 1925. Educated at Los Alamos School, New Mexico, 1939–40; Phillips Exeter Academy, New Hampshire, 1940–43. Served in the United States Army, 1943–46: Warrant Officer. Editor, E.P. Dutton, publishers, New York, 1946. Lived in Antigua, Guatemala, 1947–49, and Italy, 1967–76. Member, Advisory Board, *Partisan Review*, New Brunswick, New Jersey, 1960–71; Democratic-Liberal candidate for Congress, New York, 1960; member, President's Advisory Committee on the Arts, 1961–63; Co-Chairman, New Party, 1968–71. Recipient: Mystery Writers of America award, for television play, 1954; National Book Critics Circle award, for criticism, 1983. Address: Ravello, Salerno, Italy; or c/o Random House Inc., 201 East 50th Street, New York, New York 10022, U.S.A.

PUBLICATIONS

Novels

Williwaw. New York, Dutton, 1946; London, Panther, 1965.

In a Yellow Wood.   New York, Dutton, 1947; London, New English Library, 1967.
The City and the Pillar.   New York, Dutton, 1948; London, Lehmann, 1949; revised edition, Dutton, and London, Heinemann, 1965.
The Season of Comfort.   New York, Dutton, 1949.
Dark Green, Bright Red.   New York, Dutton, and London, Lehmann, 1950.
A Search for the King: A Twelfth Century Legend.   New York, Dutton, 1950; London, New English Library, 1967.
The Judgment of Paris.   New York, Dutton, 1952; London, Heinemann, 1953; revised edition, Boston, Little Brown, 1965; Heinemann, 1966.
Messiah.   New York, Dutton, 1954; London, Heinemann, 1955; revised edition, Boston, Little Brown, 1965; Heinemann 1968.
Three: Williwaw, A Thirsty Evil, Julian the Apostate.   New York, New American Library, 1962.
Julian.   Boston, Little Brown, and London, Heinemann, 1964.
Washington, D.C.   Boston, Little Brown, and London, Heinemann, 1967.
Myra Breckinridge.   Boston, Little Brown, and London, Blond, 1968.
Two Sisters: A Memoir in the Form of a Novel.   Boston, Little Brown, and London, Heinemann, 1970.
Burr.   New York, Random House, 1973; London, Heinemann, 1974.
Myron.   New York, Random House, 1974; London, Heinemann, 1975.
1876.   New York, Random House, and London, Heinemann, 1976.
Kalki.   New York, Random House, and London, Heinemann, 1978.
Creation.   New York, Random House, and London, Heinemann, 1981.
Duluth.   New York, Random House, and London, Heinemann, 1983.
Lincoln.   New York, Random House, and London, Heinemann, 1984.

Novels as Edgar Box

Death in the Fifth Position.   New York, Dutton, 1952; London, Heinemann, 1954.
Death Before Bedtime.   New York, Dutton, 1953; London, Heinemann, 1954.
Death Likes It Hot.   New York, Dutton, 1954; London, Heinemann, 1955.

Short Stories

A Thirsty Evil: Seven Short Stories.   New York, Zero Press, 1956; London, Heinemann, 1958.

Plays

Visit to a Small Planet (televised, 1955).   Included in *Visit to a Small Planet and Other Television Plays*, 1956; revised version (produced New York, 1957; London, 1960), Boston, Little Brown, 1957; in *Three Plays*, 1962.
Honor (televised, 1956).   Published in *Television Plays for Writers: Eight Television Plays*, edited by A.S. Burack, Boston, The Writer, 1957; revised version, as *On the March to the Sea: A Southron Comedy* (produced Bonn, Germany, 1961), in *Three Plays*, 1962.

Visit to a Small Planet and Other Television Plays (includes *Barn Burning, Dark Possession, The Death of Billy the Kid, A Sense of Justice, Smoke, Summer Pavilion, The Turn of the Screw*).   Boston, Little Brown, 1956.
The Best Man: A Play about Politics (produced New York, 1960).   Boston, Little Brown, 1960; in *Three Plays*, 1962.
Three Plays (includes *Visit to a Small Planet, The Best Man, On the March to the Sea*).   London, Heinemann, 1962.
Romulus: A New Comedy, adaptation of a play by Friedrich Dürrenmatt (produced New York, 1962).   New York, Dramatists Play Service, 1962.
Weekend (produced New York, 1968).   New York, Dramatists Play Service, 1968.
An Evening with Richard Nixon and . . . (produced New York, 1972).   New York, Random House, 1972.

Screenplays: *The Catered Affair*, 1956; *I Accuse*, 1958; *The Scapegoat*, with Robert Hamer, 1959; *Suddenly Last Summer*, with Tennessee Williams, 1960; *The Best Man*, 1964; *Is Paris Burning?*, with Francis Ford Coppola, 1966; *Last of the Mobile Hot-Shots*, 1970.

Television Plays: *Barn Burning*, from the story by Faulkner, 1954; *Dark Possession*, 1954; *Smoke*, from the story by Faulkner, 1954; *Visit to a Small Planet*, 1955; *The Death of Billy the Kid*, 1955; *A Sense of Justice*, 1955; *Summer Pavilion*, 1955; *The Turn of the Screw*, from the story by Henry James, 1955; *Honor*, 1956; *The Indestructible Mr. Gore*, 1960.

Other

Rocking the Boat (essays).   Boston, Little Brown, 1962; London, Heinemann, 1963.
Sex, Death, and Money (essays).   New York, Bantam, 1968.
Reflections upon a Sinking Ship (essays).   Boston, Little Brown, and London, Heinemann, 1969.
Homage to Daniel Shays: Collected Essays 1952–1972.   New York, Random House, 1972; as *Collected Essays 1952–1972*, London, Heinemann, 1974.
Matters of Fact and of Fiction: Essays 1973–1976.   New York, Random House, and London, Heinemann, 1977.
Sex Is Politics and Vice Versa.   Los Angeles, Sylvester and Orphanos, 1979.
Views from a Window: Conversations with Gore Vidal, with Robert J. Stanton.   Secaucus, New Jersey, Lyle Stuart, 1980.
The Second American Revolution and Other Essays 1976–1982.   New York, Random House, 1982; as *Pink Triangle and Yellow Star and Other Essays*, London, Heinemann, 1982.
Vidal in Venice.   New York, Summit, and London, Weidenfeld and Nicolson, 1985.

Editor, *Best Television Plays.*   New York, Ballantine, 1956.

*

Bibliography: *Gore Vidal: A Primary and Secondary Bibliography* by Robert J. Stanton, Boston, Hall, and London, Prior, 1978.

Manuscript Collection: University of Wisconsin, Madison.

Critical Studies: *Gore Vidal* by Ray Lewis White, New York, Twayne, 1968; *The Apostate Angel: A Critical Study of Gore*

Vidal by Bernard F. Dick, New York, Random House, 1974; *Gore Vidal* by Robert F. Kiernan, New York, Ungar, 1982.

*   *   *

Although a prolific author with recognizable stances, Gore Vidal is among the most versatile of contemporary American writers. In scholarly novels about ancient-world potentates, in doomsday fictions, in a playfully pornographic diptych of novels, in an American politics trilogy, and in a pseudonymous series of detective stories, he has played a dazzling variety of auctorial roles. No American writer of comparable stature has proven less predictable in his choice of subjects.

Vidal's first novel was *Williwaw*, set on an army transport vessel plying a course among the Aleutian Islands during World War II. In an obvious imitation of the terse, Hemingway style, Vidal tells a story of seven self-absorbed men whose enforced closeness results finally in a homicide half-accidental, half-murder, about which no one really cares. The novel is remarkable for its proficiency if one considers that Vidal was 19 years old when he wrote it. Of more lasting interest among the early novels, however, is *The City and the Pillar*, in which Vidal employs the Hemingway manner to tell the story of a young man's gradual discovery he is homosexual. Because the protagonist is stereotypically all-American, the novel was a *succès de scandale* in its day. Its obvious distinction now is in having charted the young man's discovery without resort to sentiment or sermon.

The Hemingway style that served Vidal well in *The City and the Pillar* served him less well in *In a Yellow Wood*, the story of an unimaginative clerk who is afforded a glimpse of the Manhattan demimonde, and in *Dark Green, Bright Red*, a novel of revolution and Weltschmerz in the tropics. With equally limited success, Vidal abandoned the Hemingway manner in *The Season of Comfort* to write an archly overripe tale of incest and generational conflicts in a genteel Southern family. More successful than these fumbled experiments in tone is *A Search for the King*, the first of Vidal's historical novels. Set in the 12th century and recounting the search for Richard Coeur de Lion by the troubadour Blondel De Néel, *A Search for the King* is noteworthy among early Vidal fictions for its lucid characterizations, witty contrivances, and general charm. Its experiments bore fruit in two subsequent novels of equally liberated technique: *The Judgment of Paris*, a camp updating of a Greek myth, and *Messiah*, a savagely apocalyptic novel about merchandizing a savior.

Vidal's first major novel is *Julian*, which purports to be the Emperor Julian's autobiographical memoir and private journal, as intemperately annotated 17 years after the emperor's death by the philosophers Priscus of Athens and Libanius of Antioch. In scenes complexly imagined and impressively researched, Vidal recreates Julian's path from Christianity to Mithraism and from philosophy to military science. The novel is rewarding for its rich historicity, but also for the interplay of Julian's elevated discourse with the witty phrase-making of Priscus and the pedantry of Libanius. Its loose, self-indulgent mode of narration proves hospitable to Vidal's sudden flashes of wit and his serendipitous interest in ideas. Indeed, its ventriloquistic mode of narration has proved the formula of Vidal's most accomplished fiction.

If *Julian* earned Vidal the reputation of a serious novelist, an atemporal trilogy of novels about public life in America confirmed the reputation. *Washington, D.C.*, the first novel of this sequence, is a wry comedy of political manners that focuses on two Washington families, one headed by a newspaper magnate, the other by a senator. As national events

from Pearl Harbor to Korea stage themselves in the background, the characters indulge a common taste for histrionics, and through a careful interweaving of the characters with affairs of state, Vidal suggests that an overwrought national life takes its keynote from such personal theatrics. Hollywood melodrama, he implies, *is* the national style. Even more sardonic in tone is the third novel in the sequence, *1876*, in which an old man named Charlie Schuyler returns from Europe to New York for the first time since 1837 and travels about the country in the service of a newspaper. Everywhere he sees violence and mendacity lurking behind the patriotic scrim of the nation's centenary—particularly in the scandals of the Grant Administration and the bitterly contested Hayes-Tilden presidential election.

The centerpiece of the trilogy and one of Vidal's best novels is *Burr*, an account of Aaron Burr's last days as written by the young Charlie Schuyler, whom Vidal imagines Burr employing and befriending. Schuyler's interest in Burr's life encourages the older man to give him his written account of the early days of the republic–a compelling, gossipy account in which the Founding Fathers are little more than despoilers of infant America. The alternation of Burr's own narrative with Schuyler's worshipful memoir results in a composite portrait of Burr as both an unregenerate adventurer and an elegant arbiter of political style. It also shows Vidal at his best: iconoclastic, anecdotal, intellectually and stylistically agile.

In a duo of confections entitled *Myra Breckinridge* and *Myron* Vidal indulges freely the taste for camp extravagance evident in his work as early as *The Season of Comfort*. *Myra Breckinridge* takes the form of a journal that the eponymous Myra begins when she arrives in Hollywood after a sex-change operation. Firm in her belief that film is the only art and militant in her devotion to Hollywood's Golden Age, she is no less imperious in her determination to realign the sexes—a determination rooted in her former life as Myron. The results are gaudily offensive, climaxing in her rape of a chauvinistic young man and ending (to her chagrin) in her accidental reversion into Myron. *Myron* picks up the story five years later when Myron falls into his TV set and discovers himself on a Hollywood set in 1948. As the novel progresses, Myra and Myron alternately commandeer the Breckinridge psyche, Myra bent on saving Hollywood from television, Myron on defeating Myra's revisionist imperative. Although not to everyone's taste, the books are enormously rich—a comedic feast of styles and sexualities, invention and invective. Their charm is considerable.

Vidal's greatest success in recent years has been in the historical mode. In *Creation* his central character and narrator is a fictional diplomat named Cyrus Spitama (a grandson of Zoroaster), who cuts a broad swath through the Persian-Greek wars and recounts fascinating meetings with the Buddha, Master Li, Confucius, and a host of kindred figures. Revisionist speculations and tantalizing "what ifs" energize what amounts to a Cook's Tour of the fifth century. If *Lincoln* overshadows *Creation*, it overshadows very nearly everything else in Vidal's oeuvre. A compelling, thoughtful, and well-researched portrait of America's 16th president, it renders his tragic Civil War years through candid viewpoints of his family, his political rivals, and even his future assassins. The result is a rare fusion of monumentality and intimacy, quite distinct from the idealized portraits created by romantic nationalism.

Although the historical novel seems increasingly Vidal's métier, he continues to write in a variety of modes. *Kalki* is a mordant doomsday novel, narrated with odd restraint by a bisexual aviatrix, the personal pilot of a Vietnam veteran who exterminates the human race in a belief that he is the last avatar of Vishnu. Because of its emotional coolness, the story fails to engage us except in scattered passages, as does the story in *Duluth*, a broad parody of law-and-order thinking in middle America. More interesting than these novels is the undervalued *Two Sisters*, a Chinese box of narrations in which each narrative replicates a single story-line encapsulated in a screenplay at the heart of the novel.

The greatness of Vidal's fiction lies not only with its extraordinary range but with its small-scale effects: witty, autobiographical indiscretions; aphoristic nuggets, firm and toothsome; a fine interplay of the demotic and the mannered. Indeed, he must be regarded as one of the most important stylists of contemporary American prose. His ear for cadence and his touch with syntax are sure, and few can equal his ability to layer a sentence with wit and to temper it with intelligence.

—Robert F. Kiernan

VONNEGUT, Kurt, Jr. American. Born in Indianapolis, Indiana, 11 November 1922. Educated at Cornell University, Ithaca, New York, 1940–42; Carnegie Institute, Pittsburgh, 1943; University of Chicago, 1945–47. Served in the United States Army Infantry, 1942–45: Purple Heart. Married 1) Jane Marie Cox in 1945 (divorced 1979), one son and two daughters, and three adopted sons; 2) Jill Krementz in 1979. Police reporter, Chicago City News Bureau, 1946; worked in public relations for the General Electric Company, Schenectady, New York, 1947–50. Since 1950, free-lance writer. After 1965, teacher, Hopefield School, Sandwich, Massachusetts. Visiting Lecturer, Writers Workshop, University of Iowa, Iowa City, 1965–67, and Harvard University, Cambridge, Massachusetts, 1970–71; Visiting Professor, City University of New York, 1973–74. Recipient: Guggenheim fellowship, 1967; American Academy grant, 1970. M.A.: University of Chicago, 1971; Litt. D.: Hobart and William Smith Colleges, Geneva, New York, 1974. Member, American Academy, 1973. Lives in New York City. Address: c/o Donald C. Farber, Tanner Gilbert Propp and Sterner, 99 Park Avenue, 25th Floor, New York, New York 10016, U.S.A.

PUBLICATIONS

Novels

Player Piano. New York, Scribner, 1952; London, Macmillan, 1953; as *Utopia 14*, New York, Bantam, 1954.
The Sirens of Titan. New York, Dell, 1959; London, Gollancz, 1962.
Mother Night. New York, Fawcett, 1962; London, Cape, 1968.
Cat's Cradle. New York, Holt Rinehart, and London, Gollancz, 1963.
God Bless You, Mr. Rosewater; or, Pearls Before Swine. New York, Holt Rinehart, and London, Cape, 1965.
Slaughterhouse-Five; or, The Children's Crusade. New York, Delacorte Press, 1969; London, Cape, 1970.
Breakfast of Champions; or, Goodbye, Blue Monday. New York, Delacorte Press, and London, Cape, 1973.
Slapstick; or, Lonesome No More! New York, Delacorte Press, and London, Cape, 1973.
Jailbird. New York, Delacorte Press, and London, Cape, 1979.

Deadeye Dick. New York, Delacorte Press, 1982; London, Cape, 1983.
Galápagos. New York, Delacorte Press, and London, Cape, 1985.

Short Stories

Canary in a Cat House. New York, Fawcett, 1961.
Welcome to the Monkey House: A Collection of Short Works. New York, Delacorte Press, 1968; London, Cape, 1969.

Uncollected Short Stories

"2BRO2B," in *If* (New York), January 1962.
"The Big Space Fuck," in *Again, Dangerous Visions*, edited by Harlan Ellison. New York, Doubleday, 1972; London, Millington, 1976.

Plays

Happy Birthday, Wanda June (as *Penelope*, produced Cape Cod, Massachusetts, 1960; revised version, as *Happy Birthday, Wanda June*, produced New York, 1970; London, 1977). New York, Delacorte Press, 1970; London, Cape, 1973.
The Very First Christmas Morning, in *Better Homes and Gardens* (Des Moines, Iowa), December 1962.
Between Time and Timbuktu; or, Prometheus-5: A Space Fantasy (televised, 1972; produced New York, 1976). New York, Delacorte Press, 1972; London, Panther, 1975.
Fortitude, in *Wampeters, Foma, and Granfalloons*, 1974.
Timesteps (produced Edinburgh, 1979).
God Bless You, Mr. Rosewater, adaptation of his own novel (produced New York, 1979).

Television Play: *Between Time and Timbuktu*, 1972.

Other

Wampeters, Foma, and Granfalloons: Opinions. New York, Delacorte Press, 1974; London Cape, 1975.
Sun Moon Star. New York, Harper, and London, Hutchinson, 1980.
Palm Sunday: An Autobiographical Collage. New York, Delacorte Press, and London, Cape, 1981.
Fates Worse Than Death. Nottingham, Spokesman, 1982(?).

*

Bibliography: *Kurt Vonnegut, Jr.: A Descriptive Bibliography and Annotated Secondary Checklist* by Asa B. Pieratt, Jr., and Jerome Klinkowitz, Hamden, Connecticut, Shoe String Press, 1974.

Critical Studies: *Kurt Vonnegut, Jr.*, by Peter J. Reed, New York, Warner, 1972; *Kurt Vonnegut: Fantasist of Fire and Ice* by David H. Goldsmith, Bowling Green, Ohio, Popular Press, 1972; *The Vonnegut Statement* edited by Jerome Klinkowitz and John Somer, New York, Delacorte Press, 1973, London, Panther, 1975; *Vonnegut in America: An Introduction to the Life and Work of Kurt Vonnegut* edited by Klinkowitz and Donald L. Lawler, New York, Delacorte Press, 1977, and *Kurt Vonnegut* by Klinkowitz, London, Methuen, 1982; *Kurt Vonnegut, Jr.* by Stanley Schatt, Boston, Twayne, 1976; *Kurt Vonnegut* by James Lundquist, New York, Ungar, 1977; *Vonnegut: A Preface to His Novels* by Richard Giannone, Port Washington, New York, Kennikat Press, 1977; *Kurt Vonnegut: The*

Gospel from Outer Space by Clark Mayo, San Bernardino, California, Borgo Press, 1977; *Vonnegut's Duty-Dance with Death: Theme and Structure in Slaughterhouse-Five* by Monica Loeb, Umeå, Sweden, Umeå Studies in the Humanities, 1979.

*   *   *

During the 1960's Kurt Vonnegut emerged as one of the most influential and provocative writers of fiction in America. His writing, indeed, constitutes an unremitting protest against certain horrors of our century—the unending sequence of disastrous wars, the plunging decline in the livability of the environment, and the dehumanization of the individual in a society dominated by science and technology. Such protest is by no means new or unique in literature. The peculiar force of Vonnegut's voice among so many others may be traced to its complete contemporaneity. Fantasy (usually of the science variety), black humor, a keen sense of the absurd are the ingredients of his novels and stories.

Vonnegut has quite accurately described himself as "a total pessimist." And indeed his novels and most of his other writing offer little except wry laughter to counteract despair. This is certainly true of his first novel, *Player Piano*. The time of the novel is the not-too-distant future and the place is a one-industry city, Ilium, New York, which serves as the setting for much of Vonnegut's fiction and which resembles Schenectady, New York, where Vonnegut worked in public relations. In the novel not only the local industry but industries throughout the nation have been completely mechanized. Machines supplant human workers because machines make fewer errors. All national policy is determined by huge computers located in Mammoth Cave. A small elite of scientists are in charge of all production. The masses, who are provided with all material necessities and comforts, including an impressive array of gadgetry, serve in either military or work battalions. Acutely aware of their dehumanization and worthlessness except as mere consumers of the huge output of the machines, the common people revolt under the leadership of a preacher and several renegade scientists. Though the revolt in Ilium, at least, is successful and many of the objectionable machines are destroyed, Vonnegut denies his readers any sense of satisfaction. He records that the rebels destroyed not only obnoxious machinery but also the useful and necessary technological devices such as sewage disposal plants. What is more, they soon begin to tinker with the unneeded machines with a view to making them operative again. In the face of such inveterate stupidity the leaders suicidally surrender to the government forces.

An obvious question arises: Why should Vonnegut or his readers concern themselves with the dehumanization of apparent morons? What, indeed, is there to be dehumanized? An answer is not readily forthcoming, but apparently Vonnegut considers that there is some value in attempting to save the human race from its own stupidity. In each novel there is at least one person who is aware of human folly, including his own, and thus is living proof that intellectual blindness is not universal. More frequently than not, moreover, these discerning individuals are reformers, as in *Player Piano*, who make self-sacrificing efforts to improve the lot of their fellow men. This is the case with *The Sirens of Titan*, which in plot is a rather conventional example of science fiction with an interplanetary setting. The reforming character in this book has been rendered immortal, omniscient, and virtually omnipotent by having been entrapped in a "chrono-synclastic-infundibulum." Thus endowed, he sets about uniting all nations of the world in the bonds of brotherhood by staging an abortive attack against the earth by Martians. The latter are earthlings

abducted to Mars and converted to automatons by the insertion in their skulls of radio antennae through which orders are transmitted from a central directorate. These unfortunates are thus subjected to a ruthless dehumanization and exploitation, but to a worthwhile end. The scheme is successful; the earth becomes united after the defeat of the Martian attack and the unity is cemented by the establishment of a new religion, the Church of God the Utterly Indifferent. This happy outcome is somewhat clouded, however, by the revelation that the entire history of humanity has been determined by the trivial needs of the inhabitants of the planet Tralfamadore in one of the more remote galaxies.

Cat's Cradle and *God Bless You, Mr. Rosewater* also focus upon the efforts of altruistic individuals to alleviate human misery. *Cat's Cradle* is notable for its presentation of an entirely new religion, Bokonism (named for its founder), much of the doctrine of which is written in Calypso verse. According to Bokonism, religion *should* be an opiate; its function is to deceive and, by deceiving, make people happy. It teaches that God directs human destinies and that mankind is sacred, and it promotes an ethic of love, which believers manifest by pressing the soles of their feet against those of fellow believers. Bokonism was founded and flourished on a Caribbean island oppressed by a Duvalier-type dictator. It flourished because it was outlawed, for, according to *Cat's Cradle*, at least, a religion functions most vigorously when opposed to the existing social order. There can be no doubt that Bokonism brings relief to the wretched islanders, the final horror of whose existence is that of being congealed, along with the rest of the world, by ice-nine, a discovery of an Ilium scientist. *God Bless You, Mr. Rosewater* recounts the efforts of an enormously wealthy philanthropist to alleviate human misery through the more or less random disbursement of the Rosewater Foundation's almost limitless funds. Like Bokonon, his purpose is to make existence more endurable for the masses. But he is less successful, for even with his millions he is able barely to scratch the surface of the world's wretchedness. He is taken advantage of by those whom he tries to help, and his friends and relatives consider him a lunatic. Yet he makes the effort and does achieve a degree of personal saintliness.

Two other novels, *Mother Night* and *Slaughterhouse-Five*, both of which focus upon World War II, contain no such reformers or philanthropists. In these the protagonists are never really in a position to be altruistic, even if they wish to be. In *Mother Night* Howard W. Campbell, Jr., serves schizophrenically as the Nazis' chief English-language radio propagandist at the same time that he is one of the allies' most effective spies. Years after the war he finds himself in an Israeli prison awaiting trial along with Adolf Eichmann. Here he commits suicide, even though a bizarre turn of events has ensured his acquittal. He has realized that one who has played his dual roles has betrayed beyond recovery his own humanity—a realization achieved by few Vonnegut characters in analogous situations.

Slaughterhouse-Five, perhaps Vonnegut's most powerful novel, presents two characters who can see beneath the surface to the tragic realities of human history but make no attempt to bring about change. These are the author himself, who is a frequent commentator, and the protagonist, Billy Pilgrim. The central event in the novel is the destruction of Dresden by bombs and fire storm—a catastrophe that Vonnegut himself witnessed as a prisoner of war. Billy Pilgrim's liberating insights are the outgrowth of his being freed from the prison of time and, as a result, seeing the past, present and future as one and coexistent. One consequent realization is that death is an illusion. Though his periods of release from time occur on earth, their significance is explained to him by the inhabitants of the distant planet Tralfamadore, to which he is transported on a Tralfamadorian spaceship. Though Billy finds no way to improve the tragically absurd condition of man, he does arrive at an understanding of it and a resultant deepening of compassion.

The novels after *Slaughterhouse-Five*—*Breakfast of Champions*, *Slapstick*, *Jailbird*, *Deadeye Dick*—continue to satirize human folly in its contemporary manifestations, and they still rely on fantasy, black humor, and the absurd as tools of satire, Yet their tone differs from that of the earlier fiction. The seriousness of theme and, above all, the compassion implicit in such books as *Cat's Cradle* and *Slaughterhouse-Five* are no longer noticeably present. *Slapstick*, indeed, would be appropriate as a title for any of the four. Fun and wit and laughs aplenty are not lacking, but thought is in short supply. The clown has shoved aside the thinker. But perhaps Vonnegut has concluded that is our only defense against the madness of our end-of-the-century world. In his most recent novel, *Galápagos*, however, Vonnegut achieves a subtle and effective irony. For an epigraph he quotes from Anne Frank's *Diary*: "In spite of everything, I still believe people are really good at heart." Though Vonnegut, or the narrator, declares that he agrees with this statement, the characters and events in the novel provide overwhelming evidence that most people are evil at heart. Human beings have used their "big brains"—evolution's prized gift—to destroy themselves and the world they live in. But when, by a fantastic series of events that only Vonnegut could dream up, the human species is reduced to ten individuals marooned on one of the Galápagos Islands, a reverse process of evolution sets in, the "big brains" disappear, and, after a million years, the human species has been transformed into a gentle, seal-like mammal which actually is "good at heart."

—Perry D. Westbrook

WAGONER, David (Russell). American. Born in Massillon, Ohio, 5 June 1926. Educated at Pennsylvania State University, University Park, B.A. 1947; Indiana University, Bloomington, M.A. in English 1949. Served in the United States Navy, 1944–46. Married 1) Patricia Parrott in 1961; 2) Robin Heather Seyfried in 1982. Instructor, DePauw University, Greencastle, Indiana, 1949–50, and Pennsylvania State University, 1950–54. Assistant Professor, 1954–57, Associate Professor, 1958–66, and since 1966, Professor of English, University of Washington, Seattle. Elliston Professor of Poetry, University of Cincinnati, 1968; Editor, Princeton University Press Contemporary Poetry Series, 1977–81. Since 1966, editor, *Poetry Northwest*, Seattle; since 1983, poetry editor, University of Missouri Press, Columbia. Recipient: Guggenheim fellowship, 1956; Ford fellowship, for drama, 1964; American Academy grant, 1967; Morton Dauwen Zabel Prize, 1967, Oscar Blumenthal Prize, 1974, Eunice Tietjens Memorial Prize, 1977, and English-Speaking Union Prize, 1980 (*Poetry*, Chicago); National Endowment for the Arts grant, 1969; Fels prize, 1975; Sherwood Anderson Award, 1980. Chancellor, Academy of American Poets, 1978. Address: 1918-144th SE, Mill Creek, Washington 98102, U.S.A.

PUBLICATIONS

Novels

The Man in the Middle. New York, Harcourt Brace, 1954; London, Gollancz, 1955.
Money, Money, Money. New York, Harcourt Brace, 1955.
Rock. New York, Viking Press, 1958.
The Escape Artist. New York, Farrar Straus, and London, Gollancz, 1965.
Baby, Come On Inside. New York, Farrar Straus, 1968.
Where Is My Wandering Boy Tonight? New York, Farrar Straus, 1970.
The Road to Many a Wonder. New York, Farrar Straus, 1974.
Tracker. Boston, Little Brown, 1975.
Whole Hog. Boston, Little Brown, 1976.
The Hanging Garden. Boston, Little Brown, 1980; London, Hale, 1982.

Uncollected Short Stories

"Afternoon on the Ground," in *Prairie Schooner* (Lincoln, Nebraska), Fall 1978.
"Wild Goose Chase," in *Georgia Review* (Athens), Fall 1978.
"Mr. Wallender's Romance," in *Hudson Review* (New York), Spring 1979.
"Cornet Solo," in *Boston Globe Magazine*, 20 May 1979.
"The Water Strider," in *Boston Globe Magazine*, 14 October 1979.
"Fly Boy," in *Ohio Review 25* (Athens), 1980.
"The Bird Watcher," in *Georgia Review* (Athens), Spring 1980.
"Snake Hunt," in *Western Humanities Review* (Salt Lake City), Winter 1980.
"Magic Night at the Reformatory," in *Shenandoah* (Lexington, Virginia), vol. 34, no. 4, 1981.
"The Sparrow," in *Epoch* (Ithaca, New York), Spring 1981.
"Mermaid," in *Western Humanities Review* (Salt Lake City), Summer 1981.

Plays

An Eye for an Eye for an Eye (produced Seattle, 1973).

Screenplay: *The Escape Artist*, 1981.

Verse

Dry Sun, Dry Wind. Bloomington, Indiana University Press, 1953.
A Place to Stand. Bloomington, Indiana University Press, 1958.
Poems. Portland, Oregon, Portland Art Museum, 1959.
The Nesting Ground. Bloomington, Indiana University Press, 1963.
Five Poets of the Pacific Northwest, with others, edited by Robin Skelton. Seattle, University of Washington Press, 1964.
Staying Alive. Bloomington, Indiana University Press, 1966.
New and Selected Poems. Bloomington, Indiana University Press, 1969.
Working Against Time. London, Rapp and Whiting, 1970.
Riverbed. Bloomington, Indiana University Press, 1972.
Sleeping in the Woods. Bloomington, Indiana University Press, 1974.
A Guide to Dungeness Spit. Port Townsend, Washington, Graywolf Press, 1975.
Travelling Light. Port Townsend, Washington, Graywolf Press, 1976.

Collected Poems 1956–1976. Bloomington, Indiana University Press, 1976.
Who Shall Be the Sun? Poems Based on the Lore, Legends, and Myths of Northwest Coast and Plateau Indians. Bloomington, Indiana University Press, 1978.
In Broken Country. Boston, Little Brown, 1979.
Landfall. Boston, Little Brown, 1981.
First Light. Boston, Little Brown, 1983.

Other

Editor, *Straw for the Fire: From the Notebooks of Theodore Roethke 1943–1963.* New York, Doubleday, 1972.

*

Manuscript Collections: Olin Library, Washington University, St. Louis; University of Washington, Seattle.

Critical Studies: "David Wagoner's Fiction: In the Mills of Satan" by William J. Schafer in *Critique* (Minneapolis), vol. 9, no. 1, 1965; "It Dawns on Us That We Must Come Apart," in *Alone with America* by Richard Howard, New York, Atheneum, 1969, London, Thames and Hudson, 1970, revised edition, Atheneum, 1980; "An Interview with David Wagoner," in *Crazy Horse 12* (Marshall, Minnesota), 1972; "A Conversation with David Wagoner," in *Yes* (Avoca, New York), vol. 4, no. 1, 1973; "On David Wagoner," in *Salmagundi* (Saratoga Springs, New York), Spring-Summer 1973, and "Pelting Dark Windows," in *Parnassus* (New York), Spring-Summer 1977, both by Sanford Pinsker.

David Wagoner comments:

It is almost impossible for me to comment coherently on my own fiction, except to say that I began writing poetry first and received early encouragement as a writer of fiction from Edward J. Nichols at Penn State and Peter Taylor at Indiana University, and later from Malcolm Cowley at Viking Press and Catharine Carver who was then at Harcourt Brace. I seem to have a penchant for what might be called serious farce, but whether farce can stand the serious strains I put on it, I must leave to others to say. I also recognize my tendency to write what I believe critics call "initiation" novels. I tend to dramatize or write in scenes rather than to be discursive. One clear theme would seem to be the would-be innocent protagonist *vs.* the corrupt city, perhaps a result of my having grown up between Chicago and Gary, Indiana, where the most sophisticated and effective forms of pollution were first perfected.

*   *   *

In his novels, David Wagoner has pursued the themes of innocence and corruption, of the connections between past, present and future, of the individual trapped in a violent society. The novels depict individuals corrupted by modern urban life, protagonists essentially innocent and helpless damaged by the pressures of family life and further maimed by society. Wagoner skilfully uses Dickensian comedy and drama to create a tragic myth of man stripped and abandoned by his parents and his fellows yet struggling to survive and to remain intact.

The Man in the Middle and *Money, Money, Money* describe helpless, childlike adults caught up in criminal machinations. *The Escape Artist* and *Where Is My Wandering Boy Tonight?* treat the same theme from the viewpoint of juvenile protagonists. Each novel involves criminals and corrupt politicians who pursue and persecute an innocent victim. There is a strong element of picaresque comedy in this drama of innocence adapting to a wicked world. The later novels also develop a complex sexual theme revolving around an Oedipal relationship—a child confronted and fascinated by a destructive mother figure. Each of the protagonists must overcome this infantile sexual bondage before he is free to live wholly, just as each must learn the depth of the world's wickedness before he can shed his infantile social innocence.

The Road to Many a Wonder continues Wagoner's comedy of 19th-century America (begun in *Where Is My Wandering Boy Tonight?*) and his parable of innocence and the Frontier. In it a gold-seeker, Isaac Bender, succeeds by the most improbable means, his questing innocence overcoming the money-corruption of the gold rush and the Hobbesian savagery of the raw West. The novel is marked by a comic sweetness and light that offsets the bleak portraiture of venal American character-types.

Tracker and *Whole Hog* extend Wagoner's story of the frontier and the wild west by focusing on the uncertainties of the pioneer spirit, the fragility of familial and social relations and the ultimate triumph of intelligent virtue over mindless evil. Both tales revolve around juvenile protagonists (Wagoner's type of innocence) who learn by painful experience to outwit a lawless adult world.

In *Rock* and *Baby, Come On Inside* Wagoner deals with the destructiveness of family life and the crippling effects of the past. Both stories concentrate on the conflict between leaving home and returning home: "You can't go home again" *vs.* "You *must* go home again." In each novel, the protagonist tries to recapture his past, to find a home place, but ends in confusion and further exile.

A recurrent pattern in Wagoner's novels is that of pursuit and flight, a nightmarish sense of implacable evil, and a recurrent scene is a metaphorical return to the womb, to primordial shelter. Charlie Bell in *The Man in the Middle* spends a night in a railway coin locker. Willy Grier is left in a garbage can in *Money, Money, Money.* Danny Masters in *The Escape Artist* hides out in a Goodwill Industries collection box and a US mailbox. The pattern of flight and hiding, a fragile individual pursued by a terrifying nemesis, occurs in a comic context—cynical wit and slapstick farce—for the dreamlike or mythic dimension of Wagoner's novels derives from their mixed tone. The stories encompass suspense, adventure, comedy, pathos, and a strong sense of the social and political life of midwestern cities.

In *The Hanging Garden* Wagoner returns to a detective-story format of homicidal insanity defeated by a man who is basically good but worn from personal and political struggle. Returning to nature (a holiday cottage), the protagonist is confronted with "natural evil" in the form of a sadistic killer. The tale becomes a description of survival of the intelligent, cultured man faced with the most primitive forces of the human psyche.

Wagoner's tragicomedies of violence achieve effects somewhat like François Truffaut's *Shoot the Piano Player.* The mixture of naivety, tough-guy dialogue, violence, thriller action, and insight into complex states of mind creates a fantasy world as an accurate analogue for contemporary urban life. Danny Masters, in *The Escape Artist,* muses on violence and trickery and how to escape them:

Danny felt his own life shut inside him, keeping as quiet as it could, shying away. Nobody should be able to break anybody open like a nut and clean out the insides, but some people did it, and he would never let them come close. That was why getting away was important, getting out, getting loose, because they had to make you sit still long enough so they could crack you open, otherwise it spoiled their aim. They were no good with moving targets, no good if you weren't where they thought you were. They knew a lot of tricks, and that was why you had to keep ahead of them, and then if you got a big enough lead, you could afford to let them know who you were, taunting them from a distance yet always ready to change shape to fool them.

Wagoner's novels reflect society's torments and traps and also explore the paths to freedom—self-understanding, imagination, and the uses of experience. While they detail corruption and destruction, they also reflect innocence and virtue. The possibilities in this world are tragic and comic, and the inevitable price of survival is loss of innocence.

—William J. Schafer

WAIN, John (Barrington). British. Born in Stoke-on-Trent, Staffordshire, 14 March 1925. Educated at the High School, Newcastle-under-Lyme, Staffordshire; St. John's College, Oxford, B.A. 1946, Fereday Fellow, 1946–49, M.A. 1950. Married 1) Marianne Urmston in 1947 (marriage dissolved, 1956); 2) Eirian James in 1960; three sons. Lecturer in English, University of Reading, Berkshire, 1947–55; Professor of Poetry, Oxford University, 1973–78. Churchill Visiting Professor, University of Bristol, 1967; Visiting Professor, Centre Universitaire Expérimentale, Vincennes, France, 1969. First Holder, Fellowship in Creative Arts, 1971–72, and since 1973, Supernumerary Fellow, Brasenose College, Oxford. Recipient: Maugham Award, 1958; Heinemann Award, 1975, and James Tait Black Memorial Prize, 1975, both for non-fiction; Whitbread Award, for fiction, 1982, and for children's book, 1984. Fellow, Royal Society of Literature, 1960 (resigned, 1961). C.B.E. (Commander, Order of the British Empire), 1984. Lives in Oxford. Address: c/o Macmillan and Company Ltd., 4 Little Essex Street, London WC2R 3LF, England.

PUBLICATIONS

Novels

Hurry on Down. London, Secker and Warburg, 1953; as *Born in Captivity*, New York, Knopf, 1954.
Living in the Present. London, Secker and Warburg, 1955; New York, Putnam, 1960.
The Contenders. London, Macmillan, and New York, St. Martin's Press, 1958.
A Travelling Woman. London, Macmillan, and New York, St. Martin's Press, 1959.
Strike the Father Dead. London, Macmillan, and New York, St. Martin's Press, 1962.
The Young Visitors. London, Macmillan, and New York, Viking Press, 1965.
The Smaller Sky. London, Macmillan, 1967.
A Winter in the Hills. London, Macmillan, and New York, Viking Press, 1970.
The Pardoner's Tale. London, Macmillan, 1978; New York, Viking Press, 1979.
Young Shoulders. London, Macmillan, 1982; as *The Free Zone Starts Here*, New York, Delacorte Press, 1984.

Short Stories

Nuncle and Other Stories. London, Macmillan, 1960; New York, St. Martin's Press, 1961.
Death of the Hind Legs and Other Stories. London, Macmillan, and New York, Viking Press, 1966.
The Life Guard. London, Macmillan, 1971; New York, Viking Press, 1972.
King Caliban and Other Stories. London, Macmillan, 1978.

Uncollected Short Stories

"The Snowman Maker," in *Winter's Tales 25*, edited by Caroline Hobhouse. London, Macmillan, 1979; New York, St. Martin's Press, 1980.
"Cargo," in *Encounter* (London), August-September 1980.
"The Tranquility Stone," in *Winter's Tales 28*, edited by A.D. Maclean. London, Macmillan, and New York, St. Martin's Press, 1982.
"Julia," in *American Scholar* (Washington, D.C.), Winter 1984–85.

Plays

Harry in the Night: An Optimistic Comedy (produced Stoke-on-Trent, 1975).

Radio Plays: *You Wouldn't Remember*, 1978; *A Winter in the Hills*, from his own novel, 1981; *Frank*, 1982.

Television Play: *Young Shoulders*, with Robert Smith, from the novel by Wain, 1984.

Verse

Mixed Feelings: Nineteen Poems. Reading, Berkshire, Reading University School of Art, 1951.
A Word Carved on a Sill. London, Routledge, and New York, St. Martin's Press, 1956.
A Song about Major Eatherly. Iowa City, Qara Press, 1961.
Weep Before God. London, Macmillan, and New York, St. Martin's Press, 1961.
Wildtrack: A Poem. London, Macmillan, and New York, Viking Press, 1965.
Letters to Five Artists. London, Macmillan, 1969; New York, Viking Press, 1970.
The Shape of Feng. London, Covent Garden Press, 1972.
Feng. London, Macmillan, and New York, Viking Press, 1975.
Poems for the Zodiac (12 booklets), illustrated by Brenda Stones. London, Pisces Press, 1980.
Thinking about Mr. Person. Beckenham, Kent, Chimaera Press, 1980.
Poems 1949–1979. London, Macmillan, 1981.
Twofold. Frome, Somerset, Bran's Head, 1981.

Other

Preliminary Essays. London, Macmillan, and New York, St. Martin's Press, 1957.
Gerard Manley Hopkins: An Idiom of Desperation. London, Oxford University Press, 1959.
Sprightly Running: Part of an Autobiography. London, Macmillan, 1962; New York, St. Martin's Press, 1963.
Essays on Literature and Ideas. London, Macmillan, and New York, St. Martin's Press, 1963.

The Living World of Shakespeare: A Playgoer's Guide. London, Macmillan, and New York, St. Martin's Press, 1964; revised edition, 1979.

Arnold Bennett. New York, Columbia University Press, 1967.

A House for the Truth: Critical Essays. London, Macmillan, 1972; New York, Viking Press, 1973.

Samuel Johnson. London, Macmillan, 1974; New York, Viking Press, 1975; revised edition, Macmillan, 1980.

A John Wain Selection, edited by Geoffrey Halson. London, Longman, 1977.

Professing Poetry. London, Macmillan, 1977; New York, Viking Press, 1978.

Lizzie's Floating Shop (for children). London, Bodley Head, 1981.

Samuel Johnson 1709–84, with K.K. Yung. London, Herbert Press, 1984.

Editor, *Contemporary Reviews of Romantic Poetry.* London, Harrap, and New York, Barnes and Noble, 1953.

Editor, *Interpretations: Essays on Twelve English Poems.* London, Routledge, 1955; New York, Hillary House, 1957.

Editor, *International Literary Annual.* London, Calder, and New York, Criterion, 2 vols., 1959–60.

Editor, *Fanny Burney's Diary.* London, Folio Society, 1960.

Editor, *Anthology of Modern Poetry.* London, Hutchinson, 1963.

Editor, *Pope.* New York, Dell, 1963.

Editor, *Selected Shorter Poems of Thomas Hardy.* London, Macmillan, and New York, St. Martin's Press, 1966; revised edition, 1975.

Editor, *The Dynasts,* by Thomas Hardy. London, Macmillan, and New York, St. Martin's Press, 1966.

Editor, *Selected Shorter Stories of Thomas Hardy.* London, Macmillan, and New York, St. Martin's Press, 1966.

Editor, *Shakespeare: Macbeth: A Casebook.* London, Macmillan, 1968.

Editor, *Shakespeare: Othello: A Casebook.* London, Macmillan, 1971.

Editor, *Johnson as Critic.* London, Routledge, 1973.

Editor, *Lives of the English Poets: A Selection,* by Samuel Johnson. London, Dent, and New York, Dutton, 1975.

Editor, *Johnson on Johnson: A Selection of the Personal and Autobiographical Writings of Samuel Johnson.* London, Dent, and New York, Dutton, 1976.

Editor, *The Poetry of Thomas Hardy: A New Selection.* London, Macmillan, 1977.

Editor, *An Edmund Wilson Celebration.* Oxford, Phaidon Press, 1978; as *Edmund Wilson: The Man and His Work,* New York, New York University Press, 1978.

Editor, *Personal Choice: A Poetry Anthology.* Newton Abbot, Devon, David and Charles, 1978.

Editor, *Anthology of Contemporary Poetry: Post-War to the Present.* London, Hutchinson, 1979.

Editor, *Everyman's Book of English Verse.* London, Dent, 1981.

Editor, *The Private Memoirs and Confessions of a Justified Sinner,* by James Hogg. London, Penguin, 1983.

Translator, *The Seafarer.* Warwick, Greville Press, 1980.

*

Bibliography: *John Braine and John Wain: A Reference Guide* by Dale Salwak, Boston, Hall, 1980.

Manuscript Collection: Edinburgh University Library.

Critical Studies: "John Wain et le Magie de l'Individu" by Françoise Barrière, in *Le Monde* (Paris), 8 August 1970; "John Wain: Révolte et Neutralité" by Pierre Yvard, in *Études Anglaises 23* (Paris), October-December 1970; "The New Puritanism, The New Academism, The New . . ." by Wain, in *A House for the Truth,* 1972.

*   *   *

In the middle 1950's John Wain first became widely known as a humorist and inconoclast. *Hurry on Down,* a mock-picaresque, became, in many journalistic accounts, a symbol for the irreverent rootlessness of the younger generaton, making fun of any established social designation. And Wain's novels frequently followed switches in conventional expectation, as in the epigraph quoted from Trollope at the beginning of *The Contenders:* "Success is the necessary misfortune of human life, but it is only to the very unfortunate that it comes early." Yet, beneath the irreverence and the prose that often reduced an emotion or a high-flown idea to the ordinary or the mechanical, images like "his heart lurched over and over in his breast like a cricket ball lobbed along a dry, bumpy pitch," Wain's perspective was that of the man of orthodox common-sense, the defender of a basic human dignity against the absurd pretenses of the modern world. Even the figure of despair, the central character of *Living in the Present,* about to commit suicide, decides that he cannot do so unless he also rids the world of the most loathsome and amoral creature he knows. Characteristically and appropriately, he chooses a snide, class-conscious neo-Fascist.

In his early work, Wain's central moral equation of plain English commonsense with unpretentious virtue sometimes seemed slightly insular. In satirizing the follies of English class-consciousness (the stages of the journey in *Hurry on Down* are magnifications of various designations in the English class system), Wain often attached images of the Continent or of cosmopolitanism to the class-elaboration he was momentarily deriding. The central character of *The Contenders,* whose point of view Wain generally endorses, is the rumpled, unheroic, but basically sound and humane provincial who is contrasted to his boyhood friends who reach out for worldly success and lock themselves into inhumane and debilitating competition. Competition remains one of the principal evils in Wain's fictional world, as the 17-year-old voice in the fantasy *Young Shoulders,* reporting to his sister who has been killed in a school-excursion air-crash, imagines the non-competitive paradise he will create in his "World Free Zone." Although Wain still retains a frequent focus on the fabric of specific social reference, his point of view has become far less provincial. The Welsh bard, for example, in *A Winter in the Hills,* true to his regional past, is sympathetically connected with Bretons, Canadians, all who would preserve their local humanity in opposition to the contemporary corporate world. Wain has become less the defender of the specifically English and more seriously and deeply the critic of contemporary English society.

Much of Wain's early comedy was an exaggeration of the uncomfortable, the assaults of badly behaved children, the pains inflicted by sleeping on worn-out bedsprings, the gastronomic rumblings produced by bad food. Beneath this comedy is a sense of the difficulty of survival, of the effort and consciousness necessary to defend oneself in an intrusive and demanding world. The worst of the characters is always the bully, the worst of societies the totalitarian. The central character is often the victim of these intrusive forces, an element of Wain's fiction most visible in his sympathy for the gentle eccentric who seeks only to still the furies in his own brain by living in Paddington station and is, therefore, hounded to death by contemporary society. In much of his later fiction, however, Wain's central characters are less passive victims, become much more conscious of themselves and their relationships with others. The young jazz musician in *Strike the Father Dead*, living amidst the dingy night-life of London during the Second World War, is conscious of all the ambivalent stresses in his revolt from his rigid, academic father, and the reconciliation between the two, so socially different and so personally alike, is made both moving and convincing. The central character in *A Winter in the Hills* works his past and his narrow fantasies into a more active engagement with contemporary life by helping both independent bus owner/drivers and poets to survive a little longer in a hostile world. In both these novels, the central characters are full of personal and social guilt for having survived thus far through luck and narrow self-protection. In these novels the guilt is understood and surmounted, the central character connected with others and with contemporary experience, as is the narrator in *Young Shoulders* who can help his parents assuage their own grief and pain in helping others in the same position. At times, Wain's thoughtful fiction is limited by simplicities in perspective, as in the overwhelming sexual guilts and feelings of desertion in *A Travelling Woman* or *The Pardoner's Tale* or, more superficially, in the exterior and political simplicities of *The Young Visitors*. At his best, however, Wain's sense of human dignity becomes much wider: women change from rewards or "instruments" to people with pasts, convictions, and experiences; children change from abrasive nuisances to people who need understanding and protection; morality grows beyond the mechanics of survival.

Wain's fiction also demonstrates a consistent interest in structure and the novel as metaphor. Often the novel seems a scheme devised to answer a particular question: what would it be like to resolve rationally to commit suicide or live completely within Paddington station? what are the implications, for people and nations, of surviving the Second World War? how do people manage the plots and puerile ratiocinations in a world of constantly shifting sexual attraction? how do human beings, as in *Young Shoulders*, survive pain and loss? how does a writer, as in *The Pardoner's Tale*, create fiction that both transposes and reveals himself? Sometimes the material in the novel, always thoroughly detailed, seems to overwhelm the question, and the structure or the metaphor seems too ruthlessly to limit the novel. At other times, structure and content balance more effectively and depict comically the complexities of the moral and serious man in a difficult world that expands both historically and geographically. Wain's fiction always shows this struggle for shape, this use of the conscious and intelligent effort by a man of letters (Wain is also a distinguished poet and literary critic) to give form to his perceptions and observations.

—James Gindin

WAKEFIELD, Dan. American. Born in Indianapolis, Indiana, 21 May 1932. Educated at Shortridge High School, Indianapolis, graduated 1950; Indiana University, Bloomington, 1950–51; Columbia University, New York, 1951–55, B.A. (honors) in English 1955. News editor, *Princeton Packet*, New Jersey, 1955; research assistant to C. Wright Mills, Columbia University, 1955; staff writer, *The Nation*, New York, 1956–61; contributing editor, *Atlantic Monthly*, Boston,

1968–82. Since 1983, co-chairperson of religious education, King's Chapel, Boston. Taught at Bread Loaf Writers Conference, Middlebury, Vermont, 1966, 1968, 1970; Visiting Lecturer, University of Massachusetts, Boston, 1965–67, 1981, University of Illinois, Urbana, 1968, University of Iowa, Iowa City, 1972, and Emerson College, Boston, 1982–83. Creator and story consultant, *James at 15* series, NBC Television, 1977–78. Recipient: Bread Loaf Writers Conference De Voto Fellowship, 1957; Nieman Foundation fellowship, for journalism, Harvard University, 1963; Rockefeller grant, 1968; National Endowment for the Arts award, 1968; Golden Eagle Award, for screenplay, 1983. Address: 75 Mount Vernon Street, Boston, Massachusetts 02108, U.S.A.

PUBLICATIONS

Novels

Going All the Way. New York, Delacorte Press, 1970; London, Weidenfeld and Nicolson, 1971.
Starting Over. New York, Delacorte Press, 1973; London, Hart Davis MacGibbon, 1974.
Home Free. New York, Delacorte Press, and London, Hart Davis MacGibbon, 1977.
Under the Apple Tree. New York, Delacorte Press, 1982.
Selling Out. Boston, Little Brown, 1985.

Uncollected Short Stories

"Autumn Full of Apples," in *The Best American Short Stories 1966*, edited by Martha Foley and David Burnett. Boston, Houghton Mifflin, 1966.
"Full Moon in Sagittarius," in *Atlantic* (Boston), January 1973.

Plays

Television Films: *The Seduction of Miss Leona*, 1980; *The Innocents Abroad*, 1983.

Other

Island in the City: The World of Spanish Harlem. Boston, Houghton Mifflin, 1959.
Revolt in the South. New York, Grove Press, 1961.
Between the Lines: A Reporter's Personal Journey Through Public Events. New York, New American Library, 1965.
Supernation at Peace and War. Boston, Little Brown, 1968.
All Her Children: The Making of a Soap Opera. New York, Doubleday, 1976.

Editor, *The Addict: An Anthology.* New York, Fawcett, 1963.

*

Manuscript Collection: Mugar Memorial Library, Boston University.

Dan Wakefield comments:
I believe in the novel as story, entertainment, and communication—as if those elements could be separated! One of my college English professors defined the novel as "how it was with a group of people." I believe it is that and more. I want my novels to convey interior as well as social truth. I want them to enable readers to appreciate how other people felt,

to make connections among human beings in all their diversity and in their alikeness as well. I love it when readers recognize some aspect of themselves in one of my characters and thus feel "I am not the only one!" who experienced some particular type of pain or joy. I try to write the way my characters think, the way they would express themselves, and I fear this attempt to be "plain" and open is sometimes misconstrued as an inability to write in a more self-consciously "literary" style. So be it. My aim is to convey the perception of the people I write about. I write about people I love, and in so doing I wish to honor them and celebrate our common humanity.

*　　*　　*

Dan Wakefield had already established himself as a feature journalist a decade before writing his first novel, but the unique style of his journalistic writing would lay the groundwork for his fiction. *Island in the City: The World of Spanish Harlem, Revolt in the South, Between the Lines*, and *Supernation at Peace and War* were pioneering efforts in a field which became known as "The New Journalism." Sacrificing the distance and objectivity of conventional journalism, Wakefield found the best way to write about an issue was to immerse himself within it and then write about himself. Thus he lived inside the poverty of New York City's Spanish Harlem, experienced firsthand the civil rights movement in the American south, and travelled from coast to coast talking with common citizens about the state of their nation. Moreover, the New Journalism used the techniques of realistic fiction, including characterization, narrative development, imagery, and symbolism to tell its story—conventions which had recently been discarded by the innovative novelists who wished their fiction to practice no such structuring illusions. As a result, by 1970 Dan Wakefield was prepared to write a new American novel of manners, using the traditional form of fiction to express the new semiotics of culture he had experienced firsthand as a New Journalist.

A strong sense of how the signs of culture operate pervades Wakefield's fiction, and his novels provide an excellent cross-section of the development of American manners since World War II. *Going All the Way* shows two young men returning to their homes in Indianapolis after serving in the Korean War. Anxious for their own lives to begin, they face the obstacles of being fettered by their parents' obsolescent manners and by the confusions, sexual and otherwise, being wrought by their exuberant young manhood. The times are changing as well, and within this kaleidoscope of radically different values Sonny and Gunner attempt to sort out new trends in dress, music, and social conduct. That matters do not improve with age is shown in *Starting Over*, in which a recently divorced advertising executive refashions his life in a new city, with a new profession and friends. An entirely new system of manners takes over, with innovations such as the single-person's lonely Sunday and holidays providing difficult tests of adjustment. His protagonist's mind, however, proves to be a *tabula rasa* upon which any suggestion can be planted. Therefore, readers can find an index to the manners of the times (the late 1960's and early 1970's in America) simply by watching the hero's reactions. The novel closes with him drifting into another marriage, with everyone telling him how lucky he is, as he stares wistfully after a young woman on the beach.

In Wakefield's first two novels his characters are richly imprinted by their social environment. That the radically changing times may have exhausted themselves and become as blank as the tablets of his characters is suggested by Wakefield's third novel, *Home Free*. Change has its rhythms and dynamics, and in this case the author shows how he can employ periods of lull and regression just as effectively. The protagonist begins college but is swept away by the countercultural movement of the times. When this movement fizzles out to its entropic end, he is cast adrift on a sea of nothingness. His stumuli have been ethereal—often just the suggestive lyrics of popular music—and when faced with reality, he has little ability to respond. He crosses America, but in a parody of Jack Kerouac's *On the Road*, for instead of energy Wakefield's hero draws on ennui. He winds up at the extreme edge of America, on the beach outside Los Angeles, where he lives in a situation as blank as a movie screen:

> His life.
> He'd walked into it like walking up the aisle of a movie and melting into the screen and becoming part of the picture, the story, finding out what happened as you went along, knowing from the beginning how it would end but not when. Then he'd be standing on the stage feeling silly and strange with the screen dark and the houselights on. Bright. He'd be blinking, trying to find his way out. In the meantime this was his life.

Under the Apple Tree and *Selling Out* are much fuller works because Wakefield again builds his fiction from the materials of popular culture, rather than from their lack. The first, set in a small Illinois town during the years of World War II, traces the maturation of a young boy as his older brother goes off to fight and the home community responds with a semiotic riot of patriotic support. The novel's action is a study of reading habits, as the war's far-off action is translated to the "home front" by means of advertisements, promotional campaigns, and instructive attitudes. Their signal nature is perfectly matched to the boy's innocence, and as he grows up so do popular notions toward the conflict. His own understanding of sexuality and human relations parallels this cultural development as his own ability to read his brother's and future sister-in-law's emotions rises from the comic-book level to the sophisticated.

Selling Out shows Wakefield's semiotic method in high relief, because the novel constitutes a test of it. His central character is a short-story writer named Perry Moss, who experiments with a new medium (film writing) in a new environment (Hollywood). Wakefield is judicially precise in his contrast of the bi-coastal and intermedia realities, as Perry finds the jet ride from Boston to Los Angeles has taken him into an entirely different world. The contrasts are shown to good purpose, not simply for their own value but for what they contribute to an understanding of Perry's fatal attempt at change. Yet his true allegiances remain to the printed word and life in New England, and when he returns to them at the end it is with a heightened sense of appreciation which his west coast adventures have made so obvious.

Wakefield knows that man is the sign-making animal, and his appreciation of the semiosis by which human life is conducted makes him ably qualified to describe how life is lived in America today.

—Jerome Klinkowitz

WALKER, Alice (Malsenior). American. Born in Eatonton, Georgia, 9 February 1944. Educated at Spelman College, Atlanta, 1961–63; Sarah Lawrence College, Bronxville, New

York, B.A. 1965. Married Melvyn R. Leventhal in 1967 (divorced, 1976); one daughter. Voter registration and Head Start program worker, Mississippi, and with New York City Department of Welfare, in mid-1960's; teacher, Jackson State College, 1968–69, and Tougaloo College, 1970–71, both Mississippi; lecturer, Wellesley College, Cambridge, Massachusetts, 1972–73, and University of Massachusetts, Boston, 1972–73; Associate Professor of English, Yale University, New Haven, Connecticut, after 1977. Distinguished Writer, University of California, Berkeley, Spring 1982; Fannie Hurst Professor, Brandeis University, Waltham, Massachusetts, Fall 1982. Recipient: Bread Loaf Writers Conference scholarship, 1966; *American Scholar* prize, for essay, 1967; Merrill fellowship, 1967; MacDowell fellowship, 1967, 1977; Radcliffe Institute fellowship, 1971; Lillian Smith Award, for poetry, 1973; American Academy Rosenthal Award, 1974; National Endowment for the Arts grant, 1977; Guggenheim grant, 1978; American Book Award, 1983; Pulitzer Prize, 1983. Ph.D.: Russell Sage College, Troy, New York, 1972; D.H.L.: University of Massachusetts, Amherst, 1983. Lives in San Francisco. Agent: Wendy Weil, Julian Bach Literary Agency, 747 Third Avenue, New York, New York 10017, U.S.A.

PUBLICATIONS

Novels

The Third Life of Grange Copeland.   New York, Harcourt Brace, 1970; London, Women's Press, 1985.
Meridian.   New York, Harcourt Brace, and London, Deutsch, 1976.
The Color Purple.   New York, Harcourt Brace, 1982; London, Women's Press, 1983.

Short Stories

In Love and Trouble: Stories of Black Women.   New York, Harcourt Brace, 1973; London, Women's Press, 1984.
You Can't Keep a Good Woman Down.   New York, Harcourt Brace, 1981; London, Women's Press, 1982.

Verse

Once.   New York, Harcourt Brace, 1968.
Five Poems.   Detroit, Broadside Press, 1972.
Revolutionary Petunias and Other Poems.   New York, Harcourt Brace, 1973.
Good Night, Willie Lee, I'll See You in the Morning.   New York, Dial Press, 1979.
Horses Make a Landscape Look More Beautiful.   New York, Harcourt Brace, 1984; London, Women's Press, 1985.

Other

Langston Hughes, American Poet (biography for children). New York, Crowell, 1974.
In Search of Our Mothers' Gardens: Womanist Prose.   New York, Harcourt Brace, 1983; London, Women's Press, 1984.

Editor, *I Love Myself When I am Laughing . . . and Then Again When I am Looking Mean and Impressive: A Zora Neale Hurston Reader.*   Old Westbury, New York, Feminist Press, 1979.

*   *   *

Alice Walker has written three novels, *The Third Life of Grange Copeland*, *Meridian*, and *The Color Purple*. Her third in 1983 won the Pulitzer Prize and the American Book Award. In *The Third Life of Grange Copeland* Walker presents three generations (1920–60) in the life of a tenant farm family. Grange's first life is with his wife and son; his second, after he abandons them, is first with a mistress and then in the north; and his third is with his grand-daughter, Ruth, who belongs to him while his son, Brownfield, remains in prison for the killing of his wife. Grange shoots Brownfield upon his release, when the latter threatens to take Ruth away.

Walker recounts the life of Brownfield in detail. Brought up in misery, he leaves to go north when his mother kills herself, but he coincidentally meets his father's mistress and marries her school-teacher niece. After a few ecstatic months, his marriage resembles that of his parents—hard work, drinking, beating the wife, and abusing the children. Brownfield systematically humiliates his wife so that he can feel superior to someone, and he finally kills her. Though Grange is partly responsible for his son's warped life, Walker uses him as he grows older to articulate her basic belief that a person like Ruth must not merely survive but survive whole. Blacks must take responsibility for their own lives, she implies, because attributing one's suffering to white society makes that society into an all-powerful god.

The metaphysical complexities of *Meridian* and its structure preclude its popular success, but it may yet be viewed as the most significant of Walker's novels, because of its balancing the need for revolution with the sustaining of traditional black values and its balancing the value of self-sacrifice against its destructiveness.

In *Meridian*, Walker uses her so-called "crazy quilt" approach, rather than the linear chronology and the photographic realism of her first novel. Though living in the late 1970's, the characters re-live the 1960's as they recall their lives then. As she moves back and forth in time, Walker pieces together impressionistic fragments of people and places, and she uses symbol and metaphor richly.

Truman Held arrives in Chicokemo, Mississippi, seeking Meridian Hill, his old revolutionary friend from college days. She now lives as an ascetic, sleeping on the floor of a bare room. Meridian suffers from seizures followed by lingering paralysis, and she wears a man's cap to cover her bald head. The illness is mysterious, although she was beaten over the head with police nightsticks in arrests the decade before. Working mostly among the poor on health care, nutrition, and voter registration, she has demonstrated this afternoon with little Black children who wanted to buy tickets to a trailer where they could view the mummified body of a blonde white woman, shot by her husband because of adultery. In bizarre response to the protest, the guns of the World War II tank in the town square were leveled at Meridian, who walked bravely toward the tank. Later she collapsed and loyal Blacks carried her unconscious and stiffened body home, a routine to which they had grown accustomed.

Meridian left high school to bear a baby and soon gave the infant away (to the parents of the boy who fathered it) so she could claim a college scholarship. Her mother, whose strength and education Meridian admired, denounced her abandonment of the baby. In college, Meridian's radical friends include Truman; his white Jewish wife, Lynne; and her roommate, Anne-Marion, who criticized Meridian for her lack of commitment to the movement because she refused to say she could kill. Anne-Marion continues to send critical messages to Meridian, although she herself now lives a comfortable life and writes only landscape poetry.

Lynne is raped by a friend who uses her as scapegoat for all his rage against a physical impairment and against white oppression. After the attack, Lynne loses self-respect, and her marriage founders. She is exploited by Black men as an "easy" woman and insulted by their wives, who do not credit her sincere concern and love for Black people. Later the five-year-old daughter of Truman and Lynne is raped and murdered by an unknown assailant. In all their griefs, both Lynne and Truman take Meridian's stability and strength for granted, and she unwillingly assumes emotional responsibility for their sorrows. Her guilt, pity, and conscientiousness make her vulnerable not only to their demands but to all political demands to sacrifice herself without limit. Meridian recognizes that she is dying and struggles to survive. She refuses now to sympathize fully with Truman's discontent, and expects him to work with her and then to take her place. She attends a church where she is comforted by familiar black music (though the hymns now have political words) and she responds as a human being, not as a political rescuer, to the needs of these people and to the values that sustain them. In what seems a sign of wholeness and healing, her hair begins to grow. As she leaves Truman and her work, she does not renounce revolutionary change. She expects that Lynne will arrive, like Truman, and begin to work again in the long struggle that all must share. Even Anne-Marion may someday join them.

In *The Color Purple*, an epistolary novel, Celie, the central character, at 14 writes notes to God on the dehumanizing nature of her existence and the humiliations she has suffered. These include rape by her father and two pregnancies by him, deathbed curses by her mother, the supposed killing of her babies by her father, physical abuse by the man she has married, and emotional abuse by him as he deceives her into thinking her sister Nettie is dead. Nettie's letters from Africa (where she works for the missionary couple who have adopted Celie's babies) disappoint in their stilted and relatively impersonal expression. But Celie's letters demonstrate Walker's control of Black vernacular and reveal the novelist's warm humanity. So economical is Walker's phrasing that the letters completely resist paraphrasing.

The book soon shifts from its concern with such grim events and becomes a lively fable suggesting an alternative vision of possibilities for the Black individual. The book is set in many locales and becomes crowded with diverse characters and develops many challenging themes. Chief among these individuals is Shug Avery, Celie's husband's longtime mistress and a blues singer, who comes to live with them and fascinates Celie. She teaches Celie about sexual arousal and maintains that God is not a white male but a presence to be loved in oneself and who is present in all things beautiful—especially in the color purple.

Among Walker's chief preoccupations in the book is the development of bonds of understanding among women who support one another in their artistic aspirations. Shug Avery and Mary Agnes (Squeak) have their blues singing in common, although Shug has greater experience and confidence. Sofia, the wife of Harpo, Celie's stepson, has artistic skills that Celie encourages as they make quilts together, but Sofia also enjoys expressing herself in putting roofs on barns and in doing carpentry work. Celie's creativity achieves a practical manifestation when she designs and markets women's pants.

Another of Walker's themes that adds richness to this novel is Celie's search for her true identity. Her early suffering, her supportive associations with Shug, and her own abundant resources all contribute to her development. In her first letter she had marked out the words, "I am." Later she learns to say "to everything listening ... 'I'm here'." She gains confidence when she hears her husband say approvingly of Shug,

"She bound to live her life and be herself no matter what." Celie has also learned to be her essential self.

—Margaret B. McDowell

WALKER, Margaret (Abigail). American. Born in Birmingham, Alabama, 7 July 1915. Educated at Northwestern University, Evanston, Illinois, B.A. 1935; University of Iowa, Iowa City, M.A. 1940, Ph.D. 1965; Yale University, New Haven, Connecticut (Ford Fellow), 1954. Married Firnist James Alexander in 1943; two sons and two daughters. Has worked as social worker, reporter, and magazine editor; taught at Livingstone College, Salisbury, North Carolina, 1941–42, 1945–46, and West Virginia State College, Institute, 1942–43. Since 1949, Professor of English, and since 1968, Director of the Institute for the Study of the History, Life and Culture of Black Peoples, Jackson State College, Mississippi. Recipient: Yale Series of Younger Poets Award, 1942; Rosenwald fellowship, 1944; Houghton Mifflin Literary Fellowship, 1966; Fulbright fellowship, 1971; National Endowment for the Arts grant, 1972. D.Litt: Northwestern University, 1974; Rust College, Holly Springs, Mississippi, 1974; D.F.A.: Denison University, Granville, Ohio, 1974; D.H.L.: Morgan State University, Baltimore, 1976. Address: 2205 Guynes Street, Jackson, Mississippi 39213, U.S.A.

PUBLICATIONS

Novels

Come Down from Yonder Mountain. Toronto, Longman, 1962.
Jubilee. Boston, Houghton Mifflin, 1966.

Verse

For My People. New Haven, Connecticut, Yale University Press, 1942.
Ballad of the Free. Detroit, Broadside Press, 1966.
Prophets for a New Day. Detroit, Broadside Press, 1970.
October Journey. Detroit, Broadside Press, 1973.

Recording: *The Poetry of Margaret Walker*, Folkways, 1975.

Other

How I Wrote "Jubilee." Chicago, Third World Press, 1972.
A Poetic Equation: Conversations Between Margaret Walker and Nikki Giovanni. Washington, D.C., Howard University Press, 1974.
The Daemonic Genius of Richard Wright. Washington, D.C., Howard University Press, 1982.

*   *   *

Authenticating her facts by extensive research, Margaret Walker enlarged the experiences of her great-grandmother during and after slavery into the epic novel *Jubilee*. The heroine, Vyry, is two years old when she enters the story at the childbed death of her 29-year-old mother, who has borne 15 slave children in rural Georgia for her master, John Dutton.

The 58 chapters are divided into three sections subtitled "The Ante-Bellum Years," "The Civil War Years," and "Reconstruction and Reaction."

The first section, beginning in 1837, introduces ten major characters, half of whom are removed by tragedy before the middle of the novel. The cook, Aunt Sally, irritably singing "mad-mood" songs, is sold. John Dutton, "yelling and cursing in the night," is dispatched by gangrene; and his "nigra"-hating wife, Big Missy Salina, dies ignominiously of a stroke. Young West Pointer Johnny Dutton and his pacifist brother-in-law, Kevin MacDougall, exit heroically but pitifully as war casualties. Old Brother Zeke, the slave preacher who secretly works for the Underground Railroad, succumbs later while a Union Army spy. Three other characters embody vigorous criticism of slavery and war: Lillian, Vyry's gentle white sister, who goes insane after the death of her Kevin and an assault by one of Sheridan's "bummers"; Ed Grimes, the brutal overseer, who lives to exploit his betters; and Randall Ware, proud blacksmith and freeman from birth, whose love for his wife Vyry "just got caught in the times" during his war service.

Of sections II and III, the former, replete with historical and military details, closely reflects the author's research. It introduces Innis Brown, who slowly convinces Vyry to end her seven-year wait for her husband. The title of the Reconstruction section, "Forty Years in the Wilderness," suits the ruinous adventures of Vyry, Innis, and the children building homes in Alabama. Flooded out, exploited in sharecropping, profoundly stricken when burned out by the Ku Klux Klan, Vyry becomes almost pathologically averse to building again. But by innate acts of humanity and racial dignity in Greenville, she inspires whites to help build the family's final home. An amicable understanding ensues between Innis and Randall Ware, who pays a visit with ideas like W.E.B. Du Bois's, and with money to educate the children.

The author's Dedication could have addressed her novel "to all the members of my race [not just 'family'] with all my love." The ancestry of almost every Black reader contains its own Vyry, thus revered in Chapter 57:

She was only a living sign and mark of all the best that any human being could hope to become. In her obvious capacity for love, redemptive and forgiving love, she was alive and standing on the highest peaks of her time and human personality. Peasant and slave, unlettered and untutored, she was nevertheless the best true example of the motherhood of her race, an ever present assurance that nothing could destroy a people whose sons had come from her loins.

Vyry's actions, always credible, deserve that praise.

Jubilee is rich with history. Numerous details of slaves' medical and culinary arts, clothing, shelter, and marriages are given. Their legally enforced illiteracy, the planned destruction of their normal affections for one another, their physical oppressions (ranging from the Black Codes to savage plantation punishments and Confederate murders at Andersonville) are depicted. Over a dozen episodes and circumstances reveal the slaves' aggressive feelings: repressed hatreds, aid to abolitionists, revolts, and escapes after 1861 (including all 46 Dutton field slaves) to take up either guns or tools for the Union Army. Matters transcending their focus in the slavocracy come to the fore: political events, the birth of the Confederacy, the specie crisis, 1863 analyzed as a turning point in the war, the Freedmen's Bureau, and the maneuvered return of White Home Rule.

The author aims at a realistically balanced treatment. The "good whites" are represented by Lillian and Kevin, Doc, the Shackelfords, and nameless abolitionists—Lillian centralizing the tragedy of war and the psychopathy constantly threatening decent slave-holders. Vicious Grimes has no Black counterpart, and the slave-holders perform no noble deeds like Jim's bringing Johnny home to die. Regional balance is implicit in use of the New York draft riots and the indefensible destructiveness of Union soldiers after the end of the fighting.

Jubilee is history explicit in the prototypal experience of one slave woman, issuing contemporaneously in what Innis Brown saw as "a wisdom and a touching humility," and ultimately in what the author's speech in 1968 at the National Urban League Conference in New Orleans expresses as follows: "We are still a [Black] people of spirit and soul. We are still fighting in the midst of white American Racism for the overwhelming truth of the primacy of human personality and the spiritual destiny of all mankind."

—James A. Emanuel

WARNER, Rex (Ernest). British. Born in Birmingham, Warwickshire, 9 March 1905. Educated at St. George's School, Harpenden, Hertfordshire; Wadham College, Oxford (open classical scholar), B.A. (honours) in classics and English literature 1928. Served in the Home Guard, London, 1942–45. Married 1) Frances Chamier Grove in 1929, two sons and one daughter; 2) Barbara Lady Rothschild in 1949, one daughter; 3) remarried Frances Chamier Grove in 1966. Schoolmaster in Egypt and England, 1928–45; worked for the Control Commission in Berlin, 1945, 1947; Director, British Institute, Athens, 1945–47; Tallman Professor, Bowdoin College, Brunswick, Maine, 1962–63; Professor of English, University of Connecticut, Storrs, 1964–74. Recipient: James Tait Black Memorial Prize, 1961. D.Litt.: Rider College, Trenton, New Jersey, 1968. Honorary Fellow, Wadham College, 1973. Commander, Royal Order of the Phoenix, Greece, 1963. Address: Anchor House, St. Leonard's Lane, Wallingford, Oxfordshire, England.

PUBLICATIONS

Novels

The Wild Goose Chase. London, Boriswood, and New York, Knopf, 1937.
The Professor. London, Boriswood, 1938; New York, Knopf, 1939.
The Aerodrome. London, Lane, 1941; Philadelphia, Lippincott, 1946.
Why Was I Killed? A Dramatic Dialogue. London, Lane, 1943; as *Return of the Traveller,* Philadelphia, Lippincott, 1944.
Men of Stones: A Melodrama. London, Lane, 1949; Philadelphia, Lippincott, 1950.
Escapade: A Tale of Average. London, Lane, 1953.
The Young Caesar. London, Collins, and Boston, Little Brown, 1958.
Imperial Caesar. London, Collins, and Boston, Little Brown, 1960.
Pericles the Athenian. London, Collins, and Boston, Little Brown, 1963.

The Converts. London, Bodley Head, and Boston, Little Brown, 1967.

Plays

Screenplays (documentaries): *World with End*, 1953; *The Immortal Land*, 1958.

Verse

Poems. London, Boriswood, 1937; New York, Knopf, 1938; revised edition, as *Poems and Contradictions*, London, Lane, 1945.

Other

The Kite (for children). Oxford, Blackwell, 1936; revised edition, London, Hamish Hamilton, 1963.
English Public Schools. London, Collins, 1945.
The Cult of Power: Essays. London, Lane, 1946; Philadelphia, Lippincott, 1947.
John Milton. London, Parrish, 1949; New York, Chanticleer Press, 1950.
Views of Attica and Its Surroundings. London, Lehmann, 1950.
E.M. Forster. London, Longman, 1950.
Men and Gods. London, MacGibbon and Kee, 1950; New York, Farrar Straus, 1951.
Ashes to Ashes: A Post-Mortem on the 1950–51 Tests, with Lyle Blair. London, MacGibbon and Kee, 1951.
Greeks and Trojans. London, MacGibbon and Kee, 1951.
Eternal Greece, photographs by Martin Hurlimann. London, Thames and Hudson, and New York, Viking Press, 1953.
The Vengeance of the Gods. London, MacGibbon and Kee, 1954.
Athens. London, Thames and Hudson, and New York, Studio, 1956.
The Greek Philosophers. New York, New American Library, 1958.
Look at Birds (for children). London, Hamish Hamilton, 1962.
The Stories of the Greeks. New York, Farrar Straus, 1967.
Athens at War: Retold from the History of the Peloponnesian War of Thucydides. London, Bodley Head, 1970; New York, Dutton, 1971.
Men of Athens: The Story of Fifth Century Athens. London, Bodley Head, and New York, Viking Press, 1972.

Editor, with Laurie Lee and Christopher Hassall, *New Poems 1954.* London, Joseph, 1954.
Editor, *Look Up at the Skies! Poems and Prose*, by Gerard Manley Hopkins. London, Bodley Head, 1972.

Translator, *The Medea of Euripides.* London, Lane, 1944; New York, Chanticleer Press, 1949.
Translator, *Prometheus Bound*, by Aeschylus. London, Lane, 1947; New York, Chanticleer Press, 1949.
Translator, *The Persian Expedition*, by Xenophon. London, Penguin, 1949.
Translator, *Hippolytus*, by Euripides. London, Lane, 1949; New York, Chanticleer Press, 1950.
Translator, *Helen*, by Euripides. London, Lane, 1951.
Translator, *The Peloponnesian War*, by Thucydides. London, Penguin, 1954.
Translator, *The Fall of the Roman Republic: Marius, Sulla, Crassus, Pompey, Caesar, Cicero: Six Lives*, by Plutarch. London, Penguin, 1958; revised edition, 1972.

Translator, *Poems of George Seferis.* London, Bodley Head, 1960; Boston, Godine, 1979.
Translator, *War Commentaries of Caesar.* New York, New American Library, 1960.
Translator, *Confessions of St. Augustine.* New York, New American Library, 1963.
Translator, with Th. D. Frangopoulos, *On the Greek Style: Selected Essays in Poetry and Hellenism*, by George Seferis. Boston, Little Brown, 1966.
Translator, *A History of My Times*, by Xenophon. London, Penguin, 1966.
Translator, *Moral Essays*, by Plutarch. London, Penguin, 1971.

*

Manuscript Collection: University of Connecticut, Storrs.

Critical Studies: *Rex Warner, Writer* by A.L. McLeod, Sydney, Wentworth Press, 1960, and *The Achievement of Rex Warner* (includes bibliography) edited by McLeod, Wentworth Press, 1965.

Rex Warner comments:

Most of my novels have been in some sense "political"; they have attempted to deal with contemporary problems of power, responsibility, and motivation. But they have not been "realistic." In the early novels, there is always an element of fantasy, but the later historical novels have still been dealing with the same general subjects.

*   *   *

By date of birth (1905), by education, and by accomplishment Rex Warner belongs to that unusual British generation which includes Auden, Isherwood, MacNeice, Aldous Huxley, Spender, Day Lewis, and Empson. That Warner has not been accorded the fame of many of those writers is an accident of publicity, not an indication of inferior merit. In a less cluttered time than ours, one has no question that Warner's stature would have been perceived from the outset and broadcast.

A classical scholar who has translated Aeschylus, Euripides, Thucydides, Xenophon, Caesar, and Plutarch, Warner began his career as a poet with *Poems*; it is our loss that he did not continue as poet. His first novel, *The Wild Goose Chase*, is unusual in English in that it displays the profound influence of Kafka. Although Auden and Isherwood in their early work indicated that they had read Kafka and some of the German expressionists, Warner's reaction to Kafka is without parallel in British writing unless one goes back to Carlyle's reaction to Goethe and Schiller. Warner's Kafkaesque work was not mere imitation, but an example of an original mind and temperament permeated and released by a profound influence.

Traditionally the English novelist has been concerned almost exclusively with social reality. In *The Wild Goose Chase* Warner writes expressionist allegory, a form quite foreign to the British mind and taste in prose fiction. Warner's unnamed country with its legendary frontier over which men pass at their peril comes directly from Kafka, while the three brothers and their quest for the wild goose, a symbol of man's political and spiritual hope, derive from myth and *Märchen*. Warner differs significantly from Kafka, however, in that Warner can write with humor as well as in Kafka's vein of the grotesque. At the same time Warner's themes are political and ethical, where Kafka's are suffocatingly psychological. *The Wild Goose Chase*, a near masterpiece, is flawed by the conclusion, in which the always tentative construction of reality dissolves into total expressionism, a theatrical resolution that does not in truth resolve the problems so scrupulously posed earlier on.

The Aerodrome, by contrast, written in 1941 during the war, is virtually unflawed. Kafka's influence is still discernible, but now it is totally assimilated and subordinated to a voice that is Warner's unchallenged own. The events of *The Aerodrome* simply relate the effects upon the villagers of the location of a flying field near their village. The villagers are exploited by a ruthlessness of the commanding Air Vice-Marshal, as in turn they are inevitably corrupted. Still writing in a nether region between the Kafkaesque and the realistic, Warner dramatizes the truism that war corrupts all whom it touches, while he does not fall into the expressionistic excesses of his first novel. Warner dominates any tendency to mannerism by intellectual control, and by his adaptation of a plot reminiscent of Greek myth and drama. Narrative economy and Greek directness allow him to write of subjects that in other hands often seem banal: love, hope, suffering, faith, endurance. The narrator's final words typify the qualities of the whole: "'That the world may be clean,' I remembered my father's words. Clean indeed it was and most intricate, fiercer than tigers, wonderful and infinitely forgiving." *The Aerodrome* finally is a novel of ideas presented directly and dramatically. With his conviction of the pathos in the discrepancy between goodness and simplicity, and the necessary corruption of war, Warner achieves tragedy. No better novel appeared in English in the period between 1930 and 1970.

Warner's three novels *The Professor, Why Was I Killed?*, and *Men of Stones* form a second category in his work. They resemble *The Aerodrome* in theme in that they are political and ethical, but their range is narrower, and each novel is more fully determined by style and intellectual control than by imagination and inventiveness. They are lesser only in contrast to Warner's finest work however; in no sense are they negligible.

By the late 1950's, Warner launched into his third period as a novelist in those narratives based upon historical themes. In *The Young Caesar, Imperial Caesar*, or *Pericles the Athenian* one may see the classical scholar and translator as opposed to the young Warner who invented his own sources. Warner's historical novels, that is, are valuable for their insights into classical Athens and Rome, but as works of the imagination they are inferior to his early work. Either the historical novelist is bound by his materials, or if he distorts or ignores them, he offends as frivolous. Warner's historical scholarship is impeccable, but his tendency to the expository, present throughout his career, dominated in his third phase. The historical novels emphasize other qualities apparent from the outset in Warner's work: the fact that he possesses an historical view of reality, and that his first allegiance is to rationality. That alone may account for his relative lack of popularity, for as the 20th century grows older, it becomes anti-historical and anti-rational.

Given Warner's range and special kind of intelligence (and here his essays, *The Cult of Power*, must not be ignored), given his splendid style, the clear product of his work in classics in its elaborateness, its clarity, and its suppleness, one must believe that as long as men honor rationality even slightly, Warner will be read. Certainly *The Aerodrome* must survive, and if later generations sort out our contemporary clutter, Rex Warner will be assured his proper place.

—John McCormick

WARREN, Robert Penn.   American.   Born in Guthrie, Kentucky, 24 April 1905. Educated at Guthrie High School; Vanderbilt University, Nashville, Tennessee, 1921–25, B.A. (summa cum laude) 1925; University of California, Berkeley, M.A. 1927; Yale University, New Haven, Connecticut, 1927–28; Oxford University (Rhodes Scholar), B. Litt. 1930. Married 1) Emma Brescia in 1930 (divorced, 1950); 2) Eleanor Clark, *q.v.*, in 1952, one son and one daughter. Assistant Professor, Southwestern College, Memphis, Tennessee, 1930–31, and Vanderbilt University, 1931–34; Assistant and Associate Professor, Louisiana State University, Baton Rouge, 1934–42; Professor of English, University of Minnesota, Minneapolis, 1942–50. Professor of Playwriting, 1950–56, Professor of English, 1962–73, and since 1973, Professor Emeritus, Yale University. Member of the Fugitive Group of poets: co-founding editor, *The Fugitive*, Nashville, 1923–25. Founding editor, *Southern Review*, Baton Rouge, Louisiana, 1935–42; advisory editor, *Kenyon Review*, Gambier, Ohio, 1942–63. Consultant in Poetry, Library of Congress, Washington, D.C., 1944–45; Jefferson Lecturer, National Endowment for the Humanities, 1974. Recipient: Caroline Sinkler Award, 1936, 1937, 1938; Levinson Prize, 1936, Union League Civic and Arts Foundation Prize, 1953, and Harriet Monroe Prize, 1976 (*Poetry*, Chicago); Houghton Mifflin Literary Fellowship, 1939; Guggenheim fellowship, 1939, 1947; Shelley Memorial Award, 1943; Pulitzer Prize, for fiction, 1947, for poetry, 1958, 1979; Robert Meltzer Award, Screen Writers Guild, 1949; Foreign Book Prize (France), 1950; Sidney Hillman Prize, 1957; Edna St. Vincent Millay Memorial Prize, 1958; National Book Award, for poetry, 1958; New York *Herald-Tribune* Van Doren Award, 1965; Bollingen Prize, for poetry, 1967; National Endowment for the Arts grant, 1968, and lectureship, 1974; Henry A. Bellaman Prize, 1970; Van Wyck Brooks Award, for poetry, 1970; National Medal for Literature, 1970; Emerson-Thoreau Medal, 1975; Copernicus Award, 1976; Presidential Medal of Freedom, 1980; Common Wealth Award, 1981; MacArthur Fellowship, 1981; Brandeis University Creative Arts Award, 1983. D.Litt.: University of Louisville, Kentucky, 1949; Kenyon College, Gambier, Ohio, 1952; Colby College, Waterville, Maine, 1956; University of Kentucky, Lexington, 1957; Swarthmore College, Pennsylvania, 1959; Yale University, 1960; Fairfield University, Connecticut, 1969; Wesleyan University, Middletown, Connecticut, 1970; Harvard University, Cambridge, Massachusetts, 1973; Southwestern College, 1974; University of the South, Sewanee, Tennessee, 1974; Monmouth College, Illinois, 1979; New York University, 1983; Oxford University, 1983; LL.D.: Bridgeport University, Connecticut, 1965; University of New Haven, Connecticut, 1974; Johns Hopkins University, Baltimore, 1977. Member, American Academy, and American Academy of Arts and Sciences; Chancellor, Academy of American Poets, 1972. Poet Laureate, 1986. Address: 2495 Redding Road, Fairfield, Connecticut 06430, U.S.A.

PUBLICATIONS

Novels

Night Rider.   Boston, Houghton Mifflin, 1939; London, Eyre and Spottiswoode, 1940.

At Heaven's Gate.   New York, Harcourt Brace, 1943; London, Eyre and Spottiswoode, 1946.

All the King's Men.   New York, Harcourt Brace, 1946; London, Eyre and Spottiswoode, 1948.

World Enough and Time: A Romantic Novel. New York, Random House, 1950; London, Eyre and Spottiswoode, 1951.

Band of Angels. New York, Random House, 1955; London, Eyre and Spottiswoode, 1956.

The Cave. New York, Random House, and London, Eyre and Spottiswoode, 1959.

Wilderness: A Tale of the Civil War. New York, Random House, 1961; London, Eyre and Spottiswoode, 1962.

Flood: A Romance of Our Time. New York, Random House, and London, Collins, 1964.

Meet Me in the Green Glen. New York, Random House, 1971; London, Secker and Warburg, 1972.

A Place to Come To. New York, Random House, and London, Secker and Warburg, 1977.

Short Stories

Blackberry Winter. Cummington, Massachusetts, Cummington Press, 1946.

The Circus in the Attic and Other Stories. New York, Harcourt Brace, 1948; London, Eyre and Spottiswoode, 1952.

Uncollected Short Stories

"How Willie Proudfit Came Home," in *The Best Short Stories 1939*, edited by Edward J. O'Brien. Boston, Houghton Mifflin, 1939.

"Have You Seen Sukie?," in *The Best American Short Stories 1964*, edited by Martha Foley and David Burnett. Boston, Houghton Mifflin, 1964.

"It's a Long Way from Central Park to Fiddlersburg," in *Kenyon Review* (Gambier, Ohio), Winter 1964.

"Chicago," in *Georgia Review* (Athens), Winter 1976.

Plays

Proud Flesh (in verse, produced Minneapolis, 1947; revised [prose] version, produced New York, 1947).

All the King's Men, adaptation of his own novel (as *Willie Stark: His Rise and Fall*, produced Dallas, 1958; as *All the King's Men*, produced New York, 1959). New York, Random House, 1960.

Verse

Thirty-Six Poems. New York, Alcestis Press, 1936.

Eleven Poems on the Same Theme. New York, New Directions, 1942.

Selected Poems 1923–1943. New York, Harcourt Brace, 1944; London, Fortune Press, 1952.

Brother to Dragons: A Tale in Verse and Voices. New York, Random House, 1953; London, Eyre and Spottiswoode, 1954; revised edition, Random House, 1979.

To a Little Girl, One Year Old, in a Ruined Fortress. Privately printed, 1956.

Promises: Poems 1954–1956. New York, Random House, 1957; London, Eyre and Spottiswoode, 1959.

You, Emperors, and Others: Poems 1957–1960. New York, Random House, 1960.

Selected Poems: New and Old 1923–1966. New York, Random House, 1966.

Incarnations: Poems 1966–1968. New York, Random House, 1968; London, W.H. Allen, 1970.

Audubon: A Vision. New York, Random House, 1969.

Or Else: Poem/Poems 1968–1974. New York, Random House, 1974.

Selected Poems 1923–1975. New York, Random House, and London, Secker and Warburg, 1977.

Now and Then: Poems 1976–1978. New York, Random House, 1978.

Two Poems. Winston-Salem, North Carolina, Palaemon Press, 1979.

Being Here: Poetry 1977–1980. New York, Random House, and London, Secker and Warburg, 1980.

Love. Winston–Salem, North Carolina, Palaemon Press, 1981.

Rumor Verified: Poems 1979–1980. New York, Random House, and London, Secker and Warburg, 1981.

Chief Joseph of the Nez Perce. New York, Random House, and London, Secker and Warburg, 1983.

New and Selected Poems 1923–1985. New York, Random House, 1985.

Recordings: *Robert Penn Warren Reads from His Own Works*, CMS, 1975; *Robert Penn Warren Reads Selected Poems*, Caedmon, 1980.

Other

John Brown: The Making of a Martyr. New York, Payson and Clarke, 1929.

I'll Take My Stand: The South and the Agrarian Tradition, with others. New York, Harper, 1930.

Understanding Poetry: An Anthology for College Students, with Cleanth Brooks. New York, Holt, 1938; revised edition, 1950, Holt Rinehart, 1960, 1976.

Understanding Fiction, with Cleanth Brooks. New York, Crofts, 1943; revised edition, Appleton Century Crofts, 1959; Englewood Cliffs, New Jersey, Prentice Hall, 1979; abridged edition, as *The Scope of Fiction*, 1960.

A Poem of Pure Imagination: An Experiment in Reading, in *The Rime of the Ancient Mariner*, by Samuel Taylor Coleridge. New York, Reynal, 1946.

Modern Rhetoric: With Readings, with Cleanth Brooks. New York, Harcourt Brace, 1949; revised edition, 1958, 1970, 1979.

Fundamentals of Good Writing: A Handbook of Modern Rhetoric, with Cleanth Brooks. New York, Harcourt Brace, 1950; London, Dobson, 1952.

Segregation: The Inner Conflict in the South. New York, Random House, 1956; London, Eyre and Spottiswoode, 1957.

Selected Essays. New York, Random House, 1958; London, Eyre and Spottiswoode, 1964.

Remember the Alamo! (for children). New York, Random House, 1958; as *How Texas Won Her Freedom*, San Jacinto, Texas, San Jacinto Museum of History, 1959.

The Gods of Mount Olympus (for children). New York, Random House, 1959; London, Muller, 1962.

The Legacy of the Civil War: Meditations on the Centennial. New York, Random House, 1961.

Who Speaks for the Negro? New York, Random House, 1965.

A Plea in Mitigation: Modern Poetry and the End of an Era (lecture). Macon, Georgia, Wesleyan College, 1966.

Homage to Theodore Dreiser. New York, Random House, 1971.

John Greenleaf Whittier's Poetry: An Appraisal and a Selection. Minneapolis, University of Minnesota Press, 1971.

A Conversation with Robert Penn Warren, edited by Frank Gado. Schenectady, New York, The Idol, 1972.

Democracy and Poetry (lecture). Cambridge, Massachusetts, Harvard University Press, 1975.

Robert Penn Warren Talking: Interviews 1950–1978, edited by Floyd C. Watkins and John T. Hiers. New York, Random House, 1980.

Jefferson Davis Gets His Citizenship Back. Lexington, University Press of Kentucky, 1980.

Editor, with Cleanth Brooks and John Thibaut Purser, *An Approach to Literature: A Collection of Prose and Verse with Analyses and Discussions.* Baton Rouge, Louisiana State University Press, 1936; revised edition, New York, Crofts, 1939, Appleton Century Crofts, 1952; Englewood Cliffs, New Jersey, Prentice Hall, 1975.

Editor, *A Southern Harvest: Short Stories by Southern Writers.* Boston, Houghton Mifflin, 1937.

Editor, with Cleanth Brooks, *An Anthology of Stories from the Southern Review.* Baton Rouge, Louisiana State University Press, 1953.

Editor, with Albert Erskine, *Short Story Masterpieces.* New York, Dell, 1954.

Editor, with Albert Erskine, *Six Centuries of Great Poetry.* New York, Dell, 1955.

Editor, with Albert Erskine, *A New Southern Harvest.* New York, Bantam, 1957.

Editor, with Allen Tate, *Selected Poems*, by Denis Devlin. New York, Holt Rinehart, 1963.

Editor, *Faulkner: A Collection of Critical Essays.* Englewood Cliffs, New Jersey, Prentice Hall, 1966.

Editor, with Robert Lowell and Peter Taylor, *Randall Jarrell 1914–1965.* New York, Farrar Straus, 1967.

Editor, *Selected Poems of Herman Melville.* New York, Random House, 1970.

Editor and part author, with Cleanth Brooks and R.W.B. Lewis, *American Literature: The Makers and the Making.* New York, St. Martin's Press, 2 vols., 1973.

Editor, *Katherine Anne Porter: A Collection of Critical Essays.* Englewood Cliffs, New Jersey, Prentice Hall, 1979.

*

Bibliography: *Robert Penn Warren: A Reference Guide* by Neil Nakadate, Boston, Hall, 1977; *Robert Penn Warren: A Descriptive Bibliography 1922–79* by James A. Grimshaw, Jr., Charlottesville, University Press of Virginia, 1981.

Manuscript Collection: Beinecke Library, Yale University, New Haven, Connecticut.

Critical Studies (selection): *Robert Penn Warren* (in German) by Klaus Poenicke, Heidelberg, Winter, 1959; *Robert Penn Warren: The Dark and Bloody Ground* by Leonard Casper, Seattle, University of Washington Press, 1960; *The Faraway Country* by Louis D. Rubin, Jr., Seattle, University of Washington Press, 1963; *The Hidden God* by Cleanth Brooks, New Haven, Connecticut, Yale University Press, 1963; *Robert Penn Warren* by Charles H. Bohner, New York, Twayne, 1964, revised edition, 1981; *Robert Penn Warren* by Paul West, Minneapolis, University of Minnesota Press, 1964, London, Oxford University Press, 1965; *Robert Penn Warren: A Collection of Critical Essays* edited by John Lewis Longley, Jr., New York, New York University Press, 1965; *The Burden of Time* by John Lincoln Stewart, Princeton, New Jersey, Princeton University Press, 1965; *Web of Being: The Novels of Robert Penn Warren* by Barnett Guttenberg, Nashville, Vanderbilt University Press, 1975; *Robert Penn Warren: A Vision Earned* by Marshall Walker, Edinburgh, Harris, and New York, Barnes and Noble, 1979; *Robert Penn Warren: A Collection of Critical Essays* edited by Richard Gray, Englewood Cliffs, New Jersey, Prentice Hall, 1980; *Critical Essays on Robert Penn Warren* edited by William B. Clark, Boston, Twayne, 1981; *Robert Penn Warren: Critical Perspectives* edited by Neil Nakadate, Lexington, University Press of Kentucky, 1981; *The Achievement of Robert Penn Warren* by James H. Justus, Baton Rouge, Louisiana State University Press, 1981; *Homage to Robert Penn Warren* edited by Frank Graziano, Durango, Colorado, Logbridge Rhodes, 1982; *Robert Penn Warren* by Katherine Snipes, New York, Ungar, 1983; *A Southern Renascence Man: Views of Robert Penn Warren* edited by Walter B. Edgar, Baton Rouge, Louisiana State University Press, 1984.

*   *   *

Robert Penn Warren, who was born in Guthrie, Kentucky, near the Tennessee line, in 1905, is the youngest and most talented of the Fugitives and Agrarians, a group of writers associated with Vanderbilt University and Nashville in the 1920's and 1930's. The most important of these writers, aside from Warren, are John Crowe Ransom, Donald Davidson, and Allen Tate, all poets and critics.

Warren is one of the vanishing species known as men of letters. In addition to his fiction he has published poetry, criticism, biography, history and sociology, children's books, plays, and other works. With various colleagues, especially Cleanth Brooks, he has edited a distinguished literary quarterly (the first series of the *Southern Review*) and many anthologies and textbooks, the most famous of which is *Understanding Poetry*.

Warren's first published work of fiction, "Prime Leaf" (1931), is a long story that he reforged as a powerful novel, *Night Rider*, a re-creation of the tobacco wars that occurred in Kentucky in the early 1900's. This novel exhibits distinctive earmarks of Warren's fiction: it is based on historical event and is set in the piedmont South; it contains a long subplot that adumbrates the main action; its protagonist finds himself caught in the vise of situations not of his making and often beyond his ability to affect; the conflict entails the clash of public and private values that is seen in the confrontation of rival camps; it is beautifully written, employing many voices and idioms and lush diction and metaphor; its structure, especially in the conclusion, is not quite sufficient to contain the pressing weight of circumstance, character, and idea that Warren packs into its frame, which is large and sprawling; and its thematic focus inheres in the idea of identity and selfhood.

In the powerful opening scene we see and feel the protagonist, Percy Munn, being jostled by a crowd standing around him on a train. In the same way Munn is forced by steadily gathering pressures to resist the corrupt practices of tobacco companies that fix prices. In resisting, Munn steps outside the law, as do other members of the association that he helps to form; and he is gradually alienated from his wife and then the community, and ultimately he loses his life. Munn is the archetype for characters who regularly appear in Warren's subsequent novels, especially Gerald Calhoun in *At Heaven's Gate* and Jeremiah Beaumont in *World Enough and Time*; in the same way Senator Edmund Tolliver, a politician who promises the world's fullness but does not deliver, is the ancestor of Bogan Murdock in *At Heaven's Gate*, Willie Stark in *All the King's Men*, Cassius Fort in *World Enough and Time*, and other figures who become too comfortable with the ways of the world. Except for its darkly naturalistic emphasis, *Night Rider* foreshadows much of what will come in Warren's fiction.

In "Knowledge and the Image of Man" (1955) Warren declares that "only by knowledge does man achieve his identity" and that "knowledge gives him his identity because it gives him an image of himself." In the same essay he speaks of the "unfolding process of self-definition." This process is revealed through a fine web and filigree of image, character, event, and idea that intersect in the overmastering theme of self-knowledge.

Warren's latest novel, *A Place to Come To*, explores this theme through the mind of a brilliant but dissatisfied scholar, Jedediah Tewksbury, whose worldly success in his profession is belied by his frustrations as son, husband, father, and friend—and by his continuing difficulty in establishing a profound and enduring relation with anyone but himself. Toward the novel's conclusion he is still searching for an adequate definition of life. "I cannot find an idea charged with passion," he says.

Scholarly types often appear in Warren's work, especially in *A Place to Come To* and *At Heaven's Gate*. Slim Sarrett, a learned and articulate poet who turns out to be a closet homosexual and a murderer, is an egomaniac, a romantic, and a liar, an Iago whose honest alter ego is Duckfoot Blake, an accountant with Ph.D. who is a philosopher by temperament. The person most affected by Sarrett and Blake (and even more by Bogan Murdock) is the novel's fumbling protagonist, Jerry Calhoun. In seeking his fortune Calhoun loses integrity and even allows his family to be adversely affected by the machinations of Meyers and Murdock, a brokerage firm modeled on an actual—and profoundly corrupt—company. At the end, as is often the case with Warren's fiction, his protagonist is left with nothing. "He had wanted so many things and had had all of them, and had had none of them, for what you had came wrong or too soon or too late."

Man's greed for power and his drive for money and advantage are dramatized even more urgently in *All the King's Men*, Warren's best known novel—and his best. Musing on it in 1966, he said: "I needed an efficient cause. Power moving into a vacuum. . . . The real center of gravity in the novel is the dynamics of power." The contrasting and complementary forces involving Willie Stark, the amoral political dictator, and Burden, who like many of Warren's characters turns his back on his past only to find himself immersed in that past, entail Warren's preoccupations with greed and violence and lust set within a context that involves the long reach of history and an overwhelming awareness of time. At the novel's culmination Jack says: "If you could not accept the past and its burden there was no future," and "if you could accept the past you might hope for the future."

In *World Enough and Time* Warren moves from politics in Louisiana in the 1930's to politics in Kentucky before 1861. In *Band of Angels* and *Wilderness* Warren explores the civil war as it respectively affects a woman of mixed blood and a Jew of European ancestry. The civil war novels lack the passion and scope and depth of *World Enough and Time* and of Warren's finest single work, *Brother to Dragons*, a long narrative in verse that reveals Warren's talents as poet, dramatist, and novelist.

Since the mid-1950's Warren has turned increasingly to poetry, and his poetic sequences (such as "Tale of Time," "The Day Dr. Knox Did It," and "Homage to Emerson") and his long poems (such as *Audubon*) reveal him at his best during the past 30 years. He is more successful in long works than in short (either poetry or fiction), and his short stories, collected in *The Circus in the Attic*, are among his weakest work.

The Cave, Flood, and *Meet Me in the Green Glen* are all novels dealing with the complexities of life in the modern South. Although some critics have argued for their importance, especially for the significance of *The Cave*, none rises to the level of Warren's first four novels. In retrospect it would appear that poetry got the upper hand over fiction in Warren's career after the publication of *World Enough and Time*, his most ambitious, complicated, poetic, and flawed novel. The work fails in part because Warren is presenting the anatomy of a deeply romantic mind and ego, a figure unsympathetic to Warren's realistic temperament but one that has fascinated him since his biography of John Brown (1929).

Warren is a philosophical novelist (and poet) who meets his own definition of the breed—a writer "for whom the documentation of the world is constantly striving to rise to the level of generalization about values, for whom the image strives to rise to symbol, for whom images always fall into a dialectical configuration, for whom the urgency of experience, no matter how vividly and strongly experience may enchant, is the urgency to know the meaning of experience." Such a writer, as Warren tells us, "is willing to go naked into the pit, again and again, to make the same old struggle for his truth" ("'The Great Mirage': Conrad and *Nostromo*," 1951). The thirst for knowledge and the reach for self-definition provide the enabling forces of Warren's fiction: time and again his characters struggle to achieve selfhood against the background of history. The little myth—that of character unfolding at a particular time and in a particular place (in "the convulsion of the world")—coalesces with the big myth of time ("out of history into history and the awful responsibility of Time," as he writes at the end of *All the King's Men*).

As a novelist Robert Penn Warren does not stand in the company of James, Dreiser, Hemingway, and Faulkner; but his overall achievement puts him in the front rank of modern American writers. His novels always offer a dazzling range of effects and provide compulsive reading.

—George Core

WATERHOUSE, Keith (Spencer). British. Born in Leeds, Yorkshire, 6 February 1929. Educated at Osmondthorpe Council School, Leeds. Served in the Royal Air Force. Married 1) Joan Foster in 1951 (divorced, 1968), one son and two daughters; 2) Stella Waterhouse. Since 1950, free-lance journalist and writer in Leeds and London; since 1970, columnist, *Daily Mirror*, London. Recipient (for journalism): Granada award, 1970, and special award, 1982; IPC award, 1970, 1973; British Press award, 1978. Agent: London Management, 235 Regent Street, London W1A 2JT. Address: 29 Kenway Road, London S.W.5, England.

PUBLICATIONS

Novels

There Is a Happy Land. London, Joseph, 1957.
Billy Liar. London, Joseph, 1959; New York, Norton, 1960.
Jubb. London, Joseph, 1963; New York, Putnam, 1964.
The Bucket Shop. London, Joseph, 1968; as *Everything Must Go*, New York, Putnam, 1969.
Billy Liar on the Moon. London, Joseph, 1975; New York, Putnam, 1976.
Office Life. London, Joseph, 1978.

Maggie Muggins; or, Spring in Earl's Court. London, Joseph, 1981.
In the Mood. London, Joseph, 1983.
Mrs. Pooter's Diary. London, Joseph, 1983.
Thinks. London, Joseph, 1984.
The Collected Letters of a Nobody. London, Joseph, 1986.

Plays

Billy Liar, with Willis Hall, adaptation of the novel by Waterhouse (produced London, 1960; Los Angeles and New York, 1963). London, Joseph, 1960; New York, Norton, 1961.
Celebration: The Wedding and The Funeral, with Willis Hall (produced Nottingham and London, 1961). London, Joseph, 1961.
England, Our England, with Willis Hall, music by Dudley Moore (produced London, 1962). London, Evans, 1964.
Squat Betty, with Willis Hall (produced London, 1962; New York, 1964). Included in *The Sponge Room, and Squat Betty*, 1963.
The Sponge Room, with Willis Hall (produced Nottingham and London, 1962; New York, 1964). Included in *The Sponge Room, and Squat Betty*, 1963; in *Modern Short Plays from Broadway and London*, edited by Stanley Richards, New York, Random House, 1969.
All Things Bright and Beautiful, with Willis Hall (produced Bristol and London, 1962). London, Joseph, 1963.
The Sponge Room, and Squat Betty, with Willis Hall. London, Evans, 1963.
Come Laughing Home, with Willis Hall (as *They Called the Bastard Stephen*, produced Bristol, 1964; as *Come Laughing Home*, produced Wimbledon, 1965). London, Evans, 1965.
Say Who You Are, with Willis Hall (produced London, 1965). London, Evans, 1966; as *Help Stamp Out Marriage* (produced New York, 1966), New York, French, 1966.
Joey, Joey, with Willis Hall, music by Ron Moody (produced London, 1966).
Whoops-a-Daisy, with Willis Hall (produced Nottingham, 1968). London, French, 1978.
Children's Day, with Willis Hall (produced Edinburgh and London, 1969). London, French, 1975.
Who's Who, with Willis Hall (produced Coventry, 1971; London, 1973). London, French, 1974.
Saturday, Sunday, Monday, with Willis Hall, adaptation of a play by Eduardo de Filippo (produced London, 1973; New York, 1974). London, Heinemann, 1974.
The Card, with Willis Hall, music and lyrics by Tony Hatch and Jackie Trent, adaptation of the novel by Arnold Bennett (produced Bristol and London, 1973).
Filumena, with Willis Hall, adaptation of a play by Eduardo de Filippo (produced London, 1977; New York, 1980). London, Heinemann, 1978.
Worzel Gummidge (for children), with Willis Hall, music by Denis King, adaptation of stories by Barbara Euphan Todd (produced Birmingham, 1980; London, 1981). London, French 1984.
Steafel Variations (songs and sketches), with Peter Tinniswood and Dick Vosburgh (produced London, 1982).
Lost Empires, with Willis Hall, music by Denis King, adaptation of the novel by J.B. Priestley (produced Darlington, County Durham, 1985).

Screenplays, with Willis Hall: *Whistle Down the Wind*, 1961; *The Valiant*, 1962; *A Kind of Loving*, 1963; *Billy Liar*, 1963; *West Eleven*, 1963; *Man in the Middle*, 1963; *Pretty Polly* (*A Matter of Innocence*), 1967; *Lock Up Your Daughters*, 1969.

Radio Plays: *The Town That Wouldn't Vote*, 1951; *There Is a Happy Land*, 1962; *The Woolen Bank Forgeries*, 1964; *The Last Phone-In*, 1976; *The Big Broadcast of 1922*, 1979.

Television Plays: *The Warmonger*, 1970; *The Upchat Line* series, 1977; *The Upchat Connection* series, 1978; *Charlie Muffin*, from novels by Brian Freemantle, 1979; *West End Tales* series, 1981; *The Happy Apple* series, from play by Jack Pulman, 1983; *This Office Life*, from his own novel, 1984; *Charters and Caldicott*, 1985; with Willis Hall—*Happy Moorings*, 1963; *How Many Angels*, 1964; *Inside George Webley* series, 1968; *Queenie's Castle* series, 1970; *Budgie* series, 1971–72; *The Upper Crusts* series, 1973; *Three's Company* series, 1973; *By Endeavour Alone*, 1973; *Billy Liar* series, 1973–74; *Briefer Encounter*, 1977; *Public Lives*, 1979; *Worzel Gummidge* series, from stories by Barbara Euphan Todd, 1979.

Other

The Café Royal: Ninety Years of Bohemia, with Guy Deghy. London, Hutchinson, 1955.
How to Avoid Matrimony, with Guy Deghy (as Herald Froy). London, Muller, 1957.
Britain's Voice Abroad, with Paul Cave. London, Daily Mirror Newspapers, 1957.
The Future of Television. London, Daily Mirror Newspapers, 1958.
The Joneses: How to Keep Up with Them, with Guy Deghy (as Lee Gibb). London, Muller, 1959.
The Higher Jones, with Guy Deghy (as Lee Gibb). London, Muller, 1961.
The Passing of the Third-Floor Buck (*Punch* sketches). London, Joseph, 1974.
Mondays, Thursdays (*Daily Mirror* columns). London, Joseph, 1976.
Rhubarb, Rhubarb, and Other Noises (*Daily Mirror* columns). London, Joseph, 1979.
The Television Adventures [and *More Television Adventures*] *of Worzel Gummidge* (for children), with Willis Hall. London, Penguin, 2 vols., 1979; complete edition, as *Worzel Gummidge's Television Adventures*, London, Kestrel, 1981.
Worzel Gummidge at the Fair (for children), with Willis Hall. London, Penguin, 1980.
Worzel Gummidge Goes to the Seaside (for children), with Willis Hall. London, Penguin, 1980.
The Trials of Worzel Gummidge (for children), with Willis Hall. London, Penguin, 1980.
Worzel's Birthday (for children), with Willis Hall. London, Penguin, 1981.
New Television Adventures of Worzel Gummidge and Aunt Sally (for children), with Willis Hall. London, Sparrow, 1981.
Daily Mirror Style. London, Mirror Books, 1981.
Worzel Gummidge and Aunt Sally (for children), with Willis Hall. London, Severn House, 1982.
Funny Peculiar (*Punch* columns). London, Joseph, 1983.
The Irish Adventures of Worzel Gummidge (for children), with Willis Hall. London, Severn House, 1984.
Waterhouse at Large (journalism). London, Joseph, 1985.

Editor, with Willis Hall, *Writers' Theatre*.   London, Heinemann, 1967.

*   *   *

Keith Waterhouse's fiction is distinguished by a sharp comic sense, a facility that works on closely polished verbal, imagistic, and logical incongruities. For example, in the well-known *Billy Liar*, a character who is one of the two owners of the funeral establishment where Billy works, a man who keeps a copy of Evelyn Waugh's *The Loved One* on his desk in order to get new ideas and who looks forward to the day when all coffins will be made of fiberglass, is introduced: "He was, for a start, only about twenty-five years old, although grown old with quick experience, like forced rhubarb." In *Billy Liar on the Moon*, a sequel to *Billy Liar* that both takes place and was written about 15 years after the original, and which moves Billy from his Yorkshire locale of the late 1950's to a carefully designed community of shopping malls, motels, and perplexing one-way streets that lead only to motorways, a new housing estate is a "suburb of the moon" with "a Legoland of crescents and culs-de-sac with green Lego roofs and red Lego chimney stacks." In *The Bucket Shop* Waterhouse depicts the bumbling, self-deceptive owner of a tatty antique shop, unsuccessful alike in his business, his adulteries, and his efforts to make his wife and his nine-year-old daughter, Melisande, fit his trendy definitions of "interesting" people. After a long passage developing Melisande's fantasies about herself, Waterhouse adds, "She had William's gift for candid self-assessment." That kind of reductive comment, like the discordant contemporary images, the play with clichés, and the exploitation of grammatical incongruities, suggest comparisons with the comic prose of Evelyn Waugh.

Waterhouse builds his verbal texture on plots that often begin with a kind of adolescent humor. Billy, in *Billy Liar*, invents highly improbable and inconsistent stories, weaving a net of public and fantastic lies that is bound to be discovered by parents, bosses, and the three girl-friends to whom he is simultaneously engaged. He is full of elaborate compulsions: if he can suck a mint without breaking it or if he walks in certain complex patterns he feels he will escape the consequences of his stories. He is also a powerful leader in his fantasy land of Ambrosia. The point of view of the young boy in Waterhouse's first novel, *There Is a Happy Land*, is even more childlike. The boy plays at being blind, drunk, or maimed, mimics all his elders and delights in calling out cheeky statements that annoy or embarrass adults. Neither child nor adolescent, the central character in *Jubb*, a rent-collector and youth-club leader in a planned "New Town," is also full of grandiose schemes that others always see through and mimics others' accepted pieties. All these characters, inventive, iconoclastic, and living almost wholly within their disordered imaginations, assault an adult world that pretends it's stable.

Underneath the texture of mimicry and iconoclasm, Waterhouse sometimes gradually shows a world far more sinister than the one suggested by the escapades of adolescent humor. As *There Is a Happy Land* develops, the tone shifts and the boy recognizes the sexuality, perversion, evil, and violence (including the murder of a young girl) in the abandoned quarries and behind the picture-windows of the lower-middle-class housing estate. The character of Jubb himself is gradually revealed as psychotic. Behind his fantasies and comic compulsions is the sexual impotence that has led him to become a peeping Tom, a pyromaniac, and a murderer. In *The Bucket Shop* William's incompetent management of money and women, as well as his incapacity to deal with the consequences of his fantasies, leads to the suicide of a dependent actress. Sometimes, as the humor fades from Waterhouse's novels, it leaves a melodramatic revelation of perverse and horrible humanity.

More recent novels, generally set in the anonymous world of London, focus satire or an understated pathos on more restricted treatments of contemporary life. *Office Life* centers on a worker made redundant who is absorbed into the modern corporation where everyone is sustained in a network of gossip, affairs, and shuffling papers, and nothing is produced or accomplished. *Maggie Muggins; or, Spring in Earl's Court* chronicles a day in the life of Maggie, born Margaret Moon, a promiscuous and alcoholic drifter in London for the past ten years in revolt from a square, stable Doncaster family. During the day, she learns of a close friend's suicide, her father's decision to marry and start a new family, and the fact that the father of her aborted baby could have married her, yet the clever prose, satirizing the social services and any pretense to reform, finally and tersely establishes her ratchety integrity and capacity to survive. *Thinks* is more experimental technically. Concentrating, as a deliberate fictional device, on the anxieties and fantasies in the mind of the central character, without reporting what he says, the novel charts the pressures on the last, long day of Edgar Bapty's life. Through train journeys, a visit to his doctor, a job interview he only dimly realizes he has fumbled, thoughts of his three former wives, numerous heavy meals, a visit to a prostitute, and several recognitions of his own sexual incapacity, Bapty's thoughts and fears build to "a magnificent Hallelujah chorus of sustained and bellowing rage" before his fatal heart attack. The compressed focus and the sharp writing give these novels immediacy and vitality.

The two novels concerning Billy Liar are lighter than Waterhouse's other fiction, although the persona of Billy represents Waterhouse's only perspective that attempts to alter circumstance. Billy lies less to cover horror or perversion than "to relieve the monotony of living on the moon," where the moon is his arid contemporary civic and domestic life. Both novels, as satire, also ridicule the parochial: in *Billy Liar* the target is, equally, romanticizing an old, rugged Yorkshire tradition and the "new" world of coffee bars, record shops, and the winner of the Miss Stradhoughton contest who delivers "whole sentences ready-packed in disposable tinfoil wrapper"; in *Billy Liar on the Moon* the target is civic pride, all the contemporary designs and shapes applied to experience and undermined both by their implicit fatuity and old-fashioned corruption. In both novels, Billy, the comic, the spinner of fantasies, uses the vision of "London" as his potential escape from provincial dullness, ineptitude, and self-seeking. That any "real London" is no answer for Waterhouse is clear from other novels such as *The Bucket Shop*, *Office Life*, and *Maggie Muggins*. Yet the point in both books about Billy Liar is that he cannot, more than momentarily in the second book, manage the break to London, cannot do more than mimic, scoff, and invent within the limited world he is dependent on. Both as satire and as a potential means of revealing some deeply thought or felt version of experience, Waterhouse's comedy is thin, a covering for the sense of horror in experience in *Jubb* or *Thinks*, in which the latent pain seems unmanageable and unchangeable. All the novels seem staged (and Waterhouse, in conjunction with Willis Hall, has written a number of plays characterized by sharply witty dialogue and clever invention). As Billy himself says, in *Billy Liar on the Moon*, he is still only a "juvenile lead" in a "comedy," not the central character in a "tragedy" he imagines, not equipped for any part in a drama of "real life." At the end of the novel, he returns to Ambrosia. Whatever the incapacities of his characters to alter or transcend experience, Waterhouse is invariably an excellent mimic, often cogent and terse, and has created a comic prose and a sense of the involuted logic of systematic fantasy that are strikingly effective and enjoyable.

—James Gindin

WATMOUGH, David. Canadian. Born in London, England, in 1926. Educated at the Coopers' Company School, London, 1937–43; King's College, University of London, 1945–49, degree in theology. Served in the Royal Navy, 1944–45. Reporter, *Cornish Guardian*, Bodmin, Cornwall, 1943–44; editor, Holy Cross Press, New York, 1953–54; talks producer, BBC Third Programme, London, 1955; editor, Ace Books, London, 1956; feature writer and critic, San Francisco *Examiner*, 1957–60; arts and theatre critic, Vancouver *Sun*, 1964–67; music and theatre critic, 1967–80, and host of a weekly television show ("Artslib"), 1979–80, Canadian Broadcasting Corporation, Vancouver. Recipient: Canada Council bursary, 1968, 1970, and Senior Arts Grant, 1976. Address: 3358 West First Avenue, Vancouver, British Columbia V6R 1G4, Canada.

PUBLICATIONS

Novel

No More into the Garden.   New York, Doubleday, 1978.

Short Stories

Ashes for Easter and Other Monodramas.   Vancouver, Talonbooks, 1972.
Love and the Waiting Game: Eleven Stories.   Ottawa, Oberon Press, 1975.
From a Cornish Landscape.   Padstow, Cornwall, Lodenek Press, 1975.
The Connecticut Countess.   Trumansburg, New York, Crossing Press, 1984.
Fury.   Ottawa, Oberon Press, 1984.

Uncollected Short Stories

"Terminus Victoria," in *Saturday Night* (Toronto), May 1976.
"Beyond the Mergansers, Above the Salal," in *Canadian Fiction* (Vancouver), Winter 1976.
"Nelly Moriarty and the Jewish Question," in *Matrix* (Lennoxville, Quebec), January 1981.
"All at Sea," in *Waves* (Downsview, Ontario), Spring 1981.
"The Cross Country Run," in *Origins* (Hamilton, Ontario), Spring 1981.
"An Image of New Jersey," in *Waves* (Downsview, Ontario), Spring 1985.
"I Hate Queers," in *Angles* (Vancouver), Spring 1985.

Plays

Friedhof (produced Vancouver, 1966).   Included in *Names for the Numbered Years*, 1967.
Do You Remember One September Afternoon? (produced Vancouver, 1966).   Included in *Names for the Numbered Years*, 1967.

Names for the Numbered Years: Three Plays (includes *Do You Remember One September Afternoon?*, *Friedhof*, *My Mother's House Has Too Many Rooms*).   Vancouver, Bau-Xi Gallery, 1967.

Other

A Church Renascent: A Study of Modern French Catholicism.   London, SPCK, 1951.
The Unlikely Pioneer (opera history).   Toronto, Mosaic Press, 1985.

Editor, *The Vancouver Fiction Book*.   Winlaw, British Columbia, Polestar Press, 1985.

*

Critical Studies: by Robert Fulford, in *Saturday Night* (Toronto), May 1976; "The Novel That Never Ends: David Watmough's Reminiscent Fictions," in *The World of Canadian Writing* by George Woodcock, Vancouver, Douglas and McIntyre, and Seattle, University of Washington Press, 1980; in *The Oxford Companion to Canadian Literature* edited by William Toye, Toronto, Oxford, and New York, Oxford University Press, 1983.

David Watmough comments:

In a very real sense I regard each successive volume of my fiction as part of an ongoing "novel" that will not be complete until I can no longer write. My work is an attempt to chronicle the private history of one man of Cornish ancestry living as a Canadian through the 20th century. My fictional protagonist, Davey Bryant, is depicted in childhood, adolescence, maturity, and, currently, middle age. If the work finally succeeds then it will be because I have been able to muster the kind of candour and honesty that such a confessional narrative demands. Another feature of the work is the depiction of private history—including the most intimate sexual and psychological detail—against the backdrop of public events.

*   *   *

David Watmough is a Canadian writer whose fiction has been set mostly in the land of his childhood, which is Cornwall. Up to now he has published a number of collections of short stories, and two open-ended novels, *No More into the Garden* and *Unruly Skeletons* (forthcoming). His claim is that for a decade and a half he has been engaged in writing a single novel that will take a lifetime to complete, and it is a claim that must be taken seriously, for the same central character, Davey Bryant, appears in almost all the fiction Watmough writes, whether it is short stories, novels, or the spoken and semi-dramatic fictions which he calls monodramas.

In many ways Davey Bryant resembles David Watmough, in the same way as some of his experiences parallel his creator's. Yet the character stands apart, observed with an irony and a candour that sometimes would make Watmough's monodramas as difficult for the audience to accept as the writer to read. But the observation is from within as well as from without, and each story, each chapter of the novel, is a confession of ambivalent acts, ambivalent motives.

In a way the saga of Davey Bryant is in the classic tradition of modernist fiction—a portrait of the artist as a young but ageing man or dog. But real life—from which so much undoubtedly comes—is modified by memory and changed by art, and Watmough's fictions walk a variety of tightropes—between actuality and truth, between the oral and the written way of speaking.

These fictions are all essentially ironic, with the initial nostalgia of the vision always underlaid by the nagging memory, the jarring truth, that provokes the nostalgia. Some of the most telling stories are those that evoke moments of folly or unworthiness which stir the same shameful recollections in the reader as the writer experiences, or, alternatively, make him uneasy because of the perilous closeness of the predicaments—frequently homosexual—which are delineated to the possibilities of his own life.

In the novels especially Davey Bryant is shown as both the victim of ludicrous circumstances and the perpetrator of petty moral atrocities. The victim is always seen to be seeking victory, and most personal relationships are marred by a cruelty that degrades one or other of the participants.

The recurrent themes are united on another level by a pervading elegiac consciousness. in *No More into the Garden*, for example, the longed-for garden that is never re-entered is in one sense the Cornwall of childhood happiness, and in another the state of collective innocence that all men seek to recover. The garden, however, becomes "a harvest of threats." By the novel's end the fullness of life is balanced by ever-present death, for as the mind expands in consciousness the physical possibilities narrow. Here, for Watmough, is the irony and also the elegy.

But the garden survives in the Proustian reality of memory, and Watmough's most recent collection of stories, *Fury*, returns to the world of childhood with all its innocence and brutality.

—George Woodcock

WEIDMAN, Jerome. American. Born in New York City, 4 April 1913. Educated at the City College of New York, 1931–33; Washington Square College, New York, 1933–34; New York University Law School, 1934–37. Served in the United States Office of War Information, 1942–45. Married Elizabeth Ann Payne in 1943; two sons. President, Authors League of America, 1969–74. Recipient (for drama): Pulitzer Prize, 1960; New York Drama Critics Circle Award, 1960; Tony Award, 1960. Agent: Brandt and Brandt, 1501 Broadway, New York, New York 10036. Address: 1966 Pacific Avenue, San Francisco, California 94109, U.S.A.

PUBLICATIONS

Novels

I Can Get It for You Wholesale. New York, Simon and Schuster, 1937; London, Heinemann, 1938.
What's in It for Me? New York, Simon and Schuster, 1938; London, Heinemann, 1939.
I'll Never Go There Any More. New York, Simon and Schuster, 1941; London, Heinemann, 1942.
The Lights Around the Shore. New York, Simon and Schuster, 1943; London, Hale, 1948.
Too Early to Tell. New York, Reynal, 1946.
The Price Is Right. New York, Harcourt Brace, 1949; London, Hammond, 1950.
The Hand of the Hunter. New York, Harcourt Brace, 1951; London, Cape, 1952.

Give Me Your Love. New York, Eton, 1952.
The Third Angel. New York, Doubleday, 1953; London, Cape, 1954.
Your Daughter Iris. New York, Doubleday, 1955; London, Cape, 1956.
The Enemy Camp. New York, Random House, 1958; London, Heinemann, 1959.
Before You Go. New York, Random House, 1960; London, Heinemann, 1961.
The Sound of Bow Bells. New York, Random House, 1962; London, Heinemann, 1963.
Word of Mouth. New York, Random House, 1964; London, Bodley Head, 1965.
Other People's Money. New York, Random House, and London, Bodley Head, 1967.
The Center of the Action. New York, Random House, 1969; London, Bodley Head, 1970.
Fourth Street East. New York, Random House, and London, Bodley Head, 1970.
Last Respects. New York, Random House, and London, Bodley Head, 1972.
Tiffany Street. New York, Random House, and London, Bodley Head, 1974.
The Temple. New York, Simon and Schuster, 1975; London, Bodley Head, 1976.
A Family Fortune. New York, Simon and Schuster, and London, Bodley Head, 1978.
Counselors-at-Law. New York, Doubleday, 1980; London, Bodley Head, 1981.

Short Stories

The Horse That Could Whistle "Dixie" and Other Stories. New York, Simon and Schuster, 1939; London, Heinemann, 1941.
The Captain's Tiger. New York, Reynal, 1947.
A Dime a Throw. New York, Berkley, 1957.
Nine Stories. New York, Random House, 1960.
My Father Sits in the Dark and Other Selected Stories. New York, Random House, 1961; London, Heinemann, 1963.
Where the Sun Never Sets and Other Stories. London, Heinemann, 1964.
The Death of Dickie Draper and Nine Other Stories. New York, Random House, 1965.
I, and I Alone. N.p., Pockettes, 1972.

Uncollected Short Stories

"The Absolute Darlings," in *McCall's* (New York), July 1965.
"The Friends of Mary Fowler," in *Redbook* (New York), July 1965.
"Mrs. Gregory Is in Industrial Diamonds," in *Cavalier* (Greenwich, Connecticut), August 1965.
"The Wife of the Man Who Suddenly Loved Women," in *Ladies Home Journal* (New York), June 1966.
"Second Breakfast," in *Playboy* (Chicago), February 1967.
"Good Man, Bad Man," in *Best Detective Stories of the Year 23*, edited by Anthony Boucher. New York, Dutton, and London, Boardman, 1968.

Plays

Fiorello!, with George Abbott, music and lyrics by Sheldon Harnick and Jerry Bock (produced New York, 1959; Bristol and London, 1962). New York, Random House, 1960.
Tenderloin, with George Abbott, music and lyrics by Sheldon Harnick and Jerry Bock, adaptation of the work by Samuel

Hopkins Adams (produced New York, 1960). New York, Random House, 1961.

I Can Get It for You Wholesale, music by Harold Rome, adaptation of the novel by Weidman (produced New York, 1962). New York, Random House, 1962.

Cool Off!, music by Howard Blackman (produced Philadelphia, 1964).

Pousse-Café, music by Duke Ellington, lyrics by Marshall Barer and Frank Tobias (produced New York, 1966).

Ivory Tower, with James Yaffe (produced Ann Arbor, Michigan, 1968). New York, Dramatists Play Service, 1969.

The Mother Lover (produced New York, 1969). New York, Dramatists Play Service, 1969.

Asterisk! A Comedy of Terrors (produced New York, 1969). New York, Dramatists Play Service, 1969.

Screenplays: *The Damned Don't Cry*, with Harold Medford, 1950; *The Eddie Cantor Story*, with Ted Sherdeman and Sidney Skolsky, 1953; *Slander*, 1957.

Television Plays: *The Reporter* series, 1964.

Other

Letter of Credit (travel). New York, Simon and Schuster, 1940.

Back Talk (essays). New York, Random House, 1963.

Editor, *The W. Somerset Maugham Sampler*. New York, Garden City Books, 1943; as *The Somerset Maugham Pocket Book*, New York, Pocket Books, 1944.

Editor, *Traveler's Cheque*. New York, Doubleday, 1954.

Editor, with others, *The First College Bowl Question Book*. New York, Random House, 1961.

*

Manuscript Collection: Humanities Research Center, University of Texas, Austin.

Critical Studies: introductions by the author to *The Horse That Could Whistle "Dixie" and Other Stories*, 1941, and *My Father Sits in the Dark and Other Selected Stories*, 1961; article by Edith Blicksilver, in *Twentieth-Century American–Jewish Fiction Writers* edited by Daniel Walden, Detroit, Gale, 1984.

*   *   *

Jerome Weidman freely admits that he writes primarily for money. Writers like Mark Twain and William Shakespeare clearly demonstrate that one can produce literary masterpieces for money. But Weidman is no Twain or Shakespeare. Most of his works are pieces of slick fiction full of outrageous coincidences and pat solutions to complex problems. His earlier works also include what passed for lurid sex in pre-1960 America. Moreover, the kind of moral vision that pervades the works of Twain and Shakespeare is absent from most of Weidman's works. Instead, from *I Can Get It for You Wholesale* through *Counselors-at-Law*, the author seems to condone the moral corruption that he depicts pervading American society.

Still, some of Weidman's works achieve a kind of intensity, and some even have a clear moral vision. Although Weidman claims that even his non-Jewish characters are really Jews disguised as gentiles, his works about Jews who are conscious of their Jewishness tend to be better than his other works. Even the ironically titled *A Family Fortune*, about a pair of Jewish gangsters who want their ill-gotten gains all for themselves rather than their family, holds together better than his works in which non-Jews are central.

Weidman burst on the literary scene with *I Can Get It for You Wholesale*, a novel about the meteoric rise of Harry Bogen in the New York garment industry from clerk to manufacturer. Hailed for its realistic treatment of the seamier aspects of the garment industry, it still is considered a minor classic for the insight it gives into its time.

At their best Weidman's works give a sensitive treatment of the role of the Jew in America's predominantly gentile society. Although a work of fiction, *Fourth Street East* reads like a series of memoirs of the life of a boy growing up shortly before and during World War I on Manhattan's Lower East Side. The novel captures the feeling of an era and a life-style that no longer exist. Unfortunately, Weidman decided to continue to tell the story of the life of Benny Kramer, protagonist and narrator of *Fourth Street East,* in two additional books, *Last Respects* and *Tiffany Street*, in both of which he once again becomes the writer of slick, sensationalistic fiction. *Fourth Street East* is pervaded with a warm nostalgia that refuses to be trite combined with a recognition that many things have changed for the better. Benny's father is a pillar of moral strength, trying to do what is right for the whole of humanity, even when he is ridiculed for it. The mother is much stronger in worldly terms, trying to do what is best for her family. In *Last Respects* and *Tiffany Street* the father loses whatever strength he had; he becomes a weak cuckold who eventually ends up in a wheelchair because of his wife's desire to make money and engage in extramarital sex. The mother becomes a ruthless, sexy vixen who is willing to expose her son to possible assassination and to have her husband shot in order to carry on her activities as a bootlegger. And the narrator seems to admire her for her activities.

In *The Enemy Camp* Weidman gives a sensitive treatment of the problems facing George Hurst, a Jew who marries a Christian from the Main Line in Philadelphia. He does not know his real parents. The woman he calls Aunt Tessie, who is not his relative but adopted him from an orphanage, has carefully taught him to hate all non-Jews. When she hears that he plans to marry a non-Jew, she decides that to her he is dead. Her brother Zischa, however, tells him: "Do what your heart tells you, not your religion. It's more important to be a man than a Jew." Deciding to follow Zischa's advice, George tries to deny that being Jewish makes him different from anyone else. He resorts to all kinds of subterfuges ranging from drinking coffee, which he hates, to keeping large, important segments of his past hidden from his wife. In other words, he tries to deny his Jewishness as a means of defending himself in his attempt to live in what he feels is the enemy camp. When finally forced to face his past and his Jewishness, he accuses his wife of being anti-Semitic. After his feelings come into the open, he discovers that she is no such thing. She, however, is horrified that he could think such a thing after they had lived together for many years and had two children. When she also discovers that he kept hidden from her some important events that occurred on their wedding day, she decides that their whole marriage has been a lie. George then discovers that he really does love her and that she has loved him for what he really is rather than what he pretends to be. Uncle Zischa was incorrect. George cannot be a man and not be a Jew. His Jewishness and his humanity are inextricably interwoven. To deny one is to deny both. With this new-found knowledge, he begins to rebuild his life.

The Temple too deals with the position of the Jew in America. David Dehn's initial stance is one of affirmation of Judaism

Darcy's Utopia (1990) → CBC

as a reaction against anti-Semitism. A series of episodes, beginning with the murder of his rabbi on the day of his bar mitzvah and culminating with his participation in the liberation of Buchenwald, convinces him that most non-Jews are enemies and that, to survive, Jews must work together to fight those enemies. Using money apparently illegally gotten from the SS shortly after World War II ended, David founds a Jewish community in Beechwood, Connecticut, a predominantly gentile town that he considers blatantly anti-Semitic. Until he moves there, its only Jewish residents either change their names to escape their Jewish identity or serve as what David calls "prop Jews," willing to live in the midst of an anti-Semitic culture for their own personal gain. As time passes, David grows significantly. He moves from a desire to hurt the Christian residents of Beechwood by putting a Jewish community and temple in their midst to a position in which he tries to change the whole community for the better. He establishes a drug rehabilitation center and college scholarships available to all members of the community and, after he becomes a selectman of the town, finds himself working for and winning the love and respect of the community at large, including several people he considered blatantly anti-Semitic. He initially builds the temple in Beechwood not as an act of worship but as a means of recapturing the feeling of safety he had in the synagogue of his youth in Albany, New York. As his death in the sanctuary wearing his father's tallis and saying the Shema shows, he moves to a position of genuine love for God. Still, David is far from being a saint. Especially unpleasant is his relationship with Hella Drachenfels, a Nazi employed at Buchenwald who turns prostitute after the war and supplies David not only with sexual gratification but also with "souvenirs" of Buchenwald that he puts in the cornerstone of the temple. His marriage to her is totally unexplained. Nonetheless, the marriage helps force the novel to its tragic conclusion.

Although Weidman is very prolific, a great deal of his work is forgettable. But some of his novels—*Fourth Street East, The Enemy Camp, The Temple*—are more than just pieces of formula fiction; they stand beside *I Can Get It for You Wholesale* as pieces that may endure.

—Richard Tuerk

WELDON, Fay (née Birkinshaw). British. Born in Alvechurch, Worcestershire, 22 February 1931; grew up in New Zealand. Educated at Girls' High School, Christchurch; Hampstead Girls' High School, London; St. Andrews University, Fife, 1949–52, M.A. in economics and psychology 1954. Married Ron Weldon in 1960; four sons. In late 1950's worked as writer for the Foreign Office and *Daily Mirror*, both London; later worked in advertising. Member of the Video Censorship Appeals Committee. Recipient: Writers Guild award, for radio play, 1973; Giles Cooper Award, for radio play, 1978; Society of Authors travelling scholarship, 1981. Lives in London. Agent: Phil Kelvin, Goodwin Associates, 12 Rabbit Row, Kensington Church Street, London W8 4DX. Address: c/o Hodder and Stoughton Ltd., 47 Bedford Square, London WC1B 3DP, England.

PUBLICATIONS

Novels

The Fat Woman's Joke. London, MacGibbon and Kee, 1967; as *... and the Wife Ran Away*, New York, McKay, 1968.

Down among the Women. London, Heinemann, 1971; New York, St. Martin's Press, 1972.
Female Friends. London, Heinemann, and New York, St. Martin's Press, 1975.
Remember Me. London, Hodder and Stoughton, and New York, Random House, 1976.
Words of Advice. New York, Random House, 1977; as *Little Sisters*, London, Hodder and Stoughton, 1978.
Praxis. London, Hodder and Stoughton, and New York, Summit, 1978.
Puffball. London, Hodder and Stoughton, and New York, Summit, 1980.
The President's Child. London, Hodder and Stoughton, 1982; New York, Doubleday, 1983.
The Life and Loves of a She-Devil. London, Hodder and Stoughton, 1983; New York, Pantheon, 1984.

Short Stories

Watching Me, Watching You. London, Hodder and Stoughton, and New York, Summit, 1981.
Polaris and Other Stories. London, Hodder and Stoughton, 1985.

Plays

Permanence, in *Mixed Blessings* (produced London, 1969). London, Methuen, 1970.
Time Hurries On, in *Scene Scripts*, edited by Michael Marland. London, Longman, 1972.
Words of Advice (produced London, 1974). London, French, 1974.
Friends (produced Richmond, Surrey, 1975).
Moving House (produced Farnham, Surrey, 1976).
Mr. Director (produced Richmond, Surrey, 1978).
Polaris (broadcast, 1978). Published in *Best Radio Plays of 1978: The Giles Cooper Award Winners*, London, Eyre Methuen, 1979.
Action Replay (produced Birmingham, 1978; as *Love Among the Women*, produced Vancouver, 1982). London, French, 1980.
I Love My Love (broadcast, 1981; produced Richmond, Surrey, 1982). London, French, 1984.
After the Prize (produced New York, 1981; as *Word Worm*, produced Newbury, Berkshire, 1984).
The Western Women (produced Lyme Regis, Dorset, 1984).

Radio Plays: *Spider*, 1973; *Housebreaker*, 1973; *Mr. Fox and Mr. First*, 1974; *The Doctor's Wife*, 1975; *Polaris*, 1978; *Weekend*, 1979; *All the Bells of Paradise*, 1979; *I Love My Love*, 1981.

Television Plays: *Wife in a Blonde Wig*, 1966; *The Fat Woman's Tale*, 1966; *What About Me*, 1967; *Dr. De Waldon's Therapy*, 1967; *Goodnight Mrs. Dill*, 1967; *The 45th Unmarried Mother*, 1967; *Fall of the Goat*, 1967; *Ruined Houses*, 1968; *Venus Rising*, 1968; *The Three Wives of Felix Hull*, 1968; *Hippy Hippy Who Cares*, 1968; *£13083*, 1968; *The Loophole*, 1969; *Smokescreen*, 1969; *Poor Mother*, 1970; *Office Party*, 1970; *On Trial* (*Upstairs, Downstairs* series), 1971; *Old Man's Hat*, 1972; *A Splinter of Ice*, 1972; *Hands*, 1972; *The Lament of an Unmarried Father*, 1972; *A Nice Rest*, 1972; *Comfortable Words*, 1973; *Desirous of Change*, 1973; *In Memoriam*, 1974; *Poor Baby*, 1975; *The Terrible Tale of Timothy Bagshott*, 1975; *Aunt Tatty*, from the story by Elizabeth Bowen, 1975; *Act of Rape*, 1977;

Married Love (*Six Women* series), 1977; *Act of Hypocrisy* (*Jubilee* series), 1977; *Chickabiddy* (*Send in the Girls* series), 1978; *Pride and Prejudice*, from the novel by Jane Austen, 1980; *Honey Ann*, 1980; *Life for Christine*, 1980; *Watching Me, Watching You* (*Leap in the Dark* series), 1980; *Little Mrs. Perkins*, from story by Penelope Mortimer, 1982; *Redundant! or, The Wife's Revenge*, 1983; *Time for Murder* series, with others, 1985.

Other

Simple Steps to Public Life, with Pamela Anderson and Mary Stott. London, Virago Press, 1980.
Letters to Alice: On First Reading Jane Austen. London, Joseph, 1984; New York, Taplinger, 1985.
Rebecca West. London, Viking, 1985.

Editor, with Elaine Feinstein, *New Stories 4.* London, Hutchinson, 1979.

*   *   *

Fay Weldon's concern is personal relationships in contemporary society, focussing on women, especially as mothers, and thus widening to take in relationships between the generations: "By our children, you shall know us." She amusingly traces long chains of cause and effect, inexorable as Greek tragedy, stemming from both conscious and unconscious motivation, and from chance circumstances. She looks at society with devastating clearsightedness, showing how good may spring from selfishness, evil from altruism. Her liberating clarity, embracing as many points of view as possible, is compulsively readable—if latterly becoming repetitive.

Weldon's unique narrative style highlights the contradiction between free will which her characters, like us, assume and the conditioning which we know we undergo. Her characters are continually referred to by their names, where English style would normally use a pronoun, and addressed directly in the second person by the author and assessed by her—"Lucky Lily" the author appraises a leading character in *Remember Me*, where she also "translates" passages of the characters' dialogue into what they *mean*, rather than say. Weldon's apparently disingenuous surface, with her own paragraphing lay-out, is underpinned by a whole battery of ironic devices, indicating the limitations on her characters'—and our—autonomy from cradle to grave. In *Puffball* this process is pushed back before the cradle, with sections "Inside Liffey" about the growth of the foetus and its conditioning via circumstances of the mother's life.

The Fat Woman's Joke, Weldon's first novel, follows a greedy couple on a diet. This novel originated as a television play, and Weldon hadn't fully developed her unique style. Her characteristic plangent note, that the worst can happen and does, is accompanied by a muted optimism, especially in her novels' endings: gradual progress occurs, at least for the majority if not for the unfortunate individual. *Down among the Women* concludes "We are the last of the women"—that is, the half of the population defined earlier as living "at floor level, washing and wiping."

Weldon's feminism colours all her work, and is powerful when she doesn't shrink from detailing the faults of individual women, or the way women exploit what advantages the system yields them. Men are the exploiting sex because the system favours them, and they take for granted the *status quo*. In *Female Friends*, focussing on three women friends and their mothers, Grace is shown as worthless, until perhaps the end, while Oliver and Patrick take what the system offers— and more.

The machinery of plot in *Remember Me* is ostensibly supernatural, as a dead divorced wife haunts her ex-husband's second *ménage*. Weldon's apparent reliance on the supernatural may seem unsatisfactory both here and in *Puffball*, where pregnant Liffey is "overlooked" by the local witch. But in both novels the psychology suggests something of Marjorie's realization about her "haunted" home in *Female Friends*: "it was me haunting myself, sending myself messages." Moreover, Weldon's version of "only connect," stressed in *Remember Me*, is that we should "pay attention to coincidence, and in general help the linkages along."

In *Little Sisters* Weldon turned to the very rich. This blackest of black comedies centres melodramatically on the wheelchair-bound Gemma, narrator of the story within a story. Weldon also uses this device in *The Fat Woman's Joke*, *Praxis*, and *The President's Child*, and dialogue is similarly used. The story-within-a-story device enables her to run different time-sequences simultaneously, emphasizing the interlocking of cause and effect between the generations, and also to highlight our imperfect understanding and information, through each individual's partial perception.

Praxis charts the life of a woman who served a prison sentence for killing "a poor little half-witted" baby, as we learn from one of the first-person chapters alternating at the start of the novel with the third-person chapters that subsequently take over. Weldon's female odyssey is entirely individual, though Praxis Duveen is inevitable sister to Dorothy Richardson's Miriam Henderson and May Sinclair's Mary Olivier.

Puffball, about Liffey's pregnancy in Somerset while her husband remains working in London, is as strongly feminist, incorporating much information about female physiology and pregnancy. In *The President's Child* Isabel, the mother of an American presidential candidate's illegitimate child, is ruthlessly hunted in a parody of a thriller. *The Life and Loves of a She-Devil* describes Ruth's remorseless revenge on the best-seller writer who "stole" her husband.

Increasingly in Weldon's work there is a repetitive sense— her books are unlike any other writer's but they are becoming all too similar to each other. This also applies to her two collections of short stories, *Watching Me, Watching You* and *Polaris and Other Stories*, mainly concerned, as usual, with men exploiting women in different domestic settings; an exception, the title story of the second volume, is the best. Despite—or perhaps because of—her unique style, Fay Weldon could become almost a victim of her own success.

—Val Warner

WELTY, Eudora. American. Born in Jackson, Mississippi, 13 April 1909. Educated at Mississippi State College for Women, Columbus, 1926–27; University of Wisconsin, Madison, B.A. 1929; Columbia University School for Advertising, New York, 1930–31. Staff member, *New York Times Book Review*, during World War II. Honorary Consultant in American Letters, Library of Congress, Washington, D.C., 1958. Recipient: Bread Loaf Writers Conference fellowship, 1940; O. Henry Award, 1942, 1943, 1968; Guggenheim fellowship, 1942, 1948; American Academy grant, 1944, Howells Medal,

1955, and Gold Medal, 1972; Ford fellowship, for drama; Brandeis University Creative Arts Award, 1965; Edward MacDowell Medal, 1970; Pulitzer Prize, 1973; National Medal for Literature, 1980; Presidential Medal of Freedom, 1980; American Book Award, for paperback, 1983; Bobst Award, 1984; Common Wealth Award, 1984. D.Litt.: Denison University, Granville, Ohio, 1971; Smith College, Northampton, Massachusetts; University of Wisconsin, Madison; University of the South, Sewanee, Tennessee; Washington and Lee University, Lexington, Virginia. Member, American Academy, 1971. Address: 1119 Pinehurst Street, Jackson, Mississippi 39202, U.S.A.

PUBLICATIONS

Novels

The Robber Bridegroom. New York, Doubleday, 1942; London, Lane, 1944.
Delta Wedding. New York, Harcourt Brace, 1946; London, Lane, 1947.
The Ponder Heart. New York, Harcourt Brace, and London, Hamish Hamilton, 1954.
Losing Battles. New York, Random House, 1970; London, Virago Press, 1982.
The Optimist's Daughter. New York, Random House, 1972; London, Deutsch, 1973.

Short Stories

A Curtain of Green. New York, Doubleday, 1941; London, Lane, 1943.
The Wide Net and Other Stories. New York, Harcourt Brace, 1943; London, Lane, 1945.
Music from Spain. Greenville, Mississippi, Levee Press, 1948.
The Golden Apples. New York, Harcourt Brace, 1949; London, Lane, 1950.
Selected Stories. New York, Modern Library, 1954.
The Bride of Innisfallen and Other Stories. New York, Harcourt Brace, and London, Hamish Hamilton, 1955.
Thirteen Stories, edited by Ruth M. Vande Kieft. New York, Harcourt Brace, 1965.
The Collected Stories of Eudora Welty. New York, Harcourt Brace, 1980; London, Boyars, 1981.
Moon Lake and Other Stories. Franklin Center, Pennsylvania, Franklin Library, 1980.
Retreat. Jackson, Mississippi, Palaemon Press, 1981.

Verse

A Flock of Guinea Hens Seen from a Car. New York, Albondocani Press, 1970.

Other

Short Stories (essay). New York, Harcourt Brace, 1949.
Place in Fiction. New York, House of Books, 1957.
Three Papers on Fiction. Northampton, Massachusetts, Smith College, 1962.
The Shoe Bird (for children). New York, Harcourt Brace, 1964.
A Sweet Devouring (on children's literature). New York, Albondocani Press, 1969.
One Time, One Place: Mississippi in the Depression: A Snapshot Album. New York, Random House, 1971.

A Pageant of Birds. New York, Albondocani Press, 1975.
Fairy Tale of the Natchez Trace. Jackson, Mississippi Historical Society, 1975.
The Eye of the Storm: Selected Essays and Reviews. New York, Random House, 1975.
Ida M'Toy (memoir). Urbana, University of Illinois Press, 1979.
Miracles of Perception: The Art of Willa Cather, with Alfred Knopf and Yehudi Menuhin. Charlottesville, Virginia, Alderman Library, 1980.
Conversations with Eudora Welty, edited by Peggy Whitman Prenshaw. Jackson, University Press of Mississippi, 1984.
One Writer's Beginnings. Cambridge, Massachusetts, Harvard University Press, 1984; London, Faber, 1985.

*

Bibliography: by Noel Polk, in *Mississippi Quarterly* (Mississippi State), Fall 1973; *Eudora Welty: A Reference Guide* by Victor H. Thompson, Boston, Hall, 1976; *Eudora Welty: A Critical Bibliography* by Bethany C. Swearingen, Jackson, University Press of Mississippi, 1984.

Manuscript Collection: Mississippi Department of Archives and History, Jackson.

Critical Studies (selection): *Eudora Welty* by Ruth M. Vande Kieft, New York, Twayne, 1962; *A Season of Dreams: The Fiction of Eudora Welty* by Alfred Appel, Jr., Baton Rouge, Louisiana State University Press, 1965; *Eudora Welty* by Joseph A. Bryant, Jr., Minneapolis, University of Minnesota Press, 1968; *The Rhetoric of Eudora Welty's Short Stories* by Zelma Turner Howard, Jackson, University Press of Mississippi, 1973; *A Still Moment: Essays on the Art of Eudora Welty* edited by John F. Desmond, Metuchen, New Jersey, Scarecrow Press, 1978; *Eudora Welty: Critical Essays* edited by Peggy Whitman Prenshaw, Jackson, University Press of Mississippi, 1979; *Eudora Welty: A Form of Thanks* edited by Ann J. Abadie and Louis D. Dollarhide, Jackson, University Press of Mississippi, 1979; *Eudora Welty's Achievement of Order* by Michael Kreyling, Baton Rouge, Louisiana State University Press, 1980; *Eudora Welty* by Elizabeth Evans, New York, Ungar, 1981; *Tissue of Lies: Eudora Welty and the Southern Romance* by Jennifer L. Randisi, Boston, University Press of America, 1982; *Eudora Welty's Chronicle: A Story of Mississippi Life* by Albert J. Devlin, Jackson, University Press of Mississippi, 1983; *With Ears Opening Like Morning Glories: Eudora Welty and the Love of Storytelling* by Carol S. Manning, Westport, Connecticut, Greenwood Press, 1985.

*   *   *

For Peggy Whitman Prenshaw's collection of tributes, I described Eudora Welty as a rare phenomenon in American letters, "a civilized writer." To explain my meaning, I must turn to Ruth M. Vande Kieft's introduction to the revised version of her *Eudora Welty.* Though Vande Kieft does not employ my term, she explains that as an artist Welty "does not seem to have felt any deep personal alienation from her culture, made no strong protests about the encroachment of industrialism or passing of the old order." Unlike the modernists, she is a writer who has accepted, as the price of civilization, its discontents.

This acceptance finds form in her still too much neglected first novel, *The Robber Bridegroom*, which comes as close as any American fiction to providing a myth of the nation's maturing as, with the passing of the frontier, the wilderness gives way to the mercantile state. "All things are double," planter Clement Musgrove observes ruefully as his own pastoral world that has replaced the Indian wild gives way in its turn to urban society. As for Jamie Lockhart, the two-faced hero of this serio-comic fantasy, Welty notes that "the outward transfer from bandit to merchant had been almost too easy to count it a change at all." The transformation is only cosmetic; merchants use the same gifts as bandits to operate legally in polite society.

Even in her first published story, "Death of a Traveling Salesman," Welty had subtly countered the Wastelanders of the 1920's and 1930's by counterpointing the death of the titular figure (that Arthur Miller would later confirm as emblematic of the dying world) with a Promethean bringer of fire as head of a family just emerging from barbarism to give promise of civilization's renewal.

The kind of memorable stories collected in Welty's first book, *A Curtain of Green*—"Why I Live at the P.O.," "Petrified Man," "A Visit of Charity," and the lilting jazz text "Powerhouse"—had been enthusiastically received by Cleanth Brooks's and Robert Penn Warren's *Southern Review*, house organ of the New Criticism that flourished on ironic portrayals of the differences between people's expectations and their fulfillment. Unlike other writers, however, Welty was able to expand her vision with changing times. With two stories in her next collection, *The Wide Net*, employing such historical figures as Aaron Burr ("First Love") and the bandit Murrell, the Man of God Lorenzo Dow, and the naturalist Audubon in "A Still Moment," Welty seemed embarked (as in *The Robber Bridegroom*) on creating a mythology that earlier aspirants had failed to produce for the emerging nation. In "A Still Moment" she had indeed captured as tellingly as Melville in *Billy Budd* the awful cost of civilization in the destruction of beauty as the quiet naturalist-artist horrifies the two wild men into whose company he has fallen by his cool shooting of a beautiful heron to use as a model for a painting.

Welty did not linger in the distant past, but returned with her next novel, *Delta Wedding*, to the world where she best found her voice (as she describes the climactic step in her development in the autobiographical *One Writer's Beginnings*), the Mississippi of her own lifetime where outsiders were beginning to challenge the rule of imperiously aristocratic family-clans that had dominated the society. Against the most tranquil background that Welty could summon up, she depicts the struggle of an uncle's bride and a niece's groom from what the Fairchilds regard as an inferior class to claim their spouses from a deeply loving but overprotective and tradition-ridden family.

Family dominates also *The Golden Apples*. Welty includes this work in her *Collected Stories*, but it is really what Forrest Ingram calls "a short-story cycle," a novel composed of tales that can be read individually but that gain additional meaning when considered in relationship to each other. Welty explains in *One Writer's Beginnings* how stories that she had originally written about various characters "under different names, at different periods in their lives, in situations not yet interlocking but ready for it," grew into "a shadowing of Greek mythological figures, gods and heroes that wander in various guises, at various times, in and out, emblems of the characters' heady dreams." Focused on "one location already evoked," the portentously named town of Morgana, Mississippi, the meandering tales demonstrate how these provincial versions of universal types, though some wander afar and some stay at home, all return at last to their origins.

Despite the principle of the eternal return seemingly underlying this story-sequence, Welty over the next decade began casting about to evoke what she regards as supremely important in fiction, "a sense of place," about somewhere beyond contemporary Mississippi—the Civil War in "The Burning," the Mississippi delta beyond New Orleans in "No Place for You, My Love," and dreamlike regions as far afield as Italy and Cork, Ireland, in "Going to Naples" and "The Bride of the Innisfallen," in the stories collected in the volume named for the last mentioned. None of these experiments, however, had quite the authenticity of a story included with them, "Ladies in Spring," and the separately published novelette *The Ponder Heart*, both of which take place in the rural Mississippi to which Welty returned, like her characters in *The Golden Apples*, after wandering.

The Ponder Heart, which went on to become a successful play after first being published in its entirety in one issue of the *New Yorker*, exemplifies the narrative form Welty handles with the most consummate skill, the first-person monologue of a figure with whom she by no means identifies, but whose mind she can read and whose words she can capture with the skill of the mockingbird, mimicking the sounds of its Southern "place." This tale, told by a busybody small-town hotel-keeper about the surprising outcome of the trial of her elderly uncle Daniel Ponder for literally tickling his teen-aged bride to death, appropriately won the William Dean Howells Award of the American Academy of Arts and Letters for the most distinguished work of American fiction for the years 1950–1955; for it was Howells who had in *The Rise of Silas Lapham* laid down the challenge to American writers to which Welty's work has become the major response, "... it is certain that our manners and customs go for more in life than our qualities. The price that we pay for civilization is the fine yet impassable differentiation of these. Perhaps we pay too much."

Whatever Welty's views of Howells's last speculation, after her triumphs with *The Ponder Heart*, she settled down to working in the same vein for 15 years as she was preoccupied with her longest and most complex novel, *Losing Battles*, the chronicle in many voices (that she reads aloud magically) of the reunion of an immense clan of subsistence farmers in one of the poorest backwoods regions of the northeast Mississippi hills. In part *Losing Battles* returns (as does later *The Optimist's Daughter*) to the story of an outsider bride's attempts to rescue (as she sees it) the husband for whom she has given up her own ambitions to improve her place in the world from the clutches of his dependent family. As the story takes shape, however, Julia Mortimer, the kind of schoolteacher whom Welty admits in *One Writer's Beginnings* she has most often written about, although she dies beyond the principal scenes of the novel during the day and a half of its action, takes over as the focal figure. She is the embodiment of the enlightened disciplinarian who, though constantly losing battles, has never surrendered in the war to share her illumination with her charges in the waste land at the margin of civilization. A marvelous mixture of comedy and pathos, the long folk-like tale is a remarkable tribute to the indomitability of the human spirit, especially the female spirit in the role that Howells celebrated as the poised guardian of civilized culture.

The writing of the novel was interrupted by two of Welty's most powerful stories that did not appear in book form until her stories were collected in 1980. "Where Is the Voice Coming From?," written in a single night after the shooting of Civil Rights leader Medgar Evers, is the internal monologue of his killer, for which, Welty explains in *One Writer's Beginnings*, she entered "into the mind and inside the skin of a character who could hardly have been more alien or repugnant to me."

"The Demonstrators" is an almost equally harrowing account of a small community's white doctor's involvement in some sordid affairs of the blacks during the years of the Civil Rights crises that he perceives necessitate the transformation of his traditional community. Most remarkable about the two stories is their revelation of the intensity that the most crucial experiences of her "place" can evoke from her.

Perhaps under the impact of such recent events, even Welty's good humor and civilized virtues have been sorely tried, as is suggested by her most recent novel, *The Optimist's Daughter*, in which she reverts to the ironic mode of her earliest stories to depict the plight of a woman who has lost her beloved husband, her mother, and her father as she is deprived of her inheritance and driven out of her home place by her father's young second wife, a redneck (never Welty's term) from Texas (envisioned here as beyond the edge of civilization). Despite all the honors that Welty has justifiably received and despite her avowal in *One Writer's Beginnings* that "Of all my strong emotions, anger is the one least responsible for my work," the ironically titled *The Optimist's Daughter* seems an acknowledgment that like Julia Mortimer, she and her society have been fighting losing battles, although the struggle has been worthwhile in honoring what she describes as her reverence for "the holiness of life."

—Warren French

WENDT, Albert. Samoan. Born in Apia, Western Samoa, 27 October 1939; member of the Aiga Sa-Tuala. Educated at New Plymouth Boys High School, New Zealand, graduated 1957; Ardmore Teacher's College, diploma in teaching, 1959; Victoria University, Wellington, 1960–64, M.A. (honours) in history 1964. Married Jennifer Elizabeth Whyte in 1964; two daughters and one son. Teacher, 1964–69, and Principal, 1969–73, Samoa College, Western Samoa. Senior Lecturer, 1974–75, Assistant Director of Extension Services, 1976–77, and currently Professor of Pacific Literature, University of the South Pacific, Suva, Fiji. Director, University of the South Pacific Centre, Apia, Western Samoa, after 1978. Editor, *Bulletin*, now *Samoa Times*, Apia, 1966. Coordinator, Unesco Program on Oceanic Cultures, 1975–79. Recipient: *Landfall* prize, 1963; Wattie Award, 1980. Agent: Tim Curnow, Curtis Brown (Australia) Pty. Ltd., 27 Union Street, Paddington, New South Wales 2021, Australia. Address: School of Education, University of the South Pacific, Box 1168, Suva, Fiji.

PUBLICATIONS

Novels

Sons for the Return Home. Auckland, Longman Paul, 1973.
Pouliuli. Auckland, Longman Paul, 1977; Honolulu, University Press of Hawaii, 1980.
Leaves of the Banyan Tree. Auckland, Longman Paul, 1979; London, Allen Lane, 1980; as *The Banyan*, New York, Doubleday, 1984.

Short Stories

Flying-Fox in a Freedom Tree. Auckland, Longman Paul, 1974.

The Birth and Death of the Miracle Man. London, Viking, 1986.

Plays

Comes the Revolution (produced Suva, Fiji, 1972).
The Contract (produced Apia, Western Samoa, 1972).

Verse

Inside Us the Dead: Poems 1961 to 1974. Auckland, Longman Paul, 1976.
Shaman of Visions. Auckland, Auckland University Press, 1984; Oxford, Oxford University Press, 1985.

Other

Editor, *Some Modern Poetry from Fiji* [*Western Samoa, the New Hebrides, the Solomon Islands*]. Suva, Fiji, Mana, 4 vols., 1974–75.
Editor, *Lali: A Pacific Anthology.* Auckland, Longman Paul, 1980.

*   *   *

As the Samoan novelist, short story writer, and poet, Albert Wendt, has said, he "belongs to two worlds in almost every way." For more than a decade after his early teens he experienced the difficulties of adapting himself to an alien culture in New Zealand, and his return to Samoa gave rise to a process of readjustment both to his ancestral past and to the post-independence present of his country. His writing stems in some measure from this bi-cultural predicament. It is a return to and a quest for the roots of his being. Significantly enough, "Inside Us the Dead" is the title of his volume of poems.

If his novels and short stories are the work of a self-acknowledged literary pioneer, they are much more than a welcome indication that a Polynesian literature is developing in the southwest Pacific. However difficult it may be to assess the ultimate value of productions for which in many important ways no firm basis for comparison exists, it is nonetheless clear that they achieve distinction as explorations of human relations and a way of life that have almost escaped the attention of romantic or racist outlanders.

Sons for the Return Home, Wendt's first novel, was published many years after his own return to Western Samoa. The simplicity of its plot and language is in marked contrast to the ambiguities and ironies of the pursuit of selfhood which, interwoven with a Samoan myth, provides the theme and gives substance and meaning to the narrative. Because it is mainly concerned with a Samoan family living in New Zealand, the fa'a Samoa or the Samoan way of life becomes an integral part of the novel's structure and not an intrusive element requiring unnecessary explanation. The doubts and difficulties implicit in the theme are developed in terms of incident and human relationship; and the disillusion experienced after "the return home" becomes the climax of the novel that offers no easy solution to the personal problems arising from cultural shock.

Wendt's later publications are centred on the extended families in the villages of Samoa, but they contain little to suggest that they are guide-books to an exotic and romantic island-world. In the short stories of *Flying-Fox in a Freedom Tree*, in *Pouliuli*, and in the three parts of *Leaves of the Banyan Tree* the quest for identity, the attempt to discover the true self caught between the claims of contending cultures, and the search for a precarious freedom from the dictates of competing orthodoxies are raised to a higher level. They are not merely the consequences of racial disharmony, but originate in the basic conditions of human existence. The flying-fox hangs upside-down in the freedom tree. The powerful head of an extended family rejects his past, repudiates his present, and in advanced old age seeks freedom in Pouliuli, in darkness. The rise and fall of another titled head of an aiga in *Leaves of the Banyan Tree*, his lust for power, his imitation of Papalagi (European) ways may be related to the social pollution of the islands, but have their source in a deeper corruption.

This long and powerful novel explores in myth and legend, in traditional social structure, in the changing post-independence present, not only what has happened to the fa'a Samoa, but what has happened to human beings. The comedy and the tragedy, the violence, the horror and the glory of human life, together with man's desperate search for the meaning of existence, are localised in a village setting populated by an extraordinary variety of characters. In its middle section an expanded version of *Flying-Fox in a Freedom Tree*, the novella that gives its title to the earlier volume of short stories, becomes an essential and thoroughly coordinated part of the whole book, linking the first section, "God, Money, and Success," to the third, "Funerals and Heirs," of this saga of a Samoan village.

As a Polynesian writer Wendt has not been satisfied to produce fiction that has entertainment value alone or to exploit the fa'a Samoa for the benefit of the foreign tourist. His aim has been far more ambitious, and he has taken greater risks. If at times he lays himself open to adverse critical comment and his intentions have not always been realised, his achievement is nonetheless impressive. He has set a standard that argues well for the future.

—H. Winston Rhodes

WESCOTT, Glenway. American. Born in Kewaskum, Wisconsin, 11 April 1901. Educated at the University of Chicago (President of the Poetry Society), 1917–19. Full-time writer from 1921; lived in France and Germany, 1925–33. D.Litt.: Rutgers University, New Brunswick, New Jersey, 1963. President, National Institute of Arts and Letters, 1959–62. Address: Hay-Meadows, Rosemont, New Jersey 08556, U.S.A.

PUBLICATIONS

Novels

The Apple of the Eye. New York, Dial Press, 1924; London, Butterworth, 1926.
The Grandmothers: A Family Portrait. New York, Harper, 1927; as *A Family Portrait*, London, Butterworth, 1927.
The Pilgrim Hawk: A Love Story. New York, Harper, 1940; London, Hamish Hamilton, 1946.
Apartment in Athens. New York, Harper, 1945; as *Household in Athens*, London, Hamish Hamilton, 1945.

Short Stories

. . . Like a Lover. Macon, France, Monroe Wheeler, 1926.
Good-bye Wisconsin. New York, Harper, 1928; London, Cape, 1929.

The Babe's Bed. Paris, Harrison, New York, Minton Balch, and London, Simkin, 1930.

Verse

The Bitterns: A Book of Twelve Poems. Evanston, Illinois, Monroe Wheeler, 1920.
Native of Rock: XX Poems 1921–1922. New York, Francisco Bianco, 1925.

Other

Elizabeth Madox Roberts: A Personal Note. New York, Viking Press, 1930.
Fear and Trembling (essays). New York, Harper, 1932.
A Calendar of Saints for Unbelievers. Paris, Harrison, New York, Minton Balch, and London, Simkin, 1932.
12 Fables of Aesop, Newly Narrated. New York, Museum of Modern Art, 1954.
Images of Truth: Remembrances and Criticism. New York, Harper, 1962; London, Hamish Hamilton, 1963.

Editor, *The Maugham Reader.* New York, Doubleday, 1950.
Editor, *Short Novels of Colette.* New York, Dial Press, 1951.

*

Bibliography: "Glenway Wescott: A Bibliography" by Sy Myron Kahn, in *Bulletin of Bibliography 22* (Boston), 1956.

Critical Studies: *Glenway Wescott* by William H. Rueckert, New York, Twayne, 1965; *Glenway Wescott: The Paradox of Voice* by Ira Johnson, Port Washington, New York, Kennikat Press, 1971.

* * *

Glenway Wescott's literary reputation has been overshadowed by the reputation of his fellow upper midwestern writers, most of them like him expatriates during the 1920's: Ernest Hemingway and John Dos Passos from Illinois; Scott Fitzgerald and Sinclair Lewis from Minnesota; and Idaho's Ezra Pound. He has written comparatively little, but that little often comes clos es to an almost lapidary perfection of sentence, paragraph, and scene. Like other "minor" writers, Wescott tends to be forgotten by a public overwhelmed by publishers' announcements of yet more "major" novels and novelists; when the inflated press-releases are consigned to their place as part of the history of advertising rather than as part of literary judgment, however, Glenway Wescott will take his place as one of the finest literary artists in this period's prose for—if nothing else—his novel *The Pilgrim Hawk*, a work which like Joyce's "The Dead," Ford's *The Good Soldier*, and Porter's *Noon Wine*, comes as close to perfection as literary art is liable to allow. Wescott gained an early reputation for technical skill; but we mistake Wescott if we assume his sole virtue is technique.

In his first book, *The Apple of the Eye*, Wescott tells three stories; in one the stunted natural growth of the marsh-land setting frames and parallels the stunting of human feelings, emotions, ideals of a woman who must live in that setting; in the second the girl can find escape only through suicide in the marsh, whereas her seducer goes on about the pagan sensuousness of ancient Greeks; and in the third the conflict between stunted marshy landscape and the seduction of the past as made viable in language takes place within a boy. It is the best of the stories. The theme is, like most themes in fiction, a philosophical commonplace: the problem of moderation, a quality Wescott in his essays insists is a good thing in itself. It is decorum, moderation, the perilous balance of life which are the themes of Wescott's fiction. As in the contrast of hard-drinking German immigrants in the Midwest with Alwyn Tower's grandparents' teetotal puritanism, deviation to either side (decorum can be breeched as much by haughtiness as by rowdiness) brings distortion to human character; and it brings tragedy.

In *The Apple of the Eye* the boy is confronted with the conflict of family duty (as embodied in the disagreeable orthodoxy of his pioneering aunt) and a sort of pagan exuberance in natural beauty (as suggested by a friend's teaching). Such conflicts run through Wescott's fiction. Yet once the central character of most of the fiction, Alwyn Tower, has got free of the homeplace, he finds that his freedom is compromised by memory: he must find his proper relationship to the past if he is to live successfully in the present. So Alwyn Tower sits in his hotel room in the South of France, having told Wisconsin "goodbye," only to remember his past, a process which enabled Wescott to create one of the finest novels in modern American fiction, *The Grandmothers*.

In an essay in *Images of Truth*, Wescott tells of having been impressed by the passage in the *Odyssey* where the shades are called up so that Odysseus can obtain information he needs to find his way home. This is, of course, the "germ" of *The Grandmothers*; for near Nice, Wescott heard and subsequently made Alwyn Tower hear, some drunken American sailors begin to sing "show me the way to go home," raising the question of where home is and how we truly arrive at the place—and know it, as Eliot says, for the first time. Alwyn Tower in a European hotel turns to a picture album; the visual images trigger his imaginative reconstruction of lives, his forebears from about 1840 down to his own parents: it is also a study of history and of what the past means, of the present and of how we come to know ourselves. Such a long look to the past is central to Wescott's works. In *The Pilgrim Hawk* Alwyn Tower in America looks back at a day in France; and in *Apartment in Athens* the very sight of the Acropolis from a window in the apartment's kitchen suggests the dimension of history in which a parable of freedom is played out in the 20th century.

The Pilgrim Hawk, subtitled "a love story," is a short novel in which a few people visit each other and a whole world of relationships is obliquely revealed. Wescott achieves in this novel a most difficult thing: a style which in its precision seems to be no style at all, and a technique so fused to theme and purpose that the story seems merely to tell itself. His is the art which conceals art. And he has used the first person narrator not just to tell a story, but in one sense to force upon the reader an examination of the very concept of perception—of how one perceives the world and then comes to knowledge, if at all. Wescott has made a tale of great complexity out of the simplest materials: one setting, a house and garden in France; a single afternoon in the 1920's, looked back on 20 years later; a plot consisting of triangular relationships of a small cast of characters—Alwyn Tower, the visiting American writer; his friend Alexandra Henry, owner of the house; two servants, Eva and Jean; and the Cullens, a wealthy roaming Irish couple who bring Ricketts, their chauffeur, and the pilgrim hawk. The action is quite limited. The Cullens arrive, displaying their rich eccentricity as well as their habit of preying

on each other and the world; the hawk by contrast is for the most part hooded and quiet. Cullen gets drunk, tries to free the hawk which is recaptured; the narrator discovers the servants and chauffeur in a jealous quarrel in the kitchen; the Cullens leave. Shortly thereafter the Cullens return briefly, Mrs. Cullen with a revolver she carries for her protection, and took from her husband; the revolver is thrown in the lake; again the Cullens leave, and the narrator and his hostess chat briefly about the day's incidents.

Two triangles are at once apparent: the Cullens and the hawk, a triangle which reveals love in its possessive, jealous, even violent aspects, ranging from repressed to domineering, lyrical to savage; and the servants with the chauffeur, a triangle which parallels some of the perverse but vital attachments and needs which constitute involvements of the main triangles. The servant Eva flirts with the chauffeur Ricketts; yet she later explains that her husband Jean needs to be made jealous so that he can express his love, a love otherwise the captive of his reticence. Freedom, then, is dependence, and captivity in love is liberty.

The third triangle is less dramatic, being entirely overlooked by some readers; yet it is central to the examination, in fictional terms, of the conflicts between appetitie and control. In revealing Cullen's hatred, the narrator also reveals himself, his own self-interest and captivity. For as a writer he has missed life, as bound to his art as the hooded hawk on Mrs. Cullen's arm. One must finally wonder why the narrator elects to recall this one day when he was the guest of Alexandra Henry who later became his sister-in-law. The reader is not *told* about the conflict of love and art; instead he receives it, as a powerful undercurrent in the story of an Irish couple and a hawk, which is also a story about love and art, freedom and captivity.

Apartment in Athens undertakes to present the emotions and psychology of conqueror and conquered; yet it is also an extension of the theme of freedom and captivity, now presented in terms of ideology rather than of love. The fictional approach is direct, rather than oblique as in *The Pilgrim Hawk*, so that the war-time "message" is not obscured by subtle rendering; yet that very "message" has obscured for many readers the other themes of the novel.

A German officer is housed in an apartment in the Athens home of a Greek intellectual who tries to "adjust" to this intrusion of a victor; as the two men try to understand each other, we have a paradigm of part of human experience. When the Greek expresses sympathy for the German whose wife is dead, he is imprisoned and executed for "subversive" remarks—a dark and bitter end, if we read the book as something more than a war-time tract. The long letter smuggled out of jail is for the success of the novel unfortunate, for the blatant intrusion of propaganda unbalances the book, which is really about masks of submission, the reality of masks when deception becomes the reality; about the complex accommodations life requires.

In some of the early stories and in *The Pilgrim Hawk*, the narrator is an alien American in France; in *Apartment in Athens* the alien in Greece is a German enemy. This, together with other shifts in narrative style as well as the announced war-time propagandistic aim of the book, has tended to obscure the relationship of the novel to Wescott's other fictions and concerns: the nature of freedom, the types of captivity of which man is capable (whether by a marsh in *The Apple of the Eye* or an invader in *Apartment in Athens*), the ambiguous relationship of a man to his home place (Alwyn Tower says in *Good-bye, Wisconsin* that he has no land, only a family). One hopes that in the not too distant future, Wescott's prose fiction will again be in print so that it can take its place as one of the truly distinguished achievements in 20th-century literature in English.

—James Korges

WEST, Anthony (Panther). British. Born in Hunstanton, Norfolk, 4 August 1914; son of the writers H.G. Wells and Rebecca West. Educated at Stowe School, Buckinghamshire; Central School of Art, London. Married 1) Katharine Church in 1936, one son and one daughter; 2) Lily Dulany Emmet in 1952, one son and one daughter. Dairy farmer, 1937–43; worked on the Far Eastern Desk, 1943–45, and in the Japanese Service, 1945–47, BBC, London. Staff writer, *The New Yorker*, 1950–79. Recipient: Houghton Mifflin Literary Fellowship, 1950. Agent: Wallace and Sheil Agency, 177 East 70th Street, New York, New York 10021. Address: Box 122, Fisher's Island, New York 06390, U.S.A.

PUBLICATIONS

Novels

On a Dark Night. London, Eyre and Spottiswoode, 1949; as *The Vintage*, Boston, Houghton Mifflin, 1950.
Another Kind. London, Eyre and Spottiswoode, 1951; Boston, Houghton Mifflin, 1952.
Heritage. New York, Random House, 1955; revised edition, London, Secker and Warburg, and New York, Washington Square Press, 1984.
The Trend Is Up. New York, Random House, 1960; London, Hamish Hamilton, 1961.
David Rees, Among Others. New York, Random House, and London, Hamish Hamilton, 1970.

Other

Gloucestershire. London, Faber, 1939.
D.H. Lawrence. London, Barker, 1951; revised edition, 1966.
The Crusades. New York, Random House, 1954; as *All about the Crusades*, London, W.H. Allen, 1967.
Principles and Persuasions: Literary Essays. New York, Harcourt Brace, 1957; London, Eyre and Spottiswoode, 1958.
Elizabethan England. New York, Odyssey Press, and London, Hamlyn, 1965.
Mortal Wounds: The Lives of Three Tormented Women. New York, McGraw Hill, 1973; London, Robson, 1975.
John Piper. London, Secker and Warburg, 1979.
H.G. Wells: Aspects of a Life. New York, Random House, and London, Hutchinson, 1984.

Editor, *The Galsworthy Reader.* New York, Scribner, 1968.

*   *   *

Anthony West, the son of Rebecca West and H.G. Wells, has been a painter, a breeder of Guernsey cattle, and a BBC journalist. All his works reflect his wide experience and reading. The novels depict varied scenes, many rural, with sharp visual detail; dialogue is still sharper, often combative, as characters work out West's favorite opposition: resignation to life's and one's own regrettable muddles, versus determination to use reason and freedom to achieve sense. The outcome is often doubtful.

West's first novel, *On a Dark Night*, has Wells's flair for imaginary worlds, but moralized. Wallis, a war-crimes prosecutor, has killed himself. His spirit is told it is "in an obstacle race"—the obstacles are "what you are, what you've been, what you hope for." He must discover the goal by wanting it "without prompting." Teamed with the German general he had got hanged, he samples the "good life"—a Riviera of handsome bodies, gossip, easy sex ("I did not think eternity would be vulgar"), art where every painting exactly fulfills the artist's intention, a fertile Alpine valley—but keeps meeting the women he had failed. Acceptance of pleasure and obliteration of guilty memories by drinking the clear, chill water of Lethe is urged by "Ransome," the opponent of a God who, he says, unfairly tested man by giving him free will. Wallis drinks from a murkier fountain which revivifies miserable memories, but leads him to see them as parts of "that uniquely greater thing— the mind of God." Heaven is there to grasp, if he will.

In *D.H. Lawrence* West called Lawrence's short stories "among the best in the English language" but thought the later novels not art but tracts to revolutionize the "relationship of man to woman and man to man." Studying Lawrence convinced West that a writer's life and writing must be considered together. He did this from 1950 to 1970 as *New Yorker* book reviewer; 27 reviews are collected in *Principles and Persuasions*. Many concern biographies, often evaluating the subject more than the treatment, though he scorns fanciful psychological denigrations of great men. He deplores Orwell's "remorseless pessimism" and even more Reinhold Niebuhr's "pallid pessimism" and rejection of reason, which would leave us helpless before any serious challenge.

West had imagined such a challenge in *Another Kind*. Walter Jackson, a discontented architect, is smitten by a gorgeous prostitute—also discontented. They set up house in an old mill, but his wife pursues—and becomes Anne's friend. The women make the *ménage à trois* (with two children) prosper. But Walter, feeling superfluous, plunges into black-marketing when a strike turns into civil war between republicans and Russian-backed socialists. A triumphant Red Terror leaves only Anne and Francis, Walter's 11-year old son, who vows to find the clue to distinguish good from evil: "If we don't . . . it'll always be like this." Anne, pregnant, thinks life's blacks and whites inextricable, but it will go on; "illumined by his determination to know, hers to create, it would be worth while."

Heritage is based on West's childhood between brilliant, dominating, un-married parents, each with his/her own career and love-life. "Max Town" is, entertainingly and affectionately, Wells undisguised; Rebecca West, then still living, is modified into "Naomi Savage," a classical actress. Richard grows up acting various roles in their lively dramas but, on the brink of World War II, feels he has been, in stage parlance, set "at liberty . . . not at all a bad thing." In the 1984 re-issue, West avows he named his fictional self "Richard Savage" after Johnson's biographee (whom the Countess of Macclesfield, his mother as he and Johnson believed, had tried to get hanged) to show Rebecca West he knew of her attempts to harm him.

The Trend Is Up is set first in New England, where Gavin Hatfield, of a decayed family, decides to make money, then in the Gulf Coast town he saw ripe for development and profitably helped develop. But Gavin's New England wife, who married for money, was shocked at her own sexual responsiveness, and felt a displaced person in the south, turns alcoholic and finally leaves. His son proves a ruthless entrepreneur. Two daughters have tangled love-lives. Gavin, left alone, gently rejects advances from a daughter's friend. He no longer has faith in money or in himself. The friend refuses to believe life will always be incomprehensible while she wants it to make sense. He wishes her happy, and returns to his silent house.

In *David Rees, Among Others* six short stories are re-shaped with a concluding seventh into a second semi-autobiographical childhood novel. Now the mother is a concert pianist, while the father, married to someone else, had died just after she became pregnant, and just before he could start a divorce. Thus family tensions are minimal, except that young David, ecstatic at finding "Aunti Gwen" is really his mother, is appalled when labeled "bastard" by his dying, unforgiving grandmother. Since West's *forte* is writing lively scenes, with shifting casts and often perfunctory connections, these sketches of the growing David, each focussing on some new character, are not much more episodic than former novels. As in *Heritage* the culmination, after sexual initiation, is a muted declaration of independence.

—George McElroy

WEST, Anthony C(athcart Muir). Irish. Born in County Down, Northern Ireland, 1 July 1910. Served in the Royal Air Force Pathfinder Force during World War II: air observer and navigator bomber. Married Olive Mary Burr in 1940; eleven children. Recipient: Atlantic Award, 1946. Address: c/o Midland Bank Ltd., Castle Street, Beaumaris, Anglesey, Gwynedd LL58 8AR, North Wales.

PUBLICATIONS

Novels

The Native Moment. New York, McDowell Obolensky, 1959; London, MacGibbon and Kee, 1961.
Rebel to Judgment. New York, Obolensky, 1962.
The Ferret Fancier. London, MacGibbon and Kee, 1963; New York, Simon and Schuster, 1965.
As Towns with Fire. London, MacGibbon and Kee, 1968; New York, Knopf, 1970.

Short Stories

River's End and Other Stories. New York, McDowell Obolensky, 1958; London, MacGibbon and Kee, 1960.
All the King's Horses and Other Stories. Dublin, Poolbeg Press, 1981.

*

Critical Study: *Forces and Themes in Ulster Fiction* by John Wilson Foster, Dublin, Gill and Macmillan, 1974.

Anthony C. West comments:

I have a creative and an a-political interest in the human condition, wherever and however it may be found, with the incorrigible hope for social harmony and world tolerance.

*   *   *

The fiction of Anthony C. West is filled with poignant and great tenderness, yet it is not just lyric. The main characters of his novels are all very much attuned to nature, yet *in* the world if not entirely *of* it. He handles scenes of childhood well, yet his children grow up. *As Towns with Fire*, his latest novel, creates a focus, almost a culmination, for *The Native Moment* and *The Ferret Fancier*.

As Towns with Fire is the portrait of a man and a war. Beginning New Year's Eve, 1939, it traces the experiences of Christopher MacMannan, an Irishman who has settled in London to train himself as a writer, to the day of his discharge from the R.A.F. after the war has ended. During this time he has done odd jobs and worked with the A.R.P., married, had two children, gone to Belfast where he suffered employment, unemployment, and air raids, joined the Air Force, and flown many missions as observer in Mosquitoes.

There is almost too much in this book, but all of it is good. The war scenes are vivid and suspenseful. There is a charming lyric episode when MacMannan camps out in the hills of Northern Ireland. There is mystery in that, although a long flashback traces his childhood in detail, his history stops when he leaves school; however, references throughout the story imply that between then and the beginning of the story proper, he had travelled widely and saved enough money for a free year in London, at the same time maturing without losing the sensitivity he had as a child. He refuses to submit his poetry for publication until it reaches some form of perfection known only to him. There is some sort of symbolism in his efforts to protect little ducks from the cruelty of thoughtless children.

A similar affinity with nature is in *The Native Moment*, an account of the day Simon Green goes to Dublin with a live eel in a pail; because London sales have dropped off, he is seeking an Irish market for the eels that abound in the northern lakes. He gets drunk, sleeps with a prostitute, is disappointed in a meeting with an old friend, and resolves to marry a girl made pregnant by her uncle. Yet so long as he can keep the eel alive, changing its water regularly he survives his crises. *The Ferret Fancier* is a pastoral in which the same kind of sensitive character is given a ferret as a pet when a child.

West has been compared with Joyce and Beckett, and if one does not seek word play or the broadly comic, it is possible to see the comparison. But in his feeling for nature, for the persons and places of the Irish countryside, he adds another ingredient. For all of their accomplishments this century, Irish writers have tended to be parochially Irish, or write mainly of urban settings or rural settings, but rarely both. West has broken through this barrier.

—William Bittner

WEST, Morris (Langlo). Australian. Born in Melbourne, Victoria, 26 April 1916. Educated at St. Mary's College, St. Hilda, Victoria; University of Melbourne, B.A. 1937. Served in the Australian Imperial Forces Corps of Signals, in the South Pacific, 1939–43: Lieutenant. Married Joyce Lawford in 1953; three sons and one daughter. For several years member of the Christian Brothers Order, and taught in New South Wales and Tasmania, 1933 until he left the order before taking final vows, 1939; secretary to William Morris Hughes, former Prime Minister of Australia, 1943; publicity manager, Radio Station 3 DB, Melbourne, 1944–45; founder, later managing director, Australian Radio Productions Pty. Ltd., Melbourne, 1945–54; after 1954, film and dramatic writer for the Shell Company and the Australian Broadcasting Network, and free-lance commentator and feature writer. Lived in England, 1956–58. Recipient: National Conference of Christians and Jews Brotherhood Award, 1960; James Tait Black Memorial Prize, 1960; Royal Society of Literature Heinemann Award, 1960; Dag Hammarskjold Prize, 1978; *Universe* prize, 1981. D.Litt.: University of California, Santa Clara, 1969; Mercy College, New York, 1982. Fellow, Royal Society of Literature, 1960, and World Academy of Arts and Sciences, 1964. Address: c/o Maurice Greenbaum, Rosenman Colin Freund Lewis and Cohen, 575 Madison Avenue, New York, New York 10022, U.S.A.

PUBLICATIONS

Novels

Moon in My Pocket (as Julian Morris).   Sydney, Australasian Publishing Company, 1945.
Gallows on the Sand.   Sydney, Angus and Robertson, 1956; London, Angus and Robertson, 1958.
Kundu.   Sydney and London, Angus and Robertson, and New York, Dell, 1957.
The Big Story.   London, Heinemann, 1957; as *The Crooked Road*, New York, Morrow, 1957.
The Second Victory.   London, Heinemann, 1958; as *Backlash*, New York, Morrow, 1958.
McCreary Moves In (as Michael East).   London, Heinemann, 1958; as *The Concubine*, as Morris West, London, New English Library, 1973; New York, New American Library, 1975.
The Devil's Advocate.   London, Heinemann, and New York, Morrow, 1959.
The Naked Country (as Michael East).   London, Heinemann, 1960; New York, Dell, 1961.
Daughter of Silence.   London, Heinemann, and New York, Morrow, 1961.
The Shoes of the Fisherman.   London, Heinemann, and New York, Morrow, 1963.
The Ambassador.   London, Heinemann, and New York, Morrow, 1965.
The Tower of Babel.   London, Heinemann, and New York, Morrow, 1968.
Summer of the Red Wolf.   London, Heinemann, and New York, Morrow, 1971.
The Salamander.   London, Heinemann, and New York, Morrow, 1973.
Harlequin.   London, Collins, and New York, Morrow, 1974.
The Navigator.   London, Collins, and New York, Morrow, 1976.
Proteus. London, Collins, and New York, Morrow, 1979.
The Clowns of God.   London, Hodder and Stoughton, and New York, Morrow, 1981.
The World Is Made of Glass.   London, Hodder and Stoughton, and New York, Morrow, 1983.

Plays

Daughter of Silence (produced New York, 1961).   New York, Morrow, 1962.
The Heretic (produced London, 1970).   New York, Morrow, 1969; London, Heinemann, 1970.
The World Is Made of Glass (produced New York, 1982).

Screenplays: *The Devil's Advocate*, 1977; *The Second Victory*, 1984.

Television Play: *Vendetta*, 1958 (UK).

Other

Children of the Sun.   London, Heinemann, 1957; as *Children of the Shadows: The True Story of the Street Urchins of Naples*, New York, Doubleday, 1957.
Scandal in the Assembly: A Bill of Complaints and a Proposal for Reform on the Matrimonial Laws and Tribunals of the Roman Catholic Church, with Robert Francis.   London, Heinemann, 1970.

*   *   *

Coming from an unhappy and deprived home, Morris West gained all the training that the Christian Brothers could give him, but turned his back on them just before taking his final vows: a period and a journey that resulted in his first book, *Moon in My Pocket*, notable chiefly for revealing few signs of promise. However, the two novels which followed, *Gallows on the Sand* and *Kundu*, are quite readable, though his first successful book was the non-fictional *Children of the Sun*. This documents the shocking conditions of the lives of Neapolitan slum children, and the selfless work of Father Borelli in attempting to help them.

The Second Victory deals with the ambiguities of administration in Allied-occupied Austria, a country that West came to know well in his search for cheap living as he set about the arduous task of writing while supporting a family. The novel's chief merit, as indeed of all of West's best work, is its pace; its weaknesses are also typical: the characters are not fully realized, the human relationships are unconvincing, and West relies rather heavily on coincidences for his denouement. *The Devil's Advocate* grew out of West's research for *Children of the Sun*, drawing together his interest in Italy and his interest in Catholicism. Over-ambitious, the novel suffers from West's penchant for philosophizing, as he tries to encompass too much material, though the novel's hero-victim is powerfully moving.

At this point in his career, worried about being labelled a Roman Catholic novelist, West commenced writing consciously for a non-Catholic and non-christian readership. *Daughter of Silence* involves an exploration of the classic dilemma of the law: is it an instrument of public order, or is it an instrument for dispensing absolute justice? *The Shoes of the Fisherman* starts with the death of a Pope, and was launched just a week before the death of Pope John XXIII. Unexpected media and public interest in the novel followed, and, apparently as a result of having tasted the fruits of topicality, West seems to have consistently, from this time on, researched and written stories that had some chance of hitting the headlines. *The Ambassador* is set in South Vietnam before, during and after the overthrow of President Diem, clearly identifiable in the novel as President Cung; the US Ambassador, Amberley, is fictional. Amberley has recently taken to Zen which makes him vulnerable to self-questioning, a state of being not suited to dealing with the moral crisis in which he finds himself: whether or not to set in motion a series of actions which will lead to Cung's downfall and death. Convinced that the war against the Vietcong cannot be won as long as Cung is in control, Amberley feels he has to decide against Cung, but he is shattered by the decision, and retires to a monastery to try to find peace and wholeness again. The novel was criticized for being flashy and pseudo-profound, and the Ambassador's soul-searching seems to indicate a character a little less robust than most countries would require of their diplomats, but the book renders the Vietnamese scene beautifully, conveying the feel of Saigon and the countryside after 20 years of battering, the war-weariness of the Vietnamese, and the impossibility of the American task.

Summer of the Red Wolf is a deceptively simple and underestimated novel of a journey to the Western Isles by a man who desires only some peace and quiet, but finds no escape from love and jealousy. Though this novel too has the occasional purple passage, it is written on the whole in a controlled and evocative style, quite superior to the sorts of clichés in which West often indulges—for example in *The Salamander*. This book was remarkable in that it represented West's first (and not very successful) attempt to use symbolism. In *Harlequin* the symbolism begins to be more effective though the book has a strange set of moral notions. Basil Yanko, a self-made computer man, is determined to ruin his aristocratic rival George Harlequin, a merchant banker, by selling him false programmes and then accusing him of fraud. The struggle is clearly between culture and California: culture soon draws a circle of journalists, financiers, and terrorists who start murdering people to further its interests. Yanko confesses under torture, and Harlequin (in a gesture no doubt intended to be read as magnanimous) burns the confession—though not the cheque that came with it! *Proteus* too has an outrageous plot concerning the idealistic and heroic John Spada, head of an international business concern, who leads an underground movement, snatching prisoners of conscience from all over the world. Unfolding at a cracking pace, the novel offers an entertaining and wish-fulfilling fantasy that appeals to the adolescent in all of us.

With the exception of a few specifically Roman Catholic novels, such as *The Shoes of the Fisherman*, West has been secularizing his fiction increasingly over the years. Though there are wider moral and spiritual issues even in the most secular of his work, *The Clowns of God* is his first novel to tackle a specifically religious subject in such a way as to interest those who do not take to Church matters. The Pope has a vision of the end of the world and is given the task of telling the faithful to prepare for the terrible disasters that presage the Second Coming. Since such a message would destroy teetering public confidence in social and political structures, the awesome bureaucracy of the Vatican moves swiftly to silence the Pope's proposed encyclical, and he is given the choice of abdicating or being certified insane. The novel explores his reasons for abdicating and his struggles and successes in spreading the message. His deep spirituality is rendered beautifully, though West's eschatology and theology seem surprisingly unorthodox.

With admirable consistency West has extended his range, moving from romantic and adventure stories to documentary, faction, history, and what might be called prophecy. His popularity as a novelist has been established for decades. However, with his latest novel, *The World Is Made of Glass*, West has finally made a bid for recognition as a major literary writer. The book is beautifully written, down to the tiny Europeanisations of style at the appropriate places. The story concerns Jung and Magda, who represent the two poles of modern Western values: one embodies knowledge; the other has outlived the wildest dreams of wealth and sensual variety, and discovered them wanting. This is a many-layered book, which generously repays careful reading.

—Prabhu S. Guptara

WEST, Paul (Noden). American. Born in Eckington, Derbyshire, England, 23 February 1930; moved to the United States, 1961; became citizen, 1971. Educated at the University of Birmingham, 1947–50, B.A. (1st class honours) 1950; Oxford University, 1950–52; Columbia University, New York, M.A. 1953. Served in the Royal Air Force, 1954–57: Flight Lieutenant. Assistant Professor, 1957–58, and Associate Professor of English, 1959–62, Memorial University of Newfoundland, St. John's. Associate Professor, 1962–68, and since 1968, Professor of English and Comparative Literature, and Senior Fellow, Institute for the Arts and Humanistic Studies, Pennsylvania State University, University Park. Visiting Professor of Comparative Literature, University of Wisconsin, Madison, 1965–66; Pratt Lecturer, Memorial University of Newfoundland, 1970; Crawshaw Professor of Literature, Colgate University, Hamilton, New York, Fall 1972; Virginia Woolf Lecturer, University of Tulsa, Oklahoma, 1973; Melvin Hill Visiting Professor, Hobart and William Smith Colleges, Geneva, New York, Fall 1974; Writer-in-Residence, Wichita State University, Kansas, 1982, and University of Arizona, Tucson, 1984. Contributor to *New Statesman*, London, 1954–62. Since 1962, regular contributor to *New York Times Book Review* and *Washington Post Book World*. Recipient: Canada Council Senior fellowship, 1960; Guggenheim fellowship, 1962; Aga Khan Prize (*Paris Review*), 1974; National Endowment for the Arts fellowship, 1980, 1985; Hazlett Memorial Award, 1981; American Academy award, 1985. Address: 117 Burrowes Building, Pennsylvania State University, University Park, Pennsylvania 16802, U.S.A.

PUBLICATIONS

Novels

A Quality of Mercy. London, Chatto and Windus, 1961.
Tenement of Clay. London, Hutchinson, 1965.
Alley Jaggers. London, Hutchinson, and New York, Harper, 1966.
I'm Expecting to Live Quite Soon. New York, Harper, 1970; London, Gollancz, 1971.
Caliban's Filibuster. New York, Doubleday, 1971.
Bela Lugosi's White Christmas. London, Gollancz, and New York, Harper, 1972.
Colonel Mint. New York, Dutton, 1972; London, Calder and Boyars, 1973.
Gala. New York, Harper, 1976.
The Very Rich Hours of Count von Stauffenberg. New York, Harper, 1980.
Rat Man of Paris. New York, Doubleday, 1986.

Uncollected Short Stories

"How to Marry a Hummingbird," in *Modern Occasions*. New York, Farrar Straus, 1966.
"The Season of the Single Women," in *New American Review 11*, edited by Theodore Solotaroff. New York, Simon and Schuster, 1971.
"The Man Who Ate the Zeitgeist," in *London Magazine*, April-May 1971.
"Invitation to a Vasectomy," in *Words* (Boston), Summer 1973.
"Brain Cell 99,999,999,999," in *New Directions 28*. New York, New Directions, 1974.
"The Wet-God's Macho," in *Remington Review* (Elizabeth, New Jersey), Spring 1974.

"Tan Salaam," in *Paris Review*, Spring 1974.
"The Universe and Other Fictions," in *New Directions 31*. New York, New Directions, 1975.
"The Sun in Heat," in *Remington Review* (Elizabeth, New Jersey), Spring 1975.
"The Monocycle," in *Carleton Miscellany* (Northfield, Minnesota), Spring 1975.
"Gustav Holst Composes Himself," in *New Directions 33*. New York, New Directions, 1976.
"Paganini Break," in *Tri-Quarterly* (Evanston, Illinois), Winter 1976.
"The Glass-Bottomed Boat," in *Mother Jones* (San Francisco), November 1976.
"Another Minotaur," in *New Directions 36*. New York, New Directions, 1978.
"The Basement of Kilimanjaro," in *Partisan Review* (New Brunswick, New Jersey), vol. 46, no. 4, 1979.
"Field Day for a Boy Soldier," in *Iowa Review* (Iowa City), Spring 1979.
"Villa-Lobos in Winter," in *Review* (London), Winter 1979–80.
"Those Pearls His Eyes," in *New Directions 44*. New York, New Directions, 1982.
"Dewey Canyon," in *Conjunctions* (New York), Spring 1982.
"The Destroyer of Delight," in *Paris Review*, Spring 1983.
"Occupied by a Through Passenger," in *Denver Quarterly*, Summer 1983.
"He Who Wears the Pee of the Tiger," in *Tri-Quarterly* (Evanston, Illinois), Spring 1984.
"Hopi," in *Kenyon Review* (Gambier, Ohio), Fall 1985.

Verse

(*Poems*).   Oxford, Fantasy Press, 1952.
The Spellbound Horses.   Toronto, Ryerson Press, 1960.
The Snow Leopard.   London, Hutchinson, 1964; New York, Harcourt Brace, 1965.

Other

The Fossils of Piety: Literary Humanism in Decline.   New York, Vantage Press, 1959.
The Growth of the Novel.   Toronto, Canadian Broadcasting Corporation, 1959.
Byron and the Spoiler's Art.   London, Chatto and Windus, and New York, St. Martin's Press, 1960.
The Modern Novel.   London, Hutchinson, 1963; New York, Hillary House, 1965.
I, Said the Sparrow (autobiography).   London, Hutchinson, 1963.
Robert Penn Warren.   Minneapolis, University of Minnesota Press, 1964; London, Oxford University Press, 1965.
The Wine of Absurdity: Essays in Literature and Consolation.   University Park, Pennsylvania State University Press, 1966.
Words for a Deaf Daughter.   London, Gollancz, 1969; New York, Harper, 1970.
Doubt and Dylan Thomas (lecture).   St. John's, Newfoundland, Memorial University, 1970.
Out of My Depths: A Swimmer in the Universe.   New York, Doubleday, 1983.

*

Manuscript Collections: Pattee Library, Pennsylvania State University, University Park; Mugar Memorial Library, Boston University.

Critical Studies: by John W. Aldridge, in *Kenyon Review* (Gambier, Ohio), September 1966; *New Literary History* (Charlottesville, Virginia), Spring 1970 and Spring 1976; "The Writer's Situation II" in *New American Review 10*, New York, New American Library, 1970, and "In Defense of Purple Prose," in *New York Times*, 15 December 1985, both by West; interview with George Plimpton, in *Caliban's Filibuster*, 1971; review in *New York Times Book Review*, 20 June 1971; in *Nation* (New York), 8 January 1977; article by Brian McLaughlin, in *British Novelists since 1960* edited by Jay L. Halio, Detroit, Gale, 1983.

Paul West comments:
Looking back, I see myself as a late starter who, between thirty and forty, in a sustained and intensive spell of application, set down half a lifetime's pondering and moved from a restless contentment with criticism and fairly orthodox fiction to an almost Fellini-like point of view.
Imagination, as I see it, is an alembic in limbo; it invents, and what it invents has to be added to the sum of Creation—even though nothing imagination invents is wholly its own. I think the realistic novel has served its turn. Fiction has to reclaim some of its ancient privileges, which writers like Lucian and Nashe and Rabelais and Grimmelshausen exploited to the full. I think that only the plasticity of a free-ranging imagination can do justice to late-20th-century man who, as incomplete as man ever was, keeps on arming himself with increasing amounts of data which, as ever, mean nothing at all.
My own fiction I have come to see as—I want it to be—a kind of linear mosaic, which is what my second novel, *Tenement of Clay*, was in a rudimentary form and which two recent ones—*The Very Rich Hours of Count von Stauffenberg* and *Rat Man of Paris*—are in a much more advanced and demanding way. Actually, since both vocabulary and syntax are themselves fictive I don't regard my autobiographical writing as essentially different from my fiction: they're both part of the mosaic I invent.

*   *   *

For excellent reasons, Camden, the central character in Paul West's uneven, faintly gothic first novel, *A Quality of Mercy*, feels that "what was wrong was not that life was too much but that it was just too many. There was powder in the wind when there should have been crystals immune from every wind. . . . Life was an unknown and unknowable quantity." Although now, more than 25 years later, West's fiction has grown so rich and apparently diverse that good readers will be suspicious of generalizations, it is still possible to see him as an artist working out unexpected variations on the theme Camden hints at indirectly, the problem of contingency. The final human tragedy, Santayana cooly observes, lies in our awareness that everything might just as well have been otherwise, in our consciousness that we are accidental creatures gratuitously existing in random places and forms. We might have been Caesar or we might have been a victim of the Holocaust; and in times when few can go on believing that angels were destined to be angels and stones stones, this can be a devastating insight. There are writers—Sartre, for example—who are in fact appalled by the idea; there are writers like Wallace Stevens and Iris Murdoch who are often exhilarated by the inexplicable variety of being; and there are also a few writers, like Nabokov and Paul West, who veer back and forth eloquently but uneasily between delight and disgust.

A good many of West's characters live condemned to this awareness of contingency, and to make matters worse, condemned to exist in exotic and unlovely forms. The archetypal figure is Caliban, an artist of sorts, howling for justice or at least freedom. In *A Quality of Mercy* there is Camden; in *Tenement of Clay* there are Lazarus, the defiant dwarf, and his mentor, Papa Nick, failed saint and keeper of a flophouse whose inmates he tries to reconcile to "the truth of life," and in helping them to swallow that truth to learn, himself, the proper "angle of drinking." In *Caliban's Filibuster*, there is Cal, the failed writer, and in West's finest novel Count von Stauffenberg, who must go on suffering beyond the grave for his failures. But clearest of all there is Alley Jaggers. At the start of that novel, Alley, longing for some dimly perceived beauty, is "enclosed and embattled but not closed up and defeated," but by the end he is both defeated and literally locked away. In *Bela Lugosi's White Christmas* Alley provides what is probably West's bitterest cry of rage:

> I never applied for admission to your so-called universe. I was kidnapped into it from a better place ... where it is more *optional* than it is here and now, about the time old God Almighty was in a poxdoctoring dither, not sure which day was which, and wondering why the bejesus he got involved with the whole thing in the first place. ... My own feeling is this, in case you care, want it for your little black book: if only He'd kept at it all through the seventh day and maybe for all of the next week, we'd all of us be better off. It's just the same as saying the world—your so-called universe—is just a wee bit carelessly put together, fundamentally, firmamentally, fucked up, there being whole armies of folks with club foots, hare lips, folks with spines open to the fresh air and brains blown up as big as hunchback's humps, not to mention the deaf and the blind and the straightforward deformed, the slobberers and slaverers, the daft and St. Vitus dancers, the monkey-faced and the Siamese twins, folks whose hands grow out from their shoulders and folks with no especial sex at all. Don't tell me that twenty sets of quints can make up for all that. Why, it's like asking a pharmacist for an aspirin and getting gunpowder instead. Better to scrap it in the first place if he couldn't get it right or couldn't make up his mind. ... Whatever blueprint there was, well, it was just a bit smudged. There ought to be laws against great minds bringing universes into being just for fun. There: that's AJ's first book of the bible; I could have done better myself once I'd gotten the sun to co-operate.

"Blow it all up then?" asks Alley's equally failed analyst, to which Alley replies, "*I* would, except I'd be loth to give your old universe a helping hand with a dead hand of my own."

It is natural enough to wonder where this view of things comes from, and tempting to conclude that it grew from West's experiences with his own deaf, brain-damaged daughter, Mandy. In such cases a parent's first response is often to ignore the handicap, to make it "go away"—or to make it go away by making the child go away. But there is another possible response: to see the handicap as a special kind of gift, and while trying to eliminate it still to "learn its nature by heart, as a caution." *Words for a Deaf Daughter* is the astonishing account of West's infinitely patient attempts to understand the world in which Mandy is enclosed but not, if he can help it, defeated; to grasp, by imaginative participation, the "supersensitivity" which such children often possess. The "caution," that is, the lesson, turns out to be an awareness of just how

arbitrary our definitions of sense and madness can be. The world West and his readers learn to look at through Mandy's eyes is a world in which things are seen with cleansed perception.

Words for a Deaf Daughter is "fact"; *Gala* is "fiction," or, as West puts it, "the scenario of a wish-fulfillment," in which an adolescent Mandy comes to visit her father in America and finally speaks to him. The importance of this wish-fulfillment is central to West's fiction and makes it imperative to remember that something like Alley's cry of rage is not really West's own cry. For all of the pain which these characters must endure, West sees that act of expression, of imaginative creation, as an act of defiance and achievement, a substantial addition to the sum of existing things. In a 1971 interview he remarked:

> What a gratuitous universe it is, anyway; what a bloody surd ... what with such defectives as waltzing mice, axolotls that should become salamanders but don't, children born without one of the human senses. Not that I'm harping on the universe's lapses rather than its norms; no, what impresses me finally is the scope for error within the constancy of the general set-up contrasted with the power to imagine things as otherwise—to rectify, to deform. What is man? He's the creature imaginative enough to ask that question. And although I know that the imagination had always to start with something not its own—hasn't *complete* underivedness—it can generate much pearl from little grit.

In *The Wine of Absurdity* he states even more emphatically that the imagination is "the only restorative each man has that is entirely his own. ... Imagination, trite and presumptuous as it may seem to express the fact, is the only source of meaning our lives can have." Thus imagining Mandy's visit and making her speak is a triumphant act; and having so imagined, West reports that "I can begin sentences with an *I* again, not so much glad or proud as astounded to be here on this planet as myself and not as a peppermint starfish, a thistle, an emu, a bit of quartz. Or a doorknob." It is the artist's imagination, then, which can turn Camden's irritating powder into crystals—if, of course, the artist has anything like Paul West's drive and dazzling verbal resources.

—Elmer Borklund

WHARTON, William (a pseudonym). American. Born in Philadelphia, Pennsylvania, in 1925. Educated at the University of California, Los Angeles. Married; four children. Painter and writer. Recipient: American Book Award, 1980. Lives in Paris. Address: c/o Knopf Inc., 201 East 50th Street, New York, New York 10022, U.S.A.

PUBLICATIONS

Novels

Birdy. New York, Knopf, and London, Cape, 1979.
Dad. New York, Knopf, and London, Cape, 1981.
A Midnight Clear. New York, Knopf, and London, Cape, 1982.

Scumbler.   New York, Knopf, and London, Cape, 1984.
Pride.   New York, Knopf, 1985.

*

William Wharton comments:

The main thrust of my work is the presentation of fantasy as a normal occupation and one which is present in all modes of existence. Most of my work is in the first person and present tense in order to establish immediacy and direct participation in the events, emotions, and experience by the reader.

*   *   *

In *Birdy*, William Wharton's first novel, the title character longs to fly. But this is only part of his larger goal. Birdy seeks a way to "know" his life without "knowledge," to move toward a free and unselfconscious life more in tune with the rhythms of the world and nature than the life offered him as a human male. Much of *Birdy* is taken up with meticulous descriptions of the life cycles of pigeons and canaries. It is from living as closely as possible with these birds that Birdy hopes to learn how to live his ideal life. Set in contrast to Birdy is his friend Alfonso, a wrestler who is looking to "pin" the world any way he can to gain revenge or some advantage. Both Birdy and Alfonso are drawn into World War II, and the horror of the war drives Birdy out of his human self. He begins imitating a baby bird waiting to be fed. It is Alfonso, himself damaged—physically, where it can most harm his image of himself—who tries to "feed" Birdy what he needs to know to be willing to become human again, though Alfonso is in no hurry to rejoin the race, either. So much of *Birdy* is taken up with the minute particulars of the lives of the birds that Alfonso's story is only sketchily told and this asymmetry of bird life over human life makes for tedious reading at times.

Birdy's greatest happiness during his time of involvement with his birds comes not from his attempts to fly, but during the nesting time when he helps the young birds survive and learn to fly. Birdy's involvement with the canaries is centered on the female he calls "Birdie." (He names her dark, violent mate "Alfonso.") Birdy identifies strongly with the bird's nurturing side, envies her her female role. This is a thread that is part of several other Wharton characters, most notably the title character in *Scumbler*. Scum, as he calls himself, is an aging American painter living with his family in Paris. Scum at times wishes he were a woman, even telling one young woman to teach him how to love her "as a woman would." Scum rents out a string of apartments, rooms, and shelters he has fixed up. He calls these his "nests." (He also thinks of his paintings as "nests" or "hideouts.") Scum, like Birdy, attempts to recreate his own existence: "I'm always trying to design my life . . . it has to be lived on purpose with purpose." His purpose in life is as much nesting and nurturing (though his own children hardly figure in the novel at all) as it is painting. Like *Birdy*, *Scumbler* is episodic, almost Quixotic, and relies on a string of epiphanies rather than on any plot resolution for its effect. Both novels end abruptly, with visions of the title characters' personal Utopias.

Dad is Wharton's most conventional novel, the story of three generations of men in a family. The oldest man is dying even while enjoying a period of restored youth; his son watches and thinks of himself as "next in line," while the third, not yet out of his teens, is impatient to get on with his life out from under the cautionary umbrella of his father's wishes for him. The grandfather is a grand character, full of life and honest surprise, but the others are little more than place holders, stock

figures used to illustrate the contrasts Wharton wants to establish. *Dad* is Wharton's longest novel, but brings little new insight to the generational conflict.

Set at the beginning of the Battle of the Bulge, *A Midnight Clear* is at once Wharton's most direct and believeable novel and that which most clearly illustrates the absurdity of human conflict. Two groups of soldiers, one American, one German, are holed up in a mountain valley. Using a snowman, a scarecrow, and a Christmas tree the two sides communicate their desire for peace with one another. Against all their best efforts death and war descend on the scene. Wharton's always meticulous prose takes on a hardboiled sound in *A Midnight Clear*: "My being squad leader is also another story. It's another story the way *Peter Rabbit* is another story from *Crime and Punishment*."

In *Pride* Wharton's efforts at using a nonhuman way of life to throw light on human moral questions is much more successful than in *Birdy*. The novel is set in 1938, as the Depression is easing up and unions are working their way into more industries. The young narrator's father is being threatened by unionbreakers. The family travels to the sea shore while the father sorts out his thoughts. While they are there a lion escapes from a boardwalk sideshow and kills a man who has tortured him. The double meaning of the word "pride"—honor and the family group—is manipulated by Wharton to parallel the lion's condition with that of the father. The lion, whose pride(s) has been destroyed, goes to his death because he has nowhere else to go. The father gathers his pride(s) and sets off on a course of self-reliance.

—William C. Bamberger

WHITE, Patrick (Victor Martindale).   Australian.   Born in London, England, 28 May 1912. Educated at Tudor House, Moss Vale, and other schools in Australia, 1919–25; Cheltenham College, 1925–29; King's College, Cambridge, 1932–35, B.A. in modern languages 1935. Served in the Royal Air Force, in the Middle East, 1940–45: Intelligence Officer. Travelled in Europe and the United States, and lived in London, before World War II; returned to Australia after the War. Recipient: Australian Literature Society Gold Medal, 1939; Miles Franklin Award, 1958, 1962; W.H. Smith Literary Award, 1959; National Conference of Christians and Jews Brotherhood Award, 1962; Nobel Prize for Literature, 1973. A.C. (Companion, Order of Australia), 1975 (returned). Lives in Sydney. Agent: Curtis Brown, 27 Union Street, Paddington, New South Wales 2021, Australia.

PUBLICATIONS

Novels

Happy Valley.   London, Harrap, 1939; New York, Viking Press, 1940.
The Living and the Dead.   London, Routledge, and New York, Viking Press, 1941.
The Aunt's Story.   London, Routledge, and New York, Viking Press, 1948.
The Tree of Man.   New York, Viking Press, 1955; London, Eyre and Spottiswoode, 1956.
Voss.   New York, Viking Press, and London, Eyre and Spottiswoode, 1957.

Riders in the Chariot.   New York, Viking Press, and London, Eyre and Spottiswoode, 1961.
The Solid Mandala.   New York, Viking Press, and London, Eyre and Spottiswoode, 1966.
The Vivisector.   New York, Viking Press, and London, Cape, 1970.
The Eye of the Storm.   London, Cape, 1973; New York, Viking Press, 1974.
A Fringe of Leaves.   London, Cape, 1976; New York, Viking Press, 1977.
The Twyborn Affair.   London, Cape, 1979; New York, Viking Press, 1980.
Memoirs of Many in One.   London, Cape, 1986.

Short Stories

The Burnt Ones.   New York, Viking Press, and London, Eyre and Spottiswoode, 1964.
The Cockatoos: Shorter Novels and Stories.   London, Cape, 1974; New York, Viking Press, 1975.

Plays

Return to Abyssinia (produced London, 1947).
The Ham Funeral (produced Adelaide, 1961; Crewe, Cheshire, 1969).   Included in *Four Plays*, 1965.
The Season at Sarsaparilla (produced Adelaide, 1962). Included in *Four Plays*, 1965.
A Cheery Soul (produced Melbourne, 1963).   Included in *Four Plays*, 1965.
Night on Bald Mountain (produced Adelaide, 1964). Included in *Four Plays*, 1965.
Four Plays.   London, Eyre and Spottiswoode, 1965; New York, Viking Press, 1966.
Big Toys (produced Sydney, 1977).   Sydney, Currency Press, 1978.
The Night the Prowler (screenplay).   Melbourne, Penguin, 1977.
Signal Driver (produced Adelaide, 1983).   Sydney, Currency Press, 1983.
Netherwood (produced Adelaide, 1983).   Sydney, Currency Press, 1983.

Screenplay: *The Night the Prowler*, 1979.

Verse

The Ploughman and Other Poems.   Sydney, Beacon Press, 1935.

Other

Flaws in the Glass: A Self-Portrait.   London, Cape, 1981; New York, Viking Press, 1982.

*

Bibliography: *A Bibliography of Patrick White* by Janette Finch, Adelaide, Libraries Board of South Australia, 1966.

Critical Studies (selection): *Patrick White* by Geoffrey Dutton, Melbourne, Lansdowne Press, 1961, revised edition, Melbourne, London, and New York, Oxford University Press, 1971; *Patrick White* by Robert F. Brissenden, London, Longman, 1966; *Patrick White* by Barry Argyle, Edinburgh, Oliver and Boyd, 1967; *Ten Essays on Patrick White Selected from*

Southerly edited by G.A. Wilkes, Sydney and London, Angus and Robertson, 1970; *The Mystery of Unity: Theme and Technique in the Novels of Patrick White* by Patricia A. Morley, Montreal, McGill-Queen's University Press, 1972; *Fossil and Psyche* by Wilson Harris, Austin, University of Texas, 1974; *Patrick White* by Alan Lawson, Melbourne and New York, Oxford University Press, 1974, London, Oxford University Press, 1975; *The Eye in the Mandala: Patrick White: A Vision of Man and God* by Peter Beatson, London, Elek, and New York, Barnes and Noble, 1976; *Patrick White: A General Introduction* by Ingmar Bjorksten, translated by Stanley Gerson, St. Lucia, University of Queensland Press, and Atlantic Highlands, New Jersey, Humanities Press, 1976; *Patrick White's Fiction* by William Walsh, London, Allen and Unwin, and Totowa, New Jersey, Rowman and Littlefield, 1977; *Patrick White: A Critical Symposium* edited by Ron E. Shepherd and Kirpal Singh, Bedford Park, South Australia, Flinders University Centre for Research, and Washington, D.C., Three Continents, 1978; *Patrick White* by Manly Johnson, New York, Ungar, 1980; *Patrick White* by Brian Kiernan, London, Macmillan, and New York, St. Martin's Press, 1980; *A Tragic Vision: The Novels of Patrick White* by A.M. McCulloch, St. Lucia, University of Queensland Press, 1983; *Aspects of Time, Ageing and Old Age in the Novels of Patrick White 1939–1979* by Mari-Ann Berg, Gothenberg, Gothenberg Studies in English, 1983; *Laden Choirs: The Fiction of Patrick White* by Peter Wolfe, Lexington, University Press of Kentucky, 1983; *Patrick White* by John Colmer, London, Methuen, 1984; *Patrick White* by John A. Weigel, Boston, Twayne, 1984.

*   *   *

Despite the fact that Patrick White has been publishing since 1939, he continues to be considered a difficult and obscure writer. The award of the Nobel Prize in 1973 reinforced the judgement of those who had always admired his work, and established him as a major international figure. White is a writer who makes serious demands of his readers, straining prose to the utmost poetic limits, putting severe pressure on syntax and vocabulary, and stretching credence to an unusual degree in his search for the transcendent in the lives of his idiosyncratic characters.

Although White was born in England while his parents were on a European tour, he grew up in Australia and did not return to England until he was sent to public school and university. After service in the R.A.F. in the Second World War he returned to Australia in 1948 and has lived there ever since, first on a small-holding outside Sydney and later in the city itself. His writing, although clearly dealing with universal themes, takes Australian history, Australian landscape, and Australian society as its raw material. There is a sustained and permanent core in White's fiction that allows his whole achievement to be seen as a continuing exploration of the individual search for identity and truth, reaching for a religious transcendence that is far from conventional structures imposed by established churches. Frequently his happiest and most fulfilled individuals are those who come to see their place in life as part of a larger landscape and a larger scheme.

Happy Valley, White's first published novel, has never been reprinted and the novelist is happy for it to disappear. Similarly *The Living and the Dead*, White's second novel, "should never have been written." *The Aunt's Story*, which was largely written on the steamer as he returned from Europe after the war is everything that the two earlier novels are not: witty, intensely realised, vividly evocative, and unusually poetic. The aunt is eccentric and outside normal society; she ends her life mad to all conventional judgement but her insights are sound and she understands her fellow artist, Moraitis, the cellist. Her landscape is the hard dry Australian pasture, and she rejects a wealthy suitor who would offer her sofas instead of a hard bench. The language of *The Aunt's Story* is astringent and bracing, forcing itself upon the reader and extracting a creative response.

The Tree of Man was to some extent written as a deliberately Australian gesture after White's return to Australia in 1948. Determined, as he later said, to transform "the bags and iron" of Australian life, he based *The Tree of Man* on the format of the family saga with its realistic treatment of the lives of early settlers, battling to carve out a life in the wilderness. Ritual trials of fire, flood, storm, and drought shape the lives of Stan and Amy Parker, as do the seasons and the normal cycle of youth and old age. White's unique achievement lies in transforming the comfortable saga with its realistic background by his avowed desire to find "the extraordinary behind the ordinary," and to trace the spiritual and emotional yearnings of basically inarticulate characters.

The engagement with the Australian landscape that was to emerge strongly in *The Tree of Man* becomes even more crucial in White's best-known novel, *Voss*. Ostensibly an historical fiction based on an actual explorer, Ludwig Leichhardt, who was lost in the centre of Australia in 1848, White's "scraggy" hero Voss struggles first with the prosperous and conventional Sydney bourgeoisie who finance the expedition, then with the other members of the party, and finally with the landscape itself. The harsh interior of this most inhospitable continent continues, now as then, to form the central myth in the Australian consciousness. As Voss advances towards his inevitable doom, his thoughts mingle with those of a young woman, Laura Trevelyan, whom he met in Sydney and intends to marry on his return. Their visionary dialogue emphasises the blend of psychic and physical confrontation, and ultimately the watchers in Sydney are led to see that the wilderness must be faced, both in practical and spiritual terms. The presence of the Aboriginals in *Voss* and their close involvement with the fortunes of the expedition show White's deep concern for these people, and his understanding of their unique mythology.

In *Riders in the Chariot* one of the four chief figures is an Aboriginal artist, Alf Dubbo, and he joins three other outcasts from the world of plastic and red brick in a daring symbolic exercise which blends the vision of the prophet Ezekiel with the spiritual striving of an eccentric nature lover, a German refugee, and a hymn-singing washerwoman. All are triumphantly joined in Alf Dubbo's painting *The Chariot*, providing once more a glimpse of the extraordinary behind the ordinary that White seeks to illuminate. The overall design of the novel, which includes the creation of the imaginary suburb of Sarsaparilla, is almost too demanding for the characters he creates, yet the vision is dazzling and the work must remain as one of White's greatest achievements.

The world of Sarsaparilla continues to exist as a background to White's first collection of short stories, *The Burnt Ones*, and to his next novel, *The Solid Mandala*. Here White explores a preoccupation with dualism in character that is to shape several subsequent works. Waldo and Arthur Brown are twins, and the novel is presented from the viewpoint of both the neurotic intellectual Waldo and the warm, supposedly mentally defective Arthur. The deeply rooted symbolism of the religious image of the mandala is sustained through such humble devices as the marbles Arthur likes to play with, and the clearing where he dances for his friend. White finds *The Solid Mandala* one of his three best novels; critics, disturbed by the overt symbolic patterning of the work, have not been so sure.

Controversy also arose over White's next novel, *The Vivisector*. It was inevitable that White should at some time choose to write a novel about a painter, since he had always been interested in contemporary art and was already a substantial collector and patron of young Australian artists. What was not so understandable was White's savage view of the artist as vivisector, a voyeuristic cause of suffering in others. Vividly set in contemporary Sydney, the novel uses the urban landscape as creatively as the earlier landscapes of Sarsaparilla and the outback. Hurtle Duffield, the painter, is also a pioneer, and like Stan Parker in *The Tree of Man* he also works with his hands to subdue the Australian wilderness. Duffield is also unable to articulate his feelings in words, and dies, like Stan, reaching out for an elusive God. The creation of Hurtle Duffield, who is sold as a child to a wealthy family, brings together several crucial concerns of the author: his fascination with the process by which a personal vision can be turned into paint, the exploration of the mental and physical landscapes that so dominate his own work as a writer, and a consideration of the role of the artist in contemporary Australian society.

The technical brilliance of *The Eye of the Storm* together with its deeply moving insights into the final days of an elderly woman consolidated White's achievement as a writer, and this was recognised by the award of the Nobel Prize in 1973. More humane in tone than *The Vivisector*, the swirling, cyclical narrative of *The Eye of the Storm* has at its centre the experience of the dying woman many years ago during a typhoon on an offshore island. Elizabeth Hunter's visionary moment during the lull at the centre of the storm forms the symbolic nucleus of the novel, and her memories of the "lustrous moment" illuminate the rest of her life. White's abrasive satire is reserved for her avaricious offspring who return from Europe for their mother's final days. While her son, now a famous actor, and her daughter, a French princess, both recognise that Australia offers them a spiritual reality that they may never find again, both escape to the safer personas they wear as Europeans.

The strand connecting Elizabeth Hunter in contemporary Sydney to Ellen Roxburgh on Fraser Island in *A Fringe of Leaves* may seem to be a tenuous one at first, but they both share a trial in the wilderness and both use this experience to enhance their understanding of life. This novel is perhaps White's most accessible work, structurally brilliant in its unobtrusive use of flashback and filtered memories, overlaid with a suggestive layering of recurrent motifs. Although based on a true incident involving a shipwreck off the Barrier Reef in 1836, *A Fringe of Leaves* questions and evaluates the Australian past to create a novel that is entirely contemporary. The contrasting lives of Ellen Roxburgh as a raw Cornish farm girl, then as the well-groomed young wife of a gentleman scholar in Cheltenham, as an adulterer in a landscape of violence and decay in Van Diemen's Land, and finally as a captive of the Aboriginals in Northern Queensland flow seamlessly through the work, allowing unexpected juxtapositions and surprising insights into the values of society. White uses dialect to accentuate Ellen's various personas and a complex web of comparisons emerges to explore the nature of civilisation and savagery, both European and Australian.

A Fringe of Leaves ends affirmatively with an emphasis on love and the strength of simple virtues, perhaps suggesting to some critics that White's harsh judgements were beginning to mellow. But the brittle, cutting tone of *The Twyborn Affair* goes against this view. This is White's most personal fictional work, involving memories and emotions that are expressed in a different form in his self-portrait, *Flaws in the Glass*, published shortly afterwards. In *The Twyborn Affair* the dislocation of personality that has occurred in earlier works is taken to its extreme, as the hero, Eddie Twyborn, shifts his persona from man to woman, fleeing from an intended marriage to an eligible, athletic Australian to become the transvestite mistress of an elderly Greek on the French Riviera. He returns to his masculine role in World War One, and goes back to Australia as a decorated hero. Again the Australian landscape acts as a source of truth and healing power as Eddie goes to work on the land, but he resists the pressures of those who love him and, essentially an alien, he flees to Europe for the last time. In the third section of the novel Eddie has again become a woman, the successful and extravagant brothel-keeper Mrs. Eadith Trist. Even given the strength of the evocative central section and the sophistication and wit of the European sections, the novel does seem to lack the expansive vision and breadth of *The Eye of the Storm* and *A Fringe of Leaves*.

Nevertheless, by defending his right to explore states of consciousness and even religious inspiration in such a way that they remain indefinable and open to a myriad of interpretations, opposing the propensity of the reader or critic to codify experience, White has made an enormous contribution to the contemporary novel. By pressing against the boundaries of everyday experience, as he presses against the boundaries of the prose he uses, White has charted new territory in the novel, and is continuing to do so.

—Margaret B. Lewis

WIDEMAN, John Edgar. American. Born in Washington, D.C., 14 June 1941. Educated at schools in Pittsburgh; University of Pennsylvania, Philadelphia (Franklin Scholar), B.A. 1963 (Phi Beta Kappa); New College, Oxford (Rhodes Scholar, 1963; Thouron Fellow, 1963–66), B.Phil. 1966; University of Iowa, Iowa City (Kent Fellow), 1966–67. Married Judith Ann Goldman in 1965; two sons and one daughter. Member of the English Department, Howard University, Washington, D.C., 1965; Instructor to Associate Professor of English, 1966–74, assistant basketball coach, 1968–72, and director of the Afro-American Studies Program, 1971–73, University of Pennsylvania. Since 1975, Professor of English, University of Wyoming, Laramie. Phi Beta Kappa Lecturer, 1976. Recipient: PEN-Faulkner Award, 1984. Address: Department of English, University of Wyoming, Laramie, Wyoming 82071, U.S.A.

PUBLICATIONS

Novels

A Glance Away. New York, Harcourt Brace, 1967.
Hurry Home. New York, Harcourt Brace, 1970.
The Lynchers. New York, Harcourt Brace, 1973.
Hiding Place. New York, Avon, 1981; London, Allison and Busby, 1984.
Sent for You Yesterday. New York, Avon, 1983; London, Allison and Busby, 1984.

Short Stories

Damballah. New York, Avon, 1981; London, Allison and Busby, 1984.

Other

Brothers and Keepers (memoirs). New York, Holt Rinehart, 1984; London, Allison and Busby, 1985.

*   *   *

John Edgar Wideman is one of the few novelists who emerged in the Black Power era without sacrificing the demands of art to the persuasions of radical militancy. Possibly as a result of his commitment to craft, his sizeable fictional production has attracted increasing attention and he is now considered as one of the best American writers of the younger generation.

A Glance Away retraces one day in the life of an ex-drug addict. As Eddie Lawson comes back home on Easter Sunday to be reunited with his mother, sister, and girlfriend, he realizes that his possible rebirth is hampered by confrontation with other people's expectations of him: his paralyzed mother, who crushes her daughter under her demanding will, wants Eddie to act as the responsible "man in the family"; and Alice, his lover, refuses to forgive him for his affair with a white girl. In this conflict-ridden and cruel world, Eddie's only stable friendship turns out to be with Brother Small, an albino who is having a homosexual relationship with Robert Thurley, a professor. Eddie discusses his problems with Thurley, who also suffers from a broken marriage and a castrating mother. Both men try to find their own identity and preserve their dignity in an absurd social environment. Thurley's friendship finally persuades Eddie not to cop out and, at least for the present, not to return to drugs.

Hurry Home has a similar structure, in a narrative that focuses on the consciousness of Cecil Brathwaite, a black law student who works as a janitor. Out of a sense of duty and guilt, he has married the girl who supported him but he has left her on their wedding night. He is befriended and taken to Europe by an artist, Webb, who wants to assuage his own conscience for failing to acknowledge his son by his black mistress. Observing the museums and monuments of Spain and Italy, Cecil admires Western civilization, but he remains torn between two worlds; just as Webb cannot accept his past, Cecil finds it difficult to come to terms with his history and he ends up in Africa, on the threshold of a new discovery. "Home" stands for that yet undefined cultural spring which will welcome him as he comes out of a spiritual no-man's-land. The form of the narrative is appropriately fragmented: memories, relived scenes, diary-like jottings, Esther's letters to Cecil, her attempts to write her autobiography from A to Z with the help of a dictionary make the novel a crisscrossing of events and relationships. The style is one of remarkable sophistication, a poetic texture of echoes, repetitions, and prolonged metaphors.

The Lynchers, unlike *Hurry Home*, is not a reverie. A novel in four voices, it unites a quartet of utterly dissimilar blacks who conspire in a violent attempt to attack the racial oppression in Philadelphia. "Littleman," the crippled activist, sets out, with the help of Saunder Rice and Orin Wilkerson, to murder a white policeman and his black concubine. The plot fails when, angry at being manipulated (or so he feels), Rice kills Wilkerson who had begun to crack. Although the novel is not a work of social realism, the world of the ghetto plays an important role; the street corner solidarity of the males is exemplified by the love which Sweetman feels for Orin, his son. Black history looms large in the background: there is a long account of the practice of lynching in America. But individual destinies are more important, although presented fragmentarily, as the novel forcefully explores the feelings of remorse and guilt in characters who bear similarities to those in Dostoevsky's *The Possessed.*

Damballah is a collection of stories set in the working-class black community of Homewood, in Pittsburgh. The stories focus on Lizabeth, whose faith vacillates as she pays regular visits to her son in jail, on her dignified, affectionate father in "Across the Wide Missouri," and on other descendants of the nearly mythical Sybela Owens (the family genealogy is worked out in "The Beginning of Homewood" and by means of "Begat charts"). From the 1840's to the 1960's, a long line of women carry the tradition. The title of the volume derives from the name of the good serpent of the sky and hints at harmonious communication through voodoo and at the notion of gathering up the family.

Hiding Place tells the story of Tommy who, having bungled an attempt to hold up a local shopkeeper, is wrongly charged with the murder of his accomplice and flees to Brunston Hill where his grandmother, Bess, lives as a recluse. Their initial diffidence becomes mutual trust and love; authentic dialogue reveals the deep bond established between them, but Tommy is caught and shot by the police before he can return to this haven. Again the theme is the necessity to achieve one's identity by coming to terms with one's heritage, represented by family and community. Unlike Wideman's earlier male characters, all split and lost, Tommy achieves wholeness at the last moment. The form here is again experimental, but less explicitly so, as the stream-of-consciousness of the "Clement" section is outweighed by the voice of Mother Bess, the repository of oral tradition.

Sent for You Yesterday goes on exploring the Homewood circle and the weight of the past: "Past lives in us, through us. Each of us harbors the spirit of people who walked the earth before we did, and those spirits depend on us for continuing existence just as we depend on their presence to live our lives to the fullest." Black musician Albert Wilkes, back in Homewood after seven years, realizes that the community he once entertained is now fast disappearing. After he is shot by the police, Lucy and Carl, lovers at 13, preserve his stories, rituals and magic, and the community legends, with the help of Brother Tate, a mysterious albino character who plays the dead man's songs on the piano. The main narrative is framed by a "Prologue in heaven" with Brother Tate. Wideman makes more extensive use than ever of the speech cadences, the rhythms and the songs, the idiom and customs of the black community. All his books are steeped in the folk tradition, but *Sent for You Yesterday* is in that respect a major achievement. The narrative is handled perfectly, whether in dream or memory. Voices, tones, inflections are attuned to the nuances of feeling; Afro-American life is celebrated in a sustained, convincing way without any obtrusive message.

A novelist potentially of the same stature as Ernest Gaines, Ishmael Reed, and Toni Morrison, Wideman is also a perceptive literary and social critic. *Brothers and Keepers* is a moving account of the social pressures and individual reactions that have led John Edgar Wideman to the path of success and his brother Robert to jail for murder. The two men appear as the two sides of a coin, the former more restrained and capable of playing the game and using standard English, the latter street-wise and fully absorbed in the vivid parlance and mores of the ghetto. The book reveals also the world of prisons, of brutal, underpaid guards suspicious of any black person, of their utter lack of concern for human qualities in the convicts. Finally, it is a soul-searching reflection on the writer's own distance from the black community and his debt towards it. A mixture of fact and fiction, biography and memoir, it blends social history and the confessional mode. This plea for Robert's parole does not try, says Ishmael Reed, "to reach the nation's conscience but to reach out to his brother to salvage him from grief and waste."

—Michel Fabre

WIEBE, Rudy (Henry). Canadian. Born in Fairholme, Saskatchewan, 4 October 1934. Educated at Alberta Mennonite High School; University of Alberta, Edmonton, 1953–56, 1958–60 (International Nickel Graduate Fellow, 1958–59; Queen Elizabeth Graduate Fellow, 1959–60), B.A. 1956, M.A. 1960; University of Tübingen, Germany (Rotary Fellow), 1957–58; University of Manitoba, Winnipeg, 1961; University of Iowa, Iowa City, 1964. Married Tena F. Isaak in 1958; one daughter and two sons. Research officer, Glenbow Foundation, Calgary, 1956; foreign service officer, Ottawa, 1960; high school teacher, Selkirk, Manitoba, 1961; editor, Mennonite Brethren *Herald*, Winnipeg, 1962–63; Assistant Professor of English, Goshen College, Indiana, 1963–67. Assistant Professor, 1967–70, Associate Professor, 1970–77, and since 1977, Professor of English, University of Alberta. Recipient: Canada Council arts scholarship, 1964, award, 1971, grant, 1977. Address: 5315 143rd Street, Edmonton, Alberta T6H 4E3, Canada.

PUBLICATIONS

Novels

Peace Shall Destroy Many. Toronto, McClelland and Stewart, 1962; Grand Rapids, Michigan, Eerdmans, 1964.
First and Vital Candle. Toronto, McClelland and Stewart, and Grand Rapids, Michigan, Eerdmans, 1966.
The Blue Mountains of China. Toronto, McClelland and Stewart, and Grand Rapids, Michigan, Eerdmans, 1970.
The Temptations of Big Bear. Toronto, McClelland and Stewart, 1973.
The Scorched-Wood People. Toronto, McClelland and Stewart, 1977.
The Mad Trapper. Toronto, McClelland and Stewart, 1980.
My Lovely Enemy. Toronto, McClelland and Stewart, 1983.

Short Stories

Where Is the Voice Coming From? Toronto, McClelland and Stewart, 1974.
Personal Fictions, with others, edited by Michael Ondaatje. Toronto, Oxford University Press, 1977.
Alberta: A Celebration, edited by Tom Radford. Edmonton, Alberta, Hurtig, 1979.
The Angel of the Tar Sands and Other Stories. Toronto, McClelland and Stewart, 1982.

Play

Far as the Eye Can See, with Theatre Passe Muraille. Edmonton, Alberta, NeWest Press, 1977.

Other

A Voice in the Land: Essays by and about Rudy Wiebe, edited by W.J. Keith. Edmonton, Alberta, NeWest Press, 1981.

Editor, *The Story-Makers: A Selection of Modern Short Stories.* Toronto, Macmillan, 1970.

Editor, *Stories from Western Canada: A Selection.* Toronto, Macmillan, 1972.

Editor, with Andreas Schroeder, *Stories from Pacific and Arctic Canada: A Selection.* Toronto, Macmillan, 1974.

Editor, *Double Vision: An Anthology of Twentieth-Century Stories in English.* Toronto, Macmillan, 1976.

Editor, *Getting Here: Stories.* Edmonton, Alberta, NeWest Press, 1977.

Editor, with Aritha van Herk, *More Stories from Western Canada.* Toronto, Macmillan, 1980.

Editor, with Aritha van Herk and Leah Flater, *West of Fiction.* Edmonton, Alberta, NeWest Press, 1982.

*

Manuscript Collection: University of Calgary Library, Alberta.

Critical Studies: *The Comedians: Hugh Hood and Rudy Wiebe* by Patricia A. Morley, Toronto, Clarke Irwin, 1977; *Epic Fiction: The Art of Rudy Wiebe* by W.J. Keith, Edmonton, University of Alberta Press, 1981; articles in *A Voice in the Land,* 1981, and *Journal of Commonwealth Literature* (Edinburgh), vol. 19, no. 1, 1984.

Rudy Wiebe comments:

I believe that the worlds of fiction—story—should provide pleasure of as many kinds as possible to the reader; I believe fiction must be precisely, peculiarly rooted in a particular place, in particular people; I believe writing fiction is as serious, as responsible an activity as I can ever perform. Therefore in my fiction I try to explore the world that I know: the land and people of western Canada; from my particular world view: a radical Jesus-oriented Christianity.

*   *   *

Central to all of Rudy Wiebe's writings is the Mennonite faith in which he was reared, and central to that is the "extremely individualistic approach to religion" (as he puts it in the foreword to his first novel) which motivates the actions and attitudes of all his characters. His novels, fundamentally and forthrightly Christian (neither tub-thumping nor ritualistic), probe the nature of faith. Deliberately didactic, they investigate the lives of ordinary people with ordinary abilities but passionate minds, to show the virtue of individual action, the power of commitment, and the sterility of material competitiveness and moral apathy. Sometimes the Christian parables intrude awkwardly, artificially, "unfictionalized," into the narrative line and symbolic tapestry, as in *First and Vital Candle* or in the end of *The Blue Mountains of China*, but when the blend is right, Wiebe's indirect style closes in on the intricate balance between intellect and feeling.

The first novel is the simplest in form, taking its title from *Daniel:* "he shall magnify himself in his heart, and by peace shall destroy many: But he shall be broken without hand." The ironic contrast implicit in the book, between Hitler's militant arrogance and the prairie Mennonite Deacon Block's pacifist arrogance, serves to highlight their similarities. The Deacon, certain to himself, is aware only of rules and traditions; always when young members of the community enquire as to the *nature* of the traditions they are told to uphold, routine orders rather than illuminating answers await them. The Deacon destroys his own family by such narrowness. For the central character too, young Thom Wiens—striving to sharpen his

mind, answer his conscience, weigh military service in an attractive cause against admirable but paradoxically "enforced" pacifism—the Deacon's negation is no answer either. But the prospect of abandoning his faith seems equally barren. Only the private relation with God and with man—lonely, terrifying, challenging, necessary—can arouse in him any promise of the true internal peace that governments cannot legislate nor other individuals rule.

The Blue Mountains of China, Wiebe's most ambitious book, explores compellingly exactly those traditions and histories that Thom sought to discover. Taking up again a theme from the earlier book's foreword, it traces the great Mennonite quest for paradise: "like ancient Israel, they were a religious nation without a country." In the minds of different generations recalling fragmentarily their own history and intuiting dimly their significance in the story of the community as a whole, the 100-year trek from Russia to China to Canada to Paraguay comes to life. But the novel is more than genealogy—more than *Exodus.* By positing the ambivalence of paradise, it tries to explore the impact of an ideal upon the communal mind of a people. From adolescent quarrels early in the book (over the innocence or sinfulness of sexuality), through dissatisfaction with Russian communes, Chinese deserts, Canadian commercialism, South American violence, and arid intellectual pretentiousness, routes to earthly paradises are one after the other quietly closed. Yet all the time *the people* is crossing borders, often in flight, undercover, at night, in the wilderness, or in another language (so that no-one can pinpoint the moment of crossing) and with each change there arises the possibility of metaphysical insight. The title mountains divide the Chinese winds, creating a "contrast between fertile Manchuria and arid Mongolia." As Wiebe metamorphoses them into the Canadian Rockies, they become an ambivalent marker of contemporary Canadian/Mennonite/individual choices, too, hinting that peace (in Vietnam or in the private spirit) is only possible when men surrender their will to control other men and turn to contemplating seriously their own moves and motives instead. Increasingly, for Wiebe's Canada, this means reflecting on the popular prejudices against the native Indians and acting to alter such attitudes. Above all it means acquiring faith in the basic humanity of men and pursuing one's way to the future that humane action can foster.

The attempt to cross the linguistic and cultural boundary that divides European from Indian civilization occupies much of the rest of Wiebe's fiction. From the short story "Where Is the Voice Coming From?" (revised in *The Angel of the Tar Sands*) to the novels about Big Bear and Louis Riel (*The Temptations of Big Bear* and *The Scorched-Wood People*), Wiebe has examined the sources of cultural power and cultural difference. Disputing the accuracy of historical records and philosophical systems of explanation (finding both to be arbitrary), Wiebe investigates the potency of speech in an oral society. In so doing he uses the rhetoric of the spoken word as the medium for his art. The novels are meant to be heard as much as read; their force derives from their ability to evoke tangible "presences" by means of voice, even when "documentary" evidence (the "proof" espoused by European rationalism) is absent or contradictory. Such a distinction helps to structure *The Blue Mountains,* too—distinguishing the "effective" spoken Low German vernacular which the Mennonites use amongst themselves from the usable but foreign (and therefore arbitrary) written language of the culture around them. In subsequent novels, Wiebe has used the techniques of popular adventure fiction to consider the pressures of isolation (as in *The Mad Trapper,* a reconstruction of the death of Albert Johnson); and he has adapted forms of Russian fiction (in *My Lovely*

Enemy) to his enquiry into the manysidedness (the carnality, the spirituality) of love.

—W.H. New

WILDING, Michael. British. Born in Worcester, 5 January 1942. Educated at Royal Grammar School, Worcester, 1950–59; Lincoln College, Oxford (Editor, *Isis*, 1962), B.A. 1963, M.A. 1968. Primary school teacher, Spetchley, Worcestershire, 1960; Lecturer in English, University of Sydney, 1963–66; Assistant Lecturer, 1967–68, and Lecturer in English, 1968, University of Birmingham. Senior Lecturer, 1969–72, and since 1972, Reader in English, University of Sydney. Editor, *Balcony*, Sydney, 1965–69, and *Tabloid Story*, Sydney, 1972–76; general editor, Asian and Pacific Writing series, University of Queensland Press, St. Lucia, 1972–82; director, Wild and Woolley, publishers, Sydney, 1974–79; editor, *Post-Modern Writing*, Sydney, 1979–81. Since 1971, Australian editor, *Stand*, Newcastle-upon-Tyne. Recipient: Australia Council senior fellowship, 1978. Address: Department of English, University of Sydney, Sydney, New South Wales 2006, Australia.

PUBLICATIONS

Novels

Living Together. St. Lucia, University of Queensland Press, 1974.
The Short Story Embassy. Sydney, Wild and Woolley, 1975.
Pacific Highway. Sydney, Hale and Iremonger, 1982.
The Paraguayan Experiment. Ringwood, Victoria, and London, Penguin, 1985.

Short Stories

Aspects of the Dying Process. St. Lucia, University of Queensland Press, 1972.
The West Midland Underground. St. Lucia, University of Queensland Press, 1975.
Scenic Drive. Sydney, Wild and Woolley, 1976.
The Phallic Forest. Sydney, Wild and Woolley, 1978.
Reading the Signs. Sydney, Hale and Iremonger, 1984.
The Man of Slow Feeling: Selected Short Stories. Ringwood, Victoria, Penguin, 1985.

Uncollected Short Stories

"Stevie Agonistes," in *Isis* (Oxford), 18 January 1961.
"Hnut," in *Isis* (Oxford), 8 November 1961.
"Black Velvet," in *Isis* (Oxford), 30 January 1963.
"A Little Fire in a Wide Field," in *Squire* (Sydney), April 1966.
"They Might Have Been Brother and Sister," in *Squire* (Sydney), November 1966.
"Yes, We Unzip Bananas," in *Westerly* (Nedlands, Western Australia), July 1968.
"The Glass Bridge," in *Westerly* (Nedlands, Western Australia), July 1970.

Play

Screenplay: *The Phallic Forest*, 1972.

Other

Milton's Paradise Lost. Sydney, Sydney University Press, 1969.
Cultural Policy in Great Britain, with Michael Green. Paris, Unesco, 1970.
Marcus Clarke. Melbourne and London, Oxford University Press, 1977.
Political Fictions. London, Routledge, 1980.

Editor, with Charles Higham, *Australians Abroad: An Anthology.* Melbourne, Cheshire, 1967.
Editor, *Three Tales*, by Henry James. Sydney, Hicks Smith, 1967.
Editor, *Marvell: Modern Judgements.* London, Macmillan, 1969; Nashville, Aurora, 1970.
Editor, with others, *We Took Their Orders and Are Dead: An Anti-War Anthology.* Sydney, Ure Smith, 1971.
Editor, *The Portable Marcus Clarke.* St. Lucia, University of Queensland Press, 1976.
Editor, with Stephen Knight, *The Radical Reader.* Sydney, Wild and Woolley, 1977.
Editor, *The Tabloid Story Pocket Book.* Sydney, Wild and Woolley, 1978.
Editor, *The Workingman's Paradise*, by William Lane. Sydney, Sydney University Press, 1980.
Editor, *Stories*, by Marcus Clarke. Sydney, Hale and Iremonger, 1983.

*

Critical Studies: "The Short Stories of Wilding and Moorhouse" by Carl Harrison-Ford, in *Southerly* (Sydney), no. 33, 1973; "Recent Developments in Australian Writing, with Particular Reference to Short Fiction" by Brian Kiernan, in *Caliban* (Toulouse), vol. 14, 1977; "The New Novel" by Leon Cantrell, in *Studies in the Recent Australian Novel* edited by K.G. Hamilton, St. Lucia, University of Queensland Press, 1978; "Uncertainty and Subversion in the Australian Novel," in *Pacific Moana Quarterly* (Hamilton, New Zealand), vol. 4, 1979, and "Character and Environment in Some Recent Australian Fiction," in *Waves* (Downsview, Ontario), vol. 7, 1979, both by Ken Gelder; "Laszlo's Testament, or, Structuring the Past and Sketching the Present in Contemporary Short Fiction," in *Kunapipi 1* (Mysore, India), 1979, and "A New Version of Pastoral," in *Australian Literary Studies* (Hobart, Tasmania), vol. 11, 1983, both by Bruce Clunies Ross; "The New Writing: Whodunnit?" by G.M. Gillard, in *Meanjin* (Melbourne), vol. 40, 1981; "Michael Wilding: Post-Modernism and the Australian Literary Heritage" by Hans Hauge, in *Overland* (Melbourne), no. 96, 1984.

*   *   *

Michael Wilding is one of a "new generation" of writers in Australia who began publishing in the early 1970's. Impelled to political action by Australia's involvement in the Vietnam War, Wilding has also protested in his writings against censorship, conservative social values, and a subservience to American cultural imperialism.

In the first of his four collections of stories to date, *Aspects of the Dying Process*, an English persona is attracted and bemused in several stories by the hedonistic Sydney youth culture which he encounters. The title suggests the "dying" as an immigrant changes colour with his new culture and extinguishes to some degree the old, and is a pun also on his sexual initiation rites. D.H. Lawrence and Henry James have left their mark on the writer's early style, in its rendering of the impulses and withdrawals of an observer who is not yet a participant in the new life. *The West Midland Underground*, Wilding's second volume of stories, has a free-wheeling variety of narrative modes and settings which include England, Greece, the United States, and Australia. In "Canal Run" a boy's claustrophobic world is evident in images of the English industrial midlands; at the centre of frustration is a thwarted sexuality: "Thinking back it is hard to see exactly when one's consciousness of sex began and became a desire for, a whole youth's looking for, fulfilment. Then, though, there was only a strong sense of sin and shame and dirt; no lyricism, and none of the hatred. It was wrong and furtive and C stream; which was another way of saying lower class."

Most stories in *The Phallic Forest* energetically flout "normal" sexual and social mores, or celebrate alternatives; and in a later collection, *Reading the Signs*, a more reflective consciousness draws on a background of class awareness for sharp and penetrating observations of appearance and behaviour. In Wilding's later work the term "Midlander" connotes the circumscribed spirit, against which all his writings rebel.

Wilding's first novel, *Living Together*, relates the exploits, and fantasies, of young men and women cohabiting in inner suburban Sydney. The traumas of Martin, Paul, and Ann (second names are unimportant) are related with wit and verve as they paint and decorate their house and have sex, joints, or drink with neighbours and visitors. (In a later novel, a character comments that the Pill introduced "a whole new anthropology" for the writer.) The strongest character is the irenic Ann, who, after leaving her outrageously chauvinist partner Martin half way through the novel, returns at the end to give his life some shape and order. The men are weaker and more ambivalent. Paul, the author's alter ego, has taken his sexual apprenticeship, but is unsure of his future directions. Martin's scenario of the house as a sort of "cultural centre" is never realised; its most memorable visitors are two female grotesques, the ever-ready next-door neighbour Mrs. Bilham, and Gretel Mann, of "cavernous appetite," who helps Paul out of his innocence. Late in the novel Paul has decided that "Change is the only aphrodisiac." The literary progenitor of this urban comedy of the 1970's is perhaps Thomas Love Peacock, whose miscellaneous parties of odd characters in English country houses also mix satire and romance, but where the treatment of sex is much more circumspect.

Wilding's second novel, *The Short Story Embassy*, and his third, *Pacific Highway*, contain insights into the literary process. The "Embassy," situated "halfway to the north" on Australia's east coast, approximates to the "cultural centre" envisaged by Martin in *Living Together*. The juxtaposition of culture and nature is a source of comedy, as in this version of "pot pastoral": "The people travelling up from the south rested there and stripped off and got their bodies brown before going on to the full north. They lay around by creeks and wove garlands of bush flowers around each other. They made daisy-chains around their necks and twined poppies in their pubic hairs. The cows came and gazed on them and licked them and they licked each other."

Here, as elsewhere, Wilding is both lyrical and amused; he celebrates the new freedoms and is affectionately ironic about them. While whimsy sometimes predominates, a sharper irony is evident in observations about characters' literary outlooks

and values. The middle-aged Laszlo, for instance, possessively jealous of his lover, Valda, puzzles over his generation of radicals, who read Tom Paine, while hers has been "turned on" to astrology. To Valda, Laszlo seems to use books as "leaning posts." *The Short Story Embassy* quizzically examines the "new" experimental literature of process and locates its enemy as the Thought Police. But this is Kafka without the menace. The visitor, Tichborne, who mysteriously leaves the Embassy, may be one of the enemy (his name is a reminder of the famous Tichborne impersonation case), but his departure lacks consequence. There is paranoia aplenty in this novel but "plot" in the conventional sense is missing.

The pastoral element is paramount in *Pacific Highway*. In some respects it is a 1980's version of Vance Palmer's *The Passage* (1930), in which a rural holiday retreat on the Pacific Ocean is destroyed by "progress" and "development." But the tone and style of the two novels differ markedly. In *Pacific Highway* the attempt by the narrator and his girlfriend, Lily, to recreate an idyllic world of innocence among friends who will live off the land, re-cycling their waste, is confronted by a censorious, authoritarian regime. This household (two young women and a man), is differentiated from other "hippies" by being middle-class and theoretical: escapees from the midlands. Confrontations with the wider society are often presented as wry comedy: for instance, how does a household with idealistic communist notions rationalise its employment of a cleaning woman? Another dimension is the love story—of the narrator and Lily—which contains some fine lyrical passages.

A search for utopia, implicit elsewhere, is the explicit theme of Wilding's fourth novel, *The Paraguayan Experiment*. The novel is a new departure for Wilding, who uses historical documents in his firm narration of the story of the New Australia movement. Disillusioned with the economic depression and social repression in Australia in the 1890's, William Lane led a group of 400 men, women, and children to found a New Australia in Paraguay. Using letters (especially Lane's), memos, and official documents, Wilding builds a lively account of this historic precursor to the idealistic communalists of the 1970's. Anachronisms in dialogue and commentary are evident, but these seem deliberate: in certain respects, which Wilding does not wish to conceal, this is a parable for the 1980's. Hence many of the issues which have obsessed this writer—the creation of alternative human settlements, the clash between individual and group needs, sexual politics, the use of drugs—are evident in this tale of a previous era in Australian history. In form and style, Wilding's fourth novel shows his continuing interest in literary experimentation and is rich in humour, fantasy, and sharp social observation.

—Bruce Bennett

WILLIAMS, John (Edward). American. Born in Clarksville, Texas, 29 August 1922. Educated at the University of Denver, B.A. 1949, M.A. 1950; University of Missouri, Columbia, Ph.D. 1954; Oxford University (English-Speaking Union Fellow), 1963. Served in the United States Army Air Force, 1942–45: Sergeant. Married 1) Avalon Smith in 1949, two daughters and one son; 2) Nancy Gardner in 1970, four step-children. Associate Editor, Alan Swallow, publishers, Denver, 1948–50; Instructor, University of Missouri, 1950–54. Assistant Professor, 1954–60, Director of the Workshop for

Writers, 1954–59, and of the Creative Writing Program, 1954–74, Associate Professor, 1960–64, since 1964, Professor of English, and Phipps Professor of Humanities, 1976–79, University of Denver. Writer-in-Residence, Wisconsin State University, Whitewater, summers 1964–66, 1968–69; taught at Bread Loaf Writers Conference, Vermont, 1966–72; Writer-in-Residence, Smith College, Northampton, Massachusetts, 1968; Hurst Professor of Creative Literature, Brandeis University, Waltham, Massachusetts, 1973. Editor, *Twentieth Century Literature*, Los Angeles, 1954–56, and *University of Denver Quarterly*, 1966–70. Recipient: Rockefeller grant, 1967; National Endowment for the Arts grant, 1969; National Book Award, 1973; American Academy award, 1985; Guggenheim fellowship, 1985. Agent: Marie Rodell-Frances Collin Literary Agency, 110 West 40th Street, New York, New York 10018. Address: Department of English, University of Denver, Denver, Colorado 80210, U.S.A.

PUBLICATIONS

Novels

Nothing But the Night.   Denver, Swallow, 1948.
Butcher's Crossing.   New York, Macmillan, and London, Gollancz, 1960.
Stoner.   New York, Viking Press, 1965; London, Allen Lane, 1973.
Augustus.   New York, Viking Press, 1972; London, Allen Lane, 1973.

Uncollected Short Stories

"Short Story 2," in *Story* (New York), Spring 1960.
"The Sleep of Reason," in *Ploughshares* (Cambridge, Massachusetts), October 1981.

Verse

The Broken Landscape.   Denver, Swallow, 1949.
The Necessary Lie.   Denver, Verb, 1965.

Other

Editor, *English Renaissance Poetry: A Collection of Shorter Poems from Skelton to Jonson.*   New York, Doubleday, 1963.

*

Critical Studies: "The Western Theme: Exploiters and Explorers" by Robert B. Heilman, in *Partisan Review* (New Brunswick, New Jersey), March–April 1961; "Artist of Diversity" (interview), in *Dust* (Paradise, California), Winter 1966; "Accounts of Mutual Acquaintances to a Group of Friends: The Fiction of John Williams" by Robert J. Nelson, in *Denver Quarterly*, Winter 1973; "*Butcher's Crossing*: The Husks and Shells of Exploitation" by Jack Brenner, in *Western American Literature* (Fort Collins, Colorado), February 1973; "Good Man and Foes" by C.P. Snow, in *Financial Times* (London), 24 May 1973; "John Williams: An Introduction to the Major Novels" by Rex Stamper, in *Mississippi Review* (Hattiesburg), vol. 3, no. 1, 1974; "Reassessing John Williams's *Stoner*" by Geary Hobson, in *New America* (Albuquerque), vol. 3, no. 2, 1977; "The Novels of John Williams" by John Stark, in *Hollins Critic* (Hollins College, Virginia), October 1980; article

by Craig Werner, in *American Novelists since World War II*, 2nd series, edited by James E. Kibler, Jr., Detroit, Gale, 1980.

John Williams comments:
  Though I prefer to let my work speak for itself, I shall say three things about myself as a novelist. First, I consider myself a professional rather than an amateur; that is, I do things for the thing's sake rather than for my own. Second, I write rather slowly, being that kind of writer that Thomas Mann once described as one who finds writing more difficult than most people do. And third, I try not to repeat myself from novel to novel.

*   *   *

  John Williams's fiction has revolved around the idea of history and the past's inexorable weight. In his four novels he had explored the symptoms of historical determinism from various perspectives. From *Butcher's Crossing*, set in mid-19th-century frontier America, to *Augustus*, set in Rome during Augustus Caesar's lifetime, Williams has concentrated on the individual in the context of his times.
  Butcher's Crossing deals with man and nature on the violently expanding frontier of early America. Specifically it chronicles one of the last great buffalo kills at the height of the craze for buffalo robes, an example of the mindless waste of crude free enterprise. The story encompasses an expedition by Will Andrews, an innocent easterner determined to see the wilderness and taste adventure, and an obsessed buffalo-hunter, Miller, who knows a mountain valley that shelters the last great bison herd. The party reaches the valley, slaughters some 3,000 buffalo, stacks the hides, then is trapped by winter. Surviving the fierce Rocky Mountain winter, on the hazardous return they lose the buffalo hides. When they reach the town of Butcher's Crossing, from which they began, they discover that the demand for buffalo hides is gone—the market has totally collapsed. The ironies of the story multiply: Will Andrews has found more experience than he bargained for, and Miller, the super-annuated mountain man, goes violently mad when he realizes that his heroic feat has been meaningless. As in frontier ballads like "Buffalo Skinners," there is a strong sense here of the blind rapacity of the frontier and of the despair which generated such pointless blood-lust.
  In contrast *Stoner* describes near-contemporary America, the life of a provincial university professor in the first half of our century. The story develops in sharp detail William Stoner's rise from rural poverty through a long career as a literature teacher. His life is a series of struggles and small triumphs that dissolve in losses: his wife is cold and neurotic, he fights petty battles with unscrupulous colleagues, has one brief and vivid affair with a student, and goes to his grave unrewarded for this intense devotion to learning. It is a small, minutely documented tragedy of a common man, set against the ideals of academe. Stoner is a talented but not brilliant teacher, an ethical man, but he is persistently defeated by people who do not hesitate to warp or betray ideals. In a small but distinct form, *Stoner* demonstrates the erosion of individual will in the face of apathy, malice, and neglect, a familiar theme of modern literature—and life.
  At the other end of the historical spectrum is *Augustus*, which details the rise to ultimate power of a seemingly inept and uncalculating man. Constructed as a mock-documentary of letters, journals, military orders, and memoirs, the story recounts Augustus Caesar's political ascent from the viewpoints of both allies and enemies, and it shows how the complex strands of history are interpreted subjectively by all observers. The pastiche of documents gives a strong sense of a Hobbesian world

of selfish motives and grasping egos. The man we see in this composite portrait is a complex individual skilfully manipulating the forces of his culture and shaping an ideology from the historical accidents around him. Yet *Augustus* demonstrates that the greatest power is ultimately as meaningless as the small man's impotence. *Augustus* concludes with Caesar's reflections on his career, a soliloquy summarizing his apparently matchless triumphs:

> The despair that I have voiced seems to me now unworthy of what I have done. Rome is not eternal; it does not matter. The barbarian will conquer; it does not matter. There was a moment of Rome, and it will not wholly die; the barbarian will become the Rome he conquers; the language will smooth his rough tongue; the vision of what he destroys will flow in his blood. And in time that is ceaseless as this salt sea upon which I am so frailly suspended, the cost is nothing, is less than nothing.

This small victory snatched from despair is very like Stoner's final meditation on his apparently futile career: "A kind of joy came upon him, as if borne in a summer breeze. He dimly recalled that he had been thinking of failure—as if it mattered. It seemed to him now that such thoughts were mean, unworthy of what his life had been." Like Gray's "Elegy," the two portraits bring together the mighty and the anonymous lives, demonstrating that the individual life is its own measure. A life examined from the inside is justified on its own terms, regardless of the defeats, confusions, and corrosive ironies of history.

—William J. Schafer

WILLIAMS, John A(lfred). American. Born in Jackson, Mississippi, 5 December 1925. Educated at Central High School, Syracuse, New York; Syracuse University, A.B. 1950. Served in the United States Navy, 1943–46. Married 1) Carolyn Clopton in 1947 (divorced), two sons; 2) Lorrain Isaac in 1965, one son. Member of the public relations department, Doug Johnson Associates, Syracuse, 1952–54, and Arthur P. Jacobs Company; staff member, CBS, Hollywood and New York, 1954–55; publicity director, Comet Press Books, New York, 1955–56; publisher and editor, *Negro Market Newsletter*, New York, 1956–57; staff member, Abelard-Schuman, publishers, New York, 1957–58; director of information, American Committee on Africa, New York, 1958; European correspondent, *Ebony* and *Jet* magazines, 1958–59; announcer, WOV Radio, New York, 1959; Africa correspondent, *Newsweek*, New York, 1964–65. Regents' Lecturer, University of California, Santa Barbara, 1972; Distinguished Professor of English, LaGuardia Community College, City University of New York, 1973–75; Visiting Professor, University of Hawaii, Honolulu, Summer 1974, and Boston University, 1978–79. Since 1979, Professor of English, Rutgers University, New Brunswick, New Jersey. Member of the Editorial Board, *Audience*, Boston, 1970–72; contributing editor, *American Journal*, New York, 1972. Recipient: American Academy grant, 1962; Syracuse University Outstanding Achievement Award, 1970; National Endowment for the Arts grant, 1977; Rutgers University Lindback Award, 1982; Before Columbus Foundation award, 1983. Litt.D.: Southeastern Massachusetts University, North Dartmouth, 1978. Address: 693 Forest Avenue, Teaneck, New Jersey 07666, U.S.A.

PUBLICATIONS

Novels

The Angry Ones. New York, Ace, 1960; as *One for New York*, Chatham, New Jersey, Chatham Bookseller, 1975.
Night Song. New York, Farrar Straus, 1961; London, Collins, 1962.
Sissie. New York, Farrar Straus, 1963; as *Journey Out of Anger*, London, Eyre and Spottiswoode, 1968.
The Man Who Cried I Am. Boston, Little Brown, 1967; London, Eyre and Spottiswoode, 1968.
Sons of Darkness, Sons of Light. Boston, Little Brown, 1969; London, Eyre and Spottiswoode, 1970.
Captain Blackman. New York, Doubleday, 1972.
Mothersill and the Foxes. New York, Doubleday, 1975.
The Junior Bachelor Society. New York, Doubleday, 1976.
! Click Song. Boston, Houghton Mifflin, 1982.
The Berhama Account. Far Hills, New Jersey, New Horizon Press, 1985.

Other

Africa: Her History, Lands, and People. New York, Cooper Square, 1962.
The Protectors (on narcotics agents; as J. Dennis Gregory), with Harry J. Anslinger. New York, Farrar Straus, 1964.
This Is My Country, Too. New York, New American Library, 1965; London, New English Library, 1966.
The Most Native of Sons: A Biography of Richard Wright. New York, Doubleday, 1970.
The King God Didn't Save: Reflections on the Life and Death of Martin Luther King, Jr. New York, Coward McCann, 1970; London, Eyre and Spottiswoode, 1971.
Flashbacks: A Twenty-Year Diary of Article Writing. New York, Doubleday, 1973.
Minorities in the City. New York, Harper, 1975.

Editor, *The Angry Black.* New York, Lancer, 1962.
Editor, *Beyond the Angry Black.* New York, Cooper Square, 1967.
Editor with Charles F. Harris, *Amistad I* and *II.* New York, Knopf, 2 vols., 1970–71.

*

Manuscript Collection: Syracuse University, New York.

Critical Studies: *America as Seen by a Black Man* by Robert T. Haley, unpublished thesis, San Jose State College, California, 1971; "The Art of John A. Williams" by John O'Brien, in *American Scholar* (Washington, D.C.), Summer 1973; *The Evolution of a Black Writer: John A. Williams* by Earl Cash, New York, Third Press, 1974; *American Fictions 1940–1980* by Frederick R. Karl, New York, Harper, 1983; *John A. Williams* by Gilbert H. Muller, Boston, Twayne, 1984; article by James L. de Jongh, in *Afro-American Fiction Writers after 1955* edited by Thadious M. Davis and Trudier Harris, Detroit, Gale, 1984.

John A. Williams comments:
  I think art has always been political and has served political ends more graciously than those of the muses. I consider myself to be a political novelist and writer to the extent that I am always aware of the social insufficiencies which are a result of political manipulation. The greatest art has always been

social-political, and in that sense I could be considered striving along traditional paths.

*   *   *

James Baldwin was to remind us of the descent one must make to excavate history in *Just above My Head*. And it is similar to the theme the critic Addison Gayle deals with in *The Way of the New World*: "It is to history that one looks for the best example of modern black men; there that the falsity of the old images, stereotypes, and metaphors can be seen. History, then, rewritten and corrected, holds the key to success in the war against the imagists." Within the framework of this critical thinking John A. Williams wages war against the imagists, merging history into fiction to create new dimensions for the writings of Black novelists and fresh images for Black readers to digest.

Throwing off the image of the black protagonist struggling for confirmation of his self worth, Williams creates, in *The Man Who Cried I Am*, Max Reddick, a Black man who becomes a "success" in the white world who asks himself "was it worth what it cost?" Reddick's final confirmation of "self" comes not from the white world, but from himself, "All you ever want to do is remind me that I am black. But, goddamn it, I also am," he says.

The need for this new direction in Black writing has been documented; however, few writers have matched Williams in destroying illusions of the Black man as a victim subjugated by the pressures of racial injustice in the Western World. It is without uncertainty that Williams's protagonists know history, and understand its function. In *Sons of Darkness, Sons of Light* Eugene Browning mulls over the advantages of knowing his past: "Remember when we began to discover Negro history—twenty years old and blam there it was, and it was sort of like peeling an onion, one thing leading to another, translucent, slippery, thin ... one morning I woke up and the enormity of what's been done to us was resting like a ball of badly digested lead in my stomach, but it got down, it went down, and I couldn't pretend anymore that it had meaning for me. Not only for me but for all the Negroes out there." But it is with reason and without anger, that Browning, after coming to the conclusion that civil rights and freedom marches would not bring justice to Blacks, employs Mafia tactics in the assassination of a policeman guilty of killing a 16-year-old black boy. "You could work ... with all your heart and what was left of your soul, but you also had to know finally ... that you had to obtain your goals by the same means as Chuck."

Williams's themes are the heightened level of group consciousness, self-resolve, and resourcefulness needed by blacks to eliminate racial injustices, through as Browning states, "Secrecy, apparent non-involvement, selected acts. That was the only answer." Williams leads us to the doorway of creating new values for the good of the group while unraveling Black people from a web of images, and stereotypes. "It is most imperative," Williams writes, "that the Negro be seen and seen as he is; the morality of the situation will then resolve itself, and truth, which is what we all presumably are after, will then be served." Williams does this well in leading us to the descent.

—Brenda R. Ferguson

WILLIAMS, Raymond (Henry). British. Born in Llanfihangel Crocorney, Wales, 31 August 1921. Educated at Henry VIII Grammar School, Abergavenny, 1932–39; Trinity College, Cambridge, 1939–41, 1945–46, M.A. 1946, Litt.D. 1969. Served in the Anti-Tank Regiment, Guards Armoured Division, 1941–45: Captain. Married Joy Dalling in 1942; two sons and one daughter. Editor, *Politics and Letters*, London, 1946–47. Staff Tutor in Literature, Oxford University Delegacy for Extra-Mural Studies, 1946–61. Since 1961, Fellow of Jesus College, Cambridge; Reader, 1967–74, and Professor of Drama, 1974–83, Cambridge University; now retired. Visiting Professor of Political Science, Stanford University, California, 1973. General Editor, New Thinkers Library, 1962–70, and English Literature in History series, Hutchinson, since 1983. Reviewer for *The Guardian*, London. Recipient: Welsh Arts Council prize, 1979. D. Univ.: Open University, Milton Keynes, Buckinghamshire, 1975; D.Litt.: University of Wales, Cardiff, 1980; University of Kent, Canterbury, 1984. Member, Welsh Academy. Address: Jesus College, Cambridge CB5 8BL, England.

PUBLICATIONS

Novels

Border Country.   London, Chatto and Windus, 1960; New York, Horizon Press, 1962.
Second Generation.   London, Chatto and Windus, 1964; New York, Horizon Press, 1965.
The Volunteers.   London, Eyre Methuen, 1978.
The Fight for Manod.   London, Chatto and Windus, 1979.
Loyalties.   London, Chatto and Windus, 1985.

Uncollected Short Stories

"Sack Labourer," in *English Story 1*, edited by Woodrow Wyatt.   London, Collins, 1941.
"This Time," in *New Writing and Daylight*.   London, Hogarth Press, 1943.
"A Fine Room to Be Ill In," in *English Story 7*, edited by Woodrow Wyatt.   London, Collins, 1947.

Plays

Koba, in *Modern Tragedy*.   London, Chatto and Windus, 1966.
A Letter from the Country (televised, 1966).   Published in *Stand* (Newcastle-upon-Tyne), 1971.
Public Inquiry (televised, 1967).   Published in *Stand* (Newcastle-upon-Tyne), vol. 9, no. 1, 1967.

Television Plays: *A Letter from the Country*, 1966; *Public Inquiry*, 1967; *The Country and the City* (documentary; *Where We Live Now* series), 1979.

Other

Reading and Criticism.   London, Muller, 1950.
Drama from Ibsen to Eliot.   London, Chatto and Windus, 1952; New York, Oxford University Press, 1953; revised edition, London, Penguin, 1964; as *Drama from Ibsen to Brecht*, Chatto and Windus, 1968, Oxford University Press, 1969.
Drama in Performance.   London, Muller, 1954; New York, Basic Books, 1969.
Preface to Film, with Michael Orrom.   London, Film Drama, 1954.

Culture and Society 1780–1950. London, Chatto and Windus, and New York, Columbia University Press, 1958.

The Long Revolution. London, Chatto and Windus, and New York, Columbia University Press, 1961.

Communications. London, Penguin, 1962; revised edition, London, Chatto and Windus, 1966; New York, Barnes and Noble, 1967.

The Existing Alternatives in Communications. London, Fabian Society, 1962.

Modern Tragedy. London, Chatto and Windus, and Stanford, California, Stanford University Press, 1966; revised edition, London, Verso, 1979.

The English Novel from Dickens to Lawrence. London, Chatto and Windus, and New York, Oxford University Press, 1970.

Orwell. London, Fontana, and New York, Viking Press, 1971.

The Country and the City. London, Chatto and Windus, and New York, Oxford University Press, 1973.

Television: Technology and Cultural Form. London, Fontana, 1974; New York, Schocken, 1975.

Drama in a Dramatised Society (lecture). Cambridge, University Press, 1975.

Keywords: A Vocabulary of Culture and Society. London, Croom Helm, and New York, Oxford University Press, 1976; revised edition, London, Fontana, 1983; New York, Oxford University Press, 1985.

Marxism and Literature. London and New York, Oxford University Press, 1977.

The Welsh Industrial Novel (lecture). Cardiff, University College Cardiff Press, 1979.

Politics and Letters: Interviews with "New Left Review." London, Verso, and New York, Schocken, 1979.

Problems in Materialism and Culture: Selected Essays. London, Verso, 1980; New York, Schocken, 1981.

Culture. London, Fontana, 1981; as *The Sociology of Culture*, New York, Schocken, 1982.

Socialism and Ecology. London, Socialist Environment and Resources Association, 1982(?).

Cobbett. Oxford, Oxford University Press, 1983.

Towards 2000. London, Chatto and Windus, 1983; as *The Year 2000*, New York, Pantheon, 1984.

The Arts Council: Politics and Policies. London, Arts Council, 1983(?).

Writing in Society. London, Verso, 1983(?).

Editor, *May Day Manifesto 1968.* London, Penguin, 1968.

Editor, *The Pelican Book of English Prose: From 1780 to the Present Day.* London, Penguin, 1970.

Editor, with Joy Williams, *D.H. Lawrence on Education.* London, Penguin, 1973.

Editor, *George Orwell: A Collection of Critical Essays.* Englewood Cliffs, New Jersey, Prentice Hall, 1974.

Editor, with Marie Axton, *English Drama: Forms and Development: Essays in Honour of Muriel Clara Bradbrook.* London, Cambridge University Press, 1977.

Editor, *Contact: Human Communication and Its History*, by Ferruccio Rossi-Landi and others. London, Thames and Hudson, 1981.

*

Critical Studies: by Dennis Potter, in *New Left Review* (London), 1961; Graham Martin, in *Views* (London), 1965; "Aspects of Raymond Williams' *Second Generation*" by Leonard Goldstein, in *Essays in Honour of William Gallacher* edited by P.M. Kemp-Ashraf and Jack Mitchell, Berlin, Humboldt Universität, 1966; "The Novel, Truth and Community" by James R. Bennett, in *D.H. Lawrence Review* (Fayetteville, Arkansas), 1970–71; "Idea of a People" by Jeremy Hooker, in *Planet* (Llangeitho Tregaron, Dyfed), 1979; *Raymond Williams* by J.P. Ward, Cardiff, University of Wales Press-Welsh Arts Council, 1981; "Socialist Fiction and the Education of Desire" by Kiernan Ryan, in *The Socialist Novel in Britain* edited by H. Gustav Klaus, Brighton, Harvester Press, 1982.

Raymond Williams comments:

(1972) When I came out of the army in 1945 I began writing the novel which was eventually published as *Border Country*. It went through some seven rewritings. It has been described as autobiographical, but this is in many ways misleading. For example, the central character, Harry Price, is a railway signalman, as was my father, but I found I could not get the book right until I had invented another character, his friend and opposite Morgan Rosser, who is in many ways as close to my own father as the character usually taken as based on him. In its final version, the novel had moved far enough from anything that can ordinarily be called autobiography for it to have to be seen in quite other ways. The chapter on the General Strike in *Border Country* has nothing autobiographical in it, yet it is the chapter of my novel-writing that I am most satisfied with.

During that period of writing and rewriting I completed two other novels, *A Map of Treason* and *The Grasshoppers*, which are still in the desk drawer. During the early 1960's I wrote my second published novel, *Second Generation*, which seems to be preferred to *Border Country* only in Eastern Europe, though I think it is exactly what I wanted to write as the working-class experience—personal and social rather than political—of the 1960's. Since then I have been working on two novels, *The Brothers* and *The Volunteers*. The latter, set in Europe in the 1990's, will probably be the first published. The former, which is closer to *Border Country*, should be completed during the next two years.

I find novel-writing very important and rewarding, and I have given much more time to it than my list of publications might suggest. But I revise and rework a great deal, and shall be satisfied if by the time I have finished I have five or six novels which I can feel are really my own. The fact that I also write social criticism has led to a simple formula in which my novels are seen as by-products, but the two kinds of writing have always been equally important to me, and in fact the novel-writing came first and will, I think, go on longer. Some of the themes of the novels overlap with the social criticism, but I only write in novel form what I am sure could not be written in essays and analysis. As to method, although I found *Border Country* difficult to write, I think the form and language of memory and the past are more accessible to contemporary novelists than a form and language of the true present as attempted in *Second Generation*. *The Volunteers*, set in the future, has required much more extended technical experiment; this is the main reason why it has taken so long to write.

(1981) *The Brothers* is still in progress, but meanwhile I have completed the *Border Country* trilogy with *The Fight for Manod* which tackles one of its themes. I am also beginning work on an unusual kind of historical novel in which the continuity is not of people but of a place.

(1986) Elements of *The Brothers* made their way into a new novel, *Loyalties*, which has interested me not only for its material but for its relatively unusual episodic form, which allowed me to trace continuities and discontinuities in a group of people and problems. The same method is developed in the historical novel mentioned above, to be called *People of the Black Mountains*. This is already of ordinary novel length and when complete will be a long work: I've wanted for many years to work through these particular themes.

*   *   *

In his book *The English Novel from Dickens to Lawrence*, and more recently in the series of interviews that make up the volume *Politics and Letters*, Raymond Williams has asserted that the famous controversy between Henry James and H.G. Wells about the task of the modern novelist has far from settled the issue. Williams deplores the frequent separation of the "personal" and the "social" into two mutually exclusive dimensions, and sees the consequent split of the genre into a "modernist," "psychological" novel and a "traditional," "realist" form at the root of the crisis in much contemporary English fiction.

The argument contains a key to the author's own practice as a novelist. His fiction is, among other things, an attempt to show that it is not only possible to make the necessary connections between individual lives and the social-historical process, between external events and the workings of the human mind, but that it can actually be done in an unforced and lucid way.

Border Country, Williams's first novel, was conceived as part of two distinct and yet connected kinds of enterprise. Published between *Culture and Society 1780–1950* and *The Long Revolution*, which established his reputation as an outstanding cultural thinker, it set out to look more closely at the human consequences of some of the fundamental social and cultural changes delineated in the two analytical works, and to explore the "human differences, between real people and real communities living the valuably various lives" (*The Long Revolution*). The borders that are crossed in this novel are many: from rural Wales to suburban London, from a working-class childhood to a middle-class career, from a predominantly oral culture to the world of academic scholarship, from a recent past to the present, from one generation to another. Yet in this mobile society there emerge also points of continuity: socially, in the direct way of life of the Welsh Border community, which Matthew Price, the temporarily returned university lecturer, rediscovers; individually, and more precariously, in the legacy that his dying father leaves to him.

But *Border Country* was also the first volume of a trilogy of novels, in each of which a central working-class experience is dramatised and the allegiance to this class of radical intellectuals of working-class descent is tested. Artistically, though not structurally, the General Strike sequence is the high point of the novel. Part of its success derives from the carefully differentiated attitudes and responses which the railwaymen in this remote village display under the impact of the strike. The reactions of the two central characters are given particular consideration: Harry Price, the quiet-spoken signalman, who sides instinctively but unerringly with the miners, carries on his life of self-sufficiency and moral integrity pretty much unscathed after the failure of the strike; whereas Morgan Rosser, the more militant and impatient trade-unionist of the two, gradually modifies his way of life as a result of his bitter disillusionment, and eventually turns into a small-scale capitalist—a development towards an altogether different set of values which marks yet another crossing of borders.

The device of letting contrasting characters embody different attitudes of the working class and labour movement, as well as give utterance to alternative strategies for the building of a more humane social order, is used throughout the trilogy.

Second Generation, with its larger cast and more complex plot, not only counterposes two working-class families, one settling for a withdrawn, private existence, the other devoting itself to industrial and political action, but distinguishes within the latter couple between Harold Owen's somewhat narrow, if tireless shop-floor activities and Kate's wider socialist horizon. It then contrasts this world of the car factory workers with left-wing academia as represented by two university dons, whose purely theoretical knowledge coupled with moderation and cynicism respectively is in turn challenged by the Owens' son Peter, when he decides to abandon his dry sociological Ph.D. thesis and put his intelligence at the service of his class instead. Narrowness, confusion, contradiction, and betrayal loom large in this work (which can be seen to reflect a particular left-wing climate of the early 1960's), threatening to block any meaningful socialist commitment whatsoever, even if such paralysing pressures are finally withstood by the individual members of the Owen family.

The grave personal costs of absorbing involvement in political causes are also suggested in *The Fight for Manod* with which the Welsh trilogy was concluded after a lapse of 15 years. This novel, however, appears less harrowed by hesitations and self-questioning, the greater resolution and confidence with which the two protagonists go about their work manifesting itself in the very title. Matthew Price and Peter Owen, who re-appear here alongside a number of other characters from *Second Generation*, investigate the possibilities of a new kind of government-funded settlement scheme for Mid-Wales, and soon discover a whole web of land speculation stretching from the local capitalist to an obscure international trust operating in Brussels and London. That Williams has thus integrated the crucial new economic and political realities created by the rise of the powerful multinational corporations and Britain's entry into the Common Market lifts *The Fight for Manod* onto an entirely different plane from the traditional socialist novel, with its emphasis on the working-class home and community (e.g., *Border Country*), the representation of work and of largely local conflict.

The atmosphere of suspense and secrecy which hangs over *The Fight of Manod* thickens in *The Volunteers*, which is a political thriller set in an increasingly authoritarian Britain of the late 1980's. What is new in this work, apart from the use of a popular genre, is a clipped, hardboiled diction, revealing the insensitive world of the news agencies in which the first-person narrator and protagonist moves. Where *The Volunteers* continues the concern of the earlier fiction is in its exposure of the central character to a painful process of reassessing his whole personal and social situation in order to bring him to the point of a clear political choice.

Williams's most recent novel, *Loyalties*, starts at a moment in history when such a choice appeared easy, with the issue of Fascism versus Democracy and Socialism in the open and morally clear-cut, though actually to volunteer for the International Brigades in Spain, as two of the characters in this novel do, demanded an evidently deeper level of commitment. The narrative then moves on to cover half a century of leftwing causes and struggles such as the turning point of the Labour Government in 1947, the Suez crisis of 1956, the Vietnam demonstration of 1968 and the miners' strike of 1984. Closely interwoven with these events are the lives of Welsh miners and Cambridge graduates, young people in the 1930's with communist leanings, who then, under various kinds of pressure, take different routes in the post-war period without, however, succumbing to the more obnoxious spectacle of breast-beating "confessions." At the heart of this intricate build-up, which involves three generations, is a probing into conflicting loyalties, and a confrontation with the question of which comes first: friend, family, class, nation, or political ideal. No clear preference or hierarchy of loyalties emerges, but once again the toll taken by sustained political engagement makes disturbing reading.

—H. Gustav Klaus

WILLIAMS, Wirt (Alfred, Jr.). American. Born in Goodman, Mississippi, 21 August 1921. Educated at Cleveland High School, Mississippi; Delta College, Cleveland, 1937–40, B.A. in English and American literature 1940; Louisiana State University, Baton Rouge, 1940–41, M.A. in journalism 1941; University of Iowa, Iowa City, 1950–53, Ph.D. in English and American literature 1953. Served in the United States Navy, 1942–46: Gunnery Officer and Assistant Gunnery Officer, *U.S.S. Decatur*, 1942–44; Executive Officer and Navigator, 1944–45, and Commanding Officer, 1945–46, *U.S.S. LSM 437*; since 1954, Lieutenant-Commander, United States Naval Reserve. Married Ann Meredith in 1954; one child. Correspondent, Associated Press, Cleveland, Mississippi, 1938–40; news editor, 1941–42, and capitol correspondent, 1946, Shreveport *Times*, Louisiana; reporter, special writer and city editor, New Orleans *Item*, 1946–49. Assistant Professor, 1953–57, Associate Professor, 1957–60, and since 1960, Professor of English, California State University, Los Angeles. Guest literary editor, Los Angeles *Times*, 1960–61, 1968. Recipient: ABC award, for reporting, 1949; Huntington Hartford fellowship, 1958. Address: 2022 Avenue of the Trees, Carlsbad, California 92008, U.S.A.

PUBLICATIONS

Novels

The Enemy. Boston, Houghton Mifflin, 1951; London, Corgi, 1967.
Love in a Windy Space. New York, Reynal, 1957.
Ada Dallas. New York, McGraw Hill, 1959; London, Muller, 1960.
A Passage of Hawks. New York, McGraw Hill, 1963; London, Muller, 1964.
The Trojans. Boston, Little Brown, 1966; London, Barrie and Rockliff, 1967.
The Far Side. New York, Horizon Press, 1972; London, Bantam, 1976.

Uncollected Short Stories

"Attack by Starlight," in *New Narratives 1944*, edited by Blanche Williams. New York, Appleton Century, 1944.
"The Unbeaten," in *Statement* (Los Angeles), Winter 1953.

Other

The Tragic Art of Ernest Hemingway. Baton Rouge, Louisiana State University Press, 1981.

Translator, *The Blue Angel*, by Heinrich Mann. New York, New American Library, 1959.

*

Manuscript Collection: Boston University.

Critical Studies: by Robert Kirsch, in the *Los Angeles Times*, 8 October 1959 and 17 December 1966; *The Recent Political Novel in America* by Joseph Blotner, Austin, University of Texas Press, 1966; John Raymond, in *Punch* (London), 18 August 1967; "Tragic Themes in Three Novels by Wirt Williams" by Gay Chow, unpublished dissertation, State College, Mississippi State University, 1977.

Wirt Williams comments:

(1972) A novelist should really keep his mouth shut about his work. His explanation of what he is about limits the work fatally, and necessarily is so incomplete as to be downright false. Even the most self-conscious writer *knows* only a small part of what he has done. The great artificer is the subconscious, which creates those recurring patterns of structure and symbol that tell what the writer really means. His work is only as strong as the force of that subconscious—vision, if you will.

Still and all, the conscious is a partner, too, and up to a point, the more thoroughly the writer plans, the better are his chances of giving the subpsyche a full free run. So he has at least some idea of what he is up to, and perhaps at least once he ought to say. For better or for worse, I am an extremely self-conscious writer: I can never quite forget technical principles of the art of fiction that I learned, or at least had explained to me, in the classroom—broadly speaking, the principles of Flaubert and particularly of Hemingway. The central conception of the Imagist poets (which I took from Hemingway without at first knowing where he got it) has been unquestionably the biggest force operating on, and in, my fiction. This conception is (put much too simply) that the writer sends emotion and idea, and makes reality, through sharp, hard pictures—undiluted by reflection or rhetoric. Almost paradoxically, the other "official" moderns I have learned from have been, in language, working the other side of the street—Conrad, Faulkner, and more lately Jean-Paul Sartre.

I teach a seminar in tragedy and once read a great deal of formalistic (academic) criticism, and what I write has been marked by those exposures, also.

So what I *think* I am saying, most of the time, is that we define our lives by what we do in the face of the universal and inescapable catastrophe. Or that we must take our own meaning in an operationally hostile universe without apparent meaning. The theme is scarcely original: no theme is, but this one is as old as tragedy. At the same time, nuanced differently in each case, it seems to be the pervasive statement of 20th-century fiction.

My first novels were an attempt to beat personal experience into fictional form. *The Enemy* is about destroyers and aircraft hunting submarines they never see in the North Atlantic in World War II. Some saw it as a paraphrase of Camus's central metaphor—Sisyphus rolling the stone up the hill. Fair enough, but I had never read Camus at the time I wrote it, and I think my pattern was stronger for my ignorance. *Love in a Windy Space* was a love story set in Louisiana—a simple enough tragedy, with a couple of fables beneath about the state of the South and of the forlorn man. *Ada Dallas* was concerned with Louisiana politics (which I had covered as a political correspondent), was awarely tragic, and was invested with the familiar ethical fable.

No longer finding my own experience that interesting, now I make up or find designs on the outside, and hope that by analogy, the essence of my experience will somehow infuse that design. *A Passage of Hawks*, a deliberately Jacobean story of murder and wickedness, was suggested by T.S. Eliot's examination of Thomas Middleton's *The Changeling*—an examination, of course, far more interesting than the play. *The Trojans* was a multi-purposed attempt to say something about the relationship between the artist and the world, to put forward a species of existentialism, to explore all sorts of varieties of experience, and to come up with some interesting information about motion pictures. Its subject matter in the narrowest sense came from recent history of that industry.

The day of the publisher as patron has been over for some time, and if a novelist is to be heard (that is to say, published) he must offer one level of appeal—among all his levels of statement—to a large and completely non-literary audience. I have accepted the condition and find it just: there are many fine things a novelist can do, but the finest of all is to tell a wonderful story. The abiding, unanswerable question, of course, is: wonderful to whom?

* * *

Wirt Williams is a pure example of the American novelist who came to literary maturity shortly after World War II. He is well-grounded in criticism and theory; he teaches and is fluent in the history of the genre. His literary forebears are writers in the grand traditions of prose fiction: Flaubert, Conrad, James, Hemingway. Understandably his expectation for all prose fiction is lofty; everywhere in his own work the alignments of image, action, character, and meaning are exact. Seen together his works make a larger statement than the separate titles.

From a brilliant first novel (*The Enemy*) to a probable middle-ground of development (*The Trojans*), the overall pattern is clear: *The Enemy* concerns the author's line-experience in North Atlantic anti-submarine warfare; *The Trojans* concerns art and the movie industry and is narrated from a fully dramatic perspective by a cerebral writer/artist. The motif of a protagonist overwhelmed by tragic or near-tragic circumstances often occurs; the ancillary literary resources of the novels stem variously from fable, myth, Jacobean drama, and others. In summary, the literary resources of the novels are extraordinary.

Intentionally, characterization, plot-structure, and chronology are not notably experimental. Typically, a story unfolds from multiple points of view; the author's attitude towards his materials is seldom extreme although irony, especially in dialogue, reoccurs. Thus all the novels are "open," public; there is little obscurity of either language or motivation. Williams acknowledges the influence of his sometimes literary correspondent, Ernest Hemingway.

The prose is taut, informational, and well-calculated. The finest language occurs in brief, descriptive passages of the sea, the rural South, or the city at dawn or at night. From these passages emerges a pervasive atmosphere; so great is this strength that a delicately controlled atmosphere may become an important protagonist in the story. Williams deals best with large effects; his unit of comparison is the whole novel.

To place the novels in a mainstream of American literature calls for other, extrinsic considerations. For example, Williams was born and raised in Mississippi, in the Black Belt—a region of America which changed almost not at all until after World War II. His father was a Southern-trained classical historian; on occasion Williams taught his father's classes in Roman history. In addition to this classical background, and before he completed the Ph.D. in literary studies, Williams was a newspaperman in New Orleans. *Love in a Windy Space, A Passage*

of Hawks, and *Ada Dallas* (also a film) are concerned with the provinciality, the passions, and enigmas of the South.

Not surprisingly, therefore, many of the protagonists are concerned with status, integrity of motive, and money; their often unconscious search for the lost "classical" values of valor, fidelity, friendship, and honor is a continuing criticism of modernity. These women and men come from a felt or remembered tradition and order; they are fated to live among the ruins of the 20th century. Typically these characters of above-average intelligence and education remain isolated or unresolved in the midst of apparent affluence. Too often the resolution they find is in personal oblivion, death, or patrician acceptance. Taken together, these concerns and attitudes suggest the novels are in the mainstream of the American novel of manners, the Romance of large-scale enterprise, the film industry and state-capitol politics included. Wirt Williams continues to write and to teach. His most recent work is scholarship on the subject of Hemingway's tragic vision and increasingly his own novels claim critical and exegetical attention.

—James B. Hall

WILLINGHAM, Calder (Baynard, Jr.). American. Born in Atlanta, Georgia, 23 December 1922. Educated at The Citadel, Charleston, South Carolina, 1940–41; University of Virginia, Charlottesville, 1941–43. Married 1) Helene Rothenberg in 1945 (divorced, 1951), one son; 2) Jane Marie Bennett in 1953, three sons and two daughters. Recipient (for screenplay): Writers Guild of America West award, 1968; British Film Academy award, 1969. Address: c/o Vanguard Press, 424 Madison Avenue, New York, New York 10017, U.S.A.

PUBLICATIONS

Novels

End as a Man. New York, Vanguard Press, 1947; London, Lehmann, 1952.
Geraldine Bradshaw. New York, Vanguard Press, 1950; revised edition, London, Barker, 1964.
Reach to the Stars. New York, Vanguard Press, 1951; London, Barker, 1965.
Natural Child. New York, Dial Press, 1952.
To Eat a Peach. New York, Dial Press, 1955; London, Mayflower, 1966.
Eternal Fire. New York, Vanguard Press, and London, Barker, 1963.
Providence Island. New York, Vanguard Press, and London, Hart Davis, 1969.
Rambling Rose. New York, Delacorte Press, 1972; London, Hart Davis MacGibbon, 1973.
The Big Nickel. New York, Dial Press, 1975; London, Hart Davis MacGibbon, 1976.
The Building of Venus Four. New York, Manor, 1977.

Short Stories

The Gates of Hell. New York, Vanguard Press, 1951; London, Mayflower, 1966.

Uncollected Short Stories

"What Star So Humble", in *New Yorker*, 16 January 1965.
"A Clowny Night in the Red-Eyed World," in *Playboy* (Chicago), March 1965.

Plays

End as a Man, adaptation of his own novel (produced New York, 1953).

Screenplays: *Paths of Glory*, with Stanley Kubrick and Jim Thompson, 1957; *The Strange One*, 1957; *The Vikings*, with Dale Wasserman, 1958; *One-Eyed Jacks*, with Guy Trosper, 1961; *The Graduate*, with Buck Henry, 1967; *Little Big Man*, 1970; *Thieves Like Us*, with Joan Tewkesbury, 1974.

Television Play: *Thou Shalt Not Commit Adultery*, with Del Reisman, 1978.

*

Calder Willingham comments:

(1972) At the beginning of my career, I was contemptuous and skeptical of the typical "best-seller" that pandered to public fantasies, wish-fulfillment, class or regional or national prejudices, etcetera. As my career progressed, I became equally contemptuous and skeptical of the typical "literary" novel that pandered to the aesthetic dicta and passing fashions of an intellectual elite. Thus, I have contrived as a novelist to fall cleverly between two stools: my work in general has dissatisfied or distressed the mass best-seller audience and at the same time has infuriated or bemused the so-called literary audience. Lonely and awkward as it is down here between these stools, I like to think of my achievement as a considerable and perhaps even unique feat on the current writing scene.

Fortunately, this fall between stools has not been unqualified; certain of my novels have been highly praised by the critical and certain of them have reached a substantial audience. But to support my large family through the years it has been necessary for me to resort to the writing of screenplays. There has been too much disturbing reality and irony in my novels for them to be generally acceptable as escapist pap for a mass audience and I break far too many rules of literary fashion (practically all in fact) for my work to appear of any great significance to the intelligentsia. I would rather this be so than to have written wish-fulfillment trash or the tedious, inhuman, unreadable literary monstrosities now fashionable.

The critical fraternity, I am afraid, has not known what on earth to make of my writing. I have used ironic contradiction and seemingly cruel humor in ways that are singular—or were singular, let us say; much of so-called modern "black comedy" seems to have been inspired by some off-hand stories I wrote 20 or 25 years ago. But also (and here the puzzlement of my critics deepens) my principal novels have been optimistic, fond of their characters, affirmative, hopeful, joyous toward life. A bewildering thing indeed, this. How can a man perceive the terrors and horrors of life, and still remain an optimist able to love his fellow creatures? I would grant it takes more courage and heart than can be contained in the critical faculty, which in blind cowardice can only conclude that such a man must be a liar or a fraud or a maddening incomprehensible idiot. I certainly have never yet seen any truly intelligent detailed criticism of my writing and I do not expect it to appear in my lifetime and this pleases me. So long as I can keep the analytical brethren off-balance and bewildered, I know I myself am crossing the wire.

As for my movie work, I do not regard this as real writing of my own, because here my sensibility is at the tender mercies of those with whom I am associated. The only way I could make a motion picture truly my own would be to produce and direct it as well as write it. I am looking for an insane millionaire to give me the money to make a really great film. In the meanwhile I cannot take with genuine seriousness any of the films on which I have worked.

As for the theatre, to me the theatre is an amusement rather than a major form, no doubt because my background as a novelist causes the medium to seem to me too restrictive. Besides, poetry is not my forte but rather the inter-play of characters in time and space, i.e., classic narrative.

My real work has been as a novelist and that work readily falls into three periods. The first is that of my initial novel, *End as a Man*, an adolescent effort marked by youthful fury and a rather simplistic view of the human condition. The second is the *Geraldine Bradshaw* period ending with *To Eat a Peach*—it was I suppose during this period that I (according to *The New Yorker*) "inadvertently fathered black comedy." The third period is that of my maturity and it has seen thus far publication of two major efforts, *Eternal Fire* and *Providence Island*. Doubtful as I am of the literary world, it has nonetheless been a profound astonishment to me that these novels have not received far greater recognition. I expect they will someday; it is my belief I put more of whatever gifts I have into these books than all my other work combined. Thus, on this Christmas Eve in snowy New Hampshire in this the year of Our Lord 1970, I look back on my struggle as a novelist with both frustration and satisfaction even as I plan to return to the bitter fray and write another book or two, God willing.

*   *   *

The simplest and possibly truest way to characterize the fiction of Calder Willingham is to call it the work of a 20th-century Fielding, for Willingham is a comic chronicler of iniquity, a creator of mock-novels, an enemy of hypocrisy who turns its lies and pretenses back on themselves, and a moral seer who is able to espy the good always and only in the midst of a chaos of vice and folly. His first novel, *End as a Man*, revealed as much, but the novels (and stories) which have followed it have shown him to be a Fielding possessed of such a strong sense of the absurd, of the natural disorder of being, that he has discarded even conventional form in his search for an artistic expression of the real and living world. Traditional genres collapse in his hands like a shack in a hurricane and at the same time open out to reveal the free imaginative source of all form—literary and artistic forms and, for that matter, the good, the true, and the beautiful.

His attack on the ponderous seriousness of the modern novel and short story has led him away from the path of predictable repetition that might have followed upon the success of his first novel. The very form of the serious novel failed him. He abandoned his plan to write a trilogy based upon the lives of hotel bellmen after he had finished and published the first two volumes, *Geraldine Bradshaw* and *Reach to the Stars*, only to give it a radically transformed conclusion 14 years later with *The Big Nickel*. The narrator of his fourth novel, *Natural Child*, confesses at the end that neither he nor any other of the characters could have written such a book and that "Maybe the cat wrote it." *To Eat a Peach*, his fifth novel, professes to be the tale of "a happy little summer in the mountains down in the deep South where the dogwood and the sycamore grow, and the sun shines all day long, when it isn't raining." His novels turn into tall tales, his characters become caricatures and then characters again, and the short stories in *The Gates of Hell* are more often than not hilarious "anti-stories." They collapse into playlets or take the form of brief and gloriously mindless essays. *Providence Island*, Willingham's longest and most carefully constructed novel, closes by calling itself "a seashell tale." *Rambling Rose* is a wonderfully comic and loving tale about a 19-year-old country girl who comes to work during the Great Depression for a family remarkably like Willingham's own. *The Big Nickel* is a harrowing look at a writer's nearly destructive brush with "the idiot slut Success," with its narrative alternating between the realistic story and a phantasmagoric rendering of the writer's state of mind. And most recently, *The Building of Venus Four*, his comic exploration of predatory sex, was almost completely ignored by a baffled literary establishment. The forms fail him, but he finds life in the absence of form, creates novels and stories that defy form.

Willingham's finest novel (and one of the most under-rated of modern American novels), *Eternal Fire*, is on the one hand a mock "Southern" novel full of sound and fury, and on the other a serious and meaningful novel expressing a moral sense which grows from an acceptance of the world with all its chaos and a forgiveness of it. One of its villains, Harry Diadem, is both as comical and as convincingly evil as any character in modern literature, but its simple hero manages to face up to the inescapable presence of evil even in the girl he loves, his "fallen angel," and to emerge "from eternal fire into manhood."

A master ironist, Willingham has consistently gone his own way, laughing and scratching, recoiling at the horror of the world, insisting always in the efficacy of "growth and affirmation, of moral heroism, of spiritual triumph." To be human is all Willingham asks of any of us—to be one who sees honestly what it is to be human and nonetheless accepts and affirms that humanity. His fiction, which calls everything into question, even and perhaps especially itself, offers as answer only the need to see the world in which we live and to dare to live in the world which we see. And that, laughably enough, is quite enough.

—R.H.W. Dillard

WILSON, A(ndrew) N(orman). British. Born in Stone, Staffordshire, 27 October 1950. Educated at Rugby School, Warwickshire, 1964–69; New College, Oxford (Chancellor's Essay Prize, 1971; Ellerton Theological Prize, 1975), 1969–72, M.A.; studied for priesthood, 1973–74. Married Katherine Duncan-Jones in 1971; two daughters. Assistant master, Merchant Taylors' School, London, 1975–76; Lecturer, St. Hugh's College, Oxford, 1976–82, and New College, 1977–80; literary editor, *The Spectator*, London, 1981–83. Recipient: Rhys Memorial Prize, for fiction, 1978, for biography, 1981; Maugham Award, 1981; Arts Council National Book Award, 1981; Southern Arts prize, 1981; W.H. Smith Literary Award, 1983. Fellow, Royal Society of Literature, 1981. Agent: A.D. Peters, 10 Buckingham Street, London WC2N 6BU, England.

PUBLICATIONS

Novels

The Sweets of Pimlico.   London, Secker and Warburg, 1977.

Unguarded Hours.   London, Secker and Warburg, 1978.
Kindly Light.   London, Secker and Warburg, 1979.
The Healing Art.   London, Secker and Warburg, 1980.
Who Was Oswald Fish?   London, Secker and Warburg, 1981.
Wise Virgin.   London, Secker and Warburg, 1982; New York, Viking Press, 1983.
Scandal; or, Priscilla's Kindness.   London, Hamish Hamilton, 1983; New York, Viking, 1984.
Gentlemen in England.   London, Hamish Hamilton, 1985; New York, Viking, 1986.

Other

The Laird of Abbotsford: A View of Sir Walter Scott.   Oxford and New York, Oxford University Press, 1980.
The Life of John Milton.   Oxford and New York, Oxford University Press, 1983.
Hilaire Belloc.   London, Hamish Hamilton, and New York, Atheneum, 1984.
How Can We Know? An Essay on the Christian Religion.   London, Hamish Hamilton, and New York, Atheneum, 1985.

Editor, *Ivanhoe*, by Scott.   London, Penguin, 1982.
Editor, *Dracula*, by Bram Stoker.   Oxford, Oxford University Press, 1983.

*   *   *

Two of A.N. Wilson's novels, *Wise Virgin* and *The Healing Art*, rise above the level of farcical satire, often badly written (from *Scandal*: "Derek could be *heard* implanting a slobbery kiss on a *powdered* cheek" [italics mine]) in the facile style of the clever public schoolboy who is afraid of showing emotion and being accused of sentimentality, and must therefore at all costs be flippant about what most preoccupies him. Although *Scandal* is the worst, *The Sweets of Pimlico*, *Unguarded Hours*, and *Kindly Light* are scant improvements, and *Who Was Oswald Fish?* is only a little better. The author suffers from the cultivation of a not-so-keen "satirical vein ... in place of a sense of humour." What saves him from dismissal is the undoubted intelligence at work and the flashes, even in the 4th-rate novels, of genuine insight into the acerbic personality. All is not lost if a reader can come across illuminating phrases such as the above from *Wise Virgin*.

More than any other recent writer, Wilson seems actually trying to overcome that aspect of his personality which has been soured by an innately English and painfully inane upbringing within the public school system and the institution of the Church of England, a system and an institution undoubtedly deserving of satire. But satire only works powerfully after the satirist has seen clearly his position vis-à-vis what he is satirising, and Wilson does not always see it because he is too much part of it. He is trapped by the traditions he purports to satirise, and as a result the satire has an unpleasant hysterical edge to it as well as the archness of a teenager who dares not look anyone in the eye and say, I believe ... in God, in love, in laughter, in life, in people ... in the necessity for a moral scheme of things. And yet that is what Wilson wants to do, he wants to take a moral stand. When he does, as in *Wise Virgin* and *The Healing Art*, the satire is transformed into humour and we have a sympathetic comic writer confronting and exploring themes novelists have always explored: the effect of one personality on another, the strangeness of religious belief, the need for morality, the almost imperceptible way in which love can effect the largest and most fundamental changes, the nature of that love, the action of grace in a world that no longer believes in the existence of grace.

Wilson's particular talent is to capture the moment of kindness. That people can and, given a chance, will be simply kind to one another is for Wilson miraculous, and when he allows his characters and his readers to stand in front of kindness and remain in awe of it without fidgeting or snickering, he achieves some moving writing that remains funny. In *Wise Virgin*, for example, Giles, the blind father of Tibba and lover of his research assistant Louise Agar, is constantly battling against tetchiness, snobbism, acerbity. Louise and Giles have a growing complex relationship in which what one may wish to call, cautiously, love and a mutual need and desire for companionship are inextricably bound. At the end of the novel Louise and her mother come to Giles for tea on Christmas Day, thanks to the machinations of Tibba, the wise virgin who acts not only out of the sourness of the clever adolescent but also out of a selfishness that is necessary for her to free herself from her father's dependence on her and her own dependence on him. This is the first meeting between Giles and Louise's mother, whom Tibba would have called "vulgar." When they meet, the mother thinks Giles is a pansy, makes snide comments to herself about the absence of a "nice settee," does not want to linger and miss "Christmas Night with the Stars": she has her own nastiness. And yet from the proprieties between strangers and the gratuitous kindness of the mother emerge moments that restore in Giles the ability to be happy and make him, finally, propose to Louise. Those pages are funny, well controlled, and serious, though neither solemn nor pompous. This is Wilson at his best.

In *The Healing Art* Wilson explores the possibility that kindness may be the best realisation for the theological virtue of caritas, as he shows the changes wrought in Pamela by her belief that she has only a few months to live. Her story is contrasted to the story of Dorothy who really is dying, though she does not know it. Dorothy is of the same class as Mrs. Agar in *Wise Virgin*, and her kindness, and the kindness of those who surround her, are used as a constant counterpoint to Pamela's search for a way of life that is not so imbued with selfishness as hers has been. She finds this life with Hereward, one of those "touchy bigoted figures whose hard affected tones proclaimed the mysteries with such radiance and which concealed an ocean of kindness so effectively that almost no one would have guessed it was there," but the reader is led to the conclusion that it is in some mysterious way through Dorothy that Pamela is enabled to find it, that in some way Dorothy gives up her life for Pamela: Pamela is left a china lady by Dorothy in her will, "for all its hideous, cheapened, glossy unnecessary vulgarity: a *lady*; a crinoline *lady*.... Nothing before had emphasised to Pamela so strongly that Dorothy was dead, dead ... in her place. The figurine would follow her about now like a tutelary idol, an emblem of deliverance." She has been delivered into kindness, inescapably through the miraculous existence of Dorothy who, through all her suffering, took time to remember Pamela when "it would never have crossed her mind to remember poor Dorothy in this way." And thanks to her and to Hereward Pamela has put away childish things, "archness, intolerance, brittleness," and learned how to be happy.

One hopes that A.N. Wilson may himself not succumb to the temptations of archness, intolerance, and brittleness and give us instead books that proclaim the mysteries with radiance and humour, and do not try to conceal kindness.

—M.J. Fitzgerald

WILSON, (Sir) Angus (Frank Johnstone-). British. Born in Bexhill, Sussex, 11 August 1913. Educated at Westminster School, London, 1927–31; Merton College, Oxford, B.A. (honours) in medieval and modern history 1936. Served in the Foreign Office, 1942–46. Staff member, British Museum, London, 1937–55: Deputy Superintendent of the Reading Room, 1949–55. Lecturer, 1963–66, Professor of English Literature, 1966–78, and since 1978, Professor Emeritus, University of East Anglia, Norwich. Ewing Lecturer, University of California, Los Angeles, 1960; Bergen Lecturer, Yale University, New Haven, Connecticut, 1960; Moody Lecturer, University of Chicago, 1960; Northcliffe Lecturer, University College, London, 1961; Leslie Stephen Lecturer, Cambridge University, 1962–63; Beckman Professor, University of California, Berkeley, 1967; John Hinkley Visiting Professor, Johns Hopkins University, Baltimore, 1974; Visiting Professor, University of Delaware, Newark, 1977, 1980, 1983, University of Iowa, Iowa City, 1978, 1986, Georgia State University, Atlanta, 1979, University of Michigan, Ann Arbor, 1979, University of Minnesota, Minneapolis, 1980, University of Pittsburgh, 1981, University of Missouri, Columbia, 1982, and University of Arizona, Tucson, 1984. Member of the Committee, Royal Literary Fund, 1966; member, Arts Council of Great Britain, 1966–69; Chairman, National Book League, London, 1971–74; President, Dickens Fellowship, London, 1974–75. Recipient: James Tait Black Memorial Prize, 1959; Foreign Book Prize (France), 1960; *Yorkshire Post* award, for nonfiction, 1971; Focus award, 1985. D.Litt.: University of Leicester, 1977; University of East Anglia, 1979; University of Sussex, Brighton, 1981; Litt.D.: Liverpool University, 1979; Hon. Dr.: the Sorbonne, Paris, 1983. Honorary Fellow, Cowell College, University of California, Santa Cruz, 1968. Fellow, 1958, Companion of Literature, 1972, and since 1982 President, Royal Society of Literature; Commandant, Order of Arts and Letters (France), 1972; Honorary Member, American Academy, 1980. C.B.E. (Commander, Order of the British Empire), 1968. Knighted, 1980. Address: Felsham Woodside, Bradfield St. George, Bury St. Edmund's, Suffolk, England.

PUBLICATIONS

Novels

Hemlock and After. London, Secker and Warburg, and New York, Viking Press, 1952.
Anglo-Saxon Attitudes. London, Secker and Warburg, and New York, Viking Press, 1956.
The Middle Age of Mrs. Eliot. London, Secker and Warburg, 1958; New York, Viking Press, 1959.
The Old Men at the Zoo. London, Secker and Warburg, and New York, Viking Press, 1961.
Late Call. London, Secker and Warburg, 1964; New York, Viking Press, 1965.
No Laughing Matter. London, Secker and Warburg, and New York, Viking Press, 1967.
As If by Magic. London, Secker and Warburg, and New York, Viking Press, 1973.

Setting the World on Fire. London, Secker and Warburg, and New York, Viking Press, 1980.

Short Stories

The Wrong Set and Other Stories. London, Secker and Warburg, 1949; New York, Morrow, 1950.
Such Darling Dodos and Other Stories. London, Secker and Warburg, 1950; New York, Morrow, 1951.
A Bit off the Map and Other Stories. London, Secker and Warburg, and New York, Viking Press, 1957.
Death Dance: Twenty-Five Short Stories. New York, Viking Press, 1969.

Plays

The Mulberry Bush (produced London, 1956). London, Secker and Warburg, 1956.

Television Plays: *After the Show,* 1959; *The Stranger,* 1960.

Other

Emile Zola: An Introductory Study of His Novels. London, Secker and Warburg, and New York, Morrow, 1952; revised edition, Secker and Warburg, 1965.
For Whom the Cloche Tolls: A Scrapbook of the Twenties, illustrated by Philippe Jullian. London, Methuen, and New York, Curtis, 1953.
The Wild Garden; or, Speaking of Writing. Berkeley, University of California Press, and London, Secker and Warburg, 1963.
Tempo: The Impact of Television on the Arts. London, Studio Vista, 1964; Chester Springs, Pennsylvania, Dufour, 1966.
The World of Charles Dickens. London, Secker and Warburg, and New York, Viking Press, 1970.
Dickens Memorial Lecture 1970, with Kathleen Tillotson and Sylvère Monad. London, Dickens Fellowship, 1970.
The Naughty Nineties. London, Eyre Methuen, 1976.
The Strange Ride of Rudyard Kipling: His Life and Works. London, Secker and Warburg, 1977; New York, Viking Press, 1978.
Diversity and Depth in Fiction: Selected Critical Writings, edited by Kerry McSweeney. London, Secker and Warburg, 1983; New York, Viking, 1984.
Reflections in a Writer's Eye: Writings on Travel. London, Secker and Warburg, 1986.

Editor, *A Maugham Twelve,* by W. Somerset Maugham. London, Heinemann, 1966.
Editor, *Cakes and Ale, and Twelve Short Stories,* by W. Somerset Maugham. New York, Doubleday, 1967.
Editor, *Writers of East Anglia.* London, Secker and Warburg, 1977.
Editor, *East Anglia in Verse and Prose.* London, Secker and Warburg, 1982.
Editor, *The Portable Dickens.* New York, Viking Press, and London, Penguin, 1983.
Editor, *Essays by Divers Hands.* Woodbridge, Suffolk, Boydell and Brewer, 1984.

*

Manuscript Collection: University of Iowa, Iowa City.

Critical Studies: *The Free Spirit* by C.B. Cox, London, Oxford University Press, 1963; *Angus Wilson* by Jay L. Halio, Edinburgh, Oliver and Boyd, 1964, and *Critical Essays on Angus Wilson* edited by Halio, Boston, Hall, 1985; *Angus Wilson* by K.W. Gransden, London, Longman, 1969; "*The Middle Age of Mrs. Eliot* and *Late Call*" by Valerie Shaw, in *Critical Quarterly* (London), Spring 1970; *Harvest of a Quiet Eye: The Novel of Compassion* by James Gindin, Bloomington, University of Indiana Press, 1971; *Angus Wilson: Mimic and Moralist* by Peter Faulkner, New York, Viking Press, and London, Secker and Warburg, 1980; *Four Contemporary Novelists* by Kerry McSweeney, Montreal, McGill-Queen's University Press, 1982, London, Scolar Press, 1983; *Angus Wilson* by Averil Gardner, Boston, Twayne, 1985.

Angus Wilson comments:

(1972) I shall confine this statement to noting certain received critical ideas about my work that seem to me misleading, or, at the very best, marginal. I have not seen the critical notice to appear with this statement nor do I know who is its author. If what I say disagrees with that notice, it is only necessary to point out that some people find authors' views of their own work illuminating, others misleading. The choice is with the reader.

1) My work is very frequently compared to that of E.M. Forster. In some ways I am, of course, flattered and gratified. It is also true that some of my early short stories, *Hemlock and After,* and above all my play, *The Mulberry Bush,* contain the sort of critique of liberal humanism that is to be found in Forster's novels, above all in *Howards End.* But there have always been wide divergences—above all in my deep distrust of money, property, and the sort of responsibility that goes with them; in my dislike of sentimentalism about the primitive, the unsophisticated, and the physically strong; in my acceptance, in general, of the city (London) as having values in many ways superior to, certainly equal with, the country; on the other hand in my placing great importance upon a close relation with animal and plant life (see my continuous concern with animal and flower imagery); in my acceptance of violence and uncontrolled passion as being in certain occasions a good; above all, in my open statement of the possibility of homosexual happiness within a conventional framework and my consequent, I believe, greater power of identifying truly sympathetically with my women characters. None of this is an attempt to suggest equality with Forster's work, only to underline differences, and to note a certain distaste that I feel for it—notably in the sentimentalization of Stephen Wonham, the treatment of Leonard and Jackie Bast (indeed what seems to me the whole coldhearted, withdrawn, judging quality of *Howards End*); nor do I share Forster's evolutionary optimism expressed by the end of *Howards End.* It seems to me that I am at once a more impulsive, a more bitchy, and a more compassionate author than E.M. Forster—that my humanism has less high hope for the future but more acceptance and liking for human beings as they are. I cannot share or hope to attain his curious mixture of cunning, love, withdrawal, and passivity. Of course, I except the wonderful *Passage to India* from all these criticisms, but then I have written nothing that can be seen in relation to it.

2) My early work was formally traditional. It was written out of my deep saturation in 19th-century novels and out of a certain feeling that, like many of my contemporaries, I had temporarily got all I could out of the "modernists'" experiments. I wrote one or two very ill-advised commitments to "traditionalism," which, together with a misunderstanding of my praise of Zola and Dickens, led me almost to be labelled as an anti-experimentalist, almost a social realist. Dickens and Zola for me, of course, have their value as poets, though also poets using all society to create their prose poems from. My

early work was probably somewhat sharply "traditional" in form—in restoring 19th-century forms; but this was a protest against a conformity to post-Jamesian techniques. With a too great tyranny of neo-traditionalism in English novel writing, I have increasingly, from *The Old Men at the Zoo*, experimented, above all with pastiche. In the apparently conventional *Late Call* there are innumerable jokes, alienations, pastiches, and other non-traditional techniques that the critics failed to see. With *No Laughing Matter* experiment has greatly taken over. The chief influence in my last years has been Virginia Woolf, whom I had to attack fiercely before I felt free to recognize as the very great novelist she was. But my work continues and will, I think, continue to be social in its general material though probably increasingly experimental in form—I am interested in man's personality and soul, but I tend to see him first from the outside as a political and social creature.

3) This leads me to my last point. I am often spoken of as having a very narrow range of characters or as being the satirist of the middle classes. This has only a superficial truth, I think. Compared to most contemporary English novelists my social range seems wide, and my approach to the middle classes (the centre of my work) is as sympathetic as it is critical.

All this, of course, is a statement of intention (realized or unrealized I am not supposed, as an author, to be able to judge; though I suspect that authors can guess at their success with their intentions more than academic critics allow). Certainly it is not a judgement of quality—here the novelist must be his own most harsh critic and also his own most loving admirer—and about both he must say nothing.

*   *   *

Angus Wilson is a realistic novelist, with a very sharp ear and eye for the subtleties of English social behaviour. But there is another aspect of his work, not so obvious on a casual reading but never far below the surface, in which he is a writer deeply concerned with cruelty and horror and the intrusions of the nightmarish into civilized life. He began as a short-story writer and in some ways remains one, since his novels are usually episodic in organization, and are likely to be at their most impressive in their treatment of small units of narrative. His first two collections of stories, *The Wrong Set* and *Such Darling Dodos*, were sharply drawn sketches of English middle-class life during and just after the Second World War, with heavy emphasis on snobbery, self-deception, and genteel cruelty. Technically they were very adroit, though their despairing view of human motives was altogether too black and unrelieved for complete plausibility. In one of these stories, "Raspberry Jam," Wilson shows a characteristic awareness of the way in which an extremity of violence can shockingly erupt into a familiar domestic setting.

Wilson's first three novels, *Hemlock and After*, *Anglo-Saxon Attitudes*, and *The Middle Age of Mrs. Eliot*, are like much of modern English fiction, in their traditional, unselfconscious attitude to form, their precise registration of social nuance, and the nature of their moral preoccupations. At the same time, their peculiar mixture of detached observation and underlying obsession make them works that only Angus Wilson could have written. Despite a sense of what Henry James called "felt life" and, in the first two, an almost Dickensian range of characters, certain thematic preoccupations tend to be very obtrusive. The reader is invited to dwell on responsibility and guilt, and the tension between the public life of busy achievement and the private life of spiritual cultivation. In Wilson's world moral progress lies in the steady eradication of self-deception. Such preoccupations are, of course, part of a central tradition

of the English novel, the line of Jane Austen and George Eliot and E.M. Forster. It must, however, be confessed that Angus Wilson's concern with these questions is at times a little finedrawn and even parochial. It is not altogether easy to identify with the problems of the self-flagellating homosexual novelist, Bernard Sands, in *Hemlock and After*, or the spiritually sluggish historian, Gerald Middleton, in *Anglo-Saxon Attitudes*. In *The Middle Age of Mrs. Eliot* Meg Eliot, an archetypal liberal heroine, is good-looking, sensitive, intelligent but not intellectual, and modestly complacent. Yet her husband is killed in an outbreak of casual political violence at the airport of an Asian country they are visiting; the rest of the novel shows her brave attempt to make something of her life in widowhood and poverty. Among other things, it suggests that Wilson is better at creating memorable female characters than male ones, and compared with its two predecessors it is a generally admirable and successful work.

In the first three novels Wilson's sense of nightmare appears in isolated incidents and recurring images, but in *The Old Men at the Zoo* it moves into the centre of the action. This work is unique in Wilson's *oeuvre* in being as much a fable as a work of realistic fiction. It is a prophetic fantasy of the near future, when England is at war with an alliance of European powers, and Wilson deals with larger moral dilemmas than he had projected in his earlier books. Politics impinges on private life in an un-English way. His hero, Simon Carter, secretary of the London Zoo, who is both an animal-lover and an efficient administrator, tries to carry on with his work as best he can after England has been defeated by the Europeans. In doing so he embodies the classical dilemma of the public servant in a period of defeat and oppression: should one try to keep society going and risk being labelled a collaborator, or should one keep up a possibly vain and even disastrous resistance? *The Old Men at the Zoo* is a bizarre and often violent narrative that seems to have enabled Wilson to face and, for a time at least, to subdue his own fantasies. His next novel, *Late Call*, is by contrast a work of relative serenity. In *Late Call* the sense of evil that had appeared in Wilson's earlier novels in elements of fantasy or marginal obsession is integrated with his principal strength as a novelist: his infallible sense of social fact. *Late Call* explores the spiritual desolation of life in a New Town in the English Midlands, where the gimmickry of affluence has become a way of life rather than an aid to living. Wilson employs the consciousness of Sylvia Calvert, a woman in her sixties, who has retired after a lifetime of managing small, unfashionable hotels. Accompanied by her sponging idler of a husband, who cares only for playing cards and reliving his days as a temporary officer in the First World War, she goes to live with her recently widowed son in the New Town of Carshall. Harold is a progressive headmaster and educational theorist: he welcomes his parents to his fine modern house with a great display of filial feelings. But why and how they cannot live with Harold and his three teenage daughters is the story that Wilson goes on to tell with considerable insight and sensitivity. Sylvia is one of his most successful fictional creations. She is not at all an educated woman, but she has much native shrewdness, and Wilson uses her honest but often baffled responses to make a remarkably sharp exposure of contemporary progressive attitudes. *Late Call* is better written and less diffuse than Wilson's previous novels, and despite, or perhaps because of, its deliberately limited theme, it is arguably his most uniformly successful novel.

Wilson has several times shown his interest in the pre-1914 world; it appears in several retrospective scenes in *Anglo-Saxon Attitudes* and in the prologue to *Late Call*, describing Sylvia's childhood in 1911. In *No Laughing Matter* he once more returns to it. He unfolds the fortunes of the Matthews family from 1912, when the book opens, up to 1967, when it closes. *No Laughing Matter* is a long, ambitious book with many local successes; it uses the several generations of the Matthews family to look at more than 50 years of English social history, and Wilson indulges to the full his love of the crowded fictional canvas. In comparison with his earlier fiction, his language is far more resourceful, and he uses it to convey a wider spectrum of feeling and to draw on a greater variety of technical devices. Yet the book, for all its richness, is uncomfortably episodic: one is frequently more conscious of Wilson as a brilliant short story writer than as a novelist who is really at home with an extended narrative. A similar criticism can be made of *As If by Magic*, another long and ambitious novel. It contains many characters and ranges in space rather than time, from contemporary England to India, Ceylon, Malaya, and Japan. In intention a penetrating anatomy of the modern world and its problems, this novel shows in practice a division between Wilson's large aims and his real, more restricted imaginative interests.

In *Setting the World on Fire* Wilson made a radical and courageous move away from realistic fiction into myth. The myth, alluded to in the title, is that of Phaeton, the son of Helios, who borrowed his father's chariot and nearly set the world on fire by driving too close to it. The fall of Phaeton is depicted in a magnificent ceiling painting in Tothill House, a physical and symbolic structure which is central to the novel, a superb 17th-century house which, improbably, still stands in Westminster, occupied by the same immensely rich aristocratic family who have lived in it for generations. One of the younger members of the family re-enacts the myth in his own life. *Setting the World on Fire* is an elaborately structured book, which is likely to provide work for academic commentators in the discovery of cunning parallels, convergences, and contrasts. In this novel Wilson opened his consciousness to rich imaginings of beauty, wealth, glamour, energy, and talent, giving them free rein, with just enough control to turn fantasy into art; the result can reasonably be called baroque, as in the work of John Vanbrugh, the real architect who had a hand in Wilson's imagined mansion. The fantasy is avowedly aristocratic, in contrast to the bourgeois spirit and settings of Wilson's earlier fiction. *Setting the World on Fire* is impressive but precarious and a little unreal, like the great house which is supposed to lie at its heart.

Angus Wilson remains a novelist of unusually fine intelligence, wide reading, and great sensitivity, who embodies certain traditional attitudes to life and the novel at a time when they are increasingly under attack. He is both a writer of broad middle-brow appeal and true literary seriousness, in itself a highly traditional combination, and one which makes him hard to subject to confident critical placing.

—Bernard Bergonzi

WILSON, Colin (Henry). British. Born in Leicester, 26 June 1931. Educated at Gateway Secondary Technical School, Leicester, 1942–47. Served in the Royal Air Force, 1949–50. Married 1) Dorothy Betty Troop in 1951 (marriage dissolved), one son; 2) Pamela Joy Stewart in 1960, two sons and one daughter. Laboratory assistant, Gateway School, 1948–49; tax collector, Leicester and Rugby, 1949–50; labourer and hospital porter in London, 1951–53; salesman for the magazines *Paris Review* and *Merlin*, Paris, 1953. Since 1954, full-time writer.

British Council Lecturer in Germany, 1957; Writer-in-Residence, Hollins College, Virginia, 1966–67; Visiting Professor, University of Washington, Seattle, 1968; Professor, Institute of the Mediterranean (Dowling College, New York), Mallorca, 1969; Visiting Professor, Rutgers University, New Brunswick, New Jersey, 1974. Agent: David Bolt Associates, Cedar House, High Street, Ripley, Surrey GU23 6AE; or, Albert Zuckerman, Writers House Inc., 21 West 26th Street, New York, New York 10010, U.S.A. Address: Tetherdown, Trewallock Lane, Gorran Haven, Cornwall PL26 6NT, England.

PUBLICATIONS

Novels

Ritual in the Dark.   London, Gollancz, and Boston, Houghton Mifflin, 1960.
Adrift in Soho.   London, Gollancz, and Boston, Houghton Mifflin, 1961.
The World of Violence.   London, Gollancz, 1963; as *The Violent World of Hugh Greene*, Boston, Houghton Mifflin, 1963.
Man Without a Shadow: The Diary of an Existentialist.   London, Barker, 1963; as *The Sex Diary of Gerard Sorme*, New York, Dial Press, 1963.
Necessary Doubt.   London, Barker, and New York, Simon and Schuster, 1964.
The Glass Cage: An Unconventional Detective Story.   London, Barker, 1966; New York, Random House, 1967.
The Mind Parasites.   London, Barker, and Sauk City, Wisconsin, Arkham House, 1967.
The Philosopher's Stone.   London, Barker, 1969; New York, Crown, 1971.
The Killer.   London, New English Library, 1970; as *Lingard*, New York, Crown, 1970.
The God of the Labyrinth.   London, Hart Davis, 1970; as *The Hedonists*, New York, New American Library, 1971.
The Black Room.   London, Weidenfeld and Nicolson, 1971; New York, Pyramid, 1975.
The Schoolgirl Murder Case.   London, Hart Davis MacGibbon, and New York, Crown, 1974.
The Space Vampires.   London, Hart Davis MacGibbon, and New York, Random House, 1976.
The Janus Murder Case.   London, Granada, 1984.
The Personality Surgeon.   London, New English Library, and San Francisco, Mercury House, 1986.

Short Story

The Return of the Lloigor.   London, Village Press, 1974.

Uncollected Short Story

"Timeslip," in *Aries 1*, edited by John Grant.   Newton Abbot, Devon, David and Charles, 1979.

Plays

The Metal Flower Blossom (produced Southend-on-Sea, Essex, 1958).
Viennese Interlude (produced Scarborough, Yorkshire, and London, 1960).
Strindberg (as *Pictures in a Bath of Acid*, produced Leeds, Yorkshire, 1971; as *Strindberg: A Fool's Decision*, produced London, 1975).   London, Calder and Boyars, 1970; New York, Random House, 1971.
Mysteries (produced Cardiff, 1979).

Other

The Outsider. London, Gollancz, and Boston, Houghton Mifflin, 1956.

Religion and the Rebel. London, Gollancz, and Boston, Houghton Mifflin, 1957.

The Age of Defeat. London, Gollancz, 1959; as *The Stature of Man*, Boston, Houghton Mifflin, 1959.

Encyclopaedia of Murder, with Patricia Pitman. London, Barker, 1961; New York, Putnam, 1962.

The Strength to Dream: Literature and the Imagination. London, Gollancz, and Boston, Houghton Mifflin, 1962.

Origins of the Sexual Impulse. London, Barker, and New York, Putnam, 1963.

Rasputin and the Fall of the Romanovs. London, Barker, and New York, Farrar Straus, 1964.

Brandy of the Damned: Discoveries of a Musical Eclectic. London, Baker, 1964; as *Chords and Discords: Purely Personal Opinions on Music*, New York, Crown, 1966; augmented edition, as *Colin Wilson on Music*, London, Pan, 1967.

Beyond the Outsider: The Philosophy of the Future. London, Barker, and Boston, Houghton Mifflin, 1965.

Eagle and Earwig (essays). London, Baker, 1965.

Introduction to the New Existentialism. London, Hutchinson, 1966; Boston, Houghton Mifflin, 1967; as *The New Existentialism*, London, Wildwood House, 1980.

Sex and the Intelligent Teenager. London, Arrow, 1966; New York, Pyramid, 1968.

Voyage to a Beginning (autobiography). London, Cecil and Amelia Woolf, 1966; New York, Crown, 1969.

Bernard Shaw: A Reassessment. London, Hutchinson, and New York, Atheneum, 1969.

A Casebook of Murder. London, Frewin, 1969; New York, Cowles, 1970.

Poetry and Mysticism. San Francisco, City Lights, 1969; London, Hutchinson, 1970.

The Strange Genius of David Lindsay, with E.H. Visiak and J.B. Pick. London, Baker, 1970; as *The Haunted Man*, San Bernardino, California, Borgo Press, 1979.

The Occult. New York, Random House, and London, Hodder and Stoughton, 1971.

New Pathways in Psychology: Maslow and the Post-Freudian Revolution. New York, Taplinger, and London, Gollancz, 1972.

Order of Assassins: The Psychology of Murder. London, Hart Davis, 1972.

L'Amour: The Ways of Love, photographs by Piero Rimaldi. New York, Crown, 1972.

Strange Powers. London, Latimer New Dimensions, 1973; New York, Random House, 1975.

Tree by Tolkien. London, Covent Garden Press-Inca, 1973; Santa Barbara, California, Capra Press, 1974.

Hermann Hesse. London, Village Press, and Philadelphia, Leaves of Grass Press, 1974.

Wilhelm Reich. London, Village Press, and Philadelphia, Leaves of Grass Press, 1974.

Jorge Luis Borges. London, Village Press, and Philadelphia, Leaves of Grass Press, 1974.

A Book of Booze. London, Gollancz, 1974.

The Unexplained. Lake Oswego, Oregon, Lost Pleiade Press, 1975.

Mysterious Powers. London, Aldus, and Danbury, Connecticut, Danbury Press, 1975; as *They Had Strange Powers*, New York, Doubleday, 1975; revised edition, as *Mysteries of the Mind*, with Stuart Holroyd, Aldus, 1978.

The Craft of the Novel. London, Gollancz, 1975.

Enigmas and Mysteries. Danbury, Connecticut, Danbury Press, and London, Aldus, 1976.

The Geller Phenomenon. London, Aldus, 1976.

Mysteries: An Investigation into the Occult, The Paranormal, and the Supernatural. London, Hodder and Stoughton, 1978; New York, Putnam, 1980.

Science Fiction as Existentialism. Hayes, Middlesex, Bran's Head, 1978.

The Search for the Real Arthur, with *King Arthur Country in Cornwall*, by Brenda Duxbury and Michael Williams. Bodmin, Cornwall, Bossiney, 1979.

Starseekers. London, Hodder and Stoughton, 1980; New York, Doubleday, 1981.

The War Against Sleep: The Philosophy of Gurdjieff. Wellingborough, Northamptonshire, Aquarian Press, and York Beach, Maine, Weiser, 1980; revised edition, Aquarian Press, 1986.

Frankenstein's Castle. Sevenoaks, Kent, Ashgrove Press, 1980; Salem, New Hampshire, Salem House, 1982.

Anti-Sartre, with an Essay on Camus. San Bernardino, California, Borgo Press, 1981.

The Quest for Wilhelm Reich. London, Granada, and New York, Doubleday, 1981.

Witches. Limpsfield, Surrey, Dragon's World, 1981; New York, A and W, 1982.

Poltergeist! A Study in Destructive Haunting. London, New English Library, 1981; New York, Putnam, 1983.

Access to Inner Worlds: The Story of Brad Absetz. London, Rider, 1983.

Encyclopaedia of Modern Murder 1962–1982, with Donald Seaman. London, Barker, 1983; New York, Putnam, 1985.

Psychic Detectives: The Story of Psychometry and the Paranormal in Crime Detection. London, Pan, 1984; San Francisco, Mercury House, 1985.

A Criminal History of Mankind. London, Granada, and New York, Putnam, 1984.

Lord of the Underworld: Jung and the Twentieth Century. Wellingborough, Northamptonshire, Aquarian Press, 1984.

The Essential Colin Wilson. London, Harrap, 1985.

The Bicameral Critic, edited by Howard F. Dossor. Bath, Avon, Ashgrove Press, 1985.

Rudolf Steiner: The Man and His Vision. Wellingborough, Northamptonshire, Aquarian Press, 1985.

Afterlife. London, Harrap, 1985.

Scandal! An Encyclopaedia, with Donald Seaman. London, Weidenfeld and Nicolson, 1986.

Editor, *Colin Wilson's Men of Mystery.* London, W.H. Allen, 1977; as *Dark Dimensions: A Celebration of the Occult*, New York, Everest House, 1978.

Editor, with John Grant, *The Book of Time.* Newton Abbot, Devon, David and Charles, 1980.

Editor, with John Grant, *The Directory of Possibilities.* Exeter, Webb and Bower, and New York, Rutledge Press, 1981.

*

Manuscript Collection: University of Texas, Austin.

Critical Studies: *The Angry Decade* by Kenneth Allsop, London, Owen, 1958; *The World of Colin Wilson* by Sidney Campion, London, Muller, 1963; "The Novels of Colin Wilson" by R.H.W. Dillard, in *Hollins Critic* (Hollins College, Virginia), October 1967; *Colin Wilson* by John A. Weigel, New York, Twayne, 1975; *Colin Wilson: The Outsider and Beyond* by Clifford P. Bendau, San Bernardino, California, Borgo Press, 1979; *The Novels of Colin Wilson* by Nicolas Tredell, London, Vision Press, 1982; *An Odyssey of Freedom: Four Themes in Colin Wilson's Novels* by K. Gunnar Bergström, Uppsala, Sweden, University of Uppsala, 1983.

Colin Wilson comments:

I am unashamedly a writer of ideas, in the tradition of Shaw, Wells, or Sartre; I see myself as part of a European rather than English literary tradition. My novels are based firmly upon the "new existentialism" expressed in the six volumes of the "Outsider Cycle" (1956–1966) and *Introduction to the New Existentialism*. Although I count myself an existential phenomenologist, I am in fundamental disagreement with the pessimistic European tradition of Heidegger, Jaspers, Sartre, and Camus, and my philosophical work has been an attempt to show that their pessimism is the outcome of certain serious misunderstandings of Husserlian phenomenology, notably of the intentionality of consciousness. The foundation of my position could be expressed in the form of a contradiction of Sartre: Consciousness *does* have an "inside." Sartre's position is fundamentally Humeian: he believes the mind *adds* meaning to the chaotic and fragmented world as you might add milk to a bowl of cornflakes; I hold, with Whitehead, that meaning is an objective reality, and that the problem is the curious narrowness and inefficiency of human consciousness.

My novels are basically preoccupied with the problem of meaning, with what Peirce called the problem of "values in a universe of chance." In the first, *Ritual in the Dark*, this takes the form of an exploration of "the great mystery of human boredom." The hero has always wanted freedom and hated being tied down to an office job; yet when a small legacy gives him "a room of his own," he finds himself bewildered, bored, directionless. His meeting with a man who, he comes to suspect, is a mass-murderer of women produces a powerful sense of meaning and direction, but he feels that this is inauthentic—that he should have been capable of *doing it himself*—finding freedom *without help from outside*. This problem of freedom is at the core of all my novels. Man experiences his freedom both positively and negatively: positively in moments of intensity and ecstasy (sex, for example), negatively in the face of crisis or a threat to his existence. Both experiences reveal that the main trouble with everyday consciousness is its narrowness, its obsessive preoccupation with trivialities. There is something fundamentally wrong with human consciousness, a form of short-sightedness amounting almost to blindness. This is, in a sense, a "religious" vision—closely akin to that of T.E. Hulme, who preferred to call it "original sin."

The main influences on my fiction, in my late teens and early twenties, were Joyce and Faulkner, and I felt strongly that the novel had advanced as far as possible in the direction of experimentalism, attempting, so to speak, to approximate to the condition of music. The solution I chose was based upon the notion of Brecht's "alienation effect." In the theatre, Brecht invites his audience to acknowledge that they are watching actors in a play, not reality; it seemed to me that the novel could back out of the Joycean *cul de sac* by choosing to be, on one level, entertainment within a conventional framework; using the conventions of the *roman policier*, the *Bildungsroman*, science fiction, the spy novel, as a kind of symbolic form (in Cassirer's sense) which is freely acknowledged *not* to correspond to its content. This I saw as the only reasonable escape from the Joycean-Faulknerian dilemma of trying to distort the form to *correspond* to an increasingly complex content. Hence, in my fiction, I have used the form of the detective story, science fiction, spy story, etc. as the "persona" or mask of the book. This also offers one enormous advantage. The Joyce disciples, in their attempt to "render" their precise meaning once and for all, robbed themselves of the possibility of free expansion and development. By treating the form as a kind of carnival mask, I am able to re-explore the same meaning or inner-conflict from different angles, so to speak. For example, the same basic meanings are explored in *The Killer* (in the United States, *Lingard*) and *The God of the Labyrinth* (*The Hedonists*), although the first is a clinically precise study of a sexually motivated killer, and the second a literary "detective story" with more than a touch of Thorne Smith farce.

The central statement in my work occurs near the beginning of *Man Without a Shadow*: "Human beings are grandfather clocks driven by watch-springs." This is why consciousness *appears* to have no "inside." All human beings suffer, more or less, from the complaint of Sartre's café proprietor in *Nausea*: "When his café empties, his head empties too." Our sense of values, which ought to be absolute, appears to depend completely upon stimuli from the environment. This problem is explored most exhaustively in my "spy novel" *The Black Room*, in which I pose the question: How could a spy be trained to withstand total sensory deprivation in a black room? If such a method could be found, it would also be a method for creating supermen.

It is this Carlylean-Nietzschean preoccupation with the potentialities of man—and his present unsatisfactoriness—that has led certain critics to accuse me of fascism, a curious accusation since, although my cast of mind is naturally conservative, I regard my work as wholly non-political.

*   *   *

Colin Wilson's many novels, which include psychological thrillers, mysteries, science-fiction fantasies, diary-confessions, and one of the first "beat" stories, are integral parts of an ambitious project which began in 1956 with the publication of *The Outsider*, that precocious "seminal book on the alienation of man." Although more like a collection of quotations and ideas from a youthful autodidact's notebooks than a coherently developed thesis, *The Outsider* impressed serious critics as well as journalists, who immediately exploited the colorful personality of the author and made the book a sensational best seller. Although Wilson still sees his first work as the most important book of its generation—and he may be right—the thoughtless enthusiasm for Wilson's erudition inevitably yielded to a more thoughtful skepticism. But the cruel change in mood toward his early success fortunately did not destroy the young man, who soon went to work again—less with a vengeance than a solemn determination to prove his significance.

Some 30 years and many books later, Wilson can no longer be dismissed as an amateur with only one lucky strike to his credit. Aware that he will eventually be judged as a philosopher, as the champion of a *new* existentialism which rejects the inevitability of despair, Wilson has neatly justified his fiction. "If I were to prescribe a rule," he wrote in 1958, "that all future philosophers would have to obey, it would be this: that no idea shall be expressed that cannot be expressed in terms of human beings in a novel—and perfectly ordinary human beings at that—not Peacockian brain-boxes. If an idea cannot be expressed in terms of people, it is a sure sign it is irrelevant to the real problems of life" (*Declaration*, p. 58).

As a matter of fact none of Wilson's prose has that kind of finesse which awes literary critics not interested in ideas, yet it is adequate to its purpose. The fairest way to approach Wilson's novels is to cooperate with his objectives. His apparent preoccupation with violence, sexuality, and criminality is thematically related to his concern with the outsider syndrome. Furthermore, his methodology always participates in his urgency. In a hurry to clear away debris and passionately committed to his position, he is neither a Naturalist nor a Romantic weaving word-spells. He says that he has endorsed "the Brechtian alienation effect" in his fiction, and that he has *intended* that his novels announce their forms and make no claim to reality. In that sense they may be read as parodies of the genres they represent. Whether he has succeeded, however, is still debatable.

Since Wilson hopes to live almost forever, there is plenty of time to abide with his project. Recent experiments are currently validating his dreams of freeing humanity from the pessimism that correlates with determinism and traditional existentialism—at least as Wilson sees them. He is continuing his research into the sources of human energy, and there is certainly more to come from this indefatigable worker who says that even now he is just beginning. In 1966 in *Voyage to a Beginning* Wilson evaluated himself with characteristic candor. After modestly estimating that his first twenty years of work had not taken him far he added a firm *but*: "I know that I have come further than any of my contemporaries. I would be a fool if I didn't know it, and a coward if I was afraid to say so."

—John A. Weigel

WILSON, Sloan. American. Born in Norwalk, Connecticut, 8 May 1920. Educated at Florida Adirondack School, graduated 1938; Harvard University, Cambridge, Massachusetts, A.B. 1942. Served in the United States Coast Guard, 1942–46: Lieutenant. Married 1) Elise Pickhardt in 1941 (divorced), two daughters and one son; 2) Betty Stephens in 1963, one daughter. Reporter, Providence *Journal*, Rhode Island, 1946–47; writer, Time Inc., New York, 1947–49; assistant director, National Citizens Commission for the Public Schools, New York, 1949–52; director of information services and Assistant Professor of English, University of Buffalo, New York, 1952–55; assistant director, White House Conference on Education, Washington, D.C., 1956; education editor, New York *Herald-Tribune* and *Parents' Magazine*, New York, 1956–58. Writer-in-Residence, Rollins College, Winter Park, Florida, 1980–82. Since 1983, director, Winter Park Artists Workshop, Florida. D.H.L.: Rollins College, 1982. Address: 789 Bonita Drive, Winter Park, Florida 32789, U.S.A.

PUBLICATIONS

Novels

Voyage to Somewhere. New York, Wyn, 1946.
The Man in the Gray Flannel Suit. New York, Simon and Schuster, 1955; London, Cassell, 1956.
A Summer Place. New York, Simon and Schuster, and London, Cassell, 1958.
A Sense of Values. New York, Harper, 1960; London, Cassell, 1961.

Georgie Winthrop. New York, Harper, and London, Cassell, 1963.
Janus Island. Boston, Little Brown, and London, Cassell, 1967.
All the Best People. New York, Putnam, 1970; London, Cassell, 1971.
Small Town. New York, Arbor House, 1978.
Ice Brothers. New York, Arbor House, 1979; London, Sphere, 1982.
The Greatest Crime. New York, Arbor House, 1980.
Pacific Interlude. New York, Arbor House, 1982.
The Man in the Gray Flannel Suit II. New York, Arbor House, 1984.

Uncollected Short Stories

"The Arrival of the Mail," in *New Yorker*, 18 August 1945.
"Party for the Veterans," in *New Yorker*, 20 April 1946.
"We've Got to Do Something," in *New Yorker*, 11 May 1946.
"The Best and Most Powerful Machines," in *Harper's* (New York), June 1946.
"Housewarming," in *New Yorker*, 3 May 1947.
"Drunk on the Train," in *New Yorker*, 3 January 1948.
"Reunion," in *New Yorker*, 6 March 1948.
"Bygones," in *New Yorker*, 18 June 1949.
"Hunt," in *Yale Review* (New Haven, Connecticut), March 1950.
"Alarm Clock," in *New Yorker*, 24 February 1951.
"Black Mollies," in *Harper's* (New York), December 1951.
"A Letter of Admonition," in *New Yorker*, 29 December 1951.
"Regatta," in *New Yorker*, 28 June 1952.
"School Days," in *The Best Short Stories of World War II*, edited by C.A. Fenton. New York, Viking Press, 1957.

Other

Away from It All. New York, Putnam, 1969; London, Cassell, 1970.
What Shall We Wear to This Party? The Man in the Gray Flannel Suit Twenty Years Before and After (autobiography). New York, Arbor House, 1976.

*

Manuscript Collection: Boston University.

Sloan Wilson comments:

My work consists of a running commentary on the world as I have seen it from 1944 to the present. Both my strength and my limitation derive from my determination to confine myself to firsthand experiences and observations. The Second World War is in my books because I fought through it. The worries and frustrations of business are on my pages because I suffered them for many years before I became a full-time writer. The joys, angers, desperation, and contentment which are part of many marriages are in my novels, because I have been married twice. Children appear in my books because I have four of them. The writing in my books is rather simple and straightforward because I have a story to tell and I want to get on with it. The English language, I believe, can be used for many purposes—to make the music of poetry, to give military orders, or to give the illusion of meaning without any meaning, as most politicians employ it. I use it to give my readers the thoughts and, most of all, the emotions which I have experienced. I want the readers to be deeply moved without becoming aware of the language which is transmitting the feelings of others to them. That's why I avoid "fancy writing"—it makes readers think about words instead of about human triumph or despair.

The men, women, and children in my books are concerned with bed-rock issues, such as how to stay alive in time of war without being a coward, how to make a good living in time of peace without selling one's soul cut-rate, and, most of all, how to understand and enjoy the mysteries of love without guilt and without hurting other people. Human beings in my books get tired, cross, and discouraged sometimes, but they doggedly pursue happiness and cling to a rather old-fashioned sense of honor to the best of their ability, which sometimes is not enough. Critics often believe my books are an oversimplification of life or a naive interpretation of it, but a few million readers tell me that for them my pages are mirrors.

*   *   *

The dust jacket of the American edition of Sloan Wilson's fifth novel, *Georgie Winthrop*, describes the book in these rather sensational terms: "The story of the man who lives next door to The Man in the Gray Flannel Suit—forty-five, intelligent, modest, decent, and catapulted by an extraordinary love into trying to grow up inside." Sloan Wilson has long been the victim of this kind of cliché-ridden, high-pressure advertising, of this nod toward a low-brow readership. If he enters literary history at all it will be as the creator of the man-in-the-gray-flannel-suit metaphor.

The typical Sloan Wilson protagonist is acutely aware of his Puritan ancestry, of his New England background, and tries desperately to "live in the present." Thus Ben Powers, in *Janus Island*, and George Winthrop, both 45-year-old family men, enter into relationships with younger women (in George's case a 17 year old) in vain attempts to ignore past commitments and future responsibilities. Tom Rath, before the present events of *The Man in the Gray Flannel Suit*, had a wartime love affair with an Italian girl in another futile effort to freeze the present moment. Rath has a kind of Faulknerian obsession with time, which often expresses itself lyrically: "Time was given us like jewels to spend, and it's the ultimate sacrilege to wish it away."

Wilson called one of his novels *All the Best People*, a title which would serve handsomely for almost any of his books. Despite the intended irony of the phrase, there is always a certain respect in evidence in his fiction for the established eastern seaboard families, with their yachts, their islands, and their prep school and Harvard-Yale backgrounds. Dana, the main character in *All the Best People*, at one point defiantly remarks to his wife: "Of course! They call people like us WASPS, Caroline, white Anglo-Saxon Protestants." Later on, Caroline asserts formidably and characteristically: "my parents said I had to learn how to like Jews and Negroes, but they never said I had to like Middle Westerners."

Wilson has proved to be a skilled chronicler of social and historical events, from the Depression years through the aftermath of World War II. *All the Best People*, his most historical novel, shows the eroding effect of various upheavals in American life on a group of families who own property at Paradise Point, near Lake George, New York. *A Sense of Values* and *All the Best People* have long sequences devoted to the military experiences of the principal male characters. The Second World War, if somewhat obliquely, figures crucially also in *The Man in the Gray Flannel Suit* and *A Summer Place*. *Janus Island*, which describes more recent events than most of the other novels, is concerned, in passing, with the disruptive presence of Vietnam.

There is no mistaking the richness and vitality of Sloan Wilson's fiction. Still, as certain reviewers have remarked, there is a sense of *déjà vu* for anyone who reads through all of his work. Events, characters, and symbols have a way of being reused. Thus the war experiences of Nathan in *A Sense of Values* and those of Dana in *All the Best People* are more than passingly similar. There are crotchety caretakers, all cast from the same mold, in *The Man in the Gray Flannel Suit*, *A Summer Place*, and *Janus Island*. Magicians serve rather similar symbolical functions in *All the Best People* and *A Sense of Values*. Sylvia's "fake mink coat over her bathing suit" in *A Summer Place* reappears in the form of Caroline's "mink-dyed muskrat coat" in *All the Best People*. Both Nort in *Janus Island* and Nathan in *A Sense of Values* have the nervous habit of clenching and unclenching their hands. Dana, at the end of *All the Best People*, comes, uncannily, to resemble Hopkins in *The Man in the Gray Flannel Suit*, and Annabelle, in *A Sense of Values*, is a female—and somewhat more aggressive—Hopkins.

Critics have objected to the untidiness of Sloan Wilson's novels; their structures tend to be indecisively open-ended. Most of them are unduly episodic. They are as far removed as possible from the tautness of the best post-World War II fiction. Wilson obviously prefers a more leisurely, digressive pace. There is, however, a certain appropriateness about the rather old-fashioned open form of these novels; they deal, after all, with a world which holds on to the old pieties and stubbornly resists change. The underplayed, somewhat symbolic final remark of George Winthrop—which ends the only novel in the Wilson canon with a university setting—reveals how important traditional values are: "No, thank you very much, but I have to be getting home. I have a long drive ahead."

—Melvin J. Friedman

WISEMAN, Adele. Canadian. Born in Winnipeg, Manitoba, in 1928. Taught English at MacDonald College, McGill University, Montreal. Recipient: Beta Sigma Chi award, 1957; Governor-General's award, 1957; National Conference of Christians and Jews Brotherhood Award, 1957; Guggenheim fellowship, 1957. Address: c/o Macmillan of Canada, 146 Front Street West, Suite 685, Toronto, Ontario M5J 1G2, Canada.

PUBLICATIONS

Novels

The Sacrifice. New York, Viking Press, and London, Gollancz, 1956.
Crackpot. Toronto, McClelland and Stewart, 1974.

Uncollected Short Story

"The Country of the Hungry Bird," in *Journal of Canadian Fiction* (Montreal), nos. 31–32, 1981.

Other

Old Markets, New Worlds. Toronto, Macmillan, 1964.
Testimonial Dinner. Erin, Ontario, Press Porcépic, 1976.
Old Woman at Play. Toronto, Clarke Irwin, 1978.

*   *   *

Adele Wiseman's second novel, *Crackpot*, gives animated voice to the central character, a fat prostitute named Hoda. Growing from a taunted childhood into middle age, Hoda manages a degree of optimism unusual in modern fiction. She comes to accept life with remarkable poise, even when her son (the relationship unknown to him) comes to her as a customer and she is called upon to initiate him and to engender in him a sense of worth.

If this novel can be seen as a singular study of an archetypal figure, Wiseman's first book, *The Sacrifice*, reads as a much more conventionally organized "novel of fathers and sons." It is a study of three generations of a Jewish family that emigrated from European pogroms to mid-Canadian urban stress. Living in either place has its problems, and the nature of life (of what it is to be a Jew, a Jew in Canada, or just to be) is the key question the book explores. The kosher butcher Abraham (with wife Sarah, son Isaac, and later grandson Moses) may seem too aptly named and employed to be fictionally credible, yet Wiseman deals with parallels and differences among individuals thoroughly enough (the subplots aid in such a structure) that the Old Testament references simply add mythical dimension to the problem she examines, and historical—genealogical—continuity to man's quest both for knowledge and for the ability to live with the knowledge he acquires.

The sacrifice of the title is thus many things at once, some admirable, others not—the Biblical story of Abraham's faith, the pagan ritual propitiation of angry gods, the immolation of self in the preservation of valued traditions, the ritual butchery, the education of one's sons to one's own ideas and standards, the accepted means for ceremonially renewing wonder, belief, and fear, and the fictional Abraham's murder of the prostitute Laiah in the belief that he is defeating Death and restoring vitality to his life and his community. For his act, Abraham is confined on Mad Mountain. Not content to be, he reflects later, he tried to be creator and destroyer, too, thus impinging on others' identity when the real struggle lay within himself. But understanding is its own punishment, he avers; it is the natural consequence of seeking beyond oneself—exemplified in the emigration as well as in the constant quest for knowledge—and the paradox of being human and alive.

Men occupy, however, various kinds of country—national political organizations, religious communities, families, economic and cultural groups, the world of life (at war with the world of death), the outlook of childhood, and the age of maturity. All blend in each man's separate identity, but all identities blend with each other in friendship and humane brotherhood. When Moses impulsively visits his "mad" grandfather, and sees his own hand taken in the older man's, he recognizes the continuity they represent—an affirmation of the cyclical progress of humanity and of the inevitability of men suffering understanding. Moses's friend Aaron departs at this point to help start the new (old, ancestral) country of Israel; Moses himself, who had been contemplating the same move, recognizes that he has a new country to explore already—not in Canada *per se*, but in the identity, the being, he has newly found, in his newly appreciated sense of heritage, and in the dimly lit recesses of his heart and mind. To shed light on some of those dark corners is the task Wiseman has attempted to dramatize; to arouse sympathy for the characters meeting their consciences in this way is the goal to which she has managed to win.

—W.H. New

WOIWODE, Larry (Alfred). American. Born in Carrington, North Dakota, 30 October 1941. Educated at the University of Illinois, Urbana, 1959–64, A.A. 1964. Married Carole Ann Peterson in 1965. Writer-in-Residence, University of Wisconsin, Madison, 1973–74. Member of the Executive Board, American PEN, 1972. Recipient: William Faulkner Foundation award, 1969; Guggenheim fellowship, 1971; American Academy award, 1980. D.Litt.: North Dakota State University, Fargo, 1977. Agent: Candida Donadio and Associates, 231 West 22nd Street, New York, New York 10011. Address: c/o Farrar Straus and Giroux, 19 Union Square West, New York, New York 10003, U.S.A.

PUBLICATIONS

Novels

What I'm Going to Do, I Think. New York, Farrar Straus, 1969; London, Weidenfeld and Nicolson, 1970.
Beyond the Bedroom Wall: A Family Album. New York, Farrar Straus, 1975.
Poppa John. New York, Farrar Straus, 1981.

Uncollected Short Stories

"The Deathless Lovers," in *New Yorker*, 10 July 1965.
"Near the Straights of Mackinac," in *New Yorker*, 9 April 1966.
"The Brothers," in *New Yorker*, 21 May 1966.
"The Visitation," in *New Yorker*, 10 September 1966.
"On This Day," in *New Yorker*, 9 September 1967.
"The History Lesson," in *New Yorker*, 30 September 1967.
"Pheasants," in *New Yorker*, 18 November 1967.
"An Old Man," in *New Yorker*, 20 April 1968.
"The Long Trip," in *New Yorker*, 13 July 1968.
"The Boy," in *New Yorker*, 31 August 1968.
"The Horses," in *New Yorker*, 28 December 1968.
"Don't You Wish You Were Dead," in *New American Review 7*, edited by Theodore Solotaroff. New York, New American Library, 1969.
"What Can Blow the Wind Away?," in *Mademoiselle* (New York), February 1969.
"The Contest," in *New Yorker*, 1 November 1969.
"Owen's Father," in *Partisan Review* (New Brunswick, New Jersey), vol. 37, no. 3, 1970.
"The Beginning of Grief," in *New Yorker*, 17 October 1970.
"Burning the Couch," in *Atlantic* (Boston), November 1970.
"The Suitor," in *The Best American Short Stories 1971*, edited by Martha Foley and David Burnett. Boston, Houghton Mifflin, 1971.
"Pneumonia, 1945," in *New Yorker*, 13 February 1971.
"The Old Halvorson Place," in *New Yorker*, 8 May 1971.
"Marie," in *New Yorker*, 25 December 1971.
"Burial," in *New Yorker*, 19 November 1973.
"Change," in *The Best American Short Stories 1981*, edited by Hortense Calisher and Shannon Ravenel. Boston, Houghton Mifflin, 1981.
"Firstborn," in *The Best American Short Stories 1983*, edited by Anne Tyler and Shannon Ravenel. Boston, Houghton Mifflin, 1983.

Verse

Poetry North: Five North Dakota Poets, with others. Fargo,
North Dakota Institute for Regional Studies, 1970.
Even Tide. New York, Farrar Straus, 1977.

* * *

Larry Woiwode's second novel, *Beyond the Bedroom Wall*,
is sure to be ranked as one of the great achievements of American fiction of the 1970's. It is a midwestern novel, an American
novel, a universal novel. It spans four generations, and could
be set in almost any century. The book's significant events
emerge out of the natural histories of human beings. It is about
births and deaths, love and courtship, joy and grief, motherhood and fatherhood, childhood, adolescence, old age. It is
about strength of character, spoiled character, redeemed character. It is about hardship and work, competence and incompetence, faith and distrust. It is about provincial bigotry and the
lot of a Catholic family in a town of Methodists. It is about
enduring.

Otto Neumiller emigrated from Germany in 1881. He went
all the way to the Dakota plain, where he prospered and then
lost most of what he had gained. In his old age, he is lonely
and envied and unloved by his neighbors. His son Charles
returns to the homestead to attend him at his death. In one
of the book's finest chapters, Woiwode shows Charles at work
making his father's coffin, lovingly washing and dressing his
father's body, burying him in the unhallowed ground of the
farm he loved. Like his father, Charles Neumiller has been
a devout Catholic all his life; and so is Charles's son Martin.
Most of the novel is the story of Martin, his wife Alpha, who
dies at 34, and their six children. The older children, the fourth
generation, are off on their own in the 1970's

The great strength of this novel is in Woiwode's rendering
of the commonplace. The Neumiller family may be a bit more
intelligent and perhaps possess more fortitude than the average
family, but they are not particularly special. In addition to
the virtues, there certainly are waywardness, carelessness, and
ill-considered impulsive behavior among them. Indeed, one
of the beautiful ironies in the novel is that it is the ill-considered
decision of Martin, usually so steady and prudent, to move
his family from North Dakota to Illinois that brings disaster
to the family, including ultimately his beloved wife's death.
But the fabric of the novel is made of such scenes as the father
telling stories to his children, the father's being overcome with
frustration and kicking one of his sons viciously, the acting
out of guilt feelings brought on by the nearly fatal illness of
a child. An important motif running through the novel is the
family's emotional involvement with each of the various houses
in which they live.

The marriage of Martin and Alpha is old-fashioned and
ordinary. Except for what is done by acts of nature, it is a
marriage that is not susceptible to disruption. This man and
this woman become totally entangled with each other, and
regardless of what befalls them they cannot imagine themselves
married to anyone else. To Martin and Alpha, marriage is
for better or for worse, forever.

Even in bulk Woiwode's first novel, *What I'm Going to Do,
I Think*, is not half the novel that *Beyond the Bedroom Wall*
is. It has a small cast of characters, with the focus rarely leaving
Chris or Ellen. it does not range over generations, but is concerned with only a few seasons in the lives of its young couple.
It is lyrical and symbolic; unfortunately it is also murky. Its
central situation is commonplace: the young woman is pregnant
and the couple marry. They take an extended honeymoon at

an isolated lodge up in northern Michigan. Only then does
the nature of the commitment he has made become real to
Chris. He is not single anymore; he must take account of
another person. He is uncertain about which emotions to share
and which to conceal. He experiences much anger, resentment,
frustration, but he does not know what to do with such feelings
in the new context. Their physical relationship is different
under the blanket of marriage; expectation, disappointment,
jealousy, fulfillment have a new texture. Neither Chris nor
Ellen has had an appropriate model for the roles of husband
and wife; Chris, especially, suffers as a result.

Both had unusual childhoods. Ellen's parents were killed
in an accident, and she has been raised by dour grandparents.
Chris's alienation from his parents is so severe that he hardly
ever thinks of them; he does not invite them to his wedding,
he does not attend his mother's funeral. It is the quality of
Chris's earlier life that is suggested by the title of the novel.
The words are part of a remark made by his father when Chris
has hurt himself being clumsy at a chore. What his father thinks
he is going to do is get himself a new kid.

The child Ellen is carrying is born dead. When Ellen calls
her grandmother for consolation, she is told that what has happened is the wages of sin. Chris and Ellen do not have another
child. The novel ends with the suggestion that Chris always
will be a troubled man, and the marriage will not bring fulfillment or much joy to husband or wife. The lives of Chris and
Ellen will never have the richness of the lives of Martin and
Alpha. Standing by itself, the earlier novel does not have a
meaning that clearly emerges from the interaction of character
and plot. When it is put beside *Beyond the Bedroom Wall*,
its theme is quite clear: without firm familial commitments,
modern life will exact constant feelings of despair and loss.

At his best, Woiwode renders the commonplace with such
emotional and psychological truth that all the reader's capacity
for empathy and compassion is tapped. Woiwode often demonstrates marvelous descriptive power; at his best, his readers
see and feel and learn with him making easy transfers of their
fictional experience to their own lives.

—Paul Marx

WOOLF, Douglas. American. Born in New York City, 23
March 1922. Educated at Harvard University, Cambridge,
Massachusetts, 1939–42; University of New Mexico, Albuquerque, 1949–50, A.B. 1950; University of Arizona, Tucson,
1950–54. Served in the American Field Service, 1942–43, and
the United States Air Force, 1943–45: Flight Officer. Married
1) Yvonne Elyce Stone in 1949, two daughters; 2) Sandra Bra-
man in 1973. Since 1950, free-lance writer and itinerant worker,
in the western United States, Canada, and Mexico; since 1976,
co-publisher and editor, Wolf Run Books. Address: Wolf Run
Books, P.O. Box 9620, Minneapolis, Minnesota 55440, U.S.A.

PUBLICATIONS

Novels

The Hypocritic Days. Majorca, Divers Press, 1955.
Fade Out. New York, Grove Press, 1959; London, Weiden-
feld and Nicolson, 1968.
Wall to Wall. New York, Grove Press, 1962.
John-Juan. Kyoto, Origin, 1967.
Ya! and John-Juan. New York, Harper, 1971.

On Us. Santa Barbara, California, Black Sparrow Press, 1977.
HAD. Eugene, Oregon, Wolf Run, 1977.
The Timing Chain. Bolinas, California, Tombouctou, 1985.

Short Stories

Signs of a Migrant Worrier. Eugene, Oregon, Coyote's Journal, 1965.
Spring of the Lamb, with *Broken Field Runner: A Douglas Woolf Notebook*, by Paul Metcalf. Highlands, North Carolina, Jargon, 1972.
Future Preconditional. Toronto, Coach House Press, 1978.

*

Critical Studies: by Edward Dorn, in *Kulchur* (New York), 1963; J.H. Prynne, in *Prospect* (London), 1964; I.D. Mackillop in *Delta 45* (Cambridge), 1969; "Douglas Woolf Issue" of *Review of Contemporary Fiction* (Elmwood Park, Illinois), vol. 2, no. 1, 1982.

Douglas Woolf comments:

For the writer these days there is a new urgency in the air, he is goaded to finish his present work before its reader disappears. Thus I feel privileged to have received lately three or four responses that seem to promise me some extra time. I'll nonetheless have my new novel ready soon.

*   *   *

The deserts, ghost towns and superhighways of Douglas Woolf's fiction are peopled by the maimed and exiled of the human race. Fleeing the desolation of modern existence, they find either that deliverance is not possible or that it is to be found in the bleak and desert places among others who are rejected and fleeing. Woolf paints a vivid surrealistic picture of a mechanistic society where the pressure for money and peer acceptance erases the last vestiges of humanity from hollow men. The wise run to preserve their souls and sometimes save another soul, too. Mr. Twombly of *Fade Out* induces his friend, Behemoth Brown, to forsake the beloved television set, and Al James of *Ya!* releases his teenage daughter, Joan, from the tightening bonds of materialism and superficiality.

Woolf's fine descriptive talent is especially notable given the unusual settings and characters he uses. *John-Juan*, for instance, captures dream-like experiences in a strong visual reality. Anyone who suffers in flight will find his painful symptoms faithfully recorded in "Off the Runway," one of the seven stories from *Signs of a Migrant Worrier*. In *Ya!* Woolf's depiction of Al James's Northwest odyssey combines vivid scenic descriptions with deft quick character sketches and concludes with a finely etched picture of James spending the night asleep in a hemlock tree high above the snowed-in-forest. John and Martha in "Bank Day" (*Migrant Worrier*) awake to a breakfast of cat food and eggs, an event which is clearly and economically described.

Although the themes are isolation and mankind's race toward destruction, the tone is usually humorous. In rare instances when the humor is too heavy-handed the work suffers—the short story "The Cat" is an example of this—but generally Woolf's comic writing is of a high order. In *Fade Out* there is a marvelous scene in which the old men visit a zoo where a science-fiction movie is being made with unresponsive tortoises cast as monsters.

With its fine balance of humor and human insight, *Fade Out* is a brilliant novel. Woolf details the cruelties visited on the aged by their families and society. Mr. Twombly has functioned in the middle-class mold for 50 years, but now retired he finds he is a nuisance to his family. His only friends are children and old people like himself, unwanted. Threatened with an ending in an old people's home, he takes his existence in hand and "fades out" to find a new life in an Arizona ghost town. His cross-country trip, accompanied by his ex-prize fighter friend, is wild and hilarious.

Woolf is a serious craftsman who writes from a perspective of detached sympathy. Seldom reviewed, he supports himself with itinerant work and takes off for solitary places to write when he has saved enough money. In 1963, he called his vocation "a desperate anachronism" and described his method as bringing his characters to a point where "some kind of balance is reached" so that the character and the reader can assess the character's position. Although he portrays a dismal society from which the wise can at best flee, he is obviously not quite willing to give up on humanity.

—Barbara M. Perkins

WOUK, Herman. American. Born in New York City, 27 May 1915. Educated at Townsend Harris Hall, New York, 1927–30; Columbia University, New York (Fox Prize, 1934), 1930–34, A.B. 1934. Served in the United States Naval Reserve, 1942–46: Lieutenant. Married Betty Sarah Brown in 1945; three sons (one deceased). Radio writer, 1935; scriptwriter for the comedian Fred Allen, 1936–41; consultant, United States Treasury Department, 1941. Since 1946, full-time writer. Visiting Professor of English, Yeshiva University, New York, 1952–58; Scholar-in-Residence, Aspen Institute, Colorado, 1973–74. Trustee, College of the Virgin Islands, 1961–69; member of the Board of Directors, Washington National Symphony, 1969–71, and Kennedy Center Productions, 1974–75. Recipient: Pulitzer Prize, 1952; Columbia University Medal of Excellence, 1952, and Hamilton Medal, 1980. L.H.D.: Yeshiva University, 1955; LL.D.: Clark University, Worcester, Massachusetts, 1960; D.Lit.: American International College, Springfield, Massachusetts, 1979. Lives in Washington, D.C. Agent: BSW Literary Agency, 3255 N Street, Washington, D.C. 20007. Address: c/o Little Brown, 34 Beacon Street, Boston, Massachusetts 02106, U.S.A.

PUBLICATIONS

Novels

Aurora Dawn. New York, Simon and Schuster, and London, Barrie, 1947.
The City Boy. New York, Simon and Schuster, 1948; London, Cape, 1956.
The Caine Mutiny. New York, Doubleday, and London, Cape, 1951.
Marjorie Morningstar. New York, Doubleday, and London, Cape, 1955.
Slattery's Hurricane. New York, Permabooks, 1956; London, New English Library, 1965.
Youngblood Hawke. New York, Doubleday, and London, Collins, 1962.
Don't Stop the Carnival. New York, Doubleday, and London, Collins, 1965.

The Lomokome Papers.   New York, Pocket Books, 1968.
The Winds of War.   Boston, Little Brown, and London, Collins, 1971.
War and Remembrance.   Boston, Little Brown, and London, Collins, 1978.
Inside, Outside.   Boston, Little Brown, and London, Collins, 1986.

Uncollected Short Stories

"Herbie Solves a Mystery," in *Feast of Leviathan*, edited by L.W. Schwarz.   New York, Rinehart, 1956.
"Old Flame," in *Good Housekeeping* (New York), May 1956.
"Irresistible Force," in *Fireside Treasury of Modern Humor*, edited by Scott Meredith.   New York, Simon and Schuster, 1963.

Plays

The Traitor (produced New York, 1949).   New York, French, 1949.
Modern Primitive (produced Hartford, Connecticut, 1951).
The Caine Mutiny Court-Martial (produced Santa Barbara, California, 1953; New York, 1954; London, 1956).   New York, Doubleday, 1954; London, Cape, 1956.
Nature's Way (produced New York, 1957).   New York, Doubleday, 1958.

Screenplays: *Slattery's Hurricane*, with Richard Murphy, 1949; *Confidentially Connie*, with Max Shulman, 1953.

Other

The Man in the Trench Coat.   New York, National Jewish Welfare Board, 1941.
This Is My God: The Jewish Way of Life.   New York, Doubleday, 1959; London, 1960; revised edition, London, Collins, 1973.

*

Manuscript Collection: Columbia University Library Special Collections, New York.

Critical Study: "You, Me and the Novel" by Wouk, in *Saturday Review-World* (New York), 29 June 1974.

Herman Wouk comments:
No author should be trusted to discuss his own work in an encyclopedia or a compendium until he has been dead thirty or forty years. Then, if anyone still cares, and if he can be raised at a séance, his opinion might be sufficiently detached to be worth something.

*   *   *

Herman Wouk continues to enjoy wide readership and to suffer critical attack for essentially the same reasons. He has a strong commitment to established values, which he champions only after energetic and attractive presentation of the Devil's case. Often, he plays Devil's advocate so well that the

book's concluding reversal to affirmation of the status quo suggests mere pandering to popular prejudice. When the book is done, the rebels emerge as villains and the evils rebelled against as blemishes on the face of a healthy world.

Thus *Aurora Dawn* is an attack on vulgarity and dishonesty in advertising, not on advertising itself, and the bullying boss is only a witless product of nepotism, not a true portrait of capitalism's face. Andrew Reale, who chases money at the price of his soul, finds salvation when his discarded fiancée inherits money and takes him back—after her millionaire husband gallantly releases her from a marriage made on the rebound. Thus, Andrew is saved from money-grubbing's debasements through a millionaire's generosity and an heiress' forgiveness.

In *The Caine Mutiny*, Wouk's Pulitzer-prize novel of World War II, a strong case is made out for mutiny aboard an American destroyer during a Pacific storm, when the paranoiac Captain Queeg breaks under pressure. When all is done, however, only the legal verdict goes to the rebels; morally, Lieutenant Keefer and his followers are guilty of deserting a military system which, despite its resident fascists, has protected American freedom against foreign fascism. *Marjorie Morningstar* chronicles the false emancipation of Marjorie Morgenstern from the values and authority of her hardworking Jewish parents to the glitter of the theatre and bohemian "freedom." Then, renouncing her renunciation, the beautiful, intelligent Marjorie readily accepts her suburban destiny as lawyer's wife, mother of two and community servant. Interestingly, in both novels the "intellectual" (Lt. Keefer and writer Noel Airman) is unmasked as an insubstantial fraud, while the philistine, even when vicious and insane like Queeg, is sincere and somewhat heroic. In both novels, the protagonists, Princetonian Willie Keith and Bronxite Marjorie, must learn that the old ways are the best ways: obedience, chastity before marriage, the faith of one's fathers, hard work and money, all sound dull but ring true. In form and style, Wouk is equally traditionalist, his early works ranging from parody of Fielding (*Aurora Dawn*) and Booth Tarkington (*City Boy*) to Victorian-sized melodramas (*Marjorie Morningstar*) bursting with incident and character.

His two next novels, *Youngblood Hawke* and *Don't Stop the Carnival*, also abound in plot and character but are below his best work. Wouk's gargantuan Arthur Youngblood was obviously modeled on Thomas Wolfe, then grafted onto a melodramatic plot of the artist turned businessman, with his talent destroyed by greed and scheming women. But Wouk does not succeed in portraying Wolfe-Hawke as a dedicated artist; instead, it is Wouk and Hawke who seem to blend in the intensity of "their" business interests and speculative shenanigans, so that the money parts of the book command more authority than the literary parts. In *Don't Stop the Carnival* Wouk returned to comedy with his middle-aged cardiac victim, Norman Paperman, who exchanges a Broadway press agent's life for ownership of a Caribbean hotel. Alas, on his island paradise, life proves even more frantic as foundation walls burst, typhoons rage, and mad employees decapitate others—but Norman copes. When all is under control, Paperman unaccountably sells out cheap (as Wouk seems to do) and returns to ulcer-ridden Broadway. But the novel does display the same comedic flair for oddball characters, clever dialogue, fast intercutting, and imaginative slapstick as had *Aurora Dawn, City Boy* (about a Jewish Penrod) and even *Marjorie Morningstar*.

Possibly, light comedy and fond satire are Wouk's forte, since his serious views seem uninspired and inhibited. But his two-volume series *The Winds of War* and *War and Remembrance* is surely his most ambitious work. The two books trace the lives of Navy Commander, later Admiral Victor Henry, and his family from 1939 through World War II, and the end of his marriage. The size and broad aims of the volumes suggests Tolstoy's *War and Peace*, but the quality of the writing is closer to Upton Sinclair's Lanny Budd series.

—Frank Campenni

WRIGHT, Charles (Stevenson). American. Born in New Franklin, Missouri, 4 June 1932. Educated in public schools in New Franklin and Sedalia, Missouri. Served in the United States Army, in Korea, 1952–54. Stockboy in St. Louis in late 1950's; then free-lance writer: columnist ("Wright's World"), *Village Voice*, New York. Lives in New York City. Address: c/o Farrar, Straus and Giroux, 19 Union Square West, New York, New York 10003, U.S.A.

PUBLICATIONS

Novels

The Messenger. New York, Farrar Straus, 1963; London, Souvenir Press, 1964.
The Wig: A Mirror Image. New York, Farrar Straus, 1966; London, Souvenir Press, 1967.
Absolutely Nothing to Get Alarmed About. New York, Farrar Straus, 1973.

Uncollected Short Stories

"A New Day," in *The Best Short Stories by Negro Writers*, edited by Langston Hughes. Boston, Little Brown, 1967.
"Sonny and the Sailor," in *Negro Digest* (Chicago), August 1968.

*

Charles Wright comments:

(1972) Numbers. One number has always walked through the front door of my mind. But when I was writing my first book, *The Messenger*, I did not think of numbers. I was very bitter at the time. *The Messenger* was simply a money roof. I was amused at its success. Mini-popular first published thing. A pleasant dream with the frame of reality.

The Wig was my life. And as I write this on a night of the last week in April of 1971—I have no regrets. Let me explain: A year after the publication of *The Messenger* I was thinking of that folkloric, second novel, and began a rough draft of a novel about a group of Black men, very much like the Black Panthers. But, in 1963, America was not ready for *that* type of novel, nor were they ready for *The Wig*. Ah! That is the first horror hors d'oeuvre. My agent, Candida Donadio, said: "This is a novel. Write it." I will tell you quite simply ... that I was afraid that I could not sustain the thing for say ... fifty pages.

Now it was another year, another country (Morocco). Frightened, I returned to the states and rewrote *The Wig* in twenty-nine days ... the best days of my life. The basic plot was the same but most of it was new. Thinking, working, like seven and, yes, sometimes fourteen hours a day. It took me less than three hours to make the final changes before the publishers accepted. I was *hot* ... hot for *National Desire* ... a short N.

West-type of novel very much like *The Wig*, although *Race* would not have been the theme.

And.

And. Many things have happened to me and to my country since then. The country has always been like this, I suppose. I only know that something left me. As a result ... I haven't written a novel in six years. I remember Langston Hughes saying: "Write another nice, little book like *The Messenger*. White folks don't like to know that Negroes can write books like that."

Ah, yes ... dear, dead Friend. Then. Yes. Another *Messenger*. And, what follows? Something that I've always wanted to do, something different ... say an action packed Hemingway novel and then say ... a Sackville-West novel. All I've ever wanted was a home by the sea and to be a good writer.

*   *   *

The literary output of Charles Wright has been slight in volume and promising, but not always effective, in practice. Wright's three small "novels" are each the size of Nathanael West novels, and they reflect the same mordant wit, yearning despair, and surrealistic lunacy of vintage West. Wright's world, however, is essentially a race-twisted society of black grotesques, of crippled lovers and dish-washer poets whose lives of wine, whores, and junkie-songs spell slow murder in white America.

The Messenger, The Wig, and *Absolutely Nothing to Get Alarmed About* portray an Inferno-world of sexual deviates: prostitutes (male and female), pimps, transvestites, poseurs, flower-children, sadistic cops. We meet not only lovers but pretenders, false black friends who set you up, genteel female perverts, white liberals whose children suddenly snarl "nigger," beloved black musicians who betray their heritage to gain white favor. Each novel centers around the efforts of a young protagonist ("Charles Stevenson" in the first and "Charles Wright" in the third novel) to cope with city life, where literally and metaphorically the protagonists prostitute themselves to survive. Each must dissemble, disguise, and sell himself; each finds the gimmicks and the humbling tricks to hustle an existence.

In *The Messenger*, which is heavily autobiographical, a young writer, Charles Stevenson (Wright's full name is Charles Stevenson Wright), stumbles to find himself, moving from the South to the army to New York. As a writer, he knows he must feel and record; his literal job as messenger is unimportant compared to his literary obligation to spread the word about life. As a black, however, he is torn between his compassion for outcast blacks and his emotional shield compounded of numbness, indifference, and cynicism. Although the writing occasionally slips into clichés or strained metaphor, style is the novel's chief attraction and is marvelously wedded to content. The writing is terse, the narrator-hero's manner laconic and usually guarded. Most episodes are deliberately inconclusive and undeveloped, sketchy vignettes that affect the narrator more than he acknowledges. Deeply touching are the few pages in which the spiritually exhausted young veteran is united with his warm, righteous grandmother, while his athletic command performance in a Southern police station is outrageously comic and brilliantly symbolic of racial debasement.

If *The Messenger* seems like a patch-quilt of styles and moods, *The Wig* is more consistent in tone and mood, but regrettably so. For Wright's second novel goes all-out as black comedy, but despite its wildness it is more black, or malicious, than comic. There is a similar gallery of transvestites and other disguise-wearing freaks in quest of identity without guilt, failure, or self-hatred, but they are portrayed without hope or compassion. The hero, Lester Jefferson, is, like all the other blacks, on the make: he has conked and curled his Afro hair into a beautiful white "wig" that will open the doors to the Great (White) Society. Alas, he doesn't make it but we are not even sorry, for neither he nor the author reaches Ellison's solution that "visibility" begins with confronting and accepting one's truly created self. There are two or three successful comic achievements: Jimmy Wishbone, who once "kept 100 million colored people contented for years" as a Stepin Fetchit type in movies and who now wants to sue white society and redeem his lost fleet of cadillacs; and Lester himself, crawling the streets in a feathery chicken-suit as employee of the Southern Fried Chicken King.

The last exchange of dialogue in *The Messenger* goes: "'Charles, what's wrong?' 'Nothing,' I said. 'Absolutely nothing.'" Wright's latest novelistic autobiography, *Absolutely Nothing to Get Alarmed About*, picks up from its predecessor's conclusion, although the locale has moved from mid-Manhattan to the Lower East Side. The mood is more uniformly despairing, with only a few attempts at the pathos and yearning of *The Messenger* or the caustic hilarity of *The Wig*. In place of the homosexual-junkie nightmare world of *The Messenger*, Wright's metaphor of our foundering American culture is here the yellow-black-white world of the Bowery. Appropriate to their original publication in New York's *Village Voice*, many chapters echo the vivid tone and the felt immediacy of "new journalism" prose.

—Frank Campenni

WURLITZER, Rudolph. American. Born in 1938(?). Recipient: *Atlantic* "Firsts" Award, 1966. Address: c/o Knopf Inc., 201 East 50th Street, New York, New York 10022, U.S.A.

PUBLICATIONS

Novels

Nog. New York, Random House, 1969; as *The Octopus*, London, Weidenfeld and Nicolson, 1969.
Flats. New York, Dutton, 1970; London, Gollancz, 1971.
Quake. New York, Dutton, 1972; London, Pan, 1974.
Slow Fade. New York, Knopf, 1984; London, Pan, 1985.

Uncollected Short Story

"Boiler Room," in *Atlantic* (Boston), March 1966.

Plays

Two-Lane Blacktop (screenplay), with Will Corry. New York, Award, 1971.

Screenplays: *Two-Lane Blacktop*, with Will Corry, 1971; *Glen and Randa*, with Lorenzo Mans and Jim McBride, 1971; *Pat Garrett and Billy the Kid*, 1973.

*

Theatrical Activities:
Actor: **Film**—*Pat Garrett and Billy the Kid*, 1973.

*   *   *

Rudolph Wurlitzer's four novels represent a determined attempt to escape the materials of narrative. Unwilling to suspend disbelief and create a representative world of people, places, and ideals, he discards the conventions of mimetic storytelling in favour of a flat-out style of direct address which in his later novels slowly modulates into a more naturalized manner, yet never one that attempts to counterfeit a world. Instead, Wurlitzer's later work draws upon certain artifices of conduct which by virtue of long use have a structure which appears to be naturally made. In either case, the novelist is excused from proposing an enabling structure for his work; from first to last, Rudolph Wurlitzer's novels speak with their own sense of authority, pretending to be nothing other than they are.

Nog and *Flats* are alternately diverse and spare works which rely upon the narrator's direct address for their substance and direction. Mirror-images of the same artistic vision, these novels contrast wild geographic narrative with a Beckett-like stasis of character, mood, and location, yet each ending with the same sense of voice alone. Even coherent character yields to this presence of mere voice, since in the first work Wurlitzer's narrator sometimes talks about Nog as a distinct person ("Nog, he was apparently of Finnish extraction, was one of those semi-religious lunatics you see wandering around the Sierras on bread and tea, or gulping down peyote in Nevada with the Indians") and other times speaks as Nog himself, while the narrator of *Flats* proposes a similar exchange of identities with a person he has met and has been describing. The effect of such shimmering exhanges is to efface any sense of represented identity, establishing the narrative voice as a pure speaking sound which draws its sense of character from what is being described. In *Nog* this irridescence becomes geographical, as the narrator's voice yields to the on-running panorama of place, from the desert American southwest, through the Pacific and the Panama Canal, to the eastern seaboard and New York City. *Flats* presents the precise opposite of this range, but not of this tendency: the narrator sits within a small square of wasteland, vocally defending his space against all interlopers. He and they are named by their apparent home towns—"Call me Memphis," he introduces himself—but in their little square of desert they are motionless and without any identities all the same. All that exists is their voice, which is the text of Wurlitzer's novel.

Thematically, Wurlitzer argues against representation as well. Nog prizes silence and is proud not to divulge information to other characters (and therefore to the reader): "No history," he remarks, "therefore no bondage." Rather than act, he makes lists, because "Lists don't need direction." *Flats* elevates this theme to phenomenological proportion, as the narrator strives to grasp events lest their surface take shape. "I don't care to look around, having disappeared in all directions," the narrator admits, refusing any identity at all. "There is only my momentum," which is the text's own movement. And even this is reductive: "I want to say the same words over and over. I want just the sound. I want to fill up what space I am with one note. ... I want a sound that is not involved with beginning or ending."

Wurlitzer's subsequent novels, *Quake* and *Slow Fade*, maintain their author's spare sense of prose, but now a textually self-conscious situation relieves the burden of flat narration. In *Quake* it is an earth tremor which by devastating the landscape erases any sense of conventional continuity; as the artifices of normal behavior crumble, the narrator is free to establish his own voice as the sole reality of his story. "The words around us blurred and carried no definition," and so his voice is the only anchor of authority. Yet the unreality unleashed by the earthquake is only a destruction of conventionality; what is now revealed is that "this day has given expression to what has always been latent within us." By the novel's end the narrator is reduced to gutteral sounds, his own ability to articulate having been destroyed with the world around him. Yet even before this it has proven to be a talent whose time has been eclipsed.

Slow Fade is ostensibly Wurlitzer's most conventional work, as it is set securely within a recognizable world and is peopled by characters whose consistency of motive and behavior qualifies them for the most realistic fiction. But as with *Quake*, the author's choice of circumstance allows for purely self-conscious narrative, since here the action involves scriptwriting and filming, two undertakings which lend a textual self-apparency to the novel. As the stories of film director Wesley Hardin, his children, and an intrusive entrepreneur evolve, the narrative becomes less a document of their lives than a series of filters and indirect analyses, as events are perceived not as themselves but with reference to scenes in films. This sense of intertextuality is enhanced by Wes's desire to learn the fate of his daughter, which he pursues by paying his son to write a film script which fictionalizes the details yet encodes the answer to his question. Yet as his son writes the script, he pauses to question his father about their relationship and to sort out the memory of his own wife's life and death. Soon so many layers of textuality have been sedimented upon the basic story that only text (and not any representations) remain. The climax of this layering occurs when Wes Hardin aborts his own film project and becomes the subject of a *cinema-verité* work encompassing his own breakdown as occasioned by his daughter's loss. In this respect the role of the entrepreneur, A.D. Ballou, becomes instrumental. What happens in the world, Wurlitzer concludes, is due not to direct action but by the manipulation of texts. As A.D. Ballou produces Hardin's autobiographical movie, so too does the reader produce the narrators' texts. Without either act, nothing would happen, and therefore Wurlitzer's novels place as little as possible in the way of this readerly action.

—Jerome Klinkowitz

YAFFE, James. American. Born in Chicago, Illinois, 31 March 1927. Educated at Fieldston School, graduated 1944; Yale University, New Haven, Connecticut, 1944–48, B.A. (summa cum laude) 1948 (Phi Beta Kappa). Served in the United States Navy, 1945–46. Married Elaine Gordon in 1964; two daughters and one son. Since 1968, Member of the English Department, currently Professor of English, and since 1981 Director of General Studies, Colorado College, Colorado Springs. Recipient: National Endowment for the Arts award, for drama, 1968. Address: 1215 North Cascade Avenue, Colorado Springs, Colorado 80903, U.S.A.

PUBLICATIONS

Novels

The Good-for-Nothing. Boston, Little Brown, and London, Constable, 1953.

What's the Big Hurry? Boston, Little Brown, 1954; as *Angry Uncle Dan*, London, Constable, 1955.
Nothing But the Night. Boston, Little Brown, 1957; London, Cape, 1958.
Mister Margolies. New York, Random House, 1962.
Nobody Does You Any Favors. New York, Putnam, 1966.
The Voyage of the Franz Joseph. New York, Putnam, 1970.
Saul and Morris, Worlds Apart. New York, Holt Rinehart, 1982.

Short Stories

Poor Cousin Evelyn. Boston, Little Brown, 1951; London, Constable, 1952.

Uncollected Short Stories

"Mom Knows Best," in *The Queen's Awards 7*, edited by Ellery Queen. Boston, Little Brown, and London, Gollancz, 1952.
"On the Brink," in *The Queen's Awards 8*, edited by Ellery Queen. Boston, Little Brown, and London, Gollancz, 1953.
"Mom Makes a Bet," in *Best Detective Stories of the Year 1953*, edited by David Coxe Cooke. New York, Dutton, 1953.
"Mom in the Spring," in *The Queen's Awards 9*, edited by Ellery Queen. Boston, Little Brown, and London, Gollancz, 1954.
"Mom Makes a Wish," in *The Queen's Awards 10*, edited by Ellery Queen. Boston, Little Brown, and London, Gollancz, 1955.
"Mom Sheds a Tear," in *Best Detective Stories of the Year 1955*, edited by David Coxe Cooke. New York, Dutton, 1955.
"One of the Family," in *The Queen's Awards 11*, edited by Ellery Queen. New York, Simon and Schuster, and London, Collins, 1956.
"Mom Sings an Aria," in *All-Star Lineup*, edited by Ellery Queen. New York, New American Library, 1966; London, Gollancz, 1968.
"Mom and the Haunted Mink," in *Mystery Parade*, edited by Ellery Queen. New York, New American Library, 1969.
"The Problem of the Emperor's Mushrooms," in *All But Impossible!*, edited by Edward D. Hoch. New Haven, Connecticut, Ticknor and Fields, 1981; London, Hale, 1983.
"D.I.C. (Department of Impossible Crimes)," in *Ellery Queen's Book of First Appearances*, edited by Ellery Queen and Eleanor Sullivan. New York, Dial Press, 1982.

Plays

The Deadly Game, adaptation of a novel by Friedrich Dürrenmatt (produced New York, 1960; London, 1967). New York, Dramatists Play Service, 1960.
This Year's Genie (for children), in *Eight Plays 2*, edited by Malcolm Fellows. London, Cassell, 1965.
Ivory Tower, with Jerome Weidman (produced Ann Arbor, Michigan, 1968). New York, Dramatists Play Service, 1969.
Immorality Play (produced Atlanta, 1983).
Cliffhanger (produced New York, 1985). New York, Dramatists Play Service, 1985.

Television Plays: for *U.S. Steel Hour, Studio One, G.E. Theater, Frontiers of Faith, The Defenders, Breaking Point, Alfred Hitchcock Presents, The Doctors and the Nurses,* and other series, 1953–67.

Other

The American Jews.   New York, Random House, 1968.
So Sue Me! The Story of a Community Court.   New York, Saturday Review Press, 1972.

*

James Yaffe comments:

For me, to write novels has been to create characters and to combine and juxtapose those characters, involve them in confrontations, place them in situations which challenge them, strengthen them, destroy them, transform them, test their mettle—and out of a variety of such characters, to build a world. Where do I get the raw material for my characters? From my own experience, of course—mostly from my experience of the world I was born and brought up in, the world of middle-class, second- and third-generation Jews living in New York, Chicago, Los Angeles. I have chosen to write about this world because I know it instinctively and subliminally, because it was part of me before I was old enough to doubt my perceptions.

But I have always tried to treat this experience not analytically or sociologically or philosophically but novelistically—that is, by imagining, and trying to re-create, the world as seen through each character's eyes. The greatest novelists, it seems to me, are those who succeed in merging their personalities with the lives and feelings of their people. This is the special ability shared by writers as different as Tolstoy and Jane Austen, Trollope and Joyce (to mention a few of my favorites). The attempt to follow their example may be presumptuous and doomed to failure, but it is also inevitable for anybody who wants to write novels.

*   *   *

James Yaffe is considered a leading novelist of middle-class Jewish life in America. His early collection of short stories (*Poor Cousin Evelyn*) and his first novel (*The Good-for-Nothing*) are essentially drawing room comedies set in New York. As in the novels of Jane Austen, whom Yaffe admits a special fondness for, small conflicts are closely scrutinized within a closed society—in Yaffe's case, the Jewish family, with all its attendant social hierarchies, its patriarchs, its strongmen and its failures, its pressures of shame and guilt applied by loved ones to safeguard conformity and tradition. In these earlier works, characters are simply drawn and situations directly presented, largely through dialogue.

A recurring Yaffe theme involves the "dreamer," an impractical or artistically oriented individual confronted with pressures to survive in a competitive business world of shady deals and opportunism. In *The Good-for-Nothing* this conflict is represented by two brothers, apparently very different from each other, yet mutually dependent. The one is college-educated and totally ineffectual in the business world, a charming sycophant. The other, a Certified Public Accountant, supports him, but in so doing restricts his own life. As they interact, it becomes unclear which is the "good for nothing," which the success or the failure: in different ways, both are unwilling to face responsibilities or the possibility of failure. Self-righteousness and self-indulgence, like sentimentality, are both forms of escape, excuses for not taking risks.

In a later novel, *Mister Margolies*, this pattern of self-deception is advanced to the point where the manipulation of reality becomes a life-style. Stanley Margolies, defeated in his early attempt to become a concert-pianist, yet unable to give up totally his dreams of a poetic life, withdraws into a world of fantasies. The reality of business and competition crashes in on this, and he withdraws deeper, erecting more elaborate defences. Yaffe's "dreamers" create worlds which are both sad and poetic, but they are not the demonic Rose-gardens of the totally mad. They are the tiny fantasies of little men, dreams reinforced by sympathetic and condescending friends with whom they still retain some form of contact.

Yaffe avoids several stereotypes popular in much contemporary Jewish literature: the dominant Jewish Mother, and the Jew-Gentile confrontation, particularly in matters sexual, as an expression of, or as a means of resolving feelings of inferiority. In general, he maintains a comic narrative tone—some of the scenes are funny—and though his characters are forever lecturing each other, their messages are frequently as confused as they are. The novels themselves preach little other than a deep compassion for the small man and his hopes.

The theme of the dreamer in search of his vision makes a terrifying appearance in *Nothing But the Night*, which is based on the Nathan Leopold-Richard Loeb murder case of 1924, and the celebrated defence by Clarence Darrow. The case history is seen through the eyes of one of the young men, not as an investigation of the criminal mind, but as a study of a lonely and creative child. As in Chekhov, Yaffe's characters take their emotions very seriously and ponder them deeply. They are often trapped by their own visions and the pressures to succeed imposed from outside. In their struggle to hold on to their dreams, they are destroyed, transformed, and occasionally liberated. An example of the latter is presented in *Nobody Does You Any Favors*, which despite its 1940's cinema-sounding title is perhaps his best novel. As opposed to the earlier New York novels which suggest short stories in their structural focus on a single event, *Nobody Does You Any Favors* with its time span of roughly 40 years allows for an extended development and growth in character. The confrontation between father and son is drawn with an understanding and passion valid beyond a scene of very special terror and insight. Certainly this novel is a significant contribution to American literature of the 20th century.

The Voyage of the Franz Joseph represented an epic departure from his usual drawing room style. Like *Nothing But the Night*, it is based on an historical event, the sailing of the German liner *St. Louis* in 1939 with a thousand Jewish refugees searching for a homeland.

—Paul Seiko Chihara

———————

YATES, Richard.   American.   Born in Yonkers, New York, 3 February 1926. Educated at the Avon School, Connecticut. Served in the United States Army Infantry, 1944–46. Married 1) Sheila Bryant in 1948 (divorced, 1959), two daughters; 2) Martha Speer in 1968 (divorced, 1974), one daughter. Financial reporter, United Press, New York, 1946–48; publicity writer, Remington Rand Inc., New York, 1948–50; free-lance public relations writer, 1953–60; Lecturer, New School for Social Research, New York, 1959–62, and Columbia University, New York, 1960–62; screenwriter, United Artists, Hollywood, 1962;

speech writer for Attorney-General Robert Kennedy, Washington, D.C., 1963; screenwriter, Columbia Pictures, Hollywood, 1965–66. Lecturer, 1964–65, and since 1966, Assistant Professor of English, University of Iowa, Iowa City. Writer-in-Residence, Wichita State University, Kansas, 1971–72. Recipient: *Atlantic* "Firsts" Award, 1953; Guggenheim fellowship, 1962, 1981; American Academy grant, 1963; Brandeis University Creative Arts Award, 1964; National Endowment for the Arts grant, 1966, and award, 1984; Rockefeller grant, 1967; Rosenthal Foundation award, 1976. Address: 497 Beacon Street, Boston, Massachusetts 02215, U.S.A.

PUBLICATIONS

Novels

Revolutionary Road.   Boston, Little Brown, 1961; London, Deutsch, 1962.
A Special Providence.   New York, Knopf, 1969.
Disturbing the Peace.   New York, Delacorte Press, 1975.
The Easter Parade.   New York, Delacorte Press, 1976; London, Eyre Methuen, 1978.
A Good School.   New York, Delacorte Press, 1978.
Young Hearts Crying.   New York, Delacorte Press, 1984; London, Methuen, 1986.

Short Stories

Eleven Kinds of Loneliness.   Boston, Little Brown, 1962; London, Deutsch, 1964.
Liars in Love.   New York, Delacorte Press, 1981; London, Methuen, 1982.

Uncollected Short Stories

"To Be a Hero," in *Saturday Evening Post* (Philadelphia), 25 September 1965.
"A Good and Gallant Woman," in *Prize Stories 1967: The O. Henry Awards,* edited by William Abrahams. New York, Doubleday, 1967.
"Bellevue," in *North American Review* (Cedar Falls, Iowa), Summer 1975.
"The Right Thing," in *Esquire* (New York), August 1984.

Play

Screenplay: *The Bridge at Remagen*, with William Roberts and Roger Hirson, 1969.

Other

Editor, *Stories for the Sixties.*   New York, Bantam, 1962.

*

Manuscript Collection: Boston University.

Critical Study: in *The Red-Hot Vacuum* by Theodore Solotaroff, New York, Atheneum, 1970.

Richard Yates comments:
    My books came very slowly at first, but production has picked up during the past ten years and I hope to keep on publishing at this more "professional" rate for however many years I may have left.

*   *   *

Richard Yates's fictional world is peopled with ordinary middle-class New Yorkers and suburbanites whose lives have gone awry. They come from broken homes; they naively believe that a mate, family, and material comfort make them happy. Their plans and dreams alike simply do not work out. Yates's men drink and seek solace in casual affairs; neither narcotic is sufficient to relieve the pain of their loneliness. His women have little promise: they glide easily through the moods of wifely reassurance, wife-as-mistress, and wife-as-cocktail companion. They always stop short of self-recognition and the admission that they cannot stand to be loved for the part they play, rather than for the person they are. In Yates's fictional world, there is "no settling of accounts, no resolution, no proof." People must make the best of a bad lot. Nurtured on songs about "the best of everything," his characters grow up to discover that the glow of good feeling lasts only moments and comes rarely. Their homes become prisons; their dreams, too fragile to withstand reality, become difficult to recall. They stumble through their lives.

The contours of Yates's stories are familiar—John Updike and John Cheever have written in the same vein of realism—but it is his finely tuned powers of observation coupled with an ability to elect the right detail that make his scenes come alive and give his writing its distinction. His skill, too, as a technician enables him to create a language, colloquial and deftly ironic, to render his detail with unerring honesty. Like J.D. Salinger, Yates can vividly capture the excruciating humiliations of adolescence. In *A Good School* he describes how a group of noisy adolescent boys strip their classmate, pin him in his bed, and force his genitals to fulfill their will. Later Yates depicts the victim trying to befriend his two literary idols who he learns, to his mortification, have witnessed the hazing and judged him with contempt. At this kind of scene, Yates excels as a writer, capturing precisely the subtle, contradictory emotions it evokes.

Yates's short stories and fiction both rely on some of Salinger's tricks of dialogue, situation, and character. But more important is his debt to Salinger for a way to handle point of view. Salinger's narrators in "For Esmé—With Love and Squalor" and *Raise High the Roof Beam, Carpenters* seem to have inspired Yates's rendering of Bob Prentice, the protagonist of "Builders" from *Eleven Kinds of Loneliness* and *A Special Providence.* Prentice, like Salinger's narrators, recognizes that the writer is a "sensitive person," that the sensitivity ought to be disguised lest it be too unsettling for the reader, that the piece of fiction to be recounted must be "no-nonsense fiction," and that the wives of these sensitive writers are "dead logical" or "breathtakingly level-headed women." Yates also imitates Salinger's method of selecting a detail and presenting it with a nice misanthropic turn. Mrs. Fedder's attitude towards Seymour Glass's sickness is echoed in Mrs. Giving's treatment of John's mental disorders in *Revolutionary Road.* John's candor and outspokenness also resembles Seymour's outburst when a lady looks too markedly at his bare feet in "A Perfect Day for Bananafish." Yates's interest in children, their moods, sullenness, tantrums, and jealousies also matches Salinger's. But if Yates imitates Salinger, this imitation is not slavish. He has his own voice, his own style—lucid, amusing, and artfully wrought—and his most recent book testifies to his independence from his mentor.

Revolutionary Road, A Special Providence, Disturbing the Peace, The Easter Parade, and *Young Hearts Crying* all touch on madness and suicide, and the profession which purports to treat their victims. April Wheeler in *Revolutionary Road* kills herself, helplessly confessing that she does not know who she is. In *The Easter Parade* the protagonist's plight is grimmer. She must go on living. At 50, Emily Grimes arrives at her nephew's door, turning to him to care for her, confessing she feels old and has never understood anything in her whole life. Her sister, an inveterate alcoholic and victim of her husband's beatings, dies after a fall. The novel leaves the reader and Emily with the sickening suspicion that Sarah's self-destruction was ultimately assisted by her husband's blow, that her death was not an accident but a murder. *Disturbing the Peace* is the story of John Wilder's crack-up, one from which he never mends. *A Special Providence* relates Bob Prentice's struggle for freedom from his neurotic mother. It is, finally, the humiliating and bitter experiences in a training camp that painfully teach Bob that he must stand alone if he is to survive, and that life has nothing to offer but survival. The protagonist of *Young Hearts Crying*, Yates's most recent novel, divides his life after his divorce into two periods: pre-Bellevue and post-Bellevue. He is the victim of several psychotic breakdowns; his daughter, a hippie in the early 1960's, also suffers from drugs and psychosis. Both figures scoff at Freud and psychology. *Young Hearts Crying* concludes with the rather banal observation that "Everybody's essentially alone." Once again Yates treats his reader to the theme of failed expectations.

Yates's two collections of short stories, *Eleven Kinds of Loneliness* and *Liars in Love*, and his first four novels all concern characters who fall in love with the postures of failure. Walter Henderson in "A Glutton for Punishment" is endlessly fascinated by the attitudes of collapse: as a child he loved to play at falling dead; as an adolescent, he was the best little loser, a real sport; and by the time he marries, failure has become a habit. In *Disturbing the Peace* Yates extends his study of failure to include a protagonist who leaves his wife and child to join his mistress and become the film producer he had always dreamt of being. The irony that the film he will make is one based on his own incarceration in Bellevue after an alcoholic binge is not one he feels until he is hopelessly enmeshed in his own actions. John Wilder, once a successful salesman, disintegrates, pursuing in life the role he has created for a film. His self-destruction is total. Believing that art offered a means to control his chaos, he flounders as we realize that his art is merely an extension of his chaos. *The Easter Parade* depicts the unhappy lives of Sarah and Emily Grimes, two girls from a broken home. Their dread of isolation pushes one into the arms of a handsome, brutish, uneducated man who looks like Olivier, and the other, first, into a bad marriage with a man who proves impotent and, then, into a series of affairs, one involving a writer who has lost his creativity. Three failed relationships leave Emily a confused, hurt woman whose independence, once a necessary defense, becomes intolerable. In "Saying Goodbye to Sally" (from *Liars in Love*) Yates returns to the theme of the film producer that he explored earlier in *Disturbing the Peace*. This time the protagonist, Jack Fields, a divorced alcoholic and father of two little girls, finds himself in Malibu writing a screenplay. Fantasizing himself to be another F. Scott Fitzgerald, he finds himself his Sheilah Graham, a strikingly attractive, long-legged, well-coiffed California "girl" smitten with the Hollywood aura, soft on Jack, but even more wed to the opulent Hollywood dream-home of her friend. In this story, as in many of the others in the collection, we see a tale of misalliance between two dreamers who play at being characters out of *The Last Tycoon*. The

stories in this collection are technically well crafted; Yates is adept at preserving the veneer of his realism, but the reader often wonders whether more isn't needed to give the stories purpose. The characters are weak; their world is inarticulate, suburban, and vapid; there is never a moment of self-realization or fulfillment. One admires Yates's craft but hopes for a richer story.

A Good School, perhaps the most autobiographical of Yates's writings, offers a story in which the protagonist's creativity survives. The book recounts the schooldays of William Grove at Dorset Academy. Dorset "believes in individuality" and has a reputation for accepting boys which no school, for a variety of good reasons, will accept. The story is set during World War II and the wartime economy ruins Dorset financially. William's schooldays bruise and build. Gawky, bookish, lacking in social background, William is subject to ridicule and neglect. Hanging on to what little dignity is left him after the vicious sexual attack from his virile and frustrated classmates, William befriends the editors of the *Dorset Chronicle* and ultimately becomes editor himself. The portrait of the school and William is convincing and moving. The war takes its toll on William's classmates and his school; William's awkward attempts to gain acceptance and his battles with his shyness and sexuality are told with humor and poignancy; and the novel ends with his coming of age while another age ends. In *A Good School* Yates's interest in writers is more affirmative than it had been before. He had aptly captured the syndrome of the failed writer in *The Easter Parade; A Good School* is the most forgiving story he has told. In it Yates is at once wry and ironic, light-hearted, and dumbly sad; never does he lapse into sentimentality.

Young Hearts Crying returns to the more pessimistic cast of realism typical of most of his books. Again, a writer, or rather, failed writer, is his protagonist. The book spans the life of Michael Davenport from his early years as an ambitious writer in Boston just returned from the War to his return to Boston more than 30 years and one divorce later, when he is a man of 52 who no longer cares whether his next book achieves the heights of his first writing, or whether his estranged wife returns to him. He has come home and is only a drink away from the mellow feeling that generally sees him through. Fans of Yates will admire this book along with his others. Quite simply, he writes very well. But if one is looking for tougher characters, a sharper moral vision, and a new scope, it is less likely that this will be forthcoming from Yates.

—Carol Simpson Stern

YERBY, Frank (Garvin). American. Born in Augusta, Georgia, 5 September 1916. Educated at Paine College, Augusta, A.B. 1937; Fisk University, Nashville, Tennessee, M.A. 1938; University of Chicago, 1939. Married 1) Flora Helen Claire Williams in 1941 (divorced), two sons and two daughters; 2) Blanca Calle Pérez in 1956. Instructor, Florida Agricultural and Mechanical College, Tallahassee, 1938–39, and Southern University and A. and M. College, Baton Rouge, Louisiana, 1939–41; laboratory technician, Ford Motor Company, Dearborn, Michigan, 1941–44; Magnaflux inspector, Ranger (Fairchild) Aircraft, Jamaica, New York, 1944–45; full-time writer from 1945; settled in Madrid, 1954. Recipient: O. Henry Award, 1944. Agent: Owen Laster, William Morris Agency, 1350 Avenue of the Americas, New York, New York

10019, U.S.A. Address: Edificio Torres Blancas, Apartamento 710, Avenida de America 37, 28002 Madrid, Spain.

PUBLICATIONS

Novels

The Foxes of Harrow.   New York, Dial Press, 1946; London, Heinemann, 1947.
The Vixens.   New York, Dial Press, 1947; London, Heinemann, 1948.
The Golden Hawk.   New York, Dial Press, 1948; London, Heinemann, 1949.
Pride's Castle.   New York, Dial Press, 1949; London, Heinemann, 1950.
Floodtide.   New York, Dial Press, 1950; London, Heinemann, 1951.
A Woman Called Fancy.   New York, Dial Press, 1951; London, Heinemann, 1952.
The Saracen Blade.   New York, Dial Press, 1952; London, Heinemann, 1953.
The Devil's Laughter.   New York, Dial Press, 1953; London, Heinemann, 1954.
Benton's Row.   New York, Dial Press, 1954; London, Heinemann, 1955.
Bride of Liberty.   New York, Dial Press, 1954; London, Heinemann, 1955.
The Treasure of Pleasant Valley.   New York, Dial Press, 1955; London, Heinemann, 1956.
Captain Rebel.   New York, Dial Press, 1956; London, Heinemann, 1957.
Fairoaks.   New York, Dial Press, 1957; London, Heinemann, 1958.
The Serpent and the Staff.   New York, Dial Press, 1958; London, Heinemann, 1959.
Jarrett's Jade.   New York, Dial Press, 1959; London, Heinemann, 1960.
Gillian.   New York, Dial Press, 1960; London, Heinemann, 1961.
The Garfield Honor.   New York, Dial Press, 1961; London, Heinemann, 1962.
Griffin's Way.   New York, Dial Press, 1962; London, Heinemann, 1963.
The Old Gods Laugh: A Modern Romance.   New York, Dial Press, and London, Heinemann, 1964.
An Odor of Sanctity.   New York, Dial Press, 1965; London, Heinemann, 1966.
Goat Song: A Novel of Ancient Greece.   New York, Dial Press, 1967; London, Heinemann, 1968.
Judas, My Brother: The Story of the Thirteenth Disciple.   New York, Dial Press, and London, Heinemann, 1969.
Speak Now.   New York, Dial Press, 1969; London, Heinemann, 1970.
The Dahomean.   New York, Dial Press, 1971; as *The Man from Dahomey*, London, Heinemann, 1971.
The Girl from Storyville: A Victorian Novel.   New York, Dial Press, and London, Heinemann, 1972.
The Voyage Unplanned.   New York, Dial Press, and London, Heinemann, 1974.
Tobias and the Angel.   New York, Dial Press, and London, Heinemann, 1975.
A Rose for Ana María.   New York, Dial Press, and London, Heinemann, 1976.
Hail the Conquering Hero.   New York, Dial Press, 1977; London, Heinemann, 1978.

A Darkness at Ingraham's Crest.   New York, Dial Press, 1979; London, Granada, 1981.
Western: A Saga of the Great Plains.   New York, Dial Press, 1982; London, Granada, 1983.
Devilseed.   New York, Doubleday, and London, Granada, 1984.
McKenzie's Hundred.   New York, Doubleday, 1985; London, Grafton, 1986.

Uncollected Short Stories

"The Thunder of God," in *New Anvil* (Chicago), April–May 1939.
"Health Card," in *O. Henry Memorial Award Prize Stories 1944*, edited by Herschel Brickell and Miriam Fuller.   New York, Doubleday, 1944.
"Roads Going Down," in *Common Ground* (New York), vol. 5, no. 4, 1945.
"The Homecoming," in *American Negro Short Stories*, edited by John Henrik Clarke.   New York, Hill and Wang, 1966.
"My Brother Went to College," in *Black American Literature: Fiction*.   Columbus, Ohio, Merrill, 1969.

*

Manuscript Collection: Mugar Memorial Library, Boston University.

Critical Studies: *Behind the Magnolia Mask: Frank Yerby as Critic of the South* by William Werdna Hill, Jr., unpublished thesis, Auburn University, Alabama, 1968; *The Unembarrassed Muse* by Russel B. Nye, New York, Dial Press, 1970; *Anti-Heroic Perspectives in the Life and Works of Frank Yerby* by James Lee Hill, unpublished thesis, University of Iowa, 1976.

Frank Yerby comments:
   (1972) The work has consisted mostly of historical novels written both to instruct and to entertain. In them, I've tried to correct the reader's historical perspective, wildly distorted in my youth, on such themes as Negro slavery, the Civil War South, and Reconstruction.
   To date, I have written only two modern novels, *The Old Gods Laugh*, largely an entertainment in the sense that Graham Greene uses the word, and *Speak Now*, a serious effort.
   Of my historicals, I should rate *An Odor of Sanctity, Judas, My Brother, Goat Song* and perhaps even *The Garfield Honor* as serious novels. The rest are entertainments, a fact of which I am *not* ashamed. Entertaining the reader is a legitimate function of a novelist.
   I hope, in the future, however, to concentrate upon serious work. Present day taxation makes writing "entertainments" worth neither the boredom, nor the bother.

*   *   *

Frank Yerby started by publishing poetry, then race-conscious short stories dealing with Negro pride and disillusionment, in the late 1930's. "Health Card," which won the O. Henry Award for 1944, was a bitter indictment of a white congressman who, acting on the assumption that all black girls are prostitutes, asked for the "health card" of a black GI's sweetheart. After vainly trying for several years to find a publisher for a saga with a black protagonist, Yerby accepted an editor's suggestion to make the hero a white southerner. "Having collected a handful of rejection slips for works about ill-treated factory workers or people who suffered because of their religion or the color of their skin, I arrived at the awesome conclusion that the reader cares not a snap about such questions; that, moreover, they are none of the novelist's business. ... The writer is, or should be, concerned with individuals." Thus did Yerby rationalize his launching into what he called "the costume novel." As soon as he made this change, he reached bestsellerdom. From 1946 to 1954, ten of his novels ranked between 5th and 10th on the bestseller list, *The Golden Hawk*, a story of pirates, being the all-media top US bestseller for 1948. Most of Yerby's fiction is historical, neatly structured, well researched (he claims he spent over ten years researching *Judas, My Brother*) with a nice balance of authentic detail and fabulous, fascinating imaginative departures from reality. As a result of precisely planned strategy, his books reach their goal, i.e., reach thousands of readers. But should one dismiss Yerby, as critic Robert Bone did, simply as "the prince of pulpsters," and consider his "potboilers" as significant only insofar as they exemplify the plight of the Negro writer until the 1960's, either forced to "pass" and forsake racial concerns or to perform a militant function?

Yerby's novels have often attracted adverse criticism, often from ideological quarters, without it affecting their popularity. *The Foxes of Harrow*, his initial venture into fictionalizing American history, compares not unfavorably with *Gone with the Wind*. It takes place during the decades leading up to the Civil War, not in Atlanta but in New Orleans. The protagonist, Stephen Fox, is an Irishman who, after being put off a riverboat for cheating and living in the red-light district, makes fortune and friends, then establishes a plantation at Harrow. There he marries Odalie (while his sister-in-law and his quadroon girlfriend seem to wait in the wings) and has a son, Etienne. This main plot is duplicated by that of the slave Archille marrying La Belle Sauvage who bears him a son, Inch; the Etienne-Inch relationship in many ways echoes aspects of the Dred Scott case, and, after the war, Inch occupies the stage in a way which infuriates Etienne. Yerby thus manages to make his Negro tragically heroic while, with great economy, the novel strives for historical balance by showing how the blacks participated in the conflict, as soldiers in the Union army, and as servants with the Confederates. The Louisiana world of Creoles, Cajuns, free blacks, and Anglo-Saxons is vividly evoked. Yerby's continuation to *The Foxes of Harrow*, dealing with Reconstruction, was to have been called *Ignoble Victory*, but the title became *The Vixens* to satisfy an editor's request for "more sex". This time, southern-born Laird Fournais, who fought with the Union, serves in the legislature as a sort of crusader for justice in spite of the evil deeds of the Knights of Camelia and opportunist politicians; he is helped by Inch, from the previous novel, whose knowledge of law turns him into a distinguished representative of his people. Again, the careful approach stresses that both sides are responsible for the errors and misdeeds of Reconstruction.

Last in the trilogy comes *Pride's Castle*. Set in the era of booming capitalism, from the 1870's to the early 20th century, it charts the ascent and decline of a southerner. Pride, already engaged to Sharon, accepts Esther out of his desire for money; he makes a fortune in railroads and builds a massive, ugly mansion, Pride's Castle, but his wife continues her liaison with her former fiancé, Joseph, and when, after an economic crash, Pride learns that Coppie, the only person he really loved, is not his, but Joseph's daughter, he commits suicide.

Floodtide is an ambitious, loosely structured novel set at the time of the Cuban revolution; it ranges from Mississippi to Paris and interestingly explores the pro-abolitionist feelings of the Cubans and their intricate relationships with Americans on a social scene more widely international than those depicted in the earlier stories. Over the years Yerby covered a colorful diversity of periods and places: he treated the United States in *The Garfield Honor*, *Captain Rebel*, and *Benton's Row* (all set in the south), and *The Treasure of Pleasant Valley* about the Gold Rush; early Christians in *Judas, My Brother*, the civilization of Sparta in *Goat Song*, the Middle Ages in *The Saracen Blade* and *An Odor of Sanctity*; he set *The Devil's Laughter* during the French Revolution and *The Voyage Unplanned* at the time of the anti-Nazi resistance. More recently, probably because of the greater freedom to create now available to the black writer, Yerby has used black protagonists although he had never balked at projecting a complex, dignified image of the Negro. *Speak Now* depicts an inter-racial love affair between a black American jazz musician and a white southern co-ed in the rather chaotic world of the Latin Quarter during the May 1968 Paris "revolution." Above all *The Dahomean* and *A Darkness at Ingraham's Crest* stand as a two-volume counterpart to Alex Haley's *Roots*. The more successful, *The Dahomean*, opens and closes in America but is set in Dahomey under the reign of King Gezo in the late 1830's. With great historical and ethnographical accuracy, it evokes daily African life, the protagonist's ritualistic passage to manhood, the rise and fall of his people's fortune. Nyasanu, son of Gbenu, a village chief, becomes a high-ranking vassal of Gezo until he is sold into slavery. Not only are native customs not viewed as "picturesque" but they are explained by cultural, political, or economic motives, like the custom of polygamy, and sometimes criticized, like the absolute power of the sovereign. In the following volume, which takes place in the American south, the magic powers of the beautiful and fearsome African, now become Wes Parks, are too utterly perfect to be believeable. The hero is transformed into a living myth, and beautiful, black, and regal Phoebe is the only fit companion for him, on the lust- and power-ridden plantation of Captain Wally Bibbs.

A prolific and popular writer, Frank Yerby has been systematically shunned by the critics. Yet, though his writing, like that of Dumas, tends to stick to well-established formulas, his literary sensitivity and the way he has managed to project a varied image of the black man and the American past deserve closer and more sophisticated attention.

—Michel Fabre

YGLESIAS, Helen (née Bassine). American. Born in New York City, 29 March 1915. Married 1) Bernard Cole in 1937, one son and one daughter; 2) Jose Yglesias, *q.v.*, in 1950, one son. Literary editor, *The Nation*, New York, 1965–69; Adjunct Professor, Columbia University School of the Arts, New York, 1973, and University of Iowa Writers Workshop, Iowa City, 1980. Recipient: Houghton Mifflin Literary Fellowship, 1972. Address: North Brooklin, Maine 04661, U.S.A.

PUBLICATIONS

Novels

How She Died. Boston, Houghton Mifflin, 1972; London, Heinemann, 1973.
Family Feeling. New York, Dial Press, 1976; London, Hodder and Stoughton, 1977.

Sweetsir. New York, Simon and Schuster, and London, Hodder and Stoughton, 1981.

Uncollected Short Stories

"Semi-Private," in *New Yorker*, 5 February 1972.
"Kaddish and Other Matters," in *New Yorker*, 6 May 1974.

Other

Starting: Early, Anew, Over, and Late. New York, Rawson Wade, 1978.

*   *   *

The novels of Helen Yglesias were written from her 54th year onwards. As she notes in her book of meditations, *Starting*, she had already had an active career of book-reviewing and editorial work; she was for a time the literary editor of *The Nation*. Yglesias's account of her career and of the careers of other men and women in *Starting* shows that a recurrent pattern in her novels is an expression of her own sense of what a proper career for a person is. Each person has, as the many conversations with others in *Starting* shows, the opportunity to discover his or her "true self" and initiate actions that allow that self to unfold. Or, alternately, to turn aside and spend the years in conformity to the expectations of a group and thus court defeat and stultification. As Yglesias asks in the Introduction to *Starting*: "Is there 'a true self'? Does it indeed exist and does its existence matter? Is there measureable damage in human and social terms when an impostor inhabits the corner of space and time reserved for a unique self—whatever that is? To do what one has always wanted to do—to be what one has always wanted to be—what does that mean?"

In the body of her book Yglesias devotes space to her own life as a young Jewish intellectual bucking the waves of indifference she met in the 1930's; it is a story that is repeated in her second novel, *Family Feeling*. She also relates the "starting" of her son, the novelist Rafael Yglesias, who, in his mid-teens, withdrew from society to realize *his* artistic destiny. And Yglesias moves on to many others whose diverse destinies are marked by the urgent questioning she directed at her own life. With a sort of modesty she remarks of herself: "I admit to a vast general ignorance of things physical, technological, mythical, religious, and political-social." Such remarks indicate the drive behind the novels, and they also suggest the areas that are left for other novelists to handle. The Yglesias novels are tales of struggle: chiefly female struggle in a society that imposes on such struggle a terminology invented by males. Yglesias is a connoisseur of the successes and failures that women like her heroines—and one supposes, herself—meet. These struggles are often well realized and convince not so much by their general truth as by the mass of detail that is clustering at center-stage. This gives the novels an effect of conviction that cannot be overlooked. Occasionally Yglesias abandons this area for theoretical speculation; she endows a heroine with her own former or present political loyalties and her own esthetic preferences, and the novels become temporarily less vivid. But the textures that are impelling are soon re-established.

Family Feeling is the novel that is a rough equivalent (and a successful one) to the story Yglesias tells in the opening section of *Starting*. *Sweetsir* is a negative version of the successful struggles in *Family Feeling*; the efforts of the heroine of *Sweetsir* commence and recommence but never move very far from the point where the repeated departures take place: the heroine's desire to be something, to realize in the relations of love some amorphous inner power that the heroine senses but cannot express. In contrast, the heroine of *Family Feeling* has an abundance of words to apply to each twist and turn of *her* journey. Yglesias's first novel, *How She Died*, is an account of a woman whose "starting" and its consequences lie somewhere between the distinct success and the grim failures related in the other two novels. The heroine of *How She Died*, Jean, devotes herself to a dying woman, has a love-affair with the woman's husband, neglects her own children, and realizes that her political ardor has brought her little reason for pride.

The other two novels, as suggested, are more decisive in their impact. *Family Feeling* reproduces the complex history of an immigrant Jewish family: a family that starts in poverty and that ends— for some of the members at least—in considerable prosperity and personal satisfaction. Barry Goddard is a son who ends as the owner of vast enterprises *and* an apartment that overlooks Central Park. Anne, whose intelligence is usually (but not always) the center of the story, follows a different course, one which leads her through social protest, literary projects that occasionally distract the reader, and finally to several years of a happy marriage with a WASP magazine editor who finds the Jewishness of Anne's family a constant diversion. The main concern of the moving narrative is not the social and personal goods that various characters grasp; it is the panorama of endless struggle—of "starting" and then achieving a continuation that is sometimes wasteful and sometimes admirable.

Such continuations do not appear in *Sweetsir*. This long and minutely executed novel, in which many pages are devoted to the details of legal procedures, begins with a domestic battle between Sally and Morgan Sweetsir, a battle that ends when Sally pushes a knife into the body of her brutal husband. Attention thus engaged, the reader is conducted through the considerable number of years that brought Sally Sweetsir to her fatal confrontation. If one chooses to wonder why Sally's many "startings" go nowhere in particular, answers arise again and again. Sally comes from a lower-class milieu where there is no such tradition of struggle and survival as that which gave strength to Anne Goddard in *Family Feeling*. Sally has almost no words to put to her desires, the desires that take her through two marriages and into the law courts. And she lacks the intelligence to direct the sexuality and the ambition that come and go in her. And quite beyond her control are the crudity and insensitivity of the two males in her life. It is no surprise that in Sally's "world" (as assembled by Yglesias) Sally does not have to pay a social penalty for her "crime." Her long list of failures to "start" constitutes a sufficient punishment.

Yglesias describes her novel-writing as "a happiness I could only liken to the happiness of love." Such happiness is open to the reader in long stretches of *Family Feeling*. And its absence is keenly felt elsewhere in the work of Yglesias.

—Harold H. Watts

YGLESIAS, Jose. American. Born in Tampa, Florida, 29 November 1919. Educated at Black Mountain College, North Carolina, 1946–47. Served in the United States Navy, 1942–45: Presidential Citation. Married Helen Bassine (i.e., Helen Yglesias, *q.v.*) in 1950; one son and two stepchildren. Dishwasher, bus boy, stock clerk; film critic, *Daily Worker*, New York, 1948–50; Assistant to the Vice-President, Merch Sharp and Dohme International, 1953–63; Regents' Lecturer, University of California, Santa Barbara, 1973. Recipient: Guggenheim fellowship, 1970, 1976; National Endowment for the Arts grant, 1974. Agent: Wallace and Sheil Agency, 177 East 70th Street, New York, New York 10021. Address: North Brooklin, Maine 04661, U.S.A.

PUBLICATIONS

Novels

A Wake in Ybor City. New York, Holt Rinehart, 1963.
An Orderly Life. New York, Pantheon, 1967; London, Hutchinson, 1968.
The Truth about Them. Cleveland, World, 1971.
Double, Double. New York, Viking Press, 1974.
The Kill Price. Indianapolis, Bobbs Merrill, 1976.

Uncollected Short Stories

"The Guns in the Closet," in *The Best American Short Stories 1972*, edited by Martha Foley. Boston, Houghton Mifflin, 1972.
"In the Bronx," in *American Review 19*, edited by Theodore Solotaroff. New York, Bantam, 1974.
"The American Sickness," in *The Best American Short Stories 1975*, edited by Martha Foley. Boston, Houghton Mifflin, 1975.

Other

The Goodbye Land. New York, Pantheon, 1967; London, Hutchinson, 1968.
In the Fist of the Revolution: Life in a Cuban Country Town. New York, Pantheon, 1968; as *In the Fist of the Revolution: Life in Castro's Cuba*, London, Allen Lane, 1968.
Down There (on Latin America). Cleveland, World, 1970.
The Franco Years: The Untold Human Story of Life under Spanish Fascism. Indianapolis, Bobbs Merrill, 1977.

Translator, *Island of Women*, by Juan Goytisolo. New York, Knopf, 1962; as *Sands of Torremolinos*, London, Cape, 1962.
Translator, *Villa Milo*, by Xavier Domingo. New York, Braziller, 1962.
Translator, *The Party's Over*, by Juan Goytisolo. New York, Grove Press, and London, Weidenfeld and Nicolson, 1966.

*

Manuscript Collection: Boston University.

Jose Yglesias comments:

I write to have my say. There are feelings and ideas that conversations and speeches and articles and reviews will not accommodate: these are the things that fiction, always so undiscriminating, finds room for. I thank God for the novel form.

* * *

A primary focus in all of Jose Yglesias's novels is the bearing of Hispanic heritage upon increasingly Americanized Cuban expatriates. Most especially it is the old extended family and Spanish "republican" predilections which he probes for contemporary life signs. His work always entails some marriage of these two concerns, which gives them a compelling blend of the personal and the socio-political. Moreover, he unfailingly discovers, happily or unhappily for his characters, analogical moral crises between the generations. This aspect of

his work reaches its finest, albeit pessimistic, fruition in his fourth and least ethnic novel, *Double, Double.*

Yglesias is gifted at delineating the conflicting claims of private, even mercantile, aspirations as against social and altruistic ones. The former include not only a regard for capital and personal luxury (the narrator of his third novel remarks "a shame-faced admiration for gentility"), but particularly for the wonders of sexual gratification and familial warmth. The latter include a regard for the democratic struggle in Spain, the egalitarian yearnings of Tampa's cigar workers (often mere "cafe revolutionaries"), the fight for Cuban independence, and, increasingly after the first novel, the hopes of all minorities, including student radicals. None of this is rendered at the expense of psychological or existential curiosity or verisimilitude.

Set in Tampa's Cuban ghetto in 1958, *A Wake in Ybor City* involves action ironically heightened by the reader's knowledge of the then incipiently successful Castro revolution. The major conflict concerns an affluent Cuban woman and her penurious family. She attempts to abort the wake the others are planning for her nephew, contemptuously labeling it "barbaric." And in asserting that the affair would kill her mother she misses the obvious, for eschewing the ancient custom is precisely what would do that. The foils to this figure are a political activist, Estaban, and Robert Moran, a Cuban–American artist. Robert is reluctantly won over to Estaban's commitment and in helping to deliver weapons to Cuban freedom fighters he is the first of Yglesias's protagonists to experience the ramifications of ideology. But in this first novel, the family and the morality of its tenacious affections are the focal points.

The least overtly political of the novels, *An Orderly Life* is still laced with socio-political motifs, which touch subtly upon the protagonist Rafe's curiously successful pursuit of a structured existence. Rafe's sense of order is not rigid, but "a kind of listening to music, a response to its swells, lulls and rhythms." To this end he strikes a balance between numerous but counterpointed forces. Free enterprise, sex as an end in itself, and marital love determine Rafe in half of his nature. In the other half he is directed by the influences of three very different friends. From Jerry comes his Marxist bent, sullied in Jerry's own life by his guilt-ridden capitulation with the Bitch Goddess; from Josh, a black radical gone homosexual, comes a gift for leavening too pure motives with pragmatic choices; from Mr. Sealy, a veritable "Southern Gentleman," comes aristocratic decorum, "the vision of order itself."

The pronoun in *The Truth about Them* is finely ambiguous. "They" are Spanish Americans; their truth is the integrity of their passional lives. "They" are also their myriad antagonists. The novel builds itself upon the narrator Pini's effort to elaborate and validate his familial past and to pass on to his son Ralph the "elegiac mood" it inspires in him. This mood is intensified by Pini's realization that his "*background* ... [is] the agony of others." Yet he has also known, shamefully, ethnic embarrassment and, anxiously, the fear "that in another generation this ambience might at best only linger like a scent after a beautiful woman has left the room." Expelled from Columbia after the student strike, Ralph sees Ybor City too narrowly, as only "a pacified village in Vietnam." But the past and present are fused happily when his grandmother gently wins him with a lesson in the survival instincts of his ancestors.

Four well-realized aspects of *Double, Double* make it Yglesias's best work. The plot is the primary masterstroke. From this emanate an astute psychological rendering of Seth Evergood's character, a brilliant unfolding of how the limitations (if not the sins) of the father are visited upon the son, and a lucid vision of the deadly serious ramifications of political dissent in contemporary America. The old thematic interests remain but are assimilated by broader ones. The novel exposes, often comically and pathetically, the disturbing relationships of sub-cultures and right-wing police power, as it depicts the bumbling attempts of an intellectual to act out his social consciousness. One wants to compare this work with "The Short Happy Life of Francis Macomber," but Evergood is deprived of Macomber's relatively luxurious moment of self-realization because—from the rear as it were—he is exploded into oblivion. It only remains for the good-hearted but dim hippie to misevaluate totally what has transpired.

—David M. Heaton

YOUNG, Al(bert James). American. Born in Ocean Springs, Mississippi, 31 May 1939. Educated at the University of Michigan, Ann Arbor (co-editor, *Generation* magazine), 1957–61; Stanford University, California. (Stegner Creative Writing Fellow), 1966–67; University of California, Berkeley, A.B. in Spanish 1969. Married Arline June Belch in 1963; one son. Free-lance musician, 1958–64; disc jockey, KJAZ-FM, Alameda, California, 1961–65; instructor and linguistic consultant, San Francisco Neighborhood Youth Corps Writing Workshop, 1968–69; writing instructor, San Francisco Museum of Art Teenage Workshop, 1968–69; Jones Lecturer in Creative Writing, Stanford University, 1969–74; screenwriter, Laser Films, New York, 1972, Stigwood Corporation, London and New York, 1972, Verdon Productions, Hollywood, 1976, First Artists Ltd., Burbank, California, 1976–77, and Universal, Hollywood, 1979; Writer-in-Residence, University of Washington, Seattle, 1981–82. Since 1979, Director, Associated Writing Programs. Founding editor, *Loveletter*, San Francisco, 1966–68. Since 1972, co-editor, *Yardbird Reader*, Berkeley, California; contributing editor, since 1972, *Changes*, New York, and since 1973, *Umoja*, New Mexico; since 1981, co-editor and co-publisher, *Quilt*, Berkeley. Recipient: National Endowment for the Arts grant, 1968, 1969, 1974; San Francisco Foundation Joseph Henry Jackson Award, 1969; Guggenheim fellowship, 1974; Pushcart prize, 1980; Before Columbus Foundation award, 1982. Agent: Lynn Nesbit, International Creative Management, 40 West 57th Street, New York, New York 10019. Address: 514 Bryant Street, Palo Alto, California 94301, U.S.A.

PUBLICATIONS

Novels

Snakes. New York, Holt Rinehart, 1970; London, Sidgwick and Jackson, 1971.
Who Is Angelina? New York, Holt Rinehart, 1975; London, Sidgwick and Jackson, 1978.
Sitting Pretty. New York, Holt Rinehart, 1976.
Ask Me Now. New York, McGraw Hill, and London, Sidgwick and Jackson, 1980.

Uncollected Short Stories

"My Old Buddy Shakes, Alas, and Grandmama Claude," in *Nexus* (San Francisco), May–June 1965.
"The Question Man and Why I Dropped Out," in *Nexus* (San Francisco), November–December 1965.

"Chicken Hawk's Dream," in *Stanford Short Stories 1968*, edited by Wallace Stegner and Richard Scowcroft. Stanford, California, Stanford University Press, 1968.
"Moon Watching by Lake Chapala," in *Aldebaran Review 3* (Berkeley, California), 1968.

Plays

Screenplays: *Nigger*, 1972; *Sparkle*, 1972.

Verse

Dancing. New York, Corinth, 1969.
The Song Turning Back into Itself. New York, Holt Rinehart, 1971.
Some Recent Fiction. San Francisco, San Francisco Book Company, 1974.
Geography of the Near Past. New York, Holt Rinehart, 1976.
The Blues Don't Change: New and Selected Poems. Baton Rouge, Louisiana State University Press, 1982.

Other

Bodies and Soul: Musical Memoirs. Berkeley, California, Creative Arts, 1981.
Kinds of Blue: Musical Memoirs. Berkeley, California, Creative Arts, 1984.

Editor, with Ishmael Reed, *Yardbird Lives!* New York, Grove Press, 1978.

*

Bibliography: in *New Black Voices* edited by Abraham Chapman, New York, New American Library, 1972.

Critical Studies: "Reader's Report" by Martin Levin, in *New York Times Book Review*, 17 May 1970; "Growing Up Black" by L.E. Sissman, in *New Yorker*, 11 July 1970; "Jazzed Up," in *Times Literary Supplement* (London), 30 July 1971; "Al Young's *Snakes*: Words to the Music" by Neil Schmitz, in *Paunch 35* (Buffalo), February 1972.

*   *   *

In his story "Chicken Hawk's Dream" Al Young tells of a young man who believes that as magically as in a dream he might become a jazz artist. Failing to bring even a sound out of a borrowed horn, Chicken Hawk retreats into dope and alcohol, but his delusion persists so that when the narrator meets him later on a Detroit street corner Chicken Hawk says that he is off to New York to cut a record—just as soon as he gets his instrument out of the pawnshop. The dream of Chicken Hawk with its refusal of discipline and lack of nerve represents a version of what Young terms "art as hustle." It is not titillation, he says in a "Statement on Aesthetics, Poetics, Kinetics" (in *New Black Voices*, 1972), but the touching of human beings so that both toucher and touched are changed that matters most in art as in life. Touch may be magical but before all else it is the sign of willingness to engage actual life.

Through the metaphor of touch and repudiation of attitudinizing Young explains most of his literary practice. His novels gain much of their force from his ability to limn the texture of experience. Precise detailing of speech demonstrates how individuals play roles uniquely significant to those with whom they have personal relationships, including readers; and ways of seeing, talking, becoming, in short, ways of expressing the feel of life's touch, engender the books' movement.

In his first novel, *Snakes*, Young infuses the traditional narrative of adolescent growth with a principle of fluidity affecting every aspect of structure, style, and theme. MC, whose journey to maturity is the story's subject, gets turned on to modern jazz, an art of process which illustrates that personality itself may derive from music. Stylistically the book is largely constructed out of raps, oral performances by MC's friends, and reminiscences of his grandmother. The first concur with the performance of improvisational music to convey the importance of expressive response; the latter carry process into biographical temporality where memory of past events maintains influence in the present. Style and structure together support Young's theme of the struggle to be free, outlined in MC's thoughts on a bus to New York where he, unlike Chicken Hawk, will cut a record: "For the first time in my life I don't feel trapped; I don't feel free either but I don't feel trapped and I'm going to try and make this feeling last for as long as I can."

Who Is Angelina? picks up Young's theme in the story of a young woman who must regain the sense of not being trapped. In one answer to the question posed by the title, Angelina finds herself, in the words of a Pepsi-drinking fortune teller, poised between freedom to choose what she wishes and weaknesses which hold her back. A return to roots among family and neighborhood renews a sense of love for origins in Angelina but also demonstrates that she has no choice but to accept her distinct individuality; and to make the best of it, she must learn to move with awareness through her own becoming. Young allows Angelina to try transcendental meditation as a means of renewal, but her crucial realization of self occurs as it must, in the context of mundane experience. In a tussle with a purse snatcher she impulsively ventilates feelings of outrage that offend the liberal sentiments of friends and bystanders. Thereby she wipes out, for herself, the illusions one gains by living second-hand.

A year in the life of Sidney J. Prettymon, known as Sitting Pretty or sometimes plain Sit, provides the story line for Young's third novel. Sit's literary cousin is Langston Hughes's Jesse B. Semple, a.k.a. Simple. By the world's reckoning both Sit and Simple are ordinary men, but each has a philosophy and style that raises him above the average. In Sit's case the philosophy involves getting by without harming others and without succumbing to the values that will compromise integrity or happiness; thus, living is an improvisational performance. Rendered in the voice of Sit the novel *Sitting Pretty* works as the prose equivalent of an Afro-American musical composition alternatively echoing the situations of blues and celebratory riffs that are unique to the character's expressive style. Sit, jogging through the streets of Palo Alto, putting his two cents worth in on a radio talk show, caring deeply for his former wife in her time of trouble and his children when they don't even know they have problems, is a triumphant creation who deserves a place in the popular imagination right alongside Simple and probably, as Wallace Stegner suggested, Huckleberry Finn too.

Like Ishmael Reed, his colleague in *Yardbird* enterprises, Young is impatient with expectations that Black writers should show their ethnicity in some predictable or stereotypical way. O.O. Gabugah the militant poet was Young's satirical treatment of such message writing, and O.O. makes an appearance in *Sitting Pretty* also. Usually, though, Young makes his point, as in *Ask Me Now*, by unselfconscious narrative of the human trials of his characters. What makes the books Black is that

the people, such as Woody Knight, the retired basketball player of his most recent novel, are granted a broad range of experience in which they talk and touch others in the style of Black culture. That style permits comedy right along with tribulation, the sort of love that yields happy endings and the losses that create frustration and anger. Reviewers loaded with prescriptions for the ethnic author and critics who want the message straight can be displeased, but Al Young's art will persist as a loving treatment of the versions of human process that are its source and subject.

—John M. Reilly

YOUNG, Marguerite (Vivian).   American.   Born in Indianapolis, Indiana, in 1909. Educated at Indiana University, Bloomington; Butler University, Indianapolis, B.A. 1930; University of Chicago, M.A. 1936; University of Iowa, Iowa City. Taught at Indiana University, 1942; University of Iowa, 1955–57; Columbia University, New York, 1958; New School for Social Research, New York, 1958–67; Fairleigh Dickinson University, Rutherford, New Jersey, 1960–62; Fordham University, Bronx, New York, 1966, 1967. Recipient: American Association of University Women grant, 1943; American Academy grant, 1945; Guggenheim fellowship, 1948; Newberry Library fellowship, 1951; Rockefeller fellowship, 1954. Address: 375 Bleecker Street, New York, New York 10014, U.S.A.

PUBLICATIONS

Novel

Miss MacIntosh, My Darling.   New York, Scribner, 1965; London, Owen, 1966.

Verse

Prismatic Ground.   New York, Macmillan, 1937.
Moderate Fable.   New York, Reynal, 1944.

Other

Where Is There Another? A Memorial to Paul Y. Anderson, with others.   Norman, Oklahoma, Cooperative Books, 1939.
Angel in the Forest: A Fairy Tale of Two Utopias (on the New Harmony community).   New York, Reynal, 1945; London, Owen, 1967.

*   *   *

Marguerite Young's titanic novel, *Miss MacIntosh, My Darling* (1,198 pages), was in slow generation for more than 17 years. It is a mammoth epic, a massive fable, a picaresque journey, a Faustian question, and a work of stunning magnitude and beauty. Her only published fiction to date, it is her masterwork. Its style is one of musicalizations, rhapsodies, symbolizations that repetitively roll and resound and double back upon themselves in an oceanic tumult. Its force is cumulative; its method is clarification through amassment, as in the great styles of Joyce or Hermann Broch or Faulkner. The major passages of the work are fluent and seminal and are grounded on four beings: Miss MacIntosh, once nursemaid to the voyager-narrator; Catherine Cartwheel, the narrator's "poor dreaming mother"; Mr. Spitzer, loyal companion to Catherine Cartwheel, composer of unheard, unwritten music and twin brother to a dead gambler with whose identity he is confounded; and Esther Longtree, a voluptuous waitress in a Wabash Valley cafe (the town of the novel is What Cheer, Iowa), who is cursed by an "everlasting, lonely pregnancy." These grand sections are procreative and fertile, spurting forth richly expressive and exhaustingly revealing passages of radiant prose. The minor sub-sections explore the submerged lives of several vivid and haunting personages. In these sections, the humor is folk, slapstick, Chaplinesque, melodramatic, and Satanic. *Miss MacIntosh, My Darling* is as often mischievously funny and devilishly humorous as it is incantatory and operatic. And, finally, the novel involves and depends on the basic and traditional American literary themes: smalltown, childhood memory, homesickness, nostalgia, quest.

—William Goyen

YURICK, Sol. American. Born in New York City, 18 January 1925. Educated at New York University, A.B. 1950; Brooklyn College, New York, M.A. 1961. Served in the United States Army, 1944–45. Married Adrienne Lash in 1958; one child. Librarian, New York University, 1945–53; social investigator, New York City Department of Welfare, 1954–59. Since 1959, full-time writer. Recipient: Guggenheim fellowship. Lives in Brooklyn, New York. Agent: Georges Borchardt Inc., 136 West 57th Street, New York, New York 10022, U.S.A.

PUBLICATIONS

Novels

The Warriors. New York, Holt Rinehart, 1965; London, W.H. Allen, 1966.
Fertig. New York, Simon and Schuster, and London, W.H. Allen, 1966.
The Bag. New York, Simon and Schuster, 1968; London, Gollancz, 1970.
An Island Death. New York, Harper, 1975.
Richard A. New York, Arbor House, and London, Methuen, 1982.

Short Stories

Someone Just Like You. New York, Harper, 1972; London, Gollancz, 1973.

Other

Editor, *Voices of Brooklyn: An Anthology.* Chicago, American Library Association, 1973.

*

Manuscript Collection: Tanument Library, New York University.

*   *   *

Taken singly, each of Sol Yurick's works constitutes a substantial contribution to the growing body of contemporary fiction that depicts the American megalopolis in perpetual crisis. Taken together, his novels make up the most compelling vision available to us (in fiction or in non-fiction) of the most nightmarish megalopolis of all: New York now. Yurick is (as surely befits someone who was involved for several years in attempting to construct a sound theoretical and practical base for action on the American left) not interested in formal experimentation in the novel for the novel's own sake. Yet neither is he a polemicist with little sense of artistic form. He is an extreme rarity: a social critic with broad theoretical and "street level" experience. Yet, he is at the same time an erudite novelist with solid historical knowledge of the genre and great skill in handling the form. In a deliberate and obviously self-conscious way, he consistently attempts to close the gap between the Biblical and classical Greek world so often alluded to in his works and the world of welfare, of murder, and of political power plays, the three major elements in his portrait of New York today.

The Warriors is a novel about a decimated New York teenage gang whom we first met on hostile "turf" on their way back to their "homeland" after a gang conference which has just ended in attempted murder. The opening scene is prefaced by an epigraph drawn from Xenophon: "My friends, these people whom you see are the last obstacle which stops us from being where we have so long struggled to be. We ought, if we could, to eat them up alive." The anabasis of Hinton (the gang artist), Lunkface, Bimbo, The Junior, and Hector is filled with memories of Ismael, leader of the Delancey Thrones, organizer of the citywide gang conference, and victim of the violence with which the conference had come to an abrupt close. "Ismael," we are told, "had the impassive face of a Spanish grandee, the purple-black color of an uncontaminated African, and the dreams of an Alexander, a Cyrus, a Napoleon." He will return in *The Bag* as a saturnine figure (now with only one eye), a dope pusher, rent collector for a slum landlord (Faust), and stockpiler of rifles, waiting for that moment when the downtrodden of the city will rise up and use these arms to kill their ancient oppressors. Ismael is not alone in his reappearance. Though seemingly selfcontained when read singly, the novels (much like those of Faulkner) shade from one into another. The gang artist, Hinton in *The Warriors*, reappears, for instance, as a major figure in *The Bag*. Hinton's mother, Minnie (permanently on welfare and having a new "lover"), and his brother the addict, Alonso, minor figures at the end of Hinton's anabasis, also return but now as full-fledged characters in *The Bag*.

In contrast to the lower depths of *The Warriors* and parts of *The Bag*, *Fertig* appears at first to be an exploration of a strictly middle-class New York Jewish milieu. But the death of Fertig's son as a result of indifference on the part of the staff of a New York hospital triggers such a paroxysm of grief that Fertig cold-bloodedly murders some seven people involved however tenuously in his son's death. As mass murderer, Fertig is then thrust into the company of the criminals, madmen, and junkies who populate Yurick's other two novels. We are also given our first view of the political elite of this mythical New York: Judge Mabel Crossland whose thighs have encompassed every prominent jurist in New York in her climb to the judgeship; Fertig's lawyer, Royboy, the small but handsome sexual athlete, with multiple obligations to his female admirers (including Mabel Crossland) on his way to becoming Senator Roy, a character whom we then meet in *The Bag*; and Irving Hockstaff, king-maker, the man who indirectly runs the whole political apparatus of the city. A pawn in the political games of the mighty, Fertig and Fertig's trial are painfully reminiscent of *An American Tragedy*.

The evocation in *Fertig* of another classic work of literature is an integral part of Yurick's aesthetic and political methodology. The book is shaped as a contemporary replay of a recurrent phenomenon: the destruction of "the little man" by the power elite. Fertig's name comments ironically on a phenomenon that never ends. Likewise Ismael and Faust in *The Bag* are conscious restatements on a theme as old as poverty. Minnie (referred to by Yurick as a black Cybele and as the Wyf of Bath) loves Alpha (Fertig or Omega's opposite?) who has left his wife, Helen. They share the world with Faust (a figure drawn not only from Goethe but from Kosinski's *The Painted Bird*), with Faust's daughter, the lesbian Eve, and with Faust's ambitious urban renewal project: Rebirth. Finally, Rebirth and all the little men and women are crushed as the ghetto detonates despite the best efforts of the man from Agape (love, affection), the master of the government's counter-insurgency game plan.

We know with Yurick at the end of *The Bag* (though it is never explicitly stated) that the future of this city that is all cities lies not with the Ismael's and others who seek social improvement but with the Royboys and the Hockstaffs. It is they who seem to believe: "It didn't matter how many people you killed so long as you contained it [the revolution] and cooled it and co-opted it and made it run smoothly." So it has always been says Yurick and so it will be: Alpha and Agape are Omega and Fertig. The end of Ismael in *The Bag* returns us not only to Ismael at the beginning of *The Warriors* but to the ancient admonition drawn from the *Anabasis*. The "homeland" lies permanently within sight but beyond reach. There is some doubt that, all his aesthetic skill and political acumen notwithstanding, Sol Yurick will ever get us any closer, but his portrayal of anabasis itself is worthy of comparison with its ancient counterpart.

—John Fuegi

APPENDIX

CAPOTE, Truman. American. Born Truman Streckfus Persons in New Orleans, Louisiana, 30 September 1924; took step-father's surname. Educated at Trinity School and St. John's Academy, New York; Greenwich High School, Connecticut. Worked in the art department, and wrote for "Talk of the Town," *The New Yorker* magazine; then full-time writer. Recipient: O. Henry Award, 1946, 1948, 1951; American Academy grant, 1959; Mystery Writers of America Edgar Allan Poe Award, 1966; Emmy Award, for television adaptation, 1967. Member, American Academy. *Died 25 August 1984.*

PUBLICATIONS

Novels

Other Voices, Other Rooms. New York, Random House, and London, Heinemann, 1948.
The Grass Harp. New York, Random House, 1951; London, Heinemann, 1952.

Short Stories

A Tree of Night and Other Stories. New York, Random House, 1949; London, Heinemann, 1950.
Breakfast at Tiffany's: A Short Novel and Three Stories. New York, Random House, and London, Hamish Hamilton, 1958.
A Christmas Memory. New York, Random House, 1966.

Uncollected Short Stories

"The Walls Are Cold," in *Decade of Short Stories* (Chicago), vol. 4, no. 3, 1943.
"A Mink of One's Own," in *Decade of Short Stories* (Chicago), vol. 6, no. 3, 1944.
"The Shape of Things," in *Decade of Short Stories* (Chicago), vol. 6, no. 4, 1944.
"Preacher's Legend," in *Prairie Schooner* (Lincoln, Nebraska), December 1945.
"Blind Items," in *Ladies Home Journal* (New York), January 1974.
Excerpts from *Answered Prayers*: "Mojave" June 1975, "Unspoiled Monsters" May 1976, and "Kate McCloud" December 1976, all in *Esquire* (New York), and "La Côte Basque, 1965," in *Great Esquire Fiction* edited by L. Rust Hills, New York, Viking Press, 1983.
"Hospitality," in *Mademoiselle* (New York), November 1980.

Plays

The Grass Harp, adaptation of his own novel (produced New York, 1952). New York, Random House 1952.
House of Flowers, music by Harold Arlen, lyrics by Capote and Arlen (produced Philadelphia and New York, 1954; revised version, produced New York, 1968; Edinburgh, 1985). New York, Random House, 1968.
The Thanksgiving Visitor, adaptation of his own story (televised, 1968). New York, Random House, 1968; London, Hamish Hamilton, 1969.
Trilogy (screenplay, with Eleanor Perry), in *Trilogy*, 1969.

Screenplays: *Beat the Devil*, with John Huston, 1953; *Indiscretion of an American Wife*, with others, 1954; *The Innocents*, with William Archibald and John Mortimer, 1961; *Trilogy*, with Eleanor Perry, 1969.

Television Plays and Films (includes documentaries): *A Christmas Memory*, with Eleanor Perry, from the story by Capote, 1966; *Among the Paths to Eden*, with Eleanor Perry, from the story by Capote, 1967; *Laura*, from the play by Vera Caspary, 1968; *The Thanksgiving Visitor*, from his own story, 1968; *Behind Prison Walls*, 1972; *The Glass House*, with Tracy Keenan Wynn and Wyatt Cooper, 1972; *Crimewatch*, 1973.

Other

Local Color. New York, Random House, 1950; London, Heinemann, 1955.
The Muses Are Heard: An Account of the Porgy and Bess Tour to Leningrad. New York, Random House, 1956; London, Heinemann, 1957.
Observations, photographs by Richard Avedon. New York, Simon and Schuster, and London, Weidenfeld and Nicolson, 1959.
Selected Writings, edited by Mark Schorer. New York, Random House, and London, Hamish Hamilton, 1963.
In Cold Blood: A True Account of a Multiple Murder and Its Consequences. New York, Random House, and London, Hamish Hamilton, 1966.
Trilogy: An Experiment in Multimedia, with Frank and Eleanor Perry. New York, Macmillan, 1969.
The Dogs Bark: Public People and Private Places. New York, Random House, 1973; London, Weidenfeld and Nicolson, 1974.
Then It All Came Down: Criminal Justice Today Discussed by Police, Criminals, and Correction Officers with Comments by Truman Capote. New York, Random House, 1976.
Music for Chameleons. New York, Random House, 1980; London, Hamish Hamilton, 1981.
One Christmas (memoir). New York, Random House, and London, Hamish Hamilton, 1983.
Conversations with Capote, with Lawrence Grobel. New York, New American Library, and London, Hutchinson, 1985.

*

Bibliography: *Truman Capote: A Primary and Secondary Bibliography* by Robert J. Stanton, Boston, Hall, 1980.

Manuscript Collection: Library of Congress, Washington, D.C.

Critical Studies: *The Worlds of Truman Capote* by William L. Nance, New York, Stein and Day, 1970, London, Calder and Boyars, 1973; *Truman Capote* by Helen S. Garson, New York, Ungar, 1980; *Truman Capote* by Marie Rudisill and James C. Simmons, New York, Morrow, 1983; *Footnote to a Friendship: A Memoir of Truman Capote and Others* by Donald Windham, Verona, Italy, Windham, 1983; *Capote: A Biography* by Gerald Clarke, New York, Linden Press, 1985.

Theatrical Activities:
Actor: **Film**—*Murder by Death*, 1976.

*   *   *

As a jet-setter, aesthete, and social critic, Truman Capote's public personality was so flamboyant it obscured, for many, his gift as a prose stylist and innovator of fictional forms. Capote was skillful in the variety of forms with which he worked—the gothic short story, lyrical novel, and "non-fiction novel," the last of which influenced a generation of writers.

As most of his critics have noted, his work falls into "day" and "night" modes—portrayals of the realistic, concrete everyday social world—a comic mode—and evocations of the mysterious and macabre, the world of dreams, violence, and the supernatural.

Capote began his career with short fiction, a form with which he experimented throughout his career: "Whatever control and technique I have," he remarked, "I owe entirely to the medium of the short story." Generally, although the bulk of these take place either in the south or in New York City, they deal with the archetypal journey from innocence to experience, and they portray a mixture of corrupt, exotic, and comic adventures. Repeatedly, from "The Walls Are Cold (1943) to "Mojave" (1975), Capote's youths encounter painful isolation, and at times failure, as they are initiated into the world of grotesques, eccentrics, and exotics. Typically, they persist in their journey, nevertheless, since knowledge of the self is gained through immersion in the world, and this, it would seem, is prerequisite to the ability to love and thus be free. The world, in all its boring, ridiculous, and potentially evil possibilities, necessitates that the individual achieve a moral, spiritual, psychological, and, at times, physical freedom.

The longer works, frequently called "novel-romances" (because they "engage reality without being realistic") reveal a more lyrical prose, as well as a greater sense of humor about small town life (*Other Voices, Other Rooms, The Grass Harp*) and the large city (*Breakfast at Tiffany's*). Once again Capote deals with coming of age and the human mandate to adjust to, rather than escape, the world. Gaining a sense of identity prepares one to be self-reliant—to be free—in an otherwise corrupt and corrupting world. *Other Voices* is the initiation story of 13-year-old Joel Knox, who travels from New Orleans to Skully's Landing in search of his estranged "father" (God, selfhood, lover). In their long-awaited meeting—a grotesque and ludicrous scene—the boy witnesses "a shaved head lying with invalid looseness on unsanitary pillows." The boy, writes Capote, had "been played a mean trick. Only he didn't know who or what to blame. He felt separated, without identity." Later, however, after experiencing various stages of guilt and identifying with his father, he transcends to the exuberance of self-knowledge and the existential "I am me." This dreamy and brooding novel is a powerful evocation of adolescent complexity and is noteworthy, as well, for its minute rendering of the language, life style, and values of the deep south.

Capote's skillful evocation of place and his ability to reproduce the varied rhythms of dialect recur in *The Grass Harp*. Here the 11-year-old Collin Fenwick, after his parents die, goes to live with two aunts in a southern backwoods. Less gothic and stylistically more pruned than *Other Voices*, the novel deals with the conflict between social conformity and individual dreams. Capote's aversion toward any capitulation to the boring and corrupting world of ordinary social traditions continues: "A man who doesn't dream is like a man who doesn't sweat: he stores up a lot of poison."

The first-person narrator of *Breakfast at Tiffany's* relates the frothy and fragmented experiences of the incredibly vivacious, zany, and lonely Holly Golightly, an 18-year-old innocent in quest of the romantic dream of Happiness. She makes "adjustments" (sometimes of questionable legality) in order to surmount the dreary middle-class world around her. She takes, for example, a "too romantic" job from a defrocked priest to visit a Mafia convict (Sally Tomato) each Thursday in prison (And why not? she asks. It "cheers up a lonely old man." Actually, her messages from Sally about the weather are codes regarding the narcotics racket.) Through the most outrageous of accommodations, Holly—who is, in fact, a Mrs. Lulamae

Barnes who has escaped her Tulip, Texas, horse-doctor husband and family—can survive, at least for a time, in her fashionable New York, brownstone. She can be stylish and knowledgable about everything *au courant*—and still retain her dreams, like her favorite one of waking up to have "breakfast at Tiffany's."

In *Local Color, The Muses Are Heard, In Cold Blood*, Capote realized one of his goals: "I've always had the theory that reportage is the great unexplored art form." The enormously successful "non-fiction novel" *In Cold Blood* brought Capote great popularity (and he earned $2 million from the movie and paperback rights alone). An account of the actual murders of the four members of the Clutter family in western Kansas, it appeared after nearly six years of research and 6,000 pages of interviews, including extensive communication with the murderers, Perry Smith and Richard Hickock. (Capote even escorted them to their executions.) A literary *tour de force* and heralded for its authenticity by such critics as F.W. Dupee, Rebecca West, and John Kenneth Galbraith, Capote's minute rendering of the plethora of detail surrounding these gratuitous and grotesque murders, the family, city, and the murderers themselves, along with his citations of lengthy non-edited conversations and testimony, assaulted the literary world, which didn't know whether to respond to this new form as journalism or art. The work, which Capote claimed to be entirely factual, also raised questions about American society, justice, and the relationships between men. As a literary form, Capote's work gained a following through the mid-1970's by writers as successful and different as Norman Mailer and Tom Wolfe.

Capote set aside his following project, an autobiographical work, *Answered Prayers*, in 1977. He said he had an apparently unsolvable problem: "How can a writer successfully combine within a single form—say the short story—all he knows about every other form of writing? ... all his colors, all his abilities on the same palette for mingling?" He did complete, however, *Music for Chameleons* which he defined as "conversational portraits"—in fact, non-fiction autobiographical essays. Its title piece and "Mojave" are particularly successful.

—Lois Gordon

CHEEVER, John (William). American. Born in Quincy, Massachusetts, 27 May 1912. Educated at Thayer Academy. Served in the United States Army Signal Corps, 1943–45: Sergeant. Married Mary M. Winternitz in 1941; one daughter and two sons. Full-time writer in New York City, 1930–51, Scarborough, New York, 1951–60, and Ossining, New York, after 1961. Taught at Barnard College, New York, 1956–57, Ossining Correctional Facility (Sing Sing prison), 1971–72, and University of Iowa Writers Workshop, Iowa City, 1973; Visiting Professor of Creative Writing, Boston University, 1974–75. Recipient: Guggenheim fellowship, 1951, and second fellowship; Benjamin Franklin Award, 1955; O. Henry Award, 1956, 1964; American Academy grant, 1956, and Howells Medal, 1965; National Book Award, 1958; National Book Critics Circle award, 1979; Pulitzer Prize, 1979; MacDowell Medal, 1979; American Book Award, for paperback, 1981; National Medal for Literature, 1982. Litt.D.: Harvard University, Cambridge, Massachusetts, 1978. Member, American Academy, 1958. *Died 18 June 1982.*

PUBLICATIONS

Novels

The Wapshot Chronicle.   New York, Harper, and London, Gollancz, 1957.
The Wapshot Scandal.   New York, Harper, and London, Gollancz, 1964.
Bullet Park.   New York, Knopf, and London, Cape, 1969.
Falconer.   New York, Knopf, and London, Cape, 1977.
Oh, What a Paradise It Seems.   New York, Knopf, and London, Cape, 1982.

Short Stories

The Way Some People Live: A Book of Stories.   New York, Random House, 1943.
The Enormous Radio and Other Stories.   New York, Funk and Wagnalls, and London, Gollancz, 1953.
Stories, with others.   New York, Farrar Straus, 1956; as *A Book of Stories*, London, Gollancz, 1957.
The Housebreaker of Shady Hill and Other Stories.   New York, Harper, 1958; London, Gollancz, 1959.
Some People, Places, and Things That Will Not Appear in My Next Novel.   New York, Harper, and London, Gollancz, 1961.
The Brigadier and the Golf Widow.   New York, Harper, 1964; London, Gollancz, 1965.
The World of Apples.   New York, Knopf, 1973; London, Cape, 1974.
The Stories of John Cheever.   New York, Knopf, 1978; London, Cape, 1979.
The Leaves, The Lion-Fish and the Bear.   Los Angeles, Sylvester and Orphanos, 1980.

Uncollected Short Stories

"Island," in *New Yorker*, 27 April 1981.
"Expelled," in *New Republic* (Washington, D.C.), 19–26 July 1982.

Plays

Television Plays: scripts for *Life with Father* series; *The Shady Hill Kidnapping*, 1982.

*

Bibliography: *John Cheever: A Reference Guide* by Francis J. Bosha, Boston, Hall, 1981.

Manuscript Collection: Brandeis University, Waltham, Massachusetts.

Critical Studies: *John Cheever* by Samuel Coale, New York, Ungar, 1977; *John Cheever* by Lynne Waldeland, Boston, Twayne, 1979; *Critical Essays on John Cheever* edited by R.G. Collins, Boston, Hall, 1982; *John Cheever: The Hobgoblin Company of Love* by George W. Hunt, Grand Rapids, Michigan, Eerdmans, 1983; *Home Before Dark: A Biographical Memoir of John Cheever* by Susan Cheever, Boston, Houghton Mifflin, 1984, London, Weidenfeld and Nicolson, 1985.

*   *   *

Over a period of 45 years, John Cheever published novels and, more successfully, short stories that earned him a secure and honored place in 20th-century American literature as a writer of fiction traditional in both its form and its values. For the most part, that is, he wrote realistic stories dealing with the manners and morals of the society—especially of the middle class in cities and the suburbs—he observed around him. His fictional forebears in this century were Henry James and Edith Wharton, and his like-minded contemporaries were writers like Louis Auchincloss, Mary McCarthy, Philip Roth, and John Updike. Like all of these social novelists, Cheever had recourse, on occasion, to myth, fable, and fantasy, but the major thrust of his fiction is toward verisimilitude, meaning, and moral judgment. He was clearly different from younger writers of his own time like John Barth or Thomas Pynchon, who represent the American expression of postmodernism, the movement that ran in uneasy if not hostile tandem with literary traditionalism in the last two decades of Cheever's life.

He brought to his writing a curious mixture of joy and gloom, of romantic fever and sophisticated skepticism. He had a virtually Dionysian appetite for the colors and smells of life and for the mysteries of love and beauty; the intensity of his feeling for sky, sea, nightfall, storm often carried him into the realm of exaltation. Against these sensuous possibilities of life, Cheever posed a morbid element. His stories reflect his acceptance of the Veblenian proposition that in America every man has the right to fail, and both the stories and the novels, more or less elegiac in tone, reveal the impermanence and meanness of our social arrangements in contrast to a more stable and happier time. Cheever also presented us with a mildly pessimistic view of man—entertained without any righteous indignation—as a mixed bag of good and evil, with an enlarged capacity for foolishness and concupiscence. He was not a profound Freudian, but the abnormalities of the normal interested him as a way of understanding the difference between appearance and reality, which is the historic responsibility of the novelist of manners, who must assume the authenticity of the real. Cheever gave us glimpses into the psychopathology of the every-day life of the middle class.

Since the celebration of Dionysian rites may properly take place in the presence of beings from the classical world, it is fitting that Cheever's best statement of this strain in his fiction is found in "Goodbye, My Brother" where, after lunar immensities and in soothing air, Diana and Helen emerge naked from the sea one morning, "unshy, beautiful, and full of grace." This story dramatizes the conflict between the Dionysian view and the Puritan ethic, which is intolerant of play and joy in the senses and demands absorption in useful and sensible pursuits. In much of his work, Cheever asserted his belief in the wonder and mystery of life and depicted sex not as an occasion for sin but as the most exalted experience of our physical lives.

But life as lived by Cheever's characters too seldom achieves the sensuous promise he knew it held. The men and women in his fiction are clearly unable to cope with love. If they are married, they are likely to engage in adultery or get a divorce or do both. If they have children they are likely to abuse or neglect them. As Cheever reproduced the pattern of life as lived by larger numbers of Americans, he did more than record. He judged, and he did so from a traditional respect for the sanctity of marriage and the stability of the home. He disapproved of the carnal anarchy that he faithfully recorded. He winced at the meanness that moves beneath the glossy surfaces of middle-class life. He scorned the pursuit of respectability and of success and progress. In a world he made to appear prosperous and stable, he recorded failure and displacement, and nowhere more successfully than in "The Swimmer." He documented the downward mobility of American life with some detachment, but he generally condemned the eager greediness of those who aspired to go up. He has left us a wry and accomplished social comedy which aptly details the acts of disintegration characteristic of the culture. He yearned for integration, or reintegration, but he did not understand or treat the psychic or social revolution necessary to bring it about. He was limited in ambition and perspective, and, critical as he was of America, he was incapable of perceiving the genuine terror of life here. He spoke neither yes nor no in thunder.

He had, instead, a gift for nostalgia. *The Wapshot Chronicle*, his first novel, is indeed critical of America, but its principal purpose is to present us with the paradox of eccentric vitality blooming in the midst of settled decadence. It is a loving evocation of life in the past which stands as a living rebuke to the shabby present. Despite its romantic attachment to the past, it skirts sentimentality in presenting a manly hero who loves his sons, his native place, the rituals of life, and the world of nature. He rejects modern skepticism and despair. The dignity, compassion, courage, and trust that he brings to his world make him an anachronism, and he is appropriately punished with humiliation for being out of tune with his time. He drowns himself by swimming off into the sea and leaves advice to his sons that ends, "Fear tastes like a rusty knife and do not let her into your house. ... Relish the love of a gentle woman. Trust in the Lord."

The Wapshot Scandal, which deals with the lives of these sons, is a thesis-ridden novel in which Cheever mounted a predictable attack on elements in contemporary culture that make us less than human: the failure of community, military-oriented science, plastic and glass environments. The third novel, *Bullet Park*, is a satiric attack on the suburbs in a mode we have seen more successfully presented in earlier work.

Falconer, Cheever's last novel, deals with prison life as a metaphor for human degradation. The protagonist, descendant of a patrician Yankee family, is a victim, participant in a crumbling marriage, sexual deviation, dope addiction, and violence. He demonstrates that it is virtually impossible for traditional attitudes and persons to survive in our time. But he refuses to surrender, and against all reason, does survive and gains his freedom under the open sky. The novel is unsteady in tone and marred by stereotype and sentimentality. Cheever did not have the intensity of imagination to sustain a long fiction. But he did have the courage to assert the validity of the old virtues and the rhetoric to move us to admiration for them. In our dreary time he spoke unblushingly of loving, gentle women, of stout-hearted friends, of admiring the world, of the bread and wine of life. He almost persuaded us that these goods are still available.

—Chester E. Eisinger

FARRELL, J(ames) G(ordon). British. Born in Liverpool, Lancashire, 23 January 1935. Educated at Rossall School; Brasenose College, Oxford, 1956–60, B.A. in French and Spanish 1960. Recipient: Harkness Fellowship, for residence in the United States, 1966–68; Arts Council award, 1970; Faber Memorial Prize, 1971; Booker Prize, 1973. *Died 12 August 1979.*

PUBLICATIONS

Novels

A Man from Elsewhere. London, Hutchinson, 1963.
The Lung. London, Hutchinson, 1965.
A Girl in the Head. London, Cape, 1967; New York, Harper, 1969.
Troubles. London, Cape, 1970; New York, Knopf, 1971.
The Siege of Krishnapur. London, Weidenfeld and Nicolson, 1973; New York, Harcourt Brace, 1974.
The Singapore Grip. London, Weidenfeld and Nicolson, 1978; New York, Knopf, 1979.
The Hill Station: An Unfinished Novel, and An Indian Diary, edited by John Spurling. London, Weidenfeld and Nicolson, 1981.

*

Critical Study: "Ireland Agonistes" by Elizabeth Bowen, in *Europa 1* (London), 1971.

J.G. Farrell commented:

(1972) About *Troubles*. It is a common misconception that when the historians have finished with a historical incident there remains nothing but a patch of feathers and a pair of feet; in fact, the most important things, for the very reason that they are trivial, are unsuitable for digestion by historians, who are only able to nourish themselves on the signing of treaties, battle strategies, the formation of Shadow Cabinets and so forth. These matters are quite alien to the life most people lead, which consists of catching colds, falling in love, or falling off bicycles. It is this *real* life which is the novelist's concern (though, needless to say, realism is not the only way to represent it). One of the things I have tried to do in *Troubles* is to show people "undergoing" history, to use an expression of Sartre's. The Irish troubles of 1919–1921 were chosen partly because they appeared to be safely lodged in the past; most of the book was written before the current Irish difficulties broke out, giving it an unintended topicality. What I wanted to do was to use this period of the past as a metaphor for today, because I believe that however much the superficial details and customs of life may change over the years, basically life itself does not change very much. Indeed, all literature that survives must depend on this assumption. Another reason why I preferred to use the past is that, as a rule, people have already made up their minds what they think about the present. About the past they are more susceptible to clarity of vision.

*   *   *

J.G. Farrell's rich and densely patterned comic style has familial links with other exiles such as Nabokov and Beckett. In contrast to them, however, it reveals a horrifying and revolting world of disease, death, and decay. That electrifying tension between the style and the vision is what powers all his work, which reached out in each new novel towards greater and greater artistic success.

When he died in 1979, Farrell had already established his reputation as perhaps the most talented novelist of his generation. Even his first novel, *A Man from Elsewhere*, which he later disowned, had its distinctive merits; and the story of how he became a novelist is typically Farrellian. He was a stalwart, rugger-playing hearty at Brasenose College, Oxford, when he caught polio, was put in an iron lung, and emerged thin and greying, his rugger days definitely behind him. From that experience of life-in-death emerged *The Lung*, with its semi-autobiographical, death-in-life world of the polio victim, Sands, surrounded by morbid fellow-patients, such as the ex-priest who covers up his sense of failure with a mordantly comic blasphemy. There is also old man Rivers who sits making baskets, "his mind a complete blank across which a naked woman passed from time to time." The only solaces left to men in Farrell's bizarre world are sex, humour, art and a compulsive, Sisyphean will to carry on.

His third novel, *A Girl in the Head* completed the first phase of his writing career. Its hero, Count Boris Slattery, is treated, as always, with a warmly pervasive irony which is more biting than the satire lavished lovingly on the blandly and horrifyingly normal people who surround the Count and from whom he becomes increasingly alienated. The desperate props with which people hide from the horror of reality (in this case a mindless middle-class cheerfulness) are more devastatingly demolished in his three major novels which followed.

With *Troubles*, Farrell found the distinctive setting for his gifts: the vast and decaying magnificence of the Majestic hotel, with its burgeoning tropical plants and exploding population of cats who together are taking over the hotel. The Majestic is owned by an eccentric Anglo-Irish family with which a well-meaning English major becomes involved. Baffled and dismayed by the mutual hostility of Protestant and Catholic, he comes to acquire a sense of responsibility for the Majestic and its unwanted but undismissable old ladies who freeload or pay as and when possible. As in all of Farrell's novels, there is a subtle economy with which the terror prevailing in the countryside, and indeed the world, is brought insistently closer, and culminates in a horrifying denouement which the reader has come to half-expect.

Troubles and *The Siege of Krishnapur* belong to the same period of Farrell's development: Irish references throng *The Siege of Krishnapur* just as Indian references crowd *Troubles*; and they share an essentially similar method and humour, though *Siege* has perhaps a greater narrative drive. Will the garrison be rescued from the mutinying sepoys who besiege it? Which of the well-bred English ladies and gentlemen will find the resources to survive in this extreme situation? What cost will they have paid? Farrell acknowledges the courage and passionate sincerity of that absurd little British band of Empire-builders who argue about Progress, Religion, and Technology surrounded by a vastly hostile human and physical environment.

In *The Singapore Grip*, too, Farrell explores the conflict of values. Tactfully, he points up the irony that the capitalism which has created Singapore also prevents it, by its shortsightedness, exploitativeness, and divisiveness, from uniting against the Japanese. What emerges is a new kind of novel for Farrell, not as interested in comedy, but of greater narrative range, complexity, and power. It is not as great an achievement as either *Troubles* or *The Siege of Krishnapur* but it marked a new stage in Farrell's development and promised an even larger artistic success—a promise that was betrayed by Farrell's death.

His three great novels were meticulously and thoroughly researched; but facts turn in Farrell's hands into wonderfully tall stories, shot through with the exotic colours of fairytale and the uproarious absurdity of slapstick. Farrell believed that people had, generally, already made up their minds about the present; the only means by which they could be led to alter their views was through a consideration of the past. The grim attrition of human hopes by vast and impersonal historical forces which are not even comprehended by his protagonists and actors is meant to hammer home a single vision: "the bitter-sweet knowledge that nothing is invulnerable to growth, decay and death, not even one's most fiercely guarded

memories." Farrell works by an Eastern and Irish exaggeration that scoffs at the manifestations of the Raj, whether in Ireland, India, or Singapore. And the Raj itself comes to symbolise all human pride and achievement. Nothing escapes the contemptuous probing of Farrell's scalpel—science and reason, statistics and religion, technology and sex, black men and white men: "the poor are just as stupid as the rich." But when the rot has been smilingly exposed, the reader realizes with a shock that Farrell still loves everything—the attractive exterior as much as the decaying interior—with a Buddhistic or Christian compassion. Farrell's artistic and life-sustaining affection as much as this demolition by artistic fiat of the 20th century's technological and civilized towers of Babel are, eventually, much more religious than Farrell realized or perhaps would have wished to recognize.

When Farrell's humour faltered, his art remained, though it was not enough to sustain his life. Readers will remain grateful to the life for the art; whether they are reduced to what he had left for solace depends on whether they seek, and whether they find, any substitute for the assumptions and methodology of the modern world and all its works, which Farrell rejected so thoroughly and persuasively.

—Prabhu S. Guptara

GARDNER, John (Champlin, Jr.). American. Born in Batavia, New York, 21 July 1933. Educated at DePauw University, Greencastle, Indiana, 1951–53; Washington University, St. Louis, A.B. 1955; University of Iowa (Woodrow Wilson Fellow, 1955–56), M.A. 1956, Ph.D. 1958. Married 1) Joan Louise Patterson in 1953, two children; 2) Liz Rosenberg in 1980. Taught at Oberlin College, Ohio, 1958–59; California State University, Chico, 1959–62, and San Francisco, 1962–65; Southern Illinois University, Carbondale, 1965–74; Bennington College, Vermont, 1974–76; Williams College, Williamstown, Massachusetts, and Skidmore College, Saratoga Springs, New York, 1976–77; George Mason University, Fairfax, Virginia, 1977–78; Member of the English Department, State University of New York, Binghamton, 1978–82. Visiting Professor, University of Detroit, 1970–71, and Northwestern University, Evanston, Illinois, 1973. Editor, *MSS*, and Southern Illinois University Press Literary Structures series. Recipient: Danforth fellowship, 1970; National Endowment for the Arts grant, 1972; American Academy award, 1975; National Book Critics Circle award, 1976. *Died 14 September 1982.*

PUBLICATIONS

Novels

The Resurrection.   New York, New American Library, 1966.
The Wreckage of Agathon.   New York, Harper, 1970.
Grendel.   New York, Knopf, 1971; London, Deutsch, 1972.
The Sunlight Dialogues.   New York, Knopf, 1972; London, Cape, 1973.
Jason and Medeia (novel in verse).   New York, Knopf, 1973.
Nickel Mountain: A Pastoral Novel.   New York, Knopf, 1973; London, Cape, 1974.
October Light.   New York, Knopf, 1976; London, Cape, 1977.
In the Suicide Mountains.   New York, Knopf, 1977.

Freddy's Book. New York, Knopf, 1980; London, Secker and Warburg, 1981.
Vlemk, The Box-Painter. Northridge, California, Lord John Press, 1980.
Mickelsson's Ghosts. New York, Knopf, and London, Secker and Warburg, 1982.

Short Stories

The King's Indian: Stories and Tales. New York, Knopf, 1974; London, Cape, 1975.
The Art of Living and Other Stories. New York, Knopf, 1981; London, Secker and Warburg, 1983.

Plays

William Wilson (libretto). Dallas, New London Press, 1978.
Three Libretti (includes *William Wilson, Frankenstein, Rumpelstiltskin*). Dallas, New London Press, 1979.

Verse

Poems. Northridge, California, Lord John Press, 1978.

Other

The Gawain-Poet. Lincoln, Nebraska, Cliff's Notes, 1967.
Le Mort Darthur. Lincoln, Nebraska, Cliff's Notes, 1967.
The Construction of the Wakefield Cycle. Carbondale, Southern Illinois University Press, 1974.
Dragon, Dragon and Other Timeless Tales (for children). New York, Knopf, 1975.
The Construction of Christian Poetry in Old English. Carbondale, Southern Illinois University Press, 1975.
Gudgekin the Thistle Girl and Other Tales (for children). New York, Knopf, 1976.
A Child's Bestiary (for children). New York, Knopf, 1977.
The Poetry of Chaucer. Carbondale, Southern Illinois University Press, 1977.
The Life and Times of Chaucer. New York, Knopf, and London, Cape, 1977.
The King of the Hummingbirds and Other Tales (for children). New York, Knopf, 1977.
On Moral Fiction. New York, Basic Books, 1978.
On Becoming a Novelist. New York, Harper, 1983.
The Art of Fiction: Notes on Craft for Young Writers. New York, Knopf, 1984.

Editor, with Lennis Dunlap, *The Forms of Fiction.* New York, Random House, 1962.
Editor, *The Complete Works of the Gawain-Poet in a Modern English Version with a Critical Introduction.* Chicago, University of Chicago Press, 1965.
Editor, with Nicholas Joost, *Papers on the Art and Age of Geoffrey Chaucer.* Edwardsville, Southern Illinois University Press, 1967.
Editor, *The Alliterative Morte Arthure, The Owl and the Nightingale, and Five Other Middle English Poems, in a Modernized Version, with Comments on the Poems, and Notes.* Carbondale, Southern Illinois University Press, 1971.
Editor, with Shannon Ravenel, *The Best American Short Stories 1982.* Boston, Houghton Mifflin, 1982.

Translator, with Nobuko Tsukui, *Tengu Child,* by Kikuo Itaya. Carbondale, Southern Illinois University Press, 1983.

Translator, with John Maier, *Gilgamesh.* New York, Knopf, 1984.

*

Bibliography: *John Gardner: A Bibliographical Profile* by John M. Howell, Carbondale, Southern Illinois University Press, 1980; *John Gardner: An Annotated Secondary Bibliography* by Robert A. Morace, New York, Garland, 1984.

Critical Studies: *John Gardner: Critical Perspectives* edited by Robert A. Morace and Kathryn VanSpanckeren, Carbondale, Southern Illinois University Press, 1982; *Arches and Light: The Fiction of John Gardner* by David Cowart, Carbondale, Southern Illinois University Press, 1983; *A World of Order and Light: The Fiction of John Gardner* by Gregory L. Morris, Athens, University of Georgia Press, 1984.

*   *   *

When John Gardner was killed in a motorcycle accident at the age of 49, he was one of the most widely read writers of his generation, and was in many quarters already considered a major American novelist. Gardner's canon divides into three modes: what he called "the older literature," that is, his scholarly studies of medieval and classical works, and, secondly, contemporary fictions, that is, his New England novels and stories, plus a third domain comprising his own fictive creations on the older literary models. As well as one of the most prominent novelists of his generation in America, Gardner was an accomplished and respected medieval scholar, literary critic, and historian, and, in the decade before his death, spokesman for the moral responsibilities of modern art.

To Gardner the medieval and modern periods are similar ages of ambiguity and uncertainty, and of menace to traditional values from crumbling ethical standards. He said that in writing medieval biography he used novelistic techniques to heighten effects, but as a critic "writing about Chaucer's poetry, on the other hand, I use the second side of a novelist's brain—the lobe that calculates and squints, studies older literature in hopes of understanding its methods and purposes with the greatest possible accuracy, perhaps so that someday, when it seems convenient, the novelist can steal them" (preface to *The Poetry of Chaucer*). His thefts are frequent and often brilliant enrichments of modern fiction with medieval, especially Chaucerian, techniques of structure, paradox, verbal characterization, allusive reflexivity, and dense subtextual interplay between philosophical and theological traditions.

Often irradiated with the myths and the heroic ethos of the medievals, every Gardner work is built upon a dualism that slowly either unravels or fuses, ending on one or more flawed samaritans doing their best to act responsibly in an incomprehensible world. Relative to that world, there is true moral grandeur in their pained discovery that the only answer to their many questions is somehow themselves, their individual response to their own perplexity. The pervasiveness of the Gardner dualism is apparent in his titles, obvious in *Jason and Medeia* and *The Sunlight Dialogues* wherein two characters begin in opposition but gradually exchange attributes, more subtle in *Grendel* and "The King's Indian" wherein the monster assimilates many of Beowulf's qualities like the "indian" his king's. The dissolving dualisms (culture and anarchy, youth and age, saintliness and criminality, desire and fear, wisdom and madness, ethics and amorality) seem designed to undermine easy certainties, forcing his characters to recognize their common humanity and mortality when faced with "emptiness," the bewildering and often frightening "painful universe" devoid of permanence, structure, and absolutes. Their courage and compassion save them, indeed ennoble them, in the brutal social and natural worlds whose cruelty only moral decency and the redemptive power of art can withstand.

The first novels concern a lone figure facing his nemesis (often death) in near solitude, in a room or a cell from which he rarely wanders. Gardner unpacks this tight structure in the works of the early 1970's, extending it into whole social panoramas of characters. He sometimes returned to it in the later works, wherein the social extension enters through intercalated novels being read or written by his solitaries in flight from the world that continues to fascinate them.

Increasingly divided in their assessment of his works since 1972, a division deepened by Gardner's long essay *On Moral Fiction*, almost all his readers nevertheless agree that *The Resurrection* and *The Wreckage of Agathon* are flawed beginnings of the novelistic mastery achieved in *Grendel* and *The Sunlight Dialogues*.

The first two novels exhibit Gardner's two creative modes: *The Resurrection* a contemporary fiction in what was to become his typical harsh New England landscape, *The Wreckage of Agathon* a virtuoso's tour de force in classical Greek history. James Chandler, Yankee philosopher facing death as mortal illness, and Agathon, Greek philosopher facing death as political imprisonment while dying, both reconsider their lives and question whether there is any cause for which they lived or now die. Through stages of, respectively, rather ponderous pessimism dwelling on the dehumanizing effects of technology without conscience, and a bawdy cynicism enraged at the trampling of humanistic values by the imperialistic police state (sometimes awkward metaphors for Gardner's America of 1966 and of 1970), both philosophers pass from thinking themselves wasted dupes to affirming the values their society abuses, vaguely humanistic ones of compassion and charity that appear "frail" and the already distinct treasure of humanizing art. These are the works of a young man already sure of his thematic concerns and commanding an awesome knowledge of western cultural history, which, as yet, remains something of the scholar's encrustation on the novelist's work.

No such disjunction remains in *Grendel*, Gardner's second tour de force in historical literary imagination but a fully achieved monologue presenting "the other side of the story" of the Beowulf epic. There remains some metaphorical relevance to America's "civilizing" of the Vietnam barbarian, but Gardner's primary emphasis is upon history, the Beowulf-Grendel contest as the keystone of Anglo-Saxon literary and, he implies, ethical traditions. It is a superb conception, effected with flawless control of technique, rhetorical range, tonal shadows and rhythms. That classic monster of western civilization, Grendel emerges in monologue as an endearingly haunted and sorrowing beast fascinated with the agile articulations of human speech and song, and with his own innate need to kill it or make it kill him in celebration of its stupid ignorance of him: "'Theories,' I whisper to the bloodstained ground." Grendel is the first victim of civilization's "progress," the sacrificial animal in whose slaughter we try as a society to eradicate our primitive being so splendidly outlaw and naive. It is just as important to note that Grendel is *good* as to note that he is insufficient. We are Beowulf also, through his history that we inherit and re-enact every day as a soulless society, though Gardner implies that we must pause, listen to our dragons. Grendel is a heart in duel with mere mind.

The cavernous heart is Gardner's narrative field for *The Sunlight Dialogues*, as extended over dozens of characters in Batavia, New York. The placid little society is splendidly individuated, each character speaking in Chaucerian precision the language of his station or milieu. The bumbling antagonist Police Chief Fred Clumly has managed to maintain himself in ill health and ill marriage, and to preserve the public peace despite the minor infractions typical to suburban life, until the dazzling advent of the Sunlight Man. Half brilliant and half mad, part anarchist and part saint, puzzling combination of con man and magician, the Sunlight Man was born in the town and now returns "from nowhere" to wreak death and havoc. Ostensibly a political saboteur (later revealed to be the past victim of a brutal act in the town), he gradually resembles more and more—in the lengthy dialogues with Clumly—the medieval jester as professional disturber of the moral peace, stripping away masks of hypocrisy and habit and "theoretical" order, revealing bigotry, moral corruption, callous brutality, human exploitation and sufferings. When not in dialogue, the novel consists in Clumly's and the town's long hunt to imprison the Sunlight Man, who in the end—partly because of a moment's panic—is shot through the heart. "God forgive us!" someone shouts, and Clumly affirms, "Correct." All return to lives indelibly altered. The Sunlight Man is another, one of the best, of Gardner's brilliant genius-philosophers, no longer in solitary retreat but brought into the midst of the society that he disrupts and instructs.

Grendel and the Sunlight Man are extraordinary creations and curiously opposite, a gentle brute crouched in shadow sorrowfully listening to human song and a mad caustic genius illumining vice and virtue with the skill of a Socrates, opposites eloquent of Gardner's protean imagination.

Most of his finest subsequent work remains focused upon middling lives against the New England landscape, increasingly restricted to a single rural building in a cold autumn, and often to a male-female couple. *Nickel Mountain* concerns the stoic despair and rejuvenation of Henry Soames, middle-aged overweight proprietor of the diner where he meets and marries young Callie, in a samaritan act that becomes love, and tenderly devotes himself to her and her illegitimate son. The somber shadow of Nickel Mountain dominates the valley and the other, similarly quiet groping lives of minor characters, all "nicked" (thwarted, harmed, even maimed) by unaccountable chance accidents or needless misfortunes, all bound in a common struggle for calm and rest. *October Light* is the violent, raging counterweight to that "Pastoral Novel": the couple are octogenarian brother and sister in desperate, often comic grotesque struggle to smash each other to death with apple crates or rifle butts or anything else they can wield with feeble old arms and failing eyes. In recurrent ire at the modern world, cantankerous old James blasts his sister's television with his shotgun and imprisons her in her bedroom with one of her trashy novels about sexual liberation and the women's movement. Alternately, the characters rail and muse in monologue, and we learn the tragic history of guilt and suicide that links his dead son with her dead husband, and the ghastly desire for vengeance in blind expiation. Their conflict, which has been called a psychomachy of the Protestant soul, is echoed in the lives of minor characters. These are both the spurned peacemakers who visit, and especially the zany cast of the dime novel *The Lost Souls of Smuggler's Rock*, concerning three sexually liberated gangs of interracial marijuana smugglers in orgiastic outlawry—James's and Sally's unrepressed violence writ large. The lurid intercalations reflexively situate James and Sally as contemporary America's ancestors still battling away at each other in guilty rage and tears, as the younger generation in delusions of progress continues reenacting the old tragedy of selfish and loveless lives. Though *Nickel Mountain* and *October Light* are Gardner's most naturalistic novels in conception as in technique, they are eerily pendant to one another, the first an almost serene moral odyssey through self-sacrifice and love, the second a grotesque paralysis in history and hatred.

Freddy's Book attempts for the first time, in perhaps experimental ways, to bring together many of Gardner's anterior motifs and techniques, most notably the monster-pariah, the intercalated fiction, the mad denunciatory genius, and especially Gardner's own alternation between contemporary and historical modes. History Professor Jack Winesap recounts accepting an invitation from an old historian to visit his home where his son ("I have a son who's a monster") has locked himself in his room and writes a strange book that perhaps the professor can understand. He arrives during a blizzard, meets the obese eight-foot Freddy, and begins the manuscript, *King Gustav and the Devil*, a crowded murky tale set in 16th-century Sweden, in which an upright knight manages finally to vanquish the Devil. Gardner ends on that slaying without return to the framing tale of Winesap and Freddy, and thus without clarifying its reflexive significance.

Disappointed readers of *Freddy's Book* often alluded to the essay *On Moral Fiction* by way of confirming a "slackening" of Gardner's powers as novelist and critic. But the opposite case might be made that, taken together, the two works show a gifted novelist reassessing his role and attempting finally to unite his many voices. The essay is his historical review of literature's great "moral artists" from Homer, Dante, and Tolstoy through Malamud, Bellow, Guy Davenport, Eudora Welty, that is, artists with an affirming belief in and sympathy for human possibility. The essay is marred by exaggerated counter-critiques of the "despair" promoted by Mailer, Barth, Heller, Updike, Coover, Vonnegut, Roth. "My position is not Christian," he said in an interview. "It's simpler than that. Art, like medicine, should support what's healthy. It shouldn't support despair. Is that old hat? Of course it is, outrageously so. We're getting so caught up in our complete moral corruption that we can't see what's happening." Few writers write so candidly about their own contemporaries, and Gardner provoked the very arguments that undoubtedly he sought.

At the height of that controversy, which Gardner certainly did not start in American letters but did much to intensify, he published *Mickelsson's Ghosts*, a brilliantly crafted novel that may be his finest work. Its intricate construction in multiple characterological perspectives makes it a difficult novel, invoking major philosophical and theological traditions, and achieving dramatic synthesis of Gardner's anterior moral concerns by, instead of casting them in symbolic actions among unlettered characters, treating them directly in the person of Mickelsson, a professional philosopher. Mickelsson is an ethicist, university professor, and renowned author, reader of Martin Luther and Nietzsche in particular. He inhabits the world that Nietzsche foretold as ensuing upon the death of God. Ethical standards have now entirely crumbled, and there is no way to *know* when an act is right or wrong, such as religious or political worship or murder, abortion, euthanasia, nuclear defense, all the issues that (bespoken by various characters) are ripping up traditions and therefore lives. Mickelsson is Mind that has failed: in the opening scene he is a divorced despairing drunk, using all our intellectual heritage to try to make sense of his personal anguish, and using his considerable powers of social analysis to determine why—as it seems—everyone has lost the sense of community and the old sure ways past fear and ignorance, which now in social isolates are becoming destructive rage or whimpering helplessness. American governments, religions, corporations (not universities, small towns, and other institutions based upon mutual care and work) have swollen into destructive monsters killing overtly: both the angry and the helpless dupe themselves in

obeying, thus engorging the new social monster half seriously tagged "the Reich," capable now of nuclear holocaust and toxic slaughter. Mickelsson is not taken in by any of it, as his razor logic slashes frauds everywhere, but in his way he was as guilty: he thought, he did not feel, "he'd failed, loved feebly." Still this despairing ethicist who jeers at everybody struggles to "choose right conduct, will the higher man's self-mastery," to reconcile the dualisms that bedevil him, such as the false peace of airy reason and the false peace of manual labor, the mad thirst for truths and the violent loathing for such a stupid quest. Renovating an old house and (perhaps) meeting its ghosts along with his own childhood memories and deepest feelings, Mickelsson comes to accept the multiple puzzle of himself and of the diverse human experience of time and space; and to return love as help in need and loneliness, joining a woman's tiny skirmish with oppressive dupery; all this by enforcing the mind's ideals in service of the heart's needs in what Gardner once terms "holy stupidity." Grotesque and tattered at the end, Mickelsson has indeed lost his philosopher's soul but gained the world, as community, in joining a few fellow humans in need.

Until his sudden death three months after the publication of *Mickelsson's Ghosts*, Gardner was considered a young novelist with many books ahead of him. Shocked reassessments of his canon expressed both surprise at rediscovering what a fine writer he was and, in some circles, the perennial critic's regret that the writer did not live up to the "promise" bestowed upon him, failing to write the kinds of books he was expected to write. Such recent novels as *Freddy's Book* had seemed murkey and leaden, and *Mickelsson's Ghosts* first received cool if not patronizing reviews as more of the same. As time passes and perspectives lengthen over the whole of Gardner's canon, *Mickelsson's Ghosts* is beginning to be seen as very good Gardner indeed and perhaps a major American novel.

His influence like his reputation will be lasting and steady, if not increasing, but never widespread. Unlike that of most learned novelists such as his beloved Samuel Beckett, Gardner's erudition requires of the reader more than nodding acquaintance with his sources. For the reader without grounding in the lives and works of Aristotle, Martin Luther, Nietzsche, and Wittgenstein, Mickelsson's anguished throes of ethical theory fall flat. One principal difficulty is that Gardner refuses to turn our intellectual and theological heritage to complete derision; whereas in Beckett the bitter jokes are wondrously clear, even if we do not quite get the abstruse allusions to Descartes and Spinoza, in Gardner we must laugh at their ridiculous extremes while appreciating their small but unique contribution to this vast human quest to understand ourselves. History is not dead in Gardner's world, as it is for many readers, nor is reason or logic ever merely ridiculous in a world where Nietzsche's madness equates with a whore's anguish over abortion or the perplexity of a thief robbed. Gardner asks us to care about our heritage of civilization, to know it, and to use it in our effort to understand the pain of one another.

In one of his few comic works, "The King's Indian," the jaunty narrator has a somber moment: "Caught up in a destinal vortex somehow of our own mad construction we'd intellected Eden to a soot-dark Foundry ...," Foundries are in the nature of modern life, Gardner knew, but it is the *intellection* of Eden into brutal exploitation that appalls him, that killed Grendel and the Sunlight Man, that menaced Freddy's fiction neatly divided into God and Devil with man vacillating between them, that threatened to defeat the philosopher Mickelsson, howling heroically for life in his "holy stupidity." In Freddy's text, "everything's the work of the Devil," ponders a Bishop, wondering how it is possible to enact the "commandments of a god who has not spoken to anyone sane for fifteen centuries?" Gardner's answer was always clear: by attending "the cavernous heart," eliding intellection for the more primitive and enduring human elements of lonely compassion and quiet courageous persistence past nature's hazards and society's nihilism.

—Jan Hokenson

JONES, James. American. Born in Robinson, Illinois, 6 November 1921. Educated at the University of Hawaii, Honolulu, 1942; New York University, 1945. Served in the United States Army, 1939–44: Bronze Star; Purple Heart. Married Gloria Mosolino in 1957; one son and one daughter. Lived in Paris, 1958–74. Writer-in-Residence, Florida International University, Miami, 1974–77. Recipient: National Book Award, 1952. *Died 9 May 1977.*

PUBLICATIONS

Novels

From Here to Eternity.   New York, Scribner, 1951; London, Collins, 1952.
Some Came Running.   New York, Scribner, 1957; London, Collins, 1959.
The Pistol.   New York, Scribner, and London, Collins, 1959.
The Thin Red Line.   New York, Scribner, 1962; London, Collins, 1963.
Go to the Widow-Maker.   New York, Delacorte Press, and London, Collins, 1967.
The Merry Month of May.   New York, Delacorte Press, and London, Collins, 1971.
A Touch of Danger.   New York, Doubleday, and London, Collins, 1973.
Whistle: A Work-in-Progress.   Bloomfield Hills, Michigan, Bruccoli Clark, 1974; complete version, as *Whistle*, New York, Delacorte Press, and London, Collins, 1978.

Short Stories

The Ice-Cream Headache and Other Stories.   New York, Delacorte Press, and London, Collins, 1968.

Uncollected Short Story

"Million-Dollar Wound," in *Esquire* (New York), November 1977.

Play

Screenplay: *The Longest Day*, with others, 1962.

Other

Viet Journal.   New York, Delacorte Press, 1974.
WWII, with Art Weithas.   New York, Grosset and Dunlap, and London, Cooper, 1975.

*

Bibliography: *James Jones: A Checklist* by John R. Hopkins, Detroit, Gale, 1974.

Critical Studies: *James Jones: A Friendship* by Willie Morris, New York, Doubleday, 1978; *James Jones* by James R. Giles, Boston, Twayne, 1981; *James Jones* by George Garrett, New York, Harcourt Brace, 1984; *Into Eternity: James Jones: The Life of an American Writer* by Frank MacShane, Boston, Houghton Mifflin, 1985.

*   *   *

When James Jones died in 1977, he had completed all but a few pages of *Whistle*, the last novel of the military trilogy that also includes *From Here to Eternity* and *The Thin Red Line*. It is now clear that his work was unevenly divided between these books and those in which he ventured uneasily into the swamps of civilian life. The army was home and family to Jones. He wrote about it as his contemporaries wrote about their childhoods and their marriages. The war was only the major episode in his trilogy; his abiding subject was the brotherhood of infantrymen. His tragedy was the disposal of his company by bullets and, more devastatingly, rehabilitation, reassignment, and discharge. The increasing eroticism in his fiction—a relentless summary of acts and gratifications—surely follows from his failure to find anywhere else the belief and loyalty that vanished when his company broke up.

Jones's greatest achievement was to portray infantrymen realistically and mythically, as he did best in *From Here to Eternity* and *The Thin Red Line*. Private Prewitt and Sergeant Warden are gentlemen rankers, enlisted *men*, on Oahu before Pearl Harbor. Their manhood is defined by their acceptance of discipline and military organization and by their reaction to any circumstance that threatens that acceptance. Duty, for Prewitt, does not include becoming one of the company jocks; it is, for Warden, the unsentimental command and care of a hundred and sixty men. The men of *The Thin Red Line*, a tough unit in a Pacific island campaign, are Warden's old company with curt new names—Welsh, Witt, Land—because Prewitt, indispensable as a character in the unfolding trilogy, had been killed off in Hawaii. The novel is "cheerfully dedicated to those greatest and most heroic of all human endeavors, WAR and WARFARE," and Jones, while intentionally ironic, obviously believed that they were second greatest and most heroic after the mere existence of the company itself. It is a more disciplined, less engaging novel than the first. The coherence of combat episodes deters Jones from his characteristic indulgence in catalogues of stray information. The plot consists of several men in the company being tested from moment to moment. It has the harrowing physical detail of Mailer's *The Naked and the Dead* with only those overtones that come out of the dedication.

Whistle came 15 years later, although, as Jones told his friend Willie Morris, it had been "turning on its spit in my head for nearly thirty years." The obsession has left its mark on a book in which Jones's view of the company is his despairing commentary on human existence at the same time that it is a case study of his writing defects. His fictional army company is finished with Winch (Welsh, Warden) in a padded cell, Prell (Witt, Prewitt) killed again, and Strange (Land, Stark) slipping over the side of a troop transport in mid-Atlantic incapable of moving on with a new company. He adds a significant new character in Landers, drafted out of college to become thoroughly absorbed in the company at the moment of its annihilation. Even comfortable middle-class adolescents, Jones suggests, will jump at the chance to leave all other ties for the shreds of a real unit. But in sealing the integrity of Jones's 30-year vision of the company, *Whistle* becomes like his later novels of civilian life. As in *Go to the Widow-Maker* and *The*

Merry Month of May, the effort to understand what is going on in the world gives way to a monotonous record of sexual gratification. That oral copulation is the supreme experience in his later novels seems only the logical development of Jones's thesis that his people have nothing left to seek or prove. It was ironic that a man who was as consumed by his own work as Jones was—swept up by it not long after he left the army—could not himself write about occupations and trades outside the work details that came with military service.

When he published *Some Came Running* in 1957, Jones proclaimed himself, like Don Quixote, "at last free from the damnable books of romance." He was free, actually, to attempt the insuperable task of portraying a man like himself, loose at home in the United States during the interval between World War II and the Korean War. Nothing can help Dave Hirsch write his book, just as nothing can prevent Frank Hirsch from building his shopping center. One estranged brother drifts among fellow isolates in his Illinois town, while the other is the advance guard of franchised, astroturfed America. Numbingly long, the novel still towers over *Go to the Widow-Maker* and *The Merry Month of May*. The latter novel was set during the French student revolts of 1968. Everyone seems to be sympathizing with the students, but it is soon clear that Jones himself thinks they are as foolish as their old-fashioned liberal parents. Worse, they are incompetent. In the family struggle which accompanies the strikes, the son is no match for his father in assertiveness, and the final, exclusive pursuit of the perfect orgasm. Again, Jones dismisses civilian complexity to court the ecstasy that the narrator of *The Merry Month of May* calls "happy elation."

The best of James Jones came in *From Here to Eternity* and *The Thin Red Line* before his company broke ranks.

—David Sanders

KEROUAC, Jack. American. Born Jean Louis Lebris de Kerouac in Lowell, Massachusetts, 12 March 1922. Educated at Lowell High School; Horace Mann School, New York, 1939–40; Columbia University, New York, 1940–41, 1942. Served in the United States Merchant Marine, 1942, 1943, and United States Navy, 1943. Married 1) Edie Parker in 1944 (annulled, 1945); 2) Joan Haverty in 1950 (divorced), one daughter; 3) Stella Sampas in 1966. Sports reporter, *Lowell Sun*, 1942; became a writer after the war, supporting himself by various odd jobs; worked as brakeman with the Southern Pacific Railroad, San Francisco, 1952–53; travelled throughout the United States and Mexico, 1953–56; fire lookout for the United States Agricultural Service in Washington state, 1956; full-time writer from 1957. *Died 21 October 1969.*

PUBLICATIONS

Novels

The Town and the City (as John Kerouac). New York, Harcourt Brace, 1950; London, Eyre and Spottiswoode, 1951.
On the Road. New York, Viking Press, 1957; London, Deutsch, 1958; edited by Scott Donaldson, Viking Press, 1978.
The Subterraneans. New York, Grove Press, 1958; London, Deutsch, 1960.

The Dharma Bums. New York, Viking Press, 1958; London, Deutsch, 1959.
Doctor Sax: Faust Part Three. New York, Grove Press, 1959; London, Evergreen, 1961.
Maggie Cassidy. New York, Avon, 1959; London, Panther, 1960.
Excerpts from "Visions of Cody." New York, New Directions, 1959.
Tristessa. New York, Avon, 1960.
Book of Dreams. San Francisco, City Lights, 1960.
Big Sur. New York, Farrar Straus, 1962; London, Deutsch, 1963.
Visions of Gerard. New York, Farrar Straus, 1963.
Visions of Gerard, and Tristessa. London, Deutsch, 1964.
Desolation Angels. New York, Coward McCann, 1965; London, Deutsch, 1966.
Satori in Paris. New York, Grove Press, 1966; London, Deutsch, 1967.
Vanity of Duluoz: An Adventurous Education 1935–46. New York, Coward McCann, 1968; London, Deutsch, 1969.
Pic. New York, Grove Press, 1971.
Visions of Cody. New York, McGraw Hill, and London, Deutsch, 1973.
Pic, and The Subterraneans. London, Deutsch, 1973.

Short Stories

Two Early Stories. New York, Aloe Editions, 1973.

Play

Pull My Daisy (screenplay). New York, Grove Press, 1961; London, Evergreen, 1961.

Screenplay: *Pull My Daisy*, 1959.

Verse

Mexico City Blues. New York, Grove Press, 1959.
Hymn—God Pray for Me. Privately printed, 1959.
Rimbaud. San Francisco, City Lights, 1960.
The Scripture of the Golden Eternity. New York, Totem-Corinth, 1960.
Poem. Privately printed, 1962.
A Pun for Al Gelpi. Privately printed, 1966.
Hugo Weber. New York, Portents, 1967.
Someday You'll Be Lying. Privately printed, 1968.
A Last Haiku. Privately printed, 1969.
Scattered Poems. San Francisco, City Lights, 1971.
Trip, Trap: Haiku along the Road from San Francisco to New York, 1959, with Albert Saijo and Lew Welch. Bolinas, California, Grey Fox Press, 1973.
Heaven and Other Poems, edited by Donald Allen. Bolinas, California, Grey Fox Press, 1977.

Other

Lonesome Traveler, drawings by Larry Rivers. New York, McGraw Hill, 1960; London, Deutsch, 1962.
Old Angel Midnight. Albion, New York, Booklegger, n.d.; Carmarthen, Unicorn Bookshop, 1976.
Dear Carolyn (letters to Carolyn Cassady), edited by Arthur and Kit Knight. California, Pennsylvania, TUVOTI, 1983.

*

Bibliography: *A Bibliography of Works by Jack Kerouac (Jean Louis de Kerouac) 1939–1967* by Ann Charters, New York,

Phoenix Book Shop, 1967, revised edition, 1975; *Jack Kerouac: An Annotated Bibliography of Secondary Sources 1944–1979* by Robert J. Milewski, Metuchen, New Jersey, Scarecrow Press, 1981.

Critical Studies: *No Pie in the Sky: The Hobo as American Cultural Hero in the Works of Jack London, John Dos Passos, and Jack Kerouac* by Frederick Feied, New York, Citadel Press, 1964; *Kerouac: A Biography* by Ann Charters, San Francisco, Straight Arrow, 1973, London, Deutsch, 1974; *Kerouac's Town* by Barry Gifford, Santa Barbara, California, Capra Press, 1973, revised edition, Berkeley, California, Creative Arts, 1977, and *Jack's Book: An Oral Biography* by Gifford and Lawrence Lee, New York, St. Martin's Press, 1978, London, Hamish Hamilton, 1979; *Visions of Kerouac* by Charles E. Jarvis, Lowell, Massachusetts, Ithaca Press, 1974; *Heart Beat: My Life with Jack and Neal* by Carolyn Cassady, Berkeley, California, Creative Arts, 1976; *Jack Kerouac, Prophet of the New Romanticism: A Critical Study* by Robert A. Hipkiss, Lawrence, Regents Press of Kansas, 1976; *Jack Kerouac: The New Picaroon* by Luc Gaffié, New York, Postillion Press, 1977; *Jack Kerouac* by Harry Russell Huebel, Boise, Idaho, Boise State University, 1979; *Desolate Angel: Jack Kerouac, The Beats, and America* by Dennis McNally, New York, Random House, 1979; *Kerouac's Crooked Road: The Development of a Fiction* by Tim Hunt, Hamden, Connecticut, Shoe String Press, 1981; *The Kerouac We Knew: Unposed Portraits, Action Shots* edited by John Montgomery, Kentfield, California, Fels and Firn Press, 1982; *Memory Babe: A Critical Biography of Jack Kerouac* by Gerald Nicosia, New York, Grove Press, 1983, London, Viking, 1985; "Jack Kerouac Issue" of *Review of Contemporary Fiction* (Elmwood Park, Illinois), vol. 3, no. 2, 1983; *Jack Kerouac* by Tom Clark, New York, Harcourt Brace, 1984; *Quest for Kerouac* by Chris Challis, London, Faber, 1984; *Jack Kerouac* by Warren French, Boston, Twayne, 1986.

Theatrical Activities:
Actor: **Film**—*Pull My Daisy*, 1959.

*   *   *

Regarded in modern American fiction as the authentic voice of the "beat generation," Jack Kerouac thought of himself as a story teller in the innovative tradition of Proust and Joyce. He was an authentic original, writing with the same idealism as Emerson, Thoreau, Melville, and Whitman, reasserting the American dream of romantic individualism in each of his published books, which he regarded as one vast autobiographical statement.

Twelve of these books comprise "The Legend of Duluoz," or "The Legend of Kerouac," his fictional autobiography, one of the most ambitious projects conceived by any modern writer. Kerouac intended in his old age to gather these books together under uniform binding and insert the real names of his contemporaries into the narratives, so that his larger design might be more apparent. His first published novel, *The Town and the City*, was based on the model of Thomas Wolfe, and Kerouac later dismissed it as a fiction written before he found his own voice. The autobiographical "Legend of Duluoz" begins with the novel *Visions of Gerard*, which describes the first years of Kerouac's Catholic French-Canadian childhood

in Lowell and the death of his brother Gerard in 1926, when Jack was four years old. *Doctor Sax* is a fantasy of memories and dreams about his boyhood (1930–36) in Lowell with an imaginary companion Doctor Sax, like the pulp magazine hero The Shadow, the champion of Good in a mythic battle against the forces of Evil. *Maggie Cassidy* is a more realistic novel about his adolescence in high school and his first love (1938–39). *Vanity of Duluoz* describes his years playing football at prep school and Columbia College, and his experience in the merchant marine and Navy during World War II. It was during these years (1939–46) that Kerouac met Allen Ginsberg and William Burroughs, named "Irwin Garden" and "Will Hubbard" in the novel. *On the Road*, Kerouac's most popular book, begins with his meeting the legendary Neal Cassady, called "Dean Moriarity" in the narrative, who took Kerouac ("Sal Paradise") on the road in 1947–50, hitch-hiking and riding buses and cars across the United States on a search for joyful adventure. In this book Ginsberg is "Carlo Marx," and Burroughs is "Old Bull Lee," *Visions of Cody* is what Kerouac called an "in-depth" description of this same period of his life with Cassady ("Cody Pomeray" here), a more richly humorous exercise in spontaneous prose extended narrative, considered too experimental to be published in its entirety during Kerouac's lifetime. *The Subterraneans* continues the autobiography as an intense account of an affair with a black girl in the summer of 1953; in this book Kerouac is "Leo Percepied," Ginsberg is "Adam Moorad," Burroughs is "Frank Carmody," and Gregory Corso is "Yuri Gligoric." In *Tristessa*, Kerouac describes a love affair in Mexico City during 1955–56, the same time period as *The Dharma Bums*. In *The Dharma Bums*, Kerouac ("Ray Smith") adventures in California with Ginsberg ("Alvah Goldbook"), Cassady ("Cody Pomeray"), Philip Whalen ("Warren Coughlin"), Michael McClure ("Ike O'Shay"), John Montgomery ("Henry Morely"), and Gary Snyder ("Japhy Ryder"), who taught Kerouac how to climb mountains and live as a Buddhist during the first year of the "Poetry Renaissance" in San Francisco. *Desolation Angels* picks up the narrative in 1956, where the previous book left off, and continues until Fall 1957, with the publication of *On the Road*, the novel that made Kerouac famous as the father of the "beats." *Big Sur* and *Satori in Paris* are the last books in the narrative of "The Legend of Duluoz," chronicling Kerouac's final years of alcoholism and anger at the media's distortion of his work and refusal to regard him as a serious writer.

The larger design in Kerouac's work, the integrity of his theme of individualism, his romantic optimism, and his reverence for life, as well as the humor of his novels and his remarkably abundant prose energy, were largely ignored by contemporary critics, intent upon ridiculing him as a hopelessly naive visionary or as an irresponsible "beatnik." Since his death in 1969, there has been more sympathy for his work, and greater awareness of the extent of the influence of his books on young readers. As Jess Ritter said in *The Vonnegut Statement*, "The great psychic migration of American youth since World War II can be charted by the novels they read and the novelists whose reputations they created. ... Kerouac and the Beats represent the psychic revolt of the 1950's." What has become increasingly clear in the last 30 years is that the fabric of American culture has never been the same since this revolt, since it represented a resurgence of the dominant thread of individualism that has been present in varying hues in the country's history since its beginnings. Jack Kerouac was as much an American idealist as Thoreau. What he said he wanted was the same hut as Thoreau's but in his hometown of Lowell, Massachusetts, not at Walden Pond. Something of a martyr—like Thoreau—in his own time, Jack Kerouac was a necessary hero who chronicled in his "Legend" the rewards and hazards of American romantic optimism in mid-20th century.

—Ann Charters

MACDONALD, Ross. Pseudonym for Kenneth Millar. American. Born in Los Gatos, California, 13 December 1915; brought up in Canada. Educated at the Kitchener-Waterloo Collegiate Institute, Ontario, graduated 1932; University of Western Ontario, London, 1933–38, B.A. (honors) 1938; University of Toronto, 1938–39; University of Michigan, Ann Arbor, 1941–44, 1948–49 (Graduate Fellow, 1941–42; Rackham Fellow, 1942–43), M.A. 1942, Ph.D. in English 1951. Served in the United States Naval Reserve, in the Pacific, 1944–46: Lieutenant Junior Grade. Married Margaret Sturm (i.e., Margaret Millar, *q.v.*) in 1938; one daughter (deceased). Teacher of English and History, Kitchener-Waterloo Collegiate Institute, 1939–41; Teaching Fellow, University of Michigan, 1942–44, 1948–49. Book reviewer, *San Francisco Chronicle*, 1957–60. Member, Board of Directors, 1960–61, 1964–65, and President, 1965, Mystery Writers of America. Recipient: Crime Writers Association Silver Dagger, 1965; University of Michigan Outstanding Achievement Award, 1972; Mystery Writers of America Grand Master Award, 1973; Popular Culture Association Award of Excellence, 1973; Private Eye Writers of America Life Achievement Award, 1981; Los Angeles *Times* Kirsch Award, 1982. *Died 11 July 1983.*
‹Alzheimers›

PUBLICATIONS

Novels

The Moving Target (as John Macdonald). New York, Knopf, 1949; London, Cassell, 1951; as *Harper*, New York, Pocket Books, 1966.
The Barbarous Coast. New York, Knopf, 1956; as John Ross Macdonald, London, Cassell, 1957.
The Doomsters. New York, Knopf, 1958; as John Ross Macdonald, London, Cassell, 1958.
The Galton Case. New York, Knopf, 1959; as John Ross Macdonald, London, Cassell, 1960.
The Ferguson Affair. New York, Knopf, 1960; London, Collins, 1961.
The Wycherly Woman. New York, Knopf, 1961; London, Collins, 1962.
The Zebra-Striped Hearse. New York, Knopf, 1962; London, Collins, 1963.
The Chill. New York, Knopf, and London, Collins, 1964.
The Far Side of the Dollar. New York, Knopf, and London, Collins, 1965.
Black Money. New York, Knopf, and London, Collins, 1966.
The Instant Enemy. New York, Knopf, and London, Collins, 1968.
The Goodbye Look. New York, Knopf, and London, Collins, 1969.
The Underground Man. New York, Knopf, and London, Collins, 1971.
Sleeping Beauty. New York, Knopf, and London, Collins, 1973.
The Blue Hammer. New York, Knopf, and London, Collins, 1976.

Novels as Kenneth Millar

The Dark Tunnel. New York, Dodd Mead, 1944; as *I Die Slowly*, London, Lion, 1955.
Trouble Follows Me. New York, Dodd Mead, 1946; as *Night Train*, London, Lion, 1955.
Blue City. New York, Knopf, 1947; London, Cassell, 1949.
The Three Roads. New York, Knopf, 1948; London, Cassell, 1950.

Novels as John Ross Macdonald

The Drowning Pool. New York, Knopf, 1950; as John Macdonald, London, Cassell, 1952.
The Way Some People Die. New York, Knopf, 1951; London, Cassell, 1953.
The Ivory Grin. New York, Knopf, 1952; London, Cassell, 1953; as *Marked for Murder*, New York, Pocket Books, 1953.
Meet Me at the Morgue. New York, Knopf, 1953; as *Experience with Evil*, Cassell, 1954.
Find a Victim. New York, Knopf, 1954; London, Cassell, 1955.

Short Stories

The Name Is Archer (as John Ross Macdonald). New York, Bantam, 1955.
Lew Archer, Private Investigator. Yonkers, New York, Mysterious Press, 1977.

Uncollected Short Stories

"Shock Treatment" (as Kenneth Millar), in *Manhunt* (New York), January 1953.
"Murder Is a Public Matter," in *Ellery Queen's Mystery Magazine* (New York), September 1959.
"Bring the Killer to Justice," in *Ellery Queen's Mystery Magazine* (New York), February 1962.
"The Singing Pigeon," in *Alfred Hitchcock Presents: A Month of Mystery.* New York, Random House, 1969.
"The Missing Sister Case," in *Ellery Queen's Champions of Mystery.* New York, Davis, 1977; London, Gollancz, 1978.

Uncollected Short Stories as John Ross Macdonald

"The Imaginary Blonde" February 1953, "The Guilty One" May 1953, "The Beat-Up Sister" October 1953, and "Bad Blood" April–May 1967, all in *Manhunt* (New York).

Other

On Crime Writing. Santa Barbara, California, Capra Press, 1973.
A Collection of Reviews. Northridge, California, Lord John Press, 1979.
Self-Portrait: Ceaselessly into the Past, edited by Ralph B. Sipper. Santa Barbara, California, Capra Press, 1981.

Editor, *Great Stories of Suspense.* New York, Knopf, 1974.

*

Bibliography: *Kenneth Millar/Ross Macdonald: A Descriptive Bibliography* by Matthew J. Bruccoli, Pittsburgh, University of Pittsburgh Press, 1983.

Manuscript Collection: University of California Library, Irvine.

Critical Studies: *Dreamers Who Live Their Dreams: The World of Ross Macdonald's Novels* by Peter Wolfe, Bowling Green, Ohio, Popular Press, 1976; *Ross Macdonald* by Jerry Speir, New York, Ungar, 1978; *Ross Macdonald/Kenneth Millar* by Matthew J. Bruccoli, New York, Harcourt Brace, 1984.

*   *   *

Now that his productive and painful life is over, literary critics may join with students of detective fiction in realizing that Ross Macdonald is one of the central authors of his time and place. Inheriting a wide variety of influences from a number of different sources in the past, his works provide an accurate and fascinating chronicle of the major preoccupations of contemporary America; it seems likely that future generations will read his fiction as we read, for example, Conan Doyle—to discover some important facts and truths about a bygone age. The complicated elements of his complicated books reveal a spider web of connections with literature and history, with the cultures of past and present, and with some timeless themes and patterns of human behavior.

As all readers of detective fiction must know, Macdonald's novels initially grew out of the hard-boiled fiction of the 1920's and 1930's, more specifically, from the powerful traditions established by Dashiell Hammett and Raymond Chandler. He named his private detective Lew Archer, after Sam Spade's murdered partner in *The Maltese Falcon*, and endowed him with some of the wit and compassion of Chandler's Philip Marlowe. Although his early books displayed some interesting prose, a sure sense of scene and atmosphere, and an ability to sketch out character, Macdonald came into his own when he stopped trying merely to improve upon Hammett and Chandler and began to stake out new territory in detective fiction. His humor and toughness always had the forced, false ring of a toy telephone and his style sometimes bordered on the self-consciously literary; what changed Macdonald was his own recognition of his real strengths—complexity and sorrow.

Starting—by his own reckoning—with *The Galton Case*, Macdonald began Lew Archer's long and troubled exploration of the tangled wilderness of the human heart that he embodies in the landscape of southern California. (In reality, his themes are at least roughly adumbrated in such early books as *Blue City* and *The Three Roads*.) His novels began to depart radically from the tough fiction of his original inspiration in their curiously static sense of action; instead of representing human behavior in moments of sequential violence, they generally demonstrate the continuing mysteries of the past. The most notable element in all of Macdonald's fiction is its obsessive preoccupation with the sources of human evil. Lew Archer invariably discovers that whatever crime or problem he confronts in the present has its real meaning in some previous—almost always perverse or shocking—event many years before. The immensely complicated plots of the Macdonald novels are not so much chronicles of actions as retracings of interlocking histories and personalities.

In their profuse ramifications, the plots—along with other important aspects of his fiction—demonstrate the author's significant links with a variety of writers and modes far removed from the usual backgrounds of detective stories. Like his illustrious predecessors in the form, he creates yet another version of the chivalric romance, which has always been submerged but visible beneath the dark waters of the private-eye novel. Like that of previous American writers, Hawthorne and Melville specially, his chief concern is not so much with the fact of crime as with its causes and effects. Like Dickens, whom he resembles in his penchant for intricate stories and surprising connections, he frequently builds his work around the image and reality of a betrayed, neglected, abandoned, and suffering child.

Out of his knowledge of psychology, his scholar's training in literature, and his interest in such figures as Homer, Sophocles, Coleridge, and Freud, and out of the painful personal life that he occasionally discussed with interviewers, Macdonald has made perhaps the most powerful use of the normal materials of detective fiction. With a structure and texture derived from folklore, fairy tale, romance, and myth, he confronts the age-old problems that also, quite unsurprisingly, turn out to be the major difficulties of our time: paternity, identity, the iron chains forged by violence, by sex, by blood, by guilt. The body of his fiction forms a complex picture, then, of our world and its tensions and anxieties.

Those who see his work as a sort of southern California pop sociology miss the point; that is merely the location where his subject surfaces. Those who consider him a useful reporter of the rapid changes in contemporary American society catch a bit more, but all the descriptions of aimless youths, drug users, the decadent rich and the corrupted bourgeoisie, the destruction of the environment, and so forth provide only the necessary context for more permanent concerns. Those who read his works in the future may find some more accurate creation of a special time and place, but it is more likely that in Macdonald's fiction they will be instructed in the harsh lessons of an inner reality. They will discover in the novel of crime, violence, and detection a sense of the mystery and sadness of human action, a dark and troubled picture of a dark and troubled age. Macdonald not only inherited a form and a central figure from Hammett and Chandler; he also acquired the sense of mission to continue and improve their advances in making the detective novel a significant and powerful literary form. His fiction should in the future grow to be ranked among the best and truest of his life time in America.

Macdonald's own place in the continuum of American detective fiction is as solid as that of Hammett and Chandler. His influence on later writers, beyond the superficial levels of the host of writers who imitate some of his mannerisms and themes, is more difficult to determine. Contemporary detective fiction is littered with sensitive private eyes who spend more time gazing into their navels than investigating their cases; the heritage of Lew Archer seems to include more sensitivity than a session full of psychologists, more *Weltschmerz* than a school of minor German poets, and more mawkish prose than a whole tabloid staffed with sob sisters. It still remains to be seen if detective fiction will truly learn from Macdonald's work in the ways he learned from that of Hammett and Chandler; his present imitators do not seem promising.

His work, from *Blue City* to *The Blue Hammer*, should prove to be influential, but probably not in the trivial ways it has worked so far. A real writer with a feel for the complex vision of human relationships and the literary skill to draw upon history, poetry, and psychology, not simply a hack with some facility, is the only sort of detective novelist who will be able to succeed Ross Macdonald. His greatest influence has been to add to the literary richness and possibility of his form; writers like that come along only seldom. It's hard to believe that anyone comparable will soon follow him, but his novels remain a challenging landmark in the glorious and varied landscape of detective fiction.

—George Grella

MANNING, Olivia. British. Born in Portsmouth, Hampshire in 1915. Educated in private schools. Married the radio producer Reginald Donald Smith in 1939. Press officer, United States Embassy, Cairo, 1942; press assistant, Public Information Office, Jerusalem, 1943–44, and British Council, Jerusalem, 1944–45; novel reviewer for *Spectator*, London, 1949–50, and *The Sunday Times*, London, 1965–66. Recipient: Tom-Gallon Trust award, 1949; *Yorkshire Post* award, 1977. C.B.E. (Commander, Order of the British Empire), 1976. *Died 23 July 1980.*

PUBLICATIONS

Novels

The Wind Changes. London, Cape, 1937; New York, Knopf, 1938.
Artist among the Missing. London, Heinemann, 1949.
School for Love. London, Heinemann, 1951.
A Different Face. London, Heinemann, 1953; New York, Abelard Schuman, 1957.
The Doves of Venus. London, Heinemann, 1955; New York, Abelard Schuman, 1956.
The Balkan Trilogy. London, Penguin, 1981.
   The Great Fortune. London, Heinemann, 1960; New York, Doubleday, 1961.
   The Spoilt City. London, Heinemann, and New York, Doubleday, 1962.
   Friends and Heroes. London, Heinemann, 1965; New York, Doubleday, 1966.
The Play Room. London, Heinemann, 1969; as *The Camperlea Girls*, New York, Coward McCann, 1969.
The Rain Forest. London, Heinemann, 1974.
The Levant Trilogy. London, Penguin, 1982.
   The Danger Tree. London, Weidenfeld and Nicolson, and New York, Atheneum, 1977.
   The Battle Lost and Won. London, Weidenfeld and Nicolson, 1978; New York, Atheneum, 1979.
   The Sum of Things. London, Weidenfeld and Nicolson, 1980; New York, Atheneum, 1981.

Short Stories

Growing Up: A Collection of Short Stories. London, Heinemann, and New York, Doubleday, 1948.
My Husband Cartwright. London, Heinemann, 1956.
A Romantic Hero and Other Stories. London, Heinemann, 1967.
Penguin Modern Stories 12, with others. London, Penguin, 1972.

Uncollected Short Stories

"Girls Together," in *Winter's Tales 16*, edited by A.D. Maclean. London, Macmillan, 1970; New York, St. Martin's Press, 1971.
"The Banana House," in *Winter's Tales 17*, edited by Caroline Hobhouse. London, Macmillan, 1971; New York, St. Martin's Press, 1972.

Plays

Screenplay: *The Play Room*, 1970.

Radio Plays: *The Little Ottleys*, from novels by Ada Leverson, 1964; *The Card*, from the novel by Arnold Bennett, 1964; *Futility*, 1973, and *The Polyglots*, 1977, from novels by William Gerhardie.

Other

The Remarkable Expedition: The Story of Stanley's Rescue of Emin Pasha from Equatorial Africa. London, Heinemann, 1947; as *The Reluctant Rescue*, New York, Doubleday, 1947.
The Dreaming Shore (travel). London, Evans, 1950.
Extraordinary Cats. London, Joseph, 1967.

Editor, *Northanger Abbey*, by Jane Austen. London, Pan, 1968.

*

Manuscript Collections: University of Texas, Austin; University of Tulsa, Oklahoma; British Library, London.

Critical Studies: *The Novel Today* by Anthony Burgess, London, Longman, 1963; *Tradition and Dream* by Walter Allen, London, Phoenix House, 1964, as *The Modern Novel in Britain and the United States*, New York, Dutton, 1964; article by James Parkhill Rathbone, in *Books and Bookmen* (London), August 1971; *Continuance and Change: The Contemporary British Novel Sequence* by Robert K. Morris, Carbondale, Southern Illinois University Press, 1972.

Olivia Manning commented:
(1972) When I have completed a book, I feel I have said all I can say concerning it. My subject is simply life as I have experienced it and I am happiest when writing of things I have known.

*   *   *

Olivia Manning began as a painter, and, from her first novel, *The Wind Changes*, onwards, what seems a painter's eye for the visible world enabled her to render particularly well the sensuous surface of relatively exotic places and landscapes. This is particularly apparent in *School for Love*, a novel of Jerusalem in wartime as registered through the consciousness of a 16-year-old English boy stranded there by the chances of war. An aspect of her painter's eye is a pure and exact prose style: her sentences give pleasure in themselves. At the same time, her art has sometimes seemed an art of diminishing; her exactness has seemed almost too cruel. This is apparent in *A Different Face*, in which the hero returns to the seaside town of Coldmouth, on the south coast of England, to discover that the money he has invested in a private school there has been lost. Coldmouth is vividly—and chillingly—described, but in the end the place-name seems too appropriate. Manning's world, one began to feel, was essentially the world of the defeated, and somehow it seemed that her very excellence as a novelist went towards imparting this feeling. Her work was lucid, ironic, and cold. One admired and applauded the integrity but was daunted by the detachment, which seemed, perhaps, the product of too great a fastidiousness.

But lucidity, irony, detachment, and fastidiousness are also the hall-marks of her Balkan Trilogy, and its sequel, The Levant Trilogy, certainly one of the outstanding achievements in post-war fiction. The achievement is such as to suggest that in it, for the first time, Manning was tackling a subject commensurate with her talents, and part of her success in it certainly comes from the qualities that had formerly seemed somehow to diminish her characters.

These qualities do, in fact, define the central consciousness through which the events of the series are reflected, that of Harriet Pringle, the newly married wife of Guy Pringle, who is a member of the staff of a cultural organization uncommonly like the British Council. They travel to Bucharest together, and *The Great Fortune* deals with that city during the first year of the war. The second ends with its occupation by the Germans after the fall of France, and *Friends and Heroes*, dealing with the departure of the Pringles for Greece, ends with their escape from Greece after the fall of Crete to Alexandria. The Levant Trilogy continues their adventures in wartime Cairo and the surrounding desert, with well-researched battle scenes (including the Battle of El Alamein), accounts of hospital ships, and later wanderings in Palestine and Syria. This, then, is a series on recent history, a war novel written from the point of view of an English non-combatant in countries remote from the West. The action is inevitably complex and the canvas large, and everything depends precisely on the eye of the beholder, Harriet Pringle, lucid, ironical, detached, fastidious, and also newly married to a man she scarcely understands. Harriet herself is almost totally unpolitical; she is a stranger in an exotic world. She is at once naive and shrewd, and it is this combination that gives her rendering of the fall of a nation its authority and authenticity. This, we feel, is exactly what it must have been like to be the helpless onlooker of the takeover of a country in time of war. As a recreation of history in fiction these novels are admirable; the novelist is doing her proper job, to show us the workings of historical events in living terms, to bring them to the human level. The place and the time, the sense of doom and the consequent corruption, seem caught perfectly. And the characters are drawn with delicacy and strength, etched with a fine clarity that often reduces them to absurdity but never lets us see them as anything but suffering human beings. Though the books do not indulge in sensationalism, the violence is never burked and comes over the more strongly because of Manning's almost Austenish precision. Nothing is exaggerated, and this, despite the horrors in the near background, the very real dangers which threaten Harriet and her husband and overwhelm some of their friends, makes the whole work a comedy of a very poignant kind. Everything is in the balance; we read the work with the advantage of hindsight. We might, otherwise, have been reading tragedy.

But this is not all. At the centre of the novel, the focal point that makes everything else real, is the relationship between Harriet and her husband Guy, the young man she scarcely knows, and sees in action in a world new to her. Harriet is constantly discovering new aspects of him. He is a committed man, secure, as he thinks, in his marriage. As Harriet notes: "Guy's attitude impressed her, though she had no intention of showing it. He had the advantage of an almost supernatural confidence in dealing with people. It seemed never to occur to him they might not do what he wanted. He had, she noted with surprise, authority. ... Only someone capable of giving so much could demand and receive so much. She felt proud of him."

The quotation illustrates something of Harriet's—and her creator's—objectivity; and also her fairness, for Guy Pringle is not an easy man to be married to. He seems to take Harriet for granted when he is engaged on what may be called his errands of mercy. He is a relentless do-gooder. But the word is wrong. Guy Pringle is much more than that. He is a man of great physical presence, an intellectual from the working class, who appears at times something of a saint, something

of a fool. And again it is Harriet's not wholly certain attitude towards him that convinces us of his reality. He convinces us as that most maddening of human beings, the good man, and the good man, as Dostoevsky discovered when writing *The Idiot*, was only convincing when made at least a little ridiculous. Guy Pringle is one of the most fascinating explorations of character in contemporary fiction.

So, in the background, great events: in the foreground a very subtle analysis of the relationship between a man and wife. The juxtaposition is everything. It assures us of the truth of both.

—Walter Allen

McCULLERS, (Lula) Carson (née Smith). American. Born in Columbus, Georgia, 19 February 1917. Educated at Columbus High School, graduated 1933; attended classes at Columbia University, New York, and New York University, 1934–36. Married James Reeves McCullers, Jr., in 1937 (divorced, 1941); remarried in 1945 (died, 1953). Lived in Charlotte, 1937–38, and Fayetteville, 1938–39, both North Carolina, and in New York City, 1940–44, and Nyack, New York after 1944. Recipient: Bread Loaf Writers Conference fellowship, 1940; Guggenheim fellowship, 1942, 1946; American Academy grant, 1943; *Mademoiselle* award, 1948; New York Drama Critics Circle award, 1950; Donaldson Award, for drama, 1950; Theatre Club Gold Medal, 1950; University of Mississippi grant, 1966; Henry Bellamann Award, 1967. Member, American Academy, 1952. *Died 29 September 1967.*

PUBLICATIONS

Novels

The Heart Is a Lonely Hunter. Boston, Houghton Mifflin, 1940; London, Cresset Press, 1943.
Reflections in a Golden Eye. Boston, Houghton Mifflin, 1941; London, Cresset Press, 1942.
The Member of the Wedding. Boston, Houghton Mifflin, and London, Cresset Press, 1946.
Clock Without Hands. Boston, Houghton Mifflin, and London, Cresset Press, 1961.

Short Stories

The Ballad of the Sad Café: The Novels and Stories of Carson McCullers. Boston, Houghton Mifflin, 1951; London, Cresset Press, 1952; as *Collected Short Stories*, Houghton Mifflin, 1961; as *The Shorter Novels and Stories of Carson McCullers*, London, Barrie and Jenkins, 1972.
Seven. New York, Bantam, 1954.

Plays

The Member of the Wedding, adaptation of her own novel (produced Philadelphia, 1949; New York, 1950; London, 1957). New York, New Directions, 1951.
The Square Root of Wonderful (produced Princeton, New Jersey, and New York, 1957; London, 1970). Boston, Houghton Mifflin, 1958; London, Cresset Press, 1958.

Television Plays: *The Invisible Wall*, from her story "The Sojourner," 1953; *The Sojourner*, from her own story, 1964.

Verse

The Twisted Trinity, music by David Diamond.   Philadelphia,
    Elkan Vogel, 1946.
Sweet as a Pickle and Clean as a Pig (for children).   Boston,
    Houghton Mifflin, 1964; London, Cape, 1965.

Other

The Mortgaged Heart (uncollected writings), edited by Mar-
    garita G. Smith.   Boston, Houghton Mifflin, 1971; London,
    Barrie and Jenkins, 1972.

*

Bibliography: *Katherine Anne Porter and Carson McCullers:
A Reference Guide* by Robert F. Kiernan, Boston, Hall, 1976;
*Carson McCullers: A Descriptive Listing and Annotated Biblio-
graphy of Criticism* by Adrian M. Shapiro, Jackson R. Bryer,
and Kathleen Field, New York, Garland, 1980.

Manuscript Collection: Humanities Research Center, University of Texas, Austin.

Critical Studies: *Carson McCullers: Her Life and Work* by
Oliver Evans, London, Owen, 1965, as *The Ballad of Carson
McCullers*, New York, Coward McCann, 1966; *Carson
McCullers* by Lawrence Graver, Minneapolis, University of
Minnesota Press, 1969; *Carson McCullers* by Dale Edmonds,
Austin, Texas, Steck Vaughn, 1969; *The Lonely Hunter: A
Biography of Carson McCullers* by Virginia Spencer Carr, New
York, Doubleday, 1975, London, Owen, 1977; *Carson
McCullers* by Richard M. Cook, New York, Ungar, 1975; *Car-
son McCullers* by Margaret B. McDowell, Boston, Twayne,
1980.

*   *   *

One of that group of precocious, eccentric, Southern *enfants
terribles* who flowered like rank hollyhocks in the 1940's, Carson McCullers was a unique sensibility. A celebrity at 22, she
wrote her best fiction within 6 years. With Faulkner, Tennessee
Williams, and Truman Capote, she cultivated a type of fiction
that critics labeled Southern Gothic. Hostile reviewers called
her work bizarre, morbid, extreme, decadent, "horror pornography"; others praised her for having achieved "a metaphysical fusion of horror and compassion"; McCullers herself noted
the "fusion of anguish and farce" in Southern writing that
caused reviewers to misread the seriously grotesque mode as
Poe-like Gothic horror for its own sake. Like Sherwood Anderson and Faulkner, she deliberately makes grotesque characters
expressionistic extensions of normal, universal human problems. Like Proust, she was obsessed with time and memory.
Although her overt didacticism reveals her preference for Tolstoy, McCullers is closer to Dostoevsky, with his "radically
tightened nervous tone" (her phrase). She once referred to
The Heart Is a Lonely Hunter as her Russian (Dostoevskian)
novel, *Reflections in a Golden Eye* as her short French (Flaubertian) novel, and *The Member of the Wedding* as her English
(Woolfian) novel.

"The South is a very emotional experience for me,"
McCullers once said. Physically, most of her fiction is set in
small southern towns, modelled on Columbus, Georgia; psychologically, "the labyrinth of the heart"; metaphorically, a
prison. Most of her fiction sets the mood *The Ballad of the
Sad Café* does: "The town itself is dreary ... lonesome, sad,
and like a place that is far off and estranged from all other
places in the world. ... You might as well walk down to the
Forks Fall Road and listen to the chain gang." As most events
occur in monotonous conditions of extreme heat and dryness
that exacerbate states of boredom and melancholy, McCullers
makes us feel the congruence of physical and psychological
weathers.

In *The Member of the Wedding* Frankie, this century's most
vivid symbol of the compulsion to belong, says to little John
Henry, "Not to belong to a 'we' makes you too lonesome."
All her characters are the "we" of Carson McCullers. Some
of them are autobiographical, especially Frankie and Mick (of
The Heart Is a Lonely Hunter). When McCullers said, "I
become the characters I write about," she was referring to
characters who have been called "strange, enigmatic, macabre,
fantastic, fanatic, narcissistic, perverted, malicious, desperate,
abnormal, diseased, pathological." Her response was to quote
Terence: "Nothing human is alien to me." Among her Gothic
grotesques are the physical cripples, giantess Amelia and the
hunchback dwarf Cousin Lymnon; the mental cripple, Captain
Penderton, a latent homosexual; the spiritual cripple, senile,
egocentric Judge Clane. Each of her novels depicts, as one
reviewer said, "a viper's nest of neurasthenic relationships."
If the two girls Frankie and Mick are also grotesque, it is only
in the sense that adolescence is a grotesque phase in every
person's development. Richard Wright praised McCullers for
handling "Negro characters with ... ease." Berenice and Portia
are almost as impressive as Faulkner's Dilsey. One might say
more appropriately of McCullers than of most writers that all
her work is autobiographical in the sense that whatever she
read and whatever she imagined *really happened* to her.

An omniscient narrator, somewhat like George Eliot,
McCullers roved among her characters. Much of the excellence
of her work may be attributed to the effects of the omniscient
point of view she almost always employed and to a simple
style that conjures an air of wonder, awe, and mystery. At
its worst, her style is wordy, precious, awkward, pseudo-liter-
ary, clumsy, too much in the passive voice, too epigrammatic,
cliché-ridden. At its best, what it emits is radiance. Like Sherwood Anderson, McCullers makes deliberate, controlled use
of the old-fashioned style, tone, and techniques of the tale,
as the openings of her novels suggest: "The participants of
this tragedy were two officers, a soldier, two women, and a
horse." One reviewer remarked upon the "distant Olympian
dispassionateness" of her style that makes us feel authorial
distance, most severely in *The Ballad*. Tennessee Williams asks
us to regard as deliberate McCullers's "absolute mastery of
design," the austere "Grecian purity" of form in that *tour de
force Reflections in a Golden Eye*; its aura of artificiality, styliza-
tion, and decadence is characteristic to some degree of all her
fiction. It is the use of too many of the deceptive tricks and
devices of the omniscient narrator that mars *Clock Without
Hands*, her least successful novel, as when Judge Clane delivers
a weakly motivated, double-barreled revelation concerning
Jester's father and Sherman's mother. But in *Heart* the omniscient point of view controls an aesthetic concept that embodies
theme and is structured by the hero-witness relationship that
McCullers develops between the mute John Singer and four
other characters. The novel is unified by a pattern of symbolic
motifs and a well-wrought design in which alternate sections

are devoted to the intimate viewpoints of the five major characters, with a different style for each. We encounter the blatant foreshadowing, the obvious, ironic symbolism (Singer as Christ the Savior), the static character descriptions, and the omniscient author's narrative summaries; but elements that are sometimes faults in the other works here sound a succession of almost perfect notes.

The growing social consciousness that made young McCullers attack capitalism, racism, and religion in *Heart* is rather muted in subsequent works until *Clock Without Hands*, which dramatizes the entanglement of personal with public radical dilemmas. Social problems are primarily objective correlatives for spiritual and emotional struggles. *Heart* is a realistic allegory of the paradoxical conflict between one's hunger for human understanding and one's simultaneous desire for inviolable privacy; in the context of society, both needs are frustrated. Isolated from society by its conditions and their own constitutions, each character is obsessed with one single idea, purpose, or personality disorder. If Singer is Christ, his obese feeble minded Greek beloved is his god, and the ironic cruelty of Antonapoulos's incomprehension suggests an allegorical statement about man and God and self-delusion.

That McCullers is a didactic writer is demonstrated in her compulsion to discuss theme and her vision of life directly with the reader. The lover and the beloved "come from different countries. ... And the curt truth is that ... the state of being beloved is intolerable to many. The beloved fears and hates the lover, and with the best of reasons. For the lover is forever trying to strip bare his beloved. The lover craves any possible relation with the beloved, even if this experience can cause him only pain" (*The Ballad*). McCullers develops her novels within the tensions of paradoxical polarities: characters simultaneously crave life and death, privacy and ideal assimilation of self with other; hopeless, doomed, often nonsexual attractions become cruel, violent repulsions, expressing love and hate; mismatched characters in tangled relationships remain always spiritually isolated. Some of them break out of the prison of solitude in compulsive, sudden acts of violence. Some turn against themselves; when the Greek, the object of his worship, perishes, Singer, like Richard Cory, shoots himself. For McCullers's transfixed prisoners, talk frequently substitutes for action. Seldom do McCullers's characters make physical or sexual contact. They internalize society's prohibitions, mistaking them for forces of nature. In McCullers's vision, the world itself is unfinished, incomplete, and so therefore are its creatures, who, like the trio in the ugly kitchen in *The Member of the Wedding*, play the game of life with a deck in which cards are missing. For what is missing in reality, characters compensate in impossible dreams and self-generated illusions, and out of severe need demonstrate the transcendent power of human imagination.

Carson McCullers was a poetic symbolist with a touch of the logician. Despite a certain static quality in all her work, one feels an intensity of expression, a tension of structure, and over all a sense of the magical and the mysterious that moved Dame Edith Sitwell to call her "a transcendental writer." Her characters hunger for communication, which was for McCullers the only access to love. Her aesthetics and her themes are inseparable; she had a compulsion to transform experience into the charged images of art. For her, the generators of all good writing were "love, passion, compassion." At times she consorted with the Sentimental Muse, and yet *The Heart Is a Lonely Hunter* is one of the most pessimistic novels ever written; still, the reader, beholding the transcendent artistry of McCullers's intuitive-intellectual imagination, is exhilarated. A work of art is "like a flowering dream," and

the writer is "a conscious dreamer," she said; between the writer's dream and the "logic of God," there is a "divine collusion."

—David Madden

O'CONNOR, (Mary) Flannery. American. Born in Savannah, Georgia, 25 March 1925. Educated at Peabody High School, Milledgeville, Georgia, graduated 1942; Georgia State College for Women, now Georgia College at Milledgeville, 1942–45, A.B. 1945; University of Iowa, Iowa City, 1945–47, M.F.A. 1947. Recipient: *Kenyon Review* fellowship, 1953; American Academy grant, 1957; O. Henry Award, 1957, 1963, 1964; Ford Foundation grant, 1959; National Catholic Book Award, 1966; National Book Award, 1972. D. Litt.: St. Mary's College, Notre Dame, Indiana, 1962; Smith College, Northampton, Massachusetts, 1963. *Died 3 August 1964.*

PUBLICATIONS

Novels

Wise Blood. New York, Harcourt Brace, 1952; London, Spearman, 1955.
The Violent Bear It Away. New York, Farrar Straus, and London, Longman, 1960.

Short Stories

A Good Man Is Hard to Find and Other Stories. New York, Harcourt Brace, 1955; as *The Artificial Nigger and Other Tales,* London, Spearman, 1957.
Everything That Rises Must Converge. New York, Farrar Straus, 1965; London, Faber, 1966.
The Complete Stories. New York, Farrar Straus, 1971.

Other

Mystery and Manners: Occasional Prose, edited by Sally and Robert Fitzgerald. New York, Farrar Straus, 1969; London, Faber, 1972.
The Habit of Being: Letters of Flannery O'Connor, edited by Sally Fitzgerald. New York, Farrar Straus, and London, Faber, 1979.
The Presence of Grace and Other Book Reviews, edited by Carter W. Martin and Leo J. Zuber. Athens, University of Georgia Press, 1983.

Editor, *A Memoir of Mary Ann.* New York, Farrar Straus, 1961; as *Death of a Child,* London, Burns and Oates, 1961.

*

Bibliography: *Flannery O'Connor and Caroline Gordon: A Reference Guide* by Robert E. Golden and Mary C. Sullivan, Boston, Hall, 1977; *Flannery O'Connor: A Descriptive Bibliography* by David Farmer, New York, Garland, 1981.

Manuscript Collection: Georgia College at Milledgeville.

Critical Studies (selection): *Flannery O'Connor: A Critical Essay* by Robert Drake, Grand Rapids, Michigan, Eerdmans,

1966; *Flannery O'Connor* by Stanley Edgar Hyman, Minneapolis, University of Minnesota Press, 1966; *The Added Dimension: The Art and Mind of Flannery O'Connor* edited by Melvin J. Friedman and Lewis A. Lawson, New York, Fordham University Press, 1966; *The True Country: Themes in the Fiction of Flannery O'Connor* by Carter W. Martin, Nashville, Tennessee, Vanderbilt University Press, 1969; *The World of Flannery O'Connor* by Josephine Hendin, Bloomington, Indiana University Press, 1970; *Eternal Crossroads: The Art of Flannery O'Connor* by Leon Driskell and Joan T. Brittain, Lexington, University Press of Kentucky, 1971; *The Christian Humanism of Flannery O'Connor* by David Eggenschwiler, Detroit, Wayne State University Press, 1972; *Nightmares and Visions: Flannery O'Connor and the Catholic Grotesque* by Gilbert Muller, Athens, University of Georgia Press, 1972; *Flannery O'Connor: Voice of the Peacock* by Kathleen Feeley, New Brunswick, New Jersey, Rutgers University Press, 1972; *Invisible Parade: The Fiction of Flannery O'Connor* by Miles Orvell, Philadelphia, Temple University Press, 1972; *Flannery O'Connor* by Dorothy Walters, New York, Twayne, 1973; *The Question of Flannery O'Connor* by Martha Stephens, Baton Rouge, Louisiana State University Press, 1973; *Flannery O'Connor* by Preston M. Browning, Jr., Carbondale, Southern Illinois University Press, 1974; *Flannery O'Connor* by Dorothy Tuck McFarland, New York, Ungar, 1976; *The Pruning Word: The Parables of Flannery O'Connor* by John R. May, Notre Dame, Indiana, University of Notre Dame Press, 1976; *Flannery O'Connor's Dark Comedies: The Limits of Inference* by Carol Shloss, Baton Rouge, Louisiana State University Press, 1980; *Flannery O'Connor: Her Life, Library, and Book Reviews*, 1980, and *Nature and Grace in Flannery O'Connor's Fiction*, 1982, both by Lorine M. Getz, New York, Mellen Press; *Flannery O'Connor's South* by Robert Coles, Baton Rouge, Louisiana State University Press, 1980; *Flannery O'Connor's Georgia* by Barbara McKenzie, Athens, University of Georgia Press, 1980; *The Flannery O'Connor Companion* by James A. Grimshaw, Jr., Westport, Connecticut, Greenwood Press, 1981; *Flannery O'Connor: The Imagination of Extremity* by Frederick Asals, Athens, University of Georgia Press, 1982.

*   *   *

"Belief, in my own case anyway, is the engine that makes perception operate." As a religious writer, Flannery O'Connor had to confront the lack of a shared world-picture with the majority of her readers. Declaring that "my subject in fiction is the action of grace in territory held largely by the devil," she recognized that in the average reader the "sense of evil is diluted or lacking altogether, and so he has forgotten the price of restoration." The unique vision of Flannery O'Connor—violent, apocalyptic, grotesque—resulted from her endeavor to function as a believing writer in a non-believing world.

Brought up a Catholic in the "Christ-haunted" Bible Belt of the American South, O'Connor focused on the dominant Protestant Fundamentalism of the region, "those aspects of Southern life where the religious feeling is most intense and where its outward forms are farthest from the Catholic, and most revealing of a need that only the Church can fill." As she exaggerated violence in her evocation of Georgia she accentuated the individualism of her backwoods prophets, because the Christian novelist "may well be forced to take ever more violent means to get vision across to this hostile audience."

The theme of both her novels is vocation. In a note to the second edition of *Wise Blood*, the author described "Haze"

Motes as "a Christian *malgré lui*." His preaching of "the Church Without Christ" involves him in killing a "false prophet" and is terminated by the destruction of his pulpit, his car; he blinds himself, and bears mute and solitary witness. Like all O'Connor's work, the book is tragi-comic since "the maximum amount of seriousness admits the maximum amount of comedy;" ironic use of profanity is a major source of humour.

Whereas *Wise Blood* is something of a negative spiritual odyssey, as Hazel Motes encounters the fake blind preacher, Enoch Emery, and Onnie Jay Holy, *The Violent Bear It Away* has a tighter structure; it is rooted in the relationships of Francis Marion Tarwater with his great-uncle, a prophet, and with his uncle Rayber and his little idiot cousin Bishop. The rationalist Rayber believes that the old man "needed the assurance of a call, and so he called himself." On his great-uncle's death, Tarwater tries to reject his vocation as a prophet and his "first mission" to baptize Bishop. Inexorably, he drowns Bishop, baptizing him simultaneously. He ceases to struggle with "the bleeding stinking mad shadow of Jesus," but by then he seems as unbalanced as his great-uncle was considered to be.

The key to O'Connor's technique is her use of anagogical vision, which she defined as "the kind of vision that is able to see different levels of reality in one image or one situation." The same symbols recur in both novels; for instance, the stones in Hazel Motes's shoes with the other rock leitmotifs in *Wise Blood* gradually recall St. Peter, while in *The Violent Bear It Away* Bishop plays with a stone in a wastepaper basket. An elaborate infrastructure of interlocking symbolism maintains the characteristic "interior suspense" of O'Connor's work.

The violence of her content is conveyed in a raw, angular style, whose vigour frequently hardens into violent imagery. In her critical writing, brought together posthumously in *Mystery and Manners*, she emphasized the writer's eye: "everything has its testing point in the eye. ... Judgment is something that begins in the act of vision." Imagery of the eye is outstanding in her novels and stories, with eyes likened to "two steel spikes" or "pitchfork prongs."

Adapted to the short-story form, these techniques produced stories wonderfully "long in depth," as O'Connor herself prescribed. Yet the collections of stories *A Good Man Is Hard to Find* and *Everything That Rises Must Converge* ought not to eclipse her supreme achievement, *The Violent Bear It Away*. The patterns of relationship in this novel recur in many of the stories, notably in "The Lame Shall Enter First"; another favourite relation is the mother-daughter one, where the mother runs a farm managing Negro and white trash labour. O'Connor's stress on "the mystery of personality" is delimited, at least for the humanist reader, by her invariable location of this in terms of pervasive religious symbolism. Against her usual "mythic background" of the South, "where belief can be made believable," her stories pivot on a character's acceptance or rejection of the moment of grace. In "The Artificial Nigger" the simultaneous delight of Nelson and Mr. Head at the sight of a plaster statue of a Negro reunites them after the grandfather's "denial" of Nelson to passers-by. The positive ending is unusual in *A Good Man*, while in *Everything That Rises* the element of violence is even stronger and most of the stories culminate in death.

This latter volume of stories was written while O'Connor was enduring the closing stages of chronic lupus, just before her early death. Her experience of suffering in her long illness may have reinforced her uncompromising vision. Though Flannery O'Connor was fond of quoting St. Thomas Aquinas's dictum that "a work of art is a good in itself," the generalized cathartic effect which her unique work has on most readers represents a dilution of its vision.

—Val Warner

SCOTT, Paul (Mark). British. Born in London, 25 March 1920. Educated at Winchmore Hill Collegiate School. Served in the British Army, 1940–43, and in the Indian Army, in India and Malaya, 1943–46. Married Nancy Edith Avery in 1941; two daughters. Company Secretary, Falcon Press and Grey Walls Press, London, 1946–50; Director, Pearn Pollinger and Higham, later David Higham Associates, literary agents, London, 1950–60. British Council Lecturer, India, 1972; Visiting Lecturer, University of Tulsa, Oklahoma, 1976–77. Recipient: Eyre and Spottiswoode literary fellowship, 1952; Arts Council grant, 1969; Booker Prize, 1977. Fellow, Royal Society of Literature, 1963. *Died 1 March 1978.*

PUBLICATIONS

Novels

Johnnie Sahib. London, Eyre and Spottiswoode, 1952.
The Alien Sky. London, Eyre and Spottiswoode, 1953; as *Six Days in Marapore*, New York, Doubleday, 1953.
A Male Child. London, Eyre and Spottiswoode, 1956; New York, Dutton, 1957.
The Mark of the Warrior. London, Eyre and Spottiswoode, and New York, Morrow, 1958.
The Chinese Love Pavilion. London, Eyre and Spottiswoode, 1960; as *The Love Pavilion*, New York, Morrow, 1960.
The Birds of Paradise. London, Eyre and Spottiswoode, and New York, Morrow, 1962.
The Bender: Pictures from an Exhibition of Middle Class Portraits. London, Secker and Warburg, 1963; as *The Bender*, New York, Morrow, 1963.
The Corrida of San Feliu. London, Secker and Warburg, and New York, Morrow, 1964.
The Raj Quartet. London, Heinemann, and New York, Morrow, 1976.
    The Jewel in the Crown. London, Heinemann, and New York, Morrow, 1966.
    The Day of the Scorpion. London, Heinemann, and New York, Morrow, 1968.
    The Towers of Silence. London, Heinemann, 1971; New York, Morrow, 1972.
    A Division of the Spoils. London, Heinemann, and New York, Morrow, 1975.
Staying On. London, Heinemann, and New York, Morrow, 1977.

Short Story

After the Funeral. Andoversford, Gloucestershire, Whittington Press, 1979.

Plays

Pillars of Salt, in *Four Jewish Plays*, edited by H.F. Rubinstein. London, Gollancz, 1948.

Radio Plays: *Lines of Communication*, 1951; *The Alien Sky*, 1954; *Sahibs and Memsahibs*, 1958.

Television Play: *The Mark of the Warrior*, from his own novel, 1959.

Verse

I, Gerontius. London, Favil Press, 1941.

*

Manuscript Collection: Humanities Research Center, University of Texas, Austin.

Critical Studies: by Scott, in *Essays by Divers Hands*, London, Oxford University Press, 1970; *Paul Scott: Images of India* by Patrick Swinden, London, Macmillan, 1980; *Paul Scott* by K. Bhaskara Rao, Boston, Twayne, 1980.

*   *   *

Paul Scott's considerable achievement as a novelist is best represented by the four inter-connected novels that make up *The Raj Quartet*. This tetralogy, set in the years 1939 to 1947, the final years of the Raj, was extended by a short novel, *Staying On*, set in 1972 and dealing with an elderly couple who decide to remain in India after Independence.

Each novel in *The Raj Quartet* is complete in itself, yet taken together they provide for the reader a growing understanding of India and involve him more and more intimately in the decisions and events of the period. The volumes are not consecutive; *The Day of the Scorpion*, for instance, barely advances in time from *The Jewel in the Crown*, and is concerned with the same events, the attack on Miss Crane and the rape of Daphne Manners in the Bibighar Gardens, yet the emphasis is placed at a different angle, and characters who appear in the first novel are revealed as very different people in the second. This is especially relevant in portraying the character of Merrick, District Superintendent of Police, who is presented as a pillar of the community in *The Jewel in the Crown*, with just a few vague suspicions surfacing about his actions, yet is seen to be a ruthless and prejudiced sadist in the next volume.

The Towers of Silence covers almost the same period of time, but introduces new characters, mostly female, and continues to develop the mysterious Merrick, whose sinister side seems to be recognised more readily by the Indian than by the English. Set in the hill station of Pankot, *The Towers of Silence* provides yet another veil of comment on the central incidents of the attacks on Daphne Manners and Miss Crane; here, the Brigadier who ordered his troops to fire on unarmed crowds in Mayapore, and whose pompous memoirs are so deftly pilloried in *The Jewel in the Crown*, can be dismissed as "a bit of a duffer" by the Colonel's wives sitting out the War in the mountains. The tragic figure of retired missionary teacher Barbie Batchelor is developed here, and allows Scott to bring out one of the most important themes in the novels, that of the class conflicts within the British themselves in India. Scott has said of British society, "We have our Brahmins, our workers, our untouchables." Barbie Batchelor, a friend of Miss Crane, is relentlessly insulted and snubbed by the women of higher social status in Pankot, the same women who exploit Lucy Smalley, the chief character of *Staying On*.

A Division of the Spoils is an extensive volume in two parts, dealing with the ultimate retreat of the British and the Partition of India. Violence fills the novel, as the figure who seems to bring evil wherever he goes, Robert Merrick, is savagely murdered, and Hindu and Muslim begin systematically to butcher each other as the British depart, a betrayal that Scott felt deeply about. In an interview in 1975 Scott said, "How did we walk out with such a high sense of duty performed? The Indians almost contributed to the feeling that we had done our job and it was no fault of ours that 250,000 people were massacred in road convoys and on trains. ... In the end it was a tragedy in the classical sense." Scott's sense of shame is symbolised by the use he makes of the old painting that Miss Crane uses to teach her class English, of Queen Victoria on her throne, supported by angels and receiving tribute from her loyal Indian subjects. This image of mutual love and care, of "man-bap," ironically appears for the last time as one of the effects packed with the murdered Merrick's trunk.

Technically, *The Raj Quartet* and *Staying On* share a sophisticated blend of narrative techniques: changing viewpoint, different narrative forms, time-shifts, and flashbacks. The unfolding of the story is constantly inventive; in the final volume the shadowy figure of the contemporary traveller depicts historical events by simply describing a series of cartoons in a Bombay newspaper. In *The Jewel in the Crown* the reader is drawn into a mosaic of fragmentary reportage: letters, memoirs, comments on the memoirs, a journal, a formal deposition; all invite the reader to take an evaluative stance on the events of the novel. At the end of *A Division of the Spoils* Merrick is buried with honour as "a gallant soldier"; his widow refers to him admiringly as someone who "never pretended," yet the reader has seen the strange pathways of Merrick's mind, his hidden homosexuality, his Pathan disguises and his ritual murder by the young Indian boys he exploits. But Susan is sincere in her view of her husband, and Scott convinces us of the value she places on him, thus making the reader feel the impossibility of ever really knowing the truth about another person, or of judging others impartially.

Staying On is a short, very poignant novel dealing mainly with two characters, Colonel Tusker Smalley and his wife Lucy, who never reached the top ranks of Anglo-Indian society and elected to remain in India after Partition rather than return to the pettiness and snobbery of England. Scott is particularly sensitive to the feelings of the elderly, and the novel precisely plots a relationship that functions not so much through words, but through the daily incidents that habit has made familiar.

Paul Scott's early novels contrast strongly to the lengthy, dense works of *The Raj Quartet*. Many are set in India and deal with experiences gained while he was on active service in India in World War II as an officer in an air supply unit.

His first published novel, *Johnnie Sahib*, describes the activities of such a unit and vigorously explores the strands of power and conflict that are involved in leading a small group of men. Similar themes concerned with the idea of the soldier as leader are examined in *The Mark of the Warrior*, a much slighter novel with a distressing feeling of inevitability about its plot and characters. *The Alien Sky* concerns itself with British civilians who are about to leave India in 1947 and looks with unusual honesty at the situation of the English liberal who cannot understand why he is so hated by the Indians he longs to help.

The idea of the soldier and the dilemma of command are also central to *The Chinese Love Pavilion*, which shares with several of the early novels a charismatic, mysterious character who both repels and fascinates the central figure. This time it is a dangerously independent ex-planter Brian Saxby who teaches the newly arrived Brent how to love the India that Brent's family have served for generations. *The Birds of Paradise* reveals the beginnings of the slow-paced, richly embellished prose that was to form the basis of his last works. In this novel the image of the decaying, stuffed birds of paradise in the garden of an Indian palace allows the author to explore the techniques of flashback that he was to use so effectively in *The Raj Quartet*.

Only three of Scott's 13 novels are not set in India or the Far East: *A Male Child* is a drab novel set in London just after World War II, but already there are hints of the rich characterisation that was to emerge. *The Bender* is a mildly amusing tale about a feckless poor relation with an inadequate private income and provides some satiric barbs at the fashionable society of the time. Narrative intricacy is strained to the utmost in *The Corrida of San Feliu*, set in Spain, with flashbacks to the past intercut with portions of an unfinished novel being written by the chief character, Edward Thornhill.

Critical acclaim came late to Paul Scott and only in the last years of his life did a wide readership develop for his work. Although the slow pace of his novels with their gradual accumulation of detail may be very much against the modern trend to short, elliptical novels, the reader finds in the very complexities of his later works an invitation to share in the complexities of life itself, and to emerge with an extended vision as a result.

—Margaret B. Lewis

TITLE
INDEX

The following list includes the titles of all the books listed in the Novels and Short Stories (designated "s") sections of the book, including the appendix. The name(s) in parenthesis is meant to direct the reader to the appropriate entry where full publication information is given.

Abandoned Woman (Condon), 1977
Abba Abba (Burgess), 1977
Abbess of Crewe (Spark), 1974
Aberration of Starlight (Sorrentino), 1980
Abominable Earthman (s Pohl), 1963
About a Marriage (G. Gordon), 1972
About Harry Towns (Friedman), 1974
Above Ground (Ludwig), 1968
Abracadabra! (Mankowitz), 1980
Absence of Ruins (Patterson), 1967
Absolute Hero (Humphreys), 1986
Absolutely Nothing to Get Alarmed About (Wright), 1973
Absurd Affair (C. Spencer), 1961
Acceptance World (Powell), 1955
Accident (Mosley), 1965
Accidental Man (Murdoch), 1971
Accidental Tourist (Tyler), 1985
Accounting (s Kostelanetz), 1972
Accounting (B. Marshall), 1958
Acolyte (Astley), 1972
Acre of Grass (Stewart), 1965
Acrobat Admit (Grossman), 1959
Acrobats (Richler), 1954
Across the Black Waters (Anand), 1940
Across the Bridge (s Greene), 1981
Across the Sea of Stars (Arthur C. Clarke), 1959
Across the Sea Wall (Koch), 1965
Act of Darkness (King), 1983
Action (King), 1978
Ad Infinitum (s Kostelanetz), 1973
Ada Dallas (W. Williams), 1959
Adah's Story (Emecheta), 1983
Adam of a New World (Lindsay), 1936
Adaptable Man (Frame), 1965
Adhar Ameireagenach (s I. Smith), 1973
Admiral and the Nuns (s Tuohy), 1962
Adrift in Soho (C. Wilson), 1961
Adventure in Washington (Rosten, as Ross), 1940
Adventures in the Alaskan Skin Trade (Hawkes), 1985
Adventures of Alyx (s Russ), 1983
Adventures of Augie March (Bellow), 1953
Adventures of Catullus Kelly (Salkey), 1969
Adventures of God in His Search for the Black Girl (Brophy), 1973
Adventures of Robina, by Herself (E. Tennant), 1986
Adversary in the House (I. Stone), 1947
Advertisements for Myself (s Mailer), 1959
Advise and Consent (Drury), 1959
Aerodrome (Warner), 1941
Affair of Men (Brathwaite), 1961
Affair to Remember (Cassill, as Aherne), 1957
African Horse (Pownall), 1975
African Stories (s Lessing), 1964
After Anzac Day (Cross), 1961
After Dinner's Sleep (S. Middleton), 1986
After Goliath (Cassill), 1985
After Julius (E. Howard), 1965
After Lazarus (s Coover), 1980
After Rome, Africa (Glanville), 1959
After the Act (Graham), 1965
After the Funeral (s Scott, appendix), 1979

After the Rain (Bowen), 1958
Afternoon Men (Powell), 1931
Afternoon of a Good Woman (Bawden), 1976
Against a Darkening Sky (Lewis), 1943
Against Entropy (Frayn), 1967
Against the Fall of Night (Arthur C. Clarke), 1953
Against the Season (Rule), 1971
Agatha (Colegate), 1973
Age (Aldiss), 1967
Age of the Pussyfoot (Pohl), 1969
Age of the Rainmakers (s W. Harris), 1971
Age of Thunder (Prokosch), 1945
Agent (Hinde), 1974
Agents and Patients (Powell), 1936
Agents and Witnesses (Newby), 1947
Agony and the Ecstasy (I. Stone), 1961
Agrippa's Daughter (Fast), 1964
Air Bridge (Innes), 1951
Air Disaster (Innes), 1937
Air That Kills (King), 1948
Air That Kills (Millar), 1957
Air We Breathe (Josipovici), 1981
Airport (Hailey), 1968
Airs of Earth (s Aldiss), 1963
Airships (s Hannah), 1978
Ajaiyi and His Inherited Poverty (Tutuola), 1967
Alabaster Egg (Freeman), 1970
Albatross (s S. Hill), 1971
Albatross Muff (Hanrahan), 1977
Alberta (s Wiebe), 1979
Albert's Memorial (Cook), 1972
Albino (Cope), 1964
Alchemy (s Lytle), 1979
Alex and the Gypsy (s Elkin), 1977
Alexandria Quartet (Durrell), 1962
Alfie (Naughton), 1966
Alfie, Darling (Naughton), 1970
Alibi (Kroetsch), 1983
Alice (Fast, as Cunningham), 1963
Alice Fell (E. Tennant), 1980
Alien Light (I. Smith), 1969
Alien Sky (Scott, appendix), 1953
All about H. Hatterr (Desani), 1951
All about Mr. Hatterr (Desani), 1948
All Fall Down (Herlihy), 1960
All Glorious Within (B. Marshall), 1944
All Heaven in a Rage (Duffy), 1973
All in a Lifetime (Allen), 1959
All My Friends Are Going to Be Strangers (McMurtry), 1972
All Night Long (Caldwell), 1942
All on the Never-Never (Lindsay), 1961
All Roads Lead to Friday (Innes), 1939
All Strange Away (s Beckett), 1976
All That Glitters (Anthony), 1981
All the Best People (S. Wilson), 1970
All the Good People I've Left Behind (s Oates), 1979
All the King's Horses (s Anthony C. West), 1981
All the King's Men (Warren), 1946
All the Little Live Things (Stegner), 1967
All Things Nice (Billington), 1969
Alley Cat (s Cope), 1973

Male Response (Aldiss), 1961
Malgudi Days (s Narayan), 1943
Malone Dies (Beckett), 1956
Malone meurt (Beckett), 1951
Mama's Little Girl (s Caldwell), 1932
Man and Boy (Morris), 1951
Man and Two Women (s Lessing), 1963
Man Called Jones (Symons), 1947
Man Comes Home (Heath), 1974
Man from Clinkapella (s Hardy), 1951
Man from Dahomey (Yerby), 1971
Man from Elsewhere (Farrell, appendix), 1963
Man from Next Door (Tracy), 1977
Man from the Sea (Stewart, as Innes), 1955
Man Hunt (Household), 1942
Man in His Prime (Phelps), 1955
Man in the Cellar (s J. O'Faolain), 1974
Man in the Gray Flannel Suit (S. Wilson), 1955
Man in the Middle (Wagoner), 1954
Man Made of Smoke (S. Middleton), 1973
Man Must Live (s Mphahlele), 1947
Man Next Door (Litvinoff), 1968
Man of Nazareth (Burgess), 1979
Man of Power (Colegate), 1960
Man of Slow Feeling (s Wilding), 1985
Man of the People (Achebe), 1966
Man Off Beat (Hughes), 1957
Man on Fire (Cassill, as Aherne), 1957
Man on the Rock (King), 1958
Man Overboard (Dickens), 1958
Man Plus (Pohl), 1976
Man to Conjure with (Baumbach), 1965
Man Who Ate the World (s Pohl), 1960
Man Who Cried I Am (John A. Williams), 1967
Man Who Doubted (s Cope), 1967
Man Who Grew Younger (s Charyn), 1967
Man Who Invented Sin (s S. O'Faolain), 1948
Man Who Invented Tomorrow (Hughes), 1968
Man Who Killed Himself (Symons), 1967
Man Who Knew Kennedy (Bourjaily), 1967
Man Who Looked Like the Prince of Wales (Manfred), 1965
Man Who Lost His Wife (Symons), 1970
Man Who Sold the Moon (s Heinlein), 1950
Man Who Upset the Universe (Asimov), 1955
Man Who Was Loved (s J. Stern), 1951
Man Who Was Not with It (Gold), 1956
Man Who Was There (Morris), 1945
Man Who Won the Pools (Stewart), 1961
Man Who Wrote Detective Stories (s Stewart), 1959
Man Whose Dreams Came True (Symons), 1968
Man Within (Greene), 1929
Man Without a Shadow (C. Wilson), 1963
Manchurian Candidate (Condon), 1959
Mandelbaum Gate (Spark), 1965
Man-Eater of Malgudi (Narayan), 1961
Mangan Inheritance (Moore), 1979
Maniac Responsible (Gover), 1963
Manly-Hearted Woman (Manfred), 1976
Mano Majra (Singh), 1956
Manor (Singer), 1967
Man's Estate (Cleary), 1972
Man's Estate (Humphreys), 1955
Manticore (Davies), 1972
Mantis Carol (van der Post), 1975
Mantissa (Fowles), 1982
Manual Labor (Busch), 1974

Many Coloured Coat (Callaghan), 1960
Many Slippery Errors (Grossman), 1963
Maori Girl (Hilliard), 1960
Maori Woman (Hilliard), 1974
Maquisard (Guerard), 1945
Maras Affair (Ambler, as Reed), 1953
Marathon Man (Goldman), 1974
Margaretha de la Porte (Rooke), 1974
Margie (Fast, as Cunningham), 1966
Maria (Abbas), 1972
Mariana (Dickens), 1940
Marie Beginning (Grossman), 1964
Marilee (s E. Spencer), 1981
Marilyn the Wild (Charyn), 1976
Mariner Dances (Newby), 1948
Marital Rites (Forster), 1981
Marjorie Morningstar (Wouk), 1955
Mark Coffin (Drury), 1979
Mark Lambert's Supper (Stewart), 1954
Mark of the Warrior (Scott, appendix), 1958
Mark of Vishnu (s Singh), 1950
Marked for Murder (Macdonald, as J.R. Macdonald, appendix), 1953
Marmot Drive (Hersey), 1953
Marnie (Graham), 1961
Marriage Machine (Freeman), 1975
Marriages and Infidelities (s Oates), 1972
Marriages Between Zones Three, Four, and Five (Lessing), 1980
Married Man (Read), 1979
Marry Me (Updike), 1976
Martello Tower (Haggard), 1986
Martha and the Eye of Love (Sharp), 1969
Martha, Eric, and George (Sharp), 1964
Martha in Paris (Sharp), 1962
Martha Quest (Lessing), 1952
Martian Chronicles (s R. Bradbury), 1950
Martian Way (s Asimov), 1955
Martyred (Kim), 1964
Maru (Head), 1971
Marx the First (B. Marshall), 1975
Mary Anne (du Maurier), 1954
Mary Deare (Innes), 1956
Mary O'Grady (Lavin), 1950
Marya (Oates), 1986
Mask of Dimitrios (Ambler), 1939
Mask of the Andes (Cleary), 1971
Masked Fisherman (s Brown), 1985
Masks and Faces (Lindsay), 1963
Mass (Sionil Jose), 1982
Master of Space (Arthur C. Clarke), 1961
Matchmaker (Gibbons), 1949
Mate in Three (Rubens), 1965
Matter of Conviction (E. Hunter), 1959
Matters of Chance (s Feinstein), 1980
Maundy (Gloag), 1969
Maut Se Pahlay (s Ali), 1945
Max (Fast), 1982
Max Jamison (Sheed), 1970
May We Borrow Your Husband? (s Greene), 1967
Maybe (Blechman), 1967
Mayo Sergeant (Hall), 1967
McBain Brief (s E. Hunter, as McBain), 1982
McCreary Moves In (M. West, as East), 1958
McGuffin (Bowen), 1984
McKenzie's Hundred (Yerby), 1985

Mr. Wakefield's Crusade (Rubens), 1985
Mister White Eyes (Gold), 1984
Mr. Wrong (s E. Howard), 1975
Mr. Zouch: Superman (Powell), 1934
Mrs. Blood (A. Thomas), 1967
Mrs. Bridge (Connell), 1958
Mrs. Eckdorf in O'Neill's Hotel (Trevor), 1969
Mrs. Pooter's Diary (Waterhouse), 1983
Mrs. Reinhardt (s O'Brien), 1978
Mrs. Stevens Hears the Mermaids Singing (Sarton), 1965
Mrs. Wallop (De Vries), 1970
Mittee (Rooke), 1951
Mixture of Frailites (Davies), 1958
Mobiles (s Cowan), 1979
Mobius the Stripper (s Josipovici), 1974
Moccasin Telegraph (s Kinsella), 1983
Mockery in Arms (Aldridge), 1974
Modulations (s Kostelanetz), 1975
Mog (Tinniswood), 1970
Molloy (Beckett), 1951
Molly's Dog (s A. Adams), 1983
Moment of Choice (Lindsay), 1955
Moment of Eclipse (s Aldiss), 1970
Moment of Love (Moore), 1965
Moment of Truth (Jameson), 1949
Monday Night (Boyle), 1938
Money (M. Amis), 1984
Money from Holme (Stewart, as Innes), 1964
Money Is Love (Condon), 1975
Money Is Love (Glanville), 1972
Money Men (Haggard), 1981
Money, Money, Money (Wagoner), 1955
Moneychangers (Hailey), 1975
Monk Dawson (Read), 1969
Monkey Grip (Garner), 1977
Monsieur (Durrell), 1974
Monsignor Quixote (Greene), 1982
Monsoon Victory (G. Hanley), 1946
Month in the Country (Carr), 1980
Month of Sundays (Updike), 1975
Month of the Falling Leaves (B. Marshall), 1963
Month Soon Goes (Jameson), 1963
Mooltiki (s Godden), 1957
Moon Deluxe (s F. Barthelme), 1983
Moon in My Pocket (M. West, as Morris), 1945
Moon Is a Harsh Mistress (Heinlein), 1966
Moon Is Making (Jameson), 1937
Moon Lake (s Welty), 1980
Moon Was Low (Dickens), 1940
Moonlite (Foster), 1981
Moons of Jupiter (s Munro), 1982
More Joy in Heaven (Callaghan), 1937
More Pricks Than Kicks (s Beckett), 1934
Moreau's Other Island (Aldiss), 1980
Morgan's Passing (Tyler), 1980
Morning Face (Anand), 1968
Morning in Antibes (Knowles), 1962
Morning Red (Manfred), 1956
Morning Star (Raven), 1984
Mortal and the Marble (Dutton), 1950
Mortal Flesh (Phelps), 1974
Mortal Matters (Gilliatt), 1983
Mortality and Mercy in Vienna (s Pynchon), 1976
Morte d'Urban (Powers), 1962
Mosby's Memoirs (s Bellow), 1968
Moscow Gold (Caute, as Salisbury), 1980

Moses Ascending (Selvon), 1975
Moses Migrating (Selvon), 1983
Moses, Prince of Egypt (Fast), 1958
Moses the Lawgiver (Keneally), 1975
Mosquito Coast (P. Theroux), 1981
Most Beautiful Woman in the World (s Abbas), 1968
Most Beautiful Woman in Town (s Bukowski), 1983
Most Private Intrigue (Rosten), 1967
Mother and Two Daughters (Godwin), 1982
Mother Can You Hear Me? (Forster), 1979
Mother Is a Country (Perutz), 1968
Mother Night (Vonnegut), 1962
Mothers and Daughters (E. Hunter), 1961
Mother's Kisses (Friedman), 1964
Mothersill and the Foxes (John A. Williams), 1975
Motor Boys in Ottawa (Hood), 1986
Motorbike (Kops), 1962
Mount Allegro (Mangione), 1943
Mountain Medicine (s Guthrie), 1961
Mountain Path (Arnow), 1936
Mountain Standard Time (Horgan), 1962
Mountains of Gilead (Ford), 1961
Mountolive (Durrell), 1958
Mourners Below (Purdy), 1981
Moviegoer (Percy), 1961
Movies (s Dixon), 1983
Moving On (McMurtry), 1970
Moving Out (Garner), 1983
Moving Parts (Katz), 1977
Moving Target (Macdonald, appendix), 1949
Mud on the Stars (Huie), 1942
Mugger (E. Hunter, as McBain), 1956
Mules (s E. Spencer), 1982
Mulligan Stew (Sorrentino), 1979
Multiple Orgasms (s Markfield), 1977
Mum and Mr. Armitage (s Bainbridge), 1985
Mumbo-Jumbo (Reed), 1972
Munchmeyer (A. Thomas), 1972
Mungo's Dream (Stewart), 1973
Murder at the ABA (Asimov), 1976
Murder Games (Davidson), 1978
Murder in Majorca (Moore, as Bryan), 1957
Murder in Mount Holly (P. Theroux), 1969
Murder in the Dark (s Atwood), 1983
Murder in the Navy (E. Hunter, as Marsten), 1955
Murder Is an Art (Stewart, as Innes), 1959
Murder! Murder! (s Symons), 1961
Murder of Aziz Khan (Ghose), 1967
Murder of Miranda (Millar), 1979
Murder of Quality (le Carré), 1962
Murderer (Heath), 1978
Murders at Moon Dance (Guthrie), 1943
Murdo (s I. Smith), 1981
Murphy (Beckett), 1938
Museums and Women (s Updike), 1972
Music for Mohini (Bhattacharya), 1952
Music from Spain (s Welty), 1948
Music School (s Updike), 1966
Muster of Arms (s Raddall), 1954
Mustian (Price), 1983
Mutual Friend (Busch), 1978
Mutuwhenua (Grace), 1978
Muur die pes (Brink), 1984
My American (Gibbons), 1939
My Amputations (Major), 1986
My Aunt Christina (s Stewart), 1983

Winter Kills (Condon), 1974
Winter Orchard (s J. Johnson), 1935
Winter People (Phelps), 1963
Winthrop Covenant (Auchincloss), 1976
Wise Blood (O'Connor, appendix), 1952
Wise Virgin (A. N. Wilson), 1982
Witch (s Brown), 1977
Witches of Eastwick (Updike), 1984
Witch-Herbalist of the Remote Town (Tutuola), 1981
Witch's Milk (De Vries), 1968
With My Little Eye (Fuller), 1948
With Shuddering Fall (Oates), 1964
Without a City Wall (Bragg), 1968
Without a Stitch in Time (s De Vries), 1972
Without Love (G. Hanley), 1957
Without Motive (Graham), 1936
Wives and Lovers (Millar), 1954
Wizards' Country (Rooke), 1957
Wolf Whistle (s Huie), 1959
Wolfbane (Pohl), 1959
Wolfnight (Freeling), 1982
Wolves Were in the Sledge (Gibbons), 1964
Woman Beware Woman (E. Tennant), 1983
Woman Called Fancy (Yerby), 1951
Woman in a Lampshade (s Jolley), 1983
Woman in Black (S. Hill), 1983
Woman in the House (s Caldwell), 1949
Woman in the Mirror (Graham), 1975
Woman of Character (Gloag), 1973
Woman of Her Age (Ludwig), 1973
Woman of Means (Taylor), 1950
Woman of My Age (Bawden), 1967
Woman of the Future (Ireland), 1979
Woman on the Edge of Time (Piercy), 1976
Woman with a Poet (s Callow), 1983
Woman's Age (Billington), 1979
Women (Bukowski), 1978
Women Against Men (Jameson), 1933
Women and Angels (s Brodkey), 1985
Women and God (Stuart), 1931
Women in the Wall (J. O'Faolain), 1975
Women of Brewster Place (Naylor), 1982
Women of Guinea Lane (Fielding), 1986
Women on the Wall (s Stegner), 1950
Wonder Effect (s Pohl), 1962
Wonderland (Oates), 1971
Wonder-Worker (Jacobson), 1973
Wooden Hunters (M. Cohen), 1975
Woods (Plante), 1982
Woods in Winter (Gibbons), 1970
Word Child (Murdoch), 1975
Word for World Is Forest (Le Guin), 1976
Word of Mouth (Weidman), 1964
Words (Josipovici), 1971
Words of Advice (Weldon), 1977
Words of My Roaring (Kroetsch), 1966
Work (Dixon), 1977
Works of Love (Morris), 1952
World According to Garp (Irving), 1978
World Elsewhere (Bowen), 1965
World Ends (Jameson, as Lamb), 1937
World Enough and Time (Warren), 1950
World in the Attic (Morris), 1949
World Is Made of Glass (M. West), 1983
World Is My Village (Abbas), 1983
World of Apples (s Cheever, appendix), 1973

World of Profit (Auchincloss), 1968
World of Strangers (Gordimer), 1958
World of Violence (C. Wilson), 1963
World of Windows (Benedictus), 1971
World of Wonders (Davies), 1975
World, The Flesh, and Father Smith (B. Marshall), 1945
World's End (s P. Theroux), 1980
World's Fair (Doctorow), 1985
World's Wanderer (Manfred, as Feikema), from 1949
Worm and the Ring (Burgess), 1961
Worstward Ho (s Beckett), 1983
Wort Papers (Mathers), 1972
Would-Be Saint (Jenkins), 1978
Wound of Love (Cassill), 1956
Wounds (Duffy), 1969
Wreath for a Redhead (Moore, as Bryan), 1951
Wreath for Adomo (Abrahams), 1956
Wreath for Garibaldi (s Garrett), 1969
Wreath for Maidens (Munonye), 1973
Wreck of the Cassandra (Prokosch), 1966
Wreck of the Grey Cat (Graham), 1958
Wreck of the Mary Deare (Innes), 1956
Wreckage of Agathon (Gardner, appendix), 1970
Wreckers Must Breathe (Innes), 1940
Wrong Ones in the Dock (Aluko), 1982
Wrong Set (s Angus Wilson), 1949
Wycherly Woman (Macdonald, appendix), 1961

XPD (Deighton), 1981

Y Tri Llais (Humphreys), 1958
Ya! (Woolf), 1971
Yarns of Billy Borker (s Hardy), 1965
Year Before Last (Boyle), 1932
Year in San Fernando (Anthony), 1965
Year of Living Dangerously (Koch), 1978
Year of the French (Flanagan), 1979
Year of the Hot Jock (s Faust), 1985
Year of the Lion (G. Hanley), 1953
Year of the Short Corn (s Urquhart), 1949
Year or So with Edgar (G. Higgins), 1979
Years of the City (Pohl), 1984
Yellow Back Radio Broke-Down (Reed), 1969
Yellow Flowers in the Antipodean Room (Frame), 1969
Yellow Streak (B. Marshall), 1977
Yellow Tapers for Paris (B. Marshall), 1943
Yes from No-Man's Land (Kops), 1965
Yesterday's Enemy (Haggard), 1976
Yesterday's Men (Turner), 1983
Yesterday's Spy (Deighton), 1975
Yonnondio (Olsen), 1974
You Are Now Entering the Human Heart (s Frame), 1984
You Cant Get There from Here (Hood), 1972
You Can't Keep a Good Woman Down (s A. Walker), 1981
You Can't See Around Corners (Cleary), 1947
You Could Live If They Let You (Markfield), 1974
You Make Your Own Life (s Pritchett), 1938
You Want the Right Frame of Reference (W. Cooper), 1971
Young Adolf (Bainbridge), 1978
Young Caesar (Warner), 1958
Young Die Good (Hale), 1932
Young Doctors (Hailey), 1962
Young Hearts Crying (Yates), 1984
Young in One Another's Arms (Rule), 1977
Young Man of Talent (Turner), 1959
Young May Moon (Newby), 1950

NOTES
ON
ADVISERS
AND
CONTRIBUTORS

ALLEN, Walter. See his own entry. **Essays:** Olivia Manning (appendix); V.S. Pritchett; Edward Upward.

ALTNER, Patricia. Librarian and free-lance writer. Reviewer of historical fiction for *Library Journal*; associate editor of *This Year's Scholarship in Science Fiction, Fantasy, and Horror*. **Essays:** Carol Hill; Mary Robison.

ANDERSEN, Richard. James Thurber Writer-in-Residence, Ohio State University, Columbus. Author of critical studies of William Goldman and Robert Coover, and four novels—*Muckaluck, Straight Cut Ditch, On the Run*, and *The Reluctant Hero*. **Essay:** William Goldman.

AUBERT, Alvin. Professor of English, Wayne State University, Detroit; editor of *Obsidian* magazine. Author of three books of poetry—*Against the Blues*, 1972, *Feeling Through*, 1975, and *South Louisiana*, 1985. **Essay:** Ernest J. Gaines.

BAKERMAN, Jane S. Professor of English, Indiana State University, Terre Haute. Author of numerous critical essays, interviews, and reviews; adviser and contributor, *American Women Writers 1–4*. Co-editor of *Adolescent Female Portraits in the American Novel 1961–1981*, 1983, and editor of *And Then There Were Nine: More Women of Mystery*, 1984. **Essays:** Lisa Alther; Daphne du Maurier; May Sarton.

BAMBERGER, William C. Editor and publisher of Bamberger Books, Flint, Michigan. Author of *William Eastlake: High Desert Interlocutor* (forthcoming), criticism in *Review of Contemporary Fiction*, and fiction in *CoEvolution, Ascent*, and other periodicals. **Essays:** Samuel R. Delany; Barry Hannah; Alice Hoffman; Diane Johnson; Steve Katz; David Madden; William Wharton.

BARNES, John. Reader in English, La Trobe University, Bundoora, Victoria; editor of *Meridian*. **Essay:** Peter Cowan.

BENNETT, Bruce. Associate Professor of English, University of Western Australia, Nedlands. Editor of the journal *Westerly: A Quarterly Review*, and the books *The Literature of Western Australia*, 1979, and *Cross Currents: Magazines and Newspapers in Australian Literature*, 1981. **Essay:** Michael Wilding.

BENNETT, Sally H. Free-lance writer. **Essays:** Richard Condon; James A. Michener.

BENSEN, Alice. Professor of English, Eastern Michigan University, Ypsilanti. Author of *Rose Macaulay*, 1969. **Essay:** Margery Sharp.

BERGONZI, Bernard. Professor of English, University of Warwick, Coventry. Author of *Descartes and the Animals*, 1954, *The Early H.G. Wells*, 1961, *Heroes' Twilight*, 1965 (2nd edition 1980), *The Situation of the Novel*, 1970 (2nd edition 1979), *T.S. Eliot*, 1971 (2nd edition 1978), *Gerard Manley Hopkins*, 1977, *Reading the Thirties*, 1978, *Years: Sixteen Poems*, 1979, *Poetry 1870 to 1914*, 1980, and *The Roman Persuasion* (novel), 1981. **Essays:** Anthony Burgess; Nigel Dennis; David Lodge; Julian Mitchell; Andrew Sinclair; Angus Wilson.

BEST, Marshall A. Editor, 1925–34, General Manager, 1935–55, and Editorial Vice-President, 1956–68, Viking Press, New York. Poems, reviews, and translations published in *Atlantic Monthly, Saturday Review*, and other magazines.

Translator of *Avarice House* by Julien Green, 1926. Died 1982. **Essays:** Rumer Godden; Manohar Malgonkar.

BIRNEY, Earle. See his own entry.

BITTNER, William. Late Professor of English, Acadia University, Wolfville, Nova Scotia. Author of *Poe: A Biography, The Novels of Waldo Frank*, and of articles in *Atlantic Monthly, The Nation, Saturday Review, New York Post*, and other periodicals. Died 1977. **Essays:** William Bradford Huie; Anthony C. West.

BORDEN, William. Associate Professor of English, University of North Dakota, Grand Forks. Author of the novel *Superstoe*, 1968, and plays, including *The Last Prostitute*, 1982, and *Loon Dance*, 1983. **Essay:** William Melvin Kelley.

BORKLUND, Elmer. Associate Professor of English, Pennsylvania State University, University Park. Former associate editor of *Chicago Review*. Author of *Contemporary Literary Critics*, 1977 (2nd edition 1982), and of articles in *Modern Philology, Commentary, New York Herald-Tribune Book Week*, and *Journal of General Education*. **Essays:** Brigid Brophy; Mavis Gallant; Mary McCarthy; Susan Sontag; Paul West.

BOWERS, Frederick. Associate Professor of English, University of British Columbia, Vancouver. Author of articles on Arthur Hugh Clough, Gabriel Fielding, syntax, and semantics, in *Renascence, Studies in English Literature, Orbis, Journal of Linguistics*, and other journals. **Essays:** Gabriel Fielding; Frederik Pohl.

BRADBURY, Malcolm. See his own entry. **Essay:** William Cooper.

BRADFORD, M.E. Professor of English and American Studies, University of Dallas; member of the Editorial Board of *Modern Age*. Author of *Rumors of Mortality: An Introduction to Allen Tate*, 1967, *A Better Guide Than Reason*, 1980, *Generations of the Faithful Heart: On the Literature of the South*, 1982, *A Worthy Company*, 1982, and of articles in *Bear, Man, and God*, 1971, *Allen Tate and His Work*, 1971, and *Sewanee Review, National Review, Southern Review*, and other periodicals. Editor of *The Form Discovered: Essays on the Achievement of Andrew Lytle*, 1973. **Essays:** Madison Jones; Andrew Lytle.

BRANDER, Laurence. Author of *George Orwell*, 1954, *Somerset Maugham*, 1963, *E.M. Forster*, 1968, *Aldous Huxley*, 1970, and *Four Acres of Our Own*, 1979. **Essay:** Ahmed Ali.

BROWN, Lloyd W. Member of the Department of Comparative Literature, University of Southern California, Los Angeles. Author of *Amiri Baraka*, 1980, *Women Writers in Black Africa*, 1981, and *West Indian Poetry*, 1984. Editor of *The Black Writer in Africa and the Americas*, 1973. **Essays:** Austin C. Clarke; Roy A.K. Heath; Marion Patrick Jones; Ismith Khan.

BURGESS, Anthony. See his own entry.

BURKE, Herbert C. Formerly William Morley Tweedie Professor of English, Mount Allison University, Sackville, New Brunswick; now retired. Author of articles on modern fiction and reviews in journals, and contributor of poetry and visual art to little magazines. **Essay:** Jack Ludwig.

CADOGAN, Mary. Secretary of an educational trust, governor of an international school, and free-lance writer. Author of three books on popular literature with Patricia Craig—*You're a Brick, Angela!*, 1976, *Women and Children First*, 1978, and *The Lady Investigates*, 1981—and of three volumes of *The Charles Hamilton Companion* (with John Wernham), 1976–82, and *The Morcove Companion*, 1981, and *From Wharton Lodge to Linton Hall*, 1984, both with Tommy Keen. **Essay:** Gillian Freeman.

CAMERON, Silver Donald. Free-lance writer. Author of *Faces of Leacock*, 1967, *Conversations with Canadian Novelists*, 1973, *The Education of Everett Richardson* (labour history), 1977, *Seasons in the Rain* (essays), 1978, *Dragon Lady* (novel), 1980, *The Baitchopper* (novel for young adults), 1982, *Schooner* (social history), 1984, and 26 radio plays. **Essay:** Thomas Head Raddall.

CAMPENNI, Frank. Associate Professor of English, University of Wisconsin, Milwaukee. Author of articles and reviews in periodicals. **Essays:** Barry Beckham; Howard Fast; Irvin Faust; Mark Mirsky; Leo Rosten; Michael Rumaker; Budd Schulberg; Terry Southern; Herman Wouk; Charles Wright.

CARAMELLO, Charles. Associate Professor of English, University of Maryland, College Park. Author of *Silverless Mirrors: Book, Self, and Postmodern American Fiction*, 1983, and some 25 articles and reviews. Co-editor of *Performance in Popular Culture*, 1977. **Essays:** Richard Kostelanetz; Ronald Sukenick.

CARPENTER, Frederic I. Author of *Emerson and Asia*, 1930, *Emerson Handbook*, 1953, *American Literature and the Dream*, 1955, *Robinson Jeffers*, 1962, *Eugene O'Neill*, 1964, and *Laurens van der Post*, 1969. Has taught at the University of Chicago, Harvard University, and the University of California, Berkeley. **Essay:** Laurens van der Post.

CARRUTH, Hayden. Professor of English, Syracuse University, New York; member of the Editorial Board, *Hudson Review*; former poetry editor of *Harper's*. Author of several books of poetry—the most recent being *Asphalt Georgics*, 1985—*Appendix A* (novel), 1963, a book on Camus, and two collections of essays, *Working Papers*, 1982, and *Effluences from the Sacred Caves*, 1983. **Essay:** J.F. Powers.

CHAMBERS, D.D.C. Associate Professor of English, Trinity College, Toronto. **Essays:** N. Scott Momaday; John Rechy.

CHARLES, Gerda. See her own entry. **Essays:** Chaim Bermant; Anita Brookner; Penelope Fitzgerald.

CHARTERS, Ann. Professor of English, University of Connecticut, Storrs. Author of *A Bibliography of Jack Kerouac*, 1967 (revised 1975), *Scenes Along the Road: Photographs of the Desolation Angels*, 1970 (2nd edition 1985), *Nobody: The Story of Bert Williams*, 1970, *Kerouac: A Biography*, 1973, and *I Love: The Story of Vladimir Mayakovsky and Lili Brik*, with Samuel Charters, 1979. Editor of *The Beats: Literary Bohemians in Postwar America*, 2 vols., 1983, and *The Story and Its Writer*, 1983. **Essays:** William S. Burroughs; Jack Kerouac (appendix).

CHEW, Shirley. Lecturer in English, University of Leeds. **Essays:** Patricia Grace; Salman Rushdie.

CHIHARA, Paul Seiko. Associate Professor of Music, University of California, Los Angeles. Composer of numerous works, including *Driftwood* (string quartet), 1969, *Forest Music for Orchestra*, 1970, and music for ballets and films. Author of "Revolution and Music," 1970, and other essays. **Essay:** James Yaffe.

CLANCY, Laurie. Senior Lecturer in English, La Trobe University, Bundoora, Victoria. Author of two novels—*A Collapsible Man*, 1975, and *Perfect Love*, 1983—a collection of short stories—*The Wife Specialist*, 1978—and critical books on Christina Stead, Xavier Herbert, and Nabokov. **Essays:** Murray Bail; David Foster; Elizabeth Jolley; C.J. Koch; Peter Mathers; George Turner.

CLARK, Anderson. Associate Professor of English, and Director of the International English Institute, Belmont College, Nashville. **Essays:** Shelby Foote; Jesse Hill Ford.

COHN, Ruby. Professor of Comparative Drama, University of California, Davis; co-editor of *Modern Drama, Theatre Journal*, and *Cambridge Guide to World Drama*. Author of *Samuel Beckett, The Comic Gamut*, 1962, *Currents in Contemporary Drama*, 1969, *Edward Albee*, 1969, *Dialogue in American Drama*, 1971, *Back to Beckett*, 1974, *Modern Shakespeare Offshoots*, 1976, *Just Play: Beckett's Theatre*, 1980, and *New American Dramatists 1960–1980*, 1982. **Essay:** Samuel Beckett.

COLMER, John. Jury Professor of English, University of Adelaide, Australia; general editor of *Studies in Australian Culture*. Author of *Coleridge: Critic of Society*, 1959, *Approaches to the Novel*, 1967, *E.M. Forster: "A Passage to India,"* 1967, *Forster: The Personal Voice*, 1975, *Patrick White: "Riders in the Chariot,"* 1977, *Coleridge to "Catch-22": Images of Society*, 1978, and *Patrick White*, 1984. Editor of works by Coleridge. **Essays:** Elizabeth Harrower; Shirley Hazzard.

CONROY, Mary. Senior Lecturer in English, Cambridgeshire College of Arts and Technology. **Essay:** Julian Gloag.

COOKE, Judy. Editor of *Fiction Magazine*, London. **Essays:** Martin Amis; A.L. Barker; Jennifer Dawson; Maureen Duffy; Stella Gibbons; Neil Jordan; Wolf Mankowitz; Penelope Mortimer.

CORBALLIS, Richard. Senior Lecturer in English, University of Canterbury, Christchurch, New Zealand. Author of *Stoppard: The Mystery and the Clockwork*, 1984, and *Introducing Witi Ihimaera* (with Simon Garrett), 1984. **Essays:** Graham Billing; Peter Hooper; Keri Hulme.

CORE, George. Editor of *Sewanee Review*, Sewanee, Tennessee. Author of *Writing from the Inside*, 1983. Editor, with Thomas Daniel Young, of *Selected Letters of John Crowe Ransom*, 1984. **Essay:** Robert Penn Warren.

COTTON, John. Author of many books of poetry—collections include *Old Movies*, 1971, *Day Book*, 1981, *Storyville Portraits*, 1984, and *The Crystal Zoo*, 1984—and of *British Poetry since 1965*, 1973. **Essays:** Brian Aldiss; Maggie Gee; D.M. Thomas.

CRAIG, David M. Associate Professor of English, Clarkson University, Potsdam, New York. Author of articles on Heller, Dickens, James, Stevenson, and other writers. **Essays:** Jerome Charyn; William Kennedy.

DAHLIE, Hallvard. Professor of English, University of Calgary, Alberta. Author of *Brian Moore*, 1969 and 1981, *Alice Munro and Her Works*, 1985, and *Varieties of Exile: The Canadian Experience* (forthcoming). Editor of *Literary Half-Yearly* (special Canadian issue), 1972, *The New Land* (co-editor), 1978, and *Ariel* (Exile issue), 1982. **Essays:** Robert Kroetsch; Alice Munro.

DAVIES, Barrie. Professor of English, University of New Brunswick, Fredericton. Editor of *The Selected Prose of Archibald Lampman*. **Essays:** Matt Cohen; David Helwig; C.J. Newman.

DAWSON, Terence. Free-lance writer. Former lecturer in French and Comparative Literature, University of East Anglia, Norwich. Author of articles in *Journal of European Studies* and *Seventeenth-Century French Studies*. **Essay:** Edna O'Brien.

de KOCK, Leon. Lecturer in English, University of South Africa, Pretoria. **Essays:** André Brink; Nadine Gordimer; Christopher Hope.

DESY, Peter. Member of the Department of English, Ohio University, Lancaster. Author of fiction and poetry in many journals and anthologies. **Essays:** Russell Banks; Denis Johnson; W.P. Kinsella; Susan Fromberg Schaeffer.

DICK, Margaret. Author of the novels *Point of Return*, 1958, and *Rhyme or Reason*, 1959, and of *The Novels of Kylie Tennant*, 1966. Reviewer for Sydney *Morning Herald* and *The Australian*. **Essay:** Kylie Tennant.

DILLARD, R.H.W. Professor of English and Chairman of the Graduate Program in Contemporary Literature and Creative Writing, Hollins College, Virginia; editor of *Hollins Critic*. Author of four books of poetry (the most recent being *The Greeting: New and Selected Poems*, 1981), two novels (*The Book of Changes*, 1974, and *The First Man on the Sun*, 1983), a collection of short fiction (*Omniphobia*, 1985), a screenplay, and *Horror Films*, 1976. Editor of two collections of essays. **Essays:** George Garrett; Calder Willingham.

DOEPKE, Dale K. Free-lance writer; author of essays on 19th-century American literature. **Essay:** Eleanor Clark.

DOUGHERTY, Jay. Member of the English Department, University of Connecticut, Storrs; editor of *Clock Radio* literary review. Author of *Coveringdeertrackswithwords*, 1984, articles in *D.H. Lawrence Review, The Explicator*, and *Wallace Stevens Journal*, and poems in literary magazines. **Essay:** Charles Bukowski.

DOYLE, Paul A. Professor of English, Nassau Community College, State University of New York, Garden City; editor, *Evelyn Waugh Newsletter* and *Nassau Review*; contributing editor, *Best Sellers*; consultant, *Choice* and *English Literature in Transition*. Author of studies of Pearl S. Buck, Evelyn Waugh, Sean O'Faolain, Liam O'Flaherty, and Paul Vincent Carroll, and of bibliographies of O'Flaherty and Waugh, a concordance to Joyce's poems, and works on writing skills and bibliography. Editor of *Alexander Pope's Iliad: An Examination* and *Thoreau: Studies and Commentaries*. **Essays:** Thomas Flanagan; Piers Paul Read; Anne Tyler.

DRABBLE, Margaret. See her own entry.

DUCKWORTH, Deborah. Former instructor in English and English as a Second Language, Louisiana State University, Baton Rouge. **Essay:** Elaine Dundy.

EDMANDS, Ursula. Former lecturer in English, Leeds Polytechnic; now with Sheffield City Council. **Essays:** Jack Cope; C.J. Driver; Dan Jacobson; Uys Krige.

EISINGER, Chester E. Former Professor of English, Purdue University, Lafayette, Indiana; now retired. Author of *Fiction of the Forties*, 1963, and articles in *Proletarian Writers of the Thirties*, 1968, and *Saturday Review*. Editor of *The 1940's: Profile of a Nation in Crisis*, 1969. **Essays:** Louis Auchincloss; Saul Bellow; John Cheever (appendix); Robert Coover; William H. Gass; Shirley Ann Grau; John Updike.

EMANUEL, James A. Professor of English, City College of New York; general editor of the Critics Series, Broadside Press, Detroit. Author of six books of poetry—the most recent being *The Broken Bowl*, 1983—and of *Langston Hughes*, 1967, and *How I Write 2* (with others), 1972. Editor, with Theodore L. Gross, of *Dark Symphony: Negro Literature in America*, 1968. **Essays:** James Baldwin; Ann Petry; Margaret Walker.

FABRE, Michel. Professor, University of Paris III. Author of *The Unfinished Quest of Richard Wright*, 1983, *La Rive Noire: de Harlem à la Seine*, 1985, and *The World of Richard Wright*, 1985. **Essays:** Leon Forrest; John Oliver Killens; John Edgar Wideman; Frank Yerby.

FEIN, Richard J. Professor of English, State University College at New Paltz, New York. Author of *Robert Lowell*, 1970 (revised 1979), *The Dance of Leah*, 1985, and articles on Thoreau, modern poetry, and the Jewish story. Editor and translator of *The Selected Poems of Yankev Glatshteyn*, 1986. **Essay:** Henry Roth.

FERGUSON, Brenda R. Free-lance writer. **Essay:** John A. Williams.

FIEDLER, Leslie A. See his own entry.

FIGUEROA, John J. Language Specialist, Manchester Education Committee; Honorary Lecturer, University of Manchester. Author of three books of poetry—the most recent being *Ignoring Hurts*, 1976—two books on Caribbean education, and many articles on language, poetry, cricket, and West Indian society. Editor and co-editor of *Caribbean Writers* (reference book), 1979, and anthologies of African and Caribbean writing. **Essays:** Earl Lovelace; Vic Reid.

FITZGERALD, M.J. Free-lance writer. Author of *Rope-Dancer* (short fiction),1986. **Essays:** Graham Swift; A.N. Wilson.

FOLEY, Barbara. Assistant Professor of English, Northwestern University, Evanston, Illinois. Author of articles on Dos Passos and other writers in *American Literature, Contemporary Literature, Genre, PMLA*, and *Modern Fiction Studies*. **Essay:** E.L. Doctorow.

FORSBERG, Roberta J. Professor of English, Whittier College, California. Author of *Madame de Staël and Freedom Today*, 1963, *Chief Mountain: The Story of Archdeacon S.H. Middleton and the Blackfoot Indians in Alberta, Canada*, 1964, *Madame de Staël and the English*, 1967, *The World of David*

Beaty, 1971, and *Antoine de Saint-Exupéry and David Beaty: Poets of a New Dimension*, 1974. **Essay:** David Beaty.

FOSTER, Ruel E. Benedum Professor of American Literature, West Virginia University, Morgantown. Author of *Work in Progress*, 1948, *William Faulkner: A Critical Appraisal*, 1951, *Elizabeth Madox Roberts, American Novelist* (with Harry Modean Campbell), 1956, and *Jesse Stuart*, 1968. **Essay:** John Knowles.

FRENCH, Warren. Professor of English and Director of the Center for American Studies, Indiana University-Purdue University, Indianapolis, retired 1986; member of the Editorial Board, *American Literature* and *Twentieth-Century Literature*; editor of the American Authors series for Twayne publishers. Author of *John Steinbeck*, 1961, *Frank Norris*, 1962, *J.D. Salinger*, 1963 (revised 1976), *A Companion to "The Grapes of Wrath,"* 1963, *The Social Novel at the End of an Era*, 1966, *The South in Film*, 1981, *Jack Kerouac*, 1986, and a series on American literature, *The Thirties*, 1967, *The Forties*, 1968, *The Fifties*, 1971, and *The Twenties*, 1975. **Essays:** Evan S. Connell, Jr.; R.K. Narayan; Alan Paton; Tom Robbins; Khushwant Singh; Elizabeth Spencer; Eudora Welty.

FRIEDMAN, Alan Warren. Professor of English, University of Texas, Austin; member of the Editorial Board, *Studies in Literature and Language*. Author of *Lawrence Durrell and the Alexandria Quartet*, 1970, *Multivalence: The Moral Quality of Form in the Modern Novel*, 1978, *William Faulkner*, 1984, and essays in *Seven Contemporary Authors*, 1966, and journals. **Essay:** Lawrence Durrell.

FRIEDMAN, Melvin J. Professor of Comparative Literature, University of Wisconsin, Milwaukee; advisory editor of *Journal of Popular Culture, Studies in the Novel, Renascence, Journal of American Culture, Studies in American Fiction, Fer de Lance, Contemporary Literature, Journal of Beckett Studies, International Fiction Review, Arete*, and *Yiddish*. Author of *Stream of Consciousness: A Study in Literary Method*, 1955. Author or editor of works about Beckett, Flannery O'Connor, Styron, Catholic novelists, and Ionesco. **Essays:** Raymond Federman; Robie Macauley; Wallace Markfield; Philip Roth; Sloan Wilson.

FROST, Lucy. Senior Lecturer in English, La Trobe University, Bundoora, Victoria. Author of *No Place for a Nervous Lady: Voices from the Australian Bush*, 1984, and articles on 19th- and 20th-century literature and culture. **Essay:** Frank Moorhouse.

FUEGI, John. Professor and Director of the Comparative Literature Program, University of Maryland, College Park; managing editor, *Brecht Yearbook*. Author of *The Wall* (documentary film), 1961, and *The Essential Brecht*, 1972. Editor of *Brecht Today*, 3 vols., 1972–74. **Essay:** Sol Yurick.

FULLER, Roy. See his own entry.

GALLOWAY, David. Chair of American Studies, University of the Ruhr, Bochum, West Germany. Author *The Absurd Hero*, 1966 (revised 1970 and 1981), *Henry James*, 1967, *Edward Lewis Wallant*, 1979, and four novels—the most recent being *Tamsen*, 1983. Editor of *The Selected Writings of Edgar Allan Poe*, 1967, *Ten Modern American Short Stories*, 1968, *Calamus*, 1982, and *The Other Poe*, 1983. **Essays:** Paul Bowles; James Leo Herlihy; Evan Hunter.

GATES, Norman T. Professor Emeritus of English, Rider College, Trenton, New Jersey. Author of *The Poetry of Richard Aldington*, 1974, and *A Checklist of the Letters of Richard Aldington*, 1977. **Essay:** James Stern.

GEHERIN, David J. Professor of English, Eastern Michigan University, Ypsilanti. Author of *Sons of Sam Spade*, 1980, and *John D. MacDonald*, 1982. **Essays:** Frederick Barthelme; Arthur Hailey; Robert Stone.

GINDIN, James. Professor of English, University of Michigan, Ann Arbor. Author of *Postwar British Fiction*, 1962, *Harvest of a Quiet Eye: The Novel of Compassion*, 1971, *The English Climate: An Excursion into a Biography of John Galsworthy*, 1979, and *John Galsworthy's Life and Art: An Alien's Fortress*, 1986. Editor of *The Return of the Native*, by Hardy, 1969. **Essays:** Kingsley Amis; John Bowen; Malcolm Bradbury; David Cook; Lionel Davidson; Margaret Drabble; John Fowles; Thomas Hinde; Elizabeth Jane Howard; Norman Mailer; Brian Moore; Iris Murdoch; Alan Sillitoe; David Storey; John Wain; Keith Waterhouse.

GORDON, Lois. Professor and Chairman of the Department of English and Comparative Literature, Fairleigh Dickinson University, Teaneck/Rutherford, New Jersey. Author of *Stratagems to Uncover Nakedness: The Dramas of Harold Pinter*, 1969, *Donald Barthelme*, 1981, *Robert Coover: The Universal Fictionmaking Process*, 1983, *Modern America: A Yearbook from 1920 to 1979*, and articles on Richard Eberhart, Randall Jarrell, Faulkner, T.S. Eliot, Philip Roth, Arthur Miller, and other writers. **Essays:** Donald Barthelme; Ann Beattie; Truman Capote (appendix); Raymond Carver; William Gaddis; Erica Jong.

GOYEN, William. Author of five novels (*The House of Breath*, 1950, *In a Farther Country*, 1955, *The Fair Sister*, 1962, *Come, The Restorer*, 1974, and *Arcadio*, 1983), several collections of short fiction (*The Collected Stories*, 1975, *Had I a Hundred Mouths: New and Selected Stories*, 1985), plays, poetry, and non-fiction (*Selected Writings*, 1974). Died 1983. **Essay:** Marguerite Young.

GREACEN, Robert. Author and lecturer. Author of three books of poetry—*One Recent Morning, The Undying Day*, 1948, and *A Garland for Captain Fox*, 1975—and of *The World of C.P. Snow*, 1962, and *Even Without Irene* (autobiography), 1969; reviewer for *Books and Bookmen, Tribune*, and other periodicals. **Essays:** Walter Allen; Storm Jameson; Bill Naughton.

GREENLEAF, Richard. Columnist, *The Daily World*. Author of essays on British and American literary history in *Marxism and Christianity*, 1968, *For a New America*, 1970, and in the journals *Science and Society* and *Religion in Life*. Died 1971. **Essay:** Josephine Johnson.

GRELLA, George. Associate Professor of English, Rochester University, New York. Author of studies of Ian Fleming, Ross Macdonald, and John le Carré in *New Republic*, and articles on the detective novel, film, and popular culture. **Essays:** Len Deighton; J.P. Donleavy; John Irving; Ross Macdonald (appendix).

GUERARD, Albert. See his own entry. **Essays:** John Hawkes; Janet Lewis.

GUPTARA, Prabhu S. Free-lance writer, lecturer, and broadcaster. Author of *Indian Spirituality*, 1984, and *Black British Literature: An Annotated Bibliography*, 1986. Editor of *Third Eye: The Prospects of Third World Film*, 1986. **Essays:** Ahmad Abbas; Lynne Reid Banks; J.G. Farrell (appendix); Gillian Tindall; Morris West.

HALIO, Jay L. Professor of English, University of Delaware, Newark; Chairman of the Editorial Board, University of Delaware Press. Author of *Angus Wilson*, 1964. Editor of *British Novelists since 1960*, 1983, and *Critical Essays on Angus Wilson*, 1985. **Essays:** Isaac Bashevis Singer; William Trevor.

HALL, James B. See his own entry. **Essays:** R.V. Cassill; William Eastlake; Paul Horgan; Frederick Manfred; Wirt Williams.

HANKIN, Cherry A. Reader in English, University of Canterbury, Christchurch, New Zealand. Author of *Katherine Mansfield and Her Confessional Stories*, 1983, and the introduction to the 1974 edition of Maurice Shadbolt's *The New Zealanders*. Editor of *Critical Essays on the New Zealand Novel*, 1976, *It Was So Late and Other Stories* by John Reece Cole, 1978, *Life in a Young Colony: Selections from Early New Zealand Writing*, 1981, *Critical Essays on the New Zealand Short Story*, 1982, and *The Letters of John Middleton Murry to Katherine Mansfield*, 1983. **Essays:** David Ballantyne; Maurice Shadbolt.

HARMON, Maurice. Associate Professor of Anglo-Irish Literature and Drama, University College, Dublin; editor of *Irish University Review*. Author of *Sean O'Faolain: A Critical Introduction*, 1966 (revised 1985), *Modern Irish Literature*, 1967, *The Poetry of Thomas Kinsella*, 1974, *Select Bibliography for the Study of Anglo-Irish Literature and Its Background*, 1976, and *A Short History of Anglo-Irish Literature from the Origins to the Present* (with Roger McHugh), 1982. Editor of works by or about Shakespeare, Synge, Richard Murphy, and Anglo-Irish poetry and fiction. **Essay:** Sean O'Faolain.

HARREX, S.C. Reader in English and Director of the Centre for Research in the New Literature in English, Flinders University of South Australia, Bedford Park. Author of *The Modern Indian Novel in English*, 1972, and of articles on Narayan, Markandaya, Rao, and other Indian writers. **Essay:** Bhabani Bhattacharya.

HART, James A. Associate Professor of English, University of British Columbia, Vancouver; member of the Editorial Board, *Canadian Review of American Studies* and *English Studies in Canada*. Author of articles on Alan Seeger, American poetry of World War I, E.E. Cummings, Allen Tate, Pope, and Chaucer. **Essays:** Allen Drury; Edward Hoagland.

HAWKES, John. See his own entry.

HEATON, David M. Associate Professor of English, and University Ombudsman, Ohio University, Athens. Author of poetry, poetry translations, and articles on Ted Hughes, Alan Sillitoe, Stanley Plumly, Alan Stephens, Ben Belitt, Marvin Bell, Jon Anderson, and George P. Elliott. **Essays:** Frederick Busch; Joan Didion; Toni Morrison; Hubert Selby, Jr.; Jose Yglesias.

HILL, Susan. See her own entry.

HOEFER, Jacqueline. Free-lance writer. Author of articles on Beckett and other modern writers. **Essay:** Kay Boyle.

HOKENSON, Jan. Associate Professor of Languages and Linguistics, Florida Atlantic University, Boca Raton. Author of articles on Beckett, Céline, and Proust, in *James Joyce Quarterly, L'Esprit Créateur, Far-Western Forum*, and *Samuel Beckett: An Anthology of Criticism* edited by Ruby Cohn, 1975. **Essays:** John Gardner (appendix); Bernard Malamud.

HOLM, Janis Butler. Assistant Professor of English, Ohio University, Athens. Author of articles on literary theory, textual bibliography, Tudor cultural history, and women's studies. **Essays:** Gayl Jones; Jayne Anne Phillips.

HUDZIAK, Craig. Doctoral student, University of Wisconsin, Milwaukee. **Essay:** William Humphrey.

IKIN, Van. Senior Tutor in English, University of Western Australia, Nedlands. Editor of the journal *Science Fiction: A Review of Speculative Literature* and the book *Australian Science Fiction*, 1982. **Essays:** Peter Carey; Robert Drewe; Frank Hardy; David Ireland.

JAMES, Louis. Professor of English and American Literature, Keynes College, University of Kent, Canterbury. Author of *The Islands in Between*, 1968, *Fiction for the Working Man 1830–50*, 1974, *Print and the People*, 1976, and *Jean Rhys*, 1978. **Essays:** O.R. Dathorne; Nicholas Hasluck; John Hearne; C.L.R. James; V.S. Naipaul.

JEFFARES, A. Norman. Professor of English Studies, University of Stirling, Scotland; editor of *Ariel: A Review of International English Literature*, and general editor of the Writers and Critics series and the New Oxford English series. Past editor of *A Review of English Studies*. Author of *Yeats: Man and Poet*, 1949, *Seven Centuries of Poetry*, 1956, *A Commentary on the Collected Poems* (1958) and *Collected Plays* (1957) *of Yeats, Anglo-Irish Literature*, 1982, and *A New Commentary on the Poems of W.B. Yeats*, 1984. Editor of *Restoration Comedy*, 1974, *Yeats: The Critical Heritage*, 1977, and *Poems of W.B. Yeats: A New Selection*, 1984. Chairman of the Literature Section of the Scottish Arts Council. **Essays:** Eric Ambler; Nicolas Freeling; William Haggard; Margaret Laurence; Mary Lavin; John le Carré.

JENKINS, Annibel. Associate Professor of English, Georgia Institute of Technology, Atlanta. **Essay:** Emma Smith.

KARIS, William M. Assistant Professor, Clarkson University, Potsdam, New York. **Essay:** Peter Taylor.

KEITH, Margaret. Free-lance writer and researcher; also an actress and director. **Essays:** Hugh Hood; Norman Levine.

KEITNER, Wendy Robbins. Associate Professor of English, University of New Brunswick, Fredericton. **Essay:** Jane Rule.

KEMP, Peter. Associate Lecturer, Middlesex Polytechnic, London. Author of *Muriel Spark*, 1974, and *H.G. Wells and the Culminating Ape*, 1982. **Essay:** William Golding.

KEMP, Sandra. Lecturer in English Literature, University of Glasgow. Author of *Limits and Renewals* (a forthcoming book on Kipling). Editor of a forthcoming anthology of Kipling's stories. **Essay:** Eva Figes.

KENDLE, Burton. Professor of English, Roosevelt University, Chicago. Author of articles on D.H. Lawrence, John Cheever, William March, Tennessee Williams, and others. **Essays:** Burt Blechman; Isabel Colegate; Roald Dahl; Brendan Gill; Alan Lelchuk.

KIERNAN, Brian. Senior Lecturer in English, University of Sydney. Author of *Images of Society and Nature* (on the Australian novel), 1971, and *Patrick White*, 1980. Editor of collections of short stories, criticism, and the work of Henry Lawson. **Essay:** Geoffrey Dutton.

KIERNAN, Robert F. Associate Professor of English, Manhattan College, Bronx, New York. Former associate editor of *Literary Research Newsletter*. Author of *Katherine Anne Porter and Carson McCullers: A Reference Guide*, 1976, *Gore Vidal*, 1982, *American Writing since 1945: A Critical Survey*, 1983, and *Noel Coward*, 1986. **Essays:** Mary Gordon; Gore Vidal.

KING, Bruce. Albert S. Johnston Professor of English, University of North Alabama, Florence; co-editor of Macmillan Modern Dramatists series. Author of *Dryden's Major Plays*, 1966, *Marvell's Allegorical Poetry*, 1977, *New English Literatures: Cultural Nationalism in a Changing World*, 1980, and *History of Seventeenth-Century English Literature*, 1982. Editor of *Introduction to Nigerian Literature*, 1971, *Literatures of the World in English*, 1974, *A Celebration of Black and African Writing*, 1976, and *West Indian Literature*, 1979. **Essays:** Robertson Davies; Anita Desai; Vincent Eri; Epeli Hau'ofa.

KLAUS, H. Gustav. Part-time Reader in English, University of Osnabrück, Germany. Author of *Caudwell im Kontext*, 1978, and *The Literature of Labour*, 1985. Editor of *Gulliver: German-English Yearbook*, 1976–82, and *The Socialist Novel in Britain*, 1982. **Essays:** Barry Hines; Raymond Williams.

KLEIN, H.M. Senior Lecturer in English and Comparative Literature, University of East Anglia, Norwich. Author of a study of English Renaissance poetry, and a translation and commentary of *Hamlet*. Editor of *The First World War in Fiction* and *The Second World War in Fiction*. **Essay:** J.I.M. Stewart.

KLEIN, Marcus. Professor of English, State University of New York, Buffalo. Author of *After Alienation: American Novels at Mid-Century*, 1964, and *Foreigners: The Making of American Literature 1900–1940*, 1981. Editor of *The American Novel since World War II*, 1969, and, with Robert Pack, of *Literature for Composition on the Theme of Innocence and Experience*, 1966, and *Short Stories: Classic, Modern, Contemporary*, 1967. **Essays:** Wright Morris; Richard G. Stern.

KLINKOWITZ, Jerome. Professor of English, University of Northern Iowa, Cedar Falls. Author of *Kurt Vonnegut, Jr.: A Descriptive Bibliography* (with Asa B. Pieratt, Jr.), 1974, *Literary Disruptions*, 1975 (revised 1980), *Donald Barthelme: A Comprehensive Bibliography* (with others), 1977, *The Life of Fiction*, 1977, *Kurt Vonnegut*, 1980, *The Practice of Fiction in America*, 1980, *The American 1960's*, 1980, *Peter Handke and the Postmodern Transformation* (with James Knowlton), 1983, *The Self-Apparent Word*, 1984, *Literary Subversions*, 1985, and *The New American Novel of Manners*, 1986. Editor of *Innovative Fiction*, 1972, *The Vonnegut Statement*, 1973, and *Writing under Fire: Stories of the Vietnam War*, 1978 (all

with John Somers), *Vonnegut in America* (with Donald L. Lawler), 1977, and *The Diaries of Willard Motley*, 1979. **Essays:** Walter Abish; Jonathan Baumbach; Guy Davenport; Stephen Dixon; Jerzy Kosinski; Clarence Major; Thomas McGuane; Gilbert Sorrentino; Dan Wakefield; Rudolph Wurlitzer.

KORGES, James. Free-lance writer. Editor of *Critique: Studies in Modern Fiction*, 1962–70. Author of *Erskine Caldwell*, 1969. Died 1975. **Essays:** Erskine Caldwell; Glenway Wescott.

KORNBLUTH, Martin L. Professor of English, Eastern Michigan University, Ypsilanti; associate editor, *Journal of Narrative Technique*, and review editor, *Choice*. Author of articles on Shaw, Goethe, the folk tale, and other subjects. **Essay:** Glendon Swarthout.

KOSTELANETZ, Richard. See his own entry. **Essay:** Leslie A. Fiedler.

LAY, Mary M. Associate Professor of Liberal Studies, Clarkson University, Potsdam, New York. Author of *Strategies for Technical Writing*, 1982, and articles on Margaret Drabble and Henry James. **Essays:** Gail Godwin; Maureen Howard.

LECKER, Robert. Associate Professor of English, McGill University, Montreal; editor of the journal *Essays on Canadian Writing*. Author of *On the Line*, 1982, and *Robert Kroetsch*, 1986. Editor of several works on Canadian literature and co-editor of the series *The Annotated Bibliography of Canada's Major Authors* and *Canadian Writers and Their Works*. **Essays:** Clark Blaise; Dave Godfrey; John Metcalf.

LeCLAIR, Thomas. Professor of English, University of Cincinnati. Author of articles on contemporary fiction in *Tri-Quarterly*, *Contemporary Literature*, and other journals, and reviews in *New York Times Book Review*, *New Republic*, *Washington Post*, and other periodicals. Editor, with Larry McCaffery, *Anything Can Happen: Interviews with Contemporary American Novelists*, 1983. **Essays:** Don DeLillo; Stanley Elkin; Joseph McElroy; Alexander Theroux.

LEE, Hermione. Lecturer in English, University of York. Presenter, *Book Four* television programme, 1982–85. Author of *The Novels of Virginia Woolf*, 1977, *Elizabeth Bowen: An Estimation*, 1981, *Philip Roth*, 1982, and introductions to works by Flannery O'Connor, Edith Oliver, Antonia White, Bowen, and Woolf. Editor of *Stevie Smith: A Selection*, 1983, and *The Duke's Children* by Trollope, 1983.

LEECH, Anastasia. Free-lance writer. **Essay:** Bruce Marshall.

LEHMANN, John. Founding editor of *New Writing, Daylight, Penguin New Writing, The London Magazine*, and the BBC's *New Soundings*. His most recent book of poetry is *The Reader at Night*, 1974; other recent books are *In My Own Time: Memoirs of a Literary Life, Thrown to the Woolfs: Leonard and Virginia Woolf and the Hogarth Press, Rupert Brooke: His Life and His Legend, The English Poets of the First World War*, and *Three Literary Friendships*.

LEVIN, Harry. Irving Babbitt Professor of Comparative Literature, Harvard University, Cambridge, Massachusetts. Author of many critical books, the most recent being *The Myth of the Golden Age in the Renaissance, Grounds for Comparison, Shakespeare and the Revolution of the Times*, and *Memo-*

ries of the Moderns. Editor of works by Jonson, Rochester, Joyce, Shakespeare, and Hawthorne, and of anthologies.

LEWIS, Margaret B.   Part-time tutor, Open University, and administrative assistant, University of Newcastle-upon-Tyne. **Essays:** Ruth Prawer Jhabvala; Thomas Keneally; Paul Scott (appendix); Patrick White.

LEWIS, Naomi.   Writer, critic, and broadcaster. Author of *A Visit to Mrs. Wilcox*, 1957, *Fantasy Books for Children*, 1975 (revised 1977), books for children, including *Once upon a Rainbow*, 1981, and *Come with Us*, 1982, and introductory essays to works on or by Hans Christian Andersen, E. Nesbit, Christina Rossetti, Arthur Waley, and others; contributor to *The Observer, New Statesman, Times Literary Supplement, Listener*, and other periodicals. Editor of *A Peculiar Music: Poems for Young Readers* by Emily Brontë, 1971, and the anthologies *A Footprint on the Air*, 1983, and *Messages*, 1985. **Essay:** J.L. Carr.

LEWIS, Peter.   Lecturer in English, University of Durham. Author of *The Beggar's Opera* (critical study), 1976, and *John le Carré*, 1984. Editor of *The Beggar's Opera* by John Gay, 1973, *Poems '74* (anthology of Anglo-Welsh poetry), 1974, and *Radio Drama*, 1981. **Essays:** Peter Ackroyd; Paul Bailey; A.S. Byatt; Maurice Gee; Ian McEwan; Nicholas Mosley; Emma Tennant.

LINDBERG, Stanley W.   Editor of *Georgia Review* and Professor of English, University of Georgia, Athens. Author of *The Annotated McGuffey*, 1976, and *Van Nostrand's Plain English Handbook*, 1980. Editor of *The Plays of Frederick Reynolds*, 3 vols., 1983. **Essay:** Jack Matthews.

LINDFORS, Bernth.   Professor of African and English Literature, University of Texas, Austin; founding editor, *Research in African Literatures*. Author of *Folklore in Nigerian Literature, Early Nigerian Literature*, and many articles on African literature, including essays on Richard Rive, La Guma, Achebe, Ekwensi, Tutuola, and D.O. Fagunwa. **Essays:** Peter Abrahams; Es'kia Mphahlele; Abioseh Nicol; Amos Tutuola.

LINDSAY, Jack.   See his own entry. **Essay:** James Aldridge.

LUCAS, John.   Professor and Head of the Department of English and Drama, Loughborough University, Leicestershire; advisory editor, *Victorian Studies, Literature and History*, and *Journal of European Studies*. Author of *Tradition and Tolerance in 19th-Century Fiction*, 1966, *The Melancholy Man: A Study of Dickens*, 1970, *Arnold Bennett*, 1975, *Egilssaga: The Poems*, 1975, *The Literature of Change*, 1977, *The 1930's: Challenge to Orthodoxy*, 1978, *Romantic to Modern*, 1982, and *Moderns and Contemporaries*, 1985. Editor of *Literature and Politics in the 19th Century*, 1971, and of works by George Crabbe and Jane Austen. **Essays:** David Caute; Barry Cole; Martha Gellhorn.

LYNCH, Robert E.   Professor of English, New Jersey Institute of Technology, Newark. Author of articles in *The Reader's Encyclopedia of Shakespeare*, 1966, and *The Reader's Encyclopedia of World Drama*, 1969. Editor of *The Example of Science: An Approach to College Composition*, 1981. **Essays:** Frederick Forsyth; Leonard Michaels.

MACHANN, Clinton.   Associate Professor of English, Texas A & M University, College Station. Author of *Krásná Amer-*

ika: A Study of the Texas Czechs 1851–1939, 1983, and numerous articles on British and American literature. **Essays:** Chaim Potok; Leslie Marmon Silko.

MADDEN, David.   See his own entry. **Essay:** Carson McCullers (appendix).

MAES-JELINEK, Hena.   Chargé de Cours, University of Liège, Belgium. Author of *Criticism of Society in the English Novel Between the Wars*, 1970, *The Naked Design*, 1976, *Wilson Harris*, 1982, *Heart of Darkness*, 1982, and articles on Peter Abrahams, V.S. Naipaul, Patrick White, and Wilson Harris. Editor of *Commonwealth Literature and the Modern World*, 1975, and *Explorations*. **Essay:** Wilson Harris.

MALIN, Irving.   Professor of English, City College of the City University of New York. Author of *William Faulkner: An Interpretation*, 1957, *New American Gothic*, 1962, *Jews and Americans*, 1965, *Saul Bellow's Fiction*, 1969, *Nathanael West's Novels*, 1972, and *Isaac Bashevis Singer*, 1972. Editor of casebooks and collections of essays on Bellow, Capote, Styron, Singer, and McCullers, and of *Psychoanalysis and American Fiction* and *Contemporary American-Jewish Literature*. **Essay:** James Purdy.

MARX, Paul.   Professor of English, University of New Haven, Connecticut. Editor of *12 Short Story Writers*, 1970. **Essay:** Larry Woiwode.

MATHIAS, Roland.   Poet and critic; former editor of *Anglo-Welsh Review*, and former chairman of the Welsh Arts Council Literature Committee. Author/ of six books of poetry (most recently *Burning Brambles: Selected Poems 1944–1979*, 1983), a collection of short stories, and studies of Vernon Watkins and John Cowper Powys. Editor of *Anglo-Welsh Poetry 1480–1980* (with Raymond Garlick), 1984, *A Ride Through the Wood* (forthcoming), works by Welsh authors, and a collection of essays on David Jones. **Essay:** Emyr Humphreys.

MATTHEWS, Brian E.   Reader in English, Flinders University of South Australia, Bedford Park. Author of *The Receding Wave: A Study of Henry Lawson's Prose*, 1972, and *Louisa: A Diary, A Life* (biographical study of Louisa Lawson), 1986. Editor of *Selected Stories of Henry Lawson*, 1972, and co-editor of *New Literary History of Australia* (forthcoming). **Essays:** Thea Astley; Jon Cleary.

McCONNELL, Frank D.   Associate Professor of English, Northwestern University, Evanston, Illinois. Author of *The Spoken Seen: Film and the Romantic Imagination*, 1975, *Four Postwar American Novelists*, 1978, and articles on William S. Burroughs, Byron, and Flaubert. **Essay:** Thomas Pynchon.

McCORMICK, John.   Professor of Comparative Literature, Rutgers University, New Brunswick, New Jersey. Author of *Catastrophe and Imagination* (on the modern novel), 1957, *The Complete Aficionado*, 1967, *American Literature 1919–1932: A Comparative History*, 1971, and *Fiction as Knowledge*, 1975. **Essay:** Rex Warner.

McDOWELL, Frederick P.W.   Professor of English, University of Iowa, Iowa City. Author of *Ellen Glasgow and the Ironic Art of Fiction*, 1960, *Elizabeth Madox Roberts*, 1963, *Caroline Gordon*, 1966, *Forster: An Annotated Bibliography of Writings about Him*, 1976, *E.M. Forster*, 1982, and articles on Shaw and Robert Penn Warren. **Essays:** Melvyn Bragg; John Braine; Gerda Charles; Frederic Raphael.

McDOWELL, Margaret B. Professor of Rhetoric and Women's Studies, University of Iowa, Iowa City. Author of *Edith Wharton*, 1975, and *Carson McCullers*, 1980. **Essays:** Angela Carter; Ellen Gilchrist; Jamaica Kincaid; Gloria Naylor; Tillie Olsen; Alice Walker.

McELROY, George. Lecturer at Indiana University Northwest, Gary. Author of textbooks and of articles on Edmund Burke and 19th-century light opera. **Essay:** Anthony West.

MEPHAM, John. Free-lance writer and editor. Former Lecturer in Philosophy, University of Sussex, Brighton. Co-author of *Issues in Marxist Philosophy*, 3 vols., 1979, and author of many articles on philosophy and literature. **Essays:** Gabriel Josipovici; David Malouf.

MERIVALE, Patricia. Professor of English, University of British Columbia, Vancouver. Author of articles in *Harvard Studies in Comparative Literature* and other periodicals. **Essay:** Jerzy Peterkiewicz.

MIELKE, Robert E. Instructor in English and Director of the Writing Center, Wake Forest University, Winston-Salem, North Carolina. Author of articles in *Warnings: An Anthology on the Nuclear Peril*, 1984, and *Teaching Writing: Pedagogy, Gender and Equity*, 1986, and of reviews, essays, short fiction, and poetry in journals. **Essay:** J.G. Ballard.

MITCHISON, Naomi. See her own entry. **Essay:** Fred Urquhart.

MONTAGUE, John. Lecturer in Poetry, University College, Cork. Author of many books of poetry including *The Rough Field* (collected edition 1972) and, most recently, *The Dead Kingdom*, a play, and a collection of short stories. Editor of *The Dolmen Miscellany of Irish Writing* and *The Faber Book of Irish Verse*, and translator of a collection of Irish poetry and *November* by André Frénaud. **Essay:** John McGahern.

MONTROSE, David. Free-lance writer. Regular reviewer for *New Statesman*, *Times Literary Supplement*, and *Honest Ulsterman*. **Essays:** Julian Barnes; William Boyd.

MOORE, Gerald. Editor of the Modern African Writers series. Former Professor of English, University of Jos, Nigeria. Author of *The Chosen Tongue*, 1969, *Wole Soyinka*, 1971 (revised 1978), and *Twelve African Writers*, 1980. Editor, with Ulli Beier, of *The Penguin Book of Modern African Poetry*, 1984. **Essays:** Elechi Amadi; George Lamming; Garth St. Omer.

MOORE, Harry T. Research Professor of English Emeritus, Southern Illinois University, Carbondale; editor of the Crosscurrents/Modern Critiques series. Author and editor of many books, including studies of Lawrence, Steinbeck, Forster, Rilke, Durrell, and James. Died 1981. **Essay:** Francis Stuart.

MORACE, Robert A. Associate Professor of English, Daemen College, Amherst, New York; Lecturer on American Literature, University of Warsaw, 1985–86. Author of *John Gardner: An Annotated Secondary Bibliography*, 1984, and essays on contemporary fiction and literary realism in anthologies and journals. Editor, with Kathryn VanSpanckeren, of

John Gardner: Critical Perspectives, 1982. **Essay:** Renata Adler.

MORDDEL, Anne. Free-lance writer. **Essays:** Mervyn Jones; Marilynne Robinson.

MORPURGO, J.E. Emeritus Professor of American Literature, University of Leeds. Author and editor of many books, including *The Pelican History of the United States*, 1955 (third edition 1970), and volumes on Cooper, Lamb, Trelawny, Cobbett, Barnes Wallis, the publisher Allen Lane, and on Athens, Venice and rugby football. **Essays:** A.B. Guthrie, Jr.; Hugh MacLennan.

MORRIS, Robert K. Professor of English, City College of the City University of New York. Author of *The Novels of Anthony Powell*, 1968, *The Consolations of Ambiguity: An Essay on the Novels of Anthony Burgess*, 1971, *Continuance and Change: The Contemporary British Novel Sequence*, 1972, and *Paradoxes of Order: Some Perspectives on the Fiction of V.S. Naipaul*, 1975. Editor of *The Achievement of William Styron* (with Irving Malin), 1975 (revised 1981), and *Old Lines, New Forces: Essays on the Contemporary British Novel 1960–1970*, 1976. **Essay:** Anthony Powell.

MURRAY, Christopher. Statutory Lecturer in English, University College, Dublin; member of the Executive Board, *Irish University Review*. Author of *Robert William Elliston, Manager*, 1975. Editor of *St. Stephen's Green* (an Irish Restoration comedy), 1980, and *Selected Plays of Lennox Robinson*, 1982. **Essay:** John Broderick.

MURRAY-SMITH, Stephen. Reader in Education, University of Melbourne. Founding editor of *Overland*, and former editor of *Melbourne Studies in Education*. Author of *Henry Lawson*, 1962 (2nd edition 1975), *Mission to the Islands*, 1979, and *Indirections*, 1981. Editor of *The Tracks We Travel*, 1953, *An Overland Muster*, 1965, *His Natural Life* by Marcus Clarke, 1970, *Classic Australian Short Stories* (with Judah Waten), 1974, and *The Dictionary of Australian Quotations*, 1984.

MUSSELL, Kay J. Director of the American Studies Program, American University, Washington, D.C. Author of *Women's Gothic and Romantic Fiction: A Reference Guide*, 1981, and *Fantasy and Reconciliation: Contemporary Formulas of Women's Romance Fiction*, 1984. **Essays:** Laura Z. Hobson; Fletcher Knebel.

NARAYAN, Shyamala A. Lecturer in English, Ranchi Women's College, India. Author of *Sudhin N. Ghose*, 1973, studies of Raja Rao, Nissim Ezekiel, and other Indian writers, and reviews in *The Hindu, Journal of Indian Writing in English*, and other periodicals. Compiler of the Indian section of "The Bibliography of Commonwealth Literature" published annually in *Journal of Commonwealth Literature*. **Essays:** Mulk Raj Anand; Sasthi Brata; Chaman Nahal; Nayantara Sahgal.

NEW, W.H. Professor of English, University of British Columbia, Vancouver; editor of *Canadian Literature* and associate editor of *World Literature Written in English*. Author of *Malcolm Lowry*, 1971, *Articulating West*, 1972, *Among Worlds*, 1975, *Malcolm Lowry: A Reference Guide*, 1978, *An Active Voice*, 1980, and other books and articles. Editor, with W.E. Messenger, of *A 20th Century Anthology*, 1984. **Essays:** Janet Frame; Zulfikar Ghose; W. O. Mitchell; Orlando Patterson; Randolph Stow; Rudy Wiebe; Adele Wiseman.

NORRIS, Leslie. Poet and lecturer. Christensen Fellow in the Humanities, Brigham Young University, Salt Lake City. Author of nine books of poetry (the most recent being *Walking the White Fields*, 1980), *Sliding and Other Stories*, 1976, and a study of Glyn Jones. Editor of a translation of *The Mabinogion* and of books on Vernon Watkins and Andrew Young. **Essay:** Glyn Jones.

NYE, Robert. See his own entry. **Essay:** Alan Burns.

O'HEARN, D.J. Sub-Dean, Faculty of Arts, University of Melbourne. Author of articles on Australian literature; regular fiction reviewer for Melbourne *Age* and Sydney *Australian*. **Essay:** Morris Lurie.

O'NEILL, John P. Late Associate Professor of English, Georgia Institute of Technology, Atlanta. Regular reviewer for the Atlanta *Journal and Constitution*. Died 1977. **Essay:** Sybille Bedford.

ORMOND, John. Documentary film-maker for the BBC, and poet. His films include *Under a Bright Heaven* (on Vernon Watkins), *A Bronze Mask* (on Dylan Thomas), *The Fragile Universe* (on Alun Lewis), and, most recently, *The Colliers' Crusade*, 1979. Author of several books of poetry including *Definition of a Waterfall*, 1973. **Essay:** Peter Tinniswood.

O'TOOLE, Bridget. Lecturer in English, University of Ulster, Coleraine. **Essay:** Rachel Trickett.

OZICK, Cynthia. See her own entry.

PACEY, Desmond. Late Vice-President (Academic), University of New Brunswick, Fredericton. Author of *Frederick Philip Grove*, 1945, *Creative Writing in Canada*, 1952 (revised 1962), *The Picnic and Other Stories*, 1958, *Our Literary Heritage*, 1968, and *Essays in Canadian Criticism*, 1969. Editor of *A Book of Canadian Stories*, 1947, and *Ten Canadian Poets*, 1958. Died 1975. **Essay:** Sinclair Ross.

PAGE, Malcolm. Associate Professor of English, Simon Fraser University, Burnaby, British Columbia; President, Association for Canadian Theatre History. Author of *John Arden*, 1984, *Arden on File*, 1985, *Stoppard on File*, 1986, and forthcoming books on *Richard II* and the Canadian playwright Michael Cook. **Essay:** Michael Frayn.

PARISI, Joseph. Associate Editor of *Poetry* magazine, Chicago. Editor, with Daryl Hine, of *The "Poetry" Anthology 1912–1977*, 1978. **Essays:** Janet Burroway; Colin Spencer.

PEDEN, William. Professor of English, University of Missouri, Columbia. Author of *Night in Funland and Other Stories*, 1968, *Twilight at Monticello* (novel), 1973, and *The American Short Story: Continuity and Change 1940–1975*, 1975. **Essay:** Nancy Hale.

PEHOWSKI, Marian. Free-lance writer and critic. Has taught comparative literature or journalism at five universities. **Essays:** Isaac Asimov; Harold Brodkey; Hortense Calisher; Niccolò Tucci.

PERKINS, Barbara M. Managing Editor of *Journal of Narrative Technique*, Eastern Michigan University, Ypsilanti. Author of articles in *Harper Handbook to Literature, American Literary Magazines: The Eighteenth and Nineteenth Centuries*, and other books and periodicals. **Essays:** Richard E. Kim; Jerre Mangione; Douglas Woolf.

PERKINS, George. Professor of English, Eastern Michigan University, Ypsilanti. Author or editor of *Writing Clear Prose*, 1964, *Varieties of Prose*, 1966, *The Theory of the American Novel*, 1970, *Realistic American Short Fiction*, 1972, *American Poetic Theory*, 1972, *The Practical Imagination* (with others), 1980, *The Harper Handbook to Literature* (with others), 1985, and *The American Tradition in Literature* (with others), sixth edition, 1985. **Essays:** Robert Gover; John Clellon Holmes.

PHIPPS, Frank T. Former Chairman of the Department of English, University of Akron, Ohio. **Essay:** Joseph Mitchell.

PIERCY, Marge. See her own entry. **Essays:** E.M. Broner; Joanna Russ.

PINSKER, Sanford. Professor of English, Franklin and Marshall College, Lancaster, Pennsylvania. Author of *The Schlemiel as Metaphor: Studies in the Yiddish and American-Jewish Novel*, 1971, *The Comedy That "Hoits": An Essay on the Fiction of Philip Roth*, 1975, *Still Life and Other Poems*, 1975, *The Languages of Joseph Conrad*, 1978, *Between Two Worlds: The American Novel in the 1960's*, 1978, *Memory Breaks Off and Other Poems*, 1984, *Conversations with Contemporary American Writers*, 1985, and many articles on contemporary fiction. Editor of *Critical Essays on Philip Roth*, 1982, and *America and the Holocaust* (with Jack Fischel), 1984. **Essays:** David Bradley; Bruce Jay Friedman; Johanna Kaplan; Jay Neugeboren.

PORTALES, Marco. Associate Professor of Literature, University of Houston, Clear Lake; associate editor of *MELUS*. Author of articles on Virginia Woolf, Henry James, Twain, Kate Chopin, Sarah Orne Jewett, Chicano and Native American writers, and other subjects. **Essay:** Rudolfo A. Anaya.

PORTER, Hal. Fiction writer, poet, and playwright. Author of three novels (*A Handful of Pennies, The Tilted Cross, The Right Thing*), several collections of short stories (*Selected Stories*, 1971), four plays, three books of poetry, three volumes of autobiography, and other non-fiction; a general selection, *Hal Porter*, was published in 1980. Died 1984.

POWELL, Anthony. See his own entry.

POYNTING, Jeremy. Lecturer, Thomas Danby College, Leeds. Author of articles in *Journal of Commonwealth Literature, Journal of South Asian Literature, World Literature Written in English, Kyk-over-Al*, and other periodicals. **Essays:** Michael Anthony; Ralph de Boissière; Andrew Salkey.

QUIGLY, Isabel. Free-lance writer and critic. Author of the novel *The Eye of Heaven*, 1955, *The Heirs of Tom Brown: The English School Story*, 1982, a book on Charlie Chaplin, and many articles and reviews in *The Times, The Guardian*, and other periodicals. Editor, with Susan Hill, of *New Stories 5*, 1980. Translator of works of European fiction and non-fiction. **Essays:** Lettice Cooper; Winston Graham.

RAVENSCROFT, Arthur. Retired university teacher (taught in Cape Town, Stellenbosch, Harare, and Leeds); founding editor, *Journal of Commonwealth Literature*, 1965–79. Author of *Chinua Achebe*, 1969 (revised 1977), *Nigerian Writers and* *the African Past*, 1978, and *A Guide to Twentieth-Century English, Irish and Commonwealth Literature* (with Harry Blamires and Peter Quartermain), 1983. Translator, with C.K. Johnman, of *Journal of Jan van Riebeeck*, vol. 3, 1958. **Essays:** Chinua Achebe; T.M. Aluko; I.N.C. Aniebo; Cyprian Ekwensi; Ahmed Essop; Bessie Head; John Munonye; Ngugi wa Thiong'o.

REID, J.C. Late Professor of English, University of Auckland. Author of *The Mind and Art of Coventry Patmore*, 1957, *Francis Thompson, Man and Poet*, 1959, *Thomas Hood*, 1963, and *Bucks and Bruisers: Pierce Egan and Regency England*, 1971. Died 1972. **Essay:** Errol Brathwaite.

REILLY, John M. Professor of English, State University of New York, Albany. Author of many articles on Afro-American literature, popular crime writing, and social fiction, and bibliographical essays in *Black American Writers*, 1978, and *American Literary Scholarship*. Editor of *Richard Wright: The Critical Reception*, 1978, and the reference book *Twentieth-Century Crime and Mystery Writers*, 1980 (2nd edition 1985). **Essays:** Cyrus Colter; Ralph Ellison; Dick Francis; George V. Higgins; Kristin Hunter; Paule Marshall; Peter Matthiessen; Larry McMurtry; Margaret Millar; Al Young.

REXROTH, Kenneth. Poet and critic; lecturer at the University of California, Santa Barbara. Author of many books of verse (most recently *The Morning Star*, 1979), plays (*Beyond the Mountains*, 1951), and non-fiction (most recently *The Elastic Retort*, 1973, and *Communalism*, 1975). Editor of several collections of poetry and translator of works by Asian, European, and classical authors. Died 1982.

RHODES, H. Winston. Professor of English (retired), University of Canterbury, Christchurch, New Zealand. Co-founder of *Tomorrow* and *New Zealand Monthly Review*. Author of *New Zealand Fiction since 1945*, 1968, *Frank Sargeson*, 1969, *New Zealand Novels*, 1969, *Frederick Sinclaire: A Memoir*, 1984, and other books. Editor of six volumes of Rewi Alley's prose and poetry and *I Saw in My Dream* by Sargeson, 1976. **Essays:** Dan Davin; Roderick Finlayson; Noel Hilliard; Witi Ihimaera; O.E. Middleton; Bill Pearson; Albert Wendt.

ROSS, Alan. Editor of *London Magazine* and Managing Director of London Magazine Editions. Author of several books of poetry, the most recent being *Death Valley*, 1980, and of critical works, travel books, and books for children. Editor of works by John Gay and Lawrence Durrell and of several anthologies. Translator of four French works.

ROSSET, Barney. President of Grove Press, Inc. Editor of *Evergreen Review Reader 1* and *2*, 1979.

ROYLE, Trevor. Free-lance writer and broadcaster; editor of *Lines Review*. Author of *We'll Support You Ever More: The Impertinent Saga of Scottish Fitba'*, with Ian Archer, 1976, *Jock Tamson's Bairns*, 1977, *Precipitous City: The Story of Literary Edinburgh*, 1980, *Death Before Dishonour: The Truth about Fighting Mac*, 1982, *The Macmillan Companion to Scottish Literature*, 1983, *James and Jim: The Biography of James Kennaway*, 1983, *The Kitchener Enigma*, 1985, and many articles in journals. **Essays:** Richard Adams; Nina Bawden; George Mackay Brown; Brian Glanville; Giles Gordon; Alasdair Gray; Clifford Hanley; Hammond Innes; Robin Jenkins; Benedict Kiely; Allan Massie; Robert Nye; James Plunkett; Elizabeth Smart; Iain Crichton Smith.

RUBIN, Louis D., Jr. Professor of English, University of North Carolina, Chapel Hill; general editor, Southern Literary Studies series; co-editor, *Southern Literary Journal*. Author and editor of many books, including the novel *The Golden Weather*, 1961, and, most recently, *William Elliott Shoots a Bear*, 1975, *The Wary Fugitives: Four Poets and the South*, 1978, *The American South: Portrait of a Culture*, 1979, *The Even-Tempered Angler*, 1983, and *A Gallery of Southerners*, 1984. **Essay:** William Styron.

SADLER, Geoff. Assistant Librarian, Local Studies, Chesterfield, Derbyshire. Author of western novels (as Jeff Sadler), including, most recently, *Throw of a Rope*, 1984, and *Manhunt in Chihuahua*, 1984, and the *Justus* trilogy of plantation novels (as Geoffrey Sadler), 1982. **Essays:** Stan Barstow; Rachel Billington; Clare Boylan; Desmond Hogan; Dambudzo Marechera; David Plante; David Pownall; Samuel Selvon; Rose Tremain.

SAMBROOK, Hana. Free-lance editor and writer. Author of study guides to *The Tenant of Wildfell Hall, Lark Rise to Candleford*, and *Victory*. **Essays:** Margaret Forster; Bernice Rubens.

SANDERS, David. Miller Professor of Humanities, Harvey Mudd College, Claremont, California. Author of *John Hersey*, 1967, and of articles on Hemingway and Dos Passos. **Essays:** Vance Bourjaily; Peter De Vries; Joseph Heller; John Hersey; James Jones (appendix).

SANDERSON, Stewart F. Honorary Harold Orton Fellow, University of Leeds; Chairman of the Literature Committee, Scottish Arts Council. Author of *Hemingway*, 1961 (revised 1970), and of many articles on British and comparative folklore and ethnology, and on modern literature. Editor of *The Secret Common-Wealth* by Robert Kirk, 1970, *The Linguistic Atlas of England* (with others), 1978, and *Studies in Linguistic Geography*, 1985. **Essays:** Gerald Hanley; Geoffrey Household; Simon Raven.

SCHAFER, William J. Professor of English, Berea College, Kentucky. Author of articles on David Wagoner and Ralph Ellison in *Critique* and *Satire Newsletter*. **Essays:** Elliott Baker; Stephen Becker; David Benedictus; Thomas Berger; Harry Crews; Nell Dunn; David Ely; Mark Harris; James A. McPherson; Reynolds Price; Mario Puzo; Ishmael Reed; Wilfrid Sheed; Clancy Sigal; Paul Theroux; David Wagoner; John Williams.

SCHORER, Mark. Late Professor of English, University of California, Berkeley. Author of three novels, three collections of short stories, and several critical works, including studies of Blake, Lawrence, and Sinclair Lewis. Editor of anthologies of fiction and literary criticism and of works by Capote and Lawrence. Died 1977.

SCOTT, Alexander. Reader in Scottish Literature, Glasgow University. Author of several books of verse, the most recent being *Poems in Scots*, 1978, plays, a biography of William Soutar, and *The MacDiarmid Makars 1923–1972*, 1972. Editor of works by William Jeffrey, Alexander Scott (1530–1584), and Soutar, and of anthologies of Scottish poetry. **Essay:** Naomi Mitchison.

SECOR, Cynthia. Free-lance writer. **Essay:** Daphne Rooke.

SEIDEL, Kathryn Lee. Assistant Professor of English, University of Maryland, College Park. Author of *The Southern Belle in American Fiction: Her Rise and Fall*, 1985, and articles on Joanna Russ, Marge Piercy, Ursula K. Le Guin, Faulkner's women, and Ellen Glasgow's satire. **Essay:** Marge Piercy.

SHUCARD, Alan R. Associate Professor of English, University of Wisconsin-Parkside, Kenosha. Author of three books of poetry and a study of Countée Cullen. **Essays:** James B. Hall; Kathrin Perutz; Irving Stone; Leon Uris.

SIEGEL, Ben. Professor of English, California State Polytechnic University, Pomona. Author of *The Puritan Heritage: America's Roots in the Bible*, 1964, *Biography Past and Present*, 1965, *Isaac Bashevis Singer*, 1969, *The Controversial Sholem Asch*, 1976, and articles on Israel Joshua Singer, Malamud, Philip Roth, and Bellow. **Essay:** Daniel Fuchs.

SMITH, Angela. Lecturer in Commonwealth Literature, University of Stirling. Author of study guides to *Persuasion*, *Wuthering Heights*, and *Voss*, and the chapter on writing in Mauritius in *The Writing of East and Central Africa* edited by G.D. Killam, 1985. **Essays:** Ayi Kwei Armah; Nuruddin Farah.

SMITH, Christopher. Senior Lecturer, School of Modern Languages and European History, University of East Anglia, Norwich; editor of *Seventeenth-Century French Studies*. Author of *Alabaster, Bikinis and Calvados: An ABC of Toponymous Words*, 1985, a forthcoming study of Jean Anouilh, and many articles and reviews of the performing arts. Editor of works by Antoine de Montchrestien, Jean de la Taille, and Pierre Matthieu. **Essays:** Buchi Emecheta; Penelope Gilliatt; Peter Vansittart.

SMITH, Curtis C. Professor of Humanities, University of Houston, Clear Lake. Author of *Olaf Stapledon: A Bibliography* (with Harvey J. Satty), 1984. Editor of the reference book *Twentieth-Century Science-Fiction Writers*, 1981 (2nd edition 1986). **Essays:** Ray Bradbury; Arthur C. Clarke; Ursula K. Le Guin.

SMITH, Grahame. Senior Lecturer in English Studies, University of Stirling. Author of *Dickens, Money and Society*, 1968, *The Novel and Society: Defoe to George Eliot*, 1984, and *The Achievement of Graham Greene*, 1985. **Essay:** Graham Greene.

SOLOMON, Eric. Professor of English, San Francisco State University. Author of *Stephen Crane in England*, 1963, *Stephen Crane: From Parody to Realism*, 1965, and many articles on 19th- and 20th-century British and American fiction. Editor of *The Faded Banners*, 1960, and *The Critic Agonistes*, 1985. **Essay:** Albert Guerard.

SQUIRES, Radcliffe. Former Professor of English, University of Michigan, Ann Arbor, and former editor of *Michigan Quarterly Review*. Author of several books of poetry—the most recent being *Gardens of the World*, 1981, and *The Envoy*, 1983—and of books on Robinson Jeffers, Robert Frost, Frederic Prokosch, and Allen Tate. Editor of a collection of essays on Tate. **Essay:** Frederic Prokosch.

STANFORD, Derek. Lecturer in Modern Literature, City Literary Institute, London. Author of two books of poetry, a memoir, and many books of literary criticism, including stud-

ies of John Betjeman, Muriel Spark, Stephen Spender, Louis MacNeice, and C. Day Lewis. Editor of several anthologies, including a collection of drama since 1945, and books on the 1890's. **Essay:** Alex Comfort.

STEDMAN, Jane W. Professor of English, Roosevelt University, Chicago. Author of articles and reviews in anthologies of Victorian studies, scholarly journals, and *Opera News*. Editor of *Gilbert Before Sullivan: Six Comic Plays*, 1967. **Essays:** Monica Dickens; P.D. James; Ira Levin.

STERN, Carol Simpson. Professor and Chairman of the Department of Performance Studies, Northwestern University, Evanston, Illinois; member of the advisory board, *Literature in Performance*, and research consultant, *English Literature in Transition*. Author of articles and theatre and book reviews in *Victorian Studies* and Chicago *Sun-Times*. **Essays:** A. Alvarez; Alfred Grossman; Elizabeth Hardwick; Doris Lessing; Alison Lurie; Charles Newman; Joyce Carol Oates; Judith Rossner; Richard Yates.

STEVENS, James R. Master, Confederation College, Thunder Bay, Ontario. Author of *Legends of the Sandy Lake Cree*, 1971, *Paddy Wilson's Gold Fever*, 1976, *Legends from the Forest*, 1985, and *Killing the Shamen*, 1985. **Essay:** Fred Bodsworth.

STEVENS, Joan. Professor of English, Victoria University, Wellington; now retired. Author of *The New Zealand Novel 1860–1965*, 1966, *New Zealand Short Stories: A Survey*, 1968, and articles on the Brontës, Thackeray, and Dickens. Editor of *Mary Taylor, Friend of Charlotte Brontë: Letters from New Zealand and Elsewhere*, 1972, and *The London Journal of Edward Jerningham Wakefield 1845–46*, 1972. **Essay:** Ian Cross.

STRANDBERG, Victor. Professor of English, Duke University, Durham, North Carolina. Author of *A Colder Fire: The Poetry of Robert Penn Warren*, 1965, *The Poetic Vision of Robert Penn Warren*, 1977, *A Faulkner Overview: Six Perspectives*, 1981, *Religious Psychology in American Literature: A Study in the Relevance of William James*, 1981, and "The Art of Cynthia Ozick" in *Texas Studies in Literature and Language*, Summer 1983. **Essay:** Cynthia Ozick.

STUCKEY, W.J. Professor of English, Purdue University, Lafayette, Indiana; founding editor of *Minnesota Review*, advisory editor of *Modern Fiction Studies*, and associate editor of *Journal of Narrative Technique*. Author of *Pulitzer Prize Novels*, 1966 (revised 1980), and *Caroline Gordon*, 1972. **Essays:** Walker Percy; Frank Tuohy.

SUMMERS, Judith. Free-lance writer. Author of *Dear Sister* (novel), 1985. **Essay:** Zoë Fairbairns.

SUTHERLAND, Fraser. Free-lance writer; managing editor of *Books in Canada* magazine. Author of several books, including *The Style of Innocence: A Study of Hemingway and Callaghan*, 1972, *Madwomen* (poetry), 1978, and *John Glassco: An Essay and Bibliography*, 1984, and of fiction, poetry, and criticism in journals and anthologies; poetry reviewer for Toronto *Globe and Mail*. **Essay:** Patricia Highsmith.

SUTHERLAND, John. Professor of English, California Institute of Technology, Pasadena. Author of *Bestsellers*, 1980. **Essay:** Tom Sharpe.

SYKES, Alrene. Senior Lecturer in English, University of Queensland, Brisbane. Formerly editor in the Drama Department, Australian Broadcasting Commission. Author of *Harold Pinter*, 1970, and of articles on modern drama and Australian fiction. Editor of *Five Plays for Radio* and four other anthologies of Australian plays. **Essays:** Jessica Anderson; Barbara Hanrahan.

TANNER, Tony. Reader in English, King's College, Cambridge. Author of books on Conrad and Bellow and of *The Reign of Wonder: Naivety and Reality in American Literature*, 1965, *City of Words: American Fiction 1950–1970*, 1971, *Adultery in the Novel*, 1980, *Thomas Pynchon*, 1982, and *Henry James: The Writer and His Work*, 1985. Editor of works by Jane Austen and Henry James, and of a collection of essays on James.

THOMAS, Roy. Lecturer in Education, University College of Swansea, Wales; now retired. Author of *How to Read a Poem*, 1961. **Essay:** Gwyn Jones.

TIFFIN, Chris. Senior Lecturer in English, University of Queensland, Brisbane. Author of articles on Australian and Pacific literatures. Editor of *South Pacific Images*, 1978, and *South Pacific Stories* (with H.M. Tiffin), 1980. **Essays:** Helen Garner; Colin Johnson.

TIFFIN, H.M. Senior Lecturer in English, University of Queensland, Brisbane. Author of articles on Australian and post-colonial literatures. Editor, with Chris Tiffin, of *South Pacific Stories*, 1980. **Essay:** J.M. Coetzee.

TOOMEY, Philippa. Staff member, *The Times*, London. Regular reviewer for *The Times, The Tablet, Fiction Magazine, Home and Country*, and other periodicals. **Essay:** Alice Thomas Ellis.

TOULSON, Shirley. Poet and free-lance writer. Author of several books of poems, and of guidebooks and studies of rural history and regional folklore, most recently *The Moors of the Southwest*, 2 vols., 1983–84, *The Mendip Hills*, 1984, and *Celtic Journeys*, 1985. **Essays:** John Berger; Christine Brooke-Rose; Russell Hoban; David Hughes; Bernard Kops; Jack Lindsay; Stanley Middleton,

TUERK, Richard. Professor of Literature and Languages, East Texas State University, Commerce. Author of *Central Still: Circle and Sphere in Thoreau's Prose*, 1975, and essays on Jewish-American literature, Emerson, Jacob Riis, and Twain. **Essays:** John Barth; Jerome Weidman.

TURNER, Roland. Editor of the reference book *The Grants Register*. **Essay:** Emanuel Litvinoff.

van de KAMP, Peter G.W. Lecturer in English, University College, Dublin. Author of articles on Anglo-Irish literature in *The Crane Bag* and *Yeats Annual*. **Essays:** John Banville; Aidan Higgins.

VOGLER, Thomas A. Professor of English and Comparative Literature, and Chair of the Humanities Institute, University of California, Santa Cruz. Author of *Preludes to Vision*, 1970, *Unnam'd Forms: Blake and Textuality*, 1985, and numerous essays on poetry and fiction of the 18th to 20th centuries. **Essay:** Ken Kesey.

WALSH, William. Professor of Commonwealth Literature, Chairman of the School of English, and Acting Vice-Chancellor, University of Leeds; now retired. Author of *Use of Imagination*, 1958, *A Human Idiom*, 1964, *A Manifold Voice*, 1970, and books on R.K. Narayan, V.S. Naipaul, D.J. Enright, Patrick White, F.R. Leavis, Coleridge, and Keats. **Essays:** Morley Callaghan; Kamala Markandaya.

WARNER, Val. Free-lance writer. Author of two books of poetry (*Under the Penthouse*, 1973, and *Before Lunch*, 1986), and articles and reviews in periodicals. Editor of *Charlotte Mew: Collected Poems and Prose*, 1981; translator of *Centenary Corbière*, 1974. **Essays:** Beryl Bainbridge; Caroline Blackwood; Philip Callow; Isobel English; Elaine Feinstein; Francis King; Elizabeth Mavor; Flannery O'Connor (appendix); Julia O'Faolain; Grace Paley; Gilbert Phelps; Fay Weldon.

WATTS, Harold H. Professor of English, Purdue University, Lafayette, Indiana; now retired. Author of *The Modern Reader's Guide to the Bible*, 1949, *Ezra Pound and the Cantos*, 1951, *Hound and Quarry*, 1953, *The Modern Reader's Guide to Religions*, 1964, and *Aldous Huxley*, 1969. **Essays:** Alice Adams; Frederick Buechner; Herbert Gold; William Maxwell; P.H. Newby; Harry Mark Petrakis; J.D. Salinger; Wallace Stegner; Honor Tracy; Helen Yglesias.

WEIGEL, John A. Professor of English, Miami University, Oxford, Ohio. Author of *Lawrence Durrell*, 1965, *Colin Wilson*, 1975, *B.F. Skinner*, 1977, and *Patrick White*, 1984. **Essays:** Jo Sinclair; Colin Wilson.

WELDON, Fay. See her own entry.

WELKER, Robert L. Professor of English, University of Alabama, Huntsville. **Essay:** Harriette Arnow.

WESTBROOK, Perry D. Professor of English, State University of New York, Albany; now retired. Author of *Acres of Flint: Writers of Rural New England*, 1951, *Biography of an Island*, 1958, *The Greatness of Man: An Essay on Dostoevsky and Whitman*, 1961, *Mary Ellen Chase*, 1966, and *Mary Wilkins Freeman*, 1967. **Essays:** G.V. Desani; Raja Rao; Kurt Vonnegut, Jr.

WESTON, Peter R. Free-lance writer. Editor of the science-fiction anthologies *Andromeda 1–3*, 1976–78. **Essays:** Robert A. Heinlein; Fritz Leiber.

WILLY, Margaret. Lecturer for the British Council, and at the City Literary Institute and Morley College, London. Author of two books of poetry (*The Invisible Sun*, 1946, and *Every Star a Tongue*, 1951), and several critical books, including studies of Chaucer, Traherne, Fielding, Browning, Crashaw, Vaughan, Emily Brontë, and English diarists. Editor of two anthologies and of plays by Goldsmith. **Essays:** Susan Hill; Jennifer Johnston; Rosamond Lehmann; Muriel Spark.

WOOD, Michael. Professor of English, University of Exeter, Devon. Author of *Stendhal*, 1971, and *America in the Movies*, 1975, and articles in *New York Review of Books, London Review of Books*, and other periodicals.

WOODCOCK, George. Free-lance writer, lecturer, and editor. Author of poetry (*Collected Poems*, 1983), plays, travel books, biographies, an autobiography (*Letter to the Past*, 1983), and works on history and politics; critical works include *William*

Godwin, 1946, *The Incomparable Aphra*, 1948, *The Paradox of Oscar Wilde*, 1949, *The Crystal Spirit* (on Orwell), 1966, *Hugh MacLennan*, 1969, *Odysseus Ever Returning: Canadian Writers and Writing*, 1970, *Mordecai Richler*, 1970, *Dawn and the Darkest Hour* (on Aldous Huxley), 1972, *Herbert Read*, 1972, *Thomas Merton*, 1978, and *The World of Canadian Writing*, 1980. Editor of anthologies and of works by Charles Lamb, Malcolm Lowry, Wyndham Lewis, Hardy, Meredith, and others. **Essays:** Margaret Atwood; Earle Birney; Leonard Cohen; Timothy Findley; Roy Fuller; Jack Hodgins; Mordecai Richler; Julian Symons; Audrey Thomas; David Watmough.

YABES, Leopoldo Y.   Professor Emeritus of Literature and Philippine Studies, University of the Philippines, Quezon City. Author of more than 20 books and numerous essays and articles; books include *The University and the Fear of Ideas*, 1956, *Philippine Literature in English*, 1958, *The Filipino Struggle for Intellectual Freedom*, 1959, *Jose Rizal on His Centenary*, 1963, *The Ordeal of a Man of Academe*, 1967, and *Graduate Education at the University of the Philippines*, 1975. Editor of many books, most recently *Philippine Short Stories*, 2 vols., 1975–81. Former editor of *Philippine Social Sciences and Humanities Review*. **Essay:** F. Sionil Jose.